SERIES

(ex•ploring)

1. To investigate in a systematic way: examine. 2. To search into or range over for the purpose of discovery.

SERIES

(ex•ploring)

1. To investigate in a systematic way: examine. 2. To search into or range over for the purpose of discovery.

Microsoft®

Office 2007

VOLUME 1

THIRD EDITION

Robert T. Grauer

Michelle Hulett | Cynthia Krebs | Maurie Wigman Lockley

Keith Mulbery | Judy Scheeren

Prentice Hall

Upper Saddle River, NJ

Columbus, OH

Library of Congress Cataloging-in-Publication Data
Microsoft Office 2007 / Robert T. Grauer . . . [et al.]. — 3rd ed.
p. cm. — (Exploring Microsoft Office 2007 series)
Rev. ed. of: Exploring Microsoft Office 2007. 2nd ed. 2007.
ISBN-13: 978-0-13-506250-0
ISBN-10: 0-13-506250-0
1. Microsoft Office. 2. Business—Computer programs. I. Grauer, Robert T., 1945-
HF5548.4.M525G694 2010
005.5—dc22

2008043567

VP/Editorial Director: Natalie E. Anderson
Editor-in-Chief: Michael Payne
Director, Product Development: Pamela Hersperger
Product Development Manager: Eileen Bien Calabro
Editorial Project Manager: Meghan Bisi
Editorial Assistant: Marilyn Matos
AVP/Director of Online Programs: Richard Keaveny
AVP/Director of Product Development: Lisa Strite
Editorial Media Project Manager: Alana Coles
Production Media Project Manager: Lorena Cerisano
Marketing Manager: Tori Olson Alves
Marketing Assistant: Angela Frey
Senior Managing Editor: Cynthia Zonneveld
Associate Managing Editor: Camille Trentacoste
Production Project Manager: Ruth Ferrera-Kargov
Senior Operations Director: Nick Sklitsis
Senior Art Director: Jonathan Boylan
Art Director: Anthony Gemmellaro
Cover Design: Anthony Gemmellaro
Cover Illustration/Photo: Courtesy of Getty Images/Laurent Hamels
Composition: GGS Higher Education Resources, A Division of Premedia Global, Inc.
Full-Service Project Management: GGS Higher Education Resources, A Division of Premedia Global, Inc.
Printer/Binder: RR Donnelly
Typeface: 10/12 Palatino

Credits and acknowledgments borrowed from other sources and reproduced, with permission, in this textbook appear on appropriate page within text.

Excel Data for Hospitality Capstone Exercises: David "Tug Boat" Mack, Brent "Goat Cheese" Hystead, and John "Lance" Burandt.

Photos and sound file on electronic supplements: Margaret Mills, Vicky A. Marella, Deanne M. Kulke, Frank Thompson, Doug Thompson, Karen Thompson, Dirk Meuleners, Paul Martens, Molly Harding, and Stan Peal.

Pearson Education Ltd., London
Pearson Education Singapore, Pte. Ltd.
Pearson Education, Canada, Ltd.
Pearson Education–Japan
Pearson Education Australia PTY, Limited
Pearson Education North Asia Ltd.
Pearson Educación de Mexico, S.A. de C.V.
Pearson Education Malaysia, Pte. Ltd.

Prentice Hall
is an imprint of

www.pearsonhighered.com

10 9 8 7 6 5 4 3 2 1
ISBN-13: 978-0-13-506250-0
ISBN-10: 0-13-506250-0

Dedications

I would like to dedicate this book to the memory of my grandmother, Effie Burrell Marcum. Her love, encouragement, and belief in my abilities got me to this point and help me endure every day. And also to John. 143

Michelle Hulett

I dedicate this book to those I love in thanks for the joy and support they give me: My wonderful children: Marshall, Jaron, Jenalee, and Michelle who make it all worthwhile, and Bradley Behle—my newest son and a welcome addition to our family.

My granddaughter, Ava—her baby cuddles make life a pleasure.
My parents, Neal and Zola Mulhern, who continually do all they can to make life easier.
And to those who have gone before: my father, Reed J. Olsen, and my Grandparents Waddoups.

Cynthia Krebs

I would like to express appreciation for my family's patience and support as I have worked on this project. Elizabeth, Aaron, and James were extraordinarily understanding and cooperative about letting me work. I need to acknowledge Dan Bullard for his continuing source of motivation and inspiration. Most of all, I need to thank my best friend and husband, Jim, for always believing in me.

Maurie Wigman Lockley

I would like to dedicate this book to my family and close friends who provided a strong community of emotional support as I completed my doctorate program.

Keith Mulbery

Thanks for my husband, Bill, for all the support and energy that has helped me to put ideas on paper. His encouragement made it all possible.

Thanks also to my parents who believe in learning at any age.
And, a special thanks to the following people for their contributions: Frank Lucente, colleague, friend, and mentor for sharing his tips and unique teaching style; and the students at Westmoreland County Community College who make it all worthwhile.

Judy Scheeren

About the Authors

Dr. Robert T. Grauer
Dr. Robert T. Grauer is an Associate Professor in the Department of Computer Information Systems at the University of Miami, where he has been honored with the Outstanding Teacher Award in the School of Business.

Dr. Grauer has written more than 20 books on programming and information systems. His work has been translated into three foreign languages and is used in all aspects of higher education at both national and international levels.

Dr. Grauer also has been a consultant to several major corporations including IBM and American Express. He received his Ph.D. in operations research in 1972 from the Polytechnic Institute of Brooklyn.

Michelle Hulett
Michelle Hulett received a B.S. degree in CIS from the University of Arkansas and a M.B.A. from Missouri State University. She has worked for various organizations as a programmer, network administrator, computer literacy coordinator, and educator. She currently teaches computer literacy and Web design classes at Missouri State University.

When not teaching or writing, she enjoys flower gardening, traveling (Alaska and Hawaii are favorites), hiking, canoeing, and camping with her husband, John, and dog, Dakota.

Cynthia Krebs
Cynthia Krebs is a professor in the Digital Media Department at Utah Valley University, where she has taught since 1988. Cynthia is the Business Education Director and teaches classes in basic computer proficiency, business presentations, business graphics, and introduction to multimedia. In April of 2008, Cynthia was awarded the Scholar of the Year award for the School of Technology of Computing. She has also received the Academic Excellence Award for the School of Business twice during her tenure at UVU.

Cynthia has presented locally and nationally and has coauthored a text on advanced word processing. She received her B.S. and M.S. degrees in Business Education with an Economics emphasis from Utah State University.

Cynthia lives by a creek in Springville, Utah, where she enjoys feeding ducks. She has four children and one granddaughter. When she isn't teaching or writing, she enjoys spending time with her children, spoiling her granddaughter, traveling with friends, reading, and playing computer games.

Maurie Wigman Lockley
Maurie Wigman Lockley teaches desktop applications and management information systems classes at the University of North Carolina Greensboro. She has been an instructor there since 1990.

She lives in a tiny piedmont North Carolina town with her husband, daughter, and two preschool-aged grandsons. She spends her free time playing with the boys, reading, camping, playing computer games, and singing. She serves on several not-for-profit boards and is active at her church.

Dr. Keith Mulbery

Dr. Keith Mulbery, Series Editor for the Exploring Office 2007 series, is an Associate Professor in the Information Systems and Technology Department at Utah Valley University, where he teaches computer applications, C# programming, systems analysis and design, and MIS classes. He has written more than 15 software textbooks and business communication test banks. In January 2001, he received the Utah Valley State College Board of Trustees Award of Excellence for authoring *MOUS Essentials Word 2000*. In addition to his series editor and authoring experience, he also served as a developmental editor on two word processing textbooks. In 2007, he received the UVSC School of Technology and Computing Scholar Award, and in 2008, he received the UVSC School of Technology and Computing Teaching Award.

He received his B.S. and M.Ed. (majoring in Business Education) from Southwestern Oklahoma State University and earned his Ph.D. in Education with an emphasis in Business Information Systems at Utah State University in 2006. His dissertation topic was computer-assisted instruction using TAIT to supplement traditional instruction in basic computer proficiency courses.

Judith Scheeren

Judith Scheeren is a professor of computer technology at Westmoreland County Community College in Youngwood, Pennsylvania where she received the Outstanding Teacher award. She holds an M.S.I.S. She holds an M.S. from the University of Pittsburgh and an advanced certificate in online teaching and learning from the University of California at Hayward. She has several years of experience in the computer industry with Fortune 500 companies. She has developed and written training materials for custom applications in both the public and private sectors. She also has written books on desktop publishing.

Contributing Authors

Linda Ericksen, Office Fundamentals Chapter

Linda Ericksen is Associate Professor of Software Engineering at the University of Advancing Technology in Tempe, Arizona. She is the author of over 20 college-level computer text books on topics ranging from the Internet through many software applications, writing for major publishers such as Que, Addison-Wesley, and Course Technology. She was also the author of her own popular series for Prentice Hall, the Quick Simple Series, which featured Microsoft Office 2000.

Lynn Hogan, Windows Vista Chapter

Lynn Hogan has taught computer literacy and microcomputer applications classes at Calhoun Community College for 25 years. For the past 18 years, she has served as chair of the Department of Computer Information Systems. She received Calhoun's outstanding instructor award in 2006, and currently teaches computer literacy for senior adults and web design courses. Having developed the first online computer course at Calhoun, she continues to work with the distance education program. She received an M.B.A. from the University of North Alabama and a Ph.D. from the University of Alabama.

She resides in Alabama with her husband and two daughters. Much of her free time is spent traveling to cutting horse shows and dressage shows, watching her daughters compete. In addition to working with horses, she enjoys cooking, reading, and family travel.

Jean Kotsiovos, Health Care Exercises

Jean Kotsiovos is the Assistant Dean of Curriculum for the School of Information Systems and Technology at Kaplan University. She received her B.S. degree in Information and Decision Sciences from the University of Illinois at Chicago and her M.A. in Education with an emphasis in Computer Education from Governors State University. She started her career in the IT industry as a programmer/analyst.

She has worked in various positions in higher education as an instructor, program coordinator, department chair, and assistant dean. She has developed numerous courses and programs in information technology for both online and traditional institutions. She has created training materials and presented a variety of workshops on computer applications. She resides in Illinois with her husband and two children. She enjoys traveling and spending time with her family.

LindaLee Massoud, Legal Exercises
LindaLee Massoud has been a professor at Mott Community College in Flint, Michigan for almost 29 years. She currently teaches a variety of computer software and programming classes in the Computer Information Systems program (Technology Division). She is also an attorney in private practice and a pilot.

Margo Mills, Arts and Hospitality Exercises
Margo Mills has been teaching students to use computer software in the Twin Cities for over 14 years. Very quickly she discovered that she was put on this earth to be paid to talk. After eight years in the corporate training arena she was hired as a business instructor at Minneapolis Business College where she has worked happily for the last year and has fallen completely in love with her students.
Add new contributing authors:

Julie Boyles, Technology Exercises
After 10 years of teaching business and computer courses at Southern Oregon University in Ashland, Oregon, Julie now teaches at Portland Community College. In addition to teaching, Julie is enrolled in a Ph.D. program in Public Administration and Policy and is the Assistant to the Editor of Asian Perspective academic journal. Enjoyment time includes travel to Latin America, hiking, and spending time with her grown daughter, Angela.

Alicen Flosi, Business Exercises
Alicen Flosi teaches business technology and business communications classes at Lamar University in Beaumont, Texas. Prior to teaching at Lamar, she was CFO/Assistant Superintendent for public school districts in Texas and Illinois. She earned her M.B.A. from Lamar and her M.M.I.S. and Ph.D. in Information Systems from Nova Southeastern University in Florida.

Diane L. Smith, Natural Science Exercises
Diane Smith has been a full-time instructor at Henry Ford Community College in Dearborn, Michigan, since 2004. In addition to teaching classes in introductory and advanced computer proficiency using Microsoft Office, she teaches customer service and business behavior classes. She is the lead instructor for the Customer Service Certificate of Achievement, Industrial Distribution Certificate, and Computer Software Applications Certificate.

Thanks to the love and support of her family and friends, she decided after 20+ years in the corporate world to change careers to teaching. Everyone else knew teaching is where she was meant to be. It just took one student to change her life to realize the impact she could make on the world.

Brief Contents

OFFICE

WORD

EXCEL

ACCESS

POWERPOINT

WINDOWS VISTA

CAPSTONE EXERCISES

Contents

CHAPTER ONE | Office Fundamentals: Using Word, Excel, Access, and PowerPoint 1

Microsoft Office Word 2007

CHAPTER ONE | Microsoft Word: What Will Word Processing Do for Me? 69

CHAPTER TWO | Gaining Proficiency: Editing and Formatting 131

CHAPTER THREE | Enhancing a Document: Tables and Graphics 195

CHAPTER FOUR | Share, Compare, and Document: Workgroups, Collaboration, and References 249

MICROSOFT OFFICE EXCEL 2007

CHAPTER THREE | Charts: Delivering a Message 429

CHAPTER FOUR | Working with Large Worksheets and Tables: Manipulating Worksheets and Table Management 485

Microsoft Office Access 2007

CHAPTER ONE | Introduction to Access: Finding Your Way through a Database 545

CHAPTER TWO | Relational Databases and Multi-Table Queries: Designing Databases and Using Related Data 605

CHAPTER THREE | Customize, Analyze, and Summarize Query Data: Creating and Using Queries to Make Decisions 677

CHAPTER FOUR | Create, Edit, and Perform Calculations in Reports: Creating Professional and Useful Reports 729

Microsoft Office PowerPoint 2007

CHAPTER ONE | Introduction to PowerPoint: Presentations Made Easy 793

CHAPTER TWO | Presentation Development: Planning and Preparing a Presentation 867

CHAPTER THREE | Presentation Design: Enhancing with Illustrations 929

CHAPTER FOUR | PowerPoint Multimedia Tools: Enhancing with Multimedia 1011

WINDOWS VISTA | Getting Started with Windows Vista 1077

Acknowledgments

The success of the Exploring series is attributed to contributions from numerous individuals. First and foremost, our heartfelt appreciation to Melissa Sabella, senior acquisitions editor, for providing new leadership and direction to capitalize on the strength and tradition of the Exploring series while implementing innovative ideas into the Exploring Office 2007 edition. Scott Davidson, senior marketing manager, was an invaluable addition to the team who believes in the mission of this series passionately and did an amazing job communicating its message. We'd also like to thank Michael Payne, editor-in-chief, and Tori Olson Alves, marketing manager, for their involvement with the third edition.

During the first few months of the first edition, Eileen Clark, senior editorial project manager, kept the team focused on the vision, pedagogy, and voice that has been the driving force behind the success of the Exploring series. Claire Hunter, market development editor, facilitated communication between the editorial team and the reviewers to ensure that this edition meets the changing needs of computer professors and students at the collegiate level. Keith Mulbery, series editor, reviewed manuscript submissions, provided feedback and guidance to authors, reviewed technical edits, and helped replace screenshots and data files when needed.

Jen Frew and Jenelle Woodrup, editorial project managers, masterfully managed the flow of manuscript files among the authors, editorial team, and production to ensure timely publication of the series. Laura Town, developmental editor, provided an objective perspective in reviewing the content and organization of selected chapters. Meghan Bisi, editorial project manager, facilitated workflow with the technical editors, series editor, and production team to ensure an improved level of accuracy in the third edition as well as managing corrections for reprints of previous editions and volumes. Eileen Calabro, product development manager, facilitated communication among the editorial team, authors, and production during a transitional stage. Doug Bell and the whole team at GGS worked through software delays, style changes and anything else we threw at them to bring the whole thing together. Art director Blair Brown's conversations with students and professors across the country yielded a design that addressed the realities of today's students with function and style.

A special thanks to the following for the use of their work in the PowerPoint section of the text: Cameron Martin, Ph.D., Assistant to the President, Utah Valley State College, for the use of the Institutional Policies and Procedures Approval Process flowchart; Nick Finner, Paralegal Studies, Utah Valley State College, for the use of his research relating to the elderly population residing in the prisons of Utah; Ryan Phillips, Xeric Landscape and Design (XericUtah.com), for sharing Xeric's concepts for creating beautiful, drought-tolerant landscapes and for the photographs illustrating these concepts; Jo Porter, Photographer, Mapleton, Utah, for allowing the use of her beautiful engagement and wedding photographs; and David and Ali Valeti for the photographs of their baby and their family.

The new members of the Exploring author team would like to especially thank Bob Grauer for his vision in developing Exploring and his leadership in creating this highly successful series.

Maryann Barber would like to thank Bob Grauer for a wonderful collaboration and providing the opportunities through which so much of her life has changed.

The Exploring team would like to especially thank the following instructors who drew on their experience in the classroom and their software expertise to give us daily advice on how to improve this book. Their impact can be seen on every page:

Barbara Stover, Marion Technical College

Bob McCloud, Sacred Heart University

Cassie Georgetti, Florida Technical College

Dana Johnson, North Dakota State University

Jim Pepe, Bentley College

Judy Brown, The University of Memphis

Lancie Anthony Affonso, College of Charleston

Mimi Duncan, University of Missouri – St. Louis

Minnie Proctor, Indian River Community College

Richard Albright, Goldey-Beacom College

We also want to acknowledge all the reviewers of the Exploring 2007 series. Their valuable comments and constructive criticism greatly improved this edition:

Aaron Schorr
Fashion Institute of Technology

Alicia Stonesifer
La Salle University

Allen Alexander, Delaware
Tech & Community College

Amy Williams, Abraham
Baldwin Agriculture College

Andrea Compton
St. Charles Community College

Annette Duvall
Central New Mexico Community College

Annie Brown
Hawaii Community College

Barbara Cierny
Harper College

Barbara Hearn
Community College of Philadelphia

Barbara Meguro
University of Hawaii at Hilo

Bette Pitts
South Plains College

Beverly Fite
Amarillo College

Bill Wagner
Villanova

Brandi N. Guidry
University of Louisiana at Lafayette

Brian Powell
West Virginia University – Morgantown
Campus

Carl Farrell
Hawaii Pacific University

Carl Penzuil
Ithaca College

Carole Bagley;
University of St. Thomas

Catherine Hain
Central New Mexico CC

Charles Edwards
University of Texas of the Permian Basin

Cheryl Slavik
Computer Learning Services

Christine L. Moore
College of Charleston

David Barnes
Penn State Altoona

David Childress;
Ashland Community College

David Law, Alfred
State College

Dennis Chalupa
Houston Baptist

Diane Stark
Phoenix College

Dianna Patterson
Texarkana College

Dianne Ross
University of Louisiana at Lafayette

Dr. Behrooz Saghafi
Chicago State University

Dr. Gladys Swindler
Fort Hays State University

Dr. Joe Teng
Barry University

Dr. Karen Nantz
Eastern Illinois University.

Duane D. Lintner
Amarillo College

Elizabeth Edmiston
North Carolina Central University

Erhan Uskup
Houston Community College

Fred Hills, McClellan
Community College

Freda Leonard
Delgado Community College

Gary R. Armstrong
Shippensburg University of Pennsylvania

Glenna Vanderhoof
Missouri State

Gregg Asher
Minnesota State University, Mankato

Hank Imus
San Diego Mesa College

Heidi Gentry-Kolen
Northwest Florida State College

Hong K. Sung
University of Central Oklahoma

Hyekyung Clark
Central New Mexico CC

J Patrick Fenton
West Valley College

Jana Carver
Amarillo College

Jane Cheng
Bloomfield College

Janos T. Fustos
Metropolitan State College of Denver

Jean Kotsiovos
Kaplan University

Jeffrey A Hassett
University of Utah

Jennifer Pickle
Amarillo College

Jerry Kolata
New England Institute of Technology

Jesse Day
South Plains College

John Arehart
Longwood University

John Lee Reardon
University of Hawaii, Manoa

Joshua Mindel
San Francisco State University

Karen Wisniewski
County College of Morris

Karl Smart
Central Michigan University

Kathleen Brenan
Ashland University

Kathryn L. Hatch
University of Arizona

Krista Lawrence
Delgado Community College

Krista Terry
Radford University

Laura McManamon
University of Dayton

Laura Reid
University of Western Ontario

Linda Johnsonius
Murray State University

Lisa Prince
Missouri State University

Lori Kelley
Madison Area Technical College

Lucy Parker,
California State University, Northridge

Lynda Henrie
LDS Business College

Lynn Bowen
Valdosta Technical College

Malia Young
Utah State University

Margie Martyn
Baldwin Wallace

Marianne Trudgeon
Fanshawe College

Marilyn Hibbert
Salt Lake Community College

Marjean Lake
LDS Business College

Mark Olaveson
Brigham Young University

Meg McManus
Northwest Florida State College

Nancy Sardone
Seton Hall University

Pam Chapman
Waubonsee Community College

Patricia Joseph
Slippery Rock University.

Patrick Hogan
Cape Fear Community College

Paula F. Bell
Lock Haven University of Pennsylvania

Paulette Comet
Community College of Baltimore County, Catonsville

Pratap Kotala
North Dakota State University

Richard Blamer
John Carroll University

Richard Herschel
St. Joseph's University

Richard Hewer
Ferris State University

Robert Gordon
Hofstra University

Robert Marmelstein
East Stroudsburg University

Robert Stumbur
Northern Alberta Institute of Technology

Roberta I. Hollen
University of Central Oklahoma

Roland Moreira
South Plains College

Ron Murch
University of Calgary

Rory J. de Simone
University of Florida

Ruth Neal
Navarro College

Sandra M. Brown
Finger Lakes Community College

Sharon Mulroney
Mount Royal College

Stephen E. Lunce
Midwestern State University

Steve Schwarz
Raritan Valley Community College

Steven Choy
University of Calgary

Susan Byrne
St. Clair College

Suzan Spitzberg
Oakton Community College

Thomas Setaro
Brookdale Community College

Todd McLeod
Fresno City College

Vickie Pickett
Midland College

Vipul Gupta
St Joseph's University

Vivek Shah
Texas State University - San Marcos

Wei-Lun Chuang
Utah State University

William Dorin
Indiana University Northwest

Finally, we wish to acknowledge reviewers of previous editions of the Exploring series—we wouldn't have made it to the 7th edition without you:

Alan Moltz
Naugatuck Valley Technical Community College

Alok Charturvedi
Purdue University

Antonio Vargas
El Paso Community College

Barbara Sherman
Buffalo State College

Bill Daley
University of Oregon

Bill Morse
DeVry Institute of Technology

Bonnie Homan
San Francisco State University

Carl M. Briggs
Indiana University School of Business

Carlotta Eaton
Radford University

Carolyn DiLeo
Westchester Community College

Cody Copeland
Johnson County Community College

Connie Wells
Georgia State University

Daniela Marghitu
Auburn University

David B. Meinert
Southwest Missouri State University

David Douglas
University of Arkansas

David Langley
University of Oregon

David Rinehard
Lansing Community College

David Weiner
University of San Francisco

Dean Combellick
Scottsdale Community College

Delores Pusins
Hillsborough Community College

Don Belle
Central Piedmont Community College

Douglas Cross
Clackamas Community College

Ernie Ivey
Polk Community College

Gale E. Rand
College Misericordia

Helen Stoloff
Hudson Valley Community College

Herach Safarian
College of the Canyons

Jack Zeller
Kirkwood Community College

James Franck
College of St. Scholastica

James Gips
Boston College

Jane King
Everett Community College

Janis Cox
Tri-County Technical College

Jerry Chin
Southwest Missouri State University

Jill Chapnick
Florida International University

Jim Pruitt
Central Washington University

John Lesson
University of Central Florida

John Shepherd
Duquesne University

Judith M. Fitspatrick
Gulf Coast Community College

Judith Rice
Santa Fe Community College

Judy Dolan
Palomar College

Karen Tracey
Central Connecticut State University

Kevin Pauli
University of Nebraska

Kim Montney
Kellogg Community College

Kimberly Chambers
Scottsdale Community College

Larry S. Corman
Fort Lewis College

Lynn Band
Middlesex Community College

Margaret Thomas
Ohio University

Marguerite Nedreberg
Youngstown State University

Marilyn Salas
Scottsdale Community College

Martin Crossland
Southwest Missouri State University

Mary McKenry Percival
University of Miami

Michael Hassett
Fort Hayes State University

Michael Stewardson
San Jacinto College – North

Midge Gerber
Southwestern Oklahoma State University

Mike Hearn
Community College of Philadelphia

Mike Kelly
Community College of Rhode Island

Mike Thomas
Indiana University School of Business

Paul E. Daurelle
Western Piedmont Community College

Ranette Halverson
Midwestern State University

Raymond Frost
Central Connecticut State University

Robert Spear, Prince
George's Community College

Rose M. Laird
Northern Virginia Community College

Sally Visci
Lorain County Community College

Shawna DePlonty
Sault College of Applied Arts and Technology

Stuart P. Brian
Holy Family College

Susan Fry
Boise State Universtiy

Suzanne Tomlinson
Iowa State University

Vernon Griffin
Austin Community College

We very much appreciate the following individuals for painstakingly checking every step and every explanation for technical accuracy, while dealing with an entirely new software application:

Barbara Waxer
Bill Daley
Beverly Fite
Dawn Wood
Denise Askew
Elizabeth Lockley
Excel-Soft Technologies

James Reidel
Janet Pickard
Janice Snyder
Jean Kotsiovos
Jeremy Harris
John Griffin
Joyce Neilsen

Julie Boyles
LeeAnn Bates
Lynn Bowen
Mara Zebest
Mary E. Pascarella
Michael Meyers
Sue McCrory

Preface

The Exploring Series

Exploring has been Prentice Hall's most successful Office Application series of the past 15 years. For Office 2007 Exploring has undergone the most extensive changes in its history, so that it can truly move today's student "beyond the point and click."

The goal of Exploring has always been to teach more than just the steps to accomplish a task – the series provides the theoretical foundation necessary for a student to understand when and why to apply a skill. This way, students achieve a broader understanding of Office.

Today's students are changing and Exploring has evolved with them. Prentice Hall traveled to college campuses across the country and spoke directly to students to determine how they study and prepare for class. We also spoke with hundreds of professors about the best ways to administer materials to such a diverse body of students.

Here is what we learned

Students go to college now with a different set of skills than they did 5 years ago. The new edition of Exploring moves students beyond the basics of the software at a faster pace, without sacrificing coverage of the fundamental skills that everybody needs to know. This ensures that students will be engaged from Chapter 1 to the end of the book.

Students have diverse career goals. With this in mind, we broadened the examples in the text (and the accompanying Instructor Resources) to include the health sciences, hospitality, urban planning, business and more. Exploring will be relevant to every student in the course.

Students read, prepare and study differently than they used to. Rather than reading a book cover to cover students want to easily identify what they need to know, and then learn it efficiently. We have added key features that will bring students into the content and make the text easy to use such as objective mapping, pull quotes, and key terms in the margins.

Moving students beyond the point and click

All of these additions mean students will be more engaged, achieve a higher level of understanding, and successfully complete this course. In addition to the experience and expertise of the series creator and author Robert T. Grauer we have assembled a tremendously talented team of supporting authors to assist with this critical revision. Each of them is equally dedicated to the Exploring mission of **moving students beyond the point and click.**

Key Features of the Office 2007 revision include

- **New** **Office Fundamentals Chapter** efficiently covers skills common among all applications like save, print, and bold to avoid repetition in each Office application's first chapter, along with coverage of problem solving skills to prepare students to apply what they learn in any situation.

- **New** **Moving Beyond the Basics** introduces advanced skills earlier because students are learning basic skills faster.

- **White Pages/Yellow Pages clearly** distinguish the theory (white pages) from the skills covered in the Hands-On exercises (yellow pages) so students always know what they are supposed to be doing.

- **New** **Objective Mapping** enables students to skip the skills and concepts they know, and quickly find those they don't, by scanning the chapter opener page for the page numbers of the material they need.

- **New** **Pull Quotes** entice students into the theory by highlighting the most interesting points.

- **New** **Conceptual Animations** connect the theory with the skills, by illustrating tough to understand concepts with interactive multimedia

- **New** **More End of Chapter Exercises** offer instructors more options for assessment. Each chapter has approximately 12–15 exercises ranging from Multiple Choice questions to open-ended projects.

- **New** **More Levels of End of Chapter Exercises,** including new Mid-Level Exercises, which tell students what to do, but not how to do it, and Capstone Exercises that cover all of the skills within each chapter.

- **New** **Mini Cases with Rubrics** are open ended exercises that guide both instructors and students to a solution with a specific rubric for each mini case.

- **New** **Cumulative Capstone Exercises** for each application tie application use to real-life professional situations in the business, natural science, technology, legal, health care, arts, and hospitality industries.

Instructor and Student Resources

Instructor Chapter Reference Cards

A four page color card for every chapter that includes a:

- *Concept Summary* that outlines the KEY objectives to cover in class with tips on where students get stuck as well as how to get them un-stuck. It helps bridge the gap between the instructor and student when discussing more difficult topics.

- *Case Study Lecture Demonstration Document* which provides instructors with a lecture sample based on the chapter opening case that will guide students to critically use the skills covered in the chapter, with examples of other ways the skills can be applied.

The Enhanced Instructor's Resource Center on CD-ROM includes:

- **Additional Capstone Production Tests** allow instructors to assess all the skills covered in a chapter with a single project.
- **Mini Case Rubrics** in Microsoft® Word format enable instructors to customize the assignment for their class.
- **PowerPoint® Presentations** for each chapter with notes included for online students.
- **Lesson Plans** that provide a detailed blueprint for an instructor to achieve chapter learning objectives and outcomes.
- **Student Data Files**
- **Annotated Solution Files**
- **Complete Test Bank**
- **Audio PowerPoint Presentations** for each chapter allow instructors to deliver an animated, narrated presentation to their students.

TestGen is a test generator program that lets you view and easily edit testbank questions, transfer them to tests, and print in a variety of formats suitable to your teaching situation. The program also offers many options for organizing and displaying testbanks and tests. A random number test generator enables you to create multiple versions of an exam. TestGen is available for instructor download from the online Instructor's Resource Center.

Prentice Hall's Companion Web Site

www.pearsonhighered.com/exploring offers expanded IT resources and downloadable supplements. This site also includes an online study guide for student self-study.

Online Course Cartridges

Flexible, robust and customizable content is available for all major online course platforms that include everything instructors need in one place.

Please contact your Sales Representative for information on accessing course cartridges for WebCT, Blackboard, or CourseCompass.

myitlab for Microsoft Office 2007, is a solution designed by professors that allows you to easily deliver Office courses with defensible assessment and outcomes-based training.

The new *Exploring Office 2007* System will seamlessly integrate online assessment and training with the new myitlab for Microsoft Office 2007!

Integrated Assessment and Training

To fully integrate the new myitlab into the *Exploring Office 2007* System we built myitlab assessment and training directly from the *Exploring* instructional content. No longer is the technology just mapped to your textbook.

This 1:1 content relationship between the *Exploring* text and myitlab means that your online assessment and training will work with your textbook to move your students beyond the point and click.

Advanced Reporting

With myitlab you will get advanced reporting capabilities including detailed student click stream data. This ability to see exactly what actions your students took on a test, click-by-click, provides you with true defensible grading.

In addition, myitlab for Office 2007 will feature. . .

Both Project-based and Skill-based assessment and training: Test and train students on Exploring projects, or break down assignments into individual Office application skills.

Outcomes-based training: Students train on what they don't know without having to relearn skills they already know.

Optimal performance and uptime: Provided by world-class hosting environment.

Dedicated student and instructor support: Professional technical support is available by phone, online chat, and email when you need it.

And much more!

www.myitlab.com

Visual Walk-Through

Office Fundamentals Chapter

efficiently covers skills common among all applications like save, print, and bold to avoid repetition in each 1st application chapter.

chapter 1 | Office Fundamentals

Using Word, Excel, Access, and PowerPoint

bjectives

After you read this chapter you will be able to:

1. Identify common interface components (page 4).
2. Use Office 2007 Help (page 10).
3. Open a file (page 18).
4. Save a file (page 21).
5. Print a document (page 24).
6. Select text to edit (page 31).
7. Insert text and change to the Overtype mode (page 32).
8. Move and copy text (page 34).
9. Find, replace, and go to text (page 36).
10. Use the Undo and Redo commands (page 39).
11. Use language tools (page 39).
12. Apply font attributes (page 43).
13. Copy formats with the Format Painter (page 47).

Hands-On Exercises

Exercises	Skills Covered
1. IDENTIFYING PROGRAM INTERFACE COMPONENTS AND USING HELP (page 12)	• Use PowerPoint's Office Button, Get Help in a Dialog Box, and Use the Zoom Slider • Use Excel's Ribbon, Get Help from an Enhanced ScreenTip, and Use the Zoom Dialog Box • Search Help in Access • Use Word's Status Bar • Search Help and Print a Help Topic
2. PERFORMING UNIVERSAL TASKS (page 28) Open: chap1_ho2_sample.docx Save as: chap1_ho2_solution.docx	• Open a File and Save it with a Different Name • Use Print Preview and Select Options • Print a Document
3. PERFORMING BASIC TASKS (page 48) Open: chap1_ho3_internet_docx Save as: chap_ho3_internet_solution.docx	• Cut, Copy, Paste, and Undo • Find and Replace Text • Check Spelling • Choose Synonyms and Use Thesaurus • Use the Research Tool • Apply Font Attributes • Use Format Painter

Microsoft Office 2007 Software Office Fundamentals 1

chapter 3 | **Access**

Customize, Analyze, and Summarize Query Data

Creating and Using Queries to Make Decisions

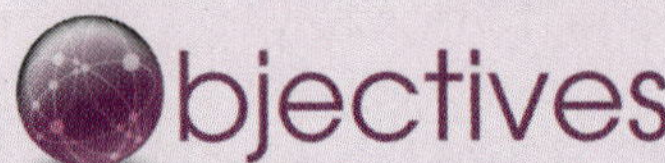

After you read this chapter you will be able to:

1. Understand the order of precedence **(page 679)**.
2. Create a calculated field in a query **(page 679)**.
3. Create expressions with the Expression Builder **(page 679)**.
4. Create and edit Access functions **(page 690)**.
5. Perform date arithmetic **(page 694)**.
6. Create and work with data aggregates **(page 704)**.

Hands-On Exercises

Exercises	Skills Covered
1. CALCULATED QUERY FIELDS (PAGE 683) **Open:** chap3_ho1-3_realestate.accdb **Save:** chap3_ho1-3_realestate_solution.accdb **Back up as:** chap3_ho1_realestate_solution.accdb	• Copy a Database and Start the Query • Select the Fields, Save, and Open the Query • Create a Calculated Field and Run the Query • Verify the Calculated Results • Recover from a Common Error
2. EXPRESSION BUILDER, FUNCTIONS, AND DATE ARITHMETIC (page 695) **Open:** chap3_ho1-3_realestate.accdb (from Exercise 1) **Save:** chap3_ho1-3_realestate_solution.accdb (additional modifications) **Back up as:** chap3_ho2_realestate_solution.accdb	• Create a Select Query • Use the Expression Builder • Create Calculations Using Input Stored in a Different Query or Table • Edit Expressions Using the Expression Builder • Use Functions • Work with Date Arithmetic
3. DATA AGGREGATES (page 707) **Open:** chap3_ho1-3_realestate.accdb (from Exercise 2) **Save:** chap3_ho1-3_realestate_solution.accdb (additional modifications)	• Add a Total Row • Create a Totals Query Based on a Select Query • Add Fields to the Design Grid • Add Grouping Options and Specify Summary Statistics

Access 2007 677

Objective Mapping

allows students to skip the skills and concepts they know and quickly find those they don't by scanning the chapter opening page for the page numbers of the material they need.

Case Study

begins each chapter to provide an effective overview of what students can accomplish by completing the chapter.

CASE STUDY

West Transylvania College Athletic Department

Case Study

The athletic department of West Transylvania College has reached a fork in the road. A significant alumni contingent insists that the college upgrade its athletic program from NCAA Division II to Division I. This process will involve adding sports, funding athletic scholarships, expanding staff, and coordinating a variety of fundraising activities.

Tom Hunt, the athletic director, wants to determine if the funding support is available both inside and outside the college to accomplish this goal. You are helping Tom prepare the five-year projected budget based on current budget figures. The plan is to increase revenues at a rate of 10% per year for five years while handling an estimated 8% increase in expenses over the same five-year period. Tom feels that a 10% increase in revenue versus an 8% increase in expenses should make the upgrade viable. Tom wants to examine how increased alumni giving, increases in college fees, and grant monies will increase the revenue flow. The Transylvania College's Athletic Committee and its Alumni Association Board of Directors want Tom to present an analysis of funding and expenses to determine if the move to NCAA Division I is feasible. As Tom's student assistant this year, it is your responsibility to help him with special projects. Tom prepared the basic projected budget spreadsheet and has asked you to finish it for him.

Your Assignment

- Read the chapter carefully and pay close attention to mathematical operations, formulas, and functions.
- Open *chap2_case_athletics*, which contains the partially completed, projected budget spreadsheet.
- Study the structure of the worksheet to determine what type of formulas you need to complete the financial calculations. Identify how you would perform calculations if you were using a calculator and make a list of formulas using regular language to determine if the financial goals will be met. As you read the chapter, identify formulas and functions that will help you complete the financial analysis. You will insert formulas in the revenue and expenditures sections for column C. Use appropriate cell references in formulas. Do not enter constant values within a formula; instead enter the 10% and 8% increases in an input area. Use appropriate functions for column totals in both the revenue and expenditures sections. Insert formulas for the Net Operating Margin and Net Margin rows. Copy the formulas.
- Review the spreadsheet and identify weaknesses in the formatting. Use your knowledge of good formatting design to improve the appearance of the spreadsheet so that it will be attractive to the Athletic Committee and the alumni board. You will format cells as currency with 0 decimals and widen columns as needed. Merge and center the title and use an attractive fill color. Emphasize the totals and margin rows with borders. Enter your name and current date. Create a custom footer that includes a page number and your instructor's name. Print the worksheet as displayed and again with cell formulas displayed. Save the workbook as **chap2_case_athletics_solution**.

380 CHAPTER 2 | Formulas and Functions

Key Terms

are called out in the margins of the chapter so students can more effectively study definitions.

Pull Quotes

entice students into the theory by highlighting the most interesting points.

Tables

A *table* is a series of rows and columns that organize data.

A *cell* is the intersection of a row and column in a table.

A *table* is a series of rows and columns that organize data effectively. The rows and columns in a table intersect to form *cells*. The table feature is one of the most powerful in Word and is an easy way to organize a series of data in a columnar list format such as employee names, inventory lists, and e-mail addresses. The Vacation Planner in Figure 3.1, for example, is actually a 4x9 table (4 columns and 9 rows). The completed table looks impressive, but it is very easy to create once you understand how a table works. In addition to the organizational benefits, tables make an excellent alignment tool. For example, you can create tables to organize data such as employee lists with phone numbers and e-mail addresses. The Exploring series uses tables to provide descriptions for various software commands. Although you can align text with tabs, you have more format control when you create a table. (See the Practice Exercises at the end of the chapter for other examples.)

The table feature is one of the most powerful in Word and is the basis for an almost limitless variety of documents. It is very easy to create once you understand how a table works.

Vacation Planner			
Item	Number of Days	Amount per Day (est)	Total Amount
Airline Ticket			449.00
Amusement Park Tickets	4	50.00	200.00
Hotel	5	120.00	600.00
Meals	6	50.00	300.00
Rental Car	5	30.00	150.00
Souvenirs	5	20.00	100.00
TOTAL EXPECTED EXPENSES			$1799.00

Figure 3.1 The Vacation Planner

In this section, you insert a table in a document. After inserting the table, you can insert or delete columns and rows if you need to change the structure. Furthermore, you learn how to merge and split cells within the table. Finally, you change the row height and column width to accommodate data in the table.

Inserting a Table

You can create a table from the Insert tab. Click Table in the Tables group on the Insert tab to see a gallery of cells from which you select the number of columns and rows you require in the table, or you can choose the Insert Table command below the gallery to display the Insert Table dialog box and enter the table composition you prefer. When you select the table dimension from the gallery or from the Insert Table dialog box, Word creates a table structure with the number of columns and rows you specify. After you define a table, you can enter text, numbers, or graphics in individual cells. Text

Tables | Word 2007 197

White Pages/ Yellow Pages

clearly distinguishes the theory (white pages) from the skills covered in the Hands-On exercises (yellow pages) so students always know what they are supposed to be doing.

Keyword for search

Collections to be searched

Type of clips to be included in results

Search results

Link to Microsoft Clip Organizer

Link to more clips online

CIS 101 Review Session

Test #2

Monday

7pm

Glass 102

Figure 3.18 The Clip Art Task Pane

You can access the Microsoft Clip Organizer (to view the various collections) by clicking Organize clips at the bottom of the Clip Art task pane. You also can access the Clip Organizer when you are not using Word; click the Start button on the taskbar, click All Programs, Micros
Clip Organizer. Once in the Organi
ous collections, reorganize the exi
add new clips (with their associate
the bottom of the task pane in Figu
and tips for finding more relevant c

Insert a Picture

In addition to the collection of clip
you also can insert your own pictu
ital camera attached to your compu
Word. After you save the picture to
on the Insert tab to locate and insert
opens so that you can navigate to t
insert the picture, there are many c
mands are discussed in the next sec

Formatting a Grap

Remember that graphical elements should enhance a document, not overpower it.

When you inse
fined size. For
very large and
resized. Most t
within the d

Step 2 Move and Resize the Clip Art Object

Refer to Figure 3.24 as you complete Step 2.

a. Click once on the clip art object to select it. Click **Text Wrapping** in the Arrange group on the Picture Tools Format tab to display the text wrapping options and then select **Square** as shown in Figure 3.24.

   You must change the layout in order to move and size the object.

b. Click **Position** in the Arrange group, and then click **More Layout Options.** Click the **Picture Position tab** in the Advanced Layout dialog box, if necessary, then click **Alignment** in the *Horizontal* section. Click the **Alignment drop-down arrow** and select **Right**. Deselect the **Allow overlap check box** in the *Options* section. Click **OK**.

c. Click **Crop** in the Size group, then hold your mouse over the sizing handles and notice how the pointer changes to angular shapes. Click the **bottom center handle** and drag it up. Drag the side handles inward to remove excess space surrounding the graphical object.

d. Click the Shape **Height box** in the Size group and type **2.77**.

   Notice the width is changed automatically to retain the proportion.

e. Save the document.

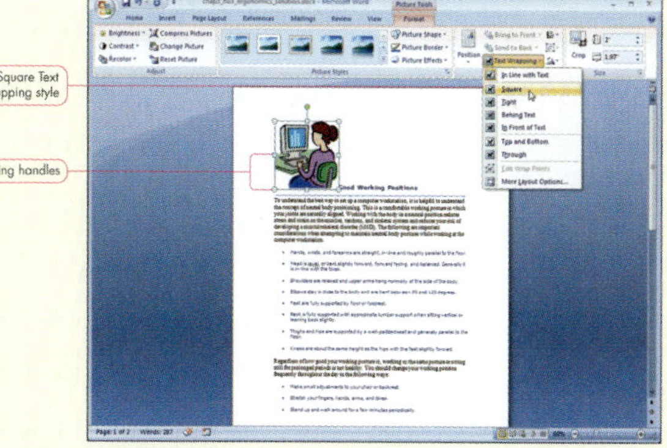

Figure 3.24 Formatting Clip Art

Step 3 Create a WordArt Object

Refer to Figure 3.25 as you complete Step 3.

a. Press **Ctrl+End** to move to the end of the document. Click the **Insert tab** and then click **WordArt** in the Text group to display the WordArt gallery.

b. Click **WordArt style 28** on the bottom row of the gallery.

   The Edit WordArt Text dialog box displays, as shown in Figure 3.25.

Summary

1. **Create a presentation using a template.** Using a template saves you a great deal of time and enables you to create a more professional presentation. Templates incorporate a theme, a layout, and content that can be modified. You can use templates that are installed when Microsoft Office is installed, or you can download templates from Microsoft Office Online. Microsoft is constantly adding templates to the online site for your use.
2. **Modify a template.** In addition to changing the content of a template, you can modify the structure and design. The structure is modified by changing the layout of a slide. To change the layout, drag placeholders to new locations or resize placeholders. You can even add placeholders so that elements such as logos can be included.
3. **Create a presentation in Outline view.** When you use a storyboard to determine your content, you create a basic outline. Then you can enter your presentation in Outline view, which enables you to concentrate on the content of the presentation. Using Outline view keeps you from getting buried in design issues at the cost of your content. It also saves you time because you can enter the information without having to move from placeholder to placeholder.
4. **Modify an outline structure.** Because the Outline view gives you a global view of the presentation, it helps you see the underlying structure of the presentation. You are able to see where content needs to be strengthened, or where the flow of information needs to be revised. If you find a slide with content that would be presented better in another location in the slide show, you can use the Collapse and Expand features to easily move it. By collapsing the slide content, you can drag it to a new location and then expand it. To move individual bullet points, cut and paste the bullet point or drag-and-drop it.
5. **Print an outline.** When you present, using the outline version of your slide show as a reference is a boon. No matter how well you know your information, it is easy to forget to present some information when facing an audience. While you would print speaker's notes if you have many details, you can print the outline as a quick reference. The outline can be printed in either the collapsed or the expanded form, giving you far fewer pages to shuffle in front of an audience than printing speaker's notes would.
6. **Import an outline.** You do not need to re-enter information from an outline created in Microsoft Word or another word processor. You can use the Open feature to import any outline that has been saved in a format that PowerPoint can read. In addition to a Word outline, you can use the common generic formats Rich Text Format and Plain Text Format.
7. **Add existing content to a presentation.** After you spend time creating the slides in a slide show, you may find that slides in the slide show would be appropriate in another show at a later date. Any slide you create can be reused in another presentation, thereby saving you considerable time and effort. You simply open the Reuse Slides pane, locate the slide show with the slide you need, and then click on the thumbnail of the slide to insert a copy of it in the new slide show.
8. **Examine slide show design principles.** With a basic understanding of slide show design principles you can create presentations that reflect your personality in a professional way. The goal of applying these principles is to create a slide show that focuses the audience on the message of the slide without being distracted by clutter or unreadable text.
9. **Apply and modify a design theme.** PowerPoint provides you with themes to help you create a clean, professional look for your presentation. Once a theme is applied you can modify the theme by changing the color scheme, the font scheme, the effects scheme, or the background style.
10. **Insert a header or footer.** Identifying information can be included in a header or footer. You may, for example, wish to include the group to whom you are presenting, or the location of the presentation, or a copyright notation for original work. You can apply footers to slides, handouts, and Notes pages. Headers may be applied to handouts and Notes pages.

Summary

links directly back to the objectives so students can more effectively study and locate the concepts that they need to focus on.

More End-of-Chapter Exercises with New Levels of Assessment

offer instructors more options for assessment. Each chapter has approximately 12-15 projects ranging from multiple choice to open-ended cases.

Practice Exercises

reinforce skills learned in the chapter with specific directions on what to do and how to do it.

New Mid-Level Exercises

assess the skills learned in the chapter by directing the students on what to do but not how to do it.

New Capstone Exercises

cover all of the skills with in each chapter without telling students how to perform the skills.

Mini Cases with Rubrics

are open-ended exercises that guide both instructors and students to a solution with a specific rubric for each Mini Case.

chapter 1 | Office Fundamentals

Using Word, Excel, Access, and PowerPoint

Objectives

After you read this chapter, you will be able to:

1. Identify common interface components **(page 4)**.
2. Use Office 2007 Help **(page 10)**.
3. Open a file **(page 18)**.
4. Save a file **(page 21)**.
5. Print a document **(page 24)**.
6. Select text to edit **(page 31)**.
7. Insert text and change to the Overtype mode **(page 32)**.
8. Move and copy text **(page 34)**.
9. Find, replace, and go to text **(page 36)**.
10. Use the Undo and Redo commands **(page 39)**.
11. Use language tools **(page 39)**.
12. Apply font attributes **(page 43)**.
13. Copy formats with the Format Painter **(page 47)**.

Hands-On Exercises

Exercises	Skills Covered
1. IDENTIFYING PROGRAM INTERFACE COMPONENTS AND USING HELP (page 12)	• Use PowerPoint's Office Button, Get Help in a Dialog Box, and Use the Zoom Slider • Use Excel's Ribbon, Get Help from an Enhanced ScreenTip, and Use the Zoom Dialog Box • Search Help in Access • Use Word's Status Bar • Search Help and Print a Help Topic
2. PERFORMING UNIVERSAL TASKS (page 28) **Open:** chap1_ho2_sample.docx **Save as:** chap1_ho2_solution.docx	• Open a File and Save it with a Different Name • Use Print Preview and Select Options • Print a Document
3. PERFORMING BASIC TASKS (page 48) **Open:** chap1_ho3_internet_docx **Save as:** chap1_ho3_internet_solution.docx	• Cut, Copy, Paste, and Undo • Find and Replace Text • Check Spelling • Choose Synonyms and Use Thesaurus • Use the Research Tool • Apply Font Attributes • Use Format Painter

CASE STUDY

Color Theory Design

Natalie Trevino's first job after finishing her interior design degree is with Color Theory Design of San Diego. Her new supervisor has asked her to review a letter written to an important client and to make any changes or corrections she thinks will improve it. Even though Natalie has used word processing software in the past, she is unfamiliar with Microsoft Office 2007. She needs to get up to speed with Word 2007 so that she can open the letter, edit the content, format the appearance, re-save the file, and print the client letter. Natalie wants to successfully complete this important first task, plus she wants to become familiar with all of Office 2007 because she realizes that her new employer, CTD, makes extensive use of all the Office products.

Case Study

In addition, Natalie needs to improve the appearance of an Excel workbook by applying font attributes, correcting spelling errors, changing the zoom magnification, and printing the worksheet. Finally, Natalie needs to modify a short PowerPoint presentation that features supplemental design information for CTD's important client.

Your Assignment

- Read the chapter and open the existing client letter, *chap1_case_design*.
- Edit the letter by inserting and overtyping text and moving existing text to improve the letter's readability.
- Find and replace text that you want to update.
- Check the spelling and improve the vocabulary by using the thesaurus.
- Modify the letter's appearance by applying font attributes.
- Save the file as **chap1_case_design_solution**, print preview, and print a copy of the letter.
- Open the *chap1_case_bid* workbook in Excel, apply bold and blue font color to the column headings, spell-check the worksheet, change the zoom to 125%, print preview, and print the workbook. Save the workbook as **chap1_case_bid_solution**.
- Open the *chap1_case_design* presentation in PowerPoint, spell-check the presentation, format text, and save it as **chap1_case_design_solution**.

Microsoft Office 2007 Software

Which software application should you choose? You have to start with an analysis of the output required.

Microsoft Office 2007 is composed of several software applications, of which the primary components are Word, Excel, PowerPoint, and Access. These programs are powerful tools that can be used to increase productivity in creating, editing, saving, and printing files. Each program is a specialized and sophisticated program, so it is necessary to use the correct one to successfully complete a task, much like using the correct tool in the physical world. For example, you use a hammer, not a screwdriver, to pound a nail into the wall. Using the correct tool gets the job done correctly and efficiently the first time; using the wrong tool may require redoing the task, thus wasting time. Likewise, you should use the most appropriate software application to create and work with computer data.

Choosing the appropriate application to use in a situation seems easy to the beginner. If you need to create a letter, you type the letter in Word. However, as situations increase in complexity, so does the need to think through using each application. For example, you can create an address book of names and addresses in Word to create form letters; you can create an address list in Excel and then use spreadsheet commands to manipulate the data; further, you can store addresses in an Access database table and then use database capabilities to manipulate the data. Which software application should you choose? You have to start with an analysis of the output required. If you only want a form letter as the final product, then you might use Word; however, if you want to spot customer trends with the data and provide detailed reports, you would use Access. Table 1.1 describes the main characteristics of the four primary programs in Microsoft Office 2007 to help you decide which program to use for particular tasks.

Word processing software is used primarily with text to create, edit, and format documents.

Spreadsheet software is used primarily with numbers to create worksheets.

Presentation graphics software is used primarily to create electronic slide shows.

Relational database software is used to store data and convert it into information.

Table 1.1 Office Products

Office 2007 Product	Application Characteristics
Word 2007	***Word processing software*** is used with text to create, edit, and format documents such as letters, memos, reports, brochures, resumes, and flyers.
Excel 2007	***Spreadsheet software*** is used to store quantitative data and to perform accurate and rapid calculations with results ranging from simple budgets to financial analyses and statistical analyses.
PowerPoint 2007	***Presentation graphics software*** is used to create slide shows for presentation by a speaker, to be published as part of a Web site, or to run as a stand-alone application on a computer kiosk.
Access 2007	***Relational database software*** is used to store data and convert it into information. Database software is used primarily for decision-making by businesses that compile data from multiple records stored in tables to produce informative reports.

In this section, you explore the common interface among the programs. You learn the names of the interface elements. In addition, you learn how to use Help to get assistance in using the software.

Identifying Common Interface Components

A ***user interface*** is the meeting point between computer software and the person using it.

A ***user interface*** is the meeting point between computer software and the person using it and provides the means for a person to communicate with a software program. Word, Excel, PowerPoint, and Access share the overall Microsoft Office 2007 interface. This interface is made up of three main sections of the screen display shown in Figure 1.1.

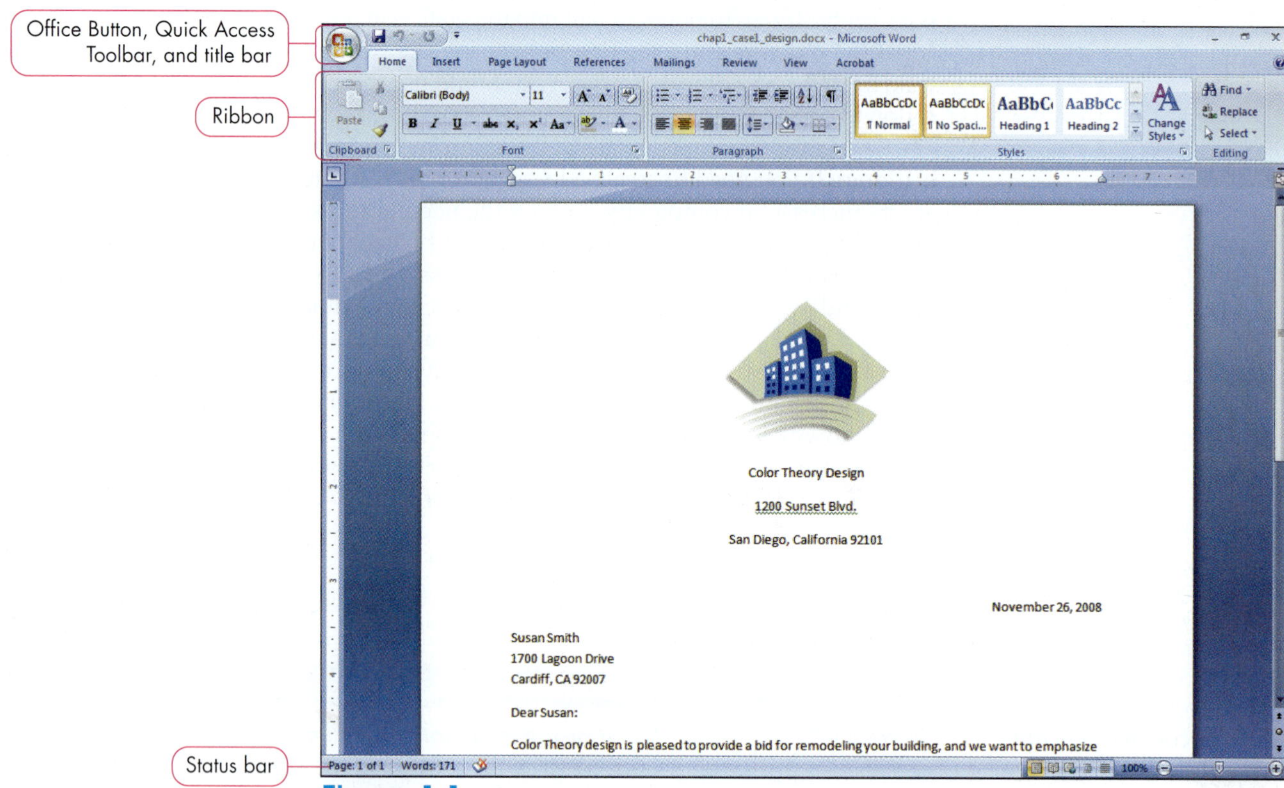

Figure 1.1 Office 2007 Interface

Use the Office Button and Quick Access Toolbar

The first section of the Office 2007 interface contains three distinct items: the Microsoft Office Button (referred to as Office Button in the Exploring series), Quick Access Toolbar, and the title bar. These three items are located at the top of the interface for quick access and reference. The following paragraphs explain each item.

Click the ***Office Button*** to display the Office menu.

The ***Office menu*** contains commands that work with an entire file or with the program.

The ***Office Button*** is an icon that, when clicked, displays the ***Office menu***, a list of commands that you can perform on the entire file or for the specific Office program. For example, when you want to perform a task that involves the entire document, such as saving, printing, or sharing a file with others, you use the commands on the Office menu. You also use the Office menu commands to work with the entire program, such as customizing program settings or exiting from the program. Some commands on the Office menu perform a default action when you click them, such as Save—the file open in the active window is saved. However, other commands open a submenu when you point to or click the command. Figure 1.2 displays the Office menu in Access 2007.

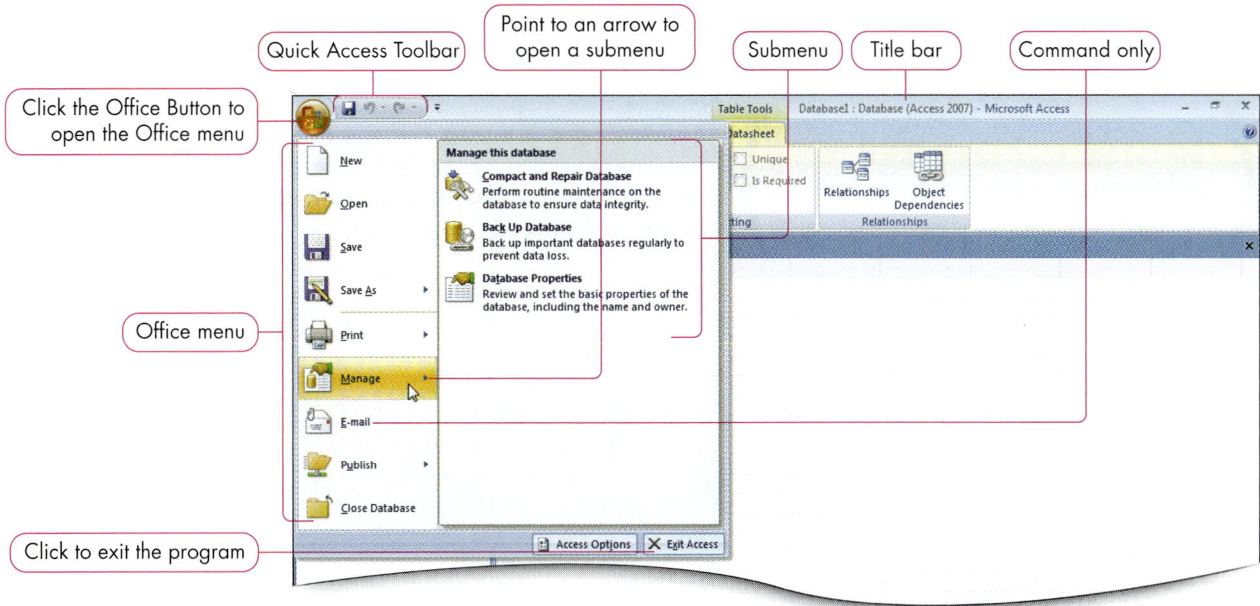

Figure 1.2 Access Office Menu

TIP
Displaying the Office Menu from the Keyboard

If you prefer to use a keyboard shortcut to display the Office menu instead of clicking the Office Button, press Alt+F.

The ***Quick Access Toolbar*** contains buttons for frequently used commands.

The second item at the top of the window is the ***Quick Access Toolbar***, which contains buttons for frequently used commands, such as saving a file or undoing an action. This toolbar keeps buttons for common tasks on the screen at all times, enabling you to be more productive in using these frequently used commands.

TIP Customizing the Quick Access Toolbar

As you become more familiar with Microsoft Office 2007, you might find that you need quick access to additional commands, such as Print Preview or Spelling & Grammar. You can easily customize the Quick Access Toolbar by clicking the Customize Quick Access Toolbar drop-down arrow on the right end of the toolbar and adding command buttons from the list that displays. You also can customize the toolbar by changing where it displays. If you want it closer to the document window, you can move the toolbar below the Ribbon.

A ***title bar*** displays the program name and file name at the top of a window.

The third item at the top of the screen is the ***title bar***, which displays the name of the open program and the file name at the top of a window. For example, in Figure 1.1, *chap1_case1_design* is the name of a document, and *Microsoft Word* is the name of the program. In Figure 1.2, *Database1* is the name of the file, and *Access 2007* is the name of the program.

The **Ribbon** is a large strip of visual commands that enables you to perform tasks.

Familiarize Yourself with the Ribbon

The second section of the Office 2007 interface is the ***Ribbon***, a large strip of visual commands that displays across the screen below the Office Button, Quick Access Toolbar, and the title bar. The Ribbon is the most important section of the interface: It is the command center of the Microsoft Office 2007 interface, providing access to the functionality of the programs (see Figure 1.3).

> The Ribbon is the command center of the Microsoft Office 2007 interface, providing access to the functionality of the programs.

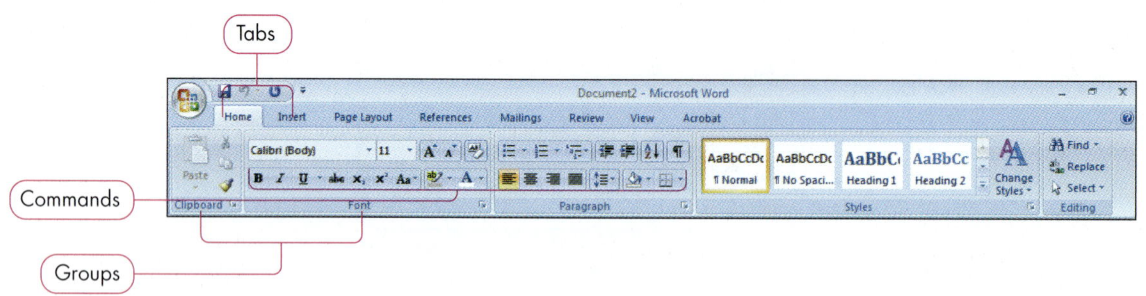

Figure 1.3 The Ribbon

The Ribbon has three main components: tabs, groups, and commands. The following list describes each component.

Tabs, which look like folder tabs, divide the Ribbon into task-oriented categories.

- ***Tabs***, which look like folder tabs, divide the Ribbon into task-oriented sections. For example, the Ribbon in Word contains these tabs: Home, Insert, Page Layout, References, Mailings, Review, and View. When you click the Home tab, you see a set of core commands for that program. When you click the Insert tab, you see a set of commands that enable you to insert objects, such as tables, clip art, headers, page numbers, etc.

Groups organize similar commands together within each tab.

- ***Groups*** organize related commands together on each tab. For example, the Home tab in Word contains these groups: Clipboard, Font, Paragraph, Styles, and Editing. These groups help organize related commands together so that you can find them easily. For example, the Font group contains font-related commands, such as Font, Font Size, Bold, Italic, Underline, Text Highlight Color, and Font Color.

A ***command*** is a visual icon in each group that you click to perform a task.

- ***Commands*** are specific tasks performed. Commands appear as visual icons or buttons within the groups on the Ribbon. The icons are designed to provide a visual clue of the purpose of the command. For example, the Bold command looks like a bolded B in the Font group on the Home tab. You simply click the desired command to perform the respective task.

The Ribbon has the same basic design—tabs, groups, and commands—across all Microsoft Office 2007 applications. When you first start using an Office 2007 application, you use the Home tab most often. The groups of commands on the Home tab are designed to get you started using the software. For example, the Home tab contains commands to help you create, edit, and format a document in Word, a worksheet in Excel, and a presentation in PowerPoint. In Access, the Home tab contains commands to save, delete, and filter records in a database table. While three of the four applications contain an Insert tab, the specific groups and commands differ by application. Regardless of the application, however, the Insert tab contains commands to *insert something*, whether it is a page number in Word, a column chart in Excel, or a shape in PowerPoint. One of the best ways to develop an understanding of the Ribbon is to study its structure in each application. As you explore each program, you will notice the similarities in how commands are grouped on tabs, and you will notice the differences specific to each application.

TIP Hiding the Ribbon

If you are creating a large document or worksheet, you might find that the Ribbon takes up too much of the screen display. Microsoft enables you to temporarily hide a large portion of the Ribbon. Double-click the active tab, such as Home, to hide all the groups and commands, greatly reducing the size of the Ribbon. When you want to display the entire Ribbon, double-click the active tab. You also can press **Ctrl+F1** to minimize and maximize the Ribbon.

The Ribbon provides an extensive set of commands that you use when creating and editing documents, worksheets, slides, tables, or other items. Figure 1.4 points out other important components of the Ribbon.

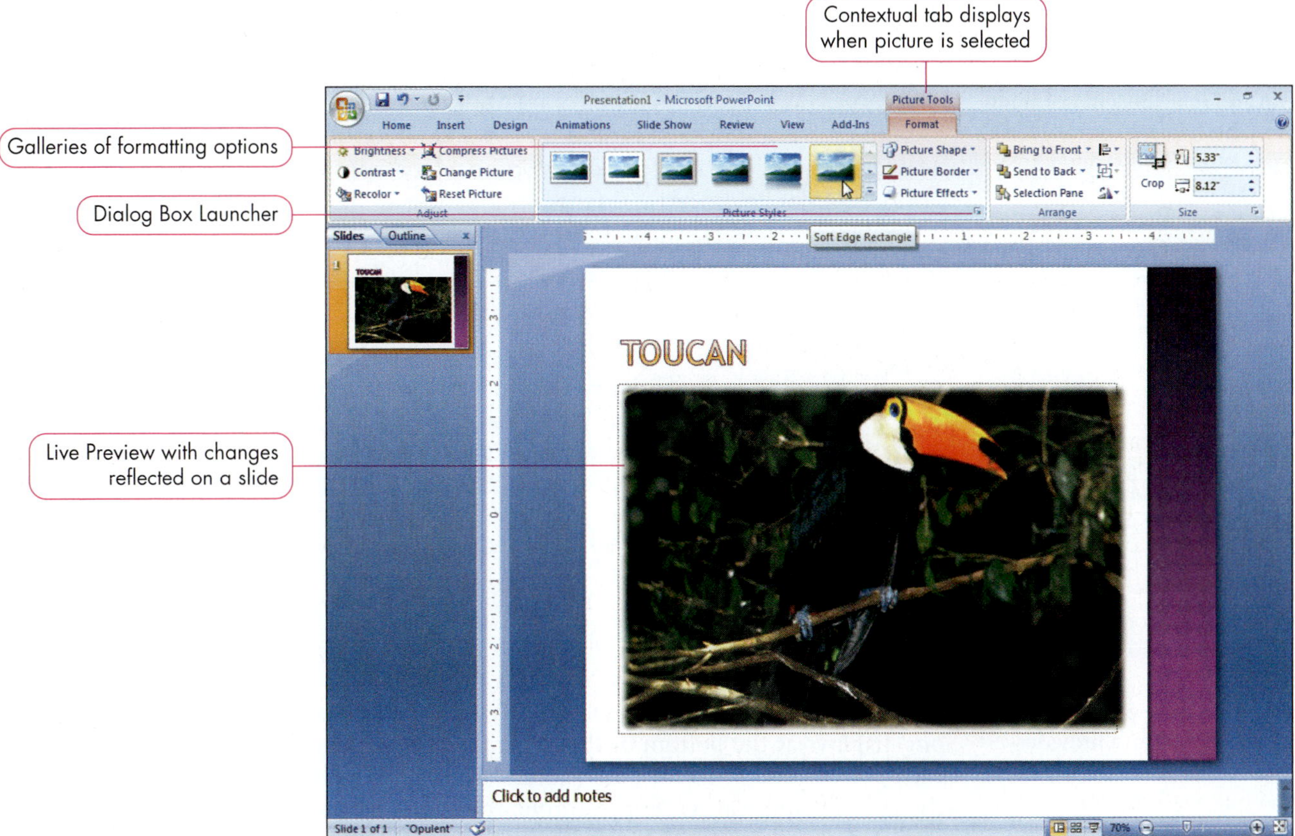

Figure 1.4 PowerPoint with Ribbon

A ***dialog box*** is a window that provides options related to a group of commands.

A ***Dialog Box Launcher*** is a small icon that, when clicked, opens a related dialog box.

A ***gallery*** is a set of options that appears as thumbnail graphics.

Live Preview provides a preview of the results for gallery options.

Figure 1.4 shows examples of four other components of the Ribbon. These components include a Dialog Box Launcher, a gallery, Live Preview, and a contextual tab. The following list describes each component:

- A ***Dialog Box Launcher*** is a small icon located on the right side of some group names that you click to open a related ***dialog box***, which is a window that provides options related to a group of commands.
- A ***gallery*** is a set of options that appear as thumbnail graphics that visually represent the option results. For example, if you create a chart in Excel, a gallery of chart formatting options provides numerous choices for formatting the chart.
- ***Live Preview*** works with the galleries, providing a preview of the results of formatting in the document. As you move your mouse pointer over the gallery

thumbnails, you see how each formatting option affects the selected item in your document, worksheet, or presentation. This feature increases productivity because you see the results immediately. If you do not like the results, keep moving the mouse pointer over other gallery options until you find a result you like.

A ***contextual tab*** is a tab that provides specialized commands that display only when the object they affect is selected.

- A *contextual tab* provides specialized commands that display only when the object they affect is selected. For example, if you insert a picture on a slide, PowerPoint displays a contextual tab on the Ribbon with commands specifically related to the selected image. When you click outside the picture to deselect it, the contextual tab disappears.

A ***Key Tip*** is the letter or number that displays over each feature on the Ribbon and Quick Access Toolbar and is the keyboard equivalent that you press.

TIP Using Keyboard Shortcuts

Many people who have used previous Office products like to use the keyboard to initiate commands. Microsoft Office 2007 makes it possible for you to continue to use keyboard shortcuts for commands on the Ribbon. Simply press Alt on the keyboard to display shortcuts, called Key Tips, on the Ribbon and Quick Access Toolbar. A ***Key Tip*** is the letter or number that displays over each feature on the Ribbon or Quick Access Toolbar and is the keyboard equivalent that you press. Notice the Key Tips that display in Figure 1.5 as a result of pressing Alt on the keyboard. Other keyboard shortcuts, such as Ctrl+C to copy text, remain the same from previous versions of Microsoft Office.

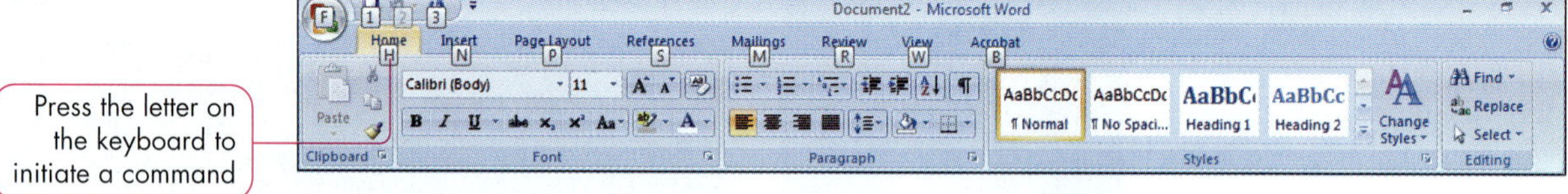

Figure 1.5 Key Tips Displayed for Ribbon and Quick Access Toolbar

Use the Status Bar

The ***status bar*** displays below the document and provides information about the open file and buttons for quick access.

The third major section of the Office 2007 user interface is the status bar. The ***status bar*** displays at the bottom of the program window and contains information about the open file and tools for quick access. The status bar contains details for the file in the specific application. For example, the Word status bar shows the current page, total number of pages, total words in the document, and proofreading status. The PowerPoint status bar shows the slide number, total slides in the presentation, and the applied theme. The Excel status bar provides general instructions and displays the average, count, and sum of values for selected cells. In each program, the status bar also includes View commands from the View tab for quick access. You can use the View commands to change the way the document, worksheet, or presentation displays onscreen. Table 1.2 describes the main characteristics of each Word 2007 view.

Table 1.2 Word Document Views

View Option	Characteristics
Print Layout	Displays the document as it will appear when printed.
Full Screen Reading	Displays the document on the entire screen to make reading long documents easier. To remove Full Screen Reading view, press the Esc key on the keyboard.
Web Layout	Displays the document as it would look as a Web page.
Outline	Displays the document as an outline.
Draft	Displays the document for quick editing without additional elements such as headers or footers.

The ***Zoom slider*** enables you to increase or decrease the magnification of the file onscreen.

The ***Zoom slider,*** located on the right edge of the status bar, enables you to drag the slide control to change the magnification of the current document, worksheet, or presentation. You can change the display to zoom in on the file to get a close up view, or you can zoom out to get an overview of the file. To use the Zoom slider, click and drag the slider control to the right to increase the zoom or to the left to decrease the zoom. If you want to set a specific zoom, such as 78%, you can type the precise value in the Zoom dialog box when you click Zoom on the View tab. Figure 1.6 shows the Zoom dialog box and the elements on Word's status bar. The Zoom dialog box in Excel and PowerPoint looks similar to the Word Zoom dialog box, but it contains fewer options in the other programs.

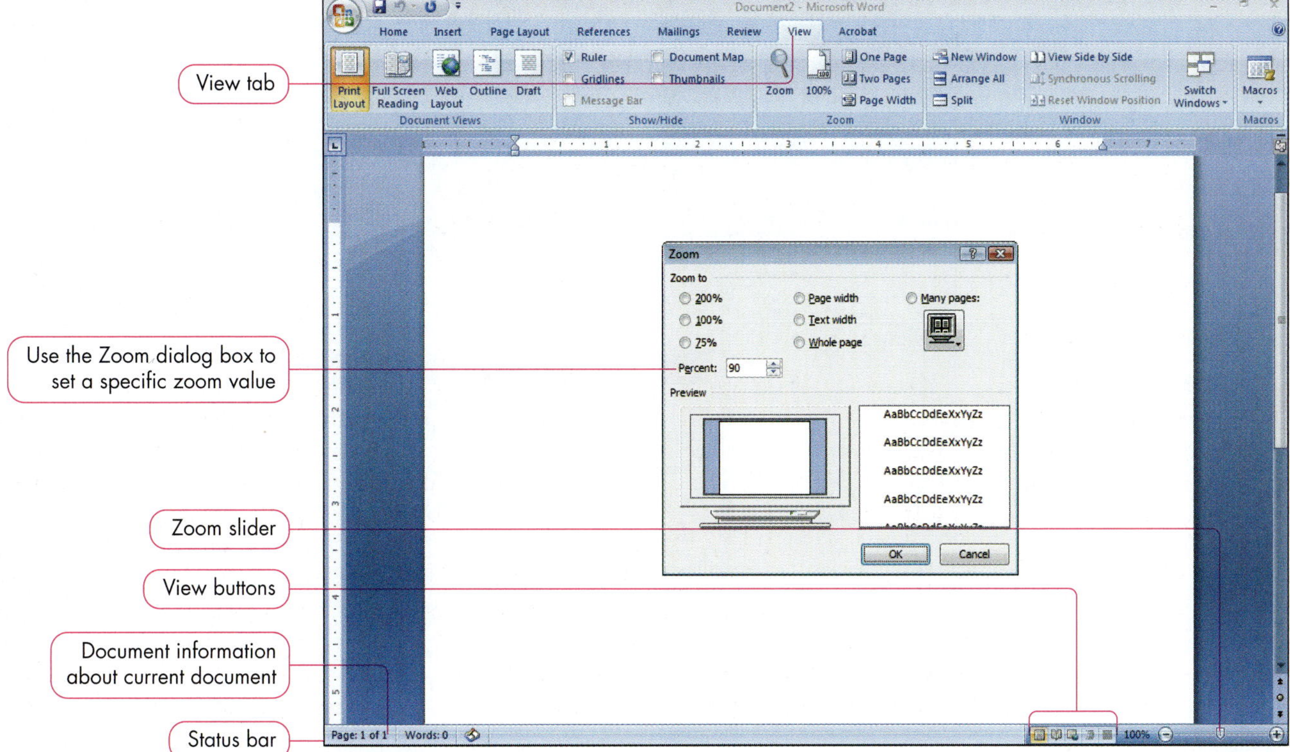

Figure 1.6 View Tab, Zoom Dialog Box, and the Status Bar in Word

Using Office 2007 Help

(Help is always available when you use any Office 2007 program.)

Have you ever started a project such as assembling an entertainment center and had to abandon it because you had no way to get help when you got stuck? Microsoft Office includes features that keep this type of scenario from happening when you use Word, Excel, Access, or PowerPoint. In fact, several methods are available to locate help when you need assistance performing tasks. Help is always available when you use any Office 2007 program. Help files reside on your computer when you install Microsoft Office, and Microsoft provides additional help files on its Web site. If you link to Microsoft Office Online, you not only have access to help files for all applications, you also have access to up-to-date products, files, and graphics to help you complete projects.

Use Office 2007 Help

To access Help, press F1 on the keyboard or click the Help button on the right edge of the Ribbon shown in Figure 1.7. If you know the topic you want help with, such as printing, you can type the key term in the Search box to display help files on that topic. Help also displays general topics in the lower part of the Help window that are links to further information. To display a table of contents for the Help files, click the Show Table of Contents icon, and after locating the desired help topic, you can print the information for future reference by clicking the Print button. Figure 1.7 shows these elements in Excel Help.

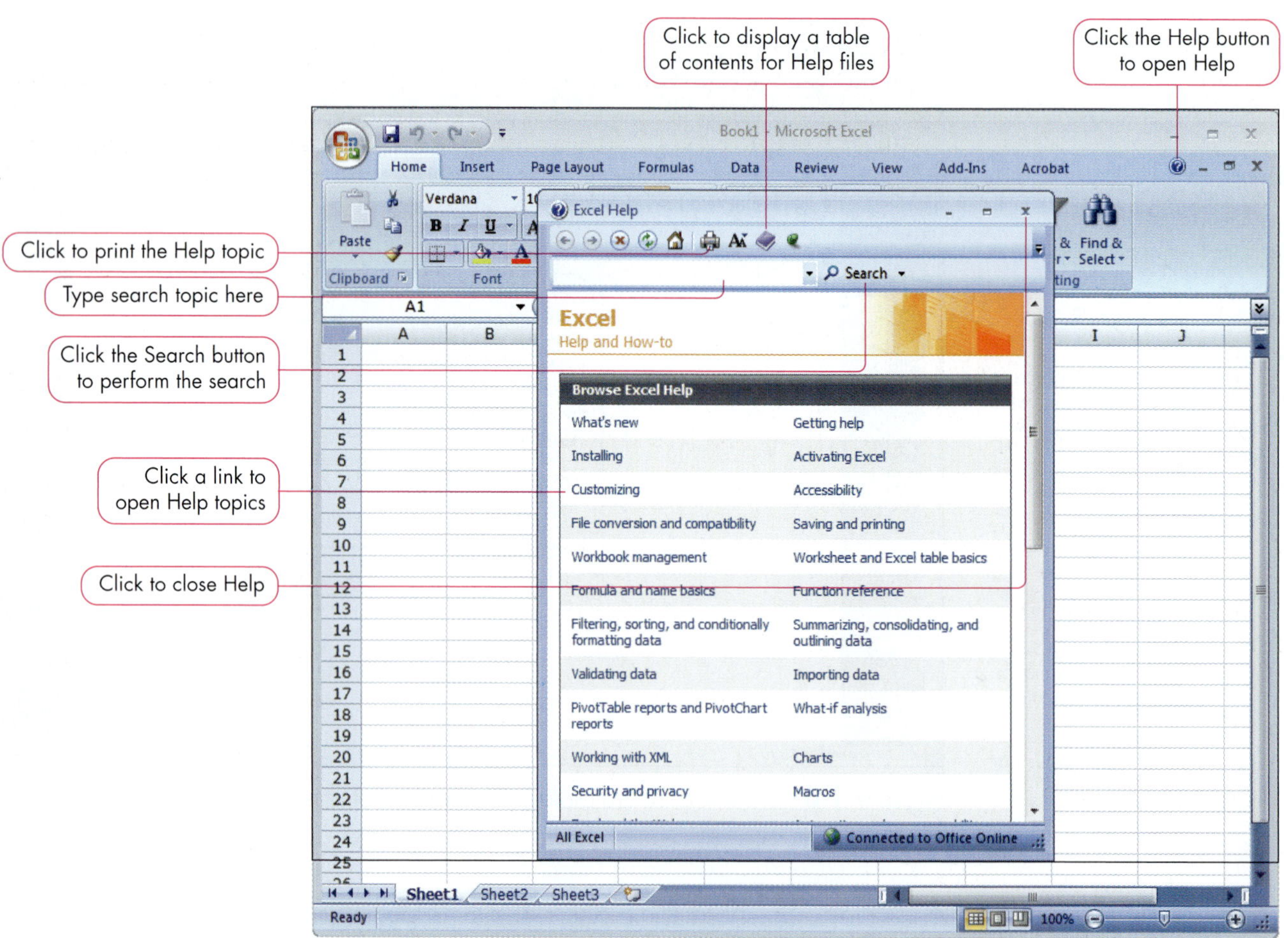

Figure 1.7 Excel Help

Use Enhanced ScreenTips

An ***Enhanced ScreenTip*** displays the name and brief description of a command when you rest the pointer on a command.

Another method for getting help is to use the Office 2007 Enhanced ScreenTips. An ***Enhanced ScreenTip*** displays when you rest the mouse pointer on a command. Notice in Figure 1.8 that the Enhanced ScreenTip provides the command name, a brief description of the command, and a link for additional help. To get help on the specific command, keep the pointer resting on the command and press F1 if the Enhanced ScreenTip displays a Help icon. The advantage of this method is that you do not have to find the correct information yourself because the Enhanced ScreenTip help is context sensitive.

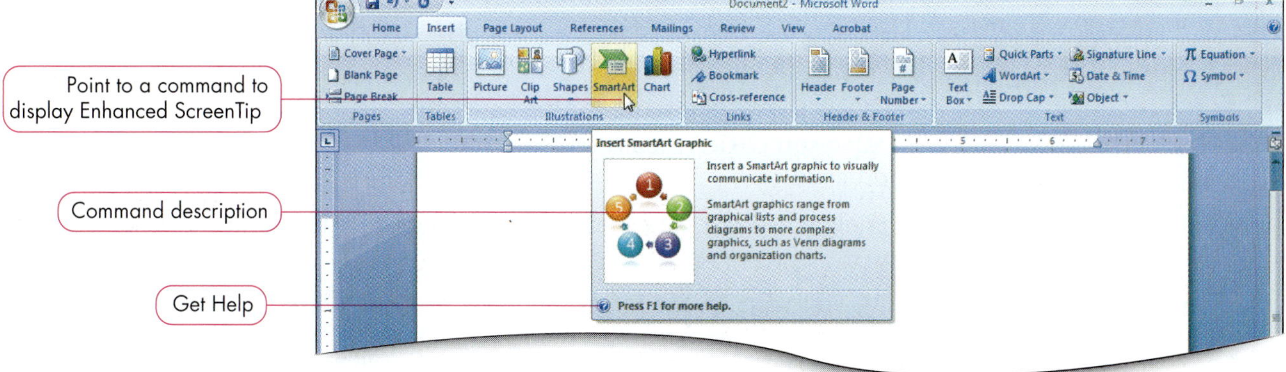

Figure 1.8 Enhanced ScreenTip

Get Help with Dialog Boxes

As you work within a dialog box, you might need help with some of the numerous options contained in that dialog box, but you do not want to close the dialog box to get assistance. For example, if you open the Insert Picture dialog box and want help with inserting files, click the Help button, which is often located on the title bar of the dialog box, to display help for the dialog box. Figure 1.9 shows the Insert Picture dialog box with Help displayed.

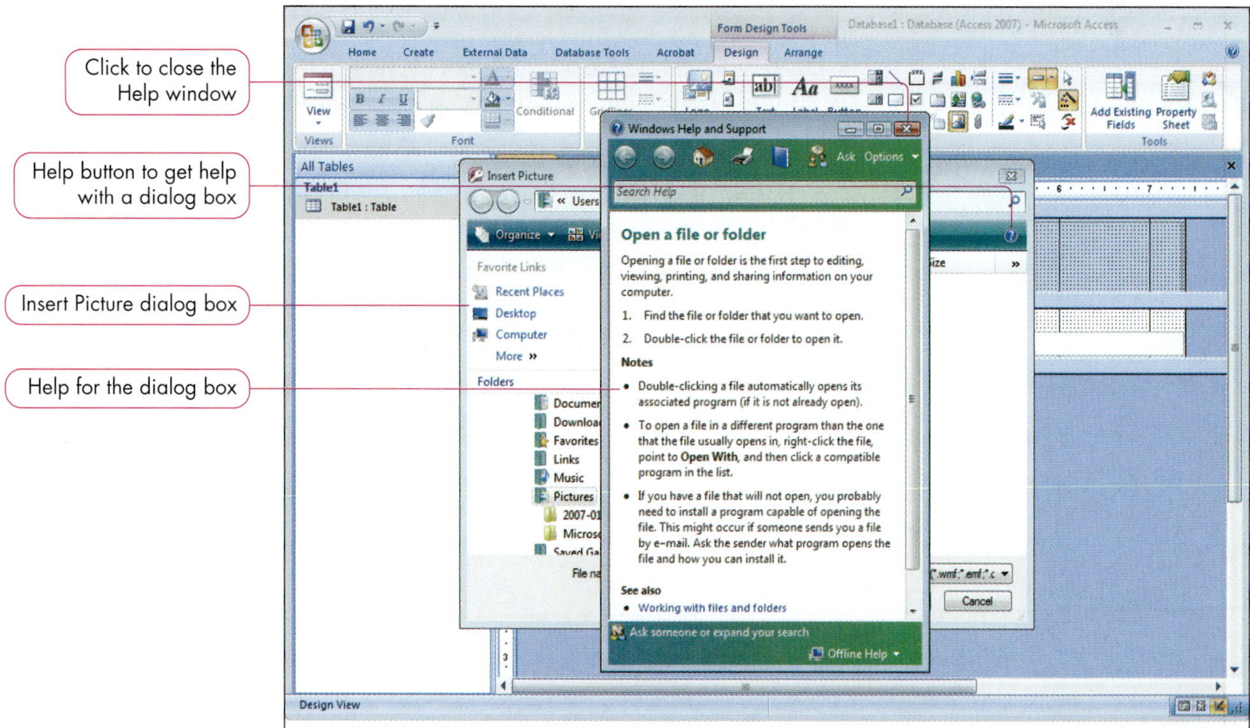

Figure 1.9 Help with Dialog Boxes

Hands-On Exercises

1 | Identifying Program Interface Components and Using Help

Skills covered: 1. Use PowerPoint's Office Button, Get Help in a Dialog Box, and Use the Zoom Slider **2.** Use Excel's Ribbon, Get Help from an Enhanced ScreenTip, and Use the Zoom Dialog Box **3.** Search Help in Access **4.** Use Word's Status Bar **5.** Search Help and Print a Help Topic

Step 1

Use PowerPoint's Office Button, Get Help in a Dialog Box, and Use the Zoom Slider

Refer to Figure 1.10 as you complete Step 1.

a. Click **Start** to display the Start menu. Click (or point to) **All Programs**, click **Microsoft Office**, then click **Microsoft Office PowerPoint 2007** to start the program.

b. Point to and rest the mouse pointer on the Office Button and then do the same to the Quick Access Toolbar.

   As you rest the mouse pointer on the Office Button, you see an Enhanced ScreenTip. As you rest the mouse pointer over a command on the Quick Access Toolbar, you see a regular ScreenTip that states the name of the command and its keyboard shortcut, such as *Save (Ctrl+S)*.

   TROUBLESHOOTING: If you do not see the Enhanced ScreenTip, keep the mouse pointer on the object a little longer.

c. Click the **Office Button** and slowly move your mouse down the list of menu options, pointing to the arrow after any command name that has one.

   The Office menu displays, and as you move the mouse down the list, submenus display for menu options that have an arrow.

d. Select **New** in the list displayed for the Office Button.

   The New Presentation dialog box displays. Depending on how Microsoft Office 2007 was installed, your screen may vary. If Microsoft Office 2007 was fully installed, you should see a thumbnail to create a Blank Presentation, and you may see additional thumbnails in the *Recently Used Templates* section of the dialog box.

e. Click the **Help button** on the title bar of the New Presentation dialog box.

   PowerPoint Help displays the topic *Why do you check to see if my software is genuine when I download a template?* Microsoft periodically changes some Help topics. The topic you see might be different from the one shown in Figure 1.10.

f. Click **Close** in the PowerPoint Help window, and click the **Cancel** button in the New Presentation dialog box.

g. Click and drag the **Zoom slider** to the right to increase the magnification. Then click and drag the **Zoom slider** back to the center point for a 100% zoom.

h. To exit PowerPoint, click the **Office Button** to display the Office menu and then click the **Exit PowerPoint button**.

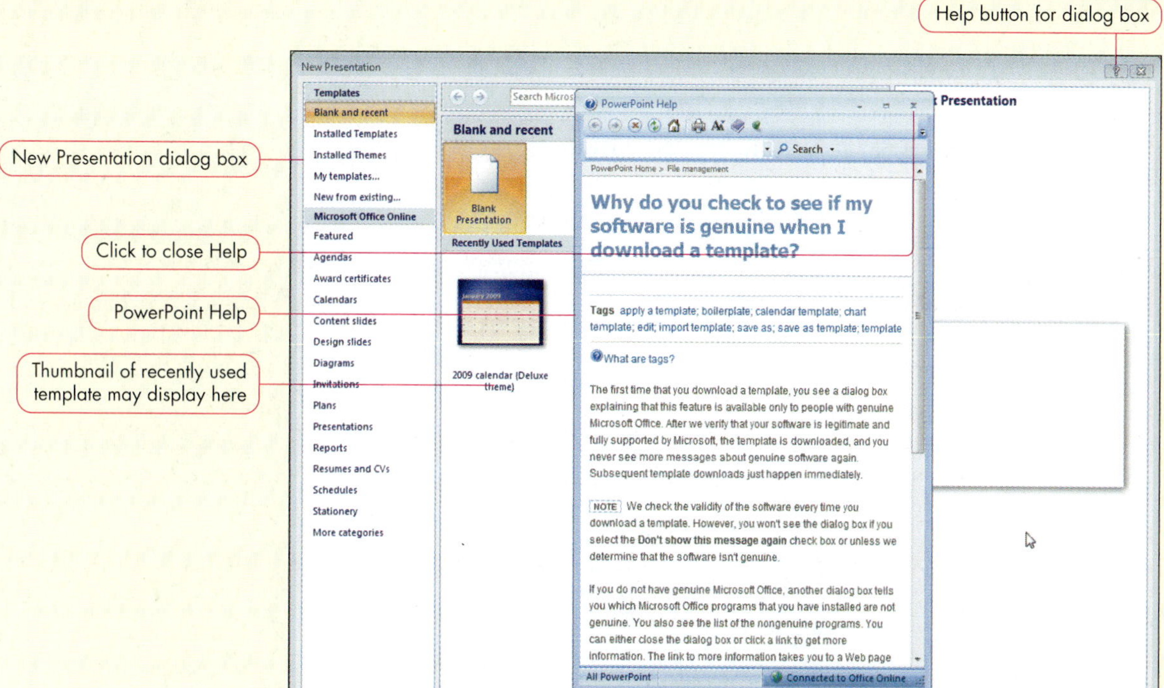

Figure 1.10 PowerPoint Help for New Presentation Dialog Box

Step 2

Use Excel's Ribbon, Get Help from an Enhanced ScreenTip, and Use the Zoom Dialog Box

Refer to Figure 1.11 as you complete Step 2.

a. Click **Start** to display the Start menu. Click (or point to) **All Programs**, click **Microsoft Office**, then click **Microsoft Office Excel 2007** to open the program.

b. Click the **Insert tab** on the Ribbon.

   The Insert tab contains groups of commands for inserting objects, such as tables, illustrations, charts, links, and text.

c. Rest the mouse on **Hyperlink** in the Links group on the Insert tab.

   The Enhanced ScreenTip for Hyperlinks displays. Notice the Enhanced ScreenTip contains a Help icon.

d. Press **F1** on the keyboard.

   Excel Help displays the *Create or remove a hyperlink* Help topic.

   TROUBLESHOOTING: If you are not connected to the Internet, you might not see the context-sensitive help.

e. Click the **Close button** in the Excel Help window.

f. Click the **View tab** on the Ribbon and click **Zoom** in the Zoom group.

   The Zoom dialog box appears so that you can change the zoom percentage.

g. Click the **200%** option and click **OK**.

   The worksheet is now magnified to 200% of its regular size.

h. Click **100%** in the Zoom group on the View tab.

   The worksheet is now restored to 100%.

i. To exit Excel, click the **Office Button** to display the Office menu and then click the **Exit Excel button**.

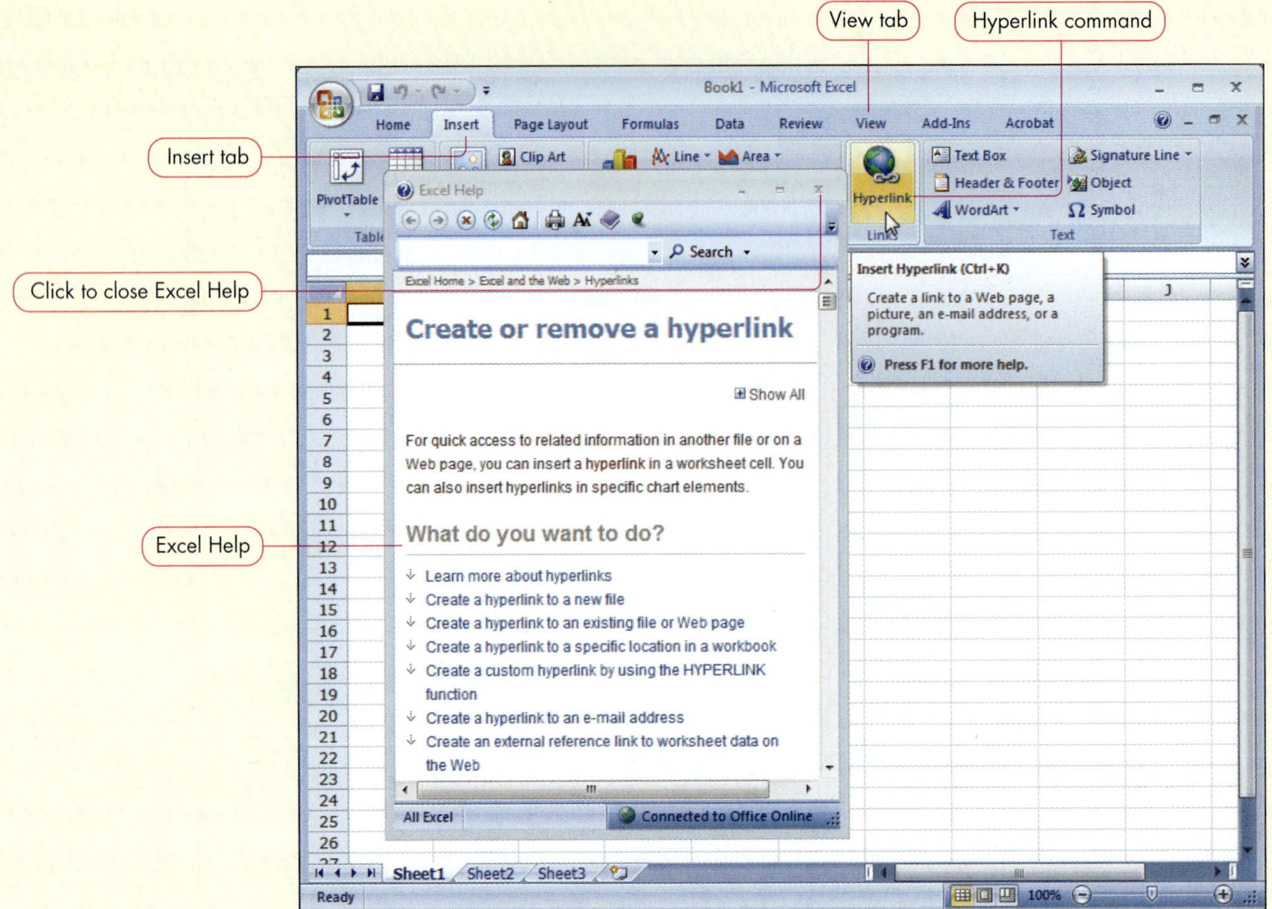

Figure 1.11 Excel Ribbon with Help

Step 3
Search Help in Access

Refer to Figure 1.12 as you complete Step 3.

a. Click **Start** to display the Start menu. Click (or point to) **All Programs**, click **Microsoft Office**, then click **Microsoft Office Access 2007** to start the program.

   Access opens and displays the Getting Started with Microsoft Office Access screen.

   TROUBLESHOOTING: If you are not familiar with Access, just use the opening screen that displays and continue with the exercise.

b. Press **F1** on the keyboard.

   Access Help displays.

c. Type **table** in the Search box in the Access Help window.

d. Click the **Search** button.

   Access displays help topics.

e. Click the topic **Create a table**.

   The *Create a table* Help topic displays.

f. Click the **Close** button on the Access Help window.

   Access Help closes.

g. To exit Access, click the **Office Button** to display the Office menu and then click the **Exit Access button**.

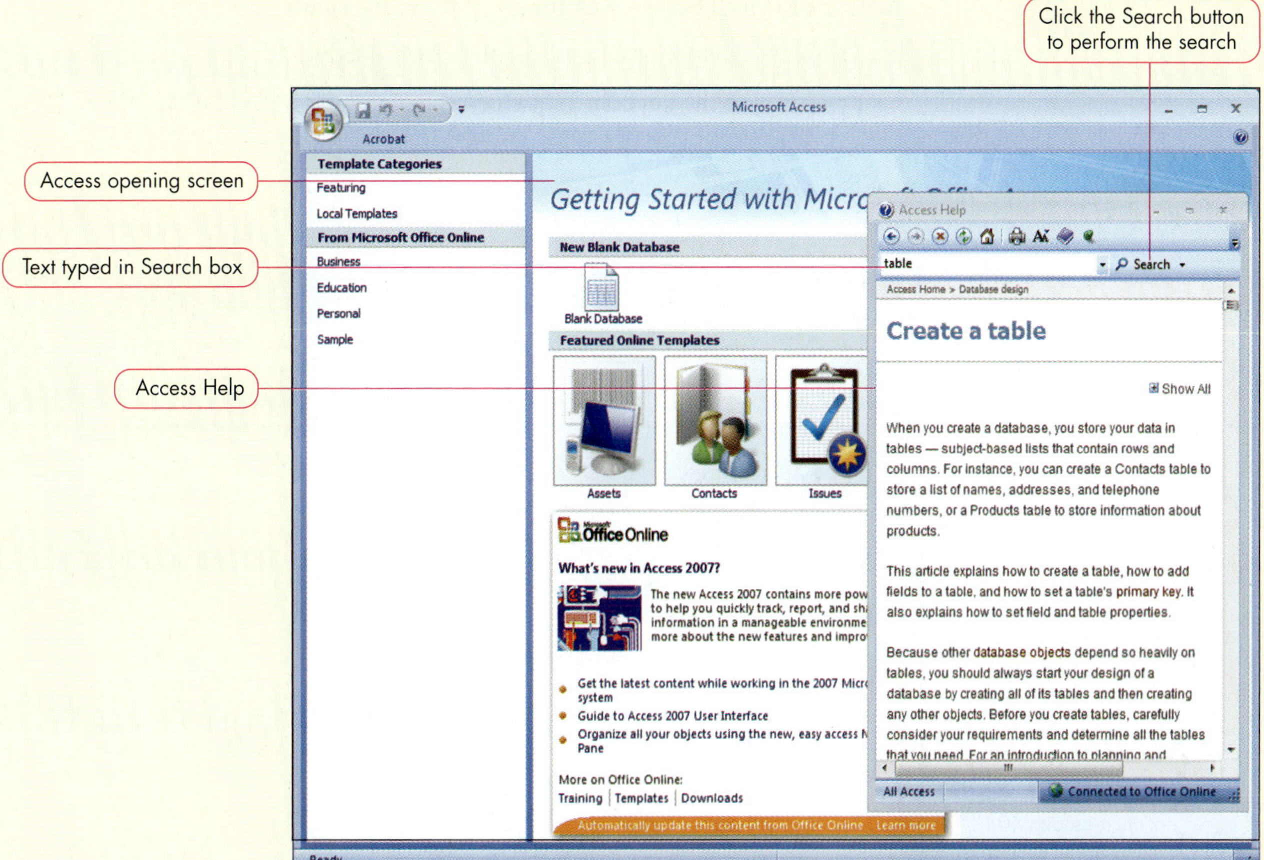

Figure 1.12 Access Help

Step 4
Use Word's Status Bar

Refer to Figure 1.13 as you complete Step 4.

a. Click **Start** to display the Start menu. Click (or point to) **All Programs**, click **Microsoft Office**, then click **Microsoft Office Word 2007** to start the program.

   Word opens with a blank document ready for you to start typing.

b. Type your first name.

   Your first name displays in the document window.

c. Point your mouse to the **Zoom slider** on the status bar.

d. Click and drag the **Zoom slider** to the right to increase the magnification.

   The document with your first name increases in size onscreen.

e. Click and drag the slider control to the left to decrease the magnification.

   The document with your first name decreases in size.

f. Click and drag the **Zoom slider** back to the center.

   The document returns to 100% magnification.

g. Slowly point the mouse to the buttons on the status bar.

   A ScreenTip displays the names of the buttons.

h. Click the **Full Screen Reading button** on the status bar.

The screen display changes to Full Screen Reading view.

i. Press **Esc** on the keyboard to return the display to Print Layout view.

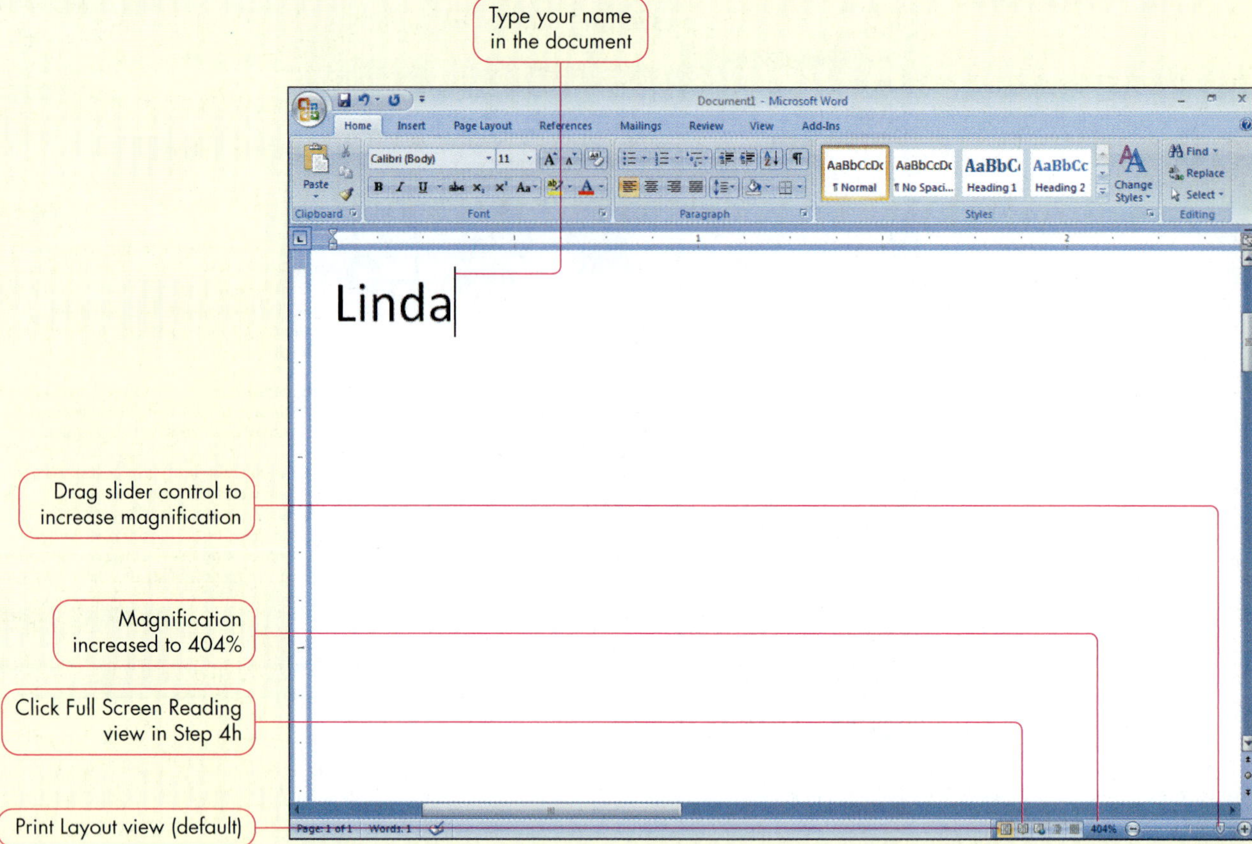

Figure 1.13 The Word Status Bar

Step 5
Search Help and Print a Help Topic

Refer to Figure 1.14 as you complete Step 5.

a. With Word open on the screen, press **F1** on the keyboard.

Word Help displays.

b. Type **zoom** in the Search box in the Word Help window.

c. Click the **Search** button.

Word Help displays related topics.

d. Click the topic **Zoom in or out of a document, presentation, or worksheet**.

The help topic displays.

TROUBLESHOOTING: If you do not have a printer that is ready to print, skip Step 5e and continue with the exercise.

e. Turn on the attached printer, be sure it has paper, and then click the Word Help **Print** button.

The Help topic prints on the attached printer.

f. Click the **Show Table of Contents** button on the Word Help toolbar.

The Table of Contents pane displays on the left side of the Word Help dialog box so that you can click popular Help topics, such as *What's new*. You can click a closed book icon to see specific topics to click for additional information, and you can click an open book icon to close the main Help topic.

g. Click the **Close** button on Word Help.

Word Help closes.

h. To exit Word, click the **Office Button** to display the Office menu and then click the **Exit Word button**.

A warning appears stating that you have not saved changes to your document.

i. Click **No** in the Word warning box.

You exit Word without saving the document.

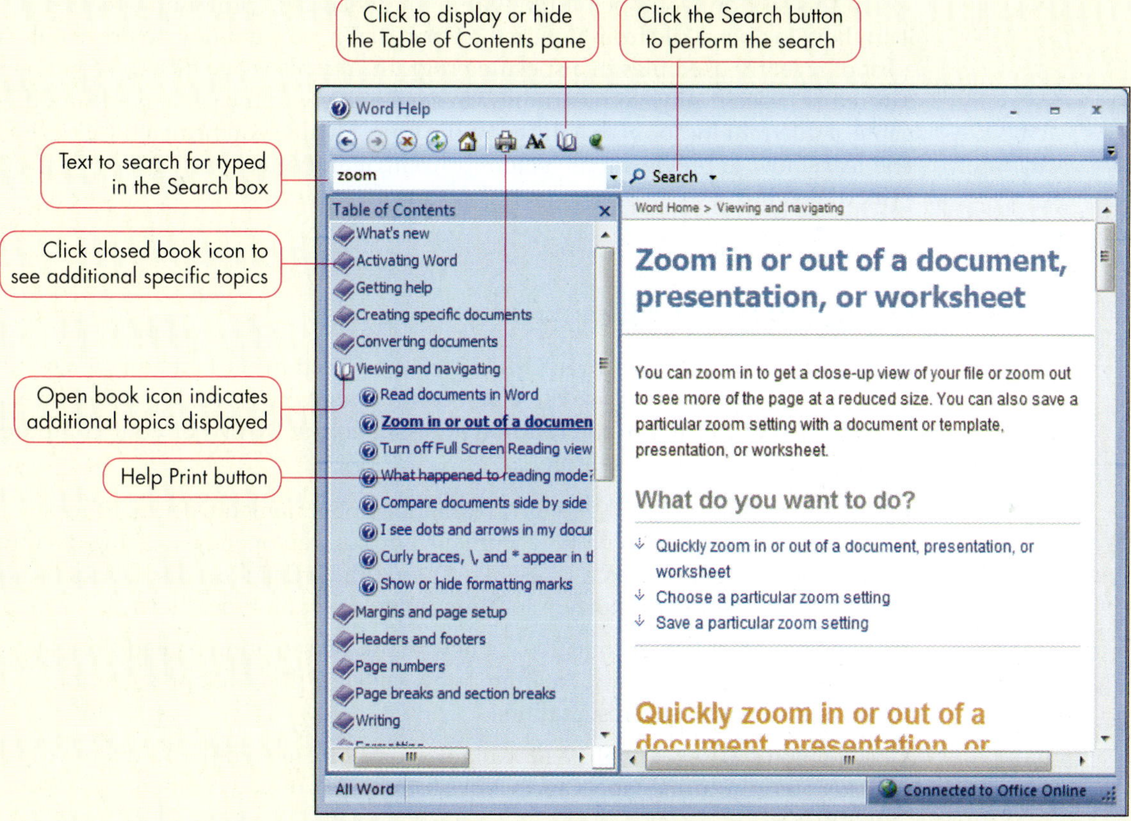

Figure 1.14 Word Help

Universal Tasks

Today, storing large amounts of information on a computer is taken for granted, but in reality computers would not have become very important if you could not save and re-use the files you create.

One of the most useful and important aspects of using computers is the ability to save and re-use information. For example, you can store letters, reports, budgets, presentations, and databases as files to reopen and use at some time in the future. Today, storing large amounts of information on a computer is taken for granted, but in reality computers would not have become very important if you could not save and re-use the files you create.

Three fundamental tasks are so important for productivity that they are considered universal to most every computer program, including Office 2007:

- opening files that have been saved
- saving files you create
- printing files

In this section, you open a file within an Office 2007 program. Specifically, you learn how to open a file from within the Open dialog box and how to open a file from a list of recently used files in a specific program. You also save files to keep them for future use. Specifically, you learn how to save a file with the same name, a different name, a different location, or a different file type. Finally, you print a file. Specifically, you learn how to preview a file before printing it and select print options within the Print dialog box.

Opening a File

When you start any program in Office 2007, you need to start creating a new file or open an existing one. You use the Open command to retrieve a file saved on a storage device and place it in the random access memory (RAM) of your computer so you can work on it. For example:

- When you start Word 2007, a new blank document named Document1 opens. You can either start typing in Document1, or you can open an existing document. The ***insertion point***, which looks like a blinking vertical line, displays in the document designating the current location where text you type displays.
- When you start PowerPoint 2007, a new blank presentation named Presentation1 opens. You can either start creating a new slide for the blank presentation, or you can open an existing presentation.
- When you start Excel 2007, a new blank workbook named Book1 opens. You can either start inputting labels and values into Book1, or you can open an existing workbook.
- When you start Access 2007—unlike Word, PowerPoint, and Excel—a new blank database is not created automatically for you. In order to get started using Access, you must create and name a database first or open an existing database.

The ***insertion point*** is the blinking vertical line in the document, cell, slide show, or database table designating the current location where text you type displays.

Open a File Using the Open Dialog Box

Opening a file in any of the Office 2007 applications is an easy process: Use the Open command from the Office menu and specify the file to open. However, locating the file to open can be difficult at times because you might not know where the file you want to use is located. You can open files stored on your computer or on a remote computer that you have access to. Further, files are saved in folders, and you might need to look for files located within folders or subfolders. The Open dialog box, shown in Figure 1.15, contains many features designed for file management; however, two features are designed specifically to help you locate files.

- **Favorite Links List**—provides shortcut links for navigating to specific folders on your computer. Click a link to select it, and the file list changes to display files and subfolders in that location.
- **Folder List**—provides a hierarchical structure of drives and folders on your computer. Click a drive or folder to display the contents of that file or folder in the file list. Table 1.3 lists and describes buttons on the Command Bar.

Table 1.3 Common Command Bar Buttons

Buttons	Characteristics
Organize	Provides methods to manage files (i.e., select, copy, move, rename, and delete) and change the layout of the dialog box.
Views	Changes icon size and detail information shown about the files and folders.
New Folder	Creates a new folder within a current folder.

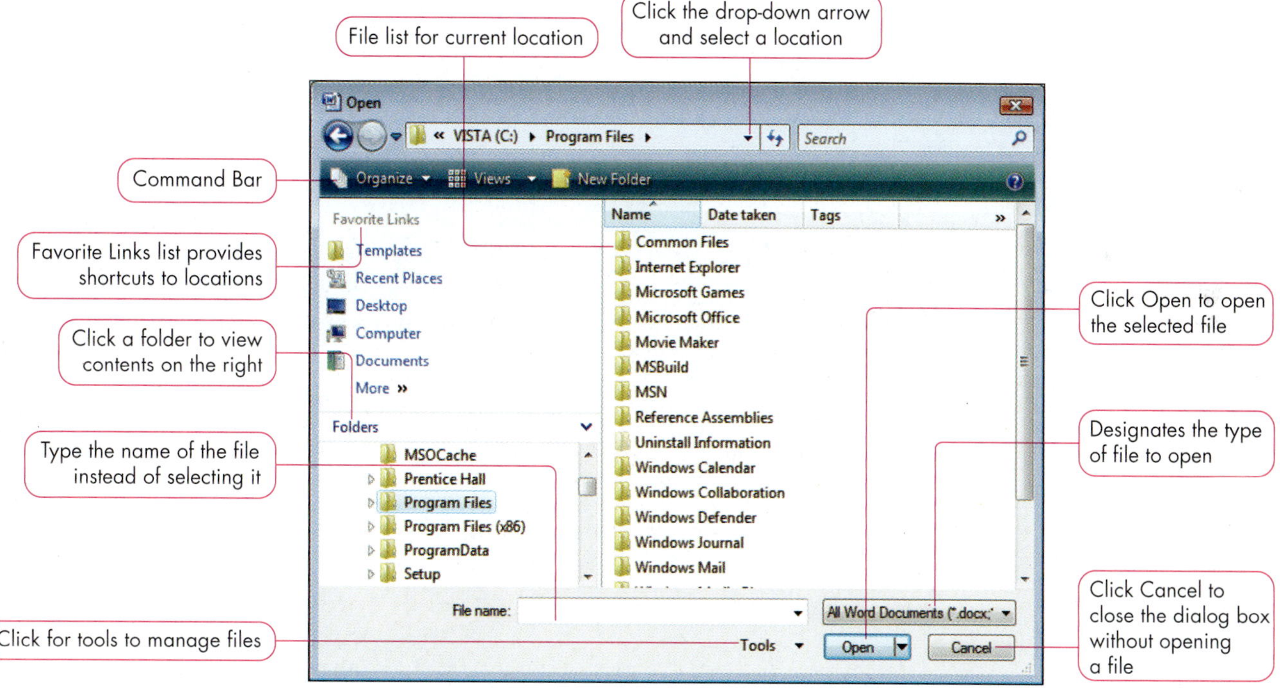

Figure 1.15 Open Dialog Box in Word

After you locate and select the file, click the Open button in the dialog box to display the file on the screen. However, if, for example, you work as part of a workgroup that shares files with each other, you might find the need to open files in a more specialized way. Microsoft Office programs provide several options for opening files when you click the drop-down arrow on the Open button. For example, if you want to keep the original file intact, you might open the file as a copy of the original. Table 1.4 describes the Open options.

Table 1.4 Open Options

Open Options	Characteristics
Open	Opens the selected file with the ability to read and write (edit).
Open Read-Only	Opens the selected file with the ability to read the contents but prevents you from changing or editing it.
Open as Copy	Opens the selected file as a copy of the original so that if you edit the file, the original remains unchanged.
Open in Browser	Opens the selected file in a Web browser.
Open with Transform	Opens a file and provides the ability to transform it into another type of document, such as an HTML document.
Open and Repair	Opens the selected file and attempts to repair any damage. If you have difficulty opening a file, try to open it by selecting Open and Repair.

Open Files Using the Recent Documents List

Office 2007 provides a quick method for accessing files you used recently. The Recent Documents list displays when the Office menu opens and provides a list of links to the last few files you used. The list changes as you work in the application to reflect only the most recent files. Figure 1.16 shows the Office menu with the Recent Documents list.

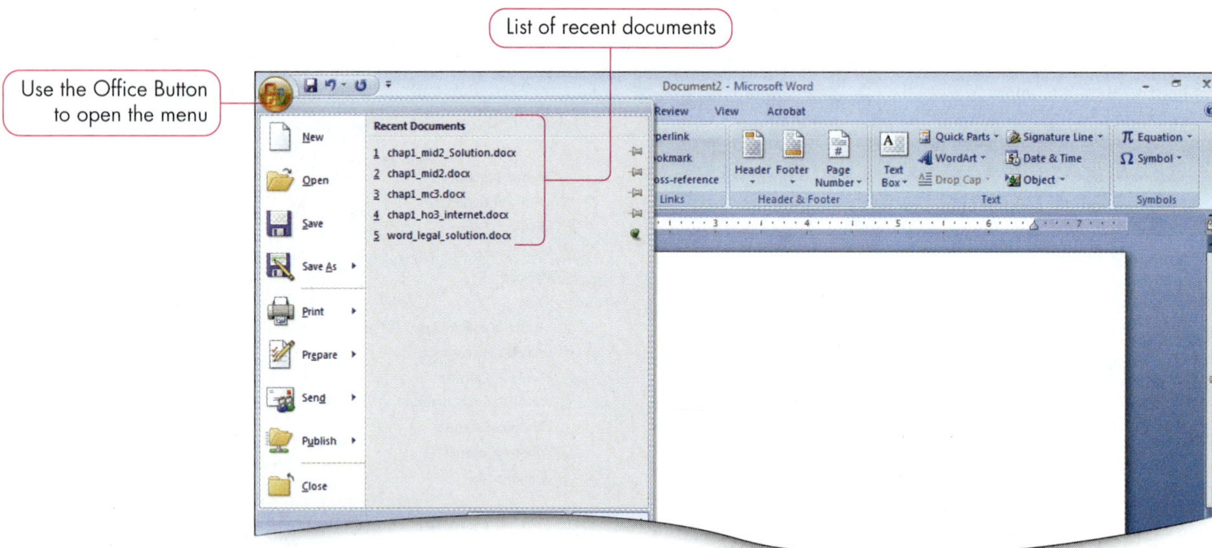

Figure 1.16 The Recent Documents List

TIP Keeping Files on the Recent Documents List

As you use the Office application and open several files, the list of Recent Documents changes; however, you can designate files to keep displayed on the Recent Documents list at all times. Notice the icon of the pushpin that displays immediately following each file name on the Recent Documents list. Just as you use pushpins to post an important notice in the real world, you use pushpins here to designate important files that you want easy access to. To pin a specific file to the Recent Documents list, click the icon of a gray pushpin. The shape of the pin changes as if pushed in, and the color of the pin changes to green designating that the file is pinned on the list. However, if later you decide to remove the file from the list, you can unpin it by simply clicking the green pushpin, changing the icon back to gray, and the file will disappear from the list over time. Notice the Recent Documents list with both gray and green pushpins in Figure 1.17.

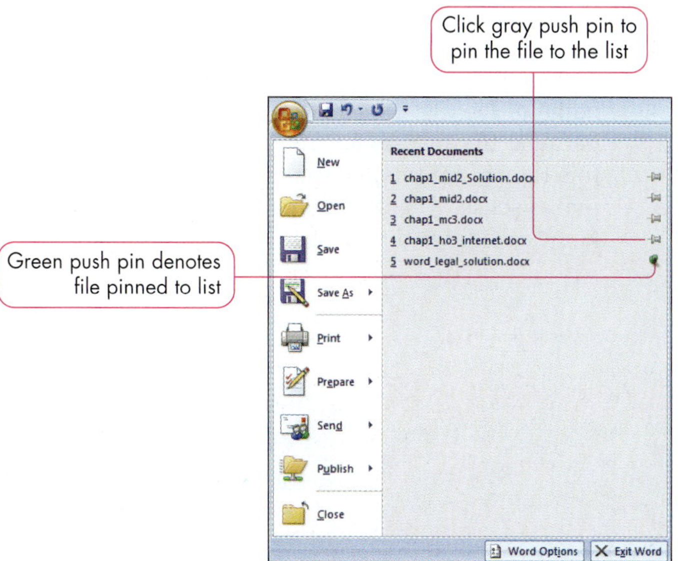

Figure 1.17 The Recent Documents List

Saving a File

As you work with any Office 2007 application and create files, you will need to save them for future use. While you are working on a file, it is stored in the temporary memory or RAM of your computer. When you save a file, the contents of the file stored in RAM are saved to the hard drive of your computer or to a storage device such as a flash drive. As you create, edit, and format a complex file such as a report, slide show, or budget, you should consider saving several versions of it as you work. For example, you might number versions or use the date in the file name to designate each version. Using this method enables you to revert to a previous version of the document if necessary. To save a file you create in Word, PowerPoint, or Excel, click the Office Button to display the Office menu. Office provides two commands that work similarly: Save and Save As. Table 1.5 describes the characteristics of these two commands.

(As you create, edit, and format a complex file such as a report, slide show, or budget, you should consider saving several versions of it as you work.)

Table 1.5 Save Options

Command	Characteristics
Save	Saves the open document: • If this is the first time the document is being saved, Office 2007 opens the Save As dialog box so that you can name the file. • If this document was saved previously, the document is automatically saved using the original file name.
Save As	Opens the Save As dialog box: • If this is the first time the document is being saved, use the Save As dialog box to name the file. • If this document was saved previously, use this option to save the file with a new name, in a new location, or as a new file type preserving the original file with its original name.

When you select the Save As command, the Save As dialog box appears (see Figure 1.18). Notice that saving and opening files are related, and that the Save As dialog box looks very similar to the Open dialog box that you saw in Figure 1.15. The dialog box requires you to specify the drive or folder in which to store the file, the name of the file, and the type of file you wish the file to be saved as. Additionally, because finding saved files is important, you should always group related files together in folders, so that you or someone else can find them in a location that makes sense. You can use the New Folder button on the Command bar to create and name a folder and then save related files to it.

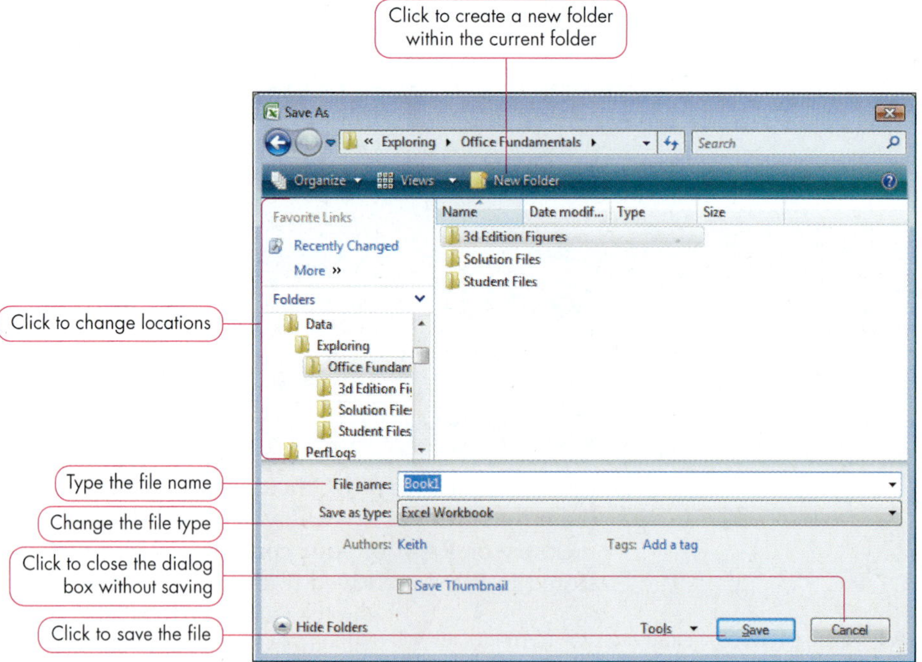

Figure 1.18 Save As Dialog Box in Excel

All subsequent executions of the Save command save the file under the assigned name, replacing the previously saved version with the new version. Pressing Ctrl+S is another way to activate the Save command. If you want to change the name of the file, use the Save As command. Word, PowerPoint, and Excel use the same basic process for saving files, which include the following options:

- naming and saving a previously unsaved file
- saving an updated file with the same name and replacing the original file with the updated one

- saving an updated file with a different name or in a different location to keep the original intact
- saving the file in a different file format

TIP Saving from the Office Menu

You should select the Save As command on the Office menu rather than pointing to the arrow that follows the command. When you point to the arrow, menu options display for saving the file in an alternative format. Always check the Save as type box in the Save As dialog box to be sure that the correct file type is specified.

A ***macro*** is a small program that automates tasks in a file.

A ***virus checker*** is software that scans files for a hidden program that can damage your computer.

A ***template*** is a file that contains formatting and design elements.

Office 2007 saves files in a different format from previous versions of the software. Office now makes use of XML formats for files created in Word, PowerPoint, and Excel. For example, in previous versions of Word, all documents were saved with the three-letter extension .doc. Now Word saves default documents with the four-letter extension .docx. The new XML format makes use of file compression to save storage space for the user. The files are compressed automatically when saved and uncompressed when opened. Another important feature is that the XML format makes using the files you create in Office 2007 easier to open in other software. This increased portability of files is a major benefit in any workplace that might have numerous applications to deal with. The new file format also differentiates between files that contain ***macros***, which are small programs that automate tasks in a file, and those that do not. This specification of files that contain macros enables a virus checker to rigorously check for damaging programs hidden in files. A ***virus checker*** is software that scans files for a hidden program that can damage your computer. Table 1.6 lists the file formats with the four-letter extension for Word, PowerPoint, and Excel, and a five-letter extension for Access.

Table 1.6 Word, PowerPoint, Excel, and Access File Extensions

File Format	Characteristics
Word	.docx—default document format .docm—a document that contains macros .dotx—a template without macros (a ***template*** is a file that contains formatting and design elements) .dotm—a template with macros
PowerPoint	.pptx—default presentation format .pptm—a presentation that contains macros .potx—a template .potm—a template with macros .ppam—an add-in that contains macros .ppsx—a slide show .ppsm—a slide show with macros .sldx—a slide saved independently of a presentation .sldm—a slide saved independently of a presentation that contains a macro .thmx—a theme used to format a slide
Excel	.xlsx—default workbook .xlsm—a workbook with macros .xltx—a template .xltm—a template with a macro .xlsb—non-XML binary workbook—for previous versions of the software .xlam—an add-in that contains macros
Access	.accdb—default database

Access 2007 saves data differently from Word, PowerPoint, and Excel. When you start Access, which is a relational database, you must create a database and define at least one table for your data. Then as you work, your data is stored automatically. This powerful software enables multiple users access to up-to-date data. The concepts of saving, opening, and printing remain the same, but the process of how data is saved is unique to this environment.

You can customize the Favorite Links bar to create a link to a folder or file you use often. To do this, display the folder, such as Chapter 1, in the right pane. Then click and drag the folder to the Favorite Links list as shown in Figure 1.19. When you release the mouse, a link to the respective folder is created, giving you quicker access to that folder in the future.

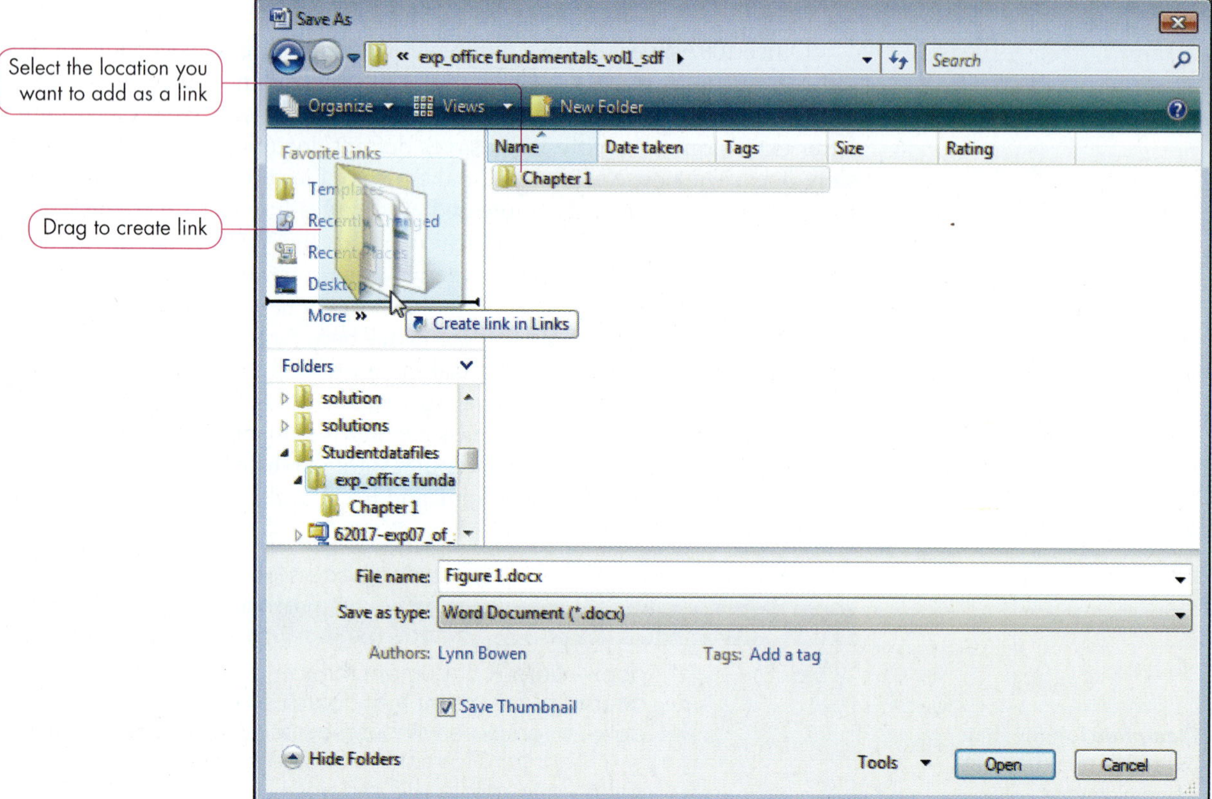

Figure 1.19 Save As Dialog Box with New Shortcut Added to My Places Bar

Printing a Document

As you work with Office 2007 applications, you will need to print hard copies of documents, such as letters to mail, presentation notes to distribute to accompany a slide show, budget spreadsheets to distribute at a staff meeting, or database summary reports to submit. Office provides flexibility so that you can preview the document before you send it to the printer; you also can select from numerous print options, such as changing the number of copies printed; or you can simply and quickly print the current document on the default printer.

Preview Before You Print

It is highly recommended that you preview your document before you print because Print Preview displays all the document elements such as graphics and formatting as they will appear when printed on paper. Previewing the document first enables you to make any changes that you need to make without wasting paper. Previewing documents uses the same method in all Office 2007 applications, that is, point to the arrow next to the Print command on the Office menu and select Print Preview to display the current document, worksheet, presentation, or database table in the Print Preview window. Figure 1.20 shows the Print Preview window in Word 2007.

It is highly recommended that you preview your document before you print because Print Preview displays all the document elements, such as graphics and formatting, as they will appear when printed on paper.

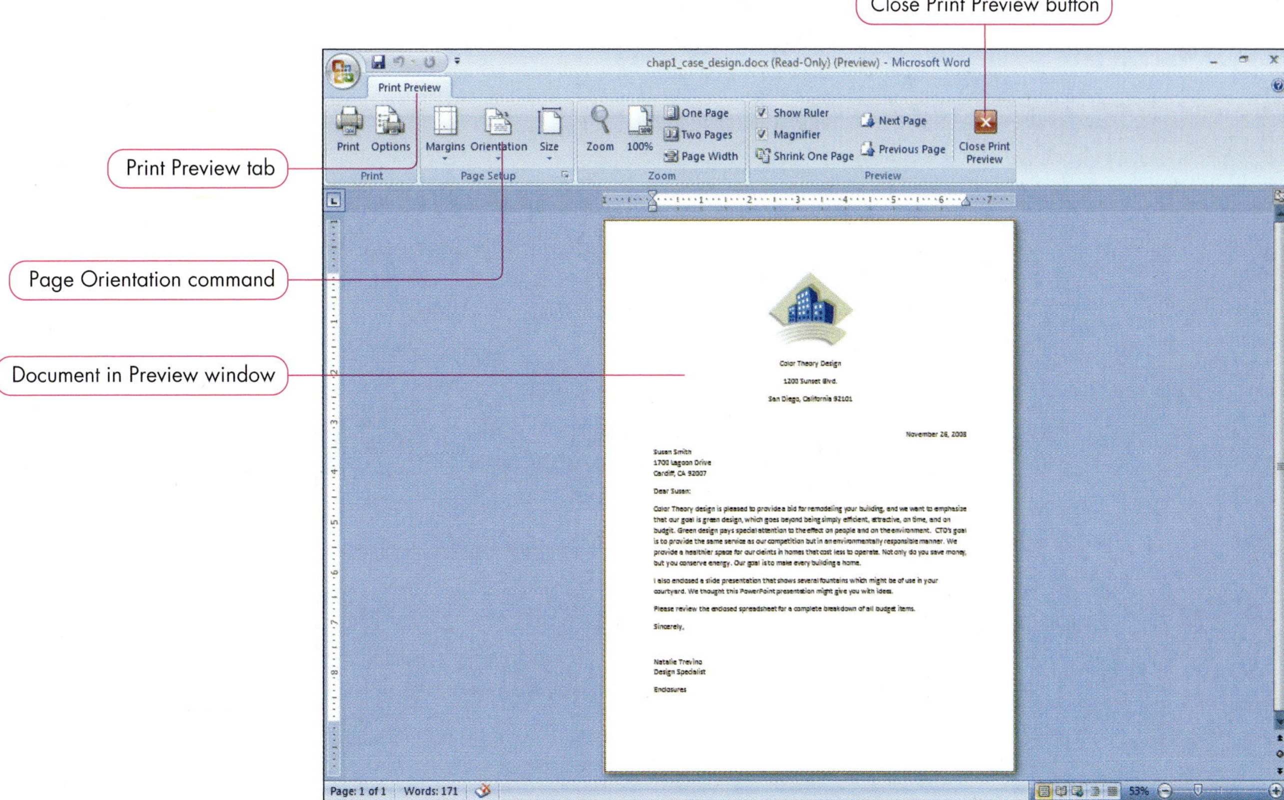

Figure 1.20 Print Preview Window

As you preview the document, you can get a closer look at the results by changing the zoom. Notice that the mouse pointer displays in the Preview window as a magnifying glass with a plus sign, so that you can simply click in the document to increase the zoom. Once clicked, the plus sign changes to a minus sign, enabling you to click in the document again to decrease the zoom. You also can use the Zoom group on the Print Preview tab or the Zoom slider on the status bar to change the view of the document.

Portrait orientation is longer than it is wide—like the portrait of a person.

Landscape orientation is wider than it is long, resembling a landscape scene.

Other options on the Print Preview tab change depending on the application that you are using. For example, you might want to change the orientation to switch from portrait to landscape. Refer to Figure 1.20. ***Portrait orientation*** is longer than it is wide, like the portrait of a person; whereas, ***landscape orientation*** is wider than it is long, resembling a landscape scene. You also can change the size of the paper or other options from the Print Preview tab.

If you need to edit the document before printing, close the Print Preview window and return to the document. However, if you are satisfied with the document and want to print, click Print in the Print group on the Print Preview tab. The Print dialog box displays. Figure 1.21 shows Word's Print dialog box.

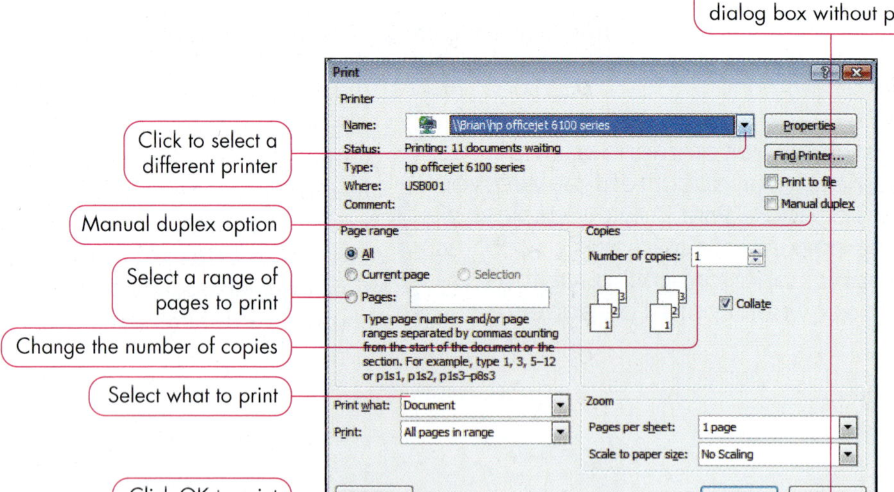

Figure 1.21 Print Dialog Box

The Print dialog box provides numerous options for selecting the correct printer, selecting what to print, and selecting how to print. Table 1.7 describes several important and often-used features of the Print dialog box.

Table 1.7 Print Dialog Box

Print Option	Characteristics
All	Select to print all the pages in the file.
Current page/slide	Select to print only the page or slide with the insertion point. This is a handy feature when you notice an error in a file, and you only want to reprint the corrected page.
Pages	Select to print only specific pages in a document. You must specify page numbers in the text box.
Number of Copies	Change the number of copies printed from the default 1 to the number desired.
Collate	Click if you are printing multiple copies of a multi-page file, and you want to print an entire first copy before printing an entire second copy, and so forth.
Print what	Select from options on what to print, varying with each application.
Selection	Select to print only selected text or objects.
Active sheet(s)	Select to print only the active worksheet(s) in Excel.
Entire workbook	Select to print all worksheets in the Excel workbook.

As you work with other Office 2007 applications, you will notice that the main print options remain unchanged; however, the details vary based on the specific task of the application. For example, the *Print what* option in PowerPoint includes options such as printing the slide, printing handouts, printing notes, or printing an outline of the presentation.

A ***duplex printer*** prints on both sides of the page.

A ***manual duplex*** operation allows you to print on both sides of the paper by printing first on one side and then on the other.

TIP Printing on Both Sides of the Paper

Duplex printers print on both sides of the page. However, if you do not have a duplex printer, you can still print on two sides of the paper by performing a ***manual duplex*** operation, which prints on both sides of the paper by printing first on one side and then on the other. To perform a manual duplex print job in Word 2007, select the Manual duplex option in the Print dialog box. Refer to Figure 1.21. With this option selected, Word prints all pages that display on one side of the paper first, then prompts you to turn the pages over and place them back in the printer tray. The print job continues by printing all the pages that appear on the other side of the paper.

Print without Previewing the File

If you want to print a file without previewing the results, select Print from the Office menu, and the Print dialog box displays. You can still make changes in the Print dialog box, or just immediately send the print job to the printer. However, if you just want to print quickly, Office 2007 provides a quick print option that enables you to send the current file to the default printer without opening the Print dialog box. This is a handy feature to use if you have only one printer attached and you want to print the current file without changing any print options. You have two ways to quick print:

- Select Quick Print from the Office menu.
- Customize the Quick Access toolbar to add the Print icon. Click the icon to print the current file without opening the Print dialog box.

Hands-On Exercises

2 | Performing Universal Tasks

Skills covered: 1. Open a File and Save It with a Different Name **2.** Use Print Preview and Select Options **3.** Print a Document

Step 1
Open a File and Save it with a Different Name

Refer to Figure 1.22 as you complete Step 1.

a. Start Word, click the **Office Button** to display the Office menu, and then select **Open**.

   The Open dialog box displays.

b. If necessary, click the **File Type List** button to locate the files for this textbook to find *chap1_ho2_sample*.

   TROUBLESHOOTING: If you have trouble finding the files that accompany this text, you may want to ask your instructor where they are located.

c. Select the file and click **Open**.

   The document displays on the screen.

d. Click the **Office Button** and then select **Save As** on the Office menu.

   The Save As dialog box displays.

e. In the *File name* box, type **chap1_ho2_solution**.

f. Check the current location at the top of the Save As dialog box. If you need to change the location to save your files, use the **Folders pane** to navigate to the correct location.

g. Make sure that the *Save as type* option is Word Document.

   TROUBLESHOOTING: Be sure that you click the **Save As** command rather than pointing to the arrow after the command, and be sure that Word Document is specified in the *Save as type* box.

h. Click the **Save** button in the dialog box to save the file under the new name.

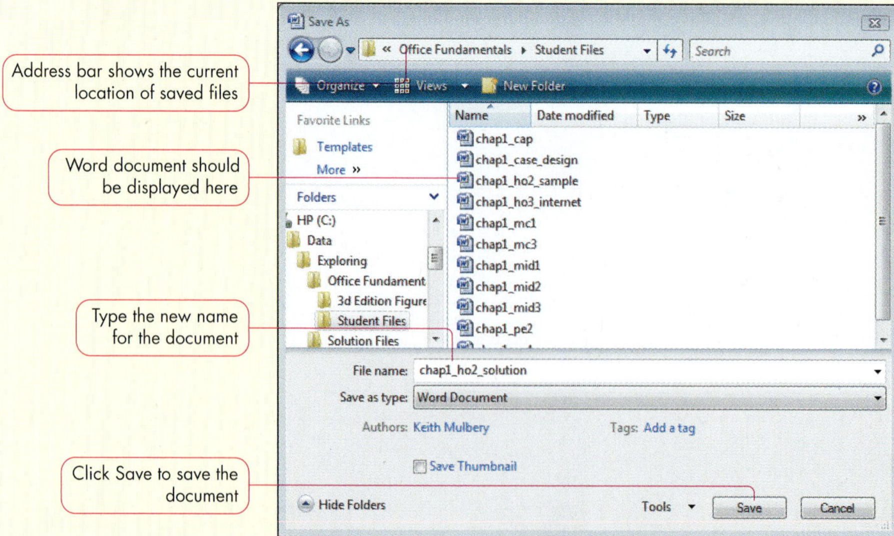

Figure 1.22 Save As Dialog Box

Step 2
Use Print Preview and Select Options

Refer to Figure 1.23 as you complete Step 2.

a. With the document displayed on the screen, click the **Office Button** and point to the arrow following **Print** on the Office menu.

   The Print submenu displays.

b. Select **Print Preview**.

   The document displays in the Print Preview window.

c. Point the magnifying glass mouse pointer in the document and click the mouse once.

   TROUBLESHOOTING: If you do not see the magnifying glass pointer, point the mouse in the document and keep it still for a moment.

   The document magnification increases.

d. Point the magnifying glass mouse pointer in the document and click the mouse again.

   The document magnification decreases.

e. Click **Orientation** in the Page Setup group on the Print Preview tab.

   The orientation options display.

f. Click **Landscape**.

   The document orientation changes to landscape.

g. Click **Orientation** a second time and then choose **Portrait**.

   The document returns to portrait orientation.

h. Click **Close Print Preview** on the Print Preview tab.

   The Print Preview window closes.

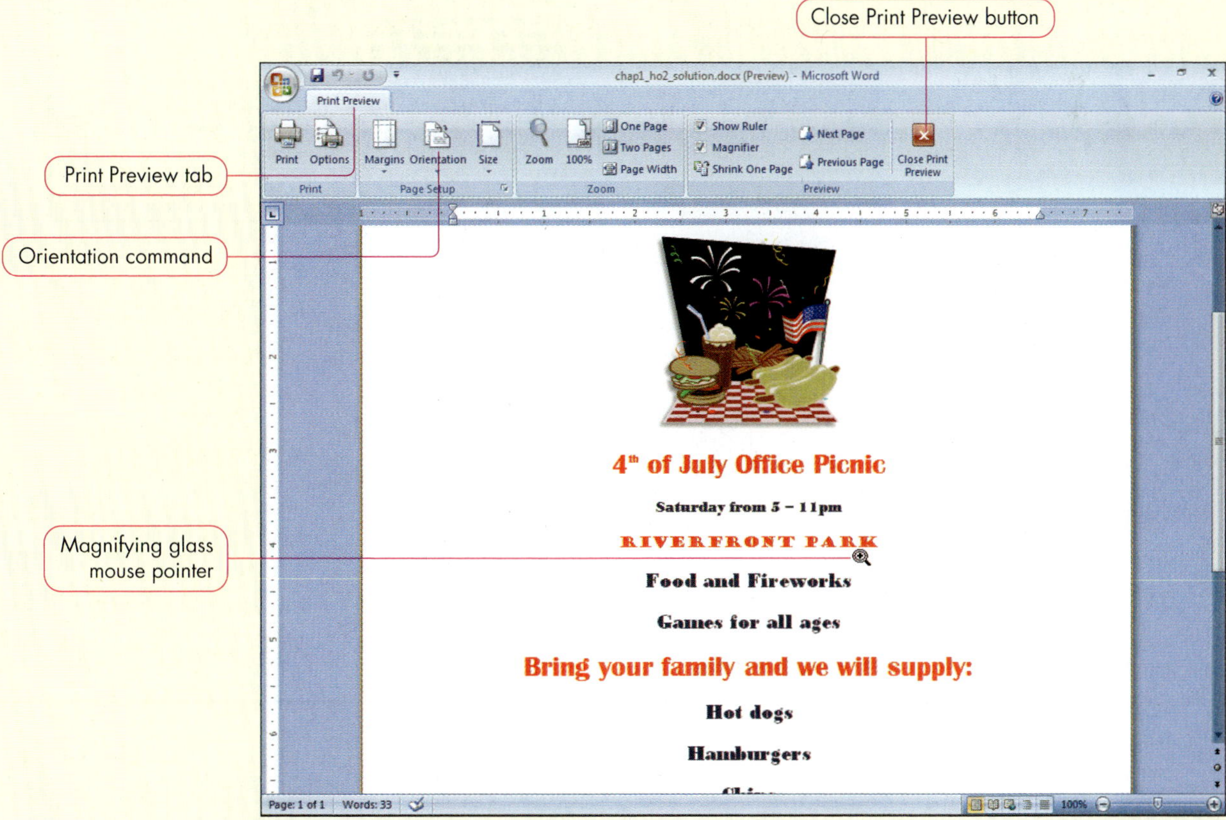

Figure 1.23 Print Preview

Step 3
Print a Document

Refer to Figure 1.24 as you complete Step 3.

a. Click the **Office Button** and then point to the arrow next to **Print** on the Office menu.

The print options display.

b. Select **Print**.

The Print dialog box displays.

TROUBLESHOOTING: Be sure that your printer is turned on and has paper loaded.

c. If necessary, select the correct printer in the **Name box** by clicking the drop-down arrow and selecting from the resulting list.

d. Click **OK**.

The Word document prints on the selected printer.

e. To exit Word, click the **Office Button** and then click the **Exit Word button**.

f. If prompted to save the file, click **No**.

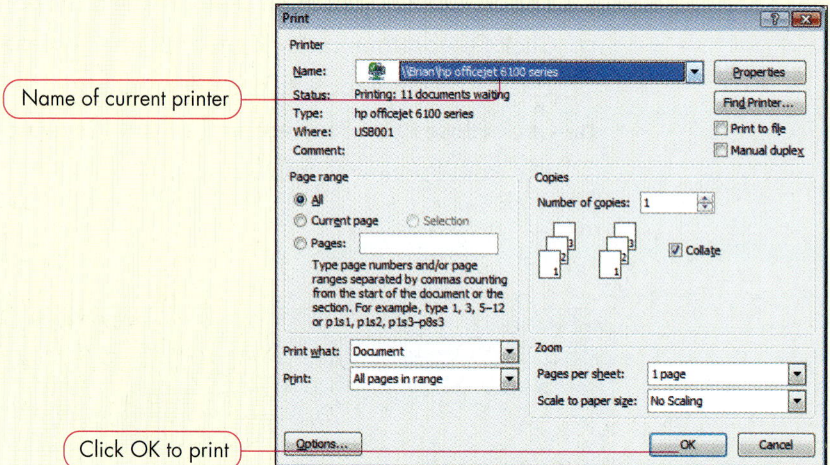

Figure 1.24 The Print Dialog Box

Basic Tasks

Many of the operations you perform in one Office program are the same or similar in all Office applications. These tasks are referred to as basic tasks and include such operations as inserting and typing over, copying and moving items, finding and replacing text, undoing and redoing commands, checking spelling and grammar, using the thesaurus, and using formatting tools. Once you learn the underlying concepts of these operations, you can apply them in different applications.

Most basic tasks in Word fall into two categories:

- editing a document
- formatting a document

Most successful writers use many word processing features to revise and edit documents, and most would agree that the revision process takes more time than the initial writing process. Errors such as spelling and grammar need to be eliminated to produce error-free writing. However, to turn a rough draft into a finished document, such as a report for a class or for a business, requires writers to revise and edit several times by adding text, removing text, replacing text, and moving text around to make the meaning clearer. Writers also improve their writing using tools to conduct research to make the information accurate and to find the most appropriate word using the thesaurus. Modern word processing applications such as Word 2007 provide these tools and more to aid the writer.

(Most successful writers use many word processing features to revise and edit documents, and most would agree that the revision process takes more time than the initial writing process.)

The second category of basic tasks is formatting text in a document. Formatting text includes changing the type, the size, and appearance of text. You might want to apply formatting to simply improve the look of a document, or you might want to emphasize particular aspects of your message. Remember that a poorly formatted document or workbook probably will not be read. So whether you are creating your résumé or the income statement for a corporation's annual report, how the output looks is important. Office 2007 provides many tools for formatting documents, but in this section, you will start by learning to apply font attributes and copy those to other locations in the document.

In this section you learn to perform basic tasks in Office 2007, using Word 2007 as the model. As you progress in learning other Office programs such as PowerPoint, Excel, and Access, you will apply the same principles in other applications.

Selecting Text to Edit

Most editing processes involve identifying the text that the writer wants to work with. For example, to specify which text to edit, you must select it. The most common method used to select text is to use the mouse. Point to one end of the text you want to select (either the beginning or end) and click-and-drag over the text. The selected text displays highlighted with a light blue background so that it stands out from other text and is ready for you to work with. The ***Mini toolbar*** displays when you select text in Word, Excel, and PowerPoint. It displays above the selected text as semitransparent and remains semitransparent until you point to it. Often-used commands from the Clipboard, Font, Paragraph, and Styles groups on the Home tab are repeated on the Mini toolbar for quick access. Figure 1.25 shows selected text with the Mini toolbar fully displayed in the document. Table 1.8 describes other methods used to select text.

The ***Mini toolbar*** displays above the selected text as semitransparent and repeats often-used commands.

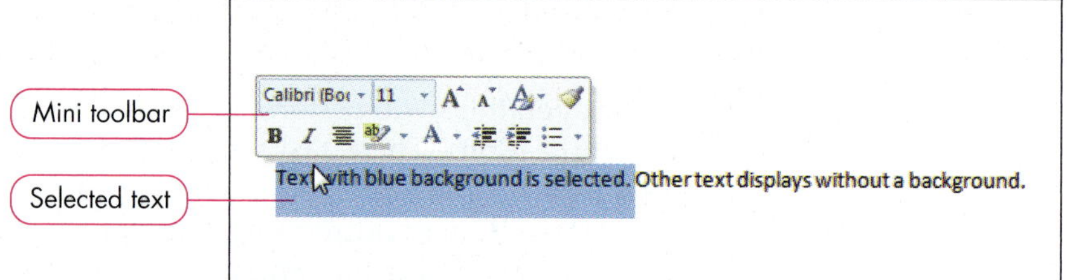

Figure 1.25 Selected Text

Table 1.8 Easy Text Selection in Word

The ***selection bar*** is the left margin white space that enables you to select document text.

Outcome Desired	Method
Select a word	Double-click the word.
One line of text	Point the mouse on the ***selection bar***, the white space to the left of the line, and when the mouse pointer changes to a right-pointing arrow, click the mouse.
A sentence	Hold down Ctrl and click in the sentence to select.
A paragraph	Triple-click the mouse in the paragraph, or double-click in the selection bar to the left of the paragraph.
Entire document	Hold down Ctrl and press A, or triple-click in the selection bar.
One character to the left of the insertion point	Hold down Shift and press the left arrow key.
One character to the right of the insertion point	Hold down Shift and press the right arrow key.

TIP Selecting Large Amounts of Text

As you edit documents, you might need to select a large portion of a document. However, as you click-and-drag over the text, you might have trouble stopping the selection at the desired location because the document scrolls by too quickly. This is actually a handy feature in Word 2007 that scrolls through the document when you drag the mouse pointer at the edge of the document window.

To select a large portion of a document, click the insertion point at the beginning of the desired selection. Then move the display to the end of the selection using the scroll bar at the right edge of the window. Scrolling leaves the insertion point where you placed it. When you reach the end of the text you want to select, hold down Shift and click the mouse. The entire body of text is selected.

Inserting Text and Changing to the Overtype Mode

Insert is adding text in a document.

As you create and edit documents using Word, you will need to ***insert*** text, which is adding text in a document. To insert or add text, point and click the mouse in the location where the text should display. With the insertion point in the location to insert the text, simply start typing. Any existing text moves to the right, making room for the new inserted text. At times you might need to add a large amount of text in a document, and you might want to replace or type over existing text instead of inserting text. This task can be accomplished two ways:

Overtype mode replaces the existing text with text you type character by character.

- Select the text to replace and start typing. The new text replaces the selected text.
- Switch to *Overtype mode*, which replaces the existing text with text you type character by character. To change to Overtype mode, select the Word Options button on the Office menu. Select the option Use Overtype Mode in the Editing Options section of the Advanced tab. Later if you want to return to Insert mode, repeat these steps to deselect the overtype mode option. Figure 1.26 shows the Word Options dialog box.

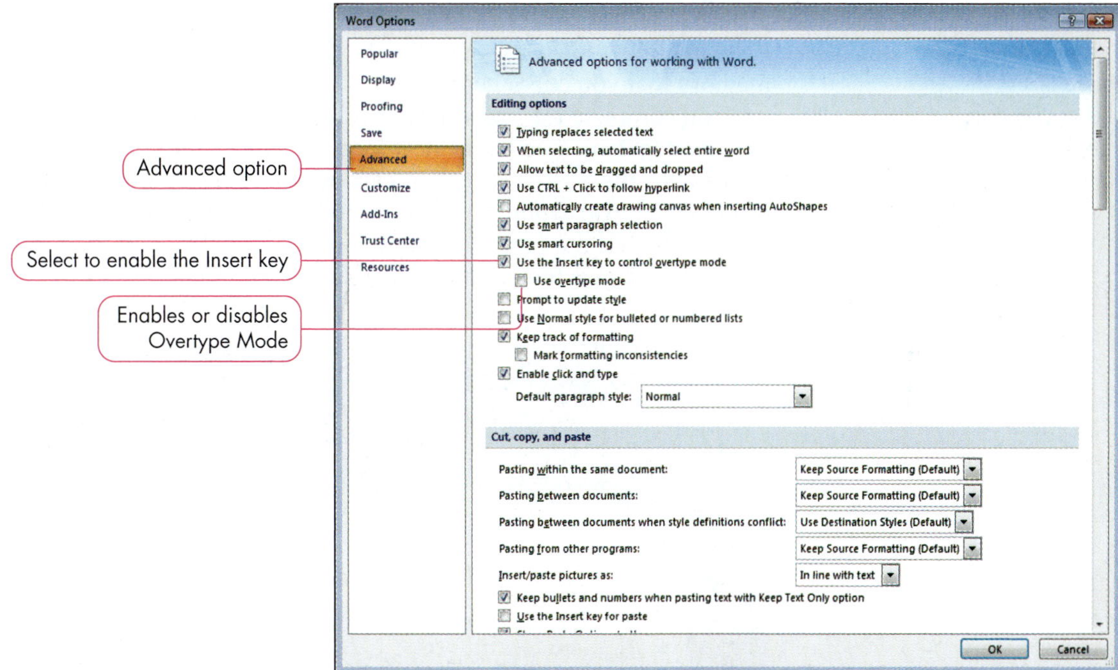

Figure 1.26 The Word Options Dialog Box

TIP Using the Insert Key on the Keyboard

If you find that you need to switch between Insert and Overtype mode often, you can enable Insert on the keyboard by clicking the Word Options button on the Office menu. Select the option Use the Insert Key to Control Overtype Mode in the Editing Options section on the Advanced tab. Refer to Figure 1.26. You can now use Insert on the keyboard to switch between the two modes, and this option stays in effect until you go back to the Word Options dialog box and deselect it.

Moving and Copying Text

As you revise a document, you might find that you need to move text from one location to another to improve the readability of the content. To move text, you must cut the selected text from its original location and then place it in the new location by pasting it there. To duplicate text, you must copy the selected text in its original location and then paste the duplicate in the desired location. To decide whether you should use the Cut or Copy command in the Clipboard group on the Home tab to perform the task, you must notice the difference in the results of each command:

Cut removes the original text or object from its current location.

Copy makes a duplicate copy of the text or object, leaving the original intact.

Paste places the cut or copied text or object in the new location.

- ***Cut*** removes the selected original text or object from its current location.
- ***Copy*** makes a duplicate copy of the text or object, leaving the original text or object intact.

Keep in mind while you work, that by default Office 2007 retains only the last item in memory that you cut or copied.

You complete the process by invoking the Paste command. ***Paste*** places the cut or copied text or object in the new location. Notice the Paste Options button displays along with the pasted text. You can simply ignore the Paste Options button, and it will disappear from the display, or you can click the drop-down arrow on the button and select a formatting option to change the display of the text you pasted. Figure 1.27 shows the options available.

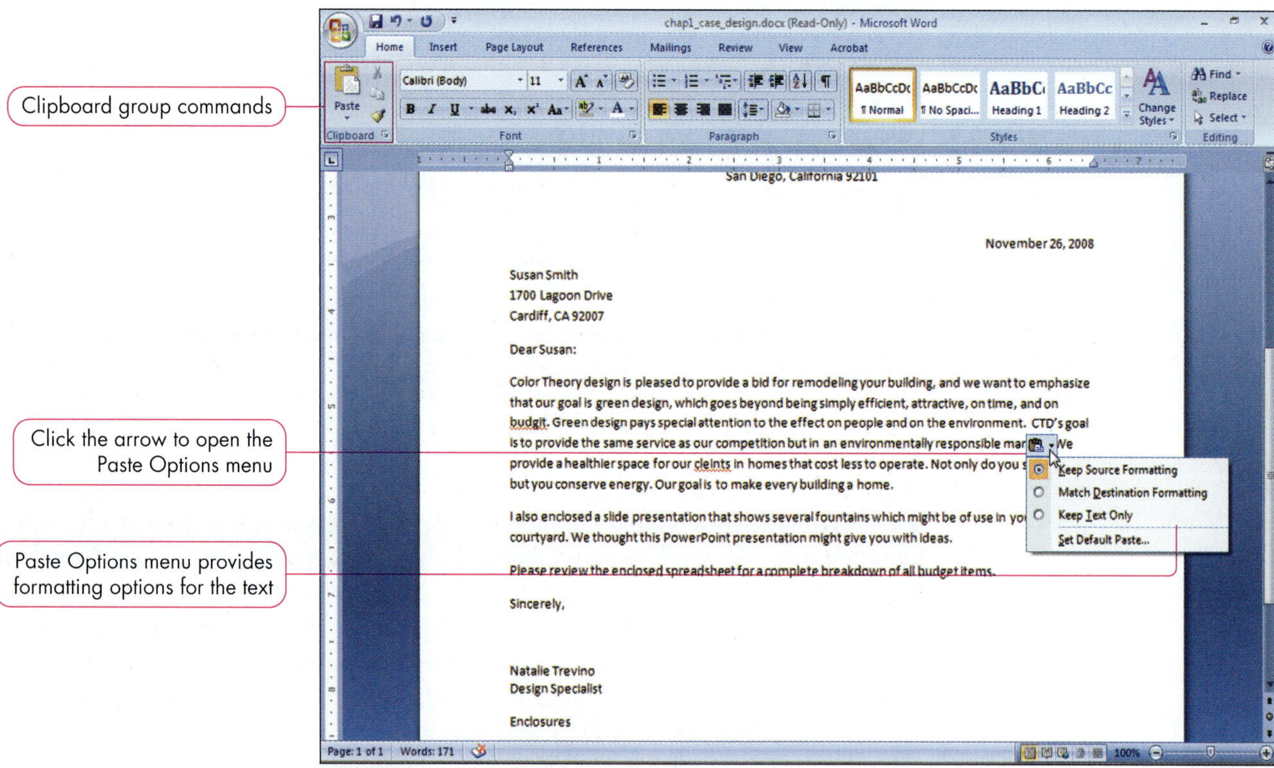

Figure 1.27 Text Pasted in the Document

TIP Moving and Copying Using Shortcuts

You can use alternative methods instead of using the commands located on the Home tab to cut, copy, and paste text. Office 2007 provides the following shortcuts:

A ***shortcut menu*** displays a list of commands that pertain to the text, object, or item you right-clicked.

- After selecting text, point back to the selected text and right-click the mouse. The ***shortcut menu*** displays a list of commands pertaining to a specific object that you right-clicked. Figure 1.34 shows an example of a shortcut menu. When you right-click selected text, you can choose Cut or Copy to remove or copy text, respectively. Move the insertion point to the desired location, right-click the mouse again, and choose Paste from the shortcut menu.
- After selecting text, use the keyboard shortcut combinations Ctrl+C to copy or Ctrl+X to cut text. Move the insertion point to the new location and press Ctrl+V to paste. These keyboard shortcuts work in most Windows applications, so they can be very useful.
- After selecting text, you can move it a short distance in the document by dragging to the new location. Point to the selected text, hold down the left mouse button, and then drag to the desired location. While you are dragging the mouse, the pointer changes to a left-pointing arrow with a box attached to it. Release the mouse button when you have placed the insertion point in the desired location, and the text displays in the new location.

Use the Office Clipboard

The ***Clipboard*** is a memory location that holds up to 24 items for you to paste into the current document, another file, or another application.

Office 2007 provides an option that enables you to cut or copy multiple items to the ***Clipboard***, which is a memory location that holds up to 24 items for you to paste into the current file, another file, or another application. The Clipboard stays active only while you are using one of the Office 2007 applications. When you exit from all Office 2007 applications, all items on the Clipboard are deleted. To accumulate items on the Clipboard, you must first display it by clicking the Dialog Box Launcher in the Clipboard group on the Home tab. When the Clipboard pane is open on the screen, its memory location is active, and the Clipboard accumulates all items you cut or copy up to the maximum 24. To paste an item from the Clipboard, point to it, click the resulting drop-down arrow, and choose Paste. To change how the Clipboard functions, use the Options button shown in Figure 1.28. One of the most important options allows the Clipboard to accumulate items even when it is not open on the screen. To activate the Clipboard so that it works in the background, click the Options button in the Clipboard and then select Collect without Showing Office Clipboard.

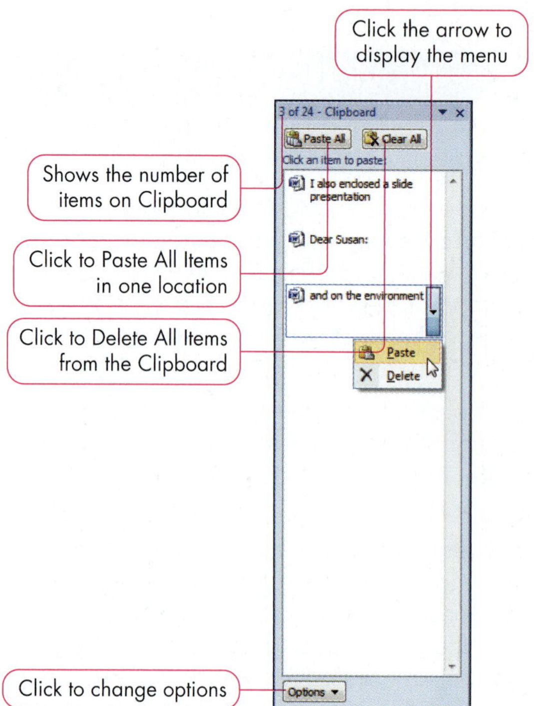

Figure 1.28 Clipboard Pane

Finding, Replacing, and Going to Text

You can waste a great deal of time slowly scrolling through a document trying to locate text or other items. Office 2007 provides features that speed up editing by automatically finding text and objects in a document, thus making you more productive. Office 2007 provides the following three related operations that all use the Find and Replace dialog box:

Find locates a word or group of words in a document.

Replace not only finds text, it replaces a word or group of words with other text.

Go To moves the insertion point to a specific location in the document.

- The ***Find*** command enables you to locate a word or group of words in a document quickly.
- The ***Replace*** command not only finds text quickly, it replaces a word or group of words with other text.
- The ***Go To*** command moves the insertion point to a specific location in the document.

Find Text

To locate text in an Office file, choose the Find command in the Editing group on the Home tab and type the text you want to locate in the resulting dialog box, as shown in Figure 1.29. After you type the text to locate, you can find the next instance after the insertion point and work through the file until you find the instance of the text you were looking for. Alternatively, you can find all instances of the text in the file at one time. If you decide to find every instance at once, the Office application temporarily highlights each one, and the text stays highlighted until you perform another operation in the file.

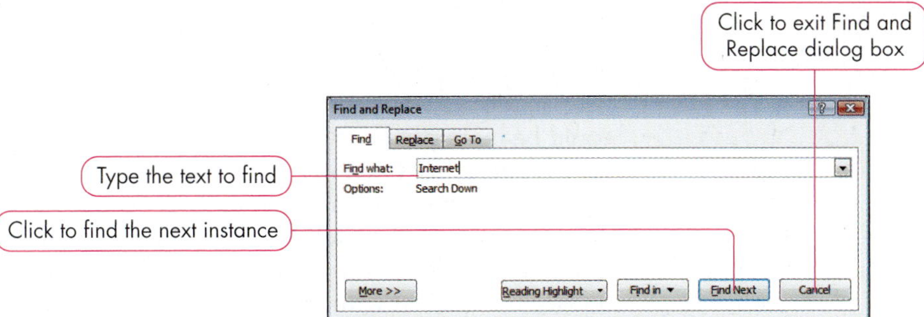

Figure 1.29 Find Tab of the Find and Replace Dialog Box

TIP Finding and Highlighting Text in Word

Sometimes temporarily highlighting all instances of text is not sufficient to help you edit the text you find. If you want Word to find all instances of specific text in a document and keep the highlighting from disappearing until you want it to, you can use the Reading Highlight option in the Find dialog box. One nice feature of this option is that even though the text remains highlighted on the screen, the document prints normally without highlighting. Figure 1.30 shows the Find and Replace dialog box with the Reading Highlight options that you use to highlight or remove the highlight from a document.

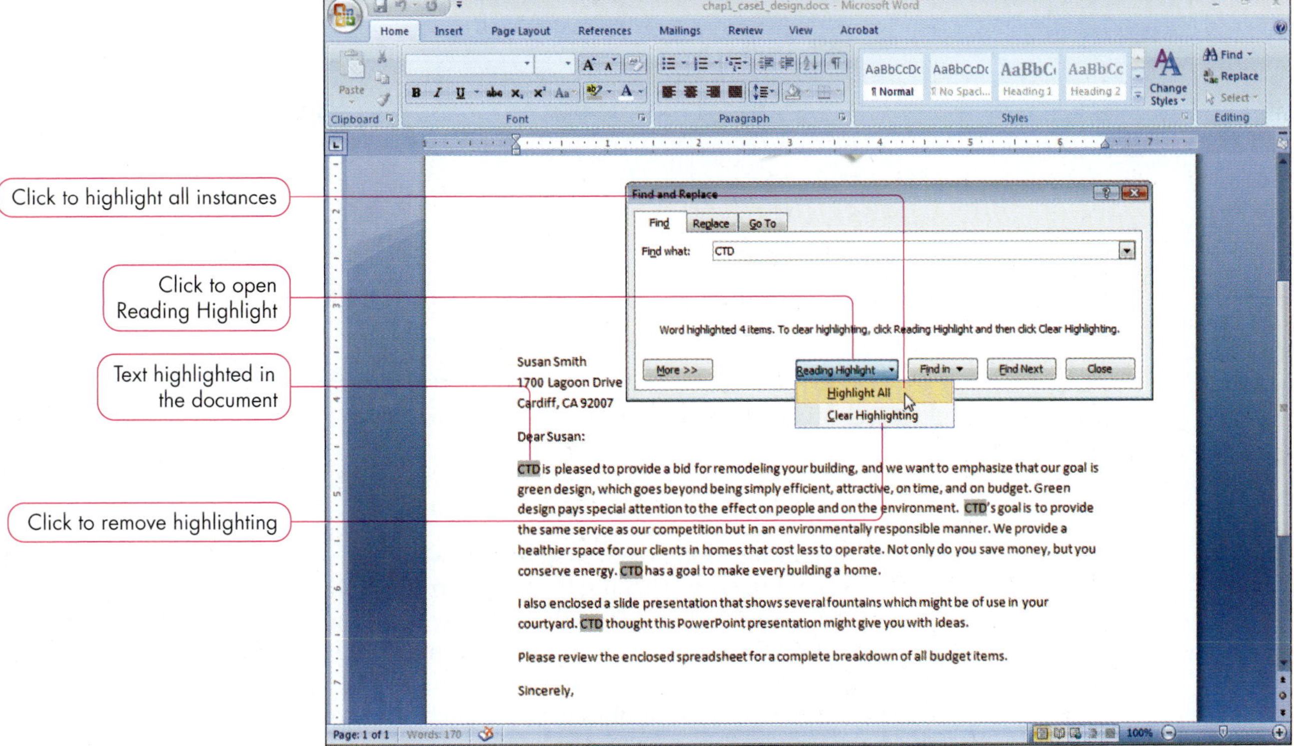

Figure 1.30 Find and Replace Dialog Box with Highlighting Options

Replace Text

While revising a file, you might realize that you have used an incorrect term and need to replace it throughout the entire file. Alternatively, you might realize that you could be more productive by re-using a letter or report that you polished and saved if you replace the previous client's or corporation's name with a new one. While you could perform these tasks manually, it would not be worth the time involved, and you might miss an instance of the old text, which could prove embarrassing. The Replace command in the Editing group on the Home tab can quickly and easily replace the old text with the new text throughout an entire file.

In the Find and Replace dialog box, first type the text to find, using the same process you used with the Find command. Second, type the text to replace the existing text with. Third, specify how you want Word to perform the operation. You can either replace each instance of the text individually, which can be time-consuming but allows you to decide whether to replace each instance one at a time, or you can replace every instance of the text in the document all at once. Word (but not the other Office applications) also provides options in the dialog box that help you replace only the correct text in the document. Click the More button to display these options. The most important one is the Find whole words only option. This option forces the application to find only complete words, not text that is part of other words. For instance, if you are searching for the word *off* to replace with other text, you would not want Word to replace the *off* in *office* with other text. Figure 1.31 shows these options along with the options for replacing text.

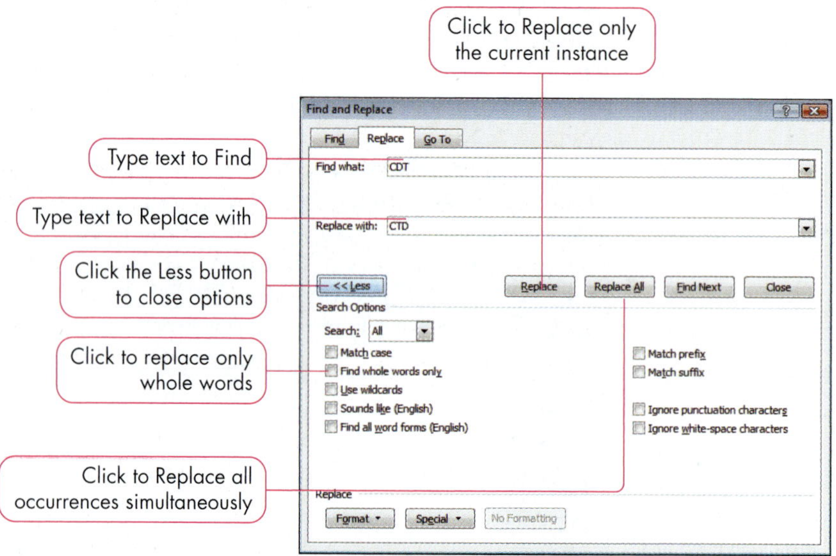

Figure 1.31 Find and Replace Dialog Box

Go Directly to a Location in a File

If you are editing a long document and want to move within it quickly, you can use the Go To command by clicking the down arrow on the Find command in the Editing group on the Home tab rather than slowly scrolling through an entire document or workbook. For example, if you want to move the insertion point to page 40 in a 200-page document, choose the Go To command and type 40 in the *Enter page number* text box. Notice the list of objects you can choose from in the Go to what section of the dialog box in Figure 1.32.

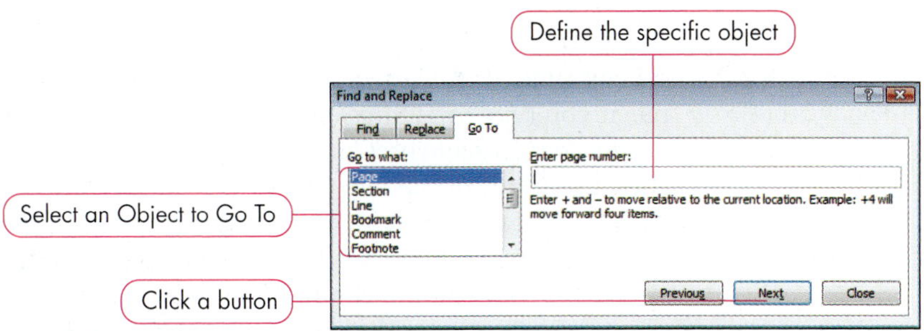

Figure 1.32 Go To Tab of the Find and Replace Dialog Box

Using the Undo and Redo Commands

The ***Undo*** command cancels your last one or more operations.

The ***Redo*** command reinstates or reverses an action performed by the Undo command.

As you create and edit files, you may perform an operation by mistake or simply change your mind about an edit you make. Office applications provide the ***Undo*** command, which can cancel your previous operation or even your last few operations. After using Undo to reverse an action or operation, you might decide that you want to use the ***Redo*** command to reinstate or reverse the action taken by the Undo command.

To undo the last action you performed, click Undo on the Quick Access Toolbar. For example, if you deleted text by mistake, immediately click Undo to restore it. If, however, you deleted some text and then performed several other operations, you can find the correct action to undo, with the understanding that all actions after that one will also be undone. To review a list of the last few actions you performed, click the Undo drop-down arrow and select the desired one from the list—Undo highlights all actions in the list down to that item and will undo all of the highlighted actions. Figure 1.33 shows a list of recent actions in PowerPoint. To reinstate or reverse an action as a result of using the Undo command, click Redo on the Quick Access Toolbar.

The ***Repeat*** command repeats only the last action you performed.

The ***Repeat*** command provides limited use because it repeats only the last action you performed. To repeat the last action, click Repeat on the Quick Access Toolbar. If the Office application is able to repeat your last action, the results will display in the document. Note that the Repeat command is replaced with the Redo command after you use the Undo command. For example, Figure 1.33 shows the Redo command after the Undo command has been used, and Figure 1.34 shows the Repeat command when Undo has not been used.

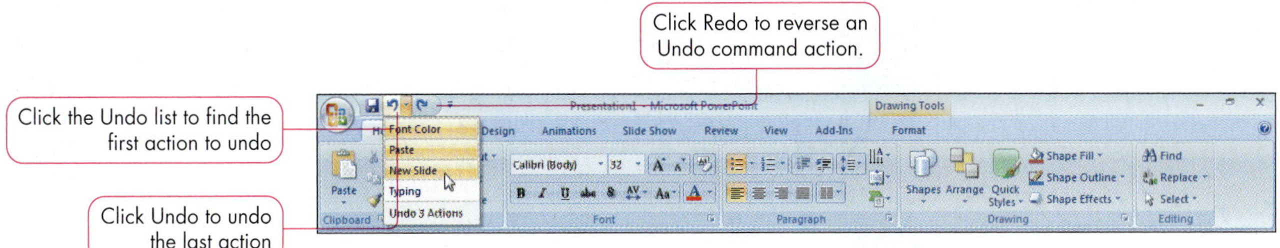

Figure 1.33 Undo and Redo Buttons

Using Language Tools

Documents, spreadsheets, and presentations represent the author, so remember that errors in writing can keep people from getting a desired job, or once on the job, can keep them from getting a desired promotion. To avoid holding yourself back, you should polish your final documents before submitting them electronically or as a hard copy. Office 2007 provides built-in proofing tools to help you fix spelling and grammar errors and help you locate the correct word or information.

AutoCorrect is a feature that makes some automatic corrections as you type.

Check Spelling and Grammar Automatically

As you type, ***AutoCorrect*** may correct some typographical errors for you. For example, if you type *teh*, Office changes it to *the*, and if you type *monday*, Office changes it to *Monday*. To see AutoCorrect options, click the Office Button, click Word Options, click Proofing on the left side of the Word Options dialog box, and then click the AutoCorrect Options button. See Help for more information on AutoCorrect.

By default, Office applications check spelling as you type and flag potential spelling errors by underlining them with a red wavy line. Word also flags potential grammar errors by underlining them with a green wavy line. You can fix these errors as you enter text, or you can ignore the errors and fix them all at once.

To fix spelling errors as you type, simply move the insertion point to a red wavy underlined word and correct the spelling yourself. If you spell the word correctly, the red wavy underline disappears. However, if you need help figuring out the correct spelling for the flagged word, then point to the error and right-click the mouse. The shortcut menu displays with possible corrections for the error. If you find the correction on the shortcut menu, click it to replace the word in the document. To fix grammar errors, follow the same process, but when the shortcut menu displays, you can choose to view more information to see rules that apply to the potential error. Notice the errors flagged in Figure 1.34. Note that the Mini toolbar also displays automatically.

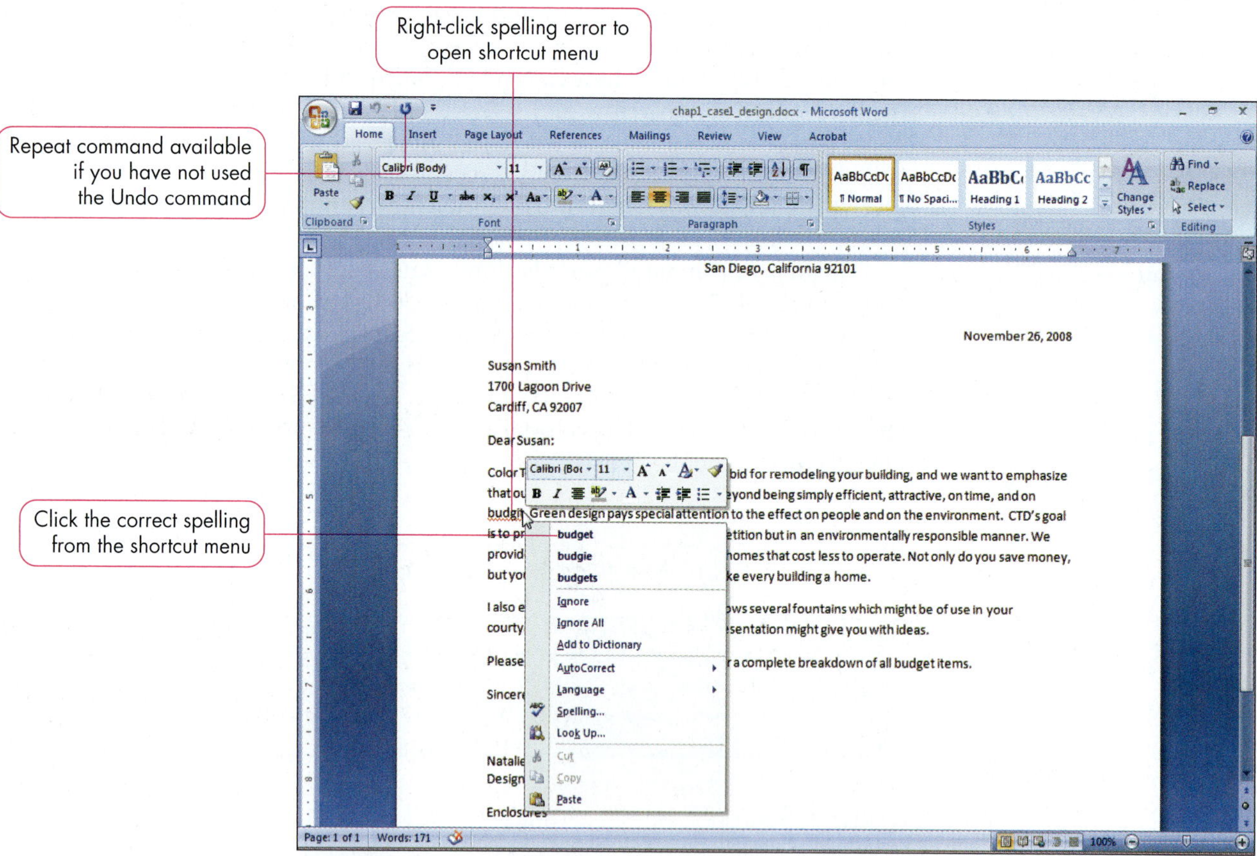

Figure 1.34 Automatic Spell and Grammar Check

Check Spelling and Grammar at Once

Some people prefer to wait until they complete typing the entire document and then check spelling and grammar at once. To check for errors, click Spelling & Grammar in Word (Spelling in Excel or PowerPoint) in the Proofing group on the Review tab. As the checking proceeds through the file and detects any spelling or grammar errors, it displays the Spelling dialog box if you are using Excel or

PowerPoint, or the Spelling and Grammar dialog box in Word. You can either correct or ignore the changes that the Spelling checker proposes to your document. For example, Figure 1.35 shows the Spelling and Grammar dialog box with a misspelled word in the top section and Word's suggestions in the bottom section. Select the correction from the list and change the current instance, or you can change all instances of the error throughout the document. However, sometimes the flagged word might be a specialized term or a person's name, so if the flagged word is not a spelling error, you can ignore it once in the current document or throughout the entire document; further, you could add the word to the spell-check list so that it never flags that spelling again.

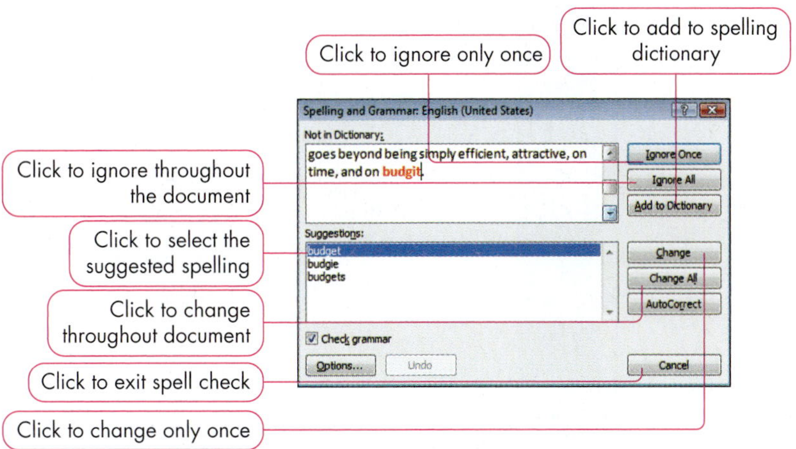

Figure 1.35 Spelling and Grammar Dialog Box

> **TIP Proofreading Your Document**
>
> The spelling and grammar checks available in Word provide great help improving your documents. However, you should not forget that you still have to proofread your document to ensure that the writing is clear, appropriate for the intended audience, and makes sense.

Use the Thesaurus

As you edit a document, spreadsheet, or presentation, you might want to improve your writing by finding a better or different word for a particular situation. For example, say you are stuck and cannot think of a better word for *big*, and you would like to find an alternative word that means the same. Word, Excel, and PowerPoint provide a built-in thesaurus, which is an electronic version of a book of synonyms. Synonyms are different words with the same or similar meaning, and antonyms are words with the opposite meaning.

The easiest method for accessing the Thesaurus in Word or PowerPoint is to point to the word in the file that you want to find an alternative for and right-click the mouse. When the shortcut menu displays, point to Synonyms, and the program displays a list of alternatives. Notice the shortcut menu and list of synonyms in Figure 1.36. To select one of the alternative words on the list, click it, and the word you select replaces the original word. If you do not see an alternative on the list that you want to use and you want to investigate further, click Thesaurus on the shortcut menu to open the full Thesaurus. You can also activate Thesaurus by clicking the Review tab on the Ribbon, and then clicking Thesaurus in the Proofing group.

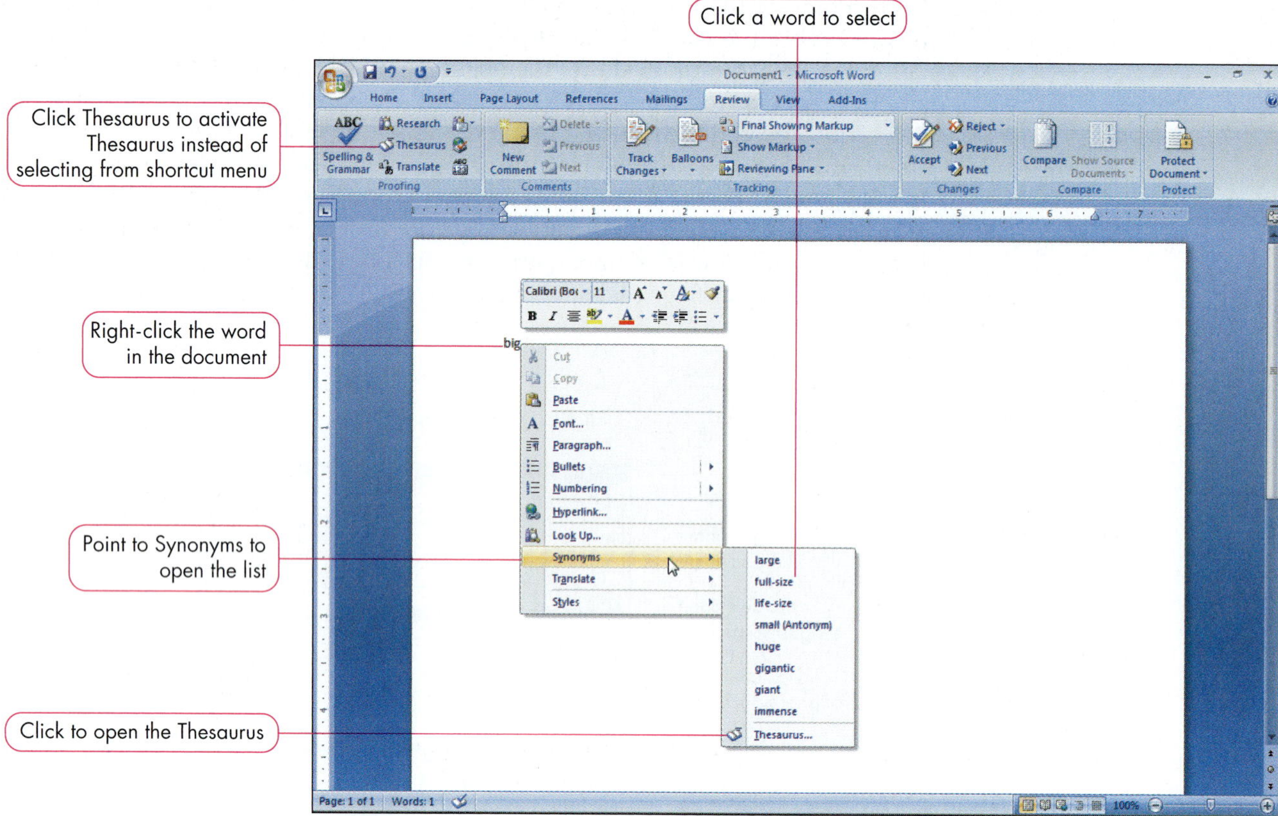
Click a word to select
Click Thesaurus to activate Thesaurus instead of selecting from shortcut menu
Right-click the word in the document
Point to Synonyms to open the list
Click to open the Thesaurus

Figure 1.36 Shortcut Menu with Synonyms

An alternative method for opening the full Thesaurus is to place the insertion point in the word you want to look up and then click the Thesaurus command in the Proofing group on the Review tab. The Thesaurus opens with alternatives for the selected word. You can use one of the words presented in the pane, or you can look up additional words. If you do not find the word you want, use the Search option to find more alternatives. Figure 1.37 shows the Thesaurus.

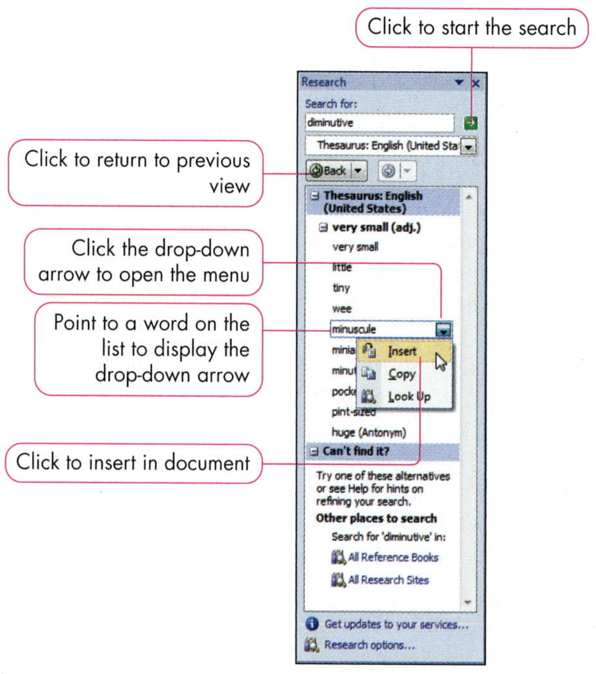
Click to start the search
Click to return to previous view
Click the drop-down arrow to open the menu
Point to a word on the list to display the drop-down arrow
Click to insert in document

Figure 1.37 The Thesaurus

Conduct Research

As you work in Word, Excel, or PowerPoint, you might need to find the definition of a word or look up an item in the encyclopedia to include accurate information. Office 2007 provides quick access to research tools. To access research tools, click the Research button in the Proofing group on the Review tab. Notice in Figure 1.38 that you can specify what you want to research and specify where to Search. Using this feature, you can choose from reference books, research sites, and business and financial sites.

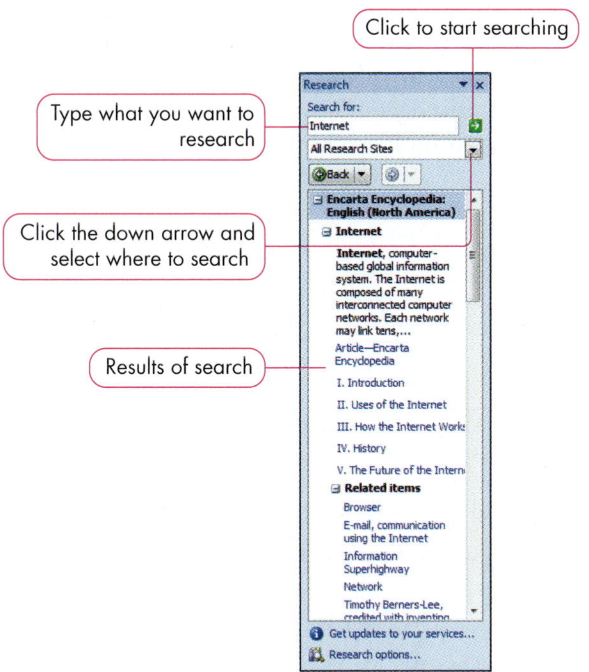

Figure 1.38 Research Task Pane

TIP Avoiding Plagiarism

If you use the research feature in Office to find information in an encyclopedia or in other locations to help you create your document, then you need to credit the source of that information. Avoid the problem of plagiarism, which is borrowing other people's words or ideas, by citing all sources that you use. You might want to check with your instructor for the exact format for citing sources.

Applying Font Attributes

> Taking the time to format text helps the reader find important information in the document by making it stand out and helps the reader understand the message by emphasizing key items.

After you have edited a document, you might want to improve its visual appeal by formatting the text. ***Formatting text*** changes an individual letter, a word, or a body of selected text. Taking the time to format text helps the reader find important information in the document by making it stand out and helps the reader understand the message by emphasizing key items. You can format the text in the document by changing the following font attributes:

Formatting text changes an individual letter, a word, or a body of selected text.

- Font face or size
- Font attributes such as bold, underline, or italic
- Font color

The Font group on the Home tab—available in Word, Excel, PowerPoint, and Access—provides many formatting options, and Office provides two methods for applying these font attributes:

- Choose the font attributes first and then type the text. The text displays in the document with the formatting.
- Type the text, select the text to format, and choose the font attributes. The selected text displays with the formatting.

You can apply more than one attribute to text, so you can select one or more attributes either all at once or at any time. Also it is easy to see which attributes you have applied to text in the document. Select the formatted text and look at the commands in the Font group on the Home tab. The commands in effect display with a gold background. See Figure 1.39. To remove an effect from text, select it and click the command. The gold background disappears for attributes that are no longer in effect.

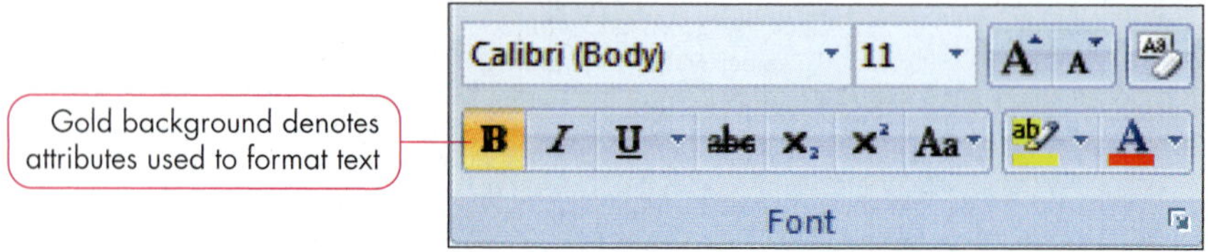

Figure 1.39 Font Group of the Home tab

Change the Font

A *font* is a named set of characters with the same design.

> Remember that more is not always better when applied to fonts, so limit the number of font changes in your document.

A *font* is a named set of characters with the same design, and Office 2007 provides many built-in fonts for you to choose from. Remember that more is not always better when applied to fonts, so limit the number of font changes in your document. Additionally, the choice of a font should depend on the intent of the document and should never overpower the message. For example, using a fancy or highly stylized font that may be difficult to read for a client letter might seem odd to the person receiving it and overpower the intended message.

One powerful feature of Office 2007 that can help you decide how a font will look in your document is Live Preview. First select the existing text, and then click the drop-down arrow on the Font list in the Font group on the Home tab. As you point to a font name in the list, Live Preview changes the selected text in the document to that font. Figure 1.40 shows the selected text displaying in a different font as a result of Live Preview. As you mouse over the different fonts, the selected text no longer appears selected. After you select a different font, the Font list closes, and you can see the text is selected.

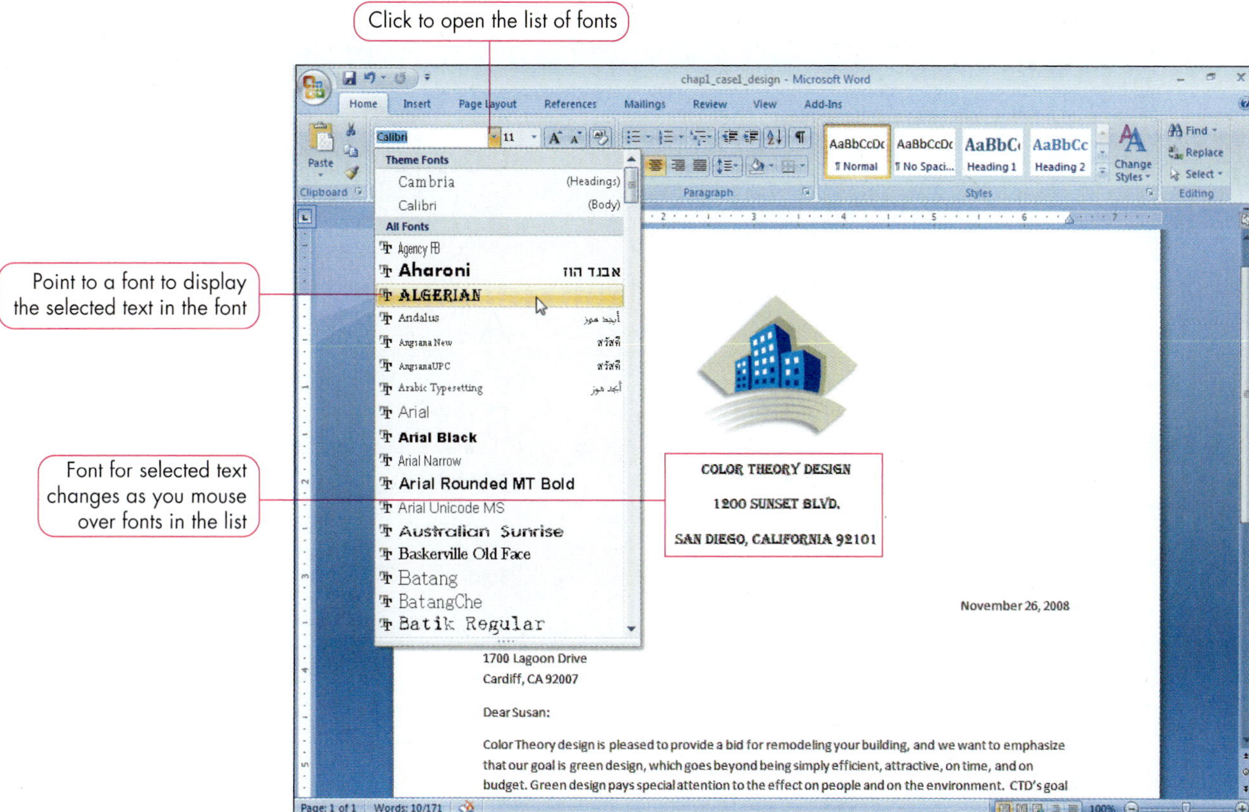

Figure 1.40 Font List

Change the Font Size, Color, and Attributes

Besides changing the font, you also can change the size, color, and other attributes of text in a document. Because these formatting operations are used so frequently, Office places many of these commands in several places for easy access:

- in the Font group on the Home tab
- on the Mini toolbar
- in the Font dialog box

Table 1.9 describes the commands that display in the Font group of the Home tab and in the Font dialog box.

Table 1.9 Font Commands

Command	Description	Example
Font	Enables you to designate the font.	Arial Comic Sans MS
Font Size	Enables you to designate an exact font size.	Size 8 Size 18
Grow Font	Each time you click the command, the selected text increases one size.	A A
Shrink Font	Each time you click the command, the selected text decreases one size.	B B
Clear Formatting	Removes all formatting from the selected text.	***Formatted*** Cleared
Bold	Makes the text darker than the surrounding text.	**Bold**
Italic	Places the selected text in italic, that is, slants the letters to the right.	*Italic*
Underline	Places a line under the text. Click the drop-down arrow to change the underline style.	Underline
Strikethrough	Draws a line through the middle of the text.	~~Strikethrough~~
Subscript	Places selected text below the baseline.	$\text{Sub}_{\text{script}}$
Superscript	Places selected text above the line of letters.	$\text{Super}^{\text{script}}$
Change Case	Changes the case of the selected text. Click the drop-down arrow to select the desired case.	lowercase UPPERCASE
Text Highlight Color	Makes selected text look like it was highlighted with a marker pen. Click the drop-down arrow to change color and other options.	Highlighted
Font Color	Changes the color of selected text. Click the drop-down arrow to change colors.	Font Color

If you have several formatting changes to make, click the Dialog Box Launcher in the Font group on the Home tab to display the Font dialog box. The Font dialog box is handy because all the formatting features display in one location, and it provides additional options such as changing the underline color. Figure 1.41 shows the Font dialog box in Word.

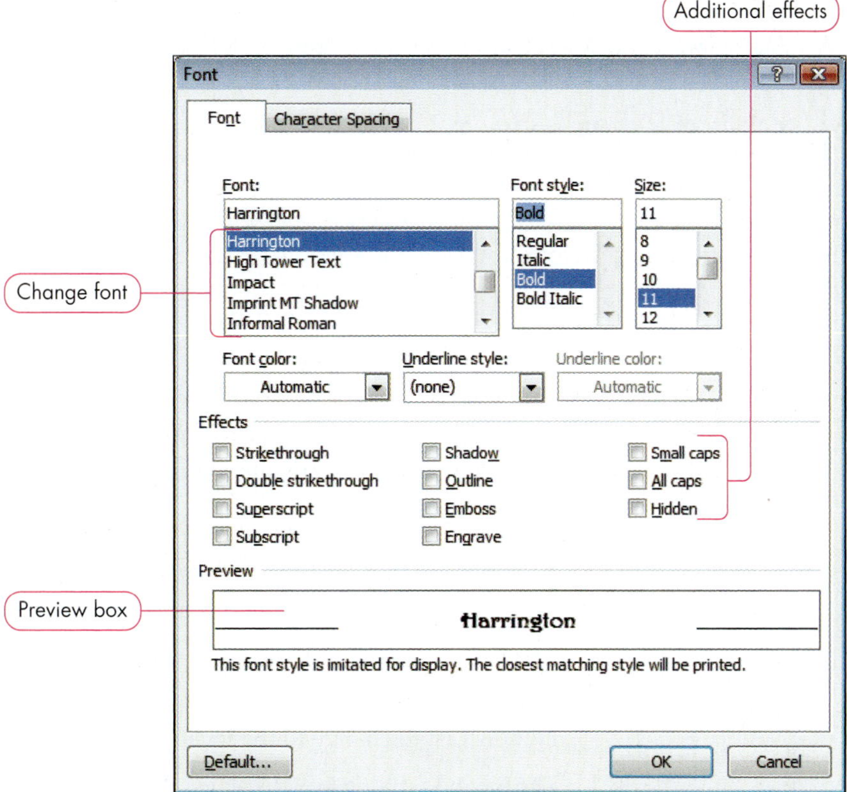

Figure 1.41 Font Dialog Box

Copying Formats with the Format Painter

The ***Format Painter*** copies the formatting of text from one location to another.

After formatting text in one part of a document, you might want to apply that same formatting to other text in a different location in the document. You could try to remember all the formatting options you selected, but that process would be time-consuming and could produce inconsistent results. Office 2007 provides a shortcut method called the ***Format Painter***, which copies the formatting of text from one location to another.

Select the formatted text you want to copy and click the Format Painter in the Clipboard group on the Home tab to copy the format. Single-click the command to turn it on to copy formatting to one location—the option turns off automatically after one copy—or double-click the command to turn it on for unlimited format copying—you must press Esc on the keyboard or single click the Format Painter button to turn it off.

Hands-On Exercises

3 | Performing Basic Tasks

Skills covered: 1. Cut, Copy, Paste, and Undo **2.** Find and Replace Text **3.** Check Spelling **4.** Choose Synonyms and Use Thesaurus **5.** Use the Research Tool **6.** Apply Font Attributes **7.** Use Format Painter

Step 1 Cut, Copy, Paste, and Undo

Refer to Figure 1.42 as you complete Steps 1 and 2.

a. Open Word and click the **Office Button**, click **Open**, and then using the Open dialog box features navigate to your classroom file location.

   TROUBLESHOOTING: If you have trouble finding the file, remember to use the Folders List to find the correct location.

b. Select the file *chap1_ho3_internet* and click the **Open** button.

   The Word document displays on the screen.

c. Click the **Office Button** and select **Save As**. If necessary, use the Favorites or Folders List to change to the location where you save files.

   The Save As dialog box displays.

d. Type the new file name **chap1_ho3_internet_solution**, be sure that *Word Document* displays in the *Save as type* box, and click **Save**.

   The file is saved with the new name.

e. Click to place the insertion point at the beginning of the second sentence in the first paragraph. Type **These developments brought together** and then press **Spacebar**.

   The text moves to the right, making room for the new inserted text.

f. Press and hold down **Ctrl** as you click this sentence below the heading The World Wide Web: *The Netscape browser led in user share until Microsoft Internet Explorer took the lead in 1999.*

g. Click **Cut** in the Clipboard group on the Home tab.

   The text disappears from the document.

h. Move the insertion point to the end of the last paragraph and click **Paste** in the Clipboard group on the Home tab.

   The text displays in the new location.

i. Reselect the sentence you just moved and click **Copy** in the Clipboard group on the Home tab.

j. Move the insertion point to the end of the first paragraph beginning *The idea* and click the right mouse button.

   The shortcut menu displays.

k. Select **Paste** from the shortcut menu.

   The text remains in the original position and is copied to the second location.

l. Click **Undo** on the Quick Access Toolbar to undo the last paste.

Step 2
Find and Replace Text

Refer to Figure 1.42 to complete Step 2.

a. Press **Ctrl + Home** to move the insertion point to the beginning of the document. Click **Replace** in the Editing group on the Home tab.

The Find and Replace dialog box displays.

b. Type **Internet** in the *Find what* box, and type **World Wide Web** in the *Replace with* box.

c. Click the **Replace All** button. Click **OK** to close the information box that informs you that Word has made seven replacements. Click **Close** to close the Find and Replace dialog box.

All instances of Internet have been replaced with World Wide Web in the document.

d. Click **Undo** on the Quick Access Toolbar.

All instances of *World Wide Web* have changed back to *Internet* in the document.

e. Click **Replace** in the Editing group on the Home tab.

The Find and Replace dialog box displays with the text you typed still in the boxes.

f. Click the **Find Next** button.

The first instance of the text *Internet* is highlighted.

g. Click the **Replace** button.

The first instance of Internet is replaced with World Wide Web, and the next instance of Internet is highlighted.

h. Click the **Find Next** button.

The highlight moves to the next instance of Internet without changing the previous one.

i. Click the **Close** button to close the Find and Replace dialog box.

The Find and Replace dialog box closes.

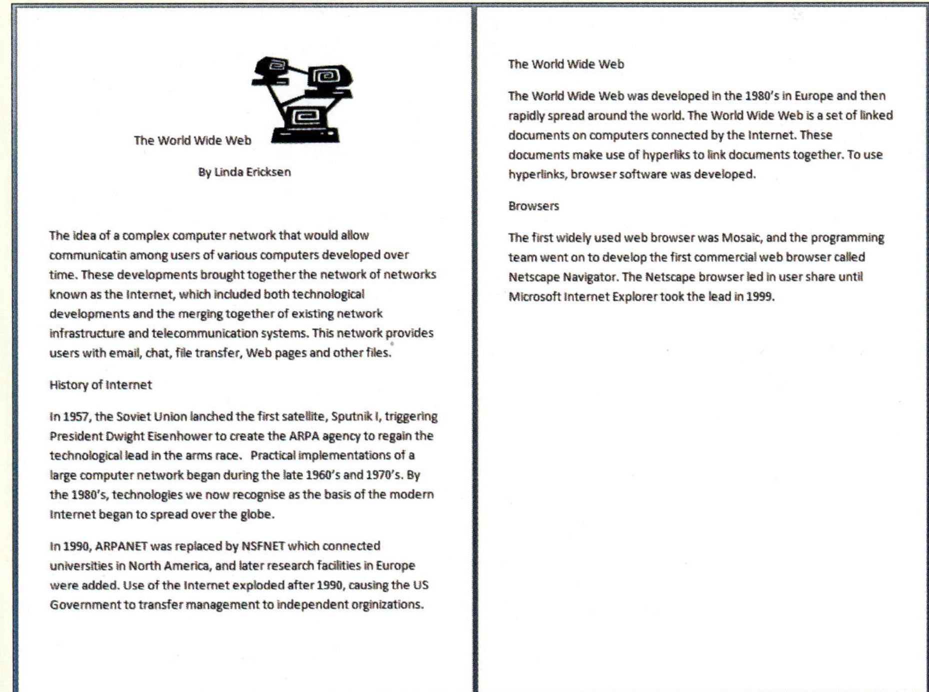

The World Wide Web

By Linda Ericksen

The idea of a complex computer network that would allow communicatin among users of various computers developed over time. These developments brought together the network of networks known as the Internet, which included both technological developments and the merging together of existing network infrastructure and telecommunication systems. This network provides users with email, chat, file transfer, Web pages and other files.

History of Internet

In 1957, the Soviet Union lanched the first satellite, Sputnik I, triggering President Dwight Eisenhower to create the ARPA agency to regain the technological lead in the arms race. Practical implementations of a large computer network began during the late 1960's and 1970's. By the 1980's, technologies we now recognise as the basis of the modern Internet began to spread over the globe.

In 1990, ARPANET was replaced by NSFNET which connected universities in North America, and later research facilities in Europe were added. Use of the Internet exploded after 1990, causing the US Government to transfer management to independent orginizations.

The World Wide Web

The World Wide Web was developed in the 1980's in Europe and then rapidly spread around the world. The World Wide Web is a set of linked documents on computers connected by the Internet. These documents make use of hyperliks to link documents together. To use hyperlinks, browser software was developed.

Browsers

The first widely used web browser was Mosaic, and the programming team went on to develop the first commercial web browser called Netscape Navigator. The Netscape browser led in user share until Microsoft Internet Explorer took the lead in 1999.

Figure 1.42 Edited Document (Shown in Full Screen Reading View)

Step 3
Check Spelling

Refer to Figure 1.43 as you complete Step 3–5.

a. Right-click the first word in the document that displays with the red wavy underline: *communicatin*.

TROUBLESHOOTING: If the first word highlighted is the author's last name, ignore it for now. The name is spelled correctly, but if it is not listed in the spell check, then Word flags it.

The shortcut menu displays with correct alternatives.

b. Click **communication** to replace the misspelled word in the document.

The incorrect spelling is replaced, and the red wavy underline disappears.

c. Click the **Review tab** and then click **Spelling & Grammar** in the Proofing group.

The Spelling and Grammar dialog box opens with the first detected error displayed.

d. Move through the document selecting the correct word from the suggestions provided and choosing to **Change** the errors.

e. Click **OK** to close the Spelling and Grammar checker when the process is complete.

Step 4
Choose Synonyms and Use Thesaurus

a. Place the insertion point in the word **complex** in the first sentence and right-click the mouse.

The shortcut menu displays.

b. Point to **Synonyms** on the shortcut menu.

The list of alternative words displays.

c. Click the alternative word **multifaceted**.

The new word replaces the word *complex* in the document.

d. Click in the word you just replaced, *multifaceted*, and click **Thesaurus** in the Proofing group on the Review tab.

The Thesaurus displays with alternatives for **multifaceted**.

e. Scroll down the list and point to the word *comprehensive*.

A box displays around the word with a drop-down arrow on the right.

f. Click the drop-down arrow to display the menu and click **Insert**.

The word *comprehensive* replaces the word in the document.

Step 5
Use the Research Tool

Refer to Figure 1.43 to complete Step 5.

a. Place the insertion point in the *Search for* text box and type **browser**.

b. Click the drop-down arrow on the **Reference** list, which currently displays the Thesaurus.

The list of reference sites displays.

c. Click **Encarta Encyclopedia: English (North America)** option.

A definition of the browser displays in the results box.

d. Click the **Close** button on the Research title bar.

The Research pane closes.

The World Wide Web

By Linda Ericksen

The idea of a comprehensive computer network that would allow communication among users of various computers developed over time. These developments brought together the network of networks known as the Internet, which included both technological developments and the merging together of existing network infrastructure and telecommunication systems. This network provides users with email, chat, file transfer, Web pages and other files.

History of Internet

In 1957, the Soviet Union lunched the first satellite, Sputnik I, triggering President Dwight Eisenhower to create the ARPA agency to regain the technological lead in the arms race. Practical implementations of a large computer network began during the late 1960's and 1970's. By the 1980's, technologies we now recognize as the basis of the modern Internet began to spread over the globe.

In 1990, ARPANET was replaced by NSFNET which connected universities in North America, and later research facilities in Europe were added. Use of the Internet exploded after 1990, causing the US Government to transfer management to independent organizations.

The World Wide Web

The World Wide Web was developed in the 1980's in Europe and then rapidly spread around the world. The World Wide Web is a set of linked documents on computers connected by the Internet. These documents make use of hyperlinks to link documents together. To use hyperlinks, browser software was developed.

Browsers

The first widely used web browser was Mosaic, and the programming team went on to develop the first commercial web browser called Netscape Navigator. The Netscape browser led in user share until Microsoft Internet Explorer took the lead in 1999.

Figure 1.43 Language Tools Improved the Document

Step 6 Apply Font Attributes

Refer to Figure 1.44 as you complete Steps 6 and 7.

a. Select the title of the document.

   The Mini toolbar displays.

b. Click **Bold** on the Mini toolbar and then click outside the title.

   TROUBLESHOOTING: If the Mini toolbar is hard to read, remember to point to it to make it display fully.

   The text changes to boldface.

c. Select the title again and click the drop-down arrow on the **Font** command in the Font group on the Home tab.

   The list of fonts displays.

d. Point to font names on the list.

   Live Preview changes the font of the selected title to display the fonts you point to.

e. Scroll down and then select the **Lucida Bright** font by clicking on the name.

   The title changes to the new font.

f. With the title still selected, click the **Font Size down arrow** and select **16**.

   The title changes to font size 16.

g. Select the byline that contains the author's name and click **Underline**, **Italic**, and **Shrink Font** once. All are located in the Font group on the Home tab.

   The author's byline displays underlined, in italic, and one font size smaller.

h. Select the first heading *History of Internet* and click the **Font Color down arrow** command in the Font group on the Home tab. When the colors display, under Standard Colors, choose **Purple** and then click outside the selected text.

   The heading displays in purple.

i. Select the heading you just formatted as purple text and click **Bold**.

Step 7
Use Format Painter

Refer to Figure 1.44 to complete Step 7.

a. Click **Format Painter** in the Clipboard group on the Home tab.

   The pointer changes to a small paintbrush.

b. Select the second unformatted heading, and repeat the process to format the third unformatted heading.

   The Format Painter formats that heading as purple and bold and automatically turns off.

c. Press **Ctrl** while you click the last sentence in the document and click the **Dialog Box Launcher** in the Font group.

d. Select **Bold** in the Font style box and **Double strikethrough** in the *Effects* section of the dialog box, then click **OK**.

e. Click outside the selected sentence to remove the selection and view the effects, and then click back in the formatted text.

   The sentence displays bold with two lines through the text. The Bold command in the Font group on the Home tab displays with a gold background.

f. Select the same sentence again and click **Bold** in the Font group on the Home tab, and then click outside the sentence.

   The Bold format has been removed from the text.

g. Click **Save** on the Quick Access Toolbar.

   The document is saved under the same name.

h. To exit Word, click the **Office Button** and then click the **Exit Word button**.

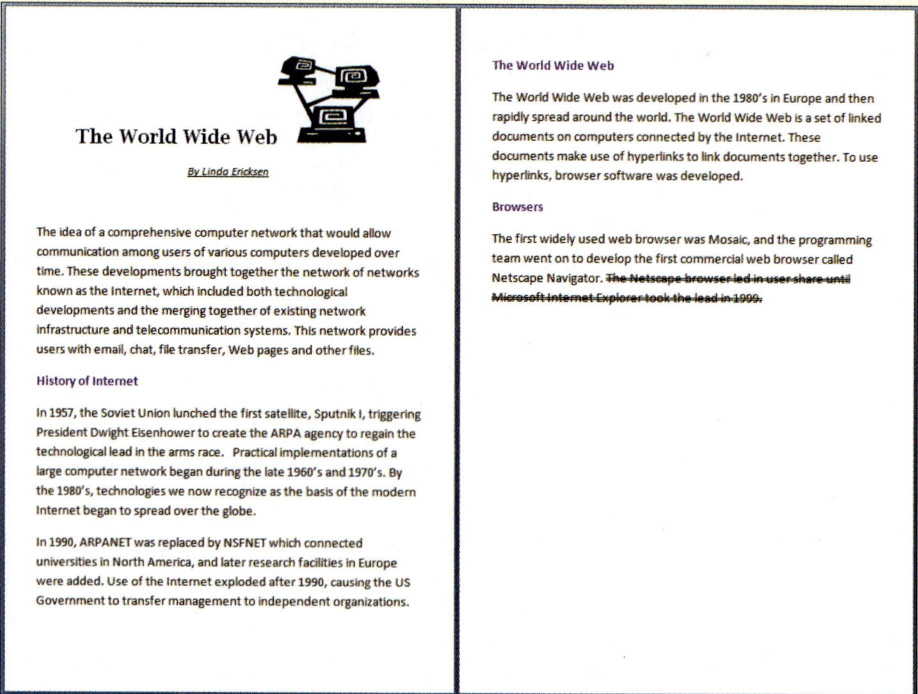

The World Wide Web

By Linda Ericksen

The idea of a comprehensive computer network that would allow communication among users of various computers developed over time. These developments brought together the network of networks known as the Internet, which included both technological developments and the merging together of existing network infrastructure and telecommunication systems. This network provides users with email, chat, file transfer, Web pages and other files.

History of Internet

In 1957, the Soviet Union lunched the first satellite, Sputnik I, triggering President Dwight Eisenhower to create the ARPA agency to regain the technological lead in the arms race. Practical implementations of a large computer network began during the late 1960's and 1970's. By the 1980's, technologies we now recognize as the basis of the modern Internet began to spread over the globe.

In 1990, ARPANET was replaced by NSFNET which connected universities in North America, and later research facilities in Europe were added. Use of the Internet exploded after 1990, causing the US Government to transfer management to independent organizations.

The World Wide Web

The World Wide Web was developed in the 1980's in Europe and then rapidly spread around the world. The World Wide Web is a set of linked documents on computers connected by the Internet. These documents make use of hyperlinks to link documents together. To use hyperlinks, browser software was developed.

Browsers

The first widely used web browser was Mosaic, and the programming team went on to develop the first commercial web browser called Netscape Navigator. ~~The Netscape browser led in user share until Microsoft Internet Explorer took the lead in 1999.~~

Figure 1.44 Formatted Document

Summary

1. **Identify common interface elements.** You learned to identify and use the common elements of the Office 2007 interface and apply them in Word, PowerPoint, Excel, and Access. The top of the application window contains the Office Button that, when clicked, displays the Office menu. The Quick Access Toolbar provides commonly used commands, such as Save and Undo. The primary command center is the Ribbon, which contains tabs to organize major tasks. Each tab contains groups of related commands. The bottom of the window contains a status bar that gives general information, view options, and the Zoom slider.

2. **Use Office 2007 Help.** When you need help to continue working with Office 2007, you can use the Help feature from your computer or get help at Microsoft Office Online. You can position the mouse pointer on a command to see an Enhanced ScreenTip. You can press F1 to display Help windows for some Enhanced ScreenTips. You can often get context-sensitive help by clicking Help within dialog boxes.

3. **Open a file.** To retrieve a file you have previously saved, you use the Open command. When you open a file, it is copied into RAM so that you can view and work on it.

4. **Save a file.** As you create and edit documents, you should save your work for future use. Use the Save or Save As command to save a file for the first time, giving it a name and location. To continue saving changes to the same file name, use Save. To assign a new name, location, or file type, use Save As.

5. **Print a document.** Producing a perfect hard copy of the document is an important task, and you can make it easier by previewing, selecting options, and printing. You can select the printer, how many copies to print, and the pages you want to print. In addition, each program has specific print options.

6. **Select text to edit.** In order to edit text, you have to identify the body of text you want to work with by selecting it first. You can select text by using the mouse.

7. **Insert text and change to the Overtype mode.** To edit text in the document, you need to be able to insert text and to replace text by typing over it. The Insert mode inserts text without deleting existing text. The Overtype mode types over existing text as you type.

8. **Move and copy text.** You can move text from one location to another to achieve a better flow in a document, worksheet, or presentation. You can use the Copy command to duplicate data in one location and use the Paste command to place the duplicate in another location.

9. **Find, Replace, and Go To text.** Another editing feature that can save you time is to find text by searching for it or going directly to a specific element in the document. You can also replace text that needs updating.

10. **Use the Undo and Redo commands.** If you make a mistake and want to undo it, you can easily correct it by using the Undo feature. If you change your mind after undoing an action, you can use the Redo command to reverse the effect of Undo. Furthermore, to save time, you can repeat the last action with the Repeat command.

11. **Use language tools.** Office 2007 provides tools to help you create and edit documents. You can use the spelling and grammar check, the built-in thesaurus, and even conduct research all from your Word document. You can check spelling and conduct research in Excel and PowerPoint as well.

12. **Apply font attributes.** Applying font formats can help make the message clearer. For example, you can select a different font to achieve a different look. In addition, you can adjust the font size and change the font color of text. Other font attributes include bold, underline, and italic.

13. **Copy formats with the Format Painter.** You might want to copy the format of text to another location or to several locations in the document. You can easily accomplish that with the Format Painter.

Key Terms

AutoCorrect 40
Clipboard 35
Command 6
Contextual tab 8
Copy 34
Cut 34
Dialog box 7
Dialog Box Launcher 7
Duplex printer 27
Enhanced ScreenTip 11
Find 36
Font 44
Format Painter 47
Formatting text 43
Gallery 7
Go To 36
Group 6
Insert 32
Insertion point 18
Key Tip 8
Landscape orientation 25
Live Preview 7
Macro 23
Manual duplex 27
Mini toolbar 31
Office Button 4
Office menu 4
Overtype mode 33
Paste 34
Portrait orientation 25
Presentation graphics software . .3
Quick Access Toolbar 5
Redo 39
Relational database software . . .3
Repeat 39
Replace 36
Ribbon 6
Selection bar 32
Shortcut menu 35
Spreadsheet software 3
Status bar 8
Tab 6
Template 23
Title bar 5
Undo 39
User interface 4
Virus checker 23
Word processing software 3
Zoom slider 9

Multiple Choice

1. Software that is used primarily with text to create, edit, and format documents is known as:
   (a) Electronic spreadsheet software
   (b) Word processing software
   (c) Presentation graphics software
   (d) Relational database software

2. Which Office feature displays when you rest the mouse pointer on a command?
   (a) The Ribbon
   (b) The status bar
   (c) An Enhanced ScreenTip
   (d) A dialog box

3. What is the name of the blinking vertical line in a document that designates the current location in the document?
   (a) A command
   (b) Overtype mode
   (c) Insert mode
   (d) Insertion point

4. If you wanted to locate every instance of text in a document and have it temporarily highlighted, which command would you use?
   (a) Find
   (b) Replace
   (c) Go To
   (d) Spell Check

5. The meeting point between computer software and the person using it is known as:
   (a) A file
   (b) Software
   (c) A template
   (d) An interface

6. Which of the following is true about the Office Ribbon?
   (a) The Ribbon displays at the bottom of the screen.
   (b) The Ribbon is only available in the Word 2007 application.
   (c) The Ribbon is the main component of the Office 2007 interface.
   (d) The Ribbon can't be used for selecting commands.

7. Which element of the Ribbon looks like folder tabs and provides commands that are task oriented?
   (a) Groups
   (b) Tabs
   (c) Status bar
   (d) Galleries

8. Which Office 2007 element provides commands that work with an entire document or file and displays by default in the title bar?
   (a) Galleries
   (b) Ribbon
   (c) Office Button
   (d) Groups

9. If you needed the entire screen to read a document, which document view would you use?
   (a) Outline view
   (b) Draft view
   (c) Print Layout
   (d) Full Screen Reading

10. The default four-letter extension for Word documents that do not contain macros is:
    (a) .docx
    (b) .pptx
    (c) .xlsx
    (d) .dotm

11. Before you can cut or copy text, you must first do which one of the following?
    (a) Preview the document.
    (b) Save the document.
    (c) Select the text.
    (d) Undo the previous command.

12. What is the name of the memory location that holds up to twenty-four items for you to paste into the current document, another document, or another application?
    (a) Places bar
    (b) Documents
    (c) Ribbon
    (d) Clipboard

...continued on Next Page

Multiple Choice Continued...

13. Word flags misspelled words by marking them with which one of the following?

(a) A green wavy underline
(b) Boldface
(c) A red wavy underline
(d) A double-underline in black

14. Which of the following displays when you select text in a document?

(a) The Mini toolbar
(b) The Quick Access Toolbar
(c) A shortcut menu
(d) The Ribbon

15. Formatting text enables you to change which of the following text attributes?

(a) The font
(b) The font size
(c) The font color
(d) All of the above

Practice Exercises

1 Using Help and Print Preview in Access 2007

a. Open Access. Click the **Office Button** and then select **Open**. Use the Folders list to find the *chap1_pe1* database and then click **Open**. If you see the Security Warning toolbar below the Ribbon, click **Options** and click the **Enable this content option** in the Microsoft Office Security Options dialog box, and click **OK**.

b. At the right side of the Ribbon, click the **Help** button. In the Help window, type **table** in the Search box. Click the **Search** button.

c. Click the topic *Create a table*. Browse the content of the Help window and then click the **Close** button in the Help window.

d. Double-click the **Courses table** in the Navigation pane on the left side of the screen. The table opens in Datasheet view.

e. Click the **Office Button**, point to the arrow after the **Print** command, and select **Print Preview** to open the Print Preview window with the Courses table displayed.

f. Point the mouse pointer on the table and click to magnify the display. Compare your screen to Figure 1.45.

g. Click the **Close Print Preview** button on the Print Preview tab.

h. Click the **Office Button** and then click the **Exit Access button**.

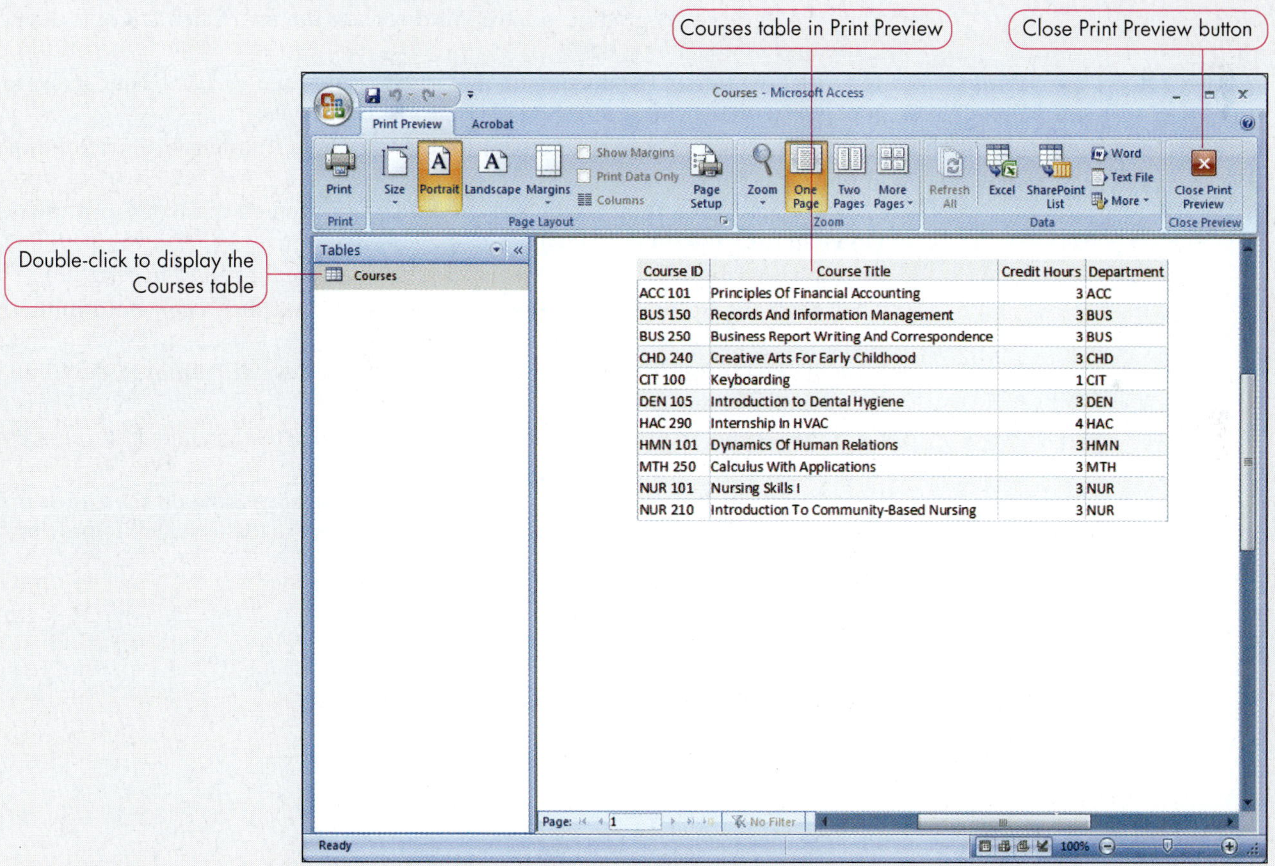

Figure 1.45 Access Print Preview

...continued on Next Page

2 Avoiding Fraud Report

As part of your Introduction to Computers course, you have prepared an oral report on phishing. You want to provide class members with a handout that summarizes the main points of your report. This handout is in the rough stages, so you need to edit it, and you also realize that you can format some of the text to emphasize the main points.

a. Start Word. Click the **Office Button** and then select **Open**. Use the Favorite Links or Folders list to find the *chap1_pe2* document and then click **Open**.
b. Click the **Office Button** and then select **Save As**. In the *File name* box, type the document name, **chap1_pe2_solution**, be sure that Word document displays in the *Save as type* box, and use the Favorite Links or Folders list to move to the location where you save your class files. Click **Save**.
c. In the document, click after the word Name and type **your name**.
d. Select your name and then click **Bold** and **Italic** on the Mini toolbar—remember to point to the Mini toolbar to make it display fully. Your name displays in bold and italic.
e. Move the insertion point immediately before the title of the document and click **Replace** in the Editing group on the Home tab.
f. In the *Find what* box of the Find and Replace dialog box, type **internet**.
g. In the *Replace with* box of the Find and Replace dialog box, type **email**.
h. Click the **Replace All** button to have Word replace the text. Click **OK** and then click **Close** to close the dialog boxes.
i. To format the title of the document, first select it and then click the **Font arrow** in the Font group on the Home tab to display the available fonts.
j. Scroll down and choose the **Impact** font if you have it; otherwise, use one that is available.
k. Place the insertion point in the word *Phishng*. Right-click the word and then click **Phishing** from the shortcut menu.
l. To emphasize important text in the list, double-click the first **NOT** to select it.
m. Click the **Font Color down arrow** and select **Red**, and then click **Bold** in the Font group on the Home tab to apply bold to the text.
n. With the first instance of NOT selected, double-click **Format Painter** in the Clipboard group on the Home tab.
o. Click the second and then the third instance of **NOT** in the list, and then press **Esc** on the keyboard to turn off the Format Painter.
p. Compare your document to Figure 1.46. Save by clicking **Save** on the Quick Access Toolbar. Close the document and exit Word or proceed to the next step to preview and print the document.

...continued on Next Page

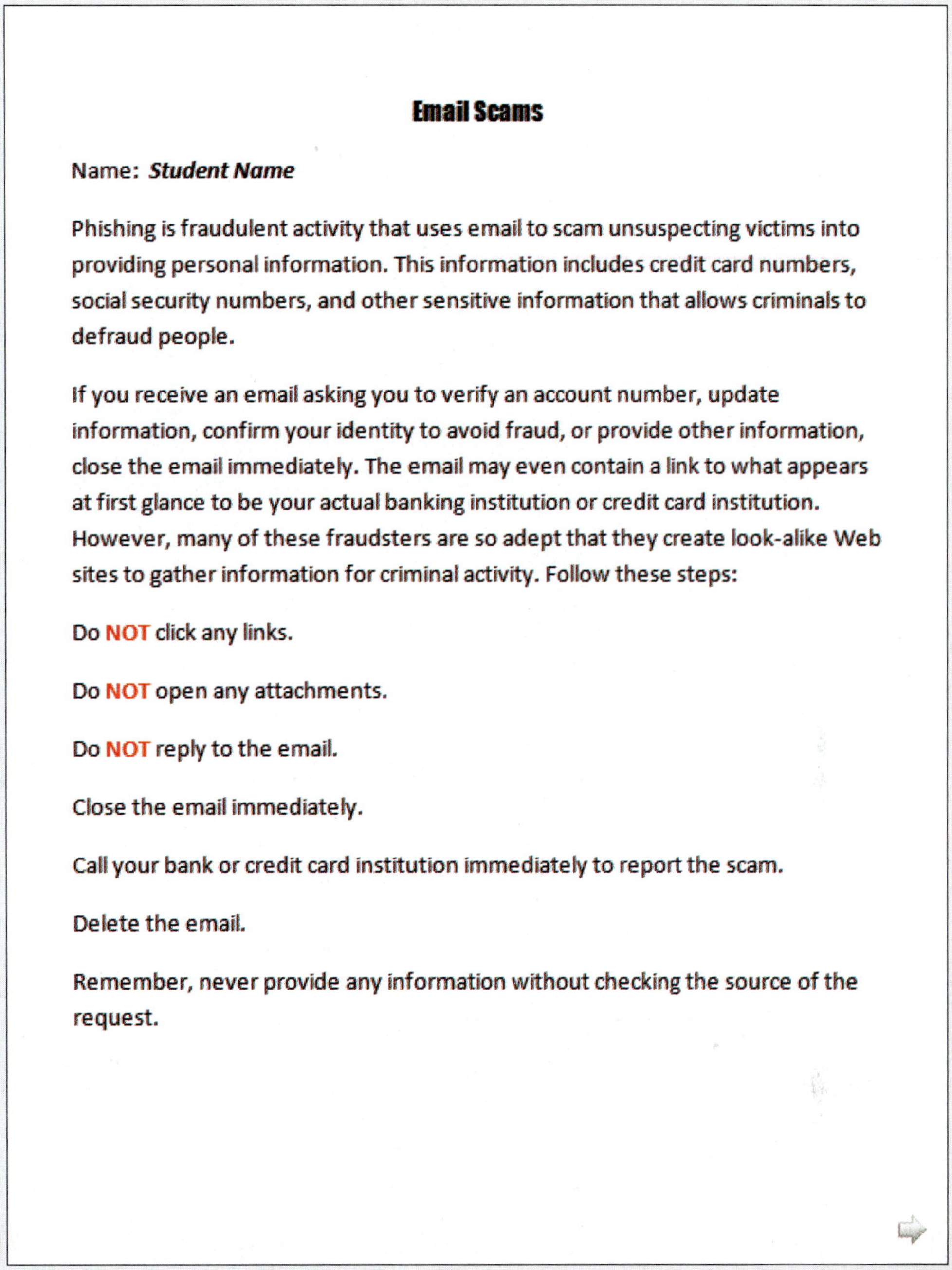

Email Scams

Name: ***Student Name***

Phishing is fraudulent activity that uses email to scam unsuspecting victims into providing personal information. This information includes credit card numbers, social security numbers, and other sensitive information that allows criminals to defraud people.

If you receive an email asking you to verify an account number, update information, confirm your identity to avoid fraud, or provide other information, close the email immediately. The email may even contain a link to what appears at first glance to be your actual banking institution or credit card institution. However, many of these fraudsters are so adept that they create look-alike Web sites to gather information for criminal activity. Follow these steps:

Do NOT click any links.

Do NOT open any attachments.

Do NOT reply to the email.

Close the email immediately.

Call your bank or credit card institution immediately to report the scam.

Delete the email.

Remember, never provide any information without checking the source of the request.

Figure 1.46 Phishing Document

3 Previewing and Printing a Document

You created a handout to accompany your oral presentation in the previous exercise. Now you want to print it out so that you can distribute it.

a. If necessary, open the *chap1_pe2_solution* that you saved in the previous exercise.
b. Click the **Office Button**, point to the arrow after the Print command, and select **Print Preview** to open the Print Preview window with the document displayed.

...continued on Next Page

c. Point the mouse pointer in the document and click to magnify the display. Click the mouse pointer a second time to reduce the display.

d. To change the orientation of the document, click **Orientation** in the Page Setup group and choose **Landscape**.

e. Click **Undo** on the Quick Access Toolbar to undo the last command, which returns the document to portrait orientation. Compare your results to the zoomed document in Figure 1.47.

f. Click **Print** on the Print Preview tab to display the Print dialog box.

g. Click **OK** to print the document.

h. Close the document without saving it.

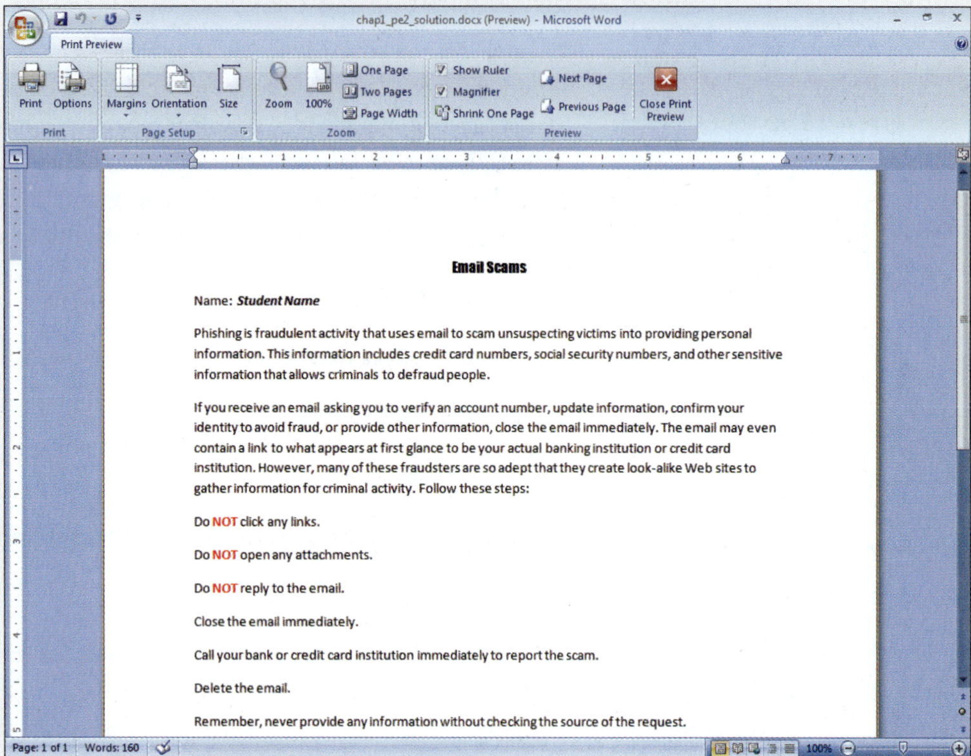

Figure 1.47 Document in Print Preview Window

4 Editing a Promotion Flyer

You work for Business Express, formerly known as Print Express, a regional company specializing in business centers that design and produce documents for local businesses and individuals. Business Express has just undergone a major transition along with a name change. Your job is to edit and refine an existing flyer to inform customers of the new changes. Proceed as follows:

a. Open Word. Click the **Office Button** and then select **Open**. Use the Favorite Links or Folders list to find the *chap1_pe4* document.

b. Click the **Office Button** again and select **Save As**. Type the document name, **chap1_pe4_solution**, be sure that Word document displays in the *Save as type* box, and use the Favorite Links or Folders list to move to the location where you save your class files.

c. Place the insertion point at the beginning of the document, and then click **Spelling & Grammar** in the Proofing group on the Review tab to open the Spelling and Grammar dialog box.

d. Click the **Change** button three times to correct the spelling errors. Click **OK** to close the completion box.

...continued on Next Page

e. Place the insertion point at the end of the first sentence of the document—just before the period. To insert the following text, press **Spacebar** and type **that offers complete business solutions**.

f. Place the insertion point in *good* in the first sentence of the third paragraph and right-click the mouse.

g. Point to **Synonyms** and then click **first-rate** to replace the word in the document.

h. Place the insertion point in *bigger* in the last sentence of the third paragraph and click **Thesaurus** in the Proofing group on the Review tab. Point to **superior** and click the drop-down arrow that displays. Click **Insert** from the menu to replace the word in the document and then click the **Close** button on the Thesaurus.

i. Select the last full paragraph of the document and click **Cut** in the Clipboard group on the Home tab to remove the paragraph from the document.

j. Place the insertion point at the beginning of the new last paragraph and click **Paste** in the Clipboard group on the Home tab to display the text.

k. Click **Undo** on the Quick Access Toolbar twice to undo the paste operation and to undo the cut operation—placing the text back in its original location.

l. Place the insertion point after the colon at the bottom of the document and type **your name**.

m. Compare your results to Figure 1.48 and then save and close the document.

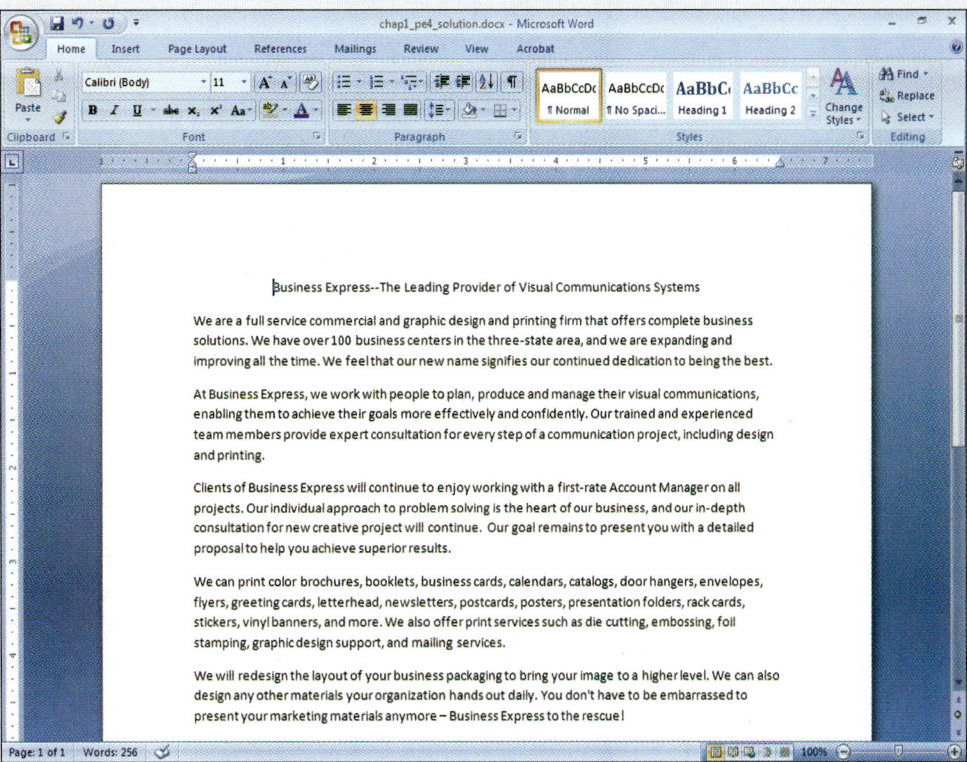

Figure 1.48 Business Flyer

Mid-Level Exercises

1 Updating a Training Document

Your position as trainer for a large building supply company involves training all new employees. It is your job to familiarize new employees with the services provided by Castle Home Building Supply. You distribute a list at the training session and you realize that it needs updating before the next session, so you decide to edit and format it.

a. Start Word. Open the *chap1_mid1* file and save it as **chap1_mid1_solution**.
b. Change the title font to Arial Rounded MT Bold size 16 and change the font color to dark brown.
c. Make the subtitle Arial Unicode MS and italic.
d. Cut the item *Help with permits* and make it the second item on the list.
e. In the first list item, insert **and** after the word *fair*.
f. Change the word *Help* in the last list item to **Assistance**.
g. Select the list of items excluding the heading, Services Provided.
h. Bold the list and change the font size to 16.
i. Save the document and compare it to Figure 1.49. Close the document.

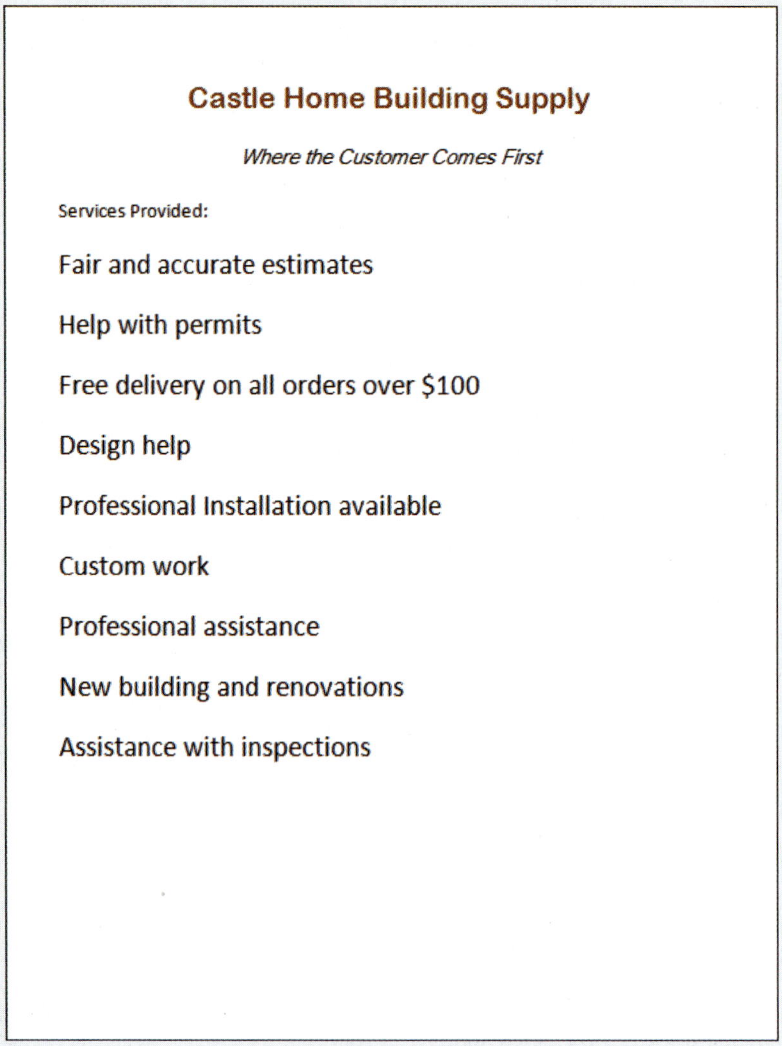

Castle Home Building Supply

Where the Customer Comes First

Services Provided:

Fair and accurate estimates

Help with permits

Free delivery on all orders over $100

Design help

Professional Installation available

Custom work

Professional assistance

New building and renovations

Assistance with inspections

Figure 1.49 Training Document

...continued on Next Page

2 Formatting a Menu

The owner of the Bayside Restaurant wants your help formatting his menu so that it is more pleasing to customers; follow the steps below:

a. Open the *chap1_mid2* document and save it as **chap1_mid2_solution**.

b. Format the menu title as Broadway size 16.

c. Format the three headings: Appetizers, Soups and Salads, and Lunch or Dinner Anytime! as Bodoni MT Black, size 12, and change the font color to Dark Red. Remember to format the first one and use the Format Painter for the second two headings.

d. Format all the dish names, such as Nachos, using the Outline Font Effects.

e. Bold all the prices in the document.

f. Preview the document, compare to Figure 1.50, and then print it.

g. Save and close the document.

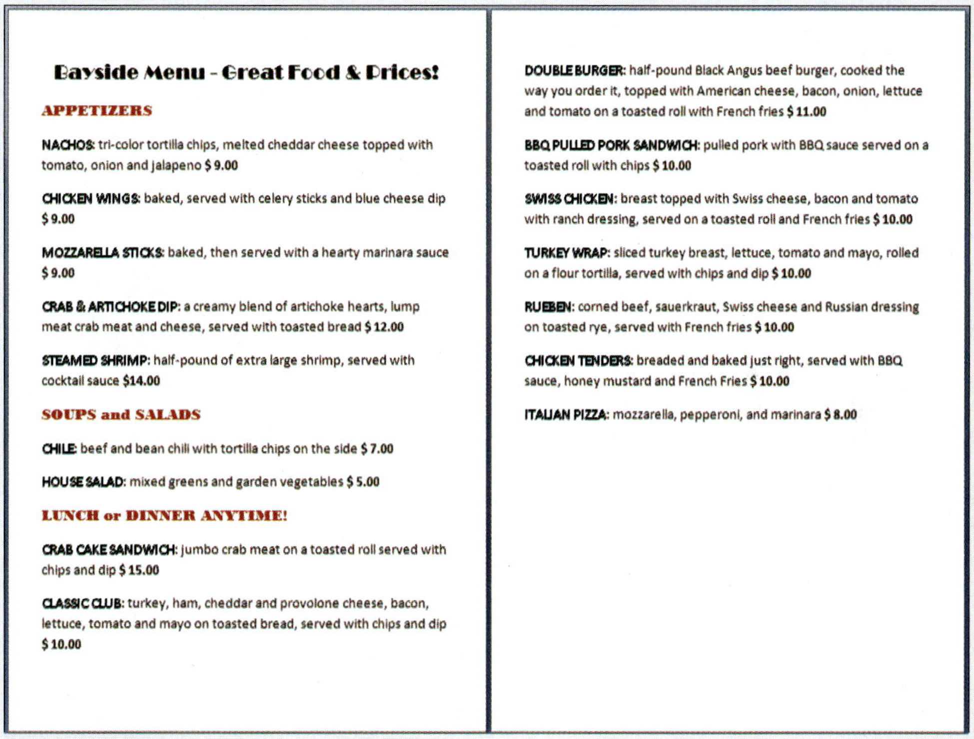

Bayside Menu - Great Food & Prices!

APPETIZERS

NACHOS: tri-color tortilla chips, melted cheddar cheese topped with tomato, onion and jalapeno **$ 9.00**

CHICKEN WINGS: baked, served with celery sticks and blue cheese dip **$ 9.00**

MOZZARELLA STICKS: baked, then served with a hearty marinara sauce **$ 9.00**

CRAB & ARTICHOKE DIP: a creamy blend of artichoke hearts, lump meat crab meat and cheese, served with toasted bread **$ 12.00**

STEAMED SHRIMP: half-pound of extra large shrimp, served with cocktail sauce **$14.00**

SOUPS and SALADS

CHILE: beef and bean chili with tortilla chips on the side **$ 7.00**

HOUSE SALAD: mixed greens and garden vegetables **$ 5.00**

LUNCH or DINNER ANYTIME!

CRAB CAKE SANDWICH: jumbo crab meat on a toasted roll served with chips and dip **$ 15.00**

CLASSIC CLUB: turkey, ham, cheddar and provolone cheese, bacon, lettuce, tomato and mayo on toasted bread, served with chips and dip **$ 10.00**

DOUBLE BURGER: half-pound Black Angus beef burger, cooked the way you order it, topped with American cheese, bacon, onion, lettuce and tomato on a toasted roll with French fries **$ 11.00**

BBQ PULLED PORK SANDWICH: pulled pork with BBQ sauce served on a toasted roll with chips **$ 10.00**

SWISS CHICKEN: breast topped with Swiss cheese, bacon and tomato with ranch dressing, served on a toasted roll and French fries **$ 10.00**

TURKEY WRAP: sliced turkey breast, lettuce, tomato and mayo, rolled on a flour tortilla, served with chips and dip **$ 10.00**

RUEBEN: corned beef, sauerkraut, Swiss cheese and Russian dressing on toasted rye, served with French fries **$ 10.00**

CHICKEN TENDERS: breaded and baked just right, served with BBQ sauce, honey mustard and French Fries **$ 10.00**

ITALIAN PIZZA: mozzarella, pepperoni, and marinara **$ 8.00**

Figure 1.50 The Formatted Menu

...continued on Next Page

3 Enhance the Insurance Letter

Your job duties at Health First Insurance, Inc., involve maintaining the correspondence. You need to update the welcome letter you send to clients to reflect the company's new name, new address, and other important elements, and then address it to a new client. Proceed as follows.

a. Open the *chap1_mid3* document and save it as **chap1_mid3_solution**.

b. Run the Spelling check to eliminate the errors.

c. Use Replace to change **University Insurance, Inc**. to **Health First Insurance, Inc**. throughout the letter.

d. Change the Address from **123 Main St**. to **1717 N. Zapata Way**.

e. Change the inside address that now has **Client name, Client Address, Client City, State and Zip Code** to **your name and complete address**. Also change the salutation to your name.

f. Move the first paragraph so that it becomes the last paragraph in the body of the letter.

g. Preview the letter to be sure that it fits on one page, compare it with Figure 1.51, and then print it.

h. Save and close the document.

Health First Insurance, Inc.

1717 N. Zapata Way

Laredo, TX 78043

Student Name

Student Address

Student City, State, and Zip Code

Dear Client name:

Welcome to the Health First Insurance, Inc. We have received and accepted your application and premium for health insurance. Please detach and the ID cards attached to this letter and keep with you at all times for identification, reference and access to emergency phone assistance and Pre Notification numbers in the event of a claim.

Enclosed you will find a Certificate of Coverage detailing the benefits, limits, exclusions and provisions of

Figure 1.51 The Updated Letter

Capstone Exercise

In this project, you work with a business plan for Far East Trading Company that will be submitted to funding sources in order to secure loans. The document requires editing to polish the final product and formatting to enhance readability and emphasize important information.

Editing the Document

This document is ready for editing, so proceed as follows:

a. Open the *chap1_cap* document. Save the document as **chap1_cap_solution**.

b. Run the Spelling and Grammar check to eliminate all spelling and grammar errors in the document.

c. Use the Thesaurus to find a synonym for the word **unique** in the second paragraph of the document.

d. Use the Go To command to move to page 3, and change the $175,000 to $250,000.

e. Move the entire second section, 2.1 Company Ownership and its paragraphs, that is currently located at the end of the document to its correct location before the 3.0 Products heading. Check and correct spacing after moving the second section to its correct location.

f. Insert the street **1879 Columbia Ave.** before Portland in the first paragraph.

g. Copy the inserted street address to section 2.3 and place it in front of Portland there also.

h. Replace the initials **FET** with **FETC** for every instance in the document.

i. Type over 1998 in the third paragraph so that it says 2008.

Formatting the Document

Next you will apply formatting techniques to the document. These format options will further increase the readability and attractiveness of your document.

a. Select the two-line title and change the font to Engravers MT, size 14, and change the color to Dark Red.

b. Select the first heading in the document: 1.0 Executive Summary, then change the font to Gautami, bold, and change the color to Dark Blue.

c. Use the Format Painter to make all the main numbered headings the same formatting, that is 2.0, 3.0, 4.0, and 5.0.

d. The first three numbered sections have subsections such as 1.1, 1.2. Select the heading 1.1 and format it for bold, italic, and change the color to a lighter blue—Aqua, Accent 5, Darker 25%.

e. Use the Format Painter to make all the numbered subsections the same formatting.

Printing the Document

To finish the job, you need to print the business plan.

a. Preview the document to check your results.

b. Print the document.

c. Save your changes and close the document.

Mini Cases

Use the rubric following the case as a guide to evaluate your work, but keep in mind that your instructor may impose additional grading criteria or use a different standard to judge your work.

A Thank-You Letter

GENERAL CASE

As the new volunteer coordinator for Special Olympics in your area, you need to send out information for prospective volunteers, and the letter you were given needs editing and formatting. Open the *chap1_mc1* document and make necessary changes to improve the appearance. You should use Replace to change the text (insert your state name), use the current date and your name and address information, format to make the letter more appealing, and eliminate all errors. Your finished document should be saved as **chap1_mc1_solution**.

Performance Elements	Exceeds Expectations	Meets Expectations	Below Expectations
Corrected All Errors	Document contains no errors.	Document contains minimal errors.	Document contains several errors.
Use of Character Formatting Features such as Font, Font Size, Font Color, or Other Attributes	Used character formatting options throughout entire document.	Used character formatting options in most sections of document.	Used character formatting options on a small portion of document.
Inserted Text where Instructed	The letter is complete with all required information inserted.	The letter is mostly complete.	Letter is incomplete.

The Information Request Letter

RESEARCH CASE

Search the Internet for opportunities to teach abroad or for internships available in your major. Have fun finding a dream opportunity. Use the address information you find on the Web site that interests you, and compose a letter asking for additional information. For example, you might want to teach English in China, so search for that information. Your finished document should be saved as **chap1_mc2_solution**.

Performance Elements	Exceeds Expectations	Meets Expectations	Below Expectations
Use of Character Formatting	Three or more character formats applied to text.	One or two character formats applied to text.	Does not apply character formats to text.
Language Tools	No spelling or grammar errors.	One spelling or grammar error.	More than one spelling or grammar error.
Presentation	Information is easy to read and understand.	Information is somewhat unclear.	Letter is unclear.

Movie Memorabilia

DISASTER RECOVERY

Use the following rubrics to guide your evaluation of your work, but keep in mind that your instructor may impose additional grading criteria.

Open the *chap1_mc3* document that can be found in the Exploring folder. The advertising document is over-formatted, and it contains several errors and problems. For example, the text has been formatted in many fonts that are difficult to read. The light color of the text also has made the document difficult to read. You should improve the formatting so that it is consistent, helps the audience read the document, and is pleasing to look at. Your finished document should be saved as **chap1_mc3_solution**.

Performance Elements	Exceeds Expectations	Meets Expectations	Below Expectations
Type of Font Chosen to Format Document	Number and style of fonts appropriate for short document.	Number or style of fonts appropriate for short document.	Overused number of fonts or chose inappropriate font.
Color of Font Chosen to Format Document	Appropriate font colors for document.	Most font colors appropriate.	Overuse of font colors.
Overall Document Appeal	Document looks appealing.	Document mostly looks appealing.	Did not improve document much.

chapter 1 | **Word**

Microsoft Word

What Will Word Processing Do for Me?

After you read this chapter, you will be able to:

1. Understand Word basics (**page 72**).
2. Use AutoText (**page 76**).
3. View a document (**page 78**).
4. Use the Mini toolbar (**page 80**).
5. Set margins and specify page orientation (**page 87**).
6. Insert page breaks (**page 88**).
7. Add page numbers (**page 90**).
8. Insert headers and footers (**page 91**).
9. Create sections (**page 92**).
10. Insert a cover page (**page 93**).
11. Use the Find and Replace commands (**page 94**).
12. Check spelling and grammar (**page 103**).
13. Use save and backup options (**page 104**).
14. Select printing options (**page 107**).
15. Customize Word (**page 108**).

Hands-On Exercises

Exercises	Skills Covered
1. INTRODUCTION TO MICROSOFT WORD (page 81) **Open:** chap1_ho1_credit.docx **Save as:** chap1_ho1_credit_solution.docx	• Open and Save a Word Document • Modify the Document • Insert AutoText • Create an AutoText Entry • Change Document Views and Zoom
2. DOCUMENT ORGANIZATION (page 96) **Open:** chap1_ho1_credit_solution.docx (from Exercise 1) **Save as:** chap1_ho2_credit_solution.docx (additional modifications)	• Set Page Margins and Orientation • Insert a Page Break • Add a Cover Page and Insert a Document Header • Insert a Section Break • Insert a Page Number in the Footer • Use Find, Replace, and Go To
3. THE FINAL TOUCHES (page 110) **Open:** chap1_ho2_credit_solution.docx (from Exercise 2) **Save as:** chap1_ho3_credit_solution.docx (additional modifications), chap1_ho3_credit2_solution.docx, and chap1_ho3_credit_solution.doc	• Perform a Spelling and Grammar Check • Run the Document Inspector and a Compatibility Check • Save in a Compatible Format • Change Word Options • Use Print Preview Features

CASE STUDY

A Question of Ethics

You would never walk into a music store, put a CD under your arm, and walk out without paying for it. What if, however, you could download the same CD from the Web for free? Are you hurting anyone? Or what if you gave a clerk a $5 bill, but received change for a $50? Would you return the extra money? Would you speak up if it was the person ahead of you in line who received change for the $50, when you clearly saw that he or she gave the clerk $5? Ethical conflicts occur all the time and result when one person or group benefits at the expense of another.

Case Study

Your Philosophy 101 instructor assigned a class project whereby students are divided into teams to consider questions of ethics and society. Each team is to submit a single document that represents the collective efforts of all the team members. The completed project is to include a brief discussion of ethical principles followed by five examples of ethical conflicts. Every member of the team will receive the same grade, regardless of his or her level of participation; indeed, this might be an ethical dilemma, in and of itself.

Your Assignment

- Read the chapter, paying special attention to sections that describe how to format a document using page breaks, headers and footers, and page numbers.
- Open the *chap1_case_ethics* document, which contains the results of your team's collaboration, but which requires further formatting before you submit it to your professor.
- Create a cover page for the document. Include the name of the report, the team members, and your course name.
- View the document in draft view and remove any unnecessary page breaks.
- Set the margins on your document to a width and height that allows for binding the document.
- Set page numbers for each page of the document except the cover page. The page numbers should display in the center of the footer. Page numbering should begin on the page that follows the cover page.
- Perform a spelling and grammar check on the document, but proofread it also.
- Save your work in a document named **chap1_case_ethics_solution.docx**.
- Run a compatibility check and then save it also in Word 97–2003 format, as **chap1_case_ethics_solution.doc**, in case your professor, who does not have Office 2007, requests a digital copy.

Introduction to Word Processing

> Word processing software is probably the most commonly used type of software. You can create letters, reports, research papers, newsletters, brochures, and other documents with Word. You can even create and send e-mail, produce Web pages, and update blogs with Word.

Word processing software is probably the most commonly used type of software. People around the world—students, office assistants, managers, and professionals in all areas—use word processing programs such as Microsoft Word for a variety of tasks. You can create letters, reports, research papers, newsletters, brochures, and other documents with Word. You can even create and send e-mail, produce Web pages, and update blogs with Word. Figure 1.1 shows examples of documents created in Word.

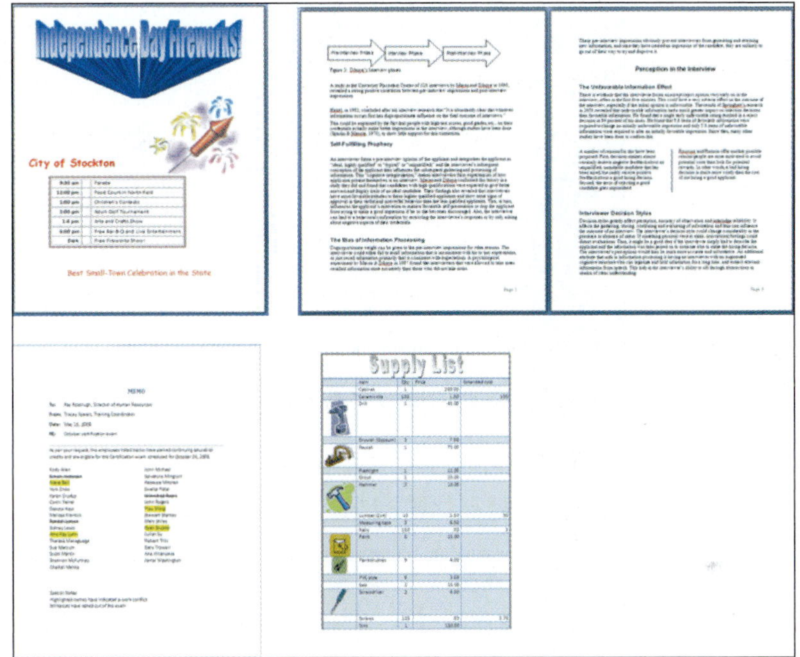

Figure 1.1 The Versatility of Microsoft Word 2007

Microsoft Word provides a multitude of features that enable you to enhance documents with only a few clicks of the mouse. You can change colors, add interesting styles of text, insert graphics, use a table to present data, track changes made to a document, view comments made about document content, combine several documents into one, and quickly create reference pages such as a table of contents, an index, or a bibliography.

This chapter provides a broad-based introduction to word processing in general and Microsoft Word in particular. All word processors adhere to certain basic concepts that must be understood to use the program effectively.

In this section, you learn about the Word interface, word wrap, and toggles. You learn how to use the AutoText feature to insert text automatically in your document, and then you change document views and learn to use the new Mini toolbar.

Understanding Word Basics

The Exploring series authors used Microsoft Word to write this book. You will use Word to complete the exercises in this chapter. When you start Word, your screen might be different. You will not see the same document shown in Figure 1.2, nor is it likely that you will customize Word in exactly the same way. You should, however, be able to recognize the basic elements that are found in the Microsoft Word window that are emphasized in Figure 1.2.

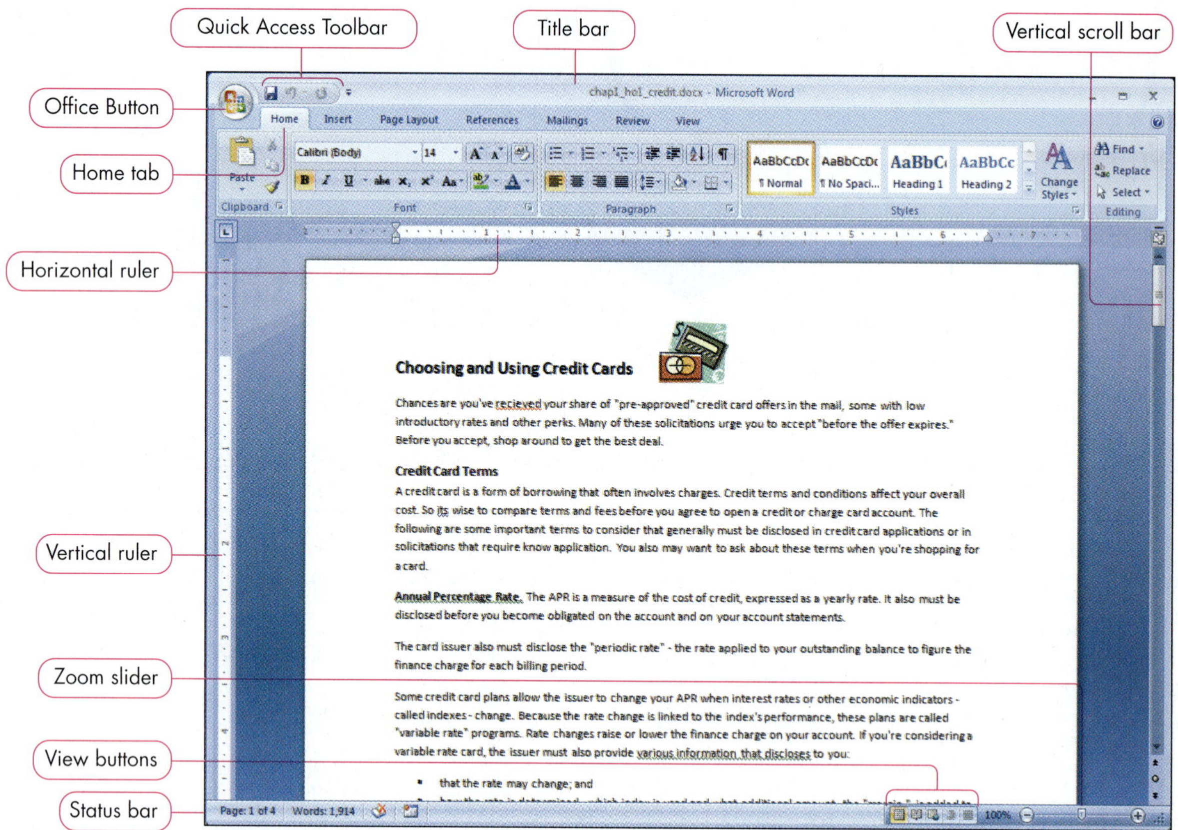

Figure 1.2 The Microsoft Word Window

Figure 1.2 displays two open windows—an application window for Microsoft Word and a document window for the specific document on which you are working. However, only one title bar appears at the top of the application window, and it reflects the application (Microsoft Word) as well as the document name (chap1_ho1_credit.docx). If you want to close the document but not the Word program, click the Office Button and select Close. To close both the document and the application, click Close in the upper-right corner.

The Quick Access Toolbar appears on the left side of the title bar. This toolbar contains commands that are used very frequently such as Save, Undo, and Repeat. Vertical and horizontal scroll bars appear at the right and bottom of a document window. You use them to view portions of a document that do not display on the screen. Each Microsoft Office application includes the Ribbon, which contains tabs that organize commands into task-oriented groups. The active tab is highlighted, and the commands on that tab display immediately below the tabs. The tabs can change according to the current task, or you can display a different tab by clicking the tab name. The tabs in Word are displayed in the Reference on the next two pages.

The status bar at the bottom of the document window displays information about the document such as the section and page where the insertion point is currently positioned, the total number of pages in the document, and the total number of words in the document. At the right side of the status bar you find View buttons that enable you to quickly change the view and zoom level of the document.

Word Tabs | Reference

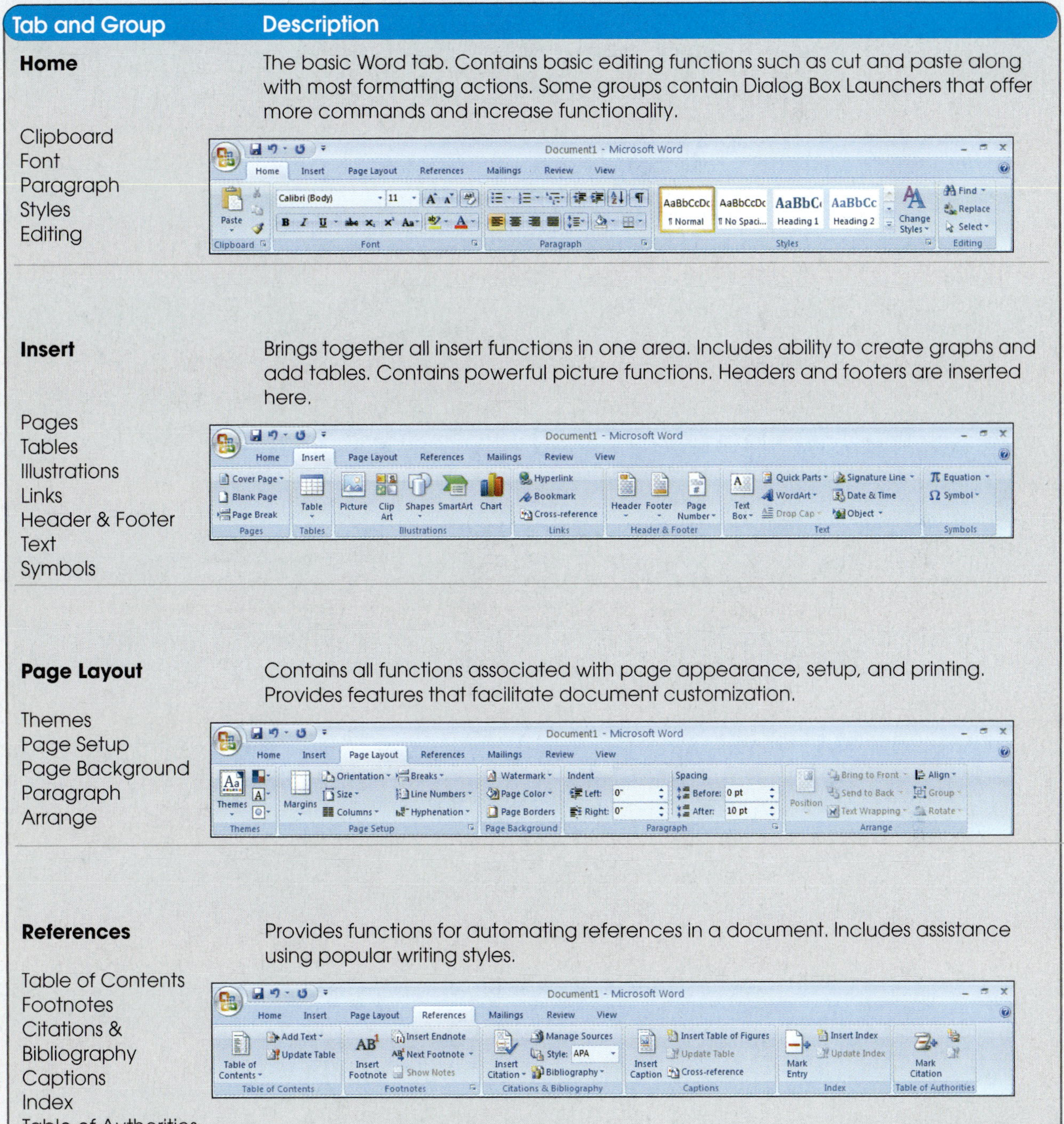

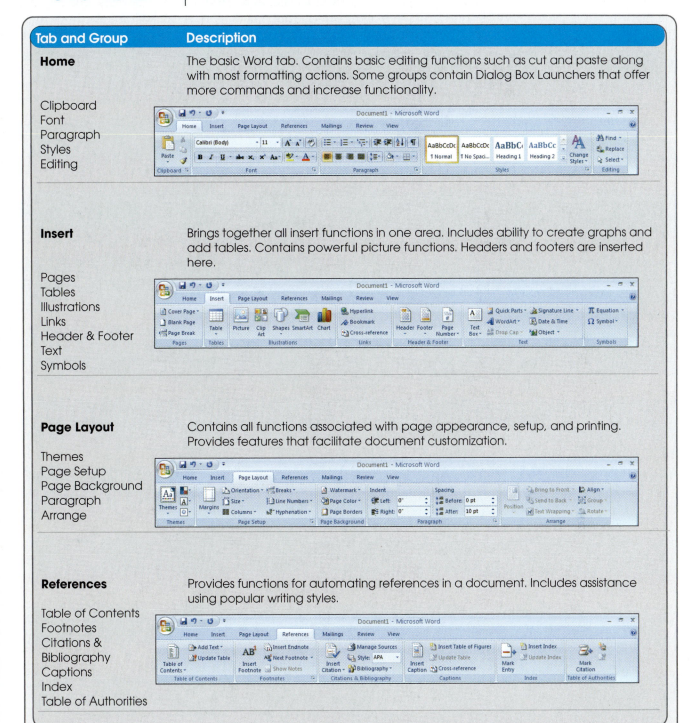

Tab and Group	Description
Home Clipboard Font Paragraph Styles Editing	The basic Word tab. Contains basic editing functions such as cut and paste along with most formatting actions. Some groups contain Dialog Box Launchers that offer more commands and increase functionality.
Insert Pages Tables Illustrations Links Header & Footer Text Symbols	Brings together all insert functions in one area. Includes ability to create graphs and add tables. Contains powerful picture functions. Headers and footers are inserted here.
Page Layout Themes Page Setup Page Background Paragraph Arrange	Contains all functions associated with page appearance, setup, and printing. Provides features that facilitate document customization.
References Table of Contents Footnotes Citations & Bibliography Captions Index Table of Authorities	Provides functions for automating references in a document. Includes assistance using popular writing styles.

Mailings

Create
Start Mail Merge
Write & Insert Fields
Preview Results
Finish

Contains commands used in the process of combining data from multiple sources and providing useful information.

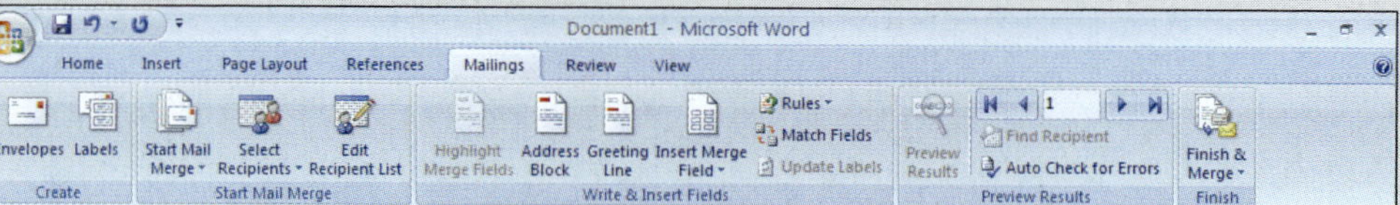

Review

Proofing
Comments
Tracking
Changes
Compare
Protect

Contains all reviewing tools in Word, including spelling and grammatical check, the management of comments, sharing, and protection.

View

Document Views
Show/Hide
Zoom
Window
Macros

Contains basic and advanced view settings. Some of these options also appear below the horizontal and vertical scroll bars.

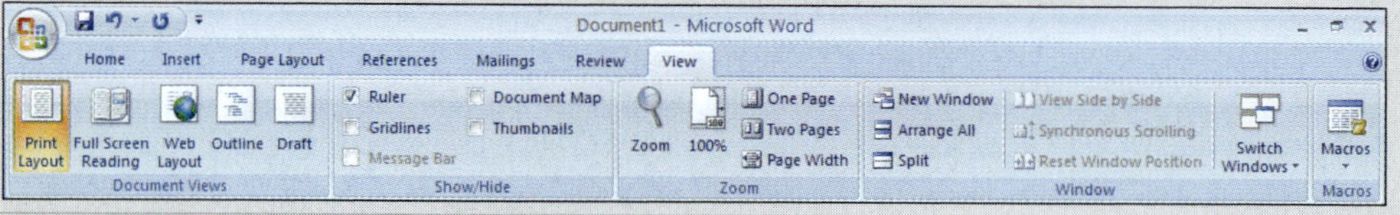

Learn about Word Wrap

Word wrap moves words to the next line if they do not fit on the current line.

A *hard return* is created when you press Enter to move the insertion point to a new line.

A *soft return* is created by the word processor as it wraps text to a new line.

A word processor is a software tool that enables you to document your thoughts or other information. Whether you are new to using a word processor or have been using one for a period of time, you will notice that certain functions seem to happen automatically. As you type, you probably don't think about how much text can fit on one line or where the sentences must roll from one line to the other. Fortunately, the word processor takes care of that for you. This function is called *word wrap* and enables you to type continually without pressing Enter at the end of a line within a paragraph. The only time you press Enter is at the end of a paragraph, or when you want the insertion point to move to the next line.

Word wrap is closely associated with another concept, that of hard and soft returns. A *hard return* is created by the user when he or she presses the Enter key at the end of a line or paragraph; a *soft return* is created by the word processor as it wraps text from one line to the next. The locations of the soft returns change automatically as a document is edited (e.g., as text is inserted or deleted, or as margins or fonts are changed). The locations of hard returns can be changed only by the user, who must intentionally insert or delete each hard return.

The paragraphs at the top of Figure 1.3 show two hard returns, one at the end of each paragraph. It also includes four soft returns in the first paragraph (one at the end of every line except the last) and three soft returns in the second paragraph. Now suppose the margins in the document are made smaller (that is, the line is made longer), as shown in the bottom paragraphs of Figure 1.3. The number of soft returns drops to three and two (in the first and second paragraphs, respectively) as more text fits on a line and fewer lines are needed. The revised document still contains the two original hard returns, one at the end of each paragraph.

Hard returns are created by pressing the Enter key at the end of a paragraph
A document with different margins contains fewer soft returns but the same hard returns
Word wrap allows you to type continuously without ever having to worry about where the line ends. A soft return is created in the document as the text is continued from one line to the next. It is not until you press the Enter key at the end of a paragraph that a hard return is entered in the document.¶
The position of the soft returns is changed automatically as you make changes in the text or the document formatting. The position of the hard returns always remains the same, unless you intentionally insert or delete them.¶
Word wrap allows you to type continuously without ever having to worry about where the line ends. A soft return is created in the document as the text is continued from one line to the next. It is not until you press the Enter key at the end of a paragraph that a hard return is entered in the document.¶
The position of the soft returns is changed automatically as you make changes in the text or the document formatting. The position of the hard returns always remains the same, unless you intentionally insert or delete them.¶

Figure 1.3 Document with Hard and Soft Returns

Use Keyboard Shortcuts to Scroll

The horizontal and vertical scrollbars frequently are used to move around in a document. However, clicking the scroll arrows does not move the insertion point; it merely lets you see different parts of the document in the document window and leaves the insertion point where it was last positioned. You can use the mouse or the keyboard to move the insertion point in a document. Table 1.1 shows useful keyboard shortcuts for moving around in a document and relocating the insertion point.

Table 1.1 Keyboard Scrolling Methods

Keys	Moves the Insertion Point	Keys	Moves the Insertion Point
Left arrow	one character to the left	Ctrl + Home	to the beginning of the document
Right arrow	one character to the right	Ctrl + End	to the end of the document
Up arrow	up one line	Ctrl + Left arrow	one word to the left
Down arrow	down one line	Ctrl + Right arrow	one word to the right
Home	to the beginning of the line	Ctrl + Up arrow	up one paragraph
End	to the end of the line	Ctrl + Down arrow	down one paragraph
PgUp	up one window or page	Ctrl + Pgup	to the top of the previous page
PgDn	down one window or page	Ctrl + PgDn	to the top of the next page

Discover Toggle Switches

Suppose you sat down at the keyboard and typed an entire sentence without pressing Shift; the sentence would be in all lowercase letters. Then you pressed the Caps Lock key and retyped the sentence, again without pressing the Shift key. This time the sentence would be in all uppercase letters. Each time you pressed the Caps Lock key, the text you type would switch from lowercase to uppercase and vice versa.

The ***toggle switch*** is a device that causes the computer to alternate between two states.

The point of this exercise is to introduce the concept of a ***toggle switch***, a device that causes the computer to alternate between two states. Caps Lock is an example of a toggle switch. Each time you press it, newly typed text will change from uppercase to lowercase and back again. In the Office Fundamentals chapter you read about other toggle switches. Some toggle switches are physical keys you press, such as the Insert key (which toggles to Overtype). Some toggle switches are software features such as the Bold, Italic, and Underline commands (which can be clicked to turn on and off).

The ***Show/Hide feature*** reveals where formatting marks such as spaces, tabs, and returns are used in the document.

Another toggle switch that enables you to reveal formatting applied to a document is the ***Show/Hide feature***. Click Show/Hide ¶ in the Paragraph group on the Home tab to reveal where formatting marks such as spaces, tabs, and hard returns are used in the document.

The Backspace and Delete keys delete one character immediately to the left or right of the insertion point, respectively. The choice between them depends on when you need to erase character(s). The Backspace key is easier if you want to delete a character (or characters) immediately after typing. The Delete key is preferable during subsequent editing.

You can delete several characters at one time by selecting (clicking and dragging the mouse over) the characters to be deleted, then pressing the Delete key. You can delete and replace text in one operation by selecting the text to be replaced and then typing the new text in its place. You can also select a block of text by clicking to place the insertion point in front of the first character, holding down Shift and then clicking to the right of the last character. Double-click a word to select it, and triple-click to select a paragraph. These forms of selecting text enable you to quickly format or delete text.

Using AutoText

The ***AutoText*** feature substitutes a predefined item for specific text but only when the user initiates it.

You learned about the AutoCorrect feature in the Office Fundamentals chapter. The ***AutoText*** feature is similar in concept to AutoCorrect in that both substitute a predefined item for a specific character string or group of characters. The difference is that the substitution occurs automatically with the AutoCorrect entry, whereas you have to take deliberate action for the AutoText substitution to take place. AutoText entries can also include significantly more text, formatting, and even clip art.

Microsoft Word includes a host of predefined AutoText entries such as days of the week and months of the year. For example, if you start typing today's date, you see a ScreenTip that displays the entire date, as shown in Figure 1.4. Press Enter while the ScreenTip is visible to insert the date automatically.

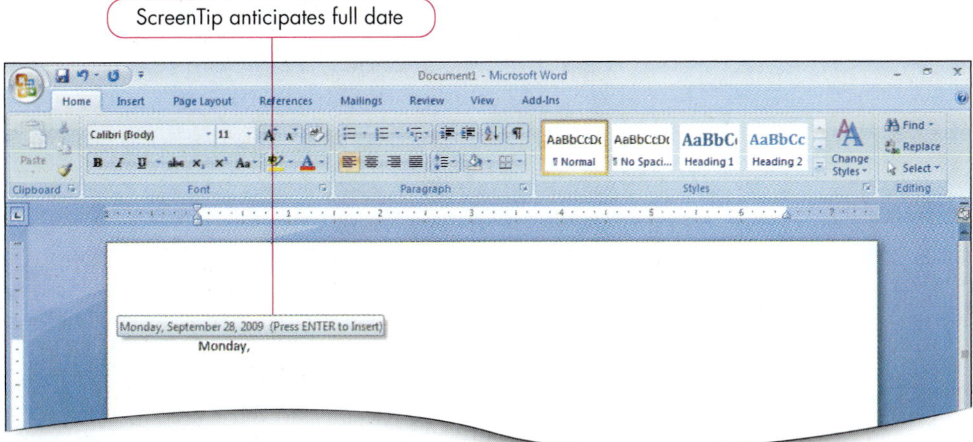

Figure 1.4 Insert AutoText

As with the AutoCorrect feature, you can define additional entries of your own. (However, you may not be able to do this in a computer lab environment.) This is advisable if you use the same piece of text frequently, such as a disclaimer, a return address, a company logo, or a cover page. You first select the text, click Quick Parts in the Text group on the Insert tab, and select Save Selection to Quick Part Gallery. In the Create New Building Block dialog box, make sure the Gallery option displays Quick Parts, and click OK. After you add entries to the Quick Parts gallery they are included in the ***Building Blocks*** library, which contains document components you use frequently, such as those mentioned above. After you add the text to the Quick Parts gallery, you can type a portion of the entry, then press F3 to insert the remainder into your document. Figure 1.5 demonstrates the creation of the AutoText entry.

Building Blocks are document components used frequently, such as disclaimers, company addresses, or a cover page.

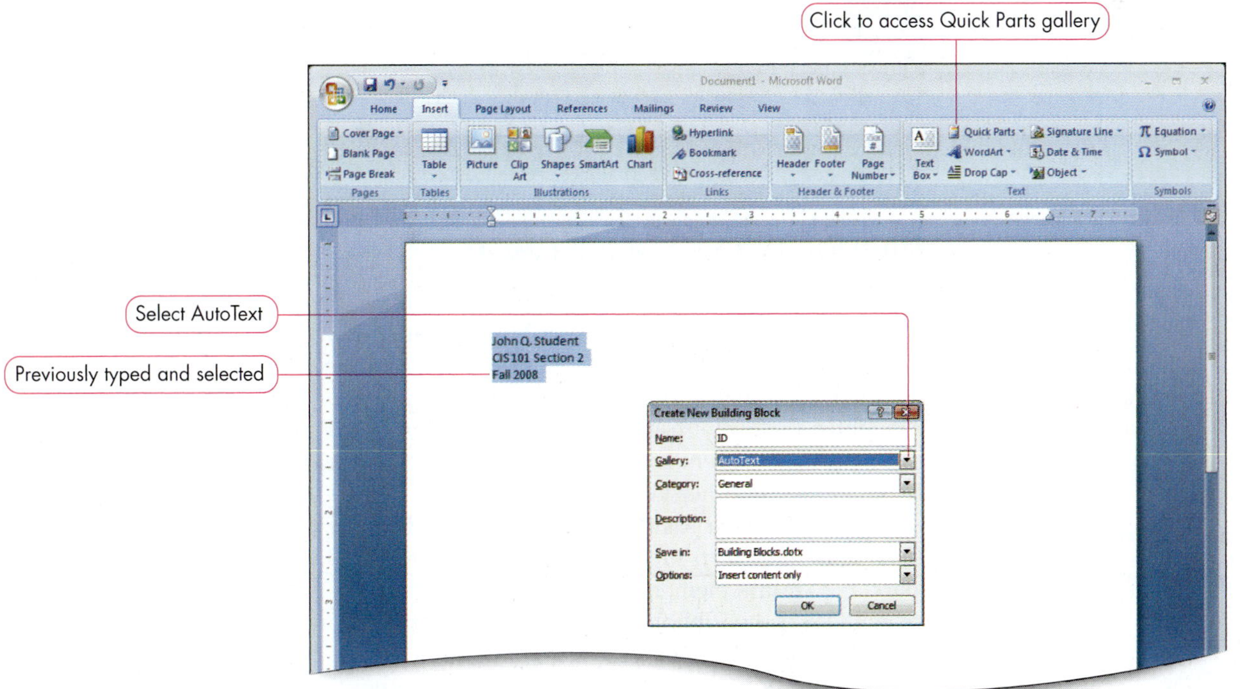

Figure 1.5 Adding an AutoText Building Block

TIP Insert the Date and Time

Some documents include the date and time they were created. A time and date stamp can help determine the most recent edition of a document, which is important if the document is updated frequently. To create a time and date stamp, click the Insert tab, click Date and Time in the Text group to display the Date and Time dialog box, then choose a format. Click the *Update automatically* check box to update the date automatically if you want your document to reflect the date on which it is opened, or clear the box to retain the date on which the date was inserted (see Figure 1.6).

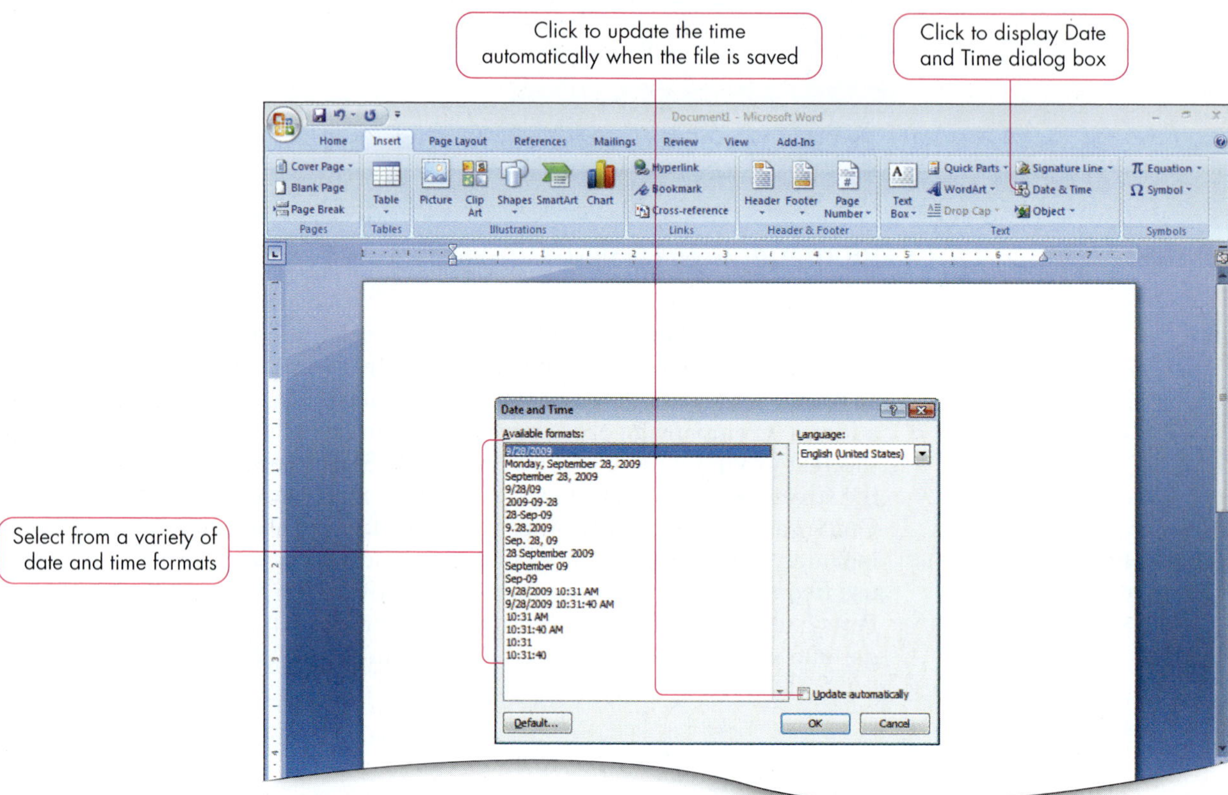

Figure 1.6 The Date and Time Dialog Box

Viewing a Document

Print Layout view is the default view and closely resembles the printed document.

Full Screen Reading view eliminates tabs and makes it easier to read your document.

Draft view shows a simplified work area, removing white space and other elements from view.

The View tab provides options that enable you to display a document in many different ways. Each view can display your document at different magnifications, which in turn determine the amount of scrolling necessary to see remote parts of a document. The ***Print Layout view*** is the default view and is the view you use most frequently. It closely resembles the printed document and displays the top and bottom margins, headers and footers, page numbers, graphics, and other features that do not appear in other views.

The ***Full Screen Reading view*** hides the Ribbon, making it easier to read your document. The ***Draft view*** creates a simple area in which to work; it removes white space and certain elements from the document, such as headers, footers, and graphics, but leaves the Ribbon. It displays information about some elements, such as page and section breaks, not easily noticed in other views. Because view options are used frequently, buttons for each also are located on the status bar as shown in Figure 1.2.

The Zoom command displays the document on the screen at different magnifications—for example, 75%, 100%, or 200%. But this command does not affect the size of the text on the printed page. It is helpful to be able to zoom in to view details or to zoom out and see the effects of your work on a full page. When you click Zoom in the Zoom group on the View tab, a dialog box displays with several zoom options (see Figure 1.7).

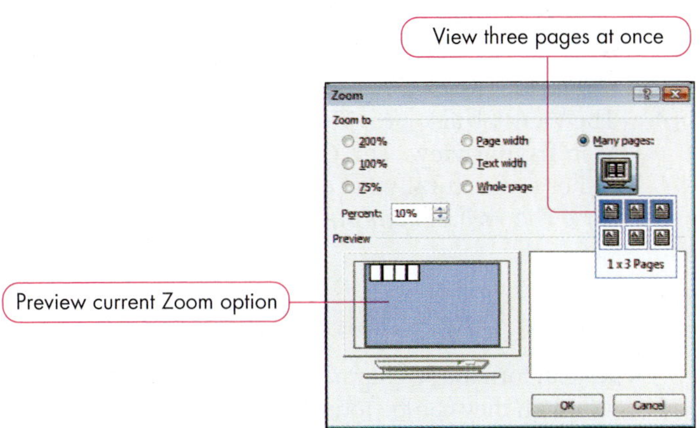

Figure 1.7 The Zoom Dialog Box

Word automatically will determine the magnification if you select one of the Zoom options—Page width, Text width, Whole page, or Many pages (Whole page and Many pages are available only in the Print Layout view). Figure 1.8, for example, displays a four-page document in Print Layout view. The 28% magnification is determined automatically after you specify the number of pages. If you use a wide screen, the magnification size might differ slightly.

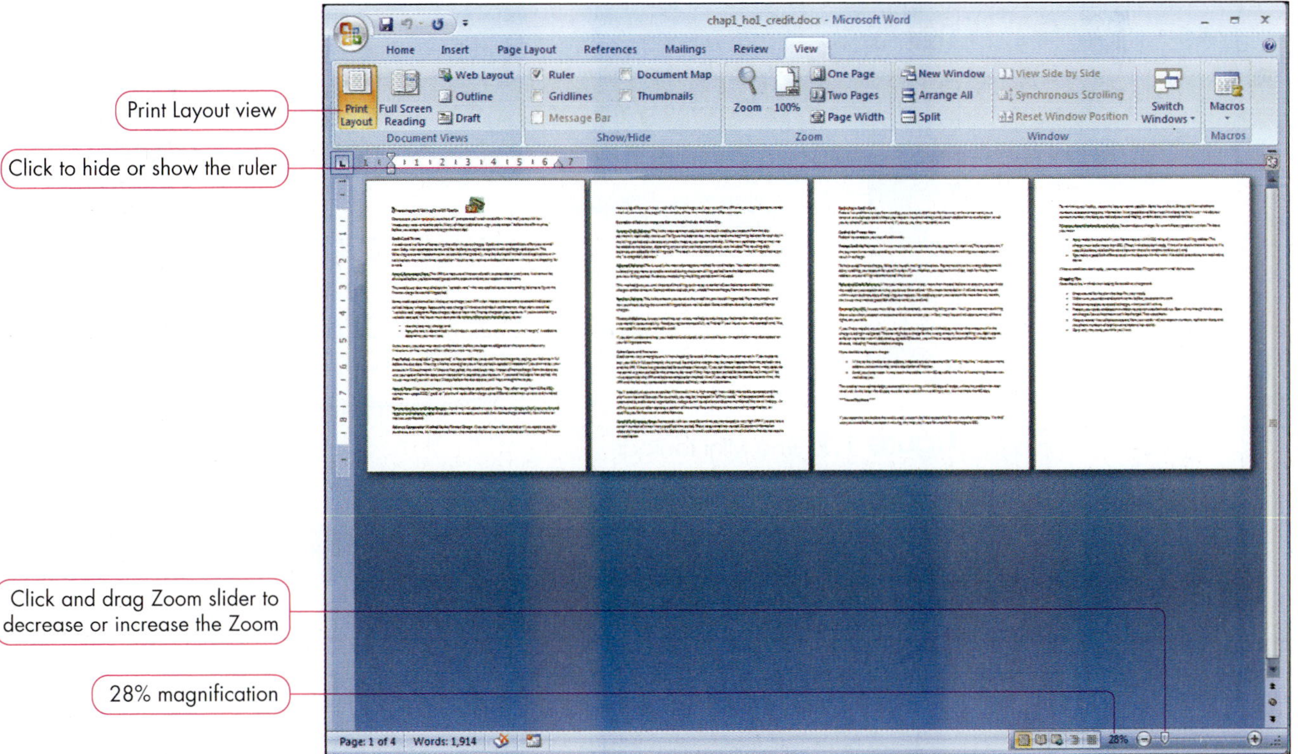

Figure 1.8 View Four Pages of Document

TIP **Use the Status Bar to Change View Options**

The status bar repeats commands from the View tab in a handy location for quick access. You can switch to Print Layout, Full Screen Reading, Web Layout, Outline, or Draft view from the buttons on the status bar. You also can use the Zoom slider to change the zoom of the current document or click the Zoom command to display the Zoom dialog box, which contains more viewing options.

The ***Outline view*** displays a structural view of the document that can be collapsed or expanded.

The ***Web Layout view*** is used when creating a Web page.

The View tab also provides access to two additional views—the Outline view and the Web Layout view. The ***Outline view*** does not display a conventional outline, but rather a structural view of a document that can be collapsed or expanded as necessary. The ***Web Layout view*** is used when you are creating a Web page.

Using the Mini Toolbar

The ***Mini toolbar*** contains frequently used formatting commands and displays when you select text.

Several formatting commands, such as Bold, Center, and Italic, are used frequently, and although they can be found on the Home tab you can also apply them using the Mini toolbar. The ***Mini toolbar*** contains frequently used formatting commands and displays when you select text or right-click selected text. The Mini toolbar displays faintly at first, then darkens as you move the mouse pointer closer to it, as shown in Figure 1.9. If you move the mouse pointer away from it, it becomes fainter; if you do not want to use the Mini toolbar and prefer it to disappear from view, press Esc when it displays. The Mini toolbar reduces the distance your mouse pointer has to travel around the screen and enables you to quickly and easily apply the most frequently used commands.

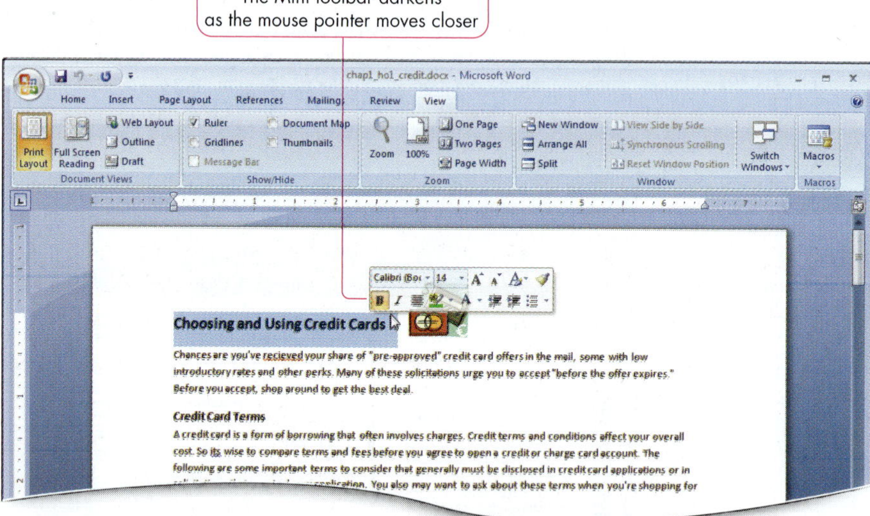

Figure 1.9 The Mini Toolbar

TIP **Learning by Doing**

Every chapter contains a series of hands-on exercises that enable you to apply what you learn at the computer. The exercises in this chapter are linked to one another in that you open and edit a simple document in Exercise 1, then you make additional modifications to that document in Exercises 2 and 3. The ability to save and open a document is critical, and you do not want to spend an inordinate amount of time entering text unless you are confident in your ability to retrieve it later.

Hands-On Exercises

1 | Introduction to Microsoft Word

Skills covered: 1. Open and Save a Word Document **2.** Modify the Document **3.** Insert AutoText **4.** Create an AutoText Entry **5.** Change Document Views and Zoom

Step 1
Open and Save a Word Document

Refer to Figure 1.10 as you complete Step 1.

a. Click **Start** to display the Start menu. Click (or point to) **All Programs**, click **Microsoft Office**, and then click **Microsoft Office Word 2007** to start the program.

b. Click the **Office Button** and select **Open**.

c. Click the appropriate drive and folder in the Folders list on the left side of the Open dialog box. Choose the location where the original data files to accompany this book are located.

d. Select ***chap1_ho1_credit***. Click **Open** to open the document.

   You should see the document containing the title *Choosing and Using Credit Cards*.

e. Click the **Office Button** and point to **Save As** and select **Word Document**.

   The Save As dialog box displays so that you can save the document in a different location, with a different name, or as a different file type. The **Exploring Word folder** is the active folder as shown in Figure 1.10.

> **TIP** Use Save and Save As
>
> You should practice saving your files often. If you open a document and you do not want to change its name, the easiest way to save it is to click Save on the Quick Access Toolbar. You can also click the Office button and select Save, but many users press the Ctrl+S keyboard command to save quickly and often. The first time you save a document, use the Save As command from the Microsoft Office menu. The command displays the Save As dialog box that enables you to assign a descriptive file name (*job cover letter*, for example) and indicate where the file will be saved. Subsequent saves will be to the same location and will update the file with new changes.

f. Click the appropriate drive and folder in the Folders list on the left side of the Save As dialog box. Choose the location where you want to save your completed files.

g. In the **File name** box, click once to position the insertion point at the end of the word *credit*. Type **_solution** to rename the document as *chap1_ho1_credit_solution*.

h. Click **Save** or press **Enter**.

   The title bar changes to reflect the new document name, *chap1_ho1_credit_solution.docx*. Depending on the user's settings, the file extension may not appear in the title bar.

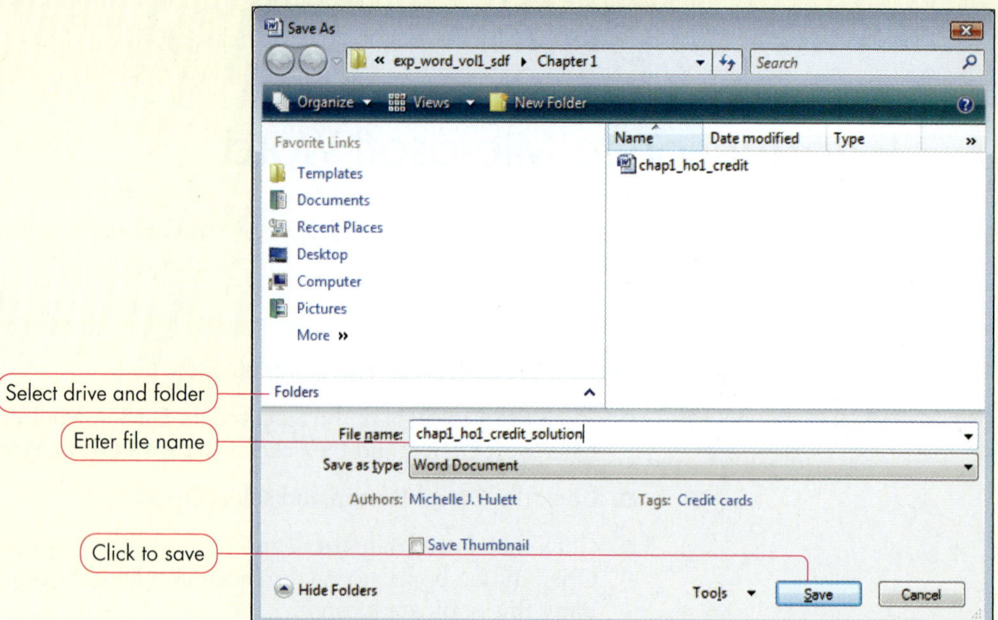

Figure 1.10 Save As Dialog Box

Step 2
Modify the Document

Refer to Figure 1.11 as you complete Step 2.

a. Use the vertical scroll bar to move down to the bottom of the third page in the document. Select the text ****Insert Text Here**** and press **Delete**.

   You will add the heading and introduction to this paragraph in the next step.

b. Click **Bold** in the Font group on the Home tab to toggle the format on, if necessary, and then type **Unauthorized Charges.**, including the period.

c. Click **Bold** in the Font group again to toggle the format off. Press **Spacebar** once to insert a space after the period typed in the step above. Then type **If your card is used without your permission, you can be held responsible for up to $50 per card**.

d. Press **Enter** after you complete the sentence. Select the *$50* that you just typed and then click **Bold** on the Mini toolbar.

   You completed the sentence using toggle switches, and you used the Mini toolbar to apply formatting.

e. Click **Show/Hide ¶** in the Paragraph group on the Home tab, if necessary, to display formatting marks in the document.

   Notice the formatting marks display to indicate where each space, tab, and soft and hard return occurs.

f. Select the hard return character that follows the sentence typed above, as shown in Figure 1.11. Press **Delete** to delete the unnecessary hard return.

   You also can place the insertion point on either side of the formatting mark and press Delete or Backspace to remove it, depending on the location of the insertion point.

g. Click **Save** on the Quick Access Toolbar.

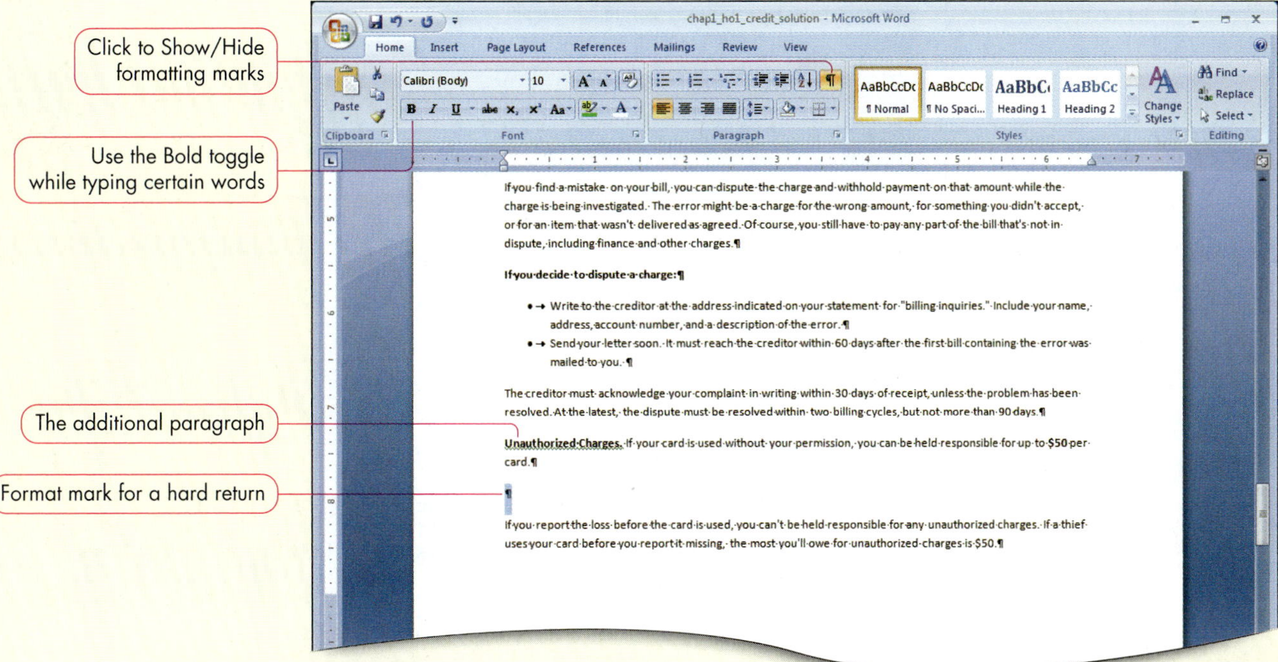

Figure 1.11 The Modified Document

Step 3
Insert AutoText

Refer to Figure 1.12 as you complete Step 3.

a. Press **Ctrl+End** to move to the end of the document and press **Enter** two times.

b. Type the first few letters of the current day of the week, such as **Tues** for *Tuesday*.

   Notice that after you type the first few letters, a ScreenTip displays the full name.

c. Press **Enter** to accept the AutoText, and then type a comma.

   Now a ScreenTip displays with the complete date—day or week, month, day, and year, as shown in Figure 1.12.

   TROUBLESHOOTING: If the complete date does not display, press **Spacebar**, then type the first few letters of the current month, such as **Oct** for October. Press **Enter** to accept the AutoText after a ScreenTip displays with the full name of the month. Then continue until a ScreenTip displays with the complete date—month, day, and year, then press **Enter** to accept and insert the date.

d. Press **Enter** to accept the date. Press **Enter** one more time to insert a hard return.

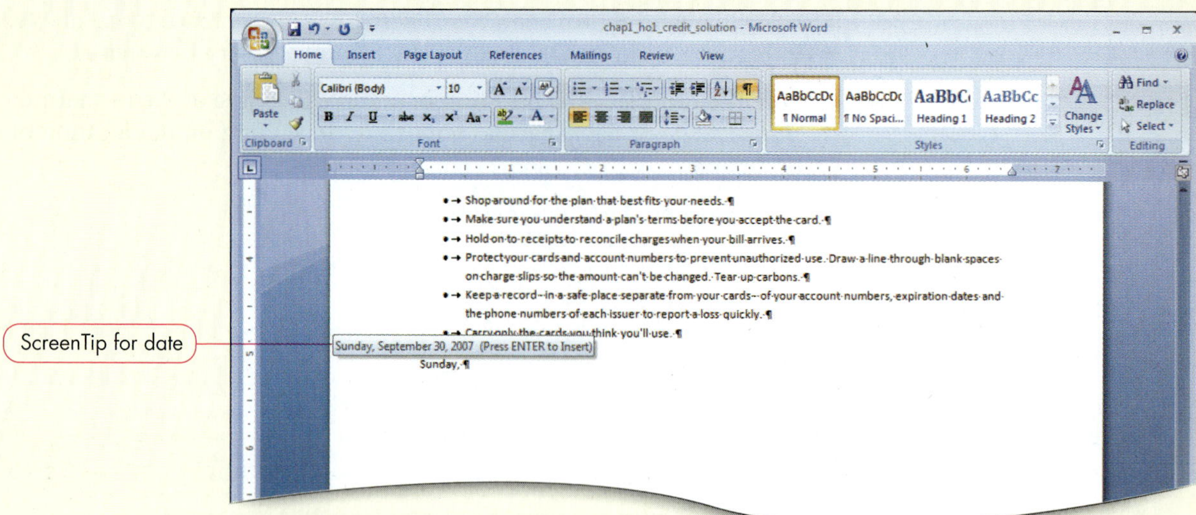

Figure 1.12 Use AutoText to Insert the Date

Step 4
Create an AutoText Entry

Refer to Figure 1.13 as you complete Step 4.

a. Type your name on the line you just added, and then select it.

b. Click the **Insert tab** and click **Quick Parts** in the Text group. Select **Save Selection to Quick Part Gallery**.

   The Create New Building Block dialog box displays.

c. In the **Name box** type your initials.

   The text in this box is what you begin to type, then press F3 to insert the actual building block content.

d. Click the **Gallery drop-down arrow**. Select **AutoText** as shown in Figure 1.13. Click **OK.**

   This procedure adds an AutoText entry to the Normal template. If you are in a lab environment, you might not have permission to add this item or save the changes to the Normal template.

e. Select your name in the document, but do not select the hard return mark, and then press **Delete** to remove it. Click **Quick Parts** and then select **Building Blocks Organizer**.

   The Building Blocks Organizer dialog box opens so that you can manage building blocks.

f. Click the **Gallery** heading at the top of the Building Blocks Organizer dialog box to sort the entries.

   The AutoText entries display first. You should be able to see your new entry near the top of the list.

g. Select your entry in the Name column. Click **Insert** at the bottom of the dialog box.

   Your name displays at the bottom of the page.

h. Click **Undo** in the Quick Access Toolbar to remove your name. Type your initials, and then press **F3**.

   Your name, as saved in the Building Block, displays. You now have experience inserting a Building Block using two different methods.

i. Click **Save** on the Quick Access Toolbar.

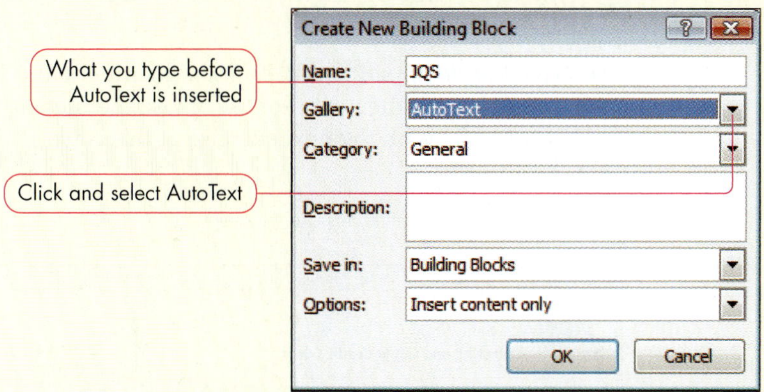

Figure 1.13 The Create New Building Block Dialog Box

Step 5
Change Document Views and Zoom

Refer to Figure 1.14 as you complete Step 5.

a. Press **Ctrl+Home** to move the insertion point to the beginning of the document. Click the **View tab** and click **Full Screen Reading** in the Document Views group.

   The document looks different, pages one and two display, the Ribbon is removed, and only a few buttons display (see Figure 1.14).

   TROUBLESHOOTING: If you do not see two pages, click **View Options** in the upper-right corner and select **Show Two Pages**.

b. Hover your mouse pointer over the arrow in the lower-right corner of the screen, and then click the arrow to scroll to the next set of pages.

   Once you pass the first page, a navigation arrow appears on the lower left side of the screen.

c. Continue navigating to the end of the document with the right arrow.

d. Click the left-pointing arrow twice to display the first two pages again.

TIP Return to Print Layout View

Press **Esc** to return to Print Layout view and close the Full Screen Reading view.

e. Click **Close** in the upper-right corner of the screen to return to the default view.

f. Click **Zoom** in the Zoom group on the View tab. Click the icon below **Many pages** and roll your mouse to select 1 × 3 Pages. Click **OK** to change the view and display three pages on the top of the screen and one page at the bottom.

Notice the Zoom slider in the lower-right corner of the window displays 39%. If you use a wide-screen monitor or do not have the Word window maximized, the size might differ slightly.

g. Save the *chap1_ho1_credit_solution* document and keep it onscreen if you plan to continue with the next exercise. Close the file and exit Word if you do not want to continue with the next exercise at this time.

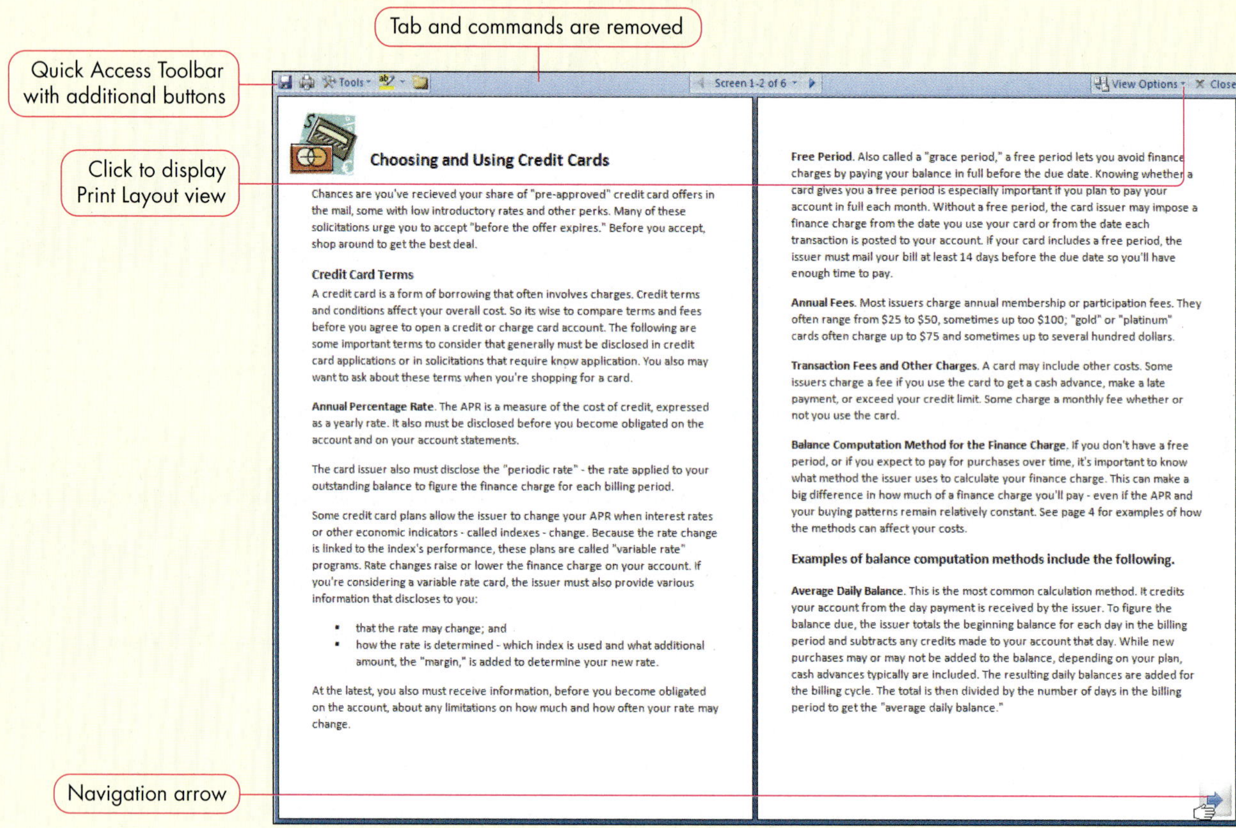

Choosing and Using Credit Cards

Chances are you've recieved your share of "pre-approved" credit card offers in the mail, some with low introductory rates and other perks. Many of these solicitations urge you to accept "before the offer expires." Before you accept, shop around to get the best deal.

Credit Card Terms

A credit card is a form of borrowing that often involves charges. Credit terms and conditions affect your overall cost. So its wise to compare terms and fees before you agree to open a credit or charge card account. The following are some important terms to consider that generally must be disclosed in credit card applications or in solicitations that require know application. You also may want to ask about these terms when you're shopping for a card.

Annual Percentage Rate. The APR is a measure of the cost of credit, expressed as a yearly rate. It also must be disclosed before you become obligated on the account and on your account statements.

The card issuer also must disclose the "periodic rate" - the rate applied to your outstanding balance to figure the finance charge for each billing period.

Some credit card plans allow the issuer to change your APR when interest rates or other economic indicators - called indexes - change. Because the rate change is linked to the index's performance, these plans are called "variable rate" programs. Rate changes raise or lower the finance charge on your account. If you're considering a variable rate card, the issuer must also provide various information that discloses to you:

- that the rate may change; and
- how the rate is determined - which index is used and what additional amount, the "margin," is added to determine your new rate.

At the latest, you also must receive information, before you become obligated on the account, about any limitations on how much and how often your rate may change.

Free Period. Also called a "grace period," a free period lets you avoid finance charges by paying your balance in full before the due date. Knowing whether a card gives you a free period is especially important if you plan to pay your account in full each month. Without a free period, the card issuer may impose a finance charge from the date you use your card or from the date each transaction is posted to your account. If your card includes a free period, the issuer must mail your bill at least 14 days before the due date so you'll have enough time to pay.

Annual Fees. Most issuers charge annual membership or participation fees. They often range from $25 to $50, sometimes up too $100; "gold" or "platinum" cards often charge up to $75 and sometimes up to several hundred dollars.

Transaction Fees and Other Charges. A card may include other costs. Some issuers charge a fee if you use the card to get a cash advance, make a late payment, or exceed your credit limit. Some charge a monthly fee whether or not you use the card.

Balance Computation Method for the Finance Charge. If you don't have a free period, or if you expect to pay for purchases over time, it's important to know what method the issuer uses to calculate your finance charge. This can make a big difference in how much of a finance charge you'll pay - even if the APR and your buying patterns remain relatively constant. See page 4 for examples of how the methods can affect your costs.

Examples of balance computation methods include the following.

Average Daily Balance. This is the most common calculation method. It credits your account from the day payment is received by the issuer. To figure the balance due, the issuer totals the beginning balance for each day in the billing period and subtracts any credits made to your account that day. While new purchases may or may not be added to the balance, depending on your plan, cash advances typically are included. The resulting daily balances are added for the billing cycle. The total is then divided by the number of days in the billing period to get the "average daily balance."

Figure 1.14 Full Screen Reading View

Document Formatting

Throughout your college and professional career, you will create a variety of documents. As you compose and edit large documents, you want to set them up so they have title pages, display a certain way when printed, or include page numbers at the top or bottom of a page. All of these options are available using features in Microsoft Word.

In this section, you make formatting changes to a Word document, such as changing the document margins and orientation. You insert page breaks, page numbers, headers and footers, sections, and cover pages. You also learn how to use the Find and Replace commands.

Setting Margins and Specifying Page Orientation

When you create a document, you consider the content you will insert, but you also should consider how you want the document to look when you print or display it. Many of the settings needed for this purpose are found on the Page Layout tab. The first setting most people change is ***margins***. Margins determine the amount of white space from the text to the edges of the page. You should adjust margins to improve the appearance and readability of your document.

Margins are the amount of white space around the top, bottom, left, and right edges of the page.

The default margins, indicated in Figure 1.15, are 1″ on the top, bottom, left, and right of the page. You can select different margin settings from the gallery that displays when you click Margins in the Page Setup group on the Page Layout tab, or you can select the Custom Margins option to enter specific settings.

> When you create a document, you consider the content you will insert, but you should also consider how you want the document to look when you print or display it. . . to have title pages, or include page numbers at the top or bottom of a page. All of these options are available using features in Microsoft Word.

When you create a short business letter, you want to increase the margins to a larger size, such as 1.5″ on all sides, so the letter contents are balanced on the printed page. When you print a long document, you might want to reduce the margins to a small amount, such as 0.3″ or 0.5″, in order to reduce the amount of paper used. If you print a formal or research paper, you want to use a 1.5″ left margin and a 1″ right margin to allow extra room for binding. The margins you choose will apply to the whole document regardless of the position of the insertion point. You can establish different margin settings for different parts of a document by creating sections. Sections are discussed later in this chapter.

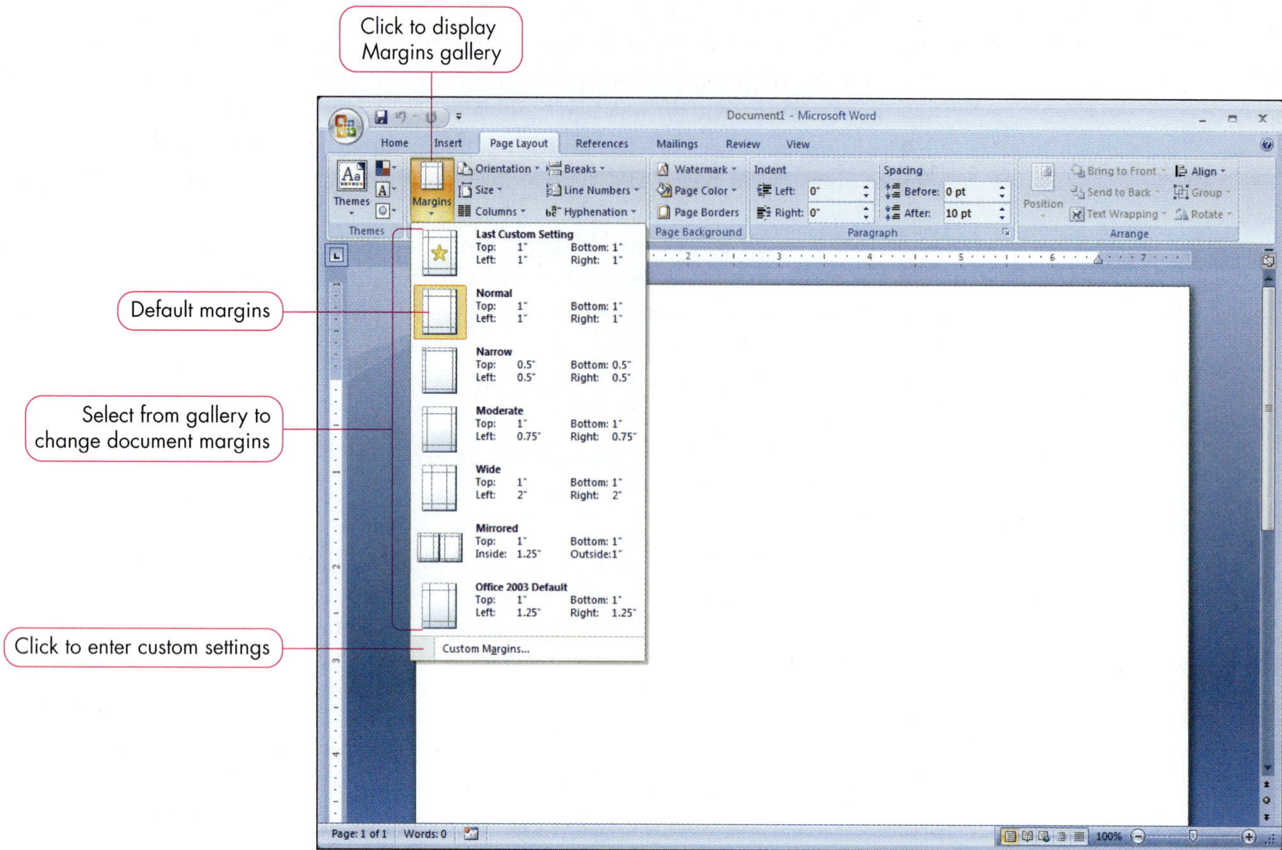

Figure 1.15 Setting Margins

Portrait orientation positions text parallel with the short side of the page.

Landscape orientation positions text parallel with the long side of the page.

Another setting to consider for a document is orientation. The Page Layout tab contains the Orientation command with two settings—portrait and landscape. ***Portrait orientation,*** the default setting, positions text parallel with the short side of the page so that the printed page is taller than it is wide. ***Landscape orientation*** flips the page 90 degrees so that text displays parallel with the longer side of the page, so that the printed page is wider than it is tall. The type of document you create and the manner in which you wish to display the information will dictate which type of orientation you use. Most documents, such as letters and research papers, use portrait orientation, but a brochure, large graphic, chart, or table might display better on a page with landscape orientation.

If you need to print a document on special paper, such as legal size (8½″ × 14″) or on an envelope, you should select the paper size before you create the document text. The Size command in the Page Setup group on the Page Layout tab contains several different document sizes from which you can choose. If you have special paper requirements, you can select More Paper Sizes to enter your own custom size. If you do not select the special size before you print, you will waste paper and find yourself with a very strange looking printout.

Inserting Page Breaks

A ***soft page break*** is inserted when text fills an entire page, then continues on the next page.

When you type more text than can fit on a page, Word continues the text on another page using soft and hard page breaks. The ***soft page break*** is a hidden marker that automatically continues text on the top of a new page when text no longer fits on the current page. These breaks adjust automatically when you add and delete text. For the most part, you rely on soft page breaks to prepare multiple-page documents. However, at times you need to start a new page before Word inserts a soft page break.

A ***hard page break*** forces the next part of a document to begin on a new page.

You can insert a ***hard page break***, a hidden marker, to force text to begin on a new page. A hard page break is inserted into a document using the Breaks command in the Page Setup group on the Page Layout tab, or Page Break in the Pages group on the Insert tab. To view the page break markers in Print Layout view, you must click Show/Hide ¶ on the Home tab, to toggle on the formatting marks as shown in Figure 1.16. You can view the page break markers without the Show/Hide toggled on when you switch to Draft view (see Figure 1.17).

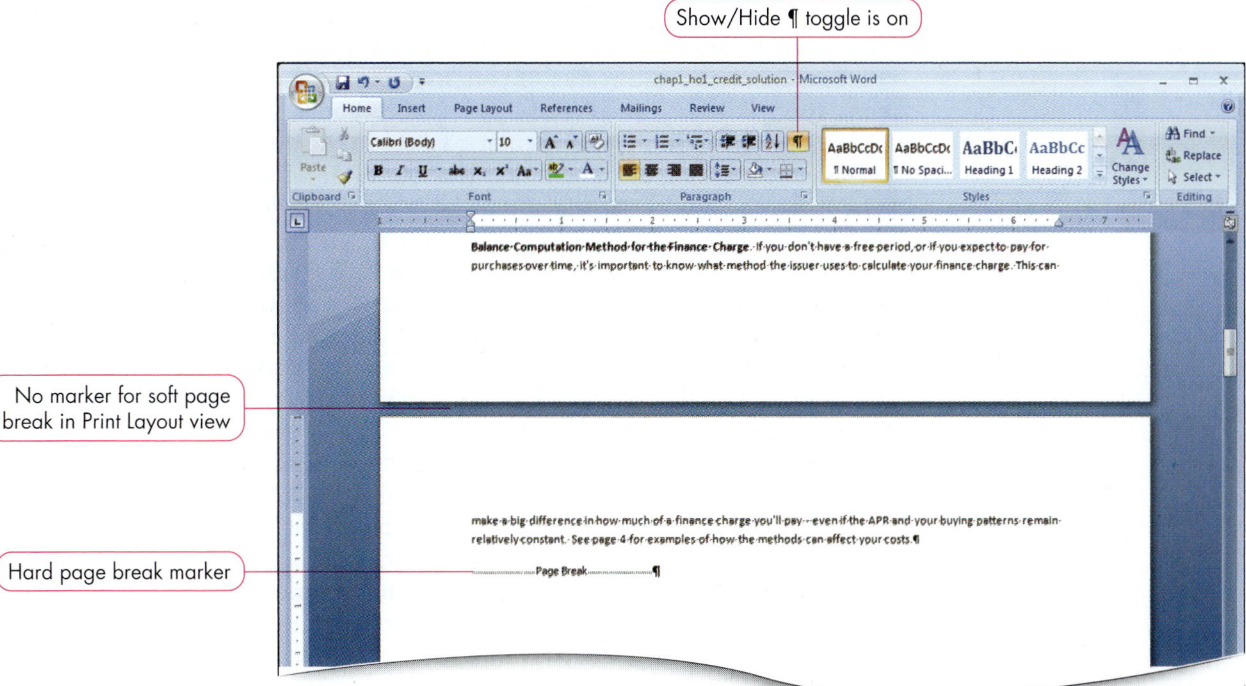

Figure 1.16 View Page Breaks in Print Layout View

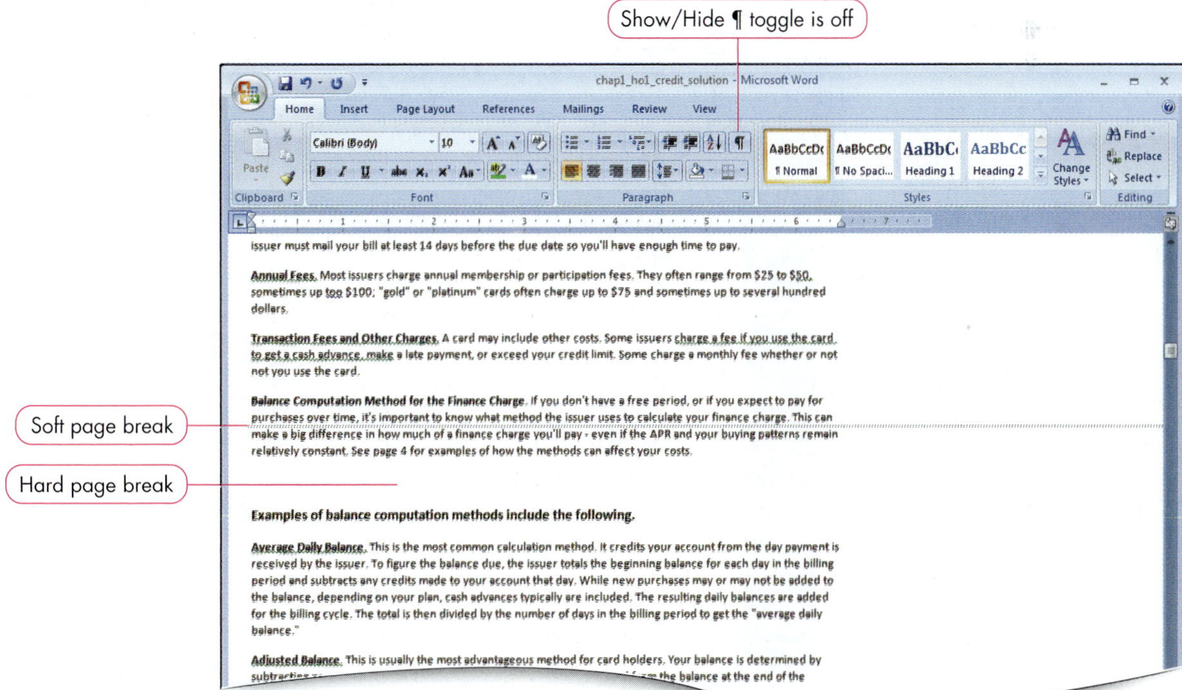

Figure 1.17 View Page Breaks in Draft View

TIP Hard Page Break Shortcut

You can use the keyboard shortcut **Ctrl+Enter** to insert a hard page break.

Adding Page Numbers

Page numbers are essential in long documents. They serve as a convenient reference point for the writer and reader. If you do not include page numbers in a long document, you will have difficulty trying to find text on a particular page or trying to tell someone where to locate a particular passage in the document. Have you ever tried to reassemble a long document that was out of order and did not have page numbers? It can be very frustrating and makes a good case for inserting page numbers in your documents.

The Page Number command in the Header & Footer group on the Insert tab is the easiest way to place page numbers into a document. When you use this feature, Word not only inserts page numbers but also automatically adjusts the page numbering when you add or delete pages. Page numbers can appear at the top or bottom of a page, and can be left, center, or right aligned. Your decision on whether to place page numbers in a header or footer might be based on personal preference, whether the writing guide for your paper dictates a specific location, or if you have other information to include in a header or footer also.

Word 2007 provides several galleries with options for formatting page numbers. New to Office 2007 is the Page Margin option, which enables you to put a page number on the side of a page. This feature adds a nice element of style to a multipage document that will be distributed as a flyer or annual report. Figure 1.18 displays a few gallery options for placing a page number at the bottom of a page.

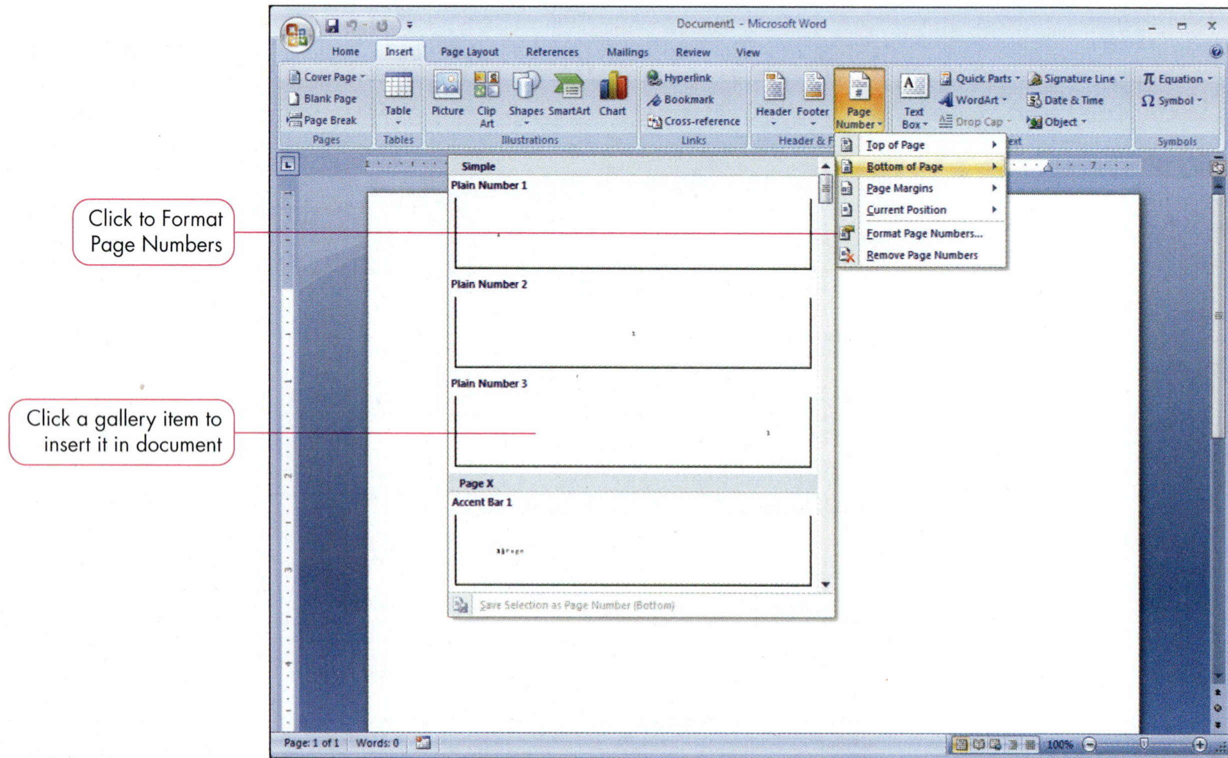

Figure 1.18 Insert Page Numbers at Bottom of Page

Word enables you to customize the number format for page numbers to use Roman rather than Arabic numerals, which often are used for preliminary or preface pages at the beginning of a book. You also can adjust the page numbering so that it starts numbering at a page other than the first. This is useful when you have a report with a cover page; you typically do not consider the cover as page one but instead begin numbering with the page that follows it. You use the Format Page Numbers command to display the Page Number Format dialog box (see Figure 1.19) where you can make these changes. If you are not satisfied with the page numbering in a document, use the Remove Page Numbers command to remove them.

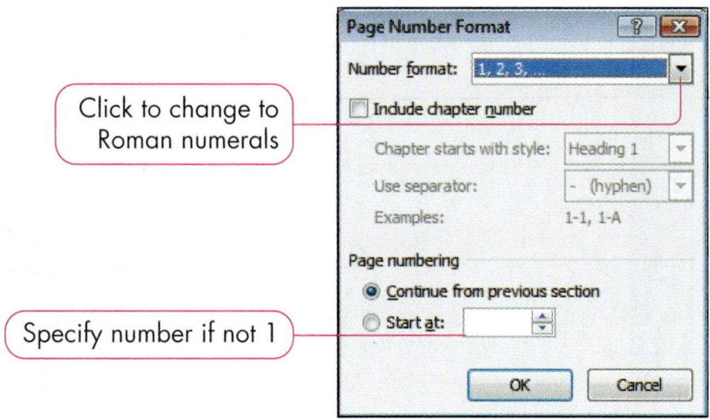

Figure 1.19 Page Number Format Dialog Box

Inserting Headers and Footers

A ***header*** is information printed at the top of document pages.

A ***footer*** is information printed at the bottom of document pages.

Headers and footers give a professional appearance to a document. A *header* consists of one or more lines that are printed at the top of a page. A *footer* is printed at the bottom of the page. A document may contain headers but not footers, footers but not headers, both headers and footers, or neither. Footers often contain the page number and a date the document was created. Headers might contain the name of an organization, author, or title of the document. Take a moment to notice the type of information you see in the headers/footers of the books or magazines you are reading.

Headers and footers are added from the Insert tab. You can create a simple header or footer by clicking Page Number, depending on whether the page number is at the top or bottom of a page. Headers and footers are formatted like any other paragraph and can be center, left or right aligned. You can format headers and footers in any typeface or point size and can include special codes to automatically insert the page number, date, and time a document is printed.

The advantage of using a header or footer (over typing the text yourself at the top or bottom of every page) is that you type the text only once, after which it appears automatically according to your specifications. In addition, the placement of the headers and footers is adjusted for changes in page breaks caused by the insertion or deletion of text in the body of the document.

Headers and footers can change continually throughout a document. Once you insert one, the Header & Footer Tools tab displays and contains many options (see Figure 1.20). For instance, you can specify a different header or footer for the first page; this is advisable when you have a cover page and do not want the header (or footer) to display on that page. You also can have different headers and footers for odd and even pages. This feature is useful when you plan to print a document that will be bound as a book. Notice the different information this book prints on the footer of odd versus even pages, and how the page numbers display in the corners of each page. If you want to change the header (or footer) midway through a document, you need to insert a section break at the point where the new header (or footer) is to begin. These breaks are discussed in the next section.

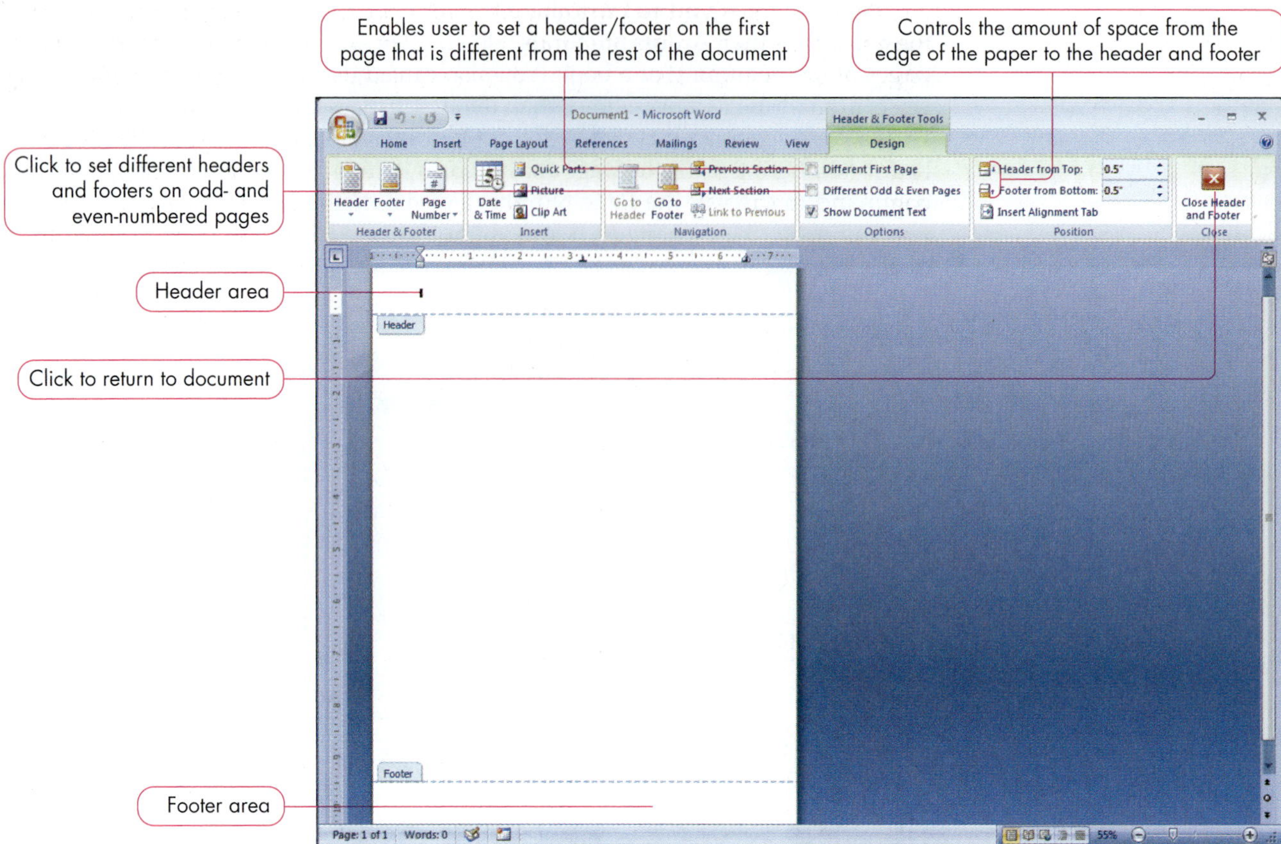

Figure 1.20 Header and Footer Tools Commands

Creating Sections

Formatting in Word occurs on three levels: character, paragraph, and section. Formatting at the section level controls headers and footers, page numbering, page size and orientation, margins, and columns. All of the documents in the text so far have consisted of a single section, and thus any section formatting applied to the entire document. You can, however, divide a document into sections and format each section independently.

A ***section break*** is a marker that divides a document into sections, thereby allowing different formatting in each section.

You determine where one section ends and another begins by clicking Breaks in the Page Setup group on the Page Layout tab. A ***section break*** is a marker that divides a document into sections. It enables you to decide how the section will be formatted on the printed page; that is, you can specify that the new section continues on the same page, that it begins on a new page, or that it begins on the next odd or even page even if a blank page has to be inserted. Formatting at the section level gives you the ability to create more sophisticated documents. You can use section formatting to do the following:

- Change the margins within a multipage letter, where the first page (the letterhead) requires a larger top margin than the other pages in the letter.
- Change the orientation from portrait to landscape to accommodate a wide table at the end of the document.
- Change the page numbering to use Roman numerals at the beginning of the document for a table of contents and Arabic numerals thereafter.
- Change the number of columns in a newsletter, which may contain a single column at the top of a page for the masthead, then two or three columns in the body of the newsletter.

Word stores the formatting characteristics of each section in the section break at the end of a section. Thus, deleting a section break also deletes the section formatting, causing the text above the break to assume the formatting characteristics of the next section.

Figure 1.21 displays a multipage view of a six-page document. The document has been divided into two sections, and the insertion point is currently on the last page of the document, which is also the first page of the second section. Note the corresponding indications on the status bar and the position of the headers and footers throughout the document.

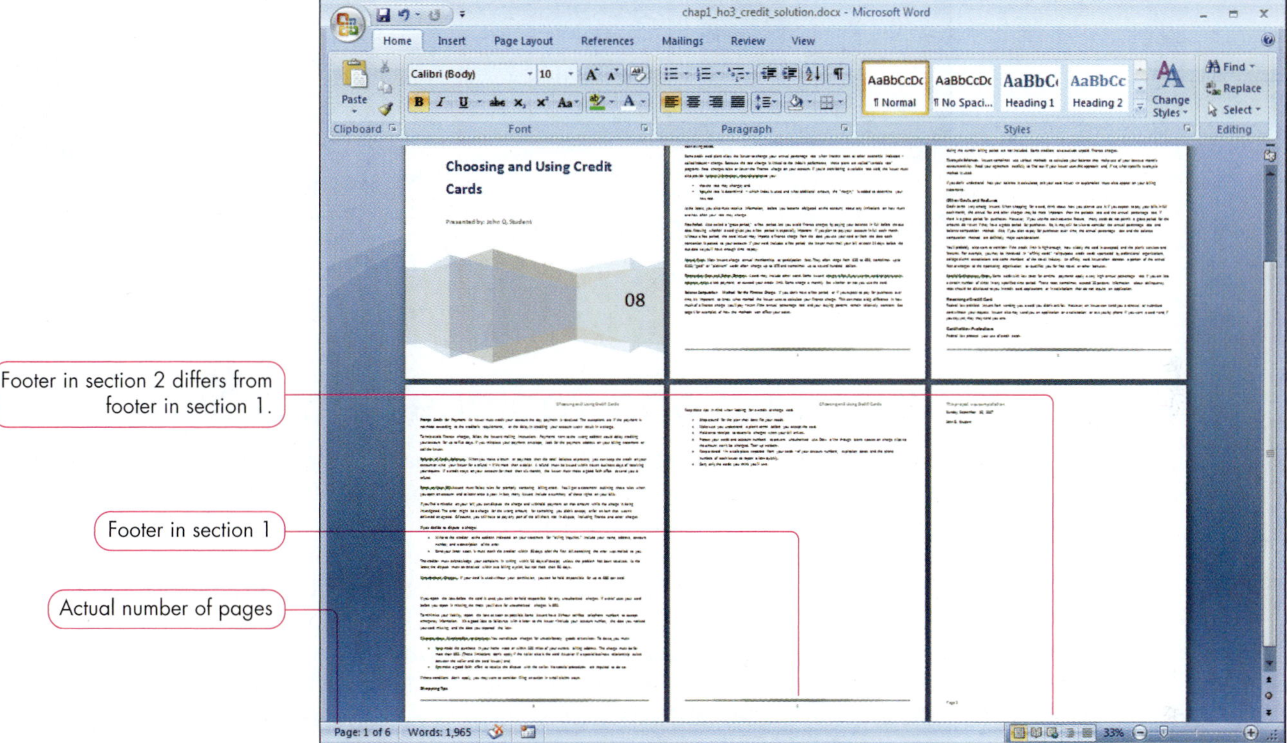

Figure 1.21 A Document with Two Sections

Inserting a Cover Page

You can use commands such as page break and keystrokes such as Ctrl+Enter, mentioned in previous sections, to create a cover page for a document. But Word 2007 offers a feature to quickly insert a preformatted cover page in your document. The Cover Page feature in the Pages group of the Insert tab includes a gallery with several designs, as shown in Figure 1.22. Each design includes building block fields, such as Document Title, Company Name, Date, and Author, which you can personalize. Additionally, the title pages already are formatted with the different first page option in the header and footer, so you don't have to change that setting after you insert the page. After you personalize and make any additional modifications of your choice, your document will include an attractive cover page.

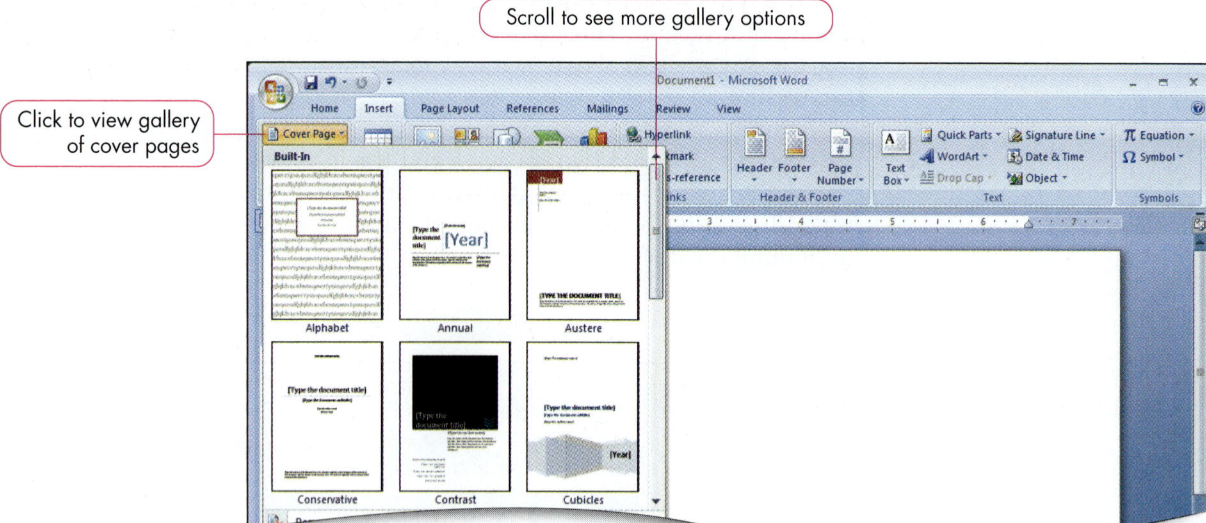

Figure 1.22 Insert a Cover Page

Using Find and Replace Commands

Even though Find and Replace have individual commands in the Editing group, on the Home tab, they share a common dialog box with different tabs for each command as well as the Go To command. The Find command locates one or more occurrences of specific text (e.g., a word or phrase). The Replace command goes one step further in that it locates the text, and then enables you to optionally replace (one or more occurrences of) that text with different text. The Go To command goes directly to a specific place (e.g., a specific page) in the document. If you use the find function and then decide you want to replace text, you can simply click the Replace tab to initiate the process. These functions are very helpful when working in a long document; you can use them to quickly locate text or jump to a different location in the document.

A ***case-sensitive search*** matches not only the text but also the use of upper- and lowercase letters.

A ***case-insensitive search*** finds a word regardless of any capitalization used.

Selective replacement lets you decide whether to replace text.

Automatic replacement makes a substitution automatically.

The search in both the Find and Replace commands is case sensitive or case insensitive. A ***case-sensitive search***, where the Match Case option is selected, matches not only the text but also the use of upper- and lowercase letters. Thus, *There* is different from *there*, and a search on one will not identify the other. A ***case-insensitive search***, where Match Case is *not* selected, is just the opposite and finds both *There* and *there*. A search also may specify whole words only to identify *there*, but not *therefore* or *thereby*. And finally, the search and replacement text also can specify different numbers of characters; for example, you could replace *flower* with *daisy*.

The Replace command implements either ***selective replacement***, which lets you examine each occurrence of the character string in context and decide whether to replace it, or ***automatic replacement***, where the substitution is made automatically. Selective replacement is implemented by clicking the Find Next command, then clicking (or not clicking) Replace to make the substitution. Automatic replacement (through the entire document) is implemented by clicking Replace All. This feature can save you a great deal of time if you need to make a replacement throughout a document, but it also can produce unintended consequences. For example, if you substitute the word *text* for *book*, the word *textbook* would become *texttext*, which is not what you had in mind.

The Find and Replace commands can include formatting and/or special characters. This command is helpful in situations where you need to make changes to the way text is formatted, but not necessarily to the text itself. You can, for example, change all italicized text to boldface, as shown in Figure 1.23, or you can change five consecutive spaces to a tab character, which makes it easier to align text. You also can use special characters in the character string such as the "any character" (consisting of ^?). For example, to find all four-letter words that begin with "f" and end with "l" (such as *fall*, *fill*, or *fail*), search for f^?^?l. (The question mark stands for any character, just like a wildcard in a card game.) You also can search for all forms of a word; for example, if you specify *am*, it will also find *is* and *are*. You can even search for a word based on how it sounds. When searching for *Marion*, for example, check the Sounds like check box, and the search will find both *Marion* and *Marian*.

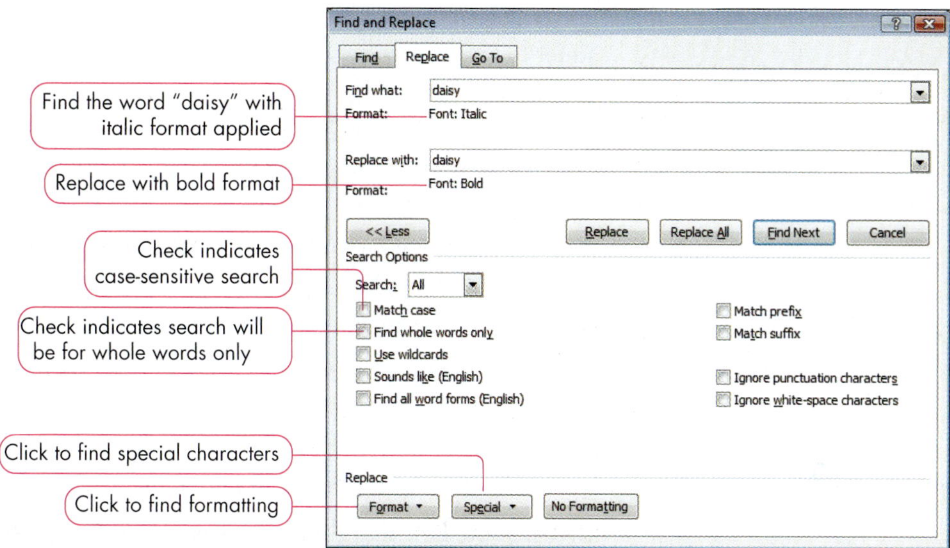

Figure 1.23 The Find and Replace Dialog Box

TIP The Go To Command

The Go To command moves the insertion point to a designated location in the document. The command is accessed by clicking the Find down arrow in the Editing group on the Home tab, by pressing **Ctrl+G**, or by clicking the page number on the status bar. After you activate the command, the Find and Replace dialog box displays the Go To tab in which you enter a page number, section, line, footnote, or other areas in the Go to what list. You also can specify a relative page number—for example, +2 to move forward two pages, or -1 to move back one page.

Hands-On Exercises

2 | Document Organization

Skills covered: 1. Set Page Margins and Orientation **2.** Insert a Page Break **3.** Add a Cover Page and Insert a Document Header **4.** Insert a Section Break **5.** Insert a Page Number in the Footer **6.** Use Find, Replace, and Go To

Step 1
Set Page Margins and Orientation

Refer to Figure 1.24 as you complete Step 1.

a. Open the *chap1_ho1_credit_solution* document if you closed it after the last hands-on exercise, and save it as **chap1_ho2_credit_solution**. Be sure you are in the single page view, which you can access by selecting **View Options** and clicking **Show One Page**.

b. Click the **Page Layout tab** and click **Margins** in the Page Setup group. Select **Custom Margins**.

   The Page Setup dialog box displays.

c. Click the **Margins tab**, if necessary. Type **.75** in the Top margin box. Press **Tab** to move the insertion point to the Bottom margin box. Type **.75** and press **Tab** to move to the Left margin box.

   0.75″ is the equivalent of ¾ of one inch.

d. Click the **Left margin down arrow** to reduce the left margin to **0.5″** and then repeat the procedure to set the right margin to **0.5″**.

   The top and bottom margins are now set at 0.75″, and the left and right margins are set at 0.5″ (see Figure 1.24).

e. Check that these settings apply to the **Whole document**, located in the lower portion of the dialog box. Click **OK**.

   You can see the change in layout as a result of changing the margins. More text displays on the first three pages, and there is only one line of text remaining on the fourth page.

f. Click **Orientation** in the Page Setup group on the Page Layout tab, and then select **Landscape**.

   The pages now display in landscape orientation. Because the document looked fine as portrait orientation, we will return to portrait orientation to prepare for the remaining exercises.

g. Click **Undo** on the Quick Access Toolbar. Save the document.

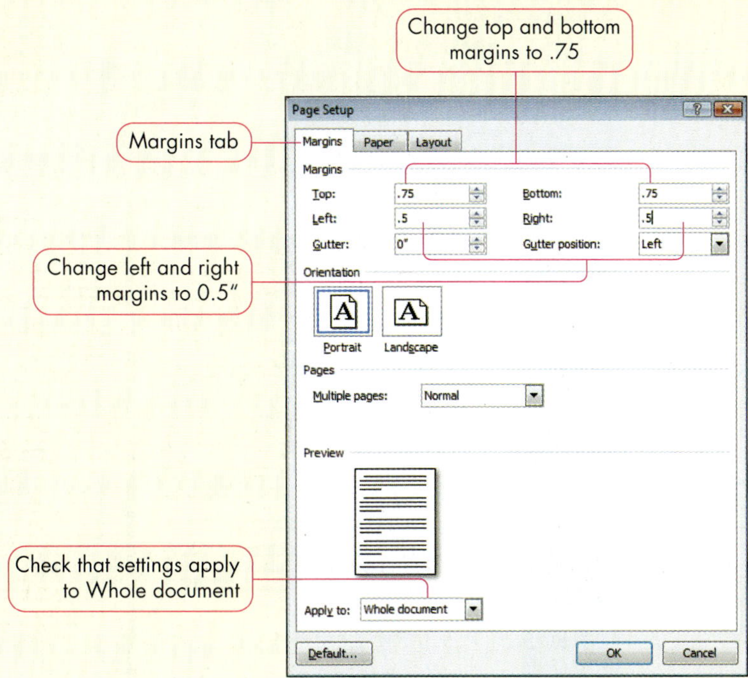

Figure 1.24 Change the Margins

Step 2
Insert a Page Break

Refer to Figure 1.25 as you complete Step 2.

a. Click the **Zoom slider** and increase the zoom to **100%**.

b. Place the insertion point on the left side of the heading *Examples of balance computation methods include the following.* on the bottom of the first page.

c. Press **Ctrl+Enter** to insert a page break.

   The heading and paragraph that follows move to the top of the second page. It leaves a gap of space at the bottom of the first page, but you will make other adjustments to compensate for that.

d. Place the insertion point on the left side of the paragraph heading *Prompt Credit for Payment.* on the bottom of the second page. Press **Enter** one time.

   The hard returns force the paragraph to relocate to the top of the next page.

e. Click the **Zoom slider** and decrease the zoom to 50%, and then display pages one and two. If necessary, click **Show/Hide ¶** in the Paragraph group on the Home tab to view formatting marks.

   Notice the marks that indicate the Page Break and hard return at the bottom of the first and second pages, as shown in Figure 1.25.

f. Save the document.

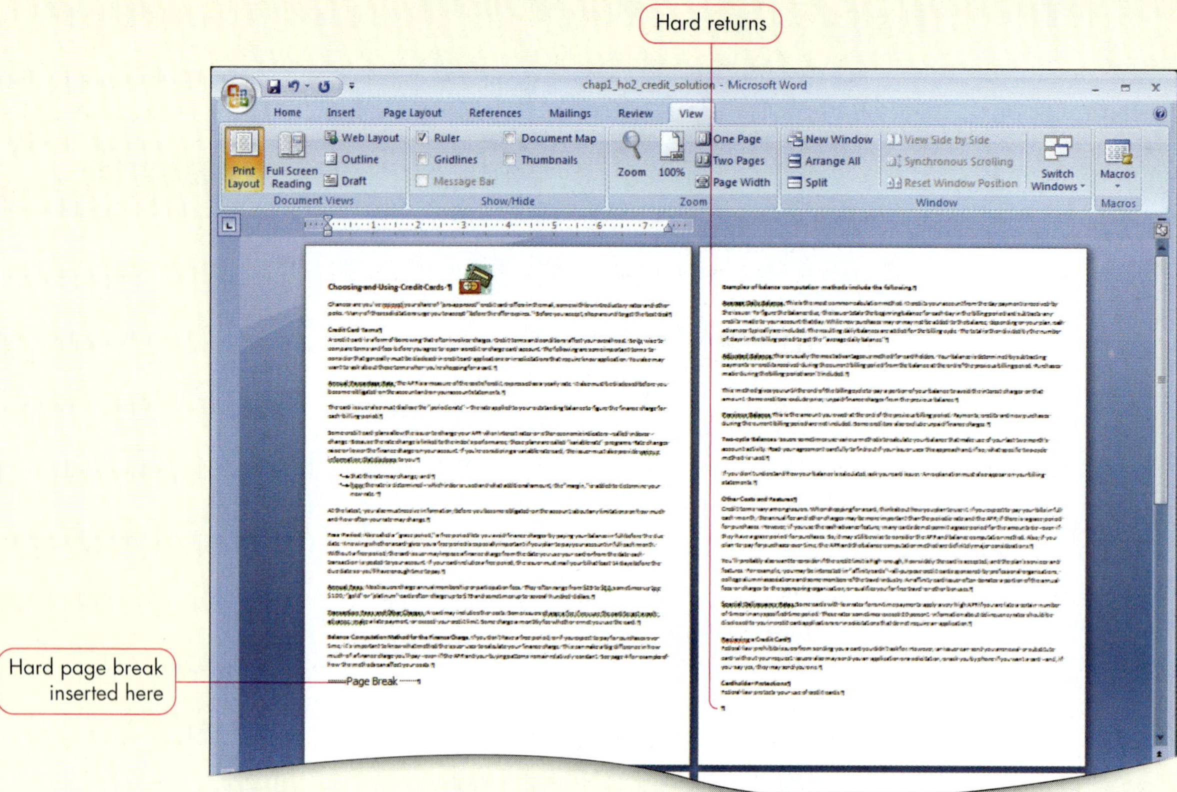

Figure 1.25 Insert a Hard Page Break

Step 3
Add a Cover Page and Insert a Document Header

Refer to Figure 1.26 as you complete Step 3.

a. Click the **Insert tab**, click **Cover Page** in the Pages group, and then click **Cubicles** from the gallery.

You now have a title page that already displays the report title, and the rest of the document begins at the top of page two. The insertion point does not have to be at the beginning of a document to insert a cover page.

TROUBLESHOOTING: If the document title does not display automatically, click the Title field and replace the text *Type the document title* with **Choosing and Using Credit Cards**.

b. Right-click the Subtitle field, *Type the document subtitle*, and select **Cut**. Right-click the Company Name field at the top of the page, and then select **Cut**. Click the Year field and type the current year. If necessary, click the Author Name field and type your name.

Due to the preset format of the title page, the date 2008 will change to 08 automatically.

c. Click the **Zoom slider** and increase the zoom to **100%**. Click **Header** on the Insert tab and select **Edit Header** at the bottom of the gallery list.

The Design tab displays, and the header area of the page is bordered by a blue line.

d. Look at the status bar on the bottom of the page to determine the page where the insertion point is located. If necessary, click **Next Section** in the Navigation group on the Design tab to place your insertion point in the header of page two. Confirm that the **Different First Page** option is selected in the Options group on the Design tab.

The cover page you created does not require a heading, and this setting prevents the heading from displaying on that page.

e. Press **Tab** two times to move the insertion point to the right side of the header. Click **Quick Parts** in the Insert group on the Design tab, point to **Document Property**, and select **Title**.

   The title of the document, *Choosing and Using Credit Cards*, displays in the header as shown in Figure 1.26.

f. Scroll down and notice the header on the remaining pages. Click **Close Header and Footer**.

g. Save the document.

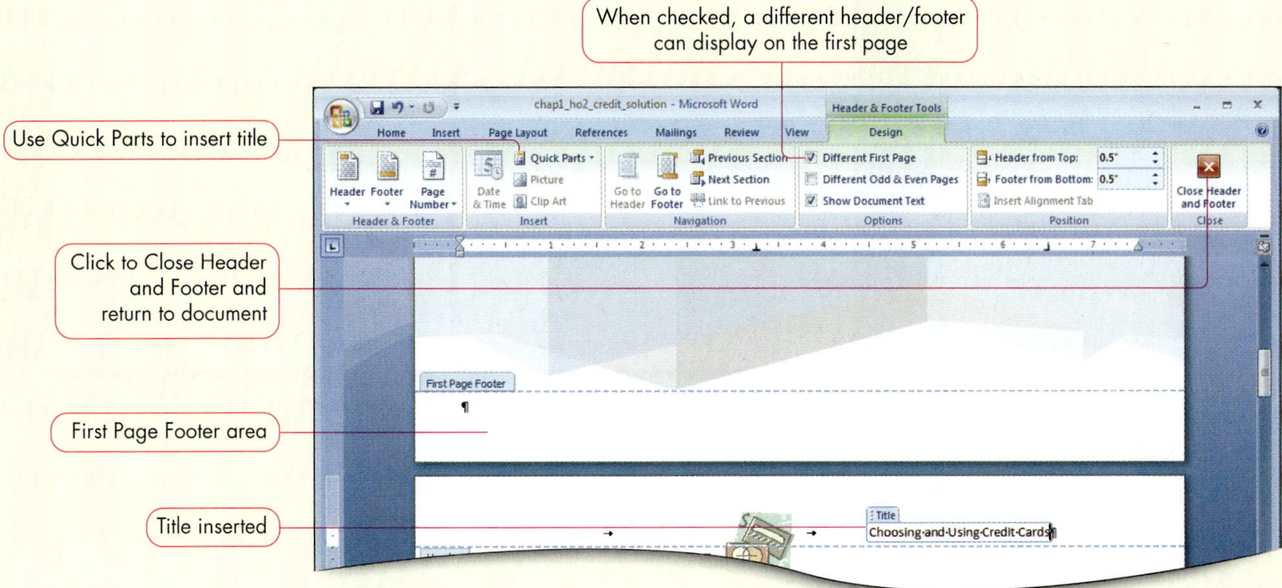

Figure 1.26 Create a Header

Step 4
Insert a Section Break

Refer to Figure 1.27 as you complete Step 4.

a. Press **Ctrl+End** to move to the end of the document, then place the insertion point on the left side of the date. Click the **Page Layout tab,** click **Breaks** in the Page Setup group, and then select **Next Page** under Section Breaks.

   By inserting this section break you are now free to make modifications to the last page without changing the previous pages.

b. Double-click in the header or footer area of the last page to display the Design tab. Click in the header of the last page and then click **Link to Previous** in the Navigation group to deselect it.

   Even though you insert a section break, the header and footer of this page take on the same formatting as the first section. When you remove that link, you can set up an independent header and/or footer.

c. In the header of the last page type **This project was completed on** as shown in Figure 1.27. Zoom two pages in order for your screen to look like figure 1.27.

d. Click **Go To Footer** in the Navigation group. Click **Link to Previous** to toggle it off. In the Position group, click the **Footer from Bottom** up arrow until **0.8"** displays.

   This footer is now independent from all other document footers, and the page number at the bottom that you will insert in the next step will print in a different location on the page.

e. Click **Close Header and Footer**. Save the document.

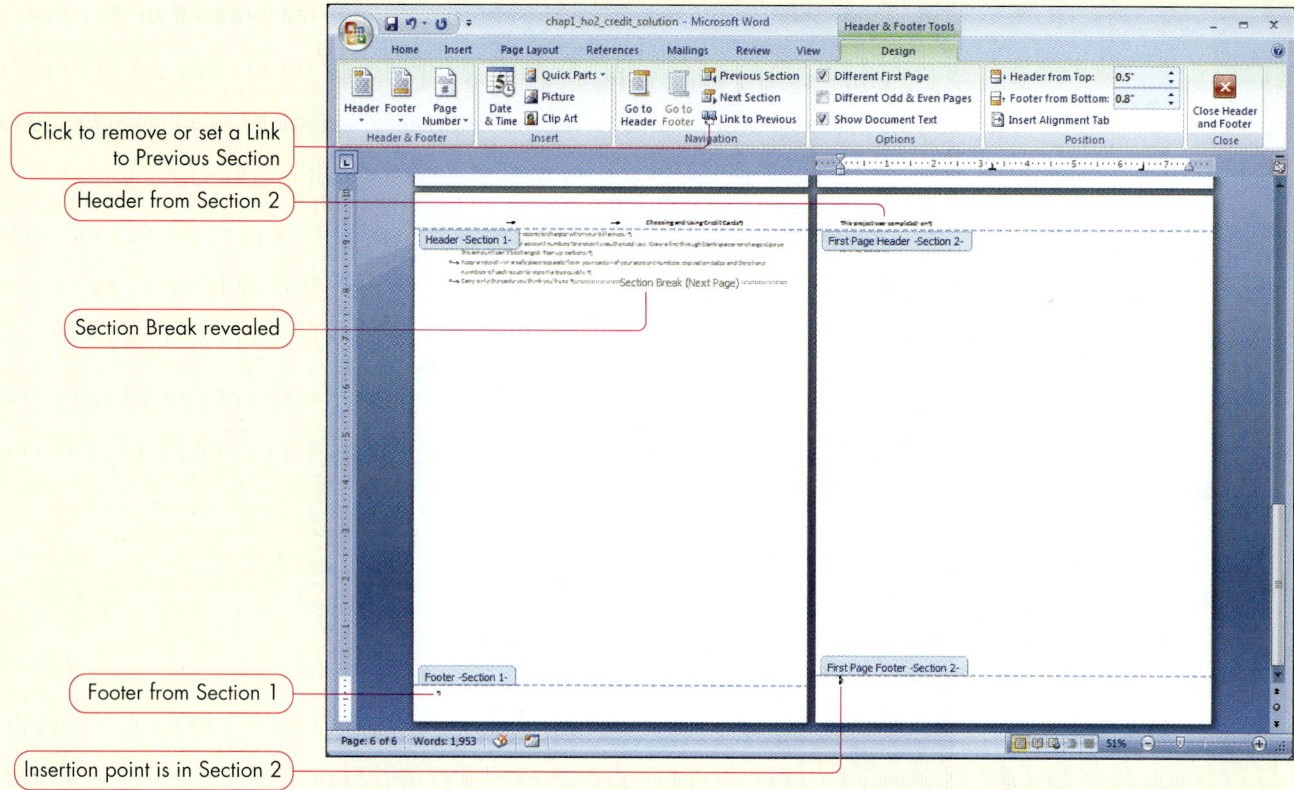

Figure 1.27 Header in Section 2

Step 5
Insert a Page Number in the Footer

Refer to Figure 1.28 as you complete Step 5.

a. Place your insertion point anywhere on the second page. Click the **Insert tab**, if necessary. Click **Page Number** in the Header & Footer group, and then point to **Bottom of Page**. Scroll down to the bottom of the gallery and click **Thick Line**.

   A dark line and the page number display on the bottom of each page except the first and last because you changed the Different First Page and Link to Previous options.

   TROUBLESHOOTING: If your insertion point was on the first page the footer will display on that page only. Click Undo on the Quick Access Toolbar, place your insertion point on page two, and repeat the step above to add the footer to the remaining pages.

b. Click **Page Number** in the Header & Footer group on the Design tab and select **Format Page Numbers**.

   The Page Number Format dialog box displays.

c. Click **Start at**, then click the down arrow until **0** displays. Click OK.

   If you begin page numbering with zero, the second page, which is the first page of content, displays as page 1.

d. Scroll to the bottom of page 6. Place the insertion point on the left side of the footer area and type **Page**, and then press **Spacebar** one time.

e. Click **Quick Parts** in the Insert group and select **Field**. Click the **Categories drop-down arrow** and select **Numbering**.

You can insert many different items in your document; use the category option to minimize the number of fields to browse through to find the one you want.

f. Select **Page** in the **Field names** list, and select the first option displayed in the Format list as shown in Figure 1.28. Click **OK**.

The end result for this operation will be similar to one that you can reach using the Page Number feature; however, this exercise demonstrates the field feature that allows you to use more customization in headers and footers by combining the field with text of your choice.

g. Click **Close Header and Footer**.

h. Save the document.

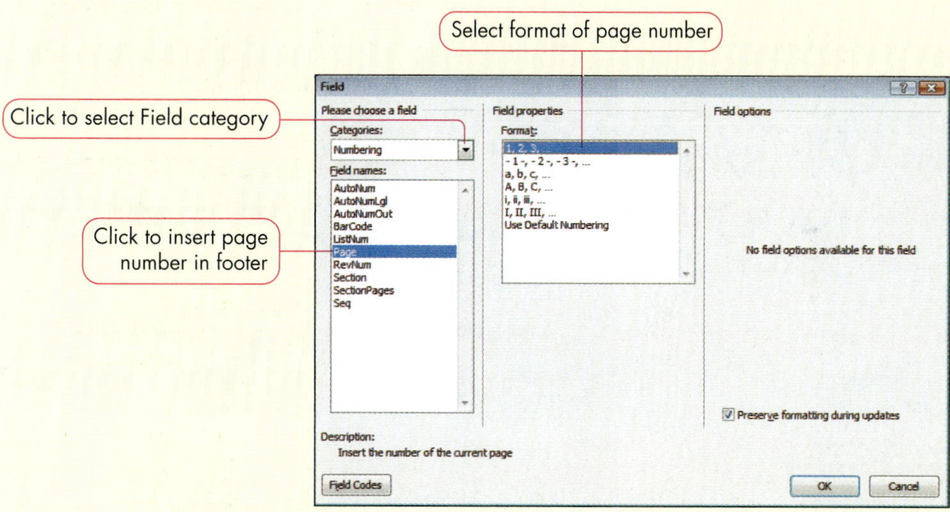

Figure 1.28 Insert a Field in a Footer

Step 6
Use Find, Replace, and Go To

Refer to Figure 1.29 as you complete Step 6.

a. Press **Ctrl+Home** to move to the beginning of the document. Click the **Home tab** and click **Find** in the Editing group.

b. Type **APR** in the *Find what* text box and then click **Find Next**.

The first occurrence of the text appears on the second page.

c. Click the **Replace tab** in the Find and Replace dialog box. Type **annual percentage rate** in the *Replace with* box. Click **Replace All**.

A dialog box displays, indicating seven replacements were made.

d. Click **OK** to remove the dialog box. In the Find what text box type **$50**. Click **More**, if necessary, then click **Format** and click **Font.** In the Find Font dialog box click **Bold** in the *Font style* list, and then click **OK**.

e. In the *Replace with* text box type **$50**. Click **Format** and click **Font.** In the Replace Font dialog box click **Regular** in the *Font style* list, and then click **OK**. Compare your window to Figure 1.29.

TROUBLESHOOTING: If you applied the Bold format to the text in the *Replace with* box instead of the *Find what* box, click **No Formatting** on the bottom of the window, then start again. Be sure the insertion point is in the desired box before you click **Format**.

f. Click **Find Next.**

The bolded occurrence of $50 displays near the bottom of the fourth page.

g. Click **Replace** to remove the formatting from the text, and then click **OK** in the dialog box that informs you Word has finished searching the document.

h. Click the **Go To tab**.

The Go To tab of the Find and Replace dialog box displays, and the insertion point is in the *Enter page number* box.

i. Type **1** in the *Enter page number* box, then click **Go To.**

The top of page 1 displays on your screen, and the Find and Replace dialog box is still onscreen.

j. Click **Section** in the **Go to what** box, type **2** in the *Enter section number* box, and then click **Go To**.

The top of page 6 displays, which is the beginning of the section you added in Step 4.

k. Click **Close**. Save the document.

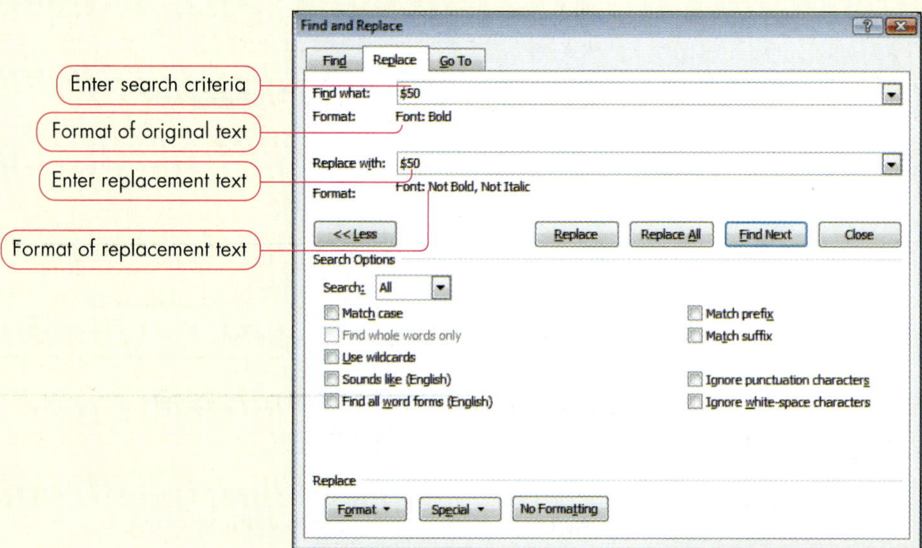

Figure 1.29 Find and Replace Text

The Final Touches

You can create a document that is, for the most part, free of typographical and grammatical errors. Word provides many features that assist in correcting a variety of grammatical mistakes.

As you work on a document you should save changes frequently. Word even has an option to create backup copies of your work periodically in case of a system failure. When you believe that your document is complete, you should take one last look and run a few diagnostics to check for mistakes in spelling and grammar. If you are sending the document to another person, you also should use the tools that locate compatibility issues your document has with older versions of Word. If you print your document, be sure to use features that avoid wasting paper.

In this section, you check for spelling and grammatical errors. You also revisit the important process of saving files as well as backup options, the Compatibility Checker, and the Document Inspector. You learn different print options, and you learn about the many customization options available in Word 2007.

Checking Spelling and Grammar

You can create a document that is, for the most part, free of typographical and grammatical errors. However, you should always proofread a document at the conclusion of your edits because it is possible the automated spelling and grammar checker did not find every error. Word provides many features that assist in correcting a variety of grammatical mistakes. In the Office Fundamentals chapter you learned how to use the Spelling and Grammar and the Thesaurus features to assist in writing and proofing. In the following paragraphs you will learn about other features that help you create error-free documents.

Perform a Spelling and Grammar Check

The ***Spelling and Grammar*** feature looks for mistakes in spelling, punctuation, writing style, and word usage.

The ***Spelling and Grammar*** feature attempts to catch mistakes in spelling, punctuation, writing style, and word usage by comparing strings of text within a document to a series of predefined rules. When located, you can accept the suggested correction and make the replacement automatically, or more often, edit the selected text and make your own changes.

You also can ask the grammar check to explain the rule it is attempting to enforce. Unlike the spell check, the grammar check is subjective, and what seems appropriate to you may be objectionable to someone else. Indeed, the grammar check is quite flexible, and can be set to check for different writing styles; that is, you can implement one set of rules to check a business letter and a different set of rules for casual writing. Many times, however, you will find that the English language is just too complex for the grammar check to detect every error, although it will find many. Depending on your reliance on the grammar check, you can set the option for it to run all the time by marking the selection in the Word Options, Proofing category.

TIP Custom Dictionaries

If you work in a field that uses technical terminology, such as nursing or aviation, you need to include those terms with the existing dictionary in the Spelling and Grammar feature. To use the custom dictionary, click the Office Button, click Word Options, click Proofing, click Custom Dictionary, and then navigate to the location where the dictionary is stored.

Check Contextual Spelling

In addition to spelling and grammar checking, Word 2007 has added a contextual spelling feature that attempts to locate a word that is spelled correctly, but used incorrectly. For example, many people confuse the usage of words such as *their* and *there*, *two* and *too*, and *which* and *witch*. The visual indication that a contextual spelling error occurs is a blue wavy line under the word as shown in Figure 1.30. By default this feature is not turned on; to invoke the command, click the Office Button, select Word Options at the bottom, select the Proofing category, then click to select the Use contextual spelling check box.

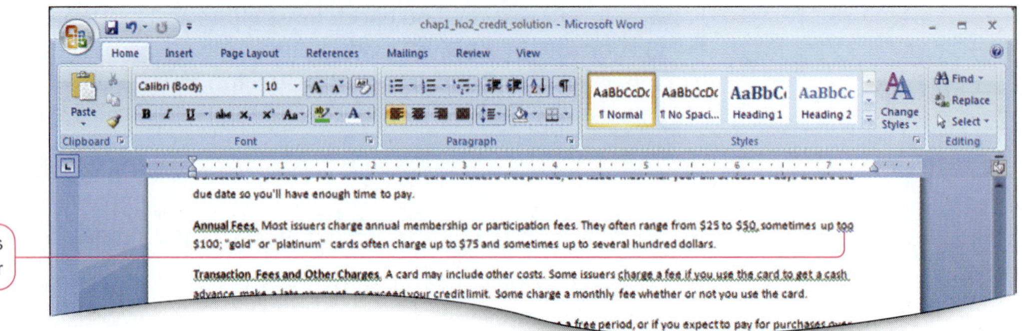

Figure 1.30 Check Contextual Spelling

Using Save and Backup Options

It's not a question of *if* it will happen but *when*. Files are lost, systems crash, and viruses infect a system. That said, we cannot overemphasize the importance of saving your work frequently. Additionally, you should use available resources to provide a backup copy (or two) of your most important documents and back up your files at every opportunity. For example, the Exploring series authors back up all of their manuscript files in case one system crashes. Graduate students periodically back up their lengthy theses and dissertations so that they do not have to recreate these research documents from scratch if one system fails.

Save a Document in Compatible Format

After reading the Office Fundamentals chapter, you know the Save and Save As commands are used to copy your documents to disk and should be used frequently in order to avoid loss of work and data. Because some people may use a different version of Microsoft Word, you should know how to save a document in a format that they can use. People cannot open a Word 2007 document in earlier versions of Word unless they update their earlier version with the Compatibility Pack that contains a converter. If you are not sure if they have installed the Compatibility Pack, it is best to save the document in an older format, such as Word 97–2003.

To save a document so that someone with a different version of Office can open it, click the Office Button and point to the arrow on the right side of the Save As command. The option to save in Word 97–2003 format appears (see Figure 1.31), and after you click it, you can use the Save As dialog box normally. The saved file will have the .doc extension instead of the Word 2007 extension, .docx. Another way to save in the older format is to double-click Save As, then select the Word 97–2003 format from the *Save as type* list in the Save As dialog box.

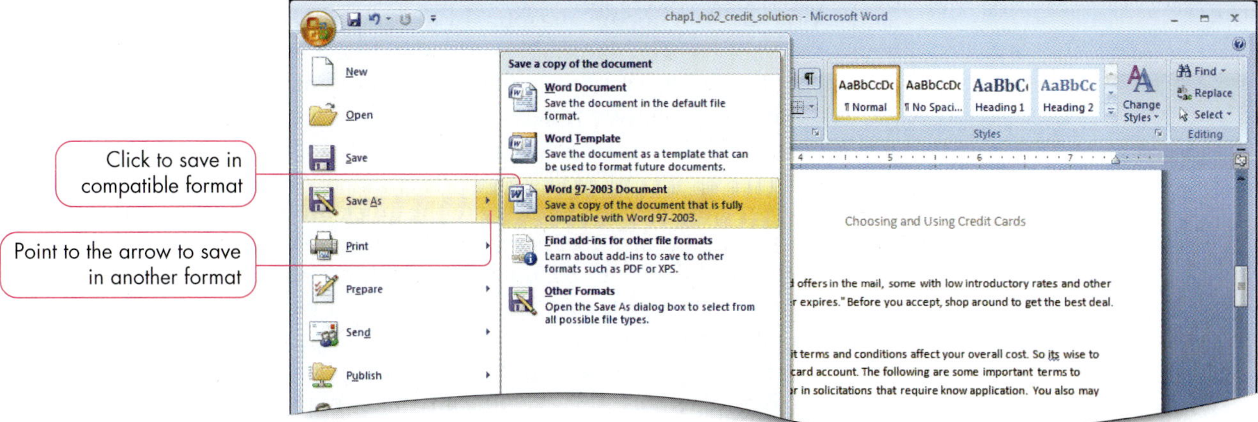

Figure 1.31 Save a File in Compatible Format

If you open a Word document created in an earlier version, such as Word 2003, the title bar will include *(Compatibility Mode)* at the top. You can still work with the document and even save it back in the same format for a Word 97–2003 user. However, some newer features of Word 2007, such as SmartArt and other graphic enhancement options used in the Cover Page and custom headers and footers, are not viewable or available for use in compatibility mode. To remove the file from compatibility mode, click the Office Button and select Convert. It will convert the file and remove the *(Compatibility Mode)* designator, but the .doc extension still displays. The next time you click Save, the extension will change to .docx, indicating that it is converted into a Word 2007 file, and then you can use all of the application features.

Understand Backup Options

Microsoft Word offers several different backup options, the most important of which is to save AutoRecover information periodically. If Microsoft Word crashes, the program will be able to recover a previous version of your document when you restart Word. The only work you will lose is anything you did between the time of the last AutoRecover operation and the time of the crash. The default *Save AutoRecover information every 10 minutes* ensures that you will never lose more than 10 minutes of work.

You also can set Word to create a backup copy in conjunction with every Save. You set these valuable backup and AutoRecover options from the Save and Advanced categories of the Word Options menu. Assume, for example, that you have created the simple document *The fox jumped over the fence*, and saved it under the name *Fox*. Assume further that you edit the document to read, *The quick brown fox jumped over the fence*, and that you saved it a second time. The second Save command changes the name of the original document from *Fox* to *Backup of Fox*, then saves the current contents of memory as *Fox*. In other words, the disk now contains two versions of the document: the current version *Fox* and the most recent previous version *Backup of Fox*.

The cycle goes on indefinitely, with *Fox* always containing the current version, and *Backup of Fox* the most recent previous version. So, if you revise and save the document a third time, *Fox* will contain the latest revision while *Backup of Fox* would contain the previous version alluding to the quick brown fox. The original (first) version of the document disappears entirely because only two versions are kept.

The contents of *Fox* and *Backup of Fox* are different, but the existence of the latter enables you to retrieve the previous version if you inadvertently edit beyond repair or accidentally erase the current *Fox* version. Should this situation occur, you can always retrieve its predecessor and at least salvage your work prior to the last save operation. But remember, this process only takes place if you enable the Always create backup copy option in the Advanced category of the Word Options dialog box.

Run the Compatibility Checker

The ***Compatibility Checker*** looks for features that are not supported by previous versions of Word.

The ***Compatibility Checker*** is a feature in Word 2007 that enables you to determine if you have used features that are not supported by previous versions. After you complete your document, click the Office Button, point to Prepare, and then select Run Compatibility Checker. If the document contains anything that could not be opened in a different version of Word, the Microsoft Office Word Compatibility Checker dialog box will list it. From this dialog box you also can indicate that you want to always check compatibility when saving this file (see Figure 1.32). If you are saving the document in a format to be used by someone with an earlier version, you will want to make corrections to the items listed in the dialog box before saving again and sending the file.

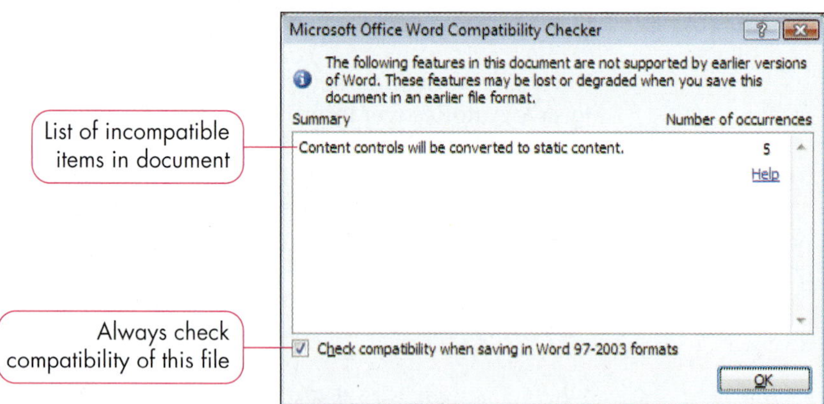

Figure 1.32 The Compatibility Checker

Run the Document Inspector

The ***Document Inspector*** checks for and removes different kinds of hidden and personal information from a document.

Before you send or give a document to another person, you should run the ***Document Inspector*** to reveal any hidden or personal data in the file. For privacy or security reasons, you might want to remove certain items contained in the document such as author name, comments made by one or more persons who have access to the document, or document server locations. Some inspectors are specific to individual Office applications, such as Excel and PowerPoint. Word provides inspectors that you can invoke to reveal different types of information, including:

- Comments, Revisions, Versions, and Annotations
- Document Properties and Personal Information
- Custom XML Data
- Headers, Footers, and Watermarks
- Hidden Text

The inspectors also can locate information in documents created in older versions of Word. Because some information that the Document Inspector might remove cannot be recovered with the Undo command, you should save a copy of your original document, using a different name, just before you run any of the inspectors. After you save the copy, click the Office Button, point to Prepare, and then select the Inspect Document option to run the inspector (see Figure 1.33). When it is complete, it will list the results and enable you to choose whether to remove the information from the document. If you forget to save a backup copy of the document, you can use the Save As command to save a copy of the document with a new name after you run the inspector.

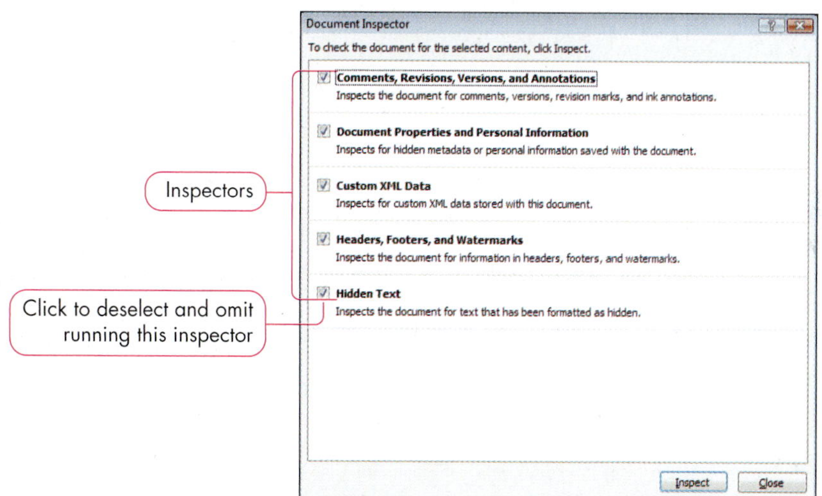

Figure 1.33 The Document Inspector

Selecting Printing Options

People often print an entire document when they want to view only a few pages. All computer users should be mindful of the environment, and limiting printer use is a perfect place to start. Millions of sheets of paper have been wasted because someone didn't take a moment to preview his or her work and then had to reprint due to a very minor error that is easily noticed in a preview window.

Click the Office Button and click the Print arrow to see three settings to consider when you are ready to print your work: Print, Quick Print, and Print Preview. You should select the Print Preview option first to see a preview of what the document will look like when you print it. In the Print Preview window you have several settings that enable you to magnify the page onscreen, display multiple pages, and even make changes to the page layout so you can view the results immediately. If you are satisfied with the document, you can launch the Print dialog box from that window.

The Quick Print option sends a document straight to the printer without prompting you for changes to the printer configuration. If you have only one printer and rarely change printer options, this is an efficient tool.

The final print option is Print, which always displays the Print dialog box and contains many useful options. For example, you can print only the page that contains the insertion point (Current page) or a specific range of pages, such as pages 3–10 (Pages). Furthermore, you can print more than one copy of the document (Number of copies), print miniature copies of pages on a single sheet of paper (Pages per sheet), or adjust the document text size to fit on a particular type of paper (Scale to paper size). If you do not have a duplex printer, you can select the option to print only even numbered pages, flip the paper over and put it back in the printer, then select the option to print only odd pages as shown in Figure 1.34. This method is used frequently by some of the Exploring authors because they do not own duplex printers and also because they want to conserve paper!

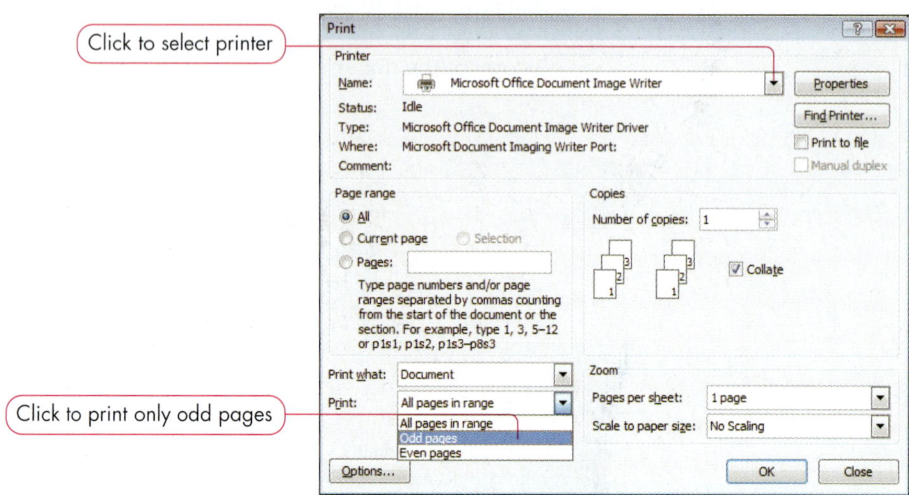

Figure 1.34 Print Options

Customizing Word

As installed, Word is set up to be useful immediately. However, you might find options that you would prefer to customize, add, or remove from the document window. For example, you can add commands to the Quick Access Toolbar (QAT) that do not currently display on any tabs. Or you can add commands that you use so frequently you prefer to access them from the always-visible QAT.

You can customize Word in many ways. To begin the process, or just to view the options available for customization, click the Office button, then select Word Options. Table 1.2 describes the main categories that you can customize and some of the features in each category. You should take some time to glance through each category as you continue to read this chapter. Keep in mind that if you are working in a school lab, you might not have permission to change options on a permanent basis.

Table 1.2 Word Options

Menu Category	Description	Sample of Options to change
Popular	Change the most popular options in Word.	Show Mini toolbar; show Enhanced ScreenTips; change color scheme; change user name and initials.
Display	Change how documents are displayed on the screen and in print.	Show white space between pages in Print Layout view; always show formatting marks such as spaces on the screen; print document properties.
Proofing	Modify how Word corrects and formats your text.	Ignore words in uppercase (don't flag as incorrect); use Spellchecker; use contextual spelling (checks for words that sound alike but are spelled differently such as two, too, and to); mark grammatical errors.
Save	Customize how documents are saved.	Default locations and format to save files; AutoRecover file location; Web server location.
Advanced	Specify editing options; cut, copy, and paste options; show document content options; display options; print options; and save options.	Allow text to be dragged and dropped; enable click and type; default paragraph style; show paste option buttons; show smart tags; number of recent documents to show in file menu; print pages in reverse order; always create backup copy; embed smart tags; update automatic links at open; compatibility options.
Customize	Customize the Quick Access Toolbar and other keyboard shortcuts.	Add or remove buttons from the QAT; determine location of QAT; customize keyboard shortcuts.
Add-Ins	View the add-ins previously installed, customize settings for add-ins, and install more add-ins.	View settings for active and inactive application add-ins; manage smart tags, templates, and disabled items.
Trust Center	View online documentation about security and privacy and change settings to protect documents from possible infections.	Enable and disable macros; change ActiveX settings; set privacy options; select trusted publishers and locations.
Resources	Provide links to Microsoft sites where you can find online resources and keep your Office application updated.	Download updates for Office; diagnose and repair problems with Office; contact Microsoft; activate your license for Office; register for free online services; view product specifications.

As you can see, you are able to customize dozens of settings in Word. Table 1.2 mentions only a small sample of them; fortunately, most users do not need to change any settings at all.

Hands-On Exercises

3 | The Final Touches

Skills covered: 1. Perform a Spelling and Grammar Check **2.** Run the Document Inspector and a Compatibility Check **3.** Save in a Compatible Format **4.** Change Word Options **5.** Use Print Preview Features

Step 1
Perform a Spelling and Grammar Check

Refer to Figure 1.35 as you complete Step 1.

a. Open the *chap1_ho2_credit_solution* document if you closed it after the last hands-on exercise, and save it as **chap1_ho3_credit_solution**.

b. Press **Ctrl+Home** to move to the beginning of the document. Click the **Review tab** and click **Spelling & Grammar** in the Proofing group.

   The Spelling and Grammar dialog box displays with the first error indicated in red text.

c. Click **Change All** to replace all misspellings of the word *recieved* with the correct *received*, then view the next error.

   TROUBLESHOOTING: If additional text is flagged, such as *you've*, click Ignore All. This indicates that Word is checking grammar and style. To do a simple spelling and grammar check, click the Office Button, click the Word Options button, click Proofing, click the Writing Style drop-down arrow, choose Grammar Only, and click OK.

d. Click **Change** to replace *its* with the correct usage, *it's*.

e. Click **Ignore Once** to keep the heading *Annual Percentage Rate*.

   Remember that not all grammar usage flagged may be incorrect. Use your best judgment for those occasions.

f. Remove the check from the **Check grammar** option.

   Most of the headings in the document will be flagged for incorrect grammar, so this will let you bypass all of them and check the spelling only.

g. Click **Change** to replace the contextual spelling error *too* with *to* near the bottom of the first page, as shown in Figure 1.35. Click **Change** to replace the incorrect spelling of Errors on the third page. Click **OK** in the box that informs you the spelling and grammar check is complete.

h. Save the document.

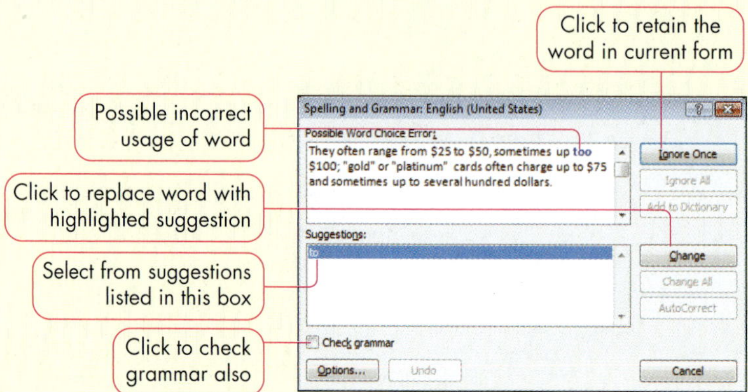

Figure 1.35 Check Spelling and Grammar

Step 2
Run the Document Inspector and a Compatibility Check

Refer to Figure 1.36 as you complete Step 2.

a. Click the **Office Button**, select **Prepare**, and then select **Run Compatibility Checker**.

   A list of any non-compatible items in the document will display in the Microsoft Office Word Compatibility Checker dialog box.

b. Click **OK** after you view the incompatible listings.

c. Click the **Office Button** and select **Save As**. Save the document as **chap1_ho3_credit2_solution**.

   Before you run the Document Inspector you save the document with a different name in order to have a backup.

d. Click the **Office Button**, point to **Prepare**, and then select **Inspect Document**.

   TROUBLESHOOTING: An informational window might display with instructions to save the document before you run the Document Inspector. You should save the document first because the Document Inspector might make changes that you cannot undo.

e. Click to select any inspector check box that is not already checked. Click **Inspect.**

   The Document Inspector results and Remove All buttons enable you to remove the items found in each category, as shown in Figure 1.36.

f. Click **Close**; do not remove any items at this time.

g. Save the document as **chap1_ho3_credit_solution**. Click **OK** to overwrite the existing file with the same name.

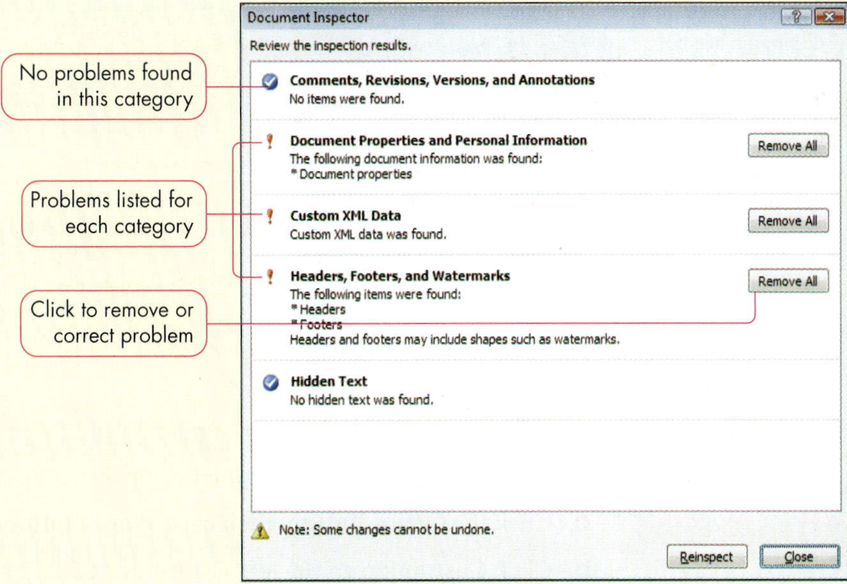

Figure 1.36 Document Inspector Results

Step 3
Save in a Compatible Format

Refer to Figure 1.37 as you complete Step 3.

a. Click the **Office Button**, point to the **Save As** arrow, and select **Word 97–2003 Document**.

b. Confirm the *Save as type* box displays **Word 97–2003 Document (*.doc)**, then click **Save**.

   The Compatibility Checker dialog box displays to confirm the compatibility issues you have seen already.

c. Click **Continue** to accept the alteration.

   The title bar displays *(Compatibility Mode)* following the file name *chap1_ho3_credit_solution.doc*. If you set the option to display file extensions on your computer, the document extension .doc displays in the title bar instead of .docx, as shown in Figure 1.37.

d. Click the **Office Button** and select **Convert**.

   The Compatibility Mode designation is removed from the title bar. If a dialog box displays stating the document will be converted to the newest file format, click OK. You can check the option that prevents the dialog box from displaying each time this situation occurs.

e. Click **Save** on the Quick Access Toolbar. Click **Save** in the Save As dialog box and click **OK** if the authorization to overwrite the current file displays.

   The document extension has been restored to .docx.

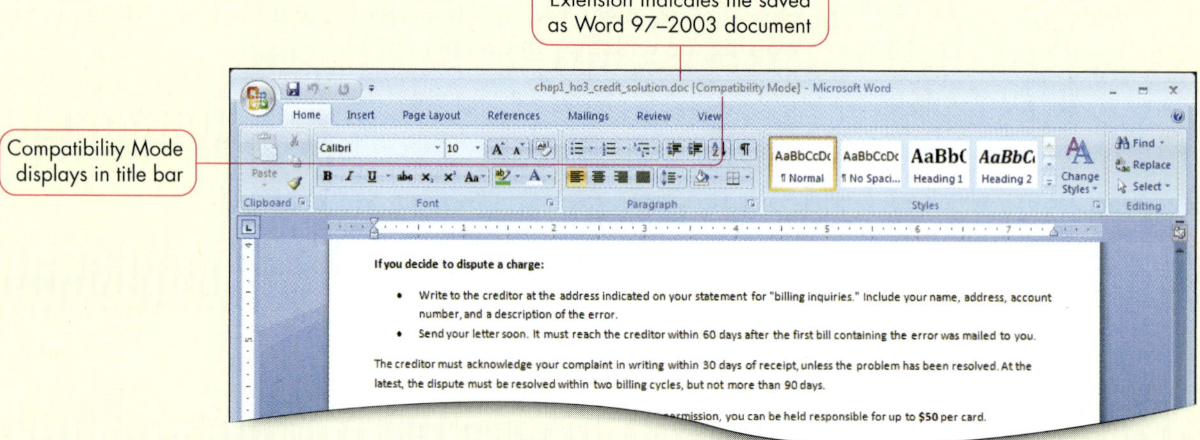

Figure 1.37 File Saved in Word 97–2003 Format

Step 4
Change Word Options

Refer to Figure 1.38 as you complete Step 4.

a. Click the **Office Button**, then click **Word Options** at the bottom of the menu.

b. Click **Customize** on the left side of the Word Options dialog box.

   Look at other Word Options also, to view the many different features you can modify.

c. Select **Print Preview** from the *Choose commands from* list and click **Add** in the middle of the dialog box.

   Print Preview displays in the Customize Quick Access Toolbar list.

d. Click the *Choose Commands from* drop-down arrow and click **Office Menu**. Scroll down the list and click **Inspect Document** from the *Choose commands from* list and click **Add**.

e. Select **Print Preview** from the Customize Quick Access Toolbar list and click **Remove**.

   Print Preview no longer displays in the list of icons for the Quick Access Toolbar, as shown in Figure 1.38.

f. Click **OK** at the bottom of the dialog box to return to the document.

   The Quick Access Toolbar includes a new icon—the Document Inspector.

   TROUBLESHOOTING: If you work in a lab environment, you might not have permission to modify the Word application. Accept any error messages you might see when saving the Word options and proceed to the next step.

g. Click the **Office Button**, click **Word Options** at the bottom of the menu, then click **Customize** on the left side of the Word Options dialog box. Select **Inspect Document** from the Customize Quick Access Toolbar list and click **Remove**. Click **OK** to close the Word Options dialog box.

   The Quick Access Toolbar returns to the default setting.

h. Save the document.

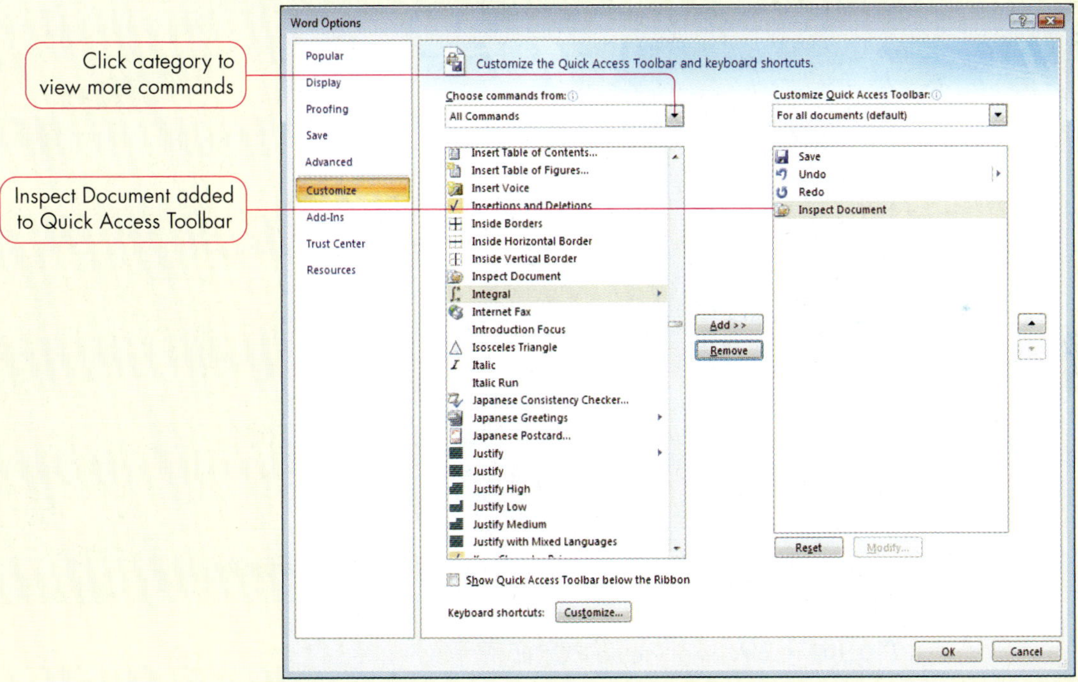

Figure 1.38 Customize the Quick Access Toolbar

Step 5
Use Print Preview Features

Refer to Figure 1.39 as you complete Step 5.

a. Click **Ctrl+Home**, if necessary, to move to the beginning of the document. Click the **Office Button**, point to the **Print** arrow, and then select **Print Preview**.

   The Print Preview window displays the first page (see Figure 1.39).

b. Click **Two Pages** in the Zoom group to view the first two pages in this document. Click the check box next to **Magnifier** in the Preview group to remove the check mark.

This step removes the magnifying glass displayed on the mouse pointer and displays the insertion point. When you remove the magnifier, you can edit the file in the Print Preview window.

c. Place the insertion point on the left side of your name and type **Presented by:**. Click anywhere on the second page to move the insertion point out of the field.

d. Click **Margins** and select the **Narrow** setting.

   Margins in section one of the document change to .5″ on each side.

e. Click **Next Page** to view each page in the document. Click **Close Print Preview** to return to the document.

f. Save the document and exit Word.

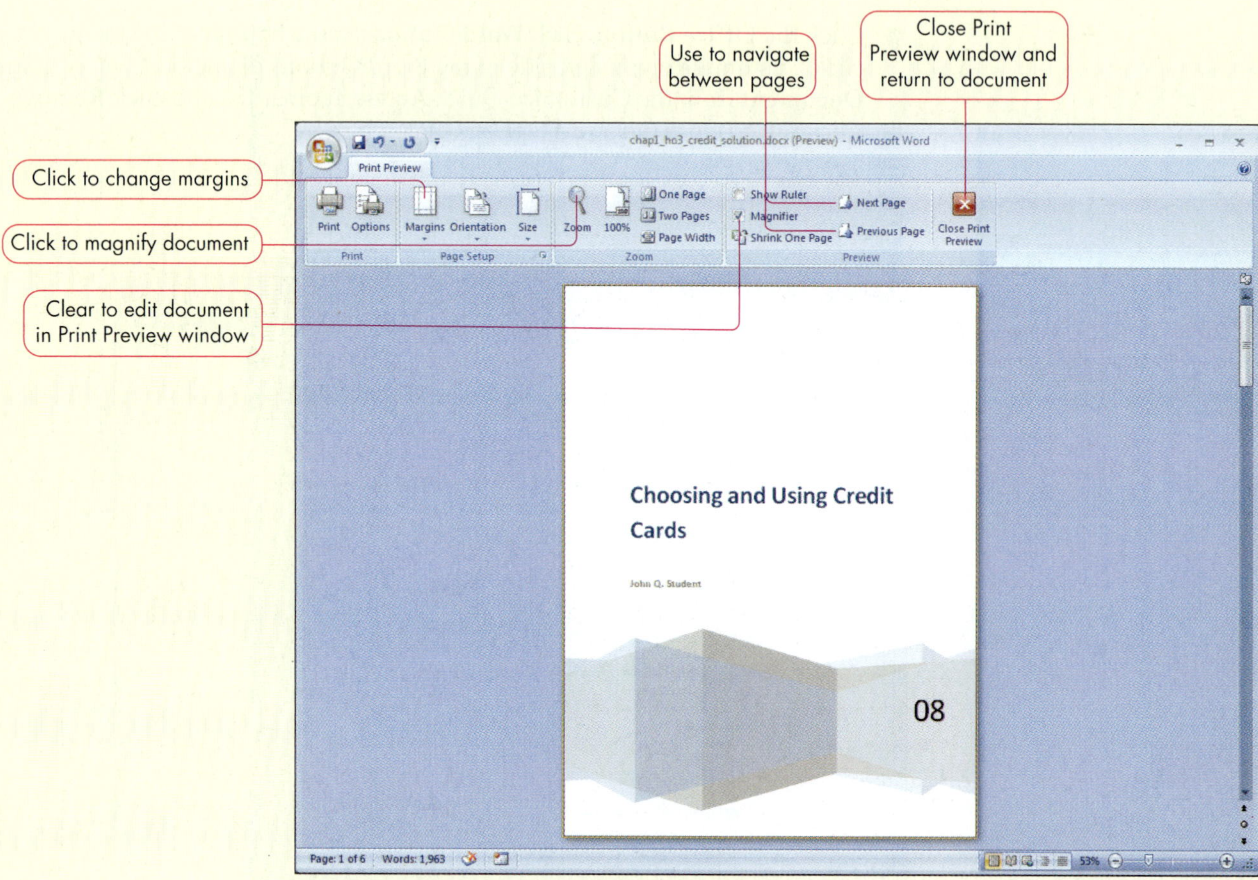

Figure 1.39 Print Preview Options

Summary

1. **Understand Word basics.** A word processing window is made up of several components including the title bar, Quick Access Toolbar, status bar, and the document area. Several tabs contain the commands that you use while working in Word, and the tabs might change according to the current task. As you type in a document, the word wrap feature automatically positions text for you using soft returns; however, you can insert a hard return to force text to the next line. Toggle switches such as the Caps Lock key or Bold feature are often used to alternate between two states while you work. The Show/Hide ¶ feature toggles on to reveal formatting marks in a document. The AutoText feature enables you to quickly insert predefined text or graphics.
2. **Use AutoText.** The AutoText feature substitutes a predefined item for specific text when the user initiates the replacement. Predefined and frequently used items, such as a logo, company name, author name, or return address, are stored as building blocks. You can type a portion of the building block entry, then press F3 to insert the remainder into your document.
3. **View a document.** The View tab provides options that enable you to display a document in many different ways. Views include Print Layout, Full Screen Reading, Web Layout, Outline, and Draft. To quickly change the view, click a button on the status bar in the lower-right corner of the window. You can use the Zoom slider to very quickly change magnification by sliding to a different percentage such as 75%. The Zoom dialog box includes options to change to whole page or multipage view.
4. **Use the Mini toolbar.** The Mini toolbar contains frequently used formatting commands such as Bold, Italic, Underline, Center, and Font Size. It displays faintly when you select text or right-click selected text, but it darkens as you move the mouse pointer closer to it. If you move the mouse pointer away from the Mini toolbar, it becomes fainter; if you do not want to use the Mini toolbar and prefer it disappears from view, press Esc when it displays.
5. **Set margins and specify page orientation.** When you create a document, you should consider how it will look when you print or display it. Margins determine the amount of white space from the text to the edge of the page. Pages can be set to display in portrait or landscape orientation. In portrait orientation, the text runs parallel to the shorter side of the paper. In landscape orientation, the text runs parallel to the longer side of the paper.
6. **Insert page breaks.** Soft page breaks occur when text no longer fits on the current page and automatically wraps to the top of a new page. The break is signified by a hidden marker that you can view using the Show/Hide ¶ feature. Hard page breaks can be used to force text onto a new page. A hard page break is inserted into a document using the Breaks command in the Page Setup group on the Page Layout tab, or Page Break in the Pages group on the Insert tab, but more easily through the Ctrl+Enter keyboard shortcut.
7. **Add page numbers.** Page numbers serve as a convenient reference point and assist in reading through a document. They can appear in the side margins, or at the top or bottom of a page, and can be left, center, or right aligned. The easiest way to place page numbers into a document is to click Page Number in the Header & Footer group on the Insert tab. When you use this feature, Word not only inserts page numbers but also adjusts automatically the page numbering when you add or delete pages.
8. **Insert headers and footers.** Headers and footers give a professional appearance to a document and are the best location to store page numbers. A header consists of one or more lines that are printed at the top of a page. A footer is printed at the bottom of a page. Footers often contain the page number and the date the document was created. Headers might contain the name of an organization, author, or title of the document. Headers and footers are added from the Insert tab. A simple header or footer also is created automatically by the Insert Page Number command.
9. **Create sections.** A section break is a marker that divides a document into sections, thereby allowing different formatting in each section. You determine where one section ends and another begins by using Breaks in the Page Setup group on the Page Layout tab. By using section breaks, you can change the margins within a multipage letter, where the first page (the letterhead) requires a larger top margin than the other pages in the letter. You also can change the page numbering within a document or even change the number of columns in a newsletter, which may contain a single column at the top of a page for the masthead, then two or three columns in the body of the newsletter.

...continued on Next Page

10. **Insert a cover page.** Word 2007 offers a feature to quickly insert a preformatted cover page in your document. The Cover Page feature includes a gallery with several designs, and each includes building block fields, such as Document Title, Company Name, Date, and Author, which you can personalize.

11. **Use the Find and Replace commands.** Find and Replace commands include settings that enable you to look for or replace specific formatting on text. They also include options to conduct a case-sensitive or case-insensitive search. You can also use automatic replacement or selective replacement where you determine on an individual basis whether to replace the text or format. You can search for formatting and special characters. The Go To command moves the insertion point to a designated location in the document. You can go to a page, a section, or specify the number of pages to move forward or backward.

12. **Check spelling and grammar.** The grammar check feature looks for mistakes in punctuation, writing style, and word usage. If it finds an error, it will underline it with a green wavy line. You also can ask the grammar check to explain the rule it is attempting to enforce. When a possible error is found, you can accept the suggested correction, or determine if it is appropriate. The contextual spelling feature attempts to locate a word that is spelled correctly but used incorrectly. For example, it looks for the correct usage of the words *there* and *their*. A contextual spelling error is underlined with a blue wavy line.

13. **Use save and backup options.** To prevent loss of data you should save and back up your work frequently. You also should be familiar with commands that enable you to save your documents in a format compatible with older versions of Microsoft Word. You can use the convert command to alter those files into Word 2007 format, which is more efficient. Several backup options can be set, including an AutoRecover setting you can customize. This feature is useful for recovering a document when the program crashes. You can also require Word to create a backup copy in conjunction with every save operation. Word 2007 includes a compatibility checker to look for features that are not supported by previous versions of Word, and it also offers a Document Inspector that checks for and removes different kinds of hidden or personal information from a document.

14. **Select printing options.** You have three options to consider when you are ready to print your work: Print, Quick Print, and Print Preview. In the Print Preview window, you have several settings that enable you to magnify the page onscreen, display multiple pages, and even make changes to the page layout so you can view the results immediately. The Quick Print option sends a document straight to the printer without prompting you for changes to the printer configuration. The Print dialog box contains many useful options including print only the current page, a specific range of pages, or a specific number of copies.

15. **Customize Word.** After installation, Word is useful immediately. However, many options can be customized. The Word Options dialog box contains nine categories of options you can change including Personalize, Proofing, and Add-Ins. You can add to or remove commands from the Quick Access Toolbar using the Customize section of the Word Options dialog box.

Key Terms

Multiple Choice

1. When entering text within a document, you normally press Enter at the end of every:
   (a) Line
   (b) Sentence
   (c) Paragraph
   (d) Page

2. How do you display the Print dialog box?
   (a) Click the Print button on the Quick Access Toolbar.
   (b) Click the Office button, and then click the Print command.
   (c) Click the Print Preview command.
   (d) Click the Home tab.

3. Which view removes all tabs from the screen?
   (a) Full Screen Reading
   (b) Print Layout
   (c) Draft
   (d) Print Preview

4. You want to add bold and italic to a phrase that is used several times in a document. What is the easiest way to make this update?
   (a) Use the Go To feature and specify the exact page for each occurrence.
   (b) Use the Find feature, then use overtype mode to replace the text.
   (c) Use the Find and Replace feature and specify the format for the replacement.
   (d) No way exists to automatically complete this update.

5. You are the only person in your office to upgrade to Word 2007. Before you share documents with co-workers you should
   (a) Print out a backup copy.
   (b) Run the Compatibility Checker.
   (c) Burn all documents to CD.
   (d) Have no concerns that they can open your documents.

6. A document has been entered into Word using the default margins. What can you say about the number of hard and soft returns if the margins are increased by 0.5″ on each side?
   (a) The number of hard returns is the same, but the number and/or position of the soft returns increases.
   (b) The number of hard returns is the same, but the number and/or position of the soft returns decreases.
   (c) The number and position of both hard and soft returns is unchanged.
   (d) The number and position of both hard and soft returns decreases.

7. Which of the following is detected by the contextual spell checker?
   (a) Duplicate words
   (b) Irregular capitalization
   (c) Use of the word *hear* when you should use *here*
   (d) Improper use of commas

8. Which option on the Page Layout tab allows you to specify that you are printing on an envelope?
   (a) Orientation
   (b) Margins
   (c) Breaks
   (d) Size

9. You need to insert a large table into a report, but it is too wide to fit on a standard page. Which of the following is the best option to use in this case?
   (a) Put the table in a separate document and don't worry about page numbering.
   (b) Insert section breaks and change the format of the page containing the table to landscape orientation.
   (c) Change the whole document to use landscape orientation.
   (d) Change margins to 0″ on the right and left.

10. What feature adds organization to your documents?
    (a) Print Preview
    (b) Orientation
    (c) Page Numbers
    (d) Find and Replace

...continued on Next Page

Multiple Choice Continued...

11. What might cause you to be unsuccessful in finding a specific block of text in your document?

(a) You are performing a case-sensitive search.

(b) You have specified formatting that is not used on the text.

(c) You are not using wildcard characters even though you are uncertain of the proper spelling of your target.

(d) All of the above.

12. Which action below is the result of using the AutoText feature?

(a) When you click the Print button on the Quick Access Toolbar, the document prints.

(b) When you select text, the Mini toolbar displays.

(c) When you press Ctrl+F, the Find dialog box displays.

(d) You start typing the date, a ScreenTip displays the date on the screen, and you press Enter to insert it.

13. If you cannot determine why a block of text starts at the top of the next page, which toggle switch should you invoke to view the formatting marks in use?

(a) Word wrap

(b) Show/Hide

(c) Bold font

(d) Caps Lock

14. If you use the margins feature frequently, what action should you take to make it more accessible?

(a) Use the Customization category of Word Options and add Margins to the Quick Access Toolbar.

(b) Use the Customization category of Word Options and add Margins to the Status bar.

(c) Use the Personalization category of Word Options and add Margins to the Quick Access Toolbar.

(d) No way exists to make it more accessible.

15. You are on page 4 of a five-page document. Which of the following is not a way to move the insertion point to the top of the first page?

(a) Press Ctrl+Home.

(b) Press Ctrl+G, type 1 in the Enter page number box, and click Go To.

(c) Press PageUp on the keyboard one time.

(d) Press Ctrl+F, click the Go To tab, type 1 in the Enter page number box, and click Go To.

16. What visual clue tells you a document is not in Word 2007 format?

(a) The status bar includes the text (Compatibility Mode).

(b) The file extension is .docx.

(c) The title bar is a different color.

(d) The title bar includes (Compatibility Mode) after the file name.

Practice Exercises

1 Impress a Potential Customer

Chapter 1 introduced you to many of the basic features and abilities of a word processor. In the following steps you use those tools to make modifications and enhancements to a letter that will be sent to a potential customer. It is important to write in a professional manner, even if the letter is casual. In this case you use Find and Replace to change a misspelled word. You also insert the date and a page number and observe the AutoCorrect feature as you misspell text while typing.

a. Start Word, if necessary, and open the *chap1_pe1_candle* document. Save the file as **chap1_pe1_candle_solution**.

b. Click **Replace** in the Editing group on the Home tab, and then type **cents** in the *Find what* box and type **Scents** in the *Replace with* box. Click **More**, if necessary, to display additional search options. **Click Find whole words only**, and then click **No Formatting**, if necessary, to remove format settings from the previous Find and Replace operation.

c. Click **Find Next** and click **Replace All** when the word is found. Click **OK** to close the dialog box that indicates Word has finished searching the document. Close the Find and Replace dialog box.

   The first sentence of the first paragraph contains the first occurrence of the word. You must select *Find whole words only* to prevent replacing the occurrences of *Scents* that are spelled correctly.

d. Move the insertion point to the left of the phrase that starts with *Take a look*. Press **Insert** to change into Insert mode, if necessary, and type the sentence **We offer teh above scented candles in four sizes, just right for any room.** As you enter the word *the*, type **teh** instead and watch as the spelling is automatically corrected.

e. Click the **Insert tab** and click **Page Number** in the Header and Footer group. Point to **Bottom of Page**, and select **Plain Number 2** from the gallery. Close Header and Footer.

f. Press **Ctrl** + **Home** to move the insertion point to the top of the page. Type the current month, then press **Enter** when the ScreenTip displays the full date.

   TROUBLESHOOTING: If you begin to type the date and the ScreenTip does not display, continue to manually type the current date.

g. Click the **View tab** and select **Full Screen Reading** in the Document Views group. Compare your document to Figure 1.40. Click **Close** to return to Print Layout view.

h. Click **Ctrl+S** to save the document. Click the **Office Button** and select **Close**.

...continued on Next Page

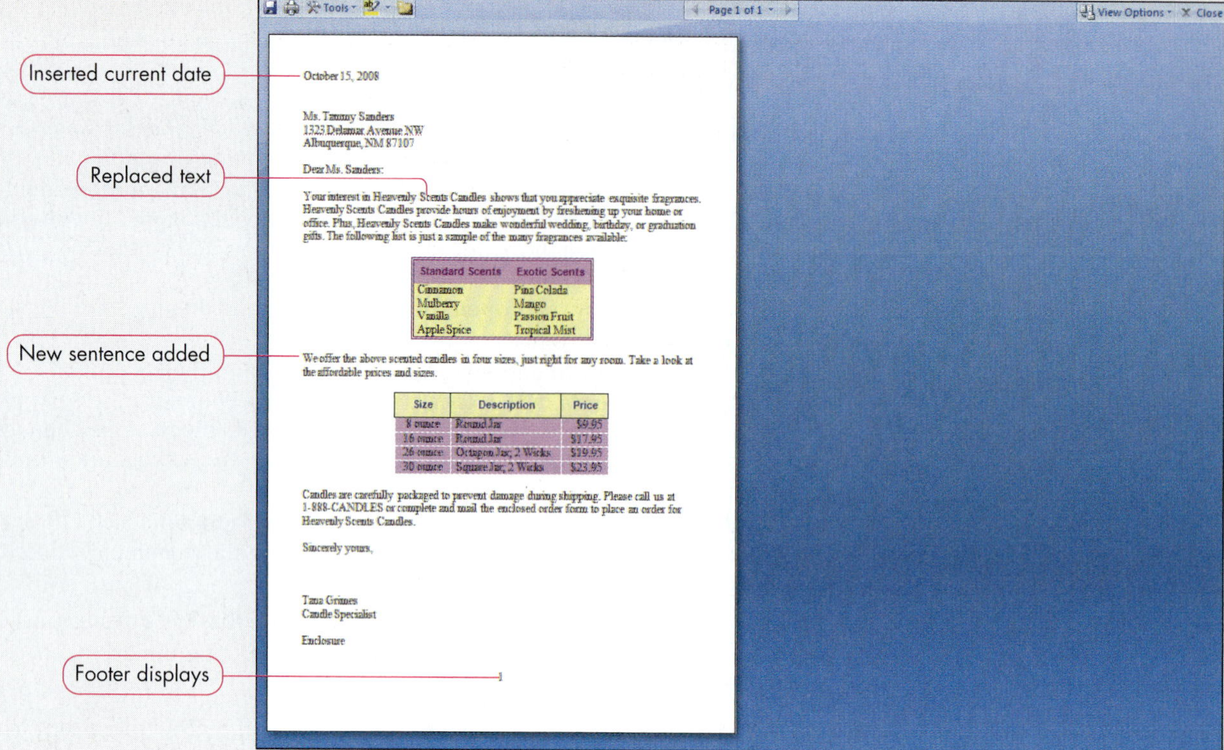

Figure 1.40 Updated Word Processing Document

2 Use Spelling and Grammar Check on a Memo

Mr. McGary, the Human Resources director of a medium-sized company, sends several memos each week to the employees in his company. It is important to communicate effectively with the employees, so he relies heavily on Word to locate errors in spelling, contextual spelling, and grammar as denoted by the wavy red, blue, and green lines, respectively. Even though Word contains these features, some mistakes may go unnoticed by the program. Mr. McGary, as well as anyone who uses a word processor, should always proofread documents carefully in addition to running the electronic spelling and grammar checkers. Your assignment is to correct the document so that it is error free and Mr. McGary can convey his message to employees without the distraction of poor spelling and grammar.

a. Open the *chap1_pe2_memo* document and save it as **chap1_pe2_memo_solution**.
b. Click the **Office Button** and click **Word Options** to display the Word Options dialog box. Click **Proofing** and click **Use contextual spelling**, if necessary, to enable that feature. Click **OK**.
c. Press **Ctrl+Home** to move to the beginning of the document. Click the **Review tab** and click **Spelling & Grammar** to check the document and correct errors. The first error displays in Figure 1.41. Use the following table to validate your corrections.

Error	**Correction**
Employeees	Employees
seminars are held inn the Cowboy Hat Hotel	seminars are held in the Cowboy Hat Hotel
managers have been instructed too allow employees in their department too attend	managers have been instructed to allow employees in their department to attend
Subrdinates	Subordinates
MEntoring	Mentoring
attend..	attend.

...continued on Next Page

d. Right-click the words *These seminars* in the last sentence of the first paragraph. Click **These seminars** to remove the extra space between the words if this error was not detected by the Spelling and Grammar checker.
e. Click the **Insert tab** and click **Footer** in the Header and Footer group. Click **Edit Footer** and select *John Q. Student*. Type your initials, then press **F3** to insert the AutoText entry that contains your name. Click **Close Header and Footer**.
f. Save and close the document.

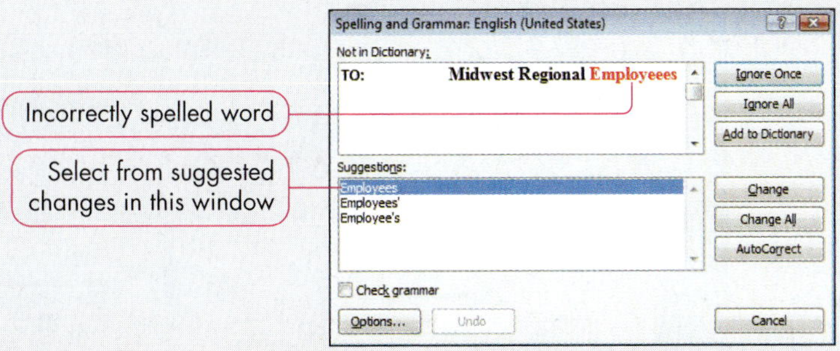

Figure 1.41 The Spell Check Process

3 Keyboard Shortcuts

Keyboard shortcuts are especially useful if you are a good typist because your hands can remain on the keyboard, as opposed to continually moving to and from the mouse. We never set out to memorize the shortcuts; we just learn them along the way as we continue to use Microsoft Office. It is much easier than you think, and the same shortcuts apply to multiple applications such as Microsoft Excel, PowerPoint, and Access.

a. Open the *chap1_pe3_shortcuts* document. Click the **Office Button** and select **Convert**. Save the document as **chap1_pe3_shortcuts_solution**, paying special attention that it is saved in Word format (*.docx).
b. Click the **Page Layout tab,** click **Margins** in the Page Setup group, and click **Normal**. Click **Orientation** and then click **Portrait**.
c. Click the **Home tab** and click **Show/Hide ¶** in the Paragraph group, if necessary, to display formatting marks.

   It will be helpful to see the formatting marks when you edit the document in the following steps.
d. Move the insertion point to the left side of the hard return mark at the end of the line containing Ctrl+B. Press **Ctrl+B,** then type the word **Bold**.
e. Move the insertion point to the left side of the hard return mark at the end of the line containing Ctrl+I. Press **Ctrl+I,** then type the word **Italic**.
f. Scroll to the bottom of the first page and place the insertion point on the left side of the title *Other Ctrl Keyboard Shortcuts*. Press **Ctrl+Enter** to insert a hard page break and keep the paragraph together on one page.
g. Click the **Insert tab**, click **Page Number** in the Header & Footer group, point to **Bottom of Page**, and select **Brackets 1** from the gallery.
h. Click **Header** in the Header & Footer group and select **Edit Header**. Click **Different First Page** in the Options group of the Design tab to insert a check mark. Place the insertion point in the header area of the second page and type **Keyboard Shortcuts**.

   Because you selected the *Different First Page* option, the header does not display on the first page as it is not needed there. However, the footer on the first page has been removed, so you will have to reinsert it.

...continued on Next Page

i. Move the insertion point to the first page footer. With the Design tab selected, click **Page Number** in the Header & Footer group, point to **Bottom of Page**, then select **Brackets 1** from the gallery. Click **Close Header and Footer**.

j. Click the **Zoom button** in the status bar, click **Many pages**, then drag to select **1 x 2 Pages**. Click **OK** to close the Zoom dialog box. Click **Show/Hide** ¶ in the Paragraph group on the Home tab to toggle off the formatting marks. Compare your document to Figure 1.42.

k. Save the document.

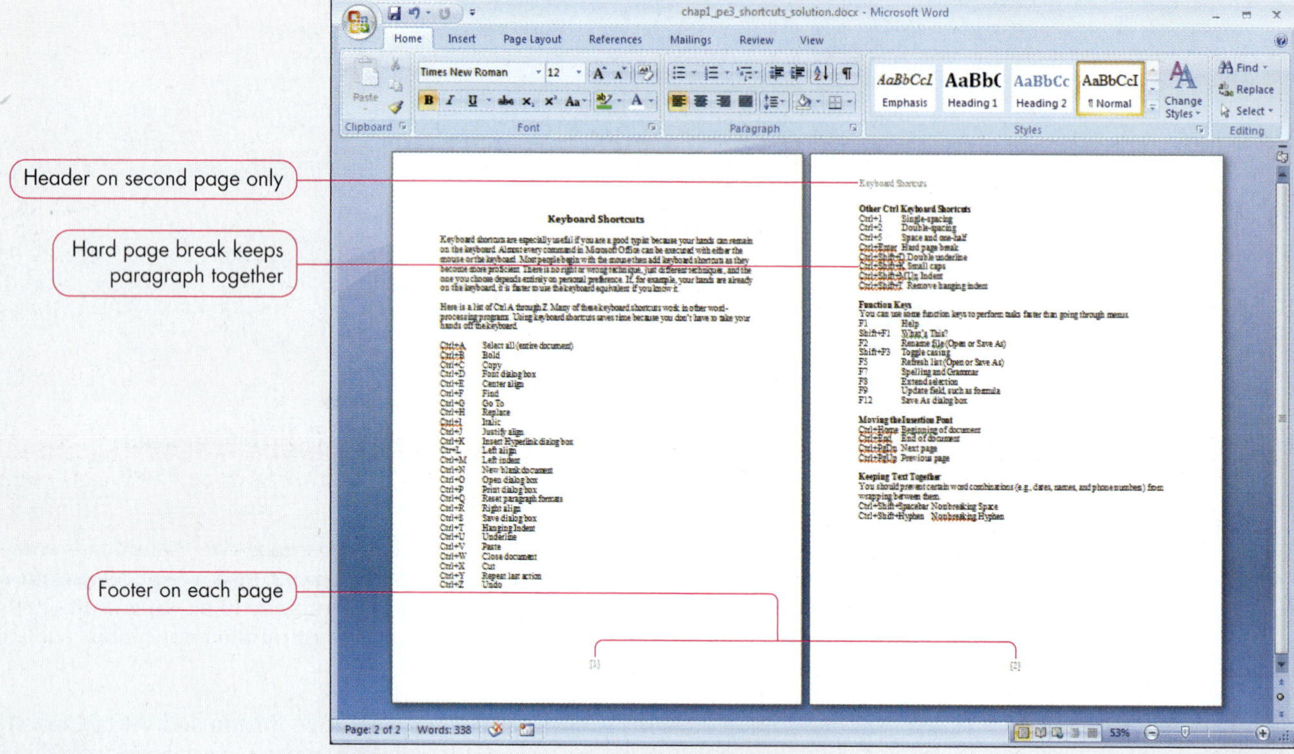

Figure 1.42 Keyboard Shortcut Document

4 Protecting Your System

The document you use in this exercise discusses computer viruses and backup procedures. It is not a question of *if* it will happen, but *when*—hard drives die, removable disks are lost, or viruses may infect a system. You can prepare for the inevitable by creating an adequate backup before the problem occurs. The advice in this document is very important; you should take it very seriously, and then protect yourself and your data.

a. Open the *chap1_pe4_virus* document and save it as **chap1_pe4_virus_solution**.

b. Click **Ctrl+H** to display the Find and Replace dialog box. In the *Find what* box, type **virus**. In the *Replace with* box, type **virus**. Click **More**, if necessary, then click the **Match case** check box.

c. Confirm that the *Replace with* text is selected or that the insertion point is in that box. Click **Format** at the bottom of the window and select **Font**. Click **Bold Italic** under the *Font Style* section, then click **OK**. Click **Replace All**, then click **OK** to confirm 17 replacements in the document. Click **Close** to remove the Find and Replace dialog box.

d. Scroll to the bottom of the first page and place the insertion point on the left side of the title *The Essence of Backup*. Press **Ctrl+Enter** to insert a hard page break. Position the insertion point at the end of the last paragraph on page 1 of the document, after the period that follows the word "programs," and press Delete two times.

   This step creates a more appropriate break and keeps the heading and content together on one page.

...continued on Next Page

e. Press **Ctrl+End** to move to the end of the document. Type your name, press **Enter**, type the name of your class, then use the mouse to select both lines of text. Click **Quick Parts** in the Text group on the **Insert tab**, then click **Save Selection to Quick Part Gallery**.

   The Create New Building Block dialog box displays, and you will add your name as an AutoText entry.

f. Replace your name in the *Name* box with the word **me**. Change the *Gallery* option to **AutoText**, and then click **OK**.

   Even though you replaced your name in the dialog box, the text that is highlighted in the document will be used when you invoke the AutoText feature.

g. Delete your name and course at the end of the document. Click **Page Number** in the Header & Footer group on the **Insert tab**, click **Bottom of Page**, and then click **Circle** from the gallery.

h. The insertion point is on the left margin of the footer. Type **Created by: me** and press **F3**.

   When you click F3, the AutoText entry should replace the text *me* with your name, and your class displays on the line below.

i. Click **Close Header and Footer**.

j. Click **Zoom** in the status bar, click **Many pages**, then drag to select **1 × 2 pages**. Click **OK** to close the Zoom dialog box. Click **Show/Hide ¶** in the Paragraph group on the Home tab to toggle off the formatting marks, if necessary. Compare your document to Figure 1.43.

k. Save the document. Click the **Office Button**, click **Prepare**, and then click **Run Compatibility Checker**.

   The results indicate that some text box positioning will change if opened in an older version of Word. It was good to check this before you save the document in Word 97–2003 format.

l. Click **OK** to close the Compatibility Checker window. Click the **Office Button**, click **Save As**, and select **Word 97–2003 Format**. Confirm the *Save as type* box displays Word 97–2003 document (*.doc), then click **Save**. Click **Continue** when the Compatibility Checker box shows the information you viewed previously.

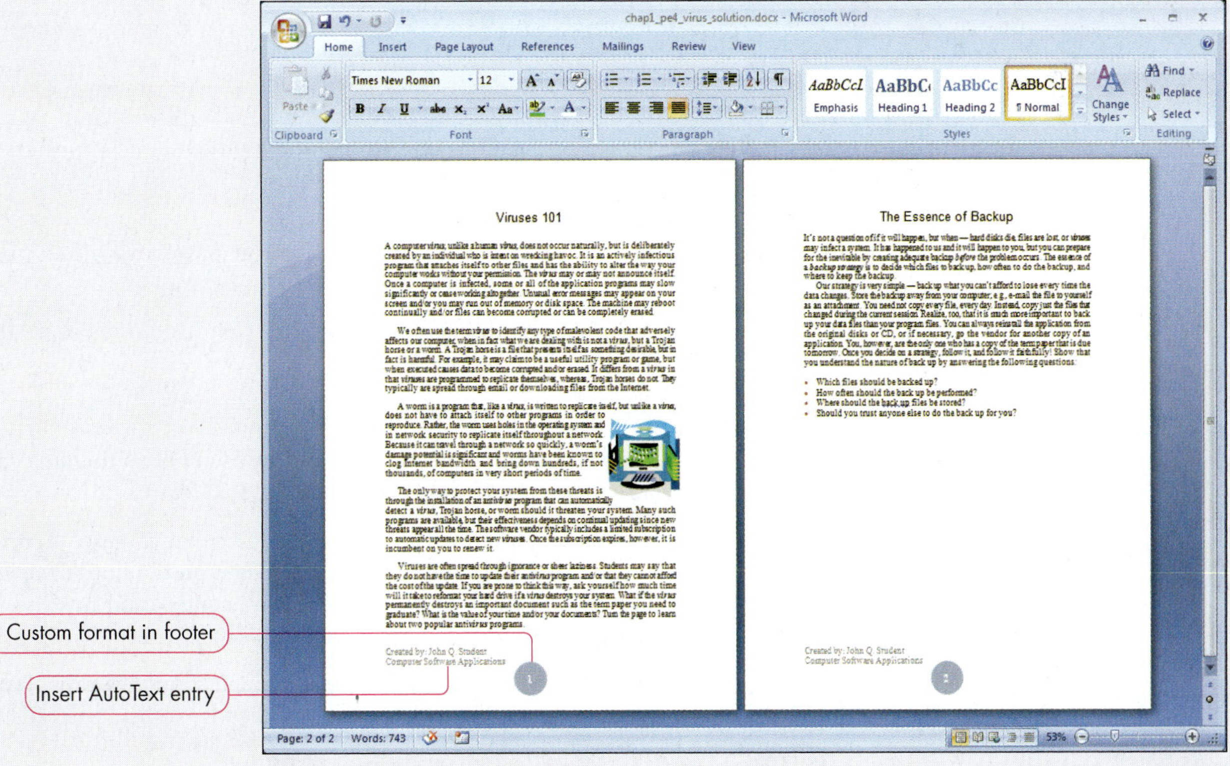

Figure 1.43 Protecting Your System

Mid-Level Exercises

1 Media-Blitz

Media-Blitz is a locally owned store that specializes in both new and used copies of popular music and movies. Its proximity to a local college campus provides a steady flow of customers during the school year. To increase sales during the typically slow summer season, it is offering discounts to students who have already enrolled in classes for the upcoming semester. You are working for the store this summer, and your assistance is needed to put the finishing touches on a flyer it wants to distribute in the area.

a. Open the *chap1_mid1_media* document and save it as **chap1_mid1_media_solution**.

b. Insert hard returns to create a list of discounts using the information below the first paragraph. Use the Mini toolbar to apply Bold and Center formatting to this group of items.

c. Perform a spelling and grammar check on the document to correct errors.

d. Create an AutoText entry for the name and address of the business. Name the entry Blitz. This entry will be useful in other documents you create for the business. Test the entry to make sure it works properly.

e. The school recently changed its name to Greene County Community College. Make appropriate changes in the flyer so each use of the name is updated and bolded.

f. Change to Full Screen Reading view, then change back to Print Layout view.

g. Display the document in the Print Preview window. Change orientation to Landscape.

h. Save and close the document.

2 Training Proposal

All About Training is an established computer training company that actively markets its services to the community. You have the opportunity to preview a document it will be sending to prospective clients and you notice several modifications that would add a professional appearance to the document. Use your skills to make the changes listed in the steps below.

a. Open the *chap1_mid2_proposal* document and save it as **chap1_mid2_proposal_solution**.

b. Insert a section break at the beginning of the document that forces the proposal to start on the second page.

c. Set 1″ margins on all sides of the whole document.

d. At the end of the last page, insert several hard returns, then type a line that says **Last Updated on:** and insert the current date using the AutoText feature.

e. Create a title page, without using the Cover Page feature, that contains a copy of the text *All About Training*. Use a 36 pt bold font and center it on the line. Type **Training Proposal** on the second line; use a 26 pt bold font, and center it on the line. Set 1.5″ margins on all sides for this page.

f. Display page numbers on the side margin. The title page should not display a page number, so page numbering should begin on the second page. (Hint: you must change a setting in the Header and Footer Design tab.)

...continued on Next Page

g. Replace each instance of the company name to display in bold, italic, and red font color. Allow the replacement only when it appears in a paragraph, not in the banner that appears at the top of the document.

h. Perform a spelling and grammar check on the document.

i. Save the document in both Word 2007 and Word 97–2003 formats so it will be available for prospective clients regardless of the version of Word they use. Close all documents.

3 Fundraiser

The organizer of a craft fair has contacted your school to request permission to conduct a fundraiser. Your work in the office of College Relations includes returning the responses from administrators on matters such as this. The response letter has been drafted, and you will complete the letter by adding the recipient's name and address; then you create an envelope in which to mail it.

a. Open a blank document and type your name on a blank line. Use your name to create a Building Block AutoText entry.

b. Open the *chap1_mid3_letter* document and save it as **chap1_mid3_letter_solution**.

c. Move the insertion point to the bottom of the letter and replace the text *Your Name Here* with your name using the AutoText entry you created in the first step.

d. Insert a Next Page Section Break at the end of the letter and apply landscape orientation to the second page.

e. Confirm that the headers and footers in the second section are not linked to the first section. Then use the AutoText entry to insert your name in the header.

f. Use copy and paste to insert the recipient's name and address from the letter in the second section. Center the address so it resembles an envelope.

g. Save and close the document.

4 Heart Disease Prevention

Millions of people suffer from heart disease and other cardiac-related illnesses. Of those people, several million will suffer a heart attack each year. Your mother volunteers for the American Heart Association and has brought you a document that explains what causes a heart attack, the signs of an attack, and what you can do to reduce your risk of having one. The information in the document is very valuable, but she needs you to put the finishing touches on this document before she circulates it in the community.

a. Open the *chap1_mid4_heart* document and save it as **chap1_mid4_heart_solution**.

b. Convert the solution file so it does not open in Compatibility Mode.

c. Create a cover page for the report. Use **Tiles** in the cover page gallery. Add text where necessary to display the report title and subtitle (use *What You Should Know* as the subtitle), and your name as author. Delete any unused fields on the cover page.

d. Change the document margins to .75″ on all sides.

e. Create a section page break between the cover page and the first page of the report. Set appropriate options to prevent a footer from displaying on the cover page. A page number should display at the bottom of the remaining pages, and you should display the number one on the first page of the report that follows the cover page.

...continued on Next Page

f. Create a header that displays the report title. It should not display on the cover or first page of the report (the page that follows the cover page). Confirm that the headers and footers in the second section are not linked to the first section.

g. Toggle the Show/Hide ¶ feature on, then select Draft view. Remove any page breaks that cause the report data to display on separate pages. Do not remove the section page break that immediately follows the cover page. View the document in Print Layout view and insert page breaks where necessary to prevent a paragraph or list from breaking across pages.

h. You are investing a lot of time in this project, so confirm that Word is performing backups every 5 minutes using the Word Options.

i. Save and close the document.

Capstone Exercise

After a hard week of work, you decide to enjoy the great outdoors by taking a canoe trip with your friends. Your friend researched the Buffalo National River and e-mailed you a document that describes the activities and preparations needed before visiting the area. You want to send the information to others who will accompany you on the trip, but the document needs some formatting modifications.

Spelling and Grammar

The first thing you notice about the report is the number of spelling and grammatical errors detected by Word. You will fix those as well as correct all references to the river that omit its status as a National River.

a. Open the file *chap1_cap_buffalo* document, found in the Exploring Word folder. Save the document as **chap1_cap_buffalo_solution**.

b. Display the document in Full Screen Reading view. Use the navigation tool to view each page. Return to Print Layout view.

c. Display the Word Options dialog box and engage the Contextual Spelling feature if it is not already in use.

d. Run the spell checker, and correct grammar and contextual spelling errors also.

e. Replace all occurrences of *Buffalo River* with **Buffalo National River**. When you make the replacements, add a bold font.

Revise Page Layout

When you zoom out to view multiple pages of the document, you notice that several lines and paragraphs break at odd places. Use formatting tools and page layout options to improve the readability of this file. Take special consideration of the picture on the last page; it seems to be too wide to display on a standard page.

a. Change the Zoom to 50% and determine where the content makes awkward breaks. Click Show/Hide ¶, if necessary, to display formatting marks that will assist you in determining which format options are in use.

b. Remove any unnecessary hard returns that interfere with word wrapping in the first paragraph.

c. Adjust margins to use the Normal setting (1″ on each side). Insert hard page breaks where necessary to keep paragraphs together.

d. Create a footer that displays page numbers. Select the **Annual** format for the page numbers.

e. Insert a Next Page Section break before the picture of the river. Change the orientation of the last page so the whole picture displays on the page.

Save in Multiple Formats

After improving the readability of the document, you remember that it has not yet been saved. Saving work is very important, and you will save it immediately. Since you will be sharing the document with friends, you also decide to save it in a format compatible with older versions.

a. Save the document again as **chap1_cap_buffalo2_solution**, then run the Compatibility Checker and Document Inspector, but do not take any suggested actions at this time.

b. Save the document in Word 97–2003 format.

c. Use the Print Preview feature to view the document before printing. Do not print unless instructed to by your teacher.

Mini Cases

Use the rubric following the case as a guide to evaluate your work, but keep in mind that your instructor may impose additional grading criteria or use a different standard to judge your work.

Letter of Appreciation

GENERAL CASE

Have you taken time to think about the people who have helped you get to where you are? For some, parents have provided encouragement and financial assistance so their children can enjoy the privileges of a higher education. Many other students receive the moral support of family but are financing their education personally. Regardless of how your education is funded, there are people who deserve your appreciation. Take this opportunity to write a letter that you can send to those people. In the letter you can give an update on your classes, tell them about your future plans, and don't forget to express your appreciation for their support. Create an attractive document using skills learned in this chapter, then save your letter as **chap1_mc1_appreciate_solution**.

Performance Elements	Exceeds Expectations	Meets Expectations	Below Expectations
Completeness	Document contains all required elements.	Document contains most required elements.	Document contains elements not specified in instructions.
Page setup	Modified or added at least three Page Layout elements.	Modified or added at least two Page Layout elements.	Did not modify or add any Page Layout elements.
Accuracy	No errors in spelling, grammar, or punctuation were found.	Fewer than two errors in spelling, grammar, or punctuation were found.	More than two errors in spelling, grammar, or punctuation were found.

Animal Concerns

RESEARCH CASE

As the population of family pets continues to grow, it is imperative that we learn how to be responsible pet owners. Very few people take the time to perform thorough research on the fundamental care of and responsibility for animal populations. Open the *chap1_mc2_animal* document and proceed to search the Internet for information that will contribute to this report on animal care and concerns. Compare information from at least three sources. Give consideration to information that is copyrighted and do not reprint it. Any information used should be cited in the document. As you enter the information and sources into the document, you will be reminded of concepts learned in Chapter 1 such as word wrap and soft returns. Use your knowledge of other formatting techniques, such as hard returns, page numbers, and margin settings, to create an attractive document. Create a cover page for the document, perform a spell check, and view the print preview before submitting this assisnment to your instructor. Create headers and/or footers to improve readability. Name your completed document **chap1_mc2_animal_solution**.

Performance Elements	Exceeds Expectations	Meets Expectations	Below Expectations
Research	All sections were completed with comprehensive information and citations.	All sections were updated but with minimal information and no citations.	Sections were not updated, no citations were given.
Page setup	Modified or added at least three Page Layout elements.	Modified or added at least two Page Layout elements.	Did not modify or add any Page Layout elements.
Accuracy	No errors in spelling, grammar, or punctuation were found.	Fewer than two errors in spelling, grammar, or punctuation were found.	More than two errors in spelling, grammar, or punctuation were found.

TMG Newsletter

DISASTER RECOVERY

The *chap1_mc3_tmgnews* document was started by an office assistant, but she quickly gave up on it after she moved paragraphs around until it became unreadable. The document contains significant errors, which cause the newsletter to display in a very disjointed way. Use your knowledge of Page Layout options and other Word features to revise this newsletter in time for the monthly mailing. Save your work as **chap1_mc3_tmgnews_solution**.

Performance Elements	Exceeds Expectations	Meets Expectations	Below Expectations
Page setup	Modified Page Layout options in such a way that newsletter displays on one page.	Few Page Layout modifications applied; newsletter displays on more than one page.	No Page Layout modifications applied; newsletter displays on more than one page.
Accuracy	No errors in spelling, grammar, or punctuation were found.	Fewer than two errors in spelling, grammar, or punctuation were found.	More than two errors in spelling, grammar, or punctuation were found.

chapter 2 | **Word**

Gaining Proficiency

Editing and Formatting

After you read this chapter, you will be able to:

1. Apply font attributes through the Font dialog box **(page 133)**.
2. Highlight text **(page 136)**.
3. Control word-wrapping with nonbreaking hyphens and nonbreaking spaces **(page 137)**.
4. Copy formats with the Format Painter **(page 139)**.
5. Set off paragraphs with tabs, borders, lists, and columns **(page 143)**.
6. Apply paragraph formats **(page 148)**.
7. Create and modify styles **(page 159)**.
8. Create a table of contents **(page 171)**.
9. Create an index **(page 171)**.

Hands-On Exercises

Exercises	Skills Covered
1. CHARACTER FORMATTING (page 140) **Open:** chap2_ho1_description.docx **Save as:** chap2_ho1_description_solution.docx	• Change Text Appearance • Insert Nonbreaking Spaces and Nonbreaking Hyphens • Highlight Text and Use Format Painter
2. PARAGRAPH FORMATTING (page 152) **Open:** chap2_ho1_description_solution.docx (from Exercise 1) **Save as:** chap2_ho2_description_solution.docx (additional modifications)	• Set Tabs in a Footer • Select Text to Format • Specify Line Spacing, Justification, and Pagination • Indent Text • Apply Borders and Shading • Change Column Structure • Insert a Section Break and Create Columns
3. STYLES (page 164) **Open:** chap2_ho3_gd.docx **Save as:** chap2_ho3_gd_solution.docx	• Apply Style Properties • Modify the Body Text Style • Modify the Heading 3 Style • Select the Outline View • Create a Paragraph Style • Create a Character Style • View the Completed Document
4. REFERENCE PAGES (page 173) **Open:** chap2_ho3_gd_solution.docx (from Exercise 3) **Save as:** chap2_ho4_gd_solution.docx (additional modifications)	• Apply a Style • Insert a Table of Contents • Define an Index Entry • Create the Index • Complete the Index • View the Completed Document

CASE STUDY

Treyserv-Pitkin Enterprises

Treyserv, a consumer products manufacturing company, has recently acquired a competitor, paving the way for a larger, stronger company poised to meet the demands of the market. Each year Treyserv generates a corporate annual report and distributes it to all employees and stockholders. You are the executive assistant to the president of Treyserv and your responsibilities include preparing and distributing the corporate annual report. This year the report emphasizes the importance of acquiring Pitkin Industries to form Treyserv-Pitkin Enterprises.

Case Study

As with most mergers or acquisitions, the newly created Treyserv-Pitkin organization will enable management to make significant changes to establish a more strategic and profitable company. Management will focus on reorganizing both companies to eliminate duplication of efforts and reduce expenses; it will reduce long-term debt when possible and combine research and development activities. The annual report always provides a synopsis of recent changes to upper management, and this year it will introduce a new Chair and Chief Executive Officer, Mr. Dewey A. Larson. The company also hired Ms. Amanda Wray as chief financial officer; both positions are very high profile and contribute to the stockholders' impression of the company's continued success. Information about these newly appointed executives and other financial data have been gathered, but the report needs to be formatted attractively before it can be distributed to employees and stockholders.

Your Assignment

- Read the chapter, paying special attention to sections that describe how to apply styles, create a table of contents, and create an index.
- Open the document, *chap2_case_treyserv*, which contains the unformatted report that was provided to you by the president of the company.
- Add format features such as borders and shading, line spacing, justification, paragraph indention, and bullet and number lists to enhance the appearance of information in the report.
- Use tabs or columns, when appropriate, to align information in the report.
- Use predefined styles, such as Heading 1 and Heading 2, to format paragraph headings throughout the document.
- Apply paragraph formats such as widow/orphan control to prevent text from wrapping awkwardly when it spans from one page to the next.
- Add a table of contents and page numbering to assist readers in locating information.
- Save your work in a document named **chap2_case_treyserv_solution**.

Text Formatting

The ultimate success of any document depends greatly on its appearance. Typeface should reinforce the message without calling attention to itself and should be consistent with the information you want to convey.

The arrangement and appearance of printed matter is called ***typography***. You also may define it as the process of selecting typefaces, type styles, and type sizes. The importance of these decisions is obvious, for the ultimate success of any document depends greatly on its appearance. Typeface should reinforce the message without calling attention to itself and should be consistent with the information you want to convey. For example, a paper prepared for a professional purpose, such as a résumé, should use a standard typeface and abstain from using one that looks funny or cute. Additionally, you want to minimize the variety of typefaces in a document to maintain a professional look.

Typography is the appearance of printed matter.

A ***typeface*** or ***font*** is a complete set of characters.

A ***serif typeface*** contains a thin line at the top and bottom of characters.

A ***sans serif typeface*** does not contain thin lines on characters.

A ***typeface*** or ***font*** is a complete set of characters—upper- and lowercase letters, numbers, punctuation marks, and special symbols. A definitive characteristic of any typeface is the presence or absence of thin lines that end the main strokes of each letter. A ***serif typeface*** contains a thin line or extension at the top and bottom of the primary strokes on characters. A ***sans serif typeface*** (sans from the French for without) does not contain the thin lines on characters. Times New Roman is an example of a serif typeface. Arial is a sans serif typeface.

Serifs help the eye to connect one letter with the next and generally are used with large amounts of text. The paragraphs in this book, for example, are set in a serif typeface. A sans serif typeface is more effective with smaller amounts of text such as titles, headlines, corporate logos, and Web pages. For example, the red heading *Text Formatting* and the pull quote by the first paragraph on this page are set in a sans serif font.

A ***monospaced typeface*** uses the same amount of horizontal space for every character.

A ***proportional typeface*** allocates horizontal space to the character.

Type style is the characteristic applied to a font, such as bold.

A second characteristic of a typeface is whether it is monospaced or proportional. A ***monospaced*** typeface (such as Courier New) uses the same amount of horizontal space for every character regardless of its width. A ***proportional*** typeface (such as Times New Roman or Arial) allocates space according to the width of the character. For example, the lowercase *m* is wider than the lowercase *i*. Monospaced fonts are used in tables and financial projections where text must be precisely lined up, one character underneath the other. Proportional typefaces create a more professional appearance and are appropriate for most documents, such as research papers, status reports, and letters. You can set any typeface in different ***type styles*** such as regular, **bold**, *italic*, or ***bold italic***.

In this section, you apply font attributes through the Font dialog box, change casing, and highlight text so that it stands out. You also control word wrapping by inserting nonbreaking hyphens and nonbreaking spaces between words. Finally, you copy formats using the Format Painter.

Applying Font Attributes Through the Font Dialog Box

In the Office Fundamentals chapter, you learned how to use the Font group on the Home tab to apply font attributes. The Font group contains commands to change the font, font size, and font color; and apply bold, italic, and underline. In addition to applying commands from the Font group, you can display the Font dialog box if you click the Font Launcher, the small icon in the right corner in the Font group, to give you complete control over the typeface, size, and style of the text in a document. Making selections in the Font dialog box before entering text sets the format of the text as you type. You also can change the font of existing text by selecting the text and then applying the desired attributes from the Font dialog box as shown in Figure 2.1.

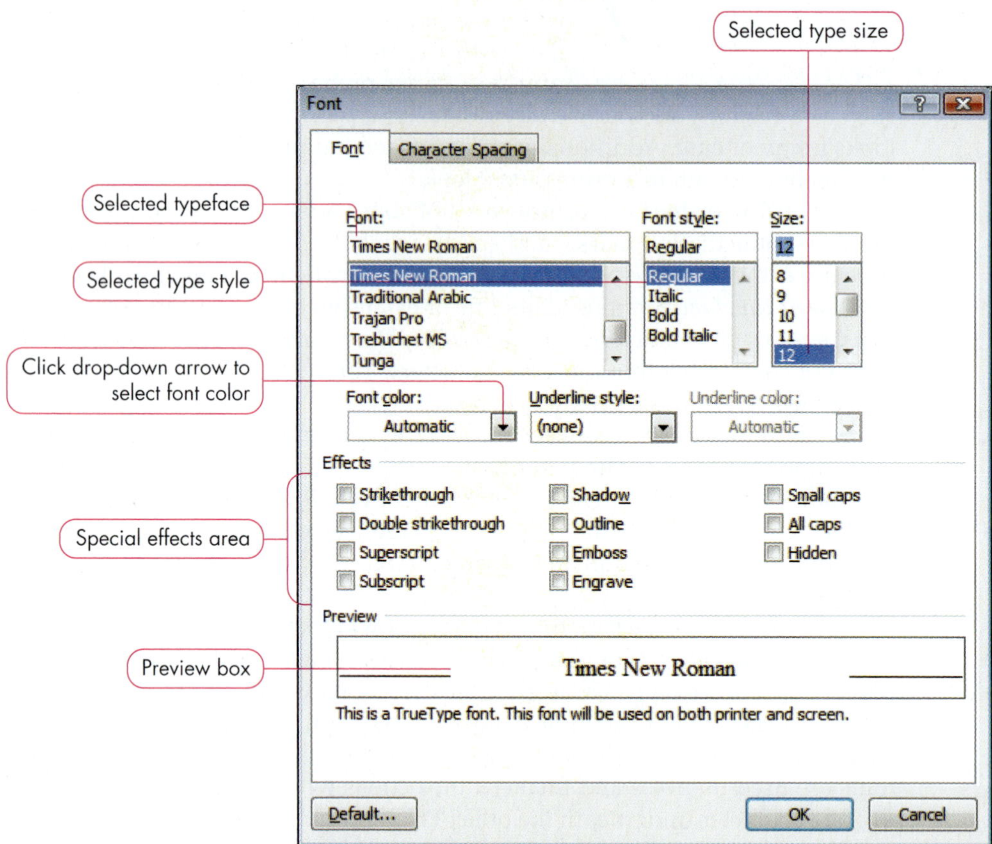

Figure 2.1 Font Dialog Box

Change Text Case (Capitalization)

Use ***Change Case*** to change capitalization of text.

To quickly change the capitalization of text in a document use ***Change Case*** in the Font group on the Home tab. When you click Change Case, the following list of options display:

- **Sentence case.** (capitalizes only the first word of the sentence or phrase)
- **lowercase** (changes the text to lowercase)
- **UPPERCASE** (changes the text to all capital letters)
- **Capitalize Each Word** (capitalizes the first letter of each word; effective for formatting titles, but remember to lowercase first letters of short prepositions, such as *of*)
- **tOGGLE cASE** (changes lowercase to uppercase and uppercase to lowercase)

This feature is useful when generating a list and you want to use the same case formatting for each item. If you do not select text first, the casing format will take effect on the text where the insertion point is located. You can toggle among uppercase, lowercase, and sentence case formats by pressing Shift+F3.

Select Font Options

In addition to changing the font, font style, and size, you can apply other font attributes to text. Although the Font group on the Home tab contains special effects commands such as strikethrough, subscript, and superscript, the *Effects* section in the Font tab in the Font dialog box contains a comprehensive set of options for applying color and special effects, such as SMALL CAPS, ^{superscripts}, or $_{\text{subscripts}}$. Table 2.1 lists and defines more of these special effects. You also can change the underline options and indicate if spaces are to be underlined or just words. You can even change the color of the text and underline.

Table 2.1 Font Effects

Effect	Description	Example
Strikethrough	Displays a horizontal line through the middle of the text	~~strikethrough~~
Superscript	Displays text in a smaller size and raised above the baseline	Super^{script}
Subscript	Displays text in a smaller size and lowered below the baseline	Sub$_{\text{script}}$
Shadow	Displays text with a 3D shadow effect	Shadow
Emboss	Displays text as if it has been raised from the page	Emboss
Engrave	Displays text as if it has been pressed down into the page	Engrave
Small caps	Displays letters as uppercase but smaller than regular-sized uppercase letters	SMALL CAPS

Hidden text does not appear onscreen.

TIP Hidden Text

Hidden text is document text that does not appear on screen, unless you click Show/Hide ¶ in the Paragraph group on the Home tab. You can use this special effect format to hide confidential information before printing documents for other people. For example, an employer can hide employees' Social Security numbers before printing a company roster.

Set Character Spacing

Character spacing is the horizontal space between characters.

Character spacing refers to the amount of horizontal space between characters. Although most character spacing is acceptable, some character combinations appear too far apart or too close together in large-sized text when printed. If so, you might want to adjust for this spacing discrepancy. The Character Spacing tab in the Font dialog box contains options in which you manually control the spacing between characters. The Character Spacing tab shown in Figure 2.2 displays four options for adjusting character spacing: Scale, Spacing, Position, and Kerning.

Scale increases or decreases text as a percentage of its size.

Scale increases or decreases the text horizontally as a percentage of its size; it does not change the vertical height of text. You may use the scale feature on justified text, which does not produce the best-looking results—adjust the scale by a low percentage (90%–95%) to improve text flow without a noticeable difference to the reader.

You may select the *Expanded* option to stretch a word or sentence so it fills more space; for example, use it on a title you want to span across the top of a page. The *Condensed* option is useful to squeeze text closer together, such as when you want to prevent one word from wrapping to another line.

Position raises or lowers text from the baseline.

Kerning allows more even spacing between characters.

Position raises or lowers text from the baseline without creating superscript or subscript size. Use this feature when you want text to stand out from other text on the same line; or use it to create a fun title by raising and/or lowering every few letters. ***Kerning*** automatically adjusts spacing between characters to achieve a more evenly spaced appearance. Kerning primarily allows letters to fit closer together, especially when a capital letter can use space unoccupied by a lowercase letter beside it. For example, you can kern the letters *Va* so the top of the *V* extends into the empty space above the *a* instead of leaving an awkward gap between them.

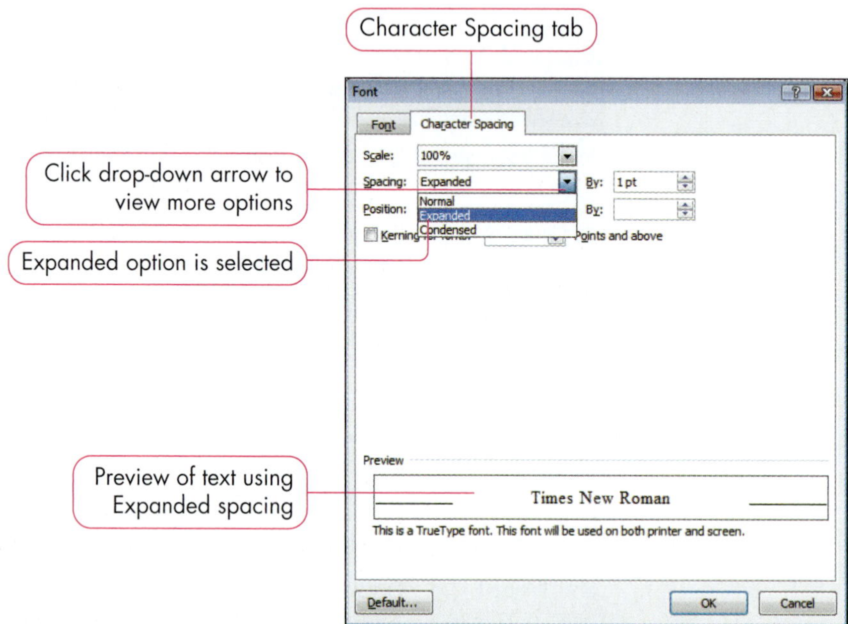

Figure 2.2 Character Spacing Tab in the Font Dialog Box

Highlighting Text

Use the ***Highlighter*** to mark text that you want to locate easily.

People often use a highlighting marker to highlight important parts of textbooks, magazine articles, and other documents. In Word you use the ***Highlighter*** to mark text that you want to stand out or locate easily. Highlighted text draws the reader's attention to important information within the documents you create, as illustrated in Figure 2.3. The Text Highlight Color command is located in the Font group on the Home tab and also on the Mini toolbar. You can click Text Highlight Color before or after selecting text. When you click Text Highlight Color before selecting text, the mouse pointer resembles a pen that you can click and drag across text to highlight it. The feature stays on so you can highlight additional text. When you finish highlighting text, press Esc to turn it off. If you select text first, click Text Highlight Color to apply the color. To remove highlights, select the highlighted text, click the Text Highlight Color arrow, and choose No Color.

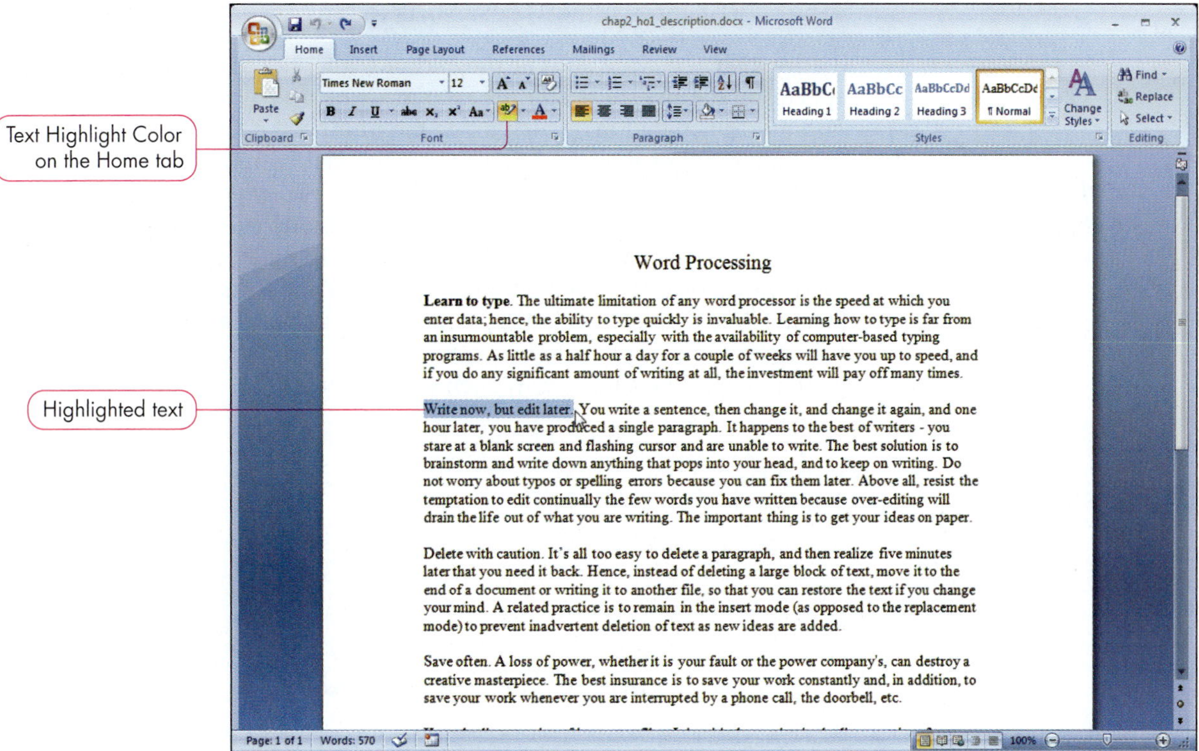

Figure 2.3 The Highlight Tool

If you use a color printer, you see the highlight colors on your printout. If you use a monochrome printer, the highlight appears in shades of gray. Be sure that you can easily read the text with the gray highlight. If not, select a lighter highlight color, and print your document again. You can create a unique highlighting effect by choosing a dark highlight color, such as Dark Blue, and applying a light font color, such as White.

TIP Impose a Time Limit

Word 2007 is supposed to save time and make you more productive. It will do exactly that, provided you use Word for its primary purpose—writing and editing. It is all too easy, however, to lose sight of that objective and spend too much time formatting the document. Concentrate on the content of your document rather than its appearance and remember that the success of a document ultimately depends on its content. Impose a limit on the amount of time you will spend on formatting.

Controlling Word Wrapping with Nonbreaking Hyphens and Nonbreaking Spaces

In Word, text wraps to the next line when the current line of text is full. Most of the time, the way words wrap is acceptable. Occasionally, however, text may wrap in an undesirable location. To improve the readability of text, you need to proofread word-wrapping locations and insert special characters. Two general areas of concern are hyphenated words and spacing within proper nouns.

Insert Nonbreaking Hyphens

A ***nonbreaking hyphen*** prevents a word from becoming separated at the hyphen.

If a hyphenated word falls at the end of a line, the first word and the hyphen may appear on the first line, and the second word may wrap to the next line. However, certain hyphenated text, such as phone numbers, should stay together to improve the readability of the text. To keep hyphenated words together, replace the regular hyphen with a nonbreaking hyphen. A ***nonbreaking hyphen*** keeps text on both sides of the hyphen together, thus preventing the hyphenated word from becoming separated at the hyphen, as shown in Figure 2.4. To insert a nonbreaking hyphen, press Ctrl+Shift+Hyphen. When you click Show/Hide ¶ in the Paragraph group on the Home tab to display formatting symbols, a regular hyphen looks like a hyphen, and a nonbreaking hyphen appears as a wider hyphen. However, the nonbreaking hyphen looks like a regular hyphen when printed.

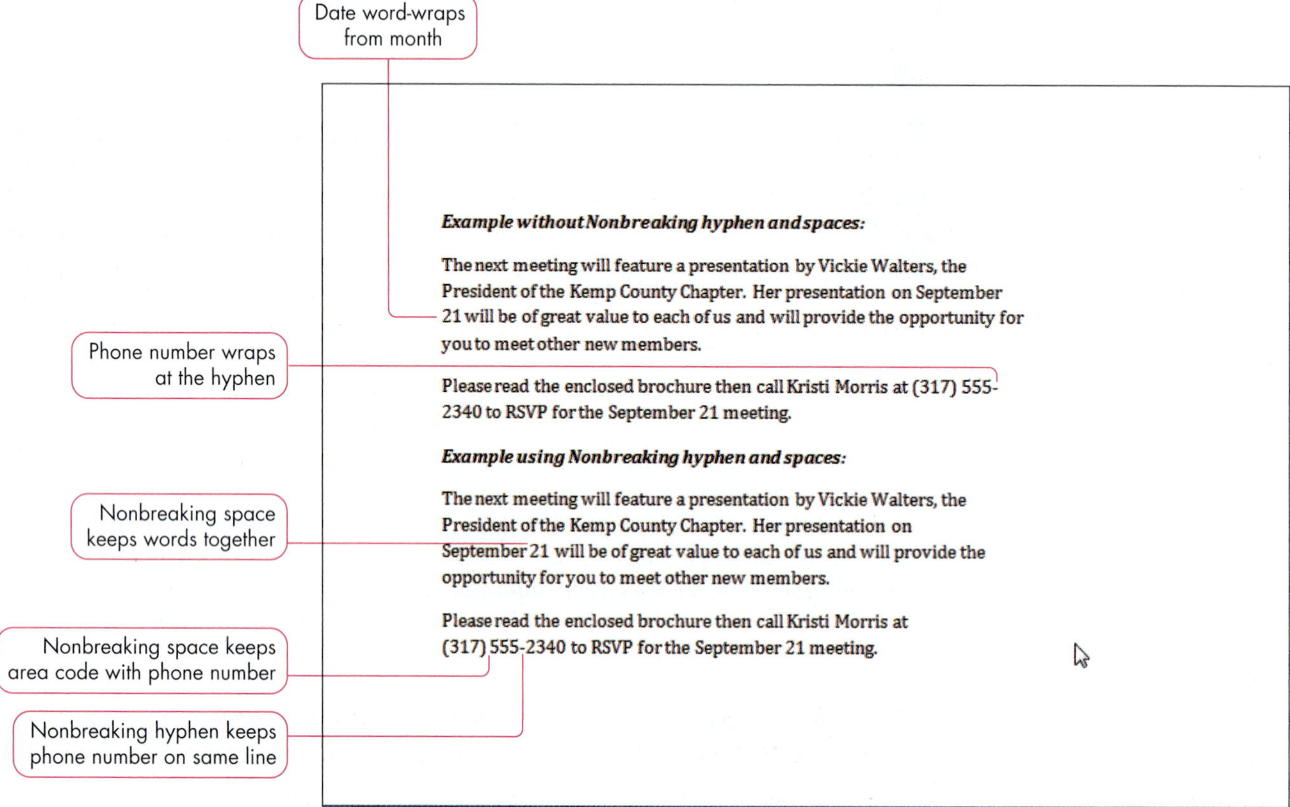

Figure 2.4 Nonbreaking Hyphens and Spaces

Insert Nonbreaking Spaces

A ***nonbreaking space*** keeps two or more words together on a line.

Because text will wrap to the next line if a word does not fit at the end of the current line, occasionally word-wrapping between certain types of words is undesirable; that is, some words should be kept together for improved readability. For example, the date *March 31* should stay together instead of word-wrapping after March. Other items that should stay together include names, such as *Ms. Stevenson*, and page references, such as *page 15*. To prevent words from separating due to the word-wrap feature, you can insert a ***nonbreaking space***—a special character that keeps two or more words together. To insert a nonbreaking space, press Ctrl+Shift+Spacebar between the two words that you want to keep together. If a space already exists, the result of pressing the Spacebar, you should delete it before you insert the nonbreaking space.

Copying Formats with the Format Painter

Use the ***Format Painter*** to copy existing text formats to other text.

You should format similar headings and text within a document with the same formatting. However, it is time-consuming to select every heading individually and apply the desired format (such as bold, underline, and font color). You can use the ***Format Painter*** to copy existing text formats to other text to ensure consistency. Using the Format Painter helps you improve your efficiency because you spend less time copying multiple formats rather than applying individual formats to each heading or block of text one at a time. When you single-click Format Painter in the Clipboard group on the Home tab, you can copy the formats only one time, then Word turns off Format Painter. When you double-click Format Painter, it stays activated so you can format an unlimited amount of text. To turn off Format Painter, click Format Painter once or press Esc.

You can use Format Painter to . . . ensure consistency . . . and improve your efficiency by spending less time copying multiple formats rather than applying individual formats to each heading or block of text one at a time.

Display Nonprinting Formatting Marks

As you type text, Word inserts nonprinting marks or symbols. While these symbols do not display on printouts, they do affect the appearance. For example, Word inserts a "code" every time you press Spacebar, Tab, and Enter. The paragraph mark ¶ at the end of a paragraph does more than just indicate the presence of a hard return. It also stores all of the formatting in effect for the paragraph. To preserve the formatting when you move or copy a paragraph, you must include the paragraph mark in the selected text. Click Show/Hide ¶ in the Paragraph group on the Home tab to display the paragraph mark and make sure it has been selected. Table 2.2 lists several common formatting marks. Both the hyphen and nonbreaking hyphen look like a regular hyphen when printed.

Table 2.2 Nonprinting Symbols

Symbol	Description	Create by
•	Regular space	Pressing Spacebar
°	Nonbreaking space	Pressing Ctrl+Shift+Spacebar
-	Regular hyphen	Pressing Hyphen
—	Nonbreaking hyphen	Pressing Ctrl+Shift+Hyphen
→	Tab	Pressing Tab
¶	End of paragraph	Pressing Enter
. . .	Hidden text	Selecting Hidden check box in Font dialog box
↵	Line break	Pressing Shift+Enter

Hands-On Exercises

1 | Character Formatting

Skills covered: 1. Change Text Appearance **2.** Insert Nonbreaking Spaces and Nonbreaking Hyphens **3.** Highlight Text and Use Format Painter

Step 1 Change Text Appearance

Refer to Figure 2.5 as you complete Step 1.

a. Start Word. Open the *chap2_ho1_description* document in the **Exploring Word folder** and save it as **chap2_ho1_description_solution**.

You must select the text for which you want to adjust the character spacing.

b. Select the heading *Word Processing*, then click the **Font Dialog Box Launcher** in the Font group on the Home tab.

The Font dialog box displays with the Font tab options.

c. Click the **Character Spacing tab** and click the **Spacing drop-down arrow**. Select **Expanded** and notice how the text changes in the preview box. Click **OK**.

Word expands the spacing between letters in the heading *Word Processing*, as shown in Figure 2.5.

d. Save the document.

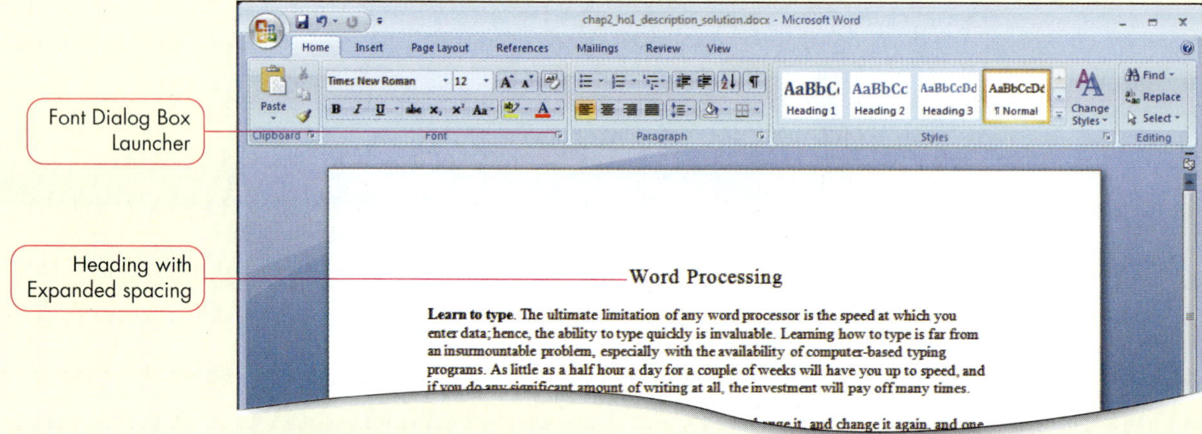

Figure 2.5 Text Formatting

Step 2 Insert Nonbreaking Spaces and Nonbreaking Hyphens

Refer to Figure 2.6 as you complete Step 2.

a. Place the insertion point between the words *you stare* in the third sentence of the second paragraph.

Before inserting a nonbreaking space, you must position the insertion point between the two words you want to keep together.

b. Delete the existing space, and then press **Ctrl+Shift+Spacebar** to insert a non-breaking space.

The nonbreaking space keeps the words *you stare* together, preventing word wrapping between the two words.

c. Select the hyphen between the text *five-minute* in the third sentence of the sixth paragraph. Delete the hyphen, and then press **Ctrl+Shift+Hyphen** to insert a nonbreaking hyphen, as shown in Figure 2.6.

TROUBLESHOOTING: If text continues word-wrapping between two words after you insert a nonbreaking space or nonbreaking hyphen, click Show/Hide ¶ in the Paragraph group on the Home tab to display symbols and then identify and delete regular spaces or hyphens that still exist between words.

d. Save the document.

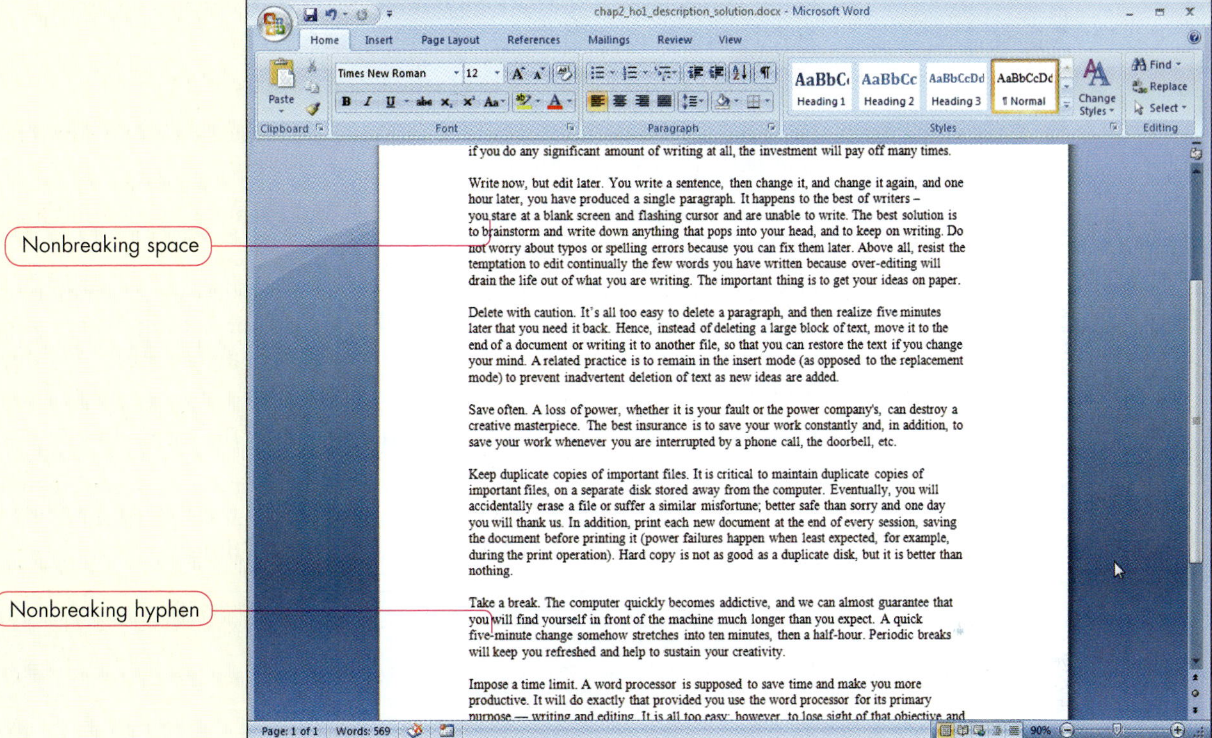

Figure 2.6 Nonbreaking Characters

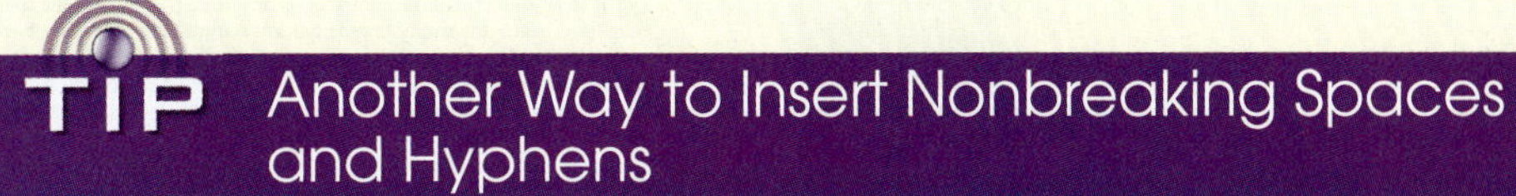

TIP Another Way to Insert Nonbreaking Spaces and Hyphens

An alternative to using keyboard shortcuts to insert nonbreaking spaces and hyphens is to use the Symbols gallery on the Insert tab. Click **More Symbols** to display the Symbol dialog box, click the Special Characters tab, select the Nonbreaking Hyphen or the Nonbreaking Space character option, and click **Insert** to insert a nonbreaking hyphen or a nonbreaking space, respectively. Close the Symbol dialog box after inserting the nonbreaking hyphen or nonbreaking space.

Step 3
Highlight Text and Use Format Painter

Refer to Figure 2.7 as you complete Step 3.

a. Select the text *Learn to type.* in the first paragraph.

b. Click **Text Highlight Color** in the Font group on the Home tab.

   Word highlighted the selected text in the default highlight color, yellow.

   TROUBLESHOOTING: If Word applies a different color to the selected text, that means another highlight color was selected after starting Word. If this happens, select the text again, click the Text Highlight Color arrow, and select Yellow.

c. Click anywhere within the sentence *Learn to type*. Double-click **Format Painter** in the Clipboard group on the Home tab. (Remember that clicking the Format Painter button once, rather than double-clicking it, enables you to copy the format only one time.)

   The mouse pointer changes to a paintbrush as shown in Figure 2.7.

d. Drag the mouse pointer over the first sentence in the second paragraph, *Write now, but edit later.*, and release the mouse.

   The formatting from the original sentence (bold font and yellow highlight) is applied to this sentence as well.

e. Drag the mouse pointer (in the shape of a paintbrush) over the remaining titles (the first sentence in each paragraph) to copy the formatting. You can click the scroll down arrow on the vertical scroll bar to display the other headings in the document.

f. Press **Esc** to turn off Format Painter after you copy the formatting to the last tip.

g. Save the *chap2_ho1_description_solution* document and keep it onscreen if you plan to continue with the next hands-on exercise. Close the file and exit Word if you will not continue with the next exercise at this time.

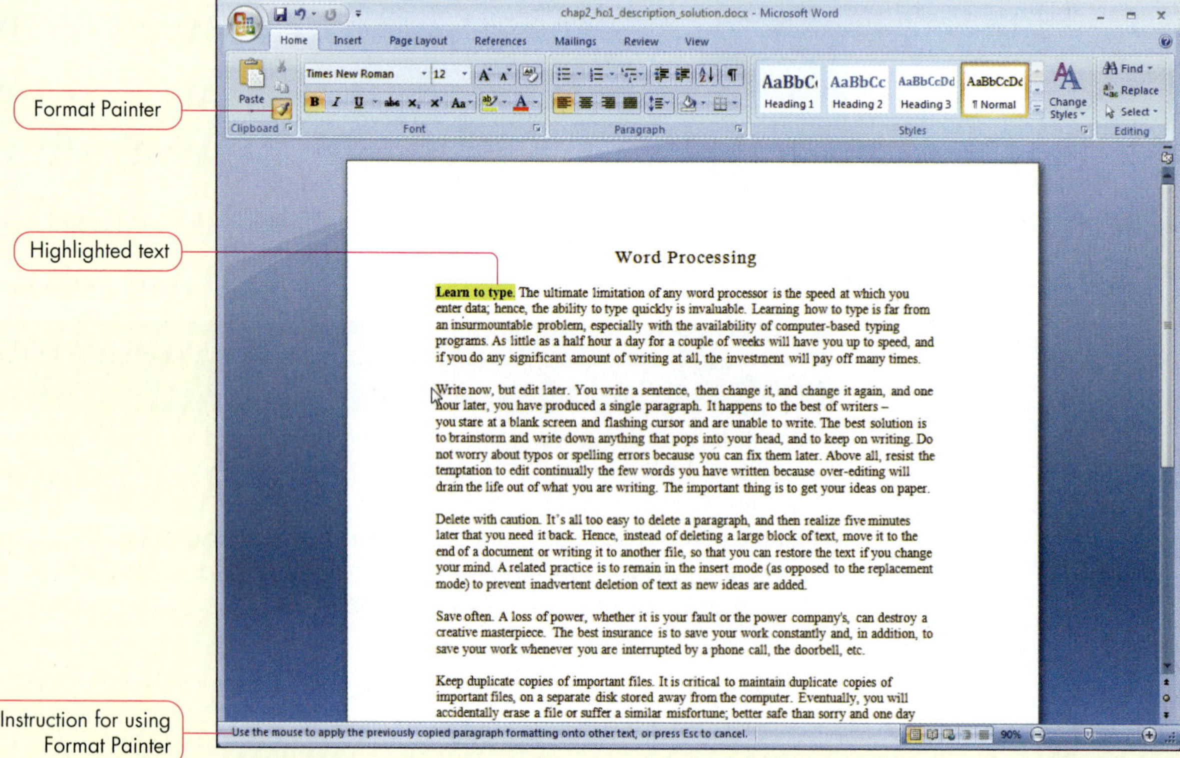

Figure 2.7 The Format Painter

Paragraph Formats

A change in typography is only one way to alter the appearance of a document. You also can change the alignment, indentation, tab stops, or line spacing for any paragraph(s) within the document. You can control the pagination and prevent the occurrence of awkward page breaks by specifying that an entire paragraph must appear on the same page, or that a one-line paragraph (e.g., a heading) should appear on the same page as the next paragraph. You can include borders or shading for added emphasis around selected paragraphs.

Word implements all of these paragraph formats for all selected paragraphs. If no paragraphs are selected, Word applies the formats to the current paragraph (the paragraph containing the insertion point), regardless of the position of the insertion point within the paragraph when you apply the paragraph formats.

(Word implements all of these paragraph formats for all selected paragraphs. If no paragraphs are selected, Word applies the feature to the current paragraph.)

In this section, you set tabs, apply borders, create lists, and format text into columns to help offset text for better readability. You also change text alignment, indent paragraphs, set line and paragraph spacing, and control pagination breaks.

Setting Off Paragraphs with Tabs, Borders, Lists, and Columns

Many people agree that their eyes tire and minds wander when they read page after page of plain black text on white paper. To break up long blocks of text or draw attention to an area of a page, you can format text with tabs, borders, lists, or columns. These formatting features enable you to modify positioning, frame a section, itemize for easy reading, order steps in a sequence, or create pillars of text for visual appeal and easy reading. For example, look through the pages of this book and notice the use of bulleted lists, tables for reference points, and borders around TIP boxes to draw your attention and enhance the pages.

Set Tabs

Tabs are markers for aligning text in a document.

Tabs are markers that specify the position for aligning text and add organization to a document. They often are used to create columns of text within a document. When you start a new document, the default tab stops are set every one-half inch across the page and are left aligned. Every time you press Tab, the insertion point moves over ½". You typically press Tab to indent the first line of paragraphs in double-spaced reports or the first line of paragraphs in a modified block style letter.

You access the Tabs feature by first clicking the Paragraph Dialog Box Launcher in the Paragraph group on the Home tab, then click the Tabs button. The Tabs dialog box displays so that you can set left, center, right, decimal, and bar tabs.

A ***left tab*** marks the position to align text on the left.

A ***center tab*** marks where text centers as you type.

A ***right tab*** marks the position to align text on the right.

A ***decimal tab*** marks where numbers align on a decimal point as you type.

A ***bar tab*** marks the location of a vertical line between columns.

- A ***left tab*** sets the start position on the left so as you type, text moves to the right of the tab setting.
- A ***center tab*** sets the middle point of the text you type; whatever you type will be centered on that tab setting.
- A ***right tab*** sets the start position on the right so as you type, text moves to the left of that tab setting and aligns on the right.
- A ***decimal tab*** aligns numbers on a decimal point. Regardless of how long the number, each number lines up with the decimal in the same position.
- A ***bar tab*** does not position text or decimals, but inserts a vertical bar at the tab setting. This bar is useful as a separator for text printed on the same line.

Instead of setting tabs in the Tabs dialog box, you can set tabs on the ruler. First, click the Tabs button to the left of the ruler (refer to Figure 2.8) until you see the tab alignment you want. Then click on the ruler in the location where you want to set the type of tab you selected. To delete a tab, click the tab marker on the ruler, then drag it down and off the ruler.

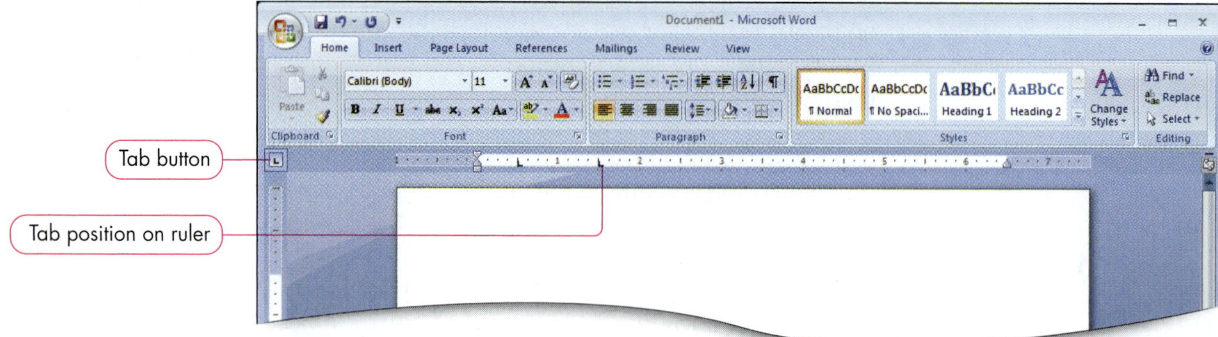

Figure 2.8 Tab Button and Ruler

TIP Deleting Default Tabs

When you set a tab on the ruler, Word deletes all of the default tab settings to the *left* of the tab you set. If you need to delete a single tab setting, click the tab marker on the ruler and drag it down. When you release the mouse, you delete the tab setting.

A ***leader character*** is dots or hyphens that connect two items.

In the Tabs dialog box you also can specify a ***leader character***, typically dots or hyphens, to draw the reader's eye across the page. For example, in a table of contents you can easily read a topic and the associated page where it is found when tab leaders connect the two, as shown in Figure 2.9. Notice also in Figure 2.9 the default tab settings have been cleared, and a right tab is set at 5".

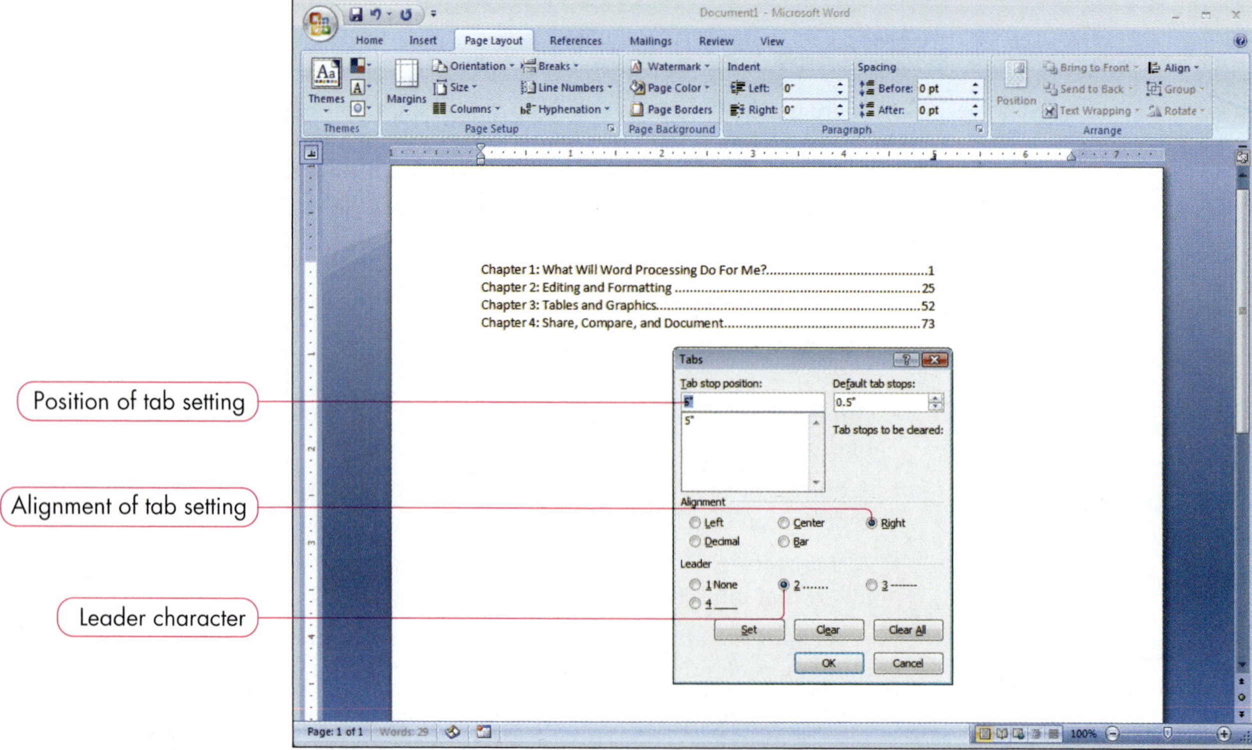

Figure 2.9 The Tabs Dialog Box

Apply Borders and Shading

A ***border*** is a line that surrounds a paragraph, a page, a table, or an image.

Shading is background color that appears behind text.

You can draw attention to a document or an area of a document by using the Borders and Shading command. A ***border*** is a line that surrounds a paragraph, a page, a table, or an image, similar to how a picture frame surrounds a photograph or piece of art. ***Shading*** is a background color that appears behind text in a paragraph, a page, or a table. You can apply specific borders, such as top, bottom, or outside, from the Border command in the Paragraph group on the Home tab. For customized borders, click the Borders arrow in the Paragraph group on the Home tab to open the Borders and Shading dialog box (see Figure 2.10). Borders or shading is applied to selected text within a paragraph, to the entire paragraph if no text is selected, to the entire page if the Page Border tab is selected. In addition, you can use the Borders tab and the Shading tab within the Borders and Shading dialog box to apply borders and shading to tables and images. You can create boxed and/or shaded text as well as place horizontal or vertical lines around different quantities of text. A good example of this practice is used in the *Exploring* series: The TIP boxes are surrounded by a border with dark shading and a white font color for the headings to attract your attention.

You can choose from several different line styles in any color, but remember you must use a color printer to display the line colors on the printed page. Colored lines appear in gray on a monochrome printer. You can place a uniform border around a paragraph (choose Box), or you can choose a shadow effect with thicker lines at the right and bottom. You also can apply lines to selected sides of a paragraph(s) by selecting a line style, then clicking the desired sides as appropriate.

The horizontal line button at the bottom of the Borders and Shading dialog box provides access to a variety of attractive horizontal line designs.

(Use page borders on . . . fliers, newsletters, and invitations, but not on formal documents such as research papers and professional reports.)

The Page Border tab enables you to place a decorative border around one or more selected pages. As with a paragraph border, you can place the border around the entire page, or you can select one or more sides. The page border also provides an additional option to use preselected clip art instead of ordinary lines. Note that it is appropriate to use page borders on documents such as fliers, newsletters, and invitations, but not on formal documents such as research papers and professional reports.

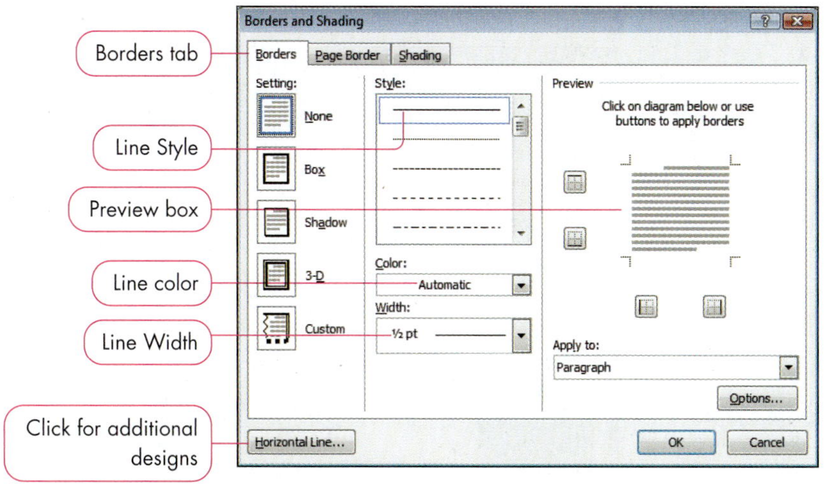

Figure 2.10 Apply a Border Around Text, Paragraphs, or Pages

Shading is applied independently of the border and is accessed from the Borders and Shading dialog box or from Shading in the Paragraph group on the Home tab. Clear (no shading) is the default. Solid (100%) shading creates a solid box where the text is turned white so you can read it. Shading of 10% or 20% generally is most effective to add emphasis to the selected paragraph (see Figure 2.11). The Borders and Shading command is implemented on the paragraph level and affects the entire paragraph unless text has been selected within the paragraph.

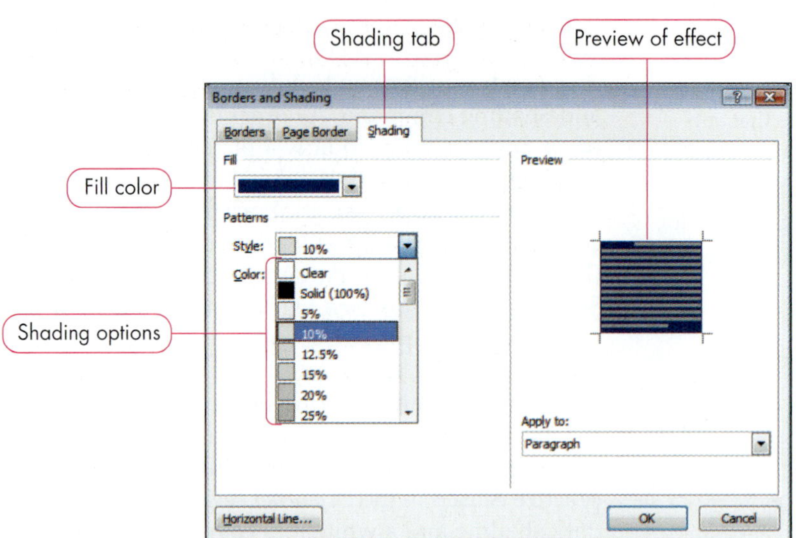

Figure 2.11 Apply Shading to Text or a Paragraph

Create Bulleted and Numbered Lists

A ***bulleted list*** itemizes and separates paragraph text to increase readability.

A ***numbered list*** sequences and prioritizes items.

A ***multilevel list*** extends a numbered list to several levels.

A list helps you organize information by highlighting important topics. A ***bulleted list*** itemizes and separates paragraphs to increase readability. A ***numbered list*** sequences and prioritizes the items and is automatically updated to accommodate additions or deletions. A ***multilevel list*** extends a numbered list to several levels, and it too is updated automatically when topics are added or deleted. You create each of these lists from the Paragraph group on the Home tab.

To apply bullet formatting to a list, click the Bullets arrow and choose one of several predefined symbols in the Bullet library (see Figure 2.12). Position your mouse over one of the bullet styles in the Bullet Library and a preview of that bullet style will display in your document. To use that style, simply click the bullet. If you want to use a different bullet symbol, click the Define New Bullet option below the Bullet Library to choose a different symbol or picture for the bullet.

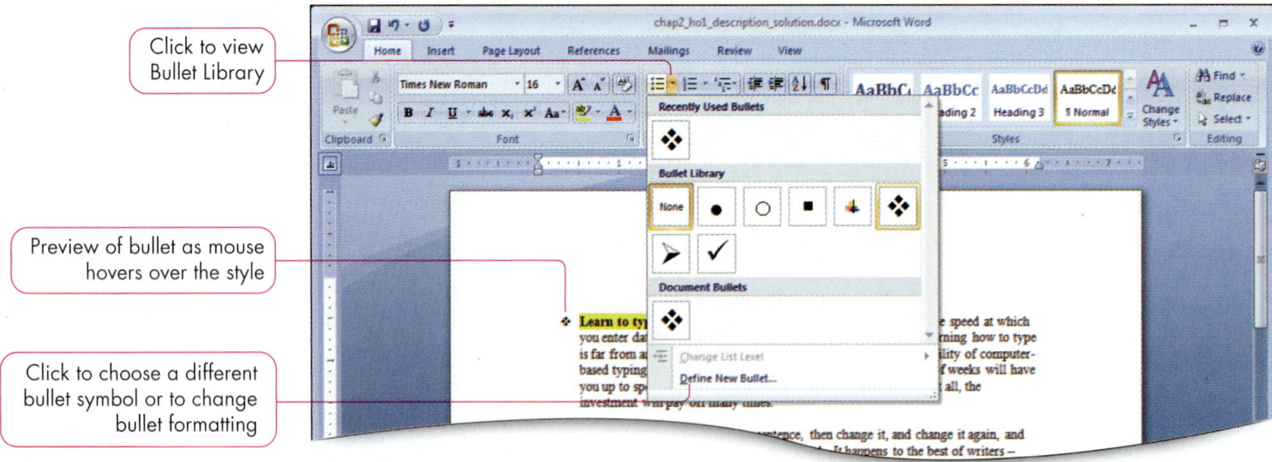

Figure 2.12 Bulleted List Options

Click the Numbering arrow in the Paragraph group to apply Arabic or Roman numerals, or upper- or lowercase letters, for a numbered list. When you position the mouse pointer over a style in the Numbering Library, you see a preview of that numbering style in your document. As with a bulleted list, you can define a new style by selecting the Define New Number Format option below the Numbering Library. Note, too, the options to restart or continue numbering found by selecting the Set Numbering Value option. These become important if a list appears in multiple places within a document. In other words, each occurrence of a list can start numbering anew, or it can continue from where the previous list left off.

The Mulitlevel List command enables you to create an outline to organize your thoughts in a hierarchical structure. As with the other types of lists, you can choose one of several default styles, and/or modify a style through the Define New Multilevel List option below the My Lists gallery. You also can specify whether each outline within a document is to restart its numbering, or whether it is to continue numbering from the previous outline.

Format Text into Columns

Columns format a section of a document into side-by-side vertical blocks.

Columns format a section of a document into side-by-side vertical blocks in which the text flows down the first column and then continues at the top of the next column. The length of a line of columnar text is shorter, enabling people to read through each article faster. To format text into columns, click the Page Layout tab and click Columns in the Page Setup group. From the Columns gallery, you can specify the number of columns or select More Columns to display the Columns dialog box. The Columns dialog box provides options for setting the number of columns and spacing between columns. Microsoft Word calculates the width of each column according to the left and right document margins on the page and the specified (default) space between columns.

The dialog box in Figure 2.13 implements a design of three equal columns. The 2" width of each column is computed based on current 1" left and right document margins and the ¼" spacing between columns. The width of each column is determined by subtracting the sum of the margins and the space between the columns (a total of 2½" in this example) from the page width of 8½". The result of the subtraction is 6", which is divided by 3 columns, resulting in a column width of 2".

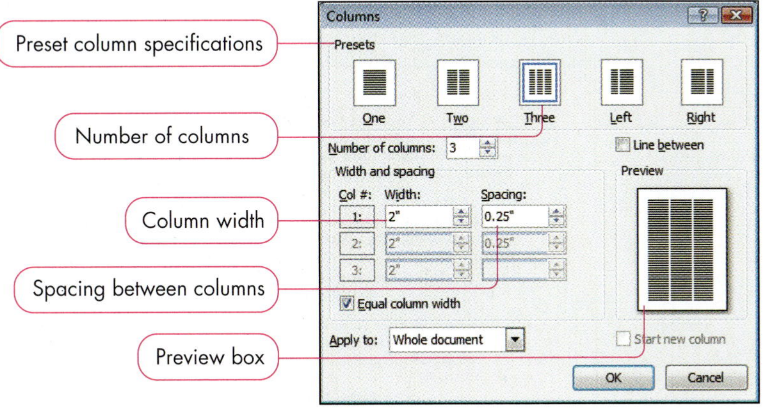

Figure 2.13 The Columns Dialog Box

One subtlety associated with column formatting is the use of sections, which control elements such as the orientation of a page (landscape or portrait), margins, page numbers, and the number of columns. All of the documents you have worked with so far have consisted of a single section, so section formatting was not an issue. It becomes important only when you want to vary an element that is formatted at the section level. You could, for example, use section formatting to create a document that has one column on its title page and two columns on the remaining pages. Creating this type of formatting requires you to divide the document into two sections by inserting a section break. You then format each section independently and specify the number of columns in each section. Table 2.3 guides you in formatting text into columns.

Table 2.3 Formatting with Columns

If your document contains . . .	And you want to apply column formatting to . . .	Do this:
only one section	the entire document	apply column formatting from anywhere within the document
two or more sections	only one section	position the insertion point in that section, and apply column formatting
one or more sections	only part of the document within a section	select the text you want to format, and then apply column formatting

Applying Paragraph Formats

The Paragraph group on the Home tab contains commands to set and control several format options for a paragraph. The options include alignment, indentation, line spacing, and pagination. These features also are found in the Paragraph dialog box. All of these formatting features are implemented at the paragraph level and affect all selected paragraphs. If no paragraphs are selected, Word applies the formatting to the current paragraph—the paragraph containing the insertion point.

Change Text Alignment

Horizontal alignment refers to the placement of text between the left and right margins.

Horizontal alignment refers to the placement of text between the left and right margins. Text is aligned in four different ways as shown in Figure 2.14. Alignment options are justified (flush left/flush right), left aligned (flush left with a ragged right margin), right aligned (flush right with a ragged left margin), or centered within the margins (ragged left and right). The default alignment is left.

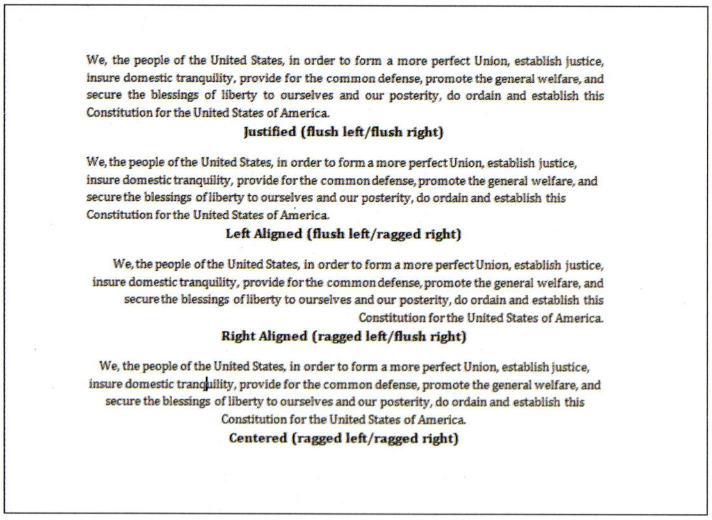

We, the people of the United States, in order to form a more perfect Union, establish justice, insure domestic tranquility, provide for the common defense, promote the general welfare, and secure the blessings of liberty to ourselves and our posterity, do ordain and establish this Constitution for the United States of America.

Justified (flush left/flush right)

We, the people of the United States, in order to form a more perfect Union, establish justice, insure domestic tranquility, provide for the common defense, promote the general welfare, and secure the blessings of liberty to ourselves and our posterity, do ordain and establish this Constitution for the United States of America.

Left Aligned (flush left/ragged right)

We, the people of the United States, in order to form a more perfect Union, establish justice, insure domestic tranquility, provide for the common defense, promote the general welfare, and secure the blessings of liberty to ourselves and our posterity, do ordain and establish this Constitution for the United States of America.

Right Aligned (ragged left/flush right)

We, the people of the United States, in order to form a more perfect Union, establish justice, insure domestic tranquility, provide for the common defense, promote the general welfare, and secure the blessings of liberty to ourselves and our posterity, do ordain and establish this Constitution for the United States of America.

Centered (ragged left/ragged right)

Figure 2.14 Horizontal Alignment

Left-aligned text is perhaps the easiest to read. The first letters of each line align with each other, helping the eye to find the beginning of each line. The lines themselves are of irregular length. Uniform spacing exists between words, and the ragged margin on the right adds white space to the text, giving it a lighter and more informal look.

Justified text, sometimes called fully justified, produces lines of equal length, with the spacing between words adjusted to align at the margins. Look closely and you will see many books, magazines, and newspapers fully justify text to add formality and "neatness" to the text. Some find this style more difficult to read because of the uneven (sometimes excessive) word spacing and/or the greater number of hyphenated words needed to justify the lines. But it also can enable you to pack more information onto a page when space is constrained.

Text that is centered or right aligned is usually restricted to limited amounts of text where the effect is more important than the ease of reading. Centered text, for example, appears frequently on wedding invitations, poems, or formal announcements. In research papers, first-level titles often are centered as well. Right-aligned text is used with figure captions and short headlines.

The Paragraph group on the Home tab contains the four alignment options: Align Text Left, Center, Align Text Right, and Justify. To apply the alignment, select text, then click the alignment option on the Home tab. You can also set alignment from the Paragraph dialog box; the Indents and Spacing tab contains an Alignment drop-down box in the General section.

TIP Alignment Keyboard Shortcuts

You can quickly apply alignment by using keyboard shortcuts. After you select the text click Ctrl+L to align left, click Ctrl+E to align center, click Ctrl+R to align right, or click Ctrl+J to justify.

Indent Paragraphs

You can indent individual paragraphs so they appear to have different margins from the rest of a document. Indentation is established at the paragraph level; thus it is possible to apply different indentation properties to different paragraphs. You can indent one paragraph from the left margin only, another from the right margin only, and a third from both the left and right margins. For example, the fifth edition of the *Publication Manual of the American Psychological Association* specifies that quotations consisting of 40 or more words should be contained in a separate paragraph that is indented ½" from the left margin. Additionally, you can indent the first line of any paragraph differently from the rest of the paragraph. And finally, a paragraph may have no indentation at all, so that it aligns on the left and right margins.

Three settings determine the indentation of a paragraph: the left indent, the right indent, and a special indent, if any (see Figure 2.15). The left and right indents are set to 0 by default, as is the special indent, and produce a paragraph with no indentation at all. Positive values for the left and right indents offset the paragraph from both margins.

A ***first line indent*** marks the location to indent only the first line in a paragraph.

A ***hanging indent*** marks how far to indent each line of a paragraph except the first.

The two types of special indentation are first line and hanging. The ***first line indent*** affects only the first line in the paragraph, and you apply it by pressing the Tab key at the beginning of the paragraph or by setting a specific measurement in the Paragraph dialog box. Remaining lines in the paragraph align at the left margin. A ***hanging indent*** aligns the first line of a paragraph at the left margin and indents the remaining lines. Hanging indents often are used with bulleted or numbered lists and to format citations on a bibliography page.

TIP Decrease Indent and Increase Indent

You can click Decrease Indent in the Paragraph group on the Home tab to decrease (bring text to the left) indented text by ½". Click Increase Indent to move text to the right for an additional ½".

Set Line and Paragraph Spacing

Line spacing is the space between the lines in a paragraph.

Paragraph spacing is the amount of space before or after a paragraph.

Line spacing determines the space between the lines in a paragraph and between paragraphs. Word provides complete flexibility and enables you to select any multiple of line spacing (single, double, line and a half, and so on). You also can specify line spacing in terms of points (1" vertical contains 72 points). Click the Line spacing command in the Paragraph group on the Home tab to establish line spacing for the current paragraph. You can also set line spacing in the *Spacing* section on the Indents and Spacing tab in the Paragraph dialog box.

Paragraph spacing is the amount of space before or after a paragraph, as indicated by the paragraph mark when you press Enter between paragraphs. Unlike line spacing that controls *all* spacing within and between paragraphs, paragraph spacing controls only the spacing between paragraphs.

Sometimes you need to single-space text within a paragraph but want to have a blank line between paragraphs. Instead of pressing Enter twice between paragraphs, you can set the paragraph spacing to control the amount of space before or after the paragraph. You can set paragraph spacing in the *Spacing* section on the Indents and Spacing tab in the Paragraph dialog box. Setting a 12-point *After* spacing creates the appearance of a double-space after the paragraph even though the user presses Enter only once between paragraphs.

The Paragraph dialog box is illustrated in Figure 2.15. The Indents and Spacing tab specifies a hanging indent, 1.5 line spacing, and justified alignment. The Preview area within the Paragraph dialog box enables you to see how the paragraph will appear within the document.

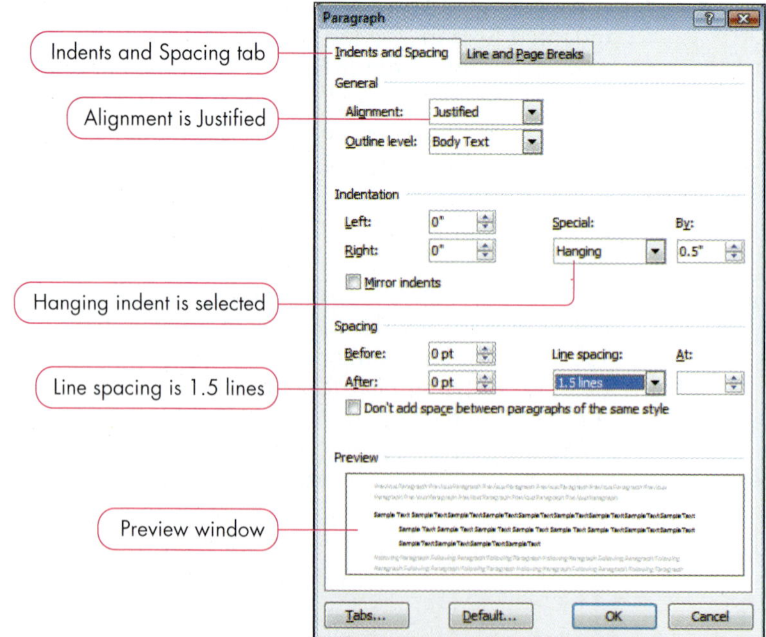

Figure 2.15 Indents and Spacing

Control Widows and Orphans

A ***widow*** is the last line of a paragraph appearing by itself at the top of a page.

An ***orphan*** is the first line of a paragraph appearing by itself at the bottom of a page.

Some lines become isolated from the remainder of a paragraph and seem out of place at the beginning or end of a multipage document. A ***widow*** refers to the last line of a paragraph appearing by itself at the top of a page. An ***orphan*** is the first line of a paragraph appearing by itself at the bottom of a page. You can prevent these from occurring by clicking the *Widow/Orphan control* check box in the *Pagination* section of the Line and Page Breaks tab of the Paragraph dialog box.

To prevent a page break from occurring within a paragraph and ensure that the entire paragraph appears on the same page use the *Keep lines together* option in the *Pagination* section of the Line and Page Breaks tab of the Paragraph dialog box. The paragraph is moved to the top of the next page if it does not fit on the bottom of the current page. Use the *Keep with next* option in the *Pagination* section to prevent a soft page break between the two paragraphs. This option is typically used to keep a heading (a one-line paragraph) with its associated text in the next paragraph. The check boxes in Figure 2.16 enable you to prevent the occurrence of awkward soft page breaks that detract from the appearance of a document.

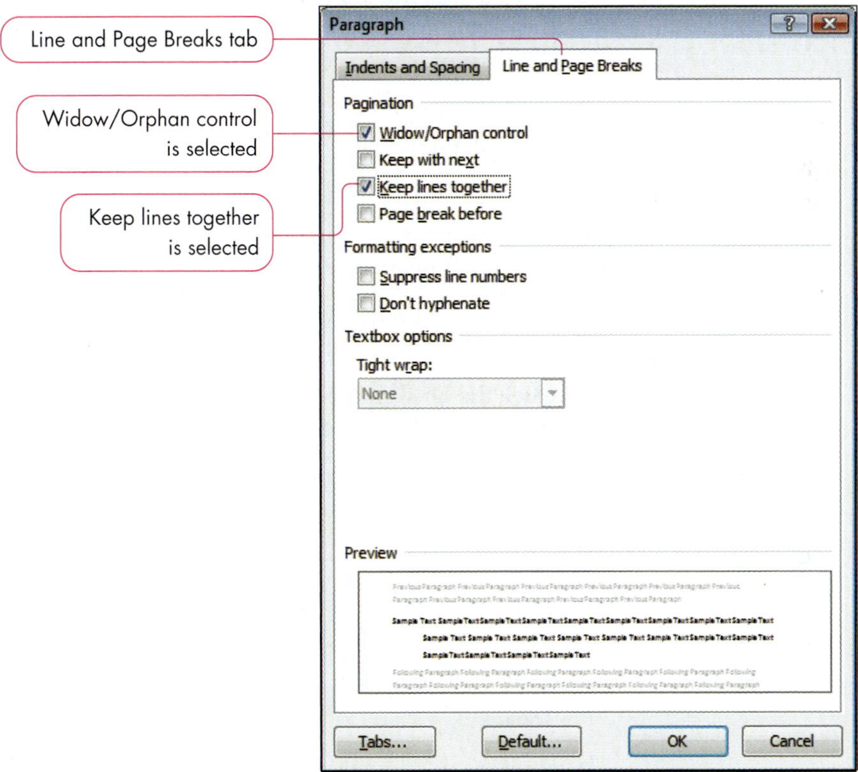

Figure 2.16 Line and Page Breaks

TIP The Section Versus the Paragraph

Line spacing, alignment, tabs, and indents are implemented at the paragraph level. Change any of these parameters anywhere within the current (or selected) paragraph(s) and you change *only* those paragraph(s). Margins, page numbering, orientation, and columns are implemented at the section level. Change these parameters anywhere within a section and you change the characteristics of every page within that section.

Hands-On Exercises

2 | Paragraph Formatting

Skills covered: 1. Set Tabs in a Footer **2.** Select Text to Format **3.** Specify Line Spacing, Justification, and Pagination **4.** Indent Text **5.** Apply Borders and Shading **6.** Change Column Structure **7.** Insert a Section Break and Create Columns

Step 1
Set Tabs in a Footer

Refer to Figure 2.17 as you complete Step 1.

a. Open the *chap2_ho1_description_solution* document if you closed it after the last hands-on exercise and save it as **chap2_ho2_description_solution**.

b. Click the **Insert tab** and then click **Footer** in the Header & Footer group. Click **Edit Footer** and notice the document text is dimmed except for the footer area.

c. Click the **Home tab** and then click the **Paragraph Dialog Box Launcher** to display the Paragraph dialog box. Click **Tabs** in the lower-left corner to display the Tabs dialog box.

   This footer contains no tab settings. You will add a 3" center tab that will be used for a page number.

d. Type **3** in the *Tab stop position* box. Click **Center** and then click **OK**.

e. Click near the bottom of your page to display the footer area, if necessary. Press **Tab** one time, type **Page** and press **Spacebar** one time.

   You reposition the insertion point to the middle of the footer area using the tab you set and type the text you want to precede the page number.

f. Click the **Design tab** and click **Quick Parts** in the Insert group, then click **Field** to open the Field dialog box. Click **Page** in the *Field names* box, then click **OK**.

   The actual page number displays in the footer as shown in Figure 2.17 and will automatically paginate for any additional pages added to your document.

   TROUBLESHOOTING: If the page number is not horizontally centered at the 3" position, double-check the tab settings on the ruler. If tab settings appear to the left of the 3" tab setting, drag the tab markers off the ruler to delete them.

g. Click **Close Header and Footer** in the Close group of the Header and Footer Tools tab.

h. Save the document.

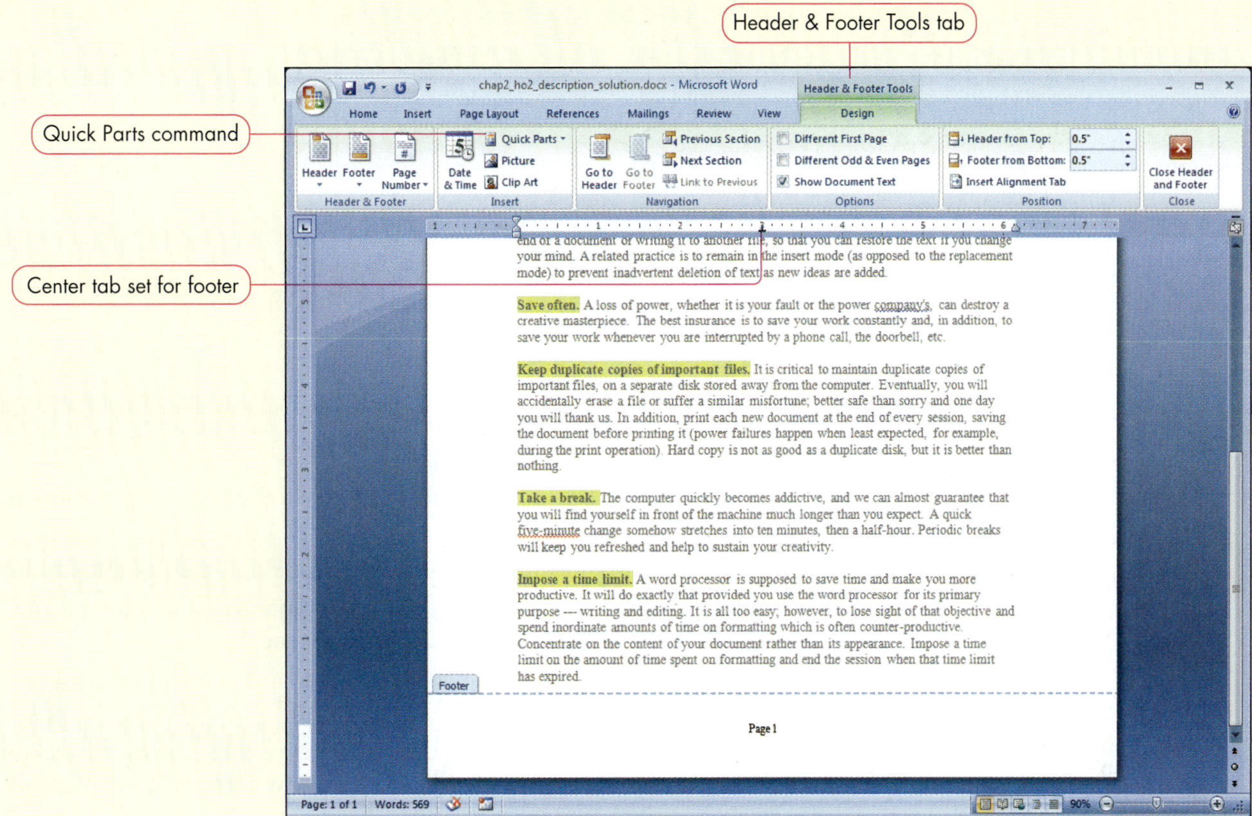

Figure 2.17 Insert Tab in Footer

Step 2
Select Text to Format

Refer to Figure 2.18 as you complete Step 2.

a. Position your insertion point at the end of the title, *Word Processing*, then press **Ctrl+Enter**.

You inserted a manual page break between the title and the list of tips.

b. Click **Zoom** in the status bar to display the Zoom dialog box. Click **Many pages** and drag to select the first two icons that represent two pages, as shown in Figure 2.18. Click **OK**.

You can see the entire document as you select text to format.

c. Select the entire second page.

d. Save the document.

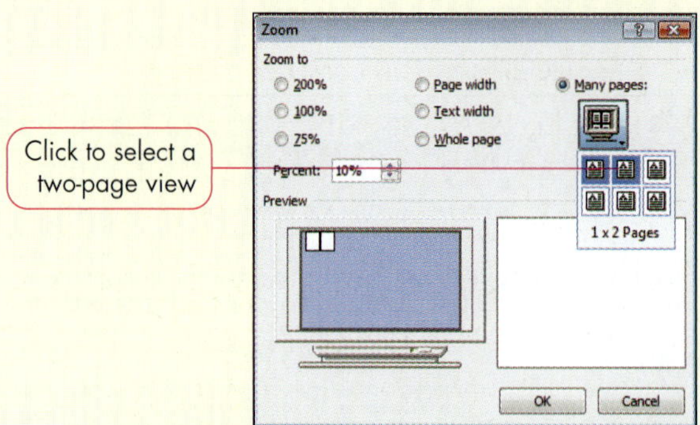

Figure 2.18 Zoom Dialog Box

Step 3
Specify Line Spacing, Justification, and Pagination

Refer to Figure 2.19 as you complete Step 3.

a. Select page 2, if necessary, and then click **Justify** in the Paragraph group on the Home tab.

b. Click **Line Spacing** in the Paragraph group on the Home tab, and then select **1.5**.

   These settings align the text on the right and left margins and add spacing before and after lines of text, making it easier to read.

c. Right-click the selected text and select **Paragraph** on the menu to display the Paragraph dialog box.

d. Click the **Line and Page Breaks tab**. Click the **Keep lines together check box** in the *Pagination* section, if necessary. Click the **Widow/Orphan control check box** in the *Pagination* section, if necessary.

e. Click **OK** to accept the settings and close the dialog box.

   These settings prevent paragraphs from being split at a page break.

f. Click anywhere in the document to deselect the text and see the effects of the formatting changes that were just specified.

   Three paragraphs now display on a third page, and none are split at the page break, as shown in Figure 2.19.

g. Save the document.

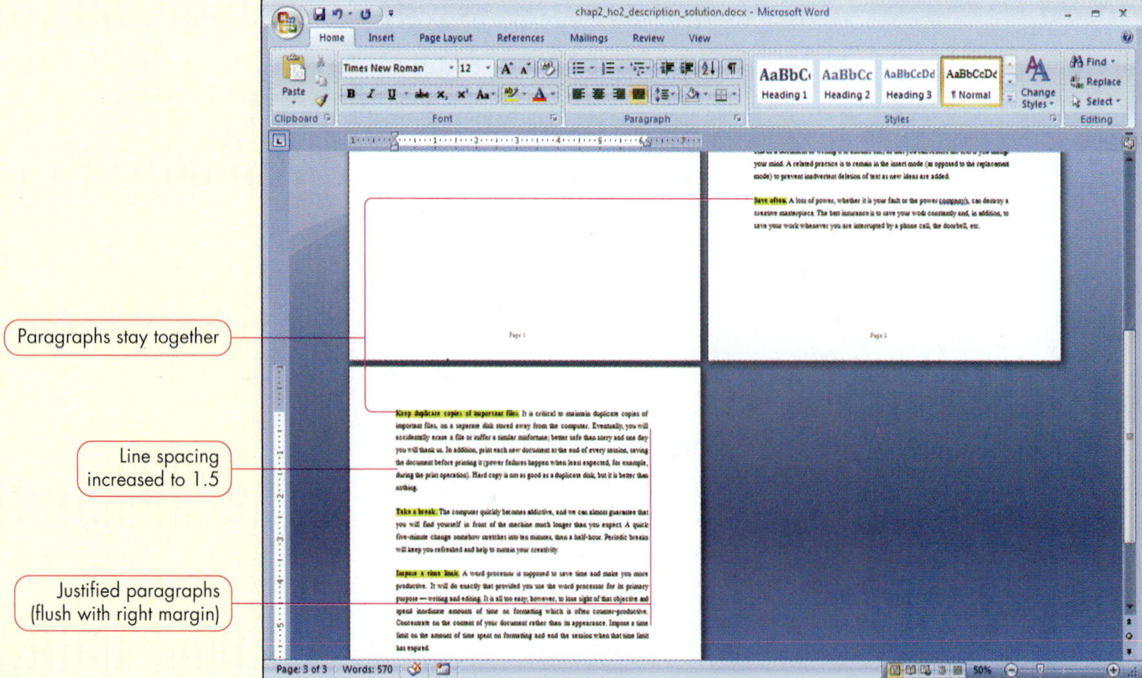

Figure 2.19 Result of Changing Line Spacing, Alignment, and Pagination

Step 4
Indent Text

Refer to Figure 2.20 as you complete Step 4.

a. Click the **Zoom slider** in the status bar and select **100%**. Select the second paragraph as shown in Figure 2.20.

   The second paragraph will not be indented yet.

b. Right-click the selected text and select **Paragraph** from the shortcut menu.

c. If necessary, click the **Indents and Spacing tab** in the Paragraph dialog box.

d. Click the **Left indentation** up arrow to display 0.5". Set the **Right indention** to 0.5" also. Click **OK**.

   Your document should match Figure 2.20.

e. Save the document.

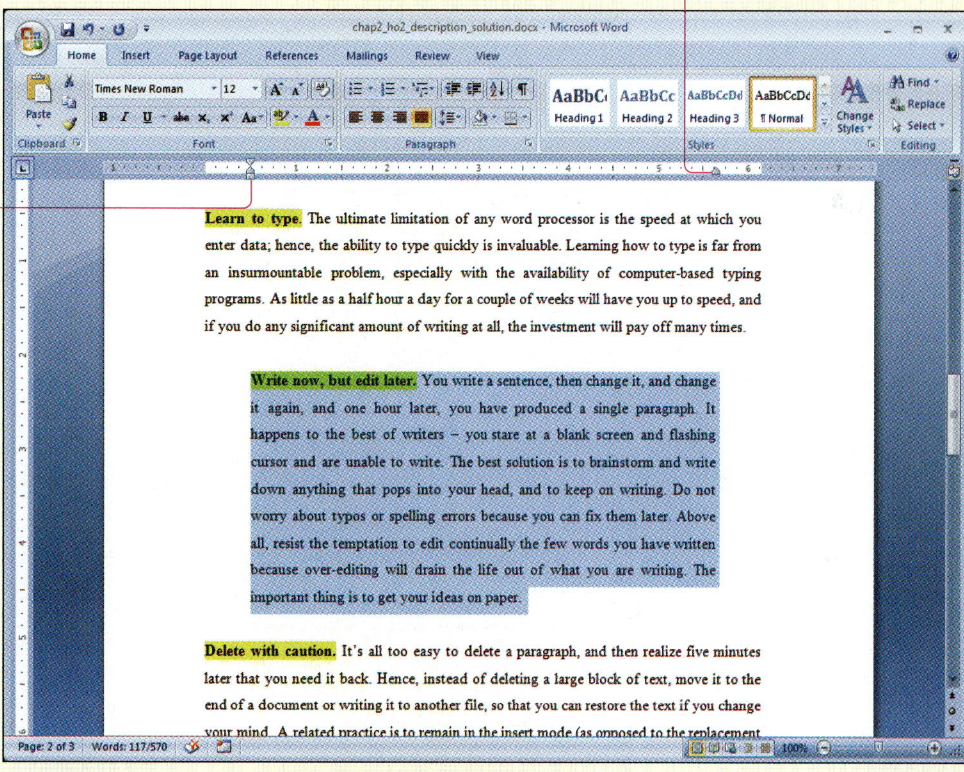

Figure 2.20 Indent

TIP Indents and the Ruler

You can use the ruler to change the special, left, and/or right indents. Select the paragraph (or paragraphs) in which you want to change indents and then drag the appropriate indent markers to the new location(s) on the ruler. If you get a hanging indent when you wanted to change the left indent, it means you dragged the bottom triangle instead of the box. Click Undo on the Quick Access Toolbar and try again. You can always use the Paragraph dialog box rather than the ruler if you continue to have difficulty.

Step 5
Apply Borders and Shading

Refer to Figure 2.21 as you complete Step 5.

a. Click the **Home tab** and click the **Borders arrow**; then click **Borders and Shading** to display the Borders and Shading dialog box shown in Figure 2.21.

b. Click the **Borders tab**, if necessary, then click the double line style in the *Style* list. Click **¾ pt** in the *Width* list, then click **Box** in the *Setting* section.

A preview of these settings will display on the right side of the window in the Preview area.

c. Click the **Shading tab**, then click the **Fill drop-down arrow** and select **Dark Blue, Text 2, Lighter 80%** from the palette. It is located in the fourth column from the left and in the second row from the top. Click **OK** to accept the settings for both Borders and Shading.

The paragraph is surrounded by a ¾ point double-line border, and a light blue shading appears behind the text.

d. Click outside the paragraph to deselect it and view your formatting changes.

e. Save the document.

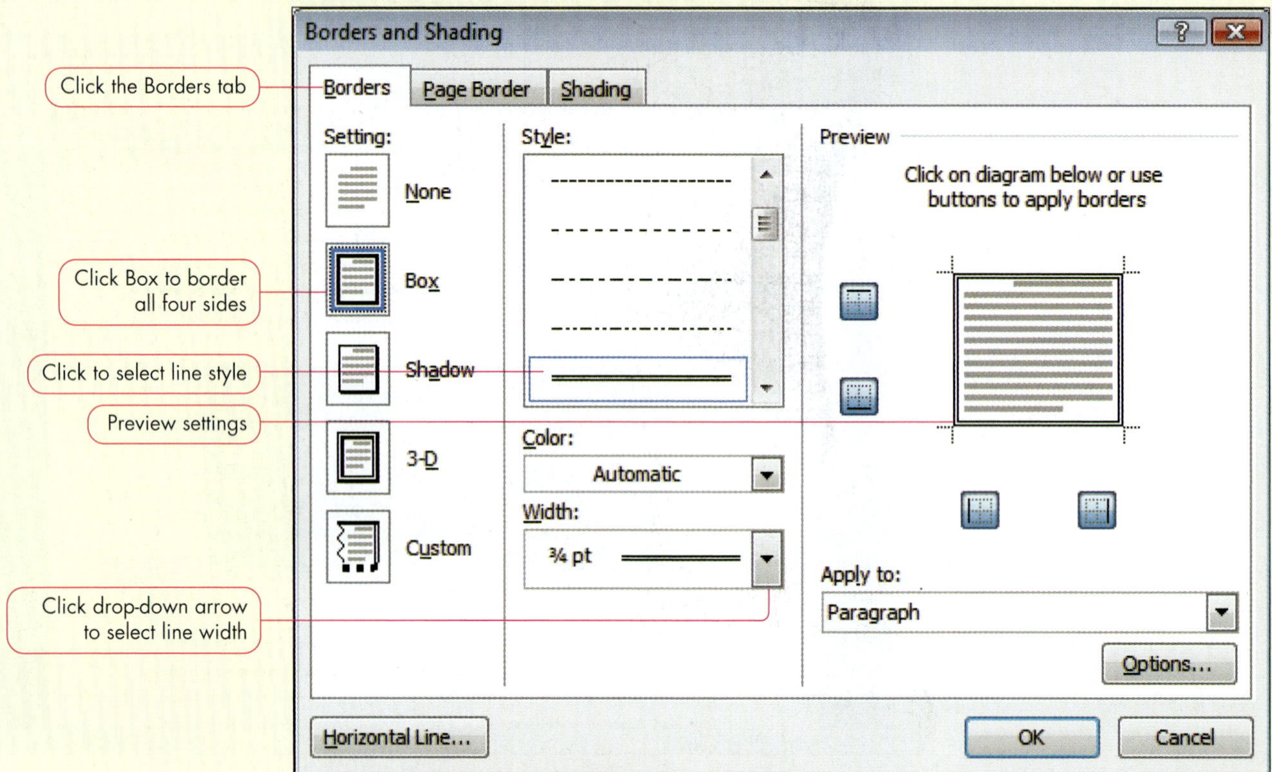

Figure 2.21 Borders and Shading Dialog Box

Step 6
Change Column Structure

Refer to Figure 2.22 as you complete Step 6.

a. Click the **Page Layout tab** and click **Margins** in the Page Setup group. Click **Custom Margins** and select the **Margins tab** if necessary.

b. Click the spin arrows to set **1"** left and right margins. Click **OK**.

The document is now formatted by 1" left, right, top, and bottom margins.

c. Click the **Zoom button** in the status bar, select **Page width,** and then click **OK**. Press **PgUp** or **PgDn** on the keyboard to scroll until the second page comes into view.

d. Click anywhere in the paragraph, *Write now, but edit later*. Right-click and select **Paragraph,** click the **Indents and Spacing tab** if necessary, then change left and right to **0"** in the *Indentation* section. Click **OK**.

These settings prepare your document for the changes you make in the next steps.

e. Click the **Page Layout tab** and click **Columns** in the Page Setup group. Click **More Columns** to display the Columns dialog box.

   Because you will change several settings related to columns, you clicked the More Columns option instead of clicking the gallery option to create three columns.

f. Click **Three** in the *Presets* section of the dialog box. The default spacing between columns is 0.5", which leads to a column width of 1.83". Change the spacing to **.25**" in the **Spacing** list, which automatically changes the column width to 2".

g. Click the **Line between check box** as shown in Figure 2.22. Click **OK**.

   The document is now formatted in three columns with 0.25" space between columns. Vertical lines appear between columns.

h. Save the document.

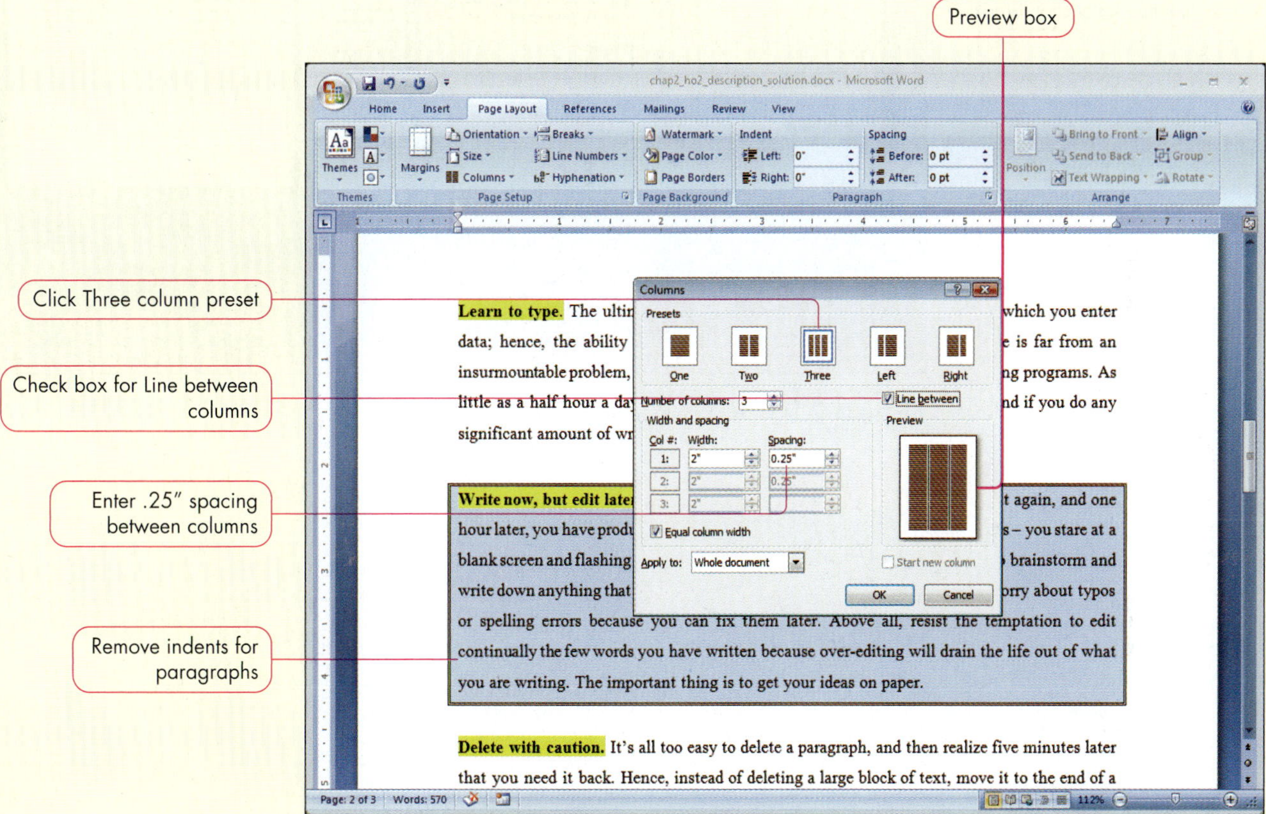

Figure 2.22 Change Column Structure

Step 7
Insert a Section Break and Create Columns

Refer to Figure 2.23 as you complete Step 7.

a. Click **Zoom** on the status bar to display the Zoom dialog box. Click **Many pages,** drag to select **1x3** pages, and then click **OK**.

   The document displays the column formatting.

b. Place the insertion point immediately to the left of the first paragraph with the *Learn to type* heading. Click the **Page Layout tab** and click **Breaks** to display the list shown in Figure 2.23. Click **Continuous** under *Section Breaks*.

c. Click anywhere on the title page, above the section break you just inserted. Click **Columns**, then click **One** to display the content in one column.

   The formatting for the first section of the document (the title page) should change to one column; the title of the document is centered across the entire page.

d. Save and close the *chap2_ho2_description_solution* document. Exit Word if you will not continue with the next exercise at this time.

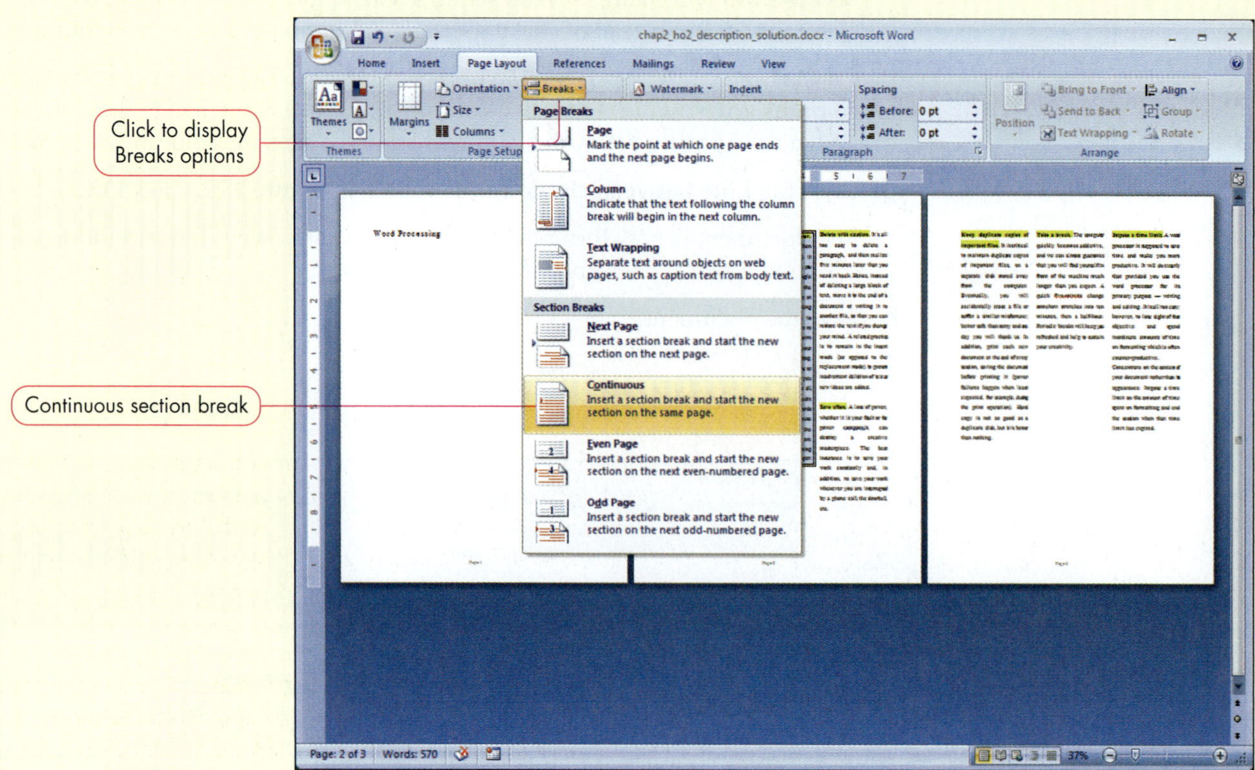

Figure 2.23 Insert a Continuous Section Break

Styles and Document References

As you complete reports, assignments, and projects for other classes or in your job, you probably apply the same text, paragraph, table, and list formatting for similar documents. Instead of formatting each document individually, you can create your own custom style to save time in setting particular formats for titles, headings, and paragraphs. Styles and other features in Word then can be used to automatically generate reference pages such as a table of contents and indexes.

In this section, you create and modify styles. You also display a document in the Outline view. Finally, you learn how to use the AutoFormat feature.

Creating and Modifying Styles

(One way to achieve uniformity throughout a document is to store the formatting information as a style. Change the style and you automatically change all text defined by that style.)

One characteristic of a professional document is the uniform formatting that is applied to similar elements throughout the document. Different elements have different formatting. For headings you can use one font, color, style, and size, and then use a completely different format design on text below those headings. The headings may be left aligned, while the text is fully justified. You can format lists and footnotes in entirely different styles.

One way to achieve uniformity throughout the document is to use the Format Painter to copy the formatting from one occurrence of each element to the next, but this step is tedious and inefficient. And if you were to change your mind after copying the formatting throughout a document, you would have to repeat the entire process all over again. A much easier way to achieve uniformity is to store all the formatting information together, which is what we refer to as a ***style***. Styles automate the formatting process and provide a consistent appearance to a document. It is possible to store any type of character or paragraph formatting within a style, and once a style is defined, you can apply it to any element within a document to produce identical formatting. Change the style and you automatically change all text defined by that style.

A ***style*** is a set of formatting options you apply to characters or paragraphs.

Styles are created on the character or paragraph level. A ***character style*** stores character formatting (font, size, and style) and affects only the selected text. A ***paragraph style*** stores paragraph formatting such as alignment, line spacing, indents, tabs, text flow, and borders and shading, as well as the font, size, and style of the text in the paragraph. A paragraph style affects the current paragraph or, if selected, multiple paragraphs. You create and apply styles from the Styles group on the Home tab as shown in Figure 2.24.

A ***character style*** stores character formatting and affects only selected text.

A ***paragraph style*** stores paragraph formatting of text.

The Normal template contains more than 100 styles. Unless you specify a style, Word uses the Normal style. The Normal style contains these settings: 11-point Calibri, 1.15 line spacing, 10-point spacing after, left horizontal alignment, and Widow/Orphan control. You can create your own styles to use in a document, modify or delete an existing style, and even add your new style to the Normal template for use in other documents.

The document in Figure 2.25 is a report about the Great Depression. Each paragraph begins with a one-line heading, followed by the supporting text. The task pane in the figure displays all of the styles used in the document. The Normal style contains the default paragraph settings (left aligned, 1.15 line spacing, 10 pt. spacing after, and 11-point Calibri font) and is assigned automatically to every paragraph unless a different style is specified. The Clear All style removes all formatting from selected text. It is the Heading 3 and Body Text styles, however, that are of interest to us, as these styles have been applied throughout the document to the associated elements.

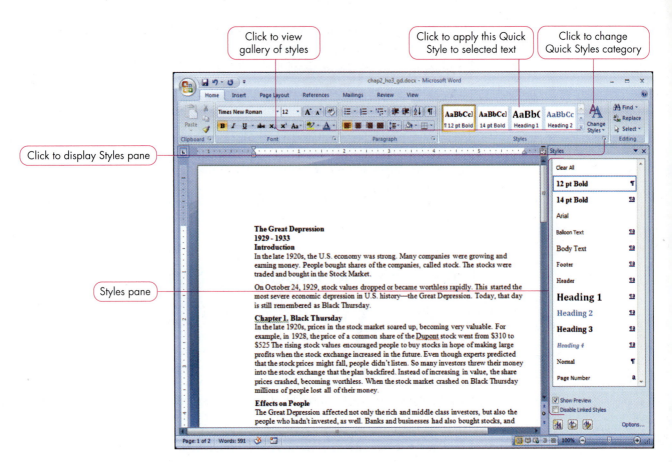

Click to view gallery of styles

Click to apply this Quick Style to selected text

Click to change Quick Styles category

Click to display Styles pane

Styles pane

Figure 2.24 The Styles Group

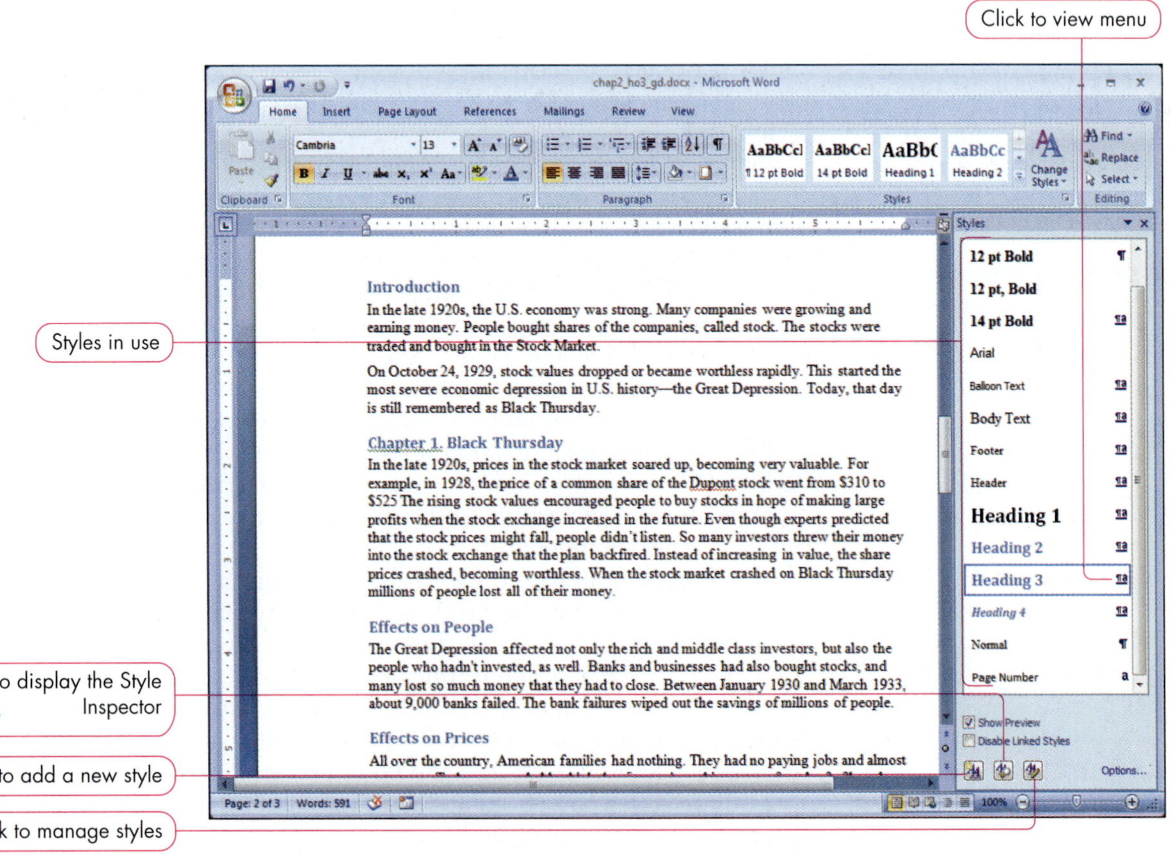

Figure 2.25 Styles Task Pane

To change the specifications of a style, click the down arrow for the particular style, then select Modify. The specifications for the Heading 3 style are shown in Figure 2.26. The current settings within the Heading 3 style use 13-point Cambria bold type with a custom color. There is a 12-point space before the text, and the heading appears on the same page as the next paragraph. The preview frame in the dialog box shows how paragraphs formatted in this style display. Click the Format button in the Modify Style dialog box to select and open other dialog boxes where you modify settings that are used in the style. And as indicated earlier, any changes to the style are reflected automatically in any text or element defined by that style.

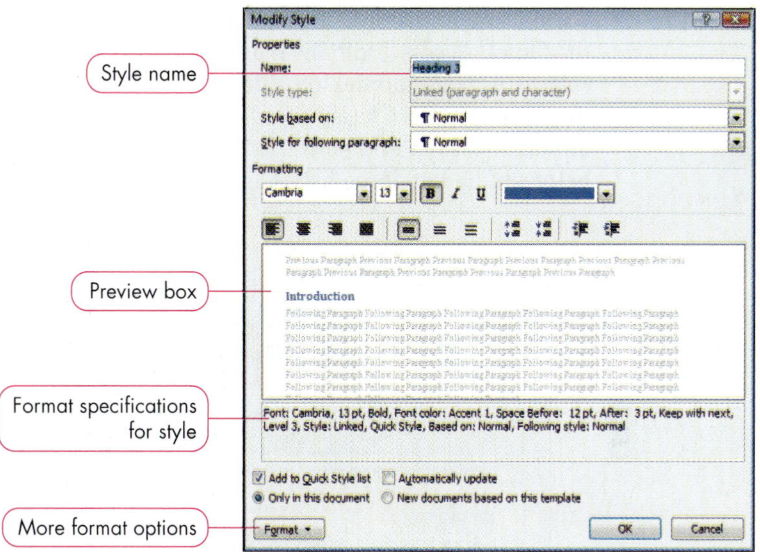

Figure 2.26 Modify a Style

TIP Styles and Paragraphs

A paragraph style affects the entire paragraph; that is, you cannot apply a paragraph style to only part of a paragraph. To apply a style to an existing paragraph, place the insertion point anywhere within the paragraph, click the Styles Dialog Box Launcher on the Home tab to display the Styles pane, then click the name of the style you want to use. The Styles pane can display in several locations. Initially it might display as a floating window, but you can drag the title bar to move it. Drag to the far left or right side, and it will dock on that side of the window.

Use the Styles Pane Options

When you display the Styles pane in your document, it might contain only the styles used in the document, as in Figure 2.25, or it might list every style in the Word document template. If the Styles pane only displays styles used in the document, you are unable to view or apply other styles. You can change the styles that display in the Styles pane by using the Styles Gallery Options dialog box which displays when you click *Options* in the lower-right corner of the Styles pane. In the *Select styles to show* box you select from several options including Recommended, In use, In current document, and All styles. Select *In use* to view only styles used in this document; select *All styles* to view all styles created for the document template as well as any custom styles you create. Other options are available in this dialog box, including how to sort the styles when displayed, and whether to show Paragraph or Font or both types of styles. To view the style names with their styles applied, click the *Show Preview* check box near the bottom of the Styles pane.

Reveal Formatting

To display complete format properties for selected text in the document, use the Reveal Formatting task pane as shown in Figure 2.27. The properties are displayed by Font, Paragraph, and Section, enabling you to click the plus or minus sign next to each item to view or hide the underlying details. The properties in each area are links to the associated dialog boxes. Click Alignment or Justification, for example, within the Paragraph area to open the Paragraph dialog box, where you can change the indicated property. This panel is often helpful for troubleshooting a format problem in a document. To view this pane, click the Styles Dialog Box Launcher on the Home tab, click Style Inspector at the bottom of the Styles pane, then click Reveal Formatting in the Style Inspector pane. If you use this feature often, you can add it to the Quick Access Toolbar. To add it, click the Office Button, then click Word Options; select *Customize* on the left side of the Word Options dialog box, then click the drop-down arrow for *Choose commands from* and select *All Commands*. Scroll down the alphabetical list and select *Reveal Formatting*, then click the Add button displayed between the two large lists. Click OK to save the addition.

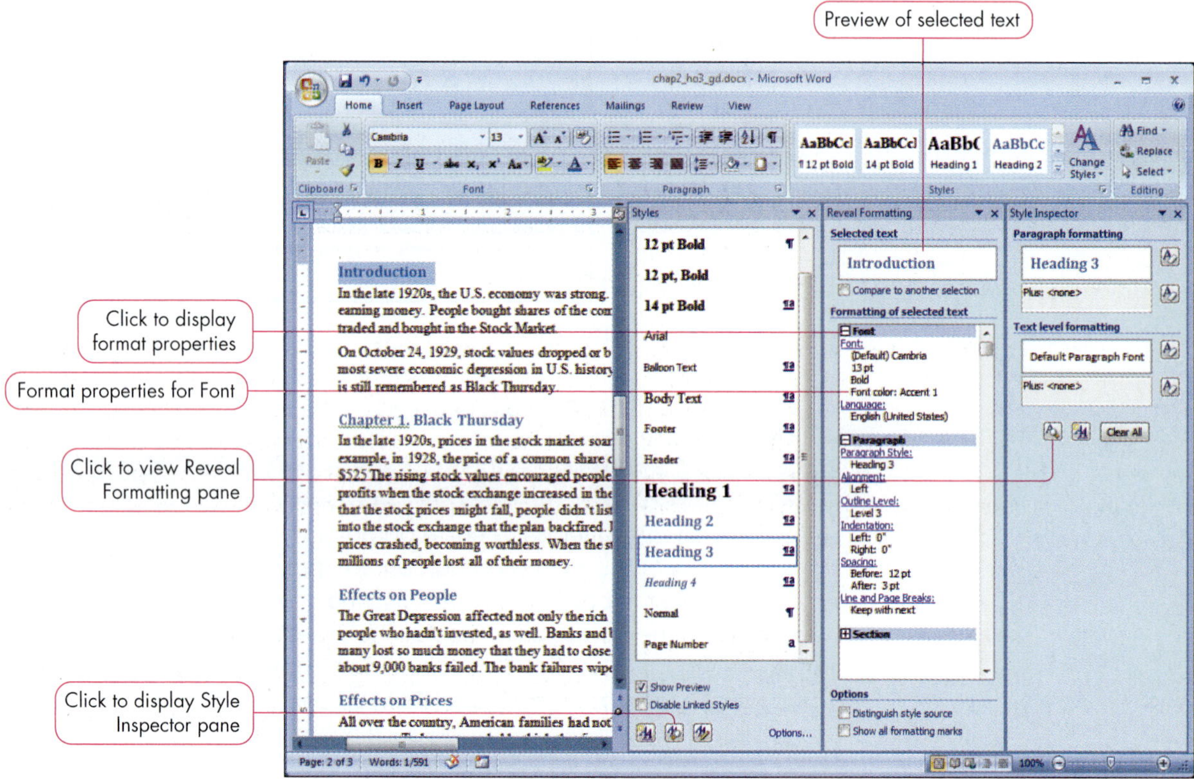

Figure 2.27 Reveal Formatting

Use the Outline View

Outline view is a structural view that displays varying amounts of detail.

One additional advantage of styles is that they enable you to view a document in the Outline view. The ***Outline view*** does not display a conventional outline, but rather a structural view of a document that can be collapsed or expanded as necessary. Consider, for example, Figure 2.28, which displays the Outline view of a report about the Great Depression. The heading for each tip is formatted according to the Heading 3 style. The text of each tip is formatted according to the Body Text style.

The advantage of Outline view is that you can collapse or expand portions of a document to provide varying amounts of detail. We have, for example, collapsed almost the entire document in Figure 2.28, displaying the headings while suppressing the body text. We also expanded the text for two sections (*Introduction* and *The New Deal)* for purposes of illustration.

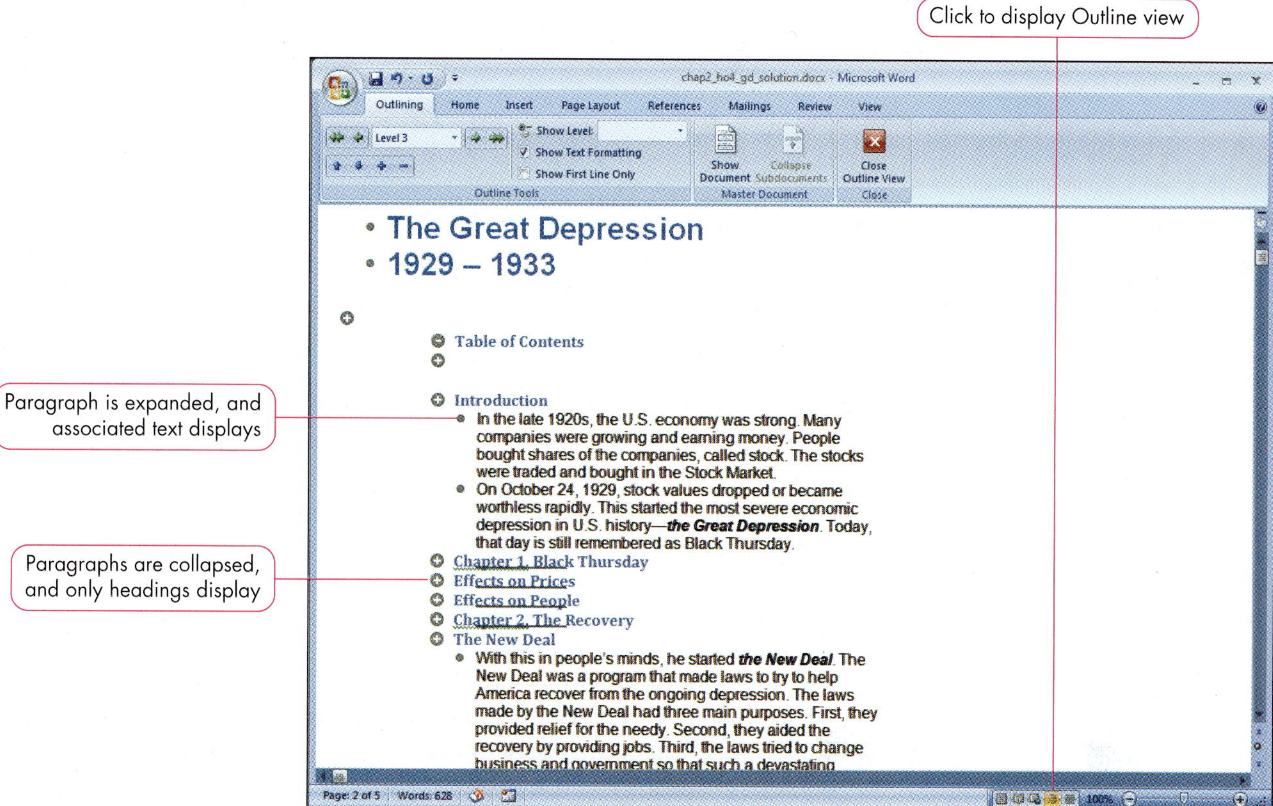

Figure 2.28 The Outline View

Now assume that you want to move one paragraph from its present position to a different position in the document. Without the Outline view, the text might stretch over several pages, making it difficult to see the text of both areas at the same time. Using the Outline view, however, you can collapse what you do not need to see, then simply click and drag headings to rearrange the text within the document. The Outline view is very useful with long documents, but it requires the use of styles throughout the document.

TIP The Outline Versus the Outline View

A conventional outline is created as a multilevel list using the Multilevel List command in the Paragraph group on the Home tab. Text for the outline is entered in the Print Layout view, *not* the Outline view. The latter provides a condensed view of a document that is used in conjunction with styles.

Use the AutoFormat Feature

Styles are extremely powerful. They enable you to impose uniform formatting within a document, and they let you take advantage of the Outline view. What if, however, you have an existing or lengthy document that does not contain any styles (other than the default Normal style, which is applied to every paragraph)? Do you have to manually go through every paragraph in order to apply the appropriate style? Fortunately, the answer is no, because the AutoFormat feature provides a quick solution. The ***AutoFormat*** feature analyzes a document and formats it for you; it evaluates an entire document and determines how each paragraph is used, then it applies an appropriate style to each paragraph. To use the AutoFormat feature, you must add it to the Quick Access Toolbar using the same procedure explained previously in the Reveal Formatting section.

The ***AutoFormat*** feature analyzes a document and formats it for you.

Hands-On Exercises

3 | Styles

Skills covered: 1. Apply Style Properties **2.** Modify the Body Text Style **3.** Modify the Heading 3 Style **4.** Select the Outline View **5.** Create a Paragraph Style **6.** Create a Character Style **7.** View the Completed Document

Step 1
Apply Style Properties

Refer to Figure 2.29 as you complete Step 1.

a. Open the document *chap2_ho3_gd* in the **Exploring Word folder** and save it as **chap2_ho3_gd_solution.**

b. Press **Ctrl+Home** to move to the beginning of the document.

   Notice the headings have been formatted with a 12-point bold font.

c. Select the first two lines, *The Great Depression* and *1929–1933*, then click **Heading 1** from the Quick Style gallery in the Styles group on the Home tab.

d. Click anywhere in the first paragraph heading, *Introduction*. Click the **Styles Dialog Box Launcher** on the Home tab. Double-click the title bar of the task pane to dock it, if necessary, so it does not float on the screen. Click the down arrow that displays when you hover over the *12 pt Bold* style listed in the Styles pane, then click **Select All 7 Instance(s).**

   All paragraph headings in this document are selected as shown in Figure 2.29.

e. Click the **More button** on the right side of the **Quick Style** gallery to display more styles, then click the **Heading 3** style.

   When you hover your mouse over the different styles in the gallery, the Live Preview feature displays the style on your selected text but will not apply it until you click on the style.

f. Save the document.

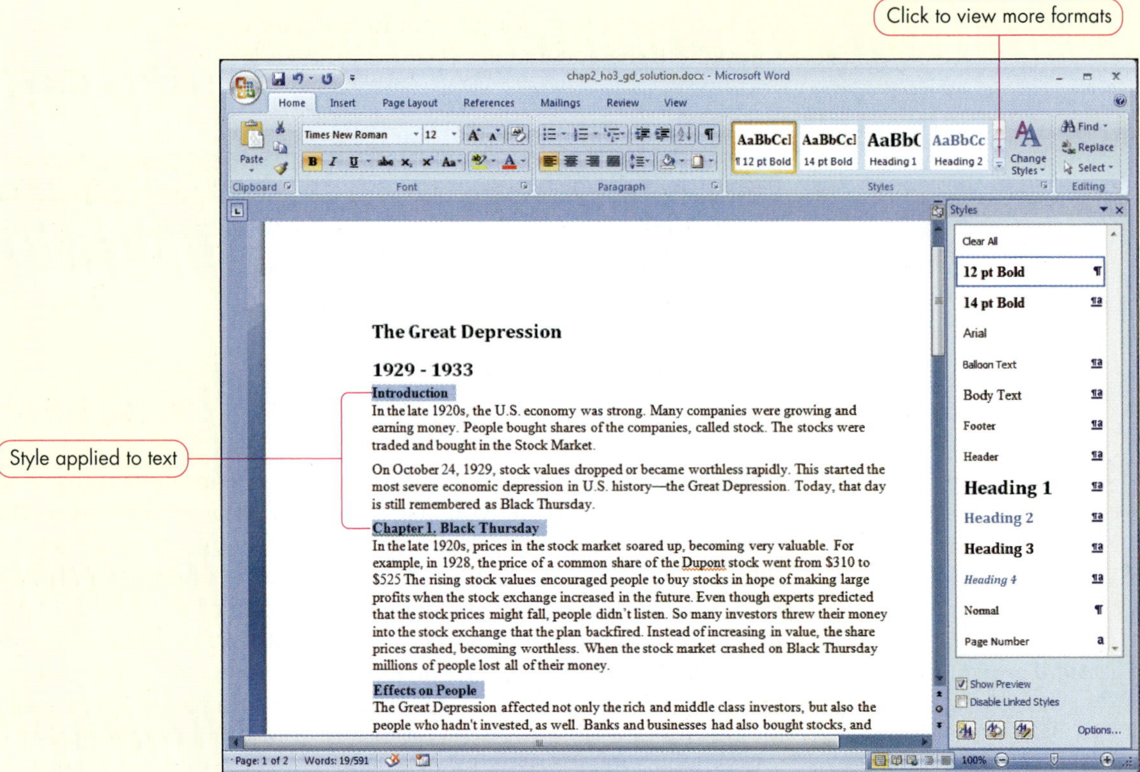

Figure 2.29 View Style Properties

Step 2
Modify the Body Text Style

Refer to Figure 2.30 as you complete Step 2.

a. Press **Ctrl+Home** to move to the beginning of the document. Place the insertion point in the first paragraph, then notice the Body Text style is selected in the Styles pane. Click the down arrow next to the style and click **Modify** to display the Modify Style dialog box.

TROUBLESHOOTING: If you click the style name instead of the down arrow, you will apply the style to the selected text instead of modifying it. Click Undo on the Quick Access Toolbar to cancel the command. Click the down arrow next to the style name to display the associated menu, and click the Modify command to display the Modify Style dialog box.

b. Change the font to **Arial**. Click **Justify** to change the alignment of every paragraph in the document formatted with the *Body Text* style.

c. Click **Format** in the lower-left corner of the window as shown in Figure 2.30, then click **Paragraph** to display the Paragraph dialog box. If necessary, click the **Line and Page Breaks tab**.

The box for Widow/Orphan control is checked by default. This option ensures that any paragraph defined by the Body Text style will not be split, leaving a single line of text at the bottom or top of a page.

d. Click the **Keep lines together check box** in the *Pagination* section.

This option is a more stringent requirement and ensures that the entire paragraph is not split.

e. Click **OK** to close the Paragraph dialog box. Click **OK** to close the Modify Style dialog box.

All of the multiline paragraphs in the document change automatically to reflect the new definition of the Body Text style, which includes full justification, a new font, and ensuring that a paragraph is not split across pages.

f. Save the document.

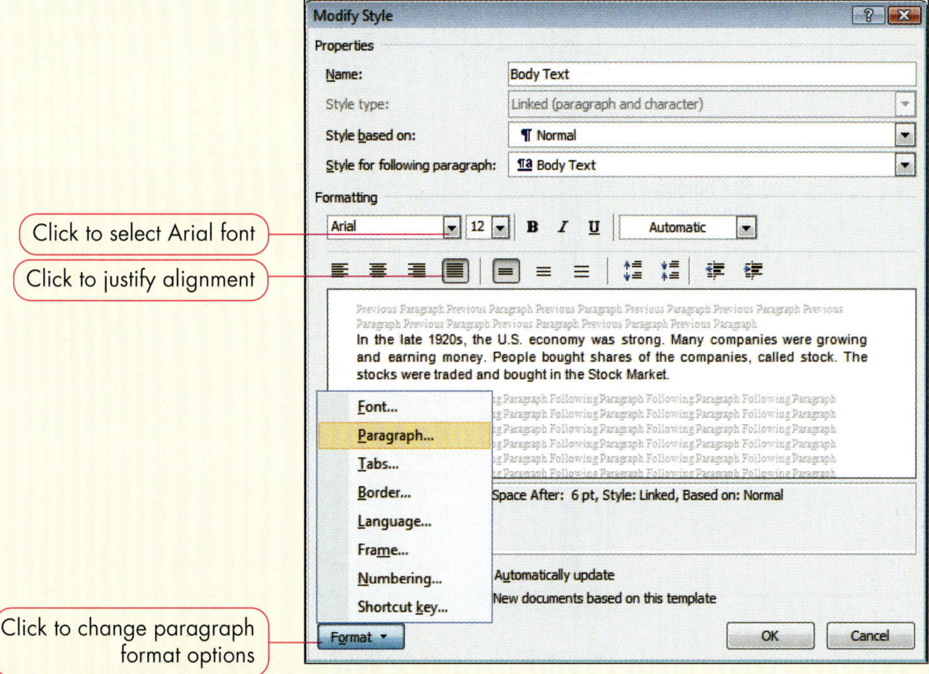

Figure 2.30 Modify the Body Text Style

Step 3
Modify the Heading 3 Style

Refer to Figure 2.31 as you complete Step 3.

a. Place the insertion point in one of the headings that has been formatted with the *Heading 3* style. Scroll, if necessary, to view *Heading 3* in the Styles pane. Hover your mouse over Heading 3, click the down arrow, then click **Modify** to display the Modify Style dialog box.

b. Click the **Font Color drop-down arrow** to display the palette in Figure 2.31. Click **Blue, Accent 1**, the blue color swatch on the first row, to change the color of all of the headings in the document.

You see a preview of the effect as you hover the mouse over the color, but the change will not take effect until you click *OK* to accept the settings and close the dialog box.

c. Click **Format** at the bottom of the dialog box, then click **Paragraph** to display the Paragraph dialog box. Click the **Indents and Spacing tab**, then change the **Spacing After** to **0**. Click **OK** to accept the settings and close the Paragraph dialog box.

You modified the style by changing the spacing after the heading to 0, which forces the paragraph text to display closer to the heading.

d. Click **OK** to close the Modify Style dialog box.

The formatting in your document has changed to reflect the changes in the Heading 3 style.

e. Save the document.

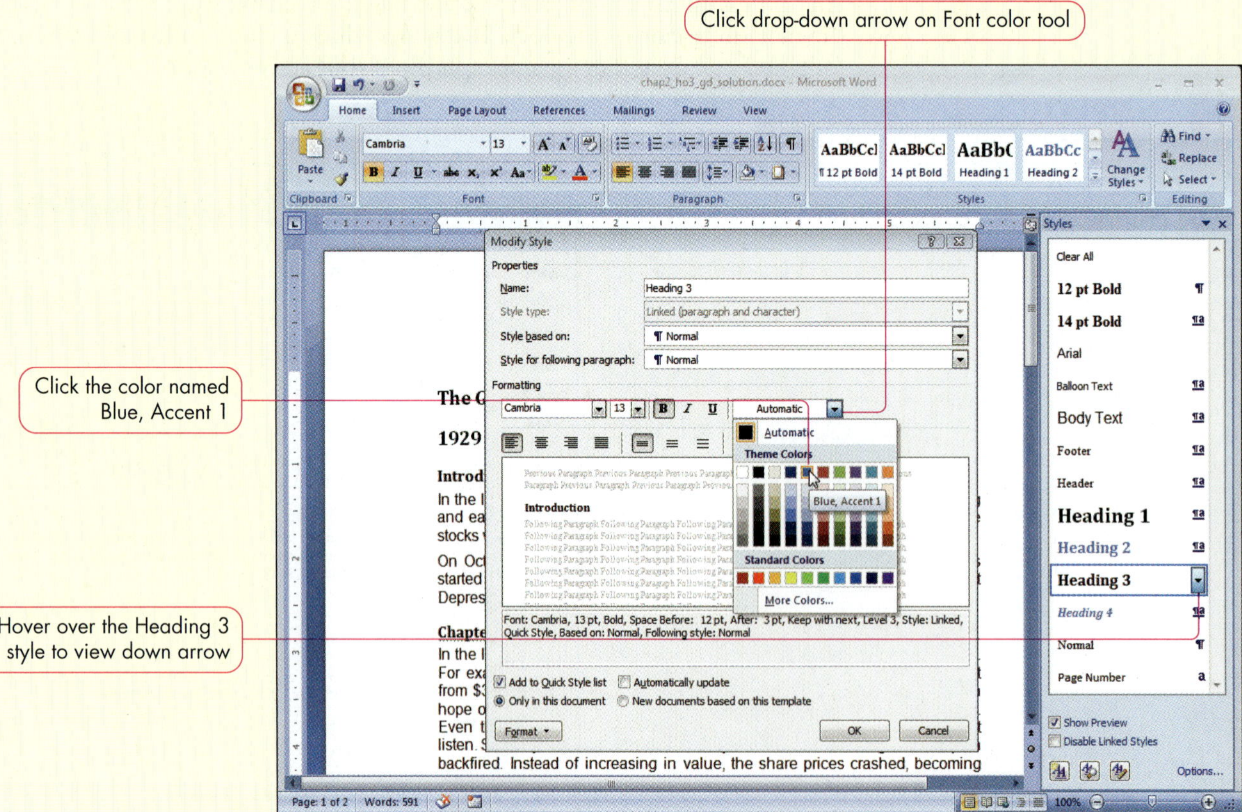

Figure 2.31 Modify the Heading 3 Style

TIP Space Before and After

Within single-spaced text, it is common practice to press the Enter key twice at the end of a paragraph (once to end the paragraph, and a second time to insert a blank line before the next paragraph). The same effect is achieved by setting the spacing before or after the paragraph using the Spacing Before or After list boxes in the Paragraph dialog box. The latter technique gives you greater flexibility in that you can specify any amount of spacing (e.g., 6 pt) to leave only half a line before or after a paragraph. It also enables you to change the spacing between paragraphs more easily because the spacing information is stored within the paragraph style.

Step 4
Select the Outline View

Refer to Figure 2.32 as you complete Step 4.

a. Close the Styles pane. Click the **View tab**, then click **Outline** to display the document in Outline view.

b. Place the insertion point to the left of the first paragraph heading, *Introduction*, and select the rest of the document. Click the **Outlining tab**, if necessary, then click **Collapse** in the Outline Tools group.

   The entire document collapses so that only the headings display.

c. Click in the heading titled *The New Deal* as shown in Figure 2.32. Click **Expand** in the Outline Tools group to see the subordinate items under this heading.

d. Select the paragraph heading *Effects on Prices*, then click **Move Up** on the Outline Tools group.

   You moved the paragraph above the paragraph that precedes it in the outline. Note that you also can drag and drop a selected paragraph.

e. Save the document.

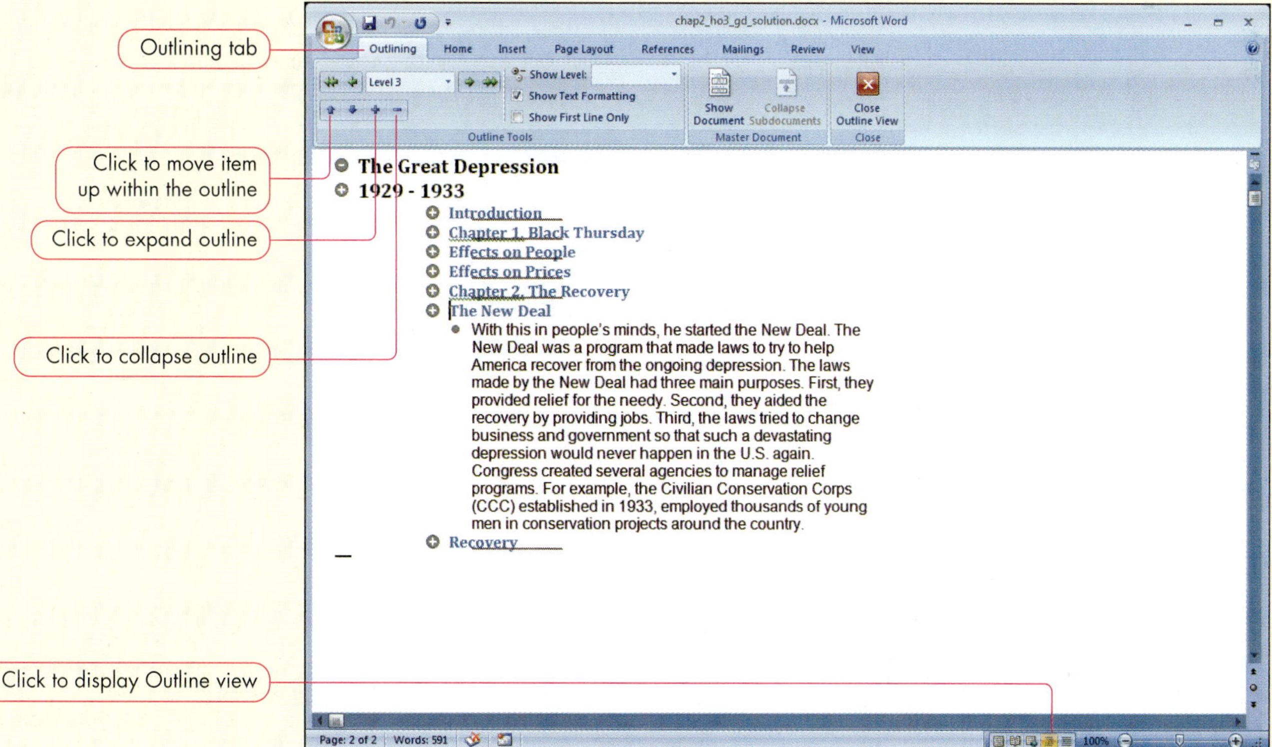

Figure 2.32 The Outline View

Step 5
Create a Paragraph Style

Refer to Figure 2.33 as you complete Step 5.

a. Click Close Outline View to change to return to Print Layout view. Click the **Home tab**, if necessary, and then click the **Styles Dialog Box Launcher** to open the Styles pane.

b. Press **Ctrl+Home** to move the insertion point to the beginning of the document, then place the insertion point to the right of *1933* and press **Ctrl+Enter**.

   Inserting a page break creates space where you can add a title page.

c. Press **Ctrl+Home** to move the insertion point to the beginning of the new page, then select both lines on the title page. Scroll up if necessary and click **Clear All** in the Styles pane. Click the **Font arrow** on the Home tab and select **Arial,** then click the **Font Size arrow** and select **24**; click **Bold** and **Center** in the Paragraph group on the Home tab. Click the **Font Color arrow** and select **Blue, Accent 1** on the color palette (the blue color swatch on the first row) to change the color of the text to blue.

   The Styles task pane displays the specifications for the text you just entered. You have created a new style, but the style is not yet named.

d. Point to the description for the title on the Styles pane (you may only be able to see the first or last few format effects such as Bold, Accent 1), hover your mouse over the description to view the down arrow, then click the down arrow as shown in Figure 2.33, and then select **Modify Style** to display the Modify Style dialog box.

e. Click in the **Name text box** in the Properties area and type **Report Title** as the name of the new style. Click **OK**.

f. Save the document.

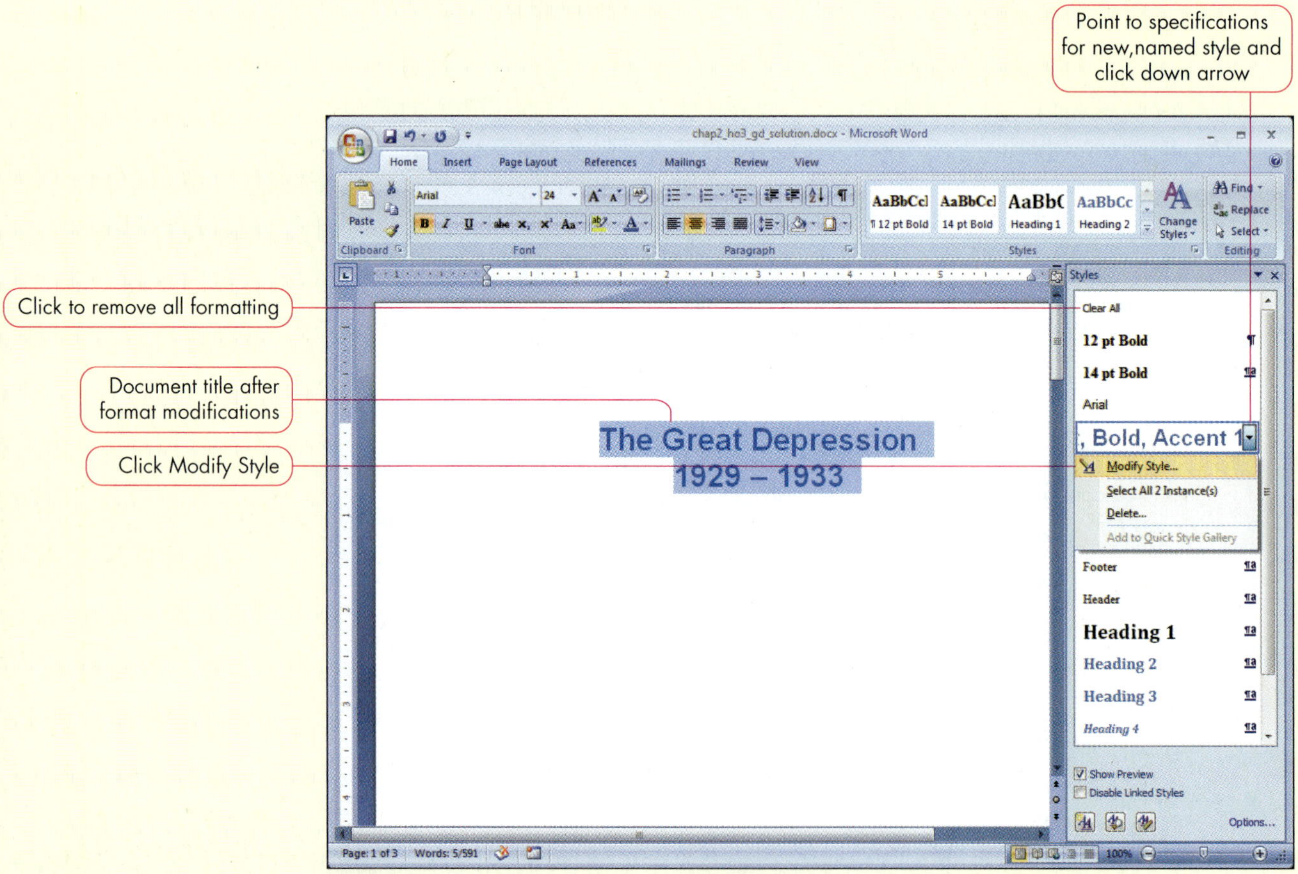

Figure 2.33 Create a Paragraph Style

Step 6
Create a Character Style

Refer to Figure 2.34 as you complete Step 6.

a. Select the words *the Great Depression* (that appear within the second paragraph of the Introduction). Click **Bold** and **Italic** in the Font group on the Home tab.

b. Click **New Style** on the bottom of the Styles pane, and then type **Emphasize** as the name of the style.

c. Click the **Style type drop-down arrow** and select **Character** (see Figure 2.34). Click **OK**.

   The style named Emphasize is listed in the Style pane and can be used throughout your document.

d. Select the words *the New Deal* in the first sentence of the *New Deal* section. Click **More** in the Quick Style gallery on the Home tab, and apply the newly created *Emphasize* character style to the selected text. Close the Styles task pane.

e. Save the document.

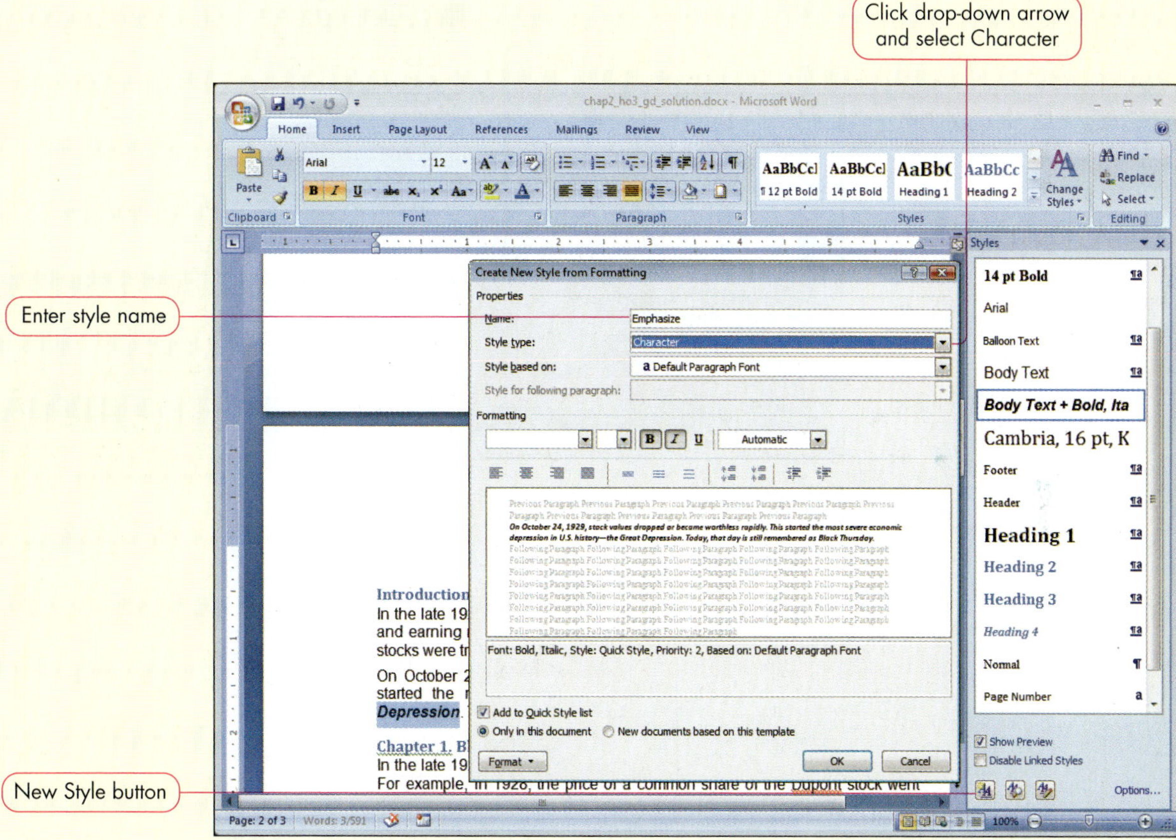

Figure 2.34 Create a Character Style

Step 7
View the Completed Document

Refer to Figure 2.35 as you complete Step 7.

a. Click **Zoom** on the status bar, click **Many pages**, then click and drag to select 1 x 3 pages. Click **OK**.

   You should see a multipage display similar to Figure 2.35. The text on the individual pages is too small to read, but you can see the page breaks and overall document flow. According to the specifications in the Body Text style, the paragraphs should all be justified, and each should fit completely on one page without spilling over to the next page.

b. Click to the left of the title on the first page and press **Enter** three times to position the title further down the page.

c. Save the *chap2_ho3_gd_solution* document and keep it onscreen if you plan to continue with the next hands-on exercise. Close the file and exit Word if you will not continue with the next exercise at this time.

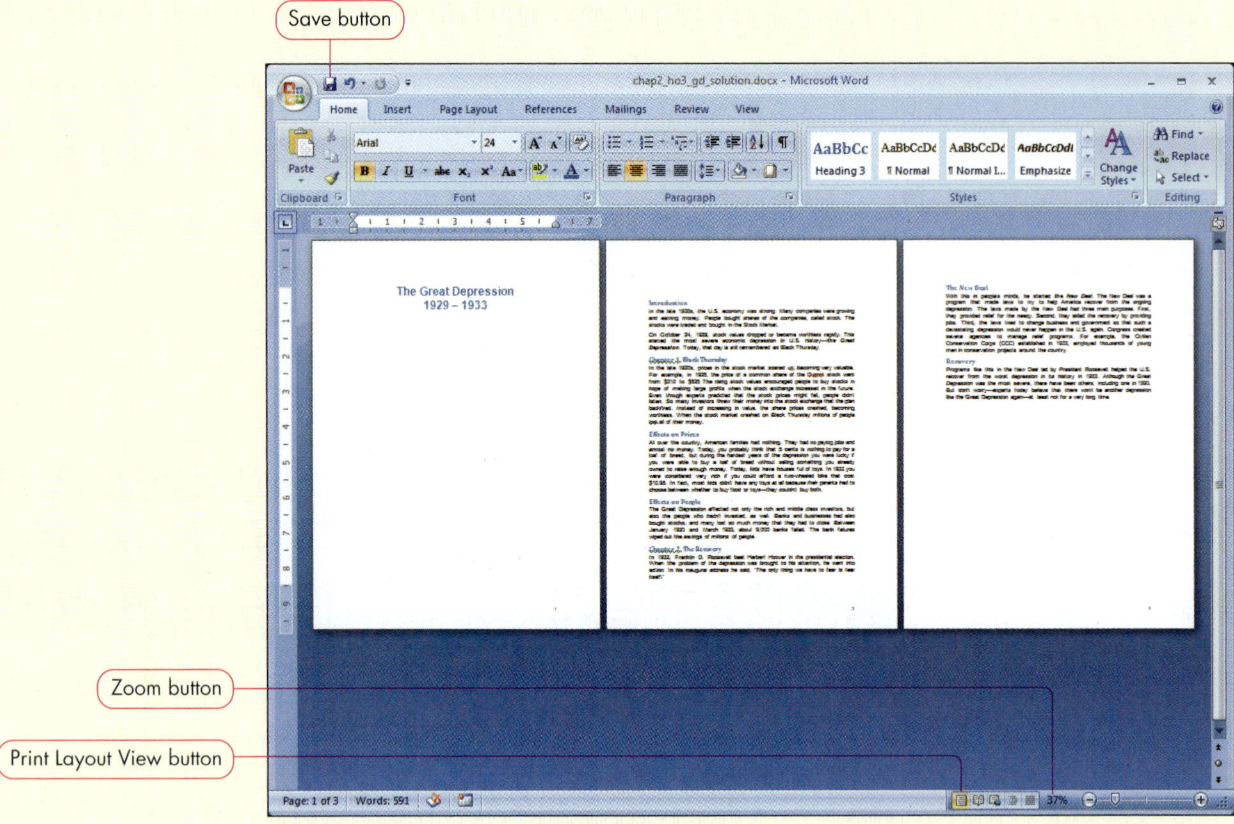

Figure 2.35 The Completed Document

Table of Contents and Indexes

Well-prepared long documents include special features to help readers locate information easily. You can use Word to help you create these supplemental document components, such as a table of contents, with minimal effort.

Well-prepared long documents include special features to help readers locate information easily. For example, people often refer to the table of contents or the index in a long document—such as a book, reference manual, or company policy—to locate particular topics within that document. You can use Word to help you create these supplemental document components with minimal effort.

In this section you generate a table of contents at the beginning of a document. You then learn how to designate text to include in an index and then generate the index at the end of a document.

Creating a Table of Contents

A ***table of contents*** lists headings and the page numbers where they appear in a document.

A ***table of contents*** lists headings in the order they appear in a document and the page numbers where the entries begin. Word can create the table of contents automatically, if you apply a style to each heading in the document. You can use built-in styles, Heading 1 through Heading 9, or identify your own custom styles to use when generating the table of contents. Word also will update the table to accommodate the addition or deletion of headings and/or changes in page numbers brought about through changes in the document.

The table of contents is located on the References tab. You can select from several predefined formats such as Classic and Formal, as well as determine how many levels to display in the table; the latter correspond to the heading styles used within the document. You can determine whether or not to right-align the page numbers; and you also can choose to include a leader character to draw the reader's eyes across the page from a heading to a page number.

Creating an Index

An ***index*** is a listing of topics and the page numbers where the topic is discussed.

An index puts the finishing touch on a long document. The ***index*** provides an alphabetical listing of topics covered in a document, along with the page numbers where the topic is discussed. Typically the index appears at the end of a book or document. Word will create an index automatically, provided that the entries for the index have been previously marked. This result, in turn, requires you to go through a document, select the terms to be included in the index, and mark them accordingly. It is not as tedious as it sounds. You can, for example, select a single occurrence of an entry and tell Word to mark all occurrences of that entry for the index. You also can create cross-references, such as "see also Internet."

After you specify the entries, create the index by choosing the Insert Index command on the References tab. You can choose a variety of styles for the index, just as you can for the table of contents. Word arranges the index entries in alphabetical order and enters the appropriate page references. You also can create additional index entries and/or move text within a document, then update the index with the click of a mouse.

Table of Contents and Index Styles

Table of Contents

TABLE OF CONTENTS 2
INTRODUCTION 2
CHAPTER 1. BLACK THURSDAY 2
EFFECTS ON PRICES 2
EFFECTS ON PEOPLE 3
CHAPTER 2. THE RECOVERY 3
THE NEW DEAL 3
RECOVERY 3

Fancy Format

INDEX

B
Bank failures, 3
Black Thursday, 2, *See* Stock Market

C
Civilian Conservation Corps, 3

D
Dupont, 2

H
Hoover, 3

N
New Deal, 3

R
Roosevelt, 3

S
Stock Market, 2

Bulleted Format

Table of Contents

Table of Contents........2
Introduction........2
Chapter 1. Black Thursday........2
Effects on Prices........2
Effects on People........3
Chapter 2. The Recovery........3
The New Deal........3
Recovery........3

Formal Format

INDEX

B
Bank failures, 3
Black Thursday, 2, *See* Stock Market

C
Civilian Conservation Corps, 3

D
Dupont, 2

H
Hoover, 3

N
New Deal, 3

R
Roosevelt, 3

S
Stock Market, 2

Classic Format

Table of Contents

Table of Contents 2
Introduction 2
Chapter 1. Black Thursday 2
Effects on Prices 3
Effects on People 3
Chapter 2. The Recovery 3
The New Deal 3
Recovery 3

Modern Format

INDEX

B
Bank failures, 3
Black Thursday, 2, *See* Stock Market

C
Civilian Conservation Corps, 3

D
Dupont, 2

H
Hoover, 3

N
New Deal, 3

R
Roosevelt, 3

S
Stock Market, 2

Fancy Format

Table of Contents

Table of Contents 2
Introduction 2
Chapter 1. Black Thursday 2
Effects on Prices 2
Effects on People 3
Chapter 2. The Recovery 3
The New Deal 3
Recovery 3

Simple Format

INDEX

B
Bank failures · 3
Black Thursday · 2, *See* Stock Market

C
Civilian Conservation Corps · 3

D
Dupont · 2

H
Hoover · 3

N
New Deal · 3

R
Roosevelt · 3

S
Stock Market · 2

Modern Format

Hands-On Exercises

4 | Reference Pages

Skills covered: 1. Apply a Style **2.** Insert a Table of Contents **3.** Define an Index Entry **4.** Create the Index **5.** Complete the Index **6.** View the Completed Document

Step 1
Apply a Style

Refer to Figure 2.36 as you complete Step 1.

a. Open the *chap2_ho3_gd_solution* document if you closed it after the last hands-on exercise, and save it as **chap2_ho4_gd_solution**.

b. Click **Zoom** in the status bar, click **Page width**, then click **OK**. Scroll to the top of the second page.

c. Click to the left of the *Introduction* title. Type **Table of Contents** and then press **Enter** two times. Press **Ctrl+Enter** to insert a page break.

   The table of contents displays on a page between the title page and the body of the document using the Heading 3 style you modified in the previous exercise.

d. Click anywhere in the *Table of Contents* heading.

   TROUBLESHOOTING: If the Heading 3 style does not display, click Heading 3 from the Quick Style gallery on the Home tab.

e. Click **Center** in the Paragraph group on the Home tab and compare your document to Figure 2.36.

f. Save the document.

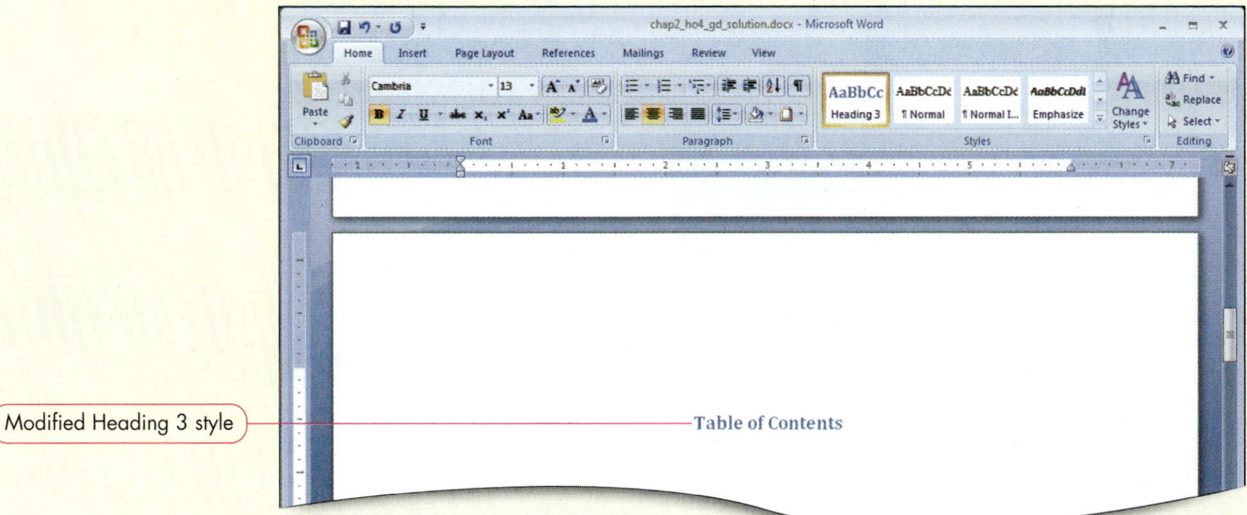

Figure 2.36 Apply a Style to a Heading

Step 2
Insert a Table of Contents

Refer to Figure 2.37 as you complete Step 2.

a. Place the insertion point immediately under the *Table of Contents* title, then click **Zoom** on the status bar. Click **Many pages**, then click and drag to select **1 x 4 Pages**. Click **OK**.

The display changes to show all four pages in the document.

b. Click the **References tab**, and then click **Table of Contents** in the Table of Contents group. Select **Insert Table of Contents.**

The Table of Contents dialog box displays (see Figure 2.37).

c. If necessary, click the **Show page numbers check box** and the **Right align page numbers check box**.

d. Click the **Formats drop-down arrow** in the *General* section and select **Distinctive**. Click the **Tab leader drop-down arrow** in the *Print Preview* section and choose a **dot leader**. Click **OK**.

Word takes a moment to create the table of contents and then displays it in the location of your insertion point.

e. Save the document.

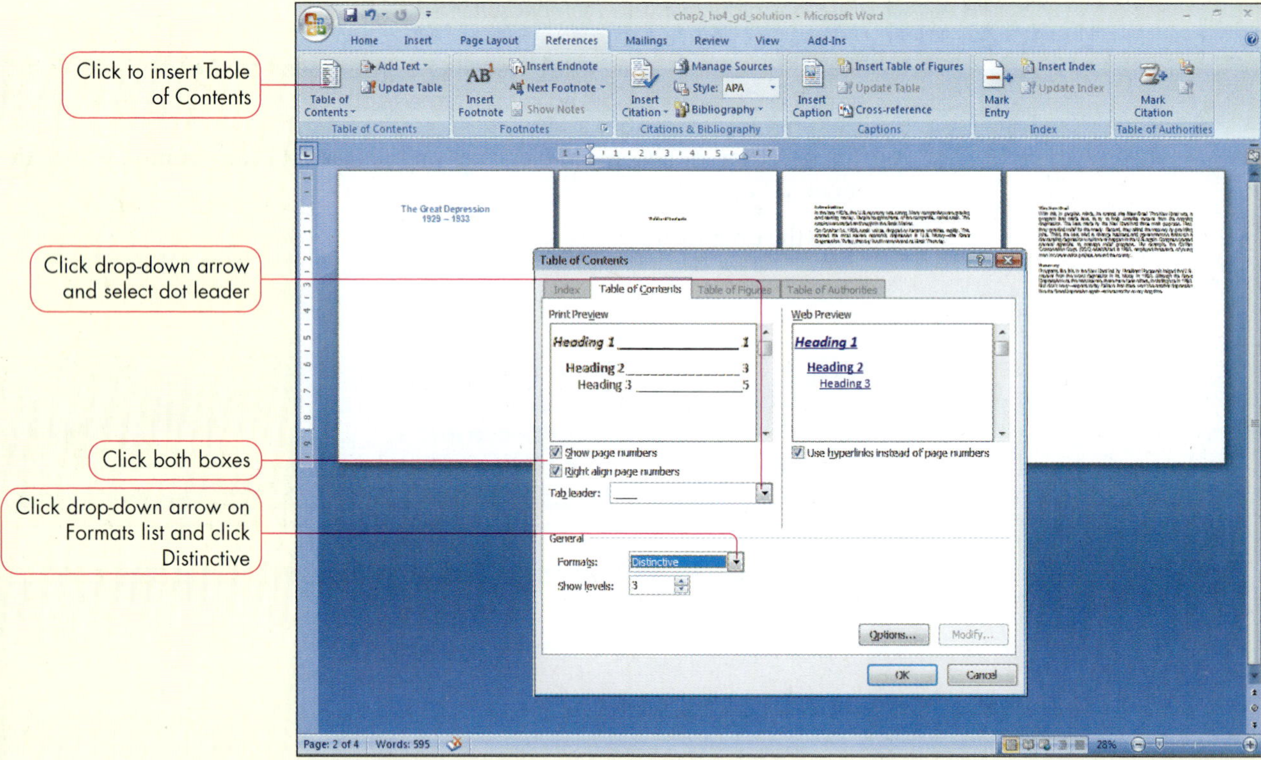

Figure 2.37 Create a Table of Contents

TIP Updating the Table of Contents

You can use a shortcut menu to update the table of contents. Point to any entry in the table of contents, then press the right mouse button to display the menu. Click **Update Field**, click **Update Entire Table**, and then click **OK**. The table of contents is adjusted automatically to reflect page number changes as well as the addition or deletion of any text defined by a style.

Step 3
Define an Index Entry

Refer to Figure 2.38 as you complete Step 3.

a. Press **Ctrl+Home** to move to the beginning of the document. Drag the Zoom Slider on the task bar to 100%. Click the **Home tab**, then click **Find** in the Editing group. Type **Black Thursday** in the *Find what* box and then click **Find Next** two times.

You click Find Next two times because the first occurrence of *Black Thursday* is in the table of contents, but that is not the occurrence you want to mark for the index.

b. Click **Cancel** to close the Find and Replace dialog box. Click **Show/Hide ¶** in the Paragraph group on the Home tab so you can see the nonprinting characters in the document.

The index entries that were created by the authors appear in curly brackets and begin with the letters XE.

c. Check that the text *Black Thursday* is selected within the document, then press **Alt+Shift+X** to display the Mark Index Entry dialog box as shown in Figure 2.38.

TROUBLESHOOTING: If you forget the shortcut, click Mark Entry on the References tab.

d. Click **Mark** to create the index entry.

After you create the index entry, you see the field code, {XE "Black Thursday"}, to indicate that the index entry is created. The Mark Index Entry dialog box stays open so that you can create additional entries by selecting additional text.

e. Click the **Cross-reference check box** in the *Options* section. Type **Stock Market** in the Cross-reference text box, then click **Mark**.

f. Click in the document, scroll down to the next paragraph, select the text *Dupont*, then click in the Mark Index Entry dialog box and notice Main entry automatically changes to Dupont. Click **Mark** to create the index entry, then close the Mark Index Entry dialog box.

g. Save the document.

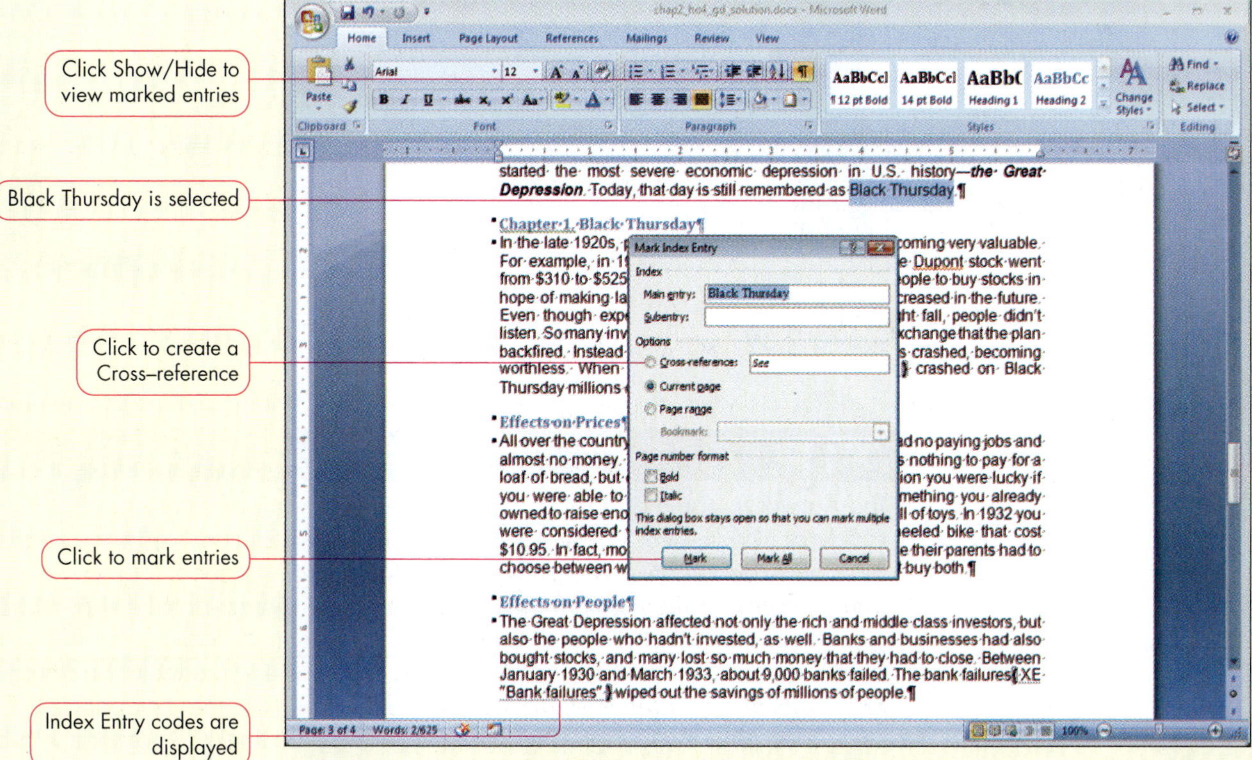

Figure 2.38 Create an Index Entry

Step 4
Create the Index

Refer to Figure 2.39 as you complete Step 4.

a. Press **Ctrl+End** to move to the end of the document, then press **Enter** to begin a new line.

This spot is where you will insert the index.

b. Click the **References tab** and then click **Insert Index** in the Index group.

The Index dialog box displays as shown in Figure 2.39.

c. Click the **Formats drop-down arrow** and select **Classic**. If necessary, click the **Columns spin box arrows** until **2** displays. Click **OK** to create the index.

TROUBLESHOOTING: Click Undo on the Quick Access Toolbar if you are not satisfied with the appearance of the index or if it does not display at the end of the document, then repeat the process.

d. Save the document.

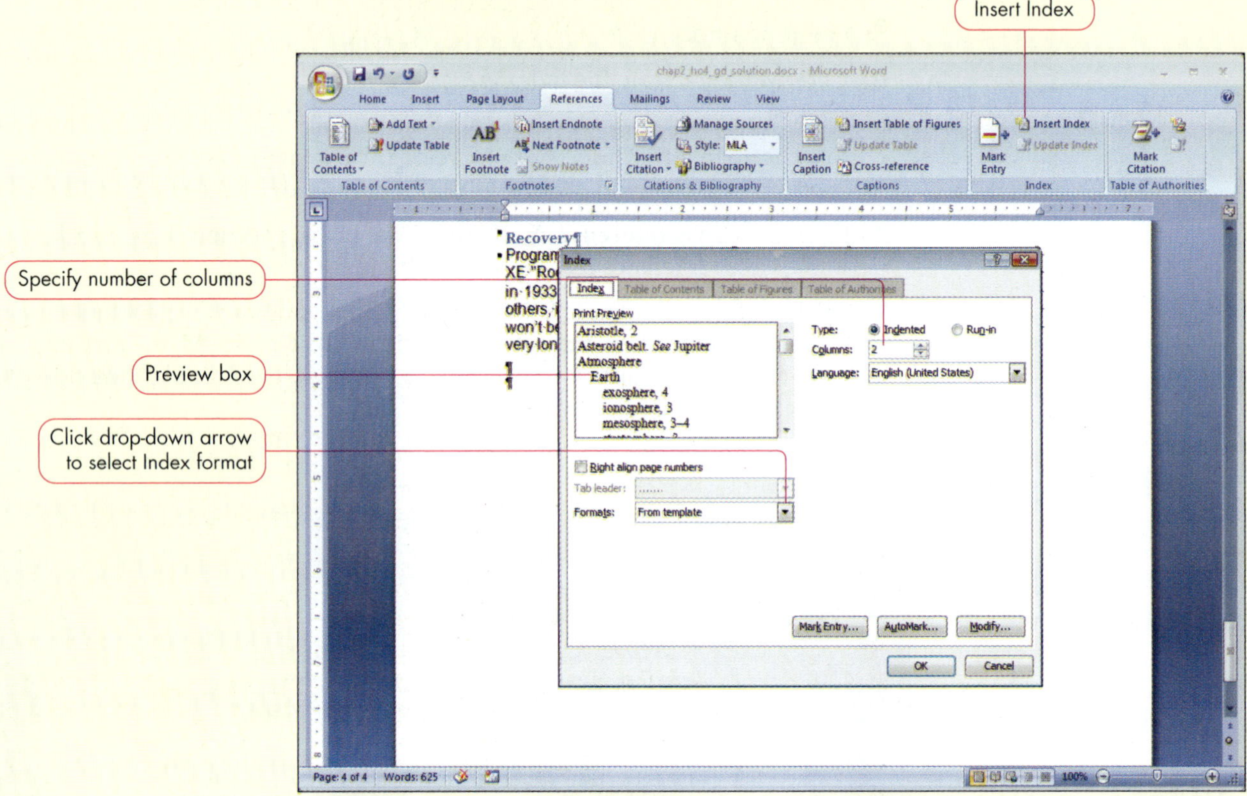

Figure 2.39 Create the Index

TIP AutoMark Index Entries

The AutoMark command will, as the name implies, automatically mark all occurrences of all entries for inclusion in an index. To use the feature, you have to create a separate document that lists the terms you want to reference, then you execute the AutoMark command from the Index dialog box. The advantage is that it is fast. The disadvantage is that every occurrence of an entry is marked in the index so that a commonly used term may have too many page references. You can, however, delete superfluous entries by manually deleting the field codes. Click **Show/Hide (¶)** in the Paragraph group of the Home tab if you do not see the entries in the document.

Step 5
Complete the Index

Refer to Figure 2.40 as you complete Step 5.

a. At the beginning of the index click to position the insertion point on the left of the letter "B".

b. Click the **Page Layout tab,** then click **Breaks** and select **Next Page**.

   The index moves to the top of a new page.

c. Click the **Insert tab**, click **Page Number** in the Header & Footer group, and then select **Format Page Numbers** to display the Page Number Format dialog box. Click **Continue from previous section**, if necessary, then click **OK**.

d. Click **Header** in the Header & Footer group, and then click **Edit Header** to display the Design tab as shown in Figure 2.40. Click **Link to Previous.**

   When you toggle the Link to Previous indicator off you create a new header for this section that is independent of and different from the header in the previous section. Notice other Header and Footer options that display in the tab.

e. Type **INDEX** in the header. Select *INDEX* then on the Mini toolbar click **Center.** Click **Close Header and Footer** in the Close group to return to the document. Click **Show/Hide (¶)** in the Paragraph group on the Home tab to turn off display of field codes.

f. Save the document.

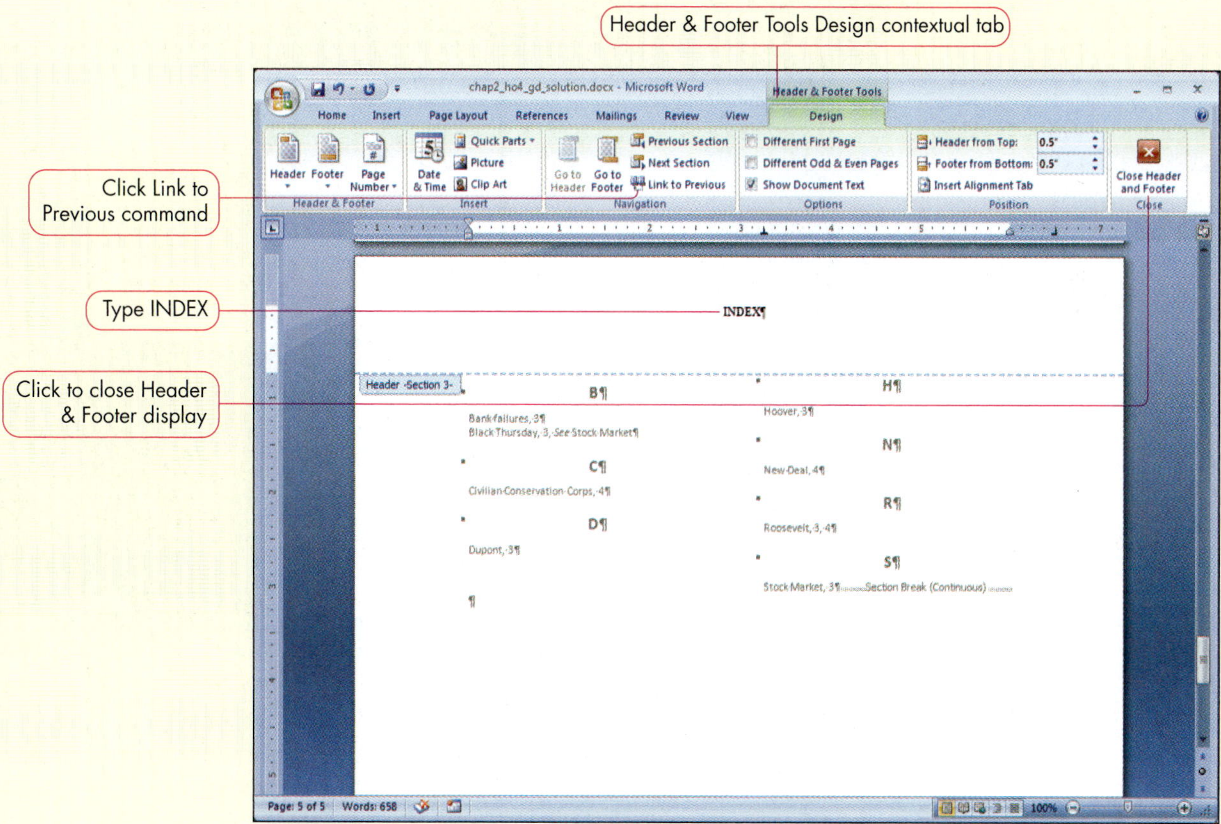

Figure 2.40 Complete the Index

TIP Check the Index Entries

Every entry in the index should begin with an uppercase letter. If this is not the case, it is because the origin entry within the body of the document was marked improperly. Click **Show/Hide ¶** in the Paragraph group on the Home tab to display the indexed entries within the document, which appear within brackets; e.g., {XE "Practice Files"}. Change each entry to begin with an uppercase letter as necessary.

Step 6 View the Completed Document

Refer to Figure 2.41 as you complete Step 6.

a. Click **Zoom** on the status bar. Click **Many pages** and drag to display **2 x 3 Pages**. Click **OK**.

   The completed document is shown in Figure 2.41. The index appears by itself on the last page of the document.

b. Save and close the *chap2_ho4_gd_solution* document.

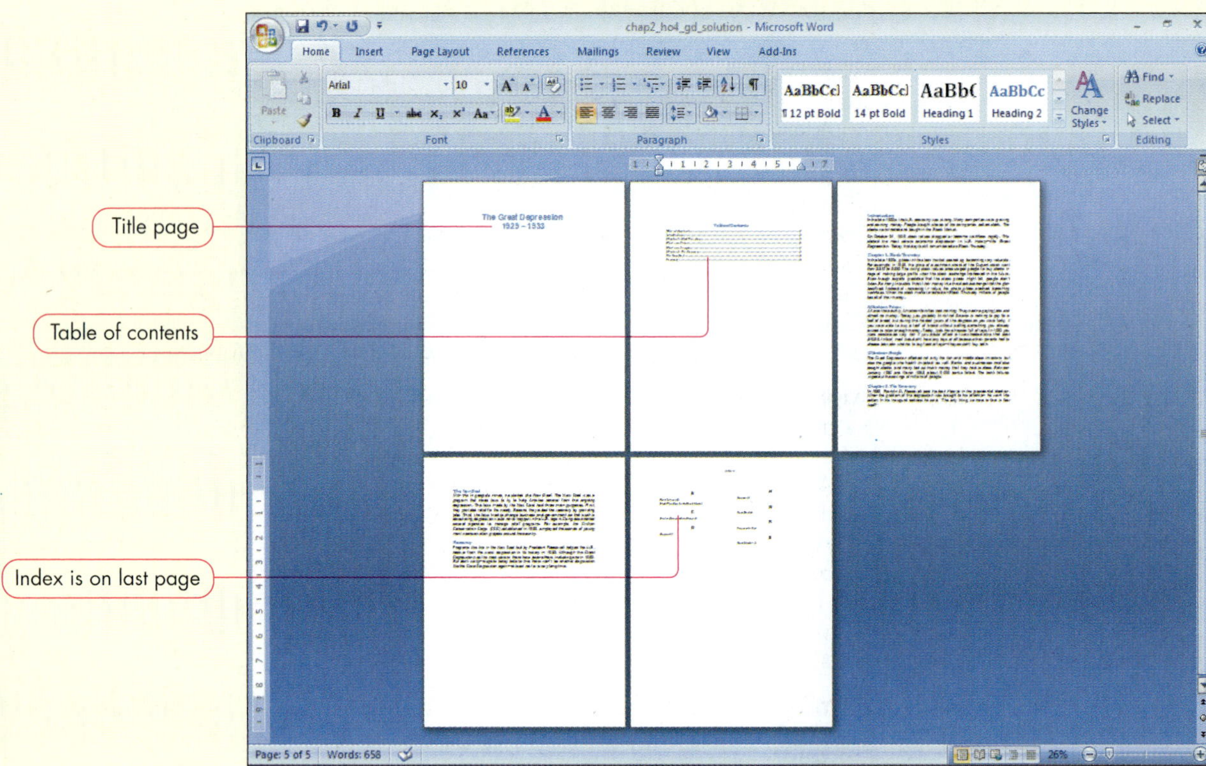

Figure 2.41 The Completed Document

Summary

1. **Apply font attributes through the Font dialog box.** Formatting occurs at the character, paragraph, or section level. The Font dialog box allows you to change spacing of the characters and also provides special formatting options for text that only appears on the screen. Through this dialog box, you can change the font and character spacing attributes including font, font size, font color, underline color, and effects. Use the character spacing options to control horizontal spacing between letters. You also can adjust the scale, position, and kerning of characters.

2. **Highlight text.** The Text Highlight Color command provides the ability to color text on screen so it stands out or resembles highlighting marks you often make in books. The Text Highlight Color command is located on the Home tab and also on the Mini toolbar that appears when you select text.

3. **Control word-wrapping with nonbreaking hyphens and nonbreaking spaces.** Occasionally, text wraps in an undesirable location in your document, or you just want to keep words together for better readability. To keep hyphenated words together on one line, use a nonbreaking hyphen to replace the regular hyphen. You insert a nonbreaking hyphen by pressing Ctrl+Shift+Hyphen in place of a hypen. You also can keep words together on one line by inserting a nonbreaking space instead of using the spacebar. To insert a nonbreaking space click Ctrl+Shift+Spacebar.

4. **Copy formats with the Format Painter.** Use the Format Painter to copy existing format features to other text for consistency in appearance. The Format Painter uses fewer clicks than formatting from scratch. You can use it one time by single-clicking Format Painter in the Clipboard group on the Home tab, then selecting the text to format. If you double-click Format Painter, it toggles on and you can select many items to format the text. To toggle off the Format Painter, press Esc or click Format Painter again.

5. **Set off paragraphs with tabs, borders, lists, and columns.** You can change the appearance and add interest to documents by using paragraph formatting options. Tabs allow you to set markers in the document to use for aligning text. Borders and shading are set at the character or paragraph level and enable you to use boxes and/or shading to highlight an area of your document. A bulleted or numbered list helps to organize information by emphasizing and/or ordering important topics. Columns add interest to a document by formatting text into side-by-side vertical blocks of text and are implemented at the section level.

6. **Apply paragraph formats.** You can use additional formatting options in the Paragraph dialog box. Paragraph alignment refers to the placement of text between the left and right margins; text can be aligned left, right, centered between, or justified, which allows it to touch both margins. Another option that incorporates the distance from margins is indention. You can specify indention from the left margin, right margin, or both, or use special indents such as hanging or first-line. Line spacing determines the space between lines in a document and can be customized as single, double, or 1.5, for example. You also can specify an amount of space to insert before or after a paragraph, which is more efficient than pressing Enter. Widow/Orphan control prevents a single line from displaying at the top or bottom of a page, separate from the rest of a paragraph.

7. **Create and modify styles.** A style is a set of formatting instructions that has been saved under a distinct name. Styles are created at the character or paragraph level and provide a consistent appearance to similar elements throughout a document. You can modify any existing style to change the formatting of all text defined by that style. You can even create a new style for use in the current or any other document. Styles provide the foundation to use other tools such as outlines and the table of contents. The Outline view displays a condensed view of a document based on styles within the document. Text may be collapsed or expanded as necessary to facilitate moving text within long documents. The Outline view does not display a conventional outline, which is created in Print Layout view using the Multilevel List command on the Home tab.

8. **Create a table of contents.** A table of contents lists headings in the order they appear in a document with their respective page numbers. Word can create it automatically, provided the built-in heading styles were applied previously to the items for inclusion.

9. **Create an index.** Word also will create an index automatically, provided that the entries for the index have been marked previously. This result, in turn, requires you to go through a document, select the appropriate text, and mark the entries accordingly.

Key Terms

Multiple Choice

1. Which of the following can be stored within a paragraph style?
   (a) Tabs and indents
   (b) Line spacing and alignment
   (c) Shading and borders
   (d) All of the above

2. What is the easiest way to change the alignment of five paragraphs scattered throughout a document, each of which is formatted with the same style?
   (a) Select the paragraphs individually, then click the appropriate alignment button.
   (b) Select the paragraphs at the same time, then click the appropriate alignment button on the Home tab.
   (c) Change the format of the existing style, which changes the paragraphs.
   (d) Retype the paragraphs according to the new specifications.

3. Which feature analyzes a document and formats it for you?
   (a) Character styles
   (b) AutoFormat
   (c) Multilevel list
   (d) Table of contents

4. Which of the following is used to create a conventional outline?
   (a) A Numbered list
   (b) The Outline view
   (c) A table of contents
   (d) An index

5. A(n) ___________ occurs when the first line of a paragraph is isolated at the bottom of a page and the rest of the paragraph continues on the next page.
   (a) widow
   (b) section break
   (c) footer
   (d) orphan

6. What is the keyboard shortcut to mark an index entry?
   (a) Index entries cannot be marked manually.
   (b) Press Ctrl+Enter
   (c) Ctrl+I
   (d) Alt+Shift+X

7. Which of the following is true regarding the formatting within a document?
   (a) Line spacing and alignment are implemented at the section level.
   (b) Margins, headers, and footers are implemented at the paragraph level.
   (c) Nonbreaking hyphens are implemented at the paragraph level.
   (d) Columns are implemented at the section level.

8. Which tab contains the Table of Contents and Index features?
   (a) Home
   (b) Insert
   (c) View
   (d) References

9. After you create and insert a table of contents into a document,
   (a) any subsequent page changes arising from the insertion or deletion of text to existing paragraphs must be entered manually.
   (b) any additions to the entries in the table arising due to the insertion of new paragraphs defined by a heading style must be entered manually.
   (c) an index can not be added to the document.
   (d) you can right-click, then select Update Field to update the table of contents.

10. Which of the following is a false statement about the Outline view?
    (a) It can be collapsed to display only headings.
    (b) It can be expanded to show the entire document.
    (c) It requires the application of styles.
    (d) It is used to create a conventional outline.

11. What is the best way to create a conventional outline in a Word document?
    (a) Use the Outline view
    (b) Use the Mulitlevel List command in the Paragraph group in Print Layout view
    (c) Use the Outlining toolbar
    (d) All of the above are equally acceptable.

...continued on Next Page

Multiple Choice Continued...

12. Which of the following is not a predefined Word style that is available in every document?

(a) Normal
(b) Heading 1
(c) Body Text
(d) Special 1

13. What happens if you modify the Body Text style in a Word document?

(a) Only the paragraph where the insertion point is located is changed.
(b) All paragraphs in the document will be changed.
(c) Only those paragraphs formatted with the Body Text style will be changed.
(d) It is not possible to change a Word default style such as Body Text.

14. Which of the following are not set at the paragraph level?

(a) Alignment
(b) Tabs and indents
(c) Line spacing
(d) Columns

15. Which of the following is a true statement regarding indents?

(a) Indents are measured from the edge of the page.
(b) The left, right, and first line indents must be set to the same value.
(c) The insertion point can be anywhere in the paragraph when indents are set.
(d) Indents must be set within the Paragraph dialog box.

16. The default tab stops are set to:

(a) Left indents every ½".
(b) Left indents every ¼".
(c) Right indents every ½".
(d) Right indents every ¼".

17. The spacing in an existing multipage document is changed from single spacing to double spacing throughout the document. What can you say about the number of hard and soft page breaks before and after the formatting change?

(a) The number of soft page breaks is the same, but the number and/or position of the hard page breaks is different.
(b) The number of hard page breaks is the same, but the number and/or position of the soft page breaks is different.
(c) The number and position of both hard and soft page breaks is the same.
(d) The number and position of both hard and soft page breaks is different.

18. Which of the following is not a valid use of the Format Painter?

(a) View formatting codes assigned to a paragraph.
(b) Copy the font style of a paragraph heading to other paragraph headings.
(c) Restore character style to a paragraph (whose style was deleted accidentally) using the style from a properly formatted paragraph.
(d) Copy the format of a paragraph that includes a hanging indent to a paragraph formatted in the Normal style.

19. If you want to be sure the phone number 555-1234 does not word-wrap what should you do?

(a) Use a nonbreaking hyphen in place of the hyphen.
(b) Use expanded spacing on the whole number.
(c) Use a nonbreaking space in place of the hyphen.
(d) Press Ctrl+Enter before you type the phone number.

Practice Exercises

1 The Purchase of a PC

You can purchase a PC from any number of vendors, each of which offers multiple models and typically enables you to upgrade individual components. You want to remember a few important tips as you shop for your next system. We have provided a few of those tips for you, but the document is difficult to read in its current state. Follow instructions to change the formatting of this document and improve readability. Refer to Figure 2.42 as you complete this exercise.

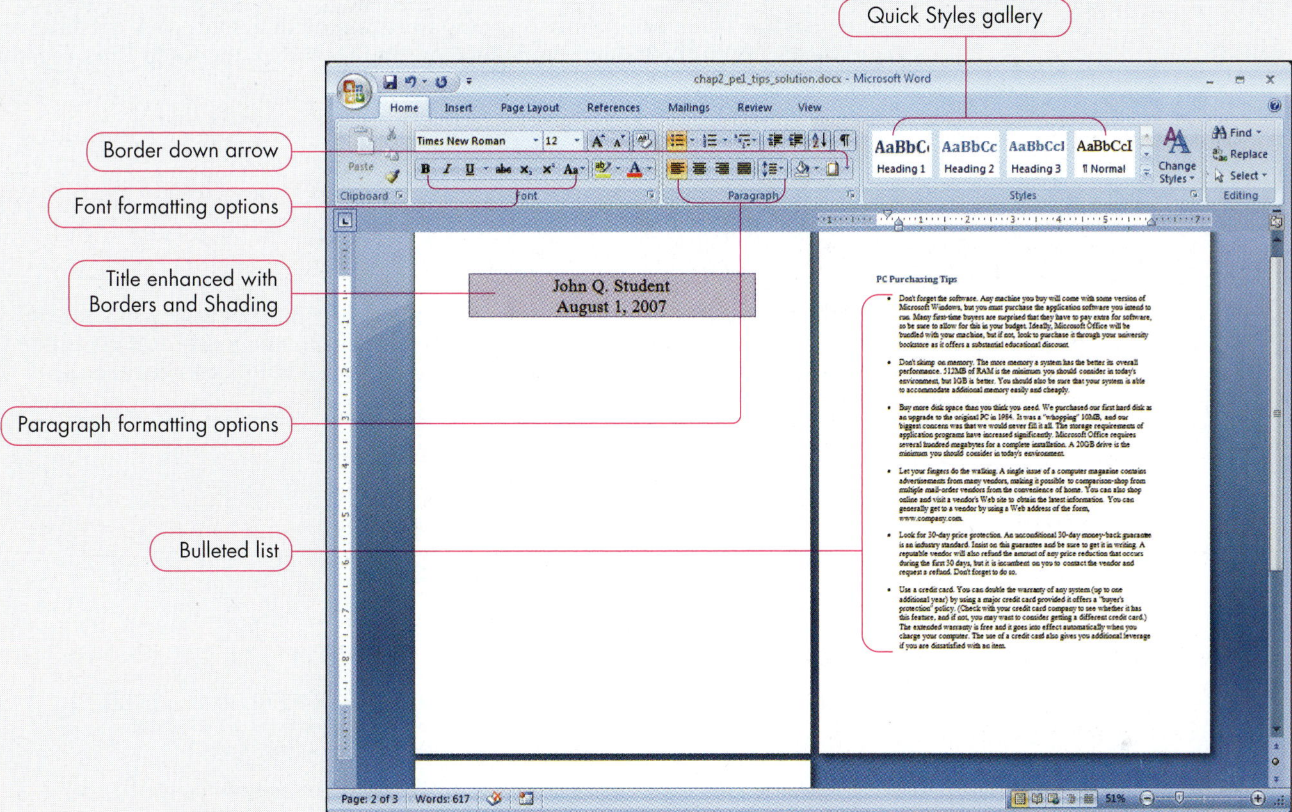

Figure 2.42 PC Purchasing Tips

a. Open the *chap2_pe1_tips* document in the Exploring Word folder and save the document as **chap2_pe1_tips_solution**.

b. Press **Ctrl+Home** to go to the beginning of the document, and then press **Ctrl+Enter** to insert a page break. Press **Ctrl+Home** to move to the beginning of the document and type your name. Press **Enter**, then type today's date. This is your title page.

c. Click the **Home tab**, select your name and date, and then click the **Borders arrow** in the Paragraph group on the Home tab. Select **Borders and Shading** to open the dialog box.

d. In the Borders tab select **Box** in the *Setting* section. Click the **Color drop-down arrow** and select **Purple, Accent 4**. Click the **Width drop-down arrow** and select **2 ¼**.

e. Click the **Shading tab.** Click the **Fill drop-down arrow,** then select **Purple, Accent 4, Lighter 60%**. Click **OK** to close the Borders and Shading dialog box.

f. Select your name again, if necessary, click the **Font size arrow** in the Font group on the Home tab, and select **26**. Click **Center** in the Paragraph group on the Home tab. Click the **Styles Dialog Box Launcher** to display the Styles Pane, then scroll to find the format applied to your name. Move your mouse over the style, then click the down arrow and select **Modify** to display the Modify Style dialog box. Type **PCTitle** in the Name box, then click **OK**.

g. Select the date, then click **PCTitle** in the Styles pane to apply the style to the second line of your title page. Close the Styles pane.

...continued on Next Page

h. The second page of the document contains various tips that we provide, but it is up to you to complete the formatting. Select the title *PC Purchasing Tips* at the top of this page. Click **Heading 1** in the Quick Styles gallery on the Home tab to format this title.
i. To create a bulleted list for the tips on this page, select all remaining text that has not been formatted, then click the **Bullets arrow** in the Paragraph group on the Home tab. Select a black circle from the bullet Style gallery.
j. The bullets help differentiate each point, but they are still spaced pretty close together. To make the document easier to read, click the **Paragraph Dialog Box Launcher**, and then click the **After spin box up arrow** until **12 pt** displays. Click the **Don't add space between paragraphs of the same style check box** (this will remove the check mark from the check box).
k. One paragraph splits between two pages. To eliminate that split, click the **Line and Page Breaks tab** in the Paragraph dialog box, and then click the **Keep lines together check box**. Click **OK**.
l. Compare your document to Figure 2.42. Save and close the document.

2 Creating a List of Job Descriptions

You work for a major book publisher, and your supervisor asked you to prepare a document that lists key personnel and their job descriptions. This information sheet will be sent to each author on the Microsoft Office 2007 team, so they will know who is responsible for different aspects of the publication process. Refer to Figure 2.43 as you complete this exercise.

Office 2007 Series

Publisher Contact	Job Description
Rachel Starkey	Executive Editor: Coordinate all books in the Office 2007 series. Contact potential authors and issue contracts to final authors. Work with all publishing personnel. Determine budgets, sales forecasts, etc.
Marilyn Kay	Development Editor: Work with author to organize topics for a final TOC. Review incoming chapters and provide suggestions for organization, content, and structure. Ensure that author correctly formats manuscript according to series specifications.
Scott Umpir	Project Manager: Coordinate the publishing process with the authors, development editors, technical editors, copy editors, and production team members.
Brittany Shaymonu	Technical Editor: Review first-draft of manuscript to ensure technical accuracy of the step-by-step lessons. Make notes of any missing or extra steps. Point out inconsistencies with menu names, options, etc., including capitalization. Make other notes from a student's perspective.
Darleen Terry	Copy Editor: Proofread manuscript and correct errors in spelling, grammar, punctuation, wording, etc. Use the tracking feature in Word to make online edits.

Figure 2.43 Publisher Job Descriptions

a. Click the **Office Button**, click **New**, and then double-click **Blank document** to open a new document. Save as **chap2_pe2_personnel_solution**.
b. Click the **Page Layout tab**, click **Margins** in the Page Setup group, and then click **Custom Margins** to display the Page Setup dialog box. Click the **Top margin spin box up arrow** until **2** displays, and then click **OK**.

...continued on Next Page

c. Type the title shown in Figure 2.43. Press **Enter** three times to triple-space after the title. Select the title and then on the Mini Toolbar click **Center**, click the **Font arrow** and select **Arial,** click the **Font size arrow** and select **16**, and click **Bold**.
d. Click the **Font Dialog Box Launcher** on the Home tab and select the **Character Spacing tab**. Click the **Spacing drop-down arrow** and select **Expanded**. Click **OK**. Click on one of the blank lines below the title to deselect it.
e. Click the **View tab** and click the **Ruler check box**, if necessary. The ruler should display at the top of your page.
f. Click on the **2"** mark on the ruler to insert a Left tab. The Left tab mark displays on the ruler.
g. Click the **Home tab**. Click the **Paragraph Dialog Box Launcher**. Click the **Special drop-down arrow** in the *Indention* section and select **Hanging**. Click in the **After text box** in the Spacing section and type **12**. Click **OK**.
h. Type the column heading **Publisher Contact**. Press **Tab** and type the column heading **Job Description**. Press **Enter** to begin on the next line. Select the column headings and on the Mini toolbar click **Bold**. Finish typing the rest of the columnar text as shown in Figure 2.43; notice the 12-point After paragraph spacing creates the equivalent of one blank line between rows.
i. Select the first job description, *Executive Editor*, and click **Underline** in the Font group on the Home tab. Double-click **Format Painter** in the Clipboard group on the Home tab, then select the remaining job descriptions to apply the Underline format to each job. After you format the last job description, press **Esc** to turn off the Format Painter.
j. Select the name of each person and apply bold formatting. Save and close the document.

3 Creating and Updating a Table of Contents and an Index

You have received an ISO 9000 document that lists standards for quality management and assurance and is used by international manufacturing and service organizations. You need to distribute the standards to your employees. It is a multipage document that does not contain a table of contents or index for easy reference. You decide to add each before making copies. After creating the table of contents, you decide only two levels of headings are necessary, so you update it to reflect your changes. After adding the index, you decide to make it more detailed, so you edit and update it as well. Refer to Figure 2.44 as you complete this exercise.

a. Open *chap2_pe3_iso* and save it as **chap2_pe3_iso_solution**.
b. Place the insertion point at the end of *ISO 9000* at the top of the first page and press **Ctrl+Enter** to insert a hard page break. The page break creates a page for the table of contents.
c. Click the **References tab**, click **Table of Contents** in the Table of Contents group, and then select **Automatic Table 1** from the gallery. Select **Update Entire Table** if the Update Table of Contents dialog box appears.
d. Click to place the insertion point on the left of the heading *I. Introduction* and press **Ctrl+Enter** to insert a hard page break.
e. Click one time anywhere in the table of contents to select it, click **Table of Contents** on the References tab, and then click **Insert Table of Contents**. Click the **Show levels spin box down arrow** until **2** displays. Click **OK**, and then click **OK** again at the prompt asking to replace the selected table of contents.
f. Before you insert the index you must mark several words as entries. Locate then select the word *quality* in the *Quality Policy* paragraph, and then press **Alt+Shift+X** to display the Mark Index Entry dialog box. Click **Mark** to create the index entry.
g. Locate and select the following words, and then click **Mark** for each one, just as you did in the previous step:

authority	In heading *Responsibility and authority*
procedures	In heading *Quality System Procedures*
supplier	First sentence under heading *Quality System Procedures*
testing	In heading *Inspection and Testing*

...continued on Next Page

h. Press **Ctrl+End** to go to the end of the document. Press **Ctrl+Enter** to insert a new page where you will display the index. Click **Insert Index** from the Index group on the References tab, and then click **OK** to create the Index.
i. You decide your index is incomplete and should include more words. Locate and select the words below. Remember to press **Alt+Shift+X** to display the Mark Index Entry dialog box and click **Mark** to create the index entry.

data control	In heading *Document and Data Control*
training	In heading *Training*
records	In heading *Control of Quality Records*

j. Close the Mark Index Entry dialog box. Position the insertion point anywhere in the index and click **Update Index** in the Index group on the References tab. Your additional entries will display in the updated index.
k. Select all entries in the index, then click **Change Case** in the Font group on the Home tab. Select **lowercase** to change the case of all entries.
l. Position the insertion point left of the section break that precedes the first index entry heading and press **Enter** two times. Move the insertion point up to the first empty line and type **INDEX**, and then select it and click **Heading 1** in the Quick Styles gallery on the Home tab.
m. Compare your results to Figure 2.44. Save and close the document.

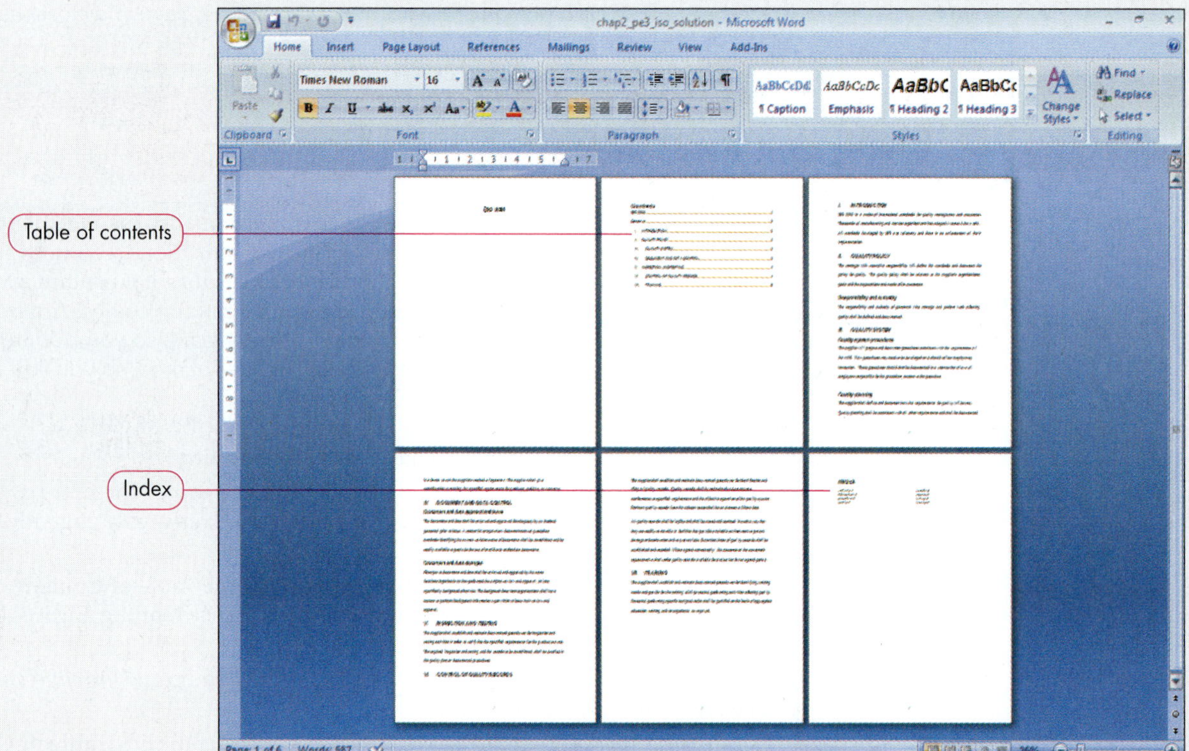

Figure 2.44 Report Including Table of Contents and Index

4 Editing a Memo to the HR Director

Tracey Spears is the training coordinator for a local company, and her responsibilities include tracking employees' continuing education efforts. The company urges employees to pursue educational opportunities that add experience and knowledge to their positions, including taking any certification exams that enhance their credentials. The human resources director has asked Ms. Spears to provide him with a list of employees who have met minimum qualifications to take an upcoming certification exam. In its present state the memo prints on two pages; you will

...continued on Next Page

format the memo using columns in order to save paper and display the entire list on one page. Refer to Figure 2.45 as you complete this exercise.

a. Open the *chap2_pe4_training* document and save it as **chap2_pe4_training_solution.**
b. Select the word *MEMO,* click **Heading 1** in the Quick Styles gallery on the Home tab, and then click **Center** in the Paragraph group on the Home tab.
c. Several employees have a work conflict and will be unable to sit for the certification exam in October. To specify the people who fall into that category scroll over *Alana Bell* to select her name, and then on the Mini toolbar click **Text Highlight Color** or click **Text Highlight Color** in the Font group on the Home tab. Repeat this process for *Amy Kay Lynn, Piau Shing,* and *Ryan Stubbs.*
d. Employees can opt out of the exam for personal reasons, and we need to specify those as well. Hold down **Ctrl** and select the following employees: *Simon Anderson, Randall Larsen,* and *Winnifred Roark.* Click the **Font Dialog Box Launcher** and then click the **Strikethrough check box** in the *Effects* section on the Font tab; click **OK** to return to the memo.
e. Now you list the employees in two columns so you can print the memo on one sheet of paper instead of two. Drag your mouse over the list of employees to select all names. Click the **Page Layout tab**, click **Columns**, and then select **Two**. The names now display in two columns, and the entire memo fits on one page as shown in Figure 2.45.
f. Save and close the document.

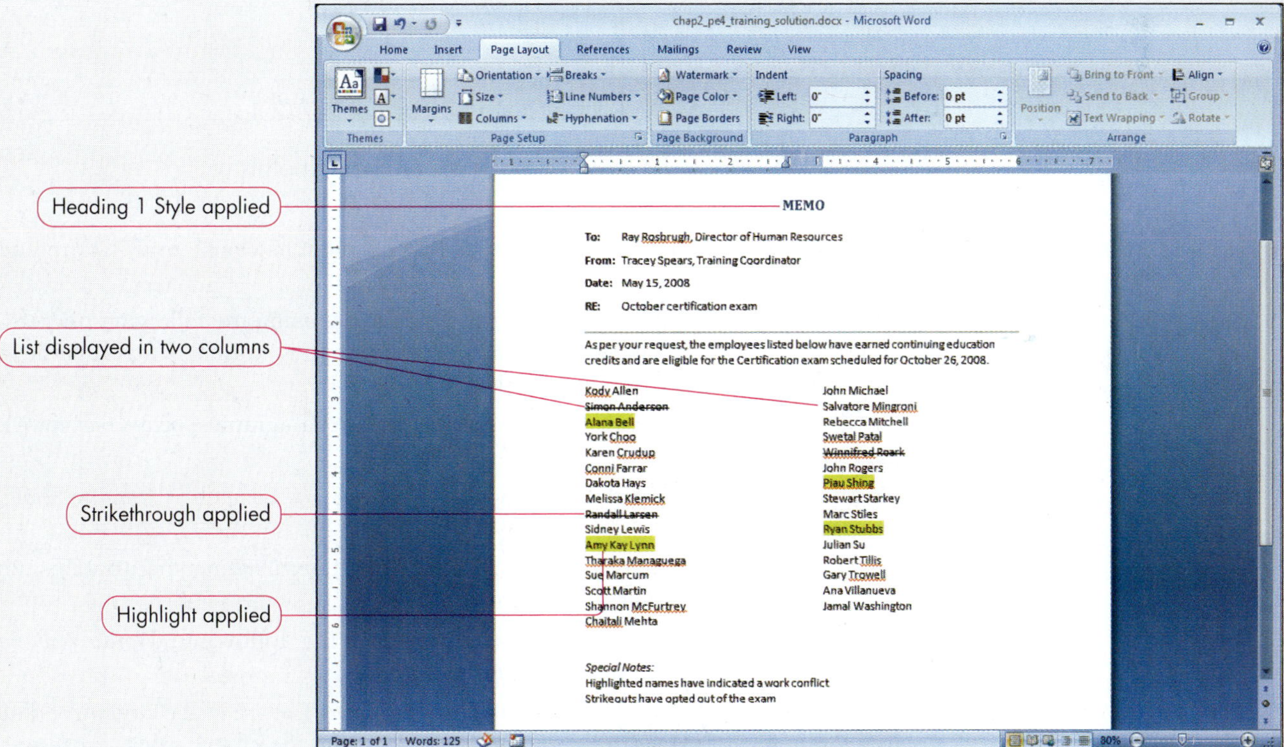

Figure 2.45 The Formatted Memo

Mid-Level Exercises

1 Creating and Applying Styles

You created a status report to inform committee members about an upcoming conference of which you are in charge. You want it to look attractive and professional, and you decide to create and apply your own styles rather than use those already available in Word. You create a paragraph style named Side Heading to format the headings and then you create a character style named Session to format the names of the conference sessions and apply these formats to document text. You then copy these two styles to the Normal template. Eventually, you delete these two styles from the Normal template. Refer to Figure 2.46 as you complete this exercise.

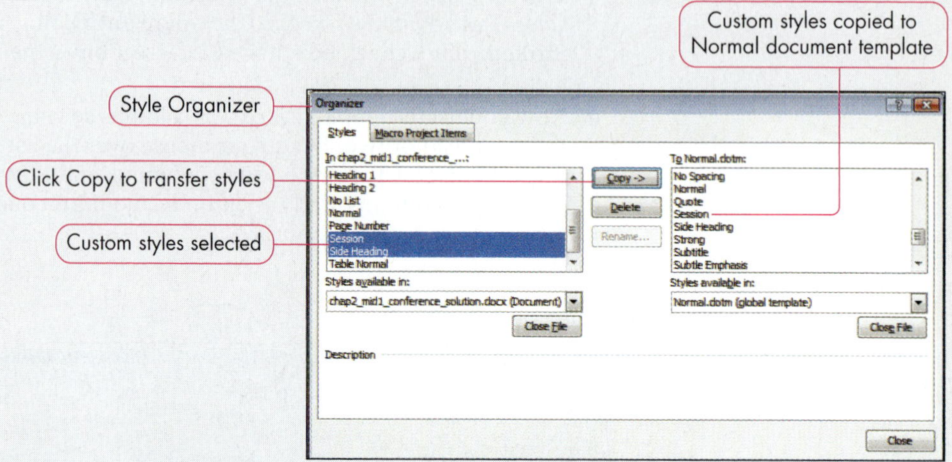

Figure 2.46 Transfer Custom Styles to the Global Template

a. Open the *chap2_mid1_conference* document and save it as **chap2_mid1_conference_solution**.
b. Create a new paragraph style named **Side Heading** using the following properties: Style based on is Normal, Style for following paragraph is Normal. Font properties are Arial, 14-pt, Bold, Red, Accent 2, Darker 50% font color.
c. Set the following paragraph formats: 12-point Before paragraph spacing, 6-point After paragraph spacing.
d. Apply the Side Heading style to the three headings *The Committee*, *Training Sessions*, and *Training Goal*.
e. Create a new character style named **Session** using the following specifications: Bold and Red, Accent 2, Darker 50% font color.
f. In the bulleted list apply the Session style to the following: *Word*, *Web Page Development*, *Multimedia*, and *Presentations Graphics*.
g. Open the Manage Styles dialog box, then click **Import/Export**. In the Organizer dialog box copy the **Side Heading** and **Session** styles from the **chap2_mid1_conference_solution.docx** list to the **Normal.dotm** list as shown in Figure 2.46. Close the Organizer dialog box.
h. Save and close *chap2_mid1_conference_solution*.
i. Open a new document. Display the Styles pane, if necessary, then verify that the Session and Side Heading styles are listed. This step proves that you copied the two styles to the Normal template so that they are available for all new documents.
j. Open the Manage Styles dialog box then click the **Import/Export button**. In the Organizer dialog box delete the two styles from the **In Normal.dotm** list. Click **Yes to All** when prompted. Close the Organizer dialog box.
k. Close the blank document without saving it.

...continued on Next Page

2 Tips for Healthy Living

As a student in the Physician Assistant program at a local university you create a document containing tips for healthier living. The facts have been typed into a Word 2007 document but are thus far unformatted. You will modify it to incorporate styles and add readability as you follow the steps below. Refer to Figure 2.47 as you complete this exercise.

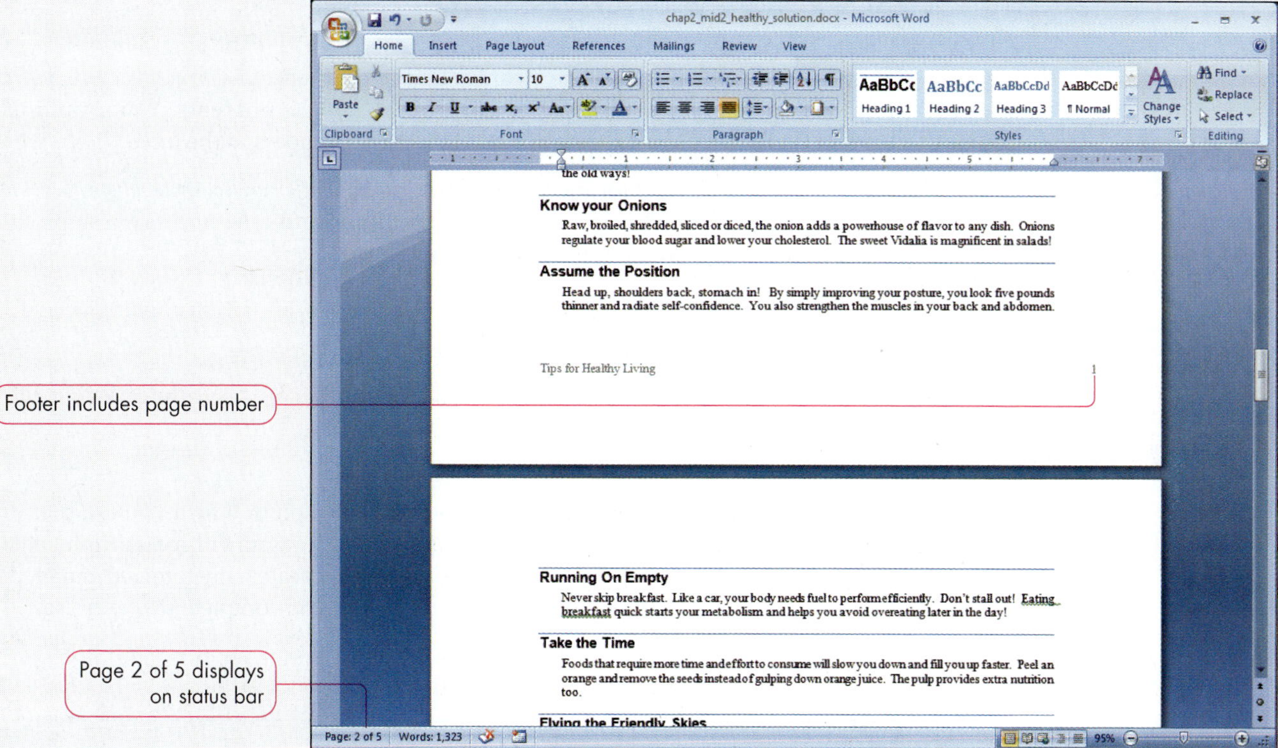

Figure 2.47 Tips for Healthy Living

a. Open the *chap2_mid2_healthy* document and save it as **chap2_mid2_healthy_solution**.

b. Apply the **Heading 1** and **Body Text** styles throughout the document. The Format Painter is a useful tool to copy formats.

c. Change the specifications for the *Body Text* and *Heading 1* styles so that your document matches the document in Figure 2.47. The Heading 1 style is 12-point Arial bold with a blue top border. The Body Text style is 10-point Times New Roman, justified, ¼" left indent, and 12-point spacing After.

d. Create a title page for the document consisting of the title, *Tips for Healthy Living*, and an additional line of text that indicates the document was prepared by you. Format the title page content using a custom style named after yourself. The custom style should contain 28-point Times New Roman font that is bold, centered, and colored in Dark Blue, Text 2 (a blue color).

e. Create a footer for the document consisting of the title, **Tips for Healthy Living**, and a page number. (You can see the footer in Figure 2.47.) The footer should not appear on the title page; that is, page 1 is actually the second page of the document. Look closely at the status bar in Figure 2.47 and you will see that you are on page 1, but that this is the second page of a five-page document.

f. Click **Outline View**, collapse the text, and view the headings only.

g. Save and close the document.

...continued on Next Page

3 Enhance the Healthy Living Document

Your modifications to the Healthy Living document in the last exercise set it up nicely for the next step in creating a comprehensive document that includes a table of contents and index.

a. Open the *chap2_mid2_healthy_solution* document you created in the last exercise and save it as **chap2_mid3_healthy_solution**. Change the document view to Print Layout so the whole document displays.

b. Create a page specifically for the table of contents, then give the page a title and generate a table of contents using the Healthy Living tip headings. Do not include the custom styles you created for the title page in the table of contents. You should use a dashed leader to connect the headings to the page numbers in the table.

c. Mark the following text for inclusion in the index: *diet, exercise, metabolism, vegetables, fat*. At the end of your document, create the index and take necessary steps so the index heading displays in the table of contents.

d. Save and close the document.

4 Editing a Welcome Letter

You composed a letter to welcome new members to an organization of which you are president. Now, you need to apply various paragraph formatting, such as alignment, paragraph spacing, and a paragraph border and shading. In addition, you want to create a customized bulleted list that describes plans for the organization. Refer to Figure 2.48 as you complete this exercise.

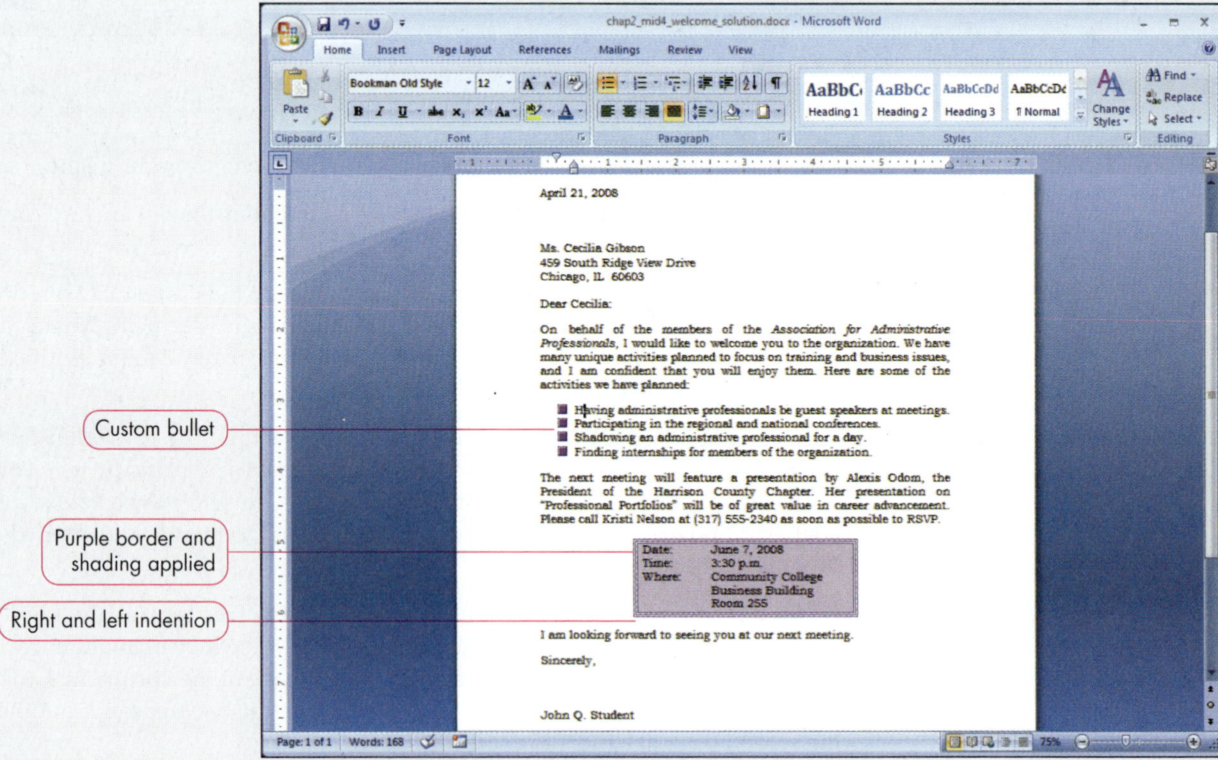

Figure 2.48 Formatted Welcome Letter

...continued on Next Page

a. Open the document *chap2_mid4_welcome* and save it as **chap2_mid4_welcome_solution**. Change Ken's name to your name in the signature block.

b. Apply Justified alignment to the entire document. Delete the asterisk (*) and create a customized bulleted list, selecting a picture bullet of your choice. Type the following items in the bulleted list:

Having administrative professionals be guest speakers at meetings.
Participating in the regional and national conferences.
Shadowing an administrative professional for a day.
Finding internships for members of the organization.

c. Select text from the salutation, *Dear Cecilia*, through the last paragraph that ends with *next meeting*. Set 12-point spacing After paragraph.

d. Select the italicized lines of text and remove the italics. For these lines of text set 1.5" left and right indents and 0-point spacing After paragraph. Apply a triple-line border, Purple, Accent 4 border color, ¾ pt border width, and Purple, Accent 4, Lighter 60% shading color.

e. Click on the line containing the text *Room 255* and set 12-point spacing After paragraph.

f. Select the entire document, and then change the Font to 12-point Bookman Old Style.

g. If needed, delete an extra tab formatting mark to the left of *Community College* to prevent it from word-wrapping. Compare your work to Figure 2.48.

h. Save and close the document.

Capstone Exercise

In this project, you work with a document prepared for managers involved in the hiring process. This report analyzes the validity of the interview process and suggests that selection doesn't depend only on quality information, but on the quality of the interpretation of information. The document requires formatting to enhance readability and important information; you will use skills from this chapter to format multiple levels of headings and figures. To make it easy for readers to locate topics in your document, create and use various supplemental document components such as a table of contents and index.

Adding Style

This document is ready for enhancements, and the styles feature is a good tool that allows you to add them quickly and easily.

a. Open the file *chap2_cap_interview* document and save it as **chap2_cap_interview_solution**.

b. Create a paragraph style named **Title_Page_1** with these formats: 22-point size, Shadow font effect, character spacing expanded by 1 point, horizontally centered, and no Widow/ Orphan control. Apply this style to the first line of the title on the title page.

c. Create a paragraph style named **Title_Page_2** based on the first style you created, with these additional formats: 20-point size, custom color 66, 4, 66. Apply this style to the subtitle on the title page.

d. Replace the * in the middle of the first page with your name. Apply the Heading 3 style to your name and the line that precedes it.

e. Apply the Body Text style to all regular paragraphs. Since this style is not a default in the gallery, you must click the Styles Dialog Box Launcher and select Body Text from the Style list.

f. Apply the Heading 2 style to the side headings, such as *Introduction* and *Pre-interview Impressions*, and the Heading 1 style to the main headings throughout the document.

Formatting the Paragraphs

Next you will apply paragraph formatting to the document. These format options will further increase the readability and attractiveness of your document.

a. Select the second paragraph in the *Introduction* section and apply these formats: 0.7" left and right indent, 6-point spacing after the paragraph, boxed 1½-point border with a custom color (31, 73, 125 RGB), and custom shading color (210, 218, 229 RGB).

b. Select the second and third paragraphs in *The Unfavorable Information Effect* section and create a two-column format with a line between the columns.

c. Use Keep Lines Together controls to prevent paragraphs from being separated across pages.

d. Insert nonbreaking spaces and nonbreaking hyphens where appropriate.

e. Apply the arrow bulleted-list format for the five-item list in the *Introduction*.

f. Apply the first numbered-list format (numbers with periods) for the three phases in the *Pre-Interview Impressions* section.

Inserting References

To put the finishing touches on your document you will add a table of contents and index. These additions enable the reader to quickly locate topics in your document and add a level of professionalism to your work.

a. Create a table of contents based on the styles you applied to paragraph headings; do not include the style you used for the title page.

b. Mark these words as index entries: behavior, favorable, impression, interview, interviewer, perceptions, personal interview, reference, unqualified. Add an index to the end of the document. Use the Classic index format.

c. A page number should display in the footer of the document. Use the **Accent Bar 4** format, but prevent it from displaying on the title page and start numbering on the page that contains the table of contents.

d. Save and close the document.

Mini Cases

Use the rubric following the case as a guide to evaluate your work, but keep in mind that your instructor may impose additional grading criteria or use a different standard to judge your work.

A Fundraising Letter

GENERAL CASE

Each year you update a letter to several community partners soliciting support for an auction. The auction raises funds for your organization, and your letter should impress your supporters by using several formatting styles and options that give it a very professional look. Open the *chap2_mc1_auction* document and make necessary changes to improve the appearance. Consider the use of columns for auction items, bullets to draw attention to the list of forms, and page borders—and that is just for starters! Your finished document should be saved as **chap2_mc1_auction_solution**.

Performance Elements	Exceeds Expectations	Meets Expectations	Below Expectations
Enhanced document using the following paragraph formatting features: columns, bullets/numbering, borders/shading	Document contains at least three of the paragraph formatting features.	Document contains at least two of the paragraph formatting features.	Document contains one or none of the paragraph formatting features.
Use of character formatting features such as Font, Font Size, Font color, or other attributes from Font dialog box.	Used character formatting options throughout entire document.	Used character formatting options in most sections of document.	Used character formatting options on a small portion of document.
Overall appearance of document	Used formatting tools to create a very attractive document that is easy to read.	Some formatting has been applied, but more updates are required for an attractive and readable document.	Minimal formatting has been applied, resulting in a plain and somewhat unattractive document.

The Invitation

RESEARCH CASE

Search the Internet for an upcoming local event at your school or in your community and produce the perfect invitation. You can invite people to a charity ball, a fun run, or to a fraternity party. Your laser printer and abundance of fancy fonts enable you to do anything a professional printer can do. Your finished document should be saved as **chap2_mc2_invitation_solution**.

Performance Elements	Exceeds Expectations	Meets Expectations	Below Expectations
Use of character formatting	Three or more character formats applied to text.	One or two character formats applied to text.	Does not apply character formats to text.
Use of styles	Created custom paragraph or character style.	Used at least two predefined styles.	Used one or no predefined style.
Use of paragraph formatting	Two or more paragraph format options used.	Used one paragraph format option.	Does not use paragraph format options.
Presentation	Invitation is formatted attractively; information is easy to read and understand.	Special formatting has been applied, but information is somewhat cluttered.	Invitation lists basic information with no special formatting for attractiveness.

Tips for Windows XP

DISASTER RECOVERY

Open the *chap2_mc3_wintips* document. The document is formatted, but it contains several errors and problems. For example, the paragraph titles are not all formatted with the same style, so they do not all display in the table of contents. You will notice most of the problems easily and you must fix them before the document can be useful. Your finished document should be saved as **chap2_mc3_wintips_solution**.

Performance Elements	Exceeds Expectations	Meets Expectations	Below Expectations
Paragraph and text formatting	Standardized style used on all paragraph text and headings.	Standardized style used on either text or headings, but not both.	Did not standardize styles on text or headings.
Table of contents	All appropriate paragraph titles are listed in the TOC.	Most paragraph titles are listed; no inappropriate titles are listed.	Some paragraph titles are not listed, and TOC contains some inappropriate titles.
Updated footer	Made all necessary updates to footer.	Made some updates to footer.	Did not update footer.

chapter 3 | **Word**

Enhancing a Document

Tables and Graphics

After you read this chapter, you will be able to:

1. Insert a table **(page 197)**.
2. Format a table **(page 205)**.
3. Sort and apply formulas to table data **(page 207)**.
4. Convert text to a table **(page 210)**.
5. Insert clip art and images into a document **(page 219)**.
6. Format a graphic element **(page 220)**.
7. Insert WordArt into a document **(page 225)**.
8. Insert symbols into a document **(page 226)**.

Hands-On Exercises

Exercises	Skills Covered
1. INSERT A TABLE **(page 201)** **Open:** Blank document **Save as:** chap3_ho1_vacation_solution.docx	• Create a Table • Insert Rows and Columns • Change Row Height and Column Width • Merge Cells to Create Header Row
2. ADVANCED TABLE FEATURES **(page 212)** **Open:** chap3_ho1_vacation_solution.docx (from Exercise 1) **Save as:** chap3_ho2_vacation_solution.docx (additional modifications) **Open:** chap3_ho2_expenses.docx (Step 7) **Save as:** chap3_ho2_expenses_solution.docx	• Apply a Table Style • Add Table Borders and Shading • Enter Formulas to Calculate Totals • Add a Row and Enter a Formula • Sort Data in a Table • Align Table and Data • Convert Text to a Table
3. CLIP ART, WORDART, AND SYMBOLS **(page 227)** **Open:** chap3_ho3_ergonomics.docx **Save as:** chap3_ho3_ergonomics_solution.docx	• Insert a Clip Art Object • Move and Resize the Clip Art Object • Create a WordArt Object • Modify the WordArt Object • Insert a Symbol

CASE STUDY

The Ozarks Science and Engineering Fair

Each spring Luanne Norgren is responsible for coordinating the Science and Engineering Fair at Southwest State University. The premier science event for the Ozarks region, attracts middle school and high school students from 28 counties. You have been hired to serve as the assistant coordinator for the event and are responsible for communications with school administrators and faculty. You prepared an informational letter that will be sent to each school explaining the event registration procedures and project criteria. At your suggestion, Luanne agreed to let you develop a one-page flyer that can be mailed independently or with the informational letter. The flyer will be an attractive source of information that will encourage participation by faculty and students at the schools.

Case Study

The event takes place April 4–6, 2008, on the university campus. The students who participate will be entered into either the Junior or Senior division, depending on their grade (7-9 in Junior, 10-12 in Senior). In both divisions students can enter a science project in any of the following categories: Biochemistry, Botany, Chemistry, Computer Science, Earth and Space Sciences, Engineering, Environmental Sciences, Physics, or Zoology.

Your Assignment

- Read the chapter, paying special attention to sections that describe how to insert and format tables and graphics.
- As assistant coordinator in charge of communications, you develop a flyer in Word that can be used as a quick source of information about the event. The flyer must include the date, divisions, and categories listed above, and contact information.
- You consider the use of a table, primarily as a placeholder for other information that you will add. Merge and split cells as necessary to create the effect you want to portray using the flyer. Use table styles to enhance color and readability of data in the table. Use borders and shading where appropriate or to supplement any table style you use.
- Insert clip art or other science-oriented graphics to add emphasis and excitement to the flyer. Use graphic formatting tools as needed to enhance colors, change styles, and compress the graphics.
- Use WordArt to create an exciting heading. Also use WordArt to enhance other places in the document as needed.
- Add a "For more information" section to the flyer and list your contact information, Phone: (555) 111-2222 and e-mail: yourname@swsu.edu.
- Save the document as **chap3_case_science_solution**.

Tables

A ***table*** is a series of columns and rows that organize data.

A ***cell*** is the intersection of a column and row in a table.

A ***table*** is a series of columns and rows that organize data effectively. The columns and rows in a table intersect to form ***cells***. The table feature is one of the most powerful in Word and is an easy way to organize a series of data in a columnar list format such as employee names, inventory lists, and e-mail addresses. The Vacation Planner in Figure 3.1, for example, is actually a 4x9 table (4 columns and 9 rows). The completed table looks impressive, and it is very easy to create once you understand how a table works. In addition to the organizational benefits, tables make an excellent alignment tool. For example, you can create tables to organize data such as employee lists with phone numbers and e-mail addresses. The Exploring series uses tables to provide descriptions for various software commands. Although you can align text with tabs, you have more format control when you create a table. (See the Practice Exercises at the end of the chapter for other examples.)

The table feature is one of the most powerful in Word and is the basis for an almost limitless variety of documents. It is very easy to create once you understand how a table works.

Vacation Planner			
Item	**Number of Days**	**Amount per Day (est)**	**Total Amount**
Airline Ticket			449.00
Amusement Park Tickets	4	50.00	200.00
Hotel	5	120.00	600.00
Meals	6	50.00	300.00
Rental Car	5	30.00	150.00
Souvenirs	5	20.00	100.00
TOTAL EXPECTED EXPENSES			$1799.00

Figure 3.1 The Vacation Planner

In this section, you insert a table in a document. After inserting the table, you can insert or delete columns and rows if you need to change the structure. Furthermore, you learn how to merge and split cells within the table. Finally, you change the row height and column width to accommodate data in the table.

Inserting a Table

You can create a table from the Insert tab. Click Table in the Tables group on the Insert tab to see a gallery of cells from which you select the number of columns and rows you require in the table, or you can choose the Insert Table command below the gallery to display the Insert Table dialog box and enter the table composition you prefer. When you select the table dimension from the gallery or from the Insert Table dialog box, Word creates a table structure with the number of columns and rows you specify. After you define a table, you can enter text, numbers, or graphics in individual cells. The text wraps itself as it is entered within a cell, so that you can add or delete text without affecting the entries in other cells.

You format the contents of an individual cell the same way you format an ordinary paragraph; that is, you change the font, apply boldface or italic, change the text alignment, or apply any other formatting command. You can select multiple cells and apply the formatting to all selected cells at once, or you can format a cell independently of every other cell.

After you insert a table in your document, use commands in the Table Tools Design and Layout tabs to modify and enhance it. Place the insertion point anywhere in the table then click either the Design or Layout tab to view the commands. In either tab just point to a command, and a ScreenTip describes its function.

TIP Tabs and Tables

The Tab key functions differently in a table than in a regular document. Press Tab to move to the next cell in the current row, or to the first cell in the next row if you are at the end of a row. Press Tab when you are in the last cell of a table to add a new blank row to the bottom of the table. Press Shift+Tab to move to the previous cell in the current row (or to the last cell in the previous row). You must press Ctrl+Tab to insert a regular tab character within a cell.

Insert and Delete Rows and Columns

You can change the structure of a table after it has been created. If you need more rows or columns to accommodate additional data in your table, it is easy to add or insert them using the Rows & Columns group on the Table Tools Layout tab. The Insert and Delete commands enable you to add new or delete existing rows or columns. When you add a column, you can specify if you want to insert it to the right or left of the current column. Likewise, you can specify where to place a new row—either above or below the currently selected row—based on where you need to add the new row.

You can delete complete rows and columns using the commands mentioned above, or you can delete only the data in those rows and columns using the Delete key on your keyboard. Keep in mind that when you insert or delete a complete row or a column, the remaining rows and columns will adjust to the positioning. For example, if you delete the third row of a 5x5 table, the data in the fourth and fifth rows move up and become the third and fourth rows. If you delete only the data in the third row, the cells would be blank and the fourth and fifth rows would not change at all.

Merge and Split Cells

You can use the Merge Cells command in the Merge group on the Table Tools Layout tab to join individual cells together (merge) to form a larger cell as was done in the first and last rows of Figure 3.1. People often merge cells to enter a main title at the top of a table. Conversely, you can use the Split Cells command in the Merge group to split a single cell into multiple cells if you require more cells to hold data.

Change Row Height and Column Width

Row height is the vertical space from the top to the bottom of a row.

Column width is the horizontal space or length of a column.

When you create a table, Word builds evenly spaced columns. Frequently you need to change the row height or column width to fit your data. ***Row height*** is the vertical distance from the top to the bottom of a row. ***Column width*** is the horizontal space or width of a column. You might increase the column width to display a wide string of text, such as first and last name, to prevent it from wrapping in the cell. You might increase row height to better fit a header that has been enlarged for emphasis.

The table command is easy to master, and as you might have guessed, you will benefit from reviewing the available commands listed in the Design and Layout tabs as shown in the reference pages. You will use many of these commands as you create a table in the hands-on exercises.

Table Tools Layout Ribbon | Reference

Group	Commands	Enables You to
Table	Select ▾ View Gridlines Properties Table	• Select particular parts of a table (entire table, column, row, or cell). • Show or hide the gridlines around the table. • Display the Table Properties dialog box to format the table.
Rows & Columns	Delete ▾ Insert Above Insert Below Insert Left Insert Right Rows & Columns	• Delete cells, columns, rows, or the entire table. • Insert rows and columns. • Display the Insert Cells dialog box.
Merge	Merge Cells Split Cells Split Table Merge	• Merge (join) selected cells together. • Split cells into additional cells. • Split the table into two tables.
Cell Size	0.22" 6.15" AutoFit ▾ Cell Size	• Adjust the row height and column width. • Adjust the column width automatically based on the data in the column. • Display the Table Properties dialog box.
Alignment	Text Direction Cell Margins Alignment	• Specify the combined horizontal and vertical alignment of text within a cell. • Change the text direction. • Set margins within a cell.
Data	Sort Repeat Heading Rows Convert to Text Formula Data	• Sort data within a table. • Repeat heading rows when tables span multiple pages. • Convert tabulated text to table format. • Insert a formula in a table.

Hands-On Exercises

1 | Insert a Table

Skills covered: 1. Create a Table **2.** Insert Rows and Columns **3.** Change Row Height and Column Width **4.** Merge Cells to Create Header Row

Step 1 Create a Table

Refer to Figure 3.2 as you complete Step 1.

a. Start Word and press **Enter** two times in the blank document; then click the **Insert tab**.

The Insert tab contains the Table command.

b. Click **Table** in the Tables group and then drag your mouse over the cells until you select 3 columns and 7 rows; you will see the table size, 3x7, displayed above the cells, as shown in Figure 3.2. Click the lower-right cell (where the 3rd column and the 7th row intersect) to insert the table into your document.

Word creates an empty table that contains three columns and seven rows. The default columns have identical widths, and the table spans from the left to the right margin.

c. Practice selecting various elements from the table, something that you will have to do in subsequent steps:

- To select a single cell, click inside the left grid line (the pointer changes to a black slanted arrow when you are in the proper position).
- To select a row, click outside the table to the left of the first cell in that row.
- To select a column, click just above the top of the column (the pointer changes to a small black downward pointing arrow).
- To select adjacent cells, drag the mouse over the cells.
- To select the entire table, drag the mouse over the table or click the table selection box that appears at the upper-left corner of the table.

d. Save the document as **chap3_ho1_vacation_solution**.

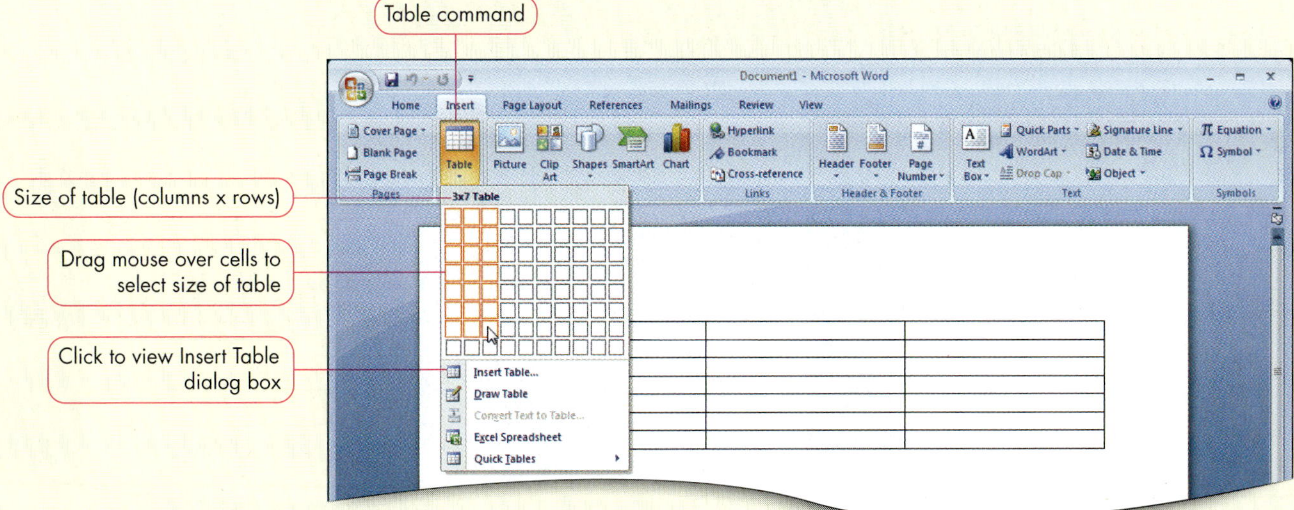

Figure 3.2 Inserting a Table

Step 2
Insert Rows and Columns

Refer to Figure 3.3 as you complete Step 2.

a. Click in the first cell of the first row and type **Vacation Planner**.

b. Click the first cell in the second row and type **Item**. Press **Tab** (or **right arrow**) to move to the next cell. Type **Number of Days**. Press **Tab** to move to the next cell, and then type **Amount per Day (est)**.

   Notice you do not have enough columns to add the last heading, *Total Amount*.

c. Click anywhere in the last column of your table, then click the **Layout tab**. Click **Insert Right** in the Rows & Columns group to add a new column to your table. Click in the second row of the new column and type **Total Amount**.

   You added a new column on the right side of the table. Notice that the column widths decrease to make room for the new column you just added.

   TROUBLESHOOTING: If the column you insert is not in the correct location within the table, click Undo on the Quick Access Toolbar, confirm your insertion point is in the last column, and then click the appropriate Insert command.

d. Select the text *Vacation Planner* in the first row. On the Mini toolbar click the **Font Size arrow** and select **18**, click **Bold,** and click **Center** to center the heading within the cell.

   The table title stands out with the larger font size, bold, and center horizontal alignment.

e. Click outside and left of the second row to select the entire row. On the Mini toolbar click the **Font Size arrow** and select **16,** and then click **Bold** and **Center**.

f. Enter the remaining data as shown in Figure 3.3. When you get to the last row and find the table is too small to hold all the data, place the insertion point in the last cell (in the Total Amount column) and press **Tab** to add a row to the end of your table. Then enter the last item and amounts.

g. Save the document.

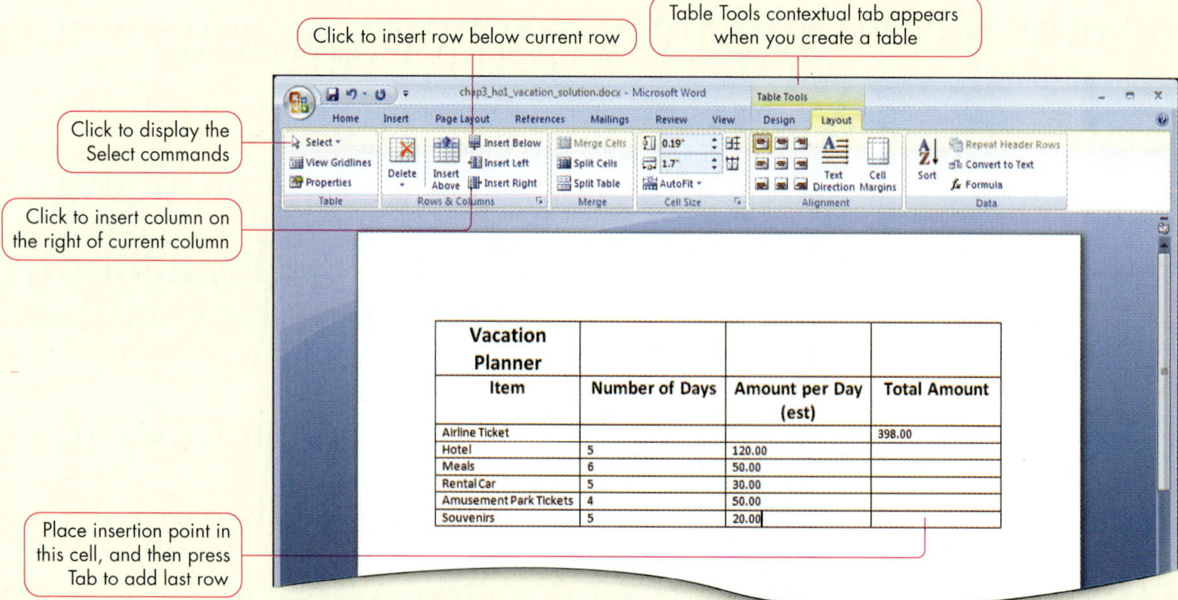

Figure 3.3 Enter the Vacation Planner Data

TIP Other Ways to Select a Table

You can click Select in the Table group on the Layout tab to display commands for selecting a cell, a column, a row, or the entire table. Figure 3.3 shows the location of the Select command.

Step 3
Change Row Height and Column Width

Refer to Figure 3.4 as you complete Step 3.

a. Hold your mouse over the second column of data until the small black arrow appears, then hold down your mouse and drag to the right to select the last three columns of the table.

b. Click the **Layout tab**, then type **1.2** in the **Width** box in the Cell Size group as shown in Figure 3.4. Click anywhere in the table or document to view the change.

   You changed the width of the last three columns so that they are each 1.2″ wide. They are now narrower, and the headings wrap even more in the cells.

c. Place the insertion point anywhere in the cell containing the text *Airline Ticket*, then click **Select** in the Table group on the Layout tab. Click **Select Row**, then hold down **Shift** and press the **down arrow** on your keyboard five times to select the remaining rows in the table. Click the **Height spin arrow** in the Cell Size group on the Layout tab to display 0.3″.

   You changed the height of the last five rows in the table to 0.3″ tall.

d. Save the document.

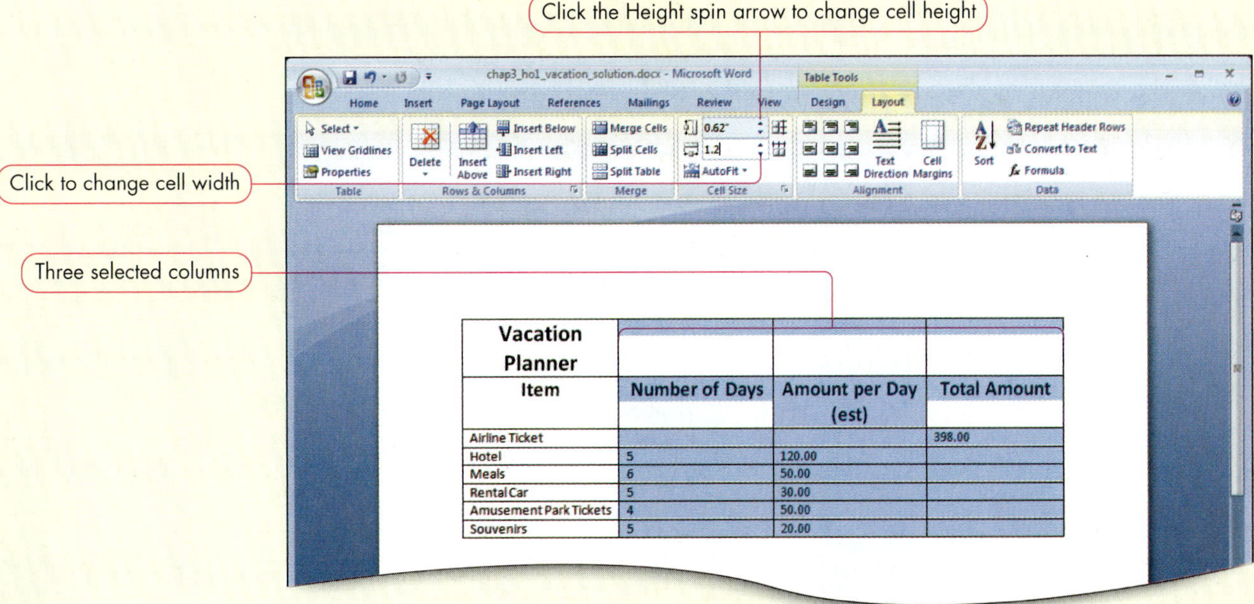

Figure 3.4 Adjust Cell Height and Width

TIP Adjusting Column Width and Row Height

If you are not certain of the exact measurements needed for row height or column width, you can use the mouse to increase or decrease the size. Position the mouse pointer on the gridline that separates the rows (or columns) until the pointer changes to a two-headed arrow. The two-headed arrow indicates you can adjust the height (or width) by clicking and dragging the gridline up or down (right or left) to resize the cell.

Step 4
Merge Cells to Create Header Row

Refer to Figure 3.5 as you complete Step 4.

a. Click outside the table to the left of the first cell in the first row to select the entire first row.

b. Click **Merge Cells** in the Merge group on the Layout tab as shown in Figure 3.5.

   You merged or joined the selected cells. The first row now contains a single cell.

c. Place the insertion point anywhere in the first row, click **Select** in the Table group on the Layout tab, then choose **Select Row**. Click the **Home tab**, click the **Font Size arrow** and select **24**. Click **Center** in the Paragraph group.

d. Click the **Layout tab**, then click the **Height spin arrow** in the Cell Size group to display **0.5″**.

   After increasing the size of the cell contents, you increased the height of the cell so the text is easier to read.

e. Save the *chap3_ho1_vacation_solution* document and keep it onscreen if you plan to continue to the next hands-on exercise. Close the file and exit Word if you do not want to continue with the next exercise at this time.

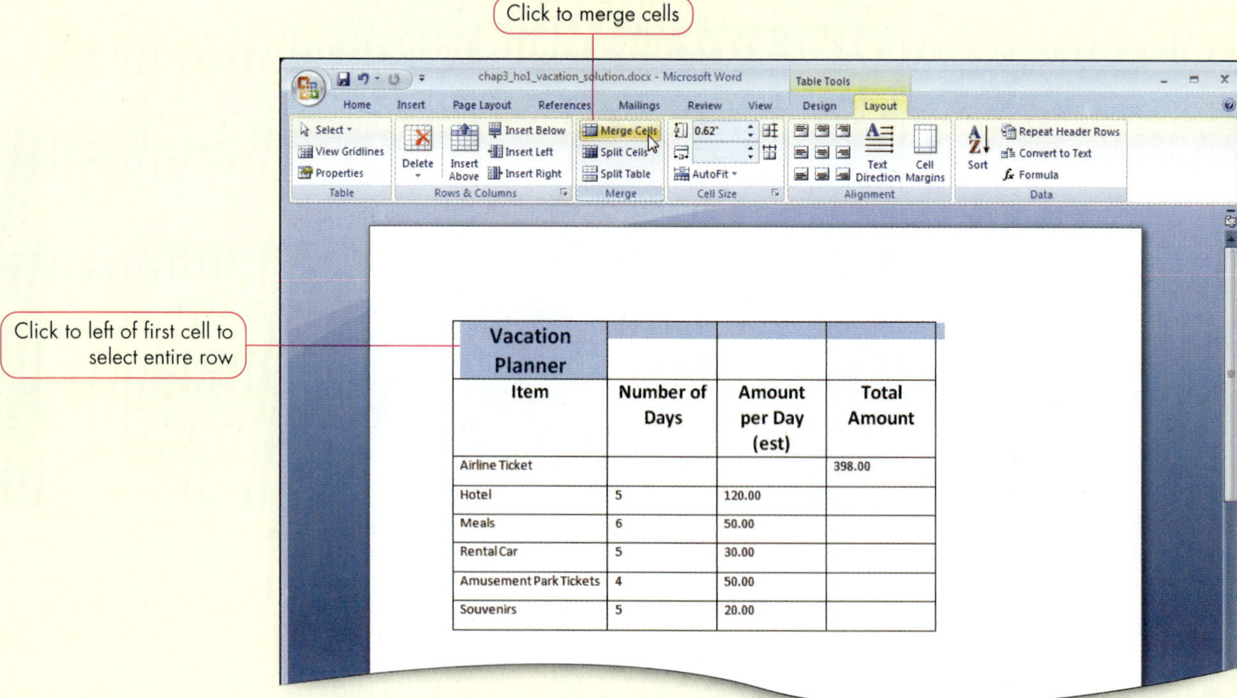

Figure 3.5 Merge First Row Cells

Advanced Table Features

After you create a basic table, you will want to enhance the appearance to create interest for the reader and improve readability. Microsoft Word 2007 provides many predefined styles, which contain borders, shading, font sizes, and other attributes that enhance a table.

You now have a good understanding of the table features and realize there are many uses for them in your Word documents. After you create the basic table, you want to enhance the appearance to create interest for the reader and improve readability. Microsoft Word 2007 includes many tools to assist with these efforts, and you will use several of them to complete the Vacation Planner table.

In this section, you learn how to format a table. Specifically, you apply borders and shading to table cells, apply table styles to the entire table, and select table alignment and position. In addition, you sort data within a table and insert formulas to perform calculations. Finally, you convert text to a table format.

Formatting a Table

Shading affects the background color within a cell.

Border refers to the line style around each cell.

You can use basic formatting options to enhance the appearance of your table. The Borders and Shading commands, for example, offer a wide variety of choices for formatting the table structure. ***Shading*** affects the background color within a cell or group of cells. Table shading is similar to the Highlight feature that places a color behind text. You often apply shading to the header row of a table to make it stand out from the data. ***Border*** refers to the line style around each cell in the table. The default is a single line, but you can choose from many styles to outline a table such as a double, triple, or a wavy line. You can even choose invisible borders if you want only data to display in your document without the outline of a table. Borders and Shading commands are located on the Design tab so you do not have to return to the Home tab to use them.

Apply Table Styles

A ***table style*** contains borders, shading, and other attributes to enhance a table.

When you do not have time to apply custom borders and shading, you will find the Table Styles feature very helpful. Microsoft Word 2007 provides many predefined ***table styles*** that contain borders, shading, font sizes, and other attributes that enhance readability of a table. The custom styles are available in the Table Styles group on the Design tab. To use a predefined table style, click anywhere in your table and then click a style from the Table Styles gallery. A few styles from the gallery display, but you can select from many others by clicking the down arrow on the right side of the gallery, as shown in Figure 3.6. The Live preview of a style displays on your table when you hover your mouse over it in the gallery. To apply a style, click it one time.

You can modify a predefined style if you wish to make changes to features such as color or alignment. You also can create your own table style and save it for use in the current document, or add it to a document template for use in other Word documents. Click the More arrow in the Table Styles group to access the Modify Table Style and New Table Style commands.

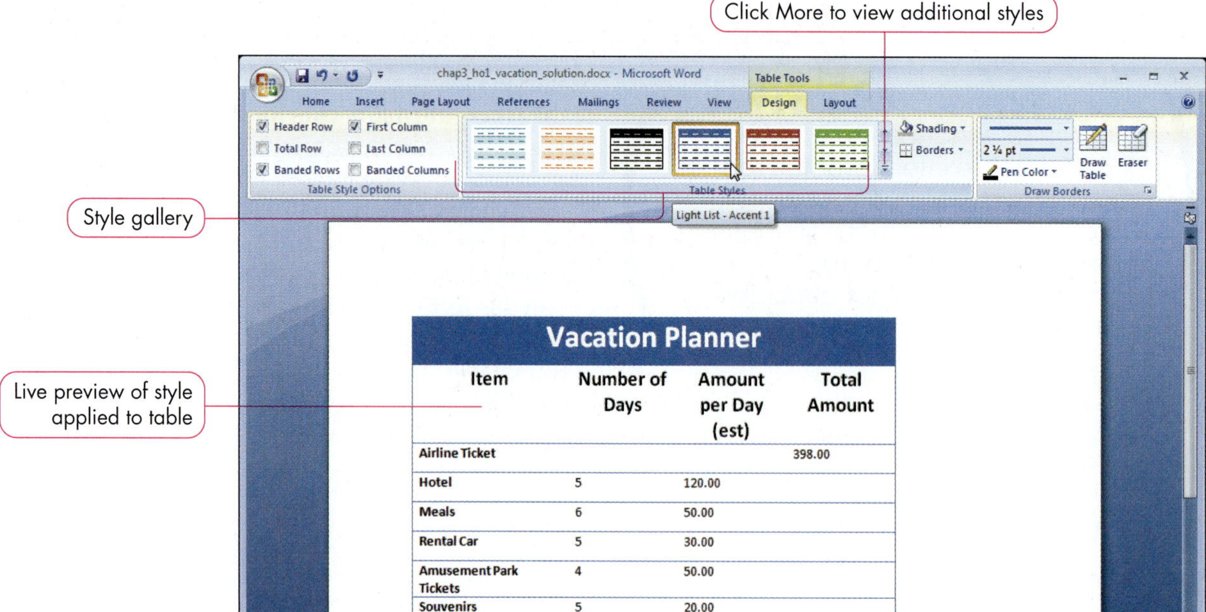

Figure 3.6 Table Styles Command

Select the Table Position and Alignment

Table alignment is the position of a table between the left and right margins.

When you insert a table, Word aligns it at the left margin by default. However, you can click Properties in the Table group on the Layout tab to change the ***table alignment***, the position of a table between the left and right document margins. For example, you might want to center the table between the margins or align it at the right margin.

You also can change alignment of the data in a table separately from the table itself using the Properties dialog box. The Layout tab includes the Alignment group that contains many options to quickly format table data.

Table data can be formatted to align in many different horizontal and vertical combinations. We often apply horizontal settings, such as center, to our data, but using vertical settings also increases readability. For example, when you want your data to be centered both horizontally and vertically within a cell so it is easy to read and does not appear to be elevated on the top or too close to the bottom, click Align Center in the Alignment group to apply that setting.

Text direction refers to the degree of rotation in which text displays.

The default ***text direction*** places text in an upright position. However, you can rotate text so it displays sideways. To change text direction, click Text Direction in the Alignment group on the Layout tab. Each time you click Text Direction, the text rotates. This is a useful tool for aligning text that is in the header row of a narrow column.

Cell margins are the amount of space between data and the cell border in a table.

The ***Cell Margins*** command in the Alignment group on the Layout tab enables you to adjust the amount of white space inside a cell as well as spacing between cells. Use this setting to improve readability of cell contents by adjusting white space around your data or between cells if they contain large amounts of text or data. If you increase cell margins, it prevents data from looking squeezed together.

TIP Right-Click for Table Formatting Options

As an alternative to using the Layout tab, you can find many table options in the context-sensitive menu that displays when you right-click the mouse. The insertion point can be anywhere in the table, and after you right-click you see several table options including Insert, Delete Cells, and Split Cells. You also can change format and alignment of table cells using the Borders and Shading, Cell Alignment, and Text Direction commands in this menu. The Table Properties option is available in the menu if you need to access features such as table alignment and cell spacing.

Sorting and Applying Formulas to Table Data

Sorting is the process of rearranging data.

Because tables provide an easy way to arrange numbers within a document, it is important to know how to use table calculations. This feature gives a Word document the power of a simple spreadsheet. Additional organization of table data is possible by the use of ***sorting***, or rearranging data based on a certain criteria. Figure 3.7 displays the vacation expenses you created previously, but this table illustrates two additional capabilities of the table feature—sorting and calculating.

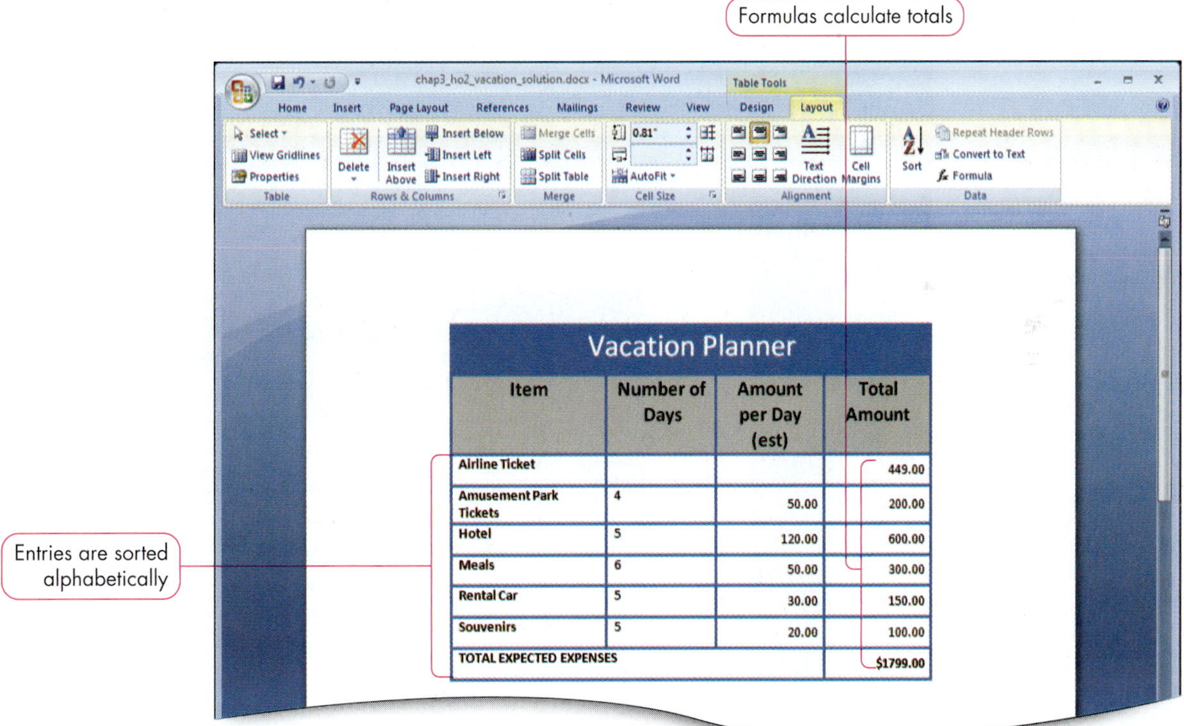

Figure 3.7 The Vacation Planner Table with Enhancements

Calculate Using Table Formulas

In this table the entries in the Total Amount column consist of formulas that were entered into the table to perform a calculation. The entries are similar to those in a spreadsheet. Thus, the rows in the table are numbered from one to nine while the columns are labeled from A to D. The row and column labels do not appear in the table, but are used in the formulas.

You know that the intersection of a row and column forms a cell. Word uses the column letter and row number of that intersection to identify the cell and to give it an address. Cell D5, for example, contains the entry to compute the total hotel expense by multiplying the number of days (in cell B5) by the amount charged per day (in cell C5). In similar fashion, the entry in cell D6 computes the total expense for meals by multiplying the values in cells B6 and C6, respectively. The formula is not entered (typed) into the cell explicitly, but is created using the Formula command in the Data group on the Layout tab.

Figure 3.8 is a slight variation of Figure 3.7 in which the field codes have been toggled on to display the formulas, as opposed to the calculated values. The cells are shaded to emphasize that these cells contain formulas (fields), as opposed to numerical values. The field codes are toggled on and off by selecting the formula and pressing Shift+F9 or by right-clicking the entry and selecting the Toggle Field Codes command.

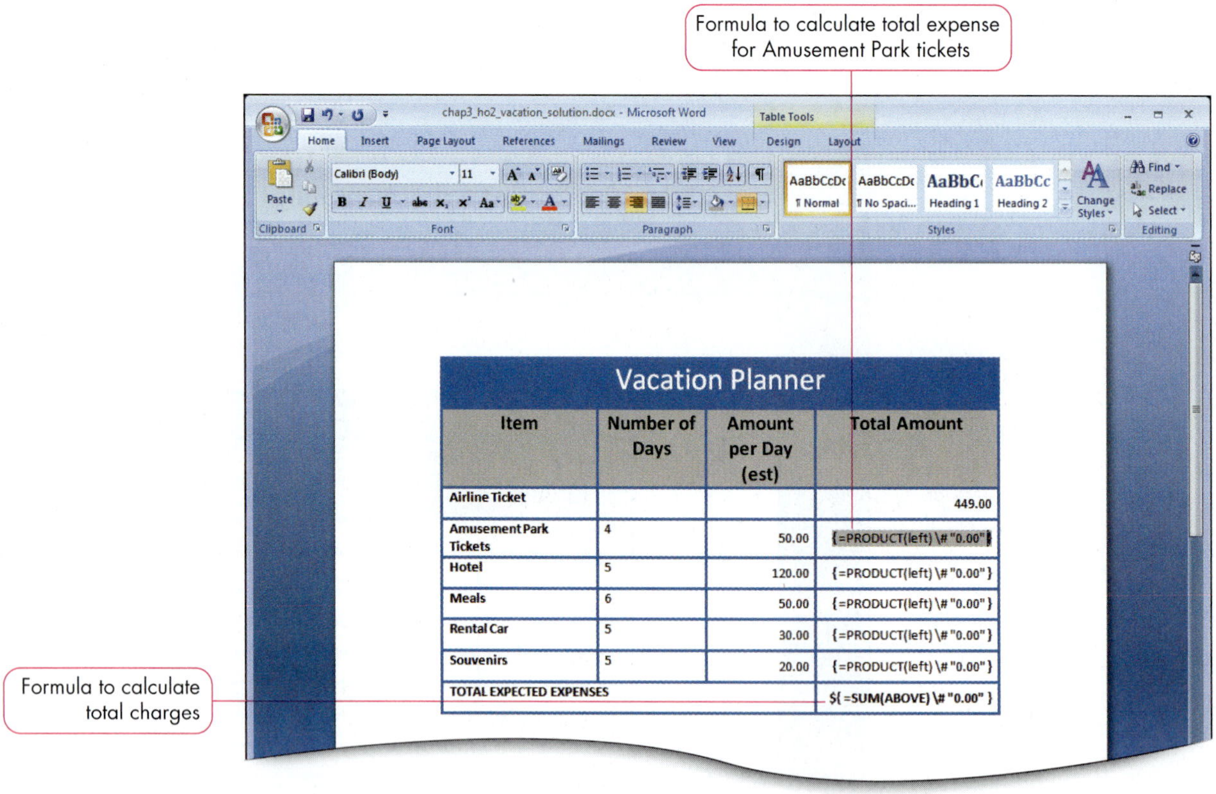

Formula to calculate total expense for Amusement Park tickets

Vacation Planner			
Item	Number of Days	Amount per Day (est)	Total Amount
Airline Ticket			449.00
Amusement Park Tickets	4	50.00	{=PRODUCT(left) \# "0.00"}
Hotel	5	120.00	{=PRODUCT(left) \# "0.00"}
Meals	6	50.00	{=PRODUCT(left) \# "0.00"}
Rental Car	5	30.00	{=PRODUCT(left) \# "0.00"}
Souvenirs	5	20.00	{=PRODUCT(left) \# "0.00"}
TOTAL EXPECTED EXPENSES			${=SUM(ABOVE) \# "0.00"}

Formula to calculate total charges

Figure 3.8 The Vacation Planner Table Displaying Formulas

The formula in cell D9 has a different syntax and adds the value of all cells directly above it. You do not need to know the syntax because Word provides a dialog box that supplies the entry for you, but once you use it to create the formula, you will find it easy to understand. It is better to use the Formula command to calculate totals than to type a number because if you add data to the table, you can use formula tools to recalculate for you.

Sort Data in a Table

Ascending order arranges data from lowest to highest.

Descending order arranges data from highest to lowest.

At times you might need to sort data in a table to enhance order or understand the data. For example, when a list of employees is reviewed, a manager would prefer to view the names in alphabetical order by last name or department. You can sort data according to the entries in a specific column or row of the table. Sort orders include ***ascending order***, which arranges text in alphabetical or sequential order starting with the lowest letter or number and continuing to the highest (A–Z or 0–9). Or you can sort in ***descending order***, where data is arranged from highest to lowest (Z–A or 9–0).

You can sort the rows in a table to display data in different sequences as shown in Figure 3.9, where the vacation items are sorted from lowest to highest expense. You also could sort the data in descending (high to low) sequence according to the Total Amount. In descending order the hotel (largest expense) displays at the top of the list, and the souvenirs (smallest expense) appear last. The second row of the table contains the field names for each column and is not included in the sort. The next six rows contain the sorted data, while the last row displays the total for all expenses and is not included in the sort.

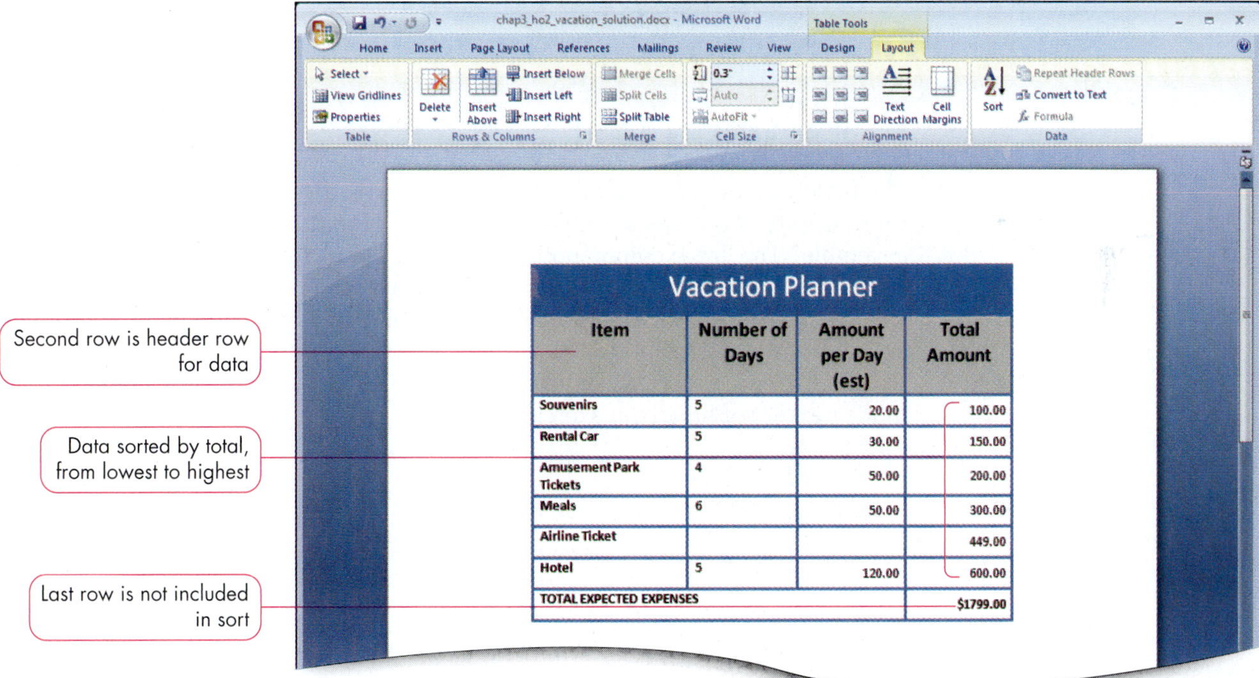

Figure 3.9 Sort the Table Data

Sorting is accomplished according to the select-then-do methodology that is used for many operations in Microsoft Word. You select the rows that are to be sorted, rows three through nine in this example, and then you click Sort in the Data group on the Layout tab. The Sort dialog box displays, as shown in Figure 3.10, which enables you to select the direction and sort criteria.

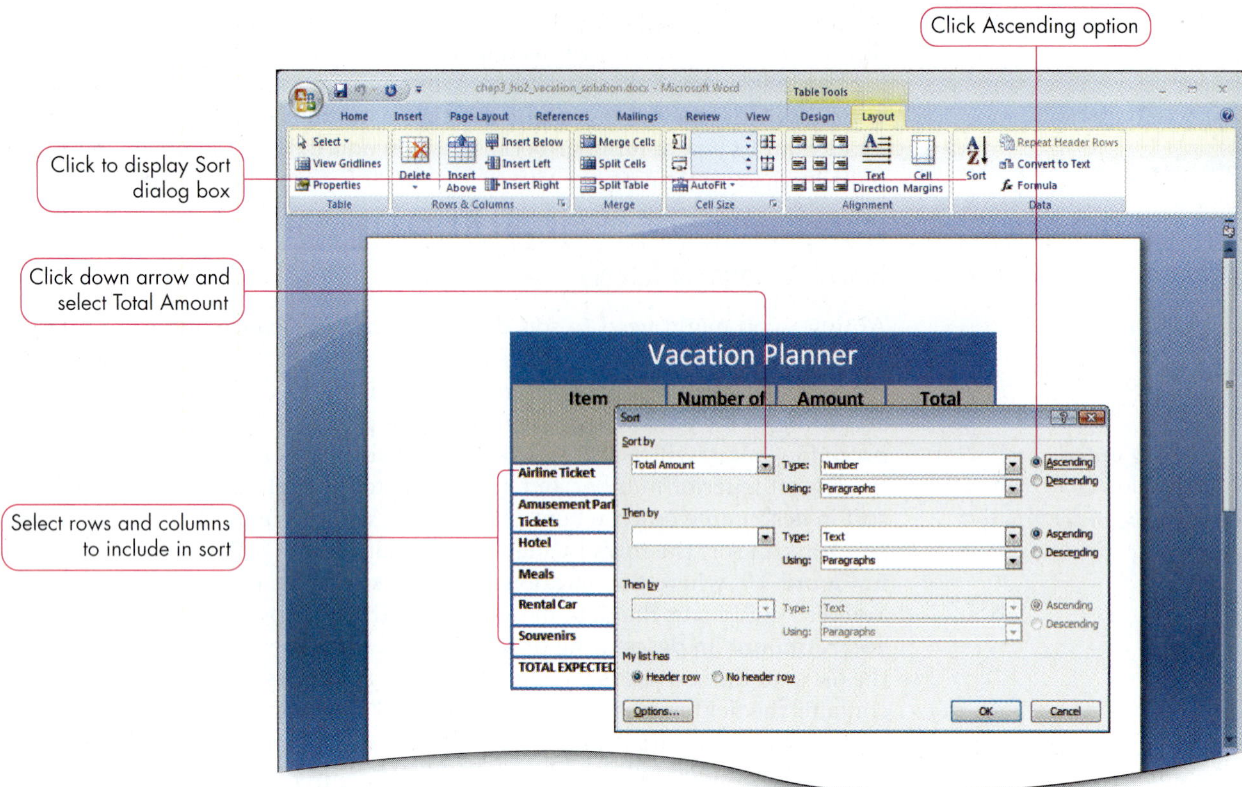

Figure 3.10 The Sort Command

Converting Text to a Table

The tables feature is outstanding. But what if you are given a lengthy list of items—for example, two items per line separated by a tab that should have been formatted as a table? The Table command on the Insert tab includes the Convert Text to Table command, and it can aid you in this transformation. After you select the text and choose this command, the Convert Text to Table dialog box displays and offers several options to assist in a quick conversion of text into a table. The command also works in reverse; you can convert a table to text. You will perform a table conversion in the next set of hands-on exercises.

Table Tools Design Ribbon | Reference

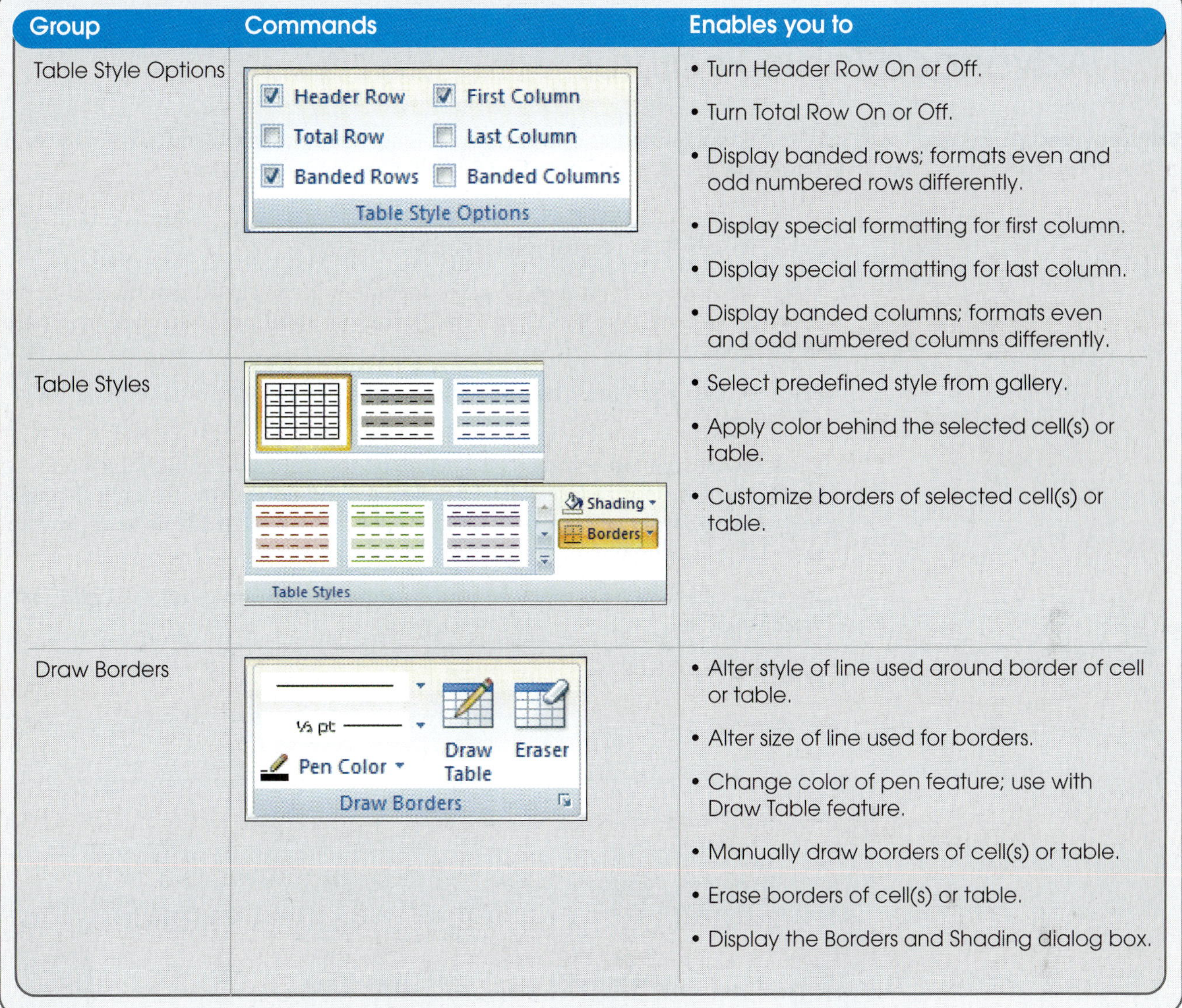

Group	Commands	Enables you to
Table Style Options	Header Row, First Column, Total Row, Last Column, Banded Rows, Banded Columns (Table Style Options)	• Turn Header Row On or Off. • Turn Total Row On or Off. • Display banded rows; formats even and odd numbered rows differently. • Display special formatting for first column. • Display special formatting for last column. • Display banded columns; formats even and odd numbered columns differently.
Table Styles	Shading, Borders (Table Styles)	• Select predefined style from gallery. • Apply color behind the selected cell(s) or table. • Customize borders of selected cell(s) or table.
Draw Borders	½ pt, Pen Color, Draw Table, Eraser (Draw Borders)	• Alter style of line used around border of cell or table. • Alter size of line used for borders. • Change color of pen feature; use with Draw Table feature. • Manually draw borders of cell(s) or table. • Erase borders of cell(s) or table. • Display the Borders and Shading dialog box.

Hands-On Exercises

2 | Advanced Table Features

Skills covered: 1. Apply a Table Style **2.** Add Table Borders and Shading **3.** Enter Formulas to Calculate Totals **4.** Add a Row and Enter a Formula **5.** Sort Data in a Table **6.** Align Table and Data **7.** Convert Text to a Table

Step 1
Apply a Table Style

Refer to Figure 3.11 as you complete Step 1.

a. Open the *chap3_ho1_vacation_solution* document if you closed it at the end of the first exercise and save it as **chap3_ho2_vacation_solution**. Then click anywhere in the table.

   The insertion point must be somewhere within the table before the Table Tools tabs display.

b. Click the **Design tab** and then click **More** on the right side of the Table Styles gallery. Hover your mouse over several styles and notice how the table changes to preview that style. Click once on the **Light List – Accent 1** style to apply it to your table as shown in Figure 3.11.

   Previous cell shading is replaced by the formatting attributes for the **Light List – Accent 1** style.

c. Save the document.

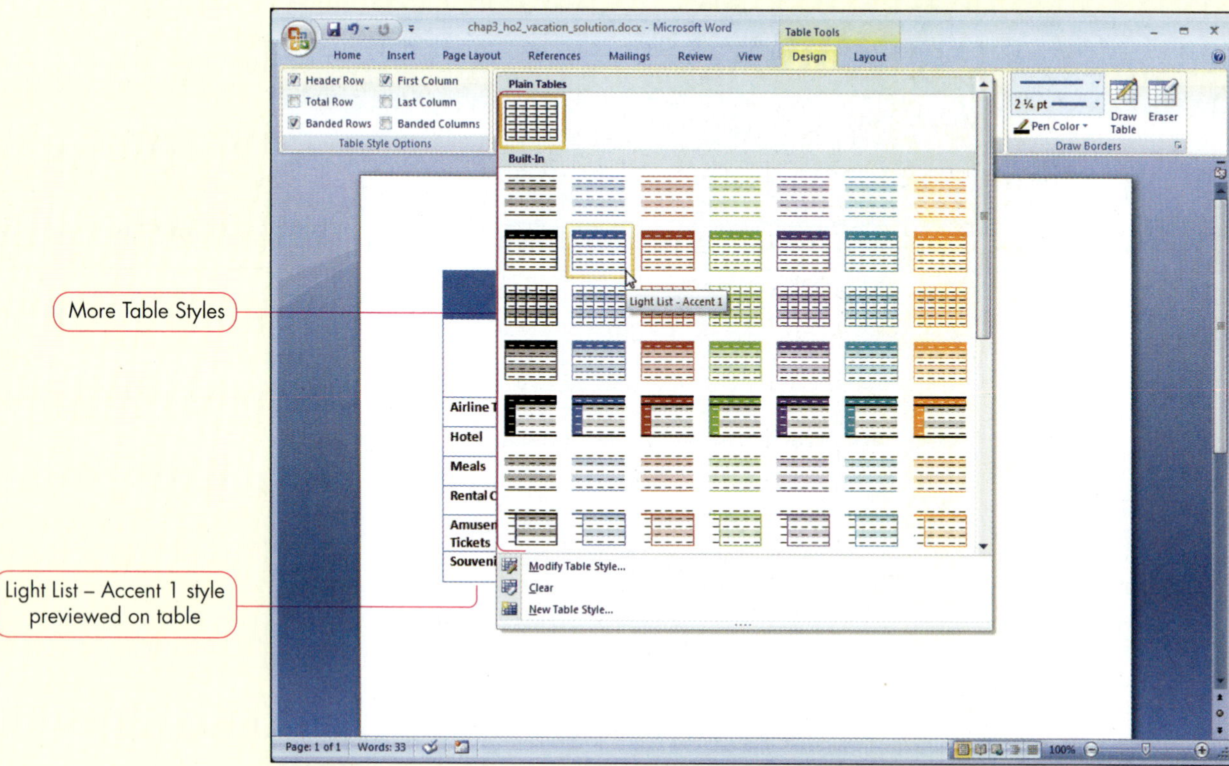

Figure 3.11 Style Applied to Vacation Planner Table

Step 2
Add Table Borders and Shading

Refer to Figure 3.12 as you complete Step 2.

a. Click anywhere in the Vacation Planner table. Click the **Borders arrow** in the Table Styles group and select **Borders and Shading**.

b. Click **All** in the *Setting* section on the left side of the Borders tab. Then click the **Width drop-down arrow** and select 2¼ pt. Click **OK** to close the Borders and Shading dialog box.

Your table has a darker blue border surrounding each cell.

c. Drag your mouse across the cells in the second row of the table to select them, then click **Shading** in the Table Styles group. Click the swatch in the fourth row of the first column named **White, Background 1, Darker 25%** as shown in Figure 3.12.

The table now displays a large, blue title row, a gray colored header row, and blue borders around the remaining data.

d. Save the document.

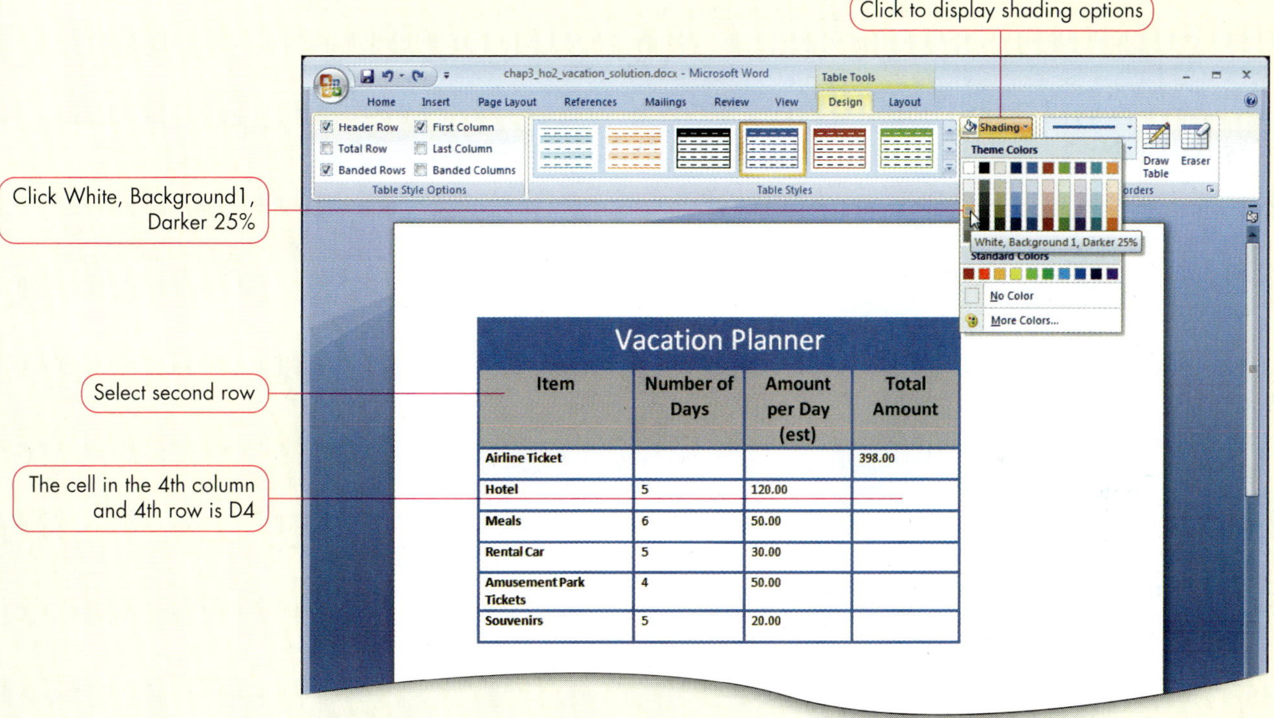

Figure 3.12 Borders and Shading Applied to Table

Step 3
Enter Formulas to Calculate Totals

Refer to Figure 3.13 as you complete Step 3.

a. Click in **cell D4**, the cell in the fourth column and fourth row. Click the **Layout tab** and click **Formula** in the Data group to display the formula box.

b. Click and drag to select the =SUM(ABOVE) function, which is entered by default. Type **=b4*c4** as shown in Figure 3.13 to replace the existing formula and compute the total hotel expense. Click the **Number format drop-down arrow** and select **0.00** and then click **OK**.

The formula is not case sensitive; you can type formula references in lowercase or capital letters. The total is computed by multiplying the number of days (in cell B4) by the amount per day (in cell C4). The result, 600, displays in a number format with two decimal places because these numbers represent a monetary value in dollars and cents.

c. Click in **cell D5**, directly below the cell you edited in the last step, then click **Formula**. In the Formula box, click and drag to select SUM(ABOVE) but do not select the equal sign, then press **Delete** to remove the formula. Click the **Paste function drop-down arrow**, and then scroll and select **PRODUCT**. Type **left** between the parentheses where the insertion point is blinking in the Formula box. Click the **Number format drop-down arrow** and select **0.00**, and then click **OK**.

   This formula performs the same function as the one you used in Step B, but it references cells to the left of the current cell instead of using actual cell addresses.

d. Calculate the total expenses for cells D6, D7, and D8 using either formula used in the previous steps.

e. Save the document.

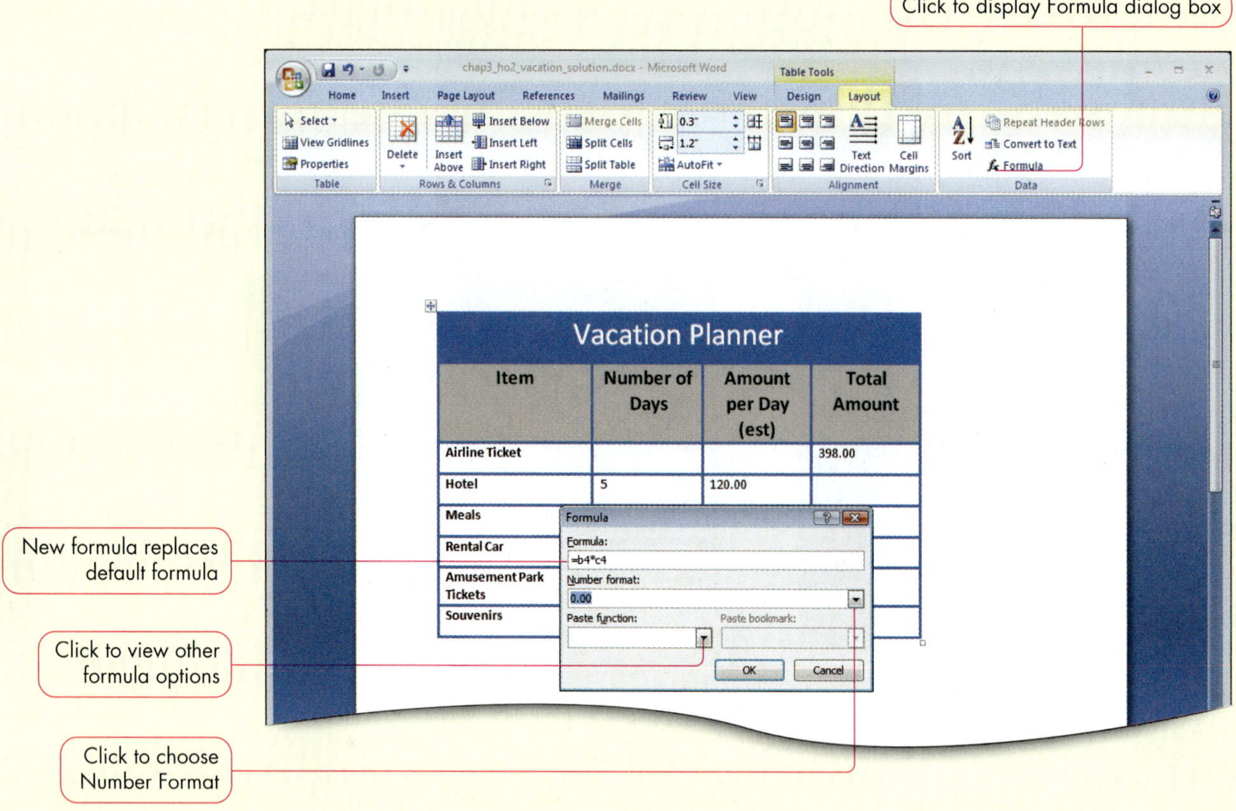

Figure 3.13 Compute a Formula in a Table

Step 4
Add a Row and Enter a Formula

Refer to Figure 3.14 as you complete Step 4.

a. Click the last cell in the table and press **Tab** to add another row to the table. Drag your mouse across all four cells in this row to select them, and then click **Merge Cells** in the Merge group on the Layout tab. Type the words **TOTAL EXPECTED EXPENSES** in the newly merged cell.

b. Click **Split Cells** in the Merge group to display the Split Cells dialog box. If necessary, click the **Number of columns spin box** to display **2**, then click **OK**.

The last row displays two cells of equal size. You will display the total vacation expense amount in the last cell, but you need to resize it to the same size as cells in the last column so the numbers will align correctly.

c. Hold your mouse over the border between the cells in the last row until a two-headed arrow displays. Then click and drag to the right until the border aligns with the border of the last column in the rows above as shown in Figure 3.14.

d. Click in the last cell of the table, click **Formula**, click the **Number format drop-down arrow**, and select **0.00**, and then click **OK** to accept the default formula, =SUM(ABOVE).

You should see 1748.00 (the sum of the cells in the last column) displayed in the selected cell.

e. Click the number, 1748.00, one time so that it is shaded in grey, then press **Shift+F9** to display the code {=SUM(ABOVE)\#"0.00"}. Press **Shift+F9** a second time to display the actual value.

f. Click in **cell D3** (the cell containing the airfare). Replace 398.00 with **449.00** and press **Tab** to move out of the cell.

The total expenses are not yet updated in cell D9.

g. Right-click on the number that displays in **cell D9** to display a shortcut menu, then select **Update Field**.

Cell D9 displays 1799.00, the updated total for all expenses.

h. Save the document.

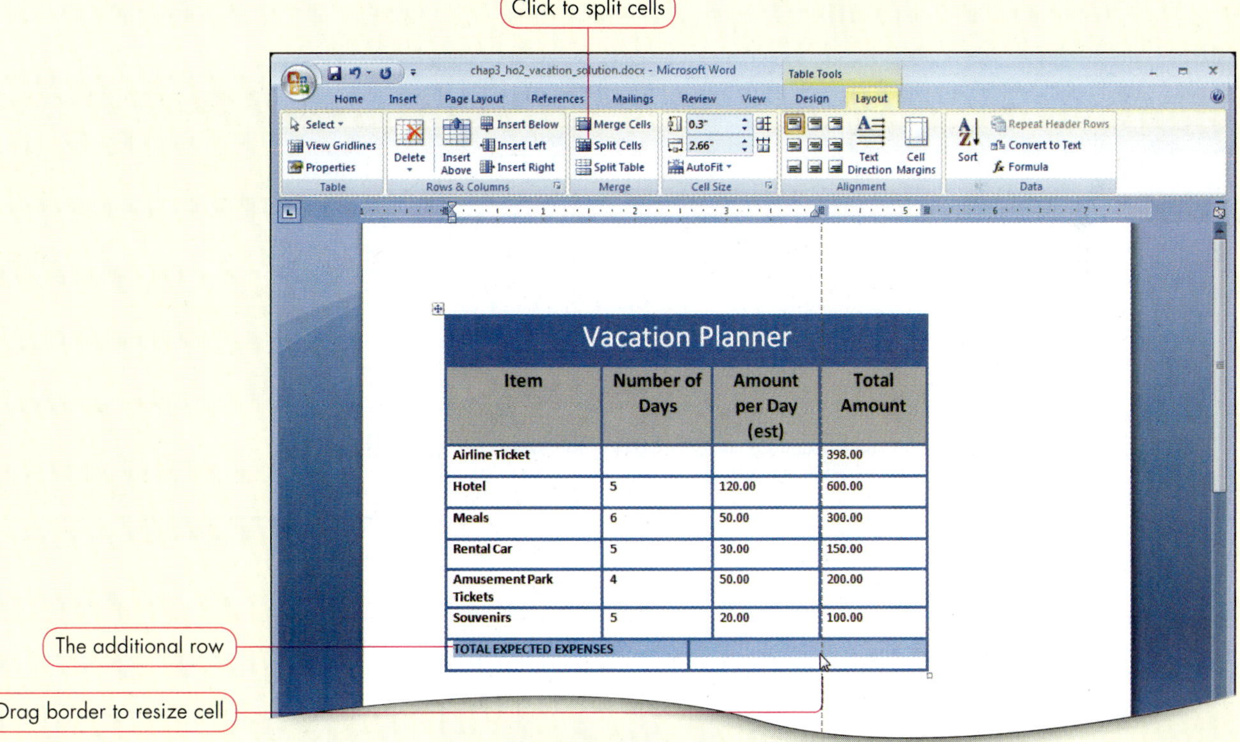

Figure 3.14 Drag to Resize Cell Width

Step 5
Sort Data in a Table

Refer to Figure 3.15 as you complete Step 5.

a. Click and drag to select rows two through eight in the table. That is, select all table rows *except* the title and total rows. Click **Sort** in the Data group on the Layout tab.

b. Click **Header row** in the *My list has* section, at the bottom of the dialog box.

c. If necessary, click the **Sort by drop-down arrow** and select **Item** (the column heading for the first column). The Ascending option is selected by default as shown in Figure 3.15. Click **OK.**

The entries in the table are rearranged alphabetically according to the entry in the Item column. The Total row remains at the bottom of the table since it was not included in the sort.

TROUBLESHOOTING: If you do not first click Header row, the headings for each column will not display in the Sort by drop-down list; instead you will see the Column numbers listed. You can sort by Column number (1, 2, 3, or 4), but it is important to click the Header row option before you leave this dialog box so the header row is not included in the sort.

d. Select rows four through six, some of which have lost formatting along the left and right borders. Click the **Design tab**, click the **Borders arrow** in the Table Styles group, then select **All Borders**.

The dark blue borders fill the left and right borders of the selected cells, matching the remainder of the table.

e. Save the document.

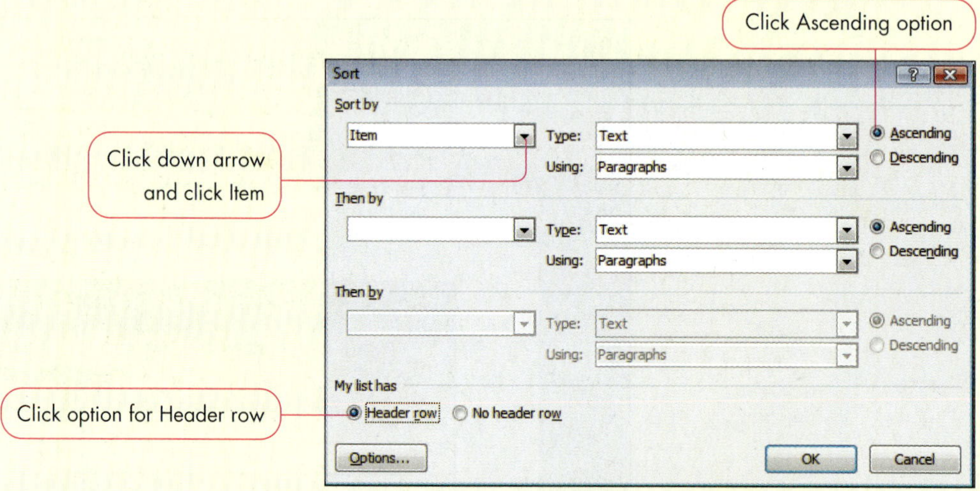

Figure 3.15 Sort Data in a Table

Step 6
Align Table and Data

Refer to Figure 3.16 as you complete Step 6.

a. Click the table selector to select the entire table. Click the **Layout tab**, then click **Properties** in the Table group.

b. Click the **Table tab**, if necessary, and then click **Center** in the *Alignment* section as shown in Figure 3.16. Click **OK**.

Your table is now centered between the left and right margins.

c. Click anywhere to deselect the whole table, then drag your mouse to select the last two columns of rows three through eight. Select entries listed under Amount Per Day (est) and Total Amount, but do not select data in the header row. Click **Align Center Right** from the Alignment group. Select the last cell in the table and click **Align Center Right** to align it with other data.

Because these columns contain numerical data, you right align them to give the effect of decimal alignment. However, the numbers are not decimal aligned, so if you display an additional digit in a value, it will result in misaligned numbers.

d. Click in the last cell and insert a dollar sign ($) in front of the amount of expected expenses.

e. Save and close the *chap3_ho2_vacation_solution* document.

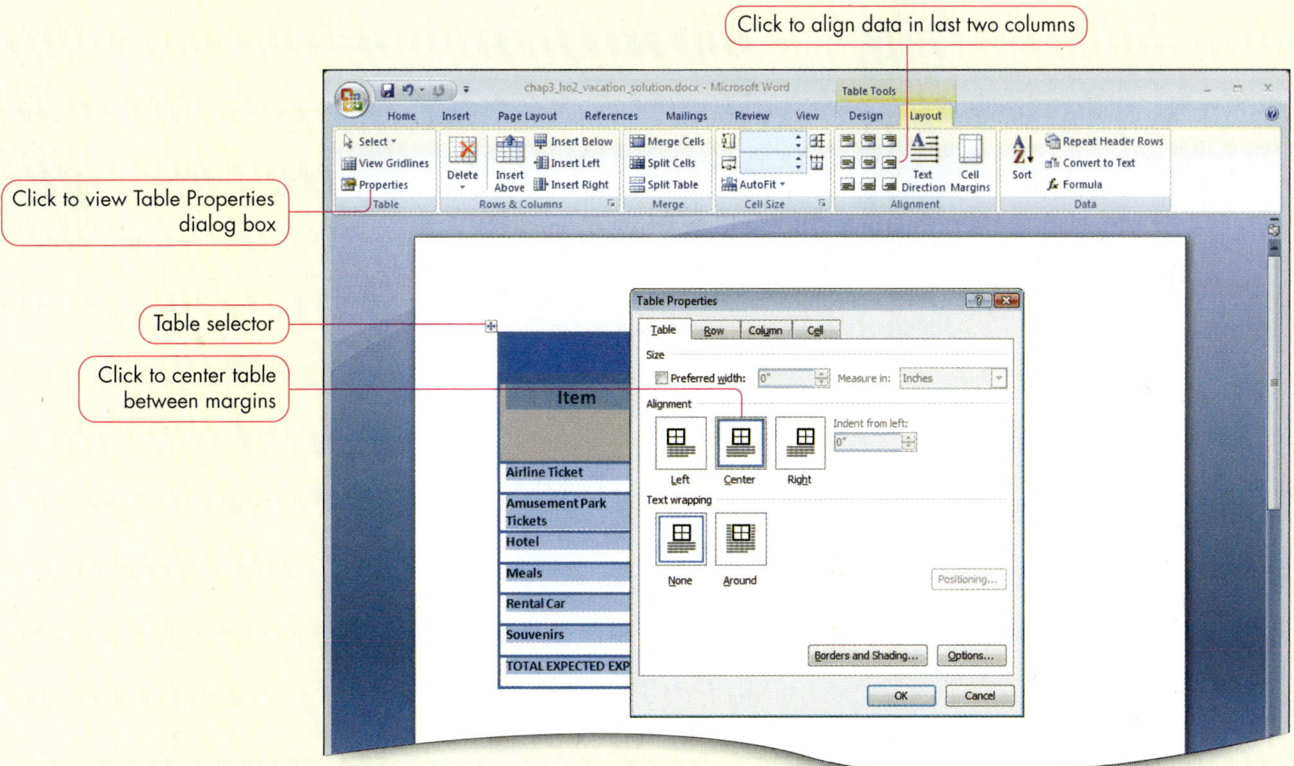

Figure 3.16 Apply Alignment to Vacation Planner Table

Step 7
Convert Text to a Table

Refer to Figure 3.17 as you complete Step 7.

a. Open the *chap3_ho2_expenses* document and save it as **chap3_ho2_expenses_solution**.

b. Press **Ctrl+A** to select all text in this document and then click the **Insert tab**.

c. Click **Table**, and then select **Convert Text to Table**. View the options in the Convert Text to Table dialog box as shown in Figure 3.17, but do not make any changes at this time. Click **OK**.

The list of items display in a table that can now be sorted and formatted.

d. Save and close the *chap3_ho2_expenses_solution* document.

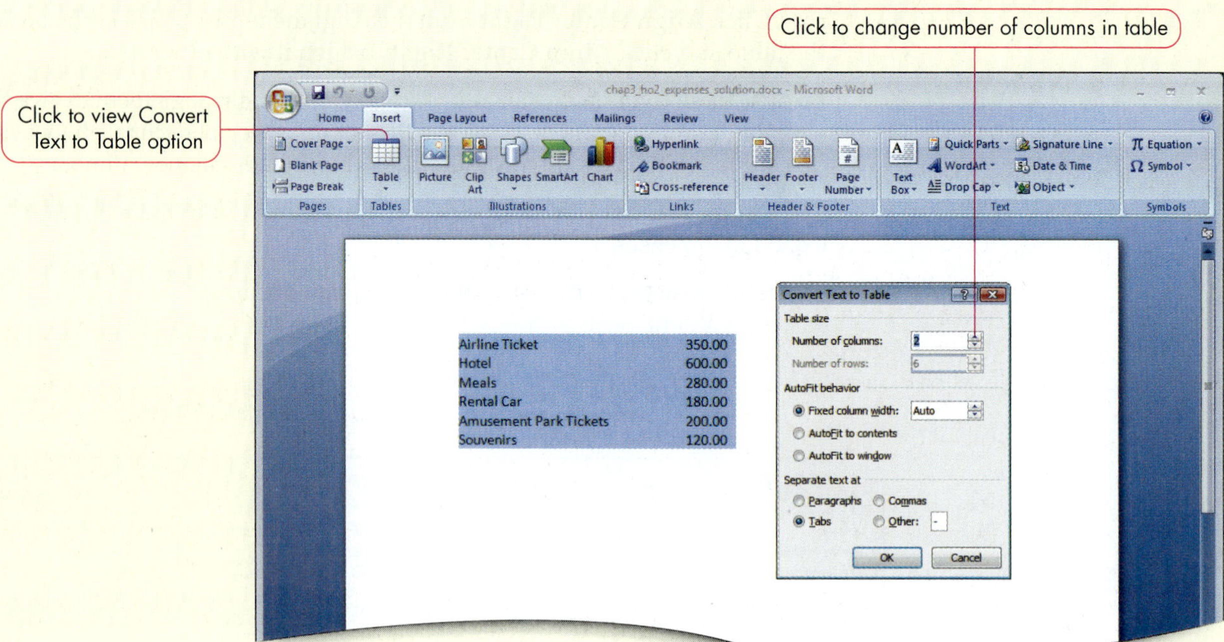

Figure 3.17 Convert Text to Table Dialog Box

Graphic Tools

Clip art is a graphical image, illustration, drawing, or sketch.

One of the most exciting features of Word is its graphic capabilities. You can use clip art, images, drawings, and scanned photographs to visually enhance brochures, newsletters, announcements, and reports. ***Clip art*** is a graphical image, illustration, drawing, or sketch. In addition to inserting clip art in a document, you can insert photographs from a digital camera or scanner, graphically shaped text, and special boxes to hold text. After inserting a graphical image or text, you can adjust size, choose placement, and perform other graphical formatting options.

One of the most exciting features of Word is its graphic capabilities. You can use clip art, images, drawings, and scanned photographs to visually enhance brochures, newsletters, announcements, and reports.

In this section, you will learn to insert a clip art and an image in a document. Then you format the image by changing the height and width, applying a text-wrapping style, applying a quick style, and adjusting graphic properties. Finally, you will insert WordArt and symbols in a document.

Inserting Clip Art and Images into a Document

Clip art and other graphical images or objects may be stored locally, purchased on a CD at a computer supply store, or downloaded from the Internet for inclusion into a document. Whether you use Microsoft's online clip gallery or purchase clip art, you should read the license agreements to know how you may legally use the images. A ***copyright*** provides legal protection to a written or artistic work, giving the author exclusive rights to its use and reproduction, except as governed under the fair use exclusion. Anything on the Internet should be considered copyrighted unless the document specifically says it is in the public domain. The Fair Use doctrine allows you to use a portion of the work for educational, nonprofit purposes, or for the purpose of critical review or commentary. All such material should be cited through an appropriate footnote or endnote. Using clip art for a purpose not allowed by the license agreement is illegal.

A ***copyright*** provides legal protection to a written or artistic work.

Manage Clips with the Microsoft Clip Organizer

The Clip Art command displays a task pane through which you can search, select, and insert clip art, photographs, sounds, and movies (collectively called clips). The clips can come from a variety of sources. They may be installed locally in the My Collections folder, in conjunction with Microsoft Office in the Office Collections folder, and/or they may have been downloaded from the Web and stored in the Web Collections folder. You can insert a specific clip into a document if you know its location. You also can search for a clip that will enhance the document on which you are working.

The ***Microsoft Clip Organizer*** catalogs pictures, sounds, and movies stored on your hard drive.

The ***Microsoft Clip Organizer*** brings you out of potential chaos by cataloging the clips, photos, sounds, and movies that are available. You enter a keyword that describes the clip you are looking for, specify the collections that are to be searched, and indicate the type of clip(s) you are looking for. The results are returned in the task pane as shown in Figure 3.18, which displays the clips that are described by the keyword *computer*. You can restrict the search to selected collections but request that all media types be displayed. If you also specify to search for items stored locally, the search is faster than one that searches online as well. When you see a clip that you want to use, click the clip to insert it into your document. For more options, point to the clip, click the down arrow that appears, and then select from the menu.

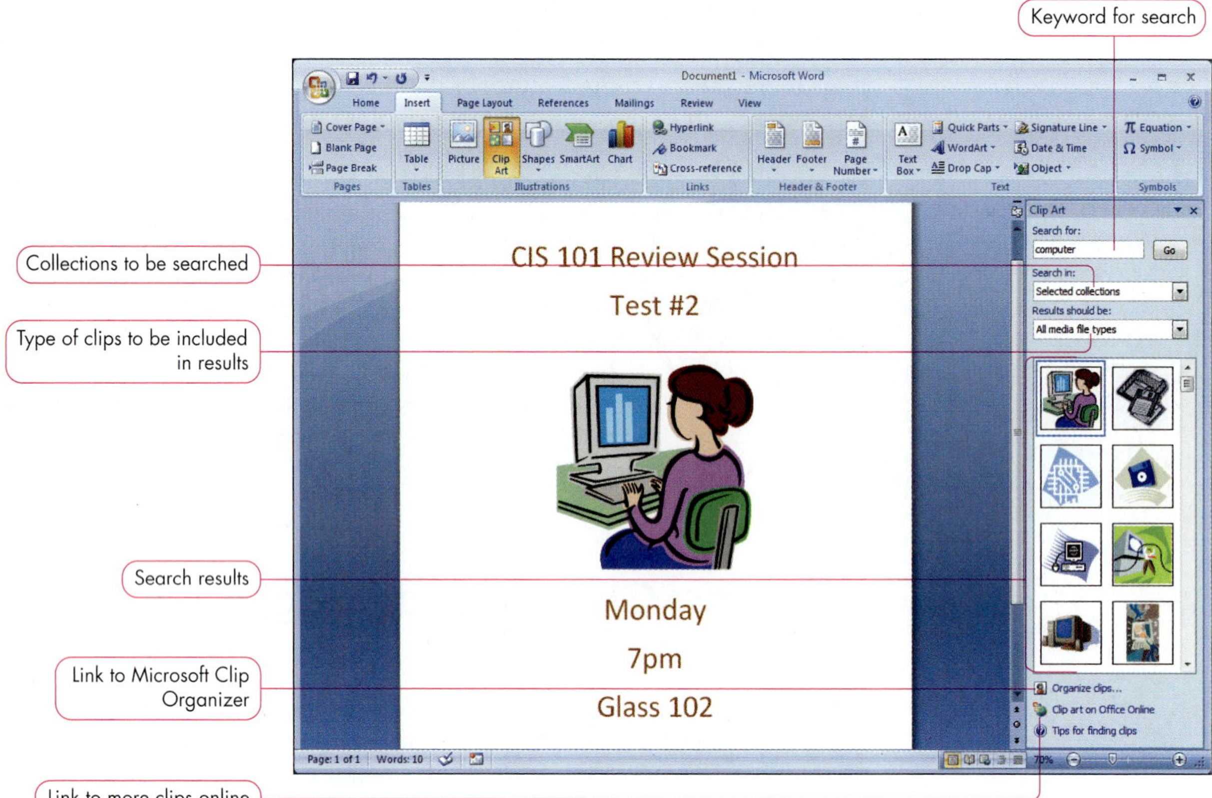

Figure 3.18 The Clip Art Task Pane

You can access the Microsoft Clip Organizer (to view the various collections) by clicking Organize clips at the bottom of the Clip Art task pane. You also can access the Clip Organizer when you are not using Word; click the Start button on the taskbar, click All Programs, Microsoft Office, Microsoft Office Tools, and Microsoft Clip Organizer. Once in the Organizer, you can search through the clips in the various collections, reorganize the existing collections, add new collections, and even add new clips (with their associated keywords) to the collections. The other links at the bottom of the task pane in Figure 3.18 provide access to additional clip art online and tips for finding more relevant clips.

Insert a Picture

In addition to the collection of clip art and pictures that you can access from Word, you also can insert your own pictures into a document. If you have a scanner or digital camera attached to your computer, you can scan or download a picture for use in Word. After you save the picture to your disk, click Picture in the Illustrations group on the Insert tab to locate and insert it in the document. The Insert Picture dialog box opens so that you can navigate to the location where the picture is saved. After you insert the picture, there are many commands you can use to format it. Those commands are discussed in the next section.

Formatting a Graphic Element

(Remember that graphical elements should enhance a document, not overpower it.)

When you insert an image in a document, it comes in a predefined size. For example the clip art image in Figure 3.18 was very large and took up much space on the page before it was resized. Most times you need to adjust an image's size so it fits within the document and does not greatly increase the document file size. Remember that graphical elements should enhance a document, not overpower it.

Adjust the Height and Width of a Graphic

Sizing handles are the small circles and squares that appear around a selected object and enable you to adjust the height and width of an object.

Word provides different tools you can use to adjust the height or width of an image, depending on how exact you want the measurements. The Picture Tools Format tab contains Height and Width commands that enable you to specify exact measurements. You can use ***sizing handles***, the small circles and squares that appear around a selected object, to size an object by clicking and dragging any one of the handles. When you use the circular sizing handles in the corner of a graphic to adjust the height (or width), Word also adjusts the width (or height) simultaneously. If needed, hold down Shift while dragging the corner sizing handle to maintain the correct proportion of the image. If you use square sizing handles on the right, left, top, or bottom, you adjust that measurement without regard to any other sides.

Adjust Text Wrapping

Text wrapping style refers to the way text wraps around an image.

When you first insert an image, Word treats it as a character in the line of text, which leaves a lot of empty space on the left or right side of the image. You may want it to align differently, perhaps allowing text to display very tightly around the object or even behind the text. ***Text wrapping style*** refers to the way text wraps around an image. Table 3.1 describes the different wrapping options.

Table 3.1 Text Wrapping Styles

Text Wrapping Style	Description
Square	Allows text to wrap around the graphic frame that surrounds the image.
Tight	Allows text to wrap tightly around the outer edges of the image itself instead of the frame.
Through	Select this option to wrap text around the perimeter and inside any open portions of the object.
Top and Bottom	Text wraps to the top and bottom of the image frame, but no text appears on the sides.
Behind Text	Allows the image to display behind the text in such a way that the image appears to float directly behind the text and does not move if text is inserted or deleted.
In Front of Text	Allows the image to display on top of the text in such a way that the image appears to float directly on top of the text and does not move if text is inserted or deleted.
In Line with Text	Graphic displays on the line where inserted so that as you add or delete text, causing the line of text to move, the image moves with it.

Apply Picture Quick Styles

The ***Picture Styles*** gallery contains preformatted options that can be applied to a graphical object.

Word 2007 introduces the ***Picture Styles*** gallery that contains many preformatted picture formats. The gallery of styles you can apply to a picture or clip art is extensive, and you also can modify the style after you apply it. The quick styles provide a valuable resource if you want to improve the appearance of a graphic but are not familiar with graphic design and format tools. For example, after you insert a graphic, with one click you can choose a style from the Quick Styles gallery that adds a border and displays a reflection of the picture. You might want to select a style that changes the shape of your graphic to an octagon, or select a style that applies a 3-D effect to the image. To apply a quick style, select the graphical object, then choose a quick style from the Picture Styles group on the Picture Tools Format tab. Other style formatting options, such as Soft Edges or 3-D Rotation, are listed in Picture Effects on the Picture Styles group as shown in Figure 3.19.

Adjust Graphic Properties

Crop or ***Cropping*** is the process of trimming the edges of an image or other graphical object.

Scale or ***scaling*** is the adjustment of height or width by a percentage of the image's original size.

Contrast is the difference between light and dark areas of an image.

Brightness is the ratio between lightness and darkness of an image.

After you insert a graphic or an image, you might find that you need to edit it before using a picture style. One of the most common changes includes ***crop*** or ***cropping***, which is the process of trimming edges or other portions of an image or other graphical object that you do not wish to display. Cropping enables you to call attention to a specific area of a graphical element while omitting any unnecessary detail. When you add images to enhance a document, you may find clip art that has more objects than you desire, or you may find an image that has damaged edges that you do not wish to appear in your document. You can solve the problems with these graphics by cropping. The cropping tool is located in the Size group on the Format tab.

Instead of cropping unused portions of a graphic, you may need to enlarge or reduce its size to fit in the desired area. The easiest method for sizing is selecting the image and dragging the selection handles. For more exact measurements, however, you can use the ***scale or scaling***, which adjusts the height or width of an image by a percentage of its original size. The scale adjustment is located in the Size dialog box, which you display by clicking the Size Dialog Box Launcher on the Format tab.

Other common adjustments to a graphical object includes contrast and/or brightness. Adjusting the ***contrast*** increases or decreases the difference in dark and light areas of the image. Adjusting the ***brightness*** lightens or darkens the overall

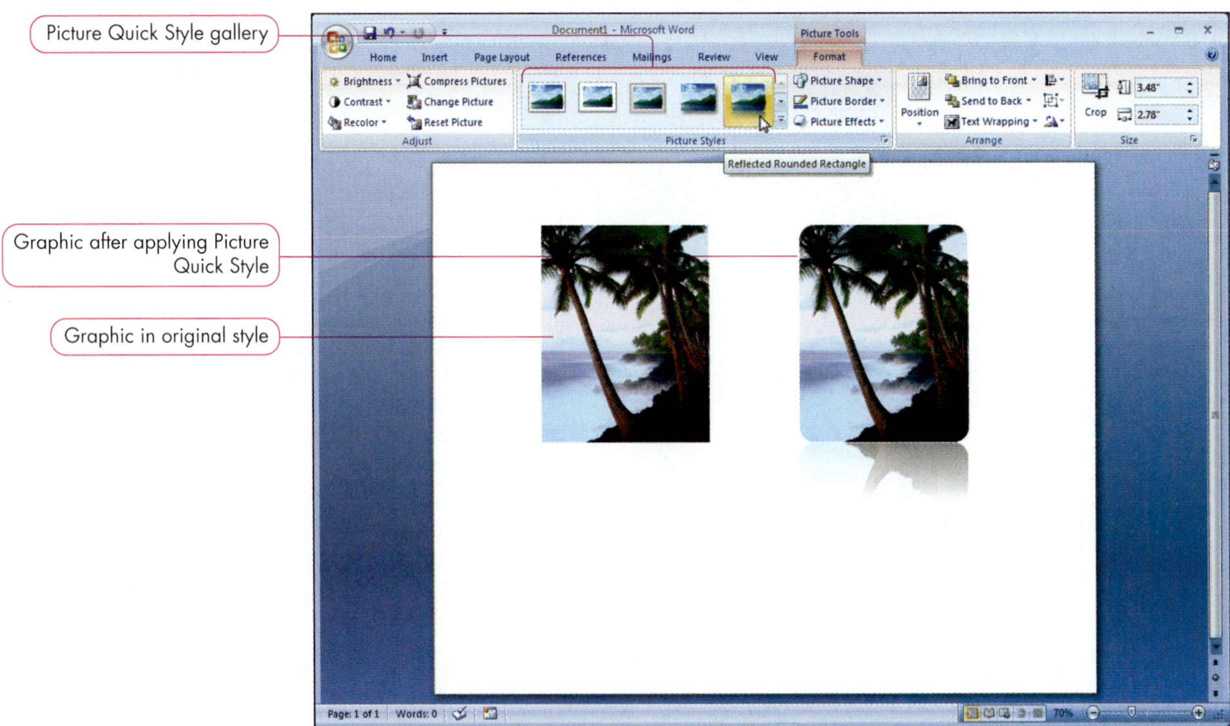

Figure 3.19 The Picture Styles Gallery

image. These adjustments often are made on a picture taken with a digital camera in poor lighting or if a clip art image is too bright or dull to match other objects in your document. Adjusting contrast or brightness can improve the visibility of subjects in a picture. You may want to increase contrast for a dramatic effect or lower contrast to soften an image. The Brightness and Contrast adjustments are in the Picture Tools group on the Format tab.

Even though graphical objects add a great deal of visual enhancement to a document, they also can increase the file size of the document. If you add several graphics to a document, you should view the file size before you copy or save it to a portable storage device, and then confirm the device has enough empty space to hold the large file. Additional consideration should be given to files you send as e-mail attachments. Many people have space limitations in their mailboxes, and a document that contains several graphics can fill their space or take a long time to download. To decrease the size a graphic occupies, you can use the ***Compress*** feature, which reduces the size of an object. When you select a graphical object, you can click the Compress Pictures command on the Picture Tools group in the Format tab, to display the Compression Settings dialog box. Here, you can select from options that allow you to reduce the size of the graphical elements, thus reducing the size of the file when you save.

Compress reduces the file size of an object.

The Picture Tools tab offers many additional graphic editing features, which are described on the following reference page.

Graphic Editing Features | Reference

Feature	Button	Description
Height		Height of an object in inches.
Width		Width of an object in inches.
Crop		Remove unwanted portions of the object from top, bottom, left, or right to adjust size.
Align		Adjust edges of object to line up on right or left margin or center between margins.
Group		Process of selecting multiple objects so you can move and format them together.
Rotate		Ability to change the position of an object by rotating it around its own center.
Text Wrapping		Refers to the way text wraps around an object.
Position		Specify location on page where object will reside.
Border		The outline surrounding an object; it can be formatted using color, shapes, or width, or can be set as invisible.
Shadow Effects		Ability to add a shadow to an object.
Compress		Reduce the file size of an object.
Brightness		Increase or decrease brightness of an object.
Contrast		Increase or decrease difference between black and white colors of an object.
Recolor		Change object to give it an effect such as washed-out or grayscale.

Inserting WordArt into a Document

Microsoft WordArt creates decorative text for a document.

Microsoft WordArt is a Microsoft Office application that creates decorative text that can be used to add interest to a document. You can use WordArt in addition to clip art, or in place of clip art if the right image is not available. You can rotate text in any direction, add three-dimensional effects, display the text vertically, slant it, arch it, or even print it upside down.

WordArt is intuitively easy to use. In essence you choose a style from the gallery (see Figure 3.20). Then you enter the specific text in the Edit WordArt Text dialog box, after which the results display (see Figure 3.21). The WordArt object can be moved and sized, just like any object. A WordArt Tools tab provides many formatting features that enable you to change alignment, add special effects, and change styles quickly. It is fun and easy, and you can create some truly unique documents.

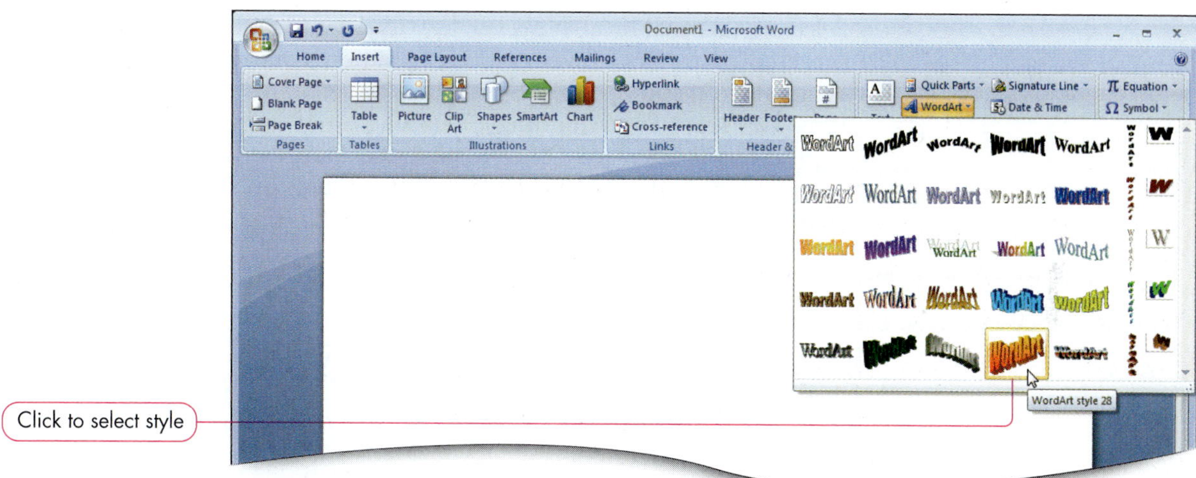

Figure 3.20 The WordArt Gallery

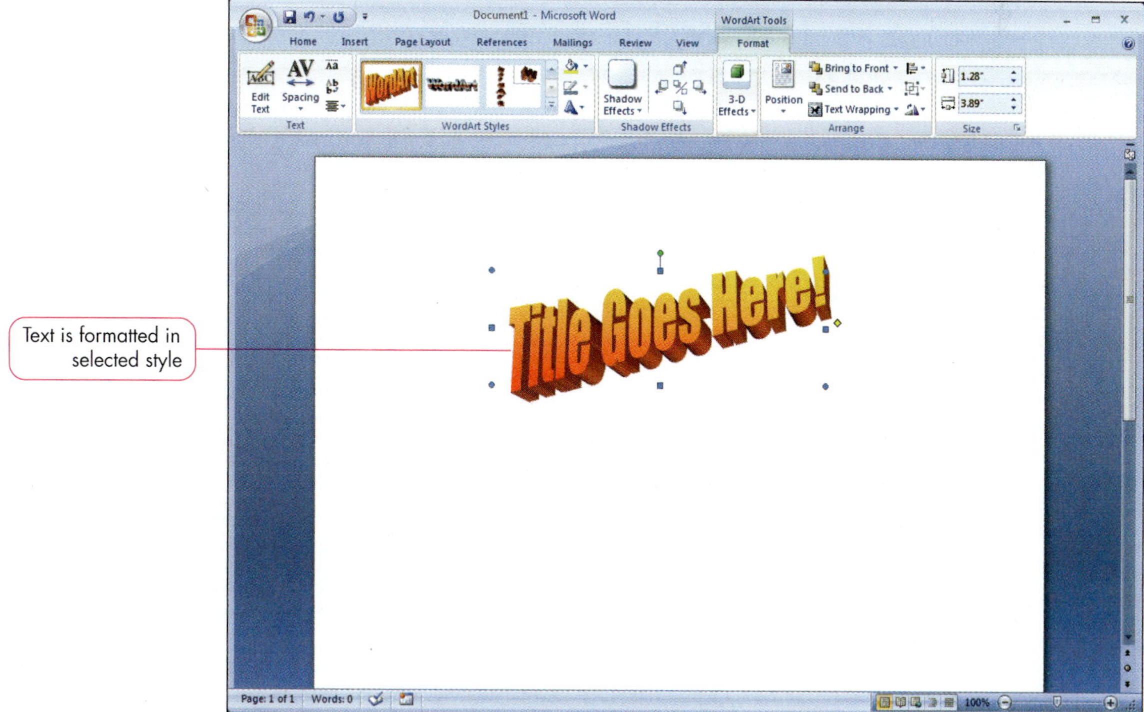

Figure 3.21 The Completed WordArt Object

Inserting Symbols into a Document

The Symbol command enables you to enter typographic symbols and/or foreign language characters into a document in place of ordinary typing—for example, ® rather than (R), © rather than (c), 1/2 and ¼, rather than 1/2 and 1/4, or é rather than e (as used in the word résumé). These special characters give a document a very professional look.

You may have already discovered that some of this formatting can be done automatically through the AutoCorrect feature that is built in to Word. If, for example, you type the letter "c" enclosed in parentheses, it will automatically be converted to the copyright symbol. You can use the Symbol command to insert other symbols, such as accented letters like the é in résumé or those in a foreign language (e.g., ¿Cómo está usted?).

The installation of Microsoft Office adds a variety of fonts onto your computer, each of which contains various symbols that can be inserted into a document. Selecting "normal text," however, as was done in Figure 3.22, provides access to the accented characters as well as other common symbols. Other fonts—especially the Wingdings, Webdings, and Symbol fonts—contain special symbols, including the Windows logo. The Wingdings, Webdings, and Symbol fonts are among the best-kept secrets in Microsoft Office. Each font contains a variety of symbols that are actually pictures. You can insert any of these symbols into a document as text, select the character and enlarge the point size, change the color, then copy the modified character to create a truly original document.

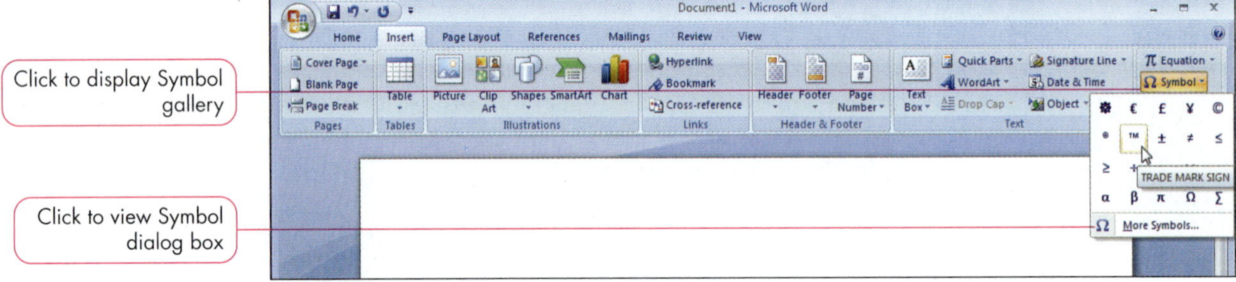

Figure 3.22 Insert Symbol Command

Hands-On Exercises

3 | Clip Art, WordArt, and Symbols

Skills covered: 1. Insert a Clip Art Object **2.** Move and Resize the Clip Art Object **3.** Create a WordArt Object **4.** Modify the WordArt Object **5.** Insert a Symbol

Step 1 Insert a Clip Art Object

Refer to Figure 3.23 as you complete Step 1.

a. Open the *chap3_ho3_ergonomics* document and save it as **chap3_ho3_ergonomics_solution**.

b. Click to move the insertion point to the beginning of the document, if necessary. Click the **Insert tab** and click **Clip Art** in the Illustrations group.

   The Clip Art task pane opens as shown in Figure 3.23.

c. Type **computer** in the **Search for box** to search for any clip art image that is indexed with this keyword. Click the **Search in drop-down arrow** and click **Office Collections**, then click to deselect My Collections and Web Collections, if necessary. Click **Go**.

   The images display in the task pane. If the Microsoft Clip Organizer displays and asks "Do you want to include thousands of additional clip art images and photos from Microsoft Office Online when you search?" click **No**.

d. Point to the first image to display a down arrow, and then click the arrow to display a menu.

e. Click **Insert** to insert the image into the document. Do not be concerned about its size or position at this time. Close the task pane.

f. Save the document.

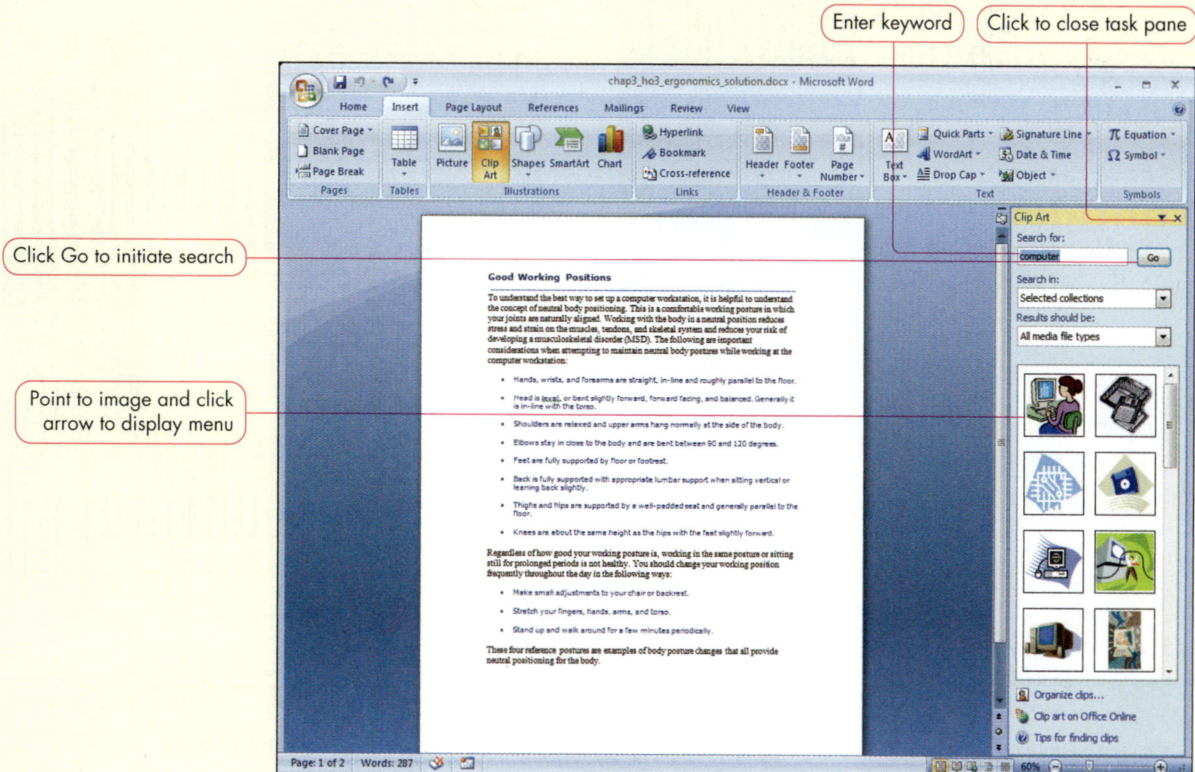

Figure 3.23 Clip Art Task Pane

Step 2

Move and Resize the Clip Art Object

Refer to Figure 3.24 as you complete Step 2.

a. Click once on the clip art object to select it. Click **Text Wrapping** in the Arrange group on the Picture Tools Format tab to display the text wrapping options and then select **Square** as shown in Figure 3.24.

   You must change the layout in order to move the object.

b. Click **Position** in the Arrange group, and then click **More Layout Options.** Click the **Picture Position tab** in the Advanced Layout dialog box, if necessary, then click **Alignment** in the *Horizontal* section. Click the **Alignment drop-down arrow** and select **Right**. Deselect the **Allow overlap check box** in the *Options* section. Click **OK.**

c. Click **Crop** in the Size group, then hold your mouse over the sizing handles and notice how the pointer changes to angular shapes. Click the **bottom center handle** and drag it up. Drag the side handles inward to remove excess space surrounding the graphical object.

d. Click the Shape **Height box** in the Size group and type **2.77**. Click anywhere in the document to view the changes.

   Notice the width is changed automatically to retain the proportion.

e. Save the document.

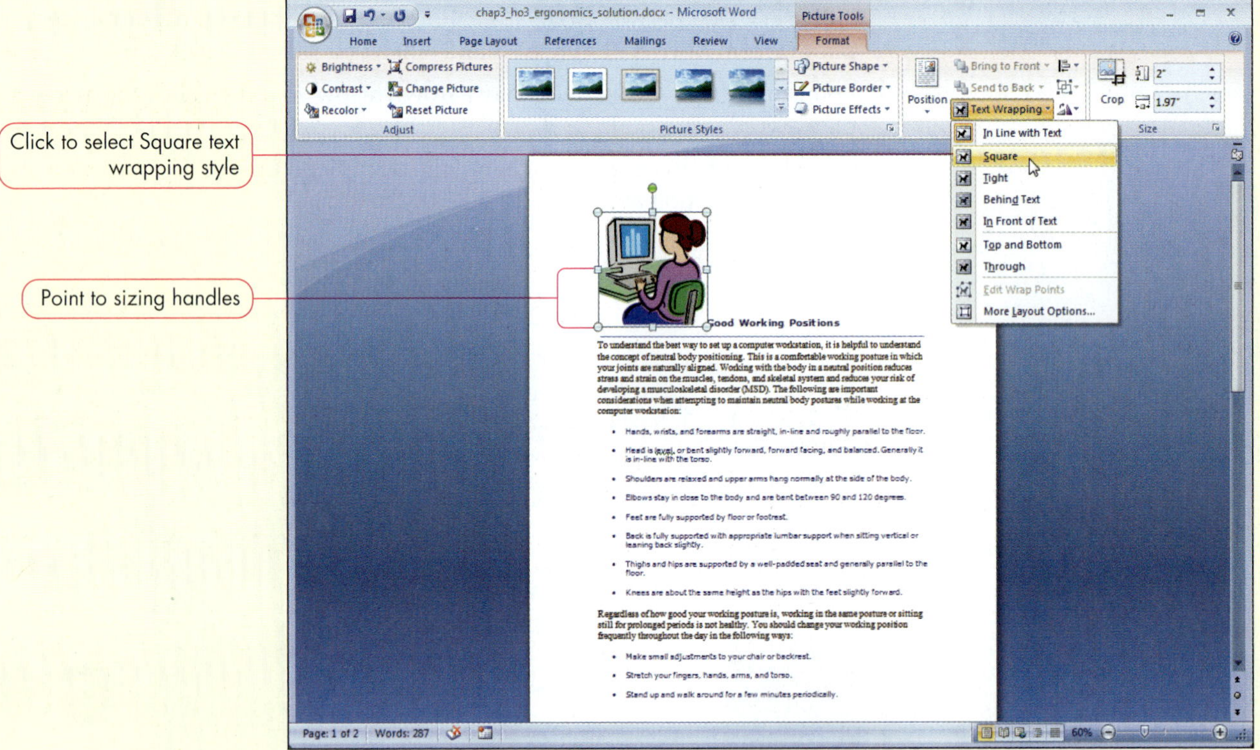

Figure 3.24 Formatting Clip Art

Step 3

Create a WordArt Object

Refer to Figure 3.25 as you complete Step 3.

a. Press **Ctrl+End** to move to the end of the document. Click the **Insert tab** and then click **WordArt** in the Text group to display the WordArt gallery.

b. Click **WordArt style 28** on the bottom row of the gallery.

   The Edit WordArt Text dialog box displays, as shown in Figure 3.25.

c. Type **WWW.OSHA.GOV** and then click OK.

The WordArt object appears in your document in the style you selected.

TROUBLESHOOTING: If the WordArt object displays on another page, you can correct it in the next steps.

d. Point to the WordArt object and right-click to display a shortcut menu. Select **Format WordArt** to display the Format WordArt dialog box.

e. Click the **Layout tab** and click **Square** in the *Wrapping style* section. Click **OK**.

It is important to select this wrapping option to facilitate placing the WordArt at the bottom of the first page.

f. Save the document.

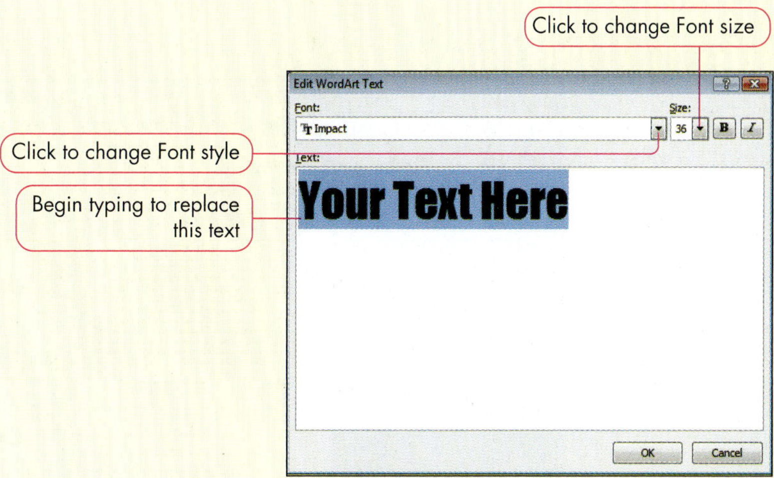

Figure 3.25 Edit WordArt Text Dialog Box

TIP Display the Format Tab Quickly

To save time and mouse clicks, you can double-click a WordArt object to quickly display the WordArt Tools Format tab.

Step 4 Modify the WordArt Object

Refer to Figure 3.26 as you complete Step 4.

a. Click and drag the WordArt object to move it to the bottom-right corner of the document, below the text.

The Format WordArt dialog box is not yet visible.

b. Point to the WordArt object, right-click to display a menu, and then click **Format WordArt** to display the Format WordArt dialog box.

Remember that many of the options in this dialog box also are displayed in the WordArt Tools Format tab.

c. Click the **Colors and Lines tab** and click the **Color drop-down arrow** in the *Fill* section to display the color palette. Click **Orange, Accent 6, Lighter 40%**, which is in the last column. Click **OK**.

This action enables you to customize the colors used in the WordArt graphic. In this case, you minimize much of the bright orange tint in the WordArt.

d. Click **3-D Effects** on the Format tab, then click **3-D Effects** to display the 3-D Effects gallery as shown in Figure 3.26. Click **3-D Style 1** from the Parallel group.

TROUBLESHOOTING: If your monitor uses a high resolution, or if you have a wide monitor, the 3-D Effects gallery might display immediately after you click 3-D Effects the first time. In that case, you will not click 3-D Effects twice, as instructed in Step D.

e. Save the document.

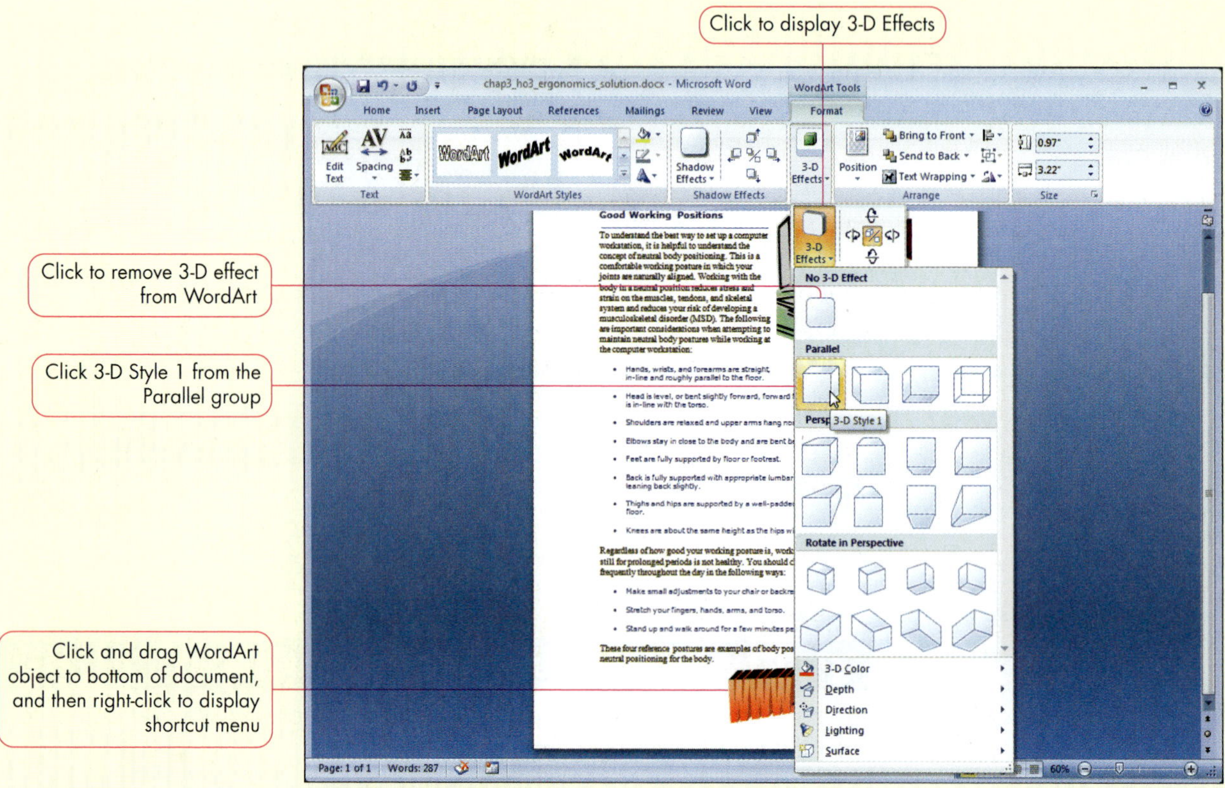

Figure 3.26 3-D Style Gallery for WordArt

Step 5
Insert a Symbol

Refer to Figure 3.27 as you complete Step 5.

a. Select the word *degrees* that displays at the end of the fourth bullet item in the document. Press **Backspace** to remove the word and the space that follows 120.

b. Click the **Insert tab,** click **Symbol** in the Symbols group, and click **More Symbols** to display the Symbol dialog box. Click the **Font drop-down arrow**, and then select **Verdana** as shown in Figure 3.27. If necessary, click the *Subset* drop-down box and select **Basic Latin.**

c. Click the **Degree symbol** (the last character in the seventh line), click **Insert**, and close the Symbol dialog box.

d. Save the *chap3_ho3_ergonomics_solution* document and close Word if you do not want to continue with the end-of-chapter exercise at this time.

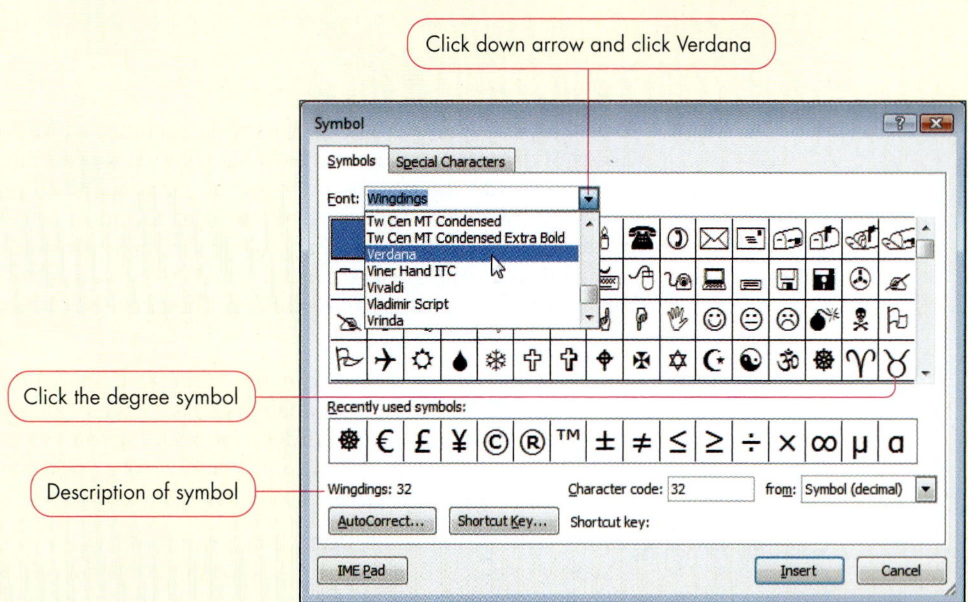

Figure 3.27 The Insert Symbol Command Symbol Dialog Box

Summary

1. **Insert a table.** Tables represent a very powerful capability within Word and are used to organize a variety of data in documents. The Table command is on the Insert tab, and tables are made up of rows and columns; the intersection of a row and column is called a cell. You can insert additional rows and columns if you need to add more data to a table, or you can delete a row or column if you no longer need data in the respective row or column. Individual cells can be merged to create a larger cell. Conversely, you can split a single cell into multiple cells. The rows in a table can be different heights and/or each column can be a different width.
2. **Format a table.** Each cell in a table is formatted independently and may contain text, numbers, and/or graphics. To enhance readability of table data, you can apply a predefined style, which Word provides, or use Borders and Shading tools to add color and enhance it. Furthermore, you can align table data—at the left margin, at the right margin, or centered between the margins. You also can change the text direction within a cell.
3. **Sort and apply formulas to table data.** You can sort the rows in a table to display the data in ascending or descending sequence, according to the values in one or more columns in the table. Sorting is accomplished by selecting the rows within the table that are to be sorted, then executing the Sort command on the Layout tab. Calculations can be performed within a table using the Formula command in the same tab.
4. **Convert text to a table.** If you have a list of tabulated items that would be easier to manipulate in a table, you can use the Convert Text to Table command. The command also works in reverse, enabling you to remove data from a table and format it as tabulated text.
5. **Insert clip art and images into a document.** You often add graphics to enhance a document. When you click the Clip Art command, Office displays a task pane where you enter a keyword to describe the clip you are looking for. The search is made possible by the Microsoft Clip Organizer, which organizes the media files available to you into collections, then enables you to limit the search to specific media types and/or specific collections. Resources (such as clip art or photographs) can be downloaded from the Web for inclusion in a Word document. Although clip art is often acceptable for educational or nonprofit use, it may not be permitted in some advertising situations. You should always assume a graphic is copyrighted unless noted otherwise.
6. **Format a graphic element.** After you insert the clip art object, you can use a variety of tools to refine the object to fit in your document, such as changing height and width, cropping, rotating, or aligning.
7. **Insert WordArt into a document.** Microsoft WordArt is an application within Microsoft Office that creates decorative text that can be used to add interest to a document. WordArt can be used in addition to clip art or in place of clip art if the right image is not available. You can rotate text in any direction, add three-dimensional effects, display the text vertically down the page, or print it upside down.
8. **Insert symbols into a document.** The Insert Symbol command provides access to special characters, making it easy to place typographic characters into a document. The symbols can be taken from any font and can be displayed in any point size.

Key Terms

Ascending order 209
Border 205
Brightness 222
Cell 197
Cell margin 206
Clip art 219
Column width 199
Compress 223
Contrast 222
Copyright 219
Crop or Cropping 222
Descending order 209
Microsoft Clip Organizer 219
Microsoft WordArt 225
Picture Style 221
Row height 199
Scale or Scaling 222
Shading 205
Sizing handle 221
Sorting 207
Table 197
Table alignment 206
Table style 205
Text direction 206
Text wrapping style 221

Multiple Choice

1. You have created a table containing numerical values and have entered the SUM(ABOVE) function at the bottom of a column. You then delete one of the rows included in the sum. Which of the following is true?
   (a) The row cannot be deleted because it contains a cell that is included in the sum function.
   (b) The sum is updated automatically.
   (c) The sum cannot be updated.
   (d) The sum will be updated provided you right-click the cell and click the Update Field command.

2. Which process below is the best option to change the size of a selected object so that the height and width change in proportion to one another?
   (a) Enter the Height and allow Word to establish the Width.
   (b) Click and drag the sizing handle on the top border, then click and drag the sizing handle on the left side.
   (c) Click and drag the sizing handle on the bottom border, then click and drag the sizing handle on the right side.
   (d) Click only the sizing handle in the middle of the left side.

3. How do you search for clip art using the Clip Organizer?
   (a) By entering a keyword that describes the image you want
   (b) By selecting the photo album option
   (c) By clicking the Clip Organizer command on the Insert tab
   (d) There is no such thing as a Clip Organizer.

4. What guideline should you remember when inserting graphics into a document?
   (a) It is distasteful to insert more than two graphics into a document.
   (b) It is not necessary to consider copyright notices if the document is for personal use.
   (c) WordArt should always be center aligned on a page.
   (d) Graphic elements should enhance a document, not overpower it.

5. Which of the following commands in the Picture Tools Format tab would you use to remove portions of a graphic that you do not wish to see in your document?
   (a) Height
   (b) Position
   (c) Crop
   (d) Reset Picture

6. Which of the following is not an example of how to use the Symbols feature in a document?
   (a) You can type (c) to insert the copyright symbol.
   (b) You can insert WordArt from the Symbol dialog box.
   (c) You can insert the Windows logo from the Symbol dialog box.
   (d) You can insert special characters from the Symbol dialog box.

7. Which of the following is true regarding objects and their associated tabs?
   (a) Clicking a WordArt object displays the WordArt Tools tab.
   (b) Right-clicking on a Picture displays the Picture Tools tab.
   (c) You can only display a tab by clicking the tab across the top of the screen.
   (d) Neither (a) nor (b).

8. Which wrap style allows text to wrap around the graphic frame that surrounds the image?
   (a) Top and Bottom
   (b) Through
   (c) Behind Text
   (d) Square

9. What provides legal protection to the author for a written or artistic work?
   (a) Copyright
   (b) Public domain
   (c) Fair use
   (d) Footnote

...continued on Next Page

Multiple Choice Continued...

10. Microsoft WordArt cannot be used to:

(a) Arch text, or print it upside down
(b) Rotate text, or add three-dimensional effects
(c) Display text vertically down a page
(d) Insert a copyright symbol

11. What happens when you press Tab from within the last cell of a table?

(a) A Tab character is inserted just as it would be for ordinary text.
(b) Word inserts a new row below the current row.
(c) Word inserts a new column to the right of the current column.
(d) The insertion point appears in the paragraph below the table.

12. What happens when you type more than one line of text into a cell?

(a) The cell gets wider to accommodate the extra text.
(b) The row gets taller as word wrapping occurs to display the additional text.
(c) The other lines are hidden by default.
(d) A new column is inserted automatically.

13. Assume you created a table with the names of the months in the first column. Each row lists data for that particular month. The insertion point is in the first cell on the third row—this row lists goals for April. You realize that you left out the goals for March. What should you do?

(a) Display the Insert tab and click the Table command.
(b) Display the Table Tools Design tab and click the Insert Cell command.
(c) Display the Table Tools Layout tab and click the Insert Left command.
(d) Display the Table Tools Layout tab and click the Insert Above command.

14. You have a list of people who were sent an invitation to a wedding. You are responsible for monitoring their responses to the invitation, whether they will attend or not, and to determine the grand total of those attending. Using skills learned in Chapter 3, what would be a good way to track this information?

(a) Use pen and paper to mark through names of those who decline the invitation and put stars by those who accept.
(b) Convert the list of names to a table; add columns that allow you to mark their response, including the number who will attend, and use a formula to add up the numbers when all responses are received.
(c) Insert wedding clip art in the document so you will know the purpose of the document.
(d) Insert a two-column table beside the names and mark the responses as declined or attending.

15. If cell A1 contains the value 2, and A2 contains the value 4, what value will be displayed if cell A3 contains the formula =PRODUCT(ABOVE)?

(a) 8
(b) 2
(c) 6
(d) This is not a valid formula.

16. What option would you use if you were given a lengthy list of items that are separated by tabs and that would be easier to format in a table?

(a) Insert Table
(b) Convert Table to Text
(c) Convert Text to Table
(d) Insert Text Box

17. Which option should you use to add color to improve the attractiveness and readability of a table?

(a) Text wrapping
(b) Sort
(c) Add column to right
(d) Borders and shading

Practice Exercises

1 The Library Station

While working as a volunteer at the local library, you are asked to create a flyer to advertise the upcoming annual book sale, as shown in Figure 3.28. You are required to use a combination of tables, clip art, WordArt, and symbols to create an informative and attractive flyer. If you are unable to find the exact same graphics, find something as similar as possible; you need not match our flyer exactly.

a. Open a new document and save it as **chap3_pe1_flyer_solution**.
b. Click the **Page Layout tab** and click **Margins** in the Page Setup group. Click **Normal**, if necessary, to set all four margins to 1".
c. Click the **Insert tab** and click **Table** in the Tables group to insert a table. Click only one cell to insert a **1x1** table.
d. Click the **Home tab**, and then click the **Font Dialog Box Launcher**. Select **Comic Sans MS** in the **Font list**, select **Bold** in the **Font style list**, and select **36** in the **Size list**. Click the **Font Color drop-down arrow** and select **Red, Accent 2, Darker 25%** (a shade of red). Click **OK** to close the Font dialog box.
e. Type **Annual Book Sale** in the table. Click **Center** in the Paragraph group to center the text within the table cell.
f. Click the **Design tab**, click the **Borders arrow**, and click **Borders and Shading**. Select **None** in the *Setting* section to remove all current borders around the table. Click the **Color drop-down arrow** and select **Red, Accent 2, Darker 50%** (at the bottom of the red column). Then click the **Width drop-down arrow** and select **3 pt**.
g. Click once on the top of the diagram in the *Preview* section to insert a top border, and then click once on the bottom of the diagram to insert a bottom border. If necessary, click the **Apply to drop-down arrow** and select **Table**, and click **OK**.
h. Click below the table to move the insertion point. Click the **Home tab**, and then click the **Font Size arrow**, and select **28**. Type the date of the sale, **March 1**, and click **Align Text Right** in the Paragraph group to move the date to the right side of the flyer.
i. Press **Enter** two times to move the insertion point down the page, click the **Insert tab,** and click **WordArt** in the Text group. Click **WordArt style 28** on the bottom row. In the Edit WordArt Text dialog box type **The Library Station** and click **OK**.
j. The WordArt object needs to be resized and relocated to have a bigger impact on our flyer. Click Position in the Arrange group on the Format tab. Select **More Layout Options** and on the Text Wrapping tab, select Tight Wrapping style. Select the Picture Position tab. Under Horizontal, select Alignment, Centered. Under Vertical, select Alignment, Centered. Click OK.
k. Click the **Height box** and type **2** to increase the height of the object. Click the **Width box** and type **6** to elongate the object. Click the uppermost handle on the top of the object and notice the insertion point changes to a curved arrow. Click this handle and hold down while rotating the object to the left so that it appears similar to Figure 3.28.
l. Click anywhere to deselect the WordArt object. Click the **Insert tab**, and then click **Clip Art**. When the Clip Art task pane displays, type **book** in the **Search for** box, click the **Search in drop-down arrow**, and click **Office Collections**. Deselect My Collections and Web Collections, if necessary, and click **Go**. Click one time on the first object to insert it in your document, then close the Clip Art task pane.
m. Click the clip art object to display the Format tab, if necessary. Click **Text Wrapping** in the Arrange group and then select **Square**. Now you can move the object anywhere in your document. Move it to the left side above the WordArt object as it appears in Figure 3.28.
n. Double-click anywhere in the bottom of your document to reposition the insertion point. Click the **Insert tab**, and then click **Table**. Drag your mouse over the cells until **2x3 Table** displays (a 2 column, 3 row table), and click to insert it in the document.
o. Click the table selector in the upper-left corner to select the whole table. Click the **Layout** tab. Click **Properties** in the Table group to display the Table Properties dialog box. Click the **Table tab**, and then click the **Preferred width check box**. Type **8** in the **Preferred width box**, and click **OK**.
p. Drag your mouse across the two cells in the first row to select it, and right-click and select **Merge Cells**. Type **Hourly Drawings for FREE Books!** in the first row.

...continued on Next Page

q. Click the **Design tab** and then click **More** in the Table Styles group. Scroll to view the **Dark List Accent 2** style. Click once to apply the style to your table.

r. Right-click the table, click **Table Properties,** click **Center** alignment, and click **OK**.

s. Select the two empty cells in the first (left) column of the table, right-click, and click **Merge Cells**. In this column enter the phrase **Discounts of 50% or More**. Select the two empty cells in the right column of the table, right-click, and select **Merge Cells** in the Alignment group. In this column type the phrase **Only at our North Glenstone Location**.

t. Click anywhere in the table, if necessary, and click the **Layout tab**. Click **Cell Margins** and click the **Allow spacing between cells check box**; then type **.1** as the spacing amount. Click **OK** and notice the improvement.

u. Select only the text in the table, but do not click the table selector; on the Mini toolbar click **Center**.

v. Make minor adjustments to each element as necessary so your flyer looks attractive and spacing is retained. Save and close the document.

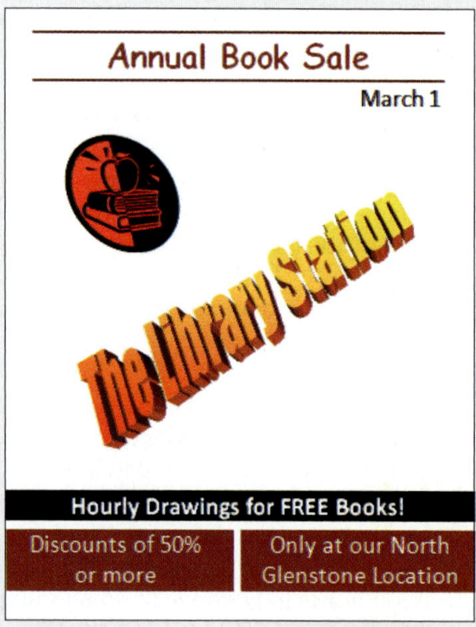

Figure 3.28 The Book Sale Flyer

2 Lost Pet

In an unfortunate mishap, your 3-year-old dog escaped from your fenced yard and is now missing. After calling local shelters and pet stores, you decide to create a flyer to post around the neighborhood and shops so that people will know whom to contact if they see her. Figure 3.29 displays a flyer that is intended to give information about your dog, Dakota, and also provide a tag with contact information that someone can pull from the flyer and take with him or her. The tag displays your name and phone number. Use a table as the basis of this document; you can use the picture of our pet or any other picture you like.

a. Open a new document and save it as **chap3_pe2_lostpet_solution**.

b. Click the **Insert tab** and click **Table** in the Tables group. Drag to select cells to create a table with 10 columns and 4 rows (**10x4 Table**), then click on the last cell to insert the table.

c. Click left of the first cell in the first row to select the entire row. Right-click the selected row and select **Merge Cells** to merge all the cells in the first row. Repeat the step to merge the cells in rows 2, and then the cells in row 3.

d. Click in the first row and enter the text **Lost Pet**. Select the text and then on the Mini toolbar click the **Font size arrow** and select **26**. The row height will increase automatically to accommodate the larger text. On the Mini toolbar click **Center** to center the text in the cell.

e. Select the cell in the second row. Click the **Design tab** and click **Shading** in the Table Styles group. Click **Black, Text 1** (the black swatch in the first row), which will place a black background in the cell.

...continued on Next Page

f. Click **Insert tab** and click **Picture** in the Illustrations group. Locate pictures of your pet or pets; we have provided a picture of Dakota, dakota.jpg, in the Exploring Word folder. When you locate the file, double-click to insert the picture. The row height will expand automatically to accommodate the picture. Click once to select the picture, if necessary, and then press **Ctrl+E** to center the picture.

g. Click in the third row and enter text to describe your pet or pets. Feel free to duplicate the information we have provided in Figure 3.29. Select the text, then on the Mini toolbar click the **Font size arrow** and select **14**, and click **Center**.

h. Type your name and phone number on two lines in the first cell of the fourth row. Display the **Layout tab**, and then click **Text Direction** one time to rotate the text (see Figure 3.29). Click **Align Top Center** to align the text vertically on the top of the cell. Right-click the cell and click **Copy**. Select the empty cells on that row, right-click, and click **Paste Cells** to populate the remaining cells with the owner information.

i. Select the entire row, right-click, and select **Borders and Shading**. Click the **Borders** tab, if necessary, and click a dashed line in the **Style list**. Click **OK**.

j. Click the **Height** box in the Cell Size group and increase the size to at least **1.5″**. The contact information now displays correctly.

k. Click **Zoom** in the task bar, click **Whole page**, and click **OK**.

l. Save and close the document.

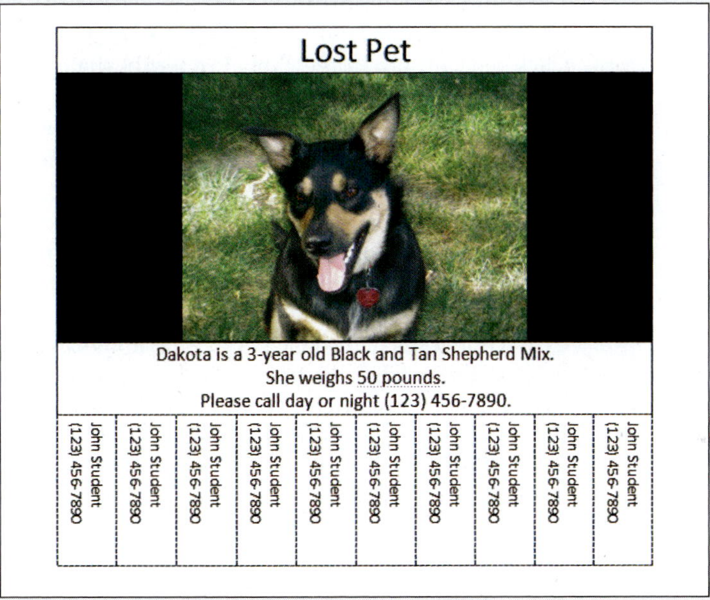

Figure 3.29 The Lost Pet Flyer

3 The Study Schedule

Your midterm grades reveal the need to set up a solid study schedule. The best way to plan your study time is to create a daily schedule, mark the times you are in class or at work, then find the needed study time. Your work in Chapter 3 of this book provided information you can use to create a document that lists days and times and allows you to establish your new study schedule. You can even add colorful borders and shading, as well as graphics, to create a document you can proudly display.

a. Open a new blank document and save it as **chap3_pe3_schedule_solution**.

b. Click the **Page Layout tab**. Click **Margins** in the Page Setup group and then click **Custom Margins** to display the Page Layout dialog box. Type **.75** in the **Top** and **Bottom** boxes, then type **.5** in the **Left** and **Right** boxes. Click **Landscape** in the *Orientation* section, and click **OK**.

...continued on Next Page

c. Click the **Insert tab** and click **Table**. Click **Insert Table** to display the Insert Table dialog box. Type **8** in the **Number of columns** box and type **12** in the **Number of rows** box. Click **OK**.

d. Click left of the first cell in the first row to select the entire first row, and **right-click** and select **Merge Cells**. Click in the merged cell, then type **Weekly Class and Study Schedule**. Select the text you typed. On the Mini toolbar click the **Font arrow** and select **Arial**, click the **Font size arrow** and select **24**, and click **Bold** and **Center**.

e. Click left of the first cell in the last row to select the entire row, then right-click and select **Merge Cells**. Click in the merged cell, type **Notes:**, then press **Enter** five times. The height of the cell increases to accommodate the blank lines.

f. Select the text you typed. On the Mini toolbar click the **Font arrow** and select **Arial**, click the **Font size arrow** and select **12**, and click **Bold**.

g. Click the second cell in the second row. Type **Monday**. Press **Tab** (or right arrow key) to move to the next cell. Type **Tuesday**. Continue until the days of the week have been entered. Select the entire row. On the Mini toolbar click the **Font arrow** and select **Arial**, click the **Font size arrow** and select **10**, and then click **Bold** and **Center**.

h. Click the first cell in the third row. Type **8:00 a.m.** Press the **down arrow key** to move to the first cell in the fourth row. Type **9:00 a.m.** Continue to enter the hourly periods up to **4:00 p.m.**

i. Select the cells containing the hours of the day, and then right-click and select **Table Properties**. Click the **Row tab**, then click the **Specify height check box**. Click the spin button until the height is **0.5″**. Click the **Row height is drop-down arrow** and select **Exactly**.

j. Click the **Cell tab** in the Table Properties dialog box, and click **Center** in the *Vertical alignment* section. Click **OK** to accept the settings and close the dialog box.

k. Select the first row, containing the title of your table. Click the **Design tab** and click **Shading**. Click **Orange, Accent 6**, the orange color at the end of the first row.

l. Click and drag to select the first four cells under Sunday, and right-click and select **Merge Cells**. Type **Reserved for services** in the new large cell. Select this text, then click the **Layout tab**. Click **Text Direction** one time to rotate the text, and then click **Align Center** to display the text as shown in Figure 3.30.

m. Click anywhere in the cell in the last row of the table. Click the **Insert tab** and click **Clip Art** to display the task pane. Type **books** in the **Search for** box, and then click **Go** or press **Enter**. Click the first clip art object to insert it in your table.

n. Click the newly inserted clip art to display the Format tab, if necessary, and click **Text Wrapping** and select **Square**. Click the sizing handle on the upper-right corner, hold down **Shift**, and drag the sizing handle to reduce the size of the object and maintain proportions. Move the object to the lower-right corner of the last row and close the Clip Art task pane.

o. Save and close the document.

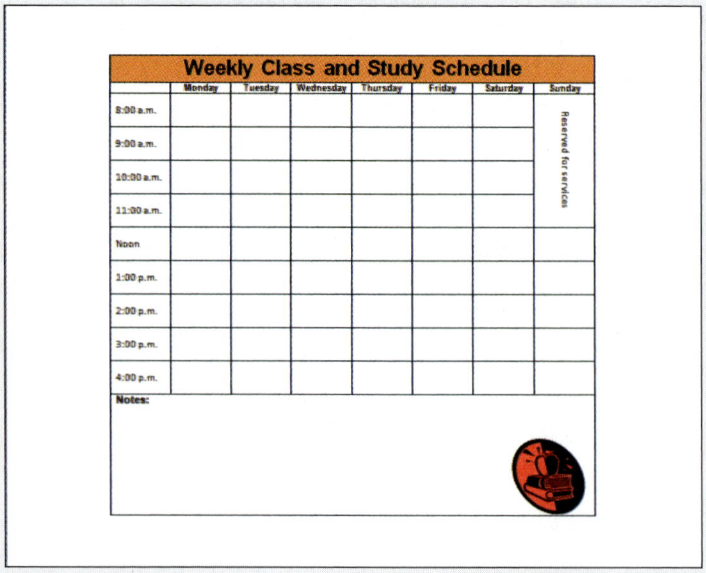

Weekly Class and Study Schedule							
	Monday	Tuesday	Wednesday	Thursday	Friday	Saturday	Sunday
8:00 a.m.							Reserved for services
9:00 a.m.							
10:00 a.m.							
11:00 a.m.							
Noon							
1:00 p.m.							
2:00 p.m.							
3:00 p.m.							
4:00 p.m.							
Notes:							

Figure 3.30 The Completed Study Schedule

...continued on Next Page

4 The Invoice

You work as a bank consultant for a software firm and must bill for services each month. Traditionally, you type the amount of your invoice in the document, but after a discussion with a coworker you discover how to use table formulas and begin to use them to calculate your total fees on the invoice. In this exercise you develop a professional-looking invoice and use formulas to calculate totals within the table.

a. Open a blank document and save it as **chap3_pe4_invoice_solution**.
b. Click the **Page Layout tab**, click **Margins**, and click **Office 2003 Default**, which sets 1.25″ left and right margins.
c. Click the **Insert tab** and click **Table**. Drag to select eight rows and two columns (**2x8 Table**).
d. Click left of the first cell in the first row to select the entire first row, right-click, and select **Merge Cells**. Click in the merged cell, and then type **Invoice.** Select the text you typed, click the **Home tab**, and click **Heading 1** from the Styles gallery. Click **Center** in the Paragraph group to complete the first row of the table.
e. Select the second and third cells in the first column, and then click the **Layout tab**. Click **Merge Cells**, click the **Height box** in the Cell Size group, and type **1** to increase the size of the cell. In this cell enter the following text:

   TO:
   Jack Hendrix Technologies
   4999 Garland Street
   Fayetteville, AR 72703

f. Select the second and third cells in the right column and click **Merge Cells**. They inherit the size from the cell on their left. Click **Align Top Right** in the Alignment group and type the following text in the cell:

   FROM:
   John Q. Student
   9444 Elton Lane
   Tulsa, OK 74147

g. Select the last five cells in the first column, then click the **Width box** in the Cell Size group and type **5**. The cells on the right might extend beyond the borders of the page, but you will fix that next. Select the five cells in the second column, then click the **Width box** and type **1.15**. Now the cells should align with the cells in the first two rows.
h. Type the following text in the third through sixth cells of the two columns, as shown in Figure 3.31:

Description	**Amount**
Consulting Fee for June	**$5640.00**
Travel Expenses	**500.00**
Supplies	**200.00**

i. In the first column of the last row type **TOTAL**. Click in the second column in the last row and click **Formula** on the Layout tab. Click **OK** to accept the formula, =SUM(ABOVE), which is correct for our calculation. The total is $6340.00.
j. Your invoice is correct, but formatting changes are needed to give it a more professional appearance. Select the third row, which contains the Description and Amount titles, and hold down **Ctrl**, and select the last row of the table. Click the **Design tab**

...continued on Next Page

and click **Shading**. Click **White, Background 1, Darker 15%** from the first column. Do not deselect the rows.

k. While the rows are selected, click the **Home tab** and click **Heading 3** from the Styles gallery. You may need to click the **More button** in the Styles group, select **Apply Styles** from the gallery, type **Heading 3** in the Apply Styles dialog box, and click **Apply**. Click anywhere to deselect the rows and view the format changes.

l. Select the last four cells in the second column, click the **Layout tab**, and click **Align Center Right** on the tab. The result gives the effect of decimal alignment. However, the numbers are not decimal aligned, so if you display an additional decimal place, it will result in misaligned numbers.

m. Select the fourth, fifth, and sixth rows, which contain the items you bill for, then click **Sort** in the Data group. Click **OK**. Deselect the rows to view the newly sorted list.

n. You determine the travel expenses were incorrect; change the amount to **550.00**. Right-click the cell that contains the formula and select **Update Field** to recalculate the total. The new total $6390.00 displays.

o. Save and close the document.

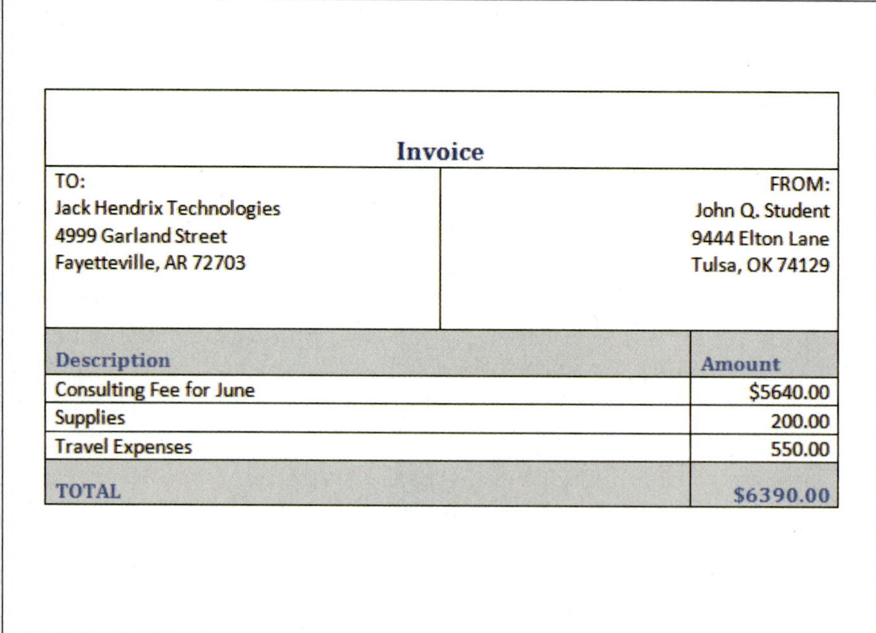

Invoice	
TO: Jack Hendrix Technologies 4999 Garland Street Fayetteville, AR 72703	FROM: John Q. Student 9444 Elton Lane Tulsa, OK 74129

Description	Amount
Consulting Fee for June	$5640.00
Supplies	200.00
Travel Expenses	550.00
TOTAL	$6390.00

Figure 3.31 The Completed Invoice

Mid-Level Exercises

1 The Résumé

Microsoft Word 2007 includes a Résumé template, but you can achieve an equally good result through the tables feature. In this exercise you create a resume for yourself using the tools learned in Chapter 3. Follow the instructions below to create a résumé similar to the document in Figure 3.32. Remember that a resume often serves as the first impression between you and a potential employer, so you must include all the information expected by an employer and display it in a manner that is easy to read and follow.

a. Open a new blank document and save it as **chap3_mid1_resume_solution**. Set margins at 1″ on the top and bottom, and 1.25″ on the left and right. Insert a 2-column, 10-row table into your document. Additional rows can be added as needed. Conversely, rows can be deleted at a later time if they are not needed.

b. Merge the two cells in the first row. Type your name in the cell and then center it. Change the font to Times New Roman, 24 pt and bold, as shown in Figure 3.32.

c. Enter your addresses in the second row. Type your campus address, telephone number, and e-mail address in the cell on the left and your permanent address and telephone number in the cell on the right. Format the text in Times New Roman, 12 pt. Left align the text in the cell on the left, and right align the text in the cell on the right.

d. Enter the categories in the left cell of each row, being sure to include the following categories: **Objective**, **Professional Accomplishments**, **Education**, **Honors**, and **References**. Format the text in Times New Roman, 12 pt, boldface, and right align the text in these cells. (Not all of these categories are visible in Figure 3.32.)

e. Enter the associated information in the right cell of each row. Be sure to include all information that would interest a prospective employer. Format the text in Times New Roman, 12 pt. Left align the text in these cells, using boldface and italics where appropriate.

f. Select rows three through ten in the first column then change the width of the cells to 1.5″. Select the same rows in the second column and increase the width of the cells until they align with the first two rows.

g. Select the entire table and remove the borders surrounding the individual cells. (Figure 3.32 displays gridlines, which—unlike borders—do not appear in the printed document.) For the first row only, set a bottom line border.

h. Save and close the document.

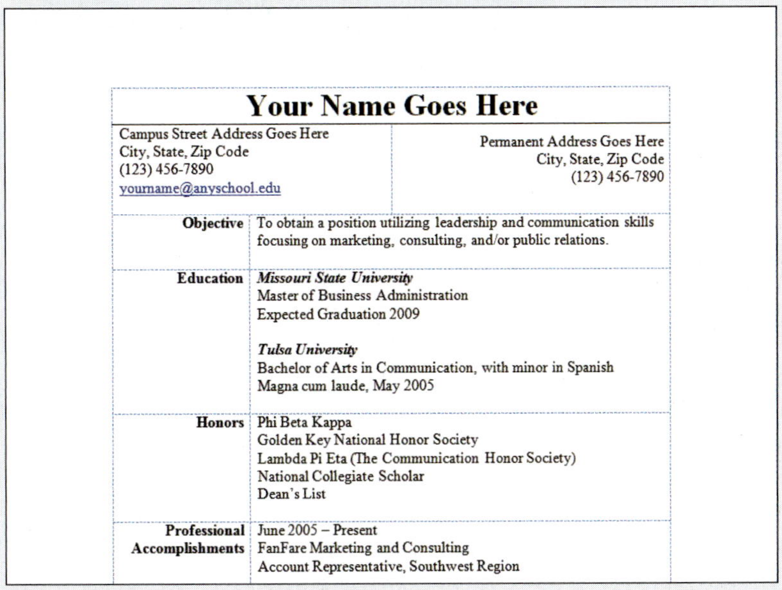

Your Name Goes Here

Campus Street Address Goes Here City, State, Zip Code (123) 456-7890 yourname@anyschool.edu	Permanent Address Goes Here City, State, Zip Code (123) 456-7890
Objective	To obtain a position utilizing leadership and communication skills focusing on marketing, consulting, and/or public relations.
Education	***Missouri State University*** Master of Business Administration Expected Graduation 2009 ***Tulsa University*** Bachelor of Arts in Communication, with minor in Spanish Magna cum laude, May 2005
Honors	Phi Beta Kappa Golden Key National Honor Society Lambda Pi Eta (The Communication Honor Society) National Collegiate Scholar Dean's List
Professional Accomplishments	June 2005 – Present FanFare Marketing and Consulting Account Representative, Southwest Region

Figure 3.32 The Completed Résumé

...continued on Next Page

2 The Employment Application

You work as an intern for the Human Resources department of a company that offers home health consulting services. Your manager mentions the need for a new employment application form and asks you to create an application form similar to the document in Figure 3.33. Use the skills you recently acquired about the tables feature in Word to follow our design and create the application form. Remember that the Tables and Borders toolbar can be used in place of the Table menu to execute various commands during the exercise. Proceed as follows:

a. Open a blank document and save it as **chap3_mid2_application_solution**.

b. Create a 3 × 8 (three columns and eight rows) table to match our design. Select the entire table after it is created initially. Change the before paragraph spacing to 6 pt. The result will drop the text in each cell half a line from the top border of the cell, and also determine the spacing between paragraphs within a cell.

c. Merge the cells in the first row to create the title for the application. Enter the text for the first line, press **Shift+Enter** to create a line break instead of a paragraph break (to minimize the spacing between lines), then enter the text on the second line. Center the text. Select the first cell and then shade the cell with the color **Black, Text 1** to create white letters on a dark background. Increase the font size of the title to 22 pt.

d. Enter the text in the next several cells as shown in Figure 3.33. Select cells individually and adjust the width to create the offsetting form fields.

e. Move down in the table until you can select the cell for the highest degree attained. Enter the indicated text, click and drag to select all four degrees, and create a custom bulleted list using the check box character in the Wingdings font.

f. Merge the cells in row 7, then enter the text that asks the applicant to describe the skills that qualify him or her for the position. Merge the cells in row 8 (these cells are not visible in Figure 3.33) to create a single cell for employment references.

g. Reduce the zoom setting to view the entire document. Change the row heights as necessary so that the completed application fills the entire page.

h. Complete the finished application as though you were applying for a job. Replace the check box next to the highest degree earned (remove the bullet) with the letter X.

i. Save and close the document.

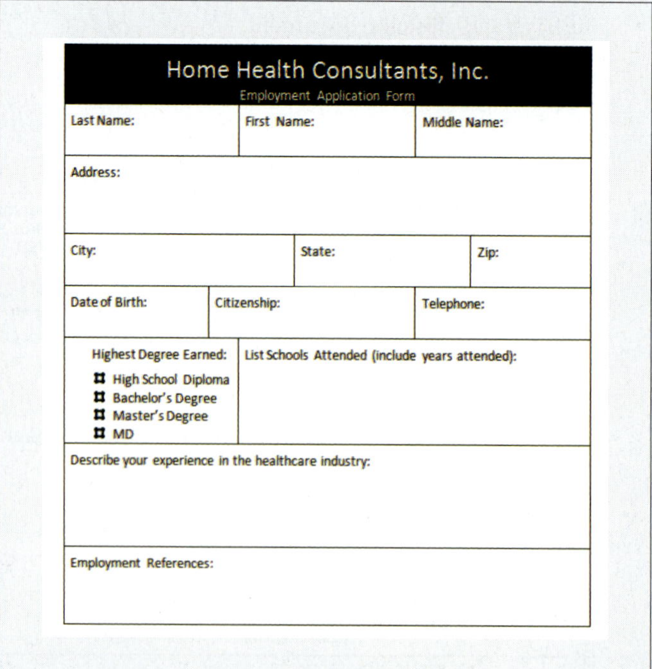

Home Health Consultants, Inc.
Employment Application Form

Last Name:	First Name:	Middle Name:
Address:		
City:	State:	Zip:
Date of Birth:	Citizenship:	Telephone:
Highest Degree Earned: ⌑ High School Diploma ⌑ Bachelor's Degree ⌑ Master's Degree ⌑ MD	List Schools Attended (include years attended):	
Describe your experience in the healthcare industry:		
Employment References:		

Figure 3.33 The Employment Application

...continued on Next Page

3 Create Company Stationery

You are the marketing manager for a private pilot flight school. Periodically you perform a review of marketing tools used in the company, then make a list of items that must be changed. In your last review you noticed the company letterhead is quite dated and should be changed. Since the change is being made, all company stationery will be replaced with the new logo. Figure 3.34 displays an envelope and matching letterhead designed by an intern. Replicate that design as closely as possible, creating both the letterhead and matching envelope.

a. Begin with the stationery. Open a blank document and save it as **chap3_mid3_stationery_solution**.
b. Click the **Narrow** margin setting, which sets 1/2″ margins all around. Enter the company name, address, telephone, and e-mail information at the top of the page. Use a larger font and distinguishing color for your name, then center all of the text at the top of the page.
c. After you type your information, convert the text into a table. Split the table into three columns so you can add a logo to each side of your information.
d. Use the Clip Organizer to locate the clip art image shown in Figure 3.34. (If you cannot find the same clip art image, use one with the same theme.) Use that image as a logo by inserting it in the first column of the table. Click the **Square** text wrapping style. Change the image height to **1″**. Crop the image to decrease width to approximately **1.1″**. Select and copy the clip art. Paste the image in the third column of the table on the right side of the page.
e. Center align the information in each cell both horizontally and vertically. Use the Borders command to add a 3-pt wide horizontal line below the text that contains your address information. Do not extend the border below the clip art images.
f. Insert a new page section break at the beginning of the document. (The result creates a new page as well as a new section. The latter enables you to change the page orientation within a document.)
g. Click on the newly inserted page and select landscape orientation. Change the **Size** to COM-10 (the standard business envelope which is 9.5" by 4.13").
h. Copy the clip art and address information from the letterhead to the envelope. Make adjustments as necessary to align your address beside the logo.
i. Save and close the document.

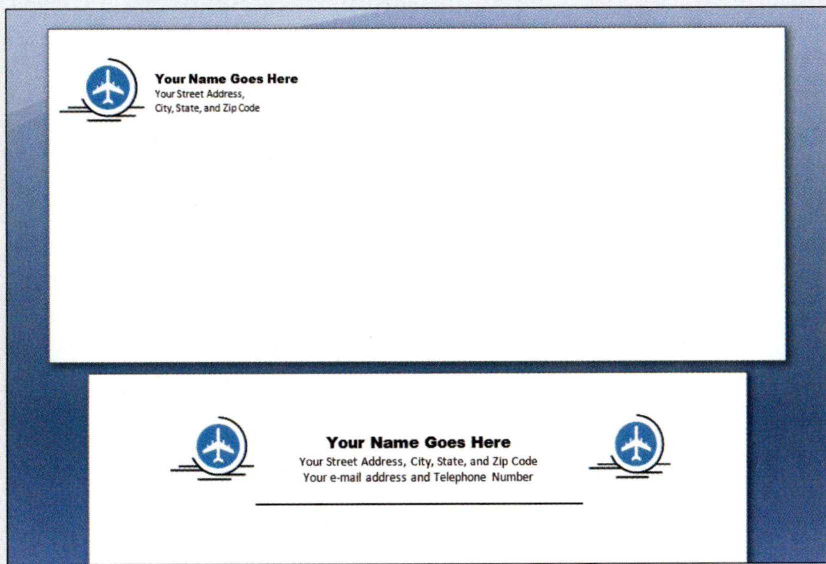

Figure 3.34 Custom Stationery

...continued on Next Page

4 July Fireworks Poster

You work as an intern for the mayor's office in City Hall. The office sponsors a yearly fireworks display near the local airport and posts informational flyers in local businesses prior to the event. The community relations director has asked for your help to create the flyers they will distribute because of your experience using Microsoft Word 2007. You are responsible for creating an exciting and attractive flyer for this year's event using the guidelines below.

a. Open a new blank document and save it as **chap3_mid4_fireworks_solution**.
b. Set the following margins: 0.6″ top, 0.3″ bottom, 0.5″ left, and 0.5″ right. If a warning appears mentioning that the margins are outside the boundary, choose the option to fix the problem.
c. Create a WordArt object with these settings: Click WordArt style 11 in the WordArt gallery. Type **Independence Day Fireworks!** in the WordArt box. Add the **3-D Style 11** effect. Change the Shape Fill, located in the WordArt Styles group of the Format tab, to use the **Linear Down** gradient color scheme. Change the height to **1.5″** and the width to **7″**, then Format the object to use **Square** text wrapping, and center it horizontally on the page.
d. Use the Clip Art task pane and search for **fireworks** in the Web Collections. Find and insert the image as shown in Figure 3.35. Adjust the height to **3″**, then crop the image to trim white space from the top and bottom of the picture. Adjust the brightness to **+20%**. Apply **Square** text wrapping, and then move the object to the right side of the flyer as shown in Figure 3.35.
e. Place the insertion point on the left side of the document and type **City of Stockton** on the left side of the clip art object. Format the text in Comic Sans MS, 26-pt size, and change the font color to **Red**.
f. Insert a table to list the events shown in Figure 3.35. Align text on the left and right as displayed. In addition to increasing cell margins, insert an extra column to create the gap between columns. Apply a **Dark Red Double-line** outside border, then left-align the table.
g. Below the table insert the text **Best Small-Town Celebration in the State** as shown in Figure 3.35. Format the text using Comic Sans MS 18-pt, change the font color to **Red**, and center the text on the page.
h. Save and close the document.

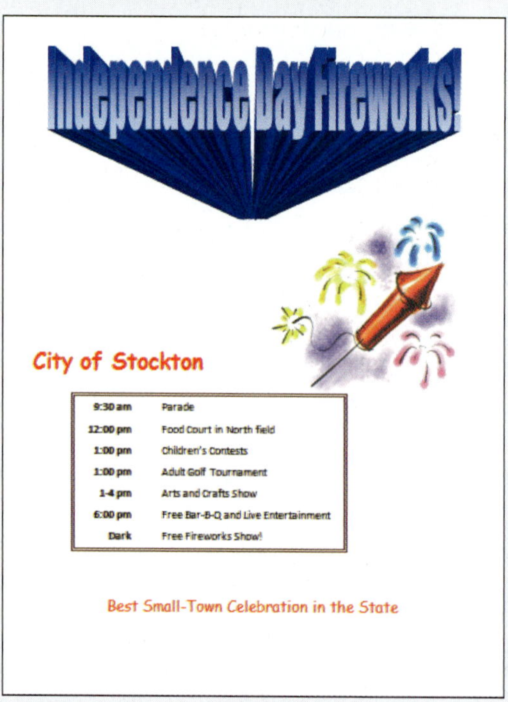

Figure 3.35 Fireworks Announcement Flyer

Capstone Exercise

You are the executive assistant to a general contractor, and your duties include listing the materials that will be used on a home remodeling project. Due to the large number of people who work on the project, from plumbers to electricians to carpenters, it is necessary to keep detailed records of the materials and supplies to use during the remodel. After the first job, you decide to provide the crew with a table of materials that includes pictures. This also might be helpful for any crewmember who does not speak English.

Create the Table

Fortunately a list of materials has been provided, which will eliminate the need for you to type a list of supplies. However, the preexisting list is weak. You decide to modify the document to increase organization and clarity by putting the list in table format, creating a header row and labels, and also adding visual enhancements with WordArt.

a. Open the *chap3_cap_construction* document and save it as **chap3_cap_construction_solution**. You wisely decide to convert this list to a three-column table so you can organize the list of materials and add more data.

b. Insert two rows at the top to use for a heading and item descriptions.
   - Create a title row on the table by merging cells in the first row.
   - Use WordArt to create a title using the phrase **Supply List**.
   - Use the second row as a header for the columns.
   - Enter an appropriate label for each column.

Format the Table

Your table is functional now, but it would look even better with additional improvements. Enhance the table of materials by aligning the data in columns, sorting the data, and using formulas to calculate costs. Since the table spans more than one page, you also should change the table properties so that the header row repeats on every page.

a. Use the Table Properties dialog box to indicate the first row should repeat as a header row at the top of each page if your table spans more than one page.

b. Align the prices of each item in the third column. The prices should appear to align on the decimal point.

c. Center the data in the second column, which displays the quantity of each item you will use in the project.

d. Sort the data in ascending order by Item.

e. Use the Split cell option to add a column to calculate the total cost of materials.

f. Use a formula to calculate the total cost of any item that has a quantity of 10 or more.

Add Visual Enhancements

Your table is very factual, but to assist members of the crew who need more visual information you will enhance the table with pictures. Insert pictures from the Clip Organizer and then use formatting tools, when appropriate, to modify the graphics so they will fit into the table cells.

a. Insert a column to the left of the first column.

b. Insert a picture of each item in the first column.
   - Use symbols, clip art, or pictures to visually describe the following materials in your table: Drill, Faucet, Hammer, Paint, Paintbrushes, Screwdriver, Toilet, and Towel holder.
   - You might not be able to locate a graphic for each item, but you should be able to find at least five to use in the table.
   - Crop or resize the graphics as necessary so they do not exceed 2" in height or width.
   - Align each graphic in the center of the cell.

TROUBLESHOOTING: If your Clip Organizer query does not return any results, click Clip art on Office Online. The Online organizer will display in a new Internet Explorer window, but you can return to Word and continue your clip art search. Your search should now return more results.

c. Apply the **Light Grid Accent 1** style to the table. Use the Borders (and Shading) feature on the Design tab to add a double-line outside border to the table. (Hint: use the **Custom** setting.) Center the table horizontally on the page. If necessary, click Table Properties and verify that the setting for the first row will repeat as a header row on the top of each page.

d. Save and close the document.

Mini Cases

Use the rubric following the case as a guide to evaluate your work, but keep in mind that your instructor may impose additional grading criteria or use a different standard to judge your work.

Holiday Greetings

GENERAL CASE

After learning how to use the creative tools in Microsoft Word 2007, you decide to create your own holiday greeting card. Your greeting card should include a picture of a family (feel free to use your own or one from the Clip Organizer) and decorative text. Use several editing features on the graphics so the greeting card reflects your personality or sentiment during the holidays. Due to printing constraints for special paper used for cards, design only the cover of your Greeting card. Save the document as **chap3_mc1_greeting_solution**. Close the document.

Performance Elements	Exceeds Expectations	Meets Expectations	Below Expectations
Use of tables and table formatting	Inserted table; applied two or more table format options.	Inserted table; applied one table format option.	Inserted table; did not apply additional formatting.
Use of graphics	Inserted at least two graphical objects and used at least three formatting options.	Inserted at least one graphical object and applied formatting.	Inserted zero or one graphical object.
Presentation	Greeting card is formatted attractively; information is easy to read and understand.	Special formatting has been applied, but information is somewhat cluttered.	Greeting card lists basic information with no special formatting for attractiveness.

Travel World

RESEARCH CASE

You have been hired at *Let's Go!* Travel Agency and asked to create a flyer to distribute on campus. Search the Internet to find a company that offers cruises to Alaska and sails through the Inside Passage. Then create a flyer that provides information about one of the cruises through the Alaska Inside Passage. You should include your name and e-mail address as the travel agent. Use a combination of clip art, photographs, and/or WordArt to make the flyer as attractive as possible. Use a table to list the Ports of Call in Alaska. Save your work as **chap3_mc2_alaska_solution**. Close the document.

Performance Elements	Exceeds Expectations	Meets Expectations	Below Expectations
Use of tables and table formatting	Inserted table; applied three or more table formats.	Inserted table; applied one or two table format options.	Inserted table; did not apply additional formatting.
Use of graphics	Inserted at least two graphical objects and applied formatting to objects.	Inserted at least two graphical objects and resized them.	Inserted zero or one graphical object.
Use of research	Two or more pieces of information are included in flyer, reflecting adequate research was performed.	Includes one piece of information reflecting research of topic.	Does not include data that indicate research was performed.
Presentation	Flyer is formatted attractively; information is easy to read and understand.	Special formatting has been applied, but information is somewhat cluttered.	Flyer lists basic information with no special formatting for attractiveness.

Payroll Report

DISASTER RECOVERY

You are assigned the job of proofreading a payroll report before it goes to the department head who issues checks. After looking at the data you find several errors that must be corrected before the report can be submitted. Open the *chap3_mc3_payroll_report* document and correct the errors. Remember to use the keyboard shortcut that reveals formulas in a table. Make further adjustments that enhance your ability to view the information easily and to make the report look more professional. Save your work as **chap3_mc3_payroll_solution**. Close the document.

Performance Elements	Exceeds Expectations	Meets Expectations	Below Expectations
Use of table formulas	Table formulas applied correctly to all entries.	Table formulas applied correctly to two entries.	Table formulas applied incorrectly to at least one item.
Use of other table formatting options	Used at least three table format options.	Used two table format options.	Does not use table format options.
Presentation	Report is formatted attractively; information is easy to read and understand.	Some report formatting corrections have been applied, but information is somewhat cluttered.	Report contains errors in formatting and presentation is poor.

chapter 4 | **Word**

Share, Compare, and Document

Workgroups, Collaboration, and References

After you read this chapter, you will be able to:

1. Insert comments into a document (**page 251**).
2. Track changes in a document (**page 254**).
3. View documents side by side (**page 263**).
4. Compare and combine documents (**page 264**).
5. Create master documents and subdocuments (**page 265**).
6. Use navigation tools (**page 267**).
7. Acknowledge a source (**page 277**).
8. Create a bibliography (**page 279**).
9. Select the writing style (**page 280**).
10. Create and modify footnotes and endnotes (**page 281**).
11. Add figure references (**page 287**).
12. Insert a table of figures (**page 288**).
13. Add legal references (**page 289**).
14. Create cross-references (**page 289**).
15. Modify document properties (**page 290**).

Hands-On Exercises

Exercises	Skills Covered
1. DOCUMENT COLLABORATION (page 258) **Open:** chap4_ho1_proposal.docx **Save as:** chap4_ho1_proposal_solution.docx	• Set User Name and Customize the Track Changes Options • Track Document Changes • View, Add, and Delete Comments • Accept and Reject Changes
2. DOCUMENT COMPARISON, MERGERS, AND NAVIGATION (page 270) **Open:** chap4_ho1_proposal_solution.docx (from Exercise 1) and chap4_ho2_proposal2.docx **Save as:** chap4_ho2_compare_solution.docx and chap4_ho2_combine_solution.docx **Open:**chap4_ho2_master.docx and chap4_ho2_background.docx **Save as:** chap4_ho2_master_solution.docx, Overview.docx, Ideology.docx, Time Frame.docx, Budget.docx, and Conclusion.docx **Open:** chap4_ho1_proposal_solution.docx (from Exercise 1) **Save as:** chap4_ho2_map_solution	• Compare and Combine Documents • View Documents Side by Side • Create Master Documents and Subdocuments • Modify Master Documents and Subdocuments • Use Document Map and Create Bookmarks
3. REFERENCE RESOURCES (page 283) **Open:** chap4_ho3_plagiarism.docx chap4_ho3_plmasterlist.xml **Save as:** chap4_ho3_plagiarism_solution.docx	• Create and Search for a Source • Select a Writing Style and Insert a Bibliography • Create and Modify Footnotes • Convert Footnotes to Endnotes and Modify Endnotes
4. ADDITIONAL REFERENCE RESOURCES (page 292) **Open:** chap4_ho4_tables.docx **Save as:** chap4_ho4_tables_solution.docx	• Add Captions and Create a Table of Figures • Create a Table of Authorities • Create a Cross-Reference • Modify Document Properties

CASE STUDY

Compiling an Employee Handbook

Case Study

After years of planning and saving, Alex Caselman has recently started his own company. He will be hiring 20 employees initially, and anticipates hiring 40 more by the end of the first fiscal year. He understands the importance of establishing goals and procedures that the employees can use to guide their efforts, so he has been working with the Small Business Development Center in his community to create these documents. The SBDC suggested Alex partner with a local business college and recruit students to assist him in writing a Staff Handbook for his employees. There are many laws which must be considered for employee hiring and management, and Alex wants to be sure his company stays in compliance with all regulations.

The two students who have volunteered to help Alex, Tanner and Elexis, have spent a number of hours researching employee handbooks and the laws that regulate hiring and employee leave in their state. They decide to assign a section to each person; after each section is written and reviewed they will combine them. Knowing they would be viewing and editing all pages for each section, each person tracked the changes in their respective documents so the person in charge of combining them can easily view the modifications. Their work has been hard and they have only completed the first five sections of the handbook, but so far everyone is pleased with their progress.

Your Assignment

- Read the chapter, paying special attention to sections that describe how to use the Track Changes and Master Document features in Word.
- Open the document *chap4_case_handbook*, which contains the opening section of the employee handbook, and save the file as **chap4_case_handbook_ solution**. This will become the master document for the handbook.
- Insert the following files, in this order, as subdocuments into the master document: *chap4_case_eligibility*, *chap4_case_employment*, *chap4_case_leave*, *chap4_case_conduct*.
- Display the document in Print Layout view, then turn on track changes. Accept all changes to the eligibility, employment, and leave sections of the document. Reject changes to the conduct section of the document.
- Renumber the conduct section so that all paragraph numbers begin with 5 instead of 7.
- Save and close the *chap4_case_handbook_solution* document.

Workgroups and Collaboration

This chapter introduces several features that go beyond the needs of the typical student and extend to capabilities that you will appreciate in the workplace, especially as you work with others on a collaborative project. This chapter opens with a discussion of workgroup editing, where suggested revisions from one or more individuals can be stored electronically within a document. This feature enables the original author to review each suggestion individually before it is incorporated into the final version of the document, and further, enables multiple people to work on the same document in collaboration with one another.

> In today's organizational environment, teams of people with diverse backgrounds, skills, and knowledge prepare documentation. When you work with a team, you can use collaboration tools in Word such as the Comment feature.

In this section you insert comments to provide feedback or to pose questions to the document author. Then you track editing changes you make so that others can see your suggested edits.

Inserting Comments in a Document

In today's organizational environment, teams of people with diverse backgrounds, skills, and knowledge prepare documentation. Team members work together while planning, developing, writing, and editing important documents. If you have not participated in a team project yet, most likely you will. When you work with a team, you can use collaboration tools in Word such as the Comments feature. A ***comment*** is a note or annotation to ask a question or provide a suggestion to another person about the content of a document. Members of the Exploring team use comments throughout the authoring process. For example, a reviewer might insert a comment to ask the author to clarify a point, or an editor might insert a comment to suggest changing the sequence of topics in a section.

A ***comment*** is a note or annotation about the content of a document.

Before you use the comment and other collaboration features, you should click the Office Button, click Word Options, and then view the Personalize section and confirm that your name is displayed as the user. Word uses this information to indicate the name of the person who uses collaboration tools, such as Comments. If you are in a lab environment, you might not have permission to modify settings or change the User name; however, you should be able to change these settings on a home computer.

Add a Comment

Add comments to a document to remind yourself (or a reviewer) of action that needs to be taken. Click in the document where you want the comment to appear, display the Review tab, and click New Comment in the Comments group to open the markup balloon (see Figure 4.1), and enter the text of the comment and click outside the comment area. ***Markup balloons*** are colored circles that contain comments, insertions, and deletions in the margin with a line drawn to where the insertion point was in the document prior to inserting the comment or editing the document. After you complete the comment, the word containing the insertion point is highlighted in the color assigned to the reviewer. If you do not select anything prior to clicking New Comment, Word selects the word or object to the left of the insertion point for the comment reference.

Markup balloons are colored circles that contain comments and display in the margins.

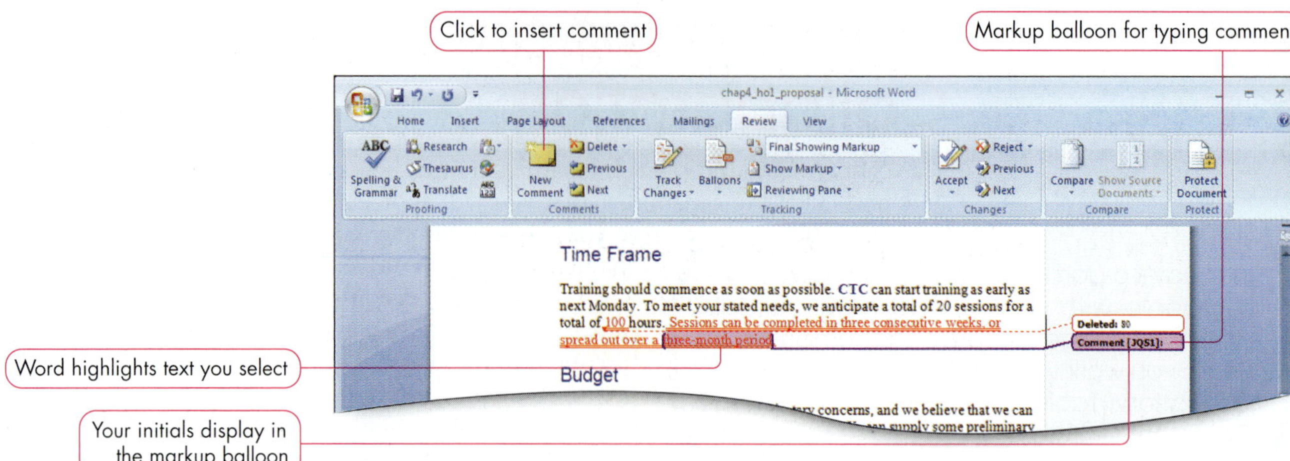

Figure 4.1 Insert a Comment

TIP Record Voice Comments

You can record voice comments if your computer contains a sound card and a microphone. The Insert Voice command is not found in a tab; therefore, you must add it to the Quick Access Toolbar using the Customize section of the Word Options command. To create the sound comment, position the insertion point where you want to insert the sound comment, click Insert Voice on the Quick Access Toolbar, click the Record button in the Sound Object dialog box, record your voice, and then click the Stop button. Click the Rewind button to rewind the sound clip, and click the Play button to hear your recording. People can listen to the voice comment by double-clicking the sound icon within the document.

View, Modify, and Delete Comments

The ***Reviewing Pane*** displays comments and changes made to a document.

Comments appear in markup balloons in Print Layout, Web Layout, and Full Screen Reading views. In Draft view comments appear as tags embedded in the document; when you hover the mouse over the tag, it displays the comment. In any view, you can display the ***Reviewing Pane***, a pane that displays all comments and editorial changes made to the main document. To display or hide the Reviewing Pane, click Reviewing Pane on the Review tab. You can display the pane vertically on the left side of the document window, as shown in Figure 4.2, or horizontally at the bottom. The Reviewing Pane is useful when the comments are too long to display completely in a markup balloon.

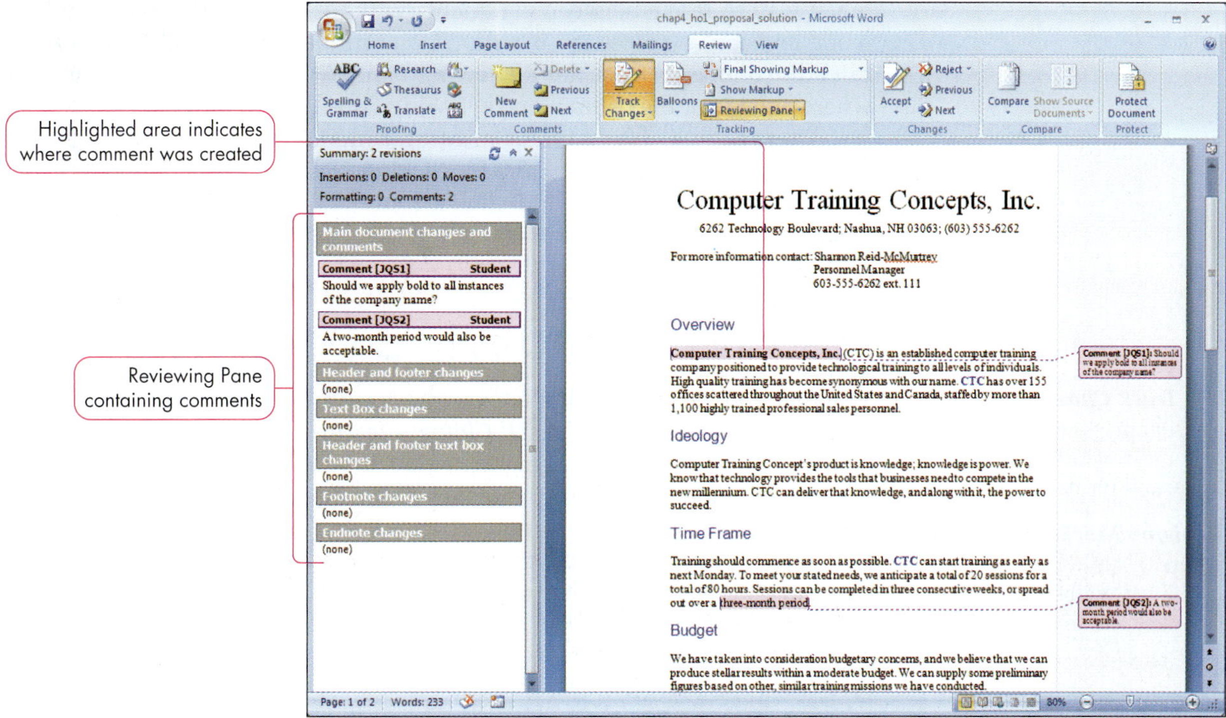
Highlighted area indicates where comment was created
Reviewing Pane containing comments

Figure 4.2 The Reviewing Pane

Show Markup enables you to view document revisions by reviewer.

If you do not see comments initially, click Show Markup on the Review tab and confirm that Comment is toggled on. The ***Show Markup*** feature enables you to view document revisions by reviewers. It also enables you to choose which type of revisions you want to view such as Comments, Ink annotations (made on a tablet PC), insertions and deletions, or formatting changes. Each can be toggled on or off, and you can view one or all at the same time. Show Markup also color codes each revision or comment with a different color for each reviewer. If you want to view changes by a particular reviewer, you simply toggle off all others in the Show Markup reviewers list as shown in Figure 4.3.

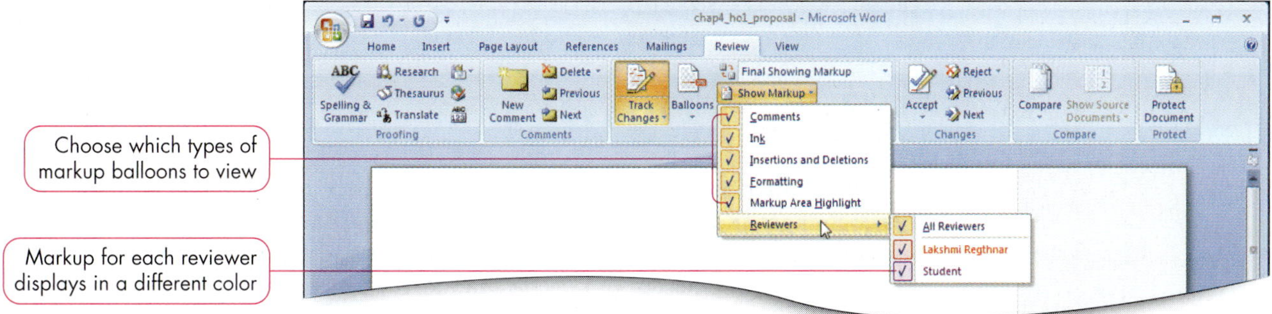
Choose which types of markup balloons to view
Markup for each reviewer displays in a different color

Figure 4.3 Show Markup Menu

You can modify comments easily. When you click inside a markup balloon, the insertion point will relocate, and you can use word processing formatting features, such as bold, italic, underline, and color, in the comment. If a document contains many comments, or the document is lengthy, you can click Previous and Next in the Comments group on the Review tab to navigate from comment to comment. This is a quick way to move between comments without scrolling through the entire document, and it also places the insertion point in the comment automatically. You also can edit comments from the Reviewing Pane. After you edit a comment, click anywhere outside of the balloon or Reviewing Pane to save the changes.

After reading, acting on, or printing comments, you can delete the comments from within the Reviewing Pane by clicking Delete in the Comments group on the Review tab. You also can right-click a comment markup balloon and select Delete Comment from the shortcut menu.

Tracking Changes in a Document

Use ***Track Changes*** to insert revision marks and markup balloons for additions, deletions, and formatting changes.

Revision Marks indicate where text is added, deleted, or formatted while the Track Changes feature is active.

Whether you work individually or with a group, you can monitor any revisions you make to a document. The ***Track Changes*** feature monitors all additions, deletions, and formatting changes you make in a document. When Track Changes is active, it applies ***Revision Marks***, which are onscreen elements that indicate locations where a person added, deleted, or formatted text. Word uses colors for different reviewers who edit a document. You can position the mouse pointer over revision marks or markup balloons to see who made the change and on what date and time, as shown in Figure 4.4. The vertical line may be on the left or right side of the screen.

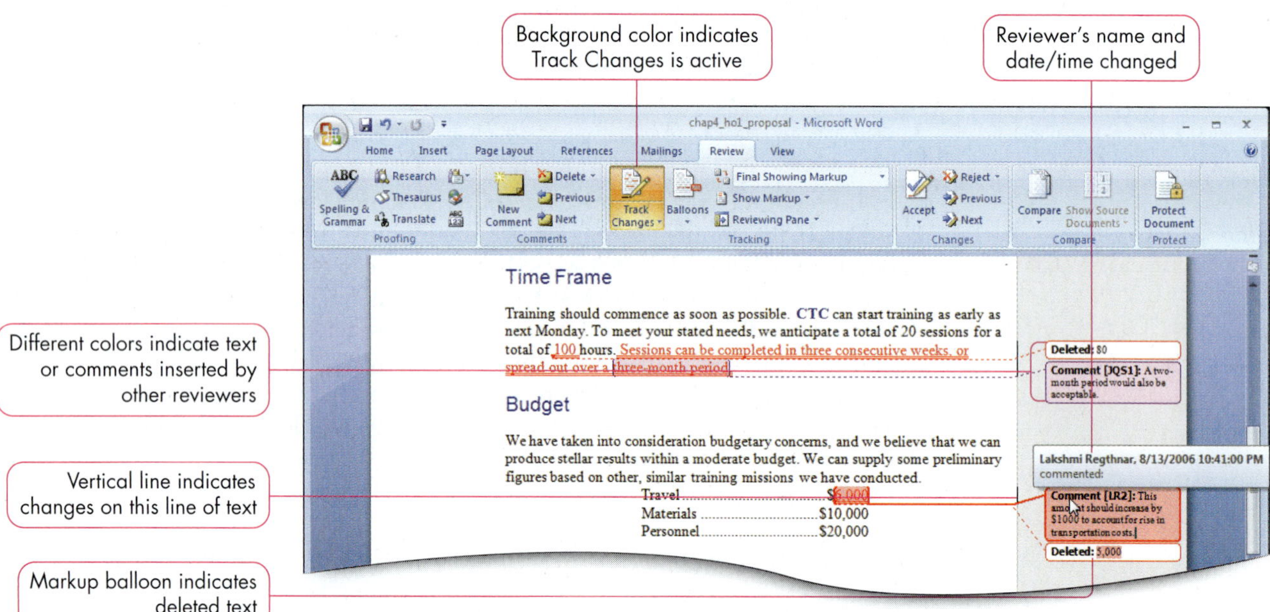

Figure 4.4 An Example of Track Changes

Word also includes markup tools, some of which enable you to accept or reject changes indicated by revision marks. The Changes group on the Review tab includes Accept to accept a suggested change and Reject to remove a suggested change. When you accept or reject a change, the revision marks and markup balloon disappear.

The Track Changes feature is useful in situations where a document must be reviewed by several people, each of whom can offer suggestions or changes, and then returned to one person who must finalize the document. The last person can view all suggestions at the same time, and then accept or reject the suggested changes with the click of a mouse. If the process takes place using paper copies of a document, it is difficult to visualize all the suggested changes at one time, and then the last person must manually change the original document. While writing the Exploring series, the authors, editors, and reviewers each inserted comments and tracked changes to the manuscript for each chapter. Each person's comments or changes displayed in different colored balloons, and because all edits were performed in one document, the Series Editor could accept and reject changes before sending the manuscript to the production department.

> **TIP Accepting or Rejecting All Changes**
>
> To accept all changes in a document at once, click the Accept arrow on the Review tab and select Accept All Changes in Document. To delete all changes in a document at once, click the Reject arrow on the Review tab and select Reject All Changes in Document.

Select Markup Views

Original Showing Markup view shows a line through deleted text and puts inserted text in a markup balloon.

Final Showing Markup view shows inserted text in the body and puts deleted text in a markup balloon.

The suggested revisions from the various reviewers display in one of two ways, as the Original Showing Markup or as the Final Showing Markup. The ***Original Showing Markup*** view shows the deleted text within the body of the document (with a line through the deleted text) and displays the inserted text in a balloon to the right of the actual document, as shown in Figure 4.5. The ***Final Showing Markup*** view is the opposite; that is, it displays the inserted text in the body of the document and shows the deleted text in a balloon. The difference is subtle and depends on personal preference with respect to displaying the insertions and deletions in a document. (All revisions fall into one of these two categories: insertions or deletions. Even if you substitute one word for another, you are deleting the original word and then inserting its replacement.) Both views display revision marks on the edge of any line that has been changed. Comments are optional and enclosed in balloons in the side margin of a document.

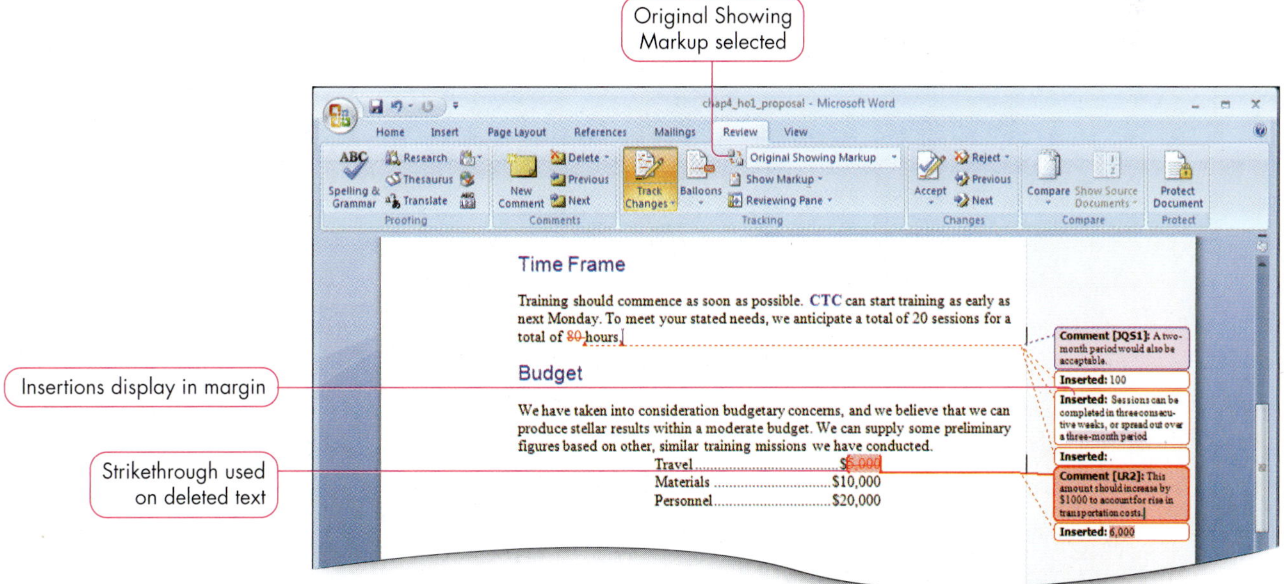

Figure 4.5 Original Showing Markup View

When you click the Display for Review arrow in the Review tab, two additional view options are listed—Final and Original. Final shows how the document looks if you accept and incorporate all tracked changes. Original shows the document prior to using the Track Changes feature.

The review process is straightforward. The initial document is sent for review to one or more individuals, who record their changes by executing the Track Changes command on the Review tab to start (or stop) the recording process. The author of the original document receives the altered document and then uses Accept and Reject in the Changes group on the Review tab to review the document and implement the suggested changes.

Customize Track Changes Options

Although the feature seems to have many options for viewing and displaying changes, you can further customize the Track Changes feature. The following reference page describes the sections and settings you can change in the Track Changes dialog box.

The beginning of this chapter mentioned that you should check the Word Options, making changes if necessary, so your name is associated with any tracked changes you make in the document. You also can access those settings from the Review tab when you click the Track Changes arrow and select Change User Name as shown in Figure 4.6. This step takes you to the Popular category of the Word Options dialog box, where you have the opportunity to enter your name and initials in the *Personalize your copy of Microsoft Office* section.

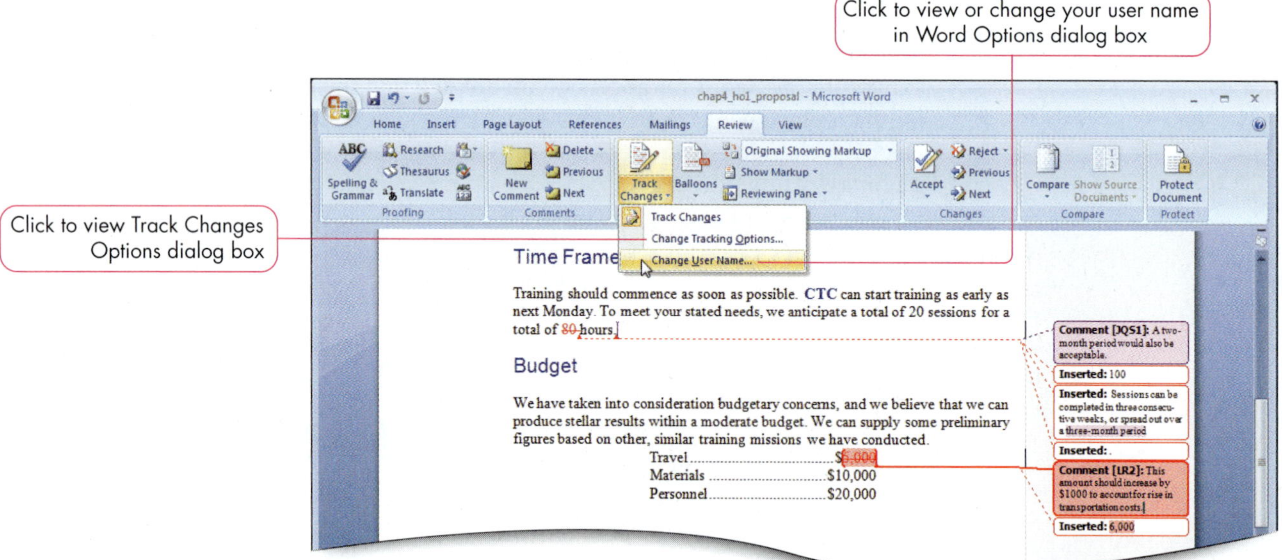

Figure 4.6 Track Changes Customization Options

Track Changes Options Dialog Box | Reference

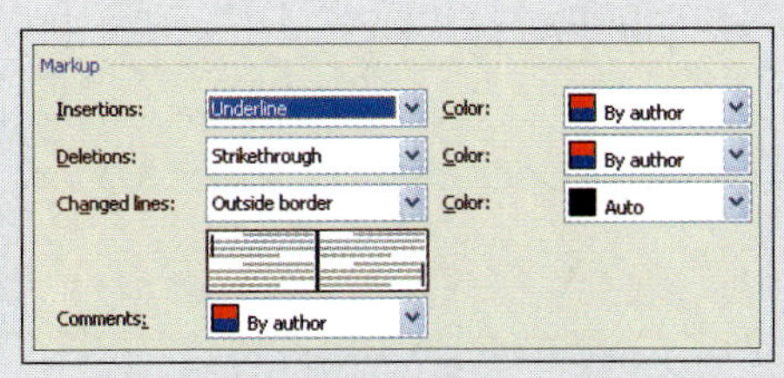

Markup

Specify format property (color, bold, italic, underline, strikethrough) used for insertions and deletions.

Specify location (left border, right border, outside border, none) of marks that indicate a change has been made to text on a line.

Specify color to use for comments, insertions, deletions, and changed lines. Select a standard color for each or assign color by author/reviewer.

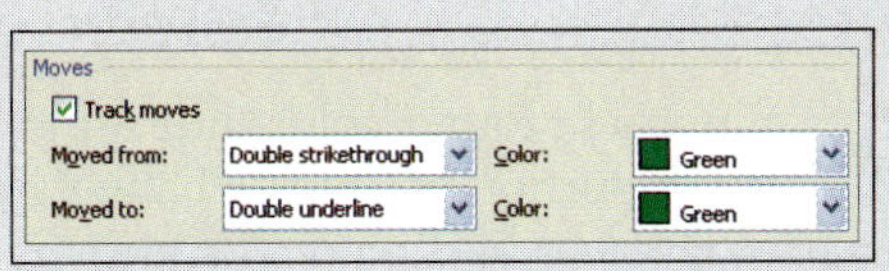

Moves

Specify format property (double strikethrough, double underline) used on text that is moved within the document.

Specify color to use for text that is moved within the document.

Select a standard color for each or assign color by author/reviewer.

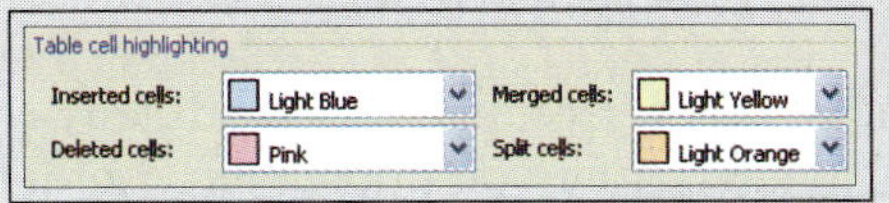

Table cell highlighting

Specify highlight color used to indicate a change in the layout of a table (insert cells, delete cells, merge or split cells).

Select a standard color for each type of modification or assign color by author/reviewer.

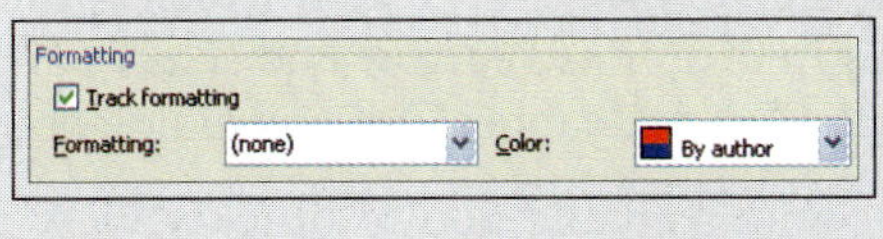

Formatting

Turn on Track formatting. Tracks any change made to the format of text or an object.

Specify format property (color, bold, italic, underline, strikethrough) used to indicate a format change.

Specify color of balloon used to indicate a format change.

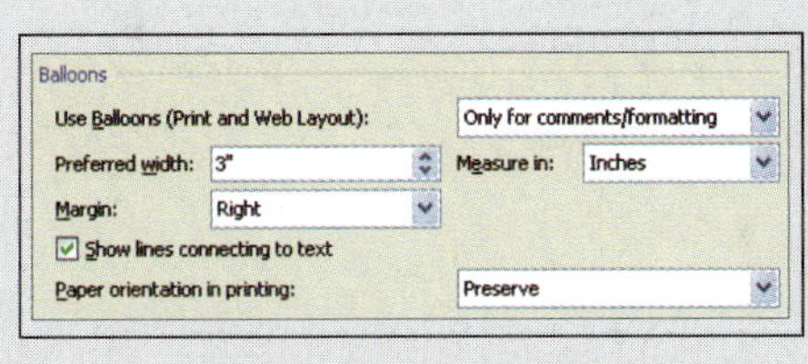

Balloons

Specify when to use balloons in Print and Web Layout views (always, never, only for comments/formatting).

Specify width of balloon.

Specify width measurement (inches or percentage of page width).

Specify in which margin (right or left) to display balloons.

Specify if lines will connect balloons to text.

Hands-On Exercises

1 | Document Collaboration

Skills covered: 1. Set User Name and Customize the Track Changes Options **2.** Track Document Changes **3.** View, Add, and Delete Comments **4.** Accept and Reject Changes

Step 1 Set User Name and Customize the Track Changes Options

Refer to Figure 4.7 as you complete Step 1.

a. Start Word. Open the *chap4_ho1_proposal* document and save it as **chap4_ho1_proposal_solution**.

b. Click the **Review tab** and click the upper portion of **Track Changes** in the Tracking group.

The command should display with an orange background color indicating the feature is turned on. When you click the upper portion of Track Changes, you toggle the feature on or off. When you click the lower portion of Track Changes, a menu of options displays, which you use in the next step.

c. Click the **Track Changes down arrow** and then select **Change User Name**. In the *Personalize your copy of Microsoft Office* section, type your name in the **User name** box and type your initials in the **Initials** box, if necessary. Click **OK** to close the Word Options dialog box.

You want to be sure your name and initials are correct before you add any comments or initiate any changes in the document. After you update the User information, your initials display with any comments or changes you make.

d. Click the **Track Changes arrow** and click **Change Tracking Options**. In the *Markup* section click the **Insertions drop-down arrow** and then click **Double underline**. In the *Formatting* section, click the **Track formatting check box**.

e. In the *Balloons* section, click the **Use Balloons (Print and Web Layout) drop-down arrow** and select **Always**, if necessary. Click the **Preferred width spin arrow** until **1.8″** displays. Click the **Margin drop-down arrow** and select **Left** as shown in Figure 4.7. Click **OK** to close the Track Changes Options dialog box.

Your revisions to the Track Changes options enable you to quickly view any additions to the document because they will be identified in balloons and insertions will display with a double underline. Additionally, you altered the location of all comment and editing balloons to display on the left side of your document instead of on the right, which is the default. You also decreased the width of the markup balloons so they will take up less space in the margins.

f. Save the document.

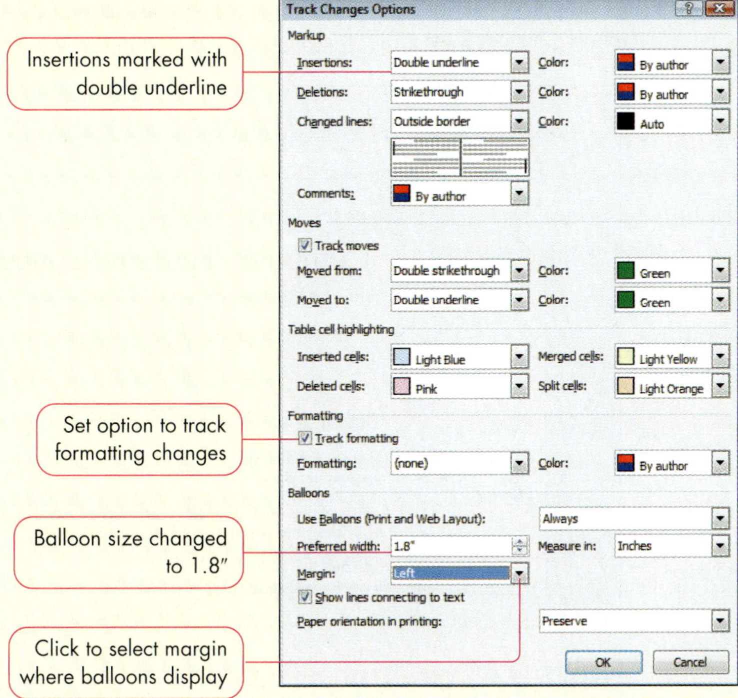

Figure 4.7 Track Changes Options Dialog Box

Step 2
Track Document Changes

Refer to Figure 4.8 as you complete Step 2.

a. Click the **Display for Review arrow** in the Tracking group on the Review tab and select **Final Showing Markup**, if necessary. Scroll down to view the bottom of the first page.

One comment and two previous changes display in balloons. Because of the changes you made in Steps 1a and 1b, any future changes you make in the document also display in balloons in the margin of the document.

b. Scroll to the top of the page, select the number *150* in the first paragraph, and replace it with **155**.

TROUBLESHOOTING: If a balloon does not display, indicating the number 150 was deleted, make sure the Track Changes is on. When on, Track Changes is highlighted in an orange color. If necessary, click Track Changes again to turn it on, then repeat Step 2b.

c. Select *Computer Training Concepts, Inc.* in the first sentence of the first paragraph and apply **Bold** from the Mini toolbar.

The changed line appears on the right side of the line you formatted, a markup balloon indicates the formatting change, and the text you inserted in Step 2b is colored with a double underline as shown in Figure 4.8.

d. Click the **Display for Review arrow** in the Tracking group and select **Final**.

The formatting change indicators do not display, and the text in the first sentence displays in bold.

e. Save the document.

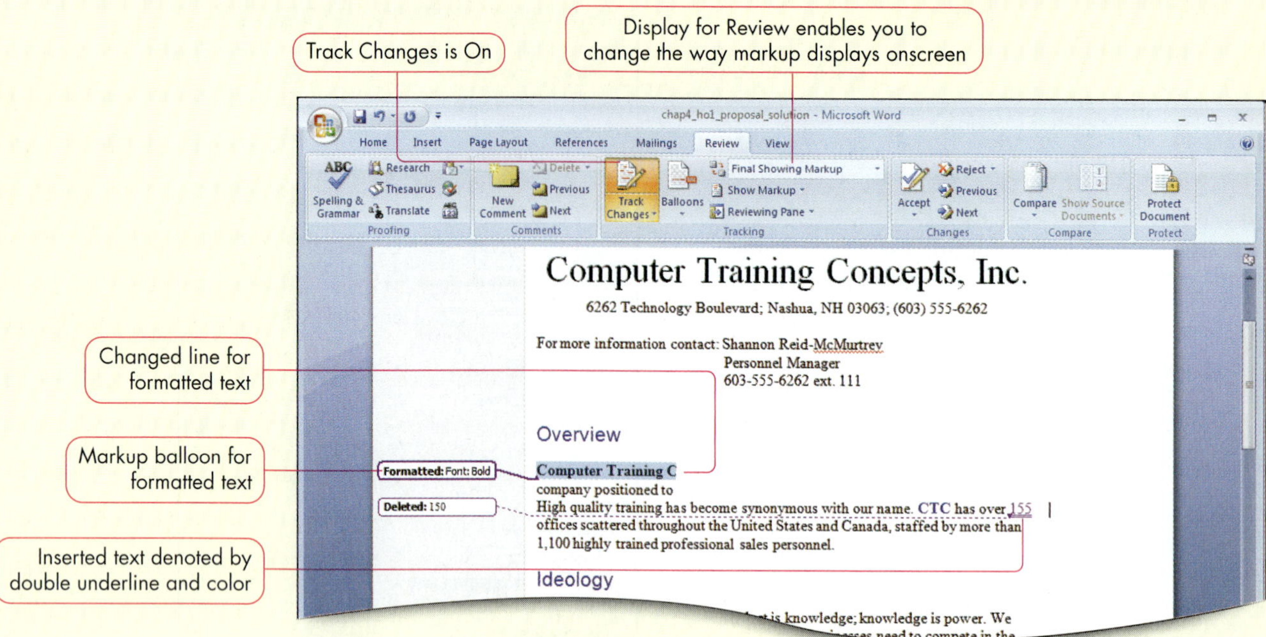

Figure 4.8 View Changes in a Document

Step 3
View, Add, and Delete Comments

Refer to Figure 4.9 as you complete Step 3.

a. Click the **Display for Review arrow** in the Tracking group and select **Final Showing Markup**.

b. Select *three-month period* at the end of the *Time Frame* paragraph. Click **New Comment** in the Comments group, and then type **A four-month period would also be acceptable.**

   If you do not select anything prior to clicking New Comment, Word selects the word or object to the left of the insertion point for the comment reference.

c. Select *Computer Training Concepts, Inc.* in the first sentence of the first paragraph. Click **New Comment**, and then type **Should we apply bold to all instances of the company name?** in the markup balloon.

d. Click inside the first markup balloon you created. Edit the comment by replacing *four-month* with **two-month**. Click outside of the balloon to deselect it.

e. Position the mouse pointer over the comment balloon in the Budget paragraph.

   When you position the mouse pointer over a markup balloon, Word displays a ScreenTip that tells you who created the comment and when.

f. Click the comment by Lakshmi Regthnar one time to select it, and then click **Delete** in the Comments group on the Review tab (see Figure 4.9).

   You removed the selected comment and the markup balloon. If you click the arrow on the right side of Delete, you can select from several options, including Delete all Comments in Document.

g. Save the document.

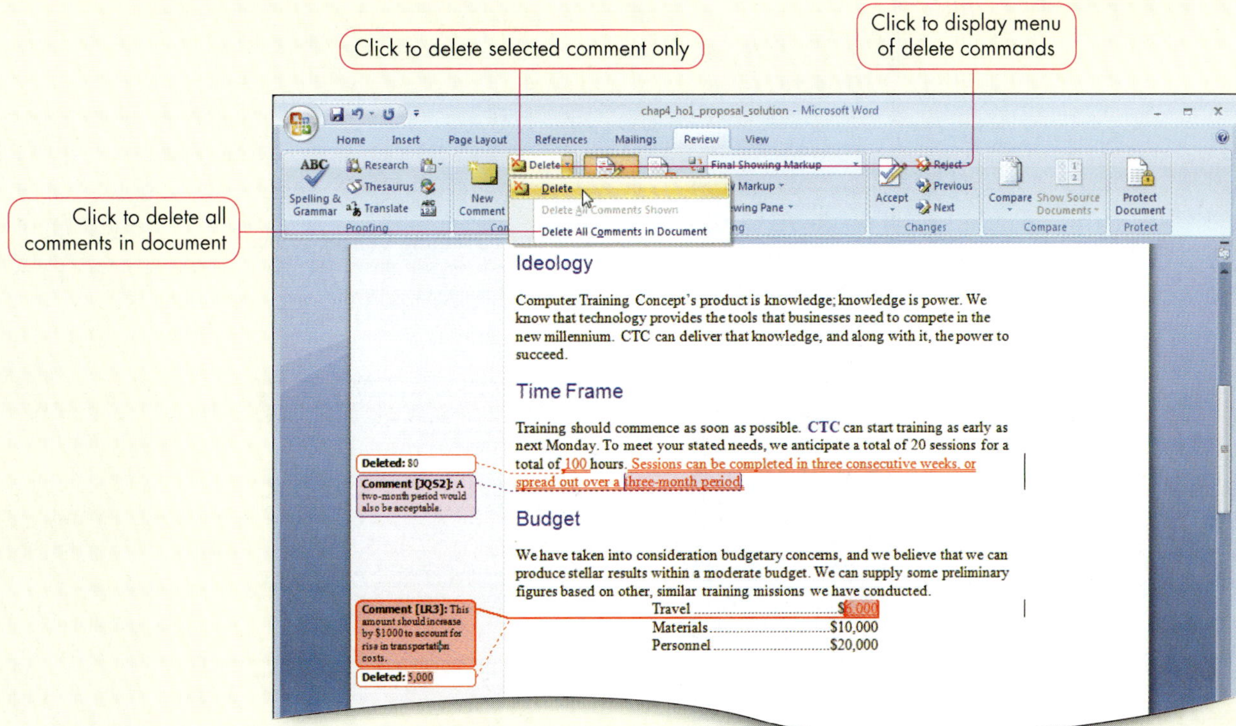

Figure 4.9 Deleting Comments

Step 4
Accept and Reject Changes

Refer to Figure 4.10 as you complete Step 4.

a. Press **Ctrl+Home** to place the insertion point at the beginning of the document.

b. Click **Next** in the Changes group to highlight the first change, and then position the mouse pointer over the tracked change.

   When you position the mouse pointer on the revision mark, a ScreenTip appears that tells you who made the change, and the date and time the change was made.

   TROUBLESHOOTING: If you click Next in the Comments group instead of Next in the Changes group, click Previous in the Comments group and then click Next in the Changes group.

c. Click **Accept** in the Changes group.

   The formatting change is accepted. When the suggested change is accepted, the markup balloons and other Track Changes markups disappear. Additionally, the markup balloon for the next change or comment is highlighted. As with other commands, you can click the upper portion of the Accept command to accept this change only, or you can click the lower portion of the command to view a menu of options for accepting changes.

d. Click **Next** in the Changes group to pass the comment and view the next markup balloon. Click **Accept** two times to accept the change to 155 offices.

e. Click **Next** in the Changes group to view the next markup balloon. Click **Reject** two times to retain the session time frame of *80 hours*.

f. Click the **Accept arrow** and click **Accept All Changes in Document**. Click the **Display for Review** arrow and select **Final**.

   Figure 4.10 shows the first page after accepting and rejecting changes.

g. Save and close *chap4_ho1_proposal_solution*. Exit Word if you will not continue with the next exercise at this time.

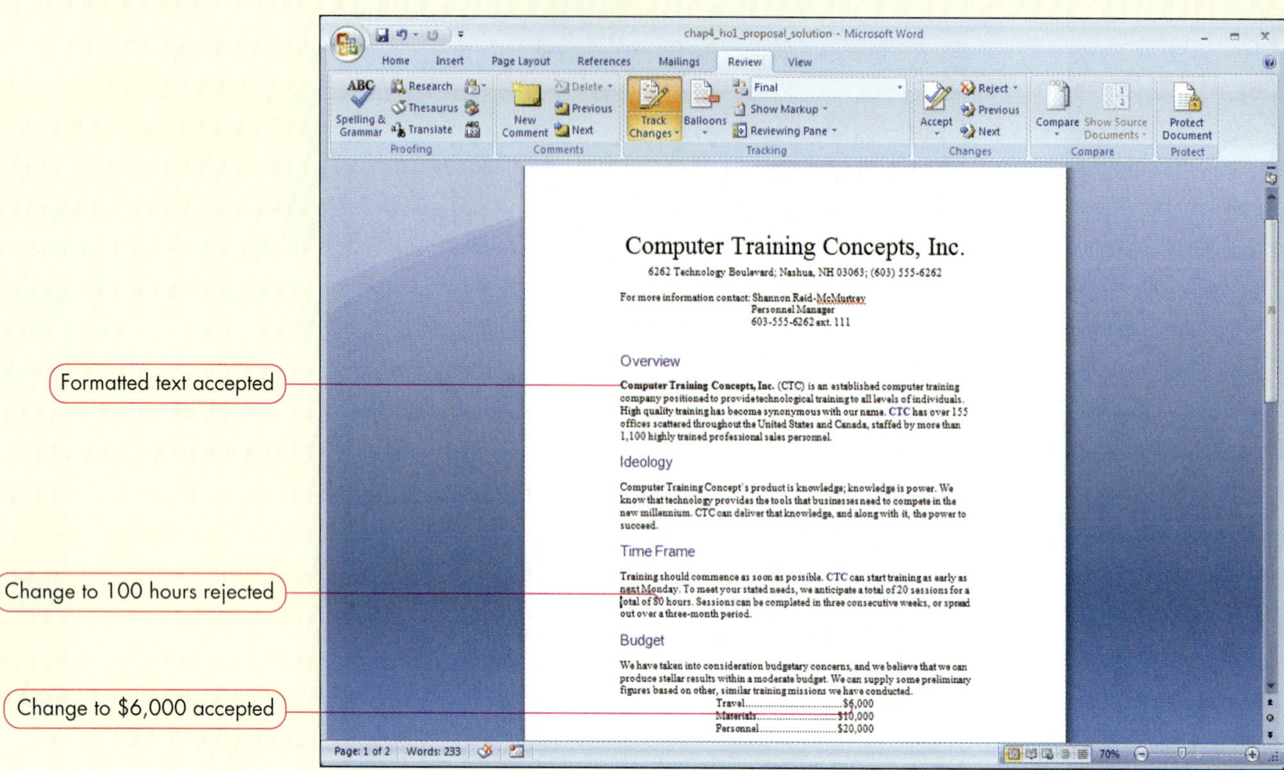

Figure 4.10 The Revised Document

Multiple Documents

Features in Word enable you to work with multiple documents simultaneously—you can view multiple documents at one time, as well as combine them into one.

The collaboration features in Word facilitate an easy exchange of ideas and revisions to a document. But some users do not use the collaboration features, which causes the process of combining information into one document to be less efficient. Fortunately, other features in Word enable you to work with multiple documents simultaneously—you can view multiple documents at one time, as well as combine them into one.

In this section, you display multiple documents side by side as well as compare and combine documents into a new file. You create a document that contains subdocuments and then use tools to navigate within lengthy documents. Finally you create an electronic marker for a location in a document and use the Go To feature.

Viewing Documents Side by Side

View Side by Side enables you to display two documents on the same screen.

The ***View Side by Side*** feature enables you to display two documents on the same screen. This is a useful tool when you want to compare an original to a revised document or when you want to cut or copy a portion from one document to another. To view two documents side by side, you must open both documents. The View Side by Side command is grayed out if only one document is open. When the documents are open, click View Side by Side in the Window group on the View tab, and the Word window will split to display each document as shown in Figure 4.11. If you have more than two documents open, the Compare Side by Side dialog box displays, and you select which document you want to display beside the active document.

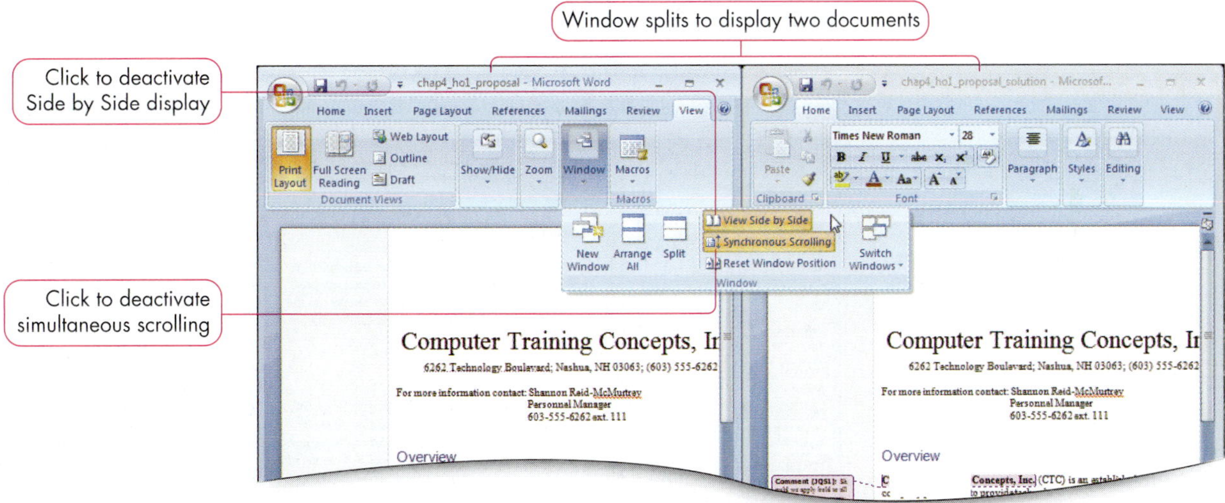

Figure 4.11 View Documents Side by Side

Synchronous scrolling enables you to simultaneously scroll through documents in Side by Side view.

When the documents display side by side, synchronous scrolling is active by default. ***Synchronous scrolling*** enables you to scroll through both documents at the same time. If you want to scroll through each document independently, click Synchronous Scrolling on the View tab to toggle it off. If you are viewing two versions of the same document, synchronous scrolling enables you to view both documents using only one scroll bar. If you scroll through each document asynchronously, you must use the respective scroll bars to navigate through each document.

While in Side by Side view, you can resize and reposition the two document windows. If you want to reset them to the original side-by-side viewing size, click Reset Window Position on the View tab. To close Side by Side view, click View Side by Side to toggle it off. The document that contains the insertion point when you close Side by Side view will display as the active document.

Comparing and Combining Documents

The ***Compare*** feature evaluates the contents of two or more documents and displays markup balloons showing the differences.

Ideally, when you have a document to submit to others for feedback, you want everyone to use the Track Changes feature in Word. However, sometimes it is necessary to have several people editing their own copy of the document simultaneously before they return it to you. When this occurs, you have several similar documents but with individual changes. Instead of compiling results from printed copies or viewing each one in Side by Side view to determine the differences, you can use a Compare feature. ***Compare*** automatically evaluates the contents of two or more documents and displays markup balloons that show the differences between the documents. You can display the differences in the original document, the revised document, or in a new document. You also can display query on the screen with the new document as shown in Figure 4.12. The Compare command is in the Compare group on the Review tab.

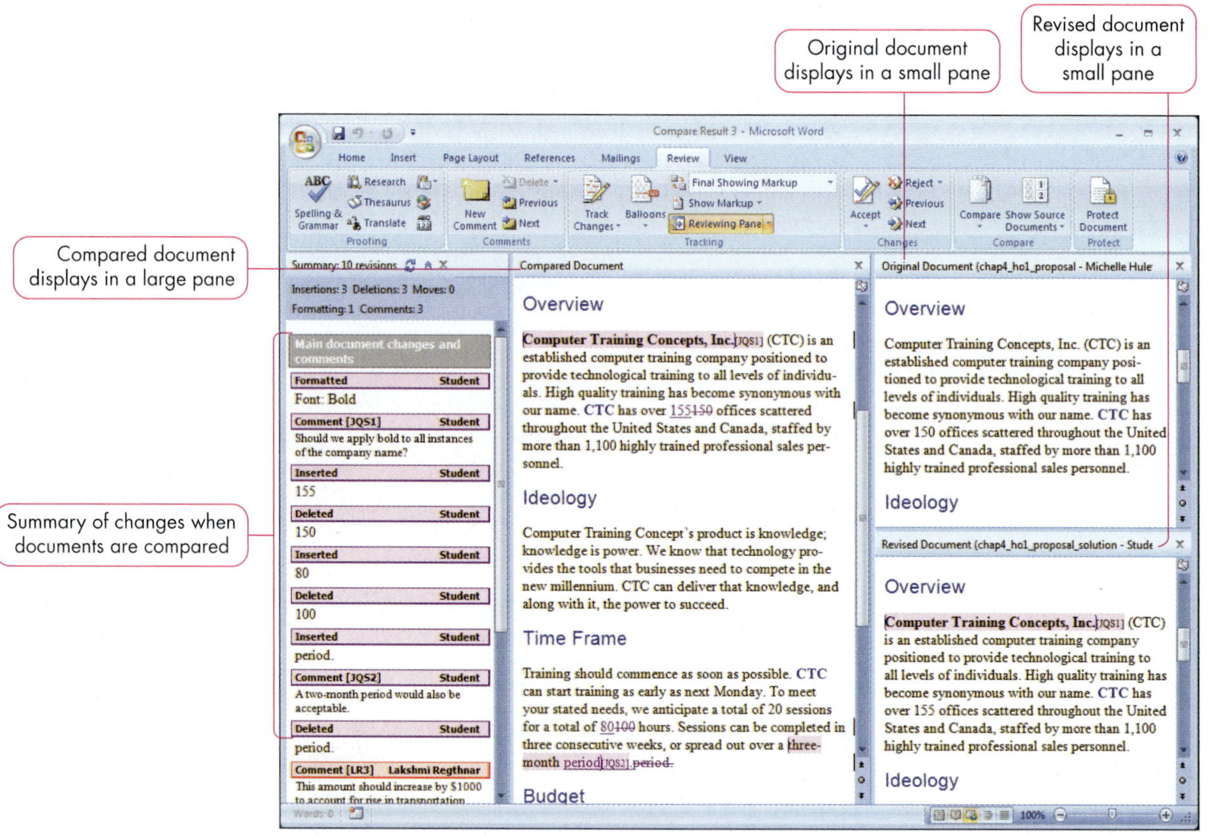

Figure 4.12 Results of Comparing Two Documents

The ***Combine*** feature incorporates all changes from multiple documents into a new document.

If you want to go a step further than just viewing the differences, you can use the ***Combine*** feature to integrate all changes from multiple documents into one document. To use the Combine feature, click the Compare arrow in the Review tab and select Combine. The Combine Documents dialog box opens displaying a variety of options you can invoke, as shown in Figure 4.13. The option you are most likely to change is in the Show Changes section, where you determine where the Combined documents will display—in the original document, the revised document, or in a new document. If you want to be certain not to modify the original documents, you should combine the changes into a new document.

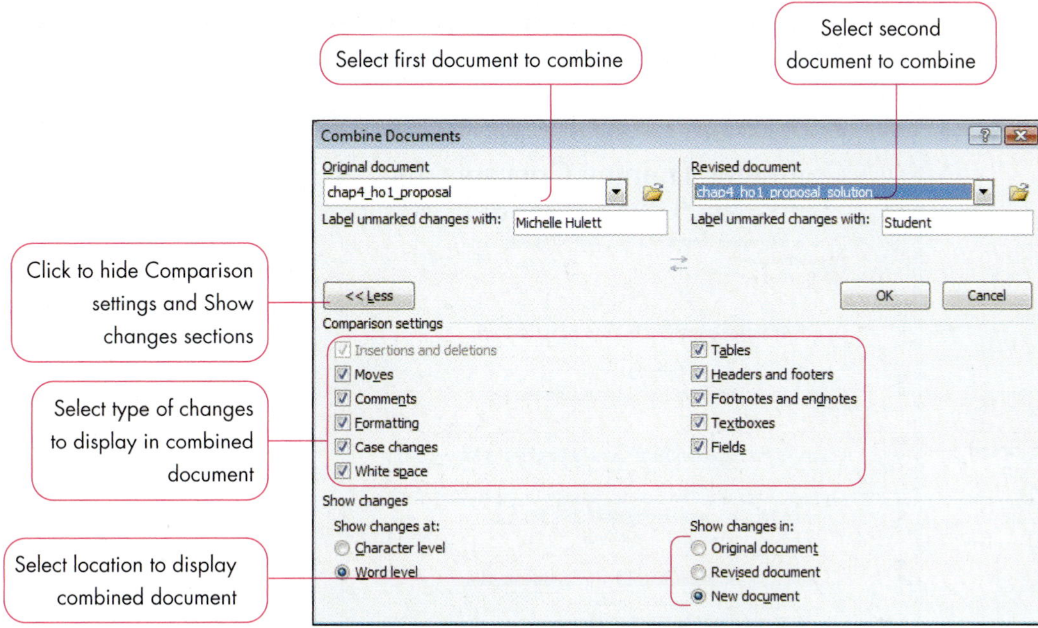

Figure 4.13 The Combine Documents Dialog Box

Creating Master Documents and Subdocuments

A ***master document*** is a document that acts like a binder for managing smaller documents.

A ***subdocument*** is a smaller document that is a part of a master document.

Working with long documents can be cumbersome. You may notice your computer slows down when you are working in a lengthy document. Scrolling, finding and replacing, editing, and formatting typically take longer. To improve this situation, you can create a ***master document***, a document that acts like a binder for managing smaller documents. A smaller document that is a part of a master document is called a ***subdocument***. The advantage of the master document is that you can work with several smaller documents, as opposed to a single large document. Thus, you edit the subdocuments individually and more efficiently than if they were all part of the same document. You can create a master document to hold the chapters of a book, where each chapter is stored as a subdocument. You also can use a master document to hold multiple documents created by others, such as a group project, where each member of the group is responsible for a section of the document.

The Outlining tab contains the Collapse and Expand Subdocuments buttons, as well as other tools associated with master documents. Figure 4.14 displays a master document with five subdocuments. The subdocuments are collapsed in Figure 4.14 and expanded in Figure 4.15. The collapsed structure enables you to see at a glance the subdocuments that comprise the master document. You can insert additional subdocuments or remove existing subdocuments from the master document. Deleting a subdocument from within a master document does not delete the actual subdocument file.

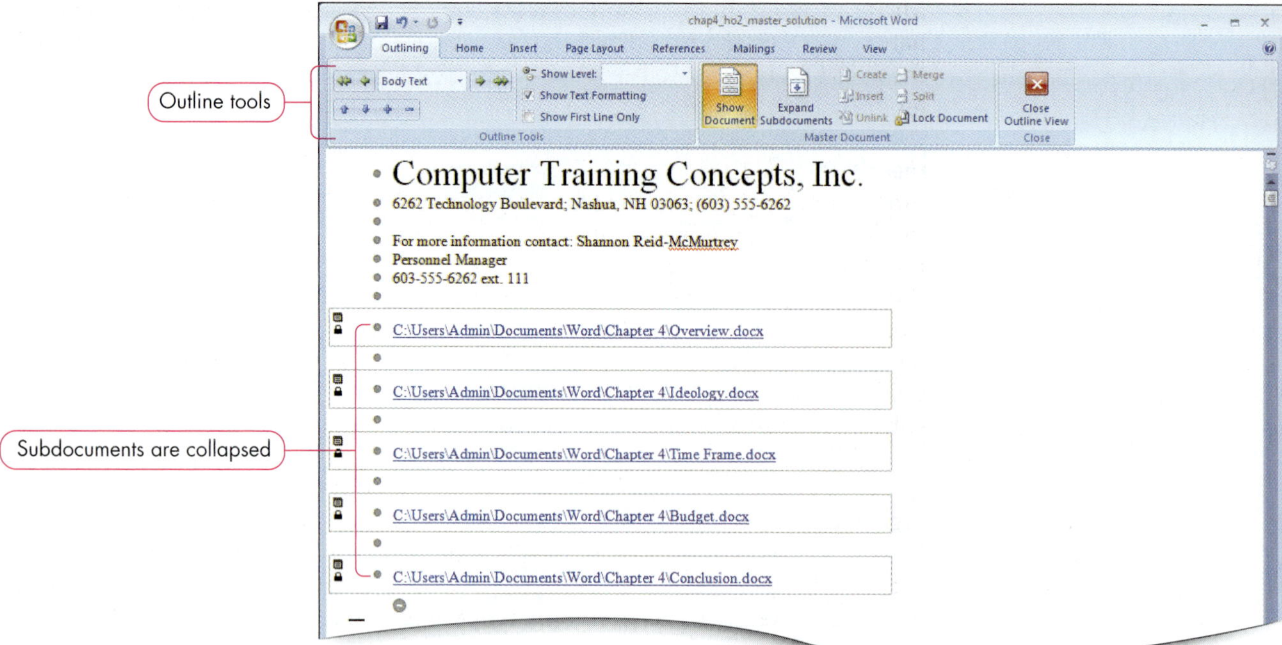

Figure 4.14 Master Document Showing Collapsed Subdocuments

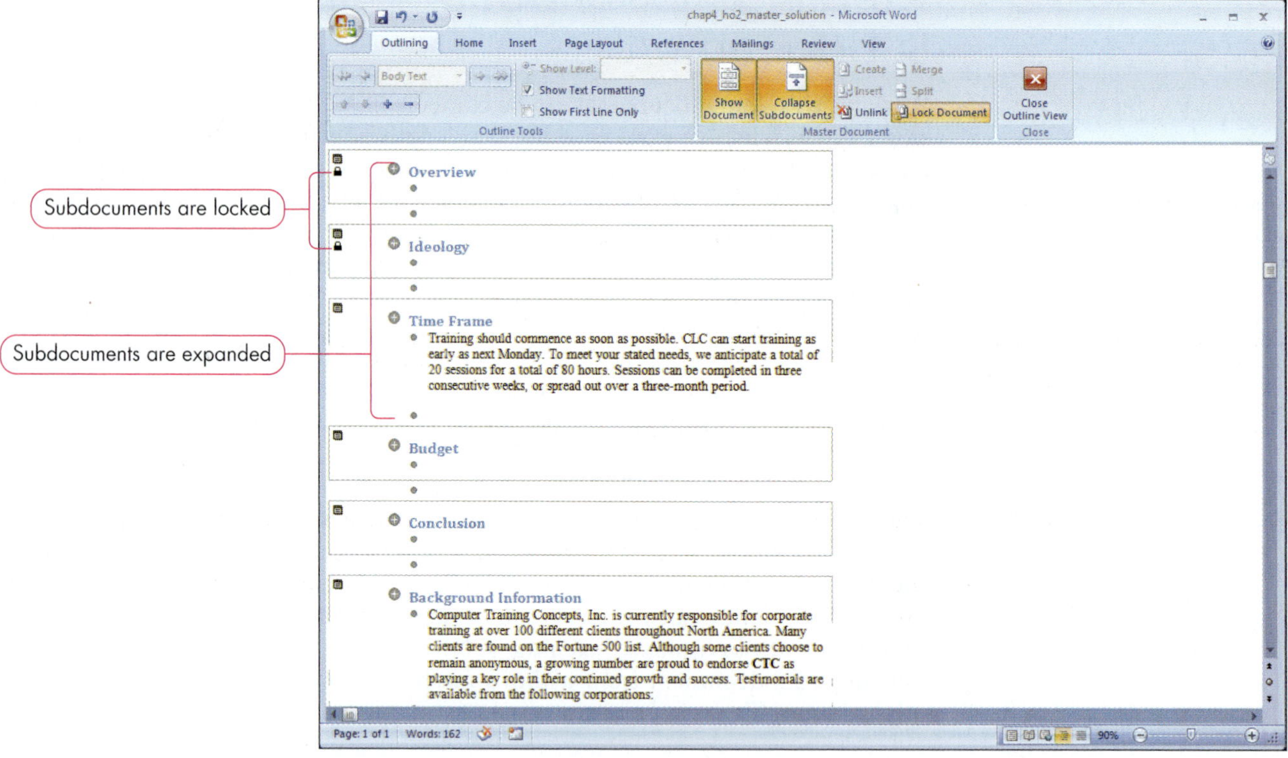

Figure 4.15 Master Document Showing Expanded Subdocuments

The expanded structure enables you to view and/or edit the contents of the subdocuments. Look carefully, however, at the subdocuments in Figure 4.15. A padlock appears to the left of the first line in the first and second subdocuments, whereas it is absent from the third and fourth subdocuments. These subdocuments are locked and unlocked, respectively. (All subdocuments are locked when collapsed as in Figure 4.14.)

You can make changes to the master document at any time. However, you can make changes to the subdocuments only when the subdocument is unlocked. Note, too, that you can make changes to a subdocument in one of two ways, either when the subdocument is expanded (and unlocked) within a master document as in Figure 4.15 or by opening the subdocument as an independent document within

Microsoft Word. Both techniques work equally well, and you will find yourself alternating between the two. You lock the subdocuments to prevent making changes to their content but also to prevent the subdocument from being deleted from the master document.

Regardless of how you edit the subdocuments, the attraction of a master document is the ability to work with multiple subdocuments simultaneously. The subdocuments are created independently of one another, with each subdocument stored in its own file. Then, when all of the subdocuments are finished, the master document is created, and the subdocuments are inserted into the master document, from where they are easily accessed. Inserting page numbers into the master document, for example, causes the numbers to run consecutively from one subdocument to the next. You also can create a table of contents or index for the master document that will reflect the entries in all of the subdocuments. And finally, you can print all of the subdocuments from within the master document with a single command.

Alternatively, you can reverse the process by starting with an empty master document and using it as the basis to create the subdocuments. This process is ideal for organizing a group project in school or at work, the chapters in a book, or the sections in a report. Start with a new document, and then enter the topics assigned to each group member. Format each topic in a heading style within the master document, and then use the Create Subdocument command to create subdocuments based on those headings. Saving the master document will automatically save each subdocument in its own file. This is the approach that you will follow in the next hands-on exercise.

TIP Printing a Master Document

If you click Print when a master document is displayed and the subdocuments are collapsed, the message *Do you want to open the subdocuments before continuing with this command?* appears. Click Yes to open the subdocuments so that they will print as one long document. Click No to print the master document that lists the subdocument filenames as they display onscreen.

Using Navigation Tools

Without a reference source, such as a table of contents, it can be difficult to locate information in a long document. Even scrolling through a long document can be inefficient if you are uncertain of the exact location that you want to view. Fortunately, Word provides navigation tools that assist the author and reader in locating content quickly and easily.

Display a Document Map and Thumbnails

The ***Document Map*** is a pane that lists the structure of headings in your document.

You can use the Find and Go To features in Word to move through a document. Another helpful navigation feature is the ***Document Map***, a pane that lists the structure of headings in your document. The headings in a document are displayed in the left pane, and the text of the document is visible in the right pane. You can click a heading in the Document Map to move the insertion point to that heading in the document. When working in long documents, the Document Map provides a way to navigate quickly to a particular topic, as shown in Figure 4.16.

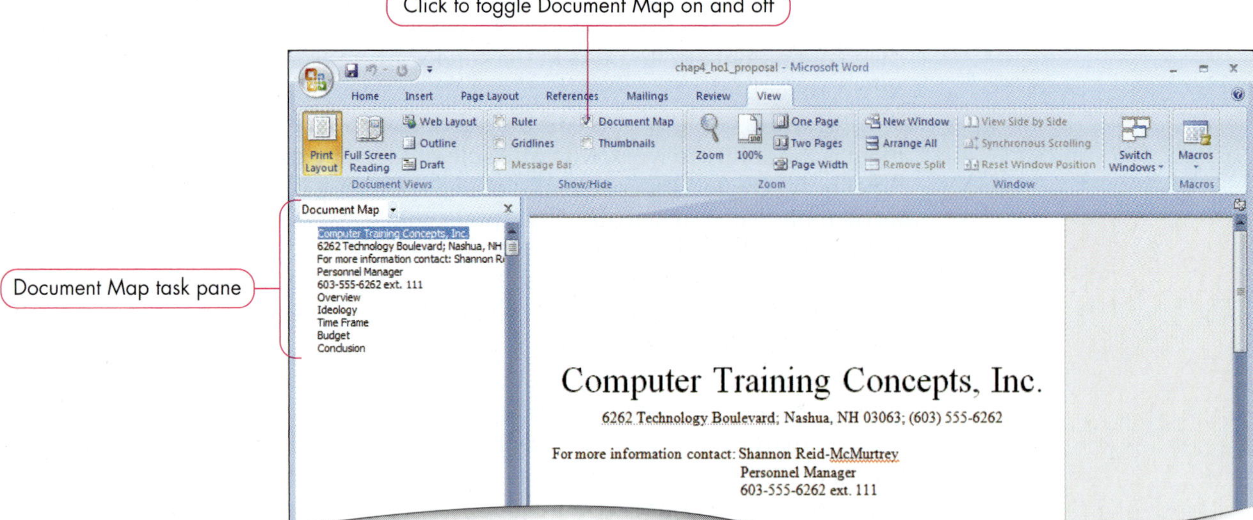

Figure 4.16 The Document Map

To display the Document Map pane, click Document Map in the Show/Hide group on the View tab. If you want to display the Document Map for a master document, be sure the master document is expanded to display the text of the subdocuments. This feature is a toggle; to close the Document Map, remove the check mark from the Document Map check box. The Document Map can be used on any document that uses the styles feature to format headings. The best way to format headings is to apply the built-in Title or Heading styles from the Styles group on the Home tab.

Thumbnails are small pictures of each page in your document that display in a separate window pane.

In lieu of the Document Map, you can display ***Thumbnails***—small pictures of each page in your document that display in a pane on the left side of the screen. As with the Document Map, you can click a thumbnail to move the insertion point to the top of that page. This is another method of navigating quickly through a document.

Even though you cannot read the text on a thumbnail, you can see the layout of a page well enough to determine if that is a location you want to display. And if you display markup, the revision marks and comments also display in the thumbnails, as shown in Figure 4.17. The Thumbnails view is a toggle; click the Thumbnails check box on the Show/Hide group on the View tab to display the pane, and remove the check to turn it off.

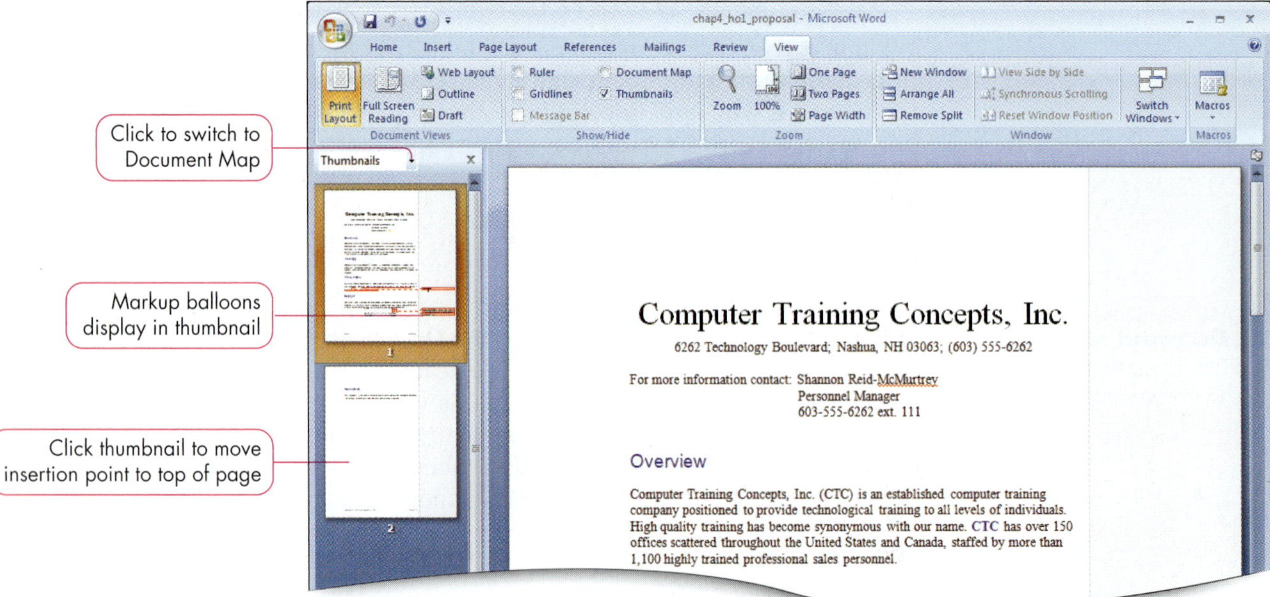

Figure 4.17 Thumbnails

Insert Bookmarks

The ***bookmark*** feature is an electronic marker for a specific location in a document

When you read a book you use a bookmark to help you return to that location quickly. Word provides the ***bookmark*** feature as an electronic marker for a specific location in a document, enabling the user to go to that location quickly. Bookmarks are helpful to mark a location where you are working. You can scroll to other parts of a document and then quickly go back to the bookmarked location. The Bookmark command is in the Links group on the Insert tab. After you click the command, the Bookmark dialog box displays, and you can designate the name of the bookmark, as shown in Figure 4.18. Bookmarks are inserted at the location of the insertion point. Bookmark names cannot contain spaces or hyphens; however, they may contain the underscore character to improve readability.

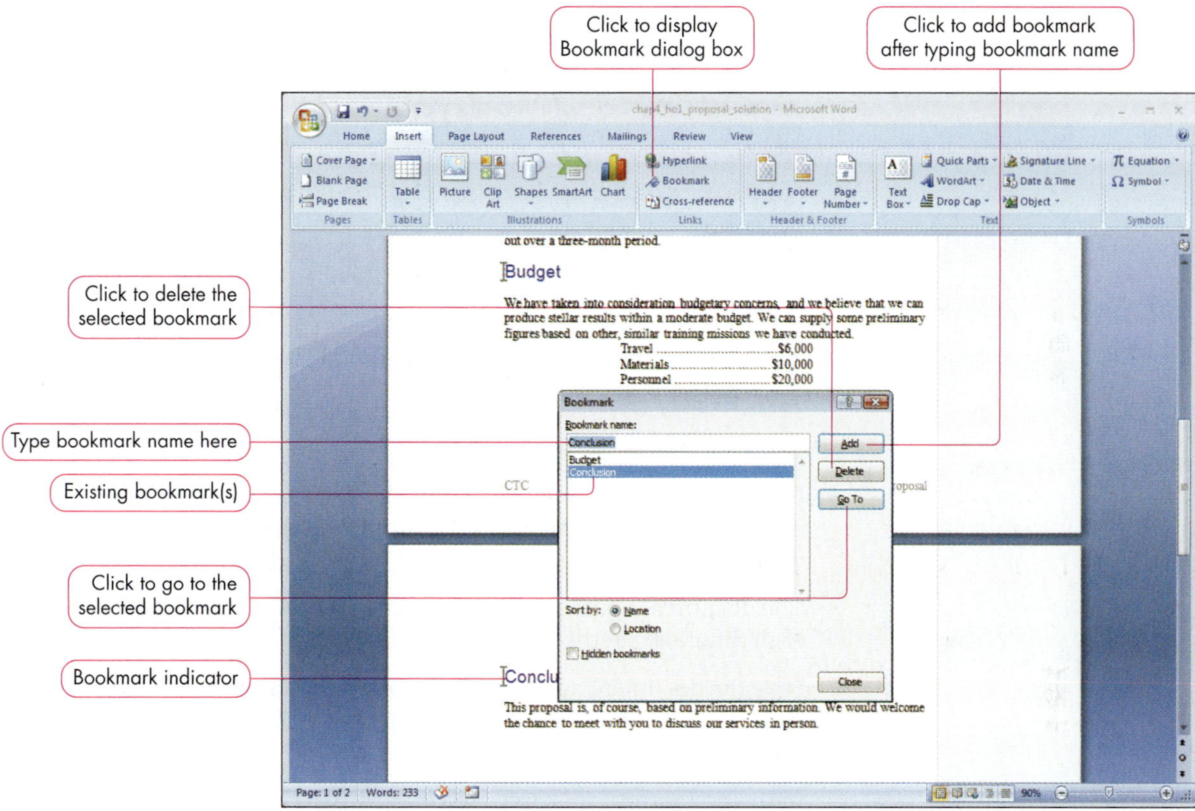

Figure 4.18 Bookmark a Location in the Document

After you insert a bookmark, you can click Bookmark on the Insert tab to see a list of bookmarks in the current document. Click a bookmark in the Bookmark name list and then click Go To to move the insertion point to that bookmarked location. You can also press Ctrl+G to open the Go To tab of the Find and Replace dialog box. When you click Bookmark in the *Go to what* section, a drop-down list of bookmarks is available to choose from.

TIP Using Numbers in Bookmark Names

You can use numbers within bookmark names, such as Quarter1. However, you cannot start a bookmark name with a number.

Hands-On Exercises

2 | Document Comparison, Mergers, and Navigation

Skills covered: 1. Compare and Combine Documents **2.** View Documents Side by Side **3.** Create Master Documents and Subdocuments **4.** Modify Master Documents and Subdocuments **5.** Use Document Map and Create Bookmarks

Step 1 Compare and Combine Documents

Refer to Figure 4.19 as you complete Step 1.

a. Click the **Review tab**. Click **Compare**, and then select **Compare** to display the Compare Documents dialog box.

b. Click the **Original document drop-down arrow** and select the *chap4_ho1_proposal_solution* document.

TROUBLESHOOTING: If the chap4_ho1_proposal_solution document does not display in the drop-down list, click the Browse for Original button to locate the document.

c. Click **Browse for Revised** beside the **Revised document** text box, and then browse to locate and open the *chap4_ho2_proposal2* document.

d. Click **More**, and then click **New document** below *Show changes in*, if necessary.

TROUBLESHOOTING: If the Comparison settings and Show changes sections do not display, click More to display them.

e. Click **OK** and then click **Yes** in the Microsoft Office Word message box that explains how the tracked changes in each document will be accepted before the document displays.

The document opens in a new window and contains markup balloons to indicate each difference in the two documents. The Reviewing Pane might also display.

f. Save the document as **chap4_ho2_compare_solution**. If the Reviewing Pane displays, click **Reviewing Pane** in the Tracking group on the Review tab to hide it.

In the first part of this exercise you compared two documents. In the next series of steps you combine the documents. Take time to notice how Word tracks the differences in compared versus combined documents.

g. Click **Compare** in the Compare group, and then select **Combine** to display the Combine Documents dialog box.

h. Click the **Original document drop-down arrow** and select the *chap4_ho1_proposal_solution* document. Click **Browse for Revised** and browse to locate the *chap4_ho2_proposal2* document.

i. Click More, and then click **New document** below *Show changes in*, if necessary. Click **OK** and then click **Continue with Merge**.

TROUBLESHOOTING: If the two documents you just merged display in small windows on the screen, click **Show Source Documents** in the Compare group on the Review tab, and then click **Hide Source Documents** to close them.

The document opens in a new window and contains markup balloons to indicate each difference in the two documents, as shown in Figure 4.19. Depending on your Track Changes settings, the balloons might display on either the left or right side of your document.

j. Save the document as **chap4_ho2_combine_solution**.

k. Leave both documents open for Step 2. If the two documents you just merged display in small windows on the screen, click **Show Source Documents** in the Compare group on the Review tab, and then click **Hide Source Documents** to close them.

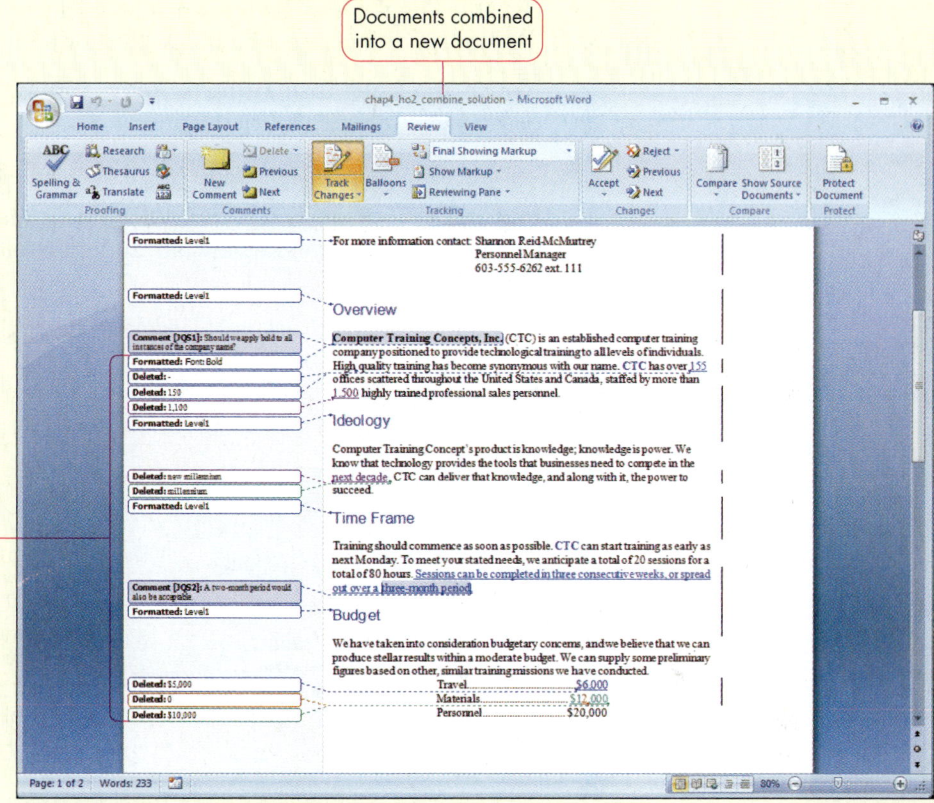

Figure 4.19 Combining Documents

Step 2
View Documents Side by Side

Refer to Figure 4.20 as you complete Step 2.

a. If *chap4_ho2_combine_solution* is not the active document, click the **View tab**, click **Switch Windows**, and then select *chap4_ho2_combine_solution* from the list. Click **View Side by Side** in the Window group.

Two windows display containing the files you created using the compare and combine features. Notice in the Window group on the View tab that Synchronous Scrolling is highlighted in an orange color to indicate the setting is on. As you scroll in one document, the other will scroll also.

TROUBLESHOOTING: If your view of one or both of the documents is insufficient, you can use the mouse to resize the window. Click and drag the border of the window until you reach an acceptable size to view the document information.

b. Scroll down to view the Time Frame paragraph and compare the differences.

In *chap4_ho2_compare_solution*, the last sentence in this section is deleted and displays in a markup balloon. In *the chap4_ho2_combine_solution*, the last sentence displays in the paragraph.

c. Click **Synchronous Scrolling** on the View tab, as shown in Figure 4.20, to turn the toggle off. Scroll down in the *chap4_ho2_combine_solution* document until the Conclusion paragraph displays.

Since the Synchronous Scrolling toggle is off, the *chap4_ho2_compare_solution* document does not scroll, and the Time Frame paragraph remains in view.

d. Scroll to the top of the page. Click the **Review tab**, click the **Tracking arrow**, click the **Display for Review arrow** (which currently shows *Final Showing Markup*), and then select **Final**. Do this for both documents.

Notice the bold formatting is only applied to the company name in the *chap4_ho2_combine_solution* document.

e. Close *chap4_ho2_compare_solution* without saving.

f. In the *chap4_ho2_combine_solution* document, click the **Accept arrow** in the Changes group on the Review tab, and then select **Accept All Changes in Document**.

g. Save and close the *chap4_ho2_combine_solution* document.

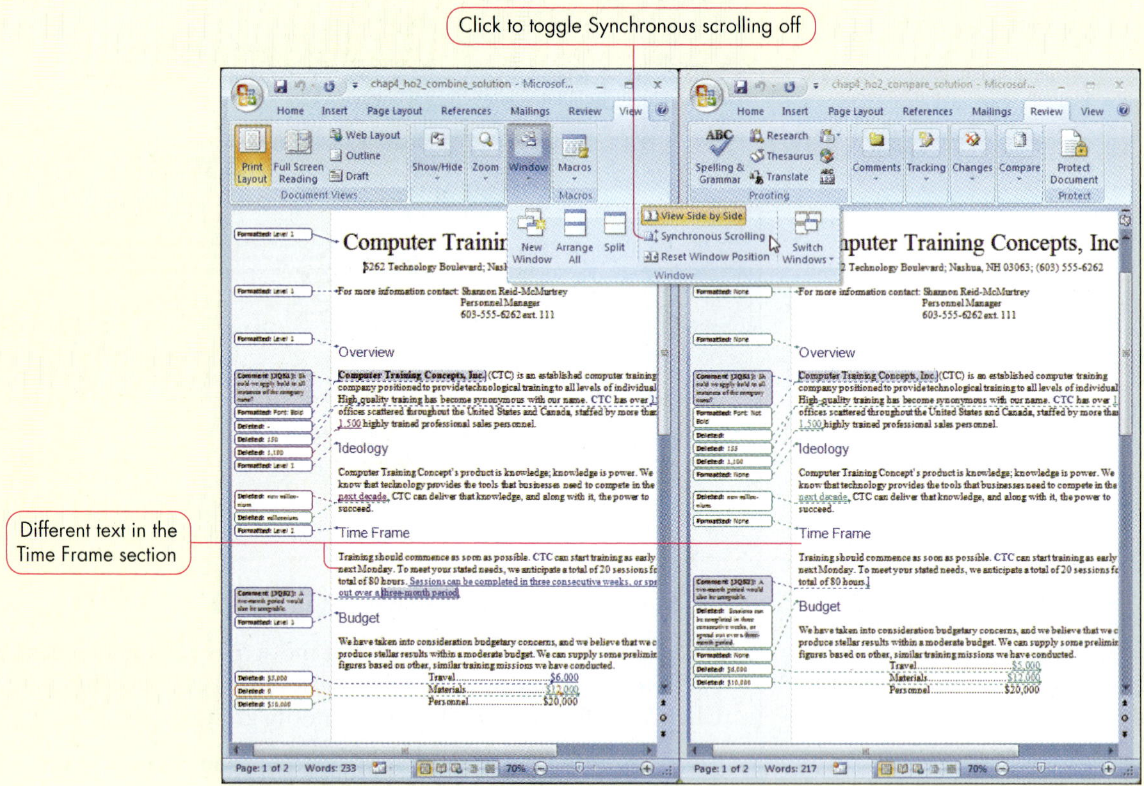

Figure 4.20 View Documents Side by Side

Step 3

Create Master Documents and Subdocuments

Refer to Figure 4.21 as you complete Step 3.

a. Open the *chap4_ho2_master* document and save it as **chap4_ho2_master_solution**.

b. Press **Ctrl+End** to move to the end of the document. Type the following headings for the subdocuments: **Overview**, **Ideology**, **Time Frame**, **Budget**, and **Conclusion**. Each word should have its own line.

c. Select the topics you just typed and then click **Heading 2** from the Quick Styles gallery on the Home tab. Click the **Outline** button on the status bar.

   The Outlining tab displays, and the document text displays in Outline view. Be sure all five headings are still selected before you perform the next step.

d. Click **Show Document** in the Master Document group to display more master document commands. Click **Create**.

   Individual subdocuments are created for the selected headings. A box surrounds each subdocument, and you see a subdocument icon in the top-left corner of each subdocument box, as shown in Figure 4.21. You also will see section breaks and other formatting marks if the Show/Hide ¶ feature is turned on.

e. Click **Collapse Subdocuments** in the Master Document group to collapse the subdocuments in the document and display the name and path where each subdocument is saved. Click **OK** if prompted to save changes to the master document.

f. Click **Expand Subdocuments** in the Master Document group to reopen and display the subdocuments.

g. Save the document.

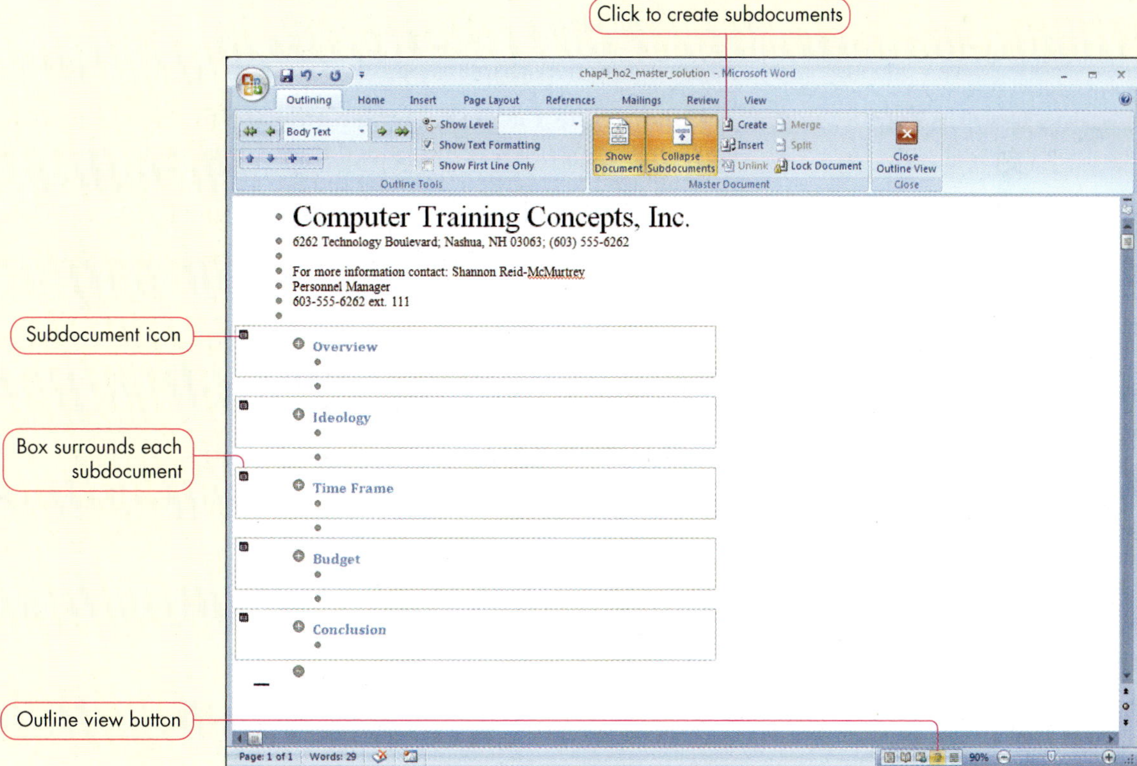

Figure 4.21 View Subdocuments in a Master Document

Step 4
Modify Master Documents and Subdocuments

Refer to Figure 4.22 as you complete Step 4.

a. Press **Ctrl+End** to move to the end of the master document.

b. Click **Insert** in the Master Document group to display the Insert Subdocument dialog box. If necessary, click the appropriate drive and folder in the Folders list on the left side of the Insert Subdocument dialog box. Choose the location where the original data files to accompany this book are located. Select *chap4_ho2_ background* and copy it to the folder where you saved *chap4_ho2_master_solution*. Select the copied file and click **Open** to insert this document into the master document. If prompted to rename the style in the subdocument, click **Yes**.

   The Background Information and Financial Statement paragraphs display as a subdocument at the bottom of the page.

c. Click within the third subdocument, Time Frame, which will eventually summarize the amount of time the company requires for training.

d. Click **Lock Document** in the Master Document group on the Outlining tab. Press the letter **a** on the keyboard.

   The padlock icon displays below the subdocument icon, and the Lock Document command is highlighted in an orange color to indicate the toggle is on. Attempts to type or edit text are not successful because the document is locked.

e. Click **Lock Document** a second time to unlock the document. Click below the Time Frame heading and type the text as shown in Figure 4.22. Then click **Save** to save changes to the Master document.

   TROUBLESHOOTING: Be sure the subdocument is unlocked so the changes you make will be reflected in the subdocument file as well.

f. Click **Close Outline View** in the Close group on the Outlining tab to return to Print Layout view.

   The document now displays on two pages.

g. Click **Show/Hide ¶** in the Paragraph group on the Home tab to display section breaks in the document, if necessary. Press **Ctrl+End** to view the end of the document. Place the insertion point on the *Section Break (Continuous)* mark that displays below the *Financial Statement* paragraph and then press **Delete**.

   The *Background Information* and *Financial Statement* paragraphs display on page one with the other subdocument headings.

   TROUBLESHOOTING: If the last two paragraphs still display on page two, position the insertion point on the left of the last paragraph mark in the document and press **Delete** to remove the empty second page.

h. Click **Show/Hide ¶** to toggle off paragraph marks.

i. Save and close the document. Exit Word if you will not continue with the next step at this time.

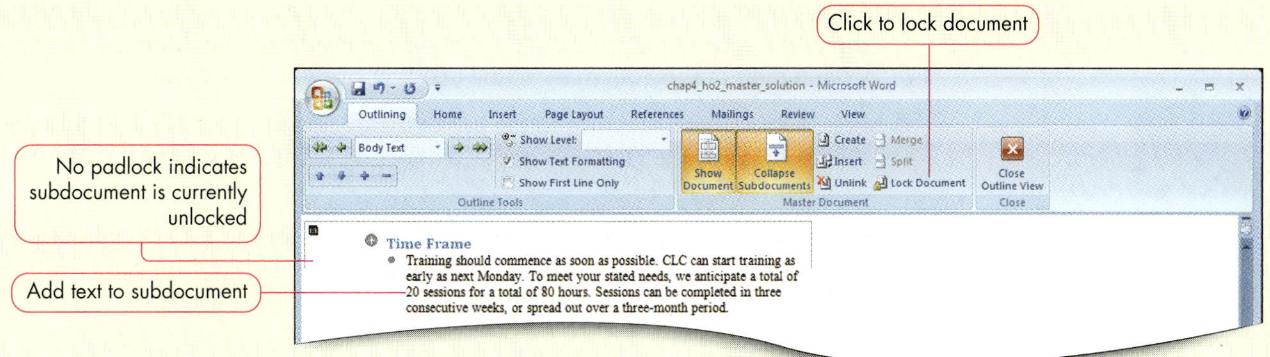

Figure 4.22 Modify a Subdocument

Step 5
Use Document Map and Create Bookmarks

Refer to Figure 4.23 as you complete Step 5.

a. Open the *chap4_ho1_proposal_solution* document you completed in Step 1 and save it as **chap4_ho2_map_solution**. Click the **View tab** and click **Thumbnails** in the Show/Hide group to display the Thumbnails pane on the left side of the screen.

   The Thumbnails appear as a separate pane on the left side of your screen. An orange border appears around the thumbnail of the currently viewed page.

b. Click the thumbnail for the second page.

   Word positions the insertion point at the beginning of the second page.

c. Click **Thumbnails** to hide the thumbnails pane. Click **Document Map**.

   The Document Map contains a list of text formatted with built-in heading styles. Like Thumbnails, it is a toggle. Clicking it again hides the Document Map pane.

d. Click **Overview** in the Document Map. Click **Computer Training Concepts, Inc.** in the Document Map.

   Because of your actions, Word moves the insertion point to the left side of the *Overview* heading near the top of the first page, and then moves it to the left of *Computer Training Concepts*. Because *Overview* and other headings are formatted with the Heading 2 style, they display in the Document Map.

e. Click **Budget** in the Document Map.

   You moved the insertion point and now you will insert a bookmark in this location.

f. Click the **Insert tab** and click **Bookmark** in the Links group. Type **Budget** in the Bookmark name text box, then click **Add**.

   Word inserts a bookmark with the name you entered. A large, gray-colored I-beam indicates the location of the bookmark.

   TROUBLESHOOTING: If you do not see the bookmark indicator, you can change a setting that enables it. Click the Office Button, then click Word Options. Click Advanced, and then scroll down and click the *Show bookmarks* check box in the Show document content section. Click OK to save the settings and return to the document.

g. Click **Conclusion** in the Document Map to position the insertion point on the top of the second page next to the *Conclusion* heading. Click **Bookmark**, type **Conclusion** in the Bookmark name text box, and then click **Add**.

h. Press **Ctrl+Home** to return to the top of the document. Press **Ctrl+G** to display the *Go To* tab of the Find and Replace dialog box. Click **Bookmark** in the *Go to what* list.

   Word displays the first bookmark name, Budget, in the Enter bookmark name text box as shown in Figure 4.23. If you click the *Enter bookmark name* drop-down arrow, the Conclusion bookmark also will display in the list.

i. Click **Go To**.

   The insertion point moves to the bookmark's location, and the Find and Replace dialog box remains onscreen in case you want to go to another bookmark.

j. Click **Close** to remove the Find and Replace dialog box. Click **Close** in the upper-right corner of the Document Map pane.

k. Save and close the file. Exit Word if you will not continue with the next exercise at this time.

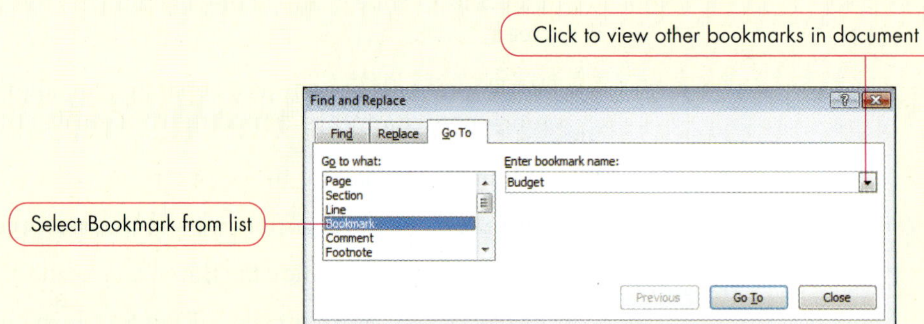

Figure 4.23 Go to a Bookmark

Reference Resources

Failure to acknowledge the source of information you use in a document is a form of plagiarism. Word includes a robust feature for tracking sources and producing the supplemental resources to display them.

Well-prepared documents often include notes that provide supplemental information or citations for sources quoted in the document. Some documents also contain other valuable supplemental components, such as a list of figures or legal references. Word 2007 includes many features that can help you create these supplemental references, as well as many others described in the following paragraphs.

In this section, you use Word to create citations used for reference pages, create a bibliography page that displays works cited in the document, and select from a list of writing styles that are commonly used to dictate the format of reference pages. You also create and modify footnote and endnote citations, which display at the bottom or end of the document.

Acknowledging a Source

Plagiarism is the act of using and documenting the ideas or writings of another as one's own.

It is common practice to use a variety of sources to supplement your own thoughts when writing a paper, report, legal brief, or many other types of document. Failure to acknowledge the source of information you use in a document is a form of plagiarism. *Webster's New Collegiate Dictionary* defines ***plagiarism*** as the act of using and documenting the ideas or writings of another as one's own. Plagiarism has serious moral and ethical implications and is taken very seriously in the academic community, and is often classified as academic dishonesty. It is also a violation of U.S. Copyright law, so it should be avoided in any professional and personal setting also.

To assist in your efforts to avoid plagiarism, which is frequently a thoughtless oversight rather than a malicious act, Word includes a robust feature for tracking sources and producing the supplemental resources to display them.

Create a Source

A ***citation*** is a note recognizing a source of information or a quoted passage.

Word provides the citation feature to track, compile, and display your research sources for inclusion in several types of supplemental references. To use this feature you use the Insert Citation command in the Citations & Bibliography group on the References tab to add data about each source, as shown in Figure 4.24. A ***citation*** is a note recognizing the source of information or a quoted passage. The Create Source dialog box includes fields to catalog information, such as author, date, publication name, page number, or Web site address, from the following types of sources:

- Book
- Book Section
- Journal Article
- Article in a Periodical
- Conference Proceedings
- Report
- Web Site
- Document from Web Site
- Electronic Source
- Art
- Sound Recording
- Performance
- Film
- Interview
- Patent
- Case
- Miscellaneous

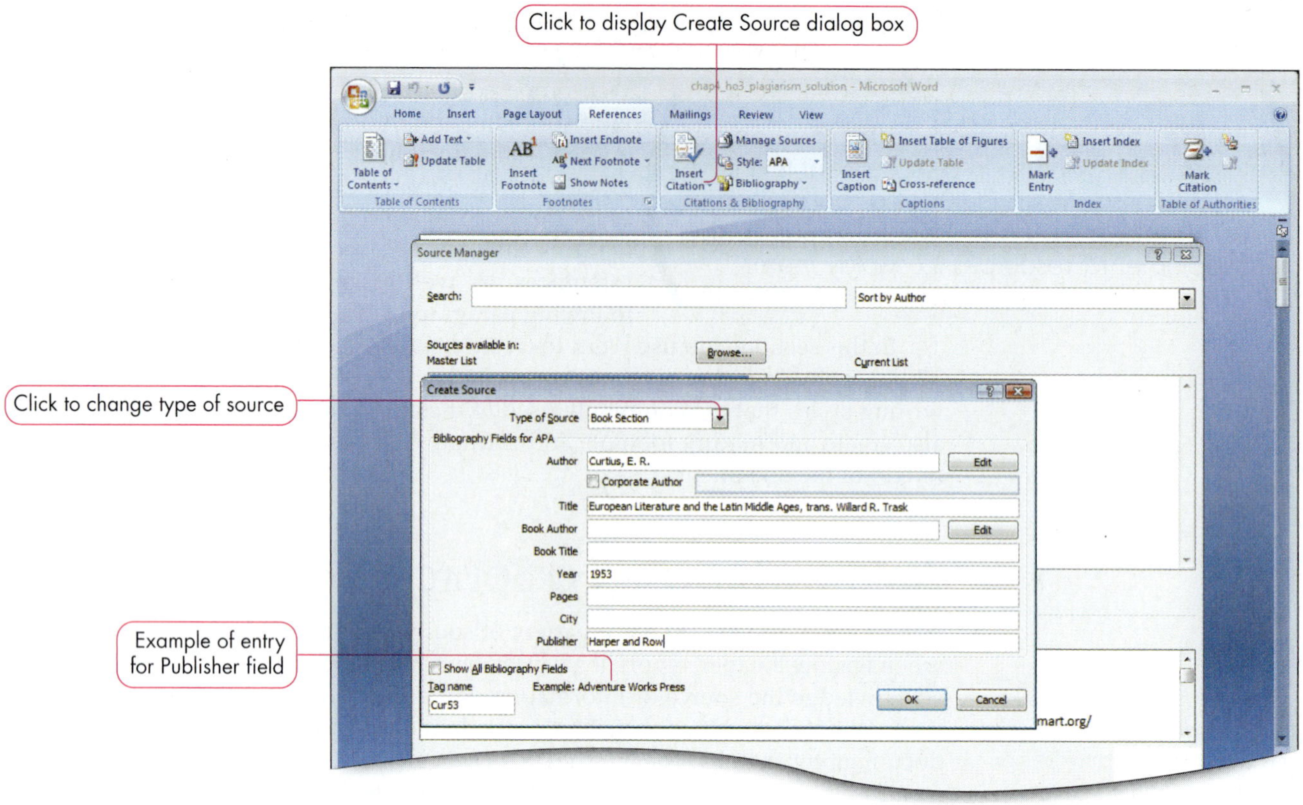

Click to display Create Source dialog box

Click to change type of source

Example of entry for Publisher field

Figure 4.24 Add a Source Citation

After you create the citation sources, you can insert them into a document using the Insert Citation command. When you click the command, a list of your sources displays; click a source from the list, and the proper citation format is inserted in your document.

Share and Search for a Source

The ***Master List*** is a database of all citation sources created in Word.

The ***Current List*** includes all citation sources you use in the current document.

After you add sources they are saved in a Master List. The ***Master List*** is a database of all citation sources created in Word on a particular computer. The source also is stored in the ***Current List***, which contains all sources you use in the current document. Sources saved in the Master List can be used in any Word document. This feature is very helpful to those who use the same sources on multiple occasions. Master Lists are stored in XML format, so you can share the Master List file with coworkers or other authors, eliminating the need to retype the information and to ensure accuracy. The Master List file is stored in \Application Data\Microsoft\Bibliography, which is a subfolder of the user account folder stored under C:\Documents and Settings. For example, a path to the Master File might be C:\Documents and Settings\John Q. Student\Application Data\Microsoft\Bibliography\Sources.xml.

The Source Manager dialog box (see Figure 4.25) displays the Master List you created, and you also can browse to find others. If you do not have access to a Master List on a local or network drive, you can e-mail the Master List file. After you open the Master List, you can copy sources to your Current List. You also can use the Research and Reference Pane to search external libraries for Master Lists of sources. If a library or host service makes its sources available in a format compatible with Office 2007, you can import its files, open the Master File, and insert a citation, avoiding the need to fill out a new Source form in Word.

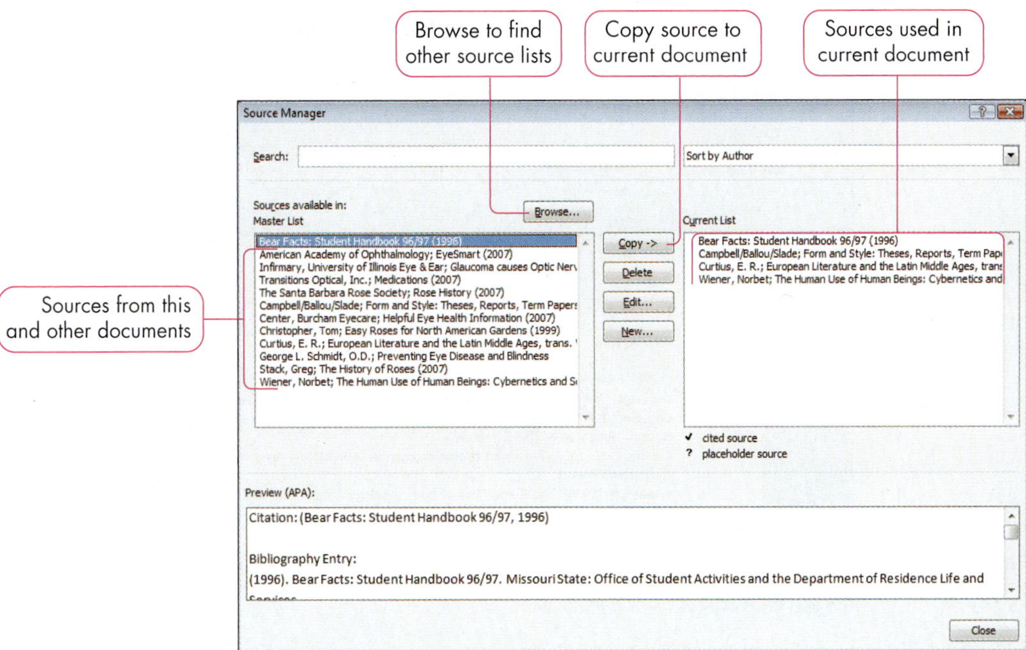

Figure 4.25 Source Manager Dialog Box

Creating a Bibliography

A ***bibliography*** is a list of works cited or consulted by an author in a document.

A ***bibliography*** is a list of works cited or consulted by an author and should be included with the document when published. Some reference manuals use the terms Works Cited or References instead of Bibliography. A bibliography is just one form of reference that gives credit to the sources you consulted or quoted in the preparation of your paper. The addition of a bibliography to your completed work demonstrates respect for the material consulted and proves that you are not plagiarizing. It also gives the reader an opportunity to validate your references for accuracy.

Word includes a bibliography feature that makes the addition of this reference page very easy. After you add the sources using the Insert Citation feature, you click Bibliography in the Citations & Bibliography group on the References tab, and then click Insert Bibliography. Any sources used in the current document will display in the appropriate format as a Bibliography, as shown in Figure 4.26.

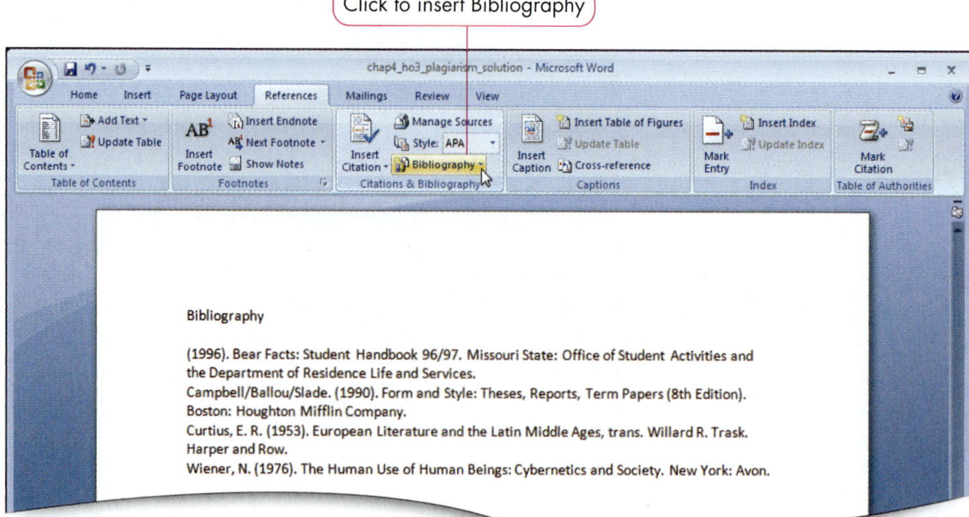

Figure 4.26 Bibliography

Selecting the Writing Style

When research papers are prepared the author often must conform to a particular writing style. The writing style, also called an editorial style, consists of rules and guidelines set forth by a publisher of a research journal to ensure consistency in presentation of research documents. Some of the presentation consistencies that a style enforces are use of punctuation and abbreviations, format of headings and tables, presentation of statistics, and citation of references. The style guidelines differ depending on the discipline the research topic comes from. For example, the APA style originates with the American Psychological Association, but many other disciplines use this style as well. Another common style is MLA, which is sanctioned by the Modern Language Association. The topic of your paper and the audience you write to will determine which style you should use while writing.

Word 2007 incorporates several writing style guidelines, which makes it easier for you to generate supplemental references in the required format. The Style list in the Citations & Bibliography group on the References tab includes the most commonly used international styles, as shown in Figure 4.27. When you select the style before creating the bibliography, the citations that appear in the bibliography will be formatted exactly as required by that style.

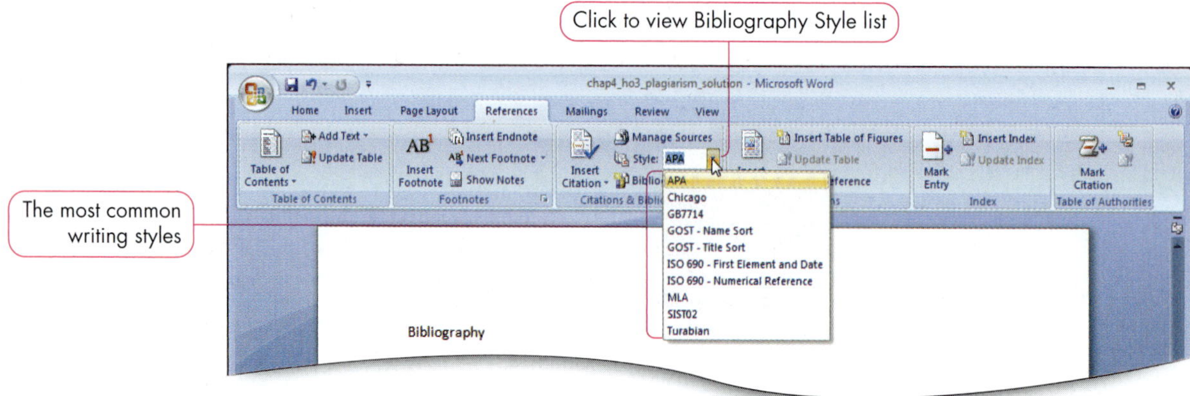

Figure 4.27 Style Options

Creating and Modifying Footnotes and Endnotes

A ***footnote*** is a citation that appears at the bottom of a page.

An ***endnote*** is a citation that appears at the end of a document.

A ***footnote*** is a citation that appears at the bottom of a page, and an ***endnote*** is a citation that appears at the end of a document. You use footnotes or endnotes to credit the sources you quote or cite in your document. You also can use footnotes or endnotes to provide supplemental information about a topic that is too distracting to include in the body of the document. Footnotes, endnotes, and bibliographies often contain the same information. Your use of one of the three options is determined by the style of paper (MLA for example) or by the person who oversees your research. When you use a bibliography, the information about a source is displayed only one time at the end of the paper, and the exact location in the document that uses information from the source may not be obvious. When you use a footnote, the information about a source displays on the specific page where a quote or information appears. When you use endnotes, the information about a source displays only at the end of the document; however, the number that identifies the endnote displays on each page, and you can use several references to the same source throughout the document.

The References tab includes the Insert Footnote and Insert Endnote commands. If you click the Footnote and Endnote Dialog Box Launcher, the Footnote and Endnote dialog box opens, and you can modify the location of the notes and the format of the numbers. By default, Word sequentially numbers footnotes with Arabic numerals (1, 2, and 3) as shown in Figure 4.28. Endnotes are numbered with lowercase Roman numerals (i, ii, and iii) based on the location of the note within the document. If you add or delete notes, Word renumbers the remaining notes automatically.

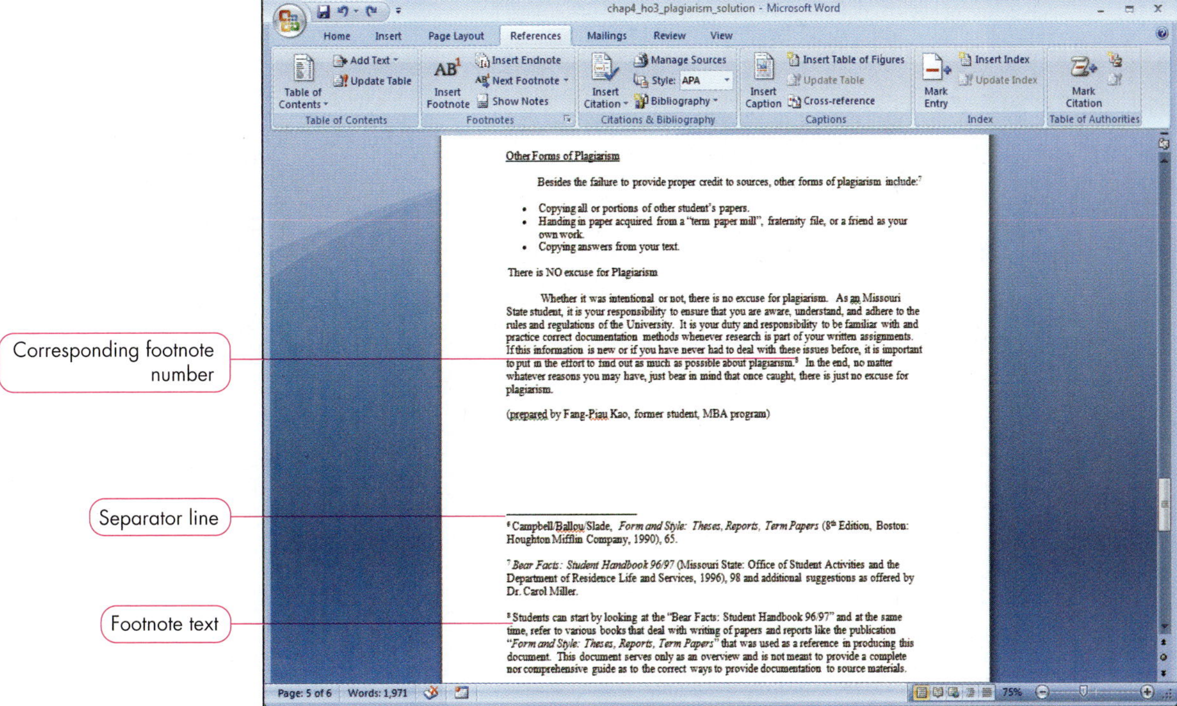

Figure 4.28 Document Containing Footnotes

You can easily make modifications to footnotes and endnotes. In Print Layout view, scroll to the bottom of the page (or for endnotes, to the end of the document or section), click inside the note, and then edit it. In Draft view, double-click the footnote or endnote reference mark to see the Footnotes or Endnotes pane, then edit the note.

TIP Relocating a Footnote or Endnote

If you created a note in the wrong location, select the note reference mark, cut it from its current location, and then paste it in the correct location within the document text. You also can use the drag-and-drop method to move a selected note reference mark to a different location.

Hands-On Exercises

3 | Reference Resources

Skills covered: 1. Create and Search for a Source **2.** Select a Writing Style and Insert a Bibliography **3.** Create and Modify Footnotes **4.** Convert Footnotes to Endnotes and Modify Endnotes

Step 1
Create and Search for a Source

Refer to Figure 4.29 as you complete Step 1.

a. Open the *chap4_ho3_plagiarism* document and save it as **chap4_ho3_ plagiarism_solution**.

b. Click the **References tab**, click **Manage Sources** in the Citations & Bibliography group, and then click **New** in the middle of the dialog box.

   Because you want to create a citation source without inserting it into the document, you use the Source Manager instead of Create Citation. After you click New in the Source Manager, the Create Source dialog box displays.

c. Click the **Type of Source drop-down arrow** and select **Book Section**. Type the source information in the Bibliography fields as shown in Figure 4.29, and then click **OK** to add the source to your document and return to the Source Manager dialog box.

d. Click **Browse** in the Source Manager dialog box to display the Open Source List dialog box. Click the appropriate drive and folder in the Folders list on the left side of the Open Source List dialog box. Choose the location where the original data files to accompany this book are located. Select *chap4_ho3_plmasterlist*, and then click **OK**.

   You return to the Source Manager dialog box, and three sources display in the *Sources available in* box.

e. Click the first source entry, if necessary, to select it. Then press and hold **Shift** and select the last entry. Click **Copy** to insert the sources into the current document.

   The three sources you copied and the one source you created display in the Current List box.

f. Click **Close** to return to the document. Save the document.

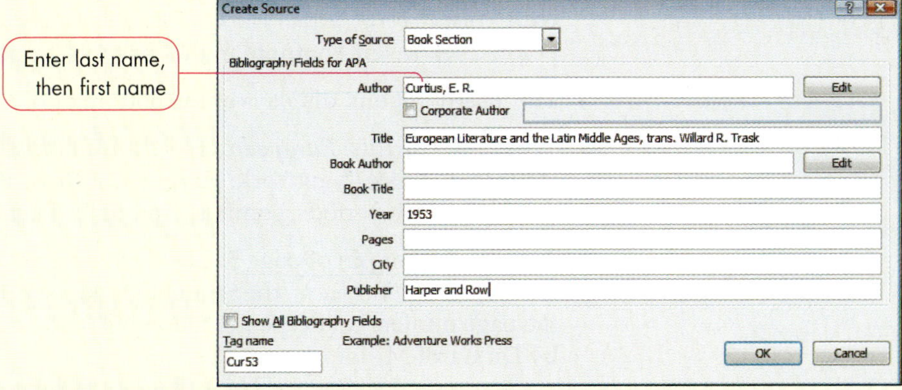

Figure 4.29 Add a New Source

Step 2
Select a Writing Style and Insert a Bibliography

Refer to Figure 4.30 as you complete Step 2.

a. Click the **Style arrow** in the Citations and Bibliography group and select **MLA**.

b. Press **Ctrl+End** to position the insertion point at the end of the document, press **Ctrl+Enter** to add a blank page, type **Bibliography** at the top of the new page, and then press **Enter** two times.

c. Click **Bibliography** in Citations and Bibliography, and then click **Insert Bibliography**.

   The sources cited in the document display in the MLA format for bibliographies, as shown in Figure 4.30.

d. Click the **Style arrow** again and select **APA**.

   The format of the bibliography changes to reflect the standards of the APA style.

e. Save the document.

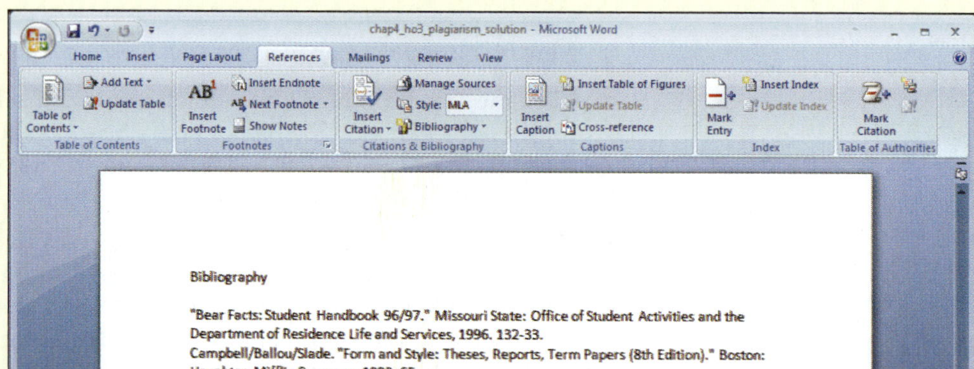

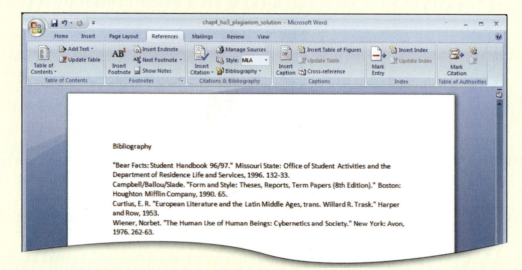

Figure 4.30 Bibliography in MLA Style

Step 3
Create and Modify Footnotes

Refer to Figure 4.31 as you complete Step 3.

a. Scroll to the top of page 3. Click one time at the end of the paragraph that begins with *Ernst Robert Curtius's term "the Latin Middle Ages"* to move the insertion point. Click **Insert Footnote** in the Footnotes group on the References tab.

   The insertion point displays at the bottom of the page, below the horizontal line.

b. Type **E. R. Curtius, *European Literature and the Latin Middle Ages*, trans. Willard R. Trask (New York: Harper and Row, 1953), 27**. Format the endnote as displayed with periods, commas, and italic. Do not bold the citation.

c. Scroll to the bottom of page 5. Click one time at the end of the seventh footnote, a reference to *Bear Facts*, the Student Handbook. Remove the period that follows the page number and type the following: **and additional suggestions as offered by Dr. Carol Miller.**

   You edited the footnote by adding text to it, as shown in Figure 4.31.

d. Save the document.

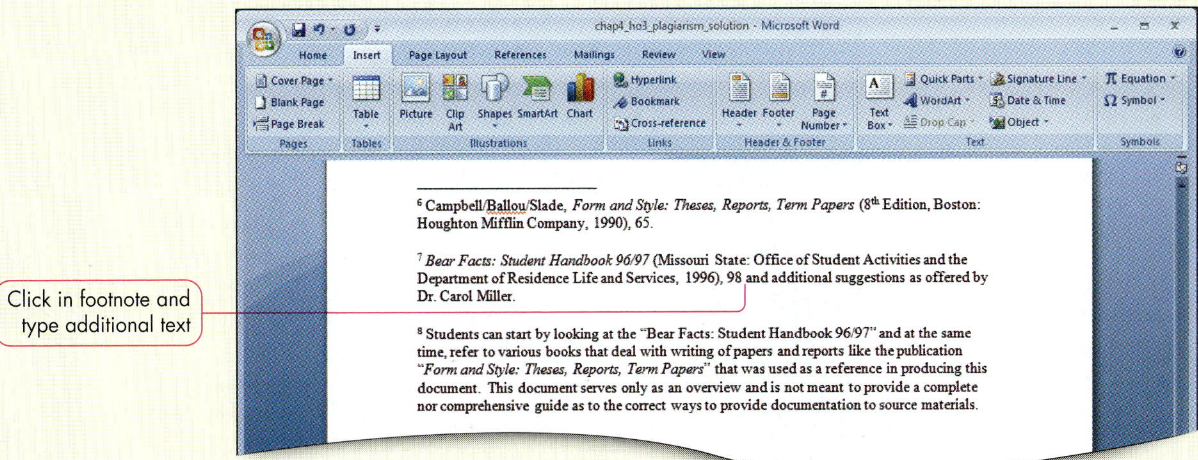

Figure 4.31 Modify a Footnote

Step 4
Convert Footnotes to Endnotes and Modify Endnotes

Refer to Figure 4.32 as you complete Step 4.

a. Click the **Footnote and Endnote Dialog Box Launcher**. Click **Convert**, click **Convert all footnotes to endnotes,** and then click **OK.** Click **Close** to close the Footnote and Endnote dialog box.

All footnotes relocate to the last page, below the Bibliography, and the number format is changed to Roman numerals.

b. Scroll to the bottom of page 3. Move the insertion point to the end of the first example paragraph, which ends with *subject to law*. Click **Insert Endnote** and type **Norbet Wiener, *The Human Use of Human Beings: Cybernetics and Society* (New York: Avon, 1976), 262–63.** Format the endnote as displayed.

The endnote displays at the end of the document and the endnote numbers adjust for the addition, as shown in Figure 4.32.

c. Save and close the document. Exit Word if you will not continue with the next exercise at this time.

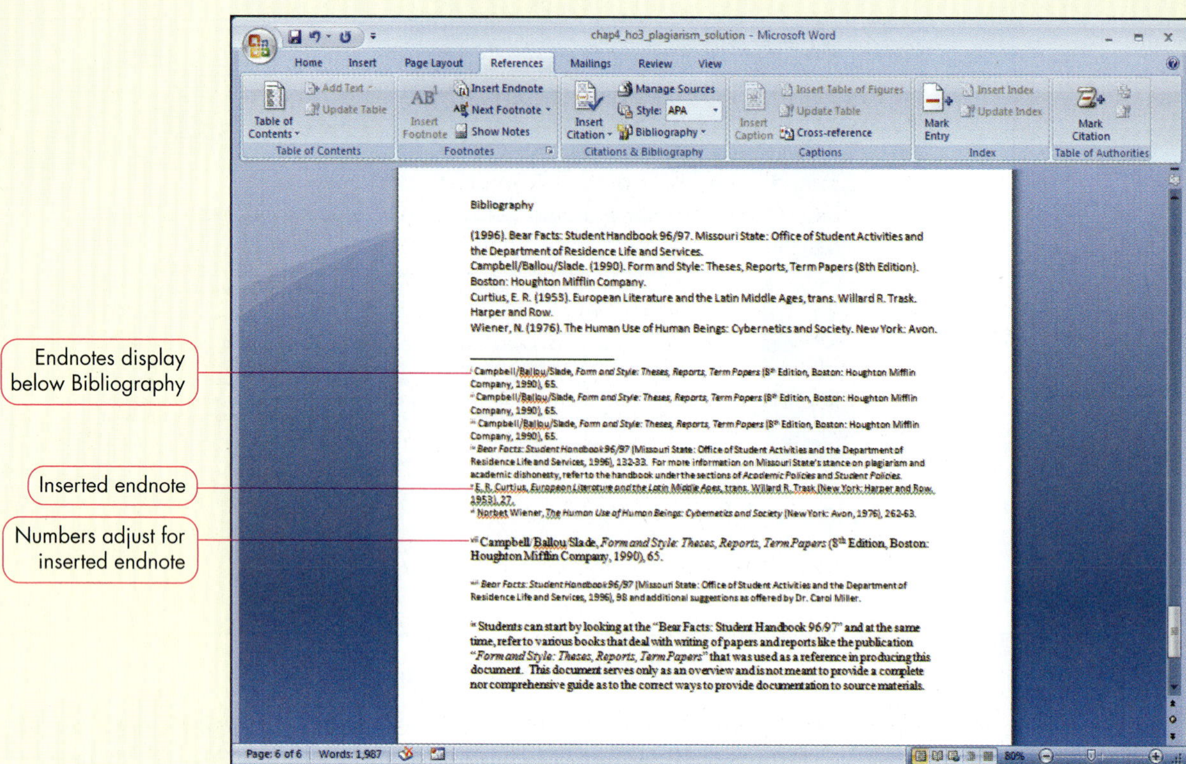
Endnotes display below Bibliography
Inserted endnote
Numbers adjust for inserted endnote

Figure 4.32 Modify an Endnote

Additional Reference Resources

The previous section mentioned several types of reference features that should be used when a document refers to outside information or sources. Some reference features are used less frequently, yet are valuable for creating professional quality documents. These supplements include a list of captions used on figures, a list of figures presented in a document, references to other locations in a document, and a list of legal sources referenced. You also can attach information that refers to the contents and origin of a document.

Some reference features are used less frequently, yet are valuable for creating professional quality documents. You also can attach information that refers to the contents and origin of a document.

In this section, you add descriptions to visual elements and create a list of the visuals used in a document. You create a cross-reference, or note that refers the reader to another location in the document, and you create a list of references from a legal document. Finally, you modify the properties associated with a document.

Adding Figure References

A ***caption*** is a descriptive title for an equation, a figure, or a table.

Documents and books often contain several images, charts, or tables. For example, this textbook contains several screenshots in each project. To help readers refer to the correct image or table, you can insert a caption. A ***caption*** is a descriptive title for an image, a figure, or a table. To add a caption click Insert Caption in the Captions group on the References tab. By default, Word assigns a number to the equation, figure, or table at the beginning of the caption. When you click Insert Caption, the Caption dialog box appears, as shown in Figure 4.33, and you can edit the default caption by adding descriptive text.

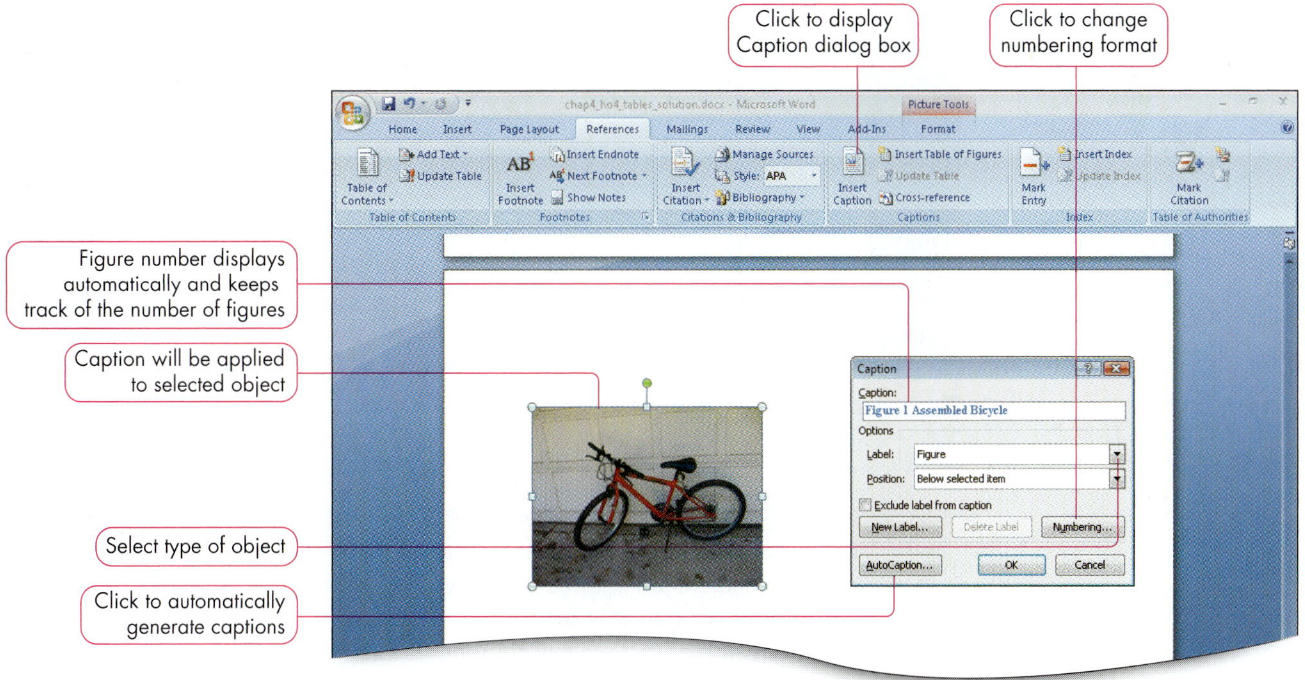

Figure 4.33 Caption Dialog Box

To automatically generate captions, click AutoCaption in the Caption dialog box. In the *Add caption when inserting* list, in the AutoCaption dialog box, click the check box next to the element type for which you want to create AutoCaptions. Specify the default caption text in the *Use label* text box, and specify the location of the caption by clicking the Position drop-down arrow. If your document will contain several captions, this feature helps you to ensure each caption is named and numbered sequentially.

Inserting a Table of Figures

A ***table of figures*** is a list of the captions in a document.

If your document includes pictures, charts and graphs, slides, or other illustrations along with a caption, you can include a ***table of figures***, or list of the captions, as a reference. To build a table of figures, Word searches a document for captions, sorts the captions by number, and displays the table of figures in the document. A table of figures is placed after the table of contents for a document. The Insert Table of Figures command is in the Captions group on the References tab. The Table of Figures dialog box, shown in Figure 4.34, enables you to select page number, format, and caption label options.

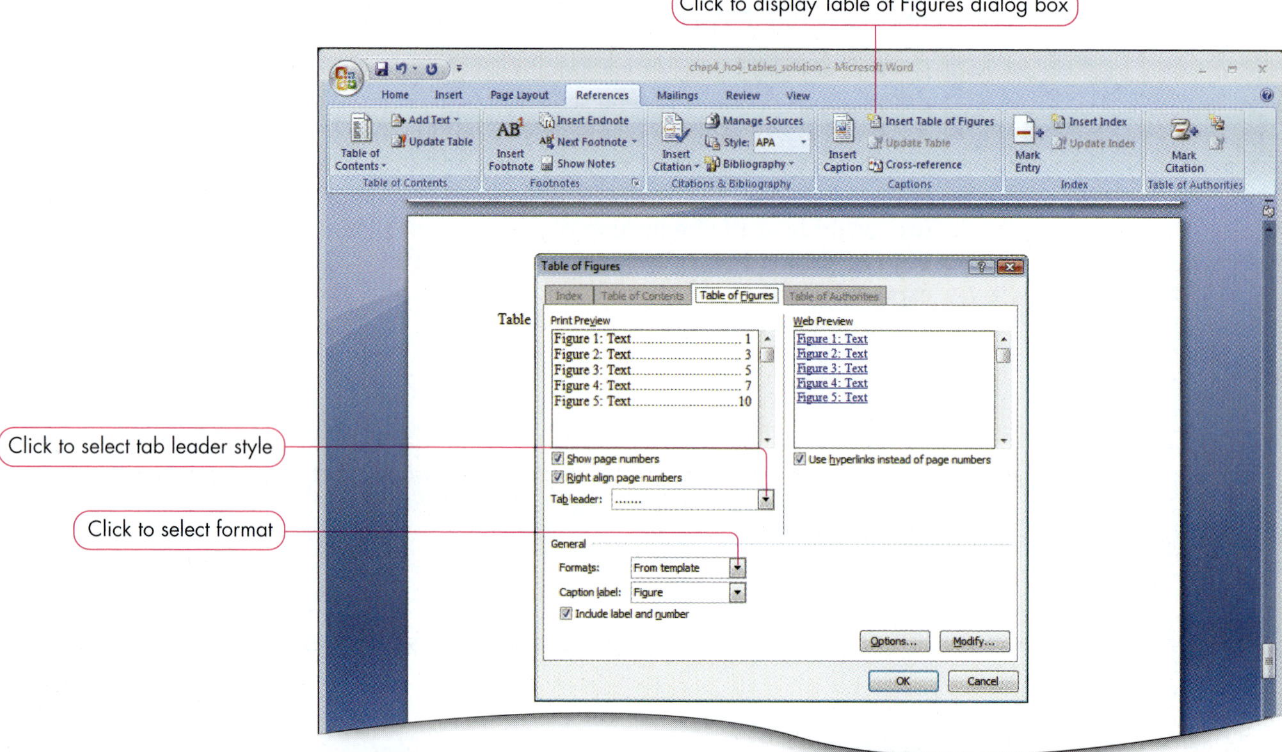

Figure 4.34 The Table of Figures Dialog Box

TIP Update a Table of Figures

If the figures or figure captions in a document change or are removed, you should update the table of figures. To update the table, right-click on any table entry to select the entire table and display a menu. Click Update Field and then choose between the options Update Page Numbers only or Update entire table. If significant changes have been made, you should update the entire table.

Adding Legal References

A ***table of authorities*** is used in legal documents to reference cases and other documents referred to in a legal brief.

A ***table of authorities*** is used in legal documents to reference cases, rules, treaties, and other documents referred to in a legal brief. You typically compile the table of authorities on a separate page at the beginning of a legal document as shown in Figure 4.35. Word's table of authorities feature enables you to track, compile, and display citations, or references to specific legal cases and other legal documents, to be included in the table of authorities. Before you generate the table of authorities, you must indicate which citations you want to include using the Mark Citation command in the Table of Authorities group on the References tab. To mark citations, select text and then click Mark Citation. After you mark the citations, click Insert Table of Authorities in the Table of Authorities group on the References tab to generate the table at the location of your insertion point.

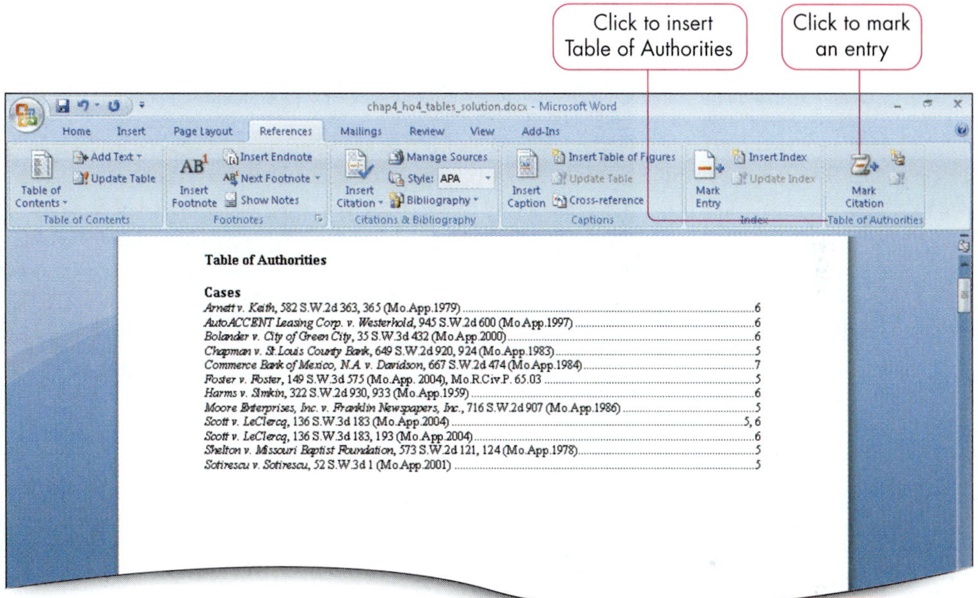

Table of Authorities

Cases

Arnett v. Keith, 582 S.W.2d 363, 365 (Mo.App.1979) 6
AutoACCENT Leasing Corp. v. Westerhold, 945 S.W.2d 600 (Mo.App.1997) 6
Bolander v. City of Green City, 35 S.W.3d 432 (Mo.App.2000) 6
Chapman v. St.Louis County Bank, 649 S.W.2d 920, 924 (Mo.App.1983) 5
Commerce Bank of Mexico, N.A. v. Davidson, 667 S.W.2d 474 (Mo.App.1984) 7
Foster v. Foster, 149 S.W.3d 575 (Mo.App. 2004), Mo.R.Civ.P. 65.03 5
Harms v. Simkin, 322 S.W.2d 930, 933 (Mo.App.1959) 6
Moore Enterprises, Inc. v. Franklin Newspapers, Inc., 716 S.W.2d 907 (Mo.App.1986) 5
Scott v. LeClercq, 136 S.W.3d 183 (Mo.App.2004) 5, 6
Scott v. LeClercq, 136 S.W.3d 183, 193 (Mo.App.2004) 6
Shelton v. Missouri Baptist Foundation, 573 S.W.2d 121, 124 (Mo.App.1978) 5
Sotirescu v. Sotirescu, 52 S.W.3d 1 (Mo.App.2001) 5

Figure 4.35 A Table of Authorities

To modify a table of authorities entry, you must display the table of authorities fields by clicking Show/Hide ¶ in the Paragraph group on the Home tab. Locate the entry that you wish to modify and edit the text inside the quotation marks. Do not change the entry in the finished table of authorities, or the next time you update the table of authorities, your changes will be lost.

To delete a table of authorities entry, select the entire entry field, including the braces {}, and press Delete. After you modify or delete a marked entry, click Update Table in the Table of Authorities group on the References tab to display the changes in the table.

Creating Cross-References

A ***cross-reference*** is a note that refers the reader to another location for more information about a topic.

A ***cross-reference*** is a note that refers the reader to another location for more information about a topic. You can create cross-references to headings, bookmarks, footnotes, endnotes, captions, and tables. A typical cross-reference looks like this: *See page 4 for more information about local recreation facilities.* For files you make available via e-mail or on an intranet, you can create an electronic cross-reference. However, if you are distributing printed copies of your document, you need printed references so the readers can find the location themselves.

To create a cross-reference, position the insertion point in the location where the reference occurs. Display the References tab and click Cross-reference in the Captions group. When the Cross-reference dialog box displays, as shown in Figure 4.36, you choose the type of reference (such as Heading, Bookmark, Figure, or Footnote) and then the reference element to display (such as page number or paragraph text). You can specify whether it displays as a hyperlink in the document, causing a ScreenTip to appear when the mouse pointer is over the cross-reference.

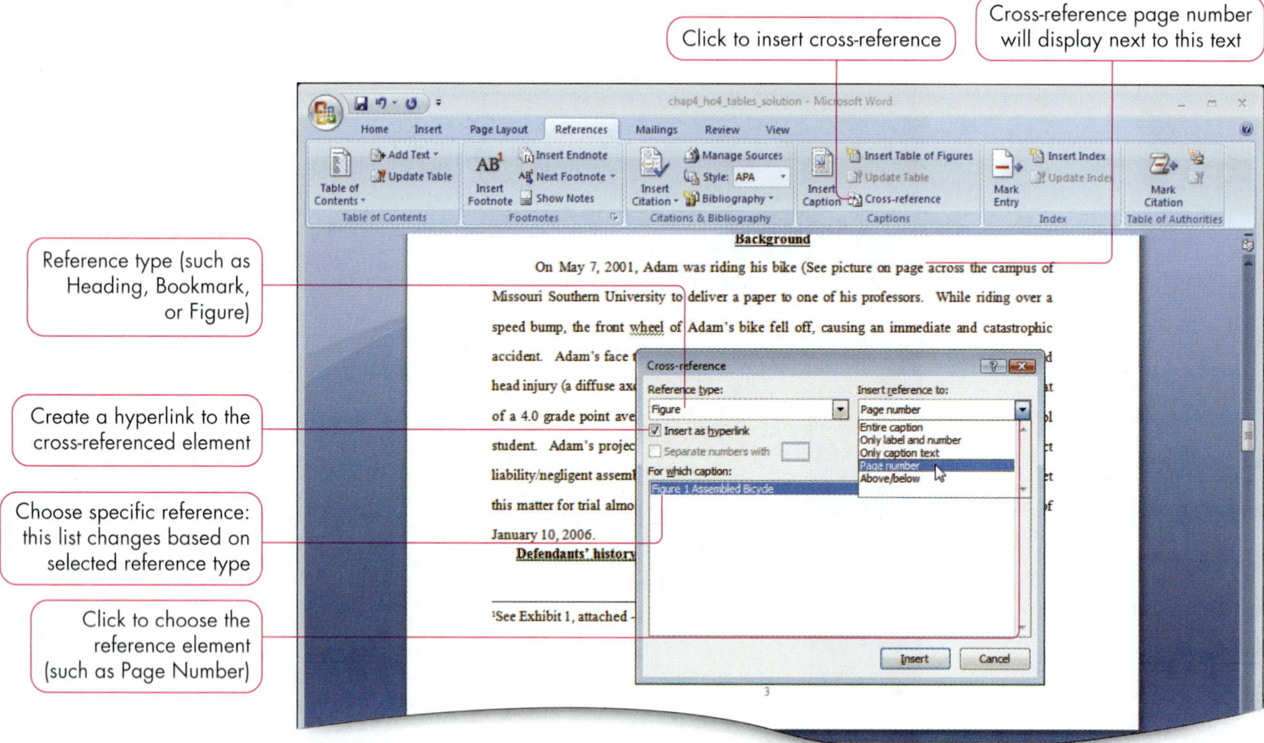

Figure 4.36 Insert a Cross-Reference

Modifying Document Properties

The ***Document Information panel*** allows you to enter descriptive information about a document.

Sometimes, you want to record information about a document but do not want to include the information directly in the document window. For example, you might want to record some notes to yourself about a document, such as the document's author, purpose, or intended audience. To help maintain documents, you can use the ***Document Information panel*** to store descriptive information about a document, such as a title, subject, author, keywords, and comments. When you create a document summary and save the document, Word saves the document summary with the document. You can update the document summary at any time by opening the Document Information panel for the respective document. To display the Document Information panel, as shown in Figure 4.37, click the Office Button, point to Prepare, and then select Properties.

Sometimes, you want to record information about a document but do not want to include the information directly in the document window . . . you can use the ***Document Information panel*** to store descriptive information about a document, such as a title, subject, author, keywords, and comments.

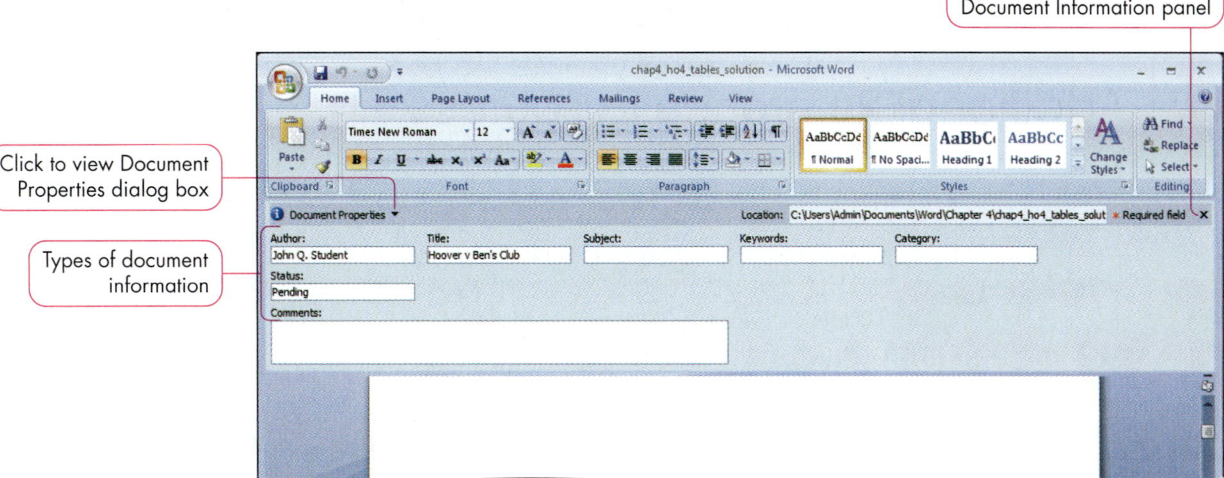

Figure 4.37 Document Information Panel

Search for a Document Using Document Properties

After you insert information into the Document Information panel, you can use it as search criteria when using the Windows search tool. The information entered as document title, comments, author, or any other field will be searched in the same manner as text that displays in the document.

Customize Document Properties

In addition to creating, modifying, and viewing a document summary, you might want to customize the document properties in the Document Information panel. When you click the arrow next to Document Properties and then click Advanced Properties, the Properties dialog box displays. The Custom tab of the Properties dialog box enables you to add other properties and assign values to those properties. For example, you might want to add the *Date completed* property and specify an exact date for reference. This date would reflect the completion date, not the date the file was last saved—in case someone opens a file and saves it without making changes. You also might create a field to track company information such as warehouse location or product numbers.

You can create and modify document summaries directly from the Open dialog box, through Windows Explorer, or in other file management windows. You do not have to create the document summary when the document is open within Microsoft Word.

Print Document Properties

You can print document properties to have hard copies to store in a filing cabinet for easy reference. To do this, display the Print dialog box, click the Print what drop-down arrow, select Document properties, and click OK.

Hands-On Exercises

4 | Additional Reference Resources

Skills covered: 1. Add Captions and Create a Table of Figures **2**. Create a Table of Authorities **3.** Create a Cross-Reference **4.** Modify Document Properties

Step 1
Add Captions and Create a Table of Figures

Refer to Figure 4.38 as you complete Step 1.

a. Open the *chap4_ho4_tables* document and save it as **chap4_ho4_ tables_solution**.

b. Press **Ctrl+End** to view the end of the document. Click once on the picture to select it. Click the **References tab** and click **Insert Caption** in the Captions group.

   The Caption dialog box displays, and the insertion point is positioned at the end of the caption text that displays automatically.

c. Press **Spacebar** to insert a space and then type **Assembled Bicycle** after the existing text in the Caption box, as shown in Figure 4.38. Click **OK**.

   The caption *Figure 1 Assembled Bicycle* displays below the picture in a text box.

d. Press **Ctrl+Home** to view page 1. Press **Ctrl+Enter** to insert a page, move your insertion point to the top of the new page and then type **Table of Figures**. Press **Enter** two times.

e. Click **Insert Table of Figures** in the Captions group to display the Table of Figures dialog box. Click **OK**.

   The table displays, showing only one entry at this time.

f. Save the document.

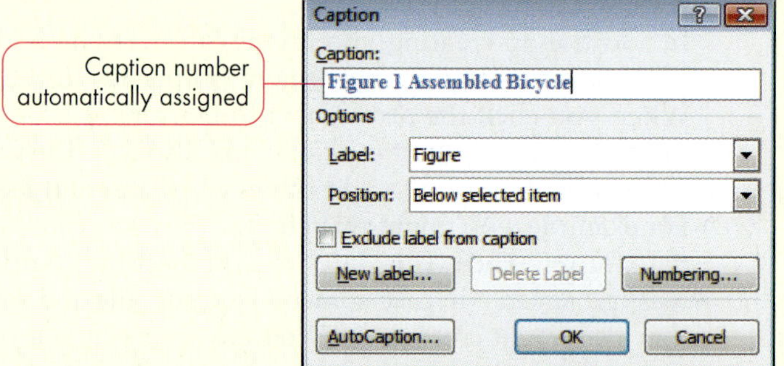

Figure 4.38 Add a Caption to a Picture

Step 2
Create a Table of Authorities

Refer to Figure 4.39 as you complete Step 2.

a. Go to page 4 in the document. Locate the *Shelton v. Missouri Baptist Foundation* case, and select the case information from *Shelton* up to and including the date *(1978)*. Select the closing parenthesis but not the comma after it. Click **Mark Citation** in the Table of Authorities group on the References tab. Click **Mark All**, as shown in Figure 4.39, and then click **Close**.

b. Search through the remainder of the document and mark all case references. Click the **Home tab**, and then click **Show/Hide ¶** in the Paragraph group to turn off display of formatting marks.

c. Press **Ctrl+Home** to position the insertion point at the beginning of the document, press **Ctrl+Enter** to add a blank page, type **Table of Authorities** at the top of the new page, and then press **Enter** one time. Click the **References tab** and then click **Insert Table of Authorities** in the Table of Authorities group. Click **OK**.

   The Table of Authorities, which lists information about the cases mentioned in the brief, is shown in Figure 4.35.

d. Save the document.

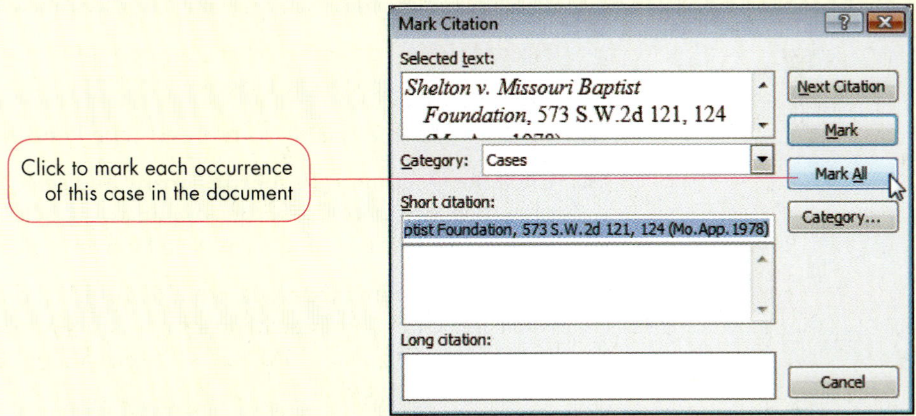

Figure 4.39 Mark Citation Dialog Box

Step 3
Create a Cross-Reference

Refer to Figure 4.40 as you complete Step 3.

a. Scroll to page 3 and place the insertion point on the right side of the word *bike* in the first sentence of the *Background* section.

b. Press **Spacebar** and type **(See picture on page**. Click the **References tab**, if necessary, and click **Cross-reference** in the Captions group. Click the **Reference type drop-down arrow** and select **Figure**, click **Figure 1** in the **For which caption** list, click the **Insert reference to drop-down arrow** and select **Page number** as shown in Figure 4.40, and then click **Insert**.

   The cross-reference displays 8, the page where the picture displays.

c. Click **Close** to close the Cross-reference dialog box. Type **)** to end the cross-reference.

   Hold your mouse over the cross-reference page number and view the ScreenTip that instructs you to press **Ctrl** while you click on the number *8* to move the insertion point to the location of the picture.

d. Save the document.

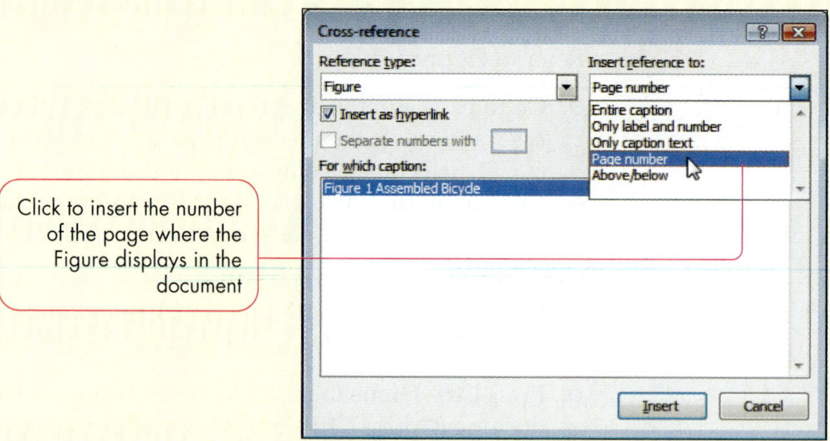

Figure 4.40 Insert Cross-Reference

Step 4 Modify Document Properties

Refer to Figure 4.41 as you complete Step 4.

a. Click the **Office Button**, select **Prepare**, and then select **Properties**.

   The Document Information panel displays above your document.

   TROUBLESHOOTING: If the Document Information panel disappears, repeat Step a. above to display it again.

b. Click one time in the *Status* box and type **Pending**.

c. Click the **Document Properties arrow** and select **Advanced Properties** to display the Document Properties dialog box. Click the **Summary tab**, click one time in the *Title* box, and then type **Hoover v Ben's Club**.

d. Click the **Custom tab,** as shown in Figure 4.41, and select **Date completed** in the *Name* list. Click the **Type drop-down arrow** and select **Date**. Type today's date in the *Value box* using MM/DD/YY format, and then click **Add**. Click **OK** to close the dialog box.

e. Save and close the document.

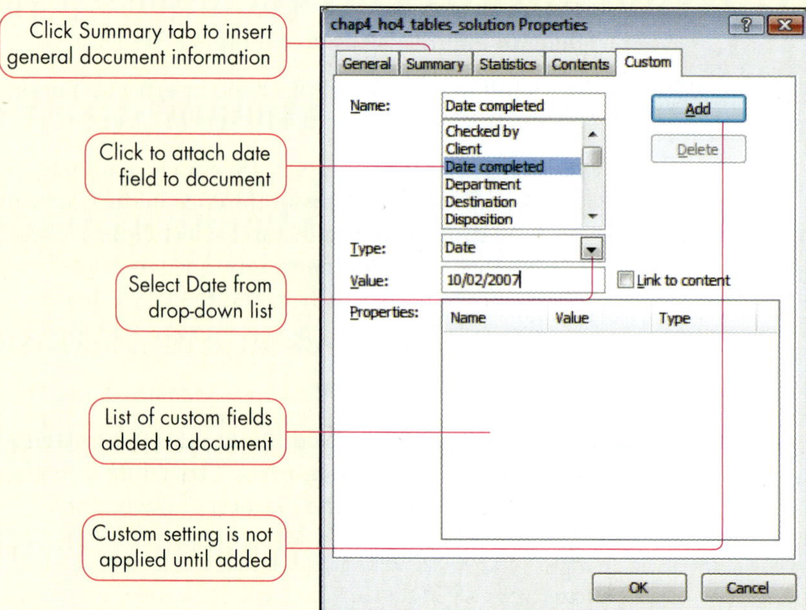

Figure 4.41 Change Document Properties

Summary

1. **Insert comments into a document.** When you work as part of a team you can use the Comment feature to collaborate. Comments enable you to ask a question or provide a suggestion to another person in a document, without modifying the content of the document. Comments are inserted using colored Markup balloons, and a different color is assigned to each reviewer. Comments appear in the Print Layout, Web Layout, and Full Screen Reading views. You can display comments in the margins of a document or in a reading pane.
2. **Track changes in a document.** This feature monitors all additions, deletions, and formatting changes you make to a document. When active, the Track Changes feature applies revision marks to indicate where a change occurs. When you move your mouse over a revision mark, it will display the name of the person who made the change as well as the date and time of change. You can use markup tools to accept or reject changes that have been tracked. These tools are especially helpful when several people make changes to the same document. If comments and tracked changes do not display initially, you can turn on the Show Markup feature to view them. You also can view the document as a final copy if all tracked changes are accepted or as the original before any changes were made and tracked. You can modify the Track Changes options to change settings such as fonts, colors, location, and size of markup balloons.
3. **View documents side by side.** This feature enables you to view two documents on the same screen. It is useful when you want to compare the contents of two documents or if you want to cut or copy and paste text from one document to another. To view two documents side by side, they must both be open in Word. While you display the two documents, you can use synchronous scrolling to move through both using only one scroll bar.
4. **Compare and combine documents.** When you have several copies of the same document submitted from different people, you can use the compare and combine features. The compare feature evaluates the contents of two or more documents and displays markup balloons that show the differences between the documents. You can determine if the differences display in the original document, a revised document, or a new document. The combine feature goes a step further and integrates all changes from multiple documents into one.
5. **Create master documents and subdocuments.** Working with long documents can be cumbersome, and a document that is very long can even slow down your computer. As an alternative to creating long documents, you can create a master document that acts like a binder for managing smaller documents. The smaller document is called a subdocument and can be edited individually at any time. It can be modified when displayed as part of the master document if it is not locked for editing. The Outlining tab contains the Collapse and Expand buttons, as well as other tools used to work on master documents. The great benefit of master and subdocuments is the ability to work with multiple subdocuments simultaneously. For example, you can create page numbers in a master document, and it will cause the numbers to run consecutively from one subdocument to the next.
6. **Use navigation tools.** When you use the Document Map feature, the headings in a document are displayed in a pane on the left, and the text of the document is visible on the right. You can click a heading in the Document Map to move the insertion point to that heading in the document. The feature is only available when headings are formatted using the styles feature. You also can use Thumbnails to navigate quickly through a document. Thumbnails are small pictures of each page that display on the left in a pane when the feature is toggled on. When you click a thumbnail, the insertion point moves to the top of that page. The bookmark feature is an electronic marker for a specific location in a document. You can designate a bookmark in a particular location in a document, then use the Go To feature to return to that bookmark.
7. **Acknowledge a source.** It is common practice to use a variety of sources to supplement your own thoughts when authoring a paper, report, legal brief, or many other types of document. Failure to acknowledge the source of information you use in a document is a form of plagiarism. Word provides the citation feature to track, compile, and display your research sources for inclusion in several types of supplemental references. After you add sources, they are saved in a Master List, a database of all citation sources created in Word on a particular computer. The source also is stored in the Current List, which contains all sources you use in the current document. These lists are stored in XML format and can be used in any Word document.

8. **Create a bibliography.** A bibliography is a list of works cited or consulted by an author and should be included with the document when published. The addition of a bibliography to your completed work demonstrates respect for the material consulted and proves that you are not plagiarizing. It also gives the reader an opportunity to validate your references for accuracy. Any sources added with the citation feature and used in the current document will display in the appropriate format as a bibliography.
9. **Select the writing style.** When research papers are prepared, the author often must conform to a particular writing style. The writing style, also called an editorial style, consists of rules and guidelines set forth by a publisher to ensure consistency in presentation of research documents. The Style list in the Citations & Bibliography group on the References tab includes the most commonly used international styles. When you select the style before creating the bibliography, the citations that appear in the bibliography will be formatted exactly as required by that style.
10. **Create and modify footnotes and endnotes.** A footnote is a citation that appears at the bottom of a page, and an endnote is a citation that appears at the end of a document. You use footnotes or endnotes to credit the sources you quote or cite in your document. If you click the Footnotes Dialog Box Launcher, the Footnotes and Endnotes dialog box opens, and you can modify the location of the notes and the format of the numbers.
11. **Add figure references.** Documents and books often contain several images, charts, or tables. To help readers refer to the correct image or table, you can insert a caption that is a descriptive title. To add a caption, click Insert Caption in the Captions group on the References tab. To automatically generate captions, click AutoCaption in the Caption dialog box.
12. **Insert a table of figures.** If your document includes pictures, charts and graphs, slides, or other illustrations along with a caption, you can include a table of figures, or list of the captions, as a reference. To build a table of figures, Word searches a document for captions, sorts the captions by number, and displays the table of figures in the document. A table of figures is commonly placed after the table of contents for a document.
13. **Add legal references.** A table of authorities is used in legal documents to reference cases, rules, treaties, and other documents referred to in a legal brief. Word's Table of Authorities feature enables you to track, compile, and display citations, or references to specific legal cases and other legal documents, to be included in the table of authorities. Before you generate the table of authorities, you must indicate which citations you want to include using the Mark Citation command. To modify a table of authorities entry, locate the entry that you wish to modify and edit the text inside the quotation marks. To delete a table of authorities entry, select the entire entry field, including the braces {}, and then press Delete. If you do not wish to use the existing categories of citations in your table of authorities, you can add or change the categories.
14. **Create cross-references.** A cross-reference is a note that refers the reader to another location for more information about a topic. You can create cross-references to headings, bookmarks, footnotes, endnotes, captions, and tables.
15. **Modify document properties.** You can create a document summary that provides descriptive information about a document, such as a title, subject, author, keywords, and comments. When you create a document summary, Word saves the document summary with the saved document. You can update the document summary at any time by opening the Document Information panel for the respective document. The Custom tab in the Document Properties dialog box enables you to add other properties and assign values to those properties. You also can print document properties from the Print dialog box.

Key Terms

Multiple Choice

1. Which of the following statements about Comments is false?
   (a) Comment balloons appear on the right side in Print Layout view by default.
   (b) A ScreenTip showing the reviewer's name and date/time of comment creation appears when the mouse pointer is over a markup balloon.
   (c) You cannot print comments with the rest of the document.
   (d) You can use the Show Markup feature on the Review tab to filter markup balloons so only comments display on the page.

2. Which dialog box gives you the ability to enter the name of the person using the computer so that person's name appears in ScreenTips for tracked changes and markup balloons?
   (a) View
   (b) File Properties
   (c) Paragraph
   (d) Word Options (located in Office menu)

3. What option enables you to see the document appearance if you accept all tracked changes?
   (a) Final Showing Markup
   (b) Final
   (c) Original Showing Markup
   (d) Original

4. Which of the document elements listed below can you find using the Go To command?
   (a) Bookmark
   (b) Hyperlink
   (c) Table of Contents
   (d) Cross-reference notation

5. Which procedure is a method used to view and edit footnote text?
   (a) By positioning the mouse pointer over the footnote reference mark and clicking inside the ScreenTip that appears
   (b) Through the Footnote and Endnote dialog box
   (c) By double-clicking the footnote reference mark and typing from within the Footnotes pane in Print Layout view
   (d) By clicking Citation on the References tab

6. When you use the styles feature to format headings, you can use this feature to view an outline of your document and click on a heading in the outline to relocate the insertion point in your document.
   (a) Bookmarks
   (b) Document Map
   (c) Thumbnails
   (d) Navigation

7. What navigation tool do you use to display images of document pages that you can click to move the insertion point to the top of a particular page?
   (a) Task pane
   (b) Document Map
   (c) Thumbnails
   (d) Zoom

8. Which option is not true about plagiarism?
   (a) It is the act of using another person's work and claiming it as your own.
   (b) It is an illegal violation of U.S. Copyright law.
   (c) It only applies to written works; ideas, spoken words, or graphics are not included.
   (d) It has serious moral and ethical implications and is taken very seriously in academic communities.

9. What document item directs a reader to another location in a document by mentioning its location?
   (a) Cross-reference
   (b) Bookmark
   (c) Endnote
   (d) Thumbnail

10. A table of figures is generated from what type of entries?
    (a) Bullets
    (b) Bookmarks
    (c) Comments
    (d) Captions

11. What does a table of authorities display?
    (a) A list of pictures, tables, and figures in a document
    (b) A list of cases, rules, treaties, and other documents cited in a legal document
    (c) A list of key words and phrases in the document
    (d) A sequential list of section headings and their page numbers

...continued on Next Page

Multiple Choice Continued...

12. What comprises a master document?

(a) Subdocuments

(b) Bibliographies

(c) Completed document

(d) Legal citations

13. Which feature enables you to attach information to a document such as author name, subject, title, keywords, and comments?

(a) Track changes

(b) Bibliography

(c) Master document

(d) Document Information panel

14. Select the sequence of events you undertake to include a bibliography in your document.

(a) Insert a citation, select writing style, insert bibliography.

(b) Type citations into document, insert bibliography, select writing style.

(c) Select writing style, mark legal references, insert bibliography.

(d) Select writing style, insert bibliography, insert citations.

15. Which feature enables you to display the differences in two documents in a separate document?

(a) Side by side view

(b) Compare documents

(c) Combo documents

(d) Subdocuments

Practice Exercises

1 Review a Document

Periodically it is helpful to step back and review the basics. In this case you have the opportunity to read and work in a document that describes the reviewing features in Word. These features are extremely helpful when working on a group project, and you should take time to evaluate and practice using these features.

a. Open *chap4_pe1_review* and *chap4_pe1_review2*. Click the **View tab** and click **View Side by Side** in the Window group. After you view the differences in the two documents, click **Window** on the View tab for the *chap4_pe1_review2* document and click **View Side by Side** to close the Side by Side view and display only one file.

b. Click the **Review tab**, click **Compare** in the Compare group, and then select **Combine**. Click **Browse for Original,** navigate to the *chap4_pe1_review* document, and then click **Open**. After you view the differences in the two documents, click **Browse for Revised**, navigate to the *chap4_pe1_review2* document, and then click **Open**. Click **OK** and then click **Continue with Merge**.

c. Save the new document as **chap4_pe1_review_solution**.

d. Click **Show Source Documents** in the Compare group on the Review tab, and then select **Hide Source Documents**, if necessary. Click **Reviewing Pane** in the Tracking group to hide the reviewing pane that displays on the left side of the screen, if necessary.

e. Click the **Track Changes arrow** and select **Change Tracking Options**. Take a moment to review the variety of options you can set in this dialog box. In the *Formatting* section, click the **Formatting drop-down arrow** and select **Double underline**, if necessary. Click the **Color drop-down arrow** in the *Formatting* section and select **Violet**. In the *Balloons* section, click the **Margin drop-down arrow** and select **Right**, if necessary. In the Balloons section click the **Preferred width spin arrow** until **1.8** displays, if necessary. Click **OK** to close the dialog box.

f. Click **Show Markup** in the Tracking group, and point to **Reviewers** to display the names of the reviewers, each of whom is displayed in a different color. Click **All Reviewers** to remove the check mark. Click **Show Markup**, point to **Reviewers**, and then click **John Doe**. Only revisions by John Doe display, as shown in Figure 4.42. Click **Show Markup**, click **Reviewers**, and then click **All Reviewers** to display all markup balloons again. Note that reviewer colors may be different on your screen.

g. Click the **Display for Review down arrow** (which currently displays *Final Showing Markup*) on the Review tab and select **Original Showing Markup**. Click the **Display for Review down arrow** again and select **Final Showing Markup**.

h. Press **Ctrl+Home** to move the insertion point to the beginning of the document, if necessary. Click **Next** in the Changes group to move to the first revision. Click **Accept** in the Changes group to accept this change. Click the **Accept arrow** and select **Accept and Move to Next**.

i. Click to place the insertion point after the letter *A* at the beginning of the second sentence. Press **Spacebar** to insert a space between *A* and *line*. Click the **Accept arrow** and select **Accept All Changes in Document**.

j. Press **Ctrl+End** to move to the end of the document. Click **New Comment** and type **Review completed by *your name* on *current date***. Substitute your name and the current date in the sentence, where appropriate.

k. Save and close the document. Close *chap4_pe1_review* and *chap4_pe1_review2* without saving.

...continued on Next Page

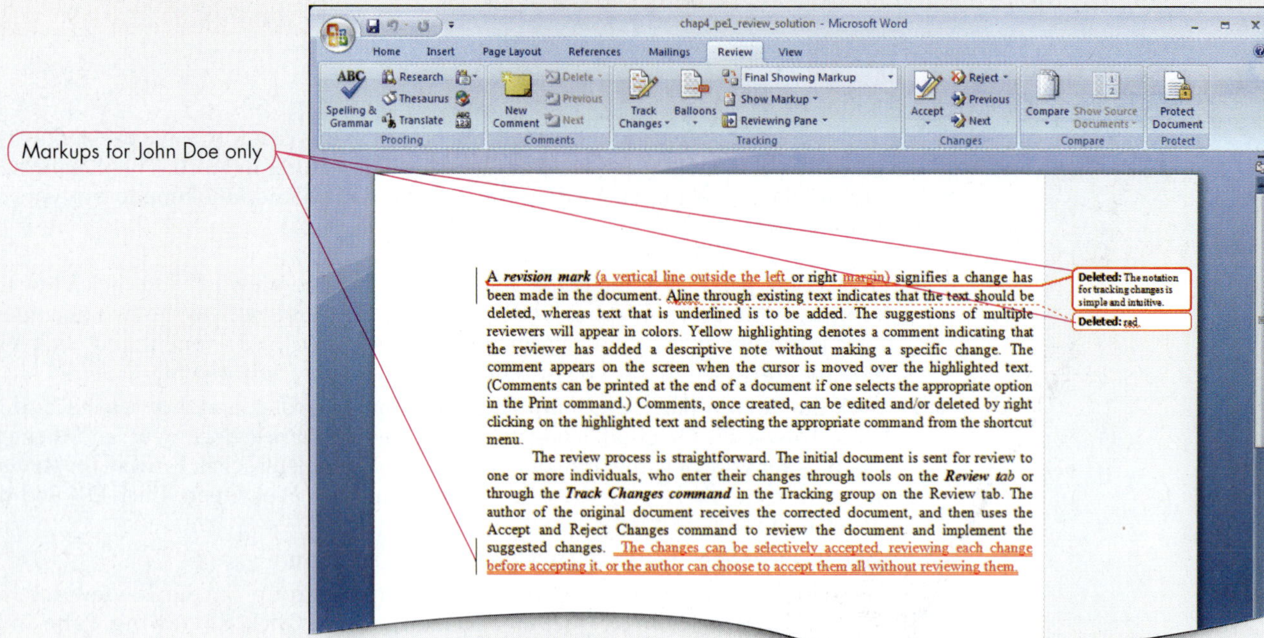

Figure 4.42 Review a Document

2 Create a Master Document

You volunteer in a middle school library and have the opportunity to observe the computer skill level of many students. You decide to create a document that contains tips for using Windows Vista for the students to use as a reference. You found three sources of information and want to combine them into one document. Fortunately, you are familiar with the Master and Subdocument features in Word, so you can easily combine the documents into one.

a. Create a new document. Click the **Outline button** on the status bar. The Outlining tab should display automatically. Save the document as **chap4_pe2_tips_solution**.

b. Type the title of the document, **Tips for Windows Vista**, and then apply **24-point Arial** and **Center** it using the Mini toolbar. Click to move the insertion point to the right side of the heading and press **Enter** two times.

c. Click **Show Document** in the Master Document group on the Outlining tab to display other features. Click **Insert**, and then open the file *chap4_pe2_tips1*. Insert two additional documents, *chap4_pe2_tips2* and *chap4_pe2_tips3*, that are stored in the same folder. When you get a Microsoft Office Word message box that asks if you want to rename the style in the subdocument, click **Yes to All**.

d. Click **Close Outline View** in the Close group on the Outlining tab, and then click the **View tab**. Click **Document Map** in the Show/Hide group to display the Document Map pane; click **Select Multiple Files** from the list in the Document Map pane as shown in Figure 4.43.

e. After the *Select Multiple Files* heading and paragraph display, click the **Insert tab**, and then click **Bookmark** in the Links group. Type **multiple** in the Bookmark name box, and then click **Add**.

f. Click the **Switch Navigation Window** arrow in the Document Map pane and click **Thumbnails**. Click the **page 6 thumbnail** and view the *Customize Windows Explorer* paragraph at the top of the page. Click **Bookmark**, type **customize** in the Bookmark name box, and then click **Add**.

g. Click **Close** in the Thumbnails pane. Press **Ctrl+G**, select **Bookmark** in the *Go to what* list, and then select **multiple**, if necessary, in the **Enter bookmark nam***e* list. Click **Go To** and view the *Select Multiple Files* paragraph. Click **Close** to remove the Find and Replace dialog box.

h. Save and close the document.

...continued on Next Page

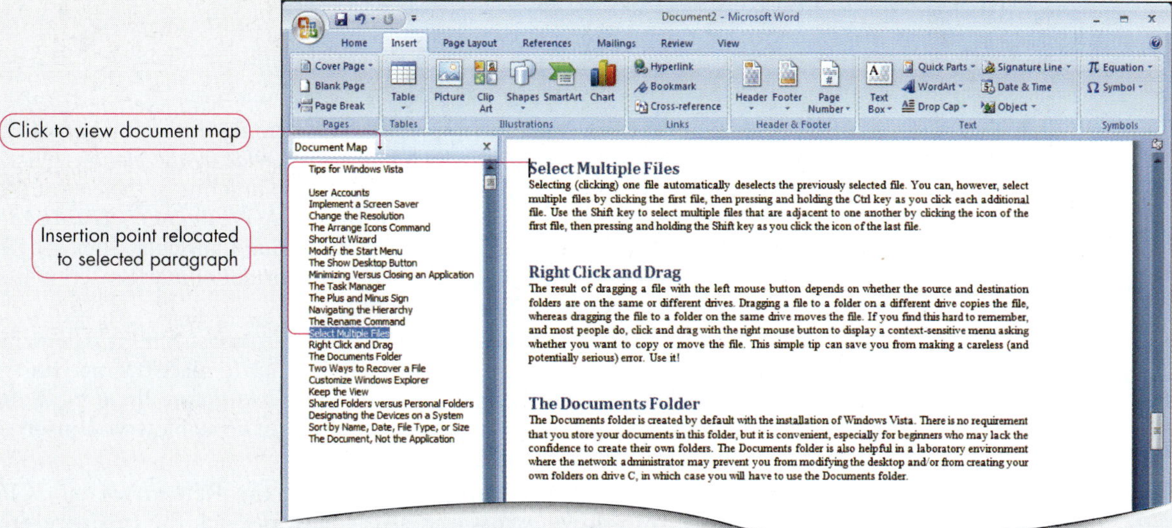

Figure 4.43 Use the Document Map

3 Planting Tulips

You are a member of the Izzard County Horticulture Society and have been asked to assist in the development of information packets about a variety of flowers and plants. You are responsible for developing an informational report about tulips that will be distributed at the fall meeting. After viewing sources of information on the Internet, in books, and in journals, you have created a short paper that includes information and pictures. In the following steps you create additional resources to accompany your report, such as a table of figures and a bibliography.

a. Open the *chap4_pe3_tulip* document and save it as **chap4_pe3_tulip_solution**.

b. Press **Ctrl+End** to view the sources at the bottom of the document. Click the **References tab**, click **Manage Sources** in the Citations & Bibliography group, and then click **New**. Click the **Type of Source drop-down arrow** and select **Article in a Periodical**. In the Author box, type **Lauren Bonar Swezey**. In the Title box, type **A Westerner's Guide to Tulips**. In the Year box, type **1999**. In the Month box, type **October**. Click **OK** to close the dialog box. Click **Close** to close the Source Manager dialog box.

c. Select the first Web site listed in the Sources list and press **Ctrl+C** to copy it to the Clipboard. Click **Insert Citation**, and then select **Add New Source**. Click the **Type of Source drop-down arrow** and click **Web site**. Click once in the URL box to move the insertion point, and then press **Ctrl+V** to paste the Web site address. Type **http://americanmeadows.com** in the Name of Web Site box, as shown in Figure 4.44. Click **OK**. Repeat this procedure for the remaining Web site sources in the list.

d. Scroll up to view the page that contains pictures of different varieties of tulips. Click one time on the first image. Click **Insert Caption** in the Captions group on the References tab. The caption number is already entered; press **Spacebar** one time and then type **Angelique** to add more detail to the caption information. Click **OK** to close the Caption dialog box. Add the following tulip classifications to the captions for the remaining images on the first row: **Beauty of Apeldoorn**, **Black Parrot**. Add the following classifications to the captions for the images on the second row: **Candela**, **Plaisir**. Remember to insert a space between the caption number and tulip classification.

e. Scroll down to the top of the page 4. Click one time on the *Planting Guide at a Glance* graphic. Click **Insert Caption**. Press **Spacebar** one time in the Caption box, which already displays *Figure 6*, and type **Planting Depth Guide**, and then click **OK**. Scroll down to the bottom of the page. Click one time on the cross-section graphic of a bulb. Click **Insert Caption**. Press **Spacebar** one time in the Caption box, which already displays *Figure 7*, type **Dissecting a Bulb**, and then click **OK**.

...continued on Next Page

f. Scroll up to page 3. Click one time to place the insertion point at the end of the third paragraph in the *Planting* section, which ends with *made by the planter*. Click **Insert Endnote** and notice the insertion point blinking on a blank line at the end of the document. Type the following: **Swezey, Lauren Bonar, A Westerner's Guide to Tulips (Sunset, October 1999)**. Click the **Footnotes Dialog Box Launcher**, click the **Number format drop-down arrow**, click **1, 2, 3** to change the format of marks used in the document to denote endnotes, and then click **Apply**.

g. Scroll to the third page and find the sentence *See the depth chart in Figure 6*, which displays in the third paragraph in the *Planting* section. Click to place the insertion point at the end of the sentence, and then add the following text before the period: **on page**. Be sure to include a space before and after the text you type. Now you insert a cross-reference to complete the sentence.

h. Click **Cross-reference** in the Captions group on the References tab. Click the **Reference type drop-down arrow** and select **Figure**. Click the **Insert reference to drop-down arrow** and select **Page Number**. Click **Figure 6** in the **For which caption** list, and then click **Insert**. The number four completes the sentence, informing the reader that the graphic is found on page 4. Click **Close** to remove the Cross-reference dialog box.

i. Place the insertion point at the end of the table of contents. Press **Ctrl+Enter** to insert a page. Type **Table of Figures.** Click at the end of the heading, and then press **Enter** two times. Click **Insert Table of Figures**, and then click **OK**. Select the *Table of Figures* heading, and then click **Heading 3** from the Styles Quick gallery in the Home tab.

j. Place the insertion point at the end of the last paragraph in the report, *Forcing Tulips*. Press **Ctrl+Enter** to insert a page. Type **Bibliography** and press **Enter** two times. Click the **References tab**. Click the **Style arrow** in the Citations & Bibliography group and click **APA**, if necessary. Click **Bibliography**, and then click **Insert Bibliography**. Select the bibliography heading, and then click **Heading 3** from the Styles Quick gallery in the Styles group on the Home tab.

k. Select the list of sources that were in the document before you inserted the bibliography and press **Delete** to remove them from the document.

l. Scroll to the second page that contains the table of contents. Click one time anywhere in the table of contents and press **F9**. Click **Update Entire Table** and then click **OK**.

m. Save and close the document.

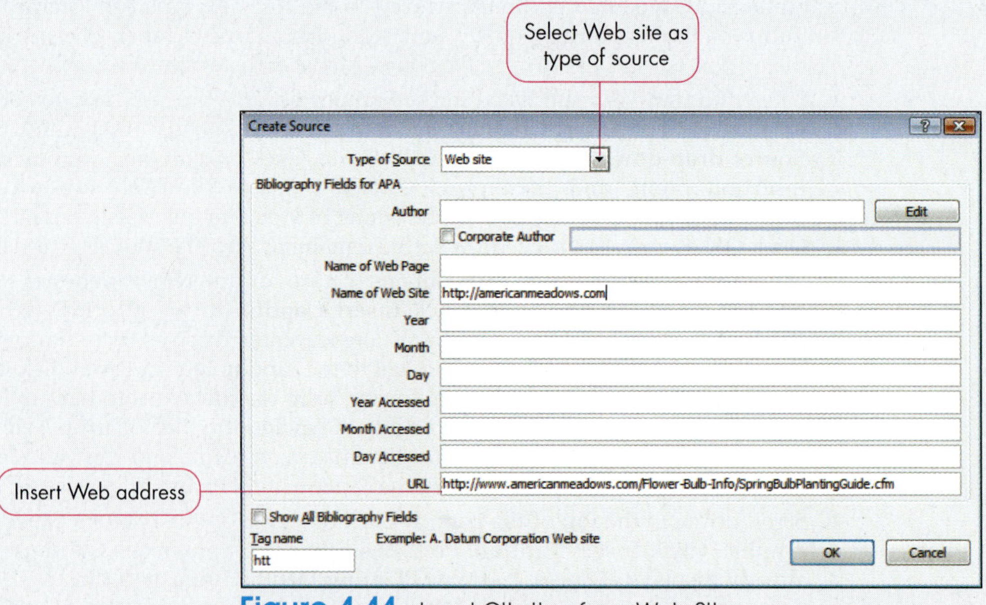

Figure 4.44 Insert Citation from Web Site

...continued on Next Page

4 Legal Brief

You work as a clerk in a law firm and are responsible for preparing documentation used in all phases of the judicial process. A senior partner in the firm asks you to complete a document by inserting a table of authorities based on the cases cited in the document. You will mark the references to other cases in the document, then prepare a table of authorities based on those cases.

a. Open *chap4_pe4_legal* and save it as **chap4_pe4_legal_solution**.
b. Press **Ctrl+Home** to move the insertion point to the beginning of the document. Display the **Page Layout tab**, click **Breaks** in the Page Setup group, and then select **Next Page** in the *Section Breaks* category.
c. Press **Ctrl+End** to move the insertion point to the end of the document. Click the **Insert tab**, click **Page Number** in the Header & Footer group, and select **Format Page Numbers**. In the Page Number Format dialog box, click the **Start at** option button to display the number **1.** Click **OK** to close the dialog box.
d. Double-click the footer area on the second page. Click **Link to Previous** in the Navigation group on the Design tab to toggle the setting off. Click **Page Number** in the Header and Footer group, point to **Bottom of Page**, and then select **Plain Number 2** from the gallery. Click **Close Header and Footer**.
e. Press **Ctrl+Home** to move the insertion point to the beginning of the document. Type the title **TABLE OF AUTHORITIES** at the top of the page. Press **Enter** twice, and then click **Align Text Left** in the Paragraph group on the Home tab, if necessary. Select the *Table of Authorities* title, and then click **Center** and **Underline** on the Home tab.
f. Select the citation *Utah Code Ann.' 33-8-34 (1994)* in the *Statutes Involved* section on the second page. Click the **References tab** and click **Mark Citation** in the Table of Authorities group. Click **Mark All** and then click **Close**. Click the **Home tab** and click **Show/Hide ¶** in the Paragraph group to turn off the display of formatting marks.
g. Scroll to the top of the document and position the insertion point on the second line following the *Table of Authorities* heading. Click **Insert Table of Authorities** in the Table of Authorities group on the References tab. In the Table of Authorities dialog box, click **Cases** in the Category list, and then click **OK** to display the table in your document, as shown in Figure 4.45.
h. Select the heading **Cases** and the three citations; click the **Home tab**, click **Line spacing** in the Paragraph group, and select **2.0** to double-space the entries in the table.
i. Click the **Office Button** and select **Prepare**. Click **Properties** to display the Document Information Panel above the document. Click one time in the **Author** box, delete the current name if necessary, and type your name. Click once in the Title box and type **Motion for Appeal**. Click once in the Comment box and type **Utah District Court**.
j. Save and close the document.

...continued on Next Page

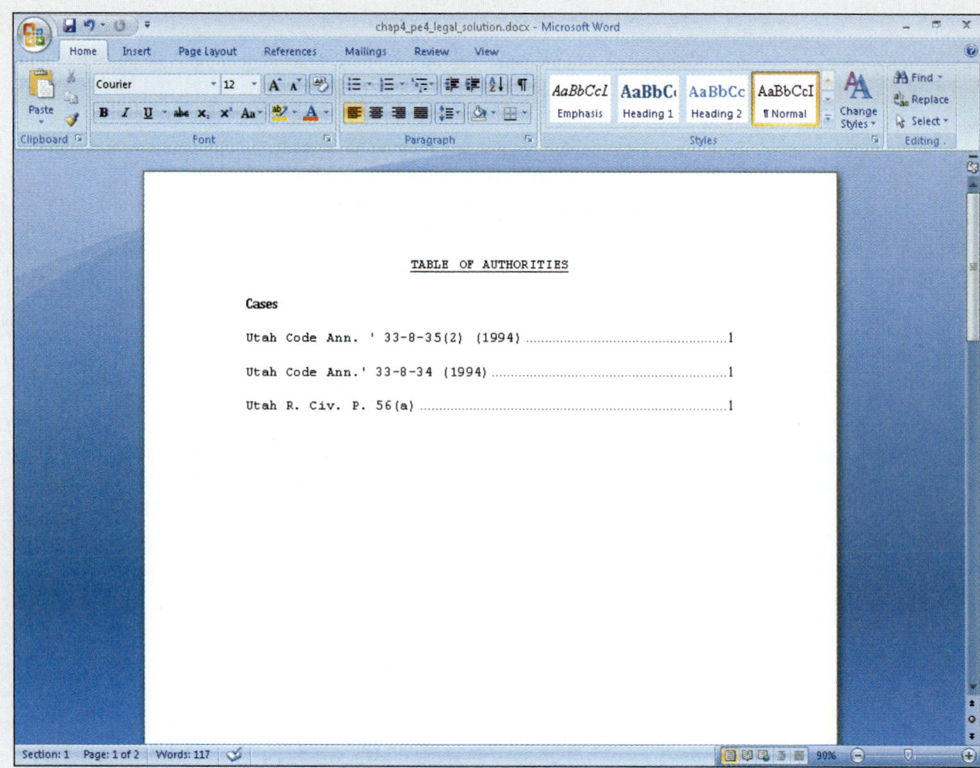

Figure 4.45 Table of Authorities

Mid-Level Exercises

1 Recipe Book

You work as a volunteer at the local humane society. The board of directors asked you to coordinate a fund-raising effort in which animal recipe books will be sold. You have been receiving recipes from several supporters via e-mail and decide to create a master document that contains all of the recipe documents. After you combine the recipes, you can print the document in preparation for the big sale.

a. Create a new master document. Save the file as **chap4_mid1_recipes_solution**.

b. At the top of the page add the title **Recipes for the Animals in Your Life** and format it using the Heading 1 style, then insert two blank lines.

c. Below the heading type the following categories on different lines: **Dogs**, **Cats**, **Birds**, and **Horses**. These category headings classify the type of recipes that follow. Format the category headings using the Heading 2 style.

d. Insert the following subdocuments into the master document below the appropriate category heading: *chap4_mid1_dogs*, *chap4_mid1_cats*, *chap4_mid1_birds*, *chap4_mid1_horses*.

e. Change the document properties and specify the following:

Title	Humane Society Animal Recipe Book
Author	Friends of the Humane Society
Comments	Distributed Fall 2008

f. Take appropriate actions so the recipes for each type of animal start on the top of a page. Remove any section breaks that create large gaps of white space within the group of recipes for a particular animal. If removal of breaks changes formatting of category headings, reapply the Heading 2 style.

g. Save and close the master document. If a window asks you to overwrite the original subdocuments, click No.

2 Sidewalk Café

Your friend Sue McCrory just purchased the Sidewalk Cafe restaurant. She prepared an information sheet to distribute to several office buildings within the neighborhood. As you review the information sheet, you annotate the document with comments. After you review your comments, you edit one comment and delete another comment. Later you receive a revision of the document from Sue. With two different documents, you use the Compare and Combine features to consolidate the documents into one final copy that Sue will distribute.

a. Open *chap4_mid2_cafe* and save it as **chap4_mid2_cafe_solution**.

b. Position the insertion point at the end of the subtitle and type the comment **Placing the italicized slogan below the restaurant name is a good idea.** Position the insertion point after *Turkey Club* and type the comment **Adding some photos of lunch items will enhance the information sheet.** In the fourth paragraph below the list, select *Sunday brunch* and insert the comment **What's on this menu?**

c. Change the Track Changes options to view markup balloons on the left side of the screen and resize the markup balloons to 1.5″ wide. Select the **Track formatting** check box, if necessary. Change the **Formatting** option to display double underline and, if necessary, change the formatting color to show **By Author**.

...continued on Next Page

d. Position the mouse pointer over the first comment markup balloon to see the comment with your name as the reviewer. Edit your second comment by adding **full-color** between *some* and *photos*. Delete the third comment.

e. Confirm the Track Changes option is toggled on. Delete the words *diverse and eclectic* on the second line of the first main paragraph, and replace them with the word **wide**. In the second paragraph, delete *on a daily basis*, including the space before *on*, but do not delete the colon at the end of that line. Italicize all instances of *Sue McCrory* and *Ken McCrory*, or any variation of their names.

f. Change the Display for Review option to Final Showing Markup, if necessary. Make appropriate adjustments so that only your changes display onscreen. Accept all of your changes.

g. Display comments and changes by all reviewers. Accept the change to delete the words *restaurant, bar, and grill*, but reject the change to delete the words *is homey and*.

h. Open the original file, **chap4_mid2_cafe,** and view it side by side with the revised file you have edited. Close the *chap4_mid2_cafe* document when your review is complete.

i. Sue made revisions to another copy of the original, named *chap4_mid2_caferevision*, and sent a copy to you. Combine that document with the *chap4_mid2_cafe_solution* and display the results in a new document named **chap4_mid2_caferevision_solution**.

j. View Sue's markups only and accept all of her changes. View all remaining markups; reject only the deletion of the phrase "is homey and" and accept all remaining changes.

k. Delete all comments.

l. Save and close all documents.

3 Web Design

You work as a Web designer at a local advertising agency and have been asked to provide some basic information to be used in a senior citizens workshop. You want to provide the basic elements of good Web design and format the document professionally. Use the basic information you have already, in a Word document, and revise it to include elements appropriate for a research-oriented paper.

a. Open *chap4_mid3_web* and save it as **chap4_mid3_web_solution**.

b. On the cover page, insert your name at the bottom.

c. Place the insertion point at the end of the *Proximity* paragraph on the page numbered 2. Insert the following text into an endnote: **Max Rebaza, <u>Effective Web Sites</u>, Chicago: Windy City Publishing, Inc. (2004): 44.**

d. Change all endnotes into footnotes.

e. In preparation for adding a bibliography to your document, create a citation using the book source from Step c. If a selection from the citation displays in the document, delete it.

f. Select the Chicago style of writing and add a bibliography at the end of the document. Use the default format and settings for the bibliography. Type a heading on the page and format it using the Heading 2 style.

g. Add captions to each graphic that displays in the paper. Allow Word to number the captions sequentially and display the caption below the graphic. Add a caption to the table on page six, and display the caption below the table.

h. Create a Table of Figures at the beginning of the document, on a separate page after the table of contents. If the Table 1 entry displays instead of figures, click the Caption label

...continued on Next Page

drop down list in the Table of Figures dialog box and select Figure. Give the page an appropriate heading and format the heading using the Heading 2 style.

i. Create bookmarks for the three major headings, *Proximity and Balance*, *Contrast and Focus*, and *Consistency*. The bookmarks should be named **proximity**, **contrast**, and **consistency**.

j. Insert a cross-reference at the end of the *Font Size and Attributes* paragraph on the seventh page. Type **See also**, then insert a **Heading** *reference type* for the **Contrast and Focus** heading. End the sentence with a period.

k. Display the Document Map and click **Table of Contents**. Update the table and select the option to update the entire table. Close the Document Map.

l. Save and close the document.

4 Table of Authorities

As the junior partner in a growing law firm, you must proofread and update all legal briefs before they are submitted to the courts. You are in the final stage of completing a medical malpractice case, but the brief cannot be filed without a Table of Authorities.

a. Open the file *chap4_mid4_authorities* and save the file as **chap4_mid4_authorities_solution**.

b. Mark all references to legal cases throughout the document.

c. Insert a Table of Authorities at the beginning of the document. Insert an appropriate header at the top of the page and format it using Heading 1 style.

d. Change document properties, insert your name as Author, title the document **Bradford v Hillcrest**, and use **Medical malpractice** as the subject.

e. Save and close the document.

Capstone Exercise

You work in a medical office where many patients have been examined or screened for cancer. The disease is a huge threat to society and a major focus of the health care system. Because of the potential risk and consequences of this disease, you decide to perform research to learn more about it, and the preventive measures you should undertake to avoid it. Your coworkers have similar concerns, and you discover they also have been researching the topic. After a few conversations, the staff of nurses and administrative assistants decide to create an informational document that can be distributed to patients. They offer to e-mail you the documents that contain information they found.

Combine Documents

You receive two documents from coworkers who searched for information about cancer on the Internet. The information is interesting and could be valuable to other people you know, so you decide to create a well-formatted document that you can distribute to anyone who expresses an interest in basic information about cancer.

a. Open the two files *chap4_cap_cancer1* and *chap4_cap_cancer2*, then view them side by side.

b. Combine the two documents into a new document. Show the source documents after you combine them into a new document.

c. The new document should contain all information from both files. Accept all insertions and reject any deletions.

d. Save the new file as **chap4_cap_cancer_solution**.

Credit Sources

You notice several places in the document where the source of the information is listed. Remembering the documentation features in Word 2007, you decide to create citations and add a bibliography to your document.

a. Insert a citation for each source posted in the document.

b. Create a footnote that displays at the end of the paragraph preceding the source listing. Cut each source listing and paste it into the footnote area. Make adjustments as necessary so the source information displays next to the number in the footnote.

c. You decide to include a bibliography as well. Use a page break to add a page to the end of the document and insert a bibliography there. Use the APA writing style for the bibliography, and provide a title formatted in the Heading 2 style. Remove any comments after creating the reference page.

Figure References

The graphics in the document are quite informative, and you want to add descriptive captions to them, and also list them on a reference page.

a. Select the first table and type the following caption: **Table 1. Cancer-related deaths from 1990–1998**. Display the captions above the graphics.

b. Select the second graphic and display the following caption above it: **Figure 1. Rate* of prostate cancer deaths, 1990–1998**.

c. Select the final graphic and display the following caption above it: **Figure 2. Rate* of female breast cancer deaths, 1990–1998**.

d. At the beginning of the document, insert a cover page using the Mod theme. Type **Cancer Information** as the document title and remove all other fields except the author name. If necessary, replace the existing author name with your own.

e. Create a blank page following the cover page and type **Table of Figures** at the top. Format the text with the Heading 2 style.

f. Below the heading insert a table of figures, using the Distinctive format. Change table of figure options so that it builds the table from captions (found in the Table of Figures Options dialog box).

Add Navigation

The document is becoming complex, and you decide to add a few bookmarks to help the reader find information quickly.

a. Display the Document Map. Click *Other primary causes of cancer include:* Place the insertion point at the left side of the heading, and then insert a bookmark named **causes**.

b. Use the Document Map to place the insertion point at the left side of the heading *What are the symptoms of cancer?* and insert a bookmark named **symptoms**.

c. Place the insertion point at the left side of the heading *Cancer treatment can take the following forms:* and insert a bookmark named **treatment**.

d. Click Go To and use the bookmarks to move the insertion point to the section about *causes*. Close the Document Map.

e. Place the insertion point to the left side of the line directly below the heading Cancer: Choosing a Treatment Program and insert a cross-reference to another paragraph heading in the document. The text for the cross-reference should begin **See also the section titled**. Allow the cross-reference to complete the statement by inserting the heading text *What are the treatments for cancer?*

f. Modify document properties and type your name in the Author field. In the Title text box type **Cancer Information**.

g. Save and close all documents.

Mini Cases

Use the rubric following the case as a guide to evaluate your work, but keep in mind that your instructor may impose additional grading criteria or use a different standard to judge your work.

Group Collaboration

GENERAL CASE

This case requires collaboration between members of a group. Two people in the group will open the *chap4_mc1_collaborate* document. Each member will turn on track changes and proceed to make corrections and add suggestions to the document. Each group member should save the modified file, adding their group number to the filename. Upon completion, the first two people will send the document to two additional group members who also will turn on Track Changes and make additional corrections and suggestions. It is acceptable to correct the previous member's corrections, but do not accept or reject changes at this time. After each member corrects the document, the group should meet together and combine the two documents using the Compare and Combine feature in Word. Combine the documents into a new document, accept and reject changes to the document, and save the final version as **chap4_mc1_collaborate_solution**. View the final version side by side with the original document. Close the documents.

Performance Elements	Exceeds Expectations	Meets Expectations	Below Expectations
Collaboration	Each member of the group participated by using the Track Changes feature while making modifications.	At least half of the members of the group participated.	Fewer than half of the members of the group participated.
Use of tools	Each member of the group used Changes feature at all times while making modifications.	The group used Track Changes at least half of the time while making modifications.	The group did not use the Track Changes feature while making modifications to the document.
Final product	The final version of the document contained proper spelling, punctuation, grammar, and well-written and complete thoughts.	The final version of the document requires additional edits to achieve proper spelling, punctuation, grammar, and well-written and complete thoughts.	The final version of the document requires vast improvements to achieve proper spelling, punctuation, grammar, and well-written and complete thoughts.

Learn to Use Writing Styles

RESEARCH CASE

Do you know someone who has been the victim of identity theft? It occurs every day. But what exactly is involved in this growing crime? Use your research skills to locate information about identity theft. You should find at least one source from the Internet, at least one source from a book, and at least one source from a journal. Use your school's library or online library resources to help locate the information sources. After you find your sources, write a two-page report, double spaced, describing identity theft. Include information about the crime, statistics, government policies, and laws that have been passed because of this crime, and the effects on victims. Cite the sources in your paper, use footnotes where appropriate, and develop a bibliography for your paper based on the APA writing style. Save the report as **chap4_mc2_idtheft_solution**. Close the document.

Performance Elements	Exceeds Expectations	Meets Expectations	Below Expectations
Research	Report cites more than one source each from a book, a journal, and an Internet site.	Report cites one source each from a book, a journal, and an Internet site.	Report cites fewer than three total sources.
Content	Report contains at least four categories of information about identity theft.	Report contains two or three topics of information about identity theft.	Report contains a minimum amount of information about identity theft.
Citations	Report includes citations, footnotes, and bibliography in APA style.	Report includes bibliography, but not in APA style. Some sources are included in footnotes, but not in bibliography.	Sources are not cited. Bibliography is missing.

Repairing Bookmarks

DISASTER RECOVERY

You work in the city's Planning and Zoning department as an analyst. You begin to prepare the Guide to Planned Developments document for posting on the city's intranet. The administrative clerk who typed the document attempted to use bookmarks for navigation purposes, but he did not test the bookmarks after inserting them. You must review the document and repair the bookmarks. Additionally, several cross-reference statements are embedded in the document, but appear to be erroneous. The cross-references are highlighted in the document so you can locate them; the highlights should be removed when you have corrected the references. Open *chap4_mc3_bookmarks* and save your revised document as **chap4_mc3_bookmarks_solution**. Close the document.

Performance Elements	Exceeds Expectations	Meets Expectations	Below Expectations
Bookmarks	All erroneous bookmarks were repaired, and links work properly.	At least half of the erroneous bookmarks were repaired, and links work properly.	Fewer than half of the erroneous bookmarks were repaired.
Cross-references	All erroneous cross-references were repaired, and links work properly.	At least half of the erroneous cross-references were repaired, and links work properly.	Fewer than half of the erroneous cross-references were repaired.

chapter 1 | **Excel**

Introduction to Excel

What Can I Do with a Spreadsheet?

After you read this chapter, you will be able to:

1. Define worksheets and workbooks (**page 314**).
2. Use spreadsheets across disciplines (**page 314**).
3. Plan for good workbook and worksheet design (**page 315**).
4. Identify Excel window components (**page 317**).
5. Enter and edit data in cells (**page 322**).
6. Describe and use symbols and the order of precedence (**page 328**).
7. Display cell formulas (**page 330**).
8. Insert and delete rows and columns (**page 331**).
9. Use cell ranges; Excel move; copy, paste, paste special; and AutoFill (**page 332**).
10. Manage worksheets (**page 340**).
11. Format worksheets (**page 341**).
12. Select page setup options for printing (**page 353**).
13. Manage cell comments (**page 356**).

Hands-On Exercises

Exercises	Skills Covered
1. INTRODUCTION TO MICROSOFT EXCEL (page 324) **Open**: none **Save as**: chap1_ho1_jake_solution.xlsx	• Plan Your Workbook • Start Microsoft Office Excel 2007 • Enter and Edit Data in Cells • Use the Save As Command and Explore the Worksheet
2. JAKE'S GYM CONTINUED (page 335) **Open**: chap1_ho2_jake.xlsx **Save as**: chap1_ho2_jake_solution.xlsx	• Open an Existing Workbook • Use Save As to Save an Existing Workbook • Insert a Row and Compute Totals • Copy the Formulas • Continue the Calculations • Insert a Column
3. FORMATTING JAKE'S GYM WORKSHEET (page 347) **Open**: chap1_ho2_jake_solution.xlsx (from Exercise 2) **Save as**: chap1_ho3_jake_solution (additional modifications)	• Manage the Workbook • Apply Number Formats • Apply Font Attributes and Borders • Change Alignment Attributes • Insert an Image
4. PRINTING JAKE'S GYM WORKSHEET (page 357) **Open**: chap1_ho3_jake_solution (from Exercise 3) **Save as**: chap1_ho4_ jake_solution (additional modifications)	• Insert a Comment • Insert Custom Header and Footer • Format to Print the Worksheet

CASE STUDY

Weddings by Grace

Grace Galia is a wedding consultant who specializes in all aspects of wedding planning for her clients. Although more and more couples are striving to cut costs by handling most of the planning on their own, Grace is successfully growing her business based on a proven history of superbly run events resulting in many happy newlyweds. She offers her clients a complete wedding package that includes the cocktail hour, dinner, and beverage (including alcohol). The client chooses the type of dinner (e.g., chicken, salmon, filet mignon, or some combination), which determines the cost per guest, and specifies the number of guests, and then the cost of the reception is obtained by simple multiplication.

Case Study

Grace provides a detailed budget to all of her clients that divides the cost of a wedding into three major categories—the ceremony, the reception (based on the package selected), and other items such as music and photography. She asks each client for their total budget, and then works closely with the client to allocate that amount over the myriad items that will be necessary. Grace promises to take the stress out of planning, and she advertises a turnkey operation, from invitations to thank-you notes. She assures her clients that their needs will be met without the clients overextending themselves financially. Grace has asked you, her manager trainee, to complete her worksheet comparing the two wedding plans she offers her clients.

Your Assignment

- Read the chapter carefully, focusing on spreadsheet formulas and basic spreadsheet commands.
- Open *chap1_case_wedding*, which contains the partially completed worksheet, and save it as **chap1_case_wedding_solution**.
- Insert formulas to calculate the cost of the reception in both options.
- Use appropriate formulas to calculate the difference in cost for each item in the two options.
- Copy the total formula to the difference column.
- Format cells as currency with no decimals. Widen or narrow columns as necessary to conform to good design principles.
- Emphasize totals with borders and separate the categories with a complementary fill color.
- Merge and center rows 1 and 2 so the headings are centered over the worksheet. Change the font, font color, and font size to match your design.
- Insert an appropriate image in the space indicated. You may have to resize to fit.
- Emphasize the category headings.
- Add your name and today's date in the footer of the worksheet.
- Choose the options you need to set from the Page Setup dialog box.

Introduction to Spreadsheets

A ***spreadsheet***, the computerized equivalent of a ledger, contains rows and columns of data. A ***spreadsheet program*** is a computer application designed to build and manipulate spreadsheets.

After word processing, a spreadsheet program is the second most common software application in use. The most popular spreadsheet program used in businesses and organizations around the world is Microsoft Excel. A ***spreadsheet***, is the computerized equivalent of a ledger. It is a grid of rows and columns enabling users to organize data, recalculate results for cells containing formulas when any data in input cells change, and make decisions based on quantitative data. A ***spreadsheet program*** is a computer application, such as Microsoft Excel, that you use to build and manipulate electronic spreadsheets. The spreadsheet has become a much more powerful tool since the first spreadsheet program, VisiCalc, was introduced in 1979.

Before the introduction of spreadsheet software, people used ledgers to track expenses and other quantitative data. Ledgers have been the basis of accounting for hundreds of years, but the accountant was always faced with the issue of making changes to correct errors or update values. The major issue, however, was the time and work involved in changing the ledger and manually calculating the results again. Figure 1.1 shows an edited ledger page that had to be recalculated. A spreadsheet makes these changes in a significantly shorter period of time and, if the data and formulas are correct, does not make errors. Any area that has numeric data is a potential area of application for a spreadsheet. Herein lies the advantage of the electronic spreadsheet: quicker, more accurate changes than were possible with a manual ledger. Further, the use of formulas and functions in Excel, along with the ability to easily copy these formulas, adds to the program's functionality and power. Figure 1.2 shows an electronic spreadsheet, and Figure 1.3 shows that the results are automatically recalculated after changing the unit price.

A spreadsheet makes these changes in a significantly shorter period of time and, if the data and formulas are correct, does not make errors.

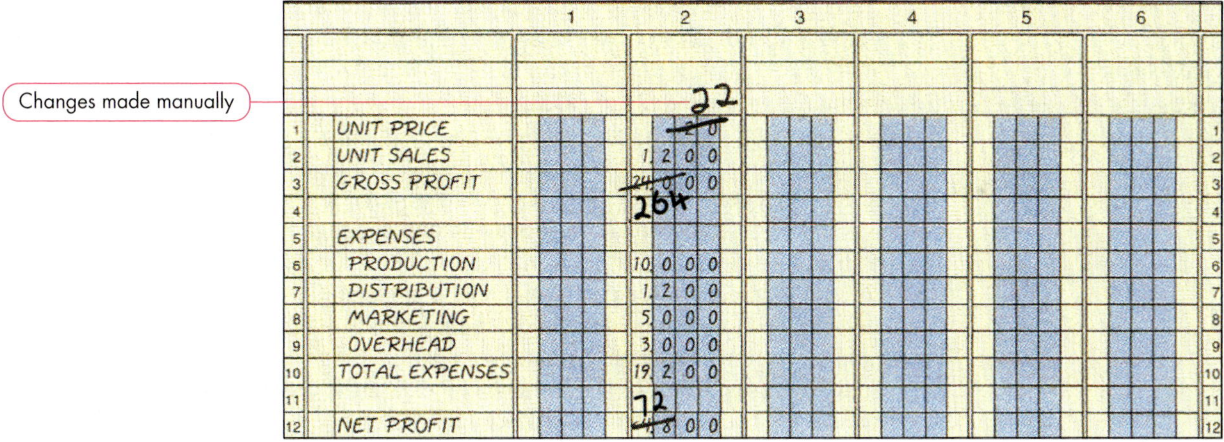

Figure 1.1 Ledger

Unit price is $20

Gross sales calculated automatically

Net profit calculated automatically

	A	B
1	Profit Projection	
2		
3	Unit Price	$20
4	Unit Sales	1,200
5	Gross Sales	$24,000
6		
7	Expenses	
8	Production	$10,000
9	Distribution	$1,200
10	Marketing	$5,000
11	Overhead	$3,000
12	Total Expenses	$19,200
13		
14	Net Profit	$4,800

Figure 1.2 Original Spreadsheet

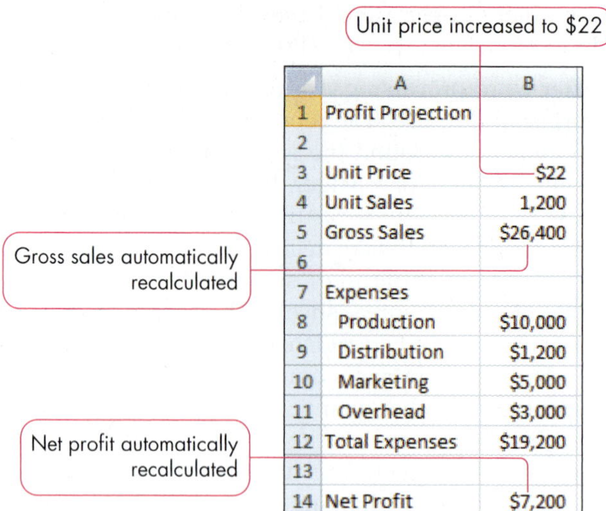

Figure 1.3 Modified Spreadsheet

In this section, you learn about workbooks and worksheets and how spreadsheets are used in various disciplines. You plan good workbook and worksheet design and identify Excel window components prior to creating a spreadsheet.

Defining Worksheets and Workbooks

A ***worksheet*** is a spreadsheet that may contain formulas, functions, values, text, and graphics.

A ***workbook*** is a file containing related worksheets.

A ***worksheet*** is a single spreadsheet consisting of a grid of columns and rows that often contain descriptive labels, numeric values, formulas, functions, and graphics. The terms worksheet and spreadsheet are often used interchangeably. A ***workbook*** is a collection of related worksheets contained within a single file. Storing multiple worksheets within one workbook helps organize related data in one file. In addition, it enables you to perform calculations among the worksheets within the workbook.

Managers often create workbooks to store an organization's annual budget. The workbook may consist of five worksheets, one for each quarter, with the fifth spreadsheet showing summary figures. Alternatively, individuals and families often create a budget workbook of 12 worksheets, one for each month, to store personal income and expenses. Instructors often create a workbook to store a grade book with individual worksheets for each class. On a personal level, you might want to list your DVD collection in one workbook in which you have a worksheet for each category, such as action, comedy, drama, etc. Within each worksheet, you list the DVD title, release date, purchase price, and so on. Regardless of the situation, you can use one workbook to contain many related worksheets.

TIP The Workbook

An Excel workbook is the electronic equivalent of the three-ring binder. A workbook contains one or more worksheets (or chart sheets), each of which is identified by a tab at the bottom of the workbook. The worksheets in a workbook are normally related to one another; for example, each worksheet may contain the sales for a specific division within a company. The advantage of a workbook is that all of its worksheets are stored in a single file, which is accessed as a unit.

Using Spreadsheets Across Disciplines

Students typically think spreadsheets are used solely for business applications. Spreadsheets are used for accounting and business planning using powerful "what-if" functions. These functions enable business planners to project different amounts of profit as other factors change. Even students can use basic "what if" analysis with a budget to determine if they can afford a particular payment or determine if they have sufficient income to buy a new car.

Spreadsheets are, however, used in many other areas. Because of the powerful graphing or charting feature of Excel, geologists and physical scientists use spreadsheets to store data about earthquakes or other physical phenomena, chart the data with a scatter chart, and then plot it on maps to predict where these phenomena might occur. Historians and social scientists have long used spreadsheets for predicting voting behavior or supporting or refuting theses such as Beard's Economic Interpretation of the Constitution. Figure 1.4 shows another use for spreadsheets—a summary of temperatures over time for several cities.

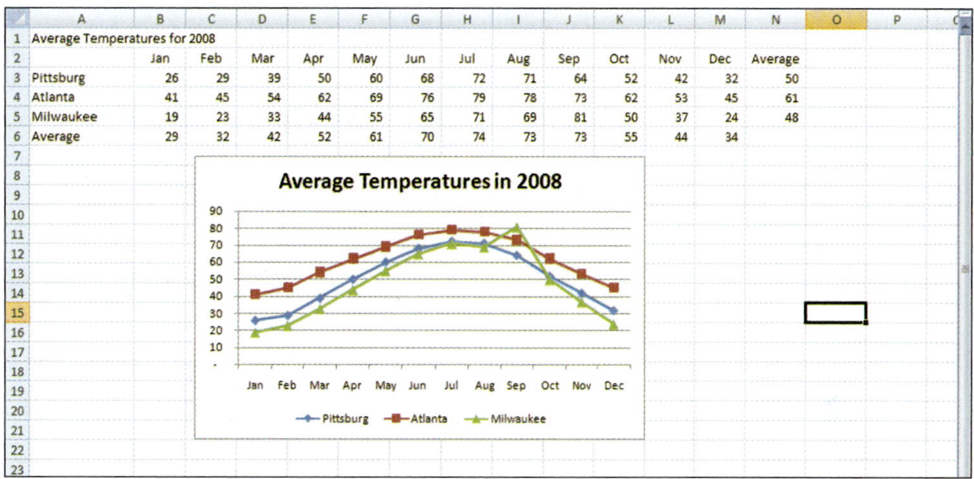

Average Temperatures for 2008													
	Jan	Feb	Mar	Apr	May	Jun	Jul	Aug	Sep	Oct	Nov	Dec	Average
Pittsburg	26	29	39	50	60	68	72	71	64	52	42	32	50
Atlanta	41	45	54	62	69	76	79	78	73	62	53	45	61
Milwaukee	19	23	33	44	55	65	71	69	81	50	37	24	48
Average	29	32	42	52	61	70	74	73	73	55	44	34	

Figure 1.4 Temperatures over Time by City Example Spreadsheet

Educators at all levels—elementary school teachers through university professors—are increasing their use of electronic spreadsheets. Many Web sites now show literally thousands of examples of how educators are using spreadsheets in their classrooms. Once both students and teachers understand the basics of Excel, the possibilities are endless. As noted, spreadsheets are widely used in education. The most common use of Excel is in creating grade book spreadsheets.

Planning for Good Workbook and Worksheet Design

Figures 1.5, 1.6, and 1.7 show three views of a teacher's grade book. The first figure shows a grade book as a teacher might keep it with paper and pencil. The second figure shows the grade book in a spreadsheet program, and the third figure shows the grade book after some changes are made. The handwritten version of the grade book has the teacher writing in grades and calculating averages with a calculator or on paper. If changes are necessary, out comes the eraser and correction fluid. The second and third examples using the electronic spreadsheet show its simplicity. The teacher can easily enter grades, change grades, use weighted items, and recalculate—that is the power of the spreadsheet. For many teachers the spreadsheet grade book is such an integral part of their work that they have never seen or cannot remember a paper grade book.

You should plan the structure of the spreadsheet before you start entering data into a new worksheet. At times it may be necessary for you to sit with paper and pencil and create the spreadsheet design on paper. See Figure 1.5 for an example of a handwritten grade book. The steps that are necessary for the design of a workbook and a worksheet include the following:

1. Figure out the purpose of the spreadsheet and how it will be constructed. For example, a professor's purpose is to create an electronic grade book to store student names and scores and to calculate student grades.

2. Make it obvious where data are to be entered. The teacher needs to store student first names, last names, and three test scores for all students in the class. See Figure 1.6 for a sample worksheet.
3. Enter data and set up formulas wherever possible. Avoid constants (raw numbers) in formulas; use cell references to cells containing numbers instead. Never do manually what Excel can do automatically. You could, for example, calculate each student's class average. Furthermore, you can calculate the class average for each test to see if the tests are too easy or too difficult.
4. Test, test, and test again to make sure the results are what you expect. It is easy to make mistakes when entering data and when constructing formulas. Make whatever changes are necessary.
5. Format the worksheet so it is attractive but not so obtrusive that the purpose of the worksheet is lost. Include a title and column headings, and center the headings. Make sure decimal points align. Add bold to headings, increase the font size for readability, and use color to draw attention to important values or to trends.
6. Document the worksheet as thoroughly as possible. Include the current date, your name, class, and semester. Include cell comments describing the formulas so you know what values are used to produce the results.
7. Save and print the finished product. Auditors and teachers may require you to print a second time with cell formulas displayed so they can verify the formulas are correct. We will discuss cell formulas more thoroughly later in the chapter.

Student	Test 1	Test 2	Final	Average
Adams	100	90	81	90.3
Baker	90	76	87	84.3
Glassman	90	78	78	82.0
Moldof	60	60	40	53.3
Walker	80	80	90	83.3
Class Average	84.0	76.8	75.2	

Walker's average grade is 83.3

Walker's final exam grade is 90

Figure 1.5 The Professor's Grade Book

	A	B	C	D	E	F
1	Student	Test 1	Test 2	Final	Average	
2						
3	Adams	100	90	81	90.3	
4	Baker	90	76	87	84.3	
5	Glassman	90	78	78	82.0	
6	Moldof	60	60	40	53.3	
7	Walker	80	80	90	83.3	
8						
9	Class Average	84.0	76.8	75.2		
10						

Walker's final exam grade is 90

Figure 1.6 Original Grades

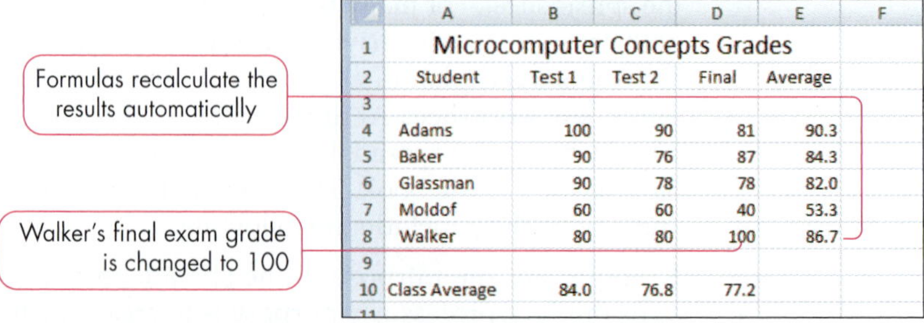

	A	B	C	D	E	F
1	Microcomputer Concepts Grades					
2	Student	Test 1	Test 2	Final	Average	
3						
4	Adams	100	90	81	90.3	
5	Baker	90	76	87	84.3	
6	Glassman	90	78	78	82.0	
7	Moldof	60	60	40	53.3	
8	Walker	80	80	100	86.7	
9						
10	Class Average	84.0	76.8	77.2		

Formulas recalculate the results automatically
Walker's final exam grade is changed to 100

Figure 1.7 Modified Spreadsheet

Identifying Excel Window Components

Each window in Excel has its own Minimize, Maximize, and Close buttons. The title bar contains the name of the application (Excel) and the name of the workbook you are using. At the bottom and right of the document window are the vertical and horizontal scroll bars. The ***active cell*** is the cell you are working in, the cell where information or data will be input. Its cell reference appears in the name box, its contents in the formula bar, and it is surrounded by a dark black box. The active cell can be changed by clicking in a different cell or using the arrow keys to move to another cell.

The ***active cell*** is the cell you are working in, the cell where information or data will be input.

The Excel window includes items that are similar to other Office applications and items that are unique to the Excel application. See Figure 1.8, the Excel window, with the parts of the window identified. The following paragraphs name and describe items in the Excel window.

- **Ribbon**: The Ribbon is made of tabs, groups, and commands.
- **Tab**: Each tab is made up of several groups so that you can see all of its functions without opening menus. The contents of each tab are shown on the reference page. This defines the tabs, the groups they contain, and their general function. You will refer to this page frequently.
- **Office Menu**: The Office menu displays when you click the Office Button in the upper left of the Excel window and contains the following commands, all of which open dialog boxes: New, Open, Save, Save As, Print, Prepare, Send, Publish, and Close. A list of recently used workbooks and an extensive Excel Options section displays. See Figure 1.9 for the contents of the Office menu.
- **Formula Bar**: The formula bar appears below the Ribbon and above the workbook screen and shows the active cell's contents. The ***formula bar*** displays the contents of cells; you can enter or edit cell contents here or directly in the active cell.

The ***formula bar*** is used to enter or edit cell contents.

- **Name Box**: The ***name box*** is another name for the cell reference of the cell currently used in the worksheet. The name box appears to the left of the formula bar and displays the active cell's address (D4) or a name it has been assigned.

The ***name box*** indicates the location or name for the active cell.

- **Sheet Tabs**: ***Sheet tabs*** are located at the bottom left of the Excel window and tell the user what sheets of a workbook are available. Three sheet tabs, initially named Sheet1, Sheet2, and Sheet3, are included when you open a new workbook in Excel. To move between sheets, click on the sheet you want to work with. You can even rename sheets with more meaningful names. If you create more sheets than can be displayed you can use the sheet tab scroll buttons to scroll through all sheet tabs.

Sheet tabs tell the user what sheets of a workbook are available.

- **Status Bar**: The status bar is located at the bottom of the Excel window. It is below the sheet tabs and above the Windows taskbar and displays information about a selected command or operation in progress. For example, it displays *Select destination and press ENTER or choose Paste* after you use the Copy command.
- **Select All Button**: The ***Select All button*** is the square at the intersection of the rows and column headings and you can use it to select all elements of the active worksheet.

The ***Select All button*** is clicked to select all elements of the worksheet.

- **Column Headings:** The letters above the columns are called column headings. Excel identifies columns by letters, such as A, B, C, and so on.
- **Row Headings:** The numbers to the left of the rows are called row headings. Excel identifies rows by numbers, such as 1, 2, 3, and so on.

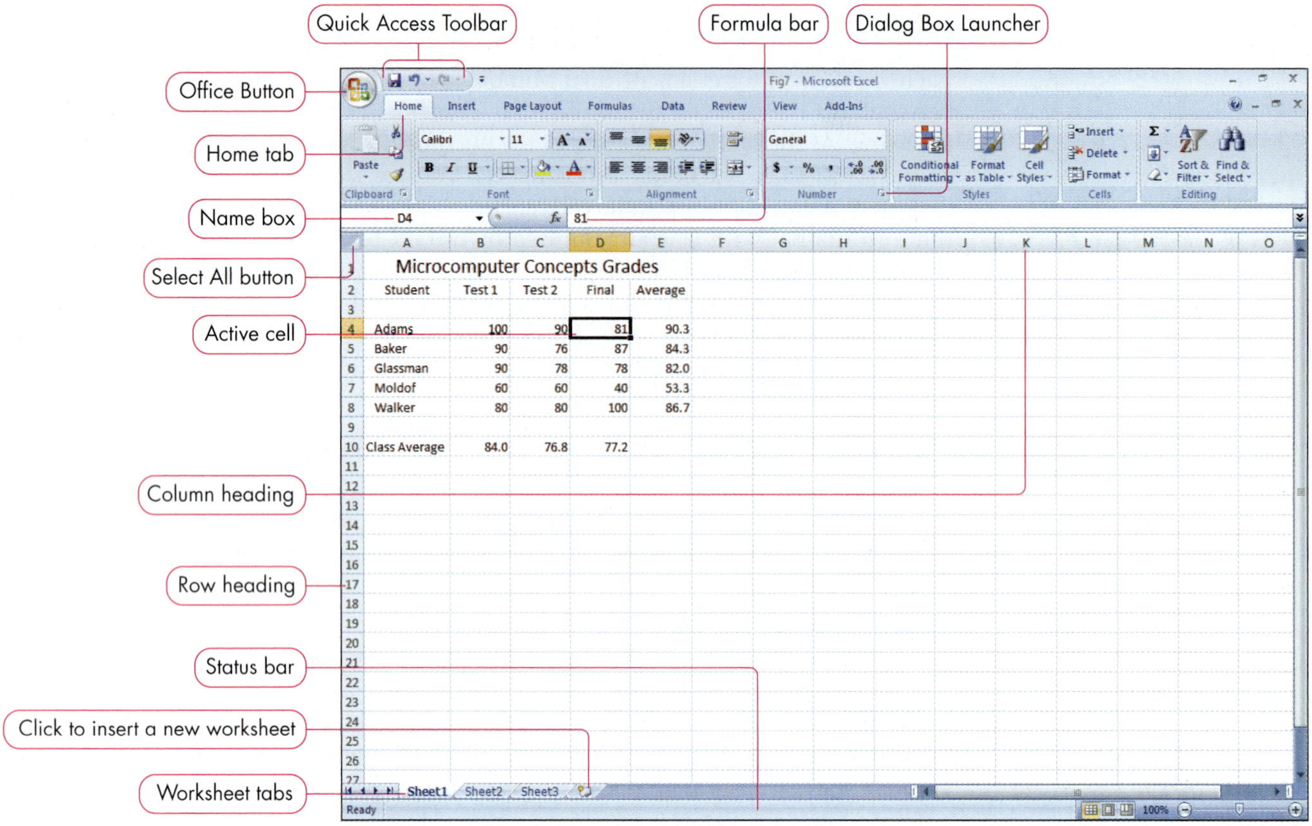

Quick Access Toolbar
Formula bar
Dialog Box Launcher
Office Button
Home tab
Name box
Select All button
Active cell
Column heading
Row heading
Status bar
Click to insert a new worksheet
Worksheet tabs

	A	B	C	D	E
1	Microcomputer Concepts Grades				
2	Student	Test 1	Test 2	Final	Average
3					
4	Adams	100	90	81	90.3
5	Baker	90	76	87	84.3
6	Glassman	90	78	78	82.0
7	Moldof	60	60	40	53.3
8	Walker	80	80	100	86.7
9					
10	Class Average	84.0	76.8	77.2	

Figure 1.8 The Excel Window

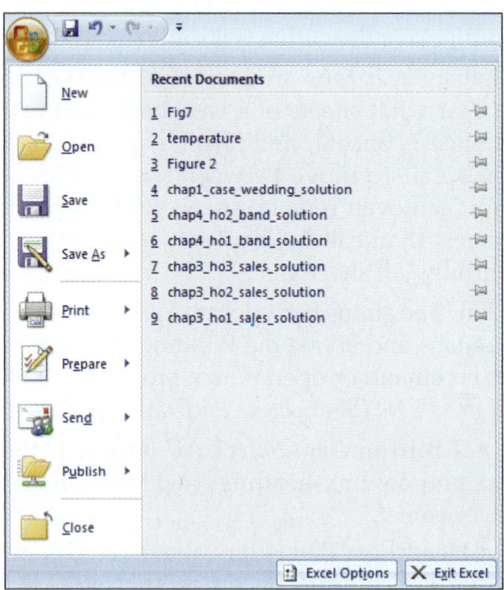

Figure 1.9 The Office Menu

Tab and Group	Description

Home

Clipboard
Font
Alignment
Number
Styles
Cells
Editing

The basic Excel tab. Contains basic editing functions such as cut and paste along with most formatting actions. As with all groups, pull-down areas are available and do increase functionality. Your Tabs may display differently depending on your screen resolution.

Insert

Tables
Illustrations
Charts
Links
Text

Brings together all insert functions in one area. Includes ability to create charts and add tables. Contains powerful picture functions. Headers and footers are inserted here.

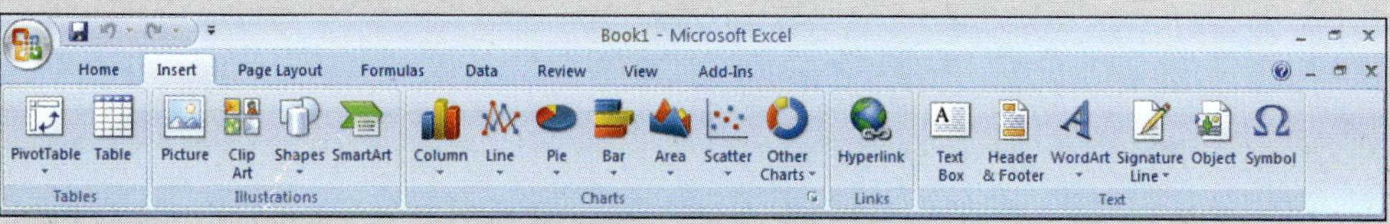

Page Layout

Themes
Page Setup
Scale to Fit
Sheet Options
Arrange

Contains all functions associated with page appearance, setup, and printing. Also controls the display of sheet options, such as gridlines and headings.

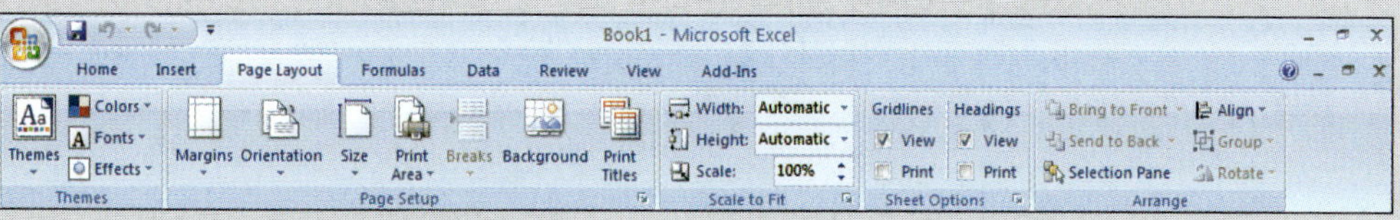

Formulas

Function Library
Defined Names
Formula Auditing
Calculation

The area that contains the mathematical backbone of Excel. Includes basic areas (Function Library) as well as more advanced (Formula Auditing).

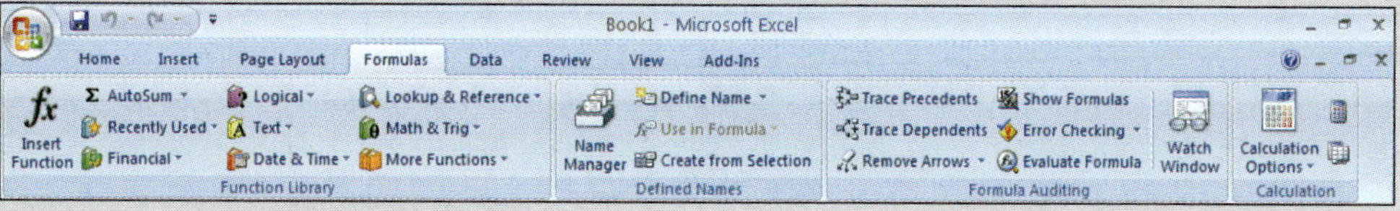

Data

Groups	Description
Get External Data Connections Sort & Filter Data Tools Outline	The heart of the database portions of Excel. While not a true relational database, it has much power and includes Goal Seek and Scenario Manager.

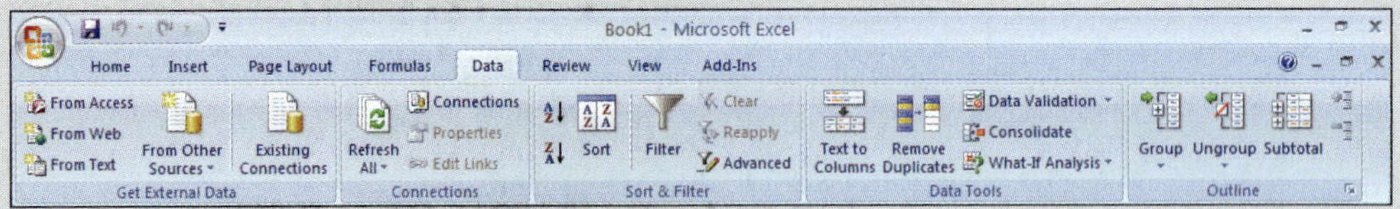

Review

Groups	Description
Proofing Comments Changes	Contains all reviewing tools in Excel, including such things as spelling, the use of comments, and sharing and protection.

View

Groups	Description
Workbook Views Show/Hide Zoom Window Macros	Contains basic and advanced view settings. Some of these options also appear below the horizontal and vertical scroll bars.

Start Excel and Create a New Worksheet

The first thing you should do is open Excel. You can do this by taking the following steps:

1. Click the Start button to display the Start menu. Position the mouse pointer over All Programs, select Microsoft Office, and then select Microsoft Office Excel 2007 from its location on the Programs menu.
2. Maximize the Excel program if necessary.

This opens a new Excel workbook with the default three worksheet tabs. When Excel is already open and you want to open a new workbook, complete the following steps:

1. Click the Office Button.
2. Select New, click Blank Workbook, and then click the Create button.

A new workbook is now open.

Identify Columns, Rows, and Cells

A spreadsheet is divided into columns and rows, with each column and row assigned a heading. Columns are assigned alphabetic headings from column A to Z, continue from AA to AZ, and then from BA to BZ until the last of the 16,384 columns is reached. Rows have numeric headings ranging from 1 to 1,048,576 (the maximum number of rows allowed).

A ***cell*** is the intersection of a column and row.

A ***cell reference*** is designated by a column letter and a row number.

The intersection of a column and row forms a ***cell***, with the number of cells in a spreadsheet equal to the number of columns times the number of rows. Each cell has a unique ***cell reference***, which is the intersection of a column and row designated by a column letter and a row number. For example, the cell at the intersection of column A and row 9 is known as cell A9. The column heading always precedes the row heading in the cell reference.

Navigate in Worksheets

Selecting cells to make them active and navigating from cell to cell are basic navigational skills in Excel. Using the mouse is probably the most convenient way to select a cell and navigate. To make a cell active, click on the desired cell. Making another cell active simply involves clicking on another cell. If the cell to be made active is not visible, use the vertical or horizontal scroll bars or the arrow keys to move so the desired cell is visible.

The other way is to use different keys to navigate through the worksheet. Table 1.1 shows keys that can be used to move in a worksheet.

Table 1.1 Keystrokes and Actions

Keystroke	Action
↑	Moves up one cell.
↓	Moves down one cell.
←	Moves left one cell.
→	Moves right one cell.
PgUp	Moves active cell up one screen.
PgDn	Moves active cell down one screen.
Home	Moves active cell to column A of current row.
Ctrl+Home	Moves active cell to cell A1.
Ctrl+End	Moves to the rightmost, lowermost active corner of the worksheet.
F5 or Ctrl+G	Displays the GoTo dialog box to enter any cell address.

Entering and Editing Data in Cells

The three types of data that can be entered in a cell in an Excel worksheet are text, values, and formulas, which also include functions. You can create very sophisticated workbooks and simple worksheets with any combination of text, values, and formulas.

Enter Text

Text includes letters, numbers, symbols, and spaces.

Text is any combination of entries from the keyboard and includes letters, numbers, symbols, and spaces. Even though text entries may be used as data, they are most often used to identify and document the spreadsheet. Text is used to indicate the title of the spreadsheet. Typically text is used for row and column labels. When you need to enter text, click in the cell where the text is to appear, type the text, and either press Enter or click the ✓ on the formula bar. Text is left-aligned by default.

Sometimes you may have a long label that does not fit well in the cell. You can insert a line break to display the label on multiple lines within the cell. To insert a line break, press Alt+Enter where you want to start the next line of text within the cell.

Enter Values

A ***value*** is a number that represent a quantity, an amount, a date, or time.

Values are numbers entered in a cell that represent a quantity, an amount, a date, or time. As a general rule, Excel can recognize if you are entering text or values by what is typed. The biggest difference between text and value entries is that value entries can be the basis of calculation while text cannot. Values are right-aligned by default.

Enter Formulas

A ***formula*** is a combination of numbers, cell references, operators, and/or functions.

Formulas (and their shorthand form, functions) are the combination of constants, cell references, arithmetic operations, and/or functions displayed in a calculation. For Excel to recognize a formula it must always start with an equal sign (=). You learn about basic formulas in this chapter. Chapter 2 provides a detailed discussion of formulas and functions. At this point it is sufficient to say that =A2+B2 is an example of a formula to perform addition.

TIP AutoComplete

As soon as you begin typing a label into a cell, Excel searches for and automatically displays any other label in that column that matches the letters you typed. AutoComplete is helpful if you want to repeat a label, but it can be distracting if you want to enter a different label that begins with the same letter. To turn the feature on (or off), click the Office Button, click Excel Options, and click the Advanced tab. Check (clear) the Enable AutoComplete for cell values check box to enable (disable) the AutoComplete feature.

Edit and Clear Cell Contents

You have several ways to edit the contents of a cell. You will probably select and stay with one technique that you find most convenient. The first method is to select the cell you want to edit, click in the formula bar, make changes, and then press Enter. The second method requires that you double-click in the cell to be edited, make the edits, and then press Enter. The third method is similar except that you select the cell, press the F2 key, and then make the edit.

You have two options to clear the contents of a cell. First, just click on a cell and press Delete. The second option involves clicking the Clear arrow in the Editing group on the Home tab. This gives you several options as to what will be cleared from the cell (see Figure 1.10).

Figure 1.10 Clear Drop-down List

Use Save and Save As

It is basic computer practice that files, including workbooks, should be saved often. If you are using a workbook and you do not want to change its name, the easiest way to save it is to click the Office Button and select Save. If you prefer keyboard shortcuts, press Ctrl+S. You also can click Save on the Quick Access Toolbar.

The first time you save a workbook, you can use the Save command or the Save As command that is located on the Office menu. For an unnamed file, either command displays the Save As dialog box. You can then assign a file name that is descriptive of the workbook (gradebook08, for example), determine the file location, and choose the file type. After selecting the appropriate options, click Save. When you use the Save command after initially saving a workbook, the subsequent changes are saved under the same workbook name and in the same location. If you want to assign a different name to a modified workbook so that you can preserve the original workbook, use the Save As command.

TIP File Management with Excel

Use the Office Button in the Open or Save As dialog box to perform basic file management within any Office application. You can select any existing file or folder, and delete it or rename it. You can also create a new folder, which is very useful when you begin to work with a large number of documents. You can also use the Views button to change the way the files are listed within the dialog box.

Hands-On Exercises

1 | Introduction to Microsoft Excel

Skills covered: 1. Plan Your Workbook **2.** Start Microsoft Office Excel 2007 **3.** Enter and Edit Data in Cells **4.** Use the Save As Command and Explore the Worksheet

Step 1 Plan Your Workbook

Refer to Figure 1.11 as you complete Step 1.

a. Prepare notes before starting Excel.

Specify or define the problem. What statistics will be produced by your spreadsheet? Do you already have the statistics, or do you need to collect them from another source? Brainstorm about what formulas and functions will be required. Experiment with paper and pencil and a calculator. The first spreadsheet you create will be a sample showing membership sales in a gym. This sample worksheet includes monthly sales by region for both first and second quarters. Also included are the calculations to determine total monthly sales, average monthly sales, total and average sales by region, and increase or decrease in sales between the first and second quarters.

b. Simplify your Excel spreadsheet for those who will enter data.

You should treat your Excel workbook like a Microsoft Word document by doing such things as adding cell comments, giving instructions, and using attractive formatting.

c. Consider these layout suggestions when designing your Excel spreadsheets:

- Reserve the first row for a spreadsheet title.
- Reserve a row for column headings.
- Reserve a column at the left for row headings.
- Do not leave blank rows and columns for white space within the spreadsheet layout.
- Widen the columns and rows and use alignment instead of leaving blank rows or columns.
- Save your work often.

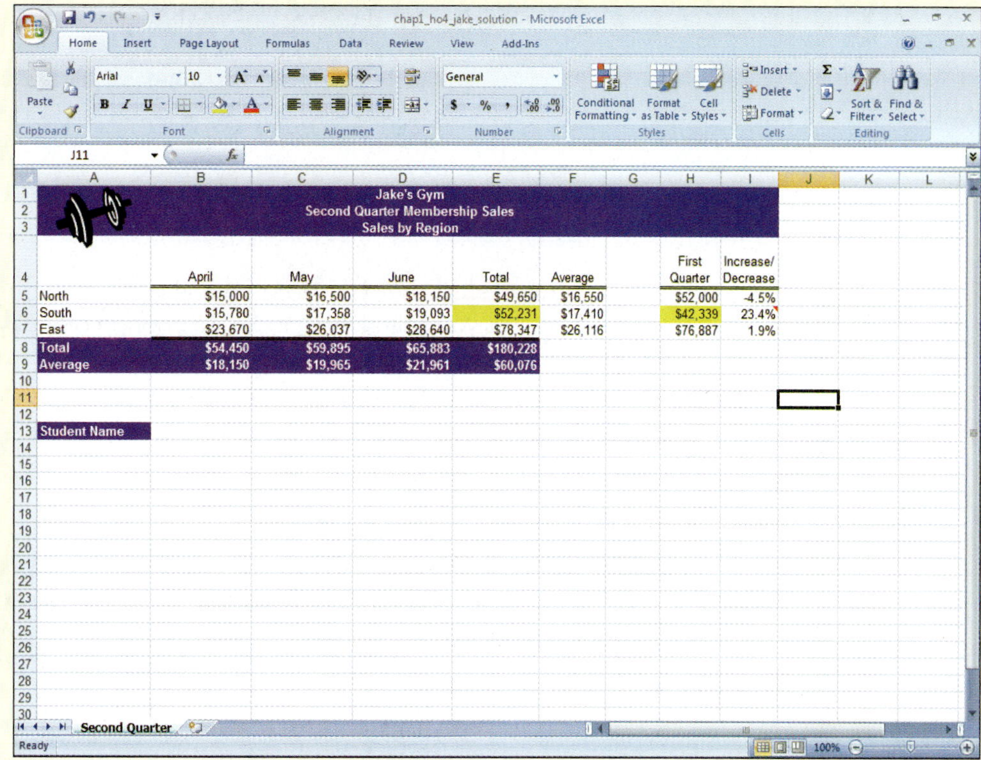

Figure 1.11 Well-Designed Spreadsheet

Step 2
Start Microsoft Office Excel 2007

a. Click the **Start button** to display the Start menu. Click (or point to) **All Programs**, click **Microsoft Office**, and then click **Microsoft Office Excel 2007** to start the program.

You should be familiar with basic file management and very comfortable moving and copying files from one folder to another. If not, you may want to review the Help material for basic file management.

b. If necessary, click the **Maximize** button in the application window so that Excel takes the entire desktop as shown in Figure 1.11. Click the **Maximize** button in the document window (if necessary) so that the workbook window is as large as possible.

Step 3
Enter and Edit Data in Cells

Refer to Figure 1.12 as you complete Step 3. The spreadsheet is shown at 120% zoom magnification so that you can see the data easier.

a. Click **cell A1**, type **Jake's Gym**, and press **Enter**.

b. In **cell A2**, type **Second Quarter Membership Sales**.

c. Click **cell B3**, type the label **April**, and press the **right arrow**.

d. Type the label **May**, and press the **right arrow**. Complete the typing for **cells D3** through **H3** as shown. Do not be concerned if the entire column label is not visible.

D3	June
E3	Total
F3	Average
G3	First Quarter
H3	Increase/Decrease

e. Enter the data for three regions as shown below, starting in **cell A4**:

	April	May	June	First Quarter
North	15000	16500	18150	31000
South	15780	17358	19093	42339
East	23670	26037	28640	76887

TROUBLESHOOTING: Data entry is important for good spreadsheet use. Verify values as you finish typing them. To change an entry, click on the cell and retype the value. To delete an entry, click on the cell and press Delete.

f. Type **Total** in **cell A7** and type **Average** in **cell A8**.

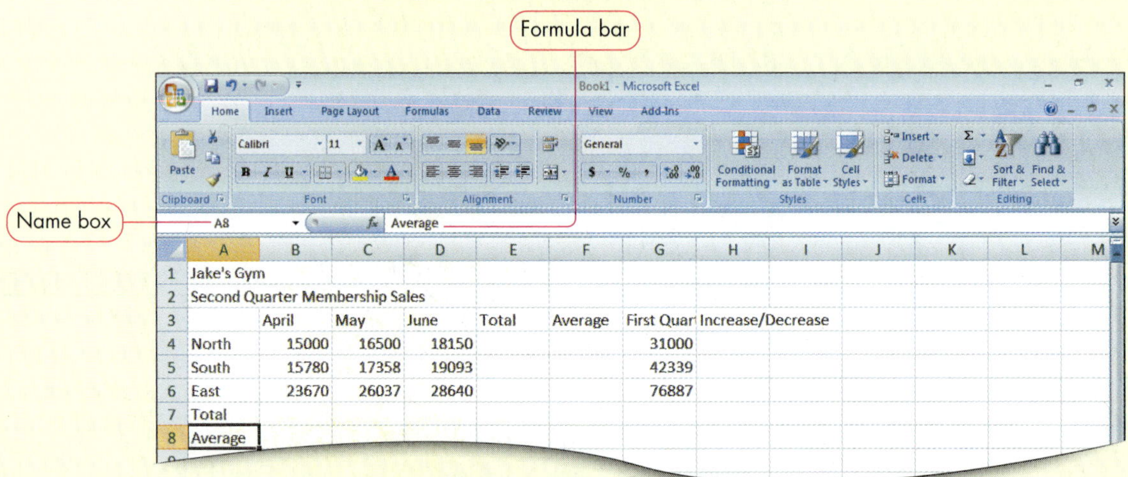

Figure 1.12 Jake's Gym Data

Step 4
Use the Save As Command and Explore the Worksheet

Refer to Figures 1.12 and 1.13 as you complete Step 4. Your Home tab may not display exactly as shown because of different screen resolutions.

a. Click the **Office Button** and click **Save As** to display the Save As dialog box shown in Figure 1.13.

b. Type **chap1_ho1_jake_solution** as the name of the new workbook.

A file name, including its path, may contain up to 255 characters. Spaces, underscores, and commas are allowed in the file name.

c. Click the appropriate drive and folder in the Folders list on the left side of the Save As dialog box. Choose the location where you want to save your completed files.

d. Click the **Save button**.

You should see the workbook as displayed in Figure 1.12.

e. Click in **cell D4**, the cell containing 18150 or the North June sales.

Cell D4 is now the active cell and is surrounded by a heavy border. The name box indicates that cell D4 is the active cell, and its contents are displayed in the formula bar.

f. Click in **cell D5** (or press the down arrow key) to make it the active cell.

The name box indicates cell D5.

g. Refer to Table 1.1 as you move around the worksheet.

h. Click the **Office Button** and select **Close** to close the *chap1_ho1_jake_solution* workbook. Keep Excel open if you plan to continue working on Hands-On Exercise 2.

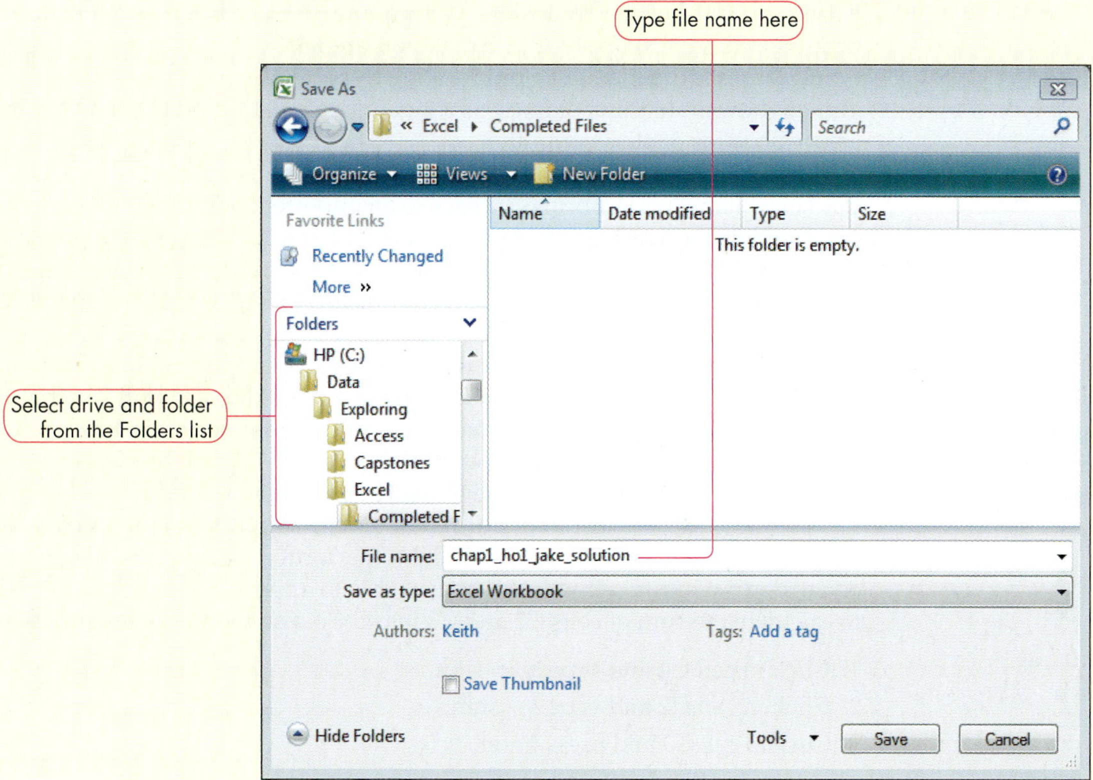

Figure 1.13 Save As Dialog Box

TIP Keyboard Shortcuts—The Dialog Box

Press Tab or Shift+Tab to move forward or backward between fields in a dialog box, or press Alt plus the underlined letter to move directly to an option. You will see underlined letters in words in dialog boxes. These are the letters you use in conjunction with the Alt key. If you do not see the underlines, press and hold down Alt until you see them. Use the spacebar to toggle check boxes on or off and the up (or down) arrow keys to move between options in a list box. Press Enter to apply selected settings and Esc to exit the dialog box without accepting the changes. These are universal shortcuts and apply to any Windows application.

Mathematics and Formulas

You have used calculators where numbers are entered, the correct arithmetic function key is pressed, and the correct answer appears. What is missing though is the knowledge of the process, or how to arrive at the correct answer. These mathematical processes are the key to understanding and using Excel. Without knowing the process and how to apply it in Excel, you are left with just numbers, not answers. Arithmetic and mathematics produce answers by calculating numbers using Excel. You might want to think of Excel as a gigantic calculating program on the most powerful calculator of all, a computer.

With Excel, when any change is made, the entire worksheet is updated based on this new value. This fact brings us back to an important question: Why use Excel when one could just as easily perform calculations on a calculator or on paper? What happens if profit is 4% rather than 5%? In the pre-Excel days, answering these questions required rewriting and retyping the whole business plan using pencil, paper, and typewriter.

(Formulas can be as simple or as complex as necessary, but always begin with an = sign and contain mathematical operators.)

In this section, you learn about the mathematical operations that are the backbone of Excel. You also will see that the order these mathematical operations are performed in can have a significant impact on the results. We touch briefly on the construction of mathematical expressions, called ***formulas***, that direct Excel to perform mathematical operations and arrive at a calculated result. Whenever you want Excel to perform a calculation you must enter an equal sign (=) in the cell where the answer is to appear. For example, if you wanted to calculate the sum of cells C2 and C3 in cell C4, you would do the following:

1. Click in cell C4 and type an = sign.
2. Click in cell C2 and type a + sign.
3. Click in cell C3 and press Enter.

This is an extremely simplified example but the principle holds true in all formulas. See Table 1.2 for examples of formulas. Formulas can be as simple or as complex as necessary, but always begin with an = sign and often contain mathematical operators.

Table 1.2 Formula Examples

Operation	Formula
Addition	=C1+C2
Subtraction	=C2-C1
Multiplication	=C1*C2
Division	=C1/C2

Describing and Using Symbols and the Order of Precedence

The four mathematical functions—addition, subtraction, multiplication, and division—are the basis of all mathematical operations. Table 1.3 lists the arithmetic operators and their purposes.

Table 1.3 Arithmetic Operators and Symbols

Operation	Common Symbol	Symbol in Excel
Addition	+	+
Subtraction	–	–
Multiplication	X	*
Division	÷	/
Exponentiation	^	^

Enter Cell References in Formulas

If this were all there was to it, Excel would be effortless for all of us, but two other things need to be done if Excel is to perform mathematical functions as it was designed to do. First, rather than entering the numbers that are contained in the cells, Excel works at its full potential if cell references (C5, B2, etc.) are used rather than the numbers themselves. See Figure 1.14 for an example.

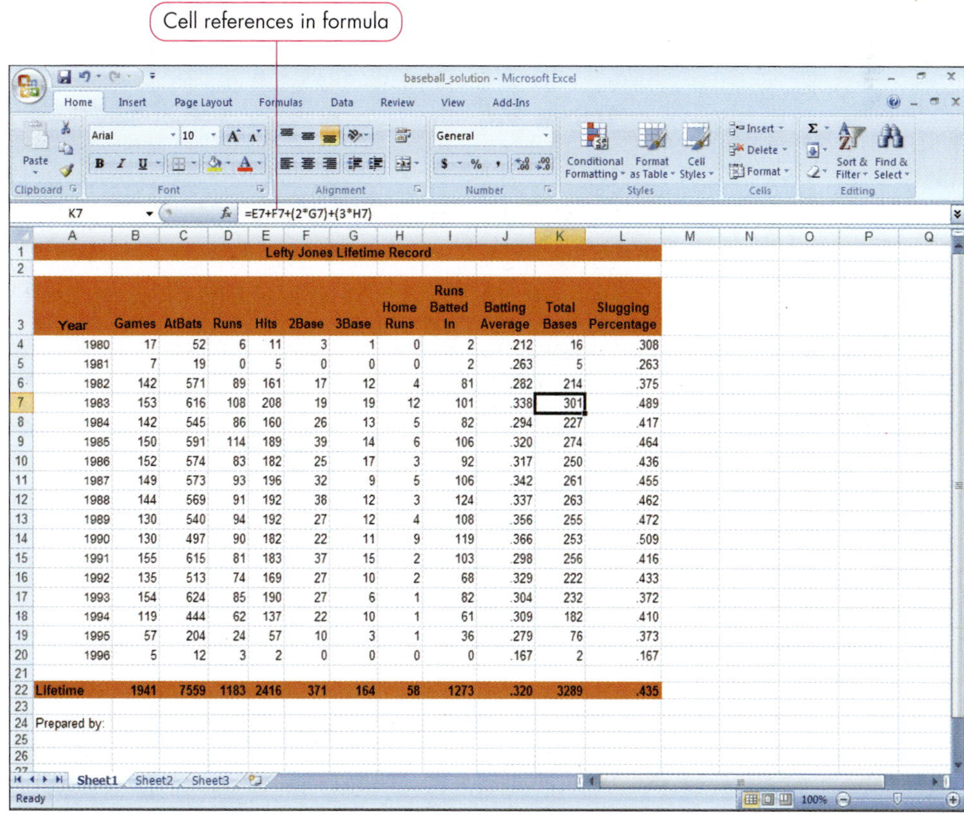

Lefty Jones Lifetime Record										
Year	Games	AtBats	Runs	Hits	2Base	3Base	Home Runs	Runs Batted In	Batting Average	Total Bases	Slugging Percentage
1980	17	52	6	11	3	1	0	2	.212	16	.308
1981	7	19	0	5	0	0	0	2	.263	5	.263
1982	142	571	89	161	17	12	4	81	.282	214	.375
1983	153	616	108	208	19	19	12	101	.338	301	.489
1984	142	545	86	160	26	13	5	82	.294	227	.417
1985	150	591	114	189	39	14	6	106	.320	274	.464
1986	152	574	83	182	25	17	3	92	.317	250	.436
1987	149	573	93	196	32	9	5	106	.342	261	.455
1988	144	569	91	192	38	12	3	124	.337	263	.462
1989	130	540	94	192	27	12	4	108	.356	255	.472
1990	130	497	90	182	22	11	9	119	.366	253	.509
1991	155	615	81	183	37	15	2	103	.298	256	.416
1992	135	513	74	169	27	10	2	68	.329	222	.433
1993	154	624	85	190	27	6	1	82	.304	232	.372
1994	119	444	62	137	22	10	1	61	.309	182	.410
1995	57	204	24	57	10	3	1	36	.279	76	.373
1996	5	12	3	2	0	0	0	0	.167	2	.167
Lifetime	1941	7559	1183	2416	371	164	58	1273	.320	3289	.435

Figure 1.14 Baseball Statistics with Cell References

The first thing to consider is how Excel (or the computer) recognizes that you want to perform a mathematical operation. For example, you decide that you need to add the contents of cells C1 and C2 and place the sum in cell C3. In C1 you have the number 5, and in C2 you have the number 3. If you enter 5+3 and press Enter, the result you see will be "5+3." This is not the answer, however, that you are looking for. You want the result of 8. Anytime you want Excel to perform a mathematical calculation, you must begin by typing =. The equal sign tells Excel "get ready to do some math." One way to get the answer of 8 is by typing =5+3 and pressing Enter to see the sum, 8, in cell C3.

If you then change the number in cell C1 from 5 to 7, you must now change the 5 to a 7 in the formula in cell C3 to calculate the new result. Excel gives you an easier and much more efficient way to update results of calculations so you do not have to change the content of cell C3 every time the values in cells C1 or C2 change. This operation is done by using cell references. Rather than using the expression =5+3 in cell C3 to get a sum, you should enter the expression =C1+C2 in cell C3. This way, even if you change the values of cell C1 or C2, the value in cell C3 remains the sum of cells C1 and C2 because you are using cell references rather than the value in the cells.

Control the Results with the Order of Precedence

The ***order of precedence*** controls the sequence in which arithmetic operations are performed, which affects the result.

Before moving on to formulas, the final mathematics concept you need to know is order of precedence. The ***order of precedence*** are rules that control the order or sequence in which arithmetic operations are performed, which in turn will change the result reported in Excel. Excel performs mathematical calculations left to right in this order: parentheses, exponentiation, multiplication or division, and finally addition or subtraction.

Review the expressions in Table 1.4 and notice how the parentheses change the value of the expression. In the second expression, the addition inside the parentheses is performed before the multiplication, changing the order of operations. Strictly following the order of mathematical operations eliminates many puzzling results when using Excel.

Table 1.4 Examples of Order of Precedence

Expression	Order to Perform Calculations	Output
= 6 + 6 * 2	Multiply first **and then** add.	18
= (6 + 6) * 2	Add the values inside the parentheses first **and then** multiply.	24
= 6 + 6 ^ 2	Simplify the exponent first: 6*6=36, **and then** add.	42
= 10/2 + 3	Divide first **and then** add.	8
= 10/(2+3)	Add first to simplify the parenthetical expression **and then** divide.	2
= 10 * 2 - 3 * 2	Multiply first **and then** subtract.	14

Displaying Cell Formulas

When you enter a formula, Excel shows the results of the formula in the spreadsheet; however, you might want to display cell formulas instead of the calculated results. When you display formulas, they will appear in the cells instead of the results of the calculation. See Figures 1.15 and 1.16. The quickest way to display cell formulas is to press Ctrl and the grave accent key (`), sometimes referred to as the tilde key. The tilde (~) key is in the upper-left corner of the keyboard, under Esc. Note: you do not press the Shift key with the tilde key to make cell formulas visible in your worksheet. You can also click Show Formulas in the Formula Auditing group on the Formulas tab to show and hide formulas.

	A	B	C	D	E	F
1	Microcomputer Concepts Grades					
2	Student	Test 1	Test 2	Final	Average	
3						
4	Adams	100	90	81	90.3	
5	Baker	90	76	87	84.3	
6	Glassman	90	78	78	82.0	
7	Moldof	60	60	40	53.3	
8	Walker	80	80	100	86.7	
9						
10	Class Average	84.0	76.8	77.2		

Figure 1.15 Spreadsheet with Values Displayed

	A	B	C	D	E
1	Microcomputer Concepts Grades				
2	Student	Test 1	Test 2	Final	Average
3					
4	Adams	100	90	81	=AVERAGE(B4:D4)
5	Baker	90	76	87	=AVERAGE(B5:D5)
6	Glassman	90	78	78	=AVERAGE(B6:D6)
7	Moldof	60	60	40	=AVERAGE(B7:D7)
8	Walker	80	80	100	=AVERAGE(B8:D8)
9					
10	Class Average	=AVERAGE(B4:B8)	=AVERAGE(C4:C8)	=AVERAGE(D4:D8)	

Figure 1.16 Spreadsheet with Formulas Displayed

Inserting and Deleting Rows and Columns

After you construct a worksheet, it is often necessary to add or delete columns or rows of information. For example, in a grade book kept by a professor, names are constantly added or deleted. This process typically involves the use of the Insert command that adds cells, rows, or columns or the Delete command that deletes cells, rows, or columns. When you use either command, the cell references in existing cells are adjusted automatically to reflect the insertion or deletion. These commands also allow sheets to be added or deleted from the workbook.

To insert a row, click in the row below where you want a row inserted (rows are always inserted above, and columns are always inserted to the left of, the selected cell), and then click the Insert down arrow in the Cells group on the Home tab. You would then select Insert Sheet Rows. To insert a column, the user would select Insert Sheet Columns. For example, if the active cell is E4, row 4 is the current row. If a column is inserted, it is inserted to the left of cell E4. To delete a row, either click the row number and click Delete in the Cells group, or click in any cell on that row, click the Delete down arrow in the Cells group, and select Delete Sheet Rows. To delete a column, either click the column letter and click Delete in the Cells group, or click in any cell in the column you want to delete, click the Delete arrow in the Cells group, and select Delete Sheet Columns.

TIP Inserting and Deleting Individual Cells

In some situations, you may need to insert and delete individual cells instead of inserting or deleting an entire row or column. To insert a cell, click in the cell where you want the new cell, click the Insert down arrow in the Cells group on the Home tab, and then click Insert Cells to display the Insert dialog box. Click the appropriate option to shift cells right or down and click OK (see Figure 1.17). To delete a cell or cells, select the cell(s), click the Delete arrow in the Cells group on the Home tab, and then click Delete Cells to display the Delete dialog box. Click the appropriate option to shift cells left or up and click OK (see Figure 1.18).

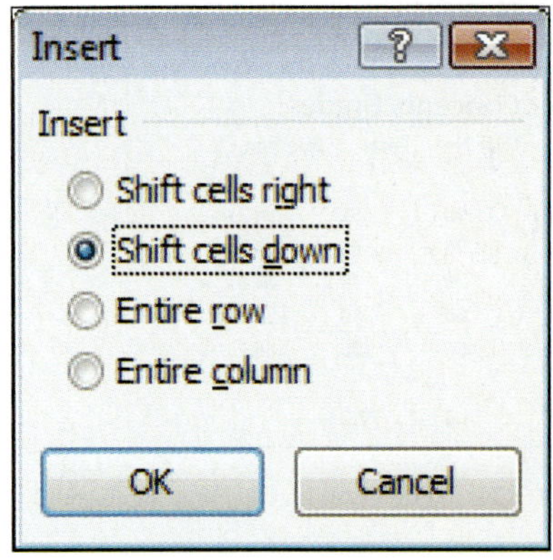

Figure 1.17 Insert Dialog Box

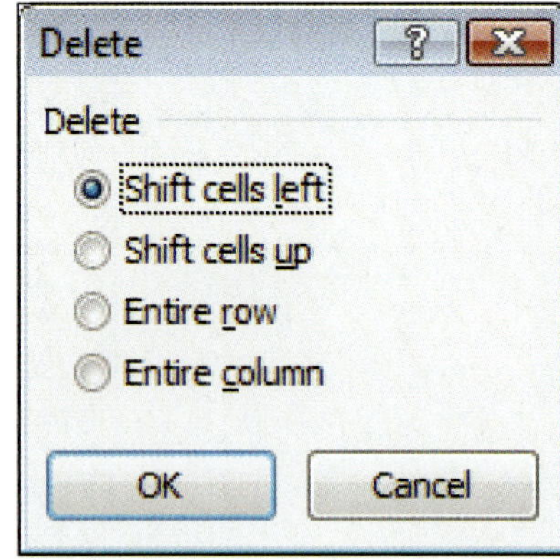

Figure 1.18 Delete Dialog Box

Using Cell Ranges; Excel Move; Copy, Paste, Paste Special; and AutoFill

Each of these topics is a basic editing function in Excel. They will be discussed in detail here, and you will be able to show your proficiency with them in Hands-On Exercise 2.

Select a Range

A ***range*** is a rectangular group of cells.

Every command in Excel applies to a rectangular group of cells known as a ***range***. A range may be as small as a single cell or as large as the entire worksheet. It may consist of a row or part of a row, a column or part of a column, or multiple rows or columns. The cells within a range are specified by indicating the diagonally opposite corners, typically the upper-left and lower-right corners of the rectangle. Many different ranges could be selected in conjunction with the worksheet shown in Figure 1.19. For example, the 1980 Player data is contained in the range B4:I4. The Lifetime totals and averages are found in the range B22:L22. The Batting Averages are found in the range J4:J20.

(A range may be as small as a single cell or as large as the entire worksheet.)

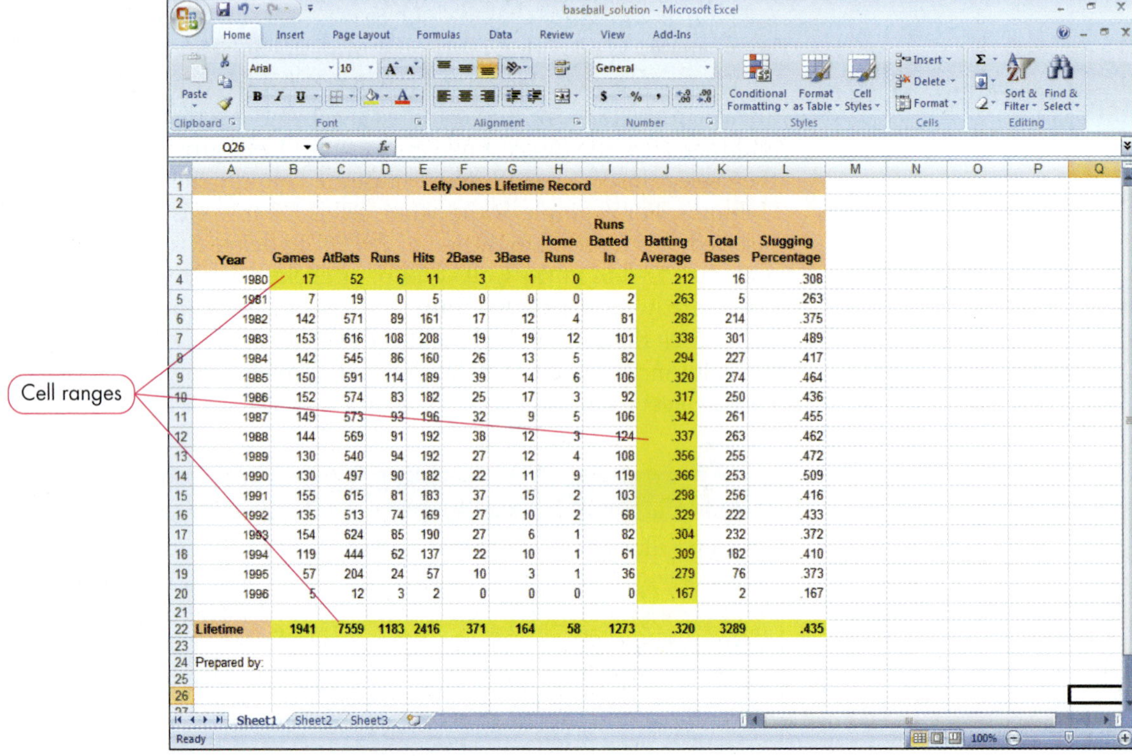

Lefty Jones Lifetime Record

Year	Games	AtBats	Runs	Hits	2Base	3Base	Home Runs	Runs Batted In	Batting Average	Total Bases	Slugging Percentage
1980	17	52	6	11	3	1	0	2	.212	16	.308
1981	7	19	0	5	0	0	0	2	.263	5	.263
1982	142	571	89	161	17	12	4	81	.282	214	.375
1983	153	616	108	208	19	19	12	101	.338	301	.489
1984	142	545	86	160	26	13	5	82	.294	227	.417
1985	150	591	114	189	39	14	6	106	.320	274	.464
1986	152	574	83	182	25	17	3	92	.317	250	.436
1987	149	573	93	196	32	9	5	106	.342	261	.455
1988	144	569	91	192	38	12	3	124	.337	263	.462
1989	130	540	94	192	27	12	4	108	.356	255	.472
1990	130	497	90	182	22	11	9	119	.366	253	.509
1991	155	615	81	183	37	15	2	103	.298	256	.416
1992	135	513	74	169	27	10	2	68	.329	222	.433
1993	154	624	85	190	27	6	1	82	.304	232	.372
1994	119	444	62	137	22	10	1	61	.309	182	.410
1995	57	204	24	57	10	3	1	36	.279	76	.373
1996	5	12	3	2	0	0	0	0	.167	2	.167
Lifetime	1941	7559	1183	2416	371	164	58	1273	.320	3289	.435

Prepared by:

Figure 1.19 Defined Ranges

The easiest way to select a range is to click and drag—click at the beginning of the range and then press and hold the left mouse button as you drag the mouse to the end of the range, where you release the mouse button. To select an entire column, click the column letter. To select an entire row, click the row number. Once selected, the range is highlighted, and its cells will be affected by any subsequent command. The range remains selected until another range is defined or until you click another cell anywhere on the worksheet.

Move a Cell's Contents

The ***move operation*** transfers the content of a cell or cell range from one location to another, with the cells where the move originated becoming empty.

The *move operation* transfers the content of a cell or cell range from one location in the worksheet to another, with the cells where the move originated becoming empty. The use of the move command can be confusing when you copy a cell containing a formula. Cell references in formulas are adjusted relative to the new location within the spreadsheet. You can use the drag-and-drop technique to move a range of cells or the cut and paste method. To use the cut and paste method:

1. Select the range of cells to be moved.
2. Click Cut in the Clipboard group on the Home tab.
3. Select the range the cells will be moved to.
4. Click Paste in the Clipboard group on the Home tab.

The ***delete operation*** removes all content from a cell or from a selected cell range.

The *delete operation* removes all content from a cell or from a selected cell range. While there are several ways to execute the delete operation, the most simple is to select a cell or range of cells and press Delete to remove the information from the cell(s).

Copy, Paste, Paste Special

The Copy, Paste, and Paste Special operations are essential editing operations in any Microsoft Office 2007 application. The Copy command enables you to begin to duplicate information in a cell or range of cells into another cell or range of cells. In order to copy material, you select the cell(s) to be copied and click Copy in the Clipboard group on the Home tab. The Paste operation enables you to duplicate cell contents that you have copied to a new location. Once the contents of a cell or range of cells have been copied, select the location on the worksheet where the material is to be copied to and click Paste in the Clipboard group on the Home tab. The Paste Special operation provides several different options when pasting material (see Figure 1.20). The power of the Copy and Paste operation is enhanced with the use of Paste Special in Excel. To display the Paste Special dialog box, click the Paste arrow in the Clipboard group on the Home tab, and then select Paste Special.

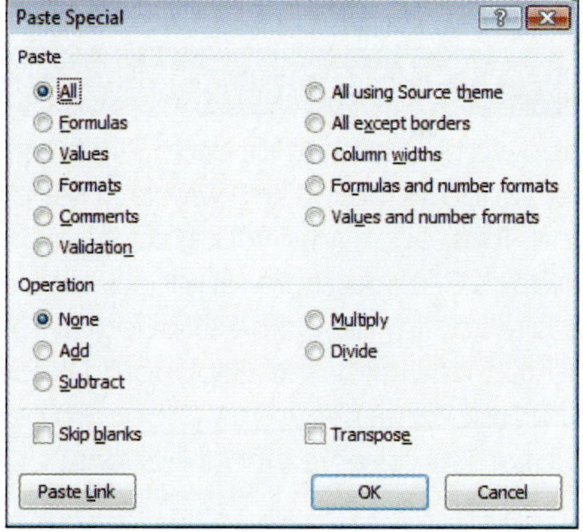

Figure 1.20 Paste Special Dialog Box

Use AutoFill

AutoFill enables you to copy the content of a cell or a range of cells by dragging the fill handle over an adjacent cell or range of cells.

The ***fill handle*** is a small black square appearing in the bottom-right corner of a cell.

AutoFill is an Excel operation that enables you to copy the content of a cell or a range of cells by dragging the ***fill handle*** (a small black square appearing in the bottom-right corner of a cell) over an adjacent cell or range of cells. AutoFill can be used in two different ways. First, you can use it to repetitively copy the contents of one cell. To do this, click the cell and use the fill handle to repeat the content. This operation is valuable for copying formulas, because the cell references are updated automatically during the AutoFill process. AutoFill also can be used to complete a sequence. For example, if you enter January in a cell, you can use AutoFill to enter the rest of the months of the year.

You can complete the quarters of a year by typing Qtr 1 in a cell and using AutoFill to fill in Qtr 2, Qtr 3, and Qtr 4 in sequence. Other sequences you can complete are weekdays and weekday abbreviations by typing the first item and using AutoFill to complete the other entries. For numeric values, however, you must specify the first two values in sequence. For example, if you want to fill in 5, 10, 15, and so on, you must enter the first two values in two cells, select the two cells, and then use AutoFill so that Excel knows to increment by 5. Figure 1.21 shows the results of filling in months, abbreviated months, quarters, weekdays, abbreviated weekdays, and the process of filling in increments of 5.

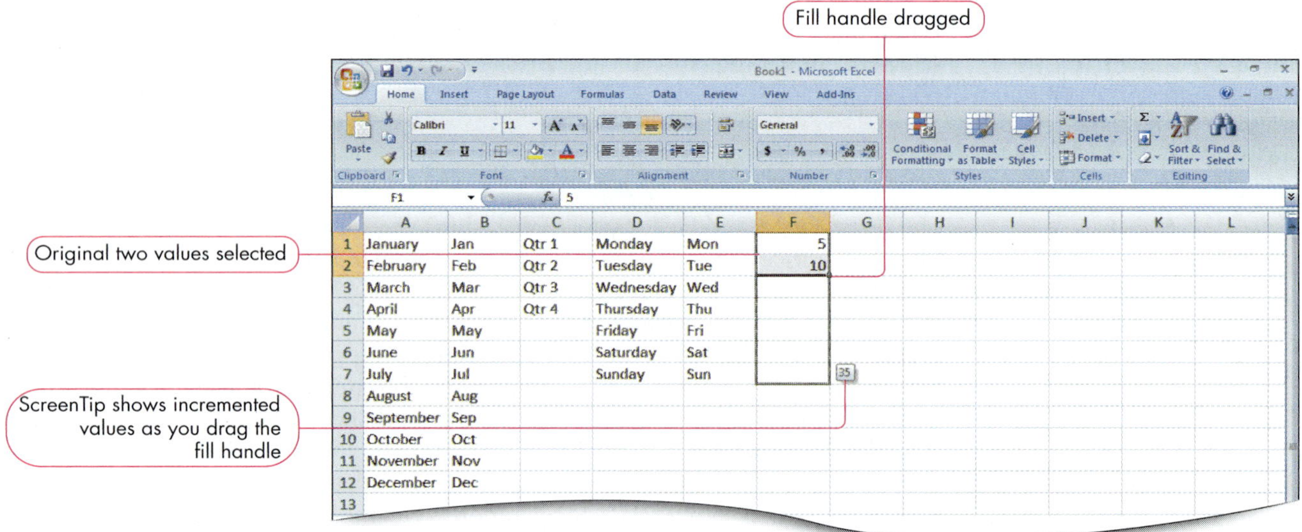

Figure 1.21 AutoFill Examples

TIP Two Different Clipboards

The Office Clipboard holds a total of up to 24 objects from multiple applications, as opposed to the Windows Clipboard, which stores only the results of the last Cut or Copy command. Thus, each time you execute a Cut or Copy command, the contents of the Windows Clipboard are replaced, whereas the copied object is added to the objects already in the Office Clipboard. To display the Office Clipboard, click the Home tab and click the Clipboard Dialog Box Launcher to display the Office Clipboard Task Pane. Leave the Clipboard open as you execute multiple cut and copy operations to observe what happens.

Hands-On Exercises

2 | Jake's Gym Continued

Skills covered: 1. Open an Existing Workbook **2.** Use Save As to Save an Existing Workbook **3.** Insert a Row and Compute Totals **4.** Copy the Formulas **5.** Continue the Calculations **6.** Insert a Column

Step 1 Open an Existing Workbook

Refer to Figure 1.22 as you complete Step 1.

a. Click the **Office Button** and select **Open**.

   You should see the Open dialog box.

b. Click the appropriate drive and folder in the Folders list on the left side of the Open dialog box. Choose the location where the original data files to accompany this book are located.

c. Click the **Views drop-down arrow** and then select **Details**.

   You changed the file list to a detailed list view, which shows more information.

d. Select *chap1_ho2_jake*. Click **Open** to open the workbook.

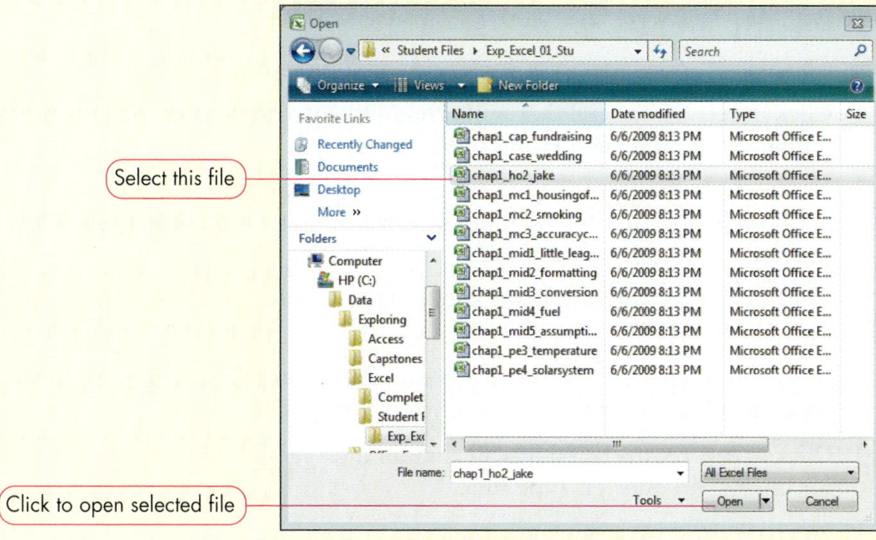

Figure 1.22 Open Dialog Box

Step 2 Use Save As to Save an Existing Workbook

a. Click the **Office Button** and select **Save As** to display the Save As dialog box.

b. Type **chap1_ho2_jake_solution** as the name of the new workbook.

   A file name and its path may contain up to 255 characters. Spaces, underscores, and commas are allowed in the file name.

c. Click the appropriate drive and folder in the Folders list on the left side of the Save As dialog box. Choose the location where you want to save your completed files.

d. Click the **Save** button.

Two identical copies of the file exist on disk: *chap1_ho2_jake* and *chap1_ho2_jake_solution*, which you just created. The title bar shows the latter name, which is the workbook currently in memory. You will work with *chap1_ho2_jake_solution* but can always return to the original *chap1_ho2_jake* if necessary.

TIP Create a New Folder

Do you work with a large number of different workbooks? If so, it may be useful to store those workbooks in different folders, perhaps one folder for each subject you are taking. Click the Office Button, select Save As to display the Save As dialog box, and then click the New Folder button. Enter the name of the folder, and then press Enter.

Step 3 Insert a Row and Compute Totals

Refer to Figure 1.23 as you complete Step 3.

a. Select **row 3**, click the **Insert arrow** in the Cells group on the Home tab, and select **Insert Sheet Rows**.

You have inserted a new row between rows 2 and 3.

b. Click in **cell A3**. Type **Sales by Region** and press **Enter**.

c. Click in **cell E5**, the cell that will contain the quarterly sales total for the North region. Type **=B5+C5+D5** and press **Enter**.

As you type the formula, color-coded borders appear around cells B5, C5, and D5, and the formula cell references appear in the same color coding. You entered the formula to compute a total.

d. Click in **cell E5**, check to make sure the formula matches the formula in the formula bar in Figure 1.23.

If necessary, click in the formula box in the formula bar and make the appropriate changes so that you have the correct formula in cell E5.

e. Click in **cell F5**, the cell that will contain the average sales for the North region for the second quarter. Type **=E5**.

You have begun to create the formula to calculate the average for the second quarter.

f. Type **/3** to calculate the average for the second quarter by dividing the total by 3, the number of months in the quarter. Press **Enter**.

Total sales, 49650, is the second quarter total, and 16550 is the average quarterly sales.

TROUBLESHOOTING: If you type an extra arithmetic symbol at the end of a formula and press Enter, Excel will display an error message box suggesting a correction. Read the message carefully before selecting Yes or No.

g. Click in **cell F5** and verify that the formula **=E5/3** is correct.

h. Type your name in **cell A13** and click **Save** on the Quick Access Toolbar to save the workbook.

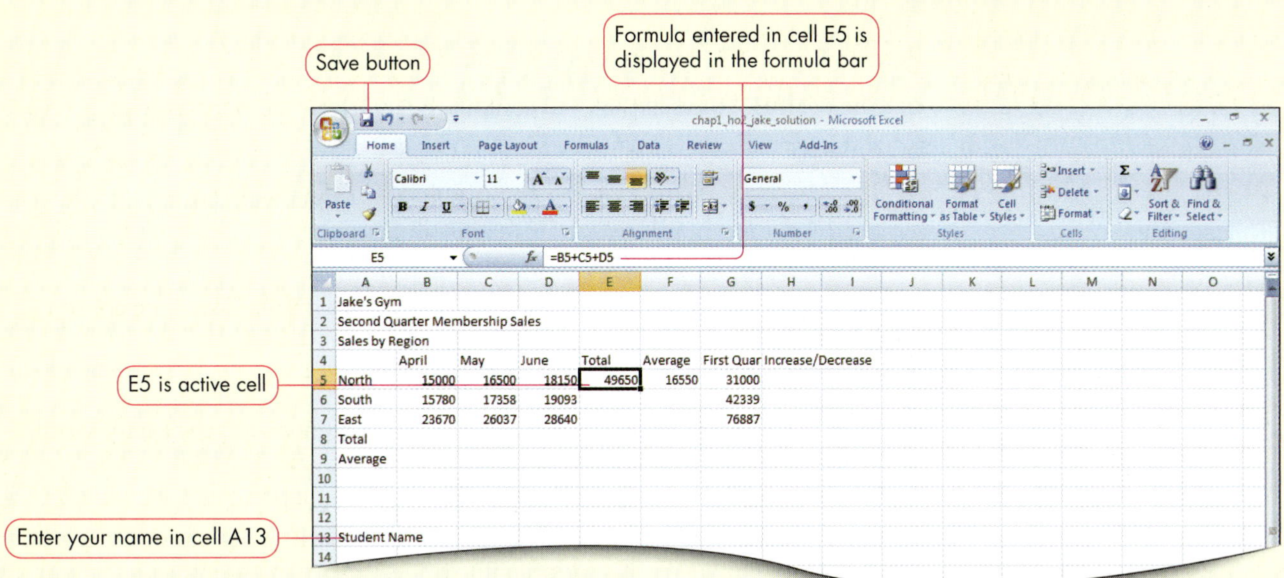

Figure 1.23 Insert Name and Compute Totals

Step 4 Copy the Formulas

Refer to Figure 1.24 as you complete Step 4.

a. Click **cell E5**.

   Point to the fill handle in the lower-right corner of cell E5. The mouse pointer changes to a thin crosshair.

b. Drag the fill handle to **cell E7** (the last cell in the region total column).

   A border appears as you drag the fill handle as shown in Figure 1.24.

c. Release the mouse button to complete the copy operation.

   The formulas for region totals have been copied to the corresponding rows for the other regions. When you click in cell E7, the cell displaying the total for the East region, you should see the formula: =B7+C7+D7.

d. Click **cell F5** and drag the fill handle to **cell F7** to copy the average sales formula down the column.

e. Save the workbook.

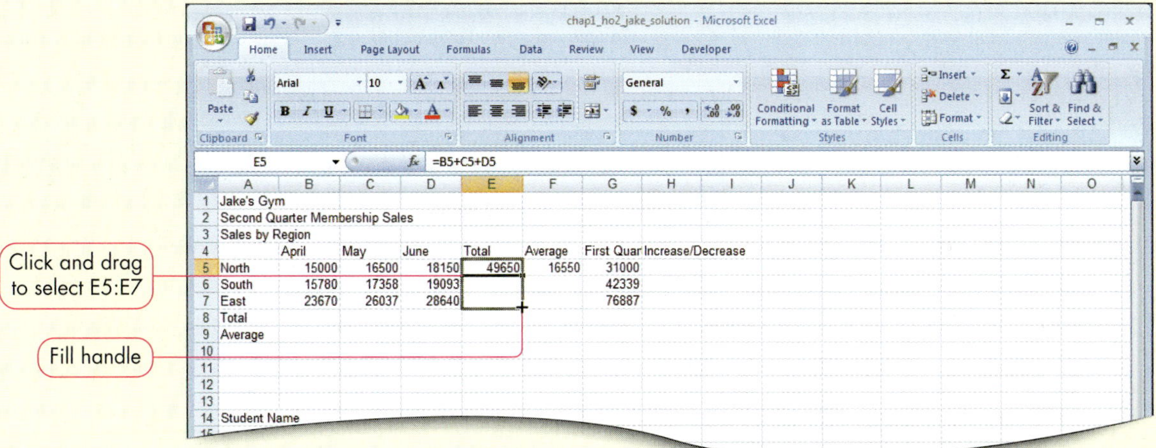

Figure 1.24 Copy the Formulas

Step 5 Continue the Calculations

Refer to Figure 1.25 as you complete Step 5.

a. Click **cell H5**, the cell that will contain the quarterly sales increase or decrease.

b. Type **=(E5–G5)/G5** and press **Enter**.

   You should see 0.601613 as the increase in sales from the first quarter to the second quarter for the North region. If this result is not correct, click cell H5 and verify that the formula =(E5-G5)/G5 is correct. Correct it in the formula bar if necessary.

c. Click **cell H5** and use the fill handle to copy the formula down the column to **cell H7**.

d. Click in **cell B8**. Type **=B5+B6+B7** and press **Enter**.

e. Click in **cell B9** to begin the formula to calculate the average sales for April. Type **=(B5+B6+B7)/3** and press Enter.

   The result 18150 displays in **cell B9**. This is an awkward method of creating a formula to calculate an average, and you will learn to use another method in Chapter 2. However, this formula illustrates the use of parentheses to control the order of precedence. Furthermore, while you typically avoid constant values such as 3 in a formula, it is sometimes acceptable if that value will never change, such as we'll always have three months in a quarter.

   TROUBLESHOOTING: The parentheses used in the formula force the addition before the division and must be used to calculate the correct value.

f. Click **cell B8** and drag through **cell B9** to select both cells. Drag the fill handle in the lower-right corner of cell B9 across through **cell E9** to copy the formulas.

   You copied the formulas to calculate both the monthly sales totals and averages for columns B through E.

g. Click in **cell G5** and type **52000,** then press **Enter**. See Figure 1.25.

   Updated information shows that the first-quarter earnings in the North region were misreported. The new number, 52000, represents a decrease in sales between the first and second quarters in the North region.

h. Save the workbook.

   You entered the formulas to calculate the appropriate totals and averages for all regions for the second quarter. You also entered the formula to determine the increase or decrease in sales from the first quarter to the second quarter.

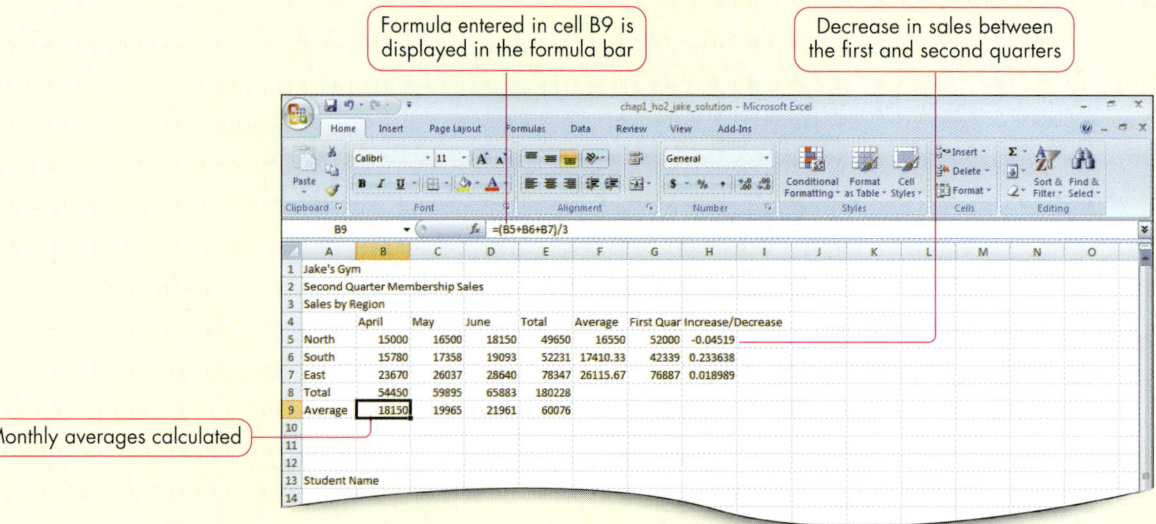

Figure 1.25 Continue the Calculations

Step 6
Insert a Column

Refer to Figure 1.26 as you complete Step 6.

a. Click the **column letter G**, the column to the right of where you want to insert a column.

   When you insert a column, it appears to the left of your initial selection, and the columns are moved to the right.

b. Click on the **Insert down arrow** in the Cells group on the Home tab.

   Figure 1.26 shows the Insert options in the Cells group.

c. Select **Insert Sheet Columns**.

   You inserted a blank column to the left of the First Quarter column or column G.

d. Save the *chap1_ho2_jake_solution* workbook and keep it onscreen if you plan to continue to the next hands-on exercise. Close the workbook and exit Excel if you do not want to continue with the next exercise at this time.

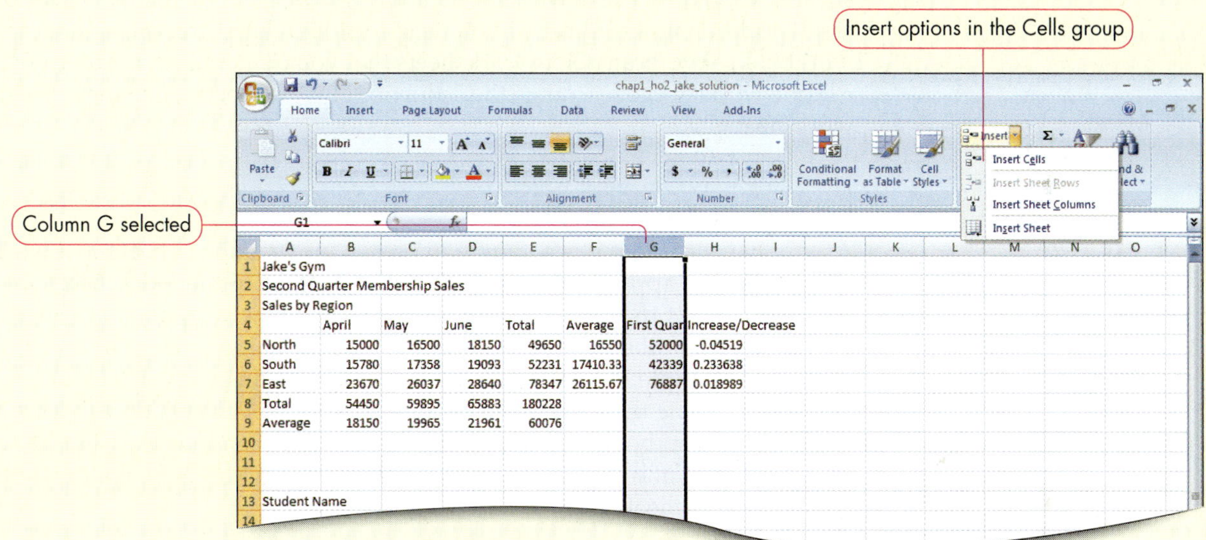

Figure 1.26 Insert a Column

TIP Using a Shortcut Menu

Another method to insert a row or column is to right-click anywhere on a row or column to show a shortcut menu. Click Insert to insert a row or a column and then select the appropriate option from the dialog box. Rows are inserted above the active cell, and columns are inserted to the left of the active cell.

Workbook and Worksheet Enhancements

At the beginning of this chapter, you learned that a worksheet or spreadsheet is a grid containing columns and rows to store numerical data. Further, you learned that a workbook is a single file that contains one or more related worksheets. So far, you have created one worksheet within a workbook. However, as you continue using Excel to develop workbooks for personal and professional use, you need to learn how to manage multiple worksheets.

In this section, you learn how to manage worksheets. Specifically, you rename worksheets and change worksheet tab colors. Furthermore, you learn how to insert, delete, add, and move worksheets.

Managing Worksheets

When you start a new blank workbook in Excel, the workbook contains three worksheets by default. These worksheets are called Sheet1, Sheet2, and Sheet3. You can insert additional worksheets if you need to store related worksheet data in the same workbook, or you can delete worksheets that you do not need. Furthermore, you can rename worksheets, rearrange the sequence of worksheets, or change the color of the worksheet tabs.

Rename Worksheets

As you have learned, it is a simple matter to move among sheets in a workbook by clicking on the appropriate sheet tab at the bottom of the worksheet window. You also learned that the default names of sheets in a new workbook are Sheet1, Sheet2, etc. To give workbook sheets more meaningful names, you will want to rename them. For example, if your budget workbook contains worksheets for each month, you should name the worksheets by month, such as *January* and *February*. A teacher who uses a workbook to store a grade book for several classes should name each sheet by class name or number, such as *MIS 1000* and *MIS 2450*. Follow these steps to rename a worksheet tab:

1. Right-click a sheet tab to show a shortcut menu.
2. Select Rename, and the sheet tab name is highlighted.
3. Type the new sheet tab name and press Enter.

Change Worksheet Tab Color

The sheet tabs are blue in color by default. The active worksheet tab is white. When you use multiple worksheets, you might find it helpful to add a color to sheet tabs in order to make the tab stand out or to emphasize the difference between sheets. For example, you might want the January tab to be blue, the February tab to be red, and the March tab to be green in a workbook containing monthly worksheets. Changing the color of the tabs in workbooks when sheets have similar names helps to identify the tab you want to work with. Follow these steps to change the worksheet tab color:

1. Right-click the Sheet1 tab.
2. Point to Tab Color.
3. Select Theme Colors, Standard Colors, No Color, or More Colors.

Move, Delete, Copy, and Add Worksheets

The fastest way to move a worksheet is to click and drag the worksheet tab. To delete a worksheet in a workbook, right-click on the sheet tab and select Delete from the shortcut menu. You can copy a worksheet in similar fashion by pressing and holding

Ctrl as you drag the worksheet tab. Move, Copy, and Delete worksheet operations also are accomplished by right-clicking the desired sheet tab and selecting the needed option from the shortcut menu.

To add a new blank worksheet, click Insert Worksheet to the right of the last worksheet tab or right-click any sheet tab, select Insert, and select Worksheet from the Insert dialog box.

You might want to move a worksheet to reorder existing sheets. For example, January is the first budget sheet, but at the end of January you move it after December so February is the sheet that opens first. If a professor is no longer teaching a course, she might delete a grade book sheet. Once a grade book sheet is created, it can be copied, modified, and used for another course.

TIP Moving and Renaming Worksheets

The fastest way to move a worksheet is to click and drag the worksheet tab. To rename a worksheet, double-click its tab to select the current name, type the new name, and press Enter.

Formatting Worksheets

Formatting worksheets allows you to change or alter the way numbers and text are presented. You can change alignment, fonts, the style of text, and the format of values, and apply borders and shading to cells, for example. These formatting procedures allow you to prepare a more eye-appealing worksheet. You format to draw attention to important areas of the worksheet, and you can emphasize totals or summary area values.

(. . . formatting procedures allow you to prepare a more eye-appealing worksheet.)

Merge and Center Labels

The ***merge and center cells*** option centers an entry across a range of selected cells.

You may want to place a title at the top of a worksheet and center it over the material contained in the worksheet. Centering helps to unify the information on the worksheet. The best way to do this is to ***merge and center cells*** into one cell across the top of the worksheet and center the content of the merged cell. See Figure 1.27, the before, and Figure 1.28, the after. The merged cells are treated as one single cell. This is a toggle command and can be undone by clicking Merge & Center a second time. To merge cells and center a title across columns A through L you would:

1. Enter the title in cell A1.
2. Select cells A1:L1.
3. Click Merge & Center in the Alignment group on the Home tab.

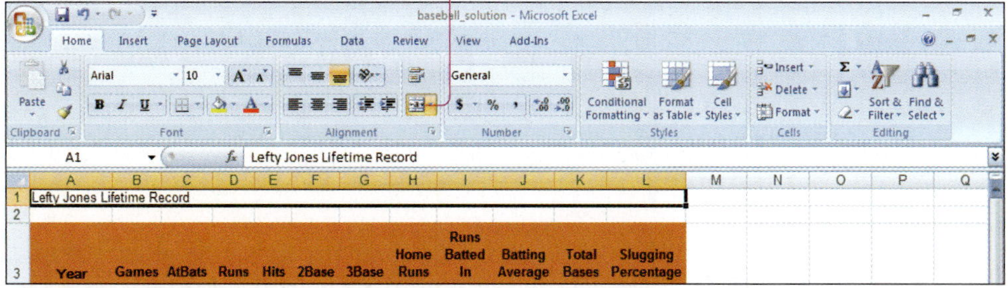

Figure 1.27 Merge and Center Title

Title merged and centered

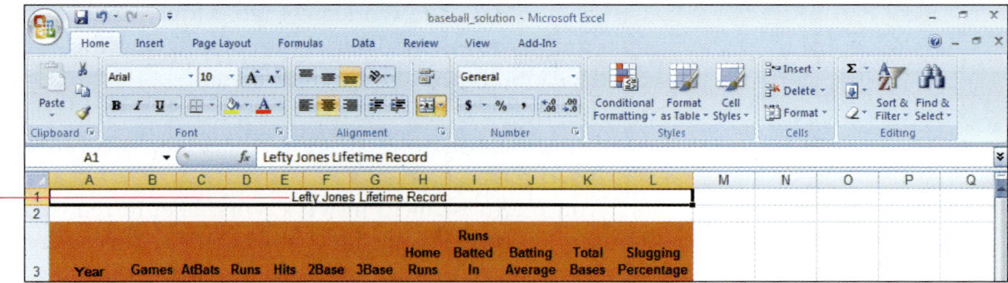

Figure 1.28 Merged and Centered Title

Adjust Cell Height and Width

It often is necessary to change the height and/or width of a cell so all of its contents are visible. When labels are longer than the cell width, they are displayed in the next cell if it is empty. If the adjacent cell is not empty, the label is truncated. Numbers appear as a series of pound signs (######) when the cell is not wide enough to display the complete number. To widen a column, drag the border between column headings to change the column width.

For example, to increase or decrease the width of column A, point to the border, and you will see a two-headed arrow. Drag the border between column headings A and B to the right or left. You also can double-click the right boundary of a column heading to change the column width to accommodate the widest entry in that column.

To increase or decrease the height of row 1, drag the border between row headings 1 and 2 down or up. You can also double-click the bottom boundary of a row heading to change the row height to accommodate entries in their entirety. Alternatively, right-click on the row number to show a shortcut menu and select Row Height. Enter an integer and click OK.

AutoFit automatically adjusts the height and width of cells.

AutoFit is an important command used when formatting a spreadsheet to automatically adjust the height and height of cells. You can choose from two types of AutoFit commands available in Format in the Cells group on the Home tab (see Figure 1.29). The AutoFit Column Width changes the column width of the selected columns to fit the contents of the column. AutoFit Row Height changes the row height of the selected row to fit the contents of the row.

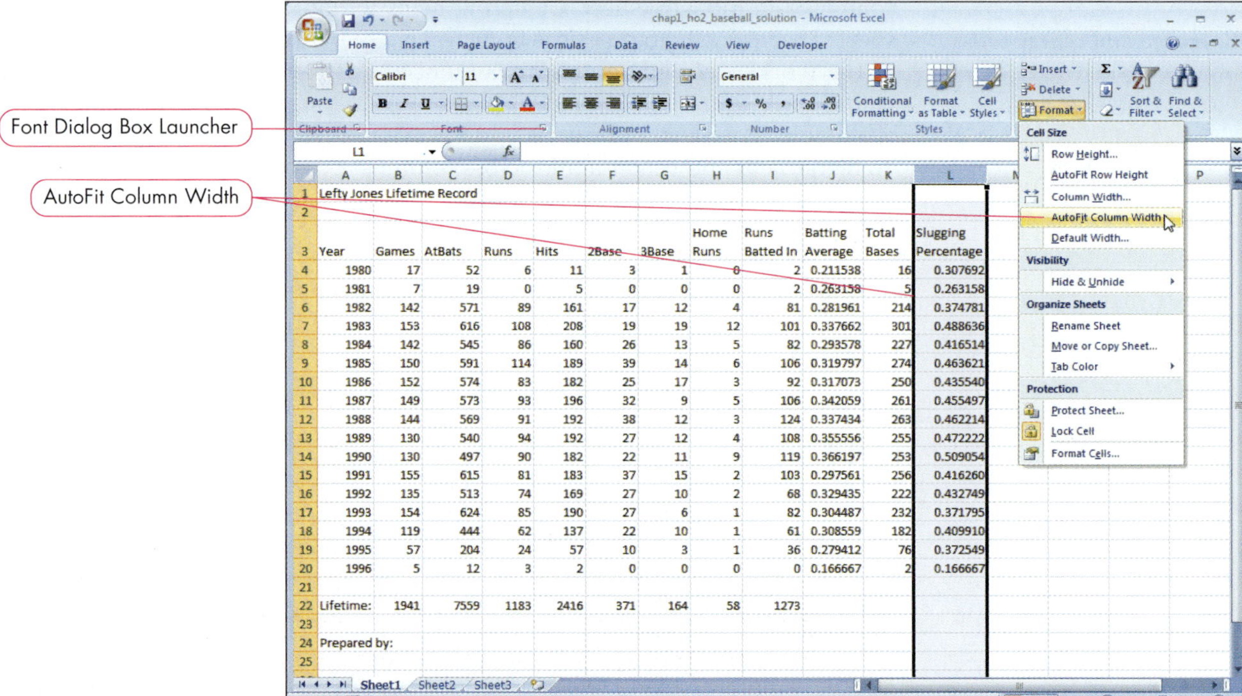

Figure 1.29 AutoFit

TIP Multiple Row Height/Column Width

To change the row height of many rows at one time, select the multiple rows and right-click to show the shortcut menu. Select Row Height and enter a number in the Row Height dialog box as shown in Figure 1.30. Click OK. To change the column width of many columns at one time, select the multiple columns and right-click to show the shortcut menu. Select Column Width and enter a number in the Column Width dialog box. Click OK.

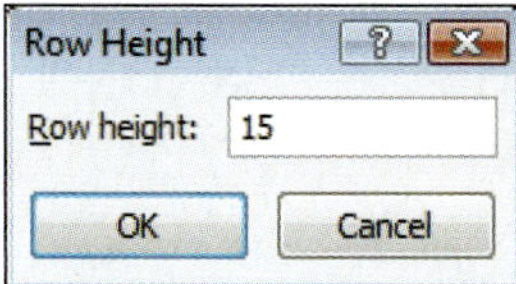

Figure 1.30 Row Height Dialog Box

Apply Borders and Shading

You have several options to choose from when adding borders to cells or applying a shade to cells. You can select a cell border from Borders in the Font group on the Home tab or you can use the Border tab in the Format Cells dialog box. Either way you can create a border around a cell (or cells) for additional emphasis. Click the Font Dialog Box Launcher in the Font group on the Home tab (see Figure 1.29) and then click the Border tab. Figure 1.31 shows the Border tab in the Format Cells dialog box. Select (click) the line style at the left of the dialog box and then click the left, right, top, and/or bottom border. It is possible to outline the entire cell or selected cells, or choose the specific side or sides; for example, thicker lines on the bottom and right sides produce a drop shadow, which can be very effective. Also, you can specify a different line style and/or a different color for the border, but a color printer is needed to see the effect on the printed output.

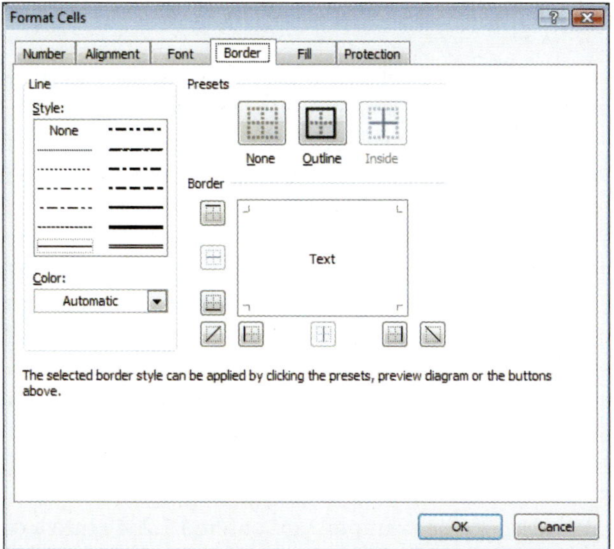

Figure 1.31 Border Tab on the Format Cells Dialog Box

You can add a shade to a cell from Fill Color in the Font group on the Home tab or you can use the Fill tab in the Format Cells dialog box. The Fill tab and Fill Color enable you to choose a different color in which to shade the cell and further emphasize its contents. The Pattern Style drop-down list lets you select an alternate pattern, such as dots or slanted lines. Click OK to accept the settings and close the dialog box. Figure 1.32 shows the Fill tab of the Format Cells dialog box.

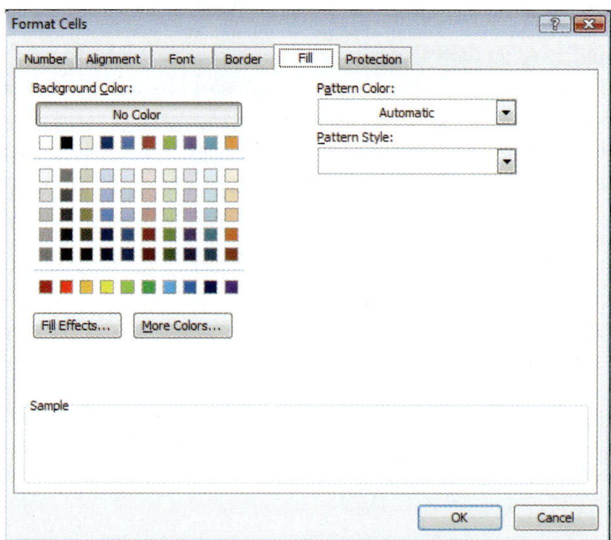

Figure 1.32 Fill Tab on the Format Cells Dialog Box

Insert Clip Art

A good way to enhance the appearance of a spreadsheet is to insert a clip art image. These images can represent the subject of the spreadsheet, the company preparing the spreadsheet, or even the personal interests of the person preparing the spreadsheet. You should use caution when inserting clip art because they can be distracting to the user of the spreadsheet or can take large amounts of disk space and slow operations on the spreadsheet. If you want to insert clip art, click Clip Art in the Illustrations group on the Insert tab to open the Clip Art task pane. Type a keyword in the Search for text box and click Go to begin the search for images matching your keyword. When you find an appropriate image, double-click it to place it in your spreadsheet. You can now move and resize the image as desired.

Format Cells

The ***Format Cells*** operation controls formatting for numbers, alignment, fonts, borders, colors, and patterns.

The ***Format Cells*** dialog box and commands on the Home tab control the formatting for numbers, alignment, fonts, borders, colors, and patterns. Execution of the command produces a tabbed dialog box in which you choose the particular formatting category and then enter the desired options. All formatting is done within the context of select-then-do. You can select the cells to which the formatting is to apply and then execute the Format Cells command. If you want to apply the same formats to an entire column or row, click the respective column letter or row number and then select the desired format. You can display the Format Cells dialog box by clicking the Dialog Box Launcher in the Font, Alignment, or Number group.

After you format a cell, the formatting remains in the cell and is applied to all subsequent values that you enter into that cell. You can, however, change the formatting by executing a new formatting command. Also, you can remove the formatting by using the options with Clear in the Editing group on the Home tab. Changing the format of a number changes the way the number is displayed, but does not change its value. If, for example, you entered 1.2345 into a cell, but displayed the number as 1.23, the actual value (1.2345) would be used in all calculations involving that cell. The numeric formats are shown and described in Table 1.5. They are accessed by clicking the Number Format down arrow in the Number group on the Home tab. The tabbed Format Cells dialog box is displayed by selecting More Number Formats.

Table 1.5 Formatting Definitions

Format Style	Definition
General	The default format for numeric entries and displays a number according to the way it was originally entered. Numbers are shown as integers (e.g., 123), decimal fractions (e.g., 1.23), or in scientific notation (e.g., 1.23E+10) if the number exceeds 11 digits.
Number	Displays a number with or without the 1000 separator (e.g., a comma) and with any number of decimal places. Negative numbers can be displayed with parentheses and/or can be shown in red.
Currency	Displays a number with the 1000 separator and an optional dollar sign (which is placed immediately to the left of the number). Negative values can be preceded by a minus sign or displayed with parentheses, and/or can be shown in red.
Accounting	Displays a number with the 1000 separator, an optional dollar sign (at the left border of the cell, vertically aligned within a column), negative values in parentheses, and zero values as hyphens.
Date	Displays the date in different ways, such as March 14, 2009, 3/14/09, or 14-Mar-09.
Time	Displays the time in different formats, such as 10:50 PM or the equivalent 22:50 (24-hour time).
Percentage	Shows when the number is multiplied by 100 for display purposes only, a percent sign is included, and any number of decimal places can be specified.
Fraction	Displays a number as a fraction, and is appropriate when there is no exact decimal equivalent. A fraction is entered into a cell by preceding the fraction with an equal sign—for example, =1/3. If the cell is not formatted as a fraction, you will see the results of the formula.
Scientific	Displays a number as a decimal fraction followed by a whole number exponent of 10; for example, the number 12345 would appear as 1.2345E+04. The exponent, +04 in the example, is the number of places the decimal point is moved to the left (or right if the exponent is negative). Very small numbers have negative exponents.
Text	Left aligns the entry and is useful for numerical values that have leading zeros and should be treated as text, such as ZIP codes.
Special	Displays a number with editing characters, such as hyphens in a Social Security number.
Custom	Enables you to select a predefined customized number format or use special symbols to create your own customized number format.

Use Fonts

You can use the same fonts in Excel as you can in any other Windows application. All fonts are WYSIWYG (What You See Is What You Get), meaning that the worksheet you see on the monitor will match the printed worksheet.

Any entry in a worksheet may be displayed in any font, style, or point size, as indicated in the Font group on the Home tab as shown in Figure 1.33. The example shows Arial, Bold, Italic, and 14 points. Special effects, such as subscripts or superscripts, are also possible. You can even select a different color, but you will need a color printer to see the effect on the printed page.

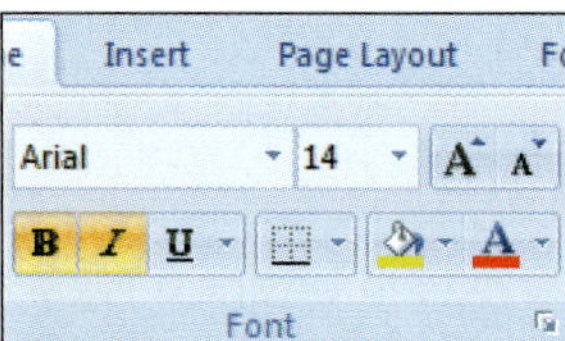

Figure 1.33 Font Group on the Home Tab

Alignment of Cell Contents

The Alignment tab in the Format Cells dialog box and the Alignment group on the Home tab together give you a wealth of options to choose from. Changing the orientation of cell contents is useful when labels are too long and widening columns is not an option. Wrapping text in a cell also reduces the need to widen a column when space is at a premium. Centering, right aligning, or left aligning text can be done for emphasis or to best display cell contents in columns. When the height of rows is changed, it is necessary to vertically adjust alignment for ease of reading. Figure 1.34 shows both the Alignment group and the Format Cells dialog box with the Alignment tab visible.

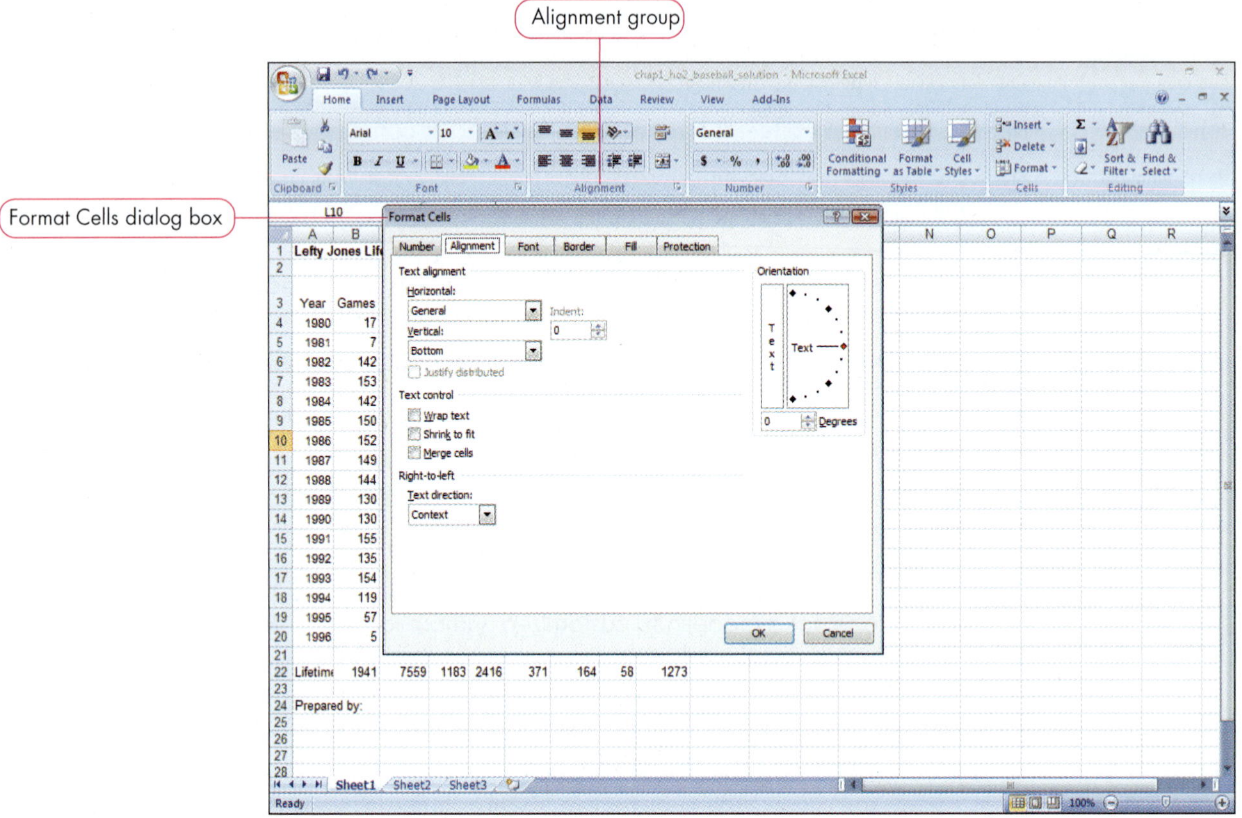

Figure 1.34 Alignment Group and Alignment Tab

TIP Use Restraint

More is not better, especially in the case of too many typefaces and styles, which produce cluttered worksheets that impress no one. Limit yourself to a maximum of two typefaces per worksheet, but choose multiple sizes or styles within those typefaces. Use boldface or italics for emphasis, but do so in moderation, because if you emphasize too many elements, the effect is lost. Figure 1.37 shows locations of number format commands.

Hands-On Exercises

3 | Formatting Jake's Gym Worksheet

Skills covered: 1. Manage the Workbook **2.** Apply Number Formats **3.** Apply Font Attributes and Borders **4.** Change Alignment Attributes **5.** Insert an Image

Step 1
Manage the Workbook

Refer to Figure 1.35 as you complete Step 1.

a. If necessary, open *chap1_ho2_jake_solution* and save it as **chap1_ho3_jake_solution**.

b. Right-click **Sheet1 tab** at the bottom of the worksheet and select **Rename** from the shortcut menu.

   You selected the generic Sheet1 tab so you can give it a more meaningful name.

c. Type **Second Quarter** and press **Enter**.

d. Right-click on the **Second Quarter** sheet tab and point to **Tab Color**.

e. Select **Aqua, Accent 5** color from the Theme Colors gallery.

   You applied a color to the Second Quarter sheet tab to make it more distinctive.

f. Right-click the **Sheet2 tab** and click **Delete**.

g. Right-click the **Sheet3 tab** and click **Delete**.

   You have deleted the unused worksheets from the workbook.

h. Save the workbook.

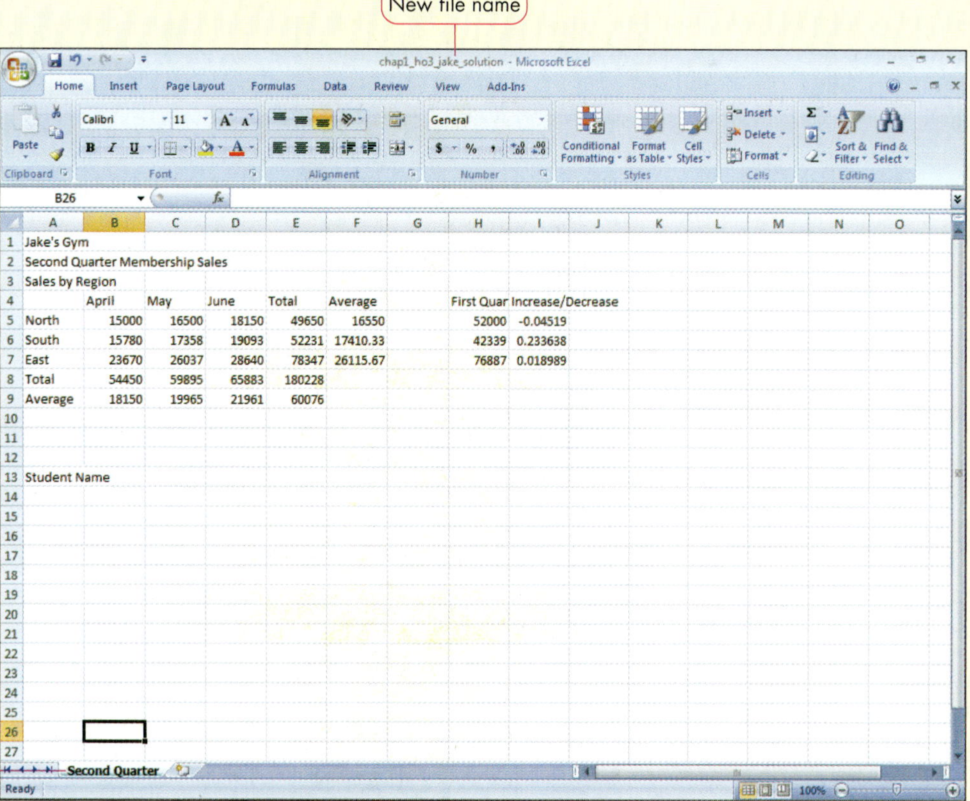

Figure 1.35 Workbook Management

Step 2
Apply Number Formats

Refer to Figure 1.36 as you complete Step 2.

a. Click and drag to select the **range I5:I7**.

   You selected the range of cells to be formatted.

b. Click the **Home tab** and click the **Number Dialog Box Launcher** in the Number group.

   The Format Cells dialog box shown in Figure 1.36 is now displayed on your screen.

c. Click the **Number tab** and select **Percentage** from the *Category* list.

d. Type **1** in the Decimal places box. Click **OK** to close the dialog box.

   You formatted the increase or decrease in sales as a percentage with 1 decimal place.

e. Click and drag to select the **range B5:H9**.

f. Click the **Number Dialog Box Launcher** in the Number group.

g. Click the **Number tab** and select **Currency** from the *Category* list.

h. Type **0** for the Decimal places box. Click **OK** to close the dialog box.

   You formatted the remaining values as currency with 0 decimal places.

i. Save the workbook.

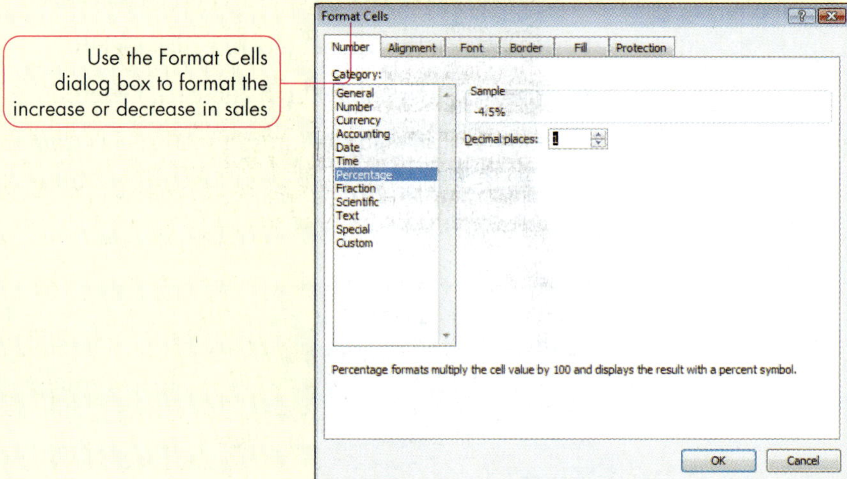

Figure 1.36 Apply Number Format

TIP Number Formats

You can change some number formats in the Number group on the Home tab. For example, you can click Accounting Number Format to display dollar signs and align decimal points for monetary amounts. You can click the Number down arrow to select various number formats, such as Number, Accounting, Date, Percentage, and Fraction. The Number group also contains commands to increase or decrease the number of decimal points. Figure 1.37 shows locations of number format commands.

Step 3 Apply Font Attributes and Borders

Refer to Figure 1.37 as you complete Step 3. Your screen display may be different depending on your screen resolution.

a. Click and drag to select the **range A1:I3**.

b. Press and hold **Ctrl** while selecting the **range A8:E9**. Continue to press and hold Ctrl while clicking **cell A13** to select it.

   You selected several ranges of noncontiguous cells and you can now apply multiple formats to these ranges.

c. Click the **Fill Color arrow** in the Font group and select the color **Purple**.

d. Click the **Font Color arrow** in the Font group and select **White, Background 1**.

   TROUBLESHOOTING: If you apply a format and change your mind, just apply another format or clear the formatting using Clear in the Editing group on the Home tab.

e. Click **Bold** in the Font group to make the text stand out.

   You formatted parts of the worksheet by using a color fill, a font color, and a font enhancement. You want to draw attention to these areas of the worksheet.

f. Select the **range B4:F4**, then press and hold **Ctrl** while selecting the **ranges H4:I4** and **B7:E7**.

g. Click **Borders arrow** in Font group and select **Bottom Double Border**.

   You again selected noncontiguous ranges of cells and then applied a double border to the bottom of the cells.

h. Select **cell E6**, press and hold **Ctrl** while selecting **cell H6**, and select **Yellow** from **Fill Color** in the Font group.

   This highlights the large increase in sales in the South region between the first and second quarter.

i. Save the workbook.

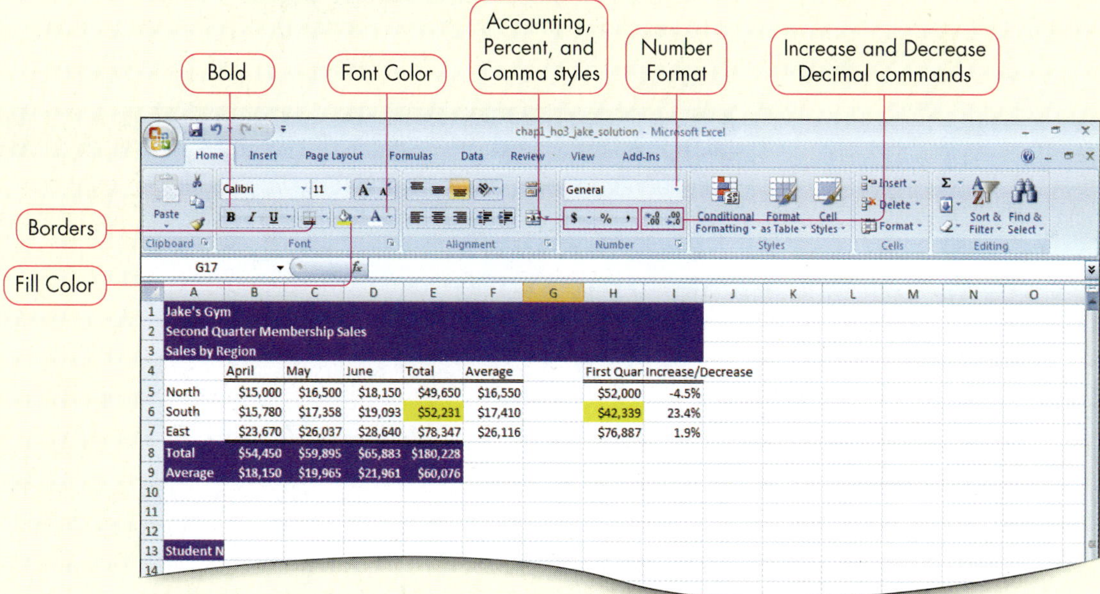

Figure 1.37 Continue Formatting Attributes and Borders

Step 4

Change Alignment Attributes

Refer to Figures 1.37 and 1.38 as you complete Step 4.

a. Click on the **Home tab** if it is not already active.

b. Click and drag to select the **range A1:I1**.

c. Click **Merge & Center** in the Alignment group on the Home tab.

d. Click and drag to select the **range A2:I2**.

e. Click **Merge & Center** in the Alignment group on the Home tab.

f. Click and drag to select the **range A3:I3**.

g. Click **Merge & Center** in the Alignment group on the Home tab.

   You have now merged cells and centered the title and two subtitles in single cells. You cannot select more than one row and merge into a single cell.

h. Click and drag to select the **range A4:I4**.

i. Right-click on the selected cell range to display a shortcut menu, then select **Format Cells** to display the dialog box.

j. Click the **Alignment tab**, and then click the **Wrap text check box** in the *Text control* section.

k. Click the **Horizontal drop-down arrow** in the *Text alignment* section, select **Center**, and click **OK** to accept the settings and close the dialog box.

   You used the shortcut menu to open the dialog box and made two enhancements to the selected text. It is more efficient to make multiple changes using a dialog box.

l. Widen column A so all text is visible.

   TROUBLESHOOTING: If your monitor is set for a high resolution or if you have a wide screen monitor, you may see text by some of the command icons. For example, you might see the words *Wrap Text* by the Wrap Text command in the Alignment group. If you want your screen to have the same resolution as the figures shown in this textbook, change your resolution to 1024 × 768.

TIP Split a Cell

If you merge too many cells or decide you no longer want cells to be merged, you can split the merged cell into individual cells again. To do this, select the merged cell and click Merge & Center in the Alignment group or deselect Merge cells on the Alignment tab in the Format Cells dialog box.

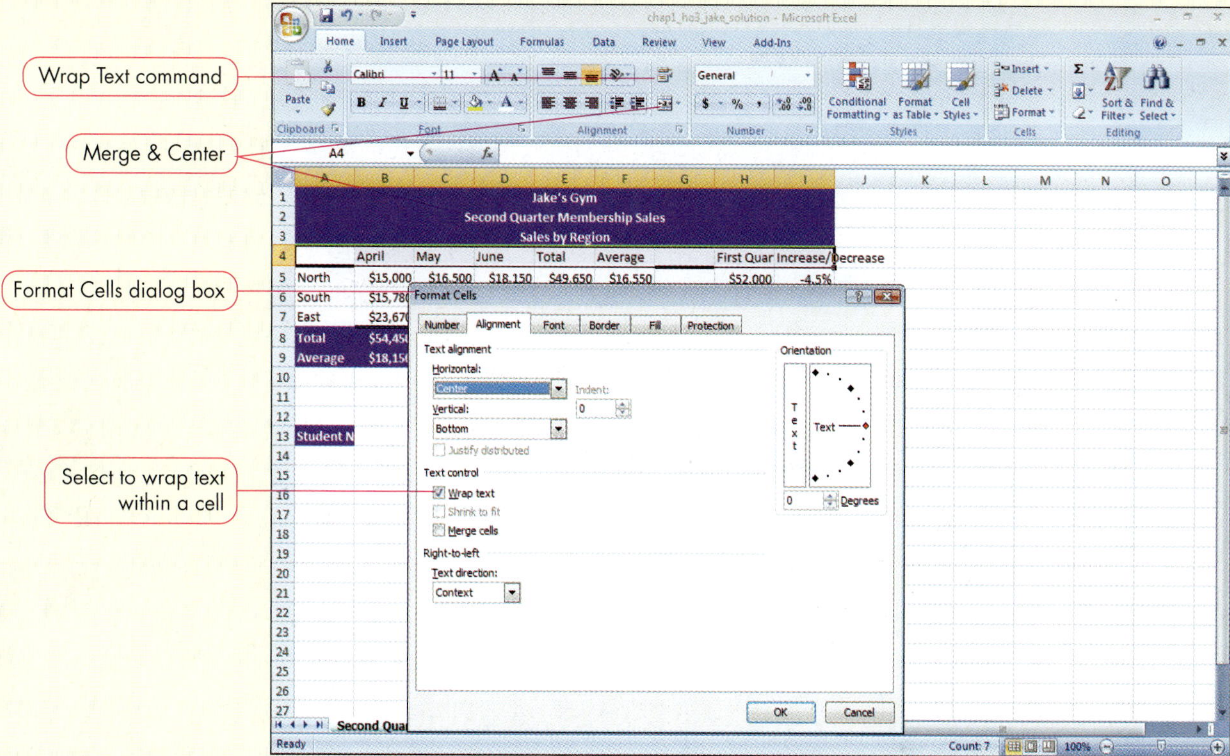

Figure 1.38 Change Alignment Attributes

Step 5
Insert an Image

Refer to Figure 1.39 as you complete Step 5.

a. Click in **cell A1**, click the **Insert tab**, and click **Clip Art** in the Illustrations group. A Clip Art task pane opens. Type **barbell** in the **Search for** box and click **Go**.

   You are going to insert a clip art image in the worksheet but must first search for an appropriate image.

b. Click to insert the image shown in Figure 1.39. Click the image to select it and drag the lower-right sizing handle to resize the image to fit the worksheet.

   When working with images, it is necessary to resize the images and widen columns or change row height.

c. Close the **Clip Art task pane**.

d. Save the *chap1_ho3_jake_solution* workbook and keep it onscreen if you plan to continue to the next hands-on exercise. Close the workbook and exit Excel if you do not want to continue with the next exercise at this time.

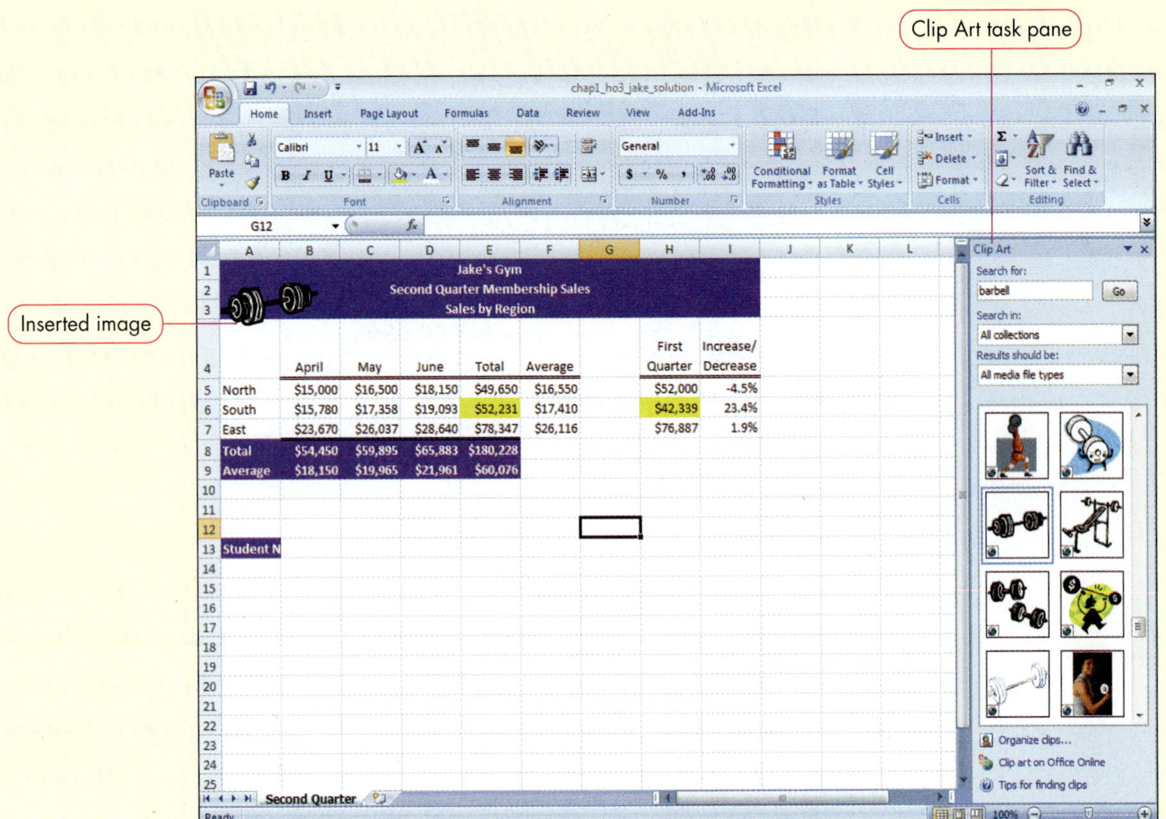

Figure 1.39 Continue to Format the Worksheet

Page Setup and Printing

The Page Setup command gives you complete control of the printed worksheet. Many of the options may not appear significant now, but you will appreciate them as you develop larger and more complicated worksheets later in the text. Workbooks and worksheets become part of auditor's reports in organizations' annual reports and quarterly reports. Spreadsheets are part of dissertations and grade books, and are the basis for budgeting both for personal use and corporate use. As you can see, printing workbooks and worksheets is an important function.

The Page Setup command gives you complete control of the printed worksheet.

In this section you select options in the Page Setup dialog box that will help make your printouts look more professional.

Selecting Page Setup Options for Printing

The Page Setup dialog box contains four tabs (see Figure 1.40). You will make selections from each to indicate the printing settings for the worksheet you want to print. The Page Setup dialog box also contains the Print Preview button. This appears on each tab, and you will use the preview feature to view your selections from each tab. Print preview is a handy and efficient way to see how the printed output will appear without wasting paper. To launch the Print Dialog box, you click the Page Setup Dialog Box Launcher from the Page Setup group on the Page Layout tab.

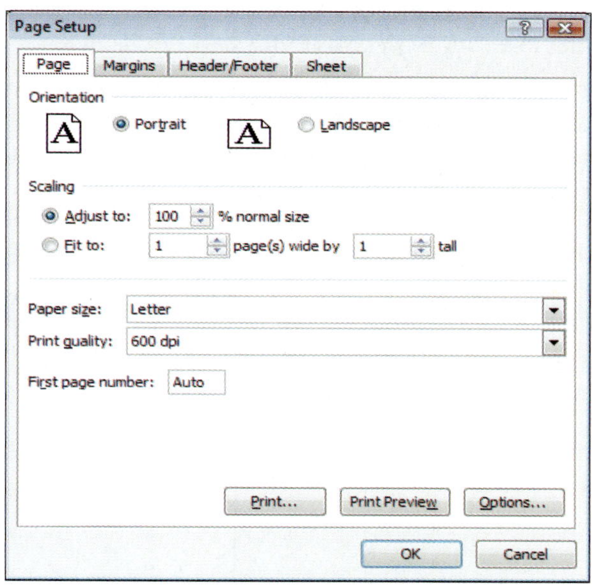

Figure 1.40 Page Setup Dialog Box

Specify Page Options with the Page Tab

The first tab in the Page Setup dialog box is the Page tab, as shown in Figure 1.41. Note that you can use the Print Preview button from any of the Page Setup dialog box tabs and that the Options button takes the user to settings for the particular printer he or she is using. The Print Preview command shows you how the worksheet will appear when printed and saves you from having to rely on trial and error.

Portrait orientation prints vertically down the page.

Landscape orientation prints horizontally across the page.

The Page orientation options determine the orientation and scaling of the printed page. ***Portrait orientation*** (8.5 × 11) prints vertically down the page. ***Landscape orientation*** (11 × 8.5) prints horizontally across the page and is used when the worksheet is too wide to fit on a portrait page. Changing the page orientation to landscape is often an acceptable solution to fit a worksheet on one page.

Scaling option buttons are used to choose the scaling factor. You can reduce or enlarge the output by a designated scaling factor, or you can force the output to fit on a specified number of pages. The latter option is typically used to force a worksheet to fit on a single page. The Paper size and Print quality lists present several options for the size paper your printer is using and the dpi (Dots Per Inch) quality of the printer.

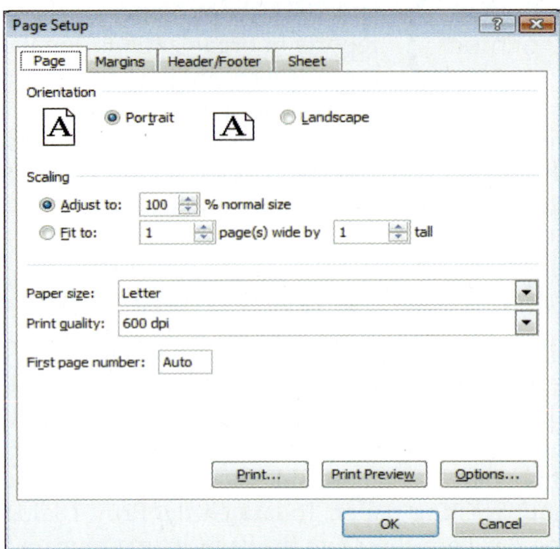

Figure 1.41 Page Tab

Use the Margins Tab to Set Margins

The Margins tab (see Figure 1.42) not only controls the margins but also centers the worksheet horizontally or vertically on the page. The Margins tab also determines the distance of the header and footer from the edge of the page. You must exercise caution in setting the margins as not all printers can accept very small margins (generally less than .25 inches). Worksheets appear more professional when you adjust margins and center the worksheet horizontally on a page.

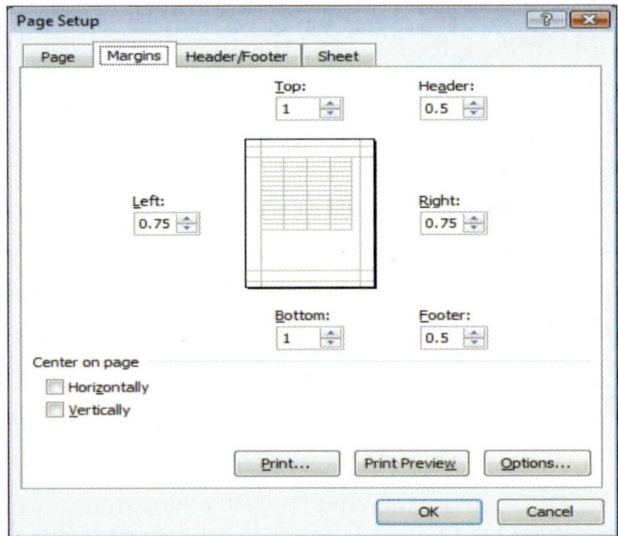

Figure 1.42 Margins

Create Headers and Footers with Header/Footer Tab

The Header/Footer tab, shown in Figure 1.43, lets you create a header and/or footer that appears at the top and/or bottom of every page. The pull-down list boxes let you choose from several preformatted entries, or alternatively, you can click the Custom Header or Custom Footer button, insert text and other objects, and then click the appropriate formatting button to customize either entry. Table 1.6 below shows a summary of buttons for headers and footers. You can use headers and footers to provide additional information about the worksheet. You can include your name, the date the worksheet was prepared, and page numbers, for example.

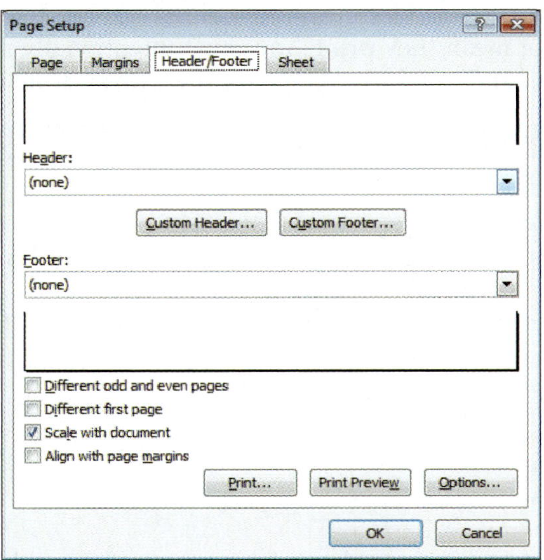

Figure 1.43 Headers and Footers

Table 1.6 Header/Footer Button Summary

Button	Name	Code Entered	Result
A	Format Text	None	Sets font, size, and text style
	Insert Page Number	&(Page)	Inserts page number
	Insert Number of Pages	&(Pages)	Indicates total number of pages
	Insert Date	&(Date)	Inserts the current date
	Insert Time	&(Time)	Inserts the current time
	Insert File Path	&(Path)&(File)	Indicates path and file name
	Insert File Name	&(File)	Indicates the file name
	Insert Sheet Name	&(Tab)	Shows the name of the active worksheet
	Insert Picture	&(Picture)	Inserts an image file
	Format Picture	None	Opens the Format Picture dialog box

Select Sheet Options from the Sheet Tab

The Sheet tab contains several additional options, as shown in Figure 1.44. The Gridlines option prints lines to separate the cells within the worksheet. The Row and column headings option displays the column letters and row numbers. Both options should be selected for most worksheets. Just because you see gridlines on the screen does not mean they print. You must intentionally select the options to print both gridlines and row and column headings if you want them to print.

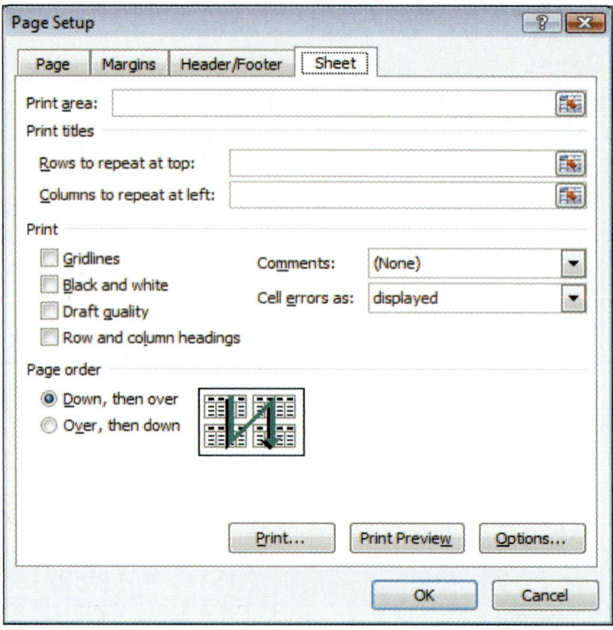

Figure 1.44 Sheet Tab

TIP Page Layout Tab

The Page Layout tab contains useful commands in the Page Setup, Scale to Fit, and Sheet Options groups. For example, you can set margins, page orientation, paper size, scaling, and gridlines.

Managing Cell Comments

A ***comment*** adds documentation to a cell.

The use of cell ***comments*** in Excel is an important yet simple way to provide documentation to others who may view the file. Comments add documentation to a cell and are inserted in a cell to explain the preparer's thoughts to or define formulas for those using the workbook. Often the creator of a file will want to provide information about a cell or cells in a worksheet without them always being visible. Inserting comments will accomplish this result. A red triangle appears in the cell containing the comment, and the comment is visible when you point at the cell. See Figure 1.45. To create a cell comment:

1. Click the cell requiring a comment.
2. On the Review tab, in the Comments group, click New Comment.
3. Enter the comment.
4. Click any other cell to complete the process.

Instead of completing the above steps, you can right-click on the cell requiring a comment and select Insert Comment from the shortcut menu.

Hands-On Exercises

4 | Printing Jake's Gym Worksheet

Skills covered: 1. Insert a Comment **2.** Insert Custom Header and Footer **3.** Format to Print the Worksheet

Step 1 Insert a Comment

Refer to Figure 1.45 as you complete Step 1.

a. Open *chap1_ho3_jake_solution* and save as **chap1_ho4_jake_solution**.

b. Click in **cell I6.**

You will type a descriptive comment in the selected cell.

c. Click the **Review tab** and click **New Comment** in the Comments group.

The name in the comment box will be different depending on the User name entered in the Excel Options dialog box.

d. Type **The largest percent of increase**.

e. Click any other cell to complete the process.

You can right-click the cell requiring a comment and select Insert Comment from the shortcut menu.

TROUBLESHOOTING: You can print your comments by first clicking in the cell containing a comment and then clicking Show All Comments in the Comments group of the Review tab. Then select As displayed on sheet from the Comments list in the Sheet tab of the Page Setup dialog box.

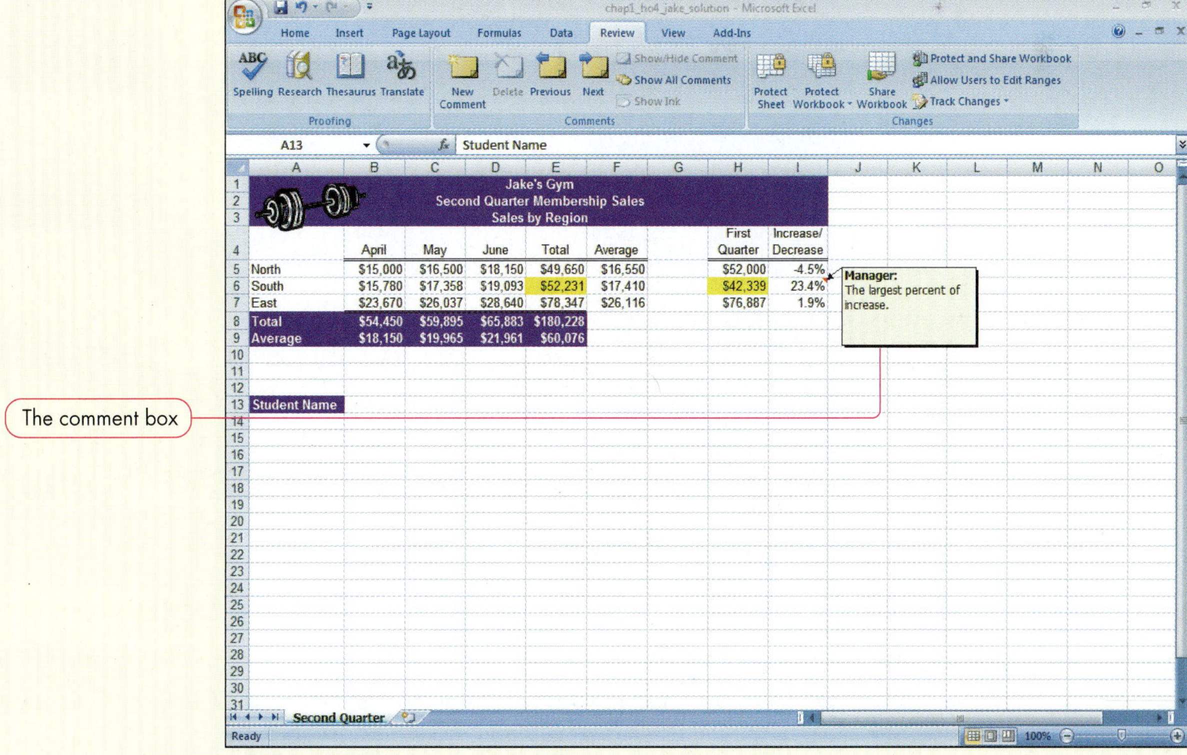

Figure 1.45 Insert a Comment

Step 2
Insert Custom Header and Footer

Refer to Figure 1.46 as you complete Step 2.

a. Click in **cell A13**, click the **Home tab**, click **Clear** in the Editing group, and select **Clear All** to delete your name and format since you will add your name to the header.

b. Click the **Page Layout tab** and click the **Page Setup Dialog Box Launcher** in the Page Setup group.

c. Click the **Header/Footer tab**.

d. Click **Custom Header** and type your name in the *Left section*.

e. Click in the *Right section* and click **Insert Page Number**. Click **OK**.

   You created a header so your name and page number will display at the top of the printed page.

f. Click **Custom Footer** and click in the *Center section*. Type your instructor's name.

g. Click in the *Right section*, click **Insert Date,** and click **OK**.

   You created a footer so your instructor's name and the date will print at the bottom of the spreadsheet page.

h. Click **Print Preview**.

   Use the preview feature to verify the placement of your header and footer. You can also see how much of the worksheet will print on a page.

i. Close **Print Preview**.

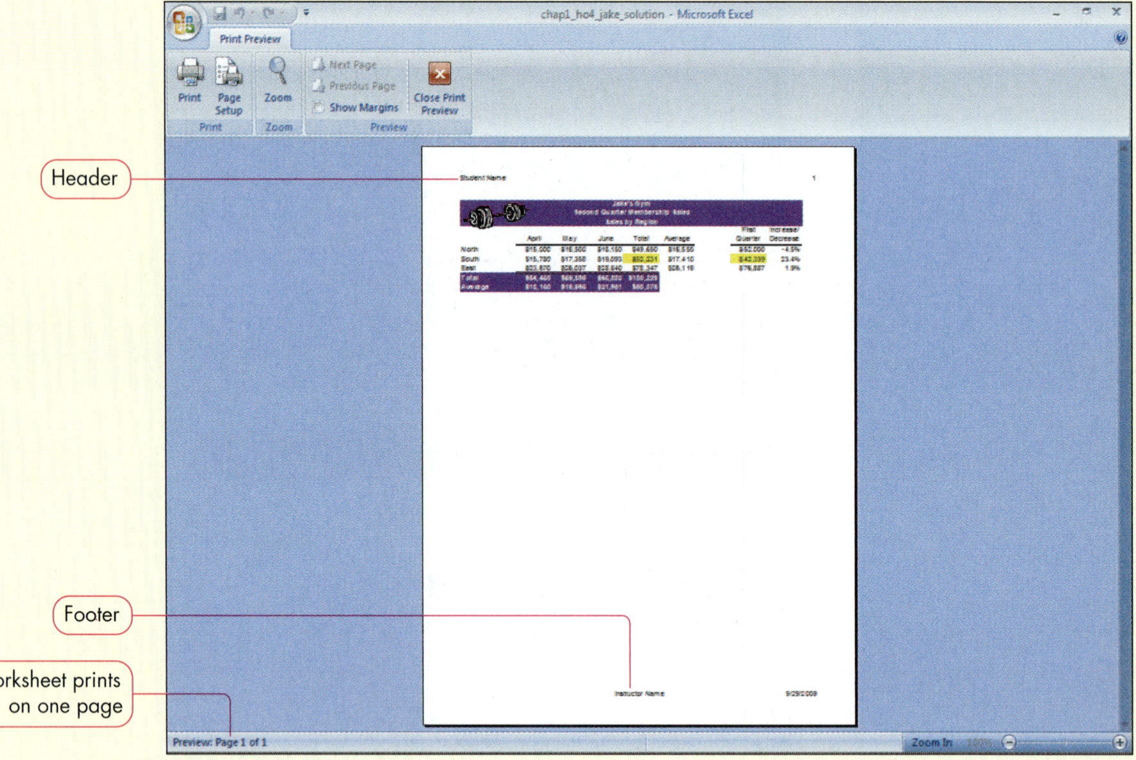

Figure 1.46 Insert a Custom Header and Footer

Step 3
Format to Print the Worksheet

Refer to Figure 1.47 as you complete Step 3.

a. Click the **Page Layout tab** if it is not the active tab. Click the **Orientation arrow** in the Page Setup group and select **Landscape**.

   You changed from portrait to landscape as one method to make sure the worksheet prints on one page if you add one or two more columns later.

b. Click the **Size arrow** in the Page Setup group, select **More Paper Sizes** and click the **Fit to option** in the *Scaling* section.

You opened the Page Setup dialog box and selected *Fit to 1 page* to force the worksheet to print on a single page, another method to print the worksheet on one page. You will continue to make selections from the Page Setup dialog box.

c. Click the **Margins tab** in the Page Setup dialog box and click the **Horizontally** and **Vertically check boxes** in the *Center on page* section.

Printing a worksheet that is centered both horizontally and vertically results in a professional-appearing document.

d. Click the **Sheet tab** in the Page Setup dialog box and click the **Row and column headings** and **Gridlines check boxes** in the *Print* section if necessary. Click the **Print Preview button** and click **Close Print Preview**.

Row and column headings and gridlines facilitate reading the data in a worksheet.

e. Click the **Office Button** and select **Print**. Click **OK** in the Print dialog box.

f. Save the workbook and press **Ctrl +** ` (the grave accent symbol) to show the cell formulas rather than the displayed values. See Figure 1.47. Adjust the column widths as necessary to print on one page and then print the worksheet a second time.

Displaying and printing cell formulas is an important task associated with worksheet creation. Formulas are the basis of many values, and it is necessary to verify the accuracy of the values. Analyzing the formulas and perhaps manually calculating the formulas is one way to verify accuracy. Printing with formulas displayed is part of worksheet documentation. (Submit assignment electronically or print as directed by your instructor.)

g. Close the workbook. Do not save the changes unless your instructor tells you to save the worksheet.

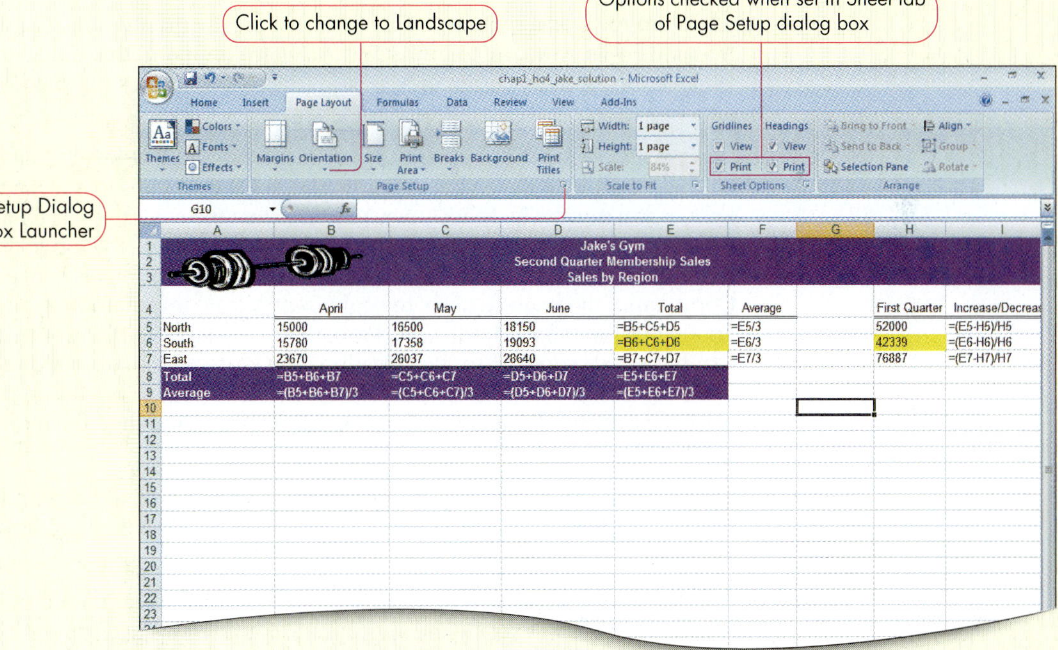

Figure 1.47 Displayed Cell Formulas

TIP Quit Without Saving

At times you may not want to save the changes to a workbook—for example, when you have edited it beyond recognition. Click the Office Button, select Close, and then click No when prompted to save the changes. Click the Office Button, click the file's name at the right of the menu to reopen the file, and then begin all over.

Summary

1. **Define worksheets and workbooks.** A spreadsheet is the computerized equivalent of an accountant's ledger. It is divided into rows and columns, with each row and column assigned a heading. The intersection of a row and column forms a cell. Spreadsheet is a generic term. Workbook and worksheet are Excel specific. An Excel workbook contains one or more worksheets.
2. **Use spreadsheets across disciplines.** Spreadsheets are used in many areas other than business. Because of the powerful graphing or charting feature of Excel, geologists and physical scientists use spreadsheets to store data about earthquakes or other physical phenomena and then graph it. Historians and social scientists have long used the power of spreadsheets for such uses as predicting voting behavior.
3. **Plan for good workbook and worksheet design.** Planning a spreadsheet before entering data into it is a necessary activity. The more prior planning that is done, the better the spreadsheet will appear, and it also will ensure that the spreadsheet shows what it is supposed to.
4. **Identify Excel window components.** The elements of the Excel window include the Ribbon, tabs, and groups. There are also quick buttons above the tabs to simplify some functions. The formula bar, sheet tabs, the status bar, and the Select All button are parts of the Excel window.
5. **Enter and edit data in cells.** You can enter three types of data in an Excel worksheet. They are text, values, and formulas. Each of these types of data has different uses in Excel.
6. **Describe and use symbols and the order of precedence.** Mathematical symbols are the base of all calculations in Excel. Understanding the order of precedence also helps clarify how mathematical calculations occur in Excel.
7. **Display cell formulas.** One of the tools that can be used to document an Excel worksheet is the ability to display cell formulas. When this tool is used, the formulas that appear in cells are shown rather than the results of the calculation.
8. **Insert and delete rows and columns.** This feature typically involves the use of the Insert command that adds cells, rows, or columns or the Delete command that deletes cells, rows, or columns. When either of these commands is used, the cell references in existing cells are automatically adjusted to reflect the insertion or deletion.
9. **Use cell ranges; Excel move; copy, paste, paste special; and AutoFill.** Each of these topics is a basic editing function in Excel. Every command in Excel applies to a rectangular group of cells known as a *range*. The Move operation transfers the content of a cell or cell range from one location on the worksheet to another with the cells where the move originated becoming empty. The Delete operation removes all content from a cell or from a selected cell range. The Copy command enables users to begin to duplicate information in a cell or range of cells into another cell or range of cells. The Paste operation enables the user to duplicate cell contents that have been copied to a new location. The Paste Special operation enables users several different options when pasting material. AutoFill is an Excel operation that enables users to copy the content of a cell or a range of cells by dragging the fill handle over another cell or range of cells.
10. **Manage worksheets.** These are operations that users of Excel should be familiar with in order to make worksheets more attractive and also to understand some basic operations that can assist in the construction of worksheets.
11. **Format worksheets.** Formatting is done within the context of select-then-do; that is, select the cell or range of cells, then execute the appropriate command. The Format Cells command controls the formatting for numbers, alignment, fonts, borders, and patterns (colors). The formatting commands on the Home tab simplify the formatting process. As you format a worksheet to improve its appearance, you might want to insert clip art as well.
12. **Select page setup options for printing.** The Page Setup command provides complete control over the printed page, enabling you to print a worksheet with or without gridlines or row and column headings. The Page Setup command also controls margins, headers and footers, centering the worksheet on a page, and orientation. The Print Preview command shows the worksheet as it will print and should be used prior to printing.
13. **Manage cell comments.** The use of comments in Excel is an important, yet simple, way to provide documentation to others who may view the file. Often the creator of a file will want to provide information about a cell or cells in a worksheet without them always being visible.

Key Terms

Multiple Choice

1. Which of the following is true?
   (a) A worksheet contains one or more workbooks.
   (b) A workbook contains one or more worksheets.
   (c) A spreadsheet contains one or more worksheets.
   (d) A worksheet contains one or more spreadsheets.

2. The cell at the intersection of the second column and third row is cell:
   (a) B3
   (b) 3B
   (c) C2
   (d) 2C

3. Which options are mutually exclusive in the Page Setup dialog box?
   (a) Portrait and landscape orientation
   (b) Cell gridlines and row and column headings
   (c) Left and right margins
   (d) Header and footer

4. Which of the following is not a symbol for a mathematical operation in Excel?
   (a) +
   (b) –
   (c) C
   (d) *

5. Which command enables you to change the margins for a printed worksheet?
   (a) View
   (b) Edit
   (c) Page Setup
   (d) Options

6. What is the effect of typing F5+F6 into a cell without a beginning equal sign?
   (a) The entry is equivalent to the formula =F5+F6.
   (b) The cell will display the contents of cell F5 plus cell F6.
   (c) The entry will be treated as a text entry and display F5+F6 in the cell.
   (d) The entry will be rejected by Excel, which will signal an error message.

7. The Save command:
   (a) Brings a workbook from disk into memory.
   (b) Brings a workbook from disk into memory and then erases the workbook on disk.
   (c) Stores the workbook in memory on disk.
   (d) Stores the workbook in memory on disk and then erases the workbook from memory.

8. Which of the following is not a basic mathematical operation?
   (a) Parentheses
   (b) Division
   (c) Multiplication
   (d) Subtraction

9. Given the formula =B5*B6+C3/D4^2, which expression would be evaluated first?
   (a) B5*B6
   (b) D4^2
   (c) C3/D4
   (d) It is impossible to determine.

10. If you see the term "C3" used in relation to Excel, this refers to what?
    (a) Absolute reference
    (b) Cell reference
    (c) Worksheet reference
    (d) Mixed reference

11. Which of the following is the correct order of mathematical operations?
    (a) Parentheses, multiplication or division, addition or subtraction
    (b) Parentheses, exponents, multiplication or division, addition or subtraction
    (c) Parentheses, exponents, addition or subtraction, multiplication or division
    (d) Multiplication or division, addition or subtraction, parentheses, exponents

12. What is the answer to =10+4*3?
    (a) 42
    (b) 22
    (c) 34
    (d) 17

...continued on Next Page

Multiple Choice Continued...

13. What is the answer to =(6*5)+4?

(a) 34
(b) 44
(c) 26
(d) 54

14. The fill handle is used to:

(a) Copy
(b) Paste
(c) Cut
(d) Select

15. The small black square in the bottom-right corner of a cell is called what?

(a) Pointer
(b) Fill handle
(c) Cross hair
(d) Select box

16. A red triangle in a cell indicates which of the following:

(a) A cell is locked.
(b) The cell contains an absolute reference.
(c) The cell contains a comment.
(d) The cell contains numeric data.

17. Which of the following is entered first when creating a formula?

(a) The equal sign
(b) A mathematical operator
(c) A function
(d) A value

18. What is the end result of clicking in a cell and then clicking Italic on the Home tab twice in a row?

(a) The cell contents are displayed in italic.
(b) The cell contents are not displayed in ordinary (non-italicized) type.
(c) The cell contents are unchanged and appear exactly as they did prior to clicking the Italic button twice in a row.
(d) Impossible to determine.

19. Which option is not available when creating a custom header or custom footer?

(a) Format Text
(b) Insert Formula
(c) Insert Number of Pages
(d) Format Picture

Practice Exercises

1 Verifying a Debit Card

One of the more common challenges beginning college students face is keeping track of their finances. The worksheet in this problem is one that you could use to verify your weekly debit card expenditures. Failure to track your debit card correctly could lead to financial disaster, as you are charged for overdrafts and could get a bad credit rating. You will use the data shown in the table below to create the worksheet. Refer to Figure 1.48 as you complete this exercise.

a. Start Excel. If Excel is already open, click the **Office Button**, select **New**, and click **Create** to display a blank workbook. Save the workbook as **chap1_pe1_debitcard_solution**.

b. Click in **cell A1** and type **Your Name Debit Card**. Do not worry about formatting at this time. Enter the labels as shown in the table below:

Cell Address	A2	B2	C2	D2	E2	F2
Label	Item #	Date	Description	Amount	Deposit	Balance

c. Click in **cell F3** and type the initial balance of **1000**. You will format the values later. Use the table below to enter the data for the first item:

Cell Reference	A4	B4	C4	D4
Data	100	6/2	Rent	575

d. Click in **cell F4** and type the formula **=F3-D4+E4** to compute the balance. The formula is entered so that the balance is computed correctly. It does not matter if an amount or deposit is entered as the transaction because Excel treats the blank cells as zeros.

e. Enter data in rows 5 through 7 as shown in Figure 1.48, but do not enter the values in the Balance column because you will calculate those. Type **Weekly Verification** in cell C8. Click in **cell F4** and use the fill handle to copy the formula to **cells F5:F7**.

f. Insert a new row above row 8 by right-clicking any cell in row 8, selecting **Insert** from the shortcut menu, clicking **Entire row** in the Insert dialog box, and then clicking **OK**.

g. Click in **cell D9** to enter the formula to total your weekly expenditure amount. Type **= D4+D6+D7** and press **Enter**. If the formula is entered correctly, you will see 670.43 in cell D9.

h. Click in **cell E9** and type **=E5** to enter the formula to total your weekly deposit. If the formula is entered correctly, you will see 250 as the total first week deposit.

i. To verify your balance, click in **cell F9,** and type **=F3-D9+E9,** and press **Enter**. If you entered the formula correctly, you will see 579.57 as the balance.

j. Right-click **cell F9** and select **Insert Comment**. Type the following comment: **Balance is equal to the initial balance minus the amounts and ATM withdrawals plus the deposits.**

k. Format the completed worksheet as shown in Figure 1.48. Click in **cell D3** and then click and drag to select the **range D3:F9**. Click the **Home tab** and click the **Number Format down arrow** in the Number group. Click **Currency** from the Number Format gallery.

l. Click and drag to select the **range B4:B7**. Click the **Number Format down arrow** in the Number group. Click **Short Date** from the Number Format gallery. Select the **range A4:A7**; press and hold **Ctrl** while dragging to select the **range A2:F2**. Click **Center** in the Alignment group on the Home tab.

m. Click and drag to select the **range A1:F2**. Click the **Fill Color arrow** in the Font group and select the color **Orange**. Click the **Font Color arrow** in the Font group and select **Blue**. Click **Bold** in the Font group.

n. Click in **cell A1** to select only this cell, click the **Font Size arrow** in the Font group on the Home tab, and **select 16**.

...continued on Next Page

o. Select the **range A2:F2** that contains the labels. Click **Borders** in the Font group on the Home tab and select **Top and Thick Bottom Border**.

p. Widen columns A through F so all text is visible by dragging the right border of each column to the right.

q. Click and drag to select the **range A1:F1**. Click **Merge & Center** in the Alignment group on the Home tab.

r. Click the **Page Layout tab** and click the **Page Setup Dialog Box Launcher** in the Page Setup group. Click the **Header/Footer tab**, click **Custom Header,** and type **Your Name** in the *Left section*. Click in the *Right section* and click **Insert File Name**. Click **OK**.

s. Click **Custom Footer** and click in the *Center section*. Type **Your Instructor's Name**. Click in the *Right section*, click **Insert Date,** and click **OK**. Click **Print Preview**. Click **Page Setup** on the Print Preview tab.

t. Click the **Margins tab** in the Page Setup dialog box and click the **Horizontally** and **Vertically check boxes** in the *Center on page* section.

u. Click the **Sheet tab** and click the **Row and column headings** and **Gridlines check boxes** in the *Print* section. Click **OK**. Click **Close Print Preview** on the Print Preview tab.

v. Click **Save** on the Quick Access Toolbar to save the workbook. Click the **Office Button,** point to **Print**, and select **Quick Print** to print the worksheet. Close the workbook.

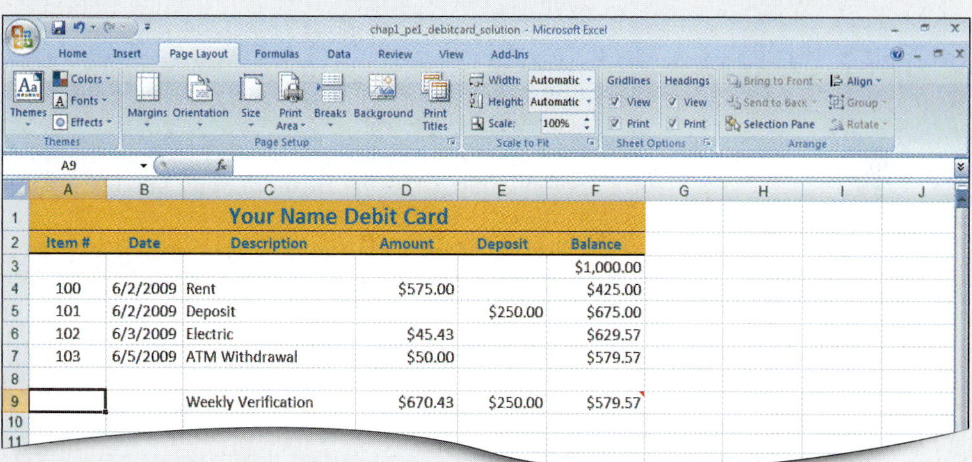

Figure 1.48 Verify Your Debit Card

2 Formatting—Create a Calendar

Excel is a spreadsheet application that gives you a row column table to work with. In this exercise, you will use the row column table to create a calendar worksheet that also demonstrates the formatting capabilities available in Excel. You will insert images representing a variety of activities in a particular month. Review Figure 1.49 to see a sample calendar page.

a. Start Excel to display a blank workbook and save as **chap1_pe2_calendar_solution**.

b. In **cell D1** enter the month for which you will create the calendar—July, for example. Click and drag to select **cells D1:F1**, then click **Merge & Center** in the Alignment group on the Home tab. Use the Font group to select **Comic Sans MS** font and **26** for the font size. Type **Your Name** in **cell D2** and press **Enter**. Click and drag to select **cells D2:F2** and merge and center as described above. Use the Font group to select **Comic Sans MS** font and **14** for the font size.

c. Right-click **row 1**, select **Row Height** from the shortcut menu, and type **39** in the Row Height dialog box to increase the row height. In similar fashion, right-click **row 2** and verify the row height is **21**.

d. Select **columns B** through **H**, right-click, select **Column Width** from the shortcut menu, and type **21.14** to change the width of the selected columns.

e. Click **cell B1**. Press and hold **Ctrl** while selecting the **ranges B1:H3, B4:B8,** and **H4:H8**. Click the **Fill Color arrow** in the Font group and select **Blue**. Click the **Font Color arrow**

...continued on Next Page

in the Font group and select **White, Background 1**. Click **Bold** in the Font group to make the text stand out.

f. Click in **cell B3**, type **Sunday**, and press **Enter**. Click **cell B3** to make it the active cell. Click and drag the fill handle from **cell B3** to **H3** to automatically enter the remaining days of the week.

g. Keeping cells B3:H3 selected, click **Center** in the Alignment group on the Home tab. Select **Comic Sans MS** as the font and **12** as the font size in the Font group on the Home tab. Increase the row height by right-clicking **row 3**, selecting **Row Height** and typing **23.25** in the Row Height dialog box, and then clicking **OK**.

h. Click **cell D4** and type **1** for the first day of the month. Type numbers for the remaining 30 days of the month in rows **4** through **8**. Increase the row height in rows 4 through 8 to **58.5**. Select rows **4** through **8** and click **Top Align** and click **Align Text Left** in the Alignment group on the Home tab. Click and drag to select **cells B4:H8**, then select **Arial, 14 point** in the Font group on the Home tab. Click and drag to select **cells B3:H8**, right-click the selected cells, select **Format Cells** to open the Format cells dialog box. Click **Border** and then click both **Outline** and **Inside** in the *Presets section*. Click **OK**.

i. Click **Clip Art** in the Illustrations group on the Insert tab and type **Fourth of July** in the **Search for** text box. Insert and resize the images as shown in Figure 1.49. Search for **Cardinal**, insert, and resize the image shown in Figure 1.49. If you create a different monthly calendar, search for, insert, and size appropriate images for holidays.

j. Right-click on the **Sheet1 tab,** select **Rename,** and type the name of the month for which you are creating the calendar. Right-click the newly renamed tab, point to **Tab Color**, and select **Red**. Delete the remaining sheets by right-clicking the sheet tab and selecting **Delete**.

k. Click the **Page Layout tab** and click the **Page Setup Dialog Box Launcher** in the Page Setup group. Click the **Header/Footer tab**. Click **Custom Footer** and type **Your Name** in the *Left section*. Click in the *Right section* and type your instructor's name. Click **OK**.

l. Click the **Margins tab** in the Page Setup dialog box and click the **Horizontally** and **Vertically check boxes** in the *Center on page* section. Click the **Page tab**, click **Landscape** in the *Orientation section*, Fit to 1 Page(s) under Scaling and click **OK**.

m. Click **Save** on the Quick Access Toolbar to save the workbook. Click the **Office Button**, point to **Print**, and select **Quick Print** to print the worksheet.

n. Close the workbook.

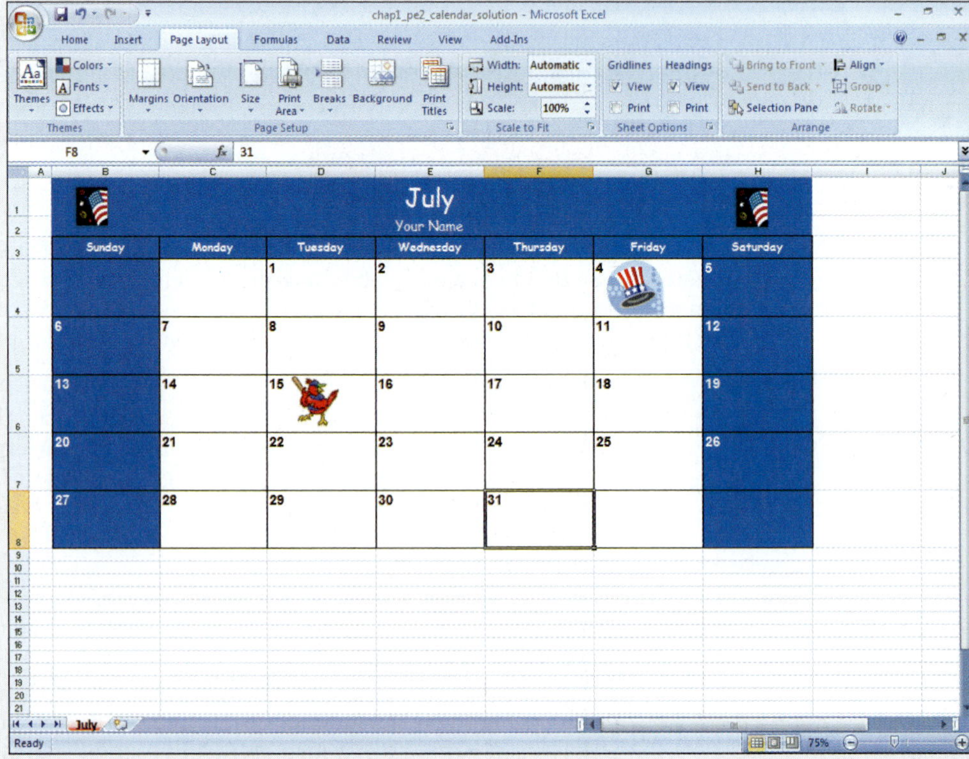

Figure 1.49 Create a Calendar

...continued on Next Page

3 Temperature Data

Your hobby is collecting, recording, and monitoring metrological data to track trends in temperature. Figure 1.50 displays the average temperature for summer in three American cities. Working with the partially completed workbook, you will create formulas, copy and paste a portion of a spreadsheet, and format both worksheets in an attractive and readable manner.

a. Open *chap1_pe3_temperature* and save as **chap1_pe3_temperature_solution** so that you can return to the original workbook if necessary.

b. Click in **cell E3**, type **=(B3+C3+D3)/3,** and press **Enter**. You entered the formula to calculate the average summer temperature for Pittsburgh. Click in **cell E3** and use the fill handle to copy the formula to **cells E4:E5**.

c. Click in **cell A6** and type **Monthly Averages**. Enter the formula to calculate the average temperature for June by clicking in **cell B6** and typing **=(B3+B4+B5)/3,** then pressing **Enter**. Click in **cell B6** and use the fill handle to copy the formula to **cells C6:D6**.

d. Click in **cell E9** and type **=(B9+C9+D9)/3,** then press **Enter** to calculate the average temperature by city for the winter months. Click in **cell E9** and use the fill handle to copy the formula to **cells E10:E11**.

e. Click in **cell A12** and type **Monthly Averages**. Click in **cell B12** and type **=(B9+B10+B11)/3,** then pressing **Enter** to calculate the average temperature for December. Click in **cell B12** and use the fill handle to copy the formula to **cells C12:D12**.

f. Format numbers in column E and rows 6 and 12 with 2 decimals by pressing and holding **Ctrl** while selecting **cells E3:E5, E9:E11**, **B6:D6**, and **B12:D12**. Click the **Number Format arrow** in the Number group on the Home tab and select **Number**. Widen **column A** to 18, and **columns B** through **E** to **11.**

g. Click in **cell A1**. Click the **Insert arrow** in the Cells group on the Home tab and select **Insert Sheet Rows** to insert a new blank row above row 1. Type the title **Temperature Comparison** in **cell A1.**

h. Select **cells A1:E1** and click **Merge & Center** in the Alignment group. Repeat for **cells A2:E2** and **cells A8:E8**. Select **cells A1:E2**. Press and hold **Ctrl** while selecting **cell A8** and then select **Light Blue** from **Fill Color** and **White, Background 1** from **Font Color** in the Font group. Change the title font and size by selecting **cell A1** and then selecting **Comic Sans MS** from the **Font** drop-down list and **18** from the **Font Size** drop-down list in the Font group.

i. Select **cells B3:E3**. Press and hold **Ctrl** while selecting **cells B9:E9** and clicking **Center** in the Alignment group.

j. Select **cells A1:E3**. Press and hold **Ctrl** while selecting **cells A7:E9** and **A13:E13** and click **Bold** in the Font group.

k. Select **cells A4:A6**. Press and hold **Ctrl** while selecting **cells A10:A12** and click **Increase Indent** in the Alignment group.

l. You will move your winter temperature data and copy the main title to a new sheet, and then rename and change the color of both sheet tabs and delete Sheet3. Select **cell A1** and click **Copy** in the Clipboard group on the Home tab.

m. Click the **Sheet2 tab**, make sure cell A1 is the active cell, and click the **Paste down arrow** in the Clipboard group, and select **Paste Special**. Select **All** from the *Paste* section of the Paste Special dialog box and then click **OK** to paste the formatted title in cell A1. Immediately open the Paste Special dialog box again and select **Column widths** from the *Paste* section. When you click **OK** to close, you will see the correct column widths.

n. Click the **Sheet1 tab**, press **Esc** to cancel the previous selected range, select **cells A8:E13,** and click **Cut** in the Clipboard group. Click the **Sheet2 tab**, make sure **cell A2** is the active cell, click **Paste** in the Clipboard group to paste the formatted portion of the worksheet in cell A2.

o. Double-click the **Sheet1 tab** and type **Summer**. Double-click the **Sheet2 tab** and type **Winter**. Right-click the **Sheet3 tab,** and select **Delete**. Right-click the **Summer tab** and select **Red** from the **Tab color palette**. Repeat but choose **Blue** for the **Winter tab**.

p. Press and hold **Ctrl** as you click the **Summer** and **Winter** worksheet tabs. This groups the worksheets. Any formatting action you take applies to both worksheets. Click the **Page Layout tab** and click the **Page Setup Dialog Box Launcher** in the Page Setup

...continued on Next Page

group. Click the **Header/Footer tab**. Click **Custom Header** and type **Your Name** in the *Left section*. Click in the *Right section* and type your course name. Click **OK**.

q. Click the **Margins tab** in the Page Setup dialog box, click **Horizontally** and **Vertically check boxes** in the *Center on page* section, and click **OK**. You centered both worksheets.

r. Print the worksheet two ways, to show both displayed values and cell formulas. Save and close the workbook.

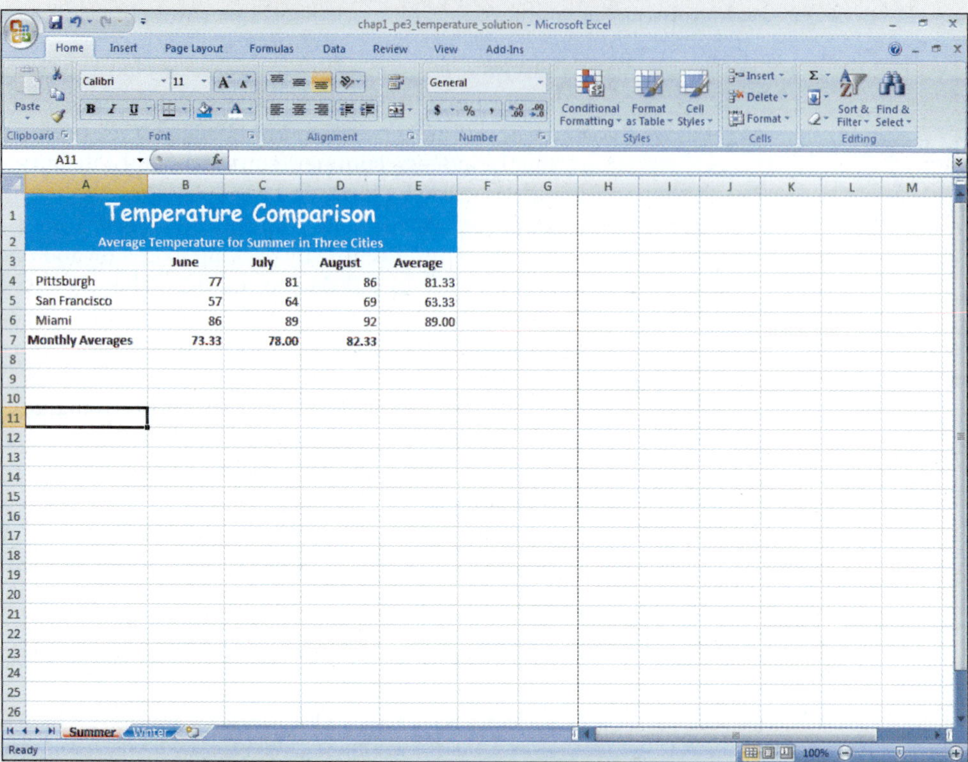

Figure 1.50 Temperature Data

4 Astronomy Lab

Figure 1.51 displays a spreadsheet with information about our solar system. Your astronomy professor asked you to complete the worksheet as part of your lab assignment. You will open the partially completed version of the workbook and complete the worksheet by developing the formulas for the first planet, copying those formulas, and then formatting the worksheet for your professor. The spreadsheet contains a Constants and Assumptions area to store two values to use in formulas. Using cell references is a better spreadsheet design than typing raw values in cells when those values might change.

a. Open *chap1_pe4_solarsystem* and save the workbook as **chap1_pe4_solarsystem_solution** so that you can return to the original workbook if necessary.

b. Click in **cell C14** and enter **150** as a weight in pounds on Earth. Click in **cell C15** and enter **3.14159**, which is the value of Pi for this worksheet.

c. Click in **cell D4** and enter the formula to compute the diameter of the first planet (Mercury). The diameter of a planet is equal to twice its radius. Type **=2*B4** and press **Enter**. In this formula, it is acceptable to use the value 2.

d. Click in **cell E4** and enter the formula to compute the circumference of a planet. The circumference is equal to the diameter times Pi. Type **=D4*$C$15** and press **Enter**. You typed *$C$15* to create an absolute or permanent reference to **cell C15**, the cell containing *3.14159*. The symbols prevent the formula from becoming C16 when copied down.

e. Click in **cell F4** and enter the formula to compute the surface area, which is equal to four times Pi times the radius squared. This is the formula to compute the surface area of a sphere, which is different from the formula to compute the area of a circle. Type **=4*$C$15*B4^2**, and press **Enter**. Using 4 and 2 in the formulas is acceptable, but it is

...continued on Next Page

easier to prevent data-entry errors on the PI value by using the cell reference rather than typing it several times.

f. Click in **cell G4** and enter the formula to compute your weight on Mercury, which is your weight on Earth times the relative gravity of Mercury compared to that of Earth. Type **=150*C4** and press **Enter**.

g. Select **cells D4:G4** and use the **fill handle** to copy the formula to **cells D5:G11**.

h. Click in **cell E14** and type **Your Name**. Apply the following formats:

- Select **cells A1:G1** and click **Merge & Center** in the Alignment group on the Home tab.
- Click the **column B heading**. Press and hold down **Ctrl** while you click the **column headings** for columns D, E, F, and G to select these columns. Click **Comma Style** in the Number group on the Home tab to format the values with commas. Click **Decrease Decimal** two times to show whole numbers only.
- Select **cells C4:C11**, click **Comma Style** in the Number group on the Home tab, and then click **Increase Decimal** in the Number group.
- Select **columns B** and **D**. Click **Format** in the Cells group on the Home tab, select **Column Width**, type **12**, and click **OK**. Set the width of column E to **14**.
- Bold rows **1, 3,** and **13**.
- Use **Dark Blue, Text 2** fill and **White, Background 1** font color for cell ranges **A1:G3, A13:C13,** and **E13:G13**.
- Click **cell B3**. Press and hold down **Ctrl** as you click **cells D3:E3**. Click **Wrap Text** in the Alignment group on the Home tab.
- Select **cells B3:G3** and click **Align Text Right** in the Alignment group.

i. Click the **Page Layout tab** and click the **Page Setup Dialog Box Launcher** to do the following:

- Click the **Page tab**, click the **Landscape option**, and click the **Fit to option**.
- Click the **Header/Footer tab**, click **Custom Header**, type your name in the *Left section,* click in the *Right section*, click **Insert File Name**, and click **OK**.
- Click the **Sheet tab**, click the **Gridlines check box**, and click the **Row and column headings check box**.
- Click the **Margins tab**, click the **Horizontally check box**, and click **OK**.

j. Print the worksheet two ways in order to show both displayed values and cell formulas. Save and close the workbook.

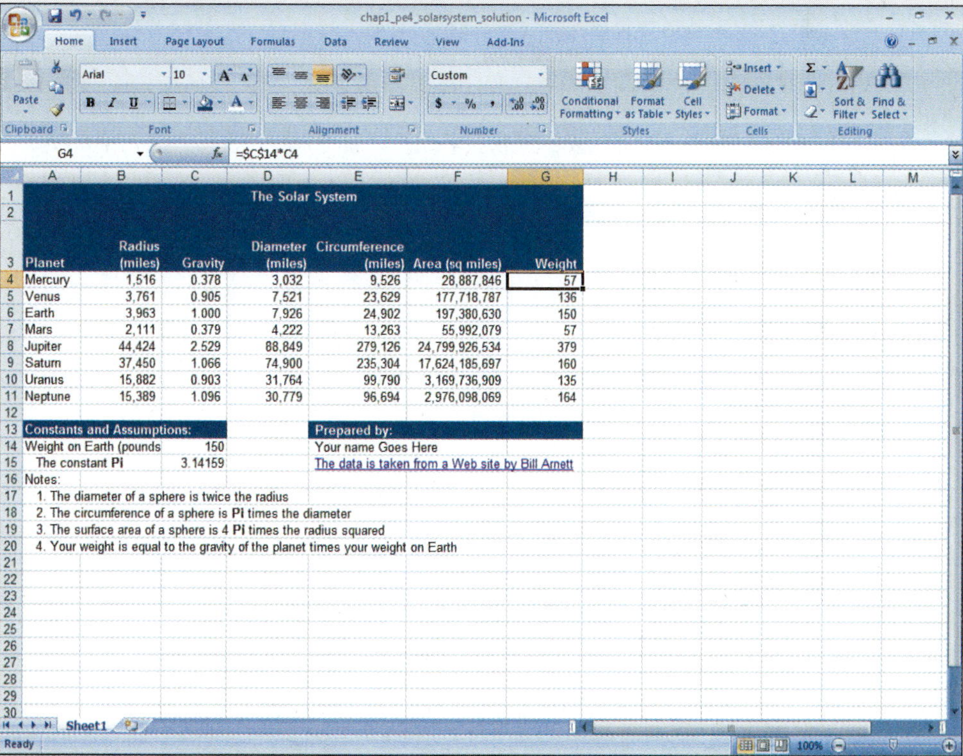

G4 =$C$14*C4

	A	B	C	D	E	F	G
1	The Solar System						
2							
3	Planet	Radius (miles)	Gravity	Diameter (miles)	Circumference (miles)	Area (sq miles)	Weight
4	Mercury	1,516	0.378	3,032	9,526	28,887,846	57
5	Venus	3,761	0.905	7,521	23,629	177,718,787	136
6	Earth	3,963	1.000	7,926	24,902	197,380,630	150
7	Mars	2,111	0.379	4,222	13,263	55,992,079	57
8	Jupiter	44,424	2.529	88,849	279,126	24,799,926,534	379
9	Saturn	37,450	1.066	74,900	235,304	17,624,185,697	160
10	Uranus	15,882	0.903	31,764	99,790	3,169,736,909	135
11	Neptune	15,389	1.096	30,779	96,694	2,976,098,069	164
12							
13	Constants and Assumptions:				Prepared by:		
14	Weight on Earth (pounds		150		Your name Goes Here		
15	The constant PI		3.14159		The data is taken from a Web site by Bill Arnett		
16	Notes:						
17	1. The diameter of a sphere is twice the radius						
18	2. The circumference of a sphere is PI times the diameter						
19	3. The surface area of a sphere is 4 PI times the radius squared						
20	4. Your weight is equal to the gravity of the planet times your weight on Earth						

Figure 1.51 Astronomy Lab

Mid-Level Exercises

1 Little League Statistician

Your mother has appointed you the family statistician for your siblings throughout their Little League career. Figure 1.52 displays the completed worksheet showing the statistical data from the last two seasons. Your task is to enter the formulas, format, and print the worksheet for your mother. You will calculate batting averages, totals for statistical data, and family totals.

a. Open the *chap1_mid1_little_league* workbook and save the workbook as **chap1_mid1_little_league_solution** so that you can return to the original workbook if necessary.

b. Click in **cell B16** and type **Your Name**. Enter the formula to compute totals in cells **C7:I7** and **C14:I14**. Click in **cell J4** and enter a formula to compute batting average, Hits/At Bats.

c. Click and drag to select the formula in **cell J4** and copy the formula to **cells J5:J7**. Enter the formula to determine the Batting Average and copy it for the 2007 season.

d. Click in **cell A18** and type **Family Batting Average**. Enter a formula in **cell B18** to calculate the family batting average. Hint: Parentheses are important here.

e. Format the worksheet exactly as shown in Figure 1.52.

f. Search for and insert the clip art image shown in the top-left corner of the worksheet.

g. Print the worksheet twice, once to show displayed values and once to show the cell formulas. Use landscape orientation and be sure that the worksheet fits on one sheet of paper. Save and close the workbook.

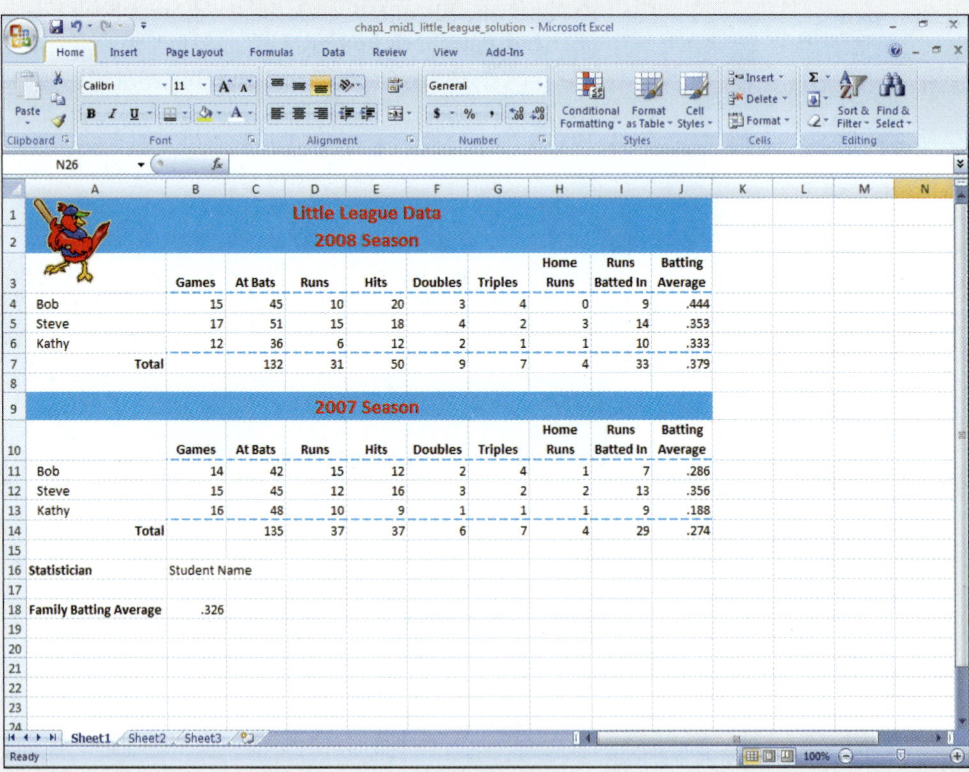

Little League Data

2008 Season

	Games	At Bats	Runs	Hits	Doubles	Triples	Home Runs	Runs Batted In	Batting Average
Bob	15	45	10	20	3	4	0	9	.444
Steve	17	51	15	18	4	2	3	14	.353
Kathy	12	36	6	12	2	1	1	10	.333
Total		132	31	50	9	7	4	33	.379

2007 Season

	Games	At Bats	Runs	Hits	Doubles	Triples	Home Runs	Runs Batted In	Batting Average
Bob	14	42	15	12	2	4	1	7	.286
Steve	15	45	12	16	3	2	2	13	.356
Kathy	16	48	10	9	1	1	1	9	.188
Total		135	37	37	6	7	4	29	.274

Statistician	Student Name
Family Batting Average	.326

Figure 1.52 Little League Statistician

...continued on Next Page

2 Exploring Formatting Options

Your computer professor has determined that you need more practice with basic formatting and cell operations in Excel. The workbook in Figure 1.53 offers this practice for you. Remember to start in cell A1 and work your way down the worksheet, using the instructions in each cell.

a. Open the *chap1_mid2_formatting* workbook and save the workbook as **chap1_mid2_formatting_solution** so that you can return to the original workbook if necessary. Click in **cell A1** and type your name, then change the formatting as indicated. Merge and center **cells A1** and **B1** into a single cell.

b. Change the width of column A to **60.71**.

c. Move to **cell A3** and format the text as indicated in the cell. Move to **cell B3** and double underline the text in Green.

d. Format **cells A4:B7** according to the instructions in the respective cells.

e. Follow the instructions in **cells A8:A14** to format the contents of **cells B8:B14**. Click in **cell B4**, click **Format Painter** in the Clipboard group on the Home tab, and then click and drag **cells A8:A14** to apply the formatting from **cell B4**.

f. Click in **cell A15**, then deselect the Merge & Center command to split the merged cell into two cells. Follow the instructions in the cell to wrap and center the text. Cell B15 should be blank when you are finished.

g. Right-click in **cell A16**, select Insert from the shortcut menu, click to shift cells down, and then click **OK**. You have inserted a new cell A16, but the contents in cell B16 should remain the same. Format **cell B16**.

h. Merge and center **cells A17** and **B17**, and then complete the indicated formatting.

i. Use the Page Setup dialog box to display gridlines and row and column headings. Change to landscape orientation and center the worksheet horizontally on the page. Add a footer that contains your name and the date and time you completed the assignment. Print the completed workbook. Save and close the workbook.

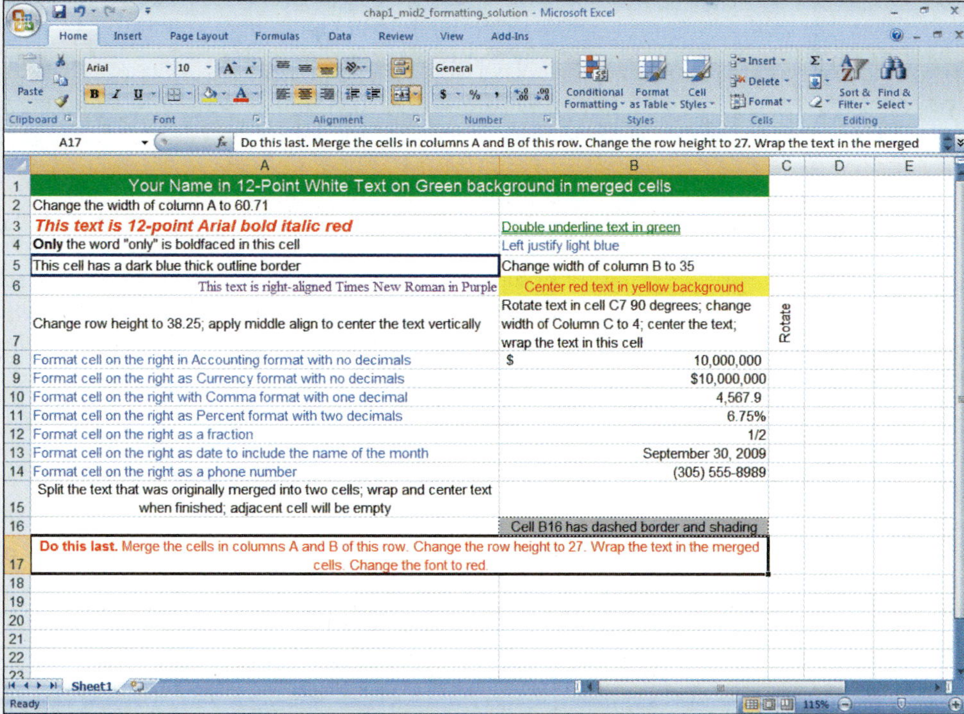

Figure 1.53 Exploring Formatting Options

...continued on Next Page

3 Measurement Conversions

You work in a testing lab for a major industrial company, and your supervisor has asked you to prepare a table of conversion factors and a table of equivalencies. You will use this as a "crib sheet" during your work and in the preparation of reports, so you want to make it as complete and as accurate as possible. The workbook in Figure 1.54 provides practice with formulas, formatting, and basic cell operations. You do have to match the formatting exactly and you must enter the identical values into column G.

a. Open the *chap1_mid3_conversion* workbook and save the workbook as **chap1_mid3_conversion_solution** so that you can return to the original workbook if necessary. Click in **cell E8** and type the formula **=1/E7**. Cell E7 contains the value to convert inches to centimeters; the reciprocal of that value will convert centimeters to inches. Enter the appropriate formula into **cell E19** to convert kilograms to pounds.

b. A kilobyte is mistakenly thought of as 1,000 bytes, whereas it is actually 1,024 (2^{10}) bytes. In similar fashion, a megabyte and a gigabyte are 2^{20} and 2^{30} bytes. Use this information to enter the appropriate formulas to display the conversion factors in cells **E21**, **E22**, and **E23**.

c. Enter the formulas for the first conversion into row 7. Click in **cell H7** and type **=C7**. Click in **cell J7** and type **=E7*G7**. Click in **cell K7** and type **=D7**. Copy the formulas in row 7 to the remaining rows in the worksheet. The use of formulas for columns H through K builds flexibility into the worksheet; that is, you can change any of the conversion factors on the left side of the worksheet, and the right side will be updated automatically.

d. Enter the values shown in column G for conversion; for example, type 12 in **cell G7** to convert 12 inches to centimeters. The result should appear automatically in **cell** J7.

e. Use Aqua, Accent 5, Lighter 80% as the fill color in **cells G7:G23** and other ranges of cells as shown in Figure 1.54.

f. Use the Merge & Center command as necessary throughout the worksheet to approximate the formatting in Figure 1.54. Change the orientation in column B so that the various labels are displayed as indicated.

g. Format the values in columns E and J to Comma style. Increase column widths if needed.

h. Display the border around the groups of cells as shown in Figure 1.54.

i. Create a header with your name on the left side and the date on the right side.

j. Print the displayed values and the cell formulas. Be sure to show the row and column headings as well as the gridlines. Use landscape orientation to be sure the worksheet fits on a single sheet of paper. Set 0.6" left and right margins.

k. Save and close the workbook.

...continued on Next Page

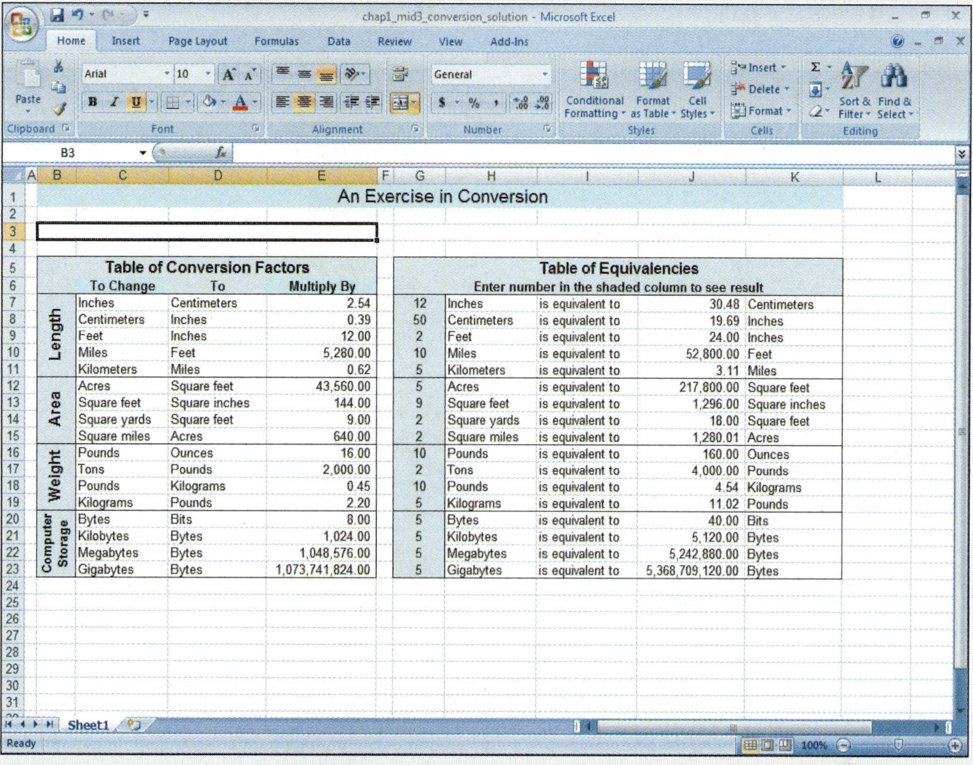

An Exercise in Conversion

Table of Conversion Factors			
	To Change	To	Multiply By
Length	Inches	Centimeters	2.54
	Centimeters	Inches	0.39
	Feet	Inches	12.00
	Miles	Feet	5,280.00
	Kilometers	Miles	0.62
Area	Acres	Square feet	43,560.00
	Square feet	Square inches	144.00
	Square yards	Square feet	9.00
	Square miles	Acres	640.00
Weight	Pounds	Ounces	16.00
	Tons	Pounds	2,000.00
	Pounds	Kilograms	0.45
	Kilograms	Pounds	2.20
Computer Storage	Bytes	Bits	8.00
	Kilobytes	Bytes	1,024.00
	Megabytes	Bytes	1,048,576.00
	Gigabytes	Bytes	1,073,741,824.00

Table of Equivalencies Enter number in the shaded column to see result				
12	Inches	is equivalent to	30.48	Centimeters
50	Centimeters	is equivalent to	19.69	Inches
2	Feet	is equivalent to	24.00	Inches
10	Miles	is equivalent to	52,800.00	Feet
5	Kilometers	is equivalent to	3.11	Miles
5	Acres	is equivalent to	217,800.00	Square feet
9	Square feet	is equivalent to	1,296.00	Square inches
2	Square yards	is equivalent to	18.00	Square feet
2	Square miles	is equivalent to	1,280.01	Acres
10	Pounds	is equivalent to	160.00	Ounces
2	Tons	is equivalent to	4,000.00	Pounds
10	Pounds	is equivalent to	4.54	Kilograms
5	Kilograms	is equivalent to	11.02	Pounds
5	Bytes	is equivalent to	40.00	Bits
5	Kilobytes	is equivalent to	5,120.00	Bytes
5	Megabytes	is equivalent to	5,242,880.00	Bytes
5	Gigabytes	is equivalent to	5,368,709,120.00	Bytes

Figure 1.54 Measurement Conversions

4 Fuel Efficiency

Your summer vacation involved traveling through several states to visit relatives and to view the scenic attractions. While traveling, you kept a travel log of mileage and gasoline purchases. Now that the vacation is over you want to determine the fuel efficiency of your automobile. The partially completed worksheet in Figure 1.55 includes the beginning mileage for the vacation trips and the amount of fuel purchased. This exercise provides practice with formulas, formatting, copying, and basic cell operations.

a. Open the *chap1_mid4_fuel* workbook and save the workbook as **chap1_mid4_fuel_solution** so that you can return to the original workbook if necessary. Click in **cell C12** and change the gallons to **9.2** because you are correcting a typing error.

b. Insert a new column between columns B and C and type **Miles Driven** in **cell C3**.

c. Select **cells A5:A12,** copy the selected range, and paste it in **cells B4:B11**. This ensures that the ending mileage for one trip is the same as the beginning mileage for the next trip. Click **cell B12** and type **34525**, the mileage at the end of the last trip.

d. Use cell references and create the formula to calculate the miles driven for each trip. Use cell references and create the formula to calculate the miles per gallon for each trip.

e. Select **cells A1:E1** and apply the Dark Blue fill color. Apply the following formats to **cell A1**: Times New Roman, 16 point, Bold, White font color. Merge and center the title over columns A through E.

f. Word-wrap the contents of **cells C3** and **E3**. Bold and center horizontally the headings in row 3. Apply the following number formats to the values in columns A and B: whole numbers, no decimals, comma format.

...continued on Next Page

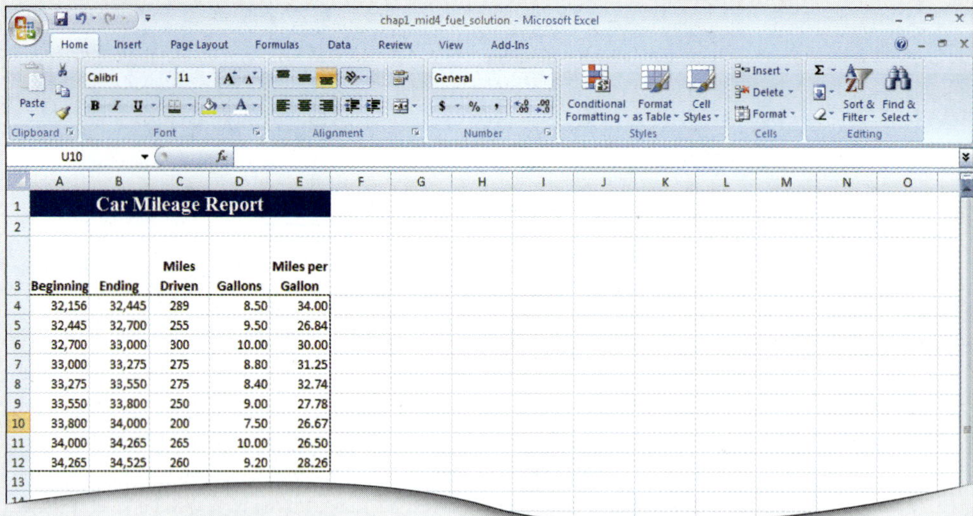

Car Mileage Report				
Beginning	Ending	Miles Driven	Gallons	Miles per Gallon
32,156	32,445	289	8.50	34.00
32,445	32,700	255	9.50	26.84
32,700	33,000	300	10.00	30.00
33,000	33,275	275	8.80	31.25
33,275	33,550	275	8.40	32.74
33,550	33,800	250	9.00	27.78
33,800	34,000	200	7.50	26.67
34,000	34,265	265	10.00	26.50
34,265	34,525	260	9.20	28.26

Figure 1.55 Fuel Efficiency

g. Format the last two columns of values as whole numbers with two decimals. Center the values in the third column. Apply a dashed border around **cells A4:E12** as shown in Figure 1.55.

h. Use the Page Setup command to display gridlines and row and column headings. Change to landscape orientation and center the worksheet horizontally and vertically on the page. Add a custom footer that contains your name and the date and time you completed the assignment. Print the workbook. Save and close the workbook.

5 Freshman Seminar Grade Book

Figure 1.56 displays your instructor's sample grade book complete with a grading scheme. Students take three exams worth 100 points each, submit a term paper and various homework assignments worth 50 points each, and then receive a grade for the semester based on their total points. The maximum number of points is 400. Your semester average is computed by dividing your total points by the maximum total points. You will complete the Freshman Seminar Grade Book worksheet so the displayed values match Figure 1.56.

a. Open the *chap1_mid5_assumption* workbook and save the workbook as **chap1_mid5_assumption_solution** so that you can return to the original workbook if necessary.

b. Click in **cell A6** and type **your name**. Enter your test scores: **98, 87, and 99**. The term paper is worth **46** and the homework **24**. Insert a column between columns D and E. Type **Exam Total** in cell **E3**. Click in **cell E4** and enter a formula to compute Smith's exam total points. Click in **cell H4** and enter a formula that will compute Smith's total points for the semester. Click in **cell I4** and enter a formula to compute Smith's semester average. Use Help to learn how to create a formula with an absolute reference to the cell containing the divisor, 400.

c. Click to select the formula in **cell E4.** Copy this formula through **cell E6**. Click and drag to select the formulas in **cells H4:I4** and copy the formulas through **cell I6**.

d. Click in **cell B7** and enter a formula that will compute the class average on the first exam. Copy this formula to **cells C7:H7**.

e. Insert a column between columns C and D and type **Percent Change in Exams** in **cell D3**. Click in **cell D4** and enter the formula to calculate the change in exam scores between the first and second exam. Copy this formula to **cells D5:D6**.

f. Format the worksheet appropriately as shown in Figure 1.56.

...continued on Next Page

g. Add your name as the grading assistant, then print the worksheet twice, once to show displayed values and once to show the cell formulas. Use landscape orientation and be sure that the worksheet fits on one sheet of paper.

h. Save and close the workbook.

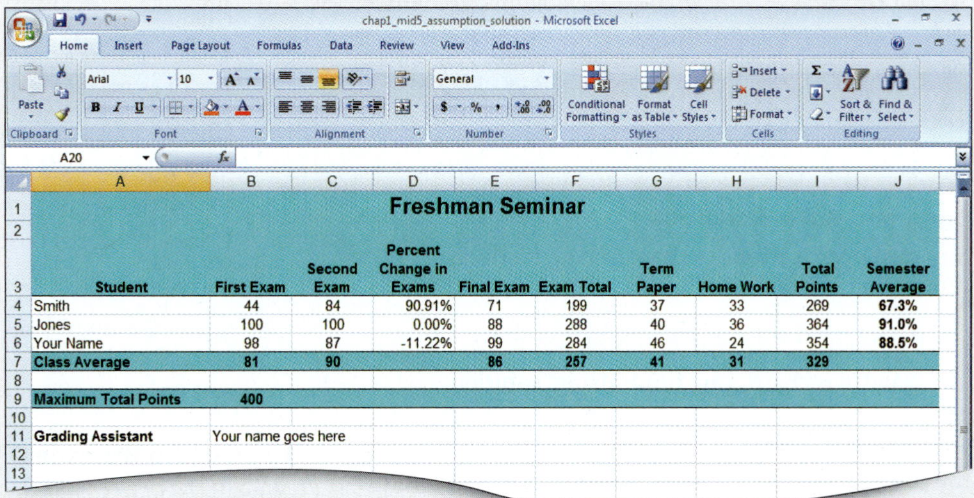

	A	B	C	D	E	F	G	H	I	J
1	Freshman Seminar									
2										
3	Student	First Exam	Second Exam	Percent Change in Exams	Final Exam	Exam Total	Term Paper	Home Work	Total Points	Semester Average
4	Smith	44	84	90.91%	71	199	37	33	269	67.3%
5	Jones	100	100	0.00%	88	288	40	36	364	91.0%
6	Your Name	98	87	-11.22%	99	284	46	24	354	88.5%
7	Class Average	81	90		86	257	41	31	329	
8										
9	Maximum Total Points	400								
10										
11	Grading Assistant	Your name goes here								
12										
13										

Figure 1.56 Freshman Seminar Grade Book

Capstone Exercise

You are the new assistant to the band director for the Upper Saddle River Marching Band and you must prepare a report showing the status of the marching band fund-raising event for the board of trustees. The report will summarize sales of all items and include the total profit to date with the amount remaining to reach the profit goal. You will open the partially completed workbook, create formulas, and format for presentation to the board of trustees.

Open and Save Workbook

You must open a worksheet that has the fund-raising sales information in it and complete the worksheet.

a. Open the *chap1_cap_fundraising* workbook.

b. Save it as **chap1_cap_fundraising_solution**.

Calculate Values

You are to create the formulas used to calculate profit per item and profit based on the number of items sold. You create a formula to calculate total profit to date and the remaining profit needed to reach the goal.

a. Enter the profit per item formula in **column C**. The profit per item is 50% of the sales price. Use Help to learn how to create an absolute reference to **cell B15** that contains the 50% profit rate.

b. Enter the profit formula in **column E**. The profit is the profit per item multiplied by the number of items sold. Copy the formula down the column.

c. Insert a blank row *below* the Lamp row. The Profit (as a percent of sales price) row is now on row 16.

d. Click in **cell E16**, and then click **Sum** in the Editing group on the Home tab to add the total profits. Edit the SUM function to change it to **=SUM(E5:E14).**

e. The formula for calculating the remaining profit to reach the goal is the goal minus the total profit to date. Enter the formula in **cell E17**.

Format the Worksheet

Now that you have finished the calculations, you must format the worksheet in a professional manner and suitable for presentation to the board of trustees of the college.

a. Insert a comment in **cell E17** and explain the formula in **cell E17**.

b. Format all money figures as Accounting style with two decimal places. Format the percentage in **cell B16** as Percent.

c. Merge and center cells on row 1. Merge and center cells on row 2. Center data within the cells on row 4.

d. Change the font to Arial and increase font size in rows 1, 2, and 3, increasing row height and column width as needed.

e. Change font color and bold rows 1, 2, 3, and 4. Change font color and bold rows 16 and 17.

f. Place borders at the top and bottom of **cells A4:E4**. Place a border at the bottom of **cells A14:E14**.

g. Change the fill color for **cells E4:E14** to **Light Green**.

h. Search for the keyword **marching band** in the Clip Art task pane. Insert an image of bass drums in **cell E2**, resizing as necessary.

Lay Out the Worksheet

Now that you have finished the major formatting you must lay out the worksheet to further separate and define areas of the worksheet. This step makes the worksheet more aesthetically pleasing and easier to read.

a. Insert new rows above **row 4**.

b. Delete sheet tabs 2 and 3.

c. Change the color of Sheet1 tab to **Purple**.

d. Rename Sheet1 as **Fundraising**.

Print the Report

Before printing the report you see it is missing the standard headers and should be printed in landscape orientation to fit on one page. You also want to show and print the cell formulas.

a. Create a custom footer with your name on the left and today's date on the right.

b. Change the page orientation to landscape.

c. Print the worksheet with displayed values.

d. Print the worksheet again with cell formulas but make sure to fit the worksheet on one page.

e. Save your changes and exit Excel.

Mini Cases

Use the rubric following the case as a guide to evaluate your work, but keep in mind that your instructor may impose additional grading criteria or use a different standard to judge your work.

Housing Office

GENERAL CASE

Your supervisor in the student housing office has asked for your help in preparing a workbook for her annual budget. Open the partially completed *chap1_mc1_housingoffice* workbook and save it as **chap1_mc1_housingoffice_solution**. This workbook is intended to compute the revenue for the dorms on campus. The revenue includes the income from single rooms, double rooms, and the associated meal plans. Your assignment is to complete the workbook. If you do the assignment correctly, the total revenue for Douglass Hall should be $5,325,000. Note that each double room has two students, each of whom is required to pay for the meal plan. Format the completed worksheet as appropriate. Place your name somewhere in the worksheet and print the worksheet two ways in order to show both displayed values and cell formulas. Be sure to use the Page Setup command to specify landscape orientation and appropriate scaling so that the entire worksheet fits on a single page. Save and close the workbook.

Performance Elements	Exceeds Expectations	Meets Expectations	Below Expectations
Create formulas	All formulas work and most efficiently stated	Formulas are correct	No formulas, numbers entered
Attractive, appropriate format	Well formatted and easy to read	Adequately formatted, difficult to read	No formatting
Print formulas and values	Prints both formulas and values	Prints either formulas or values	No printout

The Cost of Smoking

RESEARCH CASE

Smoking is hazardous to your health as well as your pocketbook. A one-pack-a-day habit, at $4.50/pack, will cost you more than $1,600 per year. Use the Web to find the current price for the items listed in the worksheet that you could purchase in one year. Open the partially completed *chap1_mc2_smoking* workbook, save it as **chap1_mc2_smoking_solution**, and compute the number of various items that you could buy over the course of a year in lieu of cigarettes. The approximate prices have been entered already, but you need not use these numbers and/or you can substitute additional items of your own. Place your name in the header and print the worksheet two ways to show both displayed values and cell. Be sure to use the Page Setup command to specify landscape orientation, and appropriate scaling so that the entire worksheet fits on a single page. Save and close the workbook.

Performance Elements	Exceeds Expectations	Meets Expectations	Below Expectations3
Research current prices	Prices current within 30 days	Prices current within 3 months	Prices more than 3 months old
Create formulas	All formulas work and most efficiently stated	Formulas are correct	No formulas, numbers entered
Format for one sheet	Formatted correctly and easy to read	Adequately formatted, difficult to read	Not formatted for one sheet
Print values and cell formulas	Values and formulas both printed	Values or formulas printed	No print

Accuracy Counts

DISASTER RECOVERY

The *chap1_mc3_accuracycounts* workbook was the last assignment completed by your predecessor prior to his unfortunate dismissal. The worksheet contains a significant error, which caused your company to underbid a contract and assume a subsequent loss of $200,000. As you look for the error, don't be distracted by the attractive formatting. The shading, lines, and other touches are nice, but accuracy is more important than anything else. Write a memo to your instructor describing the nature of the error. Include suggestions in the memo on how to avoid mistakes of this nature in the future. Open *chap1_mc3_accuracycounts* and save it as **chap1_mc3_accuracycounts_solution**. Close the workbook.

Performance Elements	Exceeds Expectations	Meets Expectations	Below Expectations
Identify and correct the error	Error correctly identified within 10 minutes	Error correctly identified within 20 minutes	Error not identified
Explain the error	Complete and correct explanation of the error	Explanation is too brief to fully explain the error	No explanation
Describe how to prevent the error	Prevention description correct	Prevention description too brief to be of any value	No prevention description

chapter 2 | **Excel**

Formulas and Functions

Math Basics for Spreadsheet Use

After you read this chapter, you will be able to:

1. Create and copy formulas (**page 381**).
2. Use relative and absolute cell addresses (**page 382**).
3. Use AutoSum (**page 389**).
4. Insert basic statistical functions (**page 390**).
5. Use date functions (**page 392**).
6. Use the IF function (**page 399**).
7. Use the VLOOKUP function (**page 400**).
8. Use the PMT function (**page 408**).
9. Use the FV function (**page 408**).

Hands-On Exercises

Exercises	Skills Covered
1. SMITHTOWN HOSPITAL RADIOLOGY DEPARTMENT PAYROLL (PAGE 384) **Open:** chap2_ho1_payroll.xlsx **Save as:** chap2_ho1_payroll_solution.xlsx	• Compute the Gross Pay • Complete the Calculations • Copy the Formulas with the Fill Handle
2. COMPLETING THE SMITHTOWN HOSPITAL RADIOLOGY DEPARTMENT PAYROLL (PAGE 394) **Open:** chap2_ho1_payroll_solution.xlsx (from Exercise 1) **Save as:** chap2_ho2_payroll_solution.xlsx (additional modifications)	• Compute the Totals • Using Other General Functions • Apply Number Formatting • Apply Font and Alignment Formatting • Insert a Comment to Complete the Worksheet
3. ATHLETIC DEPARTMENT ELIGIBILITY GRADEBOOK (PAGE 403) **Open:** chap2_ho3_gradebook.xlsx **Save as:** chap2_ho3_gradebook_solution.xlsx	• Use the IF Function • Use the VLOOKUP Function • Copy the IF and VLOOKUP Functions • Apply Page Setup Options and Print the Worksheet
4. PURCHASING A VAN FOR THE SCHOOL FOR EXCEPTIONAL CHILDREN (PAGE 410) **Open:** New workbook **Save as:** chap2_ho4_van_solution.xlsx	• Create the Worksheet • Insert the PMT Function • Format the Worksheet • Complete the Worksheet

CASE STUDY

West Transylvania College Athletic Department

Case Study

The athletic department of West Transylvania College has reached a fork in the road. A significant alumni contingent insists that the college upgrade its athletic program from NCAA Division II to Division I. This process will involve adding sports, funding athletic scholarships, expanding staff, and coordinating a variety of fundraising activities.

Tom Hunt, the athletic director, wants to determine if the funding support is available both inside and outside the college to accomplish this goal. You are helping Tom prepare the five-year projected budget based on current budget figures. The plan is to increase revenues at a rate of 10% per year for five years while handling an estimated 8% increase in expenses over the same five-year period. Tom feels that a 10% increase in revenue versus an 8% increase in expenses should make the upgrade viable. Tom wants to examine how increased alumni giving, increases in college fees, and grant monies will increase the revenue flow. The Transylvania College's Athletic Committee and its Alumni Association Board of Directors want Tom to present an analysis of funding and expenses to determine if the move to NCAA Division I is feasible. As Tom's student assistant this year, it is your responsibility to help him with special projects. Tom prepared the basic projected budget spreadsheet and has asked you to finish it for him.

Your Assignment

- Read the chapter carefully and pay close attention to mathematical operations, formulas, and functions.
- Open *chap2_case_athletics*, which contains the partially completed, projected budget spreadsheet.
- Study the structure of the worksheet to determine what type of formulas you need to complete the financial calculations. Identify how you would perform calculations if you were using a calculator and make a list of formulas using regular language to determine if the financial goals will be met. As you read the chapter, identify formulas and functions that will help you complete the financial analysis. You will insert formulas in the revenue and expenditures sections for column C. Use appropriate cell references in formulas. Do not enter constant values within a formula; instead enter the 10% revenue rate increase and 8% expense rate increase in an input area in the appropriate cells below the net margin. Use appropriate functions for column totals in both the revenue and expenditures sections. Insert formulas for the Net Operating Margin and Net Margin rows. Copy the formulas.
- Review the spreadsheet and identify weaknesses in the formatting. Use your knowledge of good formatting design to improve the appearance of the spreadsheet so that it will be attractive to the Athletic Committee and the alumni board. You will format cells as currency with 0 decimals and widen columns as needed. Merge and center the title and use an attractive fill color. Emphasize the totals and margin rows with borders. Enter your name and current date in a header. Create a custom footer that includes your instructor's name. Print the worksheet as displayed and again with cell formulas displayed. Save the workbook as **chap2_case_athletics_solution**.

Formula Basics

A ***formula*** performs mathematical operations that produce a calculated result.

Mathematical operations are the backbone of Excel. The order in which these mathematical operations are performed has a significant impact on the answers that are arrived at. We touched briefly on the construction of mathematical expressions or ***formulas*** that direct Excel to perform mathematical operations and arrive at a calculated result. A formula also may be defined as the combination of constants, cell references, and arithmetic operations displayed in a calculation. Formulas can be as simple or as complex as necessary, but they always begin with an = sign and contain mathematical operators. In this section, you learn how to use the pointing method to create formulas and the fill handle to copy formulas. Finally, you learn how to prevent a cell reference from changing when you copy a formula to other cells.

(Formulas can be as simple or as complex as necessary, but they always begin with an = sign and contain mathematical operators.)

Creating and Copying Formulas

As you recall, whenever you want Excel to perform a calculation you must enter an equal sign (=) in the cell where the answer is to appear. The equal sign indicates within Excel that a mathematical calculation is about to begin. Previously, you created formulas by typing in the cell references. Here in Chapter 2, you enter cell references to create a formula in a more efficient, straightforward way.

Point to Create a Formula

(Rather than typing a cell address . . . as you construct a formula, you can use an alternative method that involves *minimal* typing.)

Pointing uses the mouse or arrow keys to select the cell directly when creating a formula.

As previously discussed, the creation of formulas in Excel is the mathematical basis for the program, and the use of cell references is integral in the creation of formulas. However, rather than typing a cell address, such as C2, as you construct a formula, you can use an alternative method that involves *minimal* typing. ***Pointing*** uses the mouse or arrow keys to select the cell directly when creating a formula. To use the pointing technique to create a formula:

1. Click on the cell where the formula will be entered.
2. Type an equal sign (=) to start a formula.
3. Click on the cell with the value to be entered in the formula.
4. Type a mathematical operator.
5. Continue clicking on cells and typing operators to finish the formula.
6. Press Enter to complete the formula.

While the formulas may be more complex than indicated in this example, the steps are the same.

Copy Formulas with the Fill Handle

The ***fill handle*** is a small black square in the bottom-right corner of a selected cell.

Another powerful copying tool in Excel is the ***fill handle***, which is a small black solid square in the bottom-right corner of a selected cell. Using the fill handle provides another, clear-cut alternative method for copying the contents of a cell. You can use the fill handle to duplicate formulas. To copy and paste using the fill handle:

1. Click on the cell (or drag through the cells) to be copied.
2. Position the mouse pointer directly over the fill handle on the cell or cells to be copied. The pointer changes to a thin crosshair.
3. Click and hold down the left mouse button while dragging over the destination cells. Note that using the fill handle only works with contiguous or adjacent cells.

4. Release the mouse button. If the cell to be copied contained a formula, the formula is copied, the cell references are changed appropriately, and Excel performs the calculations.

TIP Contiguous Cells

In addition to using the fill handle to copy formulas, you can also use the fill handle to finish a text series. For example, you can use the fill handle to complete the days of the week, the four quarters of a year, and the month names to simplify the data-entry process. Type January in a cell, select the cell, click on the fill handle, drag to cover a total of 12 cells.

Using Relative and Absolute Cell Addresses

Excel uses three different ways to express a reference to a cell in a formula. These references are relative, absolute, and mixed, and each affects copying cell references in different ways.

A ***relative cell reference*** is a typical cell reference that changes when copied.

A ***relative cell reference*** within a formula is a cell reference that changes *relative to* the direction in which the formula is being copied. It is expressed in the form A4 (column letter, row number) and is adjusted or changed according to the direction and relative distance it is copied. When you copy a formula containing a relative cell reference over multiple columns, the column letter changes. When you copy a formula containing a relative cell reference down multiple rows, the row number changes. In Figure 2.1, the formulas in column C contain relative cell references. When the original formula =A4+B4 in cell C4 is copied down to cell C5, the copied formula is =A5+B5. Because the formula is copied down a column, the column letters in the formula stay the same, but the row numbers change, down one row number at a time. Using relative cell addresses to calculate the 2010 salary ensures that each employee's raise is added to that person's 2009 salary.

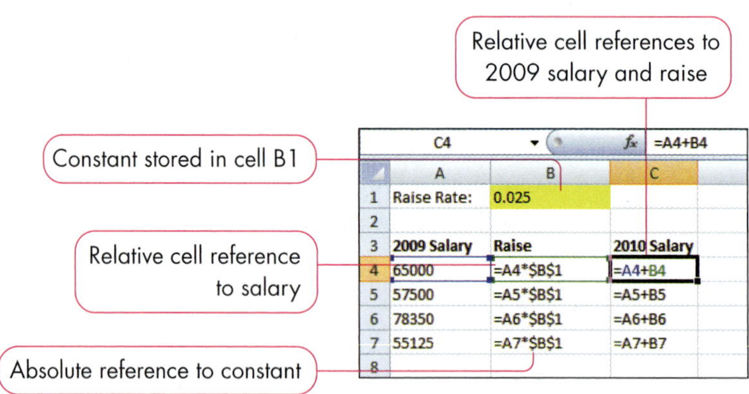

Figure 2.1 Relative and Absolute References

An ***absolute cell reference***, indicated by dollar signs before the column letter and row number, stays the same regardless of where a formula is copied.

An ***absolute cell reference*** in a formula, on the other hand, is one that stays the same no matter where you copy a formula. An absolute cell reference appears with dollar signs before both the column letter and row number ($B$1). Absolute cell references are used when the value in the cell seldom changes but the formula containing the absolute cell reference is copied. In Figure 2.1, the formulas in column B contain an absolute cell reference to the raise rate of 2.5% that is stored in cell B1.

Entering the 2.5% in an input area helps you avoid entering the 2.5% as a constant within the formulas. Cell B4 contains the formula to calculate the first person's raise: =A4*$B$1. A4 is a relative address that changes as you copy the formula down the column so that the raise is based on each employee's respective 2009 salary. That is, A4 becomes A5 on the fifth row, A6 on the sixth row, and A7 on the seventh row. $B$1 is an absolute reference to the cell containing the 2.5% cost-of-living raise. The absolute address $B$1 prevents the cell reference from changing when you copy the formula to calculate the cost-of-living raise for the other employees. That is, each employee's 2009 salary is multiplied by the constant value stored in cell B1. A benefit of an absolute cell reference is that if an input value changes, for example if the cost-of-living rate changes from 2.5% to 3% in this example, you type the new input value in only one cell, and Excel recalculates the amount of the cost-of-living raise for all the formulas. You do not have to individually edit cells containing formulas to change the raise rate value because the formulas contain an absolute cell reference to the cell containing the cost-of-living raise rate.

> A benefit of an absolute cell reference is that if an input value changes, . . . you type the new input value in only one cell, and Excel recalculates . . . all the formulas. You do not have to individually edit cells containing formulas. . . .

The ***mixed cell reference*** combines an absolute reference with a relative reference.

The third type of cell reference, the ***mixed cell reference***, occurs when you create a formula that combines an absolute reference with a relative reference. As a result, either the row number or column letter does not change when the cell is copied. Using the relative cell reference B1, it would be expressed as a mixed reference either as $B1 or B$1. In the first case, the column B is absolute, and the row number is relative; in the second case, the row 1 is absolute, and the column B is relative. In the example shown in Figure 2.1, you could change the formula in cell B4 to be =A4*B$1. Because you are copying down the same column, only the row reference 1 must be absolute; the column letter stays the same.

TIP The F4 Key

The F4 key toggles through relative, absolute, and mixed references. Click on any cell reference within a formula on the formula bar; for example, click on B4 in the formula =B4+B5. Press F4, and B4 changes to an absolute reference, $B$4. Press F4 a second time, and $B$4 becomes a mixed reference, B$4; press F4 again, and it is a different mixed reference, $B4. Press F4 a fourth time, and the cell reference returns to the original relative reference, B4.

In the first hands-on exercise, you calculate the gross pay for employees in the Smithtown Hospital's Radiology Department using the pointing method. You perform other payroll calculations and then use the fill handle to copy the formulas for the remaining employees.

Hands-On Exercises

1 | Smithtown Hospital Radiology Department Payroll

Skills covered: 1. Compute the Gross Pay **2.** Complete the Calculations **3.** Copy the Formulas with the Fill Handle

Step 1
Compute the Gross Pay

Refer to Figure 2.2 as you complete Step 1.

a. Start Excel. Open the *chap2_ho1_payroll* workbook to display the worksheet shown in Figure 2.2.

b. Save the workbook as **chap2_ho1_payroll_solution** so that you can return to the original workbook if necessary.

c. Click in **cell F4**, the cell that will contain gross pay for Dwyer. Type = to begin the formula, click **cell C4** (producing a moving border around the cell), type*, and then click **cell D4**.

You have entered the first part of the formula to compute the gross pay.

d. Type +, click **cell E4**, type *, click **cell C4**, type *, click **cell D20**, press **F4** to change the cell reference to **$D$20**, and then press **Enter**.

The formula, =C4*D4+E4*C4*$D$20, calculates the gross pay for employee Dwyer by multiplying the $8 hourly wage by 40 regular hours. This amount is added to the 8 overtime hours, multiplied by the $8 hourly wage, multiplied by the 1.5 overtime rate. Note the use of the absolute address ($D$20) in the formula. You should see 416 as the displayed value in cell F4.

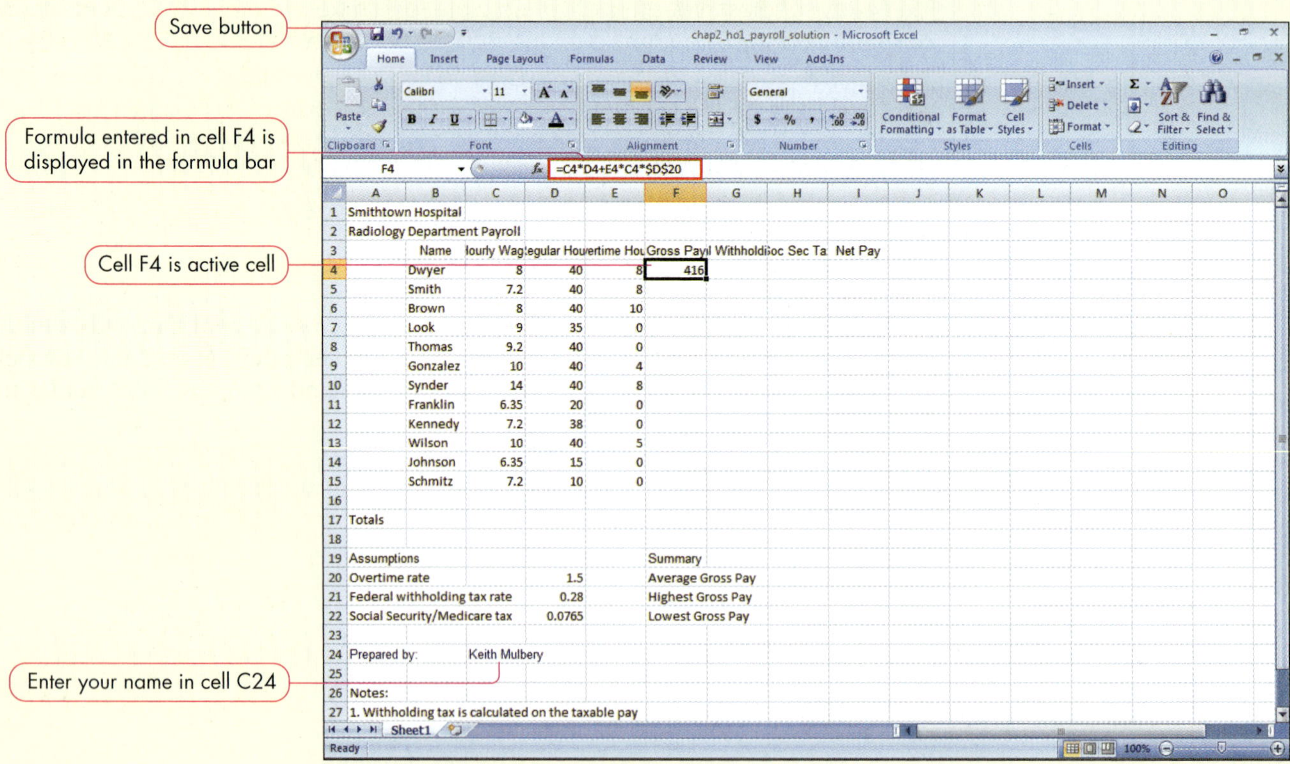

Figure 2.2 Compute the Gross Pay with Absolute Reference

e. Click in **cell F4** to be sure that the formula you entered matches the formula shown in the formula bar in Figure 2.2. If necessary, click in the formula bar and make the appropriate changes so the formula is correct in cell F4.

f. Enter your name in **cell C24** and save the workbook.

Step 2
Complete the Calculations

a. Click in **cell G4**, the cell that will contain the withholding tax for Dwyer. Type = to begin the formula, and then click **cell F4**, the cell containing the gross pay. Type * and click **cell D21**, the cell containing the federal withholding tax rate of .28 or 28%.

Cell G4 now contains the formula =F4*D21 that calculates Dwyer's withholding tax. However, if you were to copy the formula to the next row now, the copied formula would be =F5*D22, which is not correct. If a cell address is not made explicitly absolute, Excel's default relative address mode will automatically change a cell address when a formula is copied.

b. Verify that the insertion point is within or immediately to the right of cell reference D21 and press **F4**.

Pressing F4 changes the cell reference to $D$21 and explicitly makes the cell address an absolute reference. The formula can be copied and will calculate the desired result.

c. Press **Enter**.

The value in cell G4 should be 116.48. This amount is Dwyer's federal withholding tax.

d. Use the pointing method to enter the remaining formulas for Dwyer. Click in **cell H4** and enter the formula **=F4*$D$22**.

The formula calculates the employee's Social Security/Medicare tax, which is 7.65% of the gross pay. The formula uses an absolute reference ($D$22) so the cell reference will not change when you copy the formula for the other employees. The value in cell H4 should be 31.824, and this is Dwyer's Social Security/Medicare tax.

e. Click in **cell I4**, and enter the formula **=F4–(G4+H4)**. Press **Enter**.

The formula adds the federal withholding tax and Social Security/Medicare tax and then subtracts the total tax from the gross pay. The formula uses only relative cell addresses because you want the copied formulas to refer to the appropriate gross pay and tax cells for each respective employee. The value in cell I4 should be 267.696, and this amount is Dwyer's net pay.

f. Save the workbook.

Step 3
Copy the Formulas with the Fill Handle

Refer to Figure 2.3 as you complete Step 3.

a. Click and drag to select **cells F4:I4**, as shown in Figure 2.3. Point to the fill handle in the lower-right corner of cell I4. The mouse pointer changes to a thin crosshair.

You have selected the range containing formulas that you want to copy. Pointing to the fill handle triggers the display of the thin crosshair.

b. Drag the fill handle to **cell I15**, the lower-right cell in the range of employee calculations, and release the mouse to complete the copy operation.

The formulas for Dwyer have been copied to the corresponding rows. You can use Excel to calculate the gross pay, federal withholding tax, Social Security/ Medicare tax, and net pay for each employee.

c. Click in **cell F5**, the cell containing the gross pay for Smith.

You should see the formula =C5*D5+E5*C5*$D$20.

d. Click in **cell G5**, the cell containing the withholding tax for Smith.

You should see the formula =F5*$D$21, which contains a relative reference (F5) that is adjusted from one row to the next, and an absolute reference ($D$21) that remains constant from one employee to the next.

e. Save the *chap2_ho1_payroll_solution* workbook and keep it onscreen if you plan to continue to the next hands-on exercise. Save the workbook. Close the workbook and exit Excel if you do not want to continue with the next exercise at this time.

TROUBLESHOOTING: If you double-click a cell that contains a formula, Excel will display the formula, highlight the components, and allow for editing in the cell. If you double-click a cell that contains values or text, you can edit the data directly in the cell.

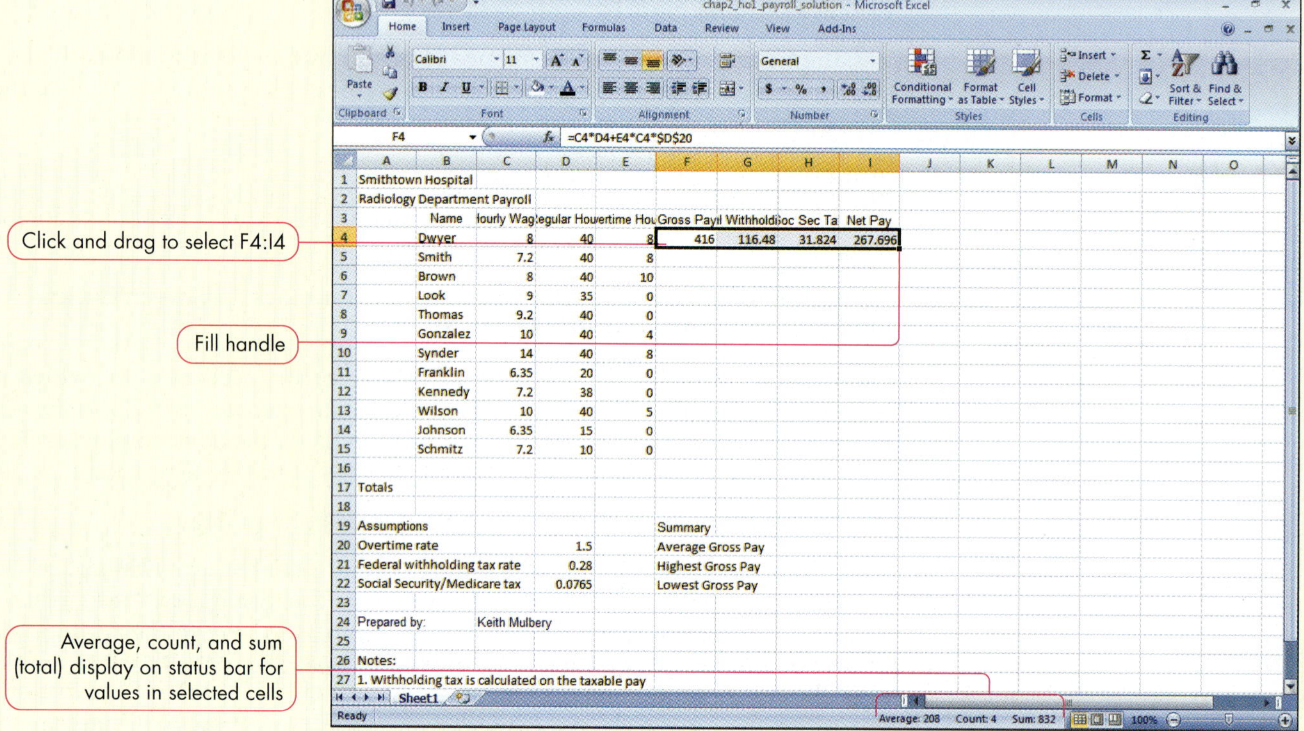

Figure 2.3 Copy the Formulas

TIP Isolate Assumptions

The formulas in a worksheet should always be based on cell references rather than specific values—for example, $D$21 rather than 0.28. The cells containing the values are clearly labeled and set apart from the rest of the worksheet. You can vary the inputs (or assumptions on which the worksheet is based) to see the effect within the worksheet. The chance for error is minimized because you are changing the contents of just a single cell instead of multiple formulas that reference those values. Excel automatically recalculates formulas when values change.

Function Basics

SUM Function | Reference

SUM(number1,number2,. . .)

A ***function*** is a preconstructed formula that makes difficult computations less complicated.

The ***SUM function***, represented by Σ or sigma, adds up or sums the numeric entries within a range of cells.

You also can construct formulas by using a *function*, a preconstructed formula that makes difficult computations less complicated. But keep in mind that functions CANNOT replace all formulas. Functions take a value or values, perform an operation, and return a value or values. The most often used function in Excel is the ***SUM function***, represented by Σ or sigma. It adds or sums numeric entries within a range of cells and then displays the result in the cell containing the function. This function is so useful that the SUM function has its own command in the Function Library group on the Formulas tab. In all, Excel contains more than 325 functions, which are broken down into categories as shown in Table 2.1.

Table 2.1 Function Category and Descriptions

Category Group	Description
Cube	Works with multi-dimensional data stored on an SQL server
Database	Analyzes data stored in Excel
Date and Time	Works with dates and time
Engineering	Returns or converts and returns values used in engineering industries.
Financial	Works with financial-related data
Information	Determines what type of data is in a cell
Logical	Calculates yes/no answers
Lookup and Reference	Provides answers after searching a table
Math and Trig	Performs standard math and trig functions
Statistical	Calculates standard statistical functions
Text	Analyzes labels

Syntax refers to the rules for constructing the function.

Arguments are values as input that perform an indicated calculation, and then return another value as output.

When you want to use a function, keep two things in mind. The first is the ***syntax*** of the function or, more simply put, the rules for constructing the function. The second is the function's ***arguments***, which are values as input that perform an indicated calculation, and then return another value as output or the data to be used in the function. While users often type functions such as =SUM(C7:C14), you may find it easier to use the Insert Function dialog box to construct functions until you learn function syntax.

Click either Insert Function to the left of the formula bar or click Insert Function in the Function Library group on the Formulas tab (see Figure 2.4) to display Insert Function dialog box (see Figure 2.5). Using the Insert Function dialog box enables you to select the function to be used (such as MAX, SUM, etc.) from the complete list of functions and specify the arguments to be used in the function. Using Insert Function greatly simplifies the construction of functions by making it easier to select and construct functions. Use the Insert Function dialog box to do the following:

> Using Insert Function greatly simplifies the construction of functions. . . .

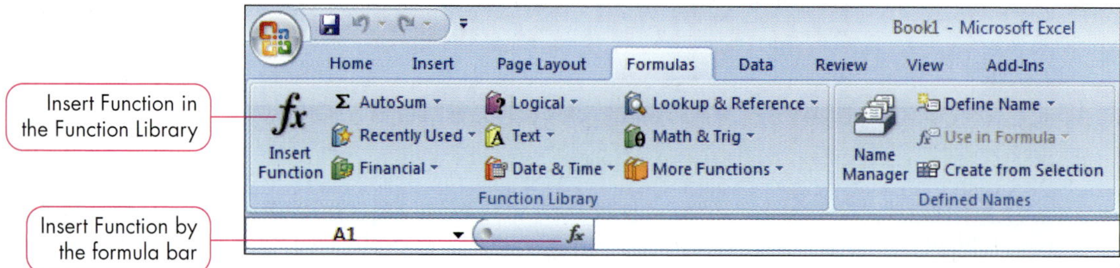

Figure 2.4 Function Library

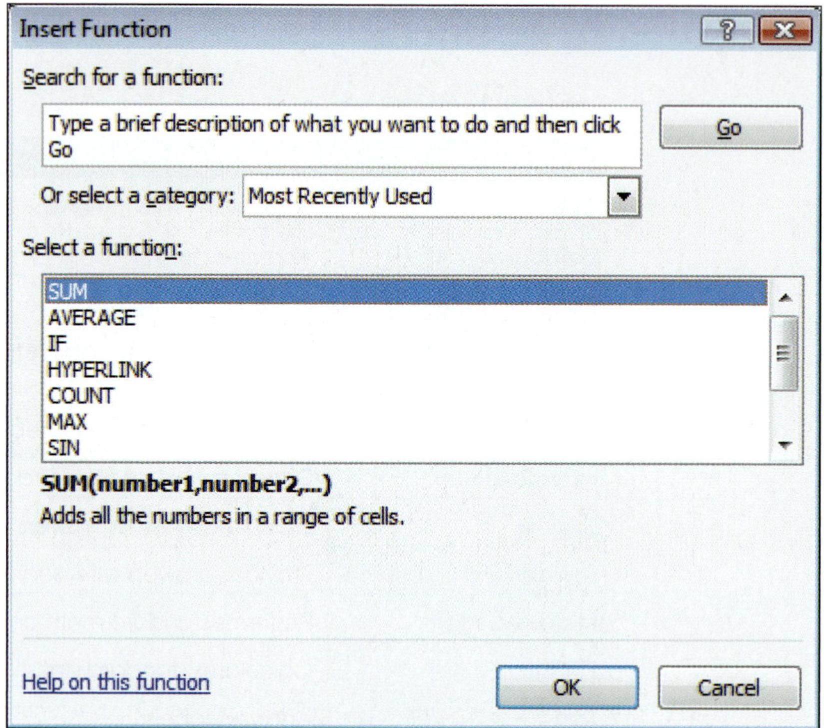

Figure 2.5 Insert Function Dialog Box

1. Search for a function by typing a brief description of what you want the function to do.
2. Select a function from the *Most Recently Used* list, from an alphabetical list within a particular category, or from an alphabetical list of *All* functions.
3. Click the function name to see the syntax and description or double-click the function name to see the function and the Function Arguments dialog box for help with adding the correct arguments. Figure 2.6 shows the Function Arguments dialog box for the SUM function.

If you know the category of the function you want to use, you can click the appropriate command in the Function Library group on the Formulas tab. Select the function and use the Function Arguments dialog box to add the arguments. See Figure 2.4 for the Function Library group.

Function Arguments

SUM

Number1 C4:E4 = {8,40,8}

Number2 = number

= 56

Adds all the numbers in a range of cells.

Number1: number1,number2,... are 1 to 255 numbers to sum. Logical values and text are ignored in cells, included if typed as arguments.

Formula result = 160.832

Help on this function

OK Cancel

Figure 2.6 Function Arguments Box

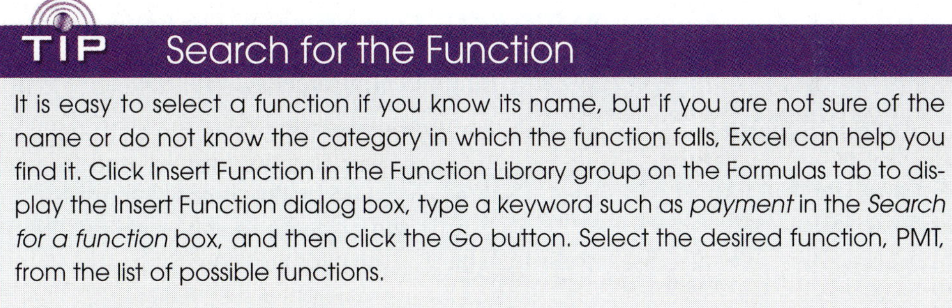

TIP Search for the Function

It is easy to select a function if you know its name, but if you are not sure of the name or do not know the category in which the function falls, Excel can help you find it. Click Insert Function in the Function Library group on the Formulas tab to display the Insert Function dialog box, type a keyword such as *payment* in the *Search for a function* box, and then click the Go button. Select the desired function, PMT, from the list of possible functions.

In this section, you insert a variety of commonly used statistical functions, such as the SUM function. In addition, you learn about two date functions.

Using AutoSum

In this chapter, you will examine several different commonly used functions, beginning with the SUM function. You can create formulas in different ways. For example, if you want to add the contents of cells C6 through C16, the formula would be written =C6+C7+C8+C9+C10+C11+C12+C13+C14+C15+C16. However, creating this type of formula manually is time-consuming and increases the probability of entering an inaccurate cell address. This process would be especially problematic if you had to add values stored in several hundred cells. Using the SUM function simplifies this operation and improves the accuracy of the addition. To create the same formula using the SUM function, you can type =SUM(C6:C16). The C6:C16 represents the cell range containing the values to be summed. Rather than typing this entire formula, you can also type =SUM(and then click and drag to select the range of cells containing values to be summed, then type the closing parenthesis. Alternatively, you can click Σ (AutoSum) in the Function Library group on the Formulas tab or in the Editing group on the Home tab. To use the AutoSum, click the cell where you want to see the results and then click AutoSum. Drag to select the cell range or values to be summed and press Enter to see the total. For example, if you use the SUM function to total the first 11 scores in Table 2.2, the result is 946.

TIP Avoiding Functions for Basic Formulas

Good spreadsheet design includes using function syntax appropriately. Therefore, you should use functions for their intended purpose, not to encapsulate basic formulas not intended by the function. For example, although =SUM(B4/C4) produces the same result as =B4/C4, the SUM function is not needed to perform the basic arithmetic division. Therefore, you should use the most appropriate, clear-cut formula, =B4/C4.

Inserting Basic Statistical Functions

In addition to using the SUM function, you should learn several other commonly used statistical functions that perform a variety of calculations to identify key values to help people make decisions. For example, you can use functions to calculate how much you spend on average per month on DVD rentals, what your highest electric bill is to control spending, and what your lowest test score is so you know what score you need to earn on your final exam to achieve the grade you desire. You can use the statistical functions to create or monitor your budget. Climatologists use statistical functions to compare rainfall averages over time in specific geographic areas.

Calculate an Average with the AVERAGE Function

AVERAGE Function | Reference

AVERAGE(number1,number2,. . .)

The ***AVERAGE function*** calculates the arithmetic mean, or average, for the values in an argument list.

The ***AVERAGE function*** calculates the arithmetic mean, or average, for the values in a range of cells. This function can be used for such calculations as the average of several scores on a test or the average score for a number of rounds of golf. The AVERAGE function appears in the form =AVERAGE(C6:C16). Using the first 11 scores in Table 2.2, the average score is 86.

Identify the Lowest Value with the MIN Function

MIN Function | Reference

MIN(number1,number2,. . .)

The ***MIN function*** determines the smallest value of all cells in a list of arguments.

The ***MIN function*** determines the smallest value of all cells in a list of arguments, such as determining the lowest score on a test. The function typically appears as =MIN(C6:C16). Although you could manually inspect a range of values to identify the lowest value, doing so is inefficient, especially in large spreadsheets. The MIN function increases your efficiency by always identifying the lowest value in the range. If you change values in the range, the MIN function will identify the new lowest value and display this value in the cell containing the MIN function. Using the first 11 scores in Table 2.2, the MIN function returns 0.

Identify the Highest Value with the MAX Function

MAX Function | Reference

MAX(number1,number2,. . .)

The ***MAX function*** determines the highest value of all cells in a list of arguments.

The ***MAX function*** analyzes an argument list to determine the highest value, as in the highest score on a test or the highest points a basketball player scored in a game in a season. This function appears as =MAX(C6:C16). Like the MIN function, when the values in the range change, the MAX function will display the new highest value within the range of cells. Generally the MIN and MAX statistical functions are discussed in concert with the AVERAGE function. These three functions are typically beginning statistical functions and are used together as a start point for more sophisticated analysis. Using the first 11 scores in Table 2.2, the MAX function returns 99.

Identify the Total Number with the COUNT and COUNTA Functions

COUNT Function | Reference

COUNT(value1,value2,. . .)

COUNTA Function | Reference

COUNTA(value1,value2,. . .)

The ***COUNT function*** counts the number of cells in a range that contain numerical data.

The ***COUNTA function*** counts the number of cells in a range that are not blank.

The two basic count functions, COUNT and COUNTA, enable a user to count the cells in a range that meet a particular criterion. The ***COUNT function*** counts the number of cells in a range that contain numerical data. This function is expressed as =COUNT(C6:C16). The ***COUNTA function*** counts the number of cells in a range that are not blank. This function is expressed as =COUNTA(C6:C16). These functions might be used to verify data entry; for example, you may need to verify that the correct type of data has been entered into the appropriate number of cells. The COUNT function is used to verify that cells have numbers in them, and the COUNTA function is used to make sure data are in every cell. Using the data in Table 2.2, both COUNT and COUNTA return 11.

Determine the Midpoint Value with the MEDIAN Function

MEDIAN Function | Reference

MEDIAN(number1,number2,. . .)

The ***MEDIAN function*** finds the midpoint value in a set of values.

Another easy basic statistical function often overlooked is the ***MEDIAN function*** that finds the midpoint value in a set of values. It is helpful to identify at what value ½ of the population is above or below. The median shows that half of the sample data are above a particular value and half are below that value. The median is particularly useful because the AVERAGE function often is influenced by extreme numbers. For example, if 10 grades are between 90 and 100 and the eleventh grade is 0, the extreme value of 0 distorts the overall average as an indicator of the set of grades. See Table 2.2 for this example. Note that 86 is the average, and 95 is the median.

Table 2.2 Compare Average and Median

Scores	
99	
98	
97	
96	
95	
95	Midpoint Score (half the scores above and half the scores below this score)
93	
92	
91	
90	
0	
86	Average Score (Equal to the sum of the values divided by the number of values)
95	Median (midpoint) Score

TIP Average, Count, and Sum

When you select a range of cells containing values, Excel displays the average, count, and sum of those values on the status bar. See Figure 2.3 at the end of Hands-On Exercise 1 for an example.

Using Date Functions

Before electronic spreadsheets, you could spend hours trying to figure out pay dates for the next year or when a new employee's probation period was up. Excel enables you to increase your productivity by using date and time functions. These functions help in two ways: by efficiently handling time-consuming procedures and by helping you analyze data related to the passing of time. For example, you can use the date and time functions to calculate when employees are eligible for certain benefits or how many days it takes to complete a project. You also can use the date functions to help you calculate if an account is 30, 60, or more days past due. Excel converts and stores dates as numbers. Using date functions enables you to calculate the difference between dates, add or subtract days from a given date, and so on.

TODAY Function | Reference

TODAY( )

The ***TODAY function*** displays the current date in a cell.

The ***TODAY function*** is a date-related function that places the current date in a cell. The function is expressed as =TODAY(). This function is updated when the worksheet is calculated or the file is opened. Unlike the statistical functions you just learned about, some date functions like TODAY() do not require cell references or data as arguments. However, you must still include the parentheses for the function to work.

NOW Function | Reference

NOW( )

The ***NOW function*** uses the computer's clock to display the current date and time side by side in a cell.

The ***NOW function*** uses the computer's clock to display the current date and time side by side in a cell. It returns the time the workbook was last opened, so the value will change every time the workbook is opened. The NOW function does the same thing as the TODAY function, except the result is formatted to display the current time as well as the current date. Both of these functions will display the current date/time when the spreadsheet file is opened. Thus date/time is always current; it is not the date/time when the function was first entered in the cell. The NOW function is expressed as =NOW(). Note that failure to insert the parentheses will cause Excel to return an error message.

TIP Function AutoComplete

Use Function AutoComplete to quickly create and edit functions, minimizing typing and syntax errors. Type an = and the beginning letters of the desired function, and Excel will display a drop-down list of valid functions, names, and text strings matching the letters. Double-click the appropriate function from the list to complete the function name automatically.

Functions Used | Reference

Name	Syntax	Definition
SUM	SUM(number1,number2, . . .)	The ***SUM function***, represented by Σ or sigma, adds up or sums the numeric entries within a range of cells.
AVERAGE	AVERAGE(number1,number2, . . .)	The ***AVERAGE function*** calculates the arithmetic mean, or average, for the values in an argument list.
MIN	MIN(number1,number2, . . .)	The ***MIN function*** determines the smallest value of all cells in a list of arguments.
MAX	MAX(number1,number2, . . .)	The ***MAX function*** determines the highest value of all cells in a list of arguments.
COUNT	COUNT(value1,value2, . . .)	The ***COUNT function*** counts the number of cells in a range that contain numerical data.
COUNTA	COUNTA(value1,value2, . . .)	The ***COUNTA function*** counts the number of cells in a range that are not blank.
MEDIAN	MEDIAN(number1,number2, . . .)	The ***MEDIAN function*** finds the midpoint value in a set of values.
NOW	NOW( )	The ***NOW function*** uses the computer's clock to display the current date and time side by side in a cell.
TODAY	TODAY( )	The ***TODAY function*** displays the current date in a cell.
IF	IF(logical_test,value_if_true,value_if_false)	The ***IF function*** is the most basic logical function in that it returns one value when a condition is met and returns another value when the condition is not met.
VLOOKUP	VLOOKUP(lookup_value,table_array, col_index_num,range_lookup)	The ***VLOOKUP function*** allows the Excel user to look up an answer from a table of possible answers.
PMT	PMT(rate,nper,pv,fv,type)	The ***PMT function*** calculates the payment on a loan.
FV	FV(rate,nper,pmt,pv,type)	The ***FV function*** returns the future value of an investment

Hands-On Exercises

2 | Completing the Smithtown Hospital Radiology Department Payroll

Skills covered: 1. Compute the Totals **2.** Using Other General Functions **3.** Apply Number Formatting **4.** Apply Font and Alignment Formatting **5.** Insert a Comment to Complete the Worksheet

Step 1 Compute the Totals

Refer to Figure 2.7 as you complete Step 1.

a. Open the *chap2_ho1_payroll_solution* workbook if you closed it after the last hands-on exercise, and save it as **chap2_ho2_payroll_solution**.

b. Click in **cell F17**, the cell that will contain the total gross pay for all employees. Click the **Formulas tab**, click **AutoSum** in the Function Library group, and click and drag over **cells F4:F15** to select the correct range.

c. Press **Enter** to complete the formula.

   Cell F17 displays the value 4144.25, and if you click in **cell F17** you will see the function, =SUM(F4:F15) in the formula bar. You have entered the SUM function to calculate the total gross pay.

d. Click and drag the fill handle in **cell F17** to **cell I17**, the remaining cells in the row. Complete the copy operation by releasing the mouse.

   Cell I17 now displays 2666.825, which is the total net pay for all employees.

e. Save the workbook.

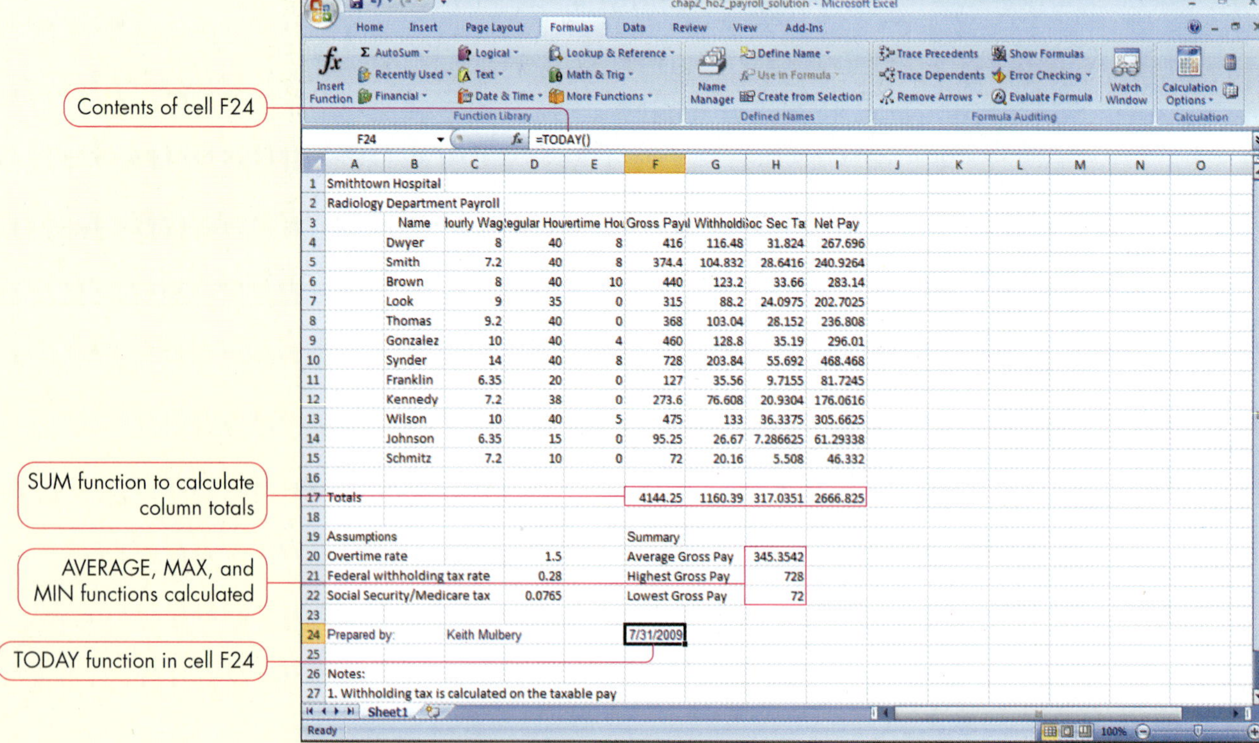

Figure 2.7 Using Functions

Step 2
Using Other General Functions

Refer to Figure 2.7 as you complete Step 2.

a. Click in **cell H20**. This cell will contain the average gross pay for all employees.

b. Type **=AVERAGE(F4:F15)** and press **Enter**.

Cell H20 displays 345.3542, which is the average gross pay for all radiology department employees.

c. In **cell H21**, type **=MAX(** and move the mouse pointer to cell **F4**. Click and drag to select cells **F4:F15**. The dashed line indicates the cells selected as you drag the mouse. Release the mouse, type **)** and press **Enter**.

Cell H21 displays the value 728, which is the highest gross pay for any employee in the radiology department.

d. In **cell H22**, type **=MIN(** and move the mouse pointer to **cell F4**. Click and drag to select cells **F4:F15**. Release the mouse, type **)** and press **Enter**.

Cell H22 displays the value 72, which is the lowest gross pay for any employee in the radiology department.

e. Click in **cell F24**, type **=TODAY()**, and press **Enter**. The current date displays in cell F24. Save the workbook.

Step 3
Apply Number Formatting

Refer to Figure 2.8 as you complete Step 3.

a. Select **cells C4:C15**. Press and hold **Ctrl** as you click and drag to select **cells F4:I15**, **cells F17:I17**, and **cells H20:H22**. Click the **Home tab,** click the **Number Format arrow** in the Number group, and then click **Currency**.

b. Click and drag to select **cells D21:D22**. Click **Percent** Style in the Number group on the Home tab and click **Increase Decimal** twice in the Number group to format each number to two decimal places.

c. Save the workbook.

Step 4
Apply Font and Alignment Formatting

Refer to Figure 2.8 as you complete Step 4.

a. Select **cells A3:I3**. Press and hold **Ctrl** as you click and drag to select **cells A19:I19**. Continue to hold **Ctrl** as you click and drag to select **cells A24:I24**.

This action will produce three rows of non-adjacent selected cells.

b. Click the **Fill Color arrow** in the Font group and select **Black, Text 1** as the fill color. Click the **Font Color arrow** in the Font group and select **White, Background 1** as the text color. Click **Bold** in the Font group so the text stands out.

c. Click and drag to select **cells A3:I3**, which also will deselect the cells in rows 19 and 24. Click **Wrap Text** in the Alignment group on the Home tab. Increase the width of column G to **11.29** so that the word *Withholding* does not wrap on two lines.

The column heading text is now centered and wraps in cells.

TROUBLESHOOTING: Excel may not automatically increase row height after you wrap text. You may have to increase the height of row 3 manually if necessary. Click and drag the dividing line between the row numbers for rows 3 and 4 to increase the height of row 3.

d. Click and drag to select **cells A1:I1**.

- Click **Fill Color** in the Font group to apply the last fill color, which is black.
- Click **Font Color** in the Font group to apply the last font color, which is white.
- Click **Bold** in the Font group so the text stands out.
- Click **Merge and Center** in the Alignment group on the Home tab.

The title, *Smithtown Hospital*, is now bold, white, and centered in a black box over the nine columns in the worksheet.

e. Click and drag to select **cells A2:I2** and apply the same four formats that you did in Step 3d.

The subtitle, *Radiology Department Payroll*, is now bold, white, and centered in a black box over the columns in the worksheet.

f. Save the workbook.

TIP The Format Painter

The Format Painter copies the formatting of the selected cell to other cells in the worksheet. Click the cell whose formatting you want to copy, then double-click Format Painter in the Clipboard group on the Home tab. The mouse pointer changes to a paintbrush to indicate that you can copy the current formatting; just click and drag the paintbrush over the cells that you want to assume the formatting of the original cell. Repeat the painting process as often as necessary, then click Format Painter a second time to return to normal editing.

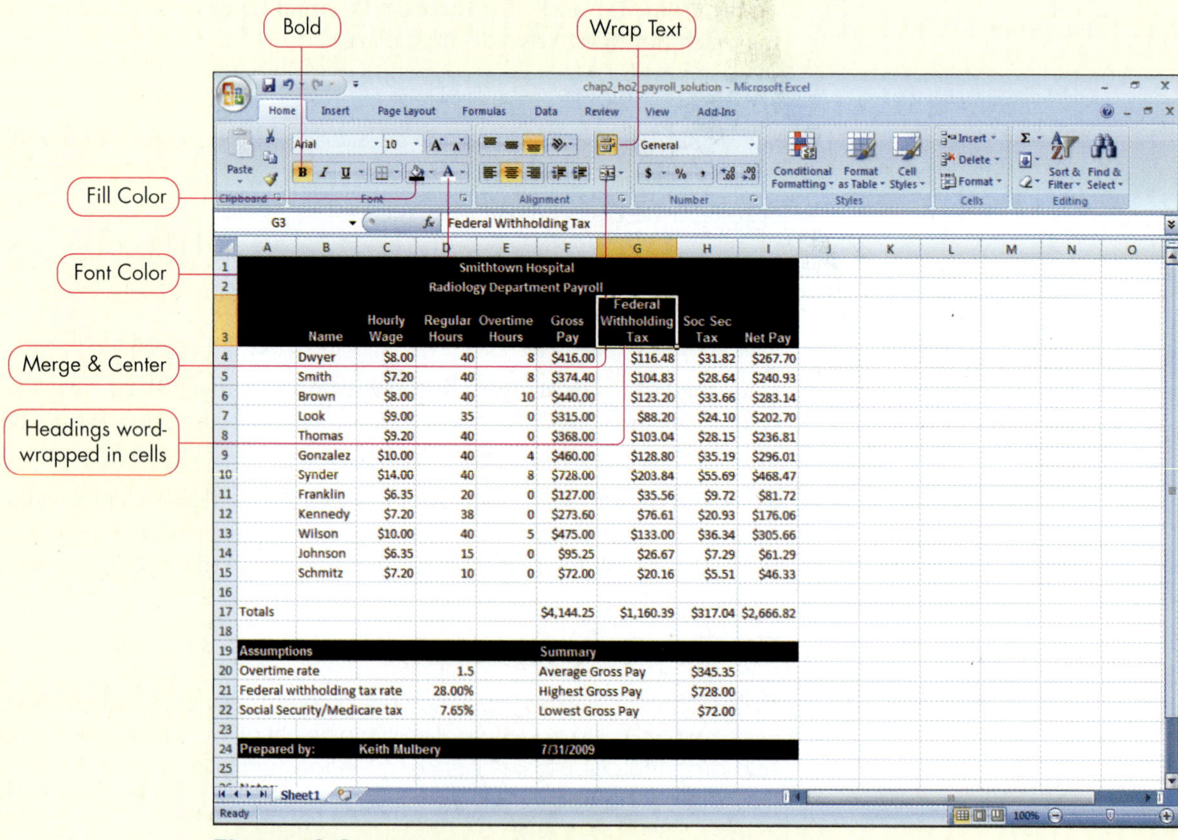

Figure 2.8 Complete the Formatting

Step 5
Insert a Comment to Complete the Worksheet

Refer to Figure 2.9 as you complete Step 5.

a. Click in **cell D21**. Click the **Review tab**, click **New Comment** in the Comments group, and type **The exercise uses a constant value for simplicity.** as shown in Figure 2.9.

   TROUBLESHOOTING: The name in the Comment box will be different on your system. The name or initials entered when registering the Microsoft Office 2007 software will appear in the comment box as the author of the comment. Use Help to learn how to change the name or initials for yourself.

b. Click any cell.

   Clicking another cell after you finish entering the comment closes the comment box. The text of the comment is no longer visible, but a tiny red triangle is visible in cell D21. When you point to cell D21, you will see the text of the comment.

c. Click the **Page Layout tab**, click **Orientation** in the Page Setup group, and select **Landscape**. Click **Size** and select **More Paper Sizes**.

   Clicking More Paper Sizes displays the Page Setup dialog box.

TIP Displaying the Page Setup Dialog Box

You also can click the Page Setup Dialog Box Launcher in the lower-right corner of the Page Setup group to display the Page Setup dialog box.

d. Click the **Page tab**, if necessary, in the Page Setup dialog box and click **Fit to 1 page** in the *Scaling* section.

e. Click the **Margins tab** and click the **Horizontally check box** in the *Center on page* section if necessary.

   This option centers worksheet data between the left and right margins.

f. Click the **Sheet tab**, click the **Row and column headings check box**, and click the **Gridlines check box** in the *Print* section. Click **OK**.

   You changed the orientation of the spreadsheet for printing as well as selected the option to force the spreadsheet on one piece of paper. The spreadsheet also will be centered horizontally with row/column headings and gridlines printed.

g. Print the worksheet. Save the *chap2_ho2_payroll_solution* workbook.

h. Press **Ctrl + `** (the grave accent key to the left of the number 1 key) to show the cell formulas rather than the displayed values. Adjust the column widths as necessary and print the worksheet a second time.

   To view the underlying formulas in your worksheet, press and hold down Ctrl while pressing ` (grave accent). This key is located above Tab on the keyboard.

i. Close the workbook without saving the view of the formulas. Exit Excel if you do not want to continue with the next exercise at this time.

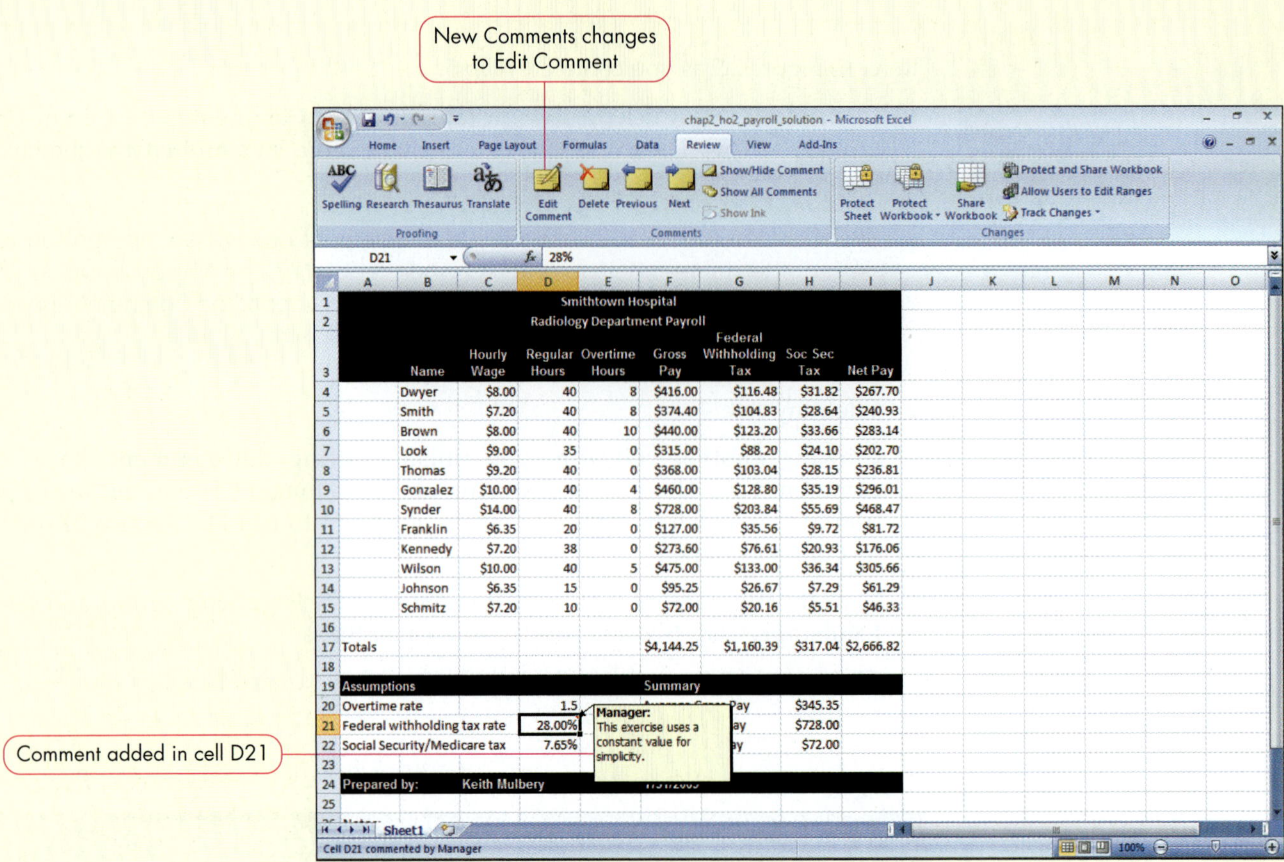

Figure 2.9 Comments and Formatting

Logical and Lookup Functions

> ... mathematics is the problem; thinking is the solution....

Several functions in Excel are designed to return an answer when a particular condition is met. These logical functions are very useful for decision-making. Excel also contains functions that search for or "look up" information in a table. These lookup functions use a designated worksheet area or table and search row by row for a match. Just remember that mathematics is the problem; thinking is the solution as you work with these functions. In this section, you use one major logical function and one major lookup function.

Using the IF Function

IF Function | Reference

IF(logical_test,value_if_true,value_if_false)

The ***IF function*** returns one value when a condition is met and returns another value when the condition is not met.

In the set of logical functions, the ***IF function*** is the most basic in that it returns one value when a condition is met and returns another value when the condition is not met. For example, you may have a display of student GPAs and want to determine if the students are eligible for the Dean's List. If the range of student GPAs were C6 through C24, the IF function would appear in cell D6 as =IF(C6>3.5, "Dean's List", "No"). This function then would be copied to cells D7 through D24. The IF function supports the decision-making capability that is used in a worksheet. The IF function has three arguments:

1. a condition that is tested to determine if it is either true or false,
2. the resulting value if the condition is true, and
3. the resulting value if the condition is false.

This function can be illustrated as:

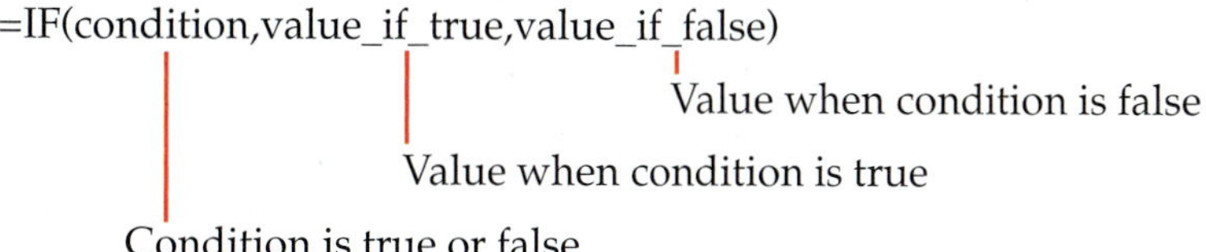

An IF function returns either the second or third argument, depending if the condition is true or false. The value_if_true and value_if_false parameters can contain text, a value, a formula, or a nested function. For example an IF function used in a gradebook might award a bonus for a student whose homework is "OK," while others do not get the bonus.

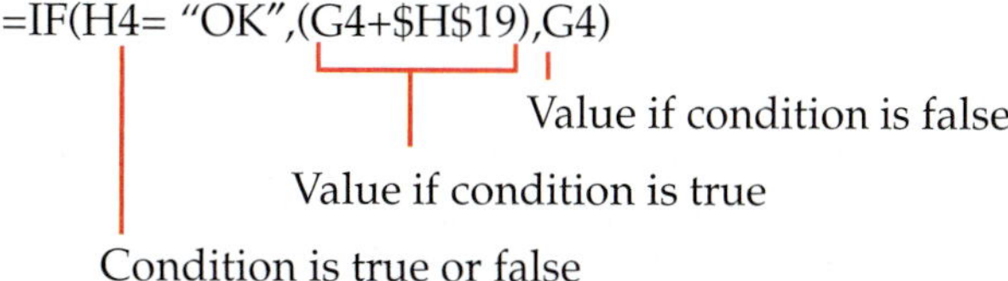

Note that when you want to compare the contents of a cell to specific text, you must enclose the comparison text in quotation marks. You also can return text in the value_if_true and value_if_false parameters by enclosing the text (but not the commas) in quotation marks.

The condition in the IF function includes one of the six comparison operators shown in Table 2.3.

Table 2.3 Comparison Operators

Operator	Description
=	Equal to
<>	Not equal to
<	Less than
>	Greater than
<=	Less than or equal to
>=	Greater than or equal to

The small sample worksheet, Figure 2.10, shows the data the IF function uses to create the examples in Table 2.4. Arguments may be numeric, cell references to display cells' contents, a formula, a function, or a text entry. Review Table 2.4 to see how Excel evaluates conditions and the results.

	A	B	C	D	E
1	10	15	April		
2	10	30	May		
3					

Figure 2.10 IF Data

Table 2.4 IF Function, Evaluation, and Result

IF Function	Evaluation	Result
=IF(A1=A2,1000,2000)	10 is equal to 10, TRUE	1000
=IF(A1<>A2,1000,2000)	10 is not equal to 10, FALSE	2000
=If(A1<>A2,B1,B2)	10 is not equal to10, FALSE	30
=IF(A1<B2,MAX(B1:B2),MIN(B1:B2))	10 is less than 30, TRUE	30
=IF(A1<A2,B1+10,B1-10)	10 is less than 10, FALSE	5
=IF(A1=A2,C1,C2)	10 is equal to 10, TRUE	April

Using the VLOOKUP Function

VLOOKUP Function | Reference

VLOOKUP(lookup_value,table_array,col_index_num,range_lookup)

The ***VLOOKUP function*** looks up an answer from a vertical table of possible answers.

When you order something on the Web or by catalog, you look up the shipping costs for your order. You find the information you want because you look up a specific piece of information (the total amount of your order) to find the associated information (the shipping cost). The VLOOKUP function works the same way. You can use the VLOOKUP function to find a company's specific tax rate from a table or look up your own tax rate. The ***VLOOKUP function*** evaluates a value and looks up this value in a vertical table to return a value, text, or formula. Use VLOOKUP to search for exact matches or for the nearest value that is less than or equal to the search value (such as assigning a shipping cost of $15.25 to an order of $300.87). Or use the VLOOKUP function to assign a B grade for an 87% class average.

Understand the VLOOKUP Function Syntax

The VLOOKUP function has the following three required arguments and one optional argument (discussed on the next page):

1. a lookup value stored in a cell,
2. a range of cells containing a lookup table, and
3. the number of the column within the lookup table that contains the value to return.

One use of a VLOOKUP function is the assignment of letter grades in a gradebook based on numeric values. Figure 2.11 shows a portion of a worksheet with a Grading Criteria Table that associates letter grades with the numerical value earned by a student. The first student's overall class average is 76.3. You can use the VLOOKUP function to identify the cell containing the student's numerical average and use that value to look up the equivalent letter grade in a table. To determine the letter grade in cell J4 based on a numeric value in cell I4, you would use the following:

=VLOOKUP(I4,$I$20:$J$24,2)

Column number containing a grade to display

Range of the table

Value to lookup (semester average)

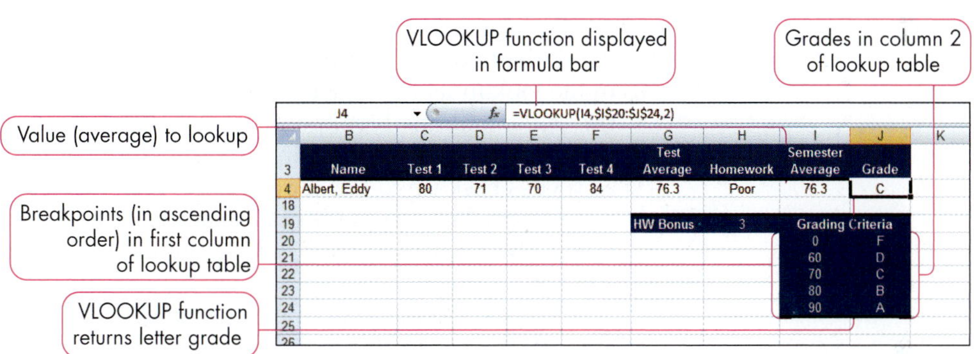

Figure 2.11 VLOOKUP Table Data

The ***lookup value*** is the value to look up in a reference table.

The ***lookup table*** is a range of cells containing the reference table.

The ***column index number*** is the column number in the lookup table that contains return values.

Cell I4 is the ***lookup value*** that represents the cell containing the value to look up in a table. In this example, the lookup value is 76.3. The table that Excel searches using a lookup function is called a ***lookup table***. In this example, the lookup table is stored in the range $I$20:$J$24. Note that an absolute reference is used so the address is not changed when the formula is copied to other cells. Furthermore, the table lookup range should *not* include the table column headings. The ***column index number***, indicated by col_index_num in the function, refers to the number of the column in the lookup table that contains the return values. In the example, the col_index_num of 2 returns the value in the second column in the lookup table that corresponds to the value being looked up.

Structure the Lookup Table

The VLOOKUP function searches the left column of a table for a specific value and returns a corresponding value from the same row but a different column. You set up the table to include unique values in the left column (for example, ranges of total amounts or numeric ranges to assign letter grades), and then Excel retrieves the associated information (for example, shipping cost or letter grade) from another column. In Figure 2.11, the lookup table extends over two columns, I and J, and five rows, 20 through 24. The table is located in the range I20:J24.

A ***breakpoint*** is the lowest numeric value for a category or series in a lookup table to produce a corresponding result for a lookup function.

You should set up the lookup table before using the VLOOKUP function. The left column, known as the lookup column, of the table includes the reference data used to look up information in the table, such as customer number, income, grade points, or the total amount range of the order. The other columns include information related to the first column, such as customer credit limit, tax rate, letter grades, or shipping cost. The values in the left or lookup column must be sorted in ascending order, from lowest to highest value. However, instead of typing an entire range, such as 80–89, for the range of B grades, you enter breakpoints only. The ***breakpoint*** is the lowest numeric value for a specific category or in a series of a lookup table to produce a corresponding result to return for a lookup function. Breakpoints are listed in ascending order in the first column of the lookup table. For example, the breakpoints in the gradebook lookup table represent the lowest numerical score to earn a particular letter grade. The breakpoints are listed in column I, and the corresponding letter grades are found in column J.

Understand How Excel Processes the Lookup

The VLOOKUP function works by searching in the left column of the lookup table until it finds an exact match or a number that is larger than the lookup value. If Excel finds an exact match, it returns the value stored in the column designated by the index number on that same row. If the table contains breakpoints for ranges rather than exact matches, when Excel finds a value larger than the lookup value, it returns the next lower value in the column designated by the col_index_num. To work accurately, the values in the first column must be in ascending order.

For example, the VLOOKUP function to assign letter grades works like this: Excel identifies the lookup value (76.3 stored in cell I4) and compares it to the values in the lookup table (stored in cells I20:J24). It tries to find an exact match; however, the table contains breakpoints rather than every conceivable numeric average. Because the lookup table is in ascending order, it notices that 76.3 is not equal to 80, so it goes back up to the 70 row. Excel then looks at the column index number of 2 and returns the letter grade of C, which is located in the second column of the lookup table. The returned grade of C is then stored in the cell J4, which contains the VLOOKUP function.

Instead of looking up values in a range, you might need to look up a value for an *exact* match. When this is the case, you must use the optional range_lookup argument in the VLOOKUP function. By default, the range_lookup is implicitly set to TRUE, which is appropriate to look up values in a range. However, to look up an exact match, you must specify FALSE in the range_lookup argument. The VLOOKUP function returns a value for the first lookup_value that matches the first column of the table_array. If no exact match is found, the function returns #N/A.

TIP HLOOKUP Function

The VLOOKUP function is arranged vertically in a table, while its counterpart, the HLOOKUP function, is arranged horizontally. Use the HLOOKUP function when your comparison values are located in a row across the top of a table of data and you want to look down a specified number of rows.

Hands-On Exercises

3 | Athletic Department Eligibility Gradebook

Skills covered: 1. Use the IF Function **2.** Use the VLOOKUP Function **3.** Copy the IF and VLOOKUP Functions **4.** Apply Page Setup Options and Print the Worksheet

Step 1
Use the IF Function

Refer to Figure 2.12 as you complete Step 1.

a. Open the *chap2_ho3_gradebook* workbook and save it as **chap2_ho3_gradebook_solution** so that you can return to the original workbook if necessary.

   The partially completed gradebook contains student test scores and their respective test averages. You need to create an IF function to determine if students have completed their homework. If they did, they receive a 3-point bonus added to their semester average. Those students who did not complete homework receive no bonus, so their semester average is the same as their test average.

b. Click in **cell I4.** Click the **Formulas tab** and click **Insert Function** in the Function Library group. Select the **IF** function from the *Select a function* list. Click **OK** to close the Insert Function dialog box and display the Function Argument dialog box.

   You will use the Function Arguments dialog box to build the IF function.

c. Click in the **Logical_test** box, keep the Function Arguments dialog box open but drag it down to view cell H4, click **cell H4** in the worksheet, and type **="OK"** to complete the logical test.

   When you use text in a function, such as to compare a cell's contents to specific text, you must enclose the text in quotation marks, such as "OK".

d. Click in the **Value_if_true** box, keep the Function Arguments dialog box open, click **cell G4** in the worksheet, type **+** and click **cell H19**. Press **F4** to change H19 to an absolute cell reference.

e. Click in the **Value_if_false** box, keep the Function Arguments dialog box open, and click **cell G4** in the worksheet.

   TROUBLESHOOTING: Text values used in arguments must be enclosed in quotes.

f. Click **OK** to insert the function into the worksheet. Save the workbook.

   Because Eddy's homework was "Poor," he did not earn the 3-point bonus. His semester average is the same as his test average, which is 76.25 in cell I4. The test average of 76.3 in cell G4 is rounded; it is really 76.25.

g. Click the **Home tab** and click **Decrease Decimal** in the Number group.

   Eddy Albert's semester average displays the rounded value of 76.3, although the true average is 76.25.

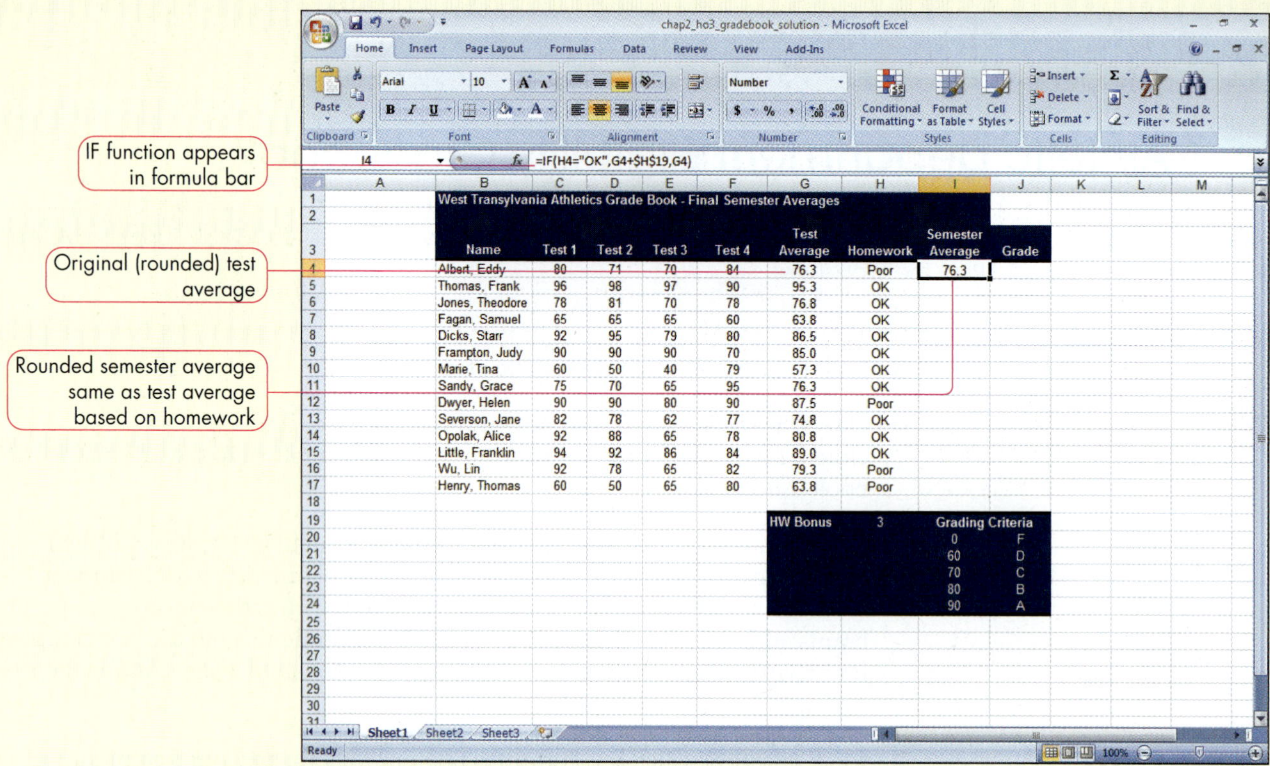

Name	Test 1	Test 2	Test 3	Test 4	Test Average	Homework	Semester Average	Grade
Albert, Eddy	80	71	70	84	76.3	Poor	76.3	
Thomas, Frank	96	98	97	90	95.3	OK		
Jones, Theodore	78	81	70	78	76.8	OK		
Fagan, Samuel	65	65	65	60	63.8	OK		
Dicks, Starr	92	95	79	80	86.5	OK		
Frampton, Judy	90	90	90	70	85.0	OK		
Marie, Tina	60	50	40	79	57.3	OK		
Sandy, Grace	75	70	65	95	76.3	OK		
Dwyer, Helen	90	90	80	90	87.5	Poor		
Severson, Jane	82	78	62	77	74.8	OK		
Opolak, Alice	92	88	65	78	80.8	OK		
Little, Franklin	94	92	86	84	89.0	OK		
Wu, Lin	92	78	65	82	79.3	Poor		
Henry, Thomas	60	50	65	80	63.8	Poor		

HW Bonus	3	Grading Criteria	
		0	F
		60	D
		70	C
		80	B
		90	A

Figure 2.12 Athletics Gradebook

Step 2
Use the VLOOKUP Function

Refer to Figure 2.13 as you complete Step 2.

a. Click in **cell J4** and click the **Lookup & Reference arrow** in the Function Library group on the Formulas tab. Select **VLOOKUP**.

You will create a VLOOKUP function using the semester average stored in column I to determine the letter grade for each student.

b. Click in the **Lookup_value** box if necessary and click **cell I4** in the worksheet.

The first student's semester average, which is stored in cell I4, is the value to look up.

c. Click in the **Table_array** box. Click **cell I20** and drag to **cell J24**, and then press **F4** to convert the entire range reference to absolute ($I$20:$J$24).

The table containing the letter grade equivalents is stored in I20:J24. You made the reference absolute so that the cell addresses do not change when you copy the function for the remaining student athletes.

d. Click in the **Col_index_num** box and type **2**.

e. Click **OK** to insert the function into the worksheet and save the workbook.

The first student's letter grade is C because his semester average of 76.3 is over 70 but less than 80.

TROUBLESHOOTING: Make sure to use an absolute reference with the table in the VLOOKUP function. You will see inaccurate results if you forget to use absolute references.

Step 3
Copy the IF and VLOOKUP Functions

Refer to Figure 2.13 as you complete Step 3.

a. Copy the IF and VLOOKUP Functions by selecting **cells I4:J4**, point to the fill handle in the lower-right corner of **cell J4**, and drag the fill handle over cells **I17:J17**.

You just copied the original IF and VLOOKUP functions for the rest of the students.

b. Check that the semester averages are formatted to one decimal place.

c. Click **cell A19** and enter your name. Click **cell A1** and type **=TODAY()** to enter today's date.

d. Click **cell A1** and hold **Ctrl** as you click **cell A19**. Click the **Home tab** and click **Bold** in the Font group. Click **Align Text Left** in the Alignment group to left-align the date. Save the workbook.

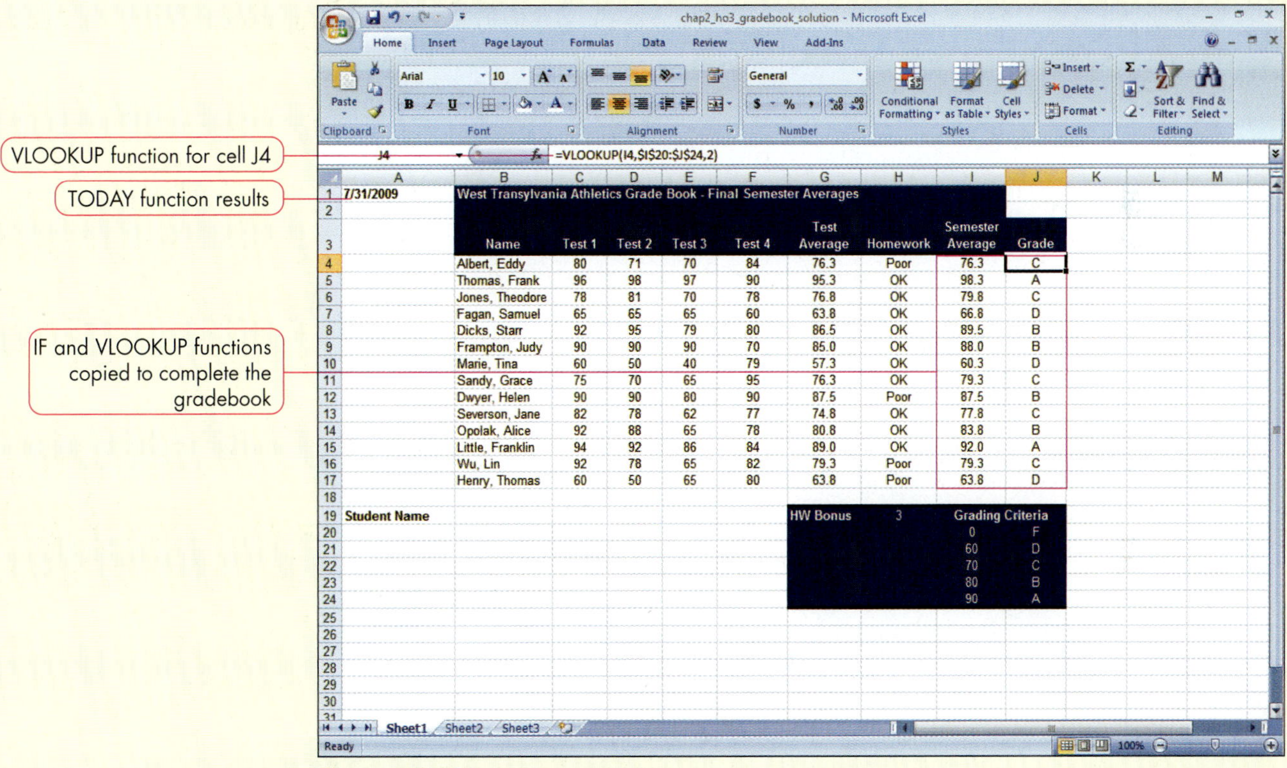

Figure 2.13 Athletics Gradebook

Step 4
Apply Page Setup Options and Print the Worksheet

a. Click the **Page Layout tab** and click **Margins** in the Page Setup group. Select **Custom Margins** to display the Margins tab in the Page Setup dialog box.

b. Click the **Horizontally check box** in the *Center on page* section to center the worksheet between the left and right margins.

c. Click the **Sheet tab**. Click the **Gridlines check box** and click the **Row and column headings check box** in the *Print* section.

d. Click **OK**. Save the workbook.

e. Click the **Office Button** and select **Print**. Click the **Preview button** to see how the workbook will print.

In Print Preview, you can see that the worksheet will print on two pages.

f. Click **Close Print Preview** in the Preview group on the Print Preview tab.

You need to change the orientation to landscape to fit on one page.

g. Click the **Page Setup Dialog Box Launcher** in the Page Setup group on the Page Layout tab, click the **Page tab**, click **Landscape**, and click **Print Preview**.

The worksheet will fit on one page now.

h. Click **Print** in the Print group on the Print Preview tab, and then click **OK** to print the worksheet. Save the workbook.

i. Press **Ctrl +** ` (grave accent) to show the cell formulas rather than the values. Adjust the column width as necessary and print the worksheet a second time. Close the workbook without saving.

Financial Functions

A spreadsheet is a tool used for decision-making. Many decisions typically involve financial situations: payments, investments, interest rates, and so on. Excel contains several financial functions to help you perform calculations with monetary values.

Review Figures 2.14, 2.15, 2.16, and 2.17 to see how a worksheet might be applied to the purchase of a car. You need to know the monthly payment, which depends on the price of the car, the down payment, and the terms of the loan. In other words:

Can you afford the monthly payment on the car of your choice?

- Can you afford the monthly payment on the car of your choice?
- What if you settle for a less expensive car and receive a manufacturer's rebate?
- What if you work next summer to earn money for a down payment?
- What if you extend the life of the loan and receive a better interest rate?
- Have you accounted for additional items such as insurance, gas, and maintenance?

The answers to these and other questions determine whether you can afford a car, and if so, which car, and how you will pay for it. The decision is made easier by developing the worksheet in Figure 2.14 and then by changing the various input values as indicated.

The availability of the worksheet lets you consider several alternatives. You realize that the purchase of a $14,999 car as shown in Figure 2.15 is prohibitive because the monthly payment is almost $476.96. Settling for a less expensive car, coming up with a substantial down payment, and obtaining a manufacturer's rebate in Figure 2.16 help, but the $317.97 monthly payment is still too high. Extending the loan to a fourth year

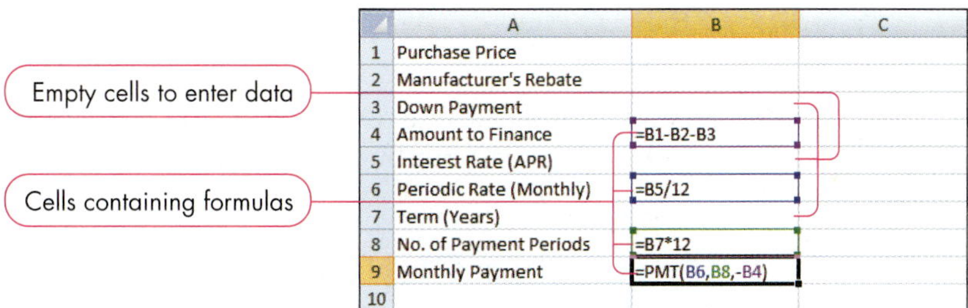

Figure 2.14 Template for Car Loan Analysis

Calculated monthly rate

Data entered

Calculated number of payment periods

Calculated monthly payment

	A	B	C
1	Purchase Price	$14,999.00	
2	Manufacturer's Rebate		
3	Down Payment		
4	Amount to Finance	$14,999.00	
5	Interest Rate (APR)	9.00%	
6	Periodic Rate (Monthly)	0.75%	
7	Term (Years)	3	
8	No. of Payment Periods	36	
9	Monthly Payment	$ 476.96	
10			

Figure 2.15 Original Data Entered: Monthly Payment Too High

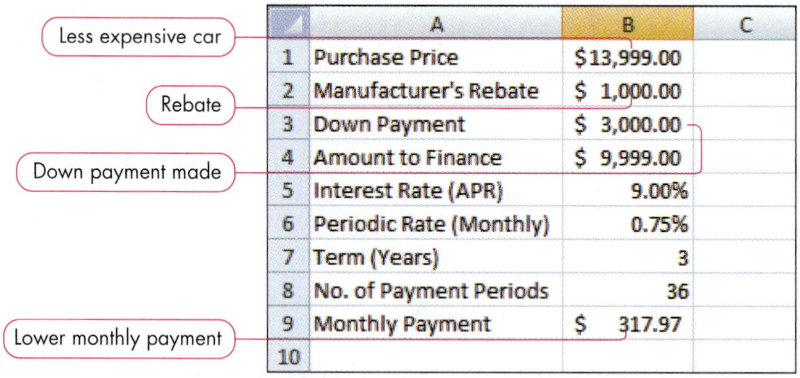

	A	B	C
1	Purchase Price	$13,999.00	
2	Manufacturer's Rebate	$ 1,000.00	
3	Down Payment	$ 3,000.00	
4	Amount to Finance	$ 9,999.00	
5	Interest Rate (APR)	9.00%	
6	Periodic Rate (Monthly)	0.75%	
7	Term (Years)	3	
8	No. of Payment Periods	36	
9	Monthly Payment	$ 317.97	
10			

Figure 2.16 Modified Data: Payment Still Too High

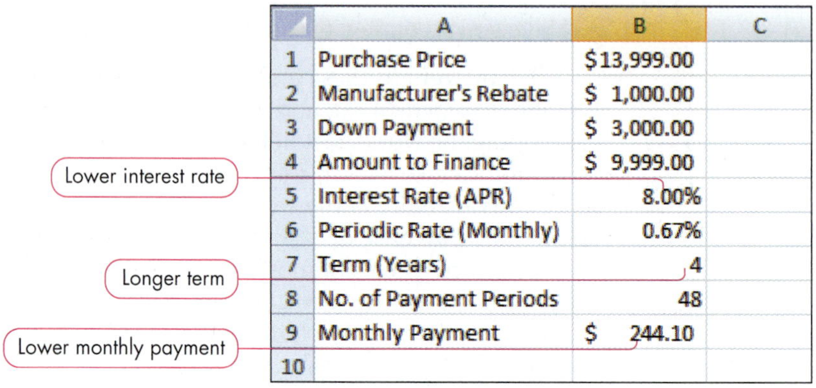

	A	B	C
1	Purchase Price	$13,999.00	
2	Manufacturer's Rebate	$ 1,000.00	
3	Down Payment	$ 3,000.00	
4	Amount to Finance	$ 9,999.00	
5	Interest Rate (APR)	8.00%	
6	Periodic Rate (Monthly)	0.67%	
7	Term (Years)	4	
8	No. of Payment Periods	48	
9	Monthly Payment	$ 244.10	
10			

Figure 2.17 Affordable Monthly Payment

at a lower interest rate as in Figure 2.17 reduces the monthly payment to $244.10, which is closer to your budgeted amount.

Using the PMT Function

The ***PMT function*** calculates the payment on a loan.

PMT Function | Reference

PMT(rate,nper,pv,fv,type)

The ***PMT function*** calculates payments for a loan that is paid off at a fixed amount at a periodic rate. The PMT function requires three arguments: the interest rate per period, the number of payment periods, and the amount of the loan, from which it computes the associated payment on a loan. The arguments are placed in parentheses and are separated by commas. Consider the PMT function as it might apply to Figure 2.15:

=PMT(.09/12,36,–14999)

- Amount of loan (as a *negative* amount)
- Number of periods (3 years × 12 months/year)
- Interest rate per period (annual rate divided by 12)

Instead of using specific values, however, you should use cell references in the PMT function arguments, so that you can easily change the input values in the individual cells instead of editing the values in the function itself. The PMT function is entered as =PMT(B6,B8,-B4) to reflect the terms of a specific loan whose arguments are in cells B4, B5, and B6. You must divide the 9% annual percentage rate (APR) by 12 months to obtain the monthly *periodic* rate. Instead of dividing the APR by 12 within the PMT function, we calculated the periodic interest rate in cell B6 and used that calculated rate in the PMT function. Next, you must multiply the 3-year term by the number of payments per year. Because you will make monthly payments, you multiply 3 by 12 months to calculate the total number of months in the term, which is 36. Instead of calculating the number of payment periods in the PMT function, we calculated the number of payment periods in cell B8 and used that calculated value in the PMT function. The amount of the loan is a minus figure because it is a debt. The loan is considered a negative because it is an outflow of cash or an expense. The amount of the loan is entered as a negative amount so the worksheet will display a positive value after calculations.

Using the FV Function

FV Function | Reference

FV(rate,nper,pmt,pv,type)

The ***FV function*** returns the future value of an investment.

The ***FV function*** returns the future value of an investment if you know the interest rate, the term, and the periodic payment. You can use the FV function to determine how much an IRA would be worth in a particular period of time. This function would be expressed as =FV(rate,nper,payment).

> (. . . more than $470,000, results from compound interest you will earn over the life of your investment of $120,000!)

Assume that you plan to contribute $3,000 a year to an IRA, that you expect to earn 7% annually, and that you will be contributing for 40 years. The future value of that investment—the amount you will have at age 65—would be $598,905! You would have contributed $120,000 ($3,000 a year for 40 years). The difference, more than $470,000, results from compound interest you will earn over the life of your investment of $120,000!

The FV function has three arguments—the interest rate (also called the rate of return), the number of periods (how long you will pay into the IRA), and the periodic investment (how much you will invest into the IRA per year). The FV function corresponding to the earlier example would be:

Amount at retirement =FV(Rate of return, Term, Periodic payment)

Computed value becomes $598,905

It is more practical, however, to enter the values into a worksheet and then use cell references within the FV function. If, for example, cells A1, A2, and A3 contained the rate of return, term, and annual contribution, respectively, the resulting FV function would be =FV(A1,A2,–A3). The periodic payment is preceded by a minus sign, just as the principal in the PMT function.

These financial functions as well as the other examples of functions provide you with the tools to perform sophisticated mathematical, statistical, and financial calculations.

TIP Financial Functions

Excel contains over 50 financial functions. To learn about these functions, display the Insert Function dialog box, click the *Or select a category* drop-down arrow, and select Financial. You can scroll through the alphabetical list of financial functions to see the syntax and purpose for each function.

Hands-On Exercises

4 | Purchasing a Van for the School for Exceptional Children

Skills covered: 1. Create the Worksheet **2.** Insert the PMT Function **3.** Format the Worksheet **4.** Complete the Worksheet

Step 1 Create the Worksheet

Refer to Figure 2.18 as you complete Steps 1-4.

a. Start a new blank workbook. Click in **cell B1** and type the title **School for Exceptional Children**. Enter the remaining labels for column B as shown in Figure 2.18.

As the transportation director, one of your responsibilities is to purchase vehicles for the school's use. You will create a worksheet, use the PMT function, and format a worksheet to show the proposed purchase price.

b. Increase the column widths to accommodate the widest entry, as necessary (other than cell B3). Enter the following as indicated below. Include the dollar sign and the percent sign as you enter the data to automatically format the cell.

Cell	Value
C4	$26,000
C5	$1,000
C6	$3,000
C8	9%
C9	3

The loan parameters have been entered into the worksheet, and you are ready to work with the PMT function.

c. Enter the formula to calculate the Amount to Finance in cell C7 by clicking in **cell C7** and typing **=C4−(C5+C6)**. Press **Enter**.

Although parentheses are not required for order of precedence, they may be used to help for understandability. You could also enter the formula **=C4−C5−C6** as an alternative.

d. Save the workbook as **chap2_ho4_van_solution**.

Step 2 Insert the PMT Function

a. Click the **Formulas tab**. Click **cell C10** and click **Financial** in the Function Library group, and click the **PMT** function. Click in the **Rate** box, if necessary, click **cell C8** of the worksheet, then type **/12**.

The Rate box contains C8/12 because interest is calculated monthly.

b. Click in the **Nper** box, click **cell C9** of the worksheet, and type ***12**.

The Nper box contains C9*12 to calculate the total number of payment periods in the loan.

c. Click in the **Pv** box, type a minus sign (–), and click **cell C7**. Click **OK** to close the Function Arguments dialog box.

The monthly payment of $699.59 is now displayed in cell C10.

d. Save the workbook.

TROUBLESHOOTING: Divide the interest rate by 12 because the rate is requested as a percentage per period. Multiply the years by 12 because the term of the loan is stated in years. It is acceptable to use 12 as a constant in these formulas since the number of months in a year is constant.

Step 3
Format the Worksheet

a. Click the **Home tab**, select **cells B1** and **C1**, and click **Merge & Center** in the Alignment group.

b. Click the **Font size arrow** in the Font group and select **12**. Click **Bold** in the Font group to boldface the title.

c. Click **cell B3**, press and hold **Ctrl** as you click **cells B10:C10**, and click **Bold**.

d. Click and drag to select **cells B4:B9**. Click **Increase Indent** in the Alignment group to indent the labels.

e. Click in **cell A12** and enter your name. Click **cell A1** and use the **TODAY** function to enter today's date. Click **cell A1** and hold **Ctrl** as you click **cell A12**. Click **Bold** and click **Align Text Left** in the Alignment group. Save the workbook.

Step 4
Complete the Worksheet

a. Click the **Page Layout tab** and click **Margins** in the Page Setup group. Click **Custom Margins** to display the Page Setup dialog box.

b. Click the **Horizontally check box** in the *Center on page* section.

c. Click the **Sheet tab** and click the **Gridlines check box** and click the **Row and column headings check box** in the *Print* section.

You used the Page Layout options to print gridlines as well as row and column headings and centered the worksheet horizontally.

d. Click **OK**. Save the workbook.

e. Click the **Office Button**, select **Print**, and click **Preview** to see how the workbook will print. Click the **Print button** and then **OK** to print the worksheet.

f. Press **Ctrl +** ` (grave accent) to show the cell formulas rather than the values. Adjust the column width as necessary and print the worksheet a second time. Close the workbook without saving the view of the cell formulas.

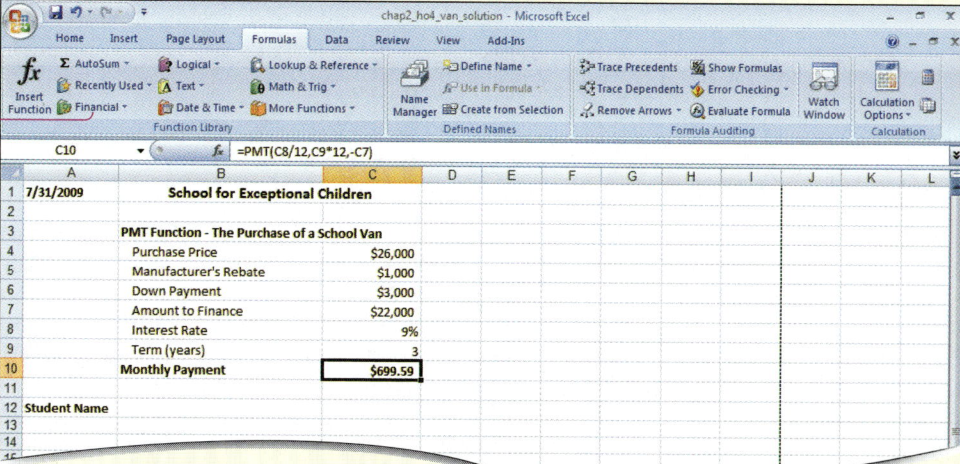

Figure 2.18 School for Exceptional Children Van

Summary

1. **Create and copy formulas.** When constructing formulas in Excel, it is more efficient to enter cell references in formulas rather than the cell contents. Entering cell references means that an addition formula should be stated as =A2+B2 rather than =1+2. By using cell references rather than cell contents, the formula does not have to be changed when the cell content changes. Pointing and using the fill handle are techniques that make the development of an Excel spreadsheet easier. The fill handle is a small black square at the lower-right corner of a selected cell(s). It is the efficient way to copy cell formulas to adjacent cells.

2. **Use relative and absolute cell addresses.** A relative reference (such as C4) changes both row and column when the cell containing the reference is copied to other worksheet cells. An absolute cell reference, such as $C$4, stays the same during the copy process. A mixed reference, such as $C4 or C$4, modifies the row or column during the copy. The use of relative and absolute references is common in the design and construction of most spreadsheets.

3. **Use AutoSum.** The AutoSum is the most often used statistical function in Excel. It is represented by the sigma and automatically sums values contained in a range of cells.

4. **Insert basic statistical functions.** Statistical functions discussed include SUM, which returns the sum of an argument list, and AVERAGE, MEDIAN, MAX, and MIN, which return the average value, the midpoint of a range of values, the highest value, and lowest value, respectively, in an argument list. The COUNT function displays the number of cells with numeric entries, and the COUNTA function displays the number of cells with numeric and/or text entries.

5. **Use date functions.** The NOW function uses the computer's clock to display the current date and time side by side in a cell. The TODAY function is another date-related function that places the current date in a cell.

6. **Use the IF function.** In the set of logical functions, the IF is the most basic. It returns one value when a condition is met and returns another value when the condition is not met. The IF function allows decision-making to be used within a worksheet. IF functions have three arguments: the condition, the result when true, and the result when false.

7. **Use the VLOOKUP function.** You can use VLOOKUP to look up an answer from a table of possible answers. The table that Excel searches using a lookup function is called a lookup table, and the value being used to search the lookup table is called a lookup value.

8. **Use the PMT function.** You can use the PMT function to calculate payments for a loan that is paid off at a fixed amount at a periodic rate. The PMT function requires three arguments: the interest rate per period, the number of periods, and the amount of the loan, from which it computes the associated payment on a loan. The arguments are placed in parentheses and are separated by commas.

9. **Use the FV function.** If you know the interest rate, the term, and the periodic payment, then you can use the FV function to return the future value of an investment. You can use the FV function to determine how much an investment would be worth at the end of a defined period of time.

Key Terms

Multiple Choice

1. After entering numbers and using the SUM function to sum the numbers, when is the function updated if one of the numbers changes?
   (a) When the file is saved
   (b) When you refresh the worksheet
   (c) When you close the file
   (d) At once

2. Which of the following returns the system date?
   (a) The Date() function
   (b) The Today() function
   (c) Date arithmetic
   (d) The Insert Date command

3. If you see the term "C3" used in relation to Excel, it refers to what?
   (a) Absolute reference
   (b) Cell reference
   (c) Worksheet reference
   (d) Mixed reference

4. The entry =PMT(C5/12,C6*12,C7):
   (a) Is invalid because the cell reference C7 is not absolute
   (b) Computes an annual payment
   (c) Divides the interest rate in C5, multiplies the number of periods in C6, and C7 is the loan amount
   (d) Is invalid because the value in C7 is negative

5. Pointing is a technique to:
   (a) Select a single cell
   (b) Select a range of contiguous cells
   (c) Select ranges of noncontiguous cells
   (d) All of the above

6. The small black square in the bottom-right corner of a cell is called what?
   (a) Pointer
   (b) Fill handle
   (c) Crosshair
   (d) Select box

7. Given the function =VLOOKUP(C6,D12:F18,3):
   (a) The entries in cells D12 through D18 are in ascending order.
   (b) The entries in cells D12 through D18 are in descending order.
   (c) The entries in cells F12 through F18 are in ascending order.
   (d) The entries in cells F12 through F18 are in descending order.

8. Which of the following must be entered when creating a formula?
   (a) The equal sign
   (b) A mathematical operator
   (c) A function
   (d) Nothing special is required.

9. Which of the following is an example of an absolute cell reference?
   (a) C4
   (b) $C$4
   (c) =C4
   (d) $C4

10. If you wanted the contents of only a column to stay the same throughout the copy process, you would use which of the following?
    (a) Relative reference
    (b) Mixed reference
    (c) Absolute reference
    (d) This is not possible

11. Which of the following references would indicate that the row would change but the column would not change during the copy process?
    (a) $C$4
    (b) =C4
    (c) $C4
    (d) C$4

12. The Σ indicates which of the following functions?
    (a) AVERAGE
    (b) MAX
    (c) MIN
    (d) SUM

...continued on Next Page

Multiple Choice Continued...

13. Which function will return the number of nonempty cells in the range A2 through A6, when the cells contain text as well as numeric entries?

(a) =COUNT(A2:A6)

(b) =COUNTA(A2:A6)

(c) =COUNT(A2,A6)

(d) =COUNTA(A2,A6)

14. The MAX function is an example of what type of function?

(a) Database

(b) Statistical

(c) Logical

(d) Lookup

15. If you want to determine the future value of an investment, what function would you use?

(a) PV

(b) FV

(c) VLOOKUP

(d) IF

Practice Exercises

1 West Transylvania Women's Basketball Season Statistics

You are the statistician for the West Transylvania Women's basketball team. You have entered basic statistics into a worksheet for the 2007–08 season. The coach wants to expand the statistics so that she can compare production for different seasons. Complete the worksheet as directed using Figure 2.19 as a guide.

a. Open the *chap2_pe1_basketball* workbook and save it as **chap2_pe1_basketball_solution** so that you can return to the original workbook if necessary.

b. The first calculation will be total points (TP). Click in **cell I5**, the cell that will contain the total points for Adams. Type = on the keyboard to begin the formula, then click **cell C5** to enter the first part of the formula to calculate total points.

c. Type **+(** and click **cell F5**, then type ***2)+(** and click **cell H5**. Type ***3)** and press **Enter**. You should see 84 as the displayed value for cell I5. Enter your name in **cell I22**. Save the workbook.

d. Click in **cell D5**, the cell that contains Adams's free throw percentage (FT%). Type = and click **cell C5**. Type **/** and click **cell B5**. Press **Enter**. You should see 0.8 in cell D5.

e. To calculate two-point field goal percentage (2-Pt FG%), click in **cell G5**, type =, click **cell F5**, type **/**, and click **cell E5**. Press **Enter** to see 0.36364 in cell G5.

f. To calculate points per game (PPG), click **cell J5** and type =. Click **cell I5**, type **/**, and click **cell C22**. Press **F4** to set cell C22 as absolute ($C$22) and press **Enter**. You should see 7 in cell J5.

g. To calculate rebounds per game (RPG), click **cell L5** and type =. Click **cell K5**, type **/**, click **cell C22**, and press **F4** to make C22 an absolute reference ($C$22). Press **Enter** and you will see 4.583333 in cell L5. Save the workbook.

h. Click in **cell D5**. Point to the fill handle in the lower-right corner of cell D5; the mouse pointer changes to a thin crosshair. Drag the fill handle to **cell D14**.

i. Release the mouse button to complete the copy operation. The formula for FT% has been copied to the corresponding rows for the other players. Repeat the above step for columns G, I, J, and L to complete all players' statistics.

j. Use statistical functions to complete the summary area below the player statistics. Click in **cell B18**, type **=AVERAGE(**, and click and drag **cells B5:B14**. Type **)** and press **Enter**. Click in **cell B19**, type **=MAX(**, and click and drag cells **B5:B14**. Type **)** and press **Enter**. Click in **cell B20**, type **=MIN(**, and click and drag cells **B5:B14**. Type **)** and press **Enter**.

k. To copy the formulas across the worksheet, click and drag over **cells B18:B20**. Point to the fill handle in the lower-right corner of cell B20; the mouse pointer changes to a thin crosshair. Drag the fill handle to **cell L20**.

l. To calculate totals in row 17, click in **cell B17**, click **AutoSum** in the Function Library group on the Formulas tab, and then click and drag **cells B5:B14**. Press **Enter** to finish the function. To copy, click **cell B17** and click **Copy** in the Clipboard group on the Home tab. Click in **cell C17** and click **Paste** in the Clipboard group on the Home tab. Click and **Paste** in **cells E17, F17, H17, I17,** and **K17** to paste the formula in the appropriate cells. Enter **=TODAY()** in cell **I23** for today's date.

m. Format the values in columns D and G as **Percent Style** with **1 decimal** place. Format columns J and L as **Number** with **1 decimal** place. Verify your calculations and format the worksheet as shown in Figure 2.19.

n. Click the **Page Layout tab**. Click **Orientation** in the Page Setup group and select **Landscape**. Click **Margins** in the Page Setup group, select **Custom Margins**, and then click the **Horizontally check box** in the *Center on page* section. Click the **Sheet tab**, click the **Gridlines check box**, and click the **Row and column headings check box** in the *Print* section. Click **OK**. Print the worksheet.

o. Save the workbook. Press **Ctrl + `** (grave accent) to show the cell formulas rather than the displayed values. Adjust the column widths as necessary and print the worksheet a second time. Save and close the workbook.

...continued on Next Page

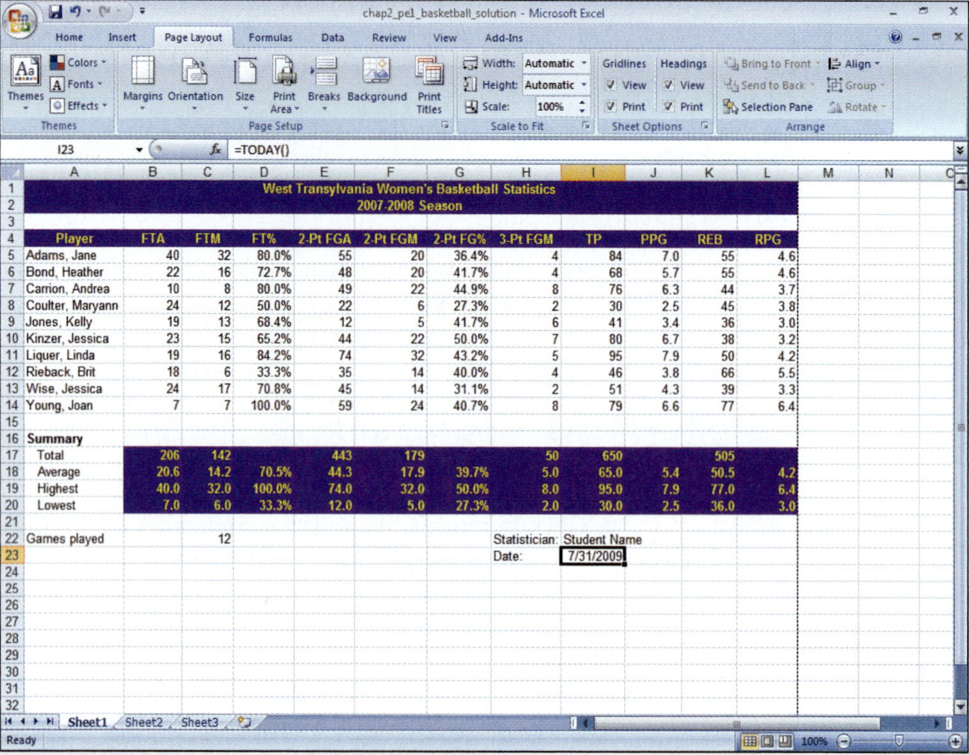

Figure 2.19 Women's Basketball Statistics

2 Predicting Retirement Income

Retirement might be years away, but it is never too soon to start planning. The Future Value function enables you to calculate the amount of money you will have at retirement, based on a series of uniform contributions. Once you reach retirement, you do not withdraw all of the money immediately, but withdraw it periodically, perhaps as a monthly pension. Your assignment is to create a new worksheet similar to the one in Figure 2.20.

a. In a new, blank workbook, enter the data for the accrual phase as shown in the following table (begin in **cell A4**):

Annual Salary	$60,000
Employee contribution	6.20%
Employer contribution	6.20%
Total contribution	
Interest Rate	6%
Years contributing	45

b. The first calculation will be the total contribution per year. Click in **cell B7**, type =, click **cell B4**, and type * and **(**. Click **cell B5**, type +, and click **cell B6**. Type **)**, and then press **Enter.** The total contribution in **cell B7** is a formula based on a percentage of your annual salary, plus a matching contribution from your employer. The 6.2% in the figure corresponds to the percentages that are currently in effect for Social Security.

c. The future value of your contributions (i.e., the amount of your "nest egg") depends on the assumptions on the left side of the worksheet. The 6% interest rate is conservative and can be achieved by investing in bonds, as opposed to equities. The

...continued on Next Page

45 years of contributions corresponds to an individual entering the work force at age 22 and retiring at 67 (the age at which today's worker will begin to collect Social Security). To calculate the future value of your nest egg, type **Future Value** in cell **A10**. Click in **cell B10**, where the future value will be calculated. Enter the FV function as follows:

- Click the **Formulas tab**, click **Financial** in the Function Library group, and click **FV**.
- Click in the **Rate** box and then click **cell B8**.
- Click in the **Nper** box and click **cell B9**.
- Click in the **Pmt** box, type a minus sign (–), and click **cell B7**.
- Click **OK** to close the Function Arguments dialog box. The future value of your nest egg is $1,582,811.74

d. The pension phase uses the PMT function to determine the payments you will receive in retirement. The formula in cell E4 is a reference to the amount accumulated in cell B10. The formula in cell E7 uses the PMT function to compute your monthly pension based on your nest egg, the interest rate, and the years in retirement. Note that accrual phase uses an *annual* contribution in its calculations, whereas the pension phase determines a *monthly* pension.

- Click **cell D3** and type **Pension Phase**. Enter the data shown below beginning in cell D4

The size of your "nest egg"	=B10
Interest rate	6%
Years in retirement	25

- Click in **cell D7** and type **Monthly Pension**. Click in **cell E7** to begin to enter the PMT function.
- Click **Financial** in the Function Library group on the Formulas tab and then click **PMT**.
- Click in the **Rate** box, click **cell E5**, and type **/12**.
- Click in the **Nper** box, click **cell E6**, and type ***12**.
- Click in the **Pv** box, type a minus sign (–), and click **cell E4**.
- Click **OK** to close the Function Arguments dialog box. The monthly pension is $10,198.08.

e. Click in **cell D10** and enter your name. Enter **=TODAY()** in **cell D11** for today's date. Verify your calculations and format the worksheet as shown in Figure 2.20.

f. Click the **Page Layout tab**, click **Orientation** in the Page Setup group, and click **Landscape**. Click **Size**, click **More Paper Sizes**, and click **Fit to 1 page** in the *Scaling* section. Click the **Margins tab** and click the **Horizontally check box** in the *Center on page* section. Click the **Sheet tab**, click the **Gridlines check box**, and click the **Row and column headings check box** in the *Print* section. Click **OK**. Print the worksheet.

g. Save the workbook as **chap2_pe2_retirement_solution.xlsx**. Press **Ctrl + `** (grave accent) to show the cell formulas rather than the displayed values. Adjust the column widths as necessary and print the worksheet a second time. Close the workbook.

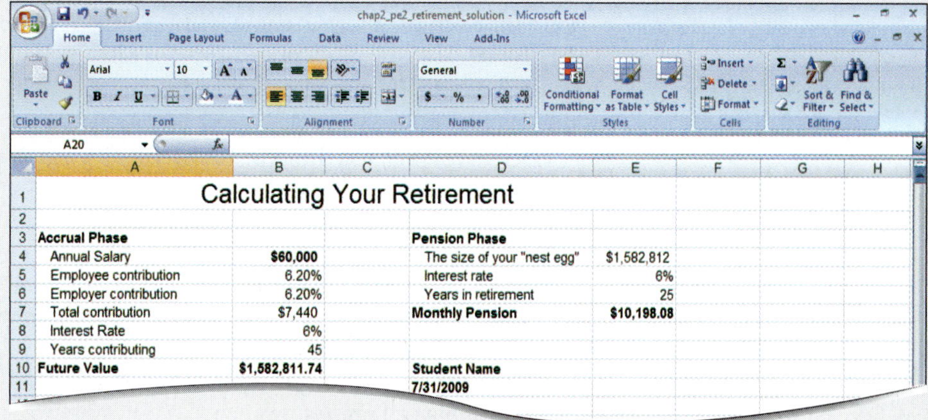

Figure 2.20 Predicting Retirement Income

...continued on Next Page

3 Election Trends

The 2004 presidential election has come and gone, but it is interesting to analyze the results of both the popular and electoral votes. You want to compare total votes and votes by state. You will find a partially completed version of the workbook shown in Figure 2.21 and enter functions to help identify election trends. Format as shown in Figure 2.21.

a. Open the *chap2_pe3_election* workbook and save it as **chap2_pe3_election_solution**.

b. Enter an appropriate IF function in cells D9 and F9 to determine the number of electoral votes for each candidate. The electoral votes are awarded on an all-or-nothing basis; that is, the candidate with the larger popular vote wins all of that state's electoral votes. The other candidate gets zero votes.
   - Click in **cell D9** to begin the first IF function. Click the **Formulas tab** and click **Insert Function** in the Function Library group.
   - Click **IF** to select the IF function and click **OK**.
   - Click in the **Logical test** box in the Function Arguments dialog box, and type **C9>E9**.
   - Click in the **Value_if_true** box and click **cell B9**.
   - Click in the **Value_if_false** box and **type ""** (quotes are needed to make empty cells).
   - Click **OK** to finish the IF function and close the dialog box.
   - Click **cell F9** to begin the second IF function.
   - Click **Insert Function** in the Function Library on the Formulas tab and click **IF** to select the IF function and click **OK**.
   - Click in the **Logical test** box, type **E9>C9**.
   - Click in the **Value_if_true** box and click **cell B9**.
   - Click in the **Value_if_false** box and **type ""** (quotes are needed to make empty cells).
   - Click **OK** to finish the IF function and close the dialog box.

c. You will now copy the entries in cells D9 and F9 to the remaining rows in the respective columns. You also will format these columns to display red and blue values, for each candidate, respectively.
   - Click in **cell D9** and drag the fill handle through **cell D59** to copy the formula.
   - To format the columns select **cells C8:D59**. Click the **Home tab**, click the **Font Color arrow** in the Font group, and click **Red**.
   - Adapt the previous two bulleted list instructions for columns E and F, substituting the appropriate column letters and applying **Blue** font color.

d. Enter a formula into cell G9 to determine the difference in the popular vote between the two candidates. The result will appear as a positive number and you will use an absolute value function. Copy this formula to the remaining rows in the column.
   - Click in **cell G9** and type **=ABS(**.
   - Click in **cell C9**, type minus (–), click in **cell E9**, type **)**, and press **Enter**.
   - Click in **cell G9** and drag the fill handle through **G59** to copy the formula.

e. You will calculate the percentage differential in the popular vote. This differential is the difference in the number of votes, divided by the total number of votes.
   - Click in **cell H9** and type **=G9/(**.
   - Click in **cell C9**, type **+**, click **cell E9**, and type **)**.
   - Click in **cell H9** and drag the fill handle through **H59** to copy the formula.

f. Enter the appropriate SUM functions in cells B4, B5, C4, and C5 to determine the electoral and popular vote totals for each candidate.
   - To calculate the total in cell B4, click in **cell B4**, click **AutoSum** in the Function Library on the Formulas tab, click and drag **cells C9:C59**, and press **Enter**.
   - To calculate the total in cell B5, click in **cell B5**, click **AutoSum** on the Formulas tab, click and drag **cells D9:D59**, and press **Enter**.
   - Repeat the first two bulleted instructions in Step f for cells **C4** and **C5** using the appropriate cell ranges.

...continued on Next Page

g. Add your name as indicated. Click the **Page Layout tab**, click **Margins** in the Page Setup group, and click **Custom Margins**. Type **0.75** in the **Top** and **Bottom** boxes to ensure the worksheet fits on one page. Adjust the column widths as necessary. Create a custom footer that shows the **date** the worksheet was printed. Print the displayed values, and then print the worksheet a second time to show the cell formulas. Save and close the workbook.

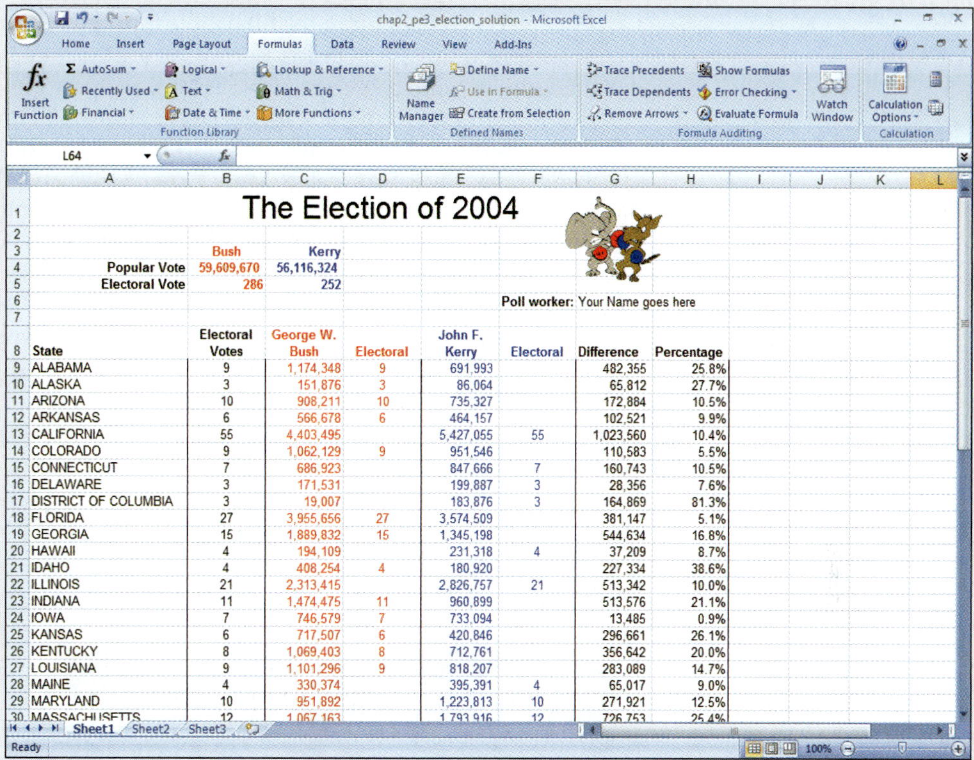

The Election of 2004

	Bush	Kerry
Popular Vote	59,609,670	56,116,324
Electoral Vote	286	252

Poll worker: Your Name goes here

State	Electoral Votes	George W. Bush	Electoral	John F. Kerry	Electoral	Difference	Percentage
ALABAMA	9	1,174,348	9	691,993		482,355	25.8%
ALASKA	3	151,876	3	86,064		65,812	27.7%
ARIZONA	10	908,211	10	735,327		172,884	10.5%
ARKANSAS	6	566,678	6	464,157		102,521	9.9%
CALIFORNIA	55	4,403,495		5,427,055	55	1,023,560	10.4%
COLORADO	9	1,062,129	9	951,546		110,583	5.5%
CONNECTICUT	7	686,923		847,666	7	160,743	10.5%
DELAWARE	3	171,531		199,887	3	28,356	7.6%
DISTRICT OF COLUMBIA	3	19,007		183,876	3	164,869	81.3%
FLORIDA	27	3,955,656	27	3,574,509		381,147	5.1%
GEORGIA	15	1,889,832	15	1,345,198		544,634	16.8%
HAWAII	4	194,109		231,318	4	37,209	8.7%
IDAHO	4	408,254	4	180,920		227,334	38.6%
ILLINOIS	21	2,313,415		2,826,757	21	513,342	10.0%
INDIANA	11	1,474,475	11	960,899		513,576	21.1%
IOWA	7	746,579	7	733,094		13,485	0.9%
KANSAS	6	717,507	6	420,846		296,661	26.1%
KENTUCKY	8	1,069,403	8	712,761		356,642	20.0%
LOUISIANA	9	1,101,296	9	818,207		283,089	14.7%
MAINE	4	330,374		395,391	4	65,017	9.0%
MARYLAND	10	951,892		1,223,813	10	271,921	12.5%
MASSACHUSETTS	12	1,067,163		1,793,916	12	726,753	25.4%

Figure 2.21 Election Trends

4 Expanded Payroll

You will revisit the payroll completed earlier in this chapter in the hands-on exercises but revise it to use a VLOOKUP function to determine the withholding tax amount based on a tax bracket, rather than a flat tax rate. Use Figure 2.22 for reference to complete the expanded payroll example. Be sure to use the appropriate combination of relative and absolute addresses so the formula in column G may be copied to the remaining rows in the worksheet.

a. Open the *chap2_pe4_exppayroll* workbook and save it as **chap2_pe4_exppayroll_ solution**.

b. Click in **cell F4**, click the **Formulas tab**, click **Lookup & Reference** in the Function Library group, and select **VLOOKUP** to display the Function Arguments dialog box.
   - Click in the **Lookup_value** box and click **cell E4**.
   - Click in the **Table_array** box, drag through **cells I20:J24**, and press **F4** to make the table references absolute.
   - Click in the **Col_index_num** box and type **2**.
   - Click **OK** to finish the VLOOKUP function and close the Function Arguments dialog box.
   - Click after the closing parenthesis for the VLOOKUP function in the formula bar, type ***E4**, and press **Enter**.

...continued on Next Page

c. Click in **cell F4** and drag the fill handle through **cell F15** to copy the formula.

d. To calculate the FICA withholding tax, click **cell G4** and type **=E4***

e. Click **cell B21**, press **F4**, and then press **Enter**.

f. Click **cell G4** and drag the fill handle through **cell G15** to copy the formula.

g. Calculate the net pay by clicking **cell H4** and type **=E4–(**.

h. Click **cell F4**, type **+**, click **cell G4**, type **)**, and press **Enter**.

i. Click in **cell H4** and drag the fill handle through **cell H15** to copy the formula.

j. Format columns F, G, and H as **Currency** with two decimal places. Replace **Student Name** with your name and use a **date function** to retrieve today's date. Verify your calculations and format the worksheet as shown in Figure 2.22.

k. Click the **Page Layout tab**, click **Orientation** in the Page Setup group, and click **Landscape**. Click **Size**, select **More Paper Sizes**, and click **Fit to 1 page** in the *Scaling* section. Click the **Margins tab** and click the **Horizontally check box** in the *Center on page* section. Click the **Sheet tab**, click the **Gridlines check box**, and click the **Row and column headings check box** in the *Print* section. Click **OK**. Print the worksheet.

l. Save the workbook. Press **Ctrl + `** (grave accent) to show the cell formulas rather than the displayed values. Adjust the column widths as necessary and print the worksheet a second time.

m. Close the workbook.

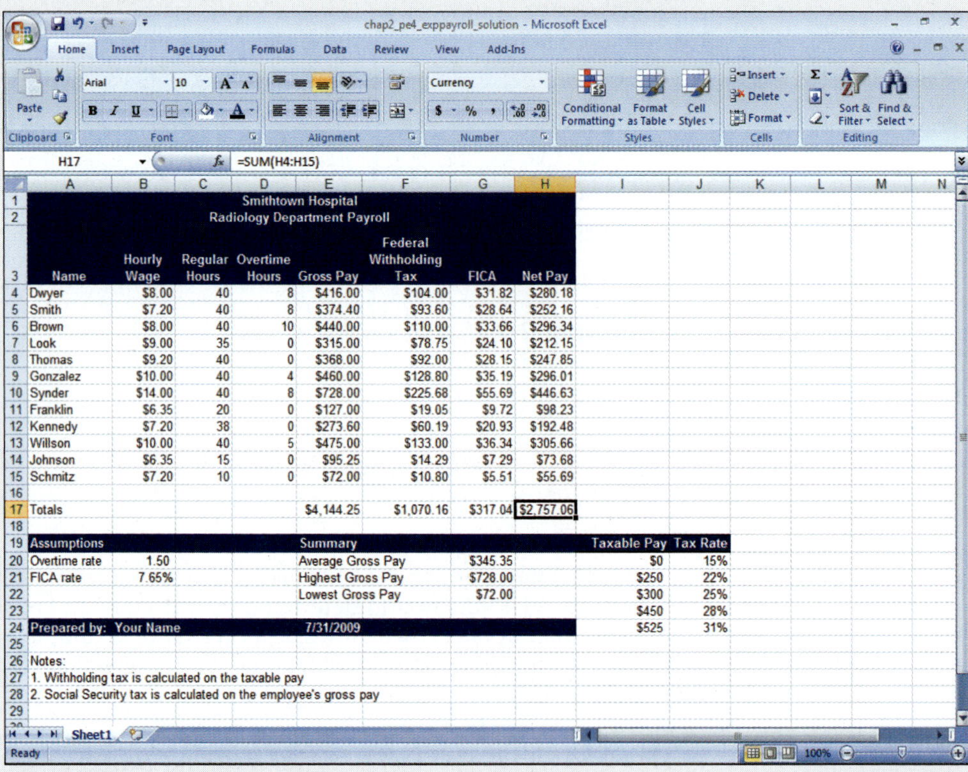

	A	B	C	D	E	F	G	H	I	J
1	Smithtown Hospital									
2	Radiology Department Payroll									
3	Name	Hourly Wage	Regular Hours	Overtime Hours	Gross Pay	Federal Withholding Tax	FICA	Net Pay		
4	Dwyer	$8.00	40	8	$416.00	$104.00	$31.82	$280.18		
5	Smith	$7.20	40	8	$374.40	$93.60	$28.64	$252.16		
6	Brown	$8.00	40	10	$440.00	$110.00	$33.66	$296.34		
7	Look	$9.00	35	0	$315.00	$78.75	$24.10	$212.15		
8	Thomas	$9.20	40	0	$368.00	$92.00	$28.15	$247.85		
9	Gonzalez	$10.00	40	4	$460.00	$128.80	$35.19	$296.01		
10	Synder	$14.00	40	8	$728.00	$225.68	$55.69	$446.63		
11	Franklin	$6.35	20	0	$127.00	$19.05	$9.72	$98.23		
12	Kennedy	$7.20	38	0	$273.60	$60.19	$20.93	$192.48		
13	Willson	$10.00	40	5	$475.00	$133.00	$36.34	$305.66		
14	Johnson	$6.35	15	0	$95.25	$14.29	$7.29	$73.68		
15	Schmitz	$7.20	10	0	$72.00	$10.80	$5.51	$55.69		
16										
17	Totals				$4,144.25	$1,070.16	$317.04	$2,757.06		
18										
19	Assumptions				Summary				Taxable Pay	Tax Rate
20	Overtime rate	1.50			Average Gross Pay		$345.35		$0	15%
21	FICA rate	7.65%			Highest Gross Pay		$728.00		$250	22%
22					Lowest Gross Pay		$72.00		$300	25%
23									$450	28%
24	Prepared by: Your Name				7/31/2009				$525	31%
25										
26	Notes:									
27	1. Withholding tax is calculated on the taxable pay									
28	2. Social Security tax is calculated on the employee's gross pay									

Figure 2.22 Expanded Payroll

Mid-Level Exercises

1 Banquet Room Inventory

Managing or tracking inventory is an important way for businesses to control operating costs. During semester breaks you work as an assistant to the manager of a banquet room facility and are responsible for updating the inventory workbook. You will create formulas and functions to illustrate how Excel is used for inventory control. Refer to Figure 2.23 as you complete the worksheet.

a. Open the *chap2_mid1_banquet* workbook. Save it as **chap2_mid1_banquet_ solution** so that you can return to the original workbook if necessary.

b. Calculate the cost by multiplying number purchased by purchase price (e.g., 200 chairs * $186.00). The total cost of inventoried items is the sum of all values. Use the **SUM function** to compute the total cost.

c. Enter the **MAX** and **MIN functions** where appropriate to determine the most and least expensive items in inventory. Use the **COUNTA function** to determine the number of categories of items in inventory.

d. Replace Student Name with your name. Add an appropriate clip art image somewhere in the worksheet. Use an appropriate date function to get today's date in your worksheet and format it as **mm/dd/yyyy**.

e. Format the worksheet in an attractive fashion, making sure to format dollar figures as currency with two decimal places. Wrap the column heading text to increase readability.

f. Print the completed worksheet twice, once with displayed values, and once to show the cell formulas. Use Page Setup for the cell formulas to switch to landscape orientation and force the output onto one page. Print gridlines and row and column headings. Save and close the workbook.

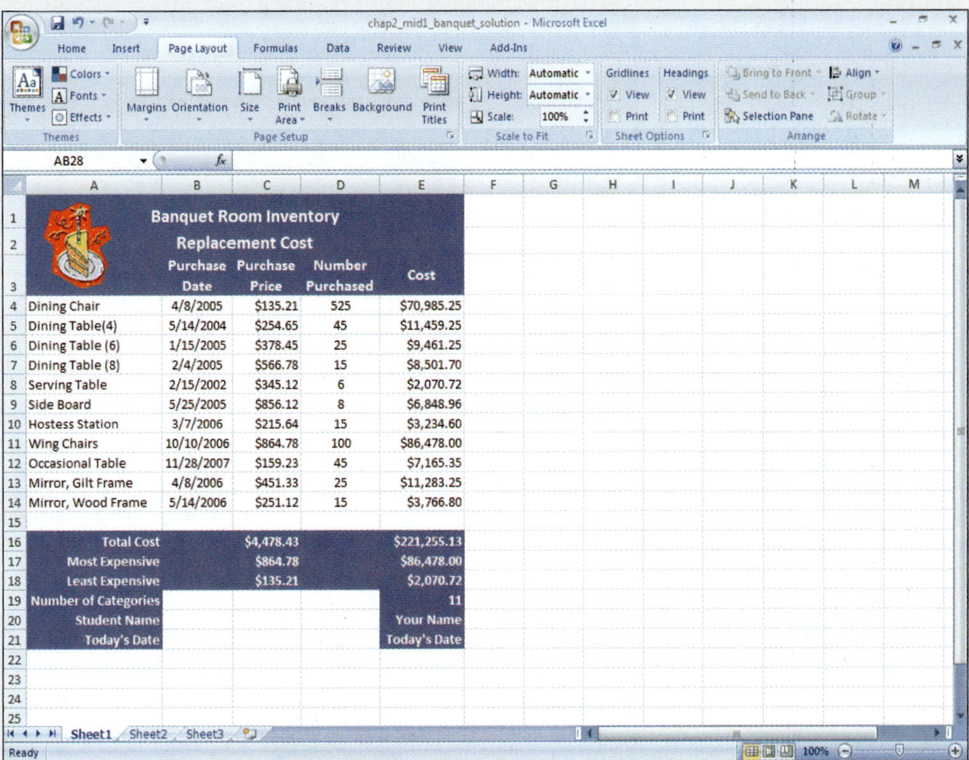

	A	B	C	D	E
1		Banquet Room Inventory			
2		Replacement Cost			
3		Purchase Date	Purchase Price	Number Purchased	Cost
4	Dining Chair	4/8/2005	$135.21	525	$70,985.25
5	Dining Table(4)	5/14/2004	$254.65	45	$11,459.25
6	Dining Table (6)	1/15/2005	$378.45	25	$9,461.25
7	Dining Table (8)	2/4/2005	$566.78	15	$8,501.70
8	Serving Table	2/15/2002	$345.12	6	$2,070.72
9	Side Board	5/25/2005	$856.12	8	$6,848.96
10	Hostess Station	3/7/2006	$215.64	15	$3,234.60
11	Wing Chairs	10/10/2006	$864.78	100	$86,478.00
12	Occasional Table	11/28/2007	$159.23	45	$7,165.35
13	Mirror, Gilt Frame	4/8/2006	$451.33	25	$11,283.25
14	Mirror, Wood Frame	5/14/2006	$251.12	15	$3,766.80
15					
16	Total Cost		$4,478.43		$221,255.13
17	Most Expensive		$864.78		$86,478.00
18	Least Expensive		$135.21		$2,070.72
19	Number of Categories				11
20	Student Name				Your Name
21	Today's Date				Today's Date

Figure 2.23 Banquet Room Inventory

...continued on Next Page

2 Real Estate Sales

The real estate market is booming, and electronic methods are necessary to keep up with the rapidly changing field. As an intern with the Duke Real Estate company, you have prepared the worksheet shown in Figure 2.24. It shows how the Duke Real Estate company uses Excel to track monthly sales and sales commissions. You will complete the Real Estate worksheet so that the displayed values match Figure 2.24.

The price per square foot is calculated by dividing the selling price by size. The percent of list price is calculated by dividing the selling price by the list price. Use an absolute reference to determine sales commission so the formula can be copied to other rows.

a. Open the *chap2_mid2_rls* workbook and save it as **chap2_mid2_rls_solution** so that you can return to the original workbook if necessary.

b. Enter the **SUM function** in **cell B14** to compute the total square feet. Copy the formula to the remaining cells in the row. Use the appropriate functions to calculate the values in the summary area.

c. Format the worksheet in an attractive manner, making sure to display all dollar amounts with the currency symbol and no decimal places. Display percentages with the percent symbol and one decimal place. Use a date function to display the current date in the cell below the heading.

d. Enter your name in **cell A17** and print the worksheet twice, once with displayed values, and once to show cell formulas. Use the Page Setup command to switch to landscape orientation and force the output onto one page. Print gridlines and row and column headings. Save and close the workbook.

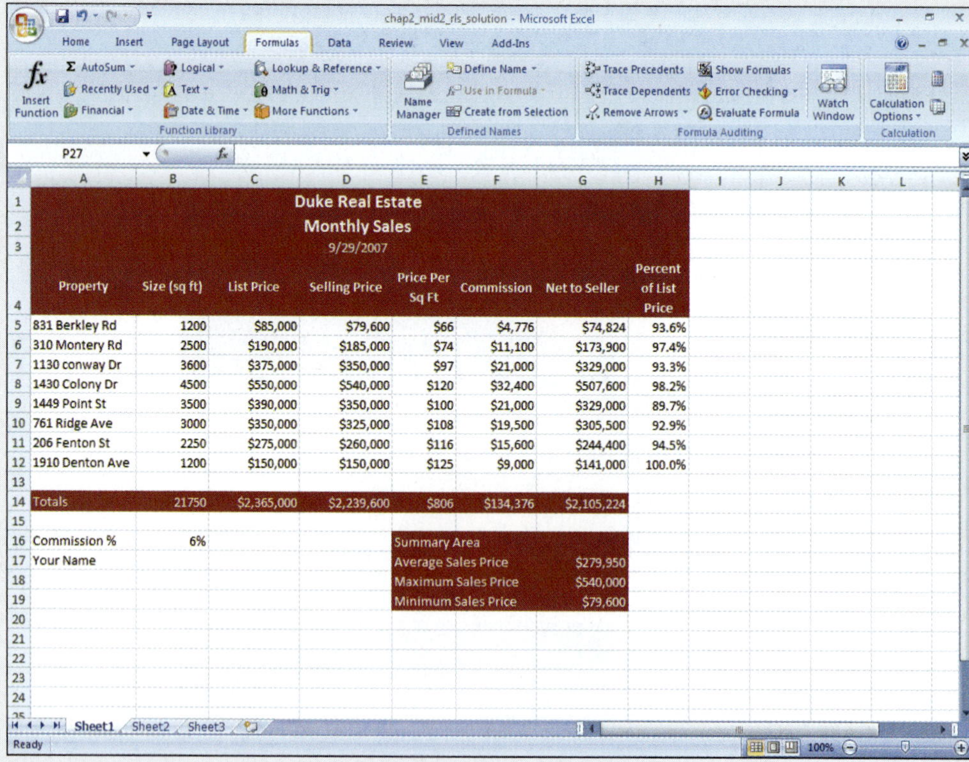

Duke Real Estate
Monthly Sales
9/29/2007

Property	Size (sq ft)	List Price	Selling Price	Price Per Sq Ft	Commission	Net to Seller	Percent of List Price
831 Berkley Rd	1200	$85,000	$79,600	$66	$4,776	$74,824	93.6%
310 Montery Rd	2500	$190,000	$185,000	$74	$11,100	$173,900	97.4%
1130 conway Dr	3600	$375,000	$350,000	$97	$21,000	$329,000	93.3%
1430 Colony Dr	4500	$550,000	$540,000	$120	$32,400	$507,600	98.2%
1449 Point St	3500	$390,000	$350,000	$100	$21,000	$329,000	89.7%
761 Ridge Ave	3000	$350,000	$325,000	$108	$19,500	$305,500	92.9%
206 Fenton St	2250	$275,000	$260,000	$116	$15,600	$244,400	94.5%
1910 Denton Ave	1200	$150,000	$150,000	$125	$9,000	$141,000	100.0%
Totals	21750	$2,365,000	$2,239,600	$806	$134,376	$2,105,224	
Commission %	6%			Summary Area			
Your Name				Average Sales Price		$279,950	
				Maximum Sales Price		$540,000	
				Minimum Sales Price		$79,600	

Figure 2.24 Real Estate Sales

...continued on Next Page

3 High School Art Collection

The Greater Latrobe School District is well known for its 70-year-old art collection. One of your duties as a summer intern is to help ready the collection for a traveling exhibition. You will use the IF function and the VLOOKUP function in Excel to determine costs associated with this art exhibition. You will complete the Greater Latrobe School District worksheet so that displayed values match Figure 2.25.

a. Open the *chap2_mid3_glsd* workbook and save it as **chap2_mid3_glsd_solution** so that you can return to the original workbook if necessary.

b. The cost of insurance is based on the value of the artwork. If the value is greater than $500, then the insurance is 25% of the value; otherwise the insurance is 10% of the value of the painting. Enter an **IF function** in G6 to compute the cost of insurance and copy the formula to the remaining cells in the column.

c. Cubic footage is calculated by multiplying height by width and dividing by 144. Enter the formula in cell H6 and copy the formula to the remaining cells.

d. The cost of the box is determined by looking up the cubic feet value in a lookup table. Use the table at **cells H25:J30** with a **VLOOKUP function** to determine the cost of a box. Remember to use absolute references for the table and copy the formula to the remaining cells in column I.

e. Use the table at **cells H25:J30** with a **VLOOKUP function** to determine the shipping cost. Remember to use absolute references for the table and copy the formula to the remaining cells in column J.

f. Calculate the total cost of insurance, box, and shipping. Copy the formula down column K. Save the workbook.

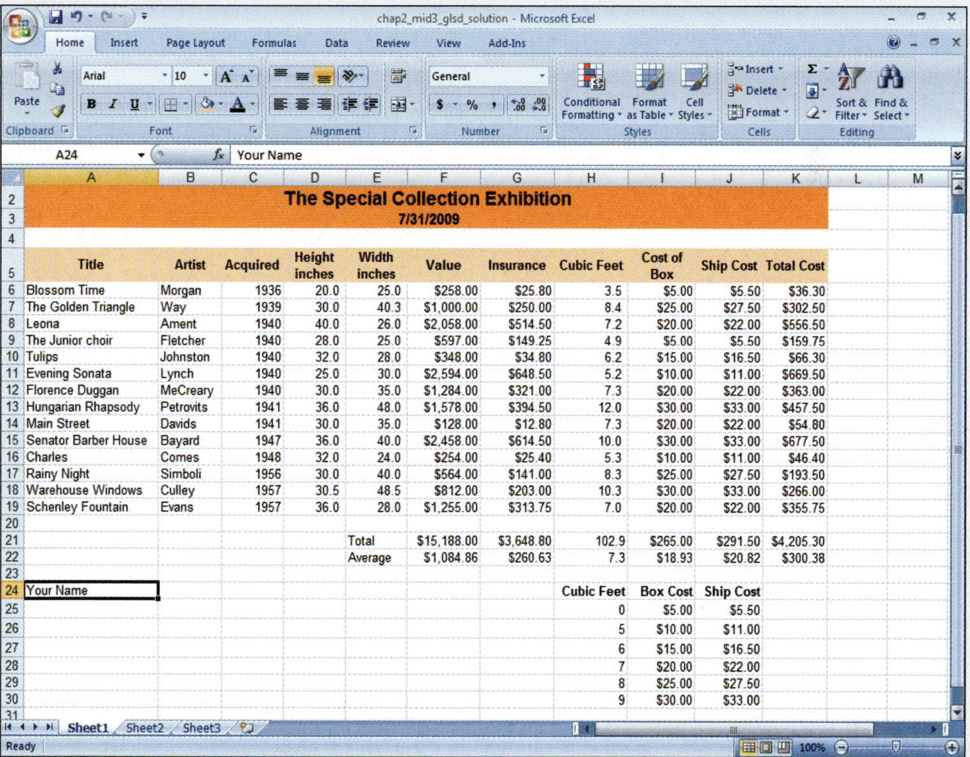

The Special Collection Exhibition

7/31/2009

Title	Artist	Acquired	Height inches	Width inches	Value	Insurance	Cubic Feet	Cost of Box	Ship Cost	Total Cost
Blossom Time	Morgan	1936	20.0	25.0	$258.00	$25.80	3.5	$5.00	$5.50	$36.30
The Golden Triangle	Way	1939	30.0	40.3	$1,000.00	$250.00	8.4	$25.00	$27.50	$302.50
Leona	Ament	1940	40.0	26.0	$2,058.00	$514.50	7.2	$20.00	$22.00	$556.50
The Junior choir	Fletcher	1940	28.0	25.0	$597.00	$149.25	4.9	$5.00	$5.50	$159.75
Tulips	Johnston	1940	32.0	28.0	$348.00	$34.80	6.2	$15.00	$16.50	$66.30
Evening Sonata	Lynch	1940	25.0	30.0	$2,594.00	$648.50	5.2	$10.00	$11.00	$669.50
Florence Duggan	MeCreary	1940	30.0	35.0	$1,284.00	$321.00	7.3	$20.00	$22.00	$363.00
Hungarian Rhapsody	Petrovits	1941	36.0	48.0	$1,578.00	$394.50	12.0	$30.00	$33.00	$457.50
Main Street	Davids	1941	30.0	35.0	$128.00	$12.80	7.3	$20.00	$22.00	$54.80
Senator Barber House	Bayard	1947	36.0	40.0	$2,458.00	$614.50	10.0	$30.00	$33.00	$677.50
Charles	Comes	1948	32.0	24.0	$254.00	$25.40	5.3	$10.00	$11.00	$46.40
Rainy Night	Simboli	1956	30.0	40.0	$564.00	$141.00	8.3	$25.00	$27.50	$193.50
Warehouse Windows	Culley	1957	30.5	48.5	$812.00	$203.00	10.3	$30.00	$33.00	$266.00
Schenley Fountain	Evans	1957	36.0	28.0	$1,255.00	$313.75	7.0	$20.00	$22.00	$355.75
				Total	$15,188.00	$3,648.80	102.9	$265.00	$291.50	$4,205.30
				Average	$1,084.86	$260.63	7.3	$18.93	$20.82	$300.38

Your Name

Cubic Feet	Box Cost	Ship Cost
0	$5.00	$5.50
5	$10.00	$11.00
6	$15.00	$16.50
7	$20.00	$22.00
8	$25.00	$27.50
9	$30.00	$33.00

Figure 2.25 Art Collection

...continued on Next Page

g. Use the **SUM function** in **cell F21** to compute the total value of the art collection. Copy the formula to the remaining cells in the row. Use the **AVERAGE function** in **cell F22** to compute the average value of a painting. Copy the formula to the remaining cells in the row.

h. Format the worksheet in an attractive manner but similar to Figure 2.25, making sure to display all dollar amounts with the currency symbol and two decimal places. Display height, width, and cubic feet with one decimal place. Use a date function to display the current date in **cell A3**.

i. Enter your name in **cell A24** and print the worksheet twice, once with displayed values, and once to show cell formulas. Use the Page Setup command to switch to landscape orientation and force the output onto one page. Print gridlines and row and column headings. Save and close the workbook.

4 Financial Functions

Your accounting professor has asked you to create a worksheet that compares interest rates and monthly payments over different time periods. Figure 2.26 is an example of how Excel is used to compare interest rates and monthly payments over different time periods. You will create this worksheet and use financial functions with relative, absolute, and mixed references.

a. Begin a new workbook by typing the following in the cells indicated:

Cell	Value
A1	Amount Borrowed
A2	Starting Interest
A5	Interest
B5	30 Years
C5	15 Years
D5	Difference
D1	100000
D2	.075
A13	Assumptions
A14	30 years
A15	15 years
B14	30
B15	15
A16	Financial Consultant
A17	Your Name

b. Save the workbook as **chap2_mid4_financial_solution**.

c. To copy the interest rate and then use it in a formula, enter the formula **=D2** in **cell A6** and enter the formula **=A6+.01** in **cell A7**. Copy the formula into **cells A8:A11**.

d. Calculate the payment for 30 years in **cell B6**. Make sure to use an absolute reference for **B14** and **D1**. Copy the formula down the column, **B7:B11**.

e. Calculate the payment for 15 years in **cell C6**. Remember to use an absolute reference for **B15** and copy the formula down the column, **C7:C11**. If any cell displays a series of #####, use AutoFit to widen the column.

...continued on Next Page

f. Calculate the difference between 15 years and 30 years in cell D6 and copy the formula down the column, **D7:D11**.

g. Format the worksheet in an attractive manner but similar to Figure 2.26, making sure to display all dollar amounts with the currency symbol and two decimal places. Use a date function to display the current date in **cell A19.**

h. Print the worksheet twice, once with displayed values, and once to show cell formulas. Use the Page Setup command to switch to landscape orientation and force the output onto one page. Print gridlines and row and column headings. Save and close the workbook.

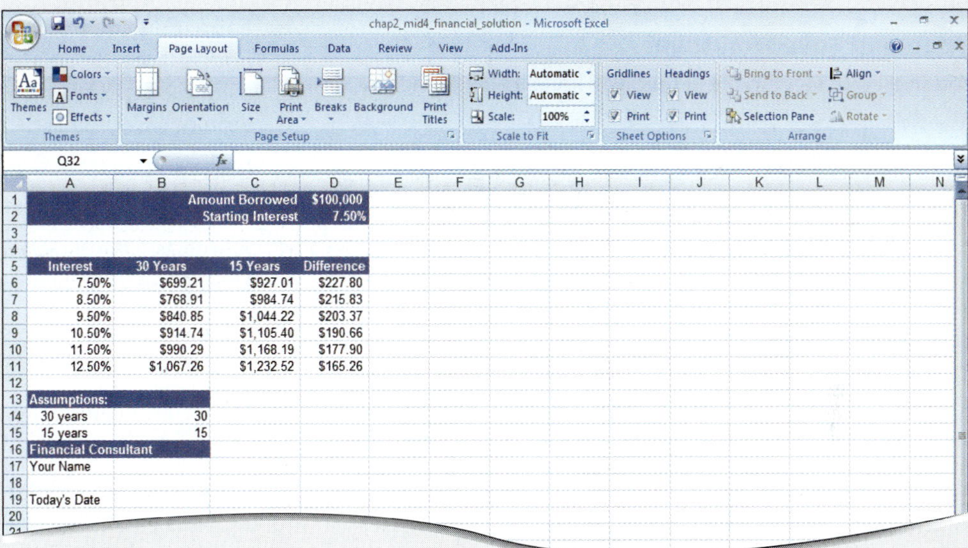

Figure 2.26 Financial Functions

Capstone Exercise

You are an intern at the First National Bank working in the loan department, and your boss has asked you to prepare the monthly "New Loan Report" for the Board of Directors. This analysis report will clearly list and summarize all new loans for residential housing in the past month. The summary area includes the loan statistics as labeled in the data file. The format of the report is appropriate for the Board of Directors for the First National Bank.

Open and Save Worksheet

You must open a worksheet that lists housing sales and finish it to complete the capstone exercise.

a. Open the file *chap2_cap_housing*.

b. Save it as **chap2_cap_housing_solution**.

c. Enter your name in **cell B28**.

Calculate Values

Functions are used to calculate the interest rate, down payment, monthly payment, and average selling price for each residential home in the worksheet. You need to create a formula to determine the down payment. Finish the calculations by using the appropriate functions to complete the Loan Statistics summary area of the worksheet.

a. Use a VLOOKUP function to determine the interest rates in column D. The interest rate is based on the term of the loan.

b. Calculate the down payment in column E. Use a VLOOKUP function to look up the term of the loan to return the percentage required for the down payment. That percentage is then multiplied by the selling price.

c. Calculate the amount financed by subtracting the down payment from the selling price. Enter the formula in column F.

d. Use a PMT function to determine the monthly payment in column G.

e. Copy all formulas as appropriate.

f. Use an AVERAGE function to calculate the average selling price in **cell B13**.

g. Use appropriate functions to determine the statistics in **cells C22:C26**.

h. Enter the TODAY function in **cell B27**.

Format the Worksheet

Now that you have finished the calculations, you must format the worksheet in a professional manner and suitable for presentation to the Board of Directors of the bank.

a. Format all money figures as currency with two decimal places. Remember to format the Loan Statistics summary figures.

b. Format the interest rates in percent style with two decimal places. Format column D and the data table columns used in the VLOOKUP functions as percent with two decimals.

c. Insert an image appropriate for a bank and representative of the housing market.

d. Apply **White, Background 1, Darker 25%** fill color, **Dark Blue** font color, and bold to the data on row 6.

e. Widen columns to display the headings but wrap the text in columns F and G. Center all column headings.

f. Merge and center the title of the report. Apply dark blue font color to the title and headings.

g. Apply thick horizontal bottom borders to rows 2, 3, 12, 17, 18, 20, and 21. Apply thin horizontal borders for the customer rows and loan term rows.

Print the Report

Before printing the report, you see it is missing the standard headers and should be printed in the landscape orientation to fit on one page.

a. Create a custom header with your name on the left and your instructor's name on the right.

b. Change the page orientation to landscape.

c. Print the worksheet with displayed values.

d. Print the worksheet again with cell formulas but make sure to fit the worksheet on one sheet.

e. Save your changes and close the workbook.

Mini Cases

Use the rubric following the case as a guide to evaluate your work, but keep in mind that your instructor may impose additional grading criteria or use a different standard to judge your work.

Corporate Salary Summary

GENERAL CASE

As a recent graduate and newly hired employee at the JAS Corporation, you are asked to complete the Annual Salary Summary Report. You are to open the *chap2_mc1_salary* workbook, save it as **chap2_mc1_salary_solution**, and complete the worksheet. You will AutoFill the months as headings, and calculate deductions, totals, and net salaries for each month. Format the worksheet for the corporate environment, making sure to use currency, no decimal places, and commas as well as percent symbols with two decimal places. Include your name in the worksheet and print displayed values and cell formulas. Close the workbook.

Performance Elements	Exceeds Expectations	Meets Expectations	Below Expectations
Create formulas	All formulas work and most efficiently stated.	Formulas are correct.	No formulas, numbers entered.
Use functions	All functions entered correctly.	One function incorrectly used.	No functions used, numbers entered.
Attractive, appropriate format	Well formatted and easy to read.	Adequately formatted, difficult to read.	No formatting.
Printing	Printed correct range and widened columns for cell formulas.	Printed correct range but did not widen columns.	Printed once (missing formula copy or worksheet copy).

Investment Club

RESEARCH CASE

As treasurer of your investment club, you must update the monthly statement for the members. Open *chap2_mc2_investment*, save it as **chap2_mc2_investment_solution**, and use the Web to find the current price per share for each of the listed stocks. Complete the worksheet, formatting as appropriate to fit on one sheet. Enter your name as treasurer, the current date as a function formatted as mm/dd/yyyy, and print displayed values as well as cell formulas, making sure to fit on one page. Close the workbook.

Performance Elements	Exceeds Expecations	Meets Expectations	Below Expectations
Research current price	All current stock prices found.	Missing two current prices.	No current prices.
Create formulas and functions	All formulas and functions correctly applied.	Two or more formulas and functions incorrectly applied.	No formulas or functions applied.
Format attractively for analysis use	Easy to read and analyze date on single sheet.	Difficult to read; lining up multiple sheets.	Lack of formatting hinders analysis.
Print values and cell formulas on one sheet	Printed correct range and widened columns for cell formulas.	Printed correct range but did not widen columns.	Printed once (missing formula copy or worksheet copy).

Peer Tutoring

DISASTER RECOVERY

As part of your service-learning project, you volunteered to tutor students in Excel. Open the spreadsheet *chap2_mc3_tutoring*, save it as **chap2_mc3_tutoring_solution**, and find five errors. Correct the errors and explain how the errors might have occurred and how they can be prevented. Include your explanation in the cells below the spreadsheet. Close the workbook.

Performance Elements	Exceeds Expectations	Meets Expectations	Below Expectations
Identify five errors	Identified all five errors.	Identified four errors.	Identified three or fewer errors.
Correct five errors	Corrected all five errors.	Corrected four errors.	Corrected three or fewer errors.
Explain the error	Complete and correct explanation of each error.	Explanation is too brief to fully explain errors.	No explanations.
Prevention description	Prevention description correct and practical.	Prevention description but obtuse.	No prevention description.

Charts

Delivering a Message

After you read this chapter, you will be able to:

1. Choose a chart type (**page 431**).
2. Create a chart (**page 438**).
3. Modify a chart (**page 450**).
4. Enhance charts with graphic shapes (**page 453**).
5. Embed charts (**page 459**).
6. Print charts (**page 460**).

Hands-On Exercises

Exercises	Skills Covered
1. THE FIRST CHART (page 443) **Open:** chap3_ho1_sales.xlsx **Save as:** chap3_ho1_sales_solution.xlsx	• Use AutoSum • Create the Chart • Complete the Chart • Move and Size the Chart • Change the Worksheet • Change the Chart Type • Create a Second Chart
2. MULTIPLE DATA SERIES (page 454) **Open:** chap3_ho1_sales_solution.xlsx (from Exercise 1) **Save as:** chap3_ho2_sales_solution.xlsx (additional modifications)	• Rename the Worksheet • Create Chart with Multiple Data Series • Copy the Chart • Change the Source Data • Change the Chart Type • Insert a Graphic Shape and Add a Text Box
3. EMBEDDING, PRINTING, AND SAVING A CHART AS A WEB PAGE (page 462) **Open:** chap3_ho2_sales_solution.xlsx (from Exercise 2) and chap3_ho3_memo.docx **Save as:** chap3_ho3_sales_solution.xlsx (additional modifications) and chap_ho3_memo_solution.docx	• Embed a Chart in Microsoft Word • Copy the Worksheet • Embed the Data • Copy the Chart • Embed the Chart • Modify the Worksheet • Update the Links • Print Worksheet and Chart • Save and View Chart as Web Page

CASE STUDY

The Changing Student Population

Case Study

Congratulations! You have just been hired as a student intern in the Admissions Office. Helen Dwyer, the dean of admissions, has asked you to start tomorrow morning to help her prepare for an upcoming presentation with the Board of Trustees in which she will report on enrollment trends over the past four years. Daytime enrollments have been steady, whereas enrollments in evening and distance (online) learning are increasing significantly. Dean Dwyer has asked for a chart(s) to summarize the data. She also would like your thoughts on what impact (if any) the Internet and the trend toward lifelong learning have had on the college population. The dean has asked you to present the information in the form of a memo addressed to the Board of Trustees with the data and graph embedded onto that page.

Dean Dwyer will be presenting her findings on "The Changing Student Population" to the Board of Trustees in two weeks. She will speak briefly and then open the floor for questions and discussion among the group. She has invited you to the meeting to answer specific questions pertaining to these trends from a student's perspective. This is an outstanding opportunity for you to participate with a key group of individuals who support the university. Be prepared to present yourself appropriately!

Your Assignment

- Read the chapter carefully and pay close attention to sections that demonstrate chart creation, chart formatting, and chart printing.
- Open the workbook *chap3_case_enrollment*, which has the enrollment statistics partially completed. You will save your workbook as **chap3_case_enrollment_solution**.
- When you review the workbook, think about the mathematical operations, formulas, and functions you would use to complete the worksheet. You will create formulas and functions to calculate annual totals and type of course totals. You also will format cells appropriately: use numbers with commas, merge and center the title, use an attractive fill color, and increase font sizes for improved readability.
- As you read the chapter, pay particular attention to the types of charts that are discussed. Some are more appropriate for presenting enrollment data than others. You will use your understanding of chart methods to determine the most appropriate charts used with the enrollment data. You will create charts to emphasize enrollment data on separate sheets. Remember to format the charts for a professional presentation that includes titles, legends, and data labels.
- As part of your presentation, you also must consider the preparation of a memo describing the enrollment information presented both in the worksheet and in the chart. The worksheet and the charts will be embedded in the final memo. The memo in Microsoft Word will summarize your enrollment data findings and include the embedded worksheet and charts. Open *chap3_case_enrollment* in Word.
- Remember that you will present the information to the university Board of Trustees, and the trustees will expect a professional, polished report. Save the memo as **chap3_case_enrollment_solution** after creating custom footers that include the page number, your name, and your instructor's name. Print the memo, the worksheet, and the charts.

A Picture Is the Message

A *chart* is a graphic representation of data.

A picture really is worth a thousand words. Excel makes it easy to create a *chart*, which is a graphic or visual representation of data. Once data is displayed in a chart, the options to enhance the information for more visual appeal and ease of analysis are almost unlimited. Because large amounts of data are available, using graphical analysis is valuable to discover what messages are hidden in the data.

In this chapter, you learn the importance of determining the message to be conveyed by a chart. You select the type of chart that best presents your message. You create and modify a chart, enhance a chart with a shape, plot multiple sets of data, embed a chart in a worksheet, and create a chart in a separate chart sheet. You enhance a chart by creating lines, objects, and 3-D shapes. The second half of the chapter explains how to create a compound document, in which a chart and its associated worksheet are dynamically linked to a memo created in Word.

In this section, you learn chart terminology and how to choose a chart type based on your needs. For example, you learn when to use a column chart and when to use a pie chart. You select the range of cells containing the numerical values and labels from which to create the chart, choose the chart type, insert the chart, and designate the chart's location.

Choosing a Chart Type

Managers know that a graphic representation of data is an attractive, clear way to convey information. Business graphics are one of the most exciting Windows applications, where charts (graphs) are created in a straightforward manner from a worksheet with just a few keystrokes or mouse clicks.

A *data point* is a numeric value that describes a single item on a chart.

A *data series* is a group of related data points.

A *category label* describes a group of data points in a chart.

A chart is based on numeric values in the cells called *data points*. For example, a data point might be the database sales for Milwaukee. A group of related data points that appear in row(s) or column(s) in the worksheet create a *data series*. For example, a data series might be a collection of database data points for four different cities. In every data series, exactly one data point is connected to a numerical value contained in a cell. Textual information, such as column and row headings (cities, months, years, product names, etc.), are used for descriptive entries called *category labels*.

The worksheet in Figure 3.1 is used throughout the chapter as the basis for the charts you create. As you can see from the worksheet, the company sells different types of software programs, and it has sales in four cities. You believe that the sales numbers are more easily grasped when they are presented graphically instead of only relying on the numbers. You need to develop a series of charts to convey the sales numbers.

	Transylvania Software Sales					
2						
3		Milwaukee	Buffalo	Harrisburg	Pittsburgh	Total
4	Word Processing	$50,000	$67,500	$200,000	$141,000	$458,500
5	Spreadsheets	$44,000	$18,000	$11,500	$105,000	$178,500
6	Database	$12,000	$7,500	$6,000	$30,000	$55,500
7	Total	$106,000	$93,000	$217,500	$276,000	

Figure 3.1 Worksheet for Charts

The sales data in the worksheet can be presented in several ways—for example, by city, by product, or by a combination of the two. Determine which type of chart is best suited to answer the following questions:

- What percentage of the total revenue comes from each city? What percentage comes from each product?
- How much revenue is produced by each city? What is the revenue for each product?

- What is the rank of each city with respect to sales?
- How much revenue does each product produce in each city?

> . . . you cannot create an effective chart unless you are sure of what that message is.

In every instance, realize that a chart exists only to deliver a message and that *you cannot create an effective chart unless you are sure of what that message is*. The next several pages discuss various types of charts, each of which is best suited to a particular type of message. After you understand how charts are used conceptually, you will create various charts in Excel.

Create Column Charts

A ***column chart*** displays data comparisons vertically in columns.

The ***X or horizontal axis*** depicts categorical labels.

The ***Y or vertical axis*** depicts numerical values.

The ***plot area*** contains graphical representation of values in data series.

The ***chart area*** contains the entire chart and all of its elements.

A ***column chart*** displays data vertically in a column formation and is used to compare values across different categories. Figure 3.2 shows total revenue by geographic area based on the worksheet data from Figure 3.1. The category labels represented by cities stored in cells B3:E3 are shown along the ***X or horizontal axis***, whereas the data points representing total monthly sales stored in cells B7:E7 are shown along the ***Y or vertical axis***. The height of each column represents the value of the individual data points. The ***plot area*** of a chart is the area containing the graphical representation of the values in a data series. The ***chart area*** contains the entire chart and all of its elements.

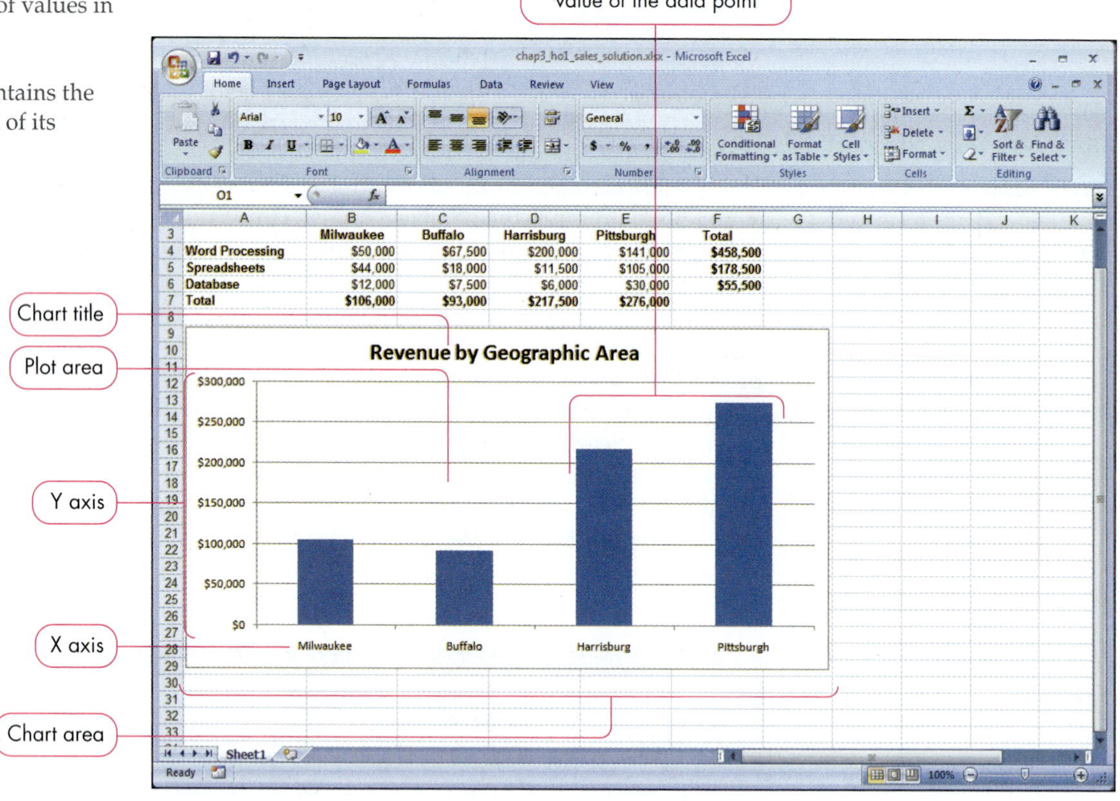

Figure 3.2 Column Chart Depicting Revenue by Geographic Area

Different types of column charts can be created to add interest or clarify the data representation. Figure 3.3 is an example of a three-dimensional (3-D) column chart. The 3-D charts present a more dynamic representation of data, as this chart demonstrates. However, the 3-D column chart is sometimes misleading. Professors often discourage students from using 3-D charts because the charts do not clearly communicate the data—the third dimension distorts data. In 3-D column charts some columns appear taller or smaller than they really are because they are either somewhat behind or at an angle to other columns. See Figure 3.3 for an example of this. For example, the Milwaukee total is $106,000, but the 3-D column chart makes it appear less than $100,000.

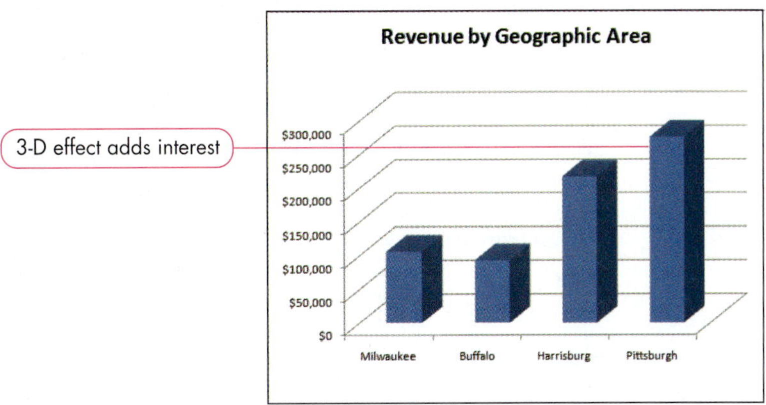

Figure 3.3 Three-Dimensional Column Chart

A ***multiple data series*** compares two or more sets of data in one chart.

Another example of the use of column charts is to compare ***multiple data series***—two or more data series—on the same chart. The concept of charting multiple data series will be discussed later in the chapter, but this concept involves the use of clustered column charts.

A ***clustered column chart*** groups similar data in columns, making visual comparison easier to determine.

A ***stacked column chart*** places (stacks) data in one column with each data series a different color for each category.

The choice of clustered versus stacked column charts depends on the intended message. If you want the audience to see the individual sales in each city or product category, the clustered column chart in Figure 3.4 is more appropriate. If, on the other hand, you want to emphasize the total sales for each city or product category, the stacked columns are preferable. The advantage of the stacked column is that the totals are shown clearly and can be compared easily. The disadvantage is that the segments within each column do not start at the same point, making it difficult to determine the actual sales for the individual categories. ***Clustered column charts*** group similar data together in columns making visual comparison of the data easier to determine. ***Stacked column charts*** place similar data in one column with each data series a different color. The effect emphasizes the total of the data series.

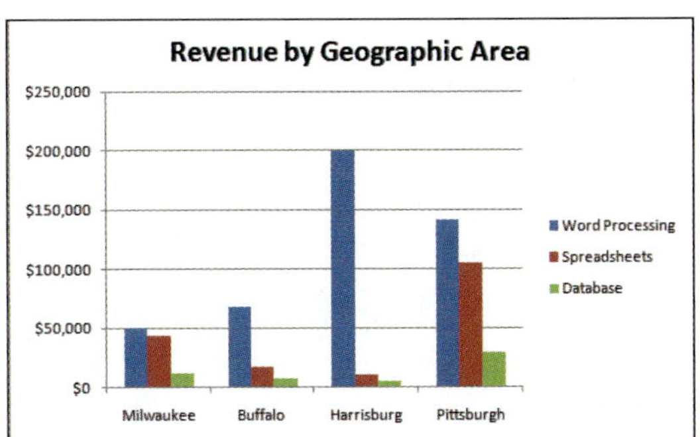

Figure 3.4 Clustered Column Chart

The scale on the Y axis is different for charts with clustered columns versus charts with stacked columns. The clustered columns in Figure 3.4 show the sales of each product category and so the Y axis goes to $250,000. The stacked columns in Figure 3.5 reflect the total sales for all products in each city, and thus the scale goes to $300,000. For a stacked column chart to make sense, its numbers must be additive. You would not convert a column chart that plots units and dollar sales side by side to a stacked column chart, because units and dollars are not additive, that is, you cannot add products and revenue. The chart in Figure 3.5 also displays a legend on the right side of the chart. A ***legend*** identifies the format or color of the data used for each series in a chart.

A ***legend*** identifies the format or color of each data series.

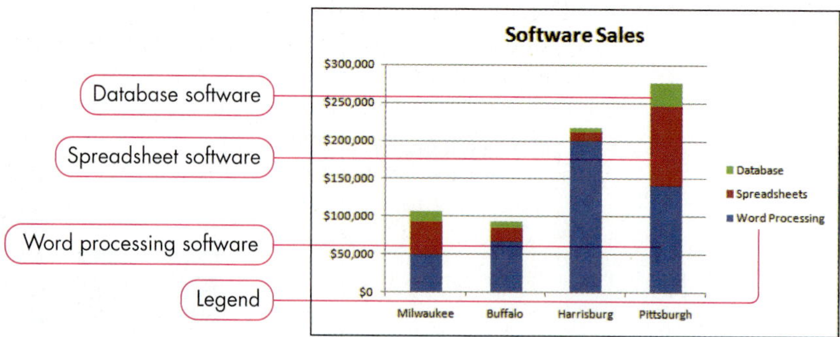

Figure 3.5 Stacked Columns

Column charts are most effective when they are limited to small numbers of categories—generally seven or fewer. If more categories exist, they end up being plotted so close together that reading and labeling become difficult or impossible.

Create a Bar Chart

A ***bar chart*** is a column chart that has been given a horizontal orientation.

A ***bar chart*** is basically a column chart that has a horizontal orientation as shown in Figure 3.6. Many people prefer this representation because it emphasizes the difference between items. Further, long descriptive labels are easier to read in a bar chart than in a column chart. Sorting the data points either from lowest to highest or highest to lowest makes a bar chart even more effective. The most basic bar chart is a clustered bar chart.

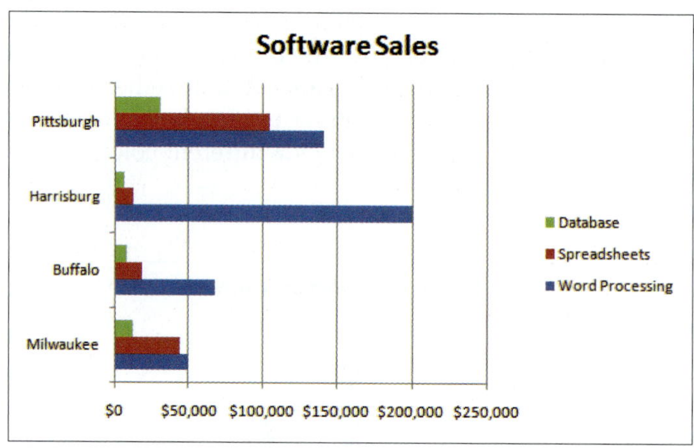

Figure 3.6 Clustered Bar Chart

TIP Keep It Simple

This rule applies to both your message and the means of conveying that message. Excel makes it easy to change fonts, styles, the shape of columns, type sizes, and colors, but such changes often detract from rather than enhance a chart. More is not necessarily better, and you do not have to use a feature just because it is there. A chart must ultimately succeed based on content alone.

Create a Pie Chart

A ***pie chart*** displays proportional relationships.

A ***pie chart*** is the most effective way to display proportional relationships. It is the type of chart to select whenever words like *percentage* or *market share* appear in the message to be delivered. The pie, or complete circle, denotes the total amount. Each slice of the pie corresponds to its respective percentage of the total.

The pie chart in Figure 3.7 divides the pie representing total sales into four slices, one for each city. The size of each slice is proportional to the percentage of total sales in that city. The chart depicts a single data series, which appears in cells B7:E7 on the associated worksheet. The data series has four data points corresponding to the total sales in each city. The data labels are placed in the wedges if they fit. If they do not fit, they are placed outside the wedge with a line pointing to the appropriate wedge.

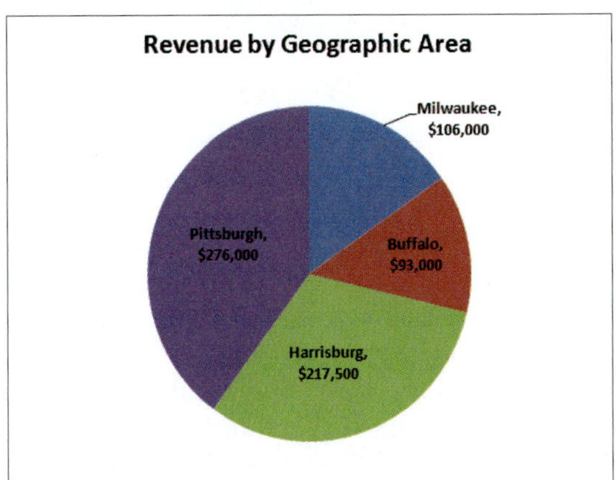

Figure 3.7 Pie Chart Showing Values

To create the pie chart, Excel computes the total sales ($692,500 in our example), calculates the percentage contributed by each city, and draws each slice of the pie in proportion to its computed percentage. Pittsburgh's sales of $276,000 account for 40% of the total, so this slice of the pie is allotted 40% of the area of the circle.

An ***exploded pie chart*** separates one or more slices of the pie chart for emphasis.

An ***exploded pie chart***, shown in Figure 3.8, separates one or more slices of the pie for emphasis. Another way to achieve emphasis in a chart is to choose a title that reflects the message you are trying to deliver. The title in Figure 3.7, *Revenue by Geographic Area*, is neutral and leaves the reader to develop his or her own conclusion about the relative contribution of each area. In contrast, the title in Figure 3.8, *Buffalo Accounts for Only 13% of the Revenue*, is more suggestive and emphasizes the problems in this office. The title could be changed to *Pittsburgh Exceeds 40% of Total Revenue* if the intent were to emphasize the contribution of Pittsburgh.

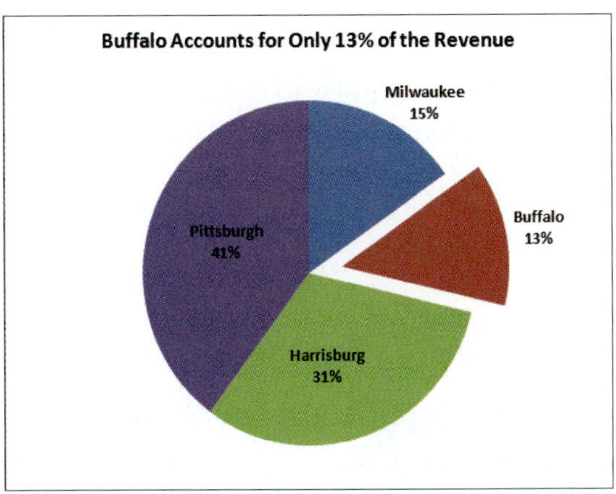

Figure 3.8 Pie Chart Showing Percentages

A ***three-dimensional pie chart*** is a pie chart that contains a three-dimensional view.

Three-dimensional pie charts may be created in exploded or unexploded format. See Figure 3.9 for an example of an unexploded pie chart. The 3-D chart is misleading because it appears as though the Harrisburg slice is larger than the Pittsburgh slice. This difference is why 3-D charts are seldom used. A pie chart is easiest to read when the number of slices is small (for example, not more than six or seven), and when small categories (percentages less than five) are grouped into a single category called *Other*.

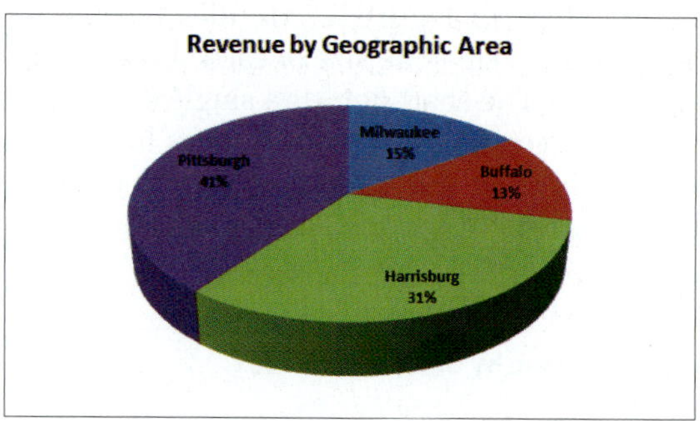

Figure 3.9 Three-Dimensional Pie Chart

Create a Line Chart

A *line chart* uses a line to connect data points in order to show trends over a long period of time.

A *line chart* shows trends over a period of time. A line connects data points. A line chart is used frequently to show stock market or economic trends. The X axis represents time, such as ten-year increments, whereas the vertical axis represents the value of a stock or quantity. The line chart enables a user to easily spot trends in the data. Figure 3.10 shows a line chart with yearly increments for four years.

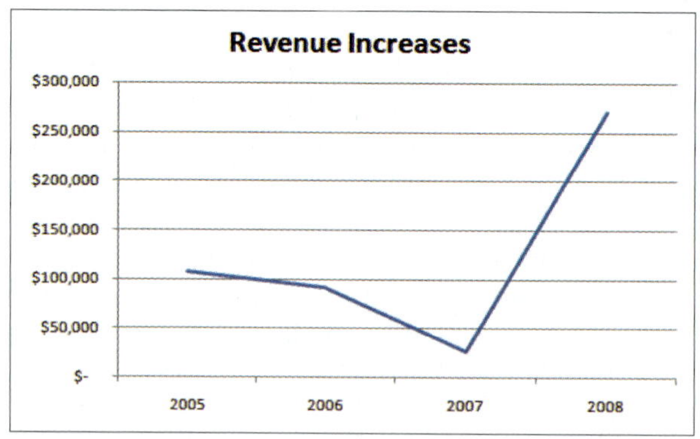

Figure 3.10 Line Chart

Create Other Chart Types

A *doughnut chart* displays values as percentages of the whole.

The *doughnut chart* is similar to a pie chart in that it shows relationship of parts to a whole, but the doughnut chart can display more than one series of data, and it has a hole in the middle (see Figure 3.11). Chart designers sometimes use the doughnut hole for titles. Each ring represents a data series. Note, however, the display of the data series in a doughnut chart can be confusing.

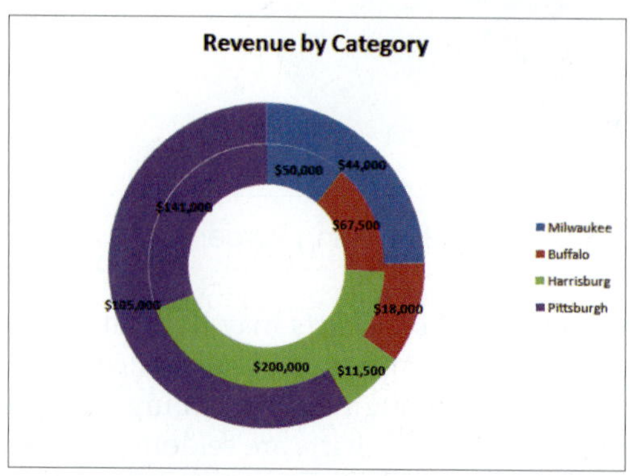

Figure 3.11 Doughnut Chart

A *scatter (XY) chart* shows a relationship between two variables.

A *scatter (XY) chart* shows a relationship between two variables. Scatter charts are used to represent the data from scientific or educational experiments that demonstrate relationships. A scatter chart is essentially the plotted dots without any connecting line. A scatter chart is used to determine if a relationship exists between two different sets of numerical data. If you plot people's wages and educational levels, you can see if a relationship between wages and education levels exists. Figure 3.12 shows a comparison of temperature over time. As the month of April passes, the temperatures rise. However, higher- and lower-than-normal temperatures affect the trend.

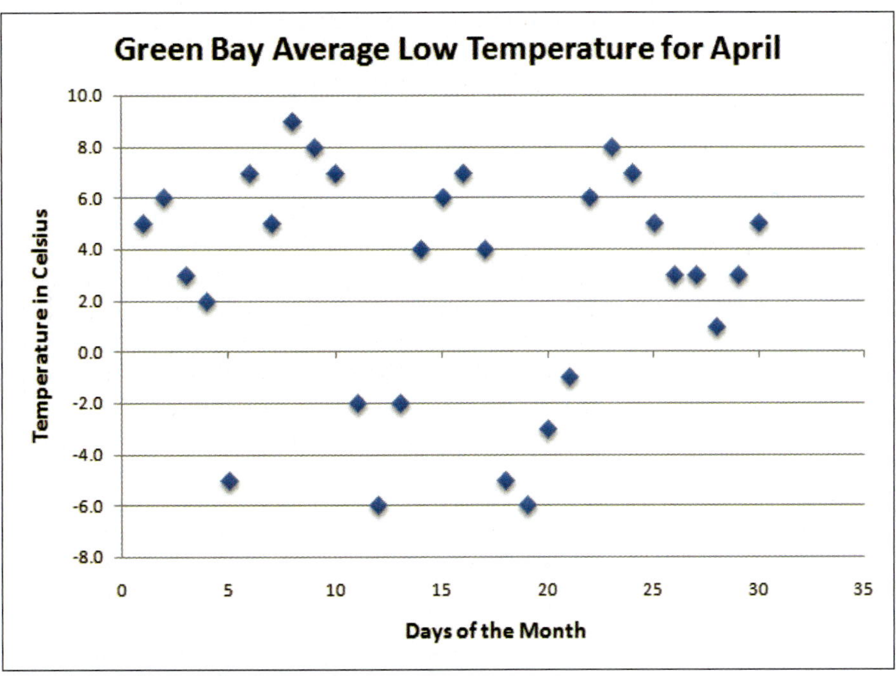

Figure 3.12 Scatter Chart

A *stock chart* shows the high, low, and close prices for individual stocks over a period of time.

Stock charts have only one major purpose: to show the high, low, and close prices for individual stocks over a period of time. While stock charts may have some other uses, such as showing a range of temperatures over a period of time, they usually are used to show stock prices. Figure 3.13 shows a stock chart that displays opening stock price, high stock price, low stock price, and closing stock price over a period of time.

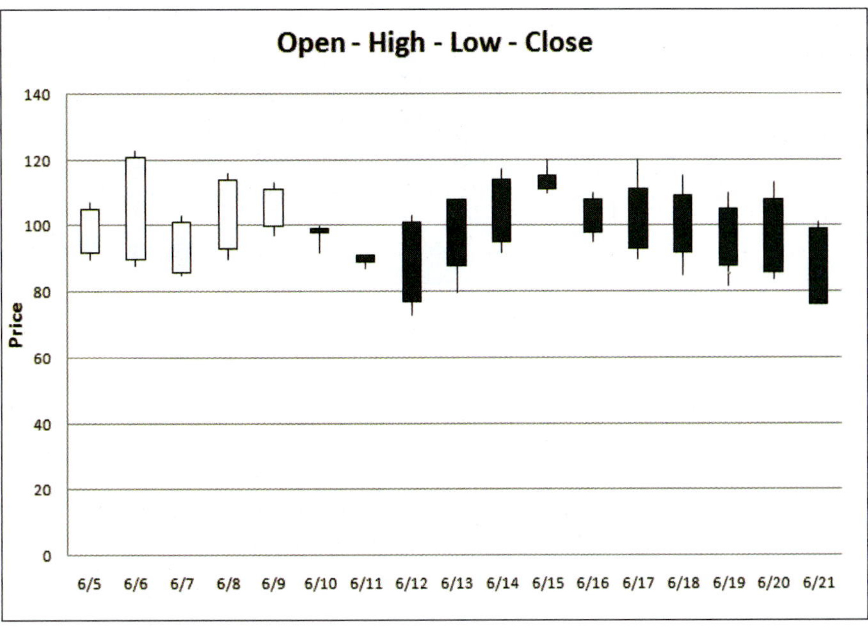

Figure 3.13 Stock Chart

Creating a Chart

Creating a chart in Excel is quick. Excel provides a variety of chart types that you can use when you create a chart. The main types of charts are described above. The six main steps to create a chart are the following:

1. Specify the data series.
2. Select the range of cells to chart.
3. Select the chart type.
4. Insert the chart and designate the chart location.
5. Choose chart options.
6. Change the chart location and size.

Specify the Data Series

For most charts, such as column and bar charts, you can plot the data in a chart that you have arranged in rows or columns on a worksheet. Some chart types, however, such as a pie chart, require a specific data arrangement. On the worksheet, select the data you want to plot as a pie chart, then select pie from the types of charts available.

The charts presented so far in the chapter displayed only a single data series, such as the total sales by location or the total sales by product category. Although such charts are useful, it is often more informative to view multiple data series, which are ranges of data values plotted as a unit in the same chart. Figure 3.14 displays the worksheet we have been using throughout the chapter. Figure 3.4 displays a clustered column chart that plots multiple data series that exist as rows (cells B4:E4, B5:E5, and B6:E6) within the worksheet. Figure 3.14 displays a chart based on the same data when the series are in columns (cells B4:B6, C4:C6, D4:D6, and E4:E6).

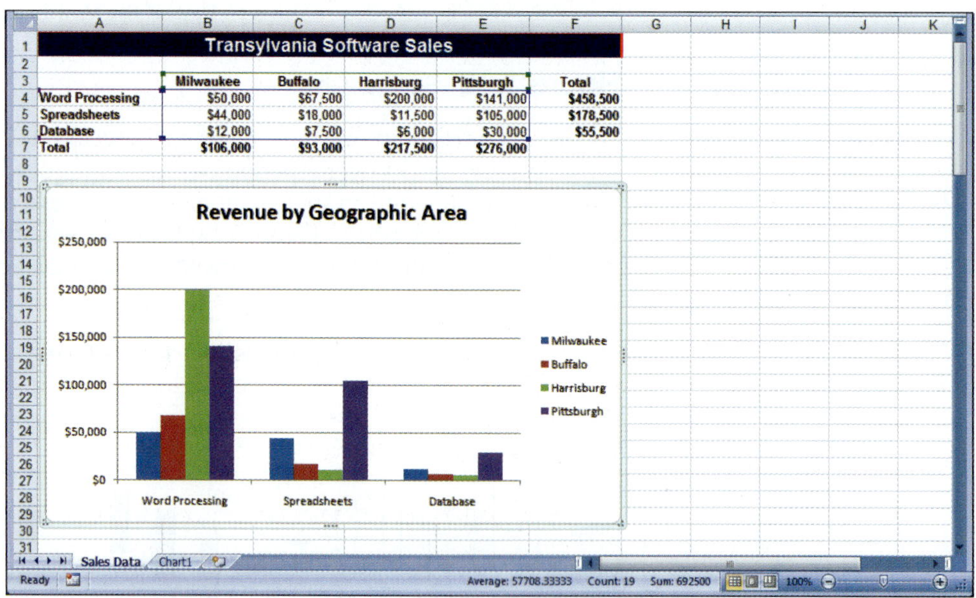

Figure 3.14 Clustered Column with Multiple Data Series as Columns

Both charts plot a total of 12 data points (three product categories for each of four locations), but they group the data differently. Figure 3.4 displays the data by city in which the sales of three product categories are shown for each of four cities. Figure 3.14 is the reverse and groups the data by product category. This time the sales in the four cities are shown for each of three product categories. The choice between the two charts depends on your message and whether you want to emphasize revenue by city or by product category. You should create the chart according to your intended purpose.

Figure 3.15 shows two charts. The one on the left plots data series in the cells B4:E4, B5:E5, and B6:E6, whereas the chart on the right plots the same data series but

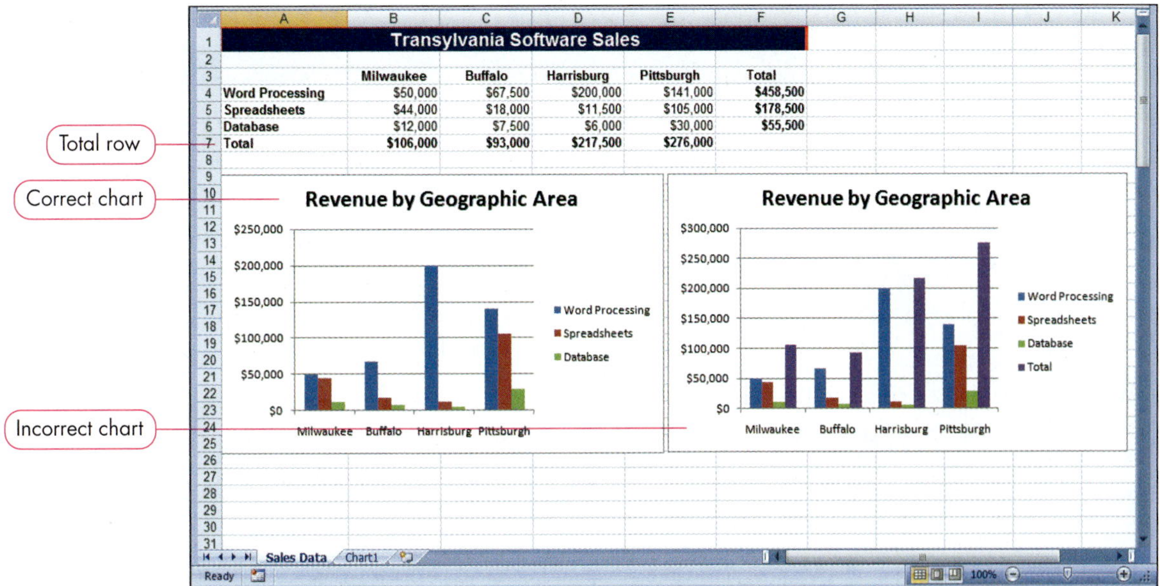

Figure 3.15

includes B7:E7, which is the total for all products. Including the total row figures (or column total figures) dramatically skews the chart, presents a misleading picture, and indicates you have selected an incorrect range for your chart. Do NOT include totals and individual data points on the same chart.

Select the Range to Chart

Too often Excel users do not put any thought into the data they select for a chart. Selecting the correct data goes hand-in-hand with having a plan for what a chart should display. For example, a user would not want to show totals in column totals that represent only several months. Even though it is a simple process to deselect cells once they have been selected, users should have a plan before selecting cells for a chart.

Table 3.1 describes different techniques for selecting cells.

Select the Chart Type

After you select the range of cells that you want to chart, your next step is to select the type of chart you want to create. Each type of chart is designed to visually illustrate a particular type of data. Table 3.2 lists the different types of charts and their purposes. Use this table as a guide for selecting the type of chart you want to use for the worksheet data.

In the Charts group on the Insert tab, do one of the following:

1. Click the chart type, and then click a chart subtype that you want to use.
2. To see all available chart types, click a chart type, and then click All Chart Types to display the Create Chart dialog box.
3. Click the arrows to scroll through all available chart types and chart subtypes, and then click the one that you want to use.

Insert the Chart and Designate the Chart Location

Excel places the chart as an embedded object on the current worksheet. You can leave the chart on the same worksheet as the worksheet data used to create the chart, or you can place the chart in a separate chart sheet. If you leave the chart in the same worksheet, you can print the worksheet and chart on the same page. If you want to print a full-sized chart, you can move the chart to its own chart sheet.

Table 3.1 Cell Selection Techniques

To Select	Do This
A single cell	Click the cell, or press the arrow keys to move to the cell.
A range of cells	Click the first cell in the range, and then drag to the last cell, or hold down Shift while you press the arrow keys to extend the selection. You also can select the first cell in the range, and then press F8 to extend the selection by using the arrow keys. To stop extending the selection, press F8 again.
A large range of cells	Click the first cell in the range, and then hold down Shift while you click the last cell in the range. You can scroll to make the last cell visible.
All cells on a worksheet	Click the Select All button. To select the entire worksheet, you also can press Ctrl+A.
Nonadjacent cells or cell ranges	Select the first cell or range of cells, and then hold down Ctrl while you select the other cells or ranges. You can also select the first cell or range of cells, and then press Shift+F8 to add another nonadjacent cell or range to the selection. To stop adding cells or ranges to the selection, press Shift+F8 again.
An entire row or column	Click the row or column heading. You can also select cells in a row or column by selecting the first cell and then pressing Ctrl+Shift+Arrow key (Right Arrow or Left Arrow for rows, Up Arrow or Down Arrow for columns).
Adjacent rows or columns	Drag across the row or column headings. Or select the first row or column, then hold down Shift while you select the last row or column.
Noncontiguous rows or columns	Click the column or row heading of the first row or column in your selection, then hold down Ctrl while you click the column or row headings of other rows or columns that you want to add to the selection.

Table 3.2 Chart Types and Purposes

Chart Type	Purpose
Column	Compares categories, shows changes over time.
Bar	Shows comparison between independent variables. Not used for time or dates.
Pie	Shows percentages of a whole. Exploded pie emphasizes a popular category.
Line	Shows change in a series over categories or time.
Doughnut	Compares how two or more series contribute to the whole.
Scatter	Shows correlation between two sets of values.
Stock	Shows high-low stock prices.

To change the location of a chart to another sheet or a new sheet:

1. Click the embedded chart or the chart sheet to select it and to display the chart tools.
2. Click Move Chart in the Location group on the Design tab.
3. In the *Choose where you want the chart to be placed* section, do one of the following:
   - Click *New sheet* to display the chart in its own chart sheet.
   - Click *Object in*, click the drop-down arrow, and select a worksheet to move the chart to another worksheet.

Choose Chart Options

When you create a chart, the Chart Tools contextual tab is available. The Design, Layout, and Format tabs are displayed in Chart Tools. You can use the commands on these tabs to modify the chart. For example, use the Design tab to display the data series by row or by column, make changes to the source data of the chart, change the location of the chart, change the chart type, save a chart as a template, or select predefined layout and formatting options. Use the Layout tab to change the display of chart elements such as chart titles and data labels, use drawing tools, or add text boxes and pictures to the chart. Use the Format tab to add fill colors, change line styles, or apply special effects. Review the Reference Page for examples of the contextual chart tools tab with the Design, Layout, and Design tabs depicted.

Chart Tools | Reference

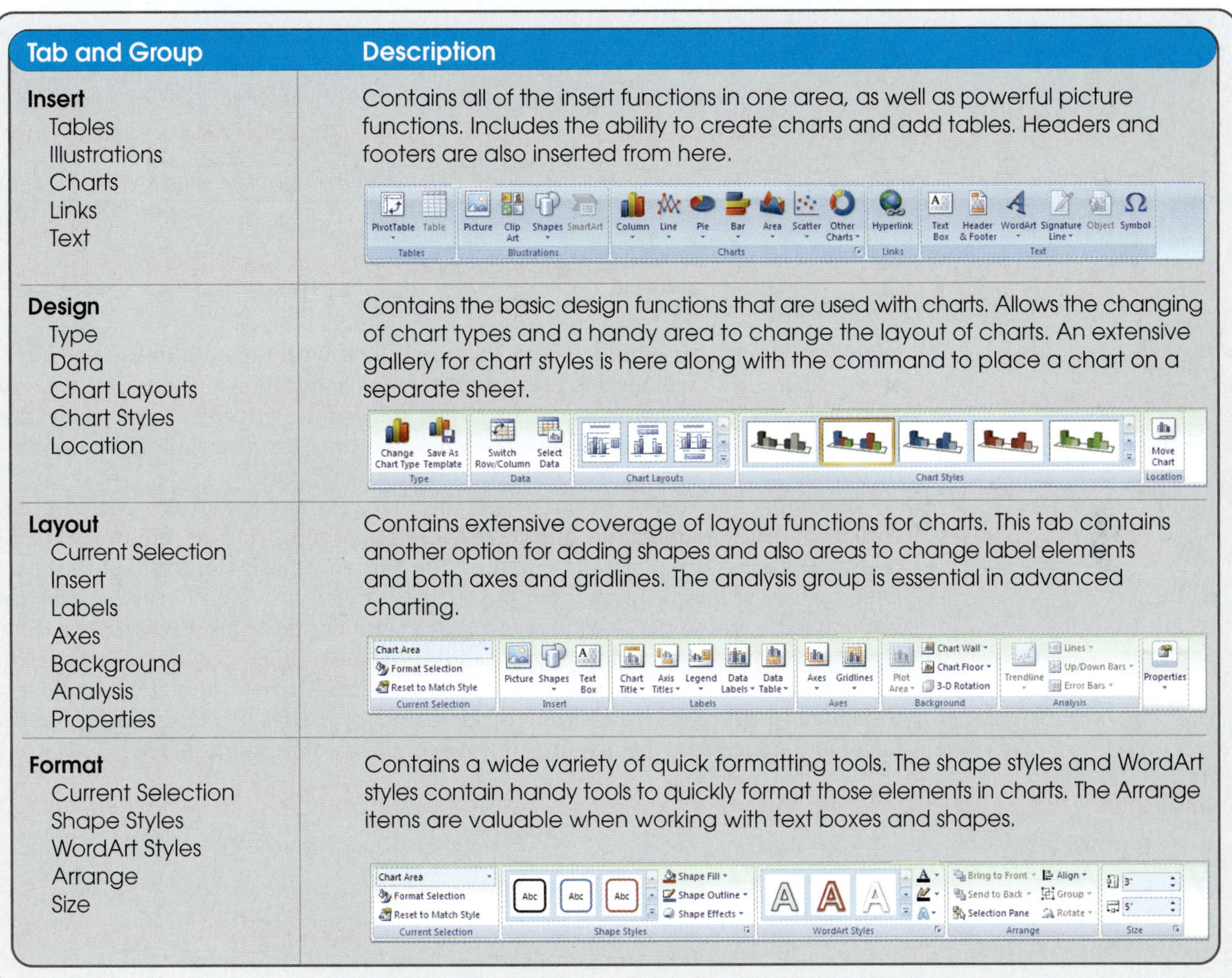

Tab and Group	Description
Insert Tables Illustrations Charts Links Text	Contains all of the insert functions in one area, as well as powerful picture functions. Includes the ability to create charts and add tables. Headers and footers are also inserted from here.
Design Type Data Chart Layouts Chart Styles Location	Contains the basic design functions that are used with charts. Allows the changing of chart types and a handy area to change the layout of charts. An extensive gallery for chart styles is here along with the command to place a chart on a separate sheet.
Layout Current Selection Insert Labels Axes Background Analysis Properties	Contains extensive coverage of layout functions for charts. This tab contains another option for adding shapes and also areas to change label elements and both axes and gridlines. The analysis group is essential in advanced charting.
Format Current Selection Shape Styles WordArt Styles Arrange Size	Contains a wide variety of quick formatting tools. The shape styles and WordArt styles contain handy tools to quickly format those elements in charts. The Arrange items are valuable when working with text boxes and shapes.

Add Graphics in Charts

You may want to add graphics, such as company logos or representative clip art, to charts to personalize the charts or make them more distinctive. In either case the procedure is simple. Again, this is a case where less is sometimes more. Be sparing in the use of graphics that can change the message being conveyed.

To add a graphic to a chart:

1. In the Illustrations group on the Insert tab, select the medium where the graphic will come from (Picture, Clip Art, Shapes, or SmartArt1).
2. Search for and insert the graphic.
3. Size and move the graphic on the chart as desired.

TIP Set a Time Limit

You can customize virtually every aspect of every object within a chart. That is the good news. It is also bad news because you can spend inordinate amounts of time for little or no gain. It is fun to experiment, but set a time limit and stop when you reach the allocated time. The default settings are often adequate to convey your message, and further experimentation might prove counterproductive.

Change the Chart Location and Size

Whether the chart is embedded on the worksheet with the data or on a separate sheet, at times you will need to move a chart or to change its size. To move a chart on any sheet, click the chart to select it. When the pointer appears as a four-headed arrow while on the margin of the chart, click and drag the chart to another location on the sheet.

To change the size of a chart, select the chart. Sizing handles are located in the corners of the chart and at the middle of the edge borders. Clicking and dragging the middle left or right sizing handle of the edge borders adjusts the width of the chart. Drag the sizing handle away from the chart to stretch or widen the chart; drag the sizing handle within the chart to decrease the width of the chart. Clicking and dragging the top or bottom middle sizing handle adjusts the height of the chart. Drag the sizing handle away from the chart to increase its height; drag the sizing handle into the chart to decrease its height. Clicking and dragging a corner sizing handle increases or decreases the height and width of the chart proportionately.

Hands-On Exercises

1 | The First Chart

Skills covered: 1. Use AutoSum **2.** Create the Chart **3.** Complete the Chart **4.** Move and Size the Chart **5.** Change the Worksheet **6.** Change the Chart Type **7.** Create a Second Chart

Step 1 Use AutoSum

Use Figure 3.16 as a guide as you work through the steps in the exercise.

a. Start Excel. Open the *chap3_ho1_sales* workbook and save it as **chap3_ho1_sales_solution**.

b. Click and drag to select **cells B7:E7** (the cells that will contain the total sales for each location). Click **AutoSum** in the Editing group on the Home tab to compute the total for each city.

c. Click and drag to select **cells F4:F6**, and then click **AutoSum**.

The SUM function is entered automatically into these cells to total the entries to the left of the selected cells.

d. Click and drag to select **cells B4:F7** and format these cells with the currency symbol and no decimal places.

e. Bold the row and column headings and the totals. Center the entries in **cells B3:F3**.

f. Save the workbook.

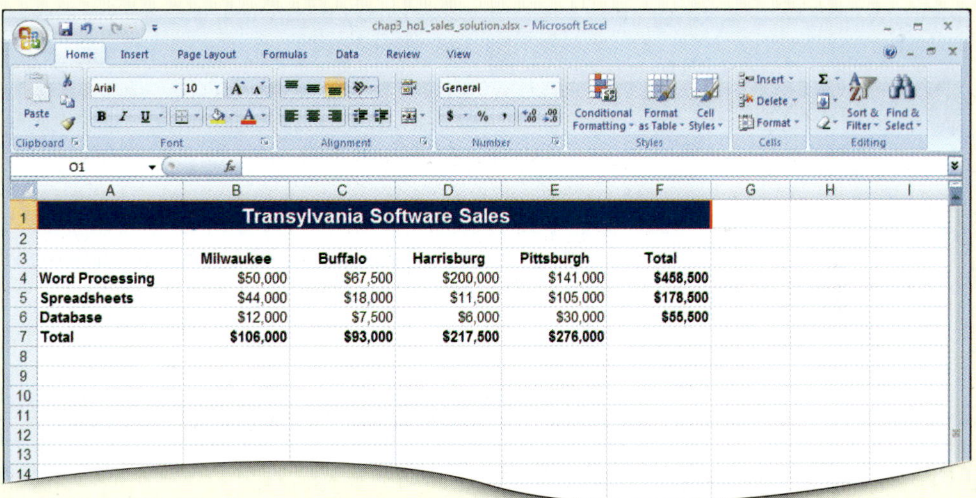

Figure 3.16 Formatted Worksheet with Totals

Step 2 Create the Chart

Refer to Figure 3.17 as you complete Step 2. Note that the colors displayed in figures may not match your screen display.

a. Select **cells B3:E3** to select the category labels (the names of the cities). Press and hold **Ctrl** as you drag the mouse over **cells B7:E7** to select the data series (the cells containing the total sales for the individual cities).

You have selected the cities that will become the X axis in your chart. You selected B7 through E7 as the values that will become the data series.

b. Check that **cells B3:E3** and **cells B7:E7** are selected. Click the **Insert tab** and click **Column** in the Charts group.

You should see the Column Chart palette as shown in Figure 3.17. When the Column chart type and Clustered column subtype are selected, the chart appears on Sheet1. Note that your default colors may differ from those displayed in your textbook.

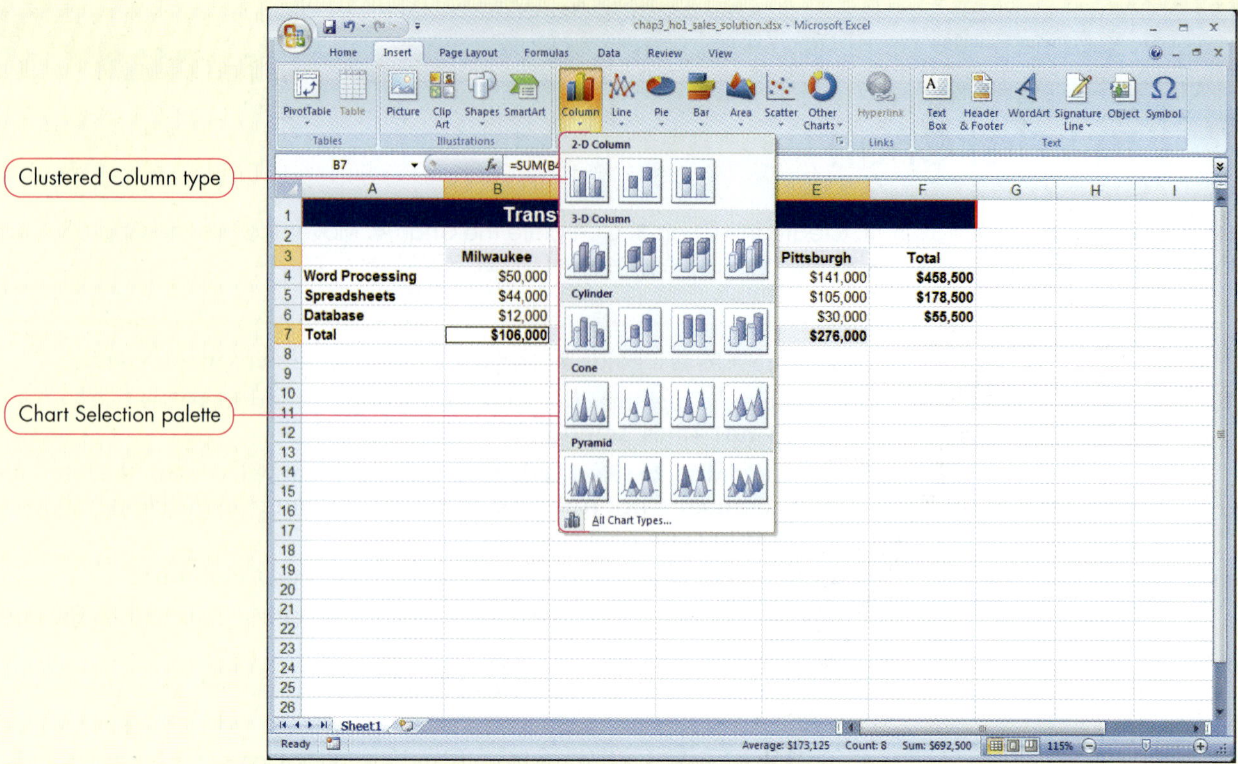

Figure 3.17 Gallery of Chart Types

TROUBLESHOOTING: If you select too little or too much data for charting purposes, you can change your data ranges. Click the Chart Tools Design tab, then click Select Data in the Data group to open the Select Data Source dialog box. Click Edit and select the correct data range.

c. Click **Clustered Column** in the *2-D Column* section to insert a chart.

As you move the mouse over the palette, a ScreenTip appears that indicates the name of the chart type.

TIP The F11 Key

The F11 key is the fastest way to create a chart in its own sheet. Select the worksheet data, including the legends and category labels, and then press F11 to create the chart. The chart displays according to the default format built into the Excel column chart. After you create the chart, you can use the Chart Tools tabs, Mini toolbars, or shortcut menus to choose a different chart type and customize the formatting.

Step 3
Complete the Chart

Refer to Figure 3.18 as you complete Step 3.

a. Click the chart object to make the chart active. Click the **Layout tab,** click **Chart Title** in the Labels group, and then click **Above Chart** to create a title for the chart.

You selected the chart and then selected the placement of the chart title using the Chart Tools Layout tab. The Layout tab indicates the selected chart element (see Figure 3.18). You can click the down arrow to display a list of chart elements and select a different element, such as Plot Area. Use the Labels group to insert and modify elements, such as the chart tile, axis titles, and legend.

b. Type **Revenue by Geographic Area** for the title and press **Enter**.

c. Click **Legend** in the Labels group on the Layout tab and select **None** to delete the legend.

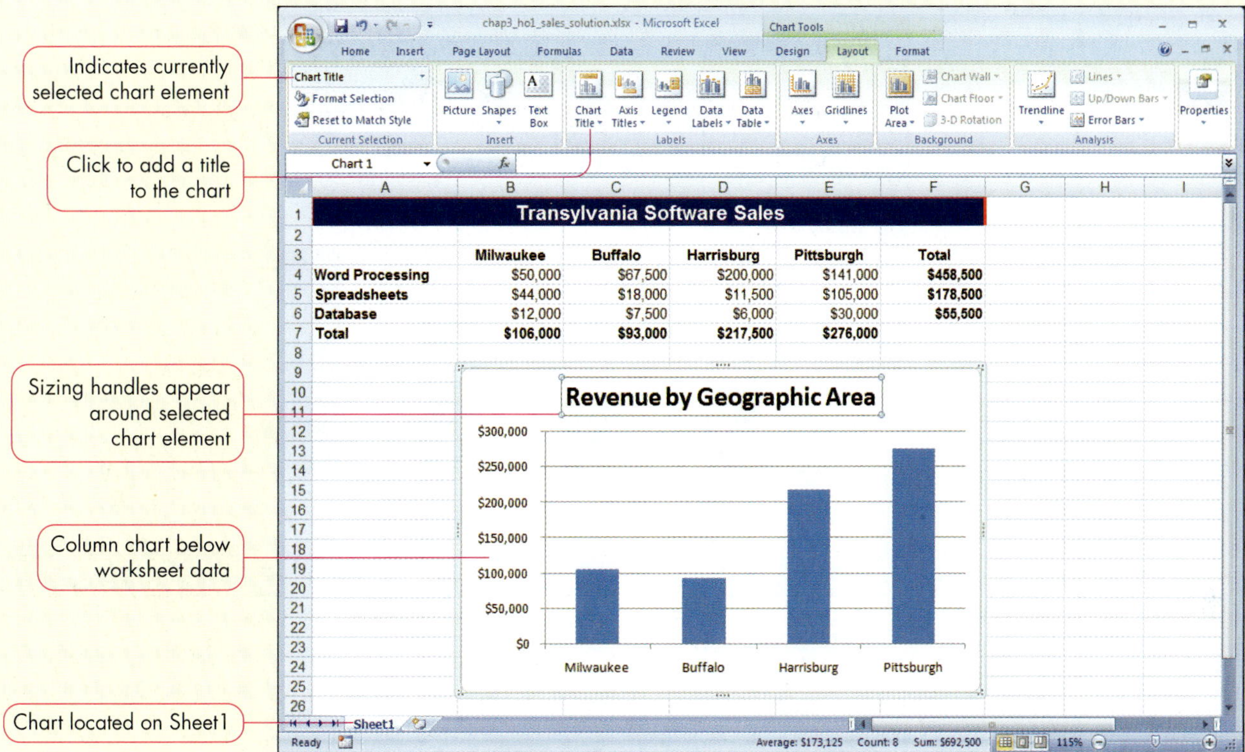

Figure 3.18 Column Chart with Title

Step 4
Move and Size the Chart

Refer to Figure 3.19 as you complete Step 4.

a. Move and size the chart just as you would any other Windows object.

You should see the completed chart in Figure 3.19. When you click the chart the sizing handles indicate the chart is selected and will be affected by subsequent commands.

1. Click the chart border to select the chart, then click on the highlighted outline of the chart and drag (the mouse pointer changes to a four-sided arrow) to move the chart so that the top left side of the chart starts in **cell A9**.

2. Drag a corner handle (the mouse pointer changes to a double arrow) to change the length and width of the chart simultaneously so that the chart covers the **range A9:G29**.

b. Click outside the chart to deselect it. The sizing handles are no longer visible.

When working with any graphic object in Excel, you can resize it by making it active and dragging sizing handles that appear at the corners and on the perimeter of the object.

c. Save the workbook.

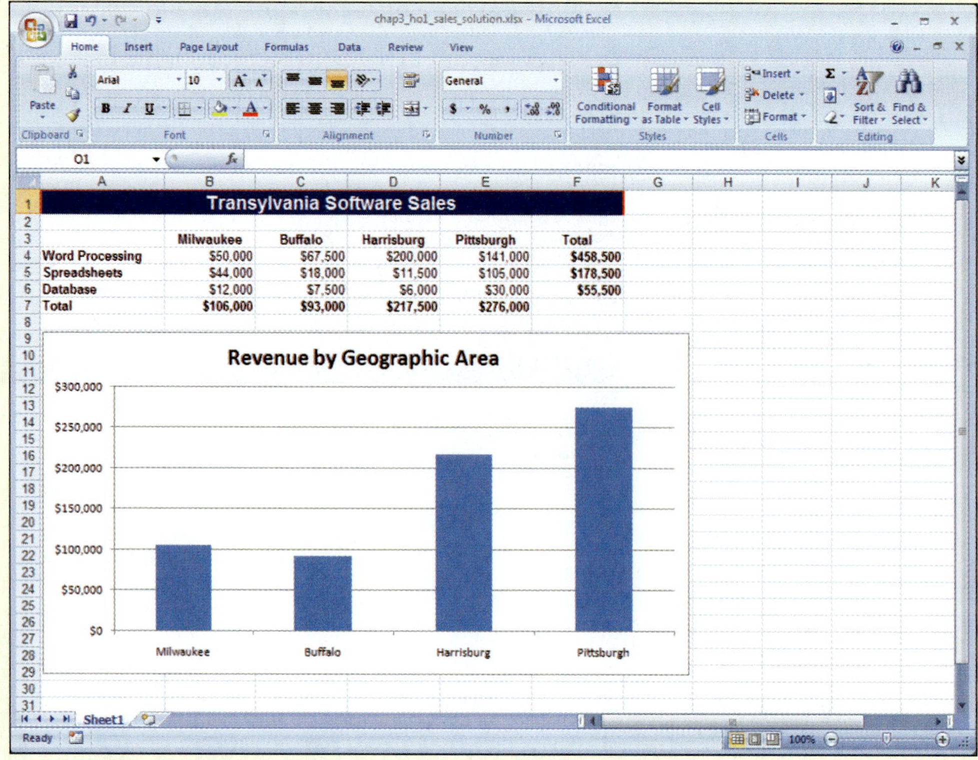

Figure 3.19 Chart Size and Location Changed

TIP Embedded Charts

An embedded chart is treated as an object that can be moved, sized, copied, or deleted just as any other Windows object. To move an embedded chart, click the border of the chart to select the chart and drag it to a new location in the worksheet. To size the chart, select it and then drag any of the eight sizing handles in the desired direction. To delete the chart, select it and press Delete. To copy the chart, select it, click Copy in the Clipboard group on the Home tab to copy the chart to the clipboard, click elsewhere in the workbook where you want the copied chart to go, and click Paste.

Step 5 Change the Worksheet

Refer to Figure 3.20 as you complete Step 5.

a. Click in **cell B4**. Change the entry to **$225,000** and press **Enter**.

   Any changes in a worksheet are automatically reflected in the associated chart. The total sales for Milwaukee in cell B7 change automatically to reflect the increased sales for word processing. The column for Milwaukee also changes in the chart and is now larger than the column for Pittsburgh.

b. Click in **cell B3**. Change the entry to **Chicago** and press **Enter**.

   The category label on the X axis changes automatically to reflect the new city name (see Figure 3.20).

c. Click **Undo** twice on the Quick Access Toolbar.

   You changed the worksheet and chart back to Milwaukee and $50,000 by clicking Undo twice. The worksheet and chart are restored to their earlier values.

d. Save the workbook.

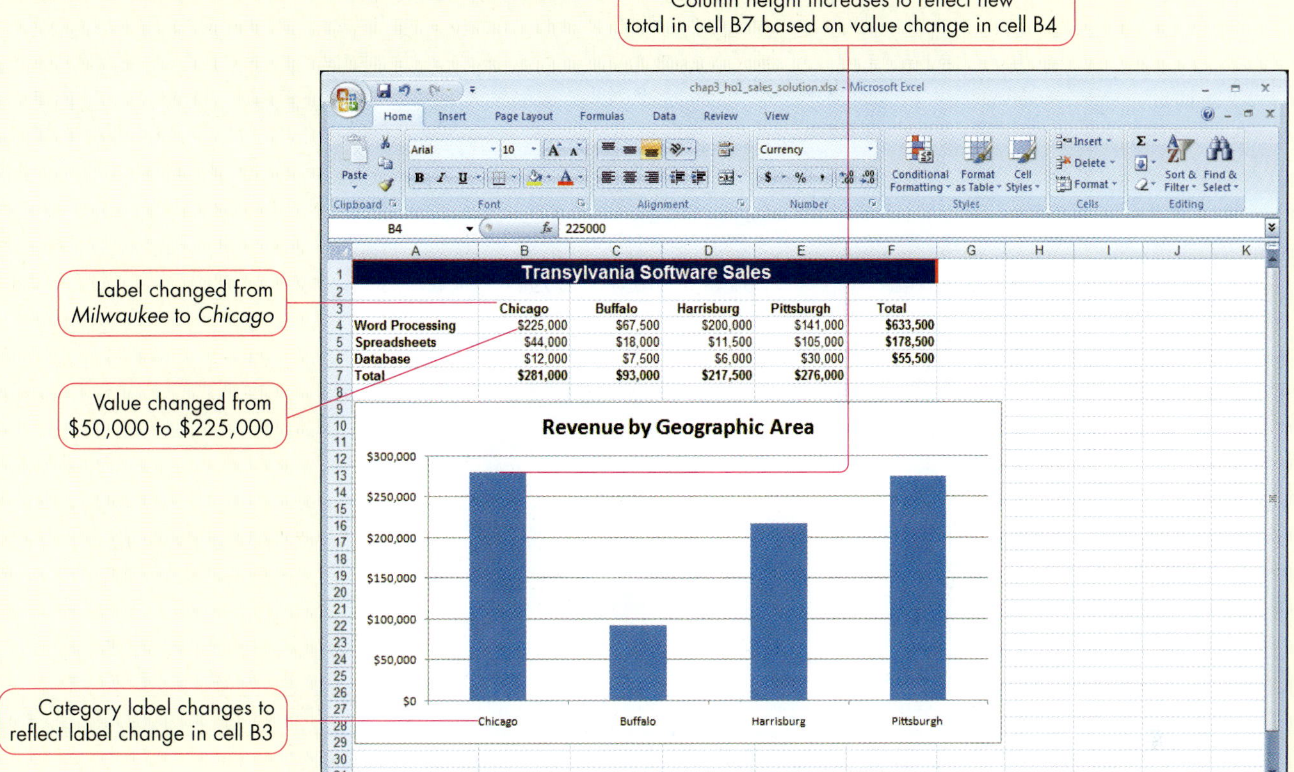

Figure 3.20 Temporary Data Changes Affect Chart

Step 6
Change the Chart Type

Refer to Figure 3.21 as you complete Step 6.

a. Click the chart border area to select the chart, click **Change Chart Type** in the Type group on the Chart Tools Design tab, click the **Pie** type, and then click **Pie** (the first button in the Pie row). Click **OK**, and the chart changes to a pie chart.

   You used the Chart Tools Design tab to change the type of chart. The following steps will guide you through adding data labels to the chart area, and formatting those data labels as percentages.

b. Point to any pie wedge, click the right mouse button to display a shortcut menu, and select **Add Data Labels**.

c. Right-click the mouse button on any pie wedge to display a shortcut menu and select **Format Data Labels** to display the Format Data Labels dialog box. Make sure **Label Options** in the left column is selected and then click the **Category Name** and **Percentage** check boxes to format the data labels. Clear the **Value** and **Show Leader Lines** check boxes.

d. Change the values in the data labels to percentages by clicking **Number** below *Label Options* on the left side of the dialog box, click **Percentage** in *Category* list, type **0** in the **Decimal places** box and click **Close** to accept the settings and close the dialog box.

   The pie chart now displays data labels as percentages. The Number format is the default when initially inserting data labels.

e. Modify each component as necessary:

   1. Click the plot area, the white area immediately surrounding the pie chart, to select the chart. Click and drag the sizing handles to increase the size of the plot area within the embedded chart.
   2. Click a label to select all data labels. Click the **Home tab**, click the **Font Size down arrow** in the Font group, and select **12**.

f. Save the workbook.

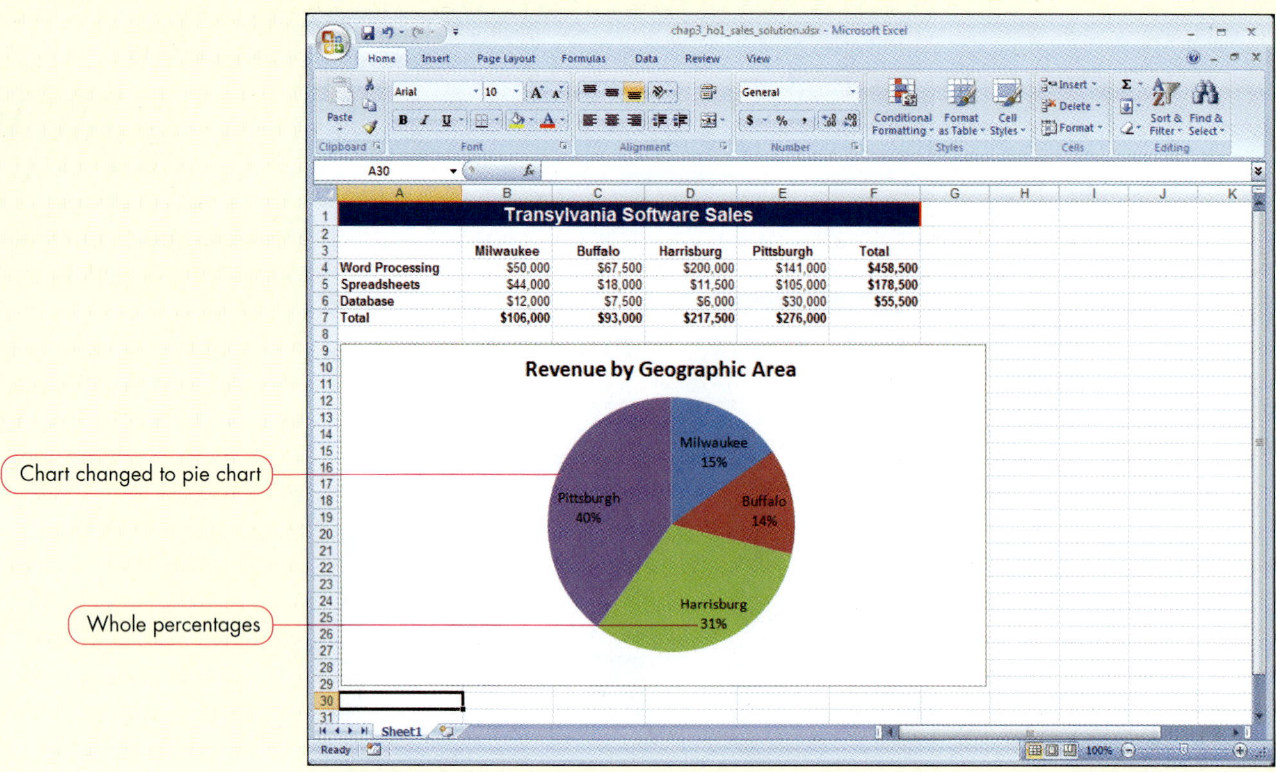

Figure 3.21 Chart Changed to Pie Chart

Step 7 Create a Second Chart

Refer to Figure 3.22 as you complete Step 7.

a. Click and drag to select **cells A4:A6** in the worksheet. Press and hold **Ctrl** as you drag the mouse to select **cells F4:F6**.

b. Click the **Insert tab**, click **Column** in the Charts group, and select **3-D Clustered Column**.

   When the Column chart type and 3-D Clustered Column subtype are selected, the chart appears on Sheet1. The values (the data being plotted) are in cells F4:F6. The category labels for the X-axis are in cells A4:A6.

c. Click **Chart Title** in the Labels group on the Layout tab and select **Centered Overlay Title.**

   The chart title overlays onto the chart without resizing the plot area. Although this option keeps the plot area larger, the title may be difficult to read when it overlaps data on the chart.

d. Type **Revenue by Product Category** for the title. Click **Legend** in the Labels group on the Layout tab and select **None** to delete the legend.

   You have created a title for your 3-D clustered column chart. You deleted the legend because you have only one data series.

e. Click the **Design tab** and click **Move Chart** in the Location group. Click **New sheet** and then click **OK** to display the chart on a new sheet and close the Move Chart dialog box.

   The 3-D column chart has been created in the chart sheet labeled Chart1 as shown in Figure 3.22.

f. Save the workbook. Exit Excel if you do not want to continue with the next exercise at this time.

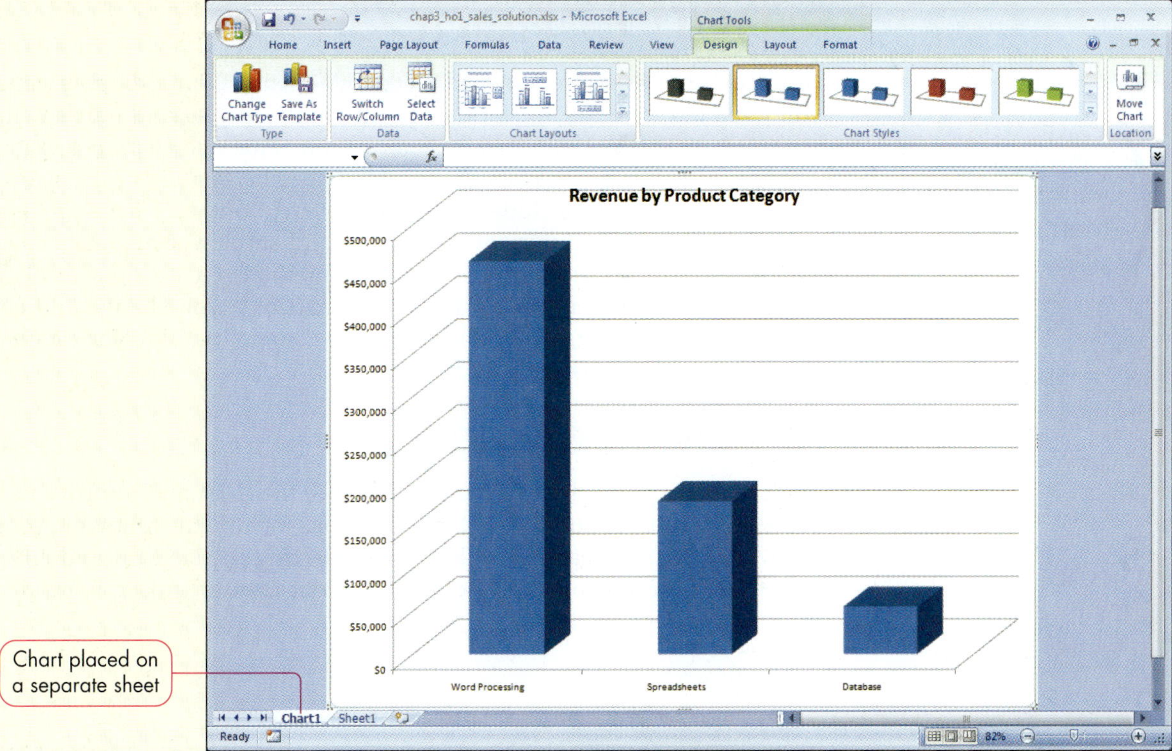

Figure 3.22 Chart Moved to Chart1 Sheet

TIP Chart Sheet Name

The default chart sheet name is Chart1, Chart2, etc. However, you can rename it before you click OK in the Move Chart dialog box, or after the sheet is created, you can double-click the chart sheet name, type a new name, and press Enter.

Chart Enhancements

Now that you already have created a chart by selecting the appropriate values and labels, you must improve the appearance of the chart. Adding and editing chart elements enhance the information value of a chart. For example, you can draw attention to a specific bar using an arrow shape that includes an appropriate text phrase. Charts are used to express information visually, and subtle visual enhancements improve comprehension while presenting a more powerful message.

(Charts are used to express information visually, and subtle visual enhancements improve comprehension while presenting a more powerful message.)

In this section you modify a chart. Specifically, you change and edit chart elements, format a chart, add data labels, and change the fill color for chart elements. Then you enhance charts by adding shapes.

Modifying a Chart

You can modify any chart element to enhance the chart and improve its appearance. Some of the most common chart modifications include the following properties: size, color, font, format, scale, or style just by selecting the element and choosing from a variety of options. Mini toolbars and shortcut menus appear as needed for you to make your selections.

TIP Anatomy of a Chart

A chart is composed of multiple components (objects), each of which can be selected and changed separately. Point to any part of a chart to display a ScreenTip indicating the name of the component, then click the mouse to select that component and display the sizing handles. You can then click and drag the object within the chart and/or right-click the mouse to display a Mini toolbar and shortcut menu with commands pertaining to the selected object.

Change and Edit Chart Elements

It is often necessary to change chart elements such as titles and axes. For example, you might need to change the title of the chart or adjust the font size of the title to balance the title text and the chart size. You can change these elements to reflect different words or edit the elements to reflect formatting changes.

On a chart, do one of the following:

- To edit the contents of a title, click the chart or axis title that you want to change.
- To edit the contents of a data label, click twice on the data label that you want to change.
- Click again to place the title or data label in editing mode, drag to select the text that you want to change, type the new text or value, and then press Enter.

To format the text, select it, and then click the formatting options that you want on the Mini toolbar. You can also use the formatting buttons in the Font group on the Home tab. To format the entire title or data label, right-click the selected text, select Format Chart Title, Format Axis Title, or Format Data Labels on the shortcut menu, and then select the formatting options that you want.

Format a Chart

The options for formatting a chart may be approached in two ways, either by using the tabs or by selecting the chart and then right-clicking and using the various format commands on the shortcut menu. Table 3.3 shows the different tabs and the formatting capabilities available with each. Figures 3.23 through 3.26 show these tabs as defined in Table 3.3.

Table 3.3 Tab and Format Features

Tab	Format Features
Insert	Insert Shapes, insert illustrations, create and edit WordArt and textboxes, Insert symbols.
Design	Change chart type, edit the data sources, change the chart style and layout, and change the location of the chart.
Layout	Again allows the insertion of shapes, graphics, and text boxes. Add or change chart title, axis title, legend, data labels, and data table. Format axis and change the background.
Format	Deals with more sophisticated control of WordArt, Shapes, and Arrangement.

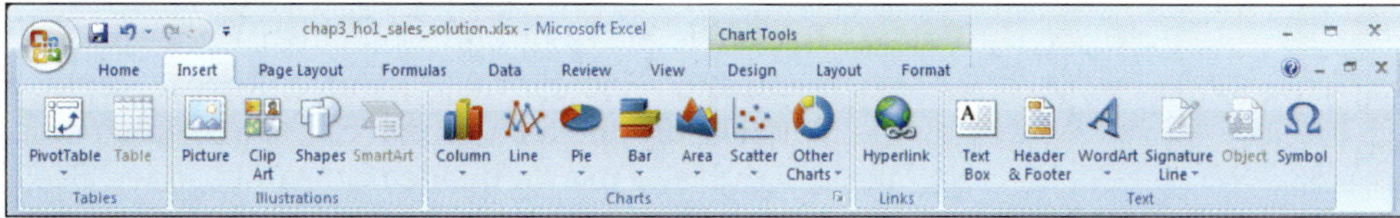

Figure 3.23 Insert Tab

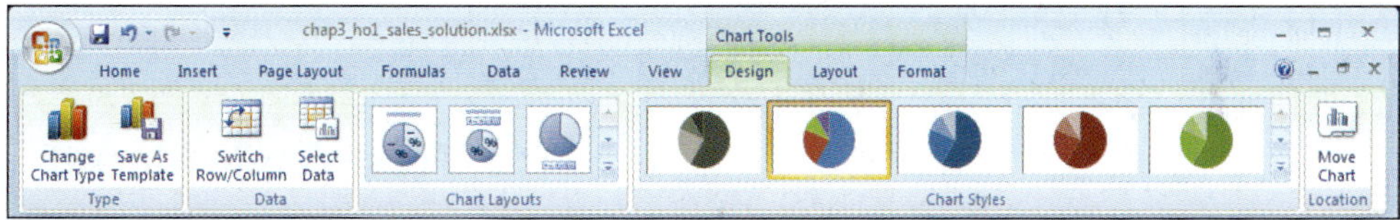

Figure 3.24 Design Tab

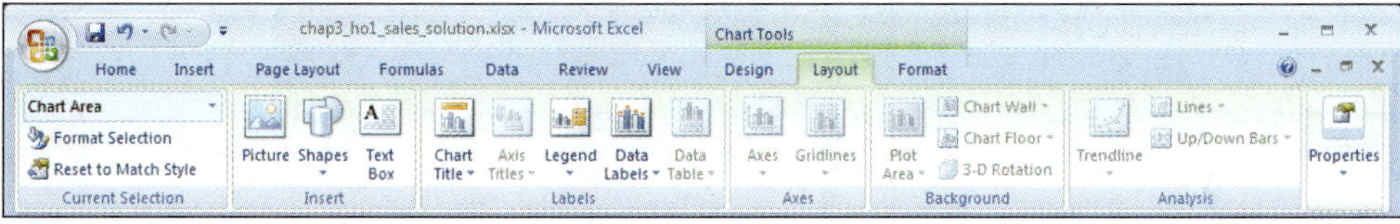

Figure 3.25 Layout Tab

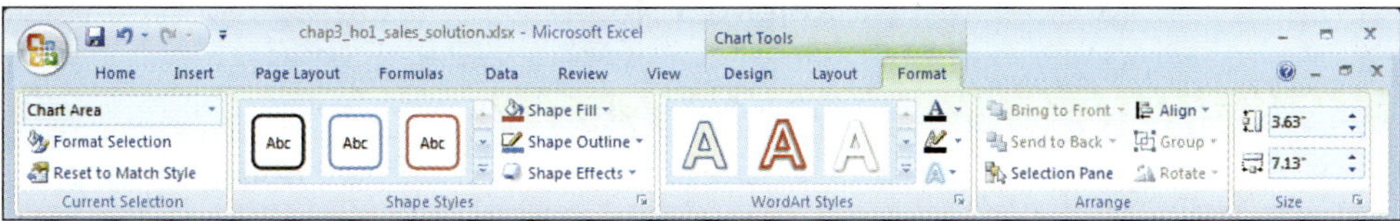

Figure 3.26 Format Tab

Add Data Labels

A ***data label*** is the value or name of a data point.

One of the features of Excel charting that does much to enhance charts is the use of ***data labels***, which are the value or name of a data point. The exact values of data shown by charts are not always clear, particularly in 3-D charts, as well as scatter charts and some line charts. It assists the readers of your charts if you label the data points with text and their values. These labels amplify the data represented in the chart by providing their numerical values on the chart. To add data labels to a chart:

1. Select the chart that will have data labels added.
2. Click Data Labels in the Labels group on the Layout tab.
3. Select the location for the data labels on the chart.

Change the Fill Color for Chart Elements

Another component you can change is the color or fill pattern of any element in the chart. Colors are used to accentuate data presented in chart form. Colors also are used to underplay data presented in chart form. Charts often are used in Microsoft PowerPoint for presentation, so you must pay attention to contrast and use appropriate colors for large screen display. Remember also that color blindness and other visual impairments can change how charts are viewed. To change the color of a data series in a column chart:

1. Right-click on any column to open the shortcut menu.
2. Select Format Data Series.
3. Select Fill in the left pane, select Solid fill, and then select a color from the Color list.
4. Click Close.

To change the color of the plot area, right-click on the plot area to open the shortcut menu and select Format Plot area. Repeat Steps 3 and 4 above.

Another unique feature you can use to enhance a chart and make the data more meaningful is to use an image in the data series. See Figure 3.27 for an example of a chart using an image of an apple to represent bushels of apples. To use an image as a data series, select the data series, click the Shape Fill down arrow in the Shape Styles group on the Format tab, and select Picture. From the Insert Picture dialog box, select the image and click Insert.

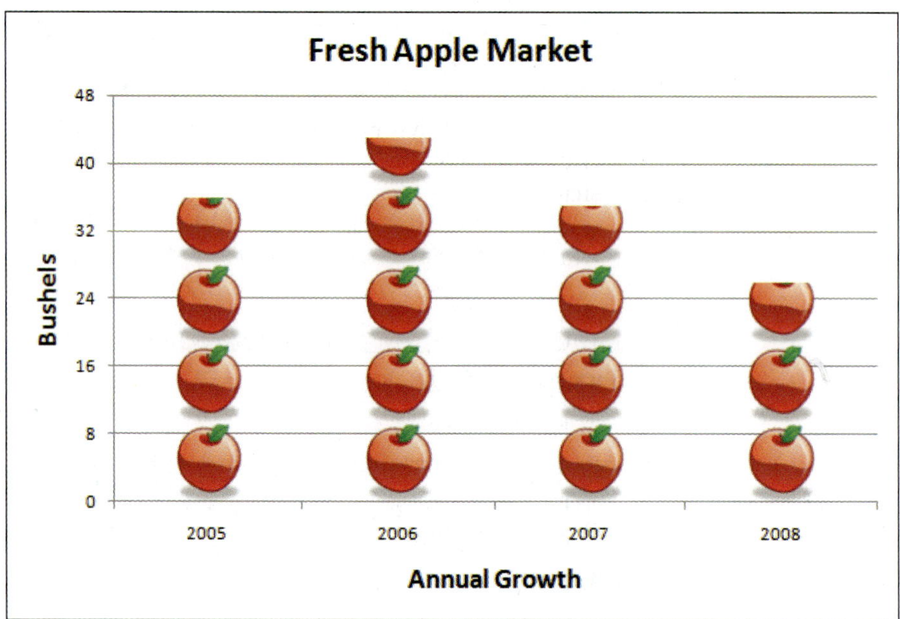

Figure 3.27 Images in Charts

TIP Quick Layout

Excel enables you to instantly change the look of a chart. After creating a chart, quickly apply a predefined layout to the chart. Choose from a variety of useful predefined layouts and then manually customize the layout of individual chart elements if desired. Select the chart before formatting. This action displays Chart Tools contextual tab, adding the Design, Layout, and Format tabs. On the Design tab, in the Chart Layouts group, click the chart layout that you want to use. To see all available layouts, click More.

TIP Shape Fill

As an alternative to right-clicking a chart element to change a fill color, you can select the specific chart element, such as one data series and click the Shape Fill down arrow in the Shape Styles group on the Format tab. You can choose specific colors, such as **Red, Accent 2, Lighter 60%** in the *Theme Colors* section, or you can select a regular color from the *Standard Colors* section.

Enhancing Charts with Graphic Shapes

Using shapes is a technique that lets you add pre-made graphics to a chart to emphasize the content of a part of a chart. Ready-made shapes come in forms such as rectangles, circles, arrows, lines, flowchart symbols, and callouts. Words also can be placed in shapes using text boxes.

Shapes can be inserted either from the Insert tab or from the Layout tab. You want to experiment with both techniques and decide which you prefer. To insert a shape using the Layout tab:

1. Click the Shapes down arrow on the Layout tab.
2. Click on the shape you want to insert.
3. Place the crosshair pointer over the location on the chart where the graphic is to be located and drag the pointer to place the shape. To constrain the drawing element to the proportion illustrated in the shapes palette, hold Shift while you drag the pointer to place the shape.
4. Release the mouse button.
5. To resize a shape, select the shape and use one of the eight selection handles to change its size.
6. Rotate the graphic by clicking the green rotation handle and dragging to rotate the shape.
7. Change the shape of the graphic by clicking the yellow diamond tool and dragging.

Hands-On Exercises

2 | Multiple Data Series

Skills covered: 1. Rename the Worksheet **2.** Create Chart with Multiple Data Series **3.** Copy the Chart **4.** Change the Source Data **5.** Change the Chart Type **6.** Insert a Graphic Shape and Add a Text Box

Step 1
Rename the Worksheet

Refer to Figure 3.28 as you complete Step 1.

a. Open *chap3_ho1_sales_solution* workbook if you closed it at the end of the previous exercise. Save the workbook as **chap3_ho2_sales_solution**.

b. Point to the workbook tab labeled Sheet1, right-click the mouse to display a shortcut menu, and then click **Rename**.

   The name of the worksheet (Sheet1) is selected.

c. Type **Sales Data** to change the name of the worksheet to the more descriptive name. Press **Enter**. Right-click the worksheet tab a second time, point to **Tab Color**, then change the color to the **Blue, Accent 1** theme color.

   You renamed the worksheet and changed the color of the sheet tab.

d. Change the name of the Chart1 sheet to **Column Chart**. Change the tab color to the **Red, Accent 2** theme color. Save the workbook.

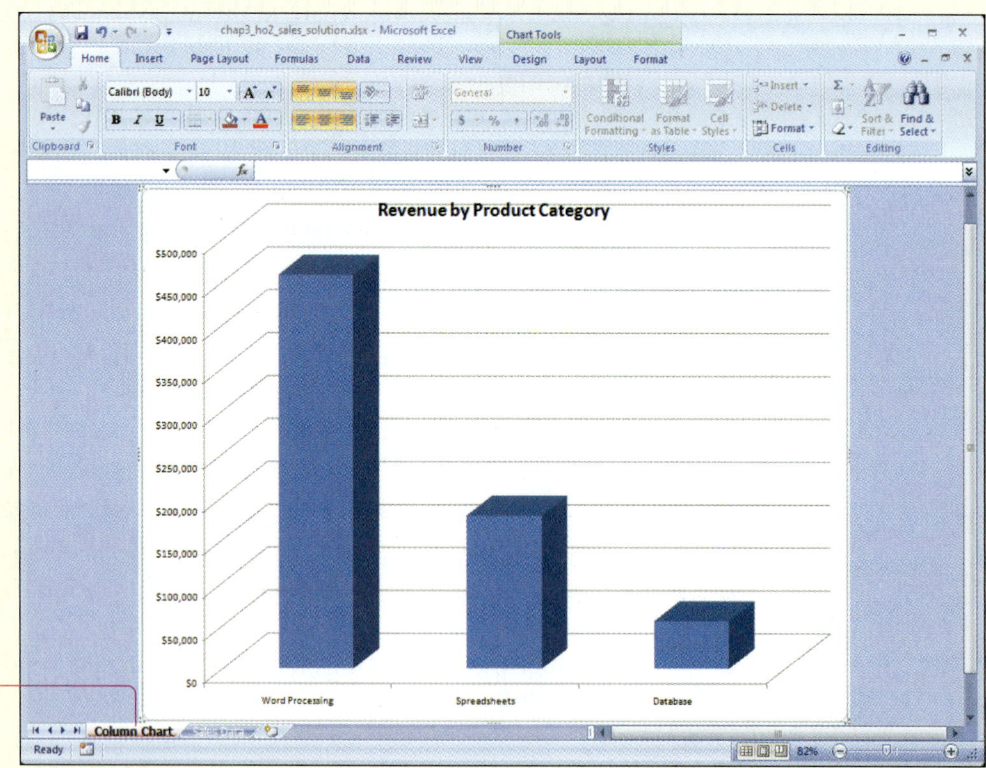

Figure 3.28 Renamed Worksheet

Step 2
Create Chart with Multiple Data Series

Refer to Figure 3.29 as you complete Step 2.

a. Click the **Sales Data tab**, then click and drag to select **cells A3:E6**.

b. Click the **Insert tab**, click **Column** in the Charts group, and select **Clustered Column** as the subtype from the gallery of column chart types.

   This type of chart is best for displaying multiple data series.

c. Click **Chart Title** in the Labels group on the Layout tab and select **Above Chart** to create a title for the chart.

d. Type **Revenue by City** for the chart title and press **Enter**.

   Using appropriate chart titles is essential as no chart should appear without a title. Viewers of your chart need to be able to quickly identify the subject of the chart.

e. Click **Move Chart** in the Location group on the Design tab. Click **New sheet**, type **Revenue by City**, and then click **OK**.

   You have moved the chart from the Sales Data sheet to a new chart sheet.

f. Right-click the **Revenue by City sheet tab**, select **Tab Color**, and select **Orange, Accent 6**. Save the workbook.

   After changing both the tab name and tab color, your chart should be similar to Figure 3.29.

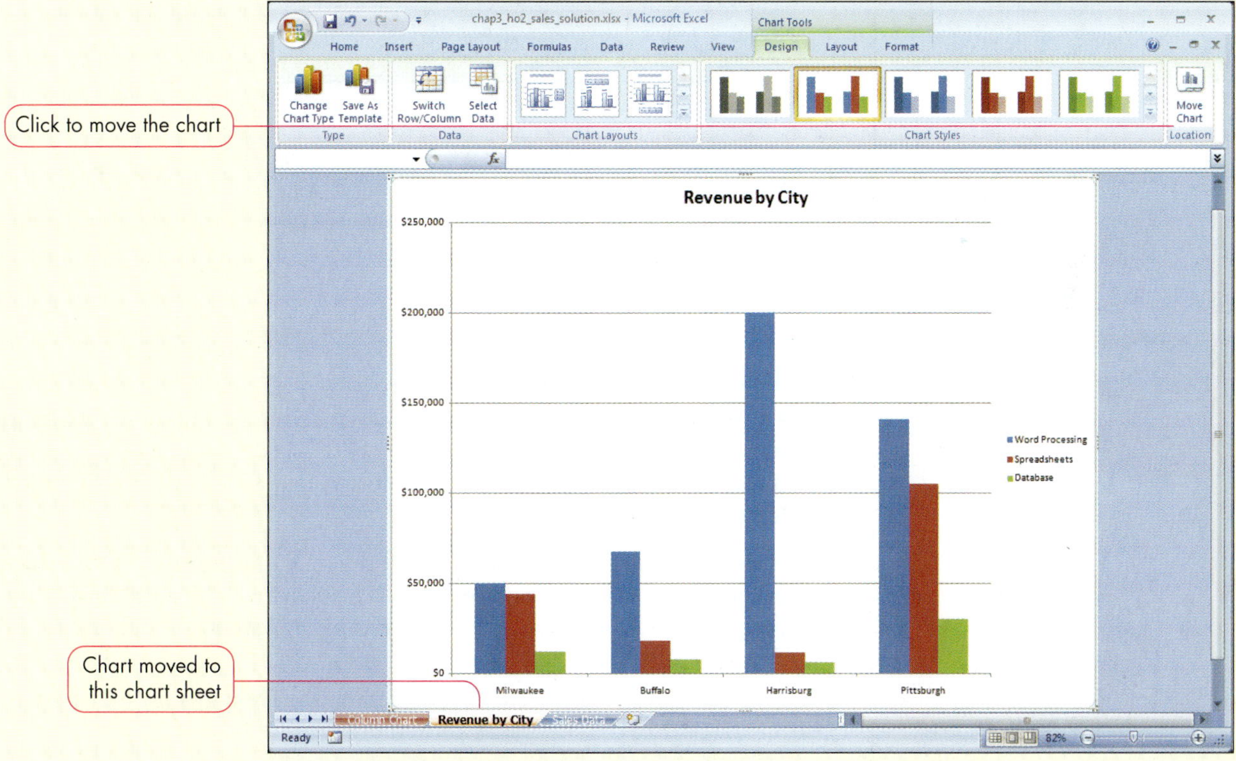

Figure 3.29 Multiple Data Series

Step 3
Copy the Chart

Refer to Figure 3.30 as you complete Step 3.

a. Click anywhere in the chart title to select the title. Click the **Font Size** list box on the Home tab and change to **24-point** type to enlarge the title.

   You changed the font size of the title to make it easier to read.

b. Point to the worksheet tab named **Revenue by City** and click to select it if it is not already selected. Then click **Format** in the Cells group of the Home tab. Click **Move or Copy Sheet** to display the dialog box shown in Figure 3.30.

c. Click **Sales Data** in the Before sheet list box. Click the **Create a copy** check box. Click **OK**.

   A duplicate worksheet called Revenue by City (2) (your sheet tab name may vary) is created and appears before or to the left of the Sales Data worksheet. You have now created a copy of the original chart and can enhance it without having to replot the data.

d. Double-click the newly created worksheet tab to select the name. Type **Revenue by Product** as the new name and save the workbook.

Figure 3.30 Move or Copy Dialog Box

Step 4
Change the Source Data

Refer to Figure 3.31 as you complete Step 4.

a. Click the **Revenue by Product tab** to make it active sheet if it is not already active. Click anywhere in the title of the chart, select the word *City*, and then type **Product Category** to replace the selected text. Click outside the title to deselect it.

   You edited the title of the chart to reflect the new data source. Before starting step b, look at the legend and the x axis. The chart was formatted by rows, so the three software categories are displayed in the legend. The four city data columns form the x axis.

b. Click the **Design tab** and click **Select Data** in the Data group to display the Select Data Source dialog box as shown in Figure 3.31.

c. Click **Switch Row/Column** in the Data group. Click **OK** to close the Select Data Source dialog box.

   Look at the legend and the x axis. After switching rows and columns, the chart is created by worksheet columns. Therefore, the city data columns in the worksheet are displayed in the legend, and the three software categories form the x axis.

d. Save the workbook.

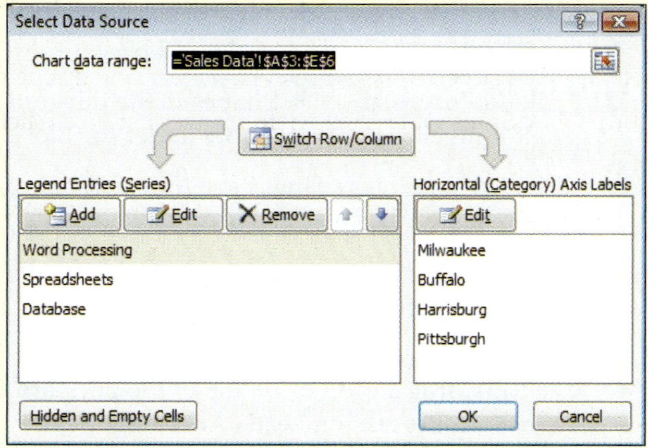

Figure 3.31 Select Data Source Dialog Box

Step 5
Change the Chart Type

Refer to Figure 3.32 as you complete Step 5.

a. Click the chart border area to select the chart, click **Change Chart Type** in the Type group on the Design tab, and click the **Stacked Column** (the second from the left in the top row of the column chart gallery). Click **OK**.

   The chart changes to a stacked column chart.

b. Right-click the legend and select **14 points** font size from the Mini toolbar.

   You increased the font size of the legend to make it more readable. Your chart should be similar to Figure 3.32.

c. Save the workbook.

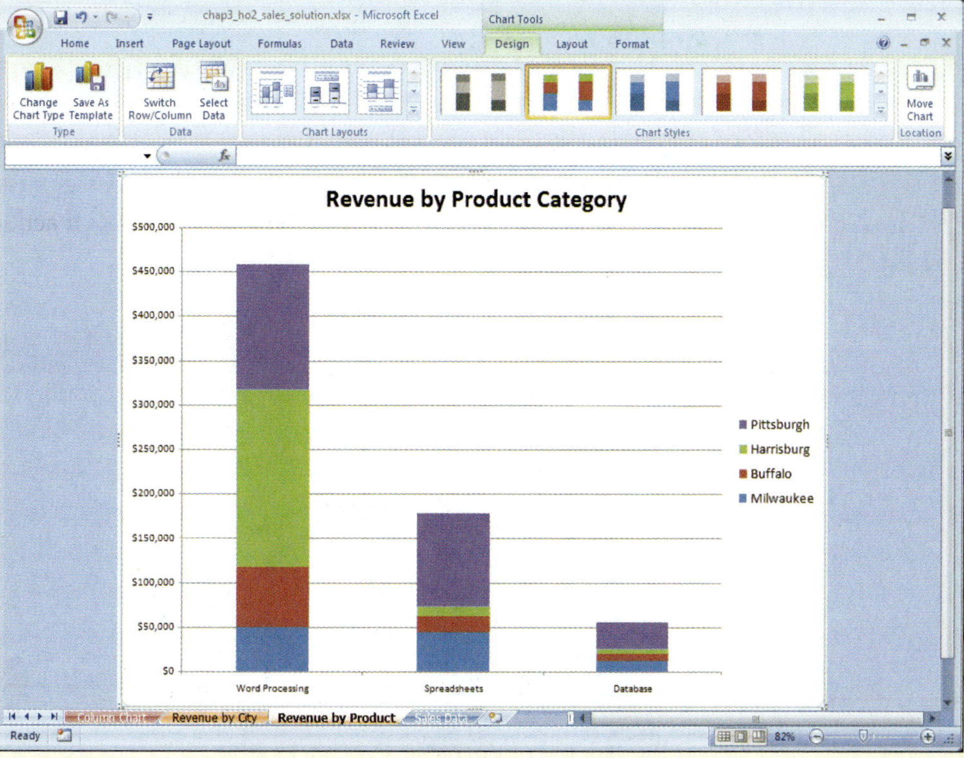

Figure 3.32 Stacked Column Chart

Step 6
Insert a Graphic Shape and Add a Text Box

Refer to Figure 3.33 as you complete Step 6.

a. Click the **Insert tab**, click **Shapes** in the Illustrations group to view the Shapes palette and click the **Left Arrow** under the Block Arrow category.

The mouse pointer changes to a thin crosshair that you will drag to "draw" the arrow shape. The crosshair appears when you click in the chart.

b. Click and drag to create a thick arrow that points to the Word Processing column. Release the mouse button. The arrow is selected, and the Format tab is displayed.

c. Click **Text Box** in the Insert Shapes group on the Format tab to insert a text box. Click and drag a text box on top of the thick arrow. Release the mouse button. Type **Word Processing Leads All Categories.**

You can use shapes to draw attention to significant trends or changes in date. The text in the shape describes the trend or change.

d. Select the text you just typed, then right-click to display a shortcut menu and Mini toolbar. Use the Mini toolbar to change the font to **12**-point bold **White, Background 1** font color.

TROUBLESHOOTING: Should you have difficulty selecting the text box, right-click on the text itself to redisplay the shortcut menu and Mini toolbar.

e. Click the title of the chart and you will see sizing handles around the title to indicate it has been selected. Click the **Font Size down arrow** on the Home tab. Click **28** to increase the size of the title. Your chart will be similar to Figure 3.33.

Increasing the size of the title enables your viewers to quickly see the subject of the chart.

f. Save the workbook, but do not print it. Exit Excel if you do not want to continue with the next exercise at this time.

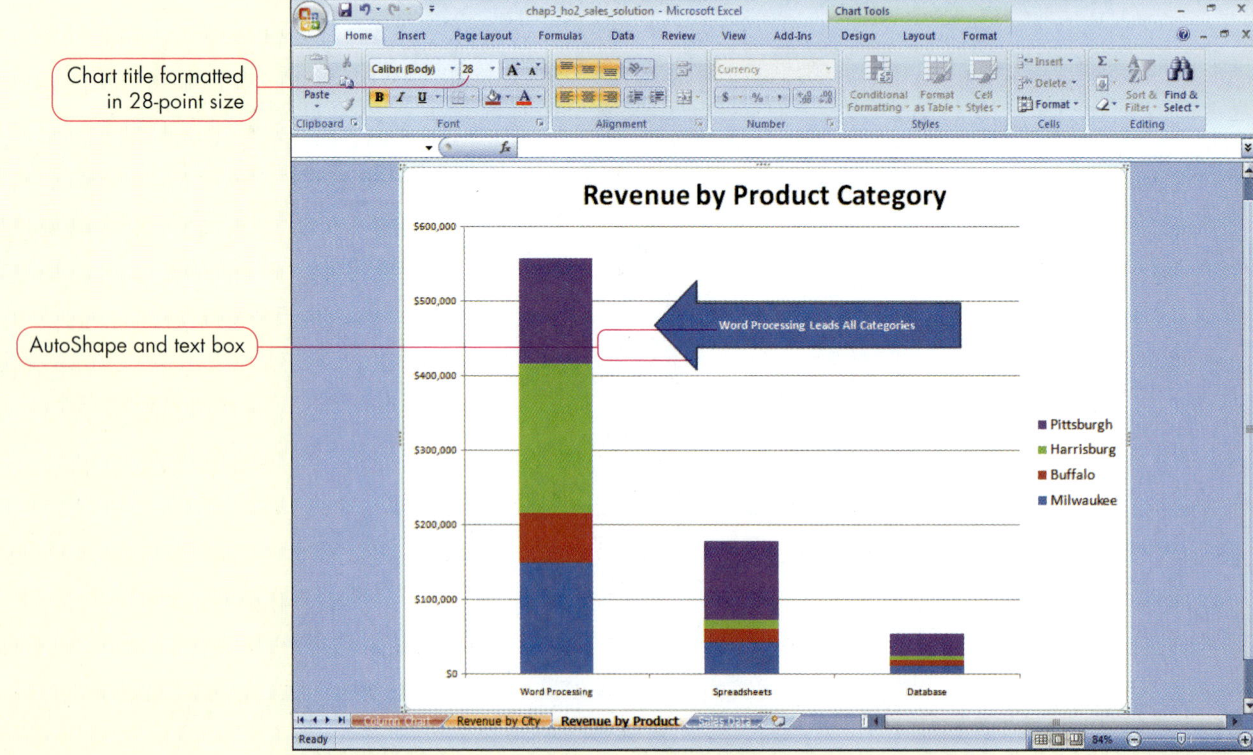

Figure 3.33 Chart with AutoShape and Text Box

Chart Distribution

> You can create visual information masterpieces that could be shared with others.

You can create visual information masterpieces that could be shared with others. Charts are used as documentation in Web pages, memos, reports, research papers, books, and a variety of other types of documents. Therefore, it is important to experience how charts are transferred to these compound documents.

In this section, you embed Excel charts in other Microsoft Office applications. Then you learn how to print the chart within a worksheet or by itself. Finally, you learn how to save a chart as a Web file.

Embedding Charts

Microsoft Excel 2007 is just one application in the Microsoft Office 2007 suite. The applications are integrated and enable for data sharing. It is straightforward to copy worksheet data and charts and paste them in Word and PowerPoint. You can then format the objects in Word or PowerPoint.

Export to Other Applications

Microsoft Office 2007 enables you to create a compound file in one application that contains data (objects) from another application. The memo in Figure 3.34, for example, was created in Word, and it contains an ***object*** (a chart) that was developed in Excel. The Excel object is linked to the Word document, so that any changes to the Excel workbook data are automatically reflected in the Word document. Formatting

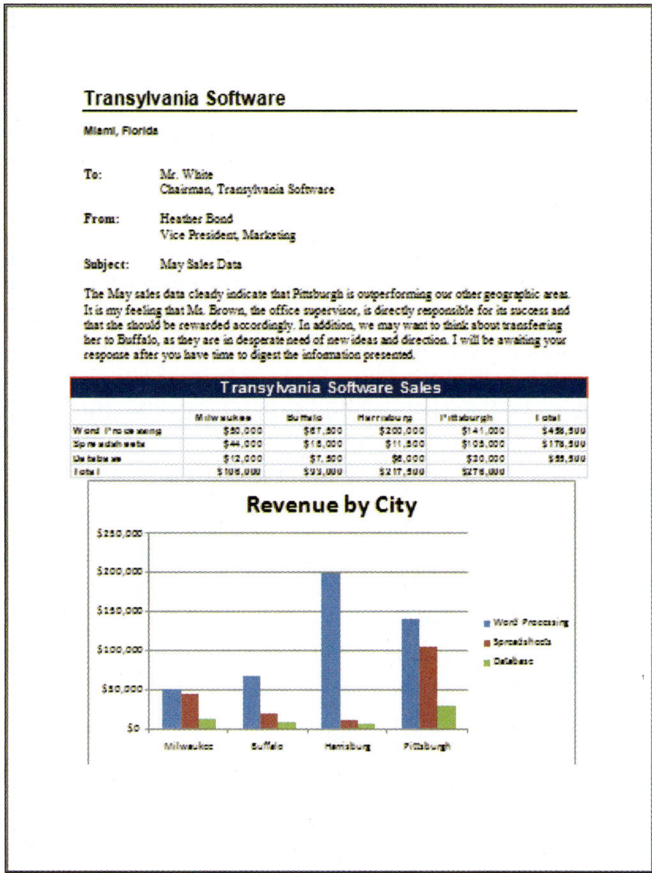

Transylvania Software

Miami, Florida

To: Mr. White
Chairman, Transylvania Software

From: Heather Bond
Vice President, Marketing

Subject: May Sales Data

The May sales data clearly indicate that Pittsburgh is outperforming our other geographic areas. It is my feeling that Ms. Brown, the office supervisor, is directly responsible for its success and that she should be rewarded accordingly. In addition, we may want to think about transfering her to Buffalo, as they are in desperate need of new ideas and direction. I will be awaiting your response after you have time to digest the infomation presented.

Transylvania Software Sales					
	Milwaukee	Buffalo	Harrisburg	Pittsburgh	Total
Word Processing	$50,000	$67,500	$200,000	$141,000	$458,500
Spreadsheets	$44,000	$18,000	$11,500	$105,000	$178,500
Database	$12,000	$7,500	$6,000	$30,000	$55,500
Total	$106,000	$93,000	$217,500	$276,000	

Figure 3.34 Memo in Microsoft Office Word

of the object in Excel after it is placed in the Word document will not be seen in the Word document. The steps to link a chart in a Word (or PowerPoint) document are:

1. Click on the chart in Excel to select it.
2. Click Copy in the Clipboard group on the Home tab.
3. Open the appropriate Word or PowerPoint document.
4. Click the Paste down arrow in the Clipboard group on the Home tab and select Paste Special.
5. Select Microsoft Office Excel Chart Object, click the Paste link option, and click OK.

Remember that changes to the worksheet data made in Excel will automatically update the chart in Excel and the other application, but changes in formatting will not be updated in the other application. To update the chart in Word, right-click the chart and select Update Link.

If you want to embed a chart without linking it back to Excel, simply click Paste in the Clipboard group on the Home tab. When you embed a chart this way, changes made to the original chart in Excel do not update at all in Word or PowerPoint; you would have to copy and paste the chart again if the data changes.

TIP Hiding and Unhiding a Worksheet

A chart delivers a message more effectively than the corresponding numeric data, and thus it may be convenient to hide the associated worksheet on which the chart is based. Click the Home tab. Then click Format in the Cells group, click Hide & Unhide, and then Hide Sheet the worksheet you want to hide. Repeat the command, selecting Unhide Sheet to make the worksheet visible again.

Printing Charts

Printing charts is a straightforward operation but requires that you closely observe the Print Preview window in the Print group on the Office menu. You have to see what will print to make sure this is what you want to print. Printing is an output that many Excel users prefer because the chart is often part of a report, research paper, or some other paper document.

Print an Object in a Worksheet

If the chart is contained on the same worksheet page as the data, you have two options, either to print only the chart or only the data table, or to print both. To print only the chart, click on the chart to ensure it is selected. You then select Print Preview from the Print group on the Office menu. Verify that only the chart is selected for printing. Then select the Page Setup options that best show the printed chart and then print the chart.

If you want to print both the chart and the data table, the above steps are followed except you must ensure that the chart is deselected. This is a case where the use of the Print Preview command is essential to ensure the correct items are being printed.

Print a Full-Page Chart

The options above can be difficult to use if a full-page printing of a chart is desired. The easier option is to place the chart on a separate sheet in the workbook and print it from there.

1. Click to select the chart.
2. Click Move Chart in the Location group on the Design tab.
3. Click the New Sheet option.
4. Select the sheet added in Step 3.
5. Use Print Preview to ensure the chart will be displayed properly when printed.
6. Select the appropriate Page Setup options and print the chart.

TIP Print Only What You Need

Why print an entire workbook if you need only a single worksheet? Press and hold the Ctrl key as you click the tab(s) of the worksheet(s) that you want to print. Click the Office Button and select Print. If it is not already selected, click Active Sheet(s) in the Print What area, and then click OK. (You also can print selected cells within a worksheet by selecting the cells, and then clicking the Selection option.)

Save as a Web Page

Excel users can place an Excel chart (and sometimes entire workbooks) on the World Wide Web. The first step to placement on the Web is to save the worksheet as a Web page. To do this:

1. Click the Office Button and select Save As.
2. Select Web Page (*.htm; *.html) from the *Save as type* drop-down list.
3. Click the Title text box to title the file appropriately and save it to the desired location. In the Publish as Web Page dialog box, click Publish.
4. You can preview the chart or workbook by opening your browser, navigating to the location of the Web page, and opening it.

Hands-on Exercises

3 | Embedding, Printing, and Saving a Chart as a Web Page

Skills covered: 1. Embed a Chart in Microsoft Word **2.** Copy the Worksheet **3.** Embed the Data **4.** Copy the Chart **5.** Embed the Chart **6.** Modify the Worksheet **7.** Update the Links **8.** Print Worksheet and Chart **9.** Save and View Chart as Web Page

Step 1
Embed a Chart in Microsoft Word

Refer to Figure 3.35 as you complete Step 1.

a. Start Word and if necessary, click the **Maximize** button in the application window so that Word takes up the entire screen.

b. Click the **Office Button** and select **Open**.

   1. Open *chap3_ho3_memo*.

   2. Save the document as **chap3_ho3_memo_solution**.

c. Set the **Zoom slider** to **100%** if necessary.

   The software memo is open.

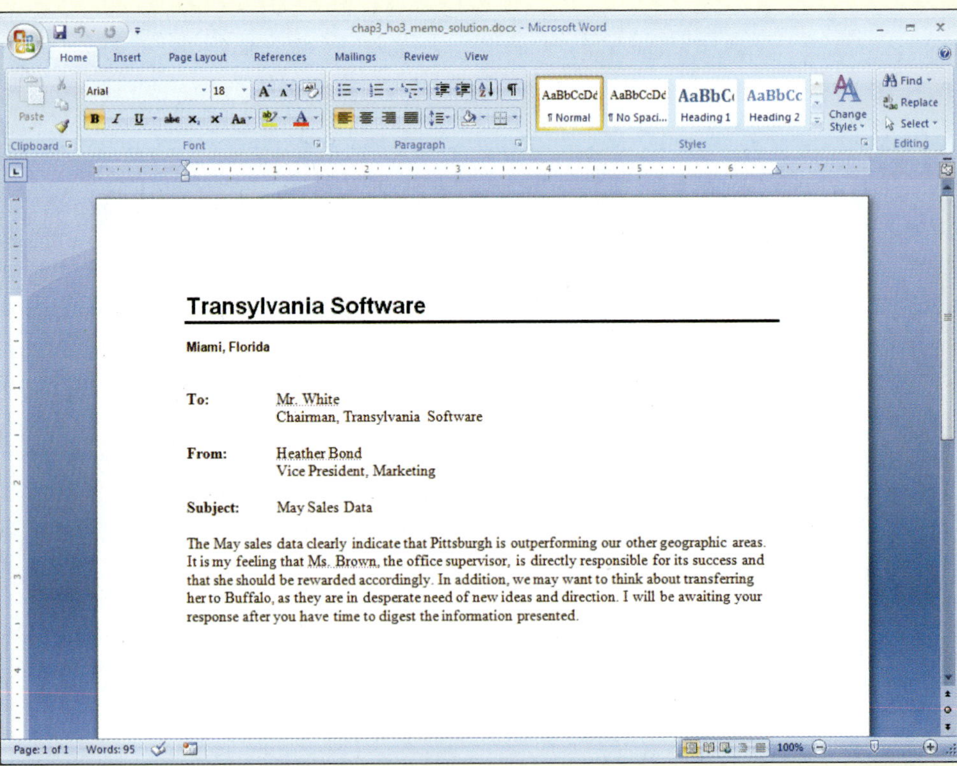

Figure 3.35 Memo in Word

Step 2
Copy the Worksheet

Refer to Figure 3.36 as you complete Step 2.

a. Open the *chap3_ho2_sales_solution* workbook from the previous exercise.

- If you did not close Microsoft Excel at the end of the previous exercise, you will see its button on the taskbar. Click the **Microsoft Excel button** to return to the *chap3_ho2_sales_solution* workbook.
- If you closed Microsoft Excel, start Excel again, and then open the *chap3_ho2_sales_solution* workbook.

b. Save the workbook as **chap3_ho3_sales_solution.**

The taskbar contains a button for both Microsoft Word and Microsoft Excel. You can click either button to move back and forth between the open applications. End by clicking the Microsoft Excel button to make it the active application.

c. Click the **Sales Data tab**. Click and drag to select **cells A1:F7** to select the entire worksheet as shown in Figure 3.36.

d. Right-click the selected area and select **Copy** from the shortcut menu.

A moving border appears around the entire worksheet, indicating that it has been copied to the clipboard.

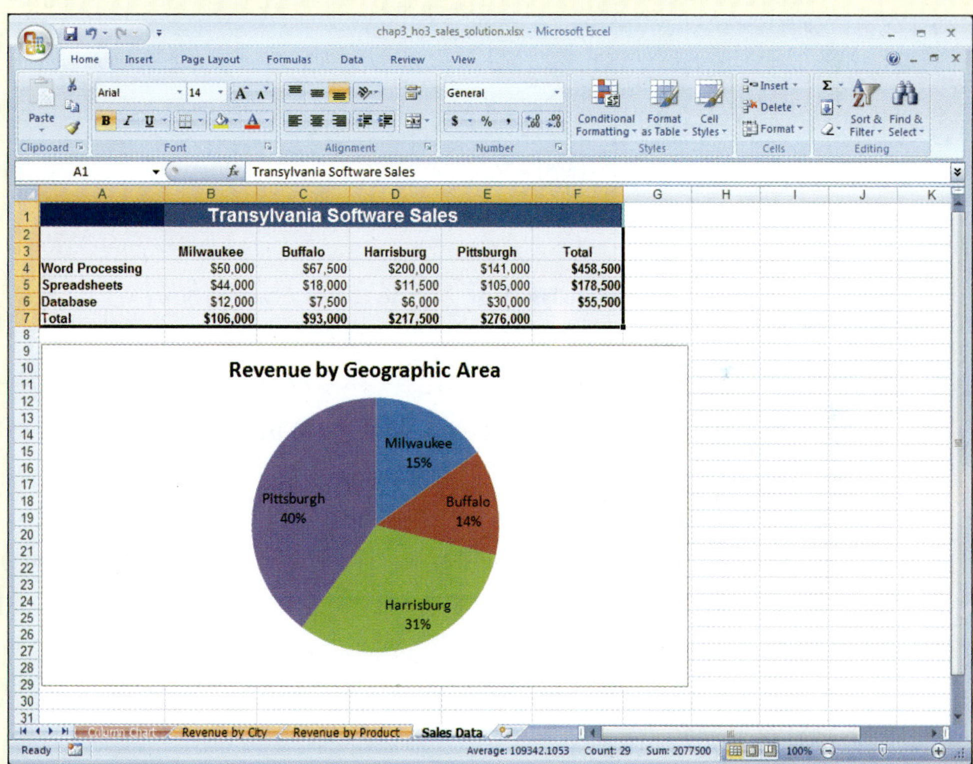

Figure 3.36 Worksheet Data to Copy

Step 3
Embed the Data

Refer to Figure 3.37 as you complete Step 3.

a. Click the **Microsoft Word button** on the taskbar to display the *chap3_ho3_memo_solution* document. Press **Ctrl+End** to move to the end of the memo, and press **Enter** to insert a blank line, which is where you will insert the Excel worksheet.

Microsoft Word is the active window, and the insertion point is at the end of the Memo document.

b. Click the **Paste down arrow** in the Clipboard group on the Home tab and select **Paste Special** to display the dialog box shown in Figure 3.37.

c. Click **Microsoft Office Excel Worksheet Object** in the list. Click **Paste link**. Click **OK** to insert the worksheet into the document.

Using the Paste Special option gives you the opportunity to paste the object and establish the link for later data editing in Excel.

d. Right-click the worksheet, select **Format Object** on the shortcut menu to display the associated dialog box, and click the **Layout tab**.

TROUBLESHOOTING: If you paste the spreadsheet only, it becomes a table in Word, not an object. You cannot format it because it is not an object with a link to Excel. You must use the Paste Special option to make sure the worksheet link is created.

e. Choose **Square** in the *Wrapping Style* section, and click **Center**. Click **OK** to accept the settings and close the dialog box. Click anywhere outside the table to deselect it. Save *chap3_ho3_memo_solution*.

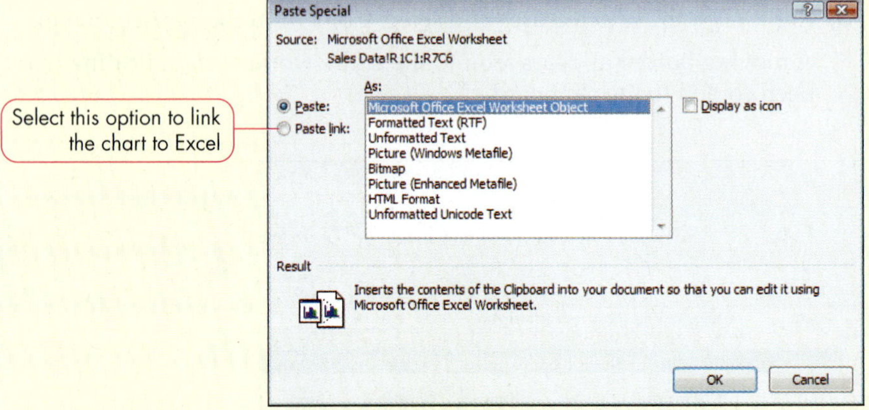

Figure 3.37 Paste Special Dialog Box

Step 4 Copy the Chart

a. Click the **Microsoft Excel button** on the taskbar to return to the worksheet.

b. Click outside the selected area to deselect the cells. Press **Esc** to remove the moving border.

c. Click the **Revenue by City tab**, and click the chart area to select the chart.

The chart is selected when you see the sizing handles on the border of the chart area.

d. Click **Copy** in the Clipboard group on the Home tab.

Step 5 Embed the Chart

Refer to Figure 3.38 as you complete Step 5.

a. Switch to **Word** and click **Paste** in the Clipboard group on the Home tab.

b. Click the **Paste Options Smart Tag** at the bottom left of the chart and verify that Chart (link to Excel data) is selected.

You pasted the chart object into your Memo. As a linked object it will be updated when the spreadsheet data is updated. The object permits chart formatting within the Word document.

TROUBLESHOOTING: If the object moves to another page, use the resize handles to shrink the object until it fits on the previous page.

c. Click on the chart if not selected, then click **Center** in the Paragraph group on the Home tab to center the chart.

d. Click the **Office Button**, point to **Print**, and then select **Print Preview**.

Your document should be similar to Figure 3.38. You use Print Preview to view your document to verify that the elements fit on one page.

e. Close Print Preview. Save the document.

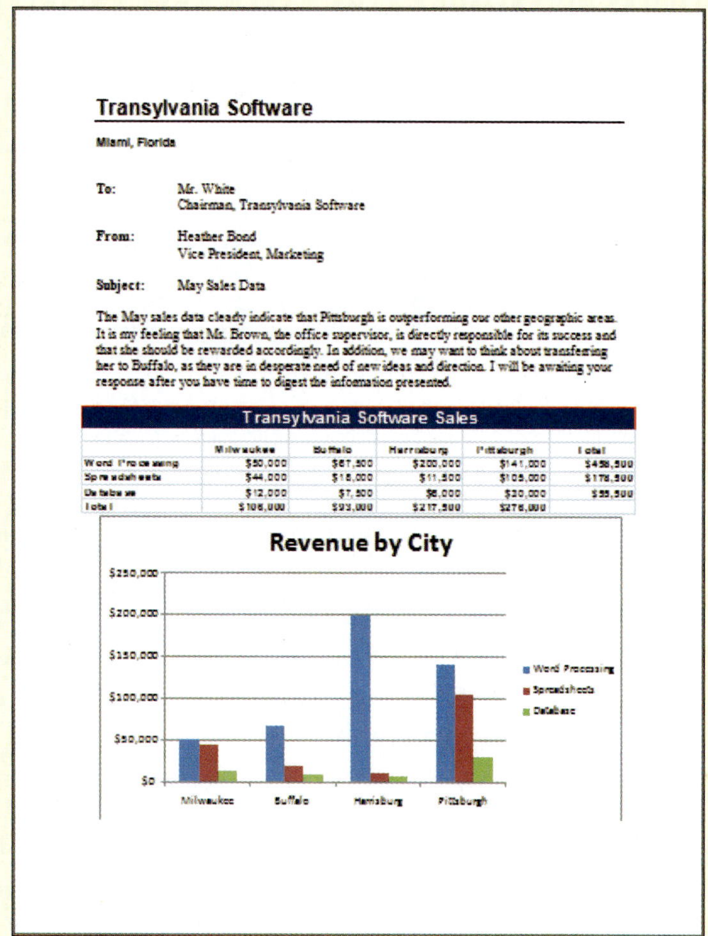

Transylvania Software

Miami, Florida

To: Mr. White
Chairman, Transylvania Software

From: Heather Bond
Vice President, Marketing

Subject: May Sales Data

The May sales data cleady indicate that Pittsburgh is outperforming our other geographic areas. It is my feeling that Ms. Brown, the office supervisor, is directly responsible for its success and that she should be rewarded accordingly. In addition, we may want to think about transfering her to Buffalo, as they are in desperate need of new ideas and direction. I will be awaiting your response after you have time to digest the infomation presented.

Transylvania Software Sales					
	Milwaukee	Buffalo	Harrisburg	Pittsburgh	Total
Word Processing	$50,000	$67,500	$200,000	$141,000	$458,500
Spreadsheets	$44,000	$18,000	$11,500	$105,000	$178,500
Database	$12,000	$7,500	$6,000	$30,000	$55,500
Total	$106,000	$93,000	$217,500	$276,000	

Figure 3.38 Chart Embedded in Memo

Step 6
Modify the Worksheet

Refer to Figure 3.39 as you complete Step 6.

a. Working in the Word document, click anywhere in the worksheet to select the worksheet and display the sizing handles.

The status bar indicates that you can double-click to edit the worksheet.

b. Double-click the worksheet to start Excel so you can change the data.

Excel starts and reopens the *chap3_ho3_sales_solution* workbook.

c. Click **Maximize** to maximize the Excel window, if needed.

d. Click the **Sales Data tab** within the workbook, if needed. Click in **cell B4**. Type **150000** and press **Enter**.

The wedge for Milwaukee shows the increase in the chart.

e. Click the **Revenue by City tab** to select the chart sheet. Save the workbook.

The chart reflects the increased sales for Milwaukee.

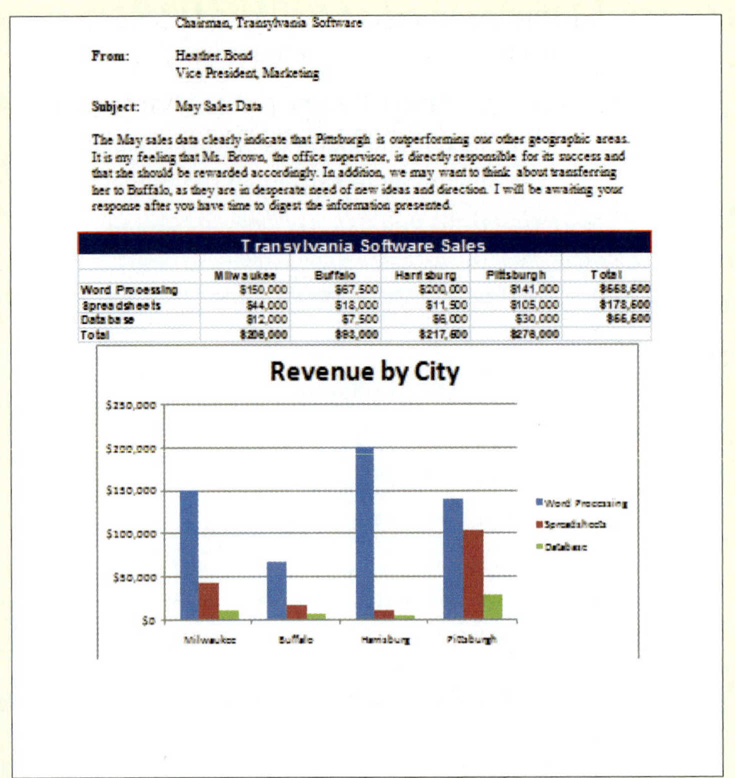

Chairman, Transylvania Software

From: Heather Bond
Vice President, Marketing

Subject: May Sales Data

The May sales data clearly indicate that Pittsburgh is outperforming our other geographic areas. It is my feeling that Ms.. Brown, the office supervisor, is directly responsible for its success and that she should be rewarded accordingly. In addition, we may want to think about transferring her to Buffalo, as they are in desperate need of new ideas and direction. I will be awaiting your response after you have time to digest the information presented.

Transylvania Software Sales					
	Milwaukee	Buffalo	Harrisburg	Pittsburgh	Total
Word Processing	$150,000	$67,500	$200,000	$141,000	$558,500
Spreadsheets	$44,000	$18,000	$11,500	$105,000	$178,500
Database	$12,000	$7,500	$6,000	$30,000	$55,500
Total	$206,000	$93,000	$217,500	$276,000	

Figure 3.39 Modified Worksheet Changes Reflected in Word Document

Step 7
Update the Links

a. Click the **Microsoft Word button** on the taskbar to display the *chap3_ho3_solution* document.

The worksheet and chart update automatically to reflect $150,000 for word processing sales in Milwaukee.

TROUBLESHOOTING: If the worksheet and chart do not automatically update, then point to the sheet object and click the right mouse button. Select Update Link from the shortcut menu.

b. Zoom to the **Whole Page** to view the completed document. Click and drag the worksheet or the chart within the memo to make any last-minute changes.

c. Save the memo again and close Word.

Step 8
Print Worksheet and Chart

Refer to Figure 3.40 as you complete Step 8.

a. Click on the **Sales Data tab** to make the Sales Data sheet active. Click the chart area to select it. Click **Move Chart** on the Design tab to display the dialog box. Click **New sheet** and click **OK** to close the dialog box.

The chart has been moved from below the spreadsheet to a new page and is displayed as full-screen view.

b. Click the **Office Button** and select **Print Preview** from the Print menu. Select or clear the **Show Margins** check box in the Preview group of the **Print Preview** toolbar to toggle the display of the margins on and off. Click **Close Print Preview** to return to the chart.

You used Print Preview and the Show Margins option to verify that the chart displays properly before printing.

c. Click **Page Setup dialog box launcher** on the Page Layout tab. Click the **Page tab** in the Page Setup dialog box if it is not displayed. Verify that **Landscape** is selected in the *Orientation* section.

d. Click the **Header/Footer tab** in the Page Setup dialog box and then click **Custom Footer** to display the Footer dialog box.

e. Click the text box for the left section and enter your name. Click the text box for the center section and enter your instructor's name.

   Headers and footers provide documentation on each page for any worksheet and chart.

f. Click the text box for the right section. Click the **Insert Date** button, press **Spacebar**, and then click the **Insert Time** button. Click **OK** to accept these settings and close the Footer dialog box. Click **OK** to close the Page Setup dialog box.

   You used the Page Setup options to change to landscape mode and create a custom footer on the page with the chart.

g. Print the workbook. Close the workbook without saving.

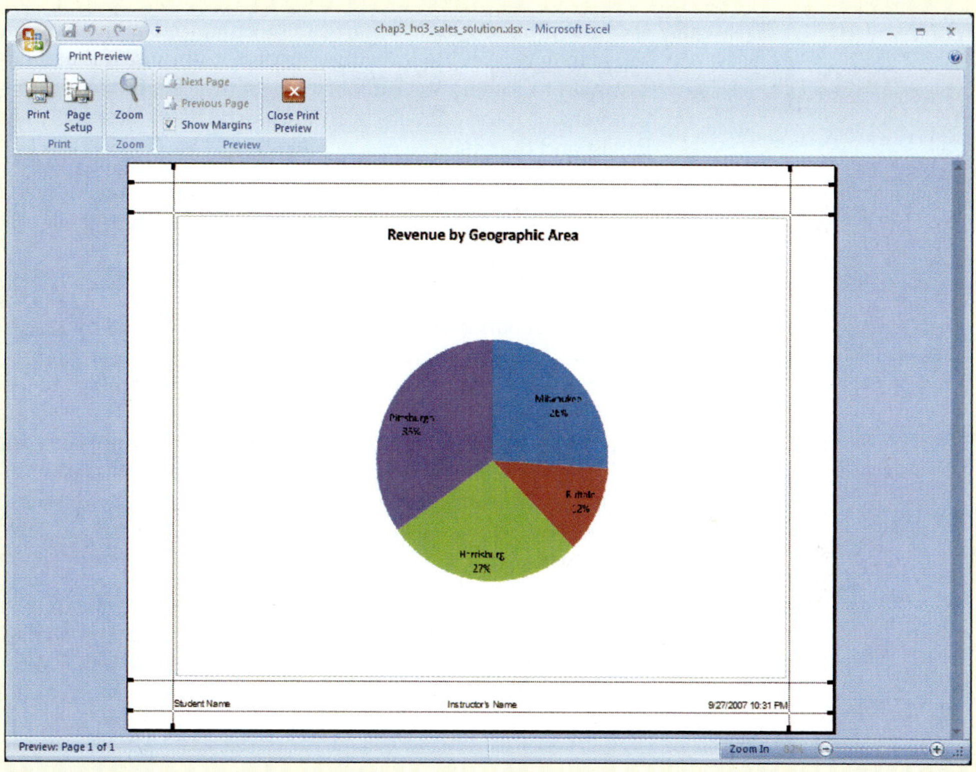

Figure 3.40 Print Preview of Chart with Custom Footers and Margin

Step 9
Save and View Chart as Web Page

a. Start Excel and open the *chap3_ho3_sales_solution* workbook.

b. Click on the **Revenue by Product tab** to make it the active sheet. Click the **Office Button** and select **Save As**.

c. Select **Web Page** from the *Save as type* list. Click **Selection: Chart**. Title the file appropriately and save it to the desired location. In the Publish as Web Page dialog box, click **Publish**.

d. You can preview the chart or workbook by opening your browser, navigating to the location of the Web page, and opening it.

Summary

1. **Choose a chart type.** A chart is a graphic representation of data in a worksheet. The type of chart chosen depends on the message to be conveyed. A pie chart is best for proportional relationships. A column or bar chart is used to show actual numbers rather than percentages. A line chart is preferable for time-related data. The choice between a clustered and a stacked column chart depends on the intended message. A clustered chart shows the contribution of each data point, but the total for each series is not as clear as with a stacked column chart. The stacked column chart, on the other hand, shows the totals clearly, but the contribution of the individual data points is obscured because the segments do not start at zero. It is important that charts are created accurately and that they do not mislead the reader. Stacked column charts should not add dissimilar quantities such as units and dollars.

2. **Create a chart.** Using the Insert tab is an effortless way to create charts. The title of a chart can help to convey the message. A neutral title such as "Revenue by City" leaves the reader to draw his or her own conclusion. Using a different title such as "Boston Leads All Cities" or "New York Is Trailing Badly" sends a very different message.

3. **Modify a chart.** Once created, a chart can be enhanced with arrows and text boxes. Multiple data series may be specified in either rows or columns. If the data are in rows, the first row is assumed to contain the category labels, and the first column is assumed to contain the legend. Conversely, if the data are in columns, the first column is assumed to contain the category labels, and the first row the legend.

4. **Enhance charts with graphic shapes.** These objects can be moved or sized and/or modified with respect to their color and other properties. The chart itself can also be modified using various tabs.

5. **Embed charts.** A chart may be embedded in a worksheet or created in a separate chart sheet. An embedded chart may be moved within a worksheet by selecting it and dragging it to its new location. An embedded chart may be sized by selecting it and dragging any of the sizing handles in the desired direction. Object embedding enables the creation of a compound document containing data from multiple applications. The essential difference between linking and embedding is whether the object is stored within the compound document (embedding) or in its own file (linking). An embedded object is stored in the compound document, which in turn becomes the only user (client) of that object. A linked object is stored in its own file, and the compound document is one of many potential users of that object. The same chart can be linked to a Word document and a PowerPoint presentation.

6. **Print charts.** Several options exist for printing charts. Users can print one chart, several charts, or a combination of the worksheet and the charts. Placing a chart on a separate sheet enables the user to print the chart in full-page format. Charts and worksheets can be saved as Web pages in HTML format and then be published to the World Wide Web (WWW).

Key Terms

Bar chart 434
Category label 431
Chart 431
Chart area 432
Clustered column chart 433
Column chart 432
Data label 451
Data point 431
Data series 431
Doughnut chart 436
Exploded pie chart 435
Legend 433
Line chart 436
Multiple data series 433
Pie chart 434
Plot area 432
Scatter (XY) chart 437
Stacked column chart 433
Stock chart 437
Three-dimensional pie chart . .435
X or horizontal axis 432
Y or vertical axis 432

Multiple Choice

1. Which type of chart is best to portray proportion or market share?
   (a) Pie chart
   (b) Line chart
   (c) Column chart
   (d) Combination chart

2. Which of the following chart types is *not* suitable to display multiple data series?
   (a) Pie chart
   (b) Horizontal bar chart
   (c) Column chart
   (d) All of the above are equally suitable.

3. Which of the following is best to display additive information from multiple data series?
   (a) A column chart with the data series stacked one on top of another
   (b) A column chart with the data series side by side
   (c) A scatter chart with two data series
   (d) A pie chart with five to ten wedges

4. A workbook can contain:
   (a) A separate chart sheet for every workbook
   (b) A separate workbook for every chart sheet
   (c) A sheet with both a workbook and chart
   (d) A separate chart sheet for every worksheet

5. Which of the following is true regarding an embedded chart?
   (a) It can be moved elsewhere within the worksheet.
   (b) It can be made larger or smaller.
   (c) Both (a) and (b)
   (d) Neither (a) nor (b)

6. Which of the following will display a shortcut menu?
   (a) Pointing to a workbook tab and clicking the right mouse button
   (b) Pointing to an embedded chart and clicking the right mouse button
   (c) Pointing to a selected cell range and clicking the right mouse button
   (d) All of the above

7. Which of the following is done *prior* to beginning to create a chart?
   (a) The data series are selected.
   (b) The location of the embedded chart within the worksheet is specified.
   (c) The workbook is saved.
   (d) The worksheet is formatted.

8. Which of the following will display sizing handles when selected?
   (a) An embedded chart
   (b) The title of a chart
   (c) A text box or arrow shape
   (d) All of the above

9. How do you switch between open applications?
   (a) Click the appropriate button on the taskbar.
   (b) Click the Start button in the taskbar.
   (c) Use Shift+Tab to cycle through the applications.
   (d) Use Crtl+~ to cycle through the applications.

10. To represent multiple data series on the same chart:
    (a) The data series must be in rows, and the rows must be adjacent to one another on the worksheet.
    (b) The data series must be in columns, and the columns must be adjacent to one another on the worksheet.
    (c) The data series may be in rows or columns so long as they are adjacent to one another.
    (d) The data series may be in rows or columns with no requirement to be next to one another.

11. If multiple data series are selected and rows are specified:
    (a) The first row will be used for the category labels.
    (b) The first row will be used for the legend.
    (c) The last column will be used for the legend.
    (d) The first column will be used for the category labels.

...continued on Next Page

Multiple Choice Continued...

12. If multiple data series are selected and columns are specified:
    (a) The first column will be used for the category (X axis) labels.
    (b) The first row will be used for the legend.
    (c) Both (a) and (b)
    (d) Neither (a) nor (b)

13. Which of the following is true about the scale on the *Y* axis in a column chart that plots multiple data series clustered versus one that stacks the values one on top of another?
    (a) The scale for the stacked columns chart contains larger values than the clustered chart.
    (b) The scale for the clustered columns contains larger values than the stacked columns.
    (c) The values on the scale will be the same for both charts.
    (d) The values will be different, but it is not possible to tell which chart has higher values.

14. A workbook includes a revenue worksheet with two embedded charts. The workbook also includes one chart in its own worksheet. How many files does it take to store this workbook?
    (a) 1
    (b) 2
    (c) 3
    (d) 4

15. You have created a Word document and embedded a linked Excel worksheet in that document. You make a change to the worksheet. What happens to the worksheet in the Word document?
    (a) It will be updated when you select the Refresh Data command.
    (b) It is unchanged.
    (c) It is automatically updated to reflect the changes.
    (d) You cannot change the worksheet because you have embedded it in a Word document.

16. You have selected cells B5:B10 as the data series for a chart and specified the data series are in columns. Which of the following is the legend text?
    (a) Cells B5 through F5
    (b) Cells C6 through F10
    (c) Cells B5 through B10
    (d) It is impossible to determine from the information given.

17. The same data range is used as the basis for an embedded pie chart, as well as a column chart in a chart sheet. Which chart(s) will change if you change the values in the data range?
    (a) The column chart
    (b) The pie chart
    (c) Both the pie chart and the column chart
    (d) Neither the pie chart nor the column chart

Practice Exercises

1 Vacation Park Admissions

Your summer job is with the professional organization representing theme parks across the country. You have gathered data on theme park admissions in four areas of the country. In this exercise you will finish the worksheet and create charts. The completed version of the worksheet is shown in Figure 3.41.

a. Open *chap3_pe1_vacation* and save as **chap3_pe1_vacation_solution**.

b. Select **cells B8:E8**. Click **AutoSum** in the Editing group on the Home tab to compute the total for each quarter. Select **cells F4:F8** and then click **AutoSum**.

c. Select **cells B4:F8** and format these cells as **Number** with commas and no decimal places. Bold the row and column headings and the totals. Center the entries in **cells B3:F3**. Select **cells A1:F1**, then click **Merge & Center** in the Alignment group on the Home tab to center the title. With the same cells selected, choose the **Blue, Accent 1** theme color from the **Fill Color** list. Increase the title font size to **14 points** and change the font color to **White, Background 1**. Select **cells B3:F3** and change the font color to **Blue, Accent 1**. Similarly change **cell A8**. Save the workbook.

d. Complete the substeps to create a column chart that shows the number of admissions for each region and for each quarter within each region and insert the graphic as shown in Figure 3.41:

- Select **cells A3:E7**. Click the **Insert tab** and click **Column** in the Charts group. Select the **Clustered Column** subtype to display the chart on the Admissions Data worksheet.
- Click the border of the chart to select it. Using the four-headed arrow, drag the chart into position below the worksheet.
- Right-click the legend and select **Bold** and **Italic** to format the legend.
- Click the **Insert tab** and click **Shapes** in the Illustrations group, and then select **Left Arrow**. Click and drag to create a thick arrow that points to the **1st Quarter South** column. Release the mouse. The arrow is selected, and the Format tab is displayed.
- Click **Text Box** in the Insert Shapes group on the Format tab to insert a text box. Click and drag a text box on top of the thick arrow. Release the mouse. Enter text by typing **South First-Quarter Admissions High**. Select the text you just typed, and use the Mini toolbar to change the font to **9-point** bold **White, Background 1**.

e. Complete the substeps to create a pie chart, in its own sheet, that shows the percentage of the total number of admissions in each region:

- Select **cells A4:A7**, then press and hold **Ctrl** while selecting cells **F4:F7**.
- Click the **Insert tab** to make it active. Click **Pie** in the Charts group, and then select **Pie** as the subtype to display the pie chart on the Admissions Data sheet. Click **Move Chart** on the Design tab, click the **New Sheet** option, type **Pie Chart**, and click **OK**.
- Right-click any pie wedge, and select **Add Data Labels** to add data labels to the chart area. Right-click any pie wedge and select **Format Data Labels** to display the Format Data Labels dialog box. Click **Label Options** and then click the **Category Name** and **Percentage check boxes** to format the data labels. Clear the **Value** check box.
- Change the values in the data labels to percentages by clicking **Number** in the left pane, click **Percentage** in the **Category** list, change the Decimal places to 0, and click **Close** to accept the settings and close the dialog box. Right-click any data label and increase the font size to **14-point** italic.

...continued on Next Page

- Click **Legend** in the Labels group on the Layout tab and select **None** to delete the legend.
- Click **Chart Title** in the Labels group on the Layout tab and select **Centered Overlay Title**. Type **Vacation Park Admissions by Region** and press **Enter**.

f. Complete the substeps to create a stacked column chart, in its own sheet, showing the number of admissions for each quarter and for each region within each quarter:

- Select **cells A3:E7** on the Admissions Data worksheet. Click the **Insert tab** and click **Column** in the Charts group. Select the **Stacked Column in 3-D** subtype to display the stacked column chart.
- Click **Move Chart** on the Design tab, click the **New sheet** option, type **Stacked Column**, and click **OK.**
- Click the border of the chart to select the entire chart. Click **Data Labels** in the Labels group on the Layout tab and select **Show**. Click **Chart Title** in the Labels group on the Layout tab and select **Centered Overlay Title**. Type **Admissions by Quarter and Region Within Quarter** and press **Enter**. Change the color of each worksheet tab to **Blue, Accent 1**.

g. Click the **Stacked Column tab** to make it the active sheet. Click the **Office Button** and select **Save As**. Select **Web Page** from the *Save as type* list. Click **Selection: Chart**. Click **Change Title** and type **Vacation Web Page**, then click **OK** and save it. In the Publish as Web Page dialog box, click **Publish**. You can preview the chart by opening your Internet browser, navigating to the location of the Web page, and opening it.

h. Click the **Pie Chart worksheet tab**. Press and hold down **Ctrl** as you click the other worksheet tabs. Create a header for the selected worksheets that includes your name, your course, and your instructor's name. Create a footer that includes the name of the worksheet tab. Print the entire workbook, consisting of the worksheet in Figure 3.41, plus the additional sheets you created. Use portrait orientation for the **Admissions Data** worksheet and landscape orientation for the other worksheets. Save and close the workbook.

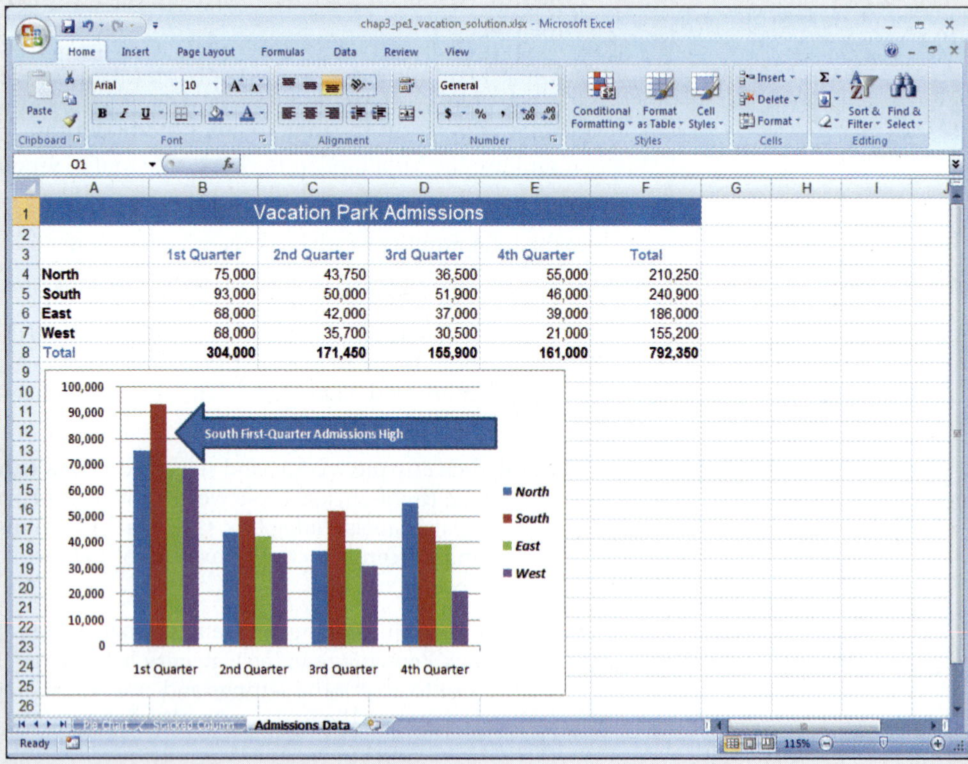

Figure 3.41 Vacation Park Charts

...continued on Next Page

2 AnytimeTalk, Inc.—Chart Formatting

The worksheet shown in Figure 3.42 shows third-quarter revenues for each salesperson at AnytimeTalk, Inc., the cellular company where you will do your internship this summer. One of your assigned duties is to complete the Fourth-Quarter Revenue worksheet and create a column chart showing a comparison of each salesperson's total sales for the fourth quarter. The chart is to be formatted for a professional presentation.

a. Open *chap3_pe2_talk* and save as **chap3_pe2_talk_solution**.
b. Click and drag to select **cells E3:E7**. Click **AutoSum** in the Editing group on the Home tab to compute the total for each salesperson. Click and drag to select **cells B8:E8** and then click **AutoSum** to compute the totals for each month and the total for the quarter.
c. Click and drag to select **cells B3:E8** and format these cells as **Currency with no decimal places**. Bold the row and column headings and the totals. Center the entries in **cells B2:E2**.
d. Select **cells A1:E1**, then click **Merge & Center** in the Alignment group on the Home tab to center the title. With the same cells selected, choose **Orange, Accent 6** from the theme colors in the **Fill Color** list. Increase the title font size to **18 points** and change the font color to **Orange, Accent 6, Darker 50%**.
e. Increase the height of row 1 as necessary to display the title. Select **cells A2:E2** and **A8**, and change the font color to the same font color used in row 1.
f. Select **cells A4:E4** and change the fill color to **Orange**, **Accent 6**, **Lighter 80%**. Save the workbook.
g. Select **cells A3:A7,** and while holding **Ctrl**, select **cells E3:E7**. Click the **Insert tab** and click **Column** in the Charts group. Select the **Clustered Cylinder** column subtype to display the chart on the Sales Data sheet.
h. Click the white background of the chart to select it and using the four-headed arrow, drag the chart into position below the worksheet data. Right-click the legend and select **Delete** to delete the legend.
i. Right-click any cylinder, and select **Add Data Labels** to add data labels to the chart area.
j. Triple-click the second cylinder to select just this column. Right-click the selected cylinder, select **Format Data Point**, click the **Fill** option in the associated dialog box, click **Gradient fill**, and then change the color of this column to a coordinating theme color. Select **Close** to close the dialog box.
k. Click in **cell A4** and enter your name. The value on the X axis changes automatically to reflect the entry in cell A4. Select the chart, and then click **Chart Title** in the Labels group on the Layout tab. Click **Above Chart** and type **Fourth-Quarter Revenues** as the title of the chart.
l. Click the **Insert tab**. Click **Shapes** in the Illustrations group, and then select **Line Callout 1**. Click and drag to create a callout that points to your cylinder. Release the mouse button. The callout is selected, and the Format tab is selected. Change the Shape Fill color and the Shape Outline color by selecting appropriate theme colors from the **Shape Fill** list and the **Shape Outline** list in the Shape Styles group on the Format tab.
m. Right-click the callout, select **Edit Text**, and type **This cylinder represents my data**. Select the text you just typed, click the **Font Size down arrow** in the Font group on the Home tab, select **10**, click the **Font Color down arrow**, and select **Automatic**.
n. Right-click the border of the chart, select **Format Chart Area**, then change the border to include rounded corners with a shadow effect. Use the Border Styles, and Shadow options to make the changes to make changes that match Figure 3.42.
o. Save the workbook and print the completed worksheet. Close the workbook.

...continued on Next Page

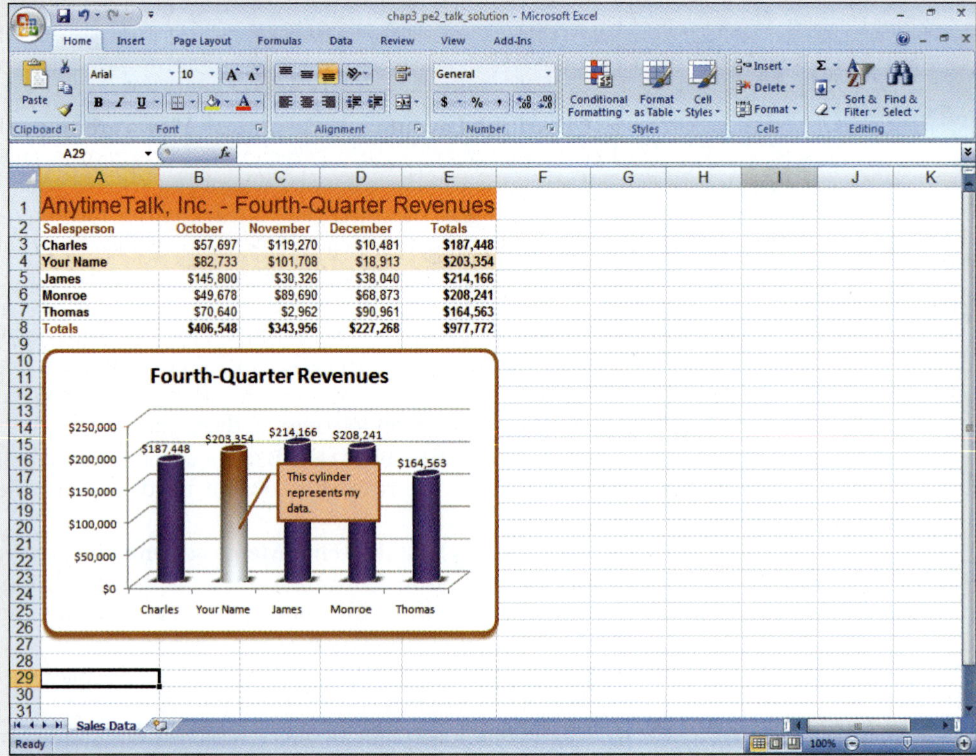

Figure 3.42 AnytimeTalk, Inc.

3 Printing Charts

Your sister asked you to chart weekly sales from her chain of mystery bookstores. As shown in Figure 3.43, stores are in four cities, and you must plot four product lines. You will create the charts as embedded objects on the worksheet. Do not be concerned about the placement of each chart until you have completed all four charts. The first chart is a clustered column and emphasizes the sales in each city (the data are in rows). The second chart is a stacked column version of the first chart. The third chart (that begins in column H of the worksheet) is a clustered column chart that emphasizes the sales in each product line (the data are in columns). The fourth chart is a stacked column version of the third chart. Figure 3.43 shows a reduced screen view of the four charts.

a. Open *chap3_pe3_print* and save as **chap3_pe3_print_solution**.
b. Select **cells A2:E6**, click **Column** in the Charts group on the Insert tab, and then click **Clustered Column** to embed a clustered column chart. With the chart selected, click **Style 16** in the Chart Styles group on the Design tab. To add a chart title, click **Layout 1** in the Chart Layouts group on the Design tab. To change the default title, select the words *Chart Title* and type **Weekly Sales by Location and Product Line**. Select the title, right-click and change the font size to **14 points**. Drag the chart into position below the workbook. Save the workbook.
c. Select the chart, click the **Home tab**, click **Copy** in the Clipboard group to copy the chart, click in **cell A27**, and click **Paste** in the Clipboard group on the Home tab. With the chart selected, click the **Design tab** and click **Change Chart Type** in the Type group. Click **Stacked Column** in the Column area of the Change Chart Type dialog box and click **OK**. Save the workbook.
d. Select the **first** chart, click the **Home tab**, click **Copy** to copy the chart, click in **cell H2**, and click **Paste**. With the chart selected, click the **Design tab** and click **Switch Row/Column** in the Data group. Save the workbook.
e. Select the third chart, click the **Home tab**, click **Copy** to copy the chart, click in **cell H19,** and click **Paste** on the Home tab. With the chart selected, click the **Design tab** and click **Change Chart Type** in the Type group. Click **Stacked Column** in the Column area of the Change Chart Type dialog box and click **OK**. Save the workbook.

...continued on Next Page

f. Click **Page Break Preview** in the Workbook Views group on the View tab. Your screen should be similar to Figure 3.43. You will see one or more dotted lines that show where the page breaks will occur. You will also see a message indicating that you can change the location of the page breaks. Click **OK** after you have read the message.

g. Click **Page Layout** in the Workbook Views group on the View tab. Click to the left of *Click to add header*, type your name, click in the middle header section, type your course, click the right header section, and type your instructor's name.

h. Click **Go to Footer** in the Navigation group on the Header & Footer Tools Design tab. Click in the left footer section, click **Current Date** in the Header & Footer Elements group, click in the middle footer section, click **File Name**, click in the right footer section, and click **Current Time**.

i. Click in the worksheet. Click the **Page Setup Dialog Box Launcher**, click **Landscape**, click the **Fit to option**, and click **OK**. Print the worksheet. Save and close the workbook.

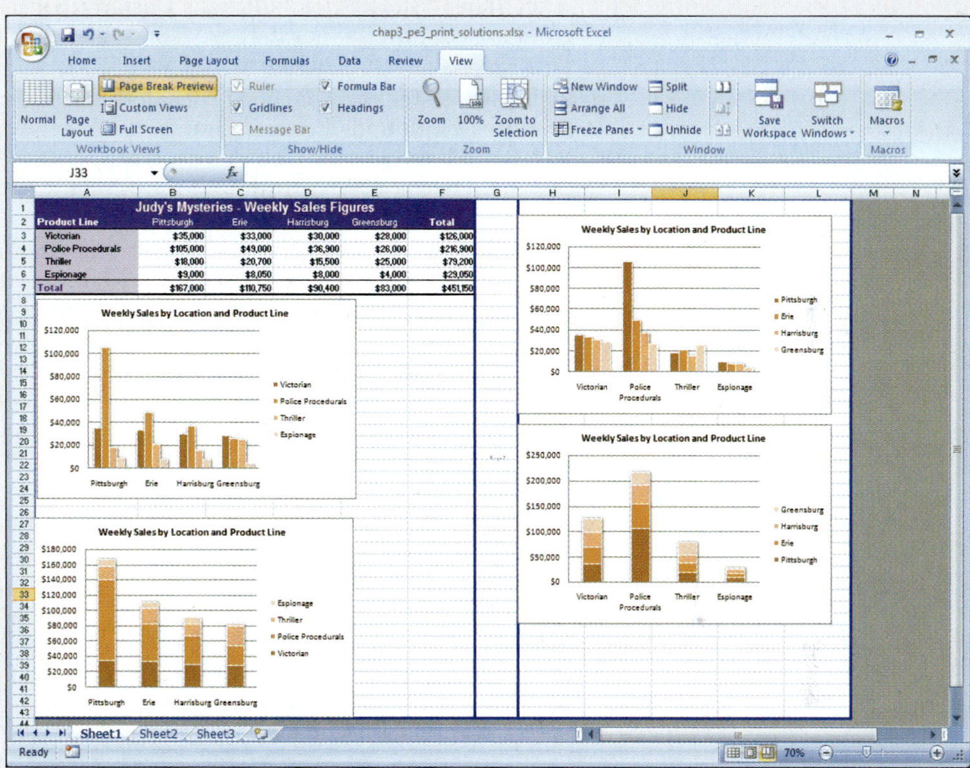

Figure 3.43 Printing Charts

4 Stock Price Comparisons

Figure 3.44 contains a combination chart to display different kinds of information on different scales for multiple data series. You start by creating a clustered column chart for the revenue and profits, and then you create a second data series to chart the stock prices as a line. Two different scales are necessary because the magnitudes of the numbers differ significantly. Your investment club asked you to make a recommendation about the purchase of the stock based on your analysis.

a. Open *chap3_pe4_stock* and save as **chap3_pe4_stock_solution**.

b. Select **cells A1:F4.** Click the **Insert tab** and click **Column** in the Charts group. Then select **Clustered Column** from the 2-D Column row. Select **Style 2** from the Design tab.

...continued on Next Page

c. Click the chart border to select the chart and using the four-headed arrow, drag the chart into position under the worksheet. Right-click the legend and select **Format Legend**. In the *Legend Options* section, click **Bottom** as the legend position, and click **Close**.

You are now going to add a secondary vertical axis to display Stock Price because the size of the numbers differs significantly from Revenue and Profit.

d. Click the chart to make it active. Click the **Format tab**. Click the **Chart Elements down arrow** in the Current Selection group and select **Series "Stock Price"** as the data series to plot on the secondary axis.

e. Click **Format Selection** in the Current Selection group and click **Secondary Axis** in *Series Options* in the Format Data Series dialog box. Click **Close** to close the dialog box. Click the **Layout tab**, click **Axes** in the Axes group, point to **Secondary Vertical Axis,** and select **Show Default Axis.**

f. Change the data series to a line chart to distinguish the secondary axis. Click the **Format tab**, click the **Chart Elements down arrow** in the Current Selection group, and select **Series "Stock Price."** Click the **Design tab**, click **Change Chart Type** in the Type group, select **Line** as the chart type, and then click the first example of a line chart. Click **OK** to view the combination chart.

g. Right-click on the chart but above the plot area, select **Format Chart Area**, click **Border Styles**, check **Rounded corners** and increase the width to 1.5 pts, click **Border Color**, click **Solid line**, click the **Color down arrow**, and select **Red, Accent 2**. Click **Shadow**, click the **Presets down arrow**, and select **Inside Center**. Click **Close** to see the customized border around the chart.

h. Deselect the chart. Click the **Page Layout tab** and open the Page Setup dialog box. Click **Landscape** for orientation, click the **Margins tab**, and click the **Horizontally** and **Vertically check boxes** to center the worksheet and chart on the page. Click the **Header/Footer tab** create a custom header for the worksheet that includes your name, your course name, and your instructor's name. Create a custom footer that contains the name of the file in which the worksheet is contained, today's date, and the current time. Save the workbook and print your worksheet. Close the workbook.

i. What do you think should be the more important factor influencing a company's stock price, its revenue (sales) or its profit (net income)? Could the situation depicted in the worksheet occur in the real world? Summarize your thoughts in a brief note to your instructor. Print the document.

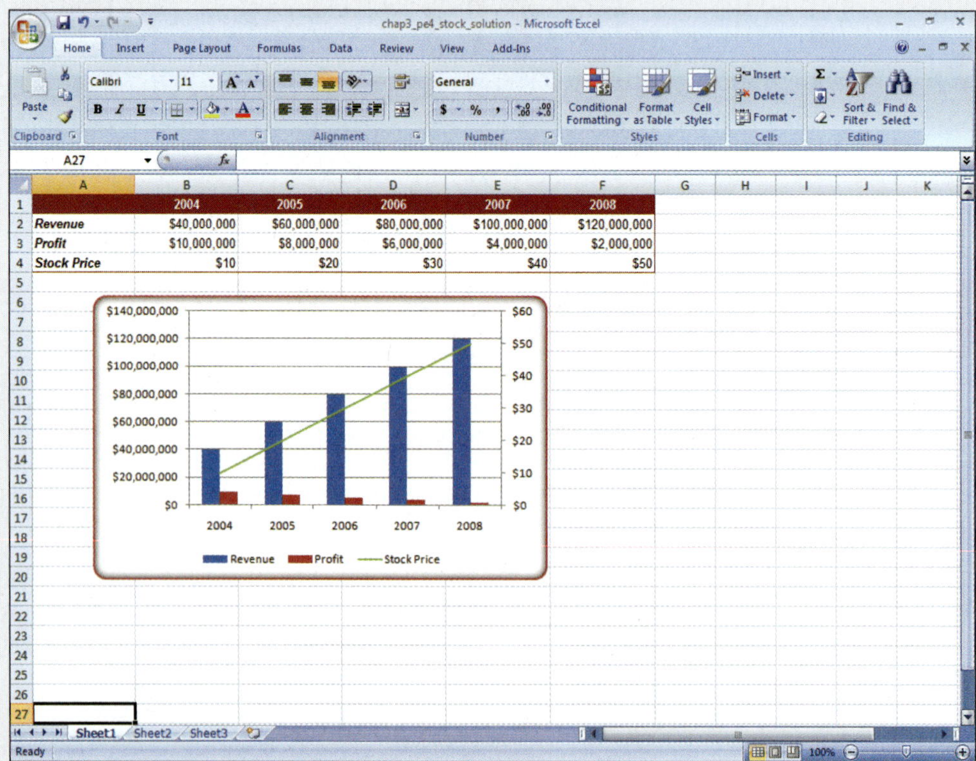

Figure 3.44 Stock Price Comparison

Mid-Level Exercises

1 The Next Car You Purchase

The Word document in Figure 3.45 displays descriptive information about a car you are interested in purchasing, a picture of the car, and a hyperlink to the Web site where the information was obtained. In addition, the document is linked to an Excel workbook that computes the car payment for you, based on the loan parameters that you provide. Your assignment is to create a similar document based on any car you choose.

a. Open *chap3_mid1_auto* and save as **chap3_mid1_auto_solution**.

b. Locate a Web site that contains information about the car you are interested in. You can go to the Web site of the manufacturer, or you can go to a general site such as autos.msn.com, which contains information about all makes and models. Select the car you want and obtain the retail price of the car.

c. Enter the price of the car, a hypothetical down payment, the interest rate of the car loan, and the term of the loan in the indicated cells. The monthly payment will be determined automatically by the PMT function that is stored in the workbook. Use Help if needed to review the PMT function. Save the workbook.

d. Select **cells A3:B9** (the cells that contain the information you want to insert into the Word document) and copy the selected range to the Clipboard.

e. Open the partially completed Word document, *chap3_mid1_auto* Microsoft Word document. Press **Ctrl+End** to position the insertion point at the end of the document. Use the Paste Special option to link the worksheet data as a link to a Microsoft Office Excel Worksheet Object. Save the Word document as **chap3_mid1_auto_solution**.

f. Use the taskbar to return to the Excel workbook. Change the amount of the down payment to **$6,500** and the interest rate for your loan to **4%**. Save the workbook. Close Excel. Return to the Word document, which should reflect the updated loan information.

g. Return to the Web page that contains the information about your car. Right-click the picture of the car that appears within the Web page and select **Save Picture As** to save the picture of the car to your computer. Use the **Insert Picture from File** command to insert the picture that you saved. Move and resize the picture as needed.

h. Complete the Word document by inserting some descriptive information about your car. Print the completed document. Save and close the document.

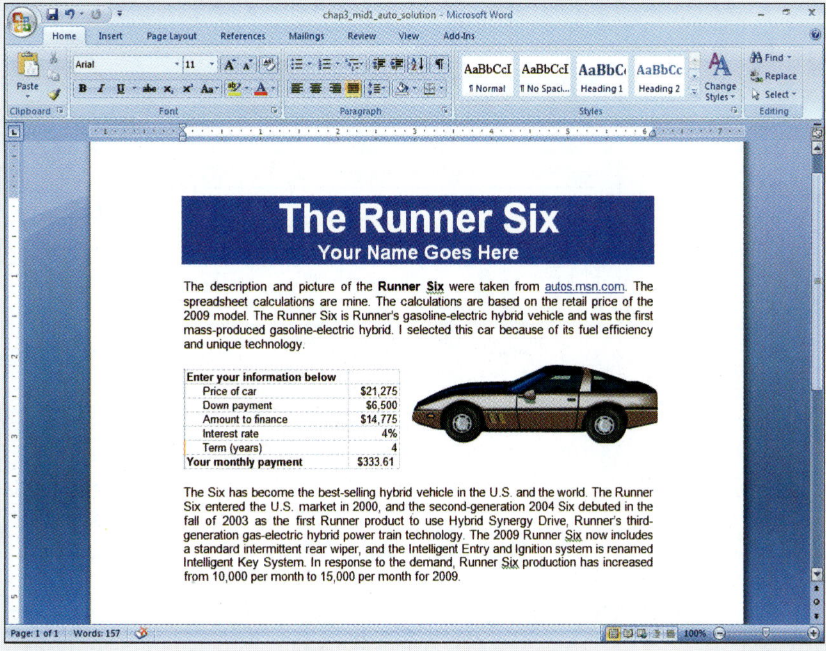

The Runner Six

Your Name Goes Here

The description and picture of the **Runner Six** were taken from autos.msn.com. The spreadsheet calculations are mine. The calculations are based on the retail price of the 2009 model. The Runner Six is Runner's gasoline-electric hybrid vehicle and was the first mass-produced gasoline-electric hybrid. I selected this car because of its fuel efficiency and unique technology.

Enter your information below	
Price of car	$21,275
Down payment	$6,500
Amount to finance	$14,775
Interest rate	4%
Term (years)	4
Your monthly payment	$333.61

The Six has become the best-selling hybrid vehicle in the U.S. and the world. The Runner Six entered the U.S. market in 2000, and the second-generation 2004 Six debuted in the fall of 2003 as the first Runner product to use Hybrid Synergy Drive, Runner's third-generation gas-electric hybrid power train technology. The 2009 Runner Six now includes a standard intermittent rear wiper, and the Intelligent Entry and Ignition system is renamed Intelligent Key System. In response to the demand, Runner Six production has increased from 10,000 per month to 15,000 per month for 2009.

Figure 3.45 The Next Car You Purchase

...continued on Next Page

2 Comparison of Rows and Columns

Figure 3.46 displays a worksheet with two similar charts detailing annual visits to different exhibits at the local Petting Zoo, one that plots data by rows and the other by columns. The distinction depends on the message you want to deliver. Both charts are correct. You collected the data at your summer job at the Petting Zoo and must now plot it for your intern supervisor as part of the analysis of the most popular animals at the zoo. You will create both charts shown and for comparison purposes create two more charts on a new sheet to determine the best presentation of data.

a. Open *chap3_mid2_zoo* and save as **chap3_mid2_zoo_solution**.

b. Use **AutoSum** to compute the total number of visits for each animal category and each quarter. Rename the Sheet1 tab as **Side by Side Columns**. Format the worksheet in an attractive manner by matching the formatting shown in Figure 3.46.

c. Create each of the charts as embedded charts on the current worksheet. The first chart specifies that the data series are in columns. The second chart specifies the data series are in rows. Apply the **Style 39** chart style to each chart.

d. Change to landscape orientation when the chart is printed. Create a custom header that includes your name, your course, and your instructor's name. Create a custom footer with the name of the worksheet, today's date, and the current time. Specify that the worksheet will be printed at 110% to create a more attractive printed page. Be sure, however, that the worksheet and associated charts fit on a single page by decreasing the bottom margin, if needed.

e. Copy the worksheet and name the duplicate worksheet as **Stacked Columns**.

f. Select the first chart in the newly created Stacked Columns worksheet. Change the chart type to Stacked Columns. Change the chart type of the second chart to Stacked Columns as well. Repeat step d for the Stacked Columns worksheet.

g. Print the completed workbook (both worksheets). Add a short note that summarizes the difference between plotting data in rows versus columns, and between clustered column charts and stacked column charts. Save and close the workbook.

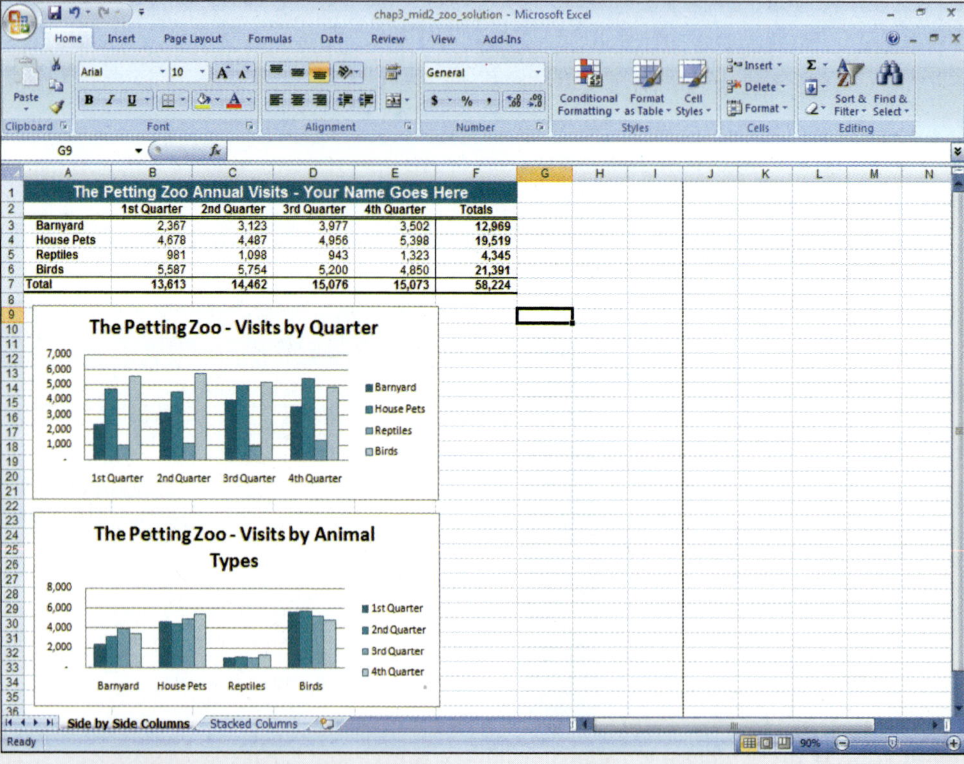

Figure 3.46 Comparison of Rows and Columns

...continued on Next Page

3 Home Arts

Your first job is as a management trainee at the Needlework Nook, a store specializing in home arts. The store manager has asked you to examine sales for the four quarters of the current year in five categories. She also has asked you to chart the sales figures. Complete the partially completed spreadsheet and create a chart that highlights quarterly product sales for the current year. Figure 3.47 shows the completed chart.

a. Open *chap3_mid3_homearts* and save as **chap3_mid3_homearts_solution**.

b. Use the **AutoSum** command to compute the totals for the quarters and categories of products. Rename Sheet1 as **Current Year**.

c. Create a stacked column chart based on the data in **cells A2:E7**. Specify that the data series are in rows so that each column represents total sales for each quarter. Display the legend on the right side of the chart. Save the chart in its own sheet called **Graphical Analysis**.

d. Experiment with variations of the chart created. Change the chart type from a stacked column to a clustered column and change the orientation of the data series from rows to columns. After experimenting with various chart types, select the stacked column chart because it is the chart most appropriate to show the sales by quarter and category. Also experiment with the placement of the legend by moving to the bottom and the top. After experimenting with the placement of the legend, place it to the right of the chart. Apply the **Style 19** chart style to the chart.

e. Add data labels to the stacks on the Graphical Analysis sheet. Change the color of the worksheet tabs to **Aqua, Accent 5** for the Current Year tab and **Aqua, Accent 5, Darker 50%** for the Graphical Analysis tab.

f. Select both worksheet tabs. Create a custom header that includes your name, your course, and your instructor's name. Create a custom footer with the name of the worksheet, today's date, and the current time.

g. Print the completed workbook consisting of two worksheets. Save and close the workbook.

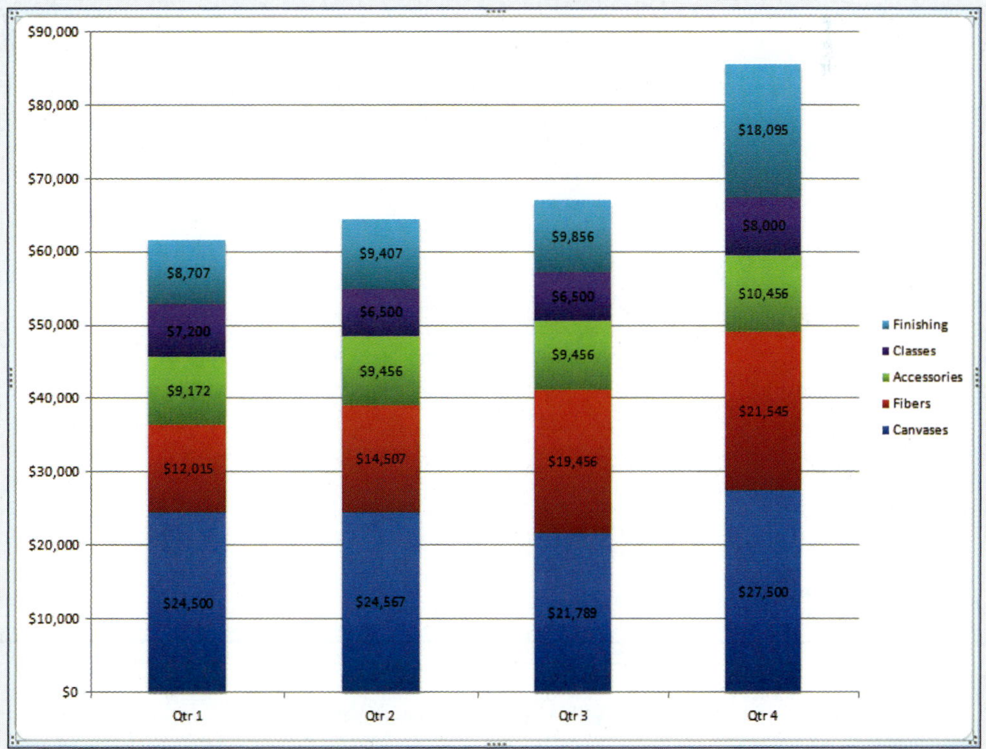

Figure 3.47 Home Arts

4 Study Analysis

Your sociology professor wants to know the correlation between time spent studying for quizzes and quiz scores, if any. You recorded the time spent studying for 10 quizzes and asked two friends to do the same thing. Now you must plot the data in a scatter chart and complete the analysis. Use the worksheet shown in Figure 3.48 and chart your data.

a. Open *chap3_mid4_scatter* and save as **chap3_mid4_scatter_solution**.

b. Insert a row above the worksheet and type the title **Test Analysis**. Center the title above the worksheet. Format the completed worksheet in an attractive manner. You do not have to duplicate our formatting exactly.

c. Create a scatter chart based on the data in **cells A2:E12**. Display the legend to the right of the chart.

d. Insert a chart title **Study Time and Quiz Scores.** Add an X-axis title **Time in Hours** and a Y-axis title **Test Score**.

e. Change the chart type to **Scatter with Smooth Lines and Markers**.

f. Add your analysis of the correlation between study time and quiz scores below the chart.

g. Delete the Sheet2 and Sheet3 tabs and rename Sheet1 as **Test Scores**. Add a tab color, **Red**, to the Test Scores tab.

h. Create a custom header that includes your name, your course, and your instructor's name. Create a custom footer with the name of the worksheet, today's date, and the current time.

i. Print the completed workbook making sure the worksheet, chart, and analysis fit on one page. Save and close the workbook.

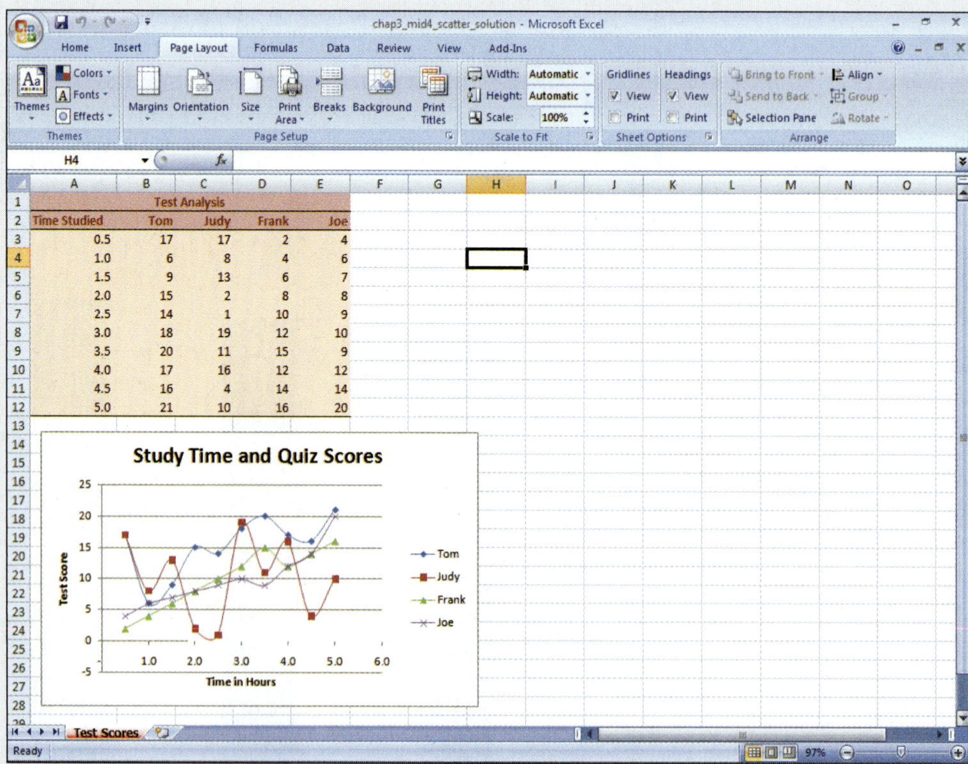

Figure 3.48 Study Analysis

5 Computer Sales Analysis

Your computer professor has asked you to provide a comparison of computer sales across the country. Complete the worksheet as shown in Figure 3.49 but include three charts to show the sales in a variety of ways. Include a summary indicating the most effective chart and why you consider it the most effective for comparing sales data.

a. Open *chap3_mid5_computer* and save as **chap3_mid5_computer_solution**.

b. Use **AutoSum** to compute the totals for the corporation in column F and row 6.

c. Format **cells B3:F6** as Currency, zero decimal places. Center the title above the worksheet. Format the completed worksheet in an attractive manner. You do not have to duplicate our formatting exactly.

d. Use the completed worksheet as the basis for a stacked column chart with the data plotted in rows.

e. Create a pie chart showing total sales by city, placing it on a separate sheet. Rename the sheet as **Sales by City.** Format the chart with the **Style 26** chart style. Add the title **Sales by City** and include data labels with category names and values in **14 point** size. Delete the legend.

f. Make a cluster column chart, placing it on a separate sheet and renaming the sheet **Sales by Product**. Format the chart with the **Style 32** chart style. Include a legend below the chart, a chart title, axes titles, and a shape to draw attention to the city with the highest notebook sales. Include an appropriate text message on the shape.

g. Select all three worksheet tabs. Create a custom footer that contains your name, the name of the worksheet, and today's date. Print the entire workbook. Save and close the workbook.

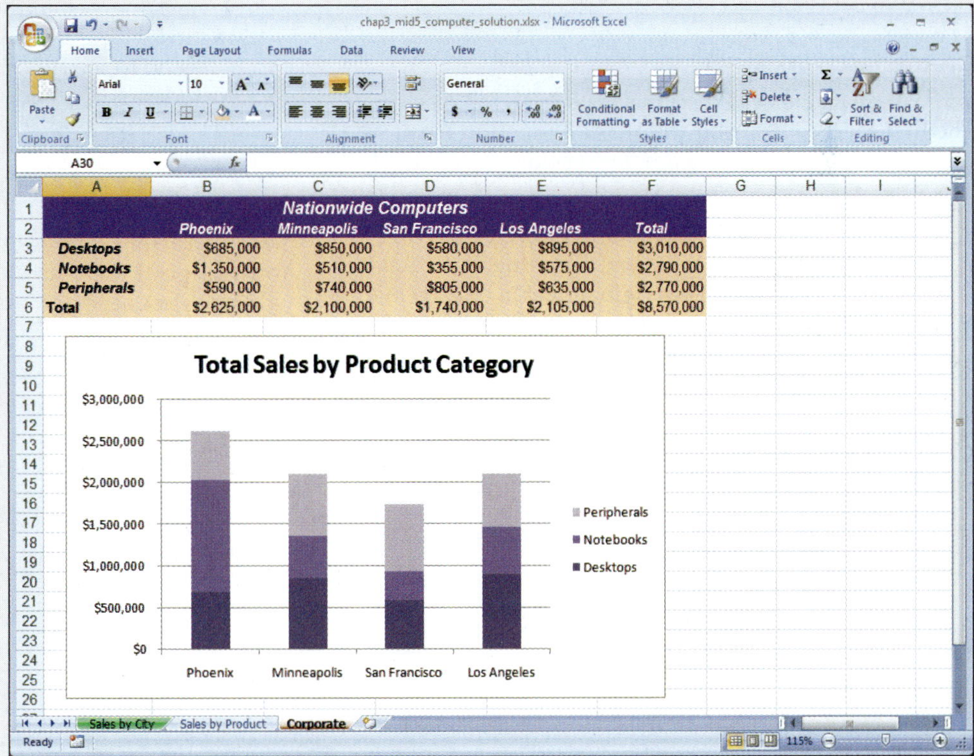

Nationwide Computers					
	Phoenix	Minneapolis	San Francisco	Los Angeles	Total
Desktops	$685,000	$850,000	$580,000	$895,000	$3,010,000
Notebooks	$1,350,000	$510,000	$355,000	$575,000	$2,790,000
Peripherals	$590,000	$740,000	$805,000	$635,000	$2,770,000
Total	$2,625,000	$2,100,000	$1,740,000	$2,105,000	$8,570,000

Figure 3.49 Computer Sales Analysis

Capstone Exercise

What if people split a dinner check using the principles of the progressive income tax that is central to our tax code? Five lifelong friends of various means meet once a week for dinner and split the $100 check according to their ability to pay. Tom, Dick, and Harry are of relatively modest means and pay $1, $4, and $9, respectively. Ben and Ken are far more prosperous and pay $18 and $68, respectively.

The friends were quite satisfied with the arrangement until the owner offered a rebate. "You are excellent customers, and I will reduce the cost of your meal by $15." The question became how to divide the $15 windfall to give everyone his fair share? The proprietor suggested that they allocate the savings according to the amount each contributed to the original check. He made a quick calculation, and then rounded each person's share to an integer, using the Integer function. For example, Tom's new bill should have been 85 cents, but it was decided he would eat for free. In similar fashion, Dick now owes $3, Harry $7, Ben $15, and Ken $60. (Ken, the most prosperous individual, made up the difference with respect to the cents that were dropped.) The new total is $85, and everyone saves money.

Once outside the restaurant the friends began to compare their savings. Tom and Dick each complained that they saved only $1. Harry grumbled that he saved only $2. Ben thought it unfair that Ken saved more than the other four friends combined. Everyone continued to pick on Ken. The next week Ken felt so uncomfortable that he did not show up, so his former friends ate without him. But when the bill came they were $60 short.

Create the Worksheet

You will create the worksheet that is the basis for the charts. The first sheet, which you will name Numerical Analysis, contains the labels and data described below.

a. Enter a title in row 1. In row three enter the following labels: **Person**, **% Paid**, **Amount**, **Projected Saving**, **New Amount**, **Actual Saving**, **% Saving**. Type **Total** in **cell A9** and type **The original total** in cell A11 and **Reduction in bill** in **cell A12**.
b. Type the names, the percent paid, and the amounts in **cells A4:C8**. This data is in the description of the problem.

Calculations and Formatting

The analysis includes calculations and formatting necessary for presentation. You will create the formulas and select appropriate formatting options.

a. Calculate the projected savings for each individual in column D, the new amount in column E, the actual savings in column F, and the percent savings in column G.
b. Calculate appropriate totals in **cells B9:G9**.
c. Enter the original total value in **cell C11** and the reduction in bill value in **cell C12**.
d. Format columns B through G as appropriate for the values displayed.
e. Format the remainder of the worksheet with appropriate colors, fonts, and font size.

Create the Charts

You will create the charts based on the worksheet values. The charts provide information visually and help you to analyze that information. You will create three charts: a pie chart, a clustered column chart, and a combination chart.

a. Create a pie chart on a separate sheet that shows the percentage of the bill each individual pays before the refund. Include descriptive titles and labels.
b. Create a column chart on a separate sheet showing the amount each individual saves. Include data labels for each data series.
c. Add a shape with text box describing the results depicted on the chart. Include descriptive titles.
d. Create a clustered column chart on a separate sheet showing the new amount of the bill and the actual savings for each individual. Include data labels formatted with Currency and zero decimal places and a legend to the right of the chart.
e. Include a shape with a text box describing the data depicted in the chart. Include descriptive titles and labels.

Footers and Printing

Your instructor requires documentation for assignments. You will print the data sheet and the three chart sheets with your name, page numbers, and your instructor's name.

a. Create a custom footer that includes your name, sheet name, and the current date on all four worksheets.
b. Print the worksheet and charts in landscape format to ensure that all charts print on separate pages.
c. Save the workbook as **chap3_cap_dinner_solution**.

Mini Cases

Use the rubric following the case as a guide to evaluate your work, but keep in mind that your instructor may impose additional grading criteria or use a different standard to judge your work.

Designer Clothing

GENERAL CASE

This assignment asks you to complete a worksheet and create an associated chart for a designer clothing boutique, and then link these Excel objects to an appropriate memo. Open the partially completed *chap3_mc1_design* workbook; compute the sales totals for each individual salesperson as well as the totals for each quarter, then format the resulting worksheet in an attractive fashion. Include your name in the title of the worksheet (cell A1). We have started the memo for you and have saved the text in the *chap3_mc1_design* Word document. Open the Word document, and then link the Excel worksheet to the Word document. Repeat the process to link the Excel chart to the Word document. Print the completed document for your instructor. Save as **chap3_mc1_design_solution.** Close the workbook.

Performance Elements	Exceeds Expectations	Meets Expectations	Below Expectations
Compute totals	Totals all correct.	Inconsistent use of SUM function.	Typed in the number.
Attractive, appropriate format	Very attractive.	Adequate.	Ugly.
Embed sheet	Sheet embedded correctly.	Sheet embedded but not in correct location.	No embedded sheet.
Embed chart	Chart embedded correctly.	Sheet embedded but not in correct location.	No embedded sheet.

The Convention Planner

RESEARCH CASE

Your first task as a convention planner is to evaluate the hotel capacity for the host city in order to make recommendations as to which hotels should host the convention. The data form can be found in the *chap3_mc2_convention* workbook, which contains a single worksheet. You are to select a city for the convention and research six different hotels in that city. For each hotel, determine the number of standard and deluxe rooms and the rate for each. Insert this information into the worksheet. Complete the worksheet by computing the total number of standard and deluxe rooms. Do not total the rates. Format the worksheet in an attractive way. Create a stacked column chart that shows the total capacity for each hotel. Move the chart to a chart sheet named *Total Capacity* and add an appropriate chart title and legend. Create a 100% stacked column chart that shows the percentage of standard and deluxe rooms for each hotel. Move the chart to a chart sheet named *Rooms*. Add an appropriate chart title. Select the worksheets, add a header with your name, course, and current date. Print the entire workbook for your instructor. Save the workbook as **chap3_mc2_convention_solution**. Close the workbook.

Performance Elements	Exceeds Expectations	Meets Expectations	Below Expectations
Research hotel information	Found six hotels and data.	Found six hotels but incomplete data.	Found fewer than six hotels with incomplete data.
Create totals	Totals all correct.	Inconsistent use of SUM function.	Typed in the number.
Format attractive	Very attractive.	Adequate.	Ugly.
Create stacked column chart	Chart created correctly.	Incorrect data used for chart.	No chart.
Create 100% stacked column chart	Chart created correctly.	Incorrect data used for chart.	No chart.
Charts on separate sheets	Both charts on separate sheets.	One chart on separate sheet.	No chart.
Printing	Three printed sheets.	Two printed sheets.	No printed output.

Peer Tutoring

DISASTER RECOVERY

As part of your service learning project you volunteer tutoring students in Excel, you will identify and correct six separate errors in the chart. Your biggest task will be selecting the correct type of chart to show the data most clearly. Open the workbook *chap3_mc3_peer* and find six errors. Correct the errors and explain how the errors might have occurred and how they can be prevented. Include your explanation in the cells below the embedded chart. Save the workbook as **chap3_mc3_peer_solution**. Close the workbook.

Performance Elements	Exceeds Expectations	Meets Expectations	Below Expectations
Identify six errors	Finds all six errors.	Finds four errors.	Finds three or fewer errors.
Explain the error	Complete and correct explanation of each error.	Explanation is too brief to fully explain error.	No explanations.
Prevention description	Prevention description correct and practical.	Prevention description but obtuse.	No prevention description.

chapter 4 | **Excel**

Working with Large Worksheets and Tables

Manipulating Worksheets and Table Management

After you read this chapter, you will be able to:

1. Freeze rows and columns (**page 488**).
2. Hide and unhide rows, columns, and worksheets (**page 489**).
3. Protect a cell, a worksheet, and a workbook (**page 490**).
4. Control calculation (**page 493**).
5. Print large worksheets (**page 493**).
6. Explore basic table management (**page 505**).
7. Sort data (**page 510**).
8. Filter and total data (**page 514**).

Hands-On Exercises

Exercises	Skills Covered
1. **MARCHING BAND ROSTER (page 497)** **Open:** chap4_ho1_band.xlsx **Save as:** chap4_ho1_band_solution.xlsx	• Freeze and Unfreeze Rows and Columns • Hide and Unhide Rows, Columns, and Worksheets • Protect a Worksheet and a Workbook and Control Calculations • Print a Large Worksheet
2. **MARCHING BAND ROSTER REVISITED (page 519)** **Open:** chap4_ho1_band_solution.xlsx (from Exercise 1) **Save as:** chap4_ho2_band_solution.xlsx (additional modifications)	• Create a Table • Add, Edit, or Delete Records, and Use Find and Replace • Format a Table • Sort a Table • Filter a Table • Create Column Totals and a Summary Report • Print the Completed Worksheet

CASE STUDY

The Spa Experts

You and Tim like to relax and went into business shortly after graduation selling spas and hot tubs. Business has been good, and your expansive showroom and wide selection appeal to a variety of customers. You and your business partner maintain a large inventory to attract the impulse buyer and currently have agreements with three manufacturers: Serenity Spas, The Original Hot Tub, and Port-a-Spa. Each manufacturer offers spas and hot tubs that appeal to different segments of the market with prices ranging from affordable to exorbitant.

The business has grown rapidly, and you need to analyze the sales data in order to increase future profits—for example, which vendor generates the most sales? Who is the leading salesperson? Do most customers purchase their spa or finance it? Are sales promotions necessary to promote business, or will customers pay the full price? You have created a simple worksheet that has sales data for the current month. Each transaction appears on a separate row and contains the name of the salesperson, the manufacturer, and the amount of the sale. You will see an indication of whether the spa was purchased or financed, and whether a promotion was in effect. You are preparing a worksheet for Tim to keep him updated on sales for the current month.

Case Study

Your Assignment

- Read the chapter carefully and pay close attention to sections that demonstrate working with data tables, sorting information, filtering data, preparing summary reports, and printing large worksheets.
- Open the *chap4_case_spa* workbook, which contains the partially completed financial worksheet, and save it as **chap4_case_spa_solution**.
- Study the structure of the worksheet. Substitute your name for Jessica Benjamin throughout the worksheet.
- Convert the range of data to a table. Sort the table in alphabetical order by sales person's first name and then by date in chronological order. Filter the table to display only the spas that were financed. Add a total row to the Amount column.
- Create a footer with your name on the left, the date in the center, and the worksheet name on the right. Set landscape orientation. Center the data horizontally and vertically on the page. Print the worksheet.
- Copy the worksheet data, insert a new worksheet named **Subtotals**, and paste the worksheet data in the new sheet. Remove the filter and convert the table back to a range of data. Insert a blank row before the column headings.
- Use the Subtotals feature to calculate the total amount by salesperson. Freeze the column heading row so that you can scroll to the last few rows while seeing the column headings. Hide column F.
- Set 0.45" left and right margins, apply the same footer as you did for the Sales Data worksheet, and display the worksheet in Print Preview. Select the option to fit the worksheet to one page. Print the worksheet.
- Save and close the workbook.

Large Worksheet Preparation

Working with large worksheets, those that are too big to display within one monitor screen, can confuse users because they are not able to view the entire worksheet at one time. When this occurs, it is necessary for you to know how to view parts of the worksheet not visible, how to keep some parts of the worksheet always in view, and how to hide selected rows and columns. These ideas are illustrated in Figure 4.1, which shows a large worksheet with cell A1 the active cell. It shows columns A through H and rows 1 through 31. Items that begin in column I or row 32 are not visible in this view.

> Working with large worksheets . . . can confuse users because they are not able to view the entire worksheet at one time.

In order to view other columns, you can click the horizontal scroll bar to view one or more columns to the right. When the active cell is in the rightmost visible column (H1 for example), pressing the right arrow key does the same thing. Clicking the down arrow in the vertical scroll bar or pressing the down arrow key when the active cell is in the bottom visible row moves the screen down one row. This is known as scrolling, but it does not address the issue of rows and columns formerly visible becoming invisible as the scrolling occurs.

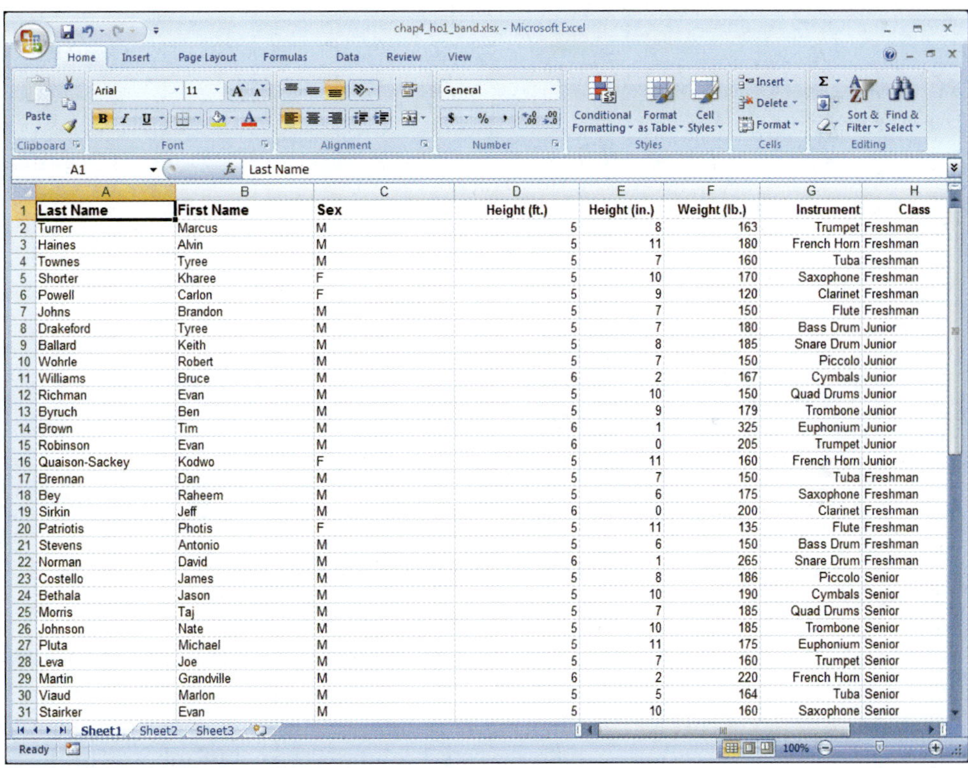

	A	B	C	D	E	F	G	H
1	Last Name	First Name	Sex	Height (ft.)	Height (in.)	Weight (lb.)	Instrument	Class
2	Turner	Marcus	M	5	8	163	Trumpet	Freshman
3	Haines	Alvin	M	5	11	180	French Horn	Freshman
4	Townes	Tyree	M	5	7	160	Tuba	Freshman
5	Shorter	Kharee	F	5	10	170	Saxophone	Freshman
6	Powell	Carlon	F	5	9	120	Clarinet	Freshman
7	Johns	Brandon	M	5	7	150	Flute	Freshman
8	Drakeford	Tyree	M	5	7	180	Bass Drum	Junior
9	Ballard	Keith	M	5	8	185	Snare Drum	Junior
10	Wohrle	Robert	M	5	7	150	Piccolo	Junior
11	Williams	Bruce	M	6	2	167	Cymbals	Junior
12	Richman	Evan	M	5	10	150	Quad Drums	Junior
13	Byruch	Ben	M	5	9	179	Trombone	Junior
14	Brown	Tim	M	6	1	325	Euphonium	Junior
15	Robinson	Evan	M	6	0	205	Trumpet	Junior
16	Quaison-Sackey	Kodwo	F	5	11	160	French Horn	Junior
17	Brennan	Dan	M	5	7	150	Tuba	Freshman
18	Bey	Raheem	M	5	6	175	Saxophone	Freshman
19	Sirkin	Jeff	M	6	0	200	Clarinet	Freshman
20	Patriotis	Photis	F	5	11	135	Flute	Freshman
21	Stevens	Antonio	M	5	6	150	Bass Drum	Freshman
22	Norman	David	M	6	1	265	Snare Drum	Freshman
23	Costello	James	M	5	8	186	Piccolo	Senior
24	Bethala	Jason	M	5	10	190	Cymbals	Senior
25	Morris	Taj	M	5	7	185	Quad Drums	Senior
26	Johnson	Nate	M	5	10	185	Trombone	Senior
27	Pluta	Michael	M	5	11	175	Euphonium	Senior
28	Leva	Joe	M	5	7	160	Trumpet	Senior
29	Martin	Grandville	M	6	2	220	French Horn	Senior
30	Viaud	Marlon	M	5	5	164	Tuba	Senior
31	Stairker	Evan	M	5	10	160	Saxophone	Senior

Figure 4.1 Large Worksheet

TIP Go to a Specific Cell

Pressing Ctrl+Home and Ctrl+End takes you to the upper-left and bottom-right cells within a worksheet, respectively. But how do you get to a specific cell? One way is to click the Find & Select in the Editing group on the Home tab and select Go To (or press F5 or press Ctrl+G) to display the Go To dialog box, enter the address of the cell in the Reference text box, then press Enter to go directly to the cell. You can also click in the Name box, type the cell reference, and press Enter.

Freezing Rows and Columns

Freezing is the process of keeping headings on the screen at all times.

When you scroll to parts of a worksheet not initially visible, some rows and columns disappear from view. It is sometimes valuable to be able to view row and column headings no matter where you scroll. This is done by ***freezing***, which is the process that enables you to keep headings on the screen as you work with large worksheets, rows, and columns as shown in Figure 4.2. Rows and columns that were not previously visible now are visible and so are the row and column headings. Figure 4.2 also shows a horizontal line and a vertical line after particular rows and columns, indicating they are frozen.

To freeze columns and rows:

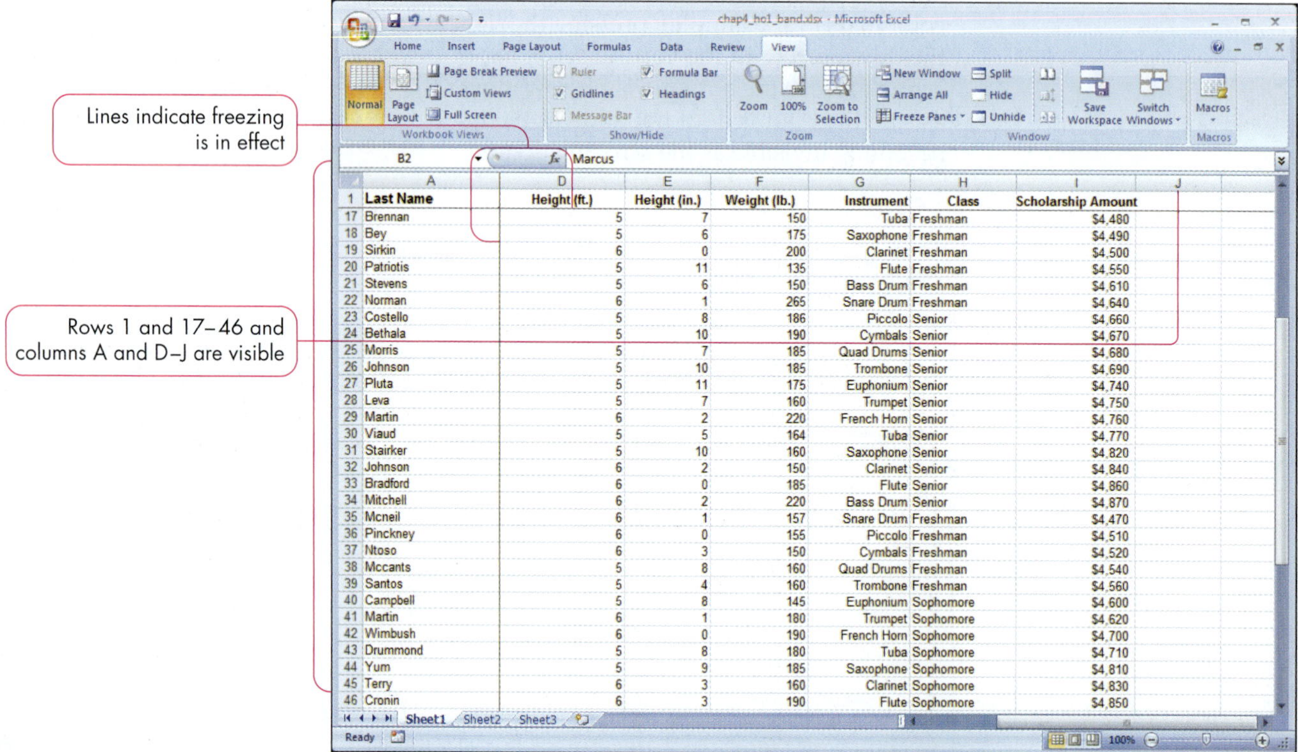

	A	D	E	F	G	H	I
1	Last Name	Height (ft.)	Height (in.)	Weight (lb.)	Instrument	Class	Scholarship Amount
17	Brennan	5	7	150	Tuba	Freshman	$4,480
18	Bey	5	6	175	Saxophone	Freshman	$4,490
19	Sirkin	6	0	200	Clarinet	Freshman	$4,500
20	Patriotis	5	11	135	Flute	Freshman	$4,550
21	Stevens	5	6	150	Bass Drum	Freshman	$4,610
22	Norman	6	1	265	Snare Drum	Freshman	$4,640
23	Costello	5	8	186	Piccolo	Senior	$4,660
24	Bethala	5	10	190	Cymbals	Senior	$4,670
25	Morris	5	7	185	Quad Drums	Senior	$4,680
26	Johnson	5	10	185	Trombone	Senior	$4,690
27	Pluta	5	11	175	Euphonium	Senior	$4,740
28	Leva	5	7	160	Trumpet	Senior	$4,750
29	Martin	6	2	220	French Horn	Senior	$4,760
30	Viaud	5	5	164	Tuba	Senior	$4,770
31	Stairker	5	10	160	Saxophone	Senior	$4,820
32	Johnson	6	2	150	Clarinet	Senior	$4,840
33	Bradford	6	0	185	Flute	Senior	$4,860
34	Mitchell	6	2	220	Bass Drum	Senior	$4,870
35	Mcneil	6	1	157	Snare Drum	Freshman	$4,470
36	Pinckney	6	0	155	Piccolo	Freshman	$4,510
37	Ntoso	6	3	150	Cymbals	Freshman	$4,520
38	Mccants	5	8	160	Quad Drums	Freshman	$4,540
39	Santos	5	4	160	Trombone	Freshman	$4,560
40	Campbell	5	8	145	Euphonium	Sophomore	$4,600
41	Martin	6	1	180	Trumpet	Sophomore	$4,620
42	Wimbush	6	0	190	French Horn	Sophomore	$4,700
43	Drummond	5	8	180	Tuba	Sophomore	$4,710
44	Yum	5	9	185	Saxophone	Sophomore	$4,810
45	Terry	6	3	160	Clarinet	Sophomore	$4,830
46	Cronin	6	3	190	Flute	Sophomore	$4,850

Figure 4.2 Visible Rows and Column Headings

1. Select the cell below the row(s) and to the right of the column(s) you want to freeze.
2. Click the View tab and click Freeze Panes in the Window group. You can freeze both rows and columns or just the top row or the first column. After making your selection, you can unfreeze rows and columns by selecting Freeze Panes. You will notice that the *Freeze* option you previously selected now displays *Unfreeze*. Click that option to unfreeze rows and columns.

Hiding and Unhiding Rows, Columns, and Worksheets

Hidden is the state of rows, columns, and sheets being invisible.

Figure 4.3 shows a worksheet with rows, columns, and a worksheet ***hidden***, which is the process of making rows, columns, and sheets invisible. The hiding of these items in a worksheet is a common practice and is done for a variety of reasons. Often, it is done to conceal nonessential information, or information not needed at a particular time. At other times, confidential information is contained in a workbook and rows, columns, or sheets must be hidden to allow nonauthorized users to view a workbook. You might also hide rows or columns to make other rows or columns visible. Row and columns containing sensitive data or data that uniquely identifies an individual or product are hidden from colleagues or competitors. Social Security Numbers, salary, or rate of pay, pricing data, and trade secret information are some examples of data used in worksheets that might be hidden. Large workbooks might include worksheets that not all employees are authorized to view because of the classified nature of the data contained in the worksheet. Trade secret information or information specifically classified by the federal government are just two examples of why worksheets may be hidden.

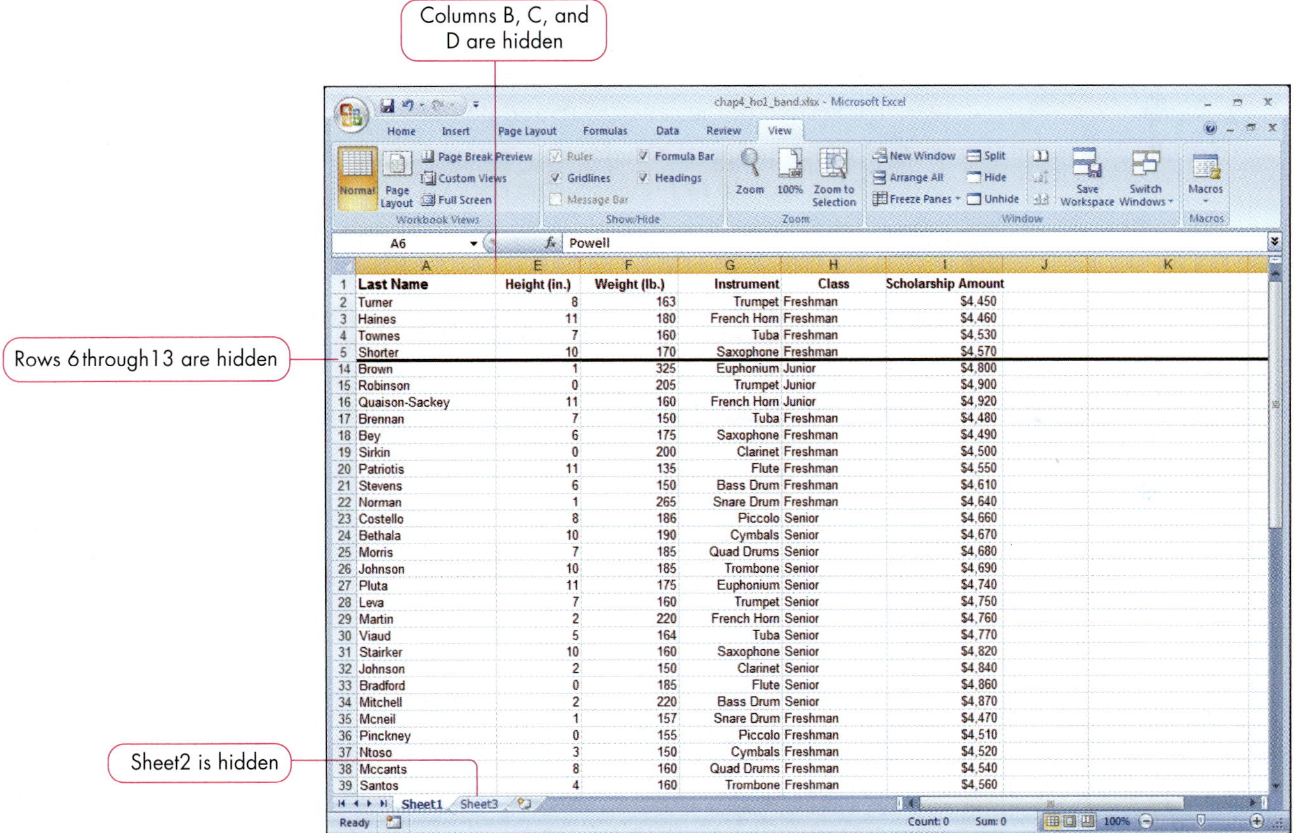

Figure 4.3 Hidden Rows, Columns, and Worksheet

Keep in mind that Hide is not a delete command. Hiding an element of a worksheet does not affect the data in that element, nor does it affect any other visible cell that might reference data in the hidden element. Formulas will still display correct results even when the references used in the formulas are hidden. To hide a particular row or column in a worksheet:

1. Select the row or column you want to hide.
2. Click the Home tab.
3. Click Format in the Cells group and point to Hide & Unhide.
4. Select the appropriate hide option.

To unhide rows or columns, repeat the above steps, except the rows or columns on either side of the hidden row or column must be selected and the appropriate unhide option is selected.

To hide a worksheet:

1. Make active the sheet you want to hide.
2. Click the Home tab.
3. Click Format in the Cells group and point to Hide & Unhide.
4. Select Hide Sheet.

To unhide a worksheet:

1. Click the Home tab.
2. Click Format in the cells group and point to Hide & Unhide.
3. Select Unhide Sheet. A dialog box appears asking which sheet is to be unhidden. Click the sheet to be unhidden and click OK.

TIP Unhiding Rows and Columns

Hiding a row or column is easy: You select the row or column(s) you want to hide, click the right mouse button, then select Hide from the shortcut menu. Unhiding a row or column is more challenging because you cannot see the target cells. To unhide a column, for example, you need to select the columns on both sides. For example, select columns A and C if you are trying to unhide column B. To unhide column A, click in the Name box and type A1. Click Format in the Cells group on the Home tab, point to Hide & Unhide, and select Unhide Columns. To unhide all hidden rows and columns, click Select All.

Protecting a Cell, a Worksheet, and a Workbook

The advent of networks and information sharing also introduced the need to protect data from being altered and from falling into the hands of the wrong person. When you post a spreadsheet on the company network, it becomes available to any user of the network. Network users can make any change to any worksheet in the workbook file. Excel has protection controls that, used with the proper restrictions, can ensure that the right people see only the right data. Unauthorized users will not be able to get into the spreadsheet. Authorized users can edit only those areas you give them access to. The formulas that calculate the visible values are confidential unless you choose to make them visible. The issue of protecting cells, worksheets, or workbooks is an important one because it can determine if users can change an element of a workbook. Generally, when a workbook is protected, the creator of the workbook controls if changes can be made to a file.

Lock and Unlock Cells

All cells in a workbook have a locked property that determines if changes can be made to a cell. This concept has no effect if a worksheet is not protected. On the other hand, once a worksheet is protected, if the locked property is on, all cells are locked, and no data can be entered. Locking cells allows you to prevent viewers of your worksheet from making any changes to the cells. You can unlock just those cells you permit others to change. For example, if you are working in a payroll department and have created an employee salary worksheet that lists pay rates, you may want to lock this data to prevent unauthorized users from changing their own pay rate. Similarly, you would want to lock the formulas for calculating gross pay. Table 4.1 illustrates the protect sheet and locked property. You can see that the Protect Sheet command must be on along with the Locked Property in order to prevent data from being entered. It is possible to allow data to be entered in some cells but not all.

1. Select the cells where entering or changing data will be allowed.
2. Click the Home tab, click Format in the Cells group, and select Format Cells to open the Format Cells dialog box.
3. Select the Protection tab, clear the Locked check box, and click OK.
4. Click the Home tab, click Format in the Cells group, and click Protect Sheet.
5. Select a password if desired and clear the *Select locked cells* check box.
6. Click OK. If you selected a password, reenter the password and click OK.

To unprotect the sheet and unlock all cells, click the Home tab, and click Format in the Cells group, and select Unprotect Sheet. If a password was set, type the password and click OK.

Table 4.1 Protect/Lock Sheet Property

Protect Sheet	Locked Property On	Locked Property Off
Yes	No data can be entered.	Data can be entered.
No	Data can be entered.	Data can be entered.

Protect and Unprotect a Worksheet

The process of protecting a worksheet can be a two-step process, because the protection can allow users to only perform certain functions in the spreadsheet or allow users to only perform certain functions in certain cells. To protect a worksheet, follow this general procedure:

1. Click the Home tab and click Format in the Cells group.
2. Click Protect Sheet.
3. Select a password if desired and click the options that users will be permitted in the worksheet. See Figure 4.4 for a display of the protect options.
4. Click OK.

It is recommended that you only use a protection password in cases requiring very tight security and that the password be placed in a safe location. Passwords can be up to 255 characters including letters, numbers, and symbols and are case sensitive. It is up to you to choose a suitably difficult password. If you forget the password, you cannot access the locked file.

To unprotect a worksheet:

1. Click the Home tab and click Format in the Cells group.
2. Select Unprotect Sheet.

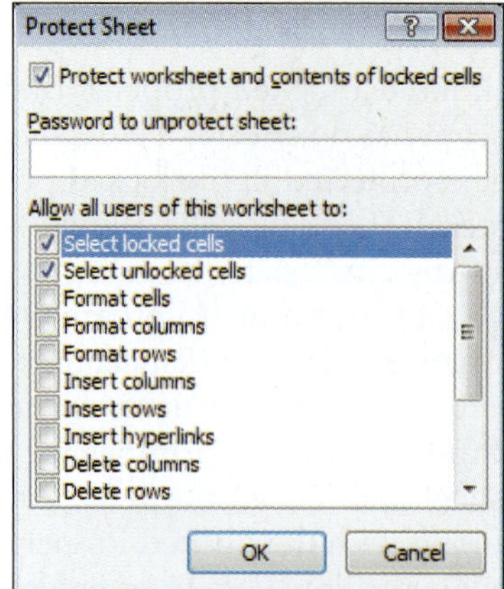

Figure 4.4 Protect Sheet Dialog Box

Protect a Workbook

Even though protecting a worksheet provides a relatively high level of protection, it does not prevent a criminal or vandal from changing the structure or windows of a workbook. This could include such things as deleting or renaming sheets. Protected workbooks prevent anyone from viewing hidden worksheets; moving, deleting, hiding, or changing the names of worksheets; and moving or copying worksheets to another workbook. The general procedure you use for protecting a workbook is as follows:

1. Click the Review tab and click Protect Workbook in the Changes group.
2. Click the boxes for the protection desired as shown in Figure 4.5.
3. Enter a password if desired in the Protect Workbook dialog box.
4. Click OK. If you selected a password, reenter the password and click OK.

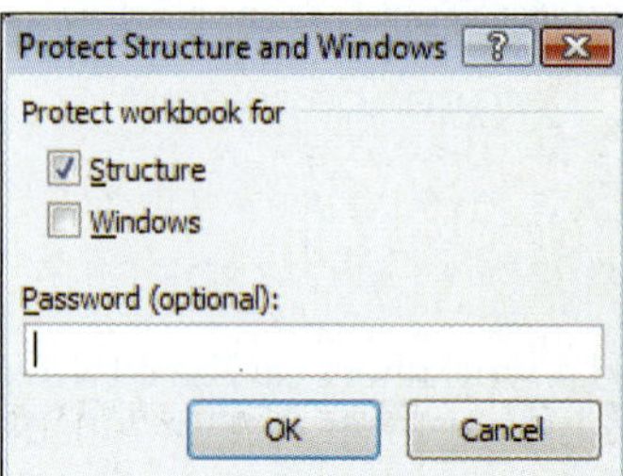

Figure 4.5 Protect Structure and Windows Dialog Box

TIP Protect the Formulas

The formulas in a well-designed worksheet should be based on a set of assumptions and initial conditions that are grouped together for ease of change. The user can change any of the initial values and see the effect ripple throughout the spreadsheet. The user need not, however, have access to the formulas, and thus the formulas should be protected. Remember, protection is a two-step process. First, you unlock the cells that you want to be able to change after the worksheet has been protected, and then you protect the worksheet.

Controlling Calculation

Calculation is the computing of formulas and the display of the results or values in the cells that contain the formulas. In Excel, the default recalculation takes place when the cells formulas refer to change. This default recalculation can be changed as circumstances warrant. Table 4.2 illustrates different recalculation schemes. These schemes all begin by clicking the Office Button, clicking Excel Options, and then clicking the Formulas category.

Table 4.2 Formula Recalculation Schemes

Recalculation Action	Steps
All dependent formulas every time a change is made to a value, formula, or name.	Click **Automatic** under Calculation Options in the Calculation group.
All dependent formulas except data tables, every time a change is made to a value, formula, or name.	Click **Automatic Except for Data Tables** under Calculate Options in the Calculation group.
Turn off automatic recalculation and recalculate open workbooks only when desired.	Click **Manual** under Calculate Options in the Calculation group.
Manually recalculate.	Click **Calculate Now** in the Calculation group on the Formulas tab, or press F9.

Printing Large Worksheets

Printing all or parts of a large worksheet presents special challenges to even veteran users of Excel. It is easy for you to make erroneous assumptions about what will print and be unpleasantly surprised. You must consider such things as Page Breaks, Page Orientation, Printing a selection, and the order in which pages print when printing all or part of a large worksheet. Figure 4.6 shows a worksheet that prints on four pieces of paper with just three columns printing on page 3 and one row printing on pages 2 and 4. You can adjust column widths, margins, and page orientation before printing to avoid wasting paper.

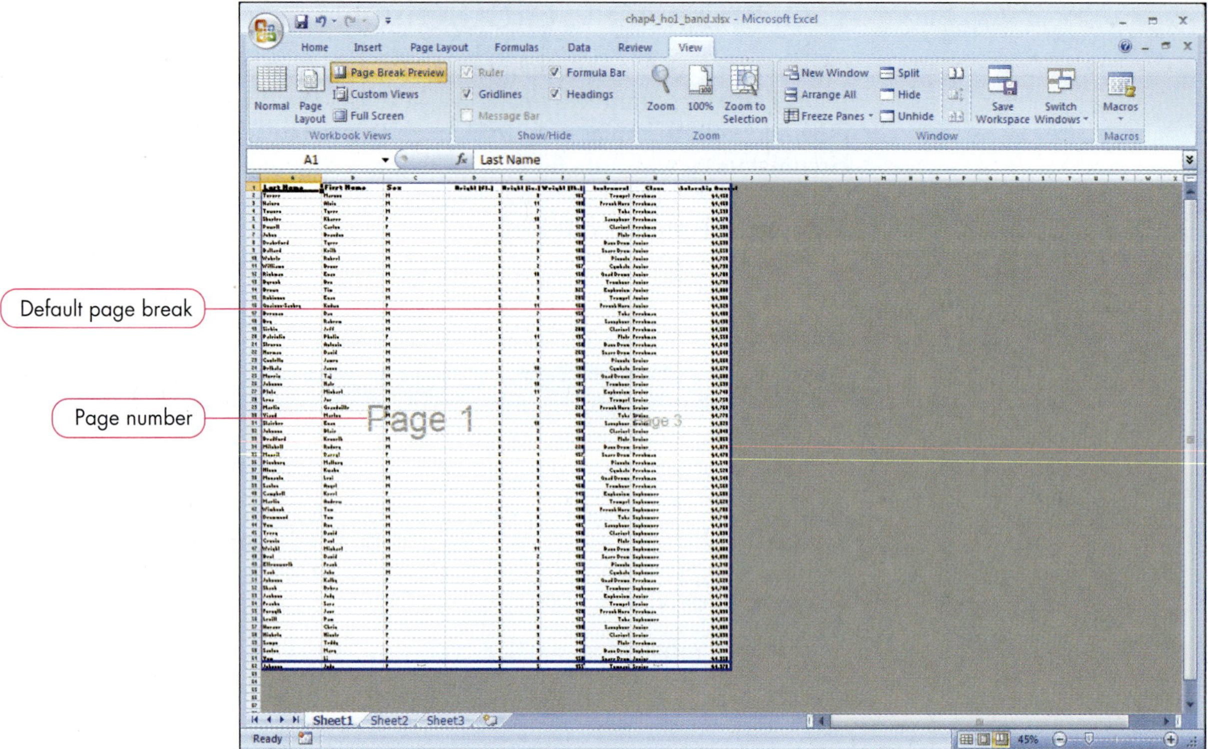

Figure 4.6 Page Break Preview

Manage Page Breaks

The ***Page Break Preview*** shows where page breaks occur and gives you the opportunity to change where the page breaks.

The *Page Break Preview* shows you where page breaks currently occur and gives you the opportunity to change where the page breaks occur when a worksheet is printed. Figure 4.6 displays a worksheet in Page Break Preview. The dashed blue line indicates where the default page breaks occur. To see and adjust page breaks:

1. Click Page Break Preview on the status bar. If the Welcome to Page Break Preview message box appears, check the *Do not show this dialog again* box and click OK.
2. A watermark shows the page numbers.
3. Move the dashed blue lines as appropriate to adjust the page breaks.

Change Page Orientation

Printing an entire worksheet on a single piece of paper is more efficient in terms of paper use and provides the reader with the whole picture. The reader does not have to shuffle pages in order to get to the totals or perhaps the summary portion of the spreadsheet. One of the more efficient ways to have more of a worksheet printed on a page is to change the page orientation. Page orientation can be either Portrait (tall) or Landscape (wide). To change page orientation to print more of a worksheet on a page:

1. Click Orientation in the Page Setup group on the Page Layout tab.
2. Select Portrait or Landscape.

Print a Selection

Excel users working with large spreadsheets sometimes want to print only a portion of a worksheet. Printing a portion of a worksheet involves selecting an area to print prior to actually printing. Figure 4.7 shows a selected area of a worksheet and the Print dialog box with Selection as the print range. Complete the following steps to print a selection or range of a worksheet:

1. Select the portion of the worksheet you want to print.
2. Click the Page Layout tab, and then click the Page Setup Dialog Box Launcher in the Page Setup group.
3. Click Print, and then click Selection in the *Print what* section.
4. Verify the selection using Preview.
5. Click Print in the Print group on the Print Preview tab.

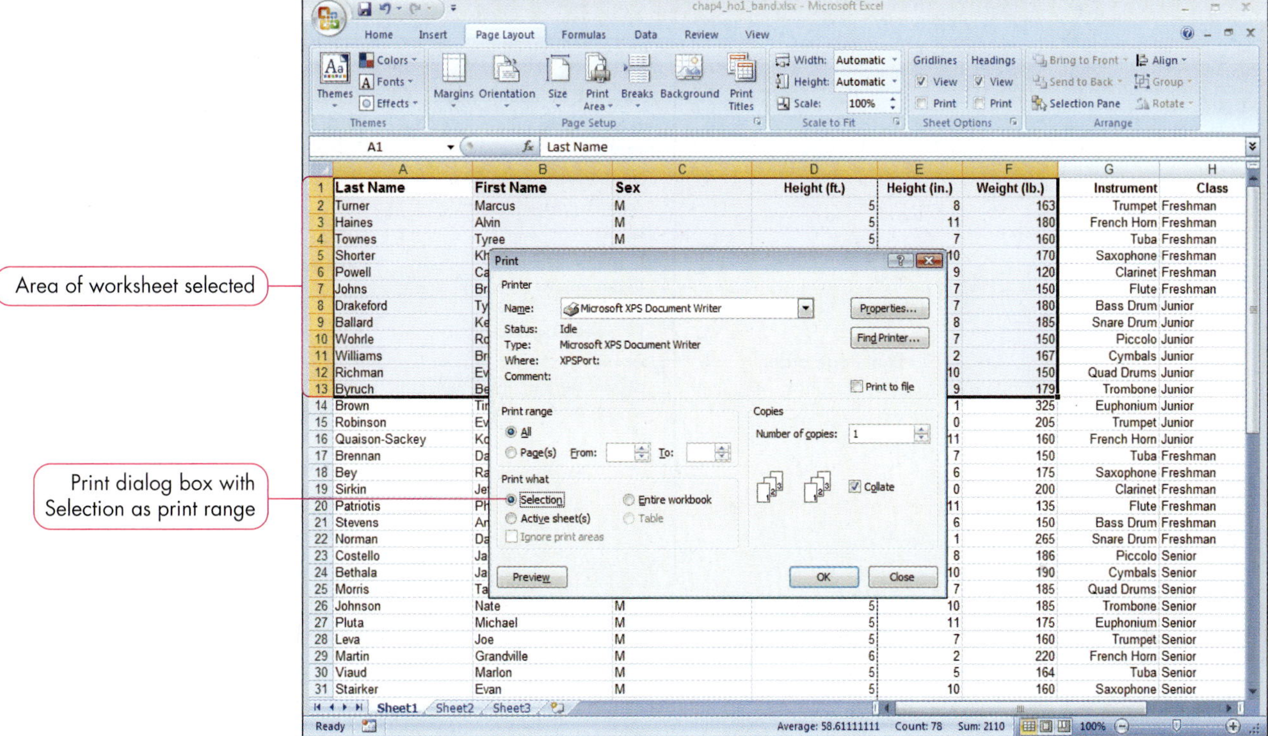

Figure 4.7 Printing a Selection

TIP Set Print Areas

To set print areas, press and hold Ctrl as you click and drag to select one or more areas in the worksheet, and then click Print Area and select Set Print Area in the Page Setup group on the Page Layout tab. The print area is highlighted. The next time you execute the Print command, you will print just the print area(s) selected, with each print area appearing on a separate page. To clear the print area, click Print Area in the Page Setup group on the Page Layout tab, and then select Clear Print Area.

Control Print Page Order

The complexity of large spreadsheets sometimes makes it necessary for you to change the order that pages will print. The print order may be changed because the data will make more sense if the order of pages printed is changed or to keep like data together. When you have four pages to print you can print left to right, 1–2 and then 3–4, or you can print top to bottom, 1–3 and then 2–4. You choose which order to print based on your worksheet; data may be arranged wider than it is tall. You control the order in which pages are numbered and printed. To change the order of the printing of pages:

1. Click the Page Setup Dialog Box Launcher on the Page Layout tab.
2. Click the Sheet tab.
3. Change the *Page order* options, as appropriate, as shown in Figure 4.8.
4. Click OK.

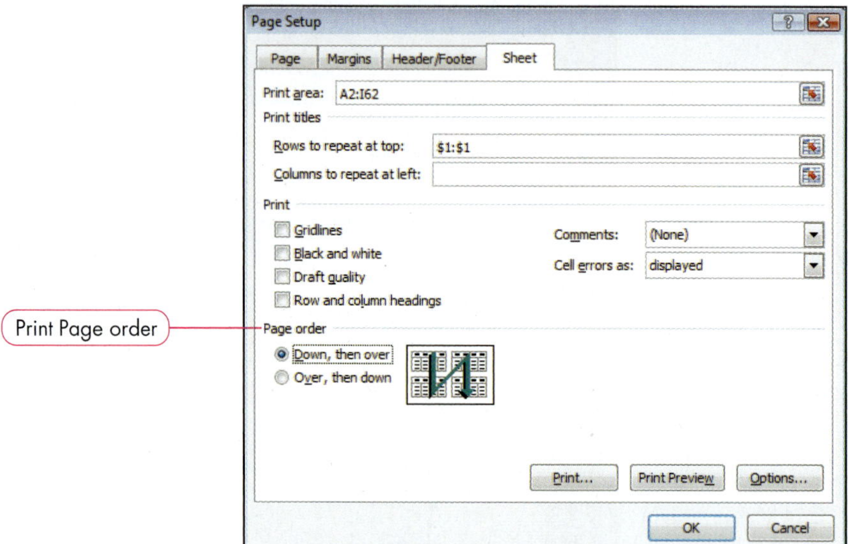

Figure 4.8 Page Setup Dialog Box

Hands-On Exercises

1 | Marching Band Roster

Skills covered: 1. Freeze and Unfreeze Rows and Columns **2.** Hide and Unhide Rows, Columns, and Worksheets **3.** Protect a Worksheet and a Workbook and Control Calculations **4.** Print a Large Worksheet

Step 1
Freeze and Unfreeze Rows and Columns

Refer to Figure 4.9 as you complete Step 1.

a. Start Excel. Open the *chap4_ho1_band* workbook and save it as **chap4_ho1_band_solution** so that you can return to the original workbook if necessary.

   As you use the horizontal scroll bar to view the worksheet, note that some columns disappear. Rows also disappear when you use the vertical scroll bar. The worksheet is too large to fit on one screen and you must use Freeze Panes to keep parts of the worksheet in constant view.

b. Click **cell B2**, the cell below the row you need to freeze. Click the **View tab**, click **Freeze Panes** in the Window group, and select **Freeze Top Row**.

   Use the vertical scroll bar to see that the row data becomes visible while the headings on the first row are "frozen" and do not scroll off the screen.

c. Click **cell B2**, the cell to the right of the column you need to freeze. Click the **View tab**, click **Freeze Panes** in the Window group, and select **Freeze First Column**.

   Use the horizontal scroll bar to see that the first column data are always visible as the other columns become visible.

d. Click the **Freeze Panes** in the Window group and select **Unfreeze Panes**.

   Now that the panes are no longer frozen, use either scroll bar to see that the worksheet is again too large to view on one screen.

   TROUBLESHOOTING: The screen resolution settings in Windows may change your view of the spreadsheet and make freezing more or less important.

e. Enter and format a heading:

   - Select **row 1**, click the **Home tab**, and click **Insert** in the Cells group to insert a new row.
   - Click in **cell A1** and type **State University Marching Band Roster**.
   - Select **cells A1:I1** and click **Merge & Center** in the Alignment group on the Home tab.
   - Point to the title and right-click the mouse to display the Mini toolbar. Click the **Bold** button and select a font size of **14**.
   - Click the **Font Color down arrow** in the Font group and select **Dark Blue** from Standard Colors; similarly, open **Fill Color** and select the complement, **Blue, Accent 1, Lighter 80%** from the blue theme colors.

f. Click in **cell B3**, click the **View tab**, click **Freeze Panes** in the Window group, and select **Freeze Panes**. Save the workbook.

g. Press **Page Down** and scroll to the right to see column I. Compare your screen to Figure 4.9.

   Note that column A and rows 1 and 2 are visible as you scroll around the worksheet.

h. Click **Freeze Panes** and select **Unfreeze Panes** to unfreeze the panes. Save the workbook.

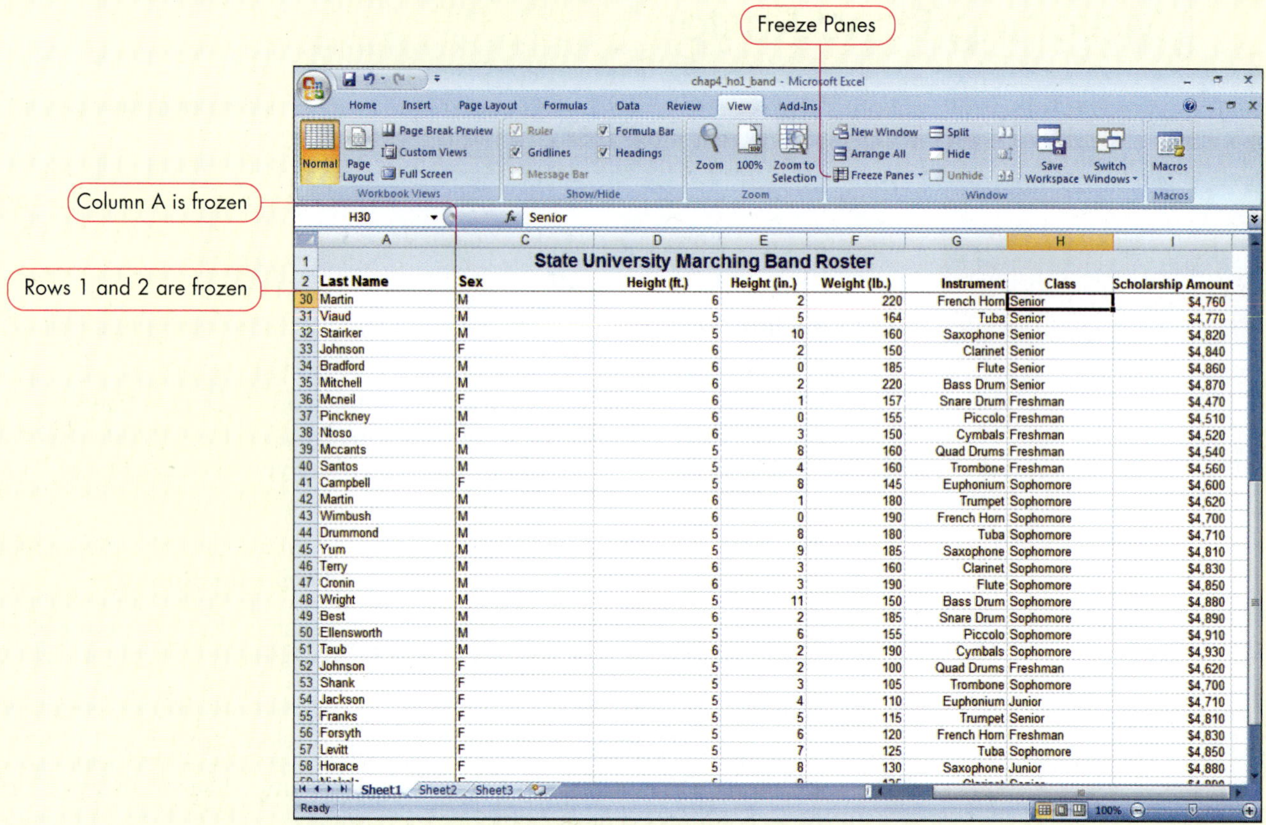

Figure 4.9 Freeze and Unfreeze Rows and Columns

Step 2
Hide and Unhide Rows, Columns, and Worksheets

Refer to Figure 4.10 as you complete Step 2.

a. Select **column F**. Click the **Home tab** if necessary, click **Format** in the Cells group, point to **Hide & Unhide**, and select **Hide Columns**.

   Column F is hidden, and a thick black line appears between columns E and G, indicating the location of the hidden column. When you begin the next step, the line disappears.

b. Select **row 6** and click **Format** in the Cells group, point to **Hide & Unhide**, and select **Hide Rows**.

   Row 6 is hidden, and a thick black line appears between rows 5 and 7, indicating the location of the hidden row.

c. Right-click the **Sheet2 tab** and select **Hide** to hide the sheet.

   When a sheet is hidden, the sheet and sheet tab disappear, and there is no indication that a sheet is hidden, unlike a hidden row or column. Refer to Figure 4.10 and note the hidden row, column, and sheet.

d. Click the **Sheet1 tab**, select **columns E** and **G**, click **Format** in the Cells group, point to **Hide & Unhide**, and select **Unhide Columns** to display the column again.

TROUBLESHOOTING: Note that the columns on both sides of the hidden columns must be selected prior to unhiding. Rows above and below hidden rows must be selected prior to unhiding.

e. Select **rows 5** and **7**, click the **Home tab,** click **Format** in the Cells group, point to **Hide & Unhide**, and select **Unhide Rows** to display row 6 again.

f. Click **Format** in the Cells group, point to **Hide & Unhide**, select **Unhide Sheet** to display the Unhide dialog box, select **Sheet2**, and click **OK** to display Sheet2 again. Save the workbook.

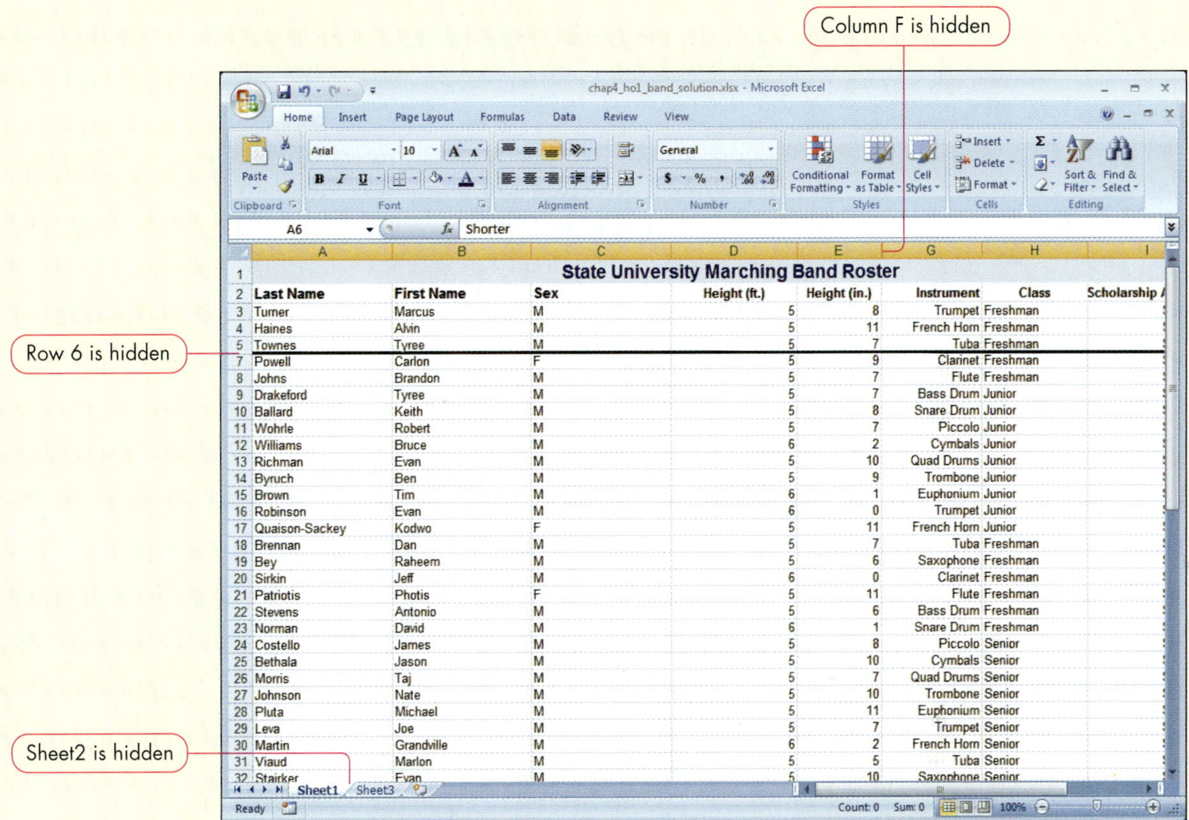

Last Name	First Name	Sex	Height (ft.)	Height (in.)	Instrument	Class	Scholarship
Turner	Marcus	M	5	8	Trumpet	Freshman	
Haines	Alvin	M	5	11	French Horn	Freshman	
Townes	Tyree	M	5	7	Tuba	Freshman	
Powell	Carlon	F	5	9	Clarinet	Freshman	
Johns	Brandon	M	5	7	Flute	Freshman	
Drakeford	Tyree	M	5	7	Bass Drum	Junior	
Ballard	Keith	M	5	8	Snare Drum	Junior	
Wohrle	Robert	M	5	7	Piccolo	Junior	
Williams	Bruce	M	6	2	Cymbals	Junior	
Richman	Evan	M	5	10	Quad Drums	Junior	
Byruch	Ben	M	5	9	Trombone	Junior	
Brown	Tim	M	6	1	Euphonium	Junior	
Robinson	Evan	M	6	0	Trumpet	Junior	
Quaison-Sackey	Kodwo	F	5	11	French Horn	Junior	
Brennan	Dan	M	5	7	Tuba	Freshman	
Bey	Raheem	M	5	6	Saxophone	Freshman	
Sirkin	Jeff	M	6	0	Clarinet	Freshman	
Patriotis	Photis	F	5	11	Flute	Freshman	
Stevens	Antonio	M	5	6	Bass Drum	Freshman	
Norman	David	M	6	1	Snare Drum	Freshman	
Costello	James	M	5	8	Piccolo	Senior	
Bethala	Jason	M	5	10	Cymbals	Senior	
Morris	Taj	M	5	7	Quad Drums	Senior	
Johnson	Nate	M	5	10	Trombone	Senior	
Pluta	Michael	M	5	11	Euphonium	Senior	
Leva	Joe	M	5	7	Trumpet	Senior	
Martin	Grandville	M	6	2	French Horn	Senior	
Viaud	Marlon	M	5	5	Tuba	Senior	
Stairker	Evan	M	5	10	Saxophone	Senior	

Figure 4.10 Hiding Rows, Columns, and Worksheets

Step 3
Protect a Worksheet and a Workbook and Control Calculations

Refer to Figure 4.11 as you complete Step 3.

a. Select **Sheet1** and select **cells G3:G63**, the cells that you want to edit.
   - Click **Format** in the Cells group, and then select **Format Cells** to open the Format Cells dialog box.
   - Click the **Protection tab**, clear the **Locked check box**, and click **OK**.
   - Click **Format** in the Cells group, and then select **Protect Sheet** to display the Protect Sheet dialog box.
   - Make sure the **Select unlocked cells check box** is selected, and clear the **Select locked cells check box**, and click **OK**.
   - You unlocked cells for editing purposes and then protected or locked all other cells. The only data that you can change is a band member's instrument. Click in the **Name box**, type **A5**, and press **Enter**. Try to change the player's name, and the Microsoft Office Excel warning box informs you that the cell is protected.

You must unprotect the worksheet in order to unlock the cells you previously protected and before continuing with this exercise.

b. Click **Format** in the Cells group and select **Unprotect Sheet** to unprotect the worksheet again.

c. Click the **Review tab**, click **Protect Workbook** in the Changes group, and then select **Protect Structure and Windows**. The Protect Structure and Windows dialog box opens. Verify that the **Structure check box** is selected and click **OK** to protect the workbook.

Remember you are the creator of the workbook and can make any changes. You have protected the workbook so that others cannot make changes.

TROUBLESHOOTING: If you enter a password in any dialog box, only those who know the password will be able to change data or perhaps open the workbook. If you forget the password, you cannot edit or perhaps cannot even open the workbook.

d. To unprotect the workbook, click **Protect Workbook** in the Changes group. Click **Protect Structure and Windows** to deselect it. Save the workbook.

e. Click the **Office Button**, click **Excel Options**, and then click **Formulas** on the left side of the Excel Options dialog box.

Calculation options are displayed at the top of the Excel Options dialog box. You can use these options to change how and when Excel calculates formulas.

f. Click **Cancel** to close the Excel Options dialog box.

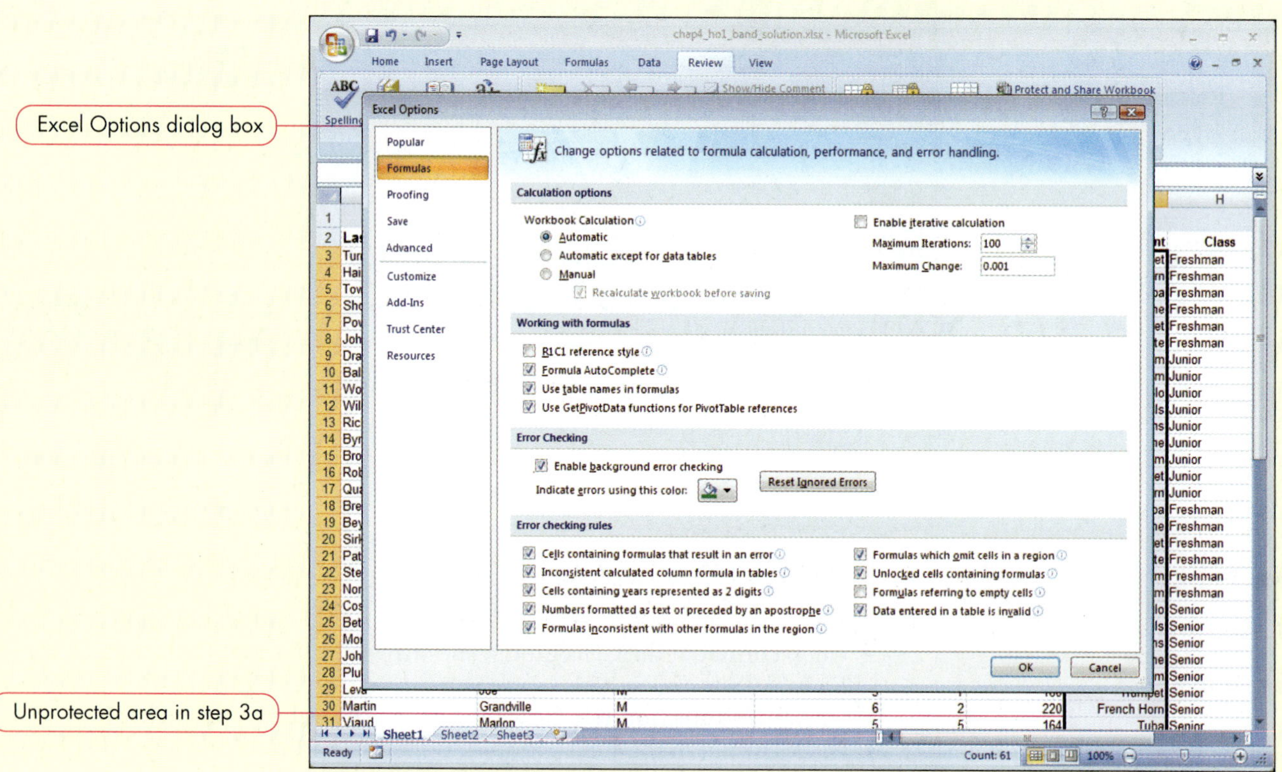

Figure 4.11 Worksheet Protection and Calculation Options

Step 4
Print a Large Worksheet

Refer to Figure 4.12 as you complete Step 4.

a. Click the **Page Break Preview** button on the status bar in the lower-right area of the window. If you see the Welcome to Page Break Preview message box, click **OK**.

   You will use the Page Break Preview command to adjust the page breaks in a large spreadsheet.

b. Move the **blue dashed line** that separates pages 1 and 3 all the way to the right to eliminate the page break.

   You might see a dashed line between columns I and J, indicating a page break. This page break occurs because part of the heading in cell I2 overlaps cell J2.

c. Click the **Normal** button on the status bar to return to Normal view.

d. Click the **Page Layout tab**, click **Orientation**, and select **Landscape** to change the page orientation.
   - Click the **Page Setup Dialog Box Launcher** on the Page Layout tab to launch the Page Setup dialog box.
   - Click the **Margins tab**, set **0.3"** top, bottom, left, and right margins.
   - Click the **Page tab** and click **Fit to**.
   - Click the **Print Preview** button and verify that the worksheet will print on one page.
   - Click **Print** in the Print group on the Print Preview tab to print the worksheet.

   Changing to landscape orientation enables the worksheet data to appear in a larger scale on one page than in portrait orientation. You used the Print Preview feature to view how much data now fits on one page before printing and then printed the worksheet.

e. Select **cells A4:H10**, then click **Print Area** in the Page Setup group on the Page Layout tab.
   - Select **Set Print Area**.
   - Click the **Page Setup Dialog Box Launcher** on the Page Layout tab to launch the Page Setup dialog box.
   - Click **Print Preview** and verify that your selection is correct.
   - Click the **Print** button, and then click **OK** in the Print dialog box to print your selection.
   - Click **Cancel** to close the Page Setup dialog box, if necessary.
   - Click **Print Area** in the Page Setup group on the Page Layout tab and select **Clear Print Area**.

   You selected just a specific portion or area of the worksheet and verified that the selection you wanted to print was correct. You then printed the selection and after printing, cleared the selection.

f. Click the **Page Setup Dialog Box Launcher**, click the **Page tab**, click the **Adjust to** option, click the spin button to display **100%**, and click **OK**.

g. Click in **cell A28**, click **Breaks** in the Page Setup group on the Page Layout tab, and select **Insert Page Break**.

h. Select **column G**, click **Breaks** on the Page Layout tab, and select **Insert Page Break**. Click **Page Break Preview** on the status bar.

You placed page breaks above cell A28 and after Column F to print the worksheet on four pages.

i. Click the **Page Setup Dialog Box Launcher** on the Page Layout tab, click the **Sheet tab**, click **Over, then down** in the *Page order* section.

j. Click the **Print Preview** button to verify that you will print four pages, click **Print** in the Print group on the Print Preview tab, and then click **OK** in the Print dialog box.

Before printing the four-page worksheet you changed the order in which the pages will print. (See Figure 4.12 and note that the Rows to repeat at top box contains the default rows to print on each page.)

k. Click **Normal** on the status bar to change back to the Normal view. Save the workbook. Close the workbook and exit Excel if you do not want to continue with the next exercise at this time.

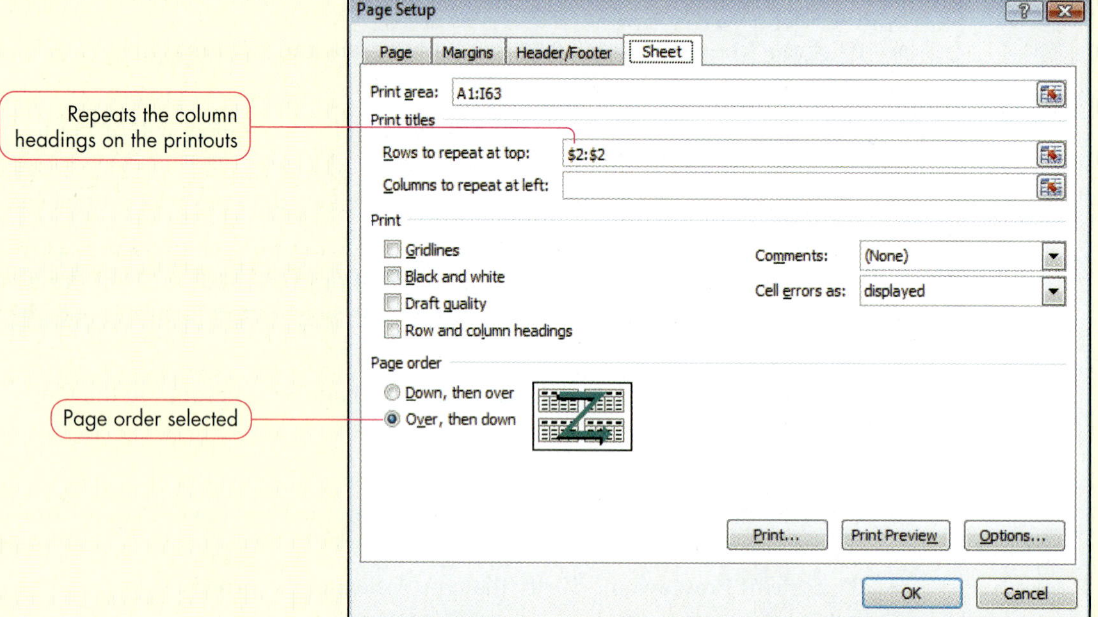

Figure 4.12 Print a Large Worksheet

Excel Data Tables

All enterprises, be they business, educational, or governmental, maintain data in the form of lists. Companies have lists of employees. Educational institutions maintain lists of students and faculty members. Governmental entities, such as the military, maintain extensive inventory lists. In this part of the chapter, we will present the fundamentals of table management, which is how Excel presents lists of data so that it can be manipulated by the program. This section begins with definitions of basic terms, such as *table*, *field*, and *record*, and then discusses the creation of tables; how to add, edit, or delete records in a table; and how to use the Find and Replace feature to change recurring data in a table. Formatting tables will be presented as well.

(All enterprises . . . maintain data in the form of lists.)

In the first part of this section, you learn how to distinguish between information and data and describe how one is converted into another. Sorting of data in tables will be explored, both in simple sorts and in multiple-level sorts. In the second part of this section, you will filter records in a table and insert column totals and summary reports with charts.

The concepts associated with tables in Excel are database concepts. These can be difficult concepts to understand in the abstract, so the following example may help to clarify things. As the Director of Human Resources at State University, you manually maintain employee data for the members of the university faculty. You maintain specifics about each employee such as name, salary, and faculty rank in an individual manila file folder that is stored in a file cabinet. The file folders have the faculty member's name on the tab, and they are sorted alphabetically by last name in the filing cabinet.

This example shows the basics of manual database management. Each item can be equated to a database term. The set of manila file folders corresponds to a file. Each folder can be equated to a record. Each item within the file folder equates to a field in a record. See Figure 4.13 for an example of a file cabinet analogy.

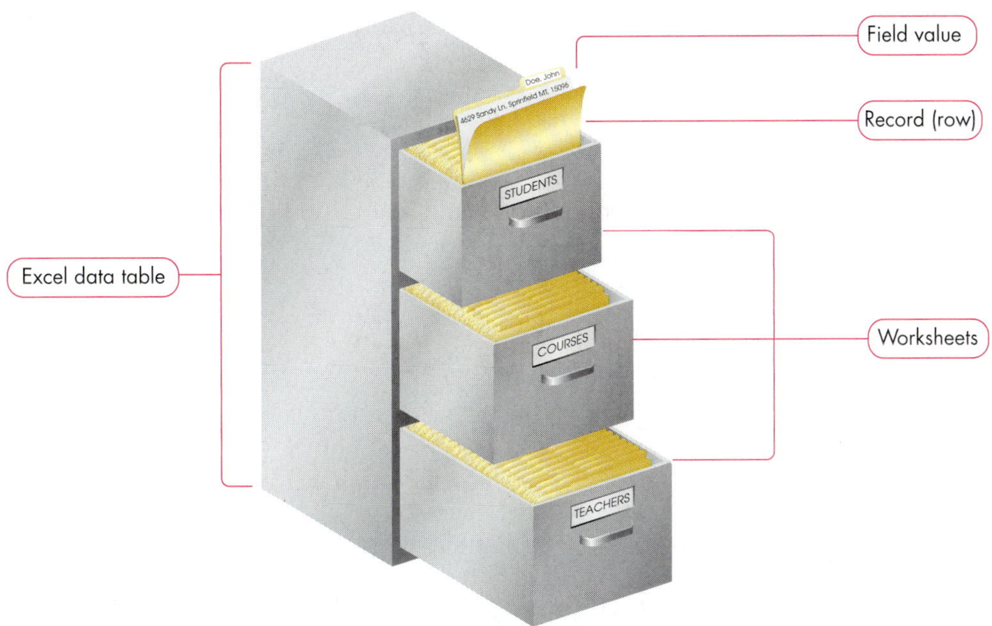

Figure 4.13 File Cabinet Analogy

A ***table*** is an area in the worksheet that contains rows and columns of related data formatted to enable data management and analysis.

A ***table*** (known as a *list* in previous versions of Excel) is an area in the worksheet that contains rows and columns of related data organized in such a way to facilitate data management and analysis. Although you can manage and analyze a range of data, a table provides many advantages over a range of data:

- Filter drop-down lists for efficient sorting and filtering
- Predefined table styles to format table rows and columns with complementary fill colors
- Ability to create and edit calculated columns
- Calculated total row enabling the user to choose from a variety of functions
- Use of structured references instead of cell references in formulas (see Help for more information)
- Ability to export the table data to a SharePoint list

A table can be used like a database table, where the rows represent the records, and the columns represent the fields. The first row contains the column labels or field names. This identifies the data that will be entered in the columns. Each row in the table contains a record. Every cell in the table area, except the field names, contains a specific value for a specific field in a specific record. Every record (row) contains the same fields (columns) in the same order as every other record.

Figure 4.14 contains a college marching band roster. This roster contains nine fields in every record: Last Name, First Name, Sex, Height (ft.), Height (in.), Weight, Instrument, Class, and Scholarship Amount. Field names should be meaningful and unique. Field names may contain up to 255 characters, but they should be kept short so the column does not become too wide and unwieldy to work with.

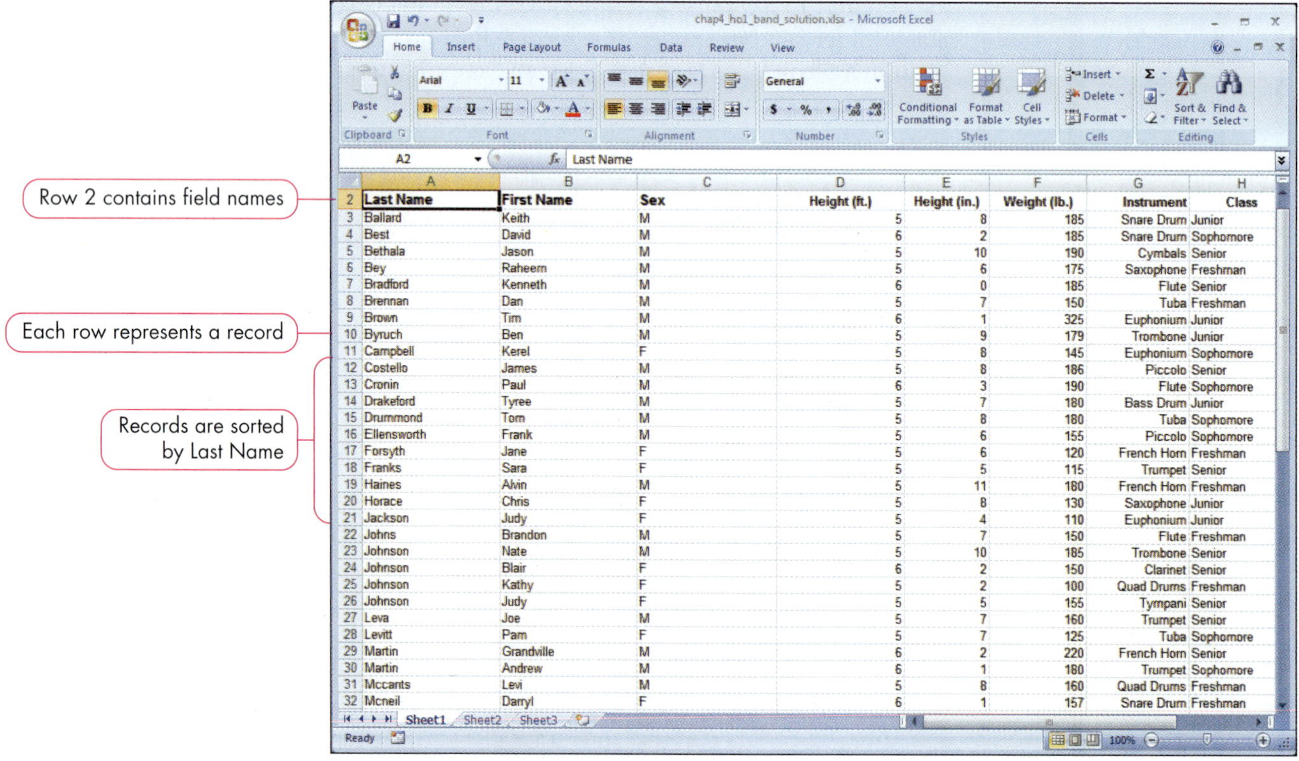

	A	B	C	D	E	F	G	H
2	Last Name	First Name	Sex	Height (ft.)	Height (in.)	Weight (lb.)	Instrument	Class
3	Ballard	Keith	M	5	8	185	Snare Drum	Junior
4	Best	David	M	6	2	185	Snare Drum	Sophomore
5	Bethala	Jason	M	5	10	190	Cymbals	Senior
6	Bey	Raheem	M	5	6	175	Saxophone	Freshman
7	Bradford	Kenneth	M	6	0	185	Flute	Senior
8	Brennan	Dan	M	5	7	150	Tuba	Freshman
9	Brown	Tim	M	6	1	325	Euphonium	Junior
10	Byruch	Ben	M	5	9	179	Trombone	Junior
11	Campbell	Kerel	F	5	8	145	Euphonium	Sophomore
12	Costello	James	M	5	8	186	Piccolo	Senior
13	Cronin	Paul	M	6	3	190	Flute	Sophomore
14	Drakeford	Tyree	M	5	7	180	Bass Drum	Junior
15	Drummond	Tom	M	5	8	180	Tuba	Sophomore
16	Ellensworth	Frank	M	5	6	155	Piccolo	Sophomore
17	Forsyth	Jane	F	5	6	120	French Horn	Freshman
18	Franks	Sara	F	5	5	115	Trumpet	Senior
19	Haines	Alvin	M	5	11	180	French Horn	Freshman
20	Horace	Chris	F	5	8	130	Saxophone	Junior
21	Jackson	Judy	F	5	4	110	Euphonium	Junior
22	Johns	Brandon	M	5	7	150	Flute	Freshman
23	Johnson	Nate	M	5	10	185	Trombone	Senior
24	Johnson	Blair	F	6	2	150	Clarinet	Senior
25	Johnson	Kathy	F	5	2	100	Quad Drums	Freshman
26	Johnson	Judy	F	5	5	155	Tympani	Senior
27	Leva	Joe	M	5	7	160	Trumpet	Senior
28	Levitt	Pam	F	5	7	125	Tuba	Sophomore
29	Martin	Grandville	M	6	2	220	French Horn	Senior
30	Martin	Andrew	M	6	1	180	Trumpet	Sophomore
31	Mccants	Levi	M	5	8	160	Quad Drums	Freshman
32	Mcneil	Darryl	F	6	1	157	Snare Drum	Freshman

Figure 4.14 Marching Band Roster

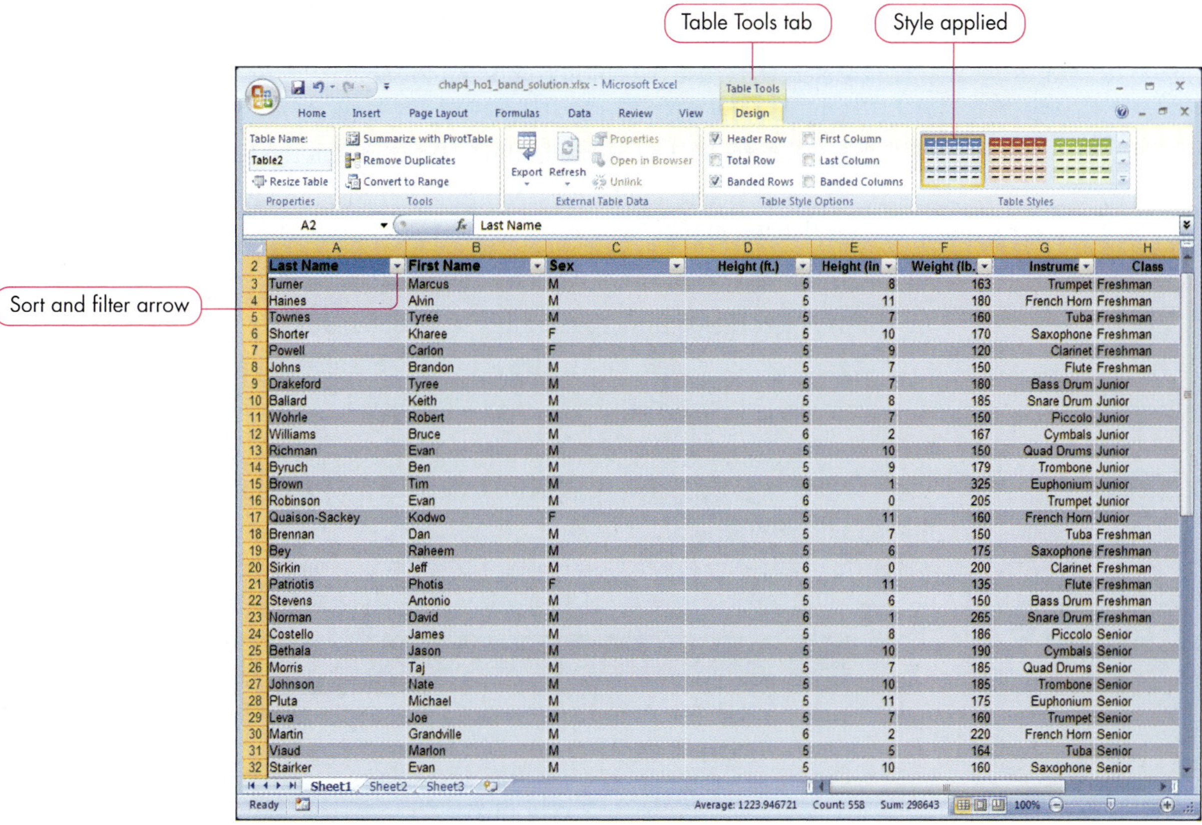

Figure 4.16 Data Table

TIP Shortcut Key

Once the table range has been selected, you can press F9 to insert a table.

Add, Edit, or Delete Records and Fields

Once you have created a table, you will add, edit, or delete records. You will use previously learned Excel commands. It is possible to edit any field in any record in the same way you change entries in a spreadsheet.

1. Click the field (cell) of the data to be edited.
2. Edit the data as desired.
3. Accept the change by pressing Enter.

To add or delete records as your data table expands or contracts, several techniques are available. To add a record:

1. Select a cell in the record below where you want the new record inserted.
2. Click the Insert down arrow in the Cells group on the Home tab.
3. Select Insert Table Rows Above.

If you want to insert a field (column) in a table, make active the field to the right of where the field is to be inserted and repeat the previous steps, except that the selection from the Insert drop-down list is Insert Table Columns to the Left.

While deleting records and fields is physically an easy operation, extreme care must be exercised to ensure that data are not erroneously deleted. If you accidentally delete data, use the Undo command immediately. To delete a record from a table:

1. Select the record to be deleted.
2. Click the Delete arrow in the Cells group on the Home tab.
3. Select Delete Table Rows. Multiple records, contiguous or noncontiguous, may be deleted in this manner.

To delete one or more fields from a table:

1. Select the column or columns to be deleted.
2. Click the Delete down arrow in the Cells group on the Home tab.
3. Select Delete Table Columns.

Again, extreme caution must be exercised when deleting records or fields. Make sure you have selected the desired row or column before initiating the delete procedures.

TIP Delete Versus Clear Contents

The Delete command in the Cells group on the Home tab deletes the selected cell, row, or column from the worksheet, and thus its execution will adjust cell references throughout the worksheet. It is very different from Clear Contents in the shortcut menu, which erases the contents (and/or formatting) of the selected cells, but does not delete the cells from the worksheet and hence has no effect on the cell references in formulas that reference those cells. Pressing Delete erases the contents of a cell and thus corresponds to the Clear Contents command.

Use Find and Replace

The Find and Replace command can be valuable when some part of the data in a table changes and there are multiple occurrences of the data. Rather than editing the data individually in each record, Find and Replace enables global editing of data. For example, Figure 4.17 shows a school marching band roster. The field shown in column H is each player's class. Rather than going to each record to edit the class, Find and Replace is used to advance the class level at the end of each school year, assuming that all juniors will become seniors.

1. Select the field that is to be edited.
2. Click Find & Select in the Editing group on the Home tab, and then select Replace.
3. Enter the data to be changed in the *Find what* box.
4. Enter the data that will replace the changed data in the *Replace with* box.
5. The user can either look at each occurrence of the data to determine if the change is appropriate or click Replace All to replace all occurrences at one time.

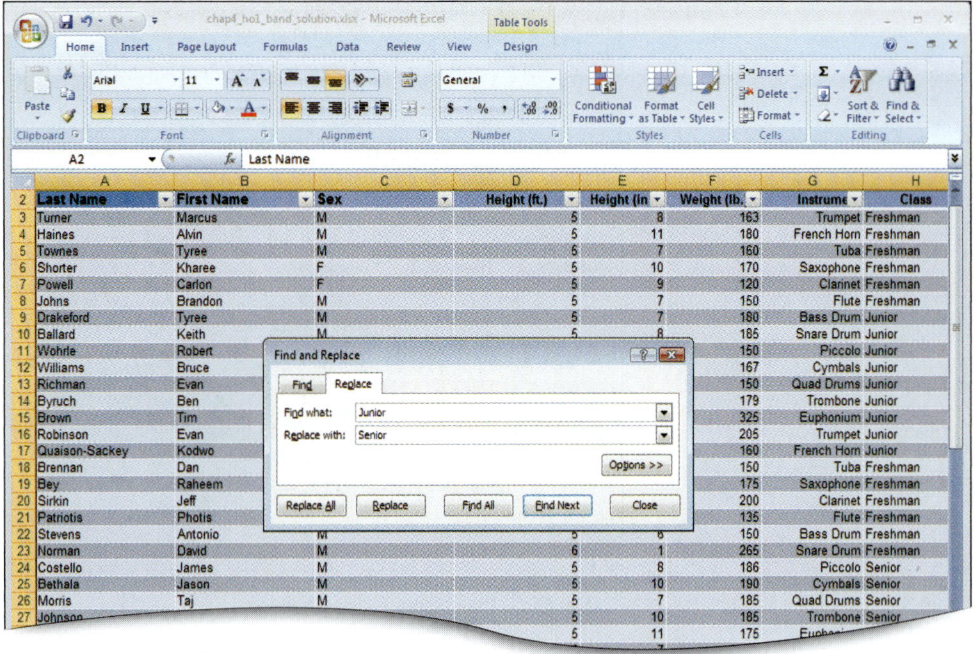

Figure 4.17 Find and Replace Data

> **TIP** Garbage In, Garbage Out (GIGO)
>
> The information produced by a system is only as good as the data on which it is based. It is absolutely critical, therefore, that you validate the data that goes into a system, or else the associated information will not be correct. No system, no matter how sophisticated, can produce valid output from invalid input. In other words, garbage in—garbage out.

Format the Table

Formatting tables can make them more attractive and easier to read, and you can emphasize data. The standard types of formatting available in worksheets are available for you to use with tables. Some of these format options, such as cell height and width, are available in the Format down arrow in the Cells group on the Home tab. Other formatting options are available in the Cell Styles gallery of the Styles group on the Home tab (see Figure 4.18). Other formatting options are present in the Number, Alignment, and Font groups on the Home tab.

One advantage that a table has over a range of data is the Table Tools Design tab is available. The Table Tools Design contextual tab provides a variety of formatting options for tables. The Table Styles group presents a selection of predefined table styles. You can see the effect of each style on a table by pointing to the style. Your table will display the style as you move the mouse across the Table Styles gallery.

The Table Style Options group, shown in Figure 4.19, contains a set of check boxes to select specific format actions in a table. Table 4.3 lists the options and the effect when each is selected. Whatever formatting and formatting effects you choose to use, avoid over-formatting the worksheet. It is not good to apply so many formatting effects that the message you want to present with the data is obscured or lost.

Figure 4.18 Cell Styles Gallery

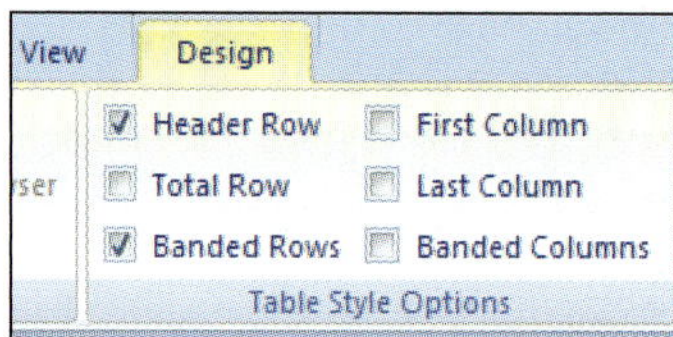

Figure 4.19 Table Style Options Group

Table 4.3 Table Style Options

Check Box Options	Action
Header Row	Turns on or off the header or top row of a table.
Totals Row	Turns on or off the totals or last row of a table.
First Column	Shows special formatting for the first column of a table.
Last Column	Shows special formatting for the last column of a table.
Banded Rows	Displays banded rows where even rows are differently formatted than odd rows.
Banded Columns	Displays banded columns where even columns are differently formatted than odd columns.

Sorting Data

The data in a table are easier to understand and work with if they are in some meaningful order. The marching band roster shown in Figure 4.20 is in no particular order, and it is difficult to locate individual band members. Parents would like the roster in alphabetical order so they can easily locate their children. Announcers and members of the media would like it arranged by name also. Instrument teachers would want it arranged by instrument so they can quickly identify the students they teach. University administrators want it arranged by scholarship amount so that they know who has been awarded how much.

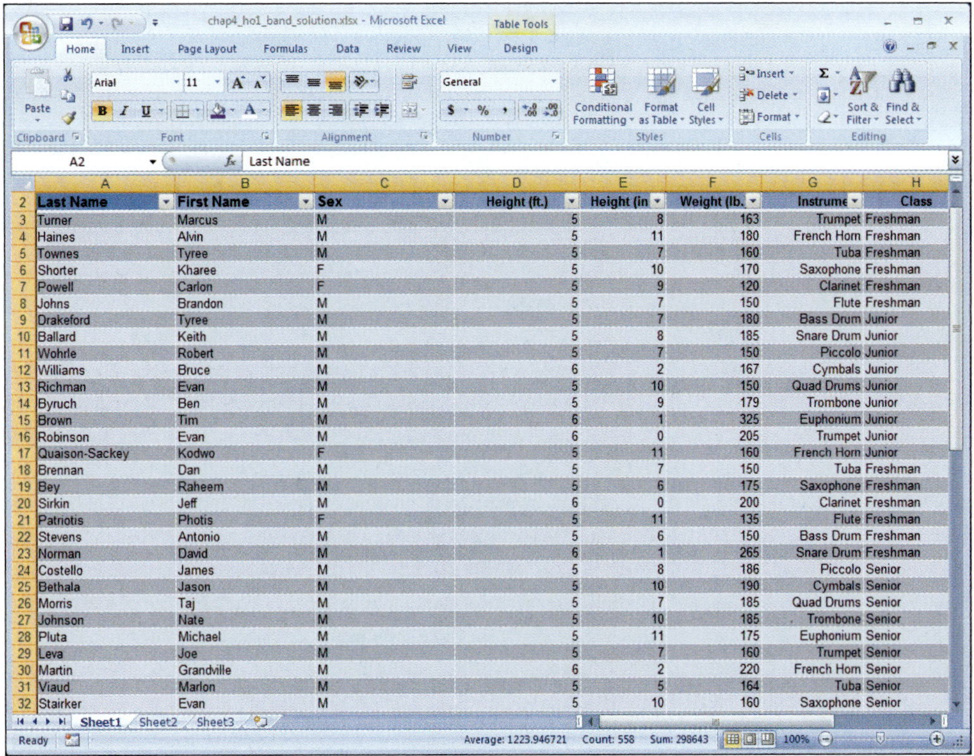

Last Name	First Name	Sex	Height (ft.)	Height (in	Weight (lb.	Instrume	Class
Turner	Marcus	M	5	8	163	Trumpet	Freshman
Haines	Alvin	M	5	11	180	French Horn	Freshman
Townes	Tyree	M	5	7	160	Tuba	Freshman
Shorter	Kharee	F	5	10	170	Saxophone	Freshman
Powell	Carlon	F	5	9	120	Clarinet	Freshman
Johns	Brandon	M	5	7	150	Flute	Freshman
Drakeford	Tyree	M	5	7	180	Bass Drum	Junior
Ballard	Keith	M	5	8	185	Snare Drum	Junior
Wohrle	Robert	M	5	7	150	Piccolo	Junior
Williams	Bruce	M	6	2	167	Cymbals	Junior
Richman	Evan	M	5	10	150	Quad Drums	Junior
Byruch	Ben	M	5	9	179	Trombone	Junior
Brown	Tim	M	6	1	325	Euphonium	Junior
Robinson	Evan	M	6	0	205	Trumpet	Junior
Quaison-Sackey	Kodwo	F	5	11	160	French Horn	Junior
Brennan	Dan	M	5	7	150	Tuba	Freshman
Bey	Raheem	M	5	6	175	Saxophone	Freshman
Sirkin	Jeff	M	6	0	200	Clarinet	Freshman
Patriotis	Photis	F	5	11	135	Flute	Freshman
Stevens	Antonio	M	5	6	150	Bass Drum	Freshman
Norman	David	M	6	1	265	Snare Drum	Freshman
Costello	James	M	5	8	186	Piccolo	Senior
Bethala	Jason	M	5	10	190	Cymbals	Senior
Morris	Taj	M	5	7	185	Quad Drums	Senior
Johnson	Nate	M	5	10	185	Trombone	Senior
Pluta	Michael	M	5	11	175	Euphonium	Senior
Leva	Joe	M	5	7	160	Trumpet	Senior
Martin	Grandville	M	6	2	220	French Horn	Senior
Viaud	Marlon	M	5	5	164	Tuba	Senior
Stairker	Evan	M	5	10	160	Saxophone	Senior

Figure 4.20 Data in No Particular Order

Sorting arranges records in a table by the value in field(s) within a table.

The ***sort command*** puts lists in ascending or descending order according to specified sort levels.

Sorting arranges records in a table by the value of one or more fields within a table. The ***sort command*** puts lists in ascending or descending order according to specified sort fields. The most basic types of sorts are ascending, or low to high, and descending high to low, sequence. Arranging table data in alphabetical order is considered an ascending sort. It is also possible to sort on more than one field at a time. An example of this with the marching band roster would be sorting alphabetically by class and then alphabetically by last name. Sort fields dictate the sequence of the records in the table; for example, if you want to put the marching band table in order by instrument, then instrument is the sort field in the sort process.

You can sort both ranges of data and tables. For both ranges and tables, you can use any of the following methods to sort data:

- Click Sort & Filter in the Editing group on the Home tab.
- Click Sort A to Z, Sort Z to A, and Sort in the Sort & Filter group on the Data tab.
- Right-click the field to sort, select Sort from the shortcut menu, and select the type of sort you want.

When data are formatted as a table, you have an additional method to sort the data. The field names appear in a header row, which contains sort and filter arrows. Click the arrow for the column you want to sort and select the type of sort you want.

Figures 4.21, 4.22, and 4.23 show the marching band roster worksheet sorted using three different sort levels. Figure 4.21 shows the roster sorted by last name. Note that the four Johnsons in the roster are not sorted in order. Figure 4.22 shows the same roster sorted by instrument. Finally, Figure 4.23 shows the roster sorted alphabetically by class in ascending order.

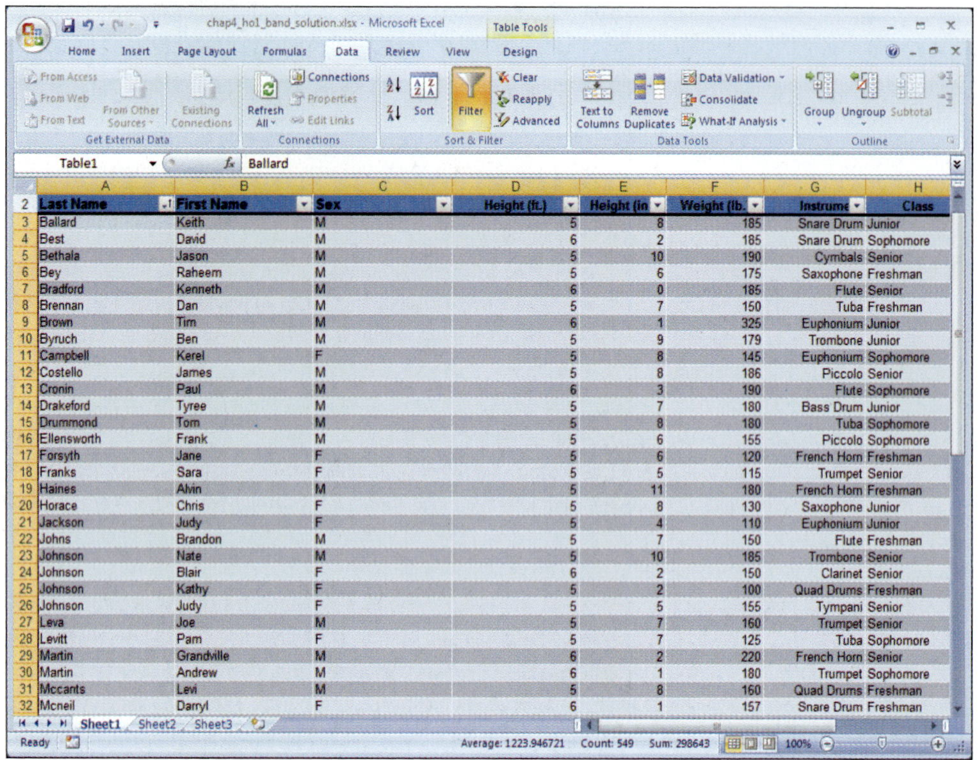

	Last Name	First Name	Sex	Height (ft.)	Height (in	Weight (lb.	Instrume	Class
3	Ballard	Keith	M	5	8	185	Snare Drum	Junior
4	Best	David	M	6	2	185	Snare Drum	Sophomore
5	Bethala	Jason	M	5	10	190	Cymbals	Senior
6	Bey	Raheem	M	5	6	175	Saxophone	Freshman
7	Bradford	Kenneth	M	6	0	185	Flute	Senior
8	Brennan	Dan	M	5	7	150	Tuba	Freshman
9	Brown	Tim	M	6	1	325	Euphonium	Junior
10	Byruch	Ben	M	5	9	179	Trombone	Junior
11	Campbell	Kerel	F	5	8	145	Euphonium	Sophomore
12	Costello	James	M	5	8	186	Piccolo	Senior
13	Cronin	Paul	M	6	3	190	Flute	Sophomore
14	Drakeford	Tyree	M	5	7	180	Bass Drum	Junior
15	Drummond	Tom	M	5	8	180	Tuba	Sophomore
16	Ellensworth	Frank	M	5	6	155	Piccolo	Sophomore
17	Forsyth	Jane	F	5	6	120	French Horn	Freshman
18	Franks	Sara	F	5	5	115	Trumpet	Senior
19	Haines	Alvin	M	5	11	180	French Horn	Freshman
20	Horace	Chris	F	5	8	130	Saxophone	Junior
21	Jackson	Judy	F	5	4	110	Euphonium	Junior
22	Johns	Brandon	M	5	7	150	Flute	Freshman
23	Johnson	Nate	M	5	10	185	Trombone	Senior
24	Johnson	Blair	F	6	2	150	Clarinet	Senior
25	Johnson	Kathy	F	5	2	100	Quad Drums	Freshman
26	Johnson	Judy	F	5	5	155	Tympani	Senior
27	Leva	Joe	M	5	7	160	Trumpet	Senior
28	Levitt	Pam	F	5	7	125	Tuba	Sophomore
29	Martin	Grandville	M	6	2	220	French Horn	Senior
30	Martin	Andrew	M	6	1	180	Trumpet	Sophomore
31	Mccants	Levi	M	5	8	160	Quad Drums	Freshman
32	Mcneil	Darryl	F	6	1	157	Snare Drum	Freshman

Figure 4.21 Sorted by Last Name

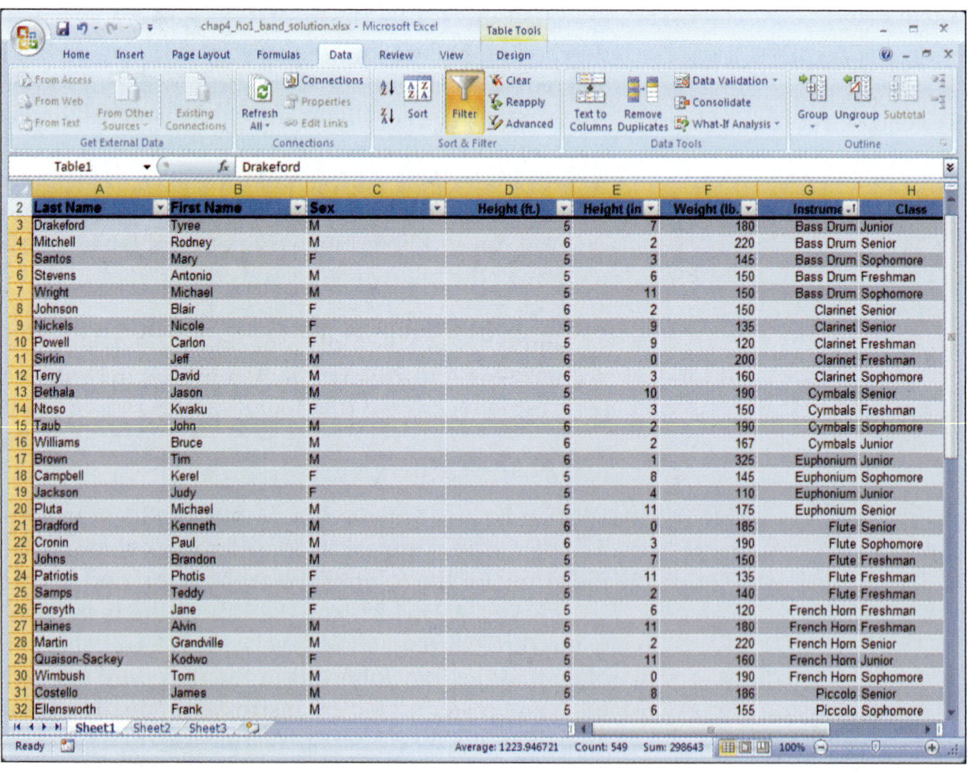

	Last Name	First Name	Sex	Height (ft.)	Height (in	Weight (lb.	Instrume	Class
3	Drakeford	Tyree	M	5	7	180	Bass Drum	Junior
4	Mitchell	Rodney	M	6	2	220	Bass Drum	Senior
5	Santos	Mary	F	5	3	145	Bass Drum	Sophomore
6	Stevens	Antonio	M	5	6	150	Bass Drum	Freshman
7	Wright	Michael	M	5	11	150	Bass Drum	Sophomore
8	Johnson	Blair	F	6	2	150	Clarinet	Senior
9	Nickels	Nicole	F	5	9	135	Clarinet	Senior
10	Powell	Carlon	F	5	9	120	Clarinet	Freshman
11	Sirkin	Jeff	M	6	0	200	Clarinet	Freshman
12	Terry	David	M	6	3	160	Clarinet	Sophomore
13	Bethala	Jason	M	5	10	190	Cymbals	Senior
14	Ntoso	Kwaku	F	6	3	150	Cymbals	Freshman
15	Taub	John	M	6	2	190	Cymbals	Sophomore
16	Williams	Bruce	M	6	2	167	Cymbals	Junior
17	Brown	Tim	M	6	1	325	Euphonium	Junior
18	Campbell	Kerel	F	5	8	145	Euphonium	Sophomore
19	Jackson	Judy	F	5	4	110	Euphonium	Junior
20	Pluta	Michael	M	5	11	175	Euphonium	Senior
21	Bradford	Kenneth	M	6	0	185	Flute	Senior
22	Cronin	Paul	M	6	3	190	Flute	Sophomore
23	Johns	Brandon	M	5	7	150	Flute	Freshman
24	Patriotis	Photis	F	5	11	135	Flute	Freshman
25	Samps	Teddy	F	5	2	140	Flute	Freshman
26	Forsyth	Jane	F	5	6	120	French Horn	Freshman
27	Haines	Alvin	M	5	11	180	French Horn	Freshman
28	Martin	Grandville	M	6	2	220	French Horn	Senior
29	Quaison-Sackey	Kodwo	F	5	11	160	French Horn	Junior
30	Wimbush	Tom	M	6	0	190	French Horn	Sophomore
31	Costello	James	M	5	8	186	Piccolo	Senior
32	Ellensworth	Frank	M	5	6	155	Piccolo	Sophomore

Figure 4.22 Sorted by Instrument

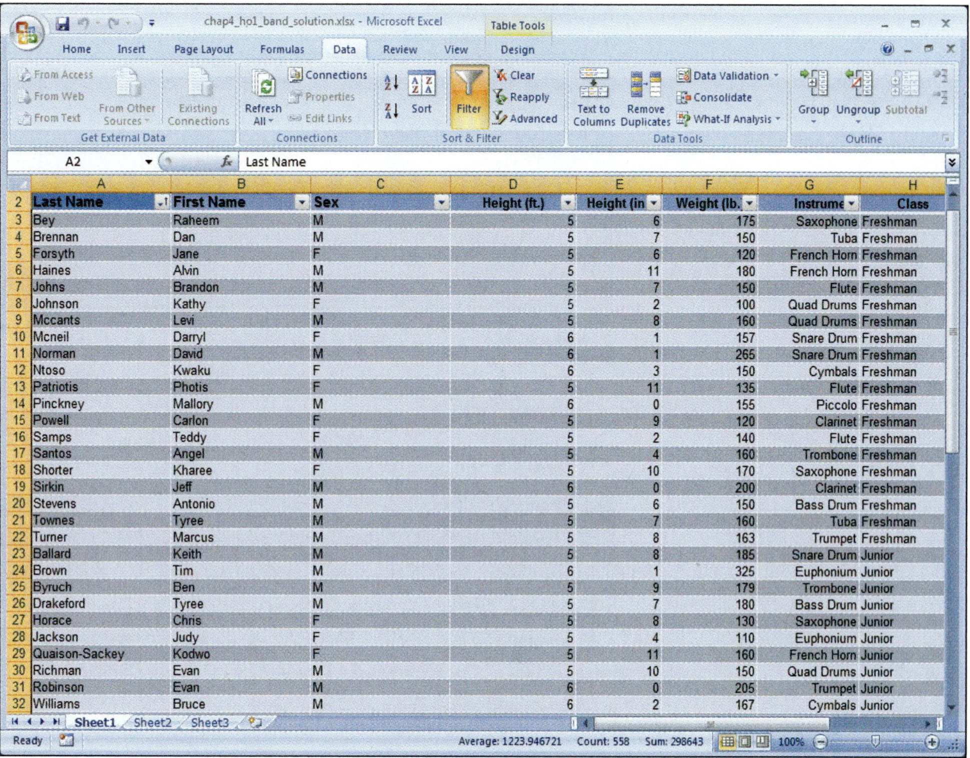

Last Name	First Name	Sex	Height (ft.)	Height (in	Weight (lb.	Instrume	Class
Bey	Raheem	M	5	6	175	Saxophone	Freshman
Brennan	Dan	M	5	7	150	Tuba	Freshman
Forsyth	Jane	F	5	6	120	French Horn	Freshman
Haines	Alvin	M	5	11	180	French Horn	Freshman
Johns	Brandon	M	5	7	150	Flute	Freshman
Johnson	Kathy	F	5	2	100	Quad Drums	Freshman
Mccants	Levi	M	5	8	160	Quad Drums	Freshman
Mcneil	Darryl	F	6	1	157	Snare Drum	Freshman
Norman	David	M	6	1	265	Snare Drum	Freshman
Ntoso	Kwaku	F	6	3	150	Cymbals	Freshman
Patriotis	Photis	F	5	11	135	Flute	Freshman
Pinckney	Mallory	M	6	0	155	Piccolo	Freshman
Powell	Carlon	F	5	9	120	Clarinet	Freshman
Samps	Teddy	F	5	2	140	Flute	Freshman
Santos	Angel	M	5	4	160	Trombone	Freshman
Shorter	Kharee	F	5	10	170	Saxophone	Freshman
Sirkin	Jeff	M	6	0	200	Clarinet	Freshman
Stevens	Antonio	M	5	6	150	Bass Drum	Freshman
Townes	Tyree	M	5	7	160	Tuba	Freshman
Turner	Marcus	M	5	8	163	Trumpet	Freshman
Ballard	Keith	M	5	8	185	Snare Drum	Junior
Brown	Tim	M	6	1	325	Euphonium	Junior
Byruch	Ben	M	5	9	179	Trombone	Junior
Drakeford	Tyree	M	5	7	180	Bass Drum	Junior
Horace	Chris	F	5	8	130	Saxophone	Junior
Jackson	Judy	F	5	4	110	Euphonium	Junior
Quaison-Sackey	Kodwo	F	5	11	160	French Horn	Junior
Richman	Evan	M	5	10	150	Quad Drums	Junior
Robinson	Evan	M	6	0	205	Trumpet	Junior
Williams	Bruce	M	6	2	167	Cymbals	Junior

Figure 4.23 Alphabetically by Class in Ascending Order

Sort in Ascending or Descending Order

The most basic sorts are those done in ascending or descending order. An ascending order sort arranges data alphabetically from A to Z, and numeric data in increasing order, or 1 to 100, for example. The descending order sort arranges data in reverse alphabetical order from Z to A, and the numeric data in decreasing order, or 100 to 1. To accomplish this:

1. Click in any cell in the column to be sorted.
2. Click either Sort A to Z or Sort Z to A in the Sort & Filter group on the Data tab.

Perform a Multiple Level Sort

At times sorting on only one field yields several records that have the same information—for example the same last name or the same class. Refer to Figure 4.21 for multiple Johnsons and Figure 4.23 for multiple members of the same class. The single sort field does not uniquely identify a record. You might need both last name and first name to uniquely identify an individual. Using multiple level sorts allows differentiation among records with the same data in the first (primary) sort level. For example, university administrators might sort on Class, Last Name, and First Name to see an alphabetical list of band members by class. Excel allows sorts on 64 different levels. To perform a multiple level sort:

1. Click in any cell in the table.
2. Click Sort in the Sort & Filter group on the Data tab. This opens the Sort dialog box.
3. Choose the primary sort level from the Sort by drop-down list, and then select the sort order from the Order drop-down list.
4. Click the Add Level button and choose the second sort level from the Then by drop-down list, and then select the sort order from the Order drop-down list.
5. Continue to click the Add Level button and add sort levels until you have entered all desired sorts. See Figure 4.24.
6. Click OK.

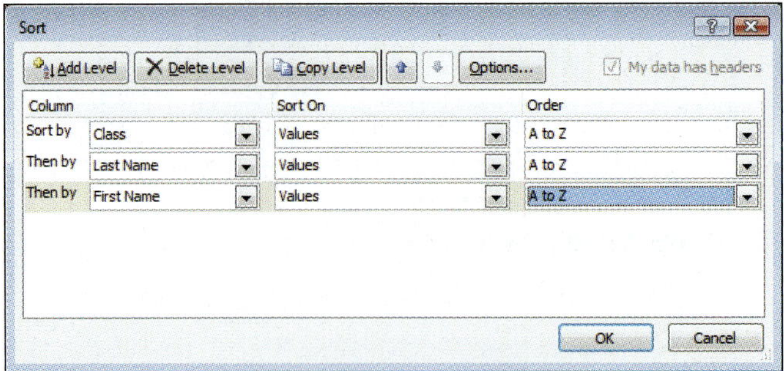

Figure 4.24 Sort Dialog Box

TIP Choose a Custom Sort Sequence

Alphabetic fields normally are arranged in strict alphabetical order. You can, however, choose a custom sort sequence such as the days of the week or the months of the year. Click Sort in the Sort & Filter group on the Data tab. Select Custom List. . . from the Order drop-down list, choose a sequence other than the alphabetic, and then close the Custom Lists dialog box.

Filtering and Totaling Data

Data refer to facts about a specific record or sets of records.

Information is data that have been arranged in some form and are viewed as useful.

Data and ***information*** are not the same thing, although you often hear the two terms used interchangeably. Data refer to facts about a specific record or sets of records, such as a band member's name, his instrument, or his weight as reflected in the marching band roster you have been using. Information is data that have been arranged in some form and is viewed as useful. With the marching band roster, an example of data would be the entire list, but information is a list of members who play the flute. In other words, data are the raw material, and information is the final output produced based on that data.

Decisions in any organization, from businesses to marching bands, are based not just on raw data but on information. The military intelligence-gathering process is an analogy to the decision making process. Many pieces of intelligence data are gathered and analyzed prior to the preparation and dissemination of intelligence information. Similarly a band director gathers data about such things as his members and their past performances before determining how many members who play different instruments need to be recruited.

In today's world, all organizations gather data that lead to information. The maintenance of data was discussed in some detail in the previous section. This final section of the chapter focuses on using data to create information.

Use AutoFilters

A ***filter*** is a condition that displays a subset of data meeting your specifications.

You can use AutoFilter to set a ***filter*** to display a subset of data from a table. The filtered data display only the records that meet the criteria you, the Excel user, specify. Records that do not meet the specified criteria are hidden: Hidden records are not deleted; they are just not displayed. Figure 4.16 depicts the marching band roster we have been using, and Figure 4.25 shows the same roster filtered to show only those members in the band who are juniors. When you created a data table, Filter in the Sort & Filter group on the Data tab was highlighted. This default option indicates that the Filter command is available. To apply a simple AutoFilter to a data table, click the filter arrow in the header row. Either Text Filters or Number Filters will display according to the type of data in the column; see Figure 4.25. Clear the Select All check box, select the filter conditions(s) to be imposed, and click OK.

If the header row with filter drop-down arrows is not visible or if you are filtering a range of data instead of a table:

1. Select the data table.
2. Click Sort & Filter in the Editing group on the Home tab.
3. Select Filter to show the filter arrows in each column header.

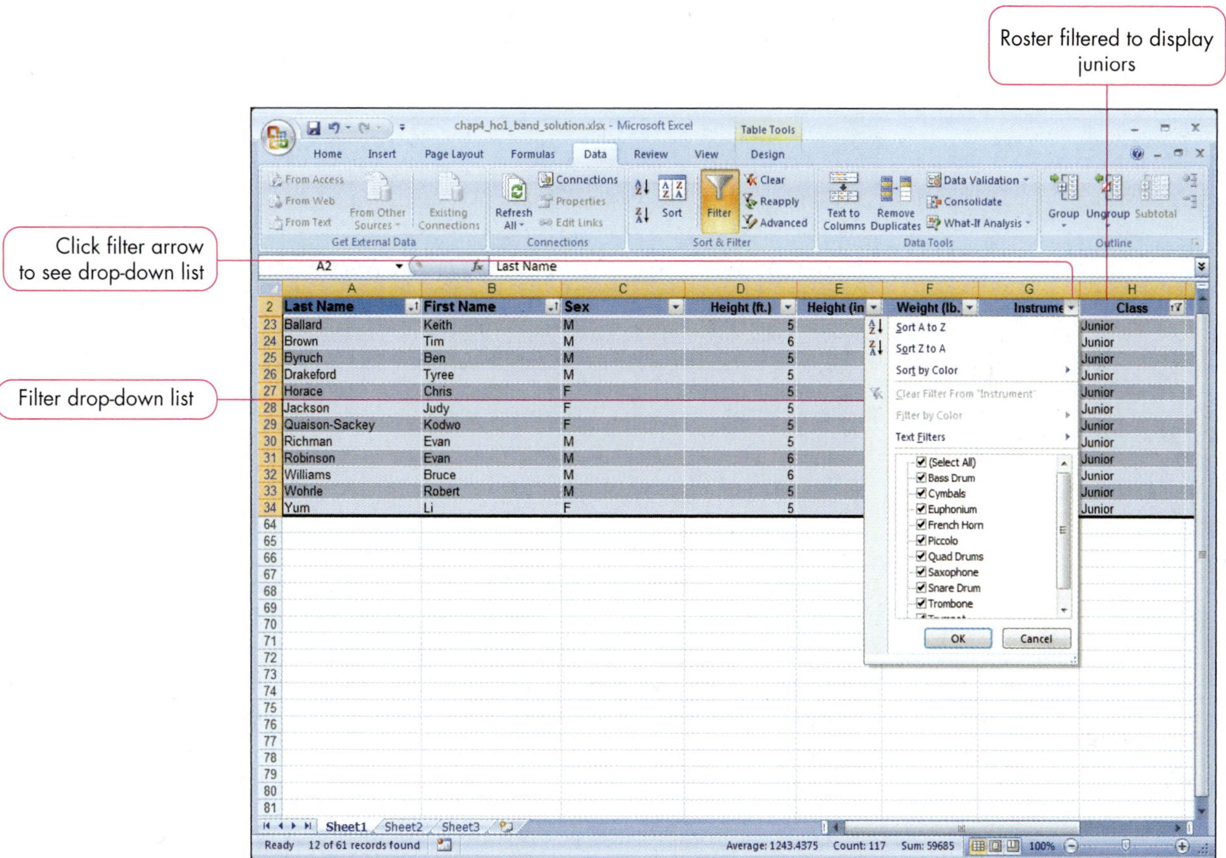

Figure 4.25 Filtered Roster

Use Multiple AutoFilters

Often Excel users need to filter on more than one criteria to display the exact information required. Multiple AutoFilters can be used to return a more specific result. With AutoFilter, you can filter more than one criteria. Filters are additive, which means that each additional filter is based on the current filtered data and further reduces a data subset. To apply multiple AutoFilters, repeat the steps described above until the subset of data is exactly what is desired. Figure 4.26 shows the marching band roster filtered to show only Snare Drum members who are also Juniors. Typically you will filter from gross to fine. For example, if you want to identify the freshman female flute players, you would filter first by class (freshman), then by sex (F), and finally by instrument (flute).

Filter arrow funnel image indicates table is filtered by this column

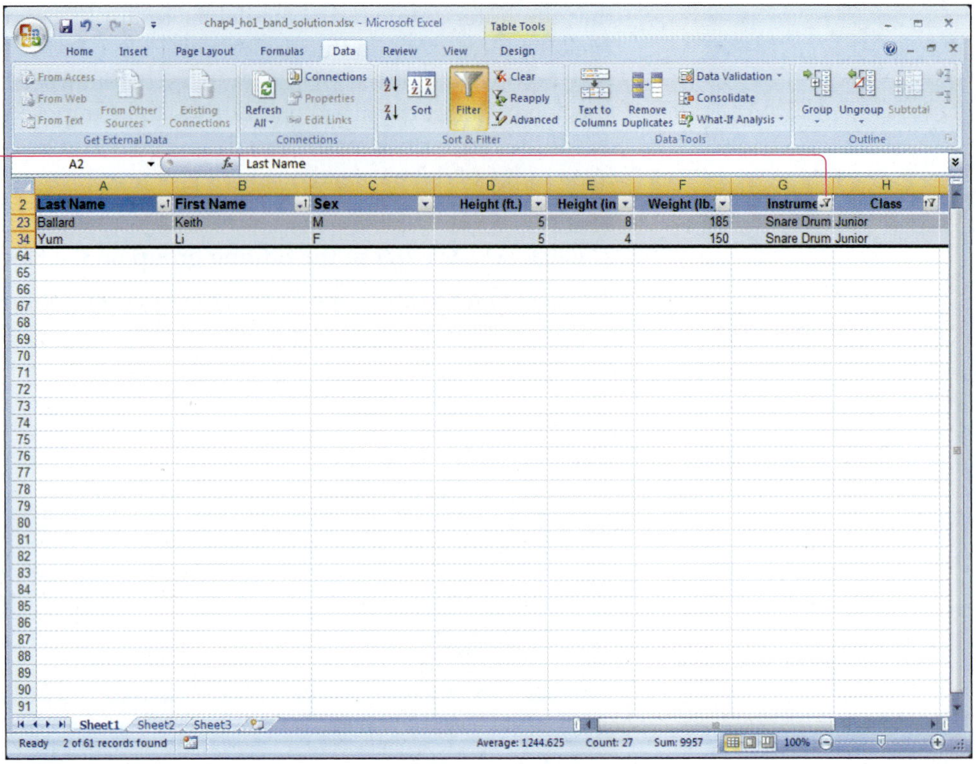

Figure 4.26 The Members Who Are Juniors and Play the Snare Drum

Insert Column Totals

Often fields exist in data tables that require calculation in order to best display some or all of the data contained in the table. You can use Help to learn more about database functions that may be used in Excel. Here, however, you will find a simple column total. The marching band roster contains a field for each member's scholarship amount. Figure 4.27 shows a column total for the scholarships awarded to marching band members. To insert column totals:

1. Ensure a cell in the table is selected so the Table Tools Design tab is available.
2. Click the Total Row check box in the Table Style Options group on the Design tab. Excel inserts a total row and totals the last column using the SUBTOTAL function.
3. Click in the total cell to see a drop-down arrow.
4. Click the drop-down arrow to select another function, such as Average, or select None to remove the total if it is not relevant to that column.
5. Click in other cells on the total row and repeat step 4 to apply totals to other columns.

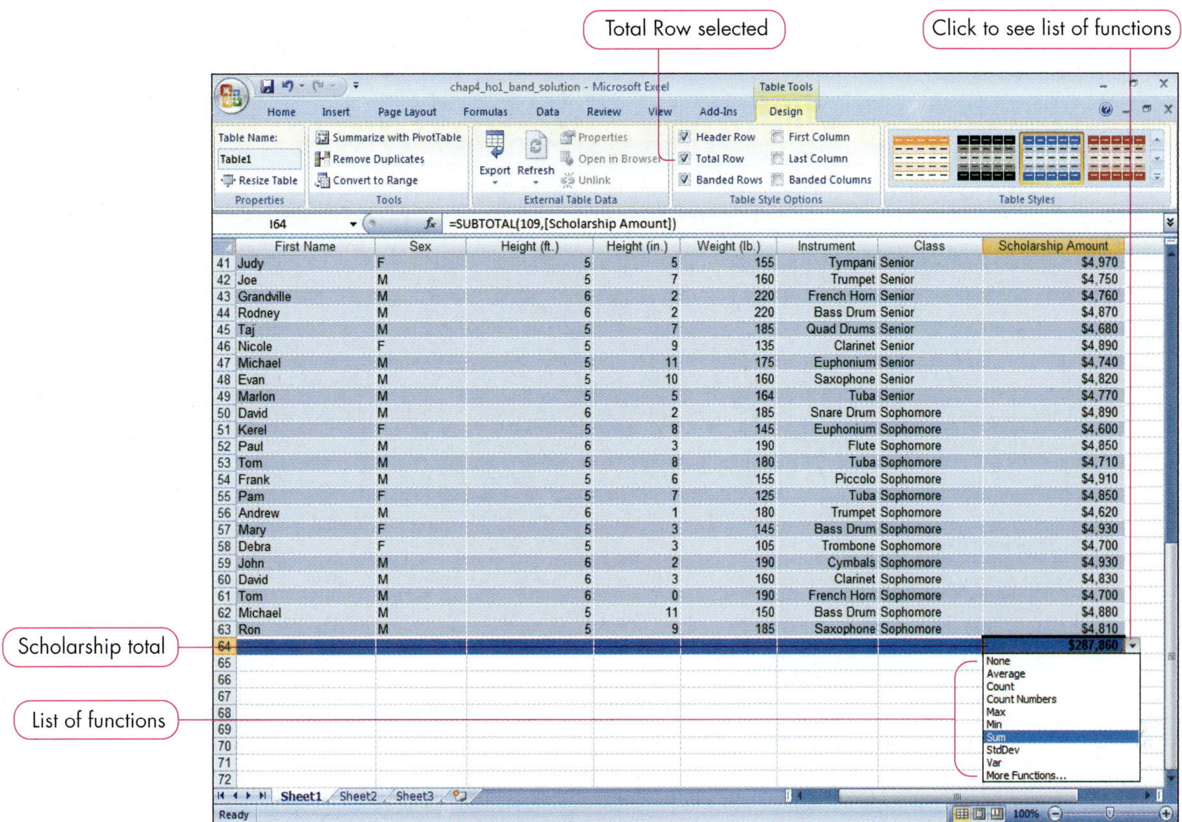

Figure 4.27 Scholarship Total

Create a Summary Report with a Chart

Creating a summary report computes subtotals for groups of records within a range of data. It is imperative you remember that the Subtotals command will not function with data in tables. The records in the range of data are grouped according to value in a specific field such as Class. The Subtotals command inserts a subtotal row into the list when the value of a designated field such as Class changes from one record to the next. Automatic row insertions are not permitted in a table.

A grand total is displayed after the last record. The list must be in sequence by the field on which the subtotals will be grouped prior to executing the Subtotals command. The data can be sorted in the data table or after the data table is converted to a list. Figure 4.28 shows a summary report for scholarship amounts by class for the marching band. To create a summary report:

1. To make sure the data are a list and not a table, click Convert to Range in the Tools group on the Design tab as necessary, and click Yes in the message box.
2. Click in the range of data, and then click Subtotal in the Outline group on the Data tab.
3. Select the appropriate options in the Subtotal dialog box, and click OK.

After you apply subtotals, you see an outline on the left side of the worksheet. Click 1 to collapse the list to the grand total only, click 2 to see the subtotals and the grand total, or click 3 to see the entire list. You can selectively collapse categories by clicking the minus sign in the outline. After collapsing the outline, you can click the + sign to selectively expand an outline.

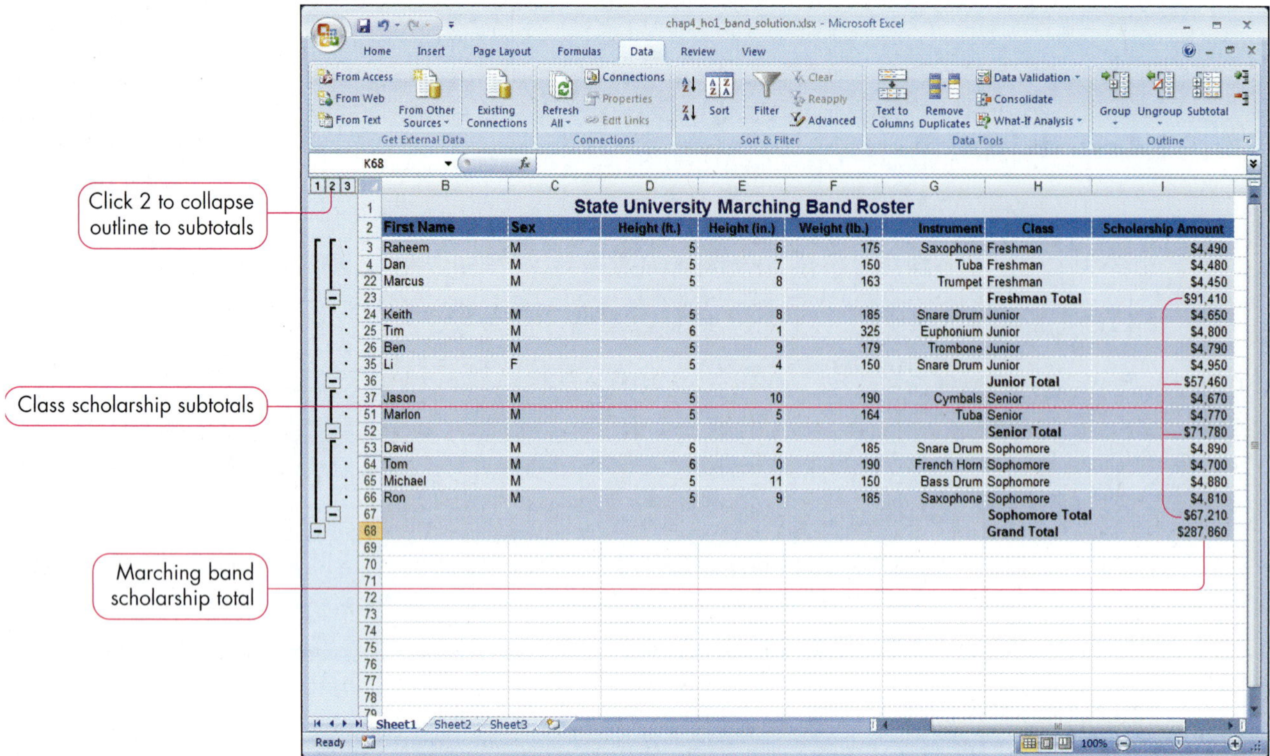

Figure 4.28 Scholarship Summary Report

A chart of the summary data is an ideal way to graphically depict the data from the summary report. See Figure 4.29 for an example of a pie chart showing the scholarship amount by class. To create a summary chart:

1. Select data fields to be charted. In the marching band example, click 2 to collapse the list to show the subtotals and grand total only to make it easier to select the class total labels and the scholarship amounts.
2. Click the Insert tab and select the type of chart appropriate for the data.
3. Format and move the chart as appropriate.

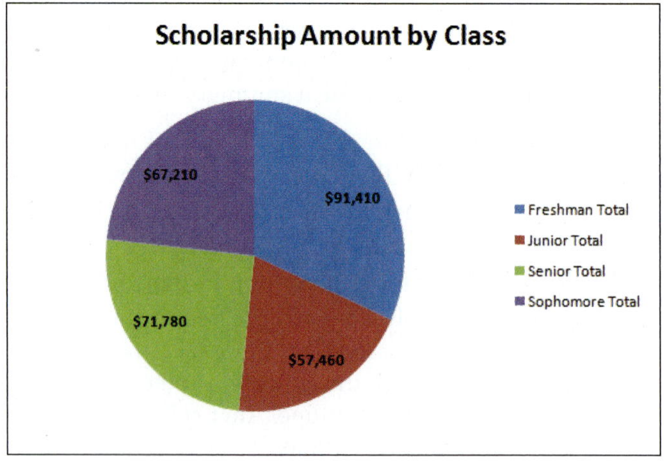

Figure 4.29 Chart of Summary Report

Hands-On Exercises

2 | Marching Band Roster Revisited

Skills covered: 1. Create a Table **2.** Add, Edit, or Delete Records, and Use Find and Replace **3.** Format a Table **4.** Sort a Table **5.** Filter a Table **6.** Create Column Totals and a Summary Report **7.** Print the Completed Worksheet

Step 1 Create a Table

Refer to Figure 4.30 as you complete Step 1.

a. Open a new blank workbook.

b. Select **cells D2:G13**.

   You have selected the area that will be defined as a table.

c. Click the **Insert tab** and click **Table** in the Tables group to display the Create Table dialog box.

d. Verify that the range of cells in the **Where is the data for your table?** box is correct, click the **My table has headers check box**, and click **OK**.

   You selected a blank area of the worksheet and formally defined it as a table. The Table Tools Design contextual tab becomes active once the table is created. Refer to the reference table to see the Table Tools Design contextual tab and groups. Also note the default style is applied to the header row with banded rows.

e. Close Book1 without saving it.

f. Open the *chap4_ho1_band_solution* workbook. Save the workbook as **chap4_ho2_band_solution**.

g. Select **cells A2:I63**, click the **Insert tab**, and click **Table**. Verify the range in the **Where is the data for your table?** box, make sure the **My table has headers check box** is selected, and click **OK**.

   The data in the selected range are converted to a table with a clearly identifiable header row. Each column header cell contains the filter arrrow that will be used later. The default table style is applied with banded rows. You will change the style later in the hands-on exercise.

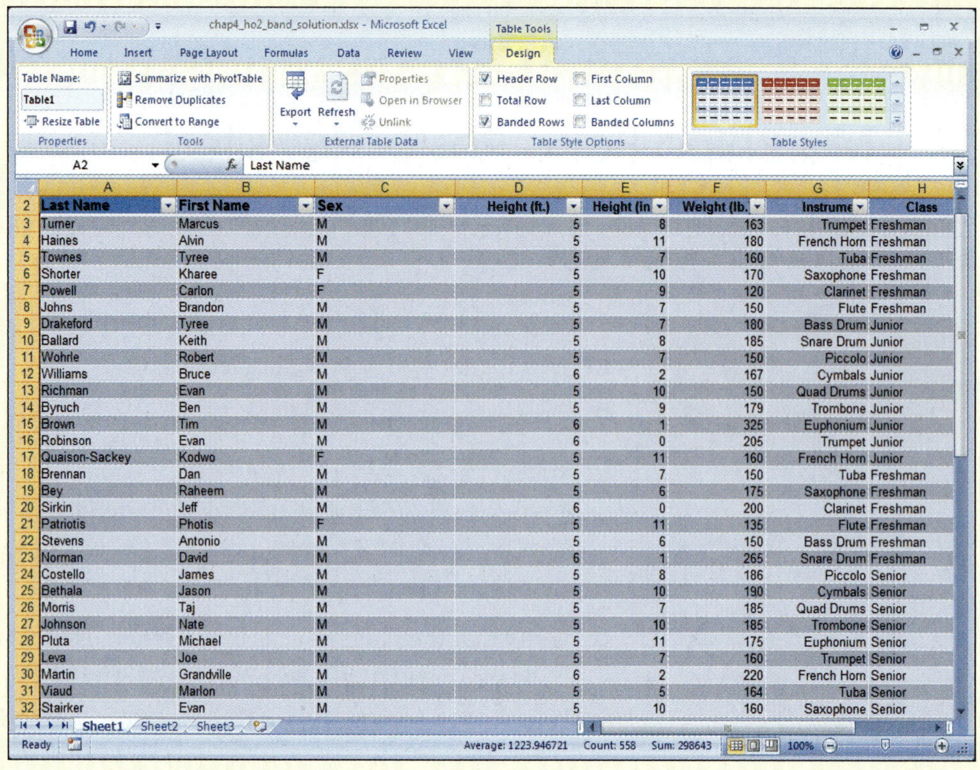

	Last Name	First Name	Sex	Height (ft.)	Height (in	Weight (lb.	Instrume	Class
3	Turner	Marcus	M	5	8	163	Trumpet	Freshman
4	Haines	Alvin	M	5	11	180	French Horn	Freshman
5	Townes	Tyree	M	5	7	160	Tuba	Freshman
6	Shorter	Kharee	F	5	10	170	Saxophone	Freshman
7	Powell	Carlon	F	5	9	120	Clarinet	Freshman
8	Johns	Brandon	M	5	7	150	Flute	Freshman
9	Drakeford	Tyree	M	5	7	180	Bass Drum	Junior
10	Ballard	Keith	M	5	8	185	Snare Drum	Junior
11	Wohrle	Robert	M	5	7	150	Piccolo	Junior
12	Williams	Bruce	M	6	2	167	Cymbals	Junior
13	Richman	Evan	M	5	10	150	Quad Drums	Junior
14	Byruch	Ben	M	5	9	179	Trombone	Junior
15	Brown	Tim	M	6	1	325	Euphonium	Junior
16	Robinson	Evan	M	6	0	205	Trumpet	Junior
17	Quaison-Sackey	Kodwo	F	5	11	160	French Horn	Junior
18	Brennan	Dan	M	5	7	150	Tuba	Freshman
19	Bey	Raheem	M	5	6	175	Saxophone	Freshman
20	Sirkin	Jeff	M	6	0	200	Clarinet	Freshman
21	Patriotis	Photis	F	5	11	135	Flute	Freshman
22	Stevens	Antonio	M	5	6	150	Bass Drum	Freshman
23	Norman	David	M	6	1	265	Snare Drum	Freshman
24	Costello	James	M	5	8	186	Piccolo	Senior
25	Bethala	Jason	M	5	10	190	Cymbals	Senior
26	Morris	Taj	M	5	7	185	Quad Drums	Senior
27	Johnson	Nate	M	5	10	185	Trombone	Senior
28	Pluta	Michael	M	5	11	175	Euphonium	Senior
29	Leva	Joe	M	5	7	160	Trumpet	Senior
30	Martin	Grandville	M	6	2	220	French Horn	Senior
31	Viaud	Marlon	M	5	5	164	Tuba	Senior
32	Stairker	Evan	M	5	10	160	Saxophone	Senior

Figure 4.30 Table Created

Step 2

Add, Edit, or Delete Records, and Use Find and Replace

Refer to Figure 4.31 as you complete Step 2.

a. Click in **cell F28**, type **195**, and press **Enter**.

   You changed Michael Pluta's weight to 195 from 175. Editing a single field is done in this manner everywhere in the table. Click the cell and type the change.

b. Click **cell A11**, click the **Home tab**, and click the **Insert down arrow** in the **Cells** group. Select **Insert Table Rows Above**. Type the following data for the new record:

Cell address	Data
A11	Thomas
B11	Joe
C11	M
D11	6
E11	3
F11	167
G11	Tuba
H11	Sophomore
I11	4550

   You inserted a blank record for row 11 and entered all the data for that record.

c. Save the workbook with the new record.

d. Select **cells A11:I11**, click the **Delete down arrow** in the Cells group, and select **Delete Table Rows.**

You deleted Joe Thomas from the data table and now see that Robert Wohrle is record 11.

TROUBLESHOOTING: If you accidentally press Delete, the entire record is deleted, but the blank row remains.

e. Select **cells H3:H63**, click the **Find and Select button** in the Editing group, and select **Replace**.

f. In the **Find what** box, type **Sophomore**; in the **Replace with** box, type **Junior**.

g. Click the **Replace All** button, and a Microsoft Office Excel message box appears, indicating the number of replacements made.

h. Click **OK** and then click **Close** to close the Replace box.

You replaced all sophomores with juniors. In a real situation, you could not assume that all students will be promoted to the next grade level. Because this is a fictitious scenario, you were exploring the Find and Replace feature to see how it works.

TROUBLESHOOTING: If no replacements were made, verify the spelling in the Find text box. Remember that using Replace All allows Excel to replace all occurrences automatically. You must click the Replace button to manually replace each instance of text you do not want to replace automatically.

i. Click **Undo** on the Quick Access Toolbar to undo the replace. Save the workbook.

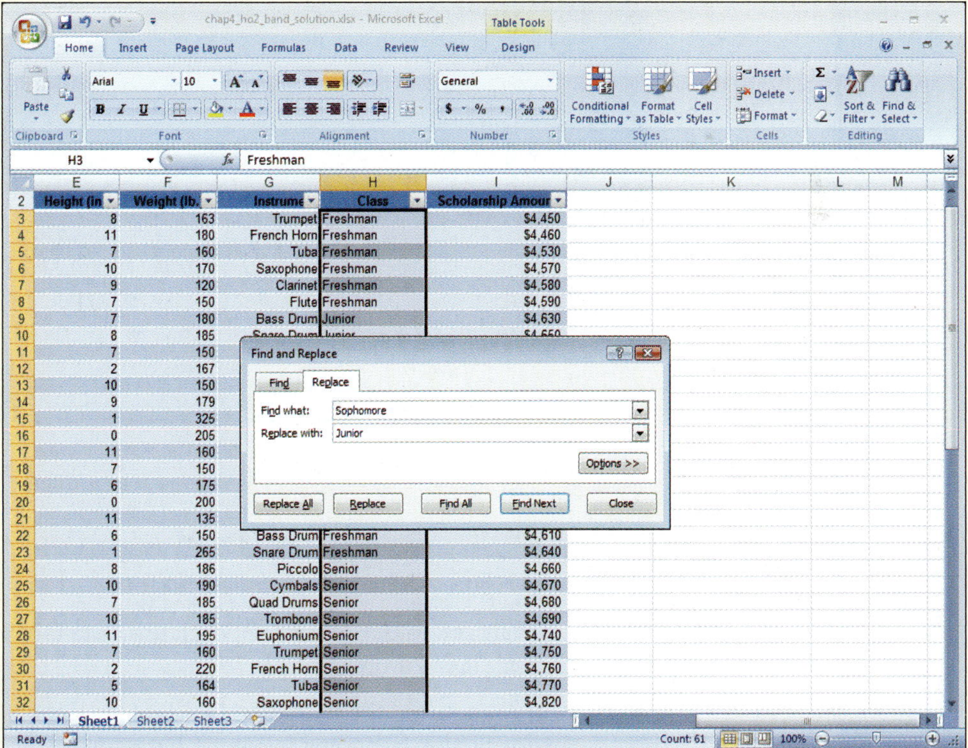

Figure 4.31 Edited Records

Step 3
Format a Table

You will explore the table style options group in this exercise by first changing the banding from rows to columns and then changing the style of the whole table. Refer to Figure 4.32 as you complete Step 3.

a. Click anywhere in the defined table, click the **Table Tools Design tab**, and select **Banded Columns** in the Table Style Options group.

b. Clear the **Banded Rows check box** in the Table Style Options group.

c. Click the **More arrow** in the Table Styles group to choose a visual style for the table from the **Gallery**.

   Move the mouse over various table styles to preview the results. The Live Preview feature is designed to provide you with a preview before making your final selection.

d. Click **Table Style Medium 7** (the last style in the first row of the Medium section).

e. Save the workbook.

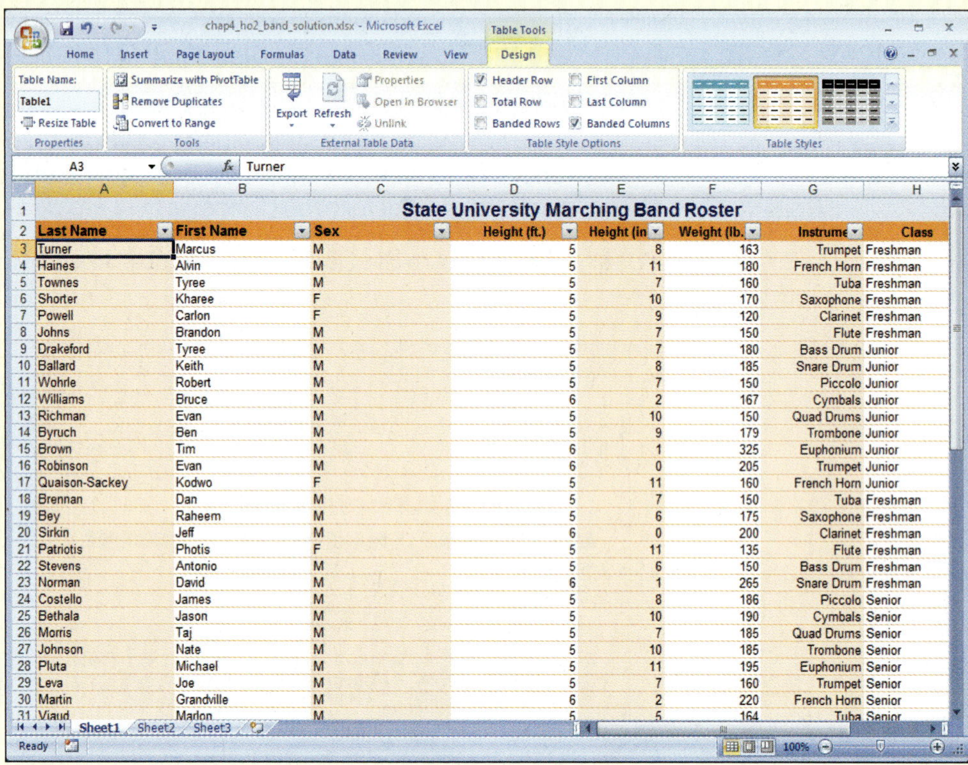

Figure 4.32 Formatting a Table

Step 4
Sort a Table

Refer to Figure 4.33 as you complete Step 4.

a. Click in any cell in **column H**, click the **Data tab**, and click **Sort A to Z** in the Sort & Filter group.

   You have sorted the marching band roster alphabetically by Class (Freshman, Junior, Senior, Sophomore). Note this is an alphabetical sort, and there are several occurrences of the same last name in the roster.

b. Click **Sort** in the Sort & Filter group on the Data tab to open the Sort dialog box.

   The Sort by Class option already exists as the primary sort field because you last sorted using the Class field.

c. Click **Add Level**, click the **Then by** drop-down arrow, and select **Last Name**.

d. Click **Add Level** again, click the **Then by drop-down arrow**, and select **First Name**. Click **OK** to perform the sort.

You sorted the marching band roster using multiple sort levels alphabetically by Class, then by Last Name, and finally by First Name.

e. Save the workbook.

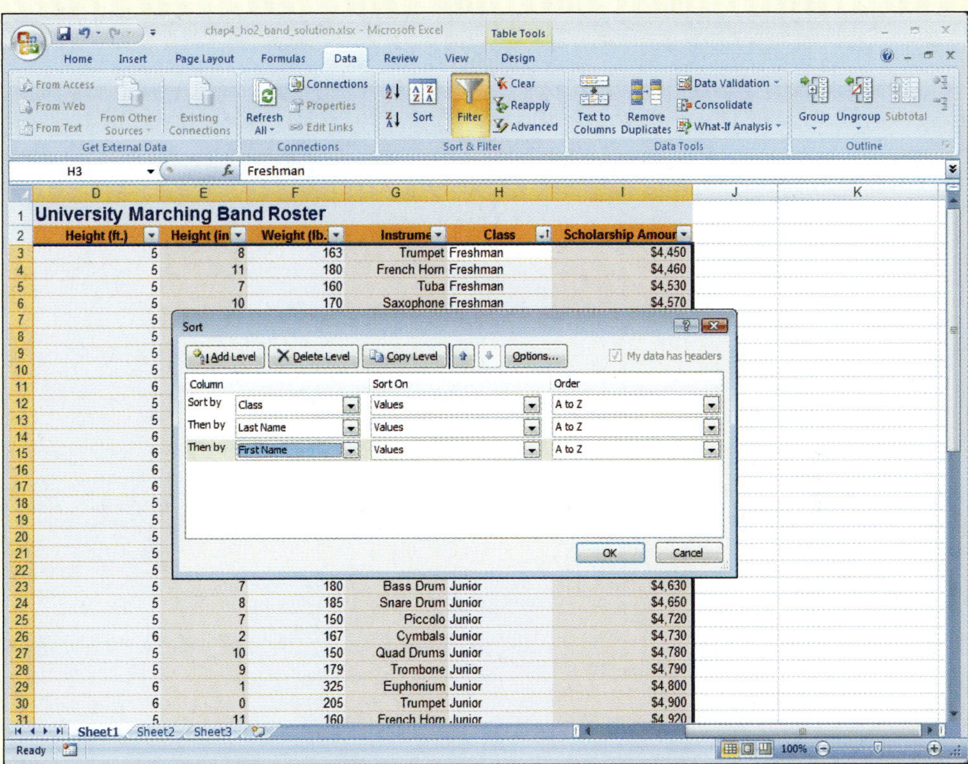

Figure 4.33 Multiple Level Sort

Step 5
Filter a Table

Refer to Figure 4.34 as you complete Step 5.

a. Click the column arrow for the **Class column** (column H). Clear the **Select All check box**. Select the **Junior check box** and click **OK**.

This filter selected just the Junior members of the band and these are now the only data rows visible.

TROUBLESHOOTING: If the column headers do not display the filter arrows, click **Sort & Filter** in the Editing group on the Home tab and select **Filter**. Or you can click **Filter** in the Sort & Filter group on the Data tab. Either way, you will make the filter arrows visible in each column header.

b. Click the **Instrument filter arrow** (column G) and clear the **Select All check box**. Select the **Euphonium check box** and click **OK**.

You have now filtered the Junior members to just those who play the Euphonium.

c. Click the **Home tab**, click **Sort & Filter** in the Editing group, and select **Clear**. Save the workbook.

The Clear command removes all filters, and all rows are now displayed.

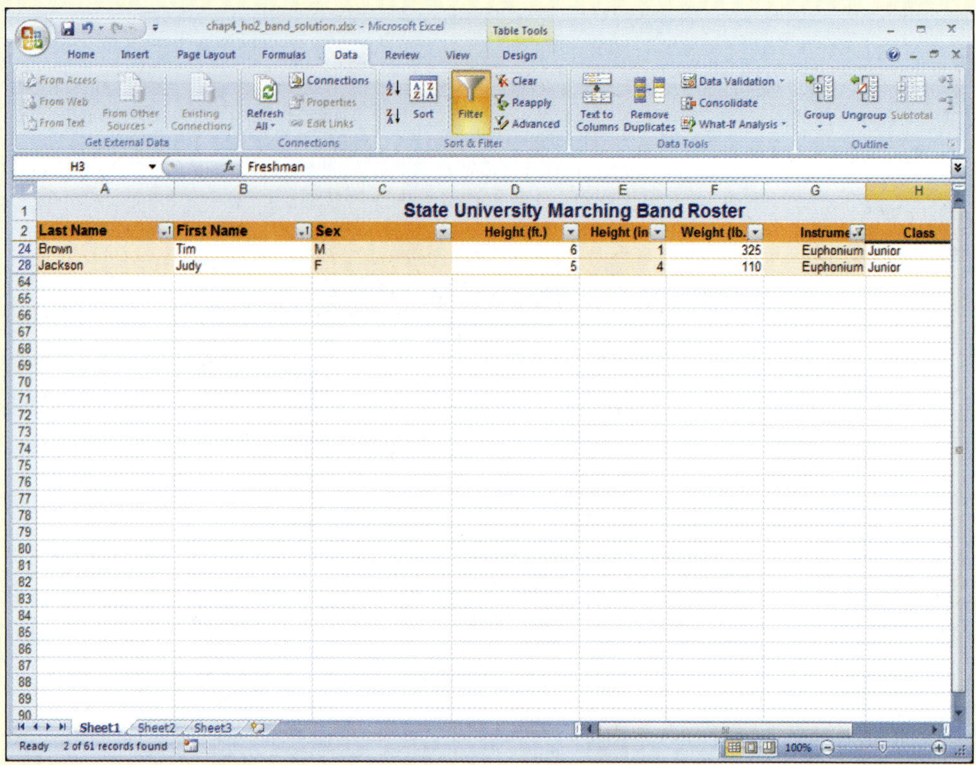

Figure 4.34 Multiple Level AutoFilter

Step 6
Create Column Totals and a Summary Report

Make sure that any cell in the table is selected and that the table is sorted by Class. Refer to Figure 4.35 as you complete Step 6. Note, some rows are hidden so you can see all subtotals.

a. Click the **Design tab**, select **Total Row** in the Table Style Options group. Save the workbook.

Scroll to see that you now have a total scholarship amount in cell I64 with a row label in A64.

b. Click **Convert to Range** in the Tools group on the Design tab. Click **Yes** in the Microsoft Office Excel message box.

TROUBLESHOOTING: You must convert the data table to a range or list to create a summary report of the data. Also note that the Table Tools contextual tab has disappeared now that you have converted the table to a list.

c. Click the **Data tab** and then click **Subtotal** in the Outline group to open the Subtotal dialog box.
- Click the **At each change in drop-down arrow** and select **Class**.
- Click the **Use function drop-down arrow** and select **Sum**.
- Make sure the **Scholarship Amount check box** is selected. If necessary, select the **Replace current subtotals** and **Summary below data check boxes**.
- Click **OK**.

Scroll through the worksheet to see the Summary Report totals for Scholarships for each Class.

d. Select **cells H23:I23**, **H36:I36**, **H52:I52,** and **H67:I67**. Click the **Insert tab**, click **Pie** in the Charts group, and select **Pie**.

   You made a pie chart because this best shows the proportion of scholarship money by class.

e. Click the **Design tab** and click **Move Chart** in Location group to open the Move Chart dialog box. Click **New sheet** and click **OK**.

f. Click the **Layout tab**, click **Data Labels** in the Labels group, and select **Inside End**.

   - Click **Chart** title in the Labels group on the Layout tab and select **Above Chart**.
   - Type **Scholarship Distribution** as the title of the chart.

   You selected just the summary report data and made a pie chart for a visual analysis of the data. You further enhanced the chart to highlight the charted data.

g. Save the workbook.

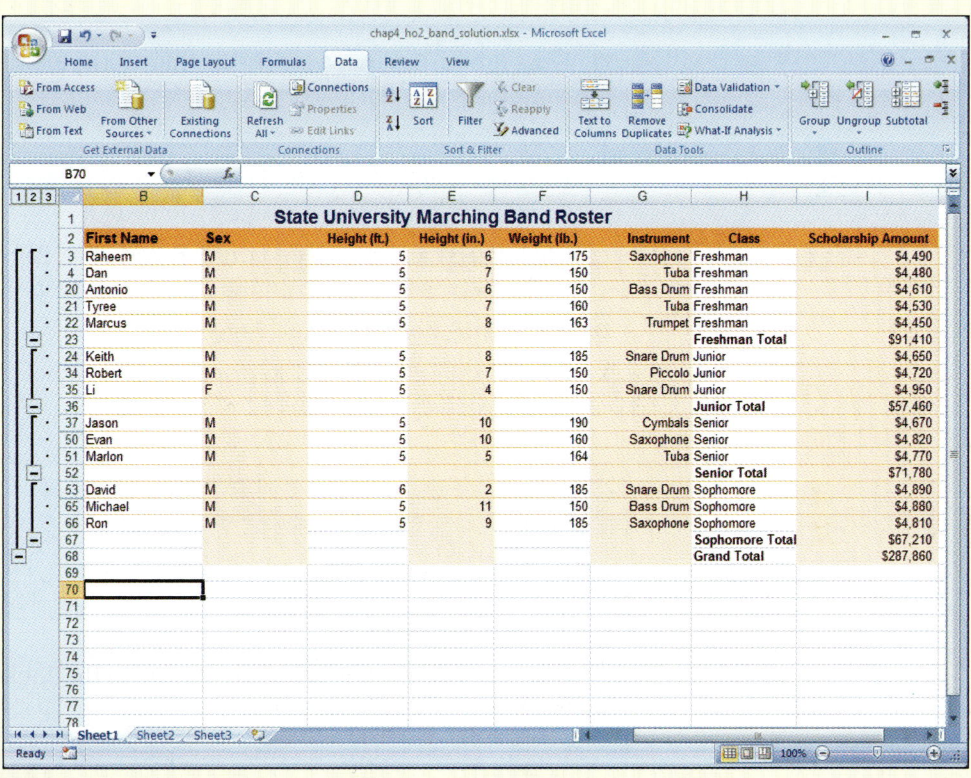

1	State University Marching Band Roster							
2	First Name	Sex	Height (ft.)	Height (in.)	Weight (lb.)	Instrument	Class	Scholarship Amount
3	Raheem	M	5	6	175	Saxophone	Freshman	$4,490
4	Dan	M	5	7	150	Tuba	Freshman	$4,480
20	Antonio	M	5	6	150	Bass Drum	Freshman	$4,610
21	Tyree	M	5	7	160	Tuba	Freshman	$4,530
22	Marcus	M	5	8	163	Trumpet	Freshman	$4,450
23							Freshman Total	$91,410
24	Keith	M	5	8	185	Snare Drum	Junior	$4,650
34	Robert	M	5	7	150	Piccolo	Junior	$4,720
35	Li	F	5	4	150	Snare Drum	Junior	$4,950
36							Junior Total	$57,460
37	Jason	M	5	10	190	Cymbals	Senior	$4,670
50	Evan	M	5	10	160	Saxophone	Senior	$4,820
51	Marlon	M	5	5	164	Tuba	Senior	$4,770
52							Senior Total	$71,780
53	David	M	6	2	185	Snare Drum	Sophomore	$4,890
65	Michael	M	5	11	150	Bass Drum	Sophomore	$4,880
66	Ron	M	5	9	185	Saxophone	Sophomore	$4,810
67							Sophomore Total	$67,210
68							Grand Total	$287,860

Figure 4.35 Summary Report

Step 7
Print the Completed Worksheet

You will format the worksheet for printing by adding a custom header and footer. You will position page breaks and select page printing order. Refer to Figure 4.36, the completed worksheet, as you complete Step 7.

a. Click the **Sheet1 tab**, click **Page Layout** on the status bar, and then reduce the Zoom view to about **70%** and scroll to view four pages.

b. Click the **Page Layout tab** and click the **Page Setup Dialog Box Launcher** to open the Page Setup dialog box.

- Click the **Header/Footer tab**, click **Custom Header**, and type your name in the *Left section*, **Marching Band Roster** in the *Center section*, and your instructor's name in the *Right section* and click **OK**.
- Click the **Custom Footer** and use the buttons to insert the date in the *Left section* and the page number in the *Right section*. Click **OK**.
- Click the **Margins tab** and select **Horizontally** and **Vertically** in the *Center on page* section.
- Click the **Sheet tab** and select **Over, then down** in the *Page order* section. Also check **Gridlines** in the *Print* section.
- Click **Print Preview** to make sure you have entered or selected the correct options.
- Click **Close Print Preview**.

It is important to view your worksheet before printing to verify your selections for headers and footers, page numbers, orientation, gridlines, and any other choices you make in the Page Setup dialog box.

c. Click **Page Break Preview** on the status bar and click **OK** in the Welcome message box, if necessary.

d. Drag the vertical page break blue line to the left so the page break is between columns E and F.

e. Drag the horizontal page break blue line so it is between rows 36 and 37.

f. Drag the bottom horizontal page break blue line to include the Sophomore Total and Grand Total rows on page 4, if needed.

g. Click **Page Layout** on the status bar and click **Page Setup Dialog Box Launcher** in the Page Setup group on the Page Layout tab.

h. Click **Print Preview** in the Page Setup dialog box to preview your spreadsheet.

i. Click **Print** and click **OK** to print your worksheet. Save the workbook and exit Excel.

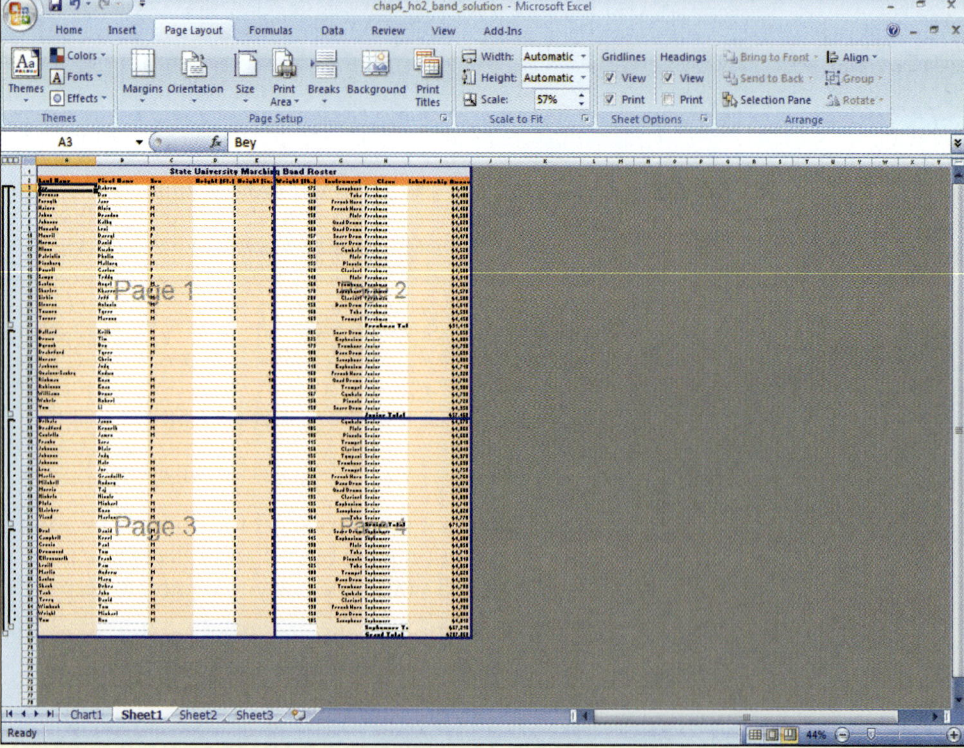

Figure 4.36 Page Layout View

Summary

1. **Freeze rows and columns.** Working with large worksheets, those that are too big for one monitor screen, can confuse users because they are not able to view the entire worksheet at one time. When working with a large worksheet, it is necessary to know how to view parts of the worksheet not visible, how to keep some parts of the worksheet always in view, and how to hide selected rows and columns. When a user is scrolling to parts of a worksheet not initially visible, some rows and columns disappear from view. It is sometimes valuable to be able to view row and column headings no matter where you scroll to, and this is done by freezing rows and columns.

2. **Hide and unhide rows, columns, and worksheets.** The hiding of rows and columns in a worksheet is a common practice and is done for a variety of reasons. It is done to conceal nonessential information, or information not needed at a particular time. There may be times when confidential information is contained in a worksheet, and rows, columns, or sheets must be hidden to allow nonauthorized users to view the worksheet.

3. **Protect a cell, a worksheet, and a workbook.** With the advent of networks and information sharing, the need evolved to protect data from change and from the wrong person. When you post a spreadsheet on the company network, it becomes available to any user of the network. They can make any change to any worksheet in the workbook file. Microsoft Excel 2007 has protection controls that, used with the proper restrictions, can ensure that the right people see only the right data.

4. **Control calculation.** Calculation is the computing of formulas and the display of the results or values in the cells that contain the formulas. In Excel, the default recalculation occurs when the cells that formulas refer to change. This default recalculation can be changed as circumstances warrant.

5. **Print large worksheets.** Printing all or parts of a large worksheet presents special challenges to even the veteran user of Excel. It is easy to make erroneous assumptions about what will print and be unpleasantly surprised. Users must consider such things as page breaks, page orientation, printing a selection, and the order in which pages will print when printing all or part of a large workbook.

6. **Explore basic table management.** Creating tables is a relatively straightforward task to complete in Excel. You choose the area in the worksheet that will contain the list, create the table, and then indicate that the table has labels or field names. Each field name must be unique to prevent confusion. Data for individual records are entered in the rows below the row of field names.

7. **Sort data.** The data in a table are often easier to understand and work with if they are in some meaningful order. Sorting arranges records in a table by the value of one or more fields within the table.

8. **Filter and total data.** Data and information are not the same thing, although you often hear the two terms used interchangeably. Data refer to facts about a specific record, such as a band member's name, his instrument, or his weight as reflected in the marching band roster you have been using. Information is data that have been arranged in some form viewed as useful. Creating a summary report computes subtotals for groups of records within a list. It is imperative that you remember that the subtotals command will not function with data in tables.

Key Terms

Data 514
Filter 514
Freezing 488
Hidden 489
Information 514
Page Break Preview 494
Sort command 511
Sorting (Sort) 511
Table 504

Multiple Choice

1. Which of the following lets you see and/or modify page breaks that will occur when the worksheet is printed?
   (a) The Page Break Preview command
   (b) The Page Setup command
   (c) The Page Breaks command
   (d) The Print Preview command

2. You are working with a large worksheet. Your row headings are in column A. Which command(s) should be used to see the row headings and the distant information in columns X, Y, and Z?
   (a) The Freeze Panes command
   (b) The Hide Rows command
   (c) The New Window command and cascade the windows
   (d) The Split Rows command

3. The command that lets you specify the order in which rows in a table appear is:
   (a) AutoFilter command
   (b) AutoFill command
   (c) Hide Rows command
   (d) Sort command

4. Columns A and B contain row headings, columns C through T contain the results of individual measurements you have taken, and columns U, V, and W contain summary and statistical information based on those measurements. What can you do to display and/or print only the row headings and the summary information?
   (a) Apply the outline feature.
   (b) Freeze rows and columns.
   (c) Hide columns C through T.
   (d) Hide columns A and B.

5. Which of the following options enables you to increase the number of columns that will be displayed on a printed worksheet?
   (a) Freezing panes
   (b) Changing from portrait to landscape orientation
   (c) Hiding columns
   (d) Using the Split command

6. You have used the AutoFilter command to display only certain rows. The other rows are not displayed. What has happened to them?
   (a) Nothing; the filtered rows are displayed in a new worksheet.
   (b) They have been written to a new worksheet.
   (c) They have been hidden.
   (d) They have been deleted.

7. All of the following statements regarding fields are true except:
   (a) Field names must be entered in the first row of the list.
   (b) Field names will change from record to record.
   (c) Field name must be unique.
   (d) Fields will be in the same order in every record.

8. Which of the following statements is true?
   (a) The Delete command can be used to delete a field, but not a record.
   (b) The Delete command can be used to delete a record, but not a field.
   (c) The Delete command erases the contents of the selected area, but does not delete it.
   (d) The Delete command can be used to delete either a record or a field.

9. You have a list of all the members of a club that you belong to. The worksheet contains other data as well. How can you be sure Excel recognizes the boundaries of the list?
   (a) Insert a comment in the upper-left corner of the list.
   (b) Insert a blank row between the field names and the data.
   (c) Insert a blank row and a blank column between the list and other data in the worksheet.
   (d) Type a row of dashes (- - -) after the last row of the list.

...continued on Next Page

Multiple Choice Continued...

10. You have a list of all the employees in your organization. The list contains employee name, office, title, and salary. You want to list all employees in each office branch. The branches should be listed alphabetically, with the employee earning the highest salary listed first in each office. Which is true of your sort order?
    (a) Branch office is the primary sort and should be in ascending order.
    (b) Salary is the primary sort and should be in descending order.
    (c) Salary is the primary sort and should be in ascending order.
    (d) Branch office is the primary sort and should be in descending order.

11. You have a list of all the employees in your organization. The list contains employee name, location, title, and salary. You want to list all employees in each location. The locations should be listed alphabetically, with the highest-paid employees listed first for each location. Which is true of your sort order?
    (a) Sort by location ascending, then by salary ascending.
    (b) Sort by location ascending, then by salary descending.
    (c) Sort by salary descending, then by location ascending.
    (d) Sort by location descending, then by salary ascending.

12. You have a list containing all the employees in your organization. You select the AutoFilter command, and then select New York from the location field. What is the result?
    (a) The list is sorted by city, with New York first.
    (b) The rows where the location is New York are written to another worksheet.
    (c) The rows where the location is not New York are deleted.
    (d) The rows where the location is not New York are hidden.

13. Which of the following statements about the AutoFilter command is true?
    (a) Records that do not meet the criteria are deleted.
    (b) If two criteria are entered, records must meet both conditions to be selected.
    (c) Records that meet the selected criteria are copied to another worksheet.
    (d) All of these statements are true.

14. How must the data be arranged before creating a summary report?
    (a) In a table
    (b) In ascending order by the contents of the first column
    (c) In either a table or a list
    (d) In a range

15. Which of the following will compute a summary function for groups of records within a range?
    (a) The Advanced Filter command
    (b) The Subtotals command
    (c) The AutoFilter command
    (d) The Totals command

16. You want to show total sales for each location. What should you do before executing the Subtotals command?
    (a) Sort by Sales, in ascending order.
    (b) Sort by Sales, in descending order.
    (c) Sort by Sales, in either ascending or descending order, then by Location.
    (d) Sort by Location, in either ascending or descending order.

Practice Exercises

1 West Transylvania Education Foundation Silent Auction

You are assisting the director of the Education Foundation as she prepares for the Chef's Table fundraising event. Your task is to record silent auction donations as they are delivered and prepare the printed report for the director. The completed worksheet is shown in Figure 4.37, and you will use this as a guide as you practice freezing panes, editing titles, protecting the worksheet, and hiding rows and columns.

a. Open *chap4_pe1_auction* and save the workbook as **chap4_pe1_auction_solution** so that you can return to the original workbook if necessary. Use the horizontal scroll bar to view the worksheet, noting that some column headings disappear. Rows may also disappear when you use the vertical scroll bar because the worksheet is too large to fit on one screen. You must use Freeze Panes to keep parts of the worksheet in constant view.

b. Click in **cell B3**, the cell below the row and the column to the right of the column you will freeze. Click the **View tab**, click **Freeze Panes** in the Window group, and select **Freeze Panes**. Use the vertical and horizontal scroll bars to see that the row and column data becomes visible while the row and column data labels remain constant.

c. Edit and format a heading:
   - Click **cell A1**, select the words **Silent Auction Donor Listing** in the Formula Bar, click the **Home tab**, and then click **Cut** in the Clipboard group.
   - Right-click **row 2**, then select **Insert** from the shortcut menu to insert a new row.
   - Right-click **cell A2** and select **Paste** from the shortcut menu.
   - Select **cells A2:L2** and click **Merge & Center** in the Alignment group on the Home tab.
   - Select **cells A1:A2**, click the **Fill Color down arrow** in the Font group on the Home tab, and choose **Light Blue** from the Standard Colors.
   - Open the **Font Color palette** in the Font group on the Home tab and choose **White, Background 1** for the title text.

d. Select **cells J4:J42**, the cells that you want to edit or protect.
   - Click **Format** in the Cells group on the Home tab and select **Format Cells** to open the Format Cells dialog box.
   - Select the **Protection tab** and clear the **Locked check box**. Click **OK**.
   - Click **Format** in the Cells group on the Home tab and select **Protect Sheet** to see the Protect Sheet dialog box.
   - Click the **Select unlocked cells check box** if necessary, and clear the **Select locked cells check box**. Click **OK**. You unlocked cells for editing purposes and then protected or locked all other cells. The only data that you can change are Item Values in column J. Try to change any donor's name or other personal information.

e. Click **Format** in the Cells group and select **Unprotect Sheet**. Click **Format** in the Cells group and select **Protect Sheet**. Clear all check marks from the *Allow all users of this worksheet to* area and click **OK**. You must unprotect the worksheet in order to unlock the cells you previously protected and before continuing with this exercise.

f. Click **Format** in the Cells group and select **Unprotect Sheet**. Click the **Review tab**, and then click **Protect Workbook** in the Changes group. Select **Protect Structure and Windows** to open the Protect Structure and Windows dialog box. Click the **Structure check box** and click **OK**.

g. Click **Protect Workbook** in the Changes group and select **Protect Structure and Windows** to deselect it. Select **columns D** through **H** and click the **Home tab**. Click **Format** in the Cells group, point to **Hide & Unhide**, and select **Hide Columns**. Columns D through H are hidden and a thick black line appears between columns C and I indicating the location of the hidden columns.

h. Select **rows 6** through **12** and click **Format** in the Cells group, point to **Hide & Unhide**, and select **Hide Rows**. Rows 6 through 12 are hidden, and a thick black line appears between rows 5 and 13, indicating the location of the hidden rows.

...continued on Next Page

i. Click the **Sheet2 tab** to make it active, click the **Home tab**, and click **Format** in the Cells group. Point to **Hide & Unhide**, and then select **Hide Sheet** to hide Sheet2.

j. Click the **Sheet1 tab** to make it active.

k. Click the **Page Layout tab**, click **Orientation** in the Page Setup group, and select **Landscape**. Click **Size**, select **More Paper Sizes**, and click **Fit to** 1 page. Click the **Margins tab**, click the **Horizontally check box** in the *Center on page section*, and set **0.75"** top and bottom margins. Click the **Header/Footer tab**, click **Custom Header**, type your name in the *Left section*, and click **OK**. Click **OK** to close the Page Setup dialog box. Print the worksheet, save the workbook, and exit Excel.

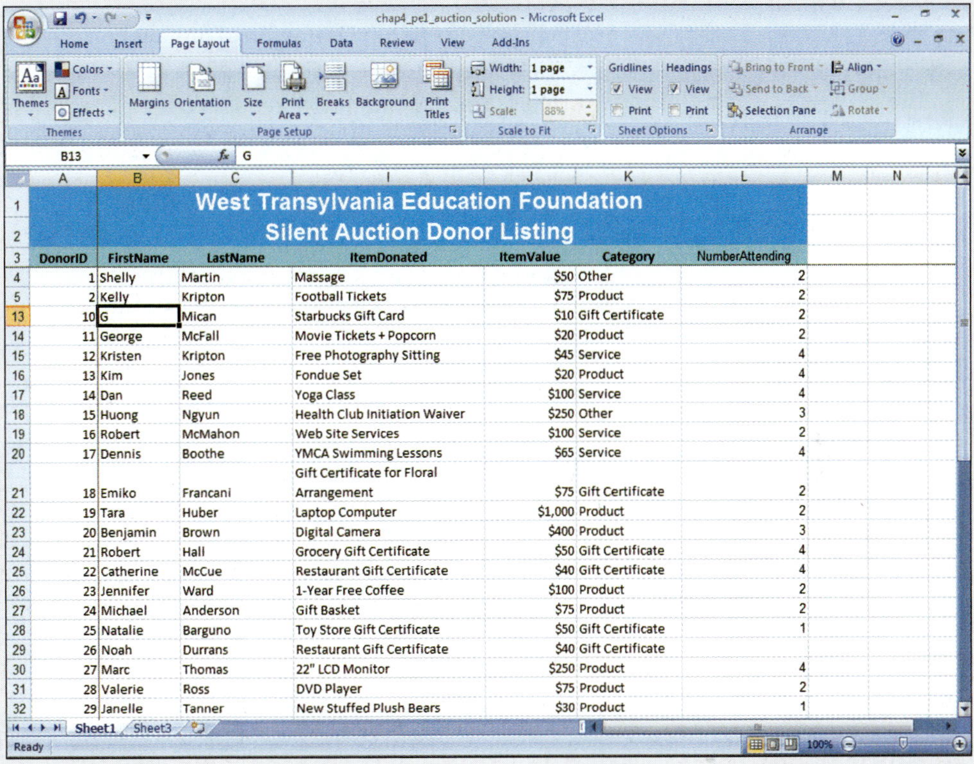

West Transylvania Education Foundation
Silent Auction Donor Listing

DonorID	FirstName	LastName	ItemDonated	ItemValue	Category	NumberAttending
1	Shelly	Martin	Massage	$50	Other	2
2	Kelly	Kripton	Football Tickets	$75	Product	2
10	G	Mican	Starbucks Gift Card	$10	Gift Certificate	2
11	George	McFall	Movie Tickets + Popcorn	$20	Product	2
12	Kristen	Kripton	Free Photography Sitting	$45	Service	4
13	Kim	Jones	Fondue Set	$20	Product	4
14	Dan	Reed	Yoga Class	$100	Service	4
15	Huong	Ngyun	Health Club Initiation Waiver	$250	Other	3
16	Robert	McMahon	Web Site Services	$100	Service	2
17	Dennis	Boothe	YMCA Swimming Lessons	$65	Service	4
18	Emiko	Francani	Gift Certificate for Floral Arrangement	$75	Gift Certificate	2
19	Tara	Huber	Laptop Computer	$1,000	Product	2
20	Benjamin	Brown	Digital Camera	$400	Product	3
21	Robert	Hall	Grocery Gift Certificate	$50	Gift Certificate	4
22	Catherine	McCue	Restaurant Gift Certificate	$40	Gift Certificate	4
23	Jennifer	Ward	1-Year Free Coffee	$100	Product	2
24	Michael	Anderson	Gift Basket	$75	Product	2
25	Natalie	Barguno	Toy Store Gift Certificate	$50	Gift Certificate	1
26	Noah	Durrans	Restaurant Gift Certificate	$40	Gift Certificate	
27	Marc	Thomas	22" LCD Monitor	$250	Product	4
28	Valerie	Ross	DVD Player	$75	Product	2
29	Janelle	Tanner	New Stuffed Plush Bears	$30	Product	1

Figure 4.37 Silent Auction Table

2 West Transylvania Education Foundation Donor List

You are assisting the director of the Education Foundation as she prepares for the major funding event of the year. Your task is to format for printing and print the list of donors and their personal information so that they can receive an acknowledgement for income tax purposes. The completed worksheet is shown in Figure 4.38, and you will use this figure as a guide as you work with page breaks, page orientation, and control print order.

a. Open *chap4_pe2_donor* and save the workbook as **chap4_pe2_donor_solution** so that you can return to the original workbook if necessary.

b. Click **Page Break Preview** on the status bar. If you see the Welcome to Page Break Preview message box, click **OK**.

c. Move the **blue dashed line** that separates pages 1 and 2 to the right to eliminate the page break. You will now see just page 1 as all page breaks have been eliminated. Click **Normal** on the status bar to return to Normal view.

d. Click the **Page Layout tab** and click **Orientation** in the Page Setup group. Select **Landscape**.

...continued on Next Page

- Click the **Page Setup Dialog Box Launcher** on the Page Layout tab to open the Page Setup dialog box.
- Click the **Page tab** and click **Fit to 1 page**.
- Click the **Header/Footer tab** and create a custom footer with your name in the *Center section*. Click **OK**.
- Click **Print Preview** and verify that the worksheet will print on one page.
- Click **Print**. Click **OK** to print the worksheet.

e. Click in **cell A16**, click **Breaks** on the Page Layout tab, and select **Insert Page Break**. Select **column H**, click **Breaks** on the Page Layout tab, and select **Insert Page Break**. Click **Page Break Preview** on the status bar.

f. Click the **Page Setup Dialog Box Launcher** on the Page Layout tab.
- Click the **Page tab** and click **Adjust to**. Increase the scaling to **100%**.
- Click **Sheet tab** and click the **Over, then down** option in the *Page order* section.
- Click **Print Preview** and verify that you will print four pages.
- Click **Print**. Click **OK**.

g. Save and close the workbook.

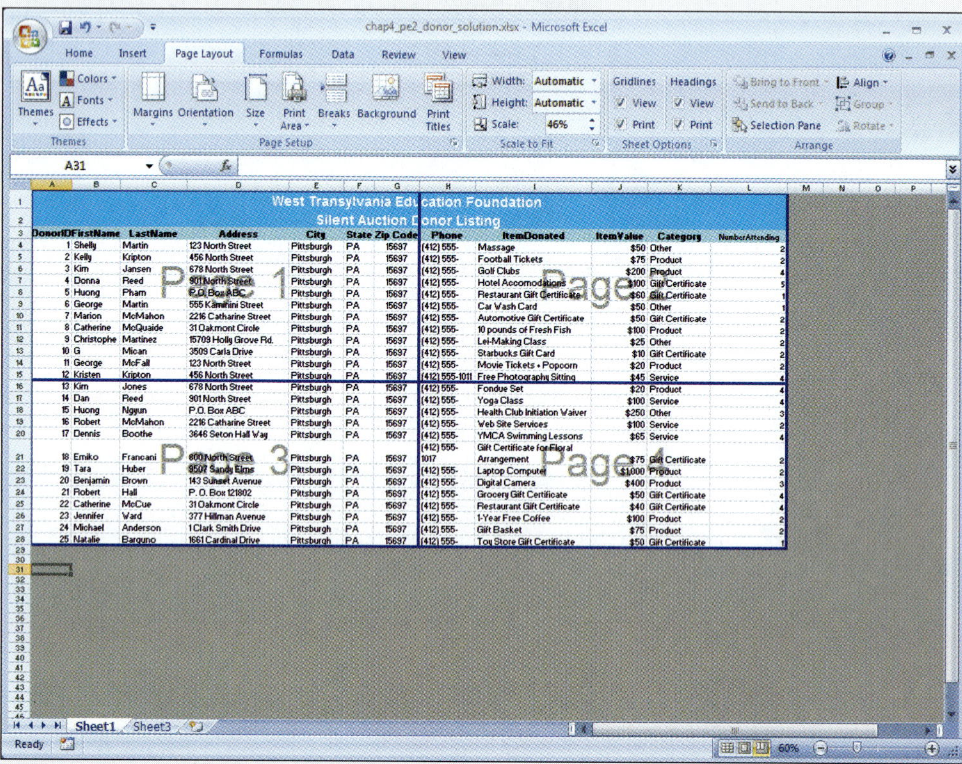

Figure 4.38 Education Foundation Donor Table

3 XYZ Corporation Employee Table

Your summer internship in the XYZ Corporation human resources department gives you the opportunity to practice your Excel skills. You are tasked with preparing a series of employee reports. You will create a table from a data range and sort and filter the data into reports required by management. The table you will work with is shown in Figure 4.39, and you will use this as a guide as you work with sorts and filters, but you will print several different pages.

a. Open *chap4_pe3_xyz* and save the workbook as **chap4_pe3_xyz_solution** so that you can return to the original workbook if necessary. Select **cells A1:H156**, click the **Insert tab**, and click **Table**. Verify the range in the **Where is the data for your table?** text box, click the **My table has headers check box**, and click **OK**. You defined the worksheet data as a table.

...continued on Next Page

b. Click anywhere in the defined table, click the **Design tab**, and then click **Banded Columns** in the Table Style Options group. Clear the **Banded Rows check box** in the Table Style Options group on the Design tab. Click the **More** button in the Table Styles group on the Design tab and select **Table Style Medium 12**.

c. Insert a new row above row 1 and type: **XYZ Corporation Employee List** in **cell A1**. Merge and center the title in **cells A1:H1**, and format the titles as **Comic Sans MS, 16, Bold**. Fill the title area with **Purple** color, and change the font color to **White, Background 1**. Select **cells F3:F157** and format as Currency with no decimals.

d. Select **cell A11** and click the **Insert down arrow** in the Cells group. Select **Insert Table Rows Above**. Type the following data for the new record:

Cell address	Data
A11	12378
B11	Your Last Name
C11	Your First Name
D11	Your Gender
E11	Trainee
F11	37800
G11	Kansas City
H11	Excellent

e. Select **cells A17:H17**, click the **Delete down arrow** in the Cells group on the Home tab, and select **Delete Table Rows.** You deleted Maylou Sampieri from the table.

f. Select **cells G3:G157**, click **Find & Select** in the Editing group on the Home tab, and select **Replace**. In the **Find what** box, type **Atlanta**; in the **Replace with** box, type **Miami**. The company moved its branch office. Click the **Replace All** button, and a Microsoft Office Excel message box appears indicating the number of replacements made. Click **OK** and then click **Close** to close the Find and Replace dialog box.

g. Select **cells A4:H11**, then click **Print Area** in the Page Setup group on the Page Layout tab. Click **Set Print Area**.
   - Click the **Page Setup Dialog Box Launcher** on the Page Layout tab to launch the Page Setup dialog box.
   - Click **Print Preview** and verify that your selection is correct. Click the **Print** button and click **OK** to print your selection.
   - Click **Print Area** in the Page Setup group on the Page Layout tab and select **Clear dialog Print Area**.

h. Click in any cell in column G, click the **Data tab**, and click **Sort A to Z** in the Sort & Filter group. The table is sorted by branch office location.
   - Click **Sort** in the Sort & Filter group on the Data tab to open the Sort dialog box. Click **Add Level**, click the **Then by** drop-down list, and select **Last Name**.
   - Click **Add Level** again, click the **Then by** drop-down list, and select **First Name**. Click **OK** to perform the sort. You sorted the employee list by location, last name, and finally by first name.

i. Select **cells A22:H39**, then click **Print Area** in the Page Setup group on the Page Layout tab. Select **Set Print Area**. Click the **Page Setup Dialog Box Launcher** on the Page Layout tab to display the Page Setup dialog box. Click **Print Preview** and verify that your selection is correct. Click the **Print button** and click **OK** to print your selection.

j. Click **Print Area** in the Page Setup group on the Page Layout tab and select **Clear Print Area**. Click the column arrow for **Title** (column E). Clear the **Select All check box**. Click the **Trainee check box** and click **OK**. This filter selects just the Trainees in the corporation, and these are now the only data rows visible.

...continued on Next Page

k. Click the **Performance filter arrow** (column H) and clear the **Select All check box**. Click the **Excellent check box** and click **OK**. You have reduced the Trainees to just those whose performance has been rated Excellent.

l. Click the **Page Setup Dialog Box Launcher** on the Page Layout tab to display the Page Setup dialog box. Click the **Page tab** and select **Landscape** as well as **Fit to 1 page**. Click the **Header/Footer tab** and insert a custom footer with your name in the *Center section*. Click **Print Preview**, and verify your changes. Click the **Print button** and click **OK** to print your filtered table.

m. Save and close the workbook.

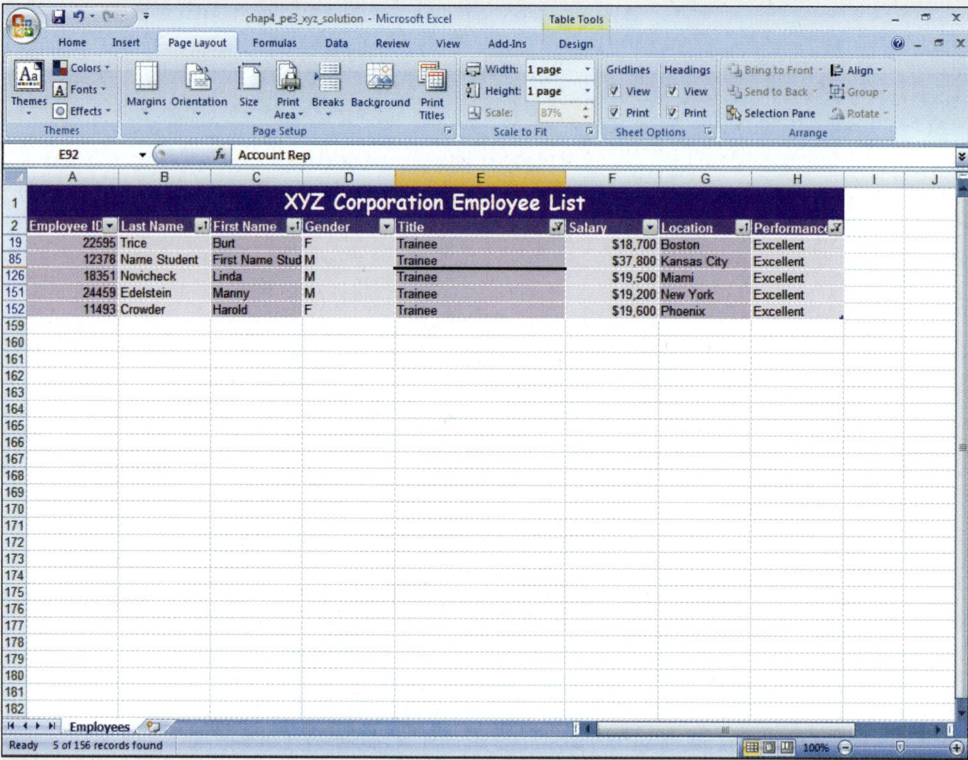

Figure 4.39 Filtered Employee Table

4 Widget Employee List

As the director of Human Resources for the Widget Group, you will complete a worksheet that will show a total of salaries paid and further break down salaries by employee title. In addition, you will create a chart that shows salaries by job title. The worksheet and chart will help you assess salary outlays. The worksheet you will work with is shown in Figure 4.40, and you will use this as a guide as you work with sorts, summary reporting, and charting.

a. Open *chap4_pe4_widget* and save the workbook as **chap4_pe4_widget_solution** so that you can return to the original workbook if necessary.

b. Click in any cell in column E, click the **Data tab**, and click **Sort A to Z** in the Sort & Filter group. The table is sorted by job title.
   - Click **Sort** in the Sort & Filter group on the Data tab to open the Sort dialog box. Click **Add Level**, click the **Then by** drop-down list, and select **Last Name**.
   - Click **Add Level** again, click the **Then by** drop-down list, and select **First Name**. Click **OK** to perform the sort. You sorted the employee list by job title, last name, and finally by first name. The sort was the necessary first step in the creation of the summary report.

c. Click in any cell in column H, click the **Design tab,** and then click the **Total Row check box** in the Table Style Options group. Scroll to see that you now have a total in cell H158 with a row label in cell A158. Make sure that any cell in the table is selected and

...continued on Next Page

that the table is sorted by Title before continuing. Click **Convert to Range** in the Tools group on the Design tab. Click **Yes** in the Microsoft Office Excel message box.

d. Click the **Data tab**, and then click **Subtotal** in the Outline group to open the Subtotal dialog box. In the **At each change in** drop-down list, select **Title**. In the **Use function** drop-down list, select **Sum**. Under **Add subtotal to**, make sure the **Salary check box** is selected. If necessary, select the **Replace current subtotals** and **Summary below data check boxes**. Click **OK**. Scroll through your list to see the Summary Report totals for Salaries for each Title group.

e. Select **cells A102:H108**, click the **Page Layout tab**, and then click **Print Area** in the Page Setup group. Select **Set Print Area**. Click the **Page Setup Dialog Box Launcher** on the Page Layout tab to display the Page Setup dialog box. Create a custom header with your name in the *Left section*, **The Widget Group** in the *Center section*, and your instructor's name in the *Right section*. Click **Print Preview** and verify that your selection is correct. Click the **Print button** and click **OK** to print your selection. Click **Print Area** in the Page Setup group on the Page Layout tab and select **Clear Print Area**.

f. Select **cells E101**, **H101**, **E108**, **H108**, **E143**, **H143**, **E161**, and **H161**. Remember to use Ctrl while selecting noncontiguous cells.

- Click the **Insert tab**, click **Column** in the Charts group, and select **Clustered Column**.
- Click the **Move Chart** button in the Location group on the **Design** tab to display the Move Chart dialog box. Click **New sheet** and click **OK**. Select the legend and delete it.

g. Click **Data Labels** in the Labels group on the Layout tab and select **Outside End**. Click **Chart** title in the Labels group on the Layout tab and select **Above Chart**. Type **Salary by Job Type** as the title of the chart. Use the Page Setup dialog box to create a custom header with your name in the *Left section*. Save the workbook and print the chart.

h. Click the **Employees tab**. Click **Page Layout** on the status bar, reduce the **Zoom** view to about **70%**, and scroll to view all of the pages. Click the **Page Setup Dialog Box Launcher** on the Page Layout tab to open the Page Setup dialog box. On the Page tab, select **Landscape**.

i. Click the **Header/Footer tab**. Click the **Custom Footer button** and use the icons to insert the date in the *Left section* and the page number in the *Right section*. Click **OK**. Click the **Margins tab** and select **Horizontally** and **Vertically** in the *Center on page* section. Set **0.25"** left and right margins, and set **1"** top and bottom margins. Click **Print Preview** to make sure you have entered or selected the correct options.

j. Click **Print**, and then click **OK** to print your worksheet. Save and close the workbook.

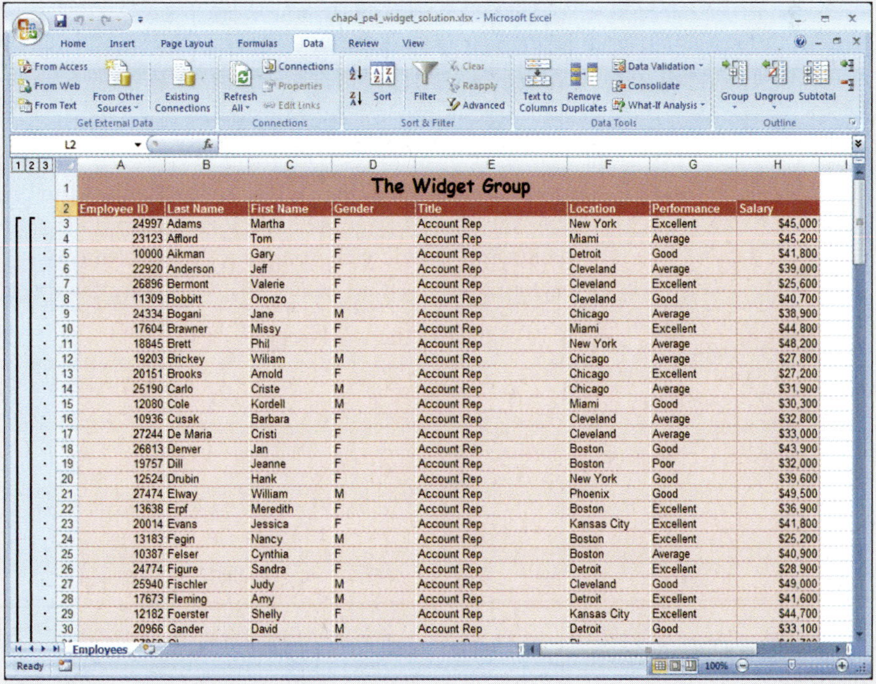

	A	B	C	D	E	F	G	H
1	The Widget Group							
2	Employee ID	Last Name	First Name	Gender	Title	Location	Performance	Salary
3	24997	Adams	Martha	F	Account Rep	New York	Excellent	$45,000
4	23123	Afflord	Tom	F	Account Rep	Miami	Average	$45,200
5	10000	Aikman	Gary	F	Account Rep	Detroit	Good	$41,800
6	22920	Anderson	Jeff	F	Account Rep	Cleveland	Average	$39,000
7	26896	Bermont	Valerie	F	Account Rep	Cleveland	Excellent	$25,600
8	11309	Bobbitt	Oronzo	F	Account Rep	Cleveland	Good	$40,700
9	24334	Bogani	Jane	M	Account Rep	Chicago	Average	$38,900
10	17604	Brawner	Missy	F	Account Rep	Miami	Excellent	$44,800
11	18845	Brett	Phil	F	Account Rep	New York	Average	$48,200
12	19203	Brickey	Wiliam	M	Account Rep	Chicago	Average	$27,800
13	20151	Brooks	Arnold	F	Account Rep	Chicago	Excellent	$27,200
14	25190	Carlo	Criste	M	Account Rep	Chicago	Average	$31,900
15	12080	Cole	Kordell	M	Account Rep	Miami	Good	$30,300
16	10936	Cusak	Barbara	F	Account Rep	Cleveland	Average	$32,800
17	27244	De Maria	Cristi	F	Account Rep	Cleveland	Average	$33,000
18	26813	Denver	Jan	F	Account Rep	Boston	Good	$43,900
19	19757	Dill	Jeanne	F	Account Rep	Boston	Poor	$32,000
20	12524	Drubin	Hank	F	Account Rep	New York	Good	$39,600
21	27474	Elway	William	M	Account Rep	Phoenix	Good	$49,500
22	13638	Erpf	Meredith	F	Account Rep	Boston	Excellent	$36,900
23	20014	Evans	Jessica	F	Account Rep	Kansas City	Excellent	$41,800
24	13183	Fegin	Nancy	M	Account Rep	Boston	Excellent	$25,200
25	10387	Felser	Cynthia	F	Account Rep	Boston	Average	$40,900
26	24774	Figure	Sandra	F	Account Rep	Detroit	Excellent	$28,900
27	25940	Fischler	Judy	M	Account Rep	Cleveland	Good	$49,000
28	17673	Fleming	Amy	M	Account Rep	Detroit	Excellent	$41,600
29	12182	Foerster	Shelly	F	Account Rep	Kansas City	Excellent	$44,700
30	20966	Gander	David	M	Account Rep	Detroit	Good	$33,100

Figure 4.40 Widget Salary Analysis

...continued on Next Page

Mid-Level Exercises

1 The Wedding Planner

Weddings by Grace is in the final stages of a wedding plan, your task as Grace's assistant is to group the guests attending the wedding by table number. The guests already have been assigned to a table based on their reception card returns. In addition, you will prepare a summary report showing how many guests will be seated at each table. You will print a report for Grace. Figure 4.41 shows the completed worksheet. Use this figure as a guide as you complete your worksheet, which will include subtotals, sorting, hiding columns, and printing a large worksheet.

a. Open the *chap4_mid1_wedding* workbook and save it as **chap4_mid1_wedding_solution** so that you can return to the original workbook if necessary.

b. Freeze rows 1 and 2 so that they are always visible. In **cell A80**, which is the first blank cell at the bottom of the list of guests, add your name and that of your guest in the appropriate columns. Type **2** as the number attending; you will be sitting at Table 01. Click in **cell A81** and enter your instructor's name and guest. Your instructor will be sitting at Table 02 and **2** will attend.

c. Combine the Names in column E, Guest Names. Use the formal forms of Address, for example; Mr. and Mrs. Joe Sutherland, Ms. Nancy Miles and Mr. Jack Wadsworth, Drs. Sam and Judy Grauer. (Hint: Use the CONCATENATE function to combine text. Use Help if needed to learn about the CONCATENATE function. Be sure the result includes spaces between words.)

d. Select columns A, B, C, and D, and then hide these columns. Widen column E to display the full guest names.

e. Sort the guests by table number in sequential order, then last name and first name in alphabetical order.

f. Use the Subtotal command to display the associated subtotal dialog box. The subtotals should be calculated at each change in table; that is, use the Sum function to add the total to the Number field. Select the check boxes to replace current subtotals and to place the summary below data.

g. Add a yellow fill color to highlight the cells that contain your name, your instructor's name, and table and number cells for you and your instructor. Merge and center the text in **cells E1:G1**. Increase the font size in the worksheet title to **36**, change the font to **Comic Sans MS**, bold the title, and then Align Right. Add a clip art image and resize columns and rows as appropriate.

h. The worksheet looks better if it is centered and printed on two pages. Display the worksheet in Page Break Preview and adjust the break so that the guests at Table 08 start the second page. Use the Page Setup dialog box to repeat rows 1 and 2 on both pages and preview the pages to be sure that two pages will print. Adjust top and bottom margins if necessary. Print the completed worksheet.

i. Save and close the workbook.

...continued on Next Page

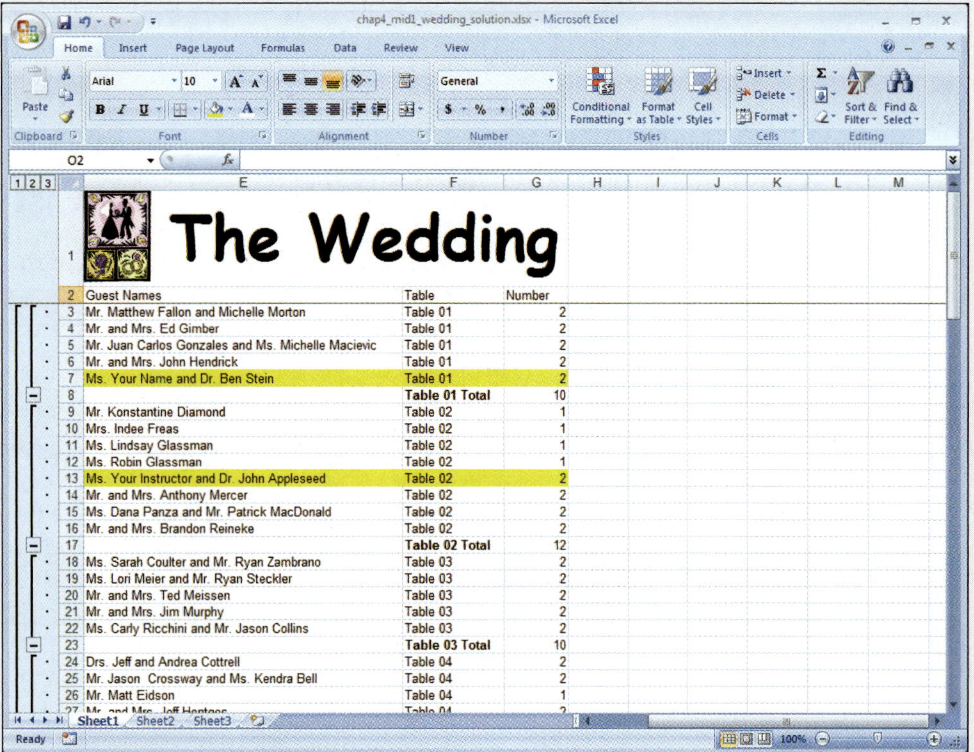

	Guest Names	Table	Number
3	Mr. Matthew Fallon and Michelle Morton	Table 01	2
4	Mr. and Mrs. Ed Gimber	Table 01	2
5	Mr. Juan Carlos Gonzales and Ms. Michelle Macievic	Table 01	2
6	Mr. and Mrs. John Hendrick	Table 01	2
7	Ms. Your Name and Dr. Ben Stein	Table 01	2
8		**Table 01 Total**	10
9	Mr. Konstantine Diamond	Table 02	1
10	Mrs. Indee Freas	Table 02	1
11	Ms. Lindsay Glassman	Table 02	1
12	Ms. Robin Glassman	Table 02	1
13	Ms. Your Instructor and Dr. John Appleseed	Table 02	2
14	Mr. and Mrs. Anthony Mercer	Table 02	2
15	Ms. Dana Panza and Mr. Patrick MacDonald	Table 02	2
16	Mr. and Mrs. Brandon Reineke	Table 02	2
17		**Table 02 Total**	12
18	Ms. Sarah Coulter and Mr. Ryan Zambrano	Table 03	2
19	Ms. Lori Meier and Mr. Ryan Steckler	Table 03	2
20	Mr. and Mrs. Ted Meissen	Table 03	2
21	Mr. and Mrs. Jim Murphy	Table 03	2
22	Ms. Carly Ricchini and Mr. Jason Collins	Table 03	2
23		**Table 03 Total**	10
24	Drs. Jeff and Andrea Cottrell	Table 04	2
25	Mr. Jason Crossway and Ms. Kendra Bell	Table 04	2
26	Mr. Matt Eidson	Table 04	1

Figure 4.41 Weddings by Grace

2 The Job Search

As the personnel director, you maintain a list of applicants. You are searching for applicants for two different positions. For the first, the position requires people who are bilingual, do not require relocation, and are judged to be experienced. The second position is a directorship requiring no relocation. You will print a report of the qualified applicants for consideration by the vice president for Human Resources. Figure 4.42 shows the completed worksheet results of the second filter, and you will use the figure as a guide as you complete your worksheet. Your work will include converting data to a table, sorting the data, applying multiple filters, formatting the table, and formatting for printing.

a. Open the *chap4_mid2_jobsearch* workbook and save the workbook as **chap4_mid2_jobsearch_solution** so that you can return to the original workbook if necessary.

b. Select **cells A2:H176** and convert the range of data to a table. Sort by last name and then by first name. Apply Table Style Medium 21 to the table.

c. Set a filter to select only those who are bilingual. Set a filter to select only those who do not have to be relocated. Finally, apply a filter to select only those who are judged to be experienced.

d. Format the title as shown in Figure 4.42.

e. Format the worksheet in an attractive fashion. Create a custom footer with your name, the date, and the name of the class you are taking. Be sure the worksheet fits on one page. Print the worksheet.

f. Clear the three filters from the worksheet in order to initiate a second search for applicants who are applying for the position of "Director" and do not require relocation. Print this worksheet for your instructor and hand in both worksheets.

g. Save and close the workbook.

...continued on Next Page

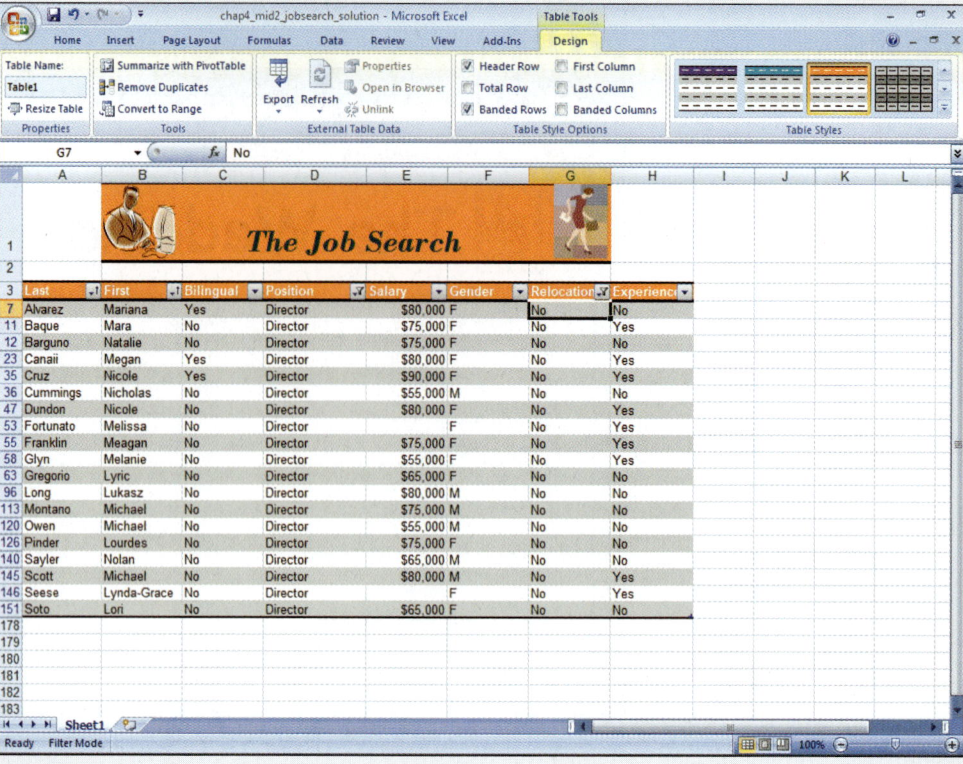

The Job Search

Row	Last	First	Bilingual	Position	Salary	Gender	Relocation	Experience
7	Alvarez	Mariana	Yes	Director	$80,000	F	No	No
11	Baque	Mara	No	Director	$75,000	F	No	Yes
12	Barguno	Natalie	No	Director	$75,000	F	No	No
23	Canaii	Megan	Yes	Director	$80,000	F	No	Yes
35	Cruz	Nicole	Yes	Director	$90,000	F	No	Yes
36	Cummings	Nicholas	No	Director	$55,000	M	No	No
47	Dundon	Nicole	No	Director	$80,000	F	No	Yes
53	Fortunato	Melissa	No	Director		F	No	Yes
55	Franklin	Meagan	No	Director	$75,000	F	No	Yes
58	Glyn	Melanie	No	Director	$55,000	F	No	Yes
63	Gregorio	Lyric	No	Director	$65,000	F	No	No
96	Long	Lukasz	No	Director	$80,000	M	No	No
113	Montano	Michael	No	Director	$75,000	M	No	No
120	Owen	Michael	No	Director	$55,000	M	No	No
126	Pinder	Lourdes	No	Director	$75,000	F	No	No
140	Sayler	Nolan	No	Director	$65,000	M	No	No
145	Scott	Michael	No	Director	$80,000	M	No	Yes
146	Seese	Lynda-Grace	No	Director		F	No	Yes
151	Soto	Lori	No	Director	$65,000	F	No	No

Figure 4.42 Job Search

3 Searching for a Doctor

You have just moved to Florida with your family and are searching for a doctor or doctors who can satisfy your family medical needs. You have obtained a list of more than 80 board-certified physicians from the state licensing agency. In this exercise, you will narrow the list using filters to a particular specialty, the city they practice in, and whether they take new patients. Furthermore, you will sort, format, and print the results for your family. Figure 4.43 shows the completed worksheet results. Use the figure as a guide as you complete your worksheet. You work will include converting a range of data to a table, sorting the data, applying multiple filters, and applying Page Setup options.

a. Open the *chap4_mid3_physicians* workbook and save the workbook as **chap4_mid3_physicians_solution** so that you can return to the original workbook if necessary.

b. Select **cells A1:H83** and convert the range of data to a table.

c. Set a filter to select only those who practice in **Fort Lauderdale**. Set a filter to select **Cardiology** and **Internal Medicine** specializations. Finally, set a filter to select only those who accept new patients (TRUE).

d. Sort by specialty, last name, and then by first name.

e. Create a custom header with your name, the date, and the name of the class you are taking. Be sure the worksheet fits on one page. Print the worksheet.

f. Save and close the workbook.

...continued on Next Page

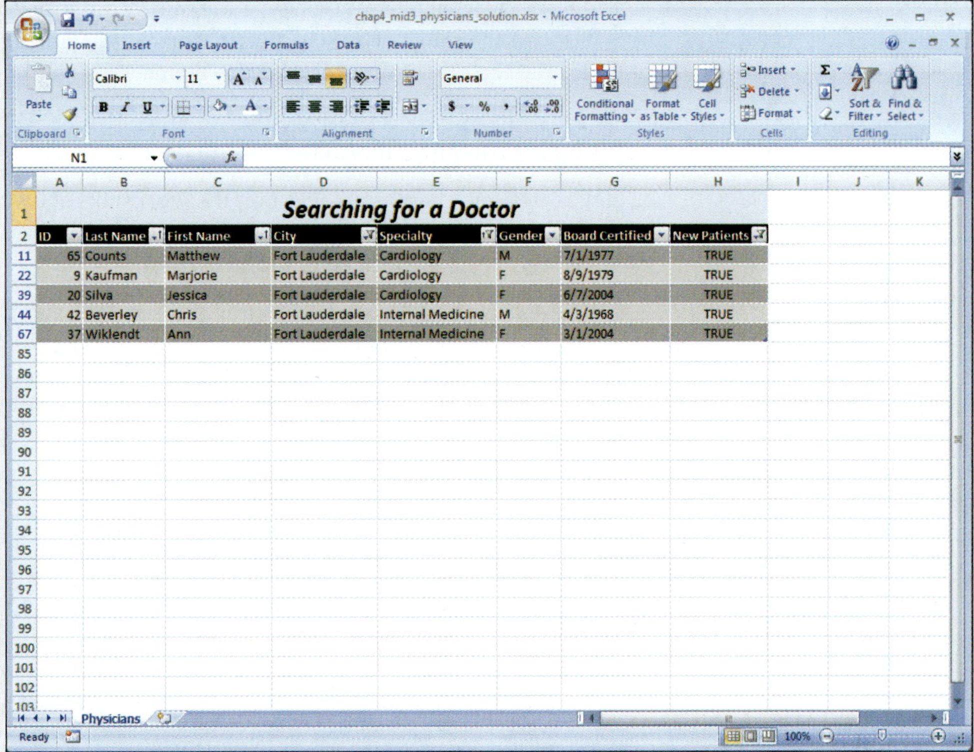

Searching for a Doctor

ID	Last Name	First Name	City	Specialty	Gender	Board Certified	New Patients
65	Counts	Matthew	Fort Lauderdale	Cardiology	M	7/1/1977	TRUE
9	Kaufman	Marjorie	Fort Lauderdale	Cardiology	F	8/9/1979	TRUE
20	Silva	Jessica	Fort Lauderdale	Cardiology	F	6/7/2004	TRUE
42	Beverley	Chris	Fort Lauderdale	Internal Medicine	M	4/3/1968	TRUE
37	Wiklendt	Ann	Fort Lauderdale	Internal Medicine	F	3/1/2004	TRUE

Figure 4.43 Searching for a Doctor

4 Population Analysis

Your geography professor has given you an assignment to analyze population data of the 50 states in the United States. In this exercise, you will determine the population density of each state, sort the states by geographic region, prepare a summary report showing the population by region, and prepare a chart illustrating the region populations. Finally, you will filter the list to show only those states in a particular geographic region and print both the chart and the filtered report. Figure 4.44 shows the filtered worksheet results with chart; use the figure as a guide as you complete your worksheet. The work you perform will include converting data to a table, sorting the data, applying multiple filters, creating a chart, formatting, and formatting for printing.

a. Open the *chap4_mid4_population* workbook and save the workbook as **chap4_mid4_population_solution** so that you can return to the original workbook if necessary.

b. Click in **cell F2** and enter the formula to calculate population density (population divided by area). Copy the formula for all states. Format the population as number with 1 decimal place.

c. Sort the range by region and then by state.

d. Create a summary report showing population subtotals by region. Use the Subtotal command to display the Subtotal dialog box. The subtotals should be calculated at each change in region. Use the **Sum** function to add the total to the Population field. Click the check boxes to replace current subtotals and to place the summary below data.

e. Add a fill color to highlight the cells that contain the region name and the region's total population. Create a clustered column chart on a separate sheet that shows total population by region. Be sure to format the chart in an aesthetically pleasing manner, include a descriptive title. Rename the Chart1 tab as **Region Chart**.

...continued on Next Page

f. Insert a row on Sheet1, then type the title **Population Statistics**. Select **cells A2:F60** and convert the range of data to a table. Format the table using Table Style Medium 12 and format the title of the worksheet to match.

g. Set a filter to select only Middle Atlantic, Middle Atlantic Total, New England, New England Total, South Atlantic, South Atlantic Total.

h. Create a pie chart as an object on the worksheet showing total population by the three geographic regions. Format the chart so it is color coordinated with your table. Add the chart title **Eastern Geographic Region**.

i. Create a custom footer with your name, the date, and the name of the class you are taking. Be sure the worksheet and chart fit on one page. Print the worksheet and the region chart.

j. Save and close the workbook.

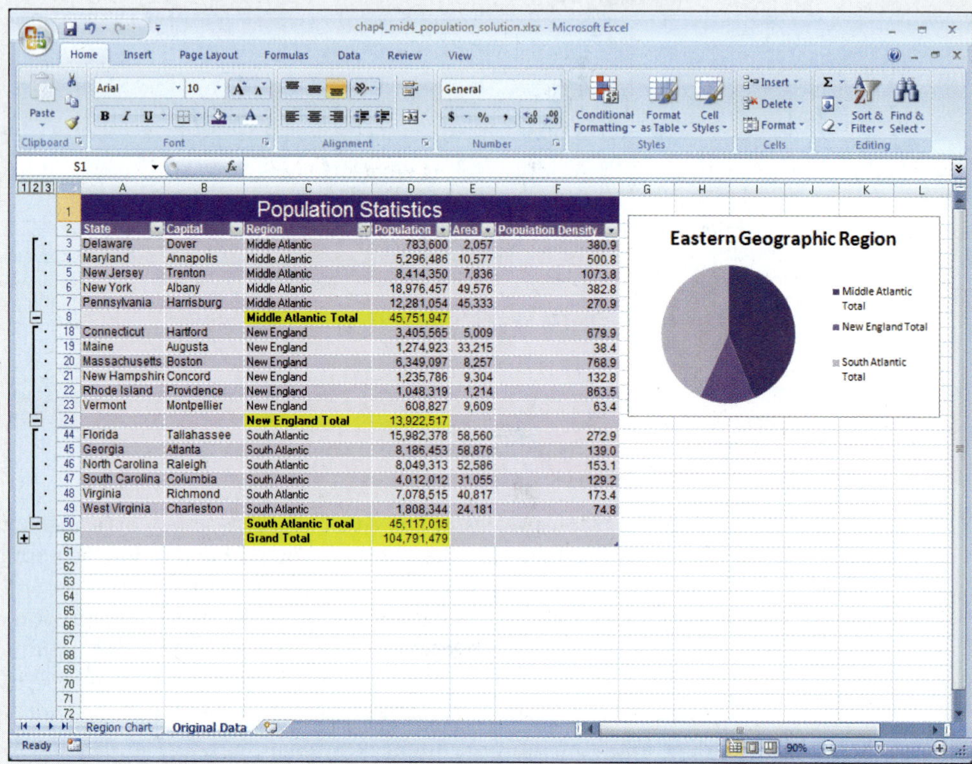

Figure 4.44 Population Analysis

Capstone Exercise

You are an intern with the Regional Realty Association and are analyzing the claim made by Alice Barr Realty that "we get your price." You have prepared a spreadsheet that shows data relating to three months' sales by Alice Barr Realty. You are going to determine the percent of asking price for each home sold that month. Determine which sales people have the most total sales and determine how many sales are made within the city of Miami. You will prepare an attractively formatted summary report for your boss and a chart showing the total sales by sales person.

Open and Save Worksheet

You must open a worksheet that lists home sales for three months.

a. Open the file *chap4_cap_barr*.

b. Save it as **chap4_cap_barr_solution**.

Calculate Percent of Asking Price and Format the Data

A formula is used to calculate the percent of asking price, and this formula is applied to all listed sales. You will format the list in an attractive and useful manner.

a. Calculate the percent of asking price by dividing the selling price by asking price. Enter the formula in column F.

b. Format columns D and E as Currency with no decimal places. Format columns G and H as dates so just the day and month (for example, 5-May) are visible. Format column F as Percentage with one decimal place.

c. Widen columns to make all data and headings visible.

d. Format the main title in Arial 24 point size, and format the subtitle in Arial 16 point size. Format the main and subtitles with Orange, Accent 6, Darker 50% font color; Orange, Accent 6, Lighter 60% fill color; and italic.

e. Bold and center the column headings.

Sort the Data and Prepare the Summary Report and Chart

In order to sort the data by asking price and sales person, you must first convert the list to a table. After you sort the data, in order to prepare the summary report, you must convert the table back into a range of data.

a. Convert the range of data to a table.

b. Sort the data by selling agent in alphabetical order and then by asking price from largest to smallest.

c. Format the table attractively.

d. Convert the table back to a range of data.

e. Prepare a summary report showing total asking price and selling price by agent.

f. Use a fill color to highlight each sales person's total asking price and selling price.

g. Prepare a column chart on a separate chart sheet that shows each sales person's total asking price and selling price. Include a title and a legend, and format the chart to complement the worksheet. Rename the chart sheet tab as **Sales Analysis**.

h. Create a custom header with your name in the *Left section* and the worksheet tab name in the *Right section*. Print the chart.

Filter the Data Table and Print the Report

Your report should list just those properties sold in Miami by agent Carey, and you will use a filter to extract this data. Further, you must format before printing to make sure the report is documented and fits on one page.

a. Copy the Sales Data worksheet. Name the duplicate worksheet as **Sales Data Table**. Arrange the worksheets in this order: Sales Data, Sales Analysis, Sales Data Table.

b. Remove the subtotals on the Sales Data Table worksheet. Convert the range of data to a table and filter the table to show only those properties sold in Miami by agent Carey.

c. Group the Sales Data and the Sales Data Table worksheets. Create a custom header with your name on the left and your instructor's name on the right. Change the orientation to landscape, center horizontally and vertically. Ungroup the worksheets.

d. Preview the Sales Data Table worksheet and make any necessary adjustments to print on one page. Display the Sales Data worksheet in Page Break Preview. Adjust the page break and repeat the column headings on all pages.

e. Save your changes and print the worksheets. Close the workbook.

Mini Cases

Use the rubric following the case as a guide to evaluate your work, but keep in mind that your instructor may impose additional grading criteria or use a different standard to judge your work.

Night on the Nile

GENERAL CASE

The University Museum is celebrating the 30th anniversary of founding with a glamorous "evening along the Nile River" theme that includes fine art, fine food, and lively entertainment featuring Egyptian dance and music. As a recent graduate and newly hired employee at the University Museum, you are tasked with maintaining the guest list, assigning guests to tables, and tracking payments for the fundraising dinner. Open the *chap4_mc1_nile* workbook and save it as **chap4_mc1_nile_solution**. Use the CONCATENATE function to construct complete guest names in column E. Watch to ensure proper spaces. Convert the range of data to a table and sort the table by table number and then by last name in alphabetical order. Create a formula to calculate the total amount of revenue; if the guest has paid, the amount paid is based on the number of guests and the price per person (shown in cell I2). Otherwise, the amount paid is 0. Freeze the column headings and last names from scrolling offscreen. Filter the table to display those guests who have not paid yet. Copy the worksheet data to Sheet2, remove the filter, and filter the data by those who have paid. Use the CONCATENATE function to construct complete guest names in column E. Watch to ensure proper spaces. Convert the range of data to a table and sort the table by table number, and convert the copied table to a range of data. Move the title to cell E1 and merge and center it over the remaining columns. Hide columns A, B, C, and D. You will create a summary report to determine revenue by table and highlight the table totals. Create a custom header with your name, the worksheet tab, and your instructor's name. Repeat the title rows on all pages, and center vertically and horizontally. Adjust the page break as needed. Print the report. Save and close the workbook.

Performance Elements	Exceeds Expectations	Meets Expectations	Below Expectations
Create and sort table	Table created correctly with headings.	Table created without headings.	No table created.
Create formula	Formula entered correctly.	Formula incorrectly used.	No formulas, numbers entered.
Summary report	Well formatted and easy to find totals.	Adequately formatted, difficult to identify totals.	No summary report.
Appropriate format for printing	All print format requirements met.	All but one print format requirement met.	Two or more print formats missing.

Census Data

RESEARCH CASE

Open the *chap4_mc2_census* workbook and save the workbook as **chap4_mc2_census_solution**. Convert the range of data to a table and apply a table style.Your geography professor has given you an assignment to analyze population data for the last three censuses. In this exercise you use the census Web site to research the last three censuses, 1980, 1990, and 2000, to find the population for each of the 50 states. Once you determine the population of each state, you will sort the states by geographic region, prepare a summary report showing the population for all three censuses by region, and print the report. Finally, you will filter the list to show only those states in your geographic region. Prepare a chart illustrating the region populations and print both the chart and the filtered report. Close the workbook.

Performance Elements	Exceeds Expectations	Meets Expectations	Below Expectations
Research census statistics	All three censuses found.	Missing 2 censuses.	No census data.
Create and sort table	Table created correctly with headings.	Table created without headings.	No table created.
Summary report	Well formatted and easy to find totals.	Adequately formatted, difficult to identify totals.	No summary report.
Chart	Chart correctly prepared and attractively formatted.	Chart correctly prepared with no formatting.	No chart.
Printed formatted report	Both summary report and chart printed.	Either summary report or chart printed.	Nothing printed.

Peer Tutoring

DISASTER RECOVERY

Your service-learning project, tutoring students, is coming to an end, but you must provide assistance with tables, summary reports, and summary charting in your final session. The assignment your tutoring student is working to complete is for a Political Science course that is analyzing the 2004 Presidential Election. Open the spreadsheet *chap4_mc3_tutoring* and save it as **chap4_mc3_tutoring_solution**, then find four errors. Correct the errors and explain how the errors might have occurred and how they can be prevented. Include your explanation in the cells on the right side of the spreadsheet. Save and close the workbook.

Performance Elements	Exceeds Expectations	Meets Expectations	Below Expectations
Identify the errors	Identified all 4 errors.	Identified 3 errors.	Identified 2 or fewer errors.
Correct the errors	Corrected all 4 errors.	Corrected 3 errors.	Corrected 2 or fewer errors.
Explain the errors	Complete and correct explanation of each error.	Explanation is too brief to fully explain error.	No explanations.
Prevention description	Prevention description correct and practical.	Prevention description but obtuse.	No prevention description.

chapter 1 | **Access**

Introduction to Access

Finding Your Way through a Database

After reading this chapter, you will be able to:

1. Explore, describe, and navigate among the objects in an Access database **(page 547).**
2. Understand the difference between working in storage and memory **(page 554).**
3. Practice good file management **(page 555).**
4. Back up, compact, and repair Access files **(page 556).**
5. Create filters **(page 565).**
6. Sort table data on one or more fields **(page 568).**
7. Know when to use Access or Excel to manage data **(page 570).**
8. Use the Relationships window **(page 578).**
9. Understand relational power **(page 579).**

Hands-On Exercises

Exercises	Skills Covered
1. INTRODUCTION TO DATABASES (page 557) **Open:** chap1_ho1-3_traders.accdb **Copy, rename, and backup:** chap1_ho1-3_traders_solution.accdb and chap1_ho1_traders_solution.accdb	• Create a Production Folder and Copy an Access File • Open an Access File • Edit a Record • Navigate an Access Form and Add Records • Recognize the Table and Form Connectivity and Delete a Record • Back up and Compact the Database
2. DATA MANIPULATION: FILTERS AND SORTS (page 572) **Open:** chap1_ho1-3_traders_soution.accdb (from Exercise 1) **Copy, rename, and backup:** chap1_ho1-3_traders_solution.accdb (additional modifications), chap1_ho2_traders_solution.docx, and chap1_ho2_traders_solution.accdb	• Use Filter by Selection with an Equal Setting • Use Filter by Selection with a Contains Setting • Use Filter by Form with an Inequity Setting • Sort a Table
3. INTRODUCTION TO RELATIONSHIPS (page 581) **Open:** chap1_ho1-3_traders_solution.accdb (from Exercise 2) **Copy, rename, and backup:** chap1_ho1-3_traders_solution.accdb (additional modifications)	• Examine the Relationships Window • Discover that Changes in Table Data Affect Queries • Use Filter by Form with an Inequity Setting and Reapply a Saved Filter • Filter a Report • Remove an Advanced Filter

CASE STUDY

Medical Research—The Lifelong Learning Physicians Association

Case Study

Today is the first day of your information technology internship appointment with the *Lifelong Learning Physicians Association*. This medical association selected you for the internship because your résumé indicates that you are proficient with Access. Bonnie Clinton, M.D., founded the organization with the purpose of keeping doctors informed about current research and to help physicians identify qualified study participants. Dr. Clinton worries that physicians do not inform their patients about study participation opportunities. She expressed further concerns that the physicians in one field, e.g., cardiology, are unfamiliar with research studies conducted in other fields, such as obstetrics.

Because the association is new, you have very little data to manage. However, the system was designed to accommodate additional data. You will need to talk to Dr. Clinton on a regular basis to determine the association's changing information needs. You may need to guide her in this process. Your responsibilities as the association's IT intern include many items.

Your Assignment

- Read the chapter, paying special attention to learning the vocabulary of database software.
- Copy the *chap1_case_physicians.accdb* file to your production folder, rename it **chap1_case_physicians_solution.accdb**, and enable the content.
- Open the Relationships window and examine the relationships among the tables and the fields contained within each of the tables to become acquainted with this database.
- Open the Volunteers table. Add yourself as a study participant by replacing the last record with your own information. You should invent data about your height, weight, blood pressure, and your cholesterol. Examine the values in the other records and enter a realistic value. Do not change the stored birthday.
- Identify all of the volunteers who might be college freshmen (18- and 19-year-olds). After you identify them, print the table listing their names and addresses. Use a filter by form with an appropriately set date criterion to identify the correctly aged participants.
- Identify all of the physicians participating in a study involving cholesterol management.
- Open the *Studies and Volunteers Report*. Print it.
- Compact and repair the database file.
- Create a backup of the database. Name the backup **chap1_case_physicians_backup.accdb**.

Data and Files Everywhere!

You probably use databases often. Each time you download an MP3 file, you enter a database via the Internet. There you find searchable data identifying files by artist's name, music style, most frequently requested files, first lines, publication companies, and song titles. If you know the name of the song but not the recording artist or record label, you generally can find it. The software supporting the Web site helps you locate the information you need. The server for the Web site provides access to a major database that contains a lot of data about available MP3 files.

(Each time you download an MP3 file, you enter a database via the internet.)

You are exposed to other databases on a regular basis. For example, your university uses a database to support the registration process. When you registered for this course, you entered a database. It probably told you the number of available seats but not the names of the other students who enrolled in the class. In addition, Web-based job and dating boards are based on database software. Organizations rely on data to conduct daily operations, regardless of whether the organization exists as a profit or not-for-profit environment. The organization maintains data about employees, volunteers, customers, activities, and facilities. Every keystroke and mouse click creates data about the organization that needs to be stored, organized, and analyzed. Microsoft Access provides the organizational decision-maker a valuable tool facilitating data retrieval and use.

In this section, you explore Access database objects and work with table views. You also learn the difference between working in storage and memory to understand how changes to database objects are saved. Finally, you practice good file management techniques by backing up, compacting, and repairing databases.

Exploring, Describing, and Navigating Among the Objects in an Access Database

A ***field*** is a basic entity or data element, such as the name of a book or the telephone number of a publisher.

A ***record*** is a complete set of all of the data (fields) about one person, place, event, or idea.

A ***table*** is a collection of records. Every record in a table contains the same fields in the same order.

A ***database*** consists of one or more tables and the supporting objects used to get data into and out of the tables.

To understand database management effectively and to use Access productively, you should first learn the vocabulary. A ***field*** is a basic entity, data element, or category, such as book titles or telephone numbers. The field does not necessarily need to contain a value. For example, a field might store fax numbers for a firm's customers. However, some of the customers may not have a fax machine so the Fax field is blank for that record. A ***record*** is a complete set of all of the data (fields) about one person, place, event, or idea. For example, your name, homework, and test scores constitute your record in your instructor's grade book. A ***table***, the foundation of every database, is a collection of related records that contain fields to organize data. If you have used Excel, you will see the similarities between a spreadsheet and an Access table. Each column represents a field, and each row represents a record. Every record in a table contains the same fields in the same order. An instructor's grade book for one class is a table containing records of all students in one structure. A ***database*** consists of one or more tables and the supporting objects used to get data into and out of the tables.

Prior to the advent of database management software, organizations managed their data manually. They placed papers in file folders and organized the folders in multiple drawer filing cabinets. You can think of the filing cabinet in the manual system as a database. Each drawer full of folders in the filing cabinet corresponds to a table within the database. Figure 1.1 shows a college's database system from before the information age. File drawers (tables) contain student data. Each folder (record) contains facts (fields) about that student. The cabinet also contains drawers (tables) full of data about the faculty and the courses offered. Together, the tables combine to form a database system.

TIP Data Versus Information

Data and information are not synonymous although the terms often are used interchangeably. Data is the raw material and consists of the table (or tables) that comprise a database. Information is the finished product. Data is converted to information by selecting (filtering) records, by sequencing (sorting) the selected records, or by summarizing data from multiple records. Decisions in an organization are based on information compiled from multiple records, as opposed to raw data.

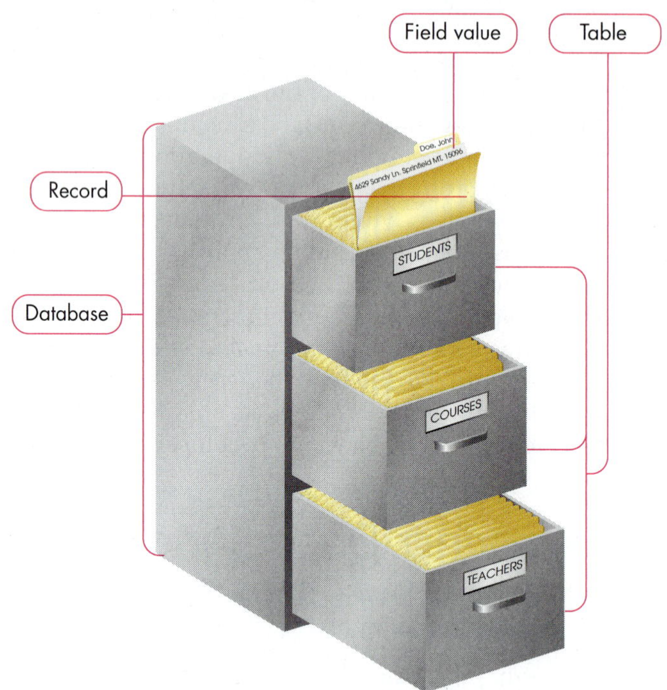

Figure 1.1 Primitive Database

Identify Access Interface Elements

Figure 1.2 shows how Microsoft Access appears onscreen. It contains two open windows—an application window for Microsoft Access and a document (database) window for the open database. Each window has its own title bar and icons. The title bar in the application window contains the name of the application (Microsoft Access) and the Minimize, Maximize (or Restore), and Close icons. The title bar in the document (database) window contains the name of the object that is currently open (Employees table). When more than one object is open at a time, the top of the document window will display tabs for each open object. The Access application window is maximized; therefore, Restore is visible. The Reference page describes the tabs and groups on the Ribbon in Access 2007.

Let's look at an example of a database for an international food distribution company—The Northwind Traders. This firm sells specialty food items to restaurants and food shops around the world. It also purchases the products it sells from diversely located firms. The Northwind Traders Company database contains eight tables: Categories, Customers, Employees, Order Details, Orders, Products, Shippers, and Suppliers. Each table, in turn, consists of multiple records, corresponding to the folders in the file cabinet.

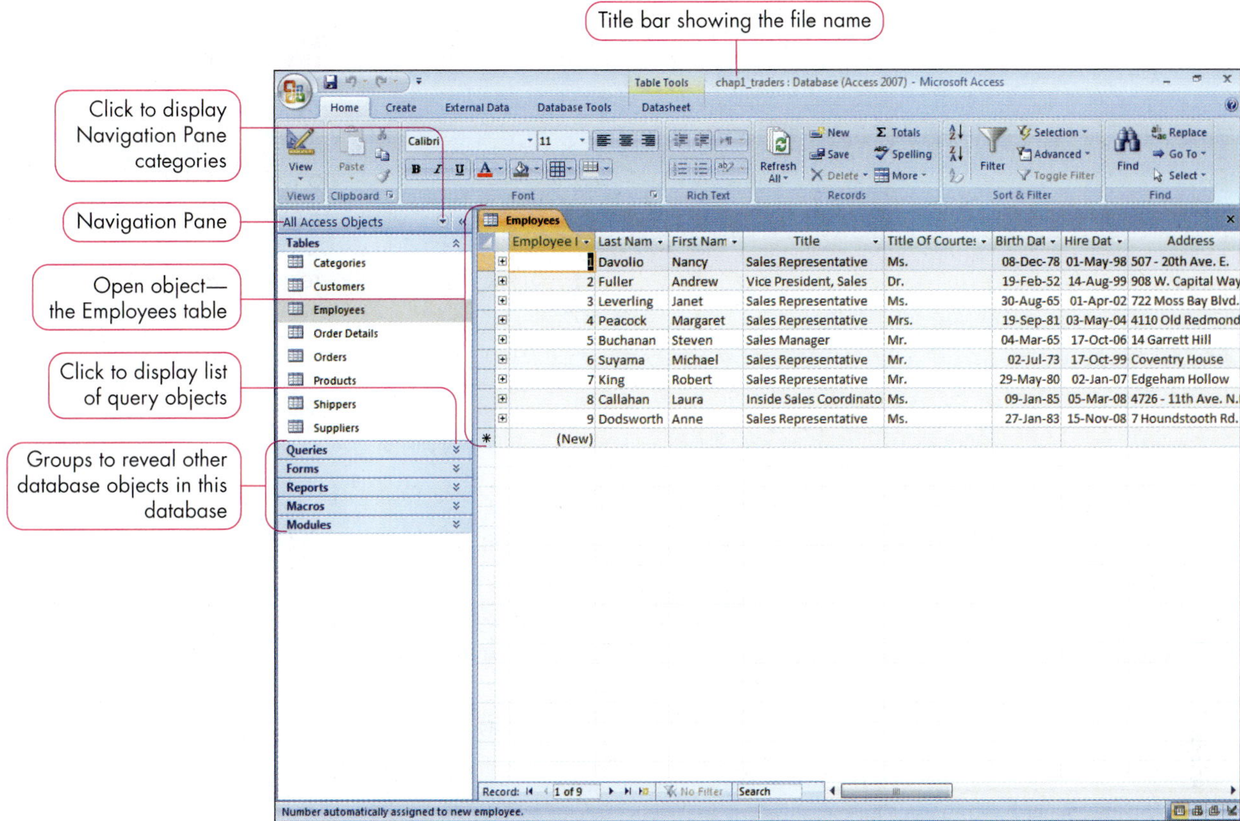

Figure 1.2 An Access Database

The Employees table, for example, contains a record for every employee. Each record in the Employees table contains 17 fields—where data about the employee's education, address, photograph, position, and so on are stored. Occasionally a field does not contain a value for a particular record. One of the employees, Margaret Peacock, did not provide a picture. The value of that field is missing. Access provides a placeholder to store the data when it is available. The Suppliers table has a record for each vendor from whom the firm purchases products, just as the Orders table has a record for each order. The real power of Access is derived from a database with multiple tables and the relationships that connect the tables.

An Access ***object*** contains the basic elements of the database.

The ***Navigation Pane*** lists database objects within groups by category.

The database window displays the various objects in an Access database. An Access ***object*** stores the basic elements of the database. Access uses six types of objects—tables, queries, forms, reports, macros, and modules. Every database must contain at least one table, and it may contain any, all, or none of the other objects. The ***Navigation Pane*** organizes and lists database objects by category (e.g., All Access Objects) and groups (e.g., Tables, Queries, Forms, Reports, Macros, and Modules). In Figure 1.2, the Tables group lists all table objects, and the other objects are hidden. Click a group name to display or hide its lists of objects. To change the category, click the current category name and select a different category from the list. When you change the category, the groups also change. For example, if you select the Tables and Related Views category, the objects are grouped by table names so that you can see which objects are related to which tables. The Navigation Pane in Figure 1.24 shows the Tables and Related Views category with the Products table group and the objects that relate to that table. Double-click an object to open it or right-click the object to display a shortcut menu.

Access Ribbon | Reference

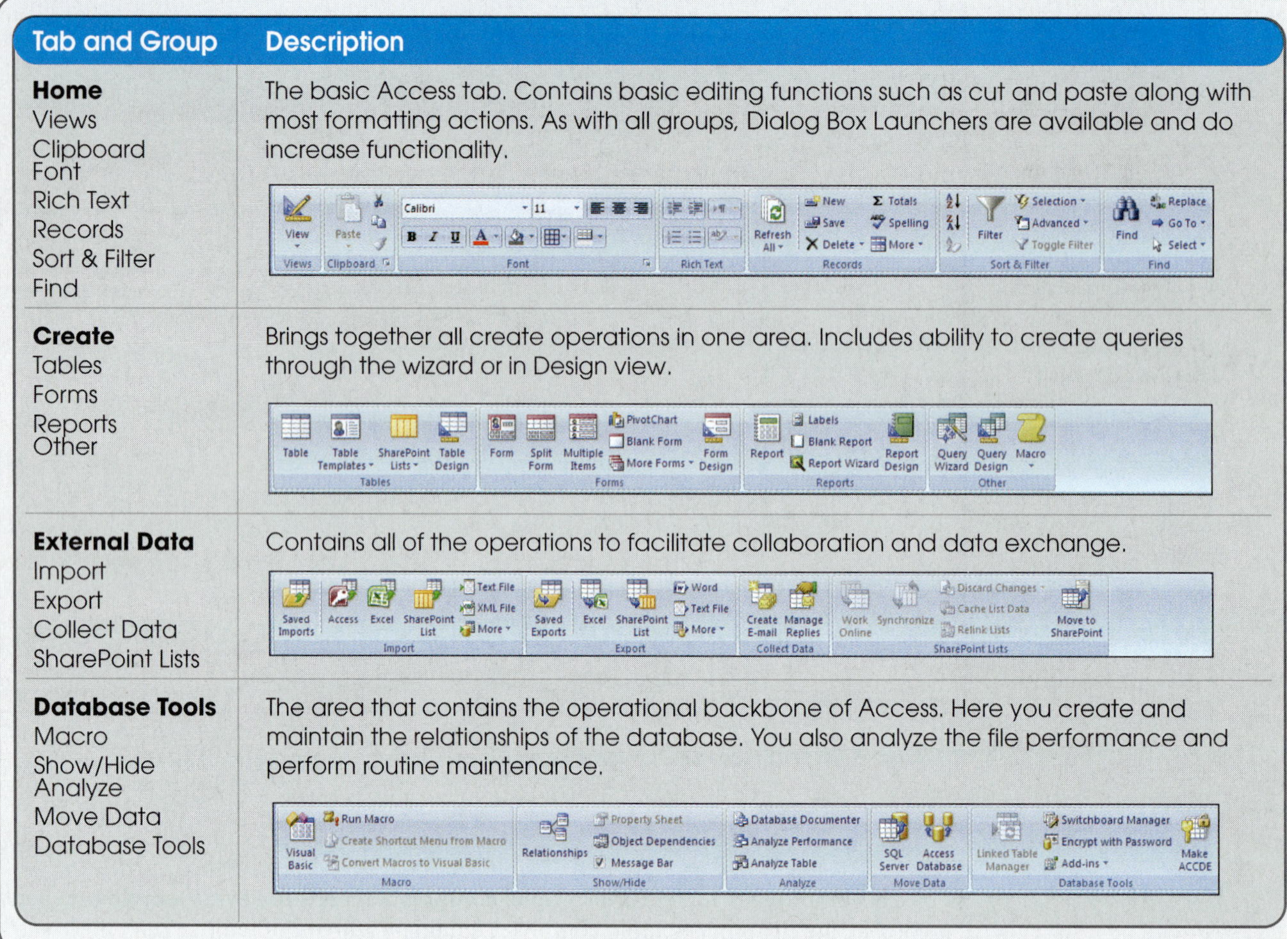

Tab and Group	Description
Home Views Clipboard Font Rich Text Records Sort & Filter Find	The basic Access tab. Contains basic editing functions such as cut and paste along with most formatting actions. As with all groups, Dialog Box Launchers are available and do increase functionality.
Create Tables Forms Reports Other	Brings together all create operations in one area. Includes ability to create queries through the wizard or in Design view.
External Data Import Export Collect Data SharePoint Lists	Contains all of the operations to facilitate collaboration and data exchange.
Database Tools Macro Show/Hide Analyze Move Data Database Tools	The area that contains the operational backbone of Access. Here you create and maintain the relationships of the database. You also analyze the file performance and perform routine maintenance.

Work with Table Views

The ***Datasheet view*** is a grid where you add, edit, and delete the records of a table.

The ***Design view*** is a different grid where you create and modify the properties of the table.

Access provides different ways in which to view a table and most other objects. The ***Datasheet view*** is a grid containing columns (fields) and rows (records), similar to an Excel spreadsheet. You can view, add, edit, and delete records of a table in the Datasheet view. You can use the ***Design view*** to create and modify the table by specifying the fields it will contain and their associated properties. The field type (for example, text or numeric data) and the field length are examples of field properties. If you need the values stored in a particular field to display as currency, you would modify the property of that field to ensure all values display appropriately.

Figure 1.3 shows the Datasheet view for the Customers table. The first row in the table displays the field names. Each additional row contains a record (the data for a specific customer). Each column represents a field (one fact about a customer). Every record in the table contains the same fields in the same order.

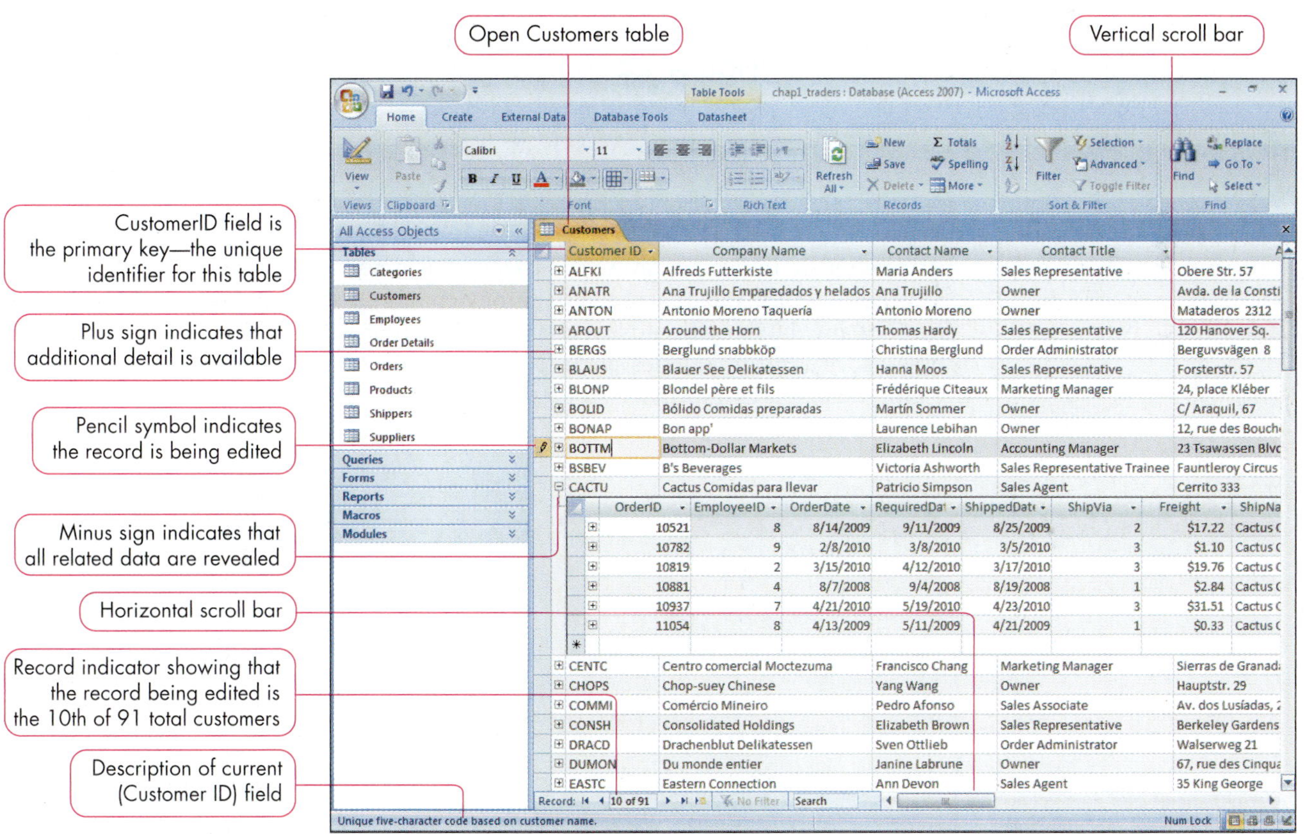

Figure 1.3 The Customers Table and Related Order Information

The ***primary key*** is the field that makes each record in a table unique.

The ***primary key*** is the field (or combination of fields) that makes each record in a table unique. The CustomerID is the primary key in the Customers table; it ensures that every record in a table is different from every other record, and it prevents the occurrence of duplicate records. Primary key fields may be numbers, letters, or a combination of both. In this case the primary key is text (letters).

The navigation bar at the bottom of Figure 1.3 shows a table with 91 records and record number 10 as the current record. You can work on only one record at a time. The vertical scroll bar at the right of the window shows that more records exist in the table than you can see at one time. The horizontal scroll bar at the bottom of the window indicates that you cannot see an entire record.

The pencil icon at the left of the record indicates that the data in the current record are being edited and that the changes have not yet been saved. The pencil icon disappears after you complete the data entry and move to another record, because Access saves data automatically as soon as you move from one record to the next.

Figure 1.4 displays the navigation buttons that you use to move within most Access objects. You may navigate using commands to go to the last and first records, advance and go back one record, and add a new record.

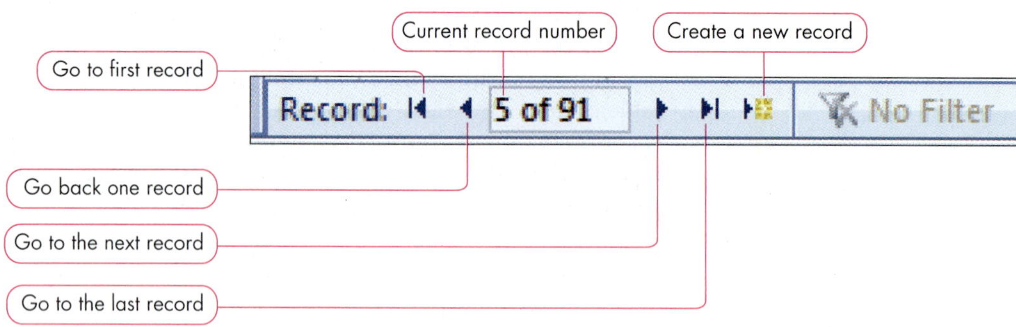

Figure 1.4 Navigation Buttons

Use Forms, Queries, and Reports

As previously indicated, an Access database is made up of different types of objects together with the tables and the data they contain. A table (or set of tables) is at the heart of any database because it contains the actual data. The other objects in a database—such as forms, queries, and reports—are based on one or more underlying tables. Figure 1.5 displays a form based on the Customers table shown earlier.

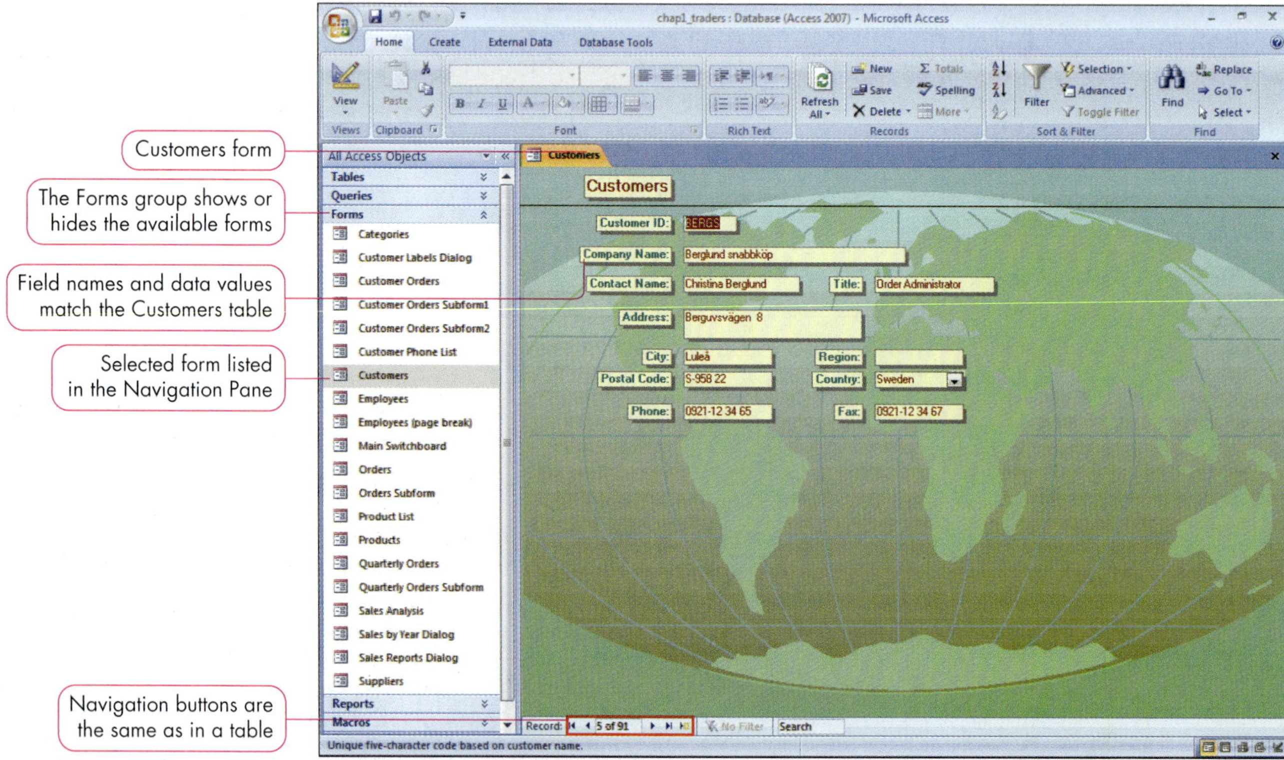

Figure 1.5 Customers Form

A *form* is an interface that enables you to enter or modify record data.

A *form* is an interface that enables you to enter or modify record data. Commands may appear in the form to add a new record, print a record, or close the form. The form provides access to all of the data maintenance operations that are available through a table. The status bar and navigation buttons at the bottom of the form are similar to those that appear at the bottom of a table. You add, delete, and edit records in Form view, but create and edit the form structure in Design view.

A *query* provides information that answers a question.

A *criterion* (*criteria*, pl) is a rule or norm that is the basis for making judgments.

Figure 1.6 displays a query that lists the products that the firm purchases from a particular supplier. A *query* provides information that answers a question based on the data within an underlying table or tables by filtering, calculating, or summarizing data. The Suppliers table, for example, contains records for many vendors, but the query in Figure 1.6 shows only the products that were supplied by a specific supplier. If you want to know the details about a specific supplier, you establish a criterion to specify which supplier you need to know about. A *criterion* (*criteria*, pl) is a rule or norm that is the basis for making judgments. If you need the names of all the suppliers in New York, you set a criterion to identify the New York suppliers. The results would yield only those suppliers from New York. Query results are similar in appearance to the underlying table, except that the query contains selected records and/or selected fields for those records. The query also may list the records in a different sequence from that of the table. (You also can use a query to add new records and modify existing records.) If you have a query open and notice an error in an address field, you can edit the record, and the edited value would immediately and permanently transfer to the table storing that record. Queries may be opened in Datasheet view or Design view. You use the Datasheet view to examine the query output and use the Design view to specify which fields and records to include in the query.

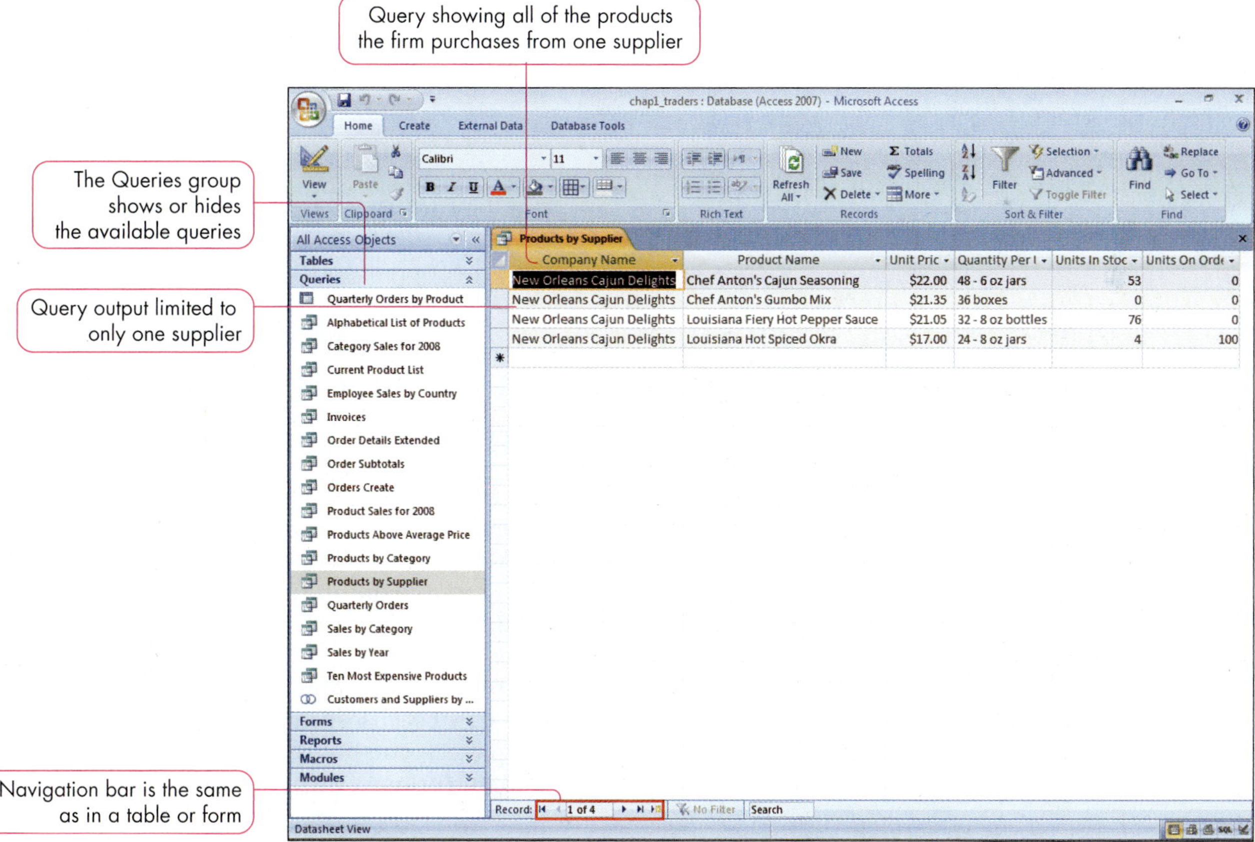

Figure 1.6 Results of a Query Shown in Datasheet View

A ***report*** presents database information professionally.

Figure 1.7 displays a report that contains the same information as the query in Figure 1.6. A ***report*** contains professionally formatted information from underlying tables or queries. Because the report information contains a more enhanced format than a query or table, you place database output in a report to print. Access provides different views for designing, modifying, and running reports. Most Access users use only the Print Preview, Print Layout, and Report views of a report.

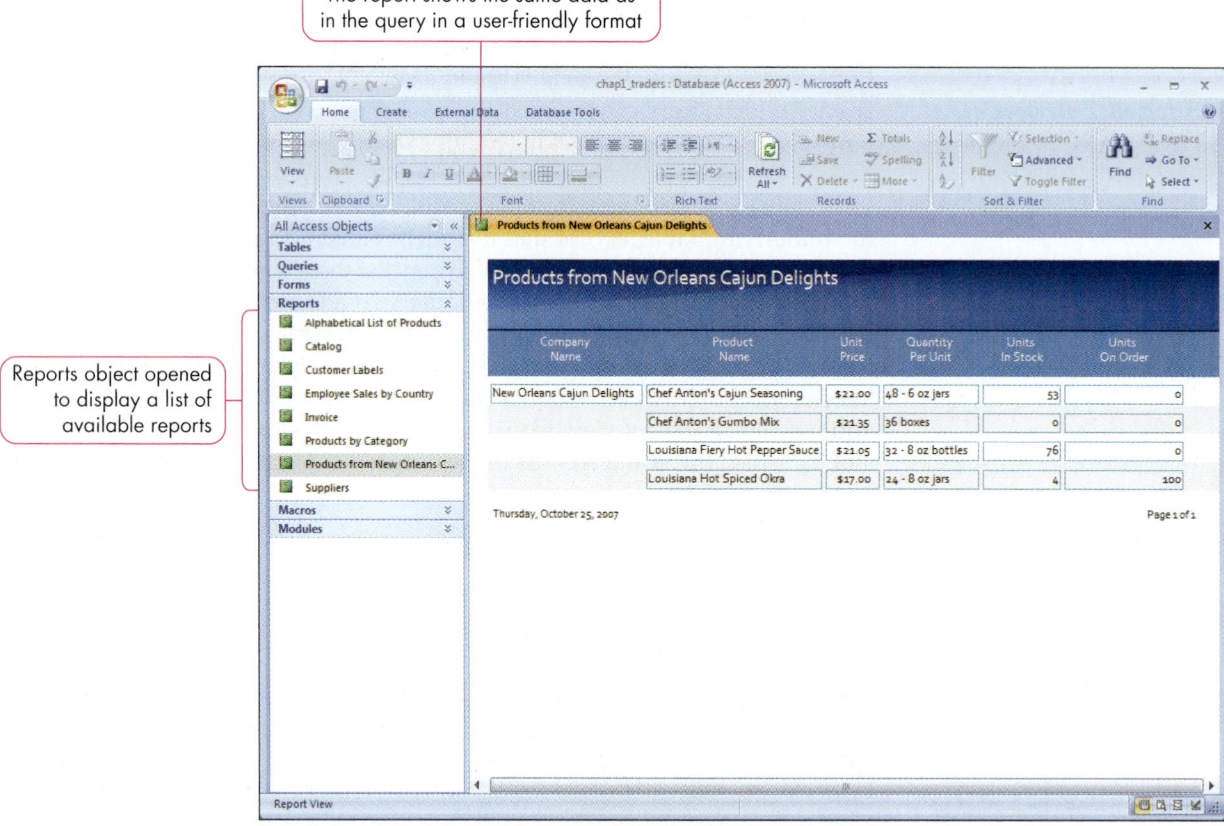

Figure 1.7 Report Displaying the Query Information from Figure 1.6

Understanding the Difference Between Working in Storage and Memory

Access is different from the other Microsoft Office applications. Word, Excel, and PowerPoint all work primarily from memory. In those applications you can easily reverse mistakes by using Undo. You make a change, discover that you dislike it, and click Undo to restore the original. These actions are possible because you work in memory (RAM) most of the time while in the other Microsoft Office applications; changes are not saved automatically to the file immediately after you make the changes. These actions are also possible because, generally, you are the only user of your file. If you work on a group project, you might e-mail the PowerPoint file to the others in the group, but you are the primary owner and user of that file. Access is *different*.

> Access is different from the other Microsoft Office applications.

Access works primarily from storage. When you make a change to a field's content in an Access table (for example, changing a customer's area code), Access saves your changes as soon as you move the insertion point to a different record; you do not need to click Save. You can click Undo to reverse several editing changes (such as changing an area code and a contact name) for a single record **immediately** after making the changes to that record. However, unlike other Office programs that let you continue

Undoing actions, you cannot use Undo to reverse edits to more than the last record you edited or to restore a field if you delete it.

Multiple users can work on the database simultaneously. As long as no two users attempt to interact with the same record at the same time, the system updates as it goes. This also means that any reports extracting the information from the database contain the most up-to-date data. The only time you need to click Save is when you are creating or changing a structural element, such as a table, query, form, or report.

TIP Save Edits While Keeping a Record Active

When you want to save changes to a record you are editing while staying on the same record, press Shift+Enter. The pencil icon, indicating an editing mode, disappears, indicating that the change is saved.

Be careful to avoid accidentally typing something in a record and pressing Enter. Doing so saves the change, and you can retrieve the original data if you are lucky enough to remember to click Undo immediately before making or editing other records. Because Access is a relational database, several other related objects (queries, reports, or forms) could also be permanently changed. In Access, one file holds everything. All of the objects—tables, forms, queries, and reports—are saved both individually and as part of the Access collection.

TIP Data Validation

No system, no matter how sophisticated, can produce valid output from invalid input. Thus, good systems are built to anticipate errors in data entry and to reject those errors prior to saving a record. Access will automatically prevent you from adding records with a duplicate primary key or entering invalid data into a numeric or date field. The database developer has the choice whether to require other types of validation, such as requiring the author's name.

Practicing Good File Management

You must exercise methodical and deliberate file management techniques to avoid damaging data. Every time you need to open a file, this book will direct you to copy the file to your production folder and rename the copied file. Name the production folder with ***Your Name Access Production***. You would not copy a real database and work in the copy often. However, as you learn, you will probably make mistakes. Following the practice of working in a copied file will facilitate mistake recovery during the learning process.

Further, it matters to which type of media you save your files. Access does not work from some media. Access runs best from a hard or network drive because those drives have sufficient access speed to support the software. Access speed measures the time it takes for the storage device to make the file content available for use. If you work from your own computer, create the production folder in the Documents folder on the hard drive. Most schools lock their hard drives so that students cannot permanently save files there. If your school provides you with storage space on the school's network, store your production folder there. The advantage to using the network is that the network administration staff backs up files regularly. If you have no storage on the school network, your next best storage option is a thumb drive, also known as USB jump drive, flash drive, Pen drive, or stick drive.

Access speed measures the time it takes for the storage device to make the file content available for use.

TIP Do Not Use This Media

Because storage space is limited, you should not use floppy disks or Zip disks. Furthermore, you should not use CDs or DVDs because Access must constantly save changes to the file, a process that does not work with storage media that have slow access speed or limited write privileges. ***Access speed*** measures the time it takes for the storage device to locate the file, open it, and transfer it to memory so that the file content is available for use. However, you may back up your work or archive it to these storage devices.

All of the objects in an Access database are stored in a single file. You can open a database from within Windows Explorer by double-clicking the file name. You also can open the database from within Access through the Recent Documents list or by clicking the Microsoft Office Button (noted as Office Button only in this textbook) and selecting Open from the Office menu. The individual objects within a database are opened from the database window.

Backing Up, Compacting, and Repairing Access Files

Data is the lifeblood of any organization. Imagine what would happen to a firm that loses the records of the orders placed but not shipped or the charity that loses the list of donor contribution records or the hospital that loses the digital records of patient X-rays. What would happen to the employee who "accidentally" deleted mission-critical data? What would happen to the other employees who did not lose the mission-critical data? Fortunately, Access recognizes how critical backup procedures are to organizations and makes backing up the database files easy.

Back Up a Database

You back up an Access file (and all of the objects it contains) with just a few mouse clicks. To back up files, click the Office Button and select Manage from the Office menu. When you select Back Up Database, the Save As dialog box opens. You may use controls in the Save As dialog box to specify storage location and file name. Access provides a default file name that is the original file name followed by the date. In most organizations, this step is useful because the Information Technology department backs up every database each day.

Compact and Repair a Database

All databases have a tendency to expand with use. This expansion will occur without new information being added. Simply using the database, creating queries and running them, or applying and removing filters may cause the file to store inefficiently. Because the files tend to be rather large to start with, any growth creates problems. Access provides another utility, Compact and Repair Database, under the Manage submenu in the Office menu that addresses this issue. The Compact and Repair utility acts much like a disk defragmenter utility. It finds related file sectors and reassembles them in one location if they become scattered from database use. You should compact and repair your database each day when you close the file. This step often will decrease file size by 50% or more. Access closes any open objects during the compact and repair procedure, so it is a good idea to close any objects in the database prior to compacting so that you will control if any design changes will be saved or not.

In the next hands-on exercise, you will work with a database from an international gourmet food distributor, the Northwind Traders. This firm purchases food items from suppliers and sells them to restaurants and specialty food shops. It depends on the data stored in the Access database to make daily decisions.

Hands-On Exercises

1 | Introduction to Databases

Skills covered: 1. Create a Production Folder and Copy an Access File **2.** Open an Access File **3.** Edit a Record **4.** Navigate an Access Form and Add Records **5.** Recognize the Table and Form Connectivity and Delete a Record **6.** Back up and Compact the Database

Step 1 Create a Production Folder and Copy an Access File

Refer to Figure 1.8 as you complete Step 1.

a. Right-click **Computer** on the desktop and select **Explore** from the shortcut menu.

   This step opens the Explore utility in a two-pane view that facilitates transferring materials between folders.

b. Determine where your production folder will reside and double-click that location. For example, double-click the **Documents** folder if that is where your files will reside.

   For the remainder of this book, it is assumed that your production folder resides in the Documents folder on the hard drive. Your folder may actually exist on another drive. What is important is that you (1) create and use the folder and (2) remember where it is.

c. Right-click anywhere on a blank spot in the right pane of the Explorer window. Select **New** and then select **Folder** from the shortcut menu.

   A new folder is created with the default name, New Folder, selected and ready to be renamed.

d. Type **Your Name Access Production** and press **Enter**.

e. Open the folder that contains the student data files that accompany this textbook.

f. Find the file named *chap1_ho1-3_traders.accdb*, right-click the file, and select **Copy** from the shortcut menu.

g. Open the newly created production folder named with your name. Right-click a blank area in the right side of the Explorer window and select **Paste**.

   You have created a copy of the original *chap1_ho1-3_traders.accdb* file. You will work with the copy. In the event that you make mistakes, the original remains intact in the student data folder. You can recopy it and rework the exercise if necessary.

h. Rename the newly copied file **your_name_chap1_ho1-3_traders_solution.accdb**.

   You need to remember to rename all of the solution files with your name. If your instructor requests that you submit your work for evaluation using a shared folder on the campus network, each file must have a unique name. You risk overwriting another student's work (or having someone overwrite your work) if you do not name your files with your name and the file designation.

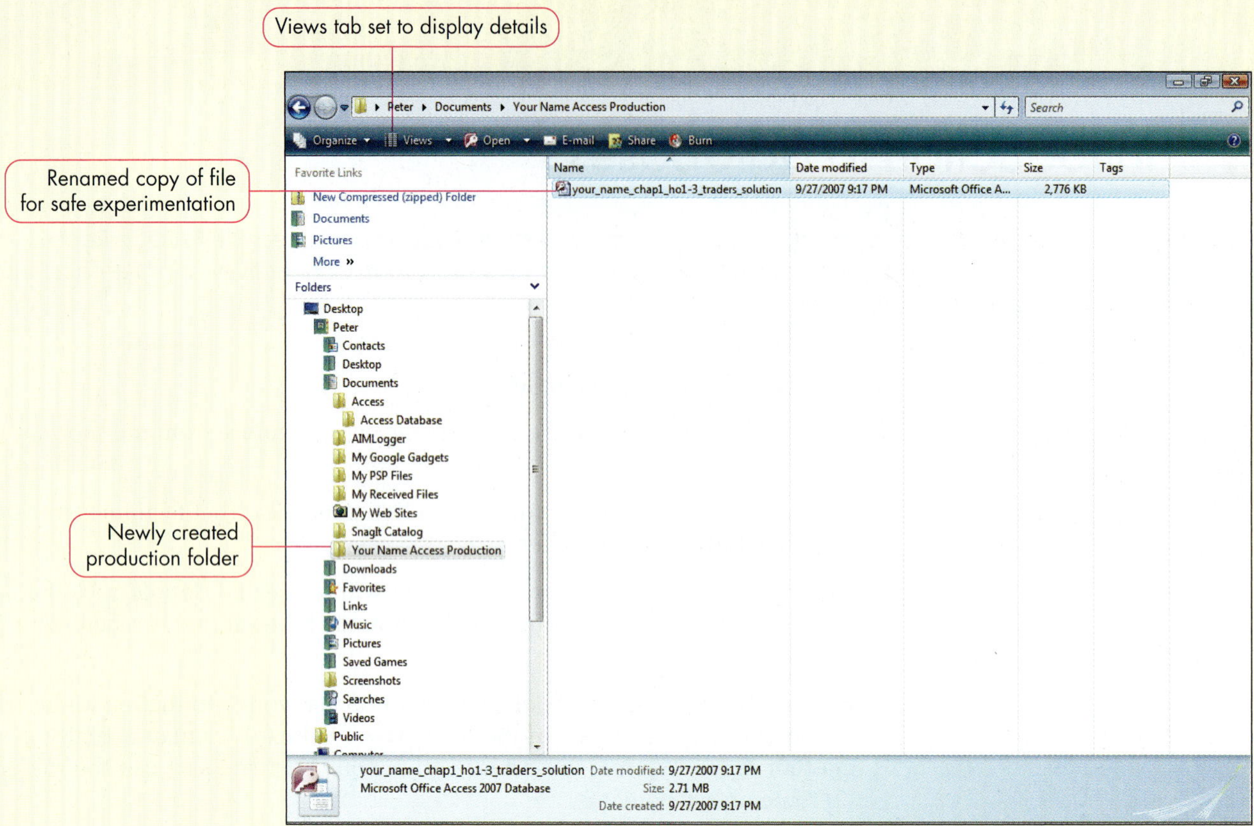

Figure 1.8 Production Folder Created Showing Copied and Renamed File

Step 2
Open an Access File

Refer to Figure 1.9 as you complete Step 2.

a. Double-click the *your_name_chap1_ho1-3_traders_solution* file to open it.

   This step launches Access and opens the database file. From now on, this book will refer to the files without the *your_name* prefix. The Security Warning toolbar may appear below the Ribbon, indicating that some database content is disabled.

b. Click **Options** on the Security Warning toolbar. See Figure 1.9.

   When you open an Access file, you may need to enable the content. Several viruses and worms may be transmitted via Access files. You may be reasonably confident of the trustworthiness of the files in this book. However, if an Access file arrives as an attachment from an unsolicited e-mail message, you should not open it. Microsoft warns all users of Access files that a potential threat exists every time the file is opened.

c. Click **Enable this content** and then click **OK**.

   You just enabled the database contents. The Microsoft Office Security Options dialog box closes, and the Security Warning toolbar disappears.

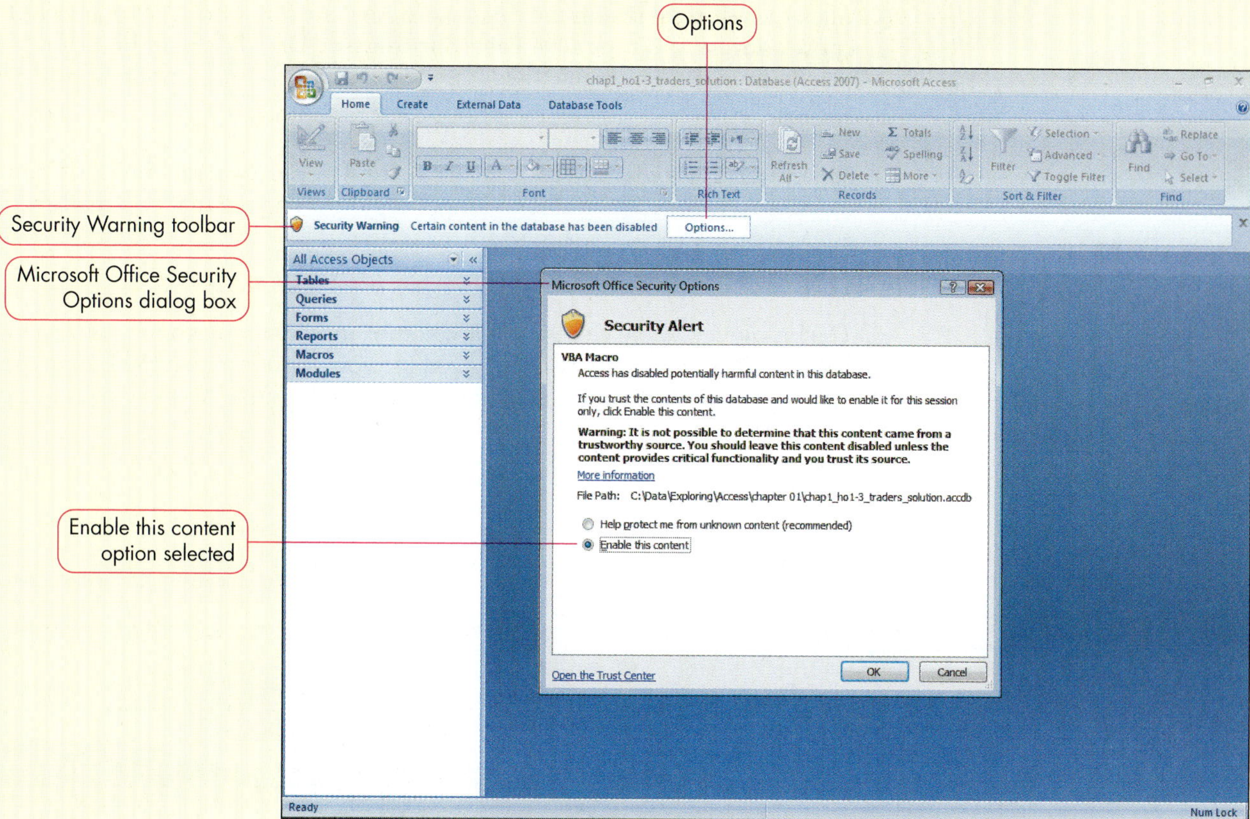

Figure 1.9 Microsoft Office Security Options Dialog Box

Step 3 Edit a Record

Refer to Figure 1.10 as you complete Step 3.

a. Click **Tables** in the Navigation Pane to expand the list of available tables.

   The list of tables contained in the database file opens.

b. Double-click the **Employees table** to open it. See Figure 1.10.

c. Click the insertion point in the fourth row. Double-click *Peacock* in the LastName field. The entire name highlights. Type **your last name** to replace *Peacock*.

   Although the column heading shows Last Name with a space, the actual field name is LastName. You will learn how to create field names without spaces but display spaces onscreen later.

d. Press **Tab** to move to the next field in the fourth row. Replace *Margaret* with **your first name**.

   You have made changes to two fields in the same record (row); the pencil displays in the row selector box.

e. Click **Undo** on the Quick Access Toolbar.

   Your first name reverts back to Margaret because you have not yet left the record.

f. Type your name again to replace *Margaret* with **your first name**. Press **Enter**.

   You should now be in the Title field and your title, *Sales Representative*, is selected. The pencil icon still displays in the row selector.

g. Click anywhere in the third row where Janet Leverling's data are stored.

   The pencil icon disappears; your changes to the table have been saved.

h. Click the address field in the first record, the one for Nancy Davolio. Select the entire address and type **4004 East Morningside Dr**. Click your insertion point into Andrew Fuller's name field.

i. Click **Undo**.

Nancy's address changes back to *507 - 20th Ave. E.* However, the Undo command is now faded. You can no longer undo the change that you made replacing Margaret Peacock's name with your own.

j. Click **Close** to close the Employees table. See Figure 1.10.

The Employees table closes. You are not prompted about saving your changes, because they have already been saved for you. If you reopen the Employees table, you will find your name, not Margaret's, because Access works in storage, not memory.

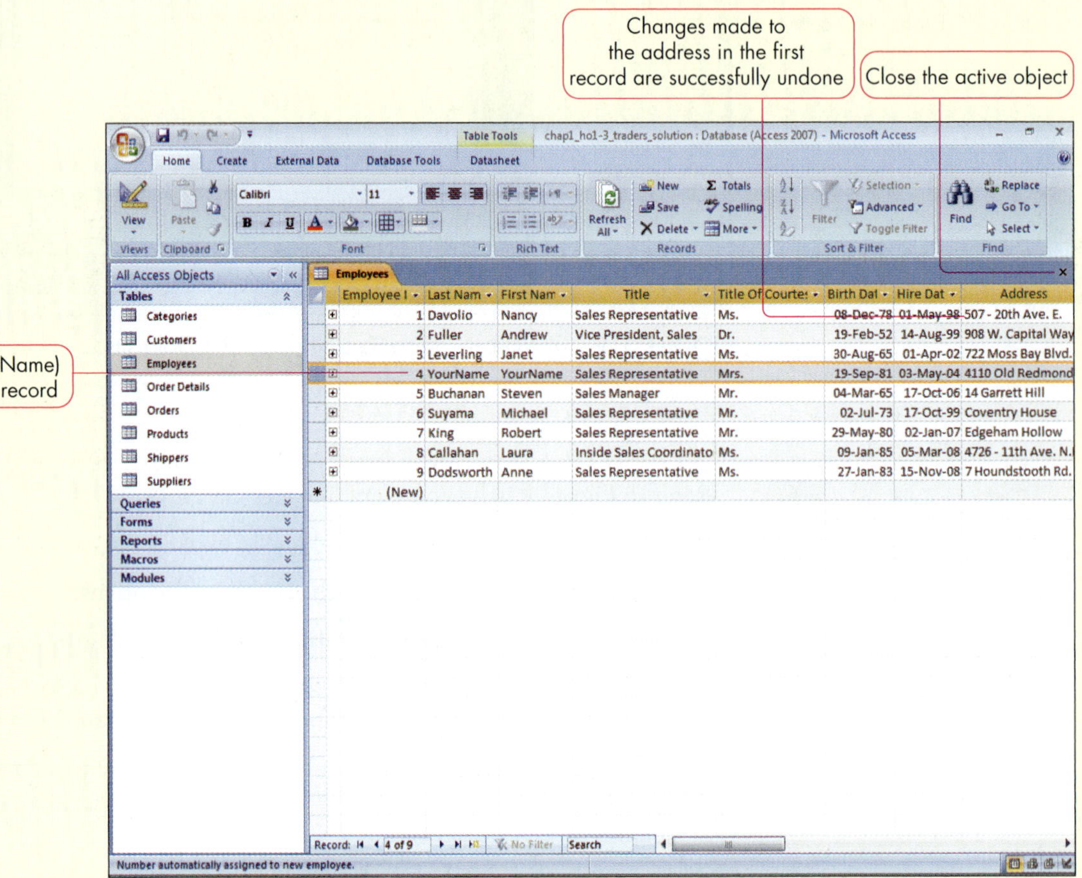

Figure 1.10 The Edited Employees Table

Step 4
Navigate an Access Form and Add Records

Refer to Figure 1.11 as you complete Step 4.

a. Click **Tables** in the Navigation Pane to close it.

The list of available tables collapses.

b. Click **Forms** in the Navigation Pane to expand the list of available form objects.

c. Double-click the **Products form** to open it.

d. Refer to Figure 1.4 and practice with the navigation buttons above the status bar to move from one record to the next. Click **Next record** and then click **Last record**.

e. Click **Find** in the Find group on the Home tab.

The Find command is an ideal way to search for specific records within a table, form, or query. You can search a single field or the entire record, match all or part of the selected field(s), move forward or back in a table, or specify a case-sensitive search. The Replace command can be used to substitute one value for another. Be careful, however, about using the Replace All option for global replacement because unintended replacements are far too common.

f. Type **ikura** in the *Find What* section of the Find and Replace dialog box. Check to make sure that the *Look In* option is set to **Product Name** and the *Match* option is set to **Whole Field**. The *Search* option should be set to **All**. Click **Find Next**.

You should see the information about *ikura*, a seafood supplied by Tokyo Traders.

g. Type **Grandma** in the *Find What* box, click the **Match drop-down arrow**, and select **Any Part of Field**. Click **Find Next**.

You should see information about Grandma's Boysenberry Spread. Setting the match option to any part of the field will return a match even if it is contained in the middle of a word.

h. Close the Find and Replace dialog box.

i. Click **New (blank) record** located on the navigation bar.

j. Enter the following information for a new product. Press **Tab** to navigate the form.

Field Name	**Value to Type**
Product Name	Your Name Pecan Pie
Supplier	Grandma Kelly's Homestead (Note, display the drop-down list to enter this information quickly)
Category	Confections (Use the drop-down box here, too)
Quantity Per Unit	1
Unit Price	25.00
Units in Stock	18
Units on Order	50
Reorder Level	20

As soon as you begin typing in the product name box, Access assigns a Product ID, in this case 78, to the record. The Product ID is used as the primary key in the Products table.

k. Click the **Office Button**, point to **Print**, and select **Print**.

The Print dialog box opens so that you can select print options.

l. Click **Selected Record(s)** and click **OK**.

You just printed the form showing the selected record.

m. Close the Products form.

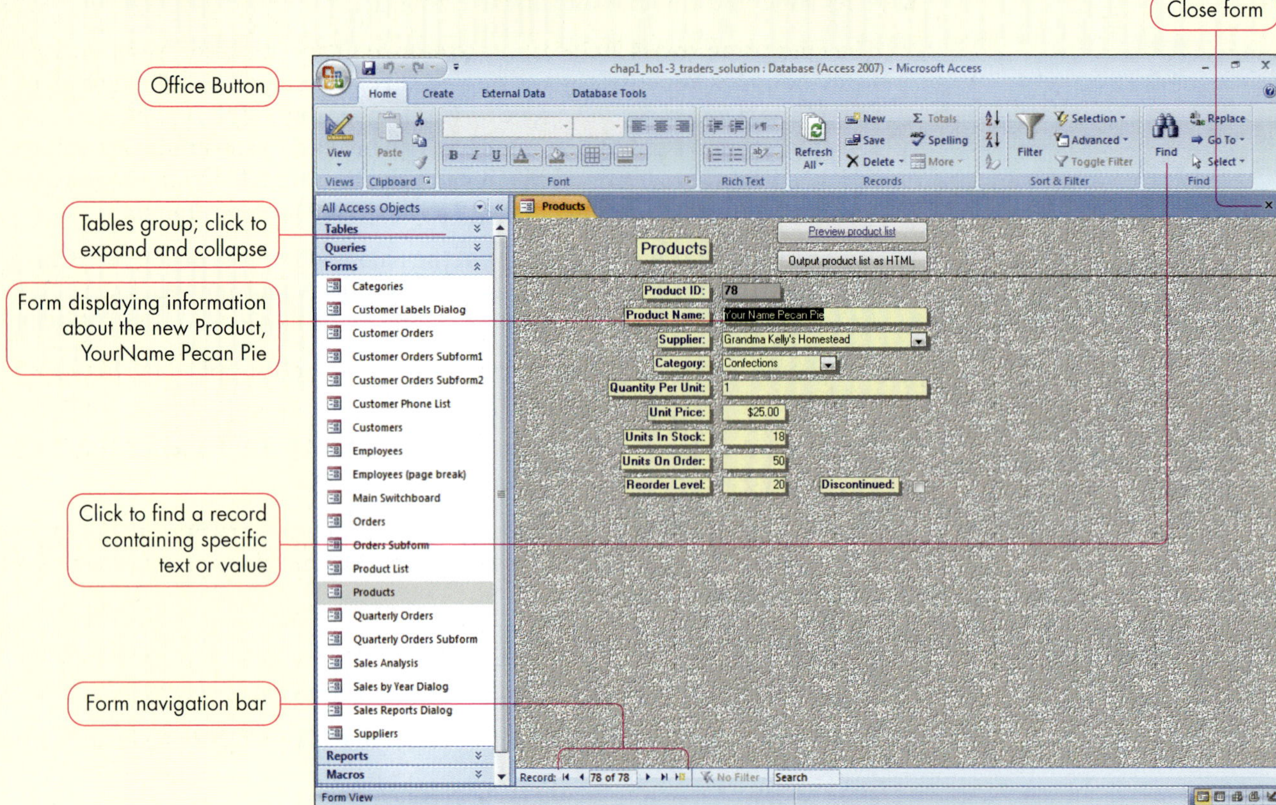

Figure 1.11 The Newly Created Record in the Products Form

TIP Create a Form

To create a form, in the Navigation Pane, select the name of the table for which you want a table created. Then click the Create tab and click Form in the Forms group. Click Save on the Quick Access Toolbar, enter a name for the form, and click OK. You can then use that form to add, modify, or delete records.

Step 5
Recognize the Table and Form Connectivity and Delete a Record

Refer to Figure 1.12 as you complete Step 5.

a. Click **Forms** in the Navigation Pane to close it.

   The list of available forms collapses.

b. Click **Tables** in the Navigation Pane to expand it.

   The list of available tables expands. You need to assure yourself that the change you made to the Products form will transfer to the Products table.

c. Double-click the **Products table** to open it.

d. Click **Last record** on the navigation bar.

   The Products form was designed to make data entry easier. It is linked to the Products table. Your newly created record about the Pecan Pie product name is stored in the Products table even though you created it in the form.

e. Navigate to the fifth record in the table, *Chef Anton's Gumbo Mix*.

f. Use the horizontal scroll bar to scroll right until you see the *Discontinued* field.

   The check mark in the Discontinued check box tells you that this product has been discontinued.

g. Click the row selector box at the left of the window (see Figure 1.12).

   The row highlights with a gold-colored border.

h. Press **Delete**.

   An error message appears. It tells you that you cannot delete this record because the table, Order Details, has related records. Even though the product is now discontinued and none of it is in stock, it cannot be deleted from the table because related records are connected to it. A customer in the past ordered this product. If you first deleted all of the orders in the Order Details table that referenced this product, you would be permitted to delete the product from the Products table.

i. Read the error message. Click **OK**.

j. Navigate to the last record. Click the *row selector* to highlight the entire row.

k. Press **Delete**. STOP. Read the error message.

   A warning box appears. It tells you that this action cannot be undone. This product can be deleted because it was just created. No customers have ever ordered it so no related records are in the system.

l. Click **No**. You do not want to delete this record.

   TROUBLESHOOTING: If you clicked Yes and deleted the record, return to Step 4j. Reenter the information for this record. You will need it later in the lesson.

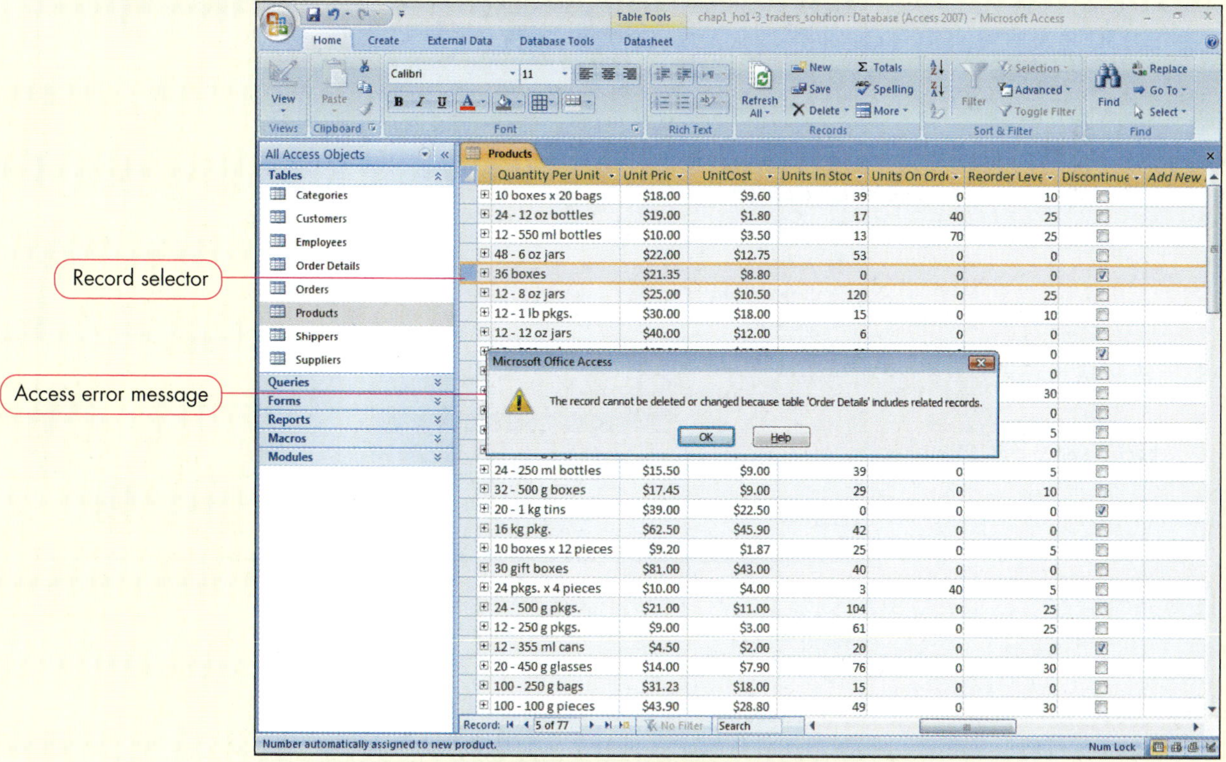

Figure 1.12 How Databases Work to Protect Data

Step 6
Back up and Compact the Database

Refer to Figure 1.13 as you complete Step 6.

a. Click the **Office Button** and select **Manage**.

   The Manage menu gives you access to three critically important tools.

b. Select **Compact and Repair Database**.

   Databases tend to get larger and larger as you use them. This feature acts as a defragmenter and eliminates wasted space. As it runs, it closes any open objects in the database.

c. Click the **Office Button**, select **Manage**, and then select **Back Up Database**.

   The Save As dialog box opens. The backup utility assigns a default name by adding a date to your file name.

d. Type **chap1_ho1_traders_solution** and click **Save**.

   You just created a backup of the database after completing the first hands-on exercise. The original database *chap1_ho1-3_traders_solution* remains onscreen. If you ruin the original database as you complete the second hands-on exercise, you can use the backup file you just created.

e. Close the file and exit Access if you do not want to continue with the next exercise at this time.

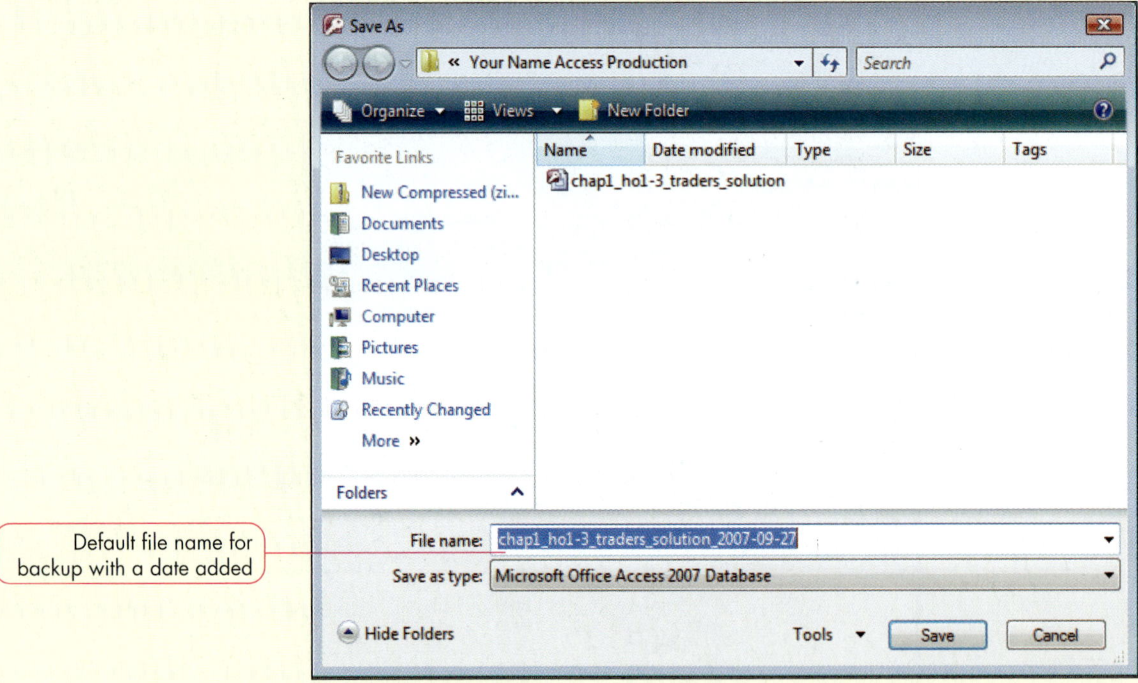

Figure 1.13 Save As Dialog Box to Back Up a Database

Filters, Sorts, and Access Versus Excel

Microsoft Office provides you with many tools that you may use to identify and extract only the records needed at the moment. For example, you might need to know which suppliers are located in New Orleans or which customers have not ordered any products in the last 60 days. You might use that information to identify possible disruptions to product deliveries or customers who may need a telephone call to see if all is well. Both Access and Excel contain powerful tools that enable you to sift through data and extract the information you need and arrange it in a way that makes sense to you. An important part of becoming a proficient computer user is recognizing when to use which tool to accomplish a task.

In this section you learn how to create filters to examine records and organize these records by sorting table data. You also will examine the logic of Access and Excel in more detail. You will investigate when to use which application to complete a given task.

Creating Filters

A ***filter*** lets you find a subset of data meeting your specifications.

In the first hands-on exercise, you used data from an existing table to obtain information from the database. You created new records and saw that the changes made in a form update data in the associated table data. You found the pecan pie, but you also saw lots of other products. When all of the information needed is contained in a single table, form, report, or query, you can open the object in the Datasheet view, and then apply a filter to display only the records of interest to you. A ***filter*** displays a subset of records; from the object according to specified criteria. You use filters to examine data. Applying a filter does not delete any records; it simply hides extraneous records from your view.

Figure 1.14 displays a Customers table with 91 records. The records in the table are displayed in sequence according to the CustomerID, which is also the primary key (the field or combination of fields that uniquely identifies a record). The navigation bar indicates that the active record is the sixth in the table. Let's explore how you would retrieve a partial list of those records, such as records of customers in Germany only.

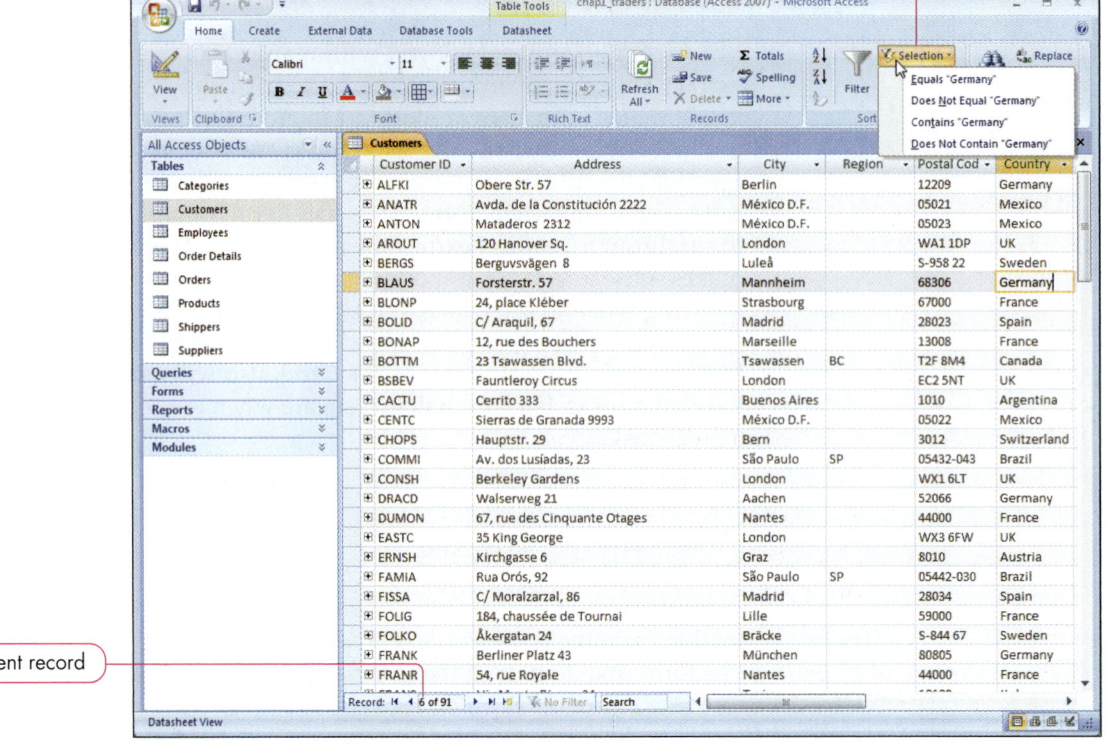

Figure 1.14 Unfiltered Table with Appropriate Sort Options Selected

Figure 1.15 displays a filtered view of the same table in which we see only the customers in Germany. The navigation bar shows that this is a filtered list and that the filter found 11 records satisfying the criteria. (The Customers table still contains the original 91 records, but only 11 records are visible with the filter applied.)

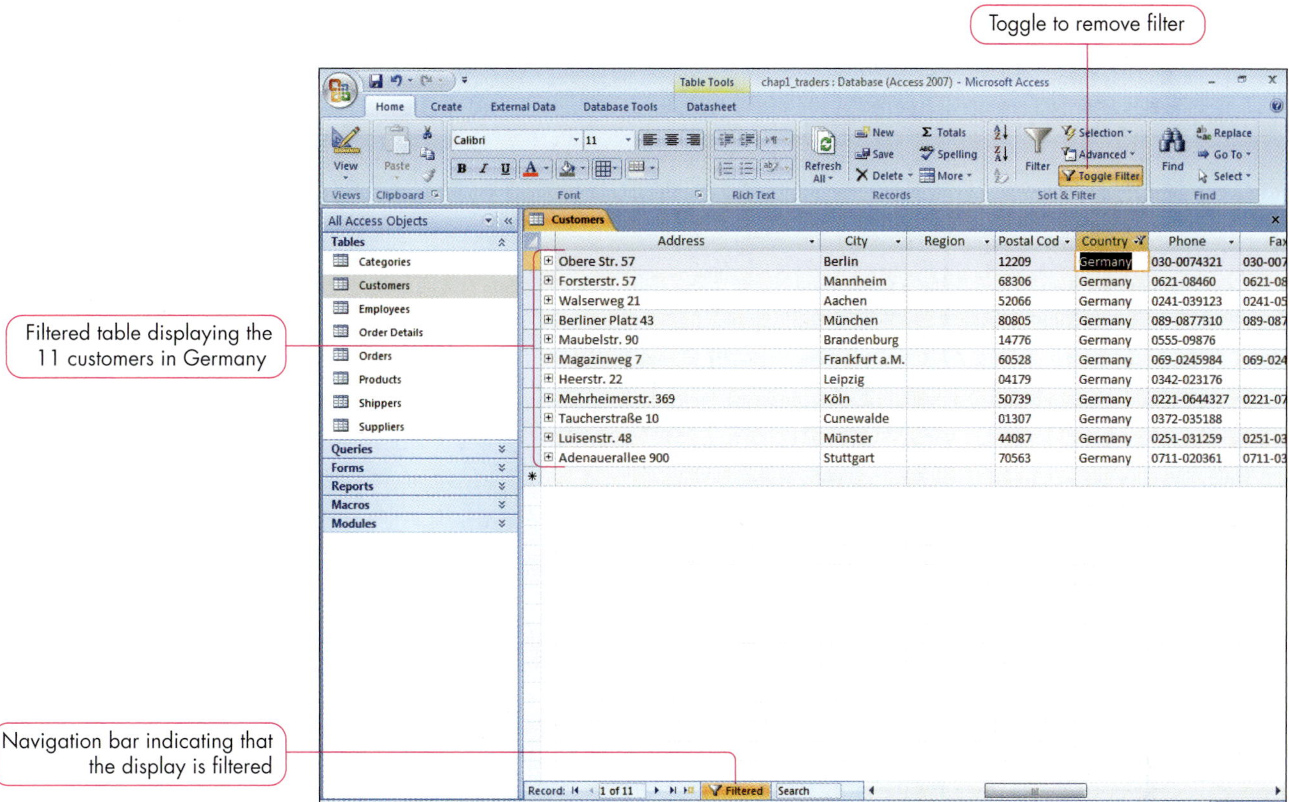

Figure 1.15 Filtered Table with Appropriate Sort Options Selected

> **TIP Use Quick Keyboard Shortcuts**
>
> Look for underlined letters in Access menus. They indicate the letters to use for the keyboard shortcuts. For example, when you click in a field and click the Selection down arrow in the Sort & Filter group, you can click the Equals "London" menu selection or simply type the letter e because the letter E in Equals is underlined, indicating a shortcut key.

Filter by Selection selects only the records that match the pre-selected criteria.

Filter by Form permits selecting criteria from a drop-down list, or applying multiple criteria.

An ***inequity*** examines a mathematical relationship such as equals, not equals, greater than, less than, greater than or equal to, or less than or equal to.

The easiest way to implement a filter is to click in any cell that contains the value of the desired criterion (such as any cell that contains *Account Rep* in the Title field), then click Filter by Selection in the Sort & Filter group. ***Filter by Selection*** selects only the records that match the pre-selected criteria.

Figure 1.16 illustrates an alternate and more powerful way to apply a filter. ***Filter by Form*** permits selecting the criteria from a drop-down list and/or applying multiple criteria simultaneously. However, the real advantage of the Filter by Form command extends beyond these conveniences to two additional capabilities. First, you can specify relationships within a criterion; for example, you can use an inequity setting to select products with an inventory level greater than (or less than) 30. An ***inequity*** examines a mathematical relationship such as equals, not equals, greater than, less than, greater than or equal to, or less than or equal to. Filter by Selection, on the other hand, requires you to specify criteria equal to an existing value. Figure 1.16 shows the filtered query setup to select Beverages with more than 30 units in stock.

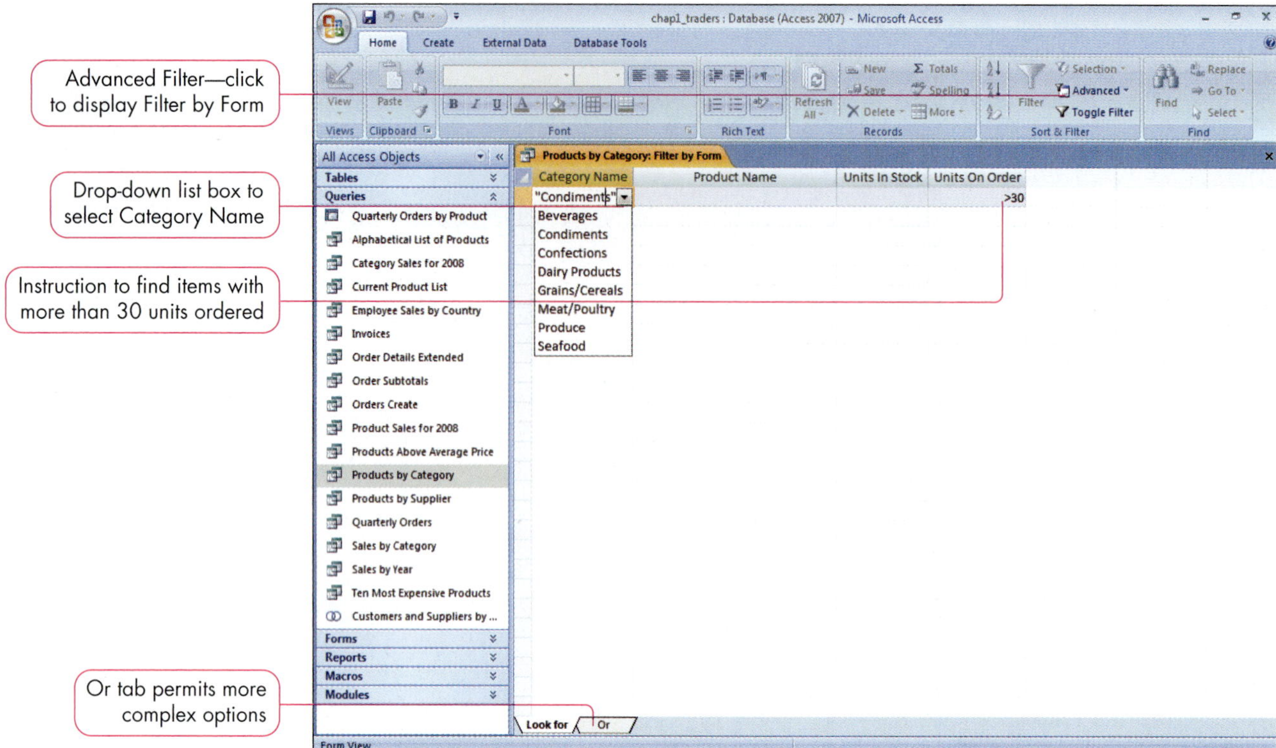

Figure 1.16 Filter by Form Design Grid

A second advantage of the Filter by Form command is that you can specify alternative criteria (such as customers in Germany or orders for over 30 units) by clicking the Or tab. (The latter capability is not implemented in Figure 1.16.) However, the availability of the various filter and sort commands enables you to obtain information from a database quickly and easily without creating a query or report.

Sorting Table Data on One or More Fields

A ***sort*** lists those records in a specific sequence, such as alphabetically by last name.

Sort Ascending provides an alphabetical list of text data or a small to large list of numeric data.

Sort Descending displays records with the highest value listed first.

You also can change the order of the information by sorting by one or more fields. A ***sort*** lists those records in a specific sequence, such as alphabetically by last name or by EmployeeID. To sort the table, click in the field on which you want to sequence the records (the LastName field in this example), then click Sort Ascending in the Sort & Filter group on the Home tab. ***Ascending*** provides an alphabetical list of text data or a small to large list of numeric data. ***Descending*** is appropriate for numeric fields such as salary, if you want to display the records with the highest value listed first. Figure 1.17 shows the Customers table sorted in alphabetical order by country. You may apply both filters and sorts to table or query information to select and order the data in the way that you need to make decisions.

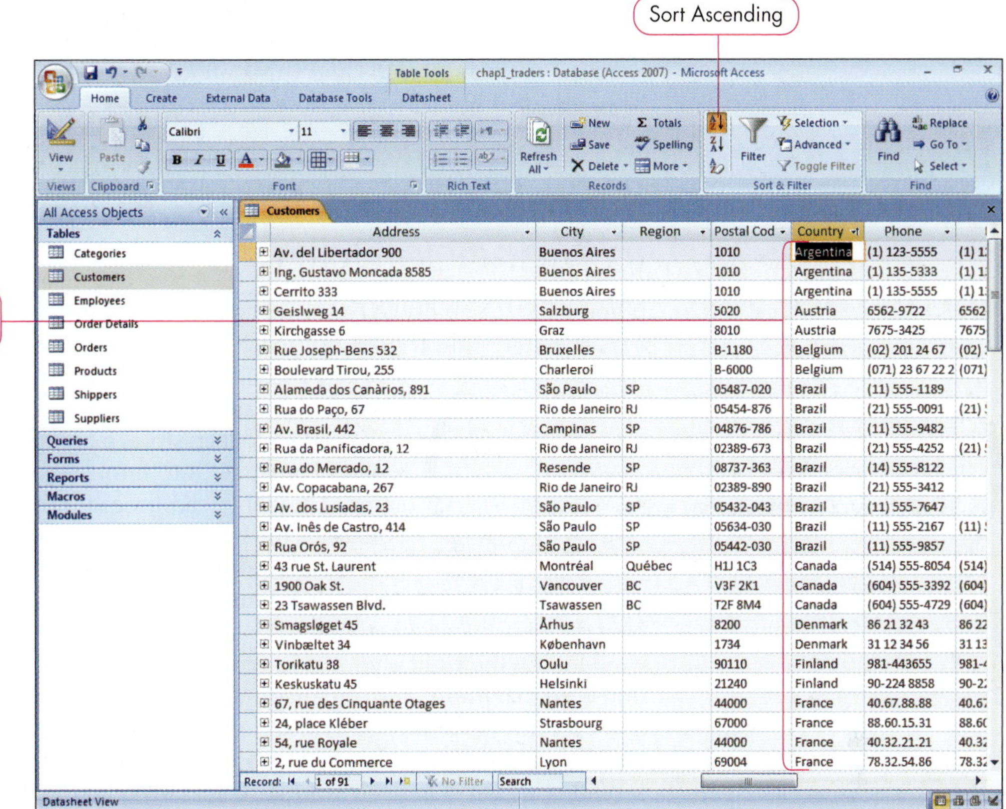

Figure 1.17 Customers Table Sorted by Country

The operations can be done in any order; that is, you can filter a table to show only selected records, then you can sort the filtered table to display the records in a different order. Conversely, you can sort a table and then apply a filter. It does not matter which operation is performed first, and indeed, you can go back and forth between the two. You can also filter the table further, by applying a second (or third) criterion; for example, click in a cell containing *USA* and apply a Filter by Selection. Then click in a record for Oregon (OR) and apply a Filter by Selection a second time to display the customers from Oregon. You also can click Toggle Filter at any time to display all of the records in the table. Filters are a temporary method for examining subsets of data. If you close the filtered table or query and reopen it, all of the records display.

TIP The Sort or Filter—Which is First?

It doesn't matter whether you sort a table and then apply a filter, or filter first and then sort. The operations are cumulative. Thus, after you sort a table, any subsequent display of filtered records for that table will be in the specified sequence. Alternatively, you can apply a filter and then sort the filtered table by clicking in the desired field and clicking the appropriate sort command. Remember, too, that all filter commands are cumulative, and hence you must remove the filter to see the original table.

You may be familiar with applying a filter, sorting data, or designing a form using Excel. The fact is, Excel can accomplish all of these activities. You need to examine your data needs and think about what your future data requirements may be to decide whether to use Access or Excel.

Knowing When to Use Access or Excel to Manage Data

If you have the ability to control data and turn it into useful information, you possess a marketable skill. It does not matter whether you are planning to become a social worker, a teacher, an engineer, an entrepreneur, a radiologist, a marketer, a day care worker, a musician, or an accountant. You will need to collect, store, maintain, manage, and protect data as well as convert it into information used to make strategic decisions. A widely used program that you probably already know is Excel. This book will help you become familiar with Access. You can accomplish many of the same things in either software. Although the two packages have much in common, they each have advantages. So, how do you choose whether to use Access or Excel?

(If you have the ability to control data and turn it into useful information, you possess a marketable skill.)

Making the right choice is critical if you want to find and update your information with maximum performance and accuracy. Ideally, your data needs and the type and amount of data used will determine how to pick the program that will work best. Sometimes organizations use Access when they probably would be better served with Excel and vice-versa. The answer to the question of which to use may depend on who you ask. An accountant probably will use Excel. The information technology professional probably will use a more sophisticated database software like Oracle, but not Access. The middle manager in the marketing or manufacturing department will probably use Access. The question remains.

Select the Software to Use

A contacts list is an example of flat data. Each column of data (names, addresses, and phone numbers) is logically related to the others. If you can store your data logically in a single table or worksheet, then do. Update your data in the same type of file. Data contained in a single page or sheet (not multiple) are called ***flat*** or ***non-relational data***. You would never store your friend's last name on a different sheet from the sheet containing the friend's cell phone number.

Data contained in a single page or sheet (not multiple) are called ***flat*** *or* ***non-relational data***.

Suppose you had a spreadsheet of club members' names and contact information. Your club decides to sell cookies as a fundraiser. You might create a new worksheet listing how many boxes of which type of cookie each member picked up to sell. Your third worksheet might show how much money each member has turned in from the cookie sales. These data are different. They are not flat. Can you imagine needing to know someone's phone number or how many cookie boxes he or she promised to sell while looking at the worksheet of data about how much money has been turned in? These data are multi-dimensional and need to be stored in more than one worksheet or table. This describes relational data. Each table holds a particular type of data (number of boxes collected, contact information, funds turned in). Relational data are best stored in Access. In this example, you would create a database with three tables. You need to adhere to the following rules about assigning data to the appropriate table.

Assign table data so that each table:

- Represents only a single subject
- Has a field(s) that uniquely identifies each record
- Does not contain duplicate fields
- Has no repetition of the same type of value
- Has no fields belonging in other tables

As the quantity and complexity of data increase, the need to organize it efficiently also increases. Access affords better data organization than Excel. Access accomplishes the organization through a system of linkages among the tables. Each record (row) should be designated with a primary key—a unique identifier that sets it apart from all of the other records in the table. The primary key might be an account number, a student identification number, or an employee access code. All data in Excel have a unique identifier—the cell address. In life, you have a Social Security Number. It's the best unique identifier you have. Ever notice how, when at the doctor's office or applying for college admission, you are asked for your Social Security Number as well as your name? Your record in its database system probably uses your Social Security Number as a unique identifier.

You still need to answer the question of when to use Access and when to use Excel.

Use Access

You should use Access to manage data when you:

- Require a relational database (multiple tables or multi-dimensional tables) to store your data or anticipate adding more tables in the future.

  For example, you may set your club membership contact list in either software, but if you believe that you also will need to keep track of the cookie sales and fund collection, use Access.
- Have a large amount of data.
- Rely on external databases to derive and analyze the data you need.

  If frequently you need to have Excel exchange data to or from Access, use Access. Even though the programs are compatible, it makes sense to work in Access to minimize compatibility issues.
- Need to maintain constant connectivity to a large external database, such as one built with Microsoft SQL Server or your organization's Enterprise Resource Planning system.
- Need to regroup data from different tables in a single place through complex queries.

  You might need to create output showing how many boxes of cookies each club member picked up and how much money they turned in along with the club member's name and phone number.
- Have many people working in the database and need strong options to update the data.

  For example, five different clerks at an auto parts store might wait on five different customers. Each clerk connects to the inventory table to find out if the needed part is in stock and where in the warehouse it is located. When the customer says, "Yes, I want that" the inventory list is instantly updated and that product is no longer available to be purchased by the other four customers.

Use Excel

You should use Excel to manage data when you:

- Require a flat or non-relational view of your data (you do not need a relational database with multiple tables).

  This idea is especially true if that data is mostly numeric—for example, if you need to maintain an expense statement.
- Want to run primarily calculations and statistical comparisons on your data.
- Know your dataset is manageable in size (no more than 15,000 rows).

  In the next exercise you will create and apply filters, perform sorts, and develop skills to customize the data presentation to answer your questions.

Hands-On Exercises

2 | Data Manipulation: Filters and Sorts

Skills covered: 1. Use Filter by Selection with an Equal Setting **2.** Use Filter by Selection with a Contains Setting **3.** Use Filter by Form with an Inequity Setting **4.** Sort a Table

Step 1
Use Filter by Selection with an Equal Setting

Refer to Figure 1.18 as you complete Step 1.

a. Open the *chap1_ho1-3_traders_solution* file if necessary, and click **Options** on the Security Warning toolbar, click the **Enable this content option** in the Microsoft Office Security Options dialog box, and click **OK**.

TROUBLESHOOTING: If you create unrecoverable errors while completing this hands-on exercise, you can delete the chap1_ho1-3_traders_solution file, copy the chap1_ho1_traders_solution backup database you created at the end of the first hands-on exercise, and open the copy of the backup database to start the second hands-on exercise again.

b. Open the **Customers table**; navigate to record 4 and replace *Thomas Hardy's* name with **your name** in the **Contact Name field**.

c. Scroll right until the **City field** is visible. Look through the record values of the field until you locate a customer in **London**, for example, the fourth record. Click in the field box to select it.

The word *"London"* will have a gold colored border around it to let you know that it is active.

d. Click **Selection** in the Sort & Filter group on the Home tab.

e. Choose **Equals "London"** from the menu.

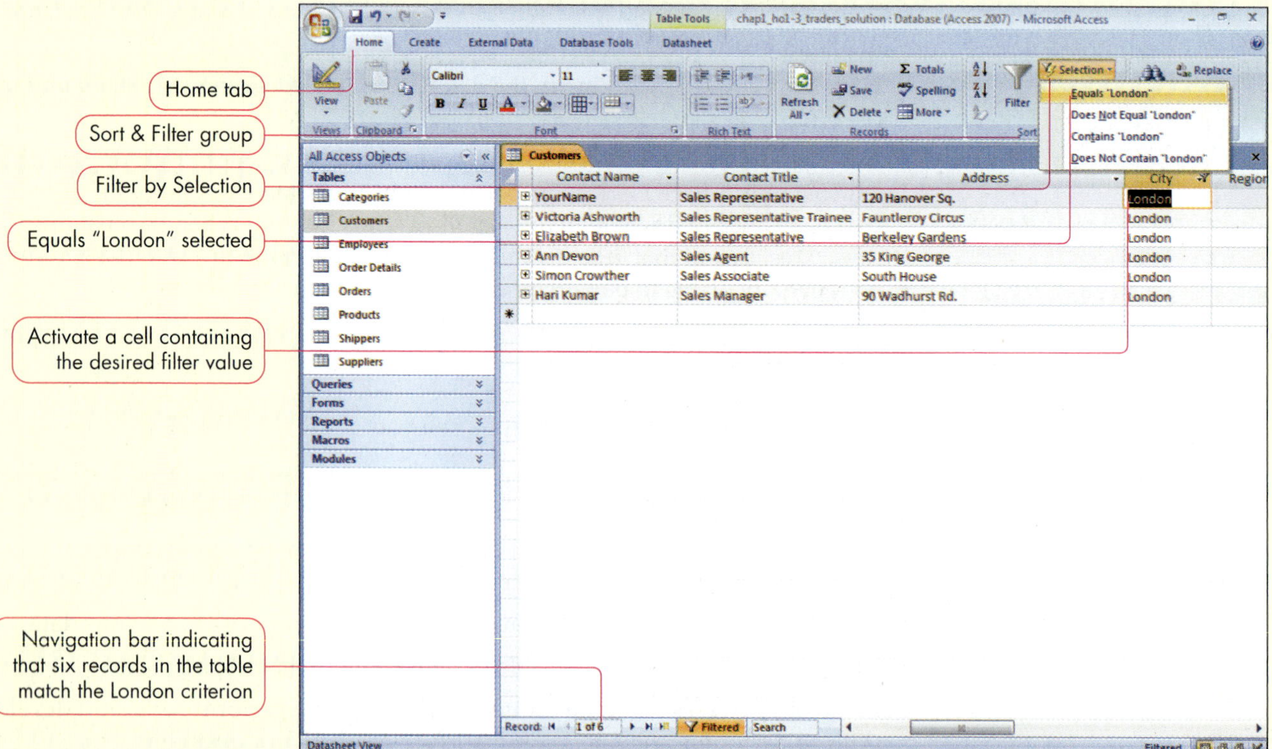

Figure 1.18 Customers Table Filtered to Display London Records Only

Step 2
Use Filter by Selection with a Contains Setting

Refer to Figure 1.19 as you complete Step 2.

a. Find a record with the value **Sales Representative** in the **Contact Title field**. Click your insertion point to activate that field. The first record has a value of *Sales Representative* for the Contact Title field.

   Sales Representative will have a gold colored border around it to let you know that it is activated.

b. Click **Selection** on the Sort & Filter group located on the Home tab.

c. Click **Contains "Sales Representative"**.

   You have applied a second layer of filtering to the customers in London. The second layer further restricts the display to only those customers who have the words Sales Representative contained in their title.

d. Scroll left until you see your name. Compare your results to those shown in Figure 1.19.

e. Click the **Office Button**, position the mouse pointer over **Print**, and then select **Quick Print**.

f. Click **Toggle Filter** in the Sort & Filter group to remove the filters.

g. Close the Customers table. Click **No** if a dialog box asks if you want to save the design changes to the Customers table.

TIP Removing Versus Deleting a Filter

Removing a filter displays all of the records that are in a table, but it does not delete the filter because the filter is stored permanently with the table. To delete the filter entirely is more complicated than simply removing it. Click Advanced on the Sort & Filter group and select the Clear All Filters option from the drop-down list box. Deleting unnecessary filters may reduce the load on the CPU and will allow the database manager to optimize the database performance.

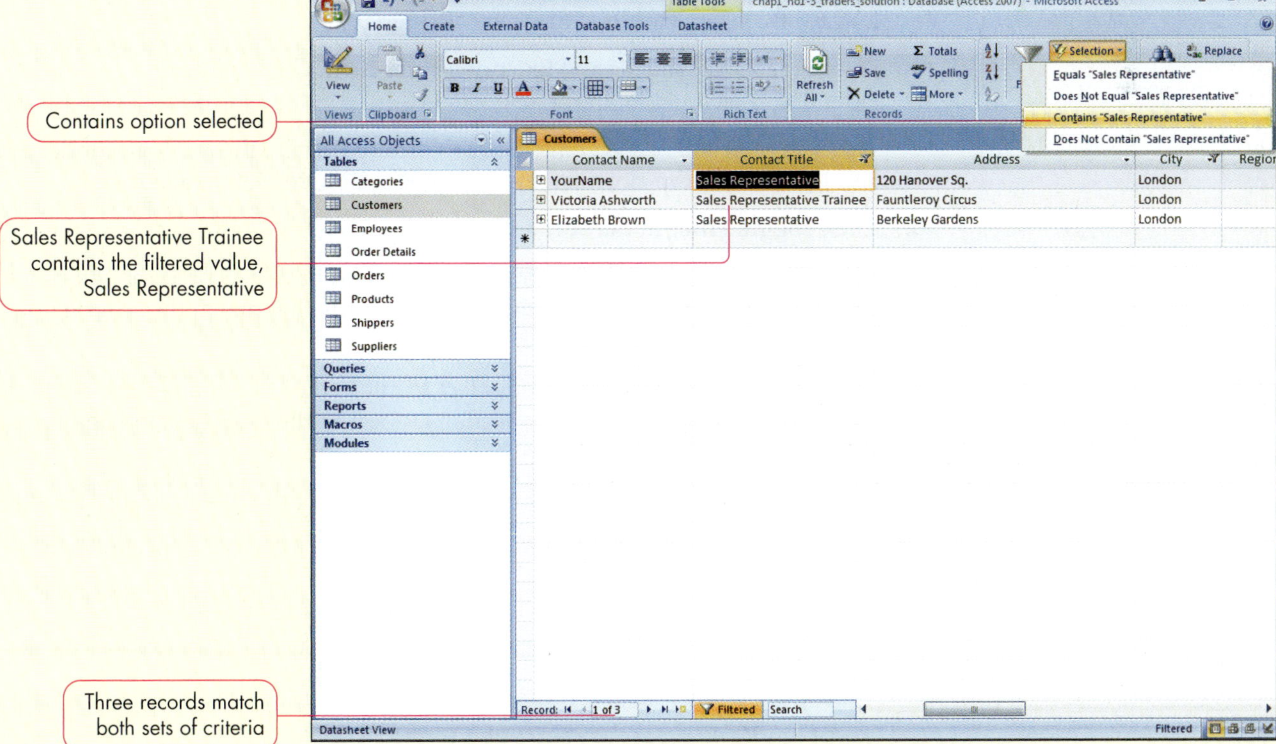

Figure 1.19 Customers Table Filtered to Display London and Sales Representative Job Titles

Step 3
Use Filter by Form with an Inequity Setting

Refer to Figure 1.20 as you complete Step 3.

a. Click **Tables** in the Navigation Pane to collapse the listed tables.

b. Click **Queries** in the Navigation Pane to expand the lists of available queries.

c. Locate and double-click the **Order Details Extended** query to open it.

   This query contains information about orders. It has fields containing information about the salesperson, the Order ID, the product name, the unit price, quantity ordered, the discount given, and an extended price. The extended price is a term used to total order information.

d. Click **Advanced** in the Sort & Filter group on the Home tab.

   The process to apply a filter by form is identical in a table or a query.

e. Select **Filter By Form** from the list.

   All of the records seem to vanish and you see only a list of field names.

f. Click in the **first row** under the **First Name** field.

   A down arrow appears at the right of the box.

g. Click the **First Name down arrow**. A list of all available first names appears.

   Your name should be on the list. It may be in a different location than that shown in Figure 1.20 because the list is in alphabetical order.

   TROUBLESHOOTING: If you do not see your name and you do see Margaret on the list, you probably skipped Steps 3c and 3d in Hands-On Exercise 1. Close the query without saving changes, turn back to the first hands-on exercise, and rework it, making sure not to omit any steps. Then you can return to this spot and work the remainder of this hands-on exercise.

h. Select **your first name** from the list.

i. Click in the *first row* under the *Last Name field* to turn on the drop-down arrow. Locate and select **your last name** by clicking it.

j. Scroll right until you see the Extended Price field. Click in the *first row* under the Extended Price field and type **<50**.

   This will select all of the items that you ordered where the total was under $50. You ignore the drop-down arrow and type the expression needed.

k. Click **Toggle Filter** in the Sort & Filter group.

   You have specified which records to include and have executed the filtering by clicking Toggle Filter. You should have 31 records that match the criteria you specified.

l. Click the **Office Button** and then select **Print**. In the Print dialog box locate the **Pages** control in the *Print Range* section. Type **1** in the *From* box and again in the *To* box. Click **OK**.

   You have instructed Access to print the first page of the filtered query results.

m. Close the query. Click **No** when asked if you want to save the design changes.

TIP Deleting Filter by Form Criterion

The Filter by Form command has all of the capabilities of the Filter by Selection command and provides two additional capabilities. First, you can use relational operators such as >, >=, <, or <= as opposed to searching for an exact value. Second, you can search for records that meet one of several conditions (the equivalent of an "Or" operation). Enter the first criterion as you normally would, then click the Or tab at the bottom of the window to display a second form in which you enter the alternate criteria. (To delete an alternate criterion, click the associated tab, and then click Delete on the toolbar.)

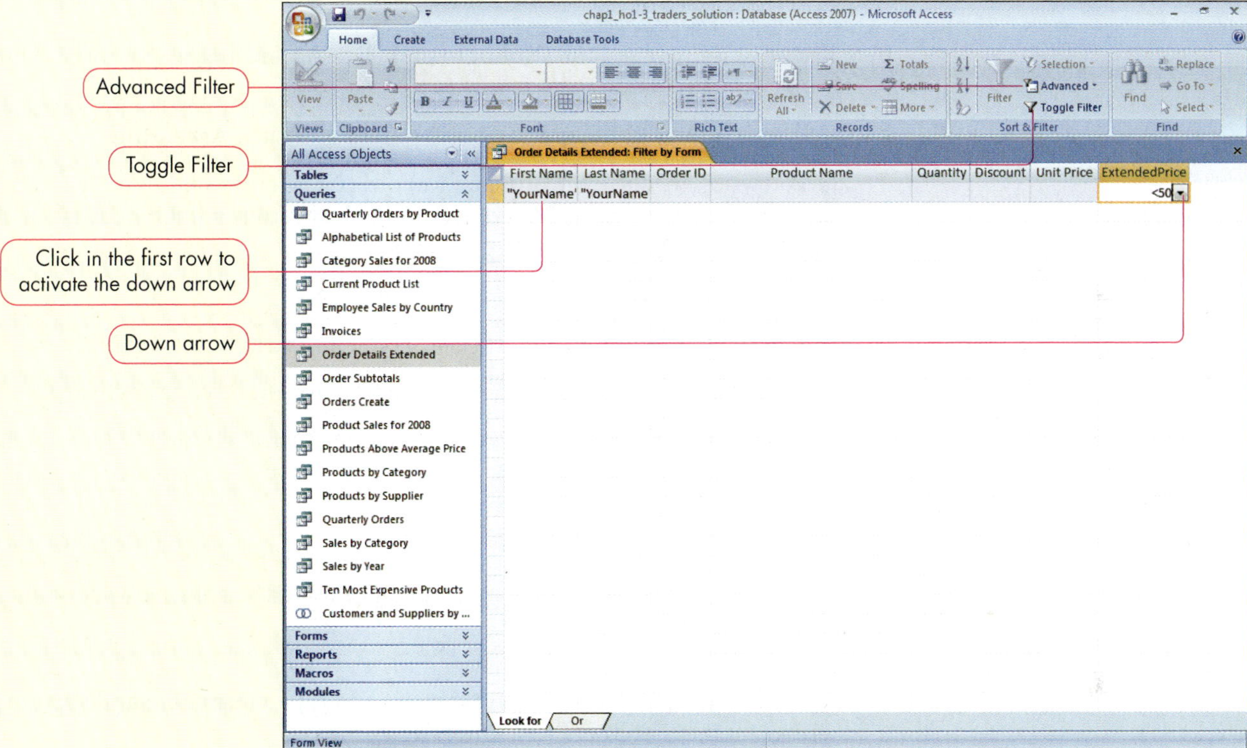

Figure 1.20 Filter by Selection Criteria Settings

Step 4 Sort a Table

Refer to Figure 1.21 as you complete Step 4.

a. Click **Queries** in the Navigation Pane to collapse the listed queries.

b. Click **Tables** in the Navigation Pane to expand the lists of available tables.

c. Locate and double-click the **Customers table** to open it.

   This table contains information about customers. It is sorted in ascending order by the Customer ID field. Because this field contains text, the table is sorted in alphabetical order.

d. Click any value in the **Customer ID field**. Click **Descending** in the Sort & Filter group on the Home tab.

   Sorting in descending order on a character field produces a reverse alphabetical order.

e. Scroll right until you can see both the **Country** and the **City fields**.

You will sort the customers by country and then by city within the countries. You can sort on more than one field as long as you sort on the primary field (in this case the country) last.

f. Click the field name for **Country**.

The entire column selects.

g. Click the **Country field name box** and hold the left mouse down.

A thick dark blue line displays on the left edge of the Country field column.

h. Check to make sure that you see the thick blue line. When you do, drag the country field to the **left**. When the thick black line moves to between the *Address and City* fields, release the mouse, and the Country field position moves to the left of the City field.

i. Click any city name in the **City field** and click **Ascending** in the Sort & Filter group.

j. Click any country name in the **Country field** and click **Ascending**.

The countries are sorted in alphabetical order. The cities within each country also are sorted alphabetically. For example, the customer in Graz, Austria, is listed before the one in Saltzburg.

k. Scroll down until you see the *UK* customers listed.

l. Scroll to the left until the *Contact Name* is the first field in the left of the screen.

m. Press **PrntScrn** located somewhere in the upper right of your keyboard.

You have captured a picture of your screen. If nothing seemed to happen, it is because the picture was saved to the Clipboard. You must retrieve the picture from the Clipboard in order to see it.

TROUBLESHOOTING: Some notebook computers have Print Screen as a function. If the words Print Screen on the key are a different color, you must press **Fn+Print Screen**.

n. Launch Word, open a *new blank document*, and type **your name and section number** on the first line. Press **Enter**.

o. Press **Ctrl+V** to paste your picture of the screenshot into the Word document. Save the document as **chap1_ho2_traders_solution.docx**. Print the Word document. Close Word.

p. Close the **Customers table**. Do not save the changes.

q. Click the **Office Button**, select **Manage**, and then select **Compact and Repair Database**.

r. Click the **Office Button** again, select **Manage**, and then select **Back Up Database**. Type **chap1_ho2_traders_solution** as the file name and click **Save**.

You just created a backup of the database after completing the second hands-on exercise. The original database *chap1_ho1-3_traders_solution* remains onscreen. If you ruin the original database as you complete the third hands-on exercise, you can use the backup file you just created.

s. Close the file and exit Access if you do not want to continue with the next exercise at this time.

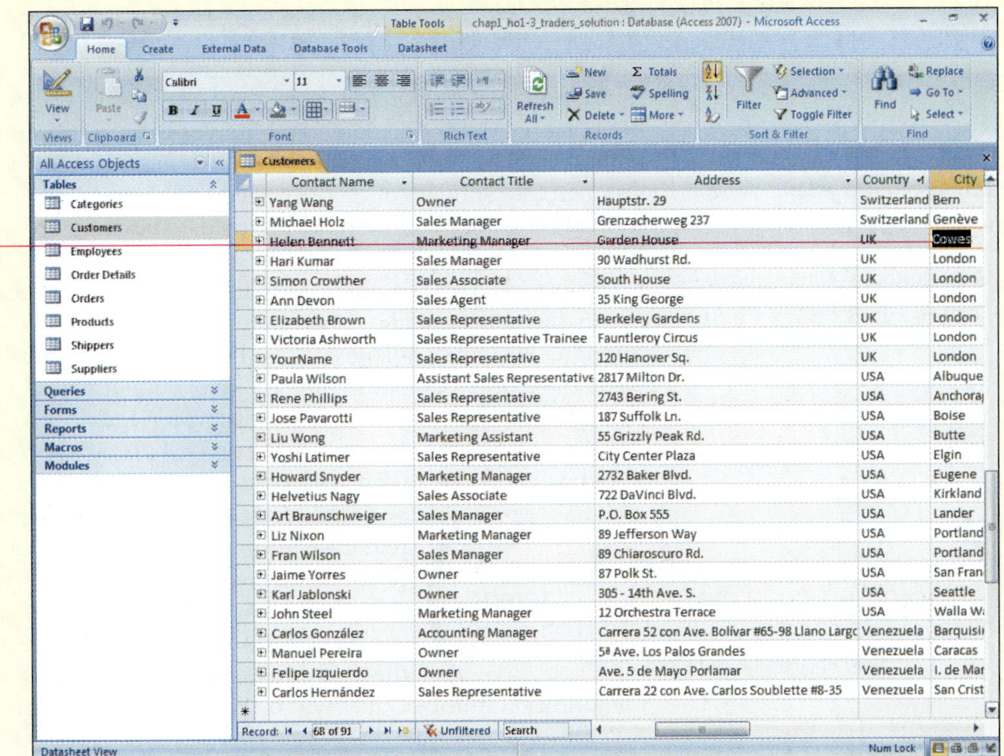
The Cowes customer lists before the London customers

Figure 1.21 The Customers Table Sorted by Country and then City

The Relational Database

A ***relational database management system*** is one in which data are grouped into similar collections, called tables, and the relationships between tables are formed by using a common field.

In the previous section you read that you should use Access when you have multidimensional data. Access derives power from multiple tables and the relationships among those tables. A ***relational database management system*** is one in which data are grouped into similar collections called tables, and the relationships between tables are formed by using a common field or fields. The design of a relational database system is illustrated in Figure 1.22. The power of a relational database lies in the software's ability to organize data and combine items in different ways to obtain a complete picture of the events the data describe. Good database design connects the data in different tables through a system of linkages. These links are the relationships that give relational databases the name. Look at Figure 1.1. The student record (folder) contains information about the student, but also contains cross-references to data stored in other cabinet drawers, such as the advisor's name or a list of courses completed. If you need to know the advisor's phone number, you can open the faculty drawer, find the advisor's record, and then locate the field containing the phone number. The cross-reference from the student file to the faculty file illustrates how a relationship works in a database. Figure 1.22 displays the cross-references between the tables as a series of lines connecting the common fields. When the database is set up properly, the users of the data can be confident that if they search a specific customer identification number, they will be given accurate information about that customer's order history and payment balances, and his/her product or shipping preferences.

(The power of a relational database lies in the software's ability to organize data and combine items in different ways to obtain a complete picture of the events the data describe.)

In this section, you will explore the relationships among tables, learn about the power of relational integrity, and discover how the software protects the organization's data.

Using the Relationships Window

A ***foreign key*** is a field in one table that also is stored in a different table as a primary key.

The relationship (the lines between the tables in Figure 1.22) is like a piece of electronic string that travels throughout the database, searching every record of every table until it finds the data satisfying the user's request. Once identified, the fields and records of interest will be tied to the end of the string, pulled through the computer and reassembled in a way that makes the data easy to understand. The first end of the string was created when the primary key was established in the Customers table. The primary key is a unique identifier for each table record. The other end of the string will be tied to a field in a different table. If you examine Figure 1.22, you will see that the CustomerID is a foreign field in the Orders table. A ***foreign key*** is a field in one table that also is stored in a different table as a primary key. Each value of the CustomerID can occur only once in the Customers table because it is a primary key. However, the CustomerID may appear multiple times in the Orders table because one customer may make many different purchases. The CustomerID field is a foreign key in the Orders table but the primary key in the Customers table.

Examine Referential Integrity

Referential integrity is the set of rules that ensure that data stored in related tables remain consistent as the data are updated.

The relationships connecting the tables will be created using an Access feature that uses referential integrity. Integrity means truthful or reliable. When ***referential integrity*** is enforced, the user can trust the "threads" running through the database and "tying" related items together. The sales manager can use the database to find the names and phone numbers of all the customers who have ordered Teatime Chocolate Biscuits (a specific product). Because referential integrity has been enforced, it will not matter that the order information is in a different table from the customer data. The invisible threads will keep the information accurately connected. The threads also provide a method of ensuring data accuracy. You cannot enter a record in the Orders table that references a CustomerID, EmployeeID, or ShipperID that does not exist elsewhere in the system. Nor can you easily delete a record in one table if it has related records in related tables.

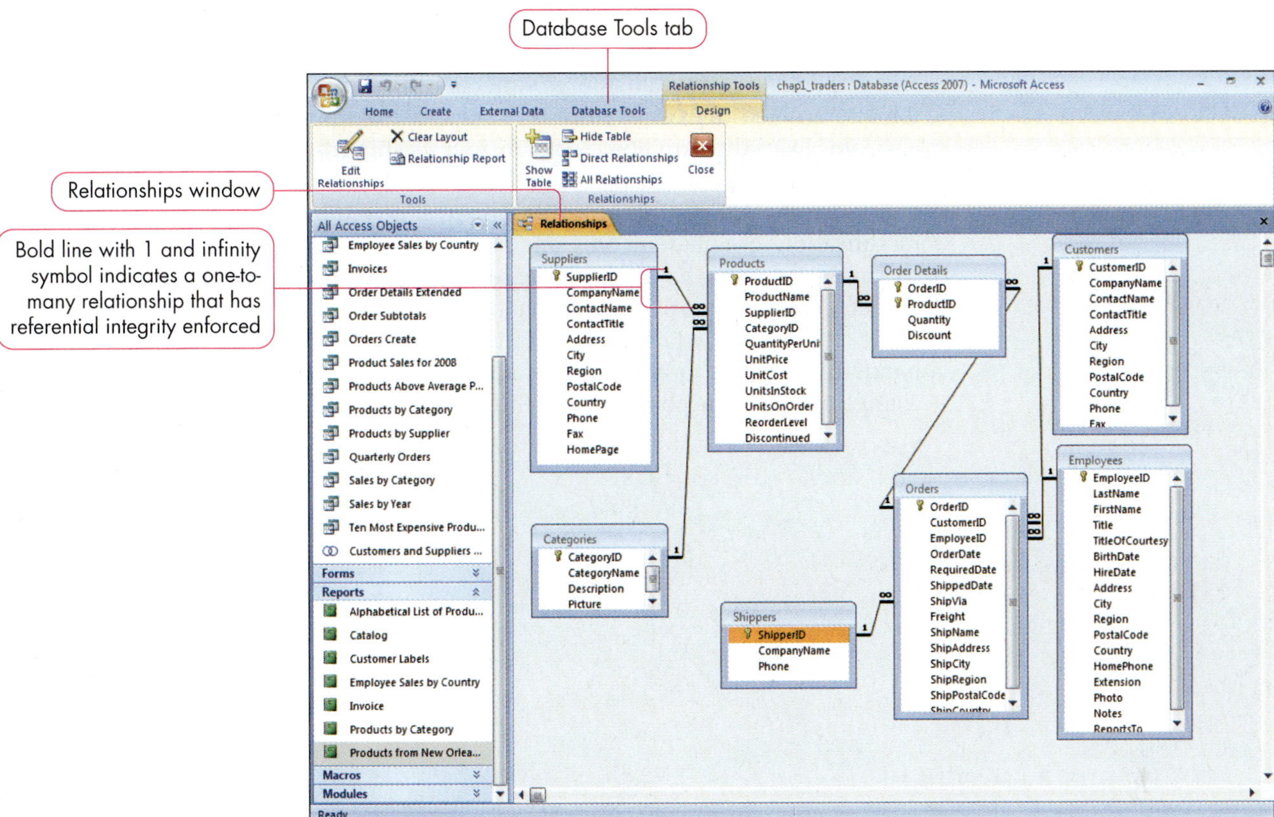

Figure 1.22 The Relationships Window Displaying Table Connections

If this were a real organization's data system, the files would be much, much larger and the data more sophisticated. When learning database skills, you should start with smaller, more manageable files. The same design principles apply regardless of the database size. A small file gives you the ability to check the tables and see if your results are correct. Even though the data amounts are small, you need to develop the work practices needed to manage large amounts of data. With only a handful of records, you can easily count the number of employees at the Washington state office. In addition to learning how to accomplish a task, you also should begin to learn to anticipate the computer's response to an instruction. As you work, ask yourself what the anticipated results should be and then verify. When you become skilled at anticipating output correctly, you are surprised less often.

(As you work, ask yourself what the anticipated results should be and then verify. When you become skilled at anticipating output correctly, you are surprised less often.)

Understanding Relational Power

In the previous section you read that you should use Access when you have multidimensional data. Access derives power from multiple tables and the relationships between those tables. This type of database is known as a relational database and is illustrated in Figure 1.22. This figure describes the database structure. Examine some of the connections. The EmployeeID is a foreign field in the Orders table. For example, you can produce a document displaying the history of each order a customer had placed and the employee's name (from the Employees table) that entered the order. The Orders table references the Order Details table where the OrderID is a foreign field. The ProductID relates to the Products table (where it is the primary key). The CategoryID is the primary key in the Categories table, but shows up as a foreign field in the Products table. The table connections, even when more than one table is involved, provide the decision-maker power. This feature gives the manager the ability to find out sales by category. How many different beverages were shipped last week? What was the total revenue generated from seafood orders last year?

Suppose a customer called to complain that his orders were arriving late. Because the ShipperID is a foreign field in the Orders table, you could look up which shipper delivered that customer's merchandise and then find out what other customers received deliveries from that shipper the same month. Are the other orders also late? Does the firm need to reconsider its shipping options? The design of a relational database enables us to extract information from multiple tables in a single query or report. Equally important, it simplifies the way data are changed in that modifications are made in only one place.

In the previous hands-on exercises, you have made modifications to table data. You created a new product, you changed an employee and customer name to your name, and you sorted data. You will trace through some of those changes in the next hands-on exercise to help you understand the power of relationships and how a change made to one object travels throughout the database file structure.

Hands-On Exercises

3 | Introduction to Relationships

Skills covered: 1. Examine the Relationships Window **2.** Discover that Changes in Table Data Affect Queries **3.** Use Filter by Form with an Inequity Setting and Reapply a Saved Filter **4.** Filter a Report **5.** Remove an Advanced Filter

Step 1 Examine the Relationships Window

Refer to Figure 1.23 as you complete Step 1.

a. Open the *chap1_ho1-3_traders_solution* file if necessary, click **Options** on the *security warning* toolbar, click the **Enable this content option** in the Microsoft Office Security Options dialog box, and click **OK**.

   TROUBLESHOOTING: If you create unrecoverable errors while completing this hands-on exercise, you can delete the *chap1_ho1-3_traders_solution* file, copy the *chap1_ho2_traders_solution* database you created at the end of the second hands-on exercise, and open the copy of the backup database to start the third hands-on exercise again.

b. Click the **Database Tools tab** and click **Relationships** in the Show/Hide group.

   Examine the relationships that connect the various tables. For example, the Products table is connected to the Suppliers, Categories, and Order Details tables.

c. Click **Show Table** in the Relationships group on the Relationship Tools Design tab.

   The Show Table dialog box opens. It tells you that there are eight available tables in the database. If you look in the Relationships window, you will see that all eight tables are in the relationship diagram.

d. Click the **Queries tab** in the Show Table dialog box.

   You could add all of the queries to the Relationships window. Things might become cluttered, but you could tell at a glance where the queries get their information.

e. Close the Show Table dialog box.

f. Click **All Access Objects** on the Navigation Pane.

g. Select **Tables and Related Views**.

   You can now see not only the tables, but also the queries, forms, and reports that connect to the table data. If a query is sourced on more than one table, it appears multiple times in the Navigation Pane. This view provides an alternate method of viewing the relationships connecting the tables.

h. Close the Relationships window.

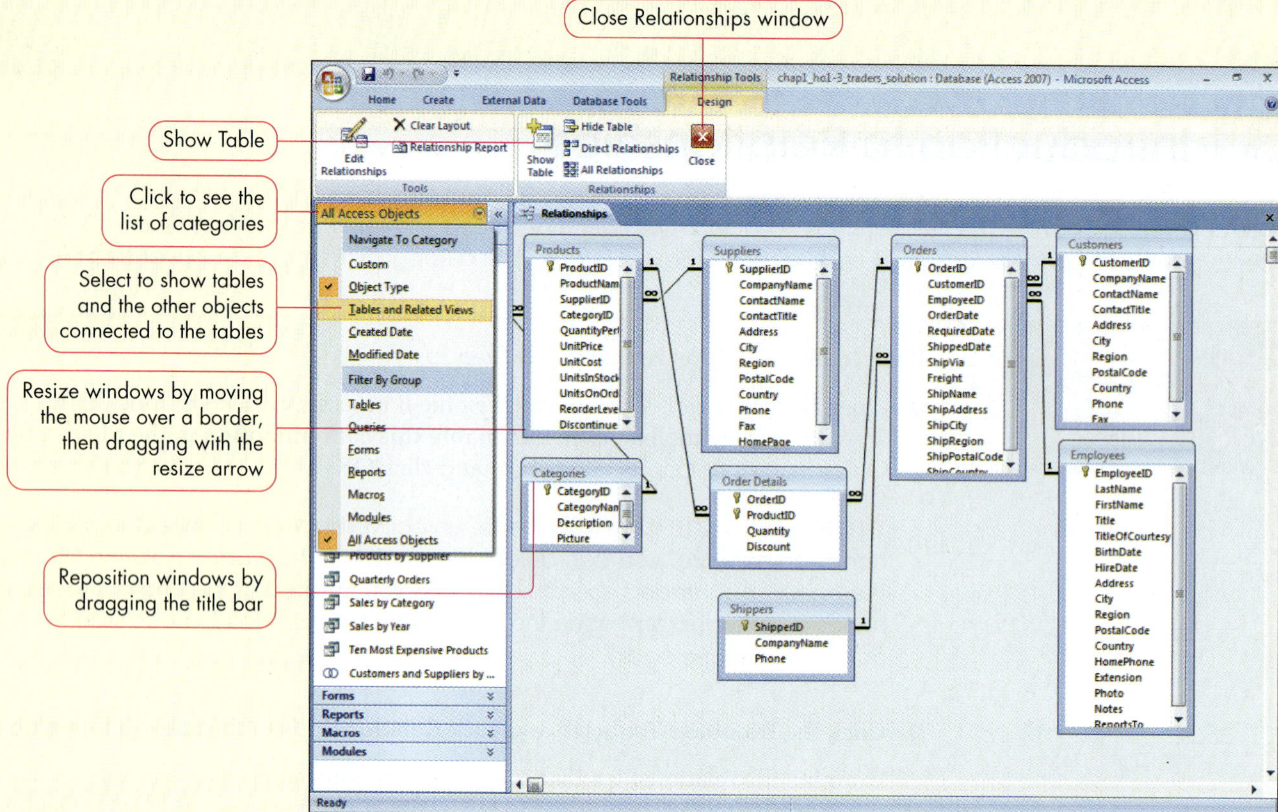

Close Relationships window
Show Table
Click to see the list of categories
Select to show tables and the other objects connected to the tables
Resize windows by moving the mouse over a border, then dragging with the resize arrow
Reposition windows by dragging the title bar

Figure 1.23 The Relationships Window Displaying the Northwind Table Relationships

Step 2
Discover that Changes in Table Data Affect Queries

Refer to Figure 1.24 as you complete Step 2.

a. Scroll in the Navigation Pane until you see the Products group. Locate and double-click the **Order Details Extended query**.

b. Examine the icons on the left edge of the Navigation Pane. Figure 1.24 identifies the object type for each of the objects.

c. Find an occurrence of *your last name* anywhere in the query (record 7 should show your name) and click your last name to make it active.

   The query contains your name because in Hands-On Exercise 1 you replaced Margaret Peacock's name in the Employees table with your name. The Employees table is related to the Orders table, the Orders table to the Order Details table, and the Order Details table to the Products table. Therefore, any change you make to the Employees table is carried throughout the database via the relationships.

d. Click **Selection** in the Sort & Filter group. Select **Equals "YourName"** from the selection menu.

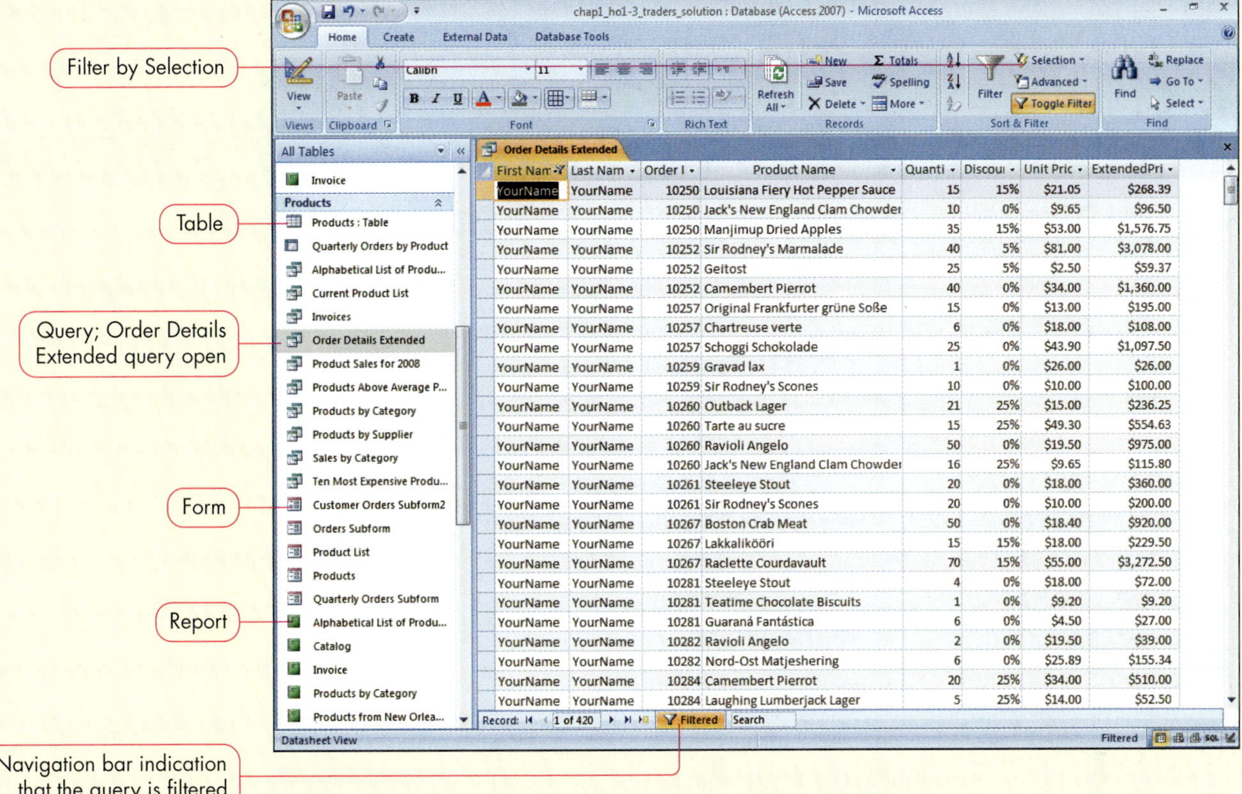

Figure 1.24 Filtered Query Results

Step 3

Use Filter by Form with an Inequity Setting and Reapply a Saved Filter

Refer to Figure 1.25 as you complete Step 3.

a. Click **Advanced Filter Options** in the Sort & Filter group.

b. Select **Filter By Form** from the drop-down list.

   Because you already applied a filter to these data, the Filter By Form design sheet opens with one criterion already filled in. Your name displays in the selection box under the Last Name field.

c. Scroll right (or press **Tab**) until the Extended Price field is visible. Click the insertion point in the **first row** under the Extended Price field.

d. Type **>2000**.

   The Extended Price field shows the purchased amount for each item ordered. If an item sold for $15 and a customer ordered 10, the Extended Price would display $150.

e. Click **Toggle Filter** in the Sort & Filter group. Examine the filtered results.

   Your inequity instruction, >2000, identified the items ordered where the extended price exceeded $2,000.

f. Press **Ctrl+S** to save the query. Close the query by clicking the X in the object window.

g. Open the **Order Details Extended query**.

   The filter disengages when you close and reopen the object. However, your filtering directions have been stored with the query design. You may reapply the filter at any time by clicking the Toggle Filter command.

h. Click **Toggle Filter** in the Sort & Filter group.

i. Compare your work to Figure 1.25. If it is correct, close the query.

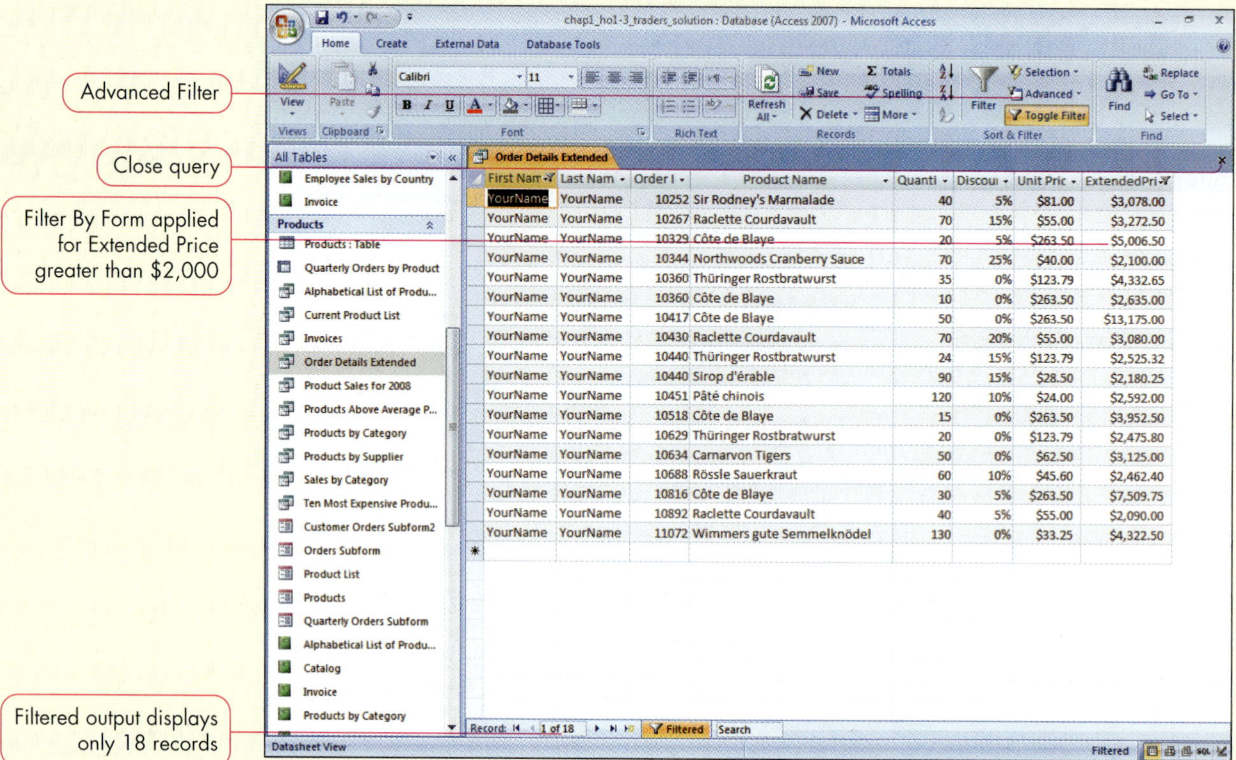

Figure 1.25 Filtered Query Results after Limiting Output to Extended Prices over $2,000

Step 4
Filter a Report

Refer to Figure 1.26 as you complete Step 4.

a. Open the **Products by Category report** located in the Products group on the Navigation Pane. You may need to scroll down to locate it.

The report should open in Print Preview with a gray stripe highlighting the report title. The Print Preview displays the report exactly as it will print. This report was formatted to display in three columns.

TROUBLESHOOTING: If you do not see the gray stripe and three columns, you probably opened the wrong object. The database also contains a Product by Category query. It is the source for the Products by Category report. Make sure you open the report (shown with the green report icon) and not the query. Close the query and open the report.

b. Examine the Confections category products. You should see **Your Name Pecan Pie**.

You created this product by entering data in a form in Hands-On Exercise 1. You later discovered that changes made to a form affect the related table. Now you see that other related objects also change when the source data changes.

c. Right-click the **gold report tab** within Products by Category. Select **Report View** from the shortcut menu.

The Report view displays the information a little differently. It no longer shows three columns. If you clicked the Print command while in Report view, the columns would print even though you do not see them. The Report view permits limited data interaction (for example, filtering).

d. Scroll down in the report until you see the title *Category: Confections*. **Right-click** the word **Confections** in the title. Select **Equals "Confections"** from the shortcut menu.

Right-clicking a selected data value in an Access table, query, form, or report activates a shortcut to a Filter by Selection menu. Alternatively, you can click the selected value, in this case, Confections, and then click Selection in the Sort & Filter group.

e. Right-click the **gold report tab** within Products by Category. Select **Print Preview** from the shortcut menu.

You need to print this report. Always view your reports in Print Preview prior to printing.

f. Click **Print** in Print group on the Print Preview tab, and then click **OK** to produce a printed copy of the filtered report.

You can bypass the Print dialog box by clicking the Office Button, positioning the mouse over Print, and then selecting Quick Print. The Quick Print command sends your work to the default printer as soon as you click it. You can use this safely when you have already viewed your work in Print Preview.

g. Save and close the report.

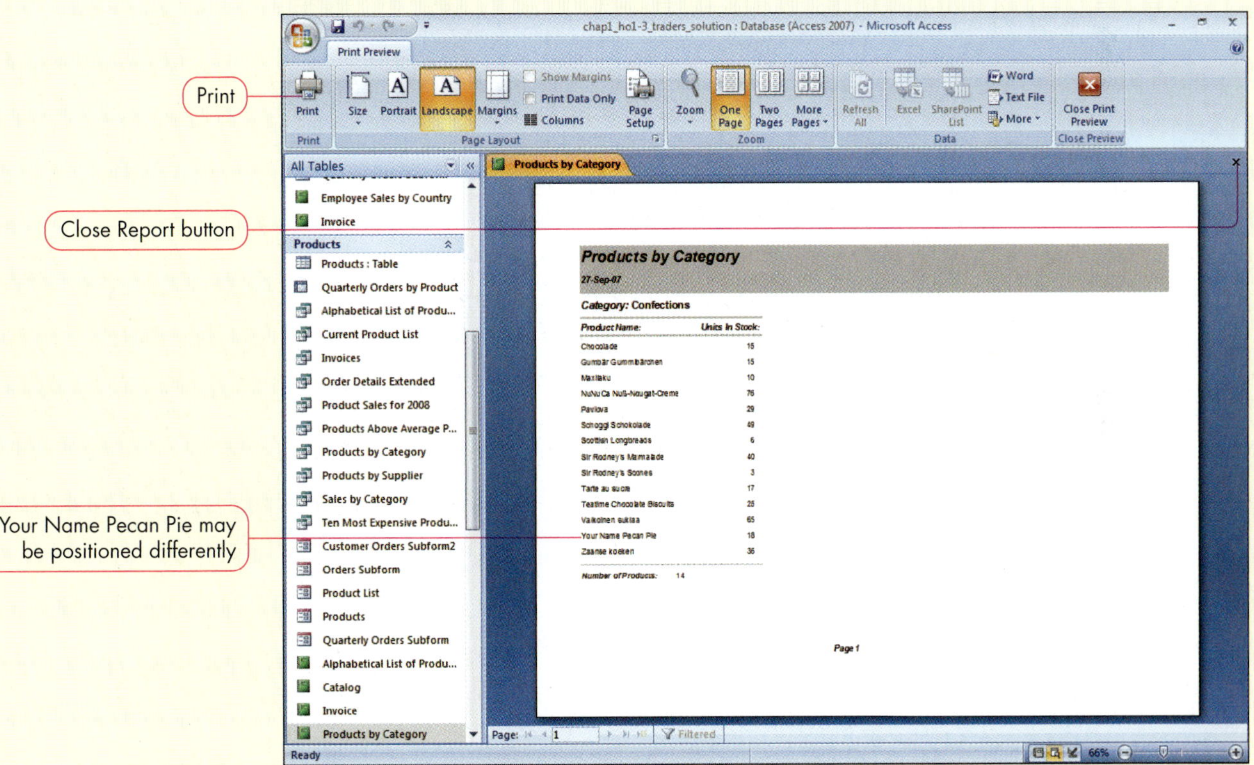

Figure 1.26 Filtered Report Results

Step 5
Remove an Advanced Filter

Refer to Figure 1.27 as you complete Step 5.

a. Open the **Order Details Extended query**.

All 2,155 records should display in the query. You have unfiltered the data. However the filter still exists.

b. Click **Toggle Filter** in the Sort & Filter group.

   You will see the same 18 filtered records that you printed in Step 3.

c. Click **Advanced** in the Sort & Filter group and click **Clear All Filters**.

d. Close the query. A dialog box opens asking if you want to save changes. Click **Yes**.

e. Open the **Order Details Extended query**.

f. Click **Advanced Filter Options** in the Sort & Filter group.

g. Check to ensure the *Clear All Filters* option is dim. Save and close the query.

h. Click the **Office Button**, select **Manage**, and select **Compact and Repair Database**. Close the file and exit Access.

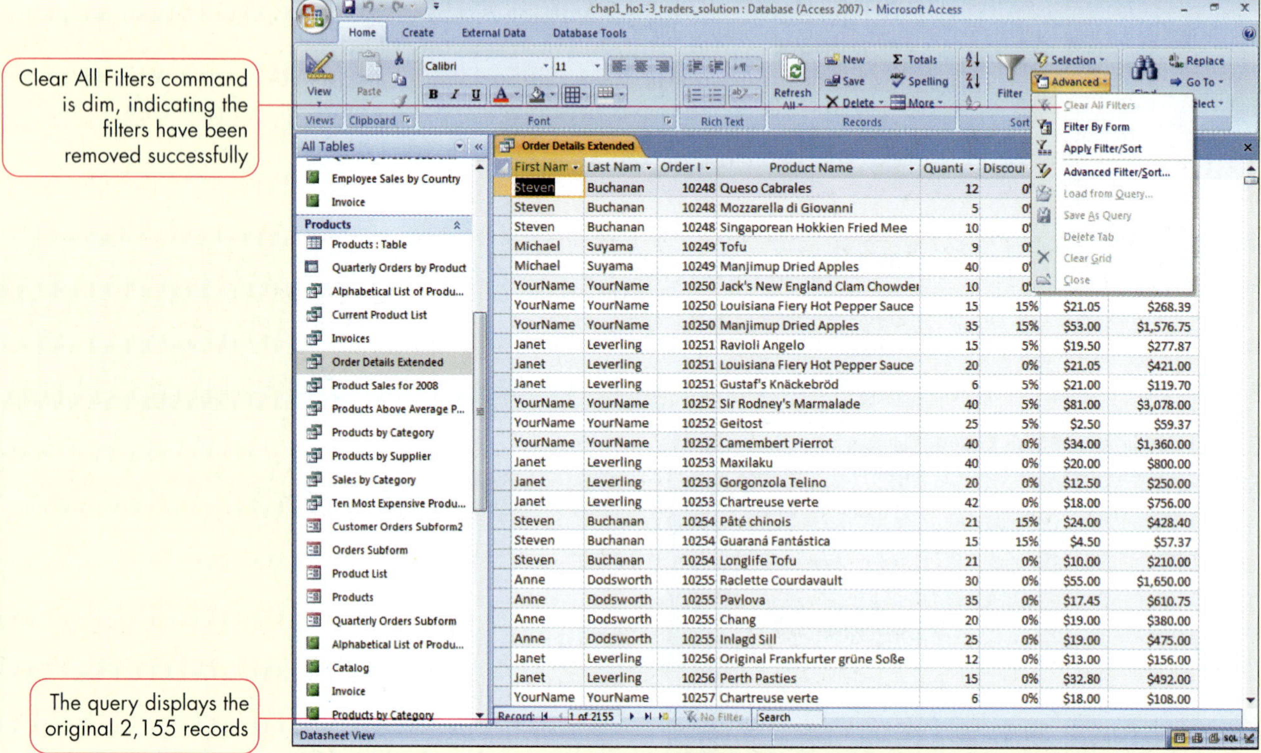

Figure 1.27 Query Results with Filters Removed

Summary

1. **Explore, describe, and navigate among objects in an Access database.** An Access database has six types of objects: tables, forms, queries, reports, macros, and modules. The database window displays these objects and enables you to open an existing object or create new objects. You may arrange these objects by type or by relationship views. The relationship view provides a listing of each table and all other objects in the database that use that table as a source. Thus, one query or report may appear several times, listed once under each table from which it derives information. Each table in the database is composed of records, and each record is in turn composed of fields. Every record in a given table has the same fields in the same order. The primary key is the field (or combination of fields) that makes every record in a table unique.

2. **Understand the difference between working in storage and memory.** Access automatically saves any changes in the current record as soon as you move to the next record or when you close the table. The Undo Current Record command cancels (undoes) the changes to the previously saved record.

3. **Practice good file management.** Because organizations depend on the data stored in databases, database users need to be intentional about exercising good file management practices. You need to be intentional about where you save your files. As you learn new Access skills, you need to make a copy of the database file and practice on the copy. This practice provides a recovery point should you make data-damaging errors.

4. **Back up, compact, and repair your database.** Because using a database tends to increase the size of the file, you should always close any database objects and compact the database prior to closing the file. This step may reduce the storage requirement by half. Adequate backup is essential when working with an Access database (or any other Office application). A duplicate copy of the database should be created at the end of every session and stored off-site (away from the computer).

5. **Create filters.** A filter is a set of criteria that is applied to a table to display a subset of the records in that table. Microsoft Access lets you Filter by Selection or Filter by Form. The application of a filter does not remove the records from the table, but simply suppresses them from view.

6. **Sort table or query data on one or more fields.** The records in a table can be displayed in ascending or descending order by clicking the appropriate command on the Home tab.

7. **Know when to use Access or Excel to manage data.** Excel data typically is flat. All of the needed information easily presents in a one-dimensional spreadsheet. Use Excel when the data are primarily numeric. Access handles multi-dimensional data more effectively. Use Access when you need to exchange data with other databases, for large amounts of data, or if your data needs are likely to expand.

8. **Use the Relationships window.** The Relationships window provides a summarizing overview of the database design. Use it to discover which fields are stored in what table. It displays the system of linkages among the table data. The Relationships window provides an excellent tool for you to become acquainted with a new database quickly.

9. **Understand relational power.** A relational database contains multiple tables and enables you to extract information from those tables in a single query. The related tables must be consistent with one another, a concept known as referential integrity. Thus, Access automatically implements additional data validation to ensure the integrity of a database. No system, no matter how sophisticated, can produce valid output from invalid input. Changes made in one object travel through the database and affect other, related objects. The relationships are based on linking primary and foreign key fields between tables.

Key Terms

Access speed 556
Criterion 553
Database 547
Datasheet view 551
Design view 551
Field 547
Filter 565
Filter by Form 567
Filter by Selection 567
Flat or non-relational data ...570
Foreign key 578
Form 553
Inequity 567
Navigation Pane 549
Object 549
Primary key 551
Query 553
Record 547
Referential integrity 578
Relational database management system 578
Report 554
Sort 568
Sort Ascending 568
Sort Descending 568
Table 547

Multiple Choice

1. Which sequence represents the hierarchy of terms, from smallest to largest?
   (a) Database, table, record, field
   (b) Field, record, table, database
   (c) Record, field, table, database
   (d) Field, record, database, table

2. Which of the following is not true regarding movement within a record (assuming you are not in the first or last field of that record)?
   (a) Press Tab or the right arrow key to move to the next field.
   (b) Press Spacebar to move to the next field to the right.
   (c) Press Shift+Tab or the left arrow key to return to the previous field.
   (d) Press the Enter key and move to the next record.

3. You're performing routine maintenance on a table within an Access database. When should you execute the Save command?
   (a) Immediately after you add, edit, or delete a record
   (b) Periodically during a session—for example, after every fifth change
   (c) Once at the end of a session
   (d) None of the above since Access automatically saves the changes as they are made

4. Which of the following objects are not contained within an Access database?
   (a) Tables and forms
   (b) Queries and reports
   (c) Macros and modules
   (d) Web sites and worksheets

5. You have opened an Access file. The left pane displays a table with forms, queries, and reports listed below a table name. Then another table and its objects display. You notice some of the object names are repeated under different tables. Why?
   (a) The Navigation Pane has been set to Object Type. The object names repeat because a query or report is frequently based on multiple tables.
   (b) The Navigation Pane has been set to Tables and Related Views. The object names repeat because a query or report is frequently based on multiple tables.
   (c) The Navigation Pane has been set to Most Recently Used View. The object names repeat because an object has been used frequently.
   (d) The database objects have been alphabetized.

6. Which of the following is not true of an Access database?
   (a) Every record in a table has the same fields as every other record. The fields are in the same order in each record.
   (b) Every table contains the same number of records as every other table.
   (c) A table containing five fields can use a different data type for each field.
   (d) All records contain the same data as all other records.

7. Which of the following is true regarding the record selector symbol?
   (a) A pencil indicates that the current record already has been saved.
   (b) An empty square indicates that the current record has not changed.
   (c) An asterisk indicates the first record in the table.
   (d) A gold border surrounds the active record.

8. You have finished an Access assignment and wish to turn it in to your instructor for evaluation. As you prepare to transfer the file, you discover that it has grown in size. It is now more than double the original size. You should:
   (a) Zip the database file prior to transmitting it to the instructor.
   (b) Turn it in; the size does not matter.
   (c) Compact and repair the database file prior to transmitting it to the instructor.
   (d) Delete extra tables or reports or fields to make the file smaller.

9. Which of the following will be accepted as valid during data entry?
   (a) Adding a record with a duplicate primary key
   (b) Entering text into a numeric field
   (c) Entering numbers into a text field
   (d) Omitting an entry in a required field

10. In a Replace command, the values for the Find and Replace commands must be:
    (a) The same length
    (b) The same case
    (c) Any part of a word
    (d) Either the same or a different length and case

...continued on Next Page

Multiple Choice Continued...

11. Which of the following capabilities is available through Filter by Selection?
    (a) The imposition of a relational condition
    (b) The imposition of an alternate (OR) condition
    (c) The imposition of an Equal condition
    (d) The imposition of a delete condition

12. You open an Access form and use it to update an address for customer Lee Fong. You exited the record and closed the form. Later you open a report that generates mailing labels. What will the address label for Lee Fong show?
    (a) The new address
    (b) The old address
    (c) The new address if you remembered to save the changes made to the form
    (d) The old address until you remember to update it in the report

13. You have created a Filter by Form in an Order Total field. You set the criterion to >25. Which of the following accurately reflects the instruction given to Access?
    (a) All orders with an Order Total of at least 25
    (b) All orders with an Order Total of less than 25
    (c) All orders with an Order Total over 25
    (d) All orders with an Order Total of 25 or less

14. You have used Find and Replace to find all occurrences of the word "his" with "his/her." You typed only his in the Find box and only his/her in the Replace box. What will the result be?
    (a) History will become His/Herstory
    (b) This will become This/Her
    (c) His will become His/Her
    (d) All of the above
    (e) None of the above

15. You are looking at an Employees table in Datasheet view. You want the names sorted alphabetically by last name and then by first name, e.g., Smith, Andrea is listed before Smith, William. To accomplish this, you must:
    (a) First sort ascending on first name and then on last name
    (b) First sort descending on first name and then on last name
    (c) First sort ascending on last name and then on first name
    (d) First sort descending on last name and then on first name

Practice Exercises

1 Comfort Insurance

The Comfort Insurance Agency is a midsized company with offices located across the country. You are the human resource director for the company. Your office is located in the home office in Miami. Each employee receives an annual performance review. The review determines employee eligibility for salary increases and the performance bonus. The employee data are stored in an Access database. This database is used by the Human Resource department to monitor and maintain employee records. Your task is to identify the employees who have a performance rating of excellent and a salary under $40,000 per year (if any). Once you identify the appropriate records, you need to sort them alphabetically by the employee's last name. Verify your work by examining Figure 1.28.

a. Copy the partially completed file in *chap1_pe1_insurance.accdb* from the Exploring Access folder to your production folder. Rename it **chap1_pe1_insurance_solution**. Double-click the file name to open it. Enable the security content by clicking the **Options** command in the Security Warning bar. Select **Enable this content** and then click **OK**.

b. Click the **Database Tools tab** and click **Relationships** in the Show/Hide group. Examine the table structure, relationships, and fields. Once you are familiar with the database, close the Relationships window.

c. Double-click the **Raises and Bonuses query** in the Navigation Pane to open it. Find *Debbie Johnson*'s name in the seventh record. Double-click *Debbie* and type your **first name**. Double-click *Johnson* and type your **last name**. Click a different record to save your change.

d. Examine the number of records in the query and remember it for future reference.

e. Find a record that has a value of *Excellent* in the *Performance field*. The record for Johnny Park (sixth record) is one. Click your insertion point in that field on the word **Excellent**.

f. Activate the **Filter by Selection** in the Sort & Filter group. Select **Equals "Excellent"** from the menu. Examine the number of records in the query and remember it for future reference.

g. Click **Advanced Filter** in the Sort & Filter group and select **Filter By Form**.

h. Position the insertion point in the first row in the *Salary field*. Type **<40000**. (Make sure you apply this number to the Salary field and not the NewSalary field.)

i. Click **Toggle Filter** in the Sort & Filter group. Examine the number of records in the query and remember it for future reference. As you add additional criteria, the number of filtered results should decrease.

j. Click **Ascending** in the Sort & Filter group on the Home tab to sort the filtered output by the employee's last name alphabetically.

k. Compare your results with Figure 1.28. Your name will be sorted into the list so your results may not match exactly. The number of records should exactly match.

l. Click the **Office Button** and position the mouse pointer over **Print**. Select **Quick Print** and click **OK**. Save the query.

m. Click the **Office Button**, select **Manage**, and select **Compact and Repair Database**. Close the file.

...continued on Next Page

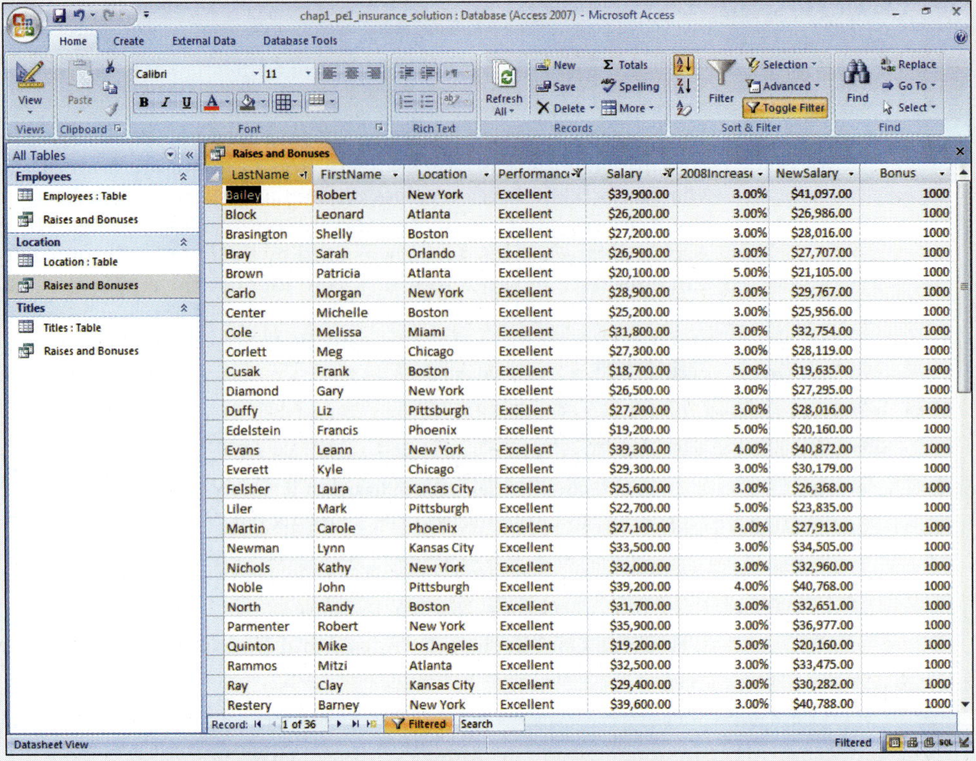

Figure 1.28 Sorted and Filtered Query Results

2 Member Rewards

The Prestige Hotel chain caters to upscale business travelers and provides state of the art conference, meeting, and reception facilities. It prides itself on its international, four-star cuisines. Last year, it began a member rewards club to help the marketing department track the purchasing patterns of its most loyal customers. All of the hotel transactions are stored in the database. Your task is to update a customer record and identify the customers who had weddings in St. Paul. Verify your work by examining Figure 1.29.

a. Copy the partially completed file in *chap1_pe2_memrewards.accdb* from the Exploring Access folder to your production folder. Rename it **chap1_pe2_memrewards_solution**. Double-click the file name to open it. Enable the security content by clicking the **Options** command in the Security Warning bar. Select **Enable this content** and then click **OK**.

b. Open the **Members Form form** and click **New (blank) record** on the navigation bar. (It has a yellow asterisk.)

c. Enter the information below in the form. Press **Tab** to move from field to field.

Field Name	Value
MemNumber	1718
LastName	Your Last Name
FirstName	Your First Name
JoinDate	7/30/2008
Address	124 West Elm Apt 12
City	Your hometown
State	Your state (2 character code)
Zip	00001

...continued on Next Page

Phone	9995551234
Email	Your e-mail
OrderID	9325
ServiceDate	8/1/2008
ServiceID	3
NoInParty	2
Location	20

d. Click **Close form** in the database window (X) to close the form.

e. Double-click the **Members table** in the Navigation Pane. Find Boyd Pegel in the first and last name field and replace his name with **your name**. Close the table.

f. Double-click the **Member Service by City query** in the Navigation Pane. Find a record that displays **St Paul** as the value in the *City field*. Click **St Paul** to select that data entry.

g. Click **Selection** in the Sort & Filter group on the Home tab. Select **Equals "St Paul"**.

h. Find a record that displays **Wedding** as the value in the *ServiceName* field. Click **Wedding** to select that data entry.

i. Click **Selection** in the Sort & Filter group on the Home tab. Select **Equals "Wedding"**.

j. Click any value in the **FirstName** field. Click **Ascending** in the Sort & Filter group on the Home tab. Click any value in the **LastName** field. Click **Ascending** in the Sort & Filter group on the Home tab.

k. Click the **Office Button**, select **Print**, and click **OK** to print the sorted and filtered query.

l. Save and close the query.

m. Click the **Office Button**, select **Manage**, and then select **Compact and Repair Database**. Close the file.

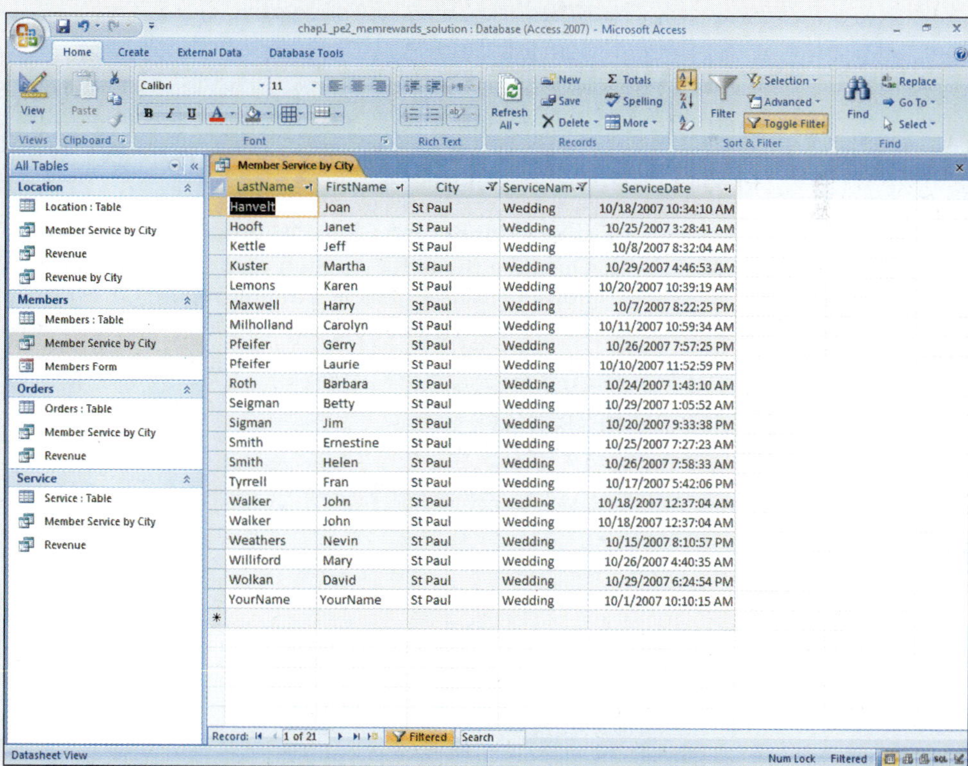

Figure 1.29 Sorted and Filtered Query Results

3 Vancouver Preschool

The Vancouver Preschool is a dynamic and exciting educational environment for young children. It launches each school year with a fundraiser that helps provide classroom supplies. Patrons are asked to donate goods and services, which are auctioned at a welcome-back-to-school dinner for students, parents, grandparents, and friends. All of the data about the donations are contained in an Access file. Your task is to make some modifications to the data and print a form and a report. Verify your work by comparing it to Figure 1.30. The report in the figure is displayed at a higher zoom percentage so that you can read the report easily. Your report may appear as a full page.

a. Copy the partially completed file *chap1_pe3_preschool.accdb* from the Exploring Access folder to your production folder. Rename it **chap1_pe3_preschool_solution.accdb**. Double-click the file name to open it. Click **Options** on the Security Warning bar, click **Enable this content**, and then click **OK**.

b. Open the **Donors form**. Navigate to a **new blank record** by clicking the navigation button with the yellow asterisk on it.

c. Enter the information below in the form.

Field Name	Value
DonorID	(New)
FirstName	Your First Name
LastName	Your Last Name
Address	124 West Elm Apt 12
City	Your hometown
State	Your state
Zip	00001
Phone	9995551234
Notes	Your e-mail
Item Donated	Car wash and hand wax
Number Attending	2
Item Value	100
Category	Service

d. Click **Print Record**. Close the form.

e. Open the **Items for Auction** report. Check to ensure that the *car wash and hand wax* donation is listed. If it is, print the report. Close Print preview.

f. Click the **Office Button**, select **Manage**, and select **Compact and Repair Database**.

g. Click the **Office Button**, select **Manage**, and select **Back Up Database**. Use the default backup file name.

h. Close the file.

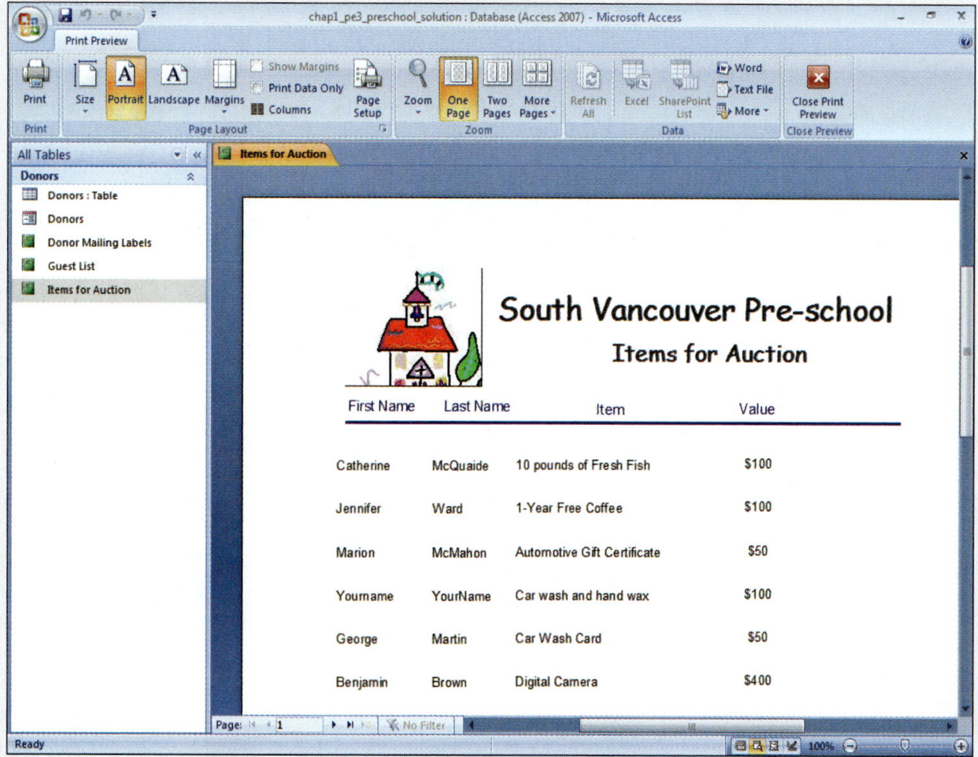

Figure 1.30 Report

4 Custom Coffee

The Custom Coffee Company is a small service organization that provides coffee, tea, and snacks to offices. Custom Coffee also provides and maintains the equipment for brewing the beverages. Although the firm is small, its excellent reputation for providing outstanding customer service has helped it grow. Part of the customer service is determined through a database the firm owner set up to organize and keep track of customer purchases. Verify your work by comparing it to Figure 1.31. The report in the figure is displayed at a higher zoom percentage so that you can read the report easily. Your report may appear as a full page.

a. Copy the partially completed file *chap1_pe4_coffee.accdb* from the Exploring Access folder to your production folder. Rename it **chap1_pe4_coffee_solution.accdb**. Double-click the file name to open the file. Click **Options** in the Security Warning bar, click **Enable this content**, and then click **OK**.

b. Click the **Navigation Pane down arrow** to change the category from Tables and Related Views to **Object Type**.

c. Examine the other objects, reports, forms, and queries in the database. Click the **Navigation Pane down arrow** and restore the **Tables and Related Views** category of looking at the objects.

d. Double-click the **Sales Reps table** to open it. Replace *YourName* with **your name** in both the LastName and FirstName fields. Close the table by clicking Close in the database window.

e. Double-click the **Customers Form** to open it. Navigate to a **new blank record** by clicking the navigation button with the yellow asterisk on it. Use **your name** for the *Customer* and *Contact* fields. Invent an address and email. Type **Miami** for the City, **FL** for the State, **33133** for the Zip Code, and **(305) 555-1234** for the Phone fields. The *Service Start Date* is **01/17/2005**. The *Credit Rating* is **A**. Type a **2** for the *Sales Rep ID*. It will convert to *S002* automatically.

f. Close the Customers Form.

g. Double-click the **Orders Form** to open it. Navigate to a new blank record by clicking the bottom navigation button with the yellow asterisk on it.

h. Type **16** as the *Customer ID*. The database will convert it to *C0016*. In the *Payment Type*, type **Cash** or select **Cash** using the drop-down arrow.

...continued on Next Page

i. Type **4** in the *Product ID box* and **2** in *Quantity*. In the next row, type **6** and **1** for *Product ID* and *Quantity*. The Product IDs will convert to P0004 and P0006. Close the form, saving changes if requested.

j. Open the **Order Details Report**. Scroll down to verify that your name appears both as a customer and as a sales rep (LastName). Right-click **your name** in the LastName field and select **Equals "Your Name"** from the shortcut menu. Right click **Miami** in the City field and select **Equals "Miami"** from the shortcut menu.

k. Click the **Office Button**, position the mouse pointer over **Print**, and select **Print Preview**. Click **Print**.

l. Click the **Office Button**, select **Manage**, and then select **Compact and Repair Database**.

m. Click the **Office Button**, select **Manage**, and then select **Back Up Database**. Use the default backup file name. Close the file.

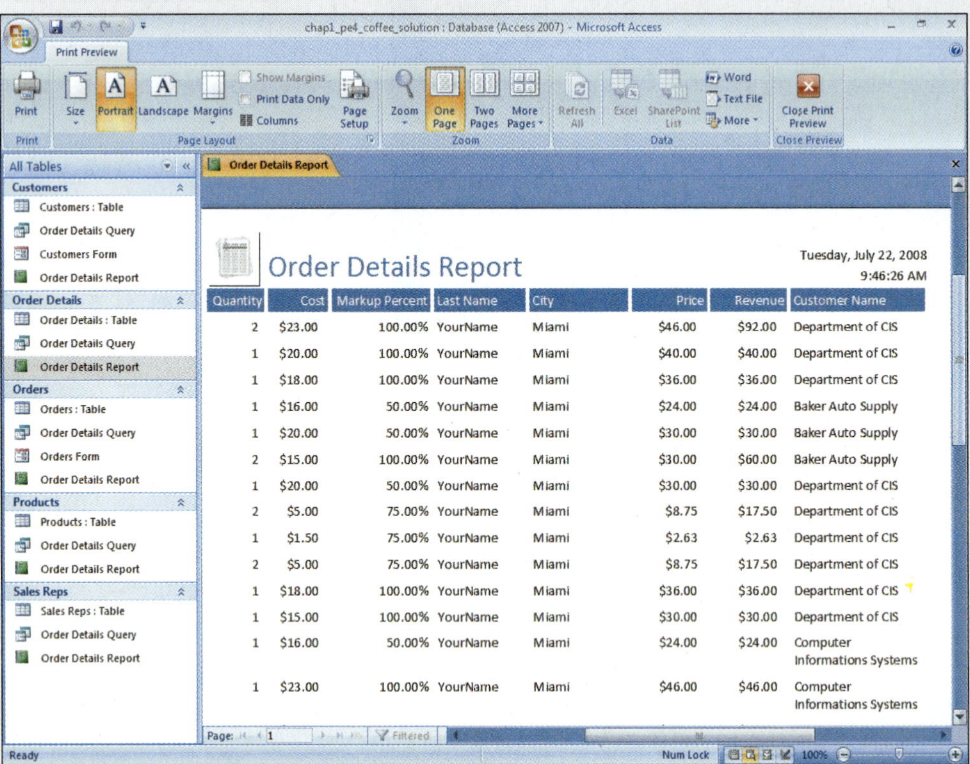

Figure 1.31 Report Showing Changes Made Using Forms

Mid-Level Exercises

1 Object Navigation, Data Entry, and Printing Database Objects

Your little sister lives to play soccer. She told her coach that you have become a computer expert. Coach (who is also the league director) called you to ask for help with the Access database file containing all of the league information. You agreed, and he promptly delivered a disc containing a copy of the league's database. The file contains information on the players, the coaches, and the teams. Players are classified by skill and experience level, with the best players described as "A." The Coaches table classifies coaching status as level 1 (head coaches) or 2 (assistant coaches). Coach asks that you add new players to the database and then identify all of the players not yet assigned to teams. He also needs you to identify the teams without coaches, the unassigned coaches, and asks that you assign each team a head and an assistant coach. Finally, Coach convinces you to volunteer as a coach in the league. Verify your work by looking at Figure 1.32.

a. Locate the file named *chap1_mid1_soccer.accdb*, copy it to your production folder, and rename it **chap1_mid1_soccer_solution.accdb**. Open the file and enable the content.

b. Open the Relationships window and examine the tables, the relationships, and the fields located in each table. Close the Relationships window.

c. Examine all of the objects in the database and think about the work Coach asked you to do. Identify which objects will assist you in accomplishing the assigned tasks.

d. Open the **Players form** and create a new record. Use your name, but you may invent the data about your address and phone. You are classified as an "A" player. Print the form containing your record. Close the form.

e. Open the **Coaches table**. Replace record 13 with **your instructor's name**. Add **yourself** as a new record. You are a *coach status* **1**.

f. Identify the players not assigned to teams. Assign each player to a team while balancing skill levels. (You would not want one team in the league to have all of the "A" skill level players because they would always win.)

g. Identify the teams without coaches and the coaches not assigned to teams. Assign a head coach and an assistant coach to each team. You may need to assign a person with head coaching qualifications to an assistant position. If you do, change his or her *status* to **2**.

h. After you assign all of the players and coaches to teams, open and print the **Master Coaching List report**.

i. After you assign all of the players and coaches to teams, open and print the **Team Rosters report**. Close the database.

...continued on Next Page

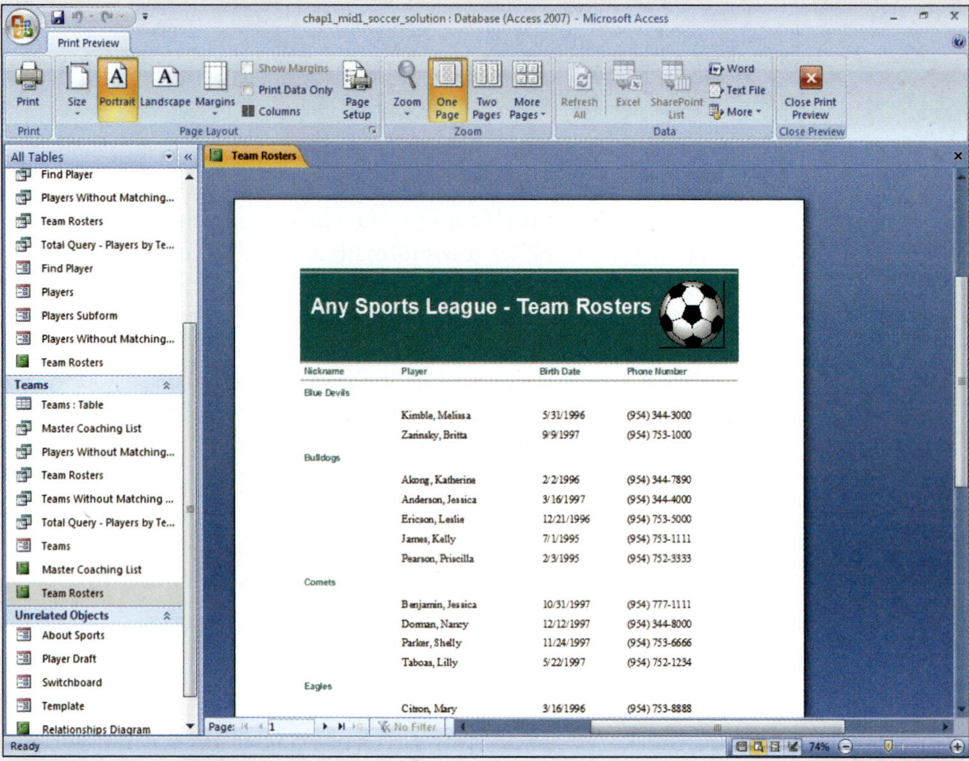

Figure 1.32 Team Roster Report

2 Sorting and Filtering Table Data Using Advanced Filters

You are the senior partner in a large, independent real estate firm that specializes in home sales. Although you still represent buyers and sellers in real estate transactions, you find that most of your time is spent supervising the agents who work for your firm. This fact distresses you because you like helping people buy and sell homes. There is a database containing all of the information on the properties your firm has listed. You believe that by using the data in the database more effectively, you can spend less time supervising the other agents and spend more time doing the part of your job that you like doing the best. Your task is to determine how many three-bedroom, two-bathroom, and garage properties your firm has listed for sale with a listing price under $400,000. Finally, you need to sort the data by list price in descending order. Refer to Figure 1.33 to verify that your results match the results shown.

a. Locate the file named *chap1_mid2_realestate.accdb*; copy it to your production folder and rename it **chap1_mid2_realestate_solution.accdb**. Open the file and enable the content. Open the **Agents table**. Find and replace *YourName* with **your name** in the first and last name fields. Close table after making the changes.

b. Create a filter by form on the data stored in the *Under 400K query*. Set the criteria to identify **three or more bedrooms**, **two or more bathrooms**, and **garage** (i.e., not a carport) properties you have listed for sale with a listing price **under $400,000**.

c. Sort the filtered results in **descending** order by the **ListPrice** field.

d. After you are sure that your results are correct, save the query.

e. Capture a screenshot of the sorted and filtered Under 400K query. With the sorted and filtered table open, press **PrintScrn**. Open Word; launch a new blank document, type **your name and section number**, and press **Enter**. Press **Ctrl+V** or click Paste. Print the

...continued on Next Page

word document. Save it as **chap1_mid2_realestate_solution. docx**. Close the Word document.

f. Compact, repair, and back up the database. Name the backup **chap1_mid2_realestate_backup.accdb**. Close the database.

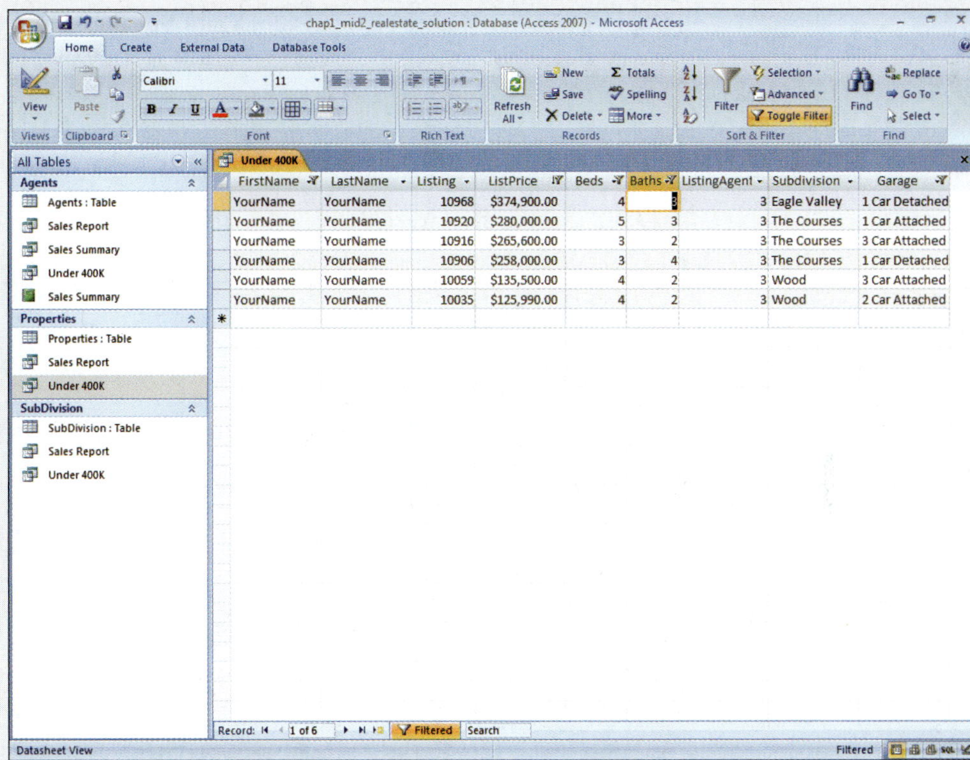

Figure 1.33 Sorted, Filtered Table

3 Sorting and Filtering Table Data Using Advanced Filters, Printing a Report

You work for the Office of Residence Life at your university as a work/study employee. The dean of student affairs, Martha Sink, PhD, placed you in this position because your transcript noted that you were enrolled in a computing class covering Microsoft Access. Dr. Sink has a special project for you. Each year the Association of Higher Education hosts a national conference to share new ideas and best practices. Next year the conference will be held on your campus, and the Office of Residence life has the responsibility of planning and organizing the events, speakers, and physical meeting spaces. To facilitate the work, the IT department has created a database containing information on the rooms, speakers, and sessions. Dr. Sink needs your assistance with extracting information from the database. Examine Figure 1.34 to verify your work.

a. Locate the file named *chap1_mid3_natconf.accdb*; copy it to your production folder and rename it **chap1_mid3_natconf_solution.accdb**. Open the file and enable the content. Open the **Speakers table**. Find and replace *YourName* with **your name**. Close the Speakers table.

...continued on Next Page

b. Open the **Speaker - Session Query** and apply a filter to identify the sessions where you or Holly Davis are the speakers. Use Filter by Form and engage the Or tab.

c. Sort the filtered results in descending order by the RoomID field.

d. Capture a screenshot of the sorted and filtered Speaker Session query. With the sorted and filtered query open on your computer press **PrintScrn**. Open Word; launch a new blank document, type **your name and section number**, and press **Enter**. Press **Ctrl+V** or click **Paste**. Print the Word document. Save it as **chap1_mid3_natconf_solution.docx**. Close the query but do not save it.

e. Open the **Master List – Sessions and Speakers report** in Report View. Apply a filter that limits the report to sessions where you are the speaker. Print the report. Close the report.

f. Compact, repair, and back up the database. Name the backup **chap1_mid3_natconf_backup.accdb**. Close the database.

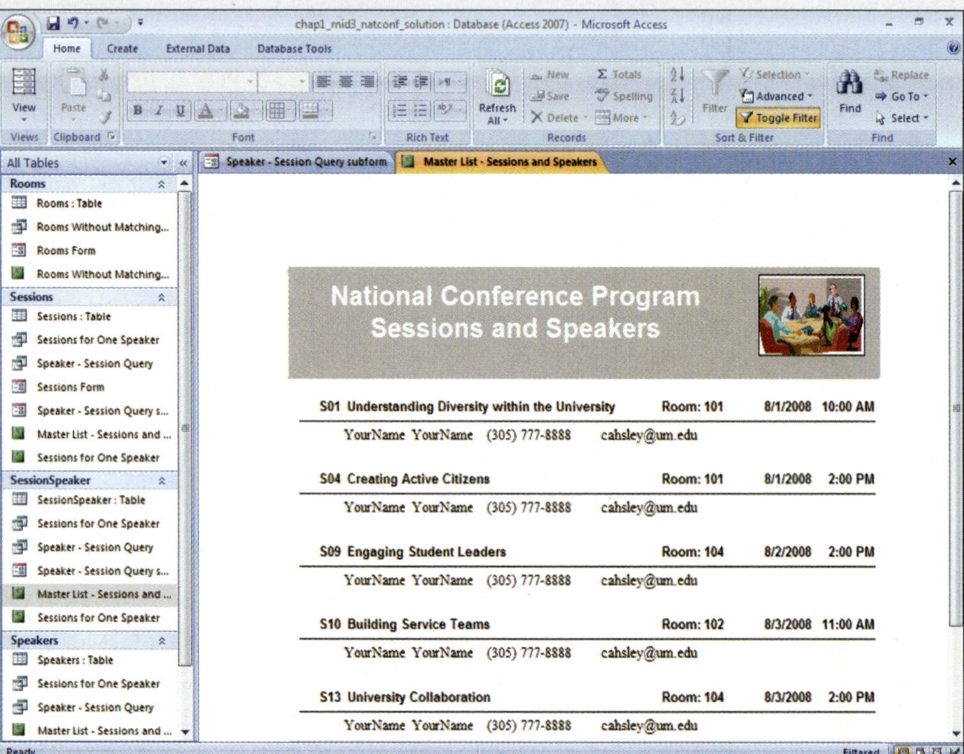

Figure 1.34 Master Sessions and Speakers Report

Capstone Exercise

Your boss expressed a concern about the accuracy of the inventory reports in the bookstore. He needs you to open the inventory database, make modifications to some records, and determine if the changes you make carry through to the other objects in the database. You will make changes to a form and then visit those changes in a table, a query, and a report. When you have verified that the changes update automatically, you will compact and repair the database and make a backup of it.

Database File Setup

You need to copy an original database file, rename the copied file, and then open the copied database to complete this capstone exercise. After you open the copied database, you will replace an existing employee's name with your name.

a. Locate the file named *chap1_cap_bookstore.accdb* and copy it to your production folder.

b. Rename the copied file as **chap1_cap_bookstore_solution.accdb**.

c. Open the *chap1_cap_bookstore_solution.accdb* file and enable the content.

d. Open the **Author Form** form.

e. Navigate to record 7 and replace *YourName* with **your name**.

f. Add a new *Title*, **Computer Wisdom II**. The *ISBN* is **0-684-80416-5**, the *PubID* is **SS**, the *PublDate* is **2007**, the *Price* is **$28.00** (just type 28, no $, period, or zeros), and *StockAmt* is **27** *units*.

g. Navigate to record 6 (or any other record). Close the form.

h. Open the **Author Form** again and navigate to record 7. The changes are there because Access works from storage, not memory. Close the form.

Sort a Query and Apply a Filter by Selection

You need to reorder a detail query so that the results are sorted alphabetically by the publisher name.

a. Open the **Publishers, Books, and Authors Query**.

b. Click in any record in the PubName field and sort the field in alphabetical order.

c. Check to make sure that two books list you as the author.

d. Click *your name* in the Author field and filter the records to show your books.

e. Close the query without saving the changes.

View a Report

You need to examine the Publishers, Books, and Authors report to determine if the changes you made to the Author form carried through to the report.

a. Open the **Publishers, Books, and Authors Report**.

b. Check to make sure that the report shows two books listing you as the author.

c. Print the report.

d. Close the report.

Filter a Table

You need to examine the Books table to determine if the changes you made to the Author form carried through to the related table. You also will filter the table to display books published after 2004 with fewer than 30 copies in inventory.

a. Open the **Books** table.

b. Click **Advanced** in the Sort & Filter group and then select **Filter by Form** from the drop-down list.

c. Create the criteria that will identify all records published after 2004 with fewer than 30 items in stock.

d. Apply the filter.

e. Print the filtered table.

f. Close the table. Do not save the design changes.

Compact and Repair a Database, Backup a Database

Now that you are satisfied that any changes made to a form, table, or query carry through the database, you are ready to compact, repair, and back up your file.

a. Select the option to compact and repair your database.

b. Select the option to create a backup copy of your database, accept the default file name, and save it.

c. Close the file.

Mini Cases

Use the rubric following the case as a guide to evaluate your work, but keep in mind that your instructor may impose additional grading criteria or use a different standard to judge your work.

Applying Filters, Printing, and File Management

GENERAL CASE

The *chap1_mc1_safebank.accdb* file contains data from a small bank. Copy the *chap1_mc1_safebank.accdb* file to your production folder, name it **chap1_mc1_safebank_solution.accdb**, and open the copied file. Use the skills from this chapter to perform several tasks. Open the Customer table, replace YourName with your name, and sort the data in alphabetical order by LastName. Print the Customer table. Open the Branch table and make yourself the manager of the Campus branch. Close both tables. Open the Branch Customers query and filter it to show only the accounts at the Campus branch with balances over $1,500.00. Print the filtered query results. Close the query but do not save it. Compact and repair the database.

Performance Elements	Exceeds Expectations	Meets Expectations	Below Expectations
Sort and print table data	Printout displays data sorted in requested order.	The table was successfully printed, but the order is incorrect.	Output missing or corrupted.
Apply filters and print query data	Appropriate filters successfully created and printed.	One of the requested filters but not both work correctly. Output created.	Output missing or corrupted.
Data entry	Data were entered correctly.	Some but not all of the requested data were entered correctly, or other data were overwritten.	Output missing or corrupted.
File management	Database was correctly compacted, repaired, and backed up.	The database was successfully compacted but not backed up or vice-versa.	Files not submitted.

Combining Name Fields

RESEARCH CASE

This chapter introduced you to the power of using Access filters and setting criteria, but you have much more to explore. Copy the file named *chap1_mc2_traders.accdb* to your production folder and rename it **chap1_mc2_traders_solution.accdb**. Open the file and enable the content. Open the Employees table and replace YourName with your first and last names. Open the Revenue report and switch to the appropriate view. Use the tools that you have learned in this chapter to filter the report. You wish to limit the output to only your sales of Seafood. You may need to use Access Help to get the filters to work. Once the report is filtered, print it. Write your instructor a letter explaining how you accomplished this step. Use a letter template in Word, your most professional writing style, and clear directions that someone could follow in order to accomplish this task. Save the document as **chap1_mc2_traders_solution.docx**. Print and close the Word document. Exit Word. Attach the printout of the name list to the letter. Turn the printouts in to the instructor if instructed to do so. Compact and repair your database.

Performance Elements	Exceeds Expectations	Meets Expectations	Below Expectations
Use online help	Appropriate articles located, and letter indicates comprehension.	Appropriate articles located, but letter did not demonstrate comprehension.	Articles not found.
Report filtered to display only your sales of seafood	Printed list attached to letter in requested format.	Printed list is attached, but the filter failed to screen one or more salespeople or categories.	List missing or incomprehensible.
Summarize and communicate	Letter clearly written and could be used as directions.	Letter text indicates some understanding but also weaknesses.	Letter missing or incomprehensible.
File management	Database was correctly compacted, repaired, and backed up.	Database was successfully compacted but not backed up or vice-versa.	Files not submitted.
Esthetics	Letter template correctly employed.	Template employed but signed in the wrong place or improperly used.	Letter missing or incomprehensible.

Coffee Revenue Queries

DISASTER RECOVERY

A co-worker called you into his office and explained that he was having difficulty with Access 2007 and asked you to look at his work. Copy the *chap1_mc3_coffee.accdb* file to your production folder, name it **chap1_mc3_coffee_solution.accdb**, and open the file. Change the Navigation Pane to the All Access Objects category. Your co-worker explains that the report is incorrect. It shows that Lockley is the sales representative for "Coulter Office Supplies" and the "Little, Joiner, and Jones" customers, when in fact you are those customers' sales representative. Make sure your name replaces YourName in the Sales Reps table. Find the source of the error and correct it. Run and print the report and turn the printout and file in to your instructor if instructed to do so. Compact and repair your database.

Performance Elements	Exceeds Expectations	Meets Expectations	Below Expectations
Error identification	Correct identification and correction of all errors.	Correct identification of all errors and correction of some errors.	Errors neither located nor corrected.
Reporting	Report opened, run, and printed successfully.	Printout submitted, but with errors.	No printout submitted for evaluation.
File management	Database was correctly compacted, repaired, and backed up.	Database was successfully compacted but not backed up or vice-versa.	Files not submitted.

Relational Databases and Multi-Table Queries

Designing Databases and Using Related Data

After you read this chapter, you will be able to:

1. Design data **(page 607)**.
2. Create tables **(page 612)**.
3. Understand table relationships **(page 625)**.
4. Share data with Excel **(page 626)**.
5. Establish table relationships **(page 630)**.
6. Create a query **(page 642)**.
7. Specify criteria for different data types **(page 645)**.
8. Copy and run a query **(page 649)**.
9. Use the Query Wizard **(page 649)**.
10. Understand large database differences **(page 653)**.

Hands-On Exercises

Exercises	Skills Covered
1. TABLE DESIGN, PROPERTIES, VIEWS, AND WIZARDS (page 618) **Open:** a new blank database **Save as:** chap2_ho1-3_safebank_solution.accdb **Back up as:** chap2_ho1_safebank_solution.accdb	• Create a New Database • Create a Table by Entering Data • Change the Primary Key, Modify Field Properties, and Delete a Field • Modify Table Fields in Design View • Create a New Field in Design View • Switch Between the Table Design and the Table Datasheet Views
2. IMPORTS AND RELATIONSHIPS (page 635) **Open:** chap2_ho1-3_safebank_solution.accdb (from Exercise 1) and chap2_ho2_safebank.xlsx **Save as:** chap2_ho1-3_safebank_solution.accdb (additional modifications) **Back up as:** chap2_ho2_safebank_solution. accdb	• Import Excel Data into an Access Table • Import Additional Excel Data • Modify an Imported Table's Design • Add Data to an Imported Table • Establish Table Relationships • Understand How Referential Integrity Protects Data
3. MULTIPLE-TABLE QUERY (page 654) **Open:** chap2_ho1-3_safebank_solution.accdb (from Exercise 2) **Save as:** chap2_ho1-3_safebank_solution.accdb (additional modifications)	• Create a Query Using a Wizard • Specify Simple Query Criteria • Change Query Data • Add a Table to a Query Using Design View and Sort a Query

CASE STUDY

National Conference

You received a work-study assignment to the Office of Student Life at your school. This morning, the dean of Student Affairs, Jackie Cole, invited you to come to her office. Dr. Cole returned from the National Conference of Student Service Providers yesterday. Thousands of educators participate in this conference annually. She volunteered your school to host the event next year. She explained that this is a wonderful opportunity to showcase your school to the rest of the education world, but that the conference details need to be planned carefully so that the scheduled events execute flawlessly. Then Dr. Cole explained that she selected you as the work-study student because of your Access skills. She explained that no one else in the office knew anything about Access. She noted that a project of this magnitude required a database to efficiently manage the data. Then she said, "We are depending on you to create and manage the database and make our school look good."

Dr. Cole asked the IT department to help you design the database. The IT staff has created a small database with a table for the speakers and a table that joins the speakers and sessions together. An Excel spreadsheet contains information about the sessions. You will need to import the Excel data into the Access file, connect it with the rest of the database, and update the data.

The IT staff did not think about the conference participants when they designed the database. You need to design a table that will hold the information about the conference participants. Think carefully about what information might be needed about each registrant. Then think about how to connect the registration information to the rest of the database. You need to establish the primary and foreign keys for the Registrant table as you plan the other fields in that table.

Your Assignment

- Copy the file named *chap2_case_natconf.accdb* to your production folder. Name the copy **chap2_case_natconf_solution.accdb**.
- Open each table and familiarize yourself with the data.
- Open the Relationships window and acquaint yourself with the tables, fields, and what will become the primary and foreign fields to create the relationships among the tables in the database.
- Import the data contained in the Excel file, *chap2_case_sessions.xlsx*. As you create the import, think about which field will be the primary key and establish appropriate properties.
- Establish a relationship between the Sessions table and the other tables in the database. Remember that a relationship may only be formed on data of like type and size.
- Replace the first record in the Speakers table with information about you.
- Create a new Session. Title it **Undergraduate Challenges**. Examine the session times and rooms and schedule this session so that it does not conflict with the other sessions.
- Create a query that will show the speaker's name, the session title, and the room number. Add parameters to limit the output to sessions conducted by **Davis**, **Kline**, and **you**. Print the query results.
- Create a table for conference participant's registrations. Carefully anticipate which fields need to be included. Participants must pay a $500 registration fee.
- Create a new record in the registration table. Add yourself as a participant.
- Capture a screenshot of the Relationships window. Paste the screenshot into a Word file. Save the file as **chap2_case_natconf_solution.docx**.
- Compact and repair your file. Back up the database as **chap2_case_natconf_solution_backup.accdb**.

Table Design, Properties, Views, and Wizards

Good database design provides the architectural framework supporting the work the database accomplishes. If the framework is flawed, the resulting work will always have flaws, too. You may remember the period leading to New Year's Eve in 1999, Y2K. Many people stocked up on groceries, withdrew cash from their checking accounts, and filled their gas tanks because they believed that the computer-operated grocery checkouts, automatic banking machines, and gasoline pumps would not function properly (if at all) on New Year's Day, 2000. These frightened people had legitimate reasons to be concerned about how computers would react when the date rolled to January 1, 2000, due to poor database design. Electronic data storage was (and remains) relatively expensive. Principles of good design dictate saving storage space when possible. As a space-saving measure, most dates in most computers prior to the mid-1990s stored the year as a two-digit number. For example, 1993 was stored as 93. The Information Systems and Computer Science professionals responsible for managing the databases in the world failed to anticipate the consequences of flawed database design.

Computers perform relatively simple arithmetic computations to measure time lapses. When subtracting 1993 from 1995, the computer knows that two years have passed. The results do not change when the dates are stored as 93 and 95. However, what would happen when the computer subtracted 99 from 01? You know that a two-year period has passed. But, the computer would believe that a *negative* 98 years had passed! Before New Year's Day, 2000, IS professionals worked extra hours correcting the design flaws in the way their systems handled and processed dates. On January 1, 2000, computerized grocery stores, ATMs, and gas pumps virtually all worked. The overtime hours combined with the new hardware and software required cost an estimated $21 billion globally to fix.

This chapter introduces the Safebank database case study to present the basic principles of table and query design. You use tables and forms to input data, and you create queries and reports to extract information from the database in a useful and organized way. The value of that information depends entirely on the quality of the underlying data, which must be both complete and accurate.

In this section, you learn about the importance of proper design and essential guidelines that are used throughout the book. After developing the design, you implement that design in Access. You create a table, and then refine its design by changing the properties of various fields. You will gain an understanding of the importance of data validation during data entry.

Designing Data

As a consumer of financial services, you know that your bank or credit union maintains data about you. Your bank has your name, address, phone number, and Social Security number. It knows if you have a credit card and what your balances are. Additionally, your bank keeps information about its branches. Think about the information your bank generates and then make a list of the data needed to produce that information. The key to the design process is to visualize the output required and to determine the input needed to produce that output. Think of the specific fields you need and characterize each field according to the type of data it contains (such as text, numbers, or dates) as well as its size (length). Figure 2.1 shows one sample list of fields. Your list may vary. The order of the fields within the table and the specific field names are not significant. What is important is that the tables contain all necessary fields so that the system can perform as intended.

Customer's Last Name–Text
Customer's First Name–Text
Customer's Identification Number–Either text or number
Address–Text
City–Text
State–Text
Postal Code–Text
Phone–Text
Branch Identification–Either text or number
Branch Manager's Name–Text
Branch Manager's Start Date–Number date formatted
Branch Location–Text
Account Number–Either text or number
Balance–Number formatted as currency

Figure 2.1 Data Needed for a Bank Database

Figure 2.1 reflects the results of a careful design process based on eight essential guidelines:

1. Include the necessary data.
2. Design for the next 100 years.
3. Design in compliance with Sarbanes Oxley.
4. Design in compliance with PNPI Regulations.
5. Store data in their smallest parts.
6. Avoid calculated data in a field.
7. Design to accommodate date arithmetic.
8. Design multiple tables.

The following paragraphs discuss these guidelines. As you proceed through the text, you will begin developing the experience necessary to design your own systems. Design is an important skill. You also must understand how to design a database and its tables to use Access effectively.

Include the Necessary Data

(. . . ask yourself what information will be expected from the system, and then determine the data required to produce that information.)

The best way to determine what data are necessary is to create a rough draft of the reports you will need, and then design tables that contain the fields necessary to create those reports. In other words, ask yourself what information will be expected from the system, and then determine the data required to produce that information. Consider, for example, the type of information that can and cannot be produced from the table in Figure 2.1:

- You can determine which branch a customer uses. You cannot, however, tell the customer with multiple accounts at different locations what the total balance of all accounts might be.

- You can calculate a total of all account balances by adding individual account balances together. You could also calculate the sum of all deposits at a branch. You cannot tell when a deposit was made because this small exercise does not store that data.
- You can determine who manages a particular branch and which accounts are located there. You cannot determine how long the customer has banked with the branch because the date that he or she opened the account is not in the table.

Whether these omissions are important depends on the objectives of the system. Of course, the data stored in a real bank's database is far more complex and much larger than the data you will use. This case has been simplified.

Design for the Next 100 Years

The ***field size property*** defines how much space to reserve for each field.

A fundamental law of information technology states that systems evolve continually and that information requirements change. Try to anticipate the future needs of the system, and then build in the flexibility to satisfy those demands. Include the necessary data at the outset, and be sure that the field sizes are large enough to accommodate future expansion. The ***field size property*** defines how many characters to reserve for a specific field.

When you include all possible elements of data that anyone might ever need, you drive up the cost of the database. Each element costs employee time to enter and maintain the data and consumes storage space. Computers have a finite amount of space. Good database design must balance the current and future needs of the system against the cost of recording and storing unnecessary data elements. Even with using data warehouses, the amount of data that we can store is limited.

> Good database design must balance the current and future needs of the system against the cost of recording and storing unnecessary data elements.

Suppose you are designing a database for your college. You would need to include students' on-campus and permanent addresses. It might be useful for someone to know other places a student might have lived or even visited during their lives. A worker in the Student Life office could help an international student connect with someone who used to live in or at least visited the international student's homeland. A student who had moved often or traveled extensively might need an extra page on his or her application form. Completing the application might take so long that the student might apply to a different college. A worker in the admissions office would need extra time to enter all the places of residence and travel into the database. The school's database file would grow and require additional storage space on the university computer system. The benefits provided to the international student from connecting him to someone who had been in his country may not justify the cost of entering, maintaining, and storing the additional data.

A ***validation rule*** checks the authenticity of the data entered in a field.

The data will prove useful only if they are accurate. You need to anticipate possible errors a data entry operator might commit. Access provides tools to protect data from user error. A ***validation rule*** restricts data entry in a field to ensure the correct type of data is entered or that the data does not violate other enforced properties, such as exceeding a size limitation. The validation rule checks the correctness of the data entered when the user exits the field. If the data entry violates the validation rule, an error message appears and prevents the invalid data from being stored in the field.

Design in Compliance with Sarbanes Oxley

Sarbanes Oxley Act (SOX) protects the general public and companies' shareholders against fraudulent practices and accounting errors.

Following the financial and accounting scandals involving Enron and World Com in 2002, the U.S. Congress passed the ***Sarbanes Oxley Act (SOX)***. Its intent is to protect the general public and companies' shareholders against fraudulent practices and accounting errors. The Securities and Exchange Commission (SEC) enforces the act. Although primarily focused on the accounting practices followed by publicly traded companies, SOX permeates corporate Information Technology policies and practices. The act requires that all business records, including electronic messages, be saved for a period of five years and be made available to the SEC on request. Penalties for non-compliance include fines, imprisonment, or both. The IT department faces the challenge of archiving all the required information in a cost-effective and efficient way.

Design in Compliance with PNPI Regulations

PNPI—Federal laws governing the safeguarding of personal, non-public information such as Social Security Numbers (SSNs), credit card or bank account numbers, medical or educational records, or other sensitive data.

Federal laws and regulations govern the safeguarding of personal, non-public information (***PNPI***), such as Social Security Numbers (SSNs), credit or bank account numbers, medical or educational records, or other sensitive, confidential or protected data (i.e., grades used in context with personally identifiable information such as name, address, or other easily traceable identifiers). Organizations must store your personal information in computer systems. For example, without your Social Security Number, the financial aid office cannot release scholarship money to pay your tuition. Your employer cannot cut a paycheck without knowing your Social Security Number. Your doctor cannot tell the student health service at your school whether you have been immunized against the measles without your written permission. The data must be stored with protected and restricted access. Congress has passed several laws to protect you from identity theft or other misuse of your private, personal information. The most important of these laws include the following:

- Family Educational Rights and Privacy Act (FERPA) [educational records]
- Gramm-Leach-Bliley Act (GLBA) [financial institution and customer data]
- Health Insurance Portability and Accountability Act (HIPAA) [health information]

Store Data in Their Smallest Parts

The design in Figure 2.1 divides a customer's name into two fields (first and last name) to reference each field individually. You might think it easier to use a single field consisting of both the first and last name, but that approach is inadequate. Consider this list in which the customer's name is stored as a single field:

- Allison Foster
- Brit Reback
- Carrie Graber
- Danielle Ferrarro
- Evelyn Adams
- Frances Coulter

The first problem in this approach is lack of flexibility: You could not easily create a salutation of the form *Dear Allison* or *Dear Ms. Foster* because the first and last names are not accessible individually. In actuality you could write a procedure to divide the name field in two, but that is beyond the capability of the Access novice.

A second difficulty is that the list of customers cannot be put into alphabetical order by last name very easily because the last name begins in the middle of the field. The names are already alphabetized by first name because sorting always begins with the left position in a field. Thus the "A" in Allison comes before the "B" in Brit, and so on. The proper way to sort the data is on the last name, which can be done more efficiently if the last name is stored as a separate field.

Think of how an address might be used. The city, state, and postal code should always be stored as separate fields. Any type of mass mailing requires you to sort on postal codes to take advantage of bulk mail. Other applications may require you to select records from a particular state or postal code, which can be done more efficiently if you store the data as separate fields. Often database users enter the postal code, and the database automatically retrieves the city and state information. You may need to direct a mailing to only a neighborhood or to a single street. The guideline is simple: Store data in their smallest parts.

Avoid Calculated Data in a Table

A ***calculated field*** is a field that derives its value from a formula that references one or more existing fields.

A ***calculated field*** produces a value from an expression—a formula or function that references an existing field or combination of fields. Although the information derived from calculations can be incredibly valuable to the decision maker, it is useful only at the moment the calculation is made. It makes no sense to store outdated data when recalculating; it will provide the decision maker with fresh, accurate information. Calculated data should not be stored in a table because they are subject to change. Storing calculated data in a table results in wasted space and can produce outdated results.

The total account balance for a customer with multiple accounts is an example of a calculated data because it is computed by adding the balances in all of the customer's accounts together. It is unnecessary to store the calculated sum of account balances in the Account table, because the table contains the fields on which the sum is based. In other words, Access is able to calculate the sum from these fields whenever it is needed, which is much more efficient than doing it manually.

Design to Accommodate Date Arithmetic

A ***constant*** is an unchanging value, like a birth date.

Date arithmetic is the process of subtracting one date from another.

A ***date/time field*** is a field that facilitates calculations for dates and times.

A person's age and date of birth provide equivalent information, as one is calculated from the other. It might seem easier, therefore, to store the age rather than the birth date to avoid the calculation. That would be a mistake because age changes continually and needs to be updated continually, but the date of birth remains ***constant***—an unchanging value. Similar reasoning applies to an employee's length of service versus date of hire. Like Excel, Access stores all dates as a serial integer. You can use ***date arithmetic*** to subtract one date from another to find out the number of days, months, or years that have lapsed between them. Access provides a special data definition for ***date/time fields*** to facilitate calculations.

Design Multiple Tables

After listing all of the data items that you want to include in the database, you need to group them into similar items. Group the customer information into one table, the branch information into another, and the account information into a third table. A well-designed database provides a means of recombining the data when needed. When the design is sound, the **referential integrity** rules ensure that consistent data is stored in a related table. For example, the Customers and Account tables are linked by relationship. Referential integrity ensures that only valid customer IDs that exist in the Customers table are used in the Account table; it prevents you from entering an invalid customer ID in the Account table.

Data redundancy occurs when unnecessary duplicate information exists in a database.

Avoid ***data redundancy***, which is the unnecessary inclusion of duplicate data among tables. You should never store duplicate information in multiple tables in a database. The information about a customer's address should only exist in a single table, the Customers table. It would be poor database design to also include the customer's address in the Account table. When duplicate information exists in a database, errors may result. Suppose the address data were stored in both the Customers and Account tables. You need to anticipate the consequences that may result when a customer moves. A likely outcome would be that the address would be updated in one but not both tables. The result would be unreliable data. Depending on which table served as the source for the output, either the new or the old address might be provided to the manager requesting the information. It is a much stronger design to have the address stored in only one table but tied to the rest of the database through the power of the relationships. See Figure 2.2.

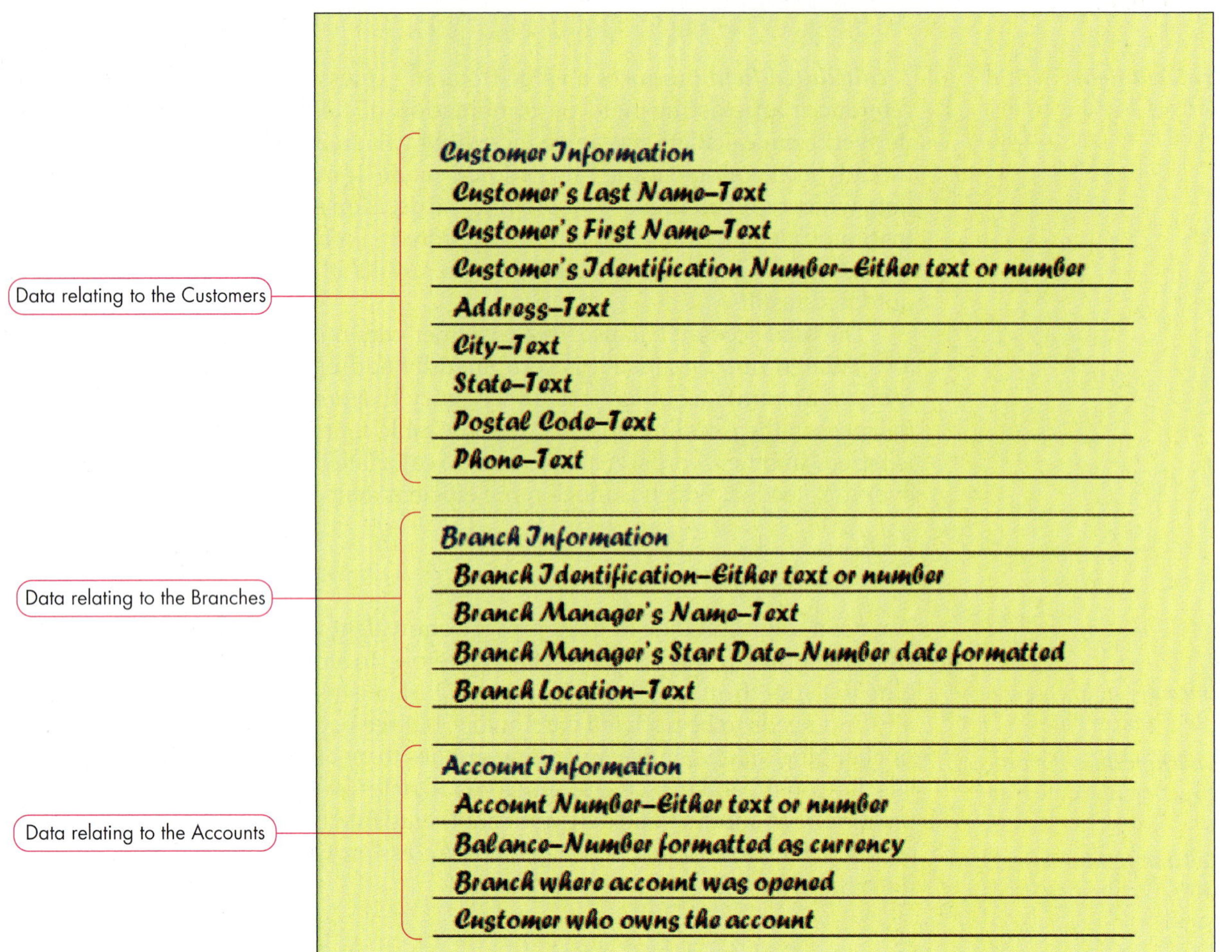

Data relating to the Customers
Customer Information
Customer's Last Name–Text
Customer's First Name–Text
Customer's Identification Number–Either text or number
Address–Text
City–Text
State–Text
Postal Code–Text
Phone–Text
Data relating to the Branches
Branch Information
Branch Identification–Either text or number
Branch Manager's Name–Text
Branch Manager's Start Date–Number date formatted
Branch Location–Text
Data relating to the Accounts
Account Information
Account Number–Either text or number
Balance–Number formatted as currency
Branch where account was opened
Customer who owns the account

Figure 2.2 Bank's Database Data Grouped to Form a Table

Creating Tables

A table and all Access objects must be created within an Access file. To create a table, you must first create the file that will house it. Access works from storage, not memory. The other Microsoft Office programs work from memory: You create first and then save. With Access you must save a file first and then create its contents. You will open a new blank database and save it to a specific storage location before you can begin creating your tables.

Access provides several ways to create a table. You can create a table by entering the table data into a field. You also can import table data from another database or application, for example, Excel. Regardless of how a table is created, you can modify it to include a new field or to delete an existing field.

CamelCase notation uses no spaces in multi-word field names, but uses uppercase letters to distinguish the first letter of each new word.

Every field has a field name to identify the data that is entered into the field. The field name should be descriptive of the data and can be up to 64 characters in length, including letters, numbers, and spaces. Actual databases employ *CamelCase notation* for fields, objects, and file names. Instead of spaces in multi-word field names, use uppercase letters to distinguish the first letter of each new word, for example, ProductCost or LastName. Access is used frequently as a user-friendly means to connect to large databases stored on mainframes. Using Access, the manager can enter the organization's databases without needing courses in specialized computer languages. The manager then can find the data needed to make a decision and convert it to information. Most large databases and most mainframe computer systems will not accept spaces in field names.

A *data type* determines the type of data that can be entered and the operations that can be performed on that data.

Every field also has a *data type* that determines the type of data that can be entered and the operations that can be performed on that data. Access recognizes 10 data types.

Illustrations of Data Types and Uses | Reference

Data Type	Description	Example
Number	A **Number** field contains a value that can be used in a calculation, such as the number of credits a student has earned. The contents of a number field are restricted to numbers, a decimal point, and a plus or minus sign.	Height
Text	A **Text** field stores alphanumeric data, such as a student's name or address. It can contain alphabetic characters, numbers, and/or special characters (i.e., an apostrophe in O'Malley). Fields that contain only numbers but are not used in a calculation (i.e., Social Security Number, telephone number, or postal code) should be designated as text fields. A text field can hold up to 255 characters.	City
Memo	A **Memo** field can be up to 65,536 characters long. Memo fields are used to hold descriptive data (several sentences or paragraphs).	Library databases that store research papers
Date/Time	A **Date/Time** field holds formatted dates or times (i.e., mm/dd/yyyy) and allows the values to be used in date or time arithmetic.	March 31, 2008
Currency	A **Currency** field can be used in a calculation and is used for fields that contain monetary values.	Your checking account balance
Yes/No	A **Yes/No** field (also known as a Boolean or Logical field) assumes one of two values, such as Yes or No, True or False, or On or Off.	Dean's list
OLE	An **OLE** Object field contains an object created by another application. OLE objects include pictures, sounds, or graphics.	Excel workbook
AutoNumber	An **AutoNumber** field is a special data type that Access uses to assign the next consecutive number each time you add a record. The value of an AutoNumber field is unique for each record in the file, and thus AutoNumber fields are frequently used as the primary key. The numbering may be sequential or random.	Customer account number
Hyperlink	A **Hyperlink** field stores a Web address (URL). All Office documents are Web-enabled so that you can click a hyperlink and display the associated Web page.	www.UNCG.edu
Attachment	The **Attachment** data type is new to Office Access 2007 .accdb files. You can attach images, spreadsheet files, charts, and other types of supported files to the records in your database.	A photo of a product

Establish a Primary Key

The **primary key** is a unique field (or combination of fields) that identifies each record in a table. Access does not require that each table have a primary key. Good database design strongly recommends the inclusion of a primary key in each table. You should select infrequently changing data for the primary key. For example, a complete address (street, city, state, and postal code) may be unique but would not make a good primary key because it is subject to change when someone moves.

You probably would not use a person's name as the primary key because many people have the same name. A Customer Identification Number, on the other hand, is unique and is a frequent choice for the primary key, as in the Customers table in this chapter. The primary key emerges naturally in many applications, such as a part number in an inventory system, or the ISBN in the Books table of a bookstore or library. At your school you have a Student ID that uniquely identifies you. No other student has the same Student ID. When no primary key occurs naturally, you can create a new field with the ***AutoNumber field*** type, and Access will assign a unique identifying number to each new record. Figure 2.3 illustrates two types of table data. In the table shown at the top of the figure, the book's ISBN is the natural primary key because no two book titles have the same ISBN. It uniquely identifies the records in the table. The lower table depicts a table where no unique identifier emerged naturally from the data, so Access automatically numbered the records in order to distinguish them.

The ***AutoNumber field*** type assigns a unique identifying number to each record.

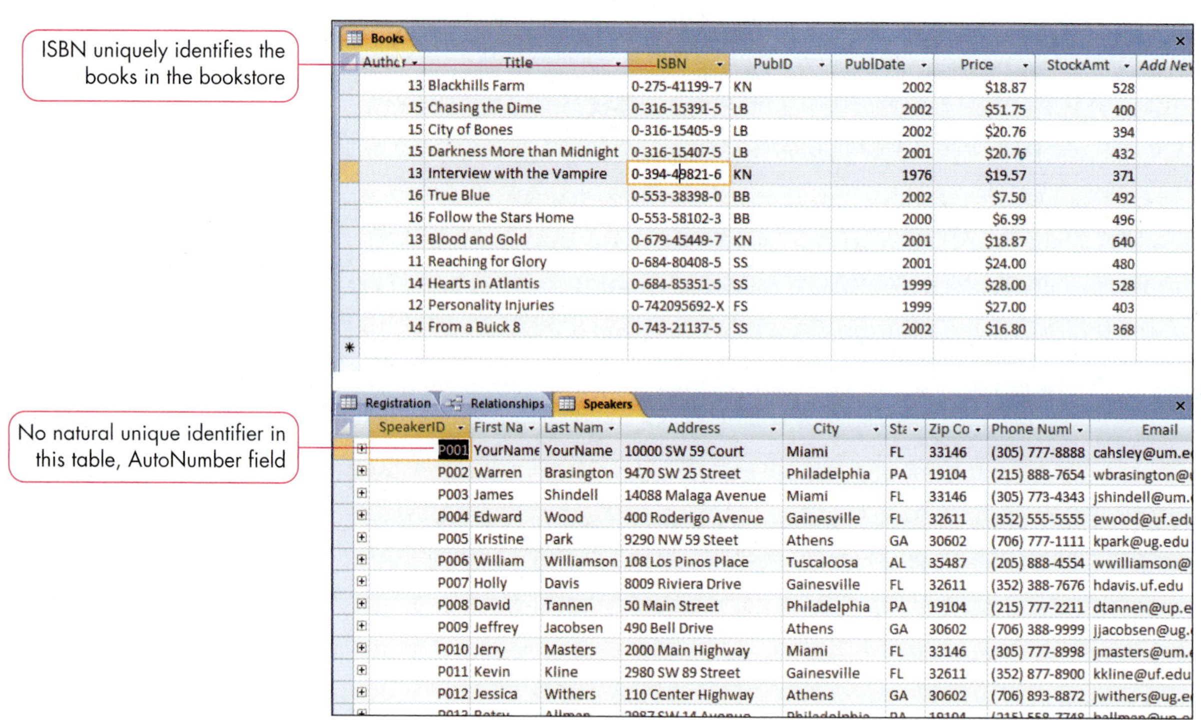

Author	Title	ISBN	PubID	PublDate	Price	StockAmt	Add New
13	Blackhills Farm	0-275-41199-7	KN	2002	$18.87	528	
15	Chasing the Dime	0-316-15391-5	LB	2002	$51.75	400	
15	City of Bones	0-316-15405-9	LB	2002	$20.76	394	
15	Darkness More than Midnight	0-316-15407-5	LB	2001	$20.76	432	
13	Interview with the Vampire	0-394-49821-6	KN	1976	$19.57	371	
16	True Blue	0-553-38398-0	BB	2002	$7.50	492	
16	Follow the Stars Home	0-553-58102-3	BB	2000	$6.99	496	
13	Blood and Gold	0-679-45449-7	KN	2001	$18.87	640	
11	Reaching for Glory	0-684-80408-5	SS	2001	$24.00	480	
14	Hearts in Atlantis	0-684-85351-5	SS	1999	$28.00	528	
12	Personality Injuries	0-742095692-X	FS	1999	$27.00	403	
14	From a Buick 8	0-743-21137-5	SS	2002	$16.80	368	

SpeakerID	First Na	Last Nam	Address	City	Sta	Zip Co	Phone Numl	Email
P001	YourName	YourName	10000 SW 59 Court	Miami	FL	33146	(305) 777-8888	cahsley@um.e
P002	Warren	Brasington	9470 SW 25 Street	Philadelphia	PA	19104	(215) 888-7654	wbrasington@
P003	James	Shindell	14088 Malaga Avenue	Miami	FL	33146	(305) 773-4343	jshindell@um.
P004	Edward	Wood	400 Roderigo Avenue	Gainesville	FL	32611	(352) 555-5555	ewood@uf.edu
P005	Kristine	Park	9290 NW 59 Steet	Athens	GA	30602	(706) 777-1111	kpark@ug.edu
P006	William	Williamson	108 Los Pinos Place	Tuscaloosa	AL	35487	(205) 888-4554	wwilliamson@
P007	Holly	Davis	8009 Riviera Drive	Gainesville	FL	32611	(352) 388-7676	hdavis.uf.edu
P008	David	Tannen	50 Main Street	Philadelphia	PA	19104	(215) 777-2211	dtannen@up.e
P009	Jeffrey	Jacobsen	490 Bell Drive	Athens	GA	30602	(706) 388-9999	jjacobsen@ug.
P010	Jerry	Masters	2000 Main Highway	Miami	FL	33146	(305) 777-8998	jmasters@um.
P011	Kevin	Kline	2980 SW 89 Street	Gainesville	FL	32611	(352) 877-8900	kkline@uf.edu
P012	Jessica	Withers	110 Center Highway	Athens	GA	30602	(706) 893-8872	jwithers@ug.e

Figure 2.3 Tables Illustrating AutoNumbered and Naturally Emerging Primary Keys

Explore Foreign Key

A **foreign key** is a primary key from one table that is used in a different table as the basis for the relationship between the tables. The Customer ID may be the primary key in the Customers table. It serves to uniquely identify each customer. It often appears as a foreign key in a related table. For example, the Order table may contain a field establishing which customer placed an individual order. Although a single Customer Identification Number can appear only one time in the Customers table, it may appear repeatedly in the Order table. A single customer may place multiple orders.

If you were the database administrator for the Youth Soccer League, you would assign a primary key to each player in the Players table and to each team in the Teams table. The Players table would have a field to show for which team the players play. The primary key in the Players table would uniquely identify the child with a PlayerID and also would show which team he or she played on using a TeamID (foreign key). Because each team has several players, you will find the TeamID repeated frequently in the Players table. Figure 2.4 depicts portions of the Players and Teams tables.

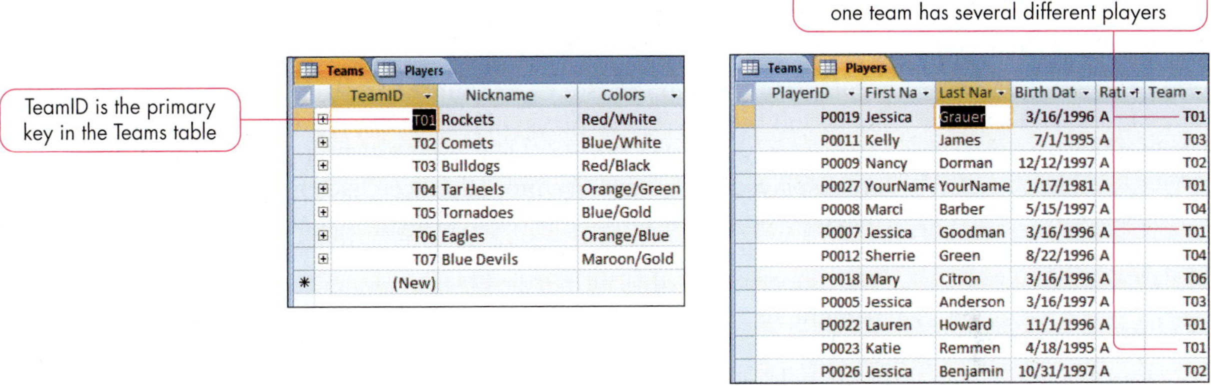

TeamID	Nickname	Colors
T01	Rockets	Red/White
T02	Comets	Blue/White
T03	Bulldogs	Red/Black
T04	Tar Heels	Orange/Green
T05	Tornadoes	Blue/Gold
T06	Eagles	Orange/Blue
T07	Blue Devils	Maroon/Gold
(New)		

PlayerID	First Na	Last Nar	Birth Dat	Rati	Team
P0019	Jessica	Grauer	3/16/1996	A	T01
P0011	Kelly	James	7/1/1995	A	T03
P0009	Nancy	Dorman	12/12/1997	A	T02
P0027	YourName	YourName	1/17/1981	A	T01
P0008	Marci	Barber	5/15/1997	A	T04
P0007	Jessica	Goodman	3/16/1996	A	T01
P0012	Sherrie	Green	8/22/1996	A	T04
P0018	Mary	Citron	3/16/1996	A	T06
P0005	Jessica	Anderson	3/16/1997	A	T03
P0022	Lauren	Howard	11/1/1996	A	T01
P0023	Katie	Remmen	4/18/1995	A	T01
P0026	Jessica	Benjamin	10/31/1997	A	T02

Figure 2.4 Tables Illustrating Primary and Foreign Keys

Use Table Views

The ***PivotTable view*** provides a convenient way to summarize and organize data about groups of records.

The ***PivotChart view*** displays a chart of the associated PivotTable View.

You may view your table in different ways. For example, you work in Datasheet view to add, edit, and delete records. The Datasheet view of an Access table resembles an Excel spreadsheet and displays data in rows (records) and columns (fields). In this chapter you will use the Design view to create and modify a table's structure, properties, and appearance. The ***PivotTable view*** provides a convenient way to summarize and organize data about groups of records. The ***PivotChart view*** displays a chart of the associated PivotTable view. Figure 2.5 displays a table in Datasheet view that corresponds to the table you saw in Figure 2.1. The Datasheet view displays the record selector symbol for the current record. It displays an asterisk in the record selector column next to the blank record at the end of the table.

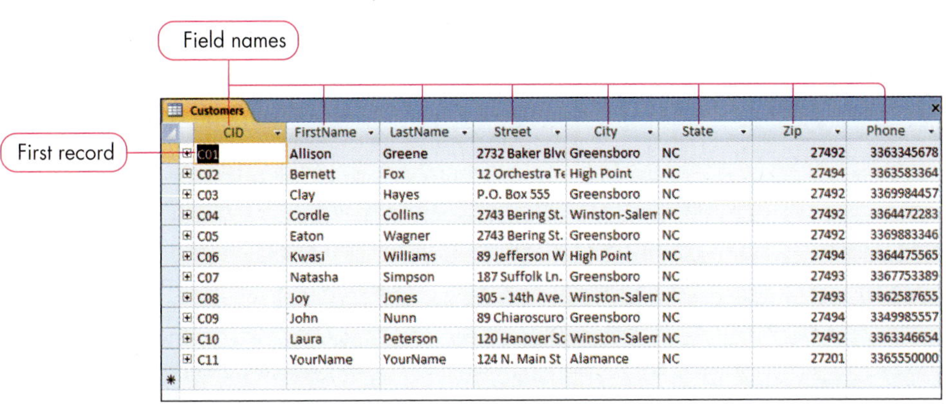

CID	FirstName	LastName	Street	City	State	Zip	Phone
C01	Allison	Greene	2732 Baker Blv	Greensboro	NC	27492	3363345678
C02	Bernett	Fox	12 Orchestra Te	High Point	NC	27494	3363583364
C03	Clay	Hayes	P.O. Box 555	Greensboro	NC	27492	3369984457
C04	Cordle	Collins	2743 Bering St.	Winston-Salem	NC	27492	3364472283
C05	Eaton	Wagner	2743 Bering St.	Greensboro	NC	27492	3369883346
C06	Kwasi	Williams	89 Jefferson W	High Point	NC	27494	3364475565
C07	Natasha	Simpson	187 Suffolk Ln.	Greensboro	NC	27493	3367753389
C08	Joy	Jones	305 - 14th Ave.	Winston-Salem	NC	27493	3362587655
C09	John	Nunn	89 Chiaroscuro	Greensboro	NC	27494	3349985557
C10	Laura	Peterson	120 Hanover Sc	Winston-Salem	NC	27492	3363346654
C11	YourName	YourName	124 N. Main St	Alamance	NC	27201	3365550000

Figure 2.5 Customers Table in Datasheet View

TIP Toggle between Datasheet and Design Views

To toggle from the Datasheet view to the Design view, click View in the Views group on the Home tab or right-click the table tab that appears above the datasheet and choose Design View from the menu. To toggle from the Design view to the Datasheet view, click View in the Views group on the Design tab or right-click the table tab that appears above the Design view grid and choose Datasheet View from the menu.

Work with Properties

A ***property*** is a characteristic or attribute of an object that determines how the object looks and behaves.

A ***property*** is a characteristic or attribute of an object that determines how the object looks and behaves. Every Access object (tables, forms, queries, and reports) has a set of properties that determine the behavior of that object. The properties for an object are displayed or changed in a property sheet. Each field has its own set of properties that determine how the data in the field are stored and displayed. The properties are set to default values according to the data type, but you can modify them if necessary. The properties are displayed in the Design view and described briefly in the following paragraphs.

A ***caption property*** specifies a label other than the field name that appears at the top of a column in Datasheet view, forms, and reports.

Exclusively using CamelCase notation provides a consistent method to name your fields, but it may make the information difficult to read and understand. Therefore, you can use the ***caption property*** to create a more readable label that appears at the top of a column in Datasheet view and in forms and reports. For example, a field named ProductCostPerUnit can have the caption *Per Unit Product Cost*. The caption displays at the top of a table or query column in Datasheet view and when the field is used in a report or form. You use the formal field name, ProductCostPerUnit, in any expressions.

In the following hands-on exercise you begin by creating a database and entering data into a table. Then you switch to the Design view to add additional fields and modify selected properties of various fields within the table.

Before launching Access, use Windows Explorer to verify that you have a folder named **Your Name Access Production** on your storage device. Remember that you cannot run Access databases from a floppy or a Zip disk or a CD, even a CD-RW. The access speed of most USB thumb drives is adequate. Access databases run best from a hard drive or network drive.

Access Table Property Types and Descriptions | Reference

Property Type	Description
Field Size	The **Field Size** property adjusts the size of a text field or limits the allowable value in a number field. Microsoft Access uses only the amount of space it needs even if the field size allows a greater number. However, Access often connects to other database programs that reserve space for the specified field length. Good practice limits the field size to reduce system storage requirements.
Format	The **Format** property changes the way a field is displayed or printed, but does not affect the stored value.
Input Mask	The **Input Mask** property facilitates data entry by displaying literal characters that are displayed but not stored, such as hyphens in a Social Security Number or slashes in a date. It also imposes data validation by ensuring that the data entered by the user fits within the mask (i.e., it prevents typing an additional digit in a phone number).
Caption	The **Caption** property specifies a label other than the field name for forms and reports. It also displays on the table's Datasheet view. It permits a more user-friendly way to view the data.
Default Value	The **Default Value** property automatically enters a designated (default) value for the field in each record that is added to the table. If 90 percent of your customers lived in North Carolina, you might consider setting the default value for the State field to NC in order to save data entry time.
Validation Rule	The **Validation Rule** property rejects any record in which the data entered does not conform to the specified rules for data entry.
Validation Text	The **Validation Text** property specifies the error message that is displayed when the validation rule is violated.
Required	The **Required** property rejects any record that does not have a value entered for this field.
Allow Zero Length	The **Allow Zero** Length property enables text or memo strings of zero length.
Indexed	The **Indexed** property increases the efficiency of a search on the designated field. (The primary key in a table is always indexed.)
Unicode Compression	The **Unicode Compression** property is set to "Yes" by default for Text, Memo, and Hyperlink fields to store the data more efficiently.
IME Mode IME Sentence Mode	The **IME Mode and IME Sentence Mode** properties refer to the Input Method Editor for East Asian languages.
Smart Tags	The properties permit advanced users to add action buttons to a field. If you were using a database offering products for sale, a Smart Tag button embedded in a product name might open an inventory file and tell the database user what products are in stock.

Hands-On Exercises

1 | Table Design, Properties, Views, and Wizards

Skills covered: 1. Create a New Database **2.** Create a Table by Entering Data **3.** Change the Primary Key, Modify Field Properties, and Delete a Field **4.** Modify Table Fields in Design View **5.** Create a New Field in Design View **6.** Switch Between the Table Design and the Table Datasheet Views

Step 1 Create a New Database

Refer to Figure 2.6 as you complete Step 1.

a. Start Microsoft Access.

   You should see the Welcome Window.

b. Click **Blank Database** in the New Blank Database section of the *Getting Started with Microsoft Office Access* window.

   The lower right corner of the window displays the Blank Database section with file management tools.

c. Click **Browse**—the little yellow folder.

d. Click the appropriate drive and folder in the Folders list on the left side of the File New Database dialog box. Choose the location where you want to save your completed files.

   You need to be intentional about where you save your database file. Otherwise you may have difficulty finding it again.

e. Click in the **File name** box and select *Database1*. Type **chap2_ho1-3_safebank_solution** to name your database and click **OK**. Click the **Create button** in the Blank Database section of the *Getting Started with Microsoft Office Access* window.

   The database window for *chap2_ho1-3_safebank_solution.accdb* should appear.

   TROUBLESHOOTING: If you skipped the instructions in Step 1d, you may have problems finding your file. From the desktop right-click Computer and select Explore from the shortcut menu. Click the Search tool. Select All Files or Folders. In the box type **chap2_ho1-3_safebank_solution.accdb.** When the search results return, copy the file, and then paste it into the appropriate folder. Open and work the remainder of the hands-on exercises from the appropriate folder.

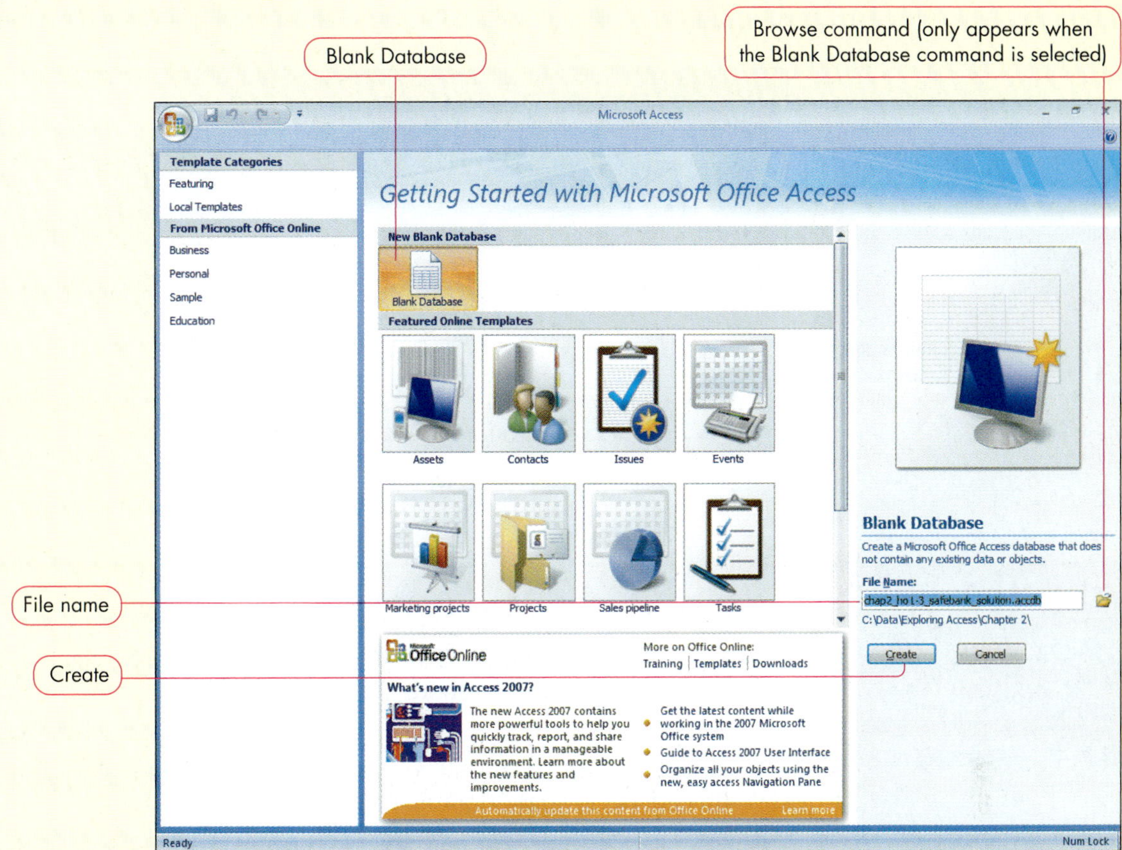

Figure 2.6 Welcome to Microsoft Office Access

Step 2
Create a Table by Entering Data

Refer to Figure 2.7 as you complete Step 2.

a. Type **B1** in the gold bordered cell and press **Enter**. The insertion point moves to the right. You also may navigate between the cells in the table by pressing **Tab** or the **arrow keys**.

b. Type **Lockley** in the first row of the third column. Press **Enter** and type **Uptown** in the next column.

c. Click in the cell below B1 and type **B2**, **Weeks**, and **Eastern**.

   If your ID numbers do not match those shown in Figure 2.7, do not be concerned. You will be deleting that field in a later step.

d. Enter the additional data for the new table as shown in Figure 2.7. Replace **YourName** with your first and last names.

e. Click **Save** on the Quick Access Toolbar. Type **Branch** in the Save As dialog box and click **OK**.

   Entering data provides an easy way to create the table initially. You can now modify the table in Design view as described in the next several steps.

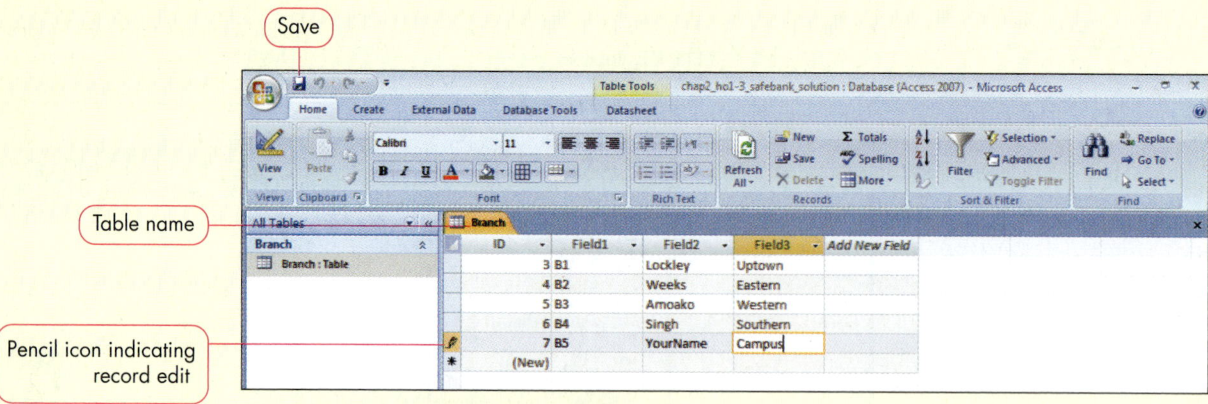

Figure 2.7 Table Data for the Branch Table

Step 3
Change the Primary Key, Modify Field Properties, and Delete a Field

Refer to Figure 2.8 as you complete Step 3.

a. Right-click the **Branch table** under All Tables in the Navigation Pane and select **Design View** from the shortcut menu.

   The fields are named ID, Field1, Field2, and Field3. These field names are not descriptive of the data, so you need to changed Field1, Field2, and Field3 to BID, Manager, and Location, respectively.

b. Click and drag *Field1* to select it and type **BID**. Replace *Field2* with **Manager** and *Field3* with **Location.**

c. Click the **row selector** to the left of the *BID* field. The entire row selects as shown in Figure 2.8.

d. Click **Primary Key** in the Tools group on the Design tab.

   You changed the primary key in this table from the automatically generated one that Access created for you to the one you intended, the BID. As soon as you identified BID as the primary key, the Indexed property updated to Yes (No Duplicates). The primary key must be a unique identifier for each record.

   TROUBLESHOOTING: A primary key must be a unique identifier for each record in the table. If you had trouble here, check to make sure the Indexed property is set to Indexed, Yes (No Duplicates). Return to Datasheet view and examine your data entry to ensure that you typed the correct values in the BID field.

e. Click the **row selector** to the left of the ID field. Click **Delete Rows** in the Tools group on the Table Tools Design tab. Click **Yes** in the warning box asking *Do you want to permanently delete the selected field(s) and all the data in the field(s)?*

TIP Shortcut Menu

You can right-click a row selector to display a shortcut menu of options to set the primary key, insert or delete rows, or display the field's properties if you prefer menus over the Ribbon.

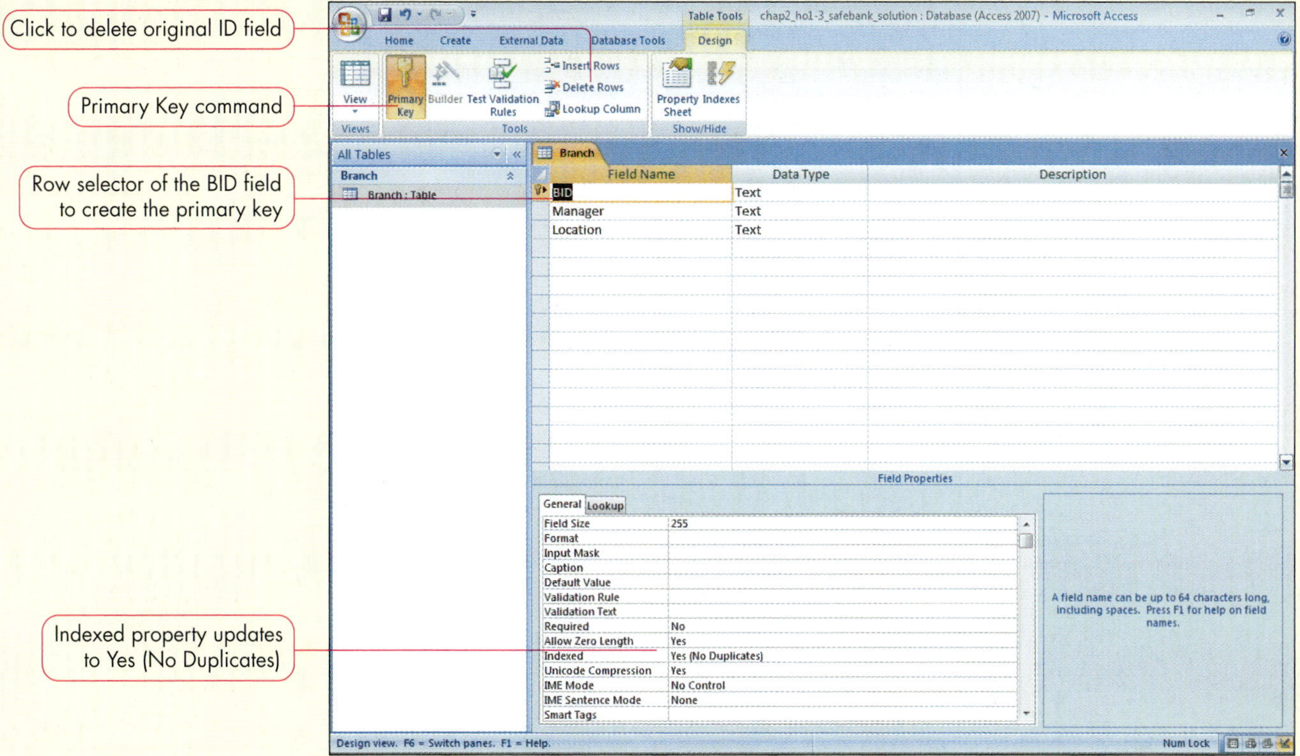

Figure 2.8 Branch Table in Design View

Step 4
Modify Table Fields in Design View

Refer to Figures 2.8 and 2.9 as you complete Step 4.

a. Modify some of the properties of the **BID** field.

1. Click in the **BID** field in the top section of the design window.
2. Click in the **Field Size** property box in the Field Properties section and type **10**.
3. Click in the **Caption** property box and type **Branch ID**.
4. Check the **Indexed** property box to make sure it is **Yes (No Duplicates)**.

If you need to change it, click in the Indexed property box. A drop-down arrow displays on the right side of the box. Scroll to select **Yes (No Duplicates)** as shown in Figure 2.8.

For the next several tasks you will toggle between the top of the design screen and the Field Properties box on the bottom of the design screen.

b. Click the **Manager** field name at the top of the window. Look in the Field Properties section. In the **Field Size** property box, replace *255* with **30**. In the **Caption** property box, type **Manager's Name**.

A caption provides a more descriptive field name. It will head the column in Datasheet view and describe data in other database objects, such as reports, forms, and queries.

c. Click the **Location** field name at the top of the window. In the **Field Size** property box, change *255* to **30**. In the **Caption** property box, type **Branch Location**.

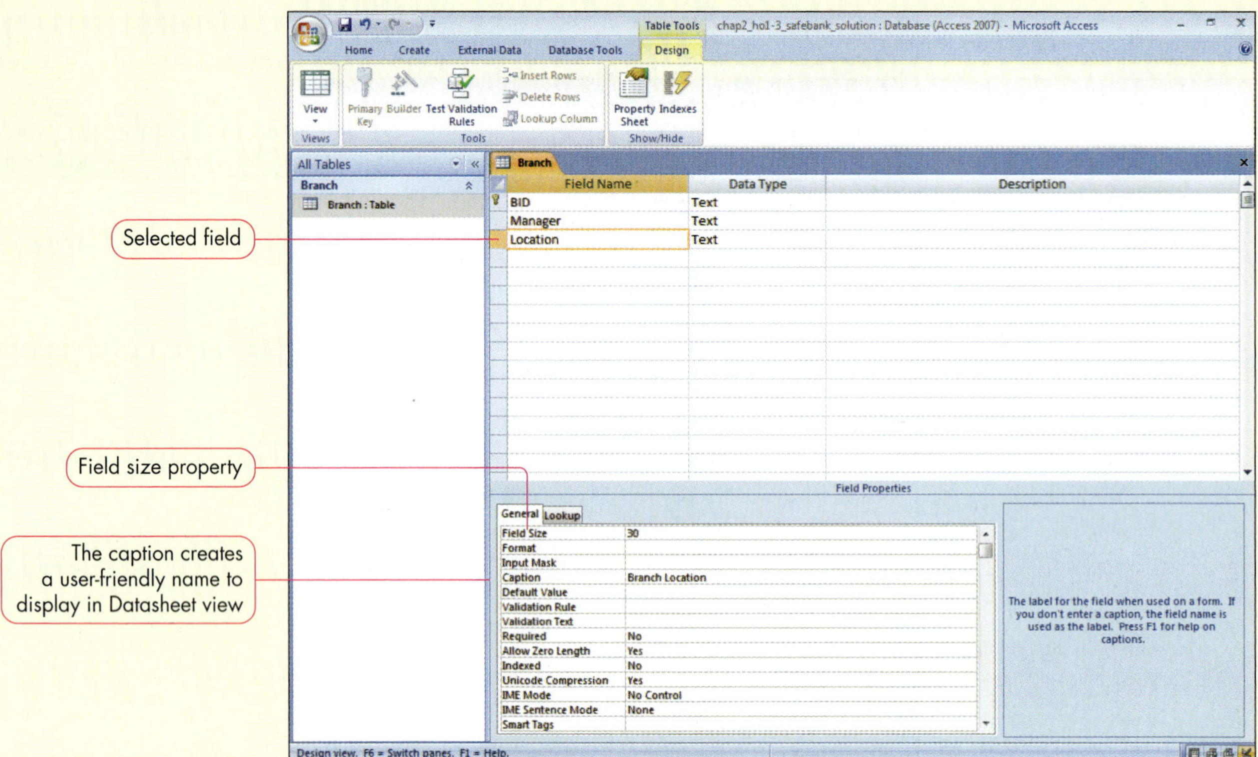

Figure 2.9 Change Field Properties to Increase Efficiency

Step 5
Create a New Field in Design View

Refer to Figure 2.10 as you complete Step 5.

a. Click the blank cell below the *Location* field name. Create a new field by typing the field name named **StartDate**.

b. Press **Tab** to move to the *Data Type* column. Click the **Data Type drop-down arrow** and select **Date/Time**.

c. Press **Tab** to move to the *Description* column and type **This date is the date the manager started working at this location.**

d. Click in the **Caption** property box and type **Manager's Start Date**.

e. Click the **Format property drop-down arrow** and select **Short Date** from the list of Date formats.

f. Click **Save** on the Quick Access Toolbar to save the Branch table within the *chap2_ho1-3_safebank_solution* database.

   A warning dialog box opens to indicate that the size of the BID, Manager, and Location field properties were shortened. It asks if you want to continue anyway. Always read the Access warnings! In this case you are OK. You changed the size of the BID field from 255 to 10 in Step 4a. You did not need 255 characters to identify the BID. Your bank only has five locations. You changed the other two field sizes in Steps 4b and 4c.

g. Click **Yes** in the warning box.

   The table Design view is useful to modify the structure of fields or to add fields to an existing table. However, tables cannot be populated in the Design view. The Datasheet view must be used to add data to a table.

TIP Keyboard Shortcut for Data Types

You also can type the first letter of the field type such as D for Date/Time, T for Text, or N for number. Click into the data type column in the field's row and, using the keyboard, type the first letter of the field type.

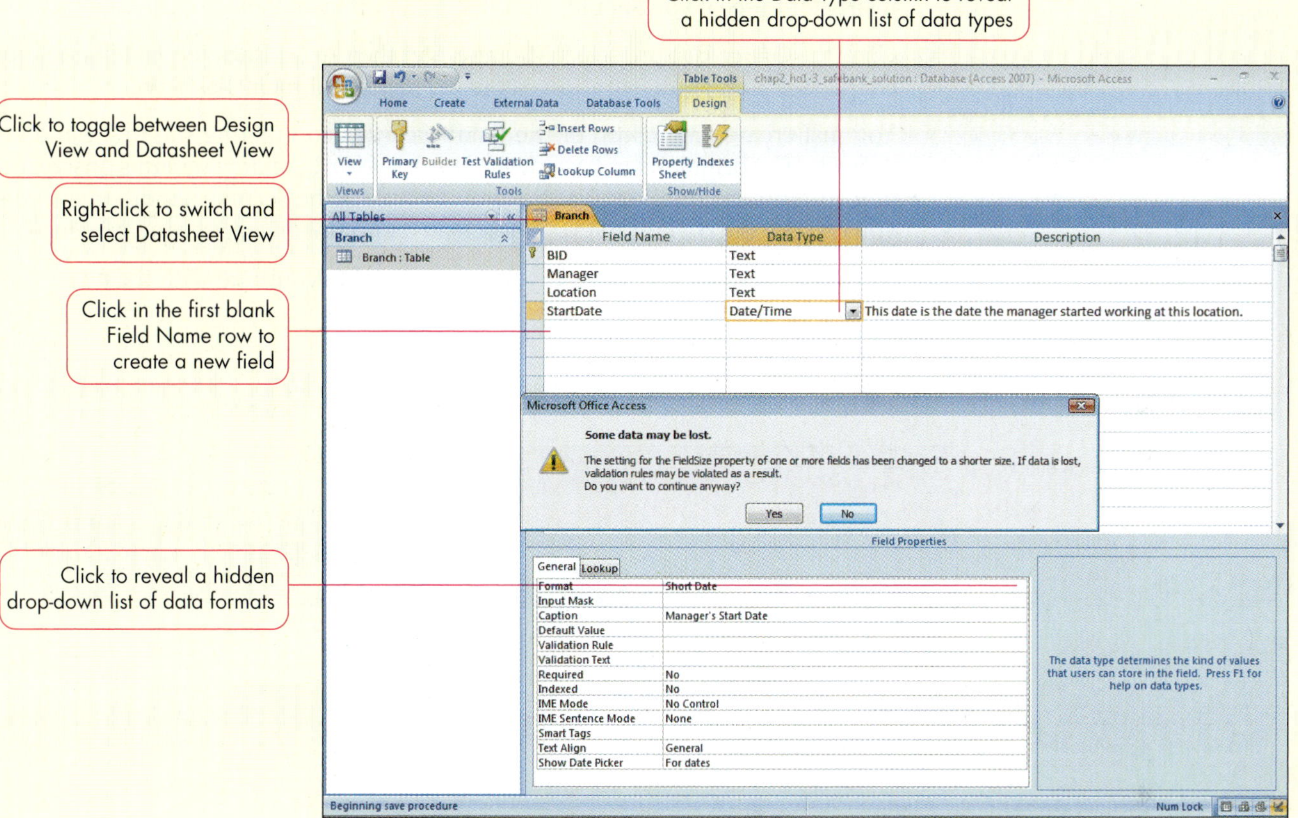

Figure 2.10 Change Field Properties to Increase Efficiency

Step 6 Switch Between the Table Design and the Table Datasheet Views

Refer to Figure 2.11 as you complete Step 6.

a. Right-click the gold tab shown in Figure 2.10 and select **Datasheet View** from the shortcut menu. (To return to the Design view, right-click the tab in Datasheet view and select Design View or click **View** in the Views group on the Design tab.)

b. Enter the dates each manager started work as shown in Figure 2.11.

   After entering the date for yourself, you remember that you started work on October 11. Therefore, you need to change the date from December 12 to October 11 using the calendar command.

c. Click the **calendar button** and click the **October 11** date on the calendar.

d. Click the table's **Close button**.

e. Double-click the **Branch table** in the Navigation Pane to open the table. Check the start dates.

   You did not save any changes you made; you closed the table without saving changes. The dates are correct because Access works from storage, not memory. As you navigate to another record, changes are saved immediately to database file.

f. Click the **Office Button**, position the mouse pointer over **Print**, and then select **Quick Print**.

   Most users do not print Access table data. Tables store and organize data and rarely generate output. People do not spend time formatting table data. Check with your instructor to see if you should submit a printed Branch table for feedback.

g. Click the **Office Button**, select **Manage**, and then select **Back Up Database**. Type **chap2_ho1_safebank_solution** as the file name and then click **Save**.

   You just created a backup of the database after completing the first hands-on exercise. The original database *chap2_ho1-3_safebank_solution* remains onscreen. If you ruin the original database as you complete the second hands-on exercise, you can use the backup file you just created and rework the second exercise.

h. Close the file and exit Access if you do not want to continue with the next exercise at this time.

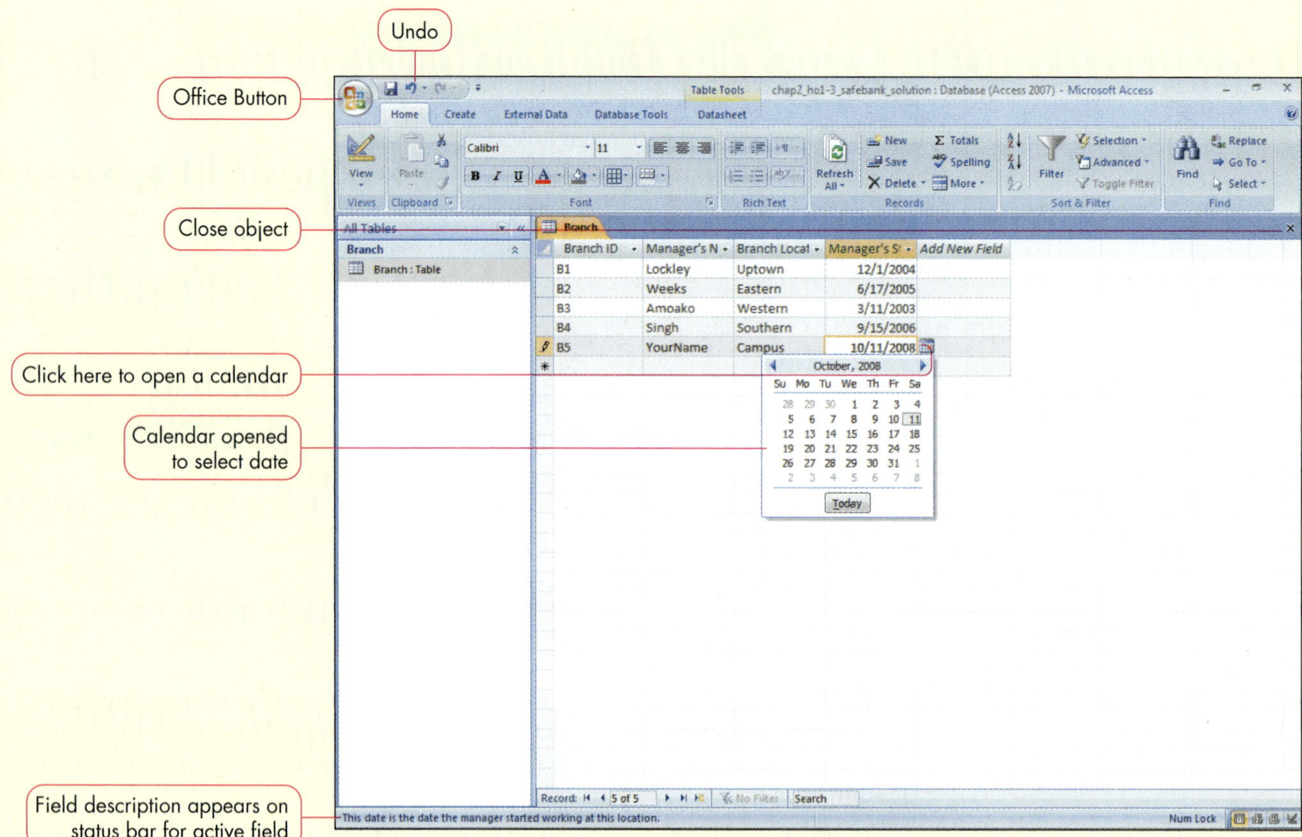

Figure 2.11 Calendar Facilitates Data Entry

Multiple Table Database

Earlier you designed a database and combined similar data items into groupings called tables. You have completed the first table in the database, the Branch table. If you reexamine your design notes and Figure 2.2, recall that you planned for two additional tables in the Safebank database. The power of a relational database lies in its ability to organize and combine data in different ways to obtain a complete picture of the events the data describe. Good database design connects the data in different tables through links. These links are the relationships that give relational databases the name. In your Safebank database one customer can have many accounts or can bank at any of the bank locations. That is, the customer's ID may be listed for many account numbers in the Accounts table, but the customer's ID is listed only one time in the Customers table. When the database is set up properly, database users can be confident that if they search for a specific customer identification number, they will be given accurate information about that customer's account balances, address, or branch preferences.

In this section, you learn about table relationships, referential integrity, indexing, and importing data from Excel.

Understanding Table Relationships

The relationship is like a piece of electronic string that travels throughout the database, searching every record of every table until it finds the events of interest. Once identified, the fields and records of interest will be tied to the end of the string, pulled through the computer, and reassembled in a way that makes the data easy to understand. The first end of the string was created when the primary key was established in the Branch table. The primary key is a unique identifier for each table record. The other end of the string ties to a field in a different table. You will include the Branch ID as a foreign field in the Accounts table. A foreign key is a field in one table that is also stored in a different table as a primary key. Each value of the Branch ID (BID) can occur only once in the Branch table because it is a primary key. However, the BID may appear multiple times in the Accounts table because many different accounts are at the same branch.

Establish Referential Integrity

The relationships will be created using an Access feature that enforces referential integrity. Integrity means truthful or reliable. When referential integrity is enforced, the user can trust the threads running through the database and tying related items together. The Campus branch manager can use the database to find the names and phone numbers of all the customers with accounts at the Campus branch. Because referential integrity has been enforced, it will not matter that the branch information is in a different table from the customer data. The invisible threads keep the information accurately connected. Managers need organized and dependable data upon which they base decisions. The threads also provide a method of ensuring data accuracy. You cannot enter a record in the Accounts table that references a Branch ID or a Customer ID that does not exist in the system. Nor can you delete a record in one table if it has related records in other tables.

(As you work, ask yourself what the anticipated results should be and then verify. When you become skilled at anticipating output correctly, you are surprised less often.)

If this were a real bank's data system, the files would be much larger and the data more sophisticated. However, the same design principles apply regardless of the database size. A small file gives you the ability to check the tables and see if your results are correct. Even though the data amounts are small, you need to develop the work practices to manage large amounts of data. With only a handful of records, you can easily count the number of accounts at the Campus branch. In addition to learning HOW to accomplish a task, you should learn to anticipate the computer's response to an instruction. Ask yourself what the anticipated results should be and then verify. When you become skilled at anticipating output correctly, you are surprised less often.

Identify Cascades

Cascades permit data changes to travel from one table to another.

Cascade delete searches the database and deletes all of the related records.

Cascade update connects a primary key change to the tables in which it is a foreign key.

Cascades help update related data across tables. In databases ***cascades*** permit data changes to travel from one table to another. The database designer may establish cascades to update or delete related records. The string tying related items together can also make global changes to the data. If one bank branch closed and the accounts were not transferred to a different branch, the ***cascade delete*** feature would search the database and delete all of the accounts and customers who banked solely at the closed branch. (This may not be an optimal business practice, but it explains how the cascade delete feature works.) If a customer with an account at one branch opens a new account at a different branch, the ***cascade update*** will travel through the databases and connect the new account to the customer's address in the Customers table and the new account balance in the Accounts table.

As a general rule, you do not want changes cascading through the database. With a click of a mouse, an inattentive data entry clerk could delete hundreds of records in various tables throughout the database. However, you need the power of a cascade occasionally. Suppose your company and another firm merged. Your firm has always stored customer account numbers as a five-digit number. The other firm has always used a three-digit account number. In this case you would turn the cascade update feature on; open the Customers table; and change all of the three digit numbers to five digit ones. The new account numbers would cascade through the database to any records in any table related to the Customers table—for example, the Payments or Orders tables.

Retrieve Data Rapidly by Indexing

The ***indexed property*** is a list that relates the field values to the records that contain the field value.

In Hands-On Exercise 1 you created the Branch table and established the BID as the primary key. Access changed the ***indexed property*** to Yes (No Duplicates). Access uses indexing exactly like you would read a book on U.S. history. If you need to know who succeeded Van Buren as president, you could start on page 1 and read the book in order page by page. Alternatively, you could go to the index and discover where the information about Van Buren may be found and open directly to that page. Using the index in a book makes finding (retrieving) information quicker. Indexing a database field has the same effect; it greatly reduces retrieval time. The actual index is a list that relates the field values to the records that contain the field value. Without an index, each row in the database would need to be scanned sequentially, an inefficient search method. The increased search time would adversely affect the performance of the database. All primary keys must be indexed. Additional table fields also may be indexed.

Sharing Data with Excel

Many Access and Excel tasks overlap. Although you are learning the highly valuable skill of using Access, more people know how to use Excel than Access. Therefore, a lot of data resides within Excel spreadsheets. Often the data stored in those spreadsheets fits well into an Access database design. Therefore, you need to be able to integrate existing Excel spreadsheet data into the organization's database. Fortunately, Access provides you with wizards that facilitate data sharing with Excel. Access can both import data from Excel and export data to Excel easily.

Figures 2.12–2.18 show how to use the Get External Data – Excel Spreadsheet wizard. You launch the wizard by clicking the External Data tab. Table 2.1 lists and describes the four groups on the External Data tab.

Table 2.1 Access and Other Applications Share Data

Process	When Used
Get External Data	Used to bring data into an Access database. The data sources include Excel, Other Access files, XML, SharePoint Lists, and Text files.
Export Data	Used to send a portion of a database to other applications. You might use this to create a Mail Merge letter and envelopes in Word. You could create an Excel file for a co-worker who does not know how to use (or does not have) Access, or could share your data over the Internet via a SharePoint List.
Collect and Update	You could create an e-mail mail merge to send e-mails to your clients and then use Access to manage the clients' responses.
Offline SharePoint Lists	This process might be used when traveling, if an immediate Internet connection is not available.

Launch the wizard by clicking the Excel command in the Get External Data Group.

Figure 2.12 shows the External Data tab that contains the Import Excel command. After you specify the data storage location, you can use the imported data to create a new table in Access, to ***append*** new records to an existing Access table, or to create a link between the Excel file and the Access table. When linked, any changes made to the Excel file will be updated automatically in the database, too.

You ***append*** records to an existing table by adding new records to the end of the table.

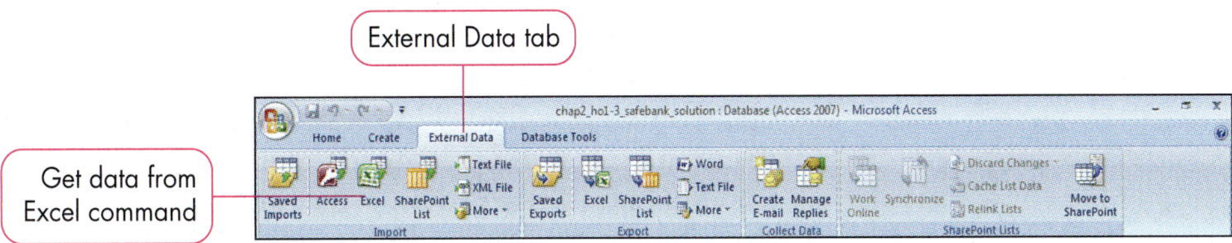

Figure 2.12 Select the Source and Destination for the Data

Figure 2.13 shows the Get External Data – Excel Spreadsheet dialog box. This feature controls where you find the data to import. It asks you to choose among three options governing what to do with the data in Access: place it in a new table, append the data to an existing table, or link the Access table to the Excel source.

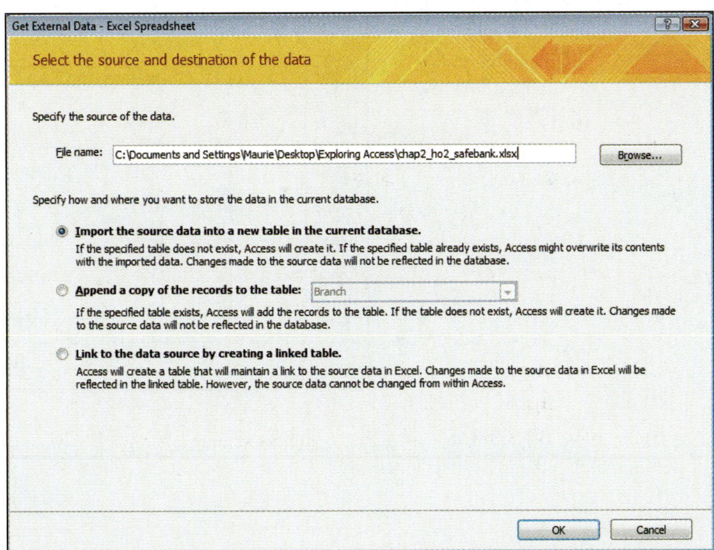

Figure 2.13 Select the Source and Destination of the Data

After you select the Excel workbook, you see the Import Spreadsheet Wizard dialog box, which displays a list of the worksheets in the specified workbook (see Figure 2.14). Use the options to specify a worksheet, in this case, the Customers worksheet. The bottom of the Import Spreadsheet Wizard dialog box displays a preview of the data stored in the specified worksheet.

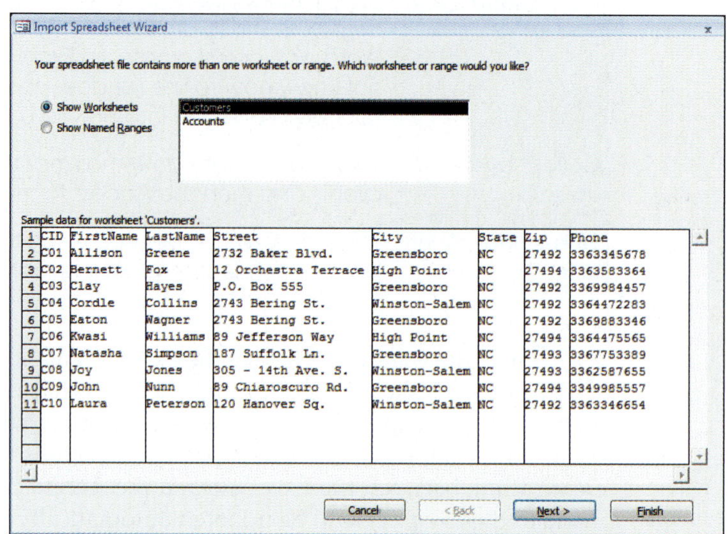

Figure 2.14 Show Available Worksheets and Preview Data

Although well-designed spreadsheets include descriptive labels, not all Excel users practice good spreadsheet design. The second window of the Import Spreadsheet Wizard dialog box contains a check box that gives you a chance to describe the data to Access (see Figure 2.15). When you find a label row in a spreadsheet, check the box. Access will use the Excel labels to generate the Access field names. When you find unlabeled data, do not check the box, and the data will import using Field1, Field2, and so on as field names.

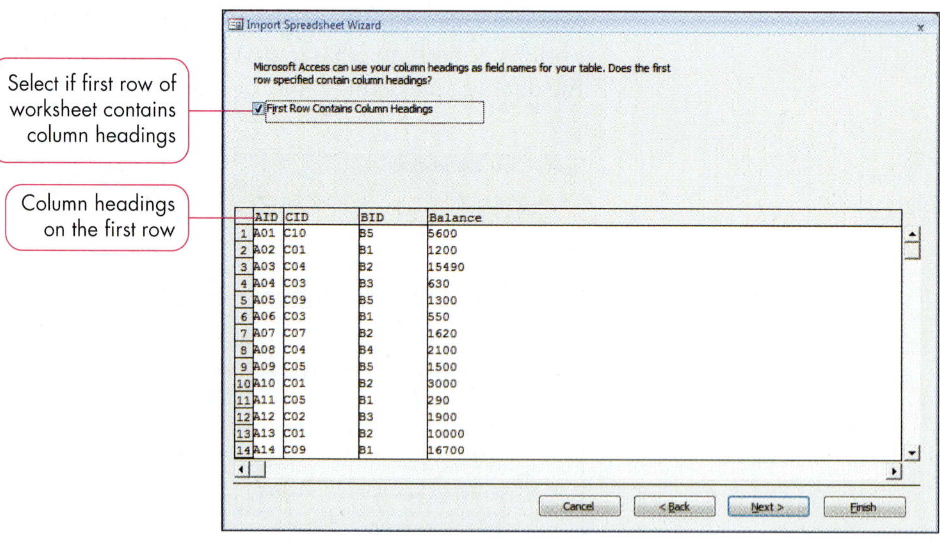

Figure 2.15 Column Headings Become Field Names

The third window of the Import Spreadsheet Wizard dialog box enables you to stipulate field properties (see Figure 2.16). The AID field is shown in the figure. Because it will become this table's primary key, you need to set the Index Property to Yes (No Duplicates). Use the Field Name box to select other fields (columns) in the worksheet and establish their properties. Not all Access table properties are supported by the wizard. You will need to open the table in Design view after importing it and make some additional property changes.

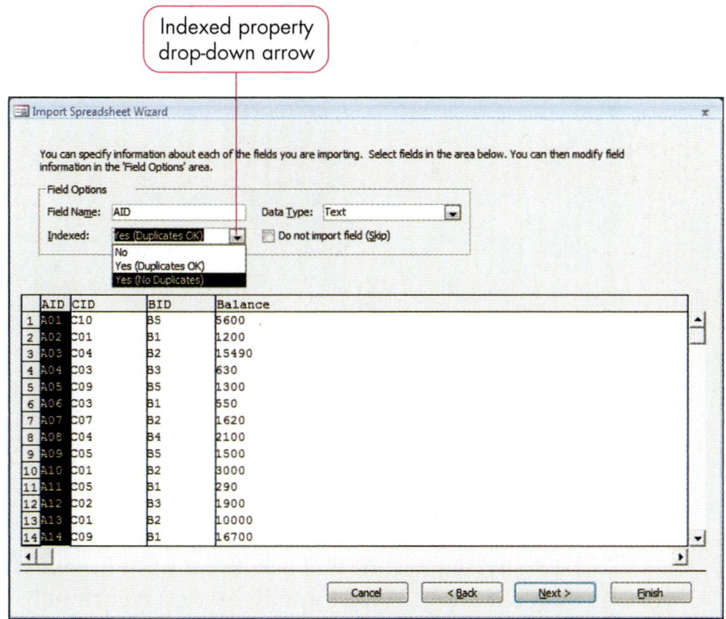

Figure 2.16 Field Options for Importing the Spreadsheet

The fourth window of the Import Spreadsheet Wizard dialog box enables you to establish the primary key before the import takes place (see Figure 2.17). If the option for *Let Access add primary key* is selected, Access will generate an AutoNumber field and designate it as the primary key. In the import described in the figure, the Excel data has a unique identifier that will become the table's primary key on import.

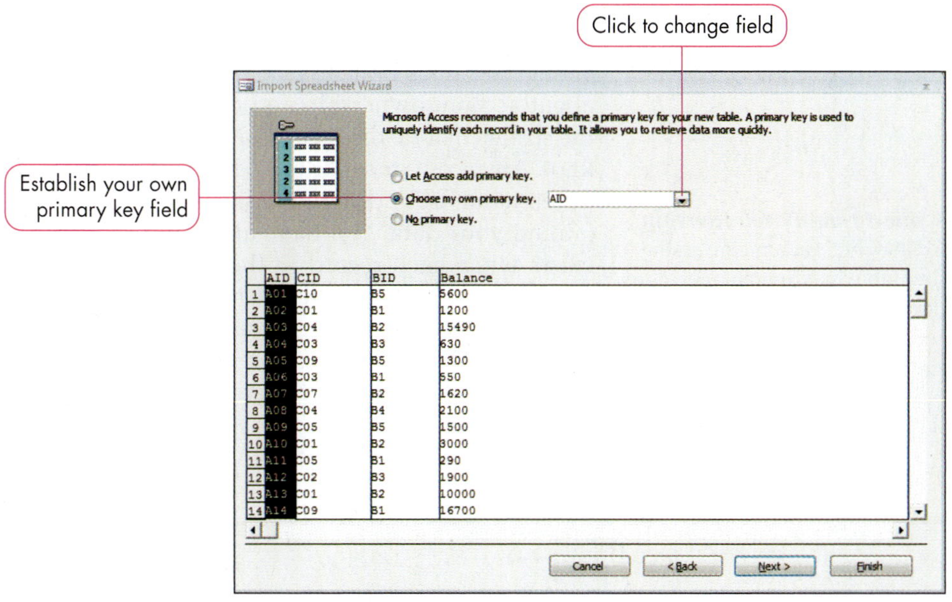

Figure 2.17 Primary Key Designation

Use the final window of the Import Spreadsheet Wizard dialog box prompts you to name the Access table. If the worksheet in the Excel workbook was named, Access uses the worksheet name as the table name (see Figure 2.18).

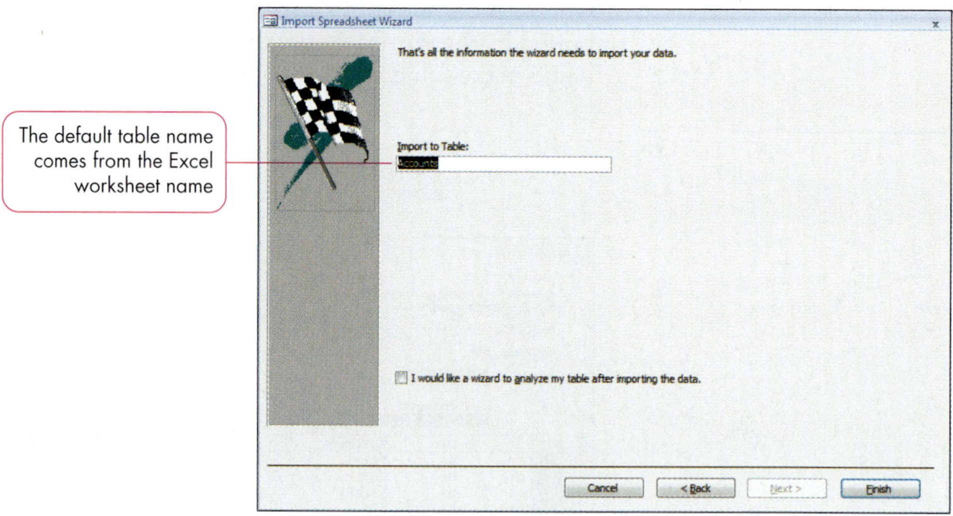

Figure 2.18 Table Name for Import Spreadsheet

Finally, the wizard will ask if you wish to save the import steps. Frequently data is shared between Access and Excel on a recurrent basis. At the close of a day or week or month, data from Excel are routinely imported and updated in Access. Saving the import steps expedites the data re-importation the next time it is needed. The imported data become a permanent part of the Access file. Access will open a final dialog box asking if you want to save the import specifications. In your hands-on exercise, the data import is a one-time only event so you do not need to save the import parameters.

Establishing Table Relationships

You should store like data items together using a logical file management structure. The customer data are stored in the Customers table. The Branch table stores data about the bank's branch, management, and location. The Accounts table stores data about account ownership and balances. You learned earlier that relationships form the strings that tie the related table data together. When you tie something, you use a knot. Any scout or sailor uses different knots for different purposes. Just as you use different knots for differing tasks, Access provides several different relationships for joining your data. You have already discovered that a ***one-to-many relationship*** exists when each record in the first table may match one, more than one, or no records in the second table. Each record in the second table matches one and only one record in the first table to establish a powerful knot or relationship. In a well-designed database you use this type of relationship most frequently. Table 2.2 lists and describes the different types of relationships you can form between Access tables.

A ***one-to-many relationship*** exists when each record in the first table may match one, more than one, or no records in the second table. Each record in the second table matches one and only one record in the first table.

Table 2.2 Relationship Types

Relationship Name	Definition
One-To-Many	This relationship is between a primary key in the first table and a foreign key in the second table. The first table must have only one occurrence of each value. That is: Each customer must have a unique identification number in the Customers table or each employee must have a unique employee identification number in the Employee table. The foreign key field in the second table may have recurrent values. For example, one customer may have many different account numbers, or one employee can provide service to many customers.
One-To-One	Two different tables use the same primary key. Exactly one record exists in the second table for each record in the first table. Sometimes security reasons require a table to be split into two related tables. For example, anyone in the company can look in the Employee table and find the employee's office number, department assignment, or telephone extension. However, only a few people need to have access to the employee's salary, Social Security Number, performance review, or marital status. Both tables use the same unique identifier to identify each employee.
Many-To-Many	This is an artificially constructed relationship giving many matching records in each direction between tables. It requires construction of a third table called a junction table. For example, a database might have a table for employees and one for projects. Several employees might be assigned to one project, but one employee might also be assigned to many different projects. When Access connects to databases using Oracle or other software, you find this relationship type. When using Access as a stand-alone software, you would specify a Multivalue field and record multiple items as legitimate entries in a single field.

Establish a One-To-Many Relationship

When you click the Database Tools tab, you see the Show/Hide group (see Figure 2.19). The first command is the tool that opens the Relationships window. If this were a long established database, the Relationships window would be populated with the related tables in the database.

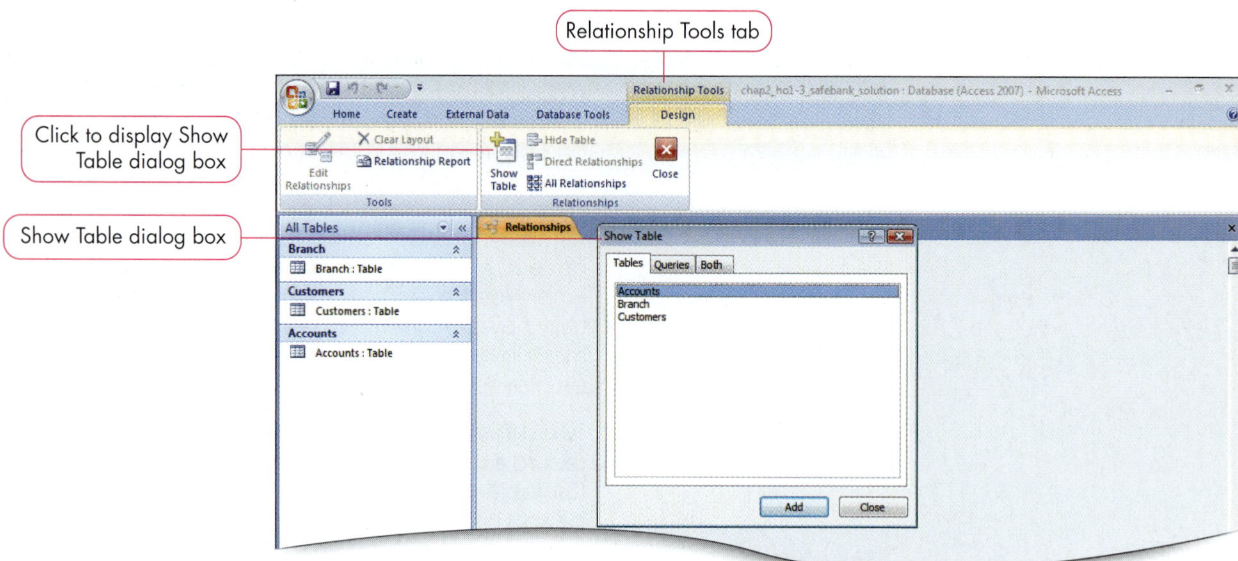

Figure 2.19 The Show/Hide Group and Show Table Dialog Box

Because the first time you will use the Relationships window you will be working in a newly created database, you must first use the Show Table dialog box to add the necessary tables to the Relationships window (see Figure 2.19). Select the tables you want to use in relation to other tables and add them to the Relationships window by clicking Add.

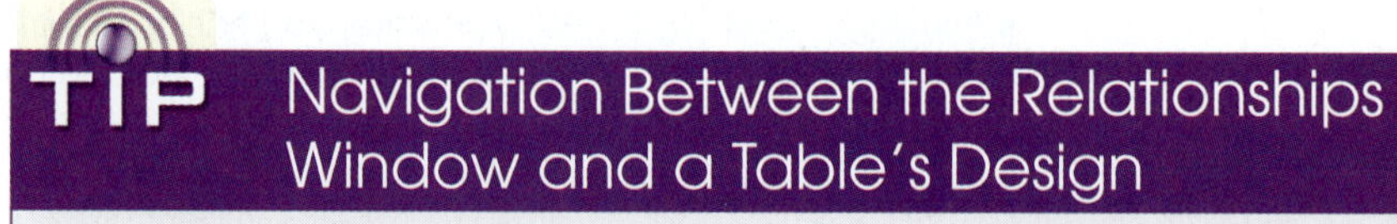

TIP Navigation Between the Relationships Window and a Table's Design

When you right-click the table title bar in the Relationships window, the shortcut menu offers you a chance to open the table in Design view. Because relationships may be established only between data with the same definition, you have a chance to check how the data in different tables have been defined.

When possible, expand the table windows to display the complete list of field names shown in the table (see Figure 2.20). You may rearrange the tables by clicking and dragging the table window title bar.

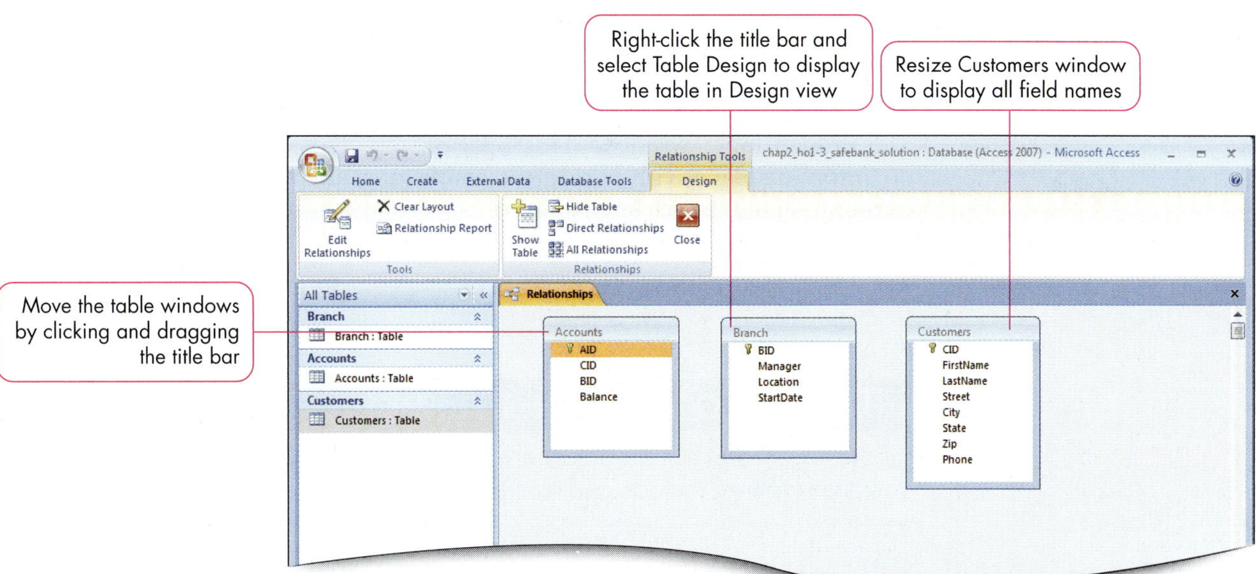

Figure 2.20 The Relationships Window with Resized Tables

Establish the relationships by clicking and dragging the field name from one table to the field name in the related table. When you release the mouse, the Edit Relationships dialog box opens (see Figure 2.21). Prior to establishing a relationship, Access runs through the table data to ensure that the rules you attempt to establish in the relationship can be met. For example, it checks to make sure that the branch identification number in the Accounts table (foreign key) exactly matches a Branch ID in the Branch table where it is the primary key. If all of the Branch IDs do not match exactly between the tables, Access cannot establish the relationship with referential integrity enforced. It will attempt to make a connection, but it will warn you that a problem exists with the data.

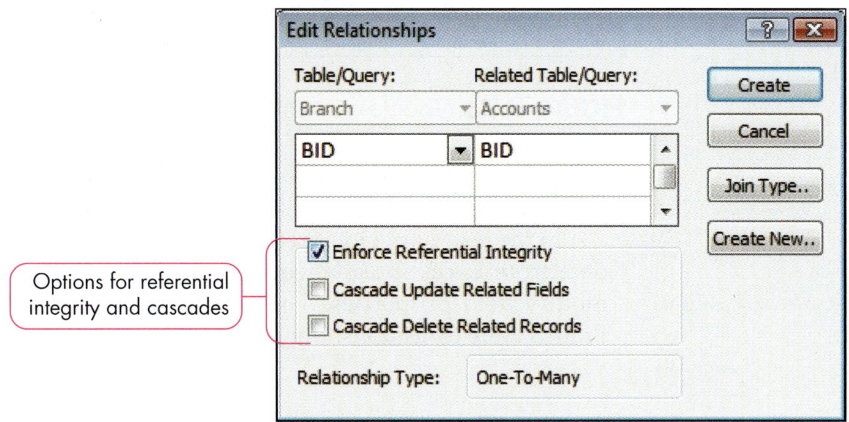

Figure 2.21 The Edit Relationships Dialog Box

Figure 2.22 shows the Relationships window for the Safebank database with all relationships created using referential integrity. The relationship between the CID field in the Customers table and CID field in the Accounts table runs behind the Branch table window. This relationship does not affect the Branch table; it simply displays with part of the connecting line obscured. You can switch the positions of the Branch and Accounts tables in the Relationships window to improve clarity.

TIP Editing a Relationship

If the relationship has already been established and you need to edit it, right-click the relationship line. You can also right-click the relationship line to delete a relationship.

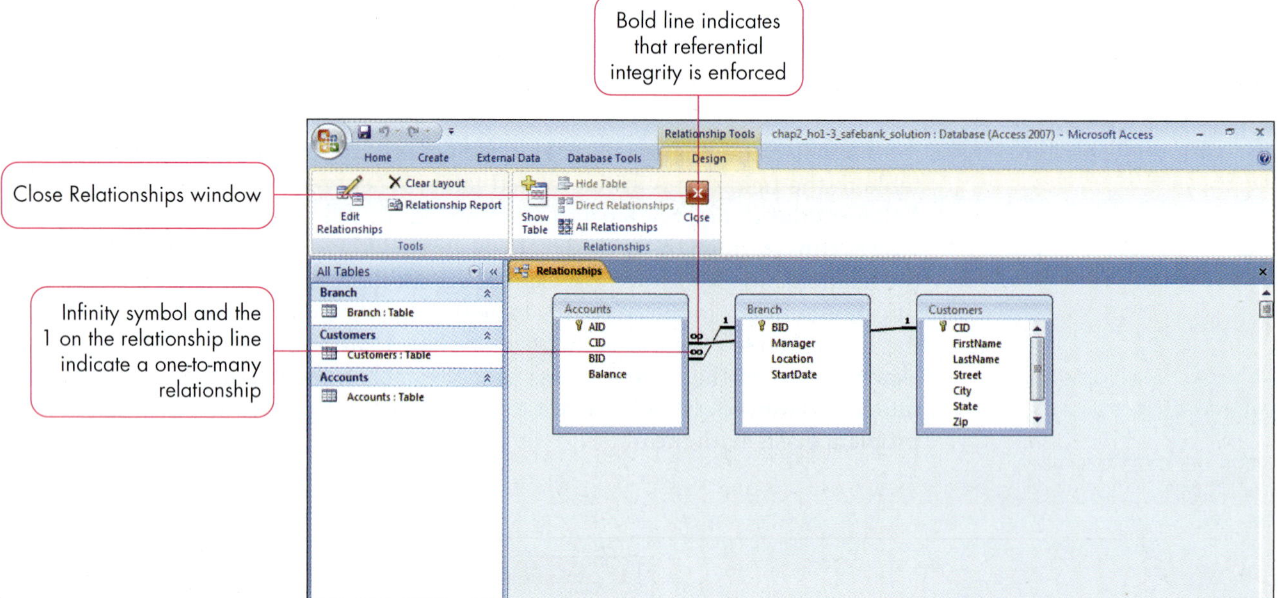

Figure 2.22 The Relationships Window Displaying One-to-Many Relationships

In the next hands-on exercise, you will create two additional tables by importing data from Excel spreadsheets into the Safebank database. You will establish and modify field properties. Then you will connect the newly imported data to the Branch table by establishing relationships between the tables.

Hands-On Exercises

2 | Imports and Relationships

Skills covered: 1. Import Excel Data into an Access Table **2.** Import Additional Excel Data **3.** Modify an Imported Table's Design **4.** Add Data to an Imported Table **5.** Establish Table Relationships **6.** Understand How Referential Integrity Protects Data

Step 1
Import Excel Data into an Access Table

Refer to Figure 2.23 and Figures 2.12 through 2.18 as you complete Step 1.

a. Open the *chap2_ho1-3_safebank_solution.accdb* file if necessary, then click **Options** on the Security Warning toolbar, click the **Enable this content option** in the Microsoft Office Security Options dialog box, and click **OK**.

   TROUBLESHOOTING: If you create unrecoverable errors while completing this hands-on exercise, you can delete the *chap2_ho1-3_safebank_solution* file, copy the *chap2_ho1_safebank_solution* database you created at the end of the first hands-on exercise, and open the copy of the backup database to start the second hands-on exercise again.

b. Click the **External Data tab** (see Figure 2.12). Click **Import Excel Spreadsheet** in the Import group to launch the Get External Data – Excel Spreadsheet wizard. Select the **Import the source data into a new table in the current database option**, if necessary, as shown in Figure 2.13.

c. Click **Browse** and go to your **Exploring Access folder**. Select the *chap2_ho2_safebank.xlsx* workbook. Click **Open**.

d. Click **OK** in the Get External Data-Excel Spreadsheet to open the **Import Spreadsheet Wizard**.

   The first window shows all of the worksheets in the workbook. This particular workbook contains only two worksheets: Accounts and Customers. The Customers worksheet is active, and a list of the data contained in the Customers worksheet displays in the Wizard.

e. Click on the **Accounts worksheet** and click **Next** (see Figure 2.14).

f. Click in the **First Row Contains Column Headings check box** to tell Access that column headings exist in the Excel file (see Figure 2.15).

   The field names, AID, CID, BID, and Balance will import from Excel along with the data stored in the rows in the worksheet.

g. Click **Next**.

   The AID (Account ID) will become the primary key in this table. It needs to be a unique identifier, so we must change the properties to disallow duplicates.

h. Click the **Indexed drop-down arrow** in the Field Options section and select **Indexed Yes (No Duplicates)**. Click **Next** (see Figure 2.16).

i. Click the **Choose my own primary key** option. Make sure that the **AID** field is selected. Click **Next** (see Figure 2.17).

   The final screen of the Import Spreadsheet Wizard asks you to name your table. The name of the Excel worksheet was Accounts and Access defaults to the worksheet name. It is an acceptable name (see Figure 2.18).

j. Click **Finish**.

A dialog box opens asking if you wish to save the parameters of this import to use again. If this were sales data that were collected in Excel and updated to the database on a weekly basis, saving the import would save time.

k. Click **Close**.

Saving these import parameters is not necessary. The new table displays in the Navigation Pane and resides in the Safebank database.

l. Open the newly imported **Accounts table** in Datasheet view, compare it to Figure 2.23, and then close the table..

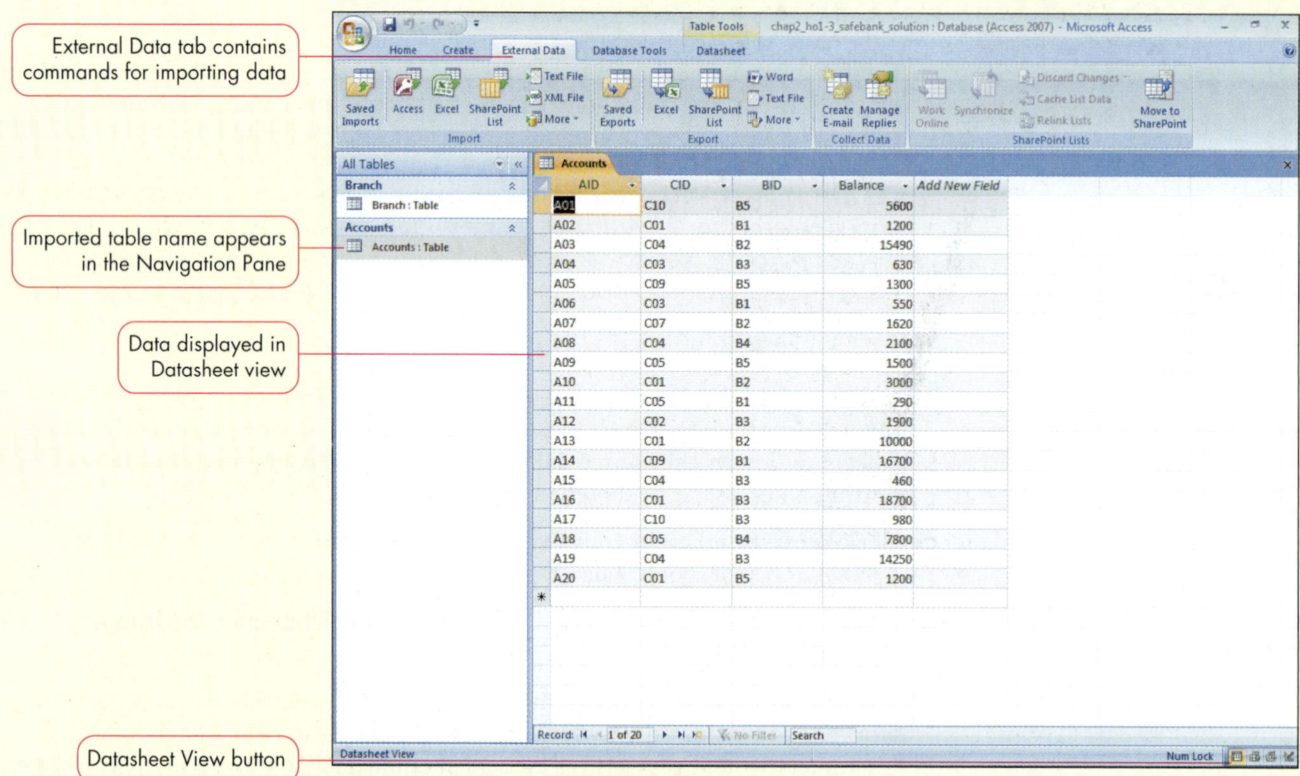

AID	CID	BID	Balance	Add New Field
A01	C10	B5	5600	
A02	C01	B1	1200	
A03	C04	B2	15490	
A04	C03	B3	630	
A05	C09	B5	1300	
A06	C03	B1	550	
A07	C07	B2	1620	
A08	C04	B4	2100	
A09	C05	B5	1500	
A10	C01	B2	3000	
A11	C05	B1	290	
A12	C02	B3	1900	
A13	C01	B2	10000	
A14	C09	B1	16700	
A15	C04	B3	460	
A16	C01	B3	18700	
A17	C10	B3	980	
A18	C05	B4	7800	
A19	C04	B3	14250	
A20	C01	B5	1200	

Figure 2.23 The Newly Imported Accounts Table

Step 2
Import Additional Excel Data

Refer to Figure 2.24 and Figures 2.13 through 2.18 as you complete Step 2.

a. Turn back to the beginning of Step 1 and repeat the instructions b through l, with the following changes.

b. Click on the **Customers worksheet** in Step 1e.

c. Change the index property of the **CID** field to **Yes (No Duplicates)** in Step 1h.

d. Identify the **CID** (Customer ID) as the primary key in Step 1i.

The default table name will be the Customers table. This is a good name so accept it.

e. Click **Finish** and click **Close**.

The Navigation Pane contains three tables: Branch, Accounts, and Customers.

f. Open the newly imported **Customers table** in Datasheet view, compare it to Figure 2.24, and then close the table.

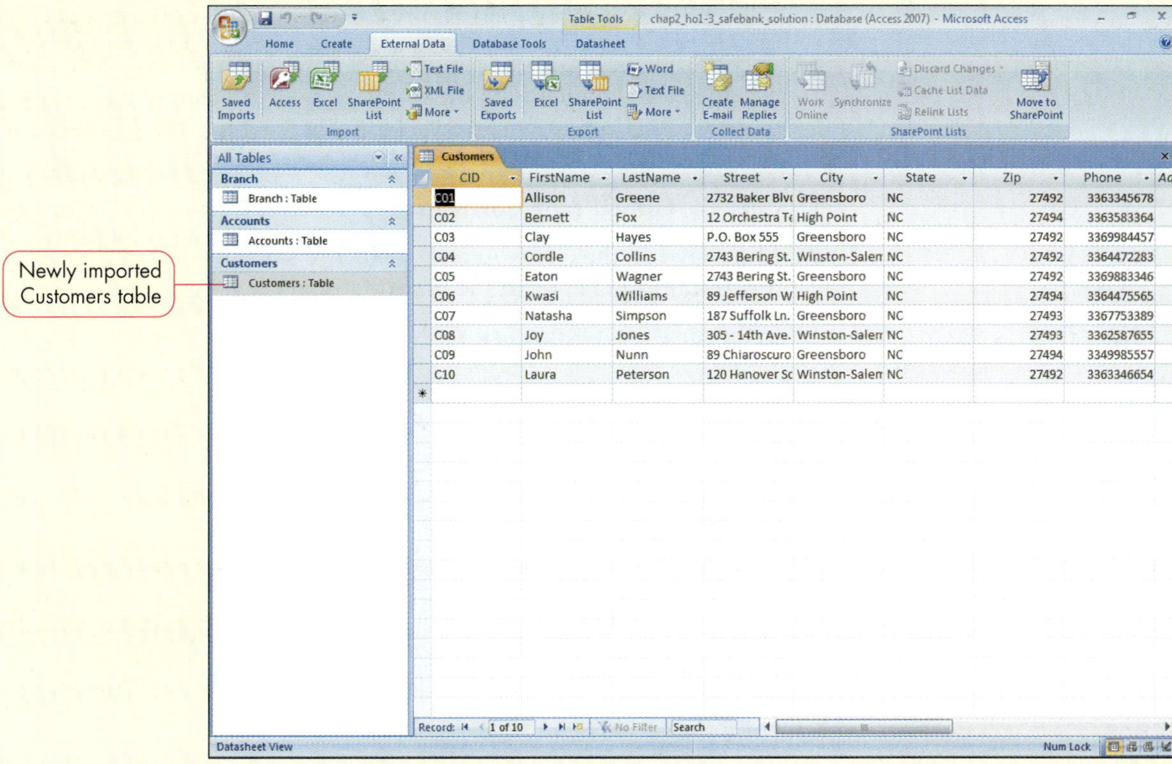

CID	FirstName	LastName	Street	City	State	Zip	Phone
C01	Allison	Greene	2732 Baker Blv	Greensboro	NC	27492	3363345678
C02	Bernett	Fox	12 Orchestra Te	High Point	NC	27494	3363583364
C03	Clay	Hayes	P.O. Box 555	Greensboro	NC	27492	3369984457
C04	Cordle	Collins	2743 Bering St.	Winston-Salen	NC	27492	3364472283
C05	Eaton	Wagner	2743 Bering St.	Greensboro	NC	27492	3369883346
C06	Kwasi	Williams	89 Jefferson W	High Point	NC	27494	3364475565
C07	Natasha	Simpson	187 Suffolk Ln.	Greensboro	NC	27493	3367753389
C08	Joy	Jones	305 - 14th Ave.	Winston-Salen	NC	27493	3362587655
C09	John	Nunn	89 Chiaroscuro	Greensboro	NC	27494	3349985557
C10	Laura	Peterson	120 Hanover Sc	Winston-Salen	NC	27492	3363346654

Figure 2.24 The Newly Imported Customers Table

Step 3 Modify an Imported Table's Design

Refer to Figure 2.25 as you complete Step 3.

a. Open the **Accounts table** in Design view and click the **AID** field if necessary.

b. Change the **AID** field size to **10**. Look at the bottom of the window in the Field Properties box.

   The field size was set at 255. Importing data from Excel saves typing but does not always create an efficiently designed database.

c. Type **Account ID** in the **Caption** property box for the AID field.

d. Click the **CID** field in the top of the Design view window to activate the Field Properties for the CID field.

e. Type **10** in the **Field Size** property box for the CID field using the Field Properties box in the bottom of the window.

f. Type **Customer ID** in the **Caption** property for the CID field.

g. Click the **BID** field in the top of the Design view window to activate the Field Properties for the BID field.

h. Type **10** in the **Field Size** property box for the BID field in the Field Properties box at the bottom of the window.

i. Type **Branch ID** in the **Caption** property box for the BID field.

j. Click the **Balance** field in the top of the Design view window to activate the Field Properties for the Balance field.

k. Click in the **Format** property box to display a drop-down arrow.

Access often hides drop-down arrows until the property is activated. As you become more familiar with the software, you will learn which properties contain these hidden drop-down arrows. In the meanwhile, develop the habit of clicking around each new screen.

l. Click the **Format drop-down arrow** and select **Currency** from the list.

m. Click **Save** on the Quick Access Toolbar to save the design changes you made to the Accounts table. **Read the Warning Box!** Click **Yes**.

In this case it is OK to click Yes because the size of three fields were shortened.

n. Open the **Customers table** in Design view. Change the **field size** of the **CID** field to **10** and add a **caption, Customer ID**.

o. Save the design changes to the Customers table.

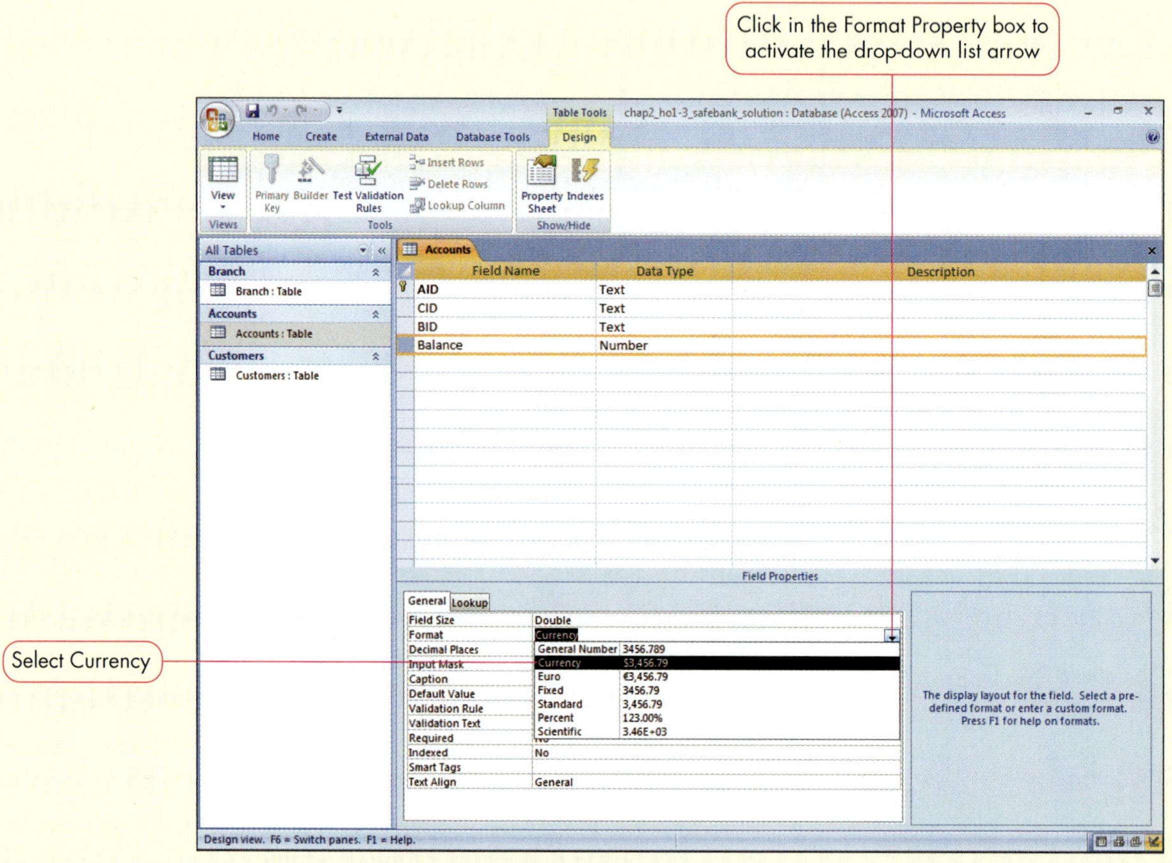

Click in the Format Property box to activate the drop-down list arrow
Select Currency

Figure 2.25 The Format Property of the Balance Field Set to Currency

Step 4
Add Data to an Imported Table

Refer to Figure 2.26 as you complete Step 4.

a. Open the **Customers table** in Datasheet view.

   The asterisk in the row selector area is the indicator of a place to enter a new record.

b. Click the **Customer ID** field in the record after C10. Type **C11**. Fill in the rest of the data using your information as the customer. You may use a fictitious address and phone number.

c. Open **Accounts table** in Datasheet view. Create a new account ID A21. Enter **C11** as the Customer ID and **B5** as the Branch ID. Use your course number and section for the Balance field value.

   If you were a student in section 04 of ISM 210, you would enter 21004 as the Balance.

d. Close all of the tables; keep the database open.

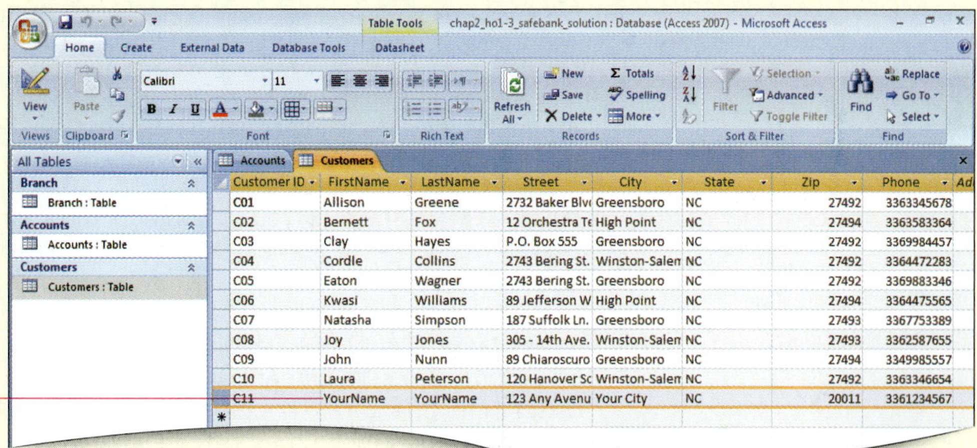
Add data about yourself

Figure 2.26 The Customers Table Displaying the New Account

Step 5
Establish Table Relationships

Refer to Figures 2.27 and 2.21 as you complete Step 5.

a. Click the **Database Tools tab**. Click **Relationships** in the Show/Hide group.

   The Relationships window opens to the Show Table dialog box.

   TROUBLESHOOTING: If the Show Table dialog box does not open, click Show Table in the Relationships group on the Design tab.

b. Double-click each of the three tables to add them to the Relationships window. (Alternatively, click a table, and then click **Add**.) Click **Close** in the Show Table dialog box.

   The Accounts and Branch table boxes are large enough to display all of the field names. The Customers table has a scroll bar because it has too many fields to display in the small space.

TROUBLESHOOTING: If you duplicate a table, you may have gotten carried away clicking and adding. The duplicate table will display in the Relationships window with a number after its name, i.e. Branch1 or Customer2. Close the Show Table dialog box. Click the title bar of the duplicated table and press Delete. This procedure also works if you add the same table twice to a Query's design grid.

c. Run your mouse over the **blue line** at the bottom of the Customers table box until its shape changes to the **resize arrow**. With the double-headed arrow showing, click the left mouse button and drag down until all the field names display and the scroll bar disappears. Move or drag each table so all the relationship lines are visible.

d. Click the **BID** field in the **Branch table**. Drag to the **BID** field in the **Accounts table** and release the mouse. The Edit Relationships dialog box opens. Check the **Enforce Referential Integrity** box. Click **Create**.

   A thick black line displays joining the two tables. It has a 1 on the end near the Branch table signifying that it is connecting the primary key (unique identifier) to an infinity symbol on the end next to the Accounts table. You have established a one-to-many relationship between the Branch and Accounts tables.

e. Click the **CID** field in the **Customers table** to select it. Drag to the **CID** field in the **Accounts table** and release the mouse. The Edit Relationships dialog box opens. Check the **Enforce Referential Integrity** box. Click **Create**.

   You have established a one-to-many relationship between the Customers and Accounts tables. A customer will have only a single Customer ID number. The same customer may have many different accounts: Savings, Checking, CDs, etc.

TROUBLESHOOTING: If you get an error message when you click Create, you possibly did not get all the field properties established correctly in Steps 3 and 4 of Hands-On Exercise 2. Relationships may be created only between like data types and sizes. Right-click the blue title bar of the Accounts window in the Relationship window and select Table Design from the shortcut menu. Click on the CID field and examine the size property. It should be set to 10. Click the BID field. It should be set to 10. Change the size property of one or both fields. Save your changes to the table design. Try to establish the relationship again. If it still does not work, check the size of the CID field in the Customers table. It should also be 10.

f. Click **Save** on the Quick Access Toolbar to save the changes to the Relationships. Close the Relationships window.

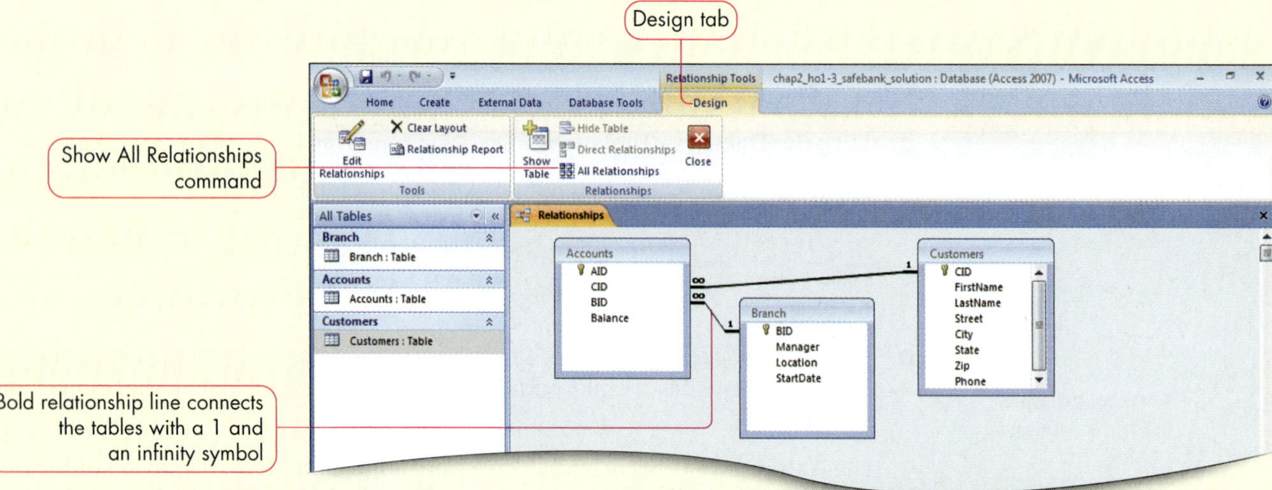

Figure 2.27 Properly Constructed Relationships Among the Tables

Step 6 Understand How Referential Integrity Protects Data

Refer to Figure 2.28 as you complete Step 6.

a. Open the **Accounts table** in Datasheet view. Add a new record: Account ID – A22; Customer ID – **C03** (Note, that is a zero, not a letter O); Branch ID – **B6**; Balance – **4000**. Press **Enter**.

   A warning box appears. This bank has five branches. A sixth branch does not exist. In this case the warning message is telling exactly what is wrong. There is no related record for B6 in the Branch table. Access does not permit data entry of unconnected data. Referential integrity was enforced between the Branch ID in the Branch table and the Branch ID in the Accounts table. Access prevents the entry of an invalid Branch ID.

b. Click **OK**. Replace *B6* with **B5** and press **Enter** twice. As soon as you move to a different record, the pencil symbol disappears, and your data are saved.

   You successfully identified a Branch ID that Access recognizes. Because referential integrity between the Accounts and Branch tables has been enforced, Access looks at each data entry item in a foreign key and matches it to a corresponding value in the table where it is the primary key. In Step 6a you attempted to enter a nonexistent Branch ID and were not allowed to make that error. In Step 6b you entered a valid Branch ID. Access examined the index for the Branch ID in the Branch table and found a corresponding value for B5.

c. Close the Accounts table. Reopen the **Accounts table** and you will find that the record you just entered for A22 has been saved.

d. Click the **Office Button**, select **Manage**, and then select **Back Up Database**. Type **chap2_ho2_safebank_solution** as the file name and click **Save**.

   You just created a backup of the database after completing the second hands-on exercise. The original database *chap2_ho1-3_safebank_solution* remains onscreen. If you ruin the original database as you complete the third hands-on exercise, you can use the backup file you just created and rework the third exercise.

e. Close the file and exit Access if you do not want to continue with the next exercise at this time.

Invalid data entry generates an error when referential integrity is enforced

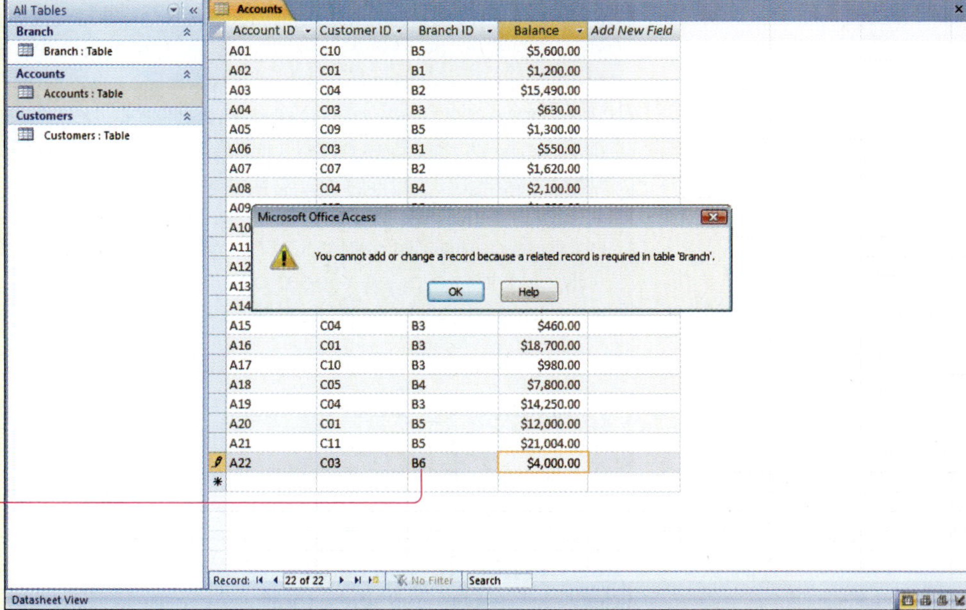

Figure 2.28 How Referential Integrity Works to Protect Data Accuracy

Queries

What if you wanted to see just the customers who bank at a specific branch or who have accounts with balances over $5,000? Perhaps you need to know the customers who have accounts at multiple branches. Maybe you will need a list of all the customers who bank with the branch managed by a specific manager. The manager's name is stored in the Branch table and the customer's name in the Customers table. In this small database, you could open both tables and mentally trace through the strings of the relationships and extract the information. But in a real world database with thousands of records, you would be unable to do this accurately. A query provides the ability to ask questions based on the data or a smaller grouping of data, and to find the answers to those questions.

A ***query*** enables you to ask questions about the data stored in a database and returns the answers from the records in the order that matches your instructions.

A *query* permits you to see the data you want arranged in the sequence that you need. It enables you to select specific records from a table (or from several tables) and show some or all of the fields for the selected records. You can perform calculations to display data that are not explicitly stored in the underlying table(s), such as the amount of interest each bank account earned during the previous month.

In this section you use the Query Wizard to create a query. You set specific conditions to display only records that meet the condition. Finally, you learn about large databases.

Creating a Query

The ***Query Wizard*** is an Access tool that facilitates new query development.

A ***dataset***, which contains the records that satisfy the criteria specified in the query, provides the answers to the user's questions.

Create a query either by using the ***Query Wizard*** or specifying the tables and fields directly in Design view. Like all of the Microsoft wizards, the Query Wizard is a method to automate your work. It facilitates new query development. The results of the query display in a ***dataset***, which contains the records that satisfy the criteria specified in the query.

A dataset looks and acts like a table, but it is not a table; it is a dynamic subset of a table that selects, sorts, and calculates records as specified in the query. A dataset is similar to a table in appearance and, like a table, it enables you to enter a new record or modify or delete an existing record. Any changes made in the dataset are reflected automatically in the underlying table.

TIP Changes Made to Query Results Overwrite Table Data

The connection between a query result and the underlying table data may create problems. On the one hand it is to your advantage that you can correct an error in data if you should happen to spot it in a query result. You save time by not having to close the query, open the table, find the record in error, fix it, and run the query again to get robust results. On the other hand, you must be careful not to accidentally click into a query record and type something. If you press Enter or Tab, whatever you accidentally typed is stored forever in the underlying table.

The ***query design grid*** displays when you select a query's Design view; it divides the window into two parts.

Return to the earlier question. How would you identify the names of all of the customers who have an account at the Campus branch? Figure 2.29 contains the ***query design grid*** used to select customers who have accounts at the Campus Branch and further, to list those customers and their account balances alphabetically. (The design grid is explained in the next section.) Figure 2.30 displays the answer to the query in the form of a dataset.

The Customers table contains 21 records. The dataset in Figure 2.30 has only six records, corresponding to the customers who have Campus branch accounts. The records in the table are ordered by the Customer ID (the primary key), whereas the records in the dataset are in alphabetical order by last name. Changing the order of data displayed in a query has no effect on the underlying table data.

TIP Examine the Record Number

An experienced Access user always examines the number of records returned in a query's results. As you add additional criteria, the number of records returned should decrease.

Create a Select Query

A ***select query*** searches the underlying tables to retrieve the data that satisfy the query parameters.

The query in Figures 2.29 and 2.30 is an example of a select query, which is the most common type of query. A ***select query*** searches the underlying tables to retrieve the data that satisfy the query parameters. The data displayed in a dataset (see Figure 2.30), which can be modified to update the data in the underlying table(s). The specifications for selecting records and determining which fields will be displayed for the selected records, as well as the sequence of the selected records, are established within the design grid of Figure 2.29. The select query is one of many different query operations Access supports.

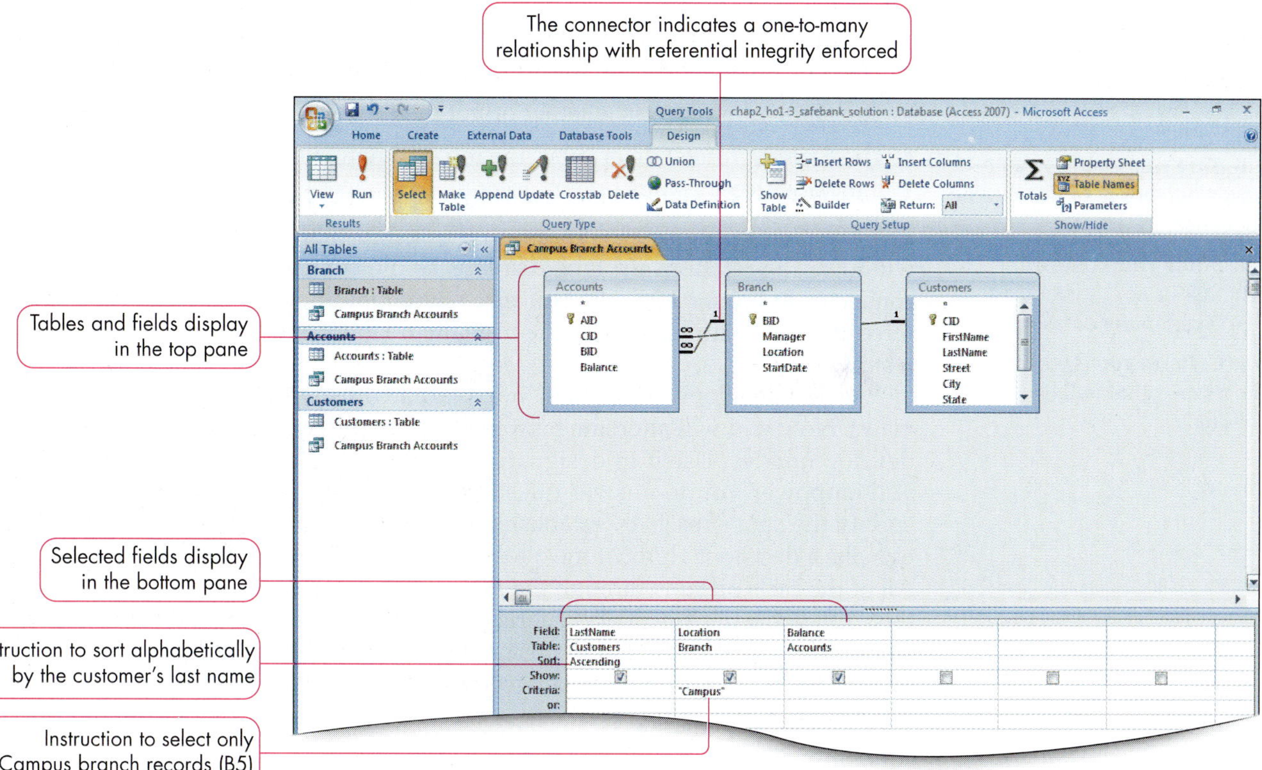

Figure 2.29 The Query Design View

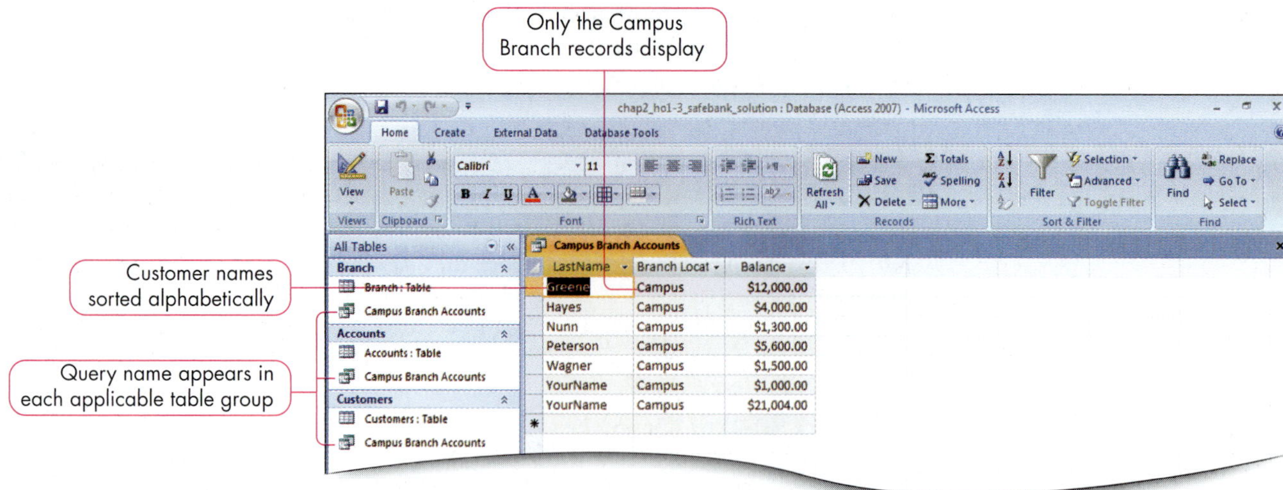

Figure 2.30 The Query Datasheet View

Use the Query Design Grid

The query design grid consists of two panes. The lower pane contains columns and rows. Each field in the query has its own column and contains multiple rows. The rows permit you to control query results.

The ***Table row*** displays the data source.

The ***Field row*** displays the field name.

The ***Sort row*** enables you to sort in ascending or descending sequence.

The ***Show row*** controls whether or not the field will be displayed in the dataset.

The ***Criteria row(s)*** determines the records that will be selected.

- The ***Table row*** displays the data source. The ***Field row*** displays the field name.
- The ***Sort row*** enables you to sort in ascending or descending sequence.
- The ***Show row*** controls whether or not the field will be displayed in the dataset.
- The ***Criteria row(s)*** determines the records that will be selected, such as customers with a Campus branch account.

The top pane contains table names in a design that resembles the Relationships window. The relationship type displays as the connector between the tables. The connector in Figure 2.29 tells you that referential integrity between the tables is in force, that the relationship is a one-to-many relation, and that we can trust the query results.

As you developed the tables, you alternated between the Design and Datasheet views. Now you will alternate between the Design view and Datasheet view as you develop queries. Use it to designate the fields and the subsets of those fields that will empower you to answer questions about the data and make decisions. You specify the data subsets by establishing criteria, which are rules or tests you can use to make a decision. Think of the query criteria as a sophisticated oil filter in your car. All of the car's oil runs through the filter. The filter collects dirt particles and strains them out of the oil. The query criteria determine the size of the filter and allow you to sift through the data to find the records of interest. The criteria operate much like a filter in a table. The difference between a filter and a query is that the query becomes a permanent part of the database. A filter gives you a temporary method to view the data.

Specifying Criteria for Different Data Types

A ***currency*** is the medium of exchange; in the United States, currency formatted values display with a dollar sign.

The field data type determines how the criteria are specified for that field. You need to enter criteria for a text field enclosed in quotation marks. To find only the records of customers with accounts at the Campus branch, you would enter "Campus" as the criteria under the Location field. You enter the criteria for number, ***currency*** (e.g., $3.00 in the United States), and counter fields as digits with or without a decimal point and/or a minus sign. (Commas and dollar signs are not allowed.) When the criterion is in a date field, you enclose the criterion in pound signs. You should enter date criteria in the mm/dd/yyyy format, such as #10/14/2008#. You enter criteria for a Yes/No field as Yes (or True) or No (or False).

Access accepts values for text and date fields in the design grid in multiple formats. You can enter the text with or without quotation marks, such as *Campus* or *"Campus."* You can enter a date with or without the pound signs, such as *1/1/2008* or *#1/1/2008#*. Access will enter the quotation marks or pound signs, respectively, for you when you move to the next cell in the design grid. Thus, text entries are always shown in quotation marks and dates in pound signs.

Use Wildcards

Select queries recognize the question mark and asterisk wildcards that enable you to search for a pattern within a text field. A question mark stands for a single character in the same position as the question mark; thus *H?ll* will return *Hall*, *Hill*, and *Hull*. An asterisk stands for any number of characters in the same position as the asterisk; for example, *S*nd* will return *Sand*, *Stand*, and *Strand*. If you search a two-letter state code field for *?C*, Access will return *NC*, *SC*, and *DC*. If you search the same field with *C, Access will return DC, NC, and SC. If you search the same field with C*, Access will return CA, CO, and CT.

Use Operands in Queries

An ***operator*** is a mathematical symbol, such as +, -, *, and /.

An ***operand*** is the portion of the mathematical expression that is being operated on.

A numeric field may be limited through standard numeric operators; ***operators*** such as plus, minus, equals, greater than, less than, multiply (*), divide (/), and not equals (<>). An ***operand*** is a portion of the mathematical expression that is being operated on, such as the value stored in a field. In Access, you use the field name as an operand, such as Date() - 30. Both the Date() field and 30 are operands.Table 2.4 shows sample expressions and discusses their results.

Table 2.4 Criteria Operands

Expression	Result
>10	For a Price field, items with a price over $10.00
<10	For a Price field, items with a price under $10.00
>=10	For a Price field, items with a price of at least $10.00
<=10	For a Price field, items with a price of $10.00 or less
=10	For a Price field, items with a price of exactly $10.00
<> 10	For a Price field, items with a price not equal to $10.00
#2/2/2008#	For a field with a Date/Time data type, such as a ShippedDate field, orders shipped on February 2, 2009
'2/2/2008'	For a text field, not a Date/Time field
Date()	For an OrderDate field, orders for today's date
Between 1/1/2007 and 3/31/2007	For a specified interval between a start and end date
Between Date( ) And DateAdd ("M", 3, Date( ))	For a RequiredDate field, orders required between today's date and three months from today's date
< Date( ) – 30	For an OrderDate field, orders more than 30 days old
Year([OrderDate]) = 2005	For an OrderDate field, orders with order dates in 2005
DatePart("q", [OrderDate]) = 4	For an OrderDate field, orders for the fourth calendar quarter
DateSerial(Year ([OrderDate]), Month ([OrderDate]) + 1, 1) – 1	For an OrderDate field, orders for the last day of each month
Year([OrderDate]) = Year(Now()) And Month([OrderDate]) = Month(Now())	For an OrderDate field, orders for the current year and month

Work with Null and Zero-Length Strings

A ***null*** value is the formal, computer term for a missing value.

Sometimes finding what is *not* known is an important part of making a decision. For example, which orders have been accepted but not shipped? Are we missing phone numbers or addresses for some of our customers? The computer term for a missing value is ***null***. Table 2.5 gives the following illustrations on how to use the Null criterion in a query.

Table 2.5 Establishing Null Criteria Expressions

Expression	Result
Is Null	For an Employee field in the Customers table when the customer has not been assigned a sales representative. (Some fields, such as primary key fields, can't contain Null.)
Is Not Null	For a ShipDate field, orders already shipped to customers
" "	For an E-mail field for customers who don't have an email address. This is indicated by a zero-length string. This is different from a Null value. Use this only when you know a customer has no e-mail, not when he or she has e-mail but you do not know what it is. You enter a zero-length string by typing two double quotation marks with no space between them (" ").

Understand Query Sort Order

The ***query sort order*** determines the order of items in the query Datasheet View.

The ***query sort order*** determines the order of items in the query Datasheet view. You can change the sort order of a query by specifying the sort order in the design grid. The sorts work from left to right. The leftmost field with a sort order specified will be the primary sort field; the next sort specified field to the right will be the secondary sort field, and so forth. Change the order of the query fields in the design grid to change the sort order of the query result. Alter the field order within the design grid by clicking in the Table row (the second row) of the design grid and specifying the table and then in the Field row and selecting a different field name. The table must be specified first because each field row drop-down list shows only the names of the fields in the specified table. You also may insert additional columns in the design grid by selecting a column and clicking Insert Columns in the Query Setup group on the Query Tools Design tab. The inserted column will insert to the left of the selected column.

TIP Reorder Query Fields

With a query open in Design view, move your mouse above a field name. The mouse pointer will change shape to a bold black arrow. When you see the bold black arrow, click the mouse. The field's column selects. Move your mouse slowly over the top of the selected area until the pointer shape changes to the move shape (a thick white arrow). When the white arrow shape shows, click and drag the field to a new position on the design grid. A thick black border moves with your mouse to tell you where the field will move. Release the mouse when the border moves to the desired position.

Establish And, Or, and Not Criteria

Until now all of the questions that you have asked the database to answer through queries have been relatively simple. Access adapts to more complex query specifications. What if you need a list of all of the customers who bank at the Campus branch and do not have accounts at any other branches? Which customers bank only at the Campus or Uptown branches? Are there customers of the Campus branch with deposits over $5,000? These questions involve multiple field interaction. The

The ***And operator*** returns only records that meet all criteria.

The ***Or operator*** returns records meeting any of the specified criteria.

The ***Not operator*** returns the opposite of the specified criteria.

moment you specify criteria in multiple fields, Access combines the fields using the And or the Or operator. When the expressions are in the same row of the query design grid, Access uses the ***And operator***. This means that only the records that meet *all* criteria in all of the fields will be returned. If the criteria are positioned in different rows of the design grid, Access uses the ***Or operator*** and will return records meeting *any* of the specified criteria. The ***Not operator*** returns the *opposite* of the specification.

Figure 2.31 shows a query in Design view that specifies an And operator. It will return all of the Campus branch accounts with balances over $5,000. Both conditions must be met for the record to be included. Figure 2.32 shows a query in Design view that specifies an Or operator. It will return all of the Campus branch accounts with any balance plus all accounts at any branch with balances over $5,000. Either condition may be met for a record to be included. Figure 2.33 shows a query in Design view that specifies a Not operator. It will return all of the accounts at all of the branches excluding the Campus branch. You may combine And, Or, and Not operators to achieve the desired result. If you need a list of the accounts with balances over $5,000 at the Campus and Uptown branches, you set the criteria so that the >5000 expression is duplicated for each location specified (see Figure 2.34).

Field:	LastName	Location	Balance
Table:	Customers	Branch	Accounts
Sort:	Ascending		
Show:	☑	☑	☑
Criteria:		"Campus"	>5000
or:			

Figure 2.31 And Criterion—Only Records Satisfying Both Conditions Will Return

Field:	LastName	Location	Balance
Table:	Customers	Branch	Accounts
Sort:	Ascending		
Show:	☑	☑	☑
Criteria:		"Campus"	
or:			>5000

Figure 2.32 Or Criterion—Records Meeting Either Condition Will Return

Field:	LastName	Location	Balance
Table:	Customers	Branch	Accounts
Sort:	Ascending		
Show:	☑	☑	☑
Criteria:		Not "Campus"	
or:			>5000

Figure 2.33 Not Criterion—Any Record Except the Matching Will Return

Field:	LastName	Location	Balance
Table:	Customers	Branch	Accounts
Sort:	Ascending		
Show:	☑	☑	☑
Criteria:		"Campus"	>5000
or:		"Uptown"	>5000

Figure 2.34 And and Or Criteria—Records Meeting Both Conditions at Both Branches Return

Copying and Running a Query

After you create a query, you may want to duplicate it to use as the basis for creating similar queries. Duplicating a query saves time in selecting tables and fields for queries that need the same structure but different criteria. After you create and save one or more queries, you can execute them whenever you need them to produce up-to-date results.

Copy a Query

Sometimes you have one-of-a-kind questions about your data. Then you create and run the query, find the answer and close it. If you create the query with the wizard, you save and name it in the last step. If you create the query in Design view, it is possible for you to exit the query without saving changes. Most queries answer recurrent questions. What were sales last week in Houston, in Dallas, in Chicago? In cases like this, you set up the query for the dates and places of interest one time, then copy it, rename the copy and establish the parameters for a different city or date.

Frequently you will need to examine multiple subsets of the data. In Hands-On Exercise 3 you will create a query displaying the names and account balances of the customers who have accounts at the Campus branch. Should you need to know the same information about the customers who have Uptown accounts, you would select the query in the Navigation Pane, and then copy and paste it to a blank space at the bottom pane. Right-click the copy and rename it Uptown. Open the newly created Uptown query in Design view and replace the Campus criterion with Uptown. When you run and save the query, the resulting dataset displays customers and account balances from the Uptown branch. Using this method takes you a few minutes to create branch specific queries for all five locations.

Run a Query

When you ***run a query***, Access processes the query instructions and displays records that meet the conditions.

After you create the query by specifying criteria and save it, you are ready to run it. You ***run a query*** by clicking the Run command (the red exclamation point) to direct Access to process the instructions specified by the query. In our databases the queries run quickly. Even in the largest database you will use in the end of chapter exercises, no query will take more than a few seconds to run. As you learn how to work with these databases, keep in mind that real-world databases can be massive. Think through the query design carefully. Include all necessary fields and tables, but do not include fields or tables that are not necessary to answer the question.

Using the Query Wizard

You may create a query directly in Design view or by using the Query Wizard. Even if you initiate the query with a wizard, you will need to learn how to modify it in Design view. Often it is much faster to copy an existing query and make slight modifications to its design than it would be to start at the beginning of the wizard. You also will need to know how to add additional tables and fields to an existing query in case you failed to think through the design thoroughly and you omitted a necessary field. To launch the Query Wizard, click the Create tab and click Query Wizard in the Other group (see Figure 2.35).

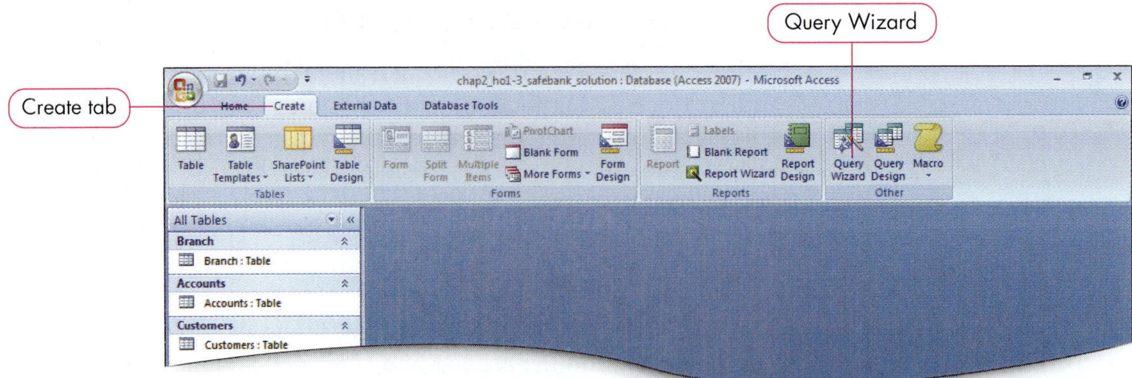

Figure 2.35 Launching the Query Wizard

Access produces many different kinds of queries. Here we will work with the most common query type, the Simple query. This is a powerful and sophisticated tool. Select the Simple Query Wizard in the first dialog box of the Query Wizard as shown in Figure 2.36.

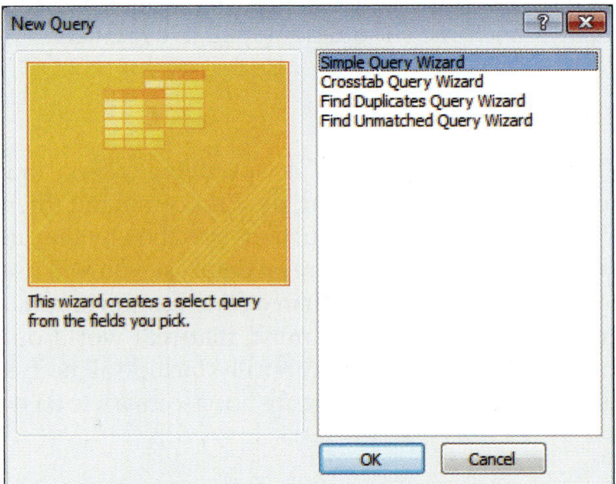

Figure 2.36 The Simple Query Wizard Step 1

In the second step of the Simple Query Wizard dialog box you specify the tables and fields needed in your query. As soon as you click on the table in the Tables/Queries drop-down box, a list of that table's fields display in the Available fields box. See Figures 2.37 and 2.38.

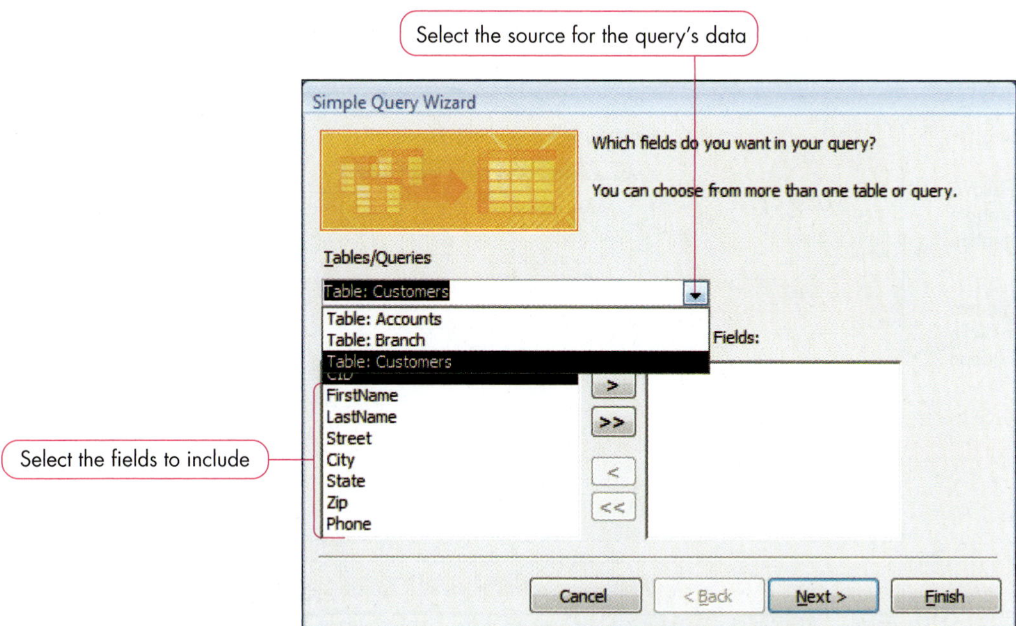

Figure 2.37 Specify which Tables or Queries to Use as Input

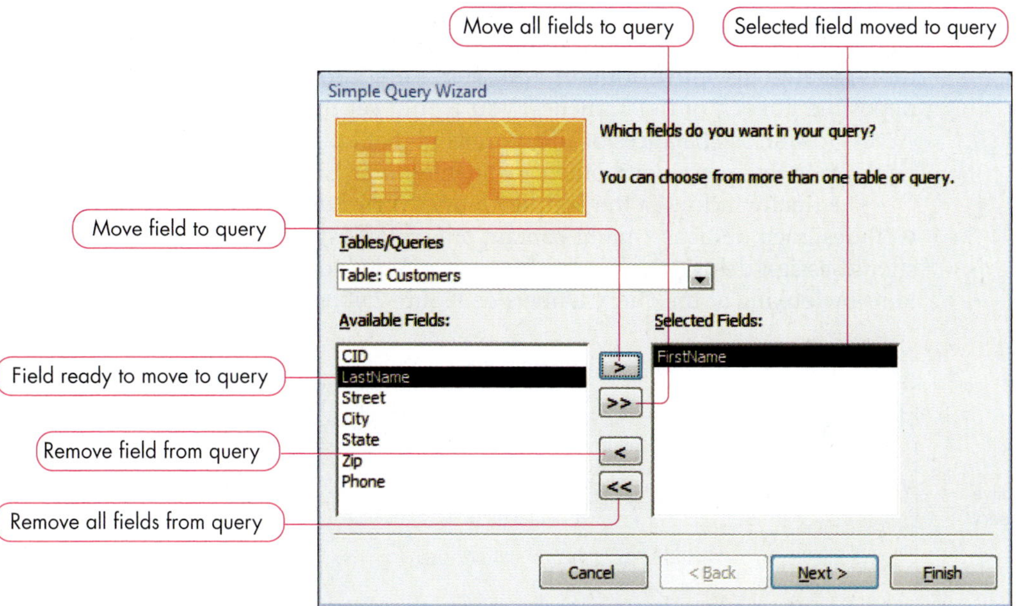

Figure 2.38 Specify the Fields for the Query

Select the necessary fields by clicking them to highlight and then using the navigation arrows described in Figure 2.39.

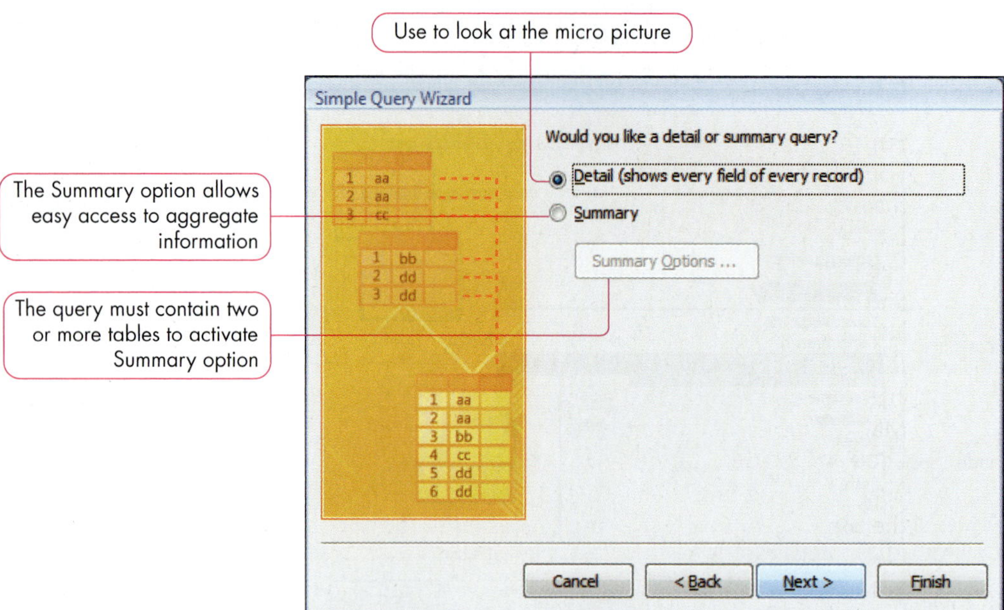

Figure 2.39 Select to Display Detail or to Summarize the Data

Aggregate means the collection of individual items into a total.

In the Simple Query Wizard, you choose between a detail or a summary query. The detail query provides every record of every field. The summary enables you to aggregate data and view only summary statistics. ***Aggregate*** means the collection of individual items into a total. If you were only interested in the total of the funds deposited at each of the branches, you would set the query to a summary and ask Access to sum the balances of all accounts in that branch. Some Access users summarize data in the queries and others do so in reports. Either approach is acceptable.

The final window in the Simple Query Wizard directs you to name the query. A well-designed database might contain only 5 tables and 500 queries. Therefore, you should assign descriptive names for your queries so that you know what each contains by looking at the query name. See Figure 2.40.

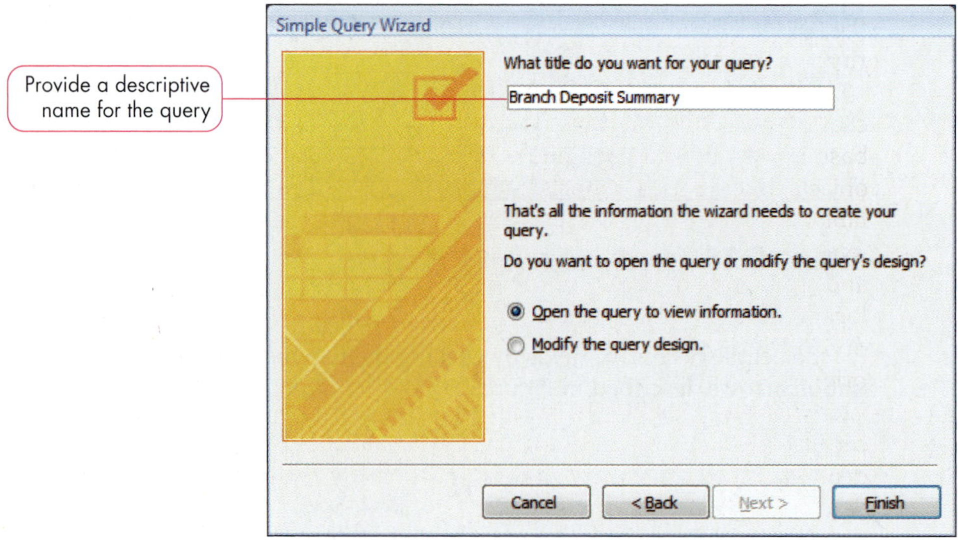

Figure 2.40 Name the Query Descriptively

Understanding Large Database Differences

Suppose you work for a large university. You need to identify all of the students at your university who are business majors, their advisor's names, and their specific majors. The Student table contains student names, identification numbers, majors, faculty advisor's identification number, class standing, addresses, and so on. The Faculty table contains faculty names, departmental affiliation, identification number, and rank. Your query needs to include fields for the student's name, major, and the advisor's name. You would not need the student's address or the faculty member's ID because those fields are unnecessary to answer the question. You need to establish criteria to select business majors: Accounting, Finance, Information Systems, Management, Marketing, and Economics.

Even if your computer is state-of-the-art, fast, powerful, and loaded with memory, this query might take up to 15 minutes to run. If you include unnecessary tables, the run time increases. At the author's university, each additional table roughly doubles the query run time. As an Access beginner, your queries might contain too much or too little information. You will make frequent modifications to the query design as you learn. As you apply your database skills to work with large databases, you will learn to carefully design queries prior to running them to minimize the time to run the queries.

In addition to the earlier mentioned size difference between real world databases and those you will use in the class, real world databases involve multiple users. Typically the organization stores the database file on the network. Multiple people may simultaneously log into the database. Each user makes changes to tables or forms. At your school, thousands of users can extract data from the university's database. Prior to meeting your advisor, you check your transcript online. You enter a database to find out how many hours you have completed and whether or not you have met the prerequisites. You have permission to view your transcript but you do not have the necessary permission to change what is recorded there. Several hundred other users have more extensive privileges in your school's database. Your Access professor can enter and probably change your grade in this class. If the securities are appropriately set on the database, your Access professor is not able to change the grade that you earned in other courses.

Most large organizations employ database administrators and managers that ensure data security, efficacy, and integrity. These professionals are well paid to make sure that no one inside or outside the firm has access to classified data or can corrupt the data resident in the system. Additionally, SOX rules mandate backup and security measures.

These positions involve a great deal of responsibility. How does someone charged with this vital role do it? One common method involves splitting the database into front and back ends. Typically the ***front end*** of a database contains the objects, like queries, reports, and forms, needed to interact with data, but not the tables where the record values reside. The tables are safely stored in the ***back end*** system where users cannot inadvertently destroy or corrupt data. Most often the front and back ends of the database are stored on different systems placed in different locations to provide an extra security measure. Users within the organization are divided into groups by their data needs. Then the groups are assigned rights and privileges. For example, a professor has privileges to record grades for students registered in his or her classes but not for other professors' classes. The financial aid officer may look at student grades and financial records, but may not alter either. The dean may look at student grades, but probably not their financial records. The student health center physician may view a student's immunization records and update it when necessary, but cannot see the student's grades.

The ***front end*** of a database contains the objects, like queries, reports, and forms, needed to interact with data, but not the tables where the record values reside.

The ***back end*** of the system protects and stores data so that users cannot inadvertently destroy or corrupt the organization's vital data.

The next hands-on exercise introduces queries as a more useful way to examine data. You use the Query Wizard to create a basic query, and then modify that query by adding an additional field and an additional table, and performing simple query criteria specifications.

Hands-On Exercises

3 | Multiple-Table Query

Skills covered: 1. Create a Query Using a Wizard **2.** Specify Simple Query Criteria **3.** Change Query Data **4.** Add a Table to a Query Using Design View and Sort a Query

Step 1
Create a Query Using a Wizard

Refer to Figure 2.41 as you complete Step 1.

a. Open the *chap2_ho1-3_safebank_solution.accdb* database from Hands-On Exercise 2 (if necessary), click **Options** on the Security Warning toolbar and click the **Enable this content option** in the Microsoft Office Security Options dialog box, and click **OK**.

   TROUBLESHOOTING: If you create unrecoverable errors while completing this hands-on exercise, you can delete the *chap2_ho1-3_safebank_solution* file, copy the *chap2_ho2_safebank_solution* database you created at the end of the second hands-on exercise, and open the copy of the backup database to start the third hands-on exercise again.

b. Click the **Create tab** and click **Query Wizard** in the Other group to launch the wizard.

   The New Query dialog box opens.

c. Simple Query Wizard is selected by default. Click **OK** to open the same.

d. Click the **Tables/Queries drop-down arrow** and select **Table: Customers**.

   This step asks you to specify the tables and fields needed in the query. A list of the fields in the Customers table displays in the Available Fields box.

e. Double-click the **FirstName** field.

   The FirstName field moves from the Available Fields box to the Selected Fields box. You can also double-click a field in the Selected Fields box to move it back to the Available box.

f. Click the **LastName** field and click the **Move Field to Query button** (see Figure 2.38).

g. Click the **Tables/Queries drop-down arrow** and select **Table: Accounts**.

h. From the list of fields in the Accounts table, select **BID** and **Balance** and move them one at a time to the Fields in Query box. Click **Next**.

   Your query should have four fields: First and Last names, BID, and Balance.

i. Select **Detail**, if necessary, to choose between a Detail and Summary Query. Click **Next**.

j. Name your query **Campus Branch Customers**. Click **Finish**.

   This name describes the data that will eventually populate the query. The default name, Customers Query, comes from the first table selected when you started the query wizard.

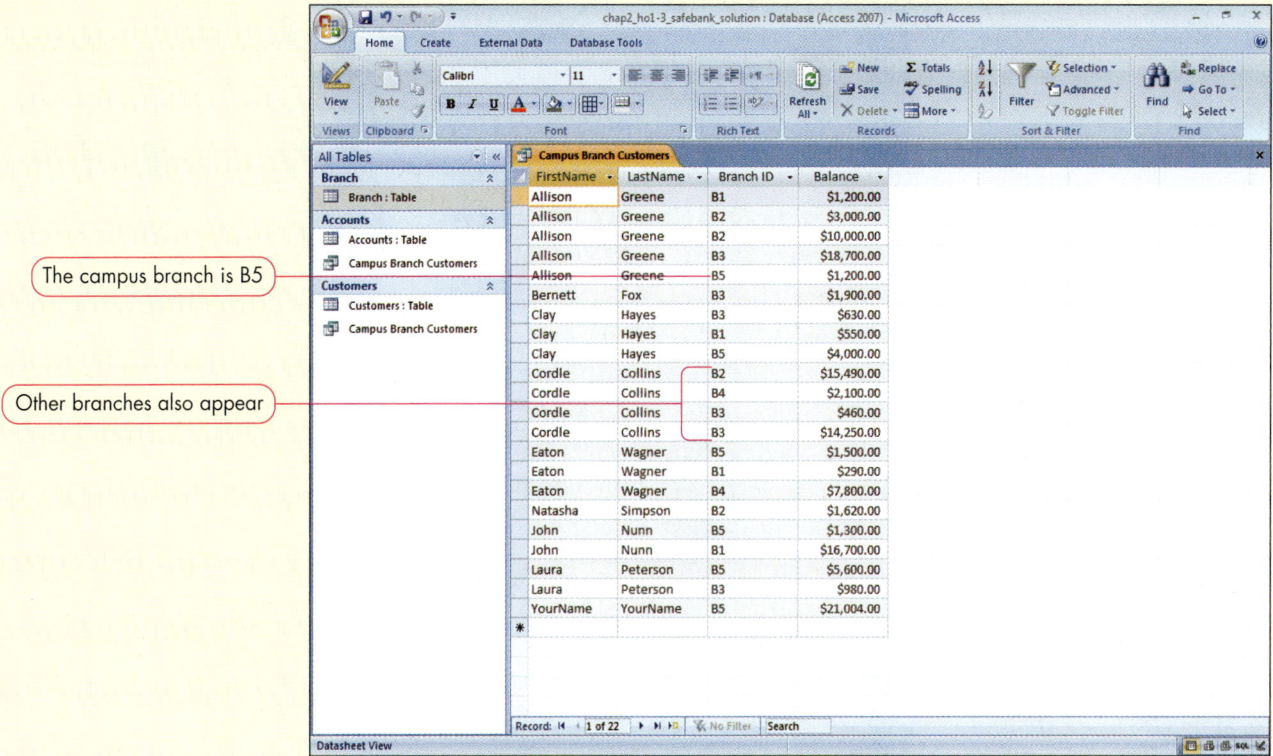
The campus branch is B5
Other branches also appear

Figure 2.41 Criteria Have Not Been Applied

Step 2
Specify Simple Query Criteria

Refer to Figure 2.42 as you complete Step 2.

a. Right-click the **Campus Branch Customers tab** and select **Design View** from the shortcut menu.

   You have created the Campus Branch Customers query to view only those customers who have accounts at the Campus branch. However, other branch's accounts also display. You need to limit the query results to only the records of interest.

b. Click in the fifth row (the **Criteria row**) under the **BID** field and type **b5**.

   Access is not case sensitive but is frequently used to connect to larger databases for which case matters.

c. Click in the **Sort row** (third row) under the **LastName field** to activate the drop-down arrow. (This is another of the hidden arrows that only provides selections when the cell is active.) Select **Ascending** from the drop-down list.

d. Click **Run** in the Results group on the Design tab.

   You should have six records in the dataset.

e. Save your query.

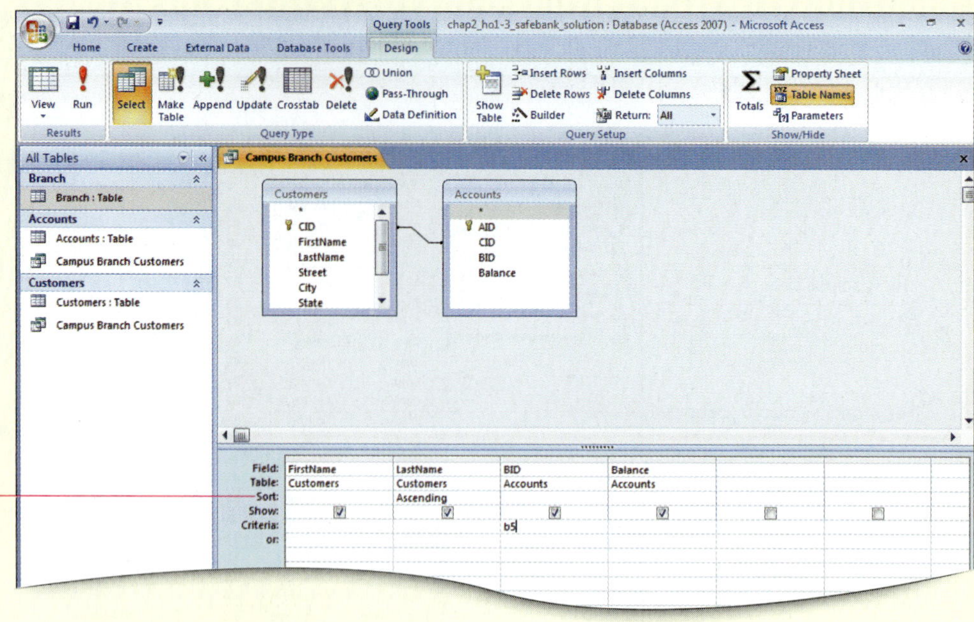

Click in the Sort row to reveal a drop-down arrow

Figure 2.42 Establishing Select Criteria and Sort Order

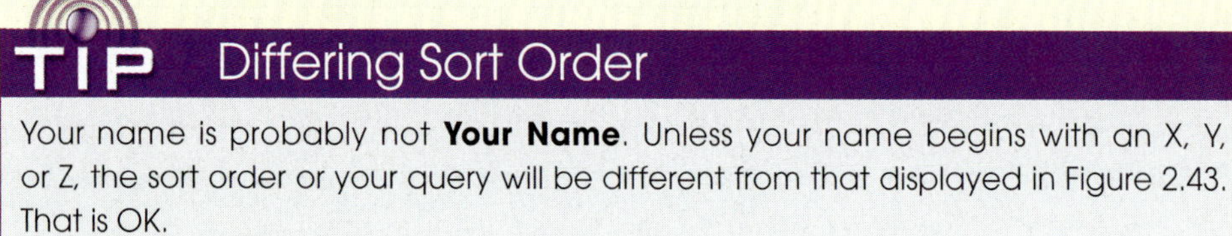

TIP Differing Sort Order

Your name is probably not **Your Name**. Unless your name begins with an X, Y, or Z, the sort order or your query will be different from that displayed in Figure 2.43. That is OK.

Step 3 Change Query Data

Refer to Figure 2.43 as you complete Step 3.

a. Click on the **Balance** field in the record for *Allison Greene's* account. Change **$1200** to **$12,000**. Press **Enter**. Close the query. Do ***not*** save your changes.

b. Open the **Accounts table**.

   Only one account shows a $12,000 balance. The Customer ID is C01.

c. Open the **Customers table**. Find the name of the customer whose Customer ID is **C01**. Close the **Customers table**.

   Allison Green's CID number is C01. The change you made in the query datasheet has permanently changed the data stored in the underlying table.

   TROUBLESHOOTING: Changes in query data change table data! As soon as you pressed Enter in Step 3a, the balance for Allison's account saved. (Remember Access works in storage, not memory.) A wise Access user is extremely careful about the position of the cursor and about typing stray characters while a table or query is open. As soon as you move to a different record, any edits are saved automatically, whether you intend the save or not!

d. Add a new record to the **Accounts table**. The Accounts table should be open. If not, open it now.

e. Type **A23**, **C11**, **B5**, and **1000**. Press **Enter**.

f. Right-click the **Campus Branch Customers query** in the Navigation Pane to open the shortcut menu and choose **Design View**. Click **Run** on the Design tab.

   You (as a bank customer) now show two accounts, one with a balance that matches your course and section number and one with a balance of $1,000.

Because you closed and reopened the query, it re-ran prior to opening. Access reruns queries to ensure that the data the query returns is the most recent in the database.

g. Close the **Accounts table**.

You successfully created a multi-table query. It does almost everything that you intended. Because this bank is so small, everybody who works there (and probably most of the customers) knows that the Campus branch is B5. But what if this were the database for a real bank? How many thousands of branches does it have? (Remember you are designing your database for 100 years.) You decide that you want to display the branch name, not the ID number. The branch name is a field in the Branch table. The Campus Branch Customers query was based on the Accounts and Customers tables. In order to display the branch name, you need to connect the Branch table to the query.

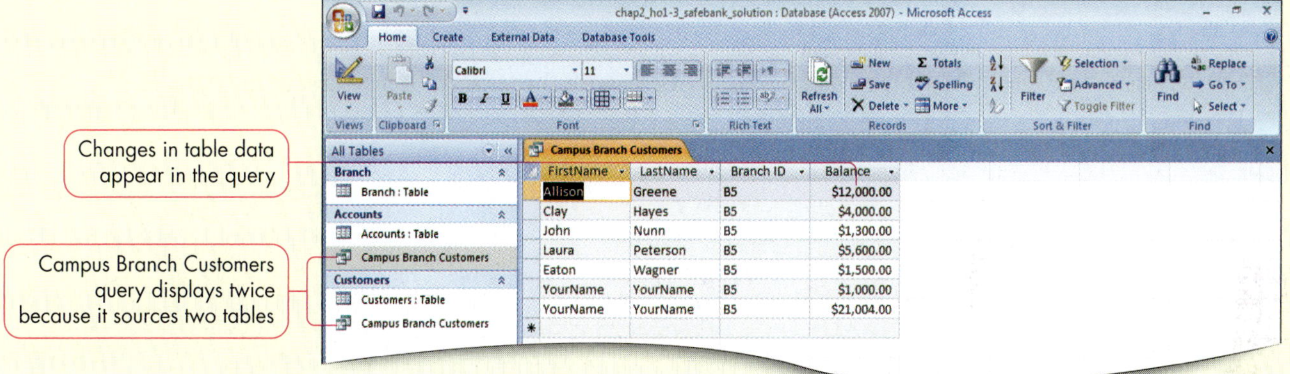

Figure 2.43 Campus Branch Customers Query Following Data Modifications

Step 4
Add a Table to a Query Using Design View and Sort a Query

Refer to Figure 2.44 as you complete Step 4.

a. Open the *Campus Branch Customers Query* if necessary. Right-click the query tab and select **Design View** from the shortcut menu.

b. Click the **Branch: Table** in the Navigation Pane.

It will turn gold to indicate that it is selected.

c. Click and drag the selected **Branch table** to the **top pane** of the Query design grid.

Your mouse pointer shape will change to a table as you drag.

d. Drop the **Branch table** next to the **Accounts table**.

The one-to-many relationship lines automatically connect the Branch table to the Accounts table. The query inherits the relationship specifications from the database design.

e. Click the **Location** field name in the Branch table and **drag** it down to the **first empty column**. It should be to the right of the Balance column.

f. Click the **Show row check box** under the **BID** field to hide this field.

The BID field is no longer needed because we have a more descriptive and easily understood name. When you save, close, and reopen the query, you will notice that Access removes the BID field since you deselected its Show check box. In some queries, you need to use a field for a criterion, but you do not want it to show. When you deselect the Show check box but enter a criterion, Access keeps that field in the design grid.

g. Remove the **B5** criterion under the Branch ID by highlighting and then deleting it.

h. Type **Campus** as a criterion in the **Location** field.

The syntax actually requires that you enter text criteria within quotation marks, such as "Campus". Access will enter these quotes for you if you forget. If you use Access to get into large databases, you may need to remember the quotation marks while setting parameters for character fields.

i. Click the word *Location*. As soon as you leave the criteria row, Access adds the missing quotes for you.

j. Click in the **Sort row** of the **Balance** field to activate the drop-down list. Select **Descending**.

The query will still be sorted alphabetically by the customer's last name because that is the left-most sort field in the design grid. You have added an additional, or secondary, sort. Customers with multiple accounts will have their accounts sorted from the largest to smallest balances.

k. Run and save your query.

Your accounts are listed with the largest balance first in the dataset.

l. Close the file and exit Access.

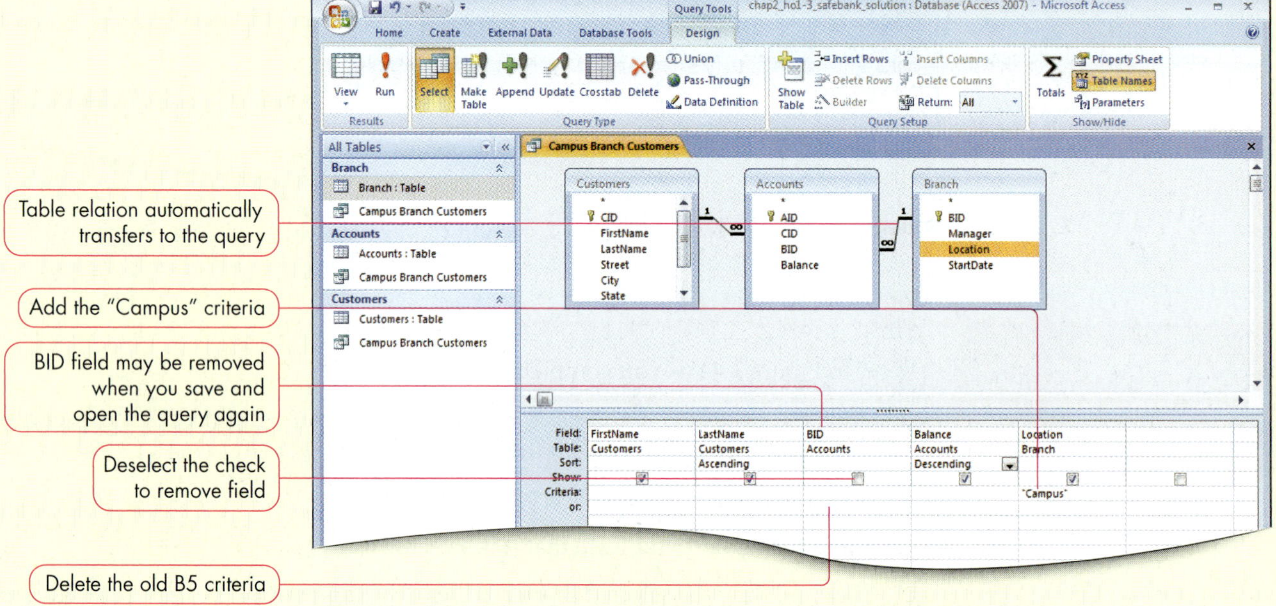

Figure 2.44 Drag and Drop the Branch Table to Add to the Query Design Grid

Summary

1. **Design data.** The architectural infrastructure that supports the database needs to be driven by the output the database will need to generate. You learned that good database design requires that you anticipate how the data will be used, both now and for a long time to come. Creating a database adds costs to the firm, and the designer must balance the costs of including data against the costs of needing it at some point in the future and not having it available. The Sarbanes Oxley Act governs how, where, and when publicly traded firms must store data. You learned that good design principles avoid storing the results of calculations in table data, that data should be stored in their smallest parts, and that like data should be grouped together to form tables.
2. **Create tables.** Access employs several ways to create a table. You can create a table yourself by entering the table data into a field. You also can import table data from another database or application, for example, Excel. You learned that each field needs a unique and descriptive name and were introduced to the CamelCase notation naming convention. Access accommodates many different types of data including: text, number, Date/Time, Yes/No, Memo, and others.
3. **Understand table relationships.** Data stored in different tables may be linked using the powerful tool of referential integrity enforcement. Typically, the primary key from one table (unique identifier) resides as a foreign key in another table. This becomes the means of creating the link.
4. **Share data with Excel.** Access facilitates data exchanges with Excel through imports and exports. You used the Import Wizard to import an Excel worksheet into an Access database table. The settings of the Import Wizard may be saved and reused when the import is recurrent.
5. **Establish table relationships.** You created links between tables in the database and attempted to enter an invalid branch number in a related table. You discovered that the enforcement of referential integrity prevented you from creating an account in a non-existent branch. Cascades give the database manager a powerful tool that facilitates updating or deleting multiple records in different tables simultaneously.
6. **Create a query.** You manipulated the data to display only those records of interest by creating a select query. Later you learned to add additional fields or tables to an existing query.
7. **Specify criteria for different data types.** Establishing criteria empowers you to see only the records that meet the criteria. Different data types require different criteria specifications. Date fields are enclosed in pound signs (#) and text fields with quote marks (""). Additionally you learned that there are powerful operators, And, Or, and Not, that return the results needed to answer complex questions. You established a sort order for arranging the query results. The Primary sort field needs to be in the left-most position in the query design grid. You may specify additional sort fields; their priority is determined by their left-to-right positions in the grid.
8. **Copy and run a query.** After specifying tables, fields, and conditions for one query, you can copy the query and modify only the criteria in the duplicate query. Copying queries saves time so that you do not have to select tables and fields again for queries that need the same structure but different criteria. After saving queries, you can run them whenever you need to display up-to-date results based on the query conditions.
9. **Use the Query Wizard.** An alternative to creating a select query is to use the Query Wizard. The wizard enables you to select tables and fields from lists. The last step of the wizard prompts you to save the query.
10. **Understand large database differences.** Large databases queries may take a long time to run. Therefore, you should think carefully about what fields and tables to include in the query prior to executing it. You learned that database administrators often split the database into front and back ends. Different users of a large database have different levels of access and privilege in order to protect the data validity.

Key Terms

Multiple Choice

1. When entering, deleting or editing table data
   (a) The table must be in Design view.
   (b) The table must be in Datasheet view.
   (c) The table may be in either Datasheet or Design view.
   (d) Data may be entered only in a form.

2. Which of the following is implemented automatically by Access?
   (a) Rejecting misspelled field entries in a record
   (b) Rejecting redundant field specifications among tables
   (c) Rejecting a record of a foreign key without a matching value in a related table
   (d) Rejecting a record in a primary key without a matching value in a related table

3. Social Security Number, phone number, and postal code should be designated as:
   (a) Number fields
   (b) Text fields
   (c) Yes/No fields
   (d) Any of the above depending on the application

4. Which of the following is true of the primary key?
   (a) Its values must be unique.
   (b) It must be defined as a text field.
   (c) It must be the first field in a table.
   (d) It can never be changed.

5. Social Security Number should not be used as a primary key because:
   (a) The Social Security Number is numeric, and primary key fields should be text.
   (b) The Social Security Number is not unique.
   (c) The Social Security Number is too long.
   (d) Using the Social Security Number may expose employees or customers to identity theft.

6. An illustration of a one-to-many relationship would be:
   (a) A unique city name relates to a single postal code.
   (b) A customer ID may be related to multiple account numbers.
   (c) A branch location may contain many branch identification numbers.
   (d) A balance field may contain many values.

7. Which of the following was not a suggested guideline for designing a table?
   (a) Include all necessary data
   (b) Store data in its smallest parts
   (c) Avoid calculated fields
   (d) Designate at least two primary keys

8. A query's specifications providing instructions about which records to include must be entered
   (a) On the Show row of the query design grid
   (b) On the Sort row of the query design grid
   (c) On the Criteria row of the query design grid
   (d) On the Table Row of the query design grid

9. Which view is used to modify field properties in a table?
   (a) Datasheet view
   (b) Design view
   (c) PivotTable view
   (d) PivotChart view

10. Which of the following is true?
    (a) Additional tables may be added to a query only by restarting the Query Wizard.
    (b) Additional tables or fields may be added to a query by clicking and dragging in the query design grid.
    (c) Access does not permit the addition of additional tables or fields to an existing query.
    (d) Additional tables may be added by copying and pasting the fields from the table to the query.

11. In which view will you see the record selector symbols of a pencil and a triangle?
    (a) Only the Datasheet view of a table
    (b) Only the Datasheet view of a query
    (c) Neither the Datasheet view of a table or query
    (d) Both the Datasheet view of a table and query

12. You attempt to make a data edit in the Datasheet view of a query by changing an account balance and then pressing Enter.
    (a) The change also must be made to the underlying table for it to be a permanent part of the database.
    (b) The change must be saved for it to be a permanent part of the database.
    (c) An error message will display because queries are used only to view data, not edit.
    (d) The change is saved, and the underlying table immediately reflects the change.

...continued on Next Page

Multiple Choice Continued...

13. Data in a Name field is stored as Janice Zook, Zachariah Allen, Tom Jones, and Nancy Allen. If the field was sorted in ascending order, which name would be last?

(a) Janice Zook
(b) Zachariah Allen
(c) Tom Jones
(d) Nancy Allen

14. Which data type appears as a check box in a table?

(a) Text field
(b) Number field
(c) Yes/No field
(d) Name field

15. Which properties would you use to provide the database user with "user-friendly" column headings in the Datasheet View of a table?

(a) Field Size and Format
(b) Input Mask, Validation Rule, and Default Value
(c) Caption
(d) Required

16. Which of the following is true with respect to an individual's hire date and years of service, both of which appear on a query that is based on an employee table?

(a) Hire date should be a calculated field; years of service should be a stored field.
(b) Hire date should be a stored field; years of service should be a calculated field.
(c) Both should be stored fields.
(d) Both should be calculated fields.

17. What is the best way to store an individual's name in a table?

(a) As a single field consisting of the last name, first name, and middle initial, in that order
(b) As a single field consisting of the first name, last name, and middle initial, in that order
(c) As three separate fields for first name, last name, and middle initial
(d) All of the above are equally suitable.

18. Which of the following would not be a good primary key?

(a) Student Number
(b) Social Security Number
(c) Employee ID
(d) A branch identification number

19. A difference between student database files and "real world" files is not:

(a) Split between front and back end storage.
(b) Many users add, delete, and change records in "real world" files.
(c) Student files tend to be much smaller than "real world" files.
(d) Students work in live databases but "real world" files have multiple copies of the database on all user's desktops.

20. Your query has a date field. If you wanted the records for the month of March 2007 returned, how would you set the criteria?

(a) <3/31/2007
(b) between 3/1/2007 and 3/31/2007
(c) >3/31/2007
(d) = March 2007

Practice Exercises

1 Martha's Vineyard Bookstore—Creation

One of your aunt's friends, Jennifer Frew, owns and operates a tiny bookstore during the tourist season on Martha's Vineyard. Jennifer asked you to help her after your aunt bragged that you are becoming quite the computer whiz because of this class. You believe that you can help Jennifer by creating a small database. She has stored information about the publication companies and the books that she sells in Excel spreadsheets. You, in consultation with Jennifer, determine that a third table—an author table— also is required. Your task is to design and populate the three tables, establish appropriate linkages between them, and enforce referential integrity. This project follows the same set of skills as used in Hands-On exercises 1 and 2 in this chapter. If you have problems, reread the detailed directions presented in the chapter. Refer to Figure 2.45 as you complete your work.

a. Start Access and click **Blank Database** in the New Blank Database section of the *Getting Started with Microsoft Office Access* window. Click **Browse**, navigate to the Your Name Access Production folder, type **chap2_pe1_bookstore_solution.accdb**, and click **OK**. Then click **Create** in the Blank Database section of the *Getting Started with Microsoft Office Access* window.

b. Enter the following data into what will become the Author table:

Field1	Field2	Field3
11	Benchloss	Michael R.
12	Turow	Scott
13	Rice	Anne
14	King	Stephen
15	Connelly	Michael
16	Rice	Luanne

c. Click **Save** on the Quick Access Toolbar. Type **Author** in the Save As dialog box and click **OK**.

d. Right-click the **Author table** in the Navigation Pane and select **Design View**. Access automatically creates a primary key; however, it is not the correct field for the primary key.

e. Click the row selector for the second row (Field1) and click **Primary Key** in the Tools group on the Design tab.

f. Check the properties of **Field1** to ensure that the *Indexed* property has been set to **Yes (No Duplicates)**, which is appropriate for a primary key. Select *Field1* and type **AuthorID** to rename the field, type **Author ID** as the caption, and check to see that **Long Integer** appears for the field size.

g. Rename *Field2* as **LastName**, type **Author's Last Name** as the caption, and type **20** as the field size. Rename *Field3* as **FirstName**, type **Author's First Name** as the caption, and type **15** as the field size.

h. Click the **ID field row selector** to select the row and click **Delete Rows** in the Tools group on the Table Tools Design tab. Click **Yes**.

i. Click **Save** on the Quick Access toolbar to save the design changes. It is safe to ignore the lost data warning because you did shorten the field sizes. Close the table.

j. Click the **External Data tab** and click **Import Excel Spreadsheet** in the Import group to launch the Get External Data - Excel Spreadsheet Wizard. Select the **Import the source data into a new table in the current database option**, click **Browse**, and go to your Exploring Access folder. Select the *chap2_pe1_bookstore.xlsx* workbook, click **Open**, and click **OK**. This workbook contains two worksheets. Do the following:

- Select the **Publishers worksheet** and click **Next**.
- Click the **First Row Contains Column Headings check box** and click **Next**.
- With the PubID field selected, click the **Indexed drop-down arrow**, select **Yes (No Duplicates)**, and click **Next**.

...continued on Next Page

- Click the **Choose my own primary key drop-down arrow**, select **PubID**, and click **Next**.
- Accept the name *Publishers* for the table name, click **Finish**, and click **Close**.

k. Repeat the Import Wizard to import the **Books worksheet** from the same file into the Access database as a table named **Books**. Set the *Indexed Field Options* property box for the ISBN to **Yes (No Duplicates)**. Set the **ISBN** as the primary field. Do not save the import steps.

l. Open the **Books table** in Design view. Make sure the **PubID** field is selected, click in the *Field Size* property, box and type **2**. Change the **ISBN** *Field size* property to **13**. Change the **Price** field *Format* property to **Currency**. Change the **AuthorCode** field *Field Size* property to **Long Integer** to create the relationship later. Click **Save** on the Quick Access toolbar to save the design changes to the **Books table**.

m. Open the **Publishers table** in Design view. Make sure the **PubID** field is selected, click in the *Field Size* property box and type **2**, and click in the *Caption* property box and type **Publisher's ID**. For **PubName** and **PubAddress** fields, click in the *Field Size* property box and type **50**. Set the *Field Size* property for **PubCity** field to **30.** Set the *Field Size* property for **PubState** field to **2**. Change the *Pub Address* field name to **PubAddress** and change the *Pub ZIP* field name to **PubZIP** (without the spaces to be consistent with the other field names). Click **Save** on the Quick Access Toolbar to save the design changes to the **Publishers table**. Close all open tables.

n. Click the **Database Tools tab** and click **Relationships** in the Show/Hide group. Double-click each table name to add it to the Relationships window. Click and drag the **AuthorID** field from the **Author table** to the **AuthorCode** field in the **Books table**. Click the **Enforce Referential Integrity check box** in the Edit Relationships dialog box. Then click **Create** to create a one-to-many relationship between the Author and Books tables.

o. Click and drag the **PubID** field from the **Publishers table** to the **PubID** field in the **Books table**. Click the three check boxes in the Edit Relationships dialog box and click **Create** to establish a one-to-many relationship between the Publishers and Books tables.

p. Click **Save** on the Quick Access Toolbar to save the changes to the Relationships window. Press **PrintScreen** to capture a screenshot. Nothing seems to happen because the screenshot is saved to the Clipboard. Launch Microsoft Word. Type **your name and section number** and press **Enter**. Paste the screenshot into the Word file, save the file as **chap2_pe1_bookstore_solution.docx**, and print it. Close Word. The Access file should still be open.

q. Close the Relationships window. Click the **Office Button,** select **Manage**, and then select **Back Up Database**. Name the backup **chap2_pe1_bookstore_solution_backup .accdb**. Close the database.

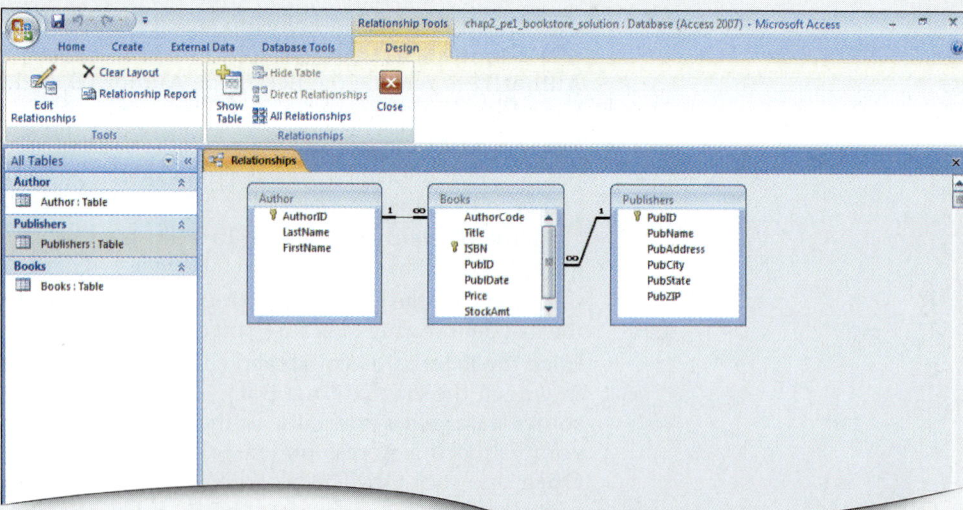

Figure 2.45 Access Relationships Window

...continued on Next Page

2 Martha's Vineyard Bookstore—Querying

Your mother's friend is thrilled with the work that you have completed on the bookstore's database. She has received additional stock and asks you to update the file with the new information. Once updated she wants you to provide a printout of all of the books in stock that were published by Simon & Shuster. **You must complete Exercise 1 before you can start this one.** This project follows the same set of skills as used in Hands-On exercise 3 in this chapter. If you have problems, reread the detailed directions presented in the chapter. Refer to Figure 2.46 as you complete your work.

a. Use Windows to copy *chap2_pe1_bookstore_solution.accdb*. Rename the copied database as **chap2_pe2_bookstore_solution.accdb**. Open *chap2_pe2_bookstore_solution*. Click **Options** in the Security Warning bar, click **Enable this content** in the Microsoft Office Security Options dialog box, and click **OK**.
b. Double-click the **Author table** in the Navigation Pane to open the table in Datasheet view. Locate the new record indicator (the one with the * in the row selector) and click the first field. Enter data for the new record using **17** as Author ID and **your name** as the first and last names. Press **Enter**. Close the Author table.
c. Open the **Books table** and click **New (blank) record** on the navigation bar. Type **17** in the AuthorCode field, **Computer Wisdom** in the Title field, **0-684-80415-5** in the ISBN field, **KN** in the PubID field, **2006** in the PublDate field, **23.50** in the Price field, and **75** in the StockAmt field. Press **Enter**. Close the Books table.
d. Click the **Create tab** and click **Query Wizard** in the Other group. Choose the **Simple Query Wizard**. From the **Author table** select the Author's **LastName** and **FirstName** fields. From the **Books table** select **Title**. Select the **PubName** field from the **Publishers table**. Name the query **Your Name Publishers, Books, and Authors**.
e. Open the query in Design view. Click in the Criteria row of the PubName field. Type **Knopf** to create a criterion to limit the output to only books published by Knopf. Click **Run** in the Results group on the Design tab.
f. Return to Design view. Click in the Sort row in the **LastName** field and select **Ascending**.
g. Move your mouse over the top of the **Title** field until the mouse pointer shape changes to a bold down arrow and then click. With the Title column selected, click and drag it to the left of the **LastName** field. Click in the Sort row in the **Title** field and select **Ascending**. You will see sort commands on both the Title and LastName fields.
h. Click **Run** in the Results group on the Design tab. Notice that because no two books have the same title, the author sort doesn't matter. It makes more sense to sort by author and then sort by title so that all books for a particular author are grouped together.
i. Click **View** in the Views group to return to Design view. Select the **Title** field like you did in step g and move it to the right of the **FirstName** field.
j. Click **Run** in the Results group on the Design tab. Notice that all of Anne Rice's books are listed together in alphabetical order. Double-click the vertical line between the **Title** and **PubName** fields to see the complete titles.
k. Save the query. Click the **Office Button**, point to **Print**, and select **Quick Print**.
l. Click the **Office Button**, select **Manage**, and then select **Compact and Repair Database**. Close the database.

...continued on Next Page

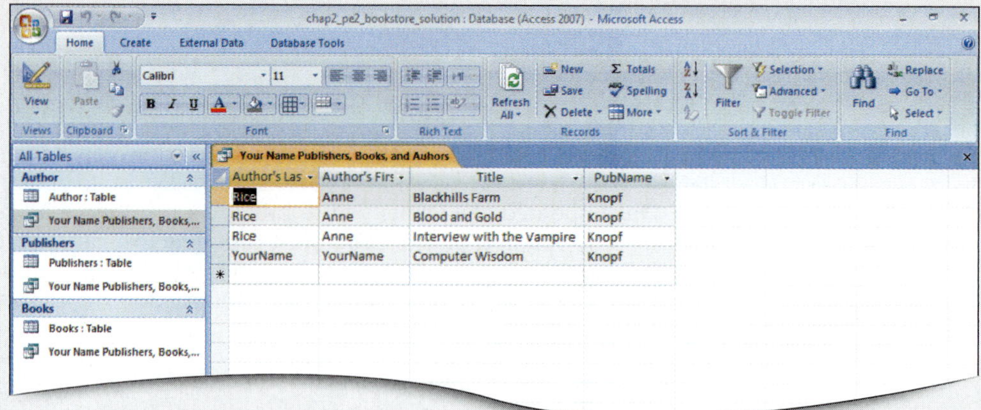

Figure 2.46 Sorted Query Results

3 Combs Insurance

The Comb's Insurance Company offers a full range of insurance services in four locations: Miami, Boston, Chicago, and Atlanta. Until now, they have stored all of the firm's Human Resource data in Excel spreadsheets. These files contain information on employee performance, salary, and education. Some of the files contain information on each of the company's job classifications, including education requirements and the salary range for that position. The firm is converting from Excel to Access to store this important data. There already is a database file containing two of the tables. You need to import the data for the third table from Excel. Once imported, you will need to modify field properties and connect the new table to the rest of the database. The Human Resources vice president is concerned that the Atlanta office ignores the salary guidelines published by the home office. He asks that you create a query to investigate the salary practices of the Atlanta office. This project follows the same set of skills as used in Hands-On Exercises 2 and 3 in this chapter. If you have problems, reread the detailed directions presented in the chapter. Refer to Figure 2.47 as you complete your work.

a. Copy the *chap2_pe3_insurance.accdb* file and rename it **chap2_pe3_insurance_solution**. Open the *chap2_pe3_insurance_solution* database, click **Options** in the Security Warning bar, click **Enable this Content**, then open and examine the data stored in the **Location** and **Titles** tables. Become familiar with the field names and the type of information stored in each table. Pay particular attention to the number of different Position titles.

b. Click the **External Data tab** and click **Import Excel Spreadsheet** in the Import group to import the *chap2_pe3_employees.xlsx* file. Select the **Employees worksheet** and click the **First Row Contains Column Headings check box**. Set the *Indexed Field Options box* for the **EmployeeID** field to **Yes (No Duplicates)**. In the next wizard screen, select the **EmployeeID** as your primary key. Name the table **Employees.**

c. Open the **Employees table** in Design view. In the top of the design window position the insertion point on the **LocationID** field. Locate the *Field Size property* in the lower portion of the table Design view window and change the Field Size for the *LocationID* to **3**. Click in the *Caption* property box and type **Location ID**. In the top of the Design view

...continued on Next Page

window, position the insertion point on the **TitleID** field. Click in the *Field Size* property box in the lower portion of the table Design view window and type **3**. Click in the *Caption* property box and type **Title ID**. Save the design changes.

d. Switch the **Employees table** to the Datasheet view and examine the data. Click any record in the Title ID field and click **Descending** in the Sort & Filter group on the Home tab. How many different position titles are in the table? Does this match the number in the Titles table?

e. Locate the new record row, the one with the * in the row selector box. Click the first field. Add yourself as a new record. Your EmployeeID is **27201**. You are a **Trainee** (T03) in the **Atlanta** (L01) office earning **$27,350**, and your performance rating is **Good**. Press **Enter**.

f. Open the **Titles table** in Datasheet view and add the missing title. The *TitleID* is **T04**, the *Title* is **Senior Account Rep**. The rest of the record is **A marketing position requiring a technical background and at least three years of experience.** It requires a **Four year degree**. The minimum salary is **$45,000**. The maximum is **$75,000**. Do not type the dollar sign or comma as you enter the salary data. Close all open tables. Answer **Yes** if prompted to save.

g. Click **Relationships** in the Show/Hide group on the Database Tools tab. Add the three tables to the Relationships window by double-clicking them one at a time (You may have to click the Show Table button to bring up the Show Table dialog box.) Close the Add Table dialog box.

h. Click the **LocationID** in the Location table and drag it to the **LocationID** in the Employees table. Drop it. In the Edit Relationships dialog box click the **Enforce referential integrity check box**. Click **Create**. Click the **TitleID** in the **Titles** table and drag it to the **TitleID** in the **Employees** table and drop it. In the Relationships dialog box, click the **Enforce Referential Integrity check box**. Click **Create**. Save the changes to the relationships and close the Relationships window.

i. Click **Query Wizard** in the Other group on the Create tab. In the first screen of the Query Wizard, select **Simple Query Wizard**. Select **Table: Location** in the Tables/Queries list. Double-click **Location** to move it to the *Selected Fields* list. Select the **Employees table** in the Tables/Queries list. Double-click **LastName**, **FirstName**, and **Salary**. Select the **Titles** table in the Tables/Queries list. Double-click **MinimumSalary** and **MaximumSalary**. Click **Next**. Select the **Detail (shows every field of every record)** option and click **Next**. Type **Your Name Atlanta** as the query title and click **Finish**.

j. Open the **Your Name Atlanta query** in Design view. Click in the Criteria row in the Location field. Type **Atlanta**. Click **Run** in the Results group on the Design tab. Check to ensure that the results display only Atlanta employees. Save and close the query.

k. Right-click the **Your Name Atlanta query** in the Navigation Pane and select **Copy**. Right-click a white space in the Navigation Pane and select **Paste**. In the Paste As dialog box, type **Your Name Boston** for the query name. Click OK.

l. Open the **Your Name Boston query** in Design view. Click in the Criteria row in the Location field. Type **Boston**. Click **Run** in the Results group on the Design Tab. Check to ensure that the results display only Boston employees. Save and close the query.

m. Open the **Your Name Atlanta** query and the **Your Name Boston** query. *Your screen should appear similar to Figure 2.47.* Print both queries.

n. Click the **Office Button**, select **Manage**, and then select **Compact and Repair Database**. Close the database.

...continued on Next Page

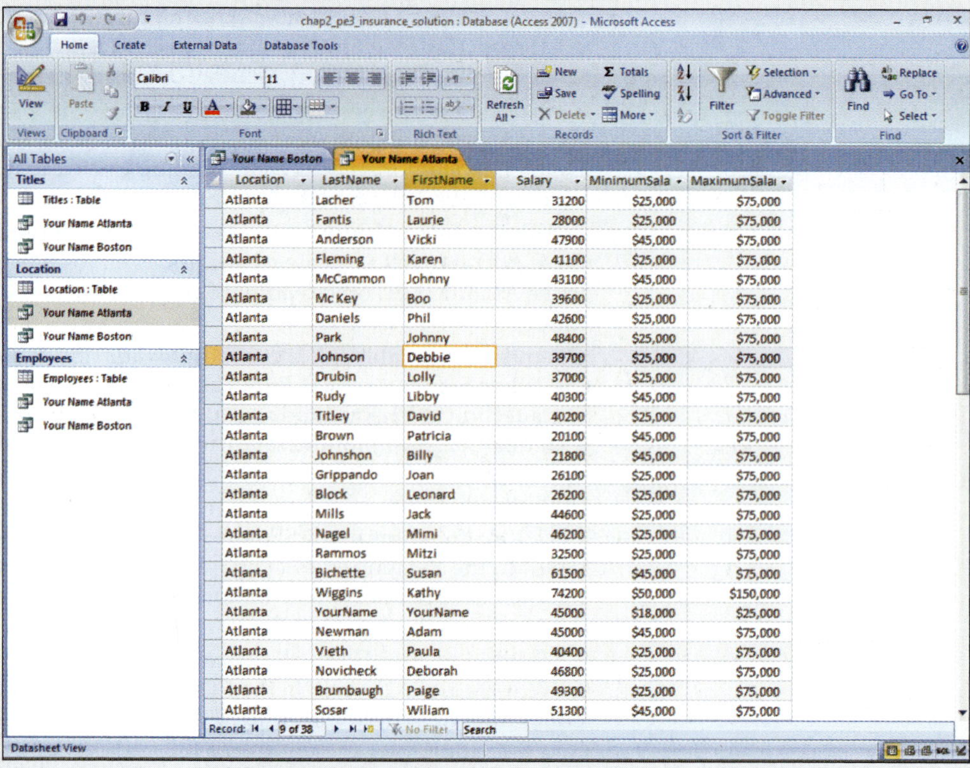

Location	LastName	FirstName	Salary	MinimumSala	MaximumSala
Atlanta	Lacher	Tom	31200	$25,000	$75,000
Atlanta	Fantis	Laurie	28000	$25,000	$75,000
Atlanta	Anderson	Vicki	47900	$45,000	$75,000
Atlanta	Fleming	Karen	41100	$25,000	$75,000
Atlanta	McCammon	Johnny	43100	$45,000	$75,000
Atlanta	Mc Key	Boo	39600	$25,000	$75,000
Atlanta	Daniels	Phil	42600	$25,000	$75,000
Atlanta	Park	Johnny	48400	$25,000	$75,000
Atlanta	Johnson	Debbie	39700	$25,000	$75,000
Atlanta	Drubin	Lolly	37000	$25,000	$75,000
Atlanta	Rudy	Libby	40300	$45,000	$75,000
Atlanta	Titley	David	40200	$25,000	$75,000
Atlanta	Brown	Patricia	20100	$45,000	$75,000
Atlanta	Johnshon	Billy	21800	$45,000	$75,000
Atlanta	Grippando	Joan	26100	$25,000	$75,000
Atlanta	Block	Leonard	26200	$25,000	$75,000
Atlanta	Mills	Jack	44600	$25,000	$75,000
Atlanta	Nagel	Mimi	46200	$25,000	$75,000
Atlanta	Rammos	Mitzi	32500	$25,000	$75,000
Atlanta	Bichette	Susan	61500	$45,000	$75,000
Atlanta	Wiggins	Kathy	74200	$50,000	$150,000
Atlanta	YourName	YourName	45000	$18,000	$25,000
Atlanta	Newman	Adam	45000	$45,000	$75,000
Atlanta	Vieth	Paula	40400	$25,000	$75,000
Atlanta	Novicheck	Deborah	46800	$25,000	$75,000
Atlanta	Brumbaugh	Paige	49300	$25,000	$75,000
Atlanta	Sosar	William	51300	$45,000	$75,000

Figure 2.47 Atlanta Query Results

4 Coffee Service Company

The Coffee Service Company provides high-quality coffee, tea, snacks, and paper products to its customers. Most of the customers are offices in the area: IT firms, insurance offices, financial services. Coffee Service employees go to the customer location and restock the coffee, tea, and snacks supplied daily. A few accounts elect to pick up the merchandise at the Coffee Service Office. You have been asked to help convert the Excel files to an Access database. Once the database is set up, you need to use queries to help the owner do some market analysis. This project follows the same set of skills as used in Hands-On Exercises 2 and 3 in this chapter. The instructions are less detailed to give you a chance to practice your skills. If you have problems, reread the detailed directions presented in the chapter. Refer to Figure 2.48 as you complete your work.

a. Copy the *chap2_pe4_coffee.accdb* file. Rename the copy **chap2_pe4_coffee_solution.accdb**. Open the copied file, then open, enable the content, and examine the data stored in the tables. Become familiar with the field names and the type of information stored in each table.

b. Click the **External Data tab** and click **Import Excel Spreadsheet** in the Import group. Select the **Import the source data into a new table in the current database** option. Click **Browse**, select the *chap2_pe4_products.xlsx* workbook, click **Open,** and then click **OK.** Select the **Products worksheet** and click **Next**. Click the **First Row Contains Column Headings check box**, and then click **Next**. Make sure the ProductID field is active. Click the **Indexed property drop-down arrow** and select to **Yes (No Duplicates)**. Click **Next**. Click the **Choose my own primary key option** and select the **ProductID**. Click **Next**, type **Products** as the table name, and then click **Finish**.

c. Open the **Products table** in Design view. In the top of the design grid, click the **ProductID** field to select it. In the bottom portion of the window change the *Field Size* property to **Long Integer**. Click in the *Caption* property box and type **Product ID**. Save the changes to the Products table. Close the Products table.

...continued on Next Page

d. Click the **Database Tools tab** and then click **Relationships** in the Show/Hide group. Click **Show Table** to open the Show Table dialog box. Double-click the **Products table** to add it to the Relationships window, if it is not already shown. Close the Show Table dialog box.

e. Click the **ProductID** in the **Products table** and drag and drop it on the **ProductID** in the **Order Details table**. When the Edit Relationships dialog box opens, click the **Enforce Referential Integrity check box**. Click **Create**. Save the changes to the Relationships window and close it.

f. Open the **Sales Reps table** and replace YourName in the *FirstName* and *LastName* fields with your first and last name, respectively.

g. Launch the **Query Wizard** in the Other group on the Create tab. Make sure **Simple Query Wizard** is selected, and click **OK**. Select the **Sales Reps table** in the Tables/Queries list. Double-click the **LastName** and **FirstName** fields to move them to the Selected Fields list. Select the **Order Details table** in the Tables/Queries list. Double-click the **Quantity** field to move it to the query. Select the **Customers table** and double-click the **CustomerName** field. Select the **Products table** in the Tables/Queries list. Double-click the **ProductName**, **RefrigerationNeeded**, and **YearIntroduced** fields to move them to the query. This is a detail query. Name the query **Product Introduction**.

h. Open the **Product Introduction query** in Design view. Move the mouse over the top of the *YearIntroduced* field until the mouse pointer shape changes to a bold down arrow, and then click. With the YearIntroduced column selected, click and drag it to the left of the *ProductName* field.

i. Click in the Sort row in the **YearIntroduced** field and select **Ascending**. Click in the Sort row of the **ProductName** field and select **Ascending**.

j. Click in the Criteria row in the LastName field and type your last name. Click in the Criteria row in the FirstName field and type your first name. Click in the Criteria row in the YearIntroduced field and type **2004**. Click into the or row (the next row down) and type **2005**. Type your first and last name in the Or criteria row for the FirstName and LastName fields. This establishes criteria so that only sales by you on products introduced in 2004 and 2005 display. If you don't enter your name on the Or criteria row, the query would show *everyone* for 2005 and your records for *only* 2004.

k. Click the **Design tab** and click **Run** in the Results group. Save the design changes to the query and close it. Right-click the query name in the Navigation Pane and select **Rename**. Rename the query **2004–5 Product Introduction by YourName**. Print the query results.

l. Click the **Office Button**, select **Manage**, and then select **Compact and Repair Database.** Close the database.

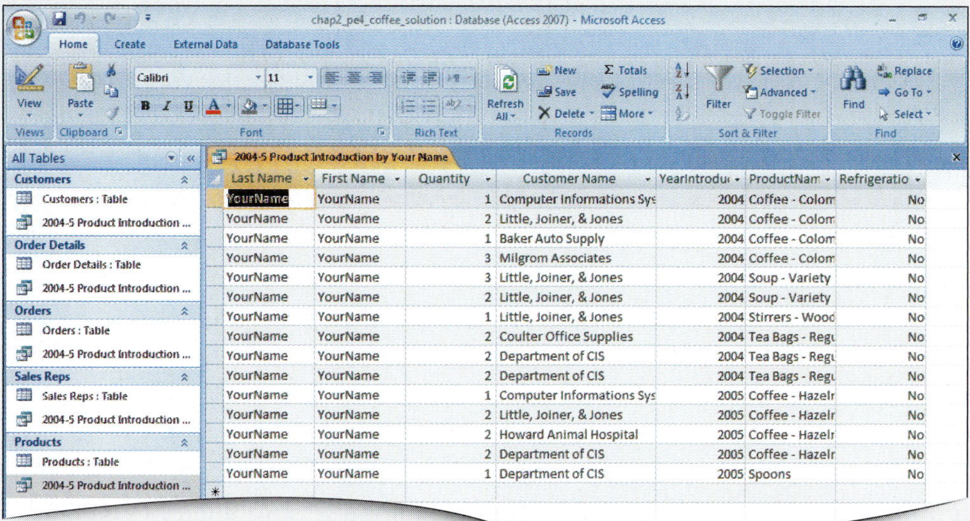

Figure 2.48 Sorted Product Introduction Query Results

Mid-Level Exercises

1 Creating a Query and Working with Criteria

You are an intern in a large, independent real estate firm that specializes in home sales. A database contains all of the information on the properties marketed by your firm. Most real estate transactions involve two agents—one representing the seller (the listing agent) and the other the buyer (the selling agent). The firm owner has asked that you examine the records of recent listings (real estate is listed when the home owner signs a contract with an agent that offers the property for sale) and sort them by subdivision (neighborhood) and the listing agent's name. The results need to include only the sold properties and be sorted by subdivision and the listing agent's last name. Refer to Figure 2.49 as you complete your work.

a. Locate the file named *chap2_mid1_realestate.accdb*; copy it to your working folder and rename it **chap2_mid1_realestate_solution.accdb**. Open the file and enable the content. Open the **Agents table.** Find and replace *Kia Hart*'s name with your name. Close the **Agents** table.

b. Create a detail query. You need the following fields: **LastName**, **FirstName**, **DateListed**, **DateSold**, **ListPrice**, **SellingAgent**, and **Subdivision**. Name the query **Your Name Sold Property by Subdivision and Agent**. Run the query and examine the number of records.

c. In Design view enter the criteria that will remove all of the properties from the Water Valley Subdivision. Run the query and examine the number of records. It should be a smaller number than in step b.

d. Rearrange the fields in the query so that the Subdivision field is in the leftmost column and the LastName field is the second from the left. Add the appropriate sort to the design grid to sort first by Subdivision and then by LastName.

e. Add a criterion that will limit the results to the properties sold after October 31, 2008.

f. Capture a screenshot of the Sales Summary query results. Have it open on your computer and press **PrintScreen** to copy a picture of what is on the monitor to the clipboard. Open Word, type your name and section number in a new blank document, press **Enter**, paste the screenshot in Word, and press **Enter** again.

g. Return to Design view and capture a screenshot of the query in Design view. Paste this screenshot below the first in the Word document. Save the Word document as **chap2_mid1_realestate_solution.docx**. Print and close the Word document. Close the database file.

...continued on Next Page

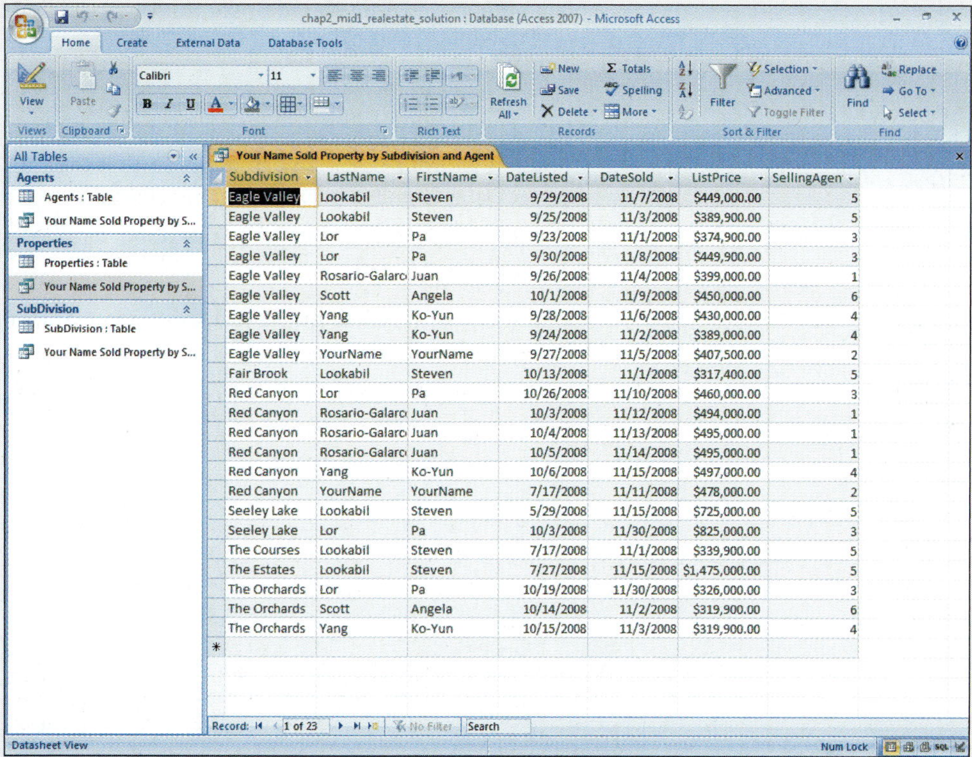

Subdivision	LastName	FirstName	DateListed	DateSold	ListPrice	SellingAgent
Eagle Valley	Lookabil	Steven	9/29/2008	11/7/2008	$449,000.00	5
Eagle Valley	Lookabil	Steven	9/25/2008	11/3/2008	$389,900.00	5
Eagle Valley	Lor	Pa	9/23/2008	11/1/2008	$374,900.00	3
Eagle Valley	Lor	Pa	9/30/2008	11/8/2008	$449,900.00	3
Eagle Valley	Rosario-Galarc	Juan	9/26/2008	11/4/2008	$399,000.00	1
Eagle Valley	Scott	Angela	10/1/2008	11/9/2008	$450,000.00	6
Eagle Valley	Yang	Ko-Yun	9/28/2008	11/6/2008	$430,000.00	4
Eagle Valley	Yang	Ko-Yun	9/24/2008	11/2/2008	$389,000.00	4
Eagle Valley	YourName	YourName	9/27/2008	11/5/2008	$407,500.00	2
Fair Brook	Lookabil	Steven	10/13/2008	11/1/2008	$317,400.00	5
Red Canyon	Lor	Pa	10/26/2008	11/10/2008	$460,000.00	3
Red Canyon	Rosario-Galarc	Juan	10/3/2008	11/12/2008	$494,000.00	1
Red Canyon	Rosario-Galarc	Juan	10/4/2008	11/13/2008	$495,000.00	1
Red Canyon	Rosario-Galarc	Juan	10/5/2008	11/14/2008	$495,000.00	1
Red Canyon	Yang	Ko-Yun	10/6/2008	11/15/2008	$497,000.00	4
Red Canyon	YourName	YourName	7/17/2008	11/11/2008	$478,000.00	2
Seeley Lake	Lookabil	Steven	5/29/2008	11/15/2008	$725,000.00	5
Seeley Lake	Lor	Pa	10/3/2008	11/30/2008	$825,000.00	3
The Courses	Lookabil	Steven	7/17/2008	11/1/2008	$339,900.00	5
The Estates	Lookabil	Steven	7/27/2008	11/15/2008	$1,475,000.00	5
The Orchards	Lor	Pa	10/19/2008	11/30/2008	$326,000.00	3
The Orchards	Scott	Angela	10/14/2008	11/2/2008	$319,900.00	6
The Orchards	Yang	Ko-Yun	10/15/2008	11/3/2008	$319,900.00	4

Figure 2.49 Sorted Product Introduction Query Results

2 Importing Excel Data, Creating, and Sorting a Query

The Prestige Hotel chain caters to upscale business travelers and provides state-of-the-art conference, meeting, and reception facilities. It prides itself on its international, four-star cuisines. Last year, it began a member rewards club to help the marketing department track the purchasing patterns of their most loyal customers. All of the hotel transactions are stored in the database. Your task is to help the manager of the Boston hotel identify the customers who used suites last year and who had more than two persons in their party. Refer to Figure 2.50 as you complete your work.

a. Copy the *chap2_mid2_memrewards.accdb* database and name the copy **chap2_mid2_memrewards_solution.accdb.** Open and tour the newly copied file. Gain an understanding of the relationships and the data contained in the different tables. Specifically look for the tables and fields containing the information you need: dates of stays in Boston suites, the member's name, and the number in the party.

b. Import the Excel file *chap2_mid2_location.xlsx* into your database as a new table. Name the table as **Location**. Use the LocationID field as the primary key. Set the field size to Double.

c. Establish a relationship between the LocationID field in the **Location table** and the Location field in the **Orders table**. Enforce referential integrity.

d. Open the **Members table** and find Fred White's name. Replace Fred's name with your own first and last name. Now find Karen Korte's name and replace it with your name.

e. Create a query that contains the fields you identified in Step a. Set a condition to limit the output to Boston, service from August–December 2007, and private parties greater than 2. Run the query and **sort** the results in descending order by the Service Date.

...continued on Next Page

Name the query **Your Name Boston Suites**. See Figure 2.50 if you need help figuring out which fields to select.

f. Examine the number of records in the status bar at the bottom of the query. It should display 23. If your number of records is different, examine the criteria.

g. Change the order of the query fields so that they display as **FirstName**, **LastName**, **ServiceDate**, **City**, **NoInParty,** and **ServiceName**.

h. Save and close the query. Copy it and in the Paste As dialog box, name the new query **Your Name Miami Suites**.

i. Open the Miami Suites query in Design view and replace the Boston criterion with Miami. Run and save the changes.

j. Print your queries if directed to do so by your instructor. Compact, repair, and back up your file. Close the database.

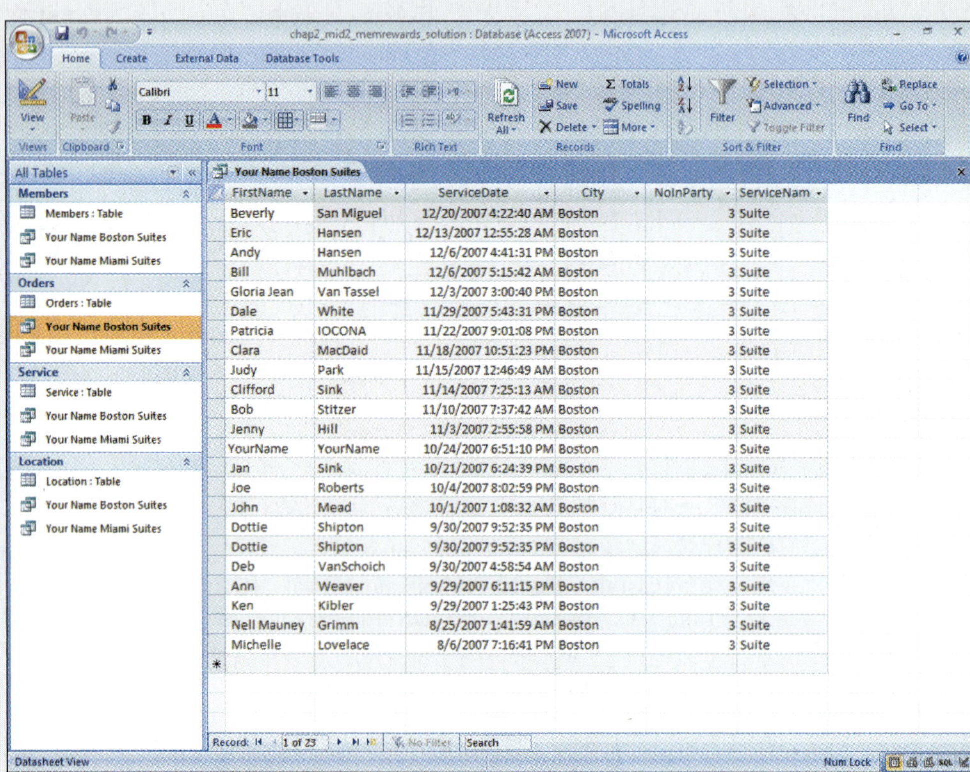

FirstName	LastName	ServiceDate	City	NoInParty	ServiceNam
Beverly	San Miguel	12/20/2007 4:22:40 AM	Boston	3	Suite
Eric	Hansen	12/13/2007 12:55:28 AM	Boston	3	Suite
Andy	Hansen	12/6/2007 4:41:31 PM	Boston	3	Suite
Bill	Muhlbach	12/6/2007 5:15:42 AM	Boston	3	Suite
Gloria Jean	Van Tassel	12/3/2007 3:00:40 PM	Boston	3	Suite
Dale	White	11/29/2007 5:43:31 PM	Boston	3	Suite
Patricia	IOCONA	11/22/2007 9:01:08 PM	Boston	3	Suite
Clara	MacDaid	11/18/2007 10:51:23 PM	Boston	3	Suite
Judy	Park	11/15/2007 12:46:49 AM	Boston	3	Suite
Clifford	Sink	11/14/2007 7:25:13 AM	Boston	3	Suite
Bob	Stitzer	11/10/2007 7:37:42 AM	Boston	3	Suite
Jenny	Hill	11/3/2007 2:55:58 PM	Boston	3	Suite
YourName	YourName	10/24/2007 6:51:10 PM	Boston	3	Suite
Jan	Sink	10/21/2007 6:24:39 PM	Boston	3	Suite
Joe	Roberts	10/4/2007 8:02:59 PM	Boston	3	Suite
John	Mead	10/1/2007 1:08:32 AM	Boston	3	Suite
Dottie	Shipton	9/30/2007 9:52:35 PM	Boston	3	Suite
Dottie	Shipton	9/30/2007 9:52:35 PM	Boston	3	Suite
Deb	VanSchoich	9/30/2007 4:58:54 AM	Boston	3	Suite
Ann	Weaver	9/29/2007 6:11:15 PM	Boston	3	Suite
Ken	Kibler	9/29/2007 1:25:43 PM	Boston	3	Suite
Nell Mauney	Grimm	8/25/2007 1:41:59 AM	Boston	3	Suite
Michelle	Lovelace	8/6/2007 7:16:41 PM	Boston	3	Suite

Figure 2.50 Boston Query Results

3 Creating and Using Queries

Northwind Traders is a small, international, specialty food company. It sells products in eight different divisions: Beverages, Confections (candy), Condiments, Dairy Products, Grains and Cereals, Meat and Poultry, Produce, and Seafood. Although most of its customers are restaurants and gourmet food shops, it has a few retail customers, too. It purchases the merchandise from a variety of suppliers. All of the order information is stored in the company's database. The marketing department uses this database to monitor and maintain sales records. You are the marketing

...continued on Next Page

manager. Your task is to identify which customers purchased Chai (tea) and Chang (Chinese Beer) in 2007. It would be valuable for you to discover the order quantities and the countries where the orders ship. After you complete the query, you will copy it and add the salesperson's name field to the copy. Refer to Figure 2.51 as you complete your work.

a. Copy the *chap2_mid3_traders.accdb* file; rename the copy **chap2_mid3_traders_solution.accdb**. Open the newly copied file and enable the content. Tour the database Relationships window to gain an understanding of the relationships and the data contained in the different tables. As you tour, specifically look for the tables and fields containing the information you need, that is, orders shipped in **2007** for the **beverages Chai** and **Chang**, the quantities purchased, the date the order shipped, and the countries the purchases were shipped to. You are interested in all of the countries *excluding* the United States.

b. After you identify the necessary fields, create a query that includes the fields of interest. Name this query **Your Name Shipping for Chai and Chang**.

c. Set the query criteria to select the records of interest—2007 orders of Chai and Chang shipped to all of the world except for the United States.

d. Sort the query results by the Company name (alphabetically) and then by the quantity ordered. (If the same company is listed twice, the largest quantity should be listed first.)

e. Print the query results. Save and close the query.

f. Copy the query and name the copy **Your Name Chai and Chang Sales by Employee**.

g. Open the **Employees table** and replace Andrew Fuller's name with your own name.

h. Add the employee's FirstName and LastName fields to the newly copied query.

i. Rearrange the fields so that the employee's LastName field is the first in the design grid and the employee's FirstName is the second. Sort the results by the employee's LastName.

j. Run, save, and print the query. Compact, repair, and back up your file. Close the database.

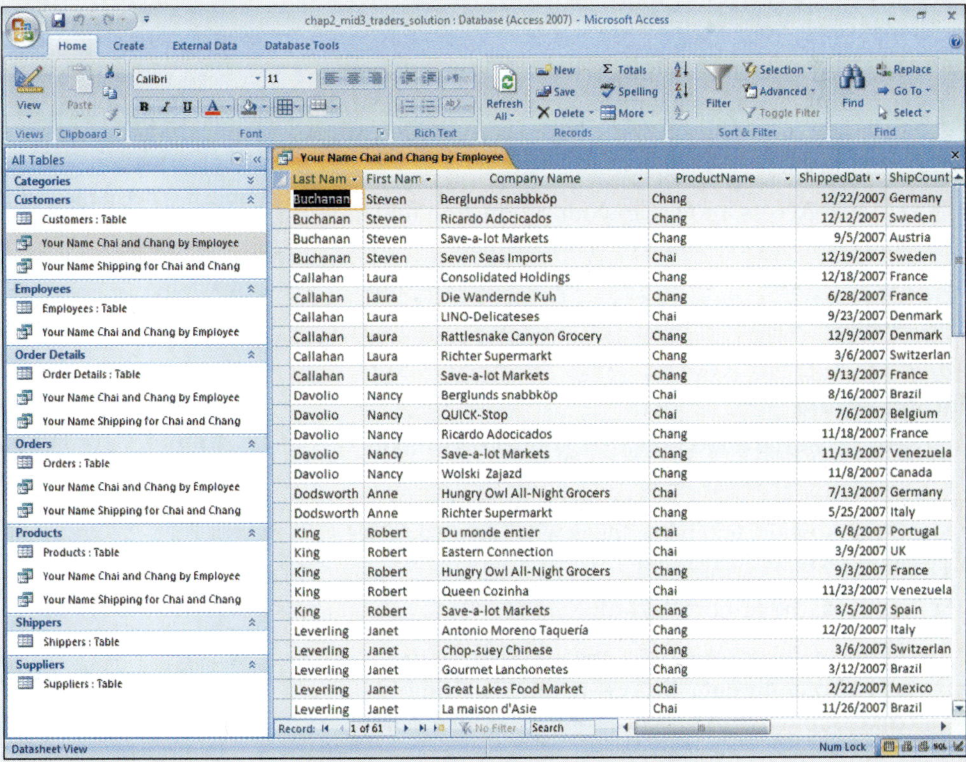

Figure 2.51 2007 Chai and Chang Sales by Employee

Capstone Exercise

The JC Raulston Arboretum at NC State University staff have been carefully saving their data in Excel for years. One particular workbook contains a worksheet that lists the names of all the Arboretum's "friends." This not-for-profit organization solicits contributions in the form of cash gifts, volunteer service, and "in-kind" gifts. An in-kind gift is a gift of a plant to the arboretum. Each year, one of the major fundraising events is the Gala. This is a formal event held on a delightful spring afternoon with cocktails, gourmet hors d'oeuvres, live music, and a silent auction featuring a plethora of unique plants and an eclectic array of many other distinctive items. As friends contribute service or funds to the Arboretum, another reward they receive are connoisseur plants. Connoisseur plants are rare new plants or hard-to-find old favorites, and they are part of the annual appeal and membership drive to benefit the Arboretum's many fine programs and its day-to-day operational expenses. These wonderful plants are sent to those who join the Friends of JC Raulston Arboretum at the Sponsor, Patron, Benefactor, or Philanthropist levels. The organization has grown. The files are too large to handle easily in Excel. Your task will be to begin the conversion of the files from Excel to Access.

Database File Setup

You need to open an Excel workbook that contains data on four named worksheets. Examine the data in the worksheets, paying attention to which fields will become the primary keys in each table and where those fields will appear as foreign keys in other tables in order to form the relationships.

a. Locate the Excel workbook named *chap2_cap_friends.xlsx* and open it.

b. Locate the Excel workbook named *chap2_cap_connplants.xlsx* and open it.

c. Examine the data, identify what will become the primary field in each table, and look for that field to reappear in other tables so that you can form relationships.

d. Launch Access, browse to your production folder, and create a new, blank database named **chap2_cap_arboretum_solution.accdb.**

e. Enable the content in *chap2_cap_arboretum_solution.accdb*.

Import Wizard

You need to use the Import Data Wizard twice to import a worksheet from each Excel workbook into Access. You need to select the worksheets, specify the primary keys, set the indexing option, and name the newly imported tables (see Figures 2.12 through 2.18).

a. Activate the Import Wizard.

b. In the first window of the wizard, identify the source of your data. Browse to the Exploring Access folder and select the *chap2_cap_friends.xlsx* workbook.

c. Set the indexing option to **Yes (No Duplicates)** for the FriendID field.

d. When prompted, select the **FriendID** as the primary key.

e. Name the table **Friends**.

f. Import the *chap2_cap_connplants.xlsx* file, set the ID field as the primary key, and name the table as **Connoisseur**.

g. In Datasheet view, examine the newly imported tables.

Create Relationships

You need to create the relationships between the tables. Identify the primary fields in each table and, using the Relationships window, connect them with their foreign key counterparts in other tables. Enforce referential integrity.

a. Close any open tables and then display the Relationships window.

b. Add the two tables to the Relationships window with the Show Table dialog box. Then, close the Show Tables dialog box.

c. Drag the FriendID from the **Friends table** to the FriendNumber field in the **Connoisseur table**. Enforce referential integrity.

d. Close the Relationships window and save your changes.

Create, Add Criteria to, and Sort a Query

You need to create a query that identifies the people who have received at least one connoisseur plant and who are not attending the Gala. Use the Query Wizard to identify the tables, Friends and Connoisseur, and fields necessary. Establish criteria that will limit the results to only records where one or more plant has been sent and there is no Gala reservation. This query will need to be sorted by the last name field.

a. Launch the Query Wizard.

b. From the **Friends table** select the NameFirst, NameLast, and the Gala fields. From the **Connoisseur table**, select the SendPlant field.

c. Name the query as **Your Name Gala No, Conn Plant Yes**.

d. Open the query in Design view and set criteria in the Gala field to **No** and in the SendPlant field to **>0**.

e. Sort the query by the NameLast field in alphabetical order.

f. Print the results. Compact, repair, and back up the file. Close the database.

Mini Cases

Use the rubric following the case as a guide to evaluate your work, but keep in mind that your instructor may impose additional grading criteria or use a different standard to judge your work.

Employee Performance Review

GENERAL CASE

The chap2_mc1_insurance.accdb file contains data from a large insurance agency. Copy the *chap2_mc1_insurance.accdb* file to your production folder, name it **chap2_mc1_insurance_solution .accdb**, and open the copied file. Use the skills from this chapter to perform several tasks. The firm's employee policy states that an employee needs to maintain a performance rating of good or excellent to maintain employment. If an employee receives an average or poor performance rating, she receives a letter reminding her of this policy and advising her to improve or suffer the consequences. You are the manager of the Atlanta office. You need to identify the employees who need a letter of reprimand. You are preparing the query so that someone else can generate a form letter to the employees. You need to include fields for the letter that contain the employees' first and last names, their position titles, and their salary. You do not need to write the letter, only assemble the data for the letter to be written. The results need to be alphabetized by the employee's names. As you work, consider the order that the fields will need to be used in the letter and order the query fields accordingly. Close the database.

Performance Elements	Exceeds Expectations	Meets Expectations	Below Expectations
Create query	All necessary and no unneeded fields included.	All necessary fields included but also unnecessary fields.	Not all necessary fields were included in the query.
Establish criteria	The query results correctly identified and selected records.	The query results correctly identified and selected records.	Incorrect criteria specifications.
Sorting	Query fields were logically ordered and appropriately sorted.	Query fields were appropriately sorted but not logically ordered.	Both the order and the sort were incorrect.
Query name	The query name described the content.	The query name partially described the content.	The query employed the default name.

Database Administrator Position

RESEARCH CASE

This chapter introduced you to the idea that employees who administer and manage databases receive high pay, but you have much more to explore. Use the Internet to search for information about database management. One useful site is published by the federal government's Bureau of Labor Statistics. It compiles an Occupational Outlook Handbook describing various positions, the type of working environment, the education necessity, salary information, and the projected growth. The Web site is **http://www.bls.gov/oco.** Your challenge is to investigate the position of Database Administrator. Use the BLS Web site and at least one other source. Write your instructor a memo describing this position. Use a memo template in Word, your most professional writing style, and specify the data sources. Save the document as **chap2_mc2_dbaseadmin_solution .docx**. Print and close the document.

Performance Elements	Exceeds Expectations	Meets Expectations	Below Expectations
Use online resources	Appropriate articles located and memo indicates comprehension.	Appropriate articles located but memo did not demonstrate comprehension.	Articles not found.
Extract useful information from the resources	Most major components of the position described accurately.	Many elements of the position described.	Many elements of the position missing or the description incomprehensible.
Summarize and communicate	Memo clearly written and free of misspellings.	Memo text indicates some understanding but also weaknesses.	Memo missing or incomprehensible.
Aesthetics	Memo template correctly employed.	Template employed but signed in the wrong place or improperly used.	Memo missing or incomprehensible.

May and Beverage Queries

DISASTER RECOVERY

A co-worker called you into his office and explained that he was having difficulty with Access 2007 and asked you to look at his work. Copy the *chap2_mc3_traders.accdb* file to your production folder, name it **chap2_mc3_traders_solution.accdb**, and open the file. It contains two queries, May 2007 Orders of Beverages and Confections and 2007 Beverage Sales by Ship Country. The May 2007 Orders of Beverages and Confections query is supposed to only have information from May. You find other dates included in the results. Your challenge is to find and correct the error(s). The 2007 Beverage Sales by Ship Country returns no results. It needs to be ordered by country. It needs to be repaired and resorted. Print the Datasheet view of both queries. Close the database.

Performance Elements	Exceeds Expectations	Meets Expectations	Below Expectations
Error identification	Correct identification and correction of all errors.	Correct identification of all errors and correction of some errors.	Errors neither located nor corrected.
May query	Correct criteria and sorted logically.	Correct criteria but inadequately sorted.	Incorrect criteria.
Beverage query	Correct criteria and sorted logically.	Correct criteria but inadequately sorted.	Incorrect criteria.

chapter 3 | **Access**

Customize, Analyze, and Summarize Query Data

Creating and Using Queries to Make Decisions

After you read this chapter, you will be able to:

1. Understand the order of precedence **(page 679)**.
2. Create a calculated field in a query **(page 679)**.
3. Create expressions with the Expression Builder **(page 689)**.
4. Create and edit Access functions **(page 690)**.
5. Perform date arithmetic **(page 694)**.
6. Create and work with data aggregates **(page 704)**.

Hands-On Exercises

Exercises	Skills Covered
1. CALCULATED QUERY FIELDS (page 683) **Open:** chap3_ho1-3_realestate.accdb **Save:** chap3_ho1-3_realestate_solution.accdb **Back up as:** chap3_ho1_realestate_solution.accdb	• Copy a Database and Start the Query • Select the Fields, Save, and Open the Query • Create a Calculated Field and Run the Query • Verify the Calculated Results • Recover from a Common Error
2. EXPRESSION BUILDER, FUNCTIONS, AND DATE ARITHMETIC (page 695) **Open:** chap3_ho1-3_realestate.accdb (from Exercise 1) **Save:** chap3_ho1-3_realestate_solution.accdb (additional modifications) **Back up as:** chap3_ho2_realestate_solution.accdb	• Create a Select Query • Use the Expression Builder • Create Calculations Using Input Stored in a Different Query or Table • Edit Expressions Using the Expression Builder • Use Functions • Work with Date Arithmetic
3. DATA AGGREGATES (page 707) **Open:** chap3_ho1-3_realestate.accdb (from Exercise 2) **Save:** chap3_ho1-3_realestate_solution.accdb (additional modifications)	• Add a Total Row • Create a Totals Query Based on a Select Query • Add Fields to the Design Grid • Add Grouping Options and Specify Summary Statistics

CASE STUDY

Replacements, Ltd.

(Replacements, Ltd exists. The data in the case file are actual data. The customer and employee information have been changed to ensure privacy. However, the inventory and sales records reflect actual transactions.)

Today is the first day in your new position as associate marketing manager at Replacements, Ltd. In preparation for your first day on the job you have spent hours browsing the Replacements Web site, www.replacements.com. There you learned that Replacements, Ltd. (located in Greensboro, N.C.) has the world's largest selection of old and new dinnerware, including china, stoneware, crystal, glassware, silver, stainless, and collectibles. Its 300,000-square-foot facilities (the size of five football fields!) house an incredible inventory of 10 million pieces in 200,000 patterns, some more than 100 years old. While interviewing for the position, you toured the show room and warehouses. You learned that Replacements provides its customers with pieces that exactly match their existing patterns of china, silver, crystal, etc. People who break a cup or accidentally drop a spoon in the disposal purchase replacement treasures.

Case Study

You have been given responsibility for managing several different patterns of merchandise. You need to maintain adequate inventory levels. On the one hand you need to have merchandise available so that when a customer wishes to purchase a fork in a specific pattern, the customer service representatives can find it and box it for shipment. To accomplish this task, you need to closely monitor past sales in the various patterns in order to understand purchasing habits and product demand. On the other hand, the firm cannot afford to stock inventory of patterns no one wishes to purchase. You exchange information with the customer service representatives and monitor their performance. If you discover that one of the patterns you manage has excess inventory, you will need to direct the buyers to stop purchasing additional pieces in that pattern and encourage the customer service representatives to suggest the pattern to customers. You will determine if and when a pattern should be discounted or if an incentive program or contest should be implemented to reward the sales associates for successfully selling the overstocked merchandise.

Your Assignment

- Copy the *chap3_case_replacement.accdb* file to your production folder. Name the copy **chap3_case_replacement_solution.accdb**.
- Open the Relationships window and acquaint yourself with the tables, fields, and relationships among the tables in the database.
- You need to convert the data into useful information. To accomplish this task, you will need to create a query that identifies the revenue generated from sales in each of the patterns you manage. Save the query as **Revenue and Commission by Employee**.
- You also must determine which patterns customers purchase most often. Save the query as **Revenue by Pattern**.
- Replacements encourages the customer service representatives by paying them bonuses based on the orders that they fill. You will calculate each customer service representative's total sales and calculate their bonuses. The bonus will be calculated based on ½% of the representative's total sales. Save the query as **Revenue and Commission by Employee**.
- Finally, you need to compare the inventory levels of each pattern piece with its sales volume. Careful monitoring of stock levels will prevent excessive inventory. For each item calculate the percent of the inventory level that was sold in the past month. For example, if there were 100 cups in a specific pattern in inventory at the beginning of the month and 18 of them were sold during the month, the sales-inventory ratio would be 18%. Set criteria so that the zero OnHandQuantity items are excluded from the calculation. Save the query as **Sales-Inventory Ratio**.

Data Summary and Analysis

Practicing good database design discourages storing results of calculations in a table. Access *can* perform arithmetic calculations using formulae and functions much like Excel. However, the calculated results do not belong in tables. Instead, calculations needed to summarize and analyze data are found in three places: queries, forms, and reports. Professionals who use Access to develop applications within organizations have very different opinions about the most appropriate placement of calculations in Access. One group assembles and manipulates data inside a query. After you establish the calculations and criteria, the data are sent to an Access report to be formatted appropriately. (This is the practice that you will employ throughout the exercises in this book.) The other group does all of the calculations inside of forms and reports. This group uses fewer queries but creates far more sophisticated reports and forms.

In this section, you learn about the order of precedence and create a calculated field in a query.

Understanding the Order of Precedence

The ***order of precedence*** establishes the sequence by which values are calculated.

The ***order of precedence*** establishes the sequence by which values are calculated in an expression. Evaluate parenthetically expressed values, then exponents, multiplication and division, and, finally, addition and subtraction. Access calculates exactly what you tell it to calculate—even if your formulae are incorrect! Table 3.1 shows some examples of arithmetic order. You must have a solid understanding of these rules in order to "teach" the computer to generate the required output. Access, like Excel, uses the following symbols:

- Addition +
- Subtraction –
- Multiplication *
- Division /
- Exponentiation ^

Table 3.1 Examples of Order of Precedence

Expression	Order to Perform Calculations	Output
= 2 + 3 * 3	Multiply first, and then add.	11
= (2 + 3) * 3	Add the values inside the parenthesis first, and then multiply.	15
= 2 + 2 ^ 3	Simplify the exponent first. 2^3 = 2*2*2 or 8. Then add.	10
= (2 + 2) ^3	Add the parenthetical values first (2 + 2 = 4), and then raise the result to the 3rd power. 4^3 = 4*4*4.	64
= 10/2 + 3	Divide first, and then add.	8
= 10/(2+3)	Add first to simplify the parenthetical expression, and then divide.	2
= 10 * 2 – 3 * 2	Multiply first, and then subtract.	14

Creating a Calculated Field in a Query

Often, you will need to perform a calculation based on values on one or more table fields. For example, a table might contain times that employees clock in and out of work. You can create a calculated field to calculate how many hours each employee worked by subtracting the ClockIn field value from the ClockOut field value. You can create a calculated field in the Design view of the query (Query Design is displayed in the Other group on the Create tab). Create the calculated field in the Field row of a blank column. You may scroll, if necessary, to find a blank column in the design grid or insert a blank column where you want the calculated field to appear. A formula used to calculate new fields from the values in existing fields is also known as an *expression*. An expression consists of a number of different items to produce the answers needed. The items used in an expression may include the following:

An ***expression*** is a formula used to calculate new fields from the values in existing fields.

- Identifiers (the names of fields, controls or properties)
- Operators (arithmetic instructions about what to do with the identifiers like + or –)
- Functions (as in Excel, Access has built-in functions to perform routine calculations, like Sum or Avg)
- ***Constants*** and values (numbers that may be used as a part of a calculation but are unlikely to change)

A ***constant*** refers to a value that does not change.

You may use the expression to perform calculations, retrieve a value from a field, set query criteria, verify data created, calculate fields or controls, and set grouping levels in reports. Access not only organizes and protects a firm's valuable data but also enables you to summarize, understand, and make decisions based on the data. Your value to an organization dramatically increases when you master the skills that surround expression building in Access.

Build Expressions with Correct Syntax

Syntax is the set of rules by which the words and symbols of an expression are correctly combined.

Enter the expression in the first row of the column. Using simple ***syntax*** rules you instruct the software to calculate the necessary values. You can create expressions to perform calculations using either field values or constants. If you use a table field, such as Balance, in the expression, you must correctly spell the field names for Access to find the appropriate values. You should assign descriptive names to the calculated fields. Access ignores spaces in calculations. The general syntax follows:

CalculatedFieldName: [InputField1] operator [InputField2]

Although this is the most appropriate format, Access enters the brackets for you if it recognizes the field name. Remember that an **operator** is a symbol, such as *, that performs some operation, such as multiplication. An **operand** is the value that is being manipulated or operated on. In calculated fields in Access, the operand is either a literal value or a field name. Figure 3.1 shows a calculated field named Interest. The calculated field first calculates the monthly interest rate by dividing the 3.5% (0.035) annual rate by 12. The monthly interest rate is then multiplied by the value in the Balance field to determine the amount of interest owed. The query

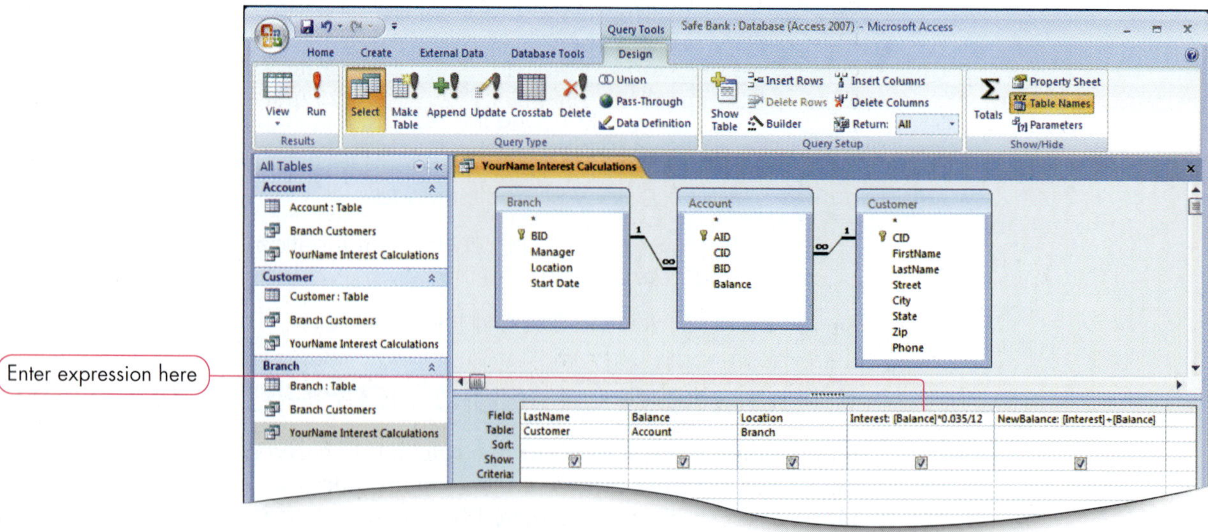

Figure 3.1 The Correct Location for a Calculated Query Expression

contains a second calculated field named NewBalance. Its value is the product of the value in the Interest field and the result of the Balance calculated field.

To help reinforce how calculated fields work, suppose you need to calculate the revenue from a purchase order. Revenue is the name of the calculated field. The following expression generates the calculated field by multiplying the unit price by the quantity ordered:

Revenue: Price*Quantity

Access enters the brackets for you and converts the expression to the following:

Revenue: [Price]*[Quantity]

For a final example of calculated fields, suppose you need to calculate a 10% price increase on all products you sell. NewPrice is the name of the calculated field. The following expression multiplies the old price by 110%:

NewPrice: Price*1.1

Access enters the brackets for you and converts the expression to the following:

NewPrice: [Price]*1.1

When you run the query, the calculated results display in the query's Datasheet view. Using the above example, Access goes to the table(s) where the prices and order quantities are stored, extracts the current data, loads it into the query, and uses the data to perform the calculation. When you direct Access to collect fields that are stored in related tables, Access uses the "strings" that form the relationship to collect the appropriate records and deliver them to the query. For example, suppose you create a query that retrieves customers' names from the Customers table and the dates that the orders were placed from the Order table. The Customers table might contain 50,000 customer records. The query will return only those customers who ordered something because the relationship integrity will limit the output to only the records of interest. After the data are assembled, you can manipulate the data in each record by entering expressions. After you run the query, you need to examine the calculated results to verify that the output is what you need. Access has the ability to process a lot of numbers very quickly. Unfortunately, Access can also return incorrectly calculated results equally quickly if the formula you create is incorrect. Remember and avoid ***GIGO***—Garbage In; Garbage Out!

(GIGO—Garbage In; Garbage Out!)

Verify Calculated Results

After your query runs, look at the values of the input field and then look at the calculated results returned. Ask yourself, "Does this answer make sense?" Use a pocket calculator or the Windows calculator to perform the same calculation using the same inputs and compare the answers. Alternatively, you can use Excel to check your calculated results. Copy and paste a few records into Excel. Repeat all of the calculations and compare the answers. The Access calculated field, the calculator, and the Excel calculations should return identical results.

After verifying the calculated results, you should save the query to run the next time you need to perform the same calculations.

Save a Query Containing Calculated Fields

Saving a query does *not* save the data. It saves only your instructions about what data to select and what to do with it once it is selected. Think of a query as a set of instructions directing Access to deliver data and the form the data are to assume at delivery. Writing a query is like placing an order with a restaurant server. You may order a medium rare steak, a baked potato, and tossed salad with blue cheese dressing. Your server writes the order and any special instructions and delivers it to the kitchen. In the kitchen the cook fills the order based on your instructions. Then the server delivers the ordered food to you. The data in a database is like the raw food in the kitchen. It is stored in the freezer or refrigerator or the cupboard (the tables). Data from the query (server's order) are assembled and "cooked." The big difference is that in the restaurant, once your steak is delivered to you, it is no longer available to other diners to order. The data in a database are *never* consumed. Data can be ordered simultaneously by multiple queries in a multiple user database environment. The data physically reside in the tables and never move from their storage location. Running the query collects the field values in the records of interest. The query contains only the instructions governing how Access selects and interacts with the data. Although not all query datasets using multiple tables can be updated, you should be careful. If you type over a data item in a query Datasheet view, the new value could automatically replace the old one in the table.

After you run, verify, and save the query, you can use the newly created calculated fields in subsequent calculations. You may use a calculated field as input for other calculated fields. However, you must first save the query so that the calculation's results will be available.

In the first hands-on exercise you will create calculated expressions, practice verification techniques, and generate and recover from a common error.

TIP Calculated Field Names

Although table field names should not have spaces, you can use spaces in calculated field names, such as New Price: (Price)*1.1. If you do not use a space in a calculated field name, such as NewPrice, you can display the Property Sheet for the calculated field and enter a name with a space in the Caption property box, similar to how you create captions in the Design view for a table.

Hands-On Exercises

1 | Calculated Query Fields

Skills covered: 1. Copy a Database and Start the Query **2.** Select the Fields, Save, and Open the Query **3.** Create a Calculated Field and Run the Query **4.** Verify the Calculated Results **5.** Recover from a Common Error

Step 1
Copy a Database and Start the Query

Refer to Figure 3.2 as you complete Step 1.

a. Use Windows Explorer to locate the file named *chap3_ho1-3_realestate.accdb*. Copy the file to your production folder and rename the copied file as **chap3_ho1-3_realestate_solution.accdb**.

b. Open the *chap3_ho1-3_realestate_solution.accdb* file.

c. Click **Options** on the Security Warning toolbar and then click **Enable this content** in the Microsoft Office Security Options dialog box, and click **OK**.

d. Click the **Create tab** and then click **Query Wizard** in the Other group.

e. Select **Simple Query Wizard** in the New Query dialog box. Click **OK**.

The Simple Query Wizard dialog box displays so that you can specify the table(s) and fields to include in the query design.

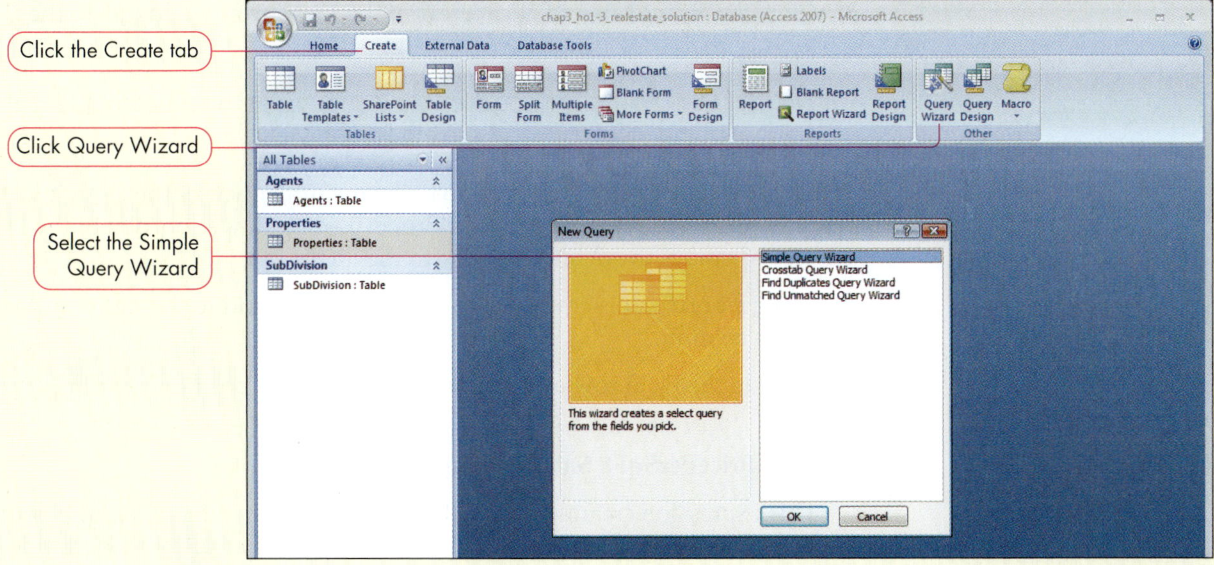

Figure 3.2 New Query Dialog Box

Step 2
Select the Fields, Save, and Open the Query

Refer to Figure 3.3 as you complete Step 2.

a. Click the **Tables/Queries drop-down arrow** and select **Table: Agents**. Double-click the **FirstName** and **LastName** fields in the **Available Fields list** to select them.

b. Click the **Tables/Queries drop-down arrow** and select **Table: Properties**. Double-click the following fields to select them: **DateListed**, **DateSold**, **ListPrice**, **SalePrice**, **SqFeet**, and **Sold**.

c. Compare your selected fields to those shown in Figure 3.3 and then click **Next**.

d. Verify that the **Detail (shows every field of every record) option** is selected in the *Would you like a detail or summary query?* screen in the Simple Query Wizard dialog box. Click **Next**.

e. Type **Your Name Sale Price per SqFt** for the query title. Click **Finish**.

The results of the query appear in the Datasheet view. Because the table fields have captions, the captions, instead of field names, appear as column headings.

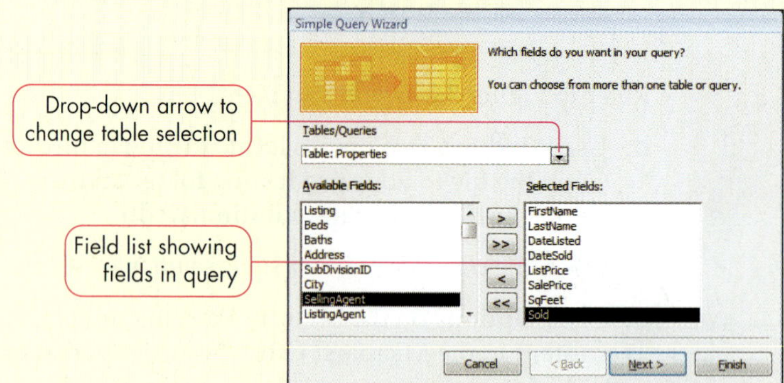

Figure 3.3 Select Fields for the Query

Step 3
Create a Calculated Field and Run the Query

Refer to Figure 3.4 as you complete Step 3.

a. Click the **Home tab** and click **View** in the View group to toggle to the Design view.

TROUBLESHOOTING: If you click View and Access does not toggle to the Design view, click the View arrow and select Design View.

This query was based on two tables, so the upper half of the Design view displays the two tables, Agents and Properties. The lower portion of the Design view displays the fields currently in the query.

b. Use the horizontal scroll bar to scroll the design grid to the right until you see a blank column.

c. Click in the Field row of the first blank column to position your insertion point there.

d. Type **PricePerSqFt: SalePrice/SqFeet** and press **Enter**.

This expression creates a new calculated field named PricePerSqFt by dividing the values in the SalePrice field by the values in the SqFeet field. In this calculated field, the operator is the division symbol (/), and the operands are the SalePrice and SqFeet fields. Look at Figure 3.4 if you need help with the syntax for the expression.

TIP Increasing Width of Columns

To increase the column width so that you can see the entire calculated field expression, double-click the vertical line in the gray area above the field names between the calculated field column and the blank column.

e. Click in the PricePerSqFt calculated field and click **Property Sheet** in the Show/Hide group on the Query Tools Design tab. Click the **Format drop-down arrow** in the Property Sheet and select **Currency**. Click in the Caption box and type **Price Per Sq Ft**. Click **Property Sheet** in the Show/Hide group to close the Property Sheet.

The Property Sheet controls how the results of the calculated field will display in Datasheet view when you run the query.

f. Click the **Design tab**, if needed, and then click **Run** in the Results group.

When you run the query, Access performs the calculations and displays the query results in Datasheet view. The calculated field values are formatted with Currency, and the column heading displays *Price Per Sq Ft* instead of the calculated field name *PricePerSqFt*.

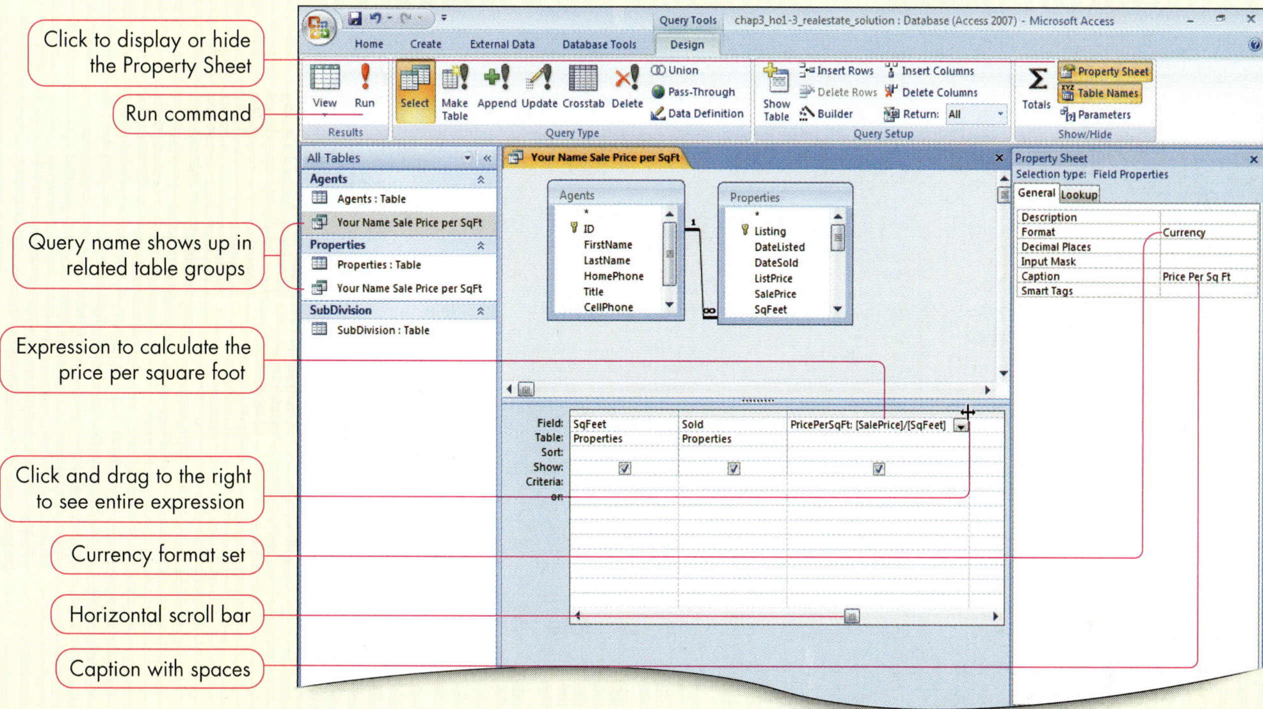

Figure 3.4 Expression Syntax and Properties for Calculated Field

Step 4
Verify the Calculated Results

Refer to Figure 3.5 as you complete Step 4.

a. Examine the results of the calculation. Ask yourself if the numbers make sense to you.

TROUBLESHOOTING: Are you having a problem? You may wish to read Step 5 now. Often a typo entered in a calculated field will result in a parameter box opening. Step 5 discusses how to recover from this error.

Look at the fourth record. The sale price is $155,000, and the number of square feet is 1,552. You can probably verify these results by dividing the values in your head. The result is about $100. The PricePerSqFt calculated field in Figure 3.5 displays $99.87.

b. Use the row selectors to select the first four records by clicking and dragging. After you select the four records, right-click them and select **Copy** from the shortcut menu.

c. Launch Excel, activate **cell A1** of a blank workbook, and paste the Access records into Excel.

The field captions appear in the first row, and the four records appear in the next four rows. The fields are located in Columns A–I. The calculated field results are pasted in Column I as values rather than as a formula.

TROUBLESHOOTING: If you see pound signs (#####) instead of numbers in an Excel column, that means the column is too narrow to display the values. Position the mouse pointer on the vertical line between the column letters, such as between D and E, and double-click the vertical line to increase the width of column D.

d. In **cell J2**, type **=F2/G2** and press **Enter**.

The formula divides the sale price by the square feet. Compare the results in the I and J columns. The numbers should be the same. If the numbers are the same, close Excel without saving the workbook and return to Access. If the values differ, look at both the Excel and Access formulae. Determine which is correct and then find and fix the error in the incorrect formula.

e. Click **Save** on the Quick Access Toolbar to save the design modifications made to the *Your Name Sale Price per SqFt* query.

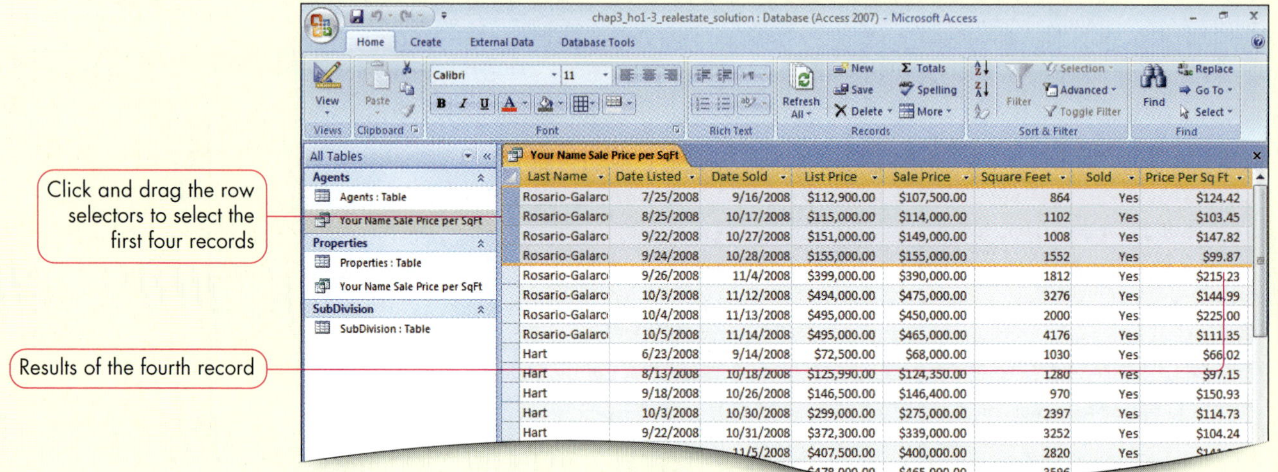

Figure 3.5 Examine Calculated Results

Step 5
Recover from a Common Error

Refer to Figure 3.6 as you complete Step 5.

a. In the *Your Name Sale Price per SqFt* query, click **View** in the Views group to switch to Design view. Scroll to the first empty column and click in the Field row to position the insertion point.

Because Access users occasionally make a typing error when creating an expression, it is useful to learn how to recover from this type of error. You will intentionally misspell a field name used in a calculation by typing the field name SalePrice as SaleSPrice and SqFeet as SqRFeet.

b. Type **WrongPricePerSqFt: SaleSPrice/SqRFeet**.

Be sure that you added the extra *S* and *R* to the field names. You are making intentional errors to learn how Access will respond.

c. Click **Run** in the Results group.

You should see the Enter Parameter Value dialog box. Examine the dialog box. What is it asking you to do? The dialog box indicates that Access could not find a value for SaleSPrice in the first record. This error occurs because the table does not contain a SaleSPrice field. Because Access is asking you to supply a value, you will type in a value.

TROUBLESHOOTING: You should carefully read the contents of a warning box or a parameter box when one appears. Access tries to tell you what is wrong. As your experience builds, the messages will become clearer to you.

d. Type **100000** in the parameter box. Before you click OK, try to anticipate what the software will do next. You intentionally misspelled *two* field names. Press **Enter** or click **OK**.

Another Enter Parameter Value dialog box displays, asking that you supply a value for SqRFeet. This error occurs because the table does not contain a SqRFeet field.

e. Type **1000** and press **Enter**.

The query has the necessary information to run and returns the results in Datasheet view.

f. Scroll right and examine the results of the calculation for WrongPricePerSqFt.

All of the records show 100. This result occurs because you entered the values 100000 and 1000, respectively, in the Enter Parameter Value dialog boxes, which used those literal values in the expression. The result of 100 appears for all records.

g. Return to Design view and correct the errors in the WrongPricePerSqFt field by changing the formula to **WrongPricePerSqFt: SalePrice/SqFeet**.

h. Click in the WrongPricePerSqFt calculated field. Click **Property Sheet** in the Show/Hide group on the Query Tools Design tab. Click the **Format drop-down arrow** in the Property Sheet and select **Currency**. Click in the Caption box and type **Wrong Price Per Sq Ft**. Click **Property Sheet** in the Show/Hide group to close the Property Sheet.

i. Run and save the query again.

The calculated values in the last two columns should be the same.

j. Close the query.

k. Click the **Office Button**, select **Manage**, and then select **Back Up Database**. Enter the file name **chap3_ho1_realestate_solution** (note *ho1* instead of *ho1-3*) and click **Save**.

You just created a backup of the database after completing the first hands-on exercise. The original database *chap3_ho1-3_realestate_solution* remains onscreen. If you ruin the original database as you complete the second hands-on exercise, you can use the backup file you just created.

l. Close the file and exit Access if you do not want to continue with the next exercise at this time.

TIP Learning Software

Following step-by-step instructions is a way to begin learning application software. If you want to become proficient in software, you must learn how to recover from errors. As you work through the rest of the Hands-On Exercises in this book, follow the instructions as presented and save your work. Then go back a few steps and make an intentional error just to see how Access responds. Read the error messages (if any) and learn from your mistakes in a safe environment.

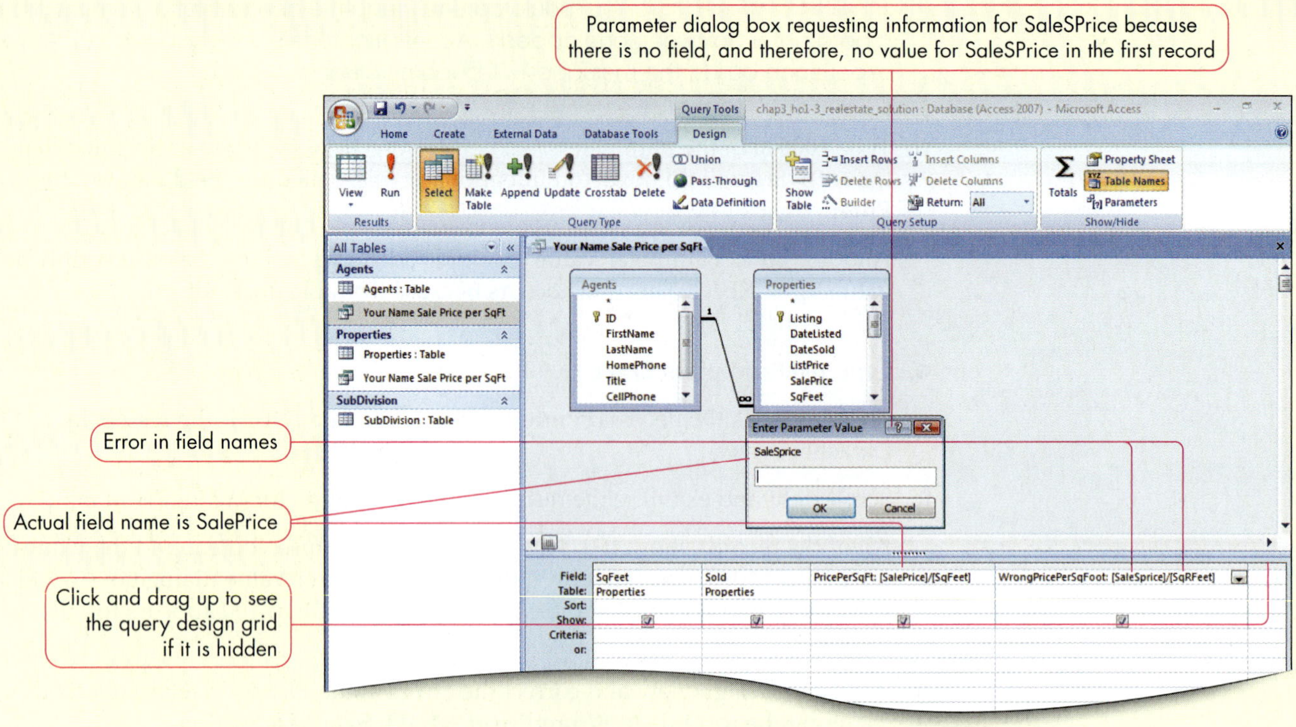

Parameter dialog box requesting information for SaleSPrice because there is no field, and therefore, no value for SaleSPrice in the first record

Error in field names

Actual field name is SalePrice

Click and drag up to see the query design grid if it is hidden

Figure 3.6 Error Recovery

TIP Displaying the Query Grid

If you open a query and do not see the query grid listing the fields and criteria, click and drag up the thick blue divider below the horizontal scroll bar. When you drag the blue divider up, the query design grid will appear. Figure 3.6 shows the blue divider.

Expression Builder

Before people used electronic database programs, decision makers were hampered because they could not find valid, timely, and accurate data on which to base decisions. In today's world data remains a problem for decision makers; however, the nature of the problem has changed. The data are current, accurate, and authentic. But because so much data are available, managers can become overwhelmed. In the last hands-on exercise, you calculated a price per square foot for real estate listings. That simple calculation can assist a decision maker to ascribe value to a property. It is a useful way to examine a complex transaction in a simplified fashion. Access enables you to calculate the value, but typing (and spelling correctly) all of those field names in the calculation is a lot of work. Fortunately, you can use the ***Expression Builder*** as an alternative, easier method to perform calculations. When you create an expression in the field text box, you must scroll to see the entire expression. The Expression Builder's size permits you to see even long, complex formulae and functions in their entirety.

The ***Expression Builder*** is a tool to help you create a formula that performs calculations easily.

In this section, you learn how to create expressions with the Expression Builder. You then learn how to create and edit functions. Finally, you perform date arithmetic.

Creating Expressions with the Expression Builder

You can use the Expression Builder in a query design grid to assist you in properly crafting the appropriate syntax. It is a blend of a calculator and a spreadsheet. You also can use the Expression Builder in other Access objects where calculations are needed. These objects include the control properties in forms and reports and table field properties. The Expression Builder requires some practice for you to learn how to use it effectively. Once you master the Expression Builder, you may use it to create a formula from scratch, or you can use it to select some pre-built expressions or functions. Additionally, the Expression Builder enables you to include useful items such as page numbers and the current date or time.

(The Expression Builder . . . is a blend of a calculator and a spreadsheet.)

Access automatically assigns placeholder names to all expressions created with the Expression Builder as Expr1, Expr2, Expr3. You need to develop the habit of running the query, verifying the calculation results and then returning to the design grid and replacing Expr1 with a descriptive field name. Good working habits will save you hours and hours when you return to your calculations in six weeks or six months.

After you save the query, the newly calculated field and descriptively named field are available to use in subsequent calculations.

Launch the Expression Builder

Open the query in Design view and display the Design tab. The Builder command is found in the Query Setup group. Figure 3.7 shows the components of the Expression Builder. The middle column contains a list of fields available in the current query. Occasionally, you may need to use a field as a calculation input that is not contained in the current query. Everything in the database is available to you through the builder. If you click the plus sign on the folder to the left of Tables or Queries in the left column, the folder will open and reveal the other tables and fields in the database. This is a wonderful feature for someone who forgot to include a needed field in a query.

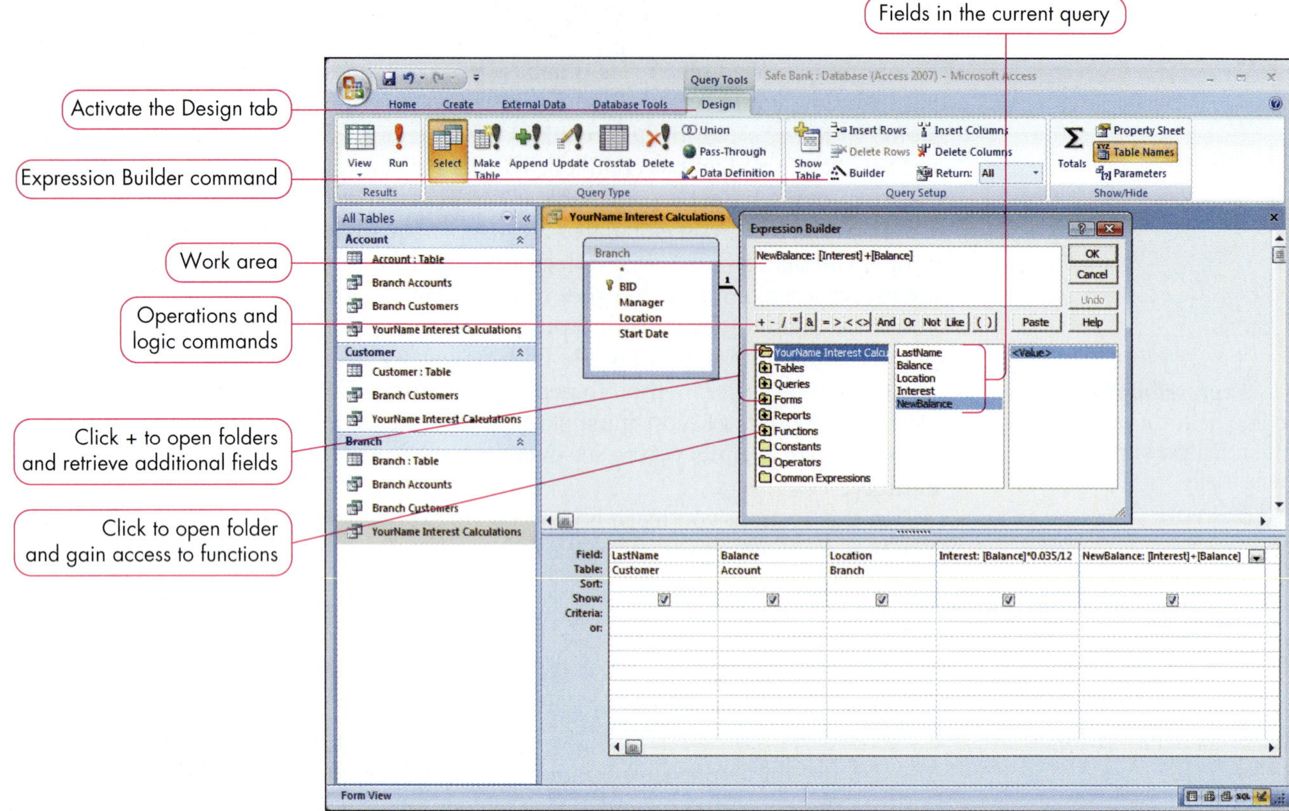

Figure 3.7 Expression Builder

The work area is the large rectangle at the top of the dialog box. Although expressions (formulas) in Excel begin with an equal sign, you do not have to start Access query expressions with an equal sign. When you need a field entered, find the field (look first in the middle column) and double-click it to add it to the expression. The field is added with the syntactically appropriate brackets inserted. Type or click operands (+, –, *, /) as needed and add additional fields to complete the expression. When you finish the expression, click OK.

Creating and Editing Access Functions

An ***Access function*** performs an operation using input supplied as arguments and returns a value.

An ***argument*** is a necessary input component required to produce the output for a function.

An *Access function* calculates commonly used expressions using predefined instructions and input values to return a calculated value. You must know the function's name and provide it arguments in order to use it. Access functions work much like Excel functions. You identify the function by its name (e.g., Avg, Sum, Pmt) and enter the required *arguments*—the input values that should be averaged, added, or calculated as a payment. They are grouped into categories of similar functions: Math, Financial, Date/Time, General, etc.

Calculate Payments with the PMT Function

The ***Pmt function*** calculates a periodic loan payment given a constant interest rate, term, and original value.

Figure 3.8 shows the *Pmt function*, which calculates a periodic loan payment given a constant interest rate, specific term of the loan, and the original value of the loan. To use this function, you need to fill in values from data stored in fields from underlying tables or supply constants in the formula.

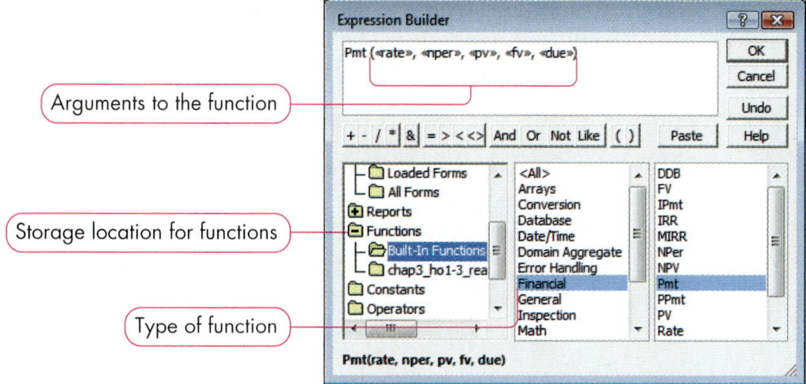

Figure 3.8 Access Function Shown in Expression Builder

The following syntax is required for the Pmt function. Table 3.2 lists and describes the arguments for the Pmt function.

Pmt(*rate*, *nper*, *pv*, *fv*, *type*)

Pmt(.065/12, 4*12, 12500,0,0)

Table 3.2

Part	Description
( )	Everything inside the parentheses is an argument to the function. The arguments are separated by commas. This function requires three arguments.
rate	Required. Expression or value specifying interest rate per period. (The period is the term of the loan payment, such as monthly or quarterly. For example, a car loan at an annual percentage rate (APR) of 6.5% with monthly payments gives the rate per period (month) of 0.065/12, or 0.005417).
nper	Required. Expression or Integer value specifying total number of payment periods in the annuity. For example, monthly payments on a four-year car loan gives a total of 4 * 12 (or 48) payment periods.
pv	Required. Expression or value specifying present value (or how much you borrow) that a series of payments to be paid in the future is worth now. For example, the loan amount is the present value to the lender of the monthly car payments.
fv	Optional. Value specifying future value or cash balance you want after you've made the final payment. For example, most loans have a future value of $0 because that's what is owed after the final payment. However, if you want to save $50,000 over 18 years for your child's education, then $50,000 is the future value.
type	Optional. Value (0 or 1) identifying when payments are due. Use 0 if payments are due at the end of the payment period (the norm), or 1 if payments are due at the beginning of the period.

Execute Actions with the IIf Function

The ***IIf function*** evaluates a condition and executes one action when the condition is true and an alternate action when the condition is false.

Another useful function is the ***IIf function***, which evaluates a condition and executes one action when the expression is true and an alternate action when the condition is false. The condition must evaluate as true or false only. For example, if balance >=10,000 or if City = "Chicago" illustrate appropriate conditions. Access evaluates the expression, determines whether it is true or false, and performs alternative actions based on the determination. For example, accounts with balances of $10,000 or more earn a 3.5% interest rate, while accounts with balances below $10,000 earn only 2.75% interest. The following syntax is required for the IIf function: IIf(expr,truepart,falsepart)

IIf(Balance >= 10000, .035, .0275)

Suppose you want to calculate the number of vacation weeks an employee is eligible to receive. The firm gives two weeks of vacation to employees with five or fewer years of employment and three weeks to employees who have worked more than five years for the firm. Your query has a field showing the number of years worked, YearsWorked. The proper syntax to calculate vacation weeks is the following:

WksVacation:IIf([YearsWorked]>5, 3,2)

This expression evaluates each record and determines if the number of years worked is more than five. When the number of years is greater than 5 (true), the expression returns the number 3 in the WksVacation field, indicating that the employee receives three weeks of vacation. If the years worked are not greater than 5 (false), the expression returns 2 in the WksVacation field, indicating that the employee receives two weeks of vacation. It is important that you write the expression so that it returns only a value of True or False for every record because Access cannot deal with ambiguities. The IIf function always evaluates both the true and false parts although the function returns only one part. When the expression, the truepart, or the falsepart references a character string (words instead of numbers), you must type the string inside of quotation marks, such as IIf([City]="Tulsa","Oklahoma","Other State").

TIP Structure IIf Logic Carefully

Even experienced Access users get surprised sometimes when using IIf functions because the false part is evaluated even when the expression is true. Occasionally this false part evaluation will result in a *divide by zero* error. You can prevent this error by rewriting the expression and reversing the operator. For example, change > to <=. You also must reverse the truepart and falsepart actions.

When you complete the expression, click OK. The Expression Builder dialog box closes, but nothing seems to happen. You have written the instruction in a form the computer understands, but you have not yet given the command to the computer to execute your instructions. The next step is to force an execution of your command by clicking Run. Your newly calculated result displays in the Datasheet view of the query. The column heading shows the default name, Expr1. Examine and verify the results of the calculation. When you are satisfied that the results are correct, return to Design view. In the design grid, double-click <Expr1> to select it, type over <Expr1> with a descriptive field name, run, and save the query.

TIP Calculated Field Availability

A calculated query field will not be available to use in subsequent calculations until after you save the query. When you need to make multiple-step calculations, you must author the steps one at a time, then run, verify, and save after each step.

Using the Expression Builder Steps | Reference

1. Open the query in Design view.
2. Position the insertion point in a blank column.
3. Click the Design tab.
4. Click Builder in the Query Setup group to launch the Expression Builder.
5. Double-click field names to add to the expression.
6. Type or click the icons for operators.
7. Double-click the Functions folder and select the type of function needed, then from the right column select the individual function.
8. Click OK to exit the Builder box.
9. Run the query.
10. Examine and verify the output.
11. Return to the Design view.
12. Highlight <Expr1> in the design grid and rename the field with a descriptive field name.
13. Run the query and save it.

Because dates are stored as sequential numbers, you can calculate an age . . . or . . . how many days past due an invoice is.

Performing Date Arithmetic

Access, like Excel, stores all dates as serial numbers. You may format the stored dates with a format that makes sense to you. In Europe, the date *November 20, 2008*, might be formatted as *20-11-2008* or *20.11.2008*. In the United States, the same date might be formatted as *11/20/2008*, and in South Asia, the date might be formatted as *20/11/2008*. ***Date formatting*** affects the date's display without changing the serial value. All dates and times in Access are stored as the number of days that have elapsed since December 31, 1899. For example, January 1, 1900, is stored as 1, indicating one day after December 31, 1899. If the time were 9:00 PM on November 20, 2008, no matter how the date or time is formatted, Access stores it as 39772.857. The 39772 represents the number of days elapsed since December 31, 1899, and the .857 reflects the fraction of the 24-hour day that has passed at 9:00 PM. This storage method may seem complicated, but it affords an Access user power and flexibility when working with date values. For example, because dates are stored as sequential numbers, you can calculate the total numbers of hours worked in a week if you record the starting and ending times for each day. Using ***date arithmetic*** you can create expressions to calculate an age in years from a birth date, or tell a business owner how many days past due an invoice is.

Date formatting affects the date's display without changing the serial value.

Using ***date arithmetic*** you can create expressions to calculate lapsed time.

Identify Partial Dates with the DatePart Function

You can look at entire dates or simply a portion of the date that is of interest. If your company increases the number of weeks of annual vacation from two weeks to three weeks after an employee has worked for five or more years, then the only part of the date of interest is the time lapsed in years. Access has a function, the ***DatePart function***, to facilitate this. Table 3.3 shows the DatePart function parameters.

The ***DatePart function*** enables users to identify a specific part of a date, such as only the year.

DatePart("yyyy",[Employees]![HireDate])

Don't let the syntax intimidate you. After you practice using the DatePart function, the syntax will get much easier to understand.

Useful date functions are:

- **Date**—Inserts the current date into an expression.
- **DatePart**—Examines a date and returns only the portion of interest.
- **DateDiff**—Measures the amount of time elapsed between two dates. This is most often today's date as determined by the date function and a date stored in a field. For example, you might calculate the number of days a payment is past due by comparing today's date with the payment DueDate.

Table 3.3 Using the DatePart Function

Function Portion	Explanation
DatePart	An Access function that examines a date and focuses on a portion of interest.
"yyyy"	The first argument, the interval, describes the portion of the date of interest. We specified the years. It could also be "dd" or "mmm".
(Employees)!(HireDate)	The second argument, the date, tells Access where to find the information. In this case, it is stored in the Employee Table in a field named HireDate.

Hands-On Exercises

2 | Expression Builder, Functions, and Date Arithmetic

Skills covered: 1. Create a Select Query **2.** Use the Expression Builder **3.** Create Calculations Using Input Stored in a Different Query or Table **4.** Edit Expressions Using the Expression Builder **5.** Use Functions **6.** Work with Date Arithmetic

Step 1 Create a Select Query

Refer to Figure 3.9 as you complete Step 1.

a. Open the *chap3_ho1-3_realestate_solution* file if necessary, click **Options** on the Security Warning toolbar and click the **Enable this content option** in the Microsoft Office Security Options dialog box, and click **OK**.

   TROUBLESHOOTING: If you create unrecoverable errors while completing this hands-on exercise, you can delete the *chap3_ho1-3_realestate_solution* file, copy the *chap3_ho1_realestate_solution* backup database you created at the end of the first hands-on exercise, and open the copy of the backup database to start the second hands-on exercise again.

b. Open the **Agents table** and replace **Angela Scott's** name with your name. Close the Agents table.

c. Click the **Create tab** and click **Query Wizard** in the Other group. Select **Simple Query Wizard** and click **OK**.

d. Select the fields (in this order) from the Agents table: **LastName** and **FirstName**. From the Properties table select **DateListed**, **DateSold**, **ListPrice**, **SalePrice**, and **SqFeet**. From the SubDivision table select the **Subdivision** field. Click **Next**.

   You have selected fields from three related tables. Because relationships exist among the tables, you can trust that the agent's name that returns when the query runs will be the agent associated with the property.

e. Check to make sure that the option **Detail** query is selected and click **Next**.

f. Name this query **Your Name Commissions** and click **Finish**.

   The query should run and open in Datasheet view. An experienced Access user always checks the number of records when a query finishes running and opens. This query should have 54 records. See Figure 3.9.

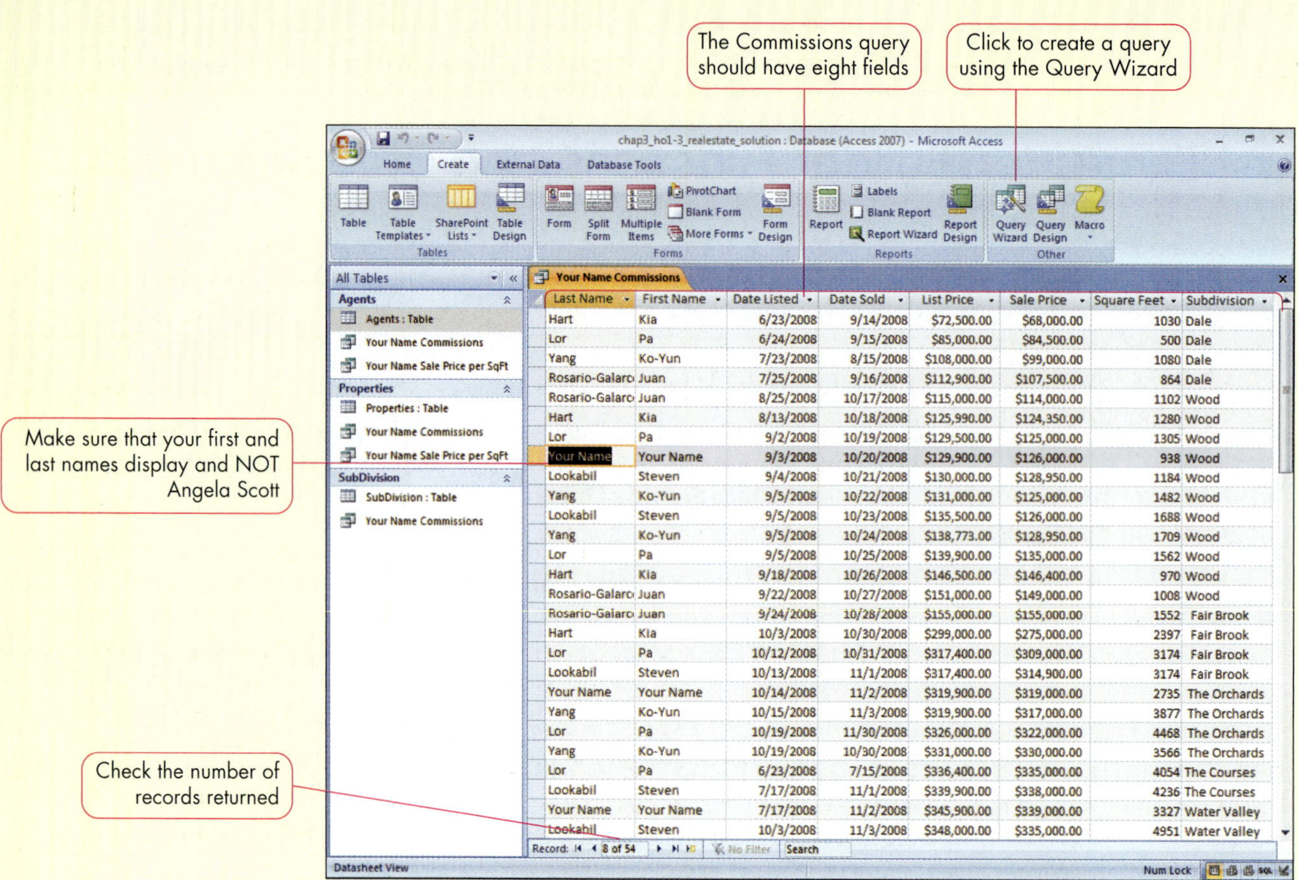
The Commissions query should have eight fields
Click to create a query using the Query Wizard
Make sure that your first and last names display and NOT Angela Scott
Check the number of records returned
Your Name Commissions

Figure 3.9 Datasheet View of the Your Name Commissions Query

Step 2
Use the Expression Builder

Refer to Figure 3.10 as you complete Step 2.

a. Click the **Home tab** and click **View** in the Views group to switch to Design view. Scroll to the right to locate the first empty column in the design grid and position your insertion point in the Field row.

b. Verify that the Design tab is selected and click **Builder** in the Query Setup group.

   The Expression Builder dialog box opens. You may click the title bar and reposition it to a more convenient location if necessary.

c. Repeat the PricePerSqFt calculation from Hands-On Exercise 1 by using the Expression Builder.

d. Locate the list of fields in the Commissions query in the middle column and double-click the **SalePrice** field.

   The work area of the Expression Builder dialog box should now display [SalePrice]. The Expression Builder adds the brackets and always spells the field names correctly.

e. Click or type the divide operator (the forward slash, /), and then double-click the **SqFeet** field name in the middle column.

   Now the work area of the expression builder will display [SalePrice] / [SqFeet].

f. Click **OK**. Run the query. Scroll right in the Datasheet view to find the newly calculated field, which is named *Expr1*.

g. Verify the results of the calculation adjusting column width if necessary.

The fifth record has values that can be rounded more easily in your head—$114,000 and 1102 Sq. Ft. That should return a result slightly higher than $100. The actual result is 103.448275862069. Once you are satisfied with the accuracy of the calculation, continue with the next step.

h. Click the **Home tab** (if necessary) and change the view to Design view by clicking **View**.

TIP Switching Between Design and Datasheet Views

An easy way to alternate views for an Access object is to right-click the object window's title bar and select the appropriate view from the shortcut menu. You can also click the views buttons in the bottom-right corner of the Access window. In this case, the object title bar says Your Name Commissions. See Figure 3.10 for instructions on where to right-click.

i. Double-click **Expr1** in the Field row of the right column. Type **PricePerSqFt**.

j. Make sure the insertion point is in the PricePerSqFt calculated field and click **Property Sheet** in the Show/Hide group on the Query Tools Design tab. Click the **Format drop-down arrow** in the Property Sheet and select **Currency**. Type **Price Per Sq Ft** in the Caption box. Click **Property Sheet** in the Show/Hide group to close the Property Sheet.

k. Run the query. Click **Save** (or press **Ctrl + S**) and return to Design view.

l. Click the insertion point in the Field row of the first empty column and activate the Expression Builder. Look in the middle column that shows the list of available fields in this query. The last listed field should be the newly saved PricePerSqFt.

TROUBLESHOOTING: Sometimes you need to edit an expression created using the Expression Builder. When you open the Expression Builder to make the edits, you will find that Access adds <Expr1> to any unsaved expressions. Locate and double-click the <Expr1> to select it and delete it prior to making the necessary edits to the expression.

TIP Expression Builder and Property Sheet

You can launch the Expression Builder by either clicking Build in the Query Setup group on the Design tab or by right-clicking in the Field row and selecting Build. Similarly, you can display the Property Sheet by clicking Property Sheet in the Show/Hide group on the Design tab or by right-clicking the Field row and selecting Properties. The exercise steps get you familiar with using the commands on the Ribbon and the shortcut menu.

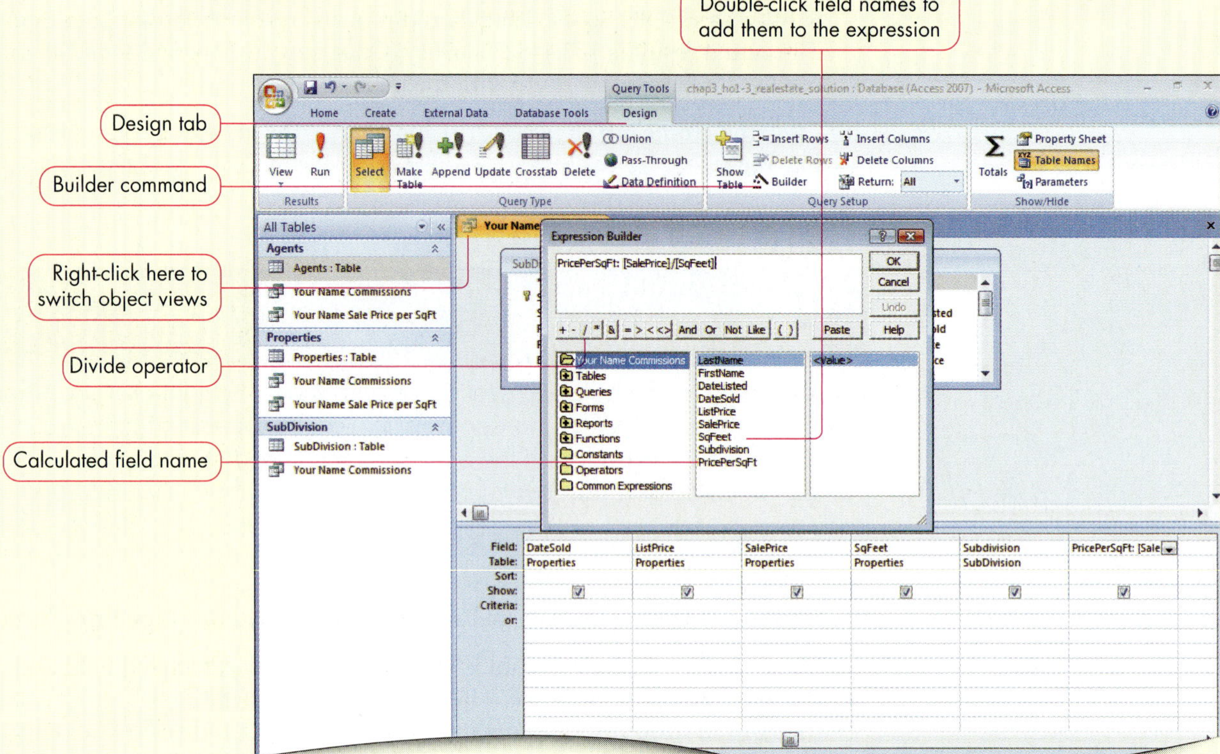

Figure 3.10 Working with the Expression Builder

Step 3
Create Calculations Using Input Stored in a Different Query or Table

Refer to Figure 3.11 as you complete Step 3.

a. With the Expression Builder dialog box open, double-click **SalePrice** in the middle column to add it to the expression. Type or click **/** (divide symbol). Your formula in the work area should be [SalePrice]/.

   In addition to calculating the price per square foot, you decide that it would be helpful if you knew the price of the sold properties per bedroom, but you did not include a field for the number of bedrooms in the query. You have two options. One, you can cancel the expression, add the missing field to the query, and then restart the expression. Two, you also can use a field in a calculation that is not resident in the query. You only need to tell Access where the field is stored.

b. Double-click the **Tables folder** in the left column of the Expression Builder.

   The Tables folder expands to reveal the table objects in the database. Because you have not yet selected a table, the middle and right columns of the Expression Builder dialog box are empty.

c. Click the **Properties table**.

   The middle column is populated with the names of the fields available from the Properties table. You will use this data to calculate the per bedroom sale price of the homes in the database.

d. Double-click the **Beds field**. Your expression will look like this:

   [SalePrice] / [Properties]![Beds].

   This expression gives Access the instruction to go to the Properties table, locate the values of the number of bedrooms for each of the records in the Commissions query, and use that value to calculate a price per bedroom value. The appropriate number of bedrooms will be returned in each calculation because relationships exist between the tables. The query will inherit the referential integrity of the source tables.

e. Click **OK**. Click **Run** in the Results group on the Design tab. Verify the calculated results.

f. Return to Design view. Double-click **Expr1** in the design grid to select it and type **PricePerBR**.

   You have renamed Expr1, but the name change does not become permanent until you save the query design.

g. Right-click the **PricePerBR** calculated field. Select **Properties** from the shortcut menu. Click the **Format drop-down arrow** in the Property Sheet and select **Currency**. Type **Price Per Bedroom** in the Caption box. Click the **X** to close the Property Sheet.

h. Save the query.

i. Position the insertion point anywhere in the Field row in the PricePerBR column.

j. Click **Builder** in the Query Setup group on the Design tab.

   The Expression Builder dialog box displays the renamed calculated field, PricePerBR, and a colon at the beginning of the expression (see Figure 3.11).

k. Click **OK** to close the Expression Builder dialog box.

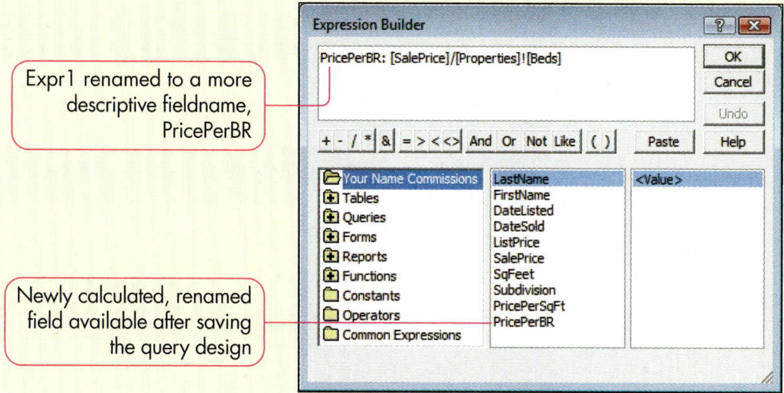

Figure 3.11 A Completed Expression

Step 4
Edit Expressions Using the Expression Builder

Refer to Figure 3.12 as you complete Step 4.

a. Click and drag to select the entire **PricePerBR** expression in the design grid. Right-click the selected expression and select **Copy**.

   Be careful that you select and copy the entire expression. You need the new field name, all of the input fields, and the operands.

   TROUBLESHOOTING: You cannot click into the next field in the design grid while the Expression Builder dialog box is open. Generally, any open dialog box in a Microsoft product is assigned top priority, and you must first deal with the dialog box before you can do anything anywhere else in the file. Close the Expression Builder dialog box if it is open.

b. Right-click in the field box of the first blank column and select **Paste**.

   Your next task is to edit the copied formula so that it reflects the price per bathroom.

c. Position the insertion point anywhere in the copied formula and click **Builder**.

d. Move the I-beam pointer over any portion of the word *Beds* in the formula. Double-click.

The entire portion of the formula, [Properties]![Beds], is highlighted.

e. Double-click the **Tables folder** in the left column, and then click the **Properties table** to open the folder and table, respectively.

Make sure that the middle column displays the field names of the available fields in the Properties table.

f. Double-click the **Baths field**.

The edited expression now displays PricePerBR: [SalePrice] / [Properties]! [Baths].

g. Drag to select the text **BR** in the *PricePerBR*. Replace BR with **Bath**.

The edited expression is PricePerBath: [SalePrice] / [Properties]! [Baths].

h. Click **OK**. Click **Run**. Click **Save**, and then return to Design view.

i. Right-click the PricePerBath calculated field. Select **Properties** from the shortcut menu. Click the **Format drop-down arrow** in the Property Sheet and select **Currency**. Type **Price Per Bathroom** in the Caption box. Click the X to close the Property Sheet.

j. Run the query. Examine the calculated results in the Datasheet view.

Do your results make sense? Which field has larger numbers in it, the price per bedroom or the price per bathroom? Do most houses have more bedrooms or bathrooms? Which number would you expect to be larger? Remember, you are dividing in these calculations. As the number on the bottom of a fraction gets larger, does the answer get larger or smaller? You do not need to write the answers to these questions on paper. You do need to develop a critical eye and force yourself to ask questions like these every time you calculate a value.

k. Click **Save**.

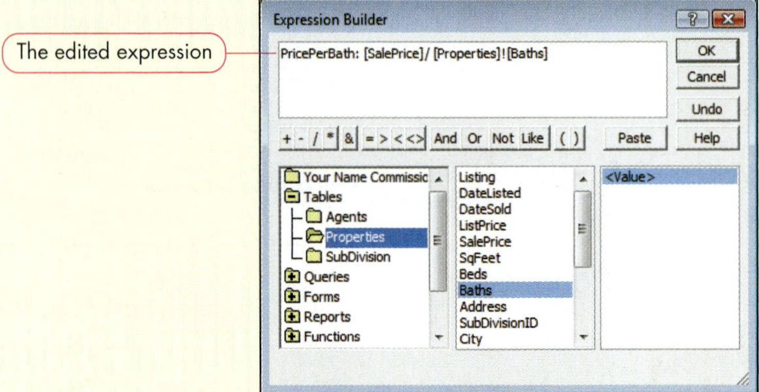

Figure 3.12 The Correctly Edited Formula

Step 5
Use Functions

Refer to Figures 3.13 and 3.14 as you complete Step 5.

a. Position the insertion point in the Field row of the first blank column of the query in Design view.

You are going to use a financial function to calculate an estimated house payment for each of the sold properties. You make the following assumptions: 90% of the sale price financed, a 30-year period, monthly payments, and a fixed 6.5% annual interest rate. The first task is to calculate the amount financed. Assume a 10% down payment means that there will be 90% of the purchase price remaining to finance.

b. Right-click in the Field box of the first blank column and select **Build** from the shortcut menu to display the Expression Builder dialog box. Type the formula **[SalePrice] * .9** and click **OK**.

You will need to use this calculated value in subsequent calculations.

c. Run and save the query, return to Design view, double-click **Expr1,** and type **AmountFinanced**.

d. Right-click the AmountFinanced calculated field and select **Properties** from the shortcut menu. Click the **Format drop-down arrow** in the Property Sheet and select **Currency**. Type **Amount Financed** in the Caption box. Click the **X** to close the Property Sheet. Save the query.

e. Position the insertion point in the field row of the next available column. Launch the Expression Builder.

f. Double-click the **Functions folder** in the left column. Click **Built-In Functions folder**.

g. Look in the middle column. Click the **Financial** function category.

h. Look in the right column. Double-click the **Pmt function**.

The Expression Builder work area displays
Pmt(<<rate>>,<<nper>>,<<pv>>,<<fv>>,<<due>>).

We are assuming monthly payments at a 6½% interest rate over 30 years with no balloon payment at the end of the 30-year period and that the finance charges are calculated at the end of each period.

i. Double-click each formula argument to select it. Substitute the appropriate information:

Argument	Replacement Value
<<rate>>	0.065/12
<<nper>>	30*12
<<pv>>	(AmountFinanced)—Click the Your Name Commissions folder to display a list of field names available to use in the query.
<<fv>>	0
<<due>>	0

TROUBLESHOOTING: If you do not see the AmountFinanced field in the list of available field names, you probably forgot to save the query after running it. Press Esc to close the Expression Builder dialog box. Click Save or press Ctrl+S to save the query design changes and re-work steps d through h.

j. Examine Figure 3.13 to make sure that you have entered the correct arguments. Click **OK**. Run the query.

The payments are all negative numbers. That is normal. You will edit the formula to return positive values.

k. Return to Design view. Click in the calculated field you just created and open the Expression Builder. Position the insertion point to the left of the left bracket, [, and type a hyphen, –. Double-click **Expr1** and type **Payment**. The expression is now:

Payment: Pmt(0.065/12, 30*12, –[AmountFinanced], 0,0). Click **OK**.

l. Right-click the **Payment** calculated field. Select **Properties** from the shortcut menu. Click the **Format drop-down arrow** in the Property Sheet and select **Currency**. Type **Payment** in the Caption box. Click the **X** to close the Property Sheet.

m. Run and save the query.

The calculated field values now appear as positive, rather than negative, values.

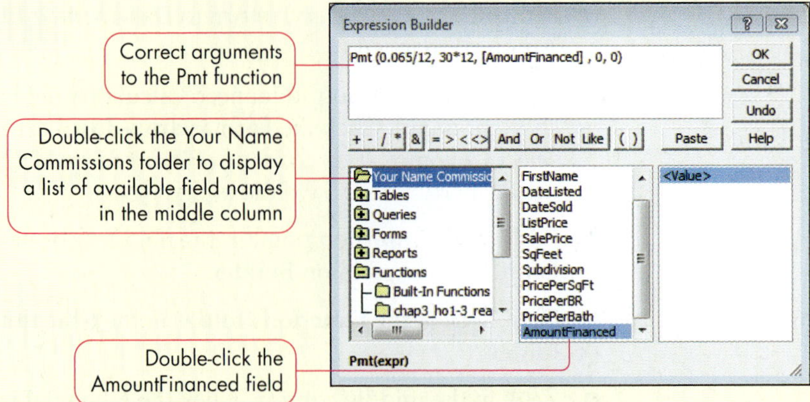

Figure 3.13 The Payment Function Arguments

Step 6 Work with Date Arithmetic

Refer to Figure 3.14 as you complete Step 6.

a. Position the insertion point in the Field row of the first blank column of the query in Design view. Launch the Expression Builder.

   You are going to calculate the number of days that each property was on the market prior to its sale.

b. Enter the formula **[DateSold] – [DateListed]** and click **OK**. Run the query. Return to Design view and replace Expr1 with **MarketDays**. Save the query. Open the Property Sheet, click the **Format drop-down arrow** and select **Fixed**, click the **Decimal Places drop-down arrow** and select **0**, and type **Days on Market** in the Caption box. Close the Property Sheet. Run the query.

   Because Access stores all dates as serial numbers, the query returns the number of days on the market. The first property was placed on the market on June 23, and it sold on September 14. Look at your query result. This property was for sale all of July, all of August, and for parts of June and September. This is about three months. Does the query result reflect about three months?

c. Create a new field in Design view. Use the Expression Builder to multiply the SalePrice field by the commission rate of 7%. The formula in the Expression Builder is **[SalePrice] * .07.** Run the query, return to Design view, and replace Expr1 with **Commission**. Save the query.

   The Commission calculated field calculates the total commission. The agent earns 7% of the sale price. The first agent's commission is $4,760.00.

d. Right-click the **Commission** calculated field. Select **Properties** from the shortcut menu. Click the **Format drop-down arrow** in the Property Sheet and select **Currency**. Type **Commission** in the Caption box. Click the **X** to close the Property Sheet.

   The values in the Commission calculated field now appear in Currency format. The first agent's commission displays as $4,760.00.

e. Click the **Office Button**, select **Manage**, and then select **Back Up Database**. Enter the file name **chap3_ho2_realestate_solution** (note *ho2* instead of *ho1-3*) and click the **Save button** in the dialog box.

   You just created a backup of the database after completing the second hands-on exercise. The original database *chap3_ho1-3_realestate_solution* remains onscreen. If you ruin the original database as you complete the third hands-on exercise, you can use the backup file you just created.

f. Close the file and exit Access if you do not want to continue with the next exercise at this time.

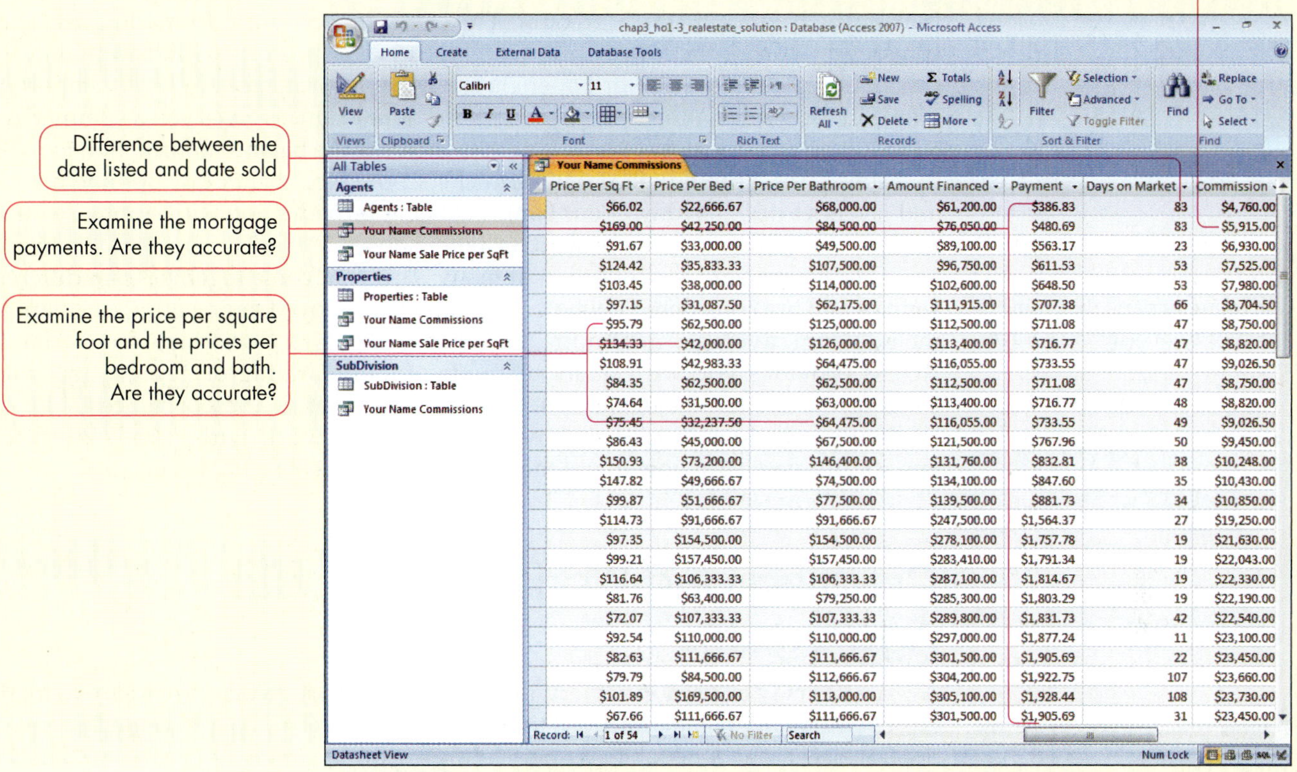
This property sold for $84,500. The commission rate is 7%. Does $5,915 reflect 7% of the sale price? Did you use a calculator or Excel to verify your calculation?
Difference between the date listed and date sold
Examine the mortgage payments. Are they accurate?
Examine the price per square foot and the prices per bedroom and bath. Are they accurate?
chap3_hol-3_realestate_solution : Database (Access 2007) - Microsoft Access
Your Name Commissions

Figure 3.14 Verify, Verify, Verify!

Data Aggregates

Assume that you have an old-fashioned bank that still sends paper statements at the end of the month through the mail. Your statement arrives at your mailbox, and you open it. What is the first thing that you examine? If you are like most people, you first look at the balance for each account. The checking account information lists each transaction during the last month, whether it is a deposit or withdrawal, and the transaction method—ATM or paper check. These records provide vitally important data. But, the information contained in the account balances gives you a summarized snapshot of your financial health. You may then use the balance information to make decisions. "Yes, I can buy those concert tickets!" or "No, I better buy nothing but gas and groceries until payday." Your bank statement provides you with summary information. Your account balances are data aggregates.

A ***data aggregate*** is a collection of many parts that come together from different sources and are considered a whole.

A ***data aggregate*** is a collection of many parts that come together from different sources and are considered a whole. Commonly employed aggregating calculations include sum, average, minimum, maximum, standard deviation, and variance. Access provides you with many methods of summarizing or aggregating data. Decision makers use the methods to help make sense of an array of choices.

In this section, you learn how to create and work with data aggregates. Specifically, you learn how to use the totals row and create a totals query.

Creating and Working with Data Aggregates

A ***total row*** displays as the last row in the Datasheet view of a table or query and provides a variety of summary statistics.

Aggregates may be used in a query, table, form, or report. Access provides two methods of adding aggregate functions to a query. A ***total row*** displays as the last row in the Datasheet view of a table or query and provides a variety of summary statistics. The first method enables you to add a total row from the Datasheet view. This method is quick and easy, works in the Datasheet view of a table or query, and has the additional advantage that it provides the total information without altering the object design. You will recall that some databases are split into front and back end portions. Different users have different levels of privileges when interacting with the database. Adding a total row to a query or table can be accomplished by the lowest-privilege-level employee because it does not alter the structure of the object. The second method enables you to alter the query design and create a totals query. This method has the advantage of permitting you to group your data into relevant subcategories. For example, you can subtotal all houses sold in a specific subdivision or by each salesperson. After the summary statistics are assembled, you can employ them to make decisions. Who is the leading salesperson? In which neighborhood do houses sell most often or least often? This method requires that the user have rights to alter the design of a query. In a large, split database, a front-end user may not be afforded the rights to create or alter a query design. The query design is generally restricted to back-end users—the IT professionals only.

Data aggregation gives the decision maker a powerful and important tool. The ability to summarize and consolidate mountains of data into a distilled and digestible format makes the Access software a popular choice for managerial users. You already have learned that data aggregates may be created in queries. Access also permits aggregation in reports. In the first section you learned that some users calculate all of their expressions in queries, whereas others perform needed calculations in forms and reports. The positioning of data aggregates also may be accomplished in a variety of ways. Some users aggregate and calculate summary statistics in queries, others in reports. You will need to learn both methods of aggregation because the practices and procedures governing database use differ among firms. Some firms allow users relatively free access to both the front and rear ends of the database; other firms grant extremely limited front-end rights only.

Create a Total Row in a Query or Table

Figure 3.15 illustrates adding the Total row to the Datasheet view. Access can total or average numeric fields only. Begin by positioning your insertion point in a numeric or currency field of any record. Then click Totals in the Records group on the Home tab. The word Total is added below the new record row of the query. The highlighted numeric field shows a box with an arrow in the Total row. You may choose from several different aggregate functions by clicking the arrow. This method works in the same way if you want to add a Total row to a numeric field in a table.

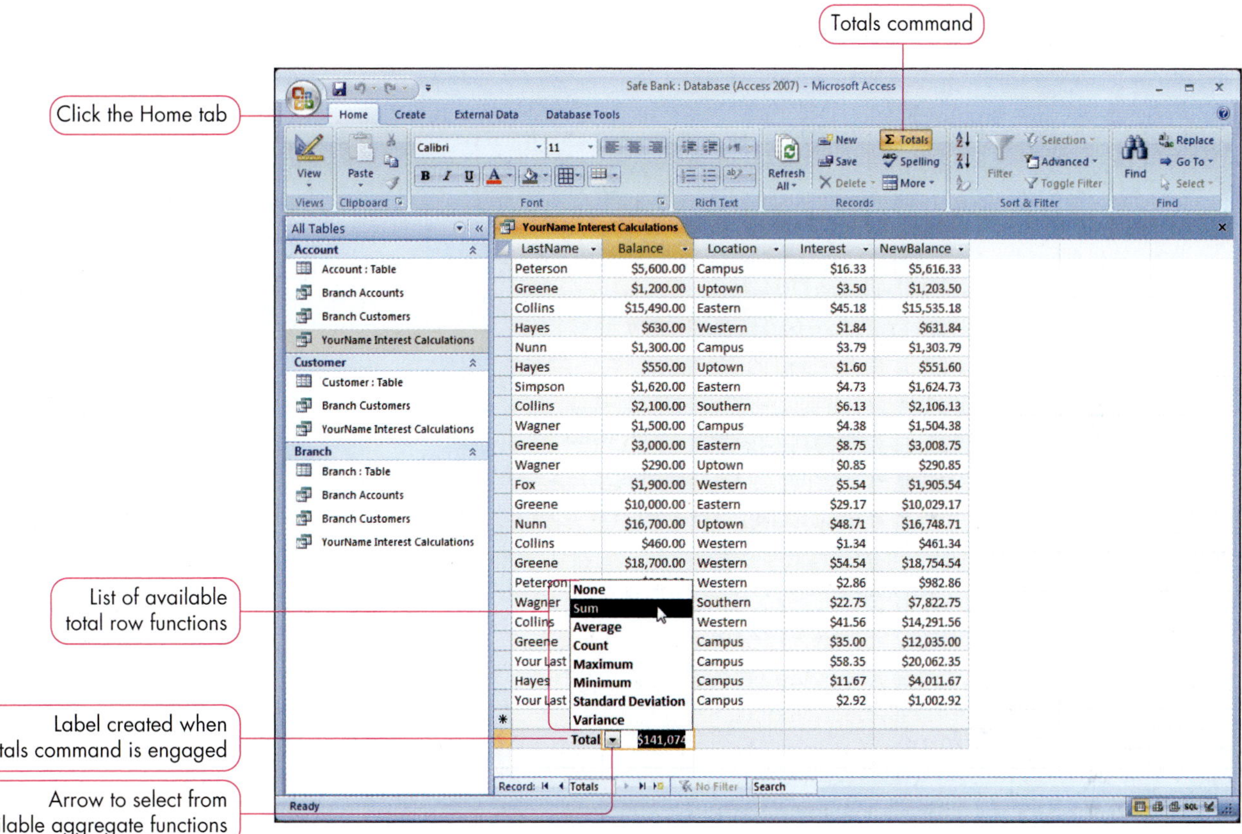

Figure 3.15 Adding a Total Row to a Query in Datasheet View

Group Totals in a Totals Query

A ***totals query*** organizes query results into groups by including a grouping field and a numeric field for aggregate calculations.

The Total row, when added to a query, provides the decision maker with useful information. However, it does not provide any method of subtotaling the data. The Total row is useful when a decision maker needs to know the totals or averages of all the data in a query or table. Sometimes knowing only the total is insufficient. The decision maker needs to know more detail. For example, knowing the total sales of houses during a period is good information. Knowing subtotals by salespeople would be more useful. Knowing subtotals by subdivision also would be useful information. Instead of using the Total row, you can create a ***totals query*** to organize the results of a query into groups to perform aggregate calculations. It contains a minimum of two fields. The first field is the grouping field, such as the salesperson's last name. The second field is the numeric field that the decision maker wishes to summarize, such as the sale price of the homes. You may add other numeric fields to a totals query to provide additional information. The totals query in Access helps you provide a more detailed snapshot of the data.

The SafeBank database that you created in Chapter 2 has five branch locations. If you need to know the total deposits by location, you would create a totals query. The two fields necessary would be the Location field in the Branch table and the Account

A totals query can only include the field or fields that you want to total and the grouping field.

Balance field in the Accounts table. After you create and run the query, you may add parameters to limit the totals query to a specific data subset. The process of adding criteria in a totals query is identical to any other query. Remember that a totals query can include only the field or fields that you want to total and one or more grouping fields. No additional descriptive fields are allowed in the totals query. If you need to see the salesperson's last name, the sale price of the house, *and* the salesperson's first name, you would need to create two queries. The first query would be the totals query summarizing the sales data by last name. Then you would need to create a second query based on the totals query and add the additional descriptive field (the first name) to the new query. Figure 3.16 shows the setup for a totals query.

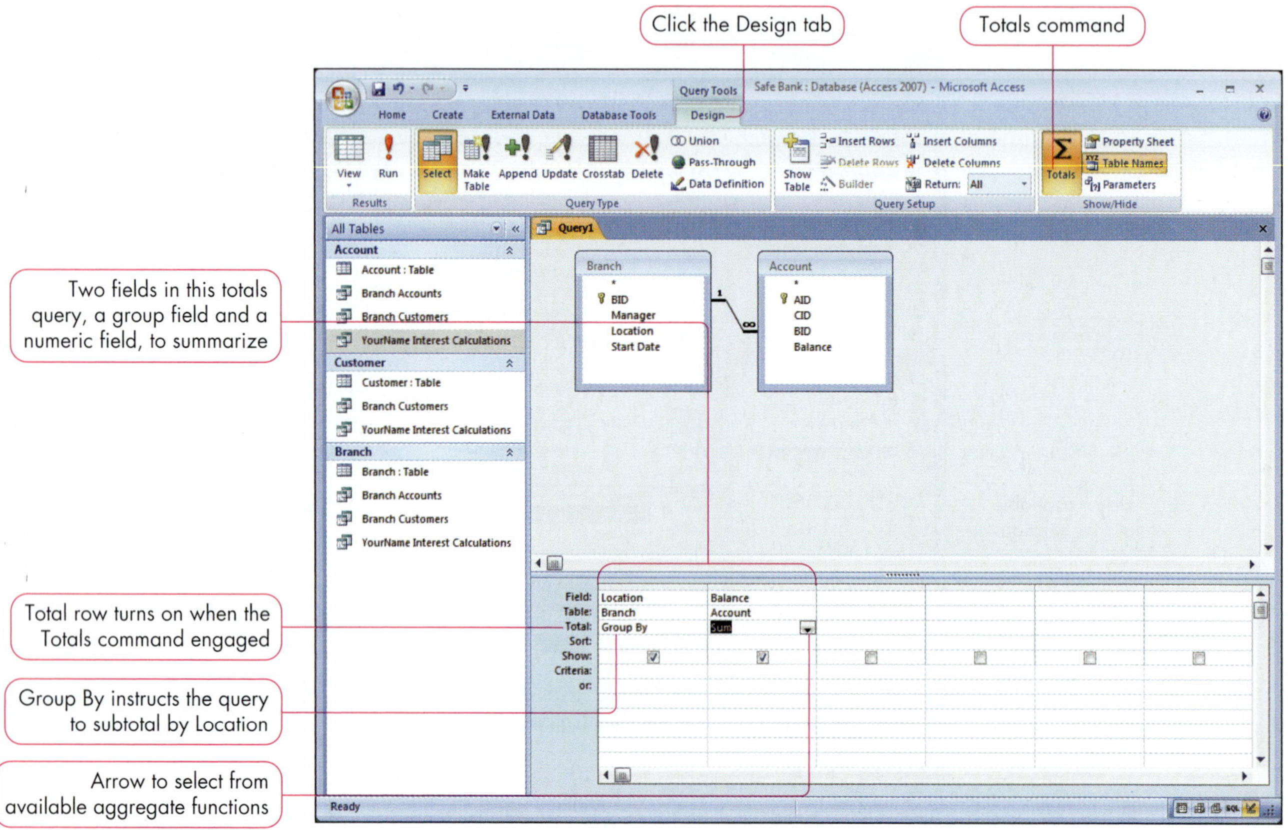

Figure 3.16 Constructing a Totals Query

Hands-On Exercises

3 | Data Aggregates

Skills covered: 1. Add a Total Row **2.** Create a Totals Query Based on a Select Query **3.** Add Fields to the Design Grid **4.** Add Grouping Options and Specify Summary Statistics

Step 1
Add a Total Row

Refer to Figure 3.17 as you complete Step 1.

a. Open the *chap3_ho1-3_realestate_solution* file if necessary, click **Options** on the Security Warning toolbar and click the **Enable this content option** in the Microsoft Office Security Options dialog box, and click **OK**.

   TROUBLESHOOTING: If you create unrecoverable errors while completing this hands-on exercise, you can delete the *chap3_ho1-3_realestate_solution* file, copy the *chap3_ho2_realestate_solution* backup database you created at the end of the second hands-on exercise, and open the copy of the backup database to start the third hands-on exercise again.

b. Open the **Your Name Commissions** query in the Datasheet view.

c. Click the **Home tab** and click **Totals** in the Records group.

   Look at the last row of the query. The Totals command is a toggle: Click it once to display the Total row. Click it again to hide the Total row. You need the Total row turned on to work the next steps.

d. Click in the cell that intersects the **Total row** and the **Sale Price** column.

   This is another place in Access that when selected, a drop-down list becomes available. Nothing indicates that the drop-down menu exists until the cell or control is active. You need to remember that this is one of those places in order to aggregate the data.

e. Click the **drop-down arrow** and select **Sum** to calculate the total of all the properties sold. Widen the Sale Price column if you can't see the entire total value.

   The total value of the properties sold is $19,936,549.00.

f. Scroll right, locate the **Subdivision field,** and click in the Total row to activate the drop-down list.

   The choices from the total list are different. You may have the summary statistics set to None or Count. Subdivision is a character field. Access recognizes that it cannot add or average words and automatically limits your options to only tasks that Access is able to do with words.

g. Select **Count** from the drop-down list in the Total row for the Subdivision field.

h. Click in the **Total row** in the **Price Per Sq Ft** column. Click the **drop-down arrow** and select **Average**.

i. Click in any record of any field. Close the query.

   A dialog box opens that asks if you wish to save the changes to the ***layout*** of the Your Name Commissions query. It does NOT ask if you wish to save the changes made to the design. Toggling a Total row on and off is a layout (cosmetic) change only and does not affect the architectural structure of the query or table design.

j. Click **Yes**. The query saves the layout changes and closes.

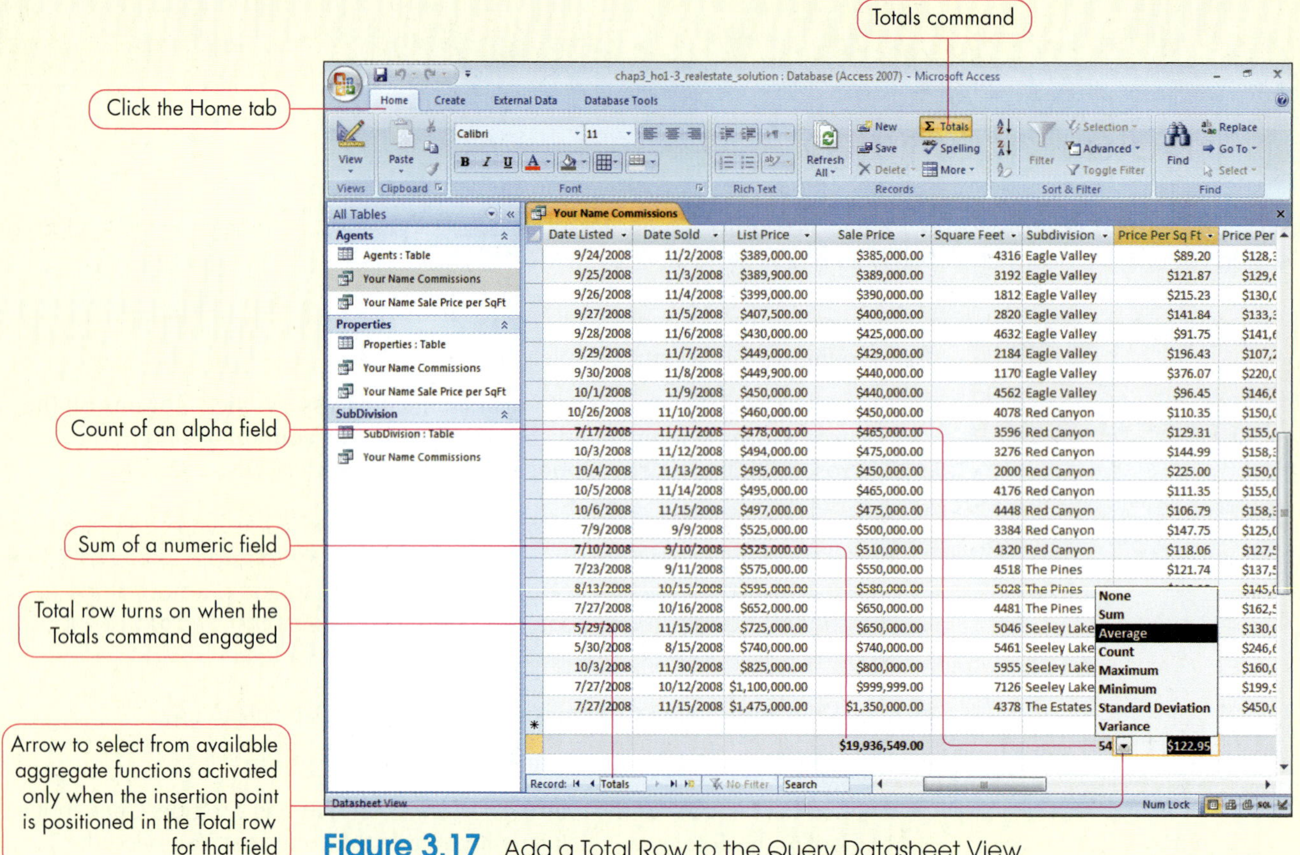

Figure 3.17 Add a Total Row to the Query Datasheet View

Step 2
Create a Totals Query Based on a Select Query

Refer to Figure 3.18 as you complete Step 2.

a. Click the **Create tab** and click **Query Design** in the Other group.

   The Show Table dialog box opens. You could source this query on the tables. However, because you already have made many useful calculations in the Commissions query, it will save you time to source the Totals query on the Commissions query.

b. Click the **Queries tab** in the Show Table dialog box.

c. Select the **Your Name Commissions** query and click **Add**.

d. Click **Close**.

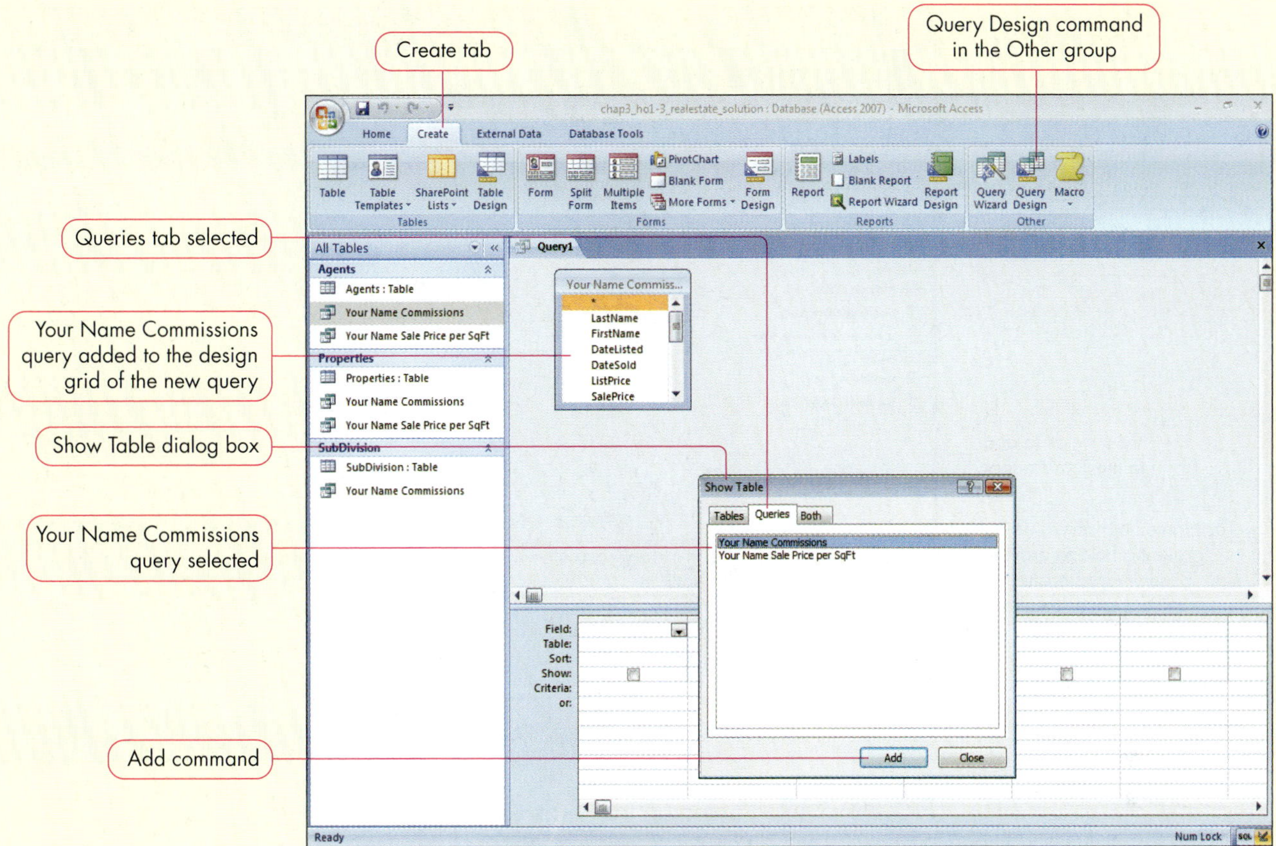

Figure 3.18 Create a Totals Query

Step 3
Add Fields to the Design Grid

Refer to Figure 3.19 as you complete Step 3.

a. Locate the **LastName** field in the Your Name Commissions field list box.

   You may add fields from the Your Name Commissions query to the new query by clicking and dragging them to the design grid or by double-clicking.

b. Double-click the **LastName** field to add it to the grid.

   You will create summary statistics based on each salesperson's activities. The LastName field is the grouping field in this totals query.

   TROUBLESHOOTING: If you attempt to double-click a field name and the computer "beeps" at you, you probably forgot to close the Show Table dialog box.

c. Double-click the **SalePrice** field to add it to the grid.

d. Scroll down in the list of available fields box and double-click **MarketDays** to add it to the new query.

e. Add the **Commission** field to the new query.

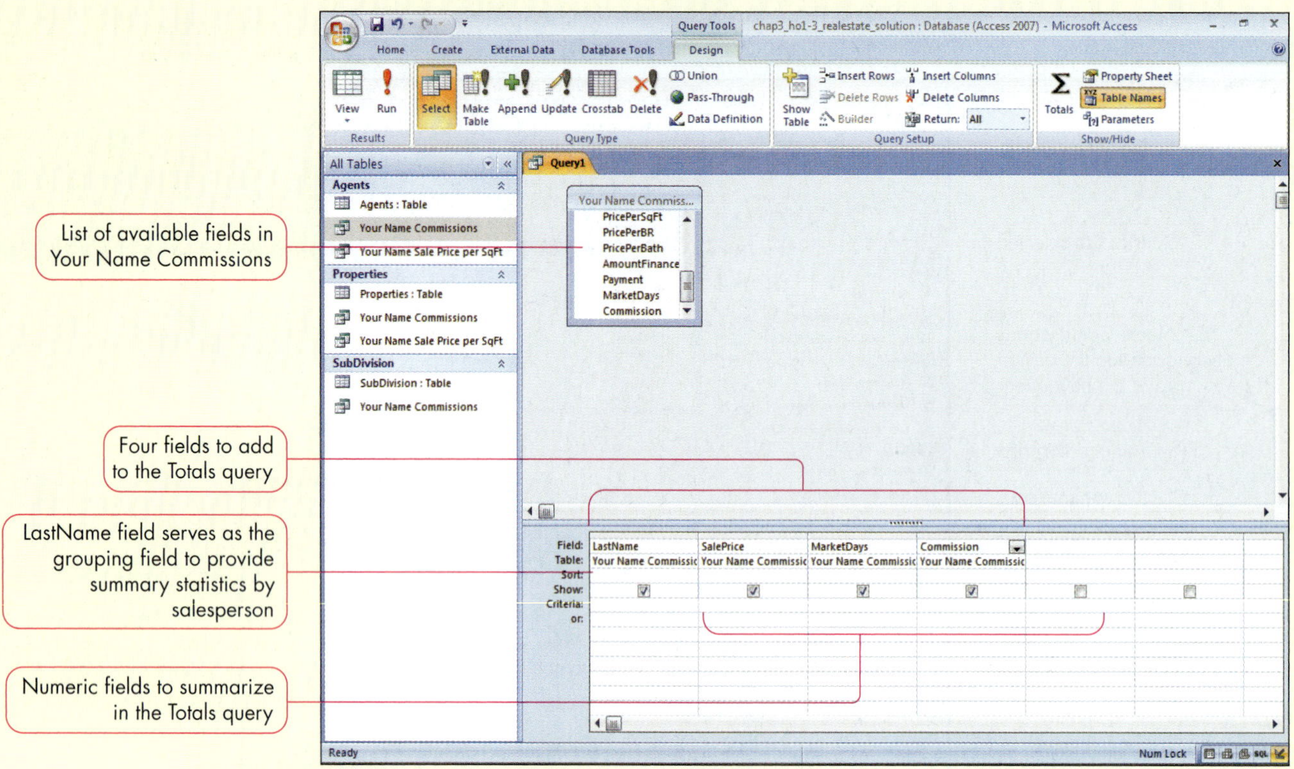

Figure 3.19 Setting up the Totals Query

Step 4
Add Grouping Options and Specify Summary Statistics

Refer to Figures 3.20 and 3.21 as you complete Step 4.

a. Click **Totals** in the Show/Hide group on the Design tab.

   Look at the lower part of the design grid. The Totals command toggles a new row between the Table and Sort rows of the design grid. When the Totals command is activated, all fields are set to Group By. You only want one Group By field, the LastName field.

b. Click in the **Total row** for the **SalePrice** field. Click the **drop-down arrow** and select **Sum** from the list.

   Here is another of those hidden drop-down lists. As you gain experience, you will learn where to look for them. For now, simply memorize that one will show up in the Total row.

c. Click in the **Total row** of the **MarketDays** field. Click the **drop-down arrow** and select **Avg**.

d. Click the **Total row** in the **Commission** field and select **Sum**.

e. Run the query. Return to Design view and set the Format property of the SalePrice and Commission fields as **Currency**. Type **Total Sale Price** and **Total Commission** in the Caption property of the SalePrice and Commission fields, respectively. Set the Format property of the MarketDays field to **Fixed**. Set the Decimal Places property to **0**. Type **Average No. of Days on Market** in the Caption property of the MarketDays field. Close the Property Sheet.

f. Verify results of the calculated summaries. Adjust column widths as needed. Save the query as **Your Name Commission Summary**.

g. Close the *chap3_ho1-3_realestate_solution* file.

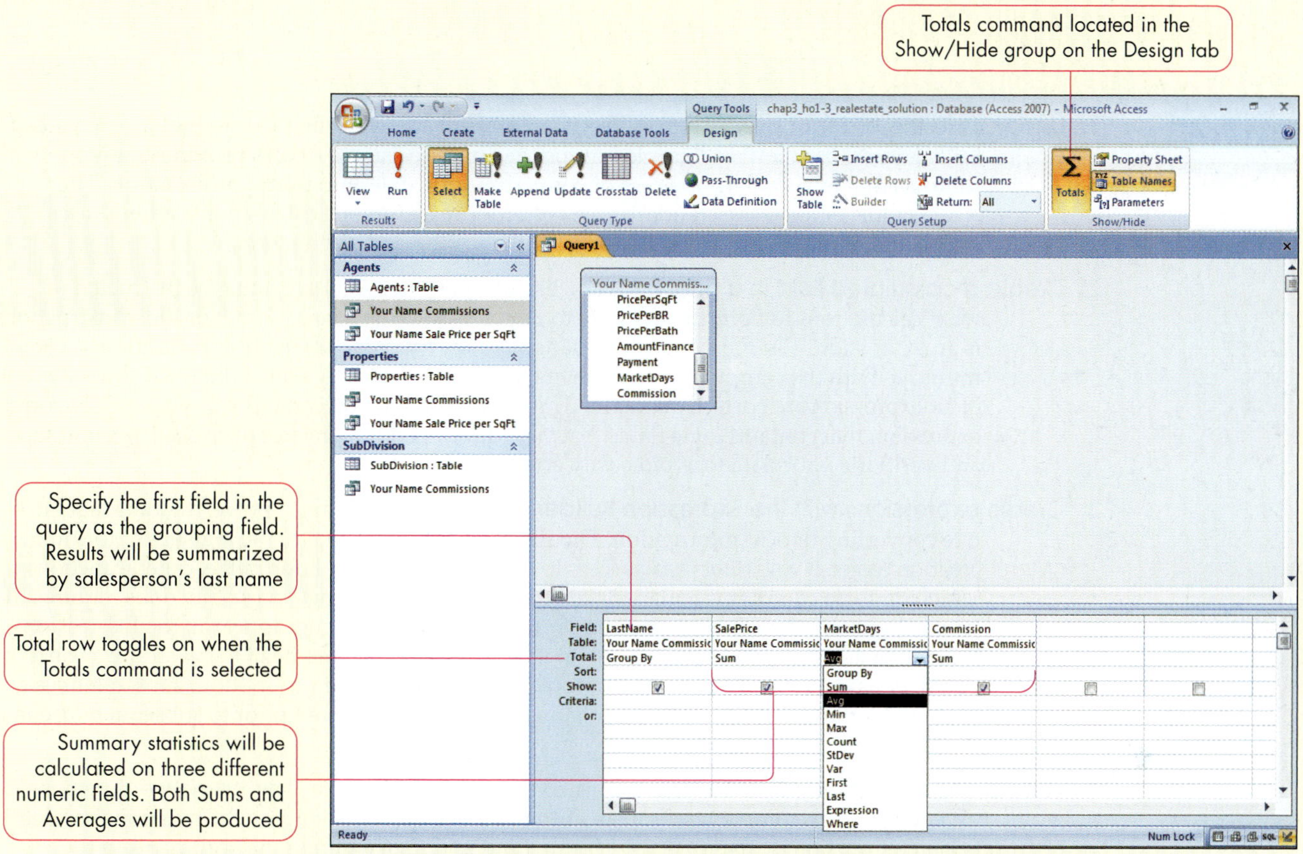

Totals command located in the Show/Hide group on the Design tab

Specify the first field in the query as the grouping field. Results will be summarized by salesperson's last name

Total row toggles on when the Totals command is selected

Summary statistics will be calculated on three different numeric fields. Both Sums and Averages will be produced

Figure 3.20 Specify Grouping Field and Summary Statistics

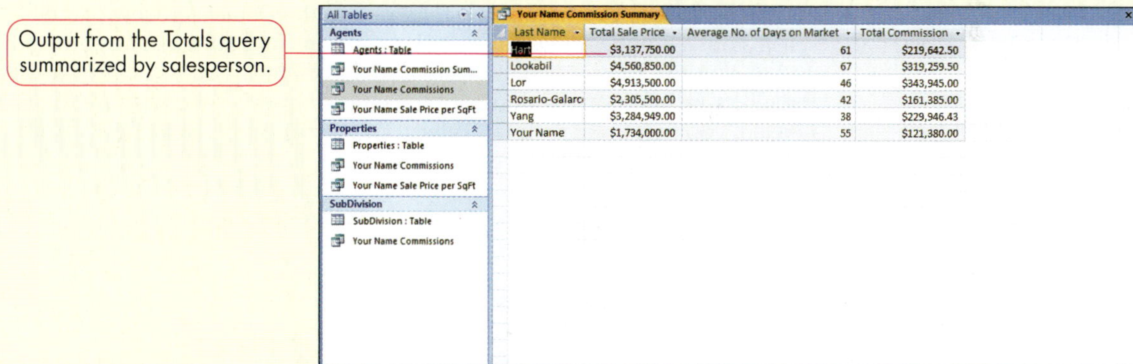

Figure 3.21 Specify Grouping Field and Summary Statistics

Summary

1. **Understand the order of precedence.** Decision makers are overwhelmed with data. They need information that they may employ to make sound decisions. Access provides many powerful tools that expedite the process of converting raw data into useful information. The Access tools employ the standard rules of order in arithmetic calculations: parentheses, exponents, multiplication and division, and addition and subtraction.
2. **Create a calculated field in a query.** Access, like all computer software, must be instructed in what calculations to perform and how to do the work. The formal name for those instructions is an expression. You must "speak the language" of the software in order to accurately communicate with the computer. Syntax refers to the set of rules by which the words and symbols of an expression are correctly combined. You learned that you can write a syntactically correct expression that contains logic flaws. You also developed the practice of critically examining and verifying your data to avoid costly errors.
3. **Create expressions with the Expression Builder.** The chapter introduced powerful tools that facilitate converting data to information. The Expression Builder makes the logistics of formula creation easier. It also offers easy access to a number of pre-built formulae, called functions, which perform complex calculations relatively painlessly. Using Access functions requires the user to know the function's name and arguments. The arguments appear in the Expression Builder enclosed in symbols (<<XXX>>) as a visual cue that you need to substitute a constant or a field name. Access can use the output of earlier calculations as input to subsequent calculations, but the expression must be renamed and the query saved prior to subsequent use in the Expression Builder.
4. **Create and edit Access functions.** You learned that Access, like Excel, has a variety of functions that can perform complex tasks in an automated fashion. You employ the functions by identifying the function by name (IIf, Avg, Sum, Pmt) and then entering the arguments in the appropriate order. Arguments are the input data Access uses to create the output. They may be field names or values.
5. **Perform date arithmetic.** Dates in Access are stored as serial numbers based on the number of days that have elapsed from an arbitrarily chosen base date, December 31, 1899. Access provides several functions to facilitate date handling. Additionally, you can simply subtract one date from another or add a number to a date to create a different date.
6. **Create and work with data aggregates.** Data aggregates provide powerful means to summarize and analyze data. You may add a Total row to the Datasheet view of a table or query and select from a number of useful summary options including count, sum, average, minimum, and maximum. These calculations require only a few mouse clicks to create. Additionally, they have no effect on the design of the table or query. When a more robust summary is needed, you may create a Totals query. This permits you to establish grouping levels for the data to make summaries more meaningful.

Key Terms

Access function .... .690
Argument .... .690
Constant .... .680
Data aggregate .... .704
Date arithmetic .... .694
Date formatting .... .694
DatePart function .... .694
Expression .... .680
Expression Builder .... .689
IIf function .... .691
Order of precedence .... .679
Pmt function .... .690
Syntax .... .680
Total row .... .704
Totals query .... .705

Multiple Choice

1. Which statement most accurately describes the differences between a table field and a calculated field?
   (a) All data entries to a table field are permanently stored, but calculated field data do not exist in the database. They appear in the datasheet, form, or report but are not a part of the dataset.
   (b) A calculated field is permanently stored in the dataset when the query, table, form, or report design is saved. Only the properties governing the data are saved when a table is saved.
   (c) Query data and Table data are dynamic, and no data are permanently stored.
   (d) None of the above

2. Which of the following correctly identify the rules of order of arithmetic operations?
   (a) Exponentiation, Parenthesis, Addition, Subtraction, Multiplication, Division
   (b) Parenthesis, Exponentiation, Addition, Subtraction, Multiplication, Division
   (c) Parenthesis, Exponentiation, Multiplication, Division, Addition, Subtraction
   (d) Addition, Subtraction, Multiplication, Division, Exponentiation, Parenthesis

3. Which set of parentheses is unnecessary in the following expression?
   = (3 * 5) + (7 / 2) – (6^2) * (36 *2)
   (a) (3 * 5)
   (b) (7 / 2)
   (c) (6^2)
   (d) (36 *2)
   (e) All of the above

4. Which statement about saving a query is true?
   (a) Data are extracted from the source table and saved in query form.
   (b) Data are duplicated from the source table and saved in query form.
   (c) Data created using expressions are saved when the query is saved, but the source data stays in the original table.
   (d) No data are saved in a query.

5. The Expression Builder command is found in the:
   (a) Manage group on the Databases Tools tab
   (b) Query Setup group on the Design tab
   (c) Database Management group on the Design tab
   (d) Design group on the Query Setup tab

6. Your database contains a Price field stored in the Products table and a Quantity field stored in the Orders table. You have created a query but forgot to add the Price field in the design. Now you need to use the price field to calculate the total for the order. The correct syntax is:
   (a) OrderTotal:(Quantity)*(Products)!(Price)
   (b) OrderTotal=(Quantity)*(Products)!(Price)
   (c) OrderTotal:[Quantity]*[Products]![Price]
   (d) OrderTotal=[Quantity]*[Products]![Price]

7. Which of the following is true about a select query?
   (a) It may reference fields from more than one table or query.
   (b) It may reference fields from a table, but not a query.
   (c) It may reference fields from either a table or a query but not both.
   (d) It may reference fields from a form.

8. You correctly calculated a value for the OrderAmount using an expression. Now you need to use the newly calculated value in another expression calculating sales tax. The most efficient method is to:
   (a) Run and save the query to make OrderAmount available as input to subsequent expressions.
   (b) Create a new query based on the query containing the calculated Order amount and then calculate the sales tax in the new query.
   (c) Close the Access file, saving the changes when asked; reopen the file and reopen the query; calculate the sales tax.
   (d) Create a backup of the database, open the backup and the query, then calculate the sales tax.

9. If state law requires that wait staff be over age 21 to serve alcohol and you have a database that stores each employee's birthdate in the Employee table, which of the following is the proper syntax to identify the employees' year of birth.
   (a) Age:DatePart("yyyy",[Employee]![BirthDate])
   (b) Age=DatePart("yyyy",[Employee]![BirthDate])
   (c) Age:DatePart("yyyy",[BirthDate]![Employee])
   (d) Age=DatePart("yyyy",[BirthDate]![Employee])

...continued on Next Page

Multiple Choice Continued...

10. You want to add a Totals row in a query Datasheet view. Where will you find the Totals command?
    (a) In the Data group on the Home tab
    (b) In the Home group on the Data tab
    (c) In the Records group on the Home tab
    (d) In the Home group on the Records tab

11. Which statement about a Totals query is true?
    (a) A Totals query may contain one or more grouping fields but several aggregating fields.
    (b) A Totals query may contain several grouping fields but only one aggregating field.
    (c) A Totals query has a limit of only two fields, one grouping field, and one aggregating field.
    (d) A Totals query can aggregate data, but to find a grand total, you must create a new query based on the Totals query and turn on the Total row in the new query.

12. You built a query expression and clicked Run. A parameter dialog box pops up on your screen. Which of the following actions is the most appropriate if you expected results to display and do not want to enter an individual value?
    (a) Click OK to make the parameter box go away.
    (b) Read the field name specified in the parameter box and look for that spelling in the calculated expression.
    (c) Type numbers in the parameter box and click OK.
    (d) Close the query without saving changes. Re-open it and try running the query again.

13. A query contains fields for StudentName and Address. You have created and run a query and are in Datasheet view examining the output. You notice a spelling error on one of the student's names. You correct the error in the query Datasheet view.
    (a) The name is correctly spelled in this query but will be misspelled in the table and all other queries based on the table.
    (b) The name is correctly spelled in the table and in all queries based on the table.
    (c) The name is correctly spelled in this query and any other queries, but will remain misspelled in the table.
    (d) You cannot edit data in a query.

14. Which of the following is not available as an aggregate function within a query?
    (a) Sum
    (b) Min
    (c) Division
    (d) Avg

15. Which of the following is not true about the rows in the query design grid?
    (a) The Total row can contain different functions for different fields.
    (b) The Total row can source fields stored in different tables.
    (c) The Total row is located between the Table and Sort rows.
    (d) The Total row can be applied only to numeric fields.

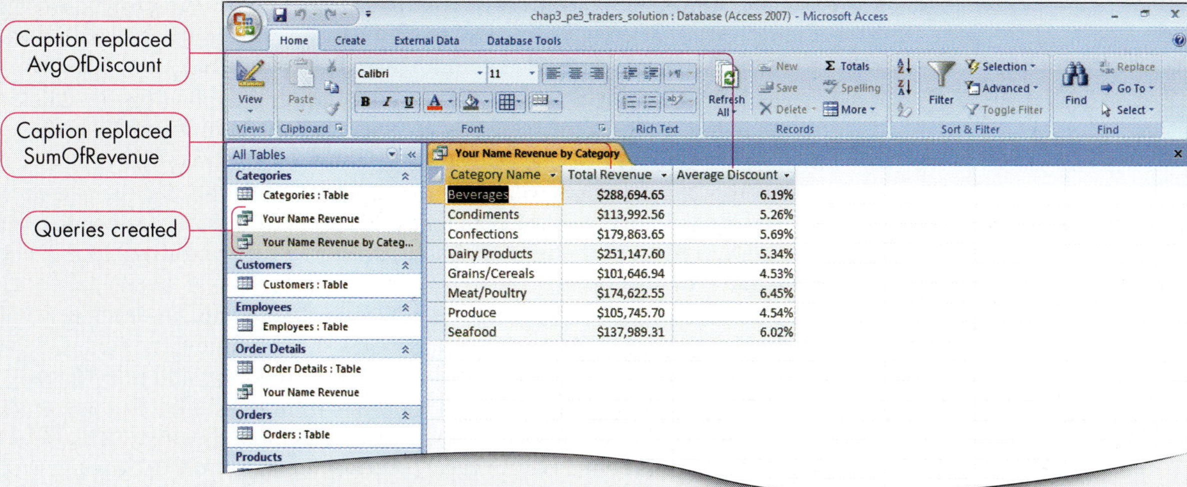

Figure 3.24 Revenue by Category

4 Member Rewards

The Prestige Hotel chain caters to upscale business travelers and provides state-of-the-art conference, meeting, and reception facilities. It prides itself on its international, four-star cuisines. Last year the chain began a member rewards club to help the marketing department track the purchasing patterns of its most loyal customers. All of the hotel transactions are stored in the database. Your task is to determine the revenue from each order and to summarize the revenue figures by location. This project follows the same set of skills as used in Hands-On Exercises 2 and 3 in this chapter. The instructions are less detailed to give you a chance to practice your skills. If you have problems, feel free to reread the detailed directions presented in the chapter. Compare your results to Figure 3.25.

a. Copy the partially completed file *chap3_pe4_memrewards.accdb* to your production folder. Rename it **chap3_pe4_memrewards_solution.accdb**, open the file, and enable the content.
b. Click the **Database Tools tab** and then click **Relationships** in the Show/Hide group. Examine the table structure, relationships, and fields. After you are familiar with the database, close the Relationships window.
c. Create a new query using the Query Wizard. Click the **Create tab** and click **Query Wizard** in the Other group. Select **Simple Query Wizard** in the first screen of the dialog box. Click **OK**.
d. Add fields to the query. From the **Location table** select the **City** field. From the **Orders** table, select the **NoInParty** field. From the **Service table** select the **PerPersonCharge** field. Click **Next**. This needs to be a detail query. Name the query **Your Name Revenue**. Click **Finish**.
e. Click **View** in the Views group to switch to Design view. Right-click **PerPersonCharge** and select **Properties** from the shortcut menu. Click the box to the right of **Format** in the Property Sheet and select **Currency**. Type **Per Person Charge** in the Caption box. Click **X** to close the Property Sheet.
f. Position the insertion point in the first blank column in the Field row. Create an expression that calculates revenue and format the field as **Currency**.

   Revenue:[NoInParty] * [PerPersonCharge]

...continued on Next Page

g. Click **Run** in the Results group on the Design tab. (If you receive the parameter dialog box, check your expression carefully for typos.) Look at the output in the Datasheet view. Verify that your answers are correct. Save and close the query.

h. Click the **Create tab** and click **Query Design** in the Other group. Click the **Queries tab** in the Show Table dialog box. Double-click the **Your Name Revenue** query to add it to the design grid. Click **Close** in the Show Table dialog box.

i. Position the insertion point in the first blank column in the Field row. Double-click the **City** field in the list of available fields in the Your Name Revenue query. Click the insertion point in the next available column in the Field row. Double-click **Revenue** to add it to the grid.

j. Click **Totals** in the Show/Hide group on the Design tab. The Total row will turn on in the design grid. This query should be grouped by the **City** field. Click in the Total row of the **Revenue** field to display the drop-down list and select **Sum**.

k. Right-click **Revenue** and select **Properties** from the shortcut menu. Click the box to the right of **Format** in the Property Sheet. From the drop-down list select **Currency**. Click in the Caption box and type **Total Revenue**. Click **X** to close the Property Sheet. Run the query.

l. Click the **Home tab** in Datasheet view. Click **Totals** in the Records group to turn on the Totals row. Click the **Total Revenue** column in the Total row. Click the drop-down arrow and select **Sum**.

m. Save this query as **Your Name Revenue by City**.

n. Run and save the query. Close the database.

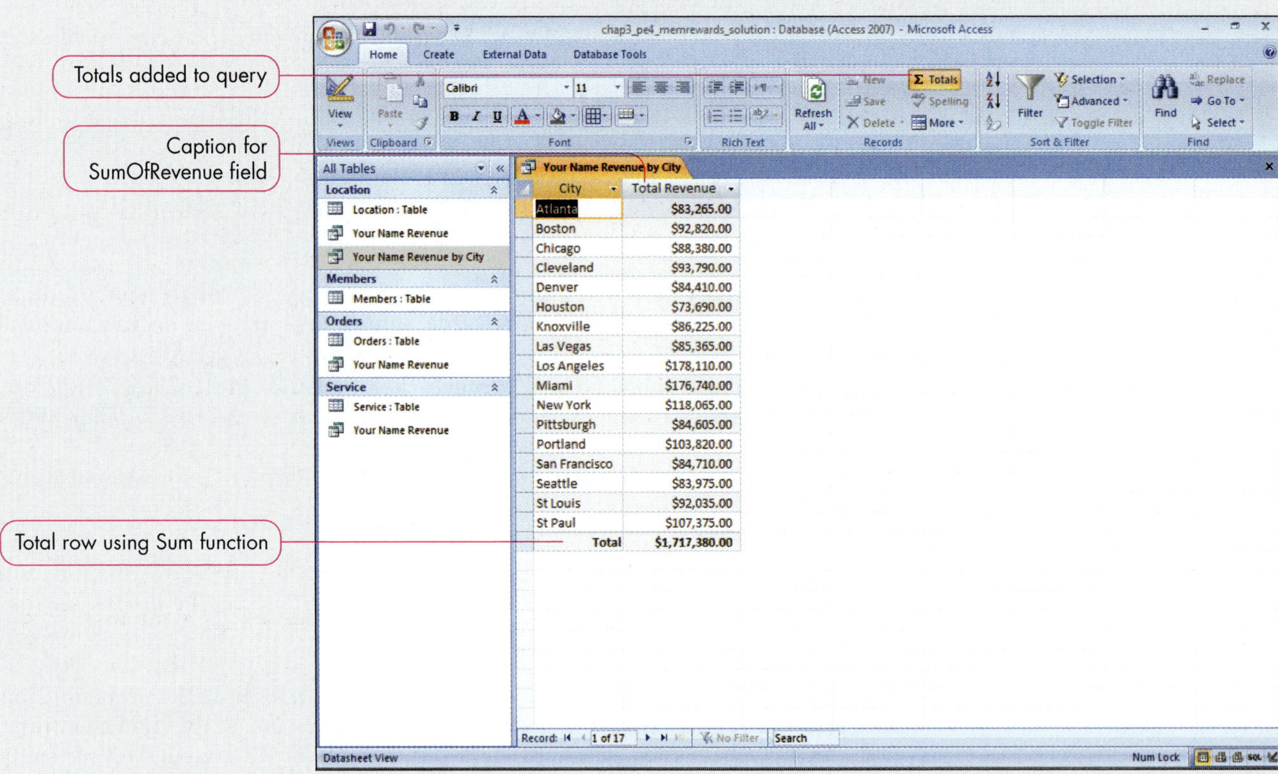

Figure 3.25 Revenue by City

Mid-Level Exercises

1 Calculating and Summarizing Specialty Food Data in a Query

Northwind Traders is a small, international, specialty food company. It sells products in eight different divisions: beverages, confections (candy), condiments, dairy products, grains and cereals, meat and poultry, produce, and seafood. Although most of its customers are restaurants and gourmet food shops, it has a few retail customers, too. The company offers discounts to some customers. Different customers receive differing discount amounts. The firm purchases merchandise from a variety of suppliers. All of the order information is stored in the company's database. This database is used by the finance department to monitor and maintain sales records. You are the finance manager. Your task is to determine the revenue and profit from each order and to summarize the revenue, profit, and discount figures by salesperson. *Revenue* is the money the firm takes in. *Profit* is the difference between revenue and costs. The salespeople may offer discounts to customers to reward loyal purchasing or to appease an angry customer when a shipment is late. Occasionally the sales people discount so deeply that the company loses money on an order, that is, the costs exceed the revenue. It is important that your calculations are correct. If the firm's profitability figures do not accurately reflect the firm's financial health, the employee's paychecks (including yours) might be returned as insufficient funds. Compare your results to Figure 3.26.

a. Locate the file named *chap3_mid1_traders.accdb*, copy it to your production folder, and rename it **chap3_mid1_traders_solution.accdb**. Open the file and enable the content. Open the **Employees table**. Find and replace **Margaret Peacock**'s name with your name. Close table.

b. Create a detail query that you will use to calculate profits for each product ordered. You will need the **LastName** field from the **Employees table**. You will also need the fields for **Quantity**, **Discount**, **OrderDate**, **ShippedDate**, **UnitPrice**, and **ProductCost** from the **Order Details**, **Orders**, and **Products** tables. Save the query as **Your Name Profit**.

c. In Design view, calculate **Revenue**, **Total Cost**, and **Profit**. Because the discounts vary, some (not all) of the profit numbers will be negative. You must factor the discount into the price as you calculate revenue. If a product price (UnitPrice) is $100 and is sold with a 20% discount, the discounted price would be $80. UnitPrice is the price for which the company sells merchandise. ProductCost is what the company pays to purchase the merchandise.

- Calculate **revenue** by multiplying the discounted price by the quantity sold.
- Calculate **total costs** by multiplying the product cost by quantity.
- Calculate **profit** by subtracting total cost from revenue.
- Format the calculated fields as **Currency** and include a caption for **Total Cost**.

d. Save, run, and close query.

e. Create a **Totals query** based on **Your Name Profit**. Group by **LastName**. Average the **Discount** field and sum the **Revenue** and **Profit** fields.

f. Format the **Discount** field as **Percent** and the **Revenue** and **Profit** fields as **Currency**. Create appropriate captions for the average and sum fields.

g. Save the totals query as **Your Name Profit by Employee** and run it.

h. With the Your Name Profit by Employee query open in Datasheet view, press **PrintScrn** to capture a screenshot. Open Word, type your name and section number in a new blank document, press **Enter**, and paste the screenshot in Word. Save the Word document as **chap3_mid1_solution**. Print the Word document. Close the Word document and close the database.

...continued on Next Page

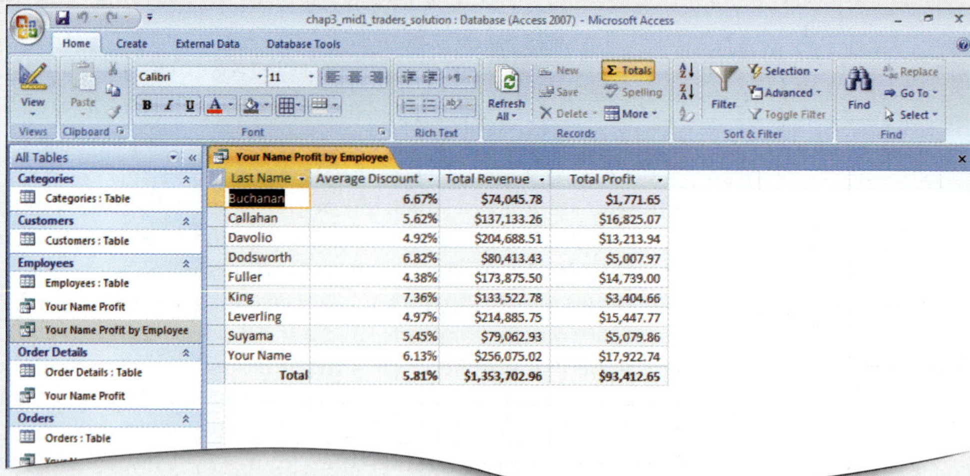

Figure 3.26 Profit by Employee

2 Calculating and Summarizing Bank Data in a Query

You are the manager of the loan department of the National Bank. Several customers have multiple loans with your institution. A single customer might have a mortgage loan, one or more car loans, and a home improvement loan. You need to monitor the total indebtedness of your customers to help them manage their debt load. Your task is to use the information stored in the database to calculate the loan payments for each loan and then to summarize the loans by customer. The Pmt function requires five arguments. The first is the interest rate per period. The interest rates in the table are annual rates, so you will need to convert them to monthly rates in the function. The second argument is the number of periods (in years). Because the payments are monthly, you also need to convert the years for each loan to months in the function. The next argument is the PV, the present value of the loan—what the loan is worth today. It tells you how much each customer has borrowed. You generally supply zeros for the last two arguments, FV, and Type. FV shows the amount the borrower will owe after the last payment has been made—the future value of the monies borrowed. Generally this is zero. The type argument tells Access whether the payment is made at the beginning or the end of the period (month). Most loans accept payments and charge interest on the unpaid balance throughout the period. Use zero as the argument for this function. See Table 3.2 for more information about the arguments to the Pmt function. Compare your results to Figure 3.27.

a. Locate the file named *chap3_mid2_nationalbank.accdb*, copy it to your production folder, and rename it **chap3_mid2_nationalbank_solution.accdb**. Open the file and enable the content. Open the **Customers table**. Find and replace **Michelle Zacco**'s name with your name.

b. Create a detail query that you will use to calculate the payments for each loan. You will need the following fields: **LastName**, **Amount**, **InterestRate**, **Term**, and **Type**. Save the query as **Your Name Loan Payment**.

...continued on Next Page

c. In Design view, use the **Pmt** function to calculate the loan payment on each loan. Divide the annual interest rate by 12 and multiply the loan's term by 12 because every year has 12 months. Include a minus sign in front of the loan amount in the expression so the result returns a positive value. The last two arguments will be zero.

d. Run the query. In the Datasheet view, add a Total row. Use it to calculate the **average** interest rate and the **sum** for the **payment**. Save and close the query.

e. Create a Totals query based on Your Name Loan Payment. **Group by LastName** and summarize the **sum** of the **Payment** field.

f. Format the **Payment** field as **Currency** and add the caption **Total Payment**.

g. Run the query. Add a total row to the Datasheet view that will sum the Total Payments. Save this query as **Your Name Payment Summary**.

h. With the Your Name Payment Summary query open in Datasheet view, press **PrintScrn** to capture a screenshot. Open Word, type your name and section number in a new blank document, press **Enter**, and paste the screenshot in Word. Save the Word document as **chap3_mid2_solution**. Print the Word document displaying the screenshot. Close the Word document and close the database.

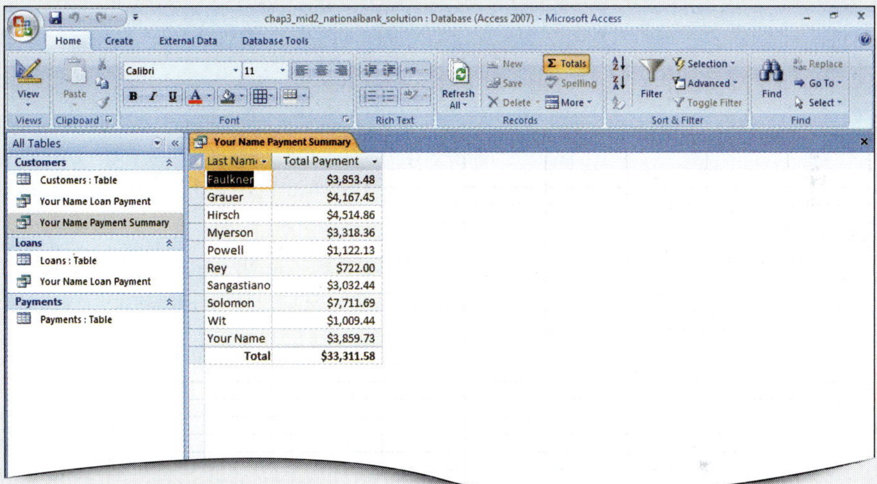

Figure 3.27 Payment Summary

3 Calculating and Summarizing Data in a Query, Working with Dates

You are the senior partner in a large, independent real estate firm that specializes in home sales. Although you still represent buyers and sellers in real estate transactions, you find that most of your time is spent supervising the agents who work for your firm. This fact distresses you because you like helping people buy and sell homes. Your firm has a database containing all of the information on the properties your firm has listed. You believe that by using the data in the database more effectively, you can spend less time supervising the other agents and spend more time doing the part of your job that you like doing the best. Your task is to determine the length of time each sold property was on the market prior to sale. Then calculate the commission from each property sale. Most real estate transactions involve two agents—one representing the seller (the listing agent) and the other the buyer (the selling agent). The two agents share the commission. Finally, you need to summarize the sales data by employee and calculate the average number of days each employee's sales were on the market prior to selling and the total commission earned by the employees. Compare your results to Figure 3.28.

a. Locate the file named *chap3_mid3_realestate.accdb*, copy it to your production folder, and rename it **chap3_mid3_realestate_solution.accdb**. Open the file and enable the content. Open the **Agents table**. Find and replace **Pa Lor**'s name with your name.

...continued on Next Page

b. Create a detail query that you will use to calculate the number of days each sold property has been on the market prior to sale. You will need the following fields: **LastName**, **DateListed**, **DateSold**, **SalePrice**, **SellingAgent**, **ListingAgent**, and **Subdivision**. Save the query as **Your Name Sales Report**.

c. In Design view, build an expression, **DaysOnMarket**, to calculate the number of days each sold property has been on the market prior to sale. Subtract the **DateListed** field from the **DateSold** field. [Hint: The answers will *never* be negative numbers!] Add an appropriate caption.

d. Calculate the commissions for the selling and listing agents using two calculated fields. Multiply the **SalePrice** by the commission rate of **3.5%**. Name the newly created fields **ListComm** and **SaleComm**. Both fields contain the same expression. They need to be named differently so that the proper agent—the listing agent or the selling agent—gets paid. Add captions and format the fields as **Currency**.

e. After you are sure that your calculations are correct, save the query. In Datasheet view, add the Total row. Use it to calculate the average number of days on the market and the sums for the **SalePrice** and commission fields. Format the **SalePrice** and commission fields as **Currency**. Save and close the query.

f. Create a Totals query based on **Your Name Sales Report**. Group by **LastName** and summarize the **DaysOnMarket** field with an **average**. Summarize the **SalePrice**, **ListComm**, and **SaleComm** fields as **sums**. Format monetary values as **Currency** and add appropriate captions.

g. Add a Total row to the Datasheet view that will sum the sale price and commission fields and average the number of days on the market. Save this query as **Your Name Sales Summary**.

h. Format the **Average Days on Market** field so that it displays only two decimal places. Format the remaining numeric fields as **Currency**. Adjust column widths and save the query.

i. With the Your Name Sales Summary query open in Datasheet view, press **PrintScrn** to capture a screenshot. Open Word, type your name and section number in a new blank document, press **Enter**, and paste the screenshot in Word. Save the Word document as **chap3_mid3_solution**. Print the Word document. Close the Word document and close the database.

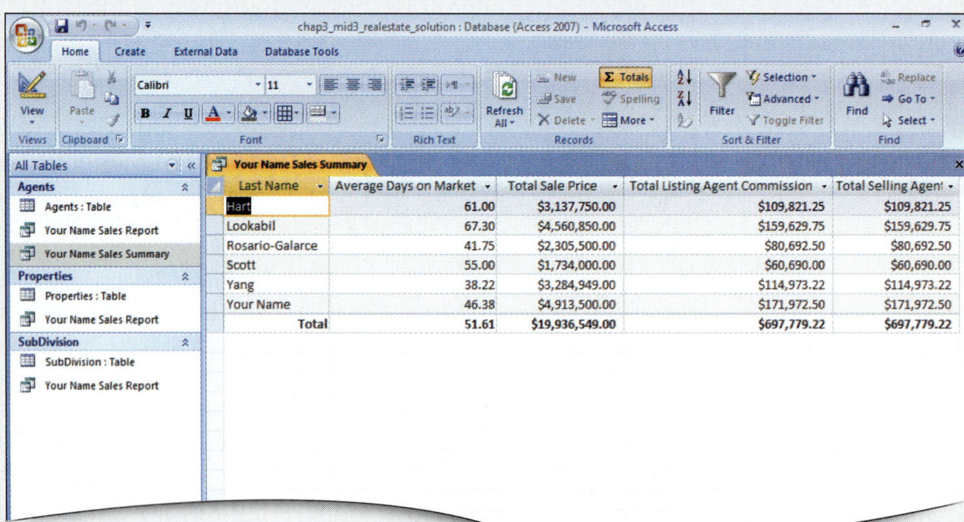

Last Name	Average Days on Market	Total Sale Price	Total Listing Agent Commission	Total Selling Agent
Hart	61.00	$3,137,750.00	$109,821.25	$109,821.25
Lookabil	67.30	$4,560,850.00	$159,629.75	$159,629.75
Rosario-Galarce	41.75	$2,305,500.00	$80,692.50	$80,692.50
Scott	55.00	$1,734,000.00	$60,690.00	$60,690.00
Yang	38.22	$3,284,949.00	$114,973.22	$114,973.22
Your Name	46.38	$4,913,500.00	$171,972.50	$171,972.50
Total	51.61	$19,936,549.00	$697,779.22	$697,779.22

Figure 3.28 Sales Summary

Capstone Exercise

Your boss expressed a concern about shipping delays. She believes that customers are not receiving the products they order in a timely fashion. Because your firm's reputation as a provider of high-quality customer service is at risk, she asks that you investigate the sales and shipping records for the last six months and report what you have discovered. In addition, the sales staff is permitted to discount the prices for some customers. Your boss is worried that the discounting erodes profits. She wants you to identify the sales staff who discount the most deeply.

Database File Setup

You need to copy an original database file, rename the copied file, and then open the copied database to complete this capstone exercise. After you open the copied database, you will replace an existing employee's name with your name.

a. Locate the file named *chap3_cap_traders.accdb* and copy it to your production folder.
b. Rename the copied file as **chap3_cap_traders_solution.accdb**.
c. Open the *chap3_cap_traders_solution.accdb* file and enable the content.
d. Open the **Employees table**.
e. Find and replace *Margaret Peacock's* name with your name.

Sales Report Query

You need to create a detail query to calculate the number of days between the date an order was placed and the date the order was shipped for each order. You also need the query to determine the amount of a discount, calculate the revenue, calculate the total cost, and calculate the profit. Furthermore, the query should calculate the employee's commission on the sale. However, before you create this query, you need to create a Totals query to determine the last shipped date. You will then use the Totals query field as a criterion for the detail query.

a. Create a **Totals** query named **Your Name Last Ship Date** to determine the last shipped date in the Orders table. Use the appropriate function from the Totals drop-down list to determine the last ship date. Save and run the query to see that date. Save and close the query.
b. Create another query that is based on the Your Name Last Ship Date query, Employees table, and other tables.
c. Include the following fields: **LastName** (from the Employees table), **OrderDate**, **ShippedDate**, **UnitPrice**, **ProductCost**, **Quantity**, and **Discount**.
d. Research the DateAdd function in Access. Insert this function as the ShippedDate criterion. Use the months abbreviation as the interval, subtract 6 months as the number of intervals, and use the MaxOfShippedDate field as the date. The criterion should then find all ship dates within the last six months of the last shipped date.
e. Save the query as **Your Name Sales Report**.
f. Create a calculated field named **DaysToShip** to calculate the number of days taken to fill each order. Subtract the OrderDate field from the ShippedDate field. (Hint: The answers will never be negative numbers.)
g. Calculate the revenue for each product ordered. Multiply the UnitPrice by the difference between 100% and the discount percent and multiply the result by Quantity.
h. Calculate TotalCost for each item ordered by multiplying ProductCost by Quantity. Calculate Profit by subtracting TotalCost from Revenue.
i. Calculate the Commission for each profitable order. When the profit on the ordered item is positive, multiply the profit by the commission rate of 3.5%. If the profit is negative (a loss), the salesperson receives no commission.
j. Use the Property Sheet to apply appropriate formats and captions for the calculated fields.
k. Sort by OrderDate. Verify that the query calculations are correct and save the query.
l. In Datasheet view, add a total row to calculate the average number of DaysToShip and the sums for the Revenue, TotalCost, Profit, and Commission fields. Format the Revenue, TotalCost, Profit, and Commission fields as Currency.

Totals Query

You need to create a totals query based on the Your Name Sales Report query. You will group the totals query by last name to provide aggregate statistics that summarize each salesperson's performance and income. It also will provide the average number of days each salesperson's orders take to ship.

a. Create a **Totals** query based on the Your Name Sales Report query. Group by **LastName** and summarize the **DaysToShip** field with an average. Format the DaysToShip field as Fixed with zero decimal places and an appropriate caption. Summarize the **Revenue**, **TotalCost**, **Profit**, and **Commission** fields as sums. Format the Revenue, TotalCost, Profit, and Commission fields as **Currency** and add appropriate captions.
b. Add a Total row to the Datasheet view that will sum the Revenue, TotalCost, Profit, and Commission fields and average the DaysToShip field.
c. Save this query as **Your Name Shipping and Commission**.
d. With the Your Name Shipping and Commission query open in Datasheet view, press **PrintScrn** to capture a screenshot. Open Word, type your name and section number in a new blank document, press **Enter**, and paste the screenshot in Word. Save the Word document as **chap3_cap_solution**. Print the Word document.
e. Close the Word document and close the database.

Mini Cases

Use the rubric following the case as a guide to evaluate your work, but keep in mind that your instructor may impose additional grading criteria or use a different standard to judge your work.

Vacation Time for Bank Employees

GENERAL CASE

The *chap3_mc1_safebank.accdb* file contains data from a small bank. Copy the *chap3_mc1_safebank.accdb* file to your production folder, name it **chap3_mc1_safebank_solution.accdb**, and open the copied file. Use the skills from this chapter to perform several tasks. The bank's employee policy states that an employee is eligible for three weeks of vacation after two years of employment. Before two full years, the employee may take two weeks of vacation. The Branch table stores the start date of each manager. You need to figure out how long each manager has worked for the bank. Once you have done that, you need to calculate the number of weeks of vacation the manager is eligible to enjoy. Set these calculations up so that when the query is opened in the future (for example, tomorrow, a month, or two years from now), the length of service and vacation values will update automatically. Add appropriate captions for the calculated fields. Save the query as **Your Name Vacation**. Create another query to summarize each customer's account balances. This summary should list the customer's name and a total of all account balances. Format the query results and add appropriate captions. Save the query as **Your Name Customer Balances**. Close the database.

Performance Elements	Exceeds Expectations	Meets Expectations	Below Expectations
Create query	All necessary and no unneeded fields included.	All necessary fields included but also unnecessary fields.	Not all necessary fields were included in the query.
Compute length of service	Calculations and methods correct.	Calculations correct but method inefficient.	Calculations incorrect and methods inefficient.
Compute vacation entitlement	Calculations and methods correct, updates automatically.	Calculations and methods correct but fail to update.	Calculations incorrect, methods inefficient, no updates.
Summarize balances	Correct method, correct totals.	Correct totals but inefficient method.	Totals incorrect or missing.

Combining Name Fields

RESEARCH CASE

This chapter introduced you to the power of using Access Expressions, but you have much more to explore. Use Access Help to search for Expressions. Open and read the articles titled *Create an expression* and *A guide to expression syntax*. Put your new knowledge to the test. Copy any of the database files that you used in this chapter and rename the copy with the prefix, **chap3_mc2**. For example, if you copy the safebank database, the file name should be **chap3_mc2_safebank_solution.accdb**. Open the file. Find a table that stores names in two fields: FirstName and LastName. Add your name to the table. Your challenge is to figure out a way of using a query to combine the last and first name fields into one field that prints the last name, a comma, a space, and then the first name. Save the query as **Last Name First Name**. Once you successfully combine the fields somewhere, alphabetize the list. Print it. Write your instructor a memo explaining how you accomplished this. Use a memo template in Word, your most professional writing style, and clear directions that someone could follow in order to accomplish this task. Attach the printout of the name list to the memo. Save the Word document as **chap3_mc2_solution**. Close the Word document, and close the database.

Performance Elements	Exceeds Expectations	Meets Expectations	Below Expectations
Use online help	Appropriate articles located and memo indicates comprehension.	Appropriate articles located but memo did not demonstrate comprehension.	Articles not found.
Prepare list of names	Printed list attached to memo in requested format.	Printed list is attached but the formatting has minor flaws.	List missing or incomprehensible.
Summarize and communicate	Memo clearly written and could be used as directions.	Memo text indicates some understanding but also weaknesses.	Memo missing or incomprehensible.
Aesthetics	Memo template correctly employed.	Template employed but signed in the wrong place or improperly used.	Memo missing or incomprehensible.

...continued on Next Page

Coffee Revenue Queries

DISASTER RECOVERY

A co-worker called you into his office and explained that he was having difficulty with Access 2007 and asked you to look at his work. Copy the *chap3_mc3_coffee.accdb* file to your production folder, name it **chap3_mc3_coffee_solution.accdb**, and open the file. It contains two queries, Your Name Revenue and Your Name Revenue by City. The Revenue query is supposed to calculate product Price (based on a markup percentage on Cost) and Revenue (the product of Price and Quantity). Something is wrong with the Revenue query. Your challenge is to find and correct the error(s). Your co-worker also tried to use the Revenue query as input for a Revenue by City query that should show revenue by city. Of course, since the Revenue query doesn't work correctly, nothing based upon it will work, either. After correcting the Revenue query, correct the Revenue by City query. Run the queries. Display all of the Revenue values as Currency, and include appropriate captions. Save the queries with your name and descriptive titles. Print the Datasheet view of the Totals by City query and turn the printout and file in to your instructor if instructed to do so. Close the database.

Performance Elements	Exceeds Expectations	Meets Expectations	Below Expectations
Error identification	Correct identification and correction of all errors.	Correct identification of all errors and correction of some errors.	Errors neither located nor corrected.
Summary query	Correct grouping options and summarization selected.	Correct grouping but some summaries incorrectly selected.	Incorrect group by option selection.
Naming	Descriptive query name selected and employed.	Query name is only partially descriptive.	Query missing or default names used.

chapter 4 | **Access**

Create, Edit, and Perform Calculations in Reports

Creating Professional and Useful Reports

After you read this chapter, you will be able to:

1. Plan a report **(page 731)**.
2. Use different report views **(page 733)**.
3. Create and edit a report **(page 737)**.
4. Identify report elements, sections, and controls **(page 747)**.
5. Add grouping levels in Layout view **(page 750)**.
6. Add fields to a report **(page 755)**.
7. Use the Report Wizard **(page 765)**.

Hands-On Exercises

Exercises	Skills Covered
1. INTRODUCTION TO ACCESS REPORTS (page 739) **Open:** chap4_ho1-3_coffee.accdb and chap4_ho1-3_coffee.gif **Save as:** chap4_ho1-3_coffee_solution.accdb **Back up as:** chap4_ho1_coffee_solution.accdb	• Create a Report Using the Report Tool • Create and Apply a Filter in a Report • Remove Fields from a Report and Adjust Column Widths • Reposition Report Objects and Insert Graphic Elements in a Report • Use AutoFormat and Format Report Elements
2. CREATE, SORT, EDIT, NEST, AND REMOVE GROUPS FROM REPORTS (page 757) **Open:** chap4_ho1-3_coffee_solution.accdb (from Exercise 1) **Save as:** chap4_ho1-3_coffee_solution.accdb (additional modifications) **Back up as:** chap4_ho2_coffee_solution.accdb	• Sort a Report • Create a Grouped Report and Sort It • Add Additional Grouping Levels and Calculate Summary Statistics • Remove Grouping Levels • Reorder Grouping Levels
3. REPORT WIZARD (page 770) **Open:** chap4_ho1-3_coffee_solution.accdb (from Exercise 2) **Save as:** chap4_ho1-3_coffee_solution.accdb (additional modifications)	• Assemble the Report Data • Create a Query-Based Report and Add Grouping • Create Summary Statistics • Select Layout and AutoFormatting • Modify the Report

CASE STUDY

Northwind Traders

Northwind Traders is a small, international, specialty food company. It sells products in eight different divisions: beverages, confections (candy), condiments, dairy products, grains and cereals, meat and poultry, produce, and seafood. Although most of its customers are restaurants and gourmet food shops, it has a few retail customers, too. All of the order information is stored in the company's database. This database is used by the finance department to monitor and maintain sales records. You are the finance manager. Your task is to determine the revenue from each order and to summarize the first-quarter revenue for each month and by each category. You need only report on gross revenue—the total amount the firm receives. This report does not need to calculate any costs or expenses. It is important that you report accurately. Figure 4.1 presents a rough layout of the report. You must identify the source data; prepare a report; and group it to match the layout.

Case Study

Your Assignment

- Copy the file named *chap4_case_traders.accdb*. Rename the copy **chap4_case_traders_solution.accdb**. Open the copied file and enable the content.
- Locate and rename the Your Name Revenue query with your first and last name. Use this query as the source for your report. It contains all the needed fields for the report plus several fields you do not need.
- Create a report based on the Your Name Revenue query. Use any report creation method you learned about in the chapter.
- Add appropriate grouping levels to produce the output shown in Figure 4.1. Name the report **Your Name First Quarter Sales by Month and Category**. You may select formatting as you want, but the grouping layout should match the design shown.
- Print the completed report.
- Compact and repair the file.
- Back up the database.

Appearances Matter

By now you know how to plan a database, create a table, establish relationships among table data, and extract, manipulate, and summarize data using queries. You generated output by printing table or query datasheets. If you look back at your earlier work, you will see that the information exists, but it is bland. You probably have worked in other application software sufficiently to wonder if Access can enhance the print files. Access provides a powerful tool, giving you the ability to organize and present selected data clearly. Most of the printed output generated by Access users comes from reports.

Enhanced data improves the functionality of database information. Just as in the other Microsoft Office applications, you can change the size, style, and placement of printed matter. You may highlight portions of output to call attention to them. You may also add graphs, pictures, or charts to help the report reader more easily convert the database data into useful information. Designing and producing clear, functional, and organized reports facilitates decision-making. Report production begins with planning the report's design.

In this section, you plan reports. First you create reports using the Report Tool, and then you edit the report by using the Layout view.

Planning a Report

A ***report*** is a printed document that displays information from a database.

A ***report*** is a printed document that displays information from a database in a manner that provides clear information to managers. You can design a report to create a catalog, a telephone directory, a financial statement, a graph showing sales by month, a shipping label, or a letter to customers reminding them about a past due payment. All documents you create using table data are Access reports. You should carefully consider what information you need and how you can optimally present it. Access provides powerful tools to help you accomplish this goal. However, if you do not take the time to plan the report in advance, the power of the tools may impede the report process. You should think through what elements you need and how they should be arranged on the printed page prior to launching the software. The time invested planning the report's appearance at the start of the process leads to fewer surprises with the end result. The report plan helps you take charge of the computer instead of the computer controlling you.

The report plan helps you take charge of the computer instead of the computer controlling you.

Draw a Paper Design

The most important tool you use to create an Access report may be a pencil. If you sketch your desired output before touching the mouse, you will be happier with the results. As you sketch, you must ask a number of questions.

- What is the purpose of the report?
- Who uses this report?
- What elements, including labels and calculations, need to be included? What formulae will produce accurate results?
- Will the results be sensitive or confidential? If so, does there need to be a warning printed on the report?
- How will the report be distributed? Will users pull the information directly from Access or will they receive it through e-mail, a fax, the Internet, Word, or Excel?

Sketch the report layout on paper. Identify the field names, their locations, their placement on the page, and other design elements as you sketch. Figure 4.1 provides a sample report layout.

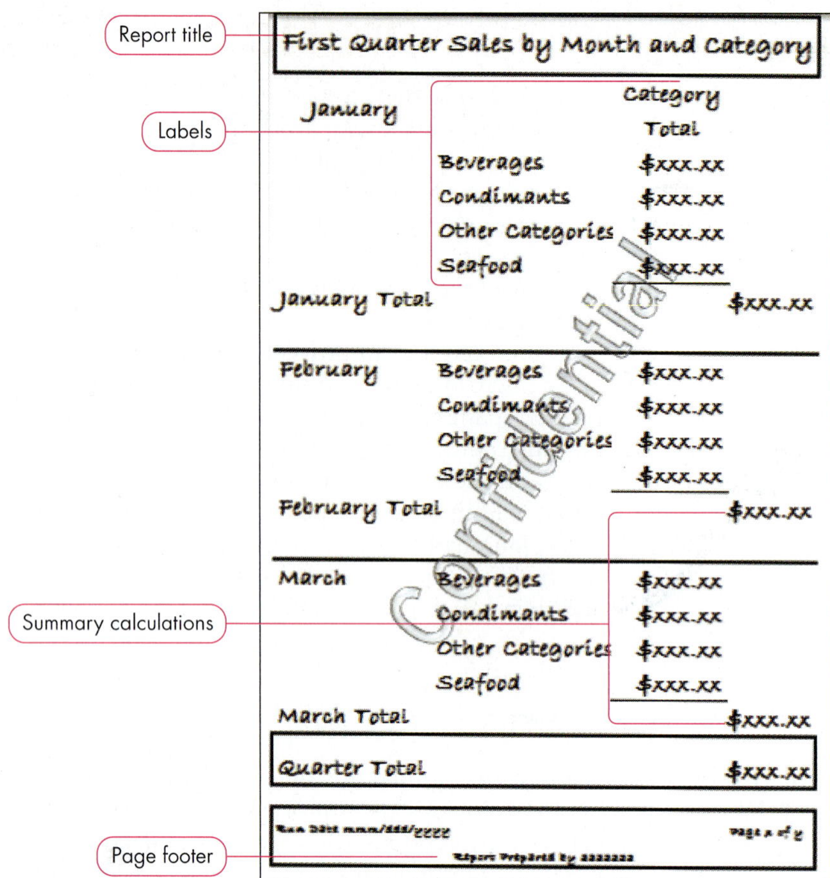

Figure 4.1 Report Plan

Identify Data Sources

In the next step of planning your report, you need to identify the data source(s) of each report element. You may use one or more tables, queries, or a combination of tables and queries as the report's source. Occasionally, a single table or query contains all of the records you need for the report. Typically, however, you need to specify several tables. When multiple tables are needed to create a report, you may assemble all necessary data in a single query and then base the report on that query. Reports frequently contain graphics as well as data. As you identify the sources of report input, you also need to specify the graphic source. Frequently, a company logo on an invoice or a watermark, indicating that the material is confidential or proprietary, is printed on the report.

Select a Reporting Tool

Access gives you several tools to facilitate report creation. Which one you select depends on the data source and complexity of the report design. Table 4.1 summarizes the available tools and their usage.

Table 4.1 Report Tools, Location, and Usage

Report Tool	Location	Data Source	Output Complexity
Report Tool	Create Tab, Reports Group, Report command	Single table or query	Limited. This creates a report showing all of the fields in the data source.
Report Wizard	Create Tab, Reports Group, Report Wizard command	Single or multiple tables or queries or a mixture of tables and queries	More sophisticated. Include (or exclude) fields. Add grouping and sorting instructions. Choose between detailed or summary data presentation.
Label Wizard	Create Tab, Reports Group, Labels command	Single or multiple tables or queries or a mixture of tables and queries	Limited. This feature only produces mailing labels (or name badges) but does so formatted to fit a variety of commercially available mailing labels. The output displays in multiple columns only in Print Preview. Filterable to exclude records.
Blank Report	Create Tab, Reports Group, Blank Report command	Single or multiple tables or queries or a mixture of tables and queries	Limited and extremely complex. Use to quickly assemble a few fields from multiple tables without stepping through the wizard. Alternatively, use to customize the most sophisticated reports with complex grouping levels and sorts.

Using Different Report Views

You have worked with Datasheet and Design views of tables and queries to perform different tasks. For example, you cannot perform data entry in an Access table in Design view, nor can you establish query criteria in Datasheet view. Similarly, Access 2007 provides different views of your report. You view and edit the report using different views depending on what you need to accomplish. Because Access reports may be more sophisticated than queries or tables, you have more views available. Each view accommodates different actions.

Use Print Preview

The ***Print Preview*** displays the report as it will be printed.

The ***Print Preview*** displays the report exactly as it will appear on the printed output. You may look at or print your reports in this view, but you cannot edit the report data. You may specify which pages to print in the Print dialog box. The default value will print all pages in the report. Figure 4.2 shows an Access report in Print Preview.

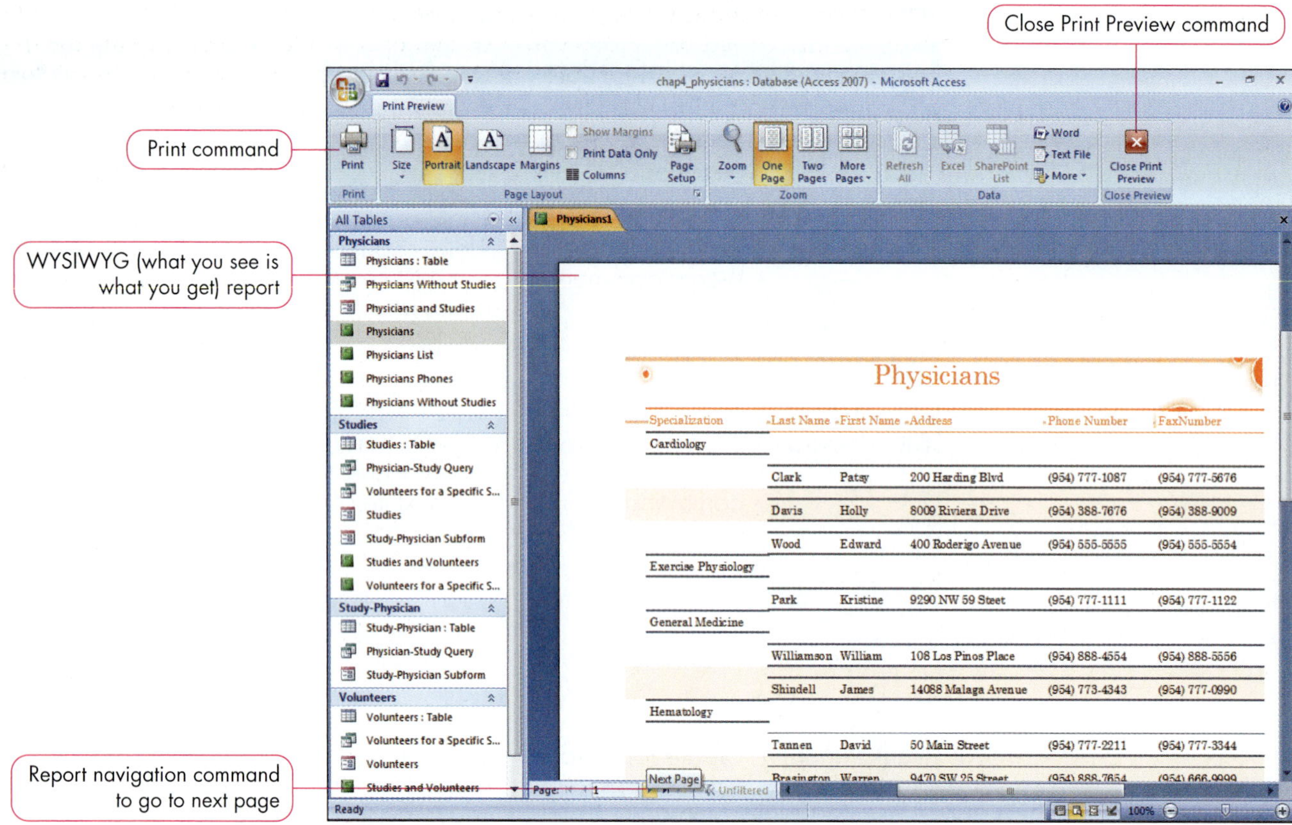

Figure 4.2 Print Preview of an Access Report

TIP Always Preview Access Reports Prior to Printing

Because databases contain a great deal of information, Access reports may become very long and may require many pages to print. Experienced Access users **always** preview their work and go to the last page of the report by using the navigation commands. Although some reports require hundreds of pages to print, many that have multiple pages may be reformatted to print on one or a few pages. The rule is preview before printing.

View and Interact with Data in Report View

Use the ***Report view*** to make temporary changes to data while viewing it as it will print.

The second way to view Access reports, the ***Report view***, provides you the ability to see what the printed report will look like and to make temporary changes to how the data are viewed. You can identify portions of the output by applying a filter. For example, if you need a list of physicians practicing Internal Medicine, you can right-click the record value and select the appropriate filtering option, *equals Internal Medicine*, from the shortcut menu. All of the other types of physicians are hidden temporarily (see Figure 4.3). If you print the filtered report, the printout will not show the hidden records. When you close and open a filtered report again, the filter disappears, and all records appear in Report view. You may reapply the filter to reproduce the filtered results. The Report view permits you to copy selected formatted records to the Clipboard and paste them in other applications. Even when the security controls on the report have been tightly set by the database administrator, this view gives the report user a measure of customization and interactivity with the data.

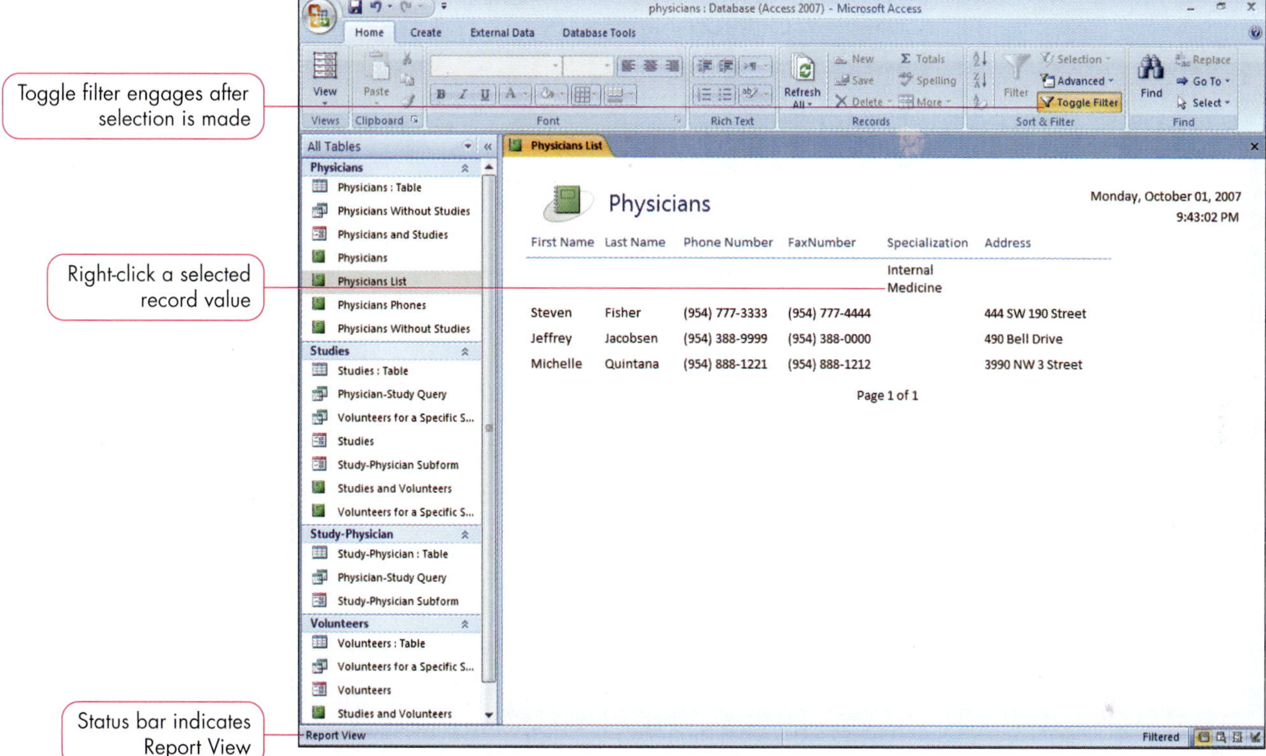

Figure 4.3 Filtered Report Output Shown in Report View

Modify Reports in Layout View

Use the ***Layout view*** to alter the report design while viewing the data.

The third (and perhaps the most useful) report view is the Layout view. Use the ***Layout view*** to alter the report design while viewing the data. You should use Layout view to add or delete fields to the report, modify field control properties, change the column widths or row height to ensure that the entire field displays without truncation, add grouping and sorting levels to a report, or to filter reported data to extract only specific records. Although the display appears as what you see is what you get (WYSIWYG), you will find sufficient variations between the Layout and Print Preview views that you will need to use Print Preview. You do most of the report's modification using Layout view. Figure 4.4 shows a report in Layout view.

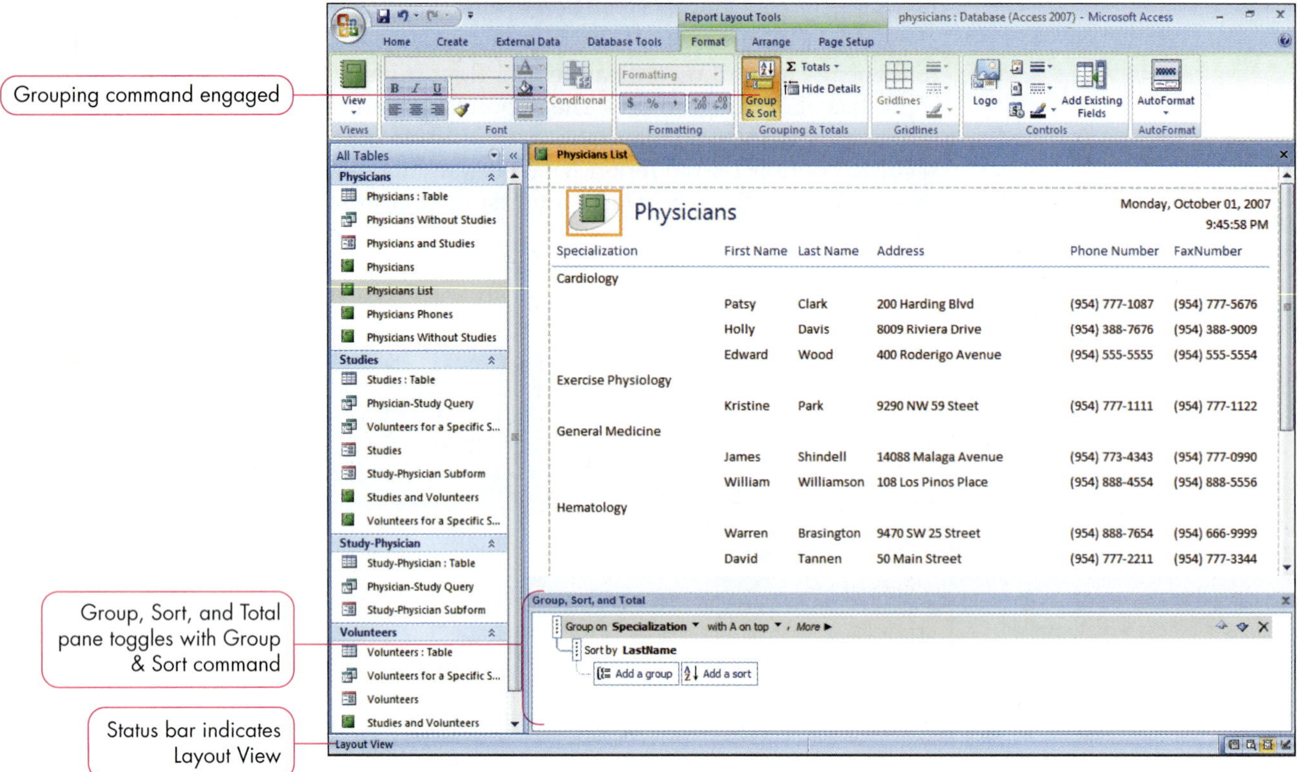

Figure 4.4 Report in Layout View with Grouping and Sorting

Perfect a Report in Design View

The ***Design view*** displays the report's infrastructure but no data.

The ***Design view*** displays the report's infrastructure design, but it does not display data. It provides you the most powerful method of viewing an Access report. You may perform many of the same tasks in Design view as you can in Layout view—add and delete fields, add and remove sorting and grouping layers, rearrange data elements, adjust column widths, and customize report elements. You do not see any of the report's data while in this view. When the report is very lengthy, hiding the data as you alter the design may be an advantage because you save time by not scrolling. However, the Design view looks so different from the final output, it may be confusing. You need to experiment with using both the Layout and Design views and decide which view fits your style. Figure 4.5 displays the Physicians report in Design view. The next section provides explanations for all of the little boxes and stripes.

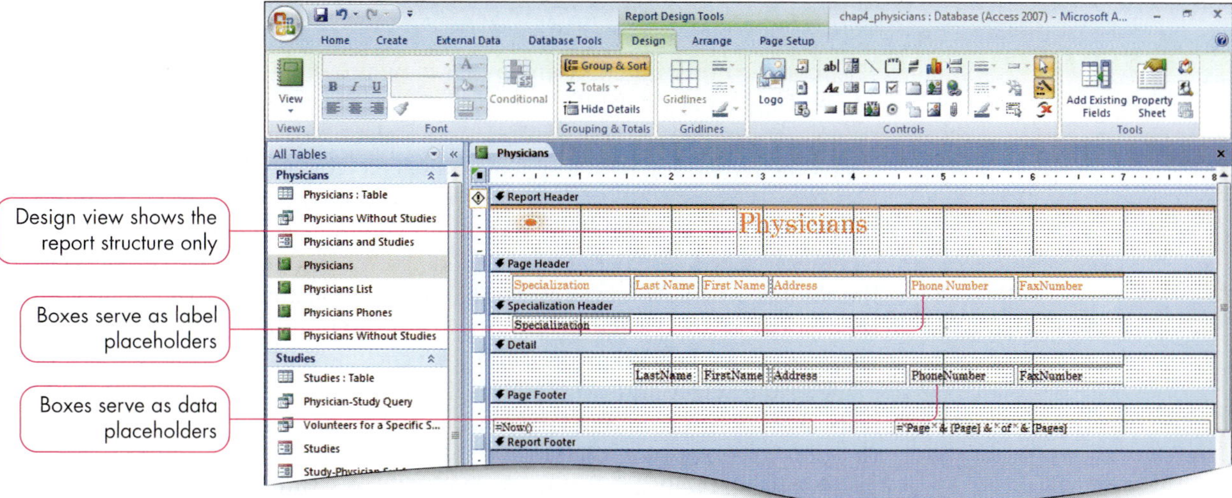
Design view shows the report structure only
Boxes serve as label placeholders
Boxes serve as data placeholders

Figure 4.5 Reports Shown in Design View Do Not Display Record Values

Create and Edit a Report

Access gives you several different methods to generate a report. You will first learn how to use the Report tool. Start by determining all of the fields needed for the report. To use the Report tool, you need to assemble all of the necessary data in one place. This tool is extremely easy to use and will adequately serve your needs much of the time. Occasionally, a table contains all of the fields for a report. More often, you will need to create or open a query containing the necessary fields. If an existing query has all of the fields needed for the report but also some unneeded fields, you will probably use the existing query. You can delete the extraneous fields.

Create a Report with the Report Tool

First you need to determine the record source for the report. Open the record source in Datasheet view. Click the Create tab and click Report in the Reports group. Access creates the report and displays it in Layout view (see Figure 4.6). If you like the look of the report, you may print, save, and close it from the Layout view. When you reopen the saved report, Access automatically returns to the record source and loads the most recent data into the report.

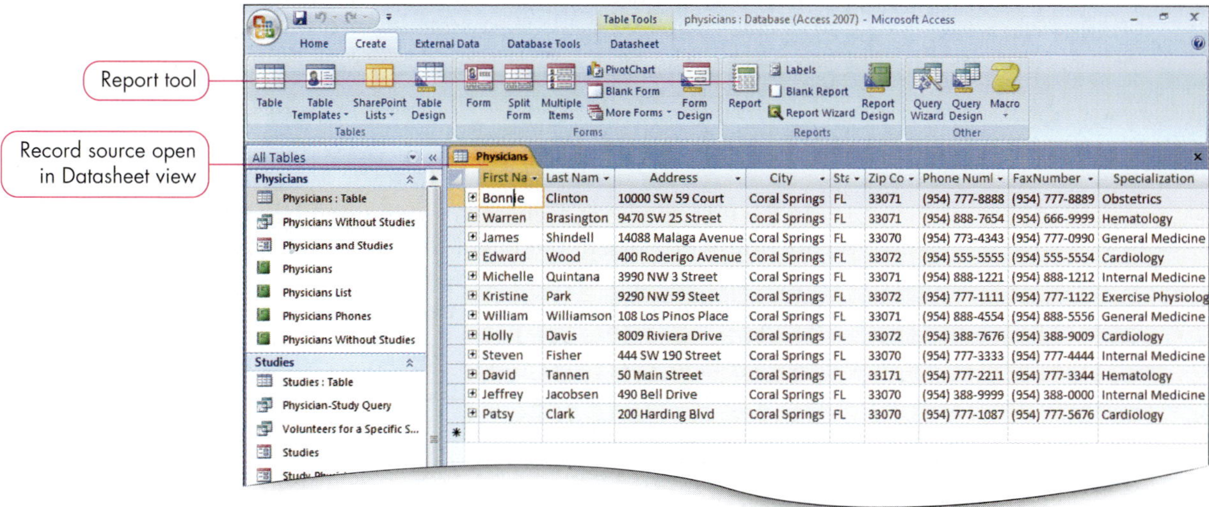
Report tool
Record source open in Datasheet view

Figure 4.6 Set Up for Using Report Tool

Edit a Report in Layout View

The report-editing functions in Layout view provide you with powerful and easy-to-use editing capabilities. If you have unnecessary fields in a report, simply click a value in the unneeded column and press Delete. Not only does the unneeded field go away; the remaining field's spacing adjusts to cover the gap where the deleted data had been. Change the column widths by clicking a value in the column and then moving your mouse over the right column boundary. When the mouse pointer shape changes to a horizontal, double-headed arrow, click and drag the boundary to adjust the column width. You may move an object by selecting it, positioning your mouse in the middle of the selection, waiting until the pointer shape changes to the move shape (the four-headed arrow), and then clicking and dragging to reposition.

Use the select-and-do method of changing font, size, color, and effects in the same way as you would in Word or Excel. Add graphic elements by clicking Logo in the Controls group on the Format tab. Then browse to the storage location of the graphic file in the Insert Picture dialog box. The editing skills you already know from working in other software applications work in essentially the same way when you edit an Access report in the Layout view. Access provides many predefined formats that you may apply to the report. Figure 4.7 shows a report in Layout view.

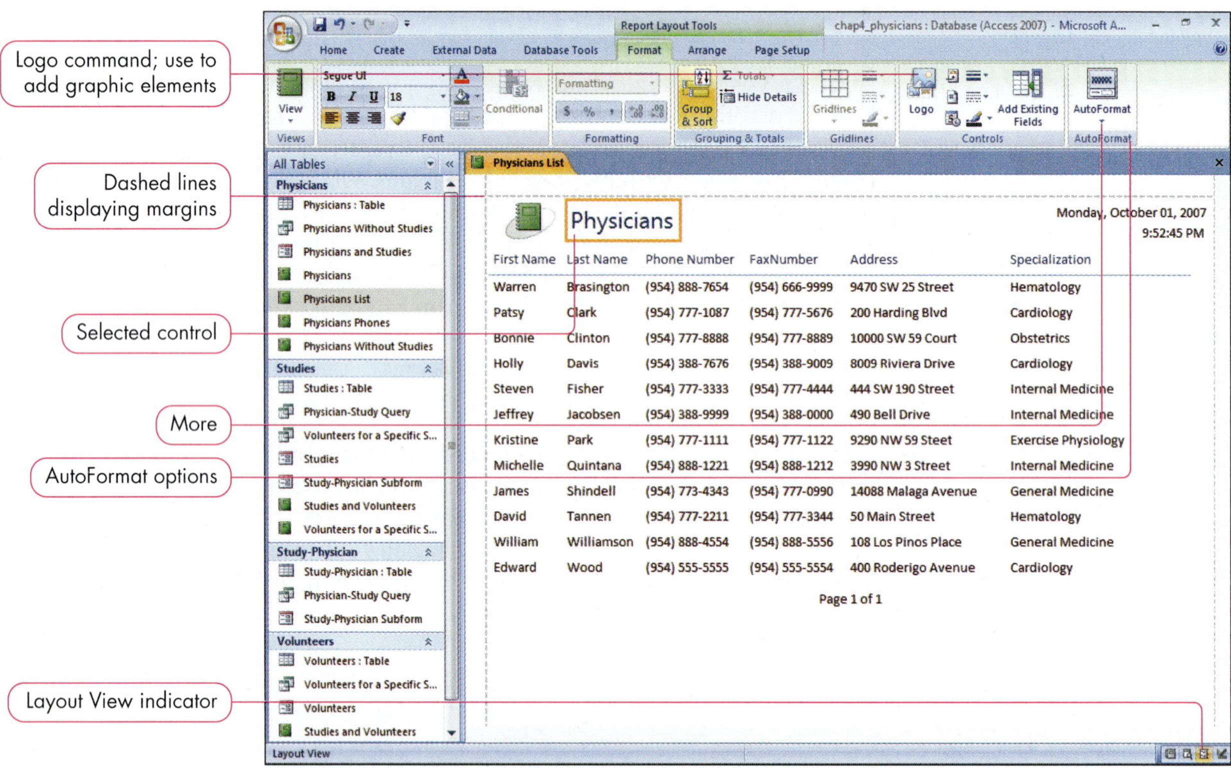

Figure 4.7 Report Layout View Elements

In the first hands-on exercise you will use the Report tool to generate an Access report. You will work in the Layout view to filter the report, remove unnecessary fields, resize and reposition columns, add graphics, apply AutoFormats to the report, and then customize the AutoFormatted results.

Hands-On Exercises

1 | Introduction to Access Reports

Skills covered: 1. Create a Report Using the Report Tool **2.** Create and Apply a Filter in a Report **3.** Remove Fields from a Report and Adjust Column Widths **4.** Reposition Report Objects and Insert Graphic Elements in a Report **5.** Use AutoFormat and Format Report Elements

Step 1
Create a Report Using the Report Tool

Refer to Figure 4.8 as you complete Step 1.

a. Use Windows Explorer to locate the file named *chap4_ho1-3_coffee.accdb*. Copy the file and rename it as **chap4_ho1-3_coffee_solution.accdb**.

b. Open the *chap4_ho1-3_coffee_solution.accdb* file.

c. Click **Options** on the Security Warning toolbar, click **Enable this content** in the Microsoft Office Security Options dialog box, and then click **OK**.

d. Open the **Sales Reps table** and replace *Your Name* with your first and last names. Close the Sales Reps table.

e. Right-click the **Your Name Revenue** query in the Navigation Pane and select **Rename**. Replace *Your Name* with your first and last names.

f. Open the **Your Name Revenue query** in Datasheet view.

g. Click the **Create tab** and then click **Report** in the Reports group.

   Access creates the report and opens it in the Layout view. The report opens with the Format tab active because you almost always need to modify the format of a newly generated report.

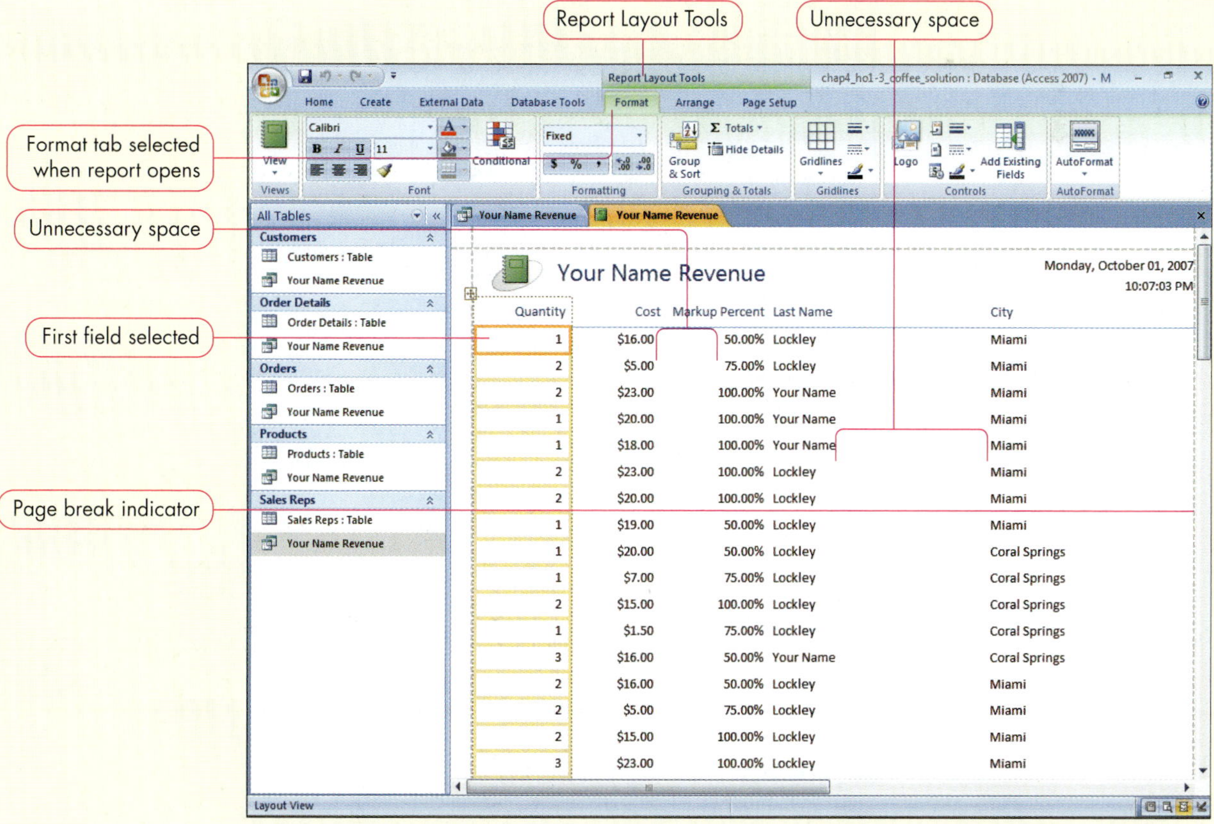

Figure 4.8 Newly Created Report Opens in Layout View

Step 2
Create and Apply a Filter in a Report

Refer to Figure 4.9 as you complete Step 2.

a. Right-click **Your Name** in the LastName field and select **Equals "Your Name"** from the shortcut menu.

You have created and applied a filter that displays only your orders. The status bar in the lower-right corner of the window tells you that the report has a filter applied. Only your records should display.

b. Right-click the word *Miami* and select **Does Not Equal "Miami"** from the shortcut menu.

Additional records are filtered out of the report, and a total for the Revenue field moves into view. Note that the total did not inherit the currency format from the source data. You may need to scroll right to see the total of the Revenue column.

c. Compare your selected fields to those shown in Figure 4.9 and then click **Save**.

The Save As dialog box opens with the default name (inherited from the source query) highlighted.

d. Type **Your Name Sales Outside of Miami**. Click **OK**.

e. Close the report and close the query.

You saved the report based on the query, so it no longer needs to be open. Although this is a small database, working with unnecessary objects open may slow your computer's response time. You should always close unnecessary objects.

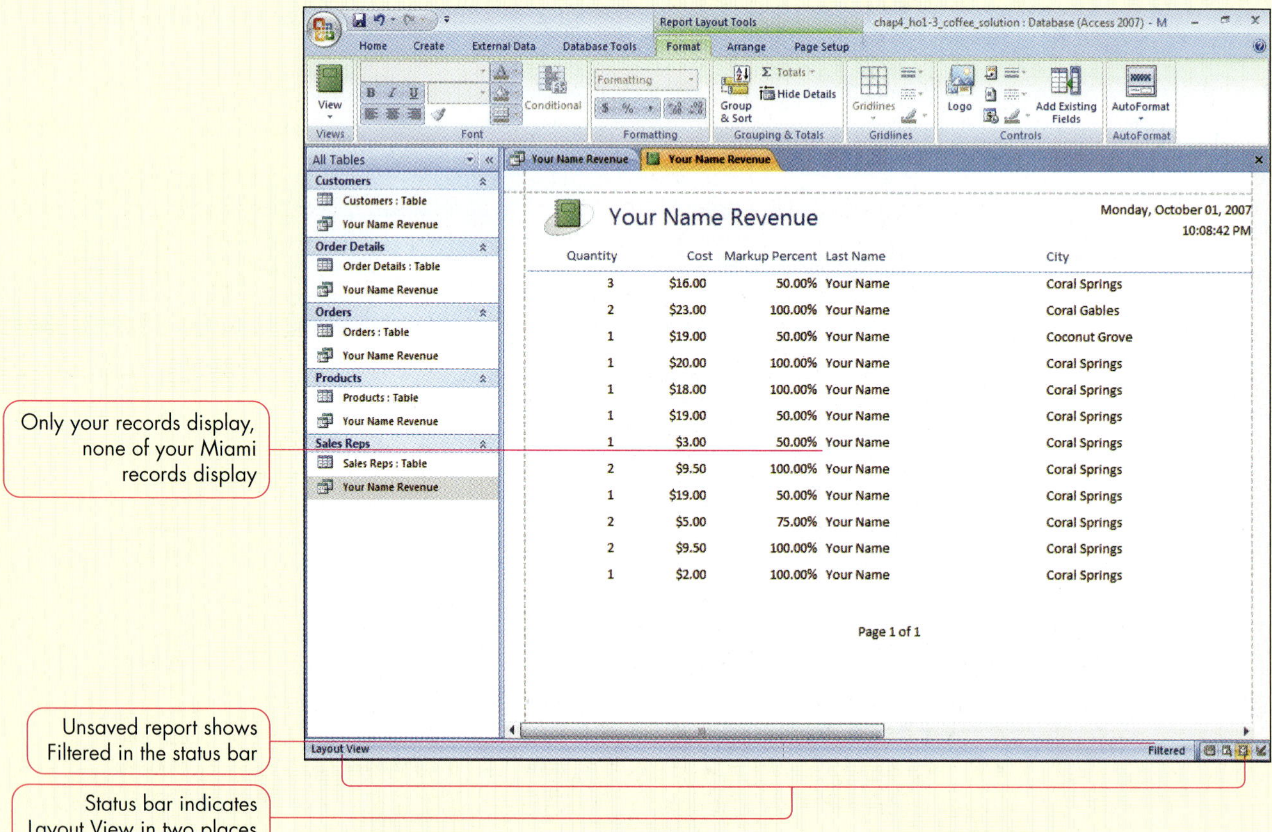

Figure 4.9 Filtered, Totaled Report

Step 3
Remove Fields from a Report and Adjust Column Widths

Refer to Figure 4.10 as you complete Step 3.

a. Open the **Your Name Sales Outside of Miami report**. Look at the left side of the status bar. It displays *Report View*. The status bar no longer indicates that the report is filtered.

   When you reopen an existing report, it opens in Report view. This view lets you look at the report and permits limited filtering capabilities. Because this view provides limited editing interaction, you need to change to Layout view.

b. Right-click the **Your Name Sales Outside of Miami tab** and select **Layout View** from the shortcut menu.

c. Click the label **Quantity**.

   A gold box surrounds the selected field name, and a dotted border surrounds the record values in the field.

   TROUBLESHOOTING: The gold box should only be around the word Quantity. If it surrounds the entire label row, you are still in Report view. Switch to Layout view and then click Quantity again.

d. Press **Delete**.

   The column disappears from the report. The remaining columns move left to fill the empty space.

e. Click **Your Name** in any record. Move your mouse to the right boundary of the gold border and, when the pointer shape changes to a double-headed arrow, click and drag the boundary to the left to decrease the column width.

f. Click a **city name** in any record. Move your mouse to the right boundary of the gold border and, when the pointer shape changes to a double-headed arrow, click and drag the boundary to the left to decrease the column width.

   The report should fit on a single page now. You notice that the column heading for the Markup Percent column is much wider than the values in the column.

g. Click the **Markup Percent** column label to activate the gold border. Single-click **Markup Percent** again to edit the label.

   You know you are in edit mode because the border color changes to black, and a flashing insertion point appears inside the border.

h. Position the insertion point to the left of the ***P*** in *Percent*. Press **Ctrl+Enter**. Click anywhere on the report to exit edit mode. Save the report.

   The Ctrl+Enter command forces a line break. The word *Percent* moves below the word *Markup*.

TIP Forced Line Break

A similar command, Alt+Enter, may be used in Excel to force a line break, when the width of the column name greatly exceeds the width of the data displayed in the column. Although word wrapping may achieve the same effect, you can more precisely control which word prints on what line by forcing the break yourself.

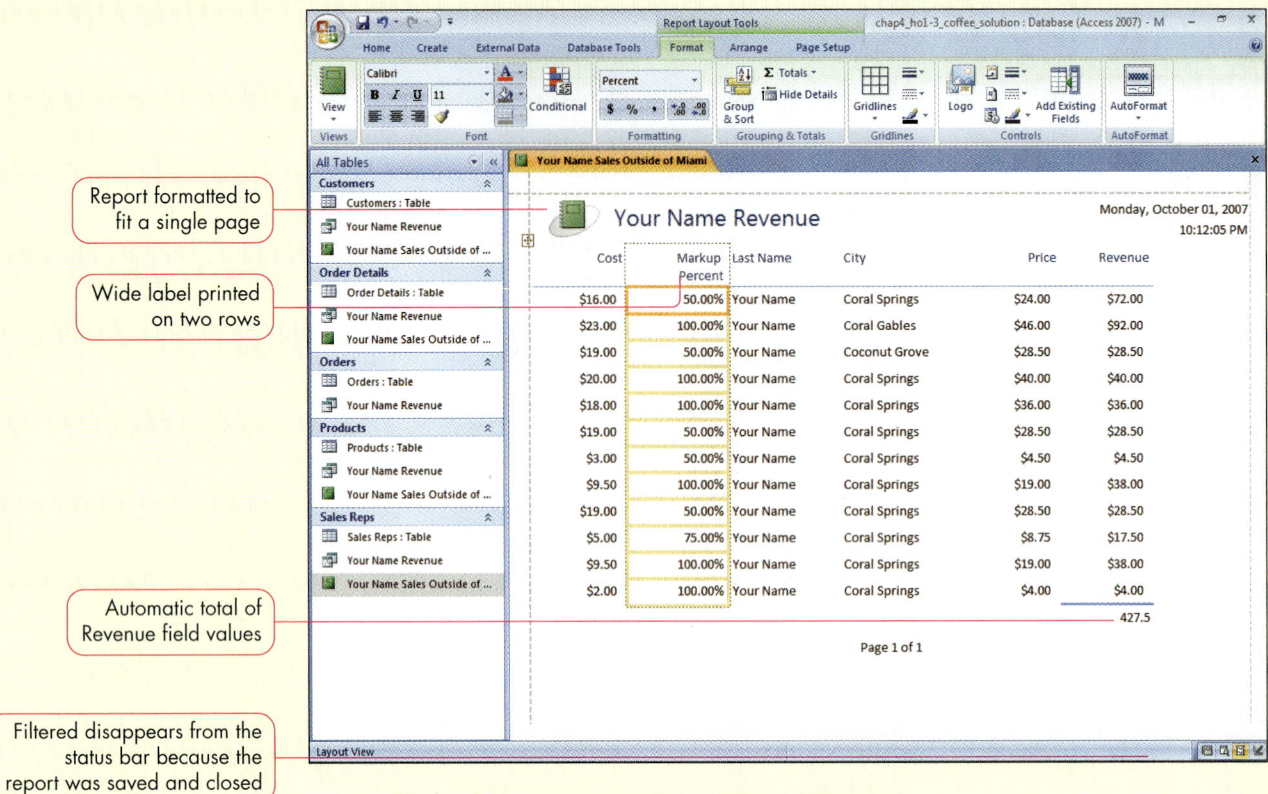

Figure 4.10 Resized Report

Step 4 Reposition Report Objects and Insert Graphic Elements in a Report

Refer to Figure 4.11 as you complete Step 4.

a. Click any record in the **City** column to select it. Move the mouse to the middle of the selected column. When the pointer shape changes to a *four-headed arrow*, click and drag to the left until the vertical gold line is on the left edge of the report. Release the mouse.

As you drag past other columns in the report, a gold line moves to tell you the column's current position. When you release the mouse, the City column moves to the first position.

TROUBLESHOOTING: When you begin to drag while located in a record, Access assumes that you want to change the height of the row until you move out of the column. While the mouse is inside the selected cell a black boundary forms across the entire row. Keep dragging left. As soon as the mouse moves outside the original boundaries, the gold line will appear.

b. Click any record in the **Last Name** column to select it. Move the mouse to the middle of the selected column. When the pointer shape changes to a *four-headed arrow*, click and drag right. Continue the drag until the vertical gold line is on the right edge of the report. Release the mouse.

The Last Name column is the last column in the report.

c. Click the report title, *Your Name Revenue*, to select it and then click it again to edit it. Type **Your Name Non–Miami Sales**.

d. Click the picture of the **report binder** to select it.

e. Click **Logo** in the Controls group on the Format tab.

The Insert Picture dialog box opens to the default folder, Pictures, but the file you need is stored in the folder with the rest of the Access files.

f. Browse to the folder that contains the student data files that accompany this textbook; locate and open the file named *chap4_ho1-3_coffee.gif*. Click **OK**.

g. Move your mouse over the lower right corner of the picture until the pointer shape changes to a diagonal, double-headed arrow. Click and drag the lower-right picture corner until the picture's size roughly doubles.

The picture enlarges, but now it covers part of your name.

TIP Use the Properties Sheet to Exactly Size an Object

If you right-click the picture and select Properties from the shortcut menu, you may use measurements to exactly size the picture. You also may add special effects, like stretch or zoom.

h. Click the report's title, *Your Name Non–Miami Sales*, to select it. Position the mouse pointer in the middle of the box. When the pointer shape changes to the four-headed move arrow, click and drag the report title right and down (see Figure 4.11).

i. Click **Save** on the Quick Access Toolbar to save the design changes to the report.

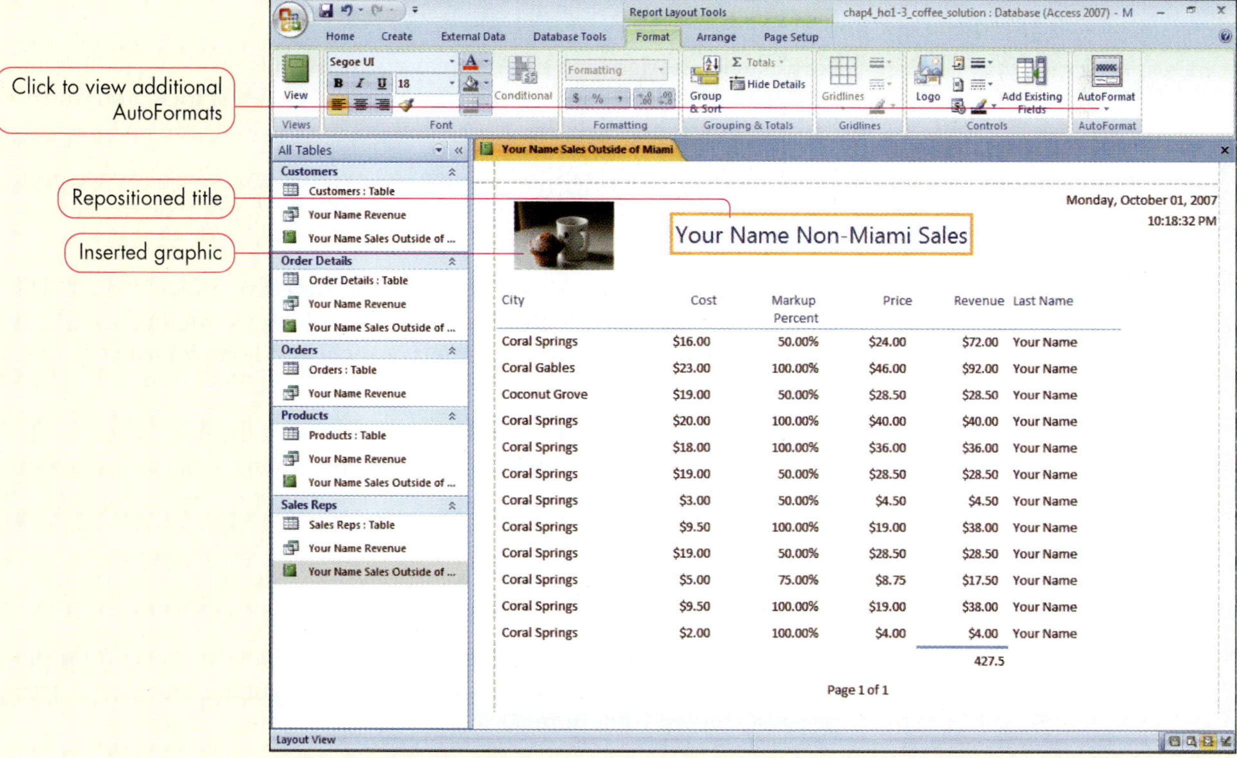

Figure 4.11 Graphic and Title Repositioned

Step 5
Use AutoFormat and Format Report Elements

Refer to Figure 4.12 as you complete Step 5.

a. Check to ensure the *Your Name Non–Miami Sales report* remains in Layout view. Right-click the **Revenue Total cell** (427.5) to select it and open the shortcut menu.

b. Select **Properties** from the shortcut menu.

The Property Sheet opens in the task pane.

c. Click the **Format tab** (if necessary), and then click the **Format drop-down arrow** in the Property Sheet and select **Currency**.

You should see the value of the Revenue field total change to $427.50.

d. Close the Property Sheet. Click **More** in the AutoFormat group on the Format tab (see Figure 4.7).

The AutoFormat gallery expands to display several formats. The last choice activates the AutoFormat Wizard.

e. Select the **Median AutoFormat** (2nd column, 3rd row) and click it.

The AutoFormat applies to the entire report. It does not matter what portion of the report you selected when you applied the AutoFormat. Every element of the report gets a format change. This effect may create problems.

f. Examine the results. Identify problems.

Although the Layout view gives you powerful editing capabilities, it does not perfectly duplicate the printed output. You need to use Print Preview to determine if the problem needs action.

g. Right-click the report tab and change to **Print Preview**. Examine the report's date and time. You should check the Report view, also. Right-click the report tab and change to **Report View**. Often, reports get copied and pasted or e-mailed directly from the Report view, so you need to make sure everything works there, too.

Fortunately, the date and time display correctly in Print Preview. You decide that you do not like how the font color looks in the Revenue total. You think it would look better if it matched the other numbers in size, font, and color.

h. Right-click the report tab and change to **Layout View**. Click any record in the **Revenue** field. Click **Format Painter** in the Font group on the Format tab. Click **$427.50**, the revenue total.

Clicking Format Painter instructs Access to save the source format. The mouse pointer has a paintbrush attached to it as you move to remind you that you will paint the stored format wherever you next click. When you reach the destination and click, the defined formats transfer.

i. Click to select the **brown** report header. Right-click the **brown area** at the top of the report and select **Properties** on the shortcut menu. Check to make sure the *Format tab* is open. Look in the *Back Color Property box*. The brown background color is color number **#775F55**. Select and **copy** the number or remember it.

You need to match the heading color to replace the blue background of the column headings. By looking up the property, you may make an exact color match.

j. Click the blue background for the **Cost heading**. Find the Back Color property on the Format sheet. Click and drag to select its contents and press **Ctrl + V** to paste the brown color number in the box. Press **Enter**.

The color change does not take effect until you move to the next row. You like the new color but decide the type font will look better larger, centered, and bold.

k. Click the **Font Size arrow** in the Font group and select **12**. Click **Bold**. Click the **Center button**.

l. Scroll in the Property Sheet for the *Cost* heading until you locate the Top Margin property. Type **0** and press **Enter**.

   The top margin might change to a slightly different setting, such as 0.0465". Do not worry about this minor difference.

m. Duplicate the format changes to the Cost heading to the other headings by double-clicking **Format Painter** in the Font group. Click the headings for *Markup Percent, Last Name, City, Price,* and *Revenue*. Press **Esc**.

   Double-clicking the Format Painter permits painting a format to multiple areas without redefining the source after each painting. Pressing Esc or clicking the Format Painter again turns the Format Painter off. You used Format Painter to copy the background color, font size, bold, center alignment, and top margin to all of the column headings.

n. Close the Property Sheet. Widen each column about a quarter inch so the entire page is filled (see Figure 4.12). Refer to Step 3e for instructions if necessary, except drag to widen rather than to narrow the column. Save your report.

   TROUBLESHOOTING: Be sure to look at the report in Print Preview. Remember, the Layout view is not perfectly WYSIWYG. It is easy to make the right column a little too wide and push the report to an extra page. Check to make sure your report is still a single page. If it is not, make the columns a little narrower.

o. Click the **Office Button**, select **Manage**, and then select **Back Up Database**. Type **chap4_ho1_coffee_solution** (note *ho1* instead of *ho1-3*) and click **Save**.

   You just created a backup of the database after completing the first hands-on exercise. The original database *chap4_ho1-3_coffee_solution* remains onscreen. If you ruin the original database as you complete the second hands-on exercise, you can use the backup file you just created.

p. Close the file and exit Access if you do not want to continue with the next exercise at this time.

TIP Learning Software

Following step-by-step instructions is a way to begin learning application software. If you want to become proficient in software, you must explore on your own. The Property Sheet contains dozens of features that you did not cover in this lesson. You have finished Hands-On Exercise 1 and saved your file. You should experiment a little. Make a copy of the report and experiment on the copy. Display the Property Sheet for a field and change properties to see the results.

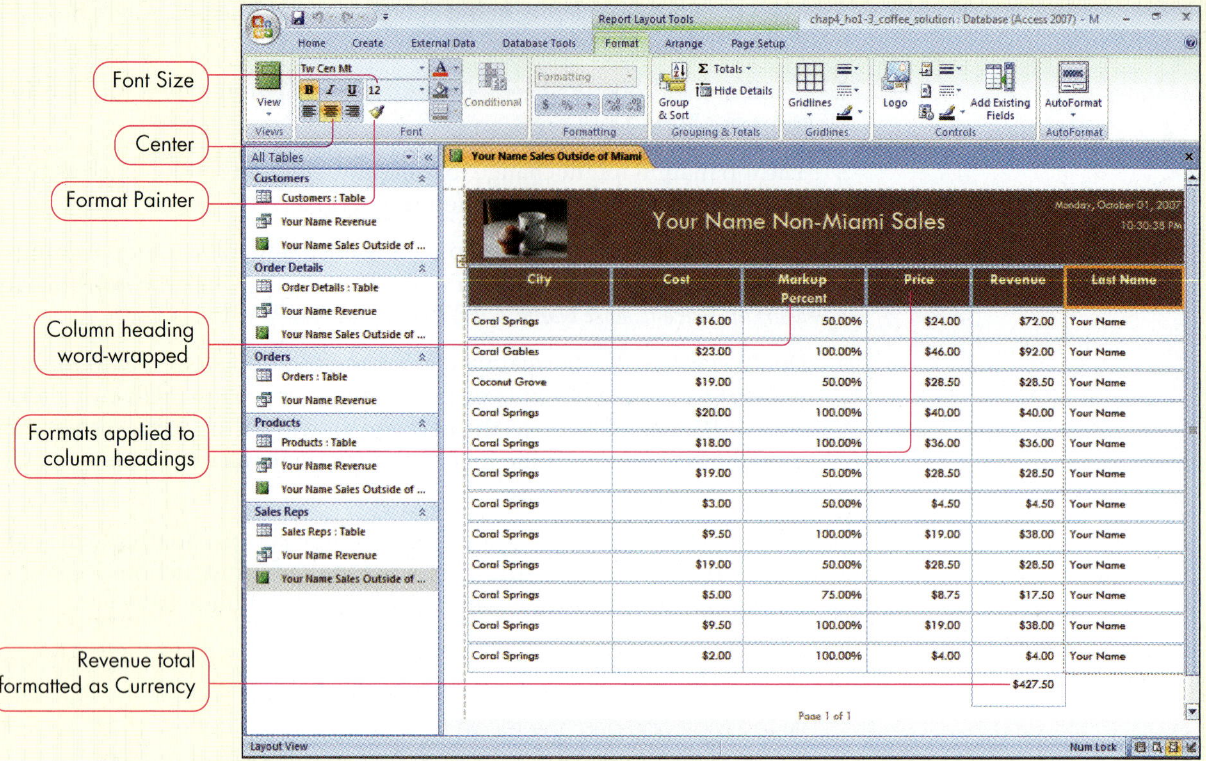

Figure 4.12 The Complete Single-Page Report

TIP Report Column Headings

If captions exist for fields in the table's Design view, the captions appear as the report column headings. The Your Name Sales Outside of Miami report is based on the Your Name Revenue query, which is based on several tables including the Products table. The Products table contains the MarkupPercent field, which includes the caption Markup Percent. Therefore, the Markup Percent caption is used for the column heading in the report.

If captions do not exist, the field names appear as the report column headings. In this situation, you need to edit the report column headings by inserting spaces between words. You will experience this method in step 5 of Hands-On Exercise 3. In that exercise, the report references the LastName field, but that field does not have a caption. Therefore, you will have to add a space to make the report's column heading look like Last Name.

The Anatomy of a Report

You have produced reasonable, sophisticated output. Look at the report design depicted in Figure 4.13. It, too, contains summary statistics but on multiple levels. The desired layout contains indents to visually classify the differing elements. The finished report will likely require several pages. It would be much easier to read if the headings repeated at the start of each new page. Access can accomplish all of this, and more.

In this section, you will learn more about a report's sections and controls. You will also learn how to group an Access report into nested sections.

Identifying Report Elements, Sections, and Controls

Access divides all reports into sections, although you only see the sectional boundaries when you display the report in Design view. You need to become familiar with the sectional areas so that you can control report output completely. For example, if you place an instruction to add field values together in the detail section, the resulting calculation will duplicate each record's value for that field. The field in the detail section contains a single value from a single record.

Understand Sectional Divisions

The ***detail section*** repeats once for each record in the underlying record source.

The ***report header section*** prints once at the beginning of each report.

The ***report footer section*** prints once at the conclusion of each report.

The ***group header section(s)*** appear once at the start of each new grouping level in the report.

The ***group footer section(s)*** appear at the end of each grouping level.

The ***detail section*** repeats once for each record in the underlying record source. If you copied the calculation and placed it in a report header or footer, the result would display the sum of all that field's values for the entire report. The ***report header section*** prints once at the beginning of each report. The ***report footer section*** prints once at the conclusion of each report. Should you find all the section bars and little boxes confusing, you still must learn something about them to accurately produce the output you desire. You will begin by learning about the section bars—the sectional boundaries.

In Figure 4.13, each blue section bar marks the upper boundary of a report area. The top bar denotes the upper boundary of the report header. The bottom bar displays the top boundary of the report's footer. The gray, grid-patterned area beneath the bars shows the space allotted to that element. Notice that the report has no space allocated to the report footer. You may change the space between areas by moving your mouse over the bottom of a bar. When the pointer shape changes to a double-headed arrow, click and drag to move the boundary. Use this method if you decide to add a footer to the report. A gray, grid-patterned work space appears as your mouse drags down. If you expand or contract the space allotment for a middle sectional boundary, the lower boundaries all move also. The ***group header section(s)*** appear once at the start of each new grouping level in the report. The ***group footer section(s)*** appear at the end of each grouping level.

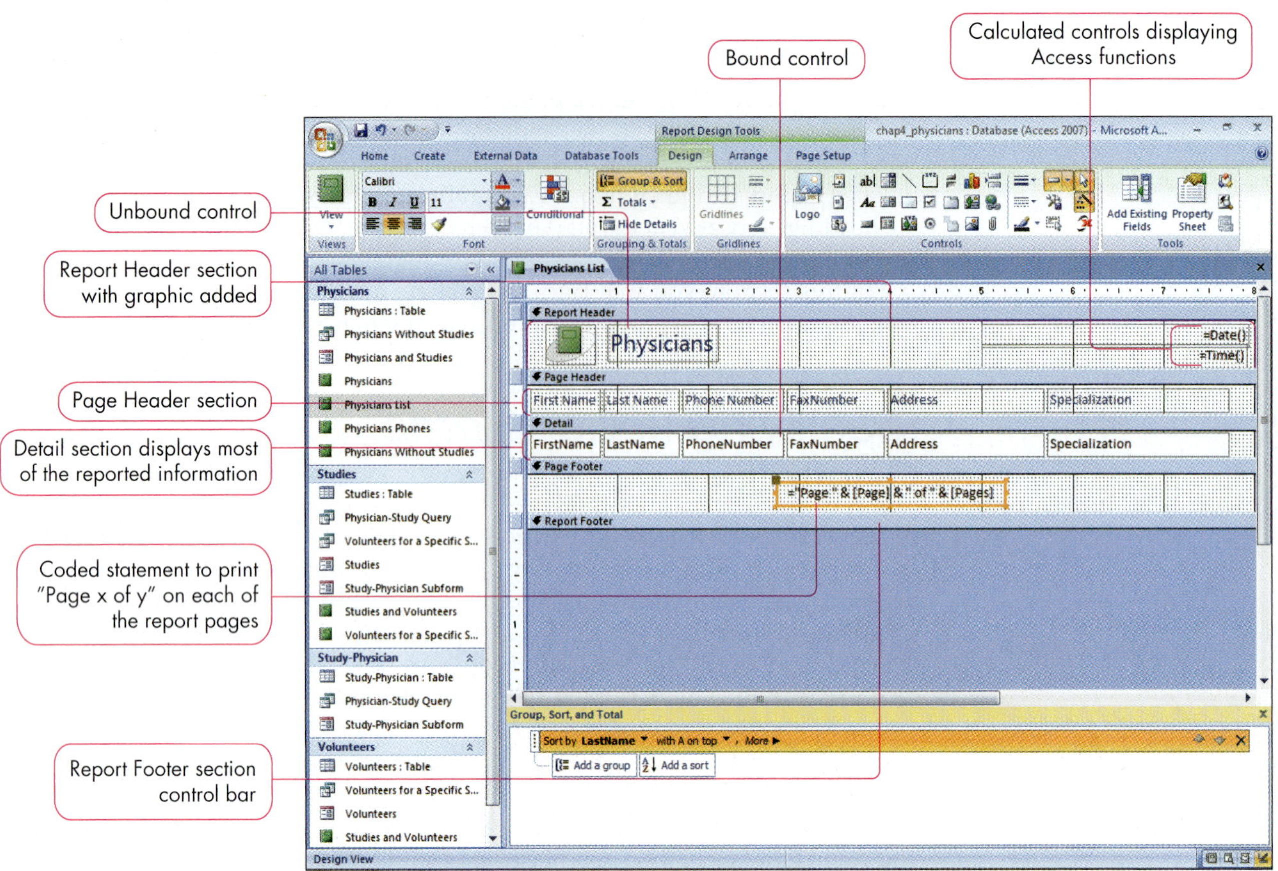

Figure 4.13 Reports Shown in Design View Do Not Display Record Values

Page headers and ***page footers*** appear once for each page in the report at the top and bottom of the pages.

If you decide that the allotted space for a particular section is not needed, you may reposition the top of the next sectional boundary so that the boundary bars touch. The element will remain in the report's design but will consume no space on the printed output and will not show in any other report view. Use the page header section to repeat column headings on the top of each new page. You will place information like page numbers in the page footer. ***Page headers*** and ***page footers*** appear once for each page in the report at the top and bottom of the report's pages, respectively.

All reports contain several different sections; see the reference page for more information about their placement and usage.

Report Tools, Location, and Usage | Reference

Design Element	Location	Frequency	Usage	Required
Report Header	Top of the report	Once	Think of the report header as the title page. It includes information like the organization's name, the report's name, and the run date.	Yes
Page Header	Top of each page	One per page	Page headers generally contain the column headings. In a multi-page report, the labels repeat at the top of each page to provide clarity	Yes
Group Header	At the start of each new group	One at the start of each new group (up to 10)	This element begins and identifies each new group. It generally contains the group name, i.e. in a report grouped by state, the state name would be the header. Any aggregating functions in a group header will summarize the group records, e.g., a SUM function will add all of the record values within the group.	No
Detail	Middle	Once per record reported	This element is repeated once for each selected record in the data source. If there were 500 records in the data source for the report, the report would have 500 detail lines. In a grouped report there may be multiple detail sections—one per group. Often, you omit the detail section entirely. You might show state total without population information showing the population per county. You might do this even when the state population was calculated by adding the county figures.	No
Group Footer	At the end of each group	Once at the end of each group (up to 10)	This element generally repeats the group name, e.g., in a report grouped by state, the state name would repeat in the footer along with a descriptor of aggregating information. An annual sales report might group by month, and one group's footer may display the Total Revenue in May. Any aggregating functions in a group's footer will summarize the group records, e.g., a SUM function will add all of the record values within the group.	No
Page Footer	Bottom of the page	Once per page in the report	Use this feature to print page numbers, page summary statistics, contact information, or report preparation/run date.	Yes, but it need not contain any data
Report Footer	End of the report	One per report	Use this feature to print grand totals or other summary information for entire project. Often the date, authorship, or contact information displays here.	Yes

TIP Report Footer Placement

In Design view, the report footer section displays below the page footer section. However, all other views and the printed output position the report footer above the page footer. Although this effect can be disconcerting the first time you notice it, it makes good sense. It ensures that the page numbers and other page footer items print in the same position on the last page of the report as on other report pages.

Work with Controls

Use ***controls*** to position, display, format, and calculate the report data.

Bound controls enable you to pull information from the underlying table or query data.

Unbound controls do not have any record source for their contents.

A ***calculated control*** uses an expression as opposed to a record value as its data source.

The position and instructions about what to do with the data once retrieved from the table or query come through the use of controls (the little boxes in Design view). You use ***controls*** to position, display, format, and calculate the report data. Access reports use different types of controls for different purposes.

You use ***bound controls*** most frequently in preparing an Access report. These controls enable you to pull information from the underlying table or query data. Like the source data, the value of a bound control may be text, dates, numbers, pictures, graphs, or Yes/No values. The latter typically displays as a check box. The binding means that the control inherits most properties—size, formatting, and relationships—from the source table. For example, a text box may display a product's price in currency format. It is bound (tied) to the UnitPrice field in the Products table, which is also set to currency format. Most bound controls display with two small boxes in the report's Design view. The left box is the control's label, the right box or text box displays the record value. A bound control's label automatically comes from the field name or caption (if one exists).

Unbound controls do not have any record source for their contents. The values contained there exist only in the report and nowhere else in the database. You use them to display information (the report's title), cosmetic elements (borders or lines to visually separate report sections), boxes, and pictures.

A ***calculated control*** uses an expression as opposed to a record value as its data source. The expression usually is bound to the record values of the fields referenced. A report expression, like a query expression, combines field names, operators, constants, and functions to instruct Access on how to perform a calculation. For example, you might use an expression to calculate a discounted price in a sales report. For example:

=[UnitPrice] * (1-[Discount] * [Quantity])

This expression would likely retrieve the UnitPrice data from the Products table, and the Discount and Quantity values from the Order Details table if you are using a retail store database that contains records for products, including unit price, selling price, and quantity.

Adding Grouping Levels in Layout View

Access provides you with several methods of creating data summaries.

- Create a Totals query by specifying a group by field and the field or fields to summarize.
- Create a grouped report using the Layout view's Sorting and Grouping tool.
- Create a grouped report using the Report Wizard and specifying the group layers within the Wizard.

Reports provide you with the same power as a Totals query and provide the added advantage of enhanced appearance. This section explores grouping and sorting in the Layout view method. The next section introduces you to the Report Wizard.

Engage the Group & Sort Tool

Open the report in Layout view. The report shown in Figure 4.14 contains over 2,000 records. Imagine that you must use this data to make decisions about your firm's operations. You would not easily identify trends and patterns by examining 50 or more printed pages. This data needs to be summarized. Begin summarizing by clicking Group & Sort in the Grouping & Totals group on the Format tab. The Group, Sort, and Total pane displays in the bottom of the report.

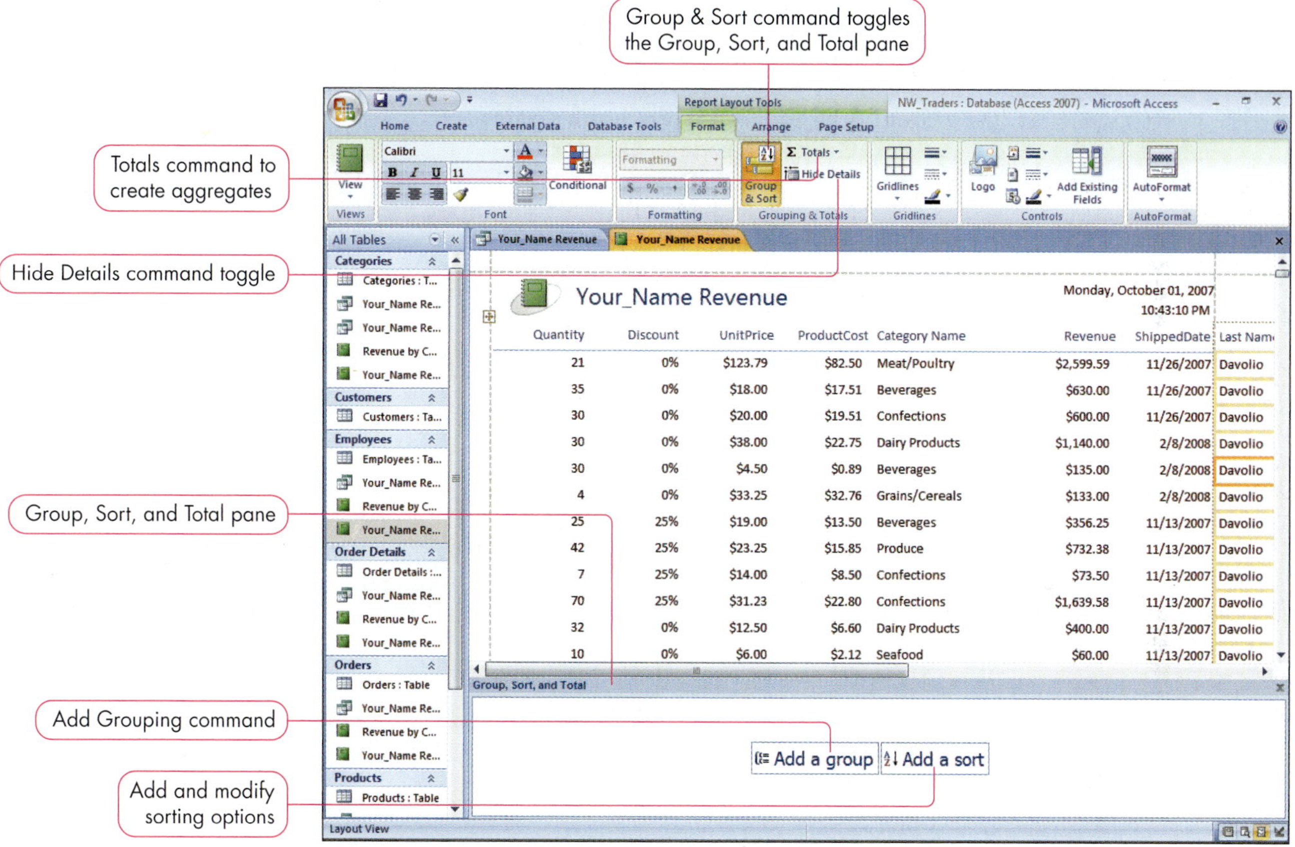

Figure 4.14 Display the Group, Sort, and Total Pane

Select the Primary Grouping Field

Nested groups provide a power-layering tool to organize information.

You may nest groups in different levels—up to 10. ***Nested groups*** provide a powerful layering tool to organize information. In this report, you need the sales figures summarized by the categories of products offered. Once created, each group contains introductory and summary information as well as the record values. Generally the group header provides identification information, for example the name of the category. You use the group footer to present summary information for the group. Figure 4.15 depicts the Add a Group command engaged with the CategoryName field selected as the primary grouping level.

After you establish the primary group, you may add additional levels. This feature works much like an outline. Suppose you needed a sales report grouped by salesperson and then by quarter. Each successive grouping layer gets tucked between the header and footer of the previous layer.

Group 1 Header — Joe Adams' Sales
Group 2 Header—Quarter 1
Many Rows of Details for Quarter 1
Group 2 Footer—Quarter 1 Summary

Group 2 Header—Quarter 2
Many Rows of Details for Quarter 2
Group 2 Footer—Quarter 2 Summary

Group 2 Header—Quarter 3
Many Rows of Details for Quarter 3
Group 2 Footer—Quarter 3 Summary

Group 2 Header—Quarter 4
Many Rows of Details for Quarter 4
Group 2 Footer—Quarter 4 Summary
Group 1 Footer—Joe Adams' Sales Totals

Group 1 Header—Brenda Smith's Sales
Group 2 Header—Quarter 1
Many Rows of Details for Quarter 1
Group 2 Footer—Quarter 1 Summary
The pattern repeats.

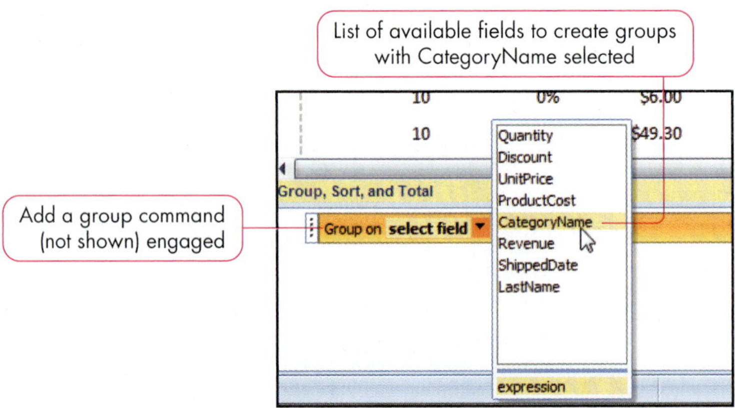

Figure 4.15 Select a Primary Grouping Level

Hide or Display Details

> . . . the less detail and more summarizing information included, the more useful the report.

You must decide if the details—the values stored in each record that report used as a source—need to be displayed in the report. Many reports only display data summaries. How you decide to display details will depend on how the report will be used. Most Access report developers follow the general rule that the less detail and more summarizing information included, the more useful the report. Access makes it easy for you to add and remove detail levels. If you omit the detail and later discover that you need it, you can easily add it back. Engage the Hide Detail command to hide or display report details (see Figure 4.16).

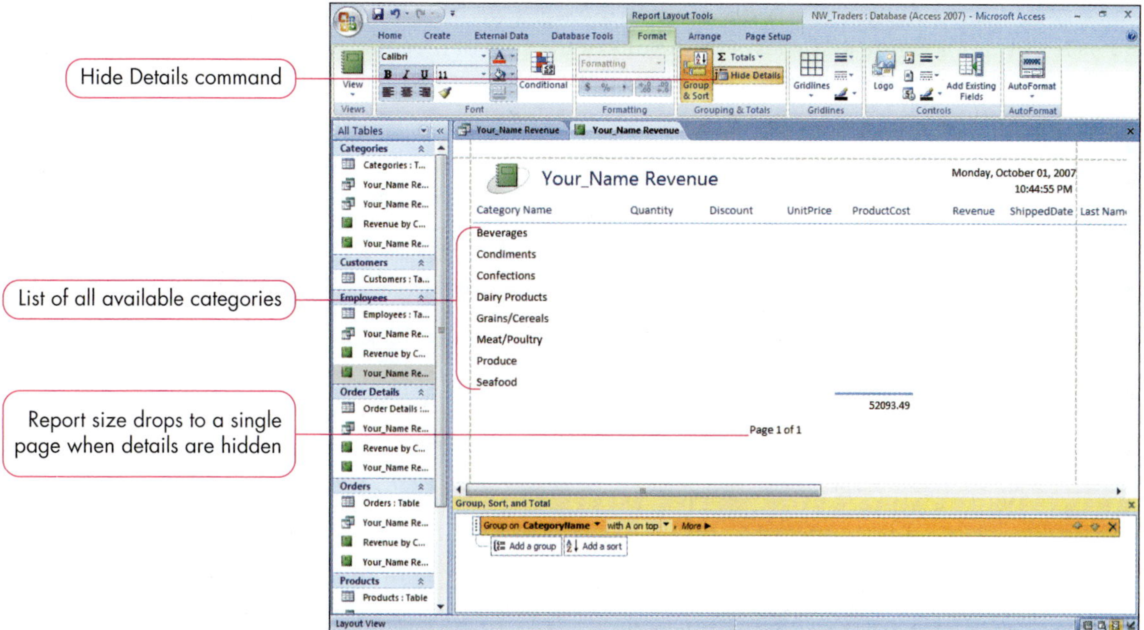

Figure 4.16 Summary Report with Details Hidden

Calculate Summary Statistics

The report in Figure 4.17 displays a list of the names of the categories of merchandise sold by the firm. The Totals command in the Grouping & Totals group helps you summarize data. First select the control label for the data you want summarized. Then click Totals and select the necessary aggregating function from the drop-down list.

Decision-makers may wish to examine the same data using different aggregating functions to answer different questions. For example, a sum of all revenue generated by each product category will tell the manager important total sales information. Changing the report to display the maximum revenue will provide the decision-maker with information about which products generated the largest revenue. After you establish the grouping levels, Access makes it easy for you to examine the output in a variety of ways.

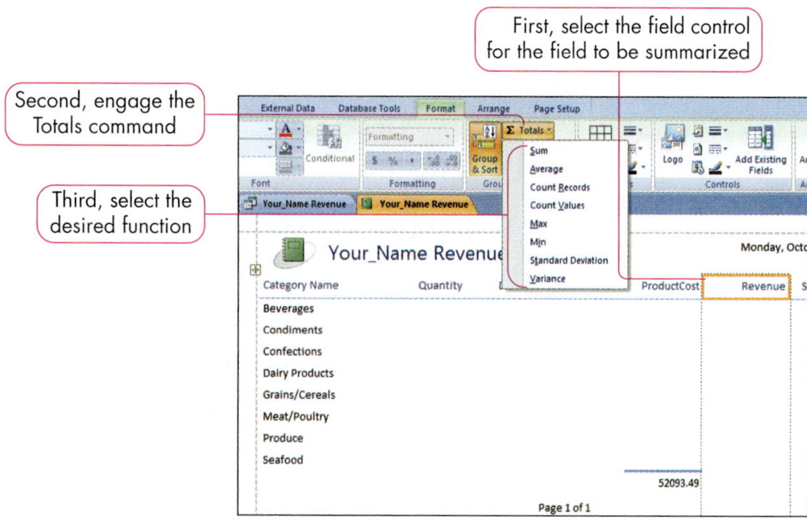

Figure 4.17 Creating a Sum of the Revenue Field

You may add summary values to additional fields using the same process. Figure 4.18 shows the results of the sum of revenue and the needed setup to calculate an average of the discounts provided customers in each product category.

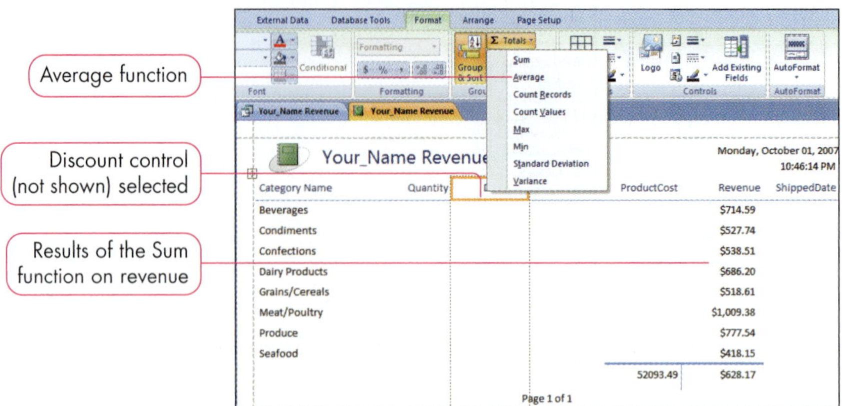

Figure 4.18 Creating an Average of the Discount Field

Add Additional Grouping Levels

You decide that having the report grouped by category is useful, but you also want to know who sells each category's products. You can add additional grouping levels to an existing report in Layout view by selecting the control that you need to group on and then clicking the Add a Group command in the Group, Sort, and Total pane. In the report displayed in Figure 4.19, you would first select the control for LastName field and then click the Add a group command. The figure displays the results of adding an additional grouping level to the report. The More command controlling the Category name group expands when selected, granting you access to additional features. The figure displays the settings necessary to display the totals (averages) for the categories below the salesperson totals.

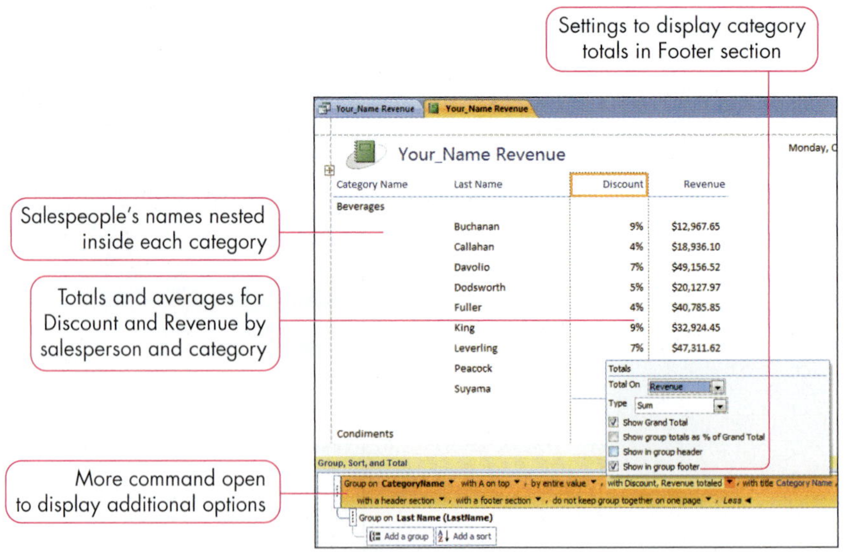

Figure 4.19 Nested Group Report with Totals Moved to Footer

Sort a Report

While working in the Layout view, you can interact with the sort order of the report's fields. Figure 4.20 shows a report with two sorting levels applied. The primary sort is the area of specialization. The secondary sort is by the physician's last name. This order groups the cardiologists together with Clark preceding Davis in the alphabetical listing.

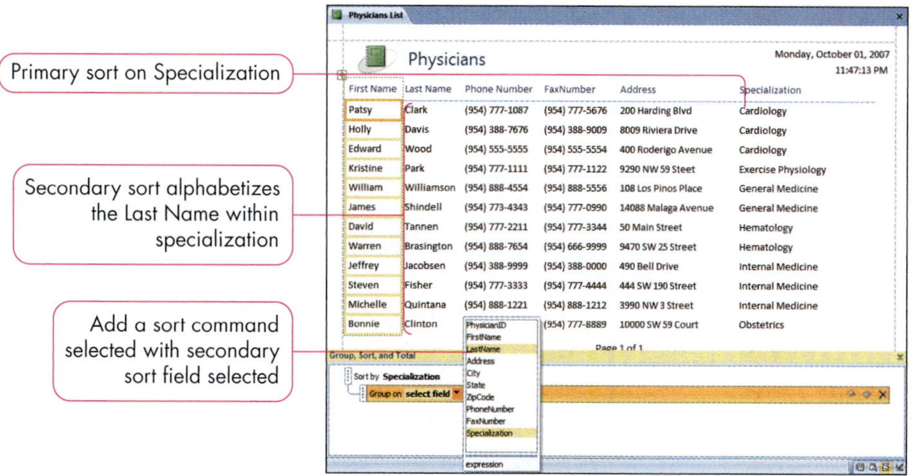

Figure 4.20 Sorted Report

Adding Fields to a Report

It is possible to omit a necessary field when designing a report. Even if a report has no errors, data needs change with time. You may need to add a new field to an existing report. Access provides an easy way to do that.

The ***Field List pane*** displays a list of all of the tables and fields in the database.

Open the report in Layout view. Activate the Format tab. Click Add Existing Fields in the Controls group. The Field List pane opens on the right side of the screen. The ***Field List pane*** displays a list of all of the tables and fields in the database. Once you locate the needed field in the Field List pane, drag and drop it on the report in the position that you want it to occupy. (Alternatively, you can double-click it.) Access creates the needed control to hold the new field, for example, a text box, and then binds the field to the newly created control (see Figure 4.21). Occasionally, you might want a different control type than the one Access creates for you. You may edit the newly created control's properties to get exactly the control you want. But, you cannot use Layout view to do so. You cannot change the control type property in Layout view. This change must be accomplished in Design view. Of course, you may only specify a control that is appropriate to that data type. For example, a Yes/No field might display as a check box, but you would rather have the words, Yes or No, display.

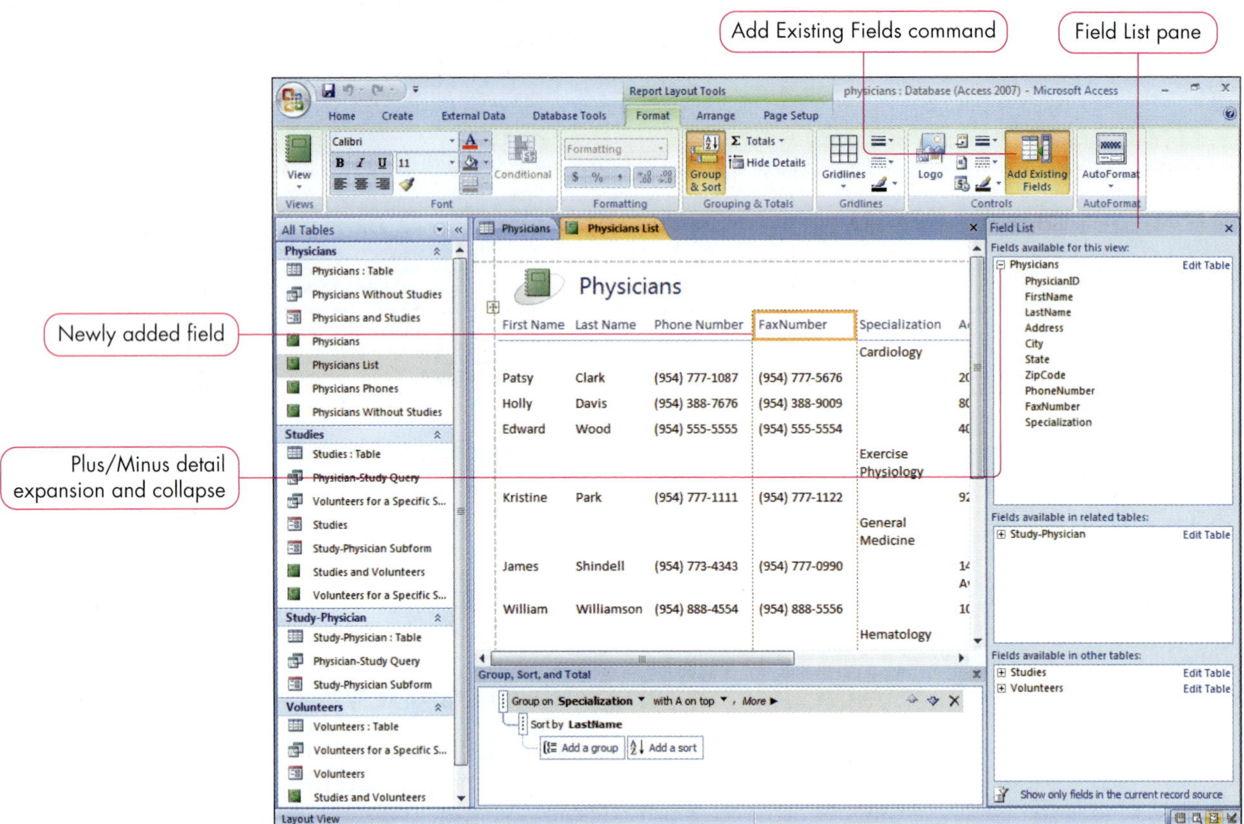

Figure 4.21 Sorted Report

In the next hands-on exercise, you will create a report, add sorting and grouping to refine the content, work with data aggregates, and add a new field to the report.

Hands-On Exercises

2 | Create, Sort, Edit, Nest, and Remove Groups from Reports

Skills covered: 1. Sort a Report **2.** Create a Grouped Report and Sort It. **3.** Add Additional Grouping Levels and Calculate Summary Statistics **4.** Remove Grouping Levels **5.** Reorder Grouping Levels

Step 1
Sort a Report

Refer to Figure 4.22 as you complete Step 1.

a. Open the *chap4_ho1-3_coffee_solution* file if necessary, click **Options** on the Security Warning toolbar, click the **Enable this content option** in the Microsoft Office Security Options dialog box, and click **OK**.

TROUBLESHOOTING: If you create unrecoverable errors while completing this hands-on exercise, you can delete the *chap4_ho1-3_coffee_solution* file, copy the *chap4_ho1_coffee_solution* backup database you created at the end of the first hands-on exercise, and open the copy of the backup database to start the second hands-on exercise again.

b. Open the **Your Name Revenue query** in Datasheet view. Click the **Create tab** and click **Report**.

c. Click **Group & Sort** in the Grouping & Totals group to turn on the Group, Sort, and Total pane at the bottom of the screen.

TROUBLESHOOTING: The Group & Sort command is a toggle. If you do not see the Group, Sort, and Total pane, click the Group & Sort command again. It may have been on, and you turned it off.

d. Click **Add a sort** in the Group, Sort, and Total pane.

A list box opens displaying the names of all the reports fields.

e. Click **LastName** from the list and select it.

Scroll through the list to see two names: Lockley and your name. If your name comes before Lockley alphabetically, your sales are reported first. If your name comes after Lockley alphabetically, Lockley's sales will be first. In the next step, you will sort the list so that your name is on the top—ascending or descending, depending on what letter your name begins with.

f. Find the **Sort with A on top drop-down arrow** in the Group, Sort, and Total pane. Click it to reveal two choices—with A on top and with Z on top. Click the choice that will position your name at the top of the list.

If your name is not on top, sort again, and select the other option.

g. Click the **Office Button**, choose **Save As**, and type **Sales by Employee and City**. Click **OK**.

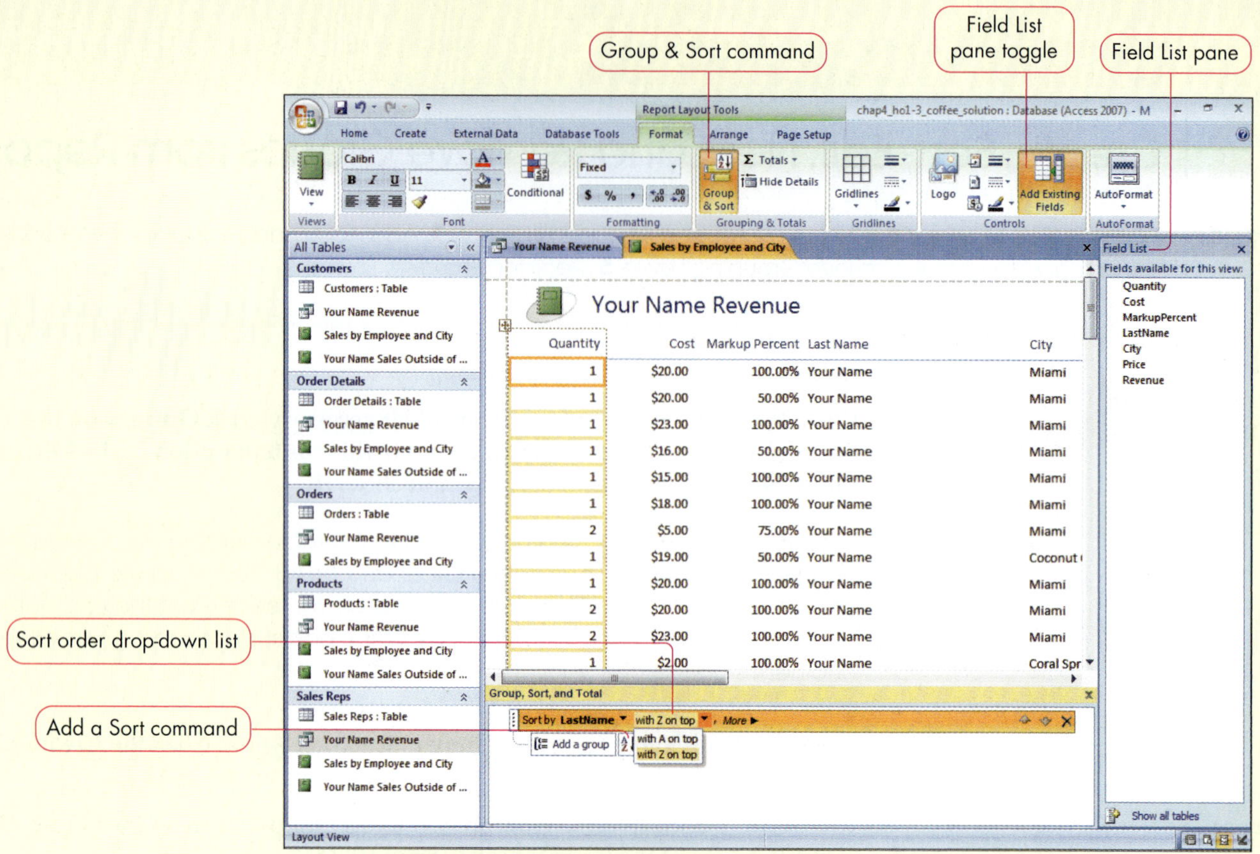

Figure 4.22 Correctly Sorted Report

Step 2
Create a Grouped Report and Sort It

Refer to Figure 4.23 as you complete Step 2.

a. Click **Add a group** in the Group, Sort, and Total pane.

A list box pops up asking you to select the field name that you want to group by.

b. Select the **LastName** field in the list box.

TROUBLESHOOTING: If your screen does not look like Figure 4.23, it may be because you selected a different group by value. Click close on the gold Group on LastName bar in the Group, Sort, and Total pane to remove the incorrect grouping. Then rework Steps 2a and 2b.

c. Scroll right until you can see the label control box for the **Revenue** field. (It is blue.) Click to select it.

d. Click the **Format tab** and click **Totals** in the Grouping & Totals group.

A drop-down list providing function options appears.

e. Click **Sum**.

f. Save the report.

A sum has been added to the Revenue field after each group. You probably cannot see it because it is scrolled off-screen. Use the scrollbar to see that your revenue is 1599.125.

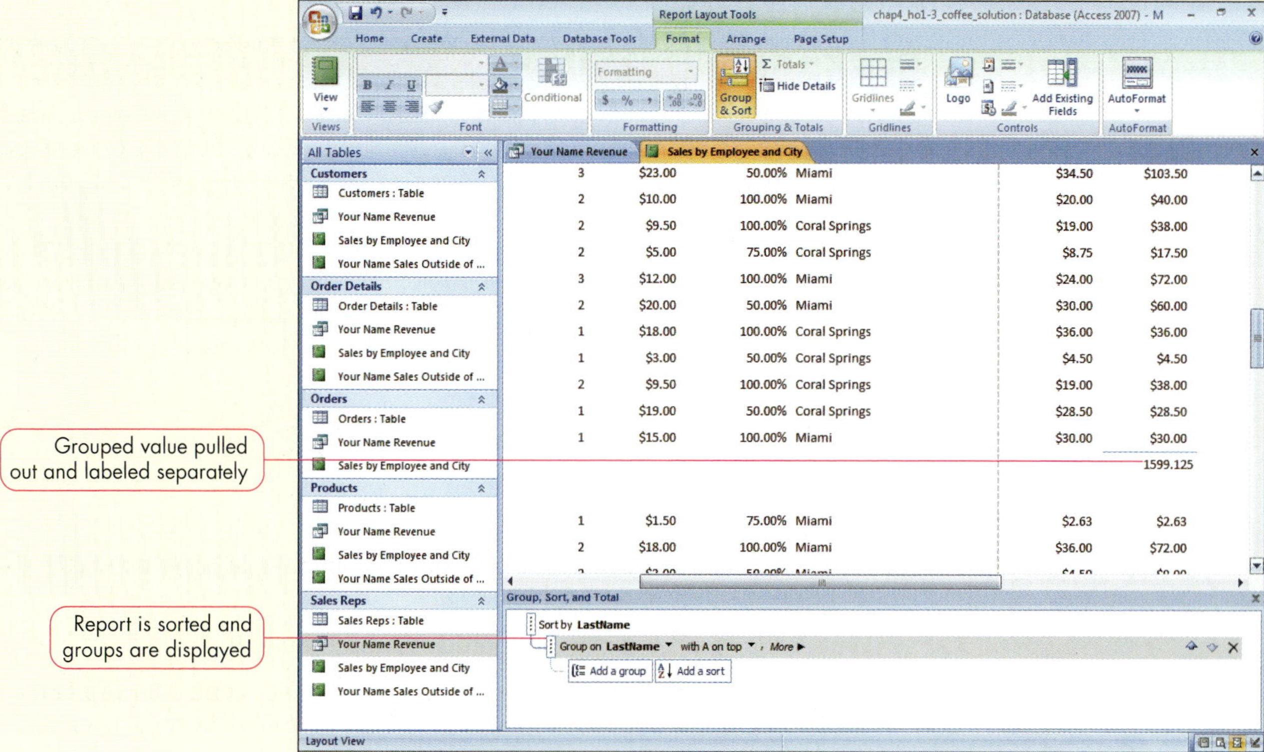
Grouped value pulled out and labeled separately
Report is sorted and groups are displayed

Figure 4.23 Correctly Sorted Report with Primary Group

Step 3
Add Additional Grouping Levels and Calculate Summary Statistics

Refer to Figure 4.24 as you complete Step 3.

a. Ensure that you are still in Layout view. Click **Add a group** in the Group, Sort, and Total pane.

b. Scroll left to locate and select the **City** field in the Field List box.

   The Primary grouping level is still the salesperson's last name. Now the customer's city is grouped together nested inside the LastName field. During this period, you sold one order to a customer in Coconut Grove, once to a customer in Coral Gables, 10 orders to customers in Coral Springs, and the rest of your orders came from Miami-based customers. You decide to create summary statistics by city and salesperson to analyze the sales information.

c. Click the **Cost** label to select it. Click **Totals** in the Grouping & Totals group. Select **Average** from the function list.

   Scroll down until you see the average cost for the orders to Coral Springs displayed. You will see the average cost of an order from a Coral Springs customer was only $12.10, while the average costs of orders to Coral Gables and Coconut Grove were much higher.

d. Scroll up and click the **City** label to select it. Click **Totals** in the Grouping & Totals group. Select **Count Records** from the function list.

   The City field is defined as a text field. Access presents different functions depending on whether the field contains text or numbers.

TIP Counting Records

If you create a report in Layout view and need to count the number of records, be sure to select a field that contains a non-null value for each record. If a report contained 20 records and you instructed Access to count a field that contained two null values, the resulting count would display 18. The missing values would not be included in the count. An easy way to fix this situation is to count only fields that have their Required property set to Yes. Alternatively, you can edit the field's control property. Select the text box containing the Count value, right-click, and select Properties. Click the Data tab. In the Control Source box, select and delete the expression and type =count(*).

e. Scroll to the last of the records from your customers (that is just above the name of the other salesperson, Lockley).

   You see the number of records of orders sold by you—39.

f. Press **Ctrl+Home** to return to the top of the report. Select the **Markup Percent** label. Click **Totals** in the Grouping & Totals group. Select **Average** from the function list.

g. Scroll to the right. Select the **Price** label. Click the **Totals** command in the Grouping & Totals group. Select **Average** from the function list. Format as currency.

   Like the Cost field, the Price field records a per-unit cost, so it does not make sense to sum it.

h. Scroll to the right. Select the **Revenue** label. Click **Totals** in the Grouping & Totals group. Select **Sum** from the function list. Check to make sure the value is formatted as currency.

   TROUBLESHOOTING: A group summary statistic should automatically inherit its formatting properties from the field's format. Occasionally the group total or average calculates correctly, but it is incorrectly formatted. To correct the format, right-click the incorrectly formatted value in the Layout view of the report and select Properties from the shortcut menu. Set the Format property to the correct value, e.g., currency, and close the Property Sheet. This action forces a format correction.

i. Narrow the first two columns so that the report fits on one page horizontally. Refer to Hands-On Exercise 1, Step 3e, if you do not remember how to do this step.

j. Save the report.

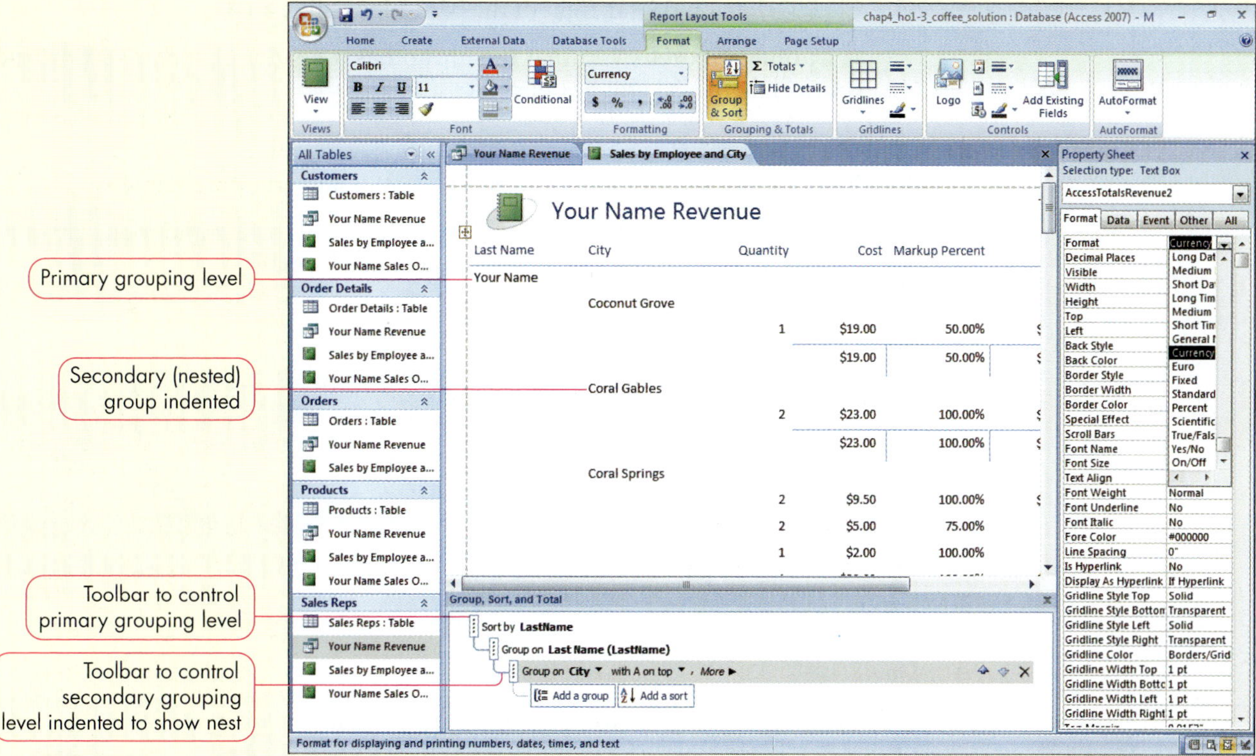

Figure 4.24 Report with Two Grouping Levels Added

Step 4
Remove Grouping Levels

Refer to Figure 4.25 as you complete Step 4.

a. Save and close the Sales by Employee and City report.

You need practice deleting grouping levels, but you need to preserve the work from Step 3. You will copy the report and delete the group levels in the copy.

b. Right-click the **Sales by Employee and City report** in the Navigation Pane. Select **Copy** from the shortcut menu. Move your mouse to a white space in the Navigation Pane, right-click, and select **Paste**.

c. Name the copy **Sales by Employee**. Click **OK**.

d. Move your mouse to a white space in the Navigation Pane. (Do this a second time.) Right-click and select **Paste**.

e. Name the copy **Sales by City**.

TROUBLESHOOTING: If your monitor resolution is set low, you may have trouble finding white space in which to paste. This file was set to display tables and related objects in the Navigation Pane. That view repeats multi-table query and report names. A view that uses less space is the Objects view. Click the Navigation Pane title bar and select Object Type. That should free up some white space for you to paste the copied report. After your copied report is pasted and renamed, switch back to the Tables and Related Views.

f. Open the **Sales by Employee report** in Layout view.

g. Click **Group & Sort** in the Grouping & Totals group on the Format tab to display the Group, Sort, and Total pane (if necessary).

h. Click the **Group on City bar** to select it.

The entire bar turns gold when selected.

i. Click **Delete** on the far right of the bar (it looks like an X).

   A warning box tells you that the group has a header or footer section and the controls there also will be deleted.

j. Click **Yes**.

   The City grouping disappears, but the LastName grouping remains.

k. Check to make sure the formats of the group totals and grand totals are appropriately formatted. If not, apply the **Currency** format.

l. Click **Save**. Close your report.

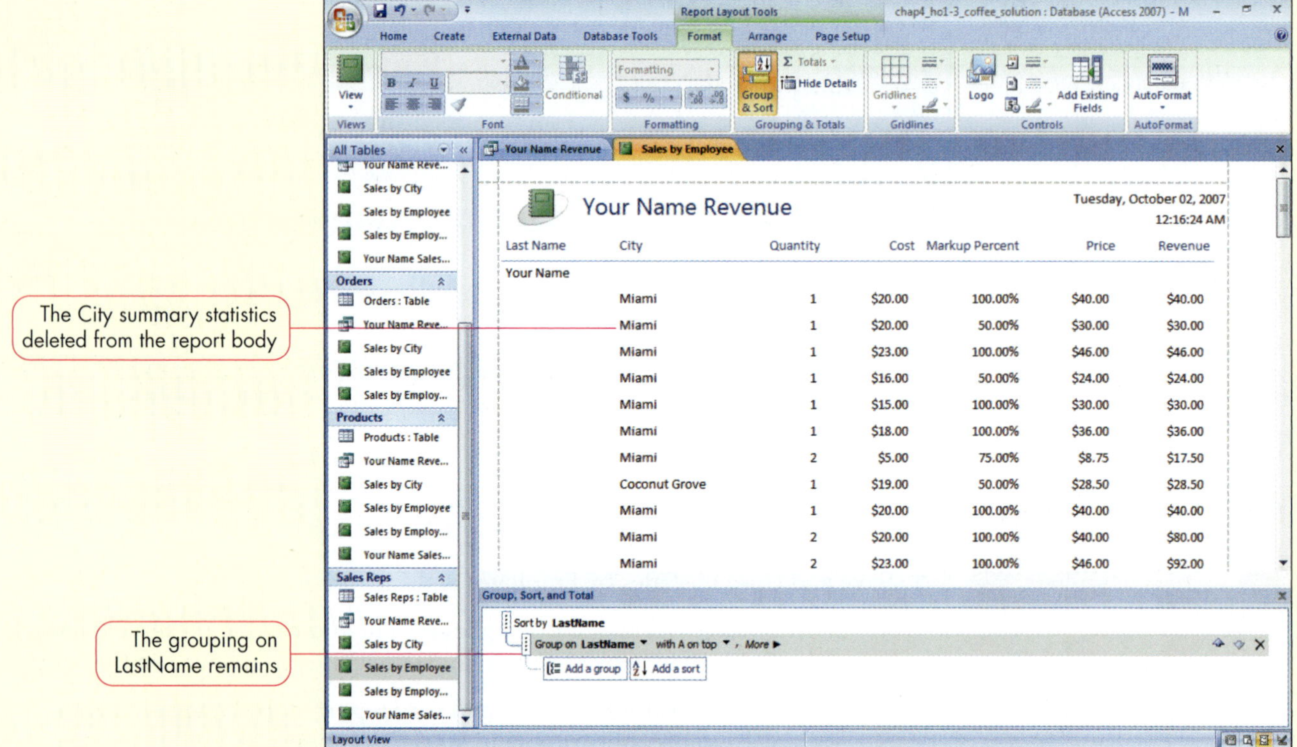

The City summary statistics deleted from the report body
The grouping on LastName remains

Figure 4.25 Sales by Employee

Step 5 Reorder Grouping Levels

Refer to Figure 4.26 as you complete Step 5.

a. Open the **Sales by City report** in Layout view.

   You are going to change the order of the grouping fields so that the primary group will be the City and the secondary group the last name.

b. Click **Group & Sort** in the Grouping & Totals group on the Format tab to display the grouping pane (if necessary).

c. Click the **Group on LastName bar** in the Group, Sort, and Total pane to select it.

d. Click the **down arrow** in the right side of the Group on LastName bar one time.

   You might have expected that the report would now be grouped by city and then by your sales and Lockley's sales grouped within each city. Your sales are together in the top of the report, Lockley's in the bottom of the report. Examine the grouping window more carefully. There is a sort in effect. It receives the top priority. So the employee sales will not group in each city.

e. Click the **Sort by LastName bar** to select it.

f. Click **Delete** on the right of the Sort by LastName bar.

When you delete the sort, the grouping prioritization changes; now, the employees are sorted within the cities as expected.

g. Check to make sure the formats of the group totals and grand totals are appropriately formatted. If not, apply the **Currency** format.

h. Click the text box containing the report title, *Your Name Revenue*. Click it again to edit it. Change the report name to **Your Name City Revenue**. Save the report.

i. Click **Group & Sort** in the Grouping & Totals group on the Format tab.

j. Click the **Office Button**, select **Manage**, and then select **Back Up Database**. Enter the file name **chap4_ho2_coffee_solution** (*note ho2 instead of ho1-3*) and click **Save**.

You just created a backup of the database after completing the second hands-on exercise. The original database *chap4_ho1-3_coffee_solution* remains onscreen. If you ruin the original database as you complete the third hands-on exercise, you can use the backup file you just created.

k. Close the file and exit Access if you do not want to continue with the next exercise at this time.

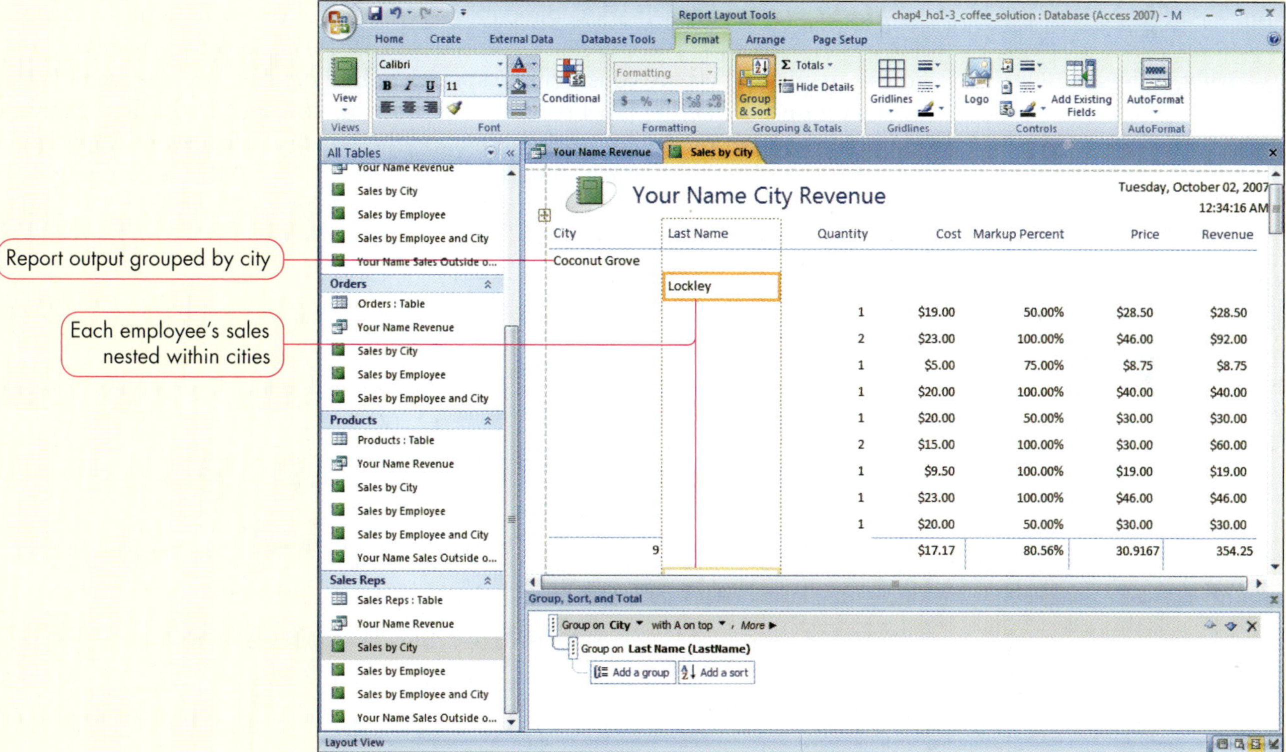

Figure 4.26 The City Report

The Report and Label Wizards

Earlier in this chapter you created a polished, professional report with grouping levels, sorts, and summary statistics by using the Report tool. You edited the report through a GUI interface and immediately saw the effect on the output. You may recall that Access provides four ways of creating a report (see Table 4.1). In this section you will create a report using the Report Wizard and edit it using both the Layout and Design views.

The ***Report Wizard*** asks you questions and then, depending on how you answer, generates the report.

The ***Report Wizard*** asks you questions and then, depending on how you answer, generates the report. Many of the wizard's dialog boxes contain commands that lead you to further levels of options. As you read this section and work through the hands-on exercise, you should explore the additional options and think about how and when you might use them. Access provides so many methods of report generation because Access users require so many differing types of reports. As you gain experience you will learn which tool is most appropriate for your tasks.

If no query exists that assembles the necessary fields for a report, the Report Wizard is probably the best option. It enables you to pull fields from multiple sources relatively easily. Access reports generated by using the Report Wizard sometimes require extensive revision to make them intelligible. Occasionally the necessary revision time greatly exceeds the time needed to assemble the needed fields in a query in order to use the Report tool. You will need to experiment with the differing methods of report generation to discover which works most effectively with your data and computing usage style.

Mailing labels are self-stick, die-cut labels that you print with names, addresses, and postal barcodes.

The ***Label Wizard*** asks you questions and then, depending on how you answer, generates the report formatted to print on mailing labels.

Mailing labels are self-stick, die-cut labels that you print with names, addresses, and postal barcodes. You purchase name-brand labels at an office supply store. In Access, mailing labels are considered a specialized report. You use the ***Label Wizard*** to help produce a mailing label report. In the wizard, you specify the label manufacturer and the label product number shown on the box of labels. For example, Avery 5660 contains 30 individual labels per sheet that are 1″ x 2⅝″. After selecting the label type, you place and format the fields in the label prototype (see Figure 4.27). The finished report is shown in Figure 4.28.

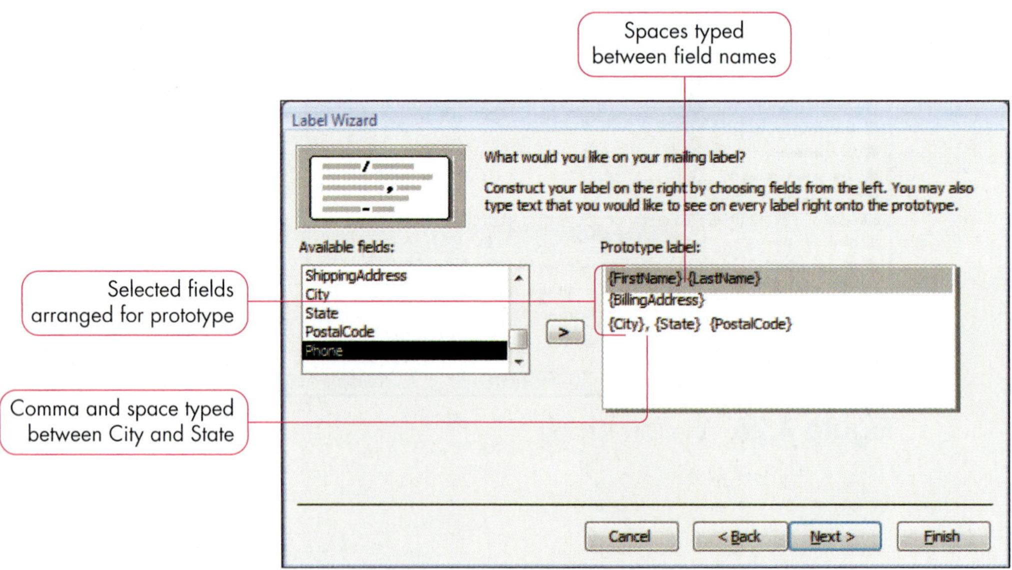

Figure 4.27 Label Prototype

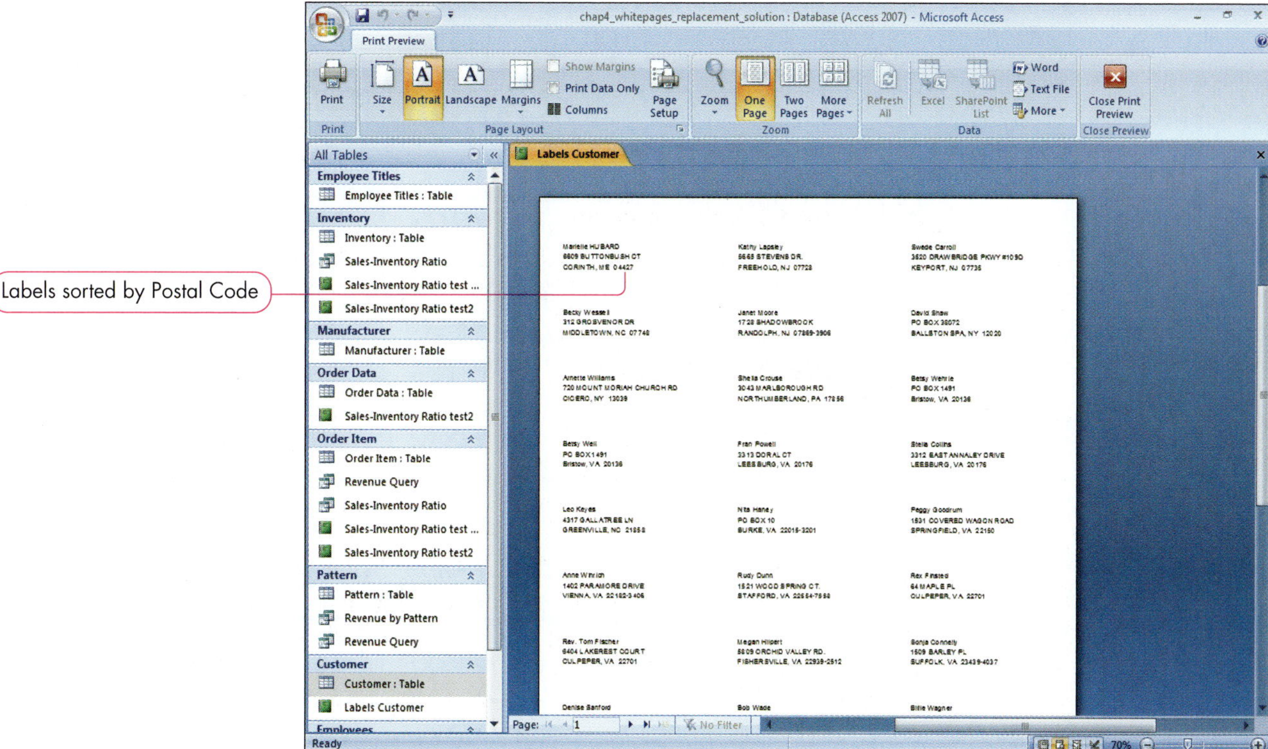

Figure 4.28 Completed Labels

Using the Report Wizard

Even when using a wizard to guide your report formation, you need to pre-plan the desired output. Suppose you needed a monthly sales report that grouped the products by category and provided summary statistics monitoring the average discounts offered to customers and the revenue generated from product sales. This report would require one grouping level and two summary calculations—one for total revenue and the other for average discount rate. Next you need to identify the report's record source. For this illustration you may assume that all necessary records exist in a query. In actual practice, you may need to first create the query assembling the needed records. Some Access users source reports directly from table data. After thinking through the design and record source, you launch the Report Wizard.

Even when using a wizard to guide your report formation, you need to pre-plan the desired output.

Start the Report Wizard

You do not need to have the report record source open to launch the Report Wizard like you do when using the Report tool. You may wish to close any open objects in your database before launching the wizard. Find the Report Wizard on the Create tab in the Reports group. The first dialog box asks you to specify the record source (see Figure 4.29).

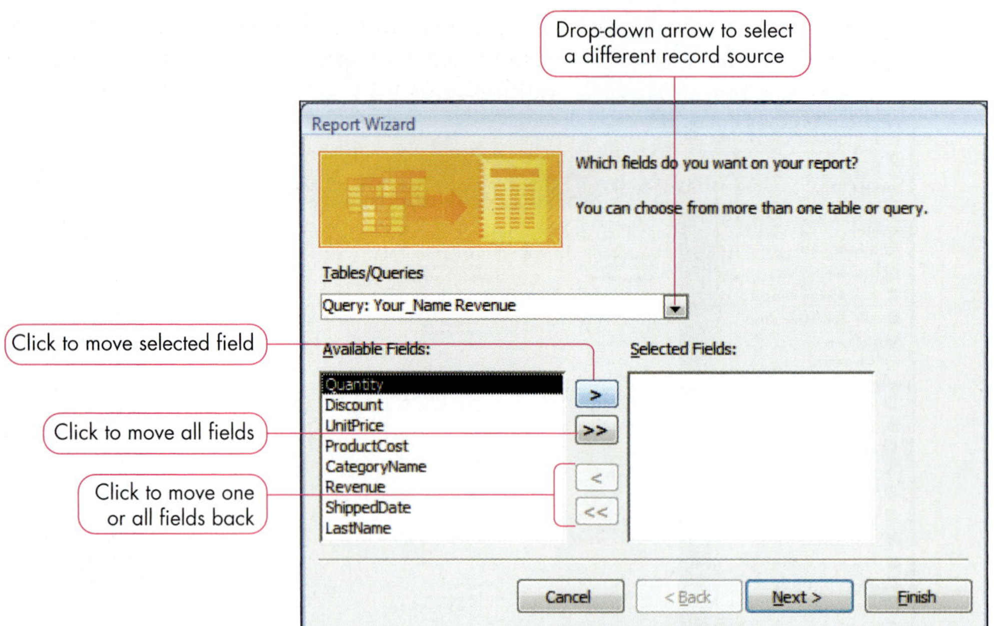

Figure 4.29 Select Records

Group Records

Grouping lets you organize and consolidate your data. You also can calculate aggregating information. In this report you need the data grouped by the CategoryName field, so in the wizard's box under "Do you want to add any grouping levels?" you would identify and double-click the CategoryName field. If you needed additional grouping levels, you would double-click those field names also. The order in which you select the groups dictates the order of nesting in the report (see Figure 4.30). The Priority commands let you change your mind and restructure the nest levels. If you select a date/time field to group by, click Grouping Options to find an interval specification box. Use it to designate the grouping interval, such as week, month, or quarter.

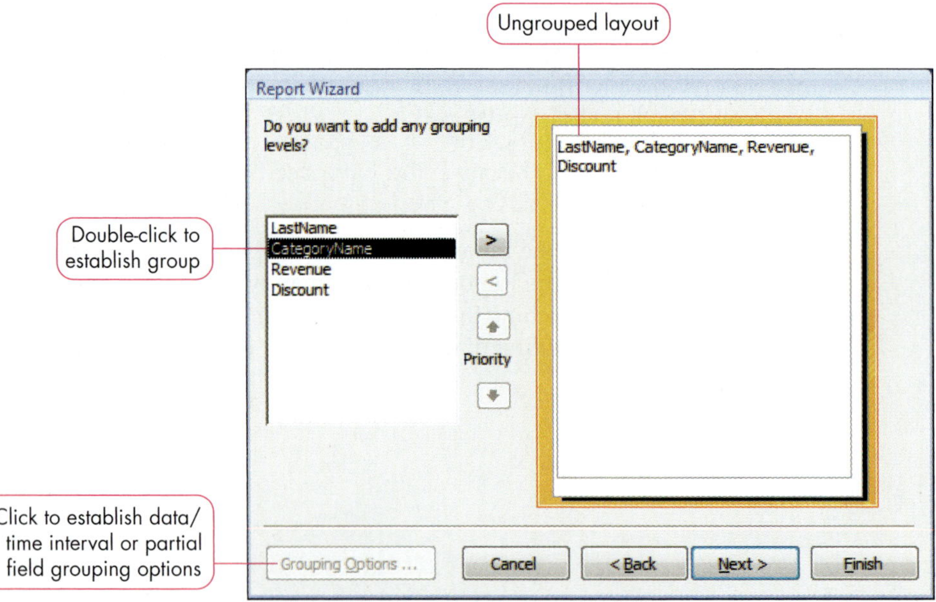

Figure 4.30 Specify Grouping Options

Figure 4.31 shows the grouping options set to group on CategoryName. Once the group is established, the Grouping Options command activates. If the group field was a date/time field, you would establish the interval in the Grouping Intervals dialog box. Because this grouping field is a text field, the intervals displayed contain portions of the field name, i.e. the first two letters. You might use this feature if you were grouping an inventory list and the inventory IDs within a category started with the same letters. For example, FJW123, FJR123, FJB123 might be inventory numbers for the fine jewelry department for watches, rings, and bracelets. If you set the grouping interval option to the two initial letters, you would include the fine jewelry department's entire inventory.

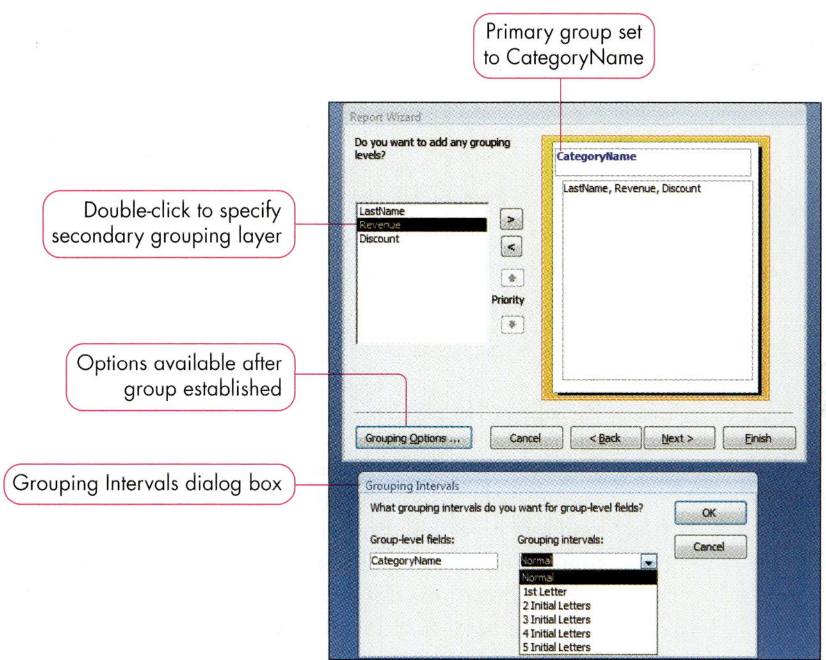

Figure 4.31 Grouping Options Set on Category

Add Sorts and Summary Instructions

The next dialog box asks "What sort order and summary information do you want for detail records?" Notice that the sorts apply only to a detail record. Some reports omit the detail, making the sort order moot. If this were a detail report, you might specify that the details be sorted first by category in ascending order and then by revenue in descending order. Because you have decided to create a summary report, you need to click the Summary Options command. This step takes you to a screen where you may choose summary statistics (sum, average, minimum, and maximum), and whether or not you want the details presented (see Figure 4.32). Clicking either OK or Cancel returns you to the Report Wizard.

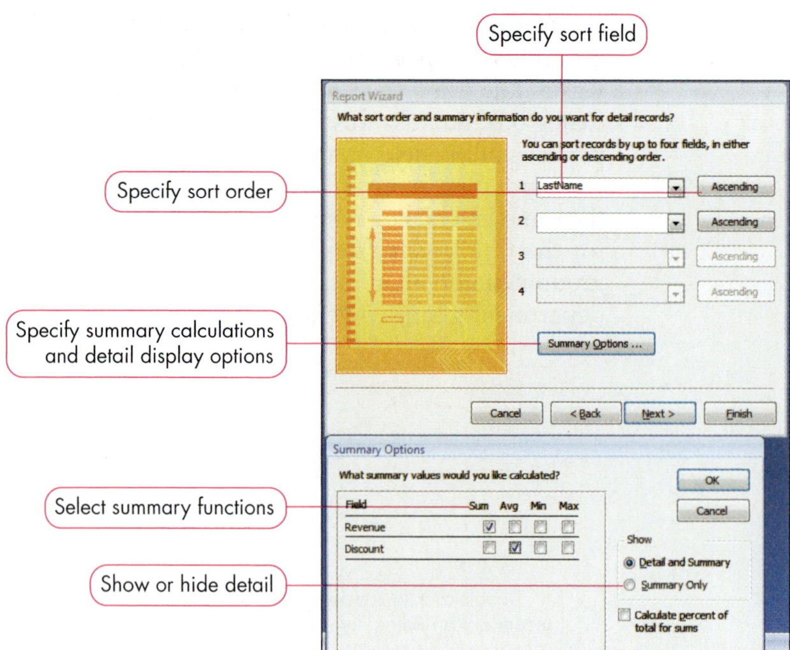

Figure 4.32 Specify Sort Options

Design the Report

The next two dialog boxes control the report's appearance. In the first you select the layout from three options. Clicking an option will give you a general preview in the preview area. The final dialog box offers you options among the AutoFormats available (see Figure 4.33). In actual organizations, the Public Relations and Graphic Communications departments dictate the design of all printed output. The organization will have one template for all internal reports and one or two others for reports generated for external consumption (e.g., an invoice).

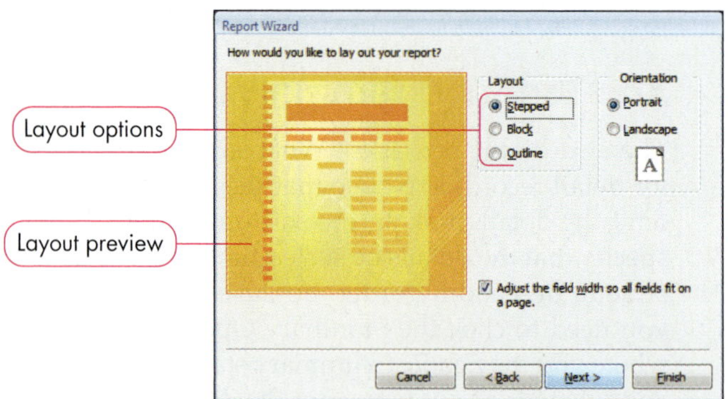

Figure 4.33 Specify Layout Options

A ***work-around*** acknowledges that a problem exists, and develops a sufficing solution.

Ironically, the design selection variety makes life more difficult for students than for real-world practitioners. On the job, you typically employ fewer than five templates. You use them all day, every day. You become intimately acquainted with all of their quirks. You develop functional work-arounds. A ***work-around*** acknowledges that a problem exists and develops a sufficing solution. In a course, you use a variety of templates and never fully understand any of them. Figure 4.34 shows AutoFormat choices.

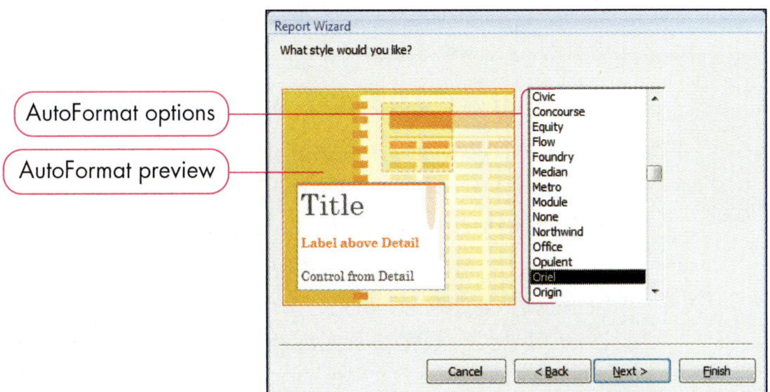

Figure 4.34 AutoFormat

Save and Name the Report

A well-designed database may contain only a few tables, but it may have many queries and reports. You should name all report objects descriptively to save you time and minimize frustration. Always name your report something that not only makes sense to you today, but also will communicate the report's contents to a co-worker or to you in six months (see Figure 4.35).

In the next hands-on exercise you will create a report using the Report Wizard and edit it using the Layout view.

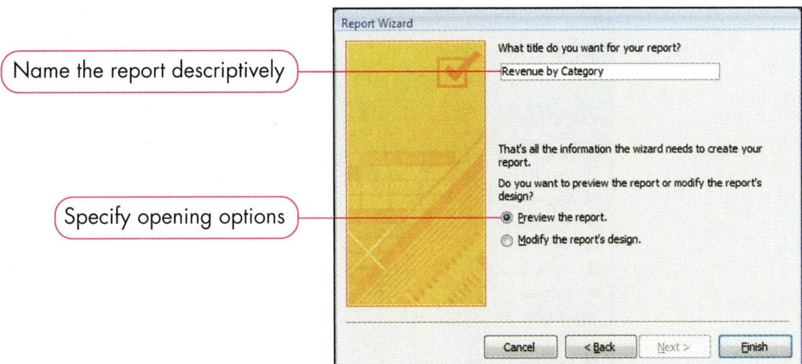

Figure 4.35 Use Descriptive Report Names

Hands-On Exercises

3 | Report Wizard

Skills covered: 1. Assemble the Report Data **2.** Create a Query-Based Report and Add Grouping **3.** Create Summary Statistics **4.** Select Layout and AutoFormatting **5.** Modify the Report

Step 1 Assemble the Report Data

Refer to Figure 4.36 as you complete Step 1.

a. Open the *chap4_ho1-3_coffee_solution* file if necessary, click **Options** on the Security Warning toolbar, click the **Enable this content option** in the Microsoft Office Security Options dialog box, and click **OK**.

   TROUBLESHOOTING: If you create unrecoverable errors while completing this hands-on exercise, you can delete the *chap4_ho1-3_coffee_solution* file, copy the *chap4_ho2_coffee_solution* backup database you created at the end of the second hands-on exercise, and open the copy of the backup database to start the third hands-on exercise again.

b. Open the **Your Name Revenue query** in Design view.

c. Add the **OrderDate** field located in the *Orders* table to the design grid by double-clicking it.

d. Add the **ProductName** field located in the *Products* table to the design grid by double-clicking it.

e. Click **Run** in the Results group on the Design tab to run the query. Scroll right to ensure that the newly added fields exist.

f. Save the changes. Close the query. Check to make sure the query name is selected in the Navigation Pane.

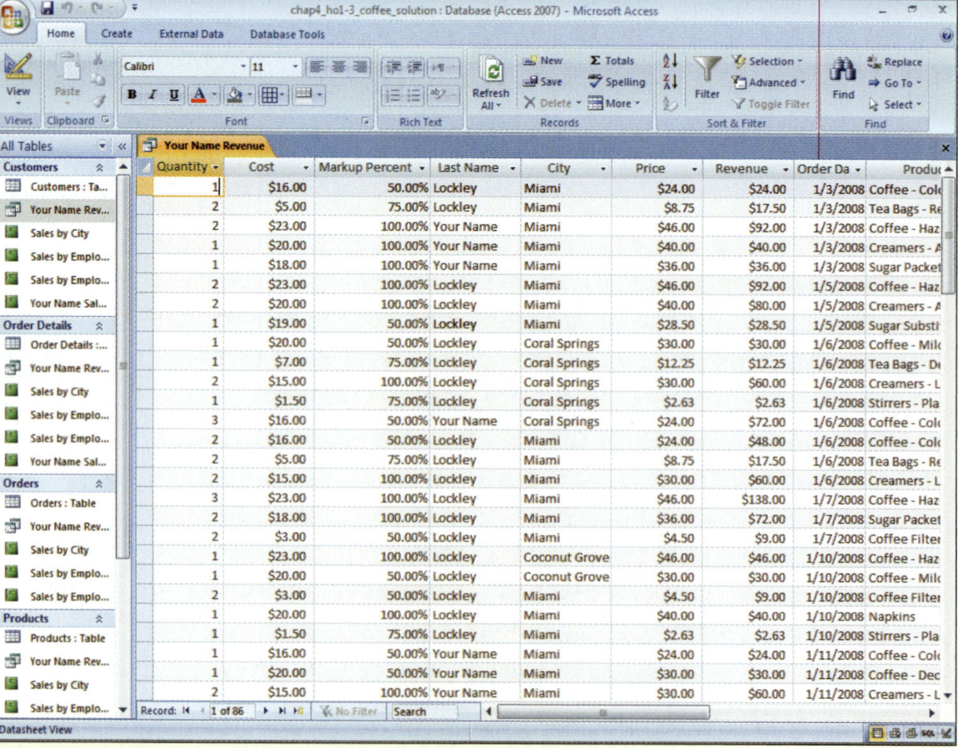

Figure 4.36 Assemble the Record Source

Step 2
Create a Query-Based Report and Add Grouping

Refer to Figure 4.37 as you complete Step 2.

a. Click the **Create tab** and click **Report Wizard** in the Reports group.

   The Report Wizard launches, and the Your Name Revenue query is the record source because it was selected when you started the wizard.

b. Click **All Fields (>>)** to move all of the query fields to the Selected Fields box. Click **Next**.

c. Double-click **OrderDate** in the grouping level box.

   The right box displays the default date grouping, OrderDate by Month. In this case you want a monthly report so you do not need to change the grouping options command.

d. Double-click the **LastName** field in the left box to add it as a grouping level.

e. Compare your grouping levels to those shown in Figure 4.37. If they match, click **Next**.

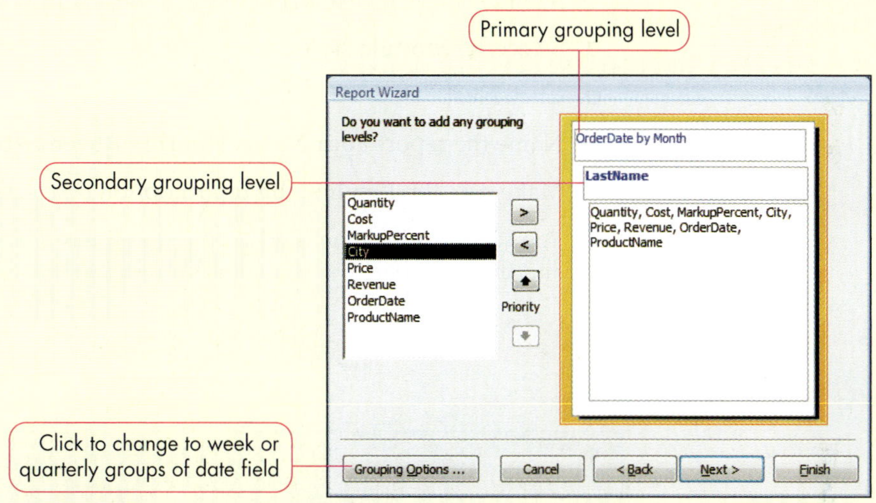

Figure 4.37 Create Groups

Step 3
Create Summary Statistics

Refer to Figure 4.38 as you complete Step 3.

a. Click the drop-down arrow beside the first sort box. Select **City** as the primary sort field.

b. Click **Summary Options**.

   TROUBLESHOOTING: As long as the Report Wizard dialog box remains open, you can click Back and revisit your work.

c. Click the **Sum** check box for the **Revenue** field.

d. Click the **Calculate percent of total for sums** check box.

e. Compare your Summary Options to those shown in Figure 4.38. If they match, click **OK** and then click **Next**.

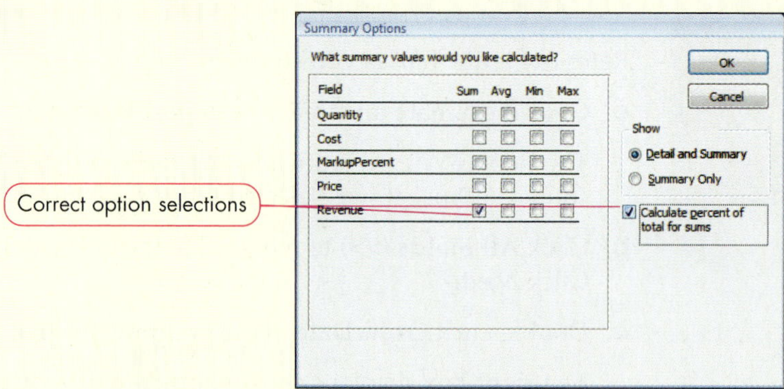

Figure 4.38 Summary Calculation Specifications

Step 4
Select Layout and AutoFormatting

Refer to Figure 4.39 as you complete Step 4.

a. Select a **Stepped** layout and a **Portrait** orientation.

b. Click **Next**.

Spend some time exploring in the Report AutoFormats of the wizard.

c. Select the **Module** style.

d. Click **Next**.

e. Name the report **Your Name Monthly Revenue by Salesperson.**

f. Make sure the **Preview the report** option is selected. Click **Finish**.

You successfully generated output, but it has flaws. Examine your work critically and then compare the problems you spot to those highlighted in Figure 4.39.

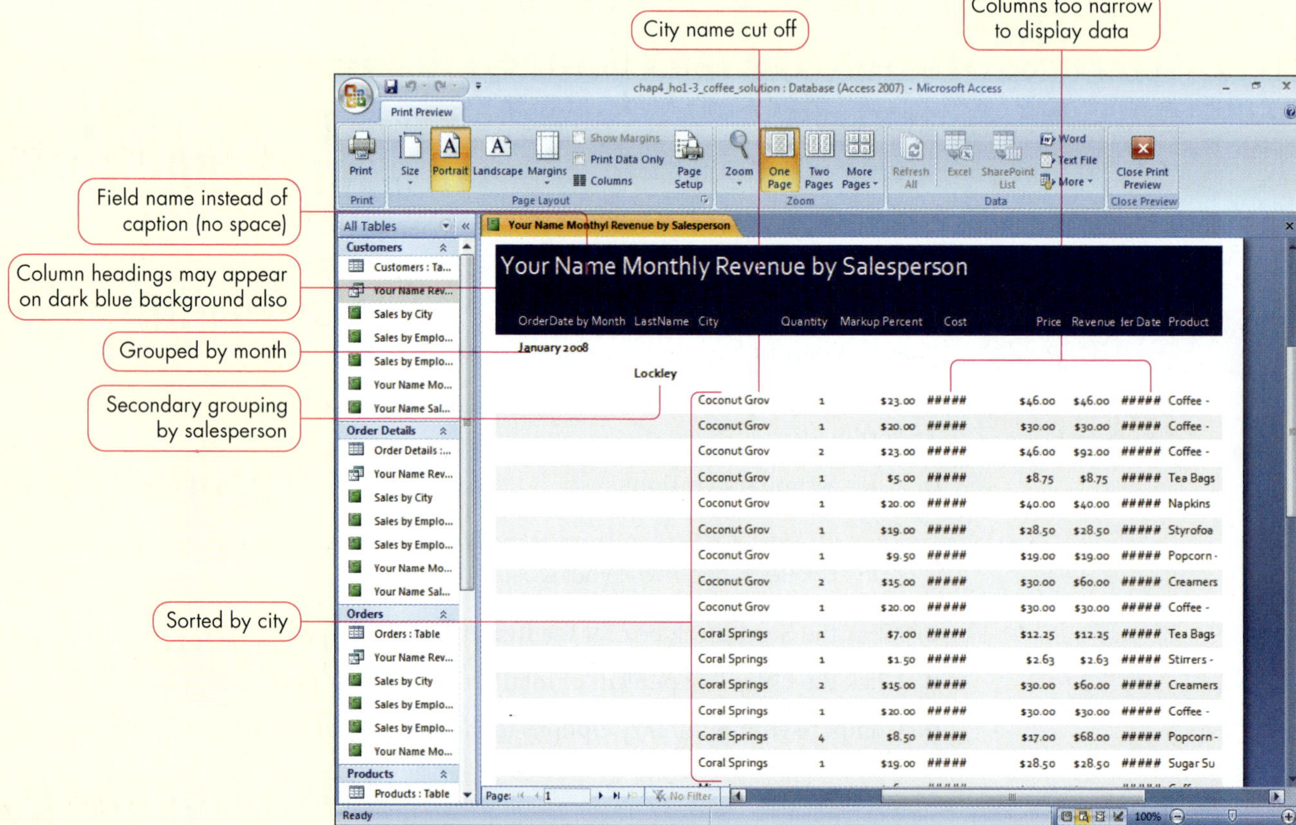

Figure 4.39 Create Groups

Step 5
Modify the Report

Refer to Figure 4.40 as you complete Step 4.

a. Right-click the report tab and select **Layout View**.

b. Select the text box for the OrderDate by Month control. Click it again to edit the text to **Order Month**. Press **Enter**.

Ideally you should save and close the report, open the Orders table, switch to Design view and add a caption for the OrderDate field. Save the design change to the table and close it. Run the query the report sources. Reopen the report. The caption will replace the field name in the text box in this and all other reports and forms that source on OrderDate. Because you also changed from OrderDate by Month to Order Month, it is excusable to make this a one-time change.

c. Ensure the **Order Month** control is still selected. Move your mouse over the right boundary and when the mouse pointer shape changes to the double-headed arrow, click and drag left about a quarter of an inch.

d. Select the text box for the **LastName** control. Click it again to edit the text. Type a **space** between Last and Name.

e. Select the **City** control text box and widen the column using the click and drag technique presented in Step 5c. Make sure the entire city name, Coconut Grove, displays.

You determine that the report is too crowded and that several fields do not need to be displayed. You decide to delete the Quantity, Markup Percent, Cost, and Price fields.

f. Click the **Quantity** field control text box and press **Delete**.

g. Delete the **Markup Percent**, **Cost**, and **Price** fields.

h. Widen the **Product Name** and **Order Date** fields.

i. Click the **Format tab** if necessary. Click **Hide Details** in the Grouping & Totals group.

The details of the report hide. This result makes it easier for you to find and edit the summary statistics.

j. Find the words, *Summary for 'LastName' = Lockley (47 detail records)*. On the line below in blue, it says Sum. Look right. You should see a small text box with some numbers or pound signs in it. The control box is too small to display the value. Click the too-small control.

k. Mouse over the control's right boundary, get the double-headed resize arrows, and then click and drag to the **right** to widen the control.

When the box is large enough you will see that the value of Lockley's total revenue is 1836.5. It is not formatted as currency.

l. Enlarge the controls for **Sum and Grand Total**. Check to see that the text boxes are large enough to display the percent values, too. Enlarge those text boxes if necessary.

m. Click the **Sum** value for Lockley, 1836.5. **Right-click** and select **Properties** from the shortcut menu. Set the **Format** property to **Currency**. With the Property Sheet still open, click the grand total and format it as **Currency**. If needed, widen the columns again after formatting the totals for Currency.

All of the sums should display in Currency format. Because there are two grouping levels, the Report Wizard repeats the grand total twice. You want to keep the bottom one because it is in the report footer along with the words, *Grand Total*.

n. Find the repeated Grand Total value (the one labeled Sum) at the bottom of the page. Select it and press **Delete**. Select and delete the word *Sum*.

o. Click **Hide Details** in the Grouping & Totals group on the Format tab to display the details to the report.

   You hid the details to format the totals. It moves them out of the way and makes it easier to format the total information.

p. Click either the **$1,836.50** or **$1,599.13 Sum control box** and drag it to the left until the values are below *Lockley* and *Your Name*, respectively. Make sure the decimal points in the Sum controls align with the decimal points in the Revenue column. Also move the **$3,435.63 grand total control** to the left to align the decimal point in the $1,599.13 control.

q. Move either the **53.45% control** or the **46.55% control** to the left to align the percent symbol (%) with the *8* in *2008* in the Order Dates column. Also move the **100.00% control** to the left to align the decimal point with the 53.45% and 46.55% controls.

r. Locate the **page number control**. If necessary, move the right boundary left so that it no longer crosses the dotted line indicating the page break.

s. Right-click the report tab and select **Print Preview**.

t. Click **Two Pages** in the Zoom group on the Print Preview tab. Use the navigation commands to preview the last page. Click **One Page**, and then click **Zoom** in the Zoom group. Print and save the report.

u. Click the **Office Button**, select **Manage**, and then select **Compact and Repair Database**.

v. Close the file and exit Access.

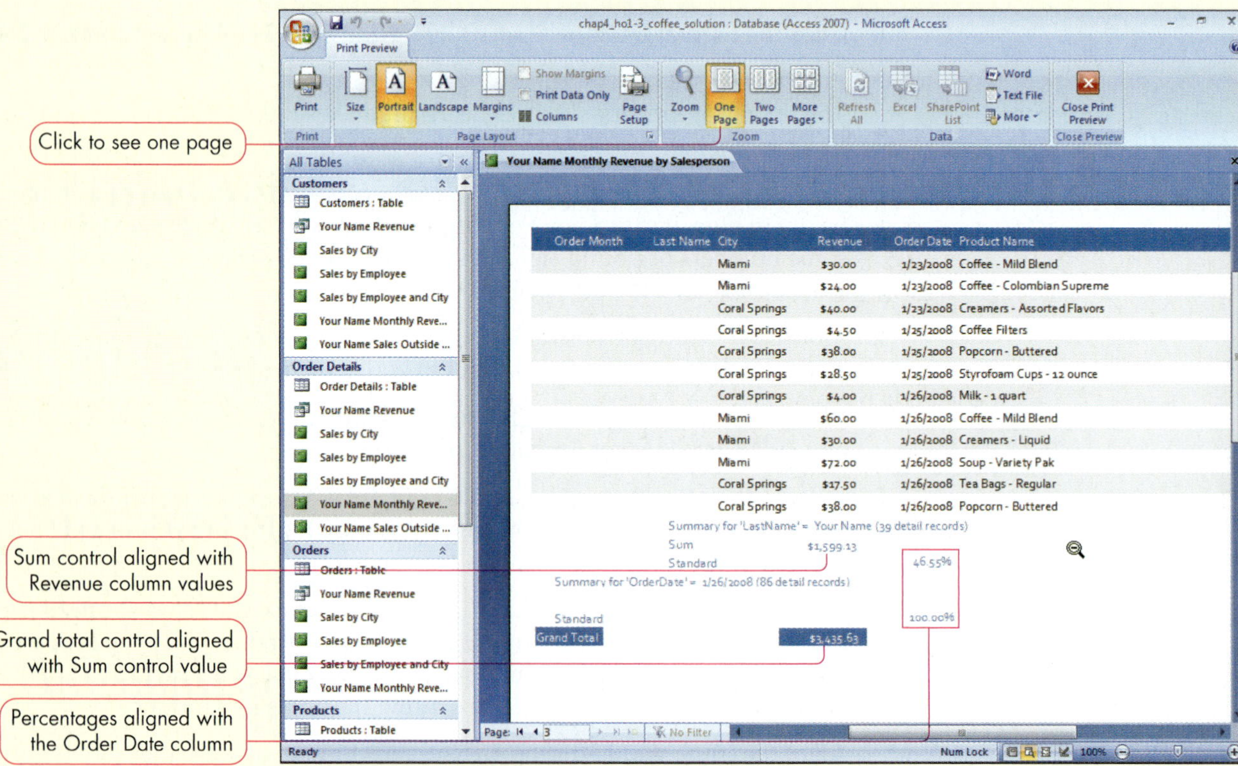

Figure 4.40 The Report in Print Preview

Summary

1. **Plan a report.** A report is a printed document that displays information from a database. Telephone directories, financial statements, shipping labels, and receipts are examples of reports. You should carefully consider what information you need and how you can optimally present it. A paper and pencil may be the best tools for planning. Develop a series of questions to ask to determine what the report should answer. Identify the data sources for the report. Select a reporting tool.

2. **Use different report views.** Access provides different views of your report depending on the operation you need to accomplish. Print Preview is an invaluable tool while designing reports. Use it liberally to preview your reports. Report view enables you to organize the data for the report by sorting and filtering it. Layout view enables you to alter the report design. This is the most powerful view and where you will spend most of your time. Design view displays the report's infrastructure design, but no data. This view has its advantages in large reports, but may be more difficult to use to make exact tweaks to the formatting.

3. **Create and edit a report.** To use the Report tool, you need to assemble all of the necessary data in one place. Occasionally, a table contains all of the necessary fields for a report. More often, you will need to create or open a query containing the necessary fields. If an existing query has all of the fields needed for the report but also some unneeded fields, you probably will use the existing query. You can delete the extraneous fields in Layout view. Access does a lot of the cosmetic work in your reports for you, by adjusting column widths as you add and remove columns. You can do the rest in Layout view.

4. **Identify report elements, sections, and controls.** Access divides all reports into sections, although you only see the sectional boundaries when you display the report in the Design view. Detail Section is the body of the report, containing each record. The Report Header (Footer) Section prints at the beginning (end) of each report. Group headers and footers appear at the tops and bottoms of each report group. Page headers and footers display at the top and bottom of each report page. You can edit these areas in the Design or Layout views. Controls display, position, format, and calculate the report data. You will use bound controls, those that are bound or tied to a source table or query, most frequently. Unbound controls have no record source in the underlying data. An example of an unbound control would be the report's title. A calculated control uses an expression as opposed to a record value as its data source. The expression usually is bound to record values of the fields referenced.

5. **Add grouping levels in Layout view.** Access provides several methods of grouping and summarizing data. You can create (1) a Totals query by specifying a group by field and the field or fields to summarize, (2) a grouped report using the Layout view's Sorting and Grouping tools, and (3) a grouped report using the Report Wizard and specifying the group layers within the wizard. Since most reports will have many thousands of records, you should sort them using the Group Sort tool. Nested groups make the report look similar to an outline. You also can hide and display details in reports and calculate summary statistics. You can add sub-groupings as needed.

6. **Add fields to a report.** Inevitably, after a report has been used, someone will say, "It would be nice to have this in the report, too." Use the Layout view to add additional fields to a report.

7. **Use the Report Wizard.** Access contains several wizards that will print common repeatedly used reports such as mailing labels. It is important that you organize your desired output for wizards just as you would if you designed the report from scratch. Unlike the Report tool, when using a Report Wizard, you should close any open objects in the data source. Like in the Report tool, you can customize the reports from the Report Wizard with groups, sorts, and summaries to tweak the overall design to best present your data. A well-designed database may only have a few tables, but dozens of queries and reports. Chances are good that they will be reused, so they should be saved and descriptively named.

Key Terms

Bound control 750
Calculated control 750
Controls 750
Design view 736
Detail section 747
Field List pane 755
Group footer section 747
Group header section 747
Label Wizard 764
Layout view 735
Mailing labels 764
Nested groups 751
Page footer 748
Page header 748
Print Preview 733
Report 731
Report footer section 747
Report header section 747
Report view 734
Report Wizard 764
Unbound controls 750
Work-around 769

Multiple Choice

1. Which statement most accurately describes the appropriate time to use a report in Access?
   (a) Entering data
   (b) Printing output for presentation
   (c) Querying data
   (d) Sorting records based on preset criteria

2. Which of the following is true?
   (I) You can edit the appearance of reports by changing fonts and styles.
   (II) You can add graphs, pictures, and charts to reports.
   (a) I but not II
   (b) II but not I
   (c) Neither I nor II
   (d) Both I and II

3. Which is an example of a report from a database?
   (a) a shipping label
   (b) a telephone directory
   (c) a sales receipt
   (d) all of the above

4. Which statement about saving a report is true?
   (a) Saved reports are static, and the data represented in a report will be the same every time you run a saved report.
   (b) Saving reports is generally not done in the real world because people rarely need the same information repeatedly.
   (c) You can edit a saved report to add additional fields at a later time.
   (d) Using a saved report can be costly and time-consuming.

5. The most important tool to create an Access report may be
   (a) the Report Grid tool
   (b) a calculator
   (c) a pencil
   (d) the Report Creator tool

6. It is always best to ask _______ questions about what the report should look like and do.
   (a) the programmer
   (b) the end user
   (c) the customer
   (d) your manager

7. Which of the following are important things to know as you create an Access report?
   (a) Access cannot calculate data in a report.
   (b) Reports can be summarized, but the summaries have to be designed in the underlying query.
   (c) Reports cannot draw data from multiple tables.
   (d) What type of delivery mechanism will be used, fax, e-mail Word, Excel, PowerPoint, Internet, or printer, and what type and size of paper will be used for the report.

8. If you want to create mailing labels from your Customers table, the fastest and easiest tool would be Access':
   (a) Report Tool
   (b) Report Wizard
   (c) Label Wizard
   (d) Mailing Wizard

9. Which of the following is the most sophisticated and flexible tool for report generation?
   (a) Report Tool
   (b) Report Wizard
   (c) Free form report
   (d) WYSIWYG report

10. Use the __________ to see what the printed report will look like before printing. This step helps with the overall layout and makes the report easy to read and understand.
    (a) Report Tool
    (b) Report Wizard
    (c) Group Wizard
    (d) Print Preview

11. You should modify column widths and row heights for a report in:
    (a) Layout view
    (b) Print Preview
    (c) Group view
    (d) Report view

12. Which of the following is true?
    (I) Access can create a report from multiple tables.
    (II) You will usually have to create a new query to create a report.
    (a) I but not II
    (b) II but not I
    (c) Both I and II
    (d) Neither I nor II

... continued on Next Page

Multiple Choice Continued...

13. What happens if you click a value in Layout view and press Delete?

(a) The entire column is deleted from the report, and column widths are adjusted to use the empty space.

(b) Nothing; you cannot change data in Layout view.

(c) The record is deleted from the report but remains in the database.

(d) An error message appears, saying that you should not attempt to manipulate records in a report.

14. Your pointer shape should be a ____________ to widen or narrow a column in Layout view.

(a) single arrow

(b) hand

(c) two-headed arrow

(d) dashed-tail arrow

15. Which of these is not a sectional division used in Access reports?

(a) Detail section

(b) Report header and footer sections

(c) Group header and footer sections

(d) Summary section

16. Bound controls are so called because they are bound or attached to:

(I) source data

(II) the report's margins

(a) I but not II

(b) II but not I

(c) Both I and II

(d) Neither I nor II

17. Which of the following is true?

(a) Unbound controls are used infrequently within reports.

(b) Unbound controls are used to display cosmetic elements in a report.

(c) Unbound controls must be saved separately because they are not part of a record.

(d) Unbound controls cannot be used with bound controls in the same report.

18. To organize your data in a highly usable and readable report, you may use:

(a) Nested tables

(b) Nested groups

(c) Nested queries

(d) Calculated fields

Practice Exercises

1 Comfort Insurance Raises and Bonuses Report

The Comfort Insurance Agency is a midsized company with offices located across the country. The Human Resource office is located in the home office in Miami. Each year, each employee receives a performance review. The review determines employee eligibility for salary increases and the annual performance bonus. The employee data are stored in an Access database, which is used by the Human Resource department to monitor and maintain employee records. Your task is to prepare a report showing the salary increase for each employee and his or her performance bonuses (if any). You are the Human Resource department manager. If you correctly report the employee salaries and bonuses, you will receive a bonus. Work carefully and check the accuracy of the calculations. This project follows the same set of skills as used in Hands-On Exercises 1 and 2 in this chapter. If you have problems, reread the detailed directions presented in the chapter. Compare your results to Figure 4.41.

a. Copy the partially completed file *chap4_pe1_insurance* to your production folder. Rename it **chap4_pe1_insurance_solution**, open the file, and enable the content.

b. Click the **Database Tools tab** and click **Relationships** in the Show/Hide group. Examine the table structure, relationships, and fields. After you are familiar with the database, close the Relationships window.

c. Rename the query with your name. Open the **Your Name Raises and Bonus query**.

d. Click the **Create tab** and click **Report** in the Reports group.

e. Click **Group & Sort** in the Grouping & Totals group, if necessary. Click **Add a sort** in the Group, Sort, and Total pane and select **LastName**.

f. Click the **LastName** label. Click it again to edit it and add a **space** between *Last* and *Name*. Click outside the text box to turn off editing. Move the mouse to the **right** control boundary, and when the pointer shape changes to the double-headed arrow click and drag the boundary about a half-inch to the left to make the column narrower.

g. Repeat Step f to add a space to the *FirstName* control and decrease its width. Also reduce the width for the *Performance* column. The report should only be one page wide. Add spaces to the *2008Increase* and *NewSalary* controls.

h. Click the **Report Graphic** (the picture in the upper left) to select it. Click **Logo** in the Controls group on the Format tab. Browse to and locate the file named *chap4_pe1_confident.jpg*. Click **OK** in the Insert Picture dialog box.

i. Click the report title *Your Name Raises and Bonuses* to select it. Point the mouse at the middle of the control box and when the pointer shape changes to the four-headed, move arrow, move the report title right.

j. Click the **Confidential graphic** and drag the **right** boundary right to enlarge the warning.

k. Right-click any number in the **New Salary** column and select **Properties** from the shortcut menu. Set the **Format property** in the Property Sheet to **Currency** and close the Property Sheet.

l. Right-click any number in the **Bonus** field and select **Properties**. Set the **Format property** to **Currency**. Close the Property Sheet.

m. Right-click the report tab and switch to **Print Preview**. Save the report as **Your Name Raises and Bonuses**.

n. Close the database.

...continued on Next Page

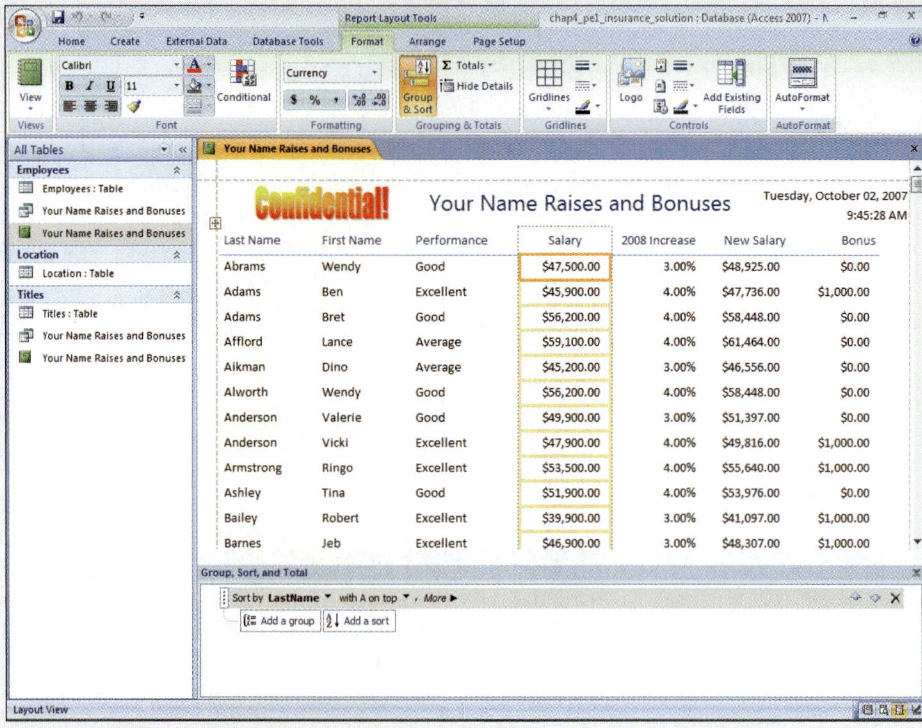

Figure 4.41 Raises and Bonuses Report

2 Comfort Insurance Raises by Location

The Comfort Insurance Agency is a midsized company with offices located across the country. The Human Resource office is located in the home office in Miami. Each year, each employee receives a performance review. The review determines employee eligibility for salary increases and the annual performance bonus. The employee data are stored in an Access database. This database is used by the Human Resource department to monitor and maintain employee records. Your task is to prepare a report showing employee raises and bonuses by city. You will need to total the payroll and bonus data for each city. You are the Human Resource department manager. If you correctly prepare the report, you will receive a bonus. This project follows the same set of skills as used in Hands-On Exercises 1 and 2 in this chapter. If you have problems, reread the detailed directions presented in the chapter. Compare your results to Figure 4.42.

a. Copy the partially completed file *chap4_pe2_insurance.accdb* to your production folder. Rename it **chap4_pe2_insurance_solution.accdb**, open the copied file, and enable the content.
b. Click the **Database Tools tab** and click **Relationships** in the Show/Hide group. Examine the table structure, relationships, and fields. After you are familiar with the database, close the Relationships window.
c. Open the **Employees Query** in Datasheet view. Click the **Create tab** and click **Report** in the Reports group.
d. Click **Add Existing Fields** in the Controls group on the Format tab. The Field List pane opens on the right. In the bottom of the Field List pane is the *Fields available in related tables pane*. Click the **Show all tables** link. The Location table is listed with a plus sign next to it. Click the **plus sign** to reveal the hidden fields available in the Location table.
e. Double-click the **Location** field (not the LocationID field) to add it to the report. Because this field is in a table not in the original record source Access asks if it is OK to create a new query that contains the Location field. Click **Yes**. The city names add to the report. The new field is selected. Close the Field List pane.
f. Click the **Location** text box at the top of the field. Move the mouse to the middle of the selected Location field and when the mouse pointer assumes the four-headed move shape, click and drag the field to the **leftmost** position in the report.

...continued on Next Page

g. Click the **LastName** text box at the top of the field to select it. Click it a second time to edit it. Type a **space** between Last and Name. Add spaces to **FirstName**, **HireDate**, **2008Increase**, **2008Raise**, **YearHired**, and **YearsWorked**.

h. Select the **Last Name** field. Move the mouse pointer over the right boundary and when the pointer shape changes to a double-headed arrow, click and drag **left** to narrow the column. Repeat this step for the **First Name** field.

i. Right-click any record in the **2008 Raise** field and select **Properties**. In the Properties Sheet, set the Format property to **Currency**. Close the Property Sheet.

j. Select the **Year Hired** field and delete it. Adjust any field column widths as necessary to make sure all the columns fit on one page.

k. Click **Group & Sort** in the Grouping & Totals group to turn on the Group, Sort, and Total pane (if necessary). Click **Add a group** in the Group, Sort, and Total pane. Click **Location** in the Group on Select field box.

l. Click the **More Options** command on the Group on Location bar. Click the drop-down arrow beside "with LastName totaled." Click the drop-down arrow in the Total On box and select **2008Raise**. Click the **Show Grand Total** and **Show in group footer** check boxes. Click anywhere outside the Total by box.

m. Click the report title and change it to **Your Name**.

n. Click the **Office Button**. Position the mouse pointer over **Print** and click **Print Preview**. Print the report.

o. Save the report as **Your Name Raises by Location**. Close the database.

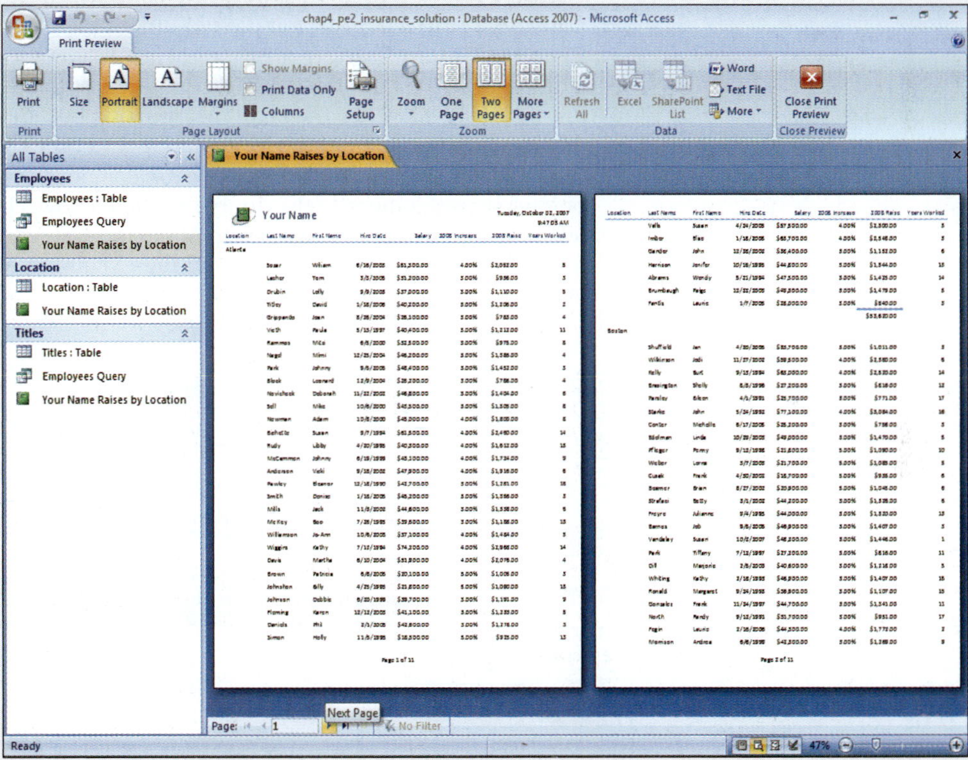

Figure 4.42 Raises by Location Shown in Print Preview

3 Northwind Traders

Northwind Traders is a small, international, specialty food company. It sells products in eight different divisions: beverages, confections (candy), condiments, dairy products, grains and cereals, meat and poultry, produce, and seafood. Although most of its customers are restaurants and gourmet food shops, it has a few retail customers, too. The firm purchases merchandise from a variety of suppliers. All of the order and inventory information is stored in the company's database. This database is used by the management to monitor and maintain records. You are the marketing manager. Your task is to prepare a report showing the profitability of the products in your inventory. You need to group the products by their categories. You also need to average the profit

...continued on Next Page

margin by category. (A profit margin is the profit divided by the price.) This project follows the same set of skills as used in Hands-On Exercises 1, 2, and 3. If you have problems, reread the detailed directions presented in the chapter. Compare your results to Figure 4.43.

a. Copy the partially completed file *chap4_pe3_traders.accdb* to your production folder. Rename it **chap4_pe3_traders_solution.accdb**, open the file, and enable the content.
b. Click the **Database Tools tab** and click **Relationships** in the Show/Hide group. Examine the table structure, relationships, and fields. After you are familiar with the database, close the Relationships window.
c. Select **Profit Margin** in the Navigation Pane. Click the **Create tab** and click **Report Wizard** in the Reports group. Select the **Profit Margin query** in the first screen of the Report Wizard. Click **All Fields (>>)** to move all of the fields in the query to the report. Click **Next**.
d. Select **by Categories** to answer the "How do you want to view your data?" question. This step creates the necessary grouping level. Click **Next**. You already have established the grouping level so click **Next** again.
e. Click **Summary Options** and indicate that you would like the **Avg** for the *ProfitMargin* field. Click **OK**, and then click **Next**.
f. Ensure that **Stepped** layout and **Portrait** orientation are selected and click **Next**.
g. Select the **Aspect** style and click **Next**. Type **Your Name Profit Margins** for the report title. Set it to open to **Preview**. Click **Finish**.
h. Right-click the report tab and select **Layout View**.
i. Click the report title to select it. Click again to edit it. Change the title to **Your Name Category Profit Margins**, if it did not inherit the title from the report name.
j. Click the **UnitsInStock** text box and click it again to edit it. Insert a **space** between Units and In. Position the insertion point left of the **S** in Stock and type **Ctrl+Enter** to force a line break. Click the **Profit Margin** text box and click it again to edit it. Position the insertion point left of the **M** in Margin and type **Ctrl+Enter** to force a line break.
k. Click the **Per Unit Profit** text box. Move the mouse over the **right boundary**. When the pointer shape changes to the double-headed arrow, click and drag the right boundary **left** to make the column narrower. Make the **Category** columns wider to display the record contents. Adjust the widths of the remaining columns as necessary to fit all on one page.

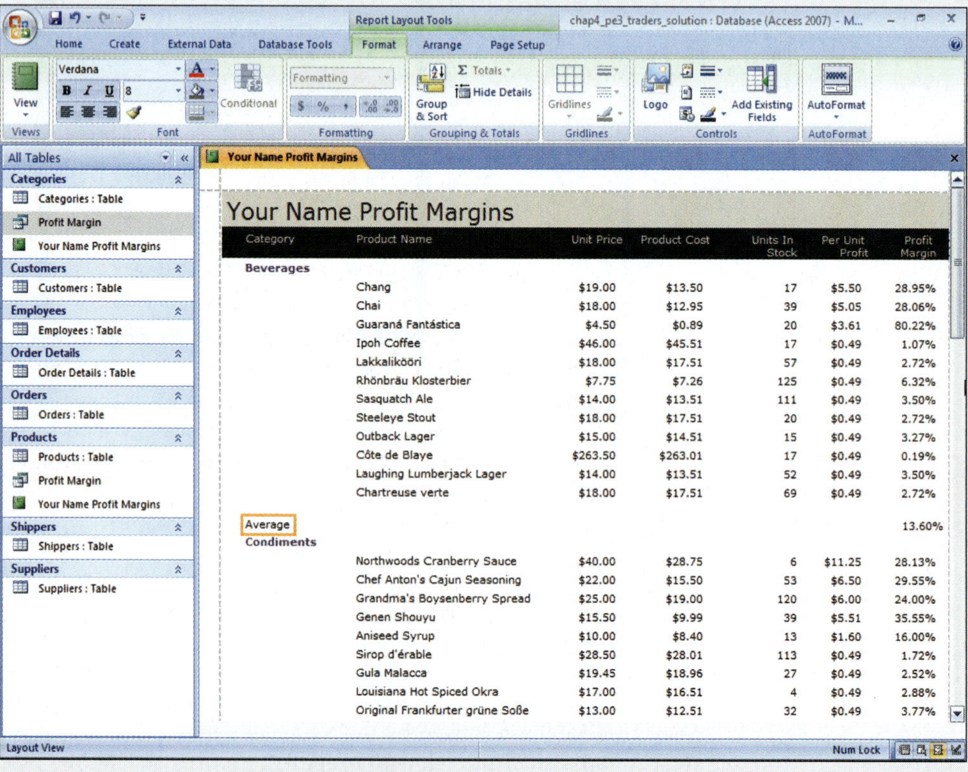

Figure 4.43 Profit Margin by Category

...continued on Next Page

l. Select the **Summary for Category Name . . .** and press **Delete**. Select **Avg** and replace it with **Average**.
m. Save the report. Print the report. Close the database.

4 Member Rewards

The Prestige Hotel chain caters to upscale business travelers and provides state-of-the-art conference, meeting, and reception facilities. It prides itself on its international, four-star cuisines. Last year, it began a member rewards club to help the marketing department track the purchasing patterns of its most loyal customers. All of the hotel transactions are stored in the database. Your task is to determine the revenue from each order and to summarize the revenue figures by location and service type. This project follows the same set of skills as used in Hands-On/Exercises 2, and 3. If you have problems, reread the detailed directions presented in the chapter. Compare your results to Figure 4.44.

a. Copy the partially completed file *chap4_pe4_memrewards.accdb* to your production folder. Rename it **chap4_pe4_memrewards_solution.accdb**, open the file, and enable the content.
b. Click the **Database Tools tab** and click **Relationships** in the Show/Hide group. Examine the table structure, relationships, and fields. After you are familiar with the database, close the Relationships window. Rename the **Your Name Revenue** query with your name.
c. Open the **Your Name Revenue** query in Datasheet view.
d. Click the **Create tab** and click **Report** in the Reports group.
e. Click **Group & Sort** in the Grouping & Totals group to turn on the Group, Sort, and Total pane (if necessary). Click **Add a group** in the Group, Sort, and Total pane. Click **City** in the Group on list box. Click **Add a group** and select **ServiceName** in the Group on list box.
f. Click **Hide Details** in the Grouping & Totals group.
g. Click **Group on ServiceName** in the Group, Sort, and Total pane to activate the group bar. Click the **More** command. Click the **with City totaled drop-down arrow**. In the **Total On** box, select **NoInParty**. In the **Type** box select **Average**. Click the **Show in group header** check box.
h. Return to the Totals dialog box, click the drop-down arrow, and click **PerPersonCharge**. Set **Type** to **Average** and check **Show in group header**.
i. Return to the **Totals** dialog box, click the drop-down arrow, and click **Revenue**. Set **Type** to **Sum** and check **Show in group header**.
j. Click **Group on City** to activate the group bar. Click **More**. Locate and click the **with City totaled drop-down arrow**. In the **Total On** box, select **NoInParty**. In the **Type** box select **Average.** Click the **Show in group footer check box.**
k. Return to the Totals dialog box, click the drop-down arrow, and click **PerPersonCharge**. Set **Type** to **Average** and check **Show in group footer.**
l. Return to the Totals dialog box, click the drop-down arrow, and click **Revenue**. Set **Type** to **Sum** and check **Show in group footer** and **Show Grand Total.**
m. Click the **ServiceName** text box and click it again to edit it. Insert a **space** between Service and Name. Click NoInParty to select and type **Number In Party**. Position the insertion point right of the **r** in Number and type **Ctrl+Enter** to force a line break. Click the **PerPerson Charge** text box and click it again to edit it. Add a space between Per and Person. Position the insertion point left of the **C** in Charge and type **Ctrl+Enter** to force a line break.

...continued on Next Page

n. Click the text box for **City**. Move the mouse over the **right boundary**. When the pointer shape changes to the double-headed arrow, click and drag the right boundary **left** to make the column narrower. Adjust the widths of the remaining columns as necessary to fit all on one page.

o. Right-click a value in the **Number in Party** field. Select **Properties** from the shortcut menu. Set the **Format** property to **Fixed**. Click the **Decimal Places** property and select **1**. Click a value in the Per Person Charge field. Set the **Format property** to **Currency**. Click a value in the Revenue field to set the **Format property** to **Currency**. Examine the formats of the city and grand totals and adjust their formats if necessary.

p. Right-click the report tab and select **Print Preview**. Save the report as **Your Name Revenue by City and Service**. Close the database.

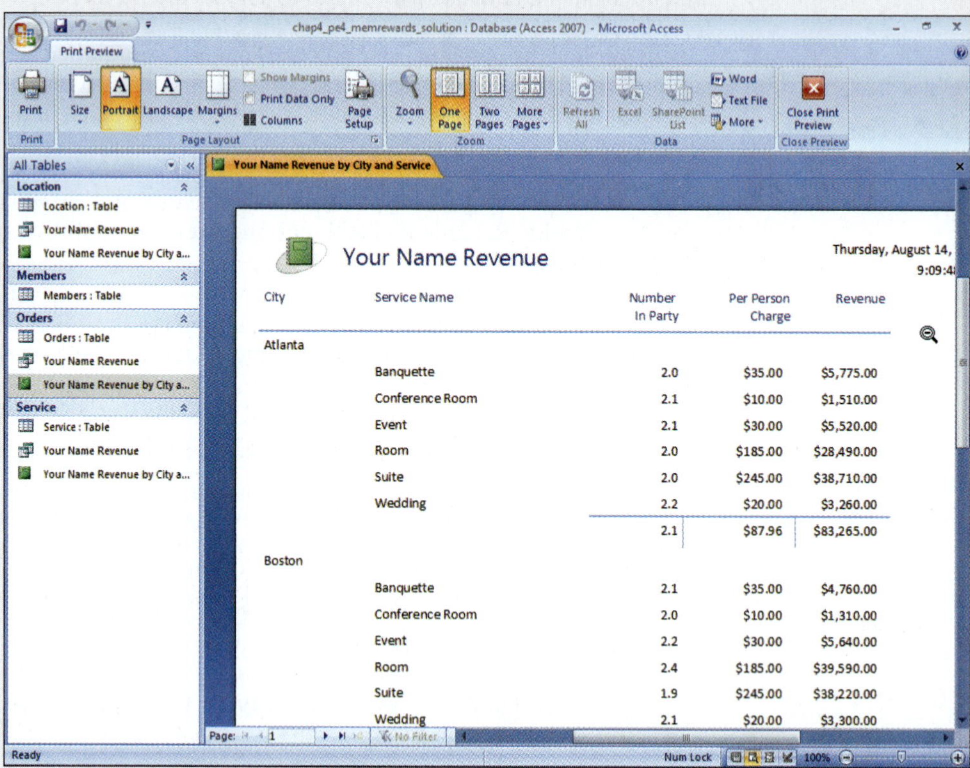

Figure 4.44 Revenue by City and Service

Mid-Level Exercises

1 Grouping and Totaling Dinnerware Revenue

(Replacements, Ltd is a real company located in Greensboro, North Carolina. The data in the case file are actual data. The customer and employee information have been changed to ensure privacy. However, the inventory and sales records reflect actual transactions.)

Today is the first day in your new position as associate marketing manager at Replacements, Ltd., which has the world's largest selection of old and new dinnerware, including china, stoneware, crystal, glassware, silver, stainless, and collectibles. In preparation for your first day on the job, you have spent hours browsing the Replacements Web site, www.replacements.com. You classify the merchandise by category number where 1 is dinnerware, 2 is crystal/glassware, and 3 is flatware (knives and forks). You are responsible for managing several different patterns of merchandise. To accomplish this task, you need to closely monitor past sales in the various patterns to understand purchasing habits and product demand. You exchange information with the customer service representatives and monitor their performance. You need to create a report that summarizes sales by pattern for the merchandise in Product Category 1, dinnerware. Compare your work to Figure 4.45.

a. Locate the file named *chap4_mid1_replacement.accdb*, copy it to your production folder, and rename it **chap4_mid1_replacement_solution.accdb**. Open the file and enable the content.

b. Open the **Revenue query**. It contains information about all three product classifications. Today, you are interested only in dinnerware. Create a report and set a filter to select only product category 1.

c. Group the report on the **LongPatName** field. Click the **More Options** command on the group bar in the Group, Sort, and Total pane. Locate the Totals drop-down arrow and select Revenue. Select the **Show Grand Total check box**. Eventually, you will hide the details, so set the total to display in the group header.

d. Hide the details. Remove all of the fields except for the LongPatName and Revenue from the report. Replace the label, *LongPatName*, with **Pattern Name**.

e. Save the report as **Your Name Revenue by Dinnerware Pattern**. Title the report appropriately.

f. Insert the *chap4_mid1_replacement.jpg* picture in the logo area. This image depicts the Spode pattern. It is copyrighted by Replacements, Ltd., and is used with permission.

g. Use the Page Setup tab to find and select the **Wide** margin setting. **Enlarge** the picture and **move the controls** in the Report Header and Footer sections to make the report a single page and attractive.

h. Right-click the total revenue and select the option to display a caption for the total value.

i. Save the report and display it in Print Preview.

j. With the *Your Name Revenue by Dinnerware Pattern* report open in Print Preview, press **PrintScrn** to capture a screenshot. Open Word, type your name and section number in a new blank document, press **Enter**, and paste the screenshot in Word. Save the Word document as **chap4_mid1_replacement_solution**. Print the Word document. Close the Word document and close the database.

...continued on Next Page

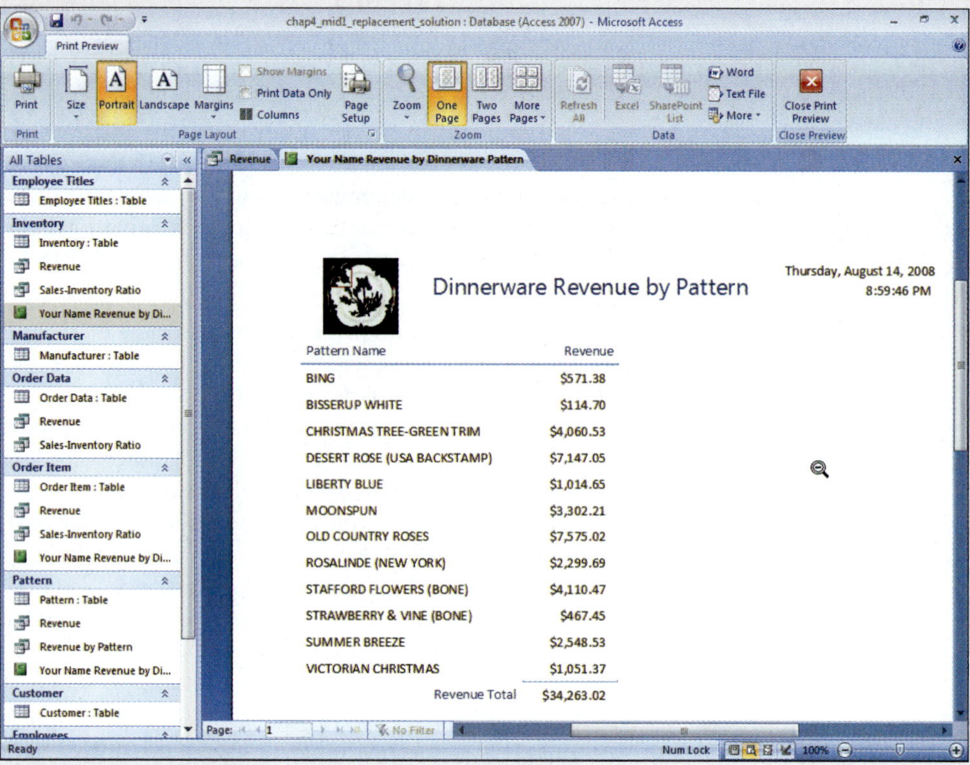

Figure 4.45 Dinnerware Revenue by Pattern

2 Calculating and Summarizing Bank Data in a Query

You are the manager of the loan department of the National Bank. Several customers have multiple loans with your institution. A single customer might have a mortgage loan, one or more car loans, and a home improvement loan. The loan department's database contains the records of all of the customer indebtedness. Your task is to use the information stored in the database to summarize the loan payments by month. Compare your results to Figure 4.46.

a. Locate the file named *chap4_mid2_nationalbank.accdb*, copy it to your production folder, and rename it **chap4_mid2_nationalbank_solution.accdb**. Open the file and enable the content. Open the **Customers table**. Find and replace **Michelle Zacco's** name with your name.

b. Open the **Payments Received** query. Use it to create a report.

c. In Report Layout view, use the Group, Sort, and Total pane to add a group. Group these data on the **PaymentDate** field.

d. Click the **More** command on the Group on PaymentDate bar in the Group, Sort, and Total pane and set the grouping interval to **Month**.

e. Click the drop-down arrow beside with Amount Received totaled to launch the Totals box. Select **AmountReceived** as the value for Totals on. Show this total in the **group footer**. Also show a **grand total**.

f. Make the name fields narrower. Save the report as **Your Name Payments Received.**

...continued on Next Page

g. Add spaces as needed to the boxes controlling the report labels. Examine the report in Print Preview. Click and drag the Zoom slider to 84%.

h. With the *Your Name Payments Received* report open in Print Preview, press **PrintScrn** to capture a screenshot. Open Word, type your name and section number in a new blank document, press **Enter**, and paste the screenshot in Word. Save the Word document as **chap4_mid2_nationalbank_solution.docx**. Print the Word document displaying the screenshot. Close the Word document and close the database.

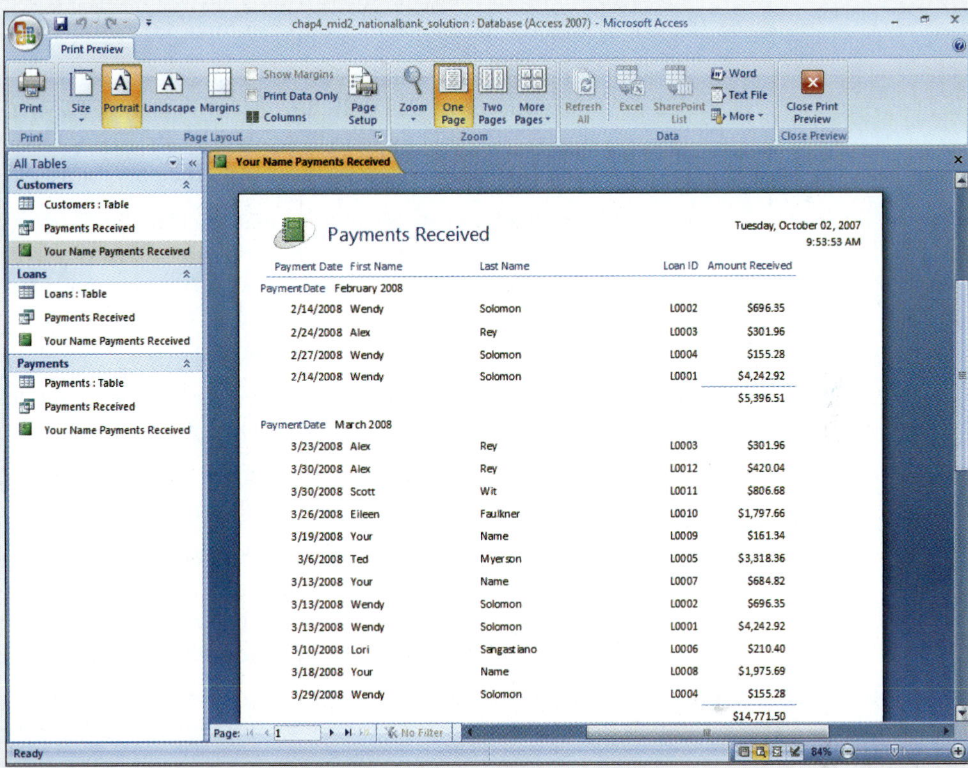

Figure 4.46 Payments Received Report

3 Real Estate Report by Month and Salesperson

You are the senior partner in a large, independent real estate firm that specializes in home sales. Although you still represent buyers and sellers in real estate transactions, you find that most of your time is spent supervising the agents who work for your firm. This fact distresses you because you like helping people buy and sell homes. Your firm has a database containing all of the information on the properties your firm has for sale. You believe that by using the data in the database more effectively, you can spend less time supervising the other agents and spend more time doing the part of your job that you like doing the best. Your task is to prepare a sales report listing all recent transactions by month and salesperson. Finally, you need to summarize the sales and commission data by employee and calculate the average number of days each employee's sales were on the market prior to selling. Compare your results to Figure 4.47.

...continued on Next Page

a. Locate the file named *chap4_mid3_realestate.accdb*, copy it to your production folder, and rename it **chap4_mid3_realestate_solution.accdb**. Open the file and enable the content. Change the Navigation Pane to display All Access Objects. Open the **Agents** table. Find and replace **Pa Lor's** name with your name.

b. Rename the **Your Name Sales Report query** with your name. Open it. Create a report. Save the report as **Your Name Sales Report**. Open it in Layout view.

c. Add **spaces** as needed in the labels in the report header. Use **Ctrl + Enter** to force a line break between *On* and *Market* in *DaysOnMarket*. Make the **Subdivision** and **LastName** fields narrower so the report fits on a single page.

d. Group the data monthly by the DateSold. Add a second group to group by LastName. Change the DateSold group heading (not column heading) to **Month Sold**.

e. Add totals to the **SalePrice** and **SaleComm** fields that sum. Calculate the average of the DaysOnMarket field. Right-click a value in the Days on Market column and add a caption. Change the caption to **Average Days**. Reduce the width of the Days on Market column so that the caption displays. Calculate grand totals for all three summary fields.

f. Use the Property Sheet to format the **DaysOnMarket** field as **Fixed** with zero decimal places. Format the **SalePrice** field as **Currency** with zero decimal places and the **SaleComm** field as **Currency** with two decimal places. Scroll through the complete report to ensure that all of the totals display fully and totals are formatted correctly. Adjust the text box widths if they do not.

g. Insert the *chap4_mid3_house.jpg* house photo as the logo. Set the margins to Normal, and adjust column widths to fit one page wide.

h. Click the AutoFormat drop-down arrow and select **AutoFormat Wizard**. In the AutoFormat box, select the Oriel format. View your report in Print Preview.

i. With the *Your Name Sales Report* open in Print Preview, press **PrintScrn** to capture a screenshot. Open Word, type your name and section number in a new blank document, press **Enter**, and paste the screenshot in Word. Save the Word document as **chap4_mid3_realestate_solution**. Print the screen. Close the Word document and close the database.

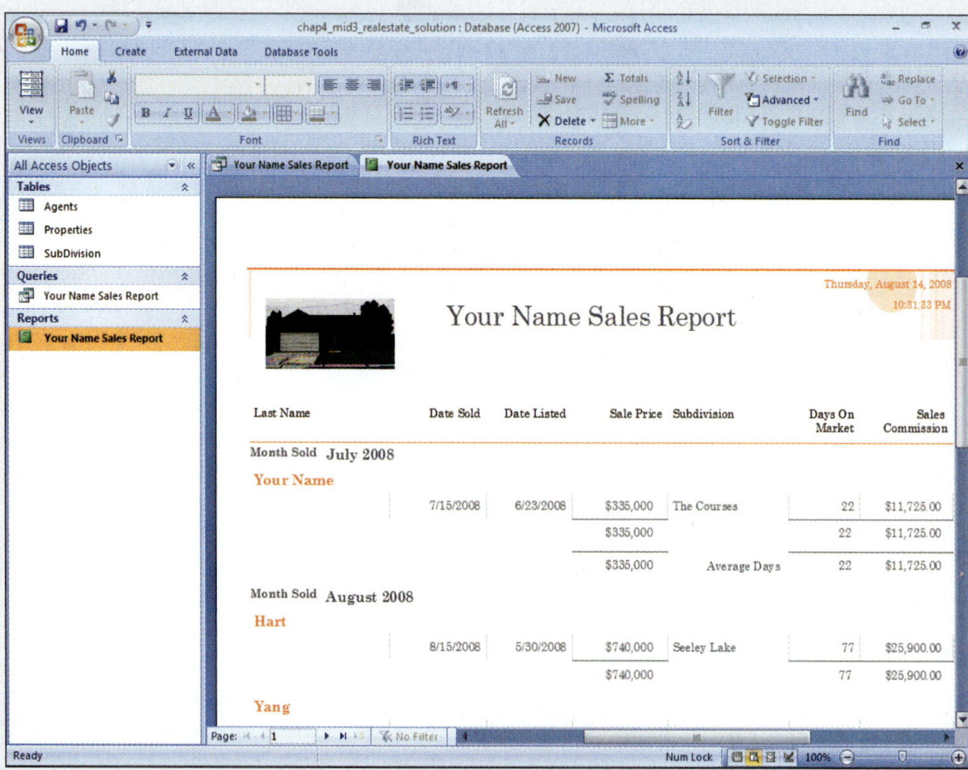

Figure 4.47 Sales Summary

Capstone Exercise

Your boss asked you to prepare a schedule for each speaker for the national conference being hosted next year on your campus. She wants to mail the schedules to the speakers so that they may provide feedback on the schedule prior to its publication. She believes that each speaker will find it easier to review his or her schedule if each speaker's schedule was printed in the same place. You assure her that you (and Access) can accomplish this task.

Database File Setup

You need to copy an original database file, rename the copied file, and then open the copied database to complete this capstone exercise. After you open the copied database, you will replace an existing employee's name with your name.

a. Locate the file named *chap4_cap_natconf.accdb* and copy it to your production folder.

b. Rename the copied file as **chap4_cap_natconf_solution.accdb**.

c. Open the *chap4_cap_natconf_solution.accdb* file and enable the content.

d. Open the **Speakers table**.

e. Find and replace **Your Name** with your name.

Report Wizard

You need to create a report based on the Speakers and Sessions with Rooms query. You decide to use the Report Wizard to accomplish this task.

a. Activate the **Report Wizard**.

b. Select **Query: Speakers and Sessions with Rooms** as the data source for the report.

c. Select all of the available fields for the report.

d. View the data by speakers.

e. Use the **LastName** and **FirstName** fields established as the primary grouping level. If they are not already moved into a box at the top of the report, double-click LastName and then FirstName to group by them.

f. Click the drop-down arrow for the first box and select **Date** as the primary sort field. Click **Next**.

g. Select the **Stepped** and **Portrait** options.

h. Choose the **Flow** style.

i. Name the report **Your Name Speaker Schedule**.

Report Edits

The report opens in the Print Preview. You need to examine the report and look for problems. Once they are identified, you will need to switch to Layout view and correct them.

a. Switch to the two-page view.

b. Display the report in Layout view.

c. Click the **Page Setup tab**. Click **Margins** in the Page Layout group. Select **Wide** from the drop-down menu.

d. Click the text box for **SessionTitle**. Insert a **space** between the words. Add a space to **RoomID**.

e. Move the **Date** field to the right of the Room ID column.

f. Resize the **FirstName** field by making it more narrow. Widen the **Session Title** field. Make the **RoomID** and **Date** fields more narrow.

g. Move the title right. Set the font size to **28 point**.

h. Insert a picture of your campus. To do this, open a browser window, navigate to your college Web site, right-click an image, and select Save As. Save the image to your production folder. Then use the Logo command to insert the image. Alternatively, insert chap4_cap_university.jpg. Resize the picture to be about the same height as the report title.

i. Apply the **Access 2007** AutoFormat style.

Additional Field

You realize the session times were not included in the query and you need them added to the report.

a. Click the Add Existing Fields Command in the Controls group.

b. Click **Show only fields in current record**, and then **Show All Tables** in the bottom of the **Field List pane**. Find and **double-click** the **StartingTime** field in the Sessions table on the top of the Field List pane.

c. Click **Yes** in the warning box. Close the Field List pane. Add a **space** between Starting and Time. Adjust columns as needed to fit all columns on one page.

d. Scroll to the end of the page. Find and select the text box for the page number and move it left so the page number prints under the Starting Time field.

e. Change the view to Report view.

f. Capture a screenshot of the Speaker Schedule report. Start a new Word document and type your name and section on the first two lines of the document. Paste the screenshot on the line below the section. Save the Word document as **chap4_cap_natconf_solution**. Print the screenshot file. Close the Word document and close the database.

...continued on Next Page

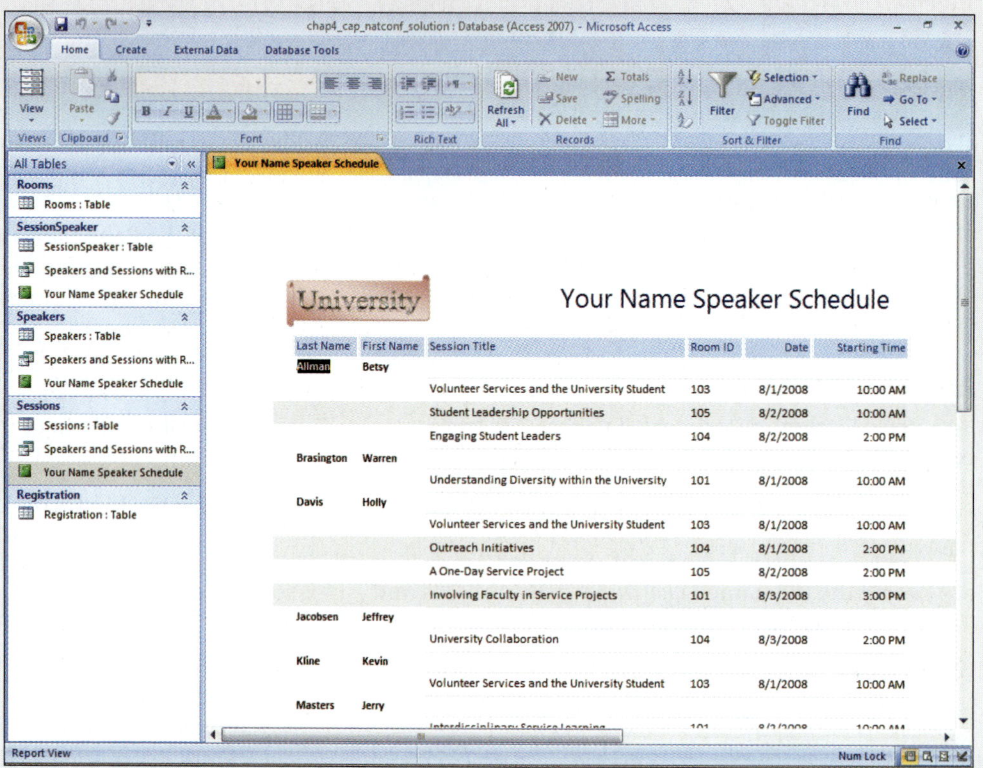

Figure 4.48 Speaker Schedule Report

Mini Cases

Use the rubric following the case as a guide to evaluate your work, but keep in mind that your instructor may impose additional grading criteria or use a different standard to judge your work.

Inventory Value

GENERAL CASE

The owner of a small bookstore called and asked for your help. Her insurance company requires that she provide the company with a report on the values of the inventory she stocks. Copy the *chap4_mc1_bookstore.accdb* file to your production folder, name it **chap4_mc1_bookstore_ solution.accdb**, and open the copied file. Use the skills from this chapter to perform several tasks. Create a report that shows the publisher's name, the author's first and last names, the book title, the book price, the number in stock, and the value of the stock. The report needs to be grouped by publisher with appropriate summary statistics calculated. The books within each publisher's group should be listed in alphabetical order by the author's last name. The report needs to contain an appropriate graphic and a grand total. The file contains a query that you may use to create the report. Close the database.

Performance Elements	Exceeds Expectations	Meets Expectations	Below Expectations
Create report	All necessary and no unneeded fields included.	All necessary fields included but also unnecessary fields.	Not all necessary fields were included.
Appropriate grouping and sorting	The grouping and sorting were correctly identified and executed.	Grouping correct but sorting incorrect or vice-versa.	Neither grouping nor sorting properly employed.
Summary statistics	Correct group aggregating information selected and appropriately displayed.	Correct group aggregating information selected, but the display had problems.	Group aggregating information not selected and/or inappropriately displayed.
Summarize balances	Correct method, correct totals.	Correct totals but inefficient method.	Totals incorrect or missing.

Producing Mailing Labels

RESEARCH CASE

This chapter introduced you to the power of using reports, but you have much more to explore. Use Access Help to search for mailing labels. Open and read the articles titled, *Use Access to Create and Print Labels* and *Learn Tips and Tricks for Creating Labels*. Put your new knowledge to the test. Copy the *chap4_mc2_arboretum.accdb* file to your production folder and rename the copy as **chap4_mc2_ arboretum_solution.accdb**. Open the file. It contains a query identifying volunteers who need to be invited to this year's gala. Your challenge is to figure out how to print the names and addresses as mailing labels. You have purchased Avery product number 5260 labels to print on. They are 1 ½″ x 2 ⅝″ with three columns of labels on each page. The mailing will be sent bulk rate, so the labels need to print sorted by postal code. After you successfully produce the report, print it on plain paper. Write your instructor a memo explaining how you accomplished this task. Use a memo template in Word, your most professional writing style, and clear directions that someone could follow in order to accomplish this task. Attach the printout of the labels to the memo. Save the Word document as **chap4_mc2_ arboretum_solution**.

Each label should be set up in this fashion:
Mr. (Dr., Ms., Mrs.,) John Doe, Jr.
Street Address
City, State Postal Code

Close the database.

Performance Elements	Exceeds Expectations	Meets Expectations	Below Expectations
Use online help	Appropriate articles located and memo indicates comprehension.	Appropriate articles located, but memo did not demonstrate comprehension.	Articles not found.
Prepare labels	Printed list attached to memo in requested format.	Printed list is attached, but the formatting has minor flaws.	List missing or incomprehensible.
Summarize and communicate	Memo clearly written and could be used as directions.	Memo text indicates some understanding but also weaknesses.	Memo missing or incomprehensible.
Aesthetics	Memo template correctly employed.	Template employed but signed in the wrong place or improperly used.	Memo missing or incomprehensible.

Real Estate Development Report

DISASTER CASE

A co-worker called you into her office, explained that she was having difficulty with Access 2007 and asked you to look at her work. Copy the *chap4_mc3_realestate.accdb* file to your working storage folder, name it **chap4_mc3_realestate_solution.accdb**, and open the file. It contains a query, Your Name Sales Report. It also contains a report based on the query. The report is supposed to show each agent's total sales with each development listed under the agent's name. There should be totals for the sales and commissions columns for each salesperson and each development. Your challenge is to find and correct the error(s) and then to produce an attractive, easy-to-read report. Close the database.

Performance Elements	Exceeds Expectations	Meets Expectations	Below Expectations
Error identification	Correct identification and correction of all errors.	Correct identification of all errors and correction of some errors.	Errors neither located nor corrected.
Grouping order	Correct grouping options and summarization selected.	Correct grouping, but some summaries incorrectly selected.	Incorrect group by option selection.
Aesthetics	Report design aids reader.	Inconsistent formatting, but all necessary data displays.	Controls improperly sized. Information obscured.

chapter 1 | PowerPoint

Introduction to PowerPoint

Presentations Made Easy

After you read this chapter, you will be able to:

1. Identify PowerPoint user interface elements (**page 799**).
2. Use PowerPoint views (**page 804**).
3. Open and save a slide show (**page 809**).
4. Get Help (**page 812**).
5. Create a storyboard (**page 817**).
6. Use slide layouts (**page 820**).
7. Apply design themes (**page 820**).
8. Review the presentation (**page 822**).
9. Add a table (**page 829**).
10. Insert clip art (**page 829**).
11. Use transitions and animations (**page 831**).
12. Run and navigate a slide show (**page 840**).
13. Print with PowerPoint (**page 842**).

Hands-On Exercises

Exercises	Skills Covered
1. INTRODUCTION TO POWERPOINT (page 813) **Open:** chap1_ho1_intro.pptx **Save as:** chap1_ho1_intro_solution.pptx	• Start PowerPoint • Open an Existing Presentation • Type a Speaker's Note • View the Presentation • Save the Presentation with a New Name • Locate Information Using Help
2. CREATING A PRESENTATION (page 823) **Open:** none **Save as:** chap1_ho2_content_solution.pptx	• Create a New Presentation • Add Slides • Check Spelling and Use the Thesaurus • Modify Text and Layout • Reorder Slides • Apply a Design Theme
3. STRENGTHENING A PRESENTATION (page 834) **Open:** chap1_ho2_content _solution.pptx (from Exercise 2) **Save as:** chap1_ho3_content_solution.pptx (additional modifications)	• Add a Table • Insert, Move, and Resize Clip Art • Apply a Transition • Animate Objects
4. NAVIGATING AND PRINTING (page 845) **Open:** chap1_ho3_content_solution.pptx (from Exercise 3) **Save as:** chap1_ho4_content_solution.pptx (additional modifications)	• Display a Slide Show • Navigate to Specific Slides • Annotate a Slide • Print Audience Handouts

CASE STUDY

Be a Volunteer

While watching television one evening, you see a public service announcement on the volunteer organization Big Brothers Big Sisters. The Big Brothers Big Sisters organization seeks to help children ages 6 through 18 reach their potential by providing mentors through their growing years. The organization matches "Bigs" (adults) with "Littles" (children) in one-on-one relationships with the goal of having the mentor make a positive impact on the child's life. Being intrigued, you attend an informational open house where volunteers and board members give an overview of the program and share personal experiences. At the open house you discover that the organization has been helping at-risk children for more than 100 years and that in 2003 Big Brothers Big Sisters was selected by *Forbes Magazine* as one of its top ten charities that it believes are worthy of donor consideration.

Case Study

You choose to answer Big Brothers Big Sisters' call to "Be a friend. Be a mentor. Just be there." You call the local organization for further information and you are invited to come in and meet representatives, introduce yourself, and complete an application. Because "Bigs" and "Littles" are matched by interests, you decide to create a presentation to introduce you and give information about your interests. Your assignment is to create a PowerPoint slide show about yourself to use in your presentation. You may want to include a slide about a mentor who has positively impacted your life. Forget modesty at this point—toot your own horn!

Your Assignment

- Read the chapter, paying special attention to how to create and enhance a presentation.
- Create a new presentation with a title slide that includes your name. Save the presentation as **chap1_case_introduction_solution**.
- Create a storyboard that includes four to six slides that introduce you, your background, and your interests. Include an introduction slide and a summary or conclusion slide as well as your main point slides introducing you.
- Use the storyboard to create a PowerPoint slide show about you.
- Apply a design theme and add a transition to at least one slide.
- Insert at least one clip art image in an appropriate location.
- Display your slide show to at least one class member, or to the entire class if asked by your instructor.
- Print handouts, four slides per page, framed.

Introduction to PowerPoint

This chapter introduces you to PowerPoint 2007, one of the major applications in Microsoft Office 2007. PowerPoint enables you to create a professional presentation without relying on others, and then lets you deliver that presentation in a variety of ways. You can show the presentation from your computer, on the World Wide Web, or create traditional overhead transparencies. You can even use PowerPoint's Package for CD feature to package your presentation with a viewer so that those without PowerPoint may still view your presentation.

A PowerPoint presentation consists of a series of slides such as those shown in Figures 1.1–1.6. The various slides contain different elements (such as text, images, and WordArt), yet the presentation has a consistent look with respect to its overall design and color scheme. Creating this type of presentation is relatively easy, and that is the power in PowerPoint. In essence, PowerPoint enables you to concentrate on the content of a presentation without worrying about its appearance. You supply the text and supporting elements and leave the formatting to PowerPoint. If, however, you wish to create your own presentation design, PowerPoint provides you with powerful tools to use in the design process.

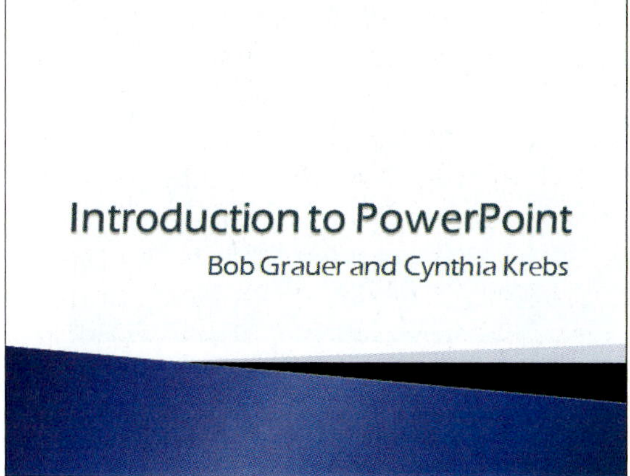
Introduction to PowerPoint
Bob Grauer and Cynthia Krebs

Figure 1.1 Title Slide

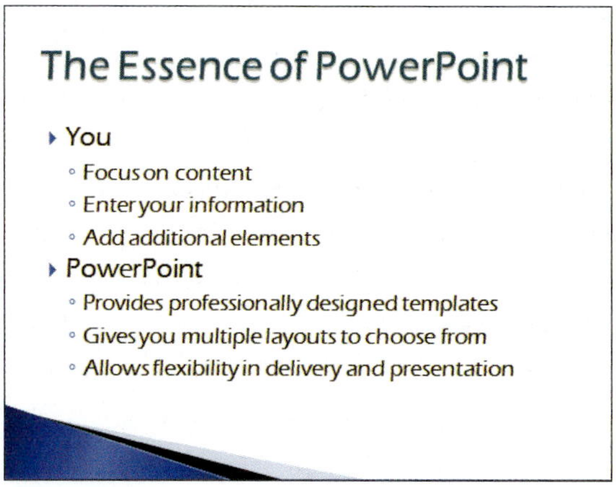

The Essence of PowerPoint

- You
  - Focus on content
  - Enter your information
  - Add additional elements
- PowerPoint
  - Provides professionally designed templates
  - Gives you multiple layouts to choose from
  - Allows flexibility in delivery and presentation

Figure 1.2 Title and Content Slide

Flexible Output

- Computer slide show
- Web-based presentation
- Audience handouts
- Outline
- Speaker notes
- Traditional transparencies

Figure 1.3 Title and Content Slide

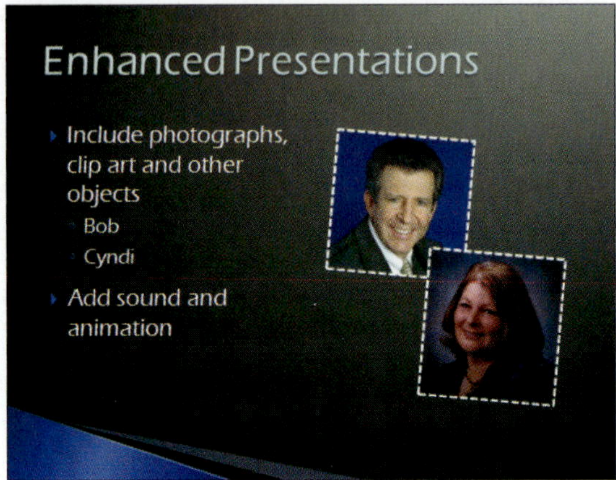

Enhanced Presentations
Include photographs, clip art and other objects
Bob
Cyndi
Add sound and animation

Figure 1.4 Two Content Slide with Images

Ease of Use

- Uses same ribbon structure as other Office 2007 applications
- Organizes and presents menus according to what you are doing
- Displays galleries with formatting and graphic options
- Shows you how your changes will look with Live Previews

Figure 1.5 Title and Content Slide

Figure 1.6 Title Slide with WordArt

In addition to helping you create the presentation, PowerPoint provides a variety of ways to deliver it. You can show the presentation on a computer monitor as a slide show or Web presentation, or you can project the slide show onto a screen or a wall for an audience. You can include sound and video in the presentation, provided your system has a sound card and speakers. You can automate the presentation and display it at a convention booth or kiosk. If you cannot show the presentation on a computer with a monitor or projector, you can easily convert it to overhead transparencies or print the presentation in various ways to distribute to your audience.

In this section, you start your exploration of PowerPoint by viewing a previously completed presentation so that you can better appreciate what PowerPoint is all about. You examine the PowerPoint interface and various views to discover the advantages of each view. You modify and save an existing presentation, and then you create your own. Finally, you use Help to obtain assistance within PowerPoint.

Delivery Tips | Reference

Practice the following delivery tips to gain confidence and polish your delivery:

- Look at the audience, not at the screen, as you speak and you will open communication and gain credibility. Use the three-second guide: look into the eyes of a member of the audience for three seconds and then scan the entire audience. Continue doing this throughout your presentation. Use your eye contact to keep members of the audience involved.
- Do not read from a prepared script or your PowerPoint Notes. Know your material thoroughly. Glance at your notes infrequently. Never post a screen full of small text and then torture your audience by saying "I know you can't read this so I will..."
- Practice or rehearse your presentation with PowerPoint at home until you are comfortable with the material and its corresponding slides.
- Speak slowly and clearly and try to vary your delivery. Show emotion or enthusiasm for your topic. If you do not care about your topic, why should the audience?
- Pause to emphasize key points when speaking.
- Speak to the person farthest away from you to be sure the people in the last row can hear you.
- Do not overwhelm your audience with PowerPoint animations, sounds, and special effects. These features should not overpower you and your message, but should enhance your message.
- Arrive early to set up so you do not keep the audience waiting while you manage equipment. Have a backup in case the equipment does not work: overhead transparencies or handouts work well. Again, know your material well enough that you can present without the slide show if necessary.
- Prepare handouts for your audience so they can relax and participate in your presentation rather than scramble taking notes.
- Thank the audience for their attention and participation. Leave on a positive note.

TIP Polish Your Delivery

The speaker is the most important part of any presentation, and a poor delivery will ruin even the best presentation. Remember that a PowerPoint slide show is a tool to aid YOU in your presentation and that YOU are the key to a good presentation. Do not use a PowerPoint slide show as a crutch for lack of preparation for a presentation. A PowerPoint presentation should not be like "karaoke," where you read your information word for word from the screen!

Identifying PowerPoint User Interface Elements

If you have completed the Exploring Series Office Fundamentals chapter on Office 2007, many of the PowerPoint 2007 interface features will be familiar to you. If this is your first experience with an Office 2007 application, you will quickly feel comfortable in PowerPoint, and because the interface is core to all of the Office 2007 applications, you will quickly be able to apply the knowledge in Word, Excel, Access, and Outlook. In Office 2007, Microsoft organizes features and commands to correspond directly to the common tasks people perform, making it possible for you to find the features you need quickly.

In PowerPoint 2007 you work with two windows: the PowerPoint application window and the document window for the current presentation. The PowerPoint application window contains the Minimize, Maximize (or Restore), and Close buttons. The PowerPoint application window also contains the title bar, which indicates the file name of the document on which you are working and the name of the application (Microsoft PowerPoint). Figure 1.7 shows the default PowerPoint view, the ***Normal view***, with three panes that provide maximum flexibility in working with the presentation. The pane on the left side of the screen shows either thumbnails or an outline of the presentation, depending on whether you select the Slides tab or the Outline tab. The Slide pane on the right displays the currently selected slide in your presentation. The final pane, the Notes pane, is located at the bottom of the screen where you enter notes pertaining to the slide or the presentation.

Normal view is the tri-pane default PowerPoint view.

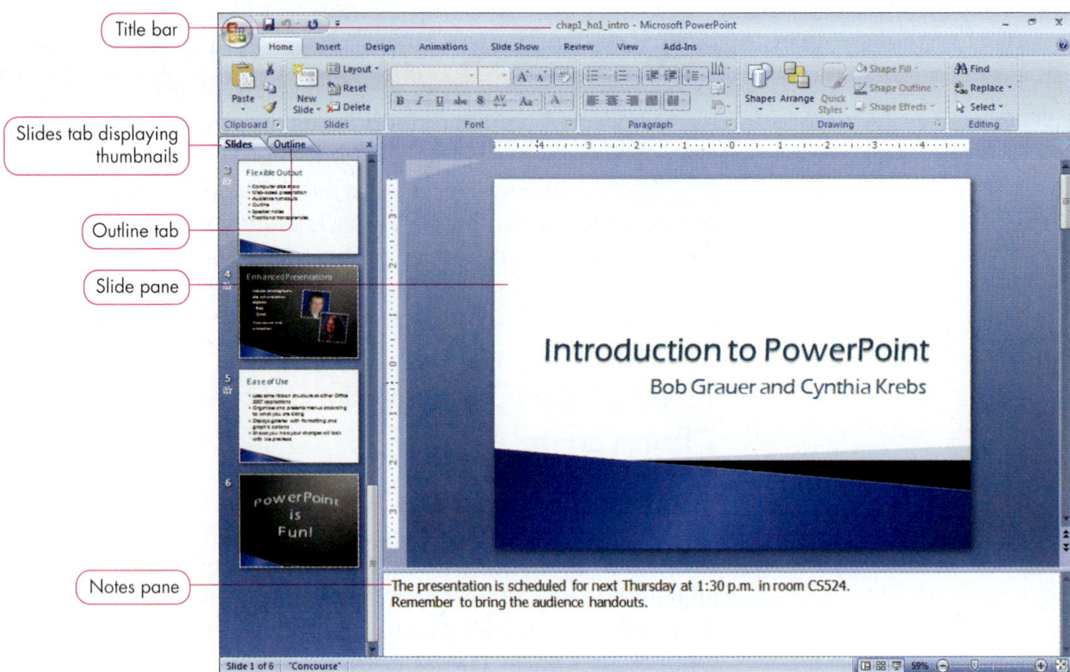

Figure 1.7 The Default PowerPoint View (Normal View)

Refer to Figure 1.8 to see the Microsoft Office Button, hereafter referred to as the Office Button, displayed below the title bar. This button provides you with an easy way to access commands for saving and printing, and includes features for finalizing your work and sharing your work with others. To the right of the Office Button is the Quick Access Toolbar, which gives you quick access to the commands that you may need at any time: Save, Undo, and Redo. You also can add other commands to the Quick Access Toolbar.

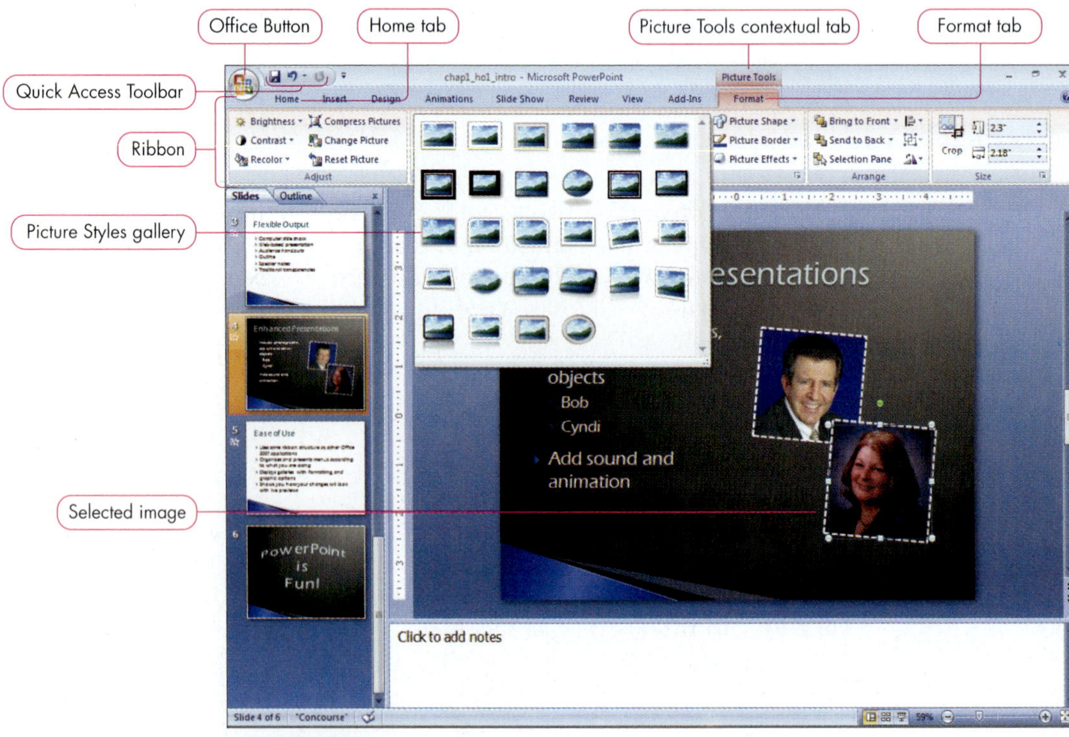

Figure 1.8 PowerPoint's Interface

The ***Ribbon*** is a command center that organizes commands into groups accessed from tabs.

Beneath the Office Button and the Quick Access Toolbar is the ***Ribbon***, a command center that organizes commands into groups. The Ribbon makes it easy for you to find the features you need. Locate the Ribbon in Figure 1.8.

TIP View Hidden Commands

If, when you look at your PowerPoint screen, it does not show all of the commands, your monitor could be set to display at a low resolution. For example, a resolution of 800 by 600 pixels used with small notebooks and older 13" CRT screens will not show all the commands. To see the hidden commands, click the ▶ on the vertical bar on the far right of the Ribbon. The remaining commands will appear. Changing your resolution to 1024 by 768 pixels or a higher resolution will enable all commands to display.

A ***tab*** sits above the Ribbon and is used to organize or group like features for quick access.

A ***tab*** sits above the Ribbon and organizes commands by grouping the most commonly used features related to your task for quick access. Once you select a tab based on the task you wish to perform, the commands that relate to one another when working on that task appear together in groups. For example, when you click the Home tab, the core PowerPoint commands appear in groups such as Clipboard, Slides, Font, Paragraph, Drawing, and Editing. PowerPoint has seven tabs: Home, Insert, Design, Animations, Slide Show, Review, and View. You may see an additional tab, Add-Ins, if you have any supplemental programs that add features to Microsoft Office. The author installed a supplemental image-capturing program, so all figures in this text display the Add-Ins tab. Table 1.1 lists each of the tabs, the groups that appear when the tab is selected, and a general description of the available commands.

TIP Minimize the Ribbon

To increase the size of the working area on your screen, you can minimize the Ribbon by clicking the Customize Quick Access Toolbar down arrow and selecting Minimize the Ribbon. To restore the Ribbon, double-click any tab. As an alternative, use the keyboard shortcut by pressing **Ctrl+F1**.

An ***object*** is any type of information that can be inserted in a slide.

A ***contextual tab*** is a specialty tab that appears only when certain types of objects are being edited.

When you add text, a graphic, a table, a chart, or any other form of information to a slide, you are adding an ***object*** to the slide. When you select certain types of objects for editing, ***contextual tabs*** containing commands specific to that object appear. The contextual tabs appear above the Ribbon and, when clicked, open a tab containing multiple tools you need. For example, in Figure 1.8, because the image of Cyndi is selected for editing, the Picture Tools contextual tab displays. Clicking the Picture Tools tab opened the Format tab. The Format tab is organized into groups related to specific tasks (Adjust, Picture Styles, Arrange, and Size).

Microsoft . . . "pick and click" formatting . . . gives you results that look good without much design effort.

As you examine Figure 1.8, notice the large box that appears on top of the Ribbon, showing a wide variety of styles that could be applied to a picture. This is the Picture Styles gallery, one of many galleries within PowerPoint. A ***gallery*** provides you with a set of visual options to choose from when working with your presentation. You click an option, and the styles in that option are applied to your object. Microsoft refers to this feature as "pick and click" formatting. "Picking and clicking" gives you results that look good without much design effort.

A ***gallery*** displays a set of predefined options that can be clicked to apply to an object.

Table 1.1 Tab, Group, Description

Tab and Group	Description
Home Clipboard Slides Font Paragraph Drawing Editing	The core PowerPoint tab. Contains basic editing functions such as cut and paste, and finding and replacing text. Includes adding slides and changing slide layout. Formatting using font, paragraph, and drawing tools is available.
Insert Tables Illustrations Links Text Media Clips	Contains all insert functions in one area. Includes ability to create tables and illustrations. Hyperlinks, text boxes, headers and footers, WordArt, and media clips are inserted here.
Design Page Setup Themes Background	Contains all functions associated with slide design including themes and backgrounds. Change page setup and slide orientation here.
Animations Preview Animations Transition to This Slide	Controls all aspects of animation including transitions, advanced options, and customizing.
Slide Show Start Slide Show Set Up Monitors	Includes slide show setup, monitor set up, and timing. Options for starting the slide show available.
Review Proofing Comments Protect	Contains all reviewing tools in PowerPoint, including such things as spelling and the use of comments.
View Presentation Views Show/Hide Zoom Color/Grayscale Window Macros	Contains Presentation Views. Advanced view options include showing or hiding slides, zooming, and available color choices. Set window arrangement here. Enables macro creation.
Add-Ins Custom Toolbars	Displays programs added to system that extend PowerPoint functionality. Does not display if supplemental programs are not installed.

A ***ScreenTip*** is a small window that describes a command.

Figure 1.9 shows a ***ScreenTip***, or small window that appears when the mouse pointer moves over a command. The ScreenTip states the name or more descriptive explanation of a command. ScreenTips can be invaluable when you need to identify a selected style. In this case, the ScreenTip gives the name of a WordArt choice, Fill–Accent 2, Warm Matte Bevel, and a preview of how it would look if selected. In some instances, an Enhanced ScreenTip appears when you position the mouse over a command. An Enhanced ScreenTip displays the message *Press F1 for more help*, so that you get additional help about that command.

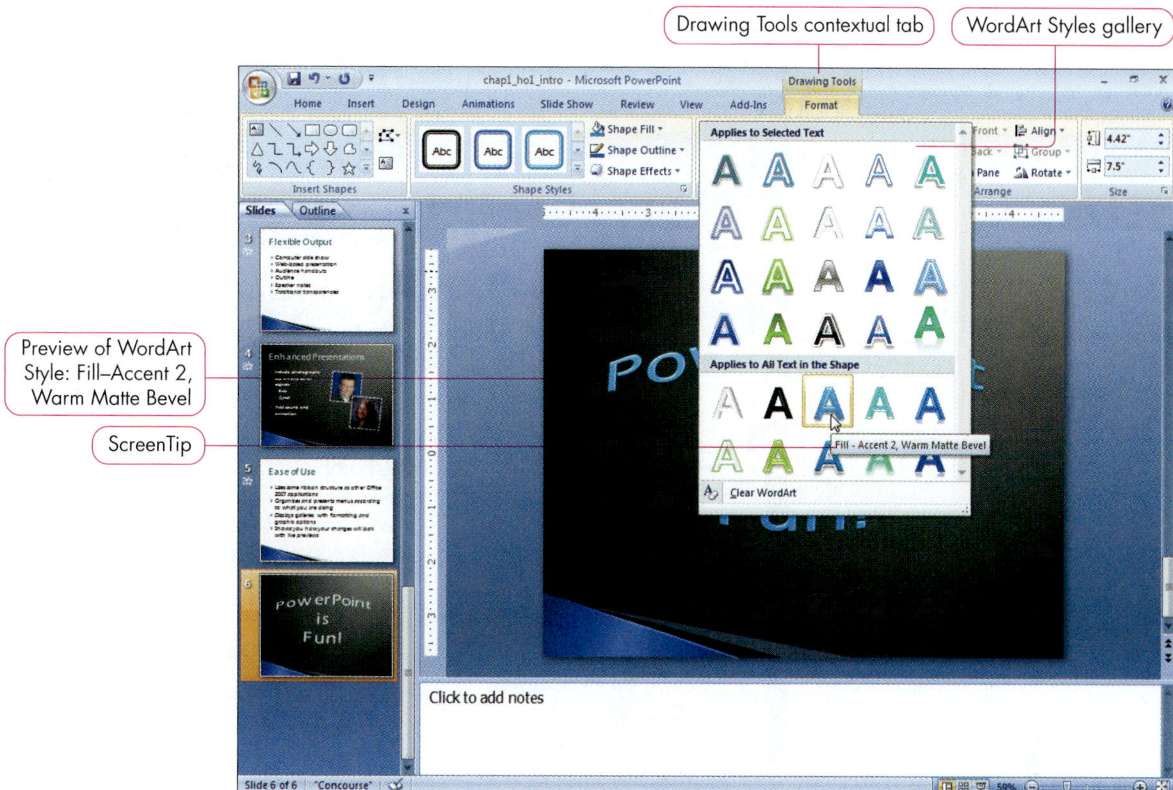

Figure 1.9 WordArt Gallery with ScreenTip

The ***Mini toolbar*** is a small, semitransparent toolbar that you can use to format text.

The ***Mini toolbar*** is a small semitransparent toolbar that appears above selected text (see Figure 1.10) and gives you quick and easy access to the formatting commands commonly applied to text (such as font, font styles, font size, text alignment, text color, indent levels, and bullet features). Because the Mini toolbar appears above the selected text, you do not have to move the mouse pointer up to the Ribbon. When you first select text, the Mini toolbar appears as a semitransparent image, but if you move the mouse pointer over the toolbar, it fades in and becomes active for your use. As the mouse pointer moves away from the toolbar, or if a command is not selected, the Mini toolbar disappears.

The ***status bar*** is a bar that contains the slide number, the Design Theme name, and view options.

Figure 1.10 also shows PowerPoint's unique ***status bar***, a bar that contains the slide number, the total number of slides, the design theme name, and options that control the view of your presentation: view buttons, the Zoom level button, the Zoom Slider, and the *Fit slide to current window* button. The status bar is located at the bottom of your screen, and can be customized. To customize the status bar, right-click the bar and then click the options you want displayed from the Customize Status Bar list.

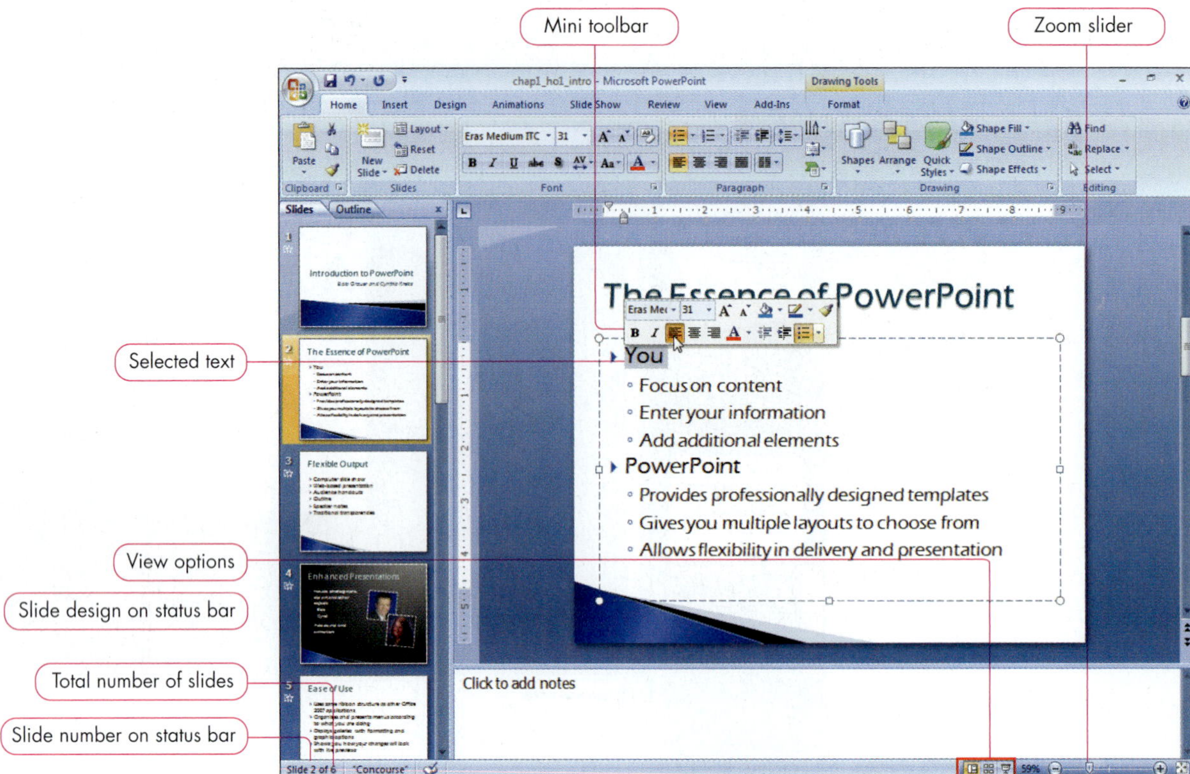

Figure 1.10 Mini Toolbar and Status Bar

Using PowerPoint Views

PowerPoint offers four primary views in which to create, modify, and deliver a presentation: Normal, Slide Sorter, Notes Page, and Slide Show. Each view represents a different way of looking at the presentation and each view has unique capabilities. (You will find some redundancy among the views in that certain tasks can be accomplished from multiple views.) The View tab gives you access to the four primary views, plus three additional views for working with masters. If you prefer, you may use the view buttons on the status bar to switch from one view to another, but only three views are available from the status bar: Normal, Slide Sorter, and Slide Show.

You looked at the default Normal view earlier in the chapter, (refer to Figure 1.7) but you will examine it in more detail now and compare it to other PowerPoint views. Knowing the benefits of each view enables to you work more efficiently. Figure 1.11 shows Normal view with the screen divided into three panes: the Outline tab pane showing the text of the presentation, the Slide pane displaying an enlarged view of one slide, and the Notes pane showing a portion of any associated speaker notes for the selected slide. The Outline tab pane provides the fastest way to type or edit text for the presentation. You type directly into the outline pane and move easily from one slide to the next. You also can use the outline pane to move and copy text from one slide to another or to rearrange the order of the slides within a presentation. The outline pane is limited, however, in that it does not show graphic elements that may be present on individual slides. Thus, you may want to switch to the Normal view that shows the Slides tab containing ***thumbnail*** images (slide miniatures) rather than the outline. In this view you can change the order of the slides by clicking and dragging a slide to a new position. The Outline and Slides tabs let you switch between the two variations of the Normal view.

A ***thumbnail*** is a miniature of a slide that appears in the Slides tab.

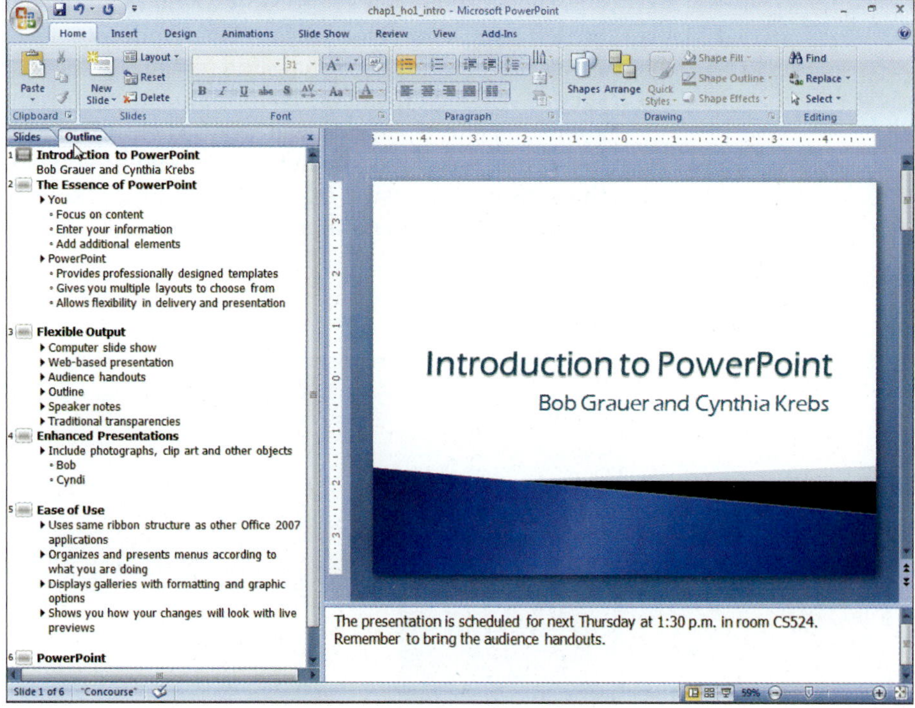

Figure 1.11 Normal View with Outline Tab Selected

The Normal view also provides access to the individual slides and speaker notes, each of which appears in its own pane. The Slide pane is the large pane on the right of the window. The Notes pane displays on the bottom of the window. You can change the size of these panes by dragging the splitter bar (border) that separates one pane from another. Figure 1.12 shows the Slides tab selected, the size of the Slide pane reduced, and the size of the Notes pane enlarged to provide for more space in which to create speaker notes.

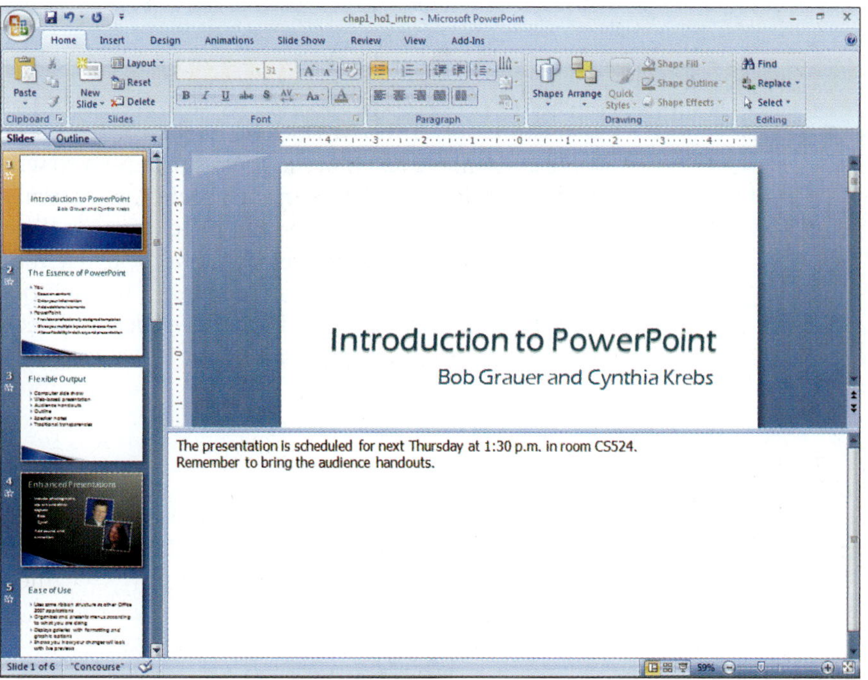

Figure 1.12 Normal View with Resized Panes

The Normal view is probably all that you need, but some designers like to close the left pane completely to see just an individual slide. This variation of the Normal view enlarges the individual slide so you can see more detail. Because the individual slide is where you change or format text, add graphical elements, or apply various animation effects, an enlarged view is helpful. Figure 1.13 shows the individual slide in Normal view with the left pane closed. If you close the left pane, you can restore the screen to its usual tri-pane view by clicking the View tab, and then clicking Normal in the Presentation Views group.

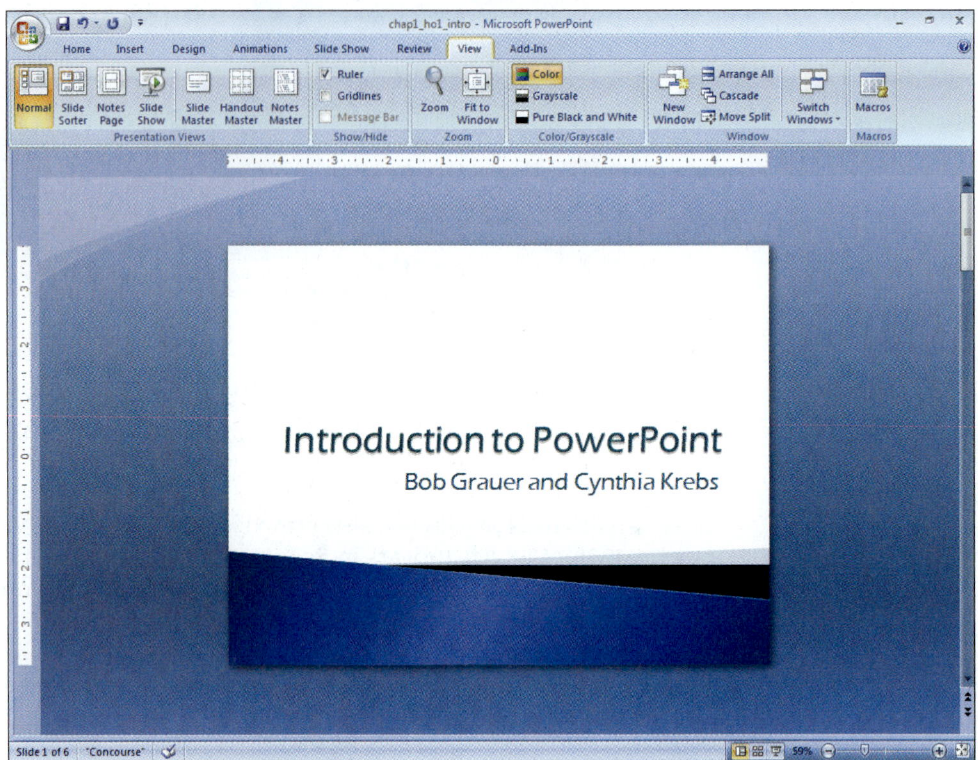

Figure 1.13 Individual Slide View

The ***Notes Page view*** is used for entering and editing large amounts of text that the speaker can refer to when presenting.

Rather than create speaker notes in the small pane available in the Normal view, you can work in the ***Notes Page view***, a view specifically created to enter and edit large amounts of text that the speaker can refer to when presenting. If you have a large amount of technical detail in the speaker notes, you also may want to print audience handouts of this view since each page contains a picture of the slide plus the associated speaker notes. The notes do not appear when the presentation is shown, but are intended to help the speaker remember the key points about each slide. To switch from Normal view to Notes Page view, click the View tab and then click Notes Page in the Presentation Views group. Figure 1.14 shows an example of the Notes Page view.

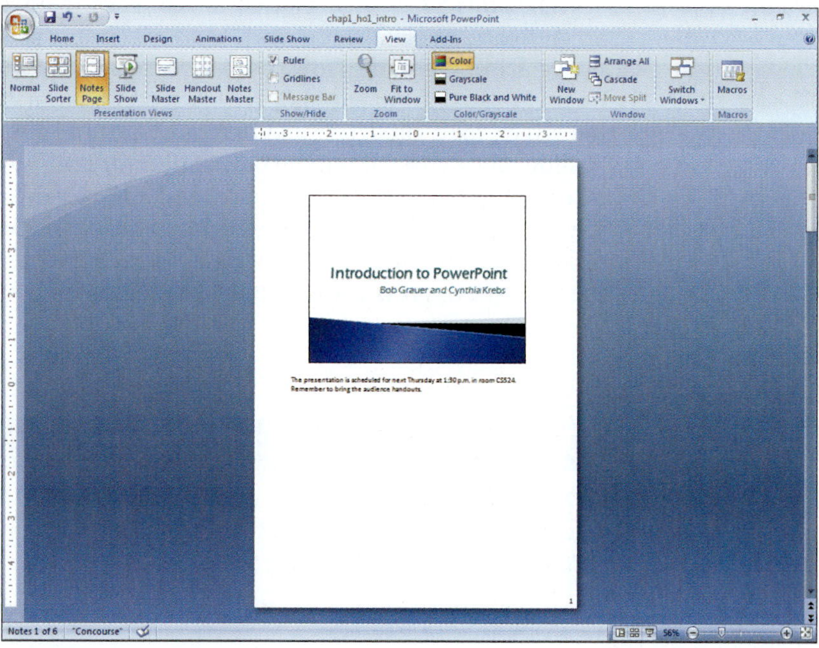

Figure 1.14 Notes Page View

The ***Slide Sorter view*** displays thumbnails of slides.

The ***Slide Sorter view*** enables you to see miniatures of your presentation slides to view multiple slides simultaneously (see Figure 1.15). This view is helpful when you wish to reorder the slides in a presentation. It also provides a convenient way to delete one or more slides. It lets you set transition effects for multiple slides. Any edit that you perform in one view is automatically updated in the other views. If, for example, you change the order of the slides in the Slide Sorter view, the changes automatically are reflected in the outline or thumbnail images within the Normal view. To switch to Slide Sorter view, click the View tab and then click Slide Sorter in the Presentation Views group. If you are in Slide Sorter view and double-click a thumbnail, PowerPoint returns to the Normal view.

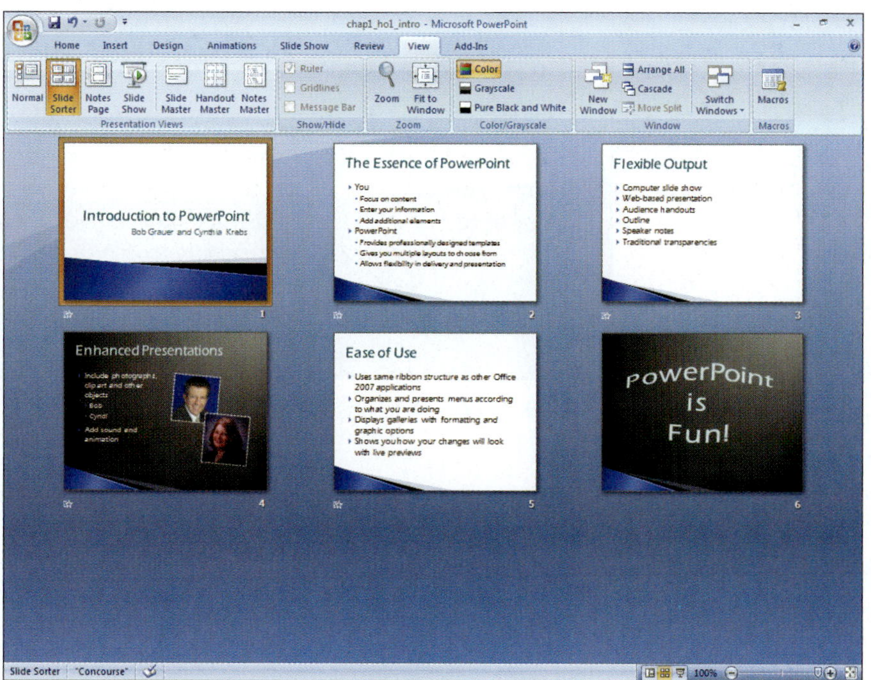

Figure 1.15 Slide Sorter View

The ***Slide Show view*** displays a full-screen view of a presentation.

The *Slide Show view* is used to deliver the completed presentation full screen to an audience, one slide at a time, as an electronic presentation on the computer (see Figure 1.16). The slide show can be presented manually, where the speaker clicks the mouse to move from one slide to the next, or automatically, where each slide stays on the screen for a predetermined amount of time, after which the next slide appears. A slide show can contain a combination of both methods for advancing. You can insert transition effects to impact the look of how one slide moves to the next. To view the presentation in Slide Show view, click the View tab and then click Slide Show in the Presentation Views group. This step begins the show with Slide 1. To end the slide show, press Escape on the keyboard.

TIP Start the Slide Show

To choose whether you start a slide show from the beginning, Slide 1, or from the current slide, click the Slide Show tab, and then click either From Beginning or From Current Slide in the Start Slide Show group.

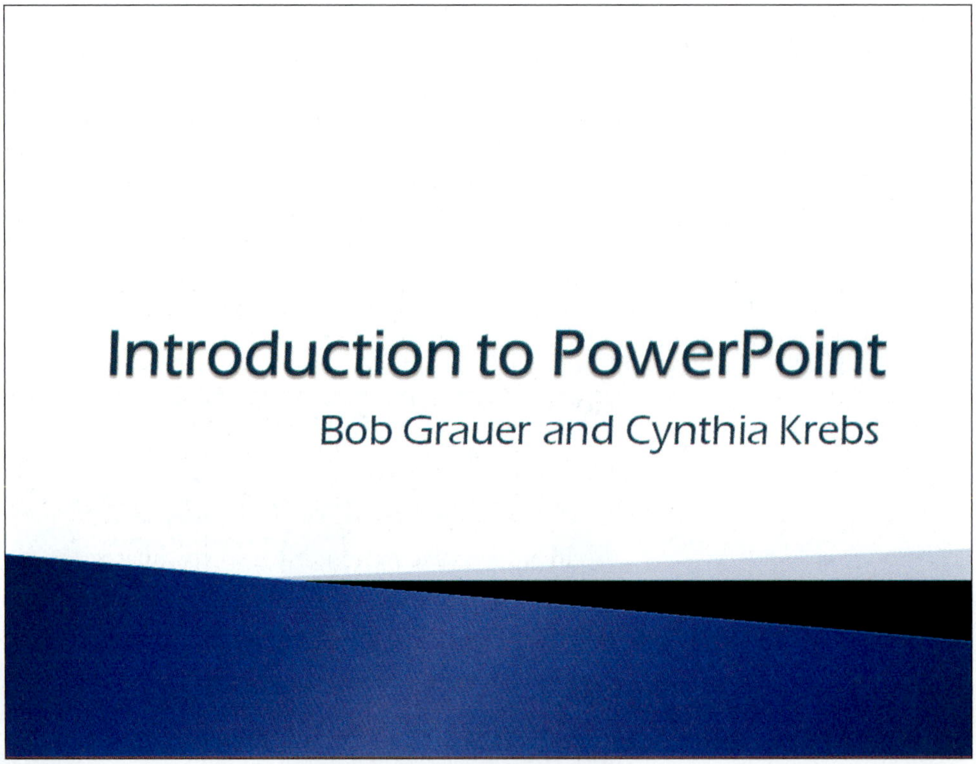

Introduction to PowerPoint
Bob Grauer and Cynthia Krebs

Figure 1.16 Slide Show View

Have you been in an audience watching a presenter use PowerPoint to deliver an electronic presentation? Did the presenter look professional at all times? While this is the desired scenario, consider another real-life scenario—the presenter holds a remote in one hand, printed speaker notes in the other hand, and is wearing a watch. The presenter is conscious of the time allotted for the presentation and attempts to look at the watch to see how much time has elapsed. Using the remote, the presenter attempts to slide a long sleeve up and reveal the watch. The remote catches on the printed speaker notes, the notes start to fall, the presenter grabs to catch them . . . and chaos results. Presenter Fumble lives! You can avoid "Presenter Fumble" by using Presenter view.

(. . . avoid "Presenter Fumble" by using Presenter view!)

Presenter view delivers a presentation on two monitors simultaneously.

Presenter view delivers a presentation on two monitors simultaneously. Typically one monitor is a projector that delivers the full-screen presentation to the audience and one monitor is a laptop or computer at the presenter's station. Having two monitors enables your audience to see your presentation at the same time you are seeing a special view of the presentation that includes the slide, speaker notes, slide thumbnails so you can jump between slides as needed, navigation arrows that advance your slide or return to the previous slide, options to enable a marking on the slide, and a timer that displays the time elapsed since you began. Figure 1.17 shows the audience view on the left side of the figure and the Presenter view on the right side.

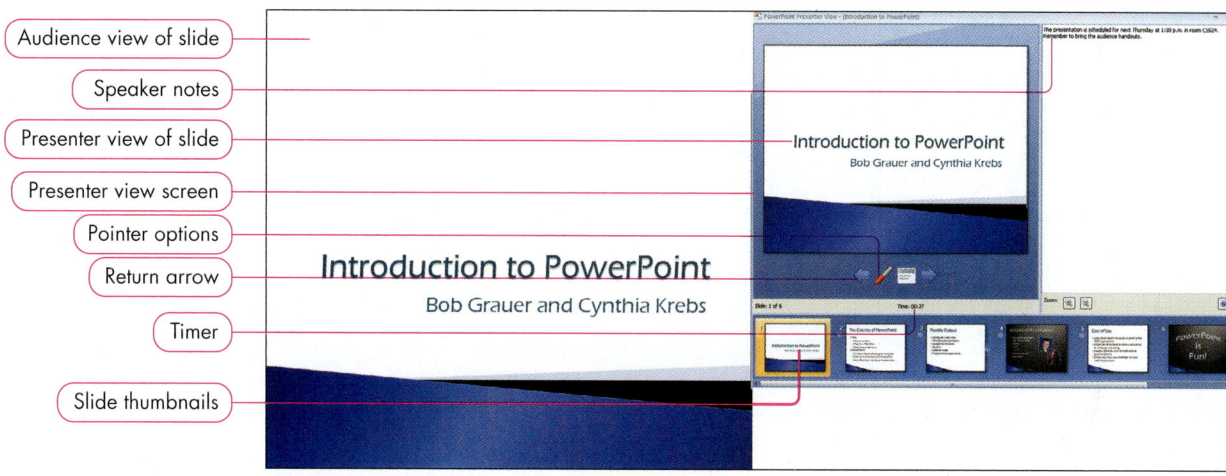

Figure 1.17 Presenter View

In order to use Presenter view, you must use a computer that has multiple monitor capability, and multiple monitor support must be turned on. If you need information about how to enable multiple monitor support, see Microsoft Windows Help. After you enable multiple monitor support, click Use Presenter View in the Monitors group on the Slide Show tab, and then click From Beginning in the Start Slide Show group under the same tab.

Opening and Saving a Slide Show

The Office Button gives you access to an important menu. The available options include the New command so that you can create a new document, in this case a presentation that is blank or that is based upon a template. You use the Open command to retrieve a presentation saved on a storage device and place it in the RAM memory of your computer so you can work on it. The Print command opens a dialog box so that you may choose print settings and then print. The Close command closes the current presentation but leaves PowerPoint open. To exit PowerPoint, click Exit PowerPoint in the Office menu or click the X located on the top right of the application window.

While you are working on a previously saved presentation, it is being saved in the temporary memory or RAM memory of your computer. The Save As command copies the presentation that you are working on to the hard drive of your computer or to a storage device such as a flash drive. When you activate the Save As command, the Save As dialog box appears (see Figure 1.18). The dialog box requires you to specify the drive or folder in which to store the presentation, the name of the presentation, and the type of file you wish the presentation to be saved as. All subsequent executions of the Save command save the presentation under the assigned name, replacing the previously saved version with the new version. If you wish to change the name of the presentation, use Save As again. Pressing Ctrl+S also displays the Save As dialog box if it is the first time you are saving the slide show.

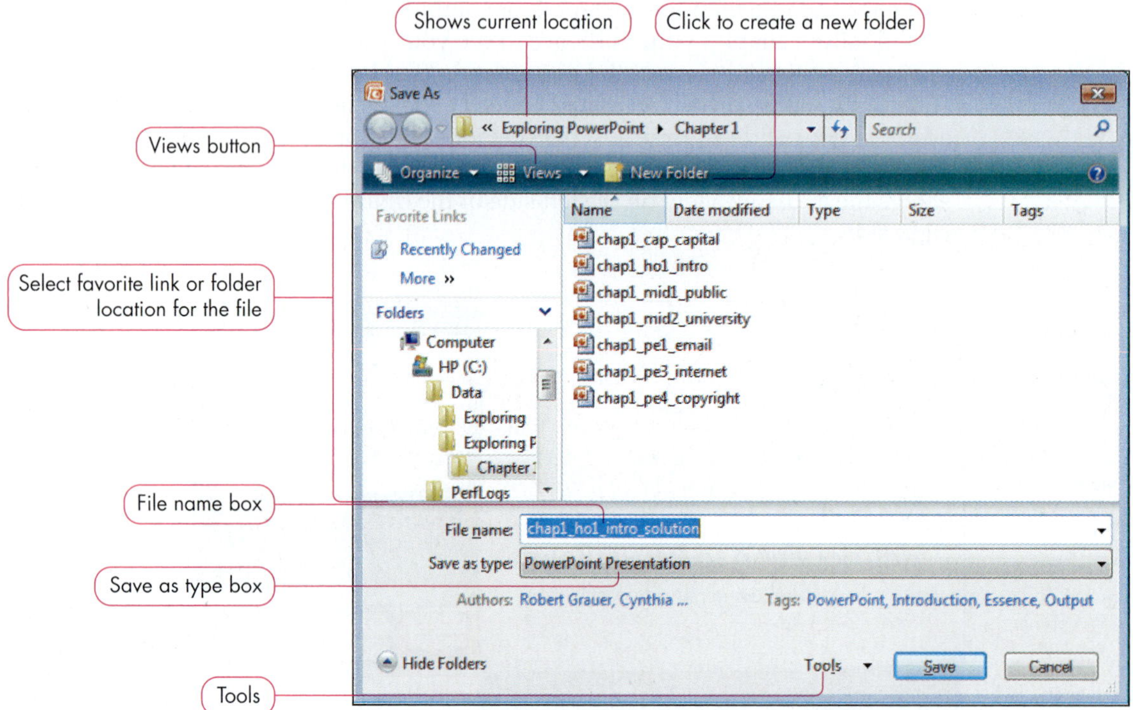

Figure 1.18 Save As Dialog Box

The file name (e.g., chap1_ho1_intro_solution) can contain up to 255 characters including spaces, commas, and/or periods. Periods are discouraged, however, since they are too easily confused with the file extensions explained in the next paragraph. Click the appropriate drive and folder in the Folders list on the left side of the Save As dialog box in which the presentation file will be saved.

The file type defaults to a PowerPoint presentation. You can save to other formats including a Web page. When you save a PowerPoint file, it is assigned a .pptx extension. This file type is an XML (Extensible Markup Language) format. This file format compresses data, which greatly reduces file sizes, thereby saving storage space on your hard drive or storage device. Another benefit of using the XML file format is that it reduces the chance of file corruption and helps you recover corrupted documents. This file format also provides increased security. One caution must be noted, however: Files created in the XML format cannot be opened in earlier versions of Microsoft Office software unless the Microsoft Office Compatibility Pack is installed. Your colleagues who share files with you should download the Compatibility Pack on all computers that may be used to open your XML files.

TIP New Folder Creation

By default, all Office documents are stored in the Documents folder. It is helpful, however, to create additional folders, especially if you work with a large number of different documents. You can create one folder for school and another for personal work, or you can create different folders for different applications. To create a folder, click the Office Button, select Save As, and then click the New Folder button. Type the name of the folder, and then press Enter to create the folder. The next time you open or save a presentation, use the Favorite Links or Folders category to navigate to that folder. For this class you may wish to create a folder with your assignment solutions for each chapter so you can quickly locate them.

The Open command retrieves a copy of an existing presentation into memory, enabling you to work with that presentation. The Open command displays the Open dialog box in which you specify the file name, the drive (and optionally the folder) that contains the file, and the file type. PowerPoint will then list all files of that type on the designated drive (and folder), enabling you to open the file you want. To aid you in selecting the correct file, click the Views button and select Extra Large Icons or Large Icons to see the first slide in a presentation, without having to open the presentation.

TIP Shortcut Menu for File Management

You can use either the Open or Save As dialog box to perform basic file management. Right-click a PowerPoint file name to see the shortcut menu. You can open, print, cut, copy, delete, or rename a file. In addition, you can display properties for a document.

Metadata are descriptive data about a document.

Document properties is the collection of metadata.

Metadata, data that describes document data, is attached to each file. The collection of metadata is referred to as the ***document properties***. General properties include file name, file type, location, size, and create/modified/accessed dates. Detailed properties include author, revision number, and so on. Figure 1.19 shows the detailed properties for the chap1_ho1_intro file.

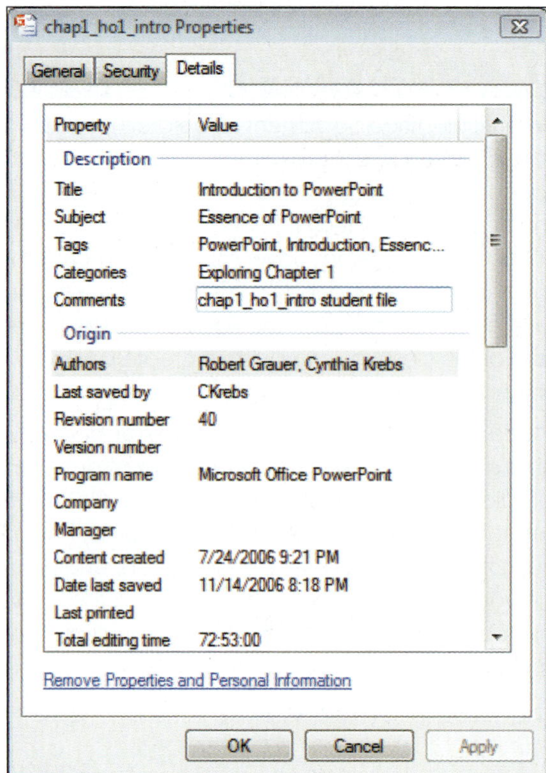

Figure 1.19 File Properties

TIP Sort by Name, Date, or File Size

The files in the Save As and Open dialog boxes can be displayed in ascending or descending sequence by name, size, file type, or date modified. Change to the Details view, then click the heading of the desired column; for example, click the Date modified column to list the files according to the date they were last changed. Click the column heading a second time to reverse the sequence—that is, to switch from ascending to descending, and vice versa.

Getting Help

Microsoft Help is designed to give you all the information you need, whether it is locating information about a specific feature, troubleshooting to solve a problem, searching for software updates, finding a template, or receiving additional training. Help is installed on your computer system at the same time your Office software applications are installed. You can use Help online or offline, depending on whether you are connected to the Internet.

To access Help, you click the Microsoft Office PowerPoint Help button located at the top right of the screen below the Close button. Or, if you prefer, you can use the Help keyboard shortcut by pressing F1. The PowerPoint Help window will appear. This window is designed to make Help easier for you to use. You can navigate and locate information by clicking one of the hyperlinked Help topics, or you can enter a topic in the Search box. The bottom portion of the Help window gives you access to Office Online where you can obtain clip art, download templates or training, or read articles. Clicking the *Up to speed with PowerPoint 2007* hyperlink and then reading the resulting Help screen will help you review the information covered thus far.

Hands-On Exercises

1 | Introduction to PowerPoint

Skills covered: **1.** Start PowerPoint **2.** Open an Existing Presentation **3.** Type a Speaker's Note **4.** View the Presentation **5.** Save the Presentation with a New Name **6.** Locate Information Using Help

Step 1 Start PowerPoint

a. Click **Start** on your Windows taskbar, and then click **All Programs**.

b. Click **Microsoft Office**, and then click **Microsoft Office PowerPoint 2007**.

You should see a blank PowerPoint presentation in Normal view.

Step 2 Open an Existing Presentation

Refer to Figure 1.20 as you complete Step 2.

a. Click the **Office Button** and select **Open**.

The Open dialog box appears.

b. Click the appropriate drive in the Folders list on the left side of the Open dialog box.

c. Double-click the **Exploring PowerPoint folder**, and then double-click the **Chapter 1** folder to make it active.

This is the folder from which you will retrieve files, and into which you will save your assignment solutions.

TROUBLESHOOTING: If you do not see an Exploring PowerPoint folder, it is possible that the student files for this text were saved to a different folder for your class. Check with your instructor to find out where to locate your student files.

d. Click the **Views button** repeatedly to cycle through the different views.

As you cycle through the views, observe the differences. Identify a reason you might use each view. Figure 1.20 is displayed in Large Icons view.

e. Double-click the *chap1_ho1_intro* presentation.

The slide show opens to the *Introduction to PowerPoint* title slide.

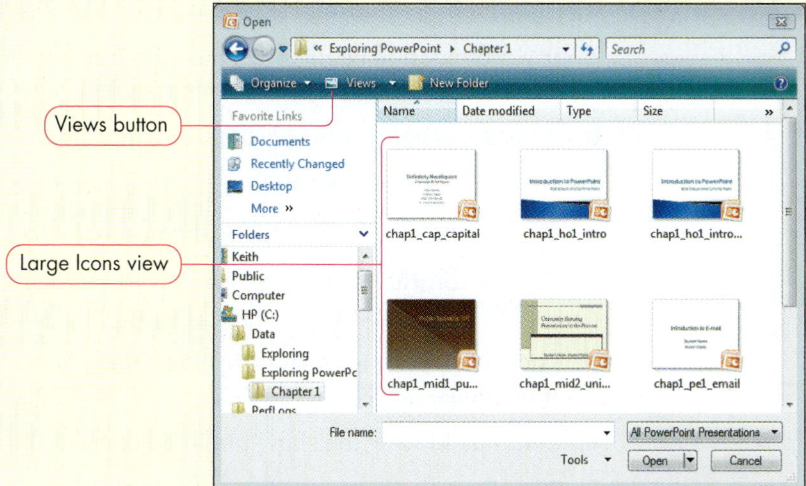

Figure 1.20 Open Dialog Box

Step 3
Type a Speaker's Note

Refer to Figure 1.21 as you complete Step 3.

a. Click the **Slide 4 thumbnail** in the Slides tab.

   Slide 4 is selected, and the slide appears in the Slide pane.

b. Drag the splitter bar between the Slide pane and the Notes pane upward to create more room in the Notes pane area.

c. Type the following information in the Notes pane: **Among the objects that can be inserted into PowerPoint are tables, clip art, diagrams, charts, hyperlinks, text boxes, headers and footers, movies, sound, and objects from other software packages**.

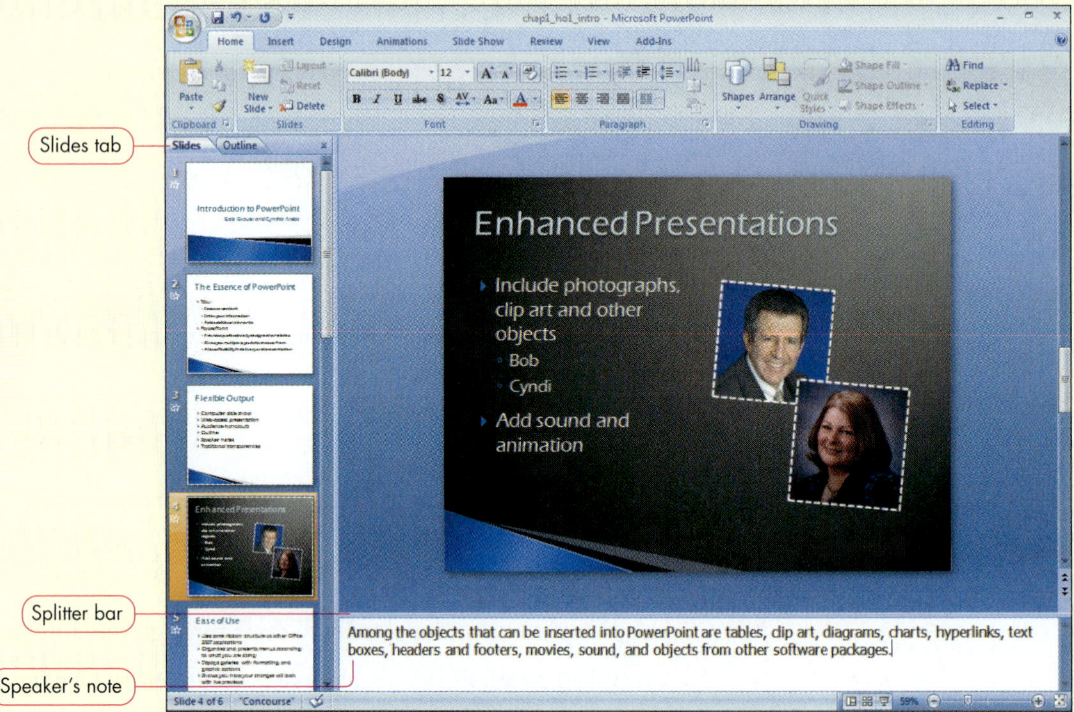

Figure 1.21 Speaker's Note

Step 4
View the Presentation

a. Click **From Beginning** in the Start Slide Show group on the Slide Show tab.

   The presentation begins with the title slide, the first slide in all slide shows. The title and subtitle have animations assigned, so they come in automatically.

b. Press **Spacebar** to advance to the second slide.

   The text on the second slide wipes down and creates each bullet point.

c. Click the left mouse button to advance to the third slide.

   The text on the third slide, and all following slides, has the same animation applied to create consistency in the presentation.

d. Click to advance to the fourth slide, which has sound added to the image animations.

e. Continue to view the show until you come to the end of the presentation.

f. Press **Esc** to return to the PowerPoint Normal view.

Step 5
Save the Presentation with a New Name

Refer to Figure 1.22 as you complete Step 3.

a. Click the **Office Button**, and then select **Save As**.

b. Click the appropriate drive and folder in the Folders list on the left side of the Save As dialog box. Choose the location where you want to save your completed files.

c. Type **chap1_ho1_intro_solution** as the file name for the presentation.

d. Click **Save**.

TIP Change the Default Folder

The default folder is where PowerPoint goes initially to open an existing presentation or to save a new presentation. You may find it useful to change the default folder if you are working on your own computer and not in a classroom lab. Click the Office Button, and then click PowerPoint Options, which enables you to modify your document settings and customize how PowerPoint behaves by default. Click Save from the frame on the left side. Click in the box that contains the default file location, enter the new drive or the new folder where you wish your files to be saved, and click OK. The next time you open or save a file, PowerPoint will go automatically to that location. This feature may not work in a classroom lab, however, if the lab has a "deep freeze" program to ensure students work from default settings.

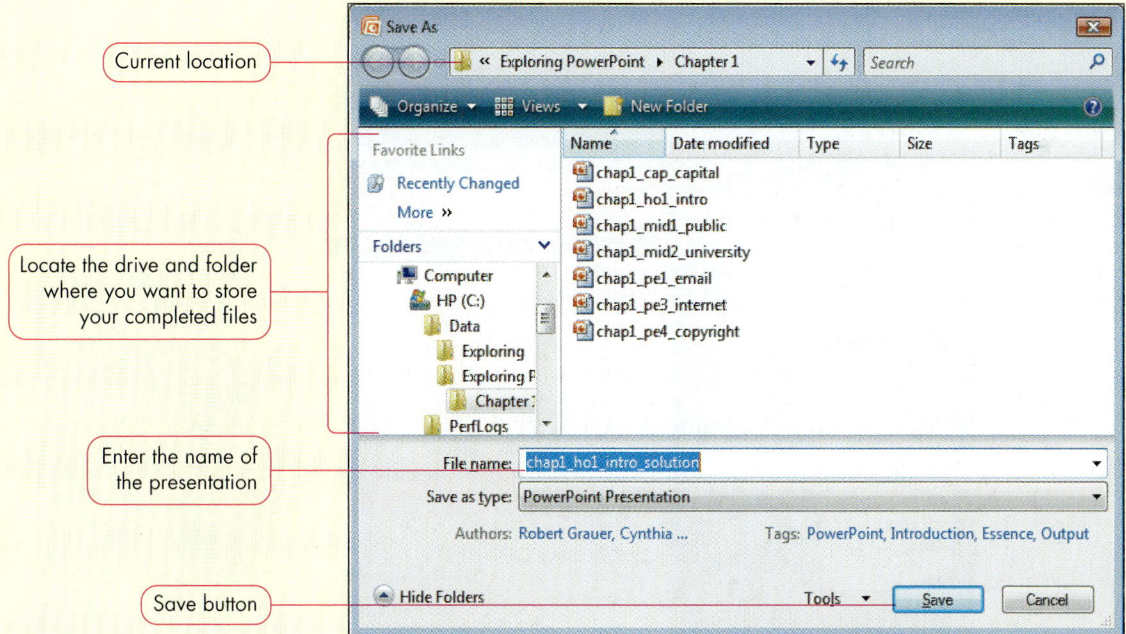

Figure 1.22 Save the Presentation with a New Name

Step 6
Locate Information Using Help

Refer to Figure 1.23 as you complete Step 6.

a. Click **Microsoft Office PowerPoint Help** on the top right side of the screen.

The PowerPoint Help window opens.

TROUBLESHOOTING: If you do not see the same Help window as displayed in Figure 1.23, you may not have an active Internet connection. If you do not have an active Internet connection, the Help feature retrieves the Help information that was installed on your computer. Also, because Help Online is a dynamic feature, Microsoft frequently adds content. Each time you open a Help Online topic, you are asked to give Microsoft feedback on the value of the topic. Due to this feature, topics may be added and links changed.

b. Click the *What's new* hyperlink, and then click the *Use the Ribbon* hyperlink.

c. Scroll to the bottom of the Help window until the *See Also* box is visible. Click *Use the keyboard to work with Ribbon programs,* and then read the article on using access keys with the Ribbon.

d. Close Help, and then press **F1** on the keyboard.

F1 is the shortcut for opening Help.

e. Type **print preview** in the Search box, and then click Search.

f. Click *Print a Help topic* and read the article.

g. Close Help, and then close the *chap1_ho1_intro_solution* presentation.

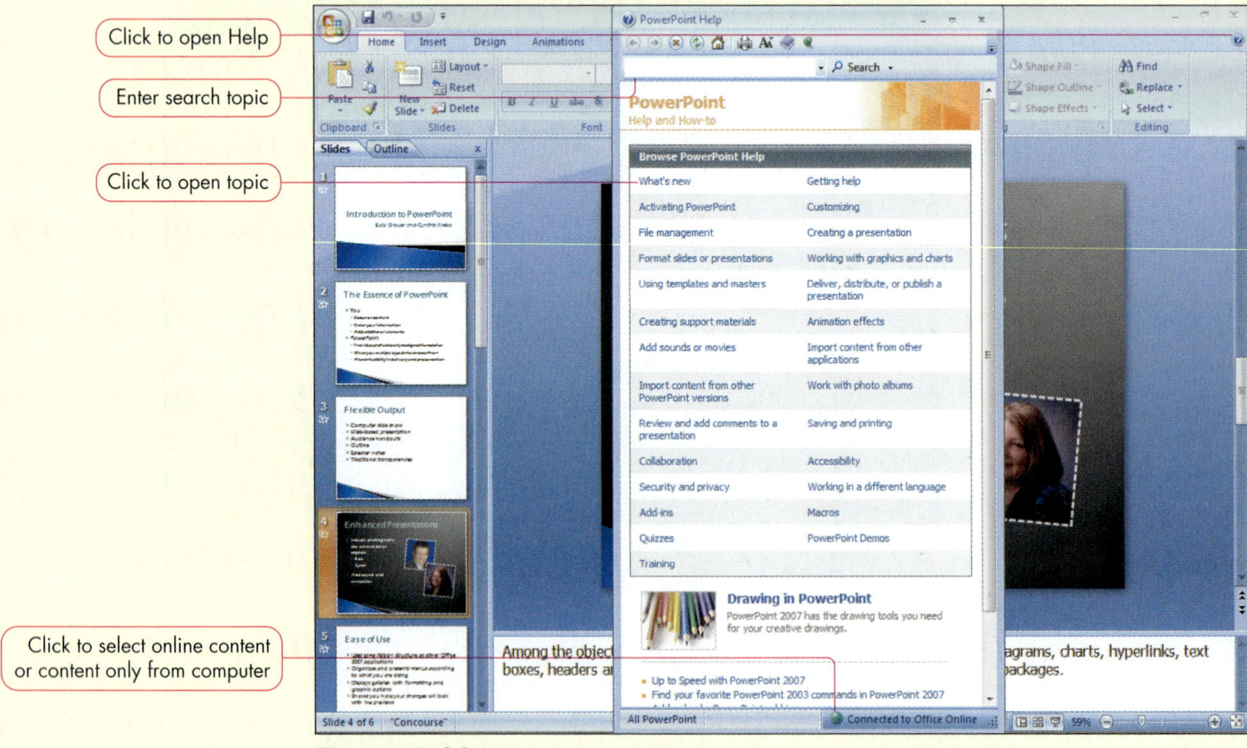

Figure 1.23 The Help Window

Presentation Creation

You are ready to create your own presentation, a process that requires you to develop its content and apply the formatting through the use of a template or design specification. You can do the steps in either order, but by starting with the content you can concentrate on your message and the structure of your message without getting distracted by the formatting and design of the presentation.

(Before you start the presentation in PowerPoint, you can complete several tasks that could make your presentation more effective and save you time.)

Before you start the presentation in PowerPoint, you can complete several tasks that could make your presentation more effective and save you time. While you know the topic you are going to present, the way you present it should be tailored to your audience. Research your audience—determine who makes up your audience, what their needs are, and what their expectations are. By tailoring your presentation to the audience, you will have a much more interesting presentation and an involved audience. After researching your audience, begin brainstorming on how to deliver your information and message to the audience. Sketch out your thoughts to help you organize them.

After you have sketched out your thoughts, enter them into the PowerPoint presentation and apply a theme to give your presentation a polished look. Review the presentation for spelling errors and word choice problems so your presentation is professional.

In this section, you create a visual plan known as a storyboard. You learn how to change layouts, apply design themes, and use the Spell Check and the Thesaurus to review your presentation for errors.

Creating a Storyboard

A ***storyboard*** is a visual plan that displays the content of each slide in the slideshow.

A ***storyboard*** is a visual plan for your presentation. It can be a very rough draft you sketch out while brainstorming, or it can be an elaborate plan that includes the text and objects drawn as they would appear on a slide. The complexity of your storyboard is your choice, but the key point is that the storyboard helps you plan the direction of your presentation. Remember the old adage, "If you don't know where you are going, you are going to end up somewhere else!"

A simple PowerPoint storyboard is divided into sections representing individual slides. The first block in the storyboard is used for the title slide. The title slide should have a short title that indicates the purpose of the presentation and introduces the speaker. Try to capture the title in two to five words. The speaker introduction information is usually included in a subtitle and can include the speaker's name and title, the speaker's organization, the organization's logo, and the date of the presentation.

While a title slide may serve as the introduction, having a separate introduction sets a professional tone for the presentation. The introduction should get the audience's attention and convince them your presentation will be worth their time. Creating an agenda showing the topics to be covered in the presentation can serve as an introduction because as you review the agenda with the audience you start them thinking about the topics. Often presenters use a thought-provoking quotation or question as the introduction, and pause for a short time to give the audience time to think. An image can be particularly moving if it relates to the topic and is displayed in silence for a moment. The presenter may then introduce the idea behind the image or question the audience to extract the meaning of the image from them, thereby inducing the audience to introduce the topic.

Following the title slide and the introduction, you have slides containing the main body of information you want your audience to have. Each key thought deserves a slide, and on that slide text bullets or other objects should develop that key thought. When preparing these slides, ask yourself what you want your audience to know that they did not know before. Ask yourself what it is you want them to remember. Create the slides to answer these questions and support these main points on the slides with facts, examples, charts or graphs, illustrations, images, or video clips.

Finally, end your presentation with a summary or conclusion. This is your last chance to get your message across to your audience. It should review main points, restate the purpose of the presentation, or invoke a call to action. The summary will solidify your purpose with the audience. Remember the old marketing maxim, "Tell 'em what you're going to tell 'em, tell 'em, then tell 'em what you told 'em,"—or in other words, "Introduction, Body, Conclusion."

After you create the storyboard, review what you wrote. Now is a good time to edit your text. Shorten complete sentences to phrases. As you present, you can expand on the information shown on the slide. The phrases on the slide help your audience organize the information in their minds. Edit phrases to use as bullet points. Review and edit the phrases so they begin with an active voice when possible to involve the user. Active voice uses action verbs—action verbs ACT! Passive verbs can be recognized by the presence of linking verbs (is, am, are, was, were).

TIP The "7 x 7" Guideline

Keep the information on your slide concise. The slide is merely a tool to help your audience "chuck into memory" the information you give. Your delivery will cover the detail. To help you remember to stay concise, follow the 7 x 7 guideline that suggests you limit the words on a visual to no more than seven words per line and seven lines per slide. This guideline gives you a total of 49 or fewer words per slide. While you may be forced to exceed this guideline on occasion, follow it as often as possible.

After you complete your planning, you are ready to prepare your PowerPoint presentation. Now instead of wasting computer time trying to decide what to say, you spend your computer time entering information, formatting, and designing. Figure 1.24 shows a working copy of a storyboard for planning presentation content. The storyboard is in rough draft form and shows changes made during the review process. The PowerPoint presentation (Figure 1.25) incorporates the changes.

Title slide

Introduction

Key topics with main points

Conclusion

Presentation Storyboard

Purpose of Presentation: Educational presentation

Audience: IAAP membership **Location:** Marriott Hotel **Date:** 9/20/08

Content	Layout	Visual Element(s)
Title Slide Planning ~~Before Creating~~ Presentation Content	Title Slide	O Shapes O Chart O Table O WordArt O Picture O Movie O Clip Art O Sound O SmartArt O ______ *Description:*
Introduction (Key Points, Quote, Image, Other) "If you don't know where you are going, you might end up someplace else." Casey Stengel	Section Header	O Shapes O Chart O Table O WordArt O Picture O Movie ☒ Clip Art O Sound O SmartArt O ______ *Description:* Stengel pic ~~confusion image~~
Support for Key Point #1 Identify Purpose ~~Selling~~ E-Commerce, Persuading Informing, Advertising, ~~Building Goodwill~~ Entertaining, Educating, Motivating	Two Content	O Shapes O Chart O Table O WordArt O Picture O Movie O Clip Art O Sound O SmartArt O ______ *Description:*
Support for Key Point #2 Define Audience Who is ~~going to be in~~ the audience? What are the ~~audience's~~ expectations? How much ~~does the audience~~ do they already know?	Title & Content	O Shapes O Chart O Table O WordArt ☒ Picture O Movie O Clip Art O Sound O SmartArt O ______ *Description:* Audience pic
Support for Key Point #3 Develop the Content Brainstorm ~~and write ideas down~~ Research ~~the topic and take notes~~ Storyboard ~~a rough draft and then refine~~	Title & Content	O Shapes O Chart O Table O WordArt O Picture O Movie O Clip Art O Sound O SmartArt O ______ *Description:* SmartArt
Support for Key Point #4 Edit the Content ~~Shorten the text from sentences to phrases~~ make text concise Make bullets parallel + use active verbs	Title & Content	O Shapes O Chart O Table O WordArt O Picture O Movie O Clip Art O Sound O SmartArt O ______ *Description:*
Summary (Restatement of Key Points, Quote, Other) The key to an effective presentation is planning ahead.	Title	O Shapes O Chart O Table O WordArt O Picture O Movie ☒ Clip Art O Sound O SmartArt O ______ *Description:* Key

Figure 1.24 Rough Draft Storyboard

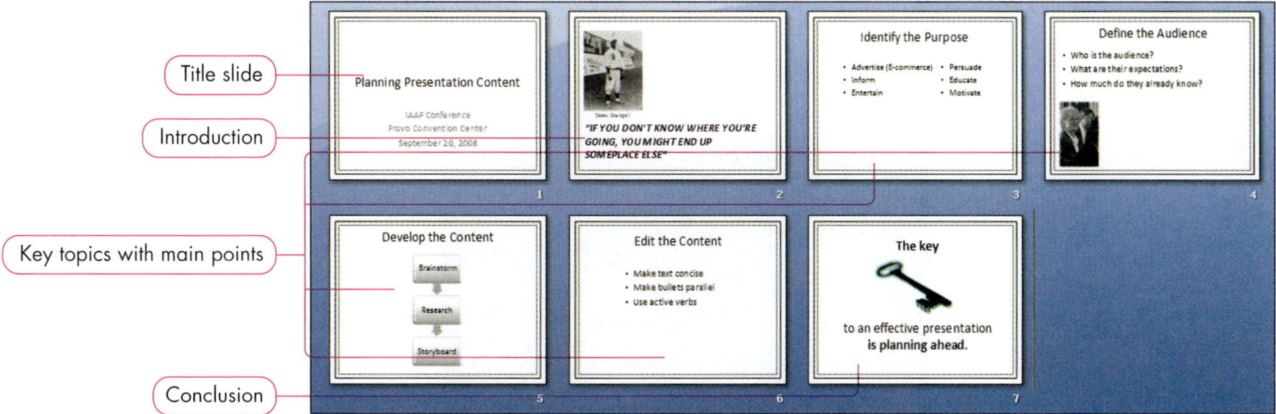

Figure 1.25 Presentation from Storyboard

TIP Storyboard Template

A sample storyboard template, *chap1_storyboard.docx*, is available in the Exploring PowerPoint Chapter 1 data files folder for you to use to help you plan your presentations.

Using Slide Layouts

When you first begin a new slide show, PowerPoint presents you with a slide for use as a title slide. New slides from that point on are typically created as content slides, consisting of a slide title and a defined area for content. You can enter content in the defined area or add new elements manually. If the slide arrangement does not meet your needs, you can change it by changing the slide layout.

A slide ***layout*** determines the position of objects containing content on the slide.

A ***placeholder*** is a container that holds content and is used in the layout to determine the position of objects on the slide.

PowerPoint provides a set of predefined slide ***layouts*** that determine the position of the objects or content on a slide. Slide layouts contain any number and combination of placeholders, and are available each time you click New Slide on the Home tab. When you click New Slide, the gallery of layouts is displayed for you to choose from. All of the layouts except the Blank layout include placeholders. ***Placeholders*** hold content and determine the position of the objects, or content, on the slide. After you select the layout, you simply click the appropriate placeholder to add the content you desire. Thus, you would click the placeholder for the title and enter the text of the title as indicated. In similar fashion, you click the placeholder for text and enter the associated text. By default, the text appears as bullets. You can change the size and position of the placeholders by moving the placeholders just as you would any object.

Applying Design Themes

A ***theme*** is a set of design elements that gives the slide show a unified, professional appearance.

PowerPoint enables you to concentrate on the content of a presentation without concern for its appearance. You focus on what you are going to say, and then utilize PowerPoint features to format the presentation attractively. The simplest method to format a slide show is to select a design theme. A design ***theme*** is a collection of formatting choices that includes colors, fonts, and special theme effects such as shadowing or glows. PowerPoint designers have created beautiful design themes for your use, and the themes are available in other Office applications, which lets you unify all of the documents you create.

When you apply a theme, the formatting implements automatically. To select and apply a theme, click the Design tab and click the More button in the Themes group. From the Themes gallery that appears, choose the theme you like. PowerPoint formats the entire presentation according to the theme you choose. Do not be afraid to apply new themes. As you gain experience with PowerPoint and design, you can rely less on PowerPoint and more on your own creativity for your design. Figures 1.26–1.29 show a title slide with four different themes applied. Note the color, font, and text alignment in each theme.

INTRODUCTION TO
POWERPOINT
Bob Grauer and Cynthia Krebs

Figure 1.26 Opulent Theme

Introduction to PowerPoint
Bob Grauer and Cynthia Krebs

Figure 1.27 Urban Theme

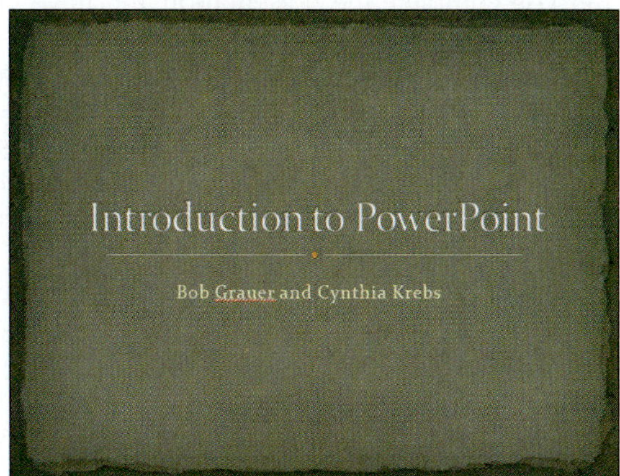
Introduction to PowerPoint
Bob Grauer and Cynthia Krebs

Figure 1.28 Paper Theme

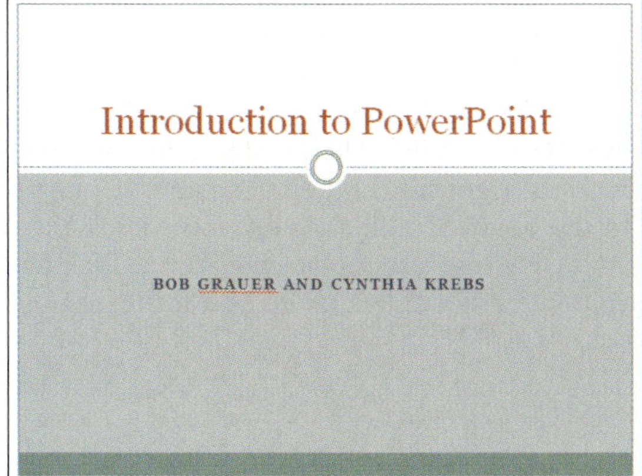
Introduction to PowerPoint
BOB GRAUER AND CYNTHIA KREBS

Figure 1.29 Civic Theme

Reviewing the Presentation

After you create the presentation, check for spelling errors and incorrect word usage. This step can be done before or after you apply the design theme, but sometimes applying the theme before checking for spelling errors helps you see errors you did not see before. It gives you a fresh look at the slide, which helps you revisualize what is displaying.

Check Spelling

A ***custom dictionary*** is a supplemental dictionary Microsoft Office uses to store items such as proper names, acronyms, or specialized words.

The first step to checking your spelling is to visually check the slide after you create the text in the placeholders. A red wavy line under a word indicates that a word is misspelled. In the case of a proper name, the word may be spelled correctly but is not in the standard dictionary shared by the software in the Microsoft Office suite. In either event, point to the underlined word and click the right mouse button to display a shortcut menu. Select the appropriate spelling from the list of suggestions. If the word does not appear in the list of suggestions, you can add the word to the ***custom dictionary***, a supplemental dictionary Microsoft Office uses to store items such as proper names, acronyms, or specialized words for your business or industry.

After you complete the presentation and have visually checked each slide, use PowerPoint's Spelling feature to check the entire presentation again. Click the Review tab, and then click Spelling in the Proofing group. If a word does not appear in the dictionary, the Spelling dialog box appears. Use the options on the right side to choose whether you wish to accept the word and resume spell checking, ignore all occurrences of the word, change the word to one of the listed choices, add the word to your custom dictionary, look at other suggested spellings, add the word to AutoCorrect, or close the dialog box.

Finally, display the presentation in Slide Show view and read each word on each slide out loud. Reading the words in the Slide Show view eliminates the distractions in PowerPoint's creation screen and enables you to concentrate fully on the text. Although the Spelling feature is a valuable tool, it does **NOT** catch commonly misused words like to, too, and two, or for, fore, and four. While proofreading three times may seem excessive to you, if you ever flash a misspelled word before an audience in full Slide Show view, you will wish you had taken the time to proofread carefully. Nothing is more embarrassing and can make you seem less professional than a misspelled word enlarged on a big screen for your audience so they cannot miss it.

Use the Thesaurus

As you proofread your presentation, or even while you are creating it, you may notice that you are using one word too often. Perhaps you find a word that doesn't seem right, but you cannot think of another word. The Thesaurus, which gives you synonyms or words with the same meaning, is ideal to use in these situations. Click the Review tab and click Thesaurus in the Proofing group. The Research task pane appears on the right side of the screen and displays synonyms for the selected word. Point to the desired replacement word, click the drop-down arrow to display a menu, and click Insert to replace the word. Click Undo on the Quick Access Toolbar to return to the original text if you prefer the original word.

TIP The Research Task Pane

Microsoft Office 2007 brings the resources of the Web directly into the application. Click Research in the Proofing group on the Review tab. Type the entry you are searching for, click the down arrow to choose a reference book, and then click the green arrow to initiate the search. You have access to reference, research, business, and financial sites. You even have an online bilingual dictionary. Research has never been easier.

Hands-On Exercises

2 | Creating a Presentation

Skills covered: 1. Create a New Presentation **2.** Add Slides **3.** Check Spelling and Use the Thesaurus **4.** Modify Text and Layout **5.** Reorder Slides **6.** Apply a Design Theme

Step 1 Create a New Presentation

Refer to Figure 1.30 as you complete Step 1.

a. Click the **Office Button**, select **New**, and then double-click **Blank Presentation**.

PowerPoint opens with a new blank presentation.

b. Click inside the placeholder containing the *Click to add title* prompt, and then type the presentation title **Creating Presentation Content**.

c. Click inside the placeholder containing the *Click to add subtitle* prompt and enter your name.

Type your name as it shows on the class roll. Do not enter a nickname or the words *Your Name*.

d. Click in the Notes pane and type today's date and the name of the course for which you are creating this slide show.

e. Save the presentation as **chap1_ho2_content_solution**.

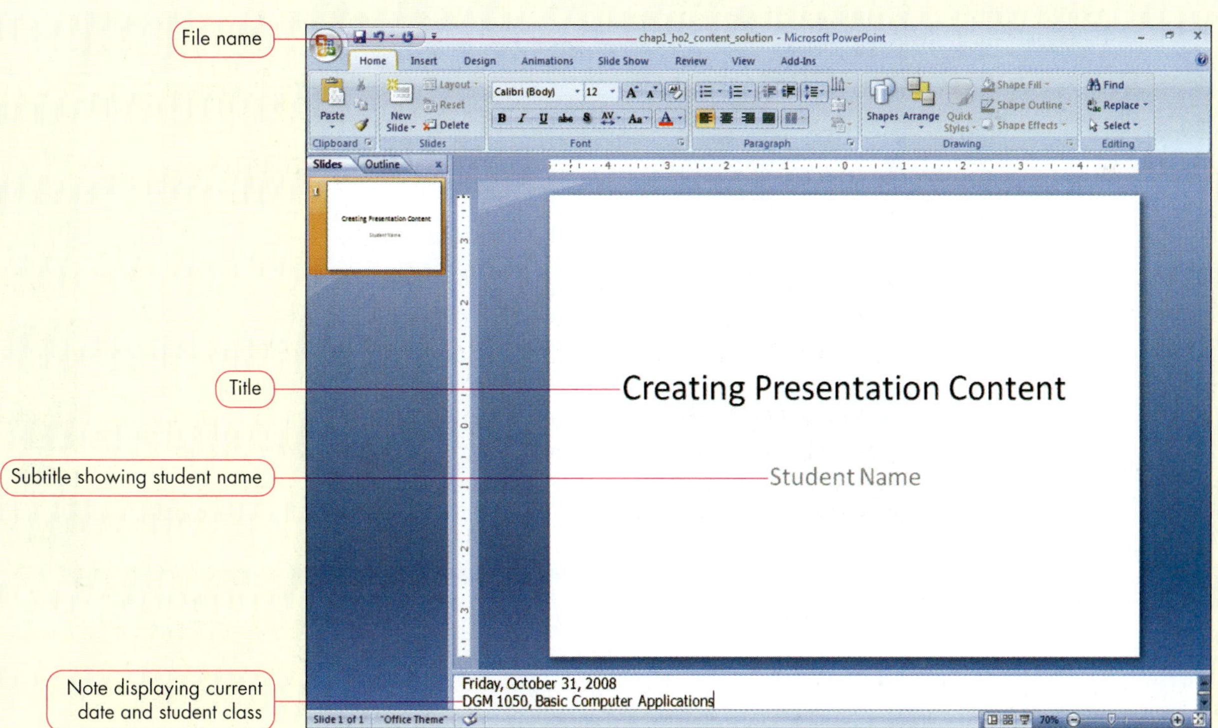

Figure 1.30 Creating Presentation Content Title Slide

Step 2
Add Slides

Refer to Figure 1.31 as you complete Step 2.

a. Click the **New Slide arrow** in the Slides group on the Home tab.

b. Select the **Title and Content** layout from the gallery.

   Slide 2 is created with two placeholders: one for the title and one for body content. You can insert an object by clicking on the bar in the center of the content placeholder, or you can enter bullets by typing text in the placeholder.

c. Type **Simplify the Content** in the title placeholder.

d. Click in the content placeholder and type **Use one main concept per slide**, and then press **Enter**.

e. Type **Use the 7 x 7 guideline** and press **Enter** again.

f. Click **Increase List Level** in the Paragraph group on the Home tab.

   Clicking Increase List Level creates a new bullet level that you can use for detail related to the main bullet. If you wish to return to the main bullet level, click Decrease List Level.

g. Type **Limit slide to seven or fewer lines** and press **Enter**.

h. Type **Limit lines to seven or fewer words**.

i. Save the *chap1_ho2_content_solution* presentation.

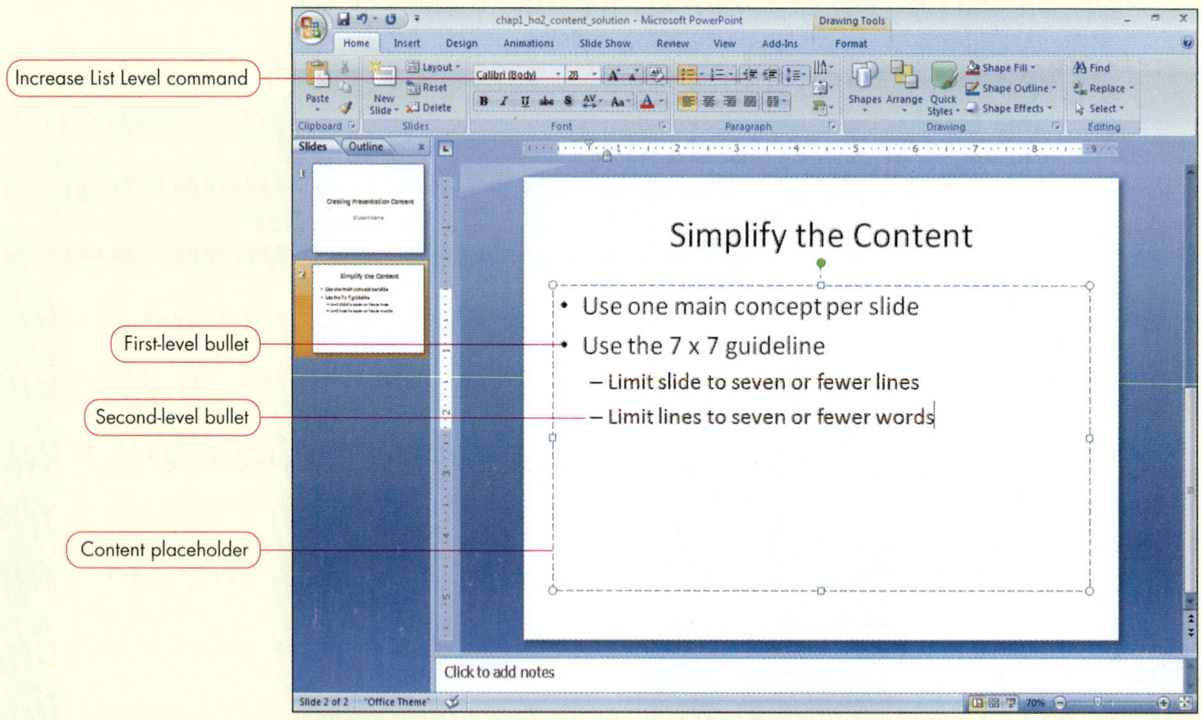

Figure 1.31 New Slide

Step 3
Check Spelling and Use the Thesaurus

Refer to Figure 1.32 as you complete Step 3.

a. Use the **New Slide** command to create four more slides with the Title and Content layout.

b. Type the following text in the appropriate slide.

Slide	Slide Title	Level 1 Bullets	Level 2 Bullets
3	Define the Audience	Who is the audience? What are their needs? What are their expectations? How much do they already know? How can you help them understand message?	
4	Develop the Content	Identify purpose Research topic Brainstorm Create storyboard	Title slide Introduction Key points Conclusion (refer to Figure 1.31)
5	Edit the Content	Make text concise Use consistent verb tense Utilize strong active verbs Eliminate excess adverbs and adjectives Use few prepositions	
6		The key to an effective presentation is planning ahead!	

c. Click **Spelling** in the Proofing group on the Review tab.

The result of the spelling check depends on how accurately you entered the text of the presentation. If the spell checker locates a word not in its dictionary, you will be prompted to resume checking, change the word, ignore the word in that occurrence or in all occurrences, or add the word to your dictionary so it isn't identified as misspelled in the future. Select one of these options and then continue checking the presentation for spelling errors, if necessary.

d. Move to **Slide 2** and click anywhere within the word *main*.

e. Click **Thesaurus** in the Proofing group on the Review tab.

The Research task pane opens and displays a list of synonyms from which to choose a replacement word.

f. Point to the word *key*, click the drop-down arrow, and click **Insert**. Close the Research task pane.

The word *main* is replaced with the word *key*.

TROUBLESHOOTING: If you click the replacement word in the Research pane list instead of clicking the drop-down arrow and choosing Insert, the replacement word you clicked will replace the original word in the Search for box, and the Research pane changes to display the synonyms of the replacement word. The word in your presentation will not change.

g. Save the *chap1_ho2_content_solution* presentation.

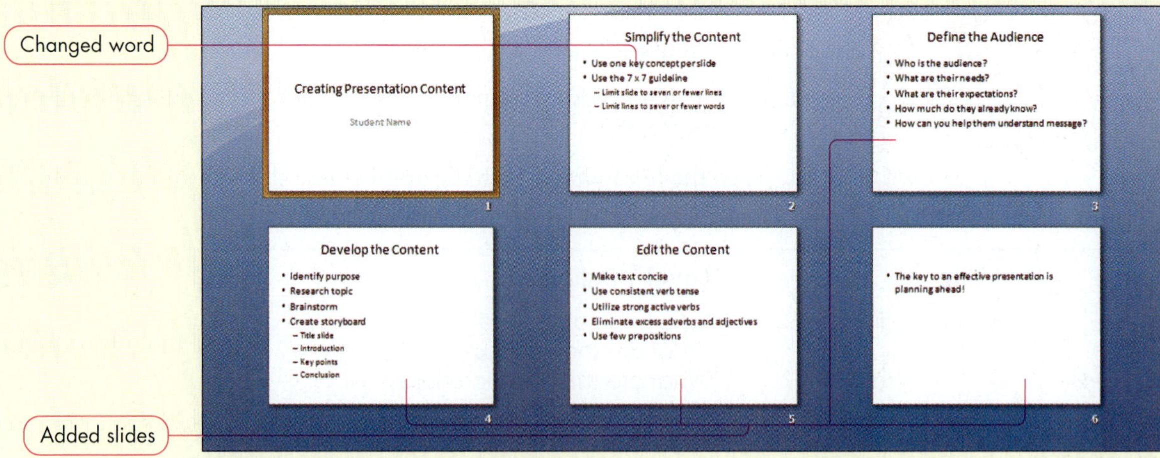

Figure 1.32 Proofed Slide Show

Step 4
Modify Text and Layout

Refer to Figure 1.33 as you complete Step 4.

a. Click the **Slide 6 thumbnail** in the Slides tab pane.

   You wish to end the slide show with a statement emphasizing the importance of planning. You created the statement in a content placeholder in a slide using the Title and Content layout. You decide to modify the text and layout of the slide to give the statement more emphasis.

b. Click the **Home tab** and click **Layout** in the Slides group.

c. Click **Title Slide**.

   The layout for Slide 6 changes to the Title Slide layout. Layouts can be used on any slide in a slide show if their format meets your needs.

d. Click the border of the Title placeholder, press **Delete** on the keyboard, and then drag the Subtitle placeholder containing your text upward until it is slightly above the center of your slide.

   The layout in Slide 6 has now been modified.

e. Drag across the text in the subtitle placeholder to select it, and then move your pointer upwards until the Mini toolbar appears.

f. Click **Bold**, and then click **Italic** on the Mini toolbar.

   Using the Mini toolbar to modify text is much faster than moving back and forth to the commands in the Font group on the Home tab to make changes.

g. Save the *chap1_ho2_content_solution* presentation.

The key to an effective presentation is planning ahead!

Figure 1.33 Slide with Modified Text and Layout

Step 5 Reorder Slides

Refer to Figure 1.34 as you complete Step 5.

a. Click the **View tab** and click **Slide Sorter** in the Presentation Views group.

The view changes to thumbnail views of the slides in the slide show with the current slide surrounded by a heavy border to indicate it is selected. Your view may differ from Figure 1.34 depending on what your zoom level is set at and screen resolution. Notice that the slides do not follow logical order. The Slide Sorter view is ideal for checking the logical sequence of slides and for changing slide position if necessary.

b. Select **Slide 2**, and then drag it so that it becomes Slide 5, the slide before the summary slide.

As you drag Slide 2 to the right, the pointer becomes a move cursor, and a vertical bar appears to indicate the position of the slide when you drop it. After you drop the slide, all slides renumber.

c. Double-click **Slide 6**.

Double-clicking a slide in the Slide Sorter view returns you to Normal view.

d. Save the *chap1_ho2_content_solution* presentation.

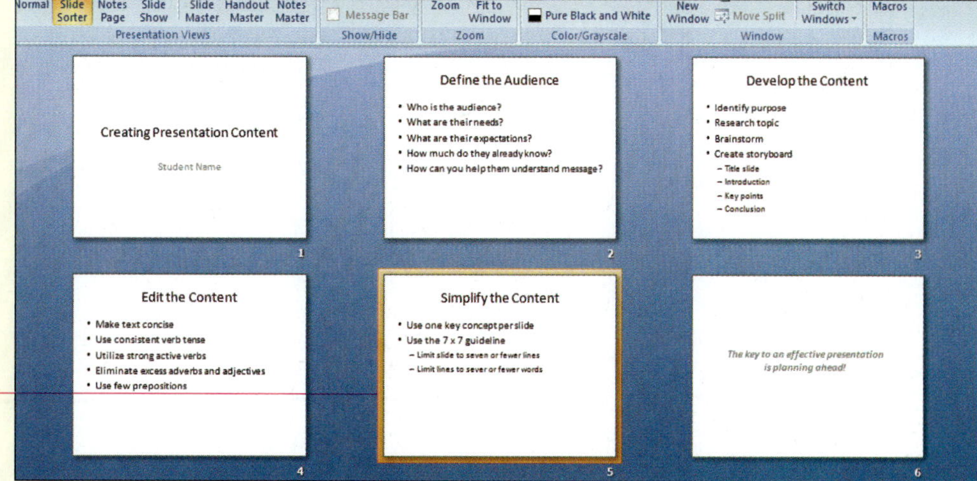

Figure 1.34 Reordered Slide Show

Step 6
Apply a Design Theme

Refer to Figure 1.35 as you complete Step 6.

a. Click the **Design tab** and click the **More button** in the Themes group.

   Point at each of the themes that appear in the gallery and note how the theme formatting impacts the text in Slide 6.

b. Click **Urban** to apply the theme to the presentation.

   The Urban theme is characterized by a clean, simple background with a business-like color scheme, making it a good choice for this presentation.

c. Drag the Slide 6 Title placeholder down and to the left, and then resize it so that it contains three lines.

   When you add the Urban theme, the background of the theme hides the text in the placeholder. You adjust the placeholder location and size to fit the theme.

   TROUBLESHOOTING: You may not see the Title placeholder on Slide 6. However, click in the middle of the dark gray area of the slide. The sizing handles appear around the placeholder when you click it. Then you can click and drag the placeholder into its new location specified by Step 6c.

d. Save the *chap1_ho2_content_solution* presentation. Close the file and exit PowerPoint if you do not want to continue to the next exercise at this time.

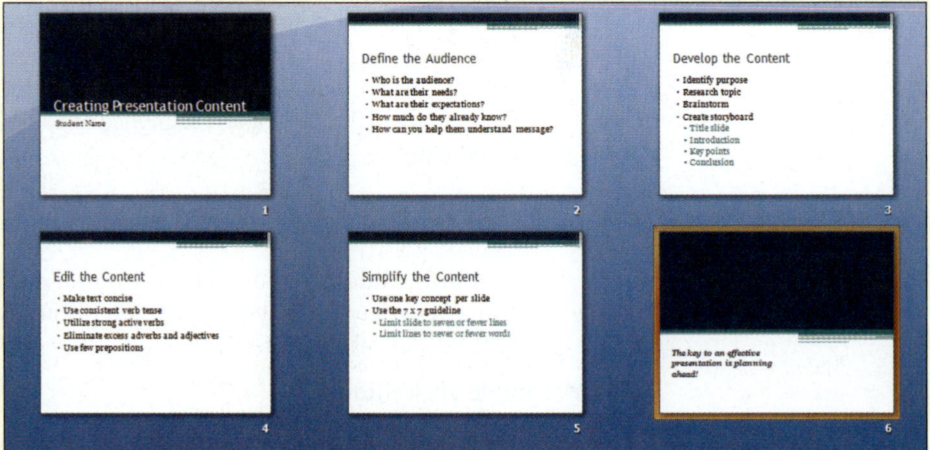

Figure 1.35 Slide Show with Urban Theme Applied

Presentation Development

Thus far our presentation is strictly text. You can strengthen your slide show by adding objects that relate to the message. PowerPoint enables you to include a variety of visual objects to add impact to your presentation. You can add clip art, images, WordArt, sound, animated clips, or video clips to increase your presentation's impact. You can add tables, charts and graphs, and diagrams to provide more information for the audience. These objects can be created in PowerPoint, or you can insert objects that were created in other applications, such as a chart from Microsoft Excel or a table from Microsoft Word.

(. . . clip art, images, WordArt, sound, animated clips, or video clips . . . increase your presentation's impact.)

In this section, you add a table to organize data in columns and rows. Then you insert clip art objects that relate to your topics. You move and resize the clip art to position it attractively on the slide. Finally, you apply transitions to your slide to control how one slide changes to another, and you apply animations to your text and clip art to help maintain your audience's attention.

Adding a Table

A ***table*** is an illustration that places information in columns and rows.

A ***table*** is an illustration that places information in columns and rows. Tables are a great way for you to present related information in an orderly manner. Tables can be simple and include just words or images, or they can be complex and include a great deal of structured numerical data. Because tables organize information for the viewer, they are a great way to augment your presentation.

You can add a table to your presentation by creating it in PowerPoint or by reusing a table created in Word or Excel. In this chapter, you create a basic table in PowerPoint. To create a table, you can select the Title and Content layout and then click the Insert Table icon on the Content bar, or you can select the Title Only layout and click the Insert tab and then click Table in the Tables group. These two options create the table with slightly different sizing, however. Figure 1.36 shows the same data entered into tables created in each of these ways.

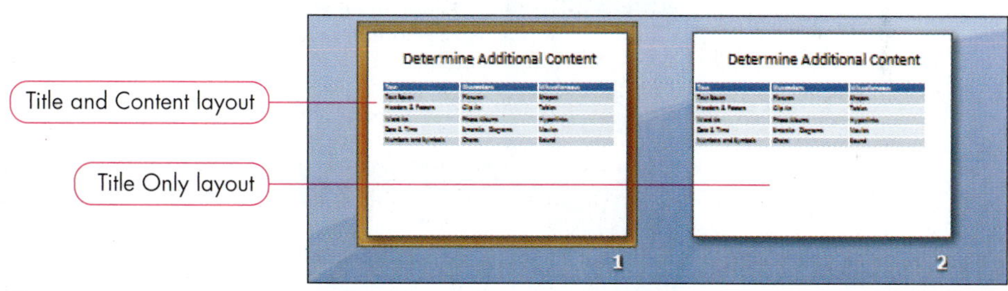

Figure 1.36 Table Layout

Inserting Clip Art

In addition to inserting tables from the Insert tab, you can insert other objects and media in your presentation. From the Illustrations group, click Picture and browse to locate a picture or image that has been saved to a storage device, click Clip Art to insert clip art from the Microsoft Clip Organizer, click Photo Album to create a photo album from images you have saved, click Shapes to insert a shape, click SmartArt to insert a diagram, or click Chart to insert a chart.

A ***clip*** is any media object that you can insert in a document.

In this chapter you concentrate on adding clip art from the Microsoft Clip Organizer, although inserting other types of clips uses the same procedure. The Microsoft Clip Organizer contains a variety of ***clips***, or media objects such as clip art, photographs, movies, or sounds, that may be inserted in a presentation. The Microsoft Clip Organizer brings order by cataloging the clips that are available to you. Clips installed locally are cataloged in the My Collections folder; clips installed in conjunction with Office are cataloged in the Office Collections folder; and clips downloaded from the Web are cataloged in the Web Collections folder. If you are connected to the Internet, clips located in Microsoft Online also display in the Clip Organizer. You can insert a specific clip into your presentation if you know its location, or you can search for a clip that will enhance your presentation.

To search for a clip, you enter a keyword that describes the clip you are looking for, specify the collections that are to be searched, and indicate the type of clip(s) you are looking for. The results are displayed in the Clip Art task pane, as shown in Figure 1.37. This figure shows clips that were located using the keyword *keys*. The example searches all collections for all media types to return the greatest number of potential clips. When you point to a clip displaying in the gallery, the clip's keywords, the clip's file size, and file format appear. When you see the clip that you want to use, point to the clip, click the drop-down arrow, and then click the Insert command from the resulting menu. You also can click the clip to insert it in the center of the slide, or drag the clip onto the slide.

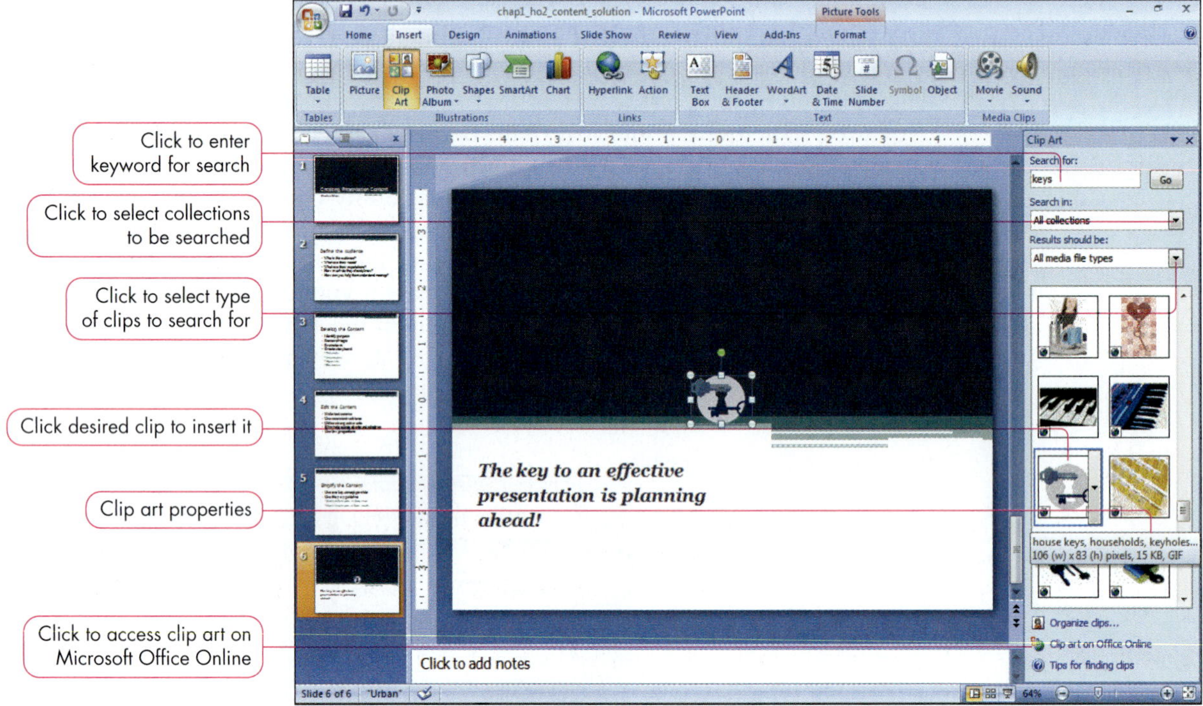

Figure 1.37 Clip Art Task Pane

TIP Reorganizing Clip Collections

You can access the Microsoft Clip Organizer (to view the various collections) by clicking the Organize clips link at the bottom of the task pane. You also can access the Clip Organizer outside of PowerPoint by clicking the Start button on the task bar, and then clicking All Programs, Microsoft Office, Microsoft Office Tools, and Microsoft Clip Organizer. Once in the Organizer, you can search through the clips in the various collections, reorganize the existing collections, add new collections, and even add new clips (with their associated keywords) to the collections.

Animate Objects

An ***animation scheme*** is a built-in, standard animation. effect.

A ***custom animation*** is an animation where the user determines the animation settings.

You can animate objects such as text, clip art, diagrams, charts, sound, and hyperlinks. You can apply a preset ***animation scheme,*** which is a built-in, standard animation created by Microsoft to simplify the animation process, or you can apply a ***custom animation*** where you determine the animation effect, the speed for the effect, the properties of the effect, and the way the animation begins. The properties available with animations are determined by the animation type. For example, if you choose a wipe animation effect, you can determine the direction property. If you choose a color wave effect, you can determine the color to be added to the object.

To apply an animation scheme, select the object you want to animate, click the Animations tab, and then click the Animate down arrow in the Animations group. A list of animation schemes opens. You can animate selected text or other objects using the options in the Animate drop-down arrow.

To apply a custom animation to an object, select the object that you want to animate and then click Custom Animation in the Animations group on the Animations tab. In the Custom Animation task pane, click Add Effect. Point to Entrance, Emphasis, Exit, or Motion Paths. Select an effect from the resulting list. Once the effect has been selected, you can determine the start, property, and speed of the transition. In this chapter you will apply an animation scheme and a basic custom animation.

The slide in Figure 1.40 shows an animation effect added to the title and the subtitle. The title will animate first, because it was selected first. A tag with the number 1 is attached to the placeholder to show it is first. The subtitle animates next, and a tag with the number 2 is attached to the subtitle placeholder. Examine the Custom Animation task pane and note the effect that was added to the subtitle, the way it will start, the direction and the speed of the animation.

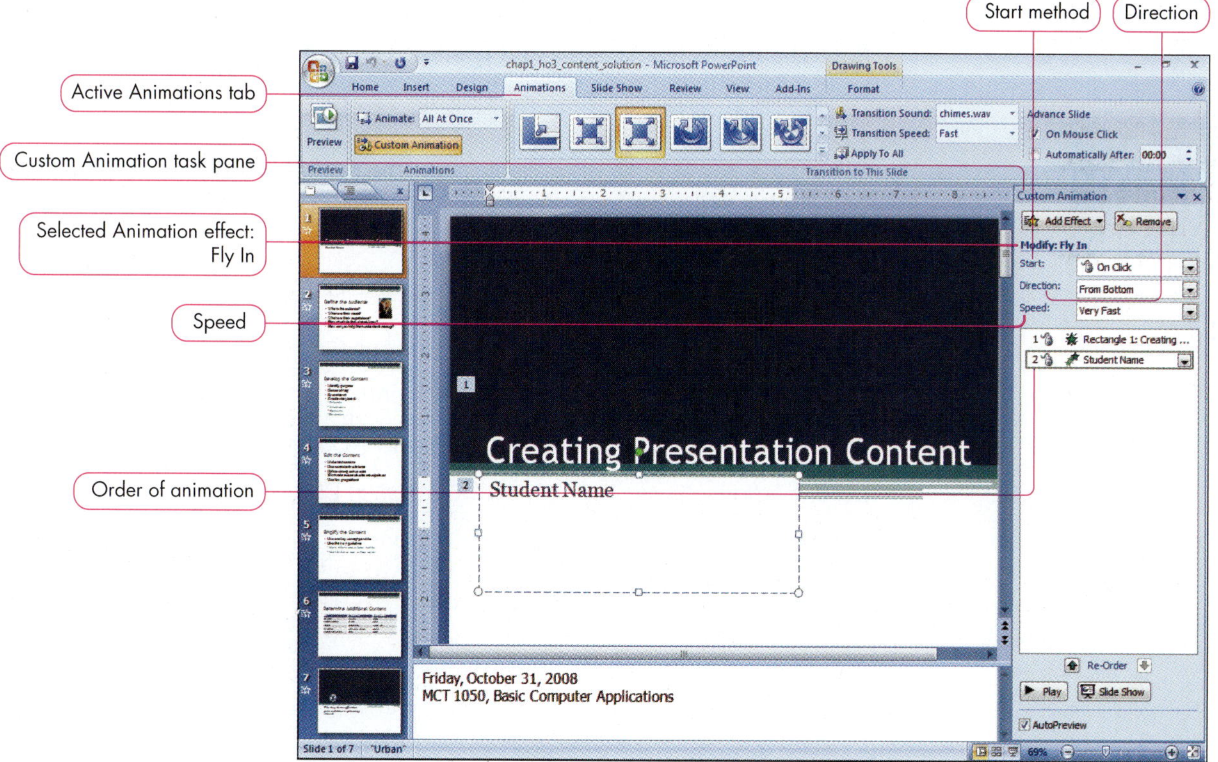

Figure 1.40 The Custom Animation Task Pane

Hands-On Exercises

3 | Strengthening a Presentation

Skills covered: **1.** Add a Table **2.** Insert, Move, and Resize Clip Art **3.** Apply a Transition **4.** Animate Objects

Step 1 Add a Table

Refer to Figure 1.41 as you complete Step 1.

a. Open the *chap1_ho2_content_solution* presentation if you closed it after the last exercise, and then save it as the **chap1_ho3_content_solution** presentation.

b. Move to **Slide 5**, click the **Home tab**, and click **New Slide** in the Slides group.

c. Click the **Title and Content** layout, if necessary.

A new slide with the Title and Content layout is inserted after Slide 5.

d. Click inside the title placeholder and type **Determine Additional Content**.

e. Click the **Insert Table icon** on the toolbar in the center of the content placeholder.

The Insert Table dialog box appears for you to enter the number of columns and the number of rows you desire.

f. Type **3** for the number of columns and **6** for the number of rows. Click **OK**.

PowerPoint creates the table and positions it on the slide. The first row of the table is formatted differently from the other rows so that it can be used for column headings.

g. Click in the top left cell of the table and type **Text**. Press **Tab** to move to the next cell and type **Illustrations**. Press **Tab** and then type **Miscellaneous** in the last heading cell.

h. Type the following text in the remaining table cells.

Text Boxes	Pictures	Shapes
Headers & Footers	Clip Art	Tables
WordArt	Photo Albums	Hyperlinks
Date & Time	SmartArt Diagrams	Movies
Numbers and Symbols	Charts	Sound

i. Save the *chap1_ho3_content_solution* presentation.

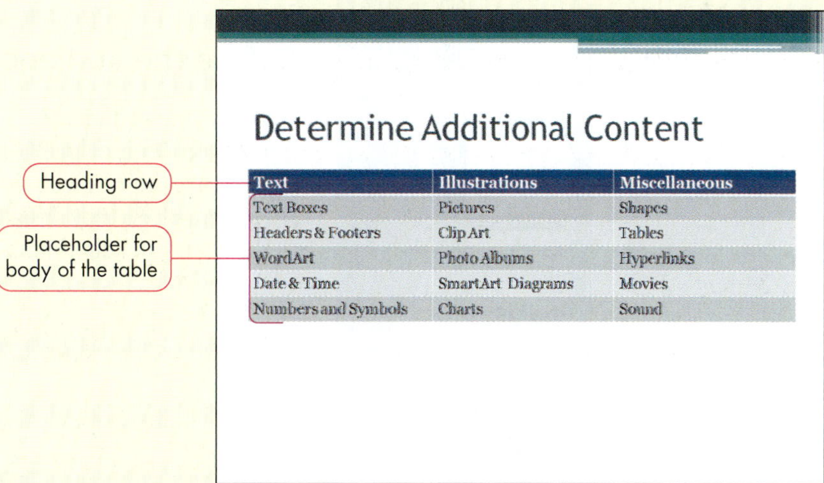

Figure 1.41 PowerPoint Table

Step 2
Insert, Move, and Resize Clip Art

Refer to Figure 1.42 as you complete Step 2.

a. Move to **Slide 2**, click the **Insert tab**, and click **Clip Art** in the Illustrations group.

b. Type **groups** in the *Search for* box. Make sure the *Search in* box is set to **All collections**.

c. Click the down arrow next to *Results should be*, deselect all options except Photographs, and then click **Go**.

d. Refer to Figure 1.42 to determine the group image to select, and then click the image to insert it in Slide 2.

   If you cannot locate the image in Figure 1.41, select another group photograph that looks like an audience.

e. Position your pointer in the center of the image and drag the image to the top right of the slide so that the top of the image touches the bars.

f. Position your pointer over the bottom-left sizing handle of the image and drag inward to reduce the size of the photograph.

   The photograph is too large. Not only is it overpowering the text, it is blocking text so that it cannot be read. As you drag the sizing handle inward, all four borders are reduced equally so the photograph no longer touches the bars.

g. If necessary, reposition the clip art image so that it is positioned attractively on the slide.

h. Move to **Slide 7**, change keyword to **keys**, change the results to show **All media types**, and then click **OK**.

i. Refer to Figure 1.42 to determine the keys clip to select and then click the image to insert it in Slide 7. Close the Clip Art task pane.

j. Reposition the clip so that it is above the word *key* but do not resize it. If you cannot find the animated clip used in the example, you may size the clip you use so it fits appropriately.

   This clip is an animated movie clip. If it is enlarged, the image will become pixelated and unattractive.

k. Save the *chap1_ho3_content_solution* presentation.

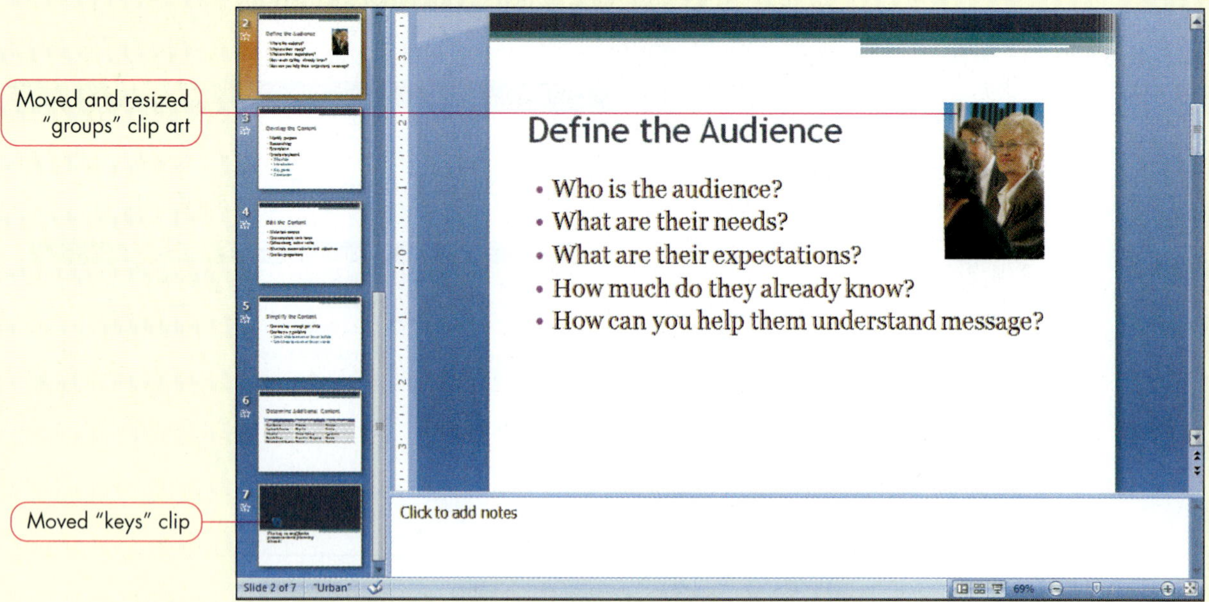

Figure 1.42 Inserted Clip Art

Step 3
Apply a Transition

Refer to Figure 1.43 as you complete Step 3.

a. Click the **Animations tab** and click **More** in the Transition to This Slide group.

b. Point at several of the transition effects to see how they impact the slide, and then click the **Box Out** wipe transition.

c. Click **Apply To All** in the Transition to This Slide group on the Animations tab.

   Apply To All will apply the transition set for the current slide to all slides in the slide show.

d. Move to **Slide 1**, click the **Transition Sound down arrow** in the Transitions To This Slide group on the Animations tab, and then click **Chime**.

   The Chime sound will play as Slide 1 enters. Presenters often use a sound or an audio clip to focus the audience's attention on the screen as the presentation begins.

e. Click **Preview** in the Preview group on the Animations tab.

   Because Slide 1 is active, you hear the chimes sound as the Box Out transition occurs.

   TROUBLESHOOTING: If you are completing this activity in a classroom lab, you may need to plug in headphones or turn on speakers to hear the sound.

f. Click the **View tab** and click **Slide Sorter** in the Presentation Views group.

   Notice the small star beneath each slide. The star indicates a transition has been applied to the slide.

g. Click any of the stars to see a preview of the transition applied to that slide.

h. Save the *chap1_ho3_content_solution* presentation.

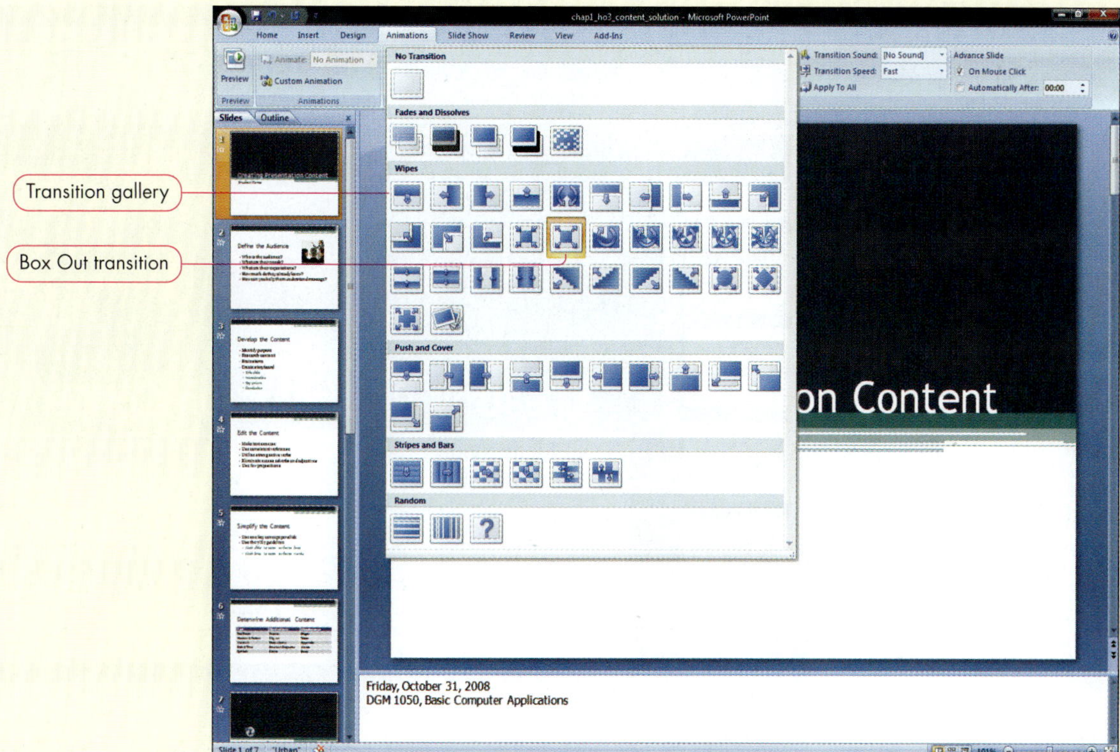

Figure 1.43 The Transition Gallery

Step 4
Animate Objects

Refer to Figure 1.44 as you complete Step 4.

a. Double-click **Slide 1** to open it in Normal view and then select the Title placeholder.

b. Click the **Animations tab** and click the **Animate down arrow** in the Animations group.

c. Click **Fade**.

The Fade animation scheme is applied to the Title placeholder. The title placeholder dissolves into the background until it is fully visible.

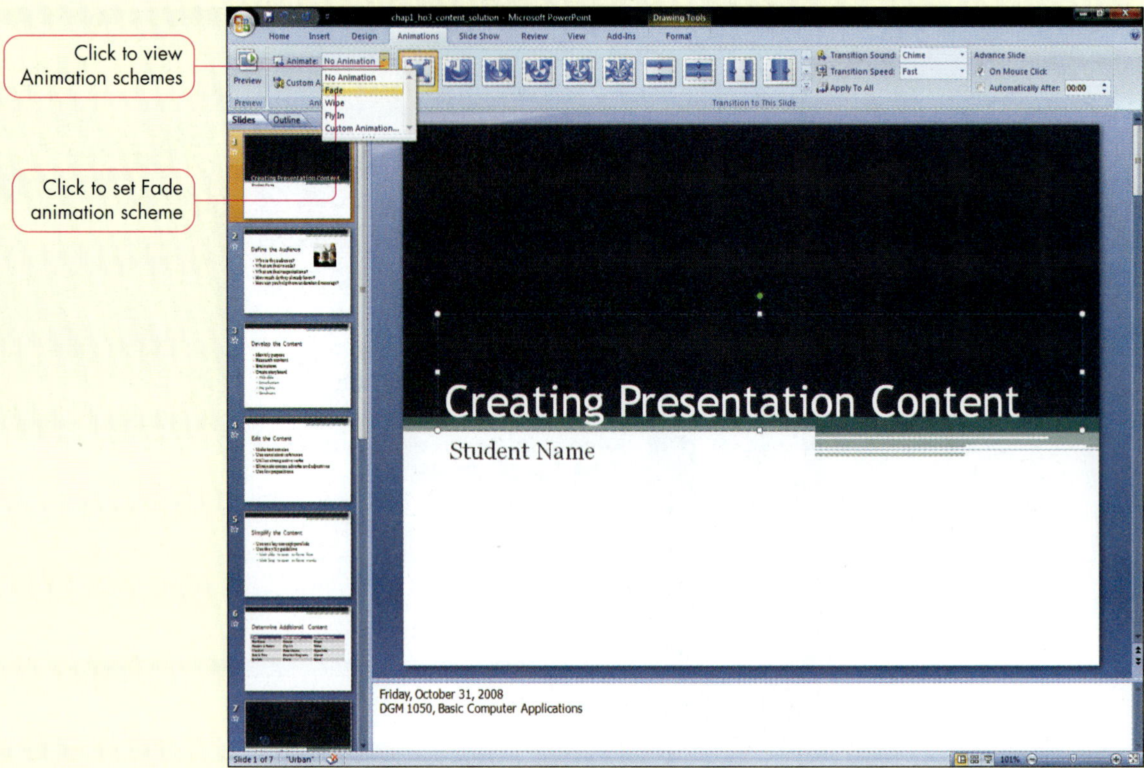

Figure 1.44 Object Animation schemes

d. Select the Subtitle placeholder on Slide 1, and then click the **Animate drop-down arrow** in the Animations group on the Animations tab.

e. Click the **All at once** button located under Fly In.

f. Move to **Slide 2** and select the photograph.

You decide to use a custom animation on the photograph so that you can have more animation choices and can control the speed with which the photograph animates.

g. Click **Custom Animation** in the Animations group on the Animations tab.

The Custom Animation task pane opens, which enables you to add an animation effect to the selected object. Refer to Figure 1.45 as you complete steps g through l.

h. Click the **Add Effect button**, point at **Entrance**, and then click **More Effects** from the animation list.

The Add Entrance Effect dialog box appears. The animation effects are separated into categories: Basic, Subtle, Moderate, and Exciting.

i. Scroll down and then select **Curve Up** in the Exciting category.

A preview of the Curve Up animation plays, but the dialog box remains open so that you can continue previewing animations until you find the one you like. Experiment with the Entrance Effects so you can see the impact they will have.

j. Select **Boomerang**, and then click **OK.**

k. Click the **Start drop-down arrow** and then select **After Previous**.

You can choose to start the animation with a mouse click, or by having the animation start automatically. If you wish to begin the animation automatically, you can choose to have it begin at the same time as a previous animation by selecting Start With Previous, or having it begin after a previous animation by selecting Start After Previous.

l. Click the **Speed drop-down arrow** and then click **Medium**.

m. Save the *chap1_ho3_content_solution* presentation. Close the file and exit PowerPoint if you do not want to continue to the next exercise at this time.

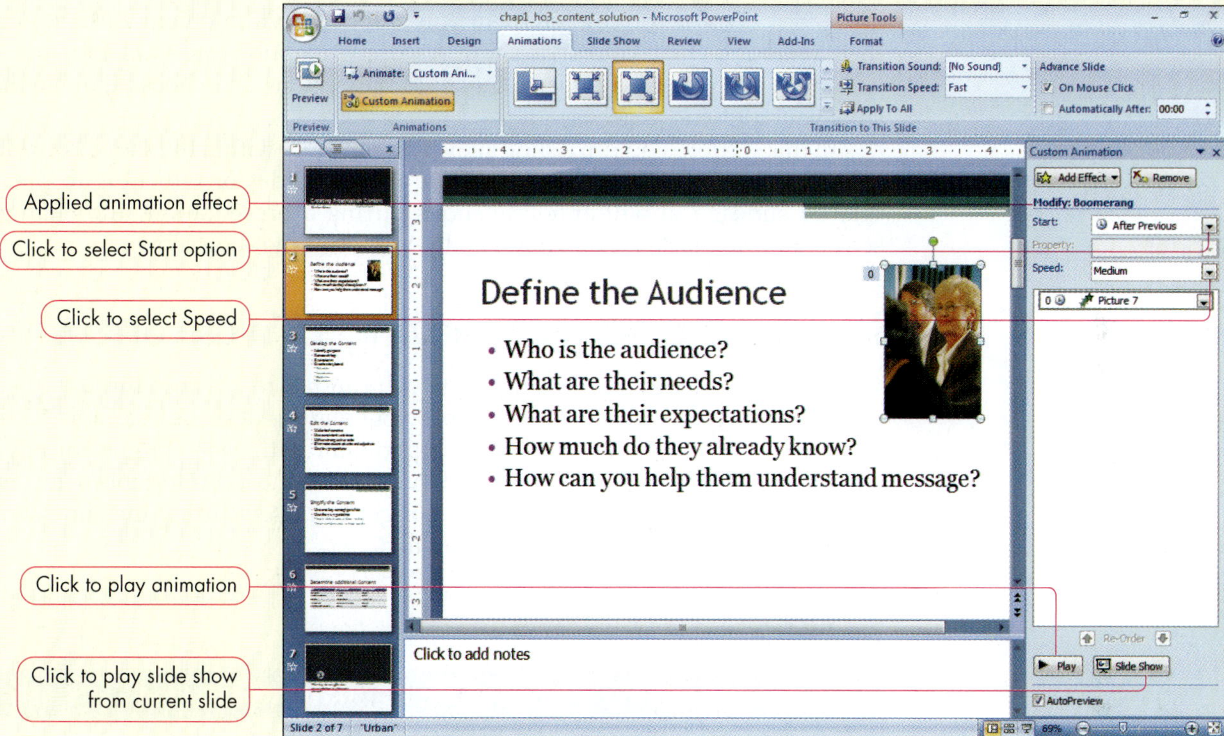

Figure 1.45 Custom Animation Task Pane

Navigation and Printing

In the beginning of this chapter you opened a slide show and advanced one by one through the slides by clicking the mouse button. This task is possible because PowerPoint is, by default, a linear software tool that advances each slide one after another in a straight line order. Audiences, however, are seldom comfortable with a linear slide show. If they are involved in the presentation, they want to ask questions. As you respond to the questions, you may find yourself needing to jump to a previous slide or needing to move to a future slide. PowerPoint's navigation options enable you to do this maneuver.

To help your audience follow your presentation, you can choose to provide them with a handout. You may give it to them at the beginning of your presentation for them to take notes on, or you tell them you will be providing them with notes and let them relax and enjoy your slide show. A variety of options are available for audience handouts. All you need do is be aware of the options and choose the one that best suits your audience's needs.

A variety of options are available for audience handouts . . . be aware of the options and choose the one that best suits your audience's needs.

In this section, you run a slide show and navigate within the show. You will practice a variety of methods for advancing to new slides or returning to previously viewed slides. You will annotate slides during a presentation, and change from screen view to black-screen view. Finally, you print the slide show.

Running and Navigating a Slide Show

PowerPoint provides multiple methods you can use to advance through your slide show. You also can go backwards to a previous slide, if desired. Use Table 1.2 to identify the navigation options, and then experiment with each method for advancing and going backwards. Find the method that you are most comfortable using and stay with that method. That way you will not get confused during the slide show and advance to a new slide before you mean to do so.

Table 1.2 Navigation Options

Navigation Option	Navigation Method
To Advance through the Slide Show	Press the Spacebar
	Press Page Down
	Press the letter **N** or **n** for next
	Press the right arrow or down arrow
	Press Enter
To Return to a Previous Slide or Animation	Right-click and choose Previous from the Popup menu
	Press the Page Up button
	Press the letter **P** or **p** for previous
	Press the left arrow or up arrow
	Press Backspace
To End the Slide Show	Press Esc on the keyboard
	Press the hyphen key
To Go to a Specific Slide	Type Slide number and press Enter
	Right-click, click Go to Slide, then click the slide desired

TIP Slide Show Controls

You can press F1 at any time during your presentation to see a list of slide show controls. Familiarize yourself with these controls before you present to a group for maximum effectiveness.

When an audience member asks a question that is answered in another slide on your slide show, you can go to that specific slide in the slide show by using the Popup menu. Right-clicking while displaying the slide show brings up a handy menu of options. Pointing to the Go to Slide command and then clicking the slide you wish to go to enables you to move to that slide. This pop-up menu also lets you end the slide show.

After the last slide in your slide show displays, the audience sees a black slide. This slide has a two-fold purpose. It enables you to end your show without having your audience see the PowerPoint design screen, and it cues the audience to expect the room lights to brighten. If you need to bring up the lights in the room while in your slide show, you can type the letter **B** or **b** for black on the keyboard, and the screen blackens. Be careful though—if you blacken the screen, you must bring up the lights. Do not stand and present in complete darkness. When you are ready to launch your slide show again, simply type the letter **B** or **b** again.

If you prefer bringing up a white screen, you can accomplish the same thing by using the letter **W** or **w** for white. White is much harsher on your audience's eyes, however, and can be very jarring. Only use white if you are in an extremely bright room, and the bright white screen is not too great of a difference in lighting. Whether using black or white, however, you are enabling the audience to concentrate on you, the speaker, without the slide show interfering.

Annotate the Slide Show

An ***annotation*** is a note that can be written or drawn on a slide for additional commentary or explanation.

You may find it helpful to add ***annotations***, or notes, to your slides. You can write or draw on your slides during a presentation. To do so, right-click to bring up the shortcut menu, and then point to Pointer Options to select your pen type. You can change the color of the pen from the Popup menu, too. To create the annotation, hold down the left mouse button as you write or draw on your slide. To erase what you have drawn, press the letter **E** or **e** on the keyboard. Keep in mind that the mouse was never intended to be an artist's tool. Your drawings or added text will be clumsy efforts at best, unless you use a tablet and pen. The annotations you create are not permanent unless you save the annotations when exiting the slide show and then save the changes upon exiting the file.

TIP Annotating Shortcuts

Press Ctrl+P to change the mouse pointer to a point, then click and drag on the slide during the presentation, much the same way your favorite football announcer diagrams a play. Use the PgDn and PgUp keys to move forward and back in the presentation while the annotation is in effect. The annotations will disappear when you exit the slide show unless you elect to keep them permanently when prompted at the end of the show. Press Ctrl+A to return the mouse pointer to an arrow.

Printing with PowerPoint

A printed copy of a PowerPoint slide show is very beneficial. It can be used by the presenter for reference during the presentation. It can be used by the audience for future reference, or as backup during equipment failure. It can even be used by students as a study guide. A printout of a single slide with text on it can be used as a poster or banner.

Print Slides

Use the Print Slides option to print each slide on a full page. One reason to print the slides as full slides is to print the slides for use as a backup. You can print the full slides on overhead transparencies that could be projected with an overhead projector during a presentation. You will be extremely grateful for the backup if your projector bulb blows out, or your computer quits working during a presentation. Using the Print Slides option also is valuable if you want to print a single slide that has been formatted as a sign or a card.

If you are printing the slides on transparencies, or on paper smaller than the standard size, be sure to set the slide size and orientation before you print. By default PowerPoint sets the slides for landscape orientation, or printing where the width is greater than the height (11 x 8.5″). If you are going to print on a transparency for an overhead projector, however, you need to set PowerPoint to portrait orientation, or printing where the height is greater than the width (8.5 x 11″).

To change your slide orientation, or to set PowerPoint to print for a different size, click the Design tab and click Page Setup in the Page Setup group to open the Page Setup dialog box. Click in the *Slides sized for* list to select the size or type of paper on which you will print. To print overhead transparency, you click Overhead. You also can set the slide orientation in this dialog box. If you wish to create a custom size of paper to print, enter the height and width. Figure 1.46 displays the Page Setup options. Note that the slide show we have been creating has been changed so that it can be printed on overhead transparencies.

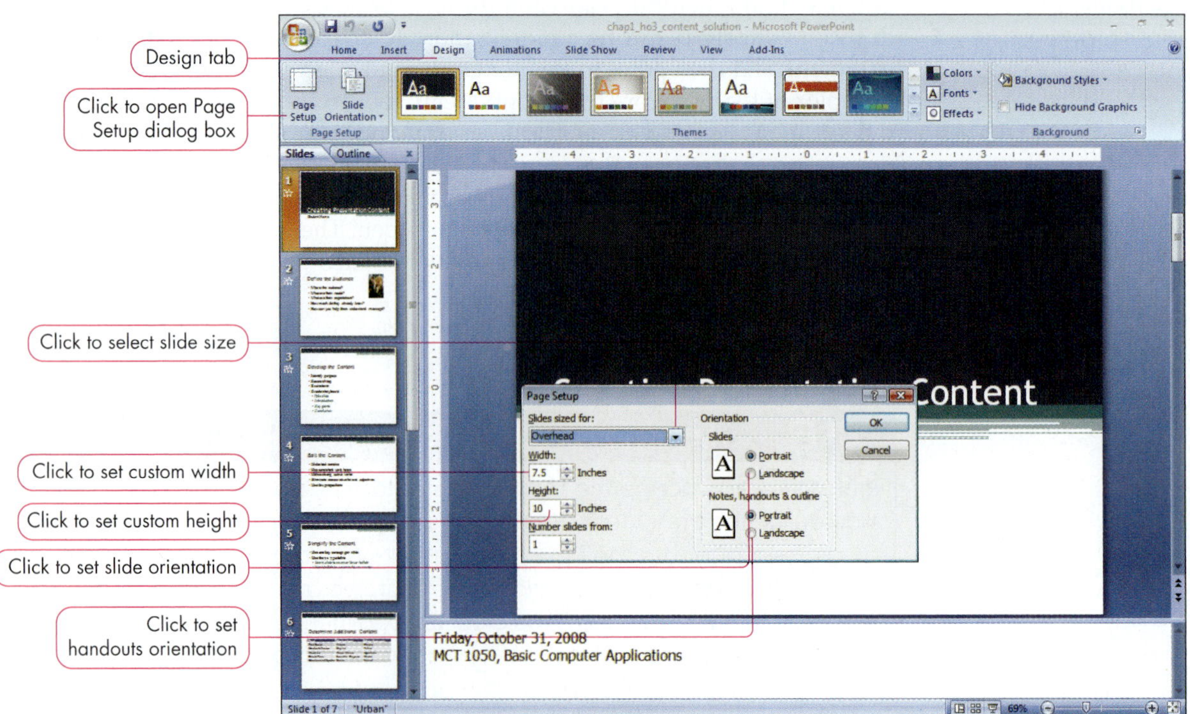

Figure 1.46 Page Setup Options

Once you have determined your page setup, you are ready to print the slides. To print, click the Office Button, select Print, and then select Print in the submenu. The Print dialog box opens so that you can select your printer, your print range, and number of copies—options available to all Office applications. In addition to the standard print options, PowerPoint has many options that tailor the printout to your needs. You can click the *Print what* drop-down arrow and select whether you want to print slides, handouts, notes pages, or outlines.

You can determine the color option with which to print. Selecting Color prints your presentation in color if you have a color printer or grayscale if you are printing on a black-and-white printer. Selecting the Grayscale option prints in shades of gray, but be aware that backgrounds do not print when using the Grayscale option. By not printing the background, you make the text in the printout easier to read and you save a lot of ink or toner. Printing with the Pure Black and White option prints with no gray fills. Try using Microsoft clip art and printing in Pure Black and White to create coloring pages for children.

If you have selected a custom size for your slide show, or if you have set up the slide show so that is it larger than the paper you are printing on, be sure to check the *Scale to fit paper* box. Doing so will ensure that each slide prints on one page. The *Frame slides* option puts a black border around the slides in the printout, giving the printout a more polished appearance. If you have applied shadows to text or objects, you may want to check the *High quality* option so that the shadows print. The final two options, *Print comments and ink markup* and *Print hidden slides*, are only active if you have used these features.

Print Handouts

The principal purpose for printing handouts is to give your audience something they can use to follow during the presentation and give them something on which to take notes. With your handout and their notes, the audience has an excellent resource for the future. Handouts can be printed with one, two, three, four, six, or nine slides per page. Printing three handouts per page is a popular option because it places thumbnails of the slides on the left side of the printout and lines on which the audience can write on the right side of the printout. Figure 1.47 shows the *Print what* option set to Handouts and the Slides per page option set to 6.

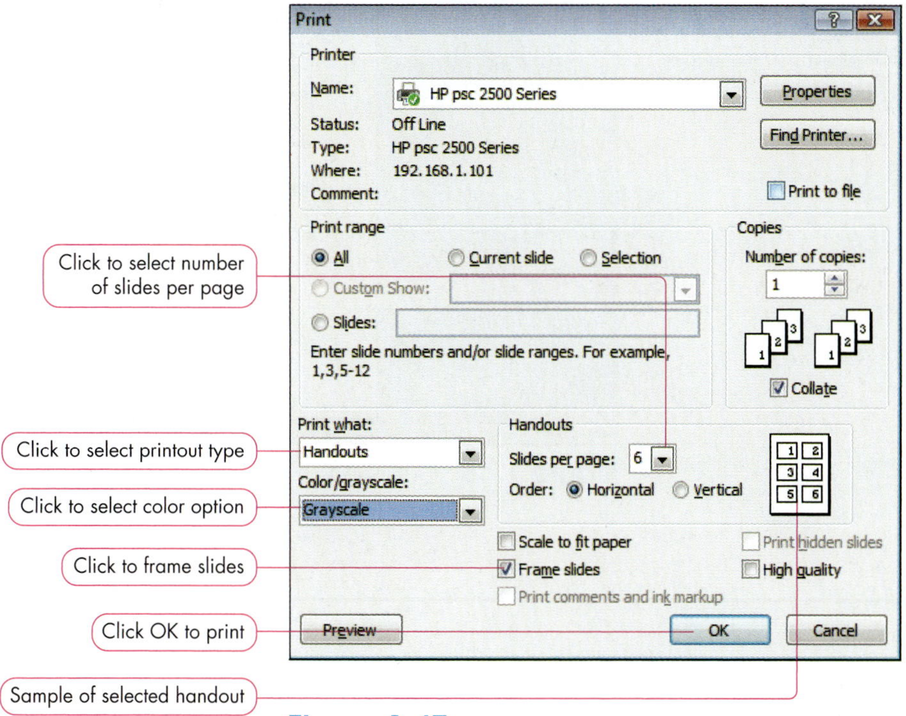

Figure 1.47 Print Dialog Box

Print Notes Pages

In the first exercise in this chapter, you created a note in the Notes pane. If you include charts or technical information in your notes, you will want to print the notes for reference. You also may want to print the detailed notes for your audience, especially if your notes contain references. To print your notes, click the Office Button, select Print, select Print from the submenu, and then click Notes Pages in the *Print what* box.

Print Outlines

You may print your presentation as an outline made up of the slide titles and main text from each of your slides. This is a good option if you only want to deal with a few pages instead of a page for each slide as is printed for Notes pages. The outline generally gives you enough detail to keep you on track with your presentation.

You can print the outline following the methods discussed for the other three printout types, but you also can preview it and print from the preview screen. To preview how a printout will look, click the Office Button, and then point to the arrow next to Print. In the list that displays, click Print Preview. Click the arrow next to the *Print what* box, and then click Outline View. If you decide to print, click Print. Figure 1.48 shows the outline for the presentation we have been creating in Print Preview.

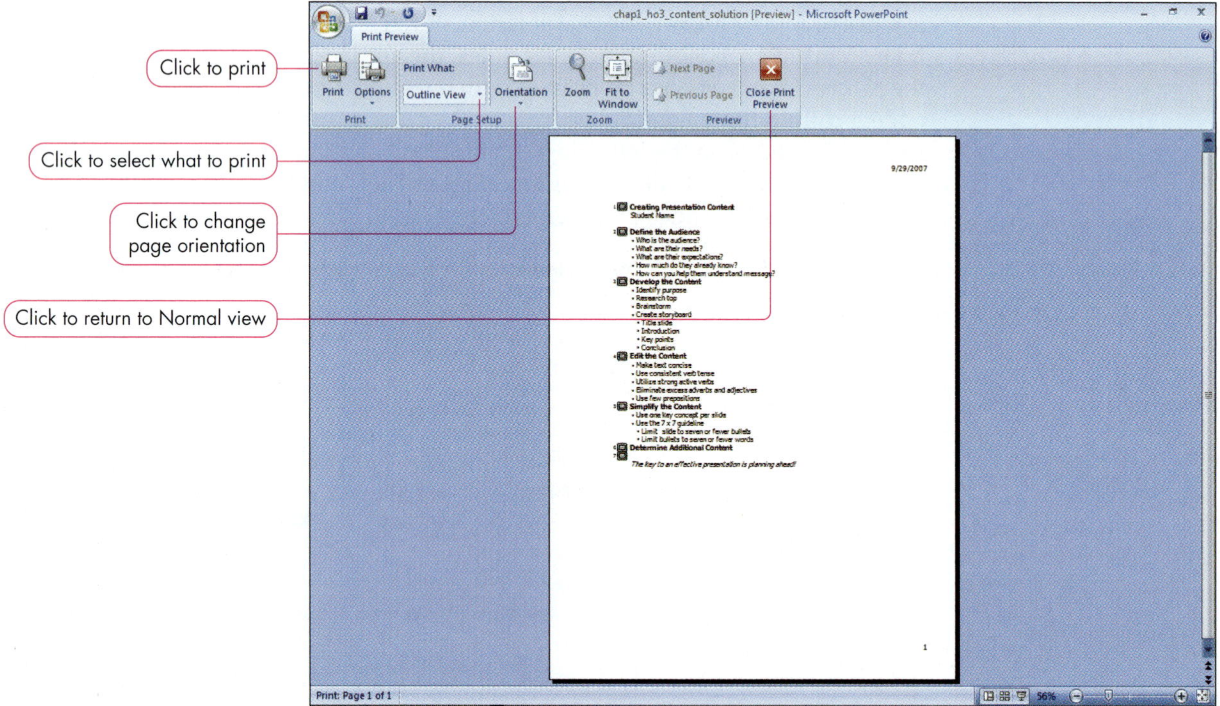

Figure 1.48 Outline View in Print Preview

Hands-On Exercises

4 | Navigating and Printing

Skills covered: 1. Display a Slide Show **2.** Navigate to Specific Slides **3.** Annotate a Slide **4.** Print Audience Handouts

Step 1
Display a Slide Show

a. Open the *chap1_ho3_content_solution* presentation if you closed it after the last exercise and then save it as the **chap1_ho4_content_solution** presentation. Type your class under your name in the subtitle placeholder.

b. Click the **Slide Show tab** and click **From Beginning** in the Start Slide Show group.

   Note the transition effect and sound you applied in Hands-On Exercise 3.

c. Press **Spacebar** to animate the title, press **Spacebar** again to animate the subtitle.

   Pressing Spacebar advances to the next animation or the next slide.

d. Click to advance to Slide 2.

   Note that the photograph animation plays automatically.

e. Press **Page Down** to advance to Slide 3.

f. Press **Page Up** to return to Slide 2.

g. Press **Enter** to advance to Slide 3.

h. Press **N** on the keyboard to advance to Slide 4.

i. Press **Backspace** to return to Slide 3.

Step 2
Navigate to Specific Slides

a. Right-click, select **Go to Slide**, and then select **5 Simply the Content**.

   Slide 5 displays.

b. Press the number **3** on the keyboard, and then press **Enter**.

   Slide 3 displays.

c. Press **F1** and read the Slide Show Help window showing the shortcut tips that are available during the display of a slide show.

d. Close the Help window.

Step 3
Annotate a Slide

a. Press **Ctrl + P**.

   The mouse pointer becomes a pen.

b. Circle and underline several words on the slide.

c. Press the letter **E**.

   The annotations erase.

d. Press the letter **B**.

   The screen blackens.

e. Press the letter **B** again.

   The slide show displays again.

f. Press **Esc** to end the slide show.

Step 4
Print Audience Handouts

a. Click the **Office Button** and select **Print**.

b. Click the **Print what drop-down arrow**, and then select **Handouts**.

c. Specify **4** slides per page and then click **OK** to print the presentation.

d. Save the *chap1_ho4_content_solution* presentation and close it.

Summary

1. **Identify PowerPoint user interface elements.** PowerPoint features are designed to aid you in creating slide shows in support of presentations you give. Slide shows are electronic presentations that enable you to advance through slides containing content that will help your audience understand your message. PowerPoint 2007 is one of the four main applications in the Office 2007 Suite that uses a new interface designed for easier access to features. PowerPoint has different views, each with unique capabilities.
2. **Use PowerPoint views.** PowerPoint contains multiple views to fit the user's needs. The Normal view is a tri-pane view that displays either thumbnail images or an outline in one pane, the slide in one pane, and a Notes pane. The Slide Sorter view displays thumbnails of multiple slides to enable the user to quickly reorder or delete slides to enhance organization. The Notes Page view displays a thumbnail of the slide and the notes the user has entered for that slide. The Slide Show view displays the slide show in full-screen view for an audience. If a presenter has multiple monitors, the Presenter's view gives the presenter options for greater control of the playback.
3. **Open and save a slide show.** Previously created slide shows can be opened so that they can be modified. After editing, they can be saved with the same file name using the Save feature, or saved with a new file name using the Save As feature. When slide shows are saved, they are assigned an extension of .pptx, indicating they are in XML (Extensible Markup Language) file format.
4. **Get Help.** PowerPoint's Help can be used to locate information about a specific feature, to troubleshoot, to search for software updates, to find a template, or to locate additional training. Help is available online or offline.
5. **Create a storyboard.** Before creating your slide show you should spend a considerable amount of time analyzing your audience, researching your message, and organizing your ideas. Organize your ideas on a storyboard, and then create your presentation in PowerPoint. After completing the slide show, you should spend a considerable amount of time practicing your presentation so that you are comfortable with your slide content and the technology you will use to present it with.
6. **Use slide layouts.** PowerPoint provides a set of predefined slide layouts that determine the position of the objects or content on a slide. Slide layouts contain any number and combination of placeholders. Placeholders hold content and determine the position of the objects on the slide.
7. **Apply design themes.** PowerPoint themes enable you to focus on the content of a presentation. You create the text and supporting elements, and then you apply a design theme to give the presentation a consistent look. The theme controls the font, background, layout, and colors.
8. **Review the presentation.** To ensure there are no typographical errors or misspelled words in a presentation, use the Check Spelling feature to complete an initial check for errors. You also need to review each slide yourself because the Check Spelling feature does not find all errors. An example of an error that the Check Spelling feature does not find is the misuse of the word "to" or "two" when the correct word is "too." Use the Thesaurus to locate synonyms for overused words in the slide show.
9. **Add a table.** Tables can be created to help organize information needed in the slide show. PowerPoint's table features can be used to specify the number of columns and rows needed in the table. Tables can be inserted from the Content bar in the Content placeholder or through the Insert tab.
10. **Insert clip art.** A variety of clips can be added to slides. Clips are media objects such as clip art, images, movies, and sound. The Microsoft Clip Organizer contains media objects you can insert, or you can locate clips and insert them through the Insert tab. Clips you gather can be added to the Microsoft Clip Organizer to help you locate them more easily.
11. **Use transitions and animations.** Transitions and animations show in Slide Show view. Transitions control the movements of slides as one slide changes to another, while an animation controls the movement of an object on the slide. Both features can aid in keeping the attention of the audience, but animations are especially valuable in directing attention to specific elements you wish to emphasize.

12. **Run and navigate within a slide show.** While displaying the slide show, you need flexibility in moving between slides. Various navigation methods advance the slide show, return to previously viewed slides, or go to specific slides. Slides can be annotated during a presentation to add emphasis or comments to slides.
13. **Print with PowerPoint.** PowerPoint has four ways to print the slideshow, each with specific benefits. The Slides method of printing prints each slide on a full page. The Handouts method prints miniatures of the slides in 1, 2, 3, 4, 6, or 9 per page format. The Notes Pages method prints each slide on a separate page and is formatted to display a single thumbnail of a slide with its associated notes. The Outline View method prints the titles and main points of the presentation in outline format.

Key Terms

Multiple Choice

1. Which of the following methods does not save changes in a PowerPoint presentation?
   (a) Click the Office Button and then click the Save As command.
   (b) Click the Save button on the Quick Access Toolbar.
   (c) Press Ctrl+S.
   (d) Press F1.

2. The Quick Access Toolbar, containing commands you may need at any time regardless of what tab is active, includes which of the following commands?
   (a) Cut and Paste
   (b) Undo and Redo
   (c) Find and Replace
   (d) Spelling and Grammar

3. You have created a very complex table with great detail on a slide. You want to give the audience a printout of the slide showing all the detail so they can review it with you during your presentation. Which of the following print methods would show the necessary detail?
   (a) Audience handout, 4 per page
   (b) Outline
   (c) Notes page
   (d) Full slide

4. While displaying a slide show, which of the following will display a list of shortcuts for navigating?
   (a) F1
   (b) F11
   (c) Ctrl+Enter
   (d) Esc

5. The predefined slide formats in PowerPoint are:
   (a) Layout views
   (b) Slide layouts
   (c) Slide guides
   (d) Slide displays

6. If you need to add an object such as clip art or a picture to a slide, which tab would you select?
   (a) Add-ins
   (b) Design
   (c) Slide
   (d) Insert

7. The Open command
   (a) Brings a presentation from a storage device into RAM memory
   (b) Removes the presentation from the storage device and brings it into RAM memory
   (c) Stores the presentation in RAM memory to a storage device
   (d) Stores the presentation in RAM memory to a storage device and then erases the presentation from RAM memory

8. The Save command
   (a) Brings a presentation from a storage device into RAM memory
   (b) Removes the presentation from the storage device and brings it into RAM memory
   (c) Stores the presentation in RAM memory to a storage device
   (d) Stores the presentation in RAM memory to a storage device and then erases the presentation from RAM memory

9. Which of the following provides a ghost image of a toolbar for use in formatting selected text?
   (a) Styles command
   (b) Quick Access Toolbar
   (c) Formatting Text gallery
   (d) Mini toolbar

10. Which of the following is a true statement?
    (a) A design theme must be applied before slides are created.
    (b) The design theme can be changed after all of the slides have been created.
    (c) Design themes control fonts and backgrounds but not placeholder location.
    (d) Placeholders positioned by a design theme cannot be moved.

11. Microsoft Clip Organizer searches
    (a) May be limited to a specific media type
    (b) Locate clips based on keywords
    (c) May be limited to specific collections
    (d) All of the above

12. Which of the following views is best for reordering the slides in a presentation?
    (a) Presenter view
    (b) Slide Show view
    (c) Reorder view
    (d) Slide Sorter view

...continued on Next Page

Multiple Choice Continued...

13. Normal view contains which of the following components?
    (a) The slide sorter pane, the tabs pane, and the slide pane
    (b) The tabs pane, the slide pane, and the slide sorter pane
    (c) The tabs pane, the slide pane, and the notes pane
    (d) The outline pane, the slide pane, and the tabs pane

14. Which of the following cannot be used to focus audience attention on a specific object on a slide during a slide show?
    (a) Apply a transition to the object
    (b) Apply an animation to the object
    (c) Use the pen tool to circle the object
    (d) Put nothing on the slide but the object

15. What is the animation effect that controls how one slide changes to another slide?
    (a) Custom animation
    (b) Animation scheme
    (c) Transition
    (d) Advance

Practice Exercises

1 Introduction to E-Mail

The exercise reviews the basics of e-mail and simultaneously provides you with practice opening, modifying, and saving an existing PowerPoint presentation. The presentation contains two slides on computer viruses and reminds you that your computer is at risk whenever you receive an e-mail message with an attachment. Notes containing explanations are included for some slides. You create a summary of what you learn and enter it as a note for the last slide. Refer to Figure 1.49 as you complete this exercise.

a. Click the **Office Button** and select **Open**. Click the appropriate drive and folder in the Folders list on the left side of the Open dialog box. Choose the location where the original data files to accompany this book are located. Select the *chap1_pe1_email* presentation and then click **Open**.
b. Click the **Slide Show tab** and click **From Beginning** in the Start Slide Show group. Read each of the slides by pressing **Spacebar** to advance through the slides. Press **Esc** to exit the Slide Show View.
c. Click in the **Slide 1 subtitle placeholder**, and then replace the words *Student Name* with your name as it appears on the instructor's rolls. Replace *Student Class* with the name of the class you are taking.
d. Click in the **Slide 10 Notes pane** and then type a short note about what you learned regarding e-mail by reviewing this slide show.
e. Click the **Slide 4 thumbnail** in the Tabs pane to move to Slide 4. Select the sample e-mail address and then type your e-mail address to replace the sample and press Enter.
f. Move to **Slide 3** and then click inside the content placeholder. Type **Inbox** and then press **Enter**. Continue typing the following bullet items: **Outbox**, **Sent items**, **Deleted items**, **Custom folders**.
g. Move to **Slide 8**, select the first protocol, *POP Client – Post Office Protocol Client*, and then move your pointer slightly upward until the Mini toolbar appears. Apply **Bold** and **Italics** to the first protocol. Repeat the process for the second protocol, *IMAP – Internet Message Access Protocol*.
h. Click the **Design tab** and click the **More button** in the Themes group.
i. Click **Technic** to apply the Technic theme to all slides in the slide show.
j. Move to **Slide 1** and adjust the size of the Title placeholder so the complete title fits on one line.
k. Click the **Office Button,** point to **Print**, and then click **Print** in the submenu. Click **Current slide** option in the *Print range* section. Click the **Frame slides check box** to activate it and then click **OK**. Slide 1 will print for your use as a cover page.
l. Open the Print dialog box again and then click the **Slides** option in the *Print range* section. Type the slide range **2–10**.
m. Click the **Print what drop-down arrow**, and then select **Handouts**. Click the **Slides per page drop-down arrow** in the *Handouts* section, and then select **3**.
n. Click the **Frame slides check box** to activate it and then click **OK**. Slides 2–10 will print 3 per page with lines for audience note taking. Staple the cover page to the handouts and then submit it to your instructor if requested to do so.
o. Click the **Office Button** and select **Save As**. Click the appropriate drive and folder in the Folders list on the left side of the Save As dialog box. Choose the location where you want to save your completed files. Type **chap1_pe1_email_solution** as the file name for the presentation. Click **Save** and close the presentation.

...continued on Next Page

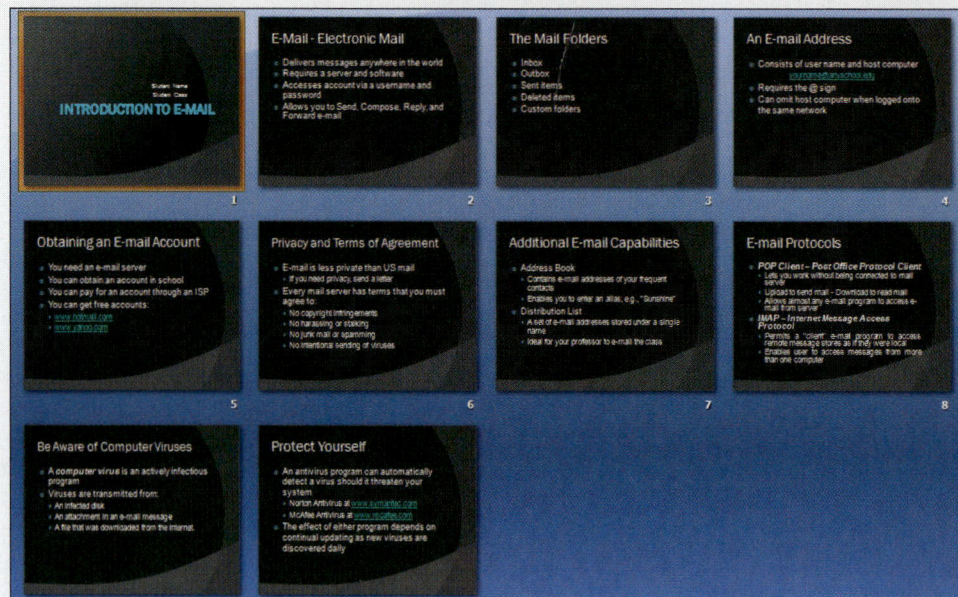

Figure 1.49 Introduction to E-Mail Presentation

2 Successful Presentations

Your employer is a successful author who often presents to various groups. He has been asked by the local International Association of Administrative Professionals (IAAP) to give the group tips for presenting successfully using PowerPoint. He created a storyboard of his presentation and has asked you to create the presentation from the storyboard. Refer to Figure 1.50 as you complete this exercise.

a. Click the **Office Button**, select **New**, click **Blank Presentation**, and then click **Create**.

b. Click the **Office Button** and select **Save As**. Click the appropriate drive and folder in the Folders list on the left side of the Save As dialog box. Choose the location where you want to save your completed files. Type **chap1_pe2_tips_solution** as the file name for the presentation. Click **Save**.

c. Click in the **Slide 1 title placeholder** and then type **Successful Presentations**. Click in the subtitle placeholder and type **Robert Grauer and your name** as it appears on the instructor's rolls.

d. Click the **Home tab**, click the **New Slide down arrow** in the Slides group, and click **Title Only**.

e. Click in the title placeholder and type **Techniques to Consider**.

f. Click **Table** in the Tables group on the Insert tab and then drag the grid to highlight two columns and five rows.

g. Type the following information in the table cells. Press **Tab** to move from cell to cell.

Feature	**Use**
Rehearse Timings	Helps you determine the length of your presentation
Header/Footer	Puts information on the top and bottom of slides, notes and handouts
Hidden Slides	Hides slides until needed
Annotate a Slide	Write on the slide

h. Click the **Home tab**, click the **New Slide down arrow** in the Slides group, and then click **Title and Content**. Type **The Delivery is Up to You**.

i. Click in the content placeholder and type the following bullet text: **Practice makes perfect, Arrive early on the big day, Maintain eye contact, Speak slowly, clearly, and with sufficient volume, Allow time for questions**.

j. Click the **Home tab**, click the **New Slide down arrow** in the Slides group, and then click **Title and Content**. Type **Keep Something in Reserve**.

...continued on Next Page

k. Click in the content placeholder and type the following bullet text: **Create hidden slides to answer difficult questions that might occur, Press Ctrl+S to display hidden slides**.
l. Click the **Home tab**, click **New Slide** in the Slides group, and then click **Title and Content**. Type **Provide Handouts.**
m. Click in the content placeholder and type the following bullet text: **Allows the audience to follow the presentation, Lets the audience take the presentation home**.
n. Click the **Review tab** and click **Spelling** in the Proofing group.
o. Correct any misspelled words Check Spelling locates. Proofread the presentation and correct any misspelled words Check Spelling missed.
p. Click the **Design tab** and click the **More button** in the Themes group.
q. Click **Oriel**.
r. Click the **Slide Show tab** and click **From Beginning** in the Start Slide Show group. Press **Page Down** to advance through the slides.
s. When you reach the end of the slide show, press the number **2**, and then press **Enter** to return to Slide 2. Press **Esc.**
t. Press **Ctrl+S** to save the *chap1_pe2_tips_solution* presentation and close the presentation.

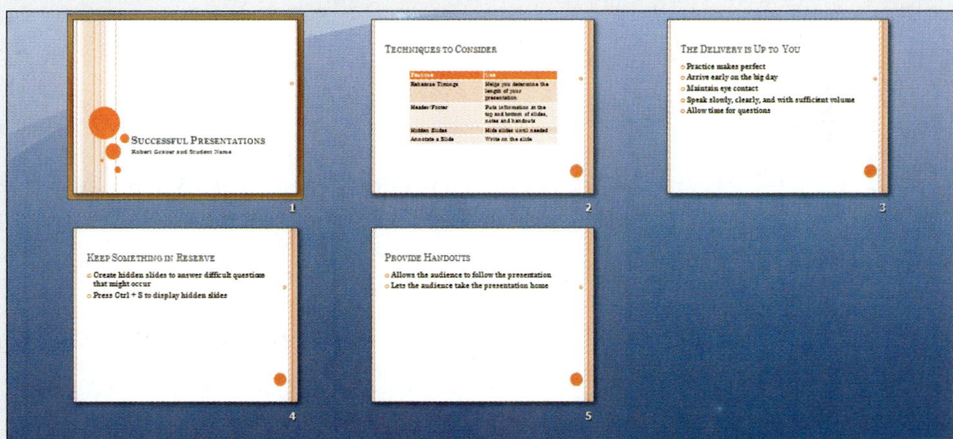

Figure 1.50 Successful Presentations Slide Show

3 Introduction to the Internet

You have been asked to give a presentation covering the basics of the Internet. You created a storyboard and entered the content in a slide show. After viewing the slide show you realize the slides are text intensive and that transitions and animations would make the show more interesting. You modify the slide show and remove some of the detail from the slides. You put the detail in the Notes pane. You add a transition and apply it to all slides, and you apply custom animations to two images. You print the Notes for you to refer to as you present. Refer to Figure 1.51 as you complete this exercise.

a. Click the **Office Button** and select **Open**. Click the appropriate drive and folder in the Folders list on the left side of the Open dialog box. Choose the location where the original data files to accompany this book are located. Click the *chap1_pe3_internet* presentation, and then click **Open**.
b. Click in the **Slide 1** title placeholder and replace the words *Your Name* with your name as it appears on the instructor's rolls. Replace *Your Class* with the name of the class you are taking.
c. Click in the **Slide 2 content placeholder** and modify the text so that it is shortened to brief, easy-to-remember chunks as displayed in Figure 1.51.

...continued on Next Page

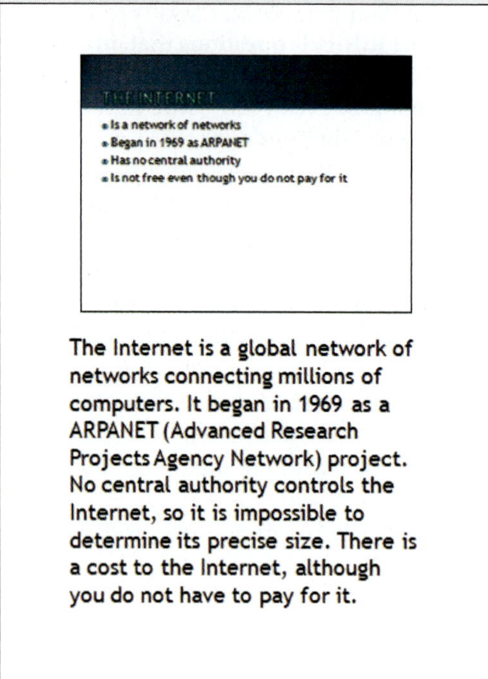

Figure 1.51 Internet Slide 2 Modifications

d. Click the **View tab**. Click **Notes Page** in the Presentation Views group, and then using Figure 1.51 as a guide, enter the notes in the Notes placeholder, which provides the appropriate place for the text omitted in the previous step.

e. Click **Normal** in the Presentation Views group on the View tab and then move to **Slide 3**. Click in the content placeholder and modify the text so that it is shortened to brief, easy-to-remember chunks as displayed in Figure 1.52.

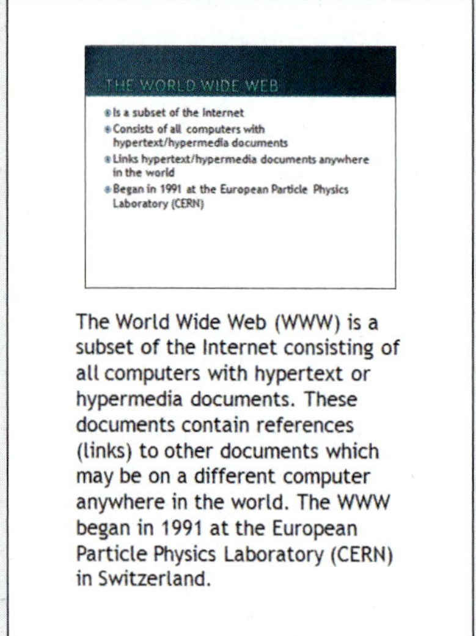

Figure 1.52 Internet Slide 3 Modifications

...continued on Next Page

f. Click the **View tab**, click **Notes Page** in the Presentation Views group, and then using Figure 1.51 as a guide, enter the notes in the Notes placeholder.
g. Click **Normal** in the Presentation Views group, and then click the **Animations tab.** Click the **More button** in the Transition to This Slide group.
h. Click the **Cover Right-Down** option and click **Apply To All**.
i. Move to **Slide 5** and then click the image of the computer network to select it.
j. Click the down arrow next to **Animate** in the Animations group on the Animations tab and then click **Fly In**. Repeat this process for the image of the modem and telephone.
k. Click the **View tab,** click **Slide Show** in the Presentation Views group, and then advance through the slide show. Press **Esc** to end the slide show after you have viewed the last slide.
l. Click the **Office Button**, select **Print**, and then select **Print Preview**.
m. Select **Notes Pages** from the Print what list and then press **Page Down** on the keyboard to advance through the slides. If your instructor asks you to print the Notes Pages, click **Print** in the Print group on the Print Preview tab. Click **Close Print Preview** in the Preview group on the Print Preview tab.
n. Click the **Office Button**, and then select **Save As**. Click the **Save in drop-down arrow** and locate the drive and folder where you are saving your file solutions. Type **chap1_pe3_internet_solution** as the file name for the presentation. Click **Save** and close the presentation.

4 Copyright and the Law

The ethics and values class you are taking this semester requires a final presentation to the class. Although a PowerPoint slide show is not required, you feel it will strengthen your presentation. You create a presentation to review basic copyright law and software licensing, and add clip art, a transition, and an animation.

a. Click the **Office Button** and select **Open**. Click the **Look in drop-down arrow** and then locate the drive and folder where your student files are saved. Select the *chap1_pe4_copyright* presentation, and then click **Open**.
b. Click the **Slide Show tab** and then click **From Beginning** in the Start Slide Show group. Read each of the slides and note the length of some bullets. Press **Esc** to return to Normal view.
c. Click the **Design tab**, click the **More button** in the Themes group, and select the **Flow theme**.
d. Click in the **Slide 1 title placeholder**, if necessary, and then replace the words *Student Name* with your name as it appears on the instructor's rolls. Replace *Student Class* with the name of the class you are taking.
e. Click the **Insert tab** and click **Clip Art** in the Illustrations group. Type **copyright** in the **Search for** box. Select the animated copyright symbol and drag it to the title slide next to your name. Refer to Figure 1.53 to help you identify the copyright logo.

TROUBLESHOOTING: If the animated copyright clip does not appear when you search for the copyright keyword, change the keyword to **law** and then select an image that relates to the presentation content and uses the same colors.

f. Click the **Animations tab** and click the **More button** in the Transition to This Slide group.
g. Click the **Fade Through Black** option and then click **Apply To All**.
h. Move to **Slide 6** and then select the blue object containing text located at the bottom of the slide.
i. Click **Custom Animation** in the Animations group on the Animations tab.
j. Click **Add Effect** in the Custom Animation task pane, click **More Effects** at the bottom of the Entrance group and then choose **Faded Zoom** from the Subtle category.
k. Click the **Start** drop-down arrow, and then click **After Previous**.

...continued on Next Page

l. Click **Play** at the bottom of the Custom Animation task pane to see the result of your custom animation.

m. Move to the last slide in the slide show, **Slide 9**, click the **Home tab**, and then click **New Slide** in the Slides group.

n. Click **Section Header** from the list of layouts.

o. Click in the title placeholder and type **Individuals who violate copyright law and/or software licensing agreements may be subject to criminal or civil action by the copyright or license owners**. Press **Ctrl + A** to select the text and change the font size to 40 pts.

p. Click the border of the subtitle placeholder and press **Delete**.

q. Drag the title placeholder downward until all of the text is visible and is centered vertically on the slide.

r. Select the text, move your pointer upward until the Mini toolbar appears, and then click the **Center Align** button.

s. Click the **Office Button** and select **Save As**. Click the **Save in drop-down arrow** and locate the drive and folder where you are saving your file solutions. Type **chap1_pe4_copyright_solution** as the file name for the presentation. Click **Save** and close the presentation.

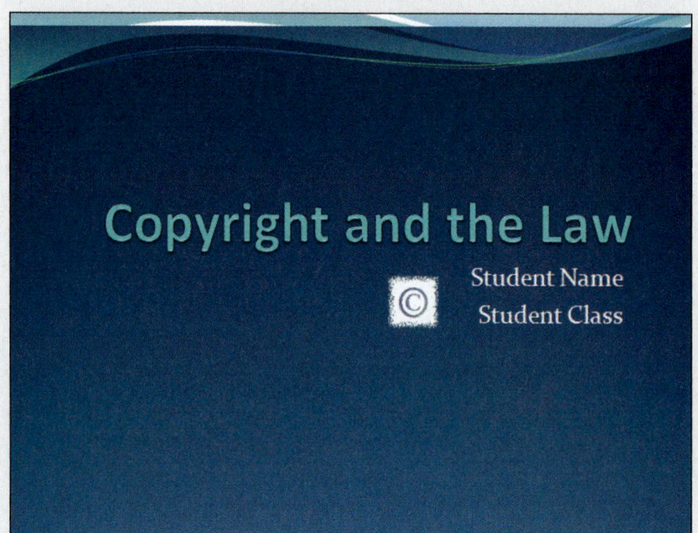

Figure 1.53 Copyright and the Law Presentation

Mid-Level Exercises

1 Public Speaking 101

PowerPoint will help you to create an attractive presentation, but the delivery is still up to you. It is easier than you think, and you should not be intimidated at the prospect of facing an audience. You can gain confidence and become an effective speaker by following the basic tenets of good public speaking. Refer to Figure 1.54 as you complete this exercise.

a. Open the *chap1_mid1_public* presentation and save it as **chap1_mid1_public_solution**.

b. Add your name and e-mail address to the title slide. Add your e-mail address to the summary slide as well.

c. Print the notes for the presentation and then view the slide show while looking at the appropriate notes for each slide. Which slides have notes attached? Are the notes redundant, or do they add something extra? Do you see how the notes help a speaker to deliver an effective presentation?

d. Which slide contains the phrase, "Common sense is not common practice"? In what context is the phrase used within the presentation?

e. Which personality said, "You can observe a lot just by watching?" In what context is the phrase used during the presentation?

f. Join a group of three or four students, and then have each person in the group deliver the presentation to his or her group. Were they able to follow the tenets of good public speaking? Share constructive criticism with each of the presenters. Constructive criticism means you identify both positive aspects of their presentations and aspects that could be improved with practice. The goal of constructive criticism is to help one another improve.

g. Summarize your thoughts about this exercise in an e-mail message to your instructor.

h. Save the *chap1_mid1_public_solution* presentation and close.

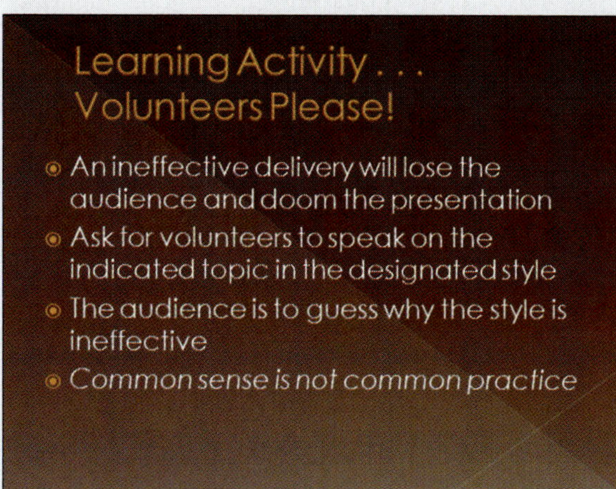

Figure 1.54 Public Speaking 101

...continued on Next Page

2 University Housing

The Provost's Office at your university manages policies and practices that affect the academic life of the university as a whole. The new provost, Dr. Richard Shaw, has asked the housing office administrator to meet with him and update him about the purpose and goals of the housing office. As a work-study student employed by the housing office, you have been asked to take the administrator's notes and prepare a presentation for the provost. Refer to Figure 1.55 as you complete this exercise.

a. Open the *chap1_mid2_university* presentation and save it as **chap1_mid2_university_solution**.

b. Add your name and the name of the class you are taking to the title slide.

c. Insert a new slide using the Title and Content layout as the second slide in the presentation. Type **Mission** as the title.

d. Type the mission in the content placeholder: **The mission of the University Housing Office is to provide a total environment that will enrich the educational experience of its residents. It seeks to promote increased interaction between faculty and students through resident masters, special programs, and intramural activities.**

e. Move to the end of the presentation and insert a new slide with the Blank layout. Insert two photograph clips related to college life from the Microsoft Clip Organizer or Office Online. Resize the photos if necessary.

f. Move to **Slide 4** and create a table using the following information:

Dorm Name	Room Revenue	Meal Revenue	Total Revenue
Ashe Hall	$2,206,010	$1,616,640	$3,822,650
Memorial	$1,282,365	$934,620	$2,216,985
Ungar Hall	$2,235,040	$1,643,584	$3,878,624
Merrick Hall	$1,941,822	$1,494,456	$3,346,278
Fort Towers	$1,360,183	$981,772	$2,341,955
Totals	$9,025,420	$6,581,072	$15,606,492

g. Select the cells containing numbers and then right-align the numbers. Select the cells containing the column titles and center-align the text.

h. Apply the **Cut** transition theme to all slides in the slide show.

i. Add the **Curve Up** custom animation to each of the images on Slide 6. Curve Up is located in the Exciting category of Entrance Effects. Set the animations so that they start automatically after the previous event.

j. Print the handouts, 3 per page, framed.

k. Save the *chap1_mid2_university_solution* presentation and close.

...continued on Next Page

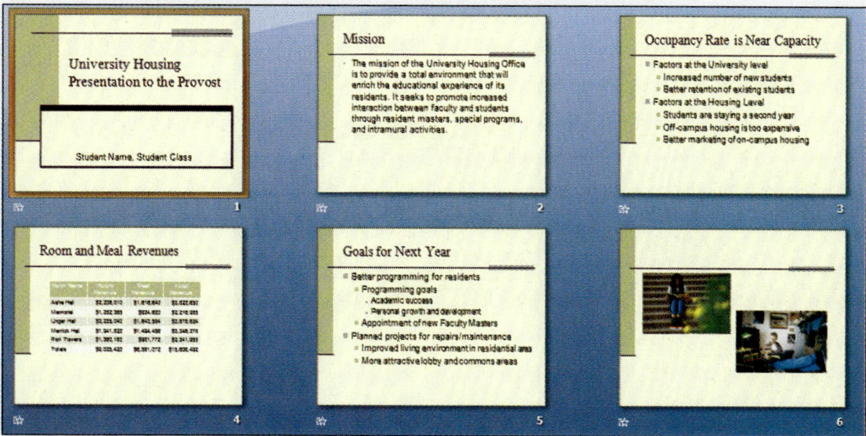

Figure 1.55 University Housing

3 PowerPoint FAQ

As a volunteer in the computer room at the local library, you get a barrage of questions about PowerPoint 2007. To help library personnel and library patrons and to reduce having to repeatedly answer the same questions, you decide to create a PowerPoint FAQ (Frequently Asked Questions) slide show that people can watch when needed. You use Help to help you prepare the FAQ slide show, and as you navigate through Help and read the associated articles, you summarize what you learn in the FAQ slide show. Refer to Figure 1.56 as you complete this exercise.

a. Create a new slide show and save it as **chap1_mid3_ppt07faq_solution**.

b. Type **PowerPoint 2007 Frequently Asked Questions** as the presentation title, and then add your name and the name of the class you are taking to the title slide.

c. Create a new slide for each of the following PowerPoint interfaces using these titles:

- What is the Microsoft Office Button?
- What is the Quick Access Toolbar?
- What is the Ribbon?
- What is a Gallery?

d. Move to **Slide 2** and open Help. Type **Office Button** as the keyword for the search and then conduct the search. When the results page displays, click the link for *What and where is the Microsoft Office Button?*

e. Read the resulting article and close the Help window. In the content placeholder, enter a summary of what you learned. For example, *The Microsoft Office Button provides access to the basic commands such as open, save, and print, and replaces the File menu.*

f. Use Help to find information about the remaining features and then enter a summary about each feature in the content placeholder of each slide.

g. Apply the **Origin** design theme to your slide show.

h. Apply the **Fade Smoothly** transition theme to all slides in the slide show.

i. Check the spelling in your presentation and then proofread carefully to catch any errors that Spelling may have missed.

j. Print the handouts as directed by your instructor.

k. Save the *chap1_mid3_ppt07faq_solution* presentation and close.

...continued on Next Page

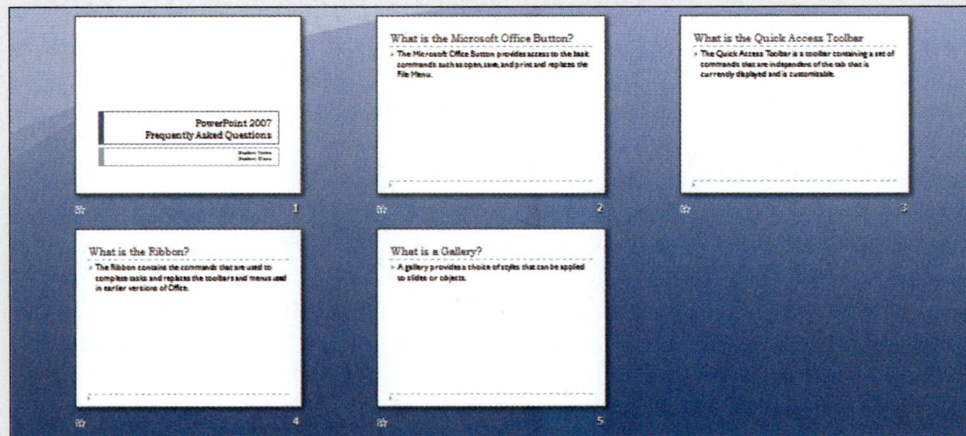

Figure 1.56 FAQ Presentation

Capstone Exercise

Definitely Needlepoint is a successful retail store owned by four close friends. One of them is your mother. The store has been in operation for three years and has increased its revenue and profit each year. The partners are looking to expand their operation by requesting venture capital. They have an important meeting scheduled next week. Help your mother prepare a PowerPoint slide show to help them present their case.

Presentation Setup

You need to open the presentation that you already started, rename the file, and save it. You add your name to the title slide and then you apply a design theme.

a. Locate the file named *chap1_cap_capital*, and then save it as **chap1_cap_capital_solution**.

b. Replace *Your Name* with your name as it appears on your instructor's roll book in the subtitle placeholder of Slide 1.

c. Apply the **Metro** design theme.

Create a Mission Statement Slide

You need to create a slide for the Definitely Needlepoint mission statement. The mission statement created by the four owners clearly reflects their personality and their attitude about their customers. This attitude is a clear factor in the success of the business, so you decide it should be preeminent in the presentation and use it as the introduction slide. (Continue with step a at the top of the next column.)

a. Insert a new slide after Slide 1 with the Title Only layout.

b. Type the following mission statement in the title placeholder: **Definitely Needlepoint provides a friendly and intimate setting in which to stitch. Our customers are not just customers, but friends who participate in a variety of social and educational activities that encourage and develop the art of needlepoint**.

c. Select the text, use the Mini toolbar to change the Font size to **28 pts**, and then apply **Italics**.

d. Reposition the placeholder so that the entire statement fits on the slide.

e. Save the *chap1_cap_capital_solution* presentation.

Create Tables

You create tables to show the increase in sales from last year to this year, the sales increase by category, and the sales increase by quarters.

a. Move to **Slide 4**, click the **Insert tab**, and then click **Table** in the Tables group.

b. Create a table with four columns and seven rows. Type the following data in your table:

Category	Last Year	This Year	Increase
Canvases	$75,915	$115,856	$39,941
Fibers	$47,404	$77,038	$29,634
Accessories	$31,590	$38,540	$6,950
Classes	$19,200	$28,200	$9,000
Finishing	$25,755	$46,065	$20,310
Totals	$199,864	$305,699	$105,835

c. Use the Mini toolbar to right-align the numbers and to bold the bottom row of totals.

d. Reposition the table on the slide so that it does not block the title. (Continue with step e in the next column.)

e. Move to **Slide 5** and insert a table of six columns and three rows.

f. Type the following data in your table:

Year	Canvases	Fibers	Accessories	Classes	Finishing
Last Year	$75,915	$47,404	$31,590	$19,200	$25,755
This Year	$115,856	$77,038	$38,540	$28,200	$46,065

g. Use the Mini toolbar to change the text font to 16 pts and then right-align the numbers.

h. Reposition the table on the slide so that it does not block the title. (Continue with step i in the next column.)

i. Move to **Slide 6** and insert a table of five columns and three rows.

j. Type the following data in your table:

...continued on Next Page

Year	Qtr 1	Qtr 2	Qtr 3	Qtr 4
Last Year	$37,761	$51,710	$52,292	$58,101
This Year	$61,594	$64,497	$67,057	$112,551

k. Spell-check the presentation, check the presentation for errors not caught by spell checking, and then carefully compare the numbers in the tables to your text to check for accuracy.

l. Save the *chap1_cap_capital_solution* presentation.

Insert Clip

Definitely Needlepoint uses a needle and thread as its logo. You decide to use a needle and thread clip on the title slide to continue this identifying image.

a. Move to **Slide 1** and open the Clip Organizer.

b. Type **stitching** in the Search for box and press **Go**.

c. Refer to Figure 1.57 to aid you in locating the needle and thread image.

d. Insert the needle and thread image and position it so that the needle is above the word *Needlepoint* and the thread appears to wrap in and out of the word.

e. Save the *chap1_cap_capital_solution* presentation.

Add Custom Animation

To emphasize the profits that Definitely Needlepoint has made over the last two years, you created two text boxes on Slide 4. You decide to animate these text boxes so that they fly in as you discuss each year. You create custom animations for each box.

a. Move to **Slide 4** and click to select the *Our first year was profitable* text box.

b. Open the Custom Animation task pane and apply a **Fly In** animation from the Entrance category.

c. Keep the text box selected and click the Add Effect button again. Apply a **Fly Out** animation from the Exit category. Note the non-printing tags now appear on the text box placeholder indicating the order of the animations.

d. Select the *Our second year was significantly better* text box and then apply a **Fly In** animation from the Entrance category.

e. Change the Start option to **With Previous**, which will cause this text box to fly in as the other text box flies out.

f. Save the *chap1_cap_capital_solution* presentation.

View and Print the Presentation

You view the presentation to proofread it without the distraction of the PowerPoint creation tools and to check to see if the transitions and animations are applied correctly. When you have proofed the presentation, you print a handout with 4 slides per page to give to the owners so they can see how the presentation is progressing.

a. Click the **Slide Show tab** and then advance through the presentation. When you get to the table slides, compare the figures with the figures in your text to ensure there are no typographical errors.

b. Exit the slide show and correct any errors.

c. Print handouts in Grayscale, 4 slides per page, and framed.

d. Save the *chap1_cap_capital_solution* presentation and close.

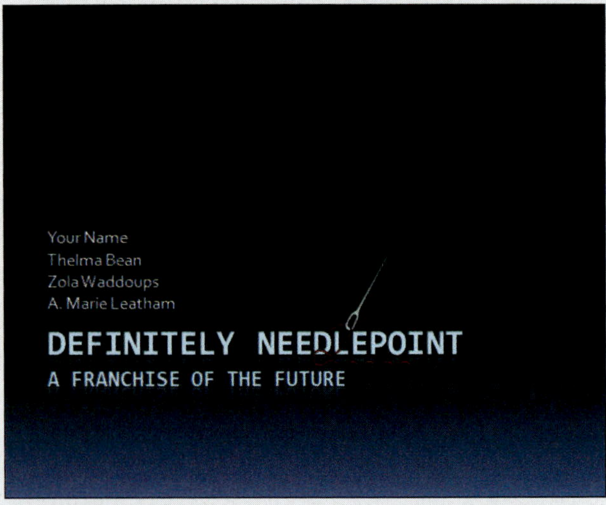

Figure 1.57 Definitely Needlepoint Title Slide

Mini Cases

Use the rubric following the case as a guide to evaluate your work, but keep in mind that your instructor may impose additional grading criteria or use a different standard to judge your work.

Green Scene Lawn Service

GENERAL CASE

You create a yard care service to help supplement your income while going to school. You name the yard service "Green Scene." You decide that one way to get your message out to potential customers is to create a presentation about your services and burn it to a CD. You'll deliver the CD to homes around your neighborhood, knowing that by delivering your message in this format, you are most likely to catch the interest of people with technological savvy—those who are busy spending their time in front of a computer instead of doing yard work.

You provide multiple services that customers can choose from. You mow once a week and cut the lawn one-third of its length at a time, you trim and edge along the foundation of the home and any fence lines, and you use a blower to remove the debris left from the trimming. You aerate the lawn in the spring to relieve soil compaction and increase water infiltration. You fertilize using natural-based, granular fertilizers and include lawn, tree, and shrub fertilization. You apply broadleaf weed control and include a surface insect control when this service is ordered. In the spring you remove winter debris, dethatch the lawn, and restock mulch beds. In the fall you remove fall leaves and you seed and mulch bare soil patches. Your tree and shrub service includes trimming and removing of trees and shrubs as well as stump removal. You treat the shrubs and trees to protect them from disease.

Create a title slide for your presentation that includes the name of your company and your name. Save your file as **chap1_mc1_greenscene_solution**. Do not worry about burning the presentation to a CD.

Slide 2 should be an introduction slide listing your services:

- Lawn Mowing, Trimming, and Edging
- Aeration, Fertilization,Weed Control
- Spring and Fall Clean-up
- Tree and Shrub Service

Create a slide for each of these topics using the Title and Content layout. The titles for the slides should match the above bullets. Use the case study introductory material to create the content for each slide. Create a summary slide using the Title Slide layout and type **Call today for a free estimate!** in the title placeholder. Include your name and telephone number in the subtitle placeholder. Insert several appropriate clips throughout the presentation and then resize and position the clips as desired. Apply the design theme of your choice. Reposition placeholders and modify text as desired. Apply a transition of your choice to all slides. Save and close the presentation.

Performance Elements	Exceeds Expectations	Meets Expectations	Below Expectations
Organization	Presentation is easy to follow because information is presented in a logical interesting sequence.	Presentation is generally easy to follow.	Presentation cannot be understood because there is no sequence of information.
Visual Aspects	Presentation background, themes, clip art, and animation are appealing and enhance the understanding of presentation purpose and content. There is a consistent visual theme.	Clip art is related to the topic. Animation enhances the presentation.	The background or theme is distracting to the topic. Clip art does not enhance understanding of the content or is unrelated.
Layout	The layout is visually pleasing and contributes to the overall message with appropriate use of headings, subheadings, bullet points, clip art, and white space.	The layout shows some structure, but placement of some headings, subheadings, bullet points, clip art, and/or white space can be improved.	The layout is cluttered and confusing. Placement of headings, subheadings, bullet points, clip art, and/or white space detracts from readability.
Mechanics	Presentation has no errors in spelling, grammar, word usage, or punctuation. No typographical errors present. Bullet points are parallel.	Presentation has no more than one error in spelling, grammar, word usage, or punctuation. Bullet points are inconsistent in no more than one slide.	Presentation readability is impaired due to repeated errors in spelling, grammar, word usage, or punctuation. Most bullet points are not parallel.

...continued on Next Page

The National Debt

RESEARCH CASE

The national debt is staggering—more than $8 trillion, or approximately $28,000 for every man, woman, and child in the United States. The annual budget is approximately $2 trillion. Use the Internet to obtain exact figures for the current year, then use this information to create a presentation about the national debt. A good place to start your research is the Web site for the United States Department of the Treasury (http://www.treas.gov) where entering National Debt in the FAQ (Frequently Asked Questions) search box brings up several interesting hyperlinks to information that you can use to develop your presentation.

Do some additional research and obtain the national debt for the years 1945 and 1967. The numbers may surprise you. For example, how does the debt for the current year compare to the debt in 1967 (at the height of the Vietnam War)? To the debt in 1945 (at the end of World War II)? Include your references on a Resources slide at the end of your presentation. Save the presentation as **chap1_mc2_debt_solution**. Close the presentation.

Performance Elements	Exceeds Expectations	Meets Expectations	Below Expectations
Organization	Presentation indicates accurate research and significant facts. Evidence exists that information has been evaluated and synthesized showing an understanding of the topic.	Presentation indicates some research has taken place and that information was included in the content.	Presentation demonstrates a lack of research or understanding of the topic. Content misinterpreted or incorrect.
Visual Aspects	Presentation background, themes, clip art, and animation are appealing and enhance the understanding of presentation purpose and content. There is a consistent visual theme.	Clip art is related to the topic. Animation is not distracting.	The background or theme is distracting to the topic. Clip art does not enhance understanding of the content or is unrelated.
Layout	The layout is visually pleasing and contributes to the overall message with appropriate use of headings, subheadings, bullet points, clip art, and white space.	The layout shows some structure, but placement of some headings, subheadings, bullet points, clip art, and/or white space can be improved.	The layout is cluttered and confusing. Placement of headings, subheadings, bullet points, clip art, and/or white space detracts from readability.
Mechanics	Presentation has no errors in spelling, grammar, word usage, or punctuation. Bullet points are parallel.	Presentation has no more than one error in spelling, grammar, word usage, or punctuation. Bullet points are inconsistent in one slide.	Presentation readability is impaired due to repeated errors in spelling, grammar, word usage, or punctuation. Most bullet points are not parallel.

Planning for Disaster

DISASTER RECOVERY

This case is perhaps the most important case of this chapter as it deals with the question of backup. Do you have a backup strategy? Do you even know what a backup strategy is? This is a good time to learn, because sooner or later you will need to recover a file. The problem always seems to occur the night before an assignment is due. You accidentally erased a file, are unable to read from a storage device like a flash drive, or worse yet, suffer a hardware failure in which you are unable to access the hard drive. The ultimate disaster is the disappearance of your computer, by theft or natural disaster.

Use the Internet to research ideas for backup strategies. Create a title slide and at least four slides related to a backup strategy or ways to protect files. Include a summary on what you plan to implement in conjunction with your work in this class. Choose the design theme, transition, and animations. Save the new presentation as **chap1_mc3_disaster_solution**. Close the presentation.

...continued on Next Page

Performance Elements	Exceeds Expectations	Meets Expectations	Below Expectations
Organization	Presentation indicates accurate research and significant facts. Evidence exists that information has been evaluated and synthesized showing an understanding of the topic.	Presentation indicates some research has taken place and the information was included in the content.	Presentation demonstrates a lack of research or understanding of the topic. Content misinterpreted or incorrect.
Visual Aspects	Presentation background, themes, clip art, and animation are appealing and enhance the understanding of presentation purpose and content. There is a consistent visual theme.	Clip art is related to the topic. Animation is not distracting.	The background or theme is distracting to the topic. Clip art does not enhance understanding of the content or is unrelated.
Layout	The layout is visually pleasing and contributes to the overall message with appropriate use of headings, subheadings, bullet points, clip art, and white space.	The layout shows some structure, but placement of some headings, subheadings, bullet points, clip art, and/or white space can be improved.	The layout is cluttered and confusing. Placement of headings, subheadings, bullet points, clip art, and/or white space detracts from readability.
Mechanics	Presentation has no errors in spelling, grammar, word usage, or punctuation. Bullet points are parallel.	Presentation has no more than one error in spelling, grammar, word usage, or punctuation. Bullet points are inconsistent in no more than one slide.	Presentation readability is impaired due to repeated errors in spelling, grammar, word usage, or punctuation. Most bullet points are not parallel.

chapter 2 | PowerPoint

Presentation Development

Planning and Preparing a Presentation

After you read this chapter, you will be able to:

1. Create a presentation using a template **(page 869)**.
2. Modify a template **(page 871)**.
3. Create a presentation in Outline view **(page 879)**.
4. Modify an outline structure **(page 881)**.
5. Print an outline **(page 882)**.
6. Import an outline **(page 887)**.
7. Add existing content to a presentation **(page 888)**.
8. Examine slide show design principles **(page 892)**.
9. Apply and modify a design theme **(page 892)**.
10. Insert a header or footer **(page 896)**.

Hands-On Exercises

Exercises	Skills Covered
1. USING A TEMPLATE (page 874) **Open:** New presentation **Insert:** chap2_ho1_photo1.tif **Save as:** chap2_ho1_nature_solution.pptx	• Create a New Presentation Based on an Installed Template • Modify Text in a Placeholder • Add a Slide and Select a Layout • Add a Picture and a Caption • Change a Layout
2. CREATING AND MODIFYING AN OUTLINE (page 883) **Open:** New presentation **Save as:** chap2_ho2_presentations_solution.pptx	• Create a Presentation in Outline View • Enter an Outline • Edit a Presentation • Modify the Outline Structure and Print
3. IMPORTING AN OUTLINE AND REUSING SLIDES (page 890) **Import:** chap2_ho3_success.docx and chap2_ho3_development.pptx **Save as:** chapt2_ho3_guide_solution.pptx	• Import a Microsoft Word Outline • Reuse Slides from Another Presentation
4. APPLYING AND MODIFYING A DESIGN THEME (page 899) **Open:** chap2_ho3_guide_solution.pptx (from Exercise 3) **Save as:** chap2_ho4_guide_solution.pptx (additional modifications)	• Apply a Theme to a Presentation • Apply a Color Scheme • Add a Font Scheme • Apply a Background Style • Hide Background Graphics on a Slide • Save Current Theme • Create a Slide Footer • Create a Handout Header and Footer

CASE STUDY

Go Back in Time

Dr. Thien Ngo, your professor in world history, has created a very interesting assignment this semester. Each student is to choose a particular voyage, trip, expedition, or journey of interest and create a 10-minute presentation from the perspective of the individual(s) who traveled. You were instructed to create the presentation as an outline in PowerPoint, and to keep it to 6–10 slides. However, Professor Ngo added a twist to the presentation—the audience you are presenting to represents the financial sponsors of your travels (i.e., those who are providing you with whatever provisions you will need to successfully complete your trip). It is up to you to convince them that your idea is worthy of their sponsorship. In addition, you need to request what you will want in return for completing a successful expedition!

Case Study

Professor Ngo cited several explorers; among them were Lewis and Clark, Amerigo Vespucci, Marco Polo, Queen Hatshepsut, Ferdinand Magellan, Neil Armstrong, Jacques Cousteau, and Christopher Columbus. You can choose from other explorers—it is up to you to determine who you would want to be and what you might like to have discovered!

Your Assignment

- Read the chapter, paying special attention to how to locate and download a template, how to create and modify an outline, and how to apply and modify theme effects in a presentation.
- Locate and download a template from Microsoft Office Online to use for your presentation. Choose a template that enhances the "exploration" theme, such as the **Spinning globe** template located in the Design slides group, Business category, or the **Papyrus extract** template, or the **Writing on the wall** template. Or, try the **Globe on water** design in the Presentations group, Design slides with content category. Create a title slide with the title **Honoring Our Explorers** and then enter your choice of explorer as the subtitle. Save the presentation as **chap2_case_explorer_solution**.
- Create an introduction slide indicating to whom the presentation will be given, slides covering main points, and a summary slide reiterating the need for the voyage. Possible slides for main points could cover the current situation, potential reasons or benefits for the voyage, a brief outline of the plan, a list of provisions, the personal qualifications needed for the leaders for this voyage or why you (as that leader) think you have what it takes to make the journey, and what you want in return for your services.
- Modify the theme color scheme or the font scheme, and then save the modified theme.
- Add at least one related clip art image and add animation to at least one slide. Apply a transition to all slides.
- Create a handout with your name in the header, and your instructor's name and your class in the footer.
- Print the Outline View.

Templates

One of the hardest things about creating a presentation is getting started. You may have a general idea of what you want to say, but the words do not come easily to you. You may know what you want to say, but you do not want to spend time designing the look for the slides. Microsoft gives you a potential solution to both of these circumstances by providing templates for your use. Microsoft's templates enable you to create very professional-looking presentations and may include content to help you decide what to say. **While previous versions of PowerPoint included an AutoContent Wizard to help you with content development, PowerPoint 2007 incorporates content within some templates to give you more freedom when developing your presentation**.

In this section, you learn how to create a presentation using a template. Second, you learn how to modify the template to create a unique appearance.

Creating a Presentation Using a Template

A ***template*** is a file that incorporates a theme, a layout, and content that can be modified.

A *template* provides for the formatting of design elements like the background, theme, and color scheme, and also font selections for titles and text boxes. Some templates include suggestions for how to modify the template. These suggestions can help you learn to use many of the features in PowerPoint. Content templates include ideas about what you could say to inform your audience about your topic.

(By visiting Microsoft Online you can quickly and easily download. . . professional templates in a variety of categories.)

PowerPoint 2007 offers professional built-in templates for you to use, but by visiting Microsoft Office Online you can quickly and easily download additional templates in a variety of categories. These templates are suitable for virtually every presentation. For example, from the Business and Legal template category at Microsoft Office Online, you can download a template for a bank loan request for a small business, a pre-incorporation agreement for a new business, or a project plan for a new business. Figure 2.1 shows four templates.

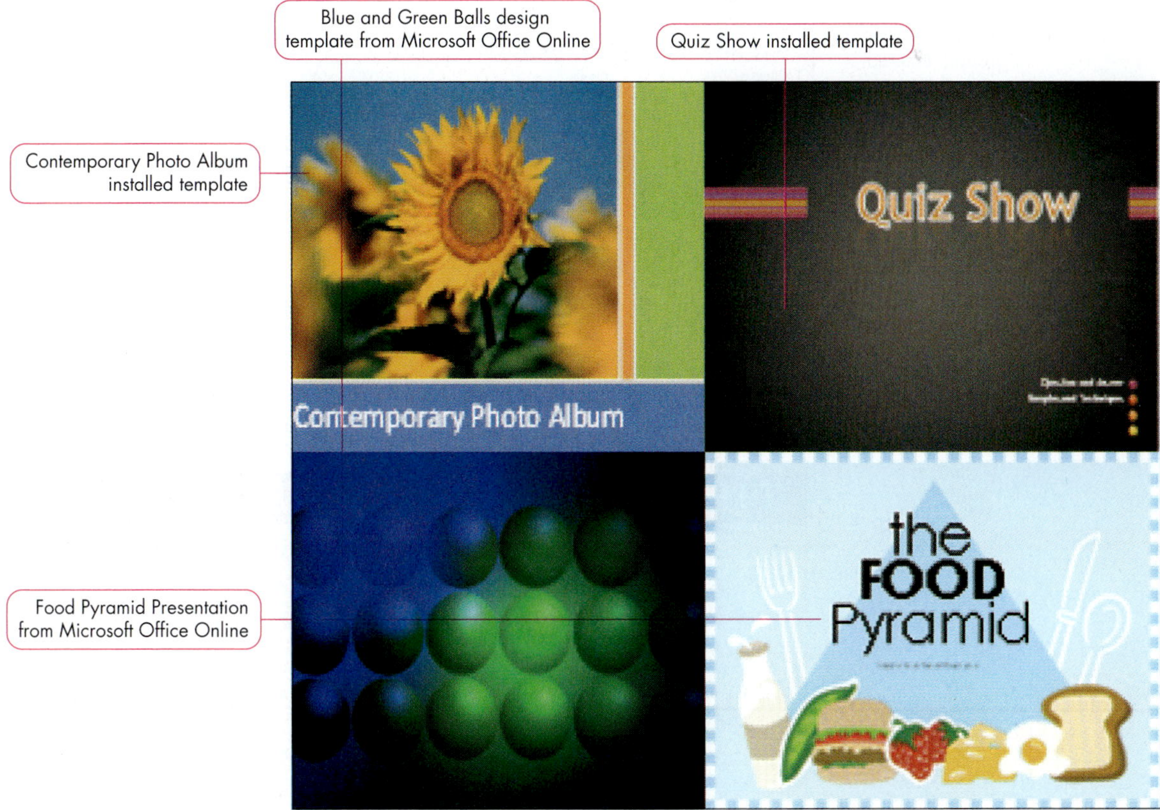

Figure 2.1 Microsoft PowerPoint Templates

Templates are available when you create a new presentation. Click the Office Button and select New. The New Presentation dialog box displays. Template categories display on the left showing the installed templates and links for categories of templates available from Microsoft Office Online. The top center of the dialog box displays the options needed to create a new blank PowerPoint presentation. The left side of the dialog box displays an option to create a new presentation from a blank presentation, from installed templates and from installed themes. Another option enables you to create a presentation from templates you have previously created and saved. Finally, you can create a presentation from an existing presentation. A preview of a selected template is displayed on the far right. Select the Featured category under the Microsoft Office Online section and hyperlinks to check for updates, training, and additional templates appear. Check with your instructor to find out if you are able to download and save Microsoft Office Online Templates in your lab. Figure 2.2 displays the New Presentation dialog box resized to show the entire box. Your dialog box may be different from Figure 2.2 because Microsoft may change its online content.

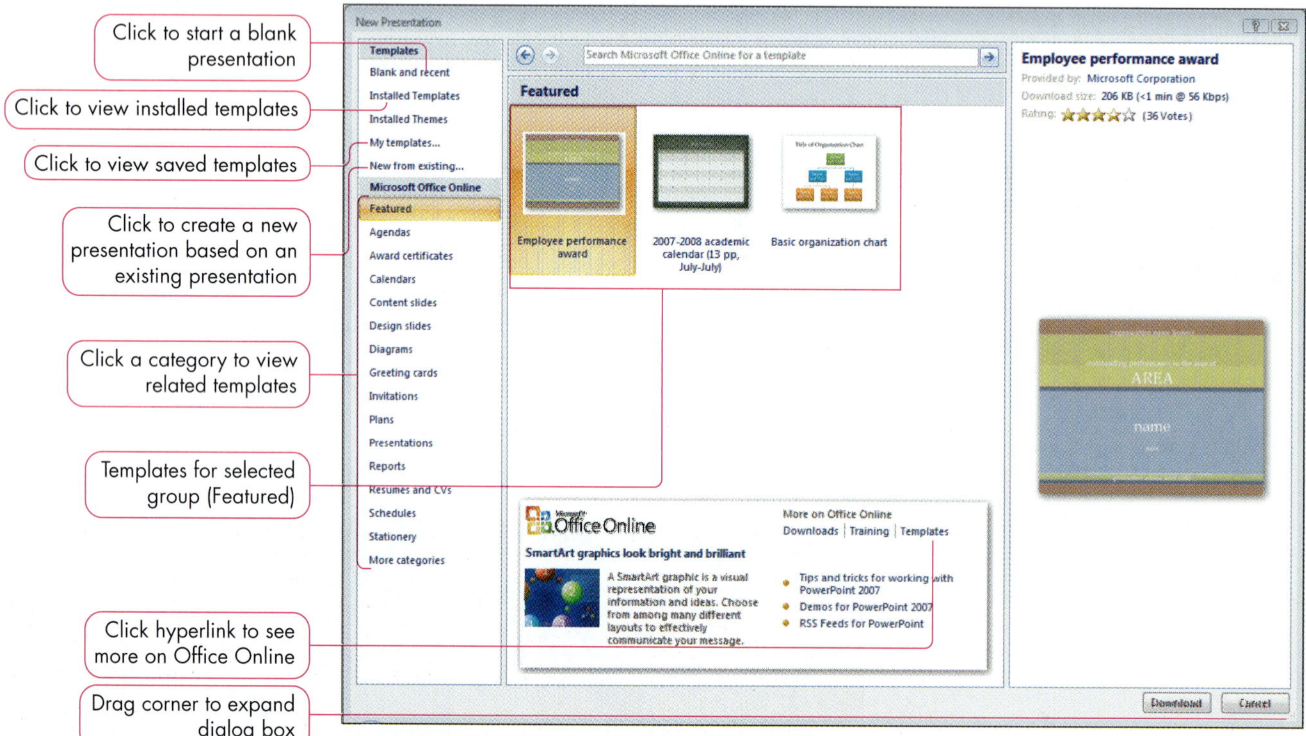

Figure 2.2 New Presentation Dialog Box

TIP Expanding a Dialog Box

To resize a dialog box to see all available options without having to use the scroll bars, position the pointer on the dots in the bottom-right corner of the dialog box. When the pointer changes to a diagonal two-headed arrow, drag until the full dialog box is visible.

When you select the Installed Templates option in the New Presentation dialog box, the templates installed with PowerPoint 2007 display. Currently, Microsoft includes six templates, but future releases of PowerPoint 2007 may install more. Figure 2.3 shows the Classic Photo Album selected and the preview of the title page for the template.

Modifying a Template

After you download an installed template, you can modify it, perhaps by adding a unifying corporate logo, changing a font style or size, or moving an object on the slide. After you modify the template, you can save it and use it over and over. This feature can save you a tremendous amount of time, as you will not have to redo your modifications the next time you use the template.

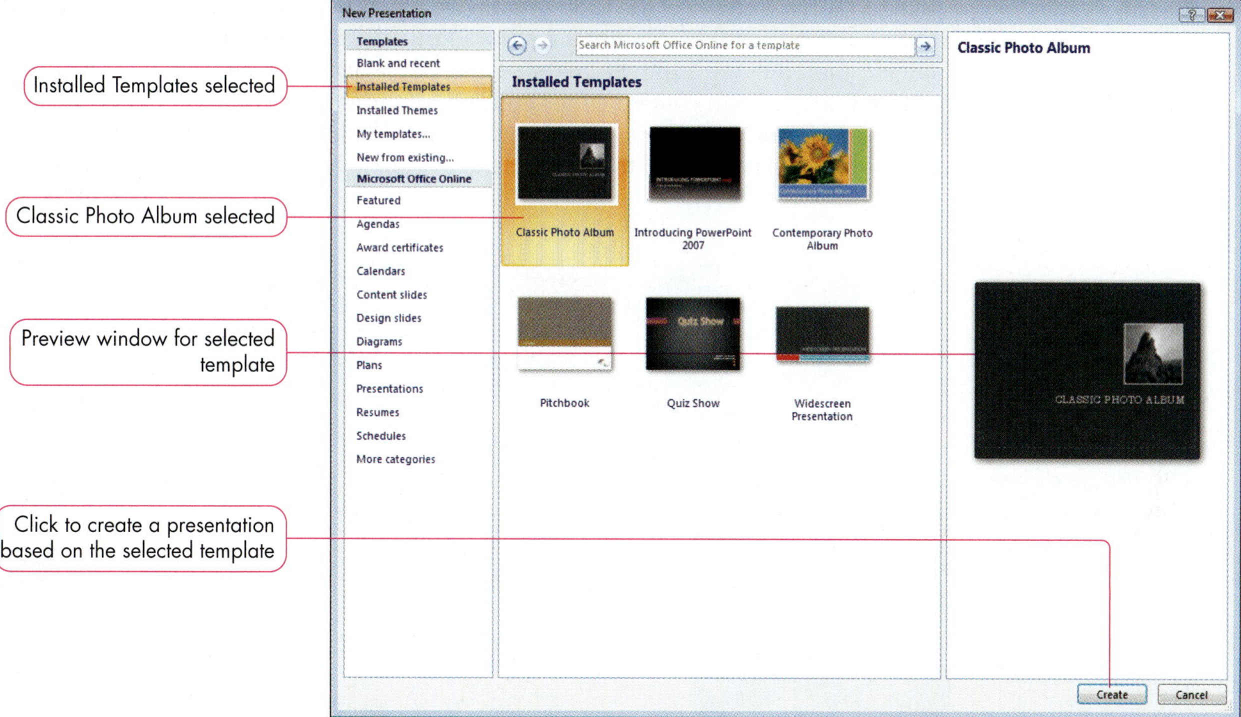

Figure 2.3 PowerPoint Installed Templates

A slide ***layout*** controls the position of objects containing content on the slide.

A ***placeholder*** is a container that holds content and is used in the layout to determine the position of objects on the slide.

When you change an object's location on a slide, you are modifying the template ***layout*** that defines, or controls, the objects on the slide. PowerPoint, as do all Microsoft Office applications, includes standard layouts for your use. The templates you download may have custom layouts unique to that particular template. To modify the location of an object, you must select the ***placeholder*** containing the object.

Placeholders contain content and are positioned in the layout of a slide. The layout can include any number or combination of placeholders, and every layout can have additional placeholders added to it. You can easily identify placeholders because they are boxes with dotted or hatch-marked borders. In addition to holding text, placeholders can contain elements such as a table, chart, clip art, diagrams, pictures, or media clips. The behavior of the content in a placeholder varies depending on the type of placeholder used. For example, a text placeholder uses internal margins to set the distance between the placeholder borders and the text, while a picture placeholder centers and crops an image that is inserted in it.

A layout may even have no placeholders. PowerPoint also includes a Blank Slide layout with no placeholders so that you can design and create your own layout. If you apply a layout that contains placeholders you do not need, you can delete the placeholder by clicking its border and then pressing Delete. If the placeholder has text, you must delete the text first, and then delete the placeholder.

Sizing handles are small circles or squares that appear at the corner and sides of a selected object.

You can resize a placeholder by clicking on the placeholder to select it and then pointing at one of the ***sizing handles*** of the placeholder. When you point at one of the sizing handles, the pointer becomes a two-headed arrow. After your pointer changes into the two-headed arrow, drag the handle until your object is the size you desire. To move a placeholder, select the placeholder and point to any of the placeholder borders. When the pointer becomes a four-headed arrow, drag the placeholder to the location you desire.

You can use text placeholders to quickly change all text contained in the placeholder. First click to select the placeholder and then click the border of the placeholder. The border changes from a dashed line to a solid line indicating that all the text is selected. After you select the text, you can change the font, size, case, color, or spacing within the placeholder. Figure 2.4 shows PowerPoint's most commonly used slide layout, the Title and Content layout. This layout has a placeholder for a title and a placeholder that can contain either bulleted text points or graphical objects available from a small icon set. The placeholder has been selected so that any change made to the text format will be applied to all text in the placeholder.

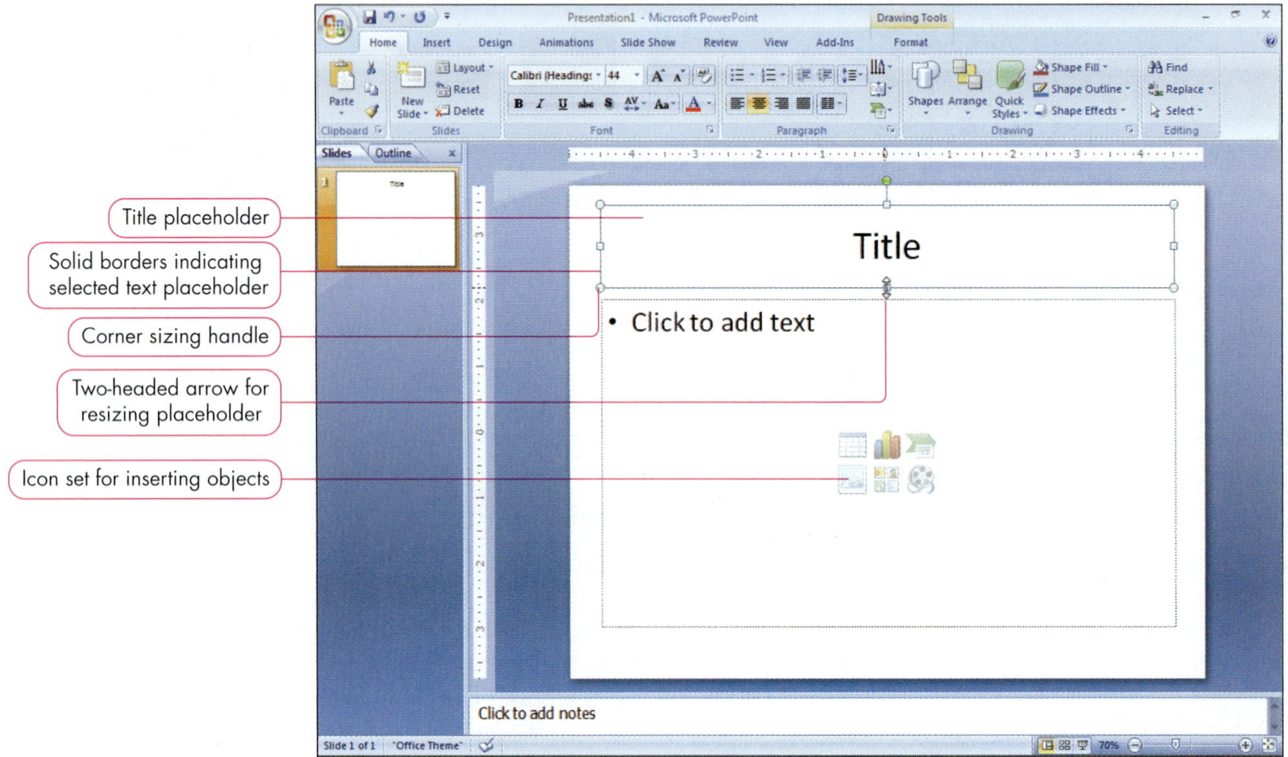

Figure 2.4 Title and Content Layout

Figure 2.5 shows the standard layouts when you open PowerPoint. By default when you launch PowerPoint, the Home tab is active and displays the Layout command in the Slides group. Click Layout to display a gallery of the standard layouts for the Office Theme, the default theme. The descriptive name indicates the types of placeholders the layout includes.

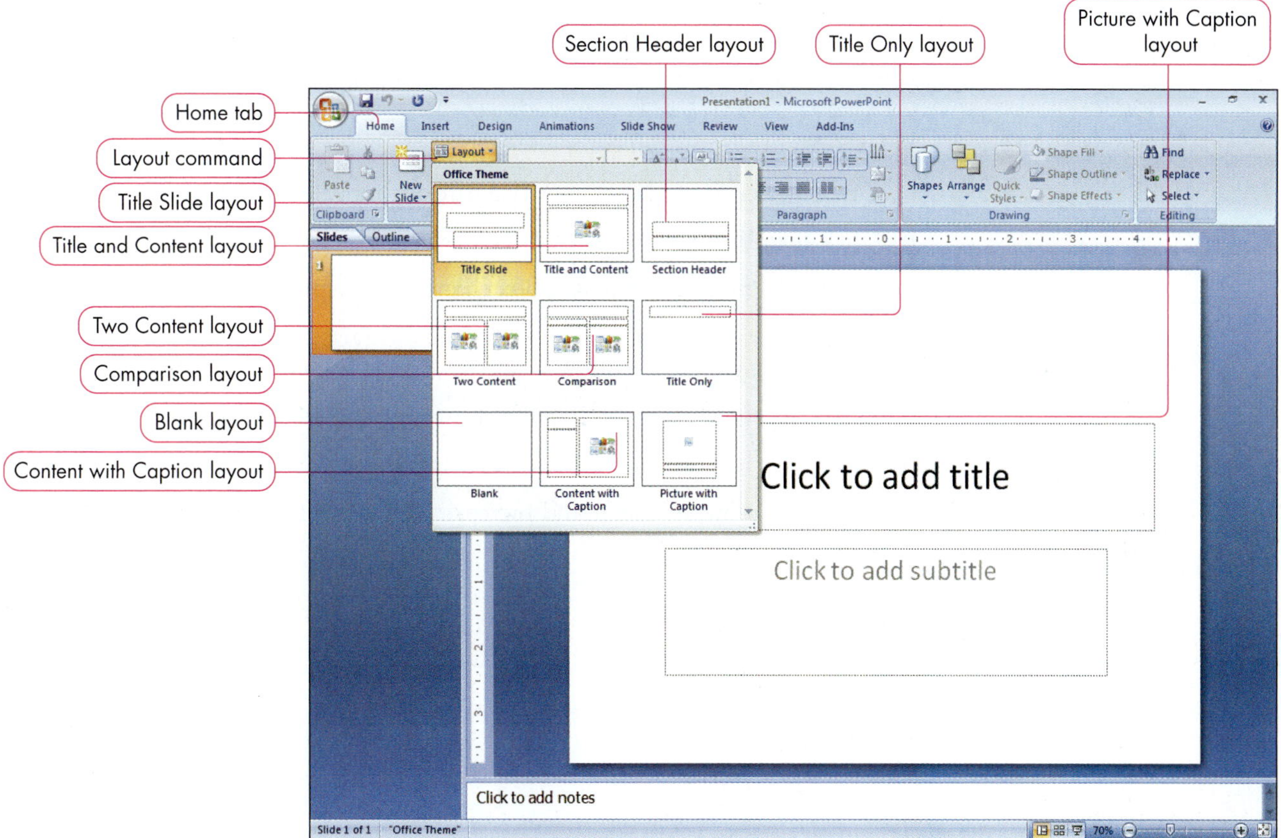

Figure 2.5 Standard Layouts

Hands-On Exercises

1 | Using a Template

Skills covered: 1. Create a New Presentation Based on an Installed Template **2.** Modify Text in a Placeholder **3.** Add a Slide and Select a Layout **4.** Add a Picture and a Caption **5.** Change a Layout

Step 1 Create a New Presentation Based on an Installed Template

Refer to Figure 2.6 as you complete Step 1.

a. Open PowerPoint, click the **Office Button**, and then select **New**.

b. Click **Installed Templates** in the Templates Category.

   The New Presentation dialog box changes to display thumbnails of the Installed Templates.

c. Select **Classic Photo Album**, if necessary, and then click **Create**.

d. Save the presentation as **chap2_ho1_nature_solution**.

e. Click the **View tab**, and then click **Fit to Window** in the Zoom group, if needed.

   The Fit to Window command increases the magnification of the current slide so that it fills most of the window. The Notes pane is barely visible.

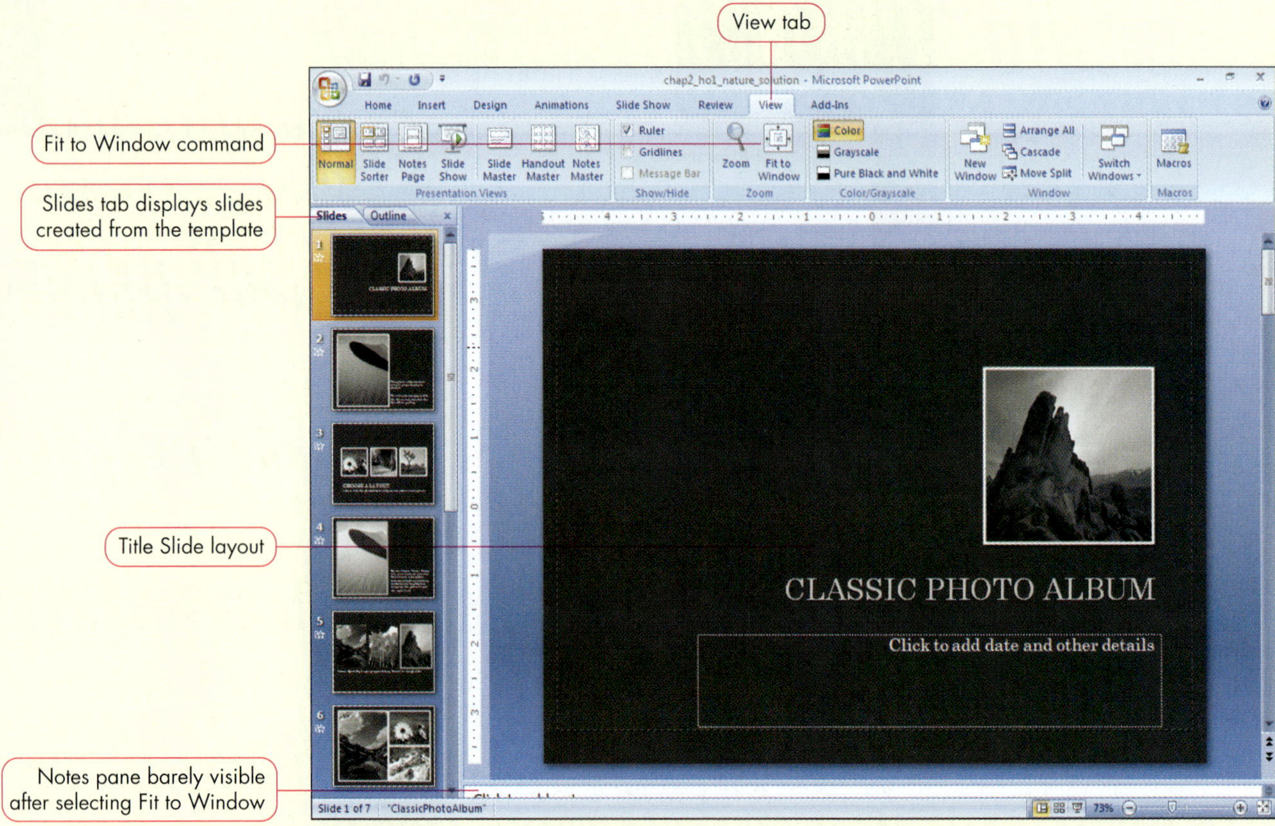

Figure 2.6 The Classic Photo Album Template

Step 2
Modify Text in a Placeholder

Refer to Figure 2.7 as you complete Step 2.

a. Select the text *CLASSIC PHOTO* in the title placeholder and then type **NATURE**.

The newly entered text replaces the selected text.

b. Replace the subtitle text, *Click to add date and other details*, with **Favorite Pictures 2009!**

c. Click the subtitle placeholder light blue dashed border.

The placeholder's dashed border is replaced with a solid border indicating that all of the content in the placeholder is selected.

d. Click the **Home tab** and click **Italic** and **Text Shadow** in the Font group.

Italic and shadowing are applied to all text in the placeholder. The shadowing is subtle, but the black shadow helps the white text stand out.

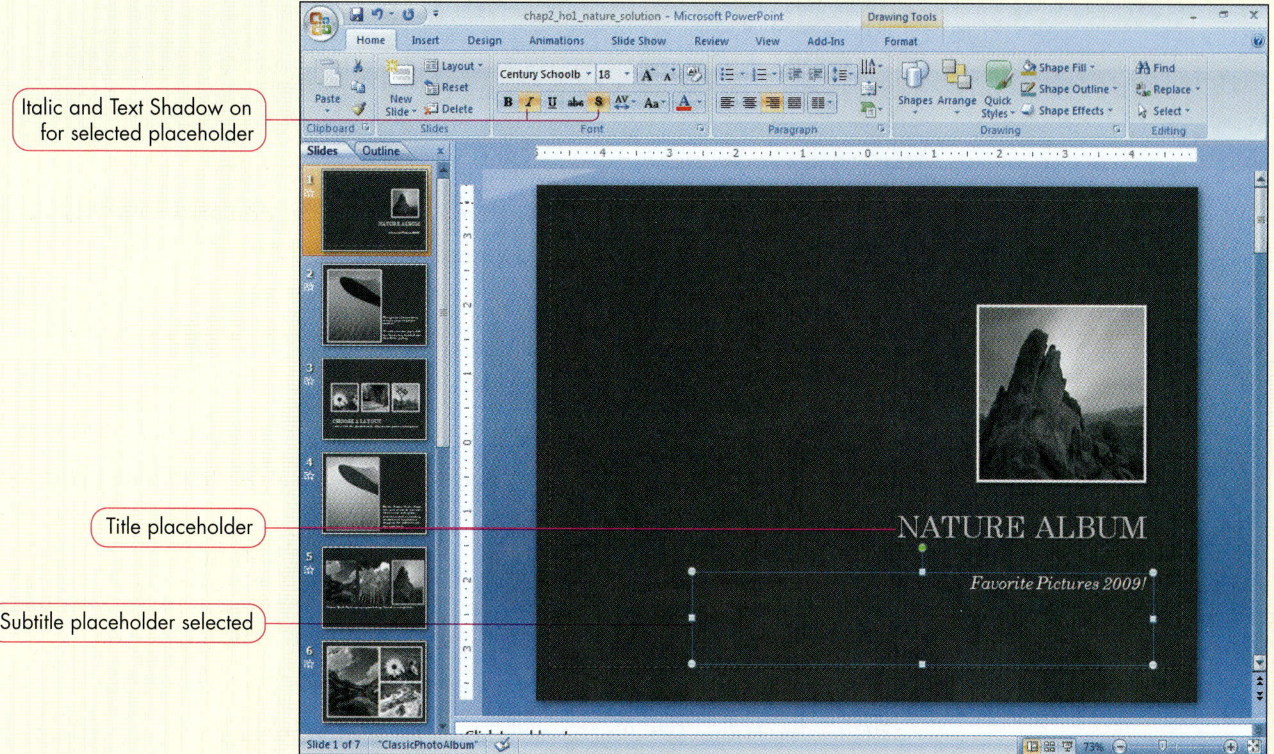

Figure 2.7 Modified Text on the Title Page

Step 3
Add a Slide and Select a Layout

Refer to Figure 2.8 as you complete Step 3.

a. Click the **Slide 2 thumbnail** displayed in the Slides tab, and then click anywhere in the text to display the placeholder.

b. Click the border of the caption placeholder, and then press **Delete**.

Pressing Delete deletes the text but not the placeholder. Because the placeholder does not print or view, you do not need to worry about it displaying. If, however, you wish to remove the placeholder, you simply click the placeholder border again and press Delete.

c. Click the **New Slide arrow** to display the Classic Photo Album template gallery.

d. Select the **Portrait with Caption** template.

A new slide is created from the template and is inserted after Slide 2.

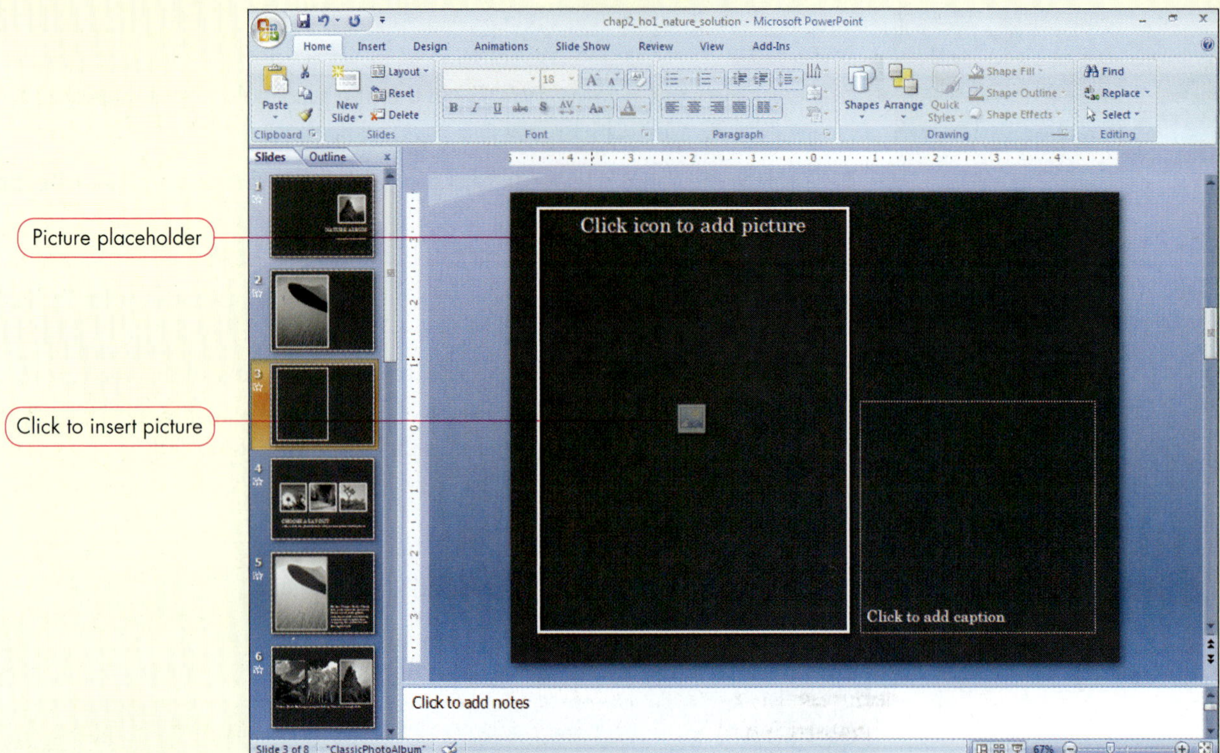

Figure 2.8 The Portrait with Caption Template

Step 4
Add a Picture and a Caption

Refer to Figure 2.9 as you complete Step 4.

a. Click the **Insert Picture from File button** located in the picture placeholder.

   The Insert Picture dialog box displays for your use as you navigate to the location of the files for your textbook.

b. Locate and select *chap2_ho1_photo1*. Click the **Insert button**.

c. Click inside the caption placeholder and type **Each moment of the year has its own beauty.** Press **Enter** twice and then type **Ralph Waldo Emerson**.

d. Click the border of the caption placeholder to select the text within.

e. Click the **Home tab**, if necessary, and click **Center** in the Paragraph group.

f. Drag the caption placeholder to the left side of the slide, and then drag the picture placeholder to the right side of the slide.

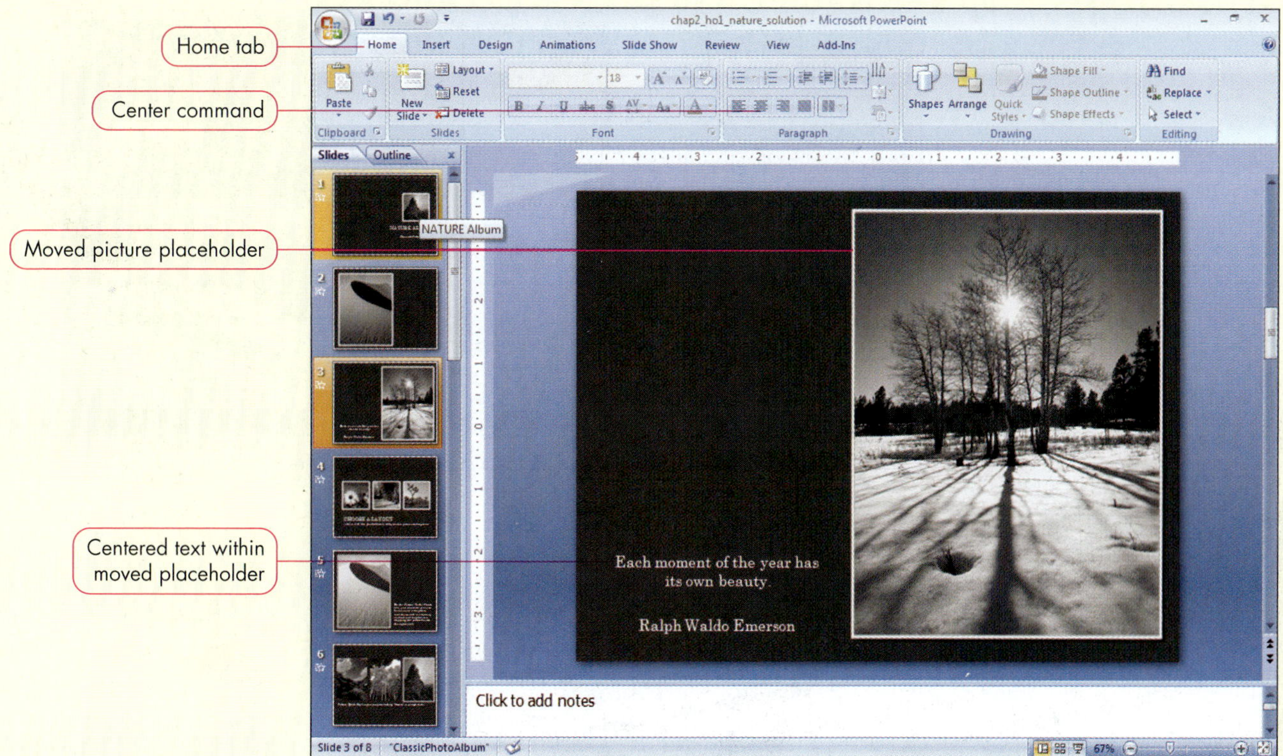

Figure 2.9 The Modified Layout

Step 5
Change a Layout

Refer to Figure 2.10 as you complete Step 5.

a. Select **Slide 4**, and then click the **Home tab**, if necessary.

b. Click **Layout** in the Slides group on the Home tab.

c. Click the **2-Up Landscape with Captions** layout to apply it to the slide.

   The Classic Photo Album includes a large number of layouts to provide you with a variety of pages in your album.

d. Select the extra photograph and press **Delete**. Select a border surrounding one of the caption placeholders and press **Delete**. Repeat selecting and deleting until all caption placeholders have been deleted.

   When you select a new layout, placeholders may not fit the new layout perfectly. You can move or delete placeholders as necessary.

e. Select the thumbnails for **Slides 5** and **6** in the Slides tab and press **Delete**.

f. Click the **Slide Show tab** and then click **From Beginning** in the Start Slide Show group to view your presentation. Press **Esc** when you are done viewing the presentation.

g. Click **Slide Sorter** in the Views buttons area on the status bar to view all the slides showing the wide variety of layouts.

h. Save the *chap2_ho1_nature_solution* presentation and close the file.

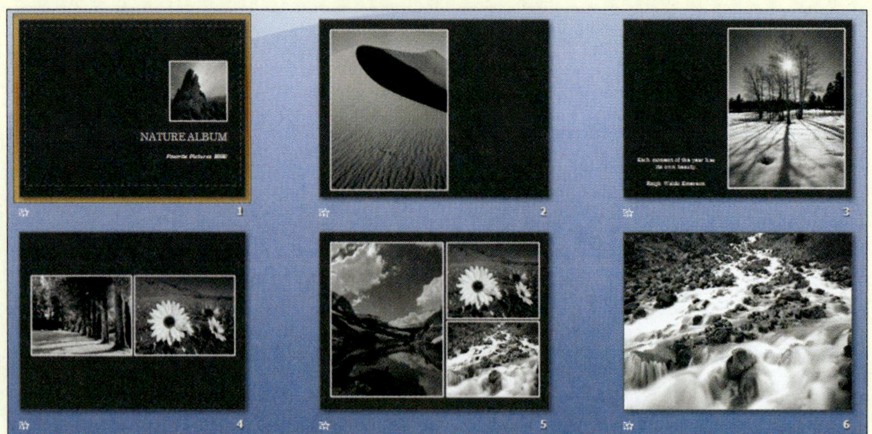

Figure 2.10 The Completed Album in Slide Sorter View

Outlines

An ***outline*** is a method of organizing text in a hierarchy to depict relationships.

A ***hierarchy*** denotes levels of importance in a structure.

Creating an ***outline*** is a method of organizing text using a ***hierarchy*** with main points and subpoints to denote the levels of importance of the text. An outline is the fastest way to enter or edit text for the presentation. Think of an outline as the road map you use to create your presentation. You created a basic outline when you created a storyboard for your presentation, and now you are ready to input the storyboard information into your presentation. Rather than having to enter the text in each placeholder on each slide separately, a time-consuming process, you type the text directly into an outline.

In this section, you create a presentation in Outline view. After creating the presentation, you modify the outline structure. Finally, you print the outline.

Creating a Presentation in Outline View

Outline view shows the presentation in an outline format with text levels.

To create an outline for your presentation you must be in Normal view, and you need to have the Outline tab selected in the pane that contains the Outline and Slides tabs. This view is considered the ***Outline view***. In this view PowerPoint shows your presentation as an outline made up of the titles and text in each slide. Each slide will display a slide icon and a slide number. The slide title appears next to the slide icon and slide number. Main text on the slide is shown indented under the slide title.

One benefit of working in the Outline view is that you can get a good overview of your presentation. While in this view, you can move easily from one slide to the next. You can copy text from one slide to another and you can rearrange the order of the slides within a presentation. You can change the sequence of the individual bullets (subpoints) in a slide, or move points to another slide. The global overview makes it easy to see relationships between points and determine where information belongs. Figure 2.11 shows a portion of a presentation in Outline view.

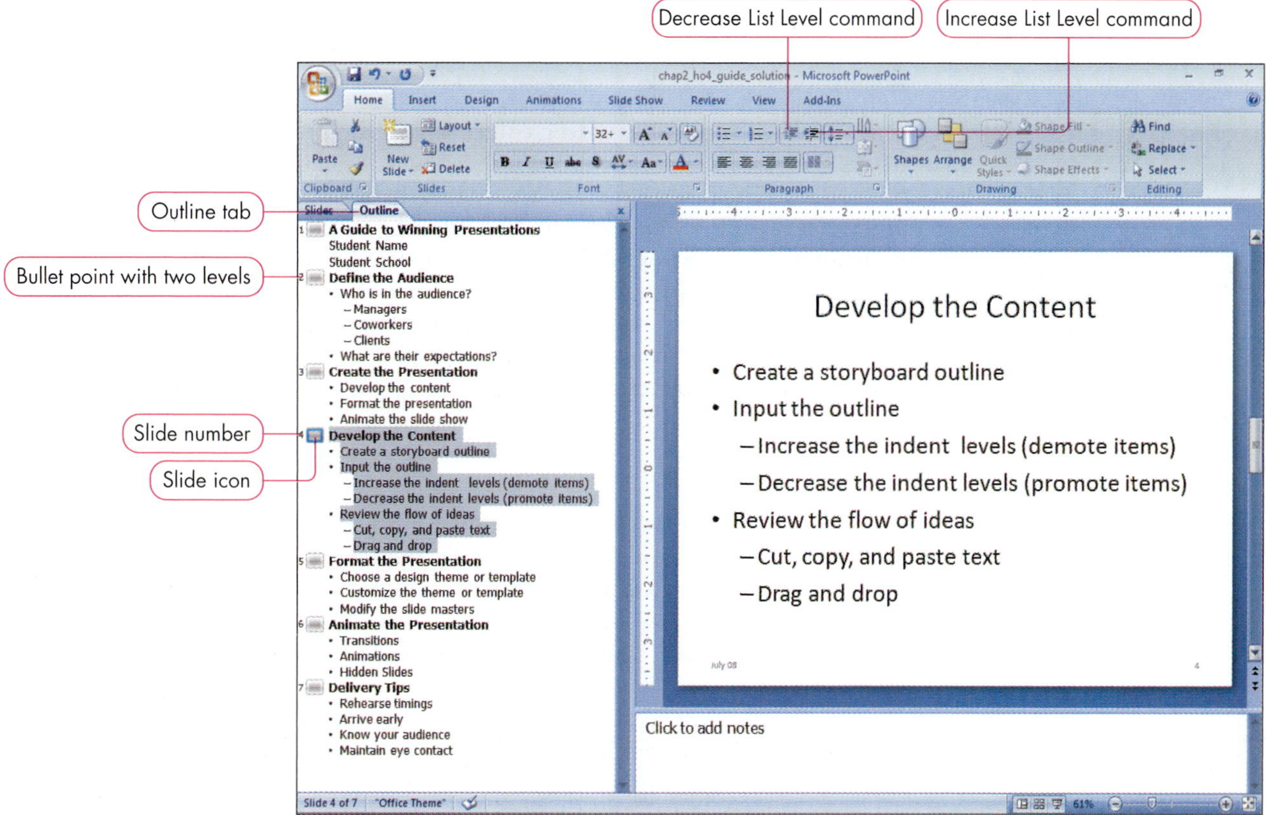

Figure 2.11 The Outline View

Remember the lower the level of an item in an outline, the greater the importance of the item.

While Figure 2.11 shows only two levels of information in the bullet points, PowerPoint 2007 accommodates nine levels of indentation. Previous versions of PowerPoint accommodated only five. Levels make it possible to show hierarchy, or importance, of the data you enter. The main points appear on Level 1. Subsidiary items are indented below the main point to which they apply. Any item can be promoted to a higher level or demoted to a lower level, either before or after the text is entered. This is accomplished clicking Increase List Level or Decrease List Level in the Paragraph group on the Home tab. Consider carefully the number of subsidiary items you add to a main point. Too many levels of hierarchy within a single slide can make the slide difficult to read or understand as the text size automatically re-sizes to a smaller size with each additional level. Remember the lower the level of an item in an outline, the greater the importance of the item. Level 1 items are your main points. Level 9 items would be insignificant in comparison.

TIP Changing List Levels in an Outline

As a quick keyboard alternative to using Increase and Decrease List Level commands on the Home tab, you can use a keyboard shortcut. Pressing Tab will demote an item or move it to the next level. The result is the same as increasing the indentation by clicking Increase List Level. Pressing Shift+Tab promotes an item or moves it back in the list. This action decreases the indentation the same as clicking Decrease List Level.

Consider, for example, Slide 4 in Figure 2.11. The title of the slide, *Develop the Content*, appears immediately after the slide number and icon. The first bullet, *Create a storyboard outline*, is indented under the title. The second bullet, *Input the outline*, has two subsidiary bullets at the next level. The next bullet, *Review the flow of ideas*, is moved back to Level 1, and it, too, has two subsidiary bullets.

Enter the Outline

The outline is an ideal way to create and edit the presentation. The insertion point marks the place where new text is entered and is established by clicking anywhere in the outline. (The insertion point automatically is placed at the title of the first slide in a new presentation.) Press Enter after typing the title or after entering the text of a bulleted item, and a new slide or bullet is created, respectively.

When you press Enter, the insertion point stays at the same indentation level as the previous one. You can continue adding more bullet points at the same level by typing the bullet information and then pressing Enter, or you can change the level of the bullet point as described above.

Edit the Outline

Editing is accomplished through the same techniques used in other Windows applications. For example, you can use the Cut, Copy, and Paste commands in the Clipboard group on the Home tab to move and copy selected text. Or, if you prefer, you can simply drag and drop text from one place to another. To locate text you wish to edit, you can click Find or Replace in the Editing group on the Home tab.

Note, too, that you can format text in the outline by using the *select-then-do* approach common to all Office applications; that is, you select the text, then you execute the appropriate command or click the appropriate command. For example, you could select the text and then apply a new font. The selected text remains highlighted and is affected by all subsequent commands until you click elsewhere in the outline.

Modifying an Outline Structure

A ***collapsed outline*** displays the title of slides only in the Outline view.

An ***expanded outline*** displays the title and content of slides in the Outline view.

Because the Outline view gives you the global picture of your presentation, you can use the view to change the structure of your outline. You can shift bullets or slides around until your outline's structure is refined. To make this process simple, you can collapse or expand your view of the outline contents. A ***collapsed outline*** view displays only the title of the slides, while the ***expanded outline*** view displays the title and the content of the slides. You can collapse or expand the content in individual slides or all slides.

Figure 2.12 displays a collapsed view of the outline, which displays only the title of each slide. When a slide is collapsed, a wavy line appears below the slide title letting you know additional levels are collapsed. Positioning the pointer over a slide icon causes it to become a four-headed arrow. To select the slide, click the icon. To move the slide, drag the icon to the desired position.

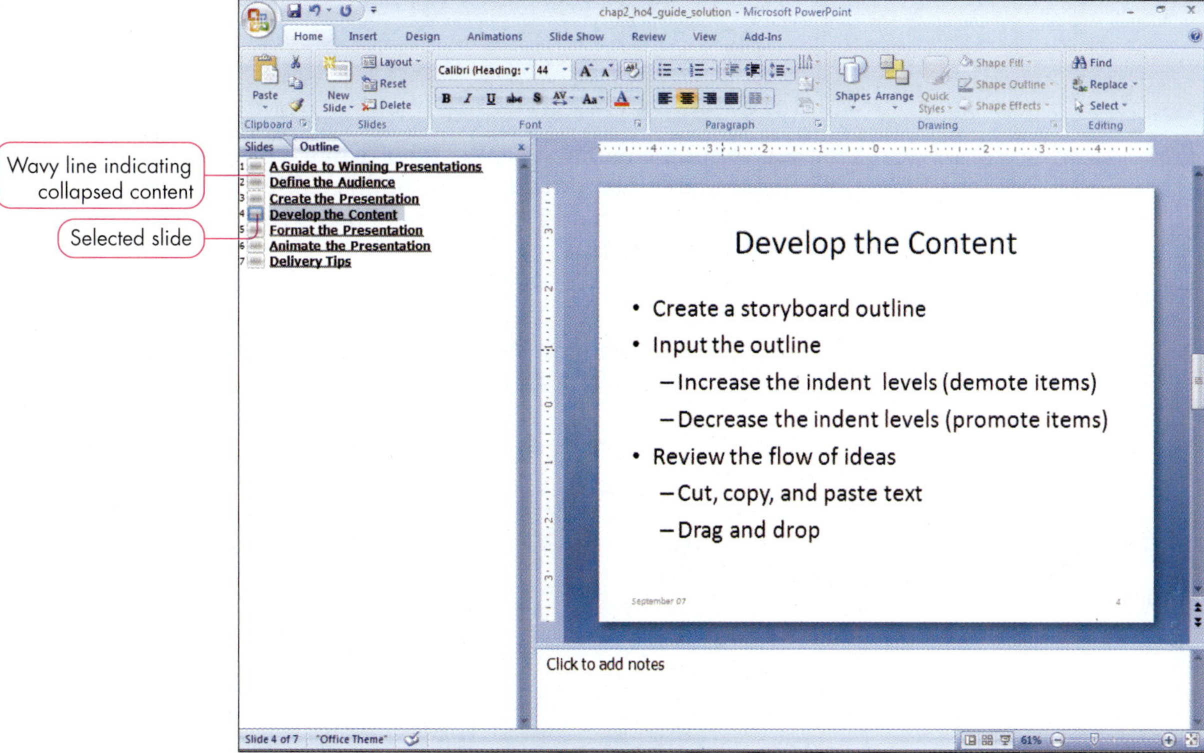

Figure 2.12 The Collapsed Outline View

To collapse a slide, select the text of the slide and right-click. The shortcut menu that appears contains the Collapse command. When you click the Collapse arrow, two new commands appear: Select Collapse or Collapse All. To expand a collapsed slide, select the slide icon and right-click. Select Expand or Expand All. See Figure 2.13 for the process involved for collapsing a slide.

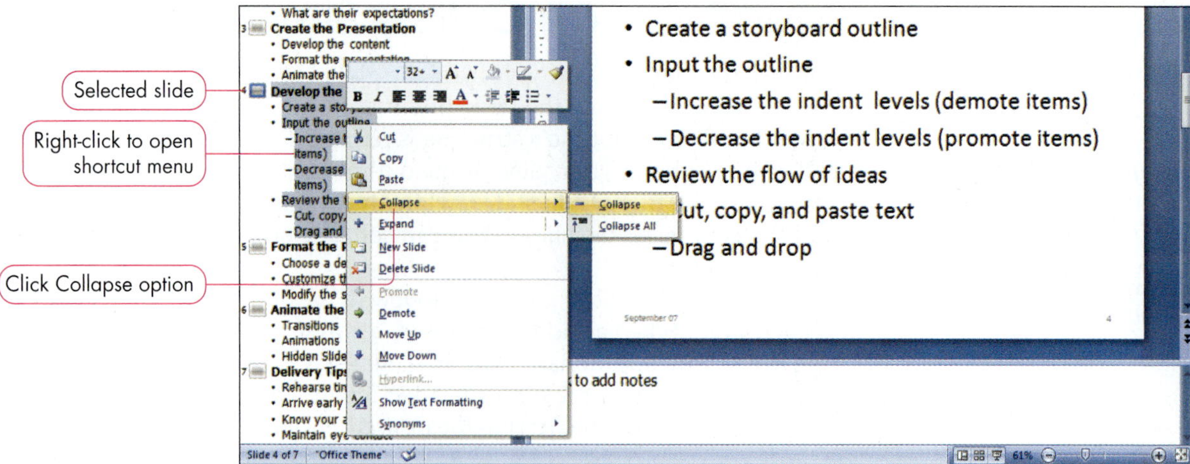

Figure 2.13 Collapse Process

Printing an Outline

You may print the outline in either the expanded or collapsed view. The slide icon and slide number will print with the outline. To print the outline, click the Office Button, point to Print, and select Print, Quick Print, or Print Preview. Figure 2.14 shows the print options.

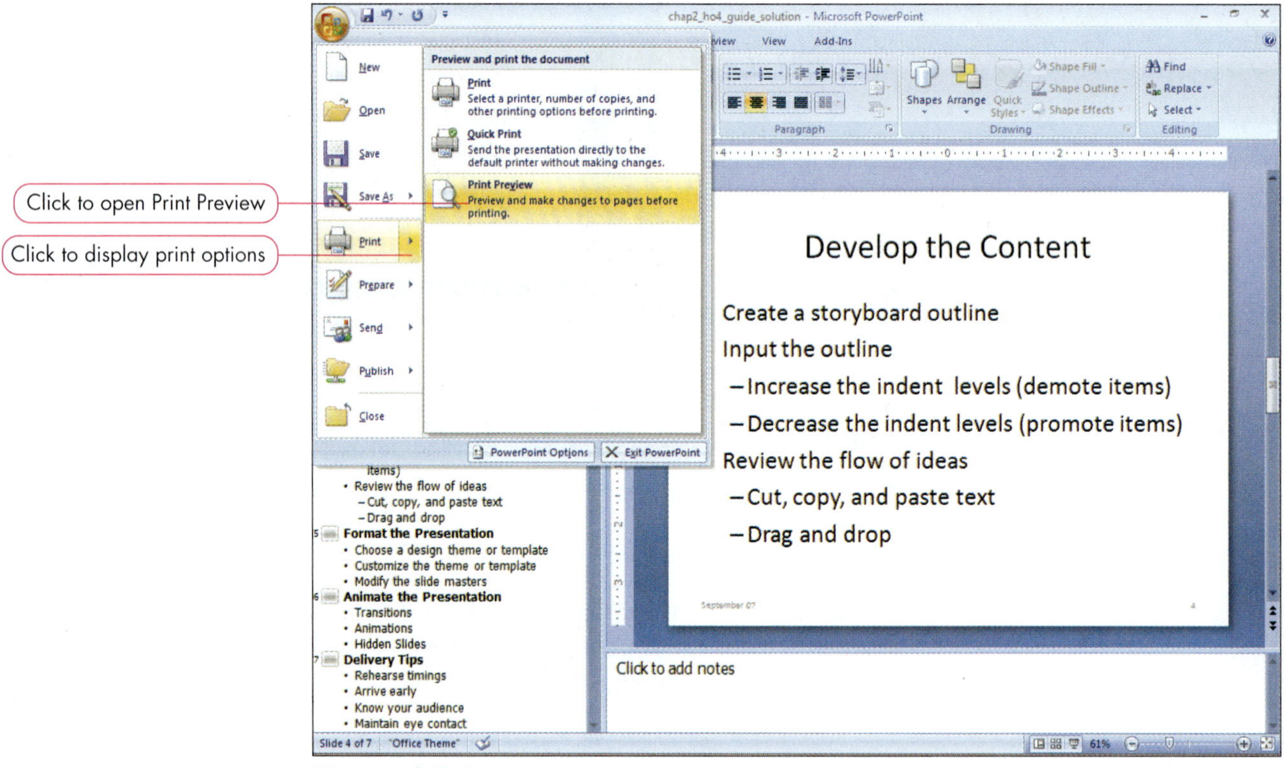

Figure 2.14 Print Options

Hands-On Exercises

2 | Creating and Modifying an Outline

Skills covered: 1. Create a Presentation in Outline View **2.** Enter an Outline **3.** Edit a Presentation **4.** Modify the Outline Structure and Print

Step 1 Create a Presentation in Outline View

Refer to Figure 2.15 as you complete Step 1.

a. Start a new presentation and click the **Outline tab** on the left side of the screen.

b. Click the **Slide 1 icon** on the Outline tab.

c. Type the title of your presentation, **A Guide to Successful Presentations** in the Outline tab pane, and then press **Enter**.

   When you pressed Enter, a new slide was created. To change the level from a new slide to a subtitle, you must increase the indent level.

d. Click **Increase List Level** in the Paragraph group on the Home tab.

e. Enter the first line of the subtitle, the words **Presented by**, and then press **Shift+Enter**.

   Pressing Shift+Enter moves the insertion point to the next line and keeps the same level.

f. Enter your name in the subtitle.

g. Save the file as **chap2_ho2_presentations_solution**.

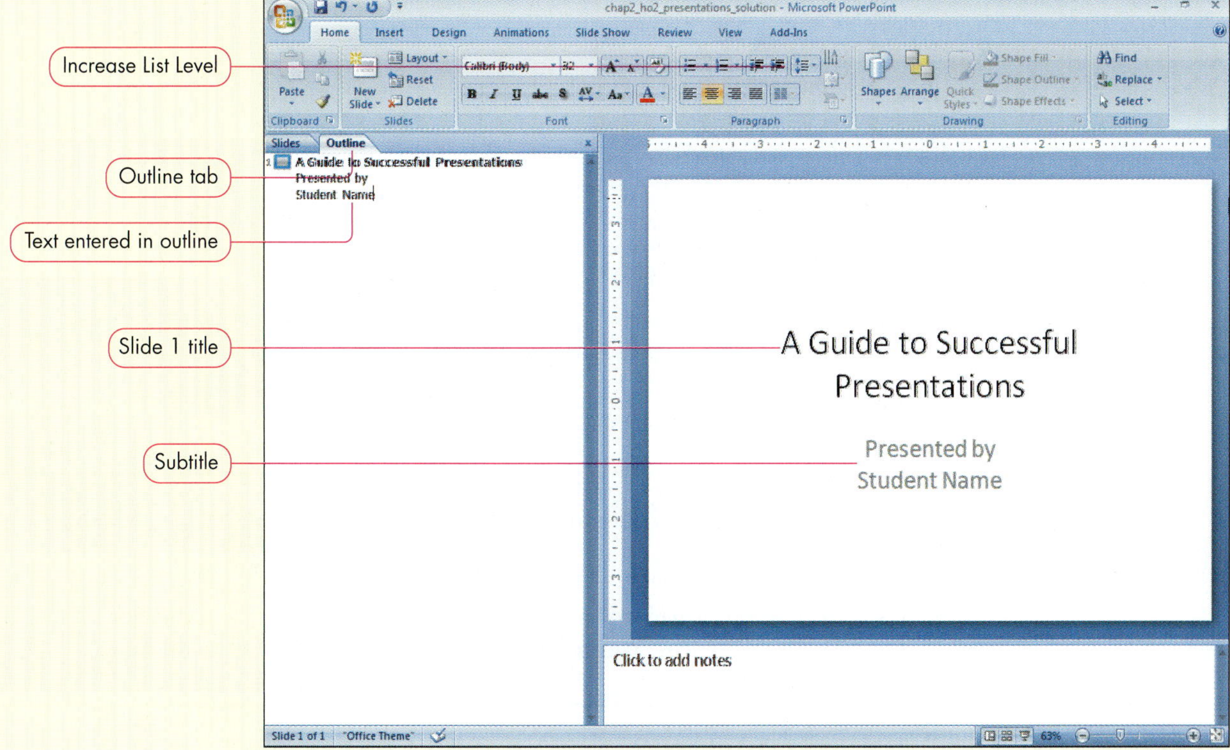

Figure 2.15 Slide 1, Title Slide

Step 2
Enter an Outline

Refer to Figure 2.16 as you complete Step 2 of the outline.

a. Press **Enter**, and then click **Decrease List Level** in the Paragraph group on the Home tab.

   A new slide, Slide 2, is created.

b. Type the title for Slide 2, **Define the Audience**, and then press **Enter**.

c. Press **Tab** to move to the next level.

   Pressing Tab is a keyboard shortcut that accomplishes the same task as clicking the Increase List Level button.

d. Type **Who is in the audience?** and then press **Enter**.

e. Press **Tab** to move to the next level and enter the text **Managers**.

   Managers becomes Level 2 text.

f. Press **Enter** and type **Coworkers**.

g. Press **Enter**, press **Shift+Tab** twice to return to the slide level, and create Slide 3.

h. Continue entering the text of the outline and then save the *chap2_ho2_presentations_solution* file. Figure 2.16 contains the text to be typed.

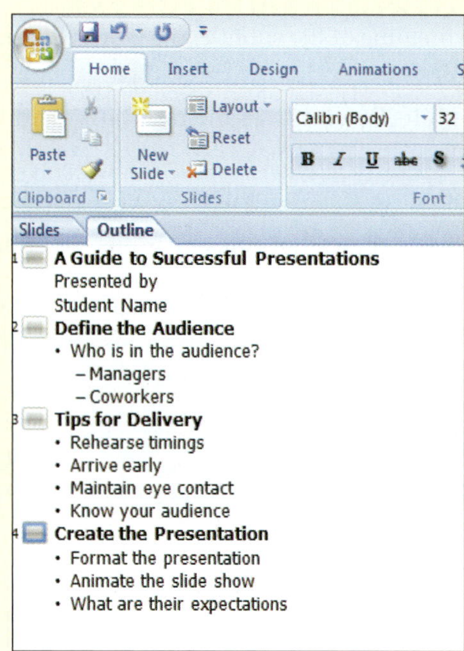

Figure 2.16 Successful Presentations Outline

Step 3
Edit a Presentation

Refer to Figure 2.17 as you complete Step 3.

a. Click at the end of the text *Coworkers* in Slide 2 of the outline.

   While proofreading your outline, you discover that you did not identify one of your audiences. You need to enter your customers as an audience.

b. Press **Enter** and type **Customers**.

   TROUBLESHOOTING: If your text does not appear in the correct position, check to see if the insertion point was in the wrong location. To enter a blank line for a new bullet, the insertion point must be at the end of an existing bullet point and not at the beginning.

c. Select the text *slide show* in the second bullet point in Slide 4 and replace it with **presentation**.

After replacing the text you notice that you left off the first step of creating a presentation—developing the content.

d. Click at the end of the title in Slide 4, and then press **Enter**.

e. Press **Tab**, type **Develop the content**, and then press **Enter**.

f. Save the *chap2_ho2_presentations_solution* file.

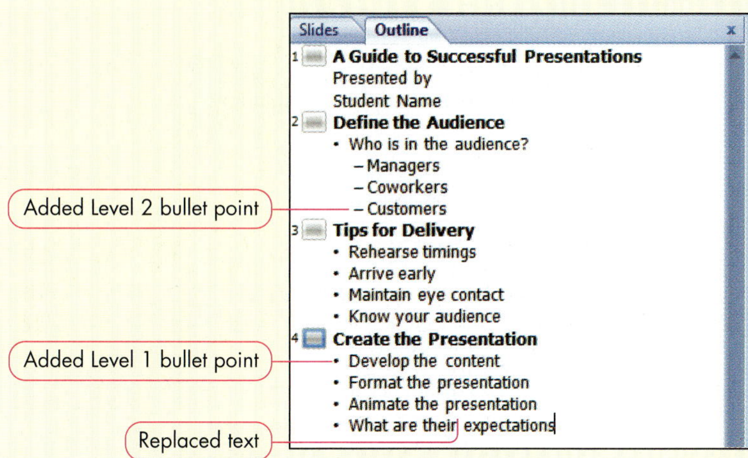

Figure 2.17 The Edited Outline

Step 4
Modify the Outline Structure and Print

Refer to Figure 2.18 as you complete Step 4.

a. Position the pointer over the last bullet in **Slide 4**. When the mouse pointer looks like a four-headed arrow, click to select the text in the bullet point, *What are their expectations*.

The last bullet in Slide 4 is out of position. It belongs at the end of Slide 2.

b. Right-click and select **Cut**.

c. Click at the end of the last bullet point in **Slide 2** and press **Enter**. Click **Decrease List Level** in the Paragraph group on the Home tab.

d. Right-click and select **Paste**. If you see another bullet after the pasted item, press **Backspace** twice to delete the bullet and position the insertion point on the right side of the pasted text. Then type a question mark at the end of the question you just moved.

In the final review of the presentation you realize that the slides are out of order. The *Tips for Delivery* slide should be the last slide in the presentation. Collapsing the bullets will make it easy to move the slide.

e. Right-click any bullet point, point at **Collapse**, and then select **Collapse All**.

f. Click the **Slide 3 icon** to select the collapsed slide.

g. Drag the **Slide 3 icon** below the Slide 4 icon and release.

h. Click the **Office Button**, point to **Print**, and then select **Print Preview**.

i. Click the **Print What down arrow** in the Page Setup group on the Print Preview tab, and then select **Outline View**.

j. Click **Orientation** in the Page Setup group on the Print Preview tab, and then select **Landscape**.

k. Click **Close Print Preview** in the Preview group and return to editing the presentation.

l. Right-click one of the slide titles in the Outline pane, point at **Expand**, and then click **Expand All**.

m. Repeat Steps 4h–j to view the presentation in Print Preview and change the orientation to **Portrait**.

n. Close Print Preview and save the *chap2_ho2_presentations_solution* file. Close the file.

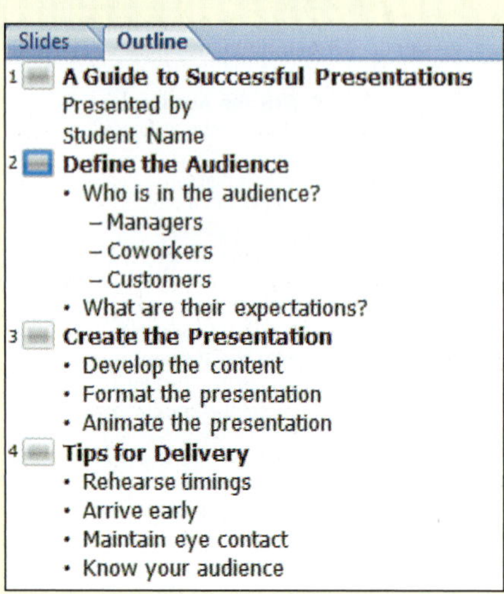

Figure 2.18 The Expanded Outline with Structural Changes

Data Imports

At some time you may receive an outline created by a colleague using Microsoft Word or another word processing program and you need to create a presentation from that outline. Or perhaps you prefer creating your outlines in a word processing program rather than within PowerPoint. This preference poses no problems as PowerPoint can create slides based on Microsoft Word outlines or outlines saved in a format that PowerPoint recognizes.

Rich Text Format (.rtf) is a file type that retains structure and most text formatting when used to transfer documents between applications or platforms.

PowerPoint recognizes outlines created and saved in a ***Rich Text Format*** (RTF), a file type you can use to transfer text documents with formatting between applications such as any word processing program and PowerPoint, or even between platforms such as Macintosh and IBM. You must save the document in the RTF format with the .rtf extension if you wish to use it in PowerPoint. When you save the document in this format, the extension .rtf is assigned to it. The outline structure and most of the text formatting is retained when you import the outline into PowerPoint.

Plain Text Format (.txt) is a file type that retains only text when used to transfer documents between applications or platforms.

PowerPoint also recognizes outlines created and saved in a ***Plain Text format*** (.txt), a file format that retains text only. When .txt outlines are imported the hierarchical structure is lost, and each line of the outline becomes a slide. No text formatting is saved. Another alternative is to import a Web document (.htm), but in this case all the text from the file appears in one placeholder on one slide.

In this section, you learn how to import an outline into a PowerPoint presentation. You also learn how to add existing content from another presentation into the current presentation.

Importing an Outline

To create a new presentation from an outline created in another format, click the Office Button, and then select Open. When the Open dialog box displays, click the All PowerPoint Presentations drop-down arrow and select All Outlines. Any files in a format PowerPoint recognizes will be listed. Double-click the document you wish to use as the basis for your presentation. Figure 2.19 displays the same outline in three different formats. All three formats appear in the list as they are all formats PowerPoint recognizes. The different icons indicate different file types.

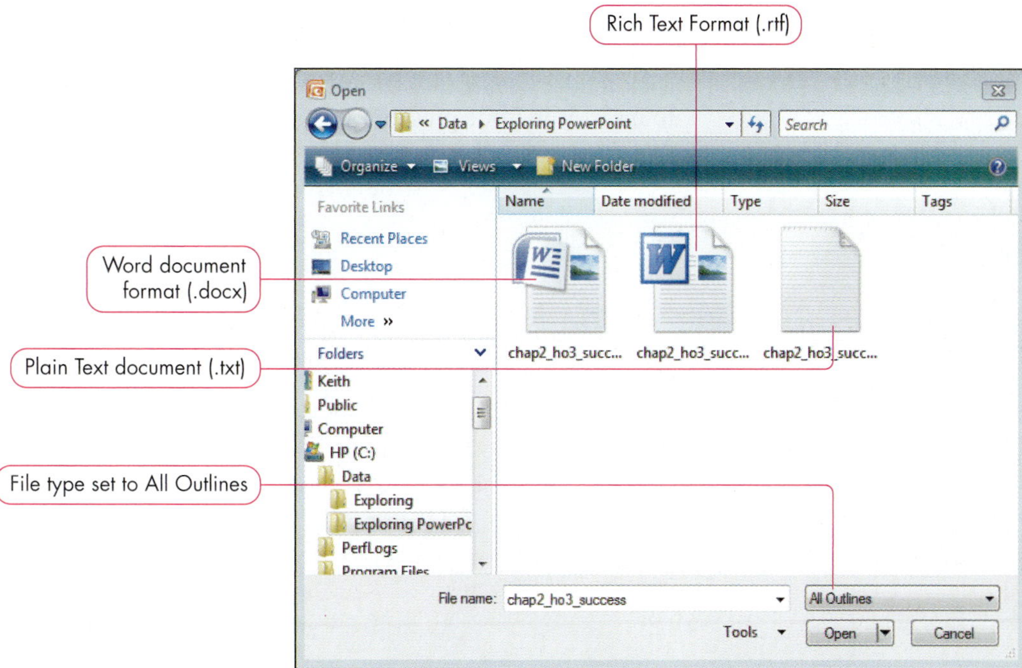

Figure 2.19 Document Formats for Importing

TIP Problems Importing a Word Outline

If you import a Word document you believe is an outline into PowerPoint and after importing, each line becomes a title for a slide, the Word document was created with bullets rather than as an outline. These two features are separate and distinct and do not import in the same manner. You may open the Word document in Word, apply outline formatting, save, and then re-import it, or you may work within the PowerPoint outline and promote and demote text until you obtain the structure you desire.

Adding Existing Content to a Presentation

(With each presentation you create, you create resources for the future!)

After you prepare a presentation, you can reuse the content in other presentations. With each presentation you create, you create resources for the future. To obtain the content from other presentations, click New Slide in the Slides group on the Home tab. The bottom of the New Slide gallery contains options for duplicating selected slides, for inserting all the slides from an existing outline, and for reusing slides you select.

When you select the Slides from Outline command, the Insert Outline dialog box displays. By default, only outlines are displayed. You can, however, change the *Files of type* to display other files. Double-click the file you wish to use, and the outline is inserted after the current slide.

For greater flexibility, however, use the Reuse Slides command to select the slides you want to use rather than insert all slides. When you select Reuse Slides, a task pane opens on the right side of your window. The Reuse Slides task pane includes a Browse button for locating the file containing the slides you wish to include in your current presentation. When you locate the file and open it, thumbnail images of your slides are displayed in the task pane. Running the pointer over a thumbnail enlarges the image so that text may be read.

At the bottom of the task pane is a check box. By default, when you insert a slide into the presentation it retains the format of the current presentation. If you wish to keep the format or the original presentation from which you are obtaining the slide, click the *Keep source formatting* check box. Finally, click the thumbnail of your choice to insert it in your presentation after the current slide. The task pane stays open for more selections. The Reuse Slides task pane is shown in Figure 2.20.

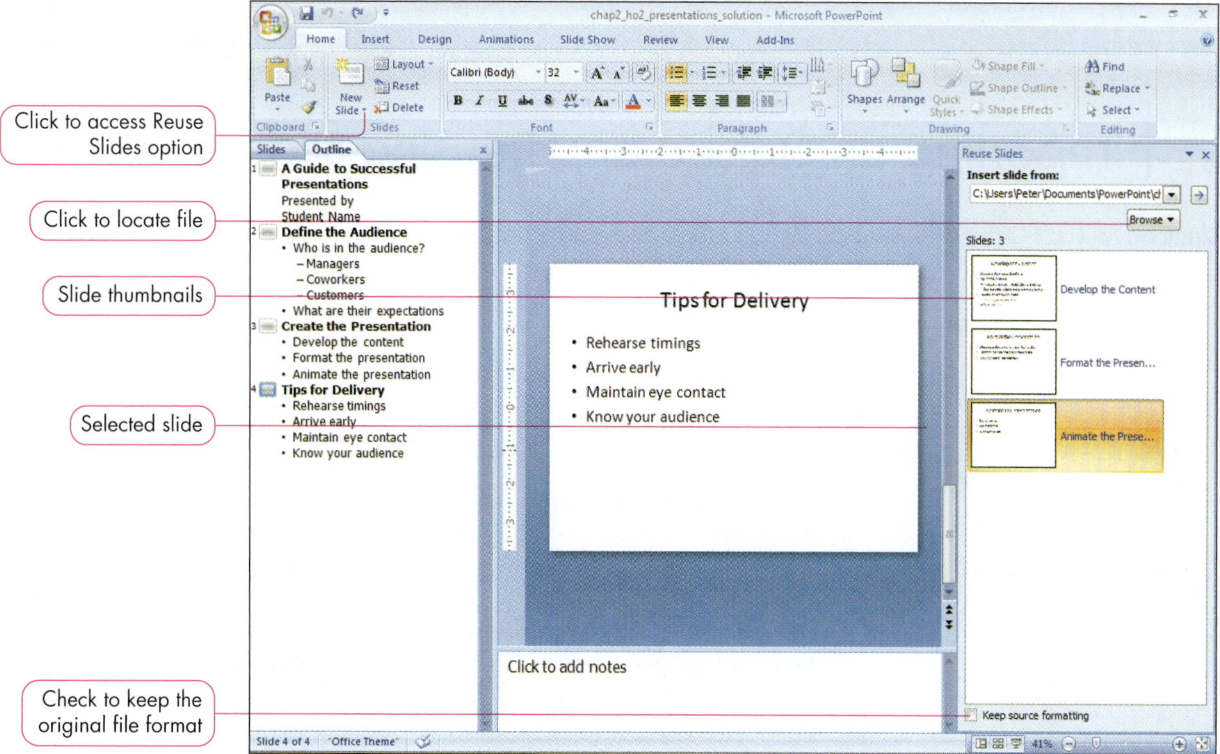

Figure 2.20 Reuse Slides Task Pane

Hands-On Exercises

3 | Importing an Outline and Reusing Slides

Skills covered: 1. Import a Microsoft Word Outline **2.** Reuse Slides from Another Presentation

Step 1
Import a Microsoft Word Outline

Refer to Figure 2.21 as you complete Step 1.

a. Click the **Office Button**, select **Open**, and then navigate to the **Chapter 2** folder within the **Exploring PowerPoint** folder.

b. Click the **All PowerPoint Presentations drop-down arrow** and select **All Outlines**.

c. Double-click to open the file *chap2_ho3_success*, a Microsoft Office Word document.

The Word outline is opened into PowerPoint, and a new presentation based upon the imported document is created. This presentation is similar to the one you created in Hands-on Exercise 1, but some of the content is slightly different. Also, notice that the font is Times New Roman based on the outline imported into the presentation.

d. Click the **Outline tab**, and select **Slide 3**, *Create the Presentation*.

e. Save the file as **chap2_ho3_guide_solution**.

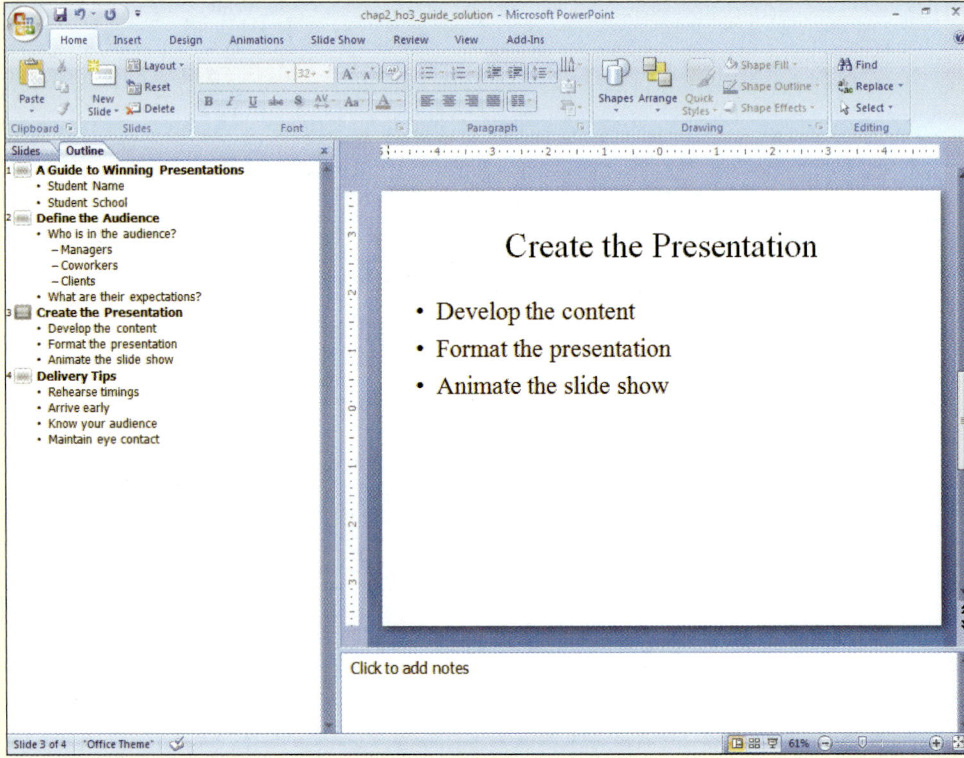

Figure 2.21 New Presentation Based on a Word Outline

Step 2
Reuse Slides from Another Presentation

Refer to Figure 2.22 as you complete Step 2.

a. Click the **Home tab** and click the **New Slide down arrow** in the Slides group.

   The New Slide gallery appears.

b. Click **Reuse Slides** at the bottom of the gallery.

   The Reuse Slides pane appears on the right side of your screen.

c. Click the **Browse button**, click **Browse File**, and locate your student files.

d. Click to select the file *chap2_ho3_development* and then click **Open**.

   TROUBLESHOOTING: If you do not see the *chap2_ho3_development* presentation, change the *Files of type* option to All PowerPoint Presentations.

e. Click each of the three successive slides in the Reuse Slides task pane to insert the slides into the slide show.

f. Close the Reuse Slides task pane.

g. Refer to Figure 2.22. Move slides as needed to obtain the correct structure, if necessary.

   Ignore font changes, as we will handle design issues in the next section of this chapter.

h. Save the *chap2_ho3_guide_solution* file and keep it onscreen if you plan to continue to the next hands-on exercise. Close the file and exit PowerPoint if you do not want to continue with the next exercise at this time.

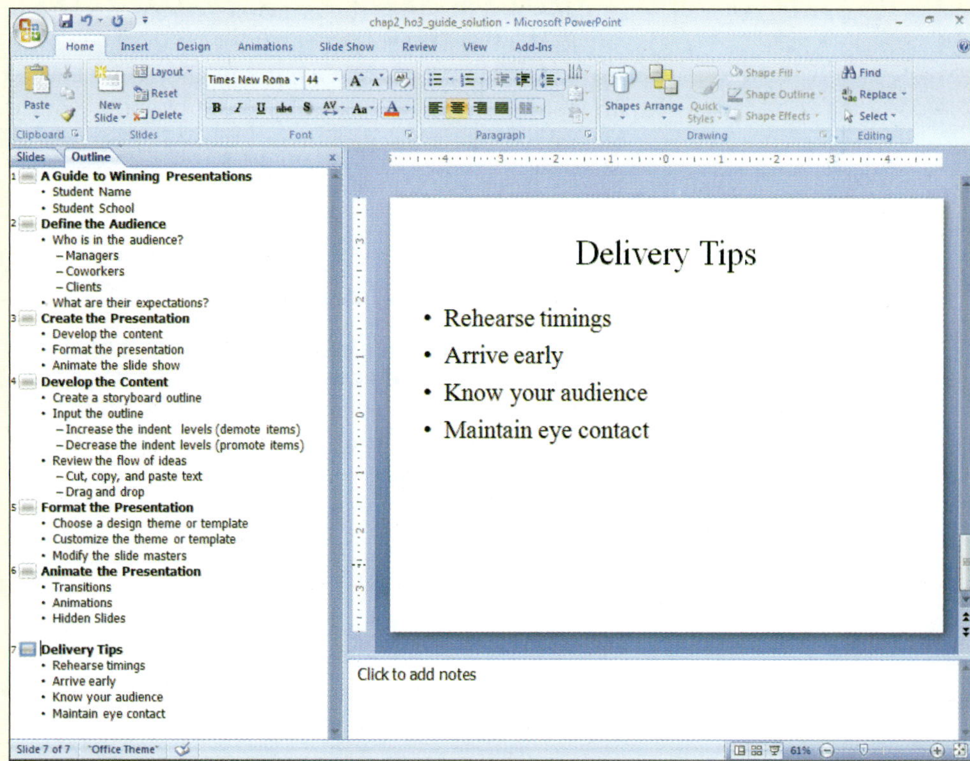

Figure 2.22 Reused Slides Added to Presentation

Design

(You should evaluate many aspects when considering the visual design of your presentation.)

When you work with the content of a presentation, it can be helpful to work with the blank template, as you did when we worked with the outlines. Working in the blank template lets you concentrate on what you want to say. After you are satisfied with the content, however, you need to consider the visual aspects of the presentation. You should evaluate many aspects when considering the visual design of your presentation. Those aspects include layout, background, typography, color, and animation.

Because the majority of people using PowerPoint are not graphic artists and do not have a strong design background, Microsoft designers created a variety of methods to help users deal with design issues. By now you should have explored themes and templates that are used to help people create an attractively designed slide show without a background in design.

In this section you explore additional Microsoft features to aid with design. After you are comfortable using these features, you can modify the design to reflect your own taste. Before doing so, however, you need to examine some basic visual design principles for PowerPoint.

Examining Slide Show Design Principles

Basic design principles are universal. When applied to a project, they can increase its appeal and professionalism. While basic principles are universal, some aspects may be applied in specific ways to the various types of modern communication: communicating through print mediums such as flyers or brochures, through audio mediums such as narrations or music, or through a visual medium such as a slide show. You will focus on a few of the principles that apply to slide shows and examine examples of slides that illustrate the principles.

Remember that these principles are guidelines. You may choose to avoid applying one of these principles, but you should be aware of the principle and why you are not following it. If you are in doubt about your design, ask a classmate or colleague to review the design and make suggestions. Fresh eyes can see things you may not.

Applying and Modifying a Design Theme

You should already have experience applying a theme. You can tweak the theme once it is applied. You can change the colors used in the theme, the fonts used, and effects used. You can even change the background styles. Each of these options is on the Design tab, and each has its own gallery. Figure 2.30 shows the locations for accessing the galleries.

Examples of Designs for Various Audiences | Reference

Figure 2.23 Examples of Choosing a Template for Audience

- All design elements should be appropriate for the audience. Carefully consider your audience and their background, and then use a design that fits the background of the audience. For example, for a presentation to elementary students you may use bright primary colors in your color scheme and cartoon-like clip art to keep their attention. Fonts should be large and easy to read. For a presentation to landscape designers, however, you may choose muted earth tones and more photographs than text to convey your message. Photographs give the slide show a more professional appearance. In a formal presentation to a group of stockholders, however, you may choose a traditional blue color scheme with tables, charts, and graphs to convey your message. Figure 2.23 shows design examples suitable for grade-schoolers and business people respectively.

Figure 2.24 Examples of a Cluttered Design (left) and a Clean Design (right)

- Keep the design neat and clean. This principle is often referred to as KISS: Keep it simple, sweetie! Figure 2.24 shows an example of cluttered and clean designs. • Avoid using multiple fonts and colors on a slide. • Too many fonts and colors make the slide look cluttered and busy. • Avoid using more than five colors on a slide and three fonts. • Avoid using multiple clip art images. • Use white space, or empty space, to open your design.

Tips for Delivery
• Rehearse timings
• Arrive early
• Maintain eye contact
• Know your audience

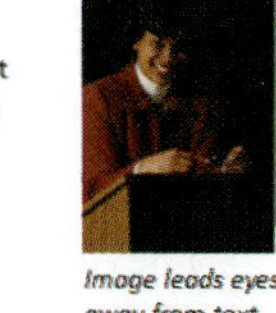

Image leads eyes away from text

Tips for Delivery
• Rehearse timings
• Arrive early
• Maintain eye contact
• Know your audience

Image leads eyes towards text

Figure 2.25 Examples of an Ineffective Focal Point (left) and an Effective Focal Point (right)

- Create a focal point, or main area of interest, on your slide and have everything else lead the viewer's eyes to that location. Images should always lead the viewer's eyes to the focal point, not away from it. Images should not be so large they detract from the focal point, unless your goal is to make the image the focal point. Figure 2.25 illustrates examples of ineffective and effective focal points.

Sans Serif **Serif**

Figure 2.26 Sans Serif and Serif Fonts

- Carefully consider the output of your presentation. If your presentation is to be delivered through a projection device, consider using sans serif fonts with short text blocks. If your presentation will be delivered as a printout, consider using a serif font, as the serifs help guide the reader's eyes across the page. You may use longer text blocks in printed presentations. Figure 2.26 displays an example of a sans serif font—a font that does not have serifs, or small lines, at the ends of letters. It also shows an example of a serif font with the serifs on the letter "S" circled. Decorative fonts are also available. When choosing a font, remember that readability is critical in a presentation.

Figure 2.27 Disjointed and Unified Design Elements

- Use a unified design for a professional look. Visual unity creates a harmony between the elements of the slide and the slides in the slide show. Unity gives the viewer a sense of order and peace. Create unity by repeating colors and shapes. Use clip art in one style so the design is unified. Figure 2.27 illustrates disjointed and unified designs.

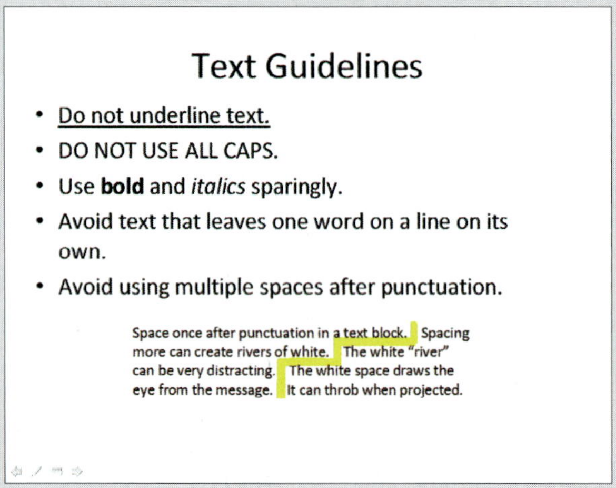

Text Guidelines

- Do not underline text.
- DO NOT USE ALL CAPS.
- Use **bold** and *italics* sparingly.
- Avoid text that leaves one word on a line on its own.
- Avoid using multiple spaces after punctuation.

Space once after punctuation in a text block. Spacing more can create rivers of white. The white "river" can be very distracting. The white space draws the eye from the message. It can throb when projected.

Figure 2.28 Appropriate and Inappropriate Text Examples

- Text is also a visual element. Figure 2.28 illustrates inappropriate text examples. Text guidelines are:
  - Do not underline text. Underlined text is harder to read, and it is generally assumed that the text is a hyperlink.
  - Avoid using all capital letters in titles, bulleted lists, or long text blocks. In addition to being difficult to read, it is considered to be yelling at the audience.
  - Use italic and bold sparingly. They can create visual clutter. Also, too much emphasis confuses the audience about what is important and creates the impression of no emphasis.
  - Avoid creating lines of text that leave a single word hanging on a line of its own.
  - Use just one space after punctuation in text blocks. This practice avoids distracting "rivers of white space" in the text block.

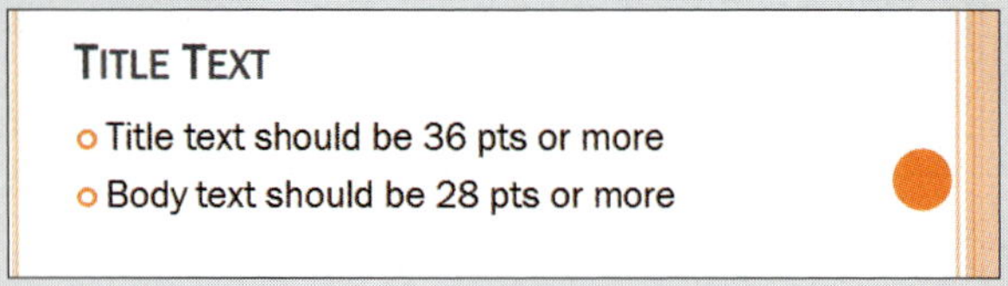

TITLE TEXT

- Title text should be 36 pts or more
- Body text should be 28 pts or more

Figure 2.29 Readable Text Guidelines

- Make text readable. Title text should use title case and be 36 pts or higher. Bullet text should be in sentence case and be 28 pts or higher. Remember the 7 × 7 guideline. When you create more than seven lines on a slide, PowerPoint automatically resizes the font to a smaller size that is difficult to read when projected. Figure 2.29 illustrates readable text.

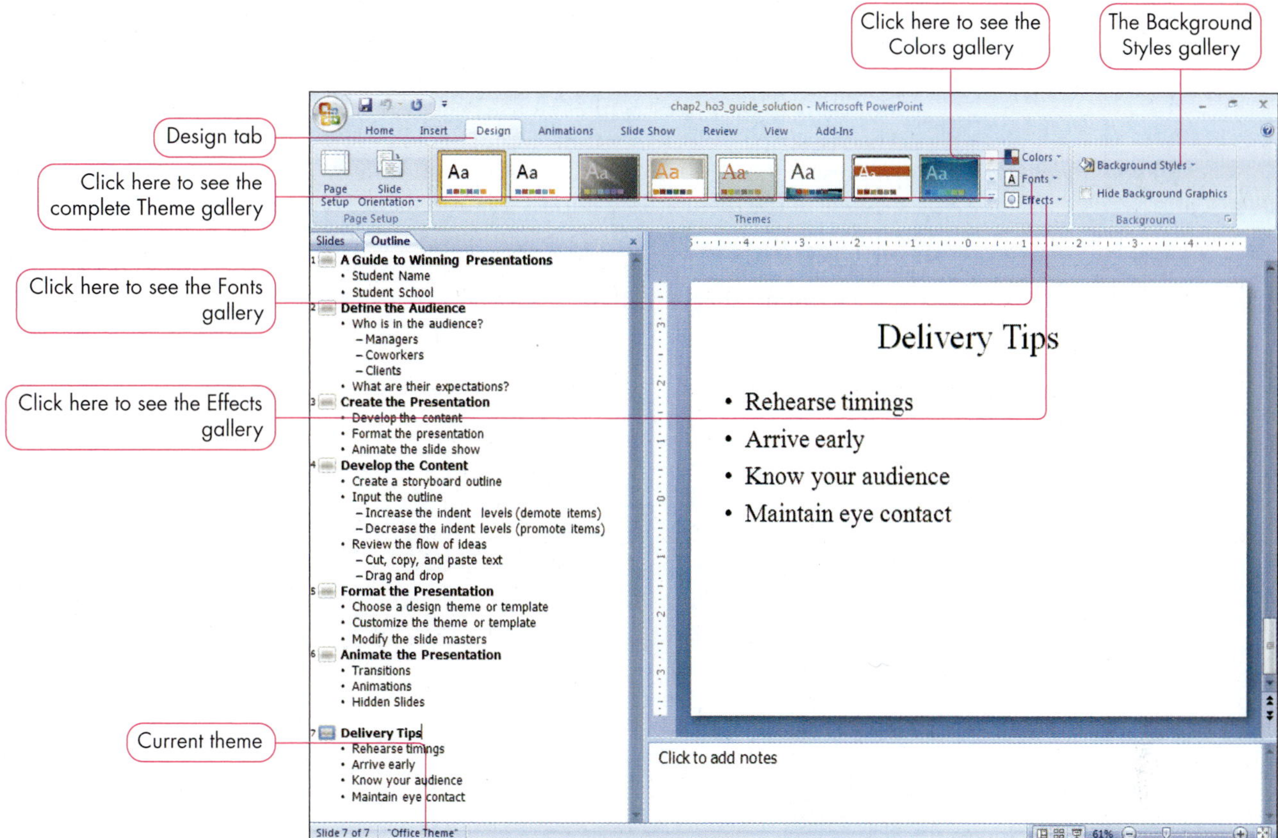

Figure 2.30 Design Galleries

The ***Colors gallery*** is a gallery with a set of colors for every available theme.

Each PowerPoint theme includes a ***Colors gallery***, a gallery that provides a set of colors. Each color in the gallery is assigned to a different element in the theme design. Once the theme is selected, you can click the Colors down arrow to display the Built-In gallery. Clicking one of the color themes applies it to the theme, thereby applying it to the presentation. You can even create your own color theme set by selecting Create New Theme Colors at the bottom of the gallery.

The ***Fonts gallery*** contains font sets for title text and body text.

Selecting a font for the title and one for the bullets or body text of your presentation can be difficult. Without a background in typography, it is hard to determine which fonts go together well. The ***Fonts gallery*** is a gallery that pairs a title font and a body font for your use. Click any of the samples in the Fonts gallery, and the font pair is applied to your theme. You do not need to select the slides because the change applies to all slides.

The ***Effects gallery*** includes a range of effects for shapes used in the presentation.

The ***Effects gallery*** is a gallery that displays a full range of special effects that can be applied to all shapes in the presentation. This aids you in maintaining the consistency of the look of your presentation. Effects in the gallery include a soft glow, soft edges to the shape, shadows, or a three-dimensional (3-D) look.

The ***Background Styles gallery*** provides both solid color and background styles for application to a theme.

You can change the background style of the theme by accessing the ***Background Styles gallery***, a gallery containing backgrounds consistent with the color theme. The backgrounds fall into one of three areas: subtle, moderate, or intense. Subtle backgrounds are a solid color, while intense backgrounds are designed with patterns such as checks, stripes, blocks, or dots. Simply changing your background style can liven up a presentation and give it your individual style.

Some of the themes, like Equity, include shapes on their background to create the design (see Figure 2.31). If the background shapes are interfering with other objects on the slide, however, you can click the Hide Background Graphics check box, and the background shapes will not display for that slide.

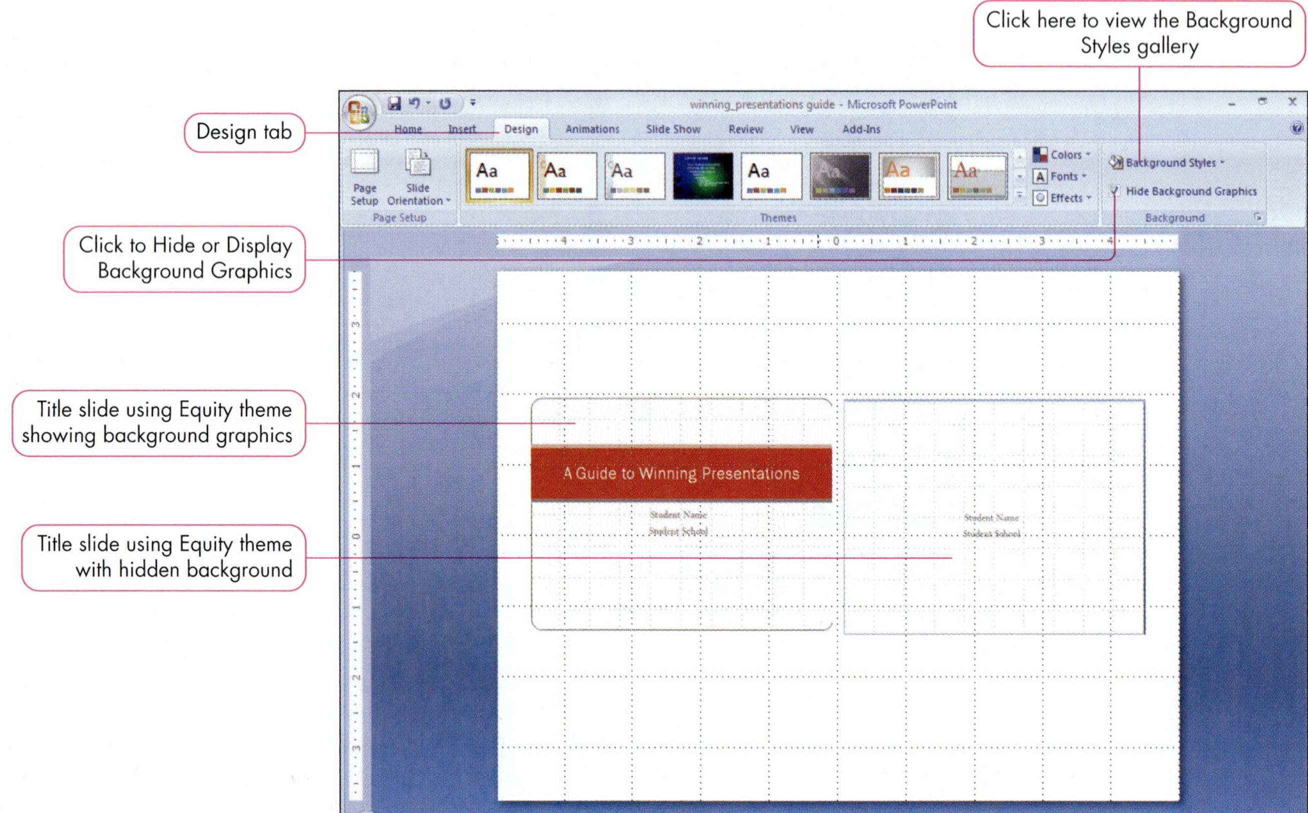

Figure 2.31 Equity Theme

Inserting a Header or Footer

A ***header*** is information that appears at the top of pages in a handout or notes page.

A ***footer*** is information that appears at the bottom of slides in a presentation, or at the bottom of pages in a handout or notes page.

You will find that many times there is information that you want to appear on every slide, handout, or notes page. As a student, your instructor may want your name on every handout you turn in, or the date you completed the assignment. Use the Header and Footer feature to do this. A ***header*** contains information that appears at the top of pages in a handout or on a notes page. A ***footer*** contains information that appears at the bottom of slides in a presentation, or at the bottom of pages in a handout or a notes page.

Common uses of headers and footers are to insert slide numbers, the time and date, a company logo, the presenter's name, or even the presentation's file name. Headers and footers can contain text or graphics. To insert text in a header or footer, you use the Header & Footer command. To insert graphics, you modify the header or footer fields in the Slide Master. For now, you will use the Header & Footer command. You can use Help to learn how to customize a Slide Master to include a logo graphic in a footer. Figure 2.32 shows an example of a title slide with a footer.

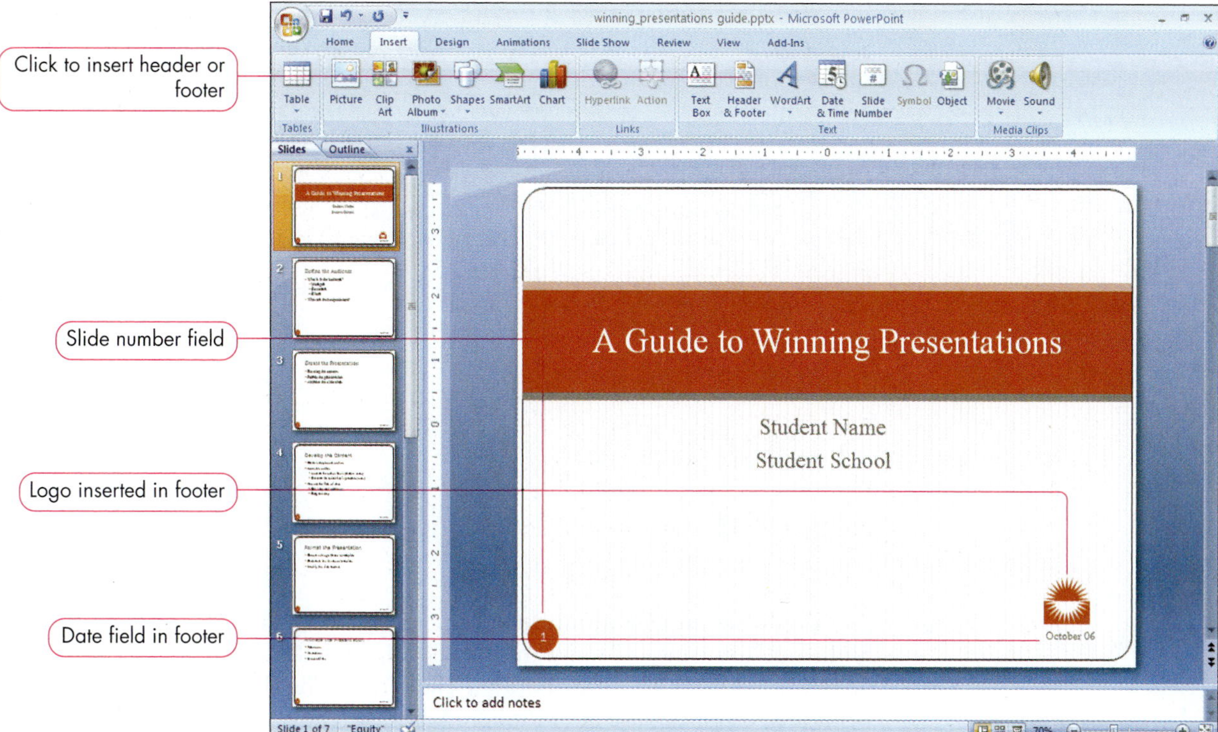

Figure 2.32 Title Slide with Footer

To create a footer for a slide, click the Insert tab, and then click Header & Footer in the Text group. Click the Slide tab when the Header and Footer dialog box displays. Click the Date and time check box in the *Include on slide* section to insert the current date and time. Click *Update automatically* if you wish the date to always be current. Once you select *Update automatically*, you can select the date format you prefer. Alternatively, you can choose the option to enter a fixed date that will not change. You use a fixed date to preserve the original date you created the presentation, which could help you keep track of versions.

A check box also activates the Slide number field. Click the Footer check box to activate the footer field. When you click the check box, the insertion point is placed inside the Footer box, and you can enter any information you desire. The Preview window lets you see the position of these fields. If you do not want the footer to appear on the title slide, click the *Don't show on title slide* check box. The last step is to click Apply to apply the footer to the selected slide, or to click Apply to All to apply the footer to every slide in the presentation. Figure 2.33 shows the Header and Footer dialog box with the Slide tab selected.

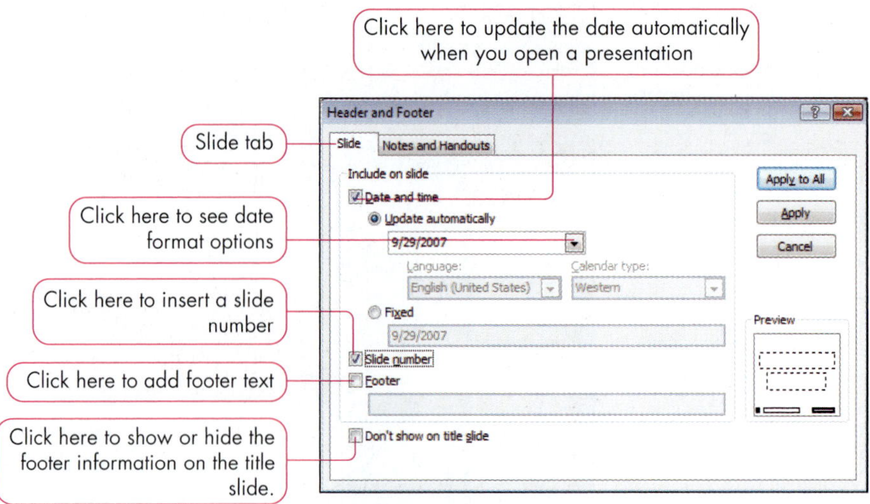

Figure 2.33 Header and Footer Dialog Box

The Notes and Handouts tab gives you many of the same options available in the Slide tab. You can add more information in this tab, however, because it gives you an extra field box for information—the Header field. Since this feature is used for printouts, the slides are not numbered, but the pages in the handout are. As you activate the fields, the preview window shows the location of the fields. The Date and Time field is located on the top right of the printout. The Header field is located on the top left. The page number is located on the bottom right, and the Footer field is on the bottom left.

4 | Applying and Modifying a Design Theme

Skills covered: 1. Apply a Theme to a Presentation **2.** Apply a Color Scheme **3.** Add a Font Scheme **4.** Apply a Background Style **5.** Hide Background Graphics on a Slide **6.** Save Current Theme **7.** Create a Slide Footer **8.** Create a Handout Header and Footer

Step 1 Apply a Theme to a Presentation

Refer to Figure 2.34 as you complete Step 1.

a. Open the *chap2_ho3_guide_solution* file if you closed it after the last hands-on exercise. Save the file as **chap2_ho4_guide_solution**.

b. Click the **Design tab** and click the **More button** in the Themes group.

   The Themes gallery opens for you to select from Themes in This Presentation, from the Built-In themes, from Office Online, or enables you to Browse for Themes you have previously created and saved.

c. Click the **Solstice theme**.

   The theme is applied to all slides in the presentation.

d. Save the *chap2_ho4_guide_solution* presentation.

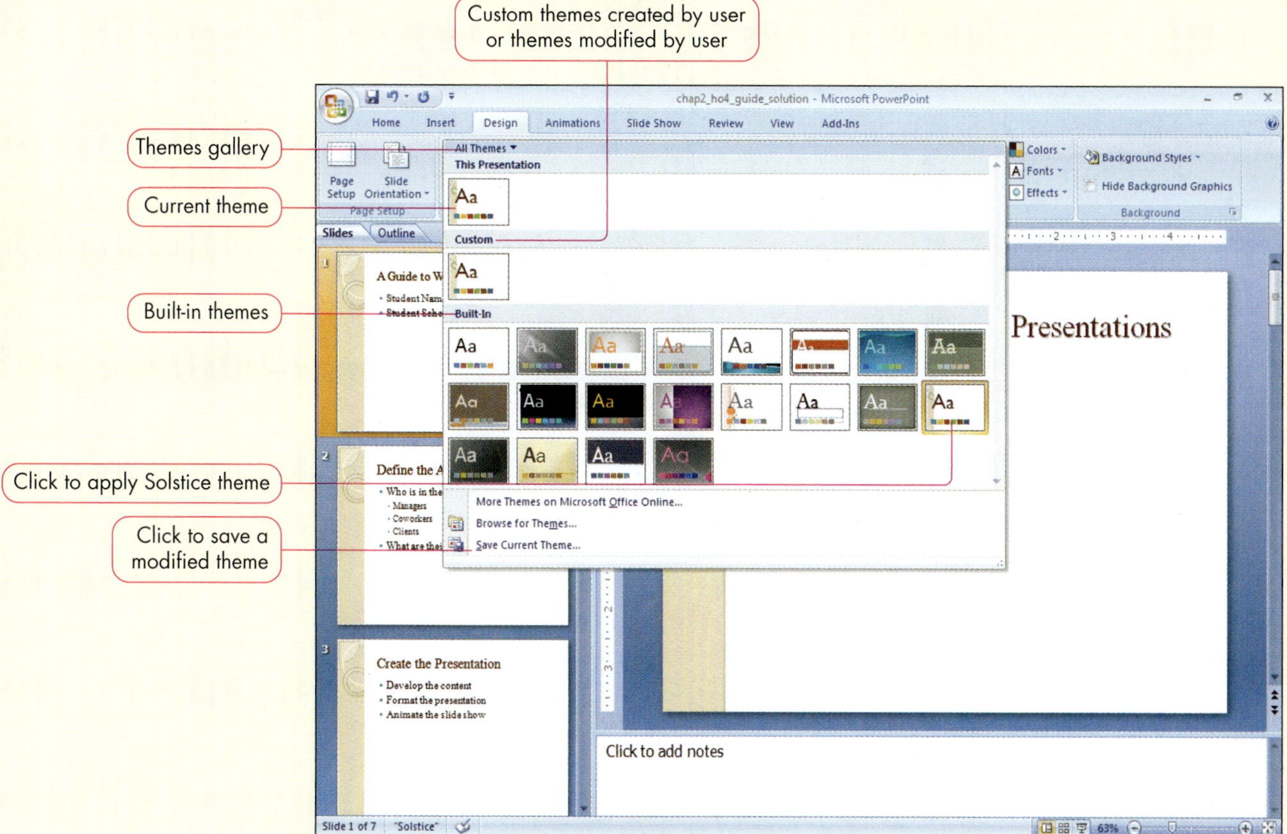

Figure 2.34 Solstice Theme

Step 2
Apply a Color Scheme

Refer to Figure 2.35 as you complete Step 2.

a. With *chap2_ho4_guide_solution* open, point at the Colors button in the Themes group.

   The Theme Colors ScreenTip shows that the currently applied color scheme is Solstice.

b. Click **Colors** in the Themes group on the Design tab to see the Built-In gallery.

c. Point to several of the color schemes to see the effects they have on the title slide.

   The color scheme is not applied until you click.

d. Click the **Origin color scheme**.

   The color scheme is applied to your presentation.

e. Save the *chap2_ho4_guide_solution* presentation.

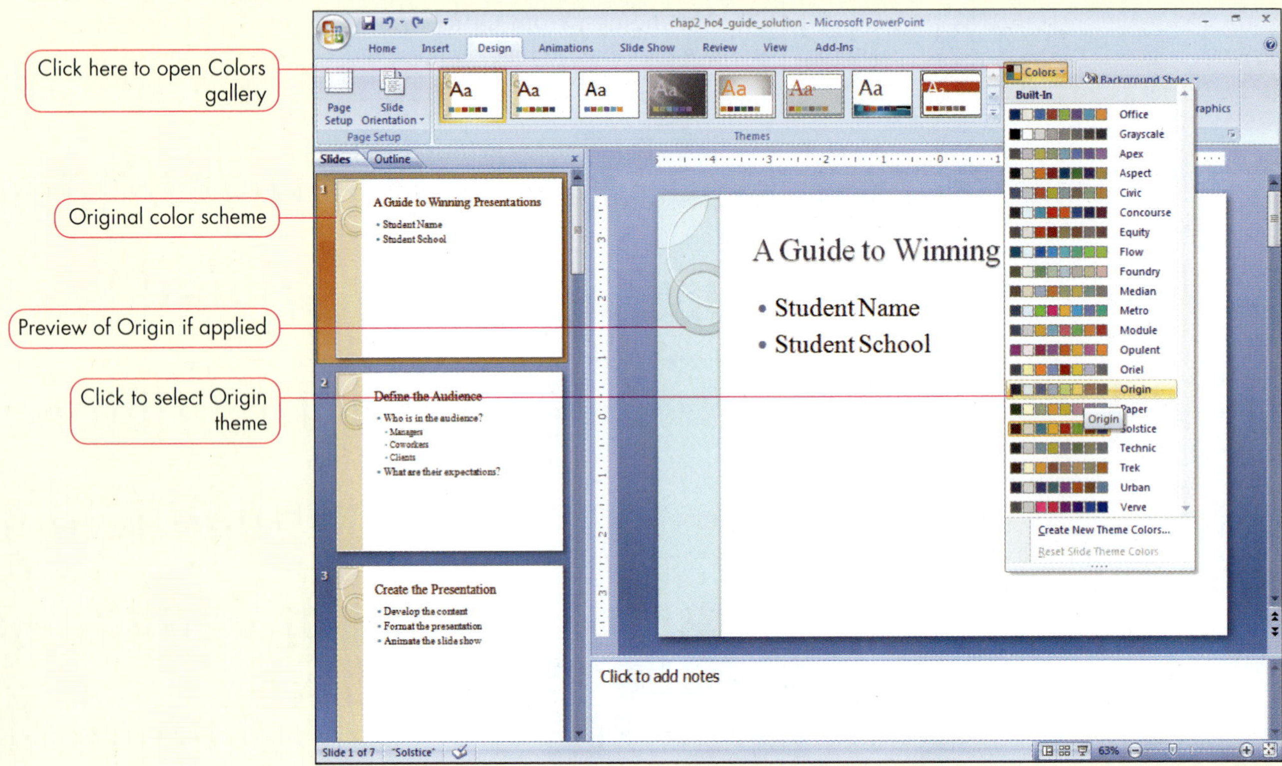

Figure 2.35 Solstice Theme with Origin Color Theme

Step 3
Add a Font Scheme

Refer to Figure 2.36 as you complete Step 3.

a. With *chap2_ho4_guide_solution* open, click the **Outline tab**.

b. Note that Slides 1, 2, 3, and 7 use different fonts than Slides 4, 5, and 6.

Slides 4, 5, and 6 were created by reusing slides from another presentation, causing the font shift. Slides 1, 2, 3, and 7 use a serif font—Times New Roman. Slides 4, 5, and 6 use a sans serif font—Gill Sans.

c. Click the **Design tab** and click **Fonts** in the Themes group.

The Built-In fonts appear in the gallery.

d. Click the **Flow font scheme** to apply it to your presentation.

The Flow font scheme applies the Calibri font to titles and the Constantia font to body text.

TROUBLESHOOTING: If the font scheme does not apply to all slides, select the slide that did not have the scheme applied and then change the title and bullets manually.

e. Save the *chap2_ho4_guide_solution* presentation.

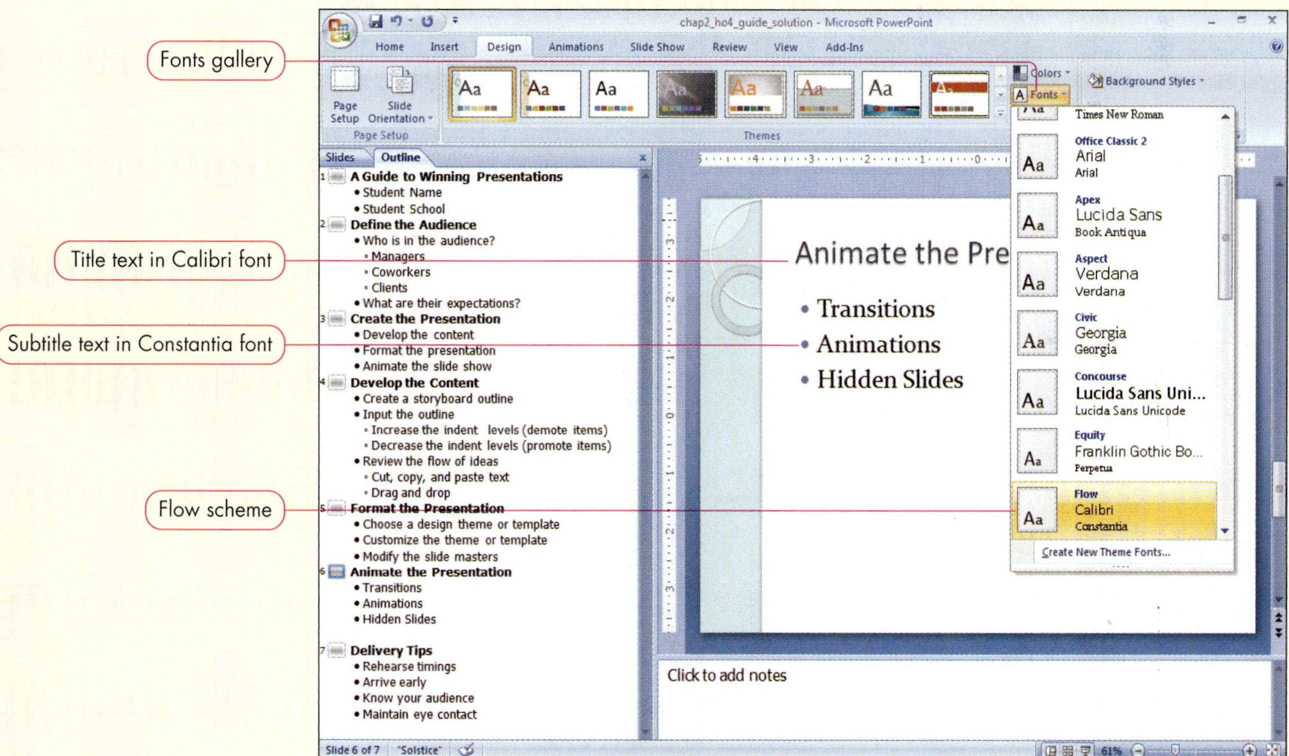

Figure 2.36 The Flow Font Scheme

Step 4
Apply a Background Style

Refer to Figure 2.37 as you complete Step 4.

a. With *chap2_ho4_guide_solution* open, click the **Slides tab**.

Changing to the Slides tab enables you to see the background style you apply on several slides.

b. Click **Background Styles** in the Background group on the Design tab.

c. Point at each of the styles and note the changes to the background graphic on the side of the slide.

> **TIP Choosing Backgrounds Based on Lighting**
>
> A dark background choice is appropriate if you will be giving your presentation in a very light room. If you use a light background in a light room, your audience may not see your text because there would not be enough contrast. If you give your presentation in a dark room, select a light background. A dark background in a dark room gives your audience an invitation to sleep!

d. Click **Style 6**.

e. Save the *chap2_ho4_guide_solution* presentation.

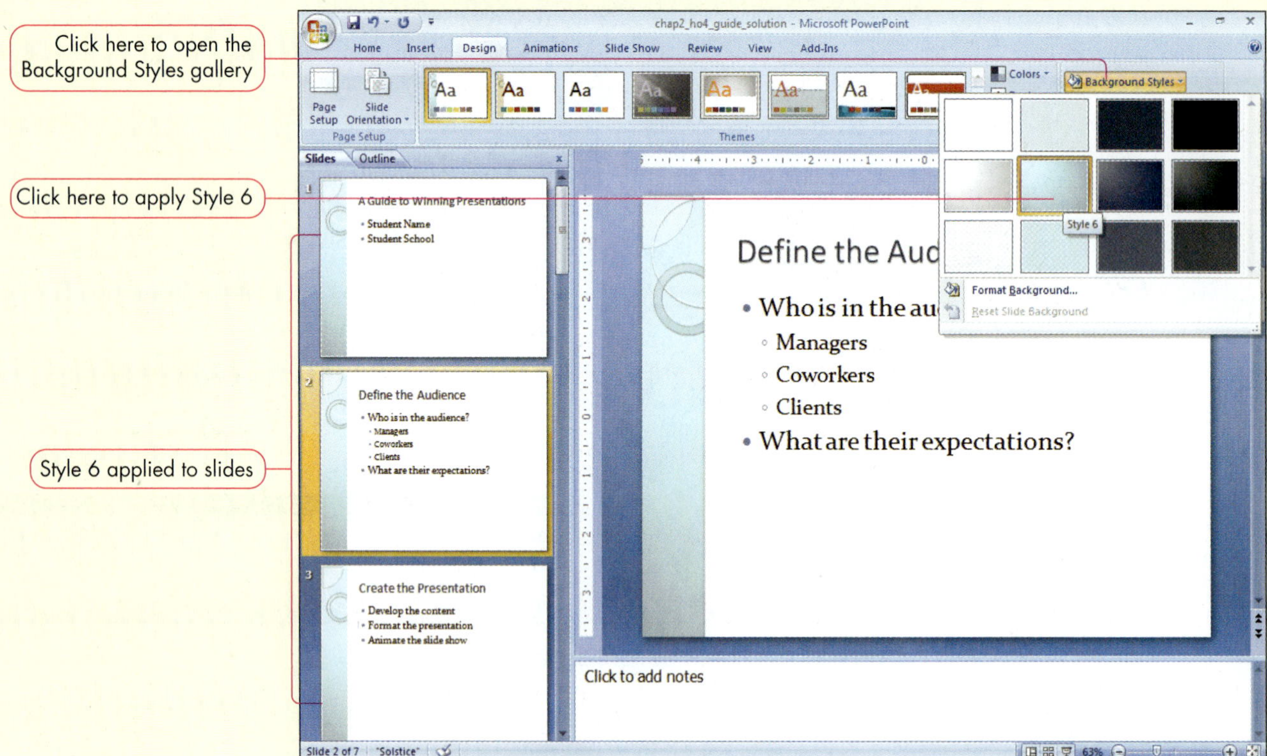

Figure 2.37 Background Style 6 Applied

Step 5
Hide Background Graphics on a Slide

Refer to Figure 2.38 as you complete Step 5.

a. With *chap2_ho4_guide_solution* open, click to select **Slide 1**, if necessary.

b. Click the **Home tab**, click **Layout** in the Slides group, and click **Title Slide**.

The first slide was formatted by the Title and Text layout when you imported the Word outline in Hands-On Exercise 2. You applied Title Slide layout to convert the bullet-list items to a subtitle.

c. Click the **Hide Background Graphics check box** in the Background group on the Design tab.

You decide to put a photograph related to presenting on the bottom of the title slide to add color. To keep the slide from being cluttered, you removed the background graphics.

d. Click the **Insert tab** and click **Clip Art** in the Illustrations group.

e. In the Clip Art task pane, type **presenter** in the **Search for** box.

f. Click the **Results should be arrow,** remove the check marks from all media types except Photographs, and then click **Go**.

g. Click the image of the presenter in the red jacket, drag it to the lower right of your slide, and then close the Clip Art task pane.

The red jacket adds more color to the title slide. Your clip art gallery may have more images if you are connected to Microsoft Online, but you can drag the scroll bar to locate this image. Figure 2.38 indicates the image to click. Because the image is positioned on the lower right, the audience's eyes would flow down to the image after reading the title. The image is looking away, which leads their eyes off the slide—a visual clue that the slide is finished. If the image was placed higher on the slide, you would flip it so that it looks inward to the focal point, the title text. Figure 2.39 displays the completed slide.

h. Save the *chap2_ho4_guide_solution* presentation.

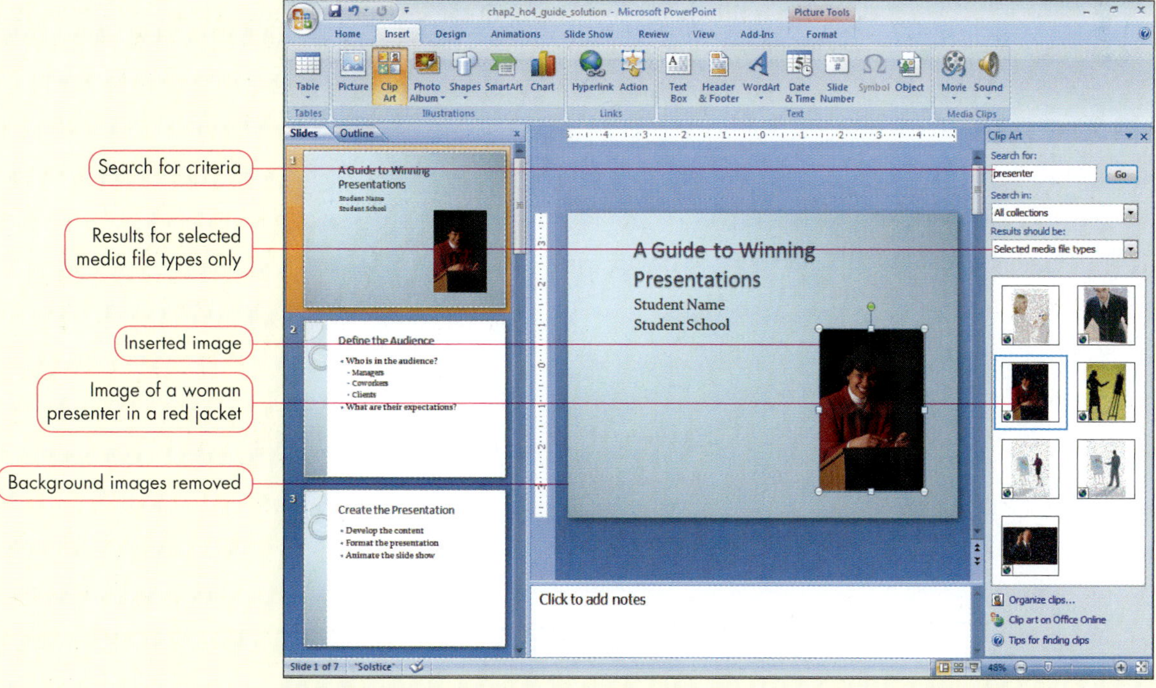

Figure 2.38 Background Image Removed and Clip Art Added

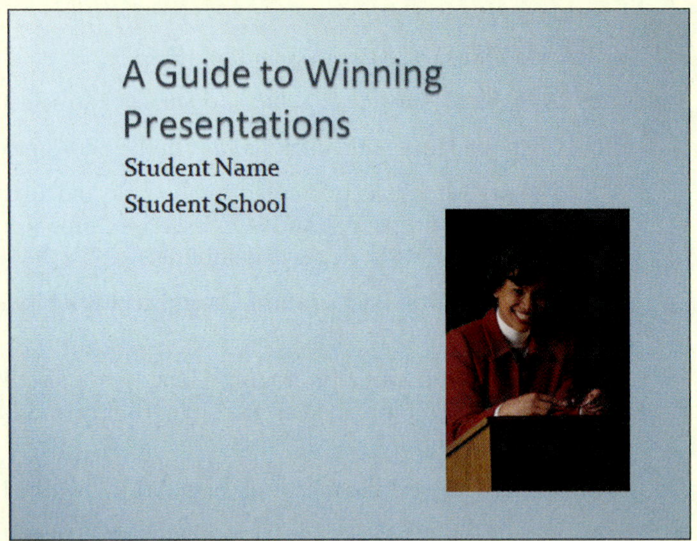

Figure 2.39 Modified Title Slide

Step 6
Save Current Theme

Refer to Figure 2.40 as you complete Step 6.

a. With *chap2_ho4_guide_solution* open, click **More** in the Themes group on the Design tab.

   To save time in the future, you save the theme you created when you customized the Solstice theme.

b. Click **Save Current Theme**.

c. Type **presenter_theme** in the **File name** box and click **Save**.

d. Click **More** in the Themes group on the Design tab.

   A new theme category has been added to the All Themes gallery—the Custom category.

e. Point at the theme displaying in the Custom category. Note the ScreenTip showing the theme name. This is the presenter_theme you just created.

f. Save the *chap2_ho4_guide_solution* presentation.

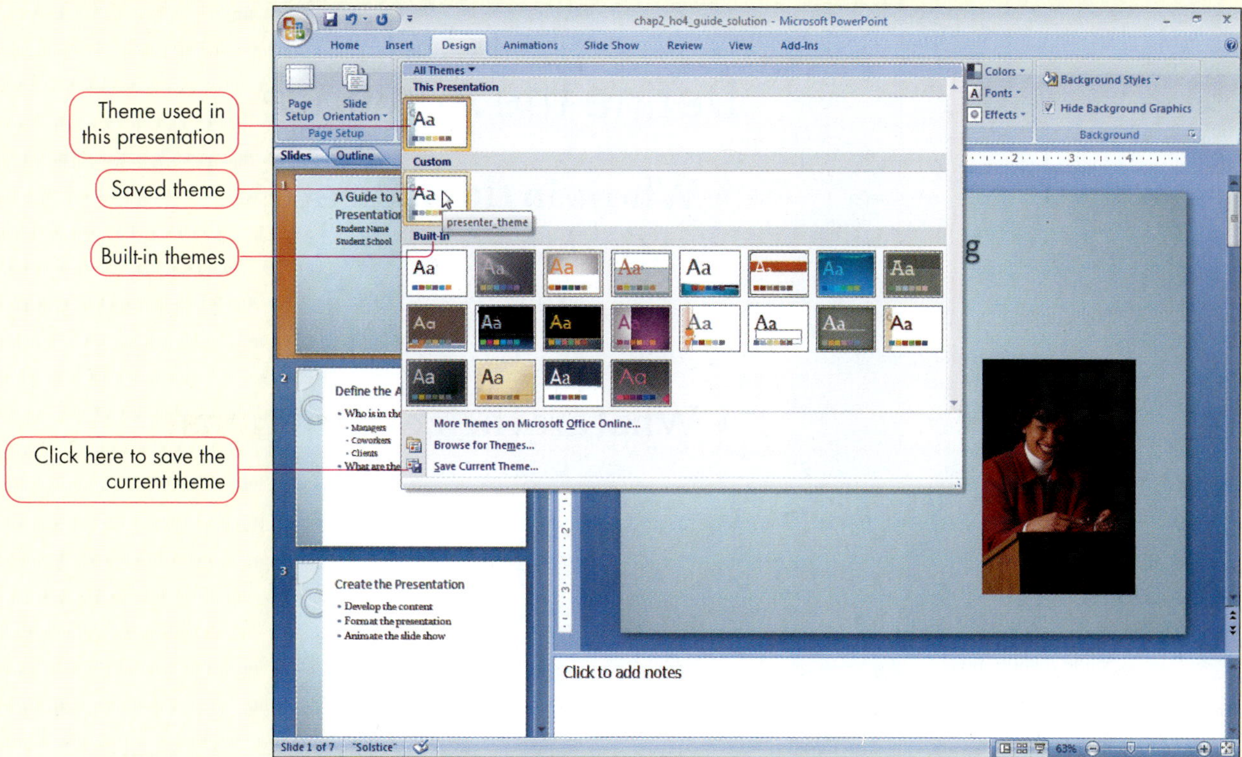

Figure 2.40 All Themes Gallery

Step 7 Create a Slide Footer

Refer to Figure 2.41 as you complete Step 7.

a. With *chap2_ho4_guide_solution* open, click the **Insert tab**, and then click **Header & Footer** in the Text group.

b. In the Header and Footer dialog box, click the **Date and time check box** in the *Include on slide* section.

c. Click **Update automatically**, if it is not already selected.

d. Click the **drop-down arrow** and select the fourth date format in the list.

   The fourth date format spells out the month and then includes the year, such as June 8, 2009.

e. Click the **Slide number check box**.

f. Click the **Don't show on title slide check box**.

   Clicking this check box adds a check mark hiding the footer on the title slide.

g. Click **Apply to All**.

h. Click the **Slide 1 thumbnail** to display the slide in the Slides pane.

   Notice that the footer does not appear on this slide because you selected the option to hide the footer on the title slide.

i. Save the *chap2_ho4_guide_solution* presentation.

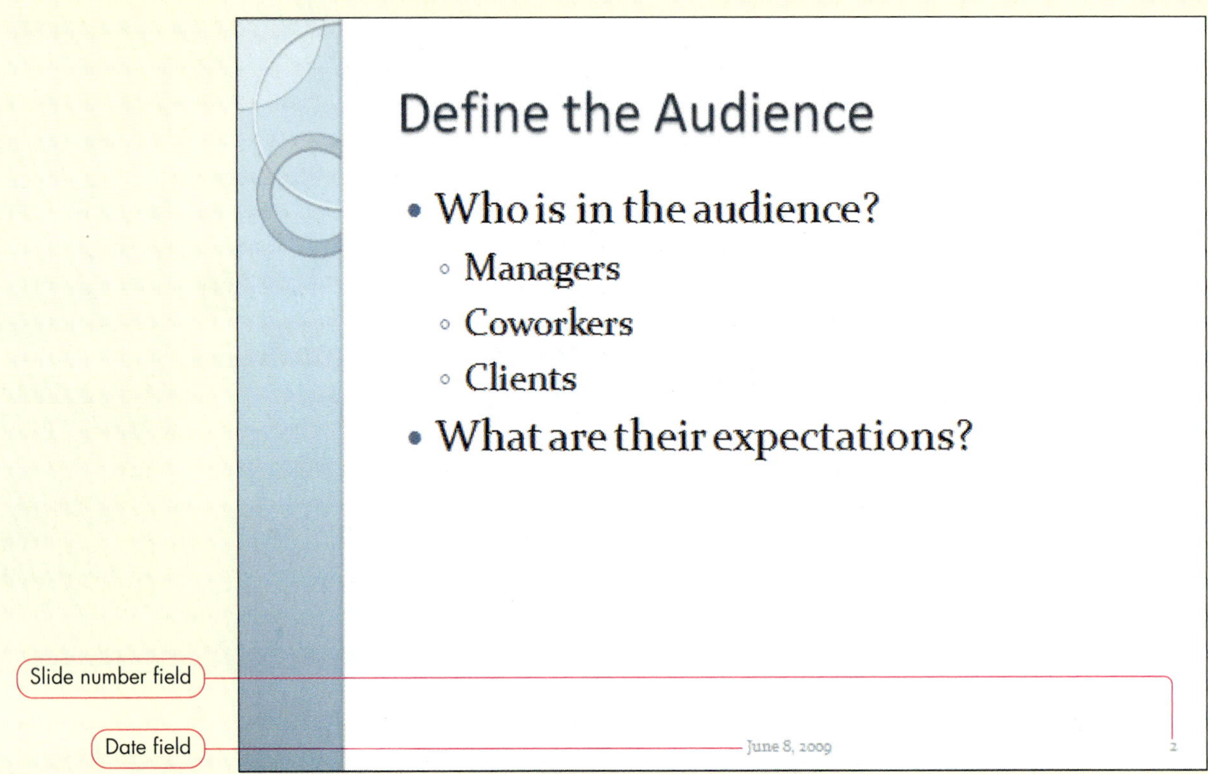

Figure 2.41 The Slide Footer

Step 8
Create a Handout Header and Footer

Refer to Figure 2.42 as you complete Step 8.

a. With *chap2_ho4_guide_solution* open, click the **Insert tab**, if necessary, and then click **Header & Footer** in the Text group.

b. Click the **Notes and Handouts tab**.

   In the previous exercise you created a footer that displays when the slide show plays. In this exercise you create a header and footer that only displays on printouts.

c. Click the **Date and time check box**.

d. Click **Update automatically**, if needed.

   By selecting the Update automatically option, you ensure that any printouts will display the current date and not the date the presentation originally was created.

e. Click the **drop-down arrow** and select the fourth date format in the list.

f. Click the **Header check box** and enter your name in the text box.

g. Click the **Footer check box** and enter your instructor's name and your class.

   Footers often are used for identifying information.

h. Click the **Apply to All button**.

i. Click the **Office Button**, point to **Print**, and then select **Print Preview**.

j. Change the *Print What* option to **Handouts (4 Slides Per Page)**.

k. Note the placement of the header, date, footer, and slide number. Click **Close Print Preview**.

l. Save the *chap2_ho4_guide_solution* presentation. Close the presentation.

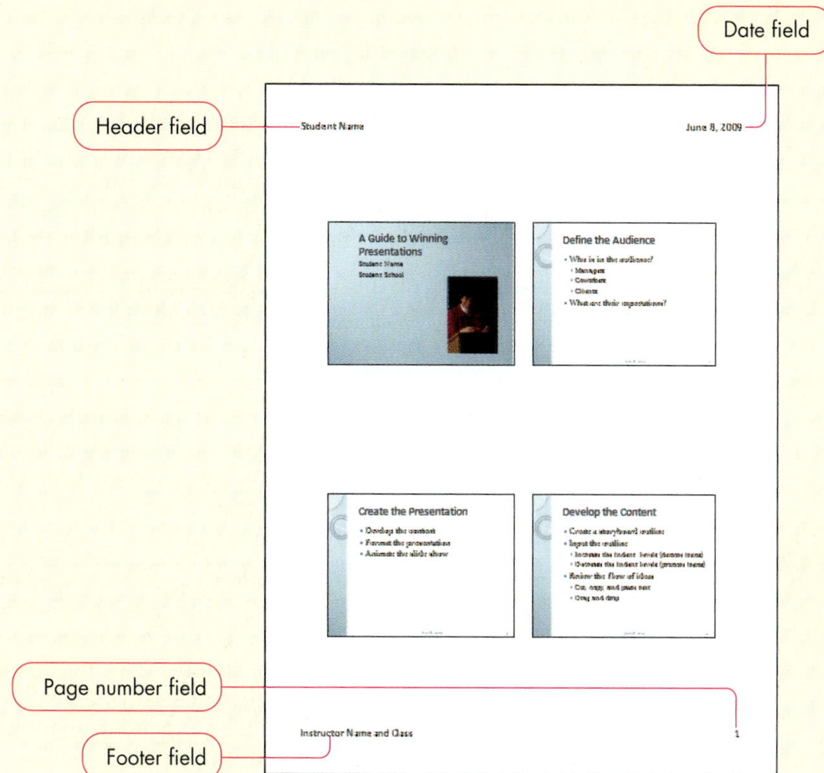

Figure 2.42 Handout Header and Footer

Summary

1. **Create a presentation using a template.** Using a template saves you a great deal of time and enables you to create a more professional presentation. Templates incorporate a theme, a layout, and content that can be modified. You can use templates that are installed when Microsoft Office is installed, or you can download templates from Microsoft Office Online. Microsoft is constantly adding templates to the online site for your use.

2. **Modify a template.** In addition to changing the content of a template, you can modify the structure and design. The structure is modified by changing the layout of a slide. To change the layout, drag placeholders to new locations or resize placeholders. You can even add placeholders so that elements such as logos can be included.

3. **Create a presentation in Outline view.** When you use a storyboard to determine your content, you create a basic outline. Then you can enter your presentation in Outline view, which enables you to concentrate on the content of the presentation. Using Outline view keeps you from getting buried in design issues at the cost of your content. It also saves you time because you can enter the information without having to move from placeholder to placeholder.

4. **Modify an outline structure.** Because the Outline view gives you a global view of the presentation, it helps you see the underlying structure of the presentation. You are able to see where content needs to be strengthened, or where the flow of information needs to be revised. If you find a slide with content that would be presented better in another location in the slide show, you can use the Collapse and Expand features to easily move it. By collapsing the slide content, you can drag it to a new location and then expand it. To move individual bullet points, cut and paste the bullet point or drag-and-drop it.

5. **Print an outline.** When you present, using the outline version of your slide show as a reference is a boon. No matter how well you know your information, it is easy to forget to present some information when facing an audience. While you would print speaker's notes if you have many details, you can print the outline as a quick reference. The outline can be printed in either the collapsed or the expanded form, giving you far fewer pages to shuffle in front of an audience than printing speaker's notes would.

6. **Import an outline.** You do not need to re-enter information from an outline created in Microsoft Word or another word processor. You can use the Open feature to import any outline that has been saved in a format that PowerPoint can read. In addition to a Word outline, you can use the common generic formats Rich Text Format and Plain Text Format.

7. **Add existing content to a presentation.** After you spend time creating the slides in a slide show, you may find that slides in the slide show would be appropriate in another show at a later date. Any slide you create can be reused in another presentation, thereby saving you considerable time and effort. You simply open the Reuse Slides pane, locate the slide show with the slide you need, and then click the thumbnail of the slide to insert a copy of it in the new slide show.

8. **Examine slide show design principles.** With a basic understanding of slide show design principles you can create presentations that reflect your personality in a professional way. The goal of applying these principles is to create a slide show that focuses the audience on the message of the slide without being distracted by clutter or unreadable text.

9. **Apply and modify a design theme.** PowerPoint provides you with themes to help you create a clean, professional look for your presentation. Once a theme is applied you can modify the theme by changing the color scheme, the font scheme, the effects scheme, or the background style.

10. **Insert a header or footer.** Identifying information can be included in a header or footer. You may, for example, wish to include the group to whom you are presenting, or the location of the presentation, or a copyright notation for original work. You can apply footers to slides, handouts, and Notes pages. Headers may be applied to handouts and Notes pages.

Key Terms

Background Styles gallery 896
Collapsed outline 881
Colors gallery 895
Effects gallery 895
Expanded outline 881
Fonts gallery 895
Footer .896
Header 896
Hierarchy 879
Layout 871
Outline 879
Outline view 879
Placeholder 871
Plain Text Format (.txt) 887
Rich Text Format (.rtf) 887
Sizing handle 872
Template 869

Multiple Choice

1. A file that incorporates a theme, a layout, and content that can be modified is known as a:
   (a) Hierarchy
   (b) Footer
   (c) Speaker note
   (d) Template

2. To create a presentation based on an installed template, click the:
   (a) File tab and then Open
   (b) Office Button and then New
   (c) Insert tab and then Add Template
   (d) Design tab and then New

3. What advantage, if any, is there to collapsing the outline so only the slide titles are visible?
   (a) More slides are displayed at one time, making it easier to rearrange the slides in the presentation.
   (b) Transition and animations can be added.
   (c) Graphical objects become visible.
   (d) All of the above

4. Which of the following is true?
   (a) Slides cannot be added to a presentation after a template has been chosen.
   (b) The slide layout must be changed before the template has been chosen.
   (c) Placeholders downloaded with a template cannot be modified.
   (d) The slide layout can be changed after the template has been chosen.

5. How do you insert identifying information on every slide in a presentation?
   (a) Click the Design tab and click Events.
   (b) Click the Insert tab and click Headers and Footers.
   (c) Click the View tab and click Headers and Footers.
   (d) Click the Home tab and click Events.

6. Which of the following is true?
   (a) PowerPoint supplies many different templates, but each template has only one color scheme.
   (b) You cannot change the color scheme of a presentation.
   (c) PowerPoint supplies many different templates, and each template in turn has multiple color schemes.
   (d) You cannot change a template once it has been selected.

7. Which of the following is the fastest and most efficient method for reusing a slide layout you have customized in another presentation?
   (a) Open the slide with the customized layout, delete the content, and enter the new information.
   (b) Open the slide with the customized layout and cut and paste the placeholders to a new slide.
   (c) Save the custom slide layout and reuse it in the new presentation.
   (d) Drag the placeholders from one slide to the next.

8. You own a small business and decide to institute an Employee of the Month award program. Which of the following would be the fastest way to create the award certificate with a professional look?
   (a) Access Microsoft Office Online and download an Award certificate template.
   (b) Select a Design Theme, modify the placeholders, and then enter the award text information.
   (c) Open Microsoft Word, insert a table, enter the award text in the table, and then add clip art.
   (d) Enter the text in the title placeholder of a slide, change the font for each line, and drag several clip art images of awards onto the slide.

9. Which of the following moves a bullet point from the first level to the second level in an outline?
   (a) Shift+Tab
   (b) Tab
   (c) Decrease List Level
   (d) Ctrl+Tab

10. The Increase List Level and Decrease List Level commands are available from which tab?
    (a) Home
    (b) Insert
    (c) Design
    (d) Slide Show

11. Which of the following formats cannot be imported to use as an outline for a presentation?
    (a) .docx
    (b) .rtf
    (c) .txt
    (d) .tiff

...continued on Next Page

Multiple Choice Continued...

12. You create a presentation for a local volunteer organization. When you arrive to present at its office, you find the room you are presenting in has many windows. Which of the following procedures should you follow?

(a) Change the theme of the presentation to a theme with a dark background.

(b) Change the background style to a dark background.

(c) Close the blinds to darken the room.

(d) Any of the above

13. Which of the following statements is a true text design guideline?

(a) Title text should be 36 pts or larger.

(b) Use underlining to emphasize key points.

(c) Create all titles in ALL CAPS.

(d) Bold all bullet points.

14. Which of the following is not a field in the Header and Footer dialog box?

(a) Date and time

(b) Slide number

(c) File name

(d) Footer

15. To add existing content to a presentation, use which of the following features?

(a) Duplicate Selected Slides

(b) Slides from Outline

(c) Reuse Slides

(d) All of the above

Practice Exercises

1 Download and Modify a Template

Figure 2.43 displays an Employee of the Year Award for Olsen Cabinets. It was created from a template downloaded from Microsoft Office Online. A small business owner who runs a cabinet shop might use an award program to motivate employees and could create this award quickly by downloading the template and modifying it. Assume you are the owner of Olsen Cabinets and you want to present your employee, Michael Mulhern, with the Employee of the Year Award.

a. Click the **Office Button** and then select **New**.
b. Click **Award certificates** in the Microsoft Office Online category.
c. Click the **Employee of the year award** and then click **Download**.
d. Save the file as **chap2_pe1_award_solution**.
e. Drag to select the text *Company Name*, and type **OLSEN CABINETS**.
f. Drag to select the text *EMPLOYEE NAME*, and type **Michael Mulhern**.
g. Select *Michael Mulhern* and move your pointer slightly upward to activate the Mini toolbar with text options.
h. Click **Bold**, and then click **Italic.**
i. Drag to select the text *Presenter's Name and Title*, and then enter your name and your class.
j. Save the *chap2_pe1_award_solution* file and close it.

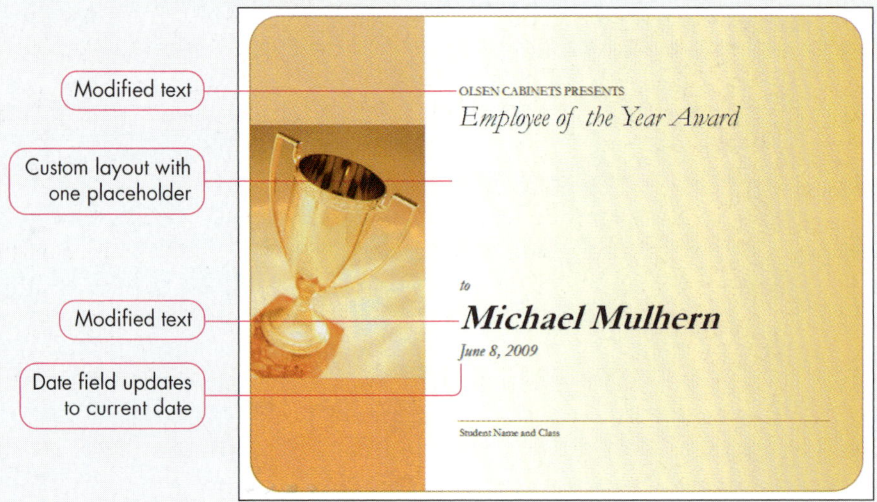

Figure 2.43 Download and Modify a Template

2 Create an Outline

The Wellness Education Center at your school promotes the overall wellness among students and employees. The center provides many services and needs to make the campus community aware of these services. You volunteer to create a presentation that can be shown to campus groups to inform them about the center and its mission. Figure 2.44 shows the outline of the presentation.

a. In a new presentation, click the **View tab** and then click **Normal** in the Presentation Views group (if necessary).
b. Click the **Outline tab.**
c. Type the title of your presentation, **Wellness Education Center**, and then press **Enter**.
d. Save the file as **chap2_pe2_center_solution**.
e. Click the **Home tab** and click **Increase List Level** in the Paragraph group.
f. Enter the first line of the subtitle, **Dedicated to.**

...continued on Next Page

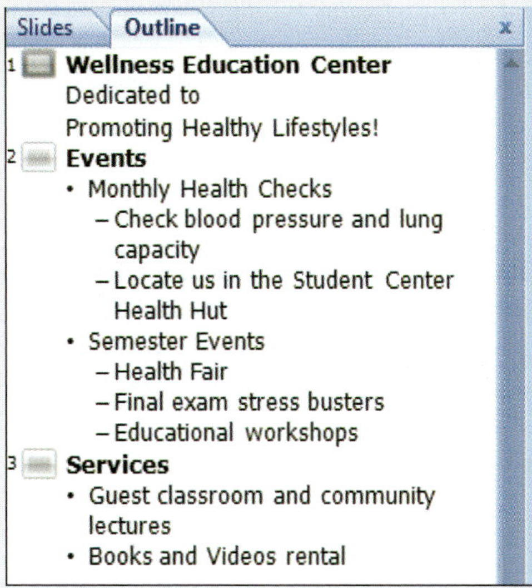

Figure 2.44 Create an Outline

g. Press **Shift+Enter** to move the insertion point to the next line of the subtitle placeholder.
h. Type the second line of the subtitle, **Promoting Healthy Lifestyles!**
i. Press **Enter** and then click **Decrease List Level** in the Paragraph group on the Home tab.
j. Type the title **Events** and then press **Enter**.
k. Press **Tab** and then type **Monthly Health Checks**.
l. Press **Enter** and then press **Tab**.
m. Type **Check blood pressure and lung capacity** and then press **Enter**.
n. Type **Locate us in the Student Center Health Hut** and then press **Enter**.
o. Press **Shift+Tab**.
p. Continue entering the text of the outline as shown in Figure 2.44.
q. Save the *chap2_pe2_center_solution* file and keep it onscreen if you plan to continue to the next exercise. Close the file and exit PowerPoint if you do not want to continue to the next exercise at this time.

3 Modify an Outline

The director at the Wellness Education Center reviews your outline. While she is pleased with its development thus far, she would like you to include more information about the Center Services, and she would like the services slide to be the second slide in the presentation. Figure 2.45 shows additional information in the outline.

a. Open the *chap2_pe2_center_solution* presentation if you closed it after the last exercise, and save it as **chap2_pe3_center_solution**.
b. Click the **Outline tab,** click at the end of the word *lectures* in Slide 3, and add **including:**
c. Proofread the bullet point you created and note that the word *including* is on a line by itself. To avoid this hanging line, remove the word *Guest* from the bullet and capitalize the word *Classroom*.
d. Position the insertion point at the end of the line, press **Enter** and then press **Tab**.
e. Type the following bullet points:
   - **Health and Fitness**
   - **Alcohol Use and Misuse**
   - **Substance/Drug Abuse**
f. Position the pointer over the bullet next to the text *Books and Videos rental* so that the pointer becomes a four-headed arrow, and then click to select the bullet.

...continued on Next Page

g. Replace the existing text by typing **Lending library**.
h. Press **Enter** and then press **Tab**.
i. Type the two bullet points for the *Lending library* as shown in Figure 2.45.
j. Right-click any line in the outline.
k. Select **Collapse**, and then select **Collapse All**.
l. Position the pointer over the slide icon for Slide 3, *Services*, and then drag *Services* above Slide 2.
m. Click the **Office Button**, point to **Print**, and then select **Print Preview**.
n. Click the **Print What arrow** in the Page Setup group, and select **Outline View**. Print the collapsed outline if directed to do so by your instructor.
o. Close Print Preview and return to the presentation.
p. Right-click any line in the outline.
q. Click **Expand** and then click **Expand All**.
r. Save the *chap2_pe3_center_solution* file and keep it onscreen if you plan to continue to the next exercise. Close the file and exit PowerPoint if you do not want to continue to the next exercise at this time.

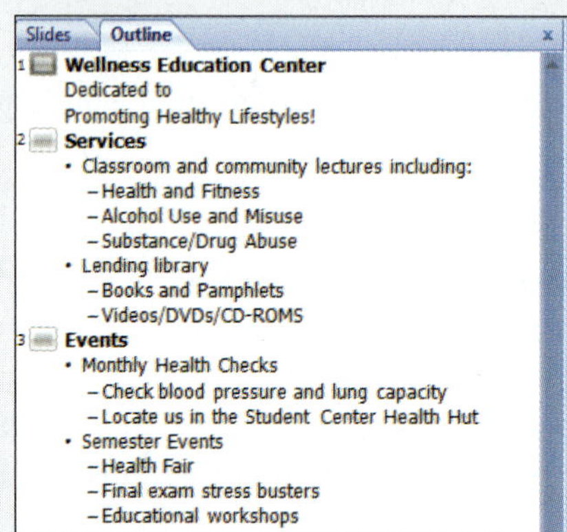

Figure 2.45 Modify an Outline

4 Add Existing Content

While reviewing the Wellness Center presentation you realize that you do not have an introduction slide or a summary slide. You remember another slide show that has slides that would fit well in this presentation. To save time and maintain consistency, you reuse these slides. Figure 2.46 shows the outline after inserting slides into the presentation.

a. Open the *chap2_pe3_center_solution* presentation if you closed it after the last exercise; then save it as **chap2_pe4_center_solution**.
b. Click the **Outline tab**, if necessary, and then click at the end of the word *Lifestyles* in Slide 1.
c. Click the **Home tab** and click **New Slide** in the Slides group.
d. Click **Reuse Slides** at the bottom of the gallery.
e. Click the **Browse button** that appears in the Reuse Slides task pane, click **Browse File**, and then navigate to the location of your student files.
f. Click to select the file *chap2_pe4_mission* and then click **Open**.
g. Click the Mission Statement thumbnail to enter it in your presentation as Slide 2.
h. Position your point of insertion at the end of your outline and then click the thumbnail for the remaining slide in the presentation, the slide beginning *We strive. . . .*
i. Close the Reuse Slides task pane.
j. Save the *chap2_pe4_center_solution* file and keep it onscreen if you plan to continue to the next exercise. Close the file and exit PowerPoint if you do not want to continue to the next exercise at this time.

...continued on Next Page

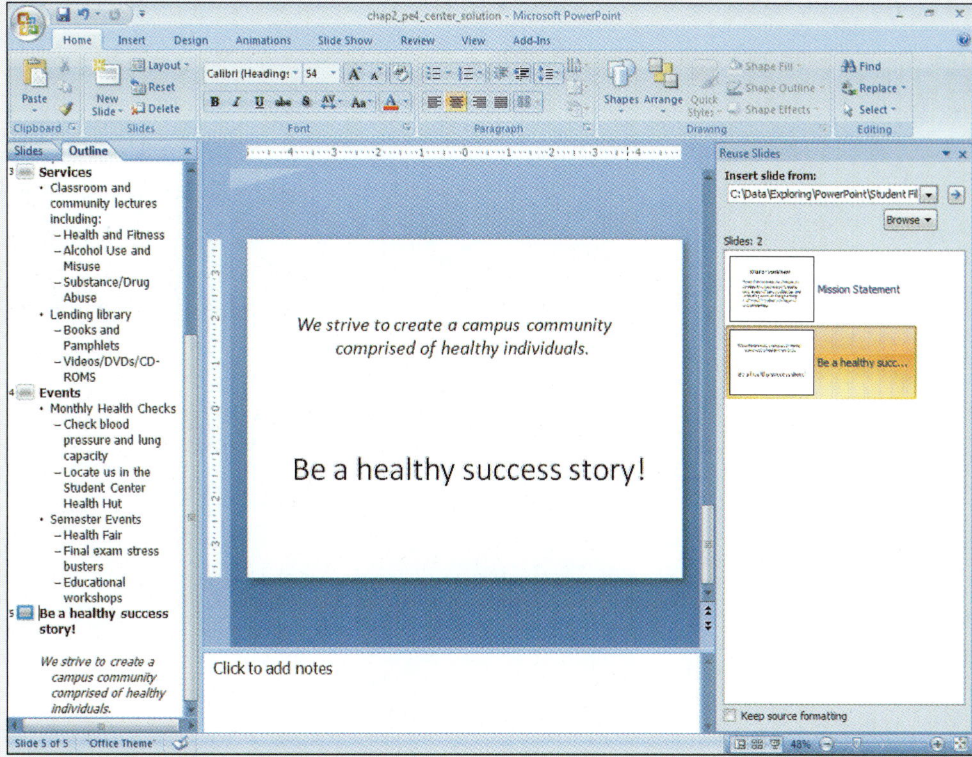

Figure 2.46 Add Existing Content

5 Apply and Modify a Theme

Both you and the director of the Wellness Education Center are satisfied with the content of the presentation, so now you concentrate on the design of the presentation. The director of the center specifies that she would like a calming blue background and a clean look. After you are satisfied with the design, you save it for future presentations you create for the center. Figure 2.47 shows the slide show after changing the theme and background color.

a. Open the *chap2_pe4_center_solution* presentation if you closed it after the last exercise; then save it as **chap2_pe5_center_solution**.
b. Click the **Design tab** and click the **More button** in the Themes group on the Design tab.
c. Click the **Trek theme**.
d. Click **Colors** in the Themes group on the Design tab.
e. Click the **Flow color scheme**.
f. Click **Fonts** in the Themes group on the Design tab.
g. Click the **Opulent font scheme**, which applies the Trebuchet MS font to the title and content placeholders.
h. Click **Background Styles** in the Background group on the Design tab.
i. Click **Style 11**.
j. Click the **More button** in the Themes group on the Design tab.
k. Click **Save Current Theme**.
l. Enter **wellness_theme** in the *File name* box and then click **Save**.
m. Save the *chap2_pe5_center_solution* file and keep it onscreen if you plan to continue to the next exercise. Close the file and exit PowerPoint if you do not want to continue to the next exercise at this time.

...continued on Next Page

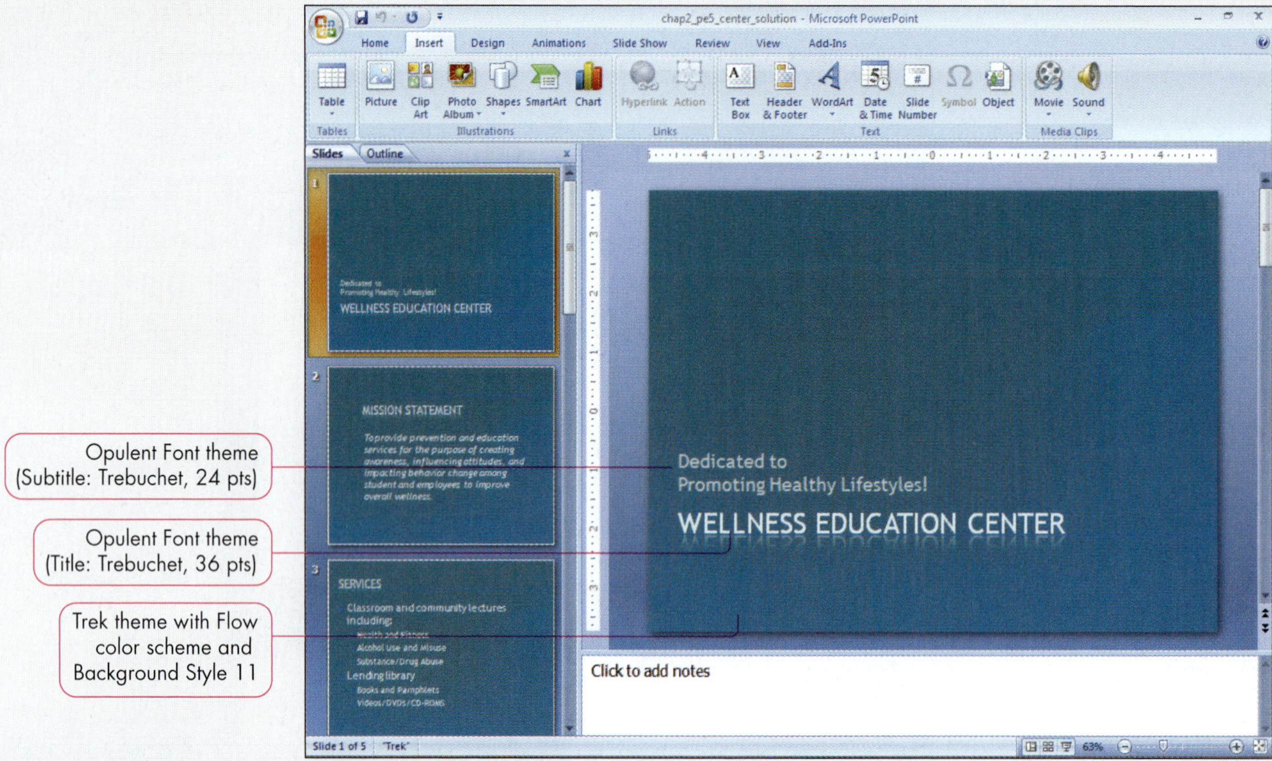

Figure 2.47 Apply and Modify a Theme

6 Create a Header and a Footer

The director of the Wellness Education Center wants to show the presentation to a colleague at a conference she is attending. Because the director does not want to bring a laptop computer on the plane, you prepare a printout using a handout format. You add a header and footer to the presentation with identifying information before printing. Figure 2.48 shows one slide with the footer, and Figure 2.49 shows the notes and handouts printout.

a. Open the *chap2_pe5_center_solution* presentation if you closed it after the last exercise; then save it as **chap2_pe6_center_solution**.
b. Click the **Insert tab** and then click **Header & Footer** in the Text group on the Insert tab.
c. Click the **Slide number check box** to insert a slide number on each slide in the presentation.
d. Click the **Footer check box** and type **Wellness Education Center**.
e. Click the **Don't show on title slide check box**, if necessary. The footer is not necessary on the title slide.
f. Click **Apply to All**. Note that this Microsoft theme moves the footer text to the top of the slide.
g. Click the **Insert tab** and click **Header & Footer** in the Text group.
h. Click the **Notes and Handouts tab**.
i. Click the **Date and time check box**.
j. Click **Update Automatically** and then click the **drop-down arrow**.
k. Click the sixth date format in the list, which is the name of the month and the last two digits of the year.
l. Click the **Header check box** and then enter your name (your name represents the director's name) in the text box.
m. Click the **Footer check box** and type **Wellness Education Center**.
n. Click **Apply to All**. Note also that the theme has a very slight change in color between the background and the Footer text causing the Footer to be almost hidden.

...continued on Next Page

o. Click the **Office Button**, point to **Print**, and then select **Print Preview**.
p. Change the **Print What** option to **Handouts** (6 slides per page).
q. Click **Print** if directed to do so by your instructor or click **Close Print Preview**.
r. Save the *chap2_pe6_center_solution* file and close the file.

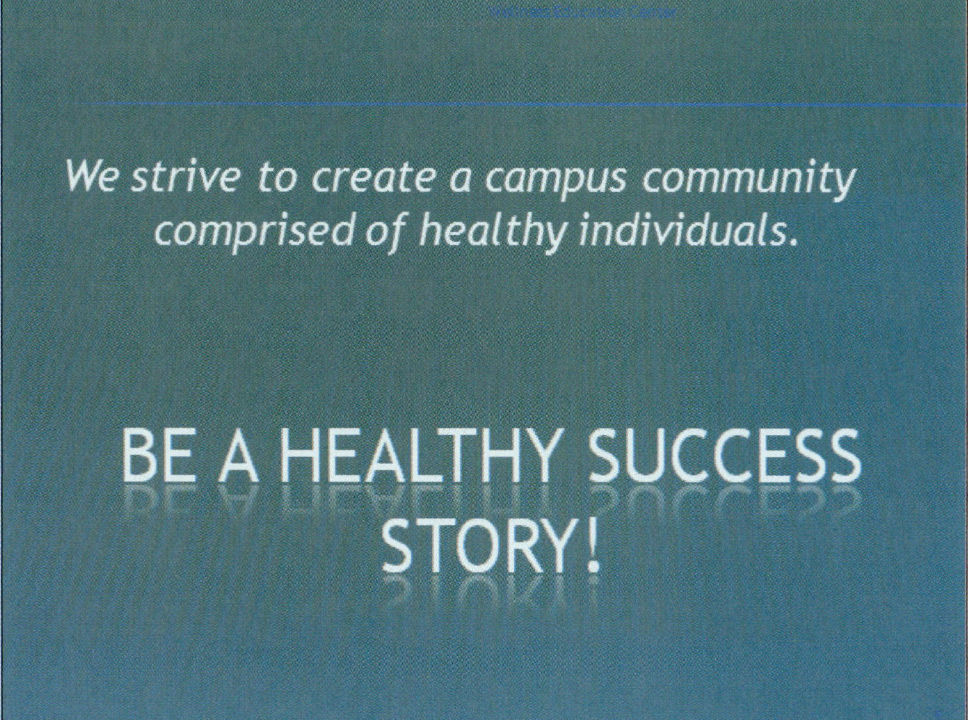

Figure 2.48 Wellness Center Slide with Footer in Blue at Top of Slide

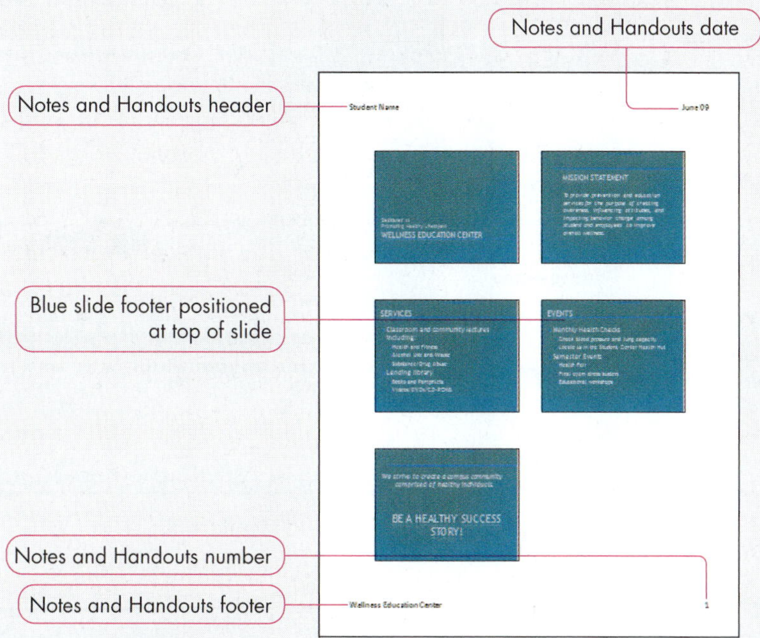

Figure 2.49 Wellness Center Handout

Mid-Level Exercises

1 USDA Food Pyramid

You have been asked to help in a local elementary school. The teacher would like you to teach the children about nutrition and healthy eating. You decide to create a presentation about the U.S. Department of Agriculture (USDA)–recommended food pyramid. (Visit http://www.mypyramid.gov.) You locate a Microsoft Office Online template based on the food pyramid that will help you organize the presentation. Figure 2.50 displays the downloaded template, and Figure 2.51 displays the conclusion slide of your presentation.

a. Download the **Food pyramid presentation**, which is available from Microsoft Office Online. It can be found in the Presentations category, Healthcare subcategory. Immediately save it as **chap2_mid1_pyramid_solution**.

b. Move to **Slide 2** and copy only the text from the lower placeholder on the slide, and then paste it into the notes area. After reading the content tips on the template slides, you think they would make excellent speaker notes for you to refer to when presenting. As you create each new slide in the rest of the exercise, copy the information on the slide and paste it to the notes as you did in this step.

c. Type the following bullet points. The completed slide is displayed in Figure 2.50.

- **Choosing the right foods helps you feel better**
- **Eating a good diet keeps you healthier**

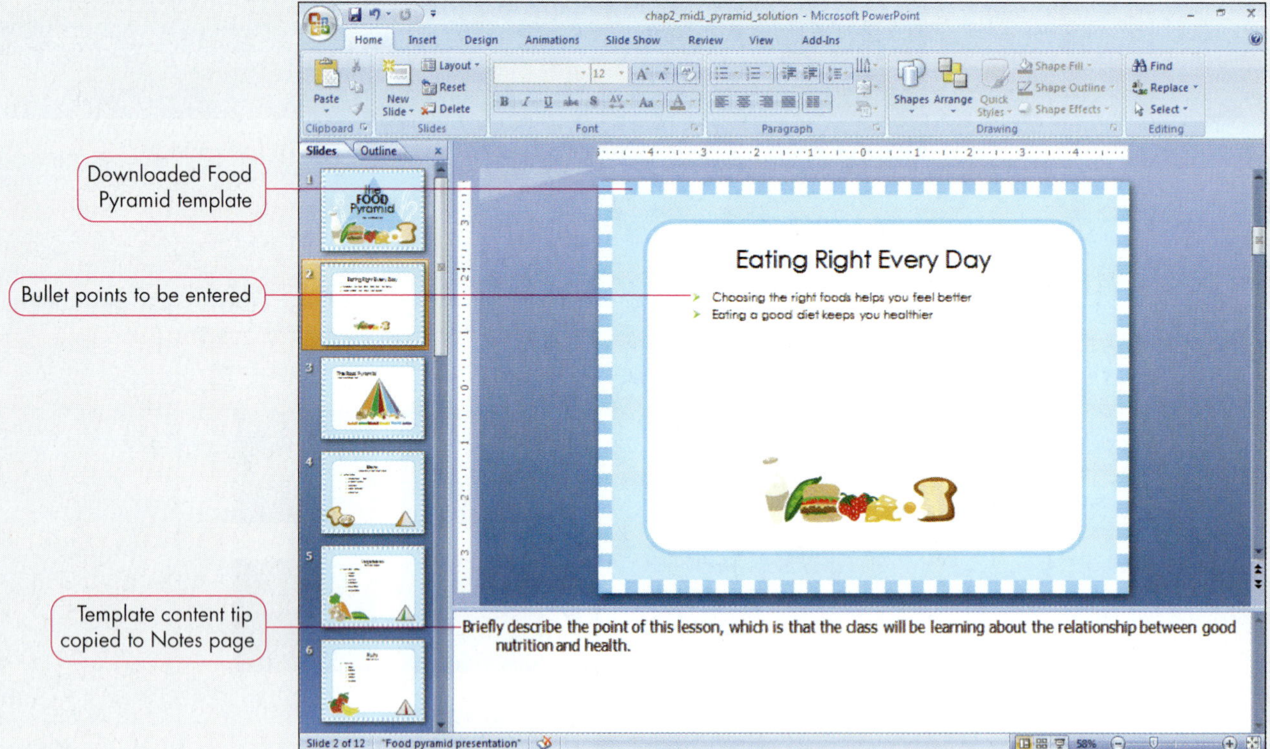

Figure 2.50 Food Pyramid Content Slide

...continued on Next Page

d. Move to **Slide 4** and type the following bullet points.

- **Great grains!**
  - **Whole-wheat flour**
  - **Cracked wheat**
  - **Oatmeal**
  - **Whole cornmeal**
  - **Brown rice**

e. Make changes to the slides as shown below.

Slide	Level 1 Bullet	Level 2 Bullets
5	Very Cool Veggies!	Broccoli Spinach Carrots Cauliflower Mushrooms Green beans
6	Fresh Fruit!	Apples Bananas Grapes Peaches Oranges
7	Only a Little Oil!	Sunflower oil Margarine Butter Mayonnaise (food containing oil)
8	Magnificent Milk!	Milk Cheese Yogurt Pudding
9	Mighty Meats and Beans!	Chicken Turkey Beef Pork Fish Beans and nuts
10	Provide bonus calories to give you energy Use for: Eat more than advised and you will gain weight.	Eating more of the foods on the list Eating higher calorie food
12	Use the MyPyramid Worksheet provided by the USDA.	
13	Follow the Food Pyramid Steps for a healthier you!	

...continued on Next Page

f. Delete **Slide 11**.

g. Change the layout for **Slide 12,** the conclusion, to a Title Slide format.

h. Delete the graphic box with the white background that was left over when you changed the layout.

i. Check the spelling of your presentation, and ignore any references to MyPyramid, the USDA worksheet name.

j. Create a handout header with your name, and a handout footer with your instructor's name and your class time. Print as required by your instructor.

k. Save the *chap2_mid1_pyramid_solution* file and close the file.

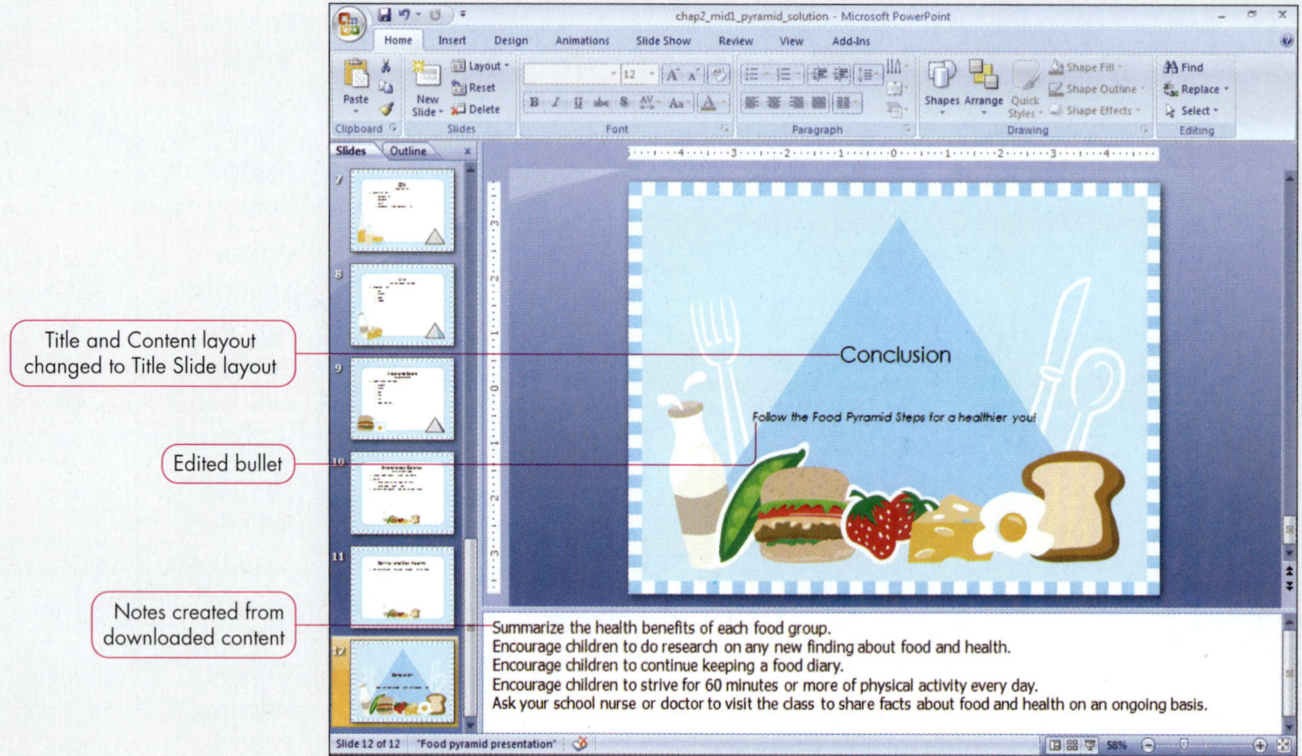

Figure 2.51 Food Pyramid Conclusion

2 Go-Digital

The local senior citizen's center has asked you to speak on photography. The center has many interested seniors—but the center has indicated to you that the seniors are unsure about whether they want information on traditional photography or digital photography. You feel that digital photography would be a good option for amateur photographers, so you decide to slant the presentation in favor of digital photography. Figure 2.52 shows the completed presentation.

a. Save a blank presentation as **chap2_mid2_digital_solution**.

b. Type the title **Go Digital, Get Creative!** so that it is on two lines in the title placeholder. Enter your name in the subtitle placeholder.

...continued on Next Page

c. Use the Outline view to create these slides.

- **Why Go Digital?**
  - **Inexpensive**
  - **Improved pictures**
  - **Instant feedback**
  - **Image sharing**
- **Inexpensive**
  - **No film cost**
  - **Free experimentation**
  - **Cameras in all price ranges**
- **Improved Pictures**
  - **Image editing with software**
    - **Remove red eye**
    - **Improve exposure**
    - **Crop the pictures**
  - **Free experimentation**
    - **Take extra pictures for practice**
    - **Try new camera settings**
- **Instant Feedback**
  - **Viewing screen**
- **Image Sharing**
  - **Traditional**
  - **Web pages/Online photo albums**
  - **E-mail**

d. Review the presentation in Outline view and note that *Free experimentation* appears in two locations, that the Instant feedback slide does not have enough information to be a slide on its own, and that the presentation does not contain a conclusion slide.

e. Move the two bullets under *Free experimentation* on **Slide 4** to the correct location on **Slide 3,** and then delete the *Free experimentation* bullet in **Slide 4**.

f. Move the information in **Slide 5** so that it becomes the first bullet point in Slide 4.

g. Spell-check your presentation.

h. Save the *chap2_mid2_digital_solution* presentation and close the file.

i. Download the **Seasons in sage** design template, which is located on Microsoft Office Online in the Design slides category, Nature subcategory.

j. Display the New Slide gallery and click **Slides from Outline**.

k. Browse to where you save your files, change *Files of type* to **All Files**, and then insert your *chap2_mid2_digital_solution* presentation.

l. Drag **Slide 1** so that it becomes the last slide of the presentation, and then type **Go Digital:** in the title placeholder, and **Unleash Your Creativity!** in the subtitle placeholder.

m. Create a handout header with your name, and a handout footer with your instructor's name and your class. Print as required by your instructor.

n. Save the **chap2_mid2_digital_solution** presentation and click **Yes** when asked if you wish to replace the original file. Close the file.

...continued on Next Page

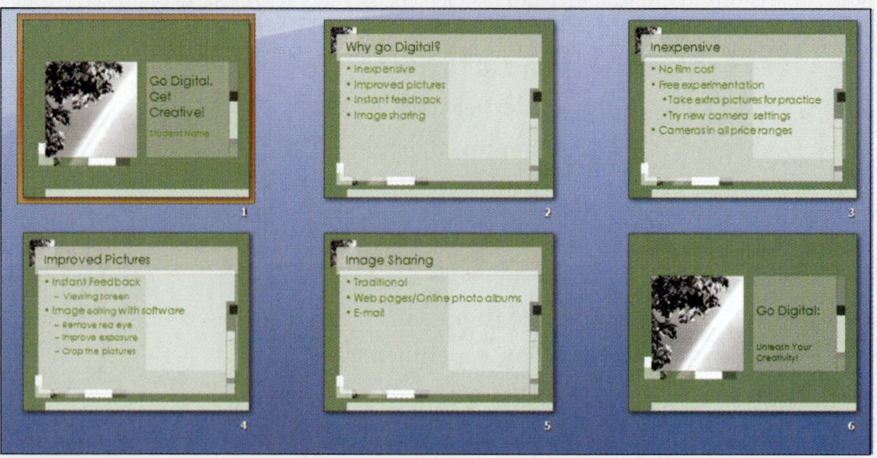

Figure 2.52 Go Digital Presentation with Seasons in Sage Template

3 The Impressionists

The paintings of the Impressionists are some of the most loved paintings in the world. Their paintings may be viewed by going to the Web page of the WebMuseum, Paris (www.ibiblio.org/wm), navigating to the Famous Artworks collections page, and then navigating to the Impressionism page. The museum is maintained by Nicolas Pioch and is not part of any official or supported project. He maintains the site for your pleasure and his. In a continuing project throughout this text you create an album celebrating the Impressionists and their works. Figure 2.53 shows the completed slide show in the Slide Sorter view.

a. Save a blank presentation as **chap2_mid3_impressionists_solution**.

b. Type the title **Impressionism**, and then enter your name in the subtitle place holder.Also include the following text in the subtitle placeholder: **All images may be viewed at The Web Museum**. (You will insert the hyperlink for the WebMuseum in a later project.)

c. Use the Outline view to create these slides.

- **Impressionist Paintings**
  - **Characterized by small brush strokes**
  - **Reproduced the artist's visual impression**
  - **Studied**
    - **Light**
    - **Atmosphere**
    - **Reflections**
    - **Color**
  - **Impressionist Artists**
    - **Claude Monet**
    - **Pierre-Auguste Renoir**
    - **Berthe Morisot**
    - **Edgar Degas**

d. Apply the **Flow theme**.

e. Apply the **Metro color theme**.

f. Insert the **Oriel font theme**. If the font theme doesn't apply to the inserted slides, manually apply the same fonts and font sizes to these slides to match the other slides.

...continued on Next Page

g. Insert the *chap2_mid3_artists* Word outline after the last slide in your presentation.

h. Rearrange the bullets in **Slide 3** so the artists are listed alphabetically by last name.

i. Collapse the outline and move **Slides 4–7** so they are listed alphabetically by last name, and then expand the outline.

j. Create a conclusion slide using the Content with Caption layout.

k. Modify the conclusion slide layout by deleting the text placeholder on the left and moving the title placeholder so that its bottom border is even with the bottom border of the large content placeholder.

l. Leave the audience with one last thought about Impressionism by entering the following text in the title placeholder on the conclusion slide: **Work at the same time on sky, water, branches, ground, keeping everything going on an equal basis . . . Don't be afraid of putting on colour . . . Paint generously and unhesitatingly, for it is best not to lose the first impression. Camille Pissarro.**

m. Italicize the Pissarro name.

n. Spell-check your presentation.

o. Create a handout header with your name, and a handout footer with your instructor's name and your class. Print as required by your instructor.

p. Save the *chap2_mid3_impressionists_solution* presentation and close the file.

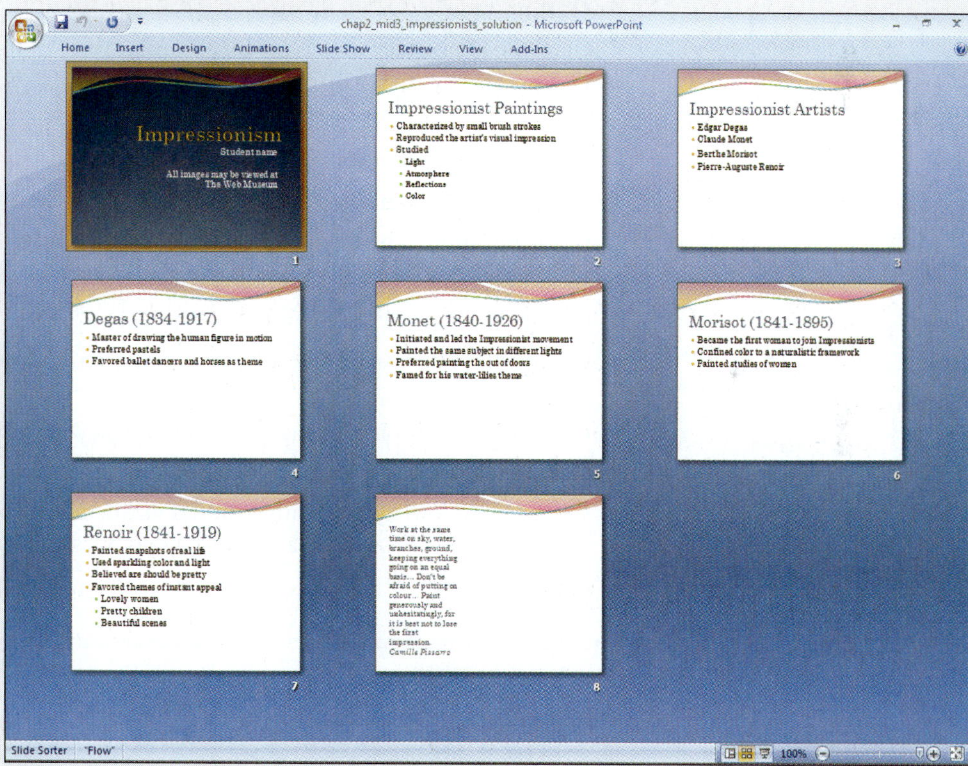

Figure 2.53 Impressionist Presentation in Slide Sorter View

4 Audience Analysis

Your community is experiencing a strong economic growth pattern, and part of this growth is because new business is encouraged and supported. Part of the support structure includes a city-sponsored Small Business Development Center (SBDC). One way the SBDC helps encourage small business owners and future business owners is to provide training on a wide variety of

...continued on Next Page

topics such as developing business plans, refining strategies, and overcoming challenges. A small business owner has requested the next training session cover giving presentations.

The SBDC maintains a list of local speakers, and as a humorous, popular speaker you are invited to address this group. You question the person issuing the invitation about the audience and find out you will be presenting to a small casual group of 8 to 10 men and women over lunch in a very informal room with no windows. You may bring your notebook computer and connect it to the center's projector. When you ask what the audience wants to get from your presentation, the SBDC representative tells you that the attendees want to know how to relax as they present. He adds that since it is a break in the middle of a busy day for them, they will probably be laughing and joking a lot. You decide to begin your presentation by addressing what you believe is the key to being a successful speaker—understanding the audience, but to do it in a humorous way. You want to show them that if a speaker knows his or her material well and analyzes the audience well, the speaker can relax while presenting and still be able to inject personality into the presentation. You also decide to create speaker notes to distribute to the group so that they can see how jotting down ideas of what to say in speaker notes can help them plan what to say to fill in around the bullet points. Figure 2.54 shows the completed slide show in Slide Sorter view.

a. Open *chap2_mid4_audience* and save it as **chap2_mid4_audience_solution**.
b. Read the Note at the bottom of Slide 1 and notice that this is a good location to keep track of when and where a presentation will be given. Move to **Slide 2** and switch to **Outline View**.
c. Click the **Home tab**, click **New Slide**, and then click **Reuse Slides**.
d. Use **Browse** in the Reuse Slides task pane and open *chap2_mid4_analysis*.
e. Insert the second slide of the *chap2_mid4_analysis* into the current slideshow and then close the Reuse Slides task pane.
f. Click the **Home tab**, click **Layout**, and then click **Comparison**.
g. Click the **Home tab**, **New Slide**, and then click **Slides from Outline**.
h. Insert the *chap2_mid4_outline* file.
i. Change the **Layout** of Slide 4 to **Title and Content**.
j. Change the title font on the slides you imported to **Comic Sans MS** and the bullets to **Calibri**.
k. Change the font color for the titles and bullets you imported to black.
l. Change **Background Styles** to **Style 5**.
m. Create a handout header with your name, and a handout footer with your instructor's name and your class. Print as required by your instructor.
n. Save the *chap2_mid 4_audience_solution* presentation and close the file.

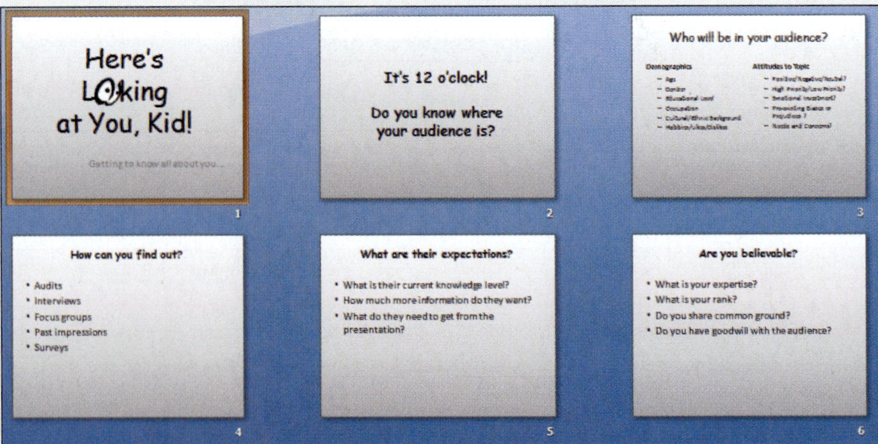

Figure 2.54 Audience Analysis Presentation in Slide Sorter View

Capstone Exercise

Your neighbors in your small southwestern subdivision are concerned about drought, fire danger, and water conservation. You volunteer to gather information about possible solutions and share the information with them at the next neighborhood association meeting. You decide a PowerPoint presentation would be an excellent way to inform them of their options. In this capstone project, you concentrate on developing the content. In later chapter capstone projects, you will enhance the project with illustrations, images, charts, and hyperlinks.

Design Template

You download a Microsoft Office Online template to create the basic design and structure for your presentation, name the presentation, and create the title slide.

a. Download the **Sun spots** design template from Microsoft Office Online, Design slides category, Abstract subcategory, Shapes subcategory.

b. Save the presentation with the file name **chap2_cap_waterwise_solution**.

c. Type **Conserve** as the title on the title slide. Reduce the font size of the title until it fits on one line.

d. Type the subtitle **Waterwise Landscaping**.

Outline and Modifications

Based on the storyboard you created after researching water conservation on the Internet, you create the outline for your presentation. As you create the outline, you also modify the outline structure.

a. Click the **Outline tab**.

b. Type **Waterwise Options** as the title for Slide 2.

c. Enter each of the following as Level 1 bullets for Slide 2: **Zeroscaping, Xeriscaping**

d. Type **Purpose of Landscaping** as the title for Slide 3.

e. Type each of the following as Level 1 bullets for Slide 3: **Beauty, Utility, Conservation**.

f. Add this speaker note to Slide 3: **With water becoming a limited resource, conservation has become a third purpose of landscaping.**

g. Modify the outline structure by reversing Slides 2 and 3.

Imported Outline

You originally started your task intending to hold two information sessions for your neighbors. You began by creating an outline on zeroscaping in Microsoft Word. You determined that using a PowerPoint slide show would let you show images, so you create a slide show on xeriscaping. After going to this work, however, you decide that it is better to make the comparison in one presentation so that homeowners are more easily able to see the overall picture. You do not want to lose the work you have already done, so you import the zeroscaping outline and reuse the xeriscaping slides.

a. Position the point of insertion at the end of the outline.

b. Use the **Slides from Outline option** to insert the *chap2_cap_zeroscaping* outline.

c. Change the layout of Slide 4 from Title and Content slide to Picture with Caption so that you may insert a picture illustrating zeroscaping later.

d. Position the point of insertion at the end of the outline.

e. Use the appropriate option to reuse slides from *chap2_cap_xeriscaping*.

f. Insert all the slides from *chap2_cap_xeriscaping*.

Design

When you preview the slide show, you note that a lack of contrast makes the text difficult to read. You decide to change the color theme and font scheme to increase the visibility of the text. You realize that you may want to use this changed theme in later presentations, so you save the theme.

a. Change the color theme to **Solstice**.

b. Change the font theme to **Trek**.

TROUBLESHOOTING: If the Picture and Caption layouts in Slides 4 and 8 do not accept the new font change because they were imported, change the caption font to Franklin Gothic Medium, 36 pts. Change the subtitle font to Franklin Gothic Medium, 32 pts.

c. Click the **More button** in the Themes group on the Design tab.

d. Save the current theme as ***heat_theme***.

e. Spell-check the presentation.

f. Apply the **Fade Through Black animation scheme** to all slides.

g. Create a handout header with your name, and a handout footer with your instructor's name and your class. Print as required by your instructor.

h. Save the *chap2_cap_waterwise_solution* presentation and close the file. Exit PowerPoint if you do not want to continue to the mini-cases at this time.

Mini Cases

Use the rubric following the case as a guide to evaluate your work, but keep in mind that your instructor may impose additional grading criteria or use a different standard to judge your work.

Identity Theft

GENERAL CASE

The partially completed *chap2_mc1_identity* presentation is intended to aid you in recognizing the global value of the outline view and how it can be used to modify the structure of a presentation. A combination of slides containing only titles and slides containing content are randomly entered as if they were created from brainstorming. Organize the presentation so there is content under each topic and that the content matches the topic in the slide title. Create an appropriate conclusion. You may add additional slides, if desired. Good resources for your presentation include the Federal Trade Commission Web site (www.consumer.gov/idtheft) and the Social Security Online Electronic Fact Sheet (www.ssa.gov/pubs/idtheft.htm).

Be sure to spell-check and carefully proof-read the content of the presentation. Save the presentation as **chap2_mc1_identity_solution**. Locate a template to use for the design and reuse the *chap2_mc1_identity_solution* presentation slides to create a new presentation. Apply a font scheme, color scheme, and background style as desired. You also may modify layouts. Add appropriate clip art to at least two slides. Remember the design guidelines as you insert the clip art. Match the colors of the clips to your background and try to locate clips that are similar—do not apply a cartoon-like clip on one slide and a professional clip on another. Apply a transition to all slides, and add a custom animation to the clip art you added. Create a handout header with your name, and a handout footer with the file name, your instructor's name, and your class. Print as directed by your instructor. Save the file as **chap2_mc1_identity_solution**, and click Yes when asked if you want to save over the original file.

Performance Elements	Exceeds Expectations	Meets Expectations	Below Expectations
Organization	Presentation is easy to follow because information is presented in a logical, interesting sequence.	Presentation is generally easy to follow.	Presentation cannot be understood because there is no sequence of information.
Visual aspects	Presentation background, themes, clip art, and animation are appealing and enhance the understanding of presentation purpose and content.	Clip art is related to topic.	The background, theme, or animation is distracting to the topic.
	There is a consistent visual theme.	Animation is not distracting.	Clip art does not enhance understanding of the content or is unrelated.
Layout	The layout is visually pleasing and contributes to the overall message with appropriate use of headings, subheadings, bullet points, clip art, and white space.	The layout shows some structure, but placement of some headings, subheadings, bullet points, clip art, and/or white space can be improved.	The layout is cluttered and confusing. Placement of headings, subheadings, bullet points, clip art, and/or white spaces detracts from readability.
Mechanics	Presentation has no errors in spelling, grammar, word usage, or punctuation.	Presentation has no more than one error in spelling, grammar, word usage, or punctuation.	Presentation readability is impaired due to repeated errors in spelling, grammar, word usage, or punctuation.
	Bullet points are parallel.	Bullet points are inconsistent in one slide.	Most bullet points are not parallel.

Accuracy Counts

RESEARCH CASE

You have a bright, creative, and energetic personality and you are using these talents in college as a senior majoring in Digital Film within the Multimedia Communication Technology Department. You hope to become a producer for a major film company, following the footsteps of your grandfather. This term you are taking MCT 4000: Administration of Studio Operations. The final project requires every student to create his or her own feature film company and present an overview of the company to the class. The presentation is to be in the form of an employee orientation: It should include the company purpose, the company's history, past and present projects, and a final slide giving the resources you used to create your presentation. Your instructor asks you to write notes for each slide.

The assignment was given at the beginning of the semester with the understanding that it would be developed as the topics were presented. It is now the end of the semester, and you, a creative procrastinator by nature, are in a real bind. You have 24 hours to complete the entire presentation before presenting it to the class. You remember Microsoft Office Online Templates and wonder if it has a template you can use. Using **film** as your keyword, search Microsoft Office Online for templates and then download a template to use in creating your presentation. You will, however, have to research what a feature film company does and add your own content to comply with the case requirements. Add clip art, transitions, and animations as desired. Create a handout header with your name, and a handout footer with your instructor's name and your class time. Print as directed by your instructor. Save the presentation as **chap2_mc2_film_solution**.

Performance Elements	Exceeds Expectations	Meets Expectations	Below Expectations
Organization	Presentation indicates accurate research and significant facts. Evidence exists that information has been evaluated and synthesized showing an understanding of the topic.	Presentation indicates some research has taken place and that information was included in the content.	Presentation demonstrates a lack of research or understanding of the topic. Content is misinterpreted or incorrect.
Visual aspects	Presentation background, themes, clip art, and animation are appealing and enhance the understanding of presentation purpose and content.	Clip art is related to the topic.	The background or theme is distracting to the topic.
	There is a consistent visual theme.	Animation is not distracting.	Clip art does not enhance understanding of the content or is unrelated.
Layout	The layout is visually pleasing and contributes to the overall message with appropriate use of headings, subheadings, bullet points, clip art, and white space.	The layout shows some structure, but placement of some headings, subheadings, bullet points, clip art, and/or white space can be improved.	The layout is cluttered and confusing. Placement of headings, subheadings, bullet points, clip art, and/or white spaces detracts from readability.
Mechanics	Presentation has no errors in spelling, grammar, word usage, or punctuation.	Presentation has no more than one error in spelling, grammar, word usage, or punctuation.	Presentation readability is impaired due to repeated errors in spelling, grammar, word usage, or punctuation.
	Bullet points are parallel.	Bullet points are inconsistent in one slide.	Most bullet points are not parallel.

My State

DISASTER RECOVERY

Your little sister prepared a report on your state for a youth organization merit badge on research, and she is going to present the information to her leader and team members. She spent a lot of time researching the state and created a presentation with the information she wants included. Unfortunately, she is frustrated because the presentation she worked so hard on looks "ugly" to her. She asks you to help her create a presentation that "won't embarrass" her. You sit down with her and show her how to download the presentation for State history report presentation template from the Microsoft Office Online site, Presentations category, Academic subcategory. Save the new presentation as **chap2_mc3_florida_solution**. You reuse her slides saved as *chap2_mc3_florida* to bring them into the new template. From there you cut and paste the images she gathered into the correct placeholders, and move bullet points to the correct slide. Resize placeholders as needed. As you edit the presentation with her, you tell your sister that mixing clip art and pictures is contributing to the cluttered look and ask her what she prefers. She cannot decide, so you use your preference, but be consistent. The template doesn't have slides for all her information, so you create new slides with appropriate layouts when needed. You remind her that although federal government organizations allow use of their images in an educational setting, your sister should give proper credit if she is going to use their data. Also give credit to the State of Florida's Web site for the information obtained from MyFlorida.com (**http://dhr.dos.state.fl.us/facts/symbols**). Give credit to the U.S. Census Bureau (**www.census.gov**) for the Quick Facts.

You delete any slide for which your sister does not have information. Be sure to spell-check and carefully proofread the content of the presentation as your sister freely admits she "wasn't worried about that stuff." You pick an animation to apply to all slides with her help, and resist her pleas to do "something different" on every slide. You explain to her that this is not an MTV music video; rather it is an informational presentation, and multiple animations are distracting. Create a handout header with your name, and a handout footer with your instructor's name and your class time. Print as directed by your instructor.

Performance Elements	Exceeds Expectations	Meets Expectations	Below Expectations.
Organization	Presentation is easy to follow because information is presented in a logical, interesting sequence.	Presentation is generally easy to follow.	Presentation cannot be understood because there is no sequence of information.
Visual aspects	Presentation background, themes, clip art, and animation are appealing and enhance the understanding of presentation purpose and content.	Clip art is related to the topic.	The background or theme is distracting to the topic.
	There is a consistent visual theme.	Animation is not distracting.	Clip art does not enhance understanding of the content or is unrelated.
Layout	The layout is visually pleasing and contributes to the overall message with appropriate use of headings, subheadings, bullet points, clip art, and white space.	The layout shows some structure, but placement of some headings, subheadings, bullet points, clip art, and/or white space can be improved.	The layout is cluttered and confusing. Placement of headings, subheadings, bullet points, clip art, and/or white spaces detracts from readability.
Mechanics	Presentation has no errors in spelling, grammar, word usage, or punctuation.	Presentation has no more than one error in spelling, grammar, word usage, or punctuation.	Presentation readability is impaired due to repeated errors in spelling, grammar, word usage, or punctuation.
	Bullet points are parallel.	Bullet points are inconsistent in one slide.	Most bullet points are not parallel.

chapter 3 | PowerPoint

Presentation Design

Enhancing with Illustrations

After you read this chapter, you will be able to:

1. Create shapes **(page 931)**.
2. Apply Quick Styles and customize shapes **(page 936)**.
3. Create SmartArt **(page 952)**.
4. Modify SmartArt diagrams **(page 955)**.
5. Create WordArt **(page 961)**.
6. Modify WordArt **(page 961)**.
7. Modify objects **(page 968)**.
8. Arrange objects **(page 975)**.

Hands-On Exercises

Exercises	Skills Covered
1. WORKING WITH SHAPES (page 944) **Open:** chap3_ho1_shapes.pptx **Save as:** chap3_ho1_shapes_solution.pptx	• Create Basic Shapes • Draw and Format Connector Lines • Modify a Freeform Shape • Apply a Quick Style and Customize Shapes • Change Shape Outlines • Change Outline, Dash, and Arrow Styles • Use Shape Effects
2. WORKING WITH SMARTART AND WORDART (page 963) **Open:** chap3_ho2_water.pptx **Save as:** chap3_ho2_water_solution.pptx	• Insert SmartArt • Modify a SmartArt Diagram • Change SmartArt Layout • Create WordArt • Modify WordArt
3. MODIFYING AND ARRANGING CLIP ART (page 980) **Open:** chap3_ho2_water_solution.pptx (from Exercise 1) **Save as:** chap3_ho3_cycle_solution.pptx (additional modifications)	• Size and Position Clip Art • Flip Clip Art • Ungroup, Modify, and Regroup Clip Art • Recolor a Picture • Reorder Shapes • Align and Distribute Clip Art

CASE STUDY

The Kelso Performing Arts Center

An appreciation for the arts is essential to the quality of life in any society, but the recent budget shortfall at every level of government has put cultural programs in jeopardy throughout the country. The city of Kelso is no exception, as its residents have tried unsuccessfully for several years to persuade the city council to build a Performing Arts Center. This year residents have a renewed sense of optimism because the political climate has changed, and there is a strong focus on revitalizing the downtown area. In addition, the Kelso family, for whom the city is named, has agreed to donate a prime five-acre site if the council will approve a $30-million bond issue to fund construction.

Case Study

Kenneth Kelso chairs the Executive Committee of the Kelso Performing Arts Center, a volunteer community board. The Executive Committee proposes organizing the Art Center with committees providing for the following functions: Finance Committee (Investments, Financial Oversite), Program Committee (Grantmaking, Distribution), and Marketing (Public Relations, Fundraising).

You are civic minded and a patron of the arts. Kenneth Kelso is also a close personal friend, and he has asked you to spearhead the effort to secure the funding. You and two colleagues from the Executive Committee are to go before the council on Monday evening to present your case. The Kelso family has worked for several hours to prepare the contents of the presentation, but it is not yet finished. Ken is counting on you to add the finishing touches. He is seeking an eye-catching, attention-grabbing, interest-keeping presentation!

Your Assignment

- Read the chapter, paying special attention to how to create SmartArt, how to change a SmartArt Layout, how to create WordArt, and how to recolor a picture.
- Open the partially completed *chap3_case_arts* presentation and save the presentation as **chap3_case_arts_solution**.
- On Slide 1, convert the title to WordArt by applying a WordArt transformation such as a glow to the text, and then recolor the picture so it matches the red tones of the curtains. Recolor the picture on the last slide so that it matches the picture in the title slide.
- Convert the bullet content in Slide 4 to a horizontal process SmartArt and apply a Quick Style that enhances the process. Change the layout of the SmartArt in Slide 5 to a pyramid layout and apply a Quick Style utilizing the colors of the presentation.
- Use a hierarchy SmartArt to create an organization chart on Slide 6. Refer to the introduction to the case study to determine the content of the chart. The Executive Committee should have the superior level, or top level, as it oversees the committees. The other committees are subordinate to the Executive Committee and as such should occupy the second level. List the functions of the committees on the third level. Apply a Quick Style.
- Create a Notes and Handouts Header and Footer with your name in the header, and your instructor's name and your class in the footer.
- Print handouts, 4 per page, grayscale, framed.

Shapes

Thus far, you have focused on presentations that consisted largely of text. In addition to entering text in presentations, you can use a variety of visual elements to add impact to a presentation. The visual effects in PowerPoint 2007 have been improved over previous versions. New effects such as 3-D, shadow, glow, warp, bevel, and others are accessible through style galleries, making it easy for you to create professional-looking graphics.

(. . . you can use a variety of visual elements to add impact to a presentation . . . 3-D, shadow, glow, warp, bevel. . . .)

A ***shape*** is a geometric or nongeometric object, such as a rectangle or an arrow.

You can include a ***shape***, a geometric or nongeometric object, as a visual element in your presentation, to create an illustration, or to highlight information. For example, after a list of items you could include a quote related to the items and create the quote inside a shape to call attention to it. Shapes also can be used as a design element. You can even combine shapes to create your own complex images or clip art. Figure 3.1 shows three PowerPoint themes utilizing shapes in each of these ways. The Equity theme uses a rectangle shape to draw attention to the information in the title placeholder. The Oriel theme utilizes circles and lines to create an interesting design. The Sunspots theme combines shapes to create a sunburst effect.

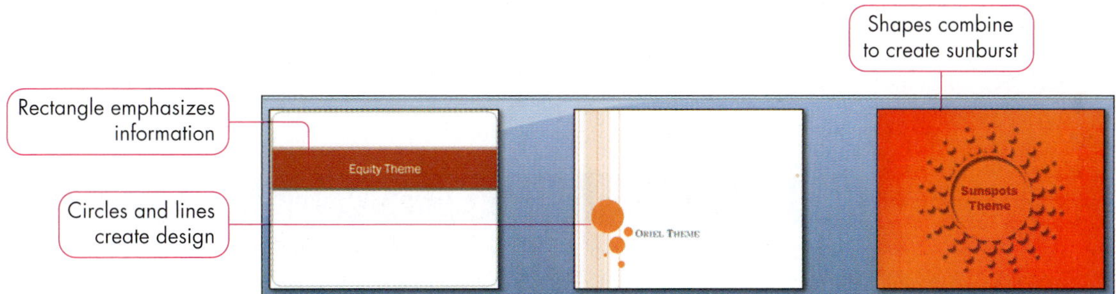

Figure 3.1 Using Shapes in Themes

In this section, you create and modify various shapes and lines. You also learn how to customize shapes and apply special effects to objects. Finally, you learn how to apply and change outline effects.

Creating Shapes

PowerPoint provides tools for creating shapes. You can insert everything from standard geometric shapes like a circle or a square to hearts and stars, equation shapes, and even banners. These are just a few of the multitude of shapes provided. After you create a shape, you can modify it and apply fills and special effects for truly spectacular graphics. To access the Shape Gallery displaying the complete list of shape tools, click the Home tab, and then click Shapes in the Drawing group (see Figure 3.2). If you have a widescreen monitor or if your monitor is set for a higher resolution, the Drawing group displays individual shapes instead of one Shapes command. If this is the case, click the More button. The Shape Gallery (see Figure 3.3) displays shapes you have recently used and all shapes available sorted into categories to make the shape you desire easy to find.

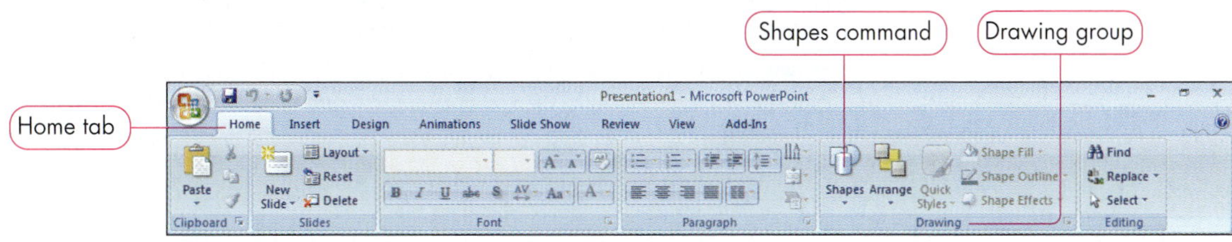

Figure 3.2 Accessing the Shape Gallery

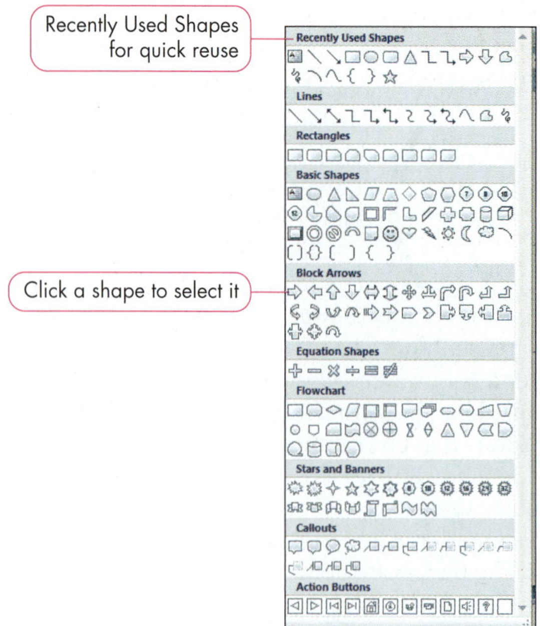

Figure 3.3 The Shape Gallery

TIP Another Location for Shapes

Shapes are also available in the Illustrations group on the Insert tab so that if the Insert tab is active, you do not have to click the Home tab to get to Shapes in the Drawing group.

The basic procedure for creating a shape is to click the shape you desire in the Shape gallery, and then click in the slide window where you wish to place the shape. The mouse pointer changes to a cross-hair to help you determine the starting and ending points of your shape. Drag the cross-hair until the shape is approximately the size you want and release. You can always resize the shape by dragging the sizing handles that surround the shape after it is created. By default, this feature deactivates after you draw one shape. If you want to add several shapes of the same type on your slide, right-click the shape you want in the Shapes gallery, and then select Lock Drawing Mode. Next, click anywhere on the slide, and then drag to create the first shape. After you create the first shape, click and drag repeatedly to create additional shapes. To release the Lock Drawing Mode, press Esc. If you do not activate the Lock Drawing Mode before creating the first shape, you have to reselect the shape each time you want to use it—a very inefficient process.

TIP Constrain a Shape

A rectangle can be constrained to form a perfect square, and an oval or ellipse can be constrained to form a perfect circle. To constrain these shapes, press and hold Shift as you drag to create the shape.

A ***callout*** is a shape that includes a line with a text box that you can use to add notes.

An ***adjustment handle*** is a control in the shape of a yellow diamond that enables you to modify a shape.

Figure 3.4 shows a series of squares created with the Lock Drawing Mode activated, a cloud created using the Cloud shape located in the Basic Shapes category, an explosion created using the Explosion 2 shape located in the Stars and Banners category, and finally a ***callout*** (a shape that includes a line with a text box that can be used to add notes, often used in cartooning) created using the Oval Callout located in the Callouts category. Notice that the callout shape is selected. The sizing handles display around the callout, and a yellow diamond shows at the bottom on the endpoint. This yellow diamond is an ***adjustment handle*** that you can drag to "reshape the shape" or change the shape. For example, if you select the Smiley Face shape and drag to create it, the shape includes a "smile" (upward curved line) with an adjustment handle attached. Drag the adjustment handle, and the smile becomes a frown (downward curved line). Your Smiley Face becomes a "Frowny Face"! Some shapes have this adjustment handle and some do not.

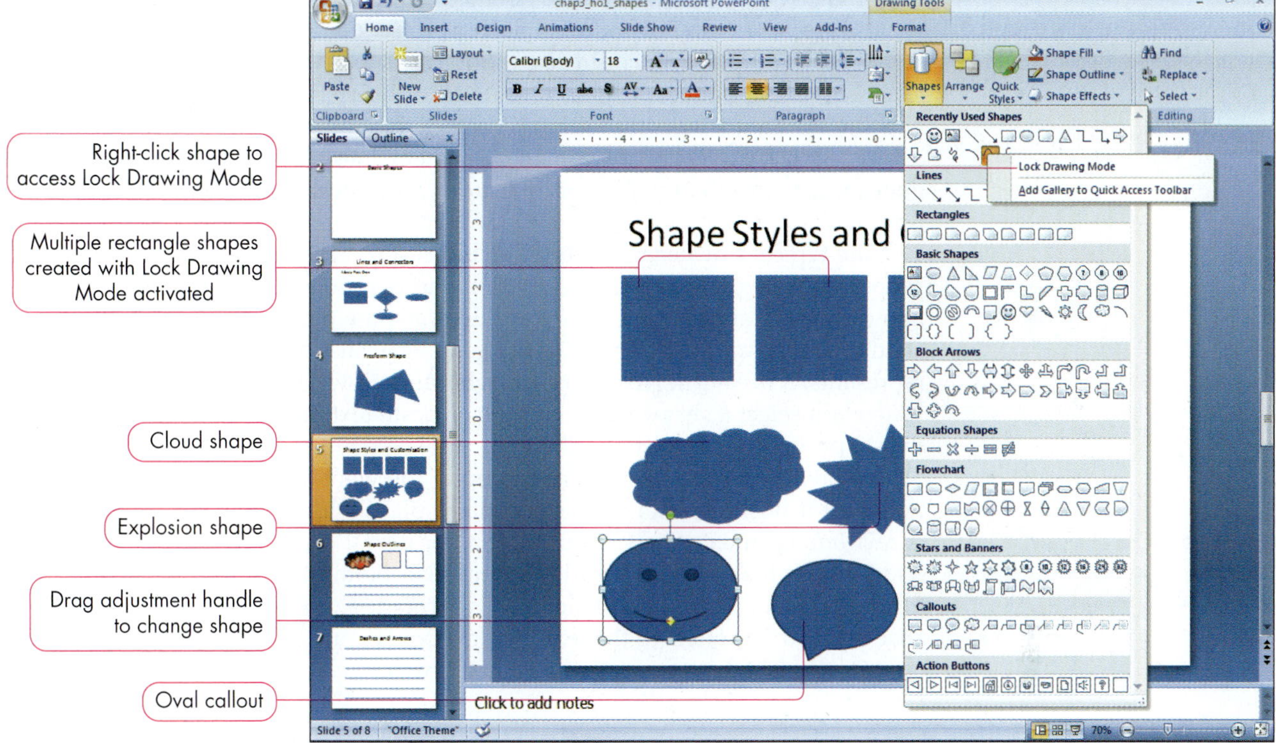

Figure 3.4 Basic Shapes

Draw Lines and Connectors

Lines, as shapes, can be used to point to information, connect shapes on a slide, or divide the slide into sections. Lines also are often used in slide design. Draw a straight line by selecting the line shape, clicking in the slide to begin the line, and then dragging to create the line. Double-click to end the line. To create a curved line, select the Curve line, click the slide where you want to start the curve, and then continue to click and move the mouse to shape the curve the way you want. As you click, you set a point for the curve to bend around. To end the curve, double-click. To draw a shape that looks like it was drawn with a pen or create smooth curves, select the Scribble shape.

TIP Create a Closed Shape

If you click near the line's starting point, the points join and create a closed shape. The advantage of joining the ends of the line and creating a closed shape is that you can include a fill.

A ***connector*** is a line that is attached to and moves with shapes.

In addition to drawing simple lines for tasks like creating dividing lines and waves, at times you may need ***connectors***, or lines that attach to the shapes you create. That way when the shapes are rearranged, the connector line moves with it. Three types of connectors are provided: straight, elbow (to create angled lines), and curved.

The first step in working with connectors is to create the shapes you want to connect with lines. After you create the shapes, select the connector line from the Shape Gallery that you wish to use. After you select the connector, red circular dots appear around the shapes if you move your pointer over them. These are the spots where you can attach the connector. You click one of the red dots and drag the line until it connects with the red circle on the next shape. The two shapes are now connected. If you move one of the shapes, the connecting line moves with it. Sometimes when you rearrange the shapes, the connectors may cross shapes and be confusing. If that happens, you can use the yellow adjustment handle to reshape the line. Select the connector line and drag the handle to obtain a clearer path.

A ***flowchart*** is an illustration showing the sequence of a project or plan.

A ***flowchart*** is an illustration that shows a sequence to be followed or a plan with steps. For example, you could use a flowchart to illustrate the sequence to be followed in taking a multiple-choice test (1. Read question and possible answers. 2. If you know the answer immediately, select the answer. 3. If you don't know the answer, skip the question and go on to the next question. 4. When finished with new questions, return to any skipped questions.). Connector lines join the shapes in the flowchart.

The typical flowchart sequence includes start and end points shown in an oval shape, steps shown in rectangle shapes, and decisions to be made shown in a diamond shape. Connectors with arrows demonstrate the order in which the sequence should be followed to accomplish the goal. Each shape is labeled to indicate what it represents. It is easy to label the shapes because PowerPoint shapes can contain text. When you select a shape and then type or paste text into it, the text becomes part of the shape and moves with the shape.

A ***text box*** is an object that enables you to place text anywhere on a slide.

If you need text on a slide (for example, you want to add a quote to a slide but do not want it positioned in the slide content placeholder), you can create a text box. A ***text box*** is an extremely useful object because it gives you the freedom to create and position text outside of slide content placeholders. Text inside a text box can be formatted just as text in placeholders is formatted. You can even add a border, fill, shadow, or a 3-D effect to the text in a text box. Figure 3.5 displays a basic flowchart created with shapes, connectors, and text boxes.

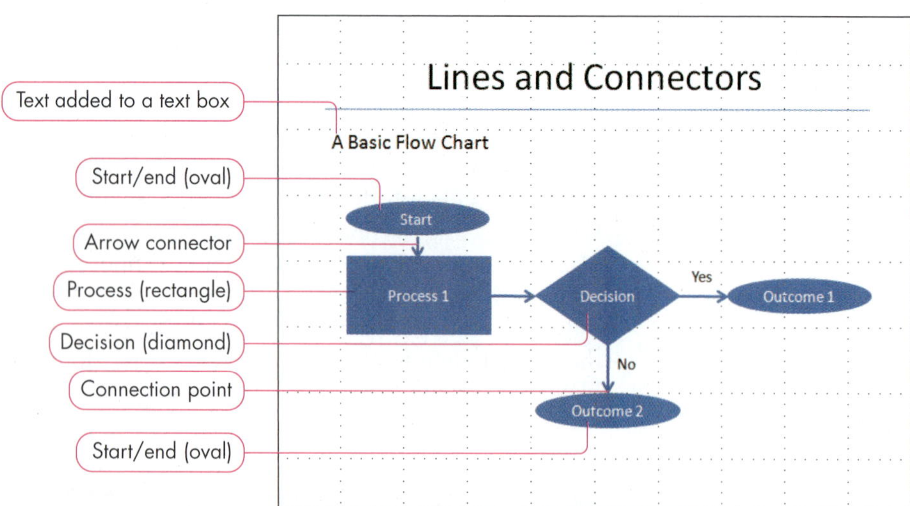

Figure 3.5 A Basic Flowchart

Create and Modify Freeform Shapes

A ***freeform shape*** is a shape that may combine both curved and straight lines to create a shape.

When you need a customized shape, you can create a *freeform shape*, a shape that may combine both curved and straight-line segments. Select the Freeform shape in the Lines category of the Shapes Gallery, and then click the slide. Drag to create curves, and click and move the mouse to draw straight lines. Double-click to end the freeform shape. If you click the starting point of the shape, you create a closed shape just as you do with lines.

A ***vertex*** is the point where a curve ends or the point where two line segments meet in a freeform shape.

To modify a freeform shape, select the shape and then under Drawing Tools, click the Format tab. In the Insert Shapes group, click Edit Shape. Finally, select Edit Points. *Vertexes*, or points where a curve ends or the point where two line segments meet, will appear, and can be moved or deleted to redefine the object's shape. The vertexes appear as black dots. Figure 3.6 shows a freeform with its vertexes displayed. Figure 3.7 shows a selected vertex dragged to a new position. When you release the left mouse button, the freeform will take the new shape.

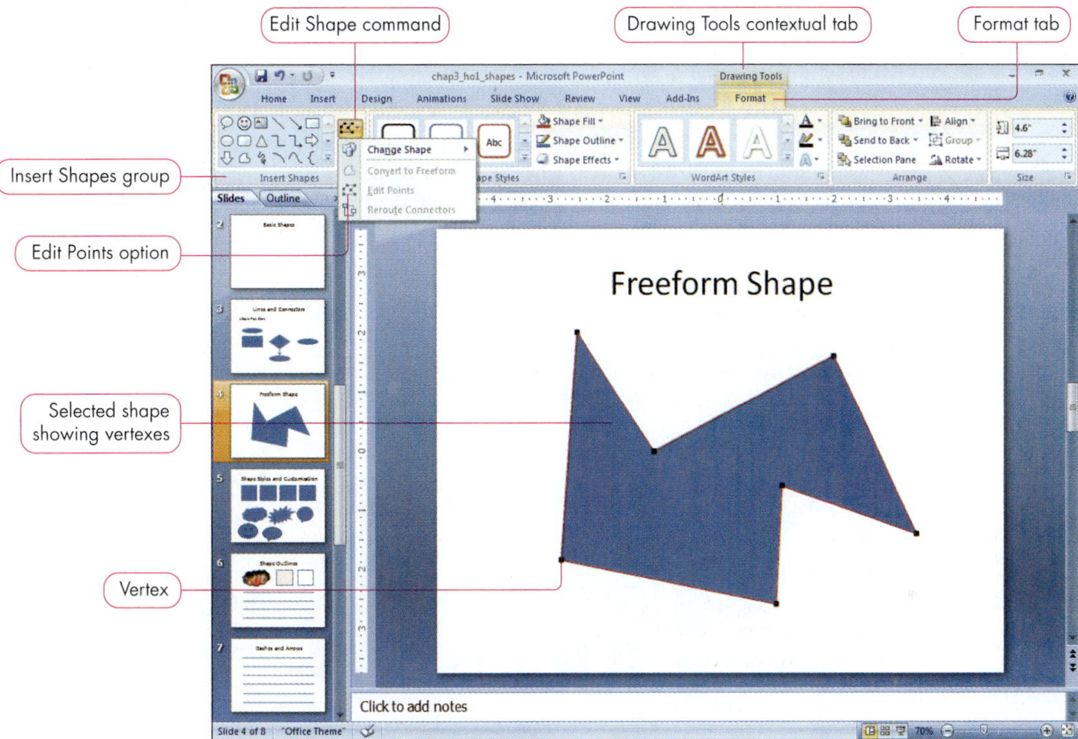

Figure 3.6 Modifying a Freeform Shape

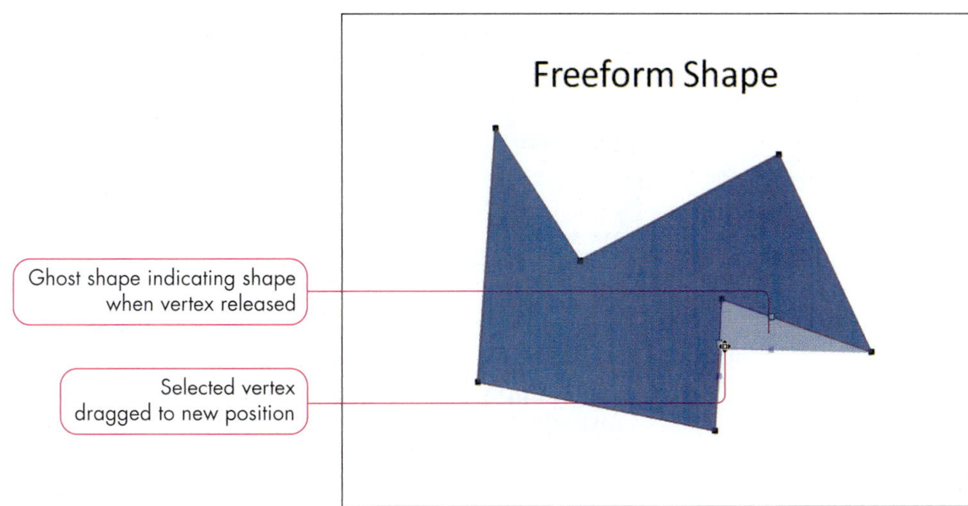

Figure 3.7 Moving a Vertex

TIP Changing a Shape

You can change any shape or freeform shape to a different shape by using the Edit Shape feature. First select the existing shape, and then click Edit Shape. Next click Change Shape. When the Shape gallery opens, click the new shape you want. The shape on the slide updates to the new shape, and any style you have applied to the original shape is retained.

Applying Quick Styles and Customizing Shapes

A ***Quick Style*** is a combination of formatting options available that can be applied to a shape or graphic.

After you create a shape, you can add a ***Quick Style*** to it. A Quick Style is a combination of different formats that can be selected from the Quick Style Gallery and applied to a shape or other objects. To see how a Quick Style would look when applied, position your pointer over the Quick Style thumbnail. When you identify the style you desire, click to apply the style. Options in the gallery include edges, shadows, line styles, gradients, and 3-D effects. Figure 3.8 shows the Quick Style gallery and several shapes with a variety of Quick Styles applied to them.

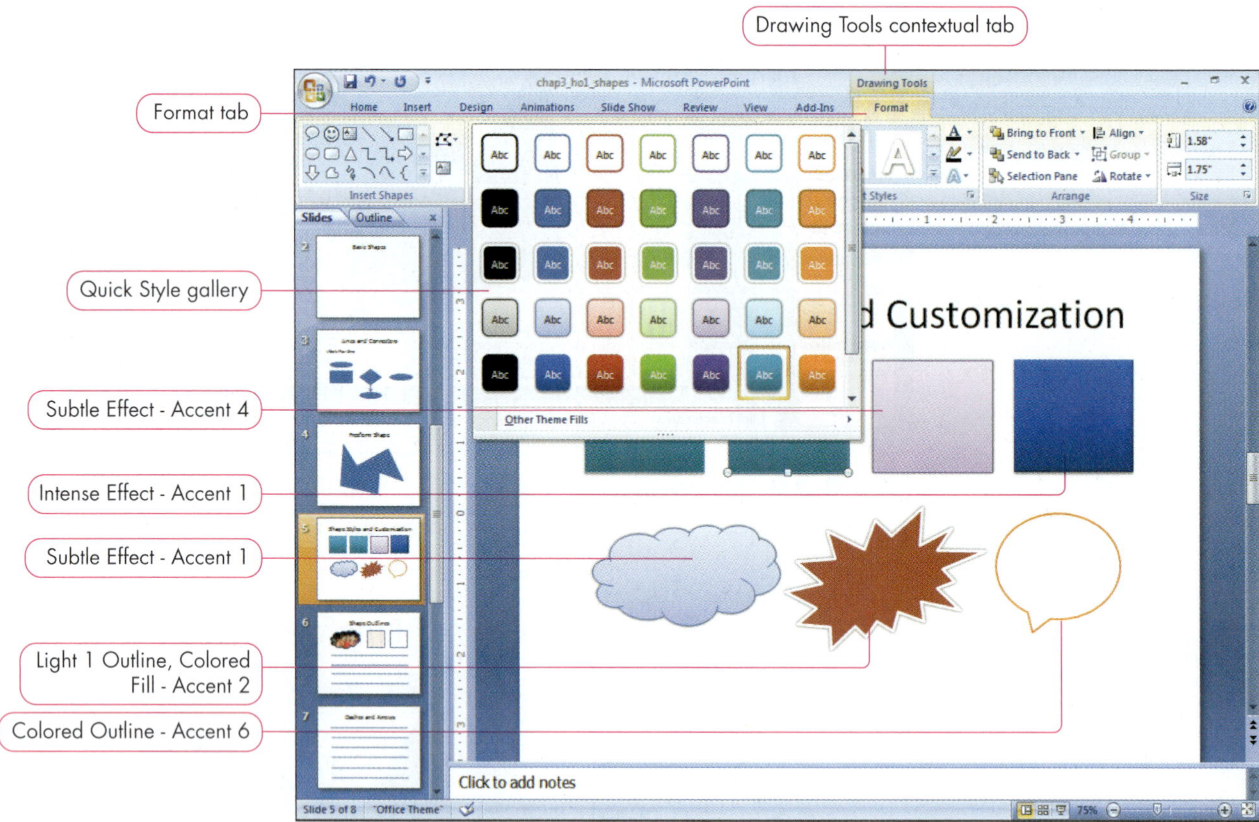

Figure 3.8 Using Quick Styles

To apply a Quick Style to a shape, select the shape. When the Drawing Tools contextual tab appears, click the Format tab. This action provides you with tools to work with as you modify the format of the selected shape. The Shape Styles group includes the More button, which enables you to apply a Quick Style, or to manually select the fill and outline of the shape and to apply special effects. When the Quick Style gallery is open, click the Quick Style you wish to apply.

TIP Apply Quick Styles and Effects to Multiple Objects

To apply a Quick Style to more than one shape or object at a time, hold down Ctrl and click each object. Each new Ctrl-click adds an object to the selection. Holding down Shift also works. When all objects are selected, choose the style or effect you desire.

A ***selection net*** selects all objects in an area defined by dragging the mouse.

Another method for selecting multiple objects on a slide is to click and then drag a ***selection net***, or marquee, around all of the objects you wish to select, and then releasing the mouse button. All objects contained in their entirety in the net, or marquee, will be selected.

Change Shape Fills

A ***fill*** refers to the inside of a shape.

A ***gradient fill*** is a blend of colors and shades.

Rather than apply a Quick Style, you may choose to customize the shape by changing the shape ***fill***, or the interior of the shape. You may choose from having a solid color fill, no fill, a picture fill, a ***gradient fill*** (a blend of one color to another color or one shade to another shade), or a texture fill. To change the fill of a selected object, click Shape Fill in the Shape Styles group on the Format tab. The Shape Fill gallery provides color choices that match the Theme Colors and color choices based on Standard Colors. Figure 3.9 shows the Shape Fill options and a shape filled with Accent 6, Lighter 60%.

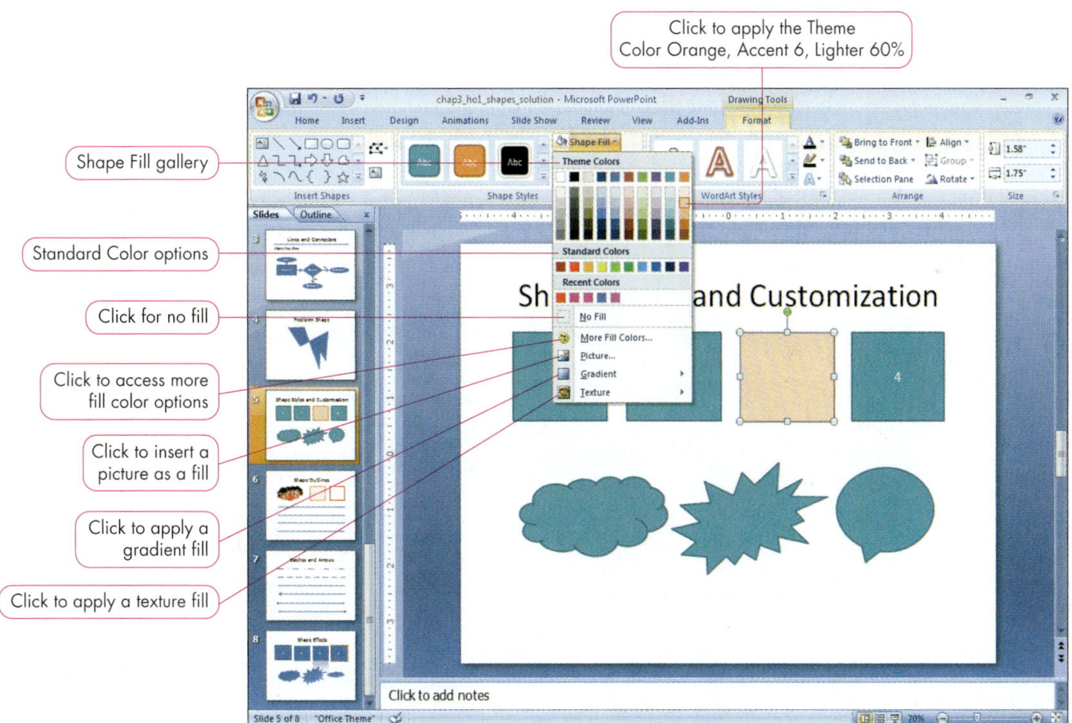

Figure 3.9 Shape Fill Options

If these color choices do not meet your needs, you can always select More Fill Colors to open the Colors dialog box where you can mix colors based on an RGB color model (Red Green Blue) or an HSL color model (Hue Saturation Luminosity). The default RGB color model gives each of the colors red, green, and blue a numeric value that ranges from 0 to 255. The combination of these values creates the color assigned to your shape. When all three RGB values are 0, you get black. When all three RGB values are 255, you get white. By using different combinations of numbers between 0 and 255, you can create almost 16 million shades of color.

Transparency refers to how much you can see through a fill.

Opaque refers to solid fill, one without transparency.

The Color dialog box also enables you to determine the amount of ***transparency***, or visibility, you wish. At 0% transparency the fill is ***opaque***, or solid, while 100% transparency is clear. The Color dialog box enables you to drag a slider to specify the percentage of transparency. Figure 3.10 shows the Color dialog box with the RGB color mode selected, Red assigned a value of 236, Green assigned a value of 32, Blue assigned a value of 148, and a transparency set at 80%.

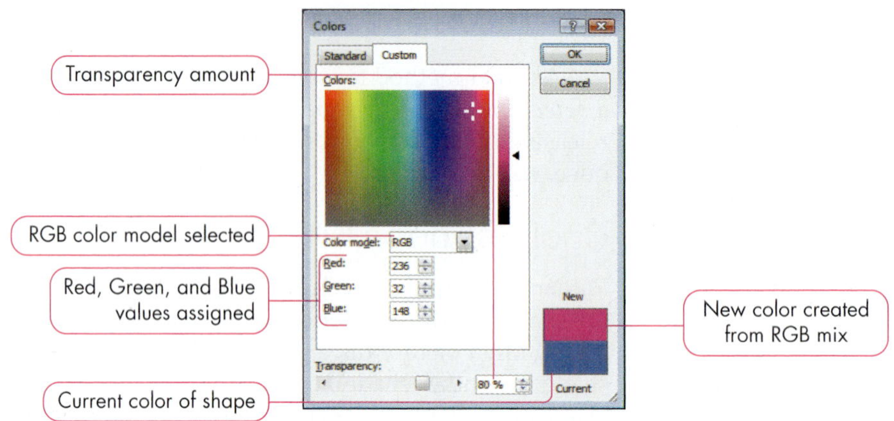

Figure 3.10 The Color Dialog Box

A ***picture fill*** inserts an image from a file into a shape.

Shapes also may be filled with images using the ***picture fill*** option. This option enables you to create unusual frames for your pictures and can be a fun way to vary the images in your presentation or create interesting frames for scrap book images. To insert a picture as a fill, click Picture in the Shape Fill gallery accessible from the Drawing Tools Format tab. Browse to locate the picture that you want to add, and then double-click the picture to insert it. Figure 3.11 shows the cloud shape filled with a casual snapshot taken with a digital camera.

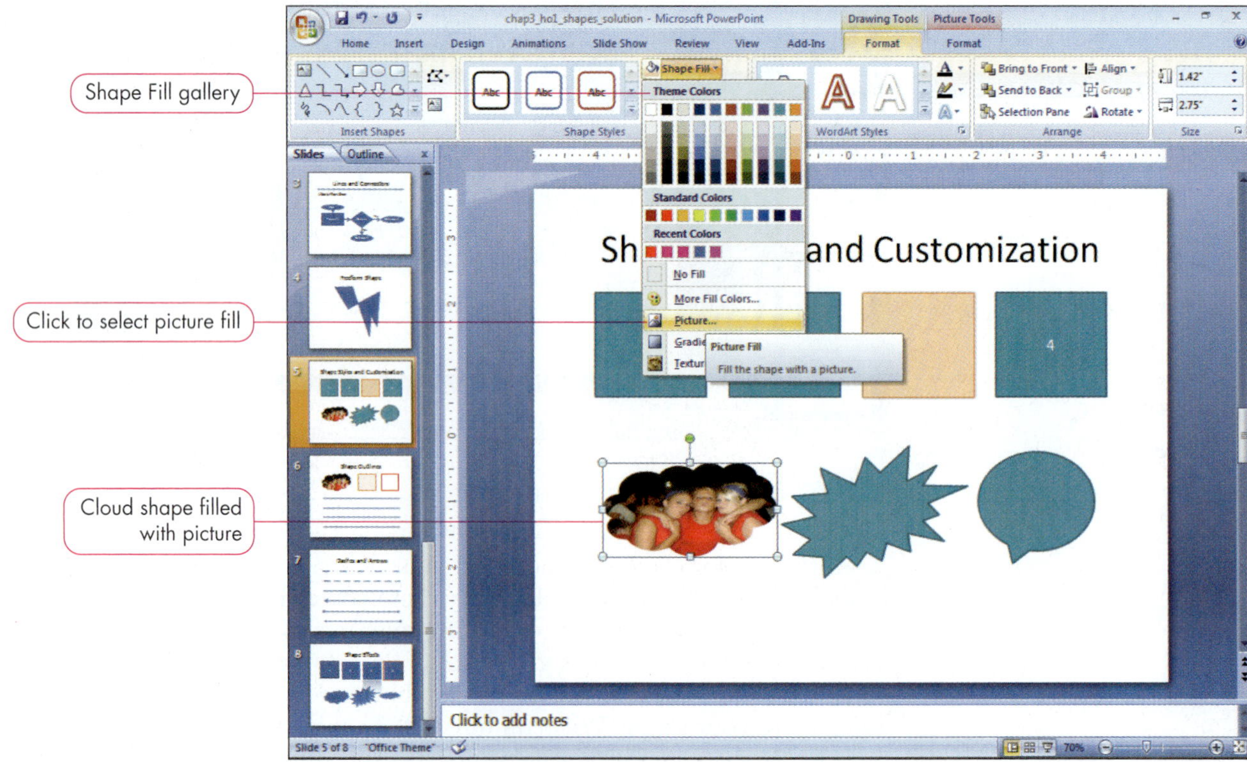

Figure 3.11 Shape Filled with a Picture

Gradient effects make interesting fills for shapes. When Gradient is selected from the Shape Fill gallery, another gallery of options appears, enabling you to select Light and Dark Variations that blend the current color with white or black in linear or radial gradients. Choosing one of these options is a quick and easy way to apply a gradient. To have more control over the gradient and have access to beautiful gradient Presets, select More Gradients at the bottom of the gallery. Figure 3.12 shows the Gradient options with a From Center gradient selected.

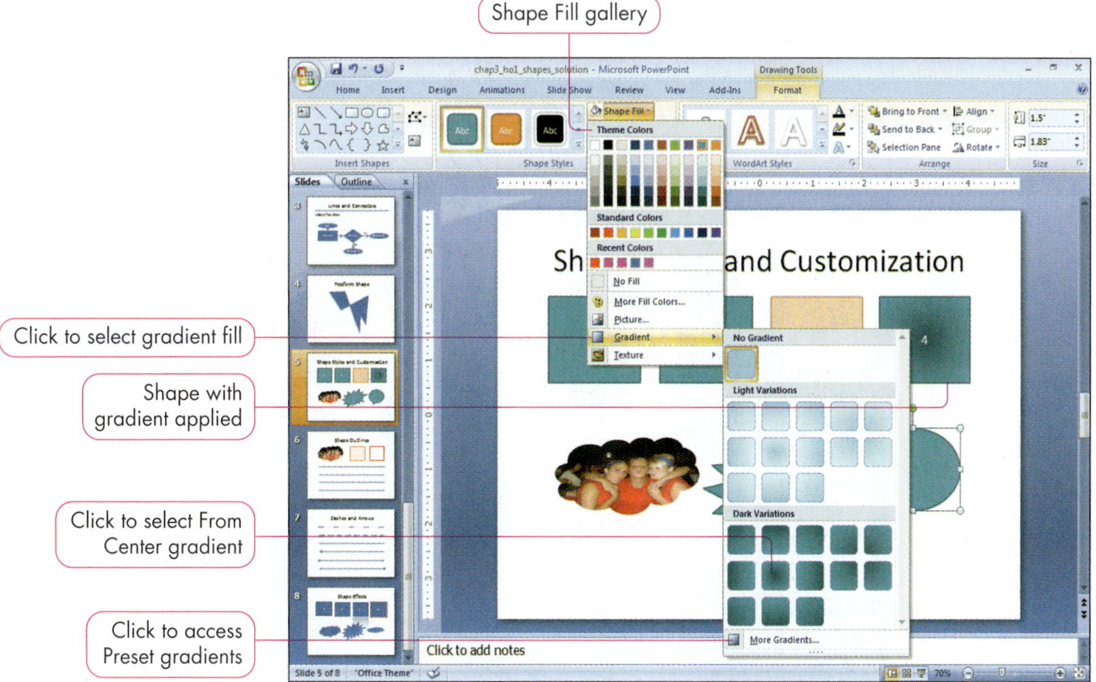

Figure 3.12 Shape Filled with the From Center Gradient Applied

When you select More Gradients, the Format Shape dialog box displays. Clicking the Gradient fill option expands to display many options you can use to customize a fill. The Preset colors gallery gives you a variety of gradients using a multitude of colors to create truly beautiful impressions. You can use other options to select a type of gradient, the direction and angle of the gradient, the number of stops used to add additional colors to a blend, and the rotate gradient option. Figure 3.13 shows the Preset colors gallery.

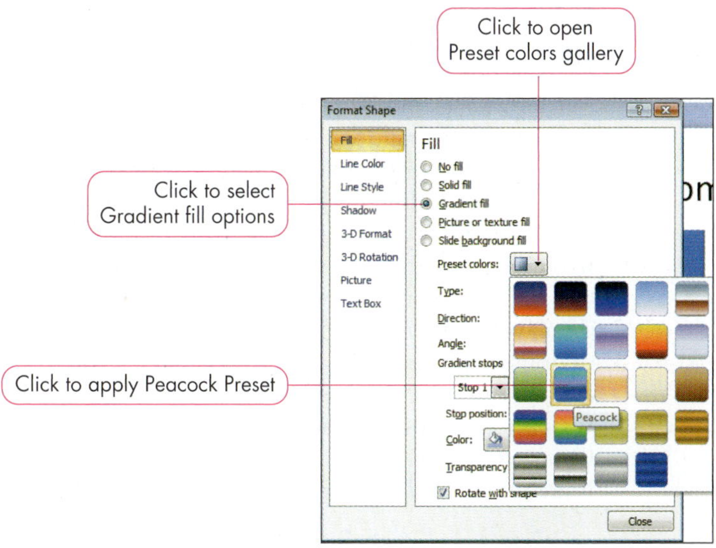

Figure 3.13 PowerPoint's Preset Color Gradients

A ***texture fill*** inserts a texture such as marble into a shape.

Selecting the Texture option from the Shape Fill Gallery gives you access to common ***texture fills*** such as canvas, denim, marble, and cork that can be used for the fill of your object. Selecting More Textures at the bottom of the Texture gallery opens the Format Shape dialog box with a multitude of options, including a tiling option. A picture can be stretched to fit the shape, or tiled so the texture is repeated to fill the shape. Tiled textures have seamless edges so that you cannot tell where one tile ends and another begins. See Figure 3.14 for the textures available in the Textures gallery.

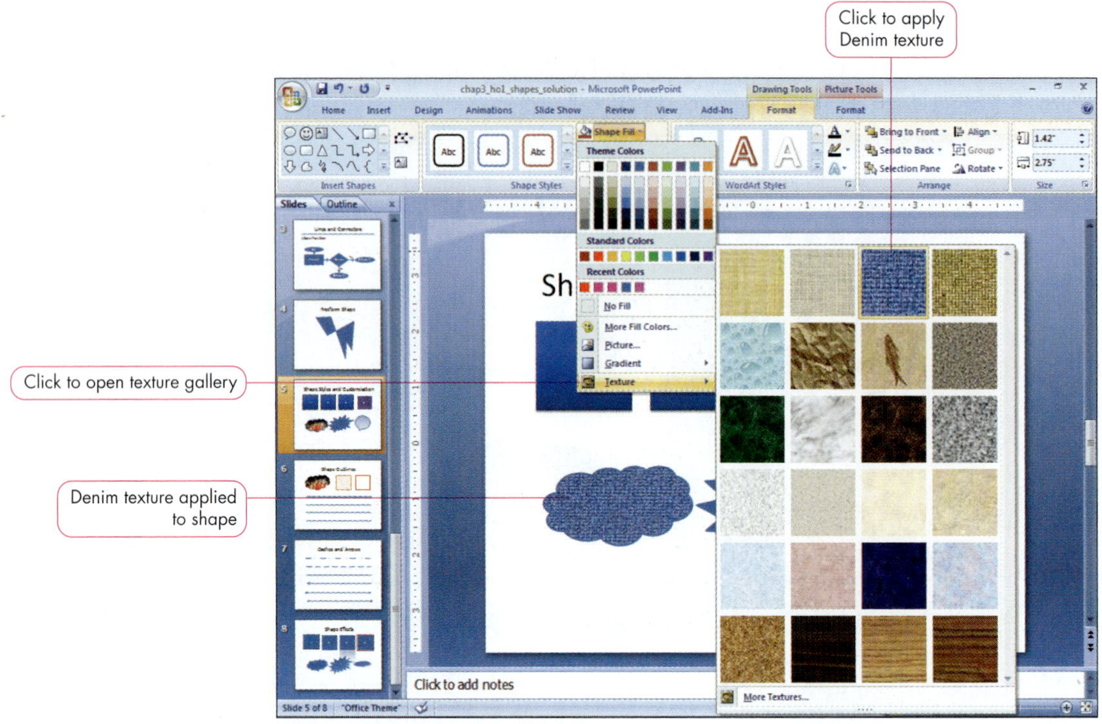

Figure 3.14 Texture Fills

Change Shape Outlines

Line weight is the width or thickness of a line.

By default, shapes have lines forming a border around the shape. You can change the style of this outline by changing its color, style, or ***line weight*** (thickness). This change can be done quickly and easily using the Shape Styles feature you are already familiar with, or by customizing using the Shape Outline options available in the Shape Styles group on the Drawing Tools Format tab. First select the line, and then open the Shape Outline gallery. The same color options detailed in changing the color of fills are available to change the color of the lines. If you wish to remove an outline, select the No Outline option. In Figure 3.15 the outline surrounding the shape with the picture fill has been removed so that it doesn't detract from the image.

The width or thickness of a line is measured in points (pts). To set the line width, click Shape Outline in the Shape Styles group on the Drawing Tools Format tab and select Weight. When you select this option, you are given choices of line weights from ¼ pt to 6 pts. One vertical inch contains 72 pts. Therefore, the thickest line you can get is 1⁄12" using this option. If you wish to change a line weight to an option not displayed, select More Lines to open the Format Shape dialog box with the Line Style options displayed. This dialog box enables you to change the line weight by selecting a weight using the spin box or by selecting the current weight and then typing in the weight you desire. You can also use the Format Shape dialog box to create Compound type outlines, which combine thick and thin lines. Figure 3.15 displays lines and an outline for a shape in various weights.

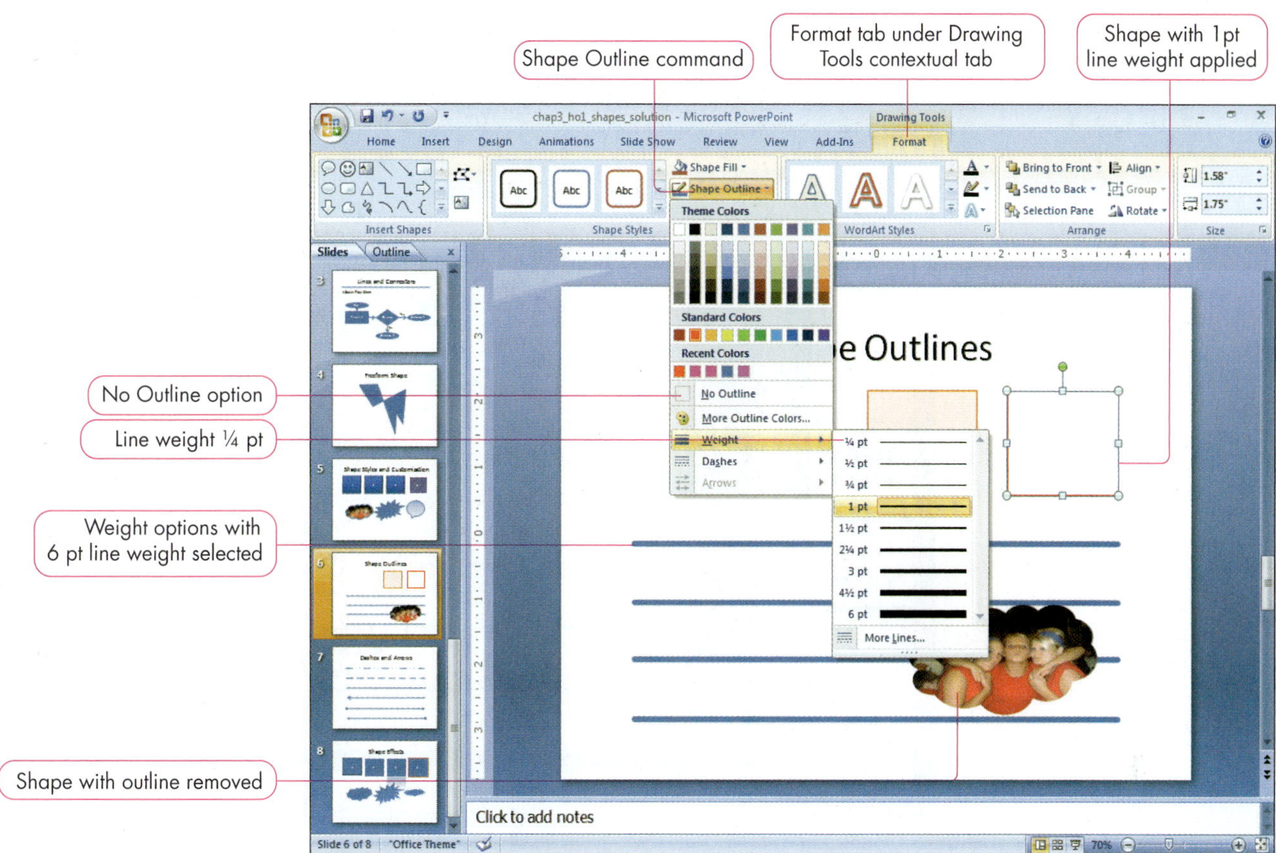

Figure 3.15 Outline Weight Options

For variety, you may wish to change the default solid line to a dashed line. Dashed lines make interesting boxes or borders for shapes and placeholders. PowerPoint lets you apply round dots, square dots, and combinations of short dashes, long dashes, and dots. To make a line dashed, select the line and then under Drawing Tools, on the Format tab, click Shape Outline. Point to the Dashes option, and then click the line style that you want. Figure 3.16 illustrates a variety of dash styles applied to 4½-pt lines.

At times you may wish to add an arrowhead to the beginning or end of a line to create an arrow that points to critical information on the slide. The Shape Outline feature enables you to create many different styles of arrows using points, circles, and diamonds. Figure 3.16 shows the arrow options as well as 4½-pt lines with arrow styles applied.

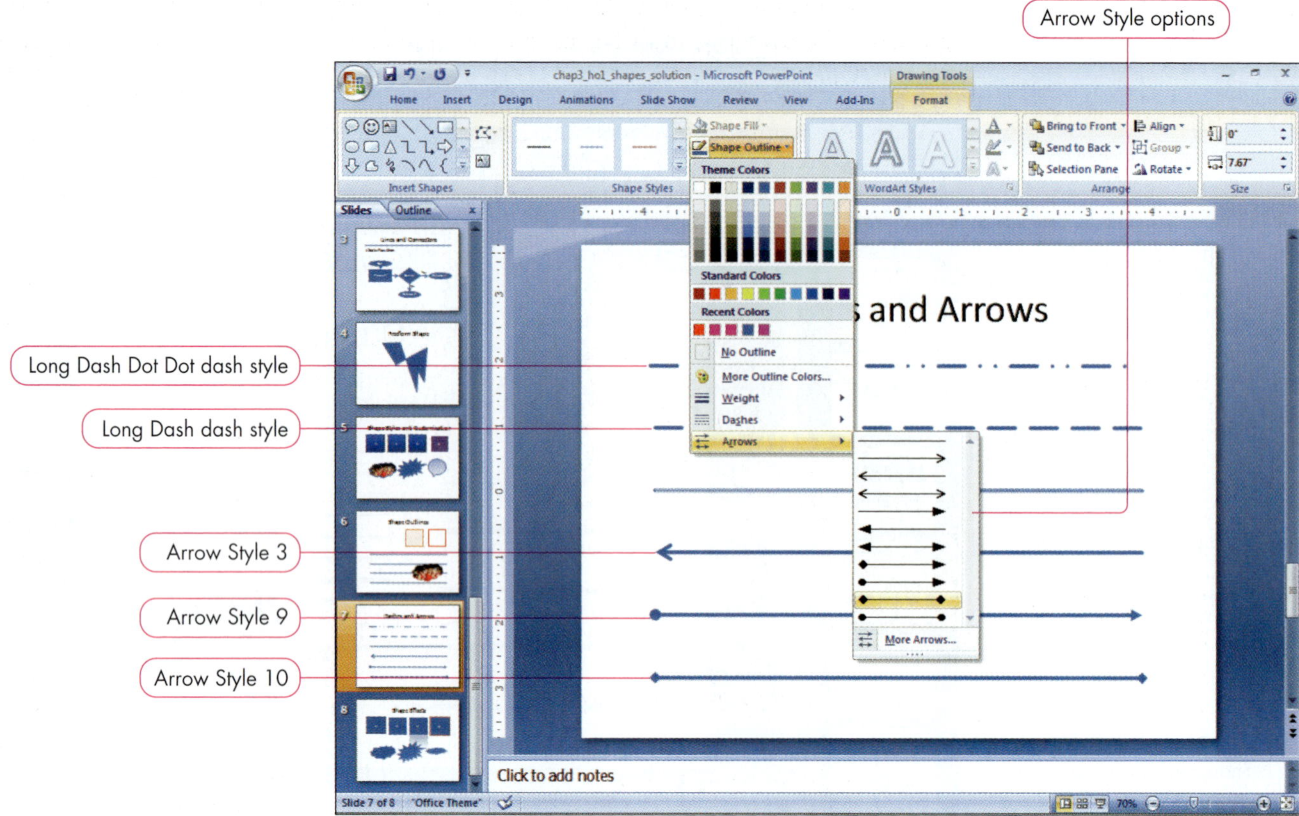

Figure 3.16 Dash and Arrow Outline Styles

> You don't need an expensive, high-powered graphics editor . . . for special effects anymore because PowerPoint 2007 enables you to apply many stunning effects to shapes. . . .

Change Shape Effects

You don't need an expensive, high-powered graphics editor such as Adobe Photoshop for special effects anymore because PowerPoint 2007 enables you to apply many stunning effects to shapes: preset three-dimensional effects, shadow effects, reflections, glows, soft edge effects, bevels, and rotations. One of the greatest strengths of PowerPoint 2007 is the ability to update any shape effects you have applied immediately when you choose a new theme. Figure 3.17 shows an example of some of the shape effects available.

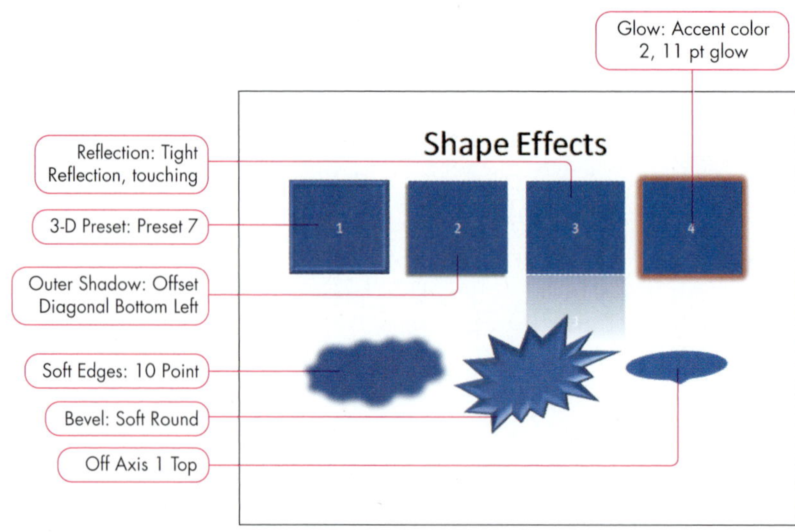

Figure 3.17 Shape Effects

To apply effects, click a shape, and then click Shape Effects in the Shape Styles group on the Drawing Tools Format tab. Point to Preset effects and select from built-in combinations of effects, or select one of the individual options underneath Preset. Or, if you prefer, you can completely customize an effect by clicking 3-D Options at the bottom of the resulting list. For example, if you click 3-D Options at the bottom of the Preset list, you open the Format Shape dialog box with the 3-D Format options available. From there you can define the bevel, depth, contours, and even the surface of the effect. Figure 3.18 displays the Material options for the surface of a shape.

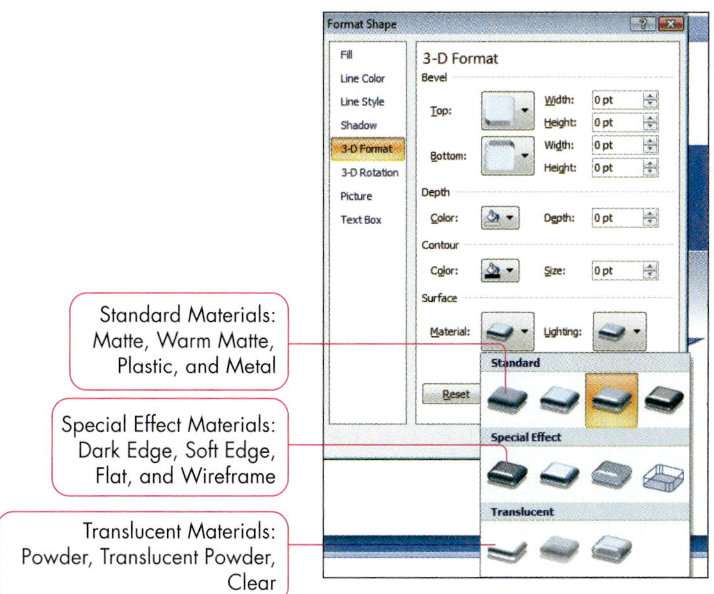

Figure 3.18 3-D Surface Options

Hands-On Exercises

1 | Working with Shapes

Skills covered: 1. Create Basic Shapes **2.** Draw and Format Connector Lines **3.** Modify a Freeform Shape **4.** Apply a Quick Style and Customize Shapes **5.** Change Shape Outlines **6.** Change Outline, Dash, and Arrow Styles **7.** Use Shape Effects

Step 1
Create Basic Shapes

Refer to Figure 3.19 as you complete Step 1.

a. Start PowerPoint, open the *chap3_ho1_shapes* presentation, and then immediately save it as **chap3_ho1_shapes_solution**.

b. Move to **Slide 2**, click the **Insert tab**, and then click **Shapes** in the Illustrations group.

c. Right-click the **Rectangle** shape in the Rectangles category, and then select **Lock Drawing Mode**.

   The Lock Drawing Mode enables you to stay in a shape creation mode so that you can create additional shapes of the same kind.

d. Hold down **Shift**, position your pointer on the upper-left side of the slide below the title, and then click to create a square. Repeat this process until you have four squares on the slide.

   Holding down Shift while clicking constrains your rectangles so they become squares. Do not worry about the size or placement of the squares at this time. You will learn how to resize and place shapes later in this chapter.

e. Click **Shapes** in the Illustrations group on the Insert tab, select **Cloud** from the Basic Shapes category, and then drag a cloud shape beneath the first square.

   The Shapes gallery opens when you click Shapes and displays the categories and shapes available so that you can locate the Cloud shape.

f. From the Shapes gallery, select **Explosion 2** from the Stars and Banners category, and then drag an explosion shape on the right side of the cloud.

g. From the Shapes gallery, select **Oval Callout** from the Callouts category, and then drag a callout on the right side of the explosion.

h. Move to **Slide 1** and enter your name and the current date in the placeholder.

i. Save the *chap3_ho1_shapes_solution* presentation.

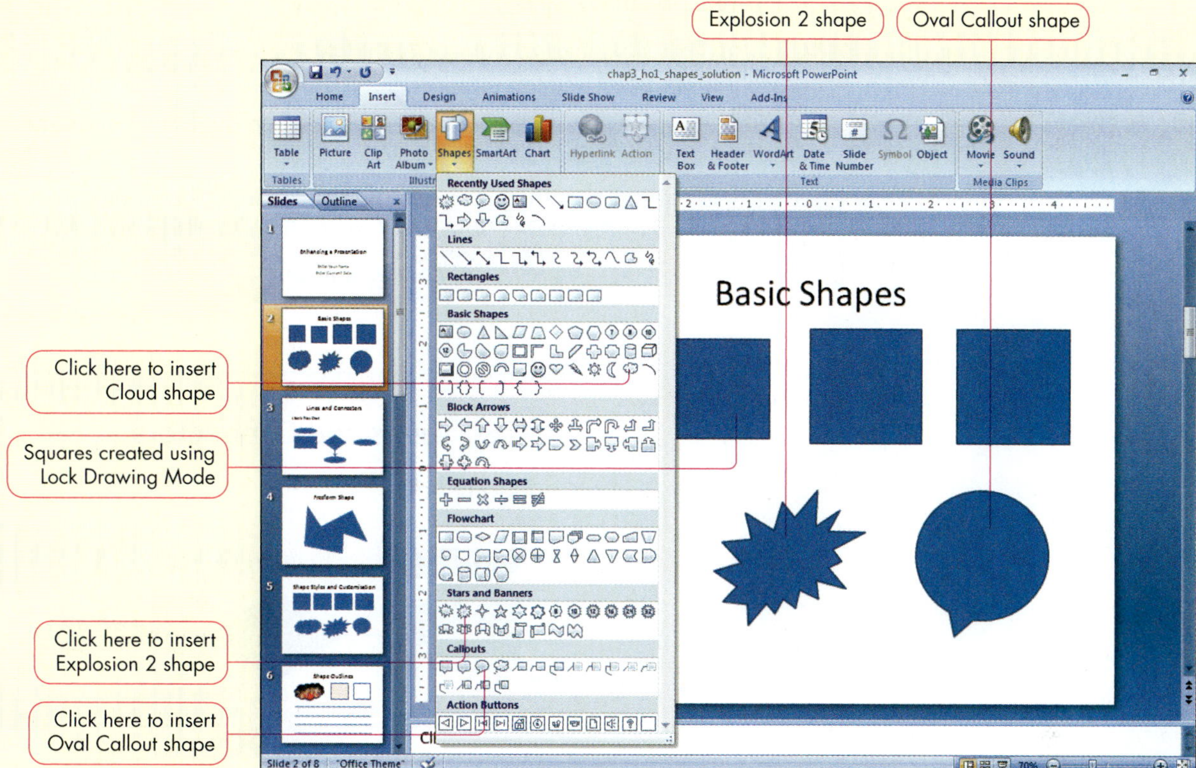

Figure 3.19 Basic Shapes

Step 2
Draw and Format Connector Lines

Refer to Figure 3.20 as you complete Step 2.

a. With *chap3_ho1_shapes_solution* onscreen, move to **Slide 3**, and then click **Shapes** in the Illustrations group on the Insert tab.

b. Click **Line** and then drag a horizontal line separating the slide title, *Lines and Connectors*, from the flowchart.

You create a line to separate the title from the flowchart. Because this line does not touch any shape, you do not need to use a connector line.

c. Select the **Elbow Arrow Connector** in the Lines category, move your pointer over the oval on the left of the slide, and then position the cross-hair on the bottom center red handle.

The shape's connector handles appear when a connector line is selected and an object is pointed at.

d. Drag a connecting line that attaches the red connecting handle on the bottom center of the oval to the top red connecting handle of the rectangle below it.

The arrowhead on the connector does not clearly show because the default line weight is very thin. You will adjust the line weight in step f.

e. Create connecting arrows that attach the rectangle to the diamond and the diamond to each of the remaining ovals as demonstrated in Figure 3.20.

f. Press and hold **Ctrl** and click all four connector lines to select them. Click the **Format tab**, click **Shape Outline** in the Shape Styles group, select **Weight**, and then select **3 pt**.

All four lines are thicker with the 3 pt weight.

g. Select the oval on the top left of the slide and type **Start**.

Selecting a shape and then entering text creates a container for text, and the text becomes part of the shape.

h. Select each of the shapes and type the text shown in Figure 3.20.

i. Click **Text Box** in the Text group on the Insert tab.

   Clicking Text Box enables you to create text that is not contained in a shape or a placeholder on the slide.

j. Position the pointer above the connector between the Decision diamond and the Outcome 1 oval, click, and then type **Yes**.

k. Repeat step j. Position the pointer to the right side of the connector between the Decision diamond and the Outcome 2 oval, click, and then type **No**.

l. Save the *chap3_ho1_shapes_solution* presentation.

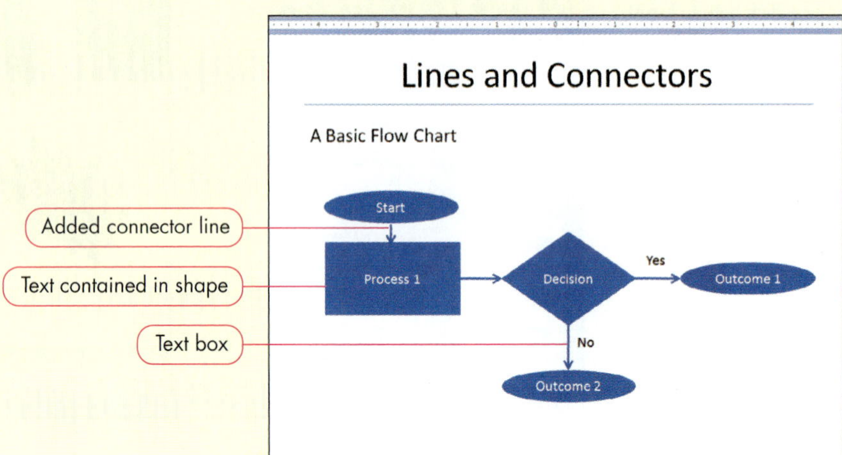

Figure 3.20 A Basic Flowchart

Step 3
Modify a Freeform Shape

Refer to Figure 3.21 as you complete Step 3.

a. With *chap3_ho1_shapes_solution* onscreen, move to **Slide 4**, and then select the freeform shape.

b. Click the **Drawing Tools Format tab**, and then click **Edit Shape** in the Insert Shapes group.

c. Click **Edit Points**.

   The freeform shape is selected—a red line surrounds its border, and the vertexes appear as black dots.

d. Select the vertex on the farthest right side of the slide and drag it to the left.

e. Select the vertex on the farthest bottom left side of the slide and drag it toward the top of the slide between the two existing vertexes.

f. Save the *chap3_ho1_shapes_solution* presentation.

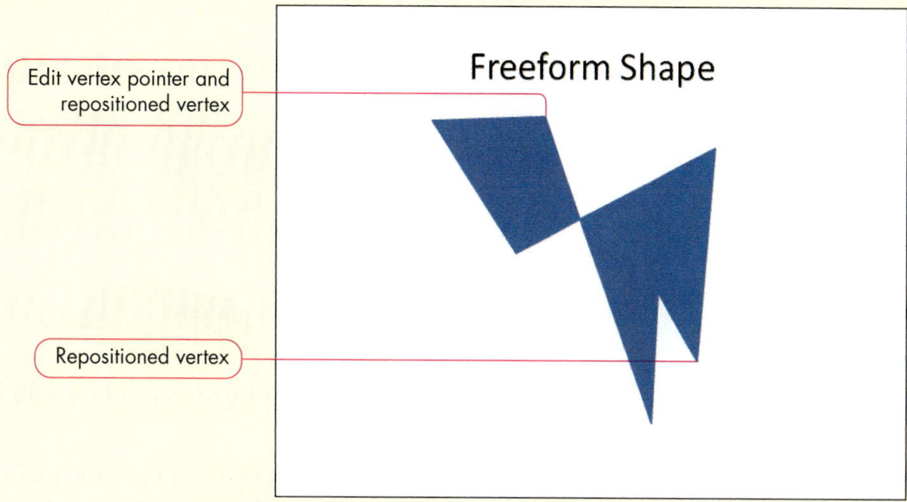

Figure 3.21 Modified Freeform Shape

Step 4
Apply a Quick Style and Customize Shapes

Refer to Figure 3.22 as you complete Step 4.

a. With *chap3_ho1_shapes_solution* onscreen, move to **Slide 5**, and then select **Rectangle 4**.

b. Click the **Drawing Tools Format tab**, if necessary, and then click the **More button** in the Shape Styles group.

c. Move your pointer over the Quick Styles, and then click **Light 1 Outline, Colored Fill – Accent 4** to apply it to Rectangle 4.

d. Click **Rectangle 1**. Press **Ctrl** as you click Rectangles 2 and 3, click the **More button** in the Shape Styles group, and then click **Intense Effect – Accent 1**.

   You can apply Quick Styles to more than one shape at a time.

e. Select the cloud shape, click **Shape Fill,** and then select **Picture**.

f. Locate the file *chap3_ho1_friends.jpg*, and then double-click to insert the picture into the shape.

g. Select the explosion shape, click **Shape Fill**, and then select **Texture**.

h. Click **Bouquet**.

i. Select the callout, click **Shape Fill**, select **Gradient**, and then select **More Gradients**.

   The Format Shape dialog box opens for your use in customizing a gradient.

j. Click **Gradient fill**, click the **Preset colors drop-down arrow**, click **Rainbow**, and then click **Close**.

k. Save the *chap3_ho1_shapes_solution* presentation.

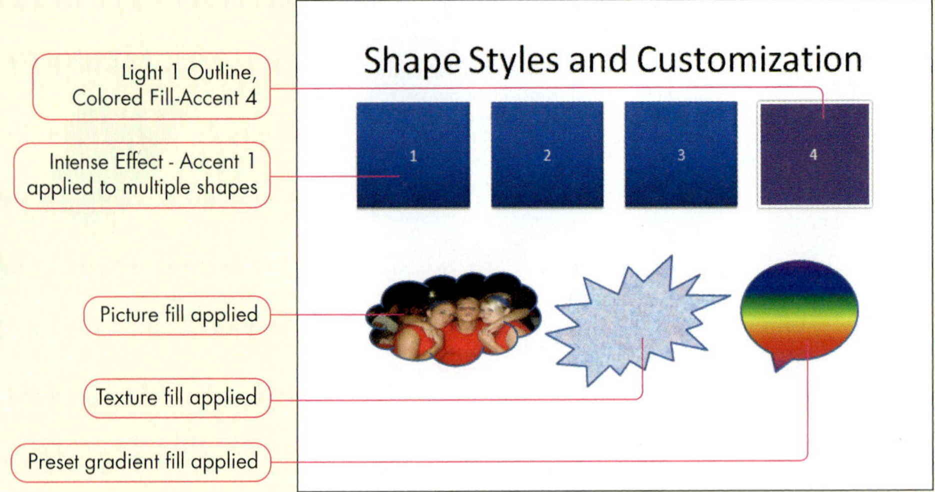

Figure 3.22 Quick Styles and Customized Fills

Step 5
Change Shape Outlines

Refer to Figure 3.23 as you complete Step 5.

a. With *chap3_ho1_shapes_solution* onscreen, select **Slide 6**, and then select the cloud shape with the picture fill.

b. Click the **Format tab** under the Drawing Tools contextual tab if necessary.

TROUBLESHOOTING: If you see two format tabs (one under Drawing Tools and one under Picture Tools), be sure to select the Format tab under Drawing Tools. The Picture Tools tab appears next to the Drawing Tools tab because of the picture fill.

c. Click **Shape Outline** in the Shape Styles group, and then select **No Outline**.

d. Select the square with the orange tint fill, click **Shape Outline**, and then click **Orange**, **Accent 6** in the Theme Colors gallery.

e. Select the square with no fill, click **Shape Outline**, and then click **More Outline Colors**. Click the custom tab if necessary.

f. Type **255** in the **Red** box, and then type **0** in the **Green** and **Blue** boxes. Click **OK**.

This selection creates a pure red outline. Leaving **Transparency** at 0% leaves the outline opaque, or solid.

g. Beginning above and to the left of the top horizontal line, drag a marquee (selection net) around the four horizontal lines.

h. Click the **Format tab**, if necessary, click **Shape Outline** in the Shape Styles group, select **Weight** and then click **6 pt**.

i. Save the *chap3_ho1_shapes_solution* presentation.

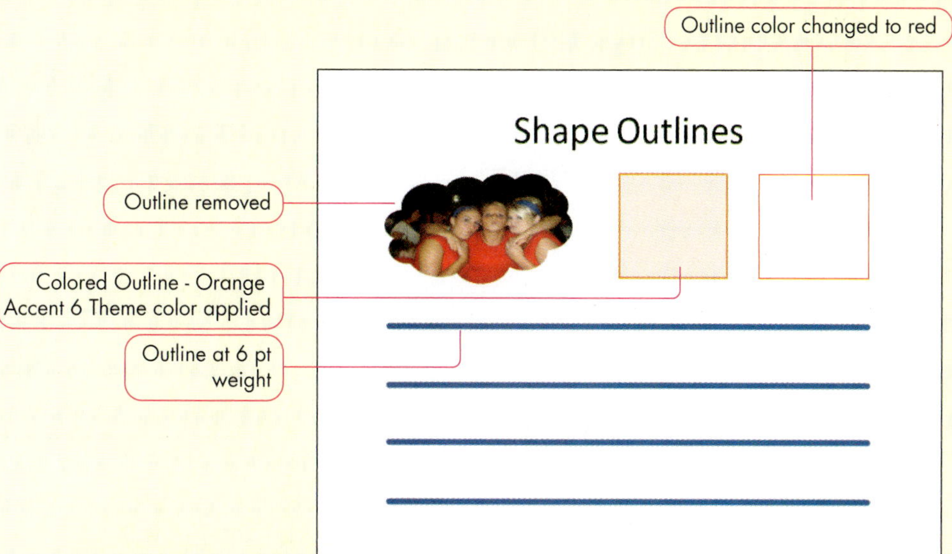

Figure 3.23 Outline Colors and Weights

Step 6
Change Outline, Dash, and Arrow Styles

Refer to Figure 3.24 as you complete Step 6.

a. With *chap3_ho1_shapes_solution* onscreen, select **Slide 7**, and then select the first horizontal line.

b. Click the **Format tab**, click **Shape Outline** in the Shape Styles group, and then point to **Dashes**.

c. Click **Long Dash Dot Dot**.

d. Select the second horizontal line, click **Shape Outline,** point to **Dashes**, and then click **Long Dash**.

e. Select the third horizontal line, click **Shape Outline**, point to **Dashes**, and then click **More Lines**.

   The Format Shape dialog box opens, providing you with options for creating custom lines including compound line types.

f. Click the **Compound type drop-down arrow**, select the last option on the list, and then click **Close**.

   This selection creates a compound line composed of three lines of different weights: one thin line, one thick line, and then one thin line.

g. Select the fourth horizontal line, click **Shape Outline**, point to **Arrows**, and then click **Arrow Style 3**.

h. Select the fifth horizontal line, click **Shape Outline**, point to **Arrows**, and then click **Arrow Style 9**.

i. Select the last horizontal line, click **Shape Outline,** point to **Arrows**, and then click **More Arrows**.

j. Click the **Begin type arrow**, then click **Stealth Arrow**.

k. Click the **End type arrow**, click **Oval Arrow**, and click **Close**

l. Save the *chap3_ho1_shapes_solution* presentation.

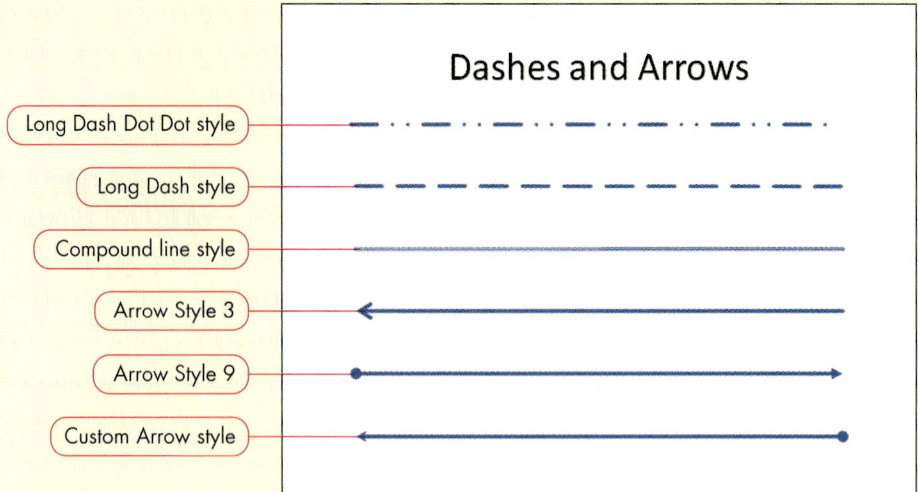

Figure 3.24 Line Dash and Arrow Styles

Step 7
Use Shape Effects

Refer to Figure 3.25 as you complete Step 7.

a. With *chap3_ho1_shapes_solution* onscreen, select **Slide 8**, and then select **Rectangle 1**.

b. Click the **Format tab**, if necessary, click **Shape Effects** in the Shape Styles group, and then click **Preset**.

c. Click **Preset 7**.

   Preset 7 combines a bevel type, a depth, contours, and a surface effect.

d. Select **Rectangle 2**, click **Shape Effects** in the Shape Styles group, click **Shadow**, and then click **Offset Diagonal Bottom Left** in the Outer category.

   The Offset Diagonal option applies a 4-pt soft shadow to the rectangle.

e. Select **Rectangle 3**, click **Shape Effects**, click **Reflection**, and then click **Tight Reflection, touching**.

f. Select **Rectangle 4**, click **Shape Effects**, click **Glow**, and then click **Accent color 2, 11 pt glow**.

g. Continue to use the **Shape Effects** options to apply effects to the remaining shapes.

Shape	**Effect**	**Style**
Cloud	Soft Edges	10 Point
Explosion	Bevel	Soft Round
Callout	3-D Rotation	Off Axis 1 Top (Parallel category)

h. Save the *chap3_ho1_shapes_solution* presentation, and close it.

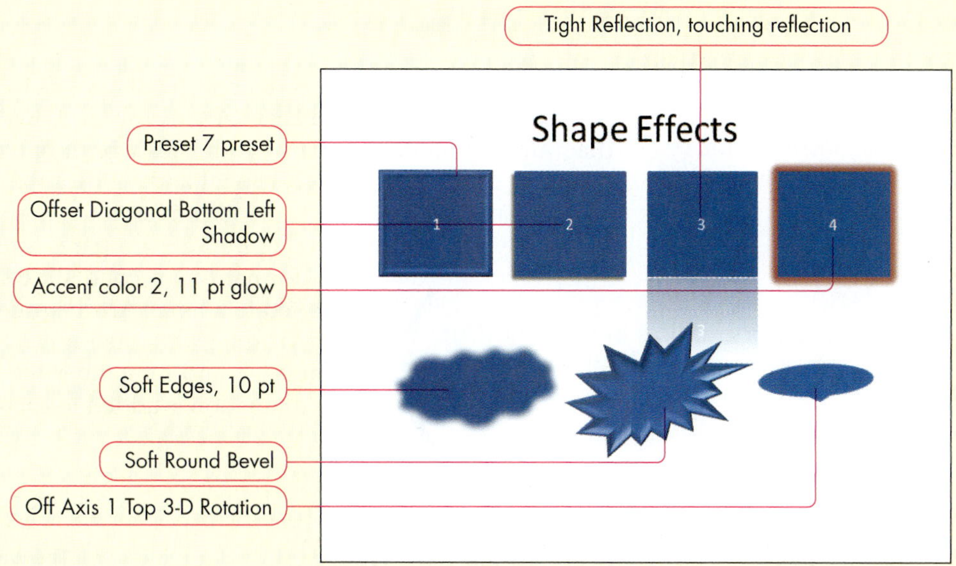

Figure 3.25 Shape Effects

SmartArt

> ***SmartArt*** is a diagram that presents information visually to effectively communicate a message.

One of the major purposes of creating shapes is to call attention to information. Recognizing this idea, the ***SmartArt*** feature in PowerPoint enables you to create a diagram and enter the text of your message in one of many existing layouts. The resulting illustration is professional and follows the theme you have selected. You also can take existing slide text and convert it to SmartArt to create a visual representation of your information. Figure 3.26 compares a text-based slide in the common bullet format to a second slide showing the same information converted to a SmartArt diagram. The arrows and colors in the SmartArt diagram make it easy for the viewer to understand the message and remember the cycle. It is especially effective when animation is added to each step.

> The arrows and colors in the SmartArt diagram make it easy for the viewer to understand the message. . . .

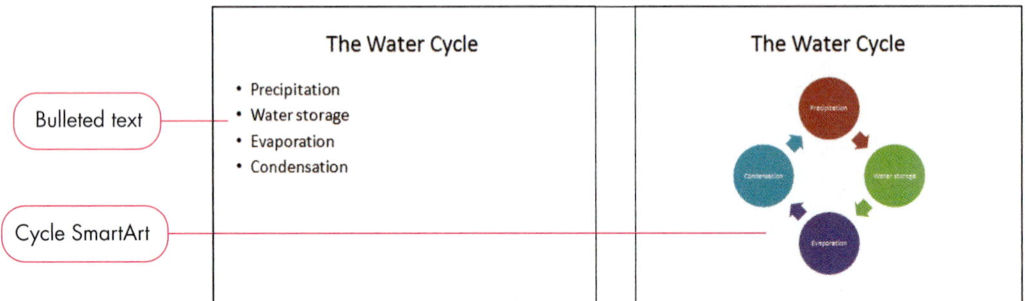

Figure 3.26 A SmartArt Depiction of the Water Cycle

Using the SmartArt feature rather than creating your own shapes is efficient and can even be inspiring when you are at a loss as to how to effectively convey your message. A SmartArt diagram creates a layout for your information, provides a Text pane for quickly entering information, automatically sizes shapes and text, and gives you the ability to switch between layouts, making it easy to choose the most effective layout. Some layouts can be used for any type of information and are designed to be visually attractive, while other layouts are created specifically for a certain type of information. For example, perhaps you have a list of items and you want to present them in an attractive way; you would select a SmartArt graphic that applies special effects but does not imply that steps must be followed in order. If, however, you have a list of steps that must be followed in order, you would select a SmartArt graphic that is numbered as well as having special effects. SmartArt includes more than 80 different layouts.

In this section, you create and modify a SmartArt diagram. Modifications include changing theme colors, using SmartArt Quick Styles, changing the layout, changing the SmartArt type, and converting text to SmartArt.

Creating SmartArt

To create a SmartArt graphic or diagram, you must choose a diagram type. The type you choose should be based on the purpose of your information and the ability of the layout for the SmartArt type to convey your message. The SmartArt gallery has seven different categories of diagrams: lists, processes, cycles, hierarchies, relationships, matrices, and pyramids. Each category includes a description of the type of information appropriate for the layouts in that category. The Reference page shows the SmartArt categories and their purposes.

SmartArt Diagram | Reference

Icon	Type	Purpose	Sample SmartArt
List	List	Use to show non-sequential information. For example: A list of items to be checked on a roof each year.	Flashing Shingles Soffits
Process	Process	Use to show steps in a process or a timeline. For example: The steps to take to wash a car.	Hose Sponge Rinse
Cycle	Cycle	Use to show a continual process. For example: The recurring business cycle.	Expansion Recovery Downturn Recession
Hierarchy	Hierarchy	Use to show a decision tree, organization chart, or pedigree. For example: A pedigree chart showing the parents of an individual.	Reed J. Olsen Ivan Olsen Gladys Jones
Relationship	Relationship	Use to illustrate connections. For example: The connection between outdoor activities.	Camping Hiking Fishing
Matrix	Matrix	Use to show how parts relate to a whole. For example: Keirsey's Temperament Theory of four groups describing human behavior	Rationals Idealists Keirsey Temperaments Artisans Guardians
Pyramid	Pyramid	Use to show proportional relationships with the largest component on the top or bottom. For example: an ecology chart.	Indirect Consumers Direct Consumers Producers

To create a SmartArt diagram, click SmartArt in the Illustrations group on the Insert tab. The Choose a SmartArt Graphic dialog box displays (see Figure 3.27) with three panes. The pane on the left side shows the types of SmartArt diagrams available. Each type of diagram includes subtypes that are displayed in the center pane. Clicking one of the subtypes enlarges the selected graphic and displays it in the preview pane on the right side. The preview pane describes purposes for which the SmartArt can be used effectively. Some of the descriptions include tips for the type of text to enter.

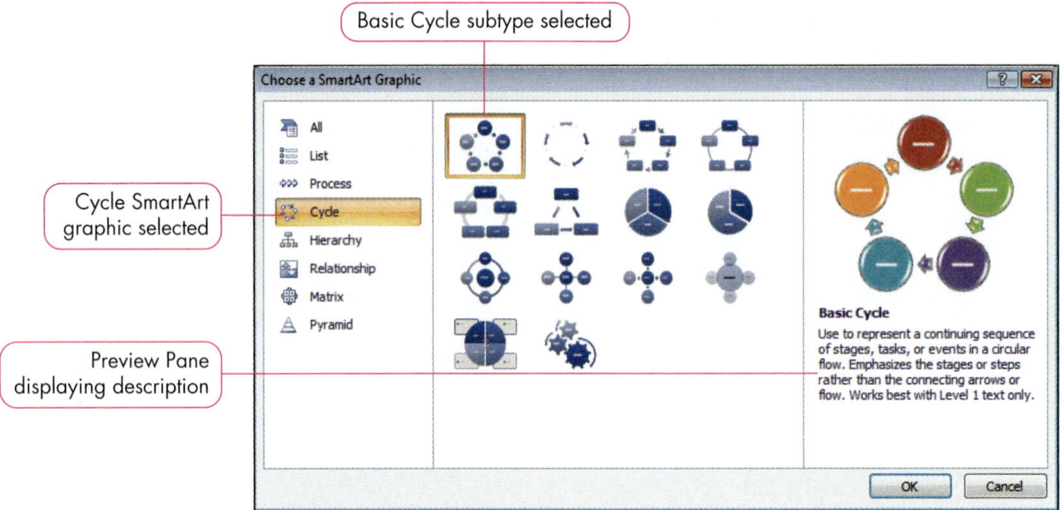

Figure 3.27 The SmartArt Gallery

TIP Text in SmartArt

The amount of text you enter in a SmartArt diagram impacts how many shapes your layout can contain. Keep your text short and limit it to key points to create a visually appealing diagram.

A ***Text pane*** is a special pane that opens up for text entry when a SmartArt diagram is selected.

Once you click to select the SmartArt diagram type and the subtype you desire, a ***Text pane*** opens for you to use to enter text. If the Text pane does not open, click Text Pane in the Create Graphic group on the Design tab. The Text pane works like an outline—enter a line of text, press Enter, and then press Tab or Shift+Tab to increase or decrease the indent level. You do not have to worry about the font size or the position of the text when you use the Text pane. The font size will decrease to fit text inside of the shape, or the shape may grow to fit the text. The layout accommodates additional shapes as you enter text—unless the type of shape is designed for a specific number of shapes, such as the Relationship Counterbalance Arrows layout, which is designed to show two opposing ideas. Figure 3.28 shows text entered into the Text pane for a Basic Cycle SmartArt diagram. Because five lines of text were created, five shapes were created.

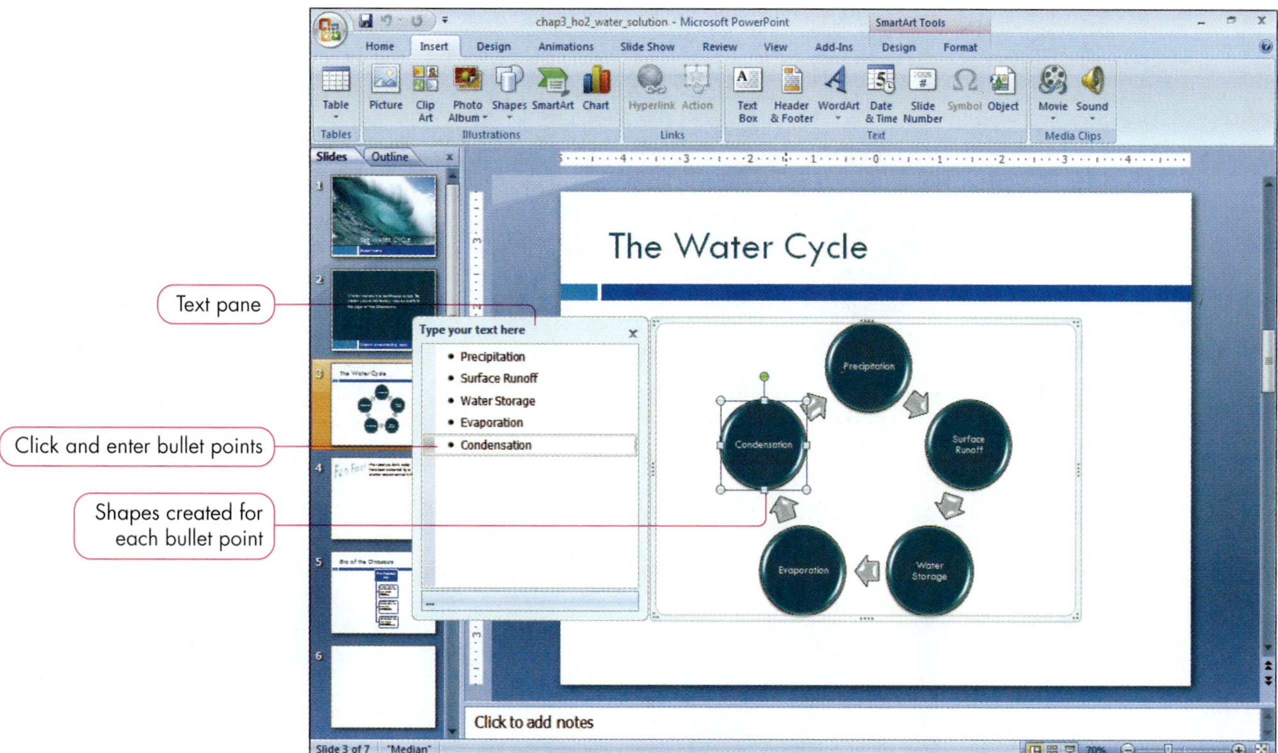

Figure 3.28 The SmartArt Text Pane

Modifying SmartArt Diagrams

Standard editing methods apply to SmartArt diagrams. For example, you can drag a SmartArt diagram by its borders to reposition it. You also can modify SmartArt text in the Text pane just as if it is in a placeholder, or you can modify the text in the shape itself. If you need an additional shape, click a shape, and then in the Text pane, position your insertion point at the beginning of the text where you want to add a shape. Type your text, and then press Enter.

An alternative method for adding shapes is to use the Add Shape command. Click an existing shape in the SmartArt diagram, and then under the SmartArt Tools contextual tab, click the Design tab. Click the Add Shape arrow in the Create Graphic group. Select Add Shape After, Add Shape Before, Add Shape Above, or Add Shape Below.

In addition to these standard methods of modifying, you also can format the SmartArt so that it really stands out. SmartArt diagrams have two galleries you use to change the look of the diagram, both of which are located under the SmartArt Tools contextual tab in the SmartArt Styles group on the Design tab. One gallery changes colors, and the other gallery applies a combination of special effects.

Change SmartArt Theme Colors

To change the color scheme of your SmartArt, click the Change Colors command to display the Colors gallery (see Figure 3.29). The gallery contains Primary Theme Colors, Colorful color choices, and color schemes based on Accent colors. Click the color variation that you want, and your SmartArt will update.

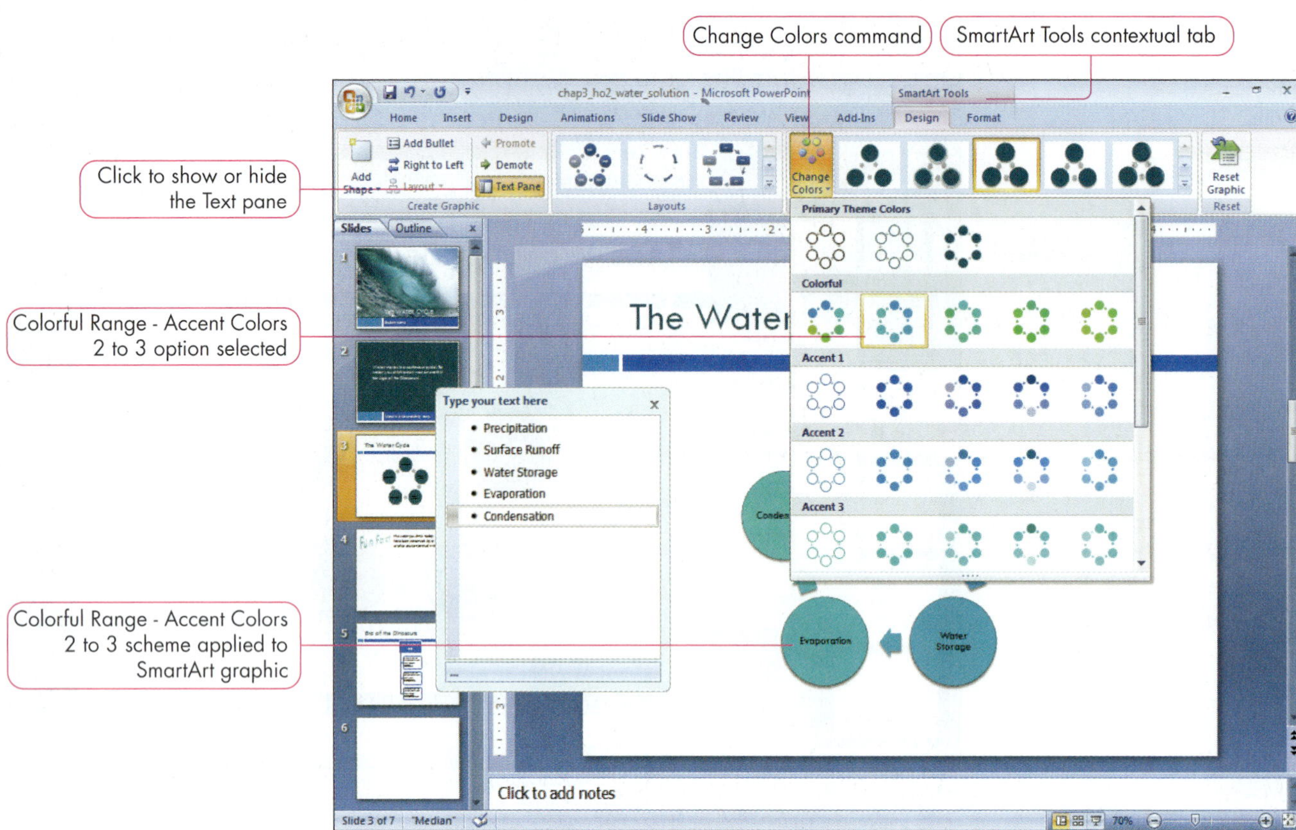

Figure 3.29 The SmartArt Color Options

Use Quick Styles with SmartArt

After creating the diagram, you can adjust the style of the diagram to match previous styles you have used in your presentation, or to make the diagram easier to understand. To apply a Quick Style to a SmartArt diagram, click your diagram and then click the Quick Style that you want from the SmartArt Styles gallery. To see the complete gallery, click the More button located in the SmartArt Styles group on the Design tab. The gallery opens and displays simple combinations of special effects, such as shadows, gradients, and 3-D effects that combine perspectives and surface styles. Figure 3.30 displays the SmartArt Quick Styles gallery.

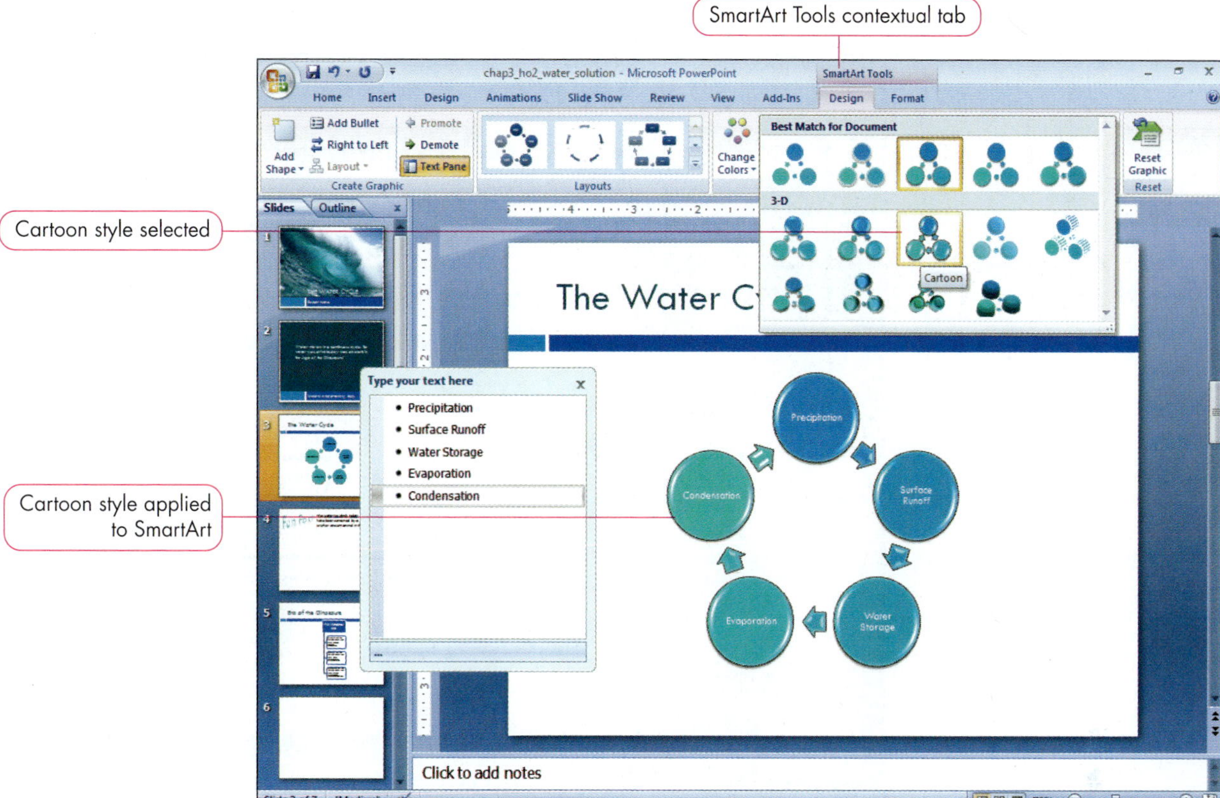

Figure 3.30 The SmartArt Quick Styles Gallery

Change the Layout

After selecting a type of SmartArt diagram, you may find the diagram fits your purpose, but the layout needs tweaking. An example would be a diagram you created that is unreadable due to the amount of text you have entered. Modifying the layout may give you more room for the text. Figure 3.31 shows a Hierarchy diagram displaying the relationship between the Mesozoic Era and its periods, along with the type of animal and dinosaur that lived during the period. In order for the text to fit, PowerPoint reduced the font size to 6 pt. Even projected on a screen, this text would be unreadable for most audience members.

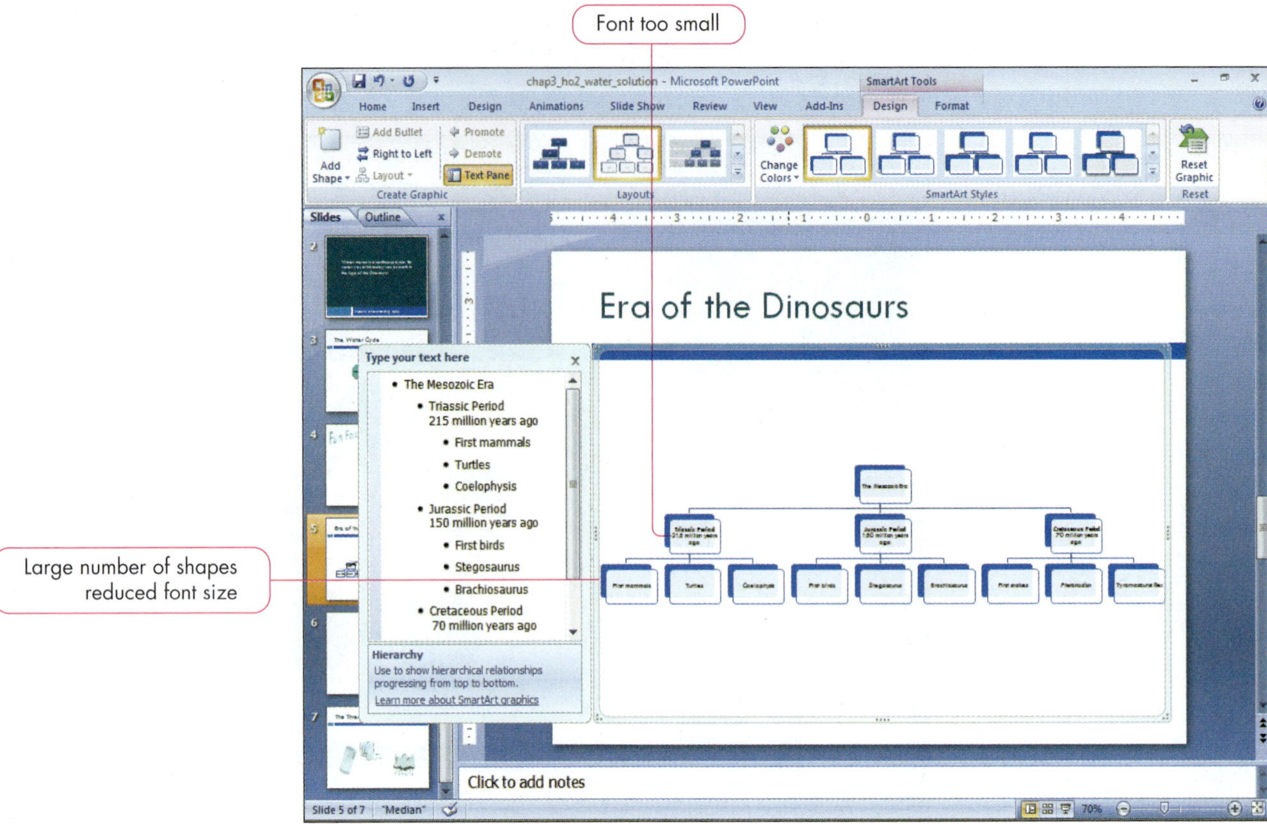

Figure 3.31 Hierarchy 1 SmartArt

By tweaking the layout, you can make the Mesozoic layout much more easily read. First, select the SmartArt diagram, and then click the SmartArt Tools Design tab. Click the More button in the Layouts group to display the Layouts gallery. Some of the layouts have special effects such as shadowing, some have fill changes, some change the box shape and border, and some change the orientation of the layout from horizontal to vertical. Test the options to determine which one provides for the greatest legibility. Figure 3.32 shows the Mesozoic information in a Hierarchy List diagram that uses a vertical orientation.

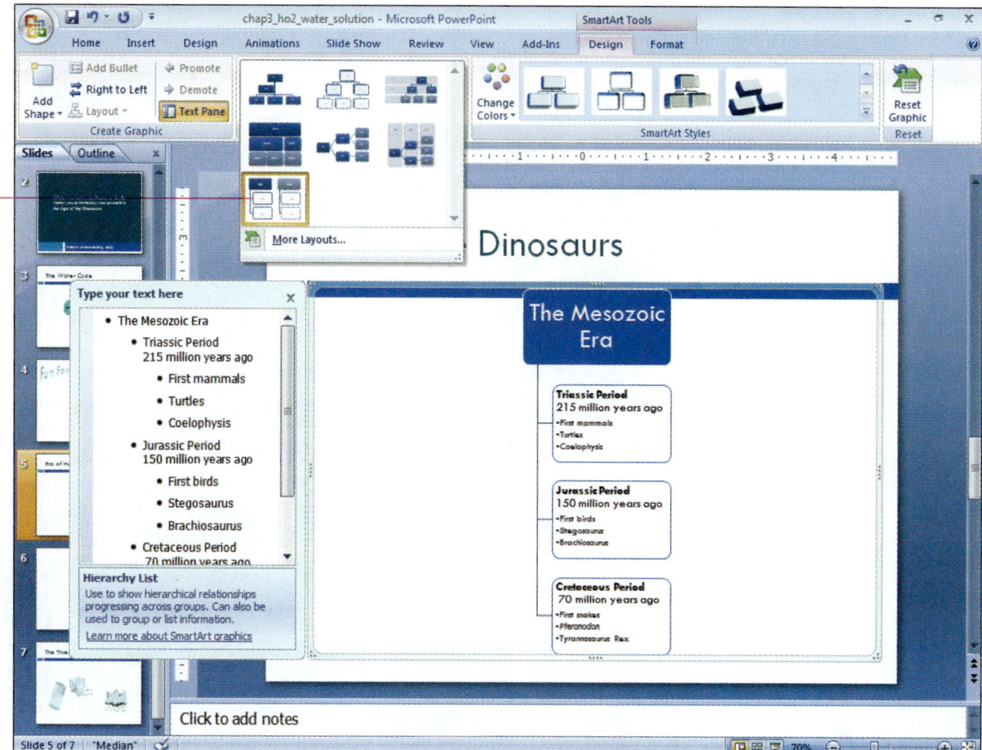

Figure 3.32 Hierarchy List SmartArt

Change SmartArt Type

You can switch a SmartArt diagram to another diagram type if you decide another SmartArt layout would better accomplish your goal. Because changing a type is similar to changing the SmartArt layout, the process is the same. To change to another SmartArt diagram, click to select the SmartArt diagram. Click the More button in the Layouts group on the SmartArt Tools Design tab, and then click More Layouts. The Choose a SmartArt Graphic gallery appears with all the categories and their layouts. Click the type and layout you desire.

Keep in mind that switching diagram types alters the layout, which may impact the audience's perception of your diagram. For example, if you have created a list of nonsequential items, switching to a cycle diagram implies a specific order to the items. Also, if you have customized the shapes, the customizations may not be transferred. Colors, line styles, and fills transfer. Rotation does not. For a complete list of which customizations will transfer and which will not, go to Help and search for *Adding charts, diagrams, or tables.*

Convert Text to a SmartArt Diagram

If you already have created text on a slide and then decide you want a SmartArt diagram, you can convert the existing text into a SmartArt illustration. Select the placeholder containing your text, and then click Convert to SmartArt Graphic in the Paragraph group on the Home tab. When the gallery appears, click the layout for the SmartArt diagram that you want (see Figure 3.33).

(. . . you can convert . . . existing text into a SmartArt illustration.)

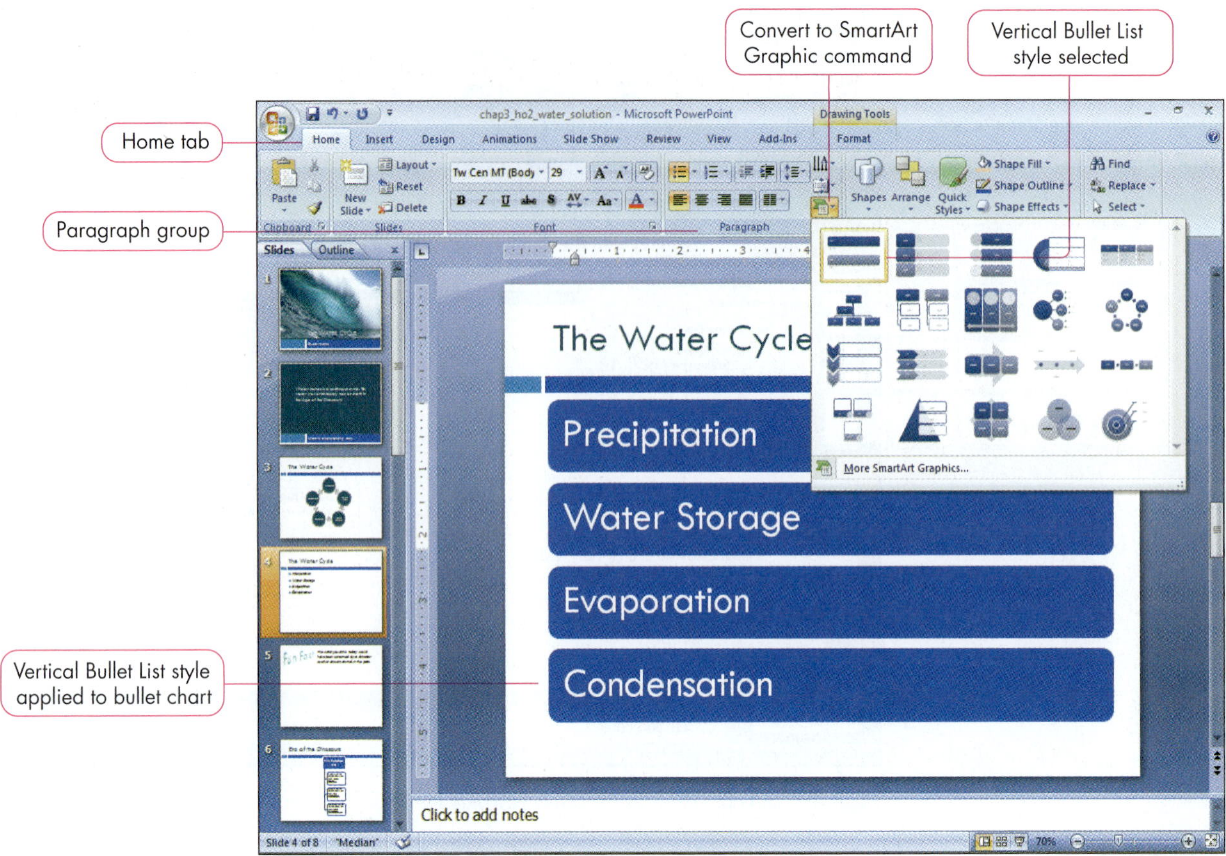

Figure 3.33 Convert to SmartArt Options

TIP Converting Text to SmartArt Using a Shortcut

For a quick method of converting text in a placeholder into SmartArt, right-click text in a placeholder and then select Convert to SmartArt. The Convert to SmartArt gallery opens so you can select a SmartArt style.

WordArt

WordArt is text that has a decorative effect applied.

WordArt is text that uses special effects based on styles in the WordArt Gallery for the purpose of calling attention to the text. While at first this may seem like WordArt is the same as SmartArt, there is a major difference. SmartArt emphasizes text by surrounding it with a container that could have special effects applied to the container. In WordArt, however, the special effect applies to the text itself, not a shape surrounding the text. For example, rather than the box surrounding text having a reflection, the text itself would have a reflection. By applying special effects directly to the text, you can create eye-catching text that emphasizes the information for your audience. Imagine text following a curve or shaped as a wave or slanted—the possibilities are endless. In this section, you explore WordArt styles to create and modify a WordArt object.

Creating WordArt

The term ***stacked*** refers to the vertical alignment of text.

WordArt has a gallery of text styles to choose from as well as options you can use to select individual settings. WordArt text even can be changed from a horizontal alignment to a ***stacked*** or vertical alignment, and can be rotated 90° to the right or left. Figure 3.34 shows WordArt text with each of these options applied.

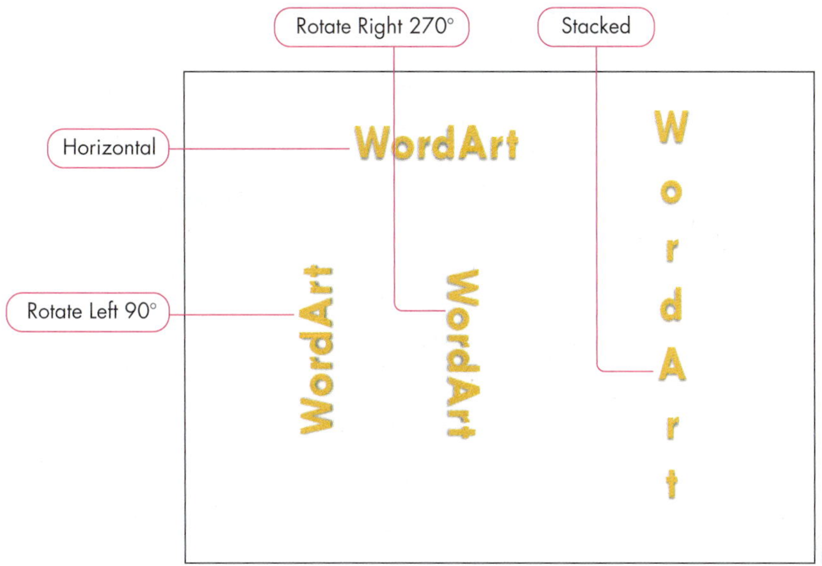

Figure 3.34 WordArt Alignment Options

You can create your text as WordArt, or you can convert existing text into WordArt. To create WordArt, click WordArt in the Text group on the Insert tab. When you click WordArt, the WordArt gallery opens with a variety of special effects to choose from. The colors reflected in the gallery match the Theme colors. Click the WordArt style of your choice and then enter your text in the WordArt placeholder.

Modifying WordArt

You can change the style of your WordArt by clicking a Quick Style located in the WordArt Styles group on the Format tab under the Drawing Tools contextual tab. Or, if you prefer, you can modify the individual elements of the WordArt by changing its fill, outline, or effects by clicking Text Fill, Text Outline, or Text Effects in the WordArt Styles group. WordArt Text Effects has a unique Transform option. Transform can rotate the WordArt text around a path, or add a warp to stretch, angle, or bloat letters. Figure 3.35 displays the WordArt Quick Styles gallery, and Figure 3.36 shows the WordArt Transform options.

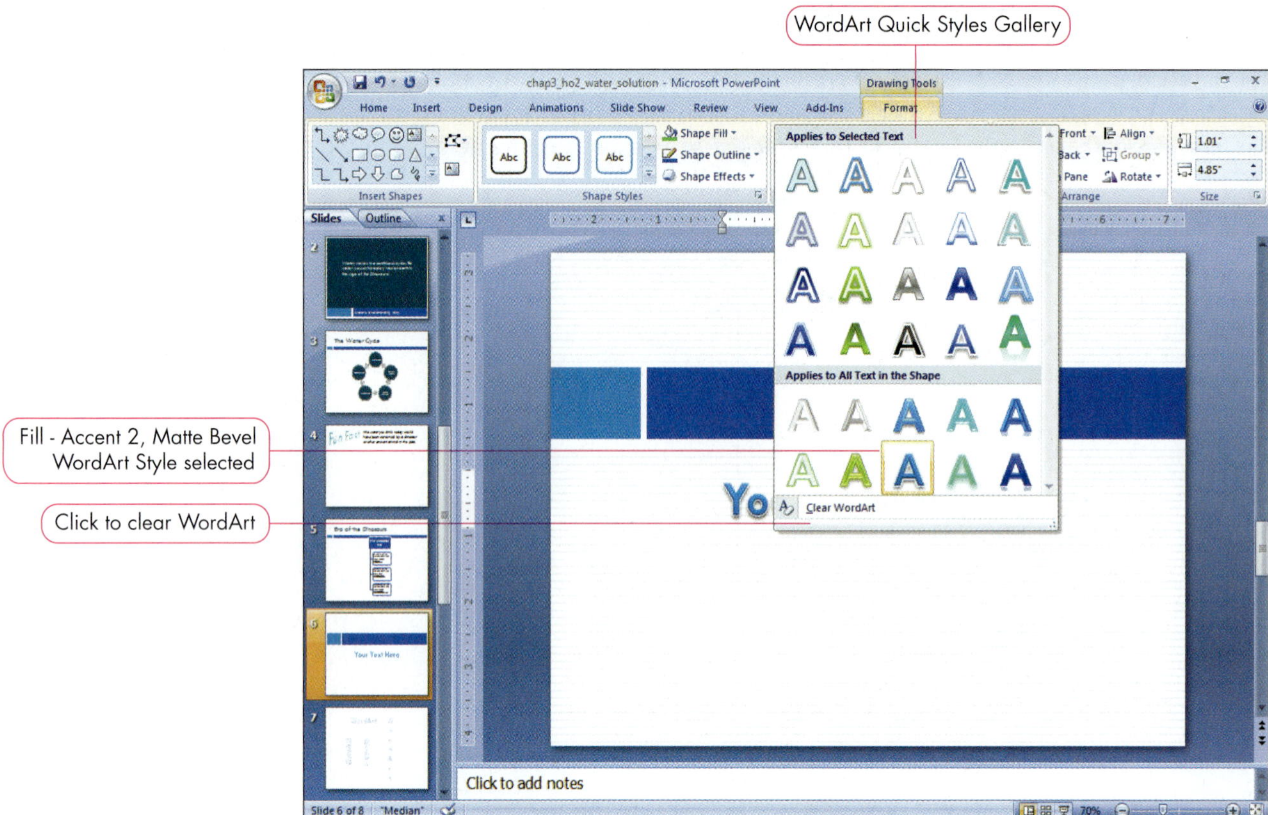

Figure 3.35 WordArt Quick Styles Gallery Options

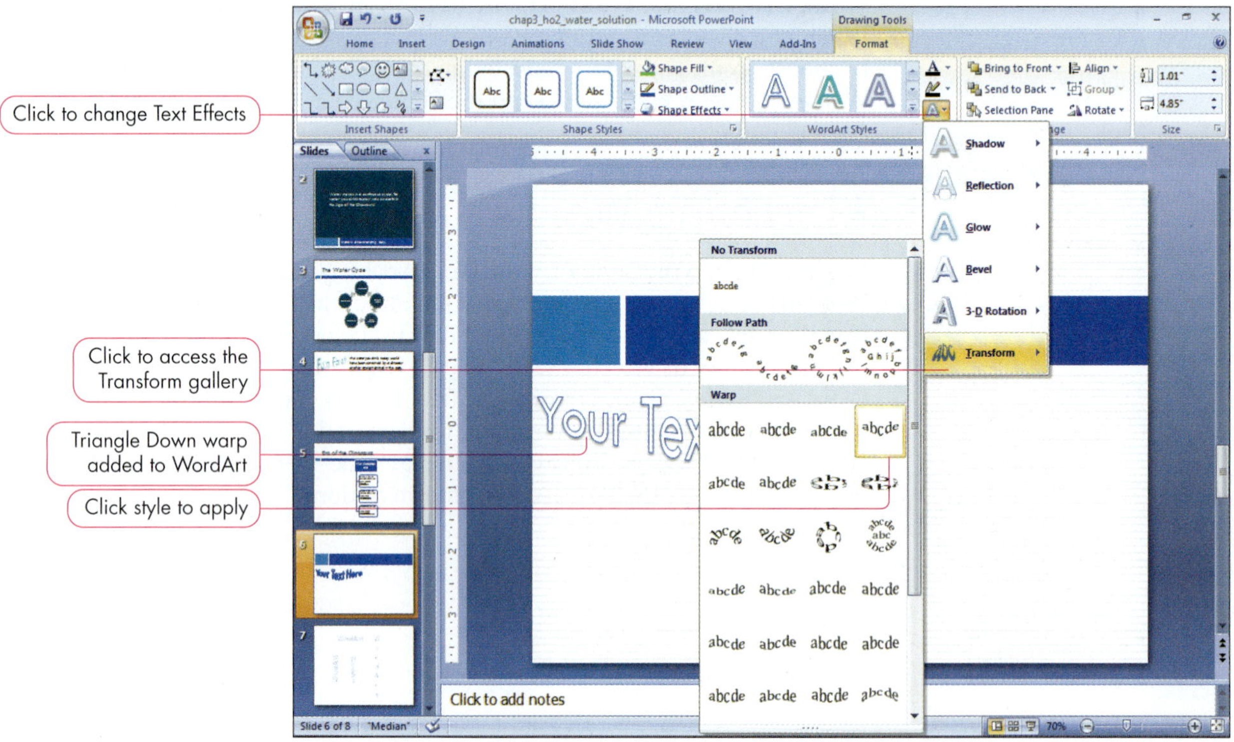

Figure 3.36 Warp Options Available with Transform

Hands-On Exercises

2 | Working with SmartArt and WordArt

Skills covered: 1. Insert SmartArt **2.** Modify a SmartArt Diagram **3.** Change SmartArt Layout **4.** Create WordArt **5.** Modify WordArt

Step 1
Insert SmartArt

Refer to Figure 3.37 as you complete Step 1.

a. Open the *chap3_ho2_water* presentation, and then immediately save it as **chap3_ho2_water_solution**.

b. Move to **Slide 3**, click the **Insert tab**, and then click **SmartArt** in the Illustrations group.

c. In the Choose a SmartArt Graphic dialog box, click **Cycle**, click the subtype **Basic Cycle,** and then click **OK**.

d. Click **Text Pane** in the Create Graphic group, if the Text pane is not displayed.

   The *Type your text here* pane opens, and your pointer is located in the first bullet location so that you can enter the text for your first cycle shape.

e. Type **Precipitation**.

   The font size for the text reduces so that the text fits inside the shape.

f. Press the **down arrow** on the keyboard to move to the second bullet and type **Water Storage**. Type the two remaining bullet points: **Evaporation** and **Condensation**.

g. Press the **down arrow** on the keyboard to move to the last bullet point and press **Backspace**.

   The extra shape in the Cycle SmartArt is removed.

h. Click the **X** on the top right of the *Type your text here* pane to close the pane.

i. Drag to reposition the SmartArt object so that it does not sit on the blue border.

j. Save the *chap3_ho2_water_solution* presentation.

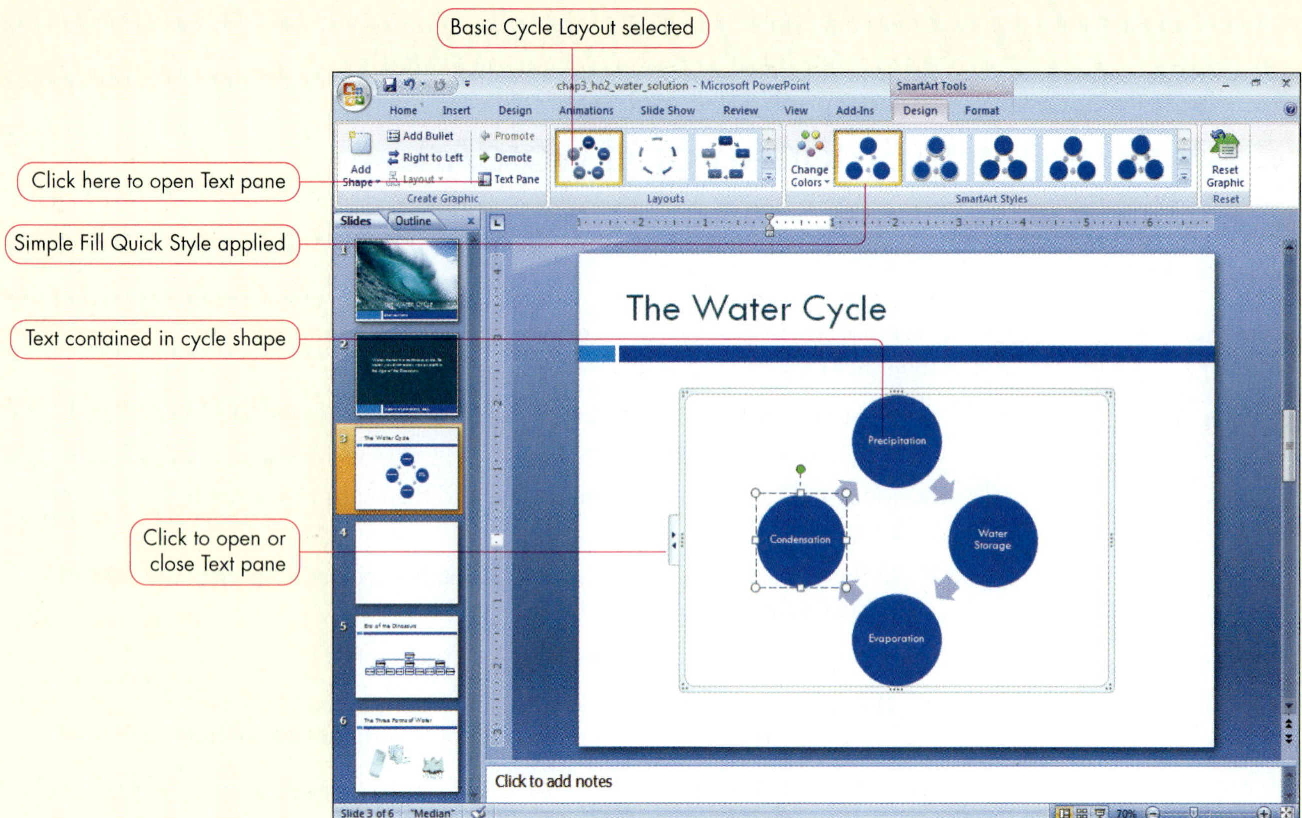

Figure 3.37 Basic Cycle SmartArt

Step 2 Modify a SmartArt Diagram

Refer to Figures 3.38 and 3.39 as you complete Step 2.

a. Click the Precipitation shape at the top of the cycle SmartArt, then click the **SmartArt Tools contextual tab**, if necessary, and click the **Design tab** (if necessary).

b. Click the lower part of **Add Shape** in the Create Graphic group on the Design tab, and then select **Add Shape After**.

Figure 3.38 shows the Add Shape options.

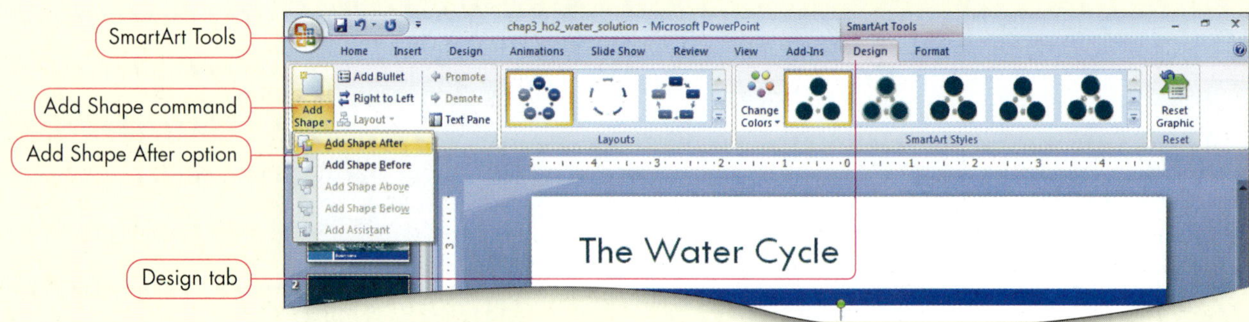

Figure 3.38 Add Shape Options

c. Type **Surface Runoff** in the new shape.

d. Click the SmartArt border to select all the shapes in your SmartArt diagram, and then click **Change Colors** in the SmartArt Styles group on the SmartArt Tools Design tab.

e. Click **Dark 2 Fill** in the Primary Theme Colors category.

f. Click the **More button** in the SmartArt Styles group.

   Move your pointer over the styles to see the impact each style has on the text in your SmartArt. Remember—the goal of graphics is to enhance your message, not make it unreadable. Your first priority should always be to make it easy for your audience to understand your message, not to decorate.

g. Click **Cartoon**.

h. Save the *chap3_ho2_water_solution* presentation.

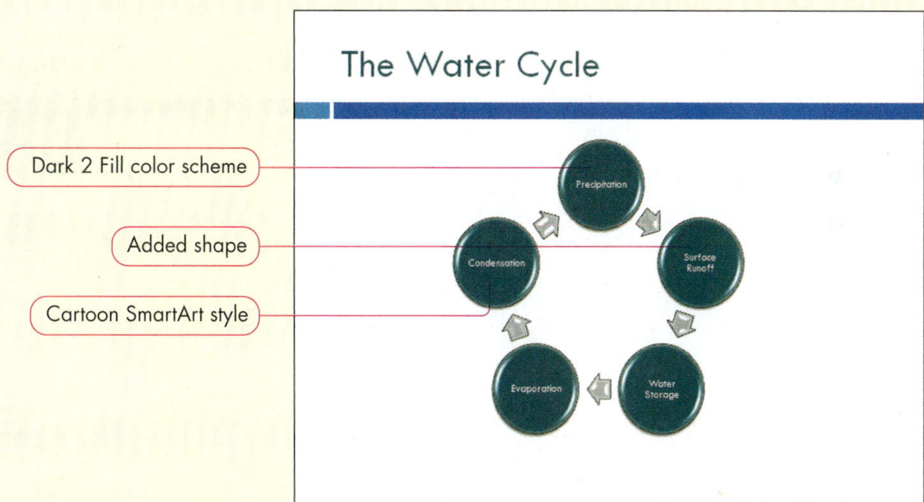

Figure 3.39 Modified SmartArt

Step 3
Change SmartArt Layout

Refer to Figure 3.40 as you complete Step 3.

a. With *chap3_ho2_water_solution* onscreen, move to **Slide 5**.

b. Click to select the SmartArt Hierarchy shape.

c. Click the **Design tab**, which is under SmartArt Tools.

d. Click the **More button** in the Layouts group, and then click **Hierarchy List** under the *Hierarchy* section.

TROUBLESHOOTING: Your screen may not match Figure 3.40 exactly. The dinosaur names have been added to the author's supplemental dictionary so wavy red lines indicating misspelled words do not appear in Figure 3.40. Your screen may display the wavy red lines.

e. Save the *chap3_ho2_water_solution* presentation.

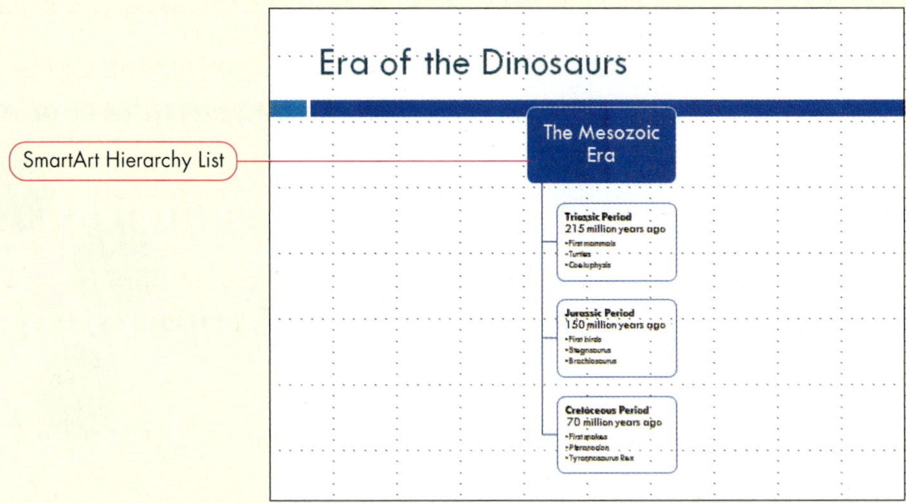

Figure 3.40 Completed SmartArt Diagram

Step 4
Create WordArt

Refer to Figure 3.41 as you complete Step 4.

a. With *chap3_ho2_water_solution* onscreen, move to **Slide 4**.

b. Click the **Insert tab** and then click **WordArt** in the Text group.

c. Click **Fill – Accent 3, Outline – Text 2**.

d. Type **Fun Fact** in the WordArt placeholder.

e. Save the *chap3_ho2_water_solution* presentation.

Figure 3.41 WordArt

Step 5
Modify WordArt

Refer to Figure 3.42 as you complete Step 5.

a. With *chap3_ho2_water_solution* onscreen, select the WordArt in Slide 4, if necessary, and then click the **Drawing Tools Format tab**.

b. Click **Text Effects** in the WordArt Styles group, and then select **Transform**.

   The Transform gallery opens showing Follow Path and Warp options.

c. Select **Cascade Up**, which is located on the bottom row, third from the left.

d. Click in the **Shape Height** box located in the Size group on the far right of the Format tab, type **1.5**, and then press **Enter**.

   The height of the WordArt shape adjusts to 1.5".

e. Drag the WordArt to the top left corner of your slide.

f. Click outside of the WordArt shape to deselect the shape.

g. Click the **Insert tab** and click **Text Box** in the Text group.

h. Click to the right of the WordArt, and then type **The water you drink today could have been consumed by a dinosaur or other ancient animal in the past**.

   The text box expands to fit the text with the result that the text is contained in one long line that flows off the slide.

i. Change the font size of the text to **28 pt**.

   TROUBLESHOOTING: If a text box extends beyond the slide boundaries, you can adjust the placeholder size until it fits on the slide. Drag the right border of the text box until the text box fits on the slide, and then reposition it to the location you desire on the slide.

j. Save the *chap3_ho2_water_solution* presentation.

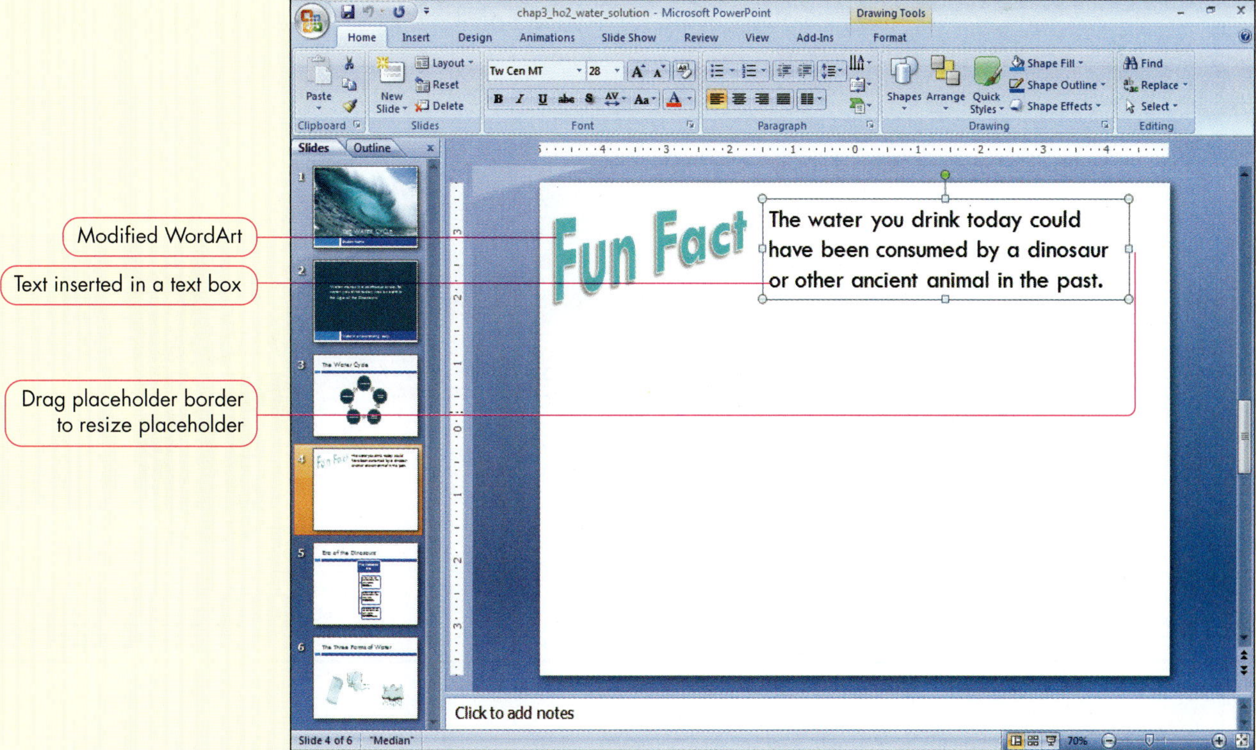

Figure 3.42 Modified WordArt

Object Manipulation

Making slides interesting is one of the goals you have been working toward thus far in this text—making the slides interesting keeps the audience's attention and increases their memory of your message. You have inserted clips, created shapes, added SmartArt, and created WordArt to accomplish this goal. As you add these objects to your slides, however, you will find that often you need to manipulate them. Perhaps you have several shapes created, and you want them to align at their left edges, or you want to arrange them by their center point and then determine the order of the shapes. Perhaps you have inserted a clip art image and the colors used in the clip art do not match the color of the SmartArt on a slide. You may even locate the perfect clip art image—except it is not perfect! It has the images you want but also includes something you do not want. For example, you locate the perfect picnic basket for your Labor Day celebration invitation, but the picnic basket is sitting on a tablecloth. You want to remove the tablecloth from the image and use just the picnic basket.

In this section you learn how to modify objects. In particular, you isolate objects you need, flip and rotate objects, group and ungroup objects, and recolor clip art. You also learn to determine the order of objects and align objects to each other and to the slide.

Modifying Objects

Examine a clip art object and you will see that the clip art image is made from a series of combined shapes. Modify existing clip art by breaking it apart into its individual shapes and then removing pieces you do not need, capturing just the shapes you need, changing or recoloring shapes, rotating shapes, and combining shapes from several clip art objects to create a new clip art object. It takes a lot of talent to create original clip art by drawing and combining shapes, but it takes only a little imagination to create a picture from existing clip art. Figure 3.43 shows a clip art image available from Microsoft Online by searching for the keyword *picnic*. The clip art was broken apart, the fireworks, flag, fries, and tablecloth removed, the hamburger, hotdogs, and milkshake flipped and resized, and finally the chocolate milkshake recolored so that it became a strawberry milkshake.

Figure 3.43 Modified Clip Art

Resizing objects is the most common modification procedure, and you already have learned to resize an object by dragging a sizing handle. You may need a more precise method of changing size, however. For example, you use PowerPoint to create an advertisement for an automobile trader magazine, and the magazine specifies that the ad must fit in a 2" by 2" space. You must size your photograph exactly to fit the requirement. You can enter an exact height and width measurement for your photographic object or an exact proportion of its original size.

To enter an exact measurement, select the object and then click Format, which is located under any of the Tools contextual tabs (such as Drawing Tools, SmartArt Tools, Picture Tools, Chart Tools, and so on). The Size group is located at the far right of any of the Format tabs and contains boxes to quickly change the Height and Width. It also contains a Size Dialog Box Launcher that opens the Size and Position dialog box with many more options.

Cropping an image means to reduce its size by removing unwanted portions of an image.

Aspect ratio refers to the ratio of width to height.

The Size tab in the Size and Position dialog box contains a section for entering exact measurements for Height and Width and a precise Rotation angle, a section for scaling an object based on its original size (note that not all clip art entered from the Clip Art task pane is brought in at full size), a section that enables you to ***crop*** unwanted parts off the image, and a section that restores the object to its original size, which you engage by clicking a Reset button. To keep the original height and width proportions of a clip, make sure the *Lock aspect ratio* check box is selected. ***Aspect ratio*** refers to the width-to-height ratio of an image. The clip art image in Figure 3.44 was sized to 265% of its original size.

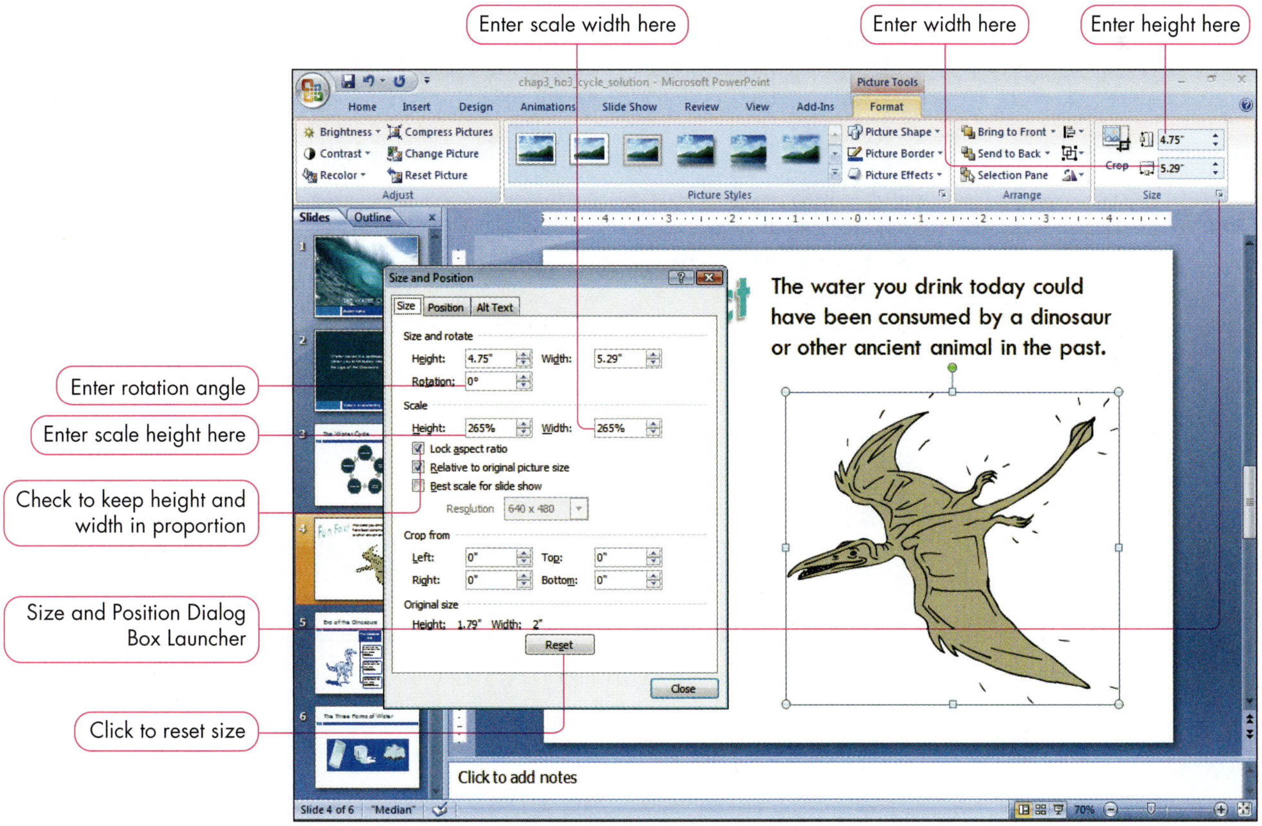

Figure 3.44 Sizing Options

Flip and Rotate

Sometimes you will find that an object is facing the wrong way. It might be facing off the slide when you need it to face text, or perhaps it is at an angle and you need it to be level. Perhaps you took a photograph with your digital camera sideways to get a full-length view, but when you download the image it is sideways. You can quickly rotate the object left or right 90°, flip it horizontally or vertically, or freely rotate it any number of degrees.

You can freely rotate a selected object by dragging the green rotation handle that appears at the top of the object in the direction that you want to rotate. To constrain the rotation to 15-degree angles, hold down Shift while dragging. To rotate exactly 90° to the left or the right, click Rotate in the Arrange group on the Format tab under the Picture Tools contextual tab. The tab name varies based on the selected object type.

When you click Rotate, you can flip the object vertically or horizontally to get a mirror-image of an object. If you prefer, you can drag one of the side sizing handles over the opposite side to flip it. If you do not drag far enough, however, you will distort the image. Figure 3.45 shows a clip art image that has been flipped.

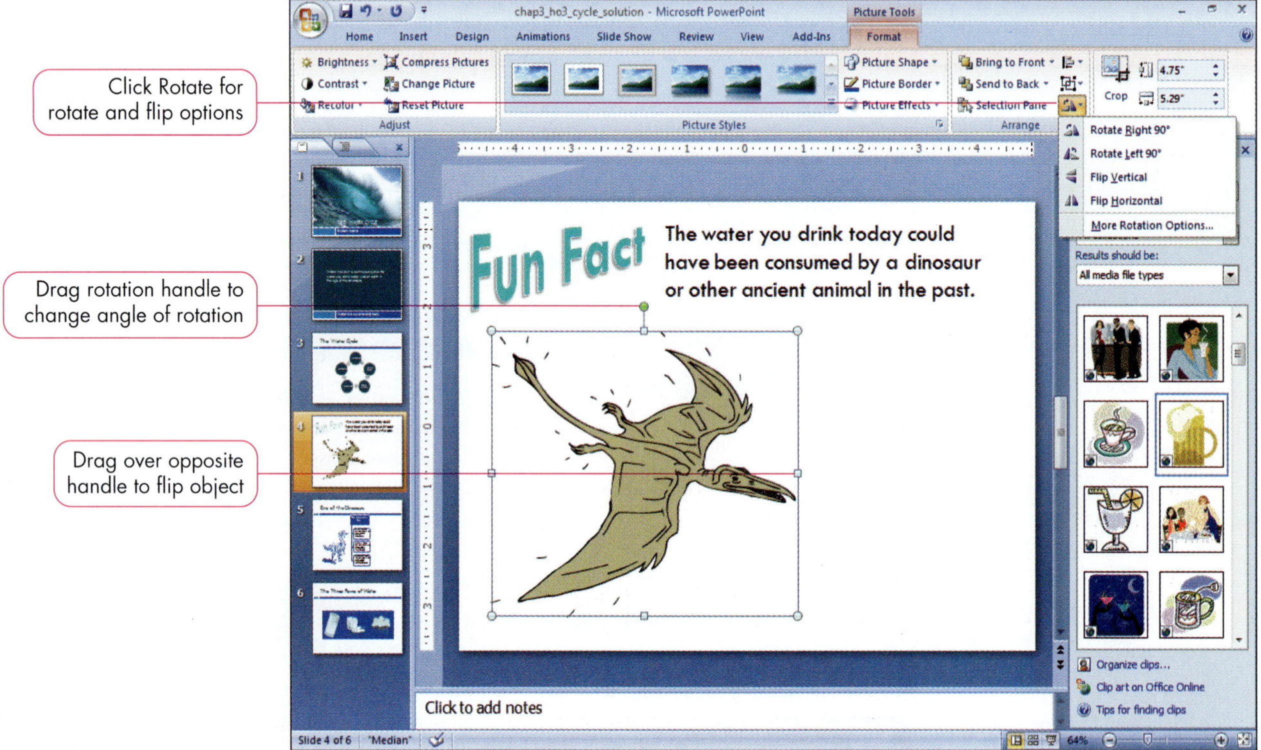

Figure 3.45 Rotating and Flipping Options

Group and Ungroup Objects

Grouping is combining two or more objects.

Ungrouping is breaking a combined object into individual objects.

*A **vector graphic*** is an object-oriented graphic based on geometric formulas.

A clip art object usually is created in pieces, layered, and then grouped to create the final clip art image. This process can be reversed. Clip art can be ungrouped, or broken apart so the individual pieces can be modified or deleted. ***Grouping*** enables multiple objects to act or move as though they were a single object, while ***ungrouping*** lets individual shapes move.

In order for a clip art image to be ungrouped and grouped, it must be created and saved as a vector graphic. ***Vector graphics*** are created using geometrical formulas to represent images and are created in drawing programs such as Adobe Illustrator and CorelDRAW. The advantage of vector files is that they can be easily edited, can be layered, and use a small amount of storage space. Microsoft's Clip Art task pane contains Microsoft Windows Metafile (.wmf) clip art, which are vector graphics.

TIP Clip Art That Will Not Ungroup

If your selected clip art image will not ungroup for editing, it is not in a vector format. The Clip Art task pane also contains clips in bitmap, .jpg, .gif, or .png formats, which are not vector-based images and cannot be ungrouped.

Clip art inserted from the Clip Art task pane needs to be converted into a drawing object as the first step of editing. Right-click the clip art image on the slide, and then click Edit Picture. A message appears asking if you want to convert the picture into a drawing object. Click Yes. This action converts and ungroups the clip so individual pieces can be modified. Complex clip art images may have more than one grouping, however. The artist may create an image from individual shapes, group it, layer it on other images, and then group it again. Figure 3.46 is an example of a complex Microsoft Windows Metafile that has multiple groups.

Fun Fact
The water you drink today could have been consumed by a dinosaur or other ancient animal in the past.
Group 1
Group 2

Figure 3.46 Complex Clip Art with Multiple Groups

To continue ungrouping, select the clip and then click Format under Drawing Tools. The Group option becomes active in the Arrange group. Click Group, and if the clip art image can be broken down further, the Ungroup option is active, and Group and Regroup are grayed out. Click Ungroup, and each individual shape is surrounded by adjustment handles. Click outside of the clip art borders to deselect the shapes, and then click the individual shape you wish to change. Figure 3.47 shows a clip art graphic that has been repeatedly ungrouped until only individual objects are left.

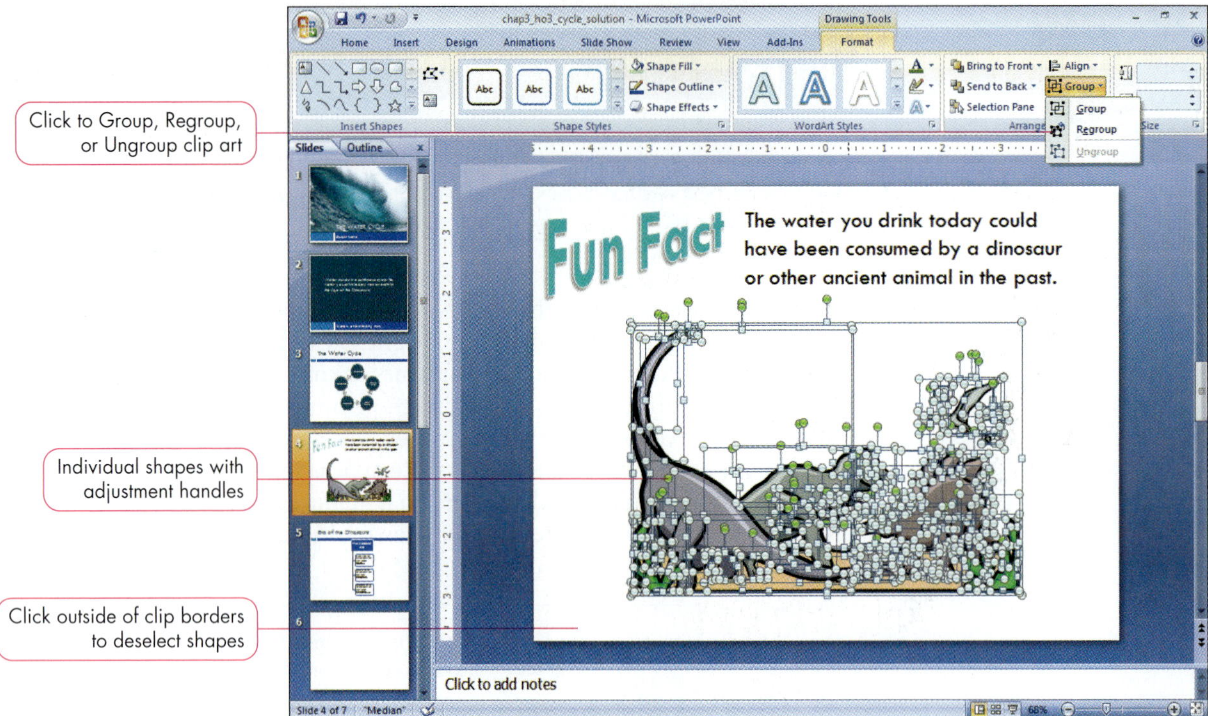

Figure 3.47 Ungrouped Complex Clip Art

When working with the individual shapes of a clip art image, it is helpful to zoom in on the clip art. Zooming helps you make sure you have the correct shape before you make your modifications. Once you select the shape, you can make all the modifications we discussed in the earlier part of this chapter. Figure 3.48 shows a selected shape that has had its fill changed to a theme color. Once you have made all of your needed changes, drag a marquee around all the shapes of the image and Group or Regroup the image. If you do not group the image, you risk moving the individual pieces inadvertently.

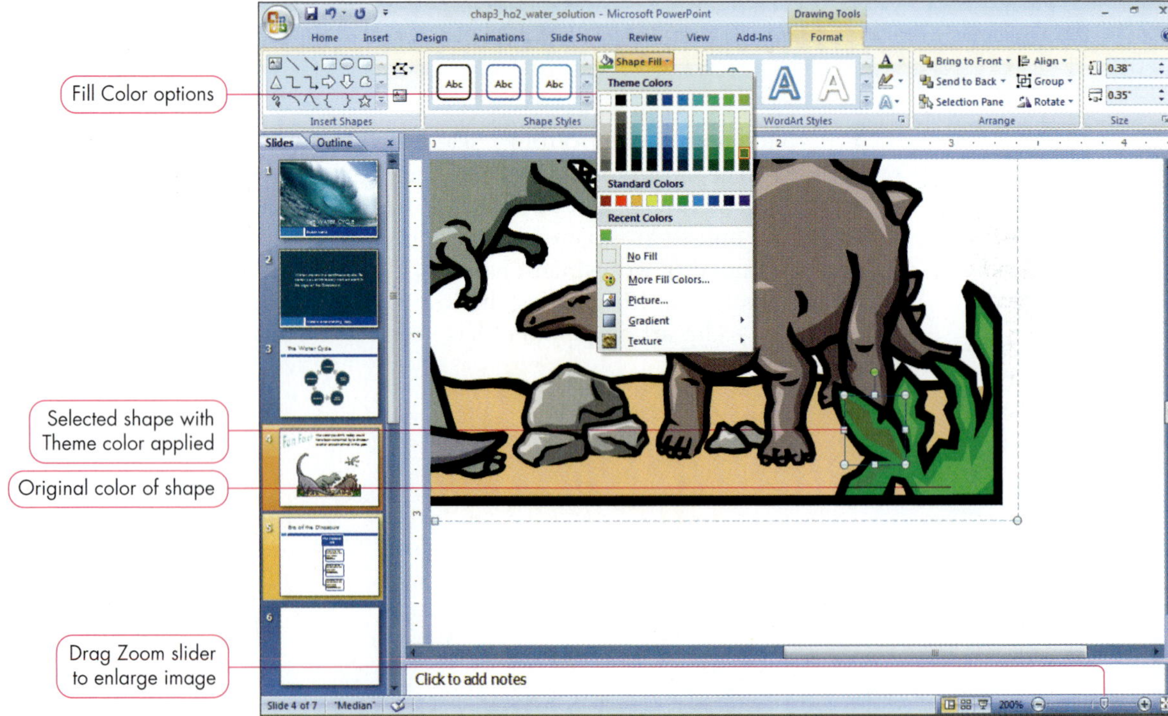

Figure 3.48 Modifying Ungrouped Shapes

Recolor Pictures

The colors in an image can be changed quickly using the Recolor Picture option. This option enables you to match your image to the color scheme of your presentation without taking the time to ungroup the image and change the color of each shape in the image. You can select either a dark or a light variation of your color scheme depending on which fits your color scheme and need.

You also can change the color mode of your picture to Grayscale, Sepia, Washout, or Black and White. Grayscale changes your picture to up to 256 shades of gray. Sepia gives you that popular golden tone often used for an "old-time" photo look. Washout is good for creating watermarks, while Black and White is a way to reduce image colors to straight black and white and simplify an image. Figure 3.49 shows two images from the Clip Art task pane that have been changed using the Recolor Picture option.

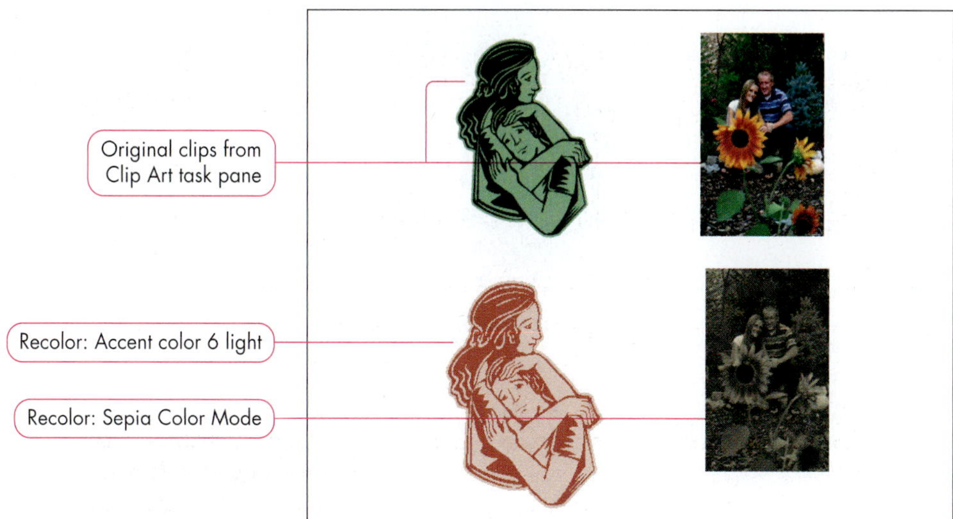

Figure 3.49 Recolored Images

To recolor clip art and pictures, click Recolor in the Adjust group on the Picture Tools Format tab. The gallery that opens provides options for Color Modes, and Dark Variations or Light Variations. It also has an option for No Recolor, which enables you to reset the picture to its original color. Click More Variations, and the color gallery opens so you can select Theme Colors, Standard Colors, or More Colors so you can customize the color used. Figure 3.50 shows the recoloring options.

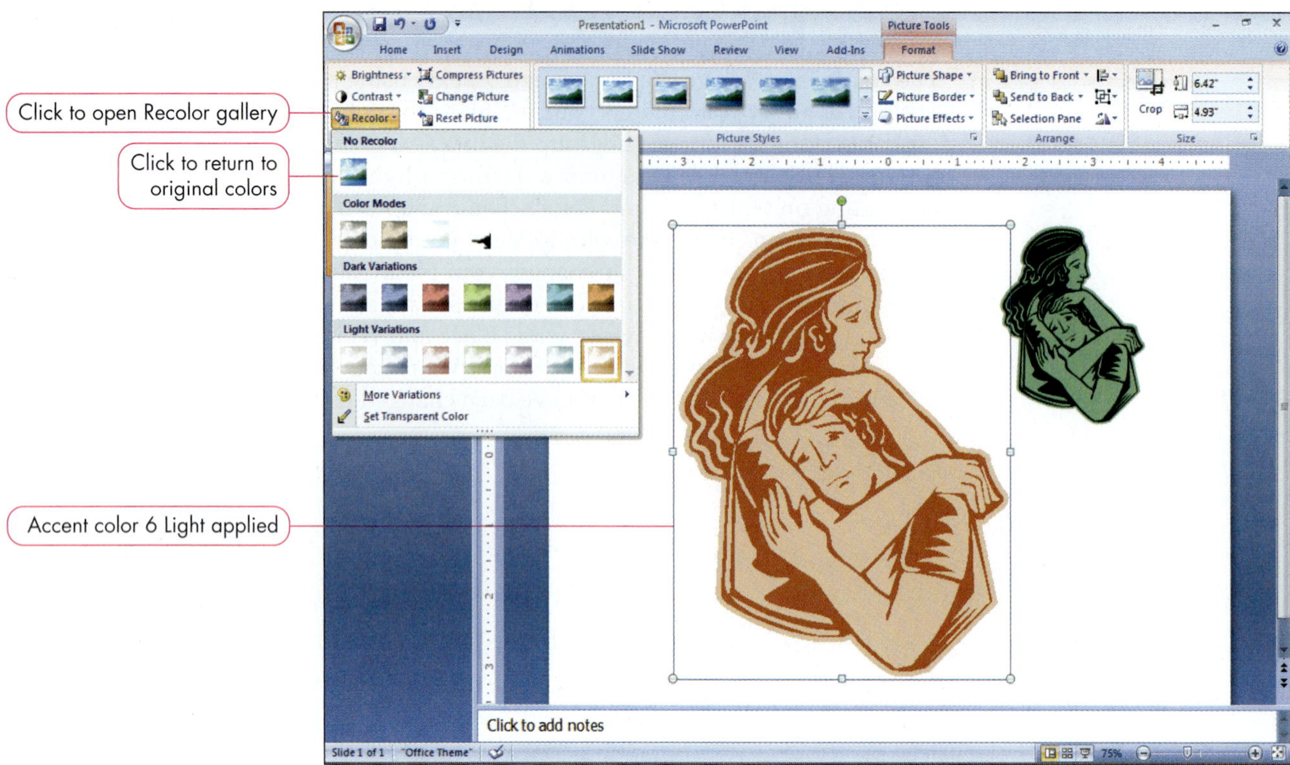

Figure 3.50 Recolored Image

The last option in the Recolor Gallery is the Set Transparent Color control. This feature is extremely valuable for creating a transparent area in most pictures. When you click Set Transparent Color, the pointer changes shape and includes an arrowhead for pointing. Drag the pointer until the arrowhead is pointing directly at the color you wish to make transparent, and then click. The color becomes transparent so that anything underneath shows through. In Figure 3.51, a frame from the Clip Art task pane has been placed on top of an image taken with a digital camera. The white background of the frame blocks the image, however. A duplicate of the image and the frame shows the result of using the Set Transparent Color option to make the white background transparent.

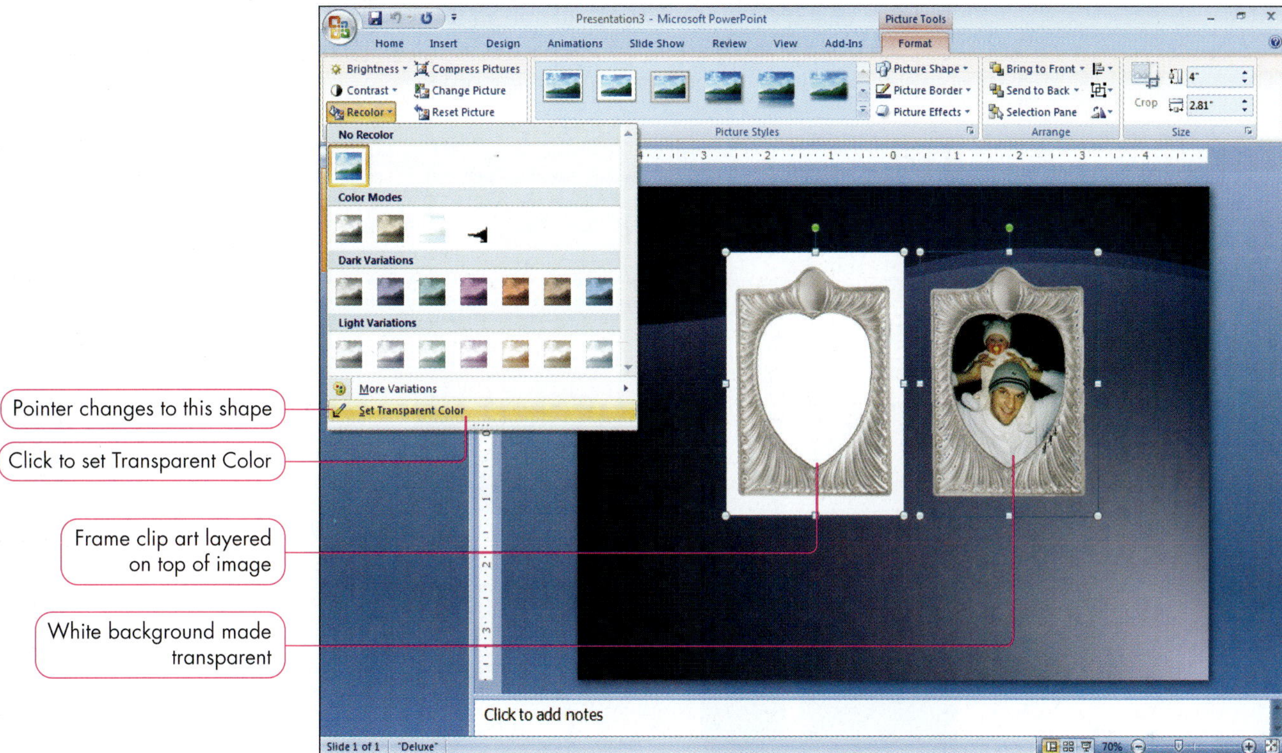

Figure 3.51 Set Transparent Color

Arranging Objects

The ***Selection Pane*** is a pane designed to help select objects.

When you have multiple objects such as placeholders, clip art, SmartArt, WordArt, or other objects on the page, it can become challenging to arrange them. Positioning the objects can be time consuming, too. Fortunately, PowerPoint has several features that will help you control the order of the objects, the position of the objects, and how the objects align to each other and the slide. Before using any of these features, however, you must select the object(s). The ***Selection Pane*** is a pane designed to help you select objects. It contains a list of all objects on the slide. You click any object on the list to select it, and once it is selected you can make the desired change. Click Selection Pane in the Arrange group on the Picture Tools Format tab to open the Selection Pane if an object is selected. If an object is not selected, click the Home tab and then click Select in the Editing group. Click Selection Pane.

Order Objects

The ***stacking order*** is the order of objects placed on top of each other.

Shapes can be placed under or on top of each other. Think of this idea as layering the objects. For example, the bottom layer of a sandwich is bread. The meat may come next or the tomato. The top layer is more bread. The order of the layers is called the ***stacking order***. PowerPoint puts shapes or other objects in a stacking order as you add them to the slide. The last shape you place on the slide is on top and is the highest in the stacking order. Clip art images are comprised of shapes that have been stacked. Once you ungroup a clip art image and modify it, you may need to change the stacking order. You can open the Selection Pane to see the order in which objects are placed. The topmost object on the list is at the top of the stacking order.

To change the order of a stack of shapes, select one of the shapes and then click the Drawing Tools Format tab. The Arrange group on the Format tab includes options for controlling the location of the shape in the stacking order. Clicking the Bring to Front arrow opens a submenu that includes the Bring to Front option, which lets you move the shape all the way to the top of the stacking order, and Bring Forward that lets you move the shape up one layer. Similarly, the Send to Back option enables you to move the shape all the way to the bottom of the stacking order or back one layer. Figure 3.52 shows the results of changing a square at the bottom of a stacking order to the top of a stacking order.

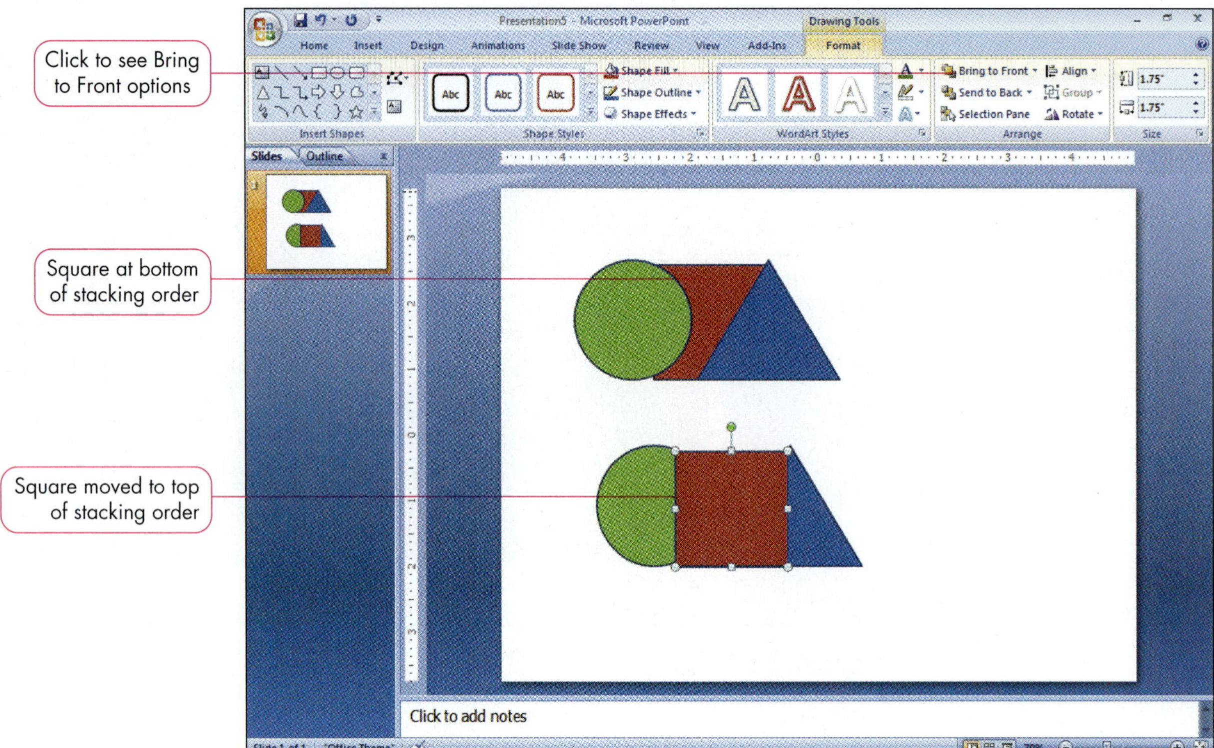

Figure 3.52 Change Stacking Order

TIP Quick Ways to Good Order

You can right-click a shape and select Bring to Front or Send to Back. Using this method you can still choose whether to move one layer or all layers. You also can open the Selection Pane, select the object, and click Up or Down Re-Order to move the object up the list or down the list.

Align Objects

Sometimes you need to position objects precisely on the slide. For example, you need a series of boxes aligned at their tops, or you need to adjust the amount of space between the boxes so that they are evenly spaced. PowerPoint has rulers, a grid, and drawing guides that enable you to complete the aligning process quickly.

A ***grid*** is a set of intersecting lines used to align objects.

Underlying each slide is a ***grid*** containing intersecting lines similar to what you would see on traditional graph paper. While normally the grid is nonprinting and nonviewable, you can activate the grid view and use the viewable grid to align your objects and to keep them evenly spaced. When you activate the grid view, the grid still will not be seen when in Slide Show view and cannot be printed. PowerPoint's rulers also can be used to help keep your objects aligned because they enable you to see the exact distance between shapes or to see size. To view the grid and the ruler, click the View tab and click the check boxes for Gridlines or Ruler.

By default, objects snap to the gridlines and measurement lines on the rulers. The Snap to feature forces an object to align with the grid by either the object's center point or the edge of the object, whichever is closest to the gridline. If you prefer, you can change the setting so that objects snap to other objects as well as or instead of the grid. You can also turn the Snap to feature off. To change the grid settings, select an object, click Align on the Drawing Tools Format tab, and then click Grid Settings. Figure 3.53 displays the Grid and Guides dialog box options.

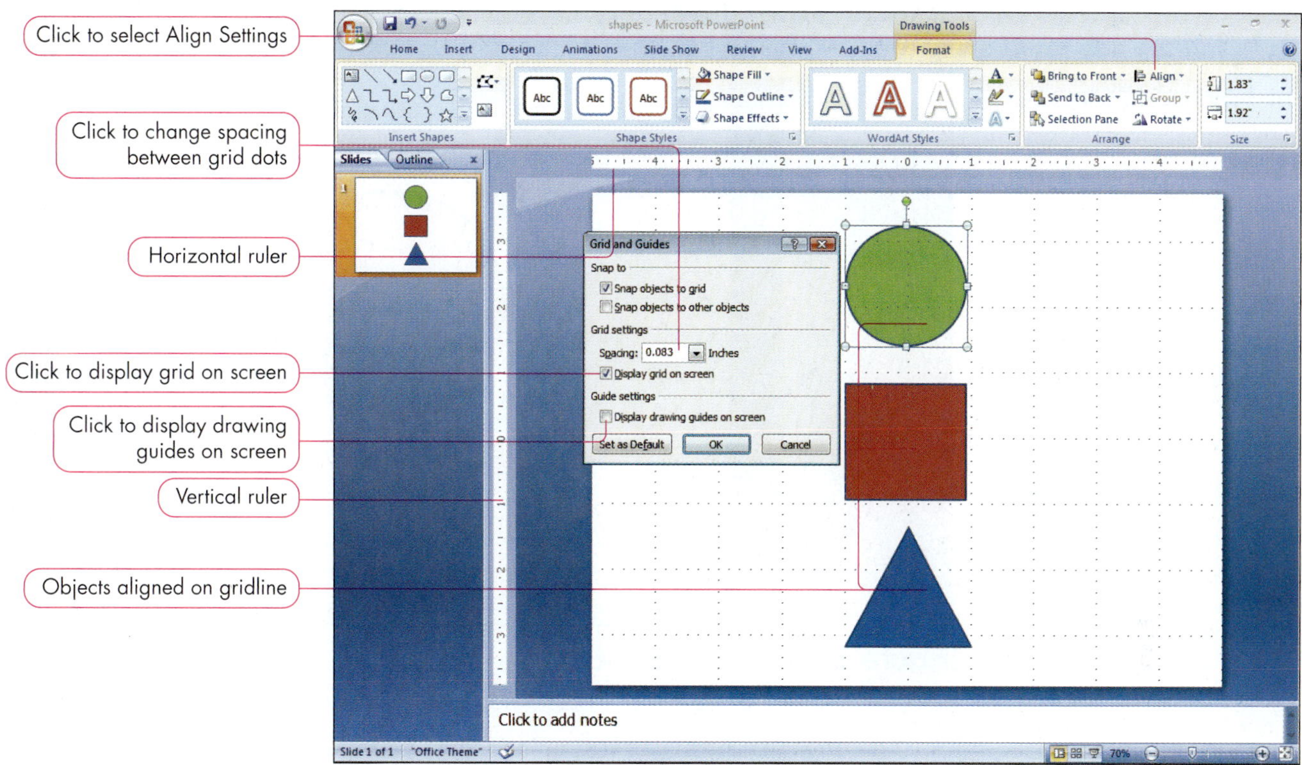

Figure 3.53 Grid and Guide Settings

TIP Overriding Snap-to

To temporarily override the snap-to feature so that you can freely drag an object to any position, press Alt as you drag.

A ***guide*** is a straight horizontal or vertical line used to align objects.

Guides are nonprinting vertical or horizontal lines that you can place on a page to help you align objects or determine regions of the slide. For example, you can use guides to mark margins on a page. When you first display the guides, you see two guides that intersect at the center of the slide (the zero setting on both the horizontal and vertical rulers). To move a guide, position your cursor over it and drag. A directional arrow will appear as well as a measurement telling you the distance from the center point you are moving the guide. To create additional guides, press Ctrl+Shift while dragging. To remove guides, drag them off the slide. Refer to Figure 3.53 to see how to display guides. Figure 3.54 displays the default guides and the creation of a new guide.

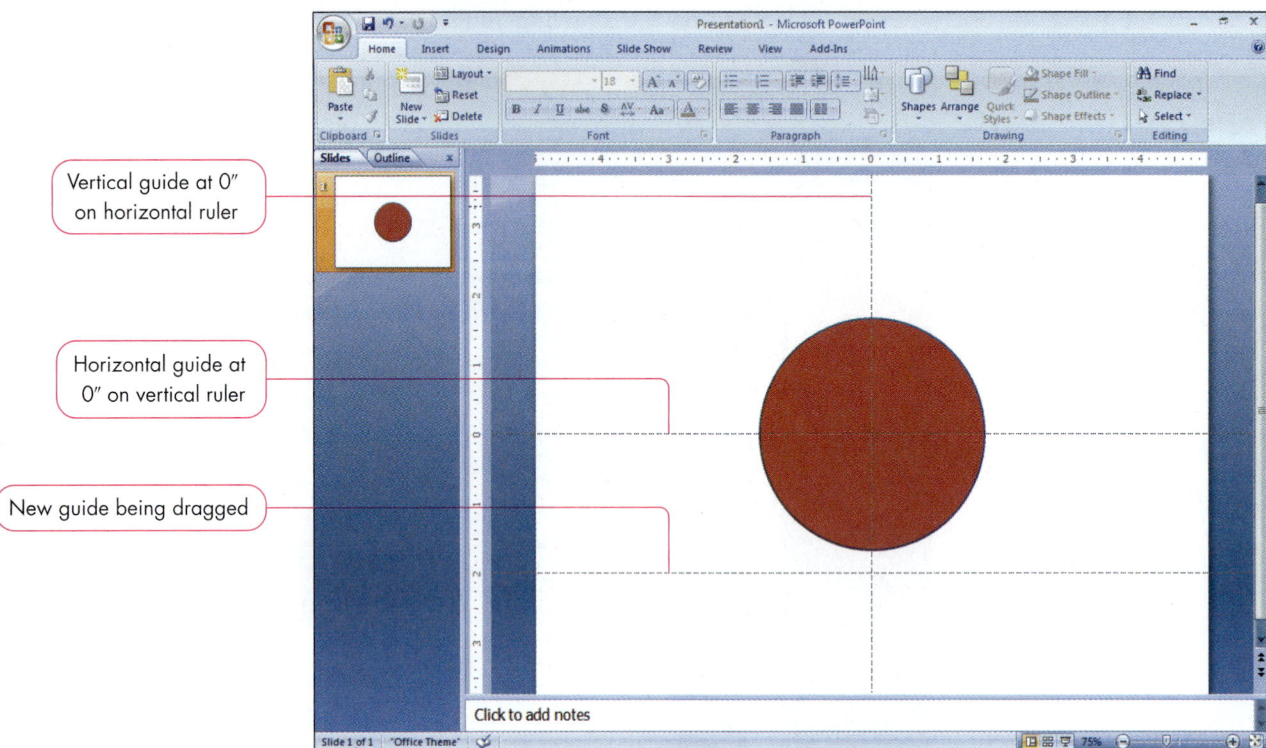

Figure 3.54 Creating a Guide

To ***align*** is to arrange in a line or so as to be parallel.

The ***Align*** feature makes it simple to line up shapes and objects in several ways. You can align with other objects by lining up the sides, middles, or top or bottom edges of objects. Or, if you have only one object or group selected, you can align in relation to the entire slide—for example, at the top or left edge of a slide. To align selected objects, click Align on the Drawing Tools Format tab. When the alignment options display, choose whether you want to align to the slide or to align objects to one another. After you have determined whether you want to align to the slide or to each other, determine how you want to align using the align options.

To ***distribute*** is to divide or evenly spread over a given area.

The Align feature also includes options to ***distribute*** selected shapes evenly over a given area. Perhaps you have shapes on the page but one is too close to another, and another is too far away. You want to have an equal amount of space between all the shapes. After selecting the shapes, click Align in the Arrange group on the Drawing Tools Format tab. Then select Distribute Horizontally or Distribute Vertically. Figure 3.55 shows three shapes that have been aligned at their middles, aligned to the middle of the slide, and distributed horizontally so that the space between them is equidistant.

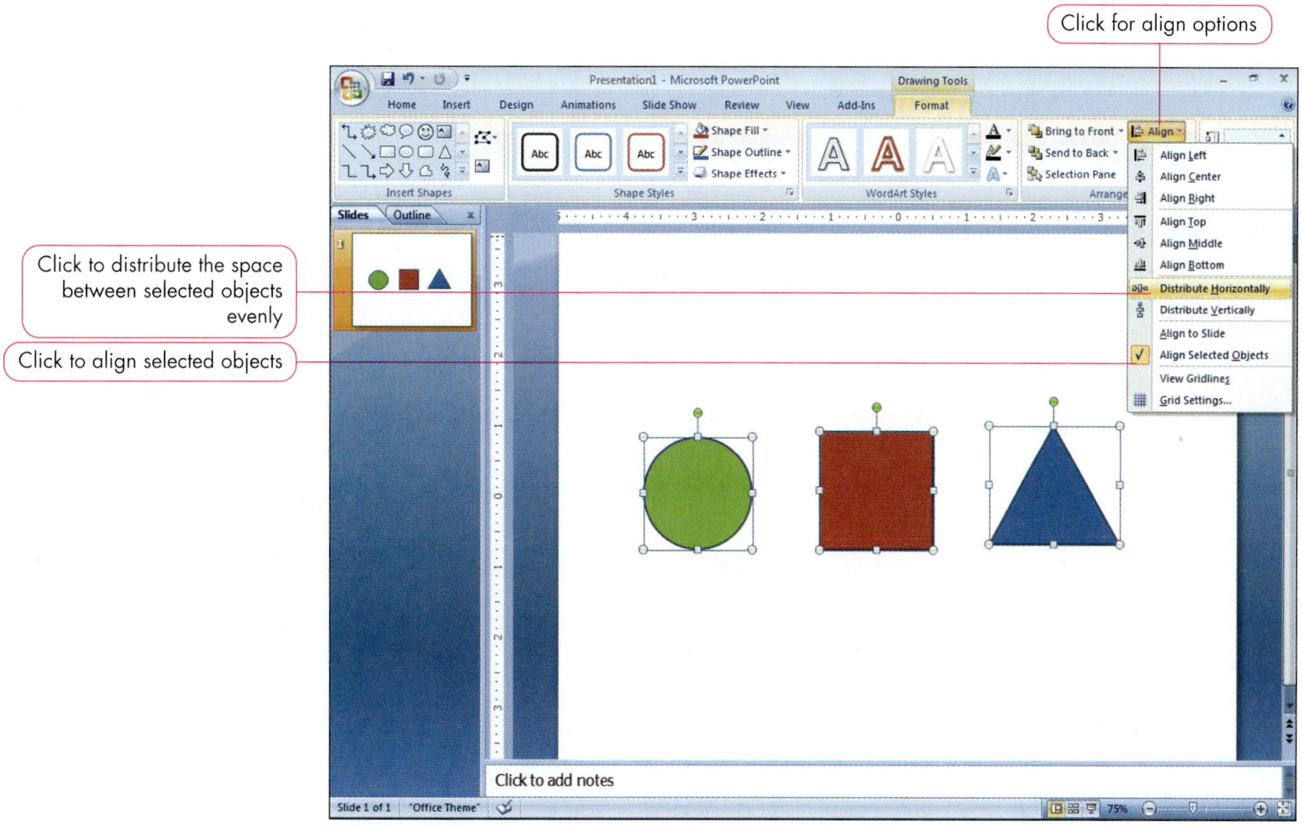

Click for align options

Click to distribute the space between selected objects evenly

Click to align selected objects

Figure 3.55 Alignment Options

Hands-On Exercises

3 | Modifying and Arranging Clip Art

Skills covered: 1. Size and Position Clip Art **2.** Flip Clip Art **3.** Ungroup, Modify, and Regroup Clip Art **4.** Recolor a Picture **5.** Reorder Shapes **6.** Align and Distribute Clip Art

Step 1
Size and Position Clip Art

Refer to Figure 3.56 as you complete Step 1.

a. Open the *chap3_ho2_water_solution* presentation, and then immediately save it as **chap3_ho3_cycle_solution**.

b. Move to **Slide 4**, click the **Insert tab**, and then click **Clip Art** in the Illustrations group.

c. Type **pterodactyls** in the **Search for** box, and then click **Go**.

   Entering the keyword *pterodactyls* narrowed your search more than entering the generic keyword *dinosaurs* would.

d. Click the clip art image containing several dinosaurs as shown in Figure 3.56, and then close the Clip Art task pane.

   The clip art image is inserted in the center of Slide 4.

e. Click to select the clip art image, if necessary, and then click the **Picture Tools Format tab**.

f. Click the **Size and Position Dialog Box Launcher** in the Size group.

   The Size and Position Dialog Box Launcher has a small arrow on it and is on the far right of the Format tab. When you click it, the Size and Position dialog box appears.

g. Type **4.5** in the **Height** box and then click in the **Width** box.

   The width of the image changes to 6.66, keeping the image in proportion. The proportion is kept because the **Lock aspect ratio** check box is checked.

h. Click the **Position tab**, and then type **1.67"** in the **Horizontal box** in the *Position on slide* section and **2.25"** in the **Vertical box**. Then click **Close**.

i. Save the *chap3_ho3_cycle_solution* presentation.

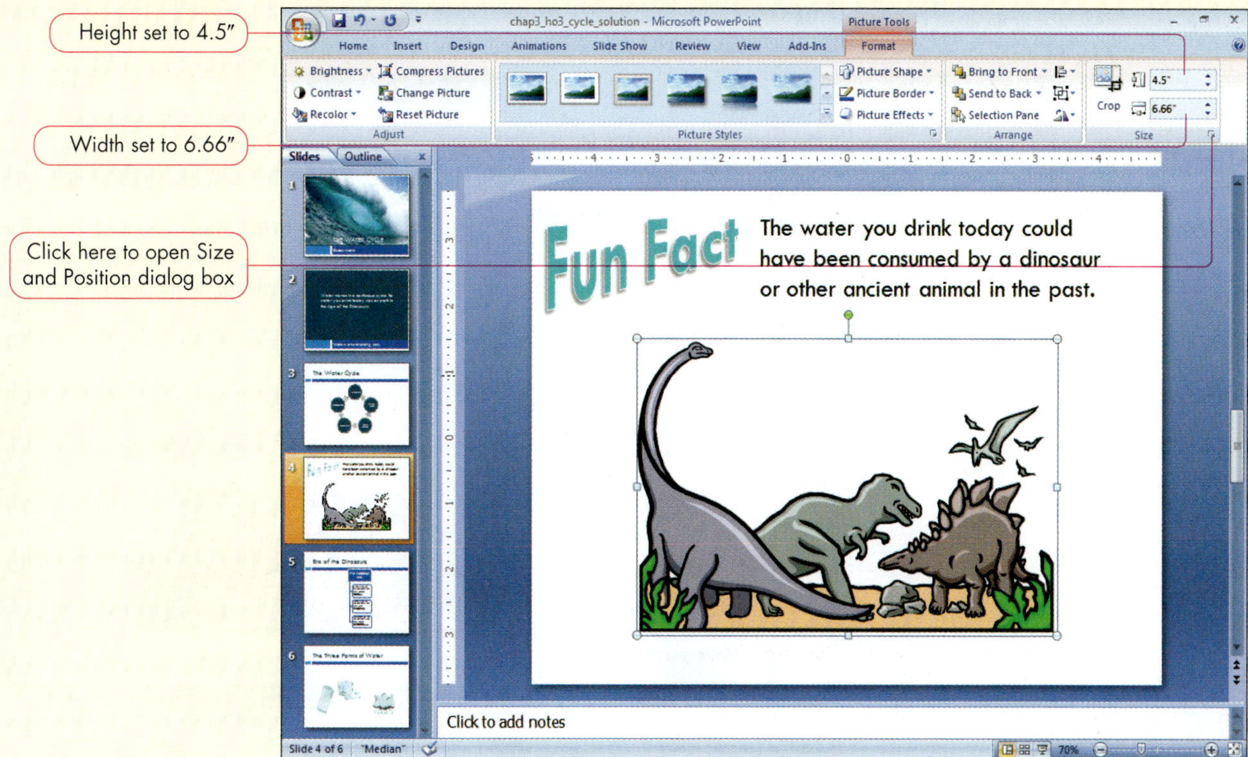
Height set to 4.5"
Width set to 6.66"
Click here to open Size and Position dialog box
Fun Fact
The water you drink today could have been consumed by a dinosaur or other ancient animal in the past.
Click to add notes

Figure 3.56 Resized and Repositioned Clip Art

Step 2
Flip Clip Art

Refer to Figure 3.57 as you complete Step 2.

a. With the *chap3_ho3_cycle_solution* presentation open, click the dinosaur clip art.

b. Click **Rotate** in the Arrange group on the Format tab under Picture Tools.

   The rotate and flip options appear.

c. Select **Flip Horizontal**.

d. Click **Rotate** in the Arrange group on the Format tab under Picture Tools, and then select **More Rotation Options**.

e. Type **180** in the **Rotation** box, and then click **Close**.

   The picture rotates upside down.

f. Click **Rotate** in the Arrange group on the Format tab under Picture Tools, and then select **Flip Vertical**.

   The clip art picture appears to be in its original position, but the rotation angle is still set at 180 degrees. You can tell when a picture has been rotated, but not when it has been flipped.

g. Save the *chap3_ho3_cycle_solution* presentation.

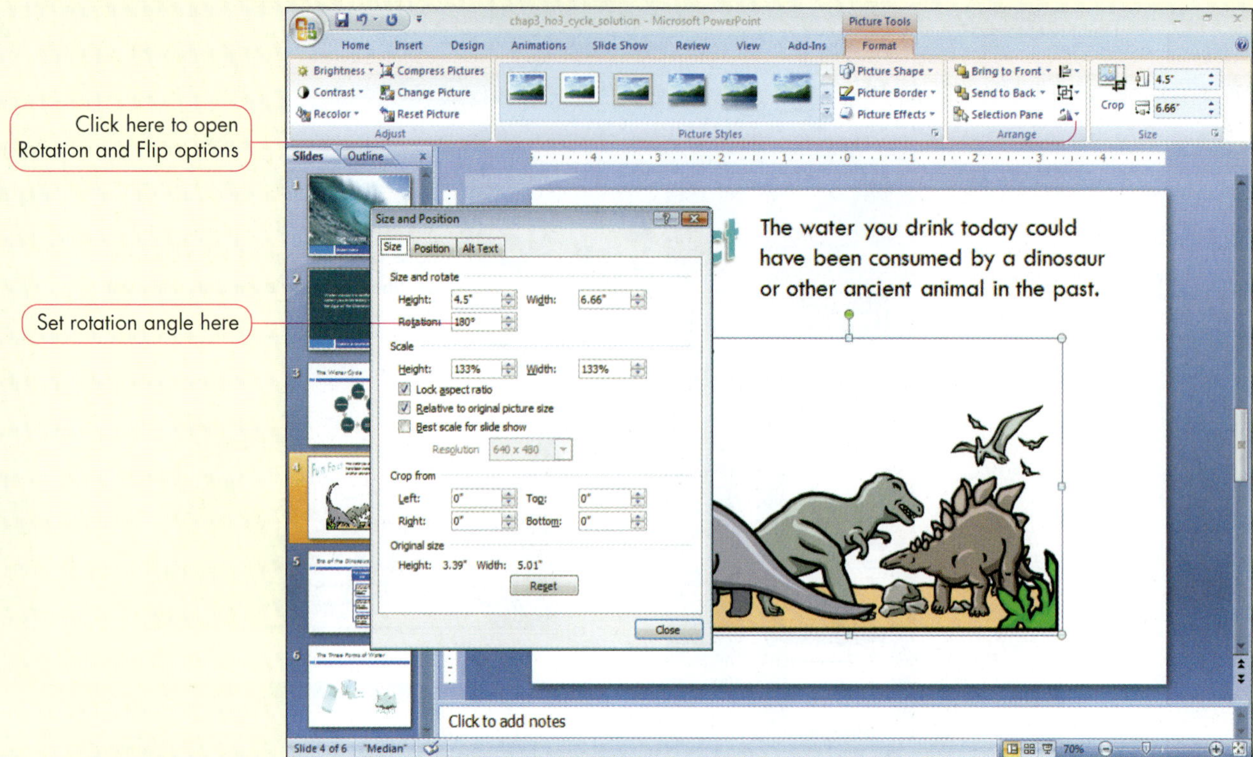
Click here to open
Rotation and Flip options
Set rotation angle here
The water you drink today could
have been consumed by a dinosaur
or other ancient animal in the past.
Click to add notes

Figure 3.57 Flipping and Rotating

Step 3 Ungroup, Modify, and Regroup Clip Art

Refer to Figures 3.58 and 3.59 as you complete Step 3.

a. With the *chap3_ho3_cycle_solution* presentation open, right-click the dinosaur clip art.

b. Select **Edit Picture**, and then click **Yes** when the Microsoft Office PowerPoint message box appears.

When you click Yes, your picture is turned into a drawing object. After this conversion you will not be able to use picture tools on the picture, but will be able to use drawing tools. The image has been converted to a drawing object, but it is still grouped. Now you must ungroup the image to modify individual pieces.

c. Click the **Drawing Tools Format tab**, and then click **Group** in the Arrange group.

d. Select **Ungroup**, and then click outside the clip art border.

When you ungroup the clip art, each shape comprising the image is selected and surrounded with adjustment handles. Clicking outside the border deselects the shapes so that you can select just the one you wish to modify.

e. Drag the **Zoom slider** to **200%**, and then drag the scroll bars to locate the plants in the bottom right of the clip art.

Zooming in makes it easier to select the individual shape you wish to modify.

f. Select one of the bright green shapes in the plant, click **Shape Fill**, in the Shape Styles group and then click **Green, Accent 5, Lighter 60%**.

You wish to change the bright green in the original clip art to a color that matches your theme color.

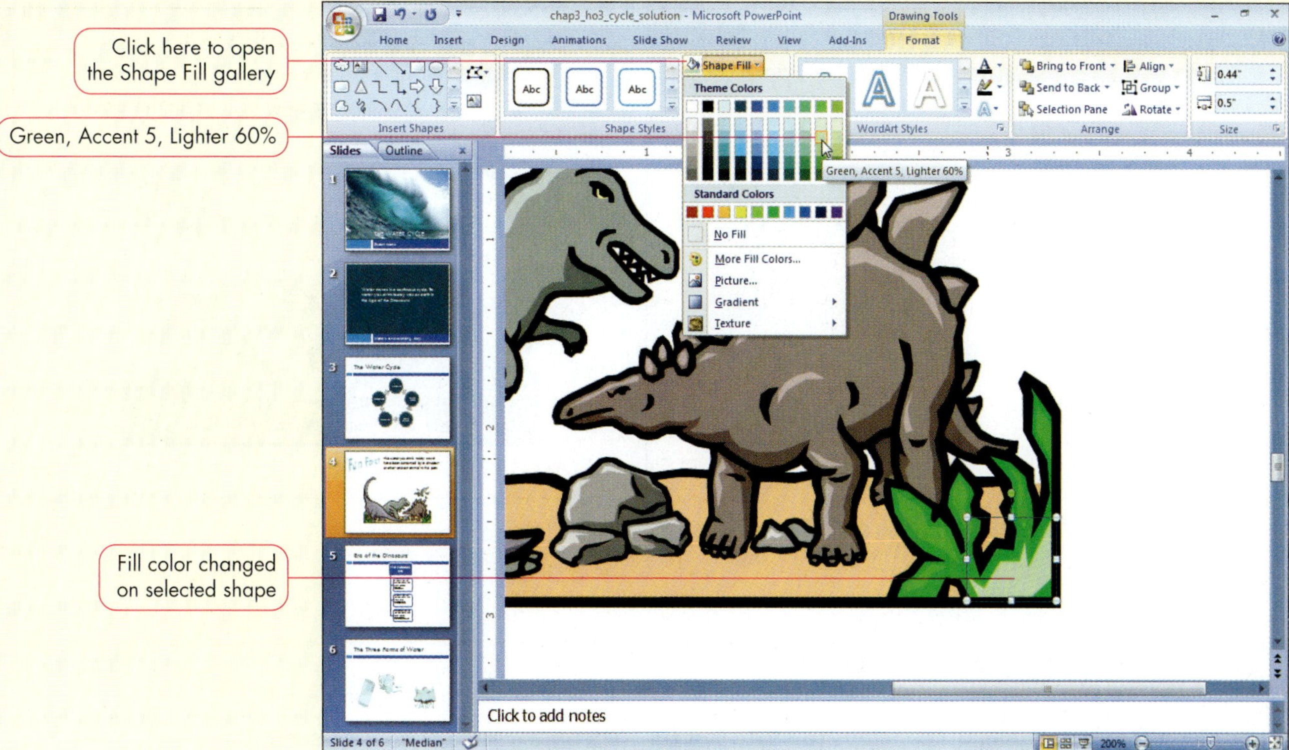

Figure 3.58 Change Fill Color

g. Change the fill color of each of the bright green shapes in the plants on both sides of the clip art to **Green, Accent 5, Lighter 60%**.

TIP Selecting Multiple Shapes

You can press Ctrl as you click several bright green shapes, and then apply the shape fill to the selected shapes at the same time.

You do not have to keep opening the Shape Fill dialog box to apply the color to your shapes. The fill bucket immediately to the left of the Shape Fill command now reflects your color choice. Simply click it to apply the color to selected shapes.

h. Click the **View tab**, and then click **Fit to Window** in the Zoom group.

i. Drag a selection net around the four pterodactyls in the clip art.

Ctrl-clicking the pterodactyls would be time consuming because of the many shapes involved. Dragging a selection net that completely encompasses shapes is a more efficient method for selecting multiple shapes.

j. Drag the pterodactyl shapes up approximately ½" to reposition them.

k. Drag a selection net around all of the shapes making the dinosaur clip art, then click the **Format tab** under Drawing Tools, select **Group**, and then select **Regroup**.

l. Save the *chap3_ho3_cycle_solution* presentation.

Figure 3.59 Modified Clip Art

Step 4
Recolor a Picture

Refer to Figure 3.60 as you complete Step 4.

a. Move to **Slide 5** of the *chap3_ho3_cycle_solution* presentation.

b. Click the **Insert tab** and click **Clip Art** in the Illustrations group.

c. Type **coelophysis** in the **Search for** box, and then click **Go**.

d. Drag the thumbnail of the Coelophysis to the bottom left of your slide and release, and then close the Clip Art task pane.

e. Click the **Format tab**.

   Because the clip art has not been converted to a drawing object, you can use the picture tools to modify it. Recoloring an image does not require clip art to be ungrouped.

f. Click **Recolor** in the Adjust group.

g. Click **Accent color 1 Light** in the Light Variations category.

   The colors in the clip art are recolored to those contained in the color theme.

h. Save the *chap3_ho3_cycle_solution* presentation.

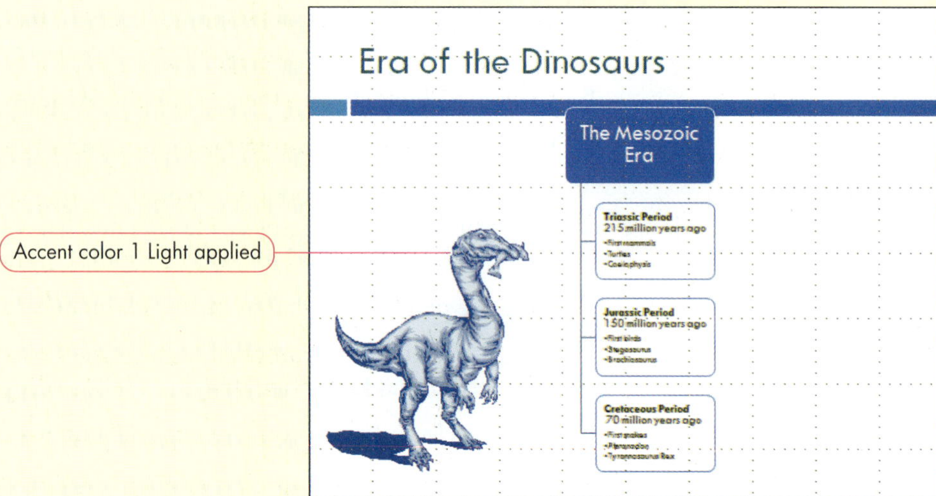

Figure 3.60 Recolored Picture

Step 5
Reorder Shapes

Refer to Figure 3.62 as you complete Step 5.

a. Move to **Slide 6** of the *chap3_ho3_cycle_solution* presentation.

b. Click the **View tab**, and then click **Ruler** in the Show/Hide group (if necessary).

   The horizontal and vertical rulers appear. We will use the rulers to help us create a shape in a specific size.

c. Click the **Home tab**, click **Shapes** in the Drawing group, and then click **Rectangle**.

d. Position the cross-hair pointer on the first 4" mark on the horizontal ruler (–4) and the first 1" mark on the vertical ruler.

   This is the beginning point for the rectangle we draw. See Figure 3.61 for help identifying the beginning location.

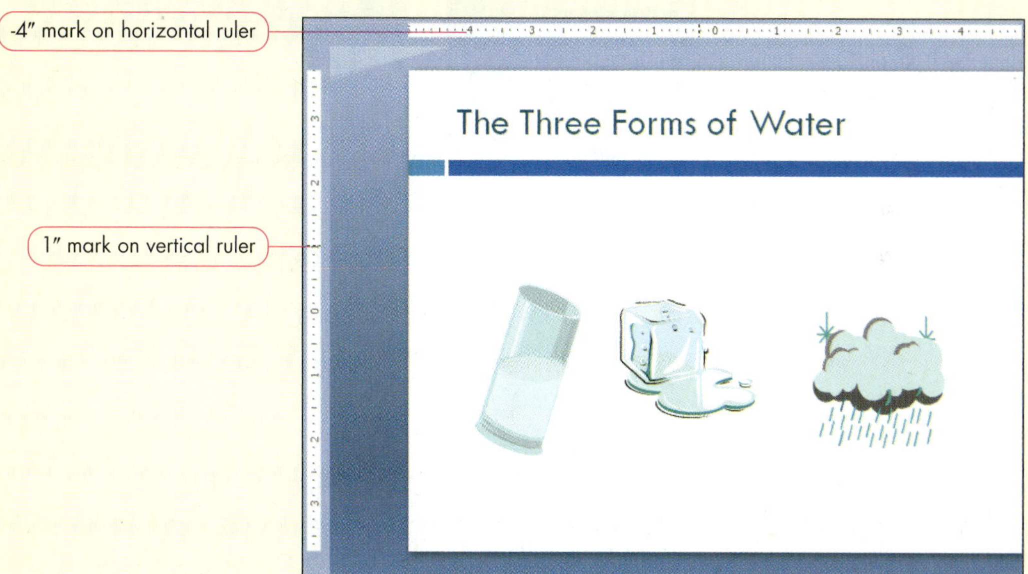

Figure 3.61 Locating Position Using Rulers

e. Drag to the last 4" mark on the horizontal ruler and the last 2" mark on the vertical ruler (–2), and then release.

   A large rectangle shape in the theme color is created on top of the clip art on the slide. You will use the rectangle as a background for the clip art. Currently it is hiding the clip art, however, and must be reordered.

f. Click **Arrange** in the Drawing group on the Home tab, and then select **Send to Back**.

g. Save the *chap3_ho3_cycle_solution* presentation.

TIP Shapes and Arrange Options

You can also insert a shape by clicking Shapes in the Illustrations group on the Insert tab. After a shape is inserted, you can click Bring to Front or Send to Back in the Arrange group on the Drawing Tools Format tab, and then select the specific option.

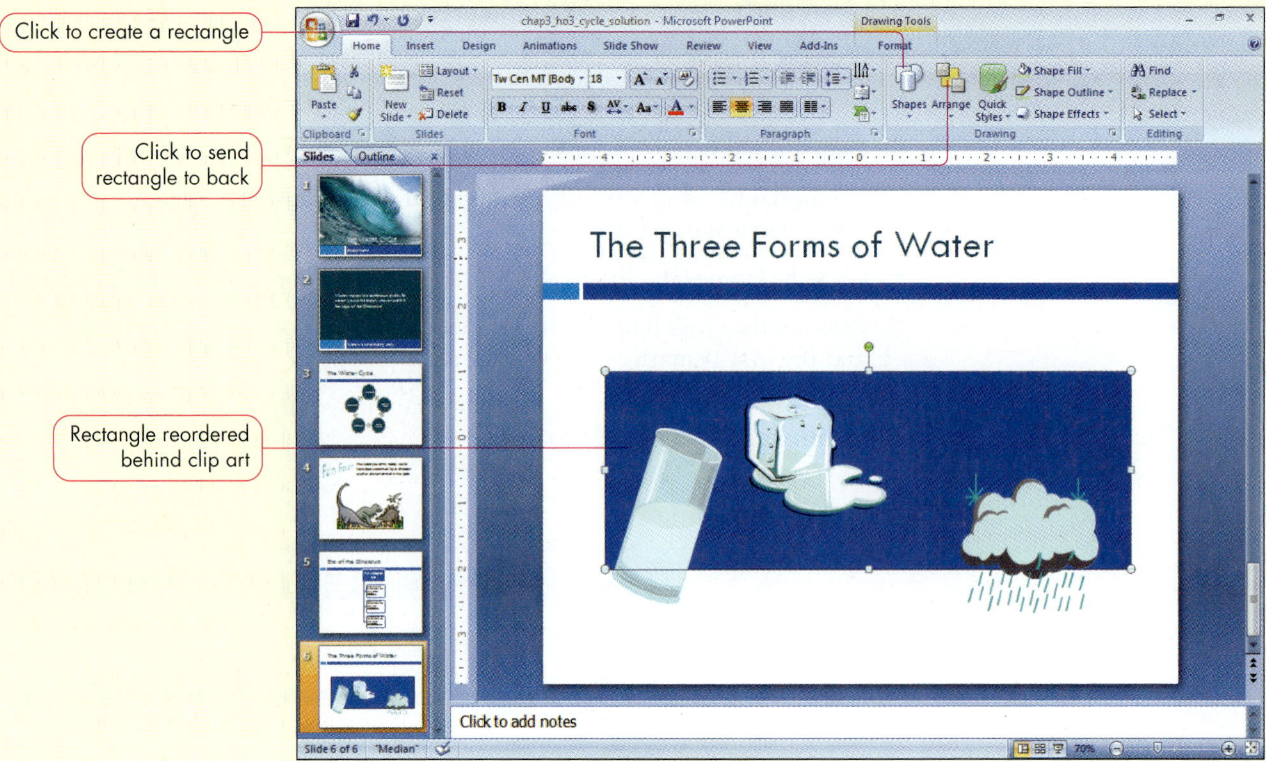

Figure 3.62 A Rectangle Background

Step 6
Align and Distribute Clip Art

Refer to Figure 3.63 as you complete Step 6.

a. With the *chap3_ho3_cycle_solution* presentation open, click the first clip art image, and then press **Ctrl** as you click each clip art image.

   Make sure the rectangle is not selected before you start selecting the clip art images. Holding down Ctrl while clicking each clip art image enables you to select all three.

b. Click **Align** in the Arrange group on the Format tab under Drawing Tools.

   The align options appear. You need to align the objects by their middles. You do not click center because that would align the objects by their centers and they would appear on top of each other.

c. Select **Align Middle**.

d. Click **Align** and select **Distribute Horizontally**.

   PowerPoint adjusts the distances between objects so that they are distributed equally.

e. Click **Group** in the Arrange group on the Drawing Tools Format tab, and then select **Group**.

   The three clip art images are grouped and become a complex picture. Individual handles around the objects are replaced with a single set of handles surrounding all three images.

f. Press **Shift**, and then click the blue rectangle.

   Pressing Shift while clicking adds the object to the selection. The rectangle and the clip art group are now both in the selection.

g. Click **Align** in the Arrange group on the Format tab under Drawing Tools, and then click **Align Middle**.

   The rectangle and grouped clip art images are aligned by the horizontal middle. This ensures the blue rectangle is behind all of the images.

h. Deselect the objects.

i. Create a Notes and Handouts Header and Footer with your name in the header, and your instructor's name and your class in the footer.

j. View the presentation and print as directed by your instructor.

k. Save the *chap3_ho3_cycle_solution* presentation, and close it.

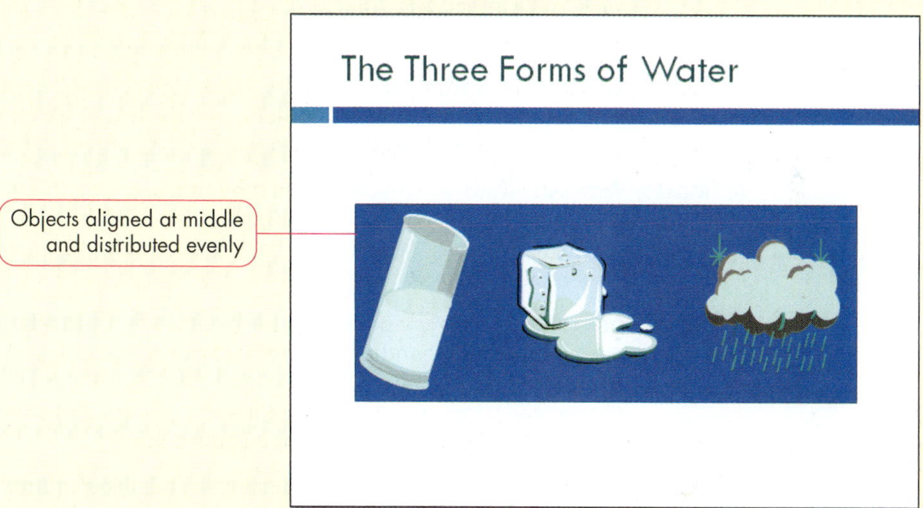

Figure 3.63 The Completed Slide

Summary

1. **Create shapes.** You can use shapes to highlight information, as a design element, or as the basis for creating clip art illustrations. PowerPoint provides tools for creating shapes as well as tools to help size and position shapes.
2. **Apply Quick Styles and customize shapes.** A shape can be customized by changing its default fill to another color, a picture, a gradient, a texture, or no fill. The shape outline color, weight, or dash style can be modified. Special effects such as shadows, reflections, and glows also may be added. Applying a Quick Style enables you to apply preset options. The vertexes of shapes also can be edited to change the form of the shape.
3. **Create SmartArt.** SmartArt graphics are diagrams that present information visually to effectively communicate your message. SmartArt graphics are organized into seven categories: lists, processes, cycles, hierarchies, relationships, matrices, and pyramids. SmartArt diagrams also may be created from existing text.
4. **Modify SmartArt diagrams.** Once created, SmartArt can be modified to include additional shapes, or to have shapes deleted, a SmartArt style applied, the color scheme revised, or special effects added. The direction of the SmartArt can be changed. SmartArt can be resized and repositioned.
5. **Create WordArt.** WordArt is text with decorative effects applied in order to draw attention to the text. Select a WordArt style and then type the text you desire. A Quick Styles gallery provides you with multiple WordArt styles that can be applied to the WordArt text.
6. **Modify WordArt.** WordArt can be modified by transforming the shape of the text, and by applying special effects and colors. The shape of the WordArt can be warped and applied to a path. The text created as WordArt can be edited. Among the many special effects available are 3-D presets and rotations.
7. **Modify objects.** Objects may be flipped horizontally or vertically, or they can be rotated by dragging the green rotation handle that appears with selected objects. Vector clip art can be ungrouped so basic shapes can be customized, and then objects can be regrouped so they can be moved as one object. Pictures can be recolored by changing their color mode or by applying a dark or light variation of a theme color or custom color.
8. **Arrange objects.** Objects are stacked in layers. The object at the top of the layer is the one that fully displays, while other objects in the stack may have some portions blocked by other objects. The stacking order of shapes can be reordered so that objects can be seen as desired. Features such as rulers, grids, guides, align, and distribute can be used to arrange objects on a slide and arrange objects in relation to one another.

Key Terms

Multiple Choice

1. Shapes are:
   (a) Images that you create by typing in a key word in the Shape Clip Organizer and then clicking the shape you desire.
   (b) A collection of graphical shapes, such as lines, arrows, and squares, that you add by using the Shapes gallery.
   (c) A category of clip art that includes pictures with a motor theme.
   (d) Shapes that you create by clicking in the Shape group under Design.

2. You insert a lightning bolt shape on your slide and want to rotate it. You:
   (a) Drag the green handle at the top of the image.
   (b) Drag one of the corner adjustment handles.
   (c) Double-click the lightning bolt and enter the number of degrees you want the shape to rotate.
   (d) Do nothing because Shapes cannot be rotated.

3. The relationship between the height and width of a shape is referred to as:
   (a) Proportion ration
   (b) Rotation aspect
   (c) Size ratio
   (d) Aspect ratio

4. Which of the following is a reason for grouping shapes?
   (a) To be able to change each shape individually
   (b) To move or modify the objects as one
   (c) To connect the shapes with connectors
   (d) To create a relationship diagram

5. Which of the following is a reason for ungrouping a clip art object?
   (a) To be able to individually change shapes used to create the composite image
   (b) To move the objects as one
   (c) To add text on top of the group
   (d) To resize the group as one piece

6. Which of the following features would you use on an ungrouped clip art image after completing your modifications?
   (a) Connector lines
   (b) Combine
   (c) Regroup
   (d) Join together

7. You have inserted a clip art image of the ocean with a palm tree on the right side of the beach. If you flip the image vertically, what would the resulting image look like?
   (a) The image would show right side up, but the palm tree would be on the left side.
   (b) The image would be upside down with the palm tree pointing down.
   (c) The image would be rotated 90 degrees, and the palm tree would be on the bottom.
   (d) The image would be rotated 270 degrees, and the palm tree would be at the top.

8. Which of the following might be a reason for changing the stacking order of shapes?
   (a) To show a relationship by placing shapes in front of or behind each other
   (b) To hide something on a shape
   (c) To uncover something hidden by another shape
   (d) All of the above

9. You stack three shapes on top of each other on a slide by inserting a large square on the page, then a small circle, and then a large triangle. Which shape will be on the top of the stacking order?
   (a) The square because you added it first
   (b) The circle because curves show above angles
   (c) The triangle because it was added last
   (d) The circle because it is small and would be hidden by the triangle

10. In the above example, how would you move the triangle to the bottom of the stacking order?
    (a) In the Arrange group, click Align, and then select Align bottom.
    (b) In the Design group, click Shape Fill, and then select Move Backward.
    (c) In the Arrange group, click Send to Back, and then select Send Backward.
    (d) In the Arrange group, click Send to Back, and then select Send to Back.

11. A Microsoft Windows Metafile (.wmf) is a vector object created by:
    (a) Rastors
    (b) Bits
    (c) Mathematical formulas
    (d) Pixels

...continued on Next Page

Multiple Choice Continued...

12. Which of the following features does not help with arranging objects on a slide?

(a) Cascade
(b) Rulers
(c) Grid
(d) Guides

13. Which of the following is not available from the SmartArt gallery?

(a) Periodic table
(b) Pyramid diagram
(c) Process graphic
(d) Matrix block

14. Which of the following SmartArt graphics displays objects in a continual process?

(a) Hierarchy
(b) Cycle
(c) List
(d) Relationship

15. You are trying to align a shape directly on top of another, but it always jumps above or below where you need to place it. What feature should you deactivate in order to accomplish this task?

(a) Align to
(b) Snap to
(c) AutoAlign
(d) Line Snap

Practice Exercises

1 Create and Modify Shapes

Your *sensei* (teacher) has asked for your aid in creating a narrated slide show on Judo that prospective students can view in a small room—a special place reserved for visitors when they first visit the *dojo* (training hall). You want to introduce visitors to the wisdom of Judo in a strong, visual way, but you want the slide show to demonstrate the principles of simplicity. To follow the principle of simplicity, you wish to avoid bullet points and text. You want the show to have empty space and a tranquil feel. Figure 3.64 displays the third slide in a slide show on Judo that uses shapes, SmartArt, and modified clip art.

a. Open *chap3_pe1_judo*, and save it as **chap3_pe1_judo_solution**.
b. Move to **Slide 3**, click the **Insert tab**, and then click **Shapes** in the Illustrations group to open the Shapes gallery.
c. Right-click the **Rounded Rectangle** shape, and then select the **Lock Drawing Mode**.
d. Position the pointer on the slide and drag to create a long rounded rectangle. Repeat this process so you have two rounded rectangles on the slide.
e. Select the rounded rectangle on the left, and type **Maximum Efficiency**.
f. Select the rounded rectangle on the right, and type **Mutual Welfare and Benefit.**
g. Select the **Elbow Double-Arrow Connector** in the Lines group of the Shapes gallery, move your pointer over the rounded rectangle on the left, and then position the crosshair on the right center red handle.
h. Drag a connecting line that attaches the right, center, red connecting handle on the left rounded rectangle to the left, center, red connecting handle on the right rounded rectangle.
i. With the connector selected, click **Shape Outline** in the Shape Styles group on the Format tab, and then click **Red, Accent 1** under Theme Colors.
j. Click **Shape Outline**, select **Weight**, and then select **1½ pt**.
k. Click the left rounded rectangle, and then press **Ctrl** as you click the right rounded rectangle.
l. Click **Shape Fill**, select **More Fill Colors**, click the **Standard tab**, and then set the **Transparency** to 20%.
m. With both shapes still selected, change the **Height** of the shapes to 3" and the **Width** to **1.5"** by clicking the spin boxes in the Size group located on the Format tab under Drawing Tools.
n. Save the *chap3_pe1_judo_solution* file and keep it onscreen if you plan to continue to the next exercise. Close the file and exit PowerPoint if you do not want to continue to the next exercise at this time.

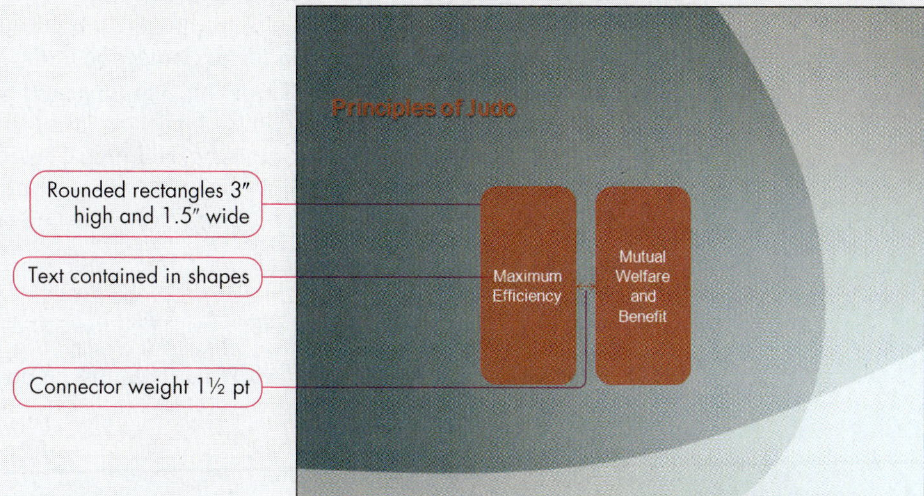

Figure 3.64 Use Shapes for Illustrations

...continued on Next Page

2 Insert and Modify SmartArt

You decide to create a slide showing the techniques used in Judo. Because Judo is a form of wrestling that emphasizes throws and pins, you create a Hierarchy SmartArt diagram to show the relationship between techniques. Figure 3.65 shows the SmartArt diagram after creation and modification.

a. Open *chap3_pe1_judo_solution* if you closed it after the last exercise and save it as **chap3_pe2_judo_solution**, and then move to **Slide 4.**
b. Click the **Home tab**, click the bottom portion of **New Slide**, and then click **Blank**.
c. Click the **Insert tab**, click **SmartArt**, in the Illustrations group and then click **Hierarchy** in the Choose a SmartArt Graphic dialog box.
d. Click the subtype **Hierarchy**, and then click **OK**.
e. Type **Judo Techniques** in the first level bullet of the Text pane.
f. Type the following Level 2 and Level 3 bullets in the Text pane:

- **Throwing (Nage)**
  - **Standing (Tachi)**
  - **Sacrifice (Sutemi)**
- **Grappling (Katame)**
  - **Holding (Osae Komi)**
  - **Choking (Shime)**
  - **Joint Locking (Kansetsu)**
- **Striking (Atemi)**
  - **Arm (Ude Ate)**
  - **Leg (Ashi Ate)**

g. Click the **More button** in the Layouts group on the Design tab under the SmartArt Tools contextual tab, and then click **Horizontal Labeled Hierarchy**.
h. Click **Format** under the SmartArt Tools contextual tab.
i. Click the **arrow** in the Size group, and then type **7** in the **Height** and **Width** boxes.
j. Drag the SmartArt to the left and up so that it fits on the slide.
k. Click the **Design tab** and then click **Change Colors** in the Quick Styles group.
l. Click **Colorful Range – Accent Colors 5 to 6**.
Because you like the effect of multiple colors, but wish to highlight the relationship between techniques, you decide to change the individual fill colors of the shapes.
m. Press **Ctrl** as you click the Throwing, Standing, and Sacrifice boxes, and then click the **Format tab**, click **Shape Fill** in the Shape Styles group, and click **Red, Accent 1**.
n. Press **Ctrl** as you click the Grappling, Holding, Choking, and Joint Locking boxes, click **Shape Fill**, and then click **Green, Accent 5**.
o. Press **Ctrl** as you click the Striking, Arm, and Leg boxes, then click **Shape Fill**, and then click **Orange, Accent 6**.
p. Click **Design** under the SmartArt Tools contextual tab, and then click **Right to Left** in the Create Graphic group.
q. Save *chap3_pe2_judo_solution* and keep it onscreen if you plan to continue to the next exercise. Close the file and exit PowerPoint if you do not want to continue to the next exercise at this time.

...continued on Next Page

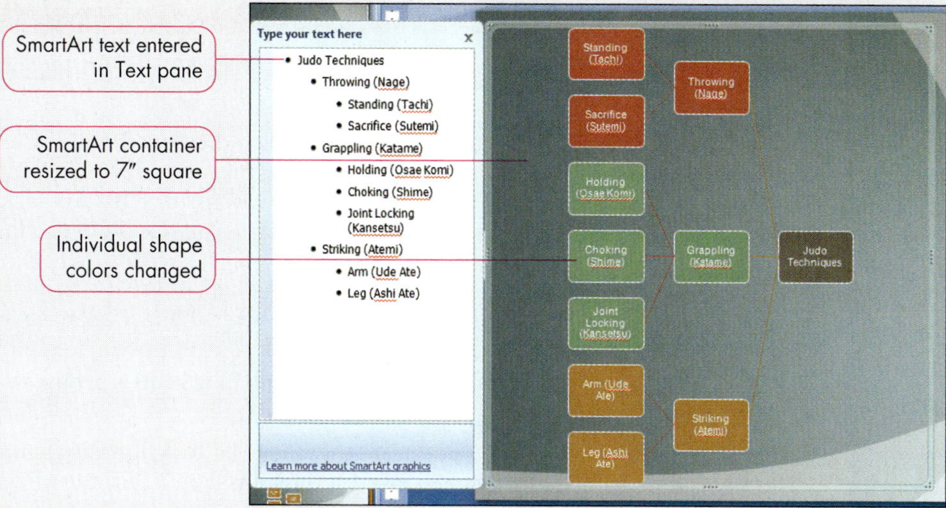

Figure 3.65 Create SmartArt

3 Convert Text to SmartArt

A Venn diagram is designed to show interconnected relationships. Using a SmartArt Venn graphic on the second slide of the slide show would emphasize how the three areas of Judo overlap to create a way of life. Figure 3.66 shows the text after it has been converted to SmartArt.

a. Open *chap3_pe2_judo_solution* if you closed it after the last exercise and save it as **chap3_pe3_judo_solution**; then move to **Slide 2.**
b. Click the placeholder containing the bullet points, and then click the **Home tab**.
c. Click **Convert to SmartArt Graphic** in the Paragraph group.
d. Click **Basic Venn**.
e. Click **Change Colors** in the SmartArt Styles group in the Design tab under SmartArt Tools.
f. Click **Colorful Range – Accent Colors 5 to 6**.
g. **Ctrl-click** each of the circles, and then click the **Format tab.**
h. Click **Text Fill** in the WordArt Styles group, and then click **White, Background 1**, which is the first option on the top row.
i. Save the *chap3_pe3_judo_solution* file and keep it onscreen if you plan to continue to the next exercise. Close the file and exit PowerPoint if you do not want to continue to the next exercise at this time.

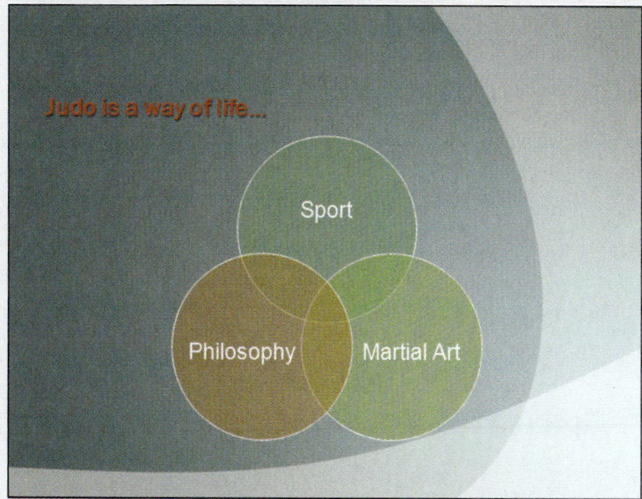

Figure 3.66 Venn Diagram

...continued on Next Page

4 Modify Clip Art

The *judogi* is the traditional uniform used for Judo practice and competition. It is constructed of heavy-weight cotton and has heavy stitching for durability. You want to show a *judogi* being worn to show its flexibility. You found a clip art image in the Microsoft Clip Art task pane, but it includes faces that you feel give a cartoony feel to the clip art. You decide to use the clip art, but want to modify it. Figure 3.67 shows the modified clip art.

a. Open *chap3_pe3_judo_solution* if you closed it after the last exercise and save it as **chap3_pe4_judo_solution**; then move to **Slide 4.**
b. Click the **Insert tab**, and then click **Clip Art** in the Illustrations group.
c. Type **judo** in the **Search for** box, and then click **Go**.
d. Refer to Figure 3.67 to help you locate the image of two fighting men in *judogi* uniforms, and then click the image to insert it on your slide. Close the Microsoft Clip Art task pane.
e. Drag the **Zoom slider** in the bottom right side of your screen to **300%**.
f. Drag the scroll bars until you can see the faces on the fighters, right-click, and then click **Edit Picture**.
g. Click **Yes** to convert the picture into a drawing object.
h. Click the **Drawing Tools Format tab**, and then click **Group** in the Arrange group.
i. Select **Ungroup**, and then click off the image to deselect the shapes.
j. **Ctrl-click** to select the lines and shapes that were used to create the eyebrows, eyes, and mouths on the two fighters, and then press **Delete**. Also delete the nose of the fighter on the right.
k. Click to select the purple shape composing the fighter on the left's hair, click **Format**, **Shape Fill** in the Shape Styles group, and then click **Red, Accent 1, Darker 50%**.
l. Change the color of the two purple shapes composing the fighter on the right's hair to the same color as you changed the fighter's hair on the left.
m. Click the **View tab** and click **Fit to Window** in the Zoom group. If necessary, drag your scroll bars until the slide is visible.
n. Drag a selection net around all the shapes composing the clip art image, and then click the **Format tab**, click **Group** in the Arrange group, and select **Regroup**.
o. Save *chap3_pe4_judo_solution* and keep it onscreen if you plan to continue to the next exercise.

Figure 3.67 Modified Clip Art

...continued on Next Page

5 Recolor a Picture

You locate a picture in the Clip Art task pane that you would like to add to the title slide. It does not match the theme color scheme, however. You use PowerPoint's Recolor feature to change the Color Mode of the image. Refer to Figure 3.68 when completing this exercise.

a. Open *chap3_pe4_judo_solution* if you closed it after the last exercise and save it as **chap3_pe5_judo_solution**; then move to **Slide 1**.
b. Click the **Insert tab** and click **Clip Art** in the Illustrations group.
c. Type **judo** in the **Search for** box, if necessary, and click **Go**.
d. Drag either the gold male or the gold female figure onto the slide, and then close the Clip Art task pane.
e. Click the **Format tab** and click **Recolor** in the Adjust group.
f. Select **Grayscale**.
g. Type **3** in the **Height** box in the Size group on the Format tab.
h. Drag the clip art picture to the right side of the screen to maintain the asymmetrical design of the title slide.
i. Save *chap3_pe5_judo_solution* and keep it onscreen if you plan to continue to the next exercise.

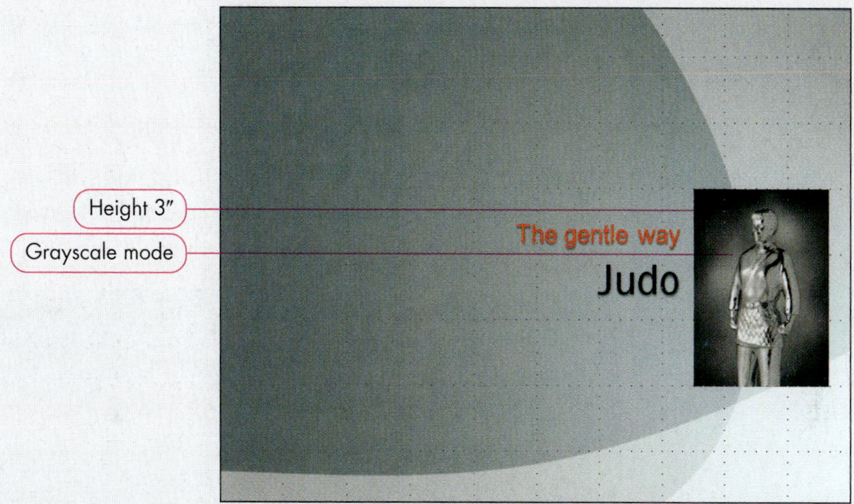

Figure 3.68 Recolored Clip Art

...continued on Next Page

6 Arrange Objects

When you viewed the judo clip art in the Clip Art task pane, you liked the three clip art images with a stained glass effect. You decide that you will add them to your slide show after the slide on techniques because they show two kicks and a throw. Refer to Figure 3.69 as you complete this exercise.

a. Open *chap3_pe5_judo_solution* if you closed it after the last exercise and save it as **chap3_pe6_judo_solution**; move to **Slide 5**, and then click the **Home tab**.
b. Click the arrow or the bottom of **New Slide** in the Slides group, and then click **Blank**.
c. Click the **Insert tab**, and then click **Clip Art** in the Illustrations group.
d. Type **judo** in the **Search for** box, if necessary, and click **Go.**
e. Drag the three stained glass judo pictures onto the slide.
f. Click the **View tab** and click **Gridlines** in the Show/Hide group.
g. Click the clip art picture of the man kicking, and then drag it until its top left corner is aligned with the -4" mark on the horizontal ruler and the zero point on the vertical ruler. The border of the clip art picture will snap in place when released, so the image itself will look like it is slightly under the gridlines.
h. Press **Ctrl** as you click the picture of the woman kicking so that it is included in the selection with the man.
i. Click **Align** on the Format tab under Picture Tools, and then click **Align Left**.
j. If the picture of the woman is blocking the picture of the man, press **Shift** and drag upward until the picture of the man is no longer blocked.
k. Drag the last picture of the two men so it aligns on a grid point between the two previously positioned pictures.
l. Create a Notes and Handouts header and footer with the date, your name in the header, and your instructor's name and your class in the footer.
m. View the slide show and print as directed by your instructor.
n. Save *chap3_pe6_judo_solution*, and close the file.

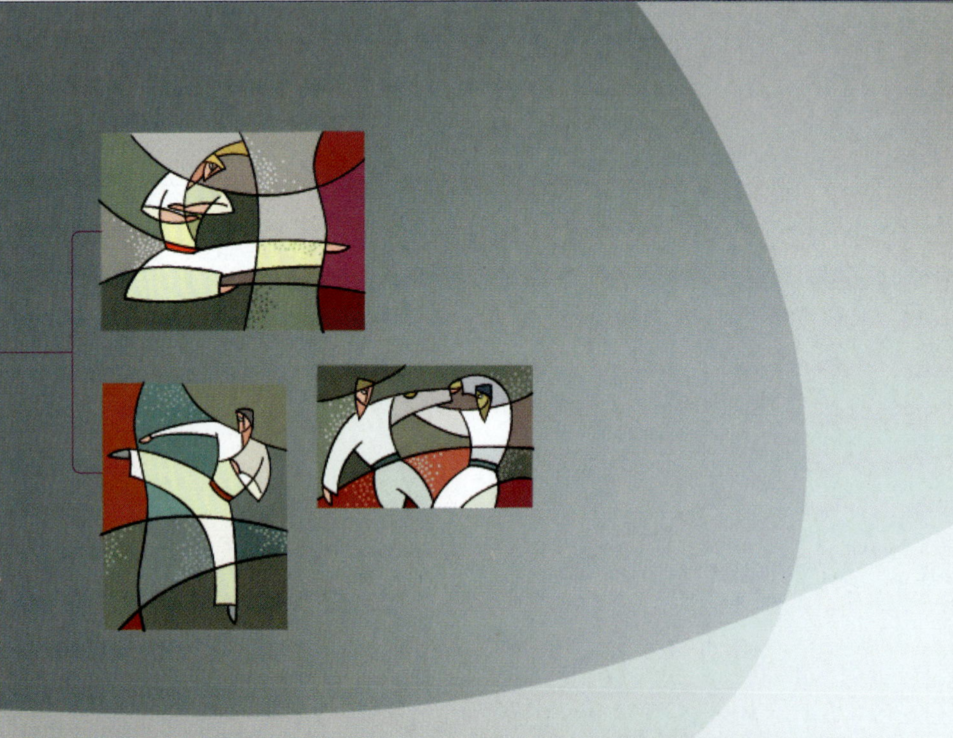

Figure 3.69 Clip Art Aligned

...continued on Next Page

Mid-Level Exercises

1 Project Management Life Cycle

You have been asked to help train the employees of a new company who seem to be having difficulty with organizing and completing company projects. Because it is a small family-owned company, many of the employees are family members who are enthusiastic and have great ideas, but who need help seeing the process a project must go through before it is complete. You start the training by reviewing the Project Management Life Cycle at the next employee meeting. Use PowerPoint's SmartArt and Shapes as needed to prepare the illustrations for this presentation. Apply Quick Styles and make customizations to create a professional look for your presentation. The partial presentation is shown in Figure 3.70.

a. Open *chap3_mid1_projmgt* and immediately save it as **chap3_mid1_projmgt_solution**.

b. Move to **Slide 2** and insert a **Process SmartArt** diagram using the **Vertical Process** style.

c. Type the following points in the Text pane, and then close the Text pane.

- **Project Initiation**
- **Project Planning**
- **Project Execution**
- **Project Completion**
- **Review and Evaluation**

d. Apply SmartArt Subtle Effect style to the SmartArt.

Refer to Figure 3.70 to complete the following steps.

e. Create two rounded rectangles to the right of the SmartArt to demonstrate the cyclical nature of project execution. Apply **Moderate Effect – Accent 1** to the rectangles, and then apply Shape Fill color **Brown, Accent 3, Darker 25%.**

f. Type **Monitor** in one rounded rectangle shape, and then type **Adjust** in the other. Change the font color to black.

g. Change the Shape Fill color of the Project Execution shape to **Brown, Accent 3, Darker 25%.**

h. Create arrows between the three rounded rectangles to indicate the cycle. Change their weight to ¾ pt.

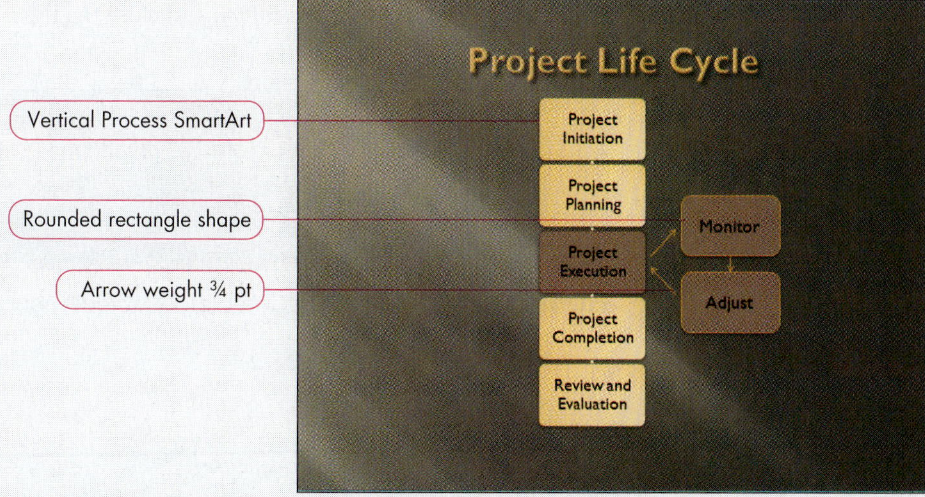

Figure 3.70 SmartArt Diagram of Project Life Cycle

...continued on Next Page

i. Move to **Slide 3** and create four shapes with the following specifications:

Shape	Fill	Position	Dimensions	Text
Rectangle 1	Subtle Effect, Accent 1	From Top Left Corner: Horizontal: 3.25" Vertical: 1.33"	Height: 3" Width: 2.17"	Project Initiation
Rectangle 2	Moderate Effect, Accent 3	From Top Left Corner: Horizontal: 1.58" Vertical: 3.83"	Height: 1.42" Width: 2.5"	Determine Project Purpose and Scope
Rectangle 3	Moderate Effect, Accent 3	From Top Left Corner: Horizontal: 4.58" Vertical: 3.83"	Height: 1.42" Width: 2.5"	Determine Boundaries
Up Arrow Callout	Moderate Effect, Accent 6	From Top Left Corner: Horizontal: 5.17" Vertical: 5.25"	Height: .92" Width: 3"	Conduct Feasibility Study

j. Move to **Slide 4** and create a **List SmartArt diagram** using the **Horizontal Bullet List style.**

k. Type the following in the Text pane:

- **Time**
  - **People**
  - **Facilities**
  - **Materials**
  - **Equipment**

l. Copy the text you entered and then paste it into the Text pane two times. Edit the first-level bullets so they read: **Time**, **Cost**, **Resources**.

m. Apply **Simple Fill** SmartArt style.

n. Create a Notes and Handouts Header and Footer with the date, your name in the header, and your instructor's name and your class in the footer. Print as required by your teacher.

o. Save *chap3_mid1_projmgt_solution*, and close the file.

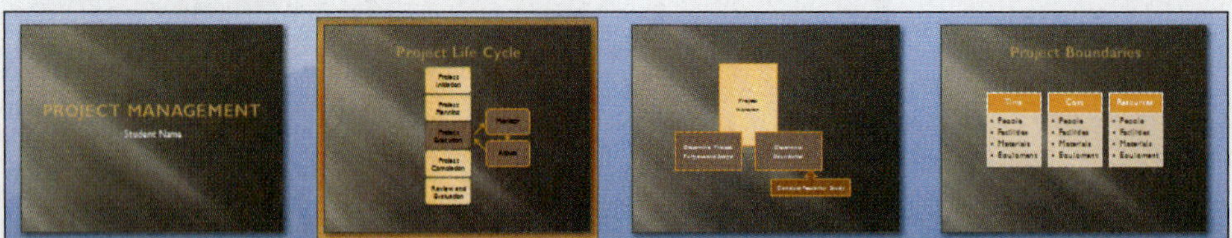

Figure 3.71 The Partially Completed Project Management Slide Show

...continued on Next Page

2 Clip Art Manipulation Experience

In this exercise you practice your clip art modification and alignment skills. Being able to quickly modify clip art to fit your theme and topic is an essential skill for a PowerPoint professional to have, and the more you practice modifying clip art, the faster you will become at it. You need to be able to ungroup or disassemble clip art, delete unwanted objects, change shape colors, reposition shapes, and then regroup the shapes so they form one coherent image. You do not have to be an artist to have fun manipulating clip art. In this exercise you manipulate a classic clip art cartoon that has been around almost as long as the microcomputer. While it serves as a humorous, fun image representing frustration on which to practice your object manipulation skills, remember that any image used in a slide show created with a message (not for practice) needs to relate to the topic. As to hitting a computer with a sledge hammer when frustrated? Don't! Violence against the computer is never a - computer problem solution and is very expensive! Refer to Figure 3.72 as you complete this exercise.

a. Open *chap3_mid2_artist*, and immediately save it as **chap3_mid2_artist_solution**.

b. Use the Slides tab to duplicate Slide 2.

c. Ungroup the Duck clip art in the new Slide 3 and convert it to a drawing object. Because this is a complex clip art image made up of a group containing the duck and a group containing the computer, and group containing the computer stand, you will need to ungroup again.

d. Drag the duck group to the upper left of the slide, and make a copy of the group. Drag the new duck group to the right side of the screen. Flip the new group horizontally.

e. Turn on the view of the grid, and drag each of the duck groups and the base of the computer table so they snap to the same grid location.

f. Change the slide title to **Flip Horizontally**.

g. Duplicate Slide 3.

h. In the new Slide 4, ungroup the original duck group until it is in individual pieces, and then change the duck's jacket to green. Change the slide title to **Change Color**.

i. Duplicate Slide 2 and drag it until it becomes Slide 4 (the Change Color slide becomes Slide 5), and change the name to *Resize*. Place the duck on top of the computer table, change the size of the computer so that it is 4" by 4", then move computer to position shown in Figure 3.72.

j. Add a sixth slide. Copy and paste one of the left facing ducks onto it. Search the Clip Art task pane for the cartoon clip of the mother kangaroo and insert it in Slide 6. Ungroup the duck. Delete all shapes except for the ones used to create the duck head. Change the line weight for the head and beak to 2 ½ pts. Group the head shapes, flip horizontally, and then tuck the head slightly above the babies in the mother kangaroo's pouch. Change slide title to **Just for Fun**.

k. Move to the title slide and delete the title and the slide title placeholder. Create a WordArt title using **Fill – Accent 3, Powder Bevel** as the WordArt Style. Type **Clip Art Artistry** in the WordArt placeholder.

l. Modify the WordArt size to 1.5" height and 6" width.

m. Position the bottom edge of the WordArt placeholder so it aligns with the zero point on the vertical ruler. Drag the left edge of the placeholder so it aligns with the 2" mark on the horizontal ruler.

n. Create a Notes and Handouts Header and Footer with the date, your name in the header, and your instructor's name and your class in the footer. Print as required by your teacher.

o. Save the *chap3_mid2_artist_solution* presentation, and close the file.

...continued on Next Page

Figure 3.72 Fun with Clip Art

3 SmartArt Ideas

The SmartArt Graphic gallery displays the categories of SmartArt diagrams available, the subtypes, and tips for the uses of the diagram. Some of the descriptions may seem difficult to understand if you do not have a great deal of experience with the various types of diagrams. To help you see an example of the type of information appropriate for each type of diagram, you create a slide show of "SmartArt ideas." You also will work extensively with sizing, placement, and fills and will be proficient with these tools by the end of the exercise. Refer to Figure 3.73 while completing this exercise.

a. Open *chap3_mid3_smartart*, and save it as **chap3_mid3_smartart_solution**.

b. On **Slide 2**, create a **Vertical Box List** SmartArt Graphic. Apply **Subtle Effect** SmartArt Style. Type the following list items:

- **List**
- **Process**
- **Cycle**
- **Hierarchy**
- **Relationship**
- **Matrix**
- **Pyramid**

c. Size the SmartArt to 7" wide, and then align it to the center of the page. Align the bottom border of the SmartArt with the last row of the gridline.

d. Move to **Slide 3**, and then create an **Upward Arrow** SmartArt graphic. Apply the **Simple Fill** SmartArt Style, and then type the following process steps:

- **Initiation and Development**
- **Institutional Review**
- **Campus Community Review**
- **Preparation for Trustees**
- **Trustees Approval**

...continued on Next Page

e. Change the height of the SmartArt to 6.17" and the width to 10". Drag the Process arrow so it fits on the slide.

f. Move to **Slide 4**, and then create a **Basic Radial** SmartArt diagram. Apply the **Intense Effect – Accent1** SmartArt Style.

g. Type **Residential College** as the center hub, and then type **Build Community, Promote Personal Growth,** and **Support Academic Success** as the spokes around the hub.

h. Set the height of the SmartArt to 5.5" and the width to 6.67", and then center the SmartArt on the slide.

i. Move to **Slide 5**, and then create a **Horizontal Hierarchy** SmartArt. Apply the **Intense Effect – Accent 1** SmartArt Style.

j. Leave the first- and second-level bullets blank in the Text pane, and then type the following in the third-level bullets: **Jones Paint & Glass**, **Quality Cleaners**, **Ames Automotive**, and **Smith Real Estate**. These are the teams in a tournament, and it is unknown who will move forward.

k. Use the Right to Left option in the Create Graphic group to change the orientation of the diagram. Drag the borders of the SmartArt graphic until it fits the page and the text is large enough to read.

l. Move to **Slide 6** and insert a **Basic Venn** SmartArt graphic. Type the following in the Text pane: ***Anesthesiology***, ***Nurses***, and ***Surgeon***.

m. Format the *Anesthesiology* shape using the right-click shortcut menu. Apply a picture fill using **doctors** as the Clip Art search keyword and include content from Office Online. Locate an appropriate photograph and then click OK and Close.

n. Format the *Anesthesiology* text with the **Fill – Text 2, Outline – Background 2** WordArt Style—the glow around the letters helps the text visibility.

o. Repeat Steps m and n to insert photographs in the remaining two shapes and to make the text visible. Use the grid to center the Venn diagram in the available space.

p. Move to **Slide 7**, create a **Basic Matrix** SmartArt graphic, apply the **Subtle Effect** SmartArt Style, and type the following text in the Text pane:

- **Urgent & Important**
- **Not Urgent & Important**
- **Urgent & Not Important**
- **Not Urgent & Not Important**

q. Move to **Slide 8**, create a **Basic Pyramid** SmartArt graphic, apply the **Subtle Effect** SmartArt Style, and type the following text in the Text pane:

- (Press **Enter** here so nothing appears in the top of the pyramid. If you type the necessary text in the SmartArt, the text size reduces until it is virtually unreadable. You will add the text for this box in a text box in a later step.)
- **Esteem**
- **Belonging and Love**
- **Safety**
- **Biological Needs**

r. Create a text box in the top shape of the pyramid and type **Self Actualization**. Drag into position. (Creating this text in the Text pane would have reduced the size of the font so that it would be close to unreadable.) Drag the border of the pyramid to enlarge it.

...continued on Next Page

s. Create a Notes and Handouts header and footer with the date, your name in the header, and your instructor's name and your class in the footer. Print as required by your instructor.

t. Save *chap3_mid3_smartart_solution*, and close the file.

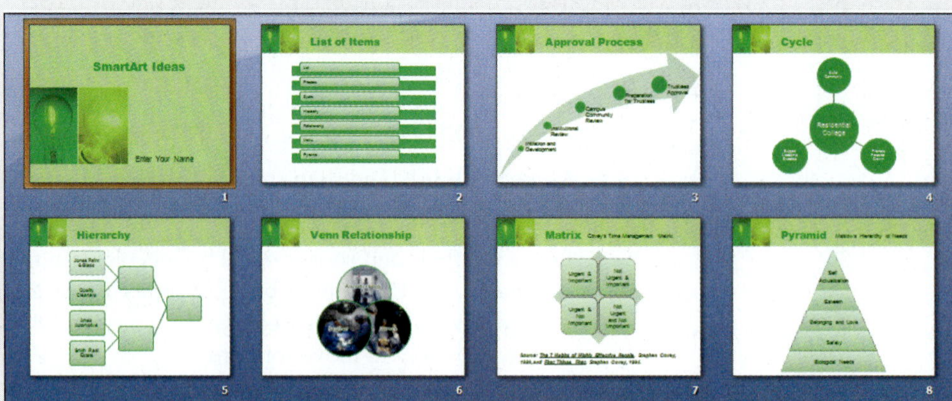

Figure 3.73 SmartArt Ideas

4 Greeting Cards

Between nieces, nephews, friend's children, and neighbor's children, you give a lot of children's birthday cards. You know that PowerPoint can be used for many types of documents in addition to slide shows. For example, you can create single sheet signs and multisheet posters. Knowing this feature, you decide to create your own card template that you can use in PowerPoint to quickly create a birthday card. After you create and save the card template, you create a birthday card for your niece who turns 1 year old next week. Refer to Figure 3.74 as you create the template, and Figure 3.75 as you create the card.

a. Open a blank presentation file and immediately save it as **chap3_mid4_card_solution**.

b. Select portrait orientation. Change slide layout to Blank.

c. Display the guides.

d. Create a text box and type **Front of Card**. Flip the text box vertically. Drag the text box to the top left quadrant of the card. This location will serve as a reminder that when the card is folded after printing, the top of the page becomes the bottom.

e. Duplicate the text box. Drag the duplicate to the top right quadrant of the card and edit the text to read **Back of Card**.

f. Drag a selection net around the two text boxes, and make a duplicate. Flip the duplicate selection vertically, and then drag the duplicate selection to the bottom quadrants of the card.

g. Edit the text on the bottom left quadrant to read **Left Inside of Card**. Edit the text on the bottom right quadrant to read **Right Inside of Card**.

h. Select the text boxes on the left side of the card (*Front of Card* and *Left Inside of Card*), and then align them at their center.

i. Select the text boxes on the right side of the card (*Back of Card* and *Right Inside of Card*), and then align them at their center.

j. Select the text boxes in the top quadrant of the card (*Front of Card* and *Back of Card*), and align them at their top.

...continued on Next Page

k. Select the text boxes in the bottom quadrant of the card (*Left Inside of Card* and *Right Inside of Card*), and then align them at their bottom.

l. Save the file as a PowerPoint Template with **chap3_mid4_cardtemplate_solution** as the file name.

m. Print the template and fold it to check the text rotation. Close the file.

n. Create a new PowerPoint Presentation based on the card template you created.

o. Locate the clip art image of a "1" candle, birthday balloons, and birthday bear. Insert the picture on the slide. Size the image so it fits in a quadrant, and then vertically flip the image. Drag the clip art image to the Front of Card quadrant and position it evenly between margins. Remember—pressing Alt while dragging temporarily releases the grid so you can move the object freely.

p. Select the Back of Card text and type **Created by**, and then enter your name.

q. Delete the text box that reads *Left Inside of Card*. Edit the *Right Inside of Card* text to read **Happy First Birthday Sweet Niece!**

r. Print as required by your instructor.

s. Save the card as **chap3_mid4_card_solution**, and close the file.

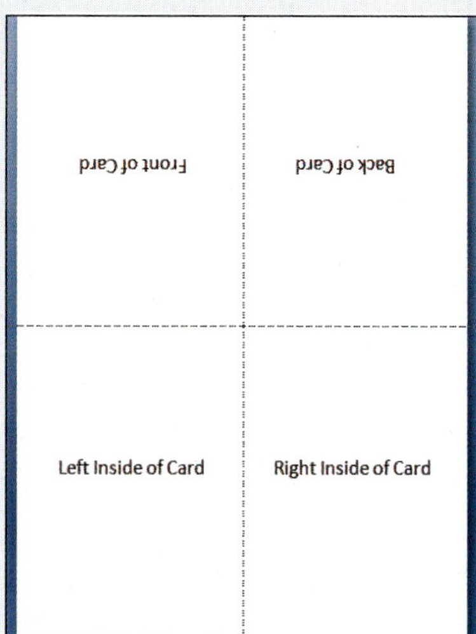

Figure 3.74 Birthday Card Template

Figure 3.75 Birthday Card

Capstone Exercise

In Chapter 2 you began a presentation on Waterwise landscaping for your neighbors in your southwestern subdivision. Previously, you concentrated on the content of the presentation, but now you are anxious to include visual elements. You also have additional information that would take a lot of text explanation, but can be presented in a much simpler and easier-to-remember format if you incorporate shapes. In this capstone exercise you will continue working on the Waterwise landscaping presentation and utilize the features you have learned in this chapter to create a new slide and revise previously created slides.

Create a "Fire Aware" Landscape

Rather than create lengthy bulleted text to explain the concept of creating zones to protect a home from fire, you decide to create a landscape using shapes and indicate the depth of the zones on the landscape. You use a combination of oval shapes, text boxes, and clip art to create the landscape.

a. Open *chap3_cap_xeriscape*, and immediately save it as **chap3_cap_xeriscape_solution**.

b. Move to **Slide 12** and create an oval on the slide.

c. Change the Shape Fill to a custom RGB color, Red:51, Green:102, and Blue:0, and a Transparency of 50%. Remove the outline from the shape.

d. Change the oval size to height 1.67" and width 6".

e. Make a copy of the oval. Change the second oval size to height 2.92" and width 8.08". Make another copy of the oval and change the third oval size to height 4" and width 10".

f. Select all three ovals and Align Center. Group the three ovals so they will move as one, and then position the group at horizontal position: 0" from top left corner and vertical position: 1" from top left corner.

g. Insert a text box, type **Zone 1**, and then drag it to the bottom center of the small oval. Apply the **Fill – White, Outline – Accent 1** WordArt Style to the text. Make two copies of the text box and edit them to read *Zone 2* and *Zone 3*. Drag Zone 2 to the bottom center of the medium sized oval, and Zone 3 to the bottom center of the large oval.

h. Locate and insert a clip art image of a house, and position it in the center of Zone 1. Size it appropriately.

i. Create arrows to indicate the depth of the zones, and label the arrows using text boxes. Zone 1's arrow should be labeled 30′, and Zones 2 and 3 should be labeled 10′. Refer to Figure 3.76 for placement of arrows and labels. Set the weight for the arrows at 1 pt. Set arrow color and text color to white.

j. Locate and insert a clip art image of a tree. Duplicate it multiple times and position a few trees in Zone 2, and more trees in Zone 3. Size trees toward the top of the slide smaller than trees nearer the bottom of the zones. Refer to Figure 3.76, but your tree and tree placement can vary.

Figure 3.76 Completed "Fire Aware" Landscaping

Convert Text to SmartArt

Now you need to go through the slide show and convert some bulleted lists to SmartArt graphics. In particular, you will convert bulleted lists to Basic Venn, Converging Arrows, and Continuous Arrow Process SmartArt graphics.

a. Move to **Slide 2**, and then convert the bulleted text to a **Basic Venn** SmartArt graphic. Refer to Figure 3.77. Apply the Simple Fill SmartArt style.

b. Move to **Slide 3**, select the Waterwise bulleted text, and convert it to a **Converging Arrow** SmartArt graphic. Resize the graphic so that the arrows almost touch to show the convergence of the methods around the theme of conserving water. Position the SmartArt in the middle of the horizontal space for Waterwise Options, and then apply the **Polished** SmartArt Style.

c. Select the Wildfire Aware Options bulleted text and convert it to a **Continuous Arrow Process** SmartArt graphic to indicate that the creation of defensible landscaping leads to zones. Apply the **Polished** SmartArt Style, and change the text color for each text block in the arrow to white. Refer to Figure 3.77.

...continued on Next Page

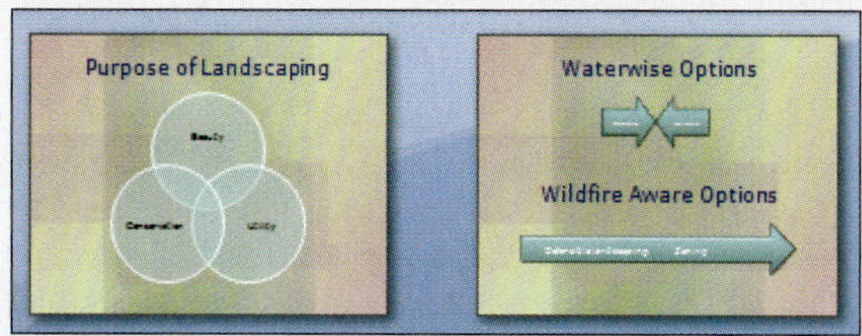

Figure 3.77 SmartArt Used to Relieve Bullet Boredom

Create SmartArt

You now need to insert a title slide, insert a text box, and create a SmartArt graphic in the form of a list.

a. Move to **Slide 12**, add a new slide with a Title Only layout, and then type **Principles for Waterwise Landscaping** as the title. Change the title font size to 32 pt and stretch the placeholder so the title displays on one line.

b. Insert a text box and type **Tips from the Office of Community Services, Fort Lewis College** inside. Center the text box under the title. Refer to Figure 3.78.

c. Create a **Vertical Block List** SmartArt to show the steps, or workflow, in the Waterwise Landscaping process. Type the following in the Text pane. The principle number should be at Level 1, and the principle should be at Level 2.

- **1 Develop Landscape Plan**
- **2 Condition Your Soil**
- **3 Limit Lawn Size**
- **4 Irrigate Efficiently**
- **5 Use Appropriate Plants**
- **6 Apply Mulches**
- **7 Maintain**

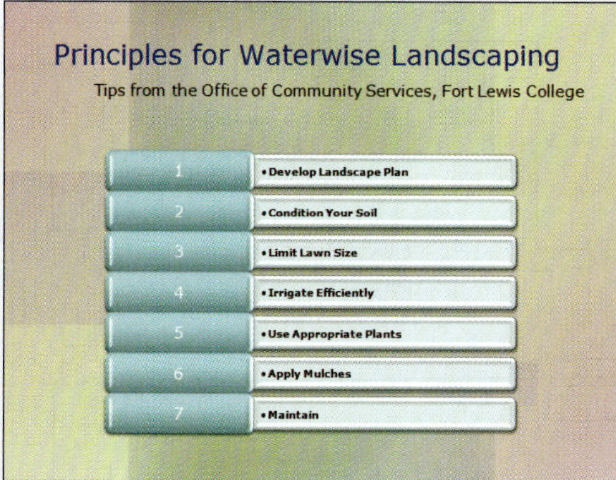

Figure 3.78 SmartArt Showing a Workflow

Convert Text to WordArt

The last graphic you want to insert is a WordArt object. After inserting the WordArt, you will apply an animation scheme and then create a Notes and Handouts header and footer.

a. Move to **Slide 1** and select the title.

b. Apply the **Gradient Fill – Accent 6, Inner Shadow** WordArt Style to the title.

c. Apply a Transform Text Effect to the title using the Chevron Up warp style.

d. Apply the **Fill – Accent 3, Outline Text 2** WordArt Style to the subtitle. Refer to Figure 3.79.

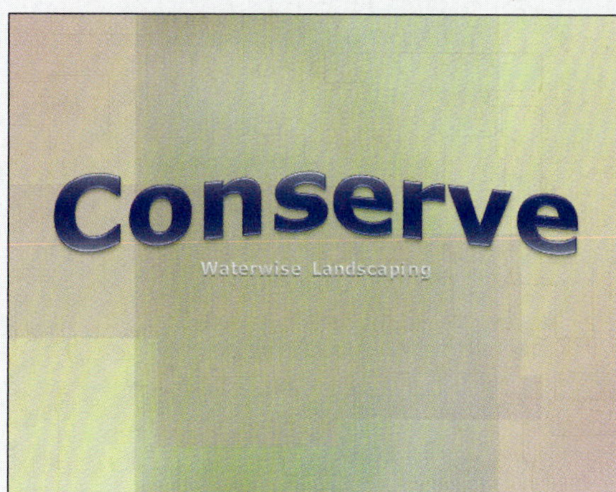

Figure 3.79 WordArt Title and Subtitle

e. Apply the Fly In animation scheme to the title, and then apply the Fade animation scheme to the subtitle.

f. Create a Notes and Handouts Header and Footer with your name in the header, and your instructor's name and your class in the footer. Print as required by your teacher.

g. Save *chap3_cap_xeriscape_solution*, and close the file.

Mini Cases

Use the rubric following the case as a guide to evaluate your work, but keep in mind that your instructor may impose additional grading criteria or use a different standard to judge your work.

Institutional Policies and Procedures Approval Process

GENERAL CASE

The president of your college has asked you to create a one-page document that shows the process that a policy or procedure must go through in order to be adopted by the college. The process involves five stages with multiple steps to be taken in each stage. You realize that this process is best shown as a flowchart. You decide to create the flowchart in PowerPoint rather than a word processor because of the convenience of grids and guides for placement, and the ease of creating shapes. You decide to use shapes instead of SmartArt so that it is easier to adjust the shapes to fit on the page. Because your output will be a printed page and a Web page, you can use smaller fonts than you could use for a presentation. Save your file as **chap3_mc1_flowchart_solution**. Figure 3.80 shows one possible solution to this task. The information you need is in the following table. Save and close the presentation.

Stage 1	Stage 2	Stage 3	Stage 4	Stage 5
Initiation and Development	Institutional Entity Review	Campus Community Review	Procedures Approval	Policy Approval
Origination	Steward	President's Council Approval for Review	President's Council Final Approval	Board of Trustees Reviews Policy
President's Council Sponsorship	Dean's Council	Posted on Intranet for Review	Procedures Approved	Policies Approved
Policy Steward Assigned	Faculty Senate		Web Manager Notifies Campus Community	Web Manager Notifies Campus Community
Policy/Procedure Development	PACE			Forward Policy to Board of Regents When Required
	Student Council			
	Others as Needed			

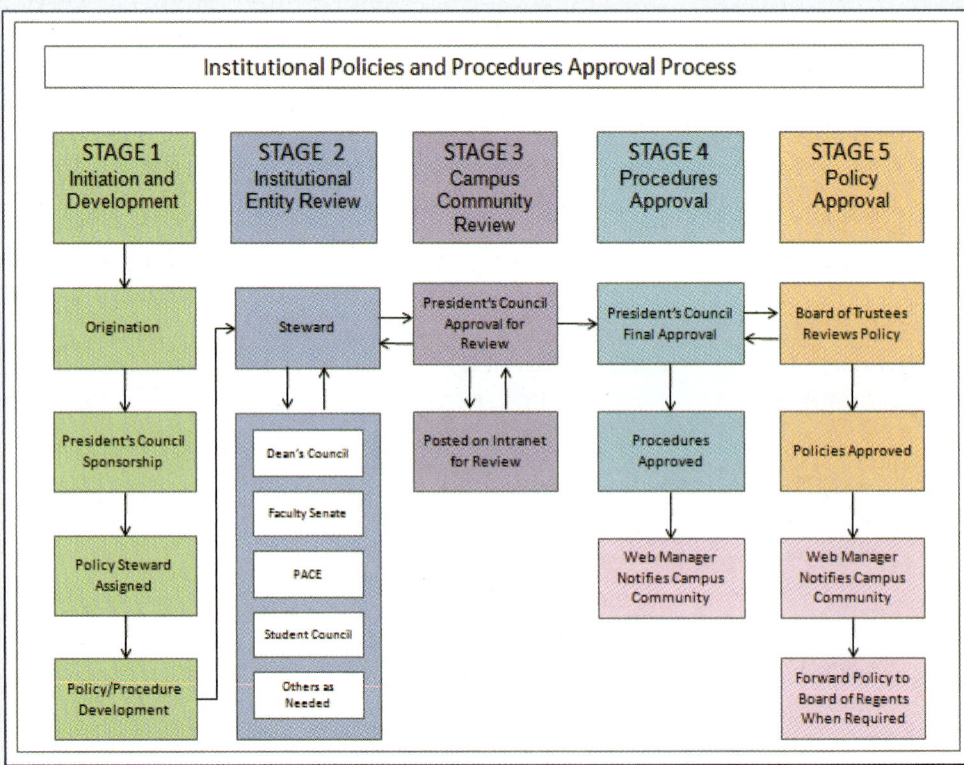

Figure 3.80 Sample Solution to Mini Case 1

Performance Elements	Exceeds Expectations	Meets Expectations	Below Expectations
Organization	Flowchart stages can be easily identified. Steps in each stage are easily identified so process is understood.	Flowchart identifies steps to be followed.	Flowchart cannot be understood because there is no sequence of information.
Visual aspects	Flowchart shapes, fills, outlines, and text are appealing and enhance understanding of the stages in flowchart process. There is a consistent visual theme.	Flowchart shapes relate to purpose and content. Text is readable.	The fills, outlines, or shapes are distracting and do not enhance understanding of the process and stages in the process.
Layout	The layout is visually pleasing and contributes to understanding the stages in the process. White space aids in separating stages in the process. Arrows indicate steps to be followed.	The layout shows some structure, but placement of some shapes, arrows, and/or white space can be improved.	The layout is cluttered and confusing. Placement of shapes, arrows, and/or white space detracts from understanding. Understanding of the process is lost.
Mechanics	Presentation has no errors in spelling, grammar, word usage, or punctuation. No typographical errors present.	Presentation has no more than one error in spelling, grammar, word usage, or punctuation.	Presentation readability is impaired due to repeated errors in spelling, grammar, word usage, or punctuation. Multiple typographical errors.

To PowerPoint or Not to PowerPoint: That Is the Question

RESEARCH CASE

This textbook has endeavored to show you the benefits of creating PowerPoint slide shows for use in presentations—but do not take the author's word for it. You need to see what industry or business professionals have to say about PowerPoint. Referring to professional Web sites can provide you with a wealth of tips and ideas for creating slide shows that move your work above the ordinary, but they also can make you aware of the dangers of relying too heavily on the software. Visit the locations shown in the table below, and then read the articles. Some locations are favorable to PowerPoint and electronic presentations, and some articles are not. Some locations are simply Web sites to aid you in your quest for PowerPoint knowledge. If a Web site is no longer active, remember that the Internet is dynamic and changes constantly. Then move on to the next article. After visiting these sites, search the Internet for articles relating to PowerPoint tips and tricks and read at least two more articles. See if you can locate an article asking if an inadvertent error in the creation of a PowerPoint presentation may have contributed to the space shuttle Columbia disaster.

Create a slide show highlighting what you learn from this experience. Your slide show might include a slide highlighting pros for using PowerPoint, a slide indicating cautions for using PowerPoint, and a slide with Tips and Tricks. Create a slide illustrating a tip you learned in your travels through the wealth of sites on PowerPoint usage. Save the presentation as **chap3_mc2_powerpoint_solution**. Close the presentation.

Professional Web Sites to Visit

Article Title	Author	Web Site
Presentation Zen	Garr Reynolds	http://presentationzen.blogs.com/presentationzen/2005/09/whats_good_powe.html
Beyond Bullets: Zen and the Art of PowerPoint	Cliff Atkinson	http://www.beyondbullets.com/2005/01/story.html
Deadly Sins of Modern PowerPoint Usage	Rick Altman	http://www.betterppt.com/editorial/archive/04mar.htm
The Gettysburg Powerpoint Presentation, 11/19/1863	Peter Norvig	http://www.norvig.com/Gettysburg/index.htm
Ask the PowerPoint experts	Microsoft Office Online	http://office.microsoft.com/en-us/powerpoint/HA011082211033.aspx?pid=CH062556591033
Microsoft PowerPoint	Indezine, compiled by Geetesh Bajaj	http://www.indezine.com/products/powerpoint/index.html

Performance Elements	Exceeds Expectations	Meets Expectations	Below Expectations
Organization	Presentation indicates accurate research and significant facts. Evidence exists that information has been evaluated and synthesized showing an understanding of the topic.	Presentation indicates some research has taken place and that information was included in the content.	Presentation demonstrates a lack of research or understanding of the topic.
Visual aspects	Presentation background, themes, clip art, and animation are appealing and enhance the understanding of presentation purpose and content. There is aconsistent visual theme.	Clip art is related to the topic. Animation is not distracting.	The background or theme is distracting to the topic. Images do not enhance understanding of the content or are unrelated.
Layout	The layout is visually pleasing and contributes to the overall message with appropriate use of headings, subheadings, bullet points, clip art, and white space.	The layout shows some structure, but placement of some headings, subheadings, bullet points, clip art, and/or white space can be improved.	The layout is cluttered and confusing. Placement of headings, subheadings, bullet points, images, and/or white space detracts from readability.
Mechanics	Presentation has no errors in spelling, grammar, word usage, or punctuation. Bullet points are parallel.	Presentation has no more than one error in spelling, grammar, word usage, or punctuation. Bullet points are inconsistent in one slide.	Presentation readability is impaired due to repeated errors in spelling, grammar, word usage, or punctuation. Most bullet points are not parallel.

Seating Chart Blues

DISASTER RECOVERY

A colleague with some knowledge of PowerPoint downloaded a Microsoft Online template for seating charts. She tried to position the shapes representing student desks on her slide in the approximate positions of desks in her classrooms, but because she does not fully understand grouping and ungrouping, she is frustrated with the process. She has grouped and ungrouped odd combinations of shapes. You offer to help her revise her seating chart. Open *chap3_mc3_seat* and save it as **chap3_mc3_seat_solution**. Revise the seating chart based on the position of desks in your computer lab. Create a shape and label for printer location, or download a printer clip art image and position it to indicate printer location. Close the presentation.

Performance Elements	Exceeds Expectations	Meets Expectations	Below Expectations
Organization	Placement of desk shapes reflects the arrangement of school computer laboratory. Printer table shape is in correct location.	Placement of desk shapes indicates arrangement of school computer laboratory.	Desk shapes do not indicate the arrangement of school computer laboratory. Printer location is incorrect or is missing.
Visual aspects	Any changes to shapes, fills, outlines, and text are appealing and enhance understanding of the classroom arrangement. There is a consistent visual theme.	Text is readable. Shape size is appropriate.	The fills, outlines, or shapes are distracting or unappealing and do not enhance understanding of the classroom arrangement.
Layout	The layout is visually pleasing and contributes to immediate understanding of desk and printer arrangement. White space indicates rows or walking space.	Layout contributes to understanding of the class room setup.	The layout is cluttered and confusing. Placement of desks and printer is incorrect, or desks are layered on top of each other, creating an impossible situation for classroom use.
Mechanics	Any added text has no errors in spelling, grammar, word usage, or punctuation. No typographical errors present.	Seating Chart has no more than one error in spelling, grammar, word usage, or punctuation.	Any added text has impaired readability due to repeated errors in spelling, grammar, word usage, or punctuation. Multiple typographical errors.

chapter 4 | PowerPoint

PowerPoint Multimedia Tools

Enhancing with Multimedia

After you read this chapter, you will be able to:

1. Insert and modify a picture **(page 1015)**.
2. Use the Internet as a resource **(page 1021)**.
3. Create a Photo Album **(page 1033)**.
4. Set Photo Album options **(page 1033)**.
5. Insert movies **(page 1038)**.
6. Set movie options **(page 1040)**.
7. Add sound **(page 1046)**.
8. Record and play narration **(page 1048)**.

Hands-On Exercises

Exercises	Skills Covered
1. USING PICTURES (page 1026) **Open:** chap4_ho1_memories.pptx **Save as:** chap4_ho1_memories_solution.pptx	• Insert Pictures • Apply and Modify a Picture Style • Adjust Brightness and Contrast • Crop and Compress • Create a Background from a Picture • Insert a Picture from the Internet
2. CREATING A PHOTO ALBUM (page 1035) **Open:** none **Save as:** chap4_ho2_album_solution.pptx, chap4_ho2_album2_solution.pptx, and chap4_ho2_album3_solution.pptx	• Select and Order Pictures • Adjust Contrast and Brightness • Set Picture Layout • Select Frame Shape • Edit Album Settings • Apply a Design Theme
3. INSERTING A MOVIE (page 1042) **Open:** chap4_ho1_memories _solution.pptx (from Exercise 1) **Save as:** chap4_ho3_memories_solution.pptx (additional modifications)	• Insert a Movie from the Clip Organizer • Insert a Movie from a File • Set Movie Options
4. ADDING SOUND (page 1051) **Open:** chap4_ho3_memories_solution.pptx (from Exercise 3) **Save as:** chap4_ho4_memories_solution.pptx (additional modifications)	• Add Sound from a File • Change Sound Settings • Insert Sound from the Clip Organizer • Add Narration

CASE STUDY

Forensics Geology Class Album

The college you attend has a strong criminal justice program culminating in a bachelor of arts degree. Graduates of the program are trained for criminal justice opportunities in law enforcement, the Drug Enforcement Agency (DEA), the Federal Bureau of Investigation (FBI), the Bureau of Alcohol, Tobacco, Firearms, and Explosives (ATF), corrections, security, investigations, immigration, and border patrol. You are newly employed in the Criminal Justice department as an aide to Professor Taume Park. She teaches a forensics geology class that provides a survey of the uses of geology in solving crime. Her class emphasizes actual criminal cases, and her students complete hands-on laboratory activities to develop their critical observation skills. During the class the students are divided into teams and assigned one of four possible presentations: identifying mineral pigments related to art forgery and cosmetics; examining and recognizing imitation amber and other gems; studying environmental pollution; or reviewing crimes in archeology.

Case Study

Professor Park takes pictures of her students on the first day of class. She brings you the memory card with the pictures of her students and asks you to print each picture. She explains to you that she writes each student's name on his or her picture to help her put the right name with the right face. With your knowledge of PowerPoint, you decide to prepare an album for Professor Park that she can copy for her students. You decide to include identifying class information, a picture of Professor Park, and a picture of her lab assistant, Katreena Castillo, on the title page of the album. Because Professor Park took the pictures of the students quickly in a poorly lit classroom with a white board behind the students, you use the album tools to improve the contrast and brightness of some pictures. You use the captions feature of the album options to add the students' names for a more professional look.

Your Assignment

- Read the chapter, paying special attention to information that explains image brightness and contrast and explains how to use PowerPoint's Photo Album feature.
- Insert all the images in the *chap4_case_images* folder except for the Professor Taume Park image and the Katreena Castillo Lab Assistant image to create a Photo Album.
- Lay out the album with four pictures per page and include captions below all pictures, thereby including the student name under the associated picture.
- Preview each picture in the album and decrease the brightness of any pictures that are especially light. Change the contrast on images that appear dim or washed out.
- Frame the pictures with the Frame shape of your choice.
- Apply the theme of your choice in either the Photo Album dialog box or in the album after it has been created.
- Include **Forensics Geology** in the title placeholder of the Title Slide. In the subtitle placeholder enter the following on separate lines: **9 a.m. MWF**; **Fall Semester**; and **your name**. Also include the pictures of Professor Park and Assistant Castillo, appropriately sized. Use a text box to insert their names beneath their pictures.
- Create a slide footer with your name, your instructor's name, and your class. Do not include the footer on the title page.
- Print the handouts, four slides per page, framed.
- Save the presentation as **chap4_case_forensics_solution**.

Pictures

Multimedia is multiple forms of media used to entertain or inform a user or audience.

Multimedia is multiple forms of media such as text, graphics, sound, animation, and video that are used to entertain or inform a user. You can utilize any of these types of media in PowerPoint by placing the multimedia object on a slide. You already have placed text and graphics in presentations, and you have applied animations to objects and transitions to slides. In this chapter you expand your experience with multimedia by inserting pictures, sound, and video in slides.

Multimedia graphics include clip art, diagrams and illustrations, pictures or photographs, scanned images, and other categories. You have worked extensively with clip art, diagrams, illustrations, and pictures from the Clip Organizer. In this section you concentrate on pictures. Pictures are one of the most popular aspects of multimedia added to PowerPoint presentations. Mark Jaremko, senior program manager in the Microsoft PowerPoint OfficeArt group, posted in the MSDN PowerPoint & OfficeArt Team Blog on June 22, 2006 ". . . Pictures are found in over 57% of all office documents, it's our single biggest graphic type and deserves some special attention."

Bitmap images are images created by bits or pixels placed on a grid that form a picture.

Pictures are bitmap images that computers can read and interpret to create a photorealistic image. Unlike clip art vector images that are created by mathematical statements, ***bitmap images*** are created by bits or pixels placed in a grid or map. Think of vector images as connect-the-dots and bitmap images as paint-by-number, and you begin to see the difference in the methods of representation.

In a bitmap image, each pixel in the image contains information about the color to be displayed. A bitmap image is required to have the realism necessary for a photograph. Each type of image has its own advantage. Vector graphics can be sized easily and still retain their clarity but are not photorealistic. Bitmap images represent a much more complex range of colors and shades, but can become pixelated (get the "jaggies") when they are enlarged. Figure 4.1 displays a pumpkin created as a vector image and one created as a bitmap image. Note the differences in realism. The boxes show a portion of the images enlarged. Note the pixelation in the enlarged portion of the bitmap image.

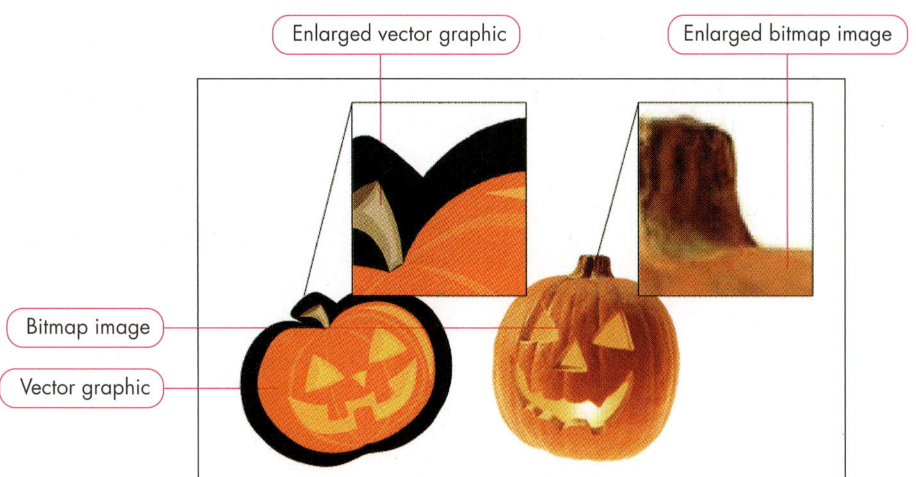

Figure 4.1 Types of Graphics

To display a photograph in a slide, you must save it in a computer bitmap format. You can accomplish this task by scanning and saving a photograph or piece of artwork, by downloading images from a digital camera, by downloading a previously created bitmap image from the Microsoft Clip Organizer or the Internet, or by creating an image in a graphics-editing software package like Photoshop. Table 4.1 displays the common types of graphic file formats that you can add to a PowerPoint slide.

Table 4.1 Types of Graphic File Formats Supported by PowerPoint 2007

File Format	Extension	Description
Computer Graphics Metafile	.cgm	Older format originally used for clip art libraries. Often used for complex engineering drawings.
Windows Enhanced Metafile	.emf	A Windows 32-bit file format.
Graphics Interchange Format	.gif	Limited to 256 colors. Effective for scanned images such as illustrations rather than for color photographs. Good for line drawings and black and white images. Supports transparent backgrounds.
Joint Photographic Experts Group	.jpg, .jpeg	Supports 16 million colors and is optimized for photographs and complex graphics. Format of choice for most photographs on the Web.
Macintosh PICT	PICT	Holds both vector and bitmap images. PICT supports 8 colors; PICT2 supports 16 million colors.
Microsoft Windows Metafile	.wmf	A Windows 16-bit file format.
Portable Network Graphics	.png	Supports 16 million colors. Approved as a standard by the World Wide Web Consortium (W3C). Intended to replace .gif format.
Tagged Image File Format	.tif, .tiff	Best file format for storing bitmapped images on personal computers. Can be any resolution. Lossless image storage creates large file sizes. Not widely supported by Web browsers.
Vector Markup Language	.vml	An XML format for vector graphics that can be embedded in Web pages in place of bitmapped .gif and .jpeg images.
Windows Bitmap (Device Independent Bitmap)	.bmp, .dib, .rle	A representation consisting of dots. The value of each dot is stored in one or more bits of data. Uncompressed and creates large file size.

In this section, you insert pictures (bitmap images) into a slide without using a content placeholder and then insert pictures using content placeholders. You apply a picture style and modify its effects. You use picture tools to adjust the brightness and contrast of a picture. You crop a picture and compress all the images in the slide show. You also create a background for a slide from a picture. Finally, you learn about using the Internet as a resource for images and review the Fair Use guidelines relating to student use of media downloaded from the Internet. You download a picture from the Internet and insert the picture into a slide show.

TIP Scanning Images

In PowerPoint 2007, if you wish to add images from a scanner or digital camera, you must first download the images to your hard drive or storage device. Once the images are downloaded, click the Insert tab, click Picture in the Illustrations group, navigate to where you stored the image, select the image, and then click Insert. As an alternative, you can scan and download images directly to your Clip Organizer. Put your image on the scanner glass and open the Clip Organizer by clicking Organize clips at the bottom of the Clip Art task pane. Click File, point to Add Clips to Organizer, and then click From Scanner or Camera. When the Insert Picture from Scanner or Camera dialog box opens, select your scanner from the Device box. Click Insert. The clip you scan appears in My Collections, not on your slide. You would then need to insert the scanned image as you do any other image from the Clip Organizer.

Inserting and Modifying a Picture

You can use several methods to insert an image on a page. To add a picture using a placeholder, select a layout with a placeholder that includes an Insert Picture from File button (see Figure 4.2). Click the Insert Picture from File button, and the Insert Picture dialog box opens. Navigate to the location of your picture files and then click the bitmap picture you want to use. Click the Insert button, and the picture is inserted in the placeholder. When you insert a picture in this manner, however, the picture is centered within the placeholder frame and is sometimes cropped to fit within the placeholder. This effect can cause unexpected results and can be startling if tops of heads are cropped off. If this situation occurs, simply undo and enlarge the placeholder and then repeat the steps for inserting an image.

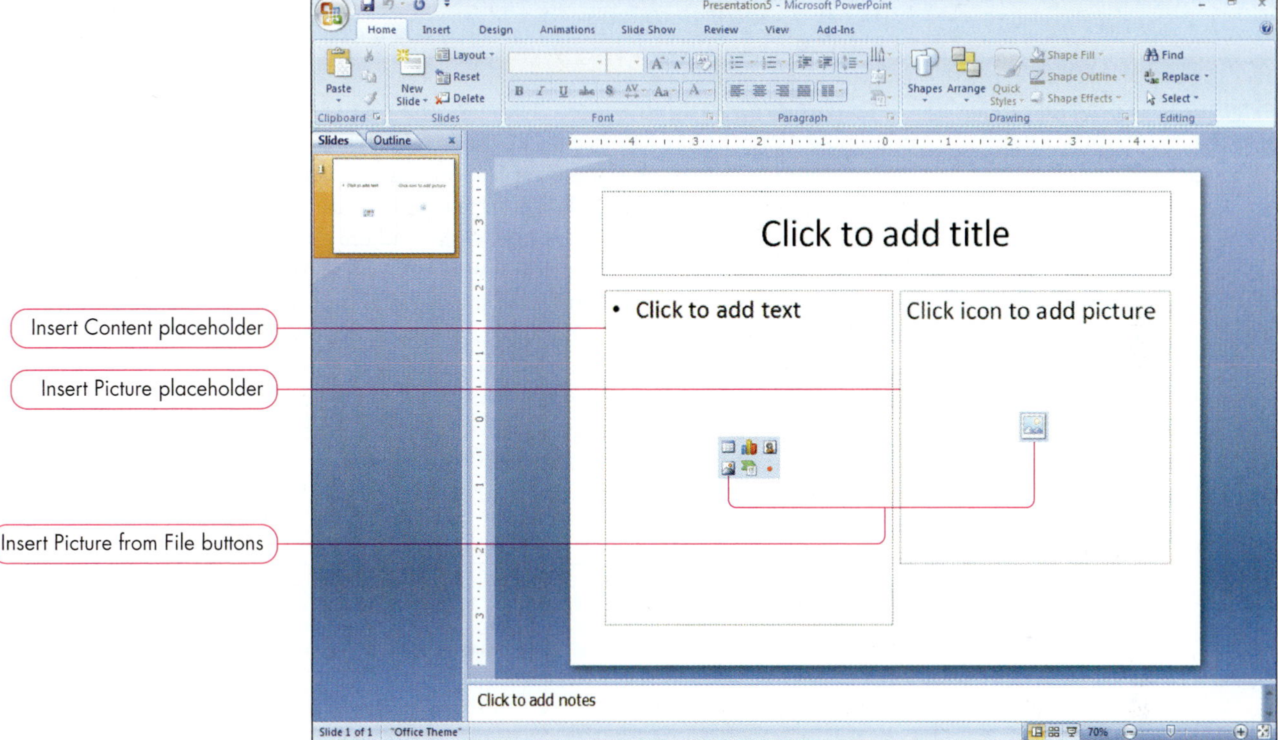

Figure 4.2 Insert Picture Using Placeholders

Another method for inserting an image is to click Picture on the Insert tab. The advantage of this method is that your image comes in at full size rather than centered and cropped in a placeholder. You can then resize the image to fit the desired area. The disadvantage is you spend time resizing and positioning the image. To insert a picture using this method, click Picture in the Illustrations group on the Insert tab. Navigate to the location of your picture files, and then click the picture you want to use. Click the Insert button, and the picture is inserted on the slide.

TIP Adding Images Using Windows Explorer

If you are adding multiple images to a slide show, you can speed up the process by opening Windows Explorer and navigating to the folder where the images are located. Position the Windows Explorer window on top of your slide show and then drag the images from the Explorer window onto the slides of your choice.

Use Picture Tools

Once you bring a picture into a slide, PowerPoint provides powerful tools that you can use to adjust the image. Some tools are designed to correct problems with a picture; others are designed to let you add stylized effects. The Picture Tools are available when you select the picture in the slide and click the Picture Tools Format tab (see Figure 4.3).

Figure 4.3 The Picture Tools

Brightness refers to the lightness or darkness of a picture.

The ***brightness*** (lightness or darkness) of a picture is often a matter of individual preference. You might need to change the brightness of your picture for reasons other than preference, however. For example, sometimes printing a picture requires different brightness than is needed when projecting an image. This situation occurs because during printing the ink may spread when placed on the page, making the picture darker. Or, you might decide you want a picture as a background and reduce the lightness so that text will show on the background. The Brightness control in the Adjust group on the Format tab enables you to adjust the brightness of your picture to your preference. You can increase or decrease the brightness in 10% increments. For increments other than 10%, select Picture Corrections Options at the bottom of the Brightness gallery, which gives you access to sliders that can be used to adjust the brightness at any increment up to 100%. Figure 4.4 shows a picture of a couple adjusted for an increase in brightness of 10%.

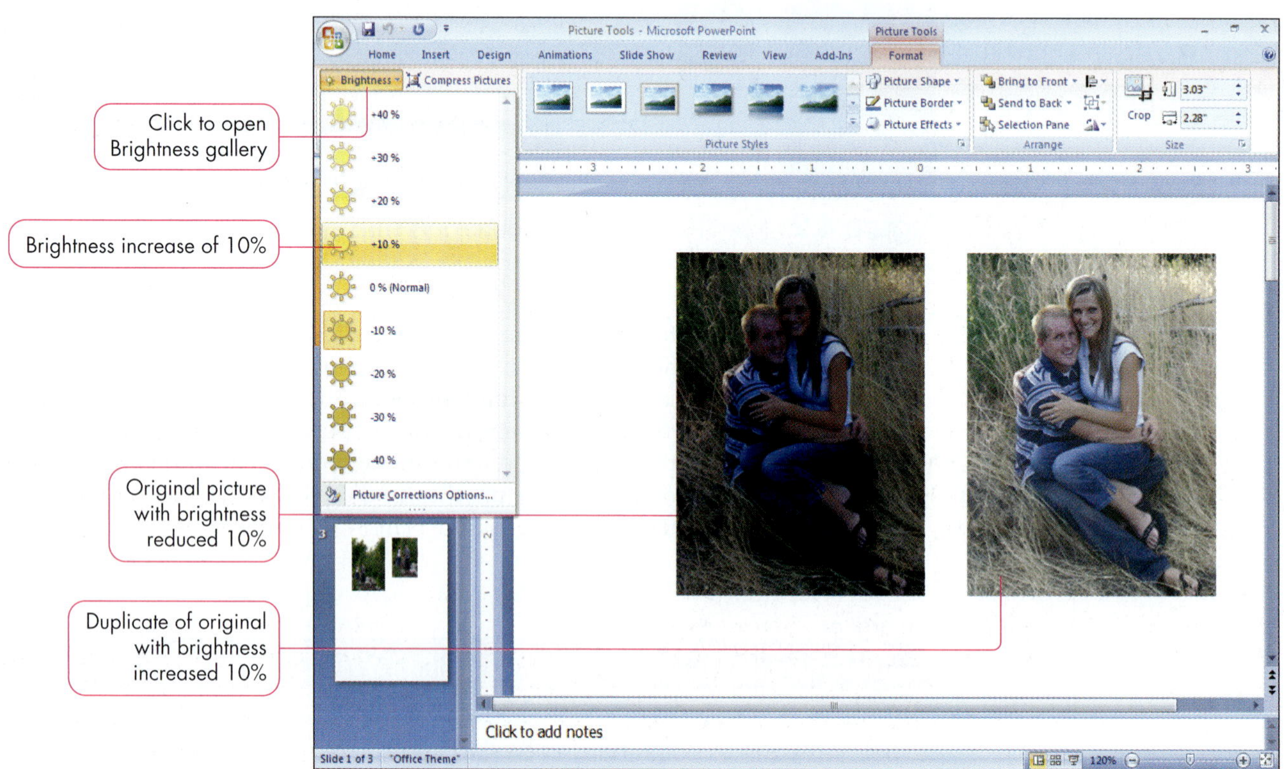

Figure 4.4 The Brightness Control

Contrast refers to the difference between the darkest and lightest areas of a picture.

Contrast refers to the difference between the darkest area (black level) and lightest area (white level). If the contrast is not set correctly, your picture can look washed out or muddy. Too much contrast and the light portion of your image will appear to explode off the screen or page. Your setting may vary depending on whether you are going to project the image or print it. Projecting impacts an image due to the light in the room. Setting the contrast adjustment in a very light room will make the image seem to need a greater contrast than setting the adjustment in a darker room. Try to set your control in the lighting that will appear when you display the presentation. Click Contrast in the Adjust group on the Format tab to change the contrast of the selected picture. Figure 4.5 shows an image adjusted for an increase in contrast of 30%. While the original actually has a good contrast setting, it appears washed out next to the image with the contrast increase. The image with the contrast increase, however, has blown out the pale blue color of the bride-to-be's shirt and would appear to throb or glow if projected.

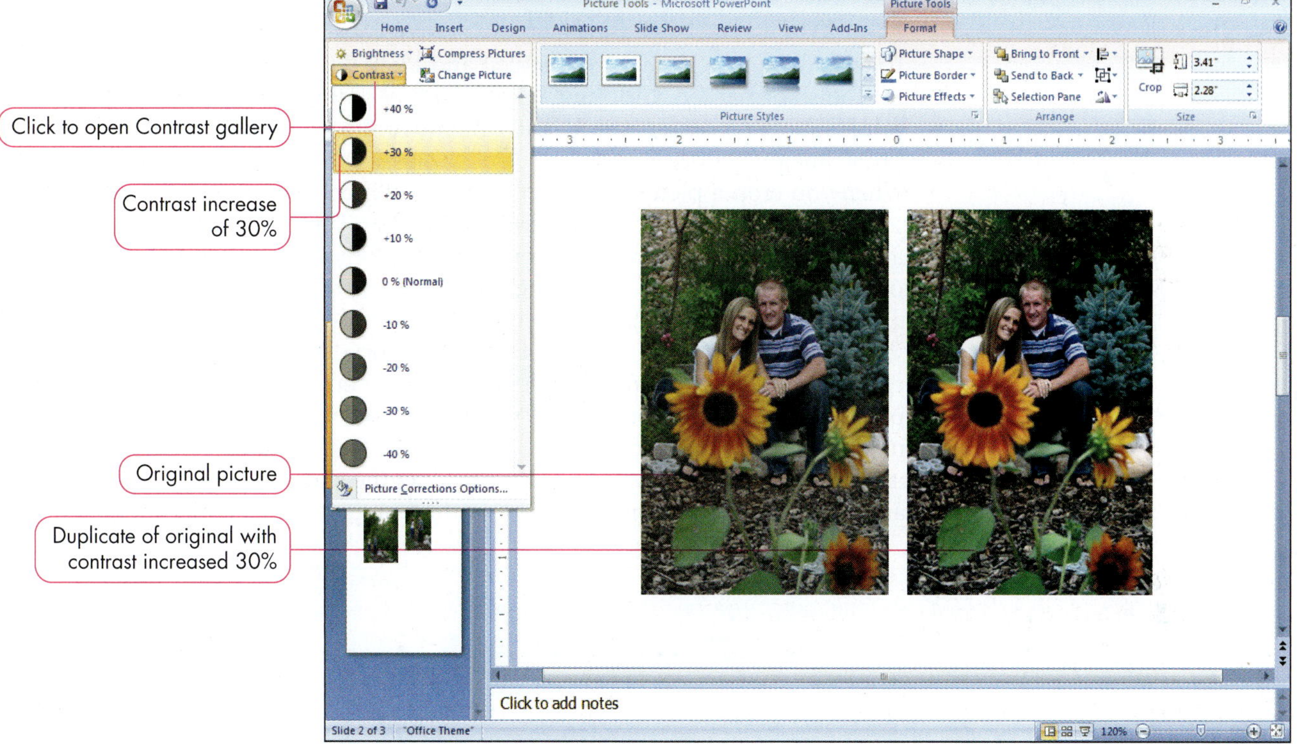

Figure 4.5 The Contrast Control

When you add pictures to your PowerPoint presentation, especially high-resolution pictures downloaded from a digital camera, the presentation file size dramatically increases. It may increase to the point that the presentation becomes slow to load and sluggish to play. The increase in the file size depends on the resolution of the pictures you add. Use the Crop tool and the Compress Pictures feature to eliminate a large part of this problem.

Cropping is the process of eliminating unwanted portions of an image.

Cropping the picture using the Crop tool lets you eliminate unwanted portions of an image, thereby focusing the viewer's attention to what it is you want him or her to see. Remember, though, that if you crop an image and try to enlarge the resulting picture, pixilation may occur that reduces the quality of the image. Figure 4.6 shows a picture that was cropped to focus attention on the young couple. The result was enlarged to an acceptable level. Further enlargement would cause unacceptable image degradation.

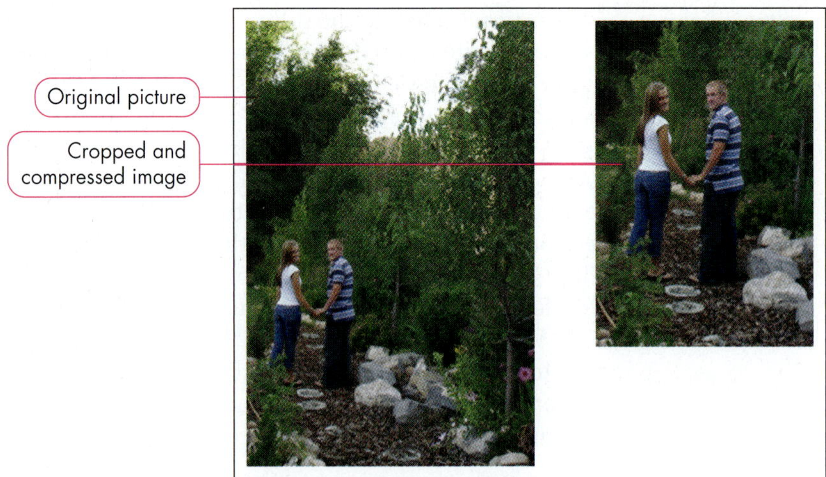

Figure 4.6 Use Crop to Focus Attention

To crop a picture, select the picture and click Crop in the Size group on the Picture Tools Format tab. Cropping handles appear around the picture. Position the cropping tool over a center handle and drag inward to eliminate the unwanted portion of the image.

When you crop a picture, the part that was cropped out does not display in the slide, but it is not removed from the presentation file. This result is in case you decide at a later date to reset the picture to its original state. When you resize an image, the resolution containing the detail of an image is retained so the file size is not reduced. The Compress Pictures option can help you manage large image files by permanently deleting the cropped areas of the selected picture or all pictures in the slide show. It also changes the resolution to a default of 220 pixels per inch (ppi), which ensures you will obtain a good quality printout. If you know, however, that you will only be displaying the slide show on screen, you can click the Options button and change your target output to 150 ppi. If you plan on e-mailing the slide show, you should change the target output to 96 ppi. Figure 4.7 shows the Compression Settings options.

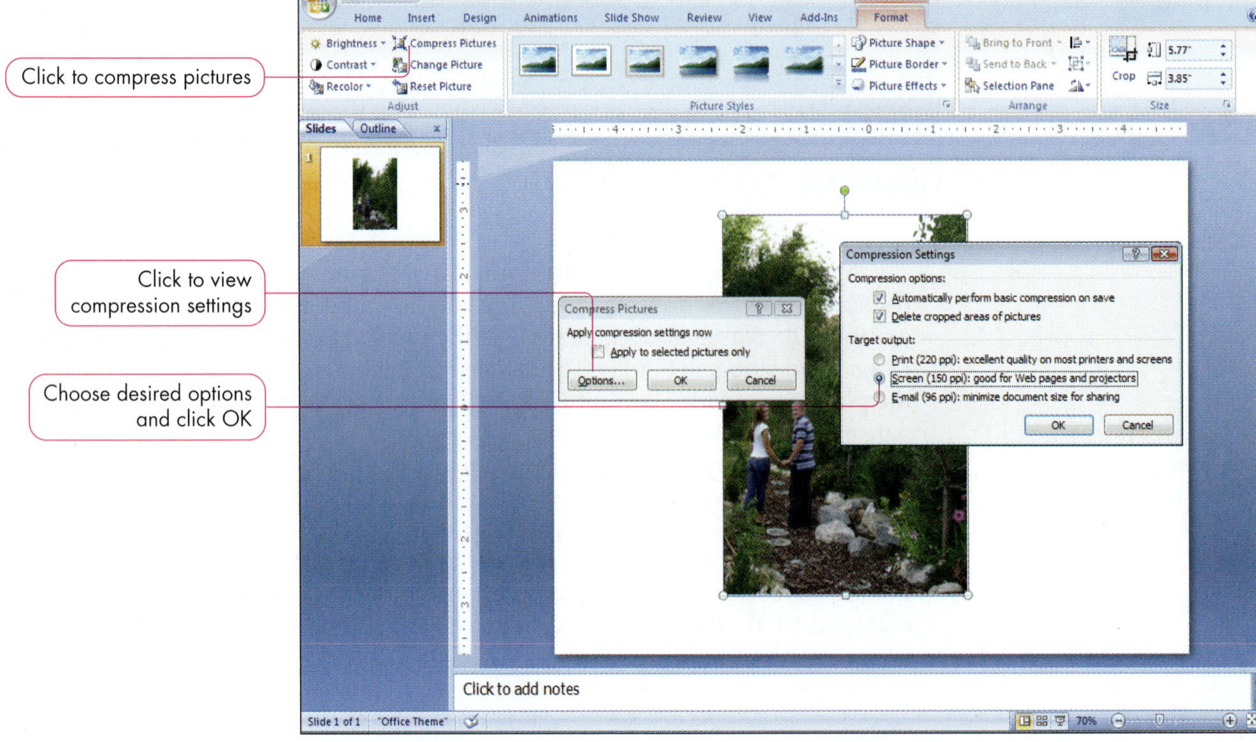

Figure 4.7 Picture Compression Options

Apply Picture Styles

> Many . . . effects are possible with Picture Styles, and when you consider that each of these effects can be modified, your creative opportunities are endless!

The Picture Styles in PowerPoint 2007 are absolutely awesome. With the new Picture Styles, you can surround your picture with attractive white frames, soften the edges of pictures, add soft shadows to the edges of pictures, apply 3-D effects to pictures, and add glossy reflections below your pictures. Many other effects are possible with Picture Styles, and when you consider that each of these effects can be modified, your creative opportunities are endless! Figure 4.8 shows a few of the possibilities.

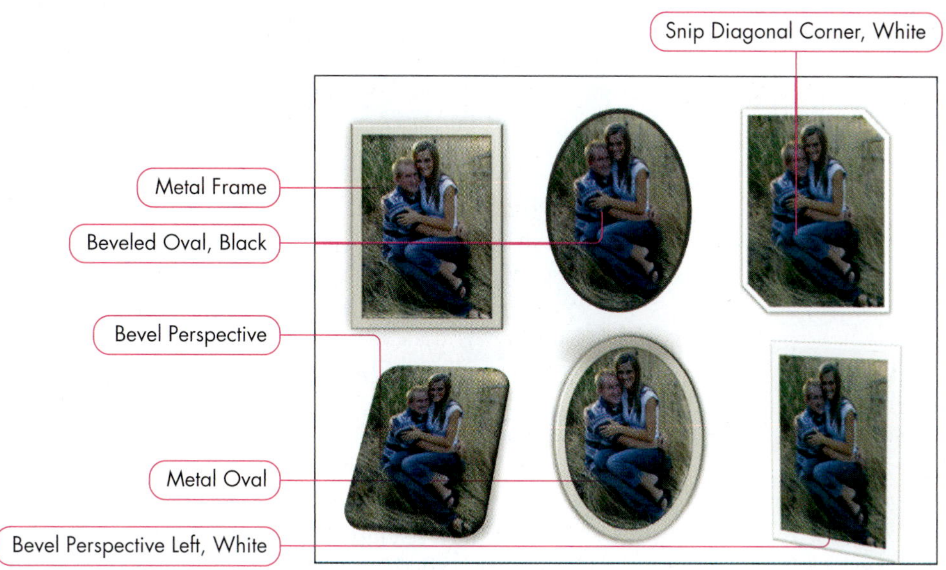

Figure 4.8 Picture Style Applications

To apply a picture style, select a picture and click a gallery image displayed in the Pictures Styles group on the Picture Tools Format tab. To see more styles, click the More button. To change the shape of the picture into any of the basic shapes available in PowerPoint, click Picture Shape in the Picture Styles group. Picture Border in the Picture Styles group enables you to select your border color, weight, or dash style. You can select from Preset, Shadow, Reflection, Glow, Soft Edges, Bevel, and 3-D Rotation effects from the Picture Effects option.

Create a Background from a Picture

Pictures can make appealing backgrounds if they are transparent enough that text can be read on top of them. Picture backgrounds personalize your presentation. To use a photograph as a background, use the Format Background command. Using the Insert Picture option involves more time because when the picture is inserted it must be resized, its transparency must be adjusted, and the order of the objects on the screen has to be changed because the photograph blocks the placeholders (see Figure 4.9).

Figure 4.9 Background from Insert Picture Option

To create a background from a picture using the Background command, click the Design tab and then click Background Styles in the Background group. When the gallery appears, click Format Background at the bottom of the gallery. The Format Background dialog box opens. Click Fill on the left side of the dialog box to see option buttons for the various fills available for backgrounds. Click Picture or texture fill, and the dialog box displays additional fill options, including a File button. Click the File button and navigate to the location where your picture is stored. Click the picture file and then click Insert. The dialog box also includes options for moving the picture by offsetting it to the left or right or the top or bottom, and for adjusting the transparency amount. Figure 4.10 shows the same picture as Figure 4.9 inserted as a background and with a transparency adjustment.

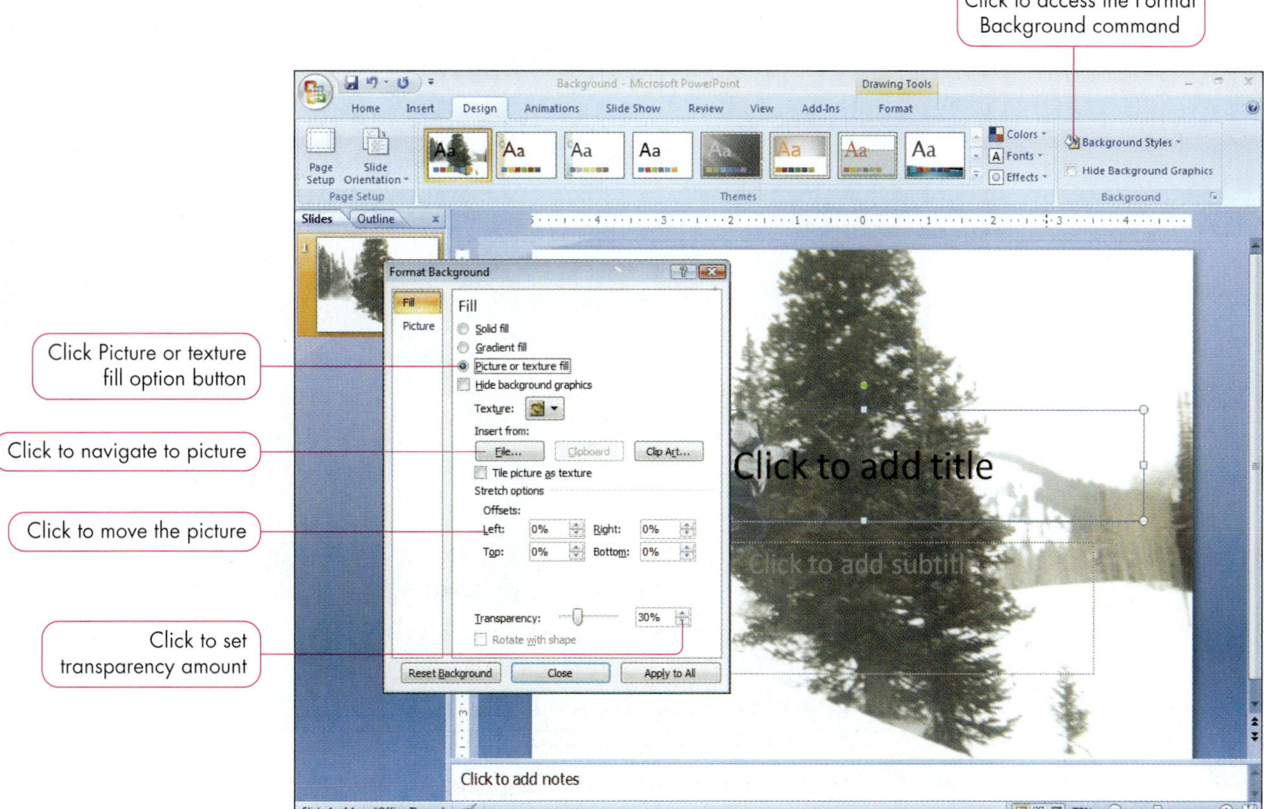

Figure 4.10 Background from Background Styles Option

Using the Internet as a Resource

The Internet and the World Wide Web are thoroughly integrated into PowerPoint, as they are throughout the Microsoft Office Suite. PowerPoint integrates with the Internet in three important ways. First, you can download resources from any Web page for inclusion in a PowerPoint presentation. Second, you can insert hyperlinks into a PowerPoint presentation, and then click those links to display the associated Web page in your Web browser. Finally, you can convert any PowerPoint presentation into a Web page. In this chapter, you will use the Internet as a resource for pictures.

Figure 4.11 illustrates how resources from the Internet can be used to enhance a PowerPoint presentation. The slide displays a photograph that was downloaded from Image*After (www.imageafter.com), a site that maintains a large, online, free photo collection that allows for free downloading of images for personal or commercial use. The photograph is displayed as an object and is typical of how most people use photographs downloaded from the Web in a presentation. To give credit to the download source, even though the site permits use, the Web site address has been entered in a text box.

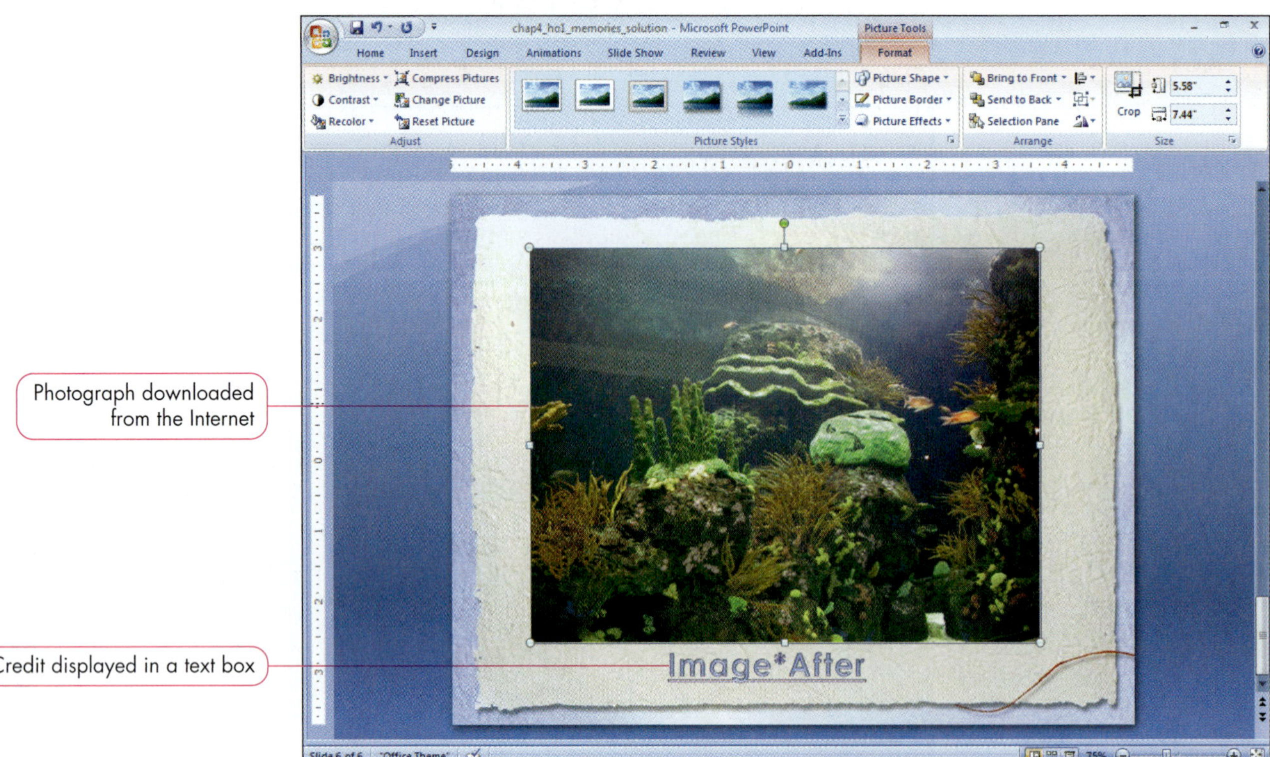

Figure 4.11 Downloaded Picture

Regardless of how you choose to use a photograph, your first task is to access the Web and locate the required image (e.g., an underwater image). After this step is done, right-click the photograph to display a shortcut menu, and then select Save Picture As to download the file to your hard drive. As an alternative, when you right-click the photograph, you can select Copy to copy the picture into the Clipboard memory.

In PowerPoint, you click Insert Picture from File in the Illustrations group on the Insert tab to insert the picture if you have downloaded it. If you copied the picture, you paste it onto your slide. You also can click Insert Hyperlink in the Links group on the Insert tab to insert a hyperlink to the resource Web site. You then can click the hyperlink during the slide show, and provided you have an Internet connection, your Web browser will display the associated page.

Microsoft makes the Internet readily accessible to you through its Research service. Click Research in the Proofing group on the Review tab, and the Research task pane opens on the right side of your screen. Enter a keyword in the Search for box, and then select the type of reference you wish to search. All Reference Books is the default for searching, but because the dictionary and thesaurus do not include images, you will speed the search process by narrowing the resources you wish to search. The Encarta Encyclopedia is a good resource that includes images. Figure 4.12 displays the Research task pane set to search for information about Cancun (Mexico) and the results of that search.

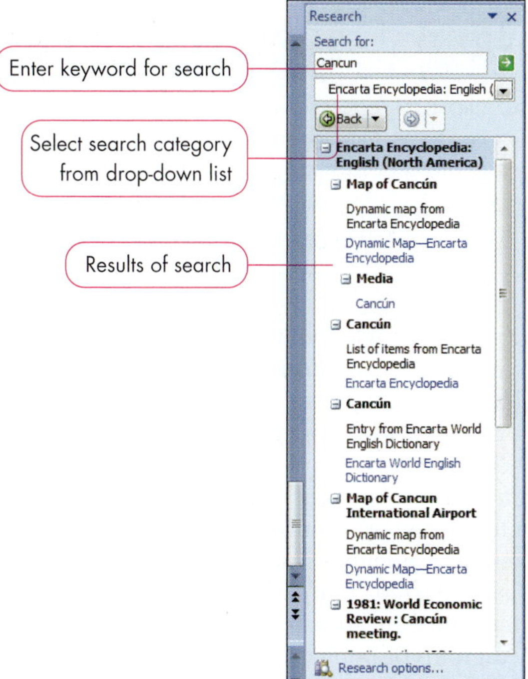

Figure 4.12 Research Task Pane

Click a link in the results area of the Research task pane, and a Web browser window opens. The Research task pane is displayed on the left side of your screen, and the article is displayed on the right. While most of the information you find using this method is free, some Web providers require a fee. If, however, the content is fee-based, a premium content icon appears by the link. You are not charged for clicking a premium content link, but you will be charged if you use the information. If you locate an image in a free area, you can download it by right-clicking the image and copying it or by downloading it as described previously.

Copyright Protection

Copyright is the legal protection afforded to a written or artistic work.

A ***copyright*** provides legal protection to a written or artistic work, including literary, dramatic, musical, and artistic works such as poetry, novels, movies, songs, computer software, and architecture. It gives the author of a work the exclusive right to the use and duplication of that work. A copyright does not, however, protect facts, ideas, systems, or methods of operation, although it may protect the way these things are expressed.

> Anything on the Internet should be considered copyrighted unless the site specifically says it is in the public domain . . .

The owner of the copyright may sell or give up a portion of his or her rights; for example, an author may give distribution rights to a publisher and/or grant movie rights to a studio. ***Infringement of a copyright*** occurs any time a right held by the copyright owner is violated without permission of the owner. Anything on the Internet should be considered copyrighted unless the site specifically says it is in the ***public domain***, in which case the author is giving everyone the right to freely reproduce and distribute the material, thereby making the work owned by the public at large. A work also may enter the public domain when the copyright of the work has expired. Does copyright protection prevent you from quoting a document found on the Web in a research paper? Does copyright protection imply that you cannot download an image for inclusion in a slide show? (Facts themselves are not covered by copyright, so you can use statistical data without fear of infringement. Images are protected unless the owner gives his or her permission for downloading.)

Infringement of copyright occurs when a right of the copyright owner is violated.

Public domain is when the rights to a literary work or property are owned by the public at large.

TIP Using Microsoft Media Elements

Photos, clip art, fonts, sounds, and movies available from Microsoft are part of Microsoft's Media Elements and are protected. To see what uses of Media Elements are prohibited, access Help, select the link for Working with graphics and charts, and then click Adding pictures, shapes, WordArt, or clip art. Select the *What uses of photos, clip art, and font images are prohibited* link and review the list of prohibited uses.

The answer to what you can use from the Web depends on many things, including the amount of the information you reference, as well as the intended use of that information. It is considered fair use, and thus not an infringement of copyright, to use a portion of a work for educational, nonprofit purposes, or for the purpose of critical review for commentary. In other words, you can use a quote, facts, or other information from the Web in an educational setting, but you should cite the original work in your footnotes, or resource, or bibliography slide. The Reference table on the next page presents guidelines students and teachers can use to help determine what multimedia can be used in an educational project based on the Proposal for Fair Use Guidelines for Educational Multimedia created in 1996. These guidelines were created by a group of publishers, authors, and educators who gathered to interpret the Copyright Act of 1976 as it applies to educational and scholarly uses of multimedia. You should note, however, that while these guidelines are part of the Congressional Record, they are not law. They can, however, help you determine when you can use multimedia materials under Fair Use principles in a non-commercial educational use.

Multimedia Copyright Guidelines for Students and Teachers | Reference

The following guidelines are based on Section 107 of the U.S. Copyright Act of 1976 and the Proposal for Fair Use Guidelines for Educational Multimedia (1996), which sets forth fair use factors for multimedia projects. These guidelines cover the use of multimedia based on Time, Portion, and Copying and Distribution Limitations. For the complete text of the guidelines, see www.uspto.gov/web/offices/dcom/olia/confu/confurep.pdf.

General Guidelines

- Student projects for specific courses may be displayed and kept in personal portfolios as examples of their academic work.
- Students in specific courses may use multimedia in projects with proper credit and citations. Full bibliographic information must be used when available.
- Students and teachers must display copyright notice if copyright ownership information is shown on the original source. Copyright may be shown in a sources or bibliographic section unless the presentation is being used for distance learning. In distance learning situations, copyright must appear on the screen when the image is viewed.
- Teachers may use media for face-to-face curriculum-based instruction, for directed self-study, in demonstrations on how to create multimedia productions, for presentations at conferences, and for distance learning. Teachers may also retain projects in their personal portfolio for personal use such as job interviews or tenure review.
- Teachers may use multimedia projects for educational purposes for up to two years, after which permission of the copyright holder is required.
- Students and teachers do not need to write for permission to use media if it falls under multimedia guidelines unless there is a possibility that the project could be broadly distributed at a later date.

Text Guidelines

- Up to 10 percent of a copyrighted work may be used, or up to 1000 words, whichever is less.
- Up to 250 words of a poem, but no more than five poems (or excerpts) from different poets or an anthology. No more than three poems (or excerpts) from a single poet.

Illustrations

- A photograph or illustration may be used in its entirety.
- Up to 15 images, but no more than 15 images from a collection.
- No more than 5 images of an artist's or photographer's work.

Motion Media

- Up to 10 percent of a copyrighted work or 3 minutes, whichever is less.
- Clip cannot be altered in any way.

Music and Sound

- Up to 10 percent of a copyrighted musical composition, not to exceed 30 seconds.
- Up to 10 percent of a sound recording, not to exceed 30 seconds.
- Alterations cannot change the basic melody or fundamental character of the work.

Distribution Limitations

- Multimedia projects should not be posted to unsecured web sites.
- No more than two copies of the original may be made, only one of which may be placed on reserve for instructional purposes.
- A copy of a project may be made for backup purposes, but may be used only when the original has been lost, damaged, or stolen.
- If more than one person created a project, each person may keep only one copy.

Hands-On Exercises

1 | Using Pictures

Skills covered: 1. Insert Pictures **2.** Apply and Modify a Picture Style **3.** Adjust Brightness and Contrast **4.** Crop and Compress **5.** Create a Background from a Picture **6.** Insert a Picture from the Internet

Step 1
Insert Pictures

Refer to Figure 4.13 as you complete Step 1.

a. Open the *chap4_ho1_memories* presentation, and then save it as **chap4_ho1_memories_solution**.

   You decide to create a memories presentation for your sister, who was recently married. You include engagement pictures, a wedding picture, and a picture to remind her of scuba diving on her honeymoon.

b. With the title slide selected, click the **Insert tab**, and click **Picture** in the Illustrations group.

   Because the Title Slide layout does not include a placeholder for content, you add a picture using the Insert Picture from File feature. The Insert Picture dialog box appears.

c. Navigate to the folder that contains the student data files that accompany this textbook and open the *chap4_ho1_memories_images* folder. Click the *chap4_ho1_1memories.jpg* file to select it and then click **Insert**.

d. Click the **Size Dialog Box Launcher** in the Size group on the Picture Tools Format tab to open the Size and Position dialog box, click in the **Height** box in the *Scale* section, and then type **38**. Click in the **Width** box in the *Scale* section and it will change to 38% automatically.

   By default the picture was sized to fit the slide and centered on the slide. You need to adjust the size and the position of the picture. Because you are adjusting both settings, it is fastest to enter the information in the dialog box. Typing 38 in the Height box automatically sets the scale for Width to 38% because the *Lock aspect ratio* check box is checked.

e. Click the **Position tab** in the still open Size and Position dialog box, and then set the **Horizontal Position on slide** options to **5″** from the **Top Left Corner**. Set the **Vertical Position on slide** options to **.3″** from the **Top Left Corner**. Click **Close**. Send the photo to the back so that the photographer credit displays.

f. Move to **Slide 2**, and then click the **Insert Picture from File button** in the large content placeholder on the left side of the screen. Open the *chap4_ho1_memories_images* folder if necessary. Click the *chap4_ho1_2memories.jpg* file to select it, and then click **Insert**.

g. Use the **Insert Picture from File buttons** in the two small content placeholders on the right side of the screen to insert *chap4_ho1_3memories.jpg* and *chap4_ho1_4memories.jpg* into your presentation.

   Note that in all three cases the images were resized to fit within the existing placeholders. While they have a "smaller" appearance, the file size is exactly the same. The resolution has not changed, and the actual image size is intact.

h. Create a Notes and Handouts Header and Footer with the date, your name in the header, and your instructor's name and your class in the footer.

i. Click **Save**.

Figure 4.13 Inserted Pictures

Step 2
Apply and Modify a Picture Style

Refer to Figure 4.14 as you complete Step 2.

a. Move to **Slide 1**, select the picture of the young couple, and then click the **Picture Tools Format tab**.

b. Click the **More button** in the Picture Styles group on the Format tab.

   The Picture Styles gallery opens showing styles using a variety of borders, shadow effects, 3-D effects, reflection effects, and more. Move your mouse over the styles and watch how each style impacts the image. Some of the styles involve extensive changes so expect a slowdown as the preview is created.

c. Select **Simple Frame, White**.

   This style applies a white border around the image, which sets the edges of the picture nicely.

d. Click **Picture Border** in the Picture Styles group on the Format tab, and then click **Indigo, Accent 4** in the Theme Colors section.

e. Click **Picture Effects** in the Picture Styles group on the Format tab, click **Bevel**, and then click **Relaxed Inset**.

   The Bevel effect applied to the outer edges of the picture make the border look as if it is raised and more like a picture frame.

f. Click **Save**.

Figure 4.14 Picture Style Applied

Step 3
Adjust Brightness and Contrast

Refer to Figure 4.15 as you complete Step 3.

a. Move to **Slide 3** and use the **Insert Picture from File buttons** in the content placeholders to insert *chap4_ho1_5memories.jpg* and *chap4_ho1_6memories.jpg* into your presentation.

   The two images were taken in different lighting conditions. You decide to adjust the brightness and contrast of one of the images to match the other. You could darken the image on the right to maintain a romantic evening mood, or you could brighten and adjust the contrast of the image on the left to show the color and detail in the image. You decide to work with the image on the left.

b. Select the image on the left, and then click **Brightness** in the Adjust group on the Picture Tools Format tab. Click **+10%**.

   The image became brighter but is muddy-looking. There needs to be greater contrast to bring out the detail.

c. Click **Contrast** in the Adjust group on the Picture Tools Format tab. Click **+10%**.

d. Click **Save**.

Figure 4.15 Brightness and Contrast Increases

Step 4
Crop and Compress

Refer to Figure 4.16 as you complete Step 4.

a. Move to **Slide 4** and examine the picture.

   The picture was inserted using the Insert Picture command, which centers it on the slide. You decide you want to focus attention on the couple by cropping the picture, but do not want to delete the wild flowers growing by the path. You decide to crop the image from the top and bottom.

b. If necessary, click the **View tab** and click **Ruler** in the Show/Hide group.

   Activating the ruler will make it easier for you to determine the area to crop.

c. Select the picture, and click the **Format tab**.

d. Click **Crop** in the Size group on the Format tab.

e. Position the Crop tool over the top, center cropping handle and drag inward until the guiding line on the vertical ruler reaches the +2″ mark.

f. Position the Crop tool over the bottom, center cropping handle and drag inward until the guiding line on the vertical ruler reaches the -2.5″ mark.

   The resulting size of the image is almost a perfect 5″ square.

g. Click **Crop** in the Size group again to toggle it off.

   The image has been resized on screen, but the file size has not been reduced. You need to compress the image to remove the unwanted portions and to lower the resolution.

h. Click **Compress Pictures** in the Adjust group on the Format tab, and then click **Options.**

   Do not check the Apply to selected pictures only option. You need to compress all the pictures you have used in the presentation to reduce the presentation file size.

   TROUBLESHOOTING: If you checked the selected pictures only option, click Cancel in the Compression Settings dialog box. You will be returned to the Compress Pictures dialog box where you can deselect the option and click Options once again.

i. Click **Screen** in the *Target output* section.

j. Click **OK**, and then click **OK** in the Compress Pictures dialog box.

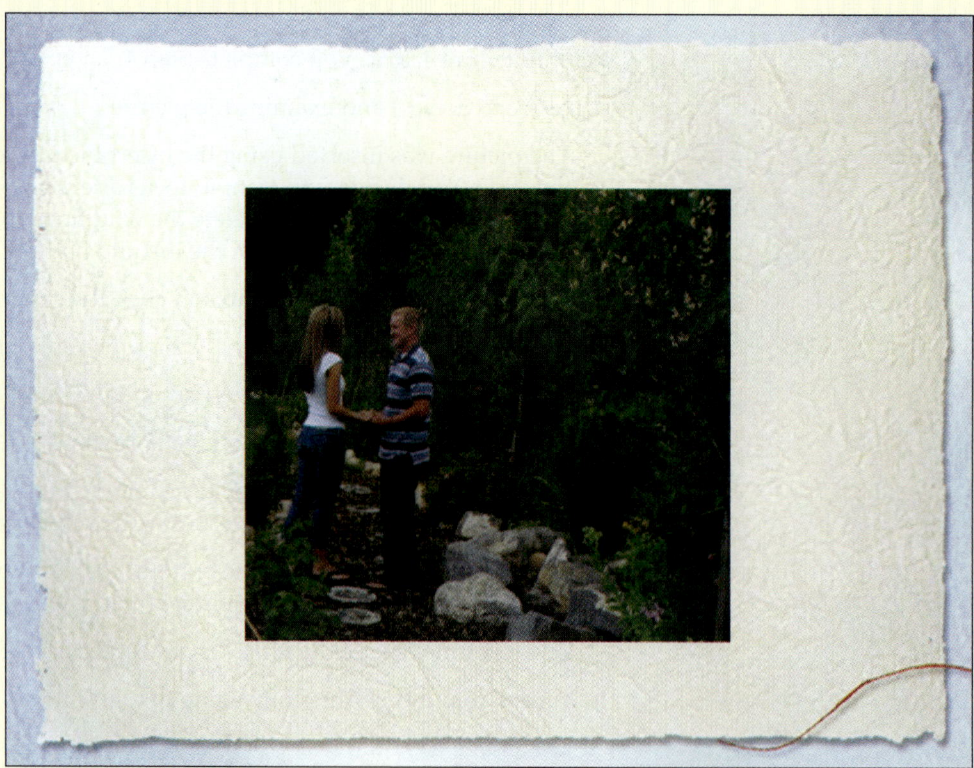

Figure 4.16 Cropped and Compressed Picture

Step 5
Create a Background from a Picture

Refer to Figure 4.17 as you complete Step 5.

a. Move to **Slide 5** and click the **Design tab**.

   The bride selected summer flowers as the wedding theme, so you decide to insert a photo of the flowers in her bouquet as a background for her bridal picture.

b. Click **Background Styles** in the Background group and then click **Format Background** at the bottom of the gallery.

c. In the Format Background dialog box, check **Hide background graphics**.

d. Click **Picture or texture fill**, click **File**, select *chap4_ho1_7memories.tif*, and then click **Insert**. Click **Close**.

   TROUBLESHOOTING: If the bouquet is not displayed, it may be blocked by the background graphics. Check **Hide Background Graphics** in the Background group on the Design tab.

e. Click **Save**.

Figure 4.17 Background from a Picture

Step 6
Insert a Picture from the Internet

Refer to Figure 4.18 as you complete Step 6.

a. Move to **Slide 6** and note the hyperlink to Image*After (imageafter.com).

   Slide 6 has a hyperlink to *Image*After*, a Web site that provides pictures free for personal or commercial use. The young couple went scuba diving in Cancun, Mexico, during their honeymoon so you want to insert a picture of an underwater scene to round off your slide show.

b. Right-click and then select **Open Hyperlink** to launch the Web site in your default browser.

   TROUBLESHOOTING: If you are not connected to the Internet, the hyperlink will not work. Connect to the Internet and then repeat Step b.

   The Image*After Web site displays the nature-underwater group and shows thumbnails of images pertaining to underwater views.

c. Point, without clicking, to each thumbnail to see a bigger image. Try to find the same image that is shown in Figure 4.18. If you do not see that image, find another image that is very similar.

d. Click the thumbnail to bring up a larger image. Right-click the image, select **Copy**, and then close the Web browser.

e. Right-click in **Slide 6** and then select **Paste**.

   Notice that because you are pasting the image instead of inserting it through the Insert Picture feature, the picture is not centered on the page.

f. Drag the picture into the approximate center of the page. Depending on the size of the image you insert, you may need to adjust the image size prior to moving it to the center.

g. Click **Save** and then close the presentation.

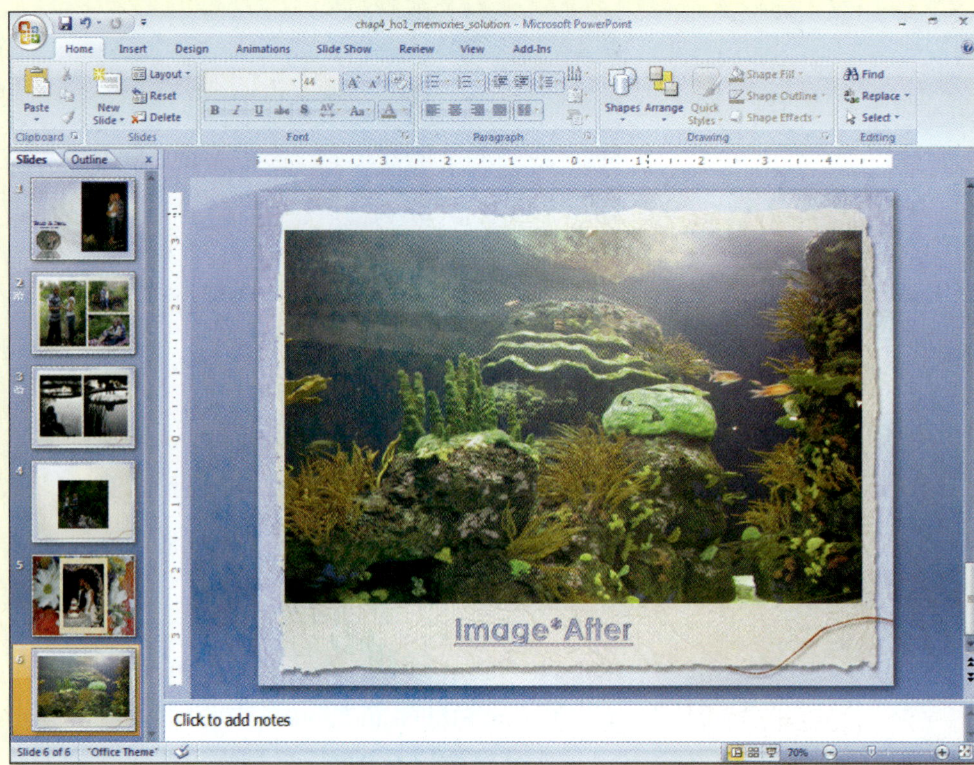

Figure 4.18 Inserted Picture from the Internet

Photo Albums

In the previous section, you created a personalized photo album containing saved photographs. While the customized product was personalized and contained images of various sizes, it was time consuming to create. PowerPoint has a Photo Album feature designed to speed this process. The feature takes the images you select and arranges them on album pages based on selections you make, saving considerable effort.

In this section you use the Photo Album feature to create an album and use the feature settings to customize your album.

Creating a Photo Album

A ***photo album*** is a presentation containing multiple pictures organized into album pages.

A Microsoft PowerPoint ***Photo Album*** is a presentation that contains multiple pictures that are imported and formatted through the Photo Album feature. Because each picture does not have to be formatted individually, you save a considerable amount of time. The photo album in Figure 4.19 contains the same images used in the first hands-on exercise. This time, however, it took less than two minutes to create the album and assign a background. Because a four-per-page layout was selected, portrait images were reduced to fit the size of the placeholder. This setting drastically reduced the size of some images, although it does create an interesting asymmetrical design on the page.

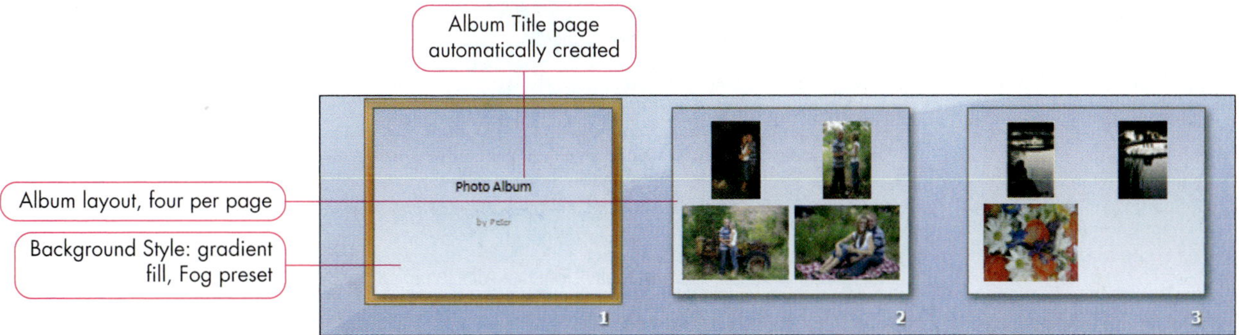

Figure 4.19 PowerPoint Photo Album

To create a photo album, click Photo Album in the Illustrations group on the Insert tab. The Photo Album dialog box opens. If you click the Photo Album arrow instead, you may choose between creating a new album or editing a previously created album. Click the File/Disk button in the Album Content section and navigate to the location of your photographs. Select the photographs you wish to include in your album—do not worry about the order of the photographs you select. You can change the order later. Once an album has been created, you can edit the album settings by clicking the Photo Album arrow in the Illustrations group on the Insert tab, and then selecting Edit Photo Album.

Setting Photo Album Options

After importing the photographs of your choice, they will appear in a list in the dialog box. Click the name of a picture, and a preview of the picture will display. This preview will help you determine the order of photographs in the album. Use the move up arrow and the move down arrow to reposition a selected photograph. You can use Ctrl or Shift to select more than one image. You can delete any unwanted photographs by selecting them and clicking the Remove button.

If you have downloaded photographs from a digital camera, you may need to rotate some of the images. Rotate buttons are included in the dialog box to accomplish this task. Contrast and brightness controls also are included so you can fine-tune your pictures within the Photo Album dialog box. You can even change the pictures to black and white. The Album Content section includes the New Text Box so that you can insert a text placeholder in the album. The text placeholder is the same size as the placeholders for pictures. The Caption option in the Album Content section will not become available until you select the layout of your album. When you select the layout, the Captions below ALL pictures option is activated. Checking this box displays the file name of the picture as a caption below the picture in the album. Figure 4.20 shows the location of these tools.

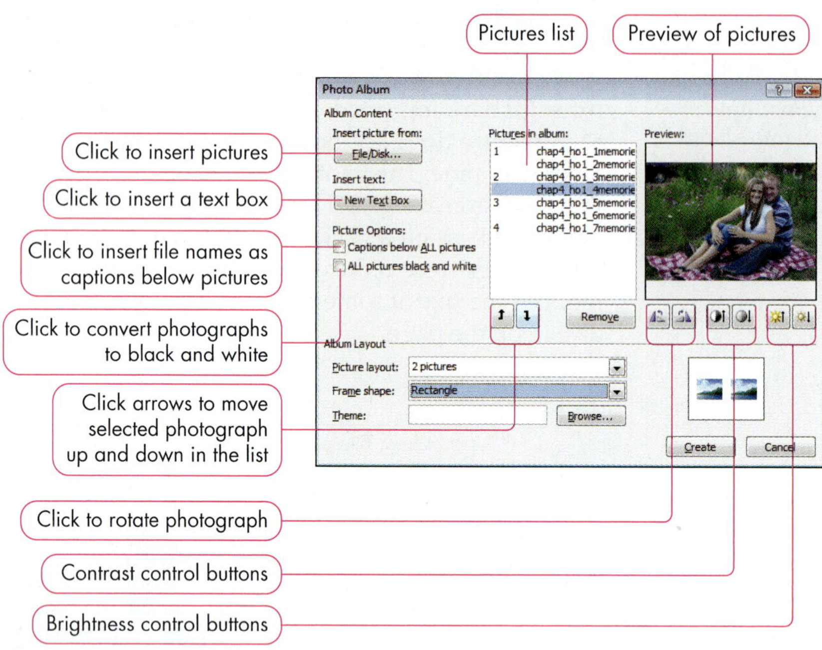

Figure 4.20 PowerPoint Photo Album Dialog Box

The Album Layout section of the Photo Album dialog box gives you your greatest opportunity for personalizing the album. First you get to select the layout for your album page. You can select from the following options: fitting a single picture on a page; one, two, or four pictures on a page; or one, two, or four pictures per page with each page including a title placeholder. When you fit a single picture per page, the image is maximized on the page. Add automatic transitions and loop the presentation, and you have a beautiful presentation for a family gathering or special event. Why not create an album of favorite family photographs through the years, burn it to a CD, and mail a copy to each family member as a holiday greeting?

> ...create an album of favorite family photographs...and mail a copy to each family member as a holiday greeting.

You can select from a variety of frame shapes in the Album Layout section. Options include rectangles, rounded rectangles, simple black or white frames, a compound black frame, a center shadow rectangle, or a soft edge rectangle. For a nostalgic "old-time" feeling picture, insert a picture into a photo album, select the ALL pictures black and white check box, and then select Simple Frame, White to create the album. Finally, change the background to a parchment theme.

You can apply a theme for the background of your album while in the Photo Album dialog box. If you are in a networked lab situation, however, it may be difficult to navigate to the location where themes are stored. If this is the case, create the album and then in the main PowerPoint window, click the Design tab and click the More button in the Themes group. Select your theme from the gallery.

Hands-On Exercises

2 | Creating a Photo Album

Skills covered: 1. Select and Order Pictures **2.** Adjust Contrast and Brightness **3.** Set Picture Layout **4.** Select Frame Shape **5.** Edit Album Settings **6.** Apply a Design Theme

Step 1 Select and Order Pictures

Refer to Figure 4.21 as you complete Step 1.

a. Click the **Insert tab**, then click **Photo Album** in the Illustrations group.

   The Photo Album dialog box opens.

b. Click **File/Disk** and navigate to the location of your student files. Open the *chap4_ho1_memories_images* folder.

c. Press **Ctrl+A** to select all pictures in the folder and then click **Insert**.

   The list of pictures displays in the Pictures in album box.

d. Use the **Move up arrow** to reposition *chap4_ho1_2memories.jpg* so that it is the first picture in the list.

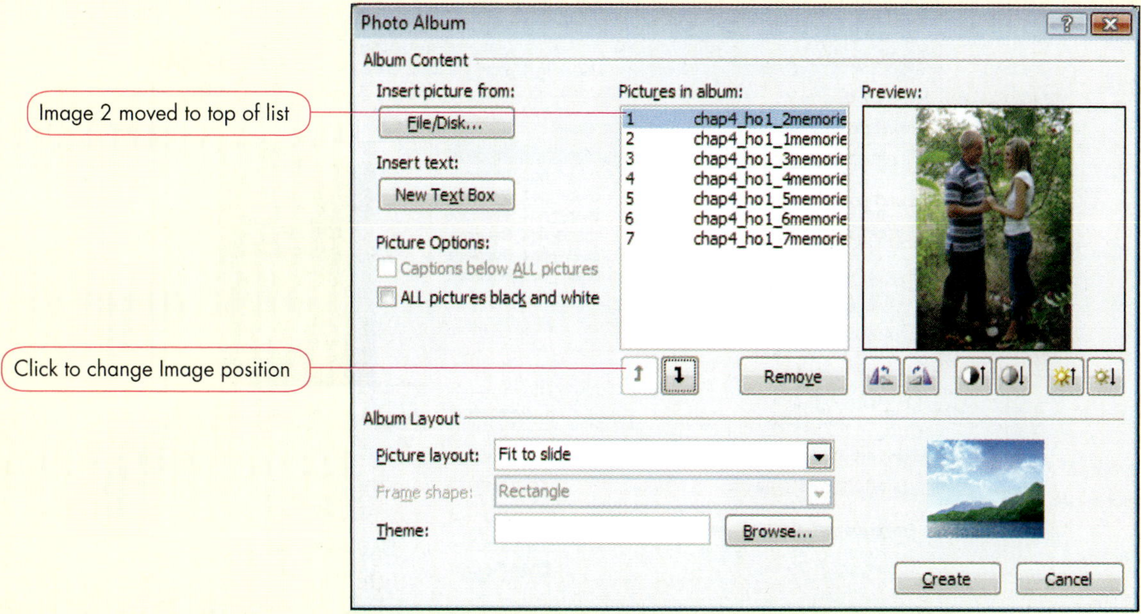

Figure 4.21 Repositioning Images in the Photo Album

Step 2 Adjust Contrast and Brightness

a. Select *chap4_ho1_5memories.jpg* in the *Pictures in Album* list.

   This image needs editing because it is too dark to see detail.

b. Click the **Increase Contrast** button four times.

c. Click the **Increase Brightness** button six times.

   Color now may be seen in the Preview window. If you had changed brightness only, the image would be washed out.

d. Select *chap4_ho1_6memories.jpg* in the list of pictures.

e. Click the **Increase Contrast** button four times and the **Increase Brightness** button six times.

Step 3
Set Picture Layout

a. Click the **Picture layout drop-down arrow** in the *Album Layout* section of the Photo Album dialog box.

b. Click each of the layouts and view the layout in the Album Layout preview window on the right.

c. Click **4 pictures**.

Clicking *4 pictures* will create an album of three pages—a title page, a page with four pictures, and a page with three pictures.

Step 4
Select Frame Shape

Refer to Figure 4.22 as you complete Step 4.

a. Click the **Frame shape drop-down arrow** in the *Album Layout* section.

b. Click each of the frames and view the preview window on the right.

c. Click **Simple Frame, White** and then click **Create**.

The album is created, but because portrait and landscape pictures are included on the same page and because portrait pictures are squeezed into small placeholders, the appearance of the album is not the best it can be.

d. Save the presentation as **chap4_ho2_album_solution**.

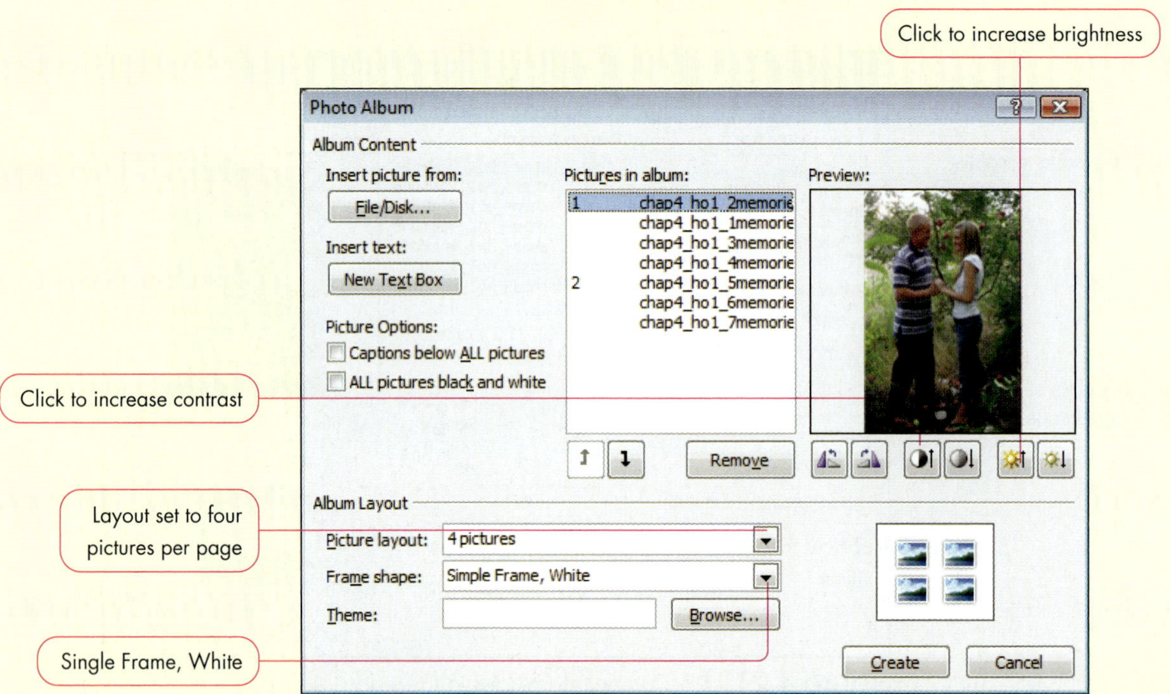

Figure 4.22 Album Setup

Step 5
Edit Album Settings

Refer to Figure 4.23 as you complete Step 5.

a. Click the **Photo Album down arrow** in the Illustrations group, and then select **Edit Photo Album**.

The Photo Album dialog box opens displaying the current settings, which you may now change. Note that the picture list has changed to indicate which pictures appear on which slide and that because you only have three images on Slide 2, a text box has been added.

b. Select the picture of the bouquet, *chap4_ho1_7memories.jpg*, in the pictures list and click the **Remove button**. Also remove the text box.

c. Click the **Picture layout drop-down arrow** and then click **2 pictures**.

d. Click the **Frame shape drop-down arrow** and select **Center Shadow Rectangle**.

e. Click **Update**.

f. Save as **chap4_ho2_album2_solution**.

The pictures now appear two per page, and the landscaped pictures are on separate pages from the portrait pictures.

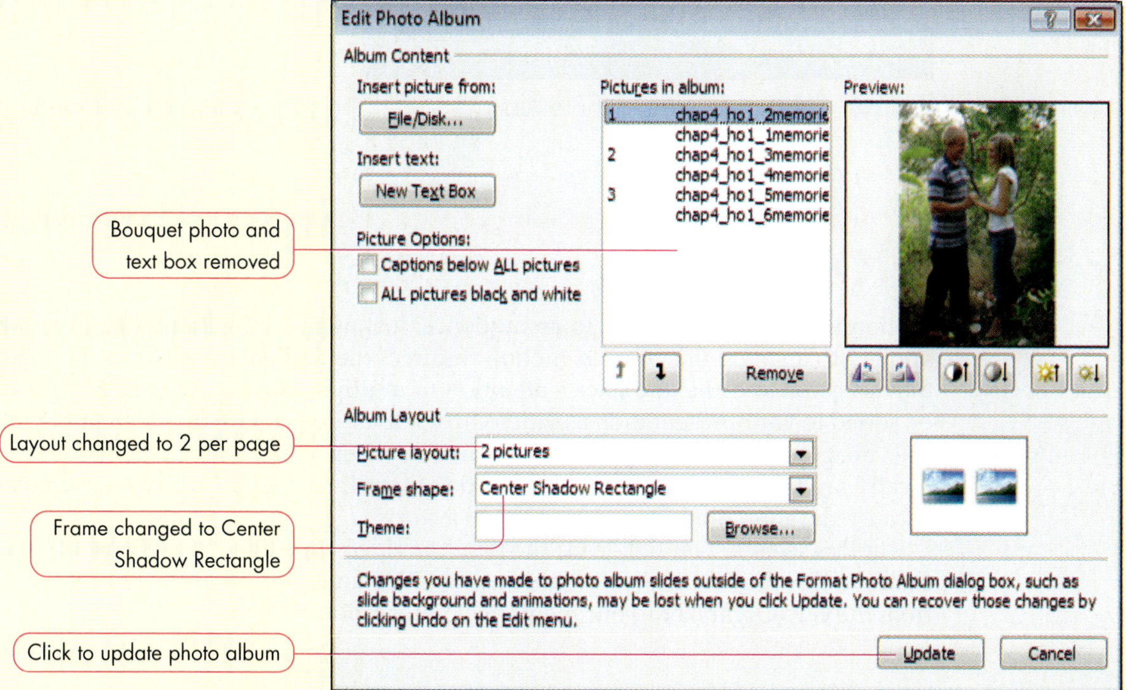

Figure 4.23 Updated Album

Step 6 Apply a Design Theme

Refer to Figure 4.24 as you complete Step 6.

a. Click the **Design tab** and then click the **More button** in the Themes group.

While you could have selected a Theme in the Photo Album dialog box, you would have needed to navigate to wherever Themes are saved on your system. This step can be quite complicated in a networked laboratory.

b. Click **Paper** to apply the theme to the presentation.

The Paper theme is characterized by a torn parchment look that goes well with the idea of memories.

c. Click **Background Styles** in the Background group on the Design tab and then click **Style 9**.

d. Create a Notes and Handouts Header and Footer with your name in the header, and your instructor's name and your class in the footer.

e. Save as **chap4_ho2_album3_solution**. Close the file and exit PowerPoint if you do not want to continue to the next exercise at this time.

Figure 4.24 Completed Photo Album

Movies

Movies are video files, or GIF files containing multiple images that stream to produce an animation.

Motion is always fascinating to an audience. Just as the animation effects we have applied to a single image used motion to direct the audience's focus to the image, movies command the audience's attention to multiple moving images. ***Movies*** can be added to your presentation as video clips or as animated GIF files containing multiple images that stream to create an animation effect. While animated GIF files technically are not movies, Microsoft includes them in the Clip Organizer as movies because the animations use motion to tell a story.

In this section, you will learn the types of video clips that PowerPoint supports, examine the options available when using video, and add an animated movie clip from the Clip Organizer to our memories presentation.

Inserting Movies

Movies are the most memorable multimedia event that you can add to your presentation. With a movie clip added to your project, you can greatly enhance and reinforce your story, and your audience can retain more of what they see. For example, a movie clip of hurricane powered water surging over levee walls and the walls collapsing beneath the pressure would stir the emotion of a viewer far more than a table listing the number of gallons of water a levee is designed to withstand. Anytime you can engage a viewer's emotions, they will remember your message.

A ***Codec*** (*co*der/*dec*oder) is a digital video compression scheme used to compress a video and decompress for playback.

Table 4.2 displays the common types of movie file formats you can use with PowerPoint. The different file formats use different types of ***codec*** (coder/decoder) software that uses an algorithm to compress or code the movie and then to decompress or decode the movie for playback. Movie playback places a tremendous demand on your computer system in terms of processing speed and memory. Using a codec reduces that demand. In order for your video file to be viewed correctly, the video player needs to have the right software installed. Because of this, even though your file extension is the same as one listed in Table 4.2 or in Help, it may not play correctly if the correct version of the codec is not installed.

Table 4.2 Types of Video File Formats Supported by PowerPoint 2007

File Format	Extension	Description
Movie file	.mpg or .mpeg	***Moving Picture Experts Group*** Evolving set of standards for video and audio compression developed by the Moving Picture Experts Group. Designed specifically for use with Video-CD and CD-i media.
Windows Media file	.asf	***Advanced Streaming Format*** Stores synchronized multimedia data. Used to stream audio and video content, images, and script commands over a network.
Windows Media Video file	.wmv	***Windows Media Video*** Compresses audio and video by using Windows Media Video compressed format. Requires a minimal amount of storage space on your computer's hard drive.
Windows Video file	.avi	***Audio Video Interleave*** Stores sound and moving pictures in Microsoft Resource Interchange File Format (RIFF) format. Common format because audio or video content that is compressed can be stored in an .avi file.

TIP Inserting a QuickTime Movie

PowerPoint 2007 does not support insertion of an Apple QuickTime movie (.mov) file. You can, however, create a hyperlink to the QuickTime movie on a PowerPoint slide. Then, while you are presenting you can click the hyperlink and QuickTime for Windows will start and automatically play the movie. When the movie is finished, you close the QuickTime window, which will return you to your slide show.

An ***embedded object*** is an object from an external source stored within a presentation.

A ***linked object*** is an object stored outside the presentation in its own file.

When you add video to your presentation, the video is linked to the presentation rather than embedded. The essential difference in embedding and linking objects is that an ***embedded object*** is placed into the presentation, whereas a linked object is stored in its own file, and the presentation is one of many potential documents that are linked to that object. The advantage of linking over embedding is that the presentation is updated automatically if the original object is changed. One caution for using linked movies—because the movie is not part of the presentation, if you move the presentation you must make sure you move a copy of the movie, too. If you change the location of the movie, you must make sure to change the link in the presentation.

To insert a movie, click the Insert tab and click the Movie down arrow in the Media Clips group. Then select Movie from File or Movie from Clip Organizer (if you click the Movie button instead of the down arrow, you go directly to the Insert Movie dialog box). When you select Movie from File, the Insert Movie dialog box displays so that you may browse to locate your file (see Figure 4.25). Locate your file and click OK. A dialog box opens to ask you how you want the movie to play inside your presentation. The movie can play automatically when the slide is displayed, or it can play when you click the mouse. You can change the settings so the movie plays after a specific time delay.

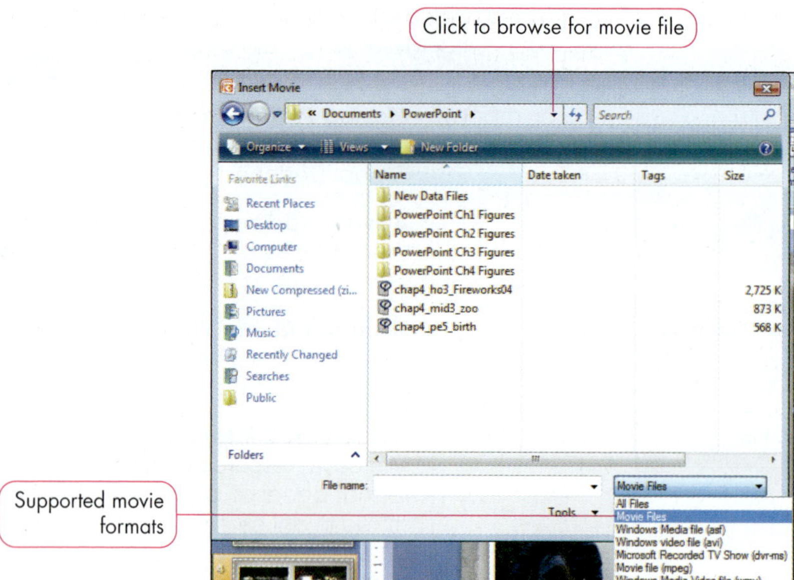

Figure 4.25 Insert Movie Dialog Box

When you click the Movie from Clip Organizer option, the Clip Organizer opens. Just as you did with clip art, you enter a keyword, indicate the type of clip you are looking for—in this case Movies—and then click Go. The results are displayed in the Clip Art task pane as shown in Figure 4.26. You can identify movie clips by the animation icon on the bottom right of the clip. The icon shows a yellow star.

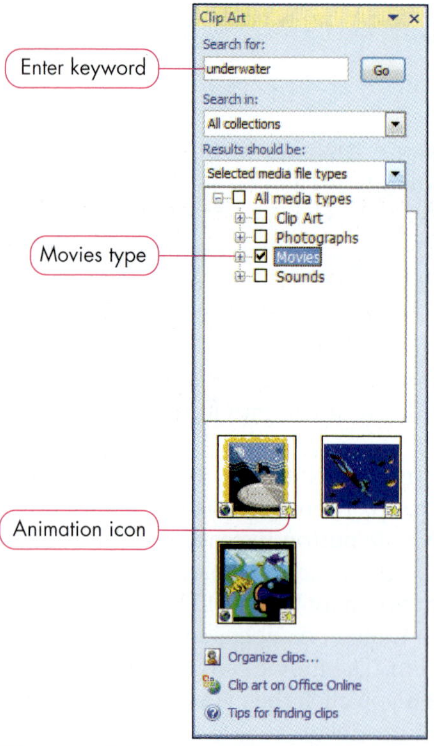

Figure 4.26 Movie from Clip Organizer

Setting Movie Options

After you insert a movie using the Movie from File option, a new contextual tab displays—Movie Tools. The Options tab beneath Movie Tools provides access to the options that enable you to preview the movie, control how your movie starts, display or hide the movie icon, play the movie full screen or not, loop the movie so it starts over after playing, and to rewind the movie after playing. Also, if your movie includes sound, the volume can be controlled through Movie Options. Figure 4.27 displays the Movie Tools and Options.

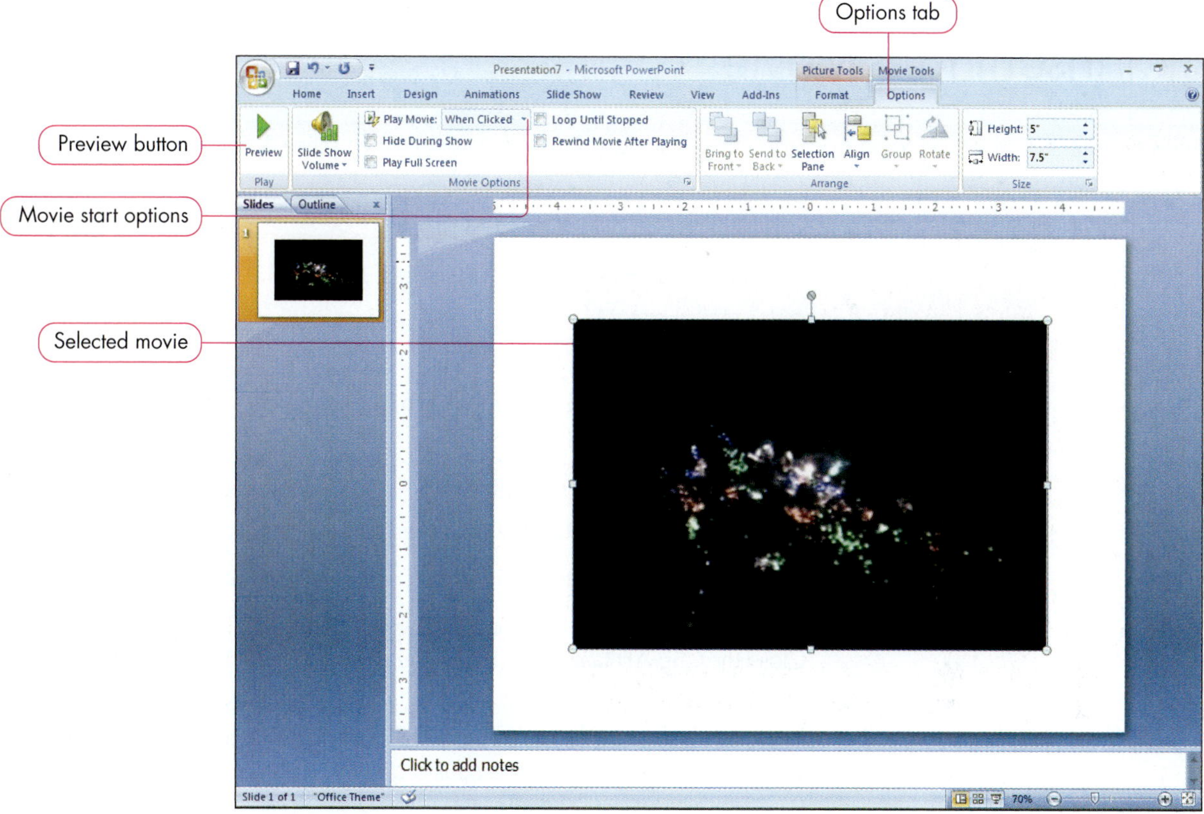

Figure 4.27 Movie Options

You may resize your movie by changing its viewing resolution. To do so, click the Size Dialog Box Launcher in the Size group on the Movie Tools Options tab. The Size and Position dialog box opens (see Figure 4.28). By default the movie is sized relative to its original picture size, but you may check Best scale for slide show, which enables you to select the desired resolution. The greater the resolution, the smaller the image size and the clearer the image. For example, a resolution of 640 x 480 fills more of the screen than a resolution of 1024 x 768, but is not as clear.

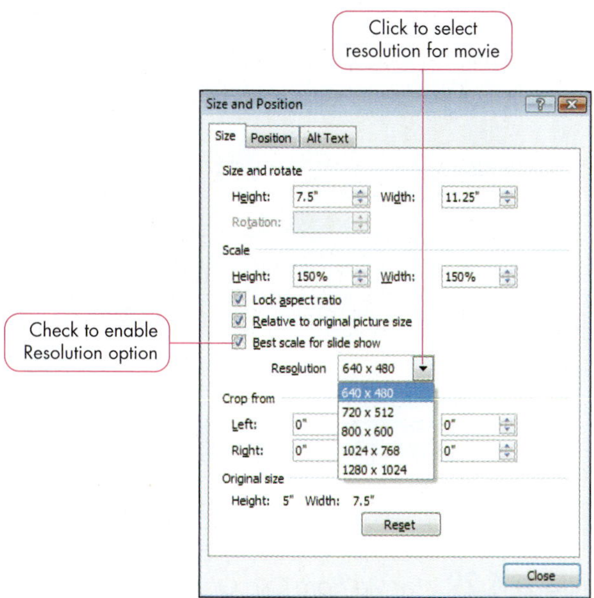

Figure 4.28 Size and Position Dialog Box

Hands-On Exercises

3 | Inserting a Movie

Skills covered: 1. Insert a Movie from the Clip Organizer **2.** Insert a Movie from a File **3.** Set Movie Options

Step 1
Insert a Movie from the Clip Organizer

Refer to Figure 4.29 as you complete Step 1.

a. Open *chap4_ho1_memories_solution* and then save as **chap4_ho3_memories_solution**.

b. Move to **Slide 6**, click the **Insert tab**, and then click the **Movie down arrow** in the Media Clips group.

c. Click **Movie from Clip Organizer**.

The Microsoft Clip Organizer opens.

d. Type **underwater** as the keyword for your search and then click **Go**.

e. Click the image of the scuba diver's head watching fish swim to insert it in your slide. Close the Clip Art task pane. Select the option to have the clip start automatically.

TROUBLESHOOTING: If you do not have a direct connection to the Internet, PowerPoint will not be able to download images from Microsoft Office Online. You will not see the image of the scuba diver watching fish swim. In that case, use **fish** as your keyword and insert a fish movie into the slide.

f. Drag the movie to the lower-right corner of your slide.

Clips are centered on the slide by default.

g. Save the presentation.

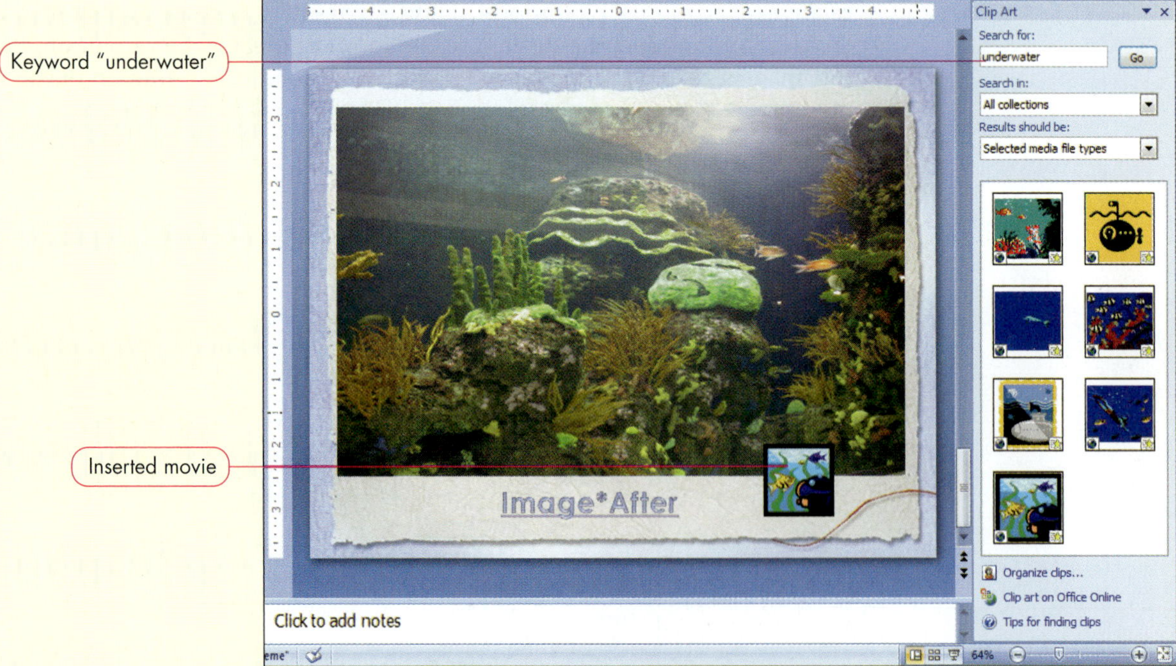

Figure 4.29 Movie from Clip Organizer

Step 2
Insert a Movie from a File

Refer to Figure 4.30 as you complete Step 2.

a. Click the **Home tab** and click the **New Slide down arrow** in the Slides group.

b. Click the **Blank** layout.

A new blank slide (Slide 7) is created and should be positioned after Slide 6. If your new slide is in a different position, drag the slide thumbnail to the end of the slides in the Slides tab.

c. Click the **Insert tab** and click the **Movie down arrow** in the Media Clips group.

The groom took digital video of the fireworks they watched on their honeymoon. You decide to add the fireworks video as the finale of your presentation.

d. Click **Movie from File** and then navigate to the location of your student files.

e. Click *chap4_ho3_fireworks04.wmv* and then click **OK**.

f. When the dialog box displays asking you how you want the movie to start in the slide, click **Automatically**.

g. If necessary, reposition the movie image so that it is positioned attractively on the slide.

h. Save the *chap4_ho3_memories_solution* presentation.

Figure 4.30 Inserted Windows Media Video File

Step 3
Set Movie Options

a. If necessary, select the movie object and then click the **Options tab** beneath the Movie Tools contextual tab in the Movie Options group.

b. Check the **Play Full Screen** option in the Movie Options group.

Enlarging the movie to play full screen causes some pixelation, but as the video is already somewhat blurry due to the speed of the fireworks, the pixelation is acceptable.

c. Check the **Rewind Movie After Playing** option in the Movie Options group.

After a movie plays, the last frame stays on the screen. Clicking Rewind rewinds the movie so that the first frame displays on the screen when the movie is over.

d. Click **Preview**.

   The movie plays on the slide for you to preview.

e. Click the **Slide Show tab** and click **From Beginning** in the Start Slide Show group.

   Advance through the slide show. Note the movie changes to full screen when playing the movie but returns to its original size and first frame when it is finished playing.

f. Save *chap4_ho3_memories_solution*. Keep the slide show open for the next hands-on exercise.

Sound

Sound can be the perfect finishing touch to a presentation, or it can be an irritating interruption. Sounds can draw on common elements of any language or culture—screams, laughs, sobs, etc. Sound can spice up your presentation, provide listening pleasure in the background, set the mood for your message, or serve as a wake-up call for the audience. People respond emotionally to sound. Harnessing the emotional impact of sound in your presentation can transform your presentation from "good" to "extraordinary." On the other hand, use sound incorrectly and you can destroy your presentation and leave the audience with a headache and confused. Just keep in mind the guideline emphasized throughout this text—any added object must enhance your message even when used for emphasis or effect—and you will not go wrong.

(Harnessing the emotional impact of sound in your presentation can transform your presentation from "good" to "extraordinary.")

Your computer needs a sound card and speakers to play sound. In a classroom or computer laboratory, however, you will need a headset or headphones for playback so that you do not disturb other students. You can play sounds and music files stored on a hard drive, flash drive, or any other storage device. You also can locate and play sounds and music stored in the Clip Organizer. If you have a CD that has an audio track you wish to play, you can direct PowerPoint to locate the audio track and play it. You can also record your own sounds, music, or narration to play from PowerPoint. Table 4.3 lists the types of Audio file formats supported by PowerPoint 2007.

Table 4.3 Types of Audio File Formats Supported by PowerPoint 2007

File Format	Extension	Description
AIFF Audio file	.aiff	***Audio Interchange File Format*** Waveform files stored in 8-bit monaural (mono or one channel) format. Not compressed. Can result in large files. Originally used on Apple and Silicon Graphics (SGI) computers.
AU Audio file	.au	***UNIX Audio*** Typically used to create sound files for UNIX computers or the Web.
MIDI file	.mid or .midi	***Musical Instrument Digital Interface*** Standard format for interchange of musical information between musical instruments, synthesizers, and computers.
MP3 Audio file	.mp3	***MPEG Audio Layer 3*** Sound file that has been compressed by using the MPEG Audio Layer 3 codec (developed by the Fraunhofer Institute).
Windows Audio file	.wav	***Wave Form*** Stores sounds as waveforms. Depending on various factors, one minute of sound can occupy as little as 644 kilobytes or as much as 27 megabytes of storage.
Windows Media Audio file	.wma	***Windows Media Audio*** Sound format used to distribute recorded music, usually over the Internet. Compressed using the Microsoft Windows Media Audio codec (developed by Microsoft).

In this section, you review the methods for inserting sound and tips for each method. You insert sound from the Clip Organizer and learn how to determine the number of times a sound clip plays, the number of slides through which the sound plays, and the method for launching the sound. Finally, you record a short narration for a presentation.

Adding Sound

To insert sound from a file, click the Insert tab, and then click Sound in the Media Clips group. If you want to insert a sound from a file, insert sound from the Clip Organizer, play a CD audio track, or record sound, click the Sound down arrow and make your selection from the list. When you select Sound from File, the Insert Sound dialog box displays. Navigate to the file location, select the file, and click OK. A message box displays, asking you how you want the sound to start in the slide show, automatically or on a mouse click. After you select how you want the sound to start, the message box disappears, and a small speaker icon representing the file appears in the center of the slide. The appearance of the icon will change depending on options you select. A number next to the icon indicates that the sound is part of an animation sequence while a hand next to the icon indicates that the sound will start with a click. You may need to display the Custom Animation task pane to see the number or hand.

To insert sound from the Clip Organizer, click the Insert tab, and then click the Sound down arrow in the Media Clips group. Select Sound from Clip Organizer, and the Clip Art task pane opens. Just as you search for pictures and movies, you insert a keyword for your search and click Go. You can point at one of the sound clips in the results pane, and a tip appears showing keywords, file size, and the sound format of the clip. To hear a preview of the clip, click the blue bar that appears on the right side of the clip when your mouse hovers over it, and then select Preview/Properties. The Preview/Properties dialog box opens, playing the sound clip and providing you with information about the clip. If you prefer, you can insert the sound clip in the slide show. Once the clip is in the slide show, you can click the Preview button in the Play group on the Sound Tools Options tab to hear it. Right-click the sound icon and you can choose Preview.

Do you have the perfect music for your presentation but it is on a CD? Do the lyrics of a song on a CD support your theme? Would the song be good background music for a slide? Do you want to welcome the audience with music as they enter the room? For all of these reasons and more, PowerPoint enables you to play sound from a CD. You can determine which track on the CD to play and whether you want the entire track to play or just a portion.

To add sound from a CD, put the CD in the CD drive of your computer and then move to the slide from which you want the sound to play. Click the Insert tab, and then click the arrow under Sound in the Media Clips group. Select Play CD Audio Track and the Insert CD Audio dialog box displays. Enter the starting and ending track numbers in the Start at track and End at track boxes under Clip Selection (see Figure 4.31). If you are playing only one track, the starting and ending number will be the same. If you want the sound to repeat, check the Loop until stopped option. When you click OK, you will be prompted to select whether you want the CD to play automatically or whether you want to click a CD icon to start the sound.

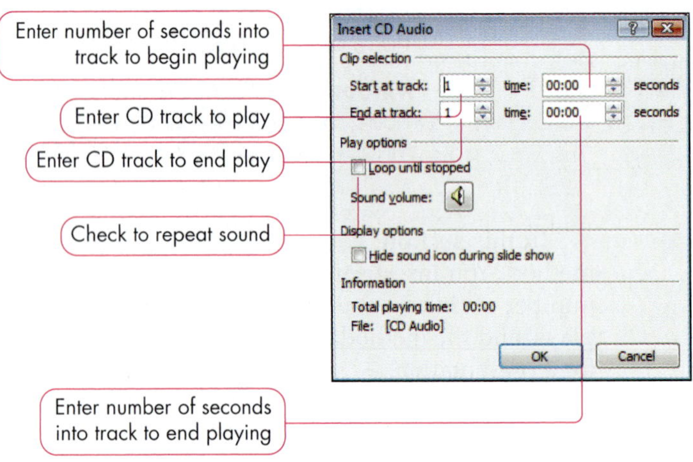

Figure 4.31 CD Audio Options

To record comments on individual slides, move to the slide in which you wish to add the comment. Click the Insert tab, click the Sound down arrow in the Media Clips group, and then select Record Sound. Click Record and start speaking (see Figure 4.32). When you stop speaking, click Stop to end the recording. Click the Play button to check the recording and continue recording until you are satisfied with the comment. In the Name box, type a name for the comment and then click OK. A sound icon will appear on your slide.

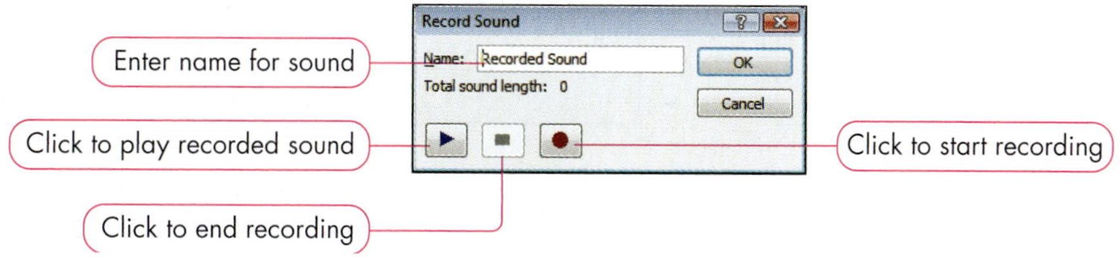

Figure 4.32 Record Sound Dialog Box

TIP Storing Sounds

Sounds that are less than 100 kb and .wav sounds are embedded in a slide show. All other sounds are linked. This link can cause problems if you take your presentation to another computer but do not take the sound files, too. One way to prevent this problem is to create a folder for your presentation. Then save the slide show, all sound files, and any other linked files like movie files to the folder for storage. Before displaying the slide show in a presentation, test it to make sure all links are working. If not, redo the links using the resource files in your folder.

Changing Sound Settings

Although only two options for starting appear in the message box that appears when you first insert sound, you have other options available through the Custom Animation task pane. You can have the sound start after a delay, or you can have the sound set up to play as part of an animation sequence. To set up for delay before the sound starts, select the sound icon and then click the Animations tab. Click Custom Animation in the Animations group. The Custom Animation task pane displays, and the selected sound will appear in the list. Click the arrow on the right side of the selected sound and select Effect Options. The Play Sound dialog box opens.

The Play Sound dialog box includes three tabs: Effect, Timing, and Sound Settings. In the Effect tab (see Figure 4.33), you can determine the start and stop settings for your sound. The Timing tab (see Figure 4.34) enables you to set the number of times a sound clip will repeat. The Sound Settings tab (see Figure 4.35) enables you to change the sound volume and hide the sound icon, and displays information about the length of the sound clip and the sound location.

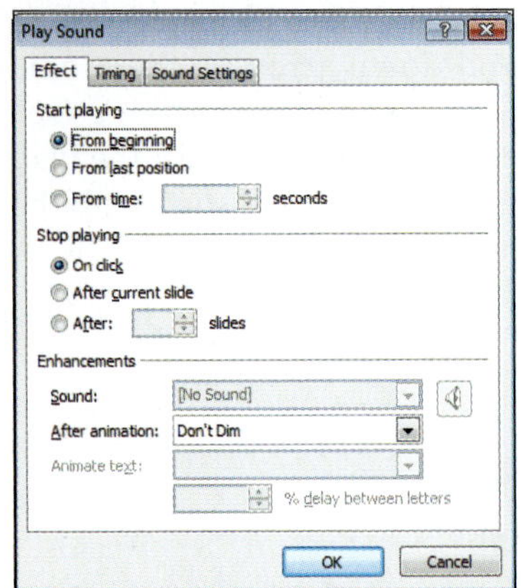

Figure 4.33 Effect Tab Settings

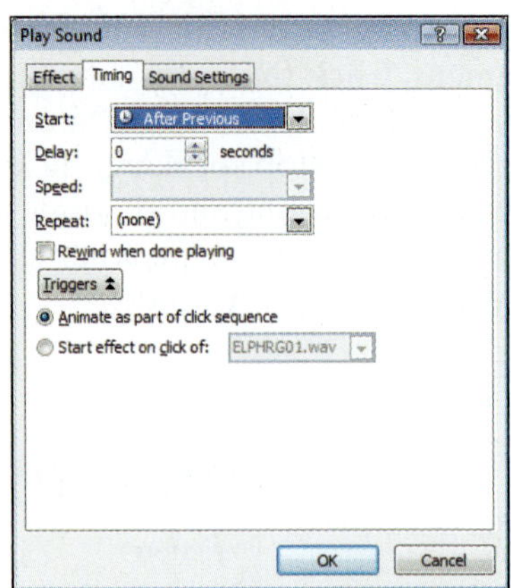

Figure 4.34 Timing Tab Settings

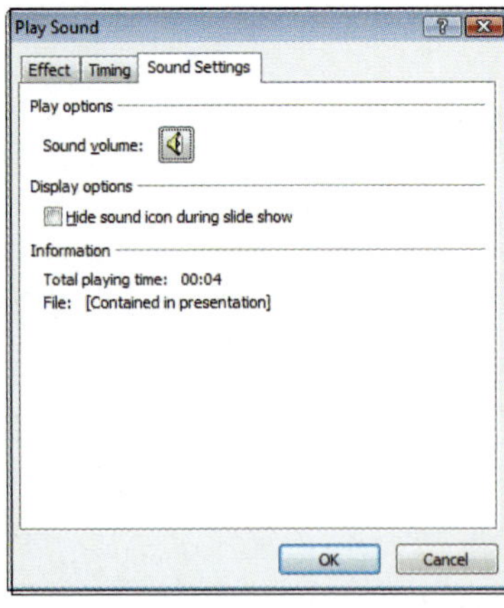

Figure 4.35 Sound Settings Tab

Play a Sound over Multiple Slides

By default, a sound plays until it ends or until the next mouse click. If you are playing background music, this default means the music ends when you click to advance to the next slide. If you would like the sound to continue as you click through slides, open the Custom Animation list, and then select the sound in the list. Click the arrow to the right of the sound, and then click Effect Options. The Play Sound dialog box appears with the Effect tab active. In the Stop playing section of the Effect tab, click the After option. Then you simply enter the number of slides you want the sound to play through. If you do not know how long the slide show will be, just enter 99! If the background music stops before you get to the last slide, you can use the Loop Until Stopped feature to keep the sound repeating. Click Loop Until Stopped in the Sound Options group on the Sound Tools Options tab.

Recording and Playing Narration

Narration is spoken commentary that is added to a project.

Sometimes you may find it helpful to add recorded ***narration***, or spoken commentary, to your slide show. One example of a need for recorded narration is when you want to create a self-running presentation, such as a presentation displaying in a kiosk at the mall. Another example would be if you are trying to create an association between words and an image on the screen, such as in a presentation to a group trying to learn a new language or for young children expanding their vocabulary. Rather than adding a narration prior to a presentation, however, you might want to create the narration during the presentation. For example, recording during a meeting would create an archive of the meeting.

You have the choice of either embedding a narration in a slide show, or linking the narration to a slide show. Embedding the narration makes for a large file size and may slow down the slide show, but you will be assured that the narration travels with the slide show. If you decide to link the narration so the narrated file is smaller and plays faster, make sure the narration is stored in a location where it can travel with or be accessed with the presentation—preferably in a folder containing the slide show and all its resources.

Before creating the narration, keep in mind the following:

- Your computer will need a sound card, speakers, and a microphone.
- Long narrations should be linked to the presentation rather than embedded.
- Comments on selected slides may be recorded rather than a narration of the entire presentation, which creates smaller file size.
- Voice narration takes precedence over any other sounds during playback.
- PowerPoint records the amount of time it takes you to narrate each slide, and if you save the slide timings, you can use them to create an automatic slide show.
- When you record your presentation, you run through the presentation and record on each slide. You can pause and resume recording during the process.

To record the narration, click the Slide Show tab, and then click Record Narration in the Set Up group (see Figure 4.36). Before recording, you need to set the microphone level to ensure that the narration can be heard. Click the Set Microphone Level button on the Record Narration dialog box. You will be asked to read a sentence to ensure the microphone is working and the volume is appropriate. When you have completed this process, click OK.

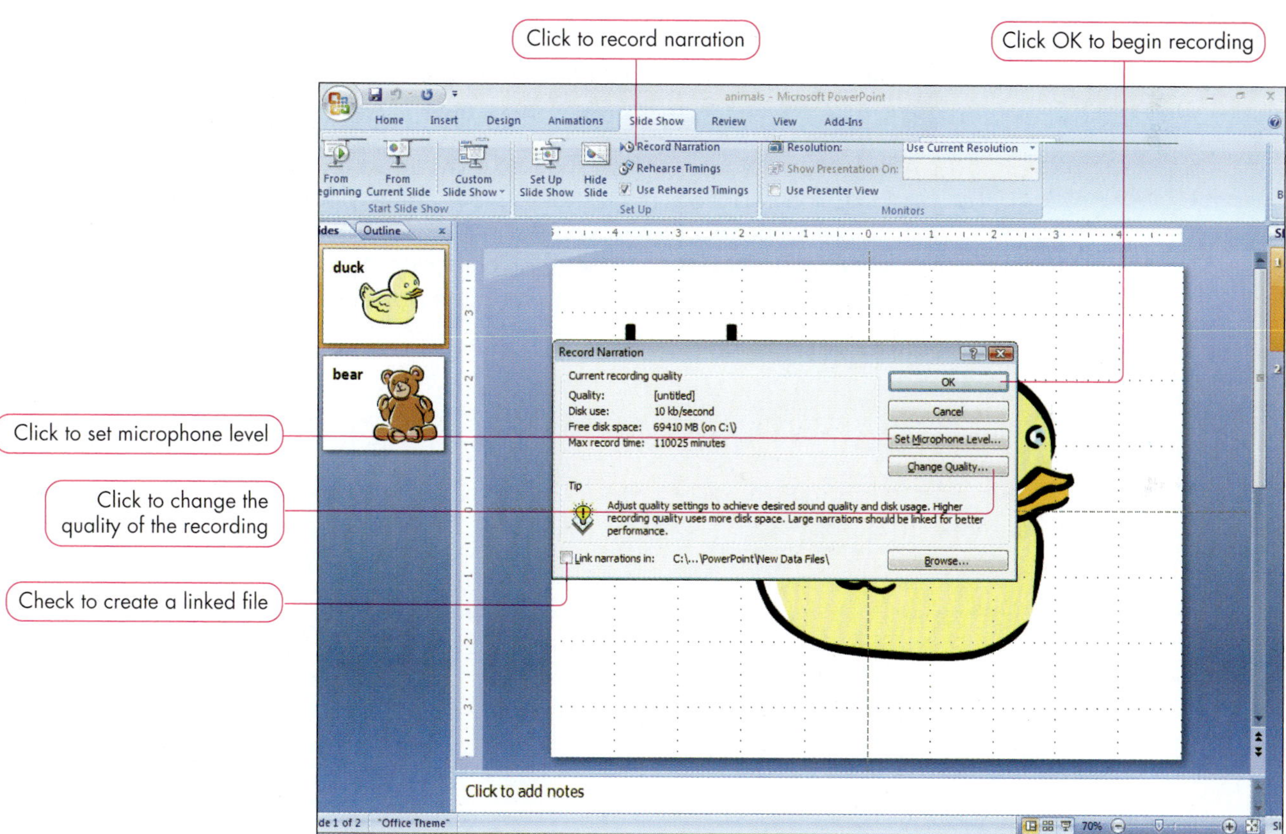

Figure 4.36 Record Narration Dialog Box

If you plan on a long narration, be sure to click the option to link the narration rather than embed the narration in the slide show. You can then navigate to the folder you wish to save the linked file in. Once again, if you have linked files in your slide show, you should create a folder for your presentation and save the slide show plus any linked files inside the folder. That way if you move the presentation to another computer, you bring all the resources with you when you copy the folder.

When you click OK at the top of the Record Narration dialog box, you enter the slide show mode and you can begin. Narrate the first slide, click to advance to the next slide, narrate, and continue advancing and narrating through the show until you reach the end. To pause during the narration and then resume again, right-click the slide, and then select either Pause Narration or Resume Narration on the shortcut menu.

When you exit the slide show, you will be asked if you want to save the show timings. PowerPoint not only recorded your voice, it recorded the amount of time you stayed on each slide. If you were creating the slide show to be self-running, you would save the timings; otherwise, there is no need to save. After making your selection, you are returned to Normal view. A sound icon appears in the lower right of the slides you narrated. View the slide show and you will hear your narrations.

To create an archive of a presentation in a meeting during which you capture your own comments and the comments of your audience, you can turn on narration before you begin your presentation.

TIP Create Notes of your Narration

A transcript of your narration should be available for those in your audience who are hearing impaired, or for those who receive a copy of your self-running slide show but do not have a sound card in their computer. Providing the transcript lets these audiences gain from your presentation, too. Putting the transcript in the PowerPoint's Notes feature and printing the Notes accomplishes this task nicely.

Hands-On Exercises

4 | Adding Sound

Skills covered: 1. Add Sound from a File **2.** Change Sound Settings **3.** Insert Sound from the Clip Organizer **4.** Add Narration

Step 1
Add Sound from a File

a. Open the *chap4_ho3_memories_solution* presentation if you closed it after the last exercise, and then save it as the **chap4_ho4_memories_solution** presentation.

b. On Slide 1, click the **Insert tab** and click the **Sound down arrow** in the Media Clips group.

c. Select **Sound from File.**

   The Insert Sound dialog box opens.

d. Navigate to the location of your student files, click *Beethoven's Symphony No. 9*, and then click **OK.**

e. When asked how you want the sound to start, click **Automatically**.

   The sound icon is displayed in the center of the slide.

f. Drag the slide icon to the bottom right.

g. Save the *chap4_ho4_memories_solution* presentation.

Step 2
Change Sound Settings

Refer to Figure 4.37 as you complete Step 2.

a. Click the **Slide Show tab** and then click **From Beginning** in the Start Slide Show group. Advance through the slides and then end the slide show.

   Note that the sound clip on Slide 1 discontinues playing as soon as you click to advance to the next slide. You will change the sound settings so the sound clip plays through several slides.

b. Select the sound icon on Slide 1.

c. Click the **Animations tab** and click **Custom Animation** in the Animations group.

d. Click the **drop-down arrow** on the right side of the sound in the animation list, and then select **Effect Options**.

e. In the *Stop playing* section of the Effect tab, type **4** in the After box, and then click **OK**.

f. Save the *chap4_ho4_memories_solution* presentation.

g. Play the slide show and note the music plays through the fourth slide.

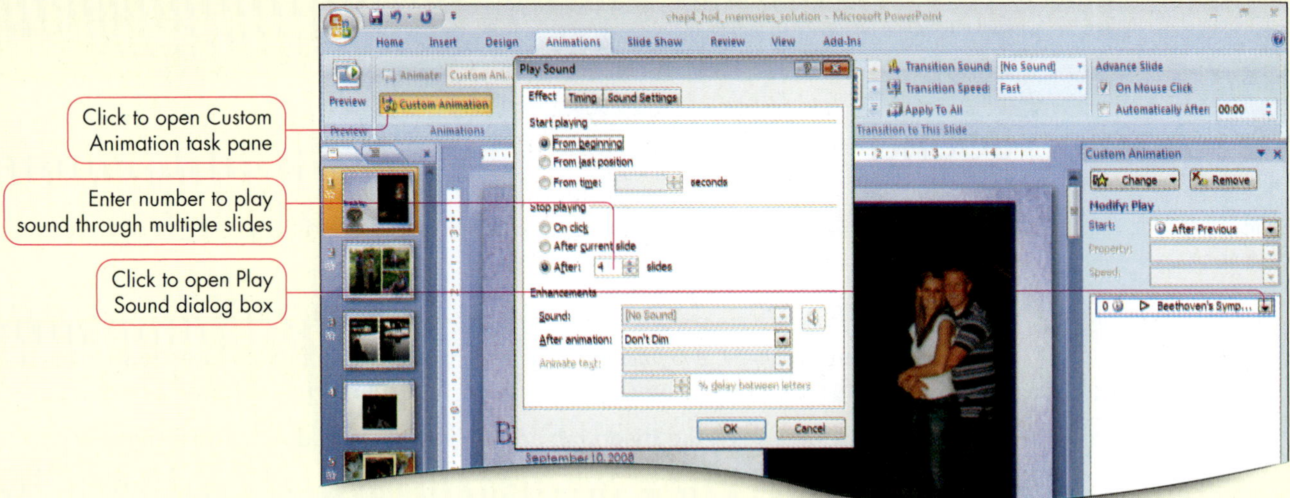

Figure 4.37 Play Sound Options

Step 3
Insert Sound from the Clip Organizer

a. Move to **Slide 5**.

b. Click the **Insert tab**, and then click the **Sound down arrow** in the Media Clips group.

c. Select **Sound from Clip Organizer**, and then type the keyword **wedding**.

d. Insert the resulting clip, Here Comes the Bride, into Slide 5 and have it start automatically.

e. Select the sound icon and drag it to the lower-right side of the screen so that it does not display during the slide show.

f. Right click the sound icon and select **Preview**.

g. Save and close the *chap4_ho4_memories_solution* presentation.

Step 4
Add Narration

a. Move to **Slide 1** and click the **Slide Show tab**.

b. Click **Record Narration** and then click **OK**.

TROUBLESHOOTING: You will not be able to complete this step without a microphone, speakers, and a sound card.

c. When the slide show displays Slide 1, read the text on Slide 1.

d. Press **Spacebar** to advance to the next slide and then press **Escape** to exit the slide show.

e. Click **Don't Save** so that slide timings are not saved with the slide show.

f. Click **From Beginning** in the Start Slide Show group so that you can hear the narration and the sounds you have added.

g. Save and close the *chap4_ho4_memories_solution* presentation.

Summary

1. **Insert and modify a picture.** Pictures are very popular for enhancing slide shows. Pictures are in a bitmap format and are realistic portrayals of what we see. They can be inserted using the Insert Picture option, which centers the image on the slide, or by using placeholders that might center and crop the image inside the placeholder. The brightness and contrast of pictures can be adjusted and the picture cropped to eliminate unwanted areas. Because bitmap images can be large files, images should be compressed.
2. **Use the Internet as a resource.** The Internet can be extremely valuable when searching for information for a presentation. Although students and teachers have rights under the Fair Use Act, care should be taken to honor all copyrights. Before inserting any information or clips into your slide show, research the copyright ownership. To be safe, contact the Web site owner and request permission to use the material. Any information used should be credited and include hyperlinks when possible, although attribution does not relieve you of the requirement to honor copyright.
3. **Create a photo album.** When you have multiple images to be inserted, using the Photo Album feature enables you to quickly insert the images into a slide show. After identifying the images you wish to use, you can rearrange the order of the pictures in the album. You also can choose among layouts for the best appearance.
4. **Utilize photo album options.** Album options for contrast and brightness enable you to make image changes without having to leave the Photo Album dialog box. In addition to adjusting contrast and brightness, you can change the pictures to black and white. File names can be turned into captions for the pictures. Frame shape can be selected and a theme applied to complete the album appearance.
5. **Insert movies.** Movies can be powerful tools when inserted into a slide show. PowerPoint plays two types of movies: digital videos and small animated clips stored in the Clip Organizer.
6. **Set movie options.** Movies can be played full screen, looped until stopped, and rewound to the first frame of the movie upon completion of the movie. You can change the movie size by changing the resolution of the movie, but pixelation can occur.
7. **Add sound.** Sound effects and music catch audience attention and add excitement to a presentation. Take care when adding sound that the sound enhances your message rather than detracts from it. All sound files except WAV files under 100 kilobytes are linked to the presentation rather than embedded. Because they are linked, you should take care to copy and move the sound files when you copy and move the presentation.
8. **Record and play narration.** You can narrate a slide show for use in a self-running presentation, or you can turn on narration during a meeting to create an archive of comments made during the presentation.

Key Terms

Multiple Choice

1. Which of the following file formats is best for photographs?
   (a) Vector
   (b) Line
   (c) Bitmap
   (d) Illustration

2. Which of the following is not a Windows graphics file format?
   (a) PICT
   (b) .jpg
   (c) .tif
   (d) .gif

3. Which of these is a feature that can be used to identify a photograph on a slide?
   (a) Frames
   (b) Captions
   (c) Labels
   (d) Full slide

4. All of the following are forms of multimedia except?
   (a) Placeholders
   (b) Video clips
   (c) Text
   (d) Sound clips

5. Which of the following file formats supports 16 million colors, is optimized for photographs and complex graphics, and is the format of choice for most photographs on the Web?
   (a) .bmp
   (b) .jpg
   (c) .gif
   (d) .tiff

6. Which procedure would you follow to change the resolution of a movie clip?
   (a) Click the Set Resolution button in the Movie Options group on the Movie Tools Options tab.
   (b) Click the Movie Options Dialog Box Launcher in the Movie Options group on the Movie Tools Options tab.
   (c) Click the Resolution button in the Arrange group on the Movie Tools Options tab.
   (d) Click the Size and Position Dialog Box Launcher in the Size group on the Movie Tools Options tab.

7. Which of the following Picture Tools would help you adjust a scanned photograph that appears muddy and does not show much difference between the light and dark areas of the image?
   (a) Brightness
   (b) Contrast
   (c) Recolor
   (d) Compress Pictures

8. Which of the following is permitted for a student project in a class?
   (a) The educational project is produced for a specific class and then retained in a personal portfolio for display in a job interview.
   (b) Only a portion of copyrighted material was used, and the portion was determined by the type of media used.
   (c) The student received permission to use copyrighted material to be distributed to classmates in the project.
   (d) All of the above uses are permitted.

9. The Photo Album dialog box enables you to make all but this edit to pictures:
   (a) Rotate
   (b) Crop
   (c) Brightness
   (d) Contrast

10. Which of the following are included in the Clip Organizer?
    (a) Windows Video Files (.avi)
    (b) Moving Picture Experts Group Movies (.mpg or .mpeg)
    (c) Animated GIF Files (.gif)
    (d) Windows Media Video files (.wmv)

11. Which of the following statements is not true?
    (a) Objects linked to a PowerPoint slide show automatically move with the slide show when its location is changed.
    (b) Embedded objects become part of a slide show.
    (c) A linked object in a slide show updates when the original object is changed.
    (d) Embedded objects do not update when the originals are changed.

...continued on Next Page

Multiple Choice Continued...

12. Which of the following sound formats may be embedded in a slide show?

(a) Windows Audio File (.wav)
(b) MIDI file (.mid or .midi)
(c) MP3 Audio file (.mp3)
(d) Windows Media Audio file (.wma)

13. All of the following can be used play a sound clip for preview except:

(a) Click the blue bar on the right side of the clip in the Clip Organizer, and then select Preview/Properties.
(b) Select the clip on the slide, and then click the Preview button in the Play group on the Options tab beneath Sound Tools.
(c) Click the clip on the slide.
(d) Right-click the sound icon and select Preview.

14. Which of the following options for inserting sound is available under the Slide Show tab rather than the Insert tab?

(a) Record Sound
(b) Sound from a File
(c) Play CD Audio Track
(d) Record Narration

15. Which of the following is a true statement regarding recording a narration?

(a) Long narrations should be embedded in the slide show.
(b) CD Audio takes precedence over voice narration on playback.
(c) The slide timings are recorded with the voice narration for use in a self-running presentation.
(d) It is not possible to pause the recording during a voice narration.

Practice Exercises

1 Adding Pictures Using Placeholders

The presentation in Figure 4.38 covers the birth and first year in the life of your niece. You were invited to her first birthday party and decided to put the presentation together as a gift for the baby. The presentation is based on the Contemporary template, so you review your skills in using a template at the same time you practice inserting pictures in Picture placeholders. You also rotate a picture.

a. Open the *chap4_pe1_birthday* presentation and then save it as **chap4_pe1_birthday_solution**.
b. On **Slide 1**, click the **Insert Picture button**.
c. Navigate to the location of your student files and open the *chap4_pe1_birthday_images* folder. Click the *chap4_pe1_birthday1.jpg* file to select it and then click **Insert**.
d. Select the text in the orange content placeholder and type **My First Year!** Click in the green placeholder and type **Happy Birthday from Uncle/Aunt and your first name**.
e. Move to **Slide 2**. Click the **Insert Picture button** in the left placeholder. In the *chap4_pe1_birthday_images* folder select and examine the *chap4_pe1_birthday2* picture.
f. Click **Insert** and then examine the image in Slide 2 and note the cropping.
g. Insert *chap4_pe1_birthday3* in the center placeholder of Slide 2 and then insert *chap4_pe1_birthday4* in the right placeholder, noting the changes that take place as the images are centered and cropped in the placeholders.
h. Select the picture in the center placeholder and click the **Format tab**, if necessary, under the Picture Tools contextual tab.
i. Click **Rotate** in the Arrange group, and then select **Rotate Right 90°**.
j. Select the text *Choose a Page Layout* and then type **July 30, 2008**. Select the text *...then click the placeholders to add your own pictures and captions* and then type **My life as a newborn—sleep, yawn, and cry!**
k. Move to **Slide 3** and read the text in the placeholder. Select the first caption text *...then* and type **Proud Papa**, and then select the second caption text and type **Loving Mama**.
l. Click the **Insert Picture button** and insert *chap4_pe1_birthday5*.
m. Save the *chap4_pe1_birthday_solution* presentation.

Figure 4.38 Birthday Presentation with Added Pictures

...continued on Next Page

2 Cropping and Compressing Pictures

You locate pictures of your niece at the Fourth of July Baby Contest. You decide to add them to your birthday presentation. One of the pictures of your niece is of her on the judging table and has a lot of distracting images, so you decide to crop the picture to focus attention to her. After cropping, you need to compress the picture to save file space. Because you plan on showing the presentation to your family at the birthday party and also on printing the presentation and putting it in a scrapbook for the baby, you compress and save one version at a resolution appropriate for printing, and then you compress and save another version at a resolution for viewing on the screen. Refer to Figure 4.39 as you complete this activity.

a. Save *chap4_pe1_birthday_solution* as **chap4_pe2_birthday_solution**.
b. Move to **Slide 4**, click the **Home tab**, and click the **New Slide down arrow**. Click **Portrait with Caption**.
c. Replace the text in the content placeholder by typing **Baby Contest** on the first line, and **July 4, 2009** on the second line.
d. Click the **Insert Picture button** and examine the landscape oriented picture *chap4_pe1_birthday6*. Click **Insert** and note that the picture is forced into the portrait-oriented placeholder and that considerable cropping took place to make this possible.
e. Click the **Insert tab** and click **Picture** in the Illustrations group. Click *chap4_pe1_birthday7* and click **Insert**.
f. Click the **View tab** and click **Ruler** in the Show/Hide group, if necessary.
g. Select the picture, click the **Picture Tools Format tab**, and then click **Crop** in the Size group on the Format tab.
h. Position the Crop tool over the top center cropping handle and drag inward until the guiding line on the vertical ruler reaches the +1" mark.
i. Position the Crop tool over the right center cropping handle and drag inward until the guiding line on the horizontal ruler reaches the +2" mark.
j. Position the Crop tool over the left center cropping handle and drag inward until the guiding line on the horizontal ruler reaches the –1" mark.
k. Click **Crop** in the Size group again to toggle it off.
l. Click the **Size Dialog Box Launcher** to open the Size and Position dialog box, and then click the **Position tab**.
m. Set the **Horizontal Position on slide** option to 6" from the **Top Left Corner**. Set the **Vertical Position on slide** option to 3.5" from the **Top Left Corner**. Click **Close**.
n. Click **Compress Pictures** in the Adjust group on the Format tab, and then click **Options**.
o. Click **Print** in the Target Output area, click **OK**, and then click **OK** in the Compress Pictures dialog box.
p. Click the **Office Button,** select **Save As**, and save the presentation as **chap4_pe2_birthdayprint_solution**.
q. Click **Compress Pictures** in the Adjust group on the Format tab, and then click **Options**.
r. Click **Screen** in the Target Output area, click **OK**, and then click **OK** in the Compress Pictures dialog box.
s. Click the **Office Button,** select **Save As**, and save the presentation as **chap4_pe2_birthday_solution**. Click **Yes** when asked if you want to replace the previous file.

...continued on Next Page

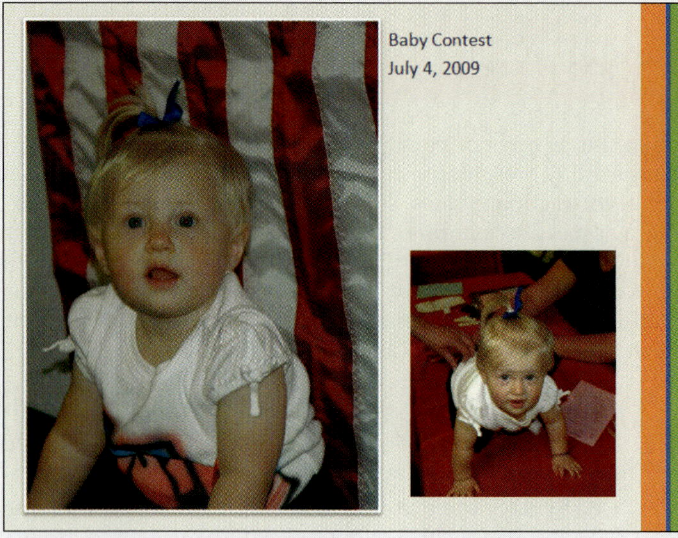

Figure 4.39 Inserted Pictures and Cropping

3 Create a Border and Apply Picture Styles

You notice that the picture you inserted does not have a border as does the picture inserted through the placeholder. You decide to add a border similar to the one on the other picture on the page. Then you decide to apply Picture Quick Styles as frames to other images in the show to add some fun variety. Refer to Figure 4.40 as you complete this activity.

a. Save *chap4_pe2_birthday_solution* as **chap4_pe3_birthday_solution**.
b. In **Slide 5**, select the small cropped picture on the right, and then click the **Picture Tools Format tab**.
c. Click **Picture Border** in the Picture Styles group, and then click **White, Background 1**.
d. Click **Picture Border** again, and then click **Weight**. Click **3 pt**.
e. Click **Picture Effects**, and then click **Shadow**. Click **Offset Center** in the Outer Shadow area.
f. Click **Picture Effects**, click **Shadow**, and then click **Shadows Options** at the bottom of the list.
g. Set the **Size** to **100%, Blur** to **5**, and the **Distance** to 2 and then click **Close**. Deselect the picture.
h. Move to **Slide 4**, select the picture on the left, and then click the **Format tab**.
i. Click **More** in the Picture Styles group.
j. Apply **Rotated, White**.
k. Select the picture in the center, click **More** in the Picture Styles group, and then click **Relaxed Perspective, White**.
l. Select the picture on the right, click **More** in the Picture Styles group, and then click **Bevel Perspective Left, White**.
m. Select the picture on the left and click the right arrow on the keyboard to shift it to the right until it fits on the slide. Select the image on the right and move it closer to the center so that the pictures in the grouping all touch.
n. Select the picture in the middle, click **Bring to Front** in the Arrange group, and then select **Bring to Front**.
o. Select the caption text, and then type **Look at me grow!** Click **Center align** on the Mini toolbar.
p. Save the *chap4_pe3_birthday_solution* presentation.

...continued on Next Page

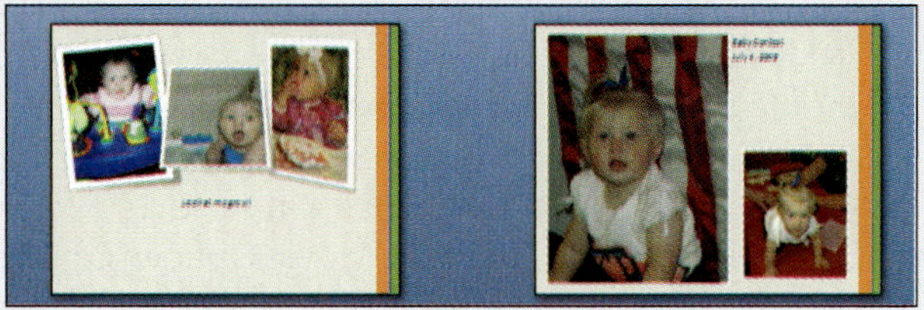

Figure 4.40 Using Picture Styles

4 Adjust Brightness and Contrast

When playing the slide show to see how it presents at this point, you notice that on the last slide, the slide showing a series of images of your niece playing with a flower, one of the photos has very dark areas because of the shadowing on a bright summer day. You decide to see if you can improve the picture using PowerPoint's Picture Tools. Refer to Figure 4.41 as you complete this activity.

a. Save the *chap4_pe3_birthday_solution* presentation as **chap4_pe4_birthday_solution.**
b. Move to **Slide 6** and select the picture of the child standing up in the lower-left corner.
c. Click the **Picture Tools Format tab**.
d. Click **Brightness** in the Picture Tools group and click +20%.
e. Click **Contrast** in the Picture Tools group and click +20%.
f. Save the *chap4_pe4_birthday_solution* presentation.

Figure 4.41 Adjusting Brightness and Contrast

5 Inserting a Movie

You decide a movie clip of your brother holding your niece on the day of her birth would enhance the presentation you are creating for your niece and the family. While the first frame of the video is all that will print in the scrapbook, the presentation will play the video because it is in Windows Media Audio/Video file format, a format PowerPoint supports. Refer to Figure 4.42 as you complete this activity.

a. Save *chap4_pe4_birthday_solution* as **chap4_pe5_birthday_solution**.
b. Move to **Slide 3** and then click the **Home tab**.
c. Click the **New Slide down arrow** in the Slides group and then click the **Blank** layout.

...continued on Next Page

d. Click **Movie** in the Media Clips group on the Insert tab, click *chap4_pe5_birth.wmv*, and click **OK**.
e. Click to play the movie **Automatically**.
f. Select the movie object, and then click the **Movie Tools Options tab**. Click **Preview** in the Play group to view the movie clip.
g. Check **Play Full Screen** in the Movie Options group.
h. Click the **Slide Show tab** and click **From Current Slide** in the Start Slide Show group.
i. Save the *chap4_pe5_birthday_solution* presentation.

Figure 4.42 Inserted Movie Clip

6 Inserting Sound

You decide to add sound to the last slide in the slide show as a finale. You use Microsoft Office Online as an Internet resource to locate happy music that you can insert in your final slide. Refer to Figure 4.43 as you complete this activity.

a. Save *chap4_pe5_birthday_solution* as **chap4_pe6_birthday_solution**.
b. Move to **Slide 7**.
c. Click the **Insert tab**, click the **Sound down arrow** in the Media Clips group, and then select **Sound from Clip Organizer**.
d. Click **Clip art on Office Online** located at the bottom of the Clip Organizer pane.
e. Enter **happy** in the Search box.
f. Click the **Search drop-down arrow** and click **Sounds.**
g. Click **Next** to move to the third page of results and locate the Humoresque sound clip.
h. Click the **Click to copy this item to your clipboard button** beneath the Humoresque sound, and then close Microsoft Office Online to return to your slide show.
i. Right-click in Slide 7 and click **Paste.**
j. Click to play the sound **Automatically.**
k. Click the **Sound Tools Options tab**.
l. Check **Hide During Show** in the Sound Options group on the Options tab.
m. Check **Loop Until Stopped** in the Sound Options group on the Options tab.
n. Click **Preview** in the Play group.
o. Create a Notes and Handouts Header and Footer with the date, your name in the header, and your instructor's name and your class in the footer.
p. Save the *chap4_pe6_birthday_solution* presentation and close the file.

...continued on Next Page

Figure 4.43 Inserted Sound Clip

7 Creating an Album

Your parents bought a small car for you to drive while going to school. While stopped at a streetlight waiting to turn right, someone driving an SUV and talking on a cell phone drives into the back of your car. A police report is filed, and the insurance companies are contacted, but you decide to use your digital camera to take pictures to keep a record of the damage. Your father wants to see the damage to the car so you think of the perfect way to show him—you quickly create an album to use as a professional record that is suitable for sending by e-mail. Refer to Figure 4.44 as you complete this activity.

a. Click the **Insert tab**, click the **Photo Album down arrow** in the Illustrations group, and then click **New Photo Album**.
b. Click **File/Disk** and navigate to the location of your student files. Open the *chap4_pe7_accident_images* folder.
c. Click one of the files, and then press **Ctrl+A** to select all pictures in the folder. Click **Insert**.
d. Click the **Picture layout drop-down arrow** in the Album Layout section.
e. Select **4 pictures**.
f. Click the **Frame shape drop-down arrow** in the Album Layout section, and then select **Rounded Rectangle**.
g. Click **Create**.
h. Move to the title slide and change the *Photo Album* text to **Accident Record**.
i. Change your name to the date of the accident, **September 7, 2008.**
j. Select one of the images in your album, click **Compress Pictures** in the Adjust group on the Format tab, and then click **Options.**
k. Click **E-mail** in the Target output section, click **OK**, and click **OK**.
l. Create a Notes and Handouts Header and Footer with the date, your name in the header, and your instructor's name and your class in the footer.
m. Save the album as **chap4_pe7_accident_solution**.

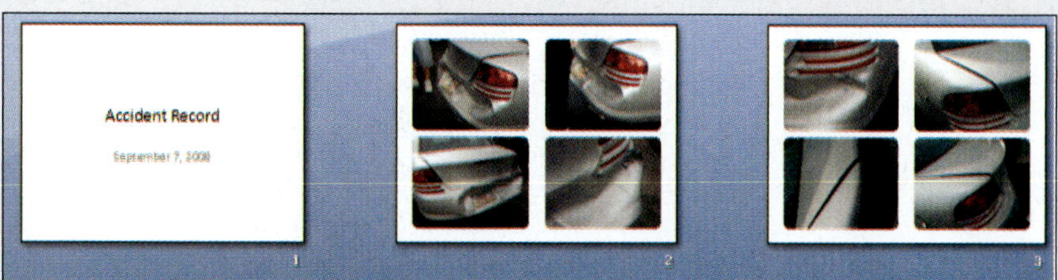

Figure 4.44 Accident Record

Mid-Level Exercises

1 Motorcycle for Sale

You have enjoyed a number of years as a motorcyclist, but now decide that you would like to sell your motorcycle and purchase a car. You added a specialized carbon fiber exhaust system to your motorcycle, have kept the bike in perfect condition, and customized the paint job. Using PowerPoint, you create a flyer advertising the motorcycle that you can reproduce and hang on bulletin boards at the college, local grocery stores, auto shops, and more. Figure 4.45 shows the completed flyer.

a. Open a blank presentation and save it as **chap4_mid1_motorcycle_solution**.

b. Change the layout to a blank layout so you have more freedom in designing your advertisement.

c. Change your slide orientation to Portrait as you will be printing a single slide to use as a flyer.

d. Search the Clip Organizer for the *For Sale* sign shown in Figure 4.45. Insert it and then change the scale to 47% of its original size. Position the sign horizontally at 0" from the Top Left Corner. Position it vertically at .33" from the Top Left Corner.

e. Create a WordArt using Gradient Fill–Accent 1 and then type **1995 Motorcycle**. Change the WordArt Text Fill to Black, Text 1. Change the WordArt font size to 44 pts. Change the Height to .8" and the Width to 3.3". Position the WordArt horizontally at 3.23" from the Top Left Corner. Position it vertically at .42" from the Top Left Corner.

f. Create a text box and type the following information inside it:

   Year: 1995
   Miles: 22,145
   Engine cc: 600
   Type: Street
   Exterior: Black
   Title: Clear

g. Position the text box horizontally at .3" from the Top Left Corner. Position it vertically at 2.17" from the Top Left Corner.

h. Navigate to the location of your student files and open the *chap4_mid1_ motorcycle_ images* folder. Insert *chap4_mid1_motorcycle1* and scale it to 60% of its original size. Drag the image so that it is to the right of the text box and beneath the WordArt.

i. Insert *chap4_mid1_motorcycle2*. Crop the photograph to get rid of unnecessary parking space area and focus in on the motorcycle. After cropping, size the Width to 2.75" and then position the image horizontally at 0" from the Top Left Corner. Position it vertically at 4.75" from the Top Left Corner.

j. Create a text box and type **Call 555-1212**. Apply WordArt Gradient Fill–Accent 1 to the text, and then apply WordArt Text Fill Black, Text 1. Drag it so it is approximately centered under the photograph above.

k. Insert *chap4_mid1_motorcycle3* and scale it to 30% of its original size. Position the photograph horizontally at 2.94" from the Top Left Corner. Position it vertically at 5.25" from the Top Left Corner.

l. Insert *chap4_mid1_motorcycle4* and scale it to 30% of its original size. Position the photograph horizontally at 5.3" from the Top Left Corner. Position it vertically at 5.25" from the Top Left Corner.

m. Create a text box and type **Custom Paint**. Apply WordArt Gradient Fill–Accent 1 to the text, and then apply WordArt Text Fill Black, Text 1. Drag it so it is approximately centered under the two photographs above.

...continued on Next Page

n. Insert *chap4_mid1_motorcycle5* and scale it to 50% of its original size. Position the photograph horizontally at 3.12" from the Top Left Corner. Position it vertically at 7.38" from the Top Left Corner.

o. Create a text box and type **Carbon Fiber Exhaust**. Apply WordArt Gradient Fill - Accent 1 to the text, and then apply WordArt Text Fill Black, Text 1. Position the text box horizontally at .42" from the Top Left Corner. Position it vertically at 8.67" from the Top Left Corner.

p. Insert an arrow that starts at *Carbon Fiber Exhaust* and points to the exhaust pipe of the motorcycle. Change the weight of the arrow to 3 pt. Change the outline color to Red, Accent 2.

q. Compress the photographs on the flyer using the default setting.

r. Create a Notes and Handouts Header and Footer with the date, your name in the header, and your instructor's name and your class in the footer.

s. Save the *chap4_mid1_motorcycle_solution* flyer and close it.

Figure 4.45 Motorcycle Sales Flyer

2 Impressionist Paintings

In this exercise you will use the Internet as a source for obtaining images of paintings by some of the masters of the Impressionist style of painting. The paintings in Figure 4.46 may be viewed at the Web Museum (www.ibiblio.org/wm), a Web museum that is maintained by Nicolas Pioch for academic and educational use. Follow the link to Explore the Web Museum unique Famous Artworks collections to the Famous Artworks exhibition page. Locate and click the Impressionism Theme (or search for Impressionist paintings or painter's names) and search for the paintings used in this assignment.

a. Open the *chap4_mid2_paintings* presentation and save it as **chap4_mid2_paintings_solution**.

b. When you locate a painting, click the thumbnail image to enlarge the painting, then right-click the painting and save the image to a new folder you create on your storage

...continued on Next Page

device named **Impressionist Paintings**. If necessary, change the name of the file to include the artist and the name of the painting. Repeat this process until you have saved each of the images of the paintings shown in Figure 4.46.

c. The painting in Slide 2 is an excellent example of the guiding principles in the Impressionist movement. It was painted by Claude Monet, and its title is *Impression: soleil levant*.

d. The painting in Slide 4 is a Degas painting, *Ballet Rehearsal*.

e. The painting in Slide 5 is a Monet painting, *Waterlilies, Green Reflection, Left Part*.

f. The painting in Slide 6 is a Morisot painting, *The Artist's Sister at a Window*.

g. The painting in Slide 7 is a Renoir painting, *On the Terrace*.

h. The painting in Slide 8 is a Pissarro painting, *Peasant Girl Drinking her Coffee*.

i. Insert Alfred Sisley's *Autumn: Banks of the Seine near Bougival* as the background of the title slide.

j. Now that you have gathered your resources, return to your slide show and insert each of the images on the appropriate artist's slide. Resize the images as needed and then position the images attractively on the page. You do not need to compress the images as they are already at a low resolution.

k. Search for **upbeat**. Find and insert *Fur Elise* in Slide 1. Hide the Sound icon during play, and loop the song. Set the song animation so it plays continuously and does not stop with the next mouse click.

l. Create a Notes and Handouts Header and Footer with the date, your name in the header, and your instructor's name and your class in the footer. Save the *chap4_mid2_paintings_solution* presentation and close it.

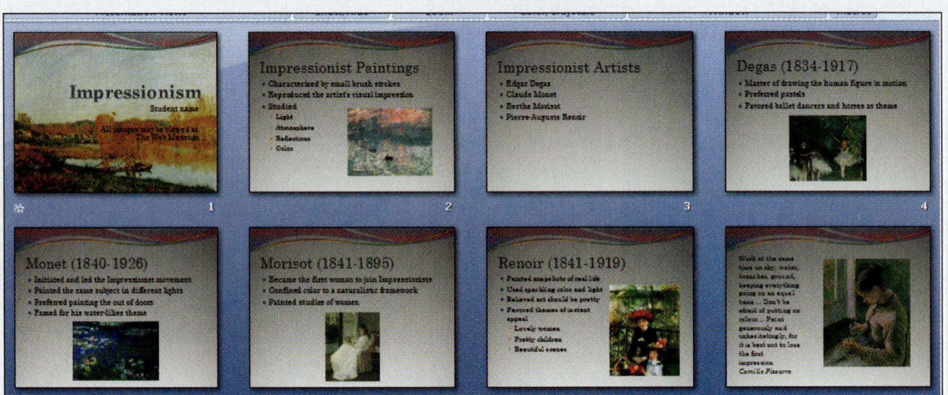

Figure 4.46 Impressionism Presentation

3 A Visit to the Zoo

As a first-grade teacher, you enjoy taking your class on field trips. Each year you take your students and parent helpers to the local zoo. The zoo has an excellent education program and is very supportive. The day your class visits, a zookeeper takes your students to specific animals and gives presentations on the animal, its habitat, its diet, and other fun facts. The keeper also teaches the children the difference between skin, fur, feathers, and scales. Because the zookeeper likes to keep the children involved by asking them questions they know the answers to now and then, the keeper asks you to teach the students about animal facts before the visit. You prepare a presentation about the coverings of some of the animals you took pictures of during last year's visit to the zoo. Refer to Figure 4.48 as you complete this activity.

a. Create a New Photo Album using the zoo photographs located in the *chap4_mid3_zoo_images* folder in your student files.

b. Use a layout of 4 pictures per album page.

...continued on Next Page

c. Because you want to include the type of covering for each animal on each slide, you must include a text box for each type of animal. Insert a text box for each animal type and use the Move Up and Move Down arrows to position the boxes for each album page (see Figure 4.47). Slide 4 should have a text box and three monkey house images. Slide 5 should have a text box, the rhinoceros image, a text box, and the elephant image. Slide 6 should have the text box, the turkey image, a text box, and the zebra image.

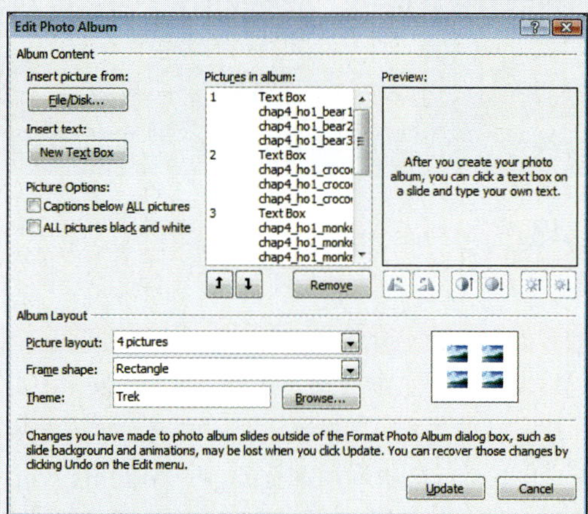

Figure 4.47

d. Use Rectangle Frames.

e. Apply the Trek theme.

f. Enter the following in the appropriate slides:

- **Black Bears are covered with fur.**
- **Crocodiles are covered with scales.**
- **Monkeys are covered with hair.**
- **Monkeys eat fruit, leaves, nuts, berries, eggs, and insects.**
- **A Rhinoceros is covered with grey skin.**
- **Elephants are covered with extremely tough skin.**
- **Turkeys are covered with feathers.**
- **Zebras are covered with striped hair.**

g. Compress the pictures for screen use.

h. Change the subtitle on Slide 1 to **Animals and Their Coverings**, and then change the title to **OUR ZOO VISIT!**

i. Record a narration for the slide show by reading the text on each slide. Do not save the slide timings.

TROUBLESHOOTING: If you do not have a microphone, you will not be able to record the narration. In that case, skip the narration recording and insert a sound from the Clip Organizer in each slide.

j. Insert the movie *chap4_mid3_zoo* in Slide 1 and have the movie start with a click.

k. Reposition the subtitle and title on Slide 1 so that they are not blocked by the movie.

l. Check the spelling in your presentation and then proofread carefully to catch any errors that Spell Checking may have missed.

m. Create a Notes and Handouts Header and Footer with the date, your name in the header, and your instructor's name and your class in the footer.

n. Save the **chap4_mid3_zoo_solution** presentation and close it.

...continued on Next Page

Figure 4.48 Zoo Presentation

4 ESL Tutor

As a tutor of ESL (English as a Second Language) students, you would like to introduce the students to the English names of common musical instruments. Your slide presentation will feature one instrument per slide, with narration of the name of the instrument and a sound button that will play the instrument's sound. The photographs and sounds of the instruments are available from Microsoft Office Online. This exercise requires a computer with a sound card, speakers or headphones, and a microphone. Refer to Figure 4.49 for an example slide.

a. Open *chap4_mid4_esl* and save it as **chap4_mid4_esl_solution**.

b. Move to **Slide 2**.

c. Use the Clip Organizer to access the Microsoft Office Online Web site.

d. Narrow your search to Photographs and then search for a photograph of a violin.

e. Mark a photograph of a violin named *j0382780.jpg* for download by clicking in the check box.

f. Change the search filter to sounds. The word *violin* should remain in the Search box. Listen to the violin sounds by clicking on the icons. Find the *Happy Violins* and mark it for download.

g. Continue by marking the following photographs and sounds for download:

Search Word	Photograph Name	Sound Name
Drums	j0402397.jpg	Drum Clash 2
Flute	j0385372.jpg	Single Flute
Harps	j0175036.jpg	Harp Up
Cymbals	j0382767.jpg	Cymbals Tag
Horn	j0382773.jpg	Short Horn Part 5

h. Click **Download 12 Items**, and then click **Download Now** to download the selected clips to the Clip Organizer. Close Microsoft Office Online.

i. Use the Clip Organizer to locate the violin photograph you downloaded and then insert the image on Slide 2.

j. Decrease the height of the violin photograph to 4.5 inches. Center the violin photograph under the title.

...continued on Next Page

k. Apply the picture style Perspective Shadow, White to the violin photograph.

l. Insert the Happy Violins sound. Set the sound to start When Clicked. Move the icon from the middle of the photograph to the lower-right side of the slide.

m. Repeat Steps i–l for each remaining instrument slide using the appropriate photograph and sound clip for each slide.

n. Compress all of pictures to Screen Target Output.

o. Move to **Slide 1**. Click the **Slide Show tab** and click **Record Narration**.

p. Click the **Set Microphone Level** button and check the sound by speaking a few words into the microphone. Move the slider to adjust the level to green. Click **OK**.

q. When the full-screen slide appears, slowly and carefully read the first slide out loud into the microphone. Click to advance to the next slide.

r. Read the instrument name slowly and clearly twice. Click to advance to the next slide. Repeat this action for each slide. At the End of the slide show screen, click to exit.

s. Don't save the slide timings.

t. Create a Notes and Handouts Header and Footer with the date, your name in the header, and your instructor's name and your class in the footer.

u. View the slide show and test each sound button. Save *chap4_mid4_esl_solution* and close the file.

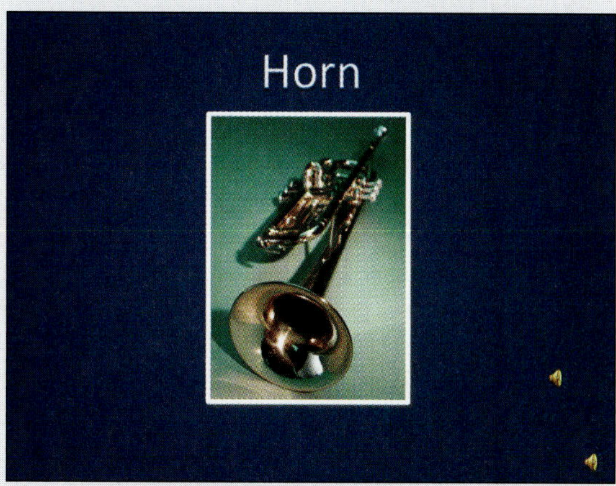

Figure 4.49 ESL Presentation

5 Birth Announcement

A close friend and her husband recently had a new baby. The father is an extremely accomplished athlete and is currently attending the university on a football scholarship. He's delighted with his "future running back." Sherry, the talented mother of your friend created handmade birth announcements that also served as an invitation to an "end zone celebration"—a luau for family and friends to meet the new baby. You attended the celebration of life and took pictures with your digital camera. You decide to record the event by putting the photographs in a PowerPoint album, print the album on heavy specialty paper, and then bind the album for the baby's first scrapbook. After viewing it, your friend's husband asks you for a copy so he can e-mail the presentation to family members who live in Tonga and were not able to attend the celebration. You modified Microsoft's Contemporary Photo Album template to resemble the invitation your friend's mother created. In this activity you will create the content, insert the photographs, and use Microsoft's picture tools to finish the project. Refer to Figure 4.50 as you complete this activity.

...continued on Next Page

a. Open *chap4_mid5_announcement* and then save it as **chap4_mid5_ announcement_solution**. Use the announcement photographs located in the *chap4_mid5_announcement_images* folder in your student files.

b. Move to **Slide 1**, modify the Title placeholder to read **IT'S A BOY!**, and then center-align the text.

c. Search the Clip Organizer for the old leather football shown in Figure 4.50. Insert it and then change the scale to 200% of its original size. Position the image horizontally at 1.83" from the Top Left Corner. Position it vertically at .13" from the Top Left Corner. Use the Set Transparent Color tool on the white background of the football so that the background shows through.

d. Move to **Slide 2** and insert *chap4_mid5_announcement1.jpg* in the picture placeholder. Enter the following text in the text placeholder, pressing Enter after each comma: **Casanova Hamani, August 22, 2008, 4:45 p.m., 6 lbs 2 oz, 19.5"**. Center-align the text and change the line spacing to **2**. Change the font for the baby's first and middle names to 28 pts.

e. Move to **Slide 3** and search the Clip Organizer using **background** as the keyword and locate the image of the lawn with a leaf on the lower left side. Insert the image and then set the image width to 10" and the height to 5.25". Position the background horizontally at 0" from the Top Left Corner. Position it vertically at 1" from the Top Left Corner.

f. Use the Crop tool to remove the leaf from the background and then arrange the background so it is aligned in the center of the slide.

g. Create a rectangle 5" wide by 4" high and apply the Intense Effect–Accent 1 Shape Style. Change the shape fill color to the Dark Blue, Text 2, Darker 50% theme color.

h. Type the following information inside it, breaking lines where appropriate: **Our future running back scored his touchdown August 22, 2008! Come join his fans in an End Zone Celebration Luau. Huddle up: August 29, 2008, 5 p.m. Dave and Alison's Home.**

i. Position the rectangle horizontally at 2.5" from the Top Left Corner. Position it vertically at 1.67" from the Top Left Corner.

j. Move to **Slide 4**. Insert *chap4_mid5_announcement2*, *chap4_mid5_announcement3*, and *chap4_mid5_announcement4* in the placeholders. Apply the Metal Oval picture style to the images of the mother and father and apply the Metal Rounded Rectangle to the image of the baby. Replace the text in the text placeholders. Type **Mother: Alison, Baby: Casanova, Father: Dave** in their respective placeholders. Center-align the text in the placeholders.

k. In **Slide 5**, insert *chap4_mid5_announcement5* in the top left corner. Change the caption to read **Mom, Dad, and cousins**. Insert *chap4_mid5_announcement6* in the top right corner. Change the caption to read **Grandma and Grandpa**. Insert *chap4_mid5_announcement7* in the bottom right corner. Change the caption to **Grandpa**. Insert *chap4_mid5_announcement8* in the bottom left corner. Change the caption to **Grandpa and Grandma**. Select the image of Grandma and Grandpa and increase the contrast 20%.

l. In **Slide 6**, starting in the top left and continuing in a clockwise order, insert *chap4_mid5_announcement9*, *chap4_mid5_announcement10*, *chap4_mid5_announcement11*, *chap4_mid5_announcement12*, and *chap4_mid5_announcement13*. Select the image of the grandfather and uncle and decrease the brightness by 10%.

m. Compress the images at print quality.

n. In **Slide 6**, create a WordArt using the Fill–Accent 2, Warm Matte Bevel style. Enter the text **End Zone Luau**. Apply the Double Wave 2 transform special effect. Change the text direction to **Rotate Left 90°**. Drag the WordArt to the right into the area not covered by text.

o. Create a Notes and Handouts Header and Footer with the date, your name in the header, and your instructor's name and your class in the footer.

p. Save the *chap4_mid5_announcement_solution* file.

q. Compress the images at E-mail quality.

r. Save the presentation as **chap4_mid5_announcement2_solution** and close it.

...continued on Next Page

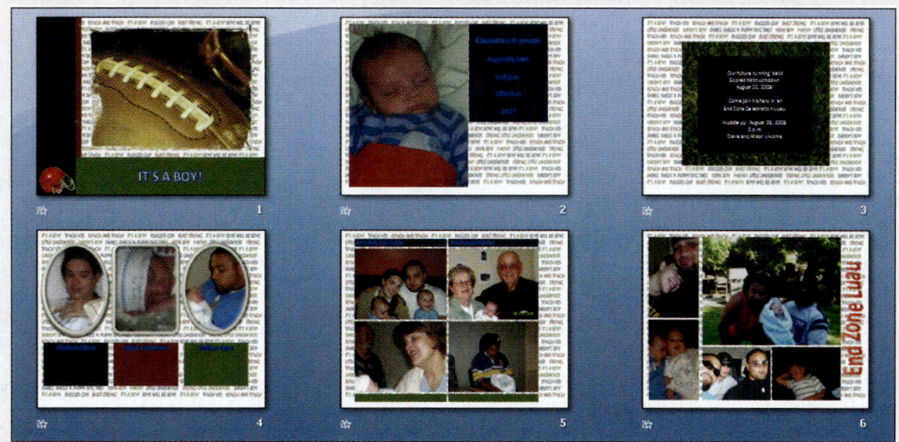

Figure 4.50 Announcement Presentation

Capstone Exercise

In Chapter 2 and Chapter 3, you developed a presentation on Waterwise Landscaping for your neighbors in your southwestern subdivision. While on a drive with your family, you saw several excellent examples of zeroscaping and captured the images on your digital camera. You are anxious to add these examples to the Waterwise presentation you have been creating. You also have been in communication with a company that you found on the Web that specializes in xeriscaping. The company, XericUtah (xericutah.com), has given you permission to use images from its Web site showing its work and demonstrating how beautiful xeriscaping can be. In this capstone exercise you will complete the Waterwise landscaping presentation.

Insert Pictures

You need to open the presentation that you already started, rename the file, and save. You insert pictures, crop, size, and then position the images.

a. Locate the file named *chap4_cap_landscape*, and then save it as **chap4_cap_landscape_solution**.

b. Create a Notes and Handouts Header and Footer with the date, your name in the header, and your instructor's name and your class in the footer.

c. Move to **Slide 4**, and then click the **Insert Picture** button in the large content placeholder. Navigate to the location of your student files and open the *chap4_cap_landscape_images* folder. Insert *chap4_cap_1landscape.jpg*.

d. Move to **Slide 5**. To create room for pictures, drag the right side of the text placeholder to the 1" position on the horizontal ruler.

e. Insert *chap4_cap_2landscape.jpg*.

f. Select the picture and activate the Crop tool.

g. Crop the green power pole from the picture (crop the left side of the image to the –3" mark on the horizontal ruler).

h. Change the width of the picture to **3"** and let the height adjust automatically.

i. Set the horizontal position to **6"** from the **Top Left Corner** and the vertical position to **4.67"** from the **Top Left Corner**.

j. Insert *chap4_cap_3landscape.jpg* in Slide 5.

k. Change the width of the image to **3"**. Let the height adjust automatically.

l. Set the horizontal position to **6"** from the **Top Left Corner** and the vertical position on slide options to **1.83"** from the **Top Left Corner**.

m. Save the *chap4_cap_landscape_solution* presentation.

Apply and Modify a Picture Style

After displaying the slide show, you decide that the pictures you inserted in Slide 5 would stand out better if they had a frame. You decide to frame the pictures by applying a Picture Style and then modifying the style.

a. On **Slide 5**, select the top picture and apply the Beveled Oval, Black picture style.

b. Apply the Picture Effect **Preset 2**.

c. Use the Format Painter to copy the effects applied to the top photograph to the bottom photograph.

d. Save the *chap4_cap_landscape_solution* presentation.

Adjust Brightness and Contrast and Compress

You insert another example of zeroscaping in your slide show, but notice it seems faded and washed out. You use the Picture Tools to adjust the brightness and contrast tools to adjust the image. After making the changes you apply an onscreen compression to all photographs.

a. Move to **Slide 7** and then insert *chap4_cap_4landscape.jpg*.

b. Decrease the image brightness to **–20%**.

c. Increase the image contrast to **+20%**.

d. Scale the height of the image to **40%**.

e. Drag the image to the bottom center of the slide.

f. Compress the images for screen output.

g. Save the *chap4_cap_landscape_solution* presentation.

Create a Background from a Picture

The title slide of your slide show is rather bland, so you determine to add a picture as a background.

a. Move to **Slide 1** and click the **Design tab**.

b. Access the Format Background options so that you can select a picture fill.

c. Insert *chap4_cap_5landscape.jpg*.

d. Save the *chap4_cap_landscape_solution* presentation.

Use the Internet as a Resource

For examples of xeriscaping you turn to the Internet and use XericUtah (*xericutah.com*) as your resource. Xeric's "goal is to create beautiful, drought-tolerant landscapes that conserve water, bring wildlife to our gardens, and breed aesthetically pleasing landscapes that appeal to all walks of life." Ryan Phillips of XericUtah has given you permission to include photos from the Web site in your presentation.

a. Connect to the Internet and go to xericutah.com. Click the link to jump to the *about us* page. Save the picture on the right side of the Web site as *xericutah1.jpg*. Images might change or be in different locations on the Web site.

...continued on Next Page

b. Insert the *xericutah.1.jpg* file in the placeholder on **Slide 8**.

c. Move to **Slide 9** and then return to the XericUtah Web site. Navigate to the *portfolio showcase* page.

d. Click the first image on Row 1 of the portfolio pieces and then position your pointer over the enlarged image on the right side of the screen. Right-click and select **Copy**. Return to the slide show and right-click, and then select **Paste**. Drag the image to the lower-left side of the slide.

e. Copy the enlargement of the third image on Row 2 of the portfolio pieces, paste it in Slide 9, and then position it in the lower middle of the slide.

f. Copy the second image on Row 3 of the portfolio pieces and then paste it in Slide 9. Drag the image to the lower-right side of the slide.

g. Select the three images, scale them to 50%, align them at their bottom, and distribute them horizontally.

h. Move to **Slide 10** and then return to the XericUtah Web site. Navigate to the *xeric plants* page and copy the image of the flowers on the left side of the screen.

i. Paste the image onto Slide 10 and drag the picture to the bottom of the slide.

j. Duplicate the image and then flip the duplicate horizontally.

k. Drag the image so the groups of white flowers overlap and the two images appear to be one, and then align their bottoms.

l. Group the two images of white flowers so they become one large bar across the bottom of the slide. Size the group to 10".

m. Search the Clip Organizer using the keyword **Petals**, and locate the image of the yellow flower. (See Figure 4.51 to help select the correct flower.) Insert the clip on Slide 11.

n. Size the image to 4" x 4" and then drag the image to the lower part of the slide in approximately the center.

o. Save the *chap4_cap_landscape_solution* presentation.

Insert a Movie

You need to create a Resource page for your presentation. Not only will this give credit to your sources, it will give your viewers the Web sites to visit for more information later. Please remember that giving credit to your source **does not** mean you are released from copyright requirements. After creating the page, you insert an animated movie clip from the Clip Organizer to recapture the attention of the audience if it is lagging. You select a clip that relates to planting.

a. Insert a slide after Slide 13 using the **Title and Content** layout.

b. Type **Resources** in the Title placeholder.

c. Click in the Content Placeholder and then type **Office of Community Services**, press **Shift+Enter**, type **Fort Lewis College**, press **Shift+Enter**, and type **http://ocs.fortlewis.edu/waterwise**.

d. Press **Enter** twice, and then type **XericUtah Landscape Design**, press **Shift+Enter**, and type **http://xericutah.com**.

e. Search the Clip Organizer for a movie using **digging** as the keyword for your search.

f. Insert the clip of the man and woman planting a tree by the title.

g. Save the *chap4_cap_landscape_solution* presentation.

Insert Sound

Your presentation is almost done, but you decide that a soft background music clip that plays continuously on Slide 1 while your neighbors enter the presentation room would help set the mood. You use the Clip Organizer to locate a soft sound clip and then you modify it to play continuously in Slide 1 and discontinue playing when you click to advance to Slide 2.

a. Search the Clip Organizer using the keyword **soft** and locate the sound clip *Soweto Underscore*.

b. Insert *Soweto Underscore* into Slide 1 and have it start automatically.

c. Set the sound options to hide the sound icon during the show.

d. Activate the **Loop Until Stopped** sound option.

e. Save the *chap4_cap_landscape_solution* presentation.

Add a Transition and Animations

To add interest to your slide show, you decide to add a transition to advance from one slide to another. To relieve you of having to constantly click to have slide objects appear, you decide to add animations. While serving as a reminder of a skill previously learned, this step completes the basic process for preparing a slide show for a presentation: create content, select design options, add objects that enhance your message, and finally add a transition and animations.

a. In Slide 1, select the **Fade Through Black** transition and apply to all slides.

b. Select the SmartArt graphic on Slide 2 and then set the animation to **Fade**, **One by one**.

...continued on Next Page

c. Select the top SmartArt graphic on Slide 3 and then set the animation to **Fly In**, **One by one**.

d. Select the bottom SmartArt graphic on Slide 3 and then set the animation to **Fly In**, **By level one by one.**

e. Select the SmartArt graphic on Slide 13 and set the animation to **Wipe**, **By level at once.**

f. Save the *chap4_cap_landscape_solution* presentation and close it.

Figure 4.51 Waterwise Presentation

Create a Photo Album

After you make your presentation to your neighbors, they are intrigued by the idea of xeriscaping but would like copies of your images to review at home. You determine the quickest way to provide them with all your images, not just those used in the presentation, is to prepare a photo album and then print copies.

a. Create a New Photo Album using the images in the *chap4_cap_landscape_images* folder.

b. Select *chap4_cap_4landscape.jpg* in the list of pictures.

c. Click the **Increase Contrast** button two times.

d. Click the **Decrease Brightness** button two times.

e. Select *4 pictures* for your album layout.

f. Use Rounded Rectangle for the **Frame Shape**.

g. Apply the **Apex** theme to the presentation.

h. Apply **Background Style 5**.

i. Enter your name as the subtitle on Slide 1. Apply the **Wipe, All at once** animation.

j. Create a Notes and Handouts Header and Footer with your name in the header, and your instructor's name and your class in the footer.

k. Save the album as **chap4_cap_landscape2_solution** and close it.

Figure 4.52 Waterwise Album

Mini Cases

Use the rubric following the case as a guide to evaluate your work, but keep in mind that your instructor may impose additional grading criteria or use a different standard to judge your work.

Multimedia Greeting Card Presentation

GENERAL CASE

Lately, you have noticed one of your friends or coworkers seems a little "down." You decide that a quick multimedia PowerPoint slide show will show that you care. Collect photographs, animations, and sounds from Internet resources (remember the copyright information). The solution to this problem is a three-to-five-slide presentation that shows you are thinking about your friend. Include at least two photographs, one movie animation, and one sound. Save your file as **chap4_mc1_greeting_solution** and close the presentation. Figure 4.53 shows one possible solution to this task.

Figure 4.53 Sample Solution to Mini Case 1

Performance Elements	Exceeds Expectations	Meets Expectations	Below Expectations
Organization	Slides follow a logical sequence with the multimedia supporting the message.	Presentation is easy to follow.	The multimedia elements are not put in a logical order and appear to be haphazardly placed.
Visual Aspects	The multimedia elements are appealing and enhance the presentation. They are consistent and blend in with the message.	Clip art is related to the topic. Animation enhances the presentation.	The multimedia does not enhance the message. The theme of the multimedia is confusing. Sounds are not well controlled.
Layout	The layout is visually pleasing and contributes to understanding the greeting. The layout is cohesive.	The layout shows structure and multimedia elements enhance the presentation.	The layout is cluttered and confusing. Understanding of the message is lost.
Mechanics	Presentation has no errors in spelling, grammar, word usage, or punctuation. No typographical errors present.	Presentation has no more than one error in spelling, grammar, word usage, or punctuation.	Presentation readability is impaired due to repeated errors in spelling, grammar, word usage, or punctuation. Multiple typographical errors.

...continued on Next Page

Netiquette Presentation

RESEARCH CASE

You have been invited back to speak about etiquette on the Internet. A surprising number of senior citizens are sending and receiving e-mail. Since this activity is new to these people, they want to make sure that they don't offend anyone. To prepare for your presentation, you complete Internet research on netiquette. Since you know how to add multimedia to presentations, include at least one movie animation. Collect images of computer users, especially older people, to add interest to your slides. Save your file as **chap4_mc2_netiquette_solution** and close the presentation. Figure 4.54 shows one possible solution to this task.

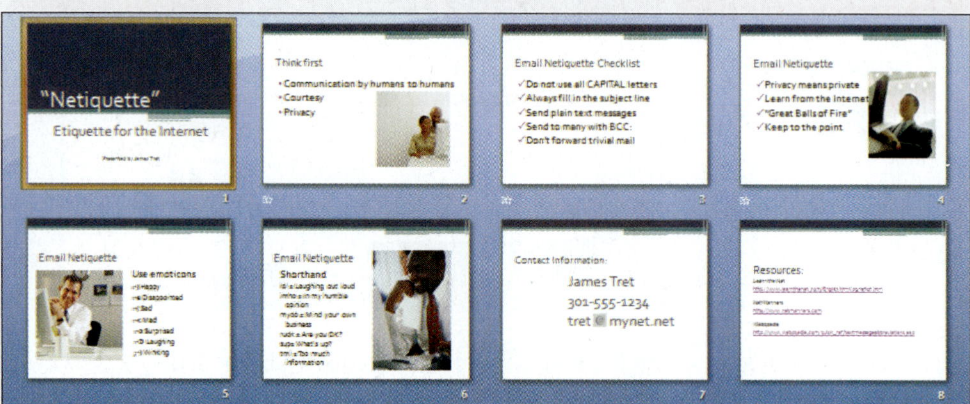

Figure 4.54 Sample Solution to Mini Case 2

Performance Elements	Exceeds Expectations	Meets Expectations	Below Expectations
Organization	Slides follow a logical sequence with the multimedia supporting the message.	Presentation indicates some research has taken place and that information was included in the content.	The multimedia elements are not placed in a logical order. The message is lost because the multimedia is distracting.
Visual Aspects	The multimedia elements are appealing and enhance the presentation. They are consistent and blend in with the message. Text is easy to read.	The multimedia elements are consistent with the message.	The multimedia does not enhance the message. The theme of the multimedia is confusing. Text is difficult to read due to size or color.
Layout	The layout is visually pleasing and contributes to understanding the topic. White space, photographs, and the movie are cohesive.	The layout shows some structure, but placement of some headings, subheadings, bullet points, multimedia elements, and/or white space can be improved.	The layout is cluttered and confusing. The multimedia elements detract from understanding.
Mechanics	Presentation has no errors in spelling, grammar, word usage, or punctuation. No typographical errors present. Sources of research are shown on an ending slide.	Presentation has no more than one error in spelling, grammar, word usage, or punctuation. Bullet points are inconsistent in one slide.	Presentation readability is impaired due to repeated errors in spelling, grammar, word usage, or punctuation. Multiple typographical errors. No resource page is included.

...continued on Next Page

Humane Society Fundraiser

DISASTER RECOVERY

On weekends you volunteer at the local humane society. You walk the dogs and play with the cats. One day when you arrived, you noticed the manager struggling with PowerPoint. The manager was trying to create a slide show that would showcase animals in positive ways to play during the annual humane society fundraiser. You offer to complete the task for the manager because you know that a PowerPoint presentation is the solution. Download photographs from Microsoft Office Online and create a 10- to 15-slide photo presentation. Include enhancements such as framing and themes to make the presentation professional looking. Save the new presentation as **chap4_mc3_humane_solution** and close the presentation. Figure 4.55 shows one possible solution to this task.

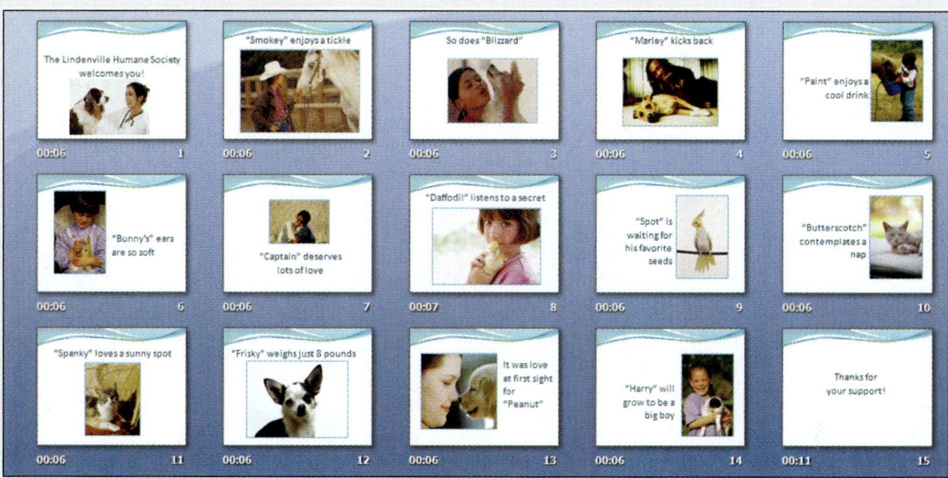

Figure 4.55 Sample Presentation for Mini Case 3

Performance Elements	Exceeds Expectations	Meets Expectations	Below Expectations
Organization	Sufficient number of photographs and slides to make the photo album interesting. Sequence of the photos leads from one type of animal to another with smooth transitions between slides.	A variety of animals are represented in the photographs.	Fewer than 10 photographs in the photo album. Photographs are not sequenced in a logical way.
Visual Aspects	There is a consistent visual theme. The contrast and brightness of the photographs is pleasing. Frame shapes enhance the photographs.	Text is readable. Frame shapes used.	The visual theme is not apparent. No frame shapes were used to enhance the photographs. Appealing photographs were not included.
Layout	The layout is visually pleasing and draws attention to the animals. Captions are added to increase the appeal of the animals.	Layout of photographs displays photographs adequately.	The layout is cluttered and confusing. Captions are not included.
Mechanics	Any added text has no errors in spelling, grammar, word usage, or punctuation. No typographical errors present.	Added text has no more than one error in spelling, grammar, word usage, or punctuation.	Any added text has impaired readability due to repeated errors in spelling, grammar, word usage, or punctuation. Multiple typographical errors.

chapter 1 | **Windows Vista**

Getting Started with Windows Vista

Objectives

After you read this chapter, you will be able to:

1. Describe Windows Vista versions and features **(page 1079)**.
2. Identify components of the Windows Vista interface **(page 1080)**.
3. Work with windows and dialog boxes **(page 1087)**.
4. Use Help and Support **(page 1091)**.
5. Manage files and folders in Windows Explorer **(page 1100)**.
6. Create, rename, and delete folders **(page 1102)**.
7. Work with files **(page 1105)**.
8. Select, copy, and move multiple files and folders **(page 1106)**.
9. Use Windows Search **(page 1114)**.
10. Manage the Recycle Bin **(page 1117)**.
11. Change computer settings through the Control Panel **(page 1118)**.

Hands-On Exercises

Exercises	Skills Covered
1. WORKING WITH WINDOWS (page 1095)	• Manage One or More Windows • Arrange Desktop Icons • Modify the Start Menu • Use Help and Support
2. WORKING WITH FILES AND FOLDERS (page 1109) **Save as:** chap1_ho2_east_kansas_highlights.rtf	• Create Folders and Subfolders • Delete a Folder • Create and Save a File • Make Backup Copies
3. WORKING WITH THE RECYCLE BIN, WINDOWS SEARCH, AND CONTROL PANEL (page 1126) **Save as:** chap1_ho3_current_price_list.rtf	• Place Files in the Recycle Bin • Manage the Recycle Bin • Use Windows Search • Work with the Control Panel

CASE STUDY

Helping Hands Outreach

Helping Hands Outreach is a nonprofit organization that collects clothing and non-perishable food items for distribution to needy families. Helping Hands operates out of three cities—Hanover, West Memphis, and Adamsville—with each branch responsible for its own inventory. Typically, inventory is subdivided into two categories—clothing and food. You have been hired to help consolidate the files from each of the branches on one computer system, while maintaining separate records of each branch's inventory. A consulting firm will develop a

Case Study

collection of files for each Helping Hands outlet, and you need to design a folder structure that logically organizes the files. You should ensure that the files are available, no matter what natural or man-made disaster might affect the physical computer housing. Therefore, your job entails not only file and folder organization, but also developing a backup strategy.

Your Assignment

- Read the chapter, paying close attention to the description of creating folders and subfolders.
- Design a folder structure that is appropriate for maintaining the database files described above. Given the organization of Helping Hands, you should design a structure that will place the files in a logical arrangement.
- Use Windows Explorer to create appropriately named folders according to your design.
- Develop a plan for backing up the folders and files. Give careful consideration to where the files will physically be placed (on what type of disk media). Using WordPad or another word processor, create a report outlining your backup plan. Include in your report a description of an appropriate folder structure for maintaining the organization's database files. Save the report as **chap1_case1_helping_hands**. Print the report.

Basics of Windows Vista

Windows Vista is the newest version of the Windows operating system.

Most new computers are configured with ***Windows Vista***, the January 2007 operating system release. Therefore, it is worth your time to explore it and learn about its computer management and security features. Microsoft has put a lot of effort into developing the most stable and secure operating system yet—one that is loaded with extra features and easy to use.

(As you consider purchasing a new computer, it is very likely that your computer will be configured with Windows Vista.)

This section explores the basics of Windows Vista. First, you learn about the different versions of Windows Vista. You also explore the Vista interface, identify components in windows and dialog boxes, and use the Help and Support feature.

Describing Windows Vista Versions and Features

Windows Defender is the Windows Vista spyware-detection program.

Windows Mail is an e-mail program that includes a junk mail filter.

Internet Explorer 7 is a Web browser that features tabbed browsing and security enhancements.

Windows Firewall blocks both unauthorized incoming Internet traffic and outgoing traffic.

Security Center is a control center that enables you to check and manage security settings.

You can choose from five versions of Windows Vista—Vista Home Basic, Vista Home Premium, Vista Business, Vista Ultimate, and Vista Enterprise. The choice you make will depend upon whether you are a home user, a multimedia enthusiast, or a high-end business user. Keep in mind that each version is priced according to its capability—you will pay more for a more powerful Vista version. Table 1.1 summarizes Windows Vista versions.

As the name suggests, Vista Home Basic focuses on standard activities such as surfing the Internet and word processing. With limited multimedia functionality and only a two-dimensional desktop, this version is a bare-bones operating system. Vista Home Basic, however, addresses the productivity, security, and entertainment goals of most home users because it includes Windows Defender, Windows Mail, Internet Explorer 7, Windows Firewall, a revamped Security Center, and Vista's enhanced parental controls. ***Windows Defender*** is Vista's antispyware program; it detects and quarantines spyware found on your computer. Spyware is software that collects personal information about you or changes computer settings without your informed consent. ***Windows Mail*** is an e-mail program with a junk mail filter. ***Internet Explorer 7*** (IE7) is a Web browser that enables you to display Web pages. IE7 features tabbed browsing and security enhancements, such as a Phishing Filter. ***Windows Firewall*** provides bidirectional support, blocking both unauthorized incoming Internet traffic and outgoing traffic. The ***Security Center*** is a control center that enables you to check for security updates, your computer's security status, manage automatic updates, and check the firewall status.

Table 1.1 Windows Vista Versions

Version	Description
Vista Home Basic	Meets the needs of most home computer users.
Vista Home Premium	Includes everything in Vista Home Basic, plus additional multimedia, mobility, and interface features.
Vista Business	Focuses on corporate needs, such as domain support, network protocols, and mobility.
Vista Enterprise	Includes everything in Vista Business, plus such features as drive encryption and multilanguage support.
Vista Ultimate	Combines all features of Vista Home Premium and Vista Enterprise, plus enhanced game performance and custom themes.

Additional features include Windows Movie Maker, Windows Media Player, Windows Photo Gallery, Windows Calendar, Windows Sidebar, and Windows Search. ***Windows Movie Maker*** is a program that enables you to create, edit, and share home movies on your computer. ***Windows Media Player 11*** is a multimedia program that enables you to work with music and movie files. ***Windows Photo Gallery*** imports images and videos, and provides tools for correcting and enhancing picture files. ***Windows Calendar*** is an organizer program that enables you to create and view appointments, and schedule tasks. ***Windows Sidebar*** appears on the right side of the Vista desktop, displaying links to local weather, stock quotes, and other news items. ***Windows Search*** is a utility program that provides an easy method for you to search for items on your computer, performing "as-you-type" searches, narrowing the results with each character that you type.

Windows Movie Maker is a program that enables you to create, edit, and share home movies on your computer.

Windows Media Player 11 is a multimedia program enabling you to work with music and movie files.

Windows Photo Gallery provides tools for correcting and enhancing picture files.

Windows Calendar is an organizer program that enables you to create and view appointments and schedule tasks.

Windows Sidebar displays links to local weather, stock quotes, and other news.

Windows Search is a utility that helps you search for items on your computer.

Vista Home Premium features Windows Vista's ***Aero Glass*** shell (a graphical user interface that includes transparencies and animations), enhanced multimedia capability, and advanced networking capabilities (peer-to-peer networks and multiple-computer parental controls). This version satisfies the computing goals of networked households, multimedia enthusiasts, and notebook users.

Aero Glass is an interface design that includes transparency effects and gives a slight three-dimensional shape to Windows features.

Vista Business includes corporate features such as built-in protection against malware and tools to make backing up files easier. With support for domains, multiple network protocols, Remote Desktop, and file and folder encryption, Vista Business is a complete business operating system. ***Remote Desktop*** is a feature that enables a computer to be run remotely from another Windows computer. Vista Business does not support enhanced multimedia activities.

Remote Desktop is a feature that enables a computer to be run remotely from another Windows computer.

Vista Ultimate combines the best of Vista Home Premium and Vista Business, maintaining the security required of business applications while supporting multimedia enjoyment. This version offers enhanced game performance, custom themes, and access to online subscription services.

Vista Enterprise includes all features of Vista Business, while facilitating drive encryption and enabling you to run old programs from earlier versions of Windows within the Enterprise environment. ***Encryption*** is the process of obscuring and protecting data, such as credit card numbers, to make them unreadable without decoding software or knowledge. Vista Enterprise is only available to volume licensing customers.

Encryption is the process of obscuring data to make it unreadable without decoding software or knowledge.

Identifying Components of the Windows Vista Interface

When you turn on the computer, you might be prompted to click a username, and enter a password if you have several user accounts created for your computer. Several individuals can share the same computer, each with a unique account with certain privileges. Each user maintains his or her individual desktop settings and is allowed a level of access designated by the computer administrator. If the computer is yours, you are the administrator. You need administrator privileges to install software or make configuration changes.

Explore the Desktop

After turning on the computer, selecting your username, and entering your password (if needed), Windows Vista loads. The first thing that you will notice about Windows Vista is the beauty of its interface, especially if the Aero Glass shell is in use. The Vista ***desktop***, the basic interface of the operating system, contains icons and a taskbar. The desktop, appearing after you boot up your computer and respond to username and password screens, offers a sweeping, transparent-glass effect that is very attractive (see Figure 1.1).

The ***desktop*** contains icons and a taskbar.

Figure 1.1 Windows Vista

Although its clarity and high-definition graphics are appealing, the desktop is much more than a simple interface through which you communicate with the operating system. It is also used for starting programs, displaying windows, managing files and folders, troubleshooting problems, and networking with other computers. Open windows have a drop shadow effect, and when you hover the mouse over a window button, the button "lights up." If Aero Glass is not in use, windows are much less translucent, with no special effects.

An ***icon*** is a pictorial element representing a program, file, Web site, or shortcut.

Just as you work at a desk at work or school, you can work on a computer desktop, which is the screen that appears each time you turn on your computer. ***Icons***, or small pictures that are displayed on the desktop, represent programs, files, or other items related to your computer. Using the mouse and clicking the icons, you can open programs or projects, similar to working with tasks on your desk. And just as you can misplace items on your desk, you can have so many computer projects on your computer desktop that you lose track of them.

Display the Windows Sidebar

Gadgets are mini-applications that display on a Windows Sidebar.

The ***taskbar*** is the horizontal bar that enables you to move among open windows and provides access to system resources.

The Windows Vista interface is more than just pretty. It includes productivity elements, such as the Windows Sidebar, that make it easy to view up-to-date information and to get a quick summary of window contents. To open the Windows Sidebar, click Start, position the mouse over All Programs, select Accessories, and then select Windows Sidebar. As Figure 1.1 shows, a Windows Sidebar contains ***gadgets***, which are actually mini-applications for such tasks as checking the weather or viewing a stock ticker. Windows Vista includes about a dozen gadgets, but more are available online. To open the Gadget Gallery, click the + at the top of the Sidebar. Open or minimized windows are displayed on the ***taskbar***, which is positioned along the bottom of the Vista desktop.

Customize the Desktop

Typical icons displayed on a desktop include the Recycle Bin, Computer, Network, and Control Panel. Although the default desktop includes only the Recycle Bin, you can customize the desktop to include other icons. Right-click the desktop, select Personalize, and click Change desktop icons. In the Desktop Icon Settings dialog box, select from the list of desktop icons, as shown in Figure 1.2, and click OK.

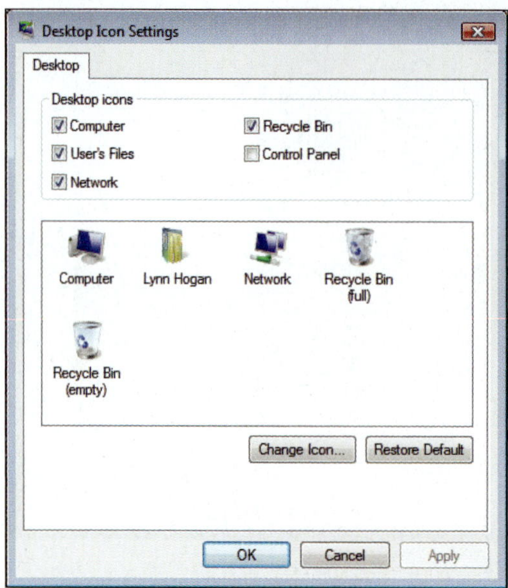

Figure 1.2 Desktop Icon Settings Dialog Box

Work with the Taskbar

The ***Start button*** provides access to programs and other system resources.

The ***Quick Launch toolbar*** contains program icons, making it possible to open programs with a single click.

The ***Notification area***, on the right side of the taskbar, displays icons for background programs and system processes.

The taskbar is located along the bottom of the desktop (see Figure 1.3). It serves several purposes, one of which is to let you know which programs are currently running in memory. It also provides a clock and a ***Start button***, which is shaped like an orb, from which you can access programs and other Windows features. You can display a ***Quick Launch toolbar*** on the taskbar, giving you one-click access to commonly used programs. If a Quick Launch toolbar does not appear on your taskbar, you can display it by right-clicking an empty area of the taskbar, pointing to Toolbars, and selecting Quick Launch toolbar. If a chevron (double arrow) appears beside the Quick Launch toolbar, click it to view more programs. The ***Notification area*** gives information on wireless connections, volume control, and programs running in the background (such as antivirus software). The Notification area prompts you to take action, such as updating Windows or safely removing hardware. If the time is incorrect on your system, you can adjust the clock by right-clicking the clock on the taskbar and selecting Adjust Date/Time. In the Date and Time dialog box, you can change the date and time and you can also change the time zone. After making the necessary changes, click OK.

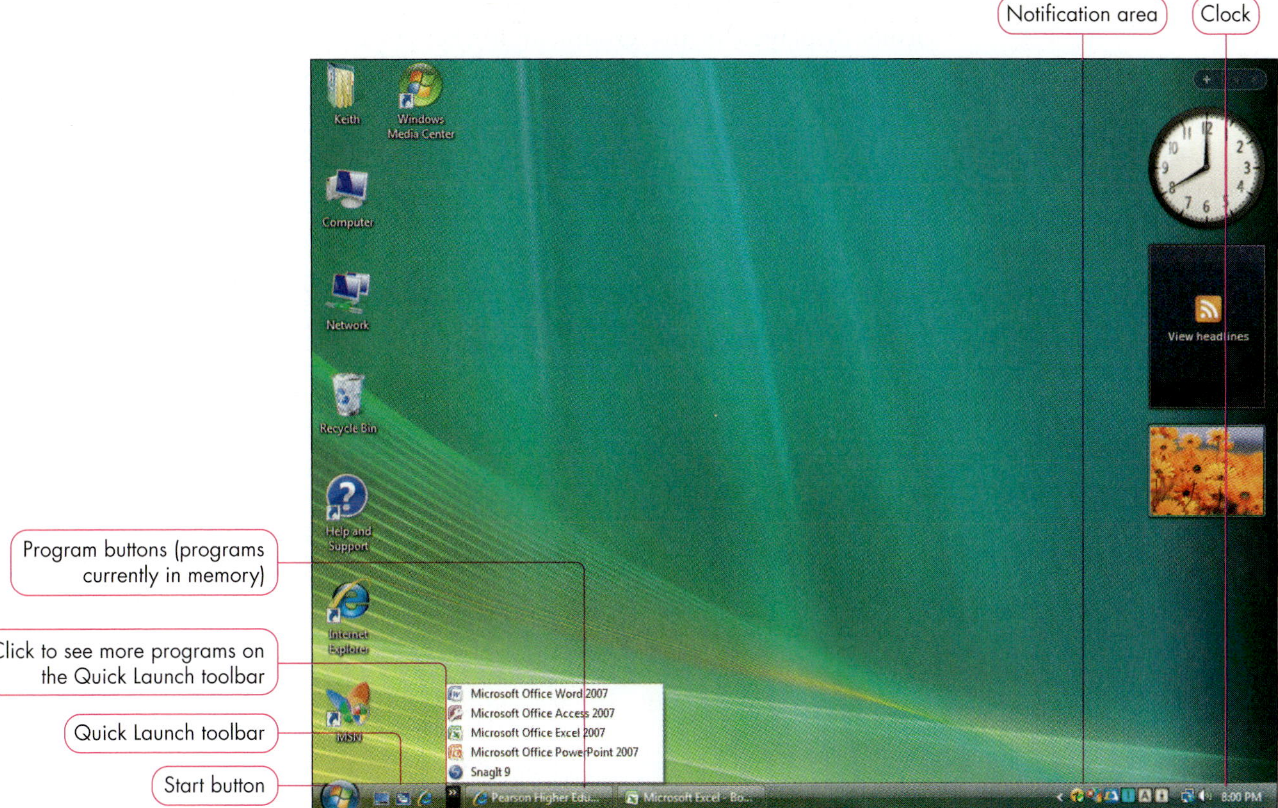

Figure 1.3 The Taskbar

You can move the taskbar to other areas of the desktop by clicking and dragging it, but most people prefer that it remain on the bottom. To make sure that your taskbar cannot be moved, you might want to lock it. To lock the taskbar, right-click an empty area of the taskbar and select Properties. The Taskbar and Start Menu Properties dialog box appears. Click the Taskbar tab, if necessary. Make sure a check mark appears beside Lock the Taskbar. If a check mark is not there, click Lock the Taskbar to select it. Notice that you can also auto-hide the taskbar from this dialog box. When you auto-hide the taskbar, the taskbar is not visible until you place the pointer over the taskbar location. Then when the pointer is moved, the taskbar goes away. Such an arrangement gives the most screen space possible for any tasks. When you have made your taskbar selections, click OK.

TIP Adjusting Taskbar Items

When the task bar is locked, no visual break appears between items on the taskbar, such as the Quick Launch toolbar and the taskbar. You can still access those areas to adjust them. Right-click the taskbar and deselect (click the check mark beside) Lock the Taskbar. Visual breaks then appear, enabling you to click and drag or otherwise modify taskbar items.

The Notification area is customizable, enabling you to control the number of icons displayed in the group. Right-click an empty area of the taskbar, select Properties, and click the Notification Area tab in the Taskbar and Start Menu Properties dialog box (see Figure 1.4). You can then choose to hide certain groups of system icons, such as Clock or Volume. Click OK after making your selections.

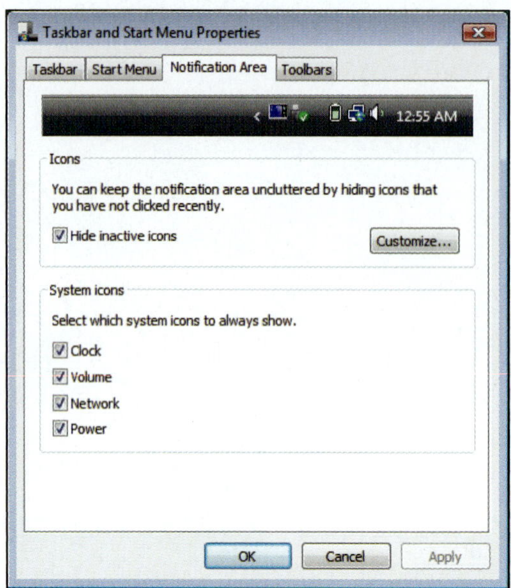

Figure 1.4 Notification Area Options

Identify Components on the Start Menu

The *Start menu* is a list of programs and utilities that displays when you click the Start button.

The Start button is the entry point to programs and resources found on your computer. The Start button appears as an orb at the left side of the taskbar. Clicking the Start button displays the ***Start menu***, a list of programs and utilities (see Figure 1.5). To the left, you will see a list of the most recently accessed programs; those used most often appear at the top of the list. Internet and e-mail items are "pinned," which means that they appear in bold and are a fixed part of the Start menu. The Instant Search box (described later in this chapter) enables you to find files and folders on your system. The bottom right side of the Start menu contains options to shut down your computer. To view programs installed on your computer, position the mouse over All Programs. Instead of a program list that flies out to the right (as in previous Windows operating systems), Vista simply converts the left side of the Start menu to a list of programs (see Figure 1.6).

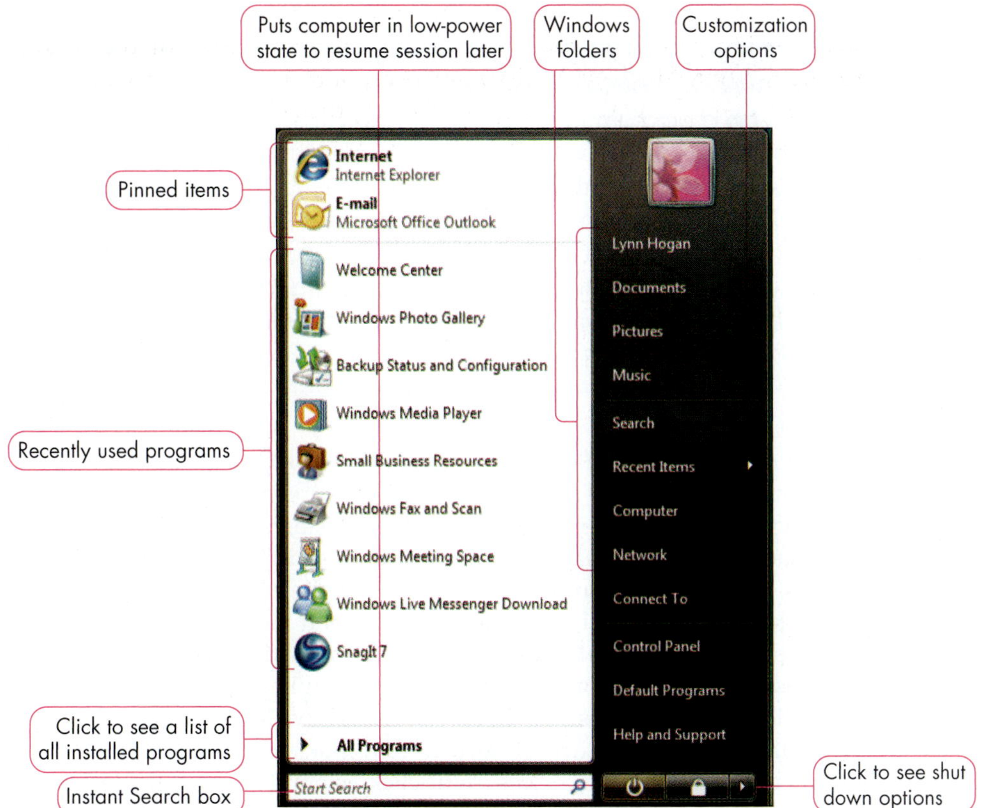

Figure 1.5 The Start Menu

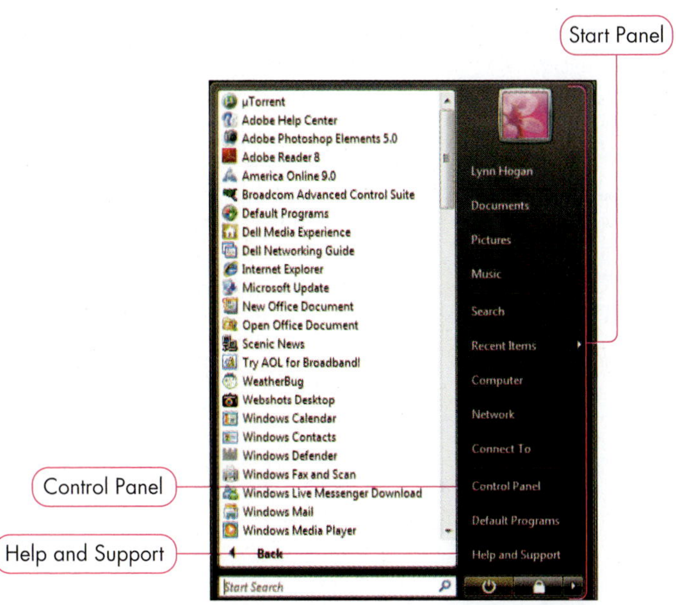

Figure 1.6 The All Programs Menu

TIP Pinning and Removing Items

You can *pin* a program to the pinned items on the Start menu so that you do not have to display the All Programs menu and submenus to start a program. To pin an item, display the All Programs menu and a submenu, if needed, to see the program name. Right-click the program name and select *Pin to Start Menu*. You can also drag and drop items onto the pinned area. If you no longer want an item in the pinned items area, right-click the pinned item and select *Unpin from the Start menu*. If you no longer want an item in the frequently used list, right-click the item and select *Remove from this list*.

The ***Start panel*** is located on the right side of the Start menu.

The right side of the Start menu, called the ***Start panel***, contains links to several common resources and folders. Items that were preceded by the word *My* in Windows XP have been renamed in Windows Vista, to drop the word *My*. For example, what was *My Computer* in Windows XP is simply *Computer* in Vista. Similarly, Pictures, Music, and Documents have dropped the *My* prefix. Along with common folders, such as Computer, Documents, Music, and Pictures, the Start Panel provides access to the ***Control Panel*** (for system customization) and ***Help and Support*** to obtain assistance and information on Windows topics.

The ***Control Panel*** enables you to change system settings, such as your background, screen saver, screen fonts, and accessibility options.

Help and Support provides assistance on Windows topics.

Earlier Windows versions displayed a slightly different Start menu, called the Classic menu. If you are accustomed to that look, you might want to change your Start menu to mimic it. To do this, right-click an empty area of the taskbar and select Properties. Click the Start Menu tab, click Classic Start menu, and click OK. To check the new look, click Start. Your menu should appear similar to the one displayed in Figure 1.7.

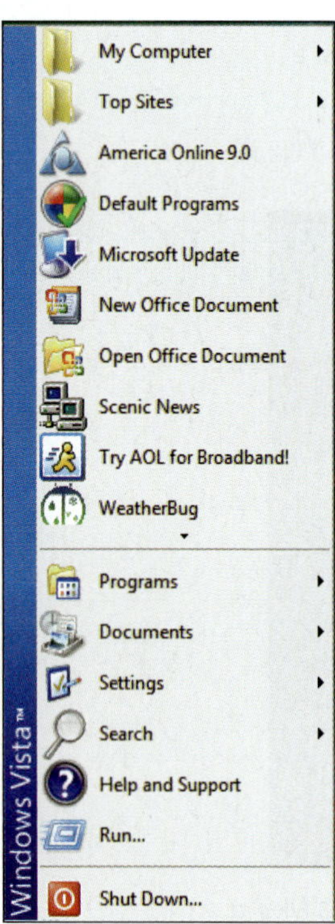

Figure 1.7 Classic Start Menu

Both the Start menu and the Quick Launch toolbar are convenient areas to place links to favorite programs. To include a favorite program on your Quick Launch toolbar, first make sure the taskbar is not locked. To do so, right-click an empty area of

A ***shortcut*** is a pointer to a file, folder, or Web site.

the taskbar and click Lock Taskbar (if a check mark appears beside it). If the Quick Launch toolbar is not visible, right-click an empty area of the taskbar, point to Toolbars, and select Quick Launch. Then, right-click and drag the program from the desktop, or from the Start menu, down to the Quick Launch toolbar. Release the mouse button and click Create Shortcuts Here to place the program link (or ***shortcut***) on the Quick Launch toolbar. From that point forward, you can simply click the program icon on the Quick Launch toolbar for immediate access to the program.

Working with Windows and Dialog Boxes

A ***window*** is an enclosed rectangular area representing a program or data.

A ***dialog box*** is a special window that requests input or presents information.

A *window* can either occupy part of your desktop or all of it, depending upon whether it is maximized. Special-purpose windows, called ***dialog boxes***, are designed for you to make selections or respond to prompts as a program is running. Although dialog boxes are considered windows, they cannot be resized. Learning to work with windows is much like managing papers on a desk. Just as you manually shift papers on a desk to work with one project or another, you can move windows on a computer desktop, closing those that you no longer need and moving or resizing others.

Understand Windows Components

When you click a folder on the Start menu, such as Computer or Documents, the folder contents open in a window. All windows share common features, as shown in Figure 1.8. The Address bar shows a hierarchical path to the current folder or window contents. The Desktop icon represents the top of the hierarchy. The second level, Lynn Hogan, represents all files and folders associated with that user account, whereas the third level, Documents, is the Documents folder for the selected user. The Address bar also contains Back and Forward buttons that enable you to visit previous windows in the same application. You can navigate to any level of the address displayed in the Address bar by clicking the folder name in the Address bar.

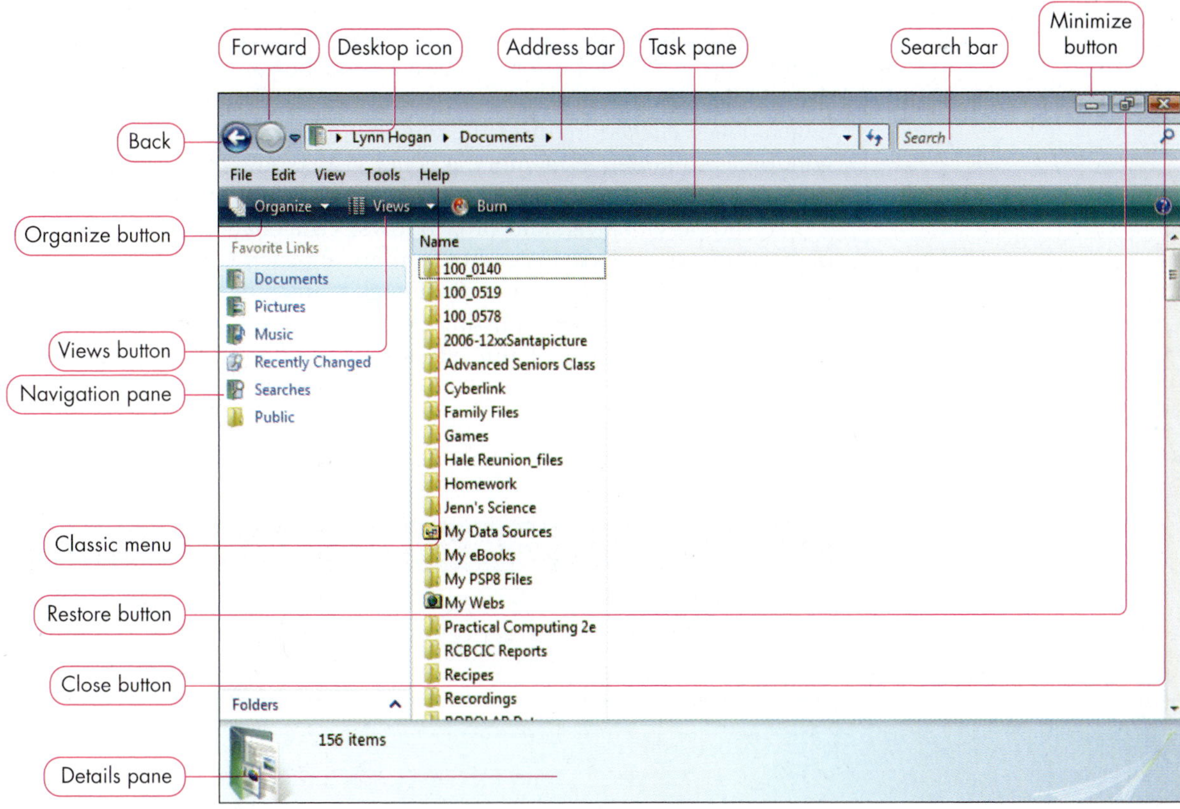

Figure 1.8 Elements of a Typical Window

To the right of the Address bar is the Search bar. Using the Search bar, you can quickly search for files within the selected folder. To conduct a search, all you need to do is type a word or phrase into the Search bar, and Vista instantly filters the folder contents to show only the files with names or contents that match the search criteria.

Beneath the Address bar is the Task pane. Although the buttons displayed on a Task pane vary with each open folder or application, the Task pane's purpose remains that of providing easy access to common tasks, such as changing the view and displaying or hiding screen elements. Regardless of the window displayed, each Task pane contains an Organize button and a Views button. The Organize button displays a menu that includes options for basic file tasks.

TIP Viewing Classic Menus

If you are familiar with, and prefer, the classic drop-down menus (Classic menus) of Windows XP, you can still display them. If you only want to view a menu once, just press Alt. Press Alt again to hide the menu. If you want Classic menus to appear in all windows even after the computer is rebooted, click Organize, select Folder and Search Options, click the View tab, and select Always Show Menus. Click OK.

Open, Size, and Move Windows

It is very easy to open multiple windows, each representing a different program or folder. Although Windows Vista has no problem dealing with several windows at once, it might become distracting for you. Thankfully, the taskbar displays a button for each open window, but even so, you will want to know how to minimize, maximize, close, resize, and move windows at will. To open a window, double-click its icon on the desktop or select it from the Start menu.

The top bar of every window contains three buttons to the far right—Minimize, Maximize (or Restore), and Close (see Figure 1.8). If the window is already displayed at full size, the middle button will be a Restore button. If the window is not at full size, the middle button will be a Maximize button. The first button is the Minimize button, which, when clicked, reduces the window to a button on the taskbar. Although the window is still open in memory, it is not visible on screen. When you want to access the window (or program) again, simply click the button on the taskbar.

As did previous versions of Windows, Vista enables you to quickly minimize all open windows at once, instead of minimizing each window individually. To do so, click the Show Desktop icon on the Quick Launch toolbar (see Figure 1.9). If you do not see the icon, or program listing, you might first have to click the double chevron that appears on the Quick Launch toolbar. Then find the icon and click it to minimize all open windows.

TIP Switch to Another Open Window

You can press Alt+Tab to make a different open window or application the active one. When you press Alt+Tab, a toolbar displays, showing icons of the open windows. Continue holding Alt and press Tab until a border displays around the window you want to be active. Then release the mouse.

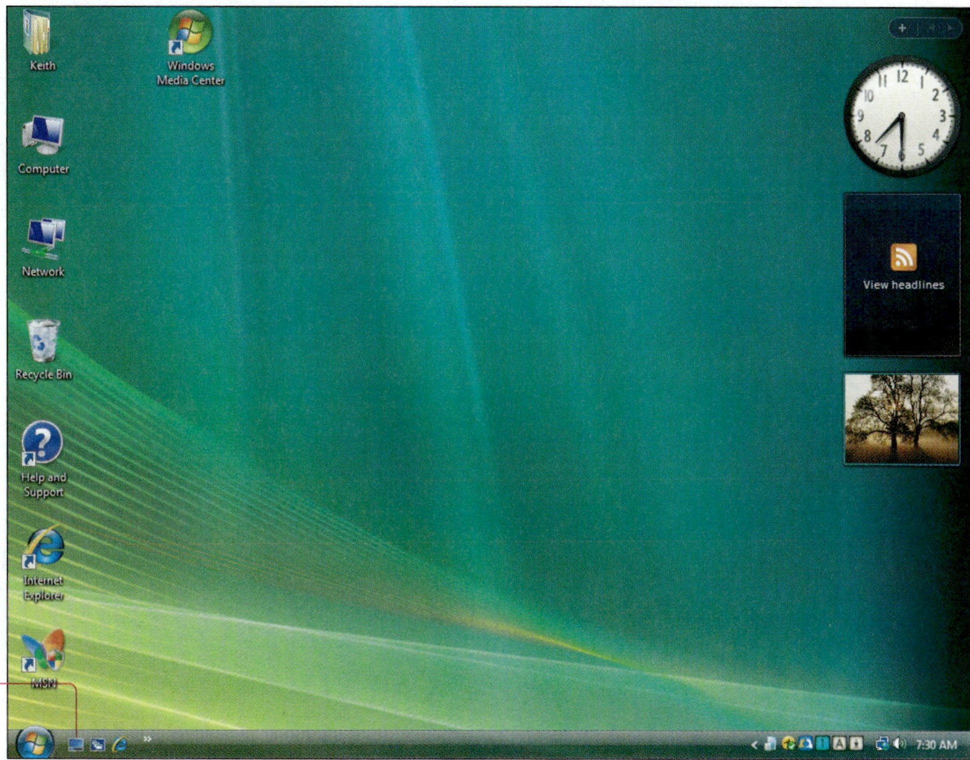

Figure 1.9 The Show Desktop Icon

The middle button is the Maximize button. Clicking it pulls the window up to full size, filling the screen. You might want to maximize a window to provide more open workspace or to display more icons. If the middle button is, instead, a Restore button (which looks like two overlapped boxes), clicking it will return the window to less than full size. Clicking the Close button, which is the one to the far right, removes the window from memory.

It is sometimes necessary to move or resize a window. Perhaps the window is obscuring a part of your desktop that is critical to your task, or maybe the window is too far to one side or the other. To move a window, click and drag the top window bar. If the window is not already maximized, it will move to the new location. Release the mouse button to position the window. To resize a window, place the pointer on a border of the window (if the window is not maximized). The pointer should become a double-headed arrow. Click and drag to make the window larger or smaller. If the pointer is on a corner of the window, forming a diagonal double-headed arrow, you can proportionally resize two adjacent sides of the window at once by clicking and dragging.

Stack and Cascade Open Windows

Stacked windows are displayed one on top of the other.

Cascaded windows are displayed such that a small section of each open window is shown behind another.

At times you might want to see part of several windows at once. To do so, you can either ***stack*** or ***cascade*** the windows. Figure 1.10 shows two windows in a cascade arrangement, while Figure 1.11 illustrates the stacked selection. To arrange several open windows on screen at once, right-click an empty area of the taskbar and select Cascade Windows to achieve the look of Figure 1.10. For the stacked arrangement of Figure 1.11, right-click an empty part of the taskbar and select Show Windows Stacked. If you want the windows to appear side by side, click Show Windows Side by Side.

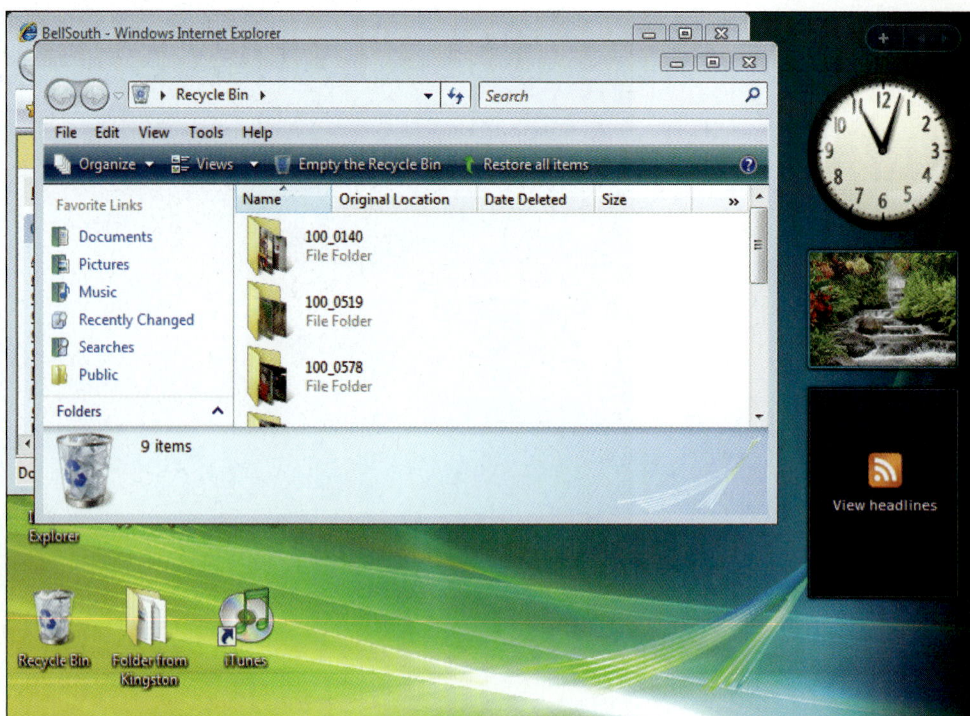

Figure 1.10 Cascaded Windows

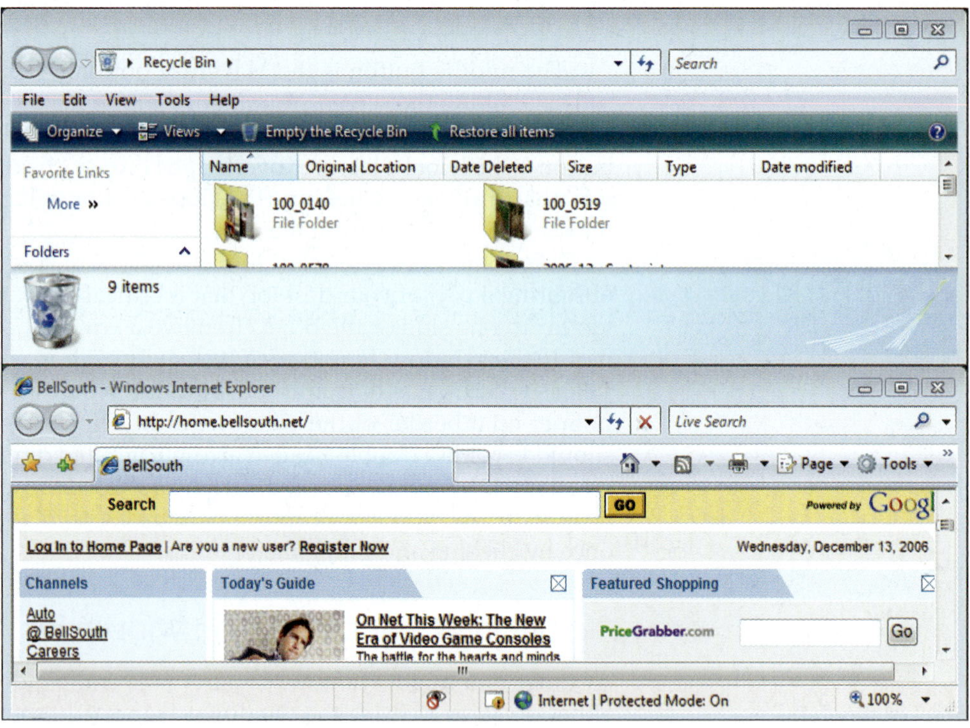

Figure 1.11 Stacked Windows

Select Options in Dialog Boxes

A dialog box is a special window that displays when an operation requires confirmation or additional information. The Print dialog box (see Figure 1.12) displays when you print a document. By responding to areas of the dialog box, you can indicate exactly what to print and how. The information is entered into the dialog box in different ways, depending on the type of information that is required.

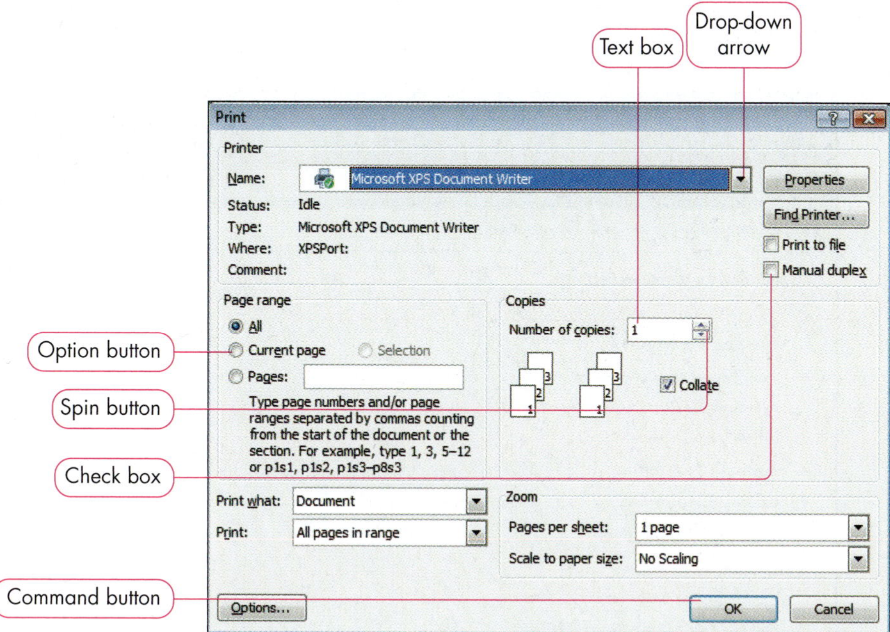

Figure 1.12 Print Dialog Box

An ***option button***, or ***radio button***, is a mutually exclusive selection in a dialog box.

A ***text box*** enables you to give an instruction by typing in a box.

A ***spin button*** is a dialog box feature whereby you can click an up or down arrow to increase or decrease a selection.

A ***check box*** enables you to select one or more items that are not mutually exclusive.

A ***list box*** presents several items, any of which can be selected.

A ***command button*** is a dialog box item that you click to accept or cancel selections.

Option buttons, sometimes called ***radio buttons***, indicate mutually exclusive choices, one of which *must* be chosen, such as the page range. In this example you can print all pages, the selection (if it is available), the current page, or a specific set of pages (such as pages 1–4), but you can choose *one and only one* option. Any time you select (click) an option, the previous option is automatically deselected.

A ***text box***, such as the one shown beside the *Pages* option in Figure 1.12, enables you to enter specific information. In this case, you could type *1–5* in the text box if you wanted only the first five pages to print. A ***spin button*** is a common component of a dialog box, providing a quick method of increasing or decreasing a setting. For example, clicking the spin button (or spinner) beside *Number of copies* enables you to increase or decrease the number of copies of the document to print. You can also enter the information explicitly by typing it into the text box beside the spin button.

Check boxes are used instead of option buttons if the choices are not mutually exclusive. You can select or clear options by clicking the appropriate check box, which toggles the operation on and off. A ***list box*** (not shown in Figure 1.12) displays some or all of the available choices, any of which can be selected by clicking the list item.

All dialog boxes also contain one or more ***command buttons*** that provide options to either accept or cancel your selections. The OK button, for example, initiates the printing process. The Cancel button does just the opposite and ignores (cancels) any changes made to the settings, closing the dialog box.

Using Help and Support

Help on almost any Windows topic is only a click away using the Help and Support Center. To access assistance, click Start and then click Help and Support. In addition, you can usually press F1 to access Help from most active windows or applications. Beneath the title bar is a navigation bar that contains Back and Forward buttons, along with links to the Help home page, print facility, and assistance from newsgroups or Microsoft IT professionals. The Search bar enables you to enter a subject and receive information. For example, suppose that you want to know about Windows Vista security features. In the Search bar, you might type Windows Security. Click the magnifying glass to the right of the Search area, or press Enter, to display results similar to those in Figure 1.13. Click any result to view additional information. Use the Back button to return to the results if you want to view another link.

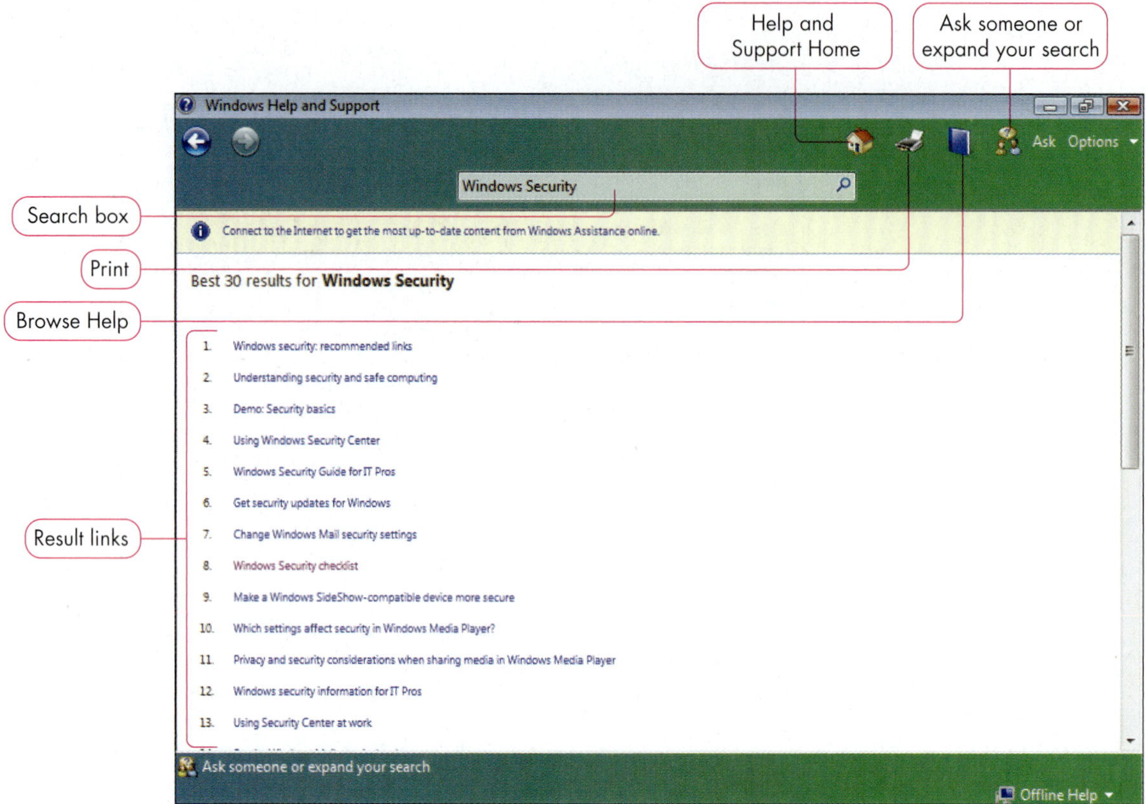

Figure 1.13 Help and Support

You can browse through Help and Support topics by clicking Browse Help, as shown in Figure 1.14. The table of contents contains topic links that you can click to display additional information. Even more assistance is available when you click Ask someone or expand your search. As Figure 1.15 shows, you can contact Microsoft Customer Support online, or post questions or answers in Windows communities. In addition, you can ask someone for help through Remote Assistance. A knowledgeable friend or computer professional can then control your computer desktop remotely, running diagnostics or otherwise determining the source of a problem. Finally, the Microsoft Knowledge Base is a large collection of articles with detailed solutions to computer problems.

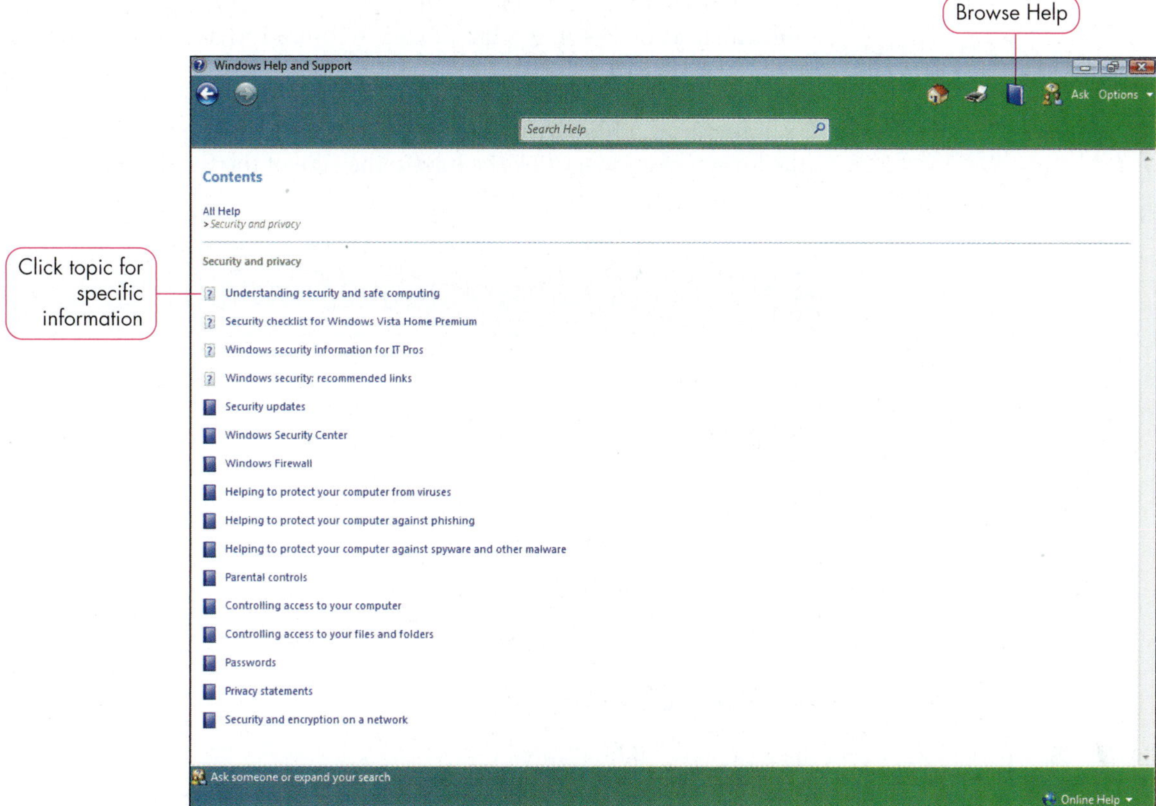

Figure 1.14 Help and Support Table of Contents

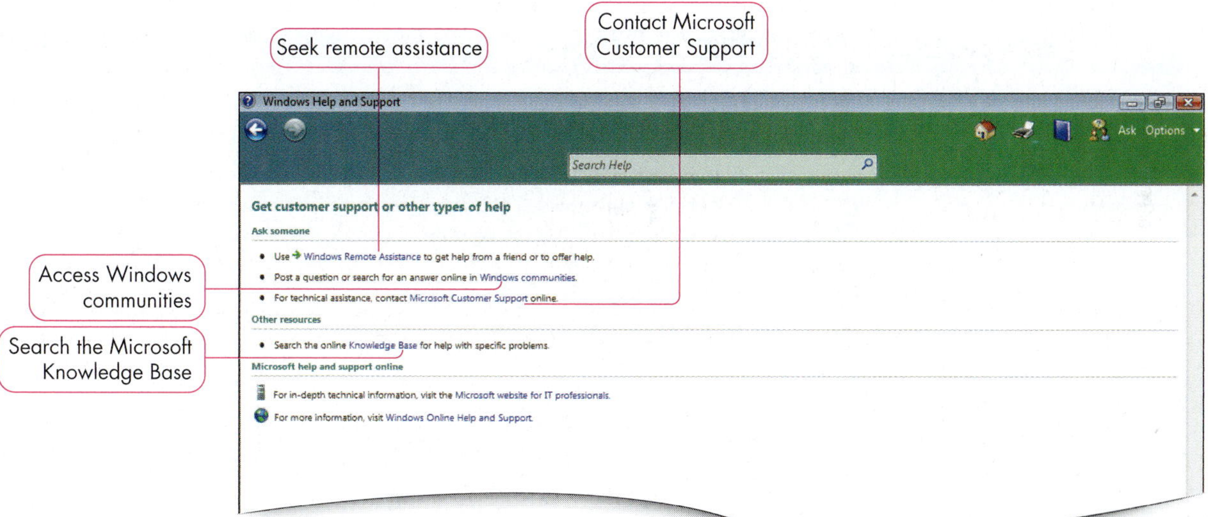

Figure 1.15 Additional Assistance Through Help and Support

Some Help topics contain a blue compass. That means that Guided Help is available. Instead of viewing a list of steps required to accomplish the task in question, you can actually see them. You can either watch and learn from the steps, or in some cases you can do them yourself with assistance from the guided tutorial. Other times, you might see a filmstrip, as shown in Figure 1.16. The filmstrip indicates a demo in the form of a movie. Click the link to the side of the filmstrip to view the video.

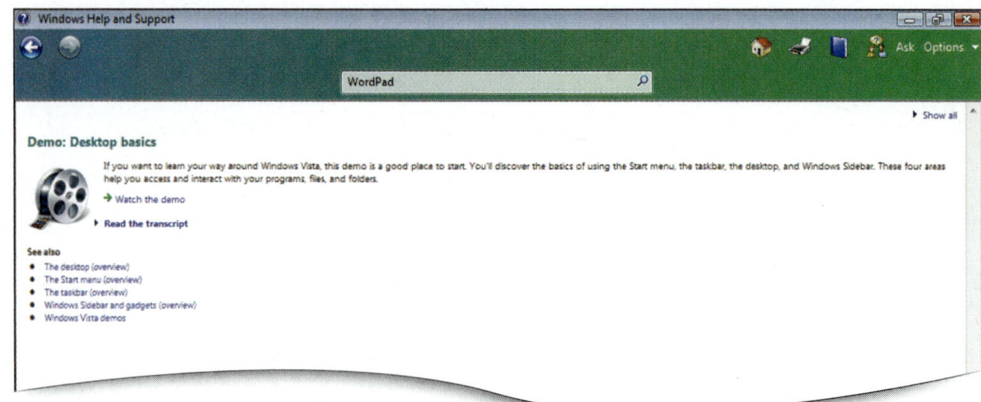

Figure 1.16 Help and Support Demo

Toolbars | Reference

Name	Icon	Purpose
Lynn Hogan	Lynn Hogan	User Folder, containing the named user's documents, music, pictures, and search results
Computer	Computer	Folder that provides access to storage devices connected to your computer, such as a hard drive, CD, DVD, flash drive, and digital camera
Network	Network	Folder that provides access to the computers and devices on your network. You can see the contents of network computers and access shared files and folders
Internet Explorer	Internet - Shortcut	Program icon that opens the Internet Explorer browser. If you have a broadband connection to the Internet, opening Internet Explorer provides a view of the Internet
Control Panel	Control Panel - Shortcut	Program icon that opens the Control Panel, which enables you to change computer settings such as the desktop background, screen saver, printer selection, system volume, and screen resolution
Recycle Bin	Recycle Bin	Program icon that provides access to the Recycle Bin, which is a temporary holding area for items deleted from the hard drive

Hands-On Exercises

1 | Working with Windows

Skills covered: 1. Manage One or More Windows **2.** Arrange Desktop Icons **3.** Modify the Start Menu **4.** Use Help and Support

Step 1 Manage One or More Windows

Refer to Figure 1.17 as you complete Step 1.

a. Click **Start** and then click **Computer**.

The Computer window displays the disk drives that are found on your computer system. Because your configuration is not likely to be exactly the same as ours, the elements on your Computer window might be different.

TROUBLESHOOTING: If your view in the left pane (Navigation pane) shows a hierarchy of devices and folders, instead of the items displayed in Figure 1.17, click the Folders drop-down arrow to change the view.

b. If the window is not already maximized (filling the entire screen), click the **Maximize** button on the right side of the top bar.

c. Click the **Restore** button to restore the window.

d. Move the pointer to a border of the window. The pointer should become a double-headed arrow. Click and drag to make the window smaller.

e. Click and drag the title bar to move the window.

f. Double-click the **Recycle Bin** icon on the desktop.

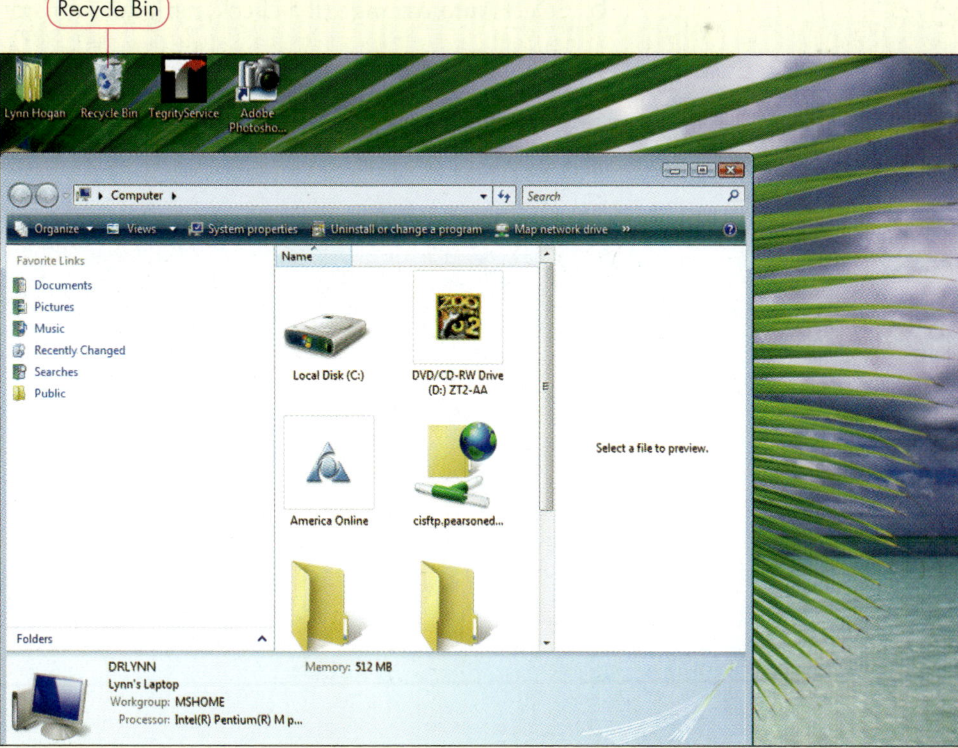

Figure 1.17 Computer Window

TROUBLESHOOTING: If you cannot see the Recycle Bin, resize or move the Computer window so that the Recycle Bin icon is visible. Sometimes a window might open in such a way that it obscures an area that is critical to your task. In that case, you must move, resize, or perhaps minimize the obstructing window. Alternatively, you could click the Show Desktop icon on the Quick Launch toolbar.

The Recycle Bin might fill the entire screen, but note the Computer button on the taskbar, indicating that the Computer window is still open in memory.

g. Right-click an empty area of the taskbar and select **Cascade Windows**.

   TROUBLESHOOTING: If the menu that appears does not include a Cascade Windows command, you clicked an occupied area of the taskbar. Be sure to right-click an *empty* part of the taskbar to display the correct menu.

h. Right-click an empty area of the taskbar and select **Show Windows Stacked**.

i. Click the **Show Desktop** icon on the Quick Launch toolbar to minimize all open windows.

   TROUBLESHOOTING: If the Quick Launch toolbar does not appear on your taskbar, open it by right-clicking an unoccupied area of the taskbar, pointing to Toolbars, and selecting Quick Launch.

j. Click the **Computer button** on the taskbar. Close the Computer window.

k. Click the **Recycle Bin button** on the taskbar. Close the Recycle Bin window.

Step 2
Arrange Desktop Icons

Refer to Figure 1.18 as you complete Step 2.

a. Right-click an empty area of the desktop and point to **View**.

b. Select **Auto Arrange** (if a check mark does not appear beside the command).

   TROUBLESHOOTING: If the **Auto Arrange** setting already has a check mark beside it, **Auto Arrange** is "on," so you do not need to select the command from the context menu. Click outside the menu to close it, if necessary.

Figure 1.18 Auto Arrange Icons

Step 3
Modify the Start Menu

Refer to Figure 1.19 as you complete Step 3.

a. Right-click a blank area of the taskbar and select **Properties**.

The Taskbar and Start Menu Properties dialog box appears.

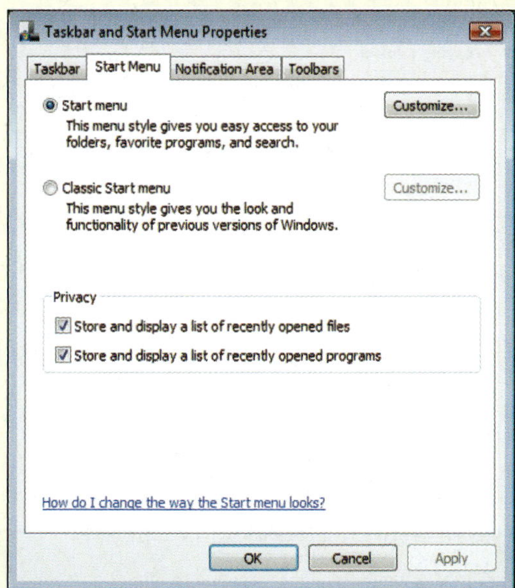

Figure 1.19 Taskbar and Start Menu Properties

b. Click the **Start Menu tab**, click the **Classic Start menu option**, and then click **OK**.

The next time that you click Start, the Start menu will display in the standard one-column Classic view rather than the Windows Vista view.

TROUBLESHOOTING: If you do not see a menu containing the Properties option, you right-clicked an occupied area of the taskbar instead of an empty part. Try the procedure again, this time being careful to click an unoccupied area.

c. Repeat Steps 3a and 3b, but click the **Start menu** option to return to the Vista Start menu. Click **OK**.

Step 4
Use Help and Support

Refer to Figure 1.20 as you complete Step 4.

a. Click **Start** and click **Help and Support**. In the Search box, type **copying a folder**. Press **Enter** or click the magnifying glass to the right of the Search area.

You will occasionally have a question about Windows and will need to use the Help and Support feature. In this case, assume that you need assistance with copying a folder from one location to another. The assistance that you get will come in handy as you explore the next section of this chapter.

b. Click **Copy a file or folder**. Read the information on copying a file or folder.

c. Click the **Print** button on the navigation bar at the top of the window. Click **Print** to print the information.

d. Close the Help and Support window.

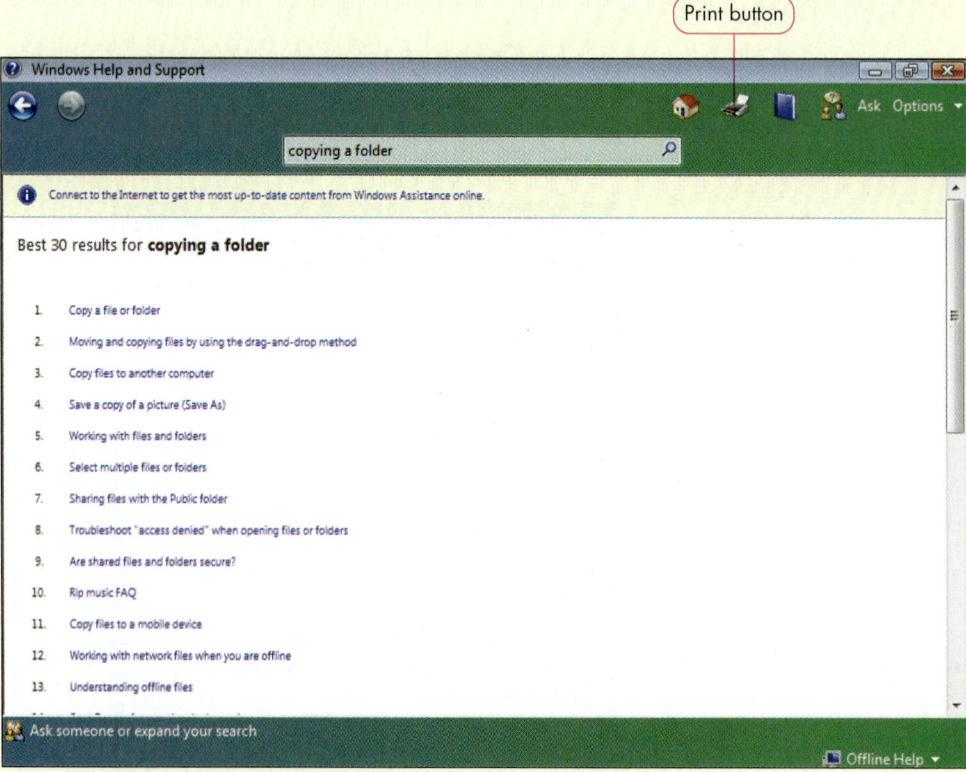

Figure 1.20 Help and Support

Files and Folders

Windows Vista provides a snapshot of your computer disk drives in the Computer folder. Click Start and click Computer to view the folder (see Figure 1.21). Along with the Address bar and Task pane, the window includes a summary of disk drives associated with your computer system. Hover the pointer over any drive to view information on the drive's free space and total space. Click System properties to find a summary of your computer's operating system, RAM size, and processor speed. Clicking Uninstall or change a program enables you to uninstall or attempt to repair programs. As always, the Back button on the Address bar is a handy way to return to previously visited screens. Click Organize, Layout to display or hide the Preview pane, Navigation pane, Details Pane, and Search pane. You can click the drop-down arrow beside the Views button to change the window view to Details, Tiles, Large Icons, or other selections, each of which is simply a different view of items contained in the window. You can also repeatedly click the Views button to cycle through available views.

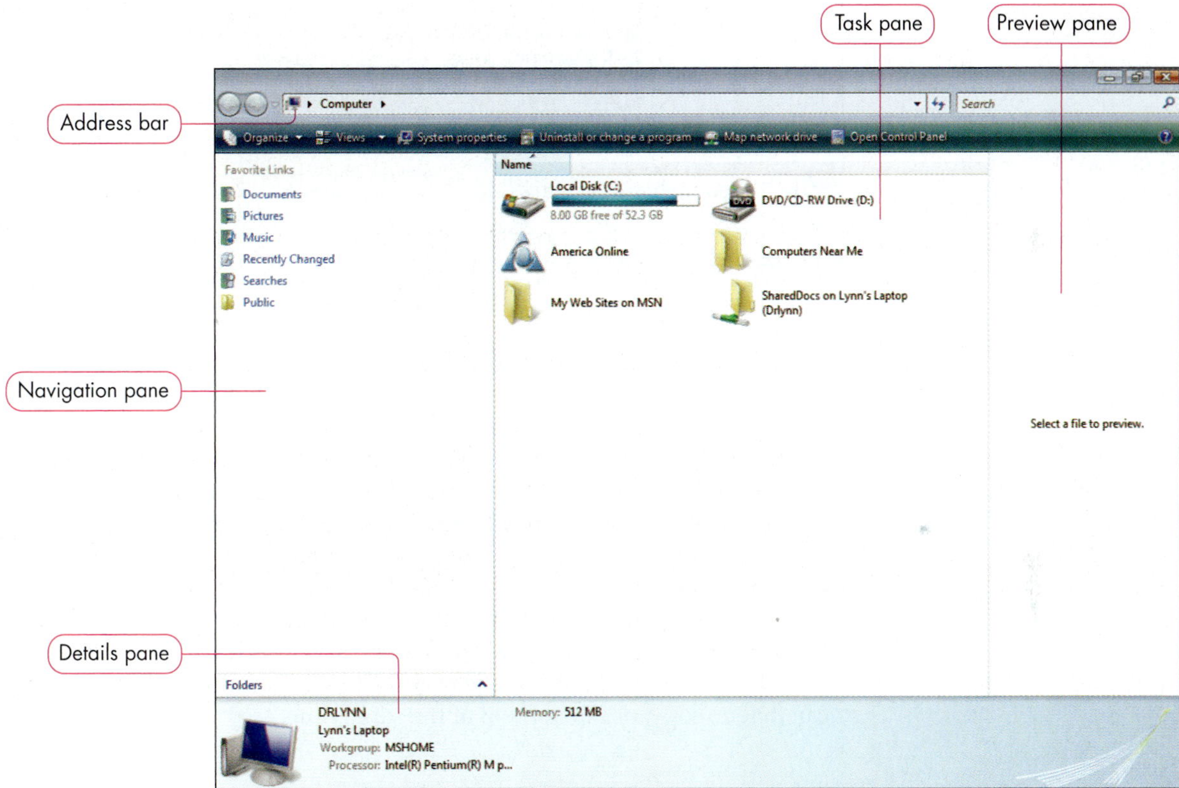

Figure 1.21 Computer Window

A ***file*** is a unit of data to which you give a name.

A ***folder*** is an object that can hold multiple files and subfolders.

A ***thumbnail*** is a miniature image of a file.

Metadata is information that describes data.

The Preview pane, usually shown at the right side of a folder window, displays the contents of the currently selected *file* (see Figure 1.22). If the item selected is a *folder*, no preview is available. The Details pane shows a ***thumbnail*** of the item, along with any ***metadata***. New to Windows Vista, metadata is information that describes data. That information could be related to any of a number of categories, including file contents, title, subject, or author. The concept of metadata is described in more detail later in this chapter. It is a major shift away from the location-centered storage design of earlier Windows versions to Vista's property-centered storage and retrieval method.

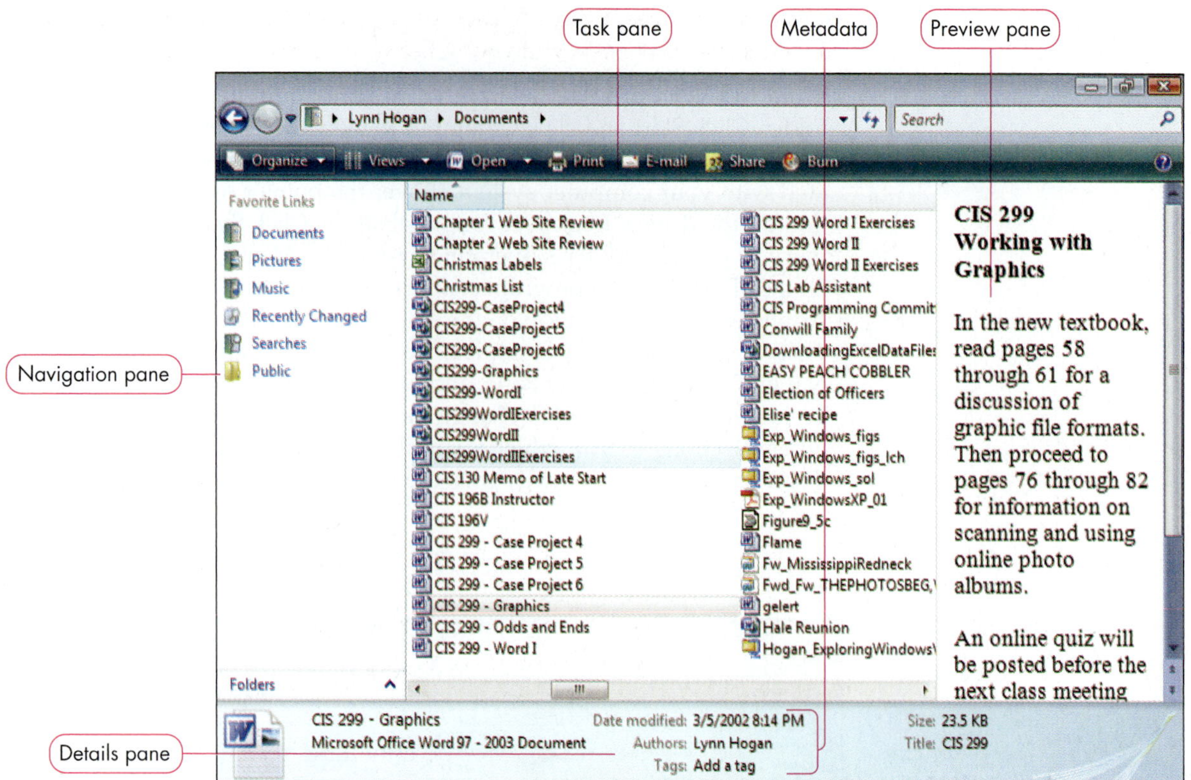

Figure 1.22 Documents Window

The Navigation pane, appearing on the left side of each folder window, provides access to the Documents, Pictures, Music, Recently Changed, and Searches folders. The first three folders are common folders found on every computer system, while the Recently Changed folder contains items from the Documents folder that have been modified in the past month. The Searches folder is actually a collection of search folders, including Recently Changed, Recent Email, and Recent Music, among others. The Searches folder also holds any searches that you have saved (as described later in this chapter).

In this section, you learn how to manage files and folders. Specifically, you learn how to create, rename, and delete folders. You also learn how to create files and add metadata to them. Finally, you learn how to select multiple files or folders so that you can delete, copy, or move them at the same time.

Managing Files and Folders in Windows Explorer

A ***data file*** is a document or item that you create and to which you give a name.

A ***program file*** is part of a software program, such as Microsoft Word.

Probably a major reason that you use a computer is to produce something of interest to you. It may be that you want to work with digital photographs, or perhaps you like to put together documents such as newsletters or reports. Your job might require the production of financial spreadsheets or databases. Anything that you create and to which you give a name is called a ***data file***. For example, when you use a word processor to write the school newsletter and save it, you will be prompted to name the newsletter, which is a data file. Some items that you create, such as digital photographs, are automatically assigned names, and are still considered data files.

(It is far too easy to lose track of data files when no orderly folder structure exists on a disk.)

A ***program file***, on the other hand, is a file that is part of a software installation. You do not create program files. Instead, they are created by software professionals and loaded onto your computer's hard drive when you install the software.

Although you have very little control over where program files are saved, you can, and should, design a storage hierarchy for your data files. Imagine a two-car garage that is so full of things that even the cars have no room. With no shelves on the walls, items in the garage are simply stacked, making it almost impossible to quickly retrieve anything. Similarly, a disk medium with no organization is difficult to manage. It is far too easy to lose track of data files when no orderly folder structure exists on a disk. In this section, you will learn to manage computer folders and files, saving files in folders that are properly named and placed in an organizational hierarchy.

Before exploring the creation of files, you should understand the concept of computer folders. Just as a folder in a filing cabinet can be labeled before any information is placed in the folder, so can a computer folder be named and positioned before files are placed in it. A computer folder is simply a labeled storage location in which data files can later be stored. A folder structure can occur across several levels. For example, you might maintain documents for several projects in the Marketing Department of your company. Your projects will include documents for Lewis Trucking Firm as well as Roundabout Children's Wear. The folder structure you create could logically include a major folder titled *Marketing Department*, with two subfolders beneath it called *Lewis Trucking* and *Roundabout Children's Wear*. The documents that you create for Lewis Trucking could then be placed and easily found in the Lewis Trucking folder. Similarly, Roundabout Children's Wear documents could be saved in the Roundabout folder.

Windows Explorer enables you to manage files and folders.

Windows Explorer is a Windows component that can be used to create and manage folders. To access Windows Explorer, click Start, then All Programs, Accessories, and Windows Explorer. Figure 1.23 shows that Windows Explorer presents the folder structure of your system in the left pane and the contents of a selected folder in the right pane. The hard drive on your computer is labeled drive C. Other drives, such as a CD or DVD, and network space are known by successive letters, such as D or F. In a classroom setting, you will most likely work with flash drives (or USB drives), which are small pocket-sized disk units that connect to a computer's USB port and act as an additional drive. Flash drives make data portable, so that you can transfer files from one computer to another. For example, you can save a report that you created at work on your flash drive, take the flash drive to your home computer, and continue to work with the report there. The drive letter assigned the removable flash drive is the next one in line. For example, if you have a hard drive and a CD drive, labeled respectively C and D, then the flash drive is the E drive. Figure 1.23 shows a flash drive (drive E:), a DVD/CD (drive D:), and a hard drive (drive C:).

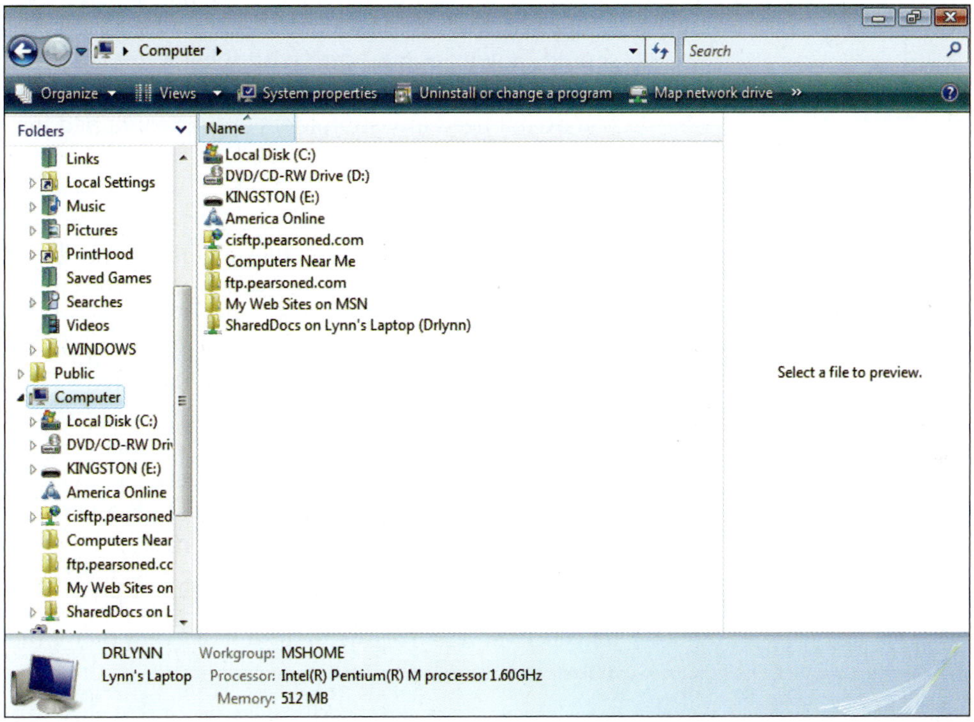

Figure 1.23 Windows Explorer Drives

TIP Opening Windows Explorer

You can open Windows Explorer by right-clicking the Start button and selecting Explore.

The hard drive is a very large storage unit. When you install software, it is saved to the hard drive. Many programs require a great deal of storage space that is quickly accessible, so the hard drive is the ideal place to house the software. Also, you are able to secure the original software CDs in a location away from the computer so that if the hard drive ever fails, you can reinstall the software on a replacement hard drive. You should take more care, however, with your data files. Those are the items that you create and that are most likely irreplaceable if you should lose them. Therefore, the hard drive, which is an unwieldy device from which to make a complete backup, is probably not the best location in which to save your data files. You are much more likely to make copies of data files stored on smaller media such as flash drives or CDs.

Along with the three control buttons (Minimize, Maximize, and Close) found in the upper-right corner of the window, Windows Explorer contains an Address bar and a Task pane. The Address bar identifies the currently selected folder or drive and includes a Search area by which you can filter the display of files. The Task pane contains several buttons that control the display of window elements. If you are familiar with previous Windows versions, you might feel comfortable with the Classic menu structure. To display the menu, press Alt. To the left is a Navigation pane that displays the hierarchy of folders on the computer. Each time you click the Views button on the Task pane, the icons are displayed in a different format and size. If, instead, you click the Views drop-down arrow, you can click and drag a slider to manually adjust the view.

Creating, Renaming, and Deleting Folders

Using Windows Explorer, it is very easy to create, rename, and delete a folder. You should, however, take care with where you create and rename a folder so that the folder structure is as you planned it. Before deleting a folder, you should make sure you do not need any subfolders or files contained inside that folder.

Create Folders

To help you organize related files together, you should create a folder or subfolder to contain the files. Doing so helps you find files later when you need them. Suppose that you want to create the Marketing Department folder on the flash drive (drive E), with Lewis Trucking and Roundabout folders placed as subfolders of the Marketing Department folder. First, connect the flash drive (USB drive) to a USB port on your computer. Wait a few seconds and examine any dialog box that subsequently opens. Most often, the dialog box provides options for viewing files stored on the flash drive. To open a Windows Explorer view, click View files and folders or Open folder to view files. If, by chance, the dialog box is an error message or provides additional information concerning the flash drive, you should respond appropriately. Alternatively, you can close the dialog box and then open Windows Explorer (click Start, All Programs, Accessories, Windows Explorer). In the Navigation pane to the left, click the small arrow to the left of Computer if the arrow is clear. If, however, the arrow is colored, the folder or disk drive is already expanded. (You might have to scroll up or down slightly to see the Computer folder.) The Computer view expands, listing storage devices on your computer system. The flash drive will be either drive E or F, as shown in Figure 1.24. Click the flash drive in the Navigation pane. (Be sure to click the drive title, not the arrow to the left.) The pane to the right will display the contents of the drive; drive E in this case. If your flash drive is empty, you will not see any files or folders in the right pane. To create the Marketing Department folder, click the Organize button on the Task pane. Then click New Folder. Type a new folder name, Marketing Department, and press Enter. The Marketing Department folder is now created on your flash drive, as shown in Figure 1.24.

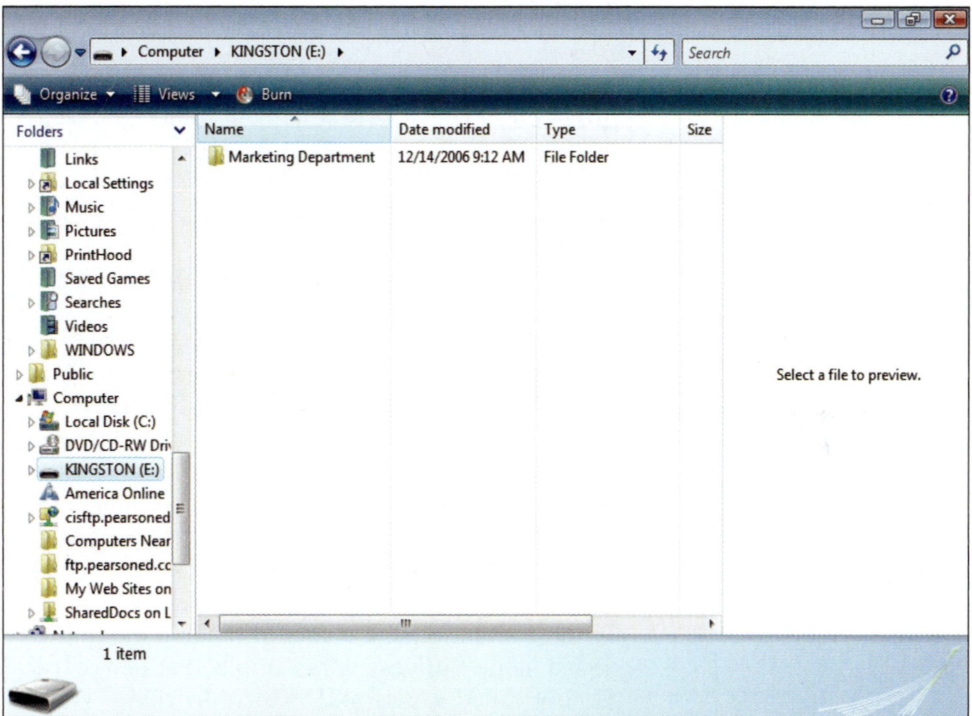

Figure 1.24 Marketing Department Folder

The two subfolders of the Marketing Department folder will be Lewis Trucking and Roundabout Children's Wear. One of the most important steps in the process of creating folders is to first select the correct folder or drive under which you want a subfolder to appear. With Windows Explorer open, click the Marketing Department folder (in the Navigation pane) because it is the folder under which you want the two subfolders to appear. If you do not see the Marketing Department folder, you may need to expand drive E by clicking the small arrow to the left of drive E. Click the Organize button. Click New Folder. Type the new folder name, Lewis Trucking, and press Enter. To be sure that the Marketing Department is the currently selected folder (so that you can create the Roundabout Children's Wear subfolder appropriately), click Marketing Department in the Address bar. The Address bar should show that the currently selected folder is Marketing Department. To create the Roundabout Children's Wear folder, click the Organize button. Click New Folder. Type Roundabout Children's Wear and press Enter. You now have two subfolders of the Marketing Department folder, as displayed in Figure 1.25.

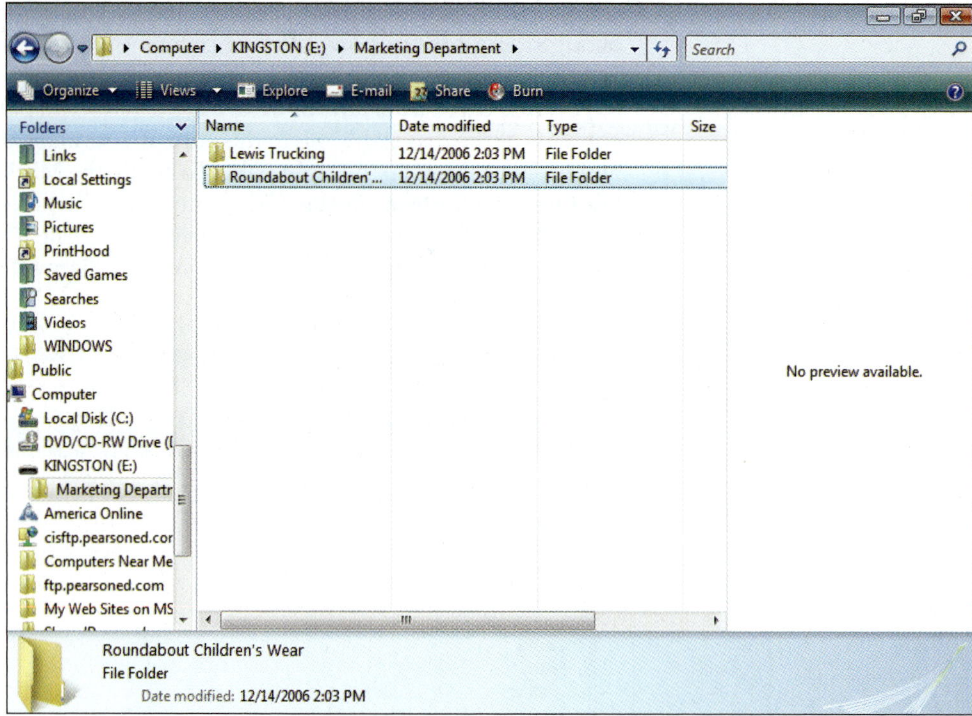

Figure 1.25 Marketing Department Subfolders

Rename Folders

At times you may find a more suitable name for a folder than the one that you gave it. Or perhaps you made a typographical mistake when you entered the folder name. In these situations, you should rename the folder to reflect the new name or corrected name. Suppose, for example, that Lewis Trucking has acquired a partner and is now called Lewis and Brown Trucking. With Windows Explorer open, click Marketing Department in the Navigation pane. If you do not see Marketing Department, you will need to click the flash drive first (probably drive E). You should see both subfolders in the right pane. Because Lewis Trucking is the folder to be renamed, click it. Click the Organize button, click Rename, type the new name, Lewis and Brown Trucking, and press Enter. Your folder is renamed!

TIP Renaming Files and Folders

You can rename a file or folder by clicking the file or folder name twice, very slowly. Then type the new name and press Enter.

Delete Folders

Be careful when deleting folders. If any files are saved in the folder to be deleted, all files are removed along with the folder. If the deleted folder comes from the hard drive, all of its contents are placed in the Recycle Bin, from which they can be retrieved later if necessary. The Recycle Bin is discussed later in this chapter. However, if the deleted folder is on a removable disk, such as a flash drive or CD, the folder and all of its files are immediately removed and cannot be retrieved. The process of deleting a folder is exactly that of renaming a folder, except that you select

Delete from the Organize button selections instead of Rename. An alternate method of deleting a folder (as well as renaming it) is to right-click the folder and make appropriate selections from the ***context menu*** that appears. The context menu is also called a ***shortcut menu***. Files are deleted in exactly the same manner as folders.

A ***context menu***, or ***shortcut menu***, contains options relative to an item or area that you clicked.

Working with Files

A file is an item that you create and to which you give a name. For example, using spreadsheet software such as Microsoft Excel, you could develop a family budget and save it to the hard drive or to a CD. During the process of saving the file, you would be required to give the file a name, such as Family Budget. Knowing about folders, you should first create a folder in which to save all family files, including the newly created family budget.

Although Windows Explorer can be used to create and manage folders, files are created and saved by specific software. Microsoft Excel is used to create Excel data files and Microsoft Word enables you to develop Word data files, for example. To create files, therefore, you must be familiar with the particular software that you are using. All applications that run under Windows Vista share a common interface, which makes it fairly easy to transition from one application to another when working with files.

Add Metadata to Files

Windows Vista encourages the use of metadata, which is information that helps categorize files and folders by content. For example, you might be enrolled in a Speech class, which requires the production of word processing outlines and PowerPoint displays to support speech topics. Most of the files, therefore, probably include the course name, Speech 101, somewhere in the title or file contents. To identify all files pertaining to your Speech class, you could apply descriptive keywords, sometimes called tags (or file properties), to the files. Such descriptive keywords are called metadata.

Although you are not required to add metadata to a file, doing so makes it possible to sort, group, stack, and filter files based on categories of metadata. To edit or create metadata for an item, first click the file to select it. If the Details Pane is not displayed, click Organize and Layout. Click Details Pane. Figure 1.26 displays the Details Pane with areas of metadata. To add descriptive data, click inside the text box beside any property that you want to add or change and type the new entry. Click Save to save your entries.

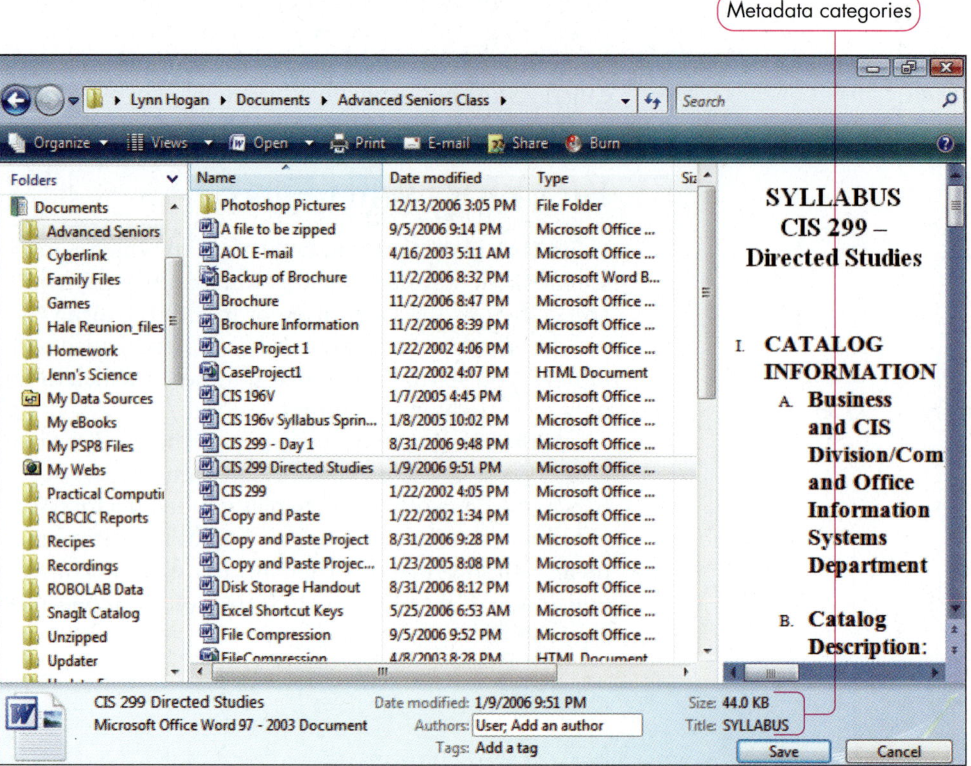

Figure 1.26 Metadata Properties

Save Files

In almost any Windows application, the method of saving a file is the same. Having created a file, perhaps by typing a memorandum or developing a slide presentation, you can save the file. Within the respective program, use the Save command. If it is the first time to save the file, you will be asked to supply a location for the save (a disk drive and perhaps a folder, if you wish) and a file name. Although specific rules apply for naming files, you are safe creating a file name of fewer than 256 characters, using only letters and numbers—no special characters, such as /, $, ?, or *. When you subsequently use the Save command, the file will be saved in the same location with the same file name. If, however, you want to save the file in another location, perhaps creating a copy or backup of the file, you should use the Save As command. You will then provide details on the location of the save and the file name for the changed file.

If you save files on a removable disk drive, such as a flash drive, you should not simply remove the drive when you are finished working with it. Doing so might cause you to lose data stored on the flash drive. Before removing the flash drive, you should click the Safely Remove Hardware button in the Notification area of the taskbar and then click the prompt to remove the appropriate device. Only then should you disconnect the disk drive. Before using a flash drive for the first time, you should read all documentation that comes with it so that you use the drive properly and minimize the risk of losing data.

Selecting, Copying, and Moving Multiple Files and Folders

In Windows Explorer, or a Windows folder, such as Documents, Music, Pictures, or Computer, you can select multiple files and folders to perform the same action at one time. For example, you might want to select a group of files to copy to a flash drive, or you might want to select files and move them to a new location or delete them. For example, you might want to select an entire group of picture files and move them from the hard drive to a CD.

Select Multiple Files and Folders

You can select several files and folders, regardless of whether they are adjacent to each other in the file list. Suppose that your digital pictures are contained in the Pictures folder. You might want to delete some of them because you have already copied them to a CD and you want to clear up some hard drive space. First, open the Pictures folder by clicking Start, and then Pictures. Each picture is displayed as a thumbnail, which is a miniature image of the picture.

Assume that you want to delete the first four pictures displayed. Because they are adjacent, you can select the first picture and each picture thereafter through the fourth picture. To do so, click the first picture (do not double-click, or it will open in an image editor), press and hold down Shift on your keyboard, and click the fourth picture. All four pictures should be bordered, indicating that they are selected. To delete the pictures, right-click any selected picture and select Delete. If you want to remove all four pictures, click Yes when asked whether you want to move all pictures to the Recycle Bin. Otherwise, click No.

If, however, you want to select only the first and fourth picture (which are not adjacent to each other) for deletion, click the first picture. Then press and hold down Ctrl while you click the fourth picture. Only the first and fourth pictures are selected. To delete the two pictures, right-click one of the pictures and select Delete. Respond to the prompt asking whether you want to move the selected pictures to the Recycle Bin.

To select all items in a folder, press and hold down Ctrl and press A on the keyboard. At that point, you can right-click any of the selected files and select from the shortcut menu. To cancel any selection, simply click in the white space outside the selection.

Windows Vista includes a new file selection technique that makes it easy to make multiple selections, regardless of whether the items are adjacent. To activate the process, click Organize and then select Folder and Search Options. The Folder Options dialog box opens. Click View, scroll down in the Advanced Settings box, click the Use check boxes to select items check box to select items (see Figure 1.27), and click OK. As you move the mouse pointer along the left side of files and folders, a check box appears. Click in the check box to select the file. In this manner, you can select multiple files and folders. If you want to quickly select all items in the folder, click the check box that appears in the Name column.

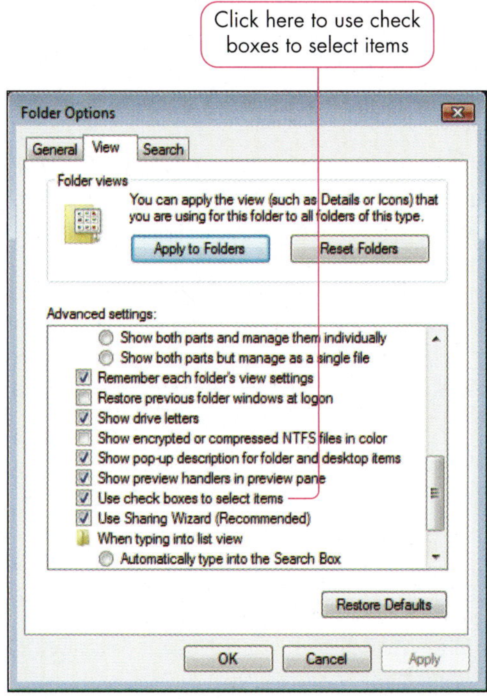

Figure 1.27 Using Check Boxes to Select Multiple Items

Copy and Move Files and Folders

A ***backup*** is a copy of a file.

When you copy or move a folder, both the folder and any files that it contains are affected. You can move or copy a folder or file to another location on the same disk or to another disk. If your purpose is to make a ***backup*** copy of an important file or folder, you will probably want to copy it to another disk.

Using a menu is one of the most foolproof ways to move or copy an item. In Windows Explorer, adjust the display so that you see the file or folder that you want to move or copy. Right-click the item and select either Cut (another word for Move) or Copy. Scroll through the Navigation pane to locate the drive or folder to which you want to move or copy the selected item. Right-click the drive or folder and select Paste. If the copied item is a folder, it should appear as a subfolder of the selected folder. If the copied item is a file, it will be placed within the selected folder.

TIP Right-Click and Drag and Drop

You can right-click a file or folder and, without releasing the mouse as you right-click, drag and drop the file or folder to another location. When you release the mouse, choose Copy Here or Move Here.

Hands-On Exercises

2 | Working with Files and Folders

Skills covered: 1. Create Folders and Subfolders **2.** Delete a Folder **3.** Create and Save a File **4.** Make Backup Copies

Step 1
Create Folders and Subfolders

Refer to Figure 1.28 as you complete Step 1.

a. Click **Computer** on the desktop, or click **Start**, click **All Programs**, select **Accessories**, and then select **Windows Explorer**. Scroll down, if necessary, in the Folders pane and click the **Computer arrow**. Click the **flash drive** (probably drive E).

   You will develop travel information for the state of Kansas. Your focus is on three major areas of the state—East, Central, and West Kansas. It makes sense to divide your folder structure accordingly. Using a flash drive, you will create a folder called Kansas Tourism.

b. Click **Organize** and then select **New Folder**.

   TROUBLESHOOTING: If, instead of **New Folder**, you see selections related to copying or moving the item, you must first click in the white area away from any file that may be listed. Then click **Organize** and **New Folder**.

c. Type **Kansas Tourism** and press **Enter**.

d. Click the **Drive E arrow** in the Navigation pane. Click **Kansas Tourism**.

   You will create three subfolders of Kansas Tourism: East Kansas, Central Kansas, and West Kansas. With the Kansas Tourism folder selected, any subfolders that you create will be subfolders of Kansas Tourism.

e. Click **Organize** and click **New Folder**. Type **East Kansas** and press **Enter**. Click in the white space outside the current folder. Check the Address bar.

   You should see that the current folder is Kansas Tourism.

f. Click **Organize** and click **New Folder**. Type **Central Kansas** and press **Enter**.

g. Create another subfolder of Kansas Tourism, titled **West Kansas**.

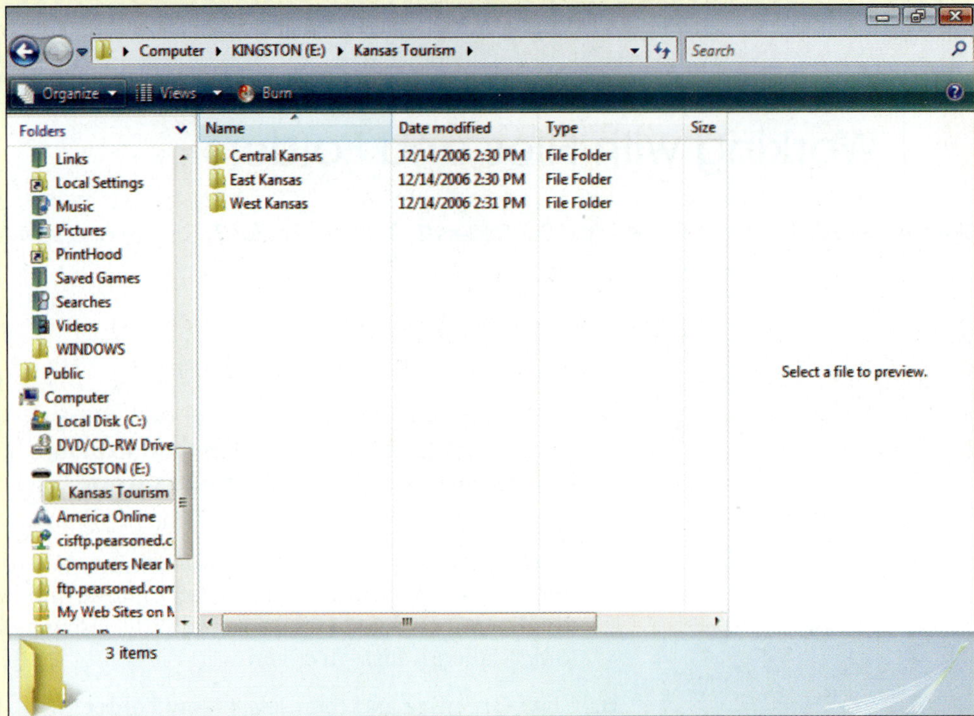

Figure 1.28 Kansas Subfolders

Step 2
Delete a Folder

Refer to Figure 1.29 as you complete Step 2.

a. Click the **Kansas Tourism arrow** (in the Navigation pane).

So far, you have created a folder called Kansas Tourism and three subfolders called West Kansas, Central Kansas, and East Kansas. Through some redistricting of the tourism group, however, Kansas is now divided into only two areas—East Kansas and West Kansas. Central Kansas should be deleted.

b. Right-click **Central Kansas** and select **Delete**. Click **Yes** when asked if you want to permanently delete Central Kansas.

You should now see only two subfolders, as shown in Figure 1.29. Central Kansas is removed.

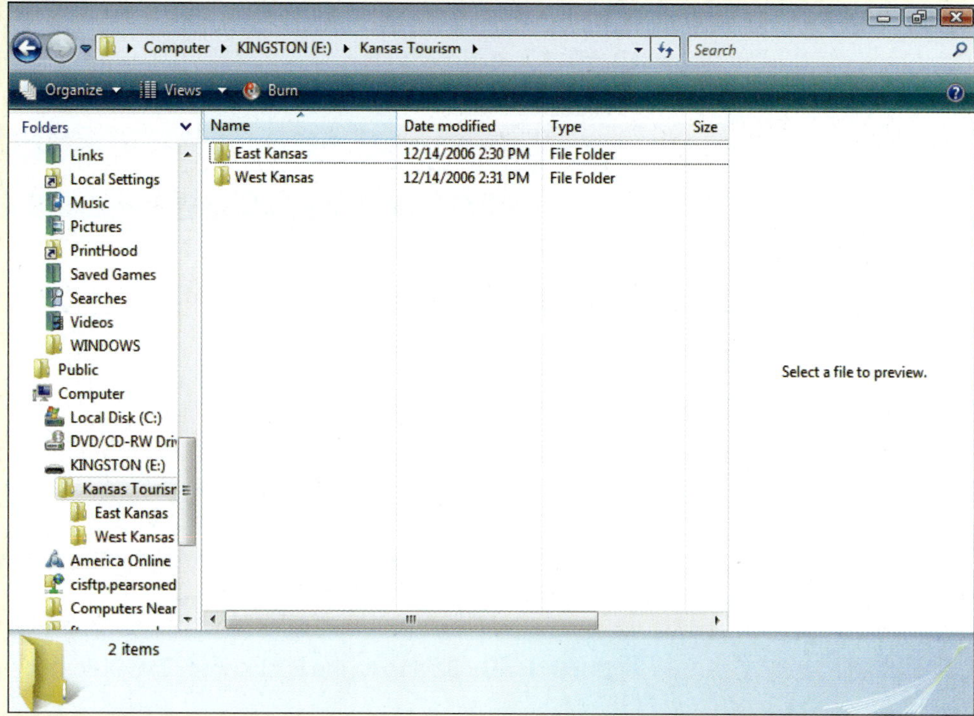

Figure 1.29 Kansas Folders (Central Kansas Deleted)

c. Click **East Kansas** (in the right pane). Click **Organize** and then click **Rename**. Type **East Kansas Travel** and press **Enter**.

   To be more descriptive, you decide to rename both subfolders to include the word Travel. East Kansas will be renamed East Kansas Travel, and West Kansas will be West Kansas Travel.

d. Right-click **West Kansas** and select **Rename**. Click again after the word *Kansas*. Press **Spacebar** and type **Travel**. Press **Enter**.

e. Close Windows Explorer.

Step 3
Create and Save a File

Refer to Figure 1.30 as you complete Step 3.

a. Click **Start**, point to **All Programs**, select **Accessories**, and select **WordPad**.

   You will create a WordPad document with a few travel highlights for East Kansas and a similar document for West Kansas. Each document will be saved in its respective folder.

b. Type **East Kansas Points of Interest**. Press **Enter** twice. Type **Eisenhower Center** and press **Enter**. Type **Natural History Museum and Biodiversity Research Center** and press **Enter**. Type **Kauffman Museum**.

c. Click **File** and select **Save**. Click **Computer** (in the left frame) and double-click the **flash drive** (probably drive E). Click the **drive E drop-down arrow** in the Address bar. Click **Kansas Tourism**. Click the **Kansas Tourism drop-down arrow** and click **East Kansas Travel**. Click in the File name box, selecting (or shading) the current file name. Type **chap1_ho2_east_kansas_highlights**. See Figure 1.30. Click **Save**. Do not close WordPad.

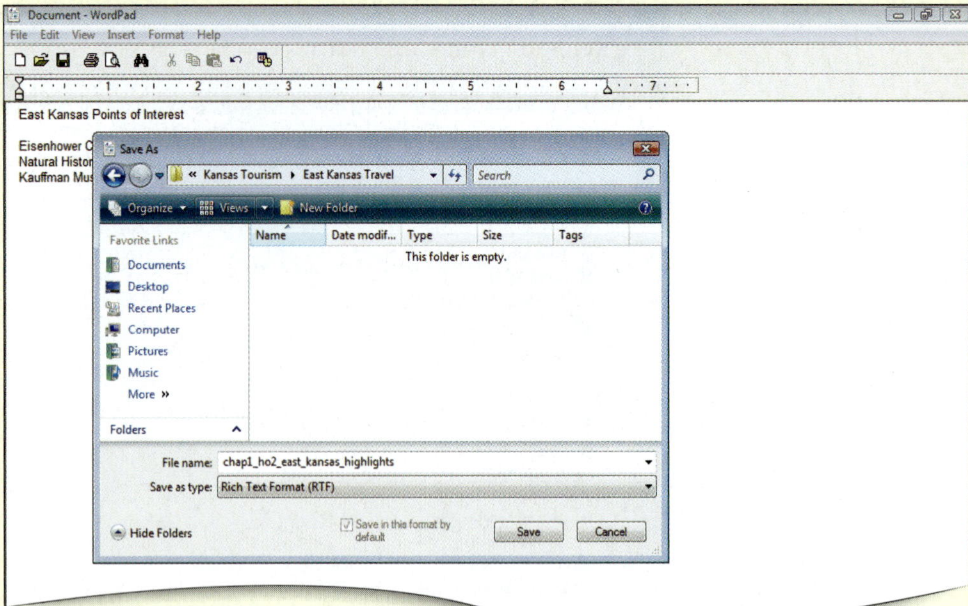

Figure 1.30 Saving to the East Kansas Travel Folder

d. Click **File** and then select **New**. Click **Rich Text Document** and click **OK**. Type **West Kansas Points of Interest** and press **Enter** twice. Type **Mid-America Air Museum** and press **Enter**. Type **Sternberg Museum of Natural History**.

e. Click **File** and select **Save**. Click the **Kansas Tourism drop-down arrow**. Click **West Kansas Travel**. Click in the file name box and type **chap1_ho2_west_kansas_highlights**. Click **Save**.

f. Close WordPad.

g. Open Windows Explorer. Scroll down, if necessary, and click the **Computer folder arrow**. Click the **flash drive arrow**. Click the **Kansas Tourism arrow**.

   To make sure the files are in the appropriate folders, you will check the contents of the flash drive. You should see the drive's folder structure in the left pane, with Kansas Tourism showing two subfolders, East Kansas Travel and West Kansas Travel.

h. Click **East Kansas Travel** in the left (Navigation) pane. To the right, you should see *chap1_ho2_east_kansas_highlights*. Click **West Kansas Travel**.

   The file titled *chap1_ho2_west_kansas_highlights* will display in the right pane.

i. Double-click **chap1_ho2_west_kansas_highlights** to open the file. Close the document without making any changes. Close Windows Explorer.

   TROUBLESHOOTING: If WordPad does not immediately close, but instead you are asked whether you want to save changes to the file, click **No** or **Don't Save**.

Step 4
Make Backup Copies

Refer to Figures 1.31 and 1.32 as you complete Step 4.

a. Click **Start**, point to **All Programs**, select **Accessories**, and select **Windows Explorer**. Scroll down and click the **Computer arrow**. Click the **flash drive arrow** in the Navigation pane. Click the **Kansas Tourism arrow**. Beneath the folder, you should see the Kansas Tourism folder structure.

   It is always a good idea to make backup copies of important files and folders. As you develop tourism information, you will make a copy of the material, preferably on another disk drive. In this example, you will copy the Kansas folder structure, including all files, to the hard drive. Copying the main folder, Kansas Tourism, will ensure that all subfolders and files are duplicated as well.

b. Right-click **Kansas Tourism** (in either the left or right pane) and select **Copy**.

c. Right-click **Local Disk C:** and select **Paste**.

d. Click the **Local Disk C: arrow** if the drive's folder structure is not already expanded. To make sure the tourism folders were copied, scroll down and click the arrow beside **Kansas Tourism**. Click **East Kansas Travel**. Note the **East Kansas Highlights** file in the right pane. Figures 1.31 and 1.32 show the folder structure of the Kansas Tourism folder on the hard drive.

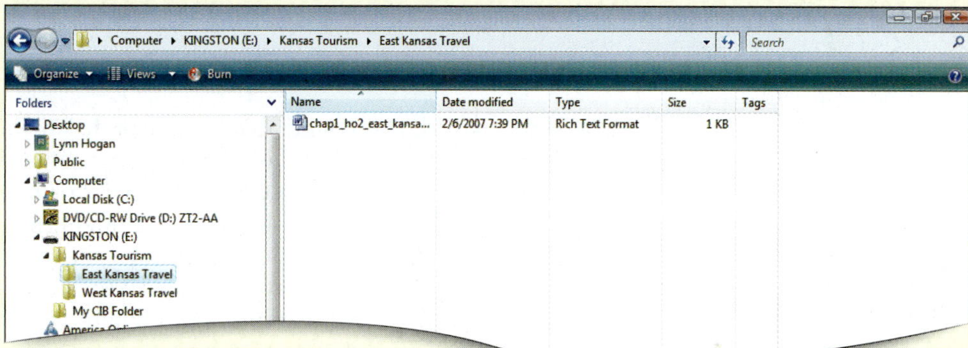

Figure 1.31 East Kansas Travel Folder

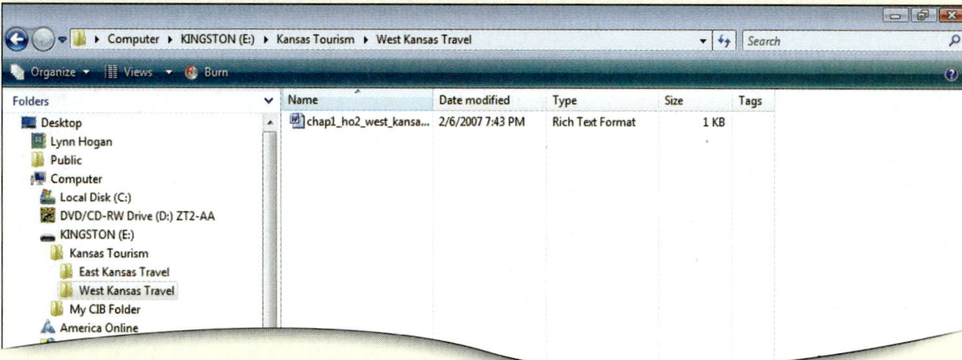

Figure 1.32 West Kansas Travel Folder

e. Right-click **Kansas Tourism** in the Navigation pane, which is a subfolder on Local Disk C:. Select **Delete.** Click **Yes**. The Kansas Tourism folder structure, along with all included files, is deleted and placed in the Recycle Bin.

f. Close all open windows.

Windows Resources: Search, Recycle Bin, and Control Panel

Windows contains a vast array of resources to help you manage your computer system and files. In the last section you learned how to create, rename, and delete folders to organize files. You also learned how to create files. As time goes by, you will store hundreds or thousands of files on your computer's hard drive or on other storage devices. When you need a file, you might not remember its name or location. However, Windows Vista contains resources to help you search through your storage devices to find the file that you need. Furthermore, as you manage your files and delete unnecessary files, you might decide you need a deleted file. The Recycle Bin helps you manage files that have been deleted from particular drives. Finally, the Control Panel contains a vast number of options to manage your system resources. You might need to use it to change default settings or to alter a particular resource.

In this section, you learn how to perform instant searches, apply advanced filtering, and save searches for the future. In addition, you learn how to manage the Recycle Bin. Finally, you learn how to use the Control Panel to manage system resources.

Using Windows Search

In a perfect world, you would always save or download files in locations that are easily recalled. In truth, though, you will often misplace files and folders and should know how to find them. Fortunately, Windows Vista makes it easy to find files and folders. You can initiate a search from several locations, including the Start menu and the Search bar area of windows such as Windows Explorer or Computer. In fact, from just about anywhere you find yourself in Vista, you can initiate a search.

(From just about anywhere you find yourself in Vista, you can initiate a search.)

The first place you will notice a Search box is on the Start menu (see Figure 1.33). As you type characters in the Search box, Vista immediately begins a search, narrowing the results even as you type. For that reason, the Search box is often referred to as the *Instant Search box*. Items that Vista searches include program names, file content and metadata, and contacts and e-mail messages. Any matching items display on the Start menu, replacing the list of pinned and recently used programs. If you see the program or file for which you are searching, click to open it.

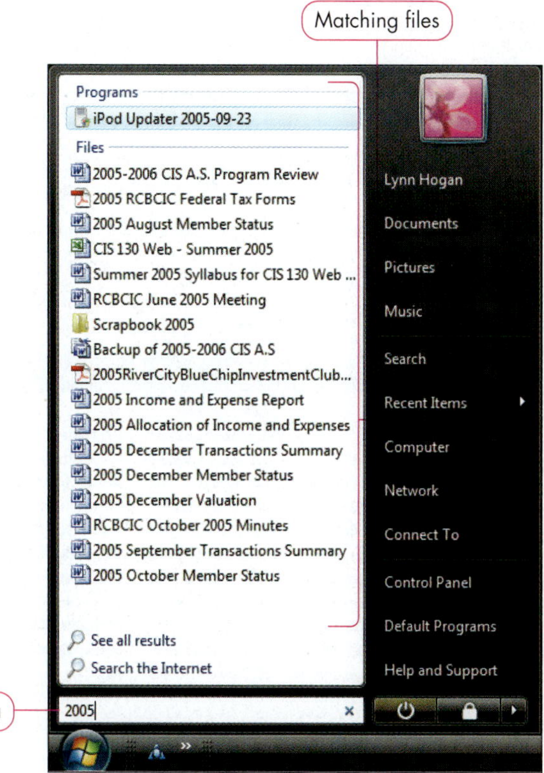

Figure 1.33 Instant Search on the Start Menu

All Windows Vista folder windows, including Windows Explorer, contain an Instant Search box. As you type, the search feature narrows the results to any files in the current folder with names or metadata that match your search text.

Apply Advanced Filters

Instant searching is effective, but sometimes time-consuming because Windows searches for all metadata as well as file contents. In addition, such searches often return far too many results to be very helpful because you might have to go through a lengthy list of results to find the one file you are looking for. In such cases, you need to know how to narrow the results to display only a certain file category or only files on a certain drive.

Advanced filtering enables you to narrow results to files of a certain category, files on a selected disk drive, or files that contain various metadata values. To begin filtering, type your search text in the Search box, click the Advanced Search drop-down arrow below the Search box, and specify additional search criteria. The *Show only* bar presents file types from which you can select. For example, you can specify that you want to show music files only. The *Location* area enables you to select a location, such as a CD or a particular folder. You can also search by other criteria, such as Date, Author, or Name. Figure 1.34 shows Advanced Filter options. Click Search to seek results based on your search criteria.

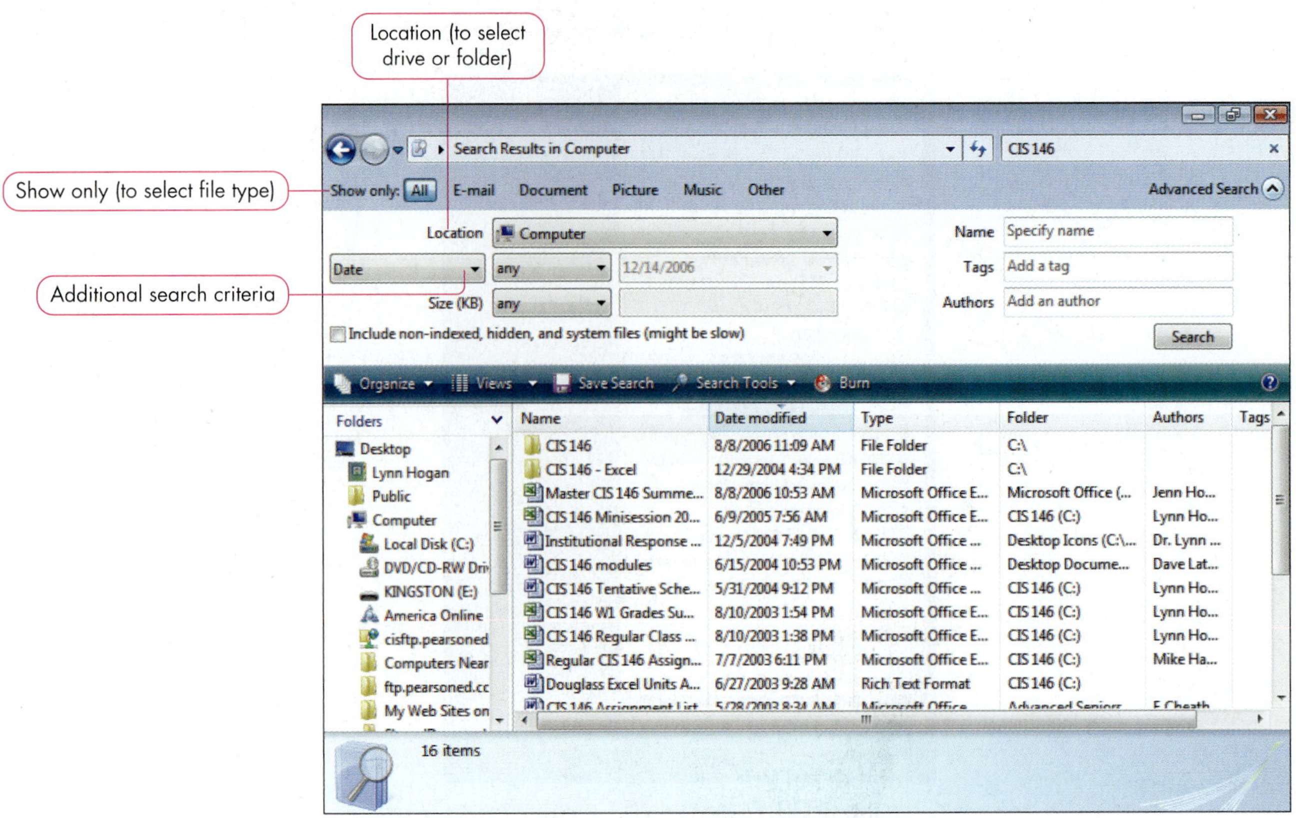

Figure 1.34 Filtering by File Category

Save Searches

So that you do not have to run the same searches time and time again, Windows Vista makes it easy to save search results in a Searches folder. After completing a search, you can save it by clicking the Save Search button in the Task pane (see Figure 1.35). When the Save As dialog box appears, type a name for the search and click Save. To run the search again, click the Searches folder in the Navigation pane and double-click the search.

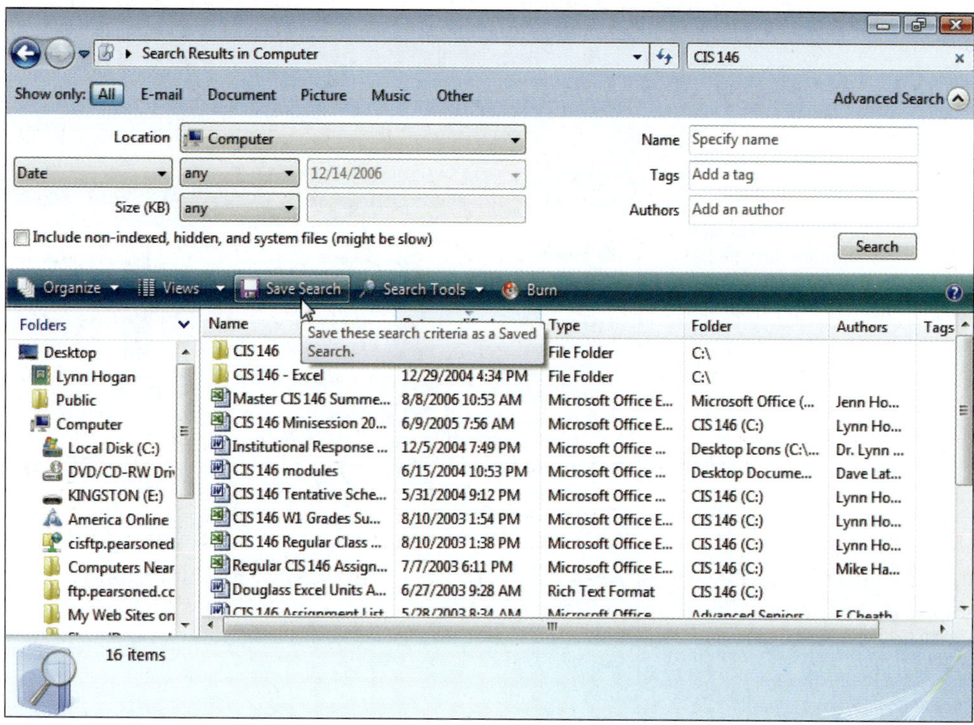

Figure 1.35 Saving a Search

Managing the Recycle Bin

The ***Recycle Bin*** is a temporary holding area for files and folders deleted from the hard drive.

When you delete a file or folder from the hard drive, the item is not immediately removed. Instead, it is placed in the ***Recycle Bin***, which is an area of space reserved on the hard drive to temporarily store deleted items. Although it is comforting to know that files and folders deleted from the hard drive are temporarily held in the Recycle Bin so that you can restore them if necessary, you should be aware that the same assurance does not apply to items deleted from removable media such as CDs and flash drives. As soon as you delete a file from a removable drive, the file is gone and you cannot retrieve it without specialized software.

You can tell if the Recycle Bin holds any items by looking at the icon on the desktop. If you see crumpled papers in the bin, deleted files are stored there. If, however, it is empty, the Recycle Bin has been emptied or was never used. Because the Recycle Bin requires hard drive space to hold deleted items, you might want to periodically empty it. You should only empty the Recycle Bin if you are certain that you will never need the files or folders stored there. You can delete all files and folders in the Recycle Bin or only selected ones. To empty the Recycle Bin, right-click the Recycle Bin icon on the desktop and select Empty the Recycle Bin or click Empty Recycle Bin from within the Recycle Bin window. When asked if you are certain, click Yes. If you want to permanently delete one or more items that are in the Recycle Bin, double-click the Recycle Bin icon. The Recycle Bin opens, as shown in Figure 1.36. Right-click any item and select Delete. The item will be permanently deleted.

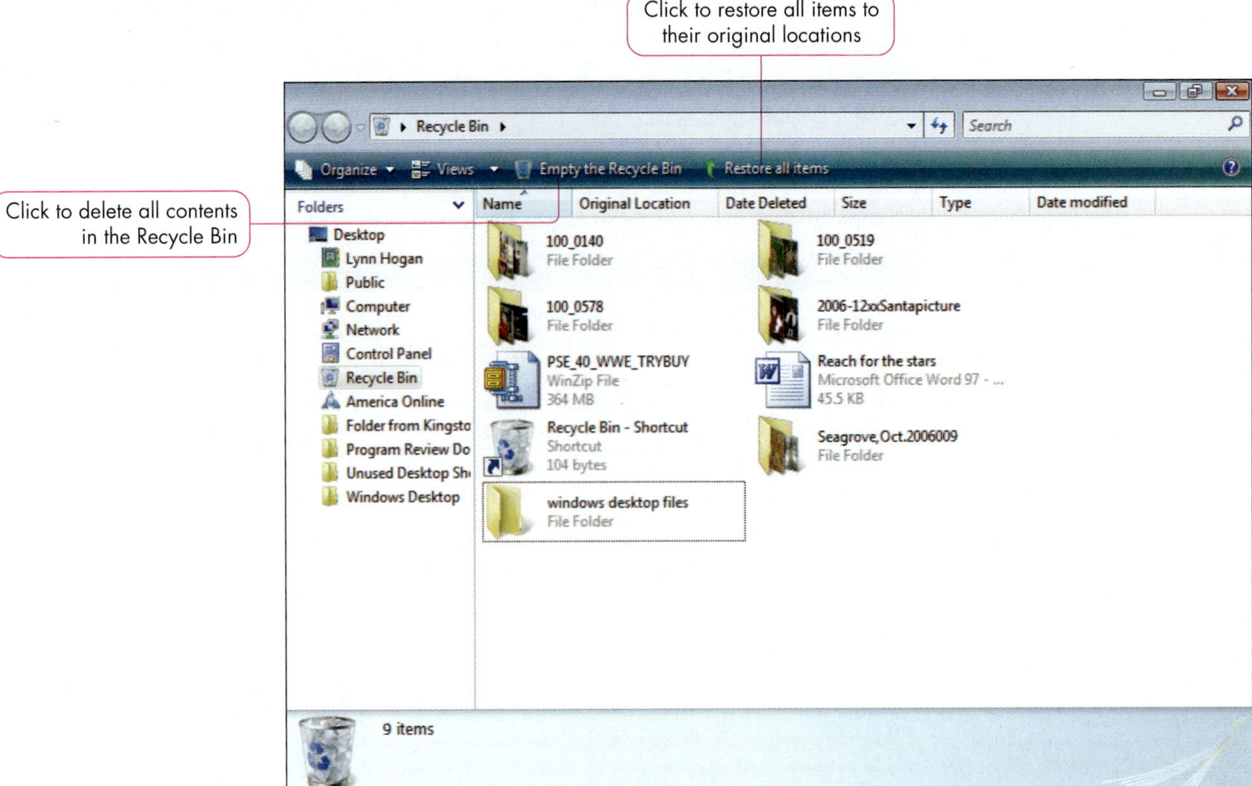

Figure 1.36 Recycle Bin

After a file is placed in the Recycle Bin, you might find that you did not intend to remove the item and want to restore it to the hard drive. That process is easy, requiring only a few clicks. Double-click the Recycle Bin on the desktop. Click Restore all items, as shown in Figure 1.36. All deleted items will be restored to the hard drive. If you only want to restore one or more items from the Recycle Bin, click any item to be restored and select Restore this Item.

Changing Computer Settings Through the Control Panel

Configuring your computer system to reflect your preferences is sure to make the time you spend at the computer more enjoyable. You can change the appearance of your display by selecting a different background or screen saver. Adjusting the mouse double-click speed and reversing the buttons if you are left-handed can make it easier to work with the mouse. You should learn how to manage printers so that you can cancel print jobs if necessary and change from one printer to another. Finally, you can create user accounts so that individuals can enjoy personalized settings and privileges.

The Control Panel enables you to customize your computer system and check system resources. Beginning with Windows XP, the Control Panel was redesigned to display a Category View, which grouped activities into ten major categories. Windows Vista continues the Category view, although with slight modifications to the categories and the way selections are accessed. To view the Control Panel, click Start and then Control Panel. Figure 1.37 shows the Control Panel.

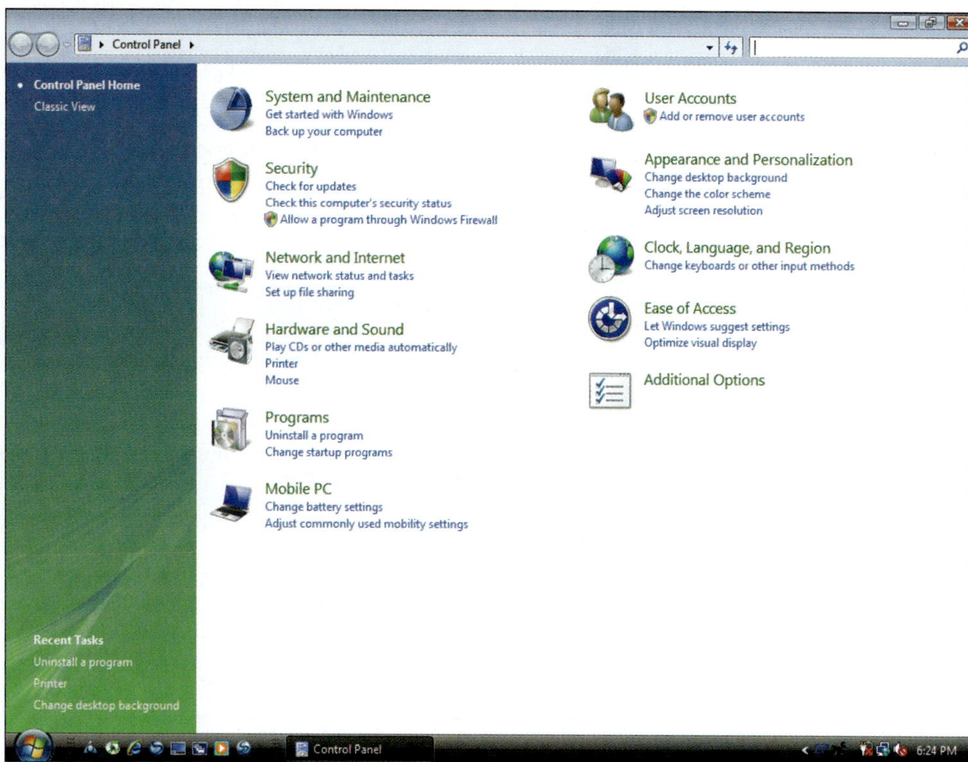

Figure 1.37 Control Panel

Change the Background

The ***background*** is the area of a display that is not covered by characters or graphics.

The desktop ***background*** can be as simple or as colorful as you like. You can select a background from choices provided by Windows Vista, or you can use a favorite photograph. To change the background, click Start and then click Control Panel. Below the Appearance and Personalization heading, click Change desktop background. Take a look at the selections, as shown in Figure 1.38. Select a background and click OK. Close any open windows. Your desktop should display your selection. If, instead, you want to display a favorite photograph as your background, follow the steps above, but instead of making a choice from the selection provided by Windows, click Browse. Navigate to the folder containing your photo and double-click it. Click OK and close any open windows.

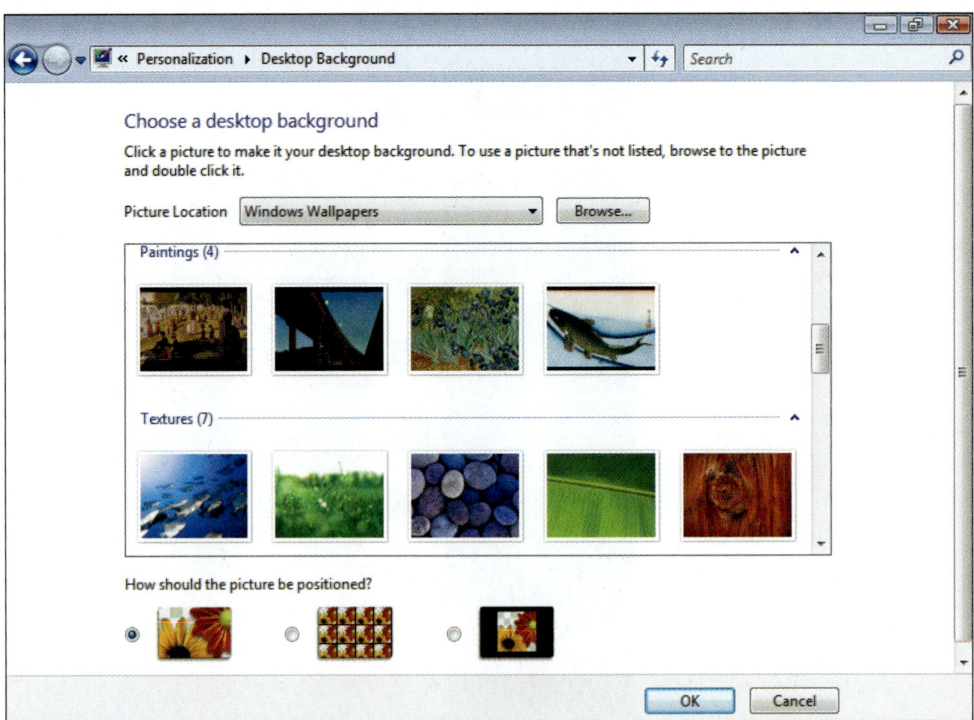

Figure 1.38 Changing a Background

Although you can use the Control Panel to change the desktop background and screen saver, you can take a shortcut. Right-click an empty area of the desktop and select Personalize. Click Desktop Background (or Screen Saver). Make a choice and click OK.

Select a Screen Saver

A ***screen saver*** is a moving image that appears on your screen when your computer has been idle for a specified period of time.

A *screen saver* is an animation that covers your screen when no mouse movement or keyboard activity occurs. Screen savers were necessary at one time to keep images from burning into a monitor. Now, however, screen savers are also used for entertainment. To set a screen saver, display the Control Panel. Click Appearance and Personalization. Click Change screen saver, which is an option under Personalization. Click the Screen saver drop-down arrow and make a selection. You can adjust the wait time if you like, which is the amount of time the computer should be idle before the screen saver begins. Click OK.

A screen saver is not only entertaining, but it can help secure your computer. You can set a password for your screen saver so that the screen saver remains on your screen until the password is entered. The screen saver password is the same password that you use when logging on to Windows. If you do not have a Windows password, you cannot protect your computer with a screen saver password. To set a password, open the Control Panel and click Appearance and Personalization. Click Change screen saver below Personalization. Click On resume, display logon screen. The next time your screen saver is activated, you can move the mouse or press a key on the keyboard. Then you must enter your Windows password to remove the screen saver.

Check System Settings

As you work with your computer, you need to be aware of such system settings as the amount of RAM and the operating system version that is installed. Understanding system information before you purchase software means that you can be certain that your computer meets the specifications required to run the software. Working with the System Properties dialog box, you can also check your processor speed, rename the computer, and allow remote access.

To view system information, display the Control Panel, click System and Maintenance, and click System. Figure 1.39 shows the System Properties dialog box. You can also view system information by clicking the System properties button on the Task pane of the Computer window.

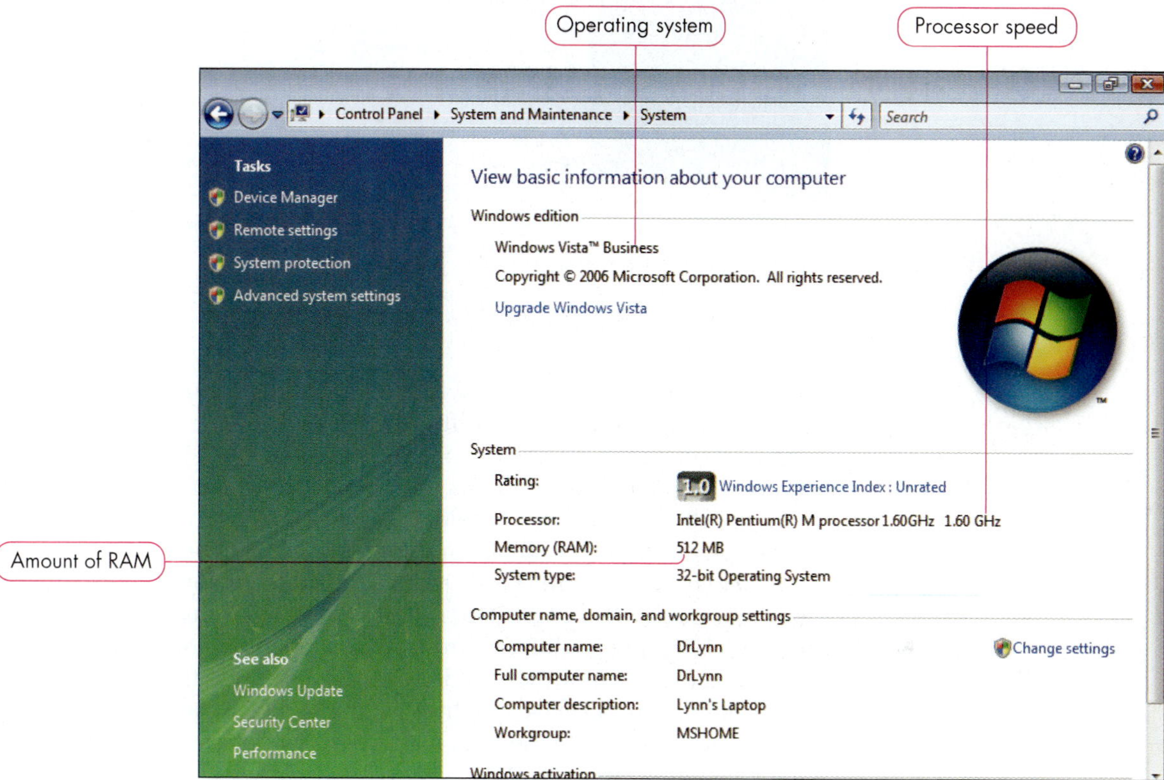

Figure 1.39 System Properties

Install and Uninstall Programs

A ***wizard*** is a step-by-step set of guided instructions.

If you own a computer, you probably purchased it because you had a purpose for it in mind. Perhaps you enjoy working with the Internet or e-mailing friends. You might use a computer to prepare documents, research family history, or prepare presentations. Whatever the purpose, you can be assured that software is available to assist you. Software that you purchase comes on a CD, usually with very little packaging or documentation. To install the software, simply place the CD in the CD drive and wait until a dialog box appears, providing a ***wizard*** to assist you in the installation process. In most cases, responding affirmatively to selections presented by the wizard results in a successful installation. Installed software appears in the All Programs list, available when you click Start, All Programs. Sometimes, a software icon will also be displayed on the desktop or in the Quick Launch toolbar.

Although working with software can be a lot of fun, you will find that it sometimes becomes obsolete or no longer interesting to you. Keeping your hard drive in top working order requires that you maximize space by removing unused files or software. For both of those reasons, you will find it necessary to uninstall software that you no longer need or enjoy. To remove software, click Start, Control Panel, and

Uninstall a program (found under Programs). Currently installed programs will display (see Figure 1.40). To remove a program, click the program name and click Uninstall or Change on the Task pane.

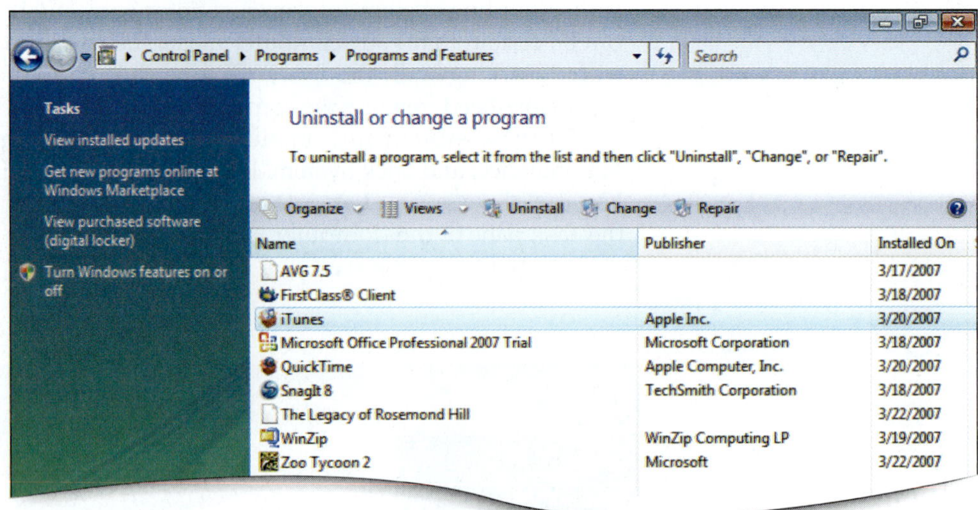

Figure 1.40 Uninstalling or Changing a Program

Manage the Mouse and Printers

Aside from the keyboard, you will spend more time using the mouse than any other piece of computer equipment. It is important that the mouse is comfortable to use and customized to meet your needs. If you are left-handed, you might want to reverse the mouse buttons so that you can use the index finger for most mouse clicks. If the speed required for a double-click is too rapid for you, you can adjust it. Both of those operations are available through the Control Panel.

Display the Control Panel and click Mouse below the Hardware and Sound heading. Click the Buttons tab, if necessary. The Mouse Properties dialog box (see Figure 1.41) might be different from yours, depending on your mouse type. Click the check box to switch primary and secondary buttons, effectively making your mouse left-handed. You can click and drag a slider to adjust the double-click speed. Double-click the sample area to the right to test the new double-click setting before accepting the changes by clicking OK.

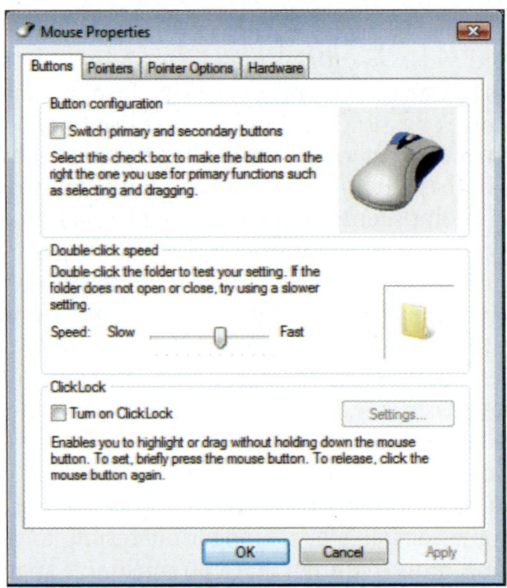

Figure 1.41 Mouse Properties

Managing a printer is a skill that you should develop early, as one of the most frustrating events is when a printer fails to print, or prints continuously without stopping. If you use more than one printer, you will need to know how to switch between printers. Make those adjustments by clicking Start, Control Panel, and Printer (under Hardware and Sound). The printer window shown in Figure 1.42 will display.

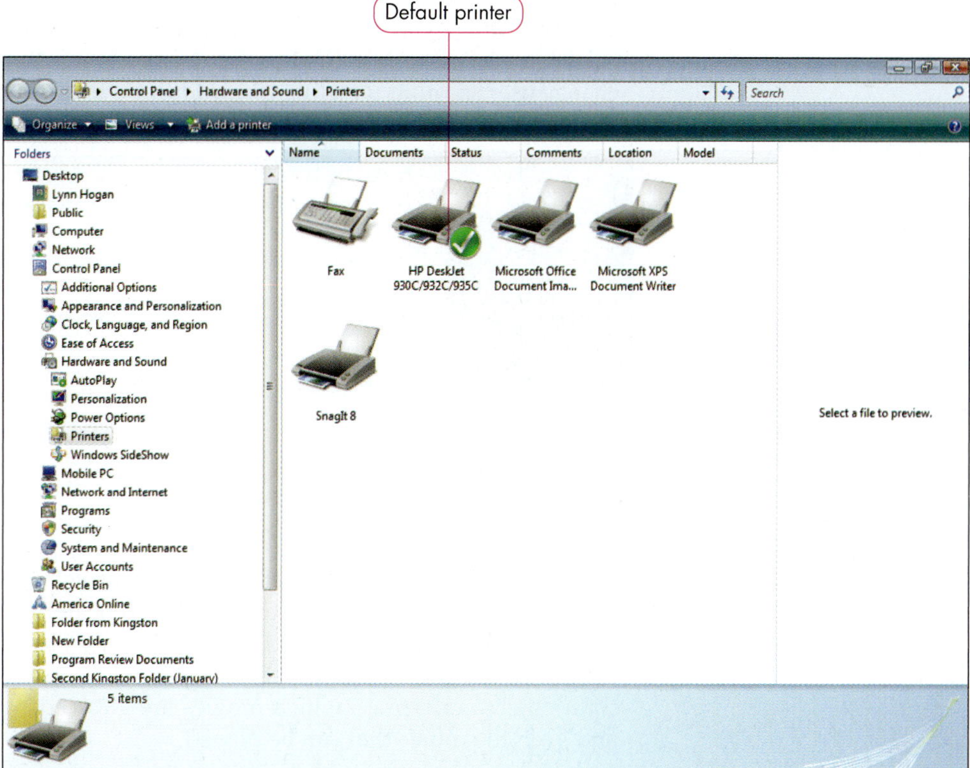

Figure 1.42 Printer Window

Your default printer (the one to which all printing is directed unless you specify otherwise) is identified by a check mark. To view the printer in more detail, double-click the printer icon. Any print job(s) being processed will be displayed, along with the status of each job—whether the job is being printed or deleted. Occasionally, you might by mistake send the same document to the printer several times. In that case, you can cancel all documents by clicking Printer, Cancel All Documents. You can also pause printing by clicking Printer, Pause Printing. Be aware, however, that print jobs are collected in a buffer, which is a holding area between the computer and printer, and even after you cancel documents, printing will likely continue for a little while before the buffer is cleared. Before printing another document, you must release the printer by following the same steps that you did to pause the printer. When you click Pause Printing a second time, the printer returns to an active state.

If you use more than one printer, you will see each of them listed in the Printers dialog box. The default printer has a check mark next to it. To change the default printer, double-click a printer without a check mark (if more than one printer is displayed), and click Printer, Set as Default Printer. Only one printer at a time can be designated as the default printer.

Create and Manage User Accounts

Windows Vista includes a user accounts feature whereby several people can use the same computer but with different accounts and varying levels of privileges. If you have only one account, it is an administrator account with full privileges. As the administrator, you can create any number of user accounts. With user accounts, each person can have a customized desktop, personal folders, and even password protection. Setting up user accounts is very easily done through the Control Panel.

To create a new user account, display the Control Panel and click User Accounts (see Figure 1.43). Then click Add or remove user accounts and click Continue. Click Create a new account, type an account name, and select either Administrator or Standard user. A standard user account can only view and work with files created by this user, customize this user's desktop, and change this user's own password, whereas an administrator can create accounts, make system-wide changes, and install programs. Click Create Account to finalize the user account. As the administrator, you can also change user accounts, deleting them, adding passwords, or changing their status.

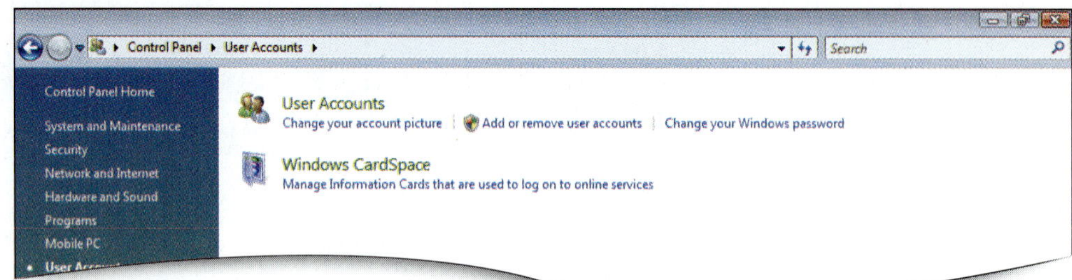

Figure 1.43 User Accounts

Parents enjoy the wealth of parental controls included in a typical Vista installation. With user accounts set up for children, parents are able to restrict Web site content and games, block specific programs, and set time limits on computer usage. Parents can control the games that are played, users who are allowed to communicate through chat or e-mail, which movies are allowed, which Web sites can be visited, and even the music that can be played.

Explore Security Settings

Security is a concern of most computer users. Microsoft has focused on enhancing security with the Vista design. To specify security settings, display the Control Panel and click Security. The Security window enables you to change settings in these major categories: Security Center, Windows Firewall, Windows Update, Windows Defender, and Internet Options (see Figure 1.44).

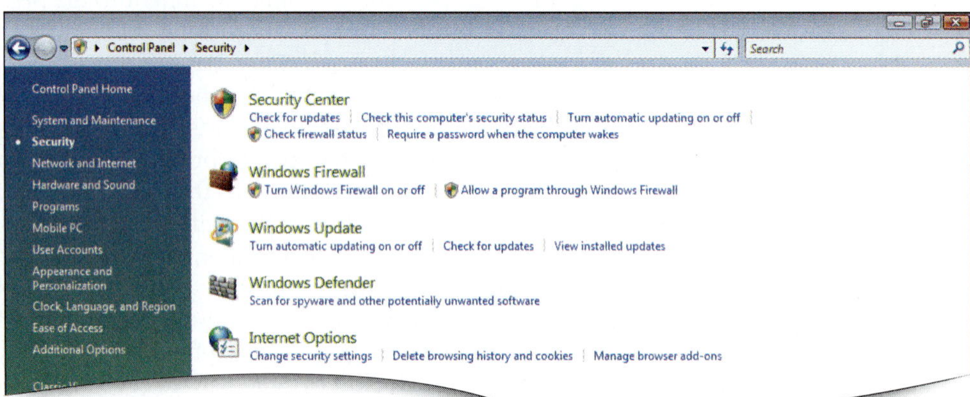

Figure 1.44 Security Window

The Security Center enables you to check the Internet for security updates, evaluate the security status of your computer, and require a password when your computer "wakes up." Windows Update enables you to turn on the automatic update feature, which will periodically check to see if your Windows Vista is up-to-date. If not, it will access Microsoft's Web site and download update files for Windows Vista while you do other work. You can specify to have the updates installed automatically or at your convenience. You can also see a list of updates you have installed for Windows Vista.

Windows Firewall and Windows Defender address unauthorized Internet traffic and spyware. Both tools are improvements over earlier Windows versions, with Firewall blocking both unauthorized incoming and outgoing traffic, whereas Defender prevents spyware from being installed on your system. A new Phishing Filter warns you if a Web page appears to be a phishing scam. Phishing is an attempt to fool you into submitting financial data on what appears to be a legitimate Web page or e-mail. The Internet Options category lets you specify security settings, delete browsing history and cookies, and manage add-ons.

Hands-On Exercises

3 | Working with the Recycle Bin, Windows Search, and Control Panel

Skills covered: 1. Place Files in the Recycle Bin **2.** Manage the Recycle Bin **3.** Use Windows Search **4.** Work with the Control Panel

Step 1
Place Files in the Recycle Bin

Refer to Figure 1.45 as you complete Step 1.

a. Click **Start**, click **All Programs**, select **Accessories**, select **Windows Explorer**. Scroll down and click the arrow to the left of Computer. Click Local Disk (C:). Click **Organize**, click **New Folder**, type **Comanche Collectibles**, and press **Enter**.

b. Close Windows Explorer.

TROUBLESHOOTING: If your folder receives a name other than **Comanche Collectibles**, you probably clicked the mouse or pressed Enter before typing the name. To correct it, right-click the folder and select **Rename**. Type the correct name and press **Enter**.

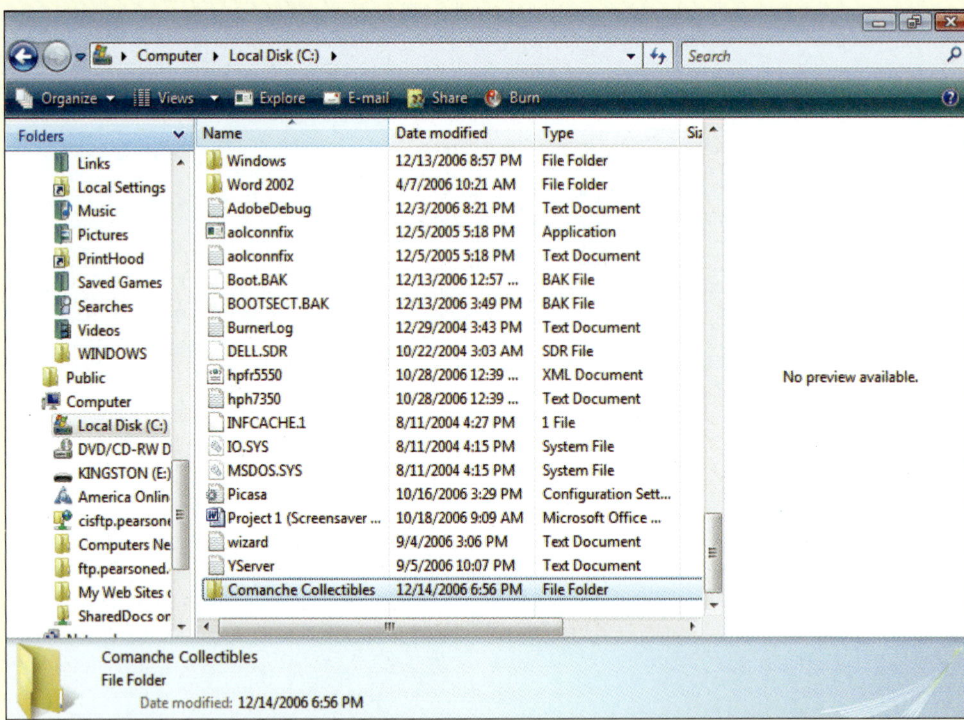

Figure 1.45 Comanche Collectibles Folder

c. Click **Start**, point to **All Programs**, select **Accessories**, and select **WordPad**. Type a short price list, making up items and prices. Press **Enter** after each line.

You will create a file to save in the folder, giving a price list of a few items in your store.

d. Click **File** and select **Save**. Scroll up or down, if necessary, and click **Computer** in the left pane. Double-click **Local Disk (C:)**. Scroll down, if necessary, and double-click **Comanche Collectibles**. Click in the file name area and change the file name to **chap1_ho3_current_price_list**. Click **Save**.

e. Click **File** and select **New**. Click **Rich Text Document** and click **OK**. Type your company name, press **Enter**, and type the company address (make it up).

   Here, you create another WordPad document, recording your business address.

f. Click **File** and select **Save**. Because the most recently accessed folder was **Comanche Collectibles**, the folder is already selected. The file name is also selected. Without clicking anywhere, type **chap1_ho3_company_address**. Click **Save**.

g. Close WordPad.

Step 2
Manage the Recycle Bin

Refer to Figure 1.46 as you complete Step 2.

a. Click **Start**, point to **All Programs**, select **Accessories**, and select **Windows Explorer**. Scroll down, if necessary, and click the arrow to the left of **Computer**. Click the arrow to the left of **Local Disk (C:)**. Scroll down, if necessary, and click **Comanche Collectibles**. To the right, you should see both files.

b. Click the first file. Hold down Shift and click the next file. With both files selected, or shaded, right-click one of the files. Select **Delete**. When asked to confirm the deletion, click **Yes**. Both files should disappear.

c. Close Windows Explorer.

d. Double-click **Recycle Bin** (on the desktop). Refer to Figure 1.46. Right-click the address file (the one containing your company address) and select **Delete**. Respond affirmatively when asked whether you want to permanently delete it.

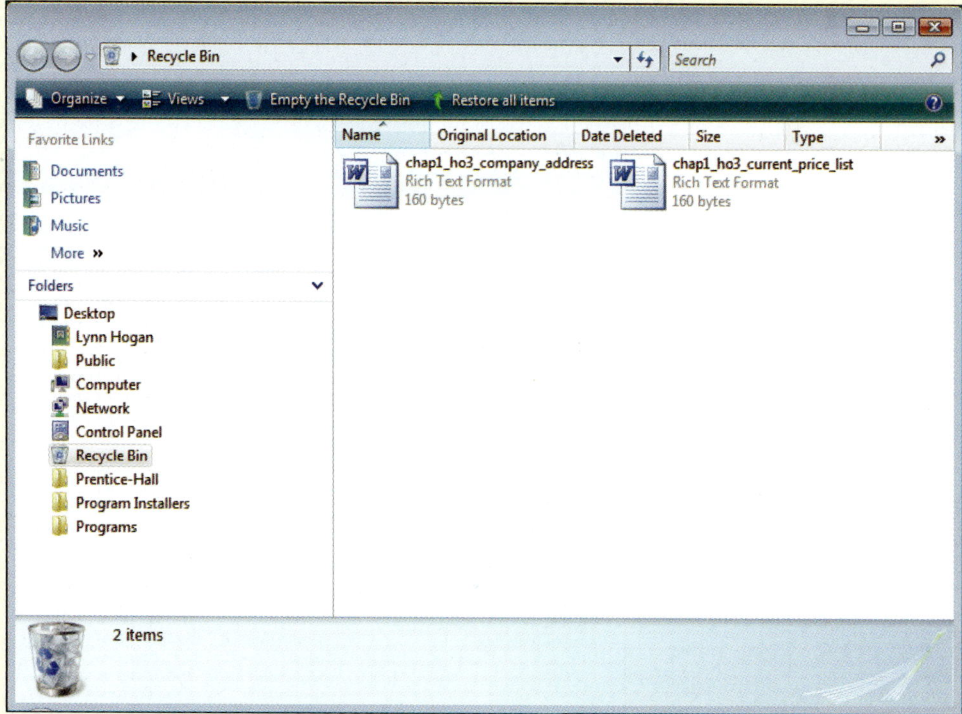

Figure 1.46 Recycle Bin

e. Click **Restore all items** (if chap1_ho3_current_price_list is the only file in the Recycle Bin). If other files are present, however, click *chap1_ho3_current_price_list* and click **Restore this item**.

   The Price List file is important to your company, so you will restore it.

f. Close the Recycle Bin.

g. Open Windows Explorer. Scroll down, if necessary, and click the arrow to the left of **Computer**. Click the arrow to the left of **Local Disk (C:)**. Right-click **Comanche Collectibles**, select **Delete**, and agree to the deletion.

   To return the hard drive to the status it was before you began this exercise, you will remove the Comanche Collectibles folder.

h. Close Windows Explorer.

i. Double-click **Recycle Bin** (on the desktop). If **Comanche Collectibles** is the only item in the Recycle Bin, click **Empty the Recycle Bin**. If, however, other items are present, right-click **Comanche Collectibles** and select **Delete**. Agree to the deletion. Close the Recycle Bin.

Step 3
Use Windows Search

Refer to Figure 1.47 as you complete Step 3.

a. Click **Start** and click **Computer** to open the Computer folder. Then click on your local disk, usually C:.

   You will conduct a search to find all files with the word "Sample" in the file title, contents, or metadata.

b. Click the **Maximize** button, if the window is less than full size.

c. Click in the Search box and type **Sample**.

   Several items are listed, each of which contains the search term within its address, contents, title, or metadata. You want to narrow the results to only picture files.

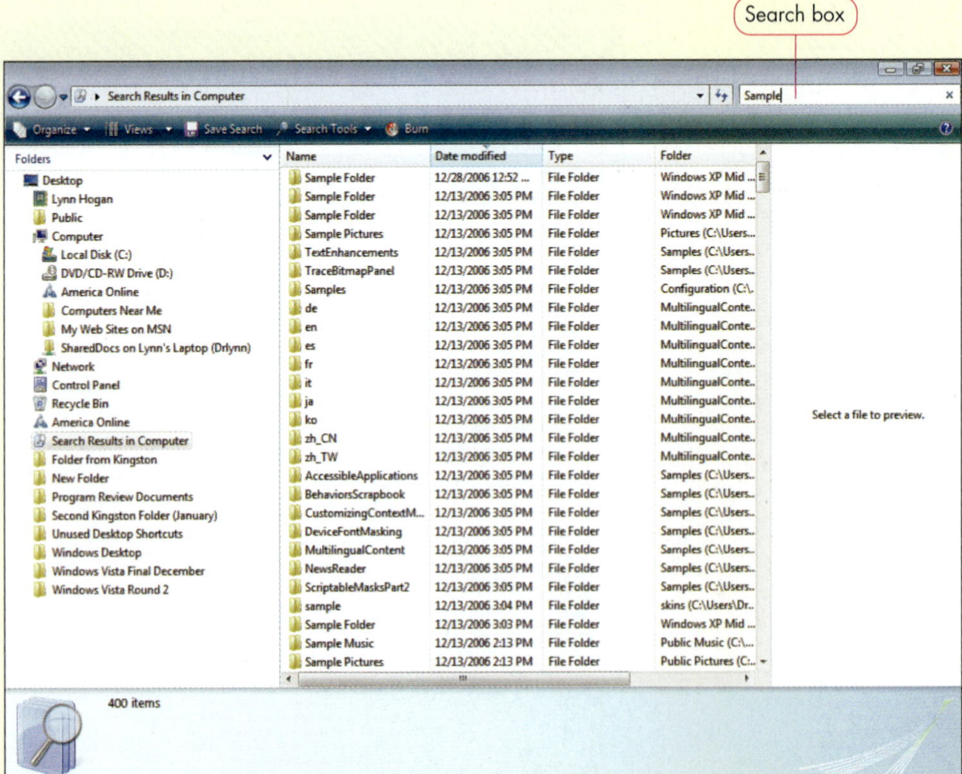

Figure 1.47 Search Criteria

d. Scroll to the bottom of the file/folder listing and click **Advanced Search** (not shown in Figure 1.47). Click **Picture** in the Show Only bar. All pictures matching the search criteria are shown.

e. Close all open windows.

Step 4
Work with the Control Panel

If you are working in a lab, before beginning this step, check with your instructor to see if it is OK to change the background and screen saver. If it is not, skip this step.

a. Click **Start**, click **Control Panel**. Click **Change desktop background** below the Appearance and Personalization heading.

b. Scroll down the list of background choices and click the large palm leaf. Click **OK**.

c. Click **Appearance and Personalization**. Click **Change screen saver**.

d. Click the **Screen saver drop-down arrow** and select **Ribbons**. Click **OK**.

e. Click **Control Panel** in the Address bar. Click **System and Maintenance**.

f. Check the amount of RAM and the operating system available on your computer system.

g. Close all open windows.

Summary

1. **Describe Windows Vista versions and features.** Windows Vista is available in five versions, some designed for home users, some for multimedia enthusiasts, and some for business applications. Some of the special features of Vista include Windows Defender, Windows Mail, Internet Explorer 7, Windows Firewall, Security Center, Windows Movie Maker, Windows Media Player, Windows Photo Gallery, and Windows Calendar. The Vista interface is one of the most striking features, especially if your computer is able to support the Aero Glass shell, a transparent glass effect. Such elements as the Windows Sidebar, complete with gadgets (mini-applications), make Vista as much fun as it is a business-oriented operating system.
2. **Identify components of the Windows Vista interface.** The main interface, called the desktop, contains shortcut icons to programs and files. The Windows Sidebar provides up-to-date information and a quick summary of window contents. The taskbar, located at the bottom of the screen, contains the Start button, Quick Launch toolbar, buttons for open programs, and the Notification area. When you click the Start button, the Start menu appears, displaying programs and options for accessing controls. You can customize the Start menu by pinning and removing items and displaying the Start menu in Classic view. The Quick Launch toolbar contains icons to quickly start programs with a single click. The button area displays buttons for open programs so that you can toggle back and forth between programs. The Notification area displays the clock and provides status icons.
3. **Work with windows and dialog boxes.** Windows open when you start programs. You can minimize, maximize, restore, and close windows. You can resize some windows by clicking and dragging the edges of windows. Dialog boxes are special windows that enable you to specify options for various tasks. Dialog box components include drop-down arrows, option buttons, text boxes, spin buttons, command buttons, and check boxes.
4. **Use Help and Support.** Windows Vista provides a Help and Support Center that provides assistance with tasks. Using Help and Support, you can learn much about Windows Vista in a very short amount of time. You can browse through topics, use the table of contents, or contact Microsoft Customer Support online. Some Help topics contain guided help to watch animated steps.
5. **Manage files and folders in Windows Explorer.** Windows Explorer displays folders and files. You can see program files and data files. Windows Explorer enables you to manage your folders and files so that you can organize them. Folders are holding areas for files and subfolders.
6. **Create, rename, and delete folders.** You can design your folder structure in any way that makes sense to you. After creating folders, you might need to rename them. When you no longer need a folder, you can delete it to clean up the listing of folders.
7. **Work with files.** To create files, you will use software, such as Microsoft Word. You can also add metadata to files. Metadata is information that helps categorize files and folders by content through keywords.
8. **Select, copy, and move multiple files and folders.** When you need to copy, move, or delete several files within one folder, you can select them and perform the action one time. To select all files, press Ctrl+A. To select adjacent files, click the first file, press and hold down Shift, and click the last file. To select nonadjacent files, press and hold down Ctrl as you click each file. It is sometimes necessary to make copies of folders and files or to move them. You might want to clear some hard drive space by moving files to a flash drive, or you might find it necessary to make a backup (copy) of a critical file on a CD.
9. **Use Windows Search.** Windows Search is built into almost every component of Windows Vista. An Instant Search box is included on the Start menu and most folder windows. As you type search keywords, Vista begins to narrow results, so that when you finish typing, all results are already displayed. Using Advanced Search, you can specify more criteria, such as the drive to search or the file type to be included in search results.

...continued on Next Page

10. **Manage the Recycle Bin.** Files that are deleted from the hard drive are not removed permanently. Instead, they are placed in the Recycle Bin, which is an area of space on the hard drive reserved for deleted items. Items deleted from a removable disk, such as a flash drive or CD-RW, are not placed in the Recycle Bin. You can recover, or restore, selected files from the Recycle Bin, or if you are sure you will never need the files, you can empty the Recycle Bin.

11. **Change computer settings through the Control Panel.** The Control Panel enables you to change the desktop appearance as well as to adjust mouse and printer settings. You can check system settings, identifying the operating system version, processor speed, and amount of RAM (memory). The Control Panel also provides access to user account settings.

Key Terms

Multiple Choice

1. A window arrangement where open windows are placed one on top of the other, with only a small segment of the background window showing, is called:
   (a) Bordered
   (b) Stacked
   (c) Tiled
   (d) Cascaded

2. A difference between a data file and a program file is that:
   (a) A program file is something that you create; a data file is provided by a software developer.
   (b) A program file is a WordPad document; a data file is an Excel document.
   (c) A data file is much larger than a program file.
   (d) A data file is something that you create; a program file is part of a software installation.

3. The Recycle Bin:
   (a) Contains files deleted from a hard drive.
   (b) Contains files deleted from a removable disk.
   (c) Is not included in Windows Vista.
   (d) Cannot be emptied.

4. The Windows Vista program that is used for creating and managing folders is:
   (a) Microsoft Defender
   (b) Computer
   (c) Windows Explorer
   (d) Windows Manager

5. An identifier, such as author or keyword, that you might give a file to describe it is called:
   (a) Title
   (b) Label
   (c) Key phrase
   (d) Metadata

6. Each window contains control buttons. They are:
   (a) Minimize, Maximize, Restore, Close
   (b) Open, Close, Resize, Move
   (c) Expand, Collapse, Open, Close
   (d) Minimize, Maximize, Open, Close

7. When a folder is copied to a different location:
   (a) The folder and all of its subfolders (including any files) are copied.
   (b) It *must* be copied to another disk.
   (c) The original folder is deleted.
   (d) The folder is renamed as it is copied to indicate that it is a duplicate.

8. One of the security features of Windows Vista is:
   (a) Monitoring spyware
   (b) Deleting crackers
   (c) Managing Windows downloads
   (d) Checking software licenses

9. A storage area that is labeled and reserved to hold files is called a:
   (a) Window
   (b) Dialog box
   (c) Bin
   (d) Folder

10. To place a program icon on the Quick Launch toolbar, you would:
    (a) Double-click and drag the program icon to the Quick Launch toolbar.
    (b) Select the program from the Quick Launch toolbar menu.
    (c) Right-click and drag the program icon to the Quick Launch toolbar.
    (d) Click Start, Quick Launch, Add.

11. The taskbar area that includes such items as volume control, background programs, and wireless connection information is the:
    (a) Preview pane
    (b) Navigation area
    (c) Contents button
    (d) Notification area

12. Which of the following is a method of placing files in the Recycle Bin? Assume that all files come from the hard drive.
    (a) Click and drag a file icon on the desktop to the Recycle Bin.
    (b) In Windows Explorer, click and drag a file to the desktop.
    (c) Right-click a file and select **Remove**.
    (d) Right-click a file and select **Erase**.

Multiple Choice Continued...

13. Small pictures on the desktop representing programs, files, folders, or shortcuts are called:

(a) Pins

(b) Icons

(c) Thumbnails

(d) Tiles

14. The Windows Vista feature that provides information on a file's metadata is:

(a) Preview pane

(b) Navigation pane

(c) Details pane

(d) Documents

15. To select multiple files that are not adjacent to one another, you would press and hold this key while clicking each file to be included.

(a) Shift

(b) Alt

(c) Ctrl

(d) Del

Practice Exercises

1 Greenview Stables

Greenview Stables is a local boarding and riding stable. The owner, Mary Sternberg, is an excellent horseback instructor but finds it difficult to keep up with the paperwork that goes along with a small business. She has recently acquired a computer with Windows Vista installed, but she has no idea how to work with it. Because you are so skilled with Windows Vista, Mary has asked you to teach her the basics so that she can begin to keep the stable's records on her computer. In preparation for the first lesson with Mary, you should practice using Windows Vista.

a. Turn on the computer and select an account, if necessary.

b. To make sure icons are set to auto-arrange, right-click an empty area of the desktop. Point to **View**. If a check mark does not appear beside **Auto Arrange**, select **Auto Arrange**. If a check mark appears beside **Auto Arrange,** click outside the menu to close it.

c. Right-click an empty area of the desktop and select **Personalize**. Click **Desktop Background**. Scroll down to find a picture of an orange flower (if you hover the mouse pointer over it, you should see that it is titled "img10").

d. Click it (or any other image, if you don't see the flower image). Click **OK**. Close the Control Panel. Close any open windows.

e. Click **Start**, select **All Programs**, select **Accessories**, and then **Paint**. Click a color in the palette at the bottom (or top) of the window. (If you do not see a color palette, click **View** and **Color Box**.) If the cursor is not shaped like a pencil, click the Pencil tool in the tool box to the right (or left). (If you do not see a tool box, click **View** and **Tool Box**.) Click and drag to write your name in cursive. Close Paint. Do not save the picture.

f. Double-click the **Recycle Bin** icon on the desktop. If the window opens as a maximized window (filling the screen), click the **Restore Down button** (the middle button). Your window should be less than full size. Make the window smaller by clicking and dragging a border or corner. Move the window by clicking and dragging the title bar. Click the **Close button** to close the Recycle Bin.

g. Click **Start** and select **Help and Support**. Click in the Search help text box and type **shut down** and press **Enter**. From the results displayed, click **Turning off your computer properly**. Read the description to learn how to shut down a computer. See Figure 1.48. Close Help and Support.

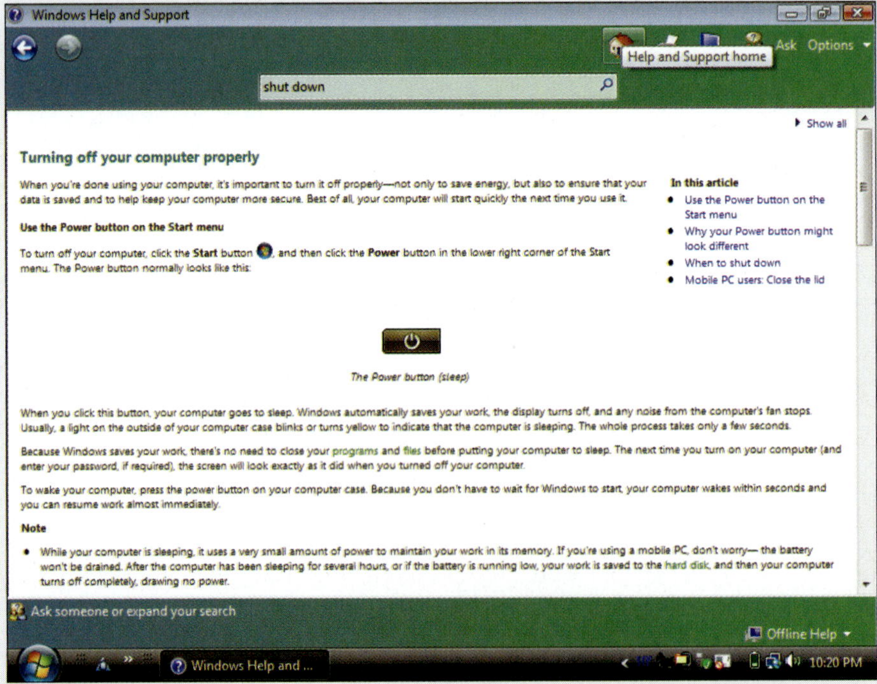

Figure 1.48 Assistance with Shutting Down

...continued on Next Page

2 Caring Holidays

The Student Government Association, of which you are a member, conducts a charity drive each year called *Caring Holidays*. One particular family has several children who are attending local schools. Because the children need access to a computer for homework and research assignments, you have found one that a friend would like to donate. Before you give the computer to the family, you want to make sure the computer is working well and that it is equipped well enough to see the children through their classes.

a. Right-click an empty area of the desktop and select **View**. Click **Large Icons**. Because the icons are too large, follow the same procedure to change them back to **Medium Icons**.

b. Click **Start**, click **Control Panel**, and click **System and Maintenance**. Click **System**. The System window should open, as shown in Figure 1.49. Which version of Windows Vista is installed on the computer? How much memory (RAM) is installed? Close all open windows.

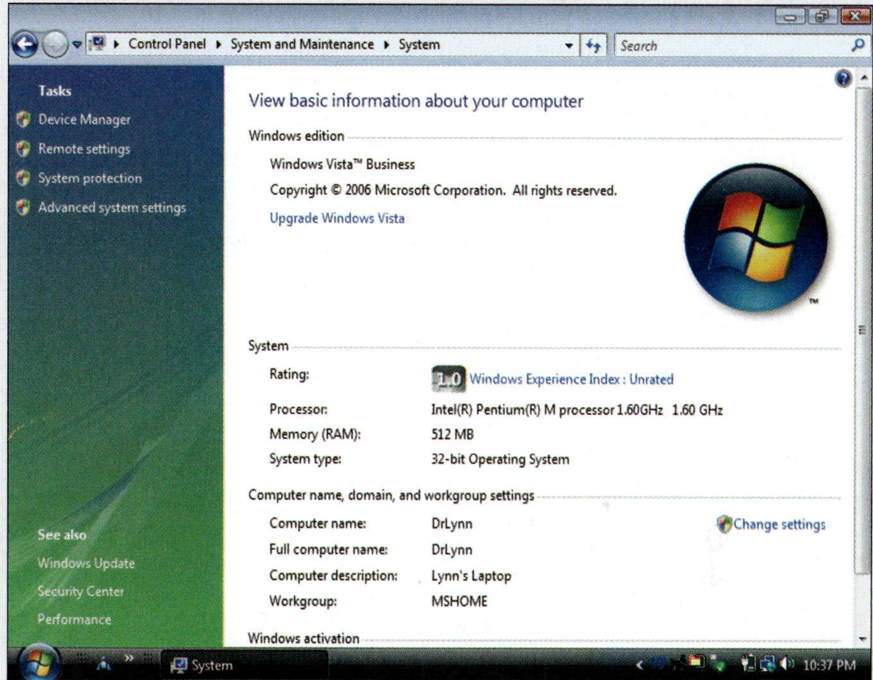

Figure 1.49 System Configuration

c. Click **Start** and click **Computer**. What type(s) of disk drives do you see? Hover the pointer over the local disk. How much disk space is available? Close Computer.

d. Just for fun, you want to set a screen saver so that when the computer is idle, a moving image obscures the screen. Click **Start** and click **Control Panel**. Click **Appearance and Personalization**. Click **Change screen saver**. Click the **Screen saver drop-down arrow** and click **Aurora** (if Aurora is not available, select another screen saver). Change the wait time to 5 minutes. Click **Preview**. Press any key to stop the screen saver. Click **OK**. Close all open windows.

e. You are not sure which programs are already installed on the system, so you want to display a complete list. Click **Start** and click **Control Panel**. Click **Uninstall a program** below the Programs heading. Wait a few seconds for the list to appear. Scroll through the list, familiarizing yourself with the programs. You will not remove any programs, but if you were actually working with a donated computer, you would click any program to remove and click **Uninstall/Change**. Close all open windows.

...continued on Next Page

3 Hobby House

As a summer job, you are working at Hobby House, a retail store specializing in home décor and crafts. The store schedules classes each weekend in various activities, including painting, scrapbooking, needlework, and seasonal crafts. The store manager has assigned you the task of organizing class files for each instructor. You will create a folder for each instructor, with subfolders for each activity. So that you can take the class files from one computer to another, you will create a folder structure on a flash (USB) drive.

a. Connect the flash drive to your computer. Close any subsequent dialog box that appears.

b. Click **Start**, select **All Programs**, select **Accessories**, and select **Windows Explorer**. Scroll down, if necessary, to locate **Computer** and click the arrow to the left to expand the view. Click the removable disk (probably drive E or F).

c. Hobby House has employed two instructors to provide instruction in Quilting, Painting, and Seasonal Crafts. To create a folder on the USB drive, click **Organize** and click **New Folder**. Type the first instructor's name, **Brown, Abby**, and press **Enter**. Check the Address bar. The removable drive should still be selected.

d. Following the procedure described in (b), create a folder on the USB drive for the second instructor, **Kress, Janice**. Although you might have several other folders on the flash drive, you should see the two that you have just created, as shown in Figure 1.50.

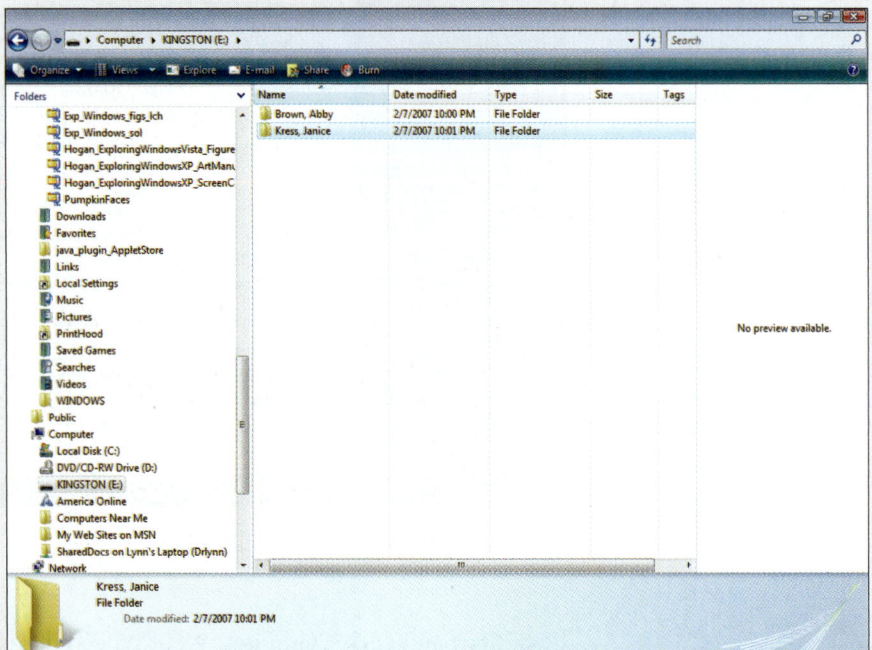

Figure 1.50 Hobby House Folders

e. Abby Brown is teaching Quilting and Painting classes, while Janice Kress is teaching Seasonal Crafts. You will create a folder for each activity assigned to an instructor so that you can later place student files in appropriate folders. Double-click the **Brown, Abby** folder in the right pane. Check the Address bar; it should show the currently selected folder as **Brown, Abby**.

f. Click **Organize** and click **New Folder**. Type the first activity assigned Ms. Brown, **Quilting**. Press **Enter**. In similar fashion, create a subfolder called **Painting** for Ms. Brown (as a subfolder of **Brown, Abby**).

g. Because Hobby House offers several Quilting classes, each focusing on a different quilt pattern, you must rename the **Quilting** folder as **Log Cabin Quilting**. Right-click the **Quilting** folder and select **Rename**. Type **Log Cabin Quilting** and press **Enter**.

...continued on Next Page

h. You will provide each instructor with a roll (listing) of students enrolled. First create a document to record students in the Log Cabin Quilting class. Click **Start**, select **All Programs**, select **Accessories**, and select **WordPad**. Type **Burns, Tammy** and press **Enter**. Type **Higgins, Hillary** and press **Enter**. Type **Johnson, Michael** and press **Enter**.

i. Click **File** and select **Save**. Click **Computer** in the left pane. Double-click the flash (USB) drive. Double-click **Brown, Abby** and double-click **Log Cabin Quilting**. Click in the file name area and type **chap1_prac3_quilting_roll_brown.** Click **Save**. Close WordPad.

j. Double-click **Log_Cabin Quilting.** You should see the **chap1_prac3_quilting_roll_brown** file in the right pane.

k. Close any open windows.

Mid-Level Exercises

1 Lawn Pro Landscape

To make a little extra money, you have taken a summer job with Lawn Pro Landscape, working in the office. Your supervisor recognizes your computer skills and has asked that you help set up a computer for the office. You must first customize the desktop and adjust a few other settings, then get a basic file structure organized for the company's billing records.

a. Customize the desktop background by selecting img22 from the categories displayed.

b. Make sure the clock on the taskbar is correct. If not, adjust it. If you are on a networked computer, you may not be able to adjust the clock.

c. Display the Quick Launch toolbar if it is not already displayed.

d. Open **Windows Explorer**. Maximize the window if it does not fill the screen. If the folder hierarchy appears in the Navigation pane (left pane), click the drop-down arrow beside Folders (at the top of the Navigation pane). Click **Pictures**. Change the view to **Details**.

e. Click **Documents**. Create a folder for billing records. The folder should be a subfolder of the Documents folder. Name the folder **Lawn Pro Billing**.

f. Delete the **Lawn Pro Billing** folder. Close Windows Explorer.

g. Create a shortcut on the Quick Launch toolbar for the Recycle Bin.

h. Get help on copying files and folders. Specifically, see what you can find about how to drag and drop files and folders from one location to another. If a printer is installed, print the help screen that explains how to copy files and folders by dragging and dropping.

i. Remove the Recycle Bin icon from the Quick Launch toolbar.

j. Close all open windows.

2 Book Club

You have recently joined a neighborhood book club. Each month, the club meets to select books to read and to discuss recent publications. Because the club is fairly new, and you know a little bit about computers, you volunteer to find some information on maintaining a successful book club.

a. You want to know what Windows can tell you about searching the Internet. In the Help and Support window, look up information on **Web Search.** Did you find any tips for searching the Internet? What is a keyboard shortcut for going to the Search box without using the mouse? Print the results of the search. Close Help and Support.

b. Connect your USB drive and create a folder called **Documents** on the drive. Then create a subfolder of **Documents** to contain the club documents that you will create each month. Name the folder **Book Club**. Close Windows Explorer.

c. Using WordPad, create a document outlining suggestions for conducting a book club meeting. Save the file in the Book Club folder on your flash drive as **chap1_mid2_books.** Close WordPad.

d. Suppose that you cannot find the **chap1_mid2_books** file. Using Windows Search, search for and locate the file. Be sure to indicate the flash drive as the location of the search. Close any open windows.

...continued on Next Page

e. You plan to upgrade some word processing software on your computer. The software requires a minimum of 10 MB of space to install and 512 MB RAM. Check your system to ensure that you have enough space for the software.

f. Delete the folders that you created in (b).

g. Close all open windows.

3 Assessment Exam

The college that you plan to attend requires that all students sit for a computer literacy assessment exam before being allowed to register. Before taking the exam, you want to refresh your memory and get a little practice. The following skills review should help.

a. Choose the Bubbles screen saver. Set the wait time to 10 minutes.

b. Auto Arrange the icons on your desktop.

c. If a Quick Launch toolbar appears on the taskbar, remove it. If it is not there, open it. Be sure to leave the taskbar as you found it by reversing your previous action.

d. Search for help on pausing printing.

e. Change the desktop background to img7 under Textures.

f. Connect your flash drive to a USB port. Create a folder on the flash drive called **Family Records**.

g. Create a subfolder of **Family Records** called **Addresses**. Create another subfolder of **Family Records** called **Birthdays**.

h. Suppose you want to locate all files modified this month. In the Search box on the Start menu, type this month (in the format xx/xxxx). Are any files listed? Open any file by clicking it.

i. Close all open windows.

Mini Cases

Use the rubric following the case as a guide to evaluate your work, but keep in mind that your instructor may impose additional grading criteria or use a different standard to judge your work.

Gadgets and the Sidebar

GENERAL CASE

One of the most appealing aspects of Windows Vista is the ability to customize your workspace. Many people enjoy including the Windows Sidebar on the desktop. The Sidebar is a vertical bar on which you can place "gadgets," which are small programs such as a clock, stock ticker, news headlines, and puzzles. In this mini case, you will learn a little about the Sidebar and how to personalize your desktop. Some gadgets are automatically placed on the Sidebar, and others are available with a typical Vista installation. You can find still others at the Microsoft Gadgets website (**www.microsoftgadgets.com**). Your task in this mini case is to develop a one- to two-page report on the use of the Windows Sidebar. Include information on how to open the Sidebar, which gadgets are available in Vista, how to customize the Sidebar so that only favorite gadgets are included, and how to find more gadgets online. A good starting place is the Vista Help and Support Center, where you can conduct a search for information on gadgets. Include information on how to organize and reorder gadgets on the Sidebar and how to remove gadgets that you no longer want. Provide a step-by-step recipe for anyone who is new to Vista, giving them all of the information they need to customize the Sidebar. Use Word or WordPad to type your report (at least one page, double-spaced), giving all of the information requested above. Save the report on your flash drive as **chap1_mc1_gadgets**.

Performance Elements	Exceeds Expectations	Meets Expectations	Below Expectations
Organization	Report is complete and well designed. All required elements are covered, including gadget selection, removing gadgets, and downloading gadgets. A step-by-step guide to working with gadgets is included in the report.	Report is of the correct length, but coverage of required topics is scant. Only some of the required topics are included, but not all.	Report is poorly researched and of insufficient length. Required topics are not addressed in an understandable manner.
Visual aspects	The report is double-spaced between paragraphs, with appropriate punctuation and formatting. It is designed with Word or WordPad.	The report contains spelling and/or grammatical errors, indicating poor preparation and proofreading. The report design is not well planned.	The report is not typed and/or is difficult to read and follow. It is obvious that it was done at the last minute, without much thought to the design.
Mechanics	The report addresses the required topics in an easy-to-read organized fashion. The student used the Help and Support Center, as suggested, to retrieve some of the required topic coverage.	The report touches on the required topics, but does not completely address each one. The sentence flow and topic description are a bit choppy and minimally address the required topics.	A section or all of the report is missing. It was not created using Word or WordPad and does not address all of the required topics.

Secure and Stable

RESEARCH CASE

Microsoft promised the most secure and stable operating system yet when it began the development of Windows Vista. Before Vista, Windows XP seemed prone to problems that kept us on edge, waiting for the next major security breach and subsequent Microsoft software patch. Your task in this mini case is to present findings related to the status of Vista security and stability. Create a two- to three-page report describing the current status of Windows security and stability. Mention the Security Center and how it can help you evaluate the essentials of your computer's security settings. Describe problems that occurred in the past and how Microsoft has designed Vista to avoid such pitfalls. In the second section of your report, explain why Microsoft claims that Vista is a very stable operating system. What has Microsoft done to improve Vista's performance, when compared to earlier operating systems? Why do experts say that Vista makes your computer less likely to fail and quicker to recover from software errors? Mention SuperFetch technology, and how it applies to Windows Vista. Your research could begin at the Microsoft website, although you are encouraged to conduct a more extensive Web search to find other sources. Use Word or WordPad to type your report (at least two pages, double-spaced), giving all of the information requested above. Save the report on your flash drive as **chap1_mc2_Vista**.

Performance Elements	Exceeds Expectations	Meets Expectations	Below Expectations
Organization	The report is well researched, addressing all required topics. Its length is appropriate.	Although the basic required elements of the report are included, they are not presented in a coherent fashion. The report is shorter than is required, with obvious effort at lengthening the report by filling it with disjointed ideas.	The report is very short, with an obvious lack of preparation. It includes little or no coverage of required topics.
Visual aspects	The report is well developed, with appropriate paragraph divisions and no typos.	The report contains a few mistakes, but the basic elements are presented in a readable manner.	The report has little or no paragraph structure, and it is difficult to identify the major points of the report. Obvious mistakes detract from the subject matter.
Mechanics	The report was developed with Word or WordPad. All required elements are addressed in the report.	The report was developed with Word or WordPad. However, the file contains several spelling and formatting mistakes and/or the file is not named as required.	The report contains multiple mistakes and is very poorly prepared with regard to sentence and paragraph structure.

volume 1 | Capstone Exercises

Using Office Beyond the Classroom

Business Exercises (Page 1147)

Application		Skills Covered
1. WORD	Page 1147	• Use AutoText • Set Margins and Specify Page Orientation • Insert Headers and Footers • Insert a Cover Page • Use the Find and Replace Commands • Check Spelling and Grammar • Apply Font Attributes Through the Font Dialog Box • Highlight Text • Copy Formats with the Format Painter • Apply Paragraph Formats • Insert a Table • Format a Table • Insert Clip Art and Images into a Document • Insert WordArt into a Document • Insert Comments into a Document • Track Changes in a Document • View Documents Side by Side • Create and Modify Footnotes and Endnotes • Modify Document Properties
2. EXCEL	Page 1151	• Enter and Edit Data in Cells • Display Cell Formulas • Insert and Delete Rows and Columns • Use Cell Ranges; Excel Move; Copy, Paste, Paste Special; and AutoFill • Manage Worksheets • Format Worksheets • Select Page Setup Options for Printing • Create and Copy Formulas • Use Relative and Absolute Cell Addresses • Use AutoSum • Insert Basic Statistical Functions • Use Date Functions • Use the IF Function • Use the PMT Function • Choose a Chart Type • Create a Chart • Modify a Chart • Enhance Charts with Graphic Shapes • Embed Charts • Print Charts • Protect a Cell, a Worksheet, and a Workbook • Sort Data • Filter and Total Data
3. ACCESS	Page 1156	• Explore, Describe, and Navigate Among the Objects in an Access Database • Back Up, Compact, and Repair Access Files • Create Filters • Sort Table Data on One or More Fields • Use the Relationships Window • Create a Query • Specify Criteria for Different Data Types • Copy and Run a Query • Use the Query Wizard • Create a Calculated Field in a Query • Create and Edit Access Functions • Perform Date Arithmetic • Create and Work with Data Aggregates • Use Different Report Views • Create and Edit a Report • Identify Report Elements, Sections, and Controls • Add Grouping Levels in Layout View • Add Fields to a Report • Use the Report Wizard
4. POWERPOINT	Page 1160	• Open and Save a Slide Show • Use Slide Layouts • Apply Design Themes • Review the Presentation • Add a Table • Insert Clip Art • Use Transitions and Animations • Run and Navigate a Slide Show • Print with PowerPoint • Add a Slide and Select a Layout • Change a Layout • Edit a Presentation • Add Existing Content to a Presentation • Apply and Modify a Design Theme • Insert a Header or Footer • Create SmartArt • Modify SmartArt Diagrams • Create WordArt • Modify WordArt • Modify Objects • Arrange Objects • Insert and Modify a Picture • Use the Internet as a Resource • Add Sound • Change Sound Settings
5. INTEGRATED	Page 1164	• Export Data from Access and Excel • Embed and Link Objects • Merge Data • Copy and Paste Between Applications • Check Spelling and Grammar

Natural Science Exercises (Page 1167)

Application		Skills Covered
1. WORD	Page 1167	• View a Document • Set Margins and Specify Page Orientation • Insert Page Breaks • Add Page Numbers • Insert Headers and Footers • Create Sections • Insert a Cover Page • Use the Find and Replace Commands • Check Spelling and Grammar • Use Save and Backup Options • Apply Font Attributes Through the Dialog Box • Set Off Paragraphs with Tabs, Borders, Lists, and Columns • Apply Paragraph Formats • Create and Modify Styles • Create a Table of Contents • Insert a Table • Format a Table • Insert Clip Art and Images into a Document • Format a Graphic Element • Insert WordArt into a Document • Insert Comments into a Document • Track Changes in a Document • Use Navigation Tools • Create and Modify Footnotes and Endnotes • Modify Document Properties
2. EXCEL	Page 1172	• Enter and Edit Data in Cells • Describe and Use Symbols and the Order of Precedence • Display Cell Formulas • Insert and Delete Rows and Columns • Use Cell Ranges; Excel Move; Copy, Paste, Paste Special; and AutoFill • Manage Worksheets • Format Worksheets • Select Page Setup Options for Printing • Create and Copy Formulas • Use Relative and Absolute Cell Addresses • Insert Basic Statistical Functions • Use Date Functions • Use the IF Function • Choose a Chart Type • Create a Chart • Modify a Chart • Embed Charts • Freeze Rows and Columns • Hide and Unhide Row, Columns, and Worksheets • Protect a Cell, a Worksheet, and a Workbook • Explore Basic Table Management • Sort Data • Filter and Total Data
3. ACCESS	Page 1177	• Explore, Describe, and Navigate Among the Objects in an Access Database • Back Up, Compact, and Repair Access Files • Create Filters • Use the Relationships Window • Understand Relational Power • Create Tables • Understand Table Relationships • Share Data with Excel • Establish Table Relationships • Create a Query • Specify Criteria for Different Data Types • Copy and Run a Query • Understand the Order of Precedence • Create a Calculated Field in a Query • Create and Edit Access Functions • Perform Date Arithmetic • Create and Work with Data Aggregates • Use Different Report Views • Create and Edit a Report • Add Grouping Levels in Layout View • Add Fields to a Report • Use the Report Wizard
4. POWERPOINT	Page 1182	• Use PowerPoint Views • Open and Save a Slide Show • Use Slide Layouts • Apply Design Themes • Add a Table • Insert Clip Art • Use Transitions and Animations • Run and Navigate a Slide Show • Print with PowerPoint • Modify an Outline Structure • Print an Outline • Add Existing Content to a Presentation • Apply and Modify a Design Theme • Insert a Header or Footer • Create SmartArt • Modify SmartArt Diagrams • Create WordArt • Modify WordArt • Modify Objects • Arrange Objects • Insert and Modify a Picture • Insert Movies • Set Movie Options • Add Sound
5. INTEGRATED	Page 1186	• Use Query Results in a Report • Export Query Results to an Excel Spreadsheet • Use a Template in Word • Insert an ExcelChart in PowerPoint • Use Comments and Markup

Technology Exercises (Page 1189)

Application		Skills Covered
1. WORD	Page 1189	• Set Margins and Specify Page Orientation • Insert Page Breaks • Add Page Numbers • Insert Headers and Footers • Create Sections • Use the Find and Replace Commands • Check Spelling and Grammar • Select Printing Options • Apply Font Attributes Through the Font Dialog Box • Highlight Text • Copy Formats with the Format Painter • Set Off Paragraphs with Tabs, Borders, Lists, and Columns • Apply Paragraph Formats • Format a Table • Convert Text to a Table • Insert Clip Art and Images into a Document • Format a Graphic Element • Insert WordArt into a Document • Insert Symbols into a Document • Insert Comments into a Document • Track Changes in a Document • Use Navigation Tools • Modify Document Properties
2. EXCEL	Page 1193	• Enter and Edit Data in Cells • Describe and Use Symbols and the Order of Precedence • Display Cell Formulas • Insert and Delete Rows and Columns • Use Cell Ranges; Excel Move; Copy, Paste, Paste Special; and AutoFill • Manage Worksheets • Format Worksheets • Select Page Setup Options for Printing • Manage Cell Comments • Create and Copy Formulas • Use Relative and Absolute Cell Addresses • Use AutoSum • Use Date Functions • Use the IF Function • Use the VLOOKUP Function • Choose a Chart Type • Create a Chart • Modify a Chart • Enhance Charts with Graphic Shapes • Embed Charts • Print Charts • Freeze Rows and Columns • Hide and Unhide Rows, Columns, and Worksheets • Protect a Cell, a Worksheet, and a Workbook • Explore Basic Table Management • Sort Data • Filter and Total Data
3. ACCESS	Page 1198	• Back Up, Compact, and Repair Access Files • Create Filters • Sort Table Data on One or More Fields • Know When To Use Access or Excel To Manage Data • Use the Relationships Window • Understand Relational Power • Create Tables • Understand Table Relationships • Share Data with Excel • Establish Table Relationships • Create a Query • Specify Criteria for Different Data Types • Copy and Run a Query • Understand the Order of Precedence • Create a Calculated Field in a Query • Create Expressions with the Expression Builder • Create and Edit Access Functions • Create and Work with Data Aggregates • Plan a Report • Use Different Report Views • Create and Edit a Report • Identify Report Elements, Sections, and Controls • Add Grouping Levels in Layout View
4. POWERPOINT	Page 1202	• Use PowerPoint Views • Open and Save a Slide Show • Create a Storyboard • Use Slide Layouts • Apply Design Themes • Review the Presentation • Insert Clip Art • Use Transitions and Animations • Run and Navigate a Slide Show • Print with PowerPoint • Create a Presentation Using a Template • Modify a Template • Print an Outline • Add Existing Content to a Presentation • Insert a Header or Footer • Create SmartArt • Modify SmartArt Diagrams • Create WordArt • Modify WordArt • Modify Objects • Arrange Objects • Insert and Modify a Picture • Use the Internet as a Resource • Add Sound
5. INTEGRATED	Page 1206	• Copy an Excel Worksheet and Paste It into PowerPoint • Create and Copy an Excel Chart and Paste It into PowerPoint • Export an Access Report to Word

Legal Exercises (Page 1209)

Application		Skills Covered
1. WORD	Page 1209	• Set Margins and Specify Page Orientation • Insert Page Breaks • Add Page Numbers • Insert Headers and Footers • Insert a Cover Page • Use the Find and Replace Commands • Check Spelling and Grammar • Use Save and Backup Options • Apply Font Attributes Through the Font Dialog Box • Control Word Wrapping with Nonbreaking Hyphens and Nonbreaking Spaces • Copy Formats with the Format Painter • Set Off Paragraphs with Tabs, Borders, Lists, and Columns • Create and Modify Styles • Insert a Table • Format a Table • Insert Clip Art and Images into a Document • Format a Graphic Element • Insert Symbols into a Document • Insert Comments into a Document • Compare and Combine Documents • Acknowledge a Source • Create and Modify Footnotes and Endnotes • Add Legal References • Modify Document Properties
2. EXCEL	Page 1215	• Plan for Good Workbook and Worksheet Design • Enter and Edit Data in Cells • Describe and Use Symbols and the Order of Precedence • Insert and Delete Rows and Columns • Use Cell Ranges; Excel Move; Copy, Paste, Paste Special; and AutoFill • Format Worksheets • Select Page Setup Options for Printing • Manage Cell Comments • Create and Copy Formulas • Use Relative and Absolute Cell Addresses • Use AutoSum • Use Date Functions • Use the IF Function • Use the VLOOKUP Function • Choose a Chart Type • Create a Chart • Modify a Chart • Embed Charts • Print Charts • Freeze Rows and Columns • Hide and Unhide Rows, Columns, and Worksheets • Protect a Cell, a Worksheet, and a Workbook • Control Calculation • Explore Basic Table Management • Sort Data • Filter and Total Data
3. ACCESS	Page 1221	• Create Filters • Sort Table Data on One or More Fields • Know When to Use Access or Excel to Manage Data • Use the Relationships Window • Design Data • Create Tables • Share Data with Excel • Establish Table Relationships • Create a Query • Use the Query Wizard • Create a Calculated Field in a Query • Perform Date Arithmetic • Create and Work with Data Aggregates • Plan a Report • Create and Edit a Report • Add Fields to a Report
4. POWERPOINT	Page 1226	• Use PowerPoint Views • Use Slide Layouts • Apply Design Themes • Insert Clip Art • Use Transitions and Animations • Run and Navigate a Slide Show • Print with PowerPoint • Modify an Outline Structure • Import an Outline • Add Existing Content to a Presentation • Apply and Modify a Design Theme • Insert a Header or Footer • Create Shapes • Apply Quick Styles and Customize Shapes • Create SmartArt • Create WordArt • Modify WordArt • Arrange Objects • Insert and Modify a Picture • Use the Internet as a Resource • Add Sound • Record and Play Narration
5. INTEGRATED	Page 1231	• Embed and Link Objects • Use Help to Research Unfamiliar Features • Apply Knowledge Gained from Help Research to Accomplish New Tasks • Merge Data/Fields into a Source File • Choose Records or Fields to Merge

Health Care Exercises (Page 1237)

Application		Skills Covered
1. WORD	Page 1237	• Use AutoText • View a Document • Use the Mini Toolbar • Set Margins and Specify Page Orientation • Insert Page Breaks • Add Page Numbers • Insert Headers and Footers • Create Sections • Insert a Cover Page • Use the Find and Replace Commands • Check Spelling and Grammar • Use Save and Backup Options • Select Printing Options • Apply Font Attributes Through the Font Dialog Box • Highlight Text • Control Word Wrapping with Nonbreaking Hyphens and Nonbreaking Spaces • Copy Formats with the Format Painter • Set Off Paragraphs with Tabs, Borders, Lists, and Columns • Apply Paragraph Formats • Create and Modify Styles • Create a Table of Contents • Insert a Table • Format a Table • Convert Text to a Table • Insert Clip Art and Images into a Document • Format a Graphic Element • Insert WordArt into a Document • Insert Symbols into a Document • Insert Comments into a Document • Track Changes in a Document • View Documents Side by Side • Compare and Combine Documents • Use Navigation Tools • Create a Bibliography • Create and Modify Footnotes and Endnotes • Add Figure References • Insert a Table of Figures • Modify Document Properties
2. EXCEL	Page 1243	• Enter and Edit Data in Cells • Describe and Use Symbols and the Order of Precedence • Display Cell Formulas • Insert and Delete Rows and Columns • Use Cell Ranges; Excel Move; Copy, Paste, Paste Special; AutoFill • Manage Worksheets • Format Worksheets • Select Page Setup Options for Printing • Create and Copy Formulas • Use Relative and Absolute Cell Addresses • Use AutoSum • Insert Basic Statistical Functions • Use Date Functions • Use the IF Function • Use the VLOOKUP Function • Choose a Chart Type • Create a Chart • Modify a Chart • Embed Charts • Print Charts • Freeze Rows and Columns • Hide and Unhide Rows, Columns, and Worksheets • Protect a Cell, a Worksheet, and a Workbook • Print Large Worksheets • Sort Data • Filter and Total Data
3. ACCESS	Page 1248	• Practice Good File Management • Back Up, Compact, and Repair Access Files • Create Filters • Sort Table Data on One or More Fields • Know When to Use Access or Excel to Manage Data • Understand Relational Power • Create Tables • Share Data with Excel • Establish Table Relationships • Create a Query • Specify Criteria for Different Data Types • Copy and Run a Query • Understand the Order of Precedence • Create a Calculated Field in a Query • Create Expressions with the Expression Builder • Create and Work with Data Aggregates • Plan a Report • Use Different Report Views • Create and Edit a Report • Identify Report Elements, Sections, and Controls • Add Grouping Levels in Layout View • Add Fields to a Report • Use the Report Wizard
4. POWERPOINT	Page 1254	• Use PowerPoint Views • Use Slide Layouts • Apply Design Themes • Add a Table • Insert Clip Art • Use Transitions and Animations • Run and Navigate a Slide Show • Print with PowerPoint • Modify an Outline Structure • Add Existing Content to a Presentation • Apply and Modify a Design Theme • Insert a Header or Footer • Create Shapes • Apply Quick Styles and Customize Shapes • Create SmartArt • Create WordArt • Modify WordArt • Arrange Objects • Insert and Modify a Picture • Use the Internet as a Resource • Insert Movies • Add Sound
5. INTEGRATED	Page 1260	• Import and Export Data Between Applications • Create Queries and Reports • Create and Format Charts • Edit a Report in Layout View • Export Data from Access to Excel

Arts Exercises (Page 1263)

Application		Skills Covered
1. WORD	Page 1263	• Use AutoText • Set Margins and Specify Page Orientation • Insert Page Breaks • Add Page Numbers • Insert Headers and Footers • Create Sections • Insert a Cover Page • Use the Find and Replace Commands • Apply Font Attributes Through the Font Dialog Box • Highlight Text • Control Word Wrapping with Nonbreaking Hyphens and Nonbreaking Spaces • Copy Formats with the Format Painter • Set Off Paragraphs with Tabs, Borders, Lists, and Columns • Apply Paragraph Formats • Create and Modify Styles • Create a Table of Contents • Create an Index • Insert a Table • Format a Table • Sort and Apply Formulas to Table Data • Convert Text to a Table • Insert Clip Art and Images into a Document • Format a Graphic Element • Insert WordArt into a Document • Insert Symbols into a Document • Insert Comments into a Document • Track Changes in a Document • View Documents Side by Side • Compare and Combine Documents • Create Master Documents and Subdocuments • Acknowledge a Source • Create a Bibliography • Select the Writing Style • Create and Modify Footnotes and Endnotes
2. EXCEL	Page 1267	• Describe and Use Symbols and the Order of Precedence • Display Cell Formulas • Insert and Delete Rows and Columns • Use Cell Ranges; Excel Move; Copy, Paste, Paste Special; and AutoFill • Create and Copy Formulas • Use Relative and Absolute Cell Addresses • Use AutoSum • Insert Basic Statistical Functions • Use Date Functions • Use the IF Function • Use the VLOOKUP Function • Use the PMT Function • Use the FV Function • Choose a Chart Type • Create a Chart • Modify a Chart • Enhance Charts with Graphic Shapes • Embed Charts • Print Charts • Freeze Rows and Columns • Hide and Unhide Rows, Columns, and Worksheets • Protect a Cell, a Worksheet, and a Workbook • Control Calculation • Print Large Worksheets
3. ACCESS	Page 1271	• Understand the Difference Between Working in Storage and Memory • Practice Good File Management • Back Up, Compact, and Repair an Access File • Create Filters • Sort Table Data on One or More Fields • Know When to Use Access or Excel to Manage Data • Use the Relationships Window • Understand Relational Power • Design Data • Create Tables • Understand Table Relationships • Share Data with Excel • Establish Table Relationships • Create a Query • Specify Criteria for Different Data Types • Copy and Run a Query • Use the Query Wizard • Understand Large Database Differences • Understand the Order of Precedence • Create a Calculated Field in a Query • Create Expressions with the Expression Builder • Create and Edit Access Functions • Perform Date Arithmetic • Create and Work with Data Aggregates • Plan a Report • Use Different Report Views • Identify Report Elements, Sections, and Controls • Add Grouping Levels in Layout View • Add Fields to a Report • Use the Report Wizard
4. POWERPOINT	Page 1276	• Identify PowerPoint User Interface Elements • Use PowerPoint Views • Open and Save a Slide Show • Get Help • Create a Storyboard • Use Slide Layouts • Apply Design Themes • Review the Presentation • Add a Table • Insert Clip Art • Use Transitions and Animations • Run and Navigate a Slide Show • Print with PowerPoint • Create a Presentation Using a Template • Modify a Template • Create a Presentation in Outline View • Modify an Outline Structure • Print an Outline • Import an Outline • Add Existing Content to a Presentation • Examine Slide Show Design Principles • Apply and Modify a Design Theme • Insert a Header or Footer • Create Shapes • Apply Quick

		Styles and Customize Shapes • Create SmartArt • Modify SmartArt Diagrams • Create WordArt • Modify WordArt • Modify Objects • Arrange Objects • Insert and Modify a Picture • Use the Internet as a Resource • Create a Photo Album • Set Photo Album Options • Insert Movies • Set Movie Options • Add Sound • Record and Play Narration
5. INTEGRATED	Page 1280	• Create a Summary Query • Export query Results to an Excel Spreadsheet • Calculate Statistics Using Min, Max, and Average Functions • Create Charts from the Data • Display the Statistics and Charts as Linked Objects in a PowerPoint Presentation • Embed Objects in Word • Use Themes Across Applications to Create Cohesive Appearance

Hospitality Exercises (Page 1283)

Application		Skills Covered
1. WORD	Page 1283	• Use AutoText • Set Margins and Specify Page Orientation • Insert Page Breaks • Add Page Numbers • Insert Headers and Footers • Create Sections • Insert a Cover Page • Use the Find and Replace Commands • Apply Font Attributes • Highlight Text • Copy Formats with the Format Painter • Set Off Paragraphs with Tabs, Borders, Lists, and Columns • Apply Paragraph Formats • Create and Modify Styles • Insert a Table • Format a Table • Sort and Apply Formulas to Table Data • Convert Text to a Table • Insert Clip Art and Images • Format a Graphic Element • Insert WordArt into a Document • Insert Symbols into a Document • Insert Comments into a Document • Track Changes in a Document • View Documents Side by Side • Compare and Combine Documents • Create Master Documents and Subdocuments • Create and Modify Footnotes and Endnotes
2. EXCEL	Page 1288	• Describe and Use Symbols and the Order of Precedence • Display Cell Formulas • Insert and Delete Rows and Columns • Use Cell Ranges; Excel Move; Copy, Paste, Paste Special; and AutoFill • Create and Copy Formulas • Use Relative and Absolute Cell Addresses • Use AutoSum • Use the IF Function • Use the VLOOKUP Function • Use the PMT Function • Choose a Chart Type • Create a Chart • Modify a Chart • Print Charts • Protect a Cell, a Worksheet, and a Workbook • Explore Basic Table Management • Sort Data • Filter and Total Data
3. ACCESS	Page 1292	• Understand the Difference Between Working in Storage and Memory • Practice Good File Management • Back Up, Compact, and Repair Access Files • Create Filters • Sort Table Data on One or More Fields • Use the Relationships Window • Understand Relational Power • Design Data • Create Tables • Understand Table Relationships • Establish Table Relationships • Create a Query • Specify Criteria for Different Data Types • Copy and Run a Query • Use the Query Wizard • Understand the Order of Precedence • Create a Calculated Field in a Query • Create Expressions with the Expression Builder • Create and Edit Access Functions • Perform Date Arithmetic • Create and Work with Data Aggregates • Plan a Report • Use Different Report Views • Identify Report Elements, Sections, and Controls • Add Grouping Levels in Layout View • Add Fields to a Report • Use the Report Wizard
4. POWERPOINT	Page 1297	• Use Slide Layouts • Apply Design Themes • Review the Presentation • Add a Table • Insert Clip Art • Use Transitions and Animations • Run and Navigate a Slide Show • Print with PowerPoint • Create a Presentation Using a Template • Modify a Template • Create a Presentation in Outline View • Modify an Outline Structure • Print an Outline • Import an Outline • Add Existing Content to a Presentation • Examine Slide Show Design Principles • Apply and Modify a Design Theme • Insert a Header or Footer • Create Shapes • Apply Quick Styles and Customize Shapes • Create SmartArt • Modify SmartArt Diagrams • Create WordArt • Modify WordArt • Modify Objects • Arrange Objects • Insert and Modify a Picture • Use the Internet as a Resource • Create a Photo Album • Set Photo Album Options • Insert Movies • Set Movie Options • Add Sound • Record and Play Narration
5. INTEGRATED	Page 1301	• Open and Save an Access Database • Create a New Query Based on an Existing Query • Export to an Excel Workbook • Create Column, Pie, and Bar Charts • Embed a Chart on Worksheets • Use Chart Layouts and Format Worksheets, Charts, and a Multilevel List • Create a Presentation from a Word Outline • Use Themes and Insert and Format Graphics • Use Comments and Markup

Managers

Use Microsoft Office Word

Background

Companies place managers in charge of various departments including public relations, research and development, finance, accounting, marketing, and production. They are responsible for planning and supervising the work of others and for accomplishing the departmental goals so that the company is successful. Managers use word processing software on a daily basis to prepare correspondence, record notes, and prepare reports and proposals. Although e-mail and messaging have replaced some written correspondence, managers still often use word processing software to prepare written documents. The following word processing skills taught in the textbook are crucial skills needed by people employed in management.

Tasks

Managers might be responsible for all types of document production. This could include the following:

- Correspondence and mailing
- Contracts
- Mailing lists
- Tables
- Brochures and flyers
- Forms and reports
- Requests for proposals

Skills

A manager should be able to do the following:

Chapter 1

- Use AutoText (page 76)
- Set margins and specify page orientation (page 87)
- Insert headers and footers (page 91)
- Insert a cover page (page 93)
- Use the Find and Replace commands (page 94)
- Check spelling and grammar (page 103)

Chapter 2

- Apply font attributes through the Font dialog box (page 133)
- Highlight text (page 136)
- Copy formats with the Format Painter (page 139)
- Apply paragraph formats (page 148)

...continued on Next Page

Chapter 3

- Insert a table (page 197)
- Format a table (page 205)
- Insert clip art and images into a document (page 219)
- Insert WordArt into a document (page 225)

Chapter 4

- Insert comments into a document (page 251)
- Track changes in a document (page 254)
- View documents side by side (page 263)
- Create and modify footnotes and endnotes (page 281)
- Modify document properties (page 290)

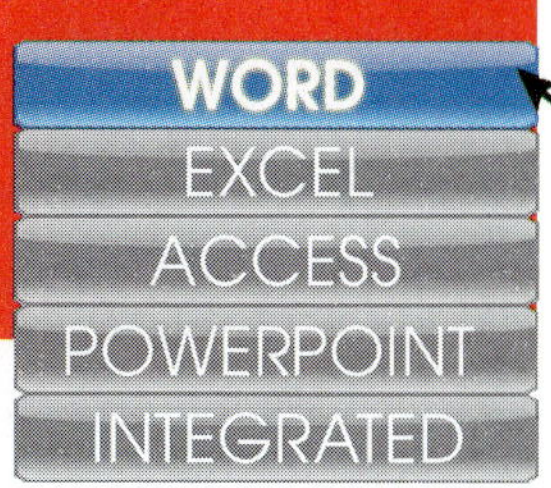

You work as the manager of the research and development department of Flat World Shoe, Inc. Your company is beginning a major marketing initiative to increase sales. Each member of the managerial team has been asked for input. You will add your changes and suggestions to the proposal that is being reviewed by all department managers. In addition, you will draft a memo to accompany the proposal and develop a letter seeking support from a critical player for the new shoe line your department is proposing.

Modify a Memorandum

Memorandums are used for correspondence within a company when the sender wants a document more formal than an e-mail. You will draft a memo to the CEO of the company to send with the finished proposal.

- Open *exp07_w_bus_cpt_memo.docx*. Save it as **exp07_w_bus_cpt_memo_solution.docx**.
- Insert **Flat World Shoe, Inc.**, as the company name in the logo box at the top.
- Replace the word *Memo* with **Interoffice Memorandum**, and align it with the word *To:*.
- Address the memo to **Mr. Shoes, CEO**.
- Insert **Hard Worker, Manager of R&D Department** in the *From:* line.
- Delete the *CC:* line; you will not be sending copies to anyone else.
- Insert the following date in the format shown: **June 17, 2008**.
- Insert **Marketing Initiative** next to *Re:*.
- Change the font from the *To* line to the end of the document to Times New Roman, 12-pt. font.
- Justify the three paragraphs.
- Add 11 pt spacing after each paragraph in the body of the memo.
- Save and close the document.

Modify a Proposal

Proposals are often used in businesses to present details about a project or to consider the benefits and disadvantages of a plan. The managers of the company have all reviewed the marketing proposal. There are currently two drafts circulating. You will combine the two drafts into one finished proposal.

- Open a new blank document. Compare and combine *exp07_w_bus_cpt_prop.docx* (the original) and *exp07_w_bus_cpt_prop2.docx*. Save it as **exp07_w_bus_cpt_prop_solution.docx**.
- Accept all changes in the document and delete the comments.
- Insert an Alphabet footer with the company name and page numbers.
- Convert the three items listed under *ADVERTISING STRATEGY AND EXECUTION* to bullets.
- In a text box at the end of the document, add the following statement: **A preliminary budget will be developed after the strategic planning meeting.**

Create and Format Table

Information is often easier to understand and read if it is presented in a table rather than buried in a paragraph. Tables can be used in any document: letters, memos, and reports.

- Create the following table below the *Messaging by Audience* section.

Targeted Consumer Demographics:

Category	Annual Sales (in millions)
Infants	$.5
Children's athletic	$.73
Children's casual	$.26
Teens athletic	$2.6
Teens casual	$.19
Women's athletic	$2.1
Women's casual	$.42
Women's dress	$1.5
Men's athletic	$3.1
Men's casual	$.28
Men's dress	$1.1

- Format the table to Table Style Simple 3.
- Sort by the *Annual Sales* column in descending order.

Insert and Format Clip Art

Add a clip art to the document.

- Search in the Clip Art Gallery for *basketball shoe* and select a clip art of your choice from these options. Position the clip art at the top-right corner of page 1 using square text wrapping.

...continued on Next Page

- Size the clip art to a width of 2.6″.
- Insert a page break before the section for *Product Comparison and Positioning*.

Create a Cover Page

Managers seldom have time to read detailed reports; however, report features such as cover pages can make it easier for managers to keep track of the many documents they receive.

- Add a next page break at the top of the proposal to create a cover page.
- Format an attractive cover page using an option from the Cover Page gallery that includes the Company Name, Date, Your Name, and the same clip art used above.

Formatting

It is important to format documents for easier readability and to correspond with company requirements. We will change the margins and delete the footer on page 1.

- Change the margins of the entire document to 1.5″ on all four sides.
- Apply the Title Style to *Flat World Shoe Inc. Marketing Plan* on the second page. Apply the Emphasis Style to the four department managers directly below the title.
- Delete the footer on the cover sheet. Start the numbering on the second page at Page 1.
- Remove the header that starts on page 2.
- Insure that the document is only three pages long.
- Include the word **Proposal** in a semitransparent, diagonal watermark.

Document Properties

The document properties make it simple to track authors and documents within the company. As department manager, you require that all documents to be routed throughout the organization include document properties.

- Set the document properties with the following:
  - Author: **Your Name**
  - Title: **Strategic Marketing Initiative**
  - Subject: **Annual Marketing Campaign**
  - Keywords: **Marketing, Initiative, Campaign**
  - Status: **Completed**

Modify a Letter

Many standard letters are used throughout the company. Using an existing standard letter template requires the user simply to change some of the information in the letter rather than to create a new letter each time. It is important to make sure that all unique information, such as names and addresses, is correct. If a letter uses pronouns, it is extremely important to make sure that the pronouns fit the recipient. You will use an existing form letter and modify it into a request to Will Smith.

- Open *exp07_w_bus_cpt_ltr.docx*. Save it as **exp07_w_bus_cpt_ltr_solution.docx**.
- Insert **Hard Worker** for the name in the first address and below the signature line.
- Insert the title **Manager of R&D Department** below the name in the first address and below the signature line.
- Insert the Street address **864 Main St.**
- Insert the following City, St, Zip: **Cody, WY 82414**
- Insert the following for the recipient: **Will Smith** (delete the title and company name lines), **3579 Fresh Prince Ln., Hollywood, CA 91611**
- Insert the Recipient Name: **Mr. Smith:** (make sure there is a colon since this is a business letter).
- Insert **Manager of Research and Development** for the title in the first paragraph.
- Insert **Flat World Shoe, Inc.**, as the organization name in the first paragraph.
- Set **Flat World Shoe, Inc.**, as Autotext.
- Change the font on the entire document to **Times New Roman**, **12-point**.
- Find the word *hat* or *hats* and replace with **shoe** or **shoes** where appropriate.
- Use WordArt **style 23**, **Californian FB**, **font size 36** to insert **Flat World Shoe, Inc.**, at the top of the letter on the right-hand side.
- Convert **The Will Smith Special** to bold text at the end of the first paragraph.
- Insert your e-mail address at the end of the last paragraph.
- Ensure that the letter prints on one page.

Check Spelling and Save the Documents

- Use the spelling checker to check the memo, letter, and proposal for errors.
- Save your documents.
- Print the documents if requested by your instructor.
- Close the documents.
- Submit the document to your instructor either electronically or printed as instructed for grading.

Managers

Use Microsoft Office Excel

Background

Managers of Accounting and Finance departments find spreadsheet software such as Microsoft Office Excel indispensible. Spreadsheets give managers the ability to manipulate data to prepare budgets and financial statements. If one number is changed in a spreadsheet, every single formula in the sheet updates. The following spreadsheet skills taught in the textbook are crucial skills needed by people employed in management.

Tasks

Managers might be responsible for creating and maintaining many types of spreadsheets. These spreadsheets could include the following:

- Revenue and expense sheets
- Budgets
- Financial statements
- Payroll documents
- Information from vendors and clients

Skills

A manager should be able to do the following:

Chapter 1

- Enter and edit data in cells (page 322)
- Display cell formulas (page 330)
- Insert and delete rows and columns (page 331)
- Use cell ranges; Excel move; copy, paste, paste special; and AutoFill (page 332)
- Manage worksheets (page 340)
- Format worksheets (page 341)
- Select page setup options for printing (page 353)

Chapter 2

- Create and copy formulas (page 381)
- Use relative and absolute cell addresses (page 382)
- Use AutoSum (page 389)
- Insert basic statistical functions (page 390)
- Use date functions (page 392)
- Use the IF function (page 399)
- Use the PMT function (page 408)

...continued on Next Page

Chapter 3

- Choose a chart type (page 431)
- Create a chart (page 438)
- Modify a chart (page 450)
- Enhance charts with graphic shapes (page 453)
- Embed charts (page 459)
- Print charts (page 460)

Chapter 4

- Protect a cell, a worksheet, and a workbook (page 490)
- Sort data (page 510)
- Filter and total data (page 514)

Managers
Volume 1 | Capstone Exercise

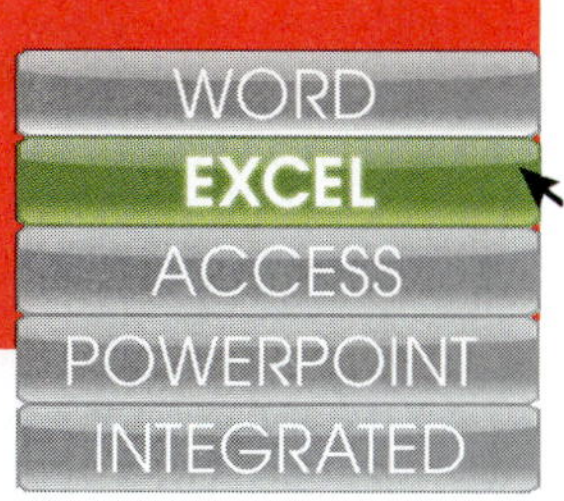

You are the manager for the Accounting and Finance departments at Flat World Shoe, Inc. In addition to ensuring that all of the day-to-day business transactions are completed accurately, you also play a key role in planning, budgeting, and reporting. As a member of the strategic management team, your input on the cost and expected benefits of the marketing initiative are invaluable. You have been asked to prepare a spreadsheet outlining the budget for the marketing plan.

Using a PMT Function to Calculate a Loan Payment

Although many expenses for the marketing plan will be variable, the company expects that one major purchase will save a great deal of time and many headaches. The company will purchase a limousine to shuttle the stars to the locations for photo shoots and promotions. The cost of the limo is $200,000. You will finance it over 5 years at an interest rate of 10%.

- Open *exp07_e_bus_cpt_bud* and save it as **exp07_e_bus_cpt_bud_solution**.
- Rename Sheet1 **Limousine**.
- Format **cell B3** for accounting and format **cell B5** for percent.
- Input the financed amount of **$200,000** in **cell B3** and the term of **5** in **cell B4**.
- Use the VLOOKUP function to insert the interest rate in **cell B5** from the lookup table in cells E2:F12.
- Use a PMT function in **cell B6** to determine the monthly payment based on a financed amount of $200,000, a 5-year loan, and an annual interest rate of 10%. Ensure that the monthly payment is a positive number.
- Use the accounting format for the cell with the solution.

Modify a List of Spokespeople

Although most of the exact costs of new projects are not known, through years of experience and knowledge in their field, Accounting Managers can develop fairly accurate estimates to be used for decision making. The major cost of the proposed marketing initiative is the cost of hiring spokespeople. You have been asked to compile a list of possible spokespeople (entertainers, athletes, and musicians) and estimated costs.

- Rename Sheet2 **Spokespeople**.
- Insert **Spokespeople for Marketing Initiative 2010** in **cell A1**.
- Merge and center the heading in **cells A2** and **B2**.
- Change the heading in **cell H2** from *Fee* to **Base Fee.**

Enter Spokespeople Information

You will input data for two spokespeople into the spreadsheet.

- Enter the following data in row 11: **Johann Bach**; **Chicago**; **IL**; **Entertainer**; **75,000**; **1**.
- Enter the following data in row 12: **Willie Nelson**; **Austin**; **TX**; **Entertainer**; **48,000**; **2**.

Enter Formulas, Formats, and Use AutoFill

To identify how much the contract will be for each spokesperson, you will multiply the base pay by the number of engagements.

- Enter a formula in **cell H3** to multiply base pay by the number of engagements.
- Use AutoFill to complete the series in **cells H4:H12**.
- Format the cells in columns F and H for accounting, no decimal places.

Use the IF Function

Some of the spokespeople have negotiated extra bonuses for special circumstances or because of their star status. You will award an additional $50,000 bonus to spokespeople who have more than four engagements. The bonus amount is listed in cell K1 so that it is convenient and can be easily changed if necessary. Also, the engagement number (4), is listed in **cell L2** for convenience.

- In **cell I3**, create an IF formula to calculate a bonus based on the table in cells **L1:M2**, so that if the celebrity appears in the number of engagements in **cell M2**, they receive the bonus in **cell M1**.
- Use AutoFill to fill in the bonuses for all spokespeople.

Create Totals

The total amount you will need to budget for each spokesperson will be the base fee multiplied by the number of engagements, plus the bonus.

- In **cell J3**, create a formula to add the contract amount and bonus.
- Use AutoFill to determine the total for each spokesperson.
- In **cell G13**, use AutoSum to add the base amounts.
- Use AutoFill in **cells H13:J13** to determine totals for each column.
- Insert **Total** as a heading in **cell A13**.
- Apply a **Top and Double Bottom** border to the total row from **cells A13:J13**.

...continued on Next Page

Format Data and Spreadsheet

The spreadsheet needs to have a professional look. You will apply the following format features to ensure that the spreadsheet is professional and easy to read.

- Change all of the fonts to **Calibri**.
- Set the title in **cell A1** to **20-point** font.
- Set the row height to **30**.
- Merge and center the title over the 10 columns.
- Use **Dark Blue, Text 2, Lighter 40%** shading for the Title.
- Apply **Dark Blue, Text 2, Lighter 60%** shading to the column headings.
- Increase column widths when necessary.
- Sort the data alphabetically by last name.
- Use **Blue Accent 1, Lighter 60%** shading for lines 4, 6, 8, 10, and 12.
- Format the accounting cells with no decimals.

Determine Averages and Maximum Amounts

Individuals from different departments often need summary information and to track spreadsheets by date created.

- Insert **Average** in **cell A15**, and insert **Highest** in **cell A16**.
- Enter formulas to determine the averages and highest numbers for columns G, H, I, and J.
- Sort the spokespeople by last name, then first name.
- Apply the accounting format with no decimal places to all dollar figures. Apply the number format with no decimal places to all other number columns.
- Format the table for ease in readability
- Protect the spreadsheet without a password, allowing users to select locked and unlocked cells.

Create a Budget

Budgets need to be set up in a manner that makes them easily understood by individuals in various departments. The typical structure is to set up the estimated costs and then return periodically and insert actual costs to make sure that you are not overspending or underspending.

- Rename Sheet3 as **Budget**
- Insert **Budget for Marketing Initiative 2010** in **cell A1** using **Calibri, 14-point** font, **bold**, **Orange, Accent 6, Darker 25%**. Extend the row height to **85.5** and middle align the title across the four columns.
- Add the following clip following the text in **cell A1**. Size the clip art appropriately.
  - Search for: **shoe**
  - Search in: **All collections**
  - Results should be: **Selected media file types, Clip Art**

- Enter a formula to insert the current date in **cell A3** so that it updates automatically. Format it as a Long Date.
- Change the font in the spreadsheet to **Calibri**.
- Center and word wrap the row headings in **cells A4:A12**.

Input Budget Data

The figures for a budget come from many different sources. As a member of the strategic management team, you work closely with all of the other departments to ensure that your budget estimates are as accurate as possible. You will use cell references as much as possible, so that as figures are updated on other sheets your budget also will be updated. To learn how to use cell references, refer to Excel Help. Search for "Create a cell reference on the same worksheet."

- Enter a cell reference in **cell B5** that will pull in the total spokesperson expense from the *Spokespeople* worksheet (**cell J13**).
- Enter **178000** for the Photographers expense in **cell B6**.
- Enter a cell reference in **cell B7** that will pull the limousine payment from the *Limousine* worksheet and multiply it by 12 since this is an annual budget.
- Enter the following expenses:
  - **Cell B8: 320000**
  - **Cell B9: 650000**
  - **Cell B10: 0**
  - **Cell B11: 0**
- Use AutoSum to determine the total budgeted expenses on row 12.
- Insert a column between columns B and C and title it **Percent of Total**.
- Format **cells C5:C12** as percent.

...continued on Next Page

- Format **cells B5:B12** and **D4:D12** as accounting with no decimals.
- Create a formula to determine the percentage of the total for **cell C5** by dividing the line item by the total budget amount.
- Use AutoFill to determine percentages for **cells C6:C11**.
- Display the cell formulas and resize the column widths to the optimal width.
- Change the page orientation to landscape. Set the left and right margins to **1.5**.

Create a Chart

Many executives and boards prefer to see charts instead of spreadsheets with details. You will prepare two charts to illustrate the budget for the Marketing proposal.

- Prepare a pie chart for the Expenses using the *Percentage* column. Use data labels to identify the percentages of each slice.
- Insert the title **Expenditure Percentages**.
- Insert a block arrow pointing to the largest section of the pie chart.
- Prepare a 2-D clustered column chart depicting the budgeted expenses for the prior year and the prior year actual amount.
- Insert the title **Budget Expenses**. Include the legend.
- Move both charts to a new worksheet called **Charts**.

Formatting the Budget

- Return to the *Budget* worksheet.
- Apply the **Top and Double Bottom** border style to row 12.
- Apply **Orange Accent 6, Darker 25% Fill Color** to the column headings in **cells A4:G4** and the total row **cells A13:D12**.
- Increase column widths when necessary.

Save the Workbook

- Save and close your workbook.
- Submit the workbook to your instructor for grading either electronically or printed as instructed.

Managers

Use Microsoft Office Access

Background

Managers use database software to assist them in maintaining and manipulating data for various purposes. The manager of the Information Systems (IS) department is often responsible for creating and maintaining databases so that the department has the information required by individuals throughout the organization in the desired format when needed. Database software gives managers the ability to manipulate data to provide output needed to prepare reports and correspondence. The IS manager serves employees in all of the departments of the company. The following database skills taught in the textbook are crucial skills needed by people employed in management.

Tasks

IS managers might be responsible for creating and maintaining many types of databases. They need to be proficient in working with the following:

- Tables
- Queries
- Forms
- Reports

Skills

An IS manager should be able to do the following:

Chapter 1

- Explore, describe, and navigate among the objects in an Access database (page 547)
- Back up, compact, and repair Access files (page 556)
- Create filters (page 565)
- Sort table data on one or more fields (page 568)
- Use the Relationships window (page 578)

Chapter 2

- Create a query (page 642)
- Specify criteria for different data types (page 645)
- Copy and run a query (page 649)
- Use the Query Wizard (page 649)

Chapter 3

- Create a calculated field in a query (page 679)
- Create and edit Access functions (page 690)

...continued on Next Page

- Perform date arithmetic (page 694)
- Create and work with data aggregates (page 704)

Chapter 4

- Use different report views (page 733)
- Create and edit a report (page 737)
- Identify report elements, sections, and controls (page 747)
- Add grouping levels in Layout view (page 750)
- Add fields to a report (page 755)
- Use the Report Wizard (page 765)

Managers
Volume 1 | Capstone Exercise

You are the manager for the Information Technology (IT) department at Flat World Shoe, Inc. In addition to overseeing hardware selection and maintenance, software selection and maintenance, and employee IT training, you create and maintain databases for all of the departments. For the most part, it is preferable for departments to use one central database rather than maintaining individuals ones. A central database limits data redundancy and errors. As a member of the strategic management team, your development of a database for the marketing initiative will prevent problems in the future. You will take the opportunity to create a more efficient database of the manufacturing plants owned and operated by the company.

Navigating Among the Objects in an Access Database

You will be working with a database designed by Flat World Shoe, Inc.

- Open *exp07_a_bus_cpt_db*. Save it as **exp_a_bus_cpt_db_solution**.
- Enable the content of the file.
- Open the table *Products*.
- Add the following record: **21, The Extreme, DE, 154.99, 86.15**.
- Sort the table by category in ascending order.
- Find the record for our Men 02 shoe and change the unit price to **129.89**.
- Close and save the *Products* table.
- Open the *Postal Codes* table.
- Create a filter by selection for all Texas postal codes.
- Remove all filters.
- Save and close the table.
- Compact and repair the database.
- Back up the database.
- Open the Relationships window.
- Show all tables in the database. Note the relationships between the tables.
- Observe the Edit Relationships dialog boxes for each relationship.
- Save and close the relationships window.

Preparing a Report

The manager of the Production department has requested a report of the children's shoes.

- Create a report on the *Products* table, filtering by category *CH*.
- Average the *Unit Price* and *Unit Cost* columns separately.
- Preview the report.
- Print the report.
- Title and save the report as **Children's Shoes** and close the report.

Create a Query

The CEO has requested a list of all of the plants that have more than 20,000 square feet.

- Create a query to display the *Plant ID*, *Plant Name*, and *Square Footage* for those plants with more than 20,000 square feet.
- Name the query **qryPlant20000SquareFeet**.
- Run, save, and close the query.

Create a Multi-Table Query

Human Resources needs the mailing addresses of the employees at the Nashville plant.

- Create a query using the *Plants* table, *Employees* table, and the *Postal Codes* table.
- Display the *Courtesy Title*, *First Name*, *Last Name*, *Address*, *City*, *State*, and *Postal Code* for those employees working in the Nashville plant (NAP).
- Sort by last name in ascending order.
- Name the query **qryNashvillePlantEmployeeAddresses.**
- Run, save, and close the query.

Create a Query and a Report with a Calculated Field

The CEO wishes to know the costs of time-and-a-half overtime, over and above the regular payroll amounts for all hourly employees in the Texas warehouses and plants.

- Create a query using the *Employees* and *Postal Codes* tables to calculate the hourly rate at time and a half for those employees in Texas who work more than 36 hours per week.
- Include the following fields: *Firstname*, *Lastname*, *Hours*, *Rate*, and *State/Region*.
- Calculate the weekly overtime costs in a column called **Overtime**. Please note: Only the hours worked over 36 hours per week count towards overtime pay.
- Name and save the query **qryTexasEmployee Overtime**.
- Create a report for the query results.
- Format the report with a title of **Texas Employee Overtime** so all columns fit on one portrait layout page.
- Format the overtime column for currency.

...continued on Next Page

- Create a Total for Overtime to calculate the cost of overtime pay to all Texas employees. Delete any other totals.
- Change the heading to **Texas Employee Overtime**.
- Save the report with the default name and close the report.

Work with Date Arithmetic

The Human Resources manager would like a list of all employees and the approximate length of time they have worked for the company.

- Create a query using the *Employees* table to calculate the length of time employees have worked for the company. Use the current date—do not adjust for days off.
- Return the results in years in a column called **Tenure**. Format the Tenure field to display only 2 decimal places.
- Include the following fields in the results: *Firstname*, *Lastname*, and *Tenure*.
- Name the query **qryEmployeeTenure**.
- Create a report from the query.
- Group by date of hire—by year.
- Sort ascending by date of hire.
- Change the title to **Employee Tenure.** Make sure all fields display appropriately.
- Save the report with the default name and close it.

Create a Query with Data Aggregates

The manager of the Accounting department would like a list of the plants that subtotals the production capacity by shoe category.

- Create a query using the *Products* table to determine the average Unit Price and average Unit Costs, grouped by *Shoe Category*.
- Name the query **qryShoeCategoryAverages**.
- Save and close the query.

Create a Query and Report

The manager of the Marketing department would like a list of the spokespeople and the shoes they promote.

- Create a query which searches for spokespeople with the last name of *Williams* using the *Spokespeople* and *Products* tables.
- Include the following fields: *FirstName*, *LastName*, and *ProductName*.
- Save the query as **qryWilliamsProducts**.
- Create a Report from the query.
- Change the heading to **Products Promoted by Williams Sisters**.
- Format the report using the Module AutoFormat.
- Save it using the default name and close the report.

Create a Report

The manager of the Production department would like a list of the products, retail prices, and unit costs.

- Create a query from the *Products* table.
- Save the query as **Product Totals by Category**.
- Use all fields but the *Spokesperson* field.
- Assume that 8 million is the maximum production capacity for each product. Calculate the revenue for each product based on 8,000,000 units. Return the result in a **Max Capacity Revenue** column. Format all dollar figures as currency.
- Create a report from the query.
- Group by Category.
- Format the report using a format from the AutoFormat Gallery.
- Remove the Logo placeholder.
- Total the revenue in the Group Footer and the Report Footer. Format the totals as currency.
- Save the report as **Product Totals by Category**.

Create a Report with Report Wizard

The CEO would like to see which plants have the largest capacity.

- Create a report using the Report Wizard.
- Use the following fields: *Plant ID, Plant Name, Capacity*.
- Sort in descending order by *Capacity*.
- Use the tabular layout and module style.
- Title the report **Plant Capacity**.

Managers

Use Microsoft Office PowerPoint

Background

Managers often use presentation graphics software to prepare sales presentations for customers, stakeholders, and employees. They also use presentation graphics software to explain procedures and projects to employees. The slide shows are often saved as Web presentations to share with individuals over the Internet. The following presentation graphic skills taught in the textbook are crucial skills needed by people employed in management.

Tasks

Managers might be responsible for all creating many different types of Microsoft Office PowerPoint presentations. These could include the following:

- Presentations
  - Slide shows for customers describing products or services
  - Slide shows for stakeholders to explain company performance or goals
- Web presentations
  - Slide shows for customers or employees who are in other locations and cannot attend presentations

Skills

A manager should be able to do the following:

Chapter 1

- Open and save a slide show (page 809)
- Use slide layouts (page 820)
- Apply design themes (page 820)
- Review the presentation (page 822)
- Add a table (page 829)
- Insert clip art (page 829)
- Use transitions and animations (page 831)
- Run and navigate a slide show (page 840)
- Print with PowerPoint (page 842)

Chapter 2

- Add a slide and select a layout (page 874)
- Change a layout (page 883)
- Edit a presentation (page 883)

...continued on Next Page

- Add existing content to a presentation (page 888)
- Apply and modify a design theme (page 892)
- Insert a header or footer (page 896)

Chapter 3

- Create SmartArt (page 952)
- Modify SmartArt Diagrams (page 955)
- Create WordArt (page 961)
- Modify WordArt (page 961)
- Modify objects (page 968)
- Arrange objects (page 975)

Chapter 4

- Insert and modify a picture (page 1015)
- Use the Internet as a resource (page 1021)
- Add sound (page 1046)
- Change sound settings (page 1051)

Managers
Volume 1 | Capstone Exercise

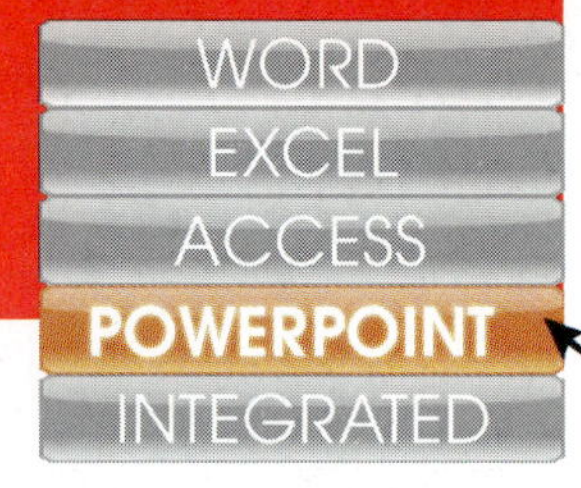

You work as the manager of the marketing department of Flat World Shoe, Inc. As part of the new marketing initiative, you have been asked to create a slideshow for the Board of Directors. Since the board has many agenda items, the slideshow must be concise, but exciting. The main part of the slideshow will be the unveiling of the Will Smith Special.

Create a Presentation

You will create a slideshow to be presented to the Board of Directors. The slideshow will present information for a new marketing initiative.

- Open *exp07_p_bus_cpt_mkting* and save the presentation as **exp07_p_bus_cpt_mkting_solution**.
- Format the presentation with the *Technic* theme.
- Insert a title slide with the title **Flat World Shoe Inc**.
- Add the subtitle **Marketing Initiative 2010** on the first slide.
- Insert the clip art shown by searching for *shoe* in *All collections*. Results should be from *clip art media file type*. Position the clip art in the lower right hand corner of the slide.

- Insert the sound clip *Bright Future* to start automatically when the presentation begins by searching in *All collections* for *sound media file type*. Place the sound icon behind the shoe clip art and hide during the show.
- Insert a title and content slide after the title slide. Title it Overview, but leave the second slide blank until you have completed the presentation. When all of the body slides are complete, come back to this slide and create an introduction slide based on the titles of the slides in the slide show.
- Convert the body of slide 3 to multilevel bullets and delete the text box that says *slide 3*.
- Insert a footer on all slides except the first one. The footer will be the company name **Flat World Shoe, Inc.**, to emphasize brand recognition.
- Change the color of the key words *Major marketing initiative* and *top 3* to **red** for emphasis on slide 4.
- Add a shadow to the key words *major marketing initiative* and *top 3* to help them stand out.
- Change *Flat World Shoe, Inc.*, to **blue** on slide 4 to match the company's color scheme on the title slide. Delete the text box identifying it as slide 4.
- Use the reuse slides feature to insert the second slide in the *exp07_p_bus_cpt_mkting_slide* file. Place it after slide 4.
- Convert the title *Product Definition* to WordArt.
- Format *Flat World Shoe, Inc.*, to **blue** to reinforce brand recognition.
- Insert several images of various types of shoes. Arrange them attractively on the slide.
- Insert a new Content and Caption slide after slide 5. The title is **Repositioning**. Change the title to **41-point** font.
- Type the following text in the text box above the title: **Now is the perfect time to reposition the company and focus on our strongest sellers.**
- Increase the size of the text box so that it expands the entire width of the slide.
- Change the text to **20-point** font.
- Resize the placeholder of the caption layout to give it more emphasis.
- Insert the following table in the content area. Use **Medium Style 2, Accent 1**; resize the table, if necessary. Center the data in the annual sales column.

Category	Annual Sales (in millions)
Men's athletic	$3.1
Teens athletic	$2.6
Women's athletic	$2.1
Women's dress	$1.5

- Modify slide 7 by using a Comparison layout. Delete the text box with the slide number.
- Move *Fabulous Feet and Shoes for Everyone* to the left and right top text boxes.
- Move the Strengths and Weaknesses bullets for *Shoes for Everyone* text to the right column.
- Modify slide 8 by using the Horizontal Bullet SmartArt for the information in the bulleted list. Delete the text box with the slide number.
- Modify slide 9 by using the Target List SmartArt. Delete the text box with the slide number.
- Add a slide titled **The Athlete Special**. Select two appropriate images from the clip art collection that fit well on the slide without having to be resized. Do not include photos of people. Once the Marketing Department sends the celebrity photos and permission slips, they will replace these clip arts.

...continued on Next Page

- Set the transition for all slides to *wipe left*.
- Add a new slide titled **Women's Dress Shoes**. Select one appropriate picture from the Internet that fits well on the slide. Do not include photos of people.
- Add a new slide titled **Athletic Shoes**. Select three appropriate images from the clip art collection that fit well on the slide without having to be resized; they may overlap. Do not include photos of people.
- Insert a conclusion slide, think of a slogan for the new campaign and use WordArt to display it on this slide.
- Add music to the conclusion slide. Play the sound automatically and hide the sound icon.
- Insert the clip art shown by searching for *shoe* in *All collections*. Results should be from *clip art media file type*. Move the clip art to the bottom-right corner of the slide.

- Animate the Clip Art so it appears to run across the bottom of the slide.
- Use spelling checker to check the presentation.
- Print handout pages with six slides per page.
- The presentation will be shown at the annual board meeting; set automatic timings appropriate to each slide.
- View the presentation and adjust the timings if necessary.
- Save and close the presentation.

Create a Web Presentation

The CEO would like to make this available online for board members who are not able to attend the annual meeting.

- Save the presentation as a *Single File Web Page*.

Integrate Microsoft Office Software

Background

Managers frequently integrate information from the various software applications. Their job is to manage and disseminate information from various sources to the groups and individuals who need it. They need to be able to find information quickly, manipulate it, and generate usable reports for decision making.

Tasks

Managers might be responsible for a variety of integrated applications. This could include the following:

- Extracting data from a Microsoft Office Access Database
- Analyzing data in Microsoft Office Excel
- Reporting information through Microsoft Office Word
- Merging Access and Word for mailings
- Preparing presentations in Microsoft Office PowerPoint for clients, employees, upper management, and other business associates

Skills

In addition to the basic application skills, a manager should be able to do the following:

- Export data from Access and Excel
- Embed and link objects
- Merge data
- Copy and paste between applications
- Check spelling and grammar

Managers
Volume 1 | Capstone Exercise

You work as the CEO of Flat World Shoe, Inc. Your company just completed a successful year with a new marketing initiative. You have been asked to prepare a report for the Board of Directors on the success of the campaign and the strategic management team's recommendations for next year. You have received input from each member of the strategic management team and will be compiling everything into a Word report for the Board of Directors. Before preparing the final report, you will need to update several documents.

Update a Database and Export Select Data to Excel

You have kept databases of the marketing promotion. You will need to update that information before exporting it to Excel.

- Open the database *exp07_i_bus_cpt_db1* and save it as **exp07_i_bus_cpt_db1_solution**.
- Add the following two records to the *Spokespeople* table:
  - **JD1, Johnny, Depp, Acting, Not Available, Male**
  - **BB1, Beach, Boys, Music, Available, Band**
- Change *George Clooney* and *Usher* to **Available**.
- Set up the relationship between the *Spokespeople* table and the *Products* table.
- Sort the *Spokesperson* table in descending order by *Available* and export the data to Excel.
- Save the workbook as **exp07_i_bus_cpt_exc_solution**.
- Return to the Access database and prepare a query using both tables.
- Include the following fields: *Spokesperson ID*, *First Name*, *Last Name*, *Available*, *Category*.
- Notice from the results that two spokespeople are not available: *Michael Jordan* and *Venus Williams*.
- Open the *Products* table and delete *MJ1* and *VW1* from the *Spokesperson* field.
- Enter **TS1** as the spokesperson for the *Dress 300*.
- Run the query again to ensure that the spokespeople endorsing a product are all available.
- Save the query as **qryAvailableReps**.
- Create a query that returns all fields of the products table and the first and last name of the spokesperson if the product has a spokesperson.
- Save the query as **qryProductSpokesperson**.
- Export the results to Excel.
- Save the workbook as **exp07_i_bus_cpt_exc_solution2**.
- Close all files.

Update a Spreadsheet and Export Select Data to Word

You have several spreadsheets you would like to include in the report. First, you need to update and format them.

- Open the workbook *exp07_i_bus_cpt_exc_solution*.
- Format cells A1:F42 as a table. Apply the Table Style Light 9 Quick Style.
- Hide the SpokesPersonID column.
- Center the data for the spokesperson ID, career, and availability columns.
- Apply a filter to display the available spokespeople.
- Resize the columns if necessary. Reformat the column headers so the entire chart fits neatly on 1 portrait oriented page.
- Open the document *exp07_i_bus_cpt_rpt* and save it as **exp07_i_bus_cpt_rpt_solution**.
- Copy the table and paste it as a link in the Word document to replace *[insert first table]* under the first paragraph under the *Background* heading.
- Save and close *exp07_i_bus_cpt_exc_solution*.
- Open the workbook *exp07_i_bus_cpt_exc_solution2*.
- Convert **cells A1:H8** to a table. Apply the Table Style Light 9 Quick Style to the table.
- Format Unit Price and Cost with the Accounting Format. Hide the Spokesperson column.
- Resize column widths if necessary, but keep them narrow enough to fit on 1 portrait layout page. You may need to play with the column headers some in order to make them fit well.
- Copy the table and paste it as a link in the Word document to replace *[insert second table]* under the second paragraph under the Background heading.
- Save and close *exp07_i_bus_cpt_exc_solution2*.

Update a Budget Document

Now that the year is over, we can input the actual expenses for the marketing plan and see how those figures compare to the budget.

- Open *exp07_i_bus_cpt_budget* and save it as **exp07_i_bus_cpt_budget_solution**.
- Input the amount **1150000** for the actual amount spent on spokespeople.
- In **cells E12** and **F12**, calculate actual expenditures and amount under or over budget. Enter a formula to determine the difference in budget to actual and the percent of total for the actual expenses in columns F and G.
- Create a bar chart that graphs budget to actual expenditures.
- Format the chart to list the Expense categories on the vertical axis and dollar figures on the horizontal axis.
- Use the Layout 3 Quick Layout and Style 3 Chart Style. Enter the title **Expenditures**.
- Copy the chart as an object and paste it to replace [*insert graph*] in the word document.

Reporting the Marketing Campaign Results

The marketing initiative was successful. You are now the second largest manufacturer of shoes. This is definitely something you want to report to the Board of Directors.

- Replace **[insert SmartArt]** with a pyramid SmartArt shape that illustrates that the following companies are in the top 3:
  - Shoes for Everyone
  - Flat World Shoe, Inc.
  - Fabulous Feet
- Insert the pinstripe footer that includes your name, the page number, and the current date.
- Make sure your report is attractive, the colors match, and everything is well formatted. Change themes or colors if it helps deliver the message in an attractive, eye-catching manner.
- Save and close your workbook.

Creating a PowerPoint Presentation of the Report

For the board meeting where you will present the fantastic news of Flat World Shoes, Inc's resurgence as an industry leader, you create a PowerPoint presentation version of the Word Report you created earlier. You have earlier tweaked your report as an outline in Word.

- Launch PowerPoint. Open the Word Document *exp07_i_bus_cpt_rpt_ppt*. Save it as a PowerPoint presentation titled **exp07_i_bus_cpt_rpt_ppt_solution**.
- Change the theme to Flow.
- Add a title slide at the beginning. Add the title **2010 Marketing Initiative Results**.
- Add a subtitle of **Flat World Shoes, Inc**.
- Change the layout of Slide 2 to Content with Caption. Paste the *Available Spokespeople* table from the spreadsheet *exp07_i_bus_cpt_exc_solution.xlsx* in the right of the slide. Resize the table for maximum readability
- Apply the Themed Style 1, Accent 1 Table Style. Emphasize the header row as you like and increase font size of the entire table. Center all Data on the table.
- On the third slide, paste the Contracted Spokespeople table from the spreadsheet *exp07_i_bus_cpt_exc_solution2.xlsx* in the lower section of the slide. Resize the table for maximum readability.
- Apply the Themed Style 1, Accent 1 Table Style. Emphasize the header row as you like and increase font size of the entire table.
- Add a new blank slide for the fourth slide. Paste the graph from the Excel workbook *exp07_i_bus_cpt_budget_solution* on this slide. Resize it to be as large as possible. Change it to Layout 5 Quick Layout and use a complementary Style from the Style Gallery. Tweak the formatting for maximum readability.
- On the fifth slide, delete the bullet points. Go to *exp07_i_bus_cpt_budget_solution* and hide columns B and C. Copy the remaining table from cells **A4:G12** to the slide and tweak the format for maximum readability. Format it similarly to the earlier two tables with a Header row and a total row.
- Copy the pyramid SmartArt listing the top three shoe manufacturers you created in the Word document *exp07_i_bus_cpt_rpt_solution* to the conclusion slide.
- Add several photos of shoes from the Clip Art Gallery to the title slide. Animate them to fade in very fast one at a time.
- Add a music sound clip from the Clip Art Gallery to play across the slides, starting at the beginning of the presentation and looping until stopped. Use business as your keyword search.
- Apply consistent transitions to all slides.
- Automatically advance slides after enough time to read the slide.
- View, save, and close the presentation.
- Turn in all work for the integrated assignment per your instructor's instructions.

Zookeepers

Use Microsoft Office Word

Background

Word processing is the most frequently used application program in almost any work environment, including a zoo. As a zookeeper or an assistant, information must be documented about the animals in your care. Reports must be produced in order to inform zoo officials about the health and well-being of the animals. It is imperative that an assistant zookeeper know the many features available in Microsoft Office Word and be comfortable using them (without having to refer regularly to a reference guide). The skills taught in these four chapters are all vitals skills in Word, in addition to other skills that would be covered at a more advanced level.

Tasks

Update a document on the status of the care of the park's baby elephants. The document will include the following elements:

- Opening a starting document
- Inserting a picture
- Inserting page numbers
- Applying a style
- Inserting a table of contents
- Updating document properties

Skills

An assistant zookeeper should be able to do the following:

Chapter 1

- View a document (page 78)
- Set margins and specify page orientation (page 87)
- Insert page breaks (page 88)
- Add page numbers (page 90)
- Insert headers and footers (page 91)
- Create sections (page 92)
- Insert a cover page (page 93)
- Use the Find and Replace commands (page 94)
- Check spelling and grammar (page 103)
- Use save and backup options (page 104)

...continued on Next Page

Chapter 2

- Apply font attributes through the Font dialog box (page 133)
- Set off paragraphs with tabs, borders, lists, and columns (page 143)
- Apply paragraph formats (page 148)
- Create and modify styles (page 159)
- Create a table of contents (page 171)

Chapter 3

- Insert a table (page 197)
- Format a table (page 205)
- Insert clip art and images into a document (page 219)
- Format a graphic element (page 220)
- Insert WordArt into a document (page 225)

Chapter 4

- Insert comments into a document (page 251)
- Track changes in a document (page 254)
- Use navigation tools (page 267)
- Create and modify footnotes and endnotes (page 281)
- Modify document properties (page 290)

Zookeepers
Volume 1 | Capstone Exercises

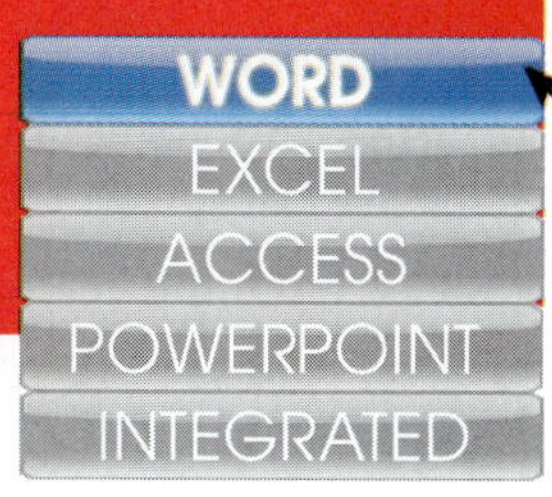

You work as a zookeeper's assistant in the elephant area of the Wild Animal Park of the Main Street Zoo. The zoo has 11 elephants currently in the exhibit, 4 of whom are babies. As an assistant zookeeper, it is your responsibility to assist the zookeeper in various duties. You might be asked to weigh, measure, and track the babies' growth progress. The zookeeper has asked you to update and correct a rough draft of a report he will forward to the head zookeeper and several zoo officials. Professionalism and accuracy are essential when making changes to this document.

Viewing a Document

- Open the *exp07_w_ns_cpt_elephant.docx* document and save it as **exp07_w_ns_cpt_elephant_solution.docx**.
- Go to the *Full Screen Reading* view and read through the document to familiarize yourself with what the zookeeper has written about the baby elephants.
- After reading through the document, change back to the *Print Layout* view.

Set Margins and Specify Page Orientation

- Change the margins of the document to the Narrow setting.
- Confirm the page orientation is set to *Portrait*.

Insert a Cover Page

With Microsoft Office Word 2007 you can easily add a professional-looking cover page to the report by using the Building Blocks feature. Each page is formatted so you can easily personalize it using the building block fields.

- Go to the top of the document and insert The Stacks cover page from the Cover Page Gallery.
- Change the document title to **Baby Elephant Report**.
- Type **Main Street Zoo** as the subtitle.
- Change the Author field to:
  - **Your Name, Assistant Zookeeper**

Insert Headers and Footers

- Insert the Stacks Header and footer styles for the body of the document. Do not show the header or footer on the cover page.
- On the right side of the footer, directly under the company name, enter the date using the Date & Time format mm/dd/yyyy.
- Set the date so it will automatically update.
- In the footer, change the company name to **Main Street Zoo**.
- Reset the page numbering so the page which starts with information about Roimba is page 1.
- Check to make sure the header appears on all pages except the cover page.

Check Spelling and Grammar

After adding a cover page and headers and footers, you move on to correcting the document itself. You notice that many words are misspelled, and the document contains a few grammatical errors.

- Run the spelling checker, and correct grammar and spelling errors.
- Choose *Ignore All* for proper names.
- Add **allomother** and **allomothers** to the dictionary.
- Proofread the report.
- Save your changes.

Use the Find and Replace Commands

- Go to the beginning of the document and select the Replace feature.
- Replace *auntie* with **allomother**.

Use Styles and Themes

The zookeeper has asked that you make the report look uniform and professional. You apply styles to the document, automating the process of uniformity.

- Select the subtitles, *Roimba, Ella, Uttam, Safi, General Health* and *Final Notes*. Apply the Heading 1 Style.
- Select the paragraph which begins *Safi has been under my care...* and the quote which begins *minor enough...* in the Uttam section. Apply the Quote Style.
- Move to the top of the report, before the subtitle *Roimba*, insert the heading **Baby Elephant Report**, and press **Enter** once.
- Apply the *Title* style to the *Baby Elephant Report* title.
- Apply the Concourse Theme to the document.
- Select all instances of the Normal style. Modify the Normal Style with these settings:
  - Fully justify paragraphs.
  - Reduce the spacing after paragraphs to 6 pts.
  - Change the font to Calibri, 11
- Apply the newly modified normal style to the body of the document.

Use Borders and Shading

To set the long quote from the veterinarian apart further, you indent it and apply shading.

- Select the paragraph beginning *Safi has been under...*
- Change the left and right margins of this paragraph to be .25 inches narrower than the rest of the document.
- Apply an Orange Accent 3, Lighter 80% shade to the paragraph.

...continued on Next Page

Use Columns

To increase readability, use 2 columns throughout the body of the report.

- Select from the heading *Roimba* to the end of the final notes.
- Apply 2 columns.

Insert a Table of Contents

To put the finishing touches on the report, you add a table of contents. The addition enables the reader to quickly locate topics in your document and adds a level of professionalism to your work.

- Go to the Title. Press **Enter** two times, then insert a section break, next page after the title. Format the title *Baby Elephant Report* as one column.
- Remove the Header from this section and make sure the pages start numbering with page 1 on the page about Roimba.
- Create a table of contents on the second page below the *Baby Elephant Report* title. Use the Automatic Table 1 style.
- Save your changes.

Insert a Table and Format a Table

The zookeeper has an addition to the report. The information he would like you to add is in a column and row format. After discussing it with him, you agree that this data would look more professional and easier to read if they were set up in a table.

- Insert the following table after the paragraph that begins *Below is the growth progress.*

Name	Height	Weight (in lbs.)	General Health
Roimba	5′4″	2640	Excellent
Ella	4′2″	864	Excellent
Uttam	3′11″	549	Excellent
Saffron	3′2″	280	Good

- Center all text in the table.
- Apply the table style *Medium List1–Accent 3.*

Insert WordArt into a Document

After inserting the table, you decided that the title needs to be enhanced a little. WordArt is a great tool for using decorative text.

- Insert a row at the top of the table and merge the cells together.
- Insert *Word Art, Style 13* (first column, third row) and change the text to **Baby Elephants** and change the font size to **18 pt**.
- Change the fill color to **Orange, Accent 3**, and center the WordArt in the center of the first row.

Add Visual Enhancements

Insert a clip art image of an elephant from the Clip Art Organizer, and use the formatting tools, when appropriate, to modify the graphic.

- Insert the following clip art image in the first paragraph about Roimba.

- Set the text wrapping to tight and position the image so the top of the elephant's head is even with the first line of the first paragraph on the right side of the column.
- Set the paragraph spacing before the heading *Roimba* to 0 pts.
- Insert the picture *safi.jpg* at the beginning of the paragraph that begins *Six-month-old Saffron.*
- Change the text wrapping to **Square**.
- Change the size of the picture to **1.41″** height with aspect ratios locked.
- Apply the picture frame style *Moderate Frame, Black.*
- Position the picture so it is even with the right side of the column and the bottom of the first paragraph about Safi.

Working with References and Citations

You know that it is a common practice to use a variety of sources to supplement your thoughts when writing a report. Failure to acknowledge the source of information is a form of plagiarism. You noticed that the zookeeper has inserted endnotes in the report but has not referenced the source of the information. You also decide that you would prefer footnotes to endnotes.

- Convert all endnotes to footnotes.
- Go to each of the footnotes in the document and insert a citation with the following information:
  - Type of Source: *Report.*
  - Author: Refer to the footnote.
  - Title: Refer to the footnote.
  - Year: **2008**.
- Press **Ctrl+End** to go to the end of the report. At that point, insert a *Section break, Next Page.* Make sure the page number in the footer continues from the previous section.
- On the last page of the report, insert a *Bibliography* using the Built-In Bibliography feature in Word.
- Change the Bibliography Style to **MLA**.

Insert Comments into a Document

You have made many changes to the report and need to document them for the zookeeper. The best way to do this is through the use of comments.

- Insert the following comments:
  - After the word *Bibliography*—Ask the zookeeper to verify that the information is correct.
  - In front of the table—Call the veterinarian to verify the figures.
  - After Final Notes—Ask the zookeeper if he has anything else that needs to be added.

...continued on Next Page

Update Table of Contents

You have added content to the report and inserted page breaks. Make sure you update the table of contents to reflect the new page numbers.

- Update the table of contents.

Update Document Properties

It is important to develop the habit of using the document properties feature for all zoo documents. Even though the documents are stored on the zoo's computer system, they will need to be easily accessed by other zoo officials.

- Open the Document Properties window and update the following information:
  - o Keywords are **baby**, **elephants**, **update**.
  - o Category: **Report**.
  - o Status: **Completed**.
  - o Comments: **Prepared for zoo officials. Formatted by Your Name**.

Track Changes in a Document

So that you know what changes have been made after the report comes back to you after the zookeeper has reviewed it, you need to turn on the track changes feature.

- Turn on *Track Changes*.
- Select *Show Revisions in Balloons*.

View, Save, and Print the Document

You want to make sure the report looks balanced and professional. An easy way to do this is to look at the document with the Thumbnails view. Also, for the convenience of other zoo officials, save a second copy of your report in the older Word 97–2003 format.

- Go to the *Thumbnails* view and review the report.
- Make any corrections you feel are necessary to make the report look professional and polished.
- Save, print, and close the report.

Zookeepers

Use Microsoft Office Excel

Background

A zookeeper's assistant will need to perform many tasks associated with the care of animals within the zoo. In addition to the general care and feeding of animals, keeping accurate records of the animal's health and well-being is another very important task. It is important for the zookeeper, veterinarians, and zoo officials to be able to access and analyze this information quickly and easily. With Microsoft Office Excel's many features, tasks are made simple. Excel's Chart tool will help give a pictorial view of data, and the Data Table feature can help sort and filter the information.

Tasks

The assistant to the zookeeper might be responsible for creating and maintaining different types of spreadsheets. These types of spreadsheets could include the following:

- Growth charts
- Tracking dietary needs
- Scheduling
- Project planning

Skills

A zookeeper's assistant should be able to do the following:

- Create a spreadsheet
- Create formulas
- Create charts
- Apply a style
- Sort and filter a data table

Chapter 1

- Enter and edit data in cells (page 322)
- Describe and use symbols and the order of precedence (page 328)
- Display cell formulas (page 330)
- Insert and delete rows and columns (page 331)
- Use cell ranges; Excel move; copy, paste, paste special; and AutoFill (page 332)
- Manage worksheets (page 340)
- Format worksheets (page 341)
- Select page setup options for printing (page 353)

...continued on Next Page

Chapter 2

- Create and copy formulas (page 381)
- Use relative and absolute cell addresses (page 382)
- Insert basic statistical functions (page 390)
- Use date functions (page 392)
- Use the IF function (page 399)

Chapter 3

- Choose a chart type (page 431)
- Create a chart (page 438)
- Modify a chart (page 450)
- Embed charts (page 459)

Chapter 4

- Freeze rows and columns (page 488)
- Hide and unhide rows, columns, and worksheets (page 489)
- Protect a cell, a worksheet, and a workbook (page 490)
- Explore basic table management (page 505)
- Sort data (page 510)
- Filter and total data (page 514)

Zookeepers
Volume 1 | Capstone Exercises

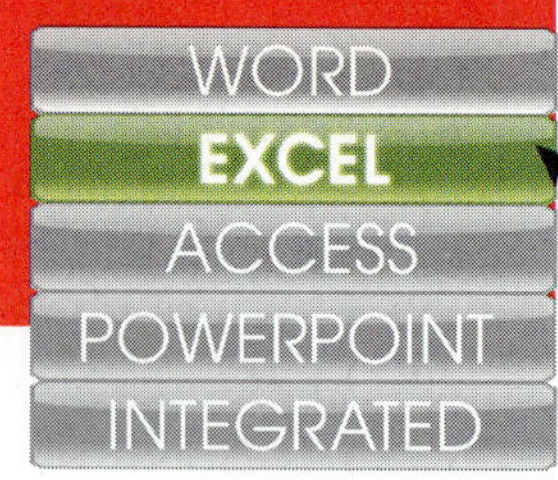

As a zookeeper's assistant, it is very important to be able to use Excel and its numerous features to create spreadsheets to track information about the animals. In this particular case, you will be tracking the baby elephants' weights and heights from birth to their most recent health exams. Accurately entering and manipulating this information is critical to the health and well-being of the elephants.

Open a Workbook

The zookeeper started a worksheet on the first baby elephant born at the zoo, but has been unable to update it. Now the zoo has four babies, and the zookeeper would like you to update the spreadsheet he started several years ago.

- Open *exp07_e_ns_cpt_elephant.xlsx* workbook.
- Save it as **exp07_e_ns_cpt_elephant_solution.xlsx**.

Update a Workbook

After looking at the workbook the zookeeper started, you see many changes that you would like to make. In addition to the changes, you need to enter the information for the three new elephants that have joined the herd.

- Starting with **Date** in **cell A2**, update the worksheet to break the Height and Weight into different sections, as shown below:

Baby Elephant		
Date	Weight In Pounds	Height In Inches
Feb-04	229	36

- Delete the sentences that are currently there and set it up in the above format.
- Adjust column widths as necessary to show all data.

Create a Formula

In the column next to *In Pounds* you would like to calculate how much weight the elephant has gained each time it has been weighed or measured.

- Add a column to the right of the Weight column.
- In the column next to *In Pounds* enter the title **Weight Gain**.
- In **cell C4**, create a formula that will calculate the elephant's weight gain or loss each time it was weighed.
- Copy the formula down to the other dates using the fill handle.
- Next to the column labeled *In Inches*, enter the title **Inches Grown**.
- In **cell E4**, create a formula that will calculate the elephant's growth in inches each time it was measured.
- Copy the formula down to the other dates using the fill handle.
- Adjust column widths as necessary to show all data.

Format Cells

- Change the title from *Baby Elephant–Roimba* to **Roimba**.
- Change the font size to **18**.
- Merge and center the title over columns A through E.
- Change the fill color of the title to **Olive Green, Accent 3, Lighter 40%**.
- Change the fill color of the heading rows to **Olive Green, Accent 3, Lighter 80%**.
- Insert a *Thick Bottom* border under the headings in row 2.
- Format the cells containing numbers to the Comma style with zero decimals.
- Bold the title and heading rows in rows 1 and 2.
- Center the headings in their own cells in row 2.

Insert Basic Statistical Functions

After showing your initial changes to the zookeeper, he is thrilled and would like to have you add more information to it. He would like to know the highest weight gain and growth, lowest weight gain and growth, and average weight gain and growth for each elephant. Being that you have completed the work in the Excel chapters of this book, you remember that Excel has functions that can help you with this: MAX, MIN, and AVERAGE. This information will help the zookeeper understand if the elephants are growing at a normal rate and what the statistics are for each baby.

- Merge and center **cells A10:B10**, **A11:B11**, **A12:B12**, and **A13:B13**. Select the newly merged cells and left justify them.
- Type the title **Average Weight Gain** in **cell A10**.
- Calculate the average weight gain for the elephant by entering the appropriate function in **cell C10**.
- Merge and center **cells D10:E10**, **D11:E11**, **D12:E12**, and **D13:E13**. Select the newly merged cells and left justify them.
- Type the title **Average Growth** in **cell D10**.
- Calculate the average growth for the elephant by entering the appropriate function in **cell F10**.
- Type the title **Maximum Weight Gain** in **cell A11**.

...continued on Next Page

- Calculate the maximum weight gain for the elephant by entering the appropriate function in **cell C11**.
- Type the tile **Maximum Growth** in **cell D11**.
- Calculate the maximum growth for the elephant by entering the appropriate function in **cell F11**.
- Type the title **Minimum Weight Gain** in **cell A12**.
- Calculate the minimum weight gain for the elephant by entering the appropriate function in **cell C12**.
- Type the tile **Minimum Growth** in **cell D12**.
- Calculate the minimum growth for the elephant by entering the appropriate function in **cell F12**.
- Bold all titles.

Use Functions

- Type the title **Average pounds gained per inch grown:** in **cell A14**.
- Using the Average Function and dividing the weight gain by the inches grown, calculate the average pounds per inch grown for the elephant in **cell A15**.
- Format the result with the comma style and 2 decimal places.
- Type the title **Date Updated:** in **cell A17**.
- Insert the function that will return the current date in **cell A18**. Format the date using type 3/14/01.
- Insert a new column between C and D. Type the title **Notes** in **cells D3** and **G3**.
- In **cell D4**, insert a function that will determine if the weight gain is less than the average weight gain. If it is less than the average, return **Weight gain below average**. If is greater than the average weight gain, return **Growth is good**.
- Copy the formula to **cells D6:D8**.
- In **cell G5**, insert a function that will determine if the inches grown are less than the average growth. If the growth is less than the average, insert the words **Below average growth**; if it is greater than the average growth, insert the words **Growth is good**.
- Copy the formula to **cells G6:G8**.
- Automatically fit the column width to accommodate all the text in these cells.

Create and Format a Chart

Now that all the figures have been entered for all the elephants, you will need to create charts based on the worksheet values. The charts provide information visually and will help the zookeeper analyze the data more easily. Some of this information will be used in a Microsoft Office PowerPoint presentation that will be given to zoo officials. It is important to select the proper chart for the information. The line chart is the best choice for tracking the elephants' weights.

- Select the *Date* and *Height In Inches* information on the worksheet in **cells A2:A7** and **E2:E7**
- Insert a *Line with Markers* chart.
- Move the chart in the worksheet below the data in **cells C16:F30**.
- Add the title **Roimba's Growth Chart** above each of the charts.
- Turn off the legend.
- Along the vertical axis add a rotated title saying **Height in Inches**.
- Change the chart style to **Style 45**.

Enhancing Charts with Graphic Shapes

Another way to enhance the appearance of a chart is to add a graphic element. As for the growth charts for the baby elephants, it would nice to add an arrow pointing out the baby's largest growth period.

- Insert the shape *Left Arrow*.
- Have the arrow point to the fastest growth period. It may look best if you rotate the arrow a bit to move it away from the chart line.
- Change the style to **Intense Effect, Accent 3**.
- Insert the text **Fastest Growth Period**.
- Center the text within the arrow.

Use Cell Ranges; Excel Move; Copy, Paste, Paste Special; and AutoFill

Since other elephants have been born since Roimba, you decide that it would be best to keep track of each calf on a different worksheet. Now that you have completed the formulas and formatting for the first elephant, you need to copy the information to the others.

- Rename Sheet 1 to **Roimba**.
- Rename Sheet 2 to **Ella**.
- Rename Sheet 3 to **Uttam**.
- Add a fourth worksheet after *Uttam* and rename that **Saffron**.
- Copy all the contents of the worksheet *Roimba*.
- Paste the contents into the other 3 sheets.
- Make the following corrections for the elephants:
    - o Ella

Date	Weight (in pounds)	Height (in inches)
09/2006	209	36
02/2007	495	47
09/2007	864	58
03/2008	1112	64
01/2009	2011	74

- o Uttam

Date	Weight (in pounds)	Height (in inches)
03/2007	249	40
09/2007	523	57
03/2008	1010	66
09/2008	1190	68
01/2009	1354	71

...continued on Next Page

- Saffron

Date	Weight (in pounds)	Height (in inches)
04/2008	280	38
05/2008	299	40
06/2008	310	42
07/2008	350	44
01/2009	600	50

- Be sure to change all appropriate titles for each of the elephants.

Select Page Setup Options for Printing

Now that you have completed all the work necessary, you will set up the print options.

- Review the Worksheets to make sure they are formatted attractively and tweak as necessary.
- Select all worksheets.
- Create a footer with your name, Assistant Zoo Keeper in the left section, the file and sheet name in center section, and page in the right section.
- Change the page orientation to **Landscape**.
- Change the margins to **Narrow**.
- Center the worksheets horizontally and vertically on the page.
- Save and print the entire workbook.
- Print the formulas of the *Roimba* worksheet.
- Close the workbook.

Open and Save a Workbook

In addition to the elephant spreadsheet, the zoo has all the elephant's information stored in a data table within zoo's Excel spreadsheet. The zookeeper would like you to add the information for the new baby elephants and run several filters for him.

- Open the workbook called *exp07_e_ns_cpt_zoo.xlsx*.
- Save it as **exp07_e_ns_cpt_zoo_solution.xlsx**.

Freeze Rows and Columns and Explore Basic Table Management

In order to work with the spreadsheet, you will need to freeze the title information so you can see what information needs to be entered into which column.

- Freeze the first two rows of the spreadsheet.
- Scroll down to the bottom of the table.
- Enter the information below:

Name	Sex	Age	Born	Weight
Roimba	Male	4	Main Street Zoo	2640
Ella	Female	2	Main Street Zoo	864
Uttam	Male	1	Main Street Zoo	549
Saffron	Female	.5	Main Street Zoo	280

Hiding and Unhiding Rows, Columns, and Worksheets

Since the zookeeper does not need to see some of the information about the elephants, he has asked you to hide certain columns before you print.

- Hide the column that lists the elephant's age.
- Adjust the column widths as necessary.

Protecting a Cell, a Worksheet, and a Workbook

Now that all of the changes have been made to the spreadsheet, the zookeeper has asked that you protect the workbook so that only approved changes can be made.

- Protect the workbook for structure.
- Enter the password **exp07**.

Filter and Sort Data

The zookeeper has asked you to run several filters on the information.

- Skip a row after the last line in the table, then enter **Your Name–Assistant Zookeeper**.
- Create a filter that displays all the male elephants that were born in South Africa.
- Sort the table by weight from largest to smallest and in ascending order by name.
- Print the results.
- Print the worksheet.
- Save your changes.

Zookeepers

Use Microsoft Office Access

Background

Zookeepers and their assistants are responsible for the care of the animals in a zoo as well as for maintaining records. They use database software to maintain animal information. Forms can be created to enter, modify, and delete animal information. Queries can be created to locate and extract information from a database. Reports can be created that display animal information in a professional-looking manner. It is imperative that a zookeeper's assistant understand the features of Microsoft Office Access and be comfortable using those features. The following database skills taught in the textbook are crucial skills that are needed for people employed at a zoo.

Tasks

Create a database of elephants at the zoo and their vital information.

- Create a database
- Enter information into the database
- Run filters for analysis
- Run queries on the data
- Create a report using the query

Skills

A zookeeper's assistant should be able to do the following:

Chapter 1

- Explore, describe, and navigate among the objects in an Access database (page 547)
- Back up, compact, and repair Access files (page 556)
- Create filters (page 565)
- Use the Relationships window (page 578)
- Understand relational power (page 579)

Chapter 2

- Create tables (page 612)
- Understand table relationships (page 625)
- Share data with Excel (page 626)
- Establish table relationships (page 630)
- Create a query (page 642)
- Specify criteria for different data types (page 645)
- Copy and run a query (page 649)

...continued on Next Page

Chapter 3

Chapter 4

Zookeepers
Volume 1 | Capstone Exercises

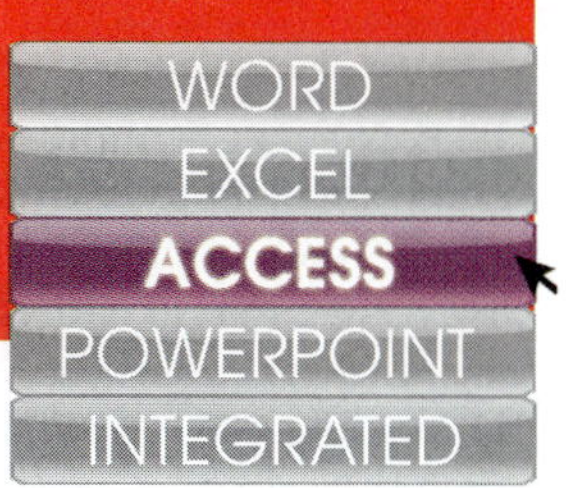

The zookeeper created a basic database several years ago when the zoo started the elephant exhibit in the Wild Animal Park. Since then, he has not had the time to update the database or even run a report. The animal database has already been set up, but you need to update it with the new baby elephants' information. The zookeeper has asked you to create a database table of the vaccines the elephants have received. He would like to compare these records with the veterinarian's records to make sure the elephants are up to date on their shots. It is important that the database is as accurate as possible. Specifically, you need to enter the baby elephants into the database, create and run a query, and prepare a report.

Exploring, Describing, and Navigating Among the Objects in an Access Database

You will need to copy the original database file, rename the copied file, and then open the copied database to complete this Capstone Exercise. After you open the copied database, you will need to enter the elephants' information.

- Open *exp07_a_ns_cpt_zoo.accdb* and save it as **exp07_a_ns_cpt_zoo_solution.accdb**.
- Enable the content.

Enter Records in a Table in the Datasheet View

In this database, there are several ways you can add records to the animal inventory table. The first way is through the Datasheet view. This view is similar to an Excel spreadsheet.

- Go to the *Datasheet* view of the *Park Animal Inventory* table.
- Enter the following new records:

ID	Animal Type	Name	Born	Location	Sex
EL0037	Elephant	Roimba	2004	Wild Animal Park	Male
EL0038	Elephant	Ella	2006	Wild Animal Park	Female
EL0039	Elephant	Uttam	2007	Wild Animal Park	Male

- Close the *Park Animal Inventory* table.

Enter Records in a Table in the Forms View

Since you forgot to enter Saffron, the zoo's newest addition to the elephant exhibit, you decide to enter her using the Form view. The Form view is just another way of entering information into a table. This view is easier than using the Datasheet view in that the information is set up in a visually appealing manner.

- Open the *Animal Inventory Form*.
- Enter the following data for new records for Saffron and for a new elephant born in 2009:

ID	Animal Type	Name	Born	Location	Sex
EL0040	Elephant	Saffron	2007	Wild Animal Park	Female
EL0041	Elephant	YOUR NAME	2000	Wild Animal Park	Male or Female

- Print the record that you created with your name on it.

Filter Records

The zookeeper would like to see a list of all the elephants and a separate list of all the elephants born after 1998.

- Open the *Park Animal Inventory* table in *Datasheet* view and filter the records to show only elephants.
- Run the filter by selection and print your results.
- Toggle filter to display all records.
- Filter records to show the elephants born after 1998.
- Print your results.
- Toggle filter to display all records.

Share Data with Excel

Several zookeepers throughout the zoo keep their animal inventory in an Excel spreadsheet. For the zoo to keep information in a consistent format, your manager has asked you to bring the spreadsheet into the current Access database.

- Use the Import External Data–Excel Spreadsheet Wizard to import the file *exp07_a_ns_cpt_excel_zoo.xlsx.*
- Append a copy of the records to the *Park Animal Inventory* table.
- Review the table to confirm the records have been imported correctly.

...continued on Next Page

Create a Table

The zookeeper is impressed with your ability to work with Access and would like for you to create a database for him to keep track of the baby elephants' vaccinations. No database has existed like this before, so you must plan the database and its tables and fields carefully. Once you have planned this out, you can create the database for him. After much thought and working with the zookeeper as to what exactly he wants in the database, you now can go through the process of building the database. After you create the database table, you need to change some properties to match the type of data to be entered for each field.

- Create a new table named **Vaccines**.
- Create the following fields and select the appropriate data types listed:

Field Name	Data Type
VacID	Text
Vaccination	Text
Manufacturer	Text
Dosage	Number
Vaccine	Text
Date_of_Vaccine	Date
Reaction	Yes/No

- Change the field size of the *Vaccination* field to **100**.
- Change the field size of VacID to **3**.
- Change the field size for the *Manufacturer* field to **20**.
- Set the primary key for this table to be VacID.
- Set the captions for each field to be the headers from the table, below.

Enter Data in a Table

Now that the table structure has been set up, you need to enter the information into the table.

- Enter the following information into the Vaccines table:

Vaccines			
Vac ID	Vaccination Name	Manufacturer	Dosage (mL) per 500lbs.
EHV	Endotheliotropic Herpesvirus	Roche	1
ENC	Encephalo-myocarditis	Merck	2
RAB	Rabies	Glaxo	3
WNV	West Nile Virus	Beyer	2

Establish Relationships

You need to establish a relationship between the Park Animal Inventory table, The Vaccination History table, and the Vaccines table.

- Establish a relationship between the *Park Animal Inventory* and the *Vaccination History* tables using the *ID* field in Park Animal Inventory and AnimalID in Vaccination History.
- Establish a relationship between the *Vaccination History* and the *Vaccines* tables on Vaccine in the *Vaccination History* table and VacID in the *Vaccines* table.
- Select *Enforce Referential Integrity*. This will create a one-to-many relationship.
- Print the relationship.
- Save the changes.

Create a Select Query

The zookeeper would like to have you run a query to find all the elephants that have received the Encephalomyocarditis vaccine and when.

- In the *Query Design* view, select all three tables for your query.
- Use the following fields for your query:
  - o *ID*—from *Park Animal Inventory* table
  - o *Name*—from *Park Animal Inventory* table
  - o *Sex*—from *Park Animal Inventory* table
  - o *Vaccination*—from *Vaccines* table
  - o *Date of Vaccine*—from *Vaccination History* table
  - o *Reaction*—from *Vaccination History* table
- Sort the query in ascending order by animal name.
- Under the criteria for vaccine enter **Encephalomyocarditis** or **enc** for VacID, but do not show the field.
- Run the query and save it as **ENC_Vaccine_Query**.
- Print your results.

Copy and Run a Query

Now that you have created a query for the Encephalomyocarditis vaccine, you need to copy it and run it for the Endotheliotropic Herpesvirus vaccine.

- Copy *ENC_Vaccine_Query* and rename it **EHV_Vaccine_Query**.
- Change the Vaccine name to **Endotheliotropic Herpesvirus**.
- Run the query.
- Print your results.
- Save the query.

Create a Calculated Field in a Query

It is time for boosters on the ENC vaccine. Create a query based on the ENC_Vaccine_Query which finds all elephants who have not had an ENC booster in the past 10 years and estimate the dosage necessary based on the weight at the last dosage.

- Make a copy of *ENC_Vaccine_Query* and rename it **ENC_Booster**.
- Edit the *ENC_Booster* query to show elephants who have not had an ENC (Encephalomyocarditis) vaccination in the past 10 years. Remove the sex field from the query because it is extraneous.

...continued on Next Page

- In a field labeled **Estimated Dose**, calculate the estimated dosage necessary for the booster by multiplying the recommended dosage (from the *Vaccines* table) per 500 pounds based on the elephants weight at last dose (from the *Vaccination History* table) plus 1,000 pounds for growth in the intervening decade or more. Of course, on the day of the vaccination, the animal will be weighed. This is just to estimate the correct quantity to order.
- Display the results in the Estimated Dose column as a number rounded to the nearest 0.01 mL.
- Save and print your results.

Create Additional Queries

The zookeeper viewed the results of your query and would like for you to run several other queries. He needs to know if any of the elephants had a reaction to the vaccine.

- Create a query named **Reactions**, returning the elephant's name, ID number, date of vaccination, name of vaccination, and if the animal had a reaction to a vaccine.
- Add a field with a calculated dosage based on weight and recommended dosage per 500 pounds for any elephants who have run a reaction to a vaccine.
- Run the query and save it.
- Print your results.

Create Data Aggregates

- Create a summary query using fields from the *Park Animal Inventory* table.
- Create a formula that will group the total number of animals you have by Animal Type under a column heading of Number of Type.
- The final result should have only 2 columns; Animal Type and the Number of each type of animal.
- Run the query and save it as **Animals_by_Type**.

Create and Edit a Report Using the Report Tool

The queries you created previously look OK, but you would like to expand on the booster program and present this information to the zookeeper in a more professional format in that these results will be forwarded on to the veterinarian and zoo officials. The reports feature within Access will help you create a professional-looking report. Appearance does matter.

- Make a copy of the *ENC_Booster* query. Modify it to include all vaccines, which are 10 years out of date.
- Save the new query as **Booster Program**.
- Create a Report based on the *Booster Program* query. Name it **Booster Program Report**.
- Group the report by the animals' names, so that if an animal needs more than one vaccine it is listed together. Sort the animals' names and vaccination names in alphabetical order.
- Delete the ID field.
- Center the Reaction column.
- Replace the generic logo with **msz_logo.jpg**.
- Apply the Concourse AutoFormat.
- Save, print, and close the report.

Use Reports to Display Aggregated Data

After creating the report using the Report tool, you would like to see if the Report Wizard is easier to use. Since the zookeeper would like you to print a report of all the animals in the park, this is a great opportunity to compare these Access features.

- Using the Report Wizard, create a report on the *Booster Program* query.
- Use all fields in the query except the Animal ID field.
- Group on Vaccination.
- Sort on Name in ascending order.
- Use a Stepped Layout on a Portrait Oriented page with the Concourse AutoFormat.
- Title the report **Booster Program Summary by Vaccine**.
- Total the estimated number of milliliters of each vaccine needed to vaccinate this group of elephants. Display the result in the footer of each group. Do not provide a grand total.
- Tweak the layout for maximum readability. Save, print, and close the report.

Add a Field to a Report

After reviewing the report, you realize you left off a field in the Booster Program Report. You will need to go back and make the necessary corrections.

- In the *Booster Program Report*, add the field **Location** after *Name* on the report.
- Preview the report.
- If the report looks good, save and print the report.

Compact and Repair a Database and Back Up a Database

Since we have been using databases, creating queries and running them, or applying and removing filers, Access might have stored information inefficiently. Use the Compact and Repair utility to take care of this. In addition to this utility, you feel it is necessary to back up the database.

- Compact and Repair the database.
- Back up the database and use the default name Access assigns it.
- Save and close any open objects, and close Access.

...continued on Next Page

Zookeepers

Use Microsoft Office PowerPoint

Background

In almost any job you might hold today, employers require employees to make presentations. These presentations can be created easily in Microsoft Office PowerPoint. At the zoo, each zookeeper makes a quarterly presentation to the zoo officials, providing them with general information regarding the animals under their care. These presentations are extremely important because the officials need to know the health and well-being of the animals and if the zookeepers have any concerns. This quarter, the zookeeper of the elephants has decided to focus on the baby elephants in the herd. Because he is not familiar with any presentation software, he asked you to help.

Tasks

To help the zookeeper, you need to create a presentation for the zoo officials on the health of the baby elephants.

- Create a presentation
- Print slides
- Reuse slides from another presentation
- Apply a theme
- Use SmartArt
- Insert pictures

Skills

A zookeeper's assistant should be able to create a presentation and do the following:

Chapter 1

- Use PowerPoint views (page 804)
- Open and save a slide show (page 809)
- Use slide layouts (page 820)
- Apply design themes (page 820)
- Add a table (page 829)
- Insert clip art (page 829)
- Use transitions and animations (page 831)
- Run and navigate a slide show (page 840)
- Print with PowerPoint (page 842)

Chapter 2

- Modify an outline structure (page 881)
- Print an outline (page 882)

...continued on Next Page

- Add existing content to a presentation (page 888)
- Apply and modify a design theme (page 892)
- Insert a header or footer (page 896)

Chapter 3

- Create SmartArt (page 952)
- Modify SmartArt diagrams (page 955)
- Create WordArt (page 961)
- Modify WordArt (page 961)
- Modify objects (page 968)
- Arrange objects (page 975)

Chapter 4

- Insert and modify a picture (page 1015)
- Insert movies (page 1038)
- Set movie options (page 1040)
- Add sound (page 1046)

Zookeepers
Volume 1 | Capstone Exercises

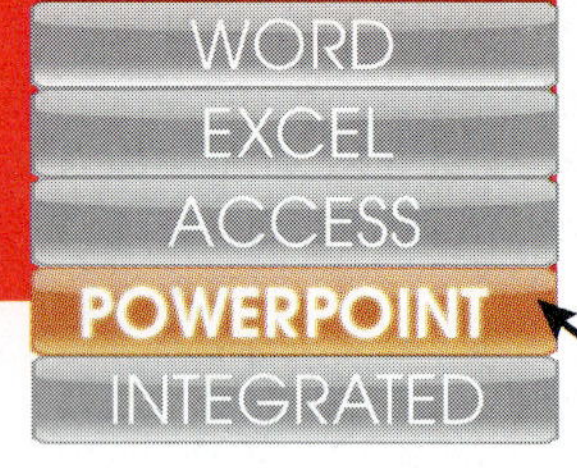

The zookeeper will present a presentation about the baby elephants to zoo officials. He has asked you to create the PowerPoint presentation. With the information you have been provided in this volume, you know how to put the ideas together and start a storyboard.

Create a Presentation and Use Slide Layouts

You worked with the head zookeeper and you decided on a basic storyboard, as follows. He will provide you the content and pictures for slides later.

Baby Elephant Presentation		
Audience: Zoo officials		
Content	Layout	Visual Elements
Title Slide	Blank	WordArt and Picture—Zoo Logo
Summary: Questions and Answers	Title only	None

- Create a new presentation based on the storyboard previously outlined.
- Apply the proper layout for each slide.
- Save the presentation as **exp07_p_ns_cpt_update_solution.pptx**.

Apply a Design Theme and Modify a Design Theme

To keep consistent with what the other zookeepers have used, you have been asked to apply a particular theme.

- Apply the *Paper* theme to the presentation.
- Change the font theme to **Aspect**.

Reuse Slides from Another Presentation

The zookeeper entered some basic information about the calves in a PowerPoint presentation. He asked if you could use the information from his slides in the presentation you have been working on. You decide to reuse the slides from the presentation he created.

- Reuse all slides located in the *exp07_p_ns_cpt_baby_elephant.pptx* file.
- Insert the four slides after *Title* slide.

Modifying an Outline Structure

You noticed that the order of the elephants is different from their birth order. In order for the presentation to flow properly, you decided to change them to birth order.

- Go to the *Outline* view and collapse each of the slides.
- Move the slides around so they are in the following order:
  - *Title*
  - *Roimba*
  - *Ella*
  - *Uttam*
  - *Saffron*
  - *Questions and Answsers*
- Expand the content for the slide for Saffron and add a last bullet that reads **Overall health is excellent**.

Insert a Footer

The zookeeper asked that you put his name and your name discretely on the bottom of every slide.

- Insert a footer that reads **By Nathan Smith, Zookeeper, and YOUR NAME, Assistant Zookeeper**.
- Be sure that the footer does not go on to two lines.

Add a Table

The zookeeper would like to see a slide added to the presentation that will show the current weight of each baby elephant.

- Insert a slide after the slide titled *Saffron*.
- Change the title of the slide to **Current Weights**.
- Insert the following table:

Name	Weight (in lbs.)	Date of Weigh-in
Roimba	2640	03/03/2008
Ella	864	03/03/2008
Uttam	549	03/03/2008
Saffron	280	06/02/2008

- Change the style of the table to **Themed Style 2, Accent 1**.

Insert ClipArt

- Search for key word *elephant*. Insert the following clip art image of an elephant in the area below the table. You might need to download the clip art from Microsoft Office online.

...continued on Next Page

- Change the size of the clip art to **2″** high and **2.25″** wide.
- Move the image to the right side of the slide.
- Copy the image and flip it horizontally.
- Move the new image to the left side of the slide.
- Align both images in the lower left and lower right of the slide.

Create SmartArt and Modify Smart Diagrams

Now that you have completed the basic presentation, there are several enhancements the zookeeper asked you to make. With the SmartArt feature and WordArt, you can make the slides more interesting. The zookeeper asked that you add a slide into the presentation that shows who the caregivers are. You need to insert a new slide and add a SmartArt object to it. After adding the SmartArt object, you will apply a Quick Style.

- Insert a new Title and Content slide after the Title slide.
- Add the title **Caregivers**.
- Insert the *Pyramid List* SmartArt object in the *Pyramid* group.
- Enter the following text in the boxes:
  - **Dr. John McTaggart, Veterinarian**
  - **Nathan Smith, Zookeeper**
  - **Your Name, Assistant Zookeeper**
- Change the SmartArt style to the **Intense Effect**.

Create and Modify WordArt

As a final touch to the presentation, you convert the title to a WordArt object.

- Go to the title slide and change the layout of the slide to Title slide. Delete the title and subtitle placeholders.
- Insert the WordArt called *Fill-Accent 2, Warm Matte Bevel* (in the fifth row, third one over).
- Enter the title **Baby Elephant Update**.
- Change the title so it shows the words **Baby Elephant** on one line and the word **Update** on the line below it.
- Center the WordArt on the slide both horizontally and vertically.
- Change the font size to **60 point**.

Apply Transitions

You decide that it would be nice to have the slides transition in.

- Choose the transition *Split Vertical Out*. Apply that one style to all slides.
- Have the slides transition on click.

Insert and Modify Pictures

The zookeeper thinks the presentation looks great but would like to see a picture of each of the babies on their respective pages.

- On the title slide insert the picture called *msz_logo_27.jpg*.
- Move the logo to the lower-right corner of the slide and set a height of 2.4″ and width of 1.52″.
- Insert the picture *Roimba.jpeg* on the left side of the slide titled *Roimba*.
- Resize the picture to a height of 2.33″ and a width of 3.5″.
- Insert the picture *Ella.jpeg* on the left side of the slide titled *Ella*.
- Resize the picture to a height of 3.5″ and a width of 2.35″.
- Insert the picture *Uttam.jpeg* on the left side of the slide titled *Uttam*.
- Resize the picture to a height of 3.5″ and a width of 3.5″.
- Insert the picture *Safi.jpeg* on the left side of the slide titled *Saffron*.
- Resize the picture to a height of 2.3″ and a width of 3.45″.

Apply Picture Styles

Now that the pictures of the elephants have been added to the slides, you would like to modify them.

- For each of the four pictures of the baby elephants, apply a different picture style:
  - For Roimba, apply the *Drop Shadow Rectangle* style.
  - For Ella, apply the *Reflected Perspective Right* style.
  - For Uttam, apply the *Beveled Oval, Black* style.
  - For Saffron, apply the *Reflected Bevel, Black* style.

Add Sound and Insert a Movie

You think it would be fun to add sound and a movie at the end of the presentation.

- Insert the sound *Applause* from the Clip Organizer on the last slide.
- The sound should start automatically.
- In the center of the slide insert a clip art movie of an elephant walking.
- Change the resolution to current resolution.

Run and Navigate a Slide Show

In order to make sure the presentation runs well, you will need to review the slide show.

- Run the slide show of the presentation.
- Make any necessary changes so the presentation flows well.

Print the Presentation

- Print the presentation as handouts with 2 slides per page.
- Print the outline of the presentation.

Zookeepers

Integrate Microsoft Office Software

Background

Each program in the Microsoft Office suite has its unique strength. Microsoft Office Word is the best program to use when creating documents, especially those requiring advanced formatting. Microsoft Office Excel is the choice when the data requires calculations, charts, or mathematical analysis. Microsoft Office PowerPoint is a presentation program that enables users to create unique, professional visual presentations and animate them. Finally, Microsoft Office Access is a database management system capable of storing and analyzing large quantities of information. All four programs work together seamlessly to help users analyze and present data most effectively.

Tasks

In a zoo, an assistant zookeeper might be asked to find data and present information using the applications in Microsoft Office 2007. This might include the following:

- Inserting an Excel chart into a Word document
- Inserting data analysis into an Excel spreadsheet
- Presenting Excel information in PowerPoint
- Making changes to information and updating it in other applications

Skills

In addition to the basic integration skills, a zookeeper's assistant might be asked to do the following:

- Use query results in a report
- Export query results to an Excel spreadsheet
- Use a template in Word
- Insert an Excel chart in PowerPoint
- Use comments and markup

Zookeepers
Volume 1 | Capstone Exercises

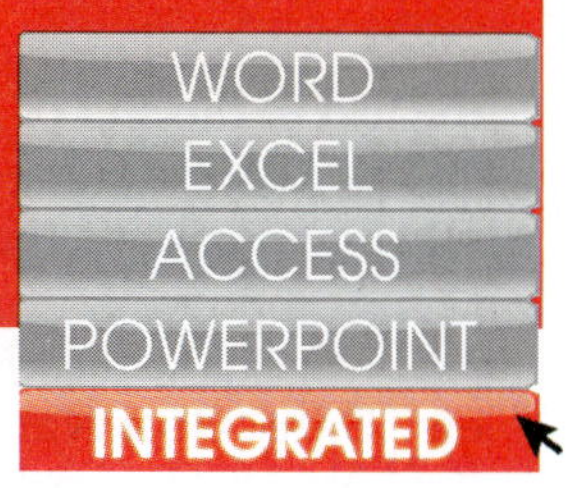

Retrieve Information from Access

A comments database has been created for the zookeepers to record information about the elephants. Documentation of the comments is critical to the care and well-being of the animals. The zookeeper has asked you to create a report that will display the comments for the animals. This information also will be exported to Excel because the vet does not have Access in his office. Since the vet does not need to see all the information, you will need to manipulate the data.

- Open Access database *exp07_i_ns_cpt_zoo_comments* and save it to your storage media as **exp07_i_ns_cpt_zoo_comments_solution**.
- Create a query based on the *Animal Behavior, Employee,* and *Park Animal Inventory* tables that will show the fields in the following order:
  - o *Date_Observed, Animal Behavior* table
  - o *Name, Park Animal Inventory* table
  - o *Medications*
  - o *Comments*
  - o *FirstName and LastName, Employee* table
- Sort the query oldest to newest.
- Run the query and save it as **Comments**.
- Create a report called **Animal Observations** based on the *Comments* query.
  - o Display the *Name, Date_Observed, Comments, Interventions, FirstName and LastName* fields, in that order, on the report.
  - o Insert the picture *Roimba.jpg* in the logo field at the top of the report.
  - o Select the Flow AutoFormat for the report.
  - o Change the title to **Animal Observations as reported by Your Name**.
  - o Change the title so that it appears only on two lines.
  - o Group the Records by Animal name and sort by observed date, oldest to newest.
  - o Adjust column widths as necessary so that all the data displays.
  - o Save and print the report.
  - o Export the *Animal Observations* report as a Rich Text File named **Animal Observations**.

Export Data to Excel

Export the Comments query to Excel. This information will be used by vetrinarians and scientists for diagnostic and research purposes.

- Export the *Comments* query to Excel.
- Save the spreadsheet as **exp07_i_ns_cpt_comments_solution.xlsx**.
- Export the data with formatting and layout.

Create an Excel Chart

- Open the *exp07_i_ns_cpt_comments_solution.xlsx* spreadsheet.
- Select the exported cells.
- Filter the table to show only the records for Kailash.
- Add an additional column to the table and label it **Weight**.
- Enter the following weights for Kailash.

Date	Weight
06/02/08	**2012**
06/05/08	**2004**
06/06/08	**1998**
06/10/08	**2000**
06/15/08	**2008**

- Create a line with markers chart showing the elephant's weight on each of the dates.
- Insert the title **Kailash's Weight**.
- Move the chart to a separate worksheet titled **Weight Chart**.
- Change the chart style to **Style 45**.
- Insert an arrow on the chart pointing at the data point for 6/6/2008.
- Change the arrow to the **Intense Effect Accent 2** style.
- Insert the text **Medication Started** in the arrow. Format the arrow attractively for the chart by resizing and rotating as necessary.
- Add a Vertical Axis Title: **In Pounds**.
- Insert a custom header with the current date in the left section and **Your Name** in the right section.
- Print the chart and save the spreadsheet.

Modify a Memo and Add Supporting Data

- Open the Word document *exp07_i_ns_cpt_vet_memo* and save it to your storage media as **exp07_i_ns_cpt_vet_memo_solution**.
- Open the Rich Text file, *Animal Observations*, you created earlier.
- Copy the section on Kailash, from the grouping with her name through the bottom record of the group. Paste it below the body of the memo.
- Convert the text to a table with tab delimiters. You will find that some of the comments and interventions

...continued on Next Page

were separated and appear on a separate row. Move the text to the end of the appropriate cells.

- Delete the first column and each of the empty rows where you moved the data.
- Merge and center *Kailash* across the top row. Add a new row below the first row. Add these column headers: **Date**, **Observations**, **Interventions**, **Observer First Name**, **Observer Last Name**.
- You should have a table of 7 rows and 5 columns, now. Apply the Light List Accent 3 table style and tweak the formatting as necessary.
- Copy the chart from the *exp07_i_ns_cpt_comments_solution.xlsx* spreadsheet. Paste it below the table.
- Add your name under the *CC:* section of the memo.
- Print, save, and close the document.

Insert Excel Charts into a PowerPoint Presentation

The last task that the zookeeper has asked you to do is to add the weight chart into a PowerPoint presentation. Since the presentation already has been created, it will be just a matter of selecting the Excel chart and pasting it into PowerPoint.

- Start PowerPoint and open the *exp07_i_ns_cpt_comments_and_concerns* presentation.
- Save it to your storage media as **exp07_i_ns_ cpt_comments_ and_concerns_solution**.
- Change the style of the design to **Module**.
- Insert a slide after *Current Status*, and choose the layout *Title only*.
- The title should be **Kailash's Weight Chart**.
- Start Excel and open the *exp07_i_ns_cpt_comments_solution* workbook.
- Copy the chart.
- In PowerPoint, paste the chart as a link.
- Resize the chart to fit completely on the slide.

Update Information with Excel and PowerPoint

After finishing the presentation, you realize that a weight is wrong in the chart. You need to correct this before the presentation to visiting animal behaviorists.

- Start Excel and bring up the *exp07_i_ns_cpt_comments_solution* workbook.
- The weight for June 5, 2008 should be **2000** lbs.
- Save and close the workbook.
- Update the links in the presentation.

Add a Comment in PowerPoint

You would like to let the zookeeper know that you have updated the presentation, so you add a comment on the slide with the Weight Chart.

- Insert a comment noting that the weight has been changed.
- Print the presentation with the comments.
- Save and close all files.

Information Training Specialists

Use Microsoft Office Word

Background

You've done it! You've landed a great job just months after finishing college! After a challenging but rewarding college career focused on technology, you have landed a dream job not only working in the technology field but also helping people develop their own technology skills.

As an information training specialist for Southern Oregon Community College (SOCC), some of your responsibilities include monitoring, maintaining, and upgrading applicable technology systems across campus; problem solving faculty technology issues; and implementing system modifications. You also support, troubleshoot, and upgrade applicable system infrastructures.

But your current focus as an information training specialist for SOCC is to ensure that faculty are well trained, knowledgeable, and efficient with software used on campus and programs that will enhance their courses. One of your tasks for the week is to develop a training schedule and to market it to faculty over the upcoming months so they can present technology portions of their class that will engage and interest students.

Tasks

An information training specialist might be responsible for developing a wide array of technology training sessions. In addition to developing course content, the position will always require a great deal of written communication created in Word such as the following:

- Memos
- Letters
- Flyers
- Proposals and reports
- Document notes
- Brochures
- Forms

Skills

An information training specialist should be able to do the following:

Chapter 1

- Set margins and specify page orientation (page 87)
- Insert page breaks (page 88)

...continued on Next Page

- Add page numbers (page 90)
- Insert headers and footers (page 91)
- Create sections (page 92)
- Use the Find and Replace commands (page 94)
- Check spelling and grammar (page 103)
- Select printing options (page 107)

Chapter 2

- Apply font attributes through the Font dialog box (page 133)
- Highlight text (page 136)
- Copy formats with the Format Painter (page 139)
- Set off paragraphs with tabs, borders, lists, and columns (page 143)
- Apply paragraph formats (page 148)

Chapter 3

- Format a table (page 205)
- Convert text to a table (page 210)
- Insert clip art and images into a document (page 219)
- Format a graphic element (page 220)
- Insert WordArt into a document (page 225)
- Insert symbols into a document (page 226)

Chapter 4

- Insert comments into a document (page 251)
- Track changes in a document (page 254)
- Use navigation tools (page 267)
- Modify document properties (page 290)

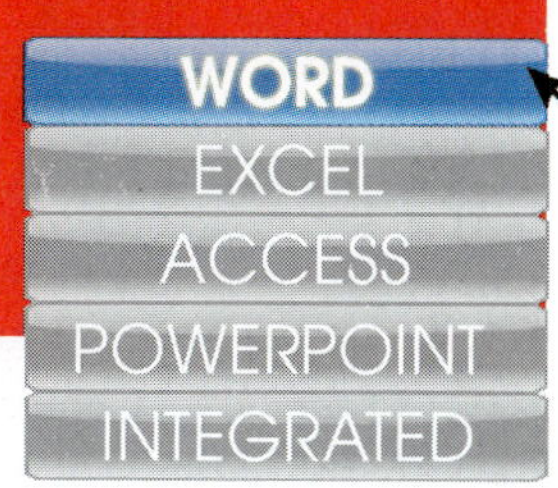

As an information training specialist at SOCC, one of your responsibilities is to develop the curriculum for training programs, market the training sessions to faculty, and be the one-and-only training instructor for a wide array of technology workshops. Your current task is to set up the workshop schedule and to market it to faculty and staff throughout the campus. You have developed the training schedule for January and February and are hoping to have it approved by your supervisor and then to start marketing it to faculty.

Your task is functional (developing the workshop schedule), but will also require a little marketing prowess (developing the flyer). After finalizing the workshop schedule, you need to create a flyer that will be distributed across campus. The flyer will be a first step to rally interest in faculty signing up for technology training. You know that the more faculty you can recruit to participate in the workshops, the less one-on-one questions and problems you will have later.

Open the File and Format the Document

You already have started the file that contains the workshop schedule, but it still needs a little polishing. The file includes the basic information for the workshops, but you will need to clean it up, format it, and enhance it.

- Open the *exp07_w_tech_cpt_workshops* document and save it as **exp07_w_tech_cpt_workshops_solution**.
- Set the right and left margins to **.75"**; top and bottom margins to **1.75"**.
- Insert a footer. Use the Alphabet style. Type **Faculty Workshops—January and February, 2009** as the footer. Notice that the page number is included automatically in this footer style.
- Select the footer text and the page number. Format as Cambria, italics, 10-point.
- Center the top three title lines of the document.

Format, Edit, and Check Spelling

Each workshop section of the document should have similar formatting. Each workshop section should look exactly the same.

- Italicize the text *WIMBA Voice Tools*. Around the section title, create a Shadow border that extends to the right margin.
- Select the newly formatted *WIMBA Voice Tools* text. Use the Format Painter to format each workshop title so they are all the same.
- Add a hard return before the *Capture your video* text in the Video Editing workshops. Add a hard return before the *Camtasia is a screenshot* text in the Camtasia workshop.
- Use the spelling checker to check your document for errors (the sentence fragment is fine if spelled correctly).

Find and Replace Text

A few editing changes still need to be made. You have decided that a 9:15 start will work better for faculty and also for the room setup. To allow yourself a half-hour break between sessions, you want to move the 12:00 session to 12:15. You have also just been informed that TE 232 will not be available and you need to use room TE 311, instead.

- Use Find and Replace to locate and replace *9:00* with **9:15**.
- Use Find and Replace to locate and replace *12:00* with **12:15**.
- Use Find and Replace to locate and replace *232* with **311**.

Create and Format Tables

Each workshop section has the data laid out, but you think they would be clearer and easier to read if they were in a table. Convert each workshop data section to a table for easy reading. In addition to being easily readable, the table needs to be visually appealing.

- Select the WIMBA Basics and WIMBA Intermediate workshop data. Be sure to select the title of the workshop as well as the nine lines of workshop data.
- Convert the text to a table (note that the text is separated at tabs).
- Format the table using **Light Shading - Accent 2** table style.
- Select the first four cells of the first row (the row of the title). Merge the cells.
- With the title row still selected, center the title and change to **14-point** font.
- Repeat these steps for each workshop so that each workshop section is formatted the same.

Create a Flyer

In addition to sending your supervisor the document that contains the list of workshops, you think it might be a good idea to include an example of a flyer that you will use to promote the workshops to faculty. The first workshop will be the WIMBA classes. You will copy the workshop table and develop a flyer from it.

- Place the insertion point at the end of the document. Insert a hard page break.
- Press **Enter** two times.
- Copy the WIMBA workshop table and paste it on the new page after the two line breaks.

Format the Flyer

The flyer would look better in landscape orientation rather than portrait. However, you want the first three pages of

...continued on Next Page

the document to remain as portrait. After the orientation change, you want to enhance the table and use WordArt to create an attractive title.

- Insert a section break at the top of the flyer page.
- Change the orientation of the flyer page to landscape.
- Select the table. Center align the table on the page.
- With the table still selected, increase the table row height to **0.5″**. Use the *AutoFit Window* option under the AutoFit icon to enlarge the table.
- Increase the font of all table data to **16-point**.
- Use the *Align Center* option to center the text in all cells of the table.
- Place the insertion point at the top of the flyer page, above the table.
- Insert WordArt with the title of the flyer: **Technology Workshops 2009**. Use WordArt style 20.
- Change the font to Tempus San ITC, bold, 36-point.
- Center the WordArt title.

Insert a Symbol and Graphic

You need to add a little more information to the flyer, including how faculty need to register for the workshops. Registration will be handled by David Ordoñez. You will need to use a symbol to correctly include his name on the flyer. Additionally, you decide a clip art image that depicts the type of workshop that will be presented will be helpful for the flyer. A clip art image of a speaker representing sound will help signify that the WIMBA Basics and WIMBA Intermediate workshops will be about using sound as a communication tool.

- Place insertion point on the blank line after the table and press **Enter** one time to enter a hard return.
- Include the following text: **Registration is required. Please send an email to David Ordo**.
- Insert the **ñ** symbol and finish the name with **ez at ordonezd@socc.edu**.
- Center the line.
- Change the font to Times New Roman, 16-point.
- Locate the following clip art image by searching for sound as the search word.

- Resize the clip art image so it is 0.7 inches high and 0.7 inches wide and move it to the left side of the flyer title.
- Change the style of the clip art image to **Colored Outline - Accent 1**.
- Copy the clip art image, paste it (knowing that it will automatically paste next to the previous image), and move the new image to the right side of the flyer title.
- Rotate the image 180 degrees so the sound waves face toward the title using the *Flip Horizontal* option on the **Rotate button** of the Arrange group located on the Format tab.

Insert a Comment

You are ready to send your finalized document to your supervisor for final approval. You have a few last-minute questions for her and decide that adding comments will be the most effective way to convey your information. However, since you have never used Track Changes, you would like to see how she is going to view the document prior to sending it to her.

- Select the first word of the document, *Southern*.
- Insert a comment with the following text: **Here is the schedule for January and February. I have created a flyer on page 4 as an example of what I will send to all faculty.**
- Select the full title of the flyer and add the following comment: **Any suggestions to this flyer?**
- In order to view how Track Changes will appear to your boss, check it for yourself with the following steps:
    - Move cursor to the beginning of the document.
    - Use the **Next Change button** to view both comments.

Insert a Bookmark

In order to jump quickly and easily to the flyer, you decide to insert a bookmark. You know it is not really necessary, but it is a nice touch!

- Select the flyer title.
- Insert a bookmark and name the bookmark as **Flyer**.

Modify Document Properties

Recording information about this and other documents will help you, as well as others, keep track of important document information. You will modify the document properties to record information about this file.

- Record the following information in the Document Properties panel:

  Author: **Geraldo Lopez**; Title: **Faculty Workshops, Jan.–Feb. 2009**; Subject: **Workshops**.

Save and Print the Document

You are ready, once again, to save your work (although you should be saving periodically throughout your work session). Although you will be sending the document along with the flyer page as an attachment with an e-mail message to your supervisor, you have decided that a printed copy will help you keep track of the scheduled workshops and help you decide if the layout and design of the flyer are appealing. You will still be able to get a clear idea of the flyer even though the comments will be included on it.

- Use the spelling checker to check the document.
- Save the document.
- Use the Print Preview option to view the full document.
- Use the shortcut keys to print the full document.

Information Training Specialists Use Microsoft Office Excel

Background

You've done it! You've landed a great job just months after finishing college! After a challenging but rewarding college career focused on technology, you have landed a dream job not only working in the technology field but also helping people develop their own technology skills.

As an information training specialist for Southern Oregon Community College (SOCC), you are responsible for hardware purchases, system upgrades, and software installation. You also support lab managers in their hardware upgrade needs.

Tasks

An information training specialist might be responsible for developing a wide array of technology worksheets. Typical worksheets that an information training specialist might create include the following:

- Budgets for computer equipment
- Training material budgets
- Budget reports of technology expenses
- Proposals and reports
- Charts to act as visual representation of data
- Faculty and staff problem logs
- System implementation schedules

Skills

An information training specialist should be able to do the following:

Chapter 1

- Enter and edit data in cells (page 322)
- Describe and use symbols and the order of precedence (page 328)
- Display cell formulas (page 330)
- Insert and delete rows and columns (page 331)
- Use cell ranges; Excel move; copy, paste, paste special; and AutoFill (page 332)
- Manage worksheets (page 340)
- Format worksheets (page 341)
- Select page setup options for printing (page 353)
- Manage cell comments (page 356)

...continued on Next Page

Chapter 2

- Create and copy formulas (page 381)
- Use relative and absolute cell addresses (page 382)
- Use AutoSum (page 389)
- Use date functions (page 392)
- Use the IF function (page 399)
- Use the VLOOKUP function (page 400)

Chapter 3

- Choose a chart type (page 431)
- Create a chart (page 438)
- Modify a chart (page 450)
- Enhance charts with graphic shapes (page 453)
- Embed charts (page 459)
- Print charts (page 460)

Chapter 4

- Freeze rows and columns (page 488)
- Hide and unhide rows, columns, and worksheets (page 489)
- Protect a cell, a worksheet, and a workbook (page 489)
- Explore basic table management (page 505)
- Sort data (page 510)
- Filter and total data (page 514)

As an information training specialist at SOCC, one of your responsibilities is to research new computer equipment for purchase by the college. Your supervisor has asked you to research new monitors to replace the current cathode ray tube (CRT) monitors in the last student computer lab to be updated. The processors are adequate, for now, but new monitors are absolutely necessary because of long and hard use of the monitors by students. After researching monitors and keyboards at some of the largest computer suppliers in the country, you have entered the data into a basic worksheet and will prepare an enhanced workbook to present to your supervisor.

Open the File and Organize the Data

You already have a file with the monitor and keyboard styles, sizes (in regard to the monitors), and prices, but it needs a little work prior to sending the information to your supervisor. The file includes the basic information for monitors and keyboards listed below. You now need to begin to organize the file, clean it up, format it, and enhance it.

- Open the *exp07_e_tech_cpt_hardware* spreadsheet and save it as **exp07_e_tech_cpt_hardware_solution**.
- Move the keyboard data in **cells B12:C18** to a new sheet, starting in **cell A4**.
- On the first worksheet containing the monitor information, insert three rows above the data.
- Move the monitor data in **cells B4:D13** to columns A, B, and C.
- Add the following column headings:
  - For the monitor data, add the following column headings in row 3: **Monitor Style**, **Size**, and **Price**.
  - For the keyboard data, add the following column headings in row 3: **Keyboard Style** and **Price**.
- Bold and italicize the column headings in both sheets.

Manage Worksheets

It is much easier to keep track of which data are on which worksheet when worksheets have appropriate names. Name and color your two worksheet tabs.

- Rename the sheet with the monitor information as **Monitors**; rename the keyboard sheet as **Keyboards**.
- Recolor the Monitors sheet tab as **Purple**; recolor the Keyboards sheet tab as **Light Blue**.
- Move the *Keyboards* worksheet to be the first worksheet.

Format Worksheets

In addition to researched data, worksheets need to be easy to read and need to look appealing. You are ready to format the worksheets.

- Widen columns to the following widths:
  - *Keyboards* worksheet: *Keyboard Style*, **90**; *Price*, **15**.
  - *Monitors* worksheet: *Monitor Style*, **60**; *Size* and *Price*, **15**.
- Apply the Accounting format to columns B and C in the *Keyboards* worksheet.
- Apply the Comma format with one decimal place in column B in the *Monitors* worksheet.
- Apply the Accounting format to column C in the *Monitors* worksheet.
- Type the following worksheet title in **cell A1** on the *Keyboards* worksheet: **SOCC Keyboard Purchase Options**.
- Type the following worksheet title in **cell A1** on the *Monitors* worksheet: **SOCC Monitor Purchase Options**.
- Merge and center the titles across each of the worksheets.
- Select merged **cell A1**, the title cell, on the *Monitors* worksheet.
- Use the Format Cells dialog box to format the selected title:
  - Bookman Old Style, Bold, Italic, 14-point font.
  - Double-outline, purple border with Yellow fill.
- Use the Format Cells dialog box to format the column titles:
  - Bookman Old Style, 12-point font.
  - All borders, automatic (black) border with Yellow fill.
- Format the monitor data with the following formats:
  - Bookman Old Style, 11-point font.
  - All borders, single outline.
- Copy all formats to the respective cells on the *Keyboards* worksheet using the Format Painter.
- Change the row height of all rows on both worksheets to **25.00**.

Sort Data

Since the college is quite price conscious, sorting the keyboard data will give a quick view of least expensive to most expensive keyboards. In addition, the monitor data can be sorted by monitor size and also by price. Using a quick filter would also be helpful for you to easily view specific data.

- Sort the keyboard data by price in ascending order.
- Sort the monitor data by size and then by price in ascending order.
- Filter the monitors data to only show the 19-inch monitors.

...continued on Next Page

Create Formulas

You have just learned that the company your college primarily deals with is currently offering a quantity discount for keyboards. A 10% discount is offered for every keyboard in your list with a purchase of at least 50. Since you know you will need at least 50, you want to add this new, discounted price to your worksheet.

- In **cell C2**, type **10%**.
- Add the following column heading in **cell C3**: **Quantity Pricing (minimum of 50)**. Format the header to match the rest of the headers and format the column of numbers to Accounting.
- Create a formula in **cell C4** to calculate the new, discounted price using the discount in **cell C2**.
- Use the fill handle to copy the formula to the other monitor rows.
- Widen column C to **25.00**.
- Use the Format Painter to format the new column with the correct formats.
- Wrap the column heading in **cell C3**.
- Change the row height of row 1 to **30**.
- In order to double-check your formulas, view the *Monitors* worksheet in Cell Formula view. After you have validated the correctness of the formulas, change it back to Normal view.
- Remove the filter on the *Monitors* worksheet.
- Adjust the formats in row 1, if necessary.

Create Report

After sufficient research you are ready to make a recommendation. Your supervisor has asked for all of the data that you have gathered, but also for a specific recommendation. You now will create a worksheet that will be the first worksheet in the workbook with the summary data.

- Insert a worksheet. Name the worksheet **Summary**. Color the tab as **Green**. Move the worksheet to be the first sheet in the workbook.
- Type the following in **cell A1**: **Keyboard and Monitor Purchase Suggestions**.
- Insert the date function in **cell A2** that shows the current date. Format the date as the month name, day, and year.
- Create the following column headings and one row total entry:
  - **Cell A4: My Hardware Suggestion.**
  - **Cell B4: Quantity to Order.**
  - **Cell C4: Total Cost.**
  - **Cell A7: Total Cost.**
- In **cell A5**, create a formula that references the Microsoft comfort curve keyboard 2000 from the *Keyboards* worksheet.
- In **cell A6**, create a formula that references the Acer AL 1916WABD from the *Monitors* worksheet.
- Widen column A to **55**; widen columns B and C to **24**.
- Enter **80** as the quantity for *keyboards*; **60** for *monitors*.
- Create formulas in the *Total Price* column for 80 keyboards at the discount price and 60 monitors.
- Sum the data for column C in **cell C7**.

Format Summary Worksheet

The new Summary report sheet needs a clean and easy-to-read format. It also needs proper number formats.

- Merge and center **cells A1:C1**. Merge and center **cells A2:C2**.
- Format the worksheet as Bookman Old Style.
- Format the following:
  - Format column B as Comma with no decimal places and column C as Accounting.
  - Select merged **cells A1** and **A2**. Format with bold, italics, 14-point font and a double-outline, purple border with yellow fill.
  - Select rows 4 and 7. Format as bold, 12-point font.
  - Select **cells A4** to **C7**. Format with All Borders.
  - Format column C as Accounting with two decimal places.
- Protect (or lock) the total cost cell of the worksheet.

Create a Chart

For the convenience of your supervisor, you will insert a pie chart that defines the expenses for keyboards from the expenses for monitors. A pie chart is the most appropriate chart, since it provides a quick visual of how the expenses will be divided out.

- Select the two hardware style cells and associated total cost cells from the Summary sheet.
- Insert a 3-D pie chart on the Summary sheet.
- Move the chart, if necessary, so it is below the summary data with the upper left corner in **cell A11**.
- Format the chart using Layout 6 and Style 6.
- Replace the chart title with **Total Cost Breakout for Hardware Purchases**.
- Create a text box on the chart with the following: **This includes 80 keyboards and 60 monitors**. Format the text as Bookman Old Style, 10-point font, and center the text in the text box.

Create VLOOKUP and IF Functions

The college has a policy that if a purchase requisition is over $10,000 additional approvals must be acquired. There are three levels of approvals needed based on the purchase requisition total. A VLOOKUP will alert you and your supervisor if approvals are required. Additionally, if you purchase in quantities of 50 or more, shipping is free for that specific line item. An IF statement will help to display clearly when shipping will and will not be included.

- Create a VLOOKUP function in **cell A9** on the *Summary* worksheet. Place the table array below the chart in columns A and B. The VLOOKUP function information follows:
  - For requisitions between $0 and $10,000—**No additional sig. req'd**; between $10,000 and $25,000—**C.I.S. Manager sig. req'd**; and $25,000 and over—**C.I.S. Mgr & Info Tech Mgr signatures req'd**.
- Use the Format Painter to format the enhancements in **cell A1** to the VLOOKUP statement cell. Be sure the outside border shows on all four sides.

...continued on Next Page

- Hide the rows of the table array.
- Insert a column between the *Quantity to Order* and the *Total Cost* columns on the *Summary* worksheet and add **Shipping** as the column heading.
- Recall that the supplier has free shipping for purchases of 50 units or more. Create an IF function in column C using the quantity needed for each item with *Free shipping* and *Additional shipping fee* as the true and false conditions.

Table Management

You have just received a call from your supervisor asking you to make sure to include quotes for several 17-inch monitors that she wants to consider for another, smaller lab on campus. Since your *Monitors* worksheet only contains information for one 17-inch monitor at the moment, you need to add more rows to your monitor table.

- On the *Monitors* worksheet, insert two additional rows. Add these two monitors to the list.
  - **I-Inc iW171ABB wide LCD, 17, 149.99.**
  - **ViewSonic VA703b LCD, 17, 189.99.**
- Reapply ascending sort by monitor size and price.
- In order for the column headings on the *Monitors* worksheet to remain on the screen when scrolling, freeze the column headings.

Save and Print

You are ready, once again, to save your work (although you should be saving periodically throughout your work session). You will attach the file and send it to your supervisor with an e-mail message, but you also want to print the summary page to make sure it will print attractively.

- Use the spelling checker to check the worksheets.
- Save the workbook.
- Use the Print Preview option to view the full data and graph.
- Change the Page Setup as follows:
  - Use **.25″** left and right margins and **.75″** top and bottom margins.
  - Use Landscape Orientation.
  - Create a Footer with your name, the file name, the worksheet name, and the current date and time.
  - Center the worksheet on the page, horizontally and vertically.
- Save, print, and close the workbook.

Information Training Specialists

Use Microsoft Office Access

Background

You've done it! You've landed a great job just months after finishing college! After a challenging but rewarding college career focused on technology, you have landed a dream job not only working in the technology field but also helping people develop their own technology skills.

As an information technology training specialist for Southern Oregon Community College (SOCC), many of your responsibilities involve faculty and staff training. But in addition to training, you are also responsible for hardware purchases and inventory. After keeping up with who has which computer, you will concern yourself primarily with using technology effectively to reduce SOCC's carbon footprint. A major initiative has come forth to replace several departments' computer hardware with Energy Star–compliant equipment. Energy Star is a joint program offered through the U.S. Environmental Protection Agency (EPA) and the U.S. Department of Energy. With the help of Energy Star, energy savings for 2007 avoided greenhouse gas emissions equivalent to those from 27 million cars—while saving $16 billion on utility bills!

Tasks

An information training specialist might be responsible for developing Microsoft Office Access files that include the following:

- Hardware purchase database information
- Hardware inventory tracking
- Faculty and staff training database information
- Sorting, filtering, and querying inventory and purchase information

Skills

An information training specialist should be able to do the following:

Chapter 1

- Back up, compact, and repair Access files (page 556)
- Create filters (page 565)
- Sort table data on one or more fields (page 568)
- Know when to use Access or Excel to manage data (page 570)
- Use the Relationship window (page 578)
- Understand relational power (page 579)

Chapter 2

- Create tables (page 612)
- Understand table relationships (page 625)

...continued on Next Page

- Share data with Excel (page 626)
- Establish table relationships (page 630)
- Create a query (page 642)
- Specify criteria for different data types (page 645)
- Copy and run a query (page 649)

Chapter 3

- Understand the order of precedence (page 679)
- Create a calculated field in a query (page 679)
- Create expressions with the Expression Builder (page 689)
- Create and edit Access functions (page 690)
- Create and work with data aggregates (page 704)

Chapter 4

- Plan a report (page 731)
- Use different report views (page 733)
- Create and edit a report (page 737)
- Identify report elements, sections, and controls (page 747)
- Add grouping levels in Layout view (page 750)

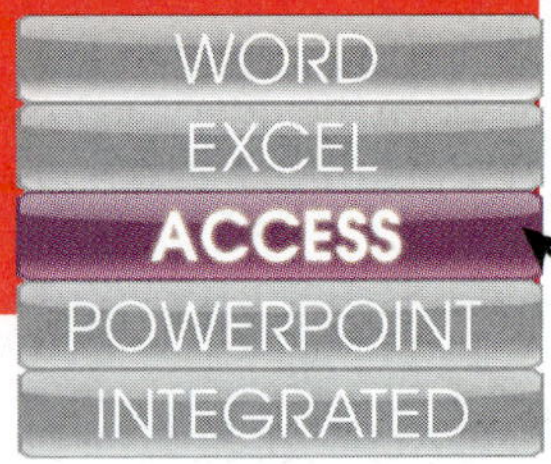

As an information training specialist at SOCC, one of your responsibilities is to make purchase recommendations for faculty and staff and to maintain the inventory database. You have researched Energy Star–compliant hardware and made purchase recommendations for new hardware for faculty and staff. The majority of the recommendations were followed, and you have a list of computers and a list of employees that you want to use together as a relational database to help you keep track of the computers' locations.

Import Database and Tables

You have a list of hardware, which the accounting department has provided you as an Excel spreadsheet, after they recorded the equipment as assets. You have a table in an Access database listing the employees. Using your knowledge of Access, you feel it would be most powerful to consolidate this data in Access. You also want to be able to create queries and reports, so your first step is to start a new database and import the Excel file into Access.

- Open *exp07_a_tech_cpt_energystar*. Save it as **exp07_a_tech_cpt_energystar_solution**.
- Import the *exp07_a_tech_cpt_hardware.xlsx* Excel workbook. The first row contains the column headings. Set the *Model Number* field to **Text**. Set the primary key to **AssetTag**. Be sure the table name is **Hardware**.
- View the data in the newly imported *Hardware* table in Datasheet view.
- Save changes to the *Hardware* table.

Change Field Properties

In a real-world application of this database, you would match computer systems appropriate to an employee's function at SOCC. This is a time-consuming process, so we have provided the employee ID number assigning each computer to an employee. Otherwise, the data headers are descriptive of the hardware purchases, but require some tweaking for Access best practices.

- In the *Hardware* table, using Design view, change any field names to eliminate disallowed spaces. Then, use captions to create easily readable headings. Include appropriate units (GB) in Memory and Hard Drive captions and (GHz) in Processor Speed captions.
- Change the decimal places in the Hard Drive captions in the *Hardware* table to **0**. Change the Field Size to **Integer**.
- Create indexes for the *Hardware* table by indexing the *Employee ID* field.
- Index the *Employee ID* field, allowing duplicates in the *Hardware* table. If other fields are listed as indexed fields, delete the index and add the *Employee ID* field as an indexed field, allowing duplicates. Create the Index Name as **Employee**.
- Save and close the table. Accept the field size change on the error warning.

Perform Database Maintenance

- Compact and repair **exp07_a_tech_cpt_energystar_solution**.
- Create a backup of *exp07_a_tech_cpt_energystar_solution*. Name it **exp07_a_tech_cpt_energystar_backup_solution**.

Modify Records

Between when you received your employee database and when the newly purchased computer hardware arrived, some personnel changes occurred.

- Open the *Employee* table. Use the Filter command to locate *Name* in the *Last Name* field. Replace the first and last name of *Your Name* with your name in the *Employee* table.
- Use the Filter command to find Stephen Jordan. Change his office number to **CS 668**.
- Close the *Employee* table.
- Open the *Hardware* table. Filter the hardware to show only Notebooks/Tablet PCs.
- Use Find and Replace to find all notebook computers with **Core2 Duo** processors. Replace with **Core2 Duo Mobile**.
- Use Find and Replace to find all desktop and notebook computers produced by **Lenovo Group Limited** and replace with **Lenovo**.

Create a Relationship

The Hardware and Employee tables should be related. Create relationships to link these tables together.

- Create a one to many relationship between the *Employee* table and the *Hardware* table with the EmployeeID as the foreign key in the *Hardware* table. Enforce referential integrity. Create and print a Relationship report.

Create Select Queries

You want to be able to see at a glance which desktop computers are for power users. These systems have 3GHz or higher processor speed, at least 160GB of hard drive space, and at least 4GB of RAM (system memory). Create a query using the Hardware table to find these systems.

- Create a query on the *Hardware* table that will return a list of systems with processor speeds in excess of 3GHz, hard drives of at least 160GB, and RAM of at least 4GB. Include all fields in the table in the default order.

...continued on Next Page

- Run the query.
- Save the query as **PowerSystems**.

Use the PowerSystems query you just built to create a new query that will return the office numbers and first and last names of the people assigned the power system computers.

- Make a copy of the *PowerSystems* query and save it as **Power Users**.
- Add the *Employees* table to the query and display First and Last Name, sorted in ascending order by last name, then first name. Include the office of these power users, but display only the asset tag number and model name for the computer in the query.
- Run and save the query.

Create a Select Query with Calculations

SOCC's standard operating procedure for purchasing desktop and notebook computers is to buy three-year extended next-business-day warranties for notebooks and two-year next-business-day warranties for all desktops. The warranty effective dates are the purchase dates. You want to calculate the warranty expiration dates for the computers in the Hardware table.

- Create a query on the *Hardware* table named **WarrantyExpiration** with asset tag, product type, purchase date, and employee ID.
- Create a calculated field to extend the purchase date to a warranty expiration date based on product type.
- Return the results in a column named **Warranty Expiration**. Sort by the nearest expiration dates.
- Run and save the query.

After creating the WarrantyExpiration query, you decide that it would be much easier to associate computers with users and office numbers.

- Create a copy of the *WarrantyExpiration* query named **WarrantyExpByUser**.
- Open the *WarrantyExpByUser* query in *Design* view. Add user first and last names and office numbers to display in the query. Do not display employee ID. Sort the query by nearest warranty expiration dates and office number. This might seem a little odd, but when you collect the computers from the offices, you will be glad to collect all the retired desktops from one floor rather to collect one on the third floor, two on the sixth floor, and so on.

Create Reports

To deploy several new computers each night, the entire Information Technology Support team will work in waves, rolling out 20 new PCs per night, two nights per week. You make reports for all the queries you created earlier for various portions of the project.

Create a Report from the PowerUser Query

- Include all fields on the report.
- Sort the report by Office in ascending order.
- Format the report so all elements fit attractively on a portrait-oriented page.
- Remove the logo.
- Retitle the report **Power Users Deployment by Office**.
- Apply a Report AutoFormat.
- Save the report as **PowerUsersReport**, print, and close your report.

Create a Warranty Expiration Report

Your supervisor wants a list of all computers whose warranty expires before 8/1/2010.

- Use the *WarrantyExpByUser* query to create a report called **WarrantyExpByUserReport** showing all fields in the query.
- Attractively format it using any AutoFormat with portrait orientation so all fields fit neatly on one page.
- Title the report **Warranty Expiration Report by Date**.
- Sort the report oldest to newest by Warranty Expiration Date, then by User's Last and First Name, in ascending order.
- Group the report on warranty expiration from oldest to newest.
- Count the asset tags and display the result in the **Group Footer** with a caption of **Warranties Expiring**.
- Keep groups together on the same page.
- Filter the report to show only systems with warranty expiration dates before 8/1/2010.
- Save, preview, print, and close the report.

Information Training Specialists

Use Microsoft Office PowerPoint

Background

You've done it! You've landed a great job just months after finishing college! After a challenging but rewarding college career focused on technology, you have landed a dream job not only working in the technology field but also helping people develop their own technology skills.

As an information training specialist for Southern Oregon Community College (SOCC), many of your responsibilities surround faculty and staff training. Training often involves software upgrades, new software site license purchases, and new hardware available throughout the campus. On occasion, your responsibilities include presenting new technology that could be advantageous to faculty and staff. A newly added responsibility is a monthly technology-update brownbag lunch session.

Tasks

An information training specialist might be responsible for developing Microsoft Office PowerPoint files that include the following:

- Slides shows as presentations to faculty and staff
- Slide show notes for faculty to leave presentations with
- Narrated presentations to run unassisted
- Visual aids as descriptions of hardware and software troubleshooting issues
- Flyers

Skills

An information training specialist should be able to do the following:

Chapter 1

- Use PowerPoint views (page 804)
- Open and save a slide show (page 809)
- Create a storyboard (page 817)
- Use slide layouts (page 820)
- Apply design themes (page 820)
- Review the presentation (page 822)
- Insert clip art (page 829)
- Use transitions and animations (page 831)
- Run and navigate a slide show (page 840)
- Print with PowerPoint (page 842)

...continued on Next Page

Chapter 2

- Create a presentation using a template (page 869)
- Modify a template (page 871)
- Print an outline (page 882)
- Add existing content to a presentation (page 888)
- Insert a header or footer (page 896)

Chapter 3

- Create SmartArt (page 952)
- Modify SmartArt diagrams (page 955)
- Create WordArt (page 961)
- Modify WordArt (page 961)
- Modify objects (page 968)
- Arrange objects (page 975)

Chapter 4

- Insert and modify a picture (page 1015)
- Use the Internet as a resource (page 1021)
- Add sound (page 1046)

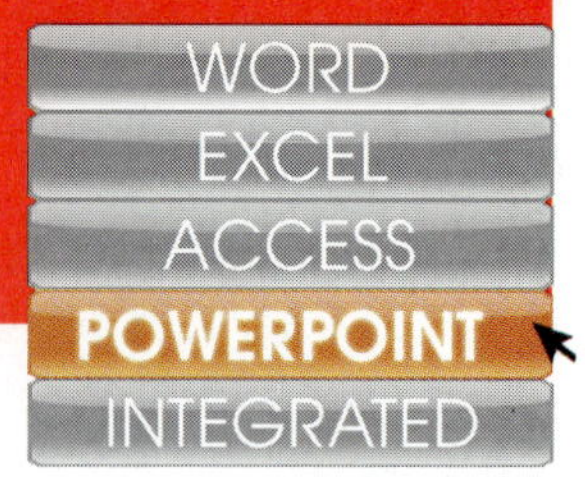

As an information training specialist at SOCC, one of your responsibilities is to organize a monthly technology update brownbag lunch session for faculty, staff, and students. It is a fairly informal setting that offers faculty, staff, and students an opportunity to update continually their technology knowledge. The sessions are meant to be light-hearted, upbeat, and enjoyable, and to offer interesting technology issues that are on the horizon.

Open the File, Select a Design, and Create a Title Slide

You have begun your PowerPoint presentation for this month. You have done your research and have had a few minutes to put some of the text into a new PowerPoint file, but you still have additional text to enter and a lot of formatting to finish before it is ready for prime time.

- Open the *exp07_p_tech_cpt_hightech* slide show and save it as **exp07_p_tech_cpt_hightech_solution**.
- Select the Flow theme. Change to Concourse color theme. Change to Verve font scheme.
- Add the following text to the title slide: **SOCC High Tech Brownbags** as the title and **Geraldo Lopez** as the subtitle.
- Format the title as **60 point** and italic. Format the subtitle as **40 point** with a shadow.

Insert a Slide and SmartArt

You would like to include a slide about the pros and the cons of online ID cards so that audience members can weigh the validity and usefulness for themselves. You also want to use SmartArt.

- Insert a new Title and Content third slide. Add the title **The Pros and Cons**.
- Insert the Vertical Bulleted List SmartArt design.
- Change the color of the SmartArt design to **Colored Fill - Accent 4**. Change the style to Cartoon.
- Add the following text to the SmartArt design:
  - In the first dark-shaded box: **Benefits**.
    - Add two items in the bulleted list under the shaded box: **Reduces phishing incidents** and **Lessens the need for multiple passwords**.
  - In the second dark-shaded box: **Concerns:**.
    - Add three items in the bulleted list under the shaded box: **Challenge of millions of web sites using the same standard**, **Privacy**, and **Identity theft**.

Insert Slides with New Content

You have information about a third fun technology topic that you want to share in the brownbag lunch seminar—Microsoft Surface. Microsoft Surface was released by Microsoft in mid-2008 and might be part of the consumer market in 2009. Microsoft Surface is the type of new technology that you want to share in this kind of environment.

- Add a new seventh Title and Content slide with the following text:
  - Title: **Microsoft Surface**.
  - Four bullets of text:
    - **Grab data with your hands and move it**.
    - **Natural movements**.
    - **30" tabletop display**.
    - **No mouse or keyboard**.
- Add a new eighth Title and Content slide with the following text:
  - Title: **Uses**.
  - Three bullets of text:
    - **Restaurants, retail, leisure and public entertainment venues**.
    - **Mounted on walls, to a mirror, or even on a refrigerator door**.
    - **International application?**
- Add a new ninth Title and Content slide with the following text:
  - Title: **Want more information?**
    - **Microsoft**.
    - **AT&T**.

Add WordArt

Of course, images enhance a presentation. You decide that a nice introduction to each technology issue would be a separate slide with the topic title. You will use WordArt objects for these. Your three topic slides will be online ID cards, the report about technology jobs, and Microsoft Surface.

- Insert a new second slide, new sixth slide, and new ninth slide.
- Change the layout of these three new slides to Section Header.
- Insert the following WordArt text on new slide 2 using **Fill - Accent 2, Warm Matt Bevel**: **Online ID Cards** which is the third option on the fifth row.
- Change the Shape Styles to **Intense Effect - Accent 4**. Change the Effect to Reflection, Half Reflection, touching.
- Copy and paste the WordArt object from slide 2 to slides 6 and 9.
- Change the text of slide 6 to **High-Tech Jobs**; change the text of slide 9 to **Microsoft Surface**.
- Center any titles that are not centered on the slide.

...continued on Next Page

Add a Footer

It will be helpful to have the current date and the slide number on the slides. This will be achieved by creating a footer.

- Add a footer to the presentation. Include a fixed date of **January 14, 2009**, and the slide number. Do not include text other than the date in the footer.
- Apply the footer to all slides. Do not include the footer on the title slide.

Add Clip Art

Every slide show needs to have a title slide and an ending slide. You decide that you want to keep the content rather clean on the slides with text, but you will add a few clip art images to add some visual interest.

- Go to the title slide and insert clip art. Type **computer** as the search word. Locate and insert the following clip art on the title slide:
- Insert two more of the same clip art. Use the Align Bottom and Distribute Horizontally options from the Align button to distribute the three clip art images across the bottom of the slide.

Add and Modify Pictures

Photographs also add a lot to a presentation. You will include a few photographs that you have on your hard drive as well as modify how they appear.

- Go to slide 9 and insert the following graphic files: *Exp_p_shipwreck*, *Exp_p_fireworks*, and *Exp_p_birds*.
- Resize the pictures and move them so all three fit below the WordArt image and above the footer.
- Select all three and change to Soft Edge Rectangle picture style.
- Rotate and overlap the three images so they are appealing and laid out on the bottom portion of the slide.
- Add the Fade animation to all three graphics with Medium speed and After Previous start. Be sure they animate from left to right.

Reuse a Slide

Since you have given brownbag presentations in the past, you have learned to not redo work that you can simply reuse. You have a one-slide file with an ending slide that you can quickly insert at the end of the presentation.

- Reuse the *ending slide.pptx* file. Be sure the slide is inserted as the final slide of the presentation.

Add Sound

Adding a small sound file to the ending slide will add a little more interest to the presentation.

- Insert the *reminder.wav* sound file to the final slide.
- Set it to play automatically.
- Hide the sound file speaker icon during the show.

Include Animation and Transitions

PowerPoint just wouldn't be PowerPoint without transitions from slide to slide and animations of text and/or graphics. You decide to add transitions to your slide show as well as animation to some of the clip art images. You know, however, that consistency is important, so you will keep the transitions and the animation styles the same throughout the presentation.

- With the prior computer clip art image selected on slide 13, use the Custom Animation task pane to add the following animation:
  - Entrance: Dissolve In with Medium speed and start set to After Previous.
  - Emphasis: Transparency with start set as After Previous with 2-second delay.
- Select the three clip art images on slide 1.
- Add the Dissolve In, Fast animation entrance effect with the After Previous setting. Make sure the images animate from left to right.
- Add the Wheel Clockwise, 3 Spokes slide transition to all slides. Change the speed to Medium.

Review the Presentation, Run the Slide Show, Print, and Save

To present a professional brownbag session, you know that you must be fully prepared. As you wrap up the presentation, you decide to print the outline, in order to take a hard copy home and study it so you will feel more prepared.

- Use spelling checker to check the presentation.
- Save the presentation.
- Print the presentation as Handouts, 6 slides per page.
- Print the outline in Expanded view.
- Run the slide show. Make any changes that are necessary and resave.

Information Training Specialists

Integrate Microsoft Office Software

Background

You've done it! You've landed a great job just months after finishing college! After a challenging but rewarding college career focused on technology, you have landed a dream job not only working in the technology field but also helping people develop their own technology skills.

As an information training specialist for Southern Oregon Community College (SOCC), you regularly meet with faculty and staff through brownbag sessions, at training workshops, or through troubleshooting their software and hardware issues. A recurring question that you hear from faculty and staff is what computer they should buy for their own personal needs. You decide to take the opportunity to inform faculty and staff about the Energy Star–compliant desktop and notebook computers that are on the market and to encourage them to first look at those models that meet the environmental standards the EPA has set. The best method of conveying the information you have gathered is through a brownbag session on campus.

Tasks

An information training specialist might be responsible for developing Microsoft Office Access files that include the following:

- Hardware purchase database information
- Hardware inventory tracking
- Faculty and staff training database information
- Sorting, filtering, and querying inventory and purchase information

Skills

An information training specialist should be able to do the following:

- Copy a Microsoft Office Excel worksheet and paste it into Microsoft Office PowerPoint
- Create and copy an Excel chart and paste it into PowerPoint
- Export an Access report to Microsoft Office Word

As an information training specialist at SOCC, one of your responsibilities is to present purchase recommendations for faculty and staff. The latest request of your supervisor is to research desktop and notebook computers for the Business Department faculty. You are not only concerned about cost, but you also want to be more considerate of the environment. You have found a database of desktop and notebook computers that are Energy Star compliant. If the list is extensive enough, you will not have to look any further—your hardware purchase recommendations can come directly from the database supplied by the U.S. Environmental Protection Agency (EPA).

Open File and Create Presentation

You already have the basics of the brownbag presentation file to serve as the start of what you want to present to the faculty. You will include some basic EPA Energy Star information.

- Open the PowerPoint slide show, **exp07_i_tech_cpt_brownbag_comp**. Two slides are ready to continue the presentation file. Save the file as **exp07_i_tech_cpt_brownbag_comp_solution**.
- Insert two new slides after slide 2. Change the layout of both of them to Title and Content.
- Add the following new content to the new slides:
  - Title: **Always Look for the Energy Star**.
    - Two following bullets: **Energy Star is a program through the U.S. Environmental Protection Agency and the U.S. Department of Energy** and **Energy savings for *just* 2007: $16 billion**.
  - Title: **Earning the Energy Star**.
    - Four following bullets: **New specifications beginning July 20, 2007**; **Only the most energy efficient computers earn the Energy Star**; **Qualified products must meet energy use guidelines for standby, sleep mode, and while in use**; and **Saves more than $1.8 billion in energy costs over 5 years**.
- Save the PowerPoint file.

Copy Excel Worksheet and Chart to PowerPoint

You know that participants are concerned about the environment, but showing them the cost savings will inspire them even more to consider only Energy Star computers for their homes. You first will include a small worksheet of the comparison, then a graph that pictorially displays the savings.

- Insert a new slide at the end of the presentation. Change the layout to Title Only.
- Add the new title: **Energy Cost Comparison: Energy Star Computer vs. Conventional**.
- Change the font size to **40**.
- Open the following Excel workbook: *exp07_i_tech_cpt_energystar_comp*. Save the file as **exp07_i_tech_cpt_energystar_comp_solution**.
- Copy **cells A1:F16**.
- Paste the cells of the worksheet to slide 5 of the presentation. Resize the worksheet data so it takes up most of the lower area of the slide and will be easier for the audience to read.
- Change the Table Style to **Themed Style 1, Accent 2** - the third style on the first row.
- In order to graphically show the savings, you want to create an Excel chart and then paste it into the presentation:
  - Select only **cells A13:A15**, **C13:C15**, and **F13:F15**. Insert a 3-D column chart.
  - Move the chart below the worksheet data and resize to the approximate width of the worksheet.
  - Format the chart with Layout 2 and delete the legend.
  - Drag each data label a little above each bar so they are all visible.
  - Change the chart title to **Cost Comparison: Energy Star vs. Conventional**.
  - Add a text box in the upper-left open area of the chart: **In addition to saving the environment, you save $177.36 over five years with an Energy Star computer!**
  - Center the text, add a solid line (retaining the default color), and draw an arrow from the text box to the $32.93 bar.
- Save the Excel workbook.
- Insert a new Title Only slide at the end of the presentation. Add **Save the Environment and Save Money!** as the title.
- Copy the Excel chart and paste it onto the slide.
- Resize the chart so it takes up most of the open area of the slide.
- Save the presentation file.

Modify Access Reports

You want the participants to leave the presentation with a list of home computers that are Energy Star compliant. You want to provide all participants with a list of Energy Star–compliant desktop and notebook computers produced by Dell, Gateway, and Lenovo. You need to modify your queries in Access a little, generate new reports, then copy them to Word in order to add more text and create

...continued on Next Page

an appealing handout for participants to refer to when they are ready to make their purchases.

- Open the *exp07_i_tech_cpt_energystar_comp* Access database file. Save it as **exp07_i_tech_cpt_energystar_comp_solution**.
- Open the *Dell/Lenovo desktops* query. Modify the query as follows:
  - Include *Gateway, Inc.* in the criteria. Run the query and notice that two Gateway computers are now added to the list.
  - Save the new query as **Dell/Gate/Len desktops.**
  - Close the query.
- Open the Dell/Lenovo desktops report and modify as follows:
  - Delete the *Processor Manufacturer* group.
  - Narrow the *Processor Speed* column to 25 characters so the report is the width of only one page.
  - Change the title of the report to **Dell, Gateway, and Lenovo Energy Star Compliant Desktops**. Change the font size to **18 point**.
  - Delete the date and time in the title area of the report.
  - Delete the page number at the bottom.
  - Save the report as **Dell/Gate/Len desktops**.
- Open the *Dell/Gate/Len notebooks* report and modify as follows:
  - Change the title of the report to **Dell, Gateway, and Lenovo Energy Star Compliant Notebooks**. Change the font size to **18 point**.
  - Delete the date in the title and the page number at the bottom.
  - Delete the count (29) at the bottom of the report.
  - Save the report.

Export an Access Report to Word

You want the participants to leave the presentation with a list of home computers that are Energy Star compliant. You will use your reports that you created in Access and copy them to Word to add more text and to create an appealing handout for participants to refer to when they are ready to make their purchases.

- Open the *Dell/Gate/Len desktops* report. Using the External Data tab, export the report to Word, leaving the Word file open after copying is complete.
- Create a hard return in the Word document after the last record of the desktop report table.
- Save the file as a Word 2007 RTF file with the name **exp07_i_tech_cpt_ES_computers**. Close the .rtf file.
- Open the *Dell/Gate/Len notebooks* report. Using the External Data tab, export the report to Word. Save the file as **exp07_i_tech_cpt_ES_notebooks**.
- Open *exp07_i_tech_cpt_ES_notebooks* and select all of the new document and copy.
- Open and go to the bottom of the *exp07_i_tech_cpt_ES_computers* file and paste the notebook report information.
- Save and close *exp07_i_tech_cpt_ES_notebooks.rtf*.
- Save *exp07_i_tech_cpt_ES_computers.rtf* as a Word 2007 file named **exp07_i_tech_cpt_ES_computers_solution.docx**.
- Close Access.

Create a Word Title Page

You want participants to leave the brownbag presentation with a list of desktop and notebook Energy Star–compliant computers, but also with a cover page that describes the information and provides your contact information.

- With the *exp07_i_tech_cpt_ES_computers_solution* Word file open, place the cursor at the beginning of the document. Insert a Next Page Section Break.
- Change all margins on the new first page to **1″**.
- Insert a Cover Page using the Motion style.
- Make the following changes to the cover page:
  - Change the year to **2009**.
  - Insert the new title as **Energy Star–Compliant Desktops and Notebooks: Dell, Gateway, and Lenovo**.
  - Replace the author name with **Geraldo Lopez**.
  - Replace the company name with **Southern Oregon Community College**.
  - Delete the date.
- Delete the current photo on the cover page.
- Insert the *exp07_i_tech_cpt_energystar_symbol.jpg* file onto the cover page.
- Move the image to the position of Middle Right with Square Text wrapping.
- Save the Word file.
- Use the Print Preview option to view the full document.
- Use the shortcut keys to print the full document.

Finalize the PowerPoint File

To wrap up the brownbag presentation, you will need a final slide. You want to include your contact information, the Energy Star Web site address, and a notation saying that you will supply all participants with a list of compliant desktop and notebook computers.

- Be sure the *exp07_i_tech_cpt_brownbag_comp_solution* file is open.
- Insert a new slide at the end of the presentation.
- Change the layout to Two Content.
- Include the following:
  - Add the title **Thank You and Keep Thinking Green!**
  - First bullet in left placeholder: **For additional information**:
    - Indent bullet: **Geraldo Lopez**.
    - Second indented bullet: **lopezg@socc.edu**.
  - Second bullet: **Energy Star information at www.energystar.gov**.
  - Third bullet: **Take home list of Energy Star computers**.
- Insert the *exp07_i_tech_cpt_energystar_symbol.jpg* file in the right placeholder.
- Use the spelling checker to check the PowerPoint file, and save it.

Paralegals

Use Microsoft Office Word

Background

Word processing is the most used Microsoft Office application program in a law office. Although legal assistants produce many of the letters that are mailed out, the paralegal creates, modifies, and disseminates a wide variety of legal documents. It is imperative that the paralegal know the many features available in Microsoft Office Word and be comfortable using them without having to refer regularly to a reference guide. Occasionally, however, the paralegal might need to refer to Microsoft Office Help to gain the knowledge needed to complete an unfamiliar task. The skills you use to complete the following tasks are taught in the four Word chapters and are all vital paralegal skills. In addition, you use other more advanced skills using Microsoft Office Help to gain proficiency in these new skills.

Tasks

In a small office, the paralegal might be responsible for all kinds of document production. This could include the following:

- Correspondence and mailings (cover letters, face sheets, copies of pleadings)
- Forms, including billing
- Memoranda
- Reports and briefs

In a larger office, the office assistant might take care of general typing duties, but the paralegal might still be responsible for the following:

- Pleadings
- Research
- Case documentation

Skills

In addition to basic formatting skills, a paralegal should be able to do the following:

Chapter 1

- Set margins and specify page orientation (page 87)
- Insert page breaks (page 88)
- Add page numbers (page 90)
- Insert headers and footers (page 91)
- Insert a cover page (page 93)
- Use the Find and Replace commands (page 94)
- Check spelling and grammar (page 103)
- Use save and backup options (page 104)

...continued on Next Page

Chapter 2

- Apply font attributes through the Font dialog box (page 133)
- Control word wrapping with nonbreaking hyphens and nonbreaking spaces (page 137)
- Copy formats with the Format Painter (page 139)
- Set off paragraphs with tabs, borders, lists, and columns (page 143)
- Create and modify styles (page 159)

Chapter 3

- Insert a table (page 197)
- Format a table (page 205)
- Insert clip art and images into a document (page 219)
- Format a graphic element (page 220)
- Insert symbols into a document (page 226)

Chapter 4

- Insert comments into a document (page 251)
- Compare and combine documents (page 264)
- Acknowledge a source (page 277)
- Create and modify footnotes and endnotes (page 281)
- Add legal references (page 289)
- Modify document properties (page 290)

Paralegal
Volume 1 | Capstone Exercises

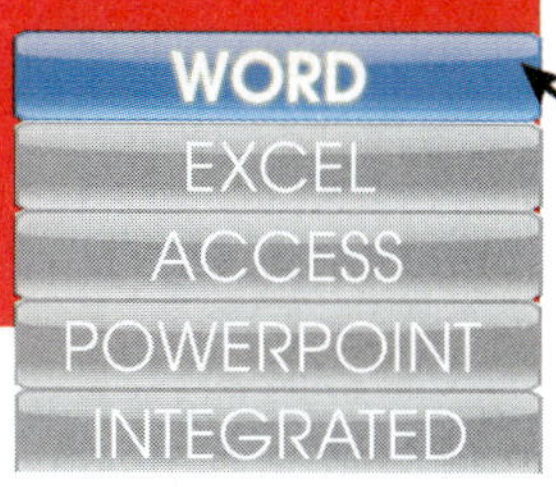

You work for a Worker's Compensation attorney who will be making a presentation at a State Bar function. He wants to prepare a document to share with the attendees that will highlight the way Worker's Compensation intersects with other areas of law. You have been provided with his raw text document to format, as well as with comments from one of his colleagues who reviewed the document. Prepare this document so that it has a professional appearance. It will be distributed in both paper and electronic form, so you will prepare it for appropriate viewing by either method.

Combine Documents

You review the document comments made by your attorney's colleague and notice that she has used a combination of methods to insert her suggestions. Your attorney has already authorized you to apply her comments to his document.

- At a blank document, use Word's Compare feature to combine *exp07_w_leg_cpt_facts1.docx* (the original document) and *exp07_w_leg_cpt_facts2.docx* (the revised document).
- Rather than keep the formatting changes from the original document, *exp07_w_leg_cpt_facts1.docx*, keep the formatting in the revised document, *exp07_w_leg_cpt_facts2.docx*.
- Accept all of Samantha's suggestions and then delete all comments.
- Save the new file as **exp07_w_leg_cpt_facts_solution.docx**.

Use Find and Replace Commands

With the Show/Hide feature active to check spacing of headings, you note that in several locations there are two spaces between words and after periods instead of the correct single space. While scanning, you also noted that a contraction was used and you wish to change it to the more formal legal style, which does not use contractions.

- Turn on the Show/Hide feature, if you have not already done so.
- Use the Replace feature to locate two spaces and replace with one space. Replace all.
- Search for the contraction *don't* and replace with **do not**.

Apply Styles and Use Format Painter

Review the outline of the document to see how it is formatted. You decide to format the title, author's name, and each paragraph heading. The paragraph and section headings in the document are currently written in Normal style with individually applied attributes (such as bold). Use the existing Heading 1 style to reformat the headings.

- Apply the Book Title style to the title of the document. Modify the style to use a font size of **16** points.
- Select the author identification line. Apply the Emphasis style.
- Select **Generally** (the 1st-level paragraph heading for the first paragraph) and then apply the Heading 1 style.
- Use the Format Painter to apply this style to the remaining 1st-level paragraph headings.

Modify Styles

The attorney prefers a more traditional color scheme, so you modify the Heading 1 style. You also modify the Normal style to include a first-line indent.

- Click in one of the headings to which you applied the Heading 1 style to open the Apply Styles dialog box. Modify the Heading 1 style so the font color applied is **Dark Blue, Text 2, Lighter 40%**.
- After changing the font color, click the **Format button** and modify the Paragraph format to include a special indention tab—a Hanging Indent.
- Click within any paragraph using the Normal style. Modify the Normal style to include a special indention tab—a First Line Indent.

Format the Document

You want the document to be formal, yet appealing. Apply several additional formatting features to improve the appearance.

- Set the left and right document margins to **1.5"**.
- Insert a header using the Pinstripes style.
- Type the header text **WORKER'S COMPENSATION: A FEW FACTS WORTH KNOWING FOR THE NON-PRACTITIONER**.
- Adjust the First Line Indent on the ruler so it is set at the margin, which moves your header to the margin.
- Insert a footer using the Pinstripes style. Type **Robert J. MacDonald**. The Pinstripes style automatically includes text on the left margin and the page number on the right margin.
- Adjust the First Line Indent on the ruler so it is set at the margin, which moves your footer to the margin.

Apply Non-Breaking Space

You review the document to see how the formatting changes you made impacted line and paragraph endings. You note on Page 4 in the paragraph headed *Collections Law* that the MCL is on one line and the actual number of the law is on the next line. You fix that by applying a non-breaking space between the parts. (The MCL will move to the next line.) NOTE: If you are using the VISTA operating system, Office 2007 will automatically add the non-breaking space.

...continued on Next Page

- Turn on the Show/Hide feature, if you have not already done so.
- Insert a non-breaking space between *MCL* and *552.625a*.
- Remove the existing space.

Add a Clip Art Image

Add a clip art image to the top of the document and position the image on the right side of the page. Add a 3-D rotation effect to the image.

- Use the Clip Art Organizer to add a graphic to the beginning of the document. In the search box, type **crutches**, and set the results to display clip art only. Choose the solid-colored clip art image of a man with a crutch (*j0292850.wmf*). Close the Clip Art task pane.
- Change the height of the graphic to **1"**. The width will change proportionately.
- Change the position of the image to **Position in Top Right with Square Text Wrapping**. (That is the choice in row 1, column 3, in the With Text Wrapping category of the Object Position gallery.)
- Apply the Perspective Contrasting Right 3-D Rotation effect to the image. (That is the choice from row 3, column 1, in the Perspective category of the 3-D Rotation gallery.)

Add a Footnote

The author's credentials currently are located at the end of the document. You decide to position the qualifications in a footnote on the first page.

- Locate the author's credentials at the end of the document, and then cut the italicized paragraph into the computer's clipboard memory.
- Move your insertion point to the end of the author's identification line on the first page of the document. Add a footnote. Paste the paragraph containing the author's credentials so it appears as the footnote on the bottom of the first page.

Check the Document Map

You want to add a document map for the convenience of your readers.

- Display the Document Map.
- Check to be sure that your headings are being displayed correctly. Check it against the original copy to be sure they all display.
- Turn off the Document Map.

Insert a Cover Page and Change the Theme Colors

As this document will be distributed at the State Bar meeting, it would be more professional to include a cover page. Because continuity gives a professional appearance, you use the Pinstripes format previously applied in your document to create the cover page. Your boss also likes the color blue, so you format the document with a blue color scheme.

- Move to the top of your document. (This is not necessary, but it is a good skill to remember!)
- Create a cover page using the Pinstripes style.
- Complete the cover page information:
    - o The title should be in place. If not, copy the title from the header of your document.
    - o Delete the subtitle.
    - o Change the date to **9/22/2010**.
    - o Change the company name to (or copy from the footnote) **MacDonald, FitzGerald & MacDonald, PC**.
    - o Change the author's name to **Robert J. MacDonald**.
- Make a copy of your graphic from page 1. Click before the page break on the cover page and paste.
- Double-click the graphic to open the formatting ribbon.
- Change the size to **2"** high. Change the position to the bottom center of the page.
- Open the theme colors; choose the Metro color scheme for the document. (Note: Change only the theme color, not the document theme.)

Mark Citations and Add a Table of Authorities

A Table of Authorities references cases, rules, treaties, and other documents referred to in a legal document. You will create a Table of Authorities for this article. The Table of Authorities will be positioned at the end of the article, although the typical location of a Table of Authorities is at the beginning of a legal document. Your Table of Authorities is positioned at the end because it is not actually part of the article. You will locate and mark only the citations on the first page of the article. Typically, after you mark several citations, you would obtain the attorney's approval of the formatting. After receiving his approval, you would mark the rest of the citations. For this capstone, however, the first page of citations is sufficient.

- Move to the first paragraph of the article. Locate the text *MCL 418.101-941*. Select the full text of the citation. Be careful not to include any extra characters or punctuation in the selection.
- Click the **References tab** and click **Mark Citation** in the Table of Authorities group. The selected text appears at the top of the dialog box. This citation is in the Statutes category. Close the dialog box. The citation will appear within the paragraph. Turn off the Show/Hide feature to hide the citation.
- Repeat for each of the citations on the first page. Mark the following as citations to be included in the Table of Authorities:
    - o **Cases:** Radecki v Worker's Disability Compensation Director, 208 Mich App 19; 526 NW2d 611 (1994)
    - o **Statutes:** IRC 104(a)(2)
    - o **Other Authorities:** IRS Publication 907
- Move to the end of the document. Insert a page break.
- Type the title **Table of Authorities** and format it with Heading 1 style. Insert two blank lines.
- Insert a Table of Authorities. Accept all defaults on the dialog box.

Add a Document Comment

You need to get the attorney's approval for the citation format in the Table of Authorities. You add a comment to the article with this request before sending the article to him.

...continued on Next Page

- Insert the following as a comment on the Table of Authorities page: **Please check the formatting of the Table of Authorities' citations. If it appears as you want, I will mark the rest of the citations.**

Update Document Properties

It is important to develop the habit of using the document properties feature for your law office documents. Even though this document will be used for outside presentation purposes, your office enforces the standard of always using the document properties section. Consistently setting the properties is a difficult habit to develop, but you'll be glad you did it later.

- Open the Document Properties window and update the information. You may retype the information or copy/paste it from other locations in the document.
  - The author is **Robert J. MacDonald**.
  - The title is **WORKER'S COMPENSATION: A FEW FACTS WORTH KNOWING FOR THE NON-PRACTITIONER**.
  - The subject is **WC overview for Attys**.
  - Keywords are **WC, General, Attorney**.
  - Category: **Presentation**.
  - Status: **Completed**.
  - Comments: **Prepared for State Bar presentation, Sept 22, 2010. Formatted by your name**.

Check Spelling and Grammar

Although a legal document contains many abbreviations and legal terms that might not be in the standard dictionary, a paralegal still should check a legal document for spelling and grammar errors. As standard abbreviations and terms are discovered, they should be added to the Custom Dictionary.

- Save your document and then run the spelling checker.
- Correct all misspelled words.
- When prompted to change the abbreviation *Mich*, ignore all.
- Add any terms you feel would be common terms in a legal office to the Custom Dictionary.

Save the Document

For the convenience of those at the State Bar, save a second copy of your document in the Word 97–2003 format.

- Save your document.
- Save the document in Word 97–2003 format for those who do not have Word 2007.
- Close the document.

Create a Table

In addition to the article, the attorney plans to distribute a table showing the Michigan State average weekly wages for the past five years.

- Create a table with six columns and six rows.
- Save the table as **exp07_w_leg_cpt_saww_solution.docx**.
- Enter the following information:

Year	SAWW	90% of SAWW (Maximum)	2/3 of SAWW	50% of SAWW (Minimum Benefit for Death Cases)	25% of SAWW (Minimum Benefit for Specific Loss and T&P
2008	$820.04	$739.00	$546.69	$410.02	$205.01
2007	$803.17	$723.00	$535.45	$401.59	$200.79
2006	$784.31	$706.00	$522.87	$392.16	$196.08
2005	$765.12	$689.00	$510.08	$382.56	$181.28
2004	$744.49	$671.00	$496.33	$362.48	$186.12

- Insert a footer using the Pinstripes style. Type **Source: Michigan State Worker's Compensation Agency**.

Format a Table

You format the table to make it easier to read and to give it a more professional appearance.

- Insert a new row above the row containing the column headings. Merge the cells in the new row and then enter the table title: **State Average Weekly Wage Chart**. Bold the title and change the font size to **22** points.
- Apply the Medium Shading 2–Accent 1 table style. (This is row 5, column 2, of the Built-in category of the Table Styles gallery.)
- Bold the column headings and change the font size to **12** points. Repeat the process with the years in the first column.
- Change the alignment for the column headings to **Bottom Center**.
- Set the alignment for rows 3 through 7 to **Top Center**.
- Position the table 2" vertically relative to the top margin.

Create WordArt

Create an eye-catching title to the page with the table using WordArt.

- Insert WordArt using WordArt Style 8. Enter the text **Michigan Worker's Compensation Agency** on two lines.

...continued on Next Page

- Nudge the shadow up once and to the left once.
- Position the WordArt in the top center with square text wrapping.

Save the Document

For the convenience of those at the State Bar, save a second copy of your document in the Word 97–2003 format.

- Save your document.
- Save the document in Word 97–2003 format for those who do not have Word 2007.
- Close the document.

Paralegals

Use Microsoft Office Excel

Background

Microsoft Office Excel is such a versatile program that an experienced paralegal can find many valuable uses for it in the law office. Rather than knowing only a prescribed list of traditional uses, a paralegal should be alert to possible creative uses of Excel. The information provided in these four chapters is an excellent starting point.

One of the tasks for which the paralegal might be responsible is recording transactions related to a trust account. A trust account is an account established by the lawyer and law firm for recording client fees and deposits. Each state has its own rules for trust account formatting and processing. For example, in Michigan, the distinction between *retainer* and *advance fees* has recently been clarified, and the distinction imposes some additional accounting requirements on the law office. The paralegal might be the person designated to set up and/or monitor the trust account. It is for this reason that an accounting topic has been chosen for this capstone exercise even though many law offices use other programs for accounting purposes.

This exercise is based on content from the "client ledger" portion of the Microsoft Office PowerPoint slide, "Three Way Reconciliation," presented at the Institute of Continuing Legal Education seminar "Ethics 2006: Practical Solutions to Real World Problems" in November 2006 by Mark A. Armitage, Esq., Deputy Director, Attorney Discipline Board of Michigan. The exercise has been modified, however, to provide you with additional practice with Excel formulas.

Tasks

In a small office, the paralegal might be responsible for all kinds of document production. This could include the following tasks:

- Completing any accounting tasks (although it is more likely that these tasks would be accomplished with third-party software, particularly a law-specific program)
- Tracking client expenditures in an extended case
- Calculating probate expenses
- Calculating real estate closure costs
- Preparing charts as trial exhibits
- Many other creative uses are possible, depending on the particular type of law practiced in the office

Skills

In addition to basic formatting skills, a paralegal should be able to do the following:

Chapter 1

- Plan for good workbook and worksheet design (page 315)
- Enter and edit data in cells (page 322)

...continued on Next Page

- Describe and use symbols and the order of precedence (page 328)
- Insert and delete rows and columns (page 331)
- Use cell ranges; Excel move; copy, paste, paste special; and AutoFill (page 322)
- Format worksheets (page 341)
- Select page setup options for printing (page 353)
- Manage cell comments (page 356)

Chapter 2

- Create and copy formulas (page 381)
- Use relative and absolute cell addresses (page 382)
- Use AutoSum (page 389)
- Use date functions (page 392)
- Use the IF function (page 399)
- Use the VLOOKUP function (page 400)

Chapter 3

- Choose a chart type (page 431)
- Create a chart (page 438)
- Modify a chart (page 450)
- Embed charts (page 459)
- Print charts (page 460)

Chapter 4

- Freeze rows and columns (page 488)
- Hide and unhide rows, columns, and worksheets (page 489)
- Protect a cell, a worksheet, and a workbook (page 490)
- Control calculation (page 493)
- Explore basic table management (page 505)
- Sort data (page 510)
- Filter and total data (page 514)

Paralegal
Volume 1 | Capstone Exercises

The attorney in your office recently attended a continuing legal education seminar that emphasized the need for individual client tracking on a trust account. Although you had maintained a trust ledger, you had not been providing individual client ledgers. (Some professionals recommend having a ledger for every client, regardless of whether any of the client's funds are in the trust account!) Rather than trying to use your formal accounting program, you asked to transfer the paper accounting method demonstrated at the seminar into a computerized equivalent in Excel as a trial process. While designing the spreadsheets, you realized that you could create the individual client ledgers and then construct the trust ledger as a set of links from the client ledgers. You realize that just as Microsoft creates templates that can be used over and over again, you can create the individual client ledger as a template and use it for each client of the attorney.

Create a Client Ledger

As you plan the worksheet to be used as the template for the individual client ledgers, you determine the information you need to record and decide each type of information should be identified with a column heading. You decide that whereas traditional accounting ledgers use the terms *debits* and *credits* for amounts that increase and decrease an account, you will use the terms *Checks* and *Deposits*. When the attorney takes a case, the client pays a retainer for the attorney's services. This creates a deposit that is added to the account. When the attorney returns funds to a client, a check is issued, which is subtracted from the account. After planning the worksheet to be used as the template, you create and name the template. Since this is a reusable template, apply all cell formatting now.

- Create a new workbook and save it as **exp07_e_leg_cpt_ledger_template_solution**.
- Type the worksheet title **Client Ledger** in **cell A1**. Type the subtitle as an asterisk (*) in **cell A2** (this cell will be used as a placeholder for the client name). The A1 and A2 title and subtitle should use the default font, **16** points, and **bold**.
- Merge and center **cells A1:J1**, and then merge and center **cells A2:J2**.
- Type **Case#** in **cell A3** using the default font, **11** points, and **bold**.
- Type the following headings on row 5 using the default font, **12** points. Use **Alt-Enter** to put the headings on two lines within the cell. Top and Center align column headings.

Client Ledger									
*									
Case #									
DATE	CLIENT	SOURCE OF DEPOSIT	PAYEE	CK #	PURPOSE	CHECKS (SUBTRACT)	DEPOSITS (ADD)	RUNNING BALANCE	MEMO

- Format **cells A6:A30** as Short Date format (month/day/year as two digits, i.e., 3/15/2009).
- Apply the Text format to **cells B6:F30**.
- Format **cells G6:I30** (Checks, Deposits, and Running Balance columns) with the Accounting format, two decimal places, and the dollar sign ($).
- Format **cells A5:J30** as a table using the Table Style Light 2 banded table format (Light section, row 1, column 3). Select the option that indicates your table has a header.
- Activate the **total row** option.
- If you are unable to see columns A–J on the screen, change the view to **75%**.
- Name the worksheet **Client Template**.

Changing the Page Layout

Set the print options for this ledger template so that worksheets created from the template are ready to be printed and inserted into the client's file. Due to the amount of information, you will change the format so that the worksheet prints in landscape.

- Set the page orientation to **Landscape**.
- Set the print area to **cells A1:J31**.
- Scale the worksheet to fit on one page.
- Use Print Preview to check that all columns display.
- Close the Print Preview window.

Create the Formulas for the Ledger

You have created this worksheet as a template for individual client ledgers. Just as you applied formats to the template, you create the formulas in the template. When a client pays the attorney a retainer, the amount is credited (added) to the running balance. When the client's account is debited for fees or costs, the amount is subtracted. Follow the bank accounting practice of adding deposits before subtracting debits.

- Type **Beginning Balance** in **cell F6**, and then enter **0** in **cell I6**.
- For **cells I7:I30**, create a formula that will calculate the running balance after that row's transaction. Ignore the *This cell is inconsistent with the column formula* warning.

...continued on Next Page

- Add formulas that will sum the Checks (G) and Deposits (H) columns in row 31.

Use the Template to Create an Individual Client Ledger

Make a copy of the worksheet template containing the individual client ledger. Use it to set up a ledger for a new client—you!

- Delete the Sheet2 and Sheet 3 worksheets in the workbook.
- Create a copy of the Client Template worksheet. Change the worksheet tab name from *Client Template (2)* to your name using this format: Last name, First name.
- Replace the asterisk (*) in the subtitle row with your name.
- Use the following figure to enter information about your account in the ledger. Enter your last name and first initial in the Client column. The column I totals will appear automatically as you complete columns G and H.
- After data entry, adjust the column widths to improve the appearance of the spreadsheet.

	A	B	C	D	E	F	G	H	I	J
1						Client Ledger				
2						Student Name				
3	Case #									
4										
5	DATE	CLIENT	SOURCE OF DEPOSIT	PAYEE	CK #	PURPOSE	CHECKS (SUBTRACT)	DEPOSITS (ADD)	RUNNING BALANCE	MEMO
6	9/9/2009	Name, Student				Beginning Balance			$ -	
7	11/14/2009	Name, Student		US Mail	3164	Send Filing Packet	$ 10.50		$ (10.50)	
8	1/5/2010	Name, Student	Ins. Co	Atty.		Settlement Proceeds		$ 10,000.00	$ 9,989.50	Check No. 1538603
9	1/15/2010	Name, Student		Atty.	3201	Fee (25%)	$ 2,500.00		$ 7,489.50	
10	1/15/2010	Name, Student		Client	3202	Balance Due Client	$ 7,489.50		$ -	

Add a Comment

Comments are useful to provide additional documentation to a cell that does not need to be visible. Add a comment about where the balance due the client was mailed.

- Insert the following comment in **cell F10**: **Sent by certified mail, return receipt, to client's vacation home.**

Save the Ledger and Print

You have created a worksheet to be used as an accounting template for the legal office. Save the workbook.

- Save **exp07_e_leg_cpt_ledger_template_solution**.
- Print the workbook as directed by your instructor.
- Close the workbook.

Create the Trust Ledger

Once the client ledgers have been set up and entries recorded, you make a trust ledger to consolidate all of the entries into one large document. This process would need to be automated if you had many clients, and you would probably use a specialized accounting program. In this small office, however, you can create the trust ledger by hand using Excel. You would need to be extremely careful using this process so that you would not introduce errors into the accounting system.

The template you created in the previous activity has been modified to include additional columns and revised column headings. The table formatting has been removed. Client ledgers have been created based on the template, and the template has been used to create a new worksheet titled **Trust Ledger, Linda Ron, P.C.** You enter the formulas for the trust ledger.

- Open *exp07_e_leg_cpt_trust_ledger* and save it as **exp07_e_leg_cpt_trust_ledger_solution**.
- Change the title of the worksheet by replacing the attorney name, *Linda Ron*, with your name.
- In **cell K12**, enter **5000** for the running balance (the amount of retainers collected from the end of the previous period).
- In **cell K13**, create a nested formula: if all the fees and charges against the account and the payment received are zero, then the value is zero; if there was a payment received, the payment should be added and any fees and charges should be subtracted from the previous value in the Running Total (cell K12). Copy the formula through row 36. The goal is to have the balance show up if there is a balance, but have nothing show up if it is the end of the entries.
- Insert today's date by function in **cell I3**.

Use the IF and VLOOKUP Functions

To help identify the type of fees charged to a client, a table was inserted at the top of each of the ledgers identifying the administrative fee code, an explanation of the fees, and the administrative fee charge. The ledgers include a column identifying the fee code and a column displaying the fee charged based on the code. Create the formula to have Excel search the table for the type of fee and then return the value for that fee. In addition, if there is no fee type specified in the ledger, the value returned should be a zero represented by a hyphen (-).

- Move to the worksheet Coolin, Tracey. Create a formula in **cell H13** that references the administrative fee code from cell G13 to look up the administrative fee. If there is no fee code, the administrative fees column should display *0*. If there is a fee code, the appropriate fee from the table should be displayed. (Note: Be sure to use absolute cell references where appropriate.)
- Copy the administrative fees formula down the column.
- Utilize the formula in the Grab, Mark; Mattox, Brian; and Client Template worksheets.

...continued on Next Page

Enter the Data

We will create links from the original client ledgers to the trust ledger. By making links, subsequent changes to the client ledgers will show up in the trust ledger. NOTE: New entries still will have to be copied by hand. Although you are familiar with copying cell contents to the clipboard, creating links with the content of the cell might be unfamiliar to you. Before completing this portion of the activity, review the Help topic "Copy specific cell contents or attributes in a worksheet."

- Select Tracey Coolin's ledger. Select **cells A13:J19** (the completed rows, but not the starter row). Copy the information.
- Switch to the Trust Ledger worksheet. Select **cell A13**, the first empty row after the starter row.
- Use the **Paste Special** option to link the pasted cells.
- Copy the contents of the next client ledger and paste the links. Correct any formatting errors that might occur after copying and pasting. Calculate the running balance.

Sort the Trust Ledger into Chronological Order and Apply Additional Formatting

Sort the trust ledger so that entries are in chronological order.

- Sort the date from oldest to newest.
- Check the check numbers to be sure they appear in numerical order. If not, you have an accounting problem that will require account auditing. (It could be an indication of embezzlement, for example.)
- Freeze the panes of the chart at **cell B12** so you can scroll down to the 100 rows you expect to have by the next accounting period (optimistic)!
- Hide the Purpose column since it is not relevant to the trust ledger.

Filter the Data to Show Deposits

You want to check the deposits (payments received) against your bank statement.

- Filter the Payment Received column to show only records that have contents greater than zero. You should have four entries remaining.
- Print this result if requested by your instructor.
- Clear the filter.

Insert a Chart of Payments and Charges

For the convenience of your attorney, insert a chart showing the payments received and the payments made (Charges and Administrative Fees) for the trust account.

- Select the column titles for columns H, I, and J. Add **cells H37 through J37**.
- Insert a bar chart of type Clustered Horizontal Cylinder.
- Move the chart below the table.
- Size the chart to a width of 7".
- Select the chart style of your choice and apply.
- Apply the Layout 2 chart layout.
- Delete the legend.
- Insert the following two-line title:
    - **Trust Account, Your Name, P.C.**
    - **Payments and Charges July–December 2010**
- Change the font color for the title to **Blue, Accent 1**.
- Center the chart between columns of the table.

Protect the Worksheet

We do not want any changes made to the Trust Ledger worksheet by mistake, so we will protect it. When we need to update the trust ledger later, we will unprotect it (not the whole file, just the Trust Ledger worksheet).

- Protect the worksheet.
- Type **ledger** as the password.
- Save the workbook.
- Note that changes cannot be made.

Print the Trust Ledger

Provide a printed copy of the trust ledger for your attorney and the accountant.

- Set the print area for the worksheet to include the ledger and the chart.
- Change the scale until the entire worksheet fits on one page width.
- Create a footer with this information: **Trust Ledger, Confidential, Page 1**.
- Center the worksheet horizontally and turn off grid lines.
- Check the final version using Print Preview. Your preview should match the following figure.
- Save and close the workbook.
- Submit as directed by your instructor.

...continued on Next Page

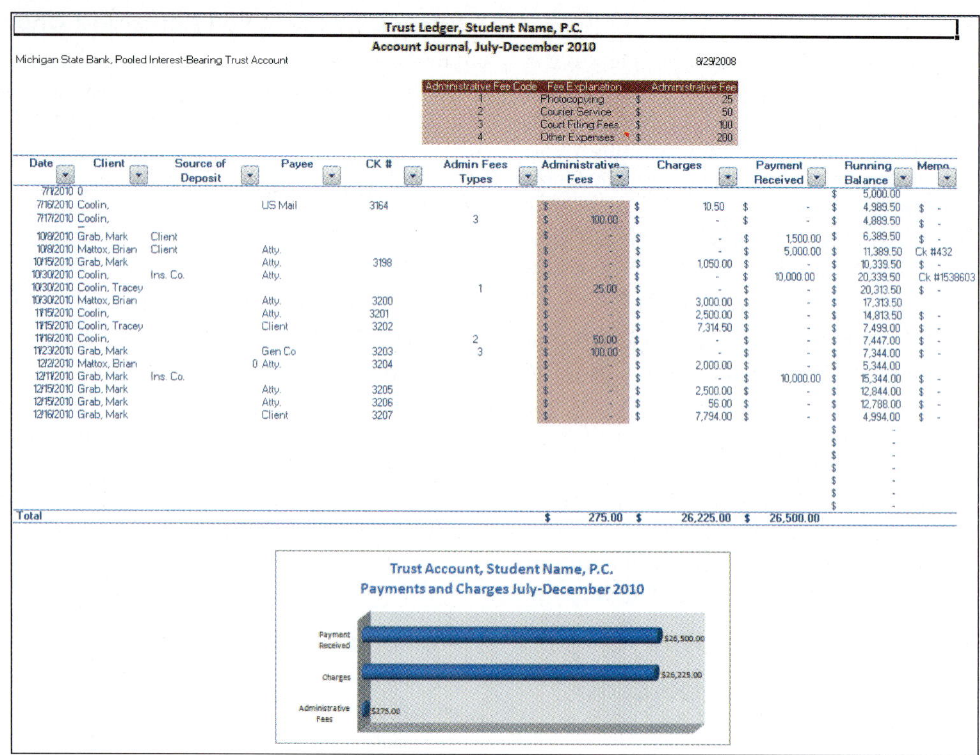

Trust Ledger, Student Name, P.C.

Account Journal, July-December 2010

Michigan State Bank, Pooled Interest-Bearing Trust Account 8/29/2008

Administrative Fee Code	Fee Explanation	Administrative Fee
1	Photocopying	$ 25
2	Courier Service	$ 50
3	Court Filing Fees	$ 100
4	Other Expenses	$ 200

Date	Client	Source of Deposit	Payee	CK #	Admin Fees Types	Administrative Fees	Charges	Payment Received	Running Balance	Memo
7/1/2010	0								$ 5,000.00	
7/16/2010	Coolin,		US Mail	3164		$ -	$ 10.50	$ -	$ 4,989.50	$ -
7/17/2010	Coolin,				3	$ 100.00	$ -	$ -	$ 4,889.50	$ -
10/8/2010	Grab, Mark	Client				$ -	$ -	$ 1,500.00	$ 6,389.50	$ -
10/8/2010	Mattox, Brian	Client	Atty.			$ -	$ -	$ 5,000.00	$ 11,389.50	Ck #432
10/15/2010	Grab, Mark		Atty.	3198		$ -	$ 1,050.00	$ -	$ 10,339.50	$ -
10/30/2010	Coolin,	Ins. Co.	Atty.			$ -	$ -	$ 10,000.00	$ 20,339.50	Ck #1538603
10/30/2010	Coolin, Tracey				1	$ 25.00	$ -	$ -	$ 20,313.50	$ -
10/30/2010	Mattox, Brian		Atty.	3200		$ -	$ 3,000.00	$ -	$ 17,313.50	
11/15/2010	Coolin,		Atty.	3201		$ -	$ 2,500.00	$ -	$ 14,813.50	$ -
11/15/2010	Coolin, Tracey		Client	3202		$ -	$ 7,314.50	$ -	$ 7,499.00	$ -
11/16/2010	Coolin,				2	$ 50.00	$ -	$ -	$ 7,447.00	$ -
11/23/2010	Grab, Mark		Gen Co	3203	3	$ 100.00	$ -	$ -	$ 7,344.00	$ -
12/2/2010	Mattox, Brian	0	Atty.	3204		$ -	$ 2,000.00	$ -	$ 5,344.00	
12/11/2010	Grab, Mark	Ins. Co.				$ -	$ -	$ 10,000.00	$ 15,344.00	$ -
12/15/2010	Grab, Mark		Atty.	3205		$ -	$ 2,500.00	$ -	$ 12,844.00	$ -
12/15/2010	Grab, Mark		Atty.	3206		$ -	$ 56.00	$ -	$ 12,788.00	$ -
12/16/2010	Grab, Mark		Client	3207		$ -	$ 7,794.00	$ -	$ 4,994.00	$ -
									$ -	
									$ -	
									$ -	
									$ -	
									$ -	
									$ -	
									$ -	
Total						$ 275.00	$ 26,225.00	$ 26,500.00		

Paralegals

Use Microsoft Office Access

Background

Much of the information used by attorneys in their offices can be tracked in a database. It is becoming more and more common to purchase an integrated case management software program to do such tracking, but many opportunities still exist for a paralegal to make good use of a Microsoft Office Access database. An Access database can be used to track every part of the law office operation, particularly in a small office that might not have purchased the larger programs due to cost. Even if an Access database is not used, the information in Chapters 1–4 will enhance one's ability to use third-party database programs more effectively.

Tasks

In a small office, the paralegal might be responsible for using Access to prepare the following:

- Client and case tracking
- Contact database, including courts and attorneys
- Trial preparation database (exhibits, documents, etc.)
- Accession file

Skills

In addition to basic formatting skills, a paralegal should be able to do the following:

Chapter 1

- Create filters (page 565)
- Sort table data on one or more fields (page 568)
- Know when to use Access or Excel to manage data (page 570)
- Use the Relationships window (page 578)

Chapter 2

- Design data (page 607)
- Create tables (page 612)
- Share data with Excel (page 626)
- Establish table relationships (page 630)
- Create a query (page 642)
- Use the Query Wizard (page 649)

...continued on Next Page

Chapter 3

- Create a calculated field in a query (page 679)
- Perform date arithmetic (page 694)
- Create and work with data aggregates (page 704)

Chapter 4

- Plan a report (page 731)
- Create and edit a report (page 737)
- Add fields to a report (page 755)

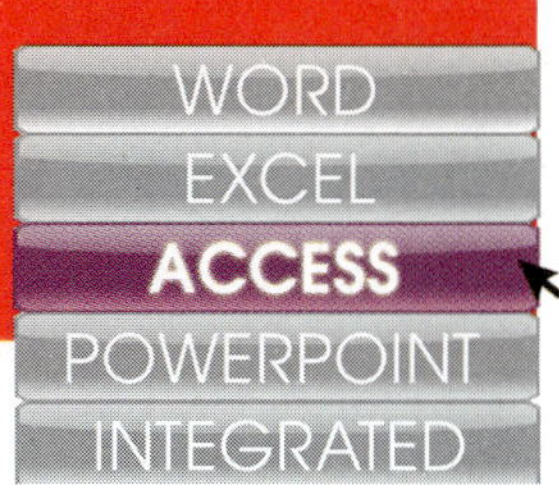

When you close a file at the end of legal representation, several steps need to be completed. The last step is to enter the case information into an accession file. The purpose of the accession file is to maintain the most basic information about a case and its storage location on the chance that the file might have to be retrieved from cold storage later. Until now, the procedure in your firm was to note closed files in a list in an Excel document. Having learned about Access, you will create a database-driven accession file for your law office.

Create the Database

There are many excellent templates available in Access, but you decide to create a new blank database for your files.

- Create a blank database and save it as **exp07_a_leg_cpt_accession_solution**.

Create the Case Type Table

Your attorney practices primarily in family law, with a little criminal law on the side, but she likes to track statistics regarding case type. After consulting with her, you create a subordinate case type table with several case type breakdowns.

- Create a new table called **CaseType**.
- Create **CaseTypeID** as the primary key.
- Add a second field named **CaseType**. It will have a Data Type of Text and field size of 25.
- Create data for your table using these case types (do not worry about alphabetical order since Access can do that for you): **Consultation**, **Separation**, **Domestic Violence**, **Divorce**, **Alimony**, **Custody**, **Child Support**, **Parenting Time**, **Paternity**, **Property Settlement**, **Misdemeanor**, **Felony**, and **Other**.

Create the County Table

Your attorney practices in several counties, although the office is centrally located. Make a subordinate table listing the counties in which your attorney practices.

- Create a new table called **County**.
- Create a field named **CountyID** as the primary key.
- Add a second field named **County**. It will have a Data Type of Text and field size of 25.
- Create data for your table using these counties: **Genesee**, **Lapeer**, **Shiawassee**, and **Oakland**.

Create the Court Table

Your attorney tries cases in multiple jurisdictions: Federal, State (civil and criminal courts), and Municipal courts. Cases are tried in Civil, Criminal, Appeals, and the Supreme Courts at each level. Create a subordinate table listing the courts in which your attorney tries cases.

- Create a new table called **Court**.
- Create a field named **CourtID** as the primary key.
- Add a second field named **Court**. It will have a Data Type of Text and field size of 25.
- Create data for your table using these courts: **Civil**, **Criminal**, **Appeals**, and **Supreme**.

Create the Case Table

The main table is the Case table. As you prepare the database field names, you recall from your studies that it is most effective *not* to put spaces in the names of objects; you choose the CapitalizeEachWord method instead. Although you could have created ID primary key fields with a specific format, you chose to allow the computer to automatically number the entries for this database.

- Create a new table in Design View named **Case**.
- Create the fields as indicated in the following figure. In the following steps, note specific instructions for each field name.

...continued on Next Page

Field Name	Data Type
CloseID	Number
OpenDate	Date/Time
CloseDate	Date/Time
CaseNo	Text
ClientLastName	Text
ClientFirstName	Text
CaseType	Number
County	Number
Court	Number
Trial	Text
Settled	Text
Summary	Text

- Type the field names and data types as indicated in the previous figure.
- Set the following field sizes:
  - Case#: **15**
  - ClientLastName: **25**
  - ClientFirstName: **20**
- Index the ClientLastName field, allowing duplicates. Close the table and save the changes.
- Create captions for field names that use CapitalizeFirstLetter notation.
- Type the Summary field with Memo Data Type.

Create and Enforce Relationships

Before importing and entering any data into the Case table, create relationships between the tables and enforce referential integrity.

- Close all tables.
- Open the Relationships window. Add the four tables to the Relationships window.
- Create a relationship between the CaseTypeID field in the *CaseType* table with the CaseType field in the *Case* table and enforce referential integrity.
- Create a relationship between the CourtID field in the *Court* table with the Court field in the *Case* table and enforce referential integrity.
- Create a relationship between the CountyID field in the *County* table with the County field in the *Case* table and enforce referential integrity.
- Attractively rearrange the tables in the Relationships window so they are easy to read.
- Close and save the Relationships window.

Import Records into the Case Table

An Excel file exists with cases closed after September 1, 2007. (Cases are "closed" only twice a month to maximize the efficiency of the operation.) Import these records into the Case table.

- Import the records in *exp07_a_leg_cpt_cases.xlsx* to the existing *Case* table.
- Open the *Case* table and replace Patricia Larkin's last name and first name with your last name and first name.

Enter Records into the Case Table Using a Form

Create a simple form using the Form wizard and then enter the data into the table as shown in the following section. If unfamiliar with creating a simple form, research it in Help.

- Create a simple form for the *Case* table. Rename it **Case Entry Form**.
- Apply the Module AutoFormat to the form.
- Open the Case Entry Form. Enter the following data records using the form:

CloseID: 10123	CloseID: 10124
Open Date: April 1, 2008	Open Date: March 18, 2009
Close Date: May 8, 2009	Close Date: September 30, 2009
Case Number: 08-499571	Case Number: 09-203381
Client Last Name: Jimenez	Client Last Name: Deheer
Party First Name: Jaime	Party First Name: William
Case Type: Divorce	Case Type: Felony
County: Genesee	County: Shiawassee
Court: 1	Court: 4
Trial: No	Trial: No
Settled: Yes	Settled: Yes
Summary: Divorce, 1 child	Summary: Possession

Create a Select Query

Create a query to locate the client *Smith* whose case was closed recently. You cannot remember the client's first name, so create a query to find all clients with the last name Smith.

- Create a query in Design View to locate all *Smiths*.
- Include all fields in the table.

...continued on Next Page

- Run the query.
- Save and close the query. Name the query **SmithCases**.

Create a Multi-Table Query

Create a query that displays all cases for Genesee County. Use the Query wizard or create it directly in Design View.

- Using the CloseID, CloseDate, CaseNo, ClientLastName, ClientFirstName fields from the *Case* table, the CaseType field from the *CaseType* table, and the County field from the *County* table, locate all cases for Genesee County.
- Close the query and name it **GeneseeCountyCases**.

Copy and Modify a Query

Now that you have a query for Genesee County, use it to create a query for Shiawassee County.

- Modify a copy of the GeneseeCountyCases query to locate all Shiawassee County cases.
- Modify the county field to locate the misspelled term *Shiawasee*.
- Run the query and note that you get no results.
- Correct the spelling of the county name by adding the second *s*: *Shiawassee*.
- Run the query and then save the results.

Calculate Case Duration

Your attorney wants to know approximately how long it takes to complete each case, sorted by court and category. You will follow up the query with a formatted report.

- Create a query in Design View using the *Case* table, the *Court* table, and the *CaseType* table.
- Add the following fields: **Court**, **CaseType**, **CaseNo**, **ClientLastName**, **ClientFirstName**.
- Create a field called **Duration in Days** and use the Expression Builder to calculate the number of days from the date opened to the date closed.
- Sort in ascending order by Court, secondarily by CaseType, and finally by ClientLastName.
- Run the query.
- Close the query. Save the query with the name **CaseDuration**.

Create an Average Duration Query

Your attorney now wants to know the average number of days it takes to complete each type of case.

- Create a query using the *Case* table and the *CaseType* table.
- Add the field **CaseType**. Sort in ascending order.
- Create a field called **Duration** and calculate the number of days from the date opened to the date closed.
- Display the Totals row. Group by CaseType and calculate the average duration for each type of case.
- Run the query and check it for accuracy.
- Close the query. Save the query with the name **AverageDuration**.

Create a Case Count Query

Create a query in which you group each case type and list how many cases of that type have been processed in the office.

- Use the CaseType field from the *CaseType* table and the CloseID field from the *Case* table to create a query for cases by case type.
- Sort the case types in ascending order.
- Display the Totals row. Group by CaseType and use the Count function in the Totals row under the CloseID field to count the number of cases.
- Save the query as **CountByCaseType**.

Plan a Report Based on the Query

Your attorney wants to know the relative percentage of cases of each type.

- Build a report based on the CountByCaseType query that groups the data by CaseType.
- Use the Summary Options feature to include the Sum and calculate the percent of total. Show both the detail and summary.
- Use the default layout and the Paper style.
- Name the report **CaseTypeReport**.
- Attractively format the report information and ensure that all data is fully visible.
- Display the CountofCloseID control from the *Detail* section in the *CaseType Header* section.
- In the *CaseType Footer* section, change the term *Sum* to **Number of Cases** and the term *Standard* to **Percentage of Cases**.
- Associate the *Number of Cases* label with the *Sum of CountofCloseID* label.
- Associate the *Percentage of Cases* label with the *Standard of CountofCloseID* label.

Compact, Repair, and Back Up the Database

Now that you have finished your work, prepare the database to be saved until you need it next. You need an original and a backup copy.

- Compact and repair your database.
- Save your database in the same location where you save your files for this textbook.
- Create a **Backups** folder in an appropriate location. Back up your database and store it in that folder. When naming the file, include today's date.

Paralegals

Use Microsoft Office PowerPoint

Background

Attorneys have historically focused on presenting their information by speaking or writing. The profession is changing rapidly with technology, however, and the use of graphical images has greatly expanded. Legal graphics are used as illustrations and exhibits, for accident reconstructions and diagrams, and in many other areas. The most common uses for graphical images might be in trial, as a supplement to a formal presentation, or for continuing education presentations. This capstone exercise, an educational presentation for a client, introduces a practical use for Microsoft Office PowerPoint within the law office. It is almost certain that the paralegal would be the proper person to prepare any kind of PowerPoint supplement that the attorney might use. These four chapters present a comprehensive introduction.

Tasks

In a small office, the paralegal might be responsible for using PowerPoint to prepare the following:

- Trial presentations and exhibits
- Formal educational presentations
- Visual aids for the attorney to use to communicate complex concepts
- Explanatory booklets

Skills

In addition to basic formatting skills, a paralegal should be able to do the following:

Chapter 1

- Use PowerPoint views (page 804)
- Use slide layouts (page 820)
- Apply design themes (page 820)
- Insert clip art (page 829)
- Use transitions and animations (page 831)
- Run and navigate a slide show (page 840)
- Print with PowerPoint (page 842)

Chapter 2

- Modify an outline structure (page 881)
- Import an outline (page 887)
- Add existing content to a presentation (page 888)
- Apply and modify a design theme (page 892)
- Insert a header or footer (page 896)

...continued on Next Page

Chapter 3

- Create shapes (page 931)
- Apply Quick Styles and customize shapes (page 936)
- Create SmartArt (page 952)
- Create WordArt (page 961)
- Modify WordArt (page 961)
- Arrange objects (page 975)

Chapter 4

- Insert and modify a picture (page 1015)
- Use the Internet as a resource (page 1021)
- Add sound (page 1046)
- Record and play narration (page 1048)

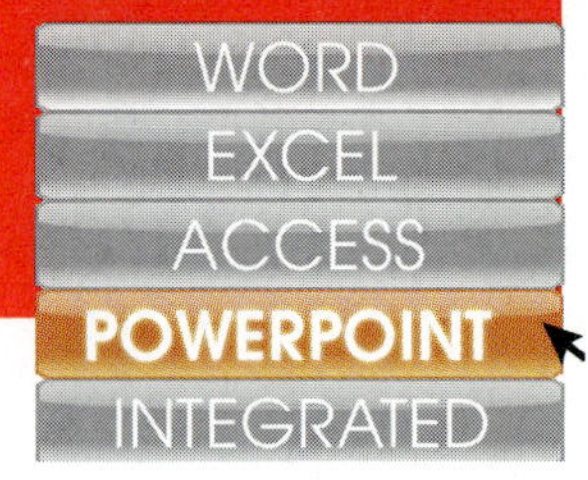

You work for Carl Bekofske, the Standing Chapter 13 Trustee for Genesee County, Michigan. He has asked you to prepare a PowerPoint presentation to explain the basics of bankruptcy to new clients prior to their first conference with him. The presentation will be based on materials he uses at his group meeting and will include narration. Use the original outline from the National Association of Chapter 13 Trustees (NACTT) to prepare this presentation.

Import an Existing Outline

The basic outline has been prepared for you in Microsoft Office Word by an office assistant. You insert the outline into a blank presentation.

- Open a blank PowerPoint presentation and save it as **exp07_p_leg_cpt_bankruptcy_solution**.
- Insert the outline *exp07_p_leg_cpt_basics.rtf* to create the basic structure of the bankruptcy presentation.
- View the slide show in full-screen mode to become familiar with the content. While reading, check the bullet points to see if they are parallel.

Modify an Outline

Presentation text is easily modified in the Outline view. Use the Outline view to edit the text you imported.

- Switch from Slides view to Outline view.
- In Slide 2, Chapter 7 and Chapter 12 have their characteristics listed as part of the 1st-level bullet, whereas the other two types of bankruptcy have their characteristics listed as 2nd-level bullets. Modify the outline so the characteristics for Chapter 7 and Chapter 12 are listed as 2nd-level bullets. Remove italics and correct punctuation.
- In Slide 3, the fourth bullet beginning with *You* does not follow parallel construction. Edit the bullet so it reads **Property may not be lost**.
- In Slide 7, two types of payments are listed with details separated from the payment plan by a hyphen. Remove the hyphens and change the detail information to 2nd-level bullets.

Apply the Design and Color Themes

Apply the basic design and color themes so you can verify the format of the slides as you work.

- Apply the Verve design theme.
- Select the Civic color theme.

Create the Title Slide

The outline did not provide a title slide for you, so you create your own on the blank slide at the beginning of the presentation.

- Format the background of Slide 1 using a picture fill. Use the keyword **burdens** and search all media file types. Then insert the first clip art image (credit cards forming a dollar sign).
- Delete the Title placeholder.
- Create the slide title using WordArt. Choose the **Gradient Fill–Accent 6, Inner Shadow style** (2nd column, 4th row).
- Type the title **BANKRUPTCY BASICS**. Change the font size to **66** pts and add shadowing. Center the Title placeholder to the slide.
- Apply a Bevel text effect using the Soft Round option in the *Bevel* section (2nd column, 2nd row).
- Change the WordArt placeholder shape fill to a complimentary color that shows up well against the graphic.
- Type **Introductory Information for Clients and Their Loved Ones** in the Subtitle placeholder. Change the font size to **bold**, **36** pts.
- Middle align the text in the placeholder.
- Apply the **Colored Outline–Accent 1** Quick Style (2nd column, 1st row).
- Center align the text in the box.

Create a Closing Slide from Existing Content

Because the majority of presentations prepared for your legal office end with contact information for the attorney, the slide has been created and saved for reuse in any presentation. Create the final slide of this bankruptcy presentation by reusing the existing contact information slide.

- Move to the last slide of the presentation, and then add a new slide reusing the *exp07_p_leg_cpt_contact* slide.
- Change the text size in the title placeholder to **40** pts.
- Use the keyword **j0222015.wmf** to locate the orange dollar sign clip art image in the Microsoft Clip Art Gallery. Insert the clip into the closing slide.
- Position the clip 1" horizontally and 5" vertically from the top-left corner.
- Modify the clip art image by changing the color of the circle surrounding the dollar sign symbol to the theme color **Red, Accent 1**. Leave the shape to the left of the circle orange. After modifying the clip, regroup the shapes.

...continued on Next Page

Insert Headers and Footers for Slides and Handouts

Create an identifying footer for the slides, and then create a header and footer for a handout to be given to the clients.

- Add a slide footer that displays on all slides but the title slide. Include the following elements:
  - An automatically updating date.
  - Slide numbers.
  - Footer text of **Bankruptcy Basics**.
- Create a Notes and Handouts header with the following elements:
  - An automatically updating date.
  - Header text of **Bankruptcy Basics—Carl Bekofske**.
  - Page numbers.

Convert Text to SmartArt

To relieve the tedium of slide after slide of bullets, often referred to as "death by PowerPoint," bulleted text can be converted to SmartArt.

- Move to Slide 2 and select the text in the Content placeholder. Because this is a list of different types of bankruptcies, convert the text to a Horizontal Bullet List.
- Resize the SmartArt to a height of **5.5"** and center it horizontally on the slide.
- Move to Slide 6. Convert the text to a Basic Chevron Process to show a progression of sorts.
- Resize the SmartArt to a width of **10"** and center it horizontally on the slide.
- Move to Slide 7. Convert the list of payments to a Vertical Picture List. Modify the SmartArt by changing the font size for the 1st level bullets to **32** pts. Change the font size for the 2nd level bullets to **24** pts.
- Resize the SmartArt to a height of **4.5"** and a width of **8"**. Center the SmartArt horizontally on the slide.

Add a Slide

It would be useful to show some statistics of the number of bankruptcy cases in Michigan.

- Create a new slide after Slide 7 using the Title and Content layout.
- Create a table with 6 columns and 7 rows.
- Go to the Web site http://www.mieb.uscourts.gov/. Choose **Court Statistics** from the menu bar on the left side of the Web page.
- Choose the newest year's statistics from the list at the bottom of the chart.
- Copy the title row and the statistics for January through June to the clipboard, and then populate the table you created with the data in the clipboard.
- Type the title **200x Bankruptcy Statistics** where *x* is the year you chose. Bold the title.

Insert and Modify Pictures

To stimulate your client's visual interest in the presentation, you add a picture and then apply a picture style to modify it. You also add pictures to one of the SmartArt diagrams you inserted earlier. While all three images are Microsoft Office images, the two images used in the SmartArt have been saved as pictures for use in the Picture placeholders.

- On Slide 3, *2008 Bankruptcy Statistics*, insert a clip art image of your choice using the keyword **worry**. Apply the Bevel Perspective picture style. Position the image on the bottom right of your slide, and then size it appropriately so it does not block any statistical information in the table.
- On Slide 8, insert *exp07_p_leg_cpt_trustee.jpg* in the Planned Payment picture placeholder. Insert *exp07_p_leg_cpt_direct.jpg* in the Direct Picture placeholder.

Add Animation

To add visual excitement to the presentation you decide to animate the pictures, SmartArt, and bullet points.

- Set the SmartArt object on Slide 2 to the Fade, One-by-one animation scheme. Modify the animation so that the animations start after previous instead of on click.
- Apply the Curve Up animation (Entrance category, *Exciting* section) to the picture in Slide 3. Animate the picture to start automatically after the table appears.
- Animate the SmartArt on Slide 7 so that it wipes left at a very slow speed. Use the After Previous setting to start the Smart Art animation.

Reorder Slides and Apply Transitions

After creating the content of a presentation, it is a good idea to review the order of the presentation in the Slide Sorter view. This allows you to check the continuity of the presentation. Then while in Slide Sorter view, you can easily set transitions for multiple slides.

- Switch to the Slide Sorter view. Adjust the Zoom level to a level where you can read the slide titles.
- Move Slide 8, *200x Bankruptcy Statistics*, after Slide 2, *Types of Bankruptcy*.
- Select Slides 4, 5, 6, and 9, the four bulleted slides. Apply the Wipe Down transition, medium speed.
- Select Slides 2, 3, 7, and 8, the three SmartArt and the table slides. Apply the Wipe Right transition, medium speed.
- Select Slides 1 and 10, the two slides using the Title Slide layout. Apply the Fade Through Black transition, fast speed.
- Switch to Slide Show view and navigate through the slide show, proofreading it.

Insert Speaker Notes and Narration

The office assistant who created the outline for this presentation also created notes and narration files for your use. She converted the original .wav sound files to the MP3 file format so that the file size would be smaller. Insert the notes and the MP3 sound files into your presentation. (As an option, if your lab is set up for sound recording, you could use the notes as a script and record your own narration.

...continued on Next Page

Review pages 1048 through 1050 for tips on recording and playing a narration if you select this option.)

- Switch to *Notes Page* view.
- Open *exp07_p_leg_cpt_notes.docx*. Copy and paste each slide's individual narration into the Notes section of its corresponding slide in your PowerPoint presentation.
- Insert *exp07_p_leg_cpt_narr01.mp3* in Slide 1 and set the sound file to play automatically.
- Position the sound icon at the top right of the slide, and then change the sound options to hide the sound icon during the slide show.
- Repeat the above two steps for each slide until the associated narrative sound file is inserted in its corresponding slide (i.e., *exp07_p_leg_cpt_narr02.mp3* in Slide 2, *exp07_p_leg_cpt_narr03.mp3* in Slide 3, etc.).

Set Automatic Timings

You decide to create the presentation as a self-running presentation using automatic timings so the client can concentrate on the content rather than advancing slide by slide. You also allow slides to be advanced by clicks so clients can quickly move past content they are familiar with. As an option, your instructor might wish for you to use Help to research the topic "Rehearse and time the delivery of a presentation" and then ask you to use the Rehearse Timings feature to set slide timing.

- Use the Advance Slide options in the Animations tab to advance the slides automatically using the following table to determine the number of seconds each slide should display. Allow the slides to advance on a mouse click if desired.

Slide 1	23 seconds	Slide 6	18 seconds
Slide 2	37 seconds	Slide 7	27 seconds
Slide 3	22 seconds	Slide 8	21 seconds
Slide 4	31 seconds	Slide 9	25 seconds
Slide 5	48 seconds	Slide 10	07 seconds

- Check your automatic timings in *Slide Sorter* view for accuracy and edit as necessary.

Set Up the Slide Show for Presentation

Because the presentation now includes automatic timings, you need to set the slide show options. You decide to set up the slide show to display with kiosk settings so it will restart automatically if the client wishes to see it additional times.

- Set the slide show using the show type *Browsed at a kiosk*.
- Advance the slides using timings.
- Leave all other default settings.

Review the Slide Show and Print a Notes Page

Before showing the presentation to the Attorney and Clients, you review it to ensure it plays correctly. Also, because you might have hearing-impaired clients in the office, prepare a print version of the slides for a person to read.

- Play the slide show to make sure it plays correctly. If there are problems, troubleshoot to correct errors.
- Print a Notes Page version of the slides.

Integrate Microsoft Office Software

Background

In addition to working with individual software programs, many opportunities exist in the law office to integrate the various applications. As the skills of the paralegal or office assistant increase, more opportunities for integration will become apparent. In many cases, the paralegal will be the one to recognize the opportunity for integration.

Tasks

Many integration projects are available between the various programs. Microsoft Office Word will frequently be the host program for the result, although Microsoft Office PowerPoint is often the host for trial exhibits. Both Microsoft Office Excel and Microsoft Office Access are good programs for creating a variety of data files to be merged and for storing data. In addition, Excel's ability to create charts from spreadsheet data could be particularly applicable in tax, probate, real estate, and trial work. Examples of law office tasks could include the following:

- Create merged documents (letters, labels, predesigned forms, pleadings, estate planning documents, etc.) from data in Excel or Access
- Embed or link Excel spreadsheets or charts into Word documents or PowerPoint slides
- Create PowerPoint presentations with various linked or embedded objects from Word and Excel

Skills

In addition to skills in each application program, a paralegal should be able to do the following:

- Embed and link objects
- Use Help to research unfamiliar features
- Apply knowledge gained from Help research to accomplish new tasks
- Merge data/fields into a source file
- Choose records or fields to merge

Paralegal
Volume 1 | Capstone Exercises

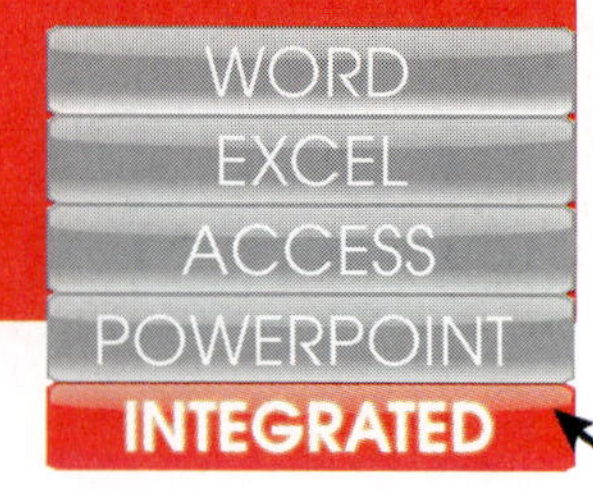

Your attorney, Donna DeWitt, has decided to run for the Family Court judicial vacancy. She will depend on you, her trusted paralegal, to prepare many of the promotional materials. You start thinking about how to integrate the various Microsoft Office software programs to produce a professional product for her.

Before starting, you decide to make a call to the Genesee County Bar Association to speak with Ms. Ramona Sain, the Executive Director. Knowing that she has many good ideas, as well as experience with several previous judicial candidates, you ask her for suggestions on what to include in the publicity announcements. She suggests that you create a database of names of possible supporters, starting with local attorneys (she can provide you with a list). Send the attorneys a personalized letter indicating that Donna is running, outlining her qualifications and including the results of the candidate survey. Ms. Sain also will provide the survey results to you. In addition to the personalized letter and survey, she suggests preparing a flyer that can be printed and distributed in various sizes. With those excellent ideas in mind, you prepare the promotional materials.

Use Help to Research Mail Merge

Ms. Sain recommended you merge a letter created with Word with a recipient list stored as an Access database. You are unfamiliar with the process, so you use Help to learn more about it.

- Use Help to search for information about conducting a mail merge.
- View the Help training exercise "Mail merge I: Use mail merge for mass mailings." Note the following terms: data source file (recipient list), main document (letter), and merge fields (placeholders).

Create a Database of Recipient Names

Ms. Sain has provided you with an Excel spreadsheet that includes the names of attorneys in the area who should be recipients of the letter announcing Donna's candidacy. (Note: For ease of use, there are only 24 names in the spreadsheet right now. The actual database of names would include many more names.) Later, you will add names of other groups and individuals, as well as add database fields to track individuals' donations or volunteer services. Right now, however, you just need the names.

- Open a new, blank Access database. Name it **exp07_i_leg_cpt_contacts_solution.accdb**.
- Import external data from the Excel spreadsheet, *exp07_i _leg_cpt_contacts.xlsx*. Complete the wizard, taking only information from Sheet 1. Indicate that the first row contains column headings. All of the fields are of type text. Let Access add the Primary key. Call the table **Contacts**. Do not save the import steps.
- Save and close the Access database.

Create a Merge Letter to Send to the Contacts

Ms. Sain indicated the first step in the campaign will be to send a letter to all attorneys thanking them for their ratings and enlisting their support. You complete the formatting of a pretyped document to serve as the main document in the merge process. You modify the format so that it fits on one page, making it possible to mail in a window envelope. Format the letter now; later, you insert a chart before completing the merge.

- Open the *exp07_i_leg_cpt_letter.docx* file. Save it as **exp07_i_leg_cpt_letter_solution.docx**.
- From the Mailings tab, start a Letters mail merge using the open letter.
- Select recipients from the *exp07_i_leg_cpt_contacts_solution.accdb* database.
- At the top of the Word document enter the following return address:

  Committee for the Election of Donna DeWitt

  PO Box 12345

  Flint, MI 48501-1234

- Enter the following e-mail address at the right margin of the *city, state, zip* line: **donnadewittforjudge@yahoo.com.**
- Apply the Metro theme to the document.
- Set *Committee for the Election of Donna DeWitt* as **WordArt Style 8** (2nd column, 2nd item). Use the default font, but make it **bold** and size it to **16** points. Center the WordArt, and then add a blank line before the first address line.
- Insert a blank line below the e-mail address and insert the date **Month, Day, Year**. Do not update automatically.
- Insert a blank line, and then insert the merge field that would create an address block using the default form of *Mr. Joshua Randall Jr.* for the recipient name. Include the three other default choices: insert company name, insert postal address, and format address.
- Insert another blank line, and then add subject line, **RE: Peer Candidate Ratings**.
- Insert an extra blank line, and then add a merge field to insert a greeting line using the format of *Dear Mr. Randall*. Use a colon after the greeting line for a formal business letter.
- Save and close the file for now. You will use it again later.

...continued on Next Page

Format the Approval Rating Spreadsheet

Ms. Sain provided you with an Excel file displaying the approval rating statistics for your attorney. Format the spreadsheet and prepare a chart depicting her ratings.

- Open the Excel file *exp07_i_leg_cpt_responses.xlsx* and save it as **exp07_i_leg_cpt_responses_solution.xlsx**.
- Merge and center the heading across columns A–I. Increase the font size to **14** and add bolding.
- Wrap the text of the column headings on columns B–H into two or three lines, as appropriate.
- Retain the same font size, but add bold to each column heading. Proofread the headings to ensure consistent title capitalization.
- Apply the same theme to the spreadsheet that you applied to the letter *Metro*.
- Format column A, Respondent #, as Text.

Add Statistics to the Approval Rating Spreadsheet

With the basic formatting in place, add statistics to the spreadsheet. Calculate averages by question and averages by person. Also calculate a final average score for the candidate. The final average score will be published in the promotional materials.

- Add the column heading **Average Rating by Person** in **cell I2**. Use Format Painter to apply the formatting from the previous column headings to the new column heading.
- Insert a formula that computes the average rating by person in **cell I3** and copy the formula to compute the rating for each respondent in the survey. Display the results to one decimal point. (Note: If Excel prompts you that adjacent cells are not part of the formula, ignore the error.)
- Insert a formula in row 138 averaging each column with respondent's ratings. Display the results to one decimal point.
- Add the row title **Averages** to row 138, and then bold the title and results in the row.
- Figure the overall average score for the candidate in **cell I138**.
- Format **cells B2:I138** as a table, and then apply the Table Style Medium 20 style. Apply banding to the last column.
- Change the column width of columns A–I to attractively accommodate the columns.
- Remove the filters from the column headings.

Create a Chart of Approval Ratings

A visual depiction of the approval ratings will be easier for most people to understand. Use the average ratings for each characteristic to format a chart for inclusion on promotional materials.

- Select the headings and averages: **cell B2:H2** and **cell B138:H138**.
- Insert a clustered 2-D bar chart.
- Approximately center the chart below the spreadsheet and size it to **3"** high by **6"** wide.
- Choose **Quick Layout #1**.
- Change the title to **Donna DeWitt, Peer Approval Ratings**.
- Change the chart title font to **12** pts.
- If necessary, switch the Row/Column data to display the category titles.
- Delete the legend.
- Apply Chart Style 7.
- Format the horizontal axis value (in Format Axis). Fix (set) the axis values: *minimum* = **0**, *maximum* = **9**, *major unit* = **5**.
- Change the properties of the numbers on the x-axis to be whole numbers (zero decimal places).
- Add an x-axis label of **Average Points, Scale of 1-9**.
- Add data labels to *Outside End*, and then remove the display of the primary horizontal axis.

Insert the Chart into the Letter

Copy the chart and paste it into the prepared letter.

- Copy the chart in the *exp07_i_leg_cpt_responses_solution.xlsx* document. Save and close the document.
- Open the Word file *exp07_i_leg_cpt_letter_solution.docx*.
- Embed the chart of approval ratings between the first and second paragraphs.
- Scale the chart proportionally to 75% of original size. Center the chart horizontally.
- Adjust the letter as necessary to fit on a single page.
- Your final letter should look like the following figure.

...continued on Next Page

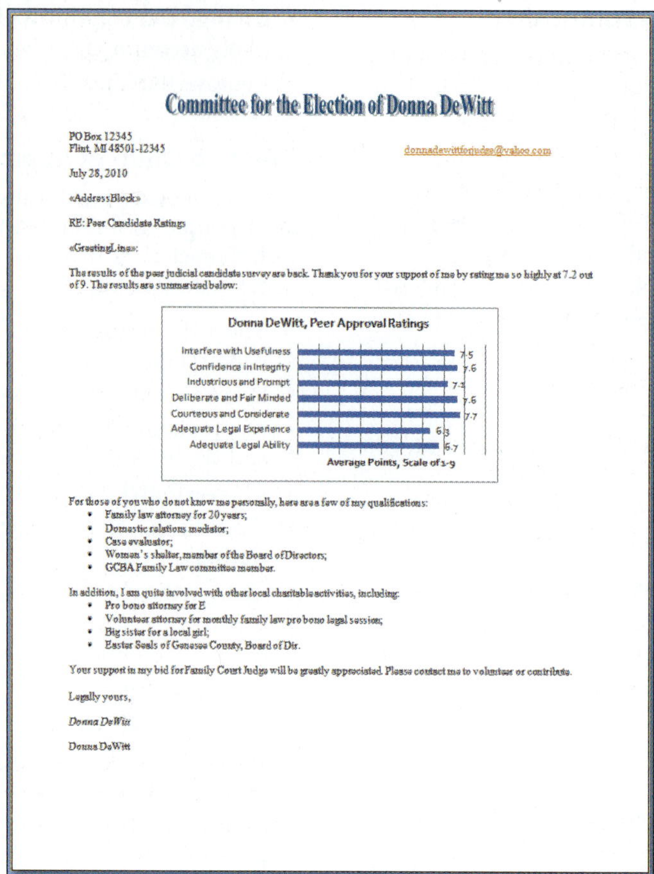

Committee for the Election of Donna DeWitt

PO Box 12345
Flint, MI 48501-12345

donnadewittforjudge@yahoo.com

July 28, 2010

«AddressBlock»

RE: Peer Candidate Ratings

«GreetingLine»:

The results of the peer judicial candidate survey are back. Thank you for your support of me by rating me so highly at 7.2 out of 9. The results are summarized below:

For those of you who do not know me personally, here are a few of my qualifications:

- Family law attorney for 20 years;
- Domestic relations mediator;
- Case evaluator;
- Women's shelter, member of the Board of Directors;
- GCBA Family Law committee member.

In addition, I am quite involved with other local charitable activities, including:

- Pro bono attorney for E
- Volunteer attorney for monthly family law pro bono legal session;
- Big sister for a local girl;
- Easter Seals of Genesee County, Board of Dir.

Your support in my bid for Family Court Judge will be greatly appreciated. Please contact me to volunteer or contribute.

Legally yours,

Donna DeWitt

Donna DeWitt

Complete the Merge

After completing the main document and the data source file, you are ready to complete the merge process.

- Using the Mailings tab, preview the results of the merge to ensure the letter fits on one page once the address block and other merge fields are inserted. Make any necessary adjustments to the letter.
- Finish and merge the main document and the data source file. Do not print the documents (there will be 24 letters). Save the merged letters as **exp07_i_leg_cpt_merge_solution**.
- Print the original letter with merge fields as directed by your instructor.
- Save the *exp07_i_leg_cpt_letter_solution* and close.

Create a Flyer in PowerPoint

You need a simple flyer that can be distributed around the city. Although simple, it should be attractive. It should outline your attorney's major qualifications. As Donna's support increases, you will hire a public relations firm to handle publicity.

- Open a new PowerPoint presentation. Save as **exp07_i_leg_cpt_flyer_solution.pptx**.
- Change the layout of Slide 1 to **Title Only**, and then change the page orientation to **Portrait**.
- Select the **Concourse** theme, and then change the color scheme to **Median** to match the colors used in your campaign letter and the approval rating spreadsheet.
- Set the background to **Background Style 1**.
- Create the following two-line main title:

  Donna DeWitt

  for Family Court Judge

- Center the title. Change the font color to **Ice Blue, Accent 1, Darker 50%**.
- Change the font of the title placeholder text to **Calibri**.
- Increase the font size of the text *Donna DeWitt* to fill the width of the title placeholder.
- Change the font size of the remainder of the title to be as wide as the line *Donna DeWitt* above.
- Select the title placeholder and apply a Quick Style of **Subtle Effect – Accent 1**.
- With the placeholder still selected, apply a shape effect of Glow, Accent color 1, 11 pt glow.
- Resize the title placeholder to a height of **2"**.
- Insert a Target List SmartArt. Add the following text, adding an extra shape when needed:
  - **Family law attorney, 20 years**
  - **Domestic relations mediator**
  - **Case evaluator**
  - **Women's Shelter, Board of Directors**
- Resize the SmartArt to **4.5"** wide. Position it so that the right edge of the SmartArt aligns with the right edge of the Title placeholder and so the top of the SmartArt is approximately 0.5" below the bottom edge of the Title placeholder.

...continued on Next Page

- Apply the White Outline SmartArt style.
- Locate and insert the picture *exp07_i_leg_cpt_dewitt.jpg*.
- Resize the picture to **3.5"** high.
- Visually align the picture with the left edge of the Title placeholder, and then use the Align feature to align it with the top edge of the SmartArt placeholder.
- Send the picture to the back so the SmartArt is overlapping it.
- Apply the Metal Oval picture style.
- Copy the *Donna DeWitt, Peer Approval Ratings* chart from the *exp07_i_leg_cpt_responses_solution.xlsx* spreadsheet, and then paste it on the slide.
- Resize the chart to **3"** high by **6"** wide. Center align the chart to the slide, and then vertically position the chart at the bottom of the slide, being careful not to let the text of the chart block the decorative edge of the theme.
- Change the shape fill of the series bars to **Ice Blue, Accent 1, Darker 50%**.
- Insert a text box at the bottom right of the flyer. Change the font size to **11** pts and the font color to **black**. Enter the following text:

  Committee for the Election of Donna DeWitt

  PO Box 12345

  Flint, MI 48501-12345

  donnadewittforjudge@yahoo.com
- Save the *exp07_i_leg_cpt_flyer_solution* and close.
- The final flyer should look like the following figure.

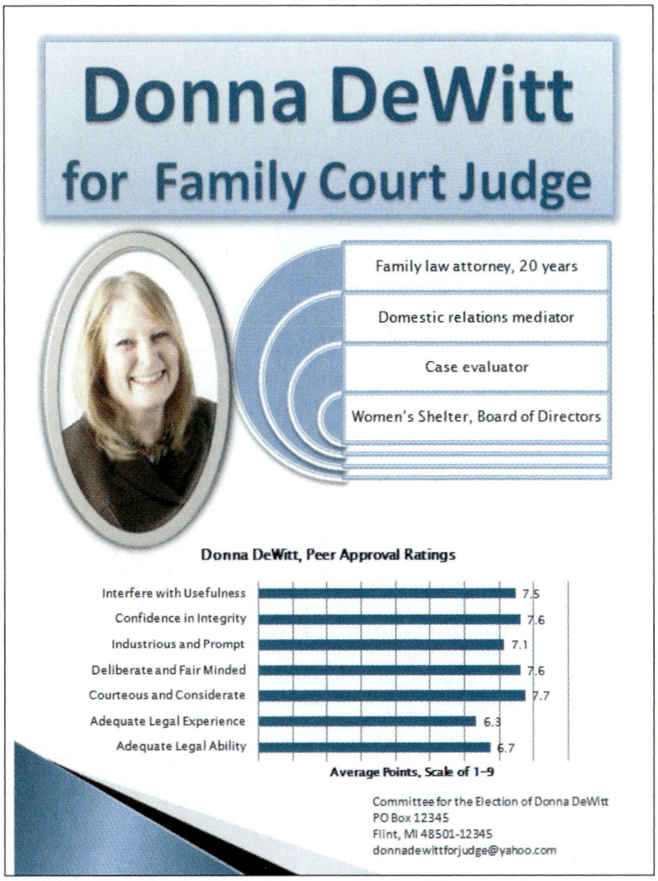

Create a Running PowerPoint Slide Show

Your attorney, Donna, is planning to have an election table at the Genesee County Fair. She asked you to make up a short PowerPoint slide presentation to run unattended at the Fair. Because of the noisy, outdoor environment, you do not use sound, but you insert animations on each slide to catch the attention of people passing by. Use the PowerPoint flyer and reconfigure it run as a short kiosk presentation.

- Save the existing flyer as **exp07_i_leg_cpt_fair_solution.pptx**.
- Change the slide orientation to Landscape, and then make three duplicates of the existing slide.
- In Slide 1, change the layout to the Title Slide layout. Delete the SmartArt, the chart, the text box, and the subtitle placeholder. Arrange the title placeholder and the picture attractively on the slide.
- Reset the picture, and then apply the Beveled Oval, Black picture style. Use the animation effect you desire on Donna DeWitt's picture, but set the animation to After Previous.
- In Slide 2, change the layout to the Blank layout. Delete the chart, the photograph, and the text box.
- Change the title placeholder text to **Qualifications**.
- Resize the SmartArt to fill the slide appropriately, and then position it attractively on the slide. Animate the SmartArt so each line fades in one by one at a medium speed.
- In Slide 3, change the layout to the Blank layout and remove all but the title placeholder and the chart.
- Change the title placeholder text to **Peer Approval Ratings**, and size it to fit on one line. Remove the chart title.
- Change the chart height to **5"** and the chart width to **8"**. Position the chart attractively on the slide. Modify the vertical axis text to **18** pts and the horizontal axis text to **12** pts.
- Animate the chart so category information wipes from the left one by one. Set the animation to start After Previous.
- Use the Title Slide layout in Slide 4, and delete the SmartArt, the chart, the picture, and the subtitle placeholder. Replace the title placeholder text with the following text:

  Vote for

  Donna DeWitt,

  Family Court Judge,

  November 6th
- Format the placeholder's text effects to resize the shape to fit the text. Position the placeholder so it is above the decorative theme design at the bottom of the slide, and center it horizontally on the slide.
- Change to the Colored Outline – Accent 1 shape style.
- Position the text box in the bottom left of the slide in the blue design element.
- From the Clip Art Gallery, insert the picture of the businesswoman that has the thumbs-up gesture in focus

...continued on Next Page

with the woman out of focus. Crop the woman's face out of the picture so only the thumb and hand remain. Position the picture at an attractive location in the bottom right of the slide.

- Apply the Light Speed entrance animation to the picture and have it animate After Previous.
- Apply the Push Down transition to all slides and advance slides automatically after 6 seconds.
- Set up the slide show to be browsed at a kiosk using automatic timings.
- Save and close the *exp07_i_leg_cpt_fair_solution* slide show.
- The final slide show should look like the following figure.

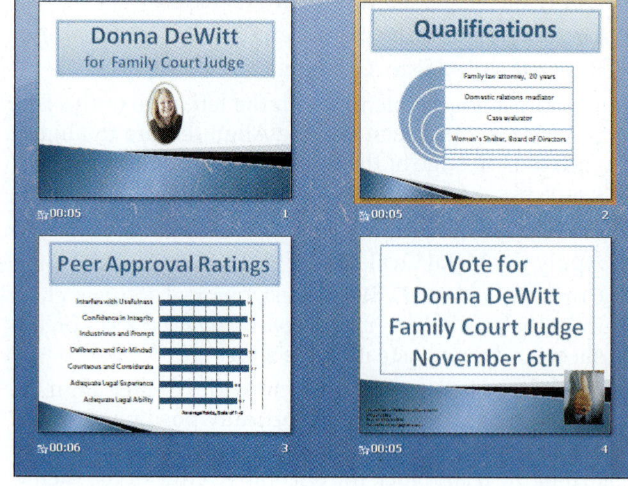

Medical Office Assistants

Use Microsoft Office Word

Background

Medical office assistants work in hospitals, clinics, and physician offices and are responsible for the administrative functions of the office. They use word processing software on a daily basis to create a wide variety of documents for physicians and patients. They transcribe dictation, prepare correspondence, and assist physicians with reports. Some documents they might develop include medical histories, patient invoices, order forms, and medical information pamphlets. It is imperative that medical office assistants understand the features of Microsoft Office Word and be comfortable using those features. The following word processing skills taught in the textbook are skills crucial to people employed in a medical office.

Tasks

Medical office assistants may be responsible for all kinds of document production. Such documents could include the following:

- Correspondence and mailing
  - Patient test results
  - Student health records
  - Medical histories
  - Memoranda and faxes
- Forms and reports
  - Patient information forms
  - Patient invoices
  - Patient schedules
  - Insurance forms
  - Lab reports
  - Purchase orders
- Brochures and pamphlets
  - Medical information brochures and pamphlets regarding health, diseases, and medicine

Skills

In addition to basic formatting skills, medical office assistants should be able to do the following:

Chapter 1

- Use AutoText (page 76)
- View a document (page 78)
- Use the Mini Toolbar (page 80)

...continued on Next Page

- Set margins and specify page orientation (page 87)
- Insert page breaks (page 88)
- Add page numbers (page 90)
- Insert headers and footers (page 91)
- Create sections (page 92)
- Insert a cover page (page 93)
- Use the Find and Replace commands (page 94)
- Check spelling and grammar (page 103)
- Use save and backup options (page 104)
- Select printing options (page 107)

Chapter 2

- Apply font attributes through the font dialog box (page 133)
- Highlight text (page 136)
- Control word wrapping with nonbreaking hyphens and nonbreaking spaces (page 137)
- Copy formats with the Format Painter (page 139)
- Set off paragraphs with tabs, borders, lists, and columns (page 143)
- Apply paragraph formats (page 148)
- Create and modify styles (page 159)
- Create a table of contents (page 171)

Chapter 3

- Insert a table (page 197)
- Format a table (page 205)
- Convert text to a table (page 210)
- Insert clip art and images into a document (page 219)
- Format a graphic element (page 220)
- Insert WordArt into a document (page 225)
- Insert symbols into a document (page 226)

Chapter 4

- Insert comments into a document (page 251)
- Track changes in a document (page 254)
- View documents side by side (page 263)
- Compare and combine documents (page 264)
- Use navigation tools (page 267)
- Create a bibliography (page 279)
- Create and modify footnotes and endnotes (page 281)
- Add figure references (page 287)
- Insert a table of figures (page 288)
- Modify document properties (page 290)

Medical Office Assistants
Volume 1 | Capstone Exercise

You work as a medical office assistant at a family practice. Your supervisor asked you to create a document about the vaccination program available to patients. You have been provided some of the text. Prepare the document so it has a friendly yet professional appearance. Include formatting, graphic elements, tables, and reference components.

Create AutoText

You often use the name of the practice, Hilltop Family Practice, in documents. Create an AutoText entry for this name. Save the entry to the Quick Part Gallery so that it is included in the Building Blocks library. (Note: AutoText is added to the Normal template. If you are in a lab environment, you might not have permission to add this name and save it to the Normal template. If this is the case, skip this step. When asked to insert the AutoText in instructions for this capstone, type the name of the family practice.)

- Type the text **Hilltop Family Practice** in a new blank document.
- Insert and save the text into the Quick Part Gallery as AutoText using **htfp** as the name.
- Close the document without saving.

Set Initial Document Formats

To ensure the vaccination guide is easy and appealing to read, you apply a larger, casual typeface and double-space the document.

- Open the *exp07_w_med_cpt_vaccinations* document and save it as **exp07_w_med_cpt_vaccinations_solution**.
- Set the top, bottom, left, and right margins to **1"**.
- Set the line spacing to double for the entire document.
- Apply **Comic Sans MS**, **14 pt**, to the entire document.
- Set the paragraph Line Spacing Options to apply 6 pt spacing before paragraphs for the entire document.

Insert a Cover Page and Change the Theme Color

You decide to insert one of Word's preformatted cover pages and then personalize the fields with your document title and physician's name.

- At the beginning of the document, insert a cover page using the Pinstripes cover page design.
- Change the document theme to Verve.
- Delete the page break at the bottom of the cover page, and then insert a Section Break (Next Page) at the same location.
- Change the document title from *DTP Vaccine* to **A Guide to Vaccinations**. Change the font to **Comic Sans MS, bold**.
- Type **For Infants, Children, and Adolescents** as the subtitle.
- Change the date to today's date.
- Change the company name to **Hilltop Family Practice** using your AutoText entry.
- Change the author's name from *Preferred Customer* to **Dr. Peter Mangas**.

Insert and Format Clip Art, WordArt, and a Symbol

Your physician, Dr. Mangas, asked that the document be very colorful and eye-catching, so you add a "colorful" image to the cover page to make it more interesting. You decide that adding WordArt also would add interest. You insert a "smiley" symbol to welcome readers to the Hilltop Family Practice immunization program.

- Insert a blank line after the physician's name, and then insert the following clip art using the following options:

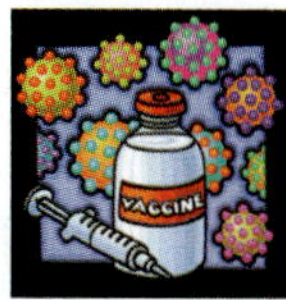

  - Search for: **vaccines**
  - Search in: **All collections**
  - Results should be: **Clip Art**
- Scale the height to **120%**.
- Set text wrapping to **Top and Bottom**.
- Align Center the clip art image.
- Position the point of insertion immediately before the section break, and then insert WordArt.
- Use WordArt Style 8 to insert the text **For more information contact Dr. Peter Mangas at (708) 555-4959.** Create the WordArt as two lines with the physician's name and phone number on the second line. Set the font to **Comic Sans MS, 14 pt**.
- Change the WordArt size to **.5"** high by **6"** wide.
- On the second page, move the point of insertion to the end of the sentence reading *Welcome to the Hilltop Family Practice immunization program*. Insert the **Wingdings:74** symbol (the smiley face). Change the symbol size to **36 pt**, and change the font color to **Pink, Accent 2**.

Add a Footer

You want page numbers to appear on every page in the document because you plan on inserting a Table of Contents. You also want the medical practice name to appear

...continued on Next Page

on every page. Add a footer to the document to accomplish both of these tasks.

- Insert a footer using the Pinstripes style. The Pinstripes style automatically includes text on the left margin and the page number on the right margin.
- Use AutoText to insert **Hilltop Family Practice** into the *Type text* field.
- Format the footer using **Comic Sans MS**, **12 pt**.

Create Sections and Apply Styles

The body of the document includes three distinct topics with information in each topic broken up as subtopics. You create sections, and then format the titles and headings in each section using existing styles.

- Apply the Title style to the title of the first section, *Immunization Basics*.
- Use Find to locate the text, *Recommended Vaccinations*, and then insert a Section Break (Next Page) at the beginning of the text. Apply the Title style to the section heading *Recommended Vaccinations*.
- Use Find to locate the text, *Suggested Schedules*, and then insert a Section Break (Next Page) at the beginning of the text. Apply the Title style to the section heading *Suggested Schedules*.
- Apply the Subtitle style to the following text in the document (use only heading text on individual lines—do not use text within paragraphs):
  - *What is a vaccine?*
  - *Are vaccines safe for my child?*
  - *What side effects could my child experience?*
  - *When should my child be vaccinated?*
  - *HBV (Hepatitis B Vaccine)*
  - *PCV (Pneumococcal Conjugate Vaccine)*
  - *DTaP (Diptheria, Tetanus, Acellular Pertussis)*
  - *Hib (Menigitis)*
  - *Influenza*
  - *MMR Vaccine*
  - *Vericella (Chickenpox)*
  - *MCV4 (Bacterial Meningitis)*
  - *Hepatitis A*
- Apply the Heading 1 style to the following text in the document (use only heading text on individual lines—do not use text within paragraphs):
  - *Diphtheria*
  - *Pertussis*
  - *Tetanus*
  - *Measles*
  - *Mumps*
  - *Rubella*

Modify Styles

After reviewing the styles you applied, you decide to modify them so the headings reflect the casual friendly "feel" that you used on the cover page. Also, because the document includes short paragraphs with subtitles and headings, you format paragraphs to control widows and orphans. Modify the styles to include the following specifications:

- Modify the Title style to use **Comic Sans MS**; **bold**; **Blue, Accent 5**. Apply Align center.
- Modify the Subtitle style to use **Comic Sans MS**; **bold**; **italic**; **16 pt**; **Pink, Accent 2**. Apply Align left. Adjust the paragraph spacing to **12 pt** before and **6 pt** after. Change paragraph settings to activate Widow/Orphan control, Keep with next, and Keep lines together.
- Modify the Heading 1 style to use **Comic Sans MS**; **bold**; **14 pt**; **Blue, Accent 5**. Adjust the paragraph spacing to **6 pt** before and **6 pt** after.

Use Find and Replace Commands

With the Show/Hide feature active to check spacing of headings, you note that in several locations there are two or three spaces between words and after periods instead of the correct single space. While scanning, you also decide that the title of one of the sections needs to be changed.

- Move to the top of the document and turn on the Show/Hide feature, if you have not already done so.
- Search for *Suggested Schedules* and replace it with **Immunization Schedules**.
- Use the Replace feature to locate all occurrences or two or three spaces and replace with one space. Replace all.

Format a Quote and a Create a Footnote

You quoted a respected authority in the introduction to the document. You format the quote using an appropriate format, and then you insert the authoring information in a footnote on the first page.

- Locate and select the quote regarding children in the United States (the second paragraph in the *Immunization Basics* section).
- Single space the quote, and then apply a **.5"** left and right indent to the paragraph.
- Italicize the quote using the Mini toolbar.
- Move your insertion point to the end of the quote. Add a footnote using the following information: **Medline Plus, a service of the U.S. National Library of Medicine and the National Institutes of Health (www.nlm.nih.gov/medlineplus/childhoodimmunization.html)**
- Apply **Century Gothic (Body)**, **11 pt** for the footnote font.

Convert Text to a Table and Format Tables

The person who gathered the initial information for this document was unsure how to format the information for the immunization schedule so she formatted one set of information as a table and one set as tabbed columns. You decide the table makes the information much easier to understand. Convert the tabbed immunization information to a table.

- Move to the end of the document. Locate and select all data after the existing table and convert the data to a table. Use three columns and separate text by tabs. (Text begins with *PPV* and ends with *Females only*.)
- Insert two rows at the top of the newly created table.

...continued on Next Page

- In the first new row at the top of the table, merge the cells, and set the alignment to Center. Change the row height to .7". Type the table's title: **Recommended Immunization Schedule for Children 7–18 Years Old**.
- Insert a footnote at the end of the title. Add the footnote text: **Centers for Disease Control and Prevention, 2008**.
- Use the Format Painter to apply the same font to this footnote as you applied to the footnote on Page 1.
- In the blank second row, type the column headings: **Vaccine**, **Age**, and **Comments**.
- Apply the Light List – Accent 5 table style to both tables in Section 3.
- Change the body of the table to a font size of **10 pt**. Do not change the title of the table. Change the line spacing to **single** for both tables in Section 3.
- Modify table format as necessary to ensure that each table appears on a single page.

Prepare the Document for Sharing and Change Document Properties

Before sending the document to your supervisor for her suggestions, you make sure there are no misspellings, and no widows or orphans. You also check the tables to make sure that ages are not displaying improperly. You insert non-breaking spaces to correct the problem.

- Check the spelling of the document and ignore all occurrences of the correct spelling of the physician's name, *Mangas*. Assume all vaccination names and disease names are spelled correctly, but add *pertussis* to the dictionary. Correct all other misspelled words.
- Proofread the document. Not all errors can be identified by using the spelling checker. Correct any errors you identify.
- Change the view to Full Screen Reading and scan the document. Change back to Print Layout view.
- Proofread the tables at the end of the document. Insert a non-breaking space between the age and the words *months* or *years* to ensure they do not separate onto two lines in the cell. Also check all parentheses to make sure they are properly used. Insert any missing parentheses.
- Set the document properties with the following information:
  - The author is **Dr. Peter Mangas**.
  - The title is **A Guide to Vaccinations**.
  - The subject is **Childhood Vaccinations**.
  - Keywords are **Vaccinations, Immunizations, Shots**.
  - Status is **Ready for Review**.

Add Highlighting and Document Comments

You need to get your supervisor's approval for the document. You create a comment asking the supervisor, Sherry Wright, to review the document in general, and two comments asking specific questions. You highlight a section to make it easier for the supervisor to identify the text to which the comment refers.

- Insert the following as a comment at the top of the Cover Page: **Please check the sections and headings to make sure I've covered everything you requested.**
- Highlight the quotation on Page 1, and then add the following comment at the end of the quote: **I added this quote from the National Institutes of Health. Do you approve?**
- Select the section title *Immunization Schedules* and add the following comment: **Are all recommended vaccinations covered?**
- Save and close *exp07_w_med_cpt_vaccinations_solution*.

Review a Document

In addition to the supervisor, the physician's assistant, JM Behle, reviewed the document. Both reviewers added comments to the document, some of which include specific instructions. You review the document using several of the reviewing features in Word to help you evaluate the changes to the document. After reviewing the document, you incorporate the changes in the document and remove all comments and highlighting.

- Open *exp07_w_med_cpt_vaccinations_solution* and *exp07_w_med_cpt_immunizations*.
- View the differences in the two documents using the View Side by Side feature. Close the documents.
- Combine *exp07_w_med_cpt_vaccinations_solution.docx* (the original document) and *exp07_w_med_cpt_immunizations.docx* (the revised document with comments).
- Rather than keep the formatting changes from the original document, keep the formatting in the revised document.
- Save the new document as *exp07_w_med_cpt_immunizations_solution.docx*.
- Remove any duplication caused by the merging of the two documents (i.e., duplicate vaccination images, WordArt, etc.)
- Use the Show Markup feature to check the names of the reviewers. Make sure that your name, as well as *Sherry Wright, Supervisor,* and *JM Behle, Physcian's Assistant,* displays.
- Accept all changes in the document.
- Format immunization additions to match document formatting, update the *Recommended Immunization Schedule for Children 0–6 Years Old* as requested in the comments, and add the footnote reference.
- Remove all comments and highlighting in the document.

Insert Supplemental Components

You create captions for the two tables and then include a table of figures page. Then, you create a table of contents for the document. You feel that not only will this make the document more professional, it will make it easier for a reader to use. After creating the table of contents and reviewing it, you realize that the supplemental components should use roman numerals for page numbers and that the document should start on page 1. You change the format and starting number for page numbers as needed.

- Create captions for each table at the end of the document. Type **Schedule for Children 0–6 Years Old** as the caption for the first table. Type **Schedule for Children 7–18 Years Old** as the caption for the second table.
- Insert a blank page between the cover page and the first page of the document (if necessary).

...continued on Next Page

- At the top of the new page type **Table of Figures** and insert two blank lines. Apply the Title style to the heading.
- Insert a table of figures using all defaults following the heading. Insert a Section Break (Next Page) between the cover page and the table of figures page.
- At the top of the new page type **Table of Contents** and insert two blank lines. Apply the Title style to the heading.
- Insert a table of contents. Change the table of contents Options to modify the Build a table of contents from settings. In the *Available styles* section, set the TOC level for Heading 1 to **3**, Heading 2 to **4**, Subtitle to **2**, and Title to **1**.
- Change the footer page number for the table of contents section to use roman numerals beginning with **i**.
- Change the footer page number for the body of the document (beginning with the *Immunization Basics* section) to use the standard number format beginning with *1*.
- Update the table of contents and the table of figures.
- Format the font for the table of contents and the table of figures to match the rest of the document, and adjust spacing as necessary.

Change the Document Properties and Save Document

- Change the status of your document to **Completed** in Document Properties.
- Print the document if requested by your instructor.
- Save and close the document.

Medical Office Assistants

Use Microsoft Office Excel

Background

Medical office assistants work in hospitals, clinics, and physician offices and are responsible for the administrative functions of the office. Medical office assistants use spreadsheet software on a daily basis. They use spreadsheets to track data, calculate data, make decisions, and create charts. It is imperative that medical office assistants understand the features of Microsoft Office Excel and be comfortable using those features. The following spreadsheet skills taught in the textbook are skills crucial to people employed in a medical office.

Tasks

Medical office assistants may be responsible for creating and maintaining all types of spreadsheets. These types of spreadsheets could include the following:

- Logs
    - Patient logs
    - Referral logs
    - Test results logs
    - Patient medication logs
    - Triage forms
    - Vaccine administration logs
- Patient schedules
- Receipt of payments

Skills

In addition to basic formatting skills, a medical office assistant should be able to do the following:

Chapter 1

- Enter and edit data in cells (page 322)
- Describe and use symbols and the order of precedence (page 328)
- Display cell formulas (page 330)
- Insert and delete rows and columns (page 331)
- Use cell ranges; Excel move; copy, paste, paste special; and AutoFill (page 332)
- Manage worksheets (page 340)
- Format worksheets (page 341)
- Select page setup options for printing (page 353)

...continued on Next Page

Chapter 2

- Create and copy formulas (page 381)
- Use relative and absolute cell addresses (page 382)
- Use AutoSum (page 389)
- Insert basic statistical functions (page 390)
- Use date functions (page 392)
- Use the IF function (page 399)
- Use the VLOOKUP function (page 400)

Chapter 3

- Choose a chart type (page 431)
- Create a chart (page 438)
- Modify a chart (page 450)
- Embed charts (page 459)
- Print charts (page 460)

Chapter 4

- Freeze rows and columns (page 488)
- Hide and unhide rows, columns, and worksheets (page 489)
- Protect a cell, a worksheet, and a workbook (page 490)
- Print large worksheets (page 493)
- Sort data (page 510)
- Filter and total data (page 514)

Medical Office Assistants
Volume 1 | Capstone Exercise

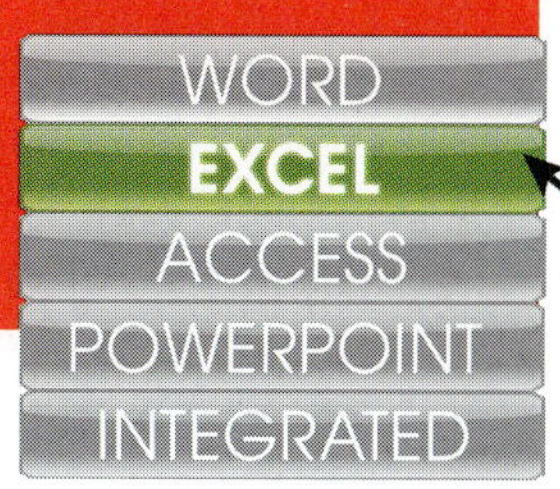

You work as a medical office assistant at the Diabetes Management Clinic at the Orland Medical Center, where patients of all ages receive diabetes specialty care. Your supervisor asked you to create a spreadsheet to log information about patients who come into the clinic for services each day. You keep track of the patient data as well as patients' insurance and payment information. The spreadsheet needs to be completed according to the following instructions.

Create a Workbook

You have a basic spreadsheet serving as a log containing patient and insurance information. Your supervisor wishes to expand the log to include payment information. The supervisor added column titles to the existing spreadsheet so that you would know the type of account information needed. Before creating the formulas and completing the log for a day's entries, you want to make sure the spreadsheet is formatted to make it attractive and easy to read.

- Open *exp07_e_med_cpt_log* and save it as **exp07_e_med_cpt_log_solution**.
- Change the font for the entire worksheet to **Calibri, 12 pt**.
- Type **Diabetes Management Clinic at Orland Medical Center** in **cell A1**.
  - Merge and center the text between columns A1 through O1.
  - Make the following changes to **cell A1**:
    - Set the style to **Bold**.
    - Set the font color to **Blue, Accent 1**.
    - Set the font size to **22 pt**.
    - Set the fill color to **White, Background 1, Darker 15%**.
- Type **Patient Log** in **cell A2**.
  - Merge and center the text between columns A2:O2.
  - Set the style to **Bold**.
  - Set the font color to **Blue, Accent 1**.
  - Set the font size to **16 pt**.
  - Set the fill color to **White, Background 1, Darker 15%**.
- Set a thick box border around **cells A1:O2**.
- Use an appropriate date function in **cell A3** to get today's date in your worksheet. Resize the column to fit the display date.
  - Format as mm/dd/yy.
  - Set the style to **Bold**.
  - Set the font size to **14 pt**.

Format Column Headings

The column headings in the document need to show organization and have a professional look. Some of the headings in the cells are overlapping or break inappropriately making the headings difficult to read. You will need to adjust the column widths.

- Type **Patient Information** in **cell A5**.
  - Merge and center the text between columns A5 through G5.
  - Make the following changes to **cell A5**:
    - Set the style to **Bold**.
    - Set the font size to **14 pt**.
- Set the fill color for **cells A5:G6** to **Dark Blue, Text 2, Lighter 60%**.
- Type **Account Information** in **cell H5**.
  - Merge and center the text between columns H5 through O5.
  - Make the following changes to **cell H5**:
    - Set the style to **Bold**.
    - Set the font size to **14 pt**.
- Set the fill color for **cells H5:O6** to **Orange, Accent 6, Lighter 60%**.
- Add these formatting features to the column headings in row 6.
  - Set the style to **Bold**.
  - Insert a thick bottom border from **cells A6:O6**.
  - AutoFit columns as needed.

Use AutoFill

The *Num* field contains the order in which the patient arrives at the clinic. Instead of entering the numbers in the rest of the rows, use AutoFill to complete the series.

- Use AutoFill to complete the series in **cells A7:A51**.

Format Data

The data in the columns need to be formatted appropriately based on the data type. The date of birth needs a date format, and the numerical data needs to be formatted as currency.

- Format **cells C7:C51** as mm/dd/yy.
- Format **cells I7:L52** and **N7:O52** to Accounting with no decimal places.
- Set a top and thick bottom border to **cells H52:O52**.

Enter Patient Information

You will input the last two patients of the day to the Patient Log spreadsheet.

- Enter the data for the second to the last patient in row 50.
  - Num: **44**.
  - Patient Name: **Olsen, Brad**.
  - Date of Birth: **February 23, 1949**.
  - Gender: **Male**.
  - Insurance Company: **Blue Cross**.

...continued on Next Page

- Insurance Type: **HMO**.
- Policy Number: **XOF-6365167**.
- Visit Code: **9211**.
- Payment/Co-Pay: **30**.
- Insurance Billing: **60**.

- Enter the data for the last patient in row 45.
  - Num: **45**.
  - Patient Name: **Kizilsac, Yusuf**.
  - Date of Birth: **June 14, 1952**.
  - Gender: **Male**.
  - Insurance Company: **None**.
  - Visit Code: **8111**.
  - Payment/Co-Pay: **100**.
  - Insurance Billing: **0**.

Use the VLOOKUP Function

The clinic has standard charges for the type of service a patient receives. The charges are stored in the Charges Lookup table. You create a VLOOKUP function using the stored information to determine the charge for the visit.

- In **cell I7**, use the table at **cells R8:S17** with a VLOOKUP function to determine the charge for the patient based on the visit code.
- Copy the formula to the remaining cells in the column.

Compute the Insurance Adjustment

Your clinic participates in a managed fee-for-service plan with the insurance companies. The service plan sets an amount a patient pays (co-pay) and a maximum charge the insurance company pays. If there is a difference between the amount your clinic charges and the total of the patient co-pay and insurance payment, the difference must be adjusted off the books.

- In **cell L7**, create a formula that adds **cell J7** (*Payment/Co-Pay*) and **cell K7** (*Insurance Billing*) together, and then subtracts that amount from **cell I7** (*Charge*).
- Copy the formula to the remaining cells in the column.

Determine Discount

Your clinic has a policy that if a patient does not have insurance and pays cash the day of the visit, a 10% discount is applied to the amount due to reduce what the patient has to pay. Use the IF function to clearly display in a column that "Yes" an adjustment is applicable or "No" an adjustment is not applicable. Then you use an IF function to determine the amount of the discount. Finally, you use an IF function to determine the total due for the visit after the insurance adjustment or cash discount are applied. In most cases, the amount remaining after the co-pay and insurance payment is written off by the medical billing agency.

- Enter an IF function in **cell M7** based on the entry in **cell E7** (*Insurance Company*). If the value is *None*, the function returns the value *Yes*. Any other value is returned as *No*.
- Copy the formula to the remaining cells in the column.
- Create an IF function in **cell N7** that returns a 10% cash discount based on the original charge (**cell I7**) if the discount is applicable. If the discount is not applicable, the discount amount should be zero.
- Copy the formula to the remaining cells in the column.
- Create a formula in **cell O7** that determines the final total due after any adjustments whether the adjustment is an insurance adjustment or a cash discount.
- Copy the formula to the remaining cells in the column.

Create Totals

Totals for each of the columns in the account information section of the spreadsheet would be useful.

- Calculate the totals for columns I, J, K, L, N, and O.

Rename the Sheet

You need to give the worksheet a more meaningful name.

- Name the current sheet **Visit Log**.
- Change the worksheet tab color to **Aqua, Accent 5**.

Create a Chart

You create a chart that displays the original charge total and the total due after adjustments so that the clinic physicians can see the impact of the adjustments on the income for that day. The chart will display in the current sheet.

- Create a 3-D Clustered Column chart that displays the *Charge* total and the *Total Due After Adjustments*.
- Size and position the chart to **cells H55:O73**.
- Set the Chart Layout to Layout 1.
- Remove the legend.
- Modify the shape fill for *Total Due After Adjustments* to **Orange, Accent 6**.
- Change the chart type to **Clustered Column** to remove the 3-D effect.
- Insert data labels on *Outside End*.
- Change the y-axis to start at **0** with an increment of 500.
- Set the chart title to **Charges After Adjustments**.

Sort Data and Hide Columns

The physician has requested to view the data in a different order. You save the requested views in new worksheets for ease of grading.

- Duplicate the *Visit Log* worksheet and name the new tab **Sort - Insurance**.
- Set the worksheet tab color to **White, Background 1**.
- Delete the chart.
- Hide the Total row and the Date of Birth and Gender columns.
- Sort the information in ascending order by *Insurance Company* and then by *Patient Name*.
- Create another duplicate of the *Visit Log* and name the new tab **Sort - Type of Visit**.
- Set the worksheet tab color to **White, Background 1**.
- Delete the chart.
- Hide row 5 and columns I:O.
- Sort the data in descending order by *Visit Code* and then by ascending order by *Insurance Company*.

...continued on Next Page

Filter Data

The physician has requested specific information regarding the number of patients with Blue Cross insurance. He also wants to know the number of patients without insurance. Filter the data.

- Duplicate the *Visit Log* worksheet and name the new tab **Filter - Insurance**.
- Set the worksheet tab color to **Orange, Accent 6**.
- Delete the chart.
- Hide the columns containing the *Lookup* table.
- Create a filter that displays all patients with Blue Cross Insurance.
- Sort the results in ascending order by *Patient Name*.
- Duplicate the *Filter - Insurance* worksheet and name the new tab **Filter - No Insurance**.
- Remove the filter.
- Create a filter that displays all patients with no insurance.
- Sort the results in ascending order by *Patient Name*.

Manage and Protect the Workbook

- Move the *Visit Log* worksheet to the first position in the workbook.
- Protect the structure of your workbook using the password **patient**.

Spell Check and Save the Workbook

- Use spelling checker to check your document for errors.
- Save your workbook.
- Print the entire workbook as required by your instructor.
- Display and print the formulas as required by your instructor.
- If instructed to do so, submit the workbook and printouts to your instructor for grading.

Medical Office Assistants

Use Microsoft Office Access

Background

Medical office assistants work in hospitals, clinics, and physician offices and are responsible for the administrative functions of the office. They use database software to maintain records, including patient, physician, and insurance information. They create queries to locate and extract information from a database. They design and create reports to display information in a professional manner. It is imperative that medical office assistants understand the features of Microsoft Office Access and be comfortable using those features. The following database skills taught in the textbook are skills crucial to people employed in a medical office.

Tasks

Medical office assistants may be responsible for creating and maintaining database information. This information could include the following:

- Creating tables and forms
  - Physician data
  - Patient data
  - Medication data
  - Test results data
  - Scheduling data
  - Insurance data
- Sorting, filtering, and querying data
- Creating a relationship between tables
- Creating reports
  - Patient schedules
  - Payments received
  - Patient balance

Skills

A medical office assistant should be able to do the following:

Chapter 1

- Practice good file management (page 555)
- Back up, compact, and repair Access files (page 556)
- Create filters (page 565)
- Sort table data on one or more fields (page 568)
- Know when to use Access or Excel to manage data (page 570)
- Understand relational power (page 579)

...continued on Next Page

Chapter 2

- Create tables (page 612)
- Share data with Excel (page 626)
- Establish table relationships (page 630)
- Create a query (page 642)
- Specify criteria for different data types (page 645)
- Copy and run a query (page 649)

Chapter 3

- Understand the order of precedence (page 679)
- Create a calculated field in a query (page 679)
- Create expressions with the Expression Builder (page 689)
- Create and work with data aggregates (page 704)

Chapter 4

- Plan a report (page 731)
- Use different report views (page 733)
- Create and edit a report (page 737)
- Identify report elements, sections, and controls (page 747)
- Add grouping levels in Layout view (page 750)
- Add fields to a report (page 755)
- Use the Report Wizard (page 765)

Medical Office Assistants
Volume 1 I Capstone Exercise

You work as a medical office assistant for Central Medical Clinics, a group of affiliated health care clinics providing patient care in many specialty areas in several locations in Chicago and nearby cities. The main office for the clinics has patient records stored in an Excel file. Information about the clinics and the physicians practicing in the clinics is stored in an Access database. Your supervisor asked you to create a relational database management system that combines the records from both resources. In addition to tracking patient, physician, and clinic information, your database management system needs to track insurance companies. The system will be able to extract data from the tables and produce reports. The database management system needs to be set up according to the instructions listed in the following text.

Create a Table and Modify Field Properties

You have an existing database that contains the records of affiliated clinics and the physicians practicing in the clinics. You need to create a table in your database that will track the insurance information. You also need to modify the existing tables for better database design.

- Copy the *exp07_a_med_cpt_medical.accdb* file and name the copy **exp07_a_med_cpt_medical_solution**.
- Create a table called *Insurance* using the following fields and properties:

Field Name	Data Type	Field Size	Comments
InsuranceID	AutoNumber		Create caption.
InsuranceName	Text	25	Create caption.
Address	Text	30	
City	Text	25	
State	Text	2	
ZipCode	Text	10	Create caption.
Phone#	Text	14	
Fax#	Text	14	

- Use Help to research how to create an input mask to enter field or control values in a specific format.
- Use the Input Mask Wizard to create an input mask for the zip code in the *Insurance* table. Use the default Input Mask format for Zip Code. Accept the underscore as the placeholder and store the data with the symbols in the mask.
- Create an input mask for the phone number and fax number using the default Input Mask format for Phone Number. Accept the underscore as the placeholder and store the data with the symbols in the mask.
- Enter the following records into the *Insurance* table in Datasheet view.

	Record 1	Record 2	Record 3	Record 4
InsuranceID	AutoNumber	AutoNumber	AutoNumber	AutoNumber
InsuranceName	United Healthcare	Aetna	Blue Cross	Humana
Address	700 River Row	1 Insurance Plaza	486 W Harrison	5873 W 68th
City	Chicago	Chicago	Chicago	Chicago
State	IL	IL	IL	IL
ZipCode	60614-3363	60290-1234	60637-4567	60645-7893
Phone#	(773) 555-2367	(312) 555-8885	(773) 555-1115	(773) 555-5465
Fax#	(773) 555-2377	(312) 555-9995	(773) 555-0550	(773) 555-0560

...continued on Next Page

- Modify the *Clinics* table by applying the following properties:

Field Name	Data Type	Field Size	Comments
ClinicID	AutoNumber	Long Integer	Make primary key. Create caption.
ClinicLocation	Text	20	Create caption.
Address#1	Text	30	
Address#2	Text	30	
City	Text	25	
State	Text	2	
ZipCode	Text	10	Create caption.
Phone#	Text	14	Use input mask.

- Modify the *Physicians* table by applying the following properties:

Field Name	Data Type	Field Size	Comments
PhysicianID	AutoNumber	Long Integer	Create caption.
FirstName	Text	20	Create caption.
LastName	Text	25	Create caption.
Specialty	Text	25	
BoardCertification	Text	50	Create caption.
Cell#	Text	14	Modify input mask to store the data with the symbols in the mask.
ClinicID	Number	Long Integer	Create caption.

Import and Modify a Table

Each day, the staff members compile the patient records in an Excel spreadsheet. Although this procedure enables the physicians and office manager to examine the patient data, your office manager recognized that bringing the data into the Access database will allow relationships to be created between the patient data, physician data, insurance data, and clinic data. With the creation of relationships between tables, complex queries can be created for data analysis.

- Import *exp07_a_med_cpt_patients.xlsx* into a new table in the current database. The first row contains the column headings. Let Access add the primary key.
- Rename the table **Patients**.
- View the data in the newly imported table in Datasheet view and adjust column widths so all data display.
- Modify the *Patients* table by applying the following properties:

Field Name	Data Type	Field Size	Comments
ID	AutoNumber	Long Integer	
FirstName	Text	20	Create caption.
LastName	Text	25	Create caption.
Phone	Text	14	Change field name to **Phone#**. Use input mask.
SSN	Text	11	Use input mask.
Address	Text	30	
City	Text	25	

...continued on Next Page

Field Name	Data Type	Field Size	Comments
State	Text	2	
ZipCode	Text	10	Create caption.
InsuranceID	Number	Long Integer	Create caption.
Policy	Text	20	
PhysicianID	Number	Long Integer	Create caption.
ClinicID	Number	Long Integer	Create caption.
Charge	Currency		
CoPay	Currency		
InsurancePayment	Currency		Create caption.

- Create a new patient record, #46, using **your name**. Make up a SSN and address information. You have no insurance, and you see physician **13** at clinic **4**. Your charge was **75** and you have no copay or insurance payment.

Modify Records

You need to make some changes in the *Patients* table. One of the patients moved to another state and no longer comes to the clinic. You need to remove her data from the *Patients* table. Another patient has the incorrect city and zip code listed in the table, and you need to update her record with the correct information.

- Locate the record for Jackie Hamilton.
- Delete the record.
- Locate the record for Melissa Smith.
- Change the city to **Rockford**.
- Change the zip code to **59910**.

Create a Relationship

You need to create the relationships between the tables. Be sure to enforce referential integrity as you create the relationships.

- Create the following relationships enforcing referential integrity:
    - *Clinics, Patients,* and *Physicians* tables: *ClinicID*.
    - *Patients* and *Physicians* tables: *PhysicianID*.
    - *Insurance* and *Patients* tables: *InsuranceID*.
- Save the relationships.

Create Queries with Criteria

The office manager would like to view a listing of the following data. Print results as directed by your instructor.

- Display a list of all patients that live in Chicago. Include last name, first name, address, city, state, zip code, and phone number. Sort alphabetically by last name and then by first name. Save as **Chicago Patients**.
- Display a complete list of all the patients (first name and last name) of Dr. Mark Bodily. Include the physician's last name and ID. Sort by patient last name in ascending order. Save as **Bodily Patients**.
- Create a query based on the *Bodily Patients* query that displays all the patients except those of Dr. Bodily. Save as **Non-Bodily Patients**.
- Display a list of all patients sorted in alphabetical order by the insurance company name and then by the last name of the patient. Include insurance ID, insurance name, last name and first name of patient, the patient policy number, and the amount of copay the patient is required to pay. Save as **Insurance by Patient**.
- Create a query that lists clinic ID and location, then the last name of the physician, first name of the physician, the specialty of the physician, and the physician's cell phone number. Filter the query so only CMC, Lake Shore locations are included. Sort by physician last name and then by specialty. Save the query as **Lake Shore Physicians**.

Use the LabelWizard

A new physician is affiliating with the Oak Brook Clinic. A postcard has been prepared that will be sent to all patients to notify them of the new physician and the physician's specialty. Your office manager asks you to prepare labels for the postcards. Print as directed by your instructor.

- Use the *Patients* table to create address labels that can be printed on Avery 5660 labels, 1″ x 2 5/6″.
- Use all fields necessary to create a standard address block.
- Save the report as **Labels Patients**.
- View the labels in Print Preview, and then switch to Design view. (Note: You can ignore the prompt telling you there is not enough horizontal space.) Change the font for all fields to **Cambria**, **9 pt**. View the labels in Print Preview.

Use the Report Wizard

The office manager would like a report that lists each physician and his or her patients. For ease, you prepare the report using the Report Wizard. Print the final report as directed by your instructor.

- Create a report and name it **Patients Grouped by Physicians**.
- Display the *LastName* and *FirstName* fields from the *Physicians* table.

...continued on Next Page

- Display the *LastName, FirstName,* and *Phone#* fields from the *Patients* table.
- Display the *InsuranceName* field from the *Insurance* table.
- Group the data by physician name.
- Sort the data by patient last name and then patient first name.
- Select the **landscape orientation** for the report.
- Select the **Civic** style for the report.
- Switch to Layout view and modify the page headers so they identify whether the names belong to the physician or the patient. Change the column widths so all data fully displays.
- Save the report.

Revise a Report Layout

The office manager would like a revised report that lists each physician and his or her patients but that displays the insurance information more predominantly. You modify the *Patients Grouped by Physicians* report and name it **Insurance Grouped by Physicians**. Print the final report as directed by your instructor.

- Revise the sort to sort first by *Physician_LastName,* then by *InsuranceName,* and then by *Patients_LastName.*
- Add a group on *Insurance Name.*

Create a Query with Calculated Field and a Report

The office manager needs a report that displays all patients with an outstanding balance. You need to create a query to find all the patients that have a balance and then create a report based on the query results. Print the report as directed by your instructor.

- Create a query named **Balance Due**.
  - Display the *FirstName, LastName, Phone#, Charge, CoPay,* and *InsurancePayment* fields in the query.
  - Create a calculated field named **Balance** to determine the remaining balance.
  - Format the *Charge, CoPay, InsurancePayment,* and *Balance* fields as Currency.
  - Set a criterion that limits the query to display only the patients that have a balance.
  - Sort the query so that the highest balances are displayed at the top of the query.
- Use the Report Tool to create a **Balance Due** report based on the *Balance Due* query.
  - Display the *LastName, FirstName, Phone#,* and *Balance* fields on the report.
  - Sort by Balance from largest to smallest.
  - Apply the Civic AutoFormat.

Back Up and Compact the Database

You compact the database to eliminate any wasted space. You also back up the database and save it as another name.

- Close any open objects in the database.
- Compact and repair the database.
- Back up the database and assign a default name by adding a date to the filename.
- Submit a copy of the *exp07_a_med_cpt_medical_solution* database and your printouts to your instructor for grading if instructed to do so.

Medical Office Assistants

Use Microsoft Office PowerPoint

Background

Medical office assistants use presentation graphics software on a regular basis. Medical presentations run the gamut from communicating research data to the scientific community to educating patients. Microsoft Office PowerPoint makes it possible for the user to create slides with graphic elements, charts and graphs, transitions, themes, and animations. It is imperative that medical office assistants understand the features of PowerPoint and be comfortable using those features. The following presentation graphics skills taught in the textbook are skills crucial to people employed in a medical office.

Tasks

Medical office assistants may be responsible for creating all types of PowerPoint presentations. These could include the following:

- Slide shows for presentation by a speaker at a conference or meeting
- Presentations that can be printed as handouts and distributed to patients and audience members at a conference
- Presentations displayed in a kiosk
- Presentations that can be distributed on a CD and viewed on a computer
- Slide shows regarding medical information that is published on a Web site

Skills

Medical office assistants should be able to do the following:

Chapter 1

- Use PowerPoint views (page 804)
- Use slide layouts (page 820)
- Apply design themes (page 820)
- Add a table (page 829)
- Insert clip art (page 829)
- Use transitions and animations (page 831)
- Run and navigate a slide show (page 840)
- Print with PowerPoint (page 842)

Chapter 2

- Modify an outline structure (page 881)
- Add existing content to a presentation (page 888)
- Apply and modify a design theme (page 892)
- Insert a header or footer (page 896)

...continued on Next Page

Chapter 3

- Create shapes (page 931)
- Apply Quick Styles and customize shapes (page 936)
- Create SmartArt (page 952)
- Create WordArt (page 961)
- Modify WordArt (page 961)
- Arrange objects (page 975)

Chapter 4

- Insert and modify a picture (page 1015)
- Use the Internet as a resource (page 1021)
- Insert movies (page 1038)
- Add sound (page 1046)

Medical Office Assistants
Volume 1 | Capstone Exercise

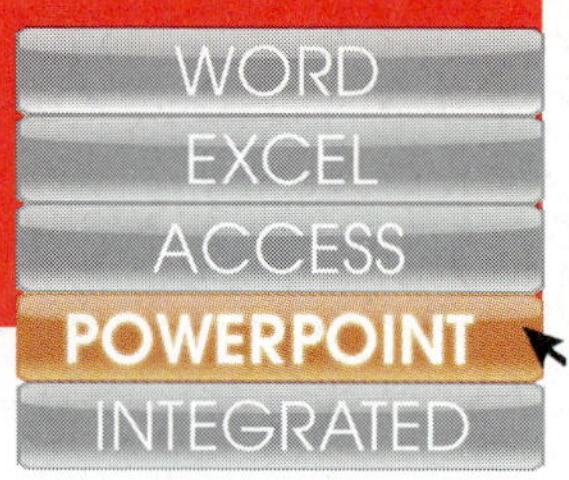

The University of Michigan Hospital is a research hospital. You work as a medical office assistant for one of the physicians, Dr. Thomas Martin. He has been asked to present to a local service organization next week. He would like to educate the group about the dangers of high blood pressure and also teach the members ways to improve their blood pressure. He has asked you to prepare a PowerPoint slide show based on a presentation he gave at a local senior citizens center. Create the slide show according to the following instructions.

Set Up the Slide Show

The outline Dr. Martin used to prepare his previous presentation was created in Microsoft Word and saved as an .rtf (rich text format) file. You insert this outline into a blank presentation.

- Create a new blank PowerPoint slide show and save it as **exp07_p_med_cpt_bloodpressure_solution**.
- Enter the following text into the placeholders:
  - Title placeholder: **HIGH BLOOD PRESSURE**.
  - Subtitle placeholder: **Presented By: Tom Martin, M.D.**
- Apply the Concourse theme.
- Change the color scheme to **Equity**.

Reuse Slides

Dr. Martin created a basic slide show about hypertension, which he presented to a local senior citizens group. His physician's assistant added speaker notes to this slide show for your use. For efficiency, you reuse this content in your slide show.

- Insert Slides 2 through 14 from *exp07_p_med_cpt_hypertension.pptx*.
- Switch to Notes Page view and read the speaker notes for each slide.
- Apply the Fade Through Black transition to all slides.
- Switch to Slide Show view, view the slide show, and then return to Normal view.

Revise the Slide Show Structure

After reviewing the slide show you realize that, although it contains a strong body of information, it is missing an introduction slide. You also feel that the conclusion slide giving references is bland. You create an introduction to the presentation using an eye-opening statement. You also modify the conclusion by adding an attractive image that you hope will serve as a call to action to encourage the viewers to become more active.

- Insert a new Slide 2 using the Section Header layout.
- Enter the following text into the placeholders:
  - Title placeholder: **The "Silent Killer" Epidemic**.
  - Subtitle placeholder: **One in three U.S. adults has high blood pressure. Because there are no symptoms, nearly one third of these people do NOT know they have it!**
- Insert the image *exp07_p_med_cpt_image1*.

- Position the image on the left side of the slide, and adjust the sizes of the text placeholders and font sizes so all text displays attractively.
- Insert a textbox following the quote to credit the resource from which you are quoting. Type **American Heart Association**.
- Enter the following notes: **High blood pressure usually has no symptoms, although sometimes headaches occur. Sometimes people only learn that they have high blood pressure AFTER it causes health problems. High blood pressure is a key risk factor for a stroke, heart attack, and kidney failure! (American Heart Association)**
- Change the layout for the conclusion slide, Slide 15, to Picture with Caption.
- Insert the picture *exp07_p_med_cpt_image4.jpg* into the picture placeholder.
- Apply the Double Frame, Black picture style to the picture.

Modify the Outline and Change Slide Layouts

To be able to concentrate on the content of the slide show you review the text in the Outline view. You check for slides with too much text and problems with parallel structure and make corrections. As a final step to reviewing the text in the document, use spelling checker and Find and Replace.

- Switch from the Slides pane to Outline pane.
- Remove all unnecessary blank lines.
- Reverse the *Diastolic Pressure* and *Systolic Pressure* families in Slide 5 so that *Systolic Pressure* and its associated bullet point appear first.

...continued on Next Page

- Move to Slide 6, *Tips for Blood Pressure Readings*, and modify the bullet points so each point begins with a verb and so that unnecessary text is removed.
- Move to Slide 13 and add the following bullet points:
    - **Rinse canned foods to reduce sodium**
    - **Choose convenience foods low in salt**
- Change the capitalization on Slide 14 so that the capitalization is consistent.
- Switch back to the Slides pane and move to Slide 4. Change the layout to **Title Only** and then delete the content placeholder and bullet point.
- Insert the picture *exp07_p_med_cpt_image3.jpg* and change the height to **6"**. Position the picture attractively on the slide.
- Move to Slide 14 and change the layout to **Two Content**. Split the list of medications evenly between the two placeholders.
- Check the spelling of the slide show and correct all misspelled words.
- Search for all occurrences of *30 minutes* and replace them with **30-minutes**.
- Carefully proofread the speaker notes for each slide and correct all errors including misspelled words and word usage errors.

Add Multimedia Objects

Recognizing that the majority of the slides are still text slides, you decide to add interest to the slide show by converting some text to SmartArt, adding shapes to illustrate points, and adding clip art.

- Insert a picture fill for the background of Slide 1. Insert *exp07_p_med_cpt_image2.jpg*. Hide the background graphics so they do not block the picture fill.
- Change the title text to the WordArt Style **Fill – Accent 2, Matte Bevel**. Add shadowing to the subtitle text.
- Convert the text in the content placeholder on Slide 11 to **Continuous Block Process** SmartArt. Apply the SmartArt style of your choice.
- In Slide 3, insert an oval and set the height to **3"** and the width to **4"**. Duplicate the oval and set the height to **2.85"** and the width to **3.8"**.
- Change the shape style of the larger oval to **Colored Fill – Accent 2**.
- To create the appearance of an artery, Align Center and Align Middle the two ovals. Group the two ovals and position them attractively on the slide.
- To illustrate pressure against the walls of an artery, insert a Left-Right Arrow shape that stretches from the left edge of the smaller oval to the right edge. Change the fill of the shape to **White, Background 1**.

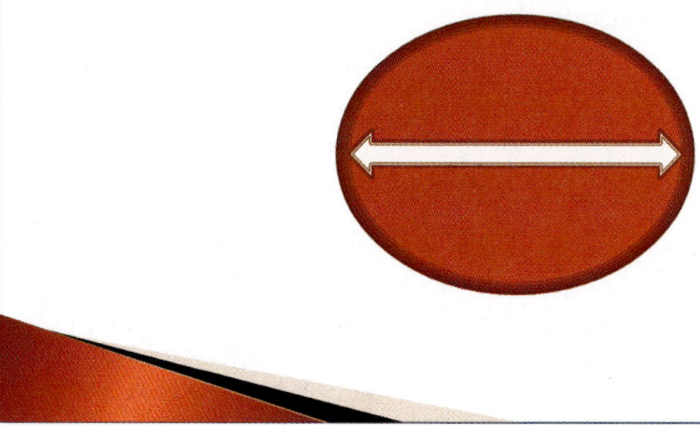

- Insert a text box on Slide 5 and type **120**. Press **Enter**, and type **80**. Change the font size to **72 pt** and apply **bold**. Center the text in the text box.
- Insert a Line shape that stretches from the left alignment point of the text box to the right alignment point of the text box. Change the shape outline theme color to **Black, Text 1** and the shape outline weight to **3 pt**.
- Insert a heart shape and apply the shape style of your choice.
- Size the heart shape to approximately the size of the textbox and position it to the left of the textbox.
- Insert the Heart Thuds sound clip using these options:
    - Search for: *heart*
    - Search in: *All collections*
    - Results should be: *Sounds*
- Start the sound automatically and hide the sound icon during the show. Loop the sound until stopped so it plays continuously until the next slide displays.

...continued on Next Page

- In Slide 8, insert the following WordArt: **Check Your Blood Pressure Regularly!** Use the Fill – Accent 1, Metal Bevel, Reflection WordArt style and change the font size to **28 pt**.
- In Slide 12, insert a photograph of your choice from the Clip Art gallery that illustrates a healthy life style. Size the image appropriately for available space, and arrange the elements on the slide in an attractive manner. Apply a picture style if desired.
- In Slide 13, insert the following Microsoft movie clip art using these options:
  - Search for: *Medical*
  - Search in: *All collections*
  - Results should be: *Movies*
- Position the movie clip beneath *Sodium* in the title to call attention to it.

Add a Table

Add a table displaying blood pressure levels.

- Insert a table with 3 columns and 5 rows in Slide 7.
- Enter the following information into the table cells:

Blood Pressure Category	Systolic	Diastolic
Normal	Less than 120	And less than 80
Prehypertension	120–139	Or 80–89
High Stage 1	140–159	Or 90–99
High Stage 2	160 or higher	Or 100 or higher

- Horizontally and vertically center the column titles.
- Resize the table to a width of **8"** and position it attractively in the white space.
- Apply the Themed Style 2 – Accent 1 table style.

Add Animation

Now that the slide show has been created, add animations to introduce elements at appropriate times and create visual interest.

- In Slide 1, apply the Ascend entrance animation to the title placeholder, having it start After Previous. Apply the same transition to the subtitle placeholder, having it start after the title placeholder has completed its animation.
- For emphasis, in Slide 3 animate the shape group to grow and shrink After Previous.
- Apply the Fly In by 1st Level Paragraphs animation scheme to the content placeholders in Slides 6, 8, 10, and 13. Animate On Click.
- Apply the Wipe One by One animation scheme to the SmartArt in Slide 11. Wipe On Click and wipe From Left.

Insert Header

Insert a Notes and Handouts header and footer that includes information about the presentation and presenter.

- Insert a header for handouts with the following features:
  - Include the date and time.
  - Insert the presenter's name, **Thomas Martin, M.D.**, in the header.
  - Include the page number.

...continued on Next Page

- Insert **Hypertension Support Group** in the footer.
- Apply these settings to all handouts.

Save and Print Presentation

Save and print the presentation.

- Save the presentation.
- Print handouts (four slides per page) as directed by your instructor.
- Submit the file to your instructor for grading if instructed to do so.

Medical Office Assistants

Integrate Microsoft Office Software

Background

You work in the billing department for the Midwest Physician Center, a group of affiliated physicians in several Midwest locations. You are asked by your supervisor to produce a report of past due accounts of all patients. You create a document that displays the accounts receivable information. The document will be distributed to all physicians during a monthly meeting. You also create a chart that depicts the past due balances grouped by clinic. The chart will be included on the document. The information will also be presented to the physicians via a PowerPoint presentation.

The patient information is stored in a Microsoft Office Access database. After preparing the report, you export the past due data to a Microsoft Office Excel spreadsheet so it can be used to create a chart. You insert the chart into a Microsoft Office PowerPoint presentation. Then you edit a memo in Microsoft Office Word and copy the accounts receivable data from Excel and the chart from PowerPoint for inclusion in the memo. You also copy the logo from the PowerPoint file so it can be incorporated at the top of the memo. The project needs to be completed according to the following instructions.

Tasks

Medical office assistants may be responsible for integrating data between Word, Excel, Access, and PowerPoint. This could include the following:

- Copying and pasting data between applications
- Exporting data to another application

Skills

In addition to basic integration skills, a medical office assistant should be able to do the following:

- Import and export data between applications.
- Create queries and reports.
- Create and format charts.
- Edit a report in Layout view
- Export data from Access to Excel

...continued on Next Page

Medical Office Assistants
Volume 1 | Capstone Exercise

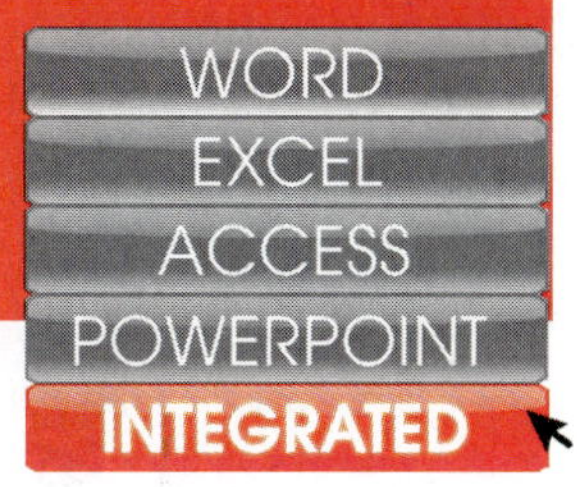

Retrieve the Past Due Account Information from Access

You use the Midwest Physician Center database to create a report that displays all patients with a balance due. Then you export the data to Excel.

- Copy the original *exp07_i_med_cpt_receivables.accdb* database. Rename the copied file as **exp07_i_med_cpt_receivables_solution.accdb**.
- Use Find to locate the following records, and then modify the records as follows.
  - Locate Jackie Bishop's record and change the payment from *$350* to **$150**. Change the insurance payment from $0 to **$8,000**.
  - Locate Scott Bianchi's record and change the payment from *$100* to **$3,350**.
  - Locate Jenalee Hulse's record and change the insurance payment from *$0* to **$750**.
- Create a query called **Patient Balance** using the *Patients* and *Physicians* tables. This query should only display patients that have a remaining balance.
  - Select the *FirstName*, *LastName*, *Charge*, *Payment*, and *Insurance Payment* fields from the *Patients* table.
  - Select the *Clinic* field from the *Physicians* table. Position the *Clinic* field between the *LastName* and *Charge* fields.
  - Calculate the Balance for each patient. Name the field **Balance**.
  - Format the *Charge*, *Payment*, *Insurance Payment*, and *Balance* fields as *Currency*.
  - Set a criterion that limits the query to display only the patients that have a balance.
  - Sort the query on the *Clinic* field (ascending) and the *Balance* field (descending).
  - Save and print the query as directed by your instructor.
- Create a report called **Patient Balance** based on the Patience Balance query.
  - Display the *Clinic*, *LastName*, *FirstName*, and *Balance* fields on the report.
  - Add a group on *Clinic*.
  - Sort the data by *Balance* in descending order.
  - Format the total as Currency.
  - Apply the Office AutoFormat to the report.
  - Save and print the report as directed by your instructor.

Export the Data to Excel

Export the *Patient Balance* query to Excel. Use the data to chart the balances of the patients.

- Use the **Export feature** in the External Data tab to export the *Patient Balance* query to Excel.
- Save the spreadsheet in the same location as the Access database solution and name it **exp07_i_med_cpt_balance_solution**.
- Export the data with formatting and layout and open the destination file after the export operation is complete.

Create the Excel Chart

Use the exported data to create a pie chart of the balances by clinic.

- Create a custom header with your name, the date, and the name of your instructor.
- AutoFit column widths.
- Create a summary report showing patient balances grouped by clinic.
- Prepare a 2D Pie Chart that shows the proportion of the total due by clinic.
- Apply Layout 1 for the Chart Layout, and size the chart so all labels appear within the pie slices.
- Set a 2-line title for the chart with **Midwest Physician Center** as the first line and **Patient Balances** as the second line.
- Move the chart to worksheet 2 and name the worksheet **Patient Balance Chart**.
- Save the spreadsheet and chart. Print as directed by your instructor.

Create the PowerPoint Slide Show

The chart you have prepared will be used as part of a presentation to the physicians by the finance department of the Midwest Physician Center. You begin this presentation by creating a logo for your department and inserting the Patient Balances chart.

- Open a blank PowerPoint presentation and save it as **exp07_i_med_cpt_midwest_solution**.
- Create a Notes and Handouts header that includes your name as the header, the date, and the name of your instructor as the footer. Create a Slide footer that displays your name and date on each slide.
- Add the title **Midwest Physician Center** and the subtitle **Finance Department**.
- Apply the Origin theme.
- Insert the clip art image of your choice using *caducei* as your keyword.
- Change the height of the clip art image to **1.5"**.
- Use WordArt to add both the center initials and department name next to the caducei. Group the WordArt and clip art to create a logo. Make other changes as desired, but do not exceed the 1.5" height requirement. Position

...continued on Next Page

the logo attractively on the slide. The following is an example of a possible logo.

- Create Slide 2 using the Blank layout.
- Copy the Excel chart and insert it into Slide 2.
- Resize the chart to a height of **6"** and position it attractively on the page.
- Apply a Fly In animation animating By Category.
- Save the slide show.
- Print the document as handouts, two per page, if directed to do so by your instructor.

Modify the Memo and Insert the Chart and Logo

Open the memo in Word and insert the information regarding the patient balances. The Excel chart will be inserted into the memo as well as the company logo from the PowerPoint slide show.

- Open the *exp07_i_med_cpt_memo.docx* file and save as **exp07_i_med_cpt_memo_solution**.
- Insert your name in the From placeholder.
- Insert the current date in the Date placeholder.
- Copy and paste the balance from the Excel spreadsheet into the first paragraph, replacing the *$xxx*.
- Copy and paste the *Midwest Physician Center Patient Balances* chart from the Excel spreadsheet below the first paragraph.
- Resize the chart height to **4"** and position the chart attractively in the white space.
- Replace the word *MEMO* with the logo from Slide 1 of the *exp07_i_med_cpt_midwest_solution* slide show.
- Save the document and print as directed by your instructor.
- Close all open documents, and if directed to do so, submit all printouts to the instructor for grading.

Production Assistants

Use Microsoft Office Word

Background

Word processing is the most used application program in a theater company business office. Production assistants create correspondence, contracts with actors, and theater rental space contracts, as well as memos, reports, press releases, and documents requiring desktop publishing. It is imperative that a production assistant becomes proficient in Microsoft Office Word and its many features.

Tasks

In a theater company's business office, a production assistant might be asked to create and edit many types of documents, including the following:

- Correspondence and mailings
- Contracts (actors and technicians of local and touring shows, crew, venue contact people)
- Mailing lists
- Tables
- Press releases
- Audition schedules
- Brochures
- Flyers

Skills

A production assistant should be able to do the following:

Chapter 1

- Use AutoText (page 76)
- Set margins and specify page orientation (page 87)
- Insert page breaks (page 88)
- Add page numbers (page 90)
- Insert headers and footers (page 91)
- Create sections (page 92)
- Insert a cover page (page 93)
- Use the Find and Replace commands (page 94)

Chapter 2

- Apply font attributes through the Font dialog box (page 133)
- Highlight text (page 136)

...continued on Next Page

- Control word wrapping with nonbreaking hyphens and nonbreaking spaces (page 137)
- Copy formats with the Format Painter (page 139)
- Set off paragraphs with tabs, borders, lists, and columns (page 143)
- Apply paragraph formats (page 148)
- Create and modify styles (page 159)
- Create a table of contents (page 171)
- Create an index (page 171)

Chapter 3

- Insert a table (page 197)
- Format a table (page 205)
- Sort and apply formulas to table data (page 207)
- Convert text to a table (page 210)
- Insert clip art and images into a document (page 219)
- Format a graphic element (page 220)
- Insert WordArt into a document (page 225)
- Insert symbols into a document (page 226)

Chapter 4

- Insert comments into a document (page 251)
- Track changes in a document (page 254)
- View documents side by side (page 263)
- Compare and combine documents (page 264)
- Create master documents and subdocuments (page 265)
- Acknowledge a source (page 277)
- Create a bibliography (page 279)
- Select the writing style (page 280)
- Create and modify footnotes and endnotes (page 281)

Production Assistants
Volume 1 | Capstone Exercises

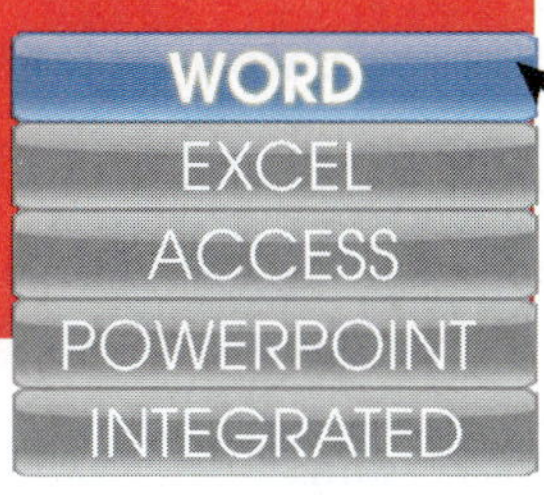

You work as a production assistant in the offices of a new company, the Green Man Theatre. You have been asked to create a press packet for Paul's Kitchen. It will include a cover page, a cover letter, a press release and a brochure advertising Paul's Kitchen.

Create the Press Packet

- Open *exp07_w_arts_cpt_press_release.docx*. Save it as **exp07_w_arts_cpt_press_release_solution.docx**.
- Set the document margins to **Normal**.
- Insert a cover page in the **Pinstripes** style. Change the document theme to **Flow**.
- Make the document title **Paul's Kitchen Press Release**.
- Change the Document Subtitle to **Presented by Green Man Theater**. Delete the company name below the date. Select today's date.
- Insert *exp07_w_arts_cpt_dat.jpg*. This JPEG file contains the company logo.
- Apply the Square text wrapping style. Place the logo in the lower right corner of the cover page.
- Create a WordArt object to the left of the logo. Its text should be Green Man Theatre. Format it attractively to complement the colors in the logo and the theme used in the rest of the document. Apply the Square text wrapping style.
- If necessary, attractively format and resize the logo and WordArt on the cover page.

Create a Cover Letter

- Add a next page section break at the top of the press release page to create a cover letter page. You might find it easiest to work with a document with many different formats and sections like this one with Show/Hide turned on. This will enable you to see the changes in formatting.
- Write a quick professional cover letter to members of the press. Do not use a return address block in the letter. Personally invite them to the show and offer two complimentary tickets to them. Make a bulleted list of the press packet contents, including:
  - o Cover Page
  - o Cover Letter
  - o Press Release
  - o Brochure
- Add the Pinstripes header to the cover letter. Deactivate the command that links the header to the previous section. Copy the WordArt you created for the cover page and resize it so it will fit attractively in the lower right side of the header. If you can't paste the WordArt, right-click in the header, and select **Remove Content Control**. Then try pasting the WordArt again in the header.
- Left-align the body of the letter.
- Add a date that will automatically update above the greeting line of the letter.
- Use the **Normal Style** to format the letter. Make sure the bulleted list has bullets after applying the style.
- Make any format changes to improve the professional appearance of the letter.
- Change the bottom margin to **1.5"**.
- Add a footer that matches the Pinstripes header. Remove the page number. In the area to type text, enter the theater's contact information displayed in two lines:

  123 Main Street, Minneapolis, MN 55404
  (612) 555–7651 www.greenmantheatre.com

- Attractively format the footer so the address is completely visible when the document prints.
- You realized that you did not include a return address at the top of the cover letter. Above the date, type a return address block using the complete contact information above. Add the address to your Quick Parts gallery as Green Man Address.
- Save the *exp07_w_arts_cpt_press_release_solution.docx* document.

Modify the Press Release

- Continue to the press release page of the press packet (page 3).
- Change *Press Release* to the **Emphasis** style.
- Change *Green Man Theater Announces the Opening of* Paul's Kitchen to the Title style.
- Change the next paragraph that starts *Paul's Kitchen . . .* to the Subtitle style.
- Change the line *Minneapolis . . .* to the Heading 1 style.
- After the body paragraph describing the basic plot of the play, add a new paragraph: **Tickets are available at the box office or online at:**.
- Use the Quick Part you created to add the contact information block.

Convert the Showtimes Table

- Convert the tab separated list below the box office information to a two-column table. Format it using the **Table Classic 1** format (top row, center).
- Autofit the content.
- Center the table horizontally on the page.
- Insert a next page section break.
- Save the *exp07_w_arts_cpt_press_release_solution.docx* document.

...continued on Next Page

Create a New Ticket Price List

- On the new page, create a new table with four columns and four rows.
- Merge the cells of the top row and create a title **Green Man Theater Ticket Price List** using the title style.
- In the second row and first column, add the following headings:

Ticket Type	At The Door	Advance Purchase	Season Tickets
Adult			
Senior			

- Add another row to accommodate **Student**.
- Enter the *At The Door* ticket prices:

Adult	$50
Senior	$25
Student	$15

- There is a 20% discount for advance purchase tickets.
- There is a 25% discount for season tickets, but you have to purchase tickets to all three plays.
- Enter formulas in the table to calculate these discounts.
- Attractively format the table so it coordinates with the document theme.
- Add a footnote explaining Season Tickets: **Season Tickets have a 25% discount on the door price. All three tickets of the season must be purchased at once to qualify for season ticket pricing.**
- Add a footnote explaining Advance Purchase: **Advance Purchase Tickets are a 20% discount on the door price and must be purchased at least two weeks before the show.**
- The Theater Shop manager asked you to include a price list of merchandise in the press packet. She gave you the name of the file. Create a link that will update if there are any price changes in the Theater Shop. The table you should link is in *exp07_w_arts_cpt_Greenman_Pricelist.docx*.
- Resize the linked table so it fits on the same page with the ticket prices.
- Save your work.

You will present this press packet to the Board of Directors before the press conference.

- Turn on **Track Changes**.
- Find all occurrences of *Theater* within *Green Man Theater* and replace with **Theatre**, so that the company name is *Green Man Theatre*.
- Go to the cover letter and make a comment on the offer of two complimentary tickets. Your comment should say: **Did we decide on two tickets or four tickets?**
- Save and close *exp07_w_arts_cpt_press_release_solution.docx*.

Make a Brochure

- Create a 2009–2010 Season Brochure. Use your judgment to format it attractively, but follow these guidelines. Use the Flow theme and have the overall appearance coordinate with the press release and the Green Man Theatre logo.
- Open *exp07_w_arts_cpt_greenman_brochure.docx* and save it as **exp07_w_arts_cpt_greenman_brochure_solution.docx**. This text should be used in the advertising brochure.
- Format the brochure so it has two folds and three panels of information on each side of the page.
- The front panel, when folded, should have the Green Man logo *exp07_w_arts_cpt_dat.jpg* and the Green Man Theatre WordArt you created earlier. It should also have *2009–2010 Season* in the same panel.
- The panel showing when you lift the front panel, with the one fold still closed, should have the information about the Green Man Theatre, which is the top paragraph in *exp07_w_arts_cpt_greenman_brochure.docx.*
- The back panel when both folds are closed should have ticket pricing information from the table you created for the press packet and the theatre's complete contact information from the Quick Parts gallery.
- When all the folds are open, the inside three panels should have pictures and information on the three plays available this season. Each panel should have information about one play. The information about the three plays are the bottom six paragraphs in *exp07_w_arts_cpt_greenman_brochure.docx*. The pictures are in the graphics directory and are labeled with the names of the plays with which they go.
- Insert a text box with the address, phone number, and Web site. Insert one shape somewhere in the brochure.
- Save and close *exp07_w_arts_cpt_greenman_brochure_solution.docx*.

Production Assistants

Use Microsoft Office Excel

Background

Microsoft Office Excel is second only to Word as the most commonly used application program in a theater company business office. Production assistants create mailing lists, budgets for upcoming shows, reports on past shows, rehearsal schedules, and display charts. Excel assists the company in analyzing data both mathematically and visually. These four chapters provide the necessary foundation to use Microsoft Excel effectively. These skills will be built upon at a more advanced level.

Tasks

In a theater company's business office, a production assistant might be asked to use spreadsheets for many purposes, including:

- Mailing lists
- Budgets for upcoming shows
- Budget reports for past shows
- Charts to act as a visual representation of data
- Rehearsal schedules
- Mileage reimbursement and other forms

Skills

A production assistant should be able to do the following:

Chapter 1

- Describe and use symbols and the order of precedence (page 328)
- Display cell formulas (page 330)
- Insert and delete rows and columns (page 331)
- Use cell ranges; Excel move; copy, paste, paste special; and AutoFill (page 332)

Chapter 2

- Create and copy formulas (page 381)
- Use relative and absolute cell addresses (page 382)
- Use AutoSum (page 389)
- Insert basic statistical functions (page 390)
- Use date functions (page 392)
- Use the IF function (page 399)
- Use the VLOOKUP function (page 400)
- Use the PMT function (page 408)
- Use the FV function (page 409)

...continued on Next Page

Chapter 3

- Choose a chart type (page 431)
- Create a chart (page 438)
- Modify a chart (page 450)
- Enhance charts with graphic shapes (page 453)
- Embed charts (page 459)
- Print charts (page 460)

Chapter 4

- Freeze rows and columns (page 488)
- Hide and unhide rows, columns, and worksheets (page 489)
- Protect a cell, a worksheet, and a workbook (page 490)
- Control calculation (page 493)
- Print large worksheets (page 493)

Production Assistants
Volume 1 | Capstone Exercises

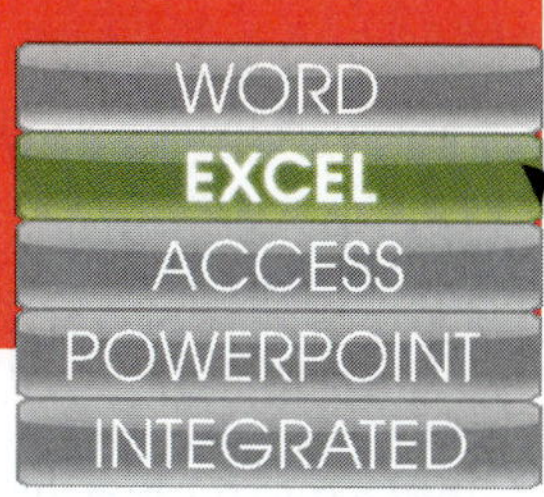

You work as a production assistant in the offices of a new company, The Green Man Theatre. You have been asked to create a packet for the director of operations. This packet will include an audition schedule, a budget for the upcoming show, Paul's Kitchen, *a spreadsheet and a chart derived from a list of costs incurred in the mounting of the current show, and a forecast of ticket sales based on past shows.*

Creating a Proposed Budget for *Paul's Kitchen*

You have been asked to compile data to create a proposed budget for the first show of the Green Man Theatre's 2009 season, *Paul's Kitchen*. You have received costs from the director, stage manager, prop master, costume designer, and tech crew. Because expenses will occur weekly, you will break the costs down on a weekly basis. *Paul's Kitchen* rehearses for four weeks, starting Monday, August 9, 2009, and opens Friday, September 4, 2009.

- Open *exp07_e_arts_cpt_greenman* and save as **exp07_e_arts_cpt_greenman_solution** so you can return to the original if necessary.
- Rename *Sheet1* as **Budget**.
- Type a formula in **cell B2** that will show the current date each time the spreadsheet is opened.
- Format the title *Budget for Paul's Kitchen* so it is centered across columns A:J with a Calibri 16 pt, White, Background 1 font and Blue, Accent 1 fill.
- Format **cells A3:J18** using a Calibri 12 pt. font. Widen columns as necessary.
- The combined actors' salaries are $1,500 per week, and the stage manager earns $200 per week. Enter these expenses in the respective rows in the budget.
- Format **cells B4:J18** as Accounting with no decimal places.
- In **cell J4**, insert the function to calculate the total salary for the director. Copy the function for the rest of the employees.
- Calculate the weekly total expense in **cell B18**. Copy the formula for the rest of the totals on row 18.

Calculate Projected Revenue and Net Profit

- Format the *Projected Ticket Sales* section. Merge and center the title across **cells A21:F21**. Use the Format Painter to copy the formatting from merged **cell A1** to merged **cell A21**.
- The Green Man Theatre decided to offer a 20% discount on advance ticket sales. Add four new cells between the Door Ticket Prices (**cells B22:B25**) and Advance Seats Sales (**cells C22:C25**).
- Click in the new **cell C22** and enter **Advance Sales Price**. Format row 22 to wrap text.
- In **cell I22**, enter **Advance Discount**. Enter **.20** in **cell I23** and apply the Percent style with no decimal places.
- In **cell C23**, create a a formula that calculates the advance purchase price for senior citizen tickets. Copy this formula for the other two groups.
- Click in **cell F23**. Create a formula that calculates total ticket revenue for all projected senior citizen ticket sales. (Hint: Sales price times quantity sold equals revenue.) Copy this formula to calculate Adult and Student Projected Revenue.
- AutoSum the total projected sales revenue in **cell F26**.
- AutoSum the total projected advance purchase tickets in **cell D26** and the tickets sold at the door in **cell E26**.
- Format **cells B23:C26** and **cells F23:F26** as Accounting with no decimal places.
- Click in **cell A28**. Format *Projected Profit* to match the section headers in **cells A1** and **A21**. This should merge **cells A28:B28**.
- In **cell B29**, create a formula to display the revenue generated from total ticket sales for *Paul's Kitchen*.
- In **cell B30**, create a formula to display the production costs (**cell J18**).
- Create a formula in **cell B31** to calculate estimated net profit (profit after expenses).
- Complete the *Paul's Kitchen Budget* worksheet by displaying all borders around the three sections of this worksheet: *Budget* (**cells A3:J18**), *Estimated Ticket Sales* (**cells A22:F26**), and *Estimated Profit* (**cells A29:B31**).
- Insert a comment in **cell J:18** that reads: **These expenses were calculated at our last tech meeting on 7/16/2009.**
- Create a header including your name, course, and instructor. Create a footer with the workbook and worksheet names and page number. Print the Budget worksheet for a budget meeting.

Use If Function

Because actors work as independent contractors, they are reimbursed for mileage. The Green Man Theatre has an optional equal mileage payment plan, which cast members can opt into to reduce the amount of paperwork. You have collected each of their round trip distances to the theater and have created an equalized mileage reimbursement based on whether they participate in the Mileage Payment Plan or not. The actors opting out of the equal mileage payment plan will turn in expense reports including their mileage logs and will receive mileage reimbursement in a lump sum at the end of the production based on their mileage logs.

- Go to the **Mileage** worksheet.
- AutoFit column width for all columns.
- In **cell B7**, create a formula to calculate miles driven by Ellen Anderson for all rehearsals and performances. The total number of rehearsals and performances is in **cell B12**. Copy the formula for the rest of the cast. Remember to use correct absolute cell references when necessary.
- Create a formula to correctly calculate total mileage reimbursement for Ellen Anderson in **cell B8**. You will

...continued on Next Page

find the reimbursement rate in **cell B11**. Copy the formula to calculate reimbursements for the rest of the cast.

- Select **cell B9**. Create an IF function that equally divides the total mileage payments across the weekly pay periods for the production cycle of the show if the cast member opts into the Mileage Equal Payment Plan. If the cast member does not participate in the Mileage Equal Payment plan, then return 0. Copy this function for the rest of the cast. The number of weeks of the production cycle is in **cell B13**.

To help accurately prepare budgets for future productions, you prepare statistics on mileage expense reimbursement for each production. Because the number of actors varies from production to production, you need statistics on mileage reimbursement for a single actor.

- In **cell A16**, type **Minimum Mileage Reimbursement**. Use a function to return the minimum total mileage reimbursement amount paid in **cell B16**.
- In **cells A17** and **B17**, prepare **Maximum Mileage Reimbursement**.
- In **cells A18** and **B18**, prepare **Average Mileage Reimbursement**.
- In **cells A19** and **B19**, prepare the total mileage expenses for the entire cast.

Use a PMT Function to Calculate a Loan Payment

Part of your responsibility in managing the budget is to make recommendations on loan expenses. The Board of Directors has voted to replace the sound system and finance the cost. A main patron is the president of a local bank. She has guaranteed an excellent interest rate of 9.75% on a five-year, unsecured loan for the sound system. The board approved the purchase of an $18,995 sound system installed. How much will the monthly payment be on the loan?

- Name *Sheet3* as **SoundSystem**. Use this worksheet to build a loan worksheet. Include an attractive title, correct formatting for all numbers displayed, and the following information to complete your worksheet.

Installed Price	$18,995
Annual Percentage Interest Rate	9.75
Length of Loan	Five years
Monthly Payment	

- Use a PMT function to solve the monthly payment. Be sure the result displays as a positive number.

Use Lookup Function

The Green Man Theatre has gained several patrons and has created an Honor Circle to thank their generous patrons. The Honor levels and required donations are listed in the table below.

Honor Levels	Individual Gifts of at least
Platinum	$10,000
Gold	$ 1,000
Silver	$ 100

One of your responsibilities is to keep track of patrons' donations and give them appropriate thanks in the play bill. You will use a lookup function to assign the appropriate Honor Level to your Patrons List.

- Go to the *Patrons* worksheet.
- Create a lookup table starting in **cell A12**, using the information in the table above.
- In **cell D3**, create a VLOOKUP function that returns silver, gold, or platinum based on each patron's gift. Copy this function for the rest of the patrons.
- Select the **Patron List** in **cells A2:D8** and turn it into a table with headers. Use the Quick Style gallery to format it with **Table Style Light 9**.
- Sort the table by **Honor Level** so Platinum Patrons are at the top of the list, followed by Gold, and finally, Silver. Sort the patrons alphabetically by last name and first name inside the Honor Level groupings.
- Save the workbook.

Create a Budget Summary

After a successful run of *Paul's Kitchen*, you create a budget summary and graphs summarizing ticket sales. Remarkably enough, the production stayed exactly on budget and Green Man Theatre's ticket sales projections were pretty accurate.

- Go to the *Budget* worksheet and copy the entire budget worksheet to a new worksheet before the *Mileage* worksheet. Name the new worksheet **Budget Summary**.
- Since *Paul's Kitchen* came in right on budget, you do not need to make any changes to the budget section. Change the header for the *Projected Ticket Sales* section to **Ticket Sales**.
- Enter these ticket sales numbers as your final sales figures, replacing the projected figures:

Ticket Type	Advance Purchase Seats	At Door Seats
Senior	202	84
Adult	604	163
Student	72	111

- From these final sales figures, construct two embedded pie charts on this worksheet to compare the percentage of ticket types at the door and advanced. One chart should show percentage by ticket type of advanced tickets sold and the other should show the percentage by ticket type of at door tickets.
- Use a layout from the gallery that displays the percentage for each pie slice for both charts.
- Create a bar chart depicting total revenue from all senior, adult, and student tickets sold.
- Move this chart to a new worksheet called **Total Sales**.
- Move the *Total Sales* worksheet to the left of the *Mileage* worksheet.
- Save and close *exp07_e_arts_cpt_greenman_solution*.

Production Assistants

Use Microsoft Office Access

Background

In order to track and analyze large amounts of information for a theater company, production assistants might use Microsoft Office Access. They create and maintain databases and create and edit queries, forms, and reports. Data will enable the company to track and analyze staff, actors, and shows, as well as create custom queries, forms, and reports to determine which staff member was in charge of a show, which actor performed in a show, and which staff members are also actors.

Tasks

In a theater company's business office, a production assistant might be asked to create and edit many types of database objects, including the following:

- Tables
- Queries
- Forms
- Reports

Skills

A Production Assistant should be able to do the following:

Chapter 1

- Understand the difference between working in storage and memory (page 554)
- Practice good file management (page 555)
- Back up, compact, and repair Access files (page 556)
- Create filters (page 565)
- Sort table data on one or more fields (page 568)
- Know when to use Access or Excel to manage data (page 570)
- Use the Relationships window (page 578)
- Understand relational power (page 579)

Chapter 2

- Design data (page 607)
- Create tables (page 612)
- Understand table relationships (page 625)
- Share data with Excel (page 626)
- Establish table relationships (page 630)
- Create a query (page 642)
- Specify criteria for different data types (page 645)

...continued on Next Page

- Copy and run a query (page 649)
- Use the Query Wizard (page 649)
- Understand large database differences (page 653)

Chapter 3

- Understand the order of precedence (page 679)
- Create a calculated field in a query (page 679)
- Create expressions with the Expression Builder (page 689)
- Create and edit Access functions (page 690)
- Perform date arithmetic (page 694)
- Create and work with data aggregates (page 704)

Chapter 4

- Plan a report (page 731)
- Use different report views (page 733)
- Identify report elements, sections, and controls (page 747)
- Add grouping levels in Layout view (page 750)
- Add fields to a report (page 755)
- Use the Report Wizard (page 765)

Production Assistants
Volume 1 | Capstone Exercises

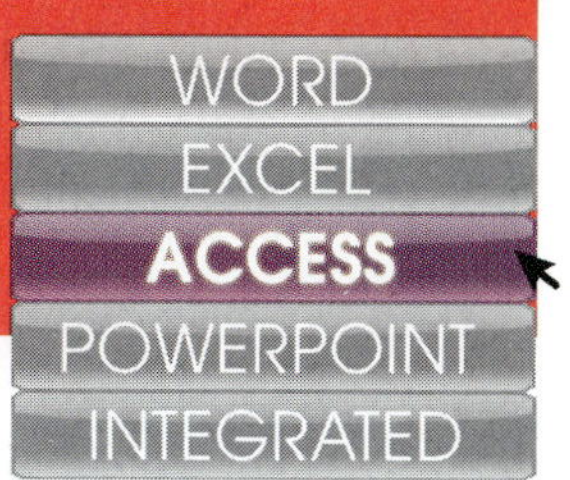

You work as a production assistant in the offices of a new company, The Green Man Theatre. One of your duties is to maintain the company database. You will create and edit tables, queries, forms, and reports as well as work with the Microsoft Access components and features. You will also be responsible for the file management of the company's documents, spreadsheets, presentations, and databases. Because you recently inherited this database, you decide to explore it.

Exploring, Describing, and Navigating Among the Objects in an Access Database

- Copy the database *exp07_a_arts_cpt_greenman.accdb*. Rename the copied file as **exp07_a_arts_cpt_greenman_solution .accdb**.
- Display the Navigation Pane in Tables and Related Views.
- Open the *tblActors* table.
- Add the following record: **26 Margo Samson, 3300 West 60th Street, New York, NY, 10003, 212-852-8900, 456-22-1094**.
- Sort the table by last name in ascending order.
- Find Stacia Henneson's record.
- Replace the last name *Henneson* with **Tandbell**.
- Create a filter by selection for all actors who live in New York City.
- Remove the filter.
- Create a filter by form for all actors who live in Queens Village, New York, who will be performing in show 200.
- Remove the filter.
- Save and close the table.
- Compact and repair the database.
- Back up the database to the drive specified by the instructor.
- Open the Relationships window.
- Show all three tables in the database. Note the relationships between the tables.
- Observe the Edit Relationships dialog box for all relationships.
- View Tables and Related Views.
- Save and close the Relationships window.

The Managing Director has requested a report of all actors who will perform in *Christmas at the Andersons'*.

- Open the *rptActorShow* report.
- Create a filter to display all actors who will perform in show 200 – *Christmas at the Andersons*.
- Preview the report.
- Print the report.
- Save and close the report.

One of your responsibilities will be to act as a liaison between the contact person at rehearsal and performance spaces and the Green Man Theatre. You have been given several scraps of paper with various bits of information on them. You will use these data to create a table.

- Create a table called **tblTheaters** in Design view that will hold information about the theaters the Green Man Theatre rents to rehearse and perform in. Use the following information to design your table.

Field Name	Caption
TheaterID	Theater ID
TheaterName	Theater Name
TheaterAddress	Theater Address
TheaterCity	Theater City
TheaterState	Theater State
TheaterZip	Theater Zip
TheaterPhone	Theater Phone
TheaterContactFirstName	Theater Contact First Name
TheaterContactLastName	Theater Contact Last Name
TheaterPricePerWeek	Weekly Theater Rental Fee
StaffID	Staff

- Change the field size for each field to an appropriate size.
- Change the data type for *TheaterPricePerWeek* to Currency, with two decimal places.

...continued on Next Page

- Save the table as **tblTheaters**.
- Enter the following records:

tblTheaters										
Theater ID	**Theater Name**	**Theater Address**	**Theater City**	**Theater State**	**Theater Zip Code**	**Theater Phone**	**Theater Contact First Name**	**Theater Contact Last Name**	**Theater Rental Fee per Week**	**Staff ID**
01	Garage Theater	123 Main Street	New York	NY	10003-	(212) 555-9999	Ted	Dawsic	$1,200.00	8900
02	8th Place Showtime	1000 West 98th Street	New York	NY	10003-	(212) 999-8888	Sharon	LeGance	$1,500.00	8901
03	People's Theater	2085 42nd Street	New York	NY	10003-	(212) 777-9999	Krystal	Sommers	$1,300.00	8900

- Close the table.

Import from Excel

Some data is stored in an Excel workbook. You want to import that data into your database, and then build relationships between the imported table and existing tables in the database.

- Import the Excel spreadsheet *exp07_a_arts_cpt_greenman_advertisers* into the database.
- Name the imported table **tblAdvertisers**.
- Add a **StaffID** field to *tblAdvertisers*. Type the following data:

StaffID
8900
8900
8900
8900
8901

- Close the table.
- Create a relationship between the staff primary key in *tblStaff* and the foreign key in *tblAdvertisers*.
- Enforce referential integrity.
- Create a relationship between the staff primary key in *tblStaff* and the foreign key of *tbltheaters*.
- Enforce referential integrity.

Queries and Reports

You need to find out which Green Man Theatre Staff person is the contact for each of the Theatres Green Man will be using this season.

- Create a query to display the following:
    - o TheaterID
    - o TheaterName
    - o StaffID
    - o StaffFirstName
    - o StaffLastName
- Name the query **qryTheaterStaffContact**.
- Save and close the query.

You will also be in charge of contracts. The next mailing that must take place is to the cast and crew of *This Was Not in the Brochure*. In order to create this mailing, you need to display just the cast and crew of that show. You decide to keep the original query intact and work with a copy.

- Copy *qryActorShow* and save the copy as **QryActorBrochure**.
- Open *qryActorBrochure*.
- Enter criteria to display only actors in the show *This Was Not in the Brochure*.
- Save and close the query.

Theater rehearsal and performance space is rented out by the week. Your managing director budgets the show on a monthly scale. You have been asked to calculate the monthly cost of each theater with which Green Man works. The managing director would like to spend no more than $1,300 per week, so you decide to display those records first.

- Modify *qryTheaterRent*. Create a calculated field using the Expression Builder to determine the cost of the space per month.
- Display only locations that cost less than $1,300 per week.
- Save and close the query.
- Create a report based on the qryTheaterRent query to display your findings. Adjust the report design to make the report readable and attractive.
- Name the report **rptTheaterRent**.

In order to calculate the cost and profit of *This Was Not in the Brochure*, you have been asked to calculate the number of days between the show's opening and closing nights.

...continued on Next Page

- Create a query called **qryRunBrochure** to calculate the number of days that *This Was Not in the Brochure* will run. Include the name of the show, the start date, and the end date of the show in the query.
- Return the results in a column called **Days in Run**.
- Save, close, and run the query.

The Board of Directors is going to vote on whether or not to invest in a vehicle for the Green Man Theatre. You have been asked to create a report listing the payment per month for three different vehicles under consideration.

- Modify *qryVehicle* to include a PMT function to determine the monthly payment of the cars up for consideration. The interest rate is 0.065, the loan will be for 60 months, and Green Man Theatre has $5,000 to use as a down payment.
- Return the result in a Monthly Payment column. Format the result as Currency with two decimal points.
- Save and close the query.
- Create a report called **rptVehiclePayment** using the Report Wizard to display the following:
  - o VehicleID
  - o VehicleYear
  - o VehicleMake
  - o VehicleModel
  - o VehicleCost
  - o Monthly Payment
- Attractively format the report so it will print on one page.
- Add the title **Vehicle Payment Report**.
- Save, print, and close the report.
- Close the database.

Production Assistants

Use Microsoft Office PowerPoint

Background

Microsoft Office PowerPoint can be a powerful tool for use in a theater company business office. Production assistants create presentations, handouts, and scripts for the presenter. It is important that a production assistant become familiar with entering text, pictures and clip art, movies, and animation to utilize the benefits of this program. The next four chapters provide the necessary foundation needed to use Microsoft PowerPoint. These skills will be built upon at a more advanced level.

Tasks

In a theater company's business office, a production assistant might be asked to create and edit many types of presentations. This could include the following:

- Creating presentations from scratch and using themes
- Animating presentations
- Creating and printing the notes page
- Using SmartArt
- Creating slides to be used as show flyers
- Editing objects
- Inserting clip art, movies, sounds, and graphic objects

Skills

A production assistant should be able to do the following:

Chapter 1

- Identify PowerPoint user interface elements (page 799)
- Use PowerPoint views (page 804)
- Open and save a slide show (page 809)
- Get Help (page 812)
- Create a storyboard (page 817)
- Use slide layouts (page 820)
- Apply design themes (page 820)
- Review the presentation (page 822)
- Add a table (page 829)
- Insert clip art (page 829)
- Use transitions and animations (page 831)
- Run and navigate a slide show (page 840)
- Print with PowerPoint (page 842)

Chapter 2

- Create a presentation using a template (page 869)
- Modify a template (page 871)
- Create a presentation in Outline view (page 879)
- Modify an outline structure (page 881)
- Print an outline (page 882)
- Import an outline (page 887)
- Add existing content to a presentation (page 888)
- Examine slide show design principles (page 892)
- Apply and modify a design theme (page 892)
- Insert a header or footer (page 896)

Chapter 3

- Create shapes (page 931)
- Apply Quick Styles and customize shapes (page 936)
- Create SmartArt (page 952)
- Modify SmartArt diagrams (page 955)
- Create WordArt (page 961)
- Modify WordArt (page 961)
- Modify objects (page 968)
- Arrange objects (page 975)

Chapter 4

- Insert and modify a picture (page 1015)
- Use the Internet as a resource (page 1021)
- Create a Photo Album (page 1033)
- Set Photo Album options (page 1033)
- Insert movies (page 1038)
- Set movie options (page 1040)
- Add sound (page 1046)
- Record and play narration (page 1048)

Production Assistants
Volume 1 | Capstone Exercises

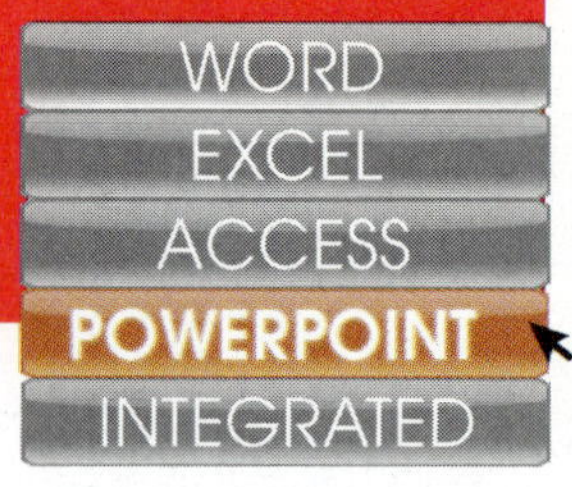

You work as a production assistant in the offices of a new company, The Green Man Theatre. You have been asked to create a presentation to display in the theater shop and box office to advertise season tickets and the current season. This will be the basis for all future presentations by Green Man Theatre.

Create a Presentation

- Open a blank PowerPoint 2007 presentation. Save the presentation as **exp07_p_arts_cpt_season_ticket_solution.pptx**.
- Format the presentation with the **Flow** theme.
- Add the title **Green Man Theatre**. Format it with a preset fire gradient fill using the Brush Script MT font. It should coordinate with the Green Man logo.
- To the right of the title, insert the **Green Man Theatre logo**, *exp07_p_arts_cpt_dat.jpg*. Format the logo with a transparent background.
- Type **2009–2010 Season** in the subtitle field of the title slide.
- Center the title and subtitle with the logo immediately to the right of the title. Adjust the objects to fit on the slide attractively.
- Insert the sound file *GreenmantheatreMP3.mp3* on slide one. Set the sound file to play automatically when slide 1 appears. Hide the sound icon behind the Green Man Theatre logo. Set it to continue playing after you advance to the next slide.
- Apply an effect for the text box object *2009–2010 season* that makes it grow, then shrink to approximately its normal size while the Green Man Theatre song plays.
- Insert a new title and content slide. Title it **Green Man Theatre Presents**. Format the title to match the Green Man title on the first slide.
- Insert a table on the slide. The table should contain:

Show	Dates
Paul's Kitchen	September 4-27, 2009
Christmas at the Andersons'	November 27, 2009–January 3, 2010
This Was Not in the Brochure	February 26–March 28, 2010

- Below the table, create a new text box, **2009–2010 Season**.
- Attractively format the slide.
- Insert a new section header slide before slide 2.
- Make the title **Green Man Theatre Mission**. Format it to match the title on the first slide.
- Add this mission statement:

  We are committed to providing the environment and the resources for new artists, musicians, actors, and dancers to create and perform new works in the Twin Cities.
- Copy the Green Man logo from slide 1. Use it on this slide two times. Make one a mirror image of the other.
- Format the slide in an attractive and consistent manner.
- Save *exp07_p_arts_cpt_season_ticket_solution.pptx*.

Create a Presentation from an Outline

You have an outline describing the three plays of the season in a Word file. You will create a new presentation from that outline, and then import those slides into the previous presentation.

- Use the Microsoft Word document *exp07_p_arts_cpt_greenman_brochure* to create a new Powerpoint Presentation.
- Apply the **Resume theme**.
- Save this presentation as **exp07_p_arts_cpt_shows_solution.pptx**.
- Save and close *exp07_p_arts_cpt_shows_solution.pptx*.
- Reuse the three slides describing the plays in *exp07_p_arts_cpt_shows_solution.pptx* in *exp07_p_arts_cpt_season_ticket_solution.pptx* as slides 4 through 6.
- Edit the newly imported slides to match the design and flow of the rest of the Season Ticket Presentation.
- There are several photographs in the student capstone folder, named *Paul's Kitchen*, *Christmas at the Andersons* and *This Was Not in the Brochure*, and a number if there is more than one. Insert these photos on the appropriate slides and format the slides attractively.
- Apply **Picture Styles** to each of the photos.
- Add a clip art image of a Christmas tree to the *Christmas at the Andersons'* slide. Tilt it so it looks like it is falling.
- Add a clip art image of a van to the *Paul's Kitchen* slide.
- Attractively format and adjust all objects on the slides as needed.
- Insert a new slide after slide 6. Apply a **Section Header** layout.
- Add the title **Season Tickets**. Add these bullets:
  - o **Available in the Box Office and Theater Shop**
  - o **25% discount on Season Ticket Purchases**
  - o **Season Tickets make great gifts.**
  - o **Ask about becoming a Patron Member of Green Man Theatre.**

...continued on Next Page

- Use the same two Green Man logos that you used on Slide 2.
- Apply a **Section Header** layout to slide 3.
- Add a new blank slide and move it to the end of the presentation. Use one of the pictures from the plays on this slide.
- Create a shape callout so the person in the picture is thinking or saying something to encourage the viewer to purchase Season Tickets. Apply a fadeout animation to the callout.
- Format the shape and picture attractively.
- Create a new Title slide. The title should match the other titles in the presentation and be titled **Patronage Levels**. Create a **Pyramid Smart Art** to display **Giving Levels**.

Patronage Level	Gifts Amount
Platinum	$10,000
Gold	$ 1,000
Silver	$ 100

- Apply consistant transition effects for all slides.
- Apply a consistent effect to all bulleted text to appear one at a time on each slide.

Modify Existing Presentation to Run at a Kiosk

- Save your work as **exp07_p_arts_cpt_season_ticket_solution**.
- Save the presentation as **exp07_p_arts_cpt_season_ticket_kiosk_solution**.
- In the *exp07_p_arts_cpt_season_ticket_kiosk_solution* file, set each slide to automatically advance to the next slide. View the presentation and adjust the timing as necessary. Make sure that all transitions are pleasing and consistent and the presentation is attractive and eye catching enough to leave running in a loop at a kiosk in the Green Man Theatre shop and in the lobby.
- Save and close *exp07_p_arts_cpt_season_ticket_kiosk_solution*.
- Return to *exp07_p_arts_cpt_season_ticket_solution*. This presentation will be used during presentations given by a presenter. Add notes to each appropriate slide for the presenter to use. The notes should contain the following information.
    - o A greeting
    - o Information on the plays including genre and directors:

Play	Genre	Director
Paul's Kitchen	Comedy	Kayla Thomas
Christmas at the Andersons'	Family Farce	Stan Peal
This Was Not in the Brochure	Drama	Sara Hill

    - o A note about Patrons
    - o A closing, thanking the audience.
- Add a footer to the presentation that includes the date and slide number.
- Save *exp07_p_arts_cpt_season_ticket_solution*.
- View both *exp07_p_arts_cpt_season_ticket_solution* and *exp07_p_arts_cpt_season_ticket_kiosk_solution* from the beginning.
- Print handouts with notes.
- Save your work and close PowerPoint.

Integrate Microsoft Office Software

Background

Each program in the Microsoft Office suite has its strength and specialty. Microsoft Office Word is the best program to use when creating documents, especially those that require advanced formatting. Microsoft Office Excel is the choice when the data require calculations, charts, or mathematical analysis. Microsoft Office PowerPoint is a presentation program. It allows users to create unique, professional presentations and animate them. Microsoft Office Access is a database management program. It is capable of storing and analyzing large quantities of information. There are times users need to use all four programs together to create the desired result.

Tasks

In a theater company's business office, a production assistant might be asked to find data and present information using all the applications in Microsoft Office 2007. This could include:

- Creating handouts for a meeting in Microsoft Word.
- Spreadsheets calculating sales in Excel
- Exporting data from Access databases
- Animated PowerPoint presentations

Skills

In addition to basic integration skills, a production assistant should be able to do the following:

- Create a summary query
- Export query results to an Excel spreadsheet
- Calculate statistics using min, max, and average functions
- Create charts from the data
- Display the statistics and charts as linked objects in a PowerPoint presentation
- Embed objects in Word
- Use themes across applications to create cohesive appearance

Production Assistants
Volume 1 | Capstone Exercises

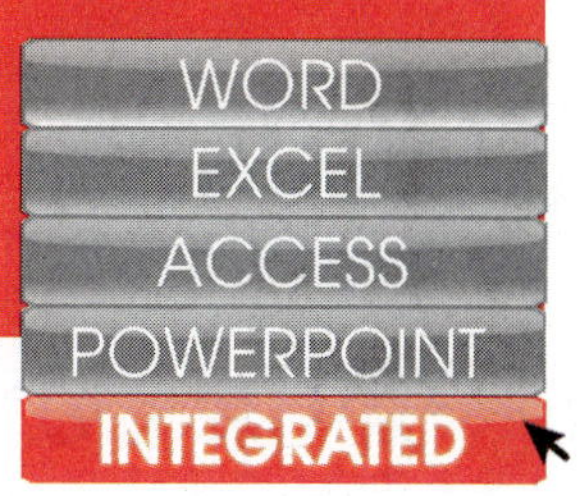

You work as a production assistant in the offices of a new company, The Green Man Theatre. You maintain the season tickets database.

The sales manager asked you to pull information that shows how many seats each season ticket holder owns for the opening weekend and put it in a Microsoft Excel spreadsheet so he can analyze sales. You exported the tables and a few queries for just the opening weekend to a test database so you do not harm production data unintentionally. If this becomes a regular function, you will move the queries into production.

- Open the Access database, *exp_i_arts_cpt_season_tickets.accdb* and save it as **exp07_i_arts_cpt_season_tickets_solution.accdb**. Season tickets are sold by the seat. Each show has its own set of seats in the run of the show. The tables of seats for each show are:

Table	Show
tblShow1	Opening Friday Night
tblShow2	Opening Saturday Night
tblShow3	Opening Sunday Matinee

- Use the Query Wizard to create a summary query to count the number of seats each ticket holder owns for opening Friday night.
- Create the same queries for Opening Saturday night and Opening Sunday Matinee.
- Export the results of all three queries to Microsoft Office Excel using **Export to Excel** in the Export group on the External Data tab.
- The results of each query should be on its own worksheet in the same workbook.

Query	Sheet
Opening Friday Night	Sheet1
Opening Saturday Night	Sheet2
Opening Sunday Matinee	Sheet3

- Save the Excel workbook as **exp07_i_arts_cpt_season_tickets_solution.xlsx**.
- Save and close **exp07_i_arts_cpt_season_tickets_solution.accdb**.

After you give the workbook *exp07_i_arts_cpt_season_tickets_solution.xlsx* to the sales manager, he comes by your office and admits he does not know what to do with it. He asks if you could please do some analysis on the buying habits of the season ticket holders. He would like a table compiling the information in the table below.

- Create a table similar to the one below on each show's worksheet.

Sales Statistics for Opening Friday Night	
Total season ticket seats sold for this show	calculation
Number of individual ticket holders for this show	calculation
Maximum number of seats owned by an individual season ticket holder	calculation
Minimum number of seats owned by an individual season ticket holder	calculation
Average number of seats owned by an individual season ticket holder	calculation

In addition to the statistical tables, he would like a chart comparing the number of seats sold for each show.

- On a new sheet, create a column chart comparing the total season tickets sold for each show on opening weekend.
- This should all be attractively formatted.
- Save your work.

After you complete this for the sales manager, he asks you to pop the chart and the sales statistics into one of those fabulous PowerPoint presentations you do so he can show it during the next board meeting. He would like the statistics for all three shows to be on one slide so the directors can view it all in one place.

- Create a new PowerPoint Presentation called **exp07_i_arts_cpt_season_tickets_solution.pptx**.
- Format it attractively using a theme that coordinates with the Green Man Theatre Logo (which you can import from *exp07_i_arts_cpt_season_tickets.docx*.) Modify the colors of the theme if necessary.
- The logo and WordArt title should appear on the title slide.
- On the second slide, object link all three opening weekend shows' statistics tables from *exp07_i_arts_cpt_season_tickets_solution.xlsx* on the first slide.
- On the third slide, Object link the chart comparing season ticket seats sold for the three opening weekend season ticket shows. Format the chart to coordinate with the PowerPoint presentation.
- Save your work.

...continued on Next Page

Finally, after you prepare the presentation, the sales manager asks you to create a Word document to e-mail to the board of directors before the meeting. This document should contain copies of the chart and the three sales statistics tables, but they should not be object linked.

- Open *exp07_i_arts_cpt_season_tickets.docx* and save it as **exp07_i_arts_cpt_season_tickets_solution.docx**.
- From the Excel workbook, *exp07_i_arts_cpt_season_tickets_solution.xlsx*, embed the Sales Statistics tables and the chart in the body of the document. Add a short introductory paragraph describing the purpose of the three tables and the chart.
- Save and close all your work.

Travel Agents

Use Microsoft Office Word

Background

Travel agents create correspondence and contracts with internal and external customers, as well as memos, reports, and documents requiring desktop publishing. It is imperative that a travel agent become proficient in Microsoft Office Word and its many features. The next four chapters are the necessary foundation needed to use Microsoft Word. These skills will be built upon at a more advanced level.

Tasks

In a travel agency a travel agent might be asked to create and edit many types of documents, including the following:

- Correspondence and mailings
- Mailing Lists
- Tables
- Flyers
- Information packets
- Agendas

Skills

A travel agent should be able to do the following:

Chapter 1

- Use AutoText (page 76)
- Set margins and specify page orientation (page 87)
- Insert page breaks (page 88)
- Add page numbers (page 90)
- Insert headers and footers (page 91)
- Create sections (page 92)
- Insert a cover page (page 93)
- Use the Find and Replace commands (page 94)

Chapter 2

- Apply font attributes through the Font dialog box (page 133)
- Highlight text (page 136)
- Copy formats with the Format Painter (page 139)
- Set off paragraphs with tabs, borders, lists, and columns (page 143)
- Apply paragraph formats (page 148)
- Create and modify styles (page 159)

...continued on Next Page

Chapter 3

- Insert a table (page 197)
- Format a table (page 205)
- Sort and apply formulas to table data (page 207)
- Insert clip art and images into a document (page 219)
- Format a graphic element (page 220)
- Insert WordArt into a document (page 225)

Chapter 4

- Create master documents and subdocuments (page 265)
- Create and modify footnotes and endnotes (page 281)

Travel Agents
Volume 1 | Capstone Exercises

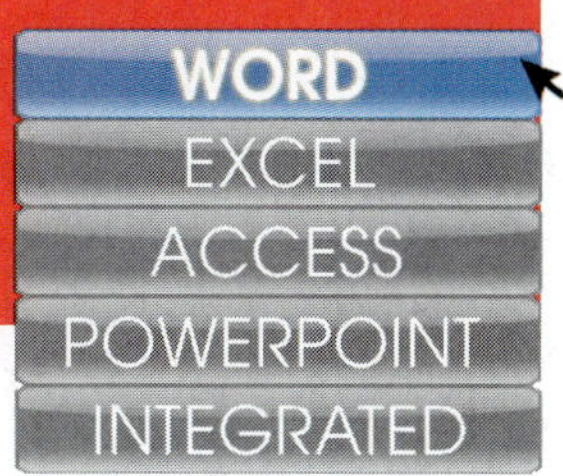

You work as a travel agent for Marella Travel. Your supervisor has asked you to create a packet for an upcoming staff meeting. This packet will consist of a cover page, an agenda, information on a new vacation package offered by the company. After the completion of this packet, you will e-mail it to your supervisor for approval.

Create a Cover Page

- Open *exp07_w_hosp_cpt_staff_meeting* and save it as **exp07_w_hosp_cpt_staff_meeting_solution**.
- Insert the Marella corporate logo (*Marella Travel Logo.bmp*).
- Insert a cover page of your choice, to complement the Marella logo.
- Move the logo to the cover sheet and format and size it attractively to complement the cover page you selected.
- Change the document theme to **Concourse**.
- Modify the colors to complement the Marella Travel logo. Save the Theme colors and the Modified theme each as **Marella_Travel**.
- Type the following title: **4th Quarter All-Staff Meeting**.
- Use the content controls on your cover page to enter:
  - o Today's date
  - o The name of the company, Marella Travel
  - o Your name as author
  - o A brief synopsis of the purpose of this document—**Quarterly Business Meeting to discuss all staff activities and upcoming promotions**
- Remove any unnecessary content controls and improve the format of the cover page as necessary.

Modify the Meeting Agenda

- Go to the second page, with Agenda at the top of the page.
- Insert a header and footer to match the style of the cover page. Note the format of the header and footer and the automatic content added.
- Modify the page numbering to begin numbering the page after the cover page as page 1.
- Remove any unnecessary content controls or content on the header or footer.
- Apply moderate margins to format the margins for the document.
- Look about ¾ of the way down the page to find *Win a Free Carribean Cruise*.
- Insert a next page section break so that *Win a Free Caribbean Cruise* goes to the top of the new page.
- Select **Agenda** at the top of the second page. Apply the Title style.
- Select from *Old Business* to the end of *choice* on the last line of the page. Apply the multilevel list command. Select the first multilevel list style after none in the list library. You should now have a list of 25 items.
- Adjust the indentation so the outline is formatted like the following image:

...continued on Next Page

1)→Old Business¶

a)→Read minutes from last week's meeting¶

i)→ Open discussion regarding minutes¶

ii)→Vote to approve/reject last week's minutes¶

b)→Follow up with volunteers for Holiday Food Drive¶

i)→ Advertising this opportunity to the company¶

(1)→Flyer in employee mailboxes¶

(2)→Edit PowerPoint presentation in main lobby¶

(3)→Prepare collection bin early and place it in the employee cafeteria¶

(4)→Ask supervisors to mention this opportunity in staff meetings between now and December 31, 2009¶

(5)→Ask supervisors to serve as an example and donate early¶

ii)→Transportation of food to Dayton Food Shelf¶

2)→New Business¶

a)→Upcoming Holiday Party¶

i)→ Date: December 12, 2009¶

ii)→Location: Wilton Hilton Ballroom¶

iii)→When: 6:00 PM – 10:00 PM¶

b)→New Vacation Package Details¶

i)→ Each package includes the following:¶

ii)→6 days, 5 nights suite accommodations in a select 3 star hotel.¶

iii)→Airfare¶

iv)→Ground Transportation to and from the airport¶

v)→Walking tours of the city¶

vi)→Three excursions of your choice¶

¶

- Add a line in the *Upcoming Holiday Party* section under *When: 6:00pm – 10:00pm* at the same outline level: **Dress Code: Holiday Semiformal Attire**.
- Under item 2b, add a table similar to the one below with field calculations to calculate:
    - The special package price, which is a 25% discount off the original price
    - The amount the customer would save

Destination	Dates	Original Package Price	Special Package Price	You Save
Cancun	March 2009	$4500.00		
Los Angeles	January 2010	$7800.00		
New York City	December 2009	$5200.00		
Paris	April 2010	$8500.00		

...continued on Next Page

- Format the first level, *New and Old Business*, of the Agenda outline using Heading 1 styles.
- Select all of the List Paragraph Style. Modify the style to increase the spacing between paragraphs to **Space Before: 6 pt, After: 12 pt**. This will give people attending the meeting room to jot down a few notes.
- Make sure that the table and item 2b are on the same page. Insert a page break to maintain the page numbering in the footer of the agenda.
- Create a new agenda item c) at the bottom of the agenda. Type the following:

  c)→Sales Promotion – Win a Free Caribbean Cruise.

  i.→The top sales person for January will win a 6 day – 5 night Caribbean Cruise.

Create a Flyer Advertising the Caribbean Cruise Sales Promotion to the Employees of Marella Travel

- Cut the last page of the agenda, all the text starting with *Win a Free Caribbean Cruise!* through the end, and paste it into a new Word document.
- Save the new document as **exp07_w_hosp_cpt_sales_promotion _ solution**.
- Save and close *exp07_w_hosp_cpt_staff_meeting_solution*.
- Apply the Marella Travel theme you created and saved earlier.
- Create a washout watermark using the Marella Travel logo.
- Create WordArt of your choice with the text **Cruise the Caribbean**. Format it to complement the Marella Travel logo.
- Place the Wordart attractively so it is large and clearly the eye catching title for the flyer.
- Format *Win A Free Caribbean Cruise* at the top of the page as a subtitle to the Wordart. You may move it to best enhance your layout.
- Format *Top Sales Agent for January Cruises the Caribbean* with intense emphasis.
- Create a footnote after *Agent*: **All sales agents employed on or before December 31, 2009, are eligible to win Cruise the Caribbean promotion.**
- Create a footnote after *Top*: **Sales contracts must be accompanied with 20% deposit to be eligible for sales promotion.**
- Create footnote after *January*: **Promotion Period begins at midnight, January 1, 2010, and ends at 11:59 pm on January 31, 2010.**
- Create SmartArt to set off the items in the cruise package individually.
- Add a clip art image of a cruise ship.
- Arrange and format all items on the page attractively.
- Save and close *exp07_w_hosp_cpt_sales_promotion_solution*.

Create a Master Document of the Quarterly Staff Meeting Agenda and Sales Promotion Flyer

- Open a new Word document. Save it as **exp07_w_hosp_cpt_marella_master_solution**.
- Format it using the Marella Travel theme you created earlier.
- Create subdocument headings of **4th Quarter Staff Meeting Agenda** and **Sales Promotion**. Format them with the **Heading 2** style.
- Switch to Outline View and add *exp07_w_hosp_cpt_staff_meeting_solution* and *exp07_w_hosp_cpt_sales_promotion_solution* as subdocuments.
- Save and close *exp07_w_hosp_cpt_marella_master_solution*.

Travel Agents

Use Microsoft Office Excel

Background

Microsoft Office Excel is an excellent tool for use in a travel agency. Travel agents can use Excel to track and calculate sales and commissions, create itineraries, calculate financing arrangements for vacation packages, and create charts to present data graphically. These data assist the company in analyzing data both mathematically and visually.

Tasks

In a travel agency business office, travel agents might be asked to create and edit many types of workbooks, including the following:

- Spreadsheets calculating sales commissions
- Payment plans for vacation packages
- Charts to act as a visual representation of data

Skills

A travel agent should be able to do the following:

Chapter 1

- Describe and use symbols and the order of precedence (page 328)
- Display cell formulas (page 330)
- Use cell ranges; Excel move; copy, paste, paste special; and AutoFill (page 332)

Chapter 2

- Create and copy formulas (page 381)
- Use relative and absolute cell addresses (page 382)
- Use AutoSum (page 389)
- Use the IF function (page 399)
- Use the VLOOKUP function (page 400)
- Use the PMT function (page 408)

Chapter 3

- Choose a chart type (page 431)
- Create a chart (page 438)
- Modify a chart (page 450)
- Print charts (page 460)

Chapter 4

Travel Agents
Volume 1 | Capstone Exercises

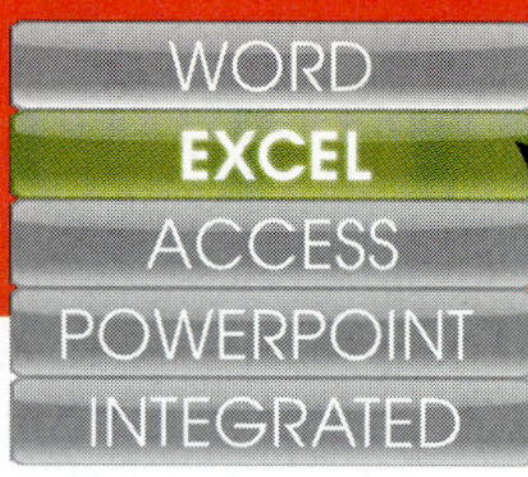

You work as a travel agent for Marella Travel. Travel agencies negotiate commission contracts with the major airlines. The travel agency receives a small percentage of the price of the airline ticket. You, as the travel agent, work on salary plus commission, which is a percentage of that portion that the agency earns from the sale of the airline ticket. You work in the corporate accounts department, where you sell mostly to business travelers seeking air travel. You enjoy a fairly healthy commission of 30% of the contracted rate for the agency. Because the rate varies among airlines, you cannot easily keep track of your expected commissions without the aid of a spreadsheet. To help plan your personal budget, you need to know how much you earn in a pay period, since your pay varies from paycheck to paycheck. You create a workbook, which enables you to calculate your commissions based on your sales for the pay period.

Creating the Spreadsheet

- Open *exp07_e_hosp_cpt_commissions* and save it as **exp07_e_hosp_cpt_commissions_solution**.
- Create a lookup function for **cell D3**, which displays the name of the airline from the table in **cells M5:O11**. Use the airline code you entered in **cell C3** to identify the correct airline. Copy the function.
- Name *Sheet1* **October**.
- In **cell F2**, create a new column header, **Contract Rate**.
- In **cell F3**, create a lookup function, which will display the contracted rate with the appropriate airline, which is found in column O of the lookup table. Copy the function.
- In **cell G2**, create a new column header, **Marella's Commission**.
- Format column G as Accounting with two decimal places.
- Create a formula in **cell G3** that will calculate the commission Marella earns from the sale of the airline ticket based on the contracted rate with that airline. Copy the function for the rest of the column.
- In **cell H2**, create a column header of **Your Name's Commission**.
- In **cell H3**, create a formula to calculate your portion (30%) of Marella's contracted rate. Put your rate in **cell N2** and use it for calculations. Copy the function for the rest of the column.
- Format the headings in row 2 so they wrap text and are bold.
- If you have completed the word assignment for Marella Travel, use the Marella Travel theme you created in Word to format the worksheet. If not, use the **Concourse** theme with **Flow Colors**. Save it as **Marella Travel**.
- Resize columns as necessary so no words break unnaturally. Center the column headings.
- Create a table from the list of ticket sales, **cells A2:H36**.
- In **cell A1**, type **Airline Ticket Commission Worksheet**. Format it to match the header row of the table and center it over the table. Increase the size of the font to be more noticeable.
- Create a total row in the table, totalling your commission and Marella's commission in the appropriate columns.
- Name the table range **Airline_Ticket_Commission_Worksheet**.
- Format the table with **Table Light Style 3**. Adjust column sizes if necessary.
- Delta announced a promotion in which they will give you five frequent flyer miles for every $20 you sell on their airline. You would really like to collect the frequent flyer miles to take a vacation during the holidays. Insert a new column on the far right of the table.
- In the header row of the new column, type **Delta Promotion Miles**.
- In the *Delta Promotion Miles* column, create a function to calculate the frequent flyer miles if it is a Delta flight. Return the number of miles earned if it is a Delta flight. Return 0 if it is not. Do not use absolute values in your formula. Use the values in cells M15:N15 in your formulas. Create a total for this column.
- Format all dollar values as accounting. Format all percentages as Percent Style with two decimal places. Format the Delta Promotion Miles as general with 2 decimal places.
- Sort the table by airline and then date, oldest to newest.
- Convert the table to a range and create a summary report of sales by sub-totalling ticket sales by airline and collapsing the table to the subtotal level.
- Create a column chart on a new sheet named **Airline Sales Chart**. The chart should graphically compare your sales for each airline. Title the chart **Ticket Sales By Airline**. Format the chart attractively.
- Delete Sheet2 and Sheet3.
- Save and close your work in *exp07_e_hosp_cpt_commissions_solution*.

Your supervisor has seen what you can do with Excel and is impressed. She confided that Marella is considering a plan to offer vacation financing where customers can pay for

...continued on Next Page

their vacations as a monthly payment over 12 months. She asked you to create a sample spreadsheet to calculate the monthly payment of a 12 month vacation payment plan with 11% annual percentage interest rate.

- Open a new workbook and save it as **exp07_e_hosp_cpt_payment_solution**.
- Enter the following information in the following cells:

  A1: Marella Travel Vacation Payment Plan

  A2: Vacation Package Price

  A3: Interest Rate

  A4: Term in Months

  A5: Monthly Payment

- Merge and center **cell A1** to **A1:B1**. Format the contents to wrap with **bold, 18 pt** font.
- Enter your loan parameters in column B. Use **$10,000** as your example package price.
- Calculate the monthly payment in **cell B5**.
- Format your spreadsheet with the Marella Travel theme. Adjust the column widths, if necessary, to ensure that all data displays attractively. Attractively tweak the formatting as needed. Use dollar and percent symbols where necessary.
- Protect this worksheet with a password of Marella so that customers cannot make changes to the worksheet without the password.
- Save and close your work in *exp07_e_hosp_cpt_payment_solution*.

Travel Agents

Use Microsoft Office Access

Background

In order to track and analyze large amounts of information, a travel agency would probably choose Microsoft Office Access. Travel agents create and maintain databases and create and edit queries, forms, and reports. This data will enable the company to track and analyze many types of data.

Tasks

In the travel industry, a travel agent might be asked to create and edit many types of database objects, including the following:

- Tables
- Queries
- Forms
- Reports

Skills

A travel agent should be able to do the following:

Chapter 1

- Understand the difference between working in storage and memory (page 554)
- Practice good file management (page 555)
- Back up, compact, and repair Access files (page 556)
- Create filters (page 565)
- Sort table data on one or more fields (page 568)
- Use the Relationships window (page 578)
- Understand relational power (page 579)

Chapter 2

- Design data (page 607)
- Create tables (page 612)
- Understand table relationships (page 625)
- Establish table relationships (page 630)
- Create a query (page 642)
- Specify criteria for different data types (page 645)
- Copy and run a query (page 649)
- Use the Query Wizard (page 649)

Chapter 3

- Understand the order of precedence (page 679)
- Create a calculated field in a query (page 679)

- Create expressions with the Expression Builder (page 689)
- Create and edit Access functions (page 690)
- Perform date arithmetic (page 694)
- Create and work with data aggregates (page 704)

Chapter 4

- Plan a report (page 731)
- Use different report views (page 733)
- Identify report elements, sections, and controls (page 747)
- Add grouping levels in Layout view (page 750)
- Add fields to a report (page 755)
- Use the Report Wizard (page 765)

Travel Agents
Volume 1 | Capstone Exercises

You work as a travel agent in the offices of Marella Travel. One of your duties is to maintain the company database. You will create and edit tables, queries, forms, and reports, as well as work with the Microsoft Office Access components and features. You are responsible for the file management of the company's documents, spreadsheets, presentations, and databases.

Exploring, Describing, and Navigating Among the Objects in an Access Database

- Copy the database *exp07_a_hosp_cpt_marella* and rename the copied file as **exp07_a_hosp_cpt_marella_solution**.
- Examine the relationships in the database.
- View Tables and Related Views.
- Open the *tblStaff* table.
- Add the following record: **8905, Margo Samson, 3300 West 60th Street, Minneapolis, MN, 55406, 612-852-8900, 456-22-1094.**
- Sort the table by **StaffLastName** in ascending order.
- Find the record for Brenda Burns.
- Replace the last name *Burns* with **Tandbell**.
- Create a filter by selection for all staff that live in St. Paul.
- Restore all table data.
- Save and close the table.
- Compact and repair the database.
- Back up the database to the drive specified by the instructor.

Marella has developed a new method of tracking sales of packaged tours. You were on the development steering team that helped develop the new database. When a travel agent makes a sale, he or she will record the sale in a Trips table, which will record who bought the trip, when they depart, when they bought it, and the travel agent who sold the packaged trip. With your skills in Access and involvement with the development steering team, your manager asked you to create a table of the vacation packages offered by Marella Travel and to create the relationships between the tables in this database system.

- Create a table called **tblPackages** in Design view.
- Type the following data and set the following properties:

Field Name	Data Type	Description	Field Size/ Decimal Places	Caption
PackageID	AutoNumber	Automatically generated package ID number here	Long Integer	Package ID
PackageName	Text	Name of the travel package	30	Package Name
PackageType	Text	Description of the package	100	Description
PackageDepPt	Text	Departure location	20	Departure Point
PackageDesPt	Text	Destination location	20	Destination Point
PackageLength	Number	Length in days	integer	Length In Days
PackagePrice	Currency	Price per person	2 decimal places	Price Per Person

- Save the table
- Type the following records:

Package ID	Package Name	Description	Departure Point	Destination Point	Length in Days	Cost per Person	Add New Field
1	The Big Apple	Tour of NYC	Minneaplolis MN	New York NY	7	$6,574.00	
2	Up, Up, and Away	Hot Air Balloon Ride	Duluth MN	Duluth MN	1	$350.00	
3	Bonjour!	Tour of Paris, France	Minnapolis MN	Paris, France	10	$8,500.00	
4	Seaside Sensaton	Cancun Vacation	Minneapolis MN	Cancun, Mexico	7	$2,890.00	
*							

...continued on Next Page

- Create relationships with enforced referential integrity between the following tables and fields:

Primary Key		Foreign Key	
Table	**Field**	**Table**	**Field**
tblPackages	PackageID	tblTrips	PackageID
tblCustomers	CustomerID	tblTrips	CustomerID
tblStaff	StaffID	tblCustomers	StaffID
		tblTrips	StaffID

- Save the database.

While you developed your portion of the new database, some other colleagues developed some of the other tables. Now it is in production. The Managing Director requested a report of all sales agents and their customers.

- Create a report using the Report Wizard.
- Use the following fields from *tblCustomers*:
  - o CustomerID
  - o CustomerFirstName
  - o CustomerLastName
- Use the following fields from *tblStaff*:
  - o StaffID
  - o StaffFirstName
  - o StaffLastName
- Group by **StaffLastName**.
- Sort ascending by **CustomerLastName**.
- Use a block layout.
- Apply the Module style.
- Enter a title in the header of **Customer Report by Travel Agent**.
- Name the report **rptCustomers**.
- View the report.
- In Layout view, delete the **Staff ID** number from the report and tweak the columns to attractively print on 1 piece of portrait letterhead.
- Save and close the report.

Your manager asked you to create a query to show all the customers of Brenda Tandbell.

- Use the Simple Query Wizard to build a query to find Brenda Tandbell's customers. Your results should return the following fields from the *Customer* table:
  - o CustomerID
  - o CustomerFirstName
  - o CustomerLastName
- Use the following fields from the *Staff* table.
  - o StaffID
  - o StaffFirstName
  - o StaffLastName
- Name the query **qryTandbellCust**.
- Run the query.
- Save and close the query.

Your manager asked you to create a sales report from the new Trips database system of tracking packaged trips. Your report will calculate the total dollar sales for a given period by agent.

- Create a query named **qryPackageSalesReport** based on the *tblTrips* table. It should also pull Customer Last Name, Staff Last Name, Package Name, and Per Person Price.
- In the *qryPackageSalesReport* query, create a formula that will calculate the extended price of each trip. Display it at the far right of the query under a heading of **Total Price**. For instance, if the customer Holmes purchased five Bonjour! trips at $8,500 per person, then you want to display how much Holmes spent on the vacation for five people.
- Create a report based on the *qrypackageSalesReport* query using the **Concourse Theme** to group and display the total sales of package vacations grouped by travel agent last name and sorted by package name. There should be:
  - o A subtotal for each travel agent
  - o Total sales for all agents
  - o Sale date for each sale
  - o A count of the number of customers buying packages and the total number sold
- Your report should have the components in the following figure. The report should look similar to this when complete.
- Format your report to display currency as displayed below.

...continued on Next Page

- Save and close your work.

Package Sales Report by Agent

Friday, August 29, 2008
12:23:24 AM

Staff Last Name	Customer Last Name	Package Name	Sale Date	Price	Quantity	Total Price
Adams						
	Holmes	Bonjour!	10/3/2009	$8,500.00	5	$42,500.00
	Chattswort	Bonjour!	10/27/2009	$8,500.00	8	$68,000.00
	Zoen	Seaside Sensation	10/7/2009	$2,890.00	7	$20,230.00
	Zoen	The Big Apple	10/15/2009	$6,574.00	4	$26,296.00
	Chattswort	Up, Up and Away	10/17/2009	$350.00	8	$2,800.00
	Holmes	Up, Up and Away	11/3/2009	$350.00	1	$350.00
	6				33	$160,176.00
Davis						

Travel Agents

Use Microsoft Office PowerPoint

Background

Microsoft Office PowerPoint can be a powerful tool in a travel agency. Travel agents create presentations, handouts, and scripts for the presenter. It is important that a travel agent become familiar with entering text, pictures, clip art, movies, and animation to utilize the benefits of this program. These four chapters are the necessary foundation needed to use PowerPoint.

Tasks

In a travel agency, travel agents might be asked to create and edit many types of presentations. This could include the following:

- Creating presentations from scratch and using themes
- Animating presentations
- Creating and printing the notes page
- Using SmartArt
- Creating slides to be used as show flyers
- Editing objects
- Inserting clip art, movies, sounds, and graphic objects

Skills

A travel agent should be able to do the following:

Chapter 1

- Use slide layouts (page 820)
- Apply design themes (page 820)
- Review the presentation (page 822)
- Add a table (page 829)
- Insert clip art (page 829)
- Use transitions and animations (page 831)
- Run and navigate a slide show (page 840)
- Print with PowerPoint (page 842)

Chapter 2

- Create a presentation using a template (page 869)
- Modify a template (page 871)
- Create a presentation in Outline view (page 879)

...continued on Next Page

- Modify an outline structure (page 881)
- Print an outline (page 882)
- Import an outline (page 887)
- Add existing content to a presentation (page 888)
- Examine slide show design principles (page 892)
- Apply and modify a design theme (page 892)
- Insert a header or footer (page 896)

Chapter 3

- Create shapes (page 931)
- Apply Quick Styles and customize shapes (page 936)
- Create SmartArt (page 952)
- Modify SmartArt diagrams (page 955)
- Create WordArt (page 961)
- Modify WordArt (page 961)
- Modify objects (page 968)
- Arrange objects (page 975)

Chapter 4

- Insert and modify a picture (page 1015)
- Use the Internet as a resource (page 1021)
- Create a Photo Album (page 1033)
- Set Photo Album options (page 1033)
- Insert movies (page 1038)
- Set movie options (page 1040)
- Add sound (page 1046)
- Record and play narration (page 1048)

Travel Agents
Volume 1 | Capstone Exercises

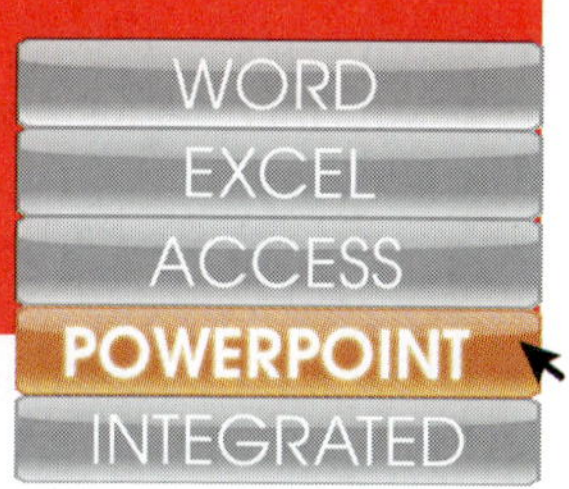

You are an employee of the Marella Travel agency, and the company is offering a new vacation package to New Zealand. You have been asked to create a PowerPoint presentation for the sales department to use at an upcoming convention. The presentation by the sales team will be given in a lecture format in an auditorium, whereas the presentation at the convention will be used at a convention to be run continuously on a computer monitor.

Create a Presentation

- Open a blank PowerPoint presentation and save it as **exp07_p_hosp_cpt_new_zealand_solution**.
- Change the layout of the first slide to **Title Slide**.
- Insert the file *NewMarellaTravel.bmp* into the bottom center of the slide. Set the white background to be the transparent color.
- Apply the Civic theme and choose a color scheme to complement the logo. Save the theme as **Marella_Travel_PPT**.
- Enter the title **New Zealand**. Attractively format it as WordArt using **Format Text Effects** with the file *MarellaTravelLogo.bmp* tiled as the text fill. Use an attractive font of your choice. Offset the title with an outline and/or shadows.
- Delete the subtitle content placeholder.
- Insert the JPEG file *New Zealand 1*. Use an attractive picture style for this and all other pictures in the slide show.
- Resize and format the elements of the title slide attractively.
- Insert a new **Title and Content** slide.
- Type the following title: **The Waters of Jade**.
- Insert the image *New Zealand 2* from the media directory.
- Resize and center the picture and apply the picture style you picked earlier.
- Copy the three paragraphs starting with *The Māori culture . . .* to *. . . but a large village.* from *exp07_p_cpt_notes.docx* to the notes page.
- Insert a new **Two Content** slide.
- Type the following title: **Welcome to the Youngest Country on Earth.**
- Insert the JPEG *New Zealand 3* from the media directory in the right placeholder. Apply the picture style and resize as necessary.
- In the Left Placeholder, type the following text: **Day One**. Format it with no bullet.
- Create a WordArt object in the upper left-hand corner of the WordArt dialog box using the text **Relax. . . .** Format the WordArt so it goes uphill from left to right and is 3-D. Otherwise, it should be attractively styled to complement the slide show's content.
- Type the following bulleted list:
  - **You will be met at the airport and ushered to your room at the Wilton Hilton.**
  - **The rest of the day is for relaxation.**
- Format the bullets using the bullets, spirals, swirls picture bullet style. You will find this bullet by searching on the keyword *Spiral* in the Bullets and Numbering Picture Bullet search box.
- Insert a new **Title and Content** slide.
- Type the following title: **Hotel Amenities**.
- Type the following bulleted list:
  - **Stunning grounds and gardens**
  - **Walking trails**
  - **Spa**
  - **Gym**
  - **Casual and fine dining restaurants**
  - **Lounge with live music nightly**
  - **24-hour room service**
- Format the bullets using the bullets, spirals, sw ture bullet style. You will find this bullet by s on the keyword *Spiral* in the Bullets and N Picture Bullet search box.
- Change the line spacing to **1.5 lines**.
- Insert the JPEG *New Zealand 4* from the med
- Resize and attractively format it with the you chose earlier to fit on the right side Rotate the picture if necessary to accomm
- Insert a new **Two Content** slide.
- Type the following title: **The Land of t Cloud**.
- Click in the right placeholder.
- Remove the first bullet.
- Type the following: **Day Two**. Forma placeholder.
- Type the following bulleted list:
  - **Viaduct Harbour**
  - **Auckland Museum**
  - **Devonport**
- Change the line spacing of the
- Insert the JPEG *New Zealand 5* Attractively resize as needed ture style you chose earlier.

- From *exp07_p_cpt_notes.docx*, copy and paste the paragraph that begins *On day two . . .* to the notes for this slide.
- Insert a new **Two Content** slide.
- Type the following title: **Bay of Plenty**.
- Click in the left placeholder.
- Type the following: **Rotorua**. Format it with no bullet.
- Type the following bulleted list, using the same bullets as earlier slides:
    - **Mt. Eden**
    - **Botanical Gardens**
    - **Polynesian Spa**

Insert the JPEG *New Zealand 6* into the right placeholder. Use the same picture style as other slides.

-m *exp07_p_cpt_notes.docx*, copy and paste the para-
h that begins *Q & A. Thank you* to the notes for this

new blank slide.

clip art of a question mark. Animate it for

p_cpt_notes.docx, copy and paste the para-
ins *Q & A. Thank you* to the notes for this

sition animation from one slide to the
the slide show.

imate the picture to fade in when

- Add a sound effect of ocean waves from the clip art gallery to the title slide. Start it automatically when the show starts. Hide the sound icon behind the Marella Logo.
- Format all bullets in the presentation as the spiral picture found in the picture gallery of the Bullets and Numbering Customize dialog box.
- Apply an animation to all the bulleted lists in the presentation so each bullet appears one at a time automatically without the speaker clicking on it.
- Use spell checker to check the presentation.
- Print Handout Pages with three slides per page.
- Save and close the presentation.

This presentation will also be shown on a monitor in the lobby of Marella Travel. You have been asked to edit the show to include automatic timings and looping.

- Open *exp07_p_hosp_cpt_new_zealand_solution* and save it as **exp07_p_hosp_cpt__automatic_solution**.
- Add automatic timings appropriate to each slide.
- Format the ocean sound to play continuously across all slides and loop when it completes.
- Set the presentation to be browsed at a kiosk and to loop until Esc, using timing.
- Add a footer with the date and **Marella Travel** at the bottom of each slide.
- View the slide show.
- Save and close the presentation.

Travel Agents

Integrate Microsoft Office Software

Background

Each program in the Microsoft Office suite has its unique strength. Microsoft Office Word is the best program to use when creating documents, especially those requiring advanced formatting. Microsoft Office Excel is the choice when the data require calculations, charts, or mathematical analysis. Microsoft Office PowerPoint is a presentation program that enables users to create unique, professional visual presentations and animate them. Finally, Microsoft Office Access is a database management system that is capable of storing and analyzing large quantities of information. All four programs work together seamlessly to help users analyze and present data most effectively.

Tasks

In a travel agency an agent might be asked to create and edit many types of files. This could include the following:

- Extracting data from an Access database
- Analyze the data in Excel
- Present the analysis visually in PowerPoint
- Present and document the analysis using Word

Skills

In addition to basic integration skills, a travel agent should be able to do the following:

- Open and save an Access database
- Create a new query based on an existing query
- Export to an Excel workbook
- Create column, pie, and bar charts
- Embed a chart on worksheets
- Use chart layouts and format worksheets, charts, and a multilevel list
- Create a presentation from a Word outline
- Use themes and insert and format graphics
- Use comments and markup

Travel Agents
Volume 1 | Capstone Exercises

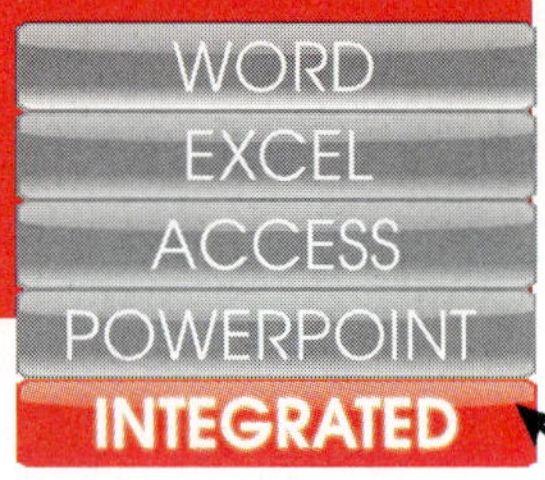

You work as a travel agent for Marella Travel. Marella has been selling packaged vacations for a long time but recently improved the tracking of the sales with an order entry system. Your supervisor asked you to pull the data of a sample group from the order entry system. She would like some analysis on sales of packaged vacations for Marella and the buying habits of those who buy packaged vacations. Once you have the analysis complete, she wants you to present your findings in a memo and a PowerPoint presentation for upper management.

Export Select Data from a Database

- Copy the database *exp07_i_hosp_cpt_marella.accdb* and rename the copied database as **exp07_i_hosp_cpt_marella_solution.accdb**.
- Examine the tables and query in the database.
- Create a query that will return the same results as *qrySalesReport* for sales between October 15, 2009, and October 31, 2009, only.
- Name the new query **qryPackageSalesReportByDate**. Run the query to verify your results.
- Export the results of the *qryPackageSalesReportByDate* query to an Excel spreadsheet using the **Export to Excel spreadsheet command** on the Export group of the External Data Tab. Transfer formatting and open the new export after exporting.
- Save the workbook as **exp07_i_hosp_cpt_export_solution.xlsx**.
- Save and close the database *exp07_i_hosp_cpt_marella_solution.accdb*. Exit Access.

Manipulate Data in Excel

For the analysis portion, you will create a summary of the sales data and make column charts comparing the sales of packaged vacations by sales person, vacation package, and customer ID.

- In *exp07_i_hosp_cpt_export_solution.xls*, rename the worksheet *qryPackageSalesReportByDate* to **By Sales Person**.
- Create a new worksheet called **By Customer**. Copy and paste the exported data to the *By Customer* worksheet.
- Create a new worksheet called **By Package**. Copy and paste the exported data to the *By Package* worksheet.

Create a Chart Depicting Sales Performance

- Return to the *By Sales Person* worksheet. Sort the data by sales person (column A, Last Name).
- Apply an outline subtotal, which subtotals the total price and changes with every change in staff last name.
- Collapse the outline to the subtotal level.
- Create a column chart that compares each individual sales person's total sales to his or her co-workers' sales.
- Format the chart as an embedded object on the same worksheet.
- Title the chart **Package Sales (in Dollars) by Sales Person**. Use a chart layout that will clearly display the title, sales person's last name, and total dollar figure he or she sold. There should be no legend.
- Tweak the formatting of all objects on the *By Sales Person* worksheet to be attractive and readable.

Create a Chart Depicting Customer Purchasing Trends

- Go to the *By Customer* worksheet. Sort the data by customer ID number.
- Apply a subtotal that sums the total sales price and changes with every change in customer ID.
- Collapse the outline to the subtotal level.
- Create a bar chart that compares the purchasing habits of the customers in the sample group. The purchasing habits here are the total spent by each customer on package vacations.
- Format the chart as an embedded object on the same worksheet.
- Title the chart **Packages (in Dollars) Purchased per Customer**.
- Use a chart layout that will clearly display the title, customer ID number, and total dollar amount he or she purchased. There should be no legend.
- Tweak the formatting of all objects on the *By Customer* worksheet to be attractive and readable.

Create Two Charts Depicting the Revenue by Product and the Number of Units Sold by Product

- Go to the *By Package* worksheet. Sort the data by package.
- Apply a subtotal that sums the total number of each package sold and the total dollar amount of each package sold.
- Collapse the outline to the subtotal level.
- Create a pie chart that compares the total quantity of each vacation package sold.
- Format the chart as an embedded object on the same sheet.
- Title the chart **Quantity of Packages Sold**.
- Use a chart layout that will clearly display the title, package name, and total quantity of each package sold. There should be no legend.

...continued on Next Page

- Tweak the formatting of all objects on the *Quantity by Package* chart to be attractive and readable.
- On the *By Package* worksheet, apply a subtotal that sums the total sales price and changes with every change in package name.
- Collapse the outline to the subtotal level.
- Create a pie chart that compares the total dollar amount of each vacation package sold.
- Format the chart as an embedded object on the same worksheet.
- Title the chart **Package Sales (in Dollars) by Package**.
- Use a chart layout that will clearly display the title, package name, and total dollar amount of each package sold. There should be no legend.
- Tweak the formatting of all objects on the *Package Sales by Package* chart to be attractive and readable.
- Save and close the workbook.

Create a Memo in Word to Distribute the Charts You Created

Now you need to write a memo that includes all the charts you just completed to distribute to the management team and Board of Directors.

- Open a new Word document and save it as **exp07_i_hosp_cpt_memo_solution.docx**.
- Create a Professional Memo to: **John Marella**, **Barb Marella**, **Keith Mulbery**, **Cynthia Krebs**, **Maurie Lockley**, **Michelle Hulett**, and **Judith Scheeren**.
- You are the author of the memo.
- Date it with today's date so it updates automatically.
- Use a professional subject line describing the contents of the memo.
- Write the body of the memo to include a short reason why you have written this memo. You wrote it to deliver the results of your analysis—the charts you created to depict the sales of the new package vacations.
- Insert all four charts in the memo. They should not update the source if altered in the Word document.
- Tweak the format and layout of the charts for maximum readability. You may find that the charts are more readable in a small format, if you remove the titles. Use captions, clearly labeling each chart if you remove titles.
- Invite the recipients of the memo distribution to a meeting to discuss the sales analysis.
- Format the memo attractively; proofread it to make sure it is free of spelling errors, typos, and grammatical errors.
- Save, print, and close *exp07_i_hosp_cpt_memo_solution*.

Create an Agenda for the Meeting

- Open a new Word document. Save it as **exp07_i_hosp_cpt_agenda_solution**.
- Type **Vacation Package Sales Analysis**.
- Format it using a title style.
- Type:
  - **Package Sales (in Dollars) by Sales Person**
  - **Packages (in Dollars) Purchased per Customer**
  - **Quantity of Packages Sold**
  - **Package Sales (in Dollars) by Package**
- Format these four lines as a multilevel list.
- Save and close *exp07_i_hosp_cpt_agenda_solution.docx*.

Create a PowerPoint Presentation to Use at the Meeting

The last part of this task is to create a PowerPoint presentation for a meeting to discuss the future sales strategies of Marella Travel. This presentation should be designed to enable everyone in a small brainstorming session to see the same information simultaneously. You will make some preliminary notes on the slideshow and have all the objects linked so that you can make changes to the original files if necessary during the meeting. While appearance always matters, this is not an advertisement, this is a vehicle to present data to a group of less than 10 corporate decision makers and you should make your presentation formatting decisions with that in mind.

- Launch PowerPoint, open the Word document *exp07_i_hosp_cpt_agenda_solution.docx*, and save it as **exp07_i_hosp_cpt_presentation_solution.pptx**.
- You should now have slides for all the charts you will discuss in the meeting.
- Change the layout of the first slide to **Title**.
- Insert the Marella Travel logo on this slide.
- If available, use the Marella Travel theme you created in the PowerPoint Marella Travel exercise. If it is not available, use the **Civic** theme with the **Flow Color** scheme and save it as **Marella_Travel_PPT**.
- On each of the appropriate slides, link the chart from the Excel workbook. Resize them to fill the slide as large as possible.
- Reformat the charts to be attractive in PowerPoint. You may find that they look better in PowerPoint slides without titles. Use a title on the slide describing the chart, if so.
- Go to slide 3, the slide presenting the sales by customer. Add a comment: **Note the two highest spending customers. Are they leaders for a large group traveling together? Perhaps a high school or college group?**
- Use a felt tip pen annotation to call out the high spending customers and the dollar amount for each.
- Adjust the formatting as necessary to be attractive and professional.
- View your presentation.
- Save and close *exp07_i_hosp_cpt_presentation_solution.pptx*.

Glossary

All key terms appearing in this book (in bold italic) are listed alphabetically in this Glossary for easy reference. If you want to learn more about a feature or concept, use the Index to find the term's other significant occurrences.

Absolute cell reference A cell reference that stays the same no matter where you copy a formula. The cell reference contains the $ symbol before the column letter and row number, such as $A$5.

Access function Predefined formula that performs an operation using input supplied as arguments and returns a value.

Access speed The amount of time it takes for the storage device to make the file content available for use.

Active cell The cell you are working in; the cell where information or data will be input.

Adjustment handle A control in the shape of a yellow diamond that enables you to modify a shape.

Aero Glass An interface design that includes transparency effects and gives a slight three-dimensional shape to Windows features.

Aggregate A collection of many parts that come together from different sources and are considered a whole.

Align To arrange in a line so as to be parallel.

And operator Returns only records that meet all criteria.

Animation Movement applied to individual elements on a single slide.

Animation scheme A built-in, standard animation effect.

Annotation A note that can be written or drawn on a slide for additional commentary or explanation.

Append Process of adding new records to the end of the table.

Argument A necessary input component required to produce the output for a function.

Ascending order Arranges data in alphabetical or sequential order from lowest to highest.

Aspect ratio The ratio of width to height.

AutoCorrect A feature that automatically corrects some typographical errors and capitalization errors as you type.

AutoFill An Excel operation that enables users to copy the content of a cell or a range of cells by dragging the fill handle over an adjacent cell or range of cells.

AutoFit The command used when formatting a spreadsheet to automatically adjust the height and width of cells.

AutoFormat A feature that evaluates an entire document, determines how each paragraph is used, then it applies an appropriate style to each paragraph.

Automatic replacement Makes a substitution automatically.

AutoNumber field A field that assigns a unique identifying number to each record.

AutoText A feature that substitutes a predefined item for specific text but only when the user initiates it.

AVERAGE function The function that determines the arithmetic mean, or average, for the values in a range of cells.

Back end Protects and stores data so that users cannot inadvertently destroy or corrupt the organization's vital data.

Background The area of a display that is not covered by characters or graphics.

Background Styles gallery Provides both solid color and background styles for application to a theme.

Bar chart A chart with a horizontal orientation that compares categories; useful when categorical labels are long.

Bar tab Does not position text or decimals, but inserts a vertical bar at the tab setting; useful as a separator for text printed on the same line.

Bibliography A list of works cited or consulted by an author and should be included with the document when published.

Bitmap image An image created by bits or pixels placed on a grid that form a picture.

Bookmark An electronic marker for a specific location in a document, enabling the user to go to that location quickly.

Border A line that surrounds a paragraph, a page, a table, or an image, similar to how a picture frame surrounds a photograph or piece of art.

Bound control A control that enables you to pull information from the underlying table or query data.

Breakpoint The lowest numeric value for a specific category or in a series of a lookup table to produce a corresponding result to return for a lookup function.

Brightness The ratio between lightness and darkness of an image.

Building Blocks Document components used frequently, such as disclaimers, company addresses, or a cover page.

Bulleted list Itemizes and separates paragraph text to increase readability.

Calculated control Uses an expression as opposed to a record value as its data source.

Calculated field A field that derives its value from a formula that references one or more existing fields.

Callout A shape that includes a line with a text box that you can use to add notes.

CamelCase notation Field-naming style that uses no spaces in multi-word field names, but uses uppercase letters to distinguish the first letter of each new word.

Caption A descriptive title for an image, a figure, or a table.

Caption property Specifies a label other than the field name that appears at the top of a column in Datasheet view, forms, and reports.

Cascade delete Searches the database and deletes all of the related records.

Cascade update Connects a primary key change to the tables in which it is a foreign key.

Cascaded windows Displayed such that a small section of each open window is shown behind another.

Cascades Permit data changes to travel from one table to another.

Case-insensitive search Finds a word regardless of any capitalization used.

Case-sensitive search Matches not only the text but also the use of upper- and lowercase letters.

Category label Textual information, such as column and row headings (cities, months, years, product names, etc.), used for descriptive entries.

Cell The intersection of a column and row in a table or in an Excel spreadsheet.

Cell margin The amount of space between data and the cell border in a table.

Cell reference The intersection of a column and row designated by a column letter and a row number.

Center tab Sets the middle point of the text you type; whatever you type will be centered on that tab setting.

Change Case Feature that enables you to change capitalization of text to all capital letters, all lowercase letters, sentence case, or toggle case.

Character spacing The horizontal space between characters.

Character style Stores character formatting (font, size, and style) and affects only the selected text.

Chart A graphic or visual representation of data.

Chart area The entire chart and all of its elements.

Check box Enables you to select one or more items that are not mutually exclusive in a dialog box.

Citation A note recognizing a source of information or a quoted passage.

Clip Any media object that you can insert in a document.

Clip art A graphical image, illustration, drawing, or sketch.

Clipboard A memory location that holds up to 24 items for you to paste into the current document, another file, or another application.

Clustered column chart A chart that groups similar data together in columns making visual comparison of the data easier to determine.

Codec Digital video compression scheme used to compress a video and decompress for playback.

Collapsed outline The PowerPoint view that displays the title of slides only in the Outline view.

Colors gallery A gallery with a set of colors for every available theme.

Column Formats a section of a document into side-by-side vertical blocks in which the text flows down the first column and then continues at the top of the next column.

Column chart A chart that displays data vertically in a column formation and is used to compare values across different categories.

Column index number A number, indicated by col_index_num in the function, that refers to the number of the column in the lookup table that contains the return values.

Column width The horizontal space or width of a column in a table or in a spreadsheet.

Combine Feature that incorporates all changes from multiple documents into a new document.

Command An icon on the Quick Access Toolbar or in a group on the Ribbon that you click to perform a task. A command can also appear as text on a menu or within a dialog box.

Commands The visual icons in each group that you click toperform a task.

Comment A private note, annotation, or additional information to the author, another reader, or to yourself.

Compare Feature that evaluates the contents of two or more documents and displays markup balloons that show the differences between the documents.

Compatibility Checker Looks for features that are not supported by previous versions of Word, Excel, PowerPoint, or Access.

Compress The process of reducing the file size of an object.

Connector A line that is attached to and moves with shapes.

Constant An unchanging value, like a birthdate.

Context menu A list of commands that pertain to the text, object, or item you right-clicked.

Contextual tab A specialty tab that appears on the Ribbon only when certain types of objects are being edited.

Contrast The difference between the darkest and lightest areas of a image.

Control Panel Windows control center that enables you to change system settings, such as your background, screen saver, screen fonts, and accessibility options.

Controls Position, display, format, and calculate the report data.

Copy The process of making a duplicate copy of the text or object leaving the original intact.

Copyright The legal protection afforded to a written or artistic work.

COUNT function The function that counts the number of cells in a range that contain numerical data.

COUNTA function The function that counts the number of cells in a range that are not blank.

Criteria row Position in a query design grid where criteria may be entered.

Criterion (criteria, pl) A rule or norm that is the basis for making judgments.

Cropping Process of reducing an image size by eliminating unwanted portions of an image.

Cross-reference A note that refers the reader to another location for more information about a topic.

Currency The medium of exchange, in the United States, currency formatted values display with a dollar sign.

Current List Includes all citation sources you use in the current document.

Custom animation An animation where the user determines the animation settings.

Custom dictionary A supplemental dictionary Microsoft Office uses to store items such as proper names, acronyms, or specialized words.

Cut Process of removing the original text or an object from its current location.

Data Facts about a specific record or sets of records.

Data aggregate A collection of many parts that come together from different sources and are considered a whole.

Data file A document or item that you create and to which you give a name.

Data label The value or name of a data point in a chart.

Data point A numeric value that describes a single item on a chart.

Data redundancy Occurs when unnecessary duplicate information exists in a database.

Data series A group of related data points that appear in row(s) or column(s) in the worksheet.

Data type Determines the type of data that can be entered and the operations that can be performed on that data.

Database A file that consists of one or more tables and the supporting objects used to get data into and out of the tables.

Dataset A container for records that satisfy the criteria specified in the query, provides the answers to the user's questions.

Datasheet view A grid containing columns (fields) and rows (records) where you add, edit, and delete records in an Access database table.

Date arithmetic A mathematical expression that calculates lapsed time.

Date formatting Affects the date's display without changing the serial value.

Date/time field A field that facilitates calculations for dates and times.

DatePart function Enables users to identify a specific part of a date, such as only the year.

Decimal tab Marks where numbers align on a decimal point as you type.

Delete operation The operation that removes all content from a cell or from a selected cell range.

Descending order Arranges data in alphabetical or sequential order from highest to lowest.

Design view Displays the infrastructure of a table, form, or report without displaying the data.

Desktop Contains icons and a taskbar.

Detail section Repeats once for each record in the underlying record source.

Dialog box A window that provides an interface for a user to select commands.

Dialog Box Launcher A small icon that, when clicked, opens a related dialog box.

Distribute To divide or evenly spread over a given area.

Document Information panel Provides descriptive information about a document, such as a title, subject, author, keywords, and comments.

Document Inspector Checks for and removes different kinds of hidden and personal information from a document.

Document Map A pane that lists the structure of headings in your document.

Document properties The collection of metadata associated with a file.

Doughnut chart A chart that displays values as percentages of the whole.

Draft view Shows a simplified work area, removing white space and other elements from view.

Duplex printer A printing device that prints on both sides of the page.

Effects gallery Includes a range of effects for shapes used in a presentation.

Embedded object An object from an external source that is stored within a presentation.

Encryption The process of obscuring data to make it unreadable without decoding software or knowledge.

Endnote A citation that appears at the end of a document.

Enhanced ScreenTip Displays when you rest the pointer on a command on the Quick Access Toolbar or Ribbon.

Expanded outline Displays the title and content of slides in the Outline view.

Exploded pie chart A chart that separates one or more slices of the pie for emphasis.

Expression A formula used to calculate new fields from the values in existing fields.

Expression Builder A tool to help you create a formula that performs calculations easily.

Field A basic entity, data element, or category, such as a book title or telephone number.

Field List pane Displays a list of all of the tables and fields in the database.

Field row The area in the query design grid that specifies fields to be used in a query.

Field size property Defines how much space to reserve for each field.

File A unit of data to which you give a name.

Fill The inside of a shape.

Fill handle A small black solid square in the bottom-right corner of a selected cell. It is used to duplicate formulas.

Filter Condition that helps you find a subset of data meeting your specifications.

Filter by Form Permits selecting the criteria from a drop-down list, or applying multiple criterion.

Filter by Selection Selects only the records that match the pre-selected criteria.

Final Showing Markup A view that displays inserted text in the body of the document and shows deleted text in a balloon.

Find Locates a word or group of words in a file.

First line indent Marks the location to indent only the first line in a paragraph.

Flat or non-relational Data contained in a single page or sheet (not multiple).

Flowchart An illustration showing the sequence of a project or plan.

Font A complete set of characters—upper- and lowercase letters, numbers, punctuation marks, and special symbols with the same design.

Fonts gallery Contains font sets for title text and body text.

Footer Information printed at the bottom of document pages.

Footnote A citation that appears at the bottom of a page.

Foreign key A field in one table that also is stored in a different table as a primary key.

Form An interface that enables you to enter or modify record data.

Format Cells Operations that control the formatting for numbers, alignment, fonts, borders, colors, and patterns in a particular cell.

Format Painter Feature that enables you to copy existing text formats to other text to ensure consistency.

Formatting text Changes an individual letter, a word, or a body of selected text.

Formula The combination of constants, cell references, arithmetic operations, and/or functions displayed in a calculation.

Formula bar The area used to enter or edit cell contents.

Freeform shape A shape that may combine both curved and straight lines to create a shape.

Freezing The process that enables you to keep headings on the screen as you work with large worksheets, rows and column.

Front end Contains the objects, like queries, reports and forms, needed to interact with data, but not the tables where the record values reside.

Full Screen Reading view Eliminates tabs and makes it easier to read your document.

Function A preconstructed formula that makes difficult computations less complicated.

FV function The function that returns the future value of an investment if you know the interest rate, the term, and the periodic payment.

Gadgets Mini-applications that display on a Windows Sidebar.

Gallery Displays a set of predefined options that can be clicked to apply to an object or to text.

Go To Moves the insertion point to a specific location in the file.

Gradient fill A blend of colors and shades.

Grid A set of intersecting lines used to align objects.

Group Categories that organize similar commands together within each tab on the Ribbon.

Group footer section(s) Appear at the end of each grouping level.

Group header section(s) Appear once at the start of each new grouping level in the report.

Grouping The process of combining two or more objects.

Guide A straight horizontal or vertical line used to align objects.

Hanging indent Aligns the first line of a paragraph at the left margin and indents the remaining lines.

Hard page break Forces the next part of a document to begin on a new page.

Hard return Created when you press Enter to move the insertion point to a new line.

Header Information printed at the top of document pages.

Help and Support Provides assistance on Windows topics.

Hidden In Excel, the process of making rows, columns, and sheets invisible.

Hidden text Document text that does not appear onscreen.

Hierarchy Denotes levels of importance in a structure.

Highlight tool Background color used to mark text that you want to stand out or locate easily.

Horizontal alignment The placement of text between the left and right margins.

IIF function (Access) The function that evaluates a condition and executes one action when the condition is true and an alternate action when the condition is false.

IF function (Excel) The function that returns one value when a condition is met and returns another value when the condition is not met.

Index An alphabetical listing of topics covered in a document, along with the page numbers where the topic is discussed.

Indexed property A list that relates the field values to the records that contain the field value.

Inequity Examines a mathematical relationship such as equals, not equals, greater than, less than, greater than or equal to, or less than or equal to.

Information Data that have been arranged or processed to view in some usable form.

Infringement of Copyright Occurs when a right of a copyright owner is violated.

Insert The process of adding text in a document, spreadsheet cell, database object, or presentation slide.

Insertion point The blinking vertical line in the document, cell, slide show, or database table designating the current location where text you type displays.

Internet Explorer 7 A Web browser that features tabbed browsing and security enhancements.

Kerning Automatically adjusts spacing between characters to achieve a more evenly spaced appearance.

Key Tip The letter or number that displays over each feature on the Ribbon and Quick Access Toolbar and is the keyboard equivalent that you press. Press Alt by itself to display Key Tips.

Label Wizard A series of dialog boxes that asks you questions and then, depending on how you answer, generates the report formatted to print on mailing labels.

Landscape orientation Page orientation is wider than it is long, resembling a landscape scene.

Layout Determines the position of objects containing content on a slide, form, report, document, or spreadsheet.

Layout view Alter the report design while viewing the data.

Leader character Typically dots or hyphens that connect two items, to draw the reader's eye across the page.

Left tab Sets the start position on the left so as you type, text moves to the right of the tab setting.

Legend The area that identifies the format or color of the data used for each series in a chart.

Line chart A chart that uses a line to connect data points in order to show trends over a long period of time.

Line spacing The vertical space between the lines in a paragraph and between paragraphs.

Line weight The width or thickness of a line.

Linked object An object stored outside the presentation in its own file.

Live Preview A feature that provides a preview of how a gallery option will affect the current text or object when the mouse pointer hovers over the gallery option.

Lookup table The table that Excel searches using a lookup function

Lookup value The location in a table that represents the cell containing the value to look up the result in a table.

Macro Small program that automates tasks in a file.

Mailing labels Self-stick, die-cut labels that you print with names, addresses, and postal barcodes.

Manual duplex Operation that enables you to print on both sides of the paper by printing first on one side and then on the other.

Margin The amount of white space around the top, bottom, left, and right edges the page.

Markup balloon Colored circles that contain comments, insertions, and deletions in the margin with a line drawn to where the insertion point was in the document prior to inserting the comment or editing the document.

Master document A document that acts like a binder for managing smaller documents.

Master List A database of all citation sources created in Word on a particular computer.

MAX function The function that determines the highest value of all cells in a list of arguments.

MEDIAN function The function that finds the midpoint value in a set of values.

Merge and center cells The action that merges the content of several cells into one cell and centers the content of the merged cell.

Metadata Data that describes other data.

Microsoft Clip Organizer Catalogs pictures, sounds, and movies stored on your hard drive.

Microsoft WordArt An application within Microsoft Office that creates decorative text that can be used to add interest to a document.

MIN function The function that determines the smallest value of all cells in a list of arguments.

Mini toolbar A semitransparent toolbar of often-used font, indent, and bullet commands that displays when you position the mouse over selected text and disappears when you move the mouse away from the selected text.

Mixed cell reference References that occur when you create a formula that combines an absolute reference with a relative reference ($C13 or C$13). As a result, either the row number or column letter does not change when the cell is copied.

Monospaced typeface Uses the same amount of horizontal space for every character.

Move operation The operation that transfers the content of a cell or cell range from one location in the worksheet to another with the cells where the move originated becoming empty.

Movie Video file, or GIF file, containing multiple images that stream to produce an animation.

Multilevel list Extends a numbered list to several levels, and is updated automatically when topics are added or deleted.

Multimedia Multiple forms of media used to entertain or inform a user or audience.

Multiple data series Series that compare two or more sets of data in one chart.

Name box Displays the cell reference of the active cell in Excel.

Narration Spoken commentary that is added to a project.

Navigation Pane In Access, a list of database objects within groups by category. Users can select how the objects are arranged within the list.

Nested groups Provide a power-layering tool to organize information.

Nonbreaking hyphen Keeps text on both sides of the hyphen together, thus preventing the hyphenated word from becoming separated at the hyphen.

Nonbreaking space A special character that keeps two or more words together.

Normal view The tri-pane default PowerPoint view.

Not operator Returns the opposite of the specified criteria.

Notes Page view Used for entering and editing large amounts of text that the speaker can refer to when presenting.

Notification area Found on the right side of the taskbar, it displays icons for background programs and system processes.

NOW function The function that uses the computer's clock to display the current date and time side by side in a cell.

Null The formal, computer term for a missing value.

Numbered list Sequences and prioritizes the items and is automatically updated to accommodate additions or deletions.

Object, Access An entity that contains the basic elements of the database. Access uses six types of objects—tables, queries, forms, reports, macros, and modules.

Object, PowerPoint Any type of information that can be inserted in slide.

Office Button Icon that, when clicked, displays the Office menu.

Office menu List of commands (such as New, Open, Save, Save As, Print, and Options) that work with an entire file or with the specific Microsoft Office program.

One-to-many relationship Exists when each record in the first table may match one, more than one, or no records in the second table. Each record in the second table matches one and only one record in the first table.

Opaque A solid fill, one without transparency.

Operand Field or value being operated or manipulated in an expression.

Operators Are plus, minus, equals, greater than, less than, multiply (*), divide (/) and not equals (<>).

Or operator Returns records meeting any of the specified criteria.

Order of precedence Rules that establish the sequence by which values are calculated.

Original Showing Markup A view that shows deleted text within the body of the document (with a line through the deleted text) and displays inserted text in a balloon to the right of the actual document.

Orphan The first line of a paragraph appearing by itself at the bottom of a page.

Outline A method of organizing text in a hierarchy to depict relationships.

Outline view Displays varying amounts of detail; a structural view of a document that can be collapsed or expanded as necessary.

Overtype mode Replaces the existing text with text you type character by character.

Page Break Preview The command that shows you where page breaks currently occur and gives you the opportunity to change where the page breaks occur when a worksheet is printed.

Page footers Appear once for each page in the report at the bottom of the pages.

Page headers Appear once for each page in the report at the top of the pages.

Paragraph spacing The amount of space before or after a paragraph.

Paragraph style Stores paragraph formatting such as alignment, line spacing, indents, as well as the font, size, and style of the text in the paragraph.

Paste Places the cut or copied text or object in the new location.

Photo Album A presentation containing multiple pictures organized into album pages.

Picture fill Inserts an image from a file into a shape.

Picture style A gallery that contains preformatted options that can be applied to a graphical object.

Pie chart A chart that is the most effective way to display proportional relationships.

PivotChart view Displays a chart of the associated PivotTable view.

PivotTable view Provides a convenient way to summarize and organize data about groups of records.

Placeholder A container that holds content and is used in the layout to determine the position of objects on the slide.

Plagiarism The act of using and documenting the ideas or writings of another as one's own.

Plain Text Format (.txt) A file type that retains only text when used to transfer documents between applications or platforms.

Plot area The area of a chart that contains the graphical representation of the values in a data series.

PMT function Calculates a periodic loan payment given a constant interest rate, term, and original value.

PNPI Federal laws governing the safeguarding of personal, non-public information such as Social Security numbers (SSNs), credit card or bank account numbers, medical or educational records, or other sensitive data.

Pointing The use of the mouse or arrow keys to select a cell directly when creating a formula.

Portrait orientation Page orientation is longer than it is wide—like the portrait of a person.

Position Raises or lowers text from the baseline without creating superscript or subscript size.

Presentation graphics software A computer application, such as Microsoft PowerPoint, that is used primarily to create electronic slide shows.

Presenter view Delivers a presentation on two monitors simultaneously.

Primary key The field that makes each record in a table unique.

Print Layout view The default view that closely resembles the printed document.

Print Preview view Displays the report as it will be printed.

Property A characteristic or attribute of an object that determines how the object looks and behaves.

Proportional typeface Allocates horizontal space to the character.

Public domain When the rights to a literary work or property are owned by the public at large.

Query A database object that enables you to ask questions about the data stored in a database and returns the answers in the order from the records that match your instructions.

Query design grid Displays when you select a query's Design view; it divides the window into two parts.

Query sort order Determines the order of items in the query datasheet view.

Query Wizard An Access tool that facilitates new query development through a series of dialog boxes.

Quick Access Toolbar A customizable row of buttons for frequently used commands, such as Save and Undo.

Quick Style A combination of formatting options available that can be applied to a shape or graphic.

Radio button See option button.

Range A rectangular group of cells. A range may be as small as a single cell or as large as the entire worksheet.

Record A complete set of all of the data (fields) about one person, place, event, or idea.

Recycle Bin A temporary holding area for files and folders deleted from the hard drive.

Redo Command that reinstates or reserves an action performed by the Undo command.

Referential Integrity The set of rules that ensure that data stored in related tables remain consistent as the data are updated.

Relational Database Management System Data are grouped into similar collections, called tables, and the relationships between tables are formed by using a common field.

Relational database software A computer application, such as Microsoft Access, that is used to store data and convert it into information.

Relative cell reference A cell reference that changes relative to the direction in which the formula is being copied.

Remote Desktop A feature that enables a computer to be run remotely from another Windows computer.

Repeat Provides limited use because it repeats only the last action you performed. The Repeat icon is replaced with the Redo icon after you use the Undo command.

Replace The process of finding and replacing a word or group of words with other text.

Report A printed document that displays information professionally from a database.

Report footer section Prints once at the conclusion of each report.

Report header section Prints once at the beginning of each report.

Report view Provides you the ability to see what the printed report will look like and to make temporary changes to how the data are viewed.

Report Wizard A series of dialog boxes that asks you questions and then, depending on how you answer, generates an Access report.

Restore Down button Returns a window to the size it was before it was maximized.

Reviewing Pane A window that displays all comments and editorial changes made to the main document.

Revision mark Indicates where text is added, deleted, or formatted while the Track Changes feature is active.

Ribbon The Microsoft Office 2007 GUI command center that organizes commands into related tabs and groups.

Rich Text Format (.rtf) A file type that retains structure and most text formatting when used to transfer documents between applications or platforms.

Right tab Sets the start position on the right so as you type, text moves to the left of that tab setting and aligns on the right.

Row height The vertical space from the top to the bottom of a row in a table or in a spreadsheet.

Run a query Access processes the query instructions and displays records that meet the conditions.

Sans serif typeface A typeface that does not contain thin lines on characters.

Sarbanes Oxley Act (SOX) A federal law passed in 2002 to protect the general public and companies' shareholders against fraudulent practices and accounting errors.

Scale or scaling Increases or decreases text or a graphic as a percentage of its size.

Scatter (xy) chart A chart that shows a relationship between two variables.

Screen saver A moving image that appears on your screen when your computer has been idle for a specified period of time.

ScreenTip A small window that describes a command when the mouse pointer is positioned over that command.

Section break A marker that divides a document into sections thereby allowing different formatting in each section.

Security Center A control center that enables you to check and manage security settings.

Select All button The square at the intersection of the rows and column headings used to select all elements in the active worksheet.

Select query Searches the underlying tables to retrieve the data that satisfy the query parameters.

Selection bar The space in the left margin area where you see a right-pointing arrow, indicating that you can select document text. For example, click once to select the current line of text.

Selection net Selects all objects in an area defined by dragging the mouse.

Selection Pane A pane designed to help select objects.

Selective replacement An option that enables you to decide whether to replace text.

Serif typeface A typeface that contains a thin line or extension at the top and bottom of the primary strokes on characters.

Shading A background color that appears behind text in a paragraph, a page, a table, or a spreadsheet cell.

Shape A geometric or nongeometric object such as a rectangle or an arrow.

Sheet tabs The tabs located at the bottom left of the Excel window that tell the user what sheets of a workbook are available.

Shortcut A pointer to a file, folder, or Web site.

Shortcut menu See context menu.

Show Markup Enables you to view document revisions by reviewer; it also allows you to choose which type of revisions you want to view such as comments, insertions and deletions, or formatting changes.

Show row Area in a query design grid that controls whether the field will display in the query results.

Show/Hide feature Reveals where formatting marks such as spaces, tabs, and returns are used in the document.

Sizing handle The small circles and squares that appear around a selected object and enable you to adjust the height and width of a selected object.

Slide Show view Used to deliver the completed presentation full screen to an audience, one slide at a time, as an electronic presentation on the computer.

Slide Sorter view Displays thumbnails of slides.

SmartArt A diagram that presents information visually to effectively communicate a message.

Soft page break Inserted when text fills an entire page then continues on the next page.

Soft return Created by the word processor as it wraps text to a new line.

Sort Lists those records in a specific sequence, such as alphabetically by last name or rearranges data based on a certain criteria.

Sort Ascending Provides an alphabetical list of text data or a small-to-large list of numeric data.

Sort command The command that puts lists in ascending or descending order according to specified sort levels.

Sort Descending Arranges the records with the highest value listed first.

Sort row The area in the query design grid in which to indicate if you want the query results sorted in ascending or descending order for a specific field.

Sorting The action that arranges records in a table by the value of one or more fields within a table.

Spelling and Grammar Feature that attempts to catch mistakes in spelling, punctuation, writing style, and word usage by comparing strings of text within a document to a series of predefined rules.

Spreadsheet The computerized equivalent of a ledger that is a grid of rows and columns enabling users to organize data, recalculate formulas when any changes in data are made, and make decisions based on quantitative data.

Spreadsheet program A computer application, such as Microsoft Excel, that is used to build and manipulate electronic spreadsheets.

Stacked The vertical alignment of text.

Stacked column chart A chart that places (stacks) data in one column with each data series a different color for each category.

Stacked windows Displayed one on top of the other.

Stacking order The order of objects placed on top of each other.

Start menu A list of programs and utilities that displays when you click the Start button.

Start panel Located on the right side of the Start menu.

Status bar The horizontal bar at the bottom of a Microsoft Office application that displays summary information about the selected window or object and contains View buttons and the Zoom slider. The Word status bar displays the page number and total words, while the Excel status bar displays the average, count, and sum of values in a selected range. The PowerPoint status bar displays the slide number and the Design Theme name.

Stock chart A chart that shows the high, low, and close prices for individual stocks over a period of time.

Storyboard A visual plan that displays the content of each slide in the slideshow.

Style A set of formatting options you apply to characters or paragraphs.

Subdocument A smaller document that is a part of a master document.

SUM function The function that adds or sums numeric entries within a range of cells and then displays the result in the cell containing the function.

Synchronous scrolling Enables you to scroll through documents at the same time in Side by Side view.

Syntax The set of rules by which the words and symbols of an expression are correctly combined.

Tab Looks like a folder tab and divides the Ribbon into task-oriented categories.

Tab, Word Markers that specify the position for aligning text and add organization to a document.

Table A series of rows and columns that organize data effectively.

Table, Access A collection of records. Every record in a table contains the same fields in the same order.

Table, Excel An area in a worksheet that contains rows and columns of related data formatted to enable data management and analysis. A table can be used as part of a database or organized collection of related data, where the worksheet rows represent the records and the worksheet columns represent the fields in a record. The first row of a table contains the column labels or field names.

Table alignment The position of a table between the left and right document margins.

Table of authorities Used in legal documents to reference cases, and other documents referred to in a legal brief.

Table of contents Lists headings in the order they appear in a document and the page numbers where the entries begin.

Table of figures A list of the captions in a document.

Table row The second row of the query design grid that specifies the tables from which the fields are selected to create a query.

Table style Contain borders, shading, font sizes, and other attributes that enhance readability of a table.

Template A file that incorporates a theme, a layout, and content that can be modified.

Text Any combination of entries from the keyboard and includes letters, numbers, symbols, and spaces.

Text box Enables you to give an instruction by typing in a box.

Text direction The degree of rotation in which text displays.

Text pane A special pane that opens up for text entry when a SmartArt diagram is selected.

Text wrapping style The way text wraps around an image.

Texture fill Inserts a texture such as marble into a shape.

Theme A set of design elements that gives the slide show a unified, professional appearance.

Three-dimensional pie chart A type of pie chart that contains a three-dimensional view.

Thumbnail A miniature image of a file.

TODAY function The function that is a date-related function that places the current date in a cell.

Toggle switch Causes the computer to alternate between two states. For example, you can toggle between the Insert mode and the Overtype mode.

Total row Displays as the last row in the Datasheet view of a table or query and provides a variety of summary statistics.

Totals query Organizes query results into groups by including a grouping field and a numeric field for aggregate calculations.

Track Changes Monitors all additions, deletions, and formatting changes you make in a document.

Transition A movement special effect that takes place as one slide replaces another in Slide Show view.

Transparency Refers to how much you can see through a fill.

Type style The characteristic applied to a font, such as bold.

Typeface A complete set of characters—upper- and lowercase letters, numbers, punctuation marks, and special symbols.

Typography The arrangement and appearance of printed matter.

Unbound controls Do not have any record source for their contents.

Undo Command cancels your last one or more operations.

Ungrouping Breaking a combined object into individual objects.

User interface The meeting point between computer software and the person using it.

Validation rule Checks the authenticity of the data entered in a field.

Value Number entered in a cell that represent a quantity, an amount, a date, or time.

Vector graphic An object-oriented graphic based on geometric formulas.

Vertex The point where a curve ends or the point where two line segments meet in a freeform shape.

View Side by Side Enables you to display two documents on the same screen.

Virus checker Software that scans files for a hidden program that can damage your computer.

VLOOKUP function The function that evaluates a value and looks up this value in a vertical table to return a value, text, or formula.

Web Layout view View to display how a document will look when posted on the Web.

Widow The last line of a paragraph appearing by itself at the top of a page.

Windows Calendar An organizer program that enables you to create and view appointments and schedule tasks.

Windows Defender The Windows Vista spyware-detection program.

Windows Explorer Enables you to manage files and folders.

Windows Firewall Blocks both unauthorized incoming Internet traffic and outgoing traffic.

Windows Mail An e-mail program that includes a junk mail filter.

Windows Media Player 11 A multimedia program enabling you to work with music and movie files.

Windows Movie Maker A program that enables you to create, edit, and share home movies on your computer.

Windows Photo Gallery Provides tools for correcting and enhancing picture files.

Windows Search A utility that helps you search for items on your computer.

Windows Sidebar Displays links to local weather, stock quotes, and other news.

Windows Vista The primary operating system (OS) for personal computers.

Wizard A step-by-step set of guided instructions.

Word processing software A computer application, such as Microsoft Word, that is used primarily with text to create, edit, and format documents.

Word wrap The feature that automatically moves words to the next line if they do not fit on the current line.

WordArt Text that has a decorative effect applied.

Work-around Acknowledges that a problem exists, and develops a sufficing solution.

Workbook A collection of related worksheets contained within a single file.

Worksheet A single spreadsheet consisting of columns and rows that may contain formulas, functions, values, text, and graphics.

X or horizontal axis The axis that depicts categorical labels.

Y or vertical axis The axis that depicts numerical values.

Zoom slider Enables you to increase or decrease the magnification of the file onscreen.

Multiple Choice Answer Keys

Office Fundamentals, Chapter 1

1. b
2. c
3. d
4. a
5. d
6. c
7. b
8. c
9. d
10. a
11. c
12. d
13. c
14. a
15. d

Word 2007, Chapter 1

1. c
2. b
3. a
4. c
5. b
6. a
7. c
8. d
9. b
10. c
11. d
12. d
13. b
14. a
15. c
16. d

Word 2007, Chapter 2

1. d
2. c
3. b
4. a
5. d
6. d
7. d
8. d
9. d
10. d
11. b
12. d
13. c
14. d
15. c
16. a
17. b
18. a
19. a

Word 2007, Chapter 3

1. d
2. a
3. a
4. d
5. c
6. b
7. a
8. d
9. a
10. d
11. b
12. b
13. d
14. b
15. a
16. c
17. d

Word 2007, Chapter 4

1. c
2. d
3. b
4. a
5. c
6. b
7. c
8. c
9. a
10. d
11. b
12. a
13. d
14. a
15. b

Excel 2007, Chapter 1

1. b
2. a
3. a
4. c
5. c
6. c
7. c
8. a
9. b
10. b
11. b
12. b
13. a
14. a
15. b
16. c
17. a
18. c
19. b

Excel 2007, Chapter 2

1. d
2. b
3. b
4. c
5. d
6. b
7. a
8. a
9. b
10. b
11. c
12. d
13. b
14. b
15. b

Excel 2007, Chapter 3

1. a
2. a
3. a
4. d
5. c
6. d
7. a
8. d
9. a
10. d
11. a
12. c
13. a
14. a
15. c
16. d
17. c

Excel 2007, Chapter 4

1. a
2. a
3. d
4. c
5. b
6. c
7. b
8. d
9. c
10. a
11. b
12. d
13. b
14. d
15. b
16. d

Access 2007, Chapter 1

1. b
2. b
3. d
4. d
5. b
6. b
7. b
8. c
9. c
10. c
11. c
12. a
13. c
14. d
15. a

Access 2007, Chapter 2

1. b
2. c
3. b
4. a
5. d
6. b
7. d
8. c
9. b
10. b
11. d
12. d
13. b
14. c
15. c
16. b
17. c
18. b
19. d
20. b

Access 2007, Chapter 3

1. a
2. c
3. e
4. d
5. b
6. c
7. a
8. a
9. a
10. c
11. a
12. b
13. b
14. c
15. d

Access 2007, Chapter 4

1. b
2. d
3. d
4. c
5. c
6. b
7. d
8. c
9. b
10. d
11. a
12. c
13. a
14. c
15. d
16. a
17. b
18. b

PowerPoint 2007, Chapter 1

1. d
2. b
3. d
4. a
5. b
6. d
7. a
8. c
9. d
10. b
11. d
12. d
13. c
14. a
15. c

PowerPoint 2007, Chapter 2

1. d
2. b
3. a
4. d
5. b
6. c
7. c
8. a
9. b
10. a
11. d
12. d
13. a
14. c
15. d

PowerPoint 2007, Chapter 3

1. b
2. a
3. d
4. b
5. a
6. c
7. b
8. d
9. c
10. d
11. c
12. a
13. a
14. b
15. b

PowerPoint 2007, Chapter 4

1. c
2. a
3. b
4. a
5. b
6. d
7. b
8. d
9. b
10. c
11. a
12. a
13. c
14. d
15. c

Windows Vista, Chapter 1

1. d
2. d
3. a
4. c
5. d
6. a
7. c
8. a
9. d
10. c
11. d
12. a
13. b
14. c
15. c

Index

A

B

C

E

F

G

H

I

J

L

M

N

Q

R

S

U

W

Z

SINGLE PC LICENSE AGREEMENT AND LIMITED WARRANTY

READ THIS LICENSE CAREFULLY BEFORE OPENING THIS PACKAGE. BY OPENING THIS PACKAGE, YOU ARE AGREEING TO THE TERMS AND CONDITIONS OF THIS LICENSE. IF YOU DO NOT AGREE, DO NOT OPEN THE PACKAGE. PROMPTLY RETURN THE UNOPENED PACKAGE AND ALL ACCOMPANYING ITEMS TO THE PLACE YOU OBTAINED THEM. *THESE TERMS APPLY TO ALL LICENSED SOFTWARE ON THE DISK EXCEPT THAT THE TERMS FOR USE OF ANY SHAREWARE OR FREEWARE ON TH E DISKETTES ARE AS SET FORTH IN THE ELECTRONIC LICENSE LOCATED ON THE DISK:*

1. GRANT OF LICENSE and OWNERSHIP: The enclosed computer programs ("Software") are licensed, not sold, to you by Prentice-Hall, Inc. ("We" or the "Company") and in consideration of your purchase or adoption of the accompanying Company textbooks and/or other materials, and your agreement to these terms. We reserve any rights not granted to you. You own only the disk(s) but we and/or our licensors own the Software itself. This license allows you to use and display your copy of the Software on a single computer (i.e., with a single CPU) at a single location for academic use only, so long as you comply with the terms of this Agreement. You may make one copy for back up, or transfer your copy to another CPU, provided that the Software is usable on only one computer.

2. RESTRICTIONS: You may not transfer or distribute the Software or documentation to anyone else. Except for backup, you may not copy the documentation or the Software. You may not network the Software or otherwise use it on more than one computer or computer terminal at the same time. You may not reverse engineer, disassemble, decompile, modify, adapt, translate, or create derivative works based on the Software or the Documentation. You may be held legally responsible for any copying or copyright infringement which is caused by your failure to abide by the terms of these restrictions.

3. TERMINATION: This license is effective until terminated. This license will terminate automatically without notice from the Company if you fail to comply with any provisions or limitations of this license. Upon termination, you shall destroy the Documentation and all copies of the Software. All provisions of this Agreement as to limitation and disclaimer of warranties, limitation of liability, remedies or damages, and our ownership rights shall survive termination.

4. DISCLAIMER OF WARRANTY: THE COMPANY AND ITS LICENSORS MAKE NO WARRANTIES ABOUT THE SOFTWARE, WHICH IS PROVIDED "AS-IS." IF THE DISK IS DEFECTIVE IN MATERIALS OR WORKMANSHIP, YOUR ONLY REMEDY IS TO RETURN IT TO THE COMPANY WITHIN 30 DAYS FOR REPLACEMENT UNLESS THE COMPANY DETERMINES IN GOOD FAITH THAT THE DISK HAS BEEN MISUSED OR IMPROPERLY INSTALLED, REPAIRED, ALTERED OR DAMAGED. THE COMPANY DISCLAIMS ALL WARRANTIES, EXPRESS OR IMPLIED, INCLUDING WITHOUT LIMITATION, THE IMPLIED WARRANTIES OF MERCHANTABILITY AND FITNESS FOR A PARTICULAR PURPOSE. THE COMPANY DOES NOT WARRANT, GUARANTEE OR MAKE ANY REPRESENTATION REGARDING THE ACCURACY, RELIABILITY, CURRENTNESS, USE, OR RESULTS OF USE, OF THE SOFTWARE.

5. LIMITATION OF REMEDIES AND DAMAGES: IN NO EVENT, SHALL THE COMPANY OR ITS EMPLOYEES, AGENTS, LICENSORS OR CONTRACTORS BE LIABLE FOR ANY INCIDENTAL, INDIRECT, SPECIAL OR CONSEQUENTIAL DAMAGES ARISING OUT OF OR IN CONNECTION WITH THIS LICENSE OR THE SOFTWARE, INCLUDING, WITHOUT LIMITATION, LOSS OF USE, LOSS OF DATA, LOSS OF INCOME OR PROFIT, OR OTHER LOSSES SUSTAINED AS A RESULT OF INJURY TO ANY PERSON, OR LOSS OF OR DAMAGE TO PROPERTY, OR CLAIMS OF THIRD PARTIES, EVEN IF THE COMPANY OR AN AUTHORIZED REPRESENTATIVE OF THE COMPANY HAS BEEN ADVISED OF THE POSSIBILITY OF SUCH DAMAGES. SOME JURISDICTIONS DO NOT ALLOW THE LIMITATION OF DAMAGES IN CERTAIN CIRCUMSTANCES, SO THE ABOVE LIMITATIONS MAY NOT ALWAYS APPLY.

6. GENERAL: THIS AGREEMENT SHALL BE CONSTRUED IN ACCORDANCE WITH THE LAWS OF THE UNITED STATES OF AMERICA AND THE STATE OF NEW YORK, APPLICABLE TO CONTRACTS MADE IN NEW YORK, AND SHALL BENEFIT THE COMPANY, ITS AFFILIATES AND ASSIGNEES. This Agreement is the complete and exclusive statement of the agreement between you and the Company and supersedes all proposals, prior agreements, oral or written, and any other communications between you and the company or any of its representatives relating to the subject matter. If you are a U.S. Government user, this Software is licensed with "restricted rights" as set forth in subparagraphs (a)-(d) of the Commercial Computer-Restricted Rights clause at FAR 52.227-19 or in subparagraphs (c)(1)(ii) of the Rights in Technical Data and Computer Software clause at DFARS 252.227-7013, and similar clauses, as applicable.

Should you have any questions concerning this agreement or if you wish to contact the Company for any reason, please contact in writing:

Multimedia Production
Higher Education Division
Prentice-Hall, Inc.
1 Lake Street
Upper Saddle River NJ 07458